Spain

Gregor Clark, Sally Davies, Duncan Garwood, Anthony Ham, Catherine Le Nevez, Isabella Noble, John Noble, Josephine Quintero, Brendan Sainsbury, Regis St Louis, Andy Symington

PLAN YOUR TRIP

PARQUE NATURAL SIERRAS DE CAZORLA P783

AITOR MUÑOZ MUÑOZ / 500PX ©

ON THE ROAD

Contents

ESB PROFESSIONAL / SHUTTERSTOCK ©

PLAZA DE ESPAÑA, SEVILLE
P648

ON THE ROAD

MAXX-STUDIO / SHUTTERSTOCK ©

ALBARRACÍN, ARAGÓN P442

Contents

UNDERSTAND

SURVIVAL GUIDE

SPECIAL FEATURES

Welcome to Spain

Passionate, sophisticated and devoted to living the good life, Spain is both a stereotype come to life and a country more diverse than you ever imagined.

An Epic Land

Spain's diverse landscapes stir the soul. The Pyrenees and the Picos de Europa are as beautiful as any mountain range, while the snowcapped Sierra Nevada rises up from the sun-baked plains of Andalucía; these are hiking destinations of the highest order. The wildly beautiful cliffs of Spain's Atlantic northwest are offset by the charming coves of the Mediterranean. And everywhere you go, villages of timeless beauty perch on hilltops, huddle in valleys and cling to coastal outcrops as tiny but resilient outposts of Old Spain. That's where the country's charms truly take hold.

A Culinary Feast

Food and wine are national obsessions in Spain, and with good reason. The touchstones of Spanish cooking are deceptively simple: incalculable variety, traditional recipes handed down through the generations, and a willingness to experiment and see what comes out of the kitchen laboratory. You may experience the best meal ever via tapas in an earthy bar, or via a meal prepared by a celebrity chef in the refined surrounds of a Michelin-starred restaurant. Either way, the breadth of gastronomic experience that awaits you is breathtaking and sure to be a highlight of your trip.

Art Imitates Life

Windswept Roman ruins, cathedrals of rare power and incomparable jewels of Islamic architecture speak of a country where the great civilisations of history have risen, fallen and left behind their indelible mark. More recently, what other country could produce such rebellious and relentlessly creative spirits as Salvador Dalí, Pablo Picasso and Antoni Gaudí and place them front and centre in public life? And here, grand monuments of history coexist alongside architectural creations of such daring that it becomes clear Spain's future will be every bit as original as its past.

Fiestas & Flamenco

For all the talk of Spain's history, this is a country that lives very much in the present and there's a reason 'fiesta' is one of the best-known words in the Spanish language – life itself is a fiesta here and everyone seems to be invited. Perhaps you'll sense it along a crowded, post-midnight street when all the world has come out to play. Or maybe that moment will come when a flamenco performer touches something deep in your soul. Whenever it happens, you'll find yourself nodding in recognition: *this* is Spain.

Why I Love Spain

By Anthony Ham, Writer

The life that courses through the streets here always gives me a feeling that this is a place where anything can happen. The passions of Spain's people are the fabric of daily life; this is a country with music in its soul, a love of fine food and wild landscapes, and a special talent for celebrating all that's good in life. Spain is home to me now, something I feel keenly whether in the night silence of a remote Castilian village built of stone or immersed in the irresistible joy of a Madrid street.

For more about our writers, see p928.

Above: Picos de Europa (p546), northern Spain

Spain

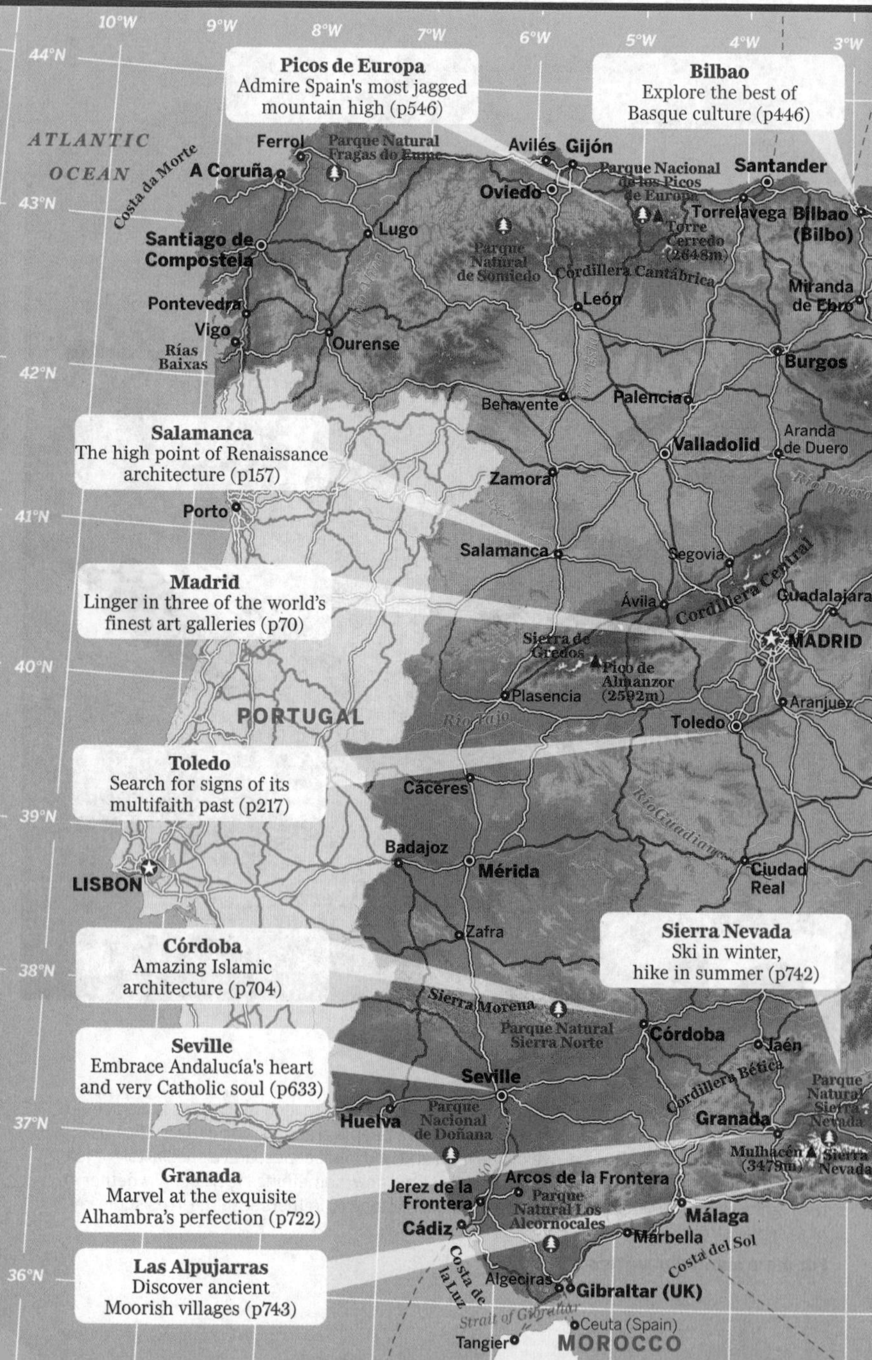

Picos de Europa
Admire Spain's most jagged mountain high (p546)
Bilbao
Explore the best of Basque culture (p446)
Salamanca
The high point of Renaissance architecture (p157)
Madrid
Linger in three of the world's finest art galleries (p70)
Toledo
Search for signs of its multifaith past (p217)
Córdoba
Amazing Islamic architecture (p704)
Seville
Embrace Andalucía's heart and very Catholic soul (p633)
Granada
Marvel at the exquisite Alhambra's perfection (p722)
Las Alpujarras
Discover ancient Moorish villages (p743)
Sierra Nevada
Ski in winter, hike in summer (p742)
10°W
9°W
8°W
7°W
6°W
5°W
4°W
3°W
44°N
43°N
42°N
41°N
40°N
39°N
38°N
37°N
36°N
ATLANTIC OCEAN
Costa da Morte
A Coruña
Ferrol
Parque Natural Fragas do Eume
Avilés
Gijón
Oviedo
Parque Nacional de los Picos de Europa
Torre Cerredo (2648m)
Santander
Torrelavega
Bilbao (Bilbo)
Santiago de Compostela
Lugo
Parque Natural de Somiedo
Cordillera Cantábrica
Miranda de Ebro
Pontevedra
Vigo
Rías Baixas
Ourense
León
Burgos
Benavente
Palencia
Valladolid
Aranda de Duero
Río Duero
Zamora
Porto
Salamanca
Segovia
Ávila
Cordillera Central
Guadalajara
MADRID
Sierra de Gredos
Pico de Almanzor (2592m)
Plasencia
Aranjuez
PORTUGAL
Río Tajo
Toledo
Cáceres
Río Guadiana
Badajoz
Mérida
Ciudad Real
LISBON
Zafra
Sierra Morena
Parque Natural Sierra Norte
Córdoba
Jaén
Cordillera Bética
Seville
Huelva
Parque Nacional de Doñana
Parque Natural Sierra Nevada
Granada
Mulhacén (3479m)
Sierra Nevada
Jerez de la Frontera
Arcos de la Frontera
Parque Natural Los Alcornocales
Cádiz
Málaga
Marbella
Costa del Sol
Costa de la Luz
Algeciras
Gibraltar (UK)
Strait of Gibraltar
Ceuta (Spain)
Tangier
MOROCCO

0 200 km
0 100 miles
FRANCE
Bay of Biscay
The Pyrenees
Hike the dramatic Pyrenean high country (p488)
Toulouse
Montpellier
Bayonne
Irún
San Sebastián
Golfe du Lion
Pyrenees
Mt Perdido (3355m)
Pico de Aneto (3404m)
Perpignan
Vitoria-Gasteiz
Pamplona (Iruña)
ANDORRA
Logroño
Parque Nacional de Ordesa y Monte Perdido
Parc Nacional d'Aigüestortes i Estany de Sant Maurici
ANDORRA LA VELLA
Figueres
Huesca
Girona
Costa Brava
Soria
Zaragoza
Lleida
Blanes
Barcelona
Tarragona
Costa Daurada
La Rioja
Meander through Spain's premier wine region (p496)
Costa del Azahar
Barcelona
Immerse yourself in Spain's style city (p249)
Teruel
Menorca
Maó
Cuenca
Castellón de la Plana (Castelló de la Plana)
Palma de Mallorca
Balearic Islands (Islas Baleares)
Valencia
Golfo de Valencia
Mallorca
Ibiza
Albacete
Ibiza Town
Formentera
Parque Natural Sierras de Cazorla, Segura y las Villas
Alicante (Alicant)
Costa Blanca
Elche (Elx)
Torrevieja
Murcia
MEDITERRANEAN SEA
Cartagena
Costa Cálida
1°E
2°E
3°E
4°E
ELEVATION
2000m
1500m
1250m
1000m
800m
600m
400m
200m
100m
0
ALGIERS
Parque Natural de Cabo de Gata-Níjar
Almería
0° (Greenwich)
1°W
2°W
ALGERIA
Oran

Spain's Top 18

1

Barcelona

1 Home to cutting-edge architecture, world-class dining and pulsating nightlife, Barcelona (p249) has long been one of Europe's most alluring destinations. Days are spent wandering the cobblestone lanes of the Gothic quarter, basking on Mediterranean beaches or marvelling at Gaudí masterpieces. By night, Barcelona is a whirl of vintage cocktail bars, gilded music halls, innovative eateries and dance-loving clubs, with the party extending well into the night. There are also colourful markets, hallowed arenas (such as Camp Nou where FC Barcelona plays), and a calendar packed with traditional Catalan festivals. *Castellers* (human castle builders; p395) perform in Plaça del Pi

Seville

2 Nowhere is as quintessentially Spanish as Seville (p633), a city of capricious moods and soulful secrets, which has played a pivotal role in the evolution of flamenco, bullfighting, baroque art and Mudéjar architecture. Blessed with year-round sunshine and fuelled culturally by a never-ending schedule of ebullient festivals, everything seems more amorous here, a feeling not lost on legions of 19th-century aesthetes, who used the city as a setting in their romantic works of fiction. Head south to the home of Carmen and Don Juan and take up the story. Casa de Pilatos (p647)

MICH SEIXAS / 500PX ©

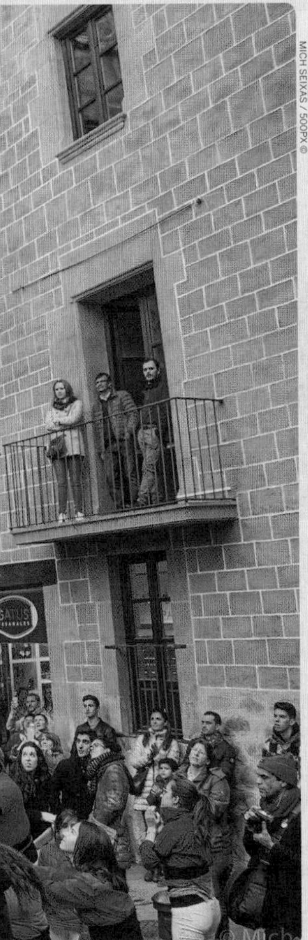

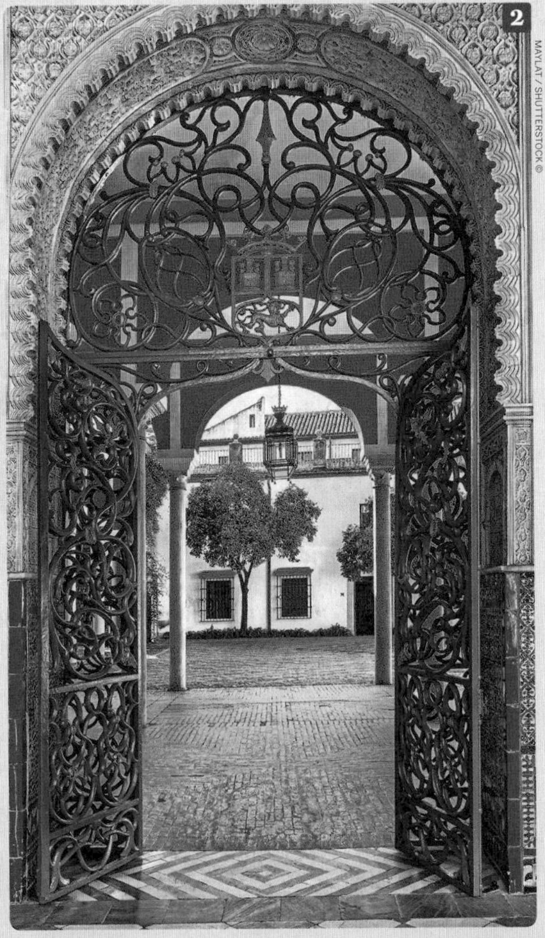

MAYLAT / SHUTTERSTOCK ©

The Alhambra

3 The palace complex of Granada's Alhambra (p722) is close to architectural perfection. It is perhaps the most refined example of Islamic art anywhere in the world, and the most enduring symbol of 800 years of Moorish rule in what was known as Al-Andalus. The red fortress towers dominate the Granada skyline, set against a backdrop of the Sierra Nevada's snowcapped peaks. Up close, the Alhambra's perfectly proportioned Generalife gardens complement the exquisite detail of the Palacio Nazaríes. Put simply, this is Spain's most beautiful monument. Palacio del Partal (p726), Alhambra

Madrid's Golden Art Triangle

4 Madrid is one of the fine-arts capitals of the world, with an extraordinary collection of art galleries concentrated in a single patch of the city-centre real estate (p75). The Museo del Prado (pictured above; p94), housing works by Goya, Velázquez, El Greco and European masters, is the showpiece, but also within a short stroll are the Centro de Arte Reina Sofía, showcasing Picasso's *Guernica*, and the Museo Thyssen-Bornemisza, which carries all the big names spanning centuries and styles.

Pintxos in San Sebastián

5 Chefs here have turned bar snacks into an art form. Sometimes called 'high cuisine in miniature', *pintxos* (Basque tapas) are piles of flavour often mounted on a slice of baguette. As you step into any bar in central San Sebastián (pictured top right; p463), the choice lined up along the counter will leave you gasping. In short, this is Spain's most memorable eating experience. Although the atmosphere is always casual, the serious business of experimenting with taste combinations (a Basque trademark) ensures that it just keeps getting better.

Córdoba's Mezquita

6 A church that became a mosque before reverting back to a church, Córdoba's stunning Mezquita (pictured above; p705) charts the evolution of Western and Islamic architecture over a 1300-year trajectory. Its most innovative features include some early horseshoe arches, an intricate *mihrab*, and a veritable 'forest' of 856 columns, many of them recycled from Roman ruins. The sheer scale of the Mezquita reflects Córdoba's erstwhile power as the most cultured city in 10th-century Europe. It was also inspiration for magnificent buildings to come, most notably in Seville and Granada.

La Sagrada Família

7 The Modernista brainchild of Antoni Gaudí, La Sagrada Família (pictured top; p274) remains a work in progress more than 90 years after its creator's death. Fanciful and profound, inspired by nature and barely restrained by a Gothic style, Barcelona's quirky temple soars skyward with an almost playful majesty. The improbable angles and departures from architectural convention will have you shaking your head in disbelief, but the detail of the decorative flourishes on the Passion Facade, Nativity Facade and elsewhere are worth studying for hours.

Camino de Santiago

8 Every year, tens of thousands of pilgrims and walkers with all manner of motivations set out to walk across northern Spain. Their destination, Santiago de Compostela (p559), is a place of untold significance for Christians, but the appeal of this epic walk (p51) goes far beyond the religious. With numerous routes to Santiago from all over the Iberian Peninsula, there's no finer way to get under Spain's skin and experience the pleasures and caprices of its natural world. And even completing one small stage will leave you with a lifetime of impressions. Hikers on the Camino de Santiago

ALEX SEGRE / 500PX ©

SHEBEKO / SHUTTERSTOCK ©

A La Playa

9 It's easy to see why Spain's beaches are Europe's favourite summer playground, but the beach is also an obsession among Spaniards in summer, when the entire country seems to head for the coast. There's so much more to Spain's coastline than the overcrowded beaches of Benidorm: the rugged coves of the Costa Brava, or Cabo de Gata (p790) in Andalucía, come close to the Mediterranean ideal, while the Atlantic beaches from Tarifa to the Portuguese frontier and the dramatic coastline of Spain's northwest are utterly spectacular. Costa Brava (p339)

Madrid Nightlife

10 Madrid is not the only European city with nightlife, but few can match its intensity and street clamour (p126). As Ernest Hemingway said, 'Nobody goes to bed in Madrid until they have killed the night'. There are wall-to-wall bars, small clubs, live venues, cocktail bars and megaclubs beloved by A-list celebrities all across the city, with unimaginable variety to suit all tastes. It's in the *barrios* (districts) of Huertas, Malasaña, Chueca and La Latina that you'll really understand what we're talking about.

Sampling Tapas

11 One of the world's most enjoyable ways to eat, tapas are as much a way of life as they are Spain's most accessible culinary superstars. These bite-sized bar snacks are the accompaniment to countless Spanish nights of revelry and come in seemingly endless variations. In Andalucía (p738), expect the best *jamón* (ham) or fine Spanish olives. In San Sebastián and elsewhere in the Basque Country – where they're called *'pintxos'* – tapas are an elaborate form of culinary art. Other great places for tapas include Madrid and Zaragoza.

Hiking in the Pyrenees

12 Spain is a walker's destination of exceptional variety, but we reckon the Pyrenees in Navarra (p488), Aragón and Catalonia offer the most special hiking country. Aragón's Parque Nacional de Ordesa y Monte Perdido (p425) is one of the high points (pun intended) of the Pyrenees, while its glories are mirrored across the regional frontier in Catalonia's Parc Nacional d'Aigüestortes i Estany de Sant Maurici (p378). It's tough but rewarding terrain, a world of great rock walls and glacial cirques, accompanied by elusive but soulful Pyrenean wildlife.

Bilbao: Spain's Northern Gem

13 It only took one building, a shimmering titanium fish called the Museo Guggenheim Bilbao (pictured right; p446), to turn Bilbao from a byword for industrial decay into a major European art centre. But while it's this most iconic of buildings that draws the visitors, it's the hard-working soul of this city that ends up captivating. There's plenty to be entranced by: riverside promenades, clanky funicular railways, superb *pintxos* bars, an iconic football team, a clutch of quality museums and, yeah OK, a shimmering titanium fish.

12

DANI MART / 500PX ©

13

© FMGB, GUGGENHEIM BILBAO MUSEOA, BILBAO 2018. PHOTO: ERIKA BARAHONA EDE

YADID LEVY / LONELY PLANET ©

Flamenco

14 The soundtrack to Europe's most passionate country, flamenco (p875) has the power to lift you out of the doldrums and stir your soul. It's as if by sharing in the pain of innumerable generations of dispossessed misfits you open a door to a secret world of musical ghosts and ancient spirits. On the other side of the coin, flamenco culture can also be surprisingly jolly, jokey and tongue-in-cheek. There's only one real proviso: you have to hear it live, preferably in its Seville–Jerez–Cádiz heartland, although anywhere in Andalucía should do.

15

KIKOSTOCK / SHUTTERSTOCK ©

16

BORIS STROUJKO / SHUTTERSTOCK ©

Semana Santa

15 Return to Spain's medieval Christian roots in the country's dramatic Easter celebrations. Religious fraternities parade elaborate *pasos* (figures) of Christ and the Virgin Mary through the streets to the emotive acclaim of the populace; the most prestigious procession is the *madrugada* (early hours) of Good Friday. Seen for the first time, it's an exotic and utterly compelling fusion of pageantry, solemnity and deep religious faith. The most extraordinary processions are in Castilla y León, Castilla La Mancha and Andalucía, but if you choose one, make it Seville (pictured top left; p651).

Costa Brava

16 Easily accessible by air and land from the rest of Europe, and filled with villages and beaches of the kind that spawned northern Europe's summer obsession with the Spanish coast, the Costa Brava (p339) in Catalonia is one of our favourite corners of the Mediterranean. Beyond this, the spirit of Salvador Dalí lends so much personality and studied eccentricity to the Costa Brava experience, from his one-time home in Port Lligat near Cadaqués to the Dalí-centric sites of Figueres and Castell de Púbol. Calella de Palafrugell (p340)

Picos de Europa

17 Jutting out in compact form just back from the rugged and ever-changing coastline of Cantabria and Asturias, the Picos de Europa (p546) comprise three dramatic limestone massifs, unique in Spain but geologically similar to the Alps and jammed with inspiring trails. These peaks and valleys form Spain's second-largest national park, with some of the most spectacular mountain scenery in the country – no small claim considering the presence of the Pyrenees and the Sierra Nevada. The Picos de Europa deservedly belong in such elite company. Lagos de Covadonga (p550)

Renaissance Salamanca

18 Luminous when floodlit, the elegant central square of Salamanca, the Plaza Mayor (p157; pictured), is possibly the most attractive in all of Spain. It is just one of many highlights in a city whose architectural splendour has few peers in the country. Salamanca is home to one of Europe's oldest and most prestigious universities, so student revelry also lights up the nights. It's this combination of grandeur and energy that makes so many people call Salamanca their favourite city in Spain and who are we to argue?

Need to Know

For more information, see Survival Guide (p879)

Currency
Euro (€)

Language
Spanish (Castilian). Also Catalan, Basque and Galician.

Visas
Generally not required for stays of up to 90 days per 180 days (visas are not required at all for members of EU or Schengen countries). Some nationalities need a Schengen visa.

Money
ATMs widely available. Credit cards accepted in most hotels and restaurants.

Mobile Phones
Local SIM cards are widely available and can be used in European and Australian mobile phones. Not compatible with many North American or Japanese systems.

Time
Central European Time (GMT/UTC plus one hour)

When to Go

High Season
(Jun–Aug, public holidays)

- ➡ Accommodation books out and prices increase by up to 50%.
- ➡ Low season in parts of inland Spain.
- ➡ Expect warm, dry and sunny weather; more humid in coastal areas.

Shoulder
(Mar–May, Sep & Oct)

- ➡ A good time to travel: mild, clear weather and fewer crowds.
- ➡ Local festivals can send prices soaring.
- ➡ Fewer hikers on trails but weather unpredictable.

Low Season
(Nov–Feb)

- ➡ Cold in central Spain; rain in the north and northwest.
- ➡ Mild temperatures in Andalucía and the Mediterranean coast.
- ➡ This is high season in ski resorts.
- ➡ Many hotels are closed in beach areas but elsewhere along the coast prices plummet.

Useful Websites

Lonely Planet (www.lonelyplanet.com/spain) Destination information, hotel bookings, traveller forums and more.

Fiestas.net (www.fiestas.net) Festivals around the country.

Tour Spain (www.tourspain.org) Culture, food and links to hotels and transport.

Turespaña (www.spain.info) Spanish tourist office's site.

Paradores (www.parador.es) Spain's finest hotel experiences with plenty to get you dreaming.

Renfe (Red Nacional de los Ferrocarriles Españoles; www.renfe.com) Spain's rail network.

Important Numbers

There are no area codes in Spain.

Spain's country code	☎34
International access code	☎00
International directory inquiries	☎11825
National directory inquiries	☎11818
Emergencies	☎112

Exchange Rates

Australia	A$1	€0.67
Canada	C$1	€0.68
Japan	¥100	€0.76
New Zealand	NZ$1	€0.61
UK	UK£1	€1.12
US	US$1	€0.85

For current exchange rates, see www.xe.com.

Daily Costs

Budget: Less than €80

- Dorm bed: €20–30
- Double room in *hostal* (budget hotel): €50–65 (€60–75 in Madrid, Barcelona and Balearics)
- Self-catering and lunch *menú del día* (set menu): €10–15

Midrange: €80–175

- Double room in midrange hotel: €65–140 (€75–200 in Madrid, Barcelona and Balearics)
- Lunch and/or dinner in local restaurant: €20–40
- Car rental: per day from €25

Top end: More than €175

- Double room in top-end hotel: €140–200 and up
- Fine dining for lunch and dinner: €150–250
- Double room in *parador*: €120–200

Opening Hours

Banks 8.30am–2pm Monday to Friday; some also open 4–7pm Thursday and 9am–1pm Saturday

Central post offices 8.30am–9.30pm Monday to Friday, 8.30am–2pm Saturday (most other branches 8.30am–2.30pm Monday to Friday, 9.30am–1pm Saturday)

Nightclubs Midnight or 1am to 5am or 6am

Restaurants Lunch 1–4pm, dinner 8.30–11pm or midnight

Shops 10am–2pm and 4.30–7.30pm or 5-8pm Monday to Friday or Saturday; big supermarkets and department stores generally open 10am–10pm Monday to Saturday

Arriving in Spain

Adolfo Suárez Madrid-Barajas Airport (Madrid) The Metro (€4.50 to €5, 30 minutes to the centre) runs from 6.05am to 1.30am; the Exprés Aeropuerto bus (30 to 40 minutes, €5) runs 24 hours between the airport and Puerta de Atocha train station or Plaza de Cibeles. There are also private minibuses or taxis (€30).

El Prat Airport (Barcelona) Buses cost €5.90 and run every five to 10 minutes from 6.10am to 1.05am; it's 30 to 40 minutes to the centre. Trains (€4.10, 25 to 30 minutes to the centre) run half-hourly from 5.42am to 11.38pm. Taxis cost €25 to €30 and reach the centre in 30 minutes.

Getting Around

Spain's public transport system is one of the best in Europe, with a fast and super-modern train system, extensive domestic air network, an impressive and well-maintained road network, and buses that connect villages in the country's remotest corners.

Train Extremely efficient rail network, from slow intercity regional trains to some of the fastest trains on the planet. More routes are added to the network every year.

Car Vast network of motorways radiating out from Madrid to all corners of the country, shadowed by smaller but often more picturesque minor roads.

Bus The workhorses of the Spanish roads, from slick express services to stop-everywhere village-to-village buses.

For much more on **getting around**, see p896

First Time Spain

For more information, see Survival Guide (p879)

Checklist

➡ With huge airfare differences, check *all* airlines before booking flights.

➡ Ask your mobile-phone provider about roaming charges (if any).

➡ Book your first night's accommodation to ensure an easy start to your trip.

➡ Check the calendar to work out which festivals to visit or avoid.

➡ Organise travel insurance.

➡ Inform your debit-/credit-card company you're heading away.

What to Pack

➡ Passport and/or national ID card (EU citizens) and carry it on you.

➡ Spanish phrasebook – not everyone speaks English.

➡ Money belt, and padlock for suitcase/backpack.

➡ Two-pin continental Europe travel plug.

➡ Earplugs for noisy Spanish nights.

➡ Renfe (train) app and a hiking one downloaded to your phone.

Top Tips for Your Trip

➡ To avoid going hungry, adjust your body clock on arrival. In no time, you'll be eating lunch at 2.30pm and dinner at 9pm.

➡ A few words of Spanish can go a long way. English is widely (but not universally) spoken.

➡ Spain is a food-obsessed country and you'll miss half the fun if you don't linger over your meals. Always ask for the local speciality.

➡ Don't be too ambitious when deciding what to cover. Spain is a large country and you'll do well to zero in on a handful of special destinations.

➡ Overnight at least once in a small village. You'll understand the country better if you do.

➡ Avoid the motorways and take scenic back roads.

➡ Get used to having less personal space and being surrounded by high-volume conversations.

Tipping

Tipping is almost always optional.

Restaurants Many Spaniards leave small change, others up to 5%, which is considered generous.

Taxis Optional, but most locals round up to the nearest euro.

Bars It's rare to leave a tip in bars (even if the bartender gives you your change on a small dish).

What to Wear

Spain has come a long way since the 1950s when visiting tourists were fined and escorted from Spanish beaches by police for wearing bikinis. Just about anything goes now, and you'll rarely feel uncomfortable because of what you're wearing. Northern Spain and much of the interior can be bitterly cold in winter – come prepared with plenty of warm clothing. You should also carry some form of wet-weather gear if you're in the northwest. Spaniards are generally quite fashion-conscious and well-dressed – in the cities in particular, they rarely dip below smart casual.

Eating

Spain is one of Europe's culinary powerhouses, a foodie destination of the highest order. So much of Spanish cuisine has colonised the world, from tapas, paella, *jamón* and *churros* to Spanish wines and olive oils. But by visiting Spain you can go to the source and enjoy Spanish cooking at its best and in all its infinite variety.

Bargaining

Haggling over prices is accepted in some markets, and shops *may* offer a small discount if you're spending a lot of money. Otherwise expect to pay the stated price.

Etiquette

Greetings Spaniards almost always greet friends and strangers alike with a kiss on each cheek, although two males only do this if they're close friends. It is customary to say *'Hola, buenos días'* or *'Hola, buenas tardes'* (in the afternoon or evening) when meeting someone or when entering a shop or bar, and *'Hasta luego'* when leaving.

Eating and drinking Spanish waiters won't expect you to thank them every time they bring you something, but they may expect you to keep your cutlery between courses in more casual bars and restaurants.

Visiting churches It is considered disrespectful to visit churches for the purposes of tourism during Mass and other worship services.

Escalators Always stand on the right to let people pass.

JUSTIN FOLKES / LONELY PLANET ©

Pintxo (Basque tapas; p454), San Sebastián

Sleeping

Spain's accommodation is generally of a high standard, and prices are reasonable, especially outside the big cities.

Hotels From boutique to family-run, with a wide range of rates.

Hostales Small, simpler hotel-style places, often with private bathrooms.

Casas Rurales Rural homes generally with rustic, simple rooms that can be reserved individually or as a block.

Paradors These state-run hotels often inhabit stunning historic buildings and can be surprisingly well priced, especially off-season.

Hostels Quality varies, but these budget spots are great places to meet other travellers.

Campsites Located across the country, amid lovely natural settings.

Reservations

Reservations for accommodation and long-distance trains are highly advisable in the main Spanish holiday seasons – Semana Santa (the week leading up to Easter Sunday), July, August and around other main public holidays.

What's New

Catalonia Cooking

Since the closure of world-renowned Costa Brava restaurant elBulli in 2011, Ferrán Adriá's culinary disciples have fanned out across the region with their own innovative projects. A fine example is Compartir in Cadaqués (p360).

Valencia Public Art

Valencia's ability to put art at the centre of its appeal grows with each passing year. Art Deco Bombas Gens (p811) has been converted into a photography and contemporary art gallery, the Iglesia de San Nicolás (p798) has restored its sumptuous painted ceiling, and the Museo de la Seda (p798) is devoted to silk.

Lorca Rebirth

Things are just about back on their feet in Lorca after the devastating 2011 earthquake, with optimism in the air and the city centre looking lovely. The majestic Colegiata de San Patricio (p842) is finally open again and is a fine symbol of the city's revival.

A New Wine Museum

The lesser-known wine region of Toro, in Castilla y León, is making a strong claim for recognition, with high-quality wines and the Pagos del Rey Wine Museum (p181).

Tabancos in Jerez

The Tabanco scene in Jerez de la Frontera (p685) has really come into its own. New owners have taken over these old sherry taverns and brought them back to life with tapas, sherry and in some cases live flamenco.

Vejer Boutique

An ever-growing number of boutique boltholes continue to make Vejer de la Frontera one of Andalucía's most attractive (and popular) overnight stops. Casa Shelly (p698) and La Fonda Antigua (p698) have joined an already-distinguished portfolio.

Catalan Veg

There's been a big rise in the number of specifically vegetarian and vegan restaurants in recent years, using Catalonia's bounty to create all kinds of meat-free delights. Tarragona's El Vergel (p396) and Girona's vegan B12 (p354) lead the way.

Casa Vicens

Gaudí's first-ever commission, Casa Vicens (p283), has had a makeover and is finally to open to the public year-round for the first time.

Toledo Hammam

Toledo has long marketed itself as the city where Muslims, Christians and Jews once lived in harmony. Medina Mudéjar (p222) beautifully captures the spirit of those times.

Steps & Ladders

Rock-climbing routes equipped with steel steps, ladders and cables are increasingly popular in the Pyrenees, but are only just starting to reach Andalucía. Via Ferrata La Mocha (p782) ascends 130m up the precipitous rocky cone La Mocha near Cazorla.

For more recommendations and reviews, see lonelyplanet.com/Spain

If You Like...

Incredible Art

Spain's artistic tradition is one of Europe's richest and most original, from local masters to Europe's finest, who flourished under Spanish royal patronage. The result? Art galleries of astonishing depth.

Museo del Prado Quite simply one of the world's best galleries. (p94)

Centro de Arte Reina Sofia Picasso's *Guernica*, Dalí and Miró. (p91)

Museo Thyssen-Bornemisza Works by seemingly every European master. (p90)

Museo Picasso Málaga More than 200 works by Picasso, Málaga's favourite son. (p753)

Museu Picasso Unrivalled collection from Picasso's early years. (p268)

Museu Nacional d'Art de Catalunya Epic collection that includes some extraordinary Romanesque frescos. (p288)

Teatre-Museu Dalí As weird and wonderful as Salvador Dalí himself. (p362)

Museo Guggenheim Bilbao Showpiece architecture and world-class contemporary art. (p446)

Museo de Bellas Artes Goya, Velázquez, El Greco, Sorolla, and they're just the start; in Valencia. (p803)

Spanish Food

Spain obsesses about food with an eating public as eager to try something new as they are wary lest their chefs stray too far from one of Europe's richest culinary traditions.

Pintxos in San Sebastián Spain's culinary capital, with more Michelin stars than Paris and the country's best *pintxos* (Basque tapas). (p469)

Paella in Valencia The birthplace of paella and still the place for the most authentic version – think chicken, beans and rabbit. (p809)

Catalan cooking in Barcelona Home city for Catalonia's legendary cooking fuelled by Spain's finest food markets. (p301)

Tapas in La Latina, Madrid Rising above Madrid's modest home-grown cuisine, this inner-city *barrio* (district) showcases the best tapas from around Spain. (p118)

Seafood in Galicia The dark arts of boiling an octopus and the Atlantic's sea creatures (goose barnacles, anyone?) are pure culinary pleasure. (p580)

Roasted meats in the interior *Cochinillo asado* (roast suckling pig) and *cordero asado lechal* (roast spring lamb) are fabulous staples. (p172)

El Celler de Can Roca Girona's finest has been named the world's best restaurant twice in recent years. (p354)

Islamic Architecture

Almost eight centuries of Muslim empires bequeathed to Spain Europe's finest accumulation of Islamic architecture, especially in Andalucía, the heartland of Al-Andalus (the Moorish-ruled areas of the Iberian Peninsula), which encompassed Granada, Córdoba and Seville.

Alhambra An extraordinary monument to the extravagance of Al-Andalus, breathtaking in scope and exquisite in detail. (p722)

Mezquita Perfection wrought in stone in Córdoba's one-time great mosque, one of Al-Andalus' finest architectural moments. (p705)

Real Alcázar Exquisite detail amid a perfectly proportioned whole in Seville. (p637)

Giralda The former minaret represents a high point in Seville's Islamic skyline. (p636)

Aljafería A rare Moorish jewel in the north. (p407)

Alcazaba Málaga's 11th-century palace-fortress. (p754)

Teruel A splendid, little-known collection of Mudéjar design, proof that Islam's influence outlasted Islamic rule. (p438)

Alcazaba Splendidly preserved fortress overlooking Almería. (p785)

Outdoor Adventure

Getting active in the Spanish wilds is getting better with each passing year, and adventure sports are growing exponentially in popularity.

Alquézar This stunning Aragonese village is brilliant for canyoning. (p433)

Tarifa Mainland Spain's southernmost tip is Spain's centre for kitesurfing and windsurfing. (p701)

Zamora Natural Kayaking in Castilla y León's west is just the start of what this outfit offers. (p184)

Aínsa Not just a beautiful hill town, but increasingly a base for mountain biking in Aragón. (p429)

Baqueira-Beret-Bonaigua Considered by many to have the Pyrenees' best snow. (p384)

Sierra Nevada Europe's southernmost ski resort with 106km of runs. (p742)

Mundaka Unreliable, but one of Europe's most celebrated waves. (p461)

Music

Spain pulsates with music wherever you go, and whether it's the soulful strains of flamenco or a vibrant music festival, Spain has your soundtrack.

Jerez de la Frontera Spine-tingling live flamenco in the cradle of the genre. (p686)

Seville One of flamenco's most prestigious stages. (p656)

Top: Mountain biking, Aragonese Pyrenees (p417)

Bottom: Palau de la Música Catalana (p265), Barcelona

Córdoba Fabulous festivals, such as the Festival de la Guitarra de Córdoba and Noche Blanca del Flamenco. (p712)

Cafe Central One of Europe's most respected jazz venues; in Madrid. (p133)

Palau de la Música Catalana Marvellous classical performances in an extraordinary Barcelonian venue. (p326)

Casa das Crechas Wednesday-night Galician folk jam sessions in Santiago de Compostela featuring bagpipes, fiddles and accordions. (p566)

Sónar World-class electronica festival in Barcelona, worth planning your trip around. (p295)

Beaches

Despite Spain's summer popularity, the country's surfeit of coastal riches means that an unspoiled beach experience remains a possibility. You just need to know where to look.

Cabo de Gata A wildly beautiful reminder of the Andalucian coast as it once was. (p790)

Costa de la Luz Unbroken stretches of sand along a beautiful coast from Tarifa to Cádiz. (p697)

Playa de la Concha One of the most beautiful city beaches anywhere in the world. (p463)

Costa Brava Rugged coast with windswept cliffs, pristine hidden coves and wide sandy beaches. (p339)

Rías Baixas Dramatic long ocean inlets and islands strung with many a fine sandy strand. (p583)

Staying Out Late

From sophisticated cocktail bars to beachside *chiringuitos* (bars), from dance-until-dawn nightclubs to outdoor *terrazas* (bars with outdoor tables), Spanish nightlife is diverse, relentless and utterly intoxicating.

Madrid Bars, nightclubs, live-music venues and nights that roll effortlessly into one another. (p126)

Valencia Barrio del Carmen and Russafa nights are famous throughout Spain, with a roaring soundtrack in the city's oldest quarter. (p812)

Barcelona Glamorous and gritty nightspots for an international crowd. (p317)

Zaragoza The heartbeat of Aragón with fabulous tapas and drinking bars that don't crank up until well after midnight. (p410)

Seville Long, hot nights and the essence of Andalucia's passion come to life. (p656)

Sitges Gay-driven, but hetero-friendly, Sitges is coastal Catalonia's party town. (p389)

Cathedrals

Catholicism stands at the heart of Spanish identity, and cathedrals, with their rich accumulation of architectural styles, form the monumental and spiritual centrepiece of many Spanish towns.

La Sagrada Família Gaudí's unfinished masterpiece rises above Barcelona like an apparition of some fevered imagination. (p274)

Catedral de Santiago de Compostela One of Spain's most sacred (and beautiful) sites, with a magnificent Romanesque portico. (p560)

Catedral de Burgos A Gothic high point with legends of El Cid lording it over the old town. (p198)

Catedral de Toledo Extravagant monument to the power of Catholic Spain in its most devout heartland. (p217)

Catedral de Sevilla Vast and very beautiful Gothic cathedral with the stunning Giralda bell tower. (p636)

Catedral de León Sublime 13th-century Gothic structure with Spain's best stained-glass windows. (p189)

Wildlife

Spain has exceptional wildlife-watching opportunities with a fine mix of charismatic carnivores, pretty pink flamingos and a bird list without peer in Europe.

Doñana Thousands of deer and wild boar, more than 300 bird species and elusive Iberian lynxes roam Andalucía's Guadalquivir wetlands. (p664)

Parque Natural Sierra de Andújar Your best chance to spot the Iberian lynx; also rare black vultures, black storks and Spanish imperial eagles. (p778)

Parque Natural de Somiedo Track brown bears high in the mountains of Asturias. (p545)

Sierra de la Culebra Home to the Iberian wolf and the best place to watch wolves in Europe. (p184)

Tarifa Watch as whales and dolphins pass through the Straits of Gibraltar. (p700)

Parque Nacional de Monfragüe Birds of prey wheel high above a dramatic canyon. (p621)

Laguna de Gallocanta *Grullas* (cranes) winter here in their thousands in Aragón. (p438)

Parque Natural Sierras de Cazorla, Segura y Las Villas Good for red and fallow deer, ibex, wild boar, mouflon, red squirrels, griffon vultures and golden eagles. (p783)

Month by Month

TOP EVENTS

Semana Santa (Holy Week), usually March or April

Las Fallas de San José, March

Bienal de Flamenco, September

Carnaval, February or March

Feria de Abril, April

January

In January, ski resorts in the Pyrenees and the Sierra Nevada are in full swing. Snow in Catalonia is usually better in the second half of January. School holidays run until around 8 January.

Three Kings

El Día de los Reyes Magos (Three Kings' Day), or simply Reyes, on 6 January, is the highlight of a Spanish kid's calendar. The evening before, politicians dress up as the three wise men and lead a sweet-distributing frenzy (Cabalgata de Reyes) through most towns.

February

This is often the coldest month, with temperatures close to freezing, especially in the north and inland regions. If you're heading to Carnaval, accommodation is at a premium in Cádiz, Sitges and Ciudad Rodrigo.

Contemporary Art Fair

One of Europe's biggest celebrations of contemporary art, Madrid's Feria Internacional de Arte Contemporánea (www.ifema.es) draws gallery reps and exhibitors from all over the world.

Carnaval

Riotously fun, Carnaval ends on the Tuesday 47 days before Easter Sunday, and involves fancy-dress parades and festivities. It's wildest in Cádiz (p675), Sitges (p390), Badajoz (p631) and Ciudad Rodrigo (p163). Other curious celebrations are held at Vilanova i la Geltrú and Solsona.

Extremadura Birds

Parque Nacional de Monfragüe has long been known to birdwatchers from across Europe, but they come in their greatest numbers in late February or early March for the Extremadura Birdwatching Fair (www.fioextremadura.es). There are seminars, hiking excursions and other twitching-related fun.

March

With the arrival of spring, Spain shakes off its winter blues (such as they are), the weather starts to warm up ever so slightly and Spaniards start dreaming of a summer by the beach.

Flamenco in Jerez

One of Spain's most important flamenco festivals takes place in the genre's heartland in late February or early March. (p684)

Las Fallas de San José

The extraordinary festival of Las Fallas consists of several days of all-night dancing and drinking, first-class fireworks and processions from 15 to 19 March. Its principal stage is Valencia city, and the festivities culminate in the ritual burning of effigies in the streets. (p807)

April

Spain has a real spring in its step, with wildflowers in full bloom, Easter

celebrations and school holidays. It requires some advance planning (book ahead), but it's a great time to be here.

Semana Santa (Holy Week)

Easter (the dates change each year) entails parades of *pasos* (holy figures), hooded penitents and huge crowds. It's extravagantly celebrated in Seville (p651), as well as Málaga (p756), Ávila (p155), Cuenca (p240), Lorca (p843) and Zamora (p183).

Catalan Food

The central Catalan town of Vic puts food at the centre of Easter celebrations, with the Mercat de Ram (www.vicfires.cat), a food and agriculture fair that's quite the spectacle.

Dance of Death

The Dansa de la Mort (Dance of Death) on Holy Thursday in the Catalan village of Verges is a chilling experience. This nocturnal dance of skeleton figures is the centrepiece of Holy Week celebrations.

Los Empalaos

On Holy Thursday, Villanueva de la Vera, in northeast Extremadura, plays out an extraordinary act of Easter self-abnegation, Los Empalaos; the devotion and self-inflicted suffering of the barefoot penitents leaves most onlookers in awe. (p618)

Feria de Abril

This week-long party, held in Seville in the second half of April, is the biggest of Andalucía's fairs. *Sevillanos* dress up in their traditional finery, ride around on horseback and in elaborate horse-drawn carriages and dance late into the night. (p651)

Moros y Cristianos (Moors & Christians)

Colourful parades and mock battles between Christian and Muslim 'armies' in Alcoy, near Alicante, make Moros y Cristianos one of the most spectacular of many such festivities staged in Valencia and Alicante provinces in late April. Other versions are held elsewhere at other times. (p835)

Romería de la Virgen

On the last Sunday in April, hundreds of thousands of people make a mass pilgrimage to the Santuario de la Virgen de la Cabeza near Andújar, in Jaén province. A small statue of the Virgin is paraded about, exciting great passion. (p778)

May

A glorious time to be in Spain, May sees the countryside carpeted with spring wildflowers and the weather can feel like summer is just around the corner.

Feria del Caballo (Horse Fair)

A colourful equestrian fair in Andalucía's horse capital, Jerez de la Frontera, the Feria del Caballo is one of Andalucía's most festive and extravagant fiestas. It features parades, horse shows, bullfights and plenty of music and dance. (p684)

Córdoba's Courtyards Open Up

Scores of beautiful private courtyards in Córdoba are opened to the public for the Fiesta de los Patios de Córdoba. It's a rare chance to see an otherwise-hidden side of Córdoba, strewn with flowers and freshly painted. (p712)

Fiesta de San Isidro

Madrid's major fiesta celebrates the city's patron saint with bullfights, parades, concerts and more. Locals dress up in traditional costumes, and some of the events, such as the bullfighting season, last for a month. (p112)

Titirimundi International Puppet Festival

For a week in the middle of May, puppet shows take over Segovia with all manner of street events throughout the city to celebrate this fine festival. (p171)

World Music in Cáceres

Cáceres hosts the annual Womad, a fabulous festival dedicated to world music and drawing top-notch musicians from across the globe to perform in the city's medieval squares. (p609)

June

By June, the north is shaking off its winter chill and the Camino de Santiago's trails are becoming crowded. In

the south, it's warming up as the coastal resorts ready themselves for the summer onslaught.

Romería del Rocío

Focused on Pentecost weekend (the seventh after Easter), this festive pilgrimage is made by up to one million people to the shrine of the Virgin in El Rocío. This is Andalucía's Catholic tradition at its most curious and compelling. (p666)

Primavera Sound

One of Spain's biggest music festivals, Primavera Sound – in Barcelona over three days in late May or early June – lures a host of international DJs and musicians. (p295)

Corpus Christi

On the Thursday in the ninth week after Easter (sometimes May, sometimes June), religious processions and celebrations take place in Toledo and other cities. The strangest celebration is the baby-jumping tradition of Castrillo de Murcia. (p222)

Electronica Festival

Performers and spectators come from all over the world for Sónar, Barcelona's two-day celebration of electronic music, which is said to be Europe's biggest festival of its kind. Dates vary each year. (p295)

Noche Blanca del Flamenco

An all-night fest of top-notch flamenco by leading song, guitar and dance artists of the genre, in picturesque venues around Córdoba. All performances are free. It all happens on a Saturday night around 20 June. (p712)

Bonfires & Fireworks

Midsummer bonfires, fireworks and roaming giants feature on the eve of the Fiesta de San Juan (24 June; Dia de Sant Joan), notably along the Mediterranean coast, particularly in Barcelona and in Ciutadella, Menorca, where you can see splendid equestrian skills in parades. (p295)

Wine Battle

Haro, one of the premier wine towns of La Rioja, enjoys the Batalla del Vino on 29 June. Participants squirt wine all over the place in one of Spain's messiest playfights, pausing only to drink the good stuff. (p501)

July

Temperatures in Andalucía and much of the interior can be fiercely hot, but July is a great time to be at the beach and is one of the best months for hiking in the Pyrenees.

Córdoba Guitar Festival

Córdoba's contribution to Spain's impressive calendar of musical events, this fine international guitar festival ranges from flamenco and classical to rock, blues and beyond. Headline performances take place in the city's theatres. (p712)

Running of the Bulls

The Fiesta de San Fermín is the weeklong nonstop festival and party in Pamplona with the daily *encierro* (running of the bulls) as its centrepiece. PETA (www.peta.org.uk) organises eye-catching protests a couple of days before. (p486)

Celtic Pride

Groups from as far off as Nova Scotia come to celebrate their Celtic roots with the *gallegos* (Galicians) at Festival Ortigueira, a bagpipe- and fiddler-filled music fest held in Galicia. (p568)

Día de la Virgen del Carmen

Around 16 July in most coastal towns, particularly in El Puerto de Santa María and Nerja, the image of the patron of fisherfolk is carried into the sea or paraded on a flotilla of small boats. (p677)

Benicàssim Music Fest

Spain is awash with outdoor concert festivals attracting big-name acts from around the country and abroad, especially in summer. This one, in the Valencian town of Benicàssim, remains one of the original and best. (p819)

Santander Summer

Semana Grande in Santander (around 25 July) is this northern Spanish town's big summer blow-out, with music, shows and plenty of partying all day and all night. (p510)

Fiestas del Apóstol Santiago

The Día de Santiago (25 July) marks the day of Spain's national saint (St

James) and is spectacularly celebrated in Santiago de Compostela. With so many pilgrims around, it's the city's most festive two weeks of the year. (p564)

August

Spaniards from all over the country join Europeans in converging on the coastal resorts of the Mediterranean. Although the weather can be unpredictable, Spain's northwestern Atlantic coast offers a more nuanced summer experience.

Classical Drama in Mérida

The peerless Roman theatre and amphitheatre in Mérida, Extremadura, become the stage for the classics of ancient Greece and Rome, and the occasional newbie such as Will Shakespeare. Performances are held most nights during July and August. (p625)

Galician Wines

The fabulous wines of Galicia are the reason for the Festa do Albariño in Cambados on the first weekend of August. Expect five days of music, fireworks and intensive consumption of Galicia's favourite fruity white wine. (p584)

Crazy for Canoeing

The Descenso Internacional del Sella takes place in Asturias on the first weekend in August when tens of thousands of people go mad for a canoeing competition between Arriondas and Ribadesella. (p536)

Galician Octopus

Galicia's passion for octopus boils over at the Festa do Pulpo de O Carballiño on the second Sunday in August. Tens of thousands converge on the town of Carballiño to eat as much of the stuff as they can. (p596)

Barcelona Street Festival

Locals compete for the most elaborately decorated street in the popular week-long Festa Major de Gràcia, held around 15 August. People pour in to listen to bands in the streets and squares, fuel up on snacks, and drink at countless street stands. (p295)

Cipotegato

In the quiet Aragonese town of Tarazona, the locals every 27 August during Cipotegato re-create a local tradition whereby a prisoner could win their freedom by trying to outrun a stone- (or these days, a tomato-) throwing mob. (p413)

Natural Cider Festival

Gijón's Fiesta de la Sidra Natural gives expression to the Asturian obsession with cider and includes an annual world-record attempt for the number of people simultaneously pouring cider in one place. It also involves musical concerts. (p532)

La Tomatina

Buñol's massive tomato-throwing festival, held in late August, must be one of the messiest get-togethers in the country. Thousands of people launch about 100 tonnes of tomatoes at one another in just an hour or so! (p816)

September

This is the month when Spain returns to work after a seemingly endless summer. Numerous festivals take advantage of the fact that weather generally remains warm until late September at least.

Fiesta de la Virgen de Guadalupe

Pretty Guadalupe in Extremadura celebrates its very own Virgin Mary during the Fiesta de la Virgen de Guadalupe. A statue is paraded about on the evening of 6 September and again on 8 September, which also happens to be Extremadura's regional feast day. (p615)

Bienal de Flamenco

There are flamenco festivals all over Spain throughout the year, but this is the most prestigious of them all. Held in Seville in even-numbered years (and Málaga every other year), it draws the biggest names in the genre. (p651)

Romans & Carthaginians

In the second half of the month, locals dress up to re-enact ancient battles during the festival of Carthagineses y Romanos in Cartagena. It's among the more original mock battles staged around Spain to honour the distant past. (p840)

Human Castles in Tarragona

Tarragona's Festival de Santa Tecla is a wonderful

chance to see Catalonia's *castells* (human 'castles') in all their glory. Teams of castellers stand on each other's shoulders to build towers up to nine levels high. (p395)

San Sebastián Film Festival

It may not be Cannes, but San Sebastián's annual two-week celebration of film is one of the most prestigious dates on Europe's film-festival circuit. It's held in the second half of the month and has been gathering plaudits since 1957. (p468)

La Rioja's Grape Harvest

Logroño celebrates the feast day of St Matthew (Fiesta de San Mateo) and the year's grape harvest. There are grape-crushing ceremonies and endless opportunities to sample the fruit of the vine in liquid form. (p497)

Barcelona's Big Party

Barcelona's co-patron saint, the Virgin of Mercy, is celebrated with fervour in the massive four-day Festes de la Mercè in September. The city stages special exhibitions, free concerts and street performers galore. (p295)

October

Autumn can be a lovely time to be in Spain, with generally mild temperatures throughout the country, although the winter chill can start to bite in central and northern parts of the country.

Sitges International Film Festival

Early October brings to the Catalan coast the world's top festival of fantasy and horror films (www.sitgesfilmfestival.com). Latest release sci-fi and scary cinema is shown in venues across town.

Fiesta de Santa Teresa

The patron saint of Ávila is honoured with 10 days of processions, concerts and fireworks around her feast day. Huddled behind medieval walls, the festival brings to life the powerful cult of personality surrounding Ávila's most famous daughter. (p155)

Fiestas del Pilar

In Zaragoza on 12 October, the faithful mix with hedonists to celebrate this festival dedicated to Our Lady of the Pillar. Festivities peak with the Ofrenda de Flores (Offering of Flowers) around the Virgin's image from the Basilica, brought out on to Plaza del Pilar. (p408)

November

A quiet time on the festival calendar, November is cool throughout the country. Depending on the year, the ski season usually begins in this month in the Pyrenees and Sierra Nevada.

Bird Migration

On Catalonia's Costa Daurada, waterbirds arrive en masse to one of Spain's most important wetlands, the Delta de l'Ebre, where the mighty Río Ebro meets the Mediterranean. Flamingos are a highlight and while many arrive in October, it's in November that the spectacle is assured. (p399)

December

The weather turns cold, but Navidad (Christmas) is on its way. There are Christmas markets, *turrón* (nougat), a long weekend at the beginning of the month and a festive period that lasts until early January.

Navidad

The main Christmas family get-together is on the night of 24 December (Noche Buena) with much feasting. Although Spanish families now celebrate both Christmas Day (when Papa Noel brings presents) and Three Kings on 6 January, the latter was traditionally the main present-giving occasion.

Noche Vieja

At midnight on New Year's Eve, all eyes turn to the television as the 12 chimes are broadcast live from Madrid's Puerta del Sol and Spaniards young and old try to eat a grape for every chime of the clock as they ring out.

Itineraries

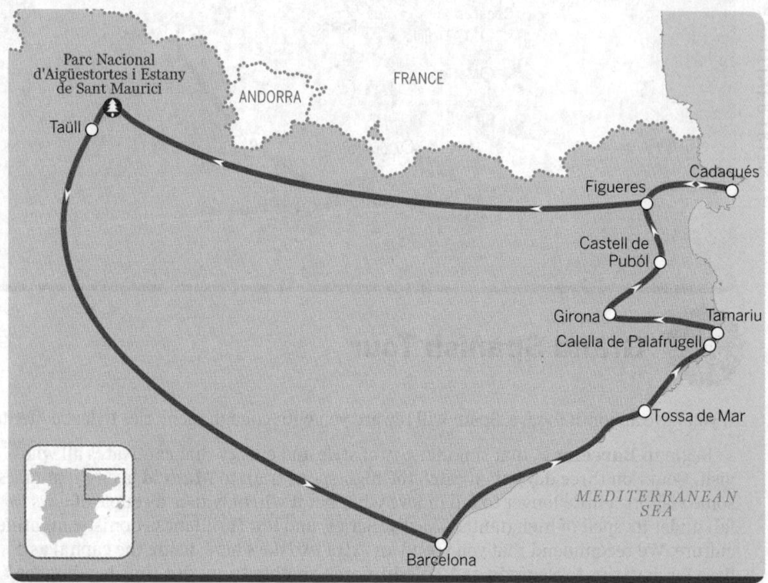

Barcelona & Around

A lifetime in Barcelona may not be enough, filled as it is with so many intensely wonderful experiences. But drag yourself away, and you'll soon discover that the wider Catalonia region is a brilliant place to explore.

You'll need a *minimum* of two days in **Barcelona** to soak up Gaudí, taste the city's culinary excellence and wander its old town. When you can tear yourself away, rent a car and head north, passing through **Tossa de Mar** and its castle-backed bay, then **Calella de Palafrugell** and **Tamariu**, two beautifully sited coastal villages, before heading inland to pass the night in wonderful **Girona**. The next day is all about Salvador Dalí, from his fantasy castle **Castell de Puból** to his extraordinary theatre-museum in **Figueres**, and then his one-time home, the lovely seaside village of **Cadaqués**. The next morning leave the Mediterranean behind and drive west in the shadow of the Pyrenees. Your reward for the long drive is a couple of nights in **Taüll**, gateway to the magnificent **Parc Nacional d'Aigüestortes i Estany de Sant Maurici**. A loop south via Lleida then east has you back in Barcelona by mid-afternoon on your final day.

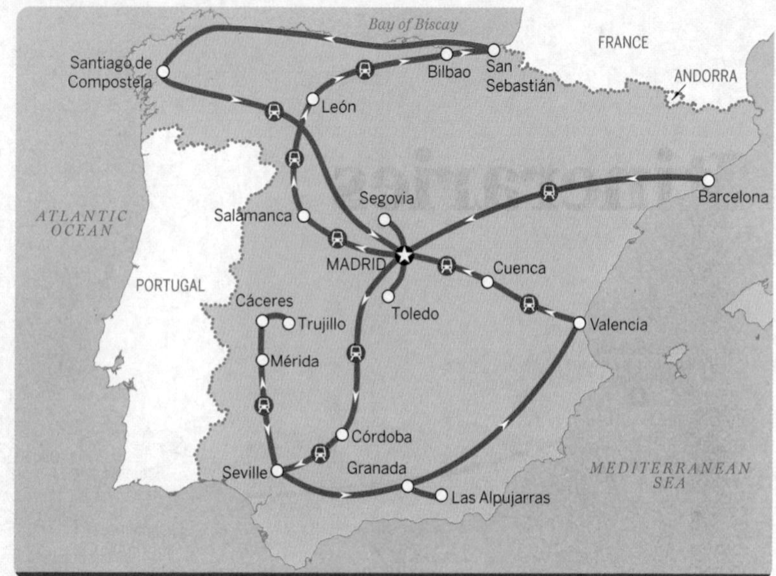

Grand Spanish Tour

If you have a month to give, Spain will reward you with enough memories to last a lifetime.

Begin in **Barcelona**, that singular city of style and energy that captivates all who visit. Count on three days, then catch the high-speed train to **Madrid**, a city that takes some visitors a little longer to fall in love with, but it will only take a couple of days to fall under its spell of high (fantastic art galleries) and low (brilliant hedonistic nightlife) culture. We recommend that you spend an extra two days here, using the capital as a base for day trips to **Segovia** and **Toledo**. Catch another train, this time heading for **Salamanca**, that plateresque jewel of Castilla y León. After a night in Salamanca, travel north by train to **León** to stay overnight and see the extraordinary stained-glass windows of its cathedral, and then continue on to **Bilbao**, home of the Museo Guggenheim Bilbao and so much that is good about Basque culture. Spend a night here, followed by another couple in splendid **San Sebastián**. A couple of days' drive on the Cantabrian, Asturian and Galician coasts will take you along Spain's most dramatic shoreline en route to **Santiago de Compostela**, where a couple of nights is a minimum to soak up this sacred city. Wherever you travel in the north, from San Sebastián to Santiago, make food a centrepiece of your visit.

Catch the train back to Madrid, then take a high-speed train to **Córdoba** for two nights and **Seville** for two nights. While you're in the area, detour north by bus or train to the Roman ruins of **Mérida** for a night, the fabulous old city of **Cáceres** for another night and medieval **Trujillo** for a third night. Return to Seville and make immediately for **Granada**; plan on two nights. Add an extra couple of nights and a rental car and you can visit the lovely villages of **Las Alpujarras**. Keep the car (or catch the train) and travel from Granada to **Valencia** to spend a couple of days enjoying its architecture, paella and irresistible energy. You've just enough time to catch the high-speed train to cliff-top **Cuenca** for a night on your way back to Madrid at journey's end.

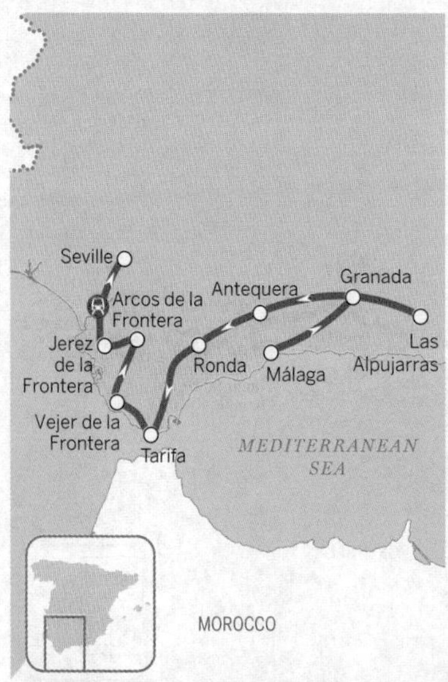

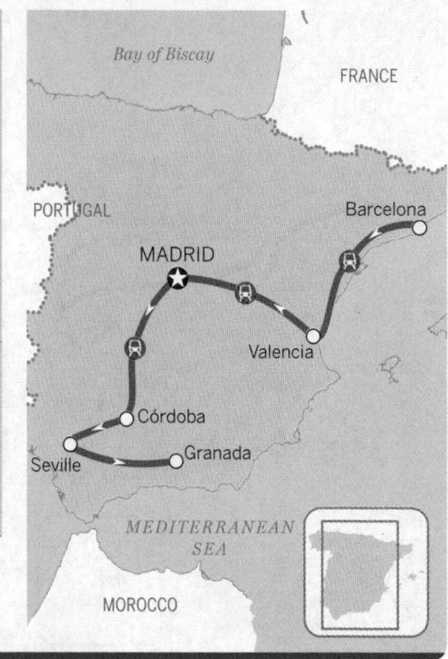

10 DAYS Andalucian Adventure

There's more to Andalucía than the monument-rich cities, although these are not to be missed. This route takes you through three iconic cities and some of the region's most beautiful villages. Begin in **Málaga**, whose airport receives flights from almost every conceivable corner of Europe. It has enough attractions to keep you occupied for one very full day. No Andalucian itinerary is complete without at least a couple of nights in peerless **Granada** with its astonishing Alhambra, gilded Capilla Real and medieval Muslim quarter of Albayzín. Rent a car and make for the other-worldly valleys of **Las Alpujarras** with their fine mountain scenery and North African–style villages. If you've kept the car, head west for three days along quiet back roads to some of Andalucía's most spectacular villages and towns: Mudéjar **Antequera**, spectacular **Ronda**, whitewashed **Tarifa**, beguiling **Vejer de la Frontera**, and **Arcos de la Frontera**, one of Andalucía's most glorious *pueblos blancos* (white villages). With three days left, leave the car and spend a night in **Jerez de la Frontera**, allowing time to visit its sherry bodegas, then catch a train north to flamenco-rich **Seville**, which is, for many, the essence of Andalucía.

2 WEEKS Essential Spain

If you want to understand why many visitors fall in love with Spain and never want to leave, look no further than its vibrant, passionate, extraordinarily beautiful cities. This itinerary takes you through the best Spain has to offer.

So many Spanish trails begin in **Barcelona**, Spain's second-biggest city and one of the coolest places on earth. Explore the architecture and sample the food, before catching the train down the coast to **Valencia** for a dose of paella, nightlife and the 21st-century wonders of the Ciudad de las Artes y las Ciencias. A fast train whisks you inland to the capital, mighty **Madrid**, for the irresistible street energy, the pretty plazas and one of the richest concentrations of art museums on the planet. Yet another fast train takes you deep into Andalucía, with **Córdoba** your entry point into this wonderful corner of Spain; the most obvious highlight is Córdoba's 8th-century Mezquita. From Córdoba it's a short hop to fabulous **Seville**. But we've saved the best until last: **Granada** boasts the extraordinary Alhambra, its soulful alter ego the Albayzín, and an eating and drinking scene that embraces Spanish culinary culture in all its variety.

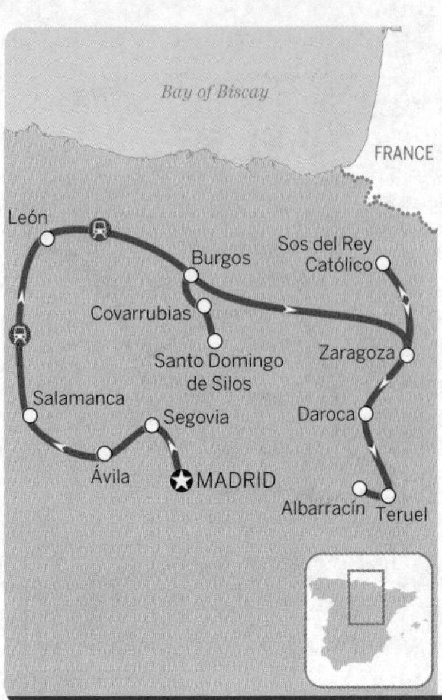

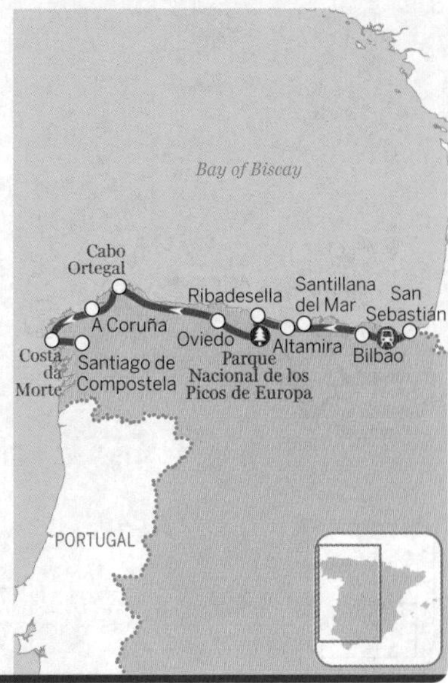

Castilla & Aragón

The Spanish interior may not fit the stereotype of sun, sand and sangría, but we love it all the more for that. This route takes in a stirring mix of lesser-known cities and stunning villages.

From **Madrid**, head to some of the loveliest towns of the Spanish heartland: **Segovia**, with its Disney-esque castle and Roman aqueduct, walled **Ávila** and vibrant **Salamanca** will occupy around four days of your time with short train rides connecting the three. Trains also connect you to **León** and **Burgos**, home to two of Spain's most extraordinary churches. Spend at least a day in each. An extra night in Burgos will allow you to take a day trip to the medieval villages of **Covarrubias** and **Santo Domingo de Silos**. Make for **Zaragoza**, one of Spain's most vibrant cities, with a wealth of monuments and great tapas – two days is a must. Rent a car and head for the hills where **Sos del Rey Católico** looks for all the world like a Tuscan hill town. Drive south for an overnight stop in dramatic **Daroca**, then on to **Teruel**, filled with Mudéjar gems. Finish your journey in **Albarracín**, one of Spain's most spectacular villages.

Northern Spain

Spain's Mediterranean Coast may get the crowds, but the country's northern coastline from San Sebastián to Santiago is one of the most spectacular in Europe.

There is no finer introduction to the north of the country than **San Sebastián**, with its dramatic setting and fabulous food. Two nights is a minimum. West of San Sebastián by train, **Bilbao** is best known as home to the showpiece Museo Guggenheim Bilbao and warrants at least a night, preferably two. To make the most of the rest of the coast, you'll need a car. Cantabria's cobblestone **Santillana del Mar**, the rock art at **Altamira** and the village of **Ribadesella** will fill one day, with another taken up by the steep valleys of the **Picos de Europa**. After a third night in irresistible **Oviedo**, tackle Galicia's coastline, one of Spain's great natural wonders, punctuated with secluded fishing villages and stunning cliffs. Don't miss **Cabo Ortegal**, dynamic **A Coruña** and the **Costa da Morte**. For the last two nights, linger in **Santiago de Compostela**, a thoroughly Galician city, a place of pilgrim footfalls, fine regional cuisine and a cathedral of rare power.

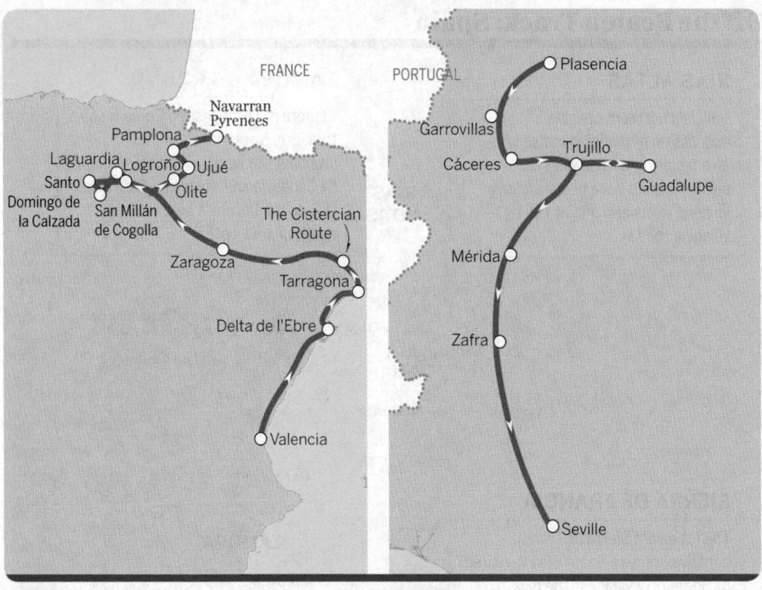

2 WEEKS Mediterranean to Mountains

This journey takes you from the shores of the Mediterranean to the deep valleys of the Pyrenees. You'll need a car to cover this in two weeks. Your reward is a chance to visit some of northwestern Spain's lesser-known jewels. Begin in **Valencia**, that most appealing of Mediterranean cities, then drive northeast, pausing in the flamingo-rich **Delta de l'Ebre** en route to **Tarragona**, one of Catalonia's most underrated destinations, with its fabulous Roman ruins. From Tarragona, head inland along the **Cistercian Route**, then cut through Aragón to vibrant and historic **Zaragoza**. After a couple of days in the Aragonese capital, and six days after leaving Valencia, pause overnight in the engaging provincial capital of **Logroño**. Continue west through the fine monastery towns of **Santo Domingo de la Calzada** and **San Millán de Cogolla** and then on into La Rioja, Spain's premier wine-producing region – **Laguardia** is a wonderful base. Head out into the eastern reaches of Navarra, for the beguiling fortress towns of **Olite** and **Ujué**, then on to pretty **Pamplona**. From here, climb into the **Navarran Pyrenees**, at their most beautiful in the Valle del Baztán and Valle del Roncal.

Extreme West

Extremadura is one of Spain's least known corners, which is all the more reason to visit.

Begin with a night in Extremadura's north, in **Plasencia**, which is jammed with notable buildings, churches and convents. From Plasencia, catch the bus or train to **Cáceres**, whose Ciudad Monumental is one of the finest surviving medieval cores in any Spanish city. After two nights here, including a half-day excursion to charming **Garrovillas**, regular buses take an hour to nearby **Trujillo**, a smaller but equally enchanting relic of the Middle Ages. Spend two nights here: one to explore the warren of cobbled lanes, and another to rent a car for a day trip to the charming hill town and pilgrims' destination of **Guadalupe**. From Trujillo it's just over an hour by bus south to **Mérida**, but the journey spans the centuries: Mérida boasts some of Spain's most impressive Roman ruins, and you'll need at least two nights here to take it all in. Further south again by bus across the plains lies whitewashed **Zafra**, a precursor to Andalucía in spirit, architecture and geography. After a night in Zafra, all roads lead to magical **Seville**, one of Andalucía's (and Spain's) most captivating cities.

Off the Beaten Track: Spain

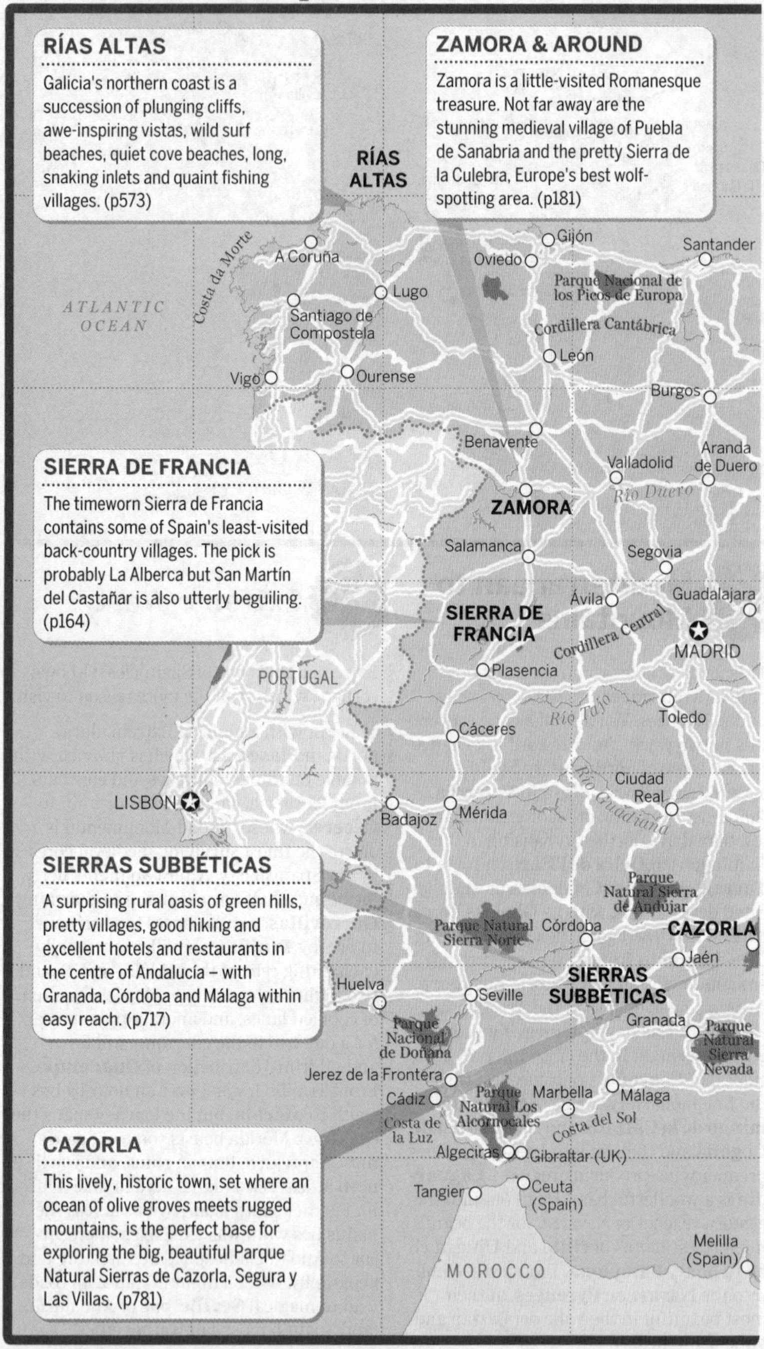

RÍAS ALTAS

Galicia's northern coast is a succession of plunging cliffs, awe-inspiring vistas, wild surf beaches, quiet cove beaches, long, snaking inlets and quaint fishing villages. (p573)

ZAMORA & AROUND

Zamora is a little-visited Romanesque treasure. Not far away are the stunning medieval village of Puebla de Sanabria and the pretty Sierra de la Culebra, Europe's best wolf-spotting area. (p181)

SIERRA DE FRANCIA

The timeworn Sierra de Francia contains some of Spain's least-visited back-country villages. The pick is probably La Alberca but San Martín del Castañar is also utterly beguiling. (p164)

SIERRAS SUBBÉTICAS

A surprising rural oasis of green hills, pretty villages, good hiking and excellent hotels and restaurants in the centre of Andalucía – with Granada, Córdoba and Málaga within easy reach. (p717)

CAZORLA

This lively, historic town, set where an ocean of olive groves meets rugged mountains, is the perfect base for exploring the big, beautiful Parque Natural Sierras de Cazorla, Segura y Las Villas. (p781)

0 200 km
0 100 miles

VALLES DE HECHO & ANSÓ

Among the least known but most beautiful of Spain's Pyrenean retreats, these twin valleys are laced with superb hikes, cosy lodgings and great meals. (p418)

CISTERCIAN ROUTE

The Cistercian Route weaves between three venerable monasteries that showcase some of Catalonia's most beautiful architecture – and the classy Priorat wine region is close by. (p398)

ALBARRACÍN

Hidden in a remote valley, pink-hued Albarracín preserves the aura of the middle ages like few villages in Spain, with remarkable monuments and wonderful spots to stay, eat and drink. (p442)

CABO DE GATA & ALMERÍA

The beach-and-cliff-strung Cabo de Gata promontory is dramatic, wild and an antidote to overdeveloped shorelines. Its gateway, Almería, is one of Spain's most agreeable smaller cities. (p790)

CARTAGENA

With a lovely waterfront and wonderful natural harbour in use for millennia, this port is one of Spain's most historically fascinating cities – an excellent surprise stop on the Mediterranean coast. (p838)

Tapas

Plan Your Trip

Eat & Drink Like a Local

For Spaniards, eating is one of life's more pleasurable obsessions. In this chapter, we'll help you make the most of this fabulous culinary culture, whether it's demystifying the dark art of ordering tapas or taking you on a journey through the regional specialities of Spanish food.

The Year in Food

Spain's relatively balmy climate ensures that, unusually for Europe, fruit and vegetables can be grown year-round.

Winter (Dec–Feb)

Across inland Spain, winter is the time for fortifying stews (such as *cocido* or *fabada*) and roasted meats, especially *cochinillo* (suckling pig) and *cordero* (spring lamb).

Winter to Spring (Nov–Apr)

Catalans salivate over *calçots*, those large spring onions that are eaten with your hands and a bib, and *romesco* (a rich red-peppers-and-ground-almond sauce). This is *pulpo* (boiled octopus) season in Galicia.

Summer (Jun–Aug)

The cold soups *gazpacho* and *salmorejo* (specialities of Andalucía) only appear in summer. Rice dishes by the Mediterranean are another key ingredient of the Spanish summer.

Autumn (Sep–Nov)

La Rioja's grape harvest gets underway in September. The Fiesta de San Mateo in Logroño (21 September) gets it all happening.

Food Experiences

Meals of a Lifetime

Arzak (p470) This San Sebastián restaurant is the home kitchen of Spain's most revered father-daughter team.

El Celler de Can Roca (p354) This Girona eatery represents everything that's good about innovative Catalan cuisine.

Tickets (p316) Barcelona restaurant headed by Albert Adrià, younger brother of Ferran, from the stable of Spain's most decorated chef.

La Terraza del Casino (p120) Located in Madrid, this is one of the country's temples to laboratory-led innovations.

Quique Dacosta (p828) Molecular gastronomy brought to the Mediterranean; in Denia.

DiverXo (p125) Madrid's only three-Michelín-starred eatery.

Food & Wine Festivals

Feria del Queso (p613) An orgy of cheese tasting and serious competition in Trujillo in late April or early May.

Feira do Viño do Ribeiro (p597) Ribadavia in Galicia's south hosts one of the region's biggest wine festivals on the first weekend of May.

Batalla del Vino (p501) A really messy wine fight, held on 29 June in Haro in La Rioja.

Festa do Pulpo de O Carballiño (p596) Carballiño in Galicia sees 70,000 people cram in for a mass octopus-eating binge on the second Sunday of August.

Fiesta de la Sidra Natural (p532) This August fiesta in Gijón includes an annual world-record attempt on the number of people simultaneously pouring cider.

Fiesta de San Mateo (p497) In Logroño, La Rioja's September grape harvest is celebrated with grape-crushing ceremonies and tastings.

Cheap Treats

Tapas or pintxos Possibly the world's most ingenious form of snacking. Madrid's La Latina *barrio* (district), Zaragoza's El Tubo and most Andalucian cities offer rich pickings, but a *pintxo* (Basque tapas) crawl in San Sebastián's Parte Vieja is one of life's most memorable gastronomic experiences.

Chocolate con churros These deep-fried doughnut strips dipped in thick hot chocolate are a Spanish favourite for breakfast, afternoon tea or at dawn on your way home from a night out. Madrid's Chocolatería de San Ginés (p126) is the most famous purveyor.

Bocadillos Rolls filled with *jamón* (cured ham) or other cured meats, cheese or (in Madrid) deep-fried calamari.

Pa amb tomaquet Bread rubbed with tomato, olive oil and garlic – a staple in Catalonia and elsewhere.

Cooking Courses

Alambique (p112) Cooking classes in Madrid covering Spanish and international themes.

Apunto (p112) Excellent range of cooking styles in Madrid.

L'Atelier (p747) Vegetarian cooking courses in Andalucía's Las Alpujarras.

Annie B's Spanish Kitchen (p698) Top-notch classes and courses in Spanish, Moroccan or seafood cuisine in Vejer de la Frontera.

Dare to Try

Oreja Pig's ear, cooked on the grill. It's a little like eating gristly bacon.

Callos Tripe cooked in a sauce of tomato, paprika, garlic and herbs. It's a speciality of Madrid.

Rabo de toro Bull's tail, or oxtail stew. It's a particular delicacy during bullfighting season in Madrid and Andalucía, when the tail comes straight from the bullring...

Percebes Goose barnacles from Galicia. The first person to try them sure was one adventurous individual, but we're glad they did.

Garrotxa Formidable Catalan cheese that almost lives up to its name.

Caracoles Snails. Much loved in Catalonia, Mallorca and Aragón.

Morcilla Blood sausage. It's blended with rice in Burgos, with onion in Asturias.

Criadillas Bull's testicles. Eaten in Andalucía.

Botillo Spanish version of haggis from Castilla y León's Bierzo region.

JAMÓN

There's no more iconic presence on the Spanish table than cured ham from the high plateau.

Jamón serrano, made from white-coated pigs, accounts for about 90% of cured ham in Spain. It's cured and dried in a climate-controlled shed for around a year.

Jamón ibérico, the elite of Spanish hams, comes from a black-coated pig indigenous to the Iberian Peninsula. Its star appeal is its ability to infiltrate fat into the muscles, producing an especially well-marbled meat. It's commonly eaten as a starter or *ración* (large tapa). Cutting it is an art form and it should be sliced so wafer-thin as to be almost transparent.

Local Specialities

Food

Spaniards love to travel in their own country, and given the riches on offer, they especially love to do so in pursuit of the perfect meal. Tell a Spaniard that you're on your way to a particular place and they'll probably start salivating at the mere thought of the local speciality, and they'll surely have a favourite restaurant at which to enjoy it.

Basque Country & Catalonia

The confluence of sea and mountains has bequeathed to the Basque Country an extraordinary culinary richness – seafood and steaks are the pillars upon which Basque cuisine was traditionally built. San Sebastián, in particular, showcases the region's diversity of culinary experiences and it was from the kitchens of San Sebastián that *nueva cocina vasca* (Basque nouvelle cuisine) emerged, announcing Spain's arrival as a culinary superpower.

Catalonia blends traditional Catalan flavours and expansive geographical diversity with an openness to influences from the rest of Europe. All manner of seafood, paella, rice and pasta dishes, as well as Pyrenean game dishes, are regulars on Catalan menus. Sauces are more prevalent here than elsewhere in Spain.

Inland Spain

The best *jamón ibérico* comes from Extremadura, Salamanca and Teruel, while *cordero asado lechal* (roast spring lamb) and *cochinillo asado* (roast suckling pig) are winter mainstays. Of the hearty stews, the king is *cocido,* a hotpot or stew with a noodle broth, carrots, cabbage, chickpeas, chicken, *morcilla* (blood sausage), beef and lard. *Migas* (breadcrumbs, often cooked with chorizo and served with grapes) are also regulars.

Percebes (goose barnacles)

Cheeses, too, are specialities here, from Extremadura's Torta del Casar (a creamy, spreadable cheese) to Castilla-La Mancha's *queso manchego* (a hard sheep's-milk cheese).

Galicia & the Northwest

Galicia is known for its bewildering array of seafood, and the star is *pulpo á feira* (spicy boiled octopus, called *pulpo a la gallega* or *pulpo gallego* in other parts of Spain), a dish whose constituent elements (octopus, oil, paprika and garlic) are so simple yet whose execution is devilishly difficult. Neighbouring Asturias and Cantabria produce Spain's best *anchoas* (anchovies).

In the high mountains of Asturias and Cantabria, the cuisine is as driven by mountain pasture as it is by the daily comings and goings of fishing fleets. Cheeses are particularly sought after, with special fame reserved for the untreated cow's-milk cheese *queso de Cabrales*. *Asturianos* (Asturians) are also passionate about their *fabada asturiana* (a stew made with pork, blood sausage and white beans) and *sidra* (cider) straight from the barrel.

Valencia, Murcia & the Balearic Islands

There's so much more to the cuisine of this region than oranges and paella, but these signature products capture the essence of the Mediterranean table. You can get a paella just about anywhere in Spain, but to get one cooked as it should be cooked, look no further than the restaurants in Valencia's waterfront Las Arenas district or La Albufera. In the Balearics, paella, rice dishes and lashings of seafood are similarly recurring themes.

Murcia's culinary fame brings us back to the oranges. The littoral is known simply as 'La Huerta' ('the garden'). Since Moorish times, this has been one of Spain's most prolific areas for growing fruit and vegetables.

Andalucía

Seafood is a consistent presence the length of the Andalucían coast. Andalucíans are famous above all for their *pescaito frito* (fried fish). A particular speciality of Cádiz, fried fish Andalucian-style means that just about anything that emerges from the sea is rolled in chickpea and wheat flour,

SECRETS OF PAELLA

Traditional Valencian paellas can have almost any ingredients, varying by region and season. The base always includes short-grain rice, garlic, olive oil and saffron. The best rice is *bomba*, which opens accordion-like when cooked, allowing for maximum absorption while remaining firm. Paella should be cooked in a large shallow pan to enable maximum contact with flavour. And for the final touch of authenticity, the grains on the bottom (and only those) should have a crunchy, savoury crust known as the *socarrat*.

Restaurants should take around 20 minutes or more to prepare rice dishes. They're usually for a minimum of two, though some places will do one for a solo diner if asked.

shaken to remove the surplus, then deep-fried ever so briefly in olive oil, just long enough to form a light, golden crust that seals the essential goodness of the fish or seafood within.

In a region where summers can be fierce, there's no better way to keep cool than with a *gazpacho andaluz* (Andalucian gazpacho), a cold soup with many manifestations. The base is almost always tomato, cucumber, vinegar and olive oil.

Wine

All of Spain's autonomous communities, with the exceptions of Asturias and Cantabria, are home to recognised wine-growing areas.

La Rioja, in the north, is Spain's best-known wine-producing region. The principal grape of Rioja is the tempranillo, widely believed to be a mutant form of the pinot noir. Its wine is smooth and fruity, seldom as dry as its supposed French counterpart. Look for the 'DOC Rioja' classification on the label and you'll find a good wine.

Not far behind are the wine-producing regions of Ribera del Duero (in Castilla y León), Navarra, Somontano (Aragón), and Valdepeñas in southern Castilla-La Mancha, which is famous for its quantities rather than quality, but is generally well priced and remains popular.

For white wines, the Ribeiro wines of Galicia are well regarded. Also from the area is one of Spain's most charming whites – albariño. This crisp, dry and refreshing drop is unusual, designated as it is by grape rather than region.

The Penedès region in Catalonia produces whites and sparkling wine such as *cava*, the traditional champagne-like toasting drink of choice for Spaniards at Christmas.

Wine Classifications

Spanish wine is subject to a complicated system of classification. If an area meets certain strict standards for a given period, covering all aspects of planting, cultivating and ageing, it receives Denominación de Origen (DO; Denomination of Origin) status. There are currently over 60 DO-recognised wine-producing areas in Spain.

An outstanding wine region gets the much-coveted Denominación de Origen Calificada (DOC), a controversial classification that some in the industry argue should apply only to specific wines, rather than every wine from within a particular region. At present, the only DOC wines come from La Rioja in northern Spain and the small Priorat area in Catalonia.

The best wines are often marked with the designation '*crianza*' (aged for one year in oak barrels), '*reserva*' (aged for two years, at least one of which is in oak barrels) and '*gran reserva*' (two years in oak and three in the bottle).

Sherry

Sherry, the unique wine of Andalucía, is Spain's national dram and is found in almost every bar, *tasca* (tapas bar) and restaurant in the land. Dry sherry, called *fino*, begins as a fairly ordinary white wine of the palomino grape, but it's 'fortified' with grape brandy. This stops fermentation and gives the wine taste and smell constituents that enable it to age into something sublime. It's taken as an *aperitivo* (aperitif) or as a table wine with seafood. *Amontillado* and *oloroso* are sweeter sherries, good for after dinner. *Manzanilla* is produced only in Sanlúcar de Barrameda near the coast in southwestern Andalucía and develops a slightly salty taste that's very appetising. It's possible to visit bodegas (wineries) in Sanlúcar, as well as in Jerez de la Frontera and El Puerto de Santa María.

How to Eat & Drink

Having joined Spaniards around the table for years, we've come to understand what eating Spanish-style is all about. If we could distil the essence of how to make food a highlight of your trip into a few simple rules, they would be these: always ask for the local speciality; never be shy about looking around to see what others have ordered before choosing; always ask the waiter for their recommendations; and, wherever possible, make your meal a centrepiece of your day.

When to Eat

Breakfast

Desayuno (breakfast) Spanish-style is generally a no-nonsense affair taken at a bar mid-morning or on the way to work. A *café con leche* (half coffee and half milk) with a *bollo* (pastry) or croissant is the typical breakfast. Another common breakfast order is a *tostada,* which is simply buttered toast.

In hotels, breakfast can begin as early as 6.30am and may continue until 10am (usually later on weekends).

Lunch

Lunch (*comida* or *almuerzo*) is the main meal of the day. During the working week few Spaniards have time to go home for lunch, so most people end up eating in restaurants, and all-inclusive three-course meals (*menús del día*) are as close as they can come to eating home-style food without breaking the bank. On weekends or in summer, Spaniards are not averse to lingering for hours over a meal with friends and family.

Lunch rarely begins before 2pm (restaurant kitchens usually open from 1.30pm until 4pm).

Dinner

Dinner (*cena*) is usually a lighter meal, although that may differ on weekends. Going out for a drink and some tapas is a popular way of eating dinner in many cities.

It does vary from region to region, but most restaurants open from 8.30pm to midnight, later on weekends.

Vegetarians & Vegans

Such is their love for meat, fish and seafood, many Spaniards, especially the older generation, don't really understand vegetarianism. As a result, dedicated vegetarian restaurants are still pretty thin on the ground outside the major cities.

That said, while vegetarians – especially vegans – can have a hard time, and while some cooked vegetable dishes can contain ham, the eating habits of Spaniards are changing; an ever-growing selection of vegetarian restaurants is springing up around the country. Barcelona and Madrid, in particular, have plenty of vegetarian restaurants to choose from.

Otherwise, salads are a Spanish staple and often are a meal in themselves. You'll also come across the odd vegetarian paella, as well as dishes such as *verduras a la plancha* (grilled vegetables); *garbanzos con espinacas* (chickpeas and spinach); and potato dishes, such as *patatas bravas* (potato chunks bathed in a slightly spicy tomato sauce) and *tortilla de patatas* (potato and onion omelette). The prevalence of legumes ensures that *lentejas* (lentils) and *judías* (beans) are also easy to track down, while *pan* (bread), *quesos* (cheeses), *alcachofas* (artichokes) and *aceitunas* (olives) are always easy to find. *Tascas* (tapas bars) usually offer more vegetarian choices than sit-down restaurants.

If vegetarians feel like a rarity among Spaniards, vegans will feel as if they've come from another planet. To make sure that you're not misunderstood, ask if dishes contain *huevos* (eggs) or *productos lácteos* (dairy).

THE TRAVELLER'S FRIEND: MENÚ DEL DÍA

One great way to cap prices at lunchtime on weekdays is to order the *menú del día,* a full three-course set menu, water, bread and wine. These meals are priced from around €10, although €12 and up is increasingly the norm. You'll be given a menu with a choice of five or six starters, the same number of mains and a handful of desserts – you choose one from each category; it's possible to order two starters, but not two mains.

Spain's Foodie Highlights

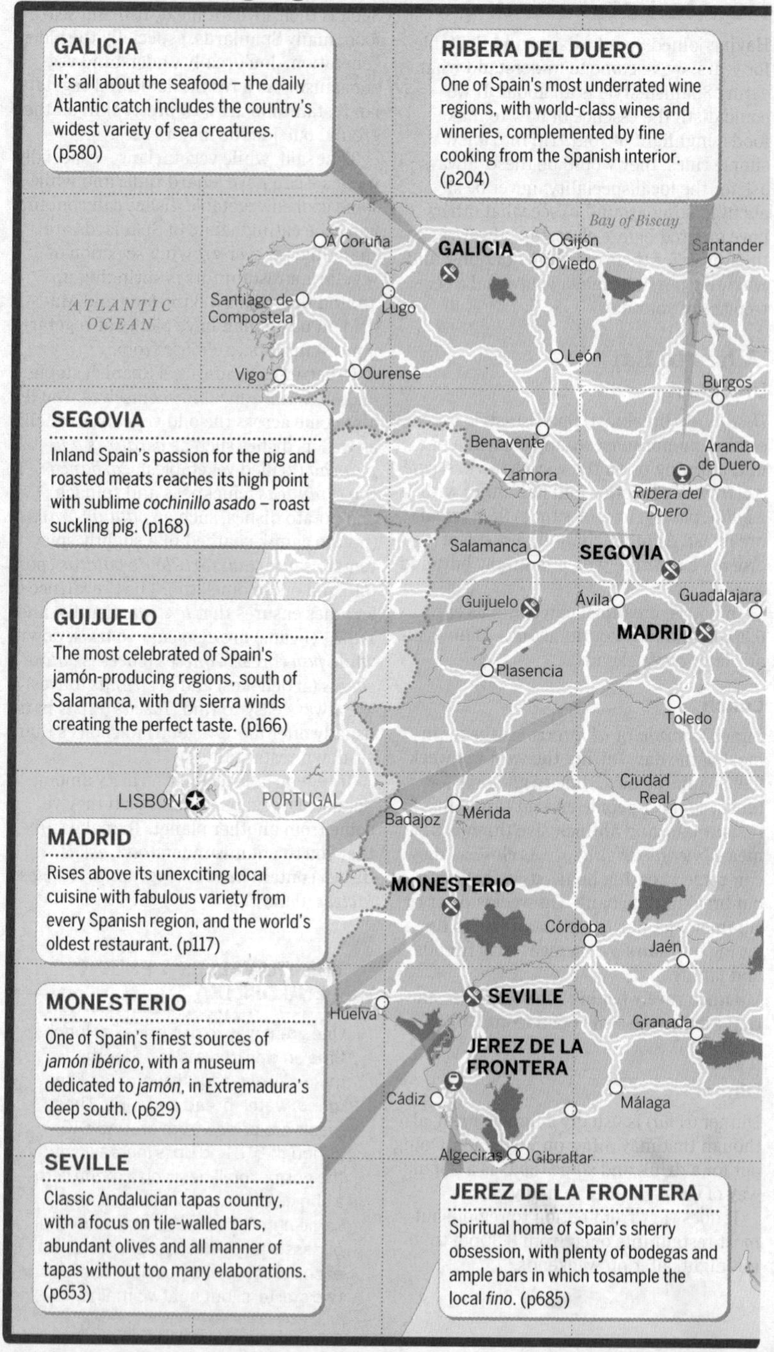
GALICIA
It's all about the seafood – the daily Atlantic catch includes the country's widest variety of sea creatures. (p580)
RIBERA DEL DUERO
One of Spain's most underrated wine regions, with world-class wines and wineries, complemented by fine cooking from the Spanish interior. (p204)
SEGOVIA
Inland Spain's passion for the pig and roasted meats reaches its high point with sublime *cochinillo asado* – roast suckling pig. (p168)
GUIJUELO
The most celebrated of Spain's jamón-producing regions, south of Salamanca, with dry sierra winds creating the perfect taste. (p166)
MADRID
Rises above its unexciting local cuisine with fabulous variety from every Spanish region, and the world's oldest restaurant. (p117)
MONESTERIO
One of Spain's finest sources of *jamón ibérico*, with a museum dedicated to *jamón*, in Extremadura's deep south. (p629)
SEVILLE
Classic Andalucian tapas country, with a focus on tile-walled bars, abundant olives and all manner of tapas without too many elaborations. (p653)
JEREZ DE LA FRONTERA
Spiritual home of Spain's sherry obsession, with plenty of bodegas and ample bars in which tosample the local *fino*. (p685)
Bay of Biscay
ATLANTIC OCEAN
A Coruña
GALICIA
Gijón
Oviedo
Santander
Santiago de Compostela
Lugo
León
Vigo
Ourense
Burgos
Benavente
Aranda de Duero
Zamora
Ribera del Duero
Salamanca
SEGOVIA
Guijuelo
Ávila
Guadalajara
MADRID
Plasencia
Toledo
Ciudad Real
LISBON
PORTUGAL
Badajoz
Mérida
MONESTERIO
Córdoba
Jaén
SEVILLE
Huelva
Granada
JEREZ DE LA FRONTERA
Cádiz
Málaga
Algeciras
Gibraltar

0 200 km
0 100 miles
SAN SEBASTIÁN
Has more Michelin stars per capita than any city on earth, and a peerless *pintxo* (Basque tapas) smorgasbord in the old town. (p469)
LA RIOJA
Spain's most celebrated wine region in the country's northeast, with an emphasis on quality reds. (p496)
SAN SEBASTIÁN
FRANCE
Bilbao
Vitoria-Gasteiz
Pamplona
ANDORRA
Logroño
LA RIOJA
Huesca
ANDORRA LA VELLA
Girona
Soria
Zaragoza
Lleida
BARCELONA
Tarragona
Golfo de Valencia
Teruel
Cuenca
Menorca
Mallorca
Maó
Palma de Mallorca
VALENCIA
Balearic Islands (Islas Baleares)
Ibiza
Albacete
Ibiza Town
Formentera
Alicante
BARCELONA
Extraordinarily rich gastronomic city and the showpiece for the superb concoctions of Catalan cooking. (p301)
Murcia
Cartagena
MEDITERRANEAN SEA
Almería
ALGIERS
VALENCIA
Paella's homeland is still the place to go for the country's best paella, whether the traditional one served with beans, rabbit and chicken, or one with seafood. (p807)
ALGERIA

ORDERING TAPAS

In the Basque Country and many bars in Madrid, Barcelona, Zaragoza and elsewhere, it couldn't be easier. With tapas varieties lined up along the bar, you either take a small plate and help yourself or point to the morsel you want.

Otherwise, many places have a list of tapas, either on a menu or posted up behind the bar.

Another way of eating tapas is to order *raciones* (literally 'rations'; large tapas servings) or *media raciones* (half-rations). After a couple of *raciones* you'll be full. In some bars you'll also get a small (free) tapa when you buy a drink.

Drinking Etiquette

Wherever you are in Spain, there'll be a bar close by. More than just places to drink, bars are centres of community life. Spaniards drink often and seem up for a drink almost any time of the day or night, but they rarely do so to excess; drinking is rarely an end in itself, but rather an accompaniment to good conversation, food or music. Perhaps they've learned that pacing themselves is the key to lasting until dawn – it's a key strategy to make the most of your Spanish night.

Where to Eat & Drink

asador Restaurant specialising in roasted meats.

bar de copas Gets going around midnight and serves hard drinks.

casa de comidas Basic restaurant serving well-priced home cooking.

cervecería The focus is on *cerveza* (beer) on tap.

horno de asador Restaurant with a wood-burning roasting oven.

marisquería Bar or restaurant specialising in seafood.

restaurante Restaurant.

taberna Usually a rustic place serving tapas and *raciones* (large tapas).

tasca Tapas bar.

terraza Open-air bar, for warm-weather tippling and tapas.

vinoteca Wine bars where you can order by the glass.

Menu Decoder

a la parrilla grilled

asado roasted or baked

bebidas drinks

carne meat

carta menu

casera homemade

ensalada salad

entrada entrée or starter

entremeses hors d'oeuvres

frito fried

menú usually refers to a set menu

menú de degustación tasting menu

pescado fish

plato combinado main-and-three-veg dish

postre dessert

raciones large-/full-plate-size serving of tapas

sopa soup

White-water rafting (p417), Aragón

Plan Your Trip

Outdoor Activities

Spain's landscapes are almost continental in their scale and variety, and they provide the backdrop to some of Europe's best hiking, most famously the Camino de Santiago. Skiing is another big draw, as are cycling, water sports, river-rafting and wildlife-watching, among other stirring outdoor pursuits.

Best Hiking

Aragón

Parque Nacional de Ordesa y Monte Perdido (June to August): the best of the Pyrenees and Spain's finest hiking.

Catalonia

Parc Nacional d'Aigüestortes i Estany de Sant Maurici (July to September): glacial lakes and mountains make a stunning backdrop to this wilderness landscape.

Cantabria & Asturias

Picos de Europa (June to August): a close second to the Pyrenees for Spain's best hiking.

Andalucía

Sierra Nevada (July to mid-September): remote peaks and snow-white villages in the Alpujarras valleys.

Pilgrimage

Camino de Santiago (Camino Francés; May to September): one of the world's favourite pilgrimages, across northern Spain from Roncesvalles to Santiago de Compostela.

Coast to Coast

GR11 (Senda Pirenáica; July and August): traverses the Pyrenees from the Atlantic to the Med.

Coastal Walks

Camiño dos Faros (May to September): an adventurous 200km trail along Galicia's spectacular Costa da Morte (Death Coast) from Malpica de Bergantiños to Cabo Fisterra.

Hiking

Spain is famous for superb walking trails that criss-cross mountains and hills in every corner of the country, from the alpine meadows of the Pyrenees to the sultry Cabo de Gata coastal trail in Andalucía. Other possibilities include conquering Spain's highest mainland peak, Mulhacén (3479m), in the Sierra Nevada above Granada; following in the footsteps of Carlos V in Extremadura; or walking along Galicia's Costa da Morte. And then there's one of the world's most famous pilgrimage trails – the route to the cathedral in Galicia's Santiago de Compostela.

When to Go

Spain encompasses a number of different climatic zones, ensuring that it's possible to hike year-round. In Andalucía conditions are at their best from March to June and in September and October; July and August are unbearable in most parts of the region (though they're the ideal months for the high Sierra Nevada). From December to February most trails remain open, except in the high mountains.

If you prefer to walk in summer, do what Spaniards have traditionally done and escape to the north. The Basque Country, Asturias, Cantabria and Galicia are best from June to September. Pyrenean passes are usually accessible from around mid-June until some time in October. August is the busiest month on the trails, so if you plan to head to popular national parks and stay in *refugios* (wilderness hostels), book ahead.

Hiking in the north can be splendid in September and into early October – the summer crowds have gone, there's (usually) still enough sunshine to go with the lovely autumn colours and there's plenty of room in the *refugios*.

Hiking Destinations

Pyrenees

For good reason, the Pyrenees, separating Spain from France, are Spain's premier walking destination. The range is utterly beautiful: prim and chocolate-box pretty on the lower slopes, wild and bleak at higher elevations, and relatively unspoilt compared to some European mountain ranges. The Pyrenees contain two outstanding national parks: Aigüestortes i Estany de Sant Maurici (p378) and Ordesa y Monte Perdido (p425). The former is home to the magnificent Carros de Foc (p380), a loop route that links nine major *refugios*.

The spectacular GR11 (Senda Pirenáica) traverses the range, connecting the Atlantic (at Hondarribia in the Basque Country) with the Mediterranean (at Cap de Creus in Catalonia). Walking the whole 35- to 50-day route is an unforgettable challenge, but there are also magnificent day hikes in the national parks and elsewhere.

Picos de Europa

Breathtaking and accessible limestone ranges with distinctive craggy peaks (usually hot rock-climbing destinations too) are the hallmark of Spain's first national park, the **Picos de Europa** (www.picosdeeuropa.com), which straddles the Cantabria, Asturias and León provinces and is firmly established as one of Spain's very best hiking areas.

A hiking itinerary known as **El Anillo de Picos** links together the Picos' most important *refugios* in several neat loops. Visit www.elanillodepicos.com for further details.

Elsewhere in Spain

To walk in mountain villages, the classic spot is Las Alpujarras (p743), near the Parque Nacional Sierra Nevada in Andalucía. The Sierras de Cazorla (p783) and Sierra de Grazalema (p690) are also outstanding. The long-distance GR7 trail traverses the first two of these regions – you can walk all or just part of the route, depending on your time and inclination.

Great coastal walking abounds, even in heavily visited areas such as the south coast.

In Galicia, the Camiño dos Faros (p570) is an adventurous 200km trail along the magnificent Costa da Morte from Malpica de Bergantiños to Cabo Fisterra (practicable in one direction only at the time of writing). Other excellent Galician routes include the Ruta Cañón do Río Mao (p599), a beautiful day hike in the inland Ribeira Sacra region, and the Camino Natural de la Ruta del Cantábrico (p582), a walking and biking trail running 154km along the northern coast from Ribadeo to the Ría de Ortigueira. The Camino Natural passes the famous Praia As Catedrais, among other places.

In Catalonia, the Parc Natural de la Zona Volcànica de la Garrotxa (p367) is another popular walking area with unique volcanic landscapes.

Another fine coastal path is the Camí de Ronda (p340), the coastal path that runs all the way up the Costa Brava and is really rather special in places.

Hiking in the Aragón Pyrenees (p417)

Information

For detailed info on walking routes in all of Spain's national parks, check out www.mapama.gob.es/es/red-parques-nacionales/nuestros-parques.

Region-specific walking (and climbing) guides are published by Cicerone Press (www.cicerone.co.uk).

Numerous bookshops around Spain sell guides and maps. The best Spanish guides are *Prames* and *Adrados*, while Editorial Alpina publishes excellent map series.

Camino de Santiago

The door is open to all, to sick and healthy, not only to Catholics but also to pagans, Jews, heretics and vagabonds.

So go the words of a 13th-century poem describing the Camino. Eight hundred years later these words still ring true. The Camino de Santiago (Way of St James) originated as a medieval pilgrimage and, for more than 1000 years, people have taken up the Camino's age-old symbols – the scallop shell and staff – and set off on

Pilgrims walking the Camino de Santiago

the adventure of a lifetime to the tomb of St James the Apostle, in Santiago de Compostela (p559), in the Iberian Peninsula's far northwest.

Today the most popular of the several *caminos* (paths) to Santiago de Compostela is the Camino Francés, which spans 775km of Spain's north from Roncesvalles (p489), on the border with France, to Santiago de Compostela in Galicia, and attracts walkers of all backgrounds and ages, from countries across the world. And no wonder: its list of assets (cultural, historical and natural) is impressive, as are its accolades. Not only is it the Council of Europe's first Cultural Itinerary and a Unesco World Heritage site but, for believers, it's a pilgrimage equal to visiting Jerusalem, and by finishing it you're guaranteed a healthy chunk of time off purgatory.

To feel, absorb, smell and taste northern Spain's diversity, for a great physical challenge, for a unique perspective on rural and urban communities, and to meet intriguing travel companions, this is an incomparable walk. *'The door is open to all'* ...so step on in.

History

In the 9th century a remarkable event occurred in the poor Iberian hinterlands: following a shining star, Pelayo, a religious hermit, unearthed the tomb of the apostle James the Greater (or, in Spanish, Santiago). The news was confirmed by the local bishop, the Asturian king and later the pope. Its impact is hard to truly imagine today, but it was instant and indelible: first a trickle, then a flood of Christian Europeans began to journey towards the setting sun in search of salvation.

Compostela became the most important destination for Christians after Rome and Jerusalem. Its popularity increased with an 11th-century papal decree granting it Holy Year status: pilgrims could receive a plenary indulgence – a full remission of your lifetime's sins – during a Holy Year. These occur when Santiago's feast day (25 July) falls on a Sunday: the next one is in 2021.

The 11th and 12th centuries marked the heyday of the pilgrimage. The Reformation was devastating for Catholic pilgrimages, and by the 19th century, the Camino had nearly died out. In its startling late 20th-century reanimation, which continues today, it's most popular as a personal and spiritual journey of discovery, rather than one necessarily motivated by religion.

Routes

Although in Spain there are many *caminos* (paths) to Santiago, by far the most popular is, and was, the Camino Francés, which originates in France, crosses the Pyrenees at Roncesvalles and then heads west for 775km across the regions of Navarra, La Rioja, Castilla y León and Galicia. Waymarked with cheerful yellow arrows and scallop shells, the 'trail' is a mishmash of rural lanes, paved secondary roads and footpaths all strung together. Starting at Roncesvalles, the Camino takes roughly two weeks to cycle or five weeks to walk.

But this is by no means the only route, and the summer crowds along the Camino Francés have prompted some to look at alternative routes: in 2005, nearly 85% of walkers took the Camino Francés; by 2016 this had fallen to 63% and four alternative routes were added to the Camino de Santiago's Unesco World Heritage listing in 2015. Increasingly popular routes include the following:

Camino de la Costa/Camino del Norte From Irún along the coasts of the Basque Country, Cantabria and Asturias, then across Galicia to Santiago.

Camino Vasco-Riojano An alternative start to the Camino Francés, beginning in Irún.

Camino Primitivo Links the Camino del Norte (from Oviedo) with Melide along the main Camino Francés.

ROCK CLIMBING

Spain offers plenty of opportunities to see the mountains and gorges from a more vertical perspective. Vie ferrate are growing fast in number and in popularity around Spain. A good source for info is the excellent (but Spanish-only) site http://deandar.com.

For an overview of Spanish rock climbing, check out the Spain information on the websites of Rockfax (www.rockfax.com) and Climb Europe (www.climb-europe.com). Both include details on the best climbs in the country. Rockfax also publishes various climbing guidebooks covering Spain.

Camino Lebaniego From either Santander or San Vicente Barquera to the important Monasterio de Santo Toribio de Liébana in Cantabria; not actually a Camino de Santiago but part of the Unesco listing nonetheless.

Camino Portugués North to Santiago through Portugal.

Vía de la Plata From Andalucía north through Extremadura, Castilla y León and on to Galicia.

A very popular alternative is to walk only the last 100km from Sarria in Galicia. This is the minimum distance allowed in order to earn a Compostella certificate of completion given out by the Catedral de Santiago de Compostela.

Camino Francés

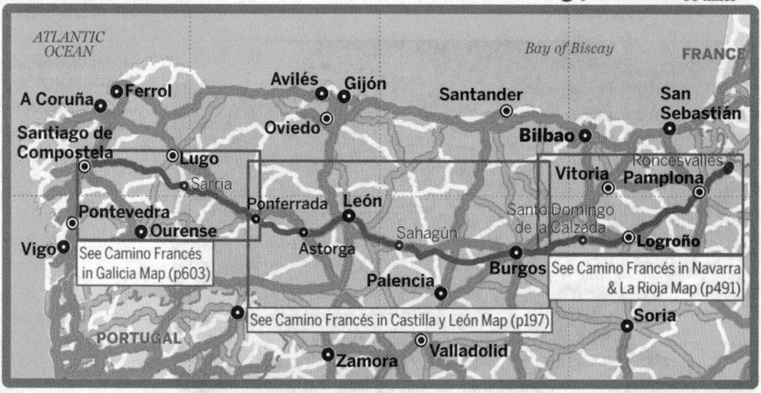

See Camino Francés in Galicia Map (p603)
See Camino Francés in Castilla y León Map (p197)
See Camino Francés in Navarra & La Rioja Map (p491)

TONO BALAGUER / SHUTTERSTOCK ©

Top: Mountain biking, Sierra Nevada (p742)

Bottom: Signage on the Camino de Santiago

Another possibility is to continue on beyond Santiago to the dramatic 'Lands End' outpost of Fisterra (Finisterre), an extra 88km, or Muxia (a further 30km still), which is considered sacred by pilgrims as it was here that the Virgin appeared (in a stone boat) before Santiago.

Information

For more information about the Credencial (like a passport for the Camino, in which pilgrims accumulate stamps at various points along the route) and the Compostella certificate, visit the website of the cathedral's Centro Internacional de Acogida al Peregrino (p567).

If you're in Santiago, the Museo das Peregrinacións e de Santiago (p563), almost alongside the cathedral, provides fascinating insights into the phenomenon of Santiago (man and city) down the centuries.

There are a number of excellent Camino websites:

Camino de Santiago (http://santiago-compostela.net) Extensive info on Camino routes as well as maps.

Mundicamino (www.mundicamino.com) Excellent, thorough descriptions and maps.

Camino de Santiago (www.caminodesantiago.me) Contains a huge selection of news groups, where you can get all of your questions answered.

When to Walk

People walk and cycle the Camino year-round. In May and June the wildflowers are glorious and the endless fields of cereals turn from green to toasty gold, making the landscapes a huge draw. July and August bring crowds of summer holidaymakers and scorching heat, especially through Castilla y León. September is less crowded and the weather is generally pleasant. From November to May there are fewer people on the road as the season can bring snow, rain and bitter winds. Santiago's feast day, 25 July, is a popular time to converge on the city.

National & Natural Parks

Much of Spain's most spectacular and ecologically important terrain – about 40,000 sq km or 8% of the entire country, if you include national hunting reserves – is under some kind of official protection. Nearly all of these areas are at least partly open to walkers, naturalists and other outdoor enthusiasts, but degrees of conservation and access vary.

The *parques nacionales* (national parks) are areas of exceptional importance and are the country's most strictly controlled protected areas. Spain has 15 national parks: 10 on the mainland, four in the Canary Islands and one in the Balearic Islands. The hundreds of other protected areas fall into at least 16 classifications and range in size from 100-sq-metre rocks off the Balearics to Andalucía's 2099-sq-km Parque Natural de Cazorla. For more information, visit www.mapama.gob.es/es/red-parques-nacionales/nuestros-parques.

Cycling

Spain has a splendid variety of cycling possibilities, from gentle family rides to challenging two-week expeditions. If you avoid the cities (where cycling can be nerve-racking), Spain is also a cycle-friendly country, with drivers accustomed to sharing the roads with platoons of Lycra-clad cyclists. The excellent network of secondary roads, usually with comfortable shoulders to ride on, is ideal for road touring.

Every Spanish region has both off-road (called BTT in Spanish, from *bici todo terreno,* meaning 'mountain bike') and touring

PILGRIM HOSTELS

There are over 300 *refugios* (simple hostels) along the Camino Francés, and numerous *refugios* on the other *caminos*. These are owned by parishes, 'friends of the Camino' associations, private individuals, town halls and regional governments. While in the early days these places were run on donations and provided little more than hot water and a bed, today's pilgrims are charged €5 to €10 and expect showers, kitchens and washing machines. Some things haven't changed though – the *refugios* still operate on a first-come, first-served basis and are intended for those doing the Camino solely under their own steam.

La Molina ski resort (p57), Catalonia

trails and routes. Mountain bikers can head to just about any sierra (mountain range) and use the extensive *pistas forestales* (forestry tracks).

In Aragón, the valleys, hills and canyons of the Sobrarbe district around Aínsa in the Pyrenees foothills are a mountain-biking paradise, with 500km of off-road tracks, many of them waymarked for riders. Here, the Zona Zero (p429) project provides masses of information and brings together service-providers such as bike-friendly accommodation, repair shops, guides and bike-transport services. Most riders bring their own bikes but there are a couple of rental outlets in Aínsa.

Galicia has set up several Centros BTT in rural areas with bikes and helmets for rent, and signposted routes in the local areas, including one in the very scenic Ribeira Sacra area. For more information, check www.turismo.gal/que-facer/centros-btt.

One highly recommended and challenging off-road excursion takes you across the snowy Sierra Nevada. Classic long-haul touring routes include the Camino de Santiago, the Ruta de la Plata and the 600km Camino del Cid, which follows in the footsteps of Spain's epic hero, El Cid, from Burgos to Valencia. Guides in Spanish exist for all of these, available at bookshops and online.

For something a little less challenging, head to the Senda del Oso, a popular, easy cycling route in Asturias. Mallorca is another popular cycling destination, with cyclists ranging from ordinary travellers to Bradley Wiggins, 2012 Tour de France winner, who trains on the mountain roads of the Serra de Tramuntana.

Information

Bike Spain (p111) in Madrid is one of the better cycling tour operators.

Most of the cycling guidebooks in publication are in Spanish:

- *España en bici*, by Paco Tortosa and María del Mar Fornés. A good overview guide, but quite hard to find.
- *Cycle Touring in Spain: Eight Detailed Routes*, by Harry Dowdell. A helpful planning tool; also practical once you're in Spain.
- *The Trailrider Guide – Spain: Single Track Mountain Biking in Spain*, by Nathan James and Linsey Stroud. Another good resource.

Surfers, Costa de la Luz (p697)

Skiing & Snowboarding

For winter powder, Spain's skiers (including the royal family) head to the Pyrenees of Aragón and Catalonia. Outside the peak periods (the beginning of December, 20 December to 6 January, Carnaval and Semana Santa), Spain's top resorts are relatively quiet, cheap and warm in comparison with their counterparts in the Alps.

The season runs from December to April, though January and February are generally the best, most reliable times for snow. However, in recent years snowfall has been a bit unpredictable.

In Aragón, two popular resorts are Formigal (p420) and Candanchú (p420). Just above the town of Jaca, Candanchú has some 60km of varied pistes (as well as 35km of cross-country track) and 25 lifts. In Catalonia, Spain's first resort, **La Molina** (www.lamolina.cat; day pass adult/child €38/30; ⊙mid-Nov–Apr), is still going strong and is ideal for families and beginners. Nearby, **Masella** is another fine ski resort and linked to La Molina by a lift. **Espot** (☎973 62 40 58; www.espotesqui.cat; Espot; day pass adult/child €32/26; ⊙Dec-Mar) and Nuria (p371) are two smaller Catalan ski resorts. Considered by many to have the Pyrenees' best snow, the 72-piste resort of Baqueira-Beret-Bonaigua (p384) boasts 30 modern lifts and 104km of downhill runs for all levels.

Spain's other major resort is Europe's southernmost: the Sierra Nevada (p742), outside Granada. The 106km of runs here are at their prime in March, and the slopes are particularly suited for families and novice-to-intermediate skiers.

Surfing

The opportunity to get into the waves is a major attraction for beginners and experts alike along many of Spain's coastal regions. The north coast of Spain has, debatably, the best surf in mainland Europe.

The main surfing region is the north coast, where numerous high-class spots can be found, but Atlantic Andalucía gets decent winter swells. Despite the flow of vans loaded down with surfboards along the north coast in the summer, it's actually autumn through to spring that's the prime time for a decent swell, with October probably the best month overall. The variety of waves along the north coast is impressive: there are numerous open, swell-exposed beach breaks for the summer months, and some seriously heavy reefs and points that only really come to life during the colder, stormier months.

VÍAS VERDES

Spain has a growing network of Vías Verdes (literally 'Green Ways', but equivalent to the 'rail trail' system in other countries), an outstanding system of decommissioned railway tracks that have been converted into bicycle (or hiking) trails. They're usually terrific cycling routes with their gentle gradients, many pass through scenic countryside and there are many bikes for rent at various points along the routes. There are more than 2400km of these trails spread across (at last count) 111 routes all across the country, and they range from 1.2km to 128km in length. Check out www.viasverdes.com for more information.

SPAIN'S BEST PARKS

PARK	FEATURES	ACTIVITIES	BEST TIME TO VISIT
Parc Nacional d'Aigüestortes i Estany de Sant Maurici (p378)	beautiful Pyrenees lake region	walking, wildlife-watching	Jun-Sep
Parque Nacional de Doñana (p664)	bird and mammal haven in Guadalquivir delta	4WD tours, walking, wildlife-watching, horse riding	year-round
Parque Nacional de Ordesa y Monte Perdido (p425)	spectacular section of the Pyrenees, with chamois, raptors and varied vegetation	walking, rock climbing, birdwatching	mid-Jun–Jul & mid-Aug–Sep
Parque Nacional de los Picos de Europa (p546)	beautiful mountain refuge for chamois, and a few wolves and bears	walking, rock climbing	May-Jul & Sep
Parques Nacional & Natural Sierra Nevada (p742)	mainland Spain's highest mountain range, with ibexes, 60 types of endemic plants and the beautiful Alpujarras valleys on its southern slopes	walking, rock climbing, mountain-biking, skiing, horse riding	year-round, depending on activity
Parque Natural Sierras de Cazorla, Segura y Las Villas (p783)	abundant wildlife, 2300 plant species and beautiful mountain scenery	walking, driving, mountain-biking, wildlife-watching, 4WD tours	Apr-Oct
Parque Natural Sierra de Grazalema (p690)	lovely, green, mountainous area with rich bird life	walking, caving, canyoning, birdwatching, paragliding, rock climbing	Sep-Jun
Parc Natural del Cadí-Moixeró (p376)	steep pre-Pyrenees range	rock climbing, walking	Jun-Sep
Parc Natural de la Zona Volcànica de la Garrotxa (p367)	beautiful wooded region with 30 volcanic cones	walking	Apr-Oct
Parque Natural de Somiedo (p345)	dramatic section of Cordillera Cantábrica	walking	Jul-Sep
Parque Natural de Cabo de Gata-Níjar (p790)	sandy beaches, volcanic cliffs, flamingo colony and semidesert vegetation	swimming, birdwatching, walking, horse riding, diving, snorkelling	year-round
Parque Natural de los Valles Occidentales (p418)	superb Pyrenean valley and mountain scenery	walking, climbing, canyoning	Jun-Sep
Parque Natural Posets-Maladeta (p430)	spectacular mountain and valley scenery including the Pyrenees' two highest peaks	walking, climbing	Jun-Sep

The most famous wave in Spain is the legendary river-mouth left at Mundaka (p461). On a good day, there's no doubt that it's one of the best waves in Europe. However, it's not very consistent, and when it's on, it's always very busy and very ugly.

Heading east, good waves can be found throughout the Basque Country. Going west, into neighbouring regions of Cantabria and Asturias, you'll also find a superb range of well-charted surf beaches, such as Rodiles (p534) in Asturias and Liencres in Cantabria; Playa de Somo (p509) in Santander is another good spot.

Galicia's beaches are an increasingly popular surfing destination. Even so, if you're looking for solitude, some isolated beaches along Galicia's beautiful Costa da Morte (p568) remain empty even in summer. In the Rías Altas, Praia de Pantín (p579), close to Cedeira, has a popular right-hander and in late August or early September it hosts the Pantín Classic, a qualifying event in the World Surf League. There are also some summer surf schools in the area.

In southwest Andalucía there are a some powerful, winter beach breaks, particularly between Tarifa and Cádiz; El Palmar (p700), just northwest of Cabo de Trafalgar, is the pick of the bunch, while weekdays off Conil de la Frontera, a little further up the coast, can be sublimely lonely.

Information

In summer a shortie wetsuit (or, in the Basque Country, just board shorts) is sufficient along all coasts except Galicia, which picks up the icy Canaries current – you'll need a light full suit here.

Surf shops abound in the popular surfing areas and usually offer board and wetsuit hire. If you're a beginner joining a surf school, ask the instructor to explain the rules and to keep you away from the more experienced surfers.

There are a number of excellent surf guidebooks to Spain.

- Lonely Planet author Stuart Butler's English-language *Big Blue Surf Guide: Spain.*
- José Pellón's Spanish-language *Guía del Surf en España.*
- Low Pressure's superb *Stormrider Guide: Europe – the Continent.*

Kitesurfing & Windsurfing

The best sailing conditions are to be found around Tarifa (p700), which has such strong and consistent winds that it's said that the town's once-high suicide rate was due to the wind turning people mad. Whether or not this is true, one thing is without doubt: Tarifa's 10km of white, sandy beaches and perfect year-round conditions have made this small town the windsurfing capital of Europe. The town is crammed with windsurfing and kitesurfing shops and schools and a huge contingent of passing surfers. However, the same wind that attracts so many devotees also makes it a less than ideal place to learn the art. Nearby, Los Caños de Meca (p699) is another fine kitesurfing spot.

If you can't make it as far south as Tarifa, then the lesser-known Empuriabrava in

Kitesurfers, near Tarifa (p700), Andalucía

Catalonia also has great conditions, especially from March to July. Speaking of Catalonia, there's also a bit of kitesurfing in the Delta de L'Ebre area and in Castelldefels. Further south, the family resort of Oliva near Valencia and Murcia's Mar Menor are worth considering. If you're looking for waves, try Spain's northwest coast, where Galicia can have fantastic conditions.

Information

An excellent guidebook to windsurfing and kitesurfing spots across Spain and the rest of Europe is Stoked Publications' *The Kite and Windsurfing Guide: Europe.*

The Spanish-language website www.windsurfesp.com gives very thorough descriptions of spots, conditions and schools all over Spain.

Kayaking, Canoeing & Rafting

Opportunities abound in Spain for taking off downstream in search of white-water fun along its 1800 rivers and streams. As most rivers are dammed for electric power

ALTERNATIVE ACTIVITIES

So you'd like to try something a little more unexpected than plain old hiking, biking, kayaking or board-riding?

How about a few hours jumping, sliding and abseiling your way down a sheer-walled canyon? Look no further than Alquézar (p433) in Aragón, one of Europe's prime locations for the sport of **canyoning** – also possible around Torla (Aragón) and Cangas de Onís (Picos de Europa), in the Sierra de Grazalema in Cádiz province, and in the Pallars Sobirà area in the Catalan Pyrenees.

Or take to the skies as a paraglider. Top flying locations include Castejón de Sos (p431) in Aragón and El Yelmo in Andalucía's Parque Natural Sierras de Cazorla, Segura y Las Villas. The Real Federación Aeronáutica España (www.rfae.es) lists clubs and events. Algodonales on the edge of Andalucía's Sierra de Grazalema is another top flying location. Paragliding Map (www.paraglidingmap.com) is good for current information on conditions at flying spots.

Though Spain doesn't have the teeming warm seas of tropical diving locations, there's still plenty of marine life in its seas, plus features such as wrecks and long cavern swim-throughs. Mediterranean dive centres cater mostly to an English-speaking market. A good starting point is the Illes Medes marine reserve (p356), off L'Estartit near Girona. Southern Spain's best diving and snorkelling is around Cabo de Gata in Andalucía, followed by Cabo de Palos in Murcia. Atlantic dive centres (in San Sebastián, Santander and A Coruña) deal mostly in Spanish: their colder waters offer a completely different, and very rewarding, underwater experience.

Like to stay on top of the water, standing on a board? Stand-up paddling (SUP) is a trend in Santander, along the Catalan coast (Sitges, Costa Brava), in the Balearics, and at plenty of spots along the Andalucian coast. There you'll find surf schools that run SUP outings and courses and there's even SUP yoga.

at some point along their flow, there are many reservoirs with excellent low-level kayaking and canoeing, where you can also hire equipment.

In general, May and June are best for kayaking, rafting, canoeing and hydrospeeding (water tobogganing). Top white-water rivers include Catalonia's turbulent Noguera Pallaresa, Aragón's Gállego and Ésera, Cantabria's Carasa and Galicia's Miño.

Zamora Natural (p184), which is known for its wolf-watching excursions, also does kayaking trips to the spectacular Parque Natural Arribes del Duero (north of Ciudad Rodrigo) and rafting at the Parque Natural Lago de Sanabria (northwest of Puebla de Sanabria). But the real highlight of its calendar is its eight- or nine-day kayaking descent of the Río Duero (or Rio Douro on the Portuguese side of the border), from close to Zamora down to Porto in Portugal, on the shores of the Atlantic. You camp by the river bank along the way and departures take place between June and October, depending on demand. Trips cost a bargain €680 per person. It has a separate website dedicated to the expedition: www.douroexpediciones.com.

In Catalonia, the Pallars Sobirà area in the Catalan Pyrenees is a big adventure sports spot, with rafting, kayaking, canyoning, horse-riding, rock-climbing and canoeing.

For fun and competition, the crazy 22km, en masse Descenso Internacional del Sella (p536) canoe race is a blast, running from Arriondas in Asturias to coastal Ribadesella. It's held on the first weekend in August.

In the Picos de Europa, kayaking and canoeing is very popular, on both the Sella (Asturias) and Deva (Cantabria) rivers.

Plan Your Trip

Travel with Children

Spain is a family-friendly destination with excellent transport and accommodation infrastructure, food to satisfy even the fussiest of eaters, and an extraordinary range of attractions that appeal to both adults and children. Visiting as a family does require careful planning, but no more than for visiting any other European country.

Spain for Kids

Spain has a surfeit of castles, horse shows, fiestas and ferias, interactive museums, flamenco shows and even the Semana Santa (Holy Week) processions, to name just a few highlights for kids.

When it comes to activities, quite a lot of adventure activities – including rafting, kayaking, canoeing, canyoning and mountain-biking – can be done at easy beginners' levels suitable for children, although check before you book in case there are age minimums. Surf and ski schools also cater to kids.

Children's Highlights

Beaches

Spain's beaches, especially those along the Mediterranean coast, are custom-made for children: many (particularly along the Costa Brava) are sheltered from the open ocean by protective coves, while most others are characterised by waveless waters that quietly lap the shore. Yes, some can get a little overcrowded in the height of summer, but there are still plenty of tranquil stretches of sand if you choose carefully.

Best Regions for Kids

Mediterranean Spain

Spain's coastline may be a summer-holiday cliché, but it's a fabulous place for a family holiday. From Catalonia in the north to Andalucía in the south, most beaches have gentle waters and numerous child-friendly attractions and activities (from water parks to water sports for older kids).

Barcelona

Theme parks, a wax museum, a chocolate museum, all manner of other museums with interactive exhibits, beaches, gardens… Barcelona is one of Spain's most child-friendly cities – even its architecture seems to have sprung from a child's imagination.

Inland Spain

Spain's interior may not be the first place you think of for a family holiday, but its concentrations of castles, tiny villages and fascinating, easily negotiated cities make it worth considering.

Playa de la Concha, San Sebastián (p463) This is Spain's most easily accessible city beach.

Aiguablava & Fornells (p347) Sheltered, beautiful Costa Brava coves.

Zahara de los Atunes Cádiz-province beach with pristine sand.

Architecture of the Imagination

Some of Spain's signature buildings look as if they emerged from some childhood fantasy, and many of these (such as the Alhambra and most art galleries) also have guidebooks aimed specifically at children. And then there's live flamenco, something that every child should see once in their lives.

Alcázar, Segovia (p169) The inspiration for Sleeping Beauty's castle.

Park Güell (p283) and Casa Batlló (p273) Gaudí's weird-and-wonderful Barcelona creations.

Castillo de Loarre, Aragón (p415) The stereotypically turreted castle.

Casas Colgadas, Cuenca (p238) Houses that hang out over the cliff.

Estadio Santiago Bernabéu (p107) and Camp Nou (p327) Football, football, football...

Museo Guggenheim Bilbao (p446) Watch them gaze in wonder.

Theme Parks & Horse Shows

Spain has seen an explosion of Disneyfied theme parks in recent years. Parks range from places that re-create the era of the dinosaurs or the Wild West to more traditional parks with rides and animals.

Dinópolis, Teruel (www.dinopolis.com; Poligano Los Planos; adult/child €28/22; ⏲10am-7pm daily Jun-Sep, Sat & Sun only rest of year; P 👪) This is a cross between Jurassic Park and a funfair.

PortAventura (www.portaventuraworld.com; adult/child €47/40, incl Ferrari Land €55/47; ⏲10am-7pm or 8pm, to midnight Jul–mid-Sep; P 👪) Fine amusement park close to Tarragona.

Terra Mítica, Benidorm (p830) Where the spirit of Disneyland meets the Med.

Oasys Mini Hollywood, Almería (p789) Wild West movie sets in the deserts.

Zoo Aquarium de Madrid (p102) Probably Spain's best zoo.

Parc d'Atraccions, Barcelona (p287) Great rides and a puppet museum.

Real Escuela Andaluza del Arte Ecuestre (☎956 31 80 08; www.realescuela.org; Avenida

EATING OUT

Food and children are two of the great loves for Spaniards, and Spanish fare is rarely spicy so kids tend to like it.

Children are usually welcome, whether in a sit-down restaurant or in a chaotically busy bar. Indeed, it's rare that you'll be made to feel uncomfortable as your children run amok, though the more formal the place, the more uncomfortable you're likely to feel. In summer the abundance of outdoor terraces with tables is ideal for families; take care, though, as it can be easy to lose sight of wandering young ones amid the scrum of people.

You cannot rely on restaurants having *tronas* (high chairs), although many do these days. Those that do, however, rarely have more than one (a handful at most), so make the request when making your reservation or as soon as you arrive.

Very few restaurants (or other public facilities) have nappy-changing facilities.

A small but growing number of restaurants offer a *menú infantil* (children's menu), which usually includes a main course (hamburger, chicken nuggets, pasta and the like), a drink and an ice cream or milkshake for dessert.

One challenge can be adapting to Spanish eating hours – when kids get hungry between meals it's sometimes possible to zip into the nearest *tasca* (tapas bar) and get them a snack, and there are also sweet shops scattered around most towns. That said, we recommend carrying emergency supplies from a supermarket for those times when there's simply nothing open.

Duque de Abrantes; training sessions adult/child €11/6.50, exhibiciones adult €21-27, child €13-17; ⌚training sessions 11am-1pm Mon, Wed & Fri, exhibiciones noon Tue & Thu) Andalucían horse shows in all their finery.

Caballerizas Reales (p711) Another excellent horse show, this time in Córdoba.

Planning

For general advice on travelling with young ones, see Lonely Planet's *Travel with Children* (2015) or visit the websites www.travelwithyourkids.com and www.familytravelnetwork.com.

Accommodation

Most hotels (but rarely budget establishments) have cots for small children, although most only have a handful, so reserve one when booking your room. If you're asking for a *cuna* (cot), it can be a good idea to ask for a larger room as many Spanish hotel or *hostal* (budget hotel) rooms can be on the small side, making for very cramped conditions. Cots sometimes cost extra, while other hotels offer them for free.

In top-end hotels you can sometimes arrange for child care, and in some places child-minding agencies cater to temporary visitors. Some top-end hotels – particularly resorts, but also some *paradores* (luxurious state-owned hotels) – have play areas or children's playgrounds, and many also have swimming pools.

What to Bring

Although you might want to bring a small supply of items that you're used to having back home (this is particularly true for baby products) in case of emergency (or a Sunday when most pharmacies and supermarkets are closed), Spain is likely to have everything you need.

➡ Baby formula in powder or liquid form, as well as sterilising solutions such as Milton, can be bought at *farmacias* (pharmacies).

➡ Disposable *pañales* (nappies or diapers) are widely available at supermarkets and *farmacias*.

➡ Fresh cow's milk is sold in cartons and plastic bottles in supermarkets in big cities, but can be hard to find in small towns, where UHT is often the only option.

Transport

Spain's transport infrastructure is world-class, and high-speed AVE trains render irrelevant the distances between many major cities. Apart from anything else, most kids love the idea that they're travelling at nearly 300km/h.

Discounts are available for children (usually under 12) on public transport. Those under four generally go free.

You can hire a *silla infantil* (car seat; usually for an additional cost) for infants and children from most car-hire firms, but you should always book them in advance. This is especially true during busy travel periods, such as Spanish school holidays, Navidad (Christmas) and Semana Santa (Holy Week).

It's extremely rare that taxis have child seats – unless you're carrying a portable version from home, you're expected to sit the child on your lap, with the seatbelt around you both.

When to Go

If you're heading for the beach, summer (especially July and August) is the obvious choice – but it's also when Spaniards undertake a mass pilgrimage to the coast, so book well ahead. It's also a good time to travel to the mountains (the Pyrenees, Sierra Nevada). The interior can be unbearably hot during the summer months, however – Seville and Córdoba regularly experience daytime temperatures of almost 50ºC.

Our favourite time for visiting Spain is in spring and autumn, particularly May, June, September and October. In all but October, you might be lucky and get weather warm enough for the beach, but temperatures in these months are generally mild and the weather often fine.

Winter can be bitterly cold in much of Spain – fine if you come prepared and even better if you're heading for the snow.

Regions at a Glance

Madrid & Around

Art
Nightlife
Food

Art's Golden Mile

Madrid is one of the world's premier cities for public art, with the Museo del Prado, the Centro de Arte Reina Sofía and the Museo Thyssen-Bornemisza all within easy walking distance of each other. And they're just the start.

Killing the Night

Nightclubs that don't really get busy until 3am. Sophisticated cocktail bars where you mingle with A-list celebrities while sipping your mojito. A dynamic live-music scene that begins with flamenco before moving on to jazz and every other genre imaginable. Welcome to one of Europe's nightlife capitals.

Tapas & Traditional Food

The world's oldest restaurant and the best in regional Spanish cooking make for memorable eating experiences, even if traditional Madrid food is nothing to get excited about. The neighbourhood of La Latina has one of the country's finest concentrations of tapas bars.

p70

Castilla y León

Medieval Towns
Villages
Food

City as Art

Rich in history, cathedrals and other grand public monuments, the splendid towns of old Castilla can be difficult to choose between. But if we had to, it would be plateresque Salamanca, fairy-tale Segovia and gorgeous León.

Quiet Pueblos

The villages of Castilla y León feel like Spain before mass tourism and the modern world arrived on Iberian shores, from the Sierra de Francia in the far southwest to medieval hamlets such as Pedraza de la Sierra, Covarrubias, Puebla de Sanabria and Calatañazor.

Hearty Inland Fare

Roasted and grilled meats are specialities in the Spanish interior, so much so that Spaniards travel here from all over the country for a winter meal. *Jamón* (cured ham) and other cured meats from Guijuelo are another regional passion.

p151

Toledo & Castilla-La Mancha

History
Literature
Villages & Castles

City of Three Faiths

In the Middle Ages, Toledo was one of the most cosmopolitan cities in Spain, as shown by some fine landmarks from that era – an evocative mosque, fine Jewish sites and a cathedral of real power adorned with works by El Greco, Zurbarán and Velázquez.

Tilting at Windmills

The Don Quijote trail through Castilla-La Mancha offers the rare opportunity to follow the terrain trod by one of literature's most eccentric figures. Windmills and sweeping plains evoke Cervantes' novel to such an extent that you can almost hear Sancho Panza's patter.

Beautiful Villages

Amid the often-empty horizons of La Mancha, pretty villages can seem like oases. Almagro and Sigüenza are our favourites, while the castles close to Toledo – this was a long-time frontier between Moorish and Christian Spain – are simply magnificent.

p215

Barcelona

Architecture
Food
Art & History

Modernista Masterpieces

From Gaudí's unfinished masterpiece – the wondrous Sagrada Família – to Domènech i Montaner's celestial Palau de la Música Catalana, Catalan visionaries have made Barcelona one of Europe's great Modernista centres, a showcase for the imaginative, surreal and captivating.

Culinary Gems

Barcelona's artistry doesn't end at the drawing board. Feasting on seafood overlooking the Mediterranean, munching on tapas at the magnificent Boqueria market, indulging in celebrated Michelin-starred restaurants – it's all part of the Barcelona experience.

Artistry of the Past

A once-vibrant settlement of ancient Rome, Barcelona has over 2000 years of history hidden in its lanes. The old Gothic centre has 14th-century churches and medieval mansions that hold more recent treasures, from a Picasso collection to pre-Columbian masterpieces.

p249

Catalonia

Food
Beaches
Hiking

The Catalan Kitchen

Vying with the Basque Country for Spain's highest per-capita ratio of celebrity chefs, Catalonia is something of a pilgrimage for gastronomes. Here, even in the smallest family establishments, cooks fuse ingredients from land and sea, always keeping faith with rich culinary traditions even as they head off in innovative new directions.

The Catalan Coast

The picturesque coastlines known as the Costa Brava and Costa Daurada are studded with postcard-pretty villages and beaches that are generally less crowded than those further south. And not far away, signposts to Salvador Dalí and the Romans make for fine day trips.

Spain's High Country

Northern Catalonia means the Pyrenees, where shapely peaks and quiet valleys offer some of the best hiking anywhere in the country.

p337

Aragón

Mountains
Villages
History

Head for the Hills

Perhaps the prettiest corner of the Pyrenees, northern Aragón combines the drama of steepling summits with the quiet pleasures of deep valleys and endless hiking trails. The Parque Nacional de Ordesa y Monte Perdido ranks among Spain's most picturesque national parks.

Stone Villages

Aragón has numerous finalists in the competition for Spain's most beautiful village, among them Aínsa, Sos del Rey Católico and Albarracín. Many sit in the Pyrenean foothills against a backdrop of snowcapped mountains.

Romans, Moors & Christians

Centred on one of Spain's most important historical kingdoms, Aragón is strewn with landmarks from the great civilisations of ancient and medieval times. Zaragoza in particular spans the millenniums with grace and fervour, and Teruel is an often-missed Mudéjar jewel.

p403

Basque Country, Navarra & La Rioja

Food
Wine
Villages

Spain's Culinary Capital

To understand the buzz surrounding Spanish food, head for San Sebastián, which is at once *pintxos* (Basque tapas) heaven and home to outrageously talented chefs. Challenging San Sebastián are Bilbao, Logroño, Vitoria and Pamplona.

The Finest Drop

La Rioja is to wine what the Basque Country is to food. Wine museums, wine tastings and vineyards stretching to the horizon make this Spain's most accessible wine region. And, of course, it accompanies every meal here.

Beautiful Villages

There are stunning villages to be found throughout the Basque Country and La Rioja, but those in the Pyrenean foothills and high valleys of Navarra are a match for anything the rest of Spain has to offer.

p444

Cantabria & Asturias

Coastal Scenery
Mountains
Food & Drink

The Scenic Coast

Wild, rocky walls encircle a beautiful sandy cove at Playa del Silencio, just one of hundreds of beaches tucked away along the rugged, emerald-green Asturian coastline, behind which rise gorgeous villages and marvellous mountainscapes.

Picos de Europa

The jagged Picos de Europa have some of the most stunning hiking country in Spain. Vertiginous precipices stretch down into the dramatic Garganta del Cares gorge, while the Naranjo de Bulnes peak beckons from beyond high mountain passes.

Cheese & Cider

Knocking back cider is Asturias' favourite pastime, particularly along Oviedo's *el bulevar de la sidra,* while the tangy Cabrales cheese from the foothills of the Picos de Europa is one of Spain's best.

p505

Santiago de Compostela & Galicia

Coastal Scenery
Food
History

The Wildest Coast

Galicia's windswept coast is one of Europe's most dramatic and stunningly beautiful. On the Rías Altas, cliffs plunge from enormous heights into turbulent Atlantic waters, interspersed with picturesque fishing villages and isolated sandy beaches.

Fruits of the Sea

Galicia has some of the world's best seafood, and fine meat from its rich pastures too. Head to Santiago de Compostela's bustling market, the Mercado de Abastos, for the best of both – and the chance to enjoy them at restaurants on the spot.

A Sacred Past

In few places are long-gone centuries as alive as they are in Santiago de Compostela. Its magnificent cathedral, churches, streets and plazas represent 1300 uninterrupted years as the goal of that great pilgrimage route, the Camino de Santiago.

p557

Extremadura

Medieval Towns
Roman Ruins
Food

Medieval Film Sets

Spain may be replete with wonderfully preserved old towns that date back to the Middle Ages, but Cáceres and Trujillo are up there with the best. Meandering along their cobblestoned lanes is a journey back into an epic past.

Roman Mérida

Spain's most beautiful Roman theatre, its longest Roman-era bridge, a breathtaking museum and a slew of other ruined glories – welcome to Emerita Augusta, now known as Mérida and Spain's finest Roman site. The fabulous bridge at Alcántara also merits a visit.

Ham & Cheese

Some of Spain's finest *jamón* comes from Extremadura, most notably from around Monesterio, which has Spain's best *jamón* museum. The Torta del Casar cheese from just north of Cáceres is another culinary star.

p604

Seville & Andalucía's Hill Towns

Music
History & Architecture
Food & Wine

Cradle of Flamenco

The towns and cities of western Andalucía pretty much invented modern flamenco. Look no further than the *bulerías* of Jerez, the *alegrías* of Cádiz and the *soleares* of Seville – all of them performed in local *tablaos* (choreographed flamenco shows) and *peñas* (flamenco clubs).

White Towns

They're all here, the famous white towns, with their ruined hilltop castles, flower boxes and small somnolent churches. Arcos, Jimena, Grazalema, Vejer...the ancient sentinels on a once-volatile frontier that divided two great civilisations.

Fish & Sherry

Where the Atlantic meets the Mediterranean you're bound to find good fish, which the Andalucians traditionally deep-fry in olive oil to create *pescaíto frito*. Then there's the sherry made from grapes that grow near the coast – a perfect pairing.

p632

Granada & South Coast Andalucía

Architecture
Beaches
Walks

Hybrid Granada

A celebrated Nasrid palace-fortress, a hilltop Moorish quarter, opulent *cármenes* (large mansions with walled gardens), and a baroque-Renaissance cathedral – the city of Granada is a magnificent collection of just about every architectural style known to European building.

Southern Beaches

The south coast's beaches are an industry, bagging more tourist euros than the rest of the region put together. Choose according to your budget and hipster-rating between Estepona, Marbella, Torremolinos, Málaga, Nerja and Almuñécar.

Wild Areas

Walk the dry, craggy coastline of Cabo de Gata, hook onto the GR7 long-distance footpath in Las Alpujarras or get lost looking for wildlife on the trails in the highlands east of Cazorla. Andalucía has its untamed side, if you know where to look.

p719

Valencia & Murcia

Fiestas
Food
Beaches

Bulls, Fire & Knights in Armour

The biggest and noisiest party is Valencia's Las Fallas in March. But almost every *pueblo* (village) has its fiesta, usually with fireworks and often with bulls. Lorca's Semana Santa (Holy Week) festivities rival those of Andalucía.

Simmering Rice

Paella first simmered over an open fire in Valencia. Rice dishes are everywhere, supplemented by fish and seafood from the Mediterranean and the freshest of vegetables grown along the fertile coastal strip down into Murcia.

Strands & Rocky Coves

From small bays to vast beaches stretching over kilometres, from tiny rocky coves to the sandy sweeps of Denia, Benidorm and Murcia's Costa Cálida (Hot Coast), there's always room to stretch out your towel.

p795

On the Road

Cantabria & Asturias
p505
Santiago de Compostela & Galicia
p557
Basque Country, Navarra & La Rioja
p444
Castilla y León
p151
Catalonia
p337
Aragón
p403
Barcelona
p249
Madrid & Around
p70
Toledo & Castilla-La Mancha
p215
Extremadura
p604
Valencia & Murcia
p795
Seville & Andalucía's Hill Towns
p632
Granada & South Coast Andalucía
p719

Madrid & Around

POP 3.17 MILLION

Includes ➡

Best Places to Eat

- ➡ Restaurante Sobrino de Botín (p118)
- ➡ DiverXo (p125)
- ➡ Estado Puro (p122)
- ➡ Bazaar (p123)
- ➡ Mercado de San Miguel (p117)

Best Places to Stay

- ➡ Central Palace Madrid (p113)
- ➡ Hotel Silken Puerta América (p117)
- ➡ Praktik Metropol (p114)
- ➡ Hotel Orfila (p117)
- ➡ ApartoSuites Jardines de Sabatini (p117)

Why Go?

Madrid is a miracle of human energy and peculiarly Spanish passions, a beguiling place with a simple message: this city knows how to live. It's true Madrid doesn't have the immediate cachet of Paris, the monumental history of Rome or the reputation for cool of that other city up the road, Barcelona. But it's a city whose contradictory impulses are legion, the perfect expression of Europe's most passionate country writ large. This city has transformed itself into one of Spain's premier style centres and its calling cards are many: astonishing art galleries, relentless nightlife, an exceptional live-music scene, a feast of fine restaurants and tapas bars, and a population that's mastered the art of the good life. It's not that other cities don't have these things: it's just that Madrid has all of them in bucketloads.

When to Go

Madrid

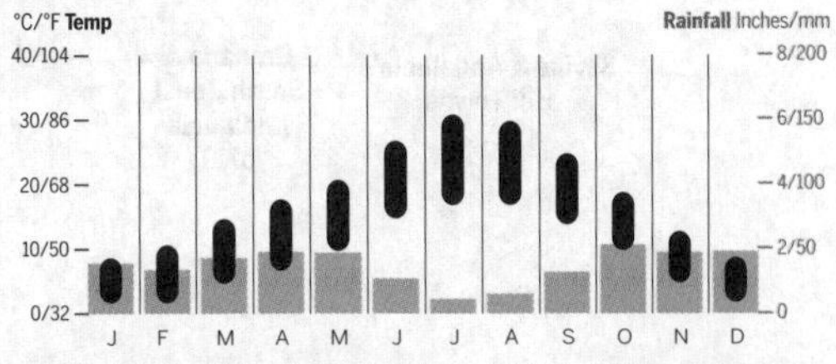

Jan–Feb Winter can be cold but glorious in Madrid when the weather is fine.

Mar–Apr Warmer spring weather brings *madrileños* (residents of Madrid) out into the city's *terrazas*.

Sep Madrid shakes off its summer torpor with (usually) lovely autumn weather.

History

When Iberia's Christians began the Reconquista (c 722) – the centuries-long campaign by Christian forces to reclaim the peninsula – the Muslims of Al-Andalus constructed a chain of fortified positions through the heart of Iberia. One of these was built by Muhammad I, emir of Córdoba, in 854, on the site of what would become Madrid. The name they gave to the new settlement was Mayrit (or Magerit), which comes from the Arabic word *majira*, meaning 'water channel'.

A Worthy Capital?

Madrid's strategic location in the centre of the peninsula saw the city change hands repeatedly, but it was not until 1309 that the travelling Cortes (royal court and parliament) sat in Madrid for the first time. Despite the growing royal attention, medieval Madrid remained dirt poor and small-scale: 'In Madrid there is nothing except what you bring with you,' observed one 15th-century writer. It simply bore no comparison with other major Spanish, let alone European, cities.

By the time Felipe II ascended the Spanish throne in 1556, Madrid was surrounded by walls that boasted 130 towers and six stone gates, but these fortifications were largely built of mud and designed more to impress than provide any meaningful defence of the city. Madrid was nonetheless chosen by Felipe II as the capital of Spain in 1561.

Madrid took centuries to grow into its new role and despite a handful of elegant churches, the imposing Alcázar and a smattering of noble residences, the city consisted of, for the most part, precarious whitewashed houses. The monumental Paseo del Prado, which now provides Madrid with so much of its grandeur, was a small creek.

During the 17th century, Spain's golden age, Madrid began to take on the aspect of a capital and was home to 175,000 people, making it the fifth-largest city in Europe (after London, Paris, Constantinople and Naples).

Carlos III (r 1759–88) gave Madrid and Spain a period of comparatively commonsense government. After he cleaned up the city, completed the Palacio Real, inaugurated the Real Jardín Botánico and carried out numerous other public works, he became known as the best 'mayor' Madrid had ever had.

Madrileños (residents of Madrid) didn't take kindly to Napoleon's invasion and subsequent occupation of Spain in 1805 and, on 2 May 1808, they attacked French troops around the Palacio Real and what is now Plaza del Dos de Mayo. The ill-fated rebellion was quickly put down by Murat, Napoleon's brother-in-law and the most powerful of his military leaders.

Wars, Franco & Terrorism

Turmoil continued to stalk the Spanish capital. The upheaval of the 19th-century Carlist Wars was followed by a two-and-a-half-year siege of Madrid by Franco's Nationalist forces from 1936 to 1939, during which the city was shelled regularly from Casa de Campo and Gran Vía became known as 'Howitzer Alley'.

After Franco's death in 1975 and the country's subsequent transition to democracy, Madrid became an icon for the new Spain as the city's young people unleashed a flood of pent-up energy. This took its most colourful form in the years of *la movida*, the endless party that swept up the city in a frenzy of creativity and open-minded freedom that has in some ways yet to abate.

On 11 March 2004, just three days before the country was due to vote in national elections, Madrid was rocked by 10 bombs on four rush-hour commuter trains heading into the capital's Atocha station. The bombs had been planted by terrorists with links to al-Qaeda, reportedly because of Spain's then support for the American-led war in Iraq. When the dust cleared, 191 people had died and 1755 were wounded, many seriously. Madrid was in shock and, for 24 hours at least, this most clamorous of cities fell silent. Then, 36 hours after the attacks, more than three million *madrileños* streamed onto the streets to protest against the bombings, making it the largest demonstration in the city's history. Although deeply traumatised, Madrid's mass act of defiance and pride began the process of healing. Visit Madrid today and you'll find a city that has resolutely returned to normal.

In the years since, Madrid has come agonisingly close in the race to host the Summer Olympics, coming third behind London and Paris in the race for 2012, second behind Rio for 2016 before falling into the also-rans for the 2020 games. And, of course, Madrid was the scene of one of the biggest celebrations in modern Spanish history when the Spanish World Cup–winning football team returned home in July 2010. These celebrations were almost matched two years later when Spain won the 2012 European Football Championships, again bringing much-needed cheer to a city affected deeply by Spain's severe economic downturn.

Madrid & Around Highlights

❶ **Museo del Prado** (p94) Watching the masterpieces of Velázquez and Goya leap off the canvas at the world-famous gallery.

❷ **El Rastro** (p82) Searching for treasure in this massive Sunday flea market, then joining the crowds in Parque del Buen Retiro.

❸ **Plaza de Santa Ana** (p86) Soaking up the buzz with a *caña* (small beer) or glass of Spanish wine on this gorgeous square.

❹ **La Latina** (p118) Going on a tapas crawl in the medieval *barrio* (district) of La Latina.

❺ **Chocolatería de San Ginés** (p126) Ordering *chocolate con churros* (deep fried doughnut strips dipped in hot chocolate) close to dawn.

❻ **Estadio Santiago Bernabéu** (p134) Making a sporting pilgrimage to see the stars of Real Madrid play.

❼ **Teatro Joy Eslava** (p126) Dancing the night away and sampling the city's world-famous nightlife.

❽ **Café de la Iberia** (p149) Feasting on roast lamb in utterly charming Chinchón.

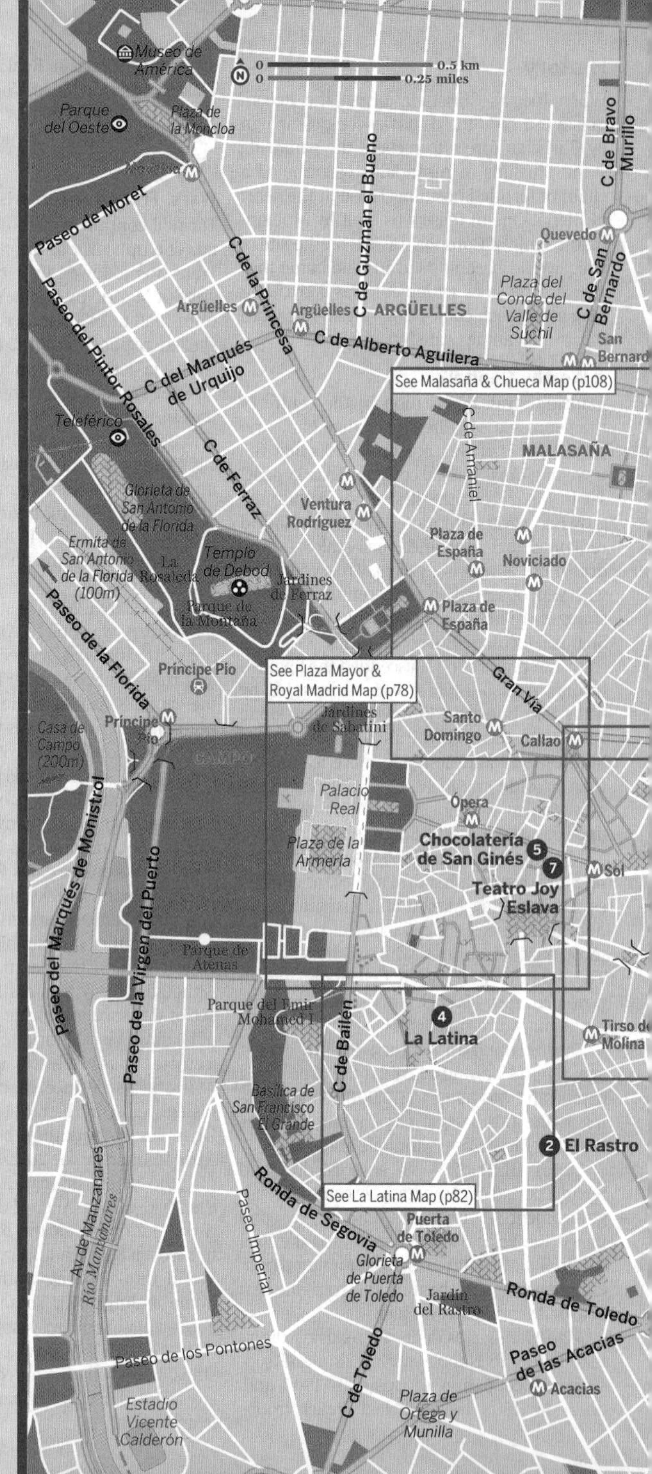

C de María de Molina
Gregorio Marañón
6 Estadio Santiago Bernabéu
Intercambiador de Avenida de América
Av de América
Glorieta del General Alvarez de Castro
C de Eloy Gonzalo
Iglesia
Paseo del General Martínez Campos
Glorieta de Emilio Castelar
CASTELLANA
C de Francisco Silvela
Plaza de Olavide
CHAMBERÍ
Estación de Chamberí
Paseo de Eduardo Dato
Rubén Darío
Núñez de Balboa
C de Juan Bravo
Diego de León
C de Luchana
C de Santa Engracia
Bilbao
ALMAGRO
SALAMANCA
Núñez de Balboa
Lista
Paseo de la Castellana
C del Príncipe de Vergara
C de Sagasta
Alonso Martínez
Museo Taurino (960m); Plaza de Toros Monumental de Las Ventas (960m)
Tribunal
Colón
Serrano
RECOLETOS
Velázquez
C de Goya
Goya
C de Hortaleza
Chueca
Paseo de los Recoletos
C de Alcalá
Goya
GOYA
Recoletos
Príncipe de Vergara
CHUECA
Recoletos
JUSTICIA
C de O'Donnell
Gran Vía
Gran Vía
Banco de España
See Salamanca Map (p104)
Sevilla
Ibiza
Paseo del Prado
Parque del Buen Retiro
Monument to Alfonso XII
RETIRO
Fuente Egipcia
Plaza de Santa Ana
3
Palacio de Velázquez
1
Museo del Prado
Palacio de Cristal
Jardines del Arquitecto Herrero Palacios
Av de Menéndez Pelayo
See Sol, Santa Ana & Huertas Map (p88)
El Ángel Caído
La Rosaleda (Rose Garden)
Plaza del Niño Jesús
La Rosaleda
Plaza de Lavapiés
Atocha
Puerta de Dante
LAVAPIÉS
Lavapiés
Café de la Iberia 8
See El Retiro & the Art Museums Map (p92)
Atocha Renfe
Av de Menéndez Pelayo
Av del Mediterráneo
Paseo de la Reina Cristina
Ronda de Valencia
Av de la Ciudad de Barcelona
Real Fábrica de Tapices
C de Cavanilles
Embajadores
Estación de Atocha
Menéndez Pelayo
C de Embajadores
Paseo de Santa María de la Cabeza
Paseo de las Delicias
C de Méndez Álvaro
Palos de la Frontera
C de Ancora
Pacífico
C del Doctor Esquerdo

Neighbourhoods at a Glance

❶ Plaza Mayor & Royal Madrid (p76)

The bustling, medieval heart of the city is where Madrid's story began and where the city became the seat of royal power. It's also where the splendour of imperial Spain was at its most ostentatious, with palaces, churches, squares and convents. It's an architectural high point of the city, with plenty of fine eating and shopping options to explore.

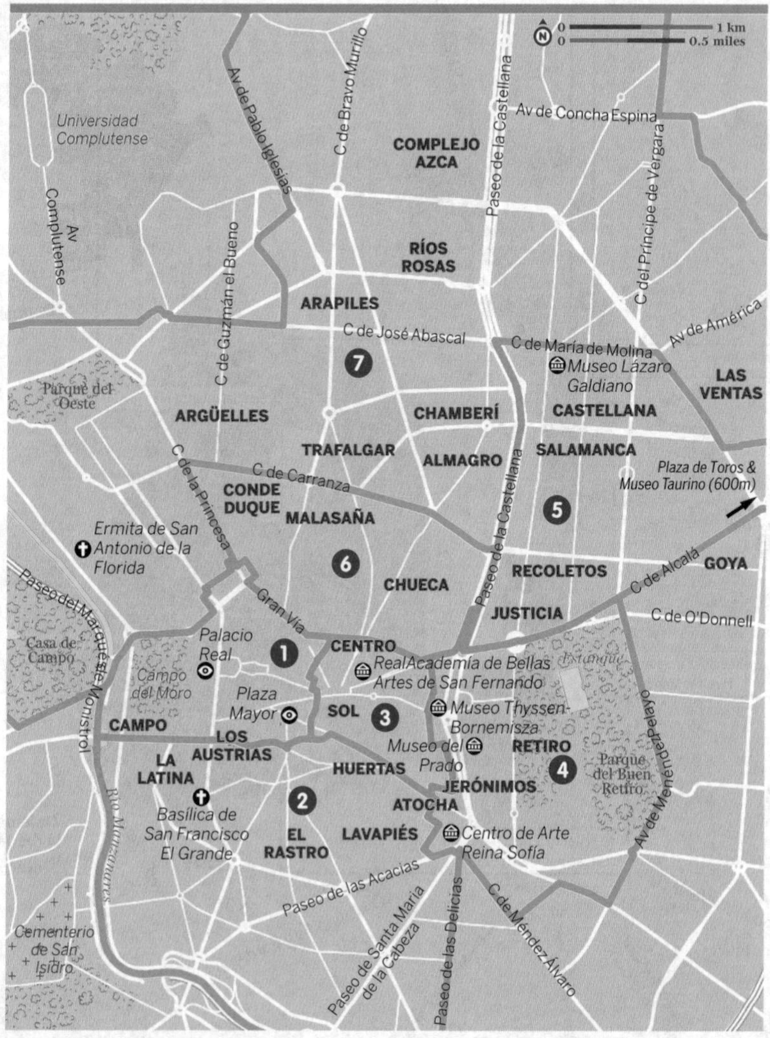

❷ La Latina & Lavapiés (p81)

La Latina combines Madrid's best selection of tapas bars, boutiques and a medieval streetscape with elegant churches; Calle de la Cava Baja is a favourite street for tapas in town. Down the hill, Lavapiés is one of the city's oldest *barrios* (districts) and the heart of multicultural Madrid. Spanning the two areas is the Sunday flea market of El Rastro.

❸ Sol, Santa Ana & Huertas (p85)

These tightly packed streets are best known for nightlife that doesn't seem to abate once the sun goes down, but there's also the beguiling Plaza de Santa Ana, a stirring literary heritage in the Barrio de las Letras and, at the Sol end of things, Madrid's beating heart, you'll find the sum total of all Madrid's personalities, with fabulous shopping, eating and entertainment options.

❹ El Retiro & the Art Museums (p87)

From Plaza de la Cibeles in the north, the buildings arrayed along Paseo del Prado read like a roll-call of Madrid's most popular attractions. Temples to high culture include the Museo del Prado, Museo Thyssen-Bornemisza and Centro de Arte Reina Sofía, which rank among the world's most prestigious art galleries. Up the hill to the east, the marvellous Parque del Buen Retiro helps to make this one of the most attractive areas of Madrid in which to spend your time.

❺ Salamanca (p103)

The *barrio* of Salamanca is Madrid's most exclusive quarter. Like nowhere else in the capital, this is where stately mansions that are set back from the street share *barrio* space with big local and international designer boutiques. Salamanca's sprinkling of fine restaurants, designer tapas bars and niche museums and galleries are also very much at home here.

❻ Malasaña & Chueca (p106)

The two inner-city *barrios* of Malasaña and Chueca are where Madrid gets up close and personal. Here, it's more an experience of life as it's lived by *madrileños* (people from Madrid) than the traditional traveller experience of ticking off from a list of wonderful, if more static, attractions. These are *barrios* with attitude and personality, where Madrid's famed nightlife, shopping and eating choices live and breathe and take you under the skin of the city.

❼ Parque del Oeste & Northern Madrid (p107)

Madrid's north contains some of the city's most attractive *barrios*, including Chamberí, which is a wonderful escape from the downtown area and offers unique insights into how locals enjoy their city. Estadio Santiago Bernabéu is a major highlight for sports fans, Parque del Oeste is a gorgeous expanse of green, while a series of fascinating sights – from Goya frescoes to an Egyptian temple – add considerable appeal.

Sights

Madrid's attractions are numerous and varied, but many of the standout highlights revolve around art – the city's art galleries are world class and you could easily spend a week exploring them. A handful of excellent museums, beautiful parks, a stunning royal palace and some of Europe's most agreeable squares provide considerable depth to the Madrid experience.

Plaza Mayor & Royal Madrid

As you'd expect from the former centrepiece of old Madrid, there are numerous highlights in this corner of the city: the royal palace, ornamental gardens (Jardines de Sabatini and the Campo del Moro), lavish convents, and storied plazas (Plaza Mayor, Plaza de la Villa, even Plaza de la Puerta del Sol) where the architecture is as beguiling as the street life that animates it. And in the absence of a cathedral worthy of the name, it's the smaller churches, including two of Madrid's oldest, that provide the focal point for those seeking the city's religious past.

★Palacio Real PALACE

(Map p78; ☎91 454 88 00; www.patrimonionacional.es; Calle de Bailén; adult/concession €11/6, guide/audioguide €4/3, EU citizens free last 2hr Mon-Thu; ⏲10am-8pm Apr-Sep, to 6pm Oct-Mar; Ⓜ Ópera) Spain's lavish Palacio Real is a jewel box of a palace, although it's used only occasionally for royal ceremonies; the royal family moved to the modest Palacio de la Zarzuela years ago.

When the *alcázar* (muslim fortress) burned down on Christmas Day 1734, Felipe V, the first of the Bourbon kings, decided to build a palace that would dwarf all its European counterparts. Felipe died before the palace was finished, which is perhaps why the Italianate baroque colossus has a mere 2800 rooms, just one-quarter of the original plan.

The official tour (self-guided tours are also possible and follow the same route) leads through 50 of the palace rooms, which hold a good selection of Goyas, 215 absurdly ornate clocks, and five Stradivarius violins still used for concerts and balls. The main stairway is a grand statement of imperial power, leading to the Halberdiers' rooms and to the sumptuous **Salón del Trono** (Throne Room), with its crimson-velvet wall coverings and Tiepolo ceiling. Shortly after, you reach the **Salón de Gasparini**, with its exquisite stucco ceiling and walls resplendent with embroidered silks.

Outside the main palace, visit the **Farmacia Real** (Map p78; Palacio Real) at the southern end of the patio known as the **Plaza de la Armería** (Plaza de Armas). Westwards across the plaza is the **Armería Real** (Royal Armoury; Map p78; www.patrimonionacional.es; Plaza de la Armería, Palacio Real; admission incl with Palacio Real entry; ⏲10am-8pm Apr-Sep, to 6pm Oct-Mar), a shiny collection of weapons and armour, mostly dating from the 16th and 17th centuries.

Plaza de Oriente SQUARE

(Map p78; Plaza de Oriente; Ⓜ Ópera) A royal palace that once had aspirations to be the Spanish Versailles. Sophisticated cafes watched over by apartments that cost the equivalent of a royal salary. The Teatro Real (p133), Madrid's opera house and one of Spain's temples to high culture. Some of the finest sunset views in Madrid… Welcome to Plaza de Oriente, a living, breathing monument to imperial Madrid.

At the centre of the plaza, which the palace overlooks, is an equestrian **statue of Felipe IV** (Map p78; Ⓜ Ópera). Designed by Velázquez, it's the perfect place to take it all in, with marvellous views wherever you look. If you're wondering how a heavy bronze statue of a rider and his horse rearing up can actually maintain that stance, the answer is simple: the hind legs are solid, while the front ones are hollow. That idea was Galileo Galilei's. Nearby are some 20 marble statues, mostly of ancient monarchs. Local legend has it that these ageing royals get down off their pedestals at night to stretch their legs when no-one's looking.

The adjacent **Jardines Cabo Naval** are a great place to watch the sunset.

Jardines de Sabatini GARDENS

(Map p78; ⏲9am-10pm May-Sep, to 9pm Oct-Apr; Ⓜ Ópera) FREE The formal French-style Jardines de Sabatini are to the north of the Palacio Real, a palace with lush gardens.

Catedral de Nuestra Señora de la Almudena CATHEDRAL

(Map p78; ☎91 542 22 00; www.catedraldelaalmudena.es; Calle de Bailén; cathedral & crypt b1y donation, museum adult/child €6/4; ⏲9am-8.30pm Mon-Sat, museum 10am-2.30pm Mon-Sat; Ⓜ Ópera) Paris has Notre Dame and Rome has St Peter's Basilica. In fact, almost every Europe-

TOP SIGHT PLAZA MAYOR

It's easy to fall in love with Madrid in the Plaza Mayor. This is the monumental heart of the city and the grand stage for so many of its most important historical events. Here, Madrid's relentless energy courses across its cobblestones beneath ochre-hued apartments, wrought-iron balconies, frescoes and stately spires.

A Grand History

Ah, the history the plaza has seen! Inaugurated in 1619, its first public ceremony was suitably auspicious – the beatification of San Isidro Labrador (St Isidro the Farm Labourer), Madrid's patron saint. Thereafter, it was as if all that was controversial about Spain took place in this square. Bullfights, often in celebration of royal weddings or births, with royalty watching on from the balconies and up to 50,000 people crammed into the plaza, were a recurring theme until 1878. Far more notorious were the *autos-da-fé* (the ritual condemnations of heretics during the Spanish Inquisition), followed by executions – burnings at the stake and deaths by garrotte on the north side of the square, hangings to the south.

A Less-Grand History

Not all the plaza's activities were grand events and, just as it is now surrounded by shops, it was once filled with food vendors. In 1673, King Carlos II issued an edict allowing the vendors to raise tarpaulins above their stalls to protect their wares and themselves from the refuse and raw sewage that people habitually tossed out of the windows above! Well into the 20th century, trams ran through Plaza Mayor.

Real Casa de la Panadería

The exquisite frescoes of the 17th-century **Real Casa de la Panadería** (Royal Bakery; Map p78; Plaza Mayor 27) rank among Madrid's more eye-catching sights. The present frescoes date to just 1992 and are the work of artist Carlos Franco, who chose images from the signs of the zodiac and gods (eg Cybele) to provide a stunning backdrop for the plaza. The frescoes were inaugurated to coincide with Madrid's 1992 spell as European Capital of Culture. The building now houses the city's main tourist office.

Spires & Slate Roofs

The plaza was designed in the 17th century by Juan Gómez de Mora who, following the dominant style of the day, adopted a Herrerian style (named after Spanish Renaissance architect Juan de Herrera). The slate spires and roofs are the most obvious expression of this pleasing and distinctively Madrid style, and their sombre hues are nicely offset by the warm colours of the uniformly ochre apartments and their 237 wrought-iron balconies.

DON'T MISS

- Spires & Slate Roofs
- Real Casa de la Panadería
- Markets

PRACTICALITIES

- Map p78
- M Sol

Plaza Mayor & Royal Madrid

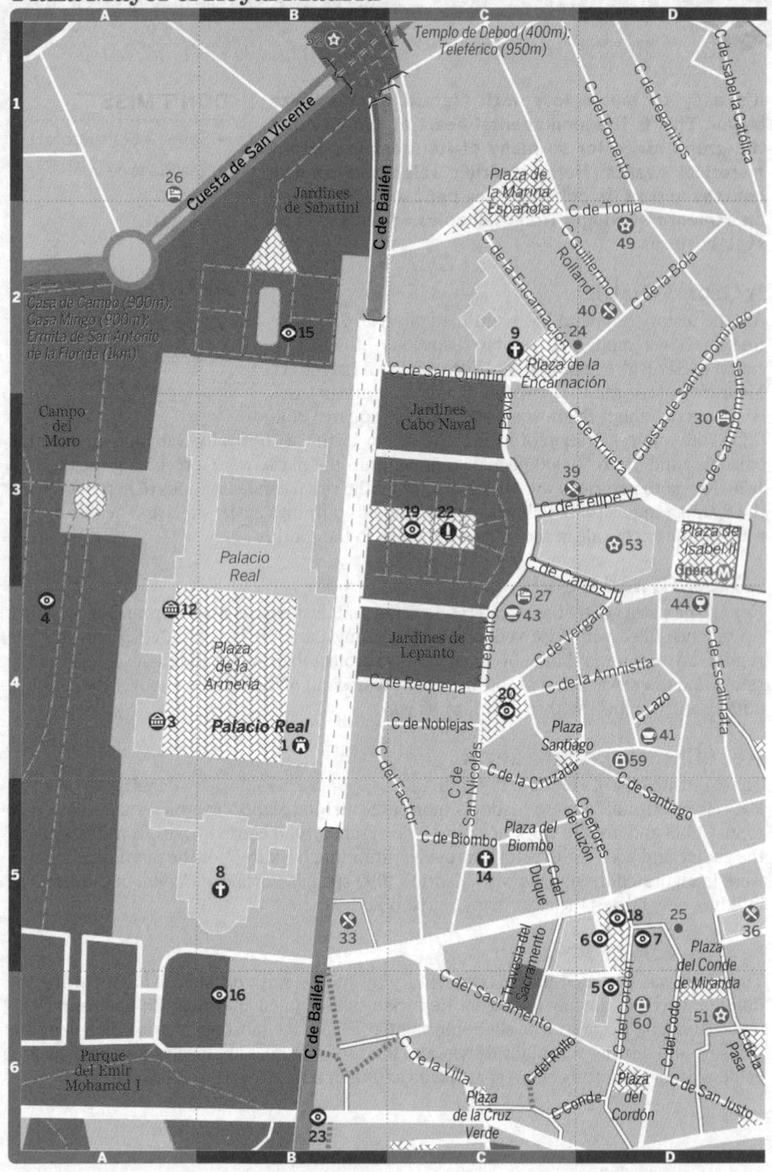

an city of stature has its signature cathedral, a standout monument to a glorious Christian past. Not Madrid. Although the exterior of the Catedral de Nuestra Señora de la Almudena sits in harmony with the adjacent Palacio Real, Madrid's cathedral is cavernous and largely charmless within; its colourful, modern ceilings do little to make up for the lack of old-world gravitas that so distinguishes great cathedrals.

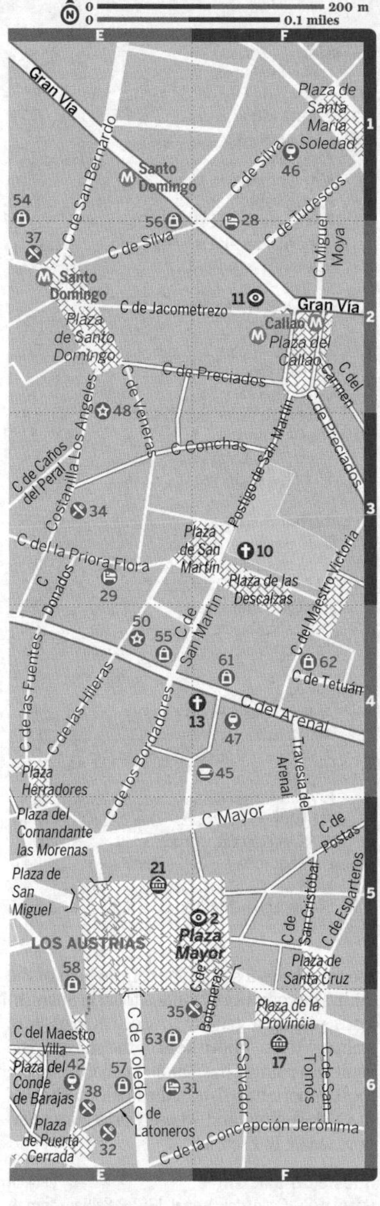

Muralla Árabe

LANDMARK

(Map p78; Cuesta de la Vega; Ⓜ Ópera) Behind the cathedral apse and down Cuesta de la Vega is a short stretch of the original 'Arab Wall', the city wall built by Madrid's early-medieval Muslim rulers. Some of it dates as far back as the 9th century, when the initial Muslim fort was raised. Other sections date from the 12th and 13th centuries, by which time the city had been taken by the Christians.

Plaza de la Villa

SQUARE

(Map p78; Plaza de la Villa; Ⓜ Ópera) The intimate Plaza de la Villa is one of Madrid's prettiest. Enclosed on three sides by wonderfully preserved examples of 17th-century *barroco madrileño* (Madrid-style baroque architecture – a pleasing amalgam of brick, exposed stone and wrought iron), it was the permanent seat of Madrid's city government from the Middle Ages until recent years, when Madrid's city council relocated to the grand Palacio de Cibeles on Plaza de la Cibeles (p101).

On the western side of the square is the 17th-century **former town hall** (Map p78; Ⓜ Ópera), in Habsburg-style baroque with Herrerian slate-tile spires. On the opposite side of the square is the Gothic **Casa de los Lujanes** (Map p78; Ⓜ Ópera), whose brickwork tower is said to have been 'home' to the imprisoned French monarch François I after his capture in the Battle of Pavia (1525). Legend has it that as the star prisoner was paraded down Calle Mayor, locals are said to have been more impressed by the splendidly attired Frenchman than they were by his more drab captor, the Spanish Habsburg emperor Carlos I, much to the chagrin of the latter. The plateresque (15th- and 16th-century Spanish baroque) **Casa de Cisneros** (Map p78; Plaza de la Villa; Ⓜ Ópera), built in 1537 with later Renaissance alterations, also catches the eye.

Palacio Gaviria

MUSEUM

(Map p88; ☎ 902 044226; Calle del Arenal 9; adult/child €12/free; ⏲ 10am-8pm Sun-Thu, to 9pm Fri & Sat; Ⓜ Sol) Until recently this 19th-century Italianate palace was a nightclub. It has since been artfully converted to a dynamic artistic space, with major temporary art exhibitions that have included an Escher retrospective and the works of Alphonse Mucha. Coupled with high-quality exhibitions is a soaring Renaissance palace with extraordinary ceiling frescoes. Put all of this together and you've one of the more exciting additions to Madrid's artistic portfolio.

Campo del Moro

GARDENS

(Map p78; ☎ 91 454 88 00; Paseo de la Virgen del Puerto; ⏲ 10am-8pm Apr-Sep, to 6pm Oct-Mar; Ⓜ Príncipe Pío) FREE These gardens beneath the Palacio Real were designed to mimic the gardens surrounding the palace at Versailles;

Plaza Mayor & Royal Madrid

Top Sights
1 Palacio Real ... B4
2 Plaza Mayor ... F5

Sights
3 Armería Real ... A4
4 Campo del Moro ... A4
5 Casa de Cisneros ... D6
6 Casa de la Villa ... D5
7 Casa de los Lujanes ... D5
8 Catedral de Nuestra Señora de la Almudena ... B5
9 Convento de la Encarnación ... C2
10 Convento de las Descalzas Reales ... F3
11 Edificio Carrión ... F2
12 Farmacia Real ... A4
13 Iglesia de San Ginés ... F4
14 Iglesia de San Nicolás de los Servitas ... C5
15 Jardines de Sabatini ... B2
16 Muralla Árabe ... B6
17 Palacio de Santa Cruz ... F6
18 Plaza de la Villa ... D5
19 Plaza de Oriente ... C3
20 Plaza de Ramales ... C4
21 Real Casa de la Panadería ... E5
22 Statue of Felipe IV ... C3
23 Viaduct & Calle de Segovia ... B6

Activities, Courses & Tours
24 Alambique ... C2
25 Bike Spain ... D5
Visitas Guiadas Oficiales ... (see 21)

Sleeping
26 ApartoSuites Jardines de Sabatini ... A1
27 Central Palace Madrid ... C4
28 Hostal Main Street Madrid ... F2
29 Hotel JC Rooms Puerta del Sol ... E3
30 Hotel Meninas ... D3
31 The Hat Madrid ... E6

Eating
32 Casa Revuelta ... E6
33 El Anciano Rey de los Vinos ... B5
34 El Pato Mudo ... E3
35 La Campana ... F6
La Ideal ... (see 35)
36 Mercado de San Miguel ... D5
37 Restaurante Sandó ... E2
38 Restaurante Sobrino de Botín ... E6
39 Taberna del Alabardero ... C3
40 Taberna La Bola ... D2

Drinking & Nightlife
41 Anticafé ... D4
42 Bodegas Ricla ... E6
43 Cafe de Oriente ... C4
44 Café del Real ... D4
45 Chocolatería de San Ginés ... F4
46 José Alfredo ... F1
47 Teatro Joy Eslava ... F4
The Sherry Corner ... (see 36)

Entertainment
48 Café Berlin ... E2
49 Café de Chinitas ... D2
50 La Coquette Blues ... E4
51 Las Carboneras ... D6
52 Las Tablas ... B1
53 Teatro Real ... D3

Shopping
54 Antigua Casa Talavera ... E1
55 Así ... E4
56 Atlético de Madrid Store ... E2
57 Casa Hernanz ... E6
58 El Arco Artesanía ... E5
59 El Flamenco Vive ... D4
60 El Jardín del Convento ... D6
61 La Madrileña ... F4
62 Maty ... F4
63 Sombrerería Medrano ... E6

nowhere is this more in evidence than along the east–west **Pradera**, a lush lawn with the Palacio Real as its backdrop. The gardens' centrepiece, which stands halfway along the Pradera, is the elegant **Fuente de las Conchas** (Fountain of the Shells), designed by Ventura Rodríguez, the Goya of Madrid's 18th-century architecture scene. The only entrance is from Paseo de la Virgen del Puerto.

Convento de las Descalzas Reales CONVENT
(Convent of the Barefoot Royals; Map p78; www.patrimonionacional.es; Plaza de las Descalzas 3; €6, incl Convento de la Encarnación €8; 10am-2pm & 4-6.30pm Tue-Sat, 10am-3pm Sun; M Ópera, Sol) The grim plateresque walls of the Convento de las Descalzas Reales offer no hint that behind the facade lies a sumptuous stronghold of the faith. The compulsory guided tour (in Spanish) leads you up a gaudily frescoed Renaissance stairway to the upper level of the cloister. The vault was painted by Claudio Coello, one of the most important artists of the Madrid School of the 17th century and whose works adorn San Lorenzo de El Escorial.

Iglesia de San Ginés CHURCH
(Map p78; Calle del Arenal 13; 8.45am-1pm & 6-9pm Mon-Sat, 9.45am-2pm & 6-9pm Sun; M Sol, Ópera) FREE Due north of Plaza Mayor, San Ginés is one of Madrid's oldest churches: it has been here in one form or another since at least the 14th century. What you see today was built in 1645 but largely reconstructed

after a fire in 1824. The church houses some fine paintings, including El Greco's *Expulsion of the Moneychangers from the Temple* (1614), which is beautifully displayed; the glass is just 6mm from the canvas to avoid reflections.

The church has stood at the centre of Madrid life for centuries. It is speculated that, prior to the arrival of the Christians in 1085, a Mozarabic community (Christians in Muslim territory) lived around the stream that later became Calle del Arenal and that their parish church stood on this site. Spain's premier playwright Lope de Vega was married here and novelist Francisco de Quevedo was baptised in its font.

Convento de la Encarnación CONVENT
(Map p78; www.patrimonionacional.es; Plaza de la Encarnación 1; €6, incl Convento de las Descalzas Reales €8; ⏲10am-2pm & 4-6.30pm Tue-Sat, 10am-3pm Sun; Ⓜ Ópera) Founded by Empress Margarita de Austria, this 17th-century mansion built in the Madrid baroque style (a pleasing amalgam of brick, exposed stone and wrought iron) is still inhabited by nuns of the Augustine order. The large art collection dates mostly from the 17th century, and among the many gold and silver reliquaries is one that contains the blood of San Pantaleón, which purportedly liquefies each year on 27 July. The convent sits on a pretty plaza close to the Palacio Real.

Iglesia de San Nicolás de los Servitas CHURCH
(Map p78; ☎91 559 40 64; Plaza de San Nicolás 6; ⏲8am-1.30pm & 5.30-8.30pm Mon, 8-9.30am & 6.30-8.30pm Tue-Sat, 9.30am-2pm & 6.30-9pm Sun & holidays; Ⓜ Ópera) Tucked away up the hill from Calle Mayor, this intimate little church is Madrid's oldest surviving building of worship; it may have been built on the site of Muslim Mayrit's second mosque. The most striking feature is the restored 12th-century Mudéjar bell tower; much of the remainder dates in part from the 15th century. The vaulting is late Gothic while the fine timber ceiling, which survived a 1936 fire, dates from about the same period. Opening hours can be unreliable.

Plaza de España SQUARE
(Map p108; Ⓜ Plaza de España) It's hard to know what to make of this curiously unprepossessing square. The square's centrepiece is a 1927 statue of Cervantes with, at the writer's feet, a bronze statue of his immortal characters Don Quijote and Sancho Panza. The 1953 **Edificio de España** (Spain Building) on the northeast side clearly sprang from the totalitarian recesses of Franco's imagination such is its resemblance to austere Soviet monumentalism. To the north stands the 35-storey **Torre de Madrid** (Madrid Tower).

Palacio de Santa Cruz HISTORIC BUILDING
(Map p78; Plaza de la Provincia; Ⓜ Sol) Just off the southeastern corner of Plaza Mayor and dominating Plaza de Santa Cruz is this baroque edifice, which houses the **Ministerio de Asuntos Exteriores** (Ministry of Foreign Affairs) and hence can only be admired from the outside. A landmark with its grey slate spires, it was built in 1643 and initially served as the court prison.

La Latina & Lavapiés

Although there are exceptions, these two *barrios* (districts) are more about experiences than traditional sights. That said, a handful of fine churches rise above La Latina, Plaza de la Paja is one of Madrid's loveliest squares, and the tangled streets of La Morería are a return to the city's distant past. And then, of course, there's El Rastro, Madrid's flea market par excellence, and the gateway to some of Madrid's most enjoyable traditions.

★**Basílica de San Francisco El Grande** CHURCH
(Map p82; Plaza de San Francisco 1; adult/concession €5/3; ⏲mass 8-10.30am Mon-Sat, museum 10.30am-12.30pm & 4-6pm Tue-Sun Sep-Jun, 10.30am-12.30pm & 5-7pm Tue-Sun Jul & Aug; Ⓜ La Latina, Puerta de Toledo) Lording it over the southwestern corner of La Latina, this imposing baroque basilica is one of Madrid's grandest old churches. Its extravagantly frescoed dome is, by some estimates, the largest in Spain and the fourth largest in the world, with a height of 56m and diameter of 33m.

Legend has it that St Francis of Assisi built a chapel on this site in 1217. The current version was designed by Francesco Sabatini, who also designed the Puerta de Alcalá (p102) and finished off the Palacio Real. He designed the church with an unusual floor plan: the nave is circular and surrounded by chapels guarded by imposing marble statues of the 12 apostles; 12 prophets, rendered in wood, sit above them at the base of the dome. Each of the chapels is adorned with frescoes and decorated according to a different historical style, but most people rush to the neo-plateresque

La Latina

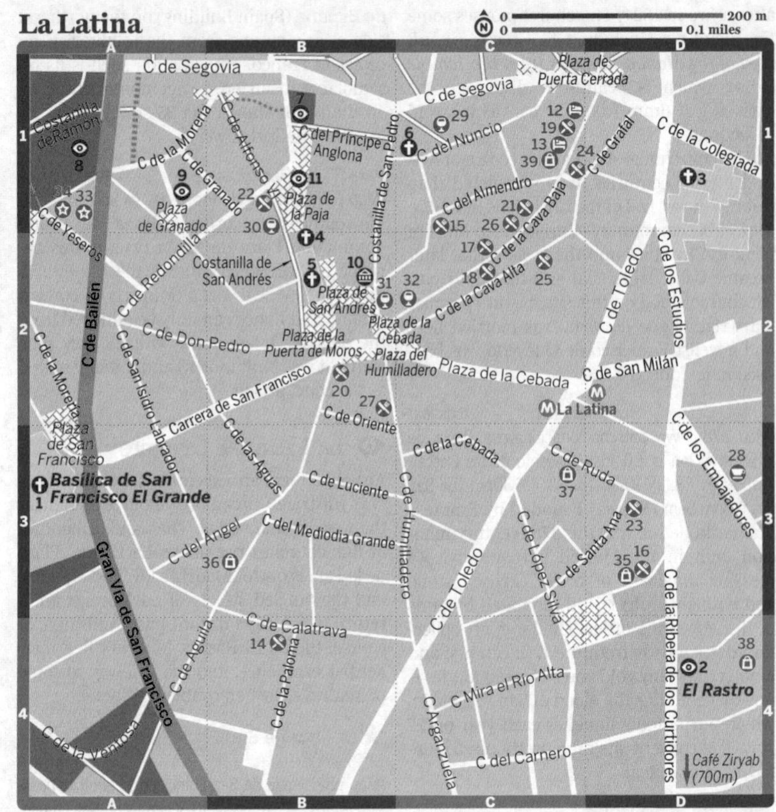

Capilla de San Bernardino, where the central fresco was painted by Goya in the early stages of his career. Unusually, Goya has painted himself into the scene (he's the one in the yellow shirt on the right).

A series of corridors behind the high altar (accessible only as part of the guided visit) is lined with works of art from the 17th to 19th centuries; highlights include a painting by Francisco Zurbarán, and another by Francisco Pacheco, the father-in-law and teacher of Velázquez. In the sacristy, watch out for the fine Renaissance *sillería* (the sculpted walnut seats where the church's superiors would meet).

A word about the opening hours: although entry is free during morning Mass times, there is no access to the museum and the lights in the Capilla de San Bernardino won't be on to illuminate the Goya. At all other times, visit is by Spanish-language guided tour (included in the admission price). Just to confuse matters, you may face a similar problem if you're here on a Friday afternoon or any time Saturday if there's a wedding taking place.

★ El Rastro MARKET

(Map p82; Calle de la Ribera de los Curtidores; ⏲8am-3pm Sun; Ⓜ La Latina) A Sunday morning at El Rastro flea market is a Madrid institution. You could easily spend an entire morning inching your way down the hill and the maze of streets. Cheap clothes, luggage, old flamenco records, even older photos of Madrid, faux designer purses, grungy T-shirts, household goods and electronics are the main fare. For every 10 pieces of junk, there's a real gem (a lost masterpiece, an Underwood typewriter) waiting to be found.

The crowded Sunday flea market was, back in the 17th and 18th centuries, largely a meat market (*rastro* means 'stain', in reference to the trail of blood left behind by animals dragged down the hill). The road

La Latina

Top Sights

1 Basílica de San Francisco El Grande A3
2 El Rastro D4

Sights

3 Basílica de Nuestra Señora del Buen Consejo D1
4 Capilla del Obispo B2
5 Iglesia de San Andrés B2
6 Iglesia de San Pedro El Viejo C1
7 Jardín del Príncipe Anglona B1
8 Jardines de Las Vistillas A1
9 La Morería A1
10 Museo de San Isidro B2
11 Plaza de la Paja B1

Sleeping

12 Posada del Dragón C1
13 Posada del León de Oro C1

Eating

14 Almacén de Vinos B4
15 Almendro 13 .... C1
16 Bar Santurce D3
17 Casa Lucas C2
18 Casa Lucio C2
19 Enotaberna del León de Oro C1
20 Juana La Loca B2
21 La Chata C1
22 La Musa Latina B1
23 Malacatín D3
24 Posada de la Villa C1
25 Taberna Matritum C2
26 Taberna Txakolina C1
27 Txirimiri B2

Drinking & Nightlife

28 Bocono Specialty Coffee D3
29 Café del Nuncio C1
30 Delic B1
31 El Bonanno B2
32 Taberna El Tempranillo C2

Entertainment

33 ContraClub A1
34 Corral de la Morería A1

Shopping

35 Aceitunas Jiménez D3
36 Botería Julio Rodríguez B3
37 De Piedra C3
38 El Rastro D4
39 Helena Rohner C1

leading through the market, Calle de la Ribera de los Curtidores, translates as 'Tanners' Alley' and further evokes this sense of a slaughterhouse past. On Sunday mornings this is the place to be, with all of Madrid (in all its diversity) here in search of a bargain.

A word of warning: pickpockets love El Rastro as much as everyone else, so keep a tight hold on your belongings and don't keep valuables in easy-to-reach pockets.

Plaza de la Paja SQUARE

(Straw Square; Map p82; Ⓜ La Latina) Around the back of the Iglesia de San Andrés, the delightful Plaza de la Paja slopes down into the tangle of lanes that once made up Madrid's Muslim quarter. In the 12th and 13th centuries, the city's main market occupied the square. At the top of the square is the **Capilla del Obispo** (Map p82; ☎ 91 559 28 74; reservascapilladelobispo@archimadrid.es; Plaza de la Paja; €2; ⏲ 6-8.30pm Mon & Wed, noon-1.30pm & 6-8.30pm Tue & Thu, noon-1.30pm & 6-9.30pm Fri, noon-1.30pm & 8-10pm Sat, noon-2pm & 6.45-8.30pm Sun; Ⓜ La Latina), while down the bottom (north side) is the walled 18th-century **Jardín del Príncipe Anglona** (Map p82; Plaza de la Paja; ⏲ 10am-10pm Apr-Oct, to 6.30pm Nov-Mar; Ⓜ La Latina), a peaceful garden.

Matadero Madrid ARTS CENTRE

(☎ 91 252 52 53; www.mataderomadrid.com; Paseo de la Chopera 14; Ⓜ Legazpi) FREE This contemporary arts centre is a stunning multipurpose space south of the centre. Occupying the converted buildings of the old Arganzuela livestock market and slaughterhouse, Matadero Madrid covers 148,300 sq metres and hosts cutting-edge drama, musical and dance performances and exhibitions on architecture, fashion, literature and cinema. It's a dynamic space and its proximity to the landscaped riverbank makes for a nontouristy alternative to sightseeing in Madrid, not to mention a brilliant opportunity to see the latest avant-garde theatre or exhibitions.

La Morería HISTORIC SITE

(Map p82; Ⓜ La Latina) The area stretching northwest from Iglesia de San Andrés to the viaduct was the heart of the *morería* (Moorish Quarter). Strain the imagination a little and the maze of winding and hilly lanes even now retains a whiff of the North African medina. This is where the Muslim population of Mayrit was concentrated in the wake of the 11th-century Christian takeover of the town.

MADRID IN...

One Day

So many Madrid days begin in the **Plaza Mayor** (p77) or nearby with a breakfast of *chocolate con churros* (chocolate with deep-fried doughnuts) at **Chocolatería de San Ginés** (p126). Drop by the **Plaza de la Villa** (p79) and **Plaza de Oriente** (p76), then stop for a coffee or wine at **Cafe de Oriente** (p126) and visit the **Palacio Real** (p76). Have lunch at **Mercado de San Miguel** (p117), one of Madrid's most innovative gastronomic spaces. Spend as much of the afternoon as you can at the **Museo del Prado** (p94). When this priceless collection of Spanish and European masterpieces gets too much, visit the **Iglesia de San Jerónimo El Real** (p103) and **Caixa Forum** (p102). To kick off the night, take in a flamenco show at **Teatro Flamenco Madrid** (p134), followed by a leisurely drink at **Café del Real** (p126) or **Anticafé** (p126). If you're up for a long night, **Teatro Joy Eslava** (p126) is an icon of the Madrid night.

Two Days

Get to the **Centro de Arte Reina Sofía** (p91) early to beat the crowds, then climb up through sedate streets to spend a couple of hours soaking up the calm of the **Parque del Buen Retiro** (p93). Wander down to admire the **Plaza de la Cibeles** (p101). After lunch at **Estado Puro** (p122), one of Madrid's most creative tapas bars, catch the metro across town to admire the Goya frescoes in the **Ermita de San Antonio de la Florida** (p107). Afterwards **Templo de Debod** (p107) and **Parque del Oeste** (p110) are fine places for a stroll. Begin the night at **Plaza de Santa Ana** (p86) for a drink or three at an outdoor table if the weather's fine. After another tipple at **La Venencia** (p127), check out if there's live jazz on offer at wonderful **Café Central** (p133). Have an after-show drink at **El Imperfecto** (p127). The night is still young – **Costello Café & Niteclub** (p134) is good if you're in the mood to dance, **La Terraza del Urban** (p128) if you're in need of more sybaritic pleasures.

Three Days

Begin the morning at the third of Madrid's world-class art galleries, the **Museo Thyssen-Bornemisza** (p90). It's such a rich collection that you could easily spend the whole morning here. If you've time to spare, consider dipping back into the Prado or Reina Sofía. Have lunch at **Platea** (p122), one of Madrid's most exciting culinary experiences. Head out east to take a tour of the **Plaza de Toros** (p103) bullring, before dipping into the **Museo Lázaro Galdiano** (p105). Spend the rest of the afternoon shopping along Calle de Serrano, Calle de José Ortega y Gasset and surrounding streets. As dusk approaches, make for La Latina and spend as long as you can picking your way among the tapas bars of **Calle de la Cava Baja** – even if you're not hungry, stop by for a beer or wine to soak up the atmosphere. A wine at **Taberna El Tempranillo** (p126) and a mojito (a rum-based cocktail) out on Plaza de la Paja at **Delic** (p126) should set you up for the night ahead.

Viaduct & Calle de Segovia HISTORIC SITE

(Map p78; Ⓜ Ópera) High above Calle de Segovia, Madrid's viaduct, which connects La Morería with the cathedral and royal palace, was built in the 19th century and replaced by a newer version in 1942; the plastic barriers were erected in the late 1990s to prevent suicide jumps. Before the viaduct was built, anyone wanting to cross from one side of the road or river to the other was obliged to make their way down to Calle de Segovia and back up the other side.

Jardines de Las Vistillas GARDENS

(Map p82; Ⓜ Ópera) West across Calle de Bailén from La Morería are the *terrazas* (open-air cafes) of Jardines de Las Vistillas, which offer one of the best vantage points in Madrid for a drink, with views towards the Sierra de Guadarrama. During the civil war, Las Vistillas was heavily bombarded by nationalist troops from the Casa de Campo, and they in turn were shelled from a republican bunker here.

Iglesia de San Andrés CHURCH
(Map p82; Plaza de San Andrés 1; ⏲9am-1pm & 6-8pm Mon-Sat, 10am-1pm Sun; Ⓜ La Latina) This proud church is more imposing than beautiful. Stern, dark columns with gold-leaf capitals against the rear wall lead your eyes up into the dome – all rose, yellow and green, and rich with sculpted floral fantasies and cherubs poking out of every nook and cranny. What you see today is the result of restoration work completed after the church was gutted during the civil war.

Museo de San Isidro MUSEUM
(Museo de los Origenes; Map p82; ☎91 366 74 15; www.madrid.es; Plaza de San Andrés 2; ⏲10am-7pm Tue-Sun mid-Jun–mid-Sep, 9.30am-8pm Tue-Sun rest of year; Ⓜ La Latina) FREE This engaging museum occupies the spot where San Isidro Labrador, patron saint of Madrid, ended his days in around 1172. A particular highlight is the large model based on Pedro Teixeira's famous 1656 map of Madrid. Of great historical interest (though not much to look at) is the 'miraculous well', where the saint called forth water to slake his master's thirst. In another miracle, the son of the saint's master fell into a well, whereupon Isidro prayed until the water rose and lifted his master's son to safety.

Basílica de Nuestra Señora del Buen Consejo CHURCH
(Catedral de San Isidro; Map p82; ☎91 369 20 37; Calle de Toledo 37; ⏲7.30am-1pm & 6-9pm; Ⓜ Tirso de Molina, La Latina) Towering above the northern end of bustling Calle de Toledo, and visible through the arches from Plaza Mayor, this imposing church long served as the city's de facto cathedral until the Catedral de Nuestra Señora de la Almudena (p76) was completed in 1992. Still known to locals as the Catedral de San Isidro, the austere baroque basilica was founded in the 17th century as the headquarters for the Jesuits.

The basilica is today home to the remains of the city's main patron saint, San Isidro (in the third chapel on your left after you walk in). His body, apparently remarkably well preserved, is only removed from here on rare occasions, such as in 1896 and 1947 when he was paraded about town in the hope he would bring rain (he did, at least in 1947).

Official opening hours aren't always to be relied upon.

Plaza de Lavapiés SQUARE
(Ⓜ Lavapiés) The triangular Plaza de Lavapiés is one of the few open spaces in Lavapiés and is a magnet for all that's good (a thriving cultural life) and bad (drugs and a high police presence) about the *barrio*. It's been cleaned up a little in recent years and the **Teatro Valle-Inclán** (☎91 505 88 01; www.cdn.mcu.es; Plaza de Lavapiés; tickets from €15; Ⓜ Lavapiés), on the southern edge of the plaza, is a striking addition to the eclectic Lavapiés streetscape.

Iglesia de San Pedro El Viejo CHURCH
(Map p82; ☎91 365 12 84; Costanilla de San Pedro; ⏲9am-12.30pm & 5-8pm Mon-Thu & Sat, 7am-9pm Fri, 9am-12.30pm Sun; Ⓜ La Latina) This fine old church is one of the few remaining windows on post-Muslim Madrid, most notably its clearly Mudéjar (a Moorish architectural style) brick bell tower, which dates from the 14th century. The church is generally closed to the public, but it's arguably more impressive from the outside; the Renaissance doorway has stood since 1525. If you can peek inside, the nave dates from the 15th century, although the interior largely owes its appearance to 17th-century renovations.

Sol, Santa Ana & Huertas

The Real Academia de Bellas Artes de San Fernando and the Plaza de Santa Ana capture two of Madrid's most enduring sources of appeal – the exceptional museums dedicated to fine art and the irresistible energy that dominates the city's streets. The charm and sense of history that define the intimate Barrio de las Letras is another completely different perspective on life, just as appealing and just as much a part of the Madrid experience.

LOCAL KNOWLEDGE

PEDRO ALMODÓVAR'S MADRID LOCATIONS

- Plaza Mayor – *La Flor de mi secreto* (The Flower of My Secret; 1995)
- El Rastro – *Laberinto de pasiones* (Labyrinth of Passion; 1982)
- Villa Rosa – *Tacones lejanos* (High Heels; 1991)
- Café del Circulo de Bellas Artes – *Kika* (1993)
- Viaducto de Segovia – *Matador* (1986)
- Museo del Jamón (Calle Mayor) – *Carne Trémula* (Live Flesh; 1997)

MUSEUM DISCOUNTS & CLOSING TIMES

Many museums (including the Museo del Prado and Centro de Arte Reina Sofía) offer free entry at selected times – check the opening hours throughout this chapter. Remember, however, that the museums can be extremely crowded during these periods.

If you plan to visit the Museo del Prado, Museo Thyssen-Bornemisza and Centro de Arte Reina Sofía while in Madrid, the **Paseo del Arte** combined ticket covers them all for €29.60 and is valid for one visit to each gallery during a 12-month period; buying separate tickets would cost €36.

★Real Academia de Bellas Artes de San Fernando MUSEUM
(Map p88; ☎91 524 08 64; www.realacademiabellasartessanfernando.com; Calle de Alcalá 13; adult/child €8/free, Wed free; ⏲10am-3pm Tue-Sun Sep-Jul; Ⓜ Sol, Sevilla) The Real Academia de Bellas Artes, Madrid's 'other' art gallery, has for centuries played a pivotal role in the artistic life of the city. As the royal fine arts academy, it has nurtured local talent, thereby complementing the royal penchant for drawing the great international artists of the day into their realm. The pantheon of former alumni reads like a who's who of Spanish art, and the collection that now hangs on the academy's walls is a suitably rich one.

★Plaza de Santa Ana SQUARE
(Map p88; Plaza de Santa Ana; Ⓜ Sevilla, Sol, Antón Martín) Plaza de Santa Ana is a delightful confluence of elegant architecture and irresistible energy. It presides over the upper reaches of the Barrio de las Letras (p86) and this literary personality makes its presence felt with the statues of the 17th-century writer Calderón de la Barca and Federíco García Lorca, and in the **Teatro Español** (Map p88; ☎91 360 14 84; www.teatroespanol.es; Calle del Príncipe 25; Ⓜ Sevilla, Sol, Antón Martín) at the plaza's eastern end. Apart from anything else, the plaza is the starting point for many a long Huertas night.

The plaza was laid out in 1810 during the controversial reign of Joseph Bonaparte (elder brother of Napoleon), giving breathing space to what had hitherto been one of Madrid's most claustrophobic *barrios*. The plaza quickly became a focal point for intellectual life, and the cafes surrounding the plaza thronged with writers, poets and artists engaging in endless *tertulias* (literary and philosophical discussions).

★Círculo de Bellas Artes ARTS CENTRE, VIEWPOINT
(La Azotea; Map p88; ☎91 360 54 00; www.circulobellasartes.com; Calle de Alcalá 42; admission to roof terrace €4; ⏲roof terrace 9am-2am Mon-Thu, to 3am Fri, 11am-3am Sat, 11am-2am Sun; Ⓜ Banco de España, Sevilla) For some of Madrid's best views, take the lift to the 7th floor of the 'Fine Arts Circle'. You can almost reach out and touch the glorious dome of the Edificio Metrópolis and otherwise take in Madrid in all its finery, including the distant mountains. Two bars, lounge music and places to recline add to the experience. Downstairs, the centre has exhibitions, concerts, short films and book readings. There's also a fine belle-époque **cafe** (Map p88; ☎91 521 69 42; Calle de Alcalá 42; ⏲9am-1am Sun-Thu, to 3am Fri & Sat; Ⓜ Banco de España, Sevilla) on the ground floor.

Barrio de las Letras AREA
(District of Letters; Map p88; Ⓜ Antón Martín) The area that unfurls down the hill east of Plaza de Santa Ana is referred to as the Barrio de las Letras, because of the writers who lived here during Spain's golden age of the 16th and 17th centuries. Miguel de Cervantes Saavedra (1547–1616), the author of *Don Quijote,* spent much of his adult life in Madrid and lived and died at **Calle de Cervantes 2** (Map p88; Ⓜ Antón Martín); a plaque (dating from 1834) sits above the door.

Sadly, the original building was torn down in the early 19th century. When Cervantes died his body was interred around the corner at the **Convento de las Trinitarias** (Map p88; Calle de Lope de Vega 16; Ⓜ Antón Martín), which is marked by another plaque. Still home to cloistered nuns, the convent is closed to the public; forensic archaeologists finally found Cervantes' remains in 2015. A commemorative Mass is held for him here every year on the anniversary of his death, 23 April. Another literary landmark is the **Casa de Lope de Vega** (Map p88; ☎91 429 92 16; www.casamuseolopedevega.org; Calle de Cervantes 11; ⏲guided tours every 30min 10am-6pm Tue-Sun; Ⓜ Antón Martín) FREE, the former home of Lope de Vega (1562–1635), Spain's premier playwright. It's now a museum containing memorabilia from Lope de Vega's life and work.

Plaza de la Puerta del Sol SQUARE

(Map p88; M Sol) The official centre point of Spain is a gracious, crowded hemisphere of elegant facades. It is, above all, a crossroads: people here are forever heading somewhere else, on foot, by metro (three lines cross here) or by bus (many lines terminate and start nearby). Hard as it is to believe now, in Madrid's earliest days, the Puerta del Sol (Gate of the Sun) was the eastern gate of the city.

The main building on the square houses the regional government of the Comunidad de Madrid. The **Casa de Correos** (Map p88; M Sol), as it is called, was built as the city's main post office in 1768. The clock was added in 1856 and on New Year's Eve people throng the square to wait impatiently for the clock to strike midnight, and at each gong swallow a grape – not as easy as it sounds! On the footpath outside the Casa de Correos is a plaque marking Spain's **Kilometre Zero**, the point from which Spain's network of roads is measured.

The semicircular junction owes its present appearance in part to the Bourbon king Carlos III (r 1759–88), whose **equestrian statue** (Map p88; M Sol) (complete with his unmistakable nose) stands in the middle. Look out for the **statue of a bear** (Map p88; M Sol) nuzzling a *madroño* (strawberry tree) at the plaza's eastern end; this is the official symbol of the city.

Casa Museo de Ratón Perez MUSEUM

(Map p88; 91 522 69 68; www.casamuseoratonperez.com; 1st fl, Calle de Arenal 8; €3; 5-8pm Mon, 11am-2pm & 5-8pm Tue-Fri, 11am-3pm & 4-8pm Sat; M Sol) The Spanish version of the tooth fairy is a cute little mouse called 'El Ratón Perez', and this small museum close to Sol takes you into a recreation of his home. Entry is by guided tour and the commentary is only in Spanish, but it's still worth a visit as you'll see his secret door, a layout of his home inside a biscuit tin and all manner of little artefacts. Entrance is via the passageway signed 'Centro Comercial Arenal 8'.

El Retiro & the Art Museums

Some of Madrid's most memorable sights inhabit this *barrio*, with most of them on or within short walking distance of the Paseo del Prado. The three world-class art museums (the Prado, Thyssen and Reina Sofía) get most of the attention, and rightly so. But the Parque del Buen Retiro is a stunning oasis in the heart of the city, at once expansively green and studded with stirring monuments. Throw in a handful of other museums and a daring exhibition space (Caixa Forum) and you've reason enough to spend two or three days in this neighbourhood alone.

WHERE ARE THEY BURIED?

While other countries have turned cemeteries and the graves of famous locals into tourist attractions, Spain has been slow to do the same. That may be because mystery surrounds the final resting places of some of Spain's most towering historical figures.

Diego Velázquez (1599–1660) According to historical records, Spain's master painter was buried in the Iglesia de San Juanito, but the church was destroyed in the early 19th century by Joseph Bonaparte to make way for what would later become the **Plaza de Ramales** (Map p78; M Ópera). Excavations in 2000 revealed the crypt of the former church, but Velázquez was nowhere to be found.

Francisco Goya (1746–1828) In 1919, 91 years after Goya's death in Bordeaux, France, his remains were entombed in the Ermita de San Antonio de la Florida (p107), the small chapel still adorned by some of Goya's most celebrate frescoes. But his head was never found.

Miguel de Cervantes Saavedra (1547–1616) Cervantes, the author of *Don Quijote*, lived much of his life in Madrid and upon his death his body was buried at the Convento de las Trinitarias (p86), in the Barrio de las Letras. In the centuries that followed, his body was somehow misplaced until, in early 2015, forensic archaeologists announced that they had discovered the bones of Cervantes in a crypt in the convent. Still home to cloistered nuns, the convent is closed to the public except for Mass.

Sol, Santa Ana & Huertas

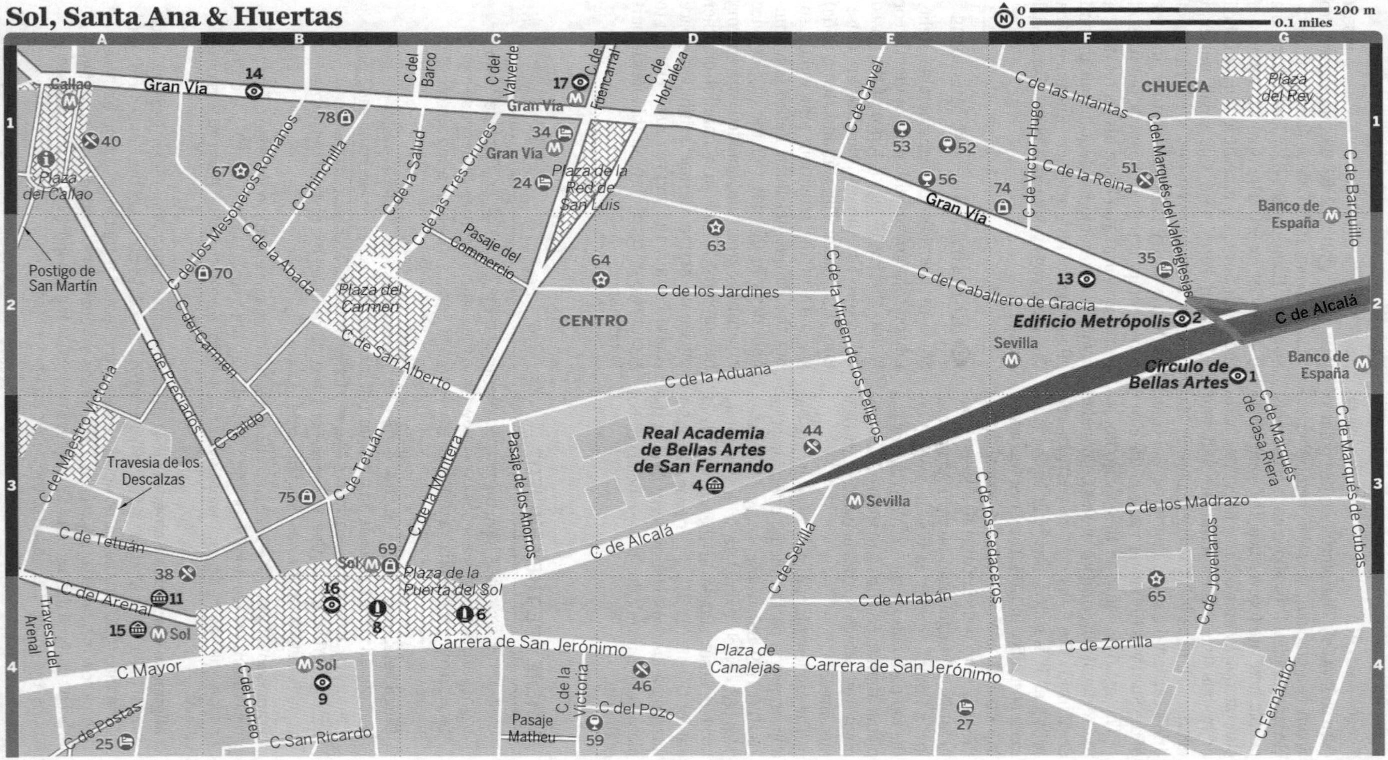

0 — 200 m
0 — 0.1 miles

A B C D E F G
1 2 3 4

Gran Vía
14
Callao
40
Plaza del Callao
Postigo de San Martín
78
67
70
C de los Mesoneros Romanos
C Chinchilla
C de la Abada
C del Carmen
C de Preciados
C del Maestro Victoria
Travesia de los Descalzas
C de Tetuán
C Galdo
75
C de la Salud
C de las Tres Cruces
C del Barco
C del Valverde
17
C de Fuencarral
C de Hortaleza
34
Gran Vía
24
Plaza de la Red de San Luis
Pasaje del Commercio
Plaza del Carmen
C de San Alberto
C de la Montera
69
Sol
Plaza de la Puerta del Sol
16
8
6
38
11
15
Sol
C del Arenal
Travesia del Arenal
C Mayor
C de Postas
25
Sol
9
C del Correo
C San Ricardo
Carrera de San Jerónimo
Pasaje Matheu
C de la Victoria
59
C del Pozo
46
Plaza de Canalejas
27
C Fernánflor
C de Zorrilla
C de Arlabán
C de Sevilla
Sevilla
C de Alcalá
Pasaje de los Ahorros
Real Academia de Bellas Artes de San Fernando
4
44
C de la Aduana
CENTRO
64
C de los Jardines
63
C de la Virgen de los Peligros
C de Clavel
53
52
56
74
C de Víctor Hugo
C de las Infantas
C de la Reina
51
C del Marqués del Valdeiglesias
CHUECA
Plaza del Rey
C de Barquillo
Banco de España
35
13
C del Caballero de Gracia
Edificio Metrópolis 2
Sevilla
Círculo de Bellas Artes 1
Banco de España
C de Marqués de Casa Riera
C de Marqués de Cubas
C de los Madrazo
C de Jovellanos
65
C de los Cedaceros

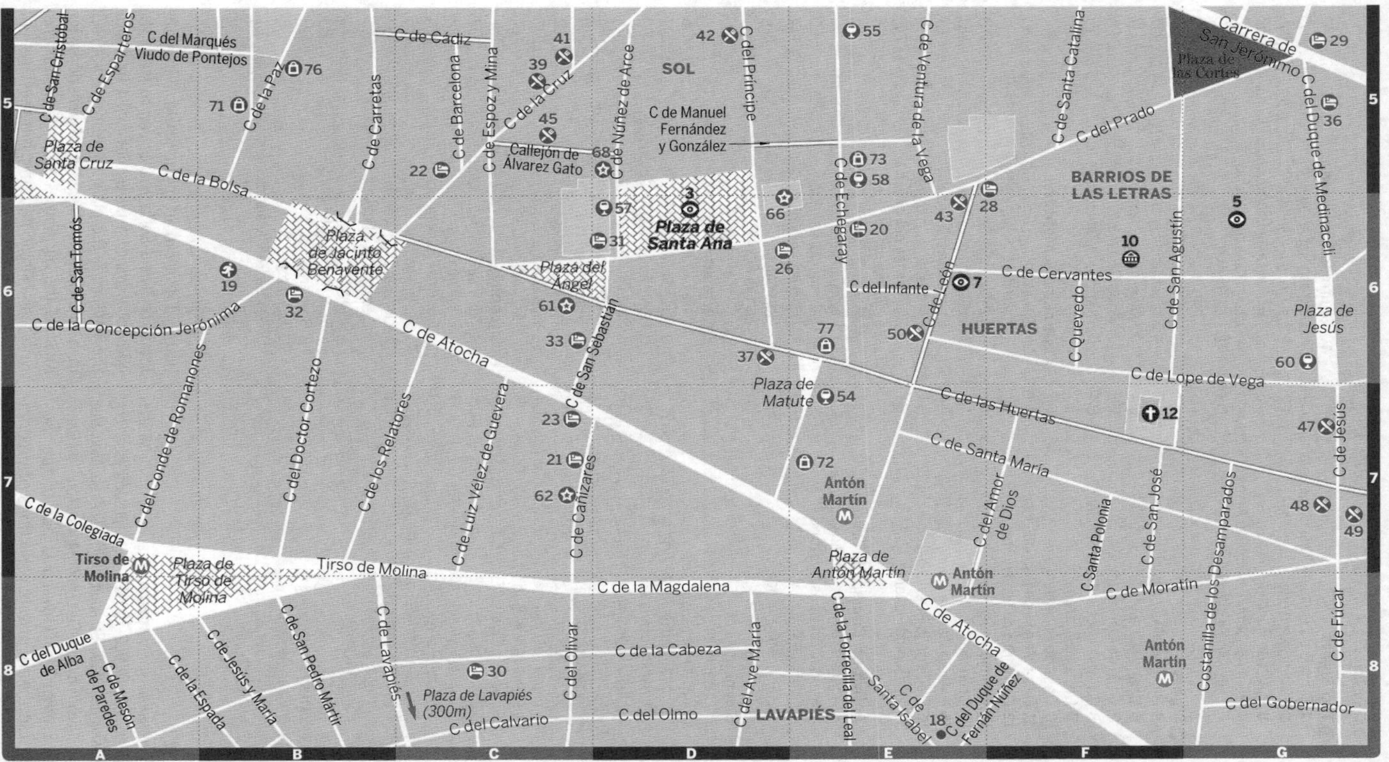
SOL
BARRIOS DE LAS LETRAS
HUERTAS
LAVAPIÉS
Plaza de Santa Ana
Plaza del Ángel
Plaza de Jacinto Benavente
Plaza de Santa Cruz
Plaza de Tirso de Molina
Plaza de Antón Martín
Plaza de Matute
Plaza de Jesús
Plaza de las Cortes
Plaza de Lavapiés (300m)
Antón Martín
Tirso de Molina
Carrera de San Jerónimo
C del Duque de Medinaceli
C del Prado
C de Santa Catalina
C de Ventura de la Vega
C de Echegaray
C del Príncipe
C de Manuel Fernández y González
C de Núñez de Arce
Callejón de Álvarez Gato
C de la Cruz
C de Espoz y Mina
C de Barcelona
C de Cádiz
C de Carretas
C de la Paz
C del Marqués Viudo de Pontejos
C de Esparteros
C de San Cristóbal
C de la Bolsa
C de San Tomás
C de la Concepción Jerónima
C del Conde de Romanones
C del Doctor Cortezo
C de Atocha
C de los Relatores
C de Luiz Vélez de Guevara
C de Cañizares
C de San Sebastián
C de las Huertas
C del Infante
C de León
C de Cervantes
C Quevedo
C de San Agustín
C de Lope de Vega
C de Jesús
C de Fúcar
C del Gobernador
Costanilla de los Desamparados
C de San José
C de Moratín
C Santa Polonia
C de Santa María
C del Amor de Dios
C del Duque de Fernán Núñez
C de Santa Isabel
C de la Torrecilla del Leal
C del Ave María
C de la Magdalena
C de la Cabeza
C del Olmo
C del Olivar
C del Calvario
C de Lavapiés
C de San Pedro Mártir
C de Jesús y María
C de la Espada
C de Mesón de Paredes
C del Duque de Alba
C de la Colegiata

Sol, Santa Ana & Huertas

Top Sights
- 1 Círculo de Bellas Artes ... G2
- 2 Edificio Metrópolis ... F2
- 3 Plaza de Santa Ana ... D6
- 4 Real Academia de Bellas Artes de San Fernando ... D3

Sights
- 5 Barrio de las Letras ... G6
- 6 Bear Statue ... C4
- 7 Calle de Cervantes 2 ... E6
- 8 Carlos III Equestrian Statue ... B4
- 9 Casa de Correos ... B4
- 10 Casa de Lope de Vega ... F6
- 11 Casa Museo de Ratón Perez ... A4
- 12 Convento de las Trinitarias ... F7
- 13 Edificio Grassy ... F2
- 14 Gran Vía ... B1
- 15 Palacio Gaviria ... A4
- 16 Plaza de la Puerta del Sol ... B4
- 17 Telefónica Building ... C1

Activities, Courses & Tours
- 18 Academia Amor de Dios ... E8
- Fundación Conservatorio Casa Patas ... (see 62)
- 19 Hammam al-Andalus ... B6

Sleeping
- 20 Catalonia Las Cortes ... E6
- 21 Cat's Hostel ... C7
- Hostal Adria Santa Ana ... (see 22)
- 22 Hostal Adriano ... C5
- 23 Hostal Fonda Horizonte ... C7
- 24 Hostal Luis XV ... C1
- 25 Hostal Madrid ... A4
- 26 Hotel Alicia ... D6
- 27 Hotel Urban ... E4
- 28 Hotel Vincci Soho ... F5
- 29 Lapepa Chic B&B ... G5
- 30 Mad Hostel ... C8
- 31 Me Melía Reina Victoria ... D6
- 32 Mola! Hostel ... B6
- 33 NH Collection Palacio de Tepa ... C6
- 34 Praktik Metropol ... C1
- 35 The Principal Madrid ... F2
- 36 Westin Palace ... G5

Eating
- 37 Casa Alberto ... D6
- 38 Casa Labra ... A3
- 39 Casa Toni ... C5
- 40 Gourmet Experience ... A1
- 41 La Casa del Abuelo ... C5
- 42 La Finca de Susana ... D5
- 43 La Mucca de Prado ... E6
- 44 La Terraza del Casino ... E3
- 45 Las Bravas ... C5
- 46 Lhardy ... D4
- 47 Los Gatos ... G7
- 48 Maceiras ... G7
- 49 Maceiras ... G7
- 50 Vinos González ... E6
- 51 Yakitoro by Chicote ... F1

Drinking & Nightlife
- 52 Bar Cock ... E1
- Café del Círculo de Bellas Artes ... (see 1)
- 53 Del Diego ... E1
- 54 El Imperfecto ... E7
- Glass Bar ... (see 27)
- La Terraza del Urban ... (see 27)
- 55 La Venencia ... E5
- 56 Museo Chicote ... E1
- 57 Radio ... D6
- 58 Salmón Gurú ... E5
- 59 Taberna Alhambra ... C4
- 60 Taberna La Dolores ... G6
- Tartân Roof ... (see 1)

Entertainment
- 61 Café Central ... C6
- 62 Casa Patas ... C7
- 63 Costello Café & Niteclub ... D2
- 64 Sala El Sol ... D2
- 65 Teatro de la Zarzuela ... F4
- 66 Teatro Español ... D6
- 67 Torres Bermejas ... B1
- 68 Villa Rosa ... D5

Shopping
- 69 Casa de Diego ... B3
- 70 Casa de Diego ... B2
- Gourmet Experience ... (see 40)
- 71 Justo Algaba ... B5
- 72 Librería Desnivel ... E7
- 73 Licores Cabello ... E5
- 74 Loewe ... F1
- 75 Real Madrid Store ... B3
- 76 Santarrufina ... B5
- 77 The Corner Shop ... E6
- 78 Tienda Real Madrid ... B1

★**Museo Thyssen-Bornemisza** MUSEUM
(Map p92; ☎902 760511; www.museothyssen.org; Paseo del Prado 8; adult/child €12/free, Mon free; ⏲10am-7pm Tue-Sun, noon-4pm Mon; Ⓜ Banco de España) The Thyssen is one of the most extraordinary private collections of predominantly European art in the world. Where the Prado or Reina Sofía enable you to study the body of work of a particular artist in depth, the Thyssen is the place to immerse yourself in a breathtaking breadth of artistic styles. Most of the big names are here, sometimes with just a single painting, but the Thyssen's

gift to Madrid and the art-loving public is to have them all under one roof. Begin on the top floor and work your way down.

➡ Second Floor

The 2nd floor, which is home to medieval art, includes some real gems hidden among the mostly 13th- and 14th-century and predominantly Italian, German and Flemish religious paintings and triptychs. Unless you've got a specialist's eye, pause in Room 5, where you'll find one work by Italy's Piero della Francesca (1410–92) and the instantly recognisable *Portrait of King Henry VIII* by Holbein the Younger (1497–1543), before continuing on to Room 10 for the evocative 1586 *Massacre of the Innocents* by Lucas Van Valckenborch. Room 11 is dedicated to El Greco (with three pieces) and his Venetian contemporaries Tintoretto and Titian, while Caravaggio and the Spaniard José de Ribera dominate Room 12. A single painting each by Murillo and Zurbarán add further Spanish flavour in the two rooms that follow, while the exceptionally rendered views of Venice by Canaletto (1697–1768) should on no account be missed.

Best of all on this floor is the extension (Rooms A to H) built to house the collection of Carmen Thyssen-Bornemisza. Room C houses paintings by Canaletto, Constable and Van Gogh, while the stunning Room H includes works by Monet, Sisley, Renoir, Pissarro and Degas.

Before heading downstairs, a detour to Rooms 19 through 21 will satisfy those devoted to 17th-century Dutch and Flemish masters, such as Anton van Dyck, Jan Brueghel the Elder, Rubens and Rembrandt (one painting).

➡ First Floor

If all that sounds impressive, the 1st floor is where the Thyssen really shines. There's a Gainsborough in Room 28 and a Goya in Room 31, but if you've been skimming the surface of this overwhelming collection, Room 32 is the place to linger over each and every painting. The astonishing texture of Van Gogh's *Les Vessenots* is a masterpiece, but the same could be said for *Woman in Riding Habit* by Manet, *The Thaw at Vétheuil* by Monet, Renoir's *Woman with a Parasol in a Garden* and Pissarro's quintessentially Parisian *Rue Saint-Honoré in the Afternoon*. Room 33 is also something special, with Cézanne, Gauguin, Toulouse-Lautrec and Degas, while the big names continue in Room 34 (Picasso, Matisse and Modigliani) and 35 (Edvard Munch and Egon Schiele).

In the 1st floor's extension (Rooms I to P), the names speak for themselves. Room K has works by Monet, Pissaro, Sorolla and Sisley, while Room L is the domain of Gauguin (including his iconic *Mata Mua*), Degas and Toulouse-Lautrec. Rooms M (Munch), N (Kandinsky), O (Matisse and Georges Braque) and P (Picasso, Matisse, Edward Hopper and Juan Gris) round out an outrageously rich journey through the masters. On your way to the stairs there's Edward Hopper's *Hotel Room*.

➡ Ground Floor

On the ground floor, the foray into the 20th century that you began in the 1st-floor extension takes over with a fine spread of paintings from cubism through to pop art.

In Room 41 you'll see a nice mix of the big three of cubism, Picasso, Georges Braque and Madrid's own Juan Gris, along with several other contemporaries. Kandinsky is the main drawcard in Room 43, while there's an early Salvador Dalí alongside Max Ernst and Paul Klee in Room 44. Picasso appears again in Room 45, another one of the gallery's standout rooms; its treasures include works by Marc Chagall and Dalí's hallucinatory *Dream Caused by the Flight of a Bee Around a Pomegranate, One Second Before Waking Up*.

Room 46 is similarly rich, with Joan Miró's *Catalan Peasant with a Guitar*, the splattered craziness of Jackson Pollock's *Brown and Silver I*, and the deceptively simple but strangely pleasing *Green on Maroon* by Mark Rothko taking centre stage. In Rooms 47 and 48 the Thyssen builds to a stirring climax, with Francis Bacon, Roy Lichtenstein, Henry Moore and Lucian Freud, Sigmund's Berlin-born grandson, all represented.

★Centro de Arte Reina Sofía MUSEUM

(Map p92; ☎91 774 10 00; www.museoreinasofia.es; Calle de Santa Isabel 52; adult/concession €10/free, 1.30-7pm Sun, 7-9pm Mon & Wed-Sat free, tickets cheaper if purchased online; ⏰10am-9pm Mon & Wed-Sat, to 7pm Sun; Ⓜ Atocha) Home to Picasso's *Guernica*, arguably Spain's most famous artwork, the Centro de Arte Reina Sofía is Madrid's premier collection of contemporary art. In addition to plenty of paintings by Picasso, other major drawcards are works by Salvador Dalí and Joan Miró. The collection principally spans the 20th century up to the 1980s. The occasional non-Spanish artist makes an appearance (including Francis

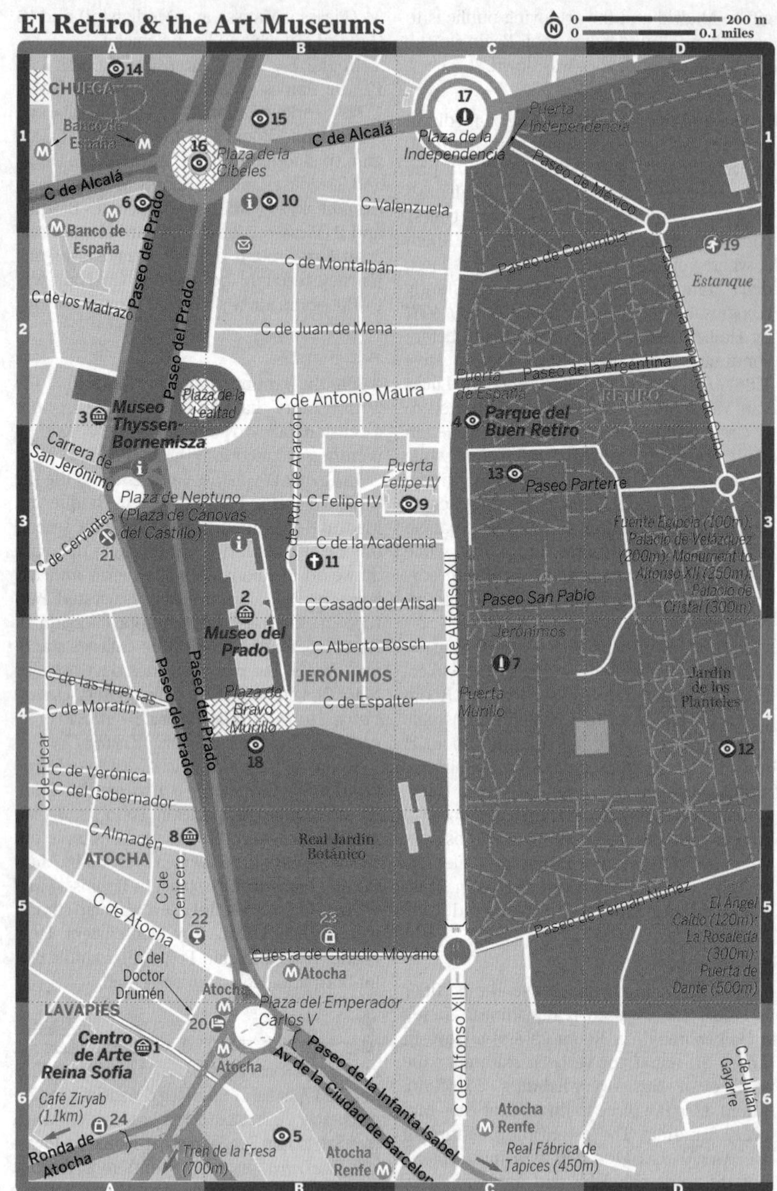

Bacon's *Lying Figure;* 1966), but most of the collection is strictly peninsular.

The permanent collection is displayed on the 2nd and 4th floors of the main wing of the museum, the Edificio Sabatini. *Guernica's* location never changes – you'll find it in Room 206 on the 2nd floor. Beyond that, the location of specific paintings can be a little confusing. The museum follows a theme-based approach, which ensures that you'll find works by Picasso or Miró, for example, spread across the two floors. The only

El Retiro & the Art Museums

Top Sights
1 Centro de Arte Reina Sofía....A6
2 Museo del Prado....B3
3 Museo Thyssen-Bornemisza....A2
4 Parque del Buen Retiro....C2

Sights
5 Antigua Estación de Atocha....B6
6 Banco de España....A1
7 Bosque del Recuerdo....C4
8 Caixa Forum....A5
9 Casón del Buen Retiro....C3
10 CentroCentro....B1
11 Iglesia de San Jerónimo El Real....B3
12 Jardín de los Planteles....D4
13 Madrid's Oldest Tree....C3
Mirador de Madrid....(see 10)
14 Palacio Buenavista....A1
15 Palacio de Linares....B1
16 Plaza de la Cibeles....A1
17 Puerta de Alcalá....C1
18 Real Jardín Botánico....B4

Activities, Courses & Tours
19 Row Boats....D2

Sleeping
20 60 Balconies Atocha....B6

Eating
21 Estado Puro....A3
Palacio de Cibeles....(see 10)

Drinking & Nightlife
22 Teatro Kapital....A5

Shopping
23 Cuesta de Claudio Moyano Bookstalls....B5
24 Librería la Central....A6

solution if you're looking for something specific is to pick up the latest copy of the *Planos de Museo* (Museum Floorplans) from the information desk just outside the main entrance; it lists the rooms in which each artist appears (although not individual paintings).

In addition to Picasso's *Guernica,* which is worth the admission fee on its own, don't neglect the artist's preparatory sketches in the rooms surrounding Room 206; they offer an intriguing insight into the development of this seminal work. If Picasso's cubist style has captured your imagination, the work of the Madrid-born Juan Gris (1887–1927) or Georges Braque (1882–1963) may appeal.

The work of Joan Miró (1893–1983) is defined by often delightfully bright primary colours, but watch out also for a handful of his equally odd sculptures. Since his paintings became a symbol of the Barcelona Olympics in 1992, his work has begun to receive the international acclaim it so richly deserves – the museum is a fine place to see a representative sample of his innovative work.

The Reina Sofía is also home to 20 or so canvases by Salvador Dalí (1904–89), of which the most famous is perhaps the surrealist extravaganza that is *El gran masturbador* (1929). Among his other works is a strange bust of a certain *Joelle,* which Dalí created with his friend Man Ray (1890–1976). Another well-known surrealist painter, Max Ernst (1891–1976), is also worth tracking down.

If you can tear yourself away from the big names, the Reina Sofía offers a terrific opportunity to learn more about sometimes lesser-known 20th-century Spanish artists. Among these are Miquel Barceló (b 1957); *madrileño* artist José Gutiérrez Solana (1886–1945); the renowned Basque painter Ignazio Zuloaga (1870–1945); Benjamín Palencia (1894–1980), whose paintings capture the turbulence of Spain in the 1930s; Barcelona painter Antoni Tàpies (1923–2012); pop artist Eduardo Arroyo (b 1937); and abstract painters such as Eusebio Sempere (1923–85) and members of the Equipo 57 group (founded in 1957 by a group of Spanish artists in exile in Paris), such as Pablo Palazuelo (1916–2007). Better known as a poet and playwright, Federico García Lorca (1898–1936) is represented by a number of his sketches.

Of the sculptors, watch in particular for Pablo Gargallo (1881–1934), whose work in bronze includes a bust of Picasso, and the renowned Basque sculptors Jorge Oteiza (1908–2003) and Eduardo Chillida (1924–2002).

★Parque del Buen Retiro GARDENS

(Map p92; Plaza de la Independencia; 6am-midnight May-Sep, to 10pm Oct-Apr; M Retiro, Príncipe de Vergara, Ibiza, Atocha) The glorious gardens of El Retiro are as beautiful as any you'll find in a European city. Littered with marble monuments, landscaped lawns, the occasional elegant building (the Palacio de Cristal is especially worth seeking out) and abundant greenery, it's quiet and contemplative during the week but comes to life on weekends. Put simply, this is one of our favourite places in Madrid.

SEAN PAVONE / SHUTTERSTOCK ©

TOP SIGHT
MUSEO DEL PRADO

Welcome to one of the world's premier art galleries. The Museo del Prado's collection is like a window onto the historical vagaries of the Spanish soul, at once grand and imperious in the royal paintings of Velázquez, darkly tumultuous in Goya's *Pinturas negras* (Black Paintings) and outward looking with sophisticated works of art from all across Europe.

Casón del Buen Retiro

This **building** (Map p92; ☎902 107077; Calle de Alfonso XII 28; ⏱hours vary; Ⓜ Retiro) overlooking the Parque del Buen Retiro is run as an academic library by the nearby Museo del Prado. The Prado runs guided visits to the stunning Hall of the Ambassadors, which is crowned by the astonishing 1697 ceiling fresco *The Apotheosis of the Spanish Monarchy* by Luca Giordano.

Edificio Jerónimos

The Prado's eastern wing (Edificio Jerónimos) is part of the Prado's stunning modern extension. Dedicated to temporary exhibitions (usually to display Prado masterpieces held in storage for decades for lack of wall space), its main attraction is the 2nd-floor cloisters. Built in 1672 with local granite, the cloisters were until recently attached to the adjacent Iglesia de San Jerónimo El Real (p103).

Edificio Villanueva

The Prado's western wing (Edificio Villanueva) was completed in 1785 as the neoclassical Palacio de Villanueva. It

DON'T MISS

- Goya
- Velázquez
- Flemish Collection
- *The Garden of Earthly Delights*
- El Greco
- *Emperor Carlos V on Horseback*
- Edificio Villanueva
- Edificio Jerónimos
- Casón del Buen Retiro

PRACTICALITIES

- Map p92
- www.museodelprado.es
- Paseo del Prado
- adult/child €15/free, 6-8pm Mon-Sat & 5-7pm Sun free, audio guide €3.50, admission plus official guidebook €24
- ⏱10am-8pm Mon-Sat, to 7pm Sun
- Ⓜ Banco de España

served as a cavalry barracks for Napoleon's troops between 1808 and 1813. In 1814 King Fernando VII decided to use the palace as a museum. Five years later the Museo del Prado opened with 311 Spanish paintings on display.

El Greco

This Greek-born artist (hence the name) is considered the finest of the Prado's Spanish Renaissance painters. The vivid, almost surreal works by this 16th-century master and adopted Spaniard, whose figures are characteristically slender and tortured, are perfectly executed. Two of his more than 30 paintings in the collection – *The Annunciation* and *The Flight into Egypt* – were painted in Italy before the artist arrived in Spain, while *The Trinity* and *Knight with His Hand on His Breast* are considered his most important works.

Emperor Carlos V on Horseback (Titian)

Considered one of the finest equestrian and royal portraits in art history, this 16th-century work is said to be the forerunner to similar paintings by Diego Rodríguez de Silva Velázquez a century later. One of the great masters of the Renaissance, Titian (1488–1576) was entering his most celebrated period as a painter when he created this, and it is widely recognised as one of his masterpieces.

Only in Madrid

Madrid must be the only city in the world where a near riot was caused by an art exhibition. John Hooper in his book *The New Spaniards* tells the story of how in 1990 the Prado brought an unprecedented number of works by Velázquez out of storage and opened its doors to the public. The exhibition was so popular that more than half a million visitors came to see the rare showing. Just before the exhibition was scheduled to end, the Prado announced that they would keep the doors open for as long as there were people wanting to enter. When the doors finally shut at 9pm, several hundred people were still outside waiting in the rain. They chanted, they shouted and they banged on the doors of this august institution with their umbrellas. The gallery was reopened, but queues kept forming and when the doors shut on the exhibition for good at 10.30pm, furious art lovers clashed with police. At midnight, there were still almost 50 people outside chanting 'We want to come in'.

TICKETS

Entrance to the Prado is via the eastern Puerta de los Jerónimos; tickets must first be purchased from the **ticket office** (Puerta de Goya; Map p92; www.museodelprado.es; Calle de Felipe IV; ⌚9.45am-7.30pm Mon-Sat, to 6.30pm Sun; Ⓜ Banco de España) at the northern end of the building, opposite the Hotel Ritz and beneath the Puerta de Goya.

The free floor plan to the Prado (available at or just inside the entrance) lists the location of 50 Prado masterpieces and gives room numbers for all major artists. It's also available online.

Goya

Francisco Goya is sometimes described as the first of the great Spanish masters and his work is found on all three floors of the Prado. Begin at the southern end of the ground or lower level where, in Rooms 64 and 65, Goya's *El dos de mayo* and *El tres de mayo* rank among Madrid's most emblematic paintings. In the adjacent rooms (66 and 67), his disturbing *Pinturas negras* (Black Paintings) are so named for the distorted animalesque appearance of their characters. The *Saturno devorando a su hijo* (Saturn Devouring His Son) is utterly disturbing, while *La romería de San Isidro* and *Aquelarre* or *El gran cabrón* (The Great He-Goat) are dominated by the compelling individual faces of the condemned souls. An interesting footnote to *Pinturas negras* is *El coloso,* a Goyaesque work hanging next to the *Pinturas negras* that was long considered part of the master's portfolio until the Prado's experts decided otherwise in 2008.

Up on the 1st floor, other masterful works include the intriguing *La família de Carlos IV,* which portrays the Spanish royal family in 1800; Goya portrayed himself in the background just as Velázquez did in *Las meninas*. Also present are *La maja vestida* (The Young Lady Dressed) and *La maja desnuda* (The Young Lady Undressed). These portraits of an unknown woman, commonly believed to be the Duquesa de Alba (who some think may have been Goya's lover), are identical save for the lack of clothing in the latter.

The Best of the Rest

No matter how long you spend in the Prado, there's always more to discover, such as the paintings by Dürer, Rafael, Tintoretto, Sorolla, Gainsborough, Fra Angelico, Tiepolo...

The Flemish Collection

The Prado's outstanding collection of Flemish art includes the fulsome figures and bulbous cherubs of Peter Paul Rubens (1577–1640). His signature works are *Las tres gracias* and *Adoración de los reyes magos*. Other fine works in the vicinity include *The Triumph of Death* by Pieter Bruegel and those by Anton Van Dyck.

Van Der Weyden's 1435 painting *El descendimiento* is unusual, both for its size and for the recurring crossbow shapes in the painting's upper corners, which are echoed in the bodies of Mary and Christ (the painting was commissioned by a Crossbow Manufacturers Brotherhood). Once the central part of a triptych, the painting is filled with drama and luminous colours.

On no account miss the weird and wonderful *The Garden of Earthly Delights* (Room 56A) by Hieronymus Bosch (c 1450–1516). No one has yet been able to provide a definitive explanation for this hallucinatory work, although many have tried. The closer you look, the harder it is to escape the feeling that he must have been doing some extraordinary drugs.

Judith at the Banquet of Holofernes, the only painting by Rembrandt in the Prado's collection, was completed in 1634; note the artist's signature and date on the arm of the chair. The painting shows a master at the peak of his powers, with an expert use of the chiaroscuro style, and the astonishing detail in the subject's clothing and face.

Museo del Prado

Velázquez

Velázquez's role as court painter means that his works provide a fascinating insight into 17th-century royal life and the Prado holds the richest collection of his works. Of all the works by Velázquez, *Las meninas* (The Maids of Honour; Room 12) is what most people come to see. Completed in 1656, it is more properly known as *La família de Felipe IV* (The Family of Felipe IV). It depicts Velázquez himself on the left and, in the centre, the infant Margarita. There's more to it than that: the artist in fact portrays himself painting the king and queen, whose images appear, according to some experts, in mirrors behind Velázquez. His mastery of light and colour is never more apparent than here. An interesting detail of the painting, aside from the extraordinary cheek of painting himself in royal company, is the presence of the cross of the Order of Santiago on his vest. The artist was apparently obsessed with being given a noble title. He received it shortly before his death, but in this oil painting he has awarded himself the order years before it would in fact be his!

The rooms surrounding *Las meninas* (Rooms 14 and 15) contain more fine paintings of various members of royalty who seem to spring off the canvas, many of them on horseback. Also nearby is his *La rendición de Breda* (The Surrender of Breda), while other Spanish painters worth tracking down in the neighbouring rooms include Bartolomé Esteban Murillo, José de Ribera and the stark figures of Francisco de Zurbarán.

Museo del Prado

PLAN OF ATTACK

Begin on the 1st floor with ❶ **Las meninas** by Velázquez. Although it alone is worth the entry price, it's a fine introduction to the 17th-century golden age of Spanish art; nearby are more of Velázquez' royal paintings and works by Zurbarán and Murillo. While on the 1st floor, seek out Goya's ❷ **La maja vestida and La maja desnuda**, with more of Goya's early works in neighbouring rooms. Downstairs at the southern end of the Prado, Goya's anger is evident in the searing ❸ **El dos de mayo and El tres de mayo**, and the torment of Goya's later years finds expression in the adjacent rooms with ❹ **Las pinturas negras** (the Black Paintings). Also on the lower floor, Hieronymus Bosch's weird and wonderful ❺ **The Garden of Earthly Delights** is one of the Prado's signature masterpieces. Returning to the 1st floor, El Greco's ❻ **Adoration of the Shepherds** is an extraordinary work, as is Peter Paul Rubens' ❼ **Las tres gracias**, which forms the centrepiece of the Prado's gathering of Flemish masters. (Note: this painting may be moved to the 2nd floor.) A detour to the 2nd floor takes in some lesser-known Goyas, but finish in the ❽ **Edificio Jerónimos** with a visit to the cloisters and the outstanding bookshop.

TOP TIPS

- Purchase your ticket online (www.museodelprado.es) and avoid the queues.
- Best time to visit is as soon as possible after opening time.
- The website (www.museodelprado.es/coleccion/que-ver) has self-guided tours for one- to three-hour visits.
- Nearby are Museo Thyssen-Bornemisza and Centro de Arte Reina Sofía. Together they form an extraordinary trio of galleries.

Las meninas (Velázquez)

This masterpiece depicts Velázquez and the Infanta Margarita. According to some experts, the images of the king and queen appear in mirrors behind Velázquez.

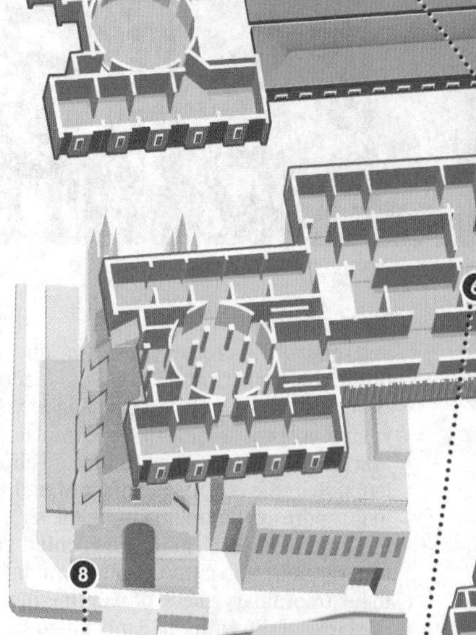

Edificio Jerónimos

Opened in 2007, this state-of-the-art extension has rotating exhibitions of Prado masterpieces held in storage for decades for lack of wall space, and stunning 2nd-floor granite cloisters that date back to 1672.

Adoration of the Shepherds (El Greco)

There's an ecstatic quality to this intense painting. El Greco's distorted rendering of bodily forms came to characterise much of his later work.

Las tres gracias (Rubens)
A late Rubens masterpiece, *The Three Graces* is a classical and masterly expression of Rubens' preoccupation with sensuality, here portraying Aglaia, Euphrosyne and Thalia, the daughters of Zeus.

La maja vestida & La maja desnuda (Goya)
These enigmatic works scandalised early-19th-century Madrid society, fuelling the rumour mill as to the woman's identity and drawing the ire of the Spanish Inquisition.

DEA PICTURE LIBRARY / GETTY IMAGES ©

DEA / G. DAGLI ORTI / GETTY IMAGES ©

El dos de mayo & El tres de mayo (Goya)
Few paintings evoke a city's sense of self quite like Goya's portrayal of Madrid's valiant but ultimately unsuccessful uprising against French rule in 1808.

Las pinturas negras (Goya)
Las pinturas negras are Goya's darkest works. *Saturno devorando a su hijo* evokes a writhing mass of tortured humanity, while *La romería de San Isidro* and *El aquelarre* are profoundly unsettling.

The Garden of Earthly Delights (Bosch)
A fantastical painting in triptych form, this overwhelming work depicts the Garden of Eden and what the Prado describes as 'the lugubrious precincts of Hell' in exquisitely bizarre detail.

KRZYSZTOF DYDYNSKI / GETTY IMAGES ©

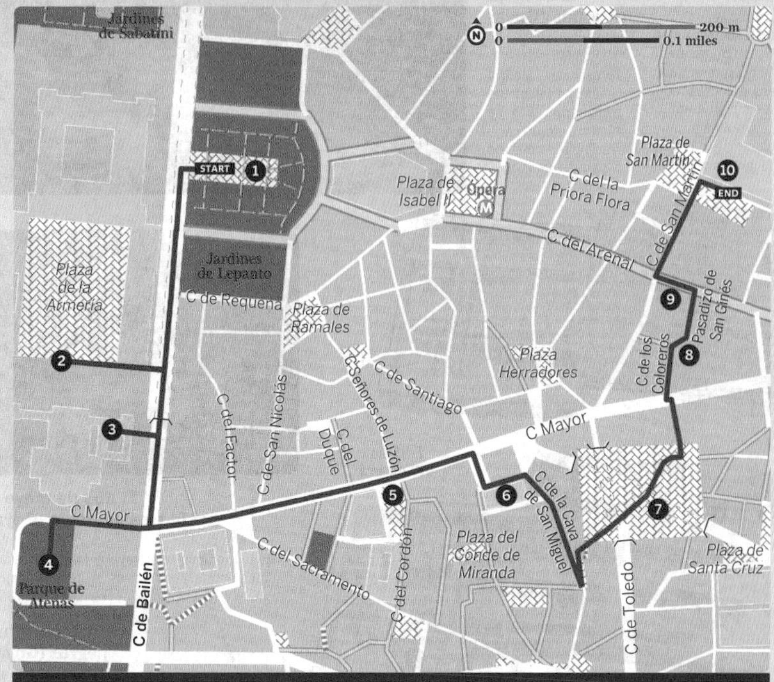

City Walk
Old Madrid

START PLAZA DE ORIENTE
END CONVENTO DE LAS DESCALZAS REALES
LENGTH 2KM; TWO HOURS

Begin in ❶ **Plaza de Oriente** (p76), a splendid arc of greenery and graceful architecture that could be Madrid's most agreeable plaza. You'll find yourself surrounded by gardens, the Palacio Real and the Teatro Real, peopled by an ever-changing cast of *madrileños* at play. Overlooking the plaza, ❷ **Palacio Real** (p76) was Spain's seat of royal power for centuries. Almost next door is ❸ **Catedral de Nuestra Señora de la Almudena** (p76); it may lack the solemnity of other Spanish cathedrals, but it's a beautiful part of the skyline.

From the cathedral, drop down to the ❹ **Muralla Árabe** (p79), a short stretch of the original 'Arab Wall', then climb gently up Calle Mayor, pausing to admire the last remaining ruins of Madrid's first cathedral, Santa María de la Almudena, then on to ❺ **Plaza de la Villa** (p79), a cosy square surrounded on three sides by some of the best examples of Madrid baroque architecture. A little further up the hill and just off Calle Mayor, ❻ **Mercado de San Miguel** (p117), one of Madrid's oldest markets, has become one of the coolest local places to eat.

Head down the hill along Cava de San Miguel, then climb up through the Arco de Cuchilleros to ❼ **Plaza Mayor** (p77), one of Spain's grandest and most beautiful plazas. Down a narrow lane north of the plaza, ❽ **Chocolatería de San Ginés** (p126) is justifiably famous for its *chocolate con churros* (deep-fried Spanish doughnuts with chocolate), the ideal Madrid indulgence at any hour of the day. Almost next door, along pedestrianised Calle del Arenal, there's the pleasing brick-and-stone ❾ **Iglesia de San Ginés** (p80), one of the longest-standing relics of Christian Madrid.

A short climb to the north, the ❿ **Convento de las Descalzas Reales** (p80) is an austere convent with an extraordinarily rich interior. In the heart of downtown Madrid, it's a great place to finish up.

Laid out in the 17th century by Felipe IV as the preserve of kings, queens and their intimates, the park was opened to the public in 1868, and ever since, when the weather's fine and on weekends in particular, *madrileños* from all across the city gather here to stroll, read the Sunday papers in the shade, take a boat ride or nurse a cool drink at the numerous outdoor *terrazas*.

The focal point for so much of El Retiro's life is the artificial *estanque* (lake), which is watched over by the massive ornamental structure of the **Monument to Alfonso XII** (Parque del Buen Retiro, Plaza de la Independencia; M Retiro) on the east side, complete with marble lions. As sunset approaches on a Sunday afternoon in summer, the crowd grows, bongos sound out across the park and people start to dance. **Row boats** (Map p92; per 45min weekdays/weekends €6/8; 10am-8.30pm Apr-Sep, to 5.45pm Oct-Mar; M Retiro) can be rented from the lake's northern shore – an iconic Madrid experience. On the southern end of the lake, the odd structure decorated with sphinxes is the **Fuente Egipcia** (Egyptian Fountain; Parque del Buen Retiro, Plaza de la Independencia; 6am-midnight May-Sep, to 10pm Oct-Apr; M Retiro); legend has it that an enormous fortune buried in the park by Felipe IV in the mid-18th century rests here. Hidden among the trees south of the lake is the **Palacio de Cristal** (91 574 66 14; www.museoreinasofia.es; Parque del Buen Retiro, Plaza de la Indepencia; 10am-10pm Apr-Sep, to 7pm Oct, to 6pm Nov-Mar; M Retiro), a magnificent metal-and-glass structure that is arguably El Retiro's most beautiful architectural monument. It was built in 1887 as a winter garden for exotic flowers and is now used for temporary exhibitions organised by the Centro de Arte Reina Sofía. Just north of here, the 1883 **Palacio de Velázquez** (www.museoreinasofia.es; Parque del Buen Retiro, Plaza de la Independencia; admission varies; 10am-10pm May-Sep, to 7pm Oct, to 6pm Nov-Apr) is also used for temporary exhibitions.

At the southern end of the park, near **La Rosaleda** (Rose Garden; Parque del Buen Retiro, Plaza de la Independencia; M Retiro, Atocha) with its more than 4000 roses, is a statue of **El Ángel Caído** (Parque del Buen Retiro, Plaza de la Independencia; M Retiro) (The Fallen Angel). Strangely, it sits 666m above sea level… The **Puerta de Dante** (Parque del Buen Retiro, Plaza de la Independencia; M Retiro), in the extreme southeastern corner of the park, is watched over by a carved mural of Dante's *Inferno*. Occupying much of the southwestern corner of the park is the **Jardín de los Planteles** (Map p92; Parque del Buen Retiro, Plaza de la Independencia; M Retiro), one of the least-visited sections of El Retiro, where quiet pathways lead beneath an overarching canopy of trees. West of here is the moving **Bosque del Recuerdo** (Memorial Garden; Map p92; Calle de Alfonso XII; 6am-10pm; M Retiro), an understated memorial to the 191 victims of the 11 March 2004 train bombings. For each victim stands an olive or cypress tree. To the north, just inside the Puerta de Felipe IV, stands what is thought to be **Madrid's oldest tree** (Map p92; Parque del Buen Retiro, Plaza de la Independencia; M Retiro), a Mexican conifer *(ahuehuete)* planted in 1633.

In the northeastern corner of the park is the **Ermita de San Isidro** (Map p104; Paseo del Quince de Mayo 62; M Retiro), a small country chapel noteworthy as one of the few, albeit modest, examples of Romanesque architecture in Madrid. When it was built, Madrid was a small village more than 2km away.

Plaza de la Cibeles SQUARE

(Map p92; M Banco de España) Of all the grand roundabouts that punctuate the Paseo del Prado, Plaza de la Cibeles most evokes the splendour of imperial Madrid. The jewel in the crown is the astonishing Palacio de Comunicaciones (p102). Other landmark buildings around the plaza's perimeter include the **Palacio de Linares and Casa de América** (Map p92; 91 595 48 00, ticket reservations 902 221424; www.casamerica.es; Plaza de la Cibeles 2; adult/student & senior/child €8/5/free; guided tours 11am, noon & 1pm Sat & Sun Sep-Jul, shorter hours Aug, ticket office 10am-3pm & 4-8pm Mon-Fri; M Banco de España), the **Palacio Buenavista** (Map p92; Plaza de la Cibeles; M Banco de España) and the national **Banco de España** (Map p92; Calle de Alcalá 48). The spectacular fountain of the goddess Cybele at the centre of the plaza is one of Madrid's most beautiful.

Ever since it was erected by Ventura Rodríguez in 1780, the fountain has been a Madrid favourite. Carlos III liked it so much he tried to have it moved to the royal gardens of the Granja de San Ildefonso, on the road to Segovia, but *madrileños* kicked up such a fuss that he let it be.

There are fine views east from Plaza de la Cibeles towards the Puerta de Alcalá or, even better, west towards the Edificio Metrópolis (p106).

WORTH A TRIP

CASA DE CAMPO

Sometimes called the 'lungs of Madrid', **Casa de Campo** (M Batán) is a 17-sq-km stand of greenery stretches west of the Río Manzanares. There are prettier and more central parks in Madrid but its scope is such that there are plenty of reasons to visit. And visit the *madrileños* do, nearly half a million of them every weekend, celebrating the fact that the short-lived Republican government of the 1930s opened the park to the public (it was previously the exclusive domain of royalty).

For city-bound *madrileños* with neither the time nor the inclination to go further afield, it has become the closest they get to nature, despite the fact that cyclists, walkers and picnickers overwhelm the byways and trails that criss-cross the park. There are tennis courts and a swimming pool, as well as the **Zoo Aquarium de Madrid** (☎902 345014; www.zoomadrid.com; Casa de Campo; adult/child €23/19; ⊙10.30am-10pm Sun-Thu, to midnight Fri & Sat Jul & Aug, shorter hours Sep-Jun; 🚌37 from Intercambiador de Príncipe Pío, M Casa de Campo) and the **Parque de Atracciones** (☎91 463 29 00; www.parquedeatracciones.es; Casa de Campo; adult/child €32/25; ⊙noon-midnight Jul & Aug, hours vary Sep-Jun). The **Teleférico** (☎91 541 11 18; www.teleferico.com; cnr Paseo del Pintor Rosales & Calle de Marqués de Urquijo; one-way/return €4.20/5.90; ⊙noon-9pm May-Aug, reduced hours Sep-Apr; M Argüelles) also takes you here with good views en route. At Casa de Campo's southern end, restaurants specialise in wedding receptions, ensuring plenty of bridal parties roaming the grounds in search of an unoccupied patch of greenery where they can take photos. Also in the park, the Andalucian-style ranch known as Batán is used to house the bulls destined to do bloody battle in the Fiestas de San Isidro Labrador.

CentroCentro ARTS CENTRE

(Map p92; ☎91 480 00 08; www.centrocentro.org; Plaza de la Cibeles 1; ⊙10am-8pm Tue-Sun; M Plaza de España) FREE One of Madrid's more surprising and diverse cultural spaces, CentroCentro is housed in the grand Palacio de Comunicaciones. It has cutting-edge exhibitions covering 5000 sq metres over four floors (floors 1, 3, 4 and 5), as well as quiet reading rooms and some stunning architecture, especially in the soaring Antiguo Patio de Operaciones on the 2nd floor. On the 8th floor is the Mirador de Madrid (p102).

Mirador de Madrid VIEWPOINT

(Map p92; www.centrocentro.org; 8th fl, Palacio de Comunicaciones, Plaza de la Cibeles; adult/child €2/0.50; ⊙10.30am-1.30pm & 4-7pm Tue-Sun; M Banco de España) The views from the summit of the Palacio de Comunicaciones are among Madrid's best, sweeping out over Plaza de la Cibeles, up the hill towards the sublime Edificio Metrópolis and out to the mountains. Buy your ticket up the stairs then take the lift to the 6th floor, from where the gates are opened every half hour. You can either take another lift or climb the stairs up to the 8th floor.

Puerta de Alcalá MONUMENT

(Map p92; Plaza de la Independencia; M Retiro) This imposing triumphal gate was once the main entrance to the city (its name derives from the fact that the road that passed under it led to Alcalá de Henares) and was surrounded by the city's walls. It was here that the city authorities controlled access to the capital and levied customs duties.

Caixa Forum MUSEUM, ARCHITECTURE

(Map p92; ☎91 330 73 00; https://obrasociallacaixa.org/en/cultura/caixaforum-madrid/que-hacemos; Paseo del Prado 36; adult/child €4/free; ⊙10am-8pm; M Atocha) This extraordinary structure is one of Madrid's most eye-catching landmarks. Seeming to hover above the ground, the brick edifice is topped by an intriguing summit of rusted iron. On an adjacent wall is the *jardín colgante* (hanging garden), a lush (if thinning) vertical wall of greenery almost four storeys high. Inside there are four floors of exhibition space awash in stainless steel and with soaring ceilings. The exhibitions here are always worth checking out and include photography, contemporary painting and multimedia shows.

Caixa Forum's shop (mostly books) is outstanding. You can visit the shop without paying the entrance fee.

Real Jardín Botánico GARDENS

(Royal Botanical Garden; Map p92; ☎91 420 04 38; www.rjb.csic.es; Plaza de Bravo Murillo 2; adult/child €4/free; ⊙10am-9pm May-Aug, to 8pm Apr & Sep, to 7pm Mar & Oct, to 6pm Nov-Feb; M Atocha) Madrid's botanical gardens are a leafy oasis in the centre of town, though they're not as expansive or as popular as the Parque del Buen Retiro. With some 30,000 species crammed into a relatively small 8-hectare area, it's more a place to wander at leisure than laze under a tree, although there are benches dotted throughout the gardens where you can sit.

Iglesia de San Jerónimo El Real CHURCH

(Map p92; ☎91 420 35 78; Calle de Ruiz de Alarcón; ⏲10am-1pm & 5-8.30pm; Ⓜ Atocha, Banco de España) FREE Tucked away behind Museo del Prado, this chapel was traditionally favoured by the Spanish royal family, and King Juan Carlos I was crowned here in 1975 upon the death of Franco. The sometimes-sober, sometimes-splendid mock-Isabelline interior is actually a 19th-century reconstruction that took its cues from Iglesia de San Juan de los Reyes in Toledo; the original was largely destroyed during the Peninsular War. What remained of the former cloisters has been incorporated into Museo del Prado.

Antigua Estación de Atocha NOTABLE BUILDING

(Old Atocha Train Station; Map p92; Plaza del Emperador Carlos V; Ⓜ Atocha Renfe) In 1992 the northwestern wing of the Antigua Estación de Atocha was given a stunning overhaul. The structure of this grand iron-and-glass relic from the 19th century was preserved, while its interior was artfully converted into a light-filled tropical garden with more than 500 plant species. The project was the work of architect Rafael Moneo, and his landmark achievement was to create a thoroughly modern space that resonates with the stately European train stations of another age.

Real Fábrica de Tapices LANDMARK

(Royal Tapestry Workshop; ☎91 434 05 50; www.realfabricadetapices.com; Calle de Fuenterrabía 2; adult/child €5/3.50; ⏲10am-2pm Mon-Fri Sep-Jul, guided tours hourly; Ⓜ Atocha Renfe, Menéndez Pelayo) If a wealthy Madrid nobleman ever wanted to impress, he went to the Real Fábrica de Tapices, where royalty commissioned the pieces that adorned their palaces and private residences. The Spanish government, Spanish royal family and the Vatican were the biggest patrons of the tapestry business: Spain alone is said to have collected four million tapestries. With such an exclusive clientele, it was a lucrative business and remains so, 300 years after the factory was founded.

Salamanca

In the *barrio* of Salamanca, the unmistakeable whiff of old money mingles comfortably with the aspirations of Spain's nouveau riche. In short, it's the sort of place to put on your finest clothes, regardless of your errand, and simply be seen. Sights are thinly spread but worth tracking down, with a focus on the arts, architecture and the very Spanish passion of bullfighting.

★Plaza de Toros STADIUM

(☎91 356 22 00; www.las-ventas.com; Calle de Alcalá 237; ⏲10am-5.30pm; Ⓜ Ventas) FREE East of central Madrid, the Plaza de Toros Monumental de Las Ventas (Las Ventas) is the most important and prestigious bullring in the world, and a visit here is a good way to gain an insight into this very Spanish tradition. The fine **Museo Taurino** (☎91 725 18 57; www.las-ventas.com; Calle de Alcalá 237; ⏲10am-5.30pm; Ⓜ Ventas) FREE is also here, and the architecture will be of interest even to those with no interest in *la corridas* (bullfights). Bullfights are still held regularly here during the season, which runs roughly mid-May to September.

One of the largest rings in the bullfighting world, Las Ventas has a grand Mudéjar exterior and a suitably coliseum-like arena surrounding the broad sandy ring. It was opened in 1931 and hosted its first fight three years later; its four storeys can seat 25,000 spectators. Like all bullrings, it evokes more a sense of a theatre than a sports stadium. It also hosts concerts.

To be carried high on the shoulders of aficionados out through the grand and decidedly Moorish Puerta de Madrid is the

GOYA IN MADRID

Madrid has the best collection of Goyas on earth. Here's where to find them:

Museo del Prado (p94)

Real Academia de Bellas Artes de San Fernando (p86)

Ermita de San Antonio de la Florida (p107)

Museo Lázaro Galdiano (p105)

Basílica de San Francisco El Grande (p81)

Museo Thyssen-Bornemisza (p90)

Salamanca

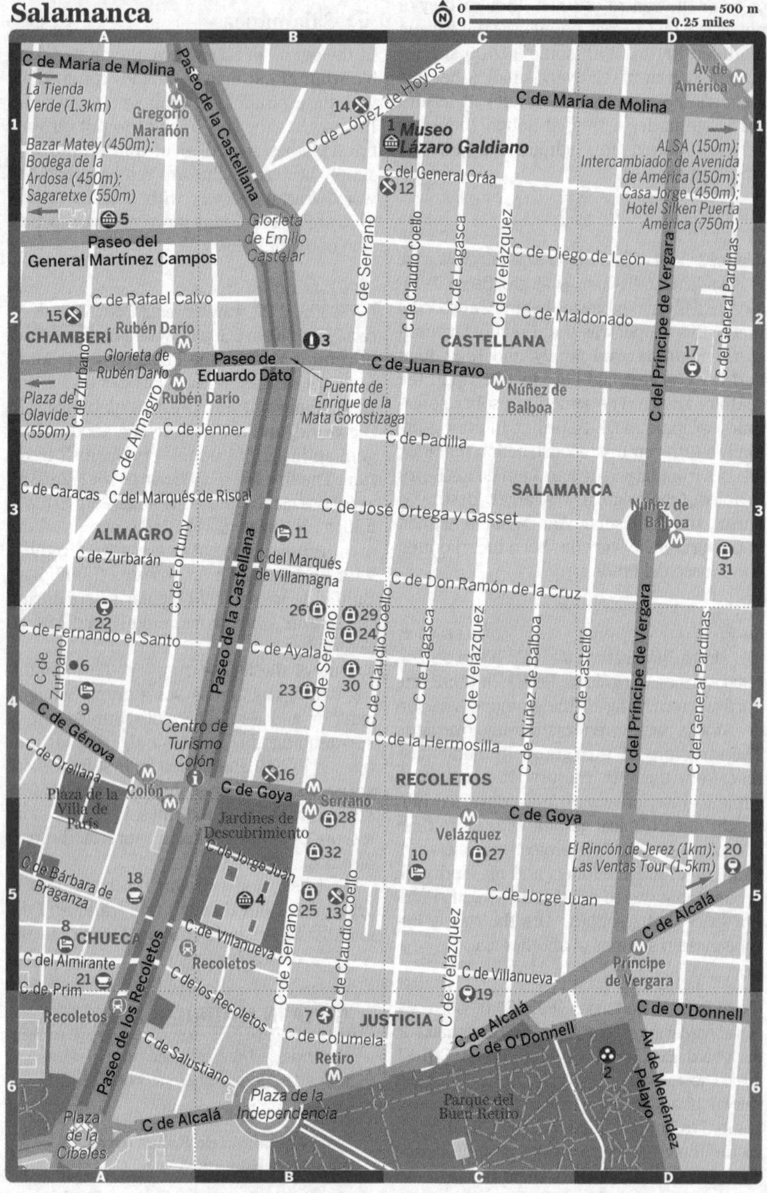

ultimate dream of any *torero* (bullfighter) – if you've made it at Las Ventas, you've reached the pinnacle of the bullfighting world. The gate is suitably known more colloquially as the 'Gate of Glory'. Guided visits (in English and Spanish) take you out onto the sand and into the royal box; tours must be booked in advance through **Las Ventas Tour** (☎687 739032; www.lasventastour.com; adult/child €13/10; ⏱10am-5.30pm, days of bullfight 10am-1.30pm; Ⓜ Ventas).

Salamanca

Top Sights
1 Museo Lázaro Galdiano C1

Sights
2 Ermita de San Isidro D6
3 Museo al Aire Libre B2
4 Museo Arqueológico Nacional B5
5 Museo Sorolla A1

Activities, Courses & Tours
6 International House A4
7 Lab Room Spa B6

Sleeping
8 60 Balconies Recoletos A5
9 Hotel Orfila A4
10 Petit Palace Art Gallery C5
11 Villa Magna B3

Eating
12 Astrolabius C1
13 Biotza B5
14 José Luis B1
15 Las Tortillas de Gabino A2
16 Platea B4

Drinking & Nightlife
17 Almonte D2
18 Café-Restaurante El Espejo A5
19 Gabana 1800 .... C6
20 Geographic Club D5
21 Gran Café de Gijón A5
22 La Vaquería Montañesa A4

Shopping
23 Agatha Ruiz de la Prada B4
24 Bombonerías Santa B4
25 Camper B5
26 De Viaje B4
27 Ekseption & Eks C5
28 Loewe B5
29 Manolo Blahnik B4
30 Mantequería Bravo B4
31 Oriol Balaguer D3
32 Purificación García B5

The Museo Taurino was closed for renovations and expansion at the time of research. When it reopens, expect a new space dedicated to bullfighting legend Manolete, as well as a curious collection of paraphernalia, costumes (the *traje de luces,* or suit of lights, is one of bullfighting's most recognisable props), photos and other bullfighting memorabilia up on the top floor above one of the two courtyards by the ring. It's a fascinating insight into the whole subculture that surrounds bullfighting.

The area where the Plaza de Toros is located is known as Las Ventas because, in times gone by, several wayside taverns (*ventas*), along with houses of ill repute, were to be found here.

★Museo Lázaro Galdiano MUSEUM

(Map p104; 91 561 60 84; www.flg.es; Calle de Serrano 122; adult/concession/child €6/3/free, last hour free; 10am-4.30pm Tue-Sat, to 3pm Sun; M Gregorio Marañón) This imposing early 20th-century Italianate stone mansion, set discreetly back from the street, belonged to Don José Lázaro Galdiano (1862–1947), a successful businessman and passionate patron of the arts. His astonishing private collection, which he bequeathed to the city upon his death, includes 13,000 works of art and objets d'art, a quarter of which are on show at any time.

Museo al Aire Libre SCULPTURE

(Map p104; Paseo de la Castellana; 24hr; M Rubén Darío) FREE This fascinating open-air collection of 17 abstract sculptures includes works by renowned Basque artist Eduardo Chillida, Catalan master Joan Miró, as well as Eusebio Sempere and Alberto Sánchez, among Spain's foremost sculptors of the 20th century. The sculptures are beneath the overpass where Paseo de Eduardo Dato crosses Paseo de la Castellana, but somehow the hint of traffic grime and pigeon shit only adds to the appeal. All but one are on the eastern side of Paseo de la Castellana.

Museo Arqueológico Nacional MUSEUM

(Map p104; 91 577 79 12; www.man.es; Calle de Serrano 13; admission €3, 2-8pm Sat & 9.30am-noon Sun free; 9.30am-8pm Tue-Sat, to 3pm Sun; M Serrano) The showpiece National Archaeology Museum contains a sweeping accumulation of artefacts behind its towering facade. Daringly redesigned within, the museum ranges across Spain's ancient history and the large collection includes stunning mosaics taken from Roman villas across Spain, intricate Muslim-era and Mudéjar handiwork, sculpted figures such as the *Dama de Ibiza* and *Dama de Elche,* examples of Romanesque and Gothic architectural styles and a partial copy of the prehistoric cave paintings of Altamira (Cantabria).

Malasaña & Chueca

Malasaña and Chueca are more for doing than seeing. But with a handful of architectural stars (the Antiguo Cuartel de Conde Duque, the Museo de Historia, the Sociedad General de Autores y Editores, and Gran Vía's marvellous facades), there's plenty to turn your head as you skip from bar to shop and back to the bar again. The neighbourhoods' squares – Plaza Dos de Mayo in particular – also provide much-needed breathing space as you wander the tightly packed streets.

Gran Vía STREET

(Map p88; Ⓜ Gran Vía, Callao) It's difficult to imagine Madrid without Gran Vía, the grand boulevard lined with towering belle-époque facades that climbs up through the centre of Madrid from Plaza de España then down to Calle de Alcalá. But it has only existed since 1910, when it was bulldozed through a labyrinth of old streets. Fourteen streets disappeared off the map, as did 311 houses, including one where Goya had once lived. In 2018, Gran Vía will be transformed into a largely pedestrian thoroughfare.

Plans for the boulevard were first announced in 1862 and so interminable were the delays that a famous *zarzuela* (Spanish mix of theatre, music and dance), *La Gran Vía,* first performed in 1886, was penned to mock the city authorities. It may have destroyed whole *barrios,* but Gran Vía is still considered one of the most successful examples of urban planning in central Madrid since the late 19th century.

One eye-catching building, the **Edificio Carrión** (Map p78; cnr Gran Vía & Calle de Jacometrezo; Ⓜ Callao) was Madrid's first pre-WWI tower-block apartment hotel. Also dominating the skyline about one-third of the way along Gran Vía is the 1920s-era **Telefónica building** (Map p88; Gran Vía; Ⓜ Gran Vía), which was for years the highest building in the city. During the civil war, when Madrid was besieged by Franco's forces and the boulevard became known as 'Howitzer Alley' due to the artillery shells that rained down upon it, the Telefónica building was a favoured target.

Among the more interesting buildings is the stunning, French-designed **Edificio Metrópolis** (Map p88; Gran Vía; Ⓜ Banco de España, Sevilla), built in 1907, which marks the southern end of Gran Vía. The winged victory statue atop its dome was added in 1975 and is best seen from Calle de Alcalá or Plaza de la Cibeles. A little up the boulevard is the **Edificio Grassy** (Map p88; Gran Vía 1; Ⓜ Banco de España, Sevilla), with the Rolex sign and built in 1916. With its circular 'temple' as a crown, and profusion of arcs and slender columns, it's one of the most elegant buildings along Gran Vía.

Otherwise Gran Vía is home to around twice as many businesses (over 1050 at last count) as homes (nearly 600); over 13,000 people work along the street; and up to 60,000 vehicles pass through every day (including almost 185 buses an hour during peak periods). There are over 40 hotels on Gran Vía, but, sadly, just three of the 15 cinemas for which Gran Vía was famous remain.

Museo de Historia MUSEUM

(Map p108; ☎ 91 701 16 86; www.madrid.es/museodehistoria; Calle de Fuencarral 78; ⏲ 10am-8pm Tue-Sun; Ⓜ Tribunal) FREE The fine Museo de Historia (formerly the Museo Municipal) has an elaborate and restored baroque entrance, raised in 1721 by Pedro de Ribera. Behind this facade, the collection is dominated by paintings and other memorabilia charting the historical evolution of Madrid. The highlights are Goya's *Allegory of the City of Madrid* (on the 1st floor); the caricatures lampooning Napoleon and the early-19th-century French occupation of Madrid (1st floor); and the expansive model of Madrid as it was in 1830 (basement).

Sociedad General de Autores y Editores ARCHITECTURE

(General Society of Authors & Editors; Map p108; Calle de Fernando VI 4; Ⓜ Alonso Martínez) This swirling, melting wedding cake of a building is as close as Madrid comes to the work of Antoni Gaudí, which so illuminates Barcelona. It's a joyously self-indulgent ode to Modernisme (an architectural and artistic style, influenced by art nouveau and sometimes known as Catalan modernism) and is virtually one of a kind in Madrid. Casual visitors are actively discouraged, but what you see from the street is impressive enough. The only exceptions are on the first Monday of October, International Architecture Day, when its interior staircase alone is reason enough to come look inside.

Museo Municipal de Arte Contemporáneo MUSEUM

(Map p108; ☎ 91 588 59 28; www.madrid.es/museoartecontemporaneo; Calle del Conde Duque 9-11; ⏲ 10am-2pm & 5.30-8.30pm Tue-Sat, 10.30am-2pm Sun; Ⓜ Ventura Rodríguez) FREE This rich collection of modern Spanish art includes mostly paintings and graphic art with a smattering of photography, sculpture and drawings. Highlights include Eduardo Arroyo and Basque sculptor Jorge Oteiza. Running throughout the collection are creative interpretations of Madrid's cityscape – avant-garde splodges and almost old-fashioned visions of modern Madrid side by side, among them a typically fantastical representation of the Cibeles fountain by one-time icon of *la movida madrileña* (the Madrid scene), Ouka Leele.

The museum is inside the **Antiguo Cuartel del Conde Duque** (Map p108; Calle del Conde Duque 9; Ⓜ Plaza de España, Ventura Rodríguez, San Bernardo).

Parque del Oeste & Northern Madrid

Madrid's north has some remarkable sights. The Ermita de San Antonio de la Florida is one of the city's richest treasures, while the Estadio Santiago Bernabéu is an icon in the world of sport. The only problem is that the many attractions are pretty far-flung, so be prepared to spend some time on the metro hopping from one to the other. The cluster of sights out west – Parque del Oeste, Faro de Madrid, Museo de América, Templo de Debod and Museo de Cerralbo – are an exception, not to mention wonderfully diverse.

★Estadio Santiago Bernabéu STADIUM

(tickets 902 324324, tours 91 398 43 00/70; www.realmadrid.com; Avenida de Concha Espina 1; tours adult/child €25/18; tours 10am-7pm Mon-Sat, 10.30am-6.30pm Sun, except match days; Ⓜ Santiago Bernabéu) Football fans and budding Madridistas (Real Madrid supporters) will want to make a pilgrimage to the Estadio Santiago Bernabéu, a temple to all that's extravagant and successful in football. Self-guided tours take you up into the stands for a panoramic view of the stadium, then through the presidential box, press room, dressing rooms, players' tunnel and even onto the pitch. The tour ends in the extraordinary Exposición de Trofeos (trophy exhibit). Better still, attend a game alongside 80,000 delirious fans.

For tours of the stadium, buy your ticket at window 10 (next to gate 7).

★Ermita de San Antonio de la Florida GALLERY

(Panteón de Goya; 91 542 07 22; www.sanantoniodelaflorida.es; Glorieta de San Antonio de la Florida 5; 9.30am-8pm Tue-Sun, hours vary Jul & Aug; Ⓜ Príncipe Pío) FREE The frescoed ceilings of the recently restored Ermita de San Antonio de la Florida are one of Madrid's most surprising secrets. The southern of the two small chapels is one of the few places to see Goya's work in its original setting, as painted by the master in 1798 on the request of Carlos IV. It's simply breathtaking.

The frescoes on the dome depict the miracle of St Anthony, who is calling on a young man to rise from the grave and absolve his father, unjustly accused of his murder. Around them swarms a typical Madrid crowd.

The painter is buried in front of the altar. His remains (minus the mysteriously missing head) were transferred in 1919 from Bordeaux (France), where he died in self-imposed exile in 1828.

Guided visits run from 9.30am to 1pm Tuesday to Friday when there are enough people.

★Templo de Debod RUINS

(Paseo del Pintor Rosales; 10am-8pm Tue-Sun; Ⓜ Ventura Rodríguez) FREE Yes, that *is* an Egyptian temple in downtown Madrid. The temple was saved from the rising waters of Lake Nasser in southern Egypt when Egyptian president Gamal Abdel Nasser built the Aswan High Dam. After 1968 it was sent block by block to Spain as a gesture of thanks to Spanish archaeologists in the Unesco team that worked to save the monuments that would otherwise have disappeared forever.

Plaza de Olavide PLAZA

(Ⓜ Bilbao, Iglesia, Quevedo) Plaza de Olavide is one of Madrid's most agreeable public spaces, a real *barrio* special. But it hasn't always had its current form. From 1934 the entire plaza was occupied by a covered, octagonal market. In November 1974, the market was demolished in a spectacular controlled explosion, opening up the plaza. To see the plaza's history told in pictures, step into Bar Méntrida at No 3 to have a drink and admire the photos on the wall.

Museo Sorolla GALLERY

(Map p104; 91 310 15 84; www.mecd.gob.es/msorolla; Paseo del General Martínez Campos 37; adult/child €3/free; 9.30am-8pm Tue-Sat, 10am-3pm Sun; Ⓜ Iglesia, Gregorio Marañón) The Valencian artist Joaquín Sorolla immortalised the clear Mediterranean light of the Valencian coast. His Madrid house, a quiet mansion surrounded by lush gardens that he designed himself, was inspired by what he had seen in Andalucía and now contains the most complete collection of the artist's works.

Malasaña & Chueca

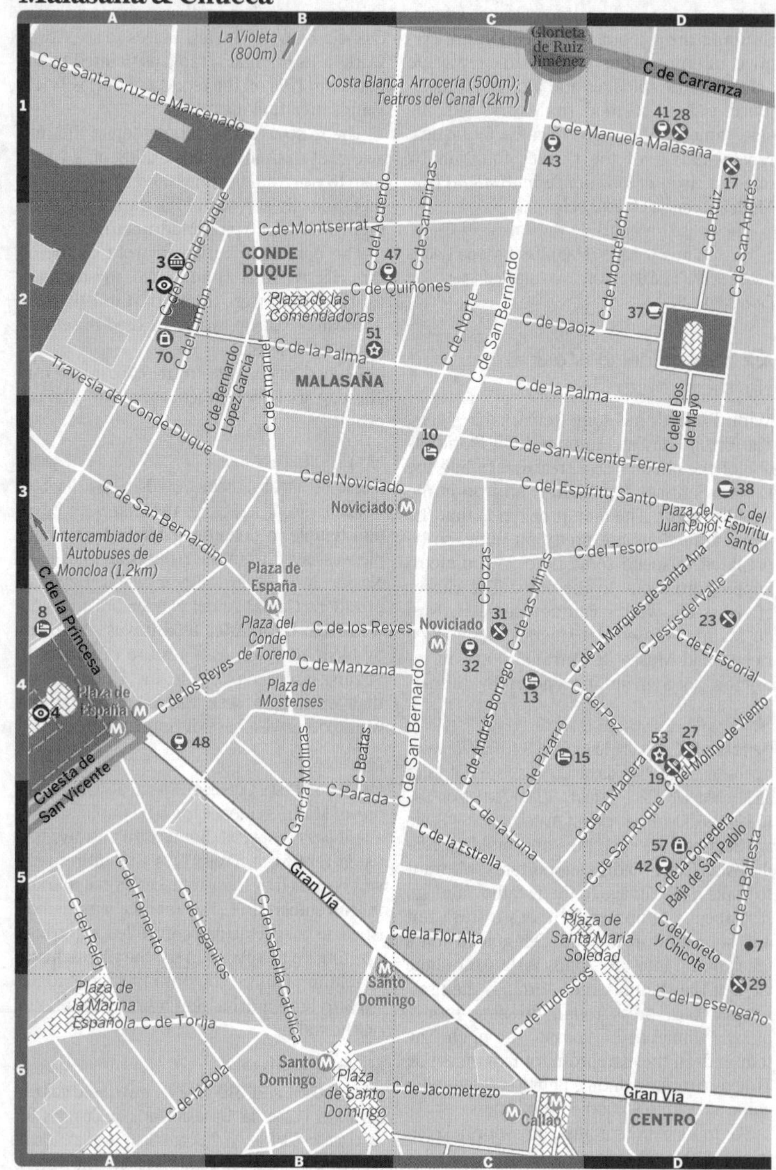

Estación de Chamberí MUSEUM

(Andén 0; www.museomadrid.com/tag/anden-0-horario; cnr Calles de Santa Engracia & de Luchana; 11am-1pm & 5-7pm Fri, 10am-2pm Sat & Sun; M Iglesia, Bilbao) FREE Estación de Chamberí, the long-lost ghost station of Madrid's metro, is now a museum piece that recreates the era of the station's inauguration in 1919 with advertisements from that time (including Madrid's then-four-digit phone numbers), ticket offices and other memorabilia almost a century old. It's an engaging journey down memory lane.

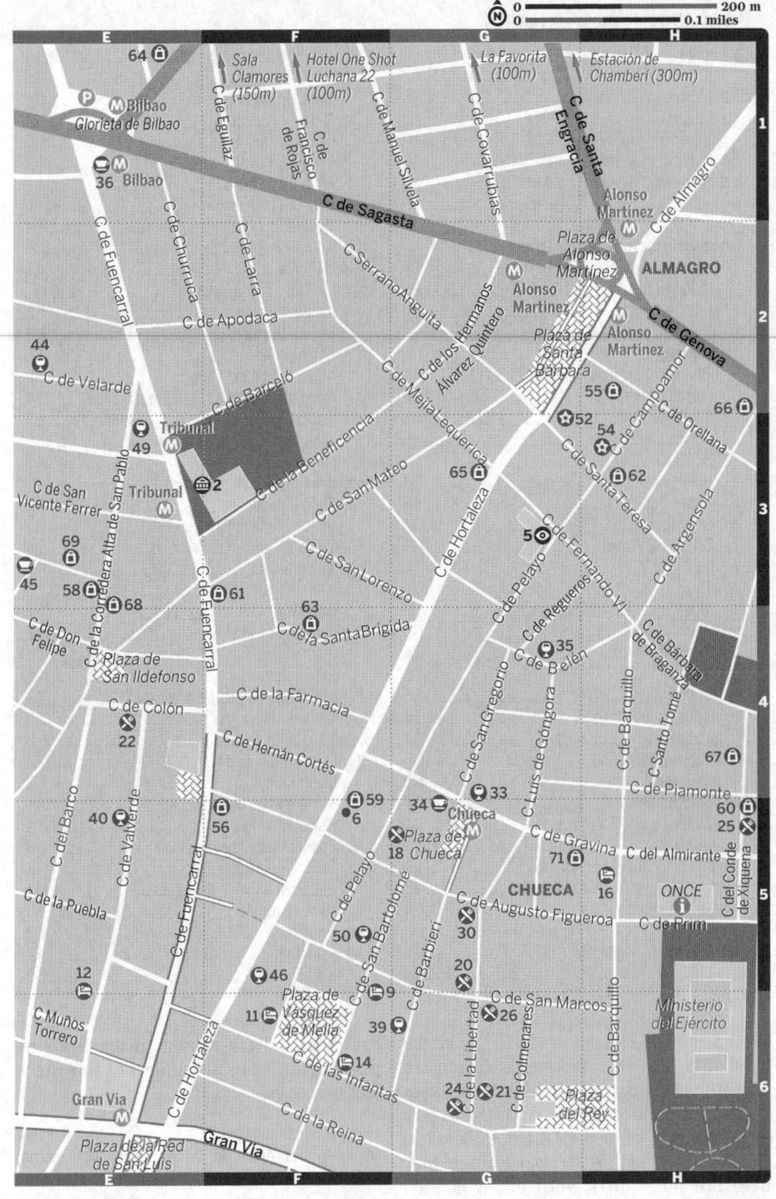

Faro de Madrid VIEWPOINT

(☎91 544 81 04; Avenida de los Reyes Católicos; adult/concession/child €3/1.50/free; ⏱9.30am-8pm Tue-Sun; Ⓜ Moncloa) After a decade closed, this supremely ugly Madrid landmark just in front of Museo de América reopened in 2015. It looks out over Parque del Oeste and has sweeping views of western Madrid. It was built in 1992 for the 500th anniversary of the discovery of America and to celebrate Madrid's role that year as the European Capital of Culture. Sunset is the perfect time to visit.

Malasaña & Chueca

Sights
1 Antiguo Cuartel del Conde Duque........A2
2 Museo de Historia........E3
3 Museo Municipal de Arte Contemporáneo........A2
4 Plaza de España........A4
5 Sociedad General de Autores y Editores........G3

Activities, Courses & Tours
6 Apunto – Centro Cultural del Gusto........F5
7 Kitchen Club........D5

Sleeping
8 Barceló Torre de Madrid........A4
9 Casa Chueca........F6
10 Flat 5 Madrid........C3
11 Hostal Don Juan........F6
12 Hostal La Zona........E5
13 Hotel Abalú........C4
14 Hotel Óscar........F6
15 Life Hotel........C4
16 Only You Hotel........H5

Eating
17 Albur........D1
18 Baco y Beto........G5
19 Bar Palentino........D4
20 Bazaar........G5
21 Bocaito........G6
22 Bodega de la Ardosa........E4
23 Casa Julio........D4
24 Celso y Manolo........G6
25 La Buena Vida........H5
26 La Carmencita........G6
27 La Mucca de Pez........D4
28 La Musa........D1
29 La Tasquita de Enfrente........D6
30 Mercado de San Antón........G5
31 Pez Tortilla........C4

Drinking & Nightlife
32 1862 Dry Bar........C4
33 Antigua Casa Ángel Sierra........G4
34 Café Acuarela........G5
35 Café Belén........G4
36 Café Comercial........E1
37 Café de Mahón........D2
38 Café Manuela........D3
39 Club 54 Studio........G6
40 Fábrica Maravillas........E5
41 Irreale........D1
42 Kikekeller........D5
43 La Tape........C1
La Terraza de Arriba........(see 14)
44 La Vía Láctea........E2
45 Lolina Vintage Café........E3
46 Mamá Inés........F5
47 Moloko Sound Club........B2
48 Nice to Meet You........A4
49 Tupperware........E3
50 Why Not?........F5

Entertainment
51 Café La Palma........B2
52 El Junco Jazz Club........G3
53 Teatro Flamenco Madrid........D4
54 Thundercat........H3

Shopping
55 Cacao Sampaka........H2
56 Camper........F5
57 El Moderno........D5
58 Flamingos Vintage Kilo........E3
59 Librería Berkana........F5
60 Lurdes Bergada........H5
61 Lurdes Bergada........F3
62 Malababa........H3
63 Monkey Garage........F4
64 Papelería Salazar........E1
65 Patrimonio Comunal Olivarero........G3
66 Poncelet........H2
67 Reserva y Cata........H4
68 Retro City........E3
69 Snapo........E3
70 Sportivo........A2
71 Xoan Viqueira........G5

Museo de América MUSEUM
(☎91 549 26 41; www.mecd.gob.es/museodeamerica/el-museo.html; Avenida de los Reyes Católicos 6; adult/concession €3/1.50, free Sun; ⌚9.30am-3pm Tue, Wed, Fri & Sat, 9.30am-7pm Thu, 10am-3pm Sun; Ⓜ Moncloa) Empire may have become a dirty word but it defined how Spain saw itself for centuries. Spanish vessels crossed the Atlantic Ocean to the Spanish colonies in Latin America, carrying adventurers one way and gold and other looted artefacts from indigenous cultures on the return journey. These latter pieces – at once the heritage of another continent and a fascinating insight into imperial Spain – are the subject of this excellent museum.

Parque del Oeste GARDENS
(Avenida del Arco de la Victoria; Ⓜ Moncloa) Sloping down the hill behind the Moncloa metro station, Parque del Oeste is quite beautiful, with plenty of shady corners where you can recline under a tree in the heat of the day and enjoy fine views out to the west towards Casa de Campo. It has been a *madrileño* favourite ever since its creation in 1906.

Activities

Lab Room Spa SPA

(Map p104; ☎91 431 21 98; www.thelabroom.com; Calle de Claudio Coello 13; ⏱11am-8pm Mon-Fri, to 7pm Sat; Ⓜ Retiro) An exclusive spa and beauty parlour whose past clients include Penélope Cruz, Jennifer Lopez, Gwyneth Paltrow and Gael García Bernal, the Lab Room is close to the ultimate in pampering for both men and women. It offers a range of make-up sessions, massages and facial and body treatments; prices can be surprisingly reasonable.

Hammam al-Andalus SPA

(Map p88; ☎91 429 90 20; http://madrid.hammamalandalus.com; Calle de Atocha 14; treatments €33-115; ⏱10am-midnight; Ⓜ Sol) Housed in the excavated cellars of old Madrid, this imitation of a traditional Arab bath offers massages and aromatherapy beneath graceful arches, accompanied by the sound of trickling water. Prices are cheapest from 10am to 4pm Monday to Friday; reservations required.

Tours

Devour Madrid Food Tour FOOD

(☎695 111832; www.madridfoodtour.com; tours €50-130) With five tours for different tastes and budgets, Devour Madrid shows you the best of Spanish food and wine in the centre of Madrid. Tours are themed: wine and tapas, flamenco, authentic local markets, history or (for the most serious foodies) the Ultimate Spanish Cuisine tour, which takes you to eight tasting stops in four hours.

Spanish Tapas Madrid FOOD

(☎672 301231; www.spanishtapasmadrid.com; per person from €70) Local boy Luis Ortega takes you through some iconic Madrid tapas bars, as well as offering tours that take in old Madrid, flamenco and the Prado.

Adventurous Appetites WALKING

(☎639 331073; www.adventurousappetites.com; 4hr tours €50; ⏱8pm-midnight Mon-Sat) English-language tapas tours through central Madrid. Prices include the first drink but exclude food.

Insider's Madrid WALKING

(☎91 447 38 66; www.insidersmadrid.com; tours from €70) An impressive range of tailor-made tours, including walking, shopping, fashion, fine arts, tapas, flamenco and bullfighting tours.

Wellington Society WALKING

(☎609 143203; www.wellsoc.org; tours from €95) A handful of quirky historical tours laced with anecdotes, led by the inimitable Stephen Drake-Jones.

Bike Spain CYCLING

(Map p78; ☎91 559 06 53; www.bikespain.info; Calle del Codo; bike rental half-/full day from €12/18, tours from €30; ⏱10am-2pm & 4-7pm Mon-Fri Mar-Oct, 10am-2pm & 3-6pm Mon-Fri Nov-Feb; Ⓜ Ópera) Bicycle hire plus English-language guided city tours by bicycle, by day or (Friday) night, as well as longer expeditions.

Visitas Guiadas Oficiales TOURS

(Official Guided Tours; Map p78; ☎902 221424; www.esmadrid.com/programa-visitas-guiadas-oficiales; Plaza Mayor 27; ⏱4pm Thu & Fri, noon Sat & Sun; Ⓜ Sol) FREE The official guided tours of the city are worth considering, although they're much reduced from what they once were. Two routes (those on Thursday and Friday) are based on Madrid's main monuments, but the two we like are the 'Madrid of Cervantes' (Saturday) and 'Women in the History of Madrid' (Sunday). Tours last for two hours and are in Spanish only.

To assure yourself of a place, turn up at (or ring) the tourist office (p143) on Plaza Mayor around 9am on the Monday before you want to take the tour.

Courses

Flamenco

Fundación Conservatorio Casa Patas DANCING

(Map p88; ☎91 429 84 71; www.fundacioncasapatas.com; Calle de Cañizares 10; 1hr class from €40; Ⓜ Antón Martín, Tirso de Molina) There's every conceivable type of flamenco instruction here, including dance, guitar, singing and much more. It's upstairs from the Casa Patas flamenco venue.

Academia Amor de Dios DANCING

(Centro de Arte Flamenco y Danza Española; Map p88; ☎91 360 04 34; www.amordedios.com; 1st fl, Calle de Santa Isabel 5; Ⓜ Antón Martín) This is the best-known course for flamenco dancing (and probably the hardest to get into). Although it's more for budding professionals (as the list of past graduates attests to) than casual visitors, it does have the odd Spanish-language *'cursillo'* (little course) that runs for a day or more. It's on the top floor of the Mercado de Antón Martín.

Even if you're not keen to immerse yourself in the flamenco world, it may be worth stopping by just for a look.

Cooking

Alambique COOKING
(Map p78; ☎91 547 42 20; www.alambique.com; Plaza de la Encarnación 2; per person from €45; Ⓜ Ópera, Santo Domingo) Most classes here last from 2½ to 3½ hours and cover a range of cuisines. Most are conducted in Spanish, but some are in English and French.

Kitchen Club COOKING
(Map p108; ☎91 522 62 63; www.kitchenclub.es; Calle de Ballesta 8; Ⓜ Gran Vía, Callao) Kitchen Club spans the globe with a range of courses just off the back of Gran Vía in the city centre. The Spanish cooking classes, conducted in Spanish, are especially popular. After each course there's time to eat what you've cooked.

Apunto – Centro Cultural del Gusto COOKING
(Map p108; ☎91 702 10 41; www.apuntolibreria.com; Calle de Hortaleza 64; per person from €55; Ⓜ Chueca) This engaging little bookstore runs fun yet professional cooking classes across a range of cuisines.

Language

Universidad Complutense LANGUAGE
(☎91 394 53 25; www.ucm.es/ccee/informacion; Secretaria de los Cursos para Extranjeros, Facultadole Filologia, Universidad Complutense; Ⓜ Cuidad Universitaria) A range of language and cultural courses throughout the year. Courses range from 120 contact hours (12 hours per week) to 200-hour courses (20 hours per week).

International House LANGUAGE
(Map p104; ☎902 141517; www.ihmadrid.es; Calle de Zurbano 8; Ⓜ Alonso Martínez) Intensive courses lasting two/four weeks cost €420/740 (20 hours per week) to €540/1040 (30 hours per week). Staff can organise accommodation with local families.

Festivals & Events

Festival Flamenco FLAMENCO
(www.deflamenco.com; ⏲May) Five days of fine flamenco music in one of the city's theatres. Big names in recent years have included Enrique Morente, Carmen Linares and Diego El Cigala. Dates are movable.

Fiestas de San Isidro Labrador CULTURAL
(www.esmadrid.com; ⏲May) Around 15 May Madrid's patron saint is honoured with a week of nonstop processions, parties and bullfights. Free concerts are held throughout the city, and this week marks the start of the city's bullfighting season.

Suma Flamenca FLAMENCO
(www.madrid.org/sumaflamenca; ⏲Jun) A soul-filled flamenco festival that draws some of the biggest names in the genre to Teatros del Canal and some of the better-known *tablaos* (flamenco venues), such as Casa Patas, Villa Rosa and Corral de la Morería.

Día del Orgullo de Gays, Lesbianas y Transexuales LGBT
(www.orgullolgtb.org; ⏲Jun) The colourful Gay Pride Parade, on the last Saturday in June, sets out from the Puerta de Alcalá in the early evening, and winds its way around the city in an explosion of music and energy, ending up at the Puerta del Sol.

Veranos de la Villa SUMMER FESTIVAL
(www.veranosdelavilla.com; ⏲Jul & Aug) Madrid's town hall stages a series of cultural events, shows and exhibitions throughout July and August, known as Summers in the City.

DCode MUSIC
(www.dcodefest.com; ⏲Sep) Held in September at Madrid's Complutense University, this terrific music festival gets better with each passing year. Franz Ferdinand, Liam Gallagher, Amaral and Kings of Convenience have been headline acts on a program that includes local and international groups.

Jazz Madrid MUSIC
(www.festivaldejazzmadrid.com; ⏲Nov) Madrid's annual jazz festival draws a prestigious cast of performers from across the globe and is an increasingly important stop on the European jazz circuit. Venues vary, from the city's intimate jazz clubs to grander theatrical stages across town.

Sleeping

Madrid has high-quality accommodation at prices that haven't been seen in the centre of other European capitals in decades. Five-star temples to good taste and a handful of buzzing hostels bookend a fabulous collection of midrange hotels; most of the midrangers are creative originals, blending high levels of comfort with an often-quirky sense of style.

Plaza Mayor & Royal Madrid

Hostal Madrid HOSTAL, APARTMENT €
(Map p88; ☎91 522 00 60; www.hostal-madrid.info; Calle de Esparteros 6; s €35-75, d €45-115, d apt €45-150; ; Ⓜ Sol) The 24 rooms at this well-run *hostal* have exposed brickwork, updated bathrooms and a look that puts many three-star hotels to shame. They also have terrific apartments (ageing in varying stages of gracefulness and ranging in size from 33 sq metres to 200 sq metres) which have fully equipped kitchens, their own sitting area and bathroom.

Hotel JC Rooms Puerta del Sol HOTEL €
(Map p78; ☎91 559 40 14; www.jchoteles-puertadelsol.com; Calle de la Flora; r €40-62; @; Ⓜ Ópera) Colourful rooms adorned with large photos of Madrid's attractions are reason enough to stay here, with the central location and outrageously reasonable prices added bonuses. Some of the rooms are a bit small, but otherwise it's an excellent choice.

★**Central Palace Madrid** HOTEL €€
(Map p78; ☎91 548 20 18; www.centralpalacemadrid.com; Plaza de Oriente 2; d without/with view €90/160; ; Ⓜ Ópera) Now here's something special. The views alone would be reason enough to come to this hotel and definitely worth paying extra for – rooms with balconies look out over the Palacio Real and Plaza de Oriente. The rooms themselves are lovely and light filled, with tasteful, subtle faux-antique furnishings, comfortable beds, light wood floors and plenty of space.

The Hat Madrid HOTEL, HOSTEL €€
(Map p78; ☎91 772 85 72; www.thehatmadrid.com; Calle Imperial 9; dm/r/apt from €20/65/110; @; Ⓜ Sol, La Latina) The Hat Madrid is an excellent choice just down the hill from Plaza Mayor that manages to span all budgets without cheapening the experience. The dorms are lovely and light-filled and you're not made to feel like a second-class citizen. Equally the rooms and apartments have a lovely fresh look. Friendly service rounds out a wonderful experience in a couldn't-be-more-central location.

Hotel Meninas BOUTIQUE HOTEL €€
(Map p78; ☎91 541 28 05; www.hotelmeninas.com; Calle de Campomanes 7; s/d from €85/95; ; Ⓜ Ópera) This is a classy, cool choice. The colour scheme is blacks, whites and greys, with dark-wood floors and splashes of fuchsia and lime green. Flat-screen TVs in every room, modern bathroom fittings, and even a laptop in some rooms, round out the clean lines and latest innovations. Past guests include Viggo Mortensen and Natalie Portman. Some rooms are on the small side.

Barceló Torre de Madrid HOTEL €€€
(Map p108; ☎91 524 23 99; www.barcelo.com; Plaza de España 18; d €180-310; @; Ⓜ Plaza de España) This five-star hotel occupies nine floors of Torre Madrid, one of the city's most iconic buildings. With views of the Royal Palace and Gran Vía, a modern design and large comfortable rooms and suites, it's for the discerning traveller. Guests can enjoy the wellness centre, and anyone can step into the bright and inviting lobby bar for a drink.

La Latina & Lavapiés

Mola! Hostel HOSTEL €
(Map p88; ☎663 624143; www.molahostel.com; Calle de Atocha 16; dm €15-20, d from €53; @; Ⓜ Sol, Tirso de Molina) This sparkling new hostel overlooking the Plaza de Jacinto Benavente in the heart of town is a terrific deal. Rooms are colourful, warmly decorated and well sized, and dorms (with four to 10 beds) are rather stylish. It's a friendly place where the staff are eager to connect you with other travellers and help you to make the most of your time in Madrid.

Hostal Fonda Horizonte HOSTAL €
(Map p88; ☎91 369 09 96; www.hostalhorizonte.com; 2nd fl, Calle de Atocha 28; s/d €45/62 with shared bathroom €33/50; ; Ⓜ Antón Martín) Billing itself as a *hostal* run by travellers for travellers, Hostal Horizonte is a well-run place. Rooms have far more character than your average *hostal,* with high ceilings, deliberately old-world furnishings and modern bathrooms. The King Alfonso XII room is especially well presented.

Mad Hostel HOSTEL €
(Map p88; ☎91 506 48 40; www.madhostel.com; Calle de la Cabeza 24; dm incl breakfast €24-30; @; Ⓜ Antón Martín) From the people who brought you **Cat's Hostel** (Map p88; ☎91 369 28 07; www.catshostel.com; Calle de Cañizares 6; dm €12-27; @; Ⓜ Antón Martín), Mad Hostel is similarly filled with life. The 1st-floor courtyard – with retractable roof – recreates an old Madrid *corrala* and is a wonderful place to chill, while the four- to eight-bed dorm rooms are smallish but clean. There's a small, rooftop bar.

★Posada del León de Oro BOUTIQUE HOTEL €€
(Map p82; ☎91 119 14 94; www.posadadelleondeoro.com; Calle de la Cava Baja 12; d/ste from €102/155; ❄📶; Ⓜ La Latina) This rehabilitated inn has muted colour schemes and generally large rooms. There's a *corrala* (traditional internal or communal patio) at its core and thoroughly modern rooms along one of Madrid's best-loved streets. The downstairs bar is terrific.

Posada del Dragón BOUTIQUE HOTEL €€
(Map p82; ☎91 119 14 24; www.posadadeldragon.com; Calle de la Cava Baja 14; s/d from €73/85; ❄📶; Ⓜ La Latina) At last a boutique hotel in the heart of La Latina. This restored 19th-century *posada* sits on one of our favourite Madrid streets, and rooms either look out over it or the pretty internal patio. Most of the rooms are on the small side but have extremely comfortable beds and bold, brassy colour schemes and designer everything. There's a terrific bar-restaurant downstairs.

Sol, Santa Ana & Huertas

Hostal Adriano HOSTAL €
(Map p88; ☎91 521 13 39; www.hostaladriano.com; 4th fl, Calle de la Cruz 26; s/d from €50/60; ❄📶; Ⓜ Sol) They don't come any better than this bright and friendly hostel wedged in the streets that mark the boundary between Sol and Huertas. Most rooms are well sized and each has its own colour scheme. Indeed, more thought has gone into the decoration than in your average *hostal*, from the bed covers to the pictures on the walls.

On the same floor, the owners run the **Hostal Adria Santa Ana** (Map p88; ☎91 521 13 39; www.hostaladriasantaana.com; 4th fl, Calle de la Cruz 26; s/d €65/75; ❄📶; Ⓜ Sol), which is a step up in price, style and comfort. Both *hostales* drop their prices in summer.

Hostal Luis XV HOSTAL €
(Map p88; ☎91 522 10 21; www.hrluisxv.net; 8th fl, Calle de la Montera 47; s/d/tr €58/73/88; ❄📶; Ⓜ Gran Vía) The spacious rooms, attention to detail and pretty much everything else make this family-run *hostal* feel pricier than it is. You'll find it hard to tear yourself away from the balconies outside every exterior room, from where the views are superb (especially from the triple in room 820). You're so high up that noise is rarely a problem.

★Praktik Metropol BOUTIQUE HOTEL €€
(Map p88; ☎91 521 29 35; www.praktikmetropol.com; Calle de la Montera 47; s/d from €90/100; ❄📶; Ⓜ Gran Vía) You'd be hard-pressed to find better value anywhere in Europe than here in this overhauled hotel. Rooms have a fresh, contemporary look with white wood furnishings, and some (especially the corner rooms) have brilliant views down to Gran Vía and out over the city. It's spread over six floors and there's a roof terrace if you don't have a room with a view.

★Hotel Alicia BOUTIQUE HOTEL €€
(Map p88; ☎91 389 60 95; www.room-matehoteles.com; Calle del Prado 2; d €125-175, ste from €200; ❄📶; Ⓜ Sol, Sevilla, Antón Martín) One of the landmark properties of the designer Room Mate chain of hotels, Hotel Alicia overlooks Plaza de Santa Ana with beautiful, spacious rooms. The style (the work of designer Pascua Ortega) is a touch more muted than in other Room Mate hotels, but the supermodern look remains intact, the downstairs bar is oh-so-cool, and the service is young and switched on.

Catalonia Las Cortes HOTEL €€
(Map p88; ☎91 389 60 51; www.hoteles-catalonia.es; Calle del Prado 6; s/d from €150/175; ❄📶; Ⓜ Antón Martín) Occupying an 18th-century palace and renovated in a style faithful to the era, this elegant hotel is a terrific choice right in the heart of Huertas. It's something of an oasis surrounded by the nonstop energy of the streets in this *barrio*. Service is discreet and attentive and the hotel gets plenty of return visitors, which is just about the best recommendation we can give.

NH Collection Palacio de Tepa HOTEL €€
(Map p88; ☎91 389 64 90; www.nh-collection.com; Calle de San Sebastián 2; d from €175; ❄📶; Ⓜ Antón Martín) Inhabiting a 19th-century palace a stone's throw from Plaza de Santa Ana, this flagship property of the respected NH chain has modern designer rooms with hardwood floors and soothing colours. Service is professional and the location is outstanding. The premium rooms and junior suites in particular have real class.

Hotel Vincci Soho HOTEL €€
(Map p88; ☎91 141 41 00; www.vinccihoteles.com; Calle del Prado 18; d from €145; ❄📶; Ⓜ Sevilla, Antón Martín) A refined sense of style permeates everything about this hotel, from the subtly lit common areas to the rooms that combine vaguely Zen aesthetics with blood-red bathrooms. As ideal a base for the museums along the Paseo del Prado as for the clamour of central Madrid, it gets most things right.

Hotel Urban LUXURY HOTEL €€€
(Map p88; ☎91 787 77 70; www.derbyhotels.com; Carrera de San Jerónimo 34; r from €230; ; Ⓜ Sevilla) This towering glass edifice is the epitome of art-inspired designer cool. It boasts original artworks from Africa and Asia; dark-wood floors and dark walls are offset by plenty of light; and the dazzling bathrooms have wonderful designer fittings – the washbasins are sublime. The rooftop swimming pool is one of Madrid's best and the gorgeous terrace is heaven on a candlelit summer's evening.

Me Melía Reina Victoria LUXURY HOTEL €€€
(Map p88; ☎91 701 60 00; www.melia.com; Plaza de Santa Ana 14; r from €175; ; Ⓜ Sol, Antón Martín) Once the landmark Gran Victoria Hotel, the Madrid home of many a famous bullfighter, this audacious hotel is a landmark of a different kind. Overlooking the western end of Plaza de Santa Ana, this luxury hotel is decked out in minimalist white with curves and comfort in all the right places.

El Retiro & the Art Museums

★ **Lapepa Chic B&B** B&B €
(Map p88; ☎648 474742; www.lapepa-bnb.com; 7th fl, Plaza de las Cortes 4; s/d from €58/64; ; Ⓜ Banco de España) A short step off Paseo del Prado and on a floor with an art-nouveau interior, this fine little B&B has lovely rooms with a contemporary, clean-line look so different from the dour *hostal* furnishings you'll find elsewhere. Modern art or even a bedhead lined with flamenco shoes gives the place personality in bucketloads. It's worth paying extra for a room with a view.

★ **60 Balconies Atocha** APARTMENT €€
(Map p92; ☎91 755 39 26; www.60balconies.com; Plaza del Emperador Carlos V 11; apt €125-255; ; Ⓜ Atocha) As convenient for Atocha train station as for the city's major art galleries, and well connected to the rest of the city on foot or by metro, 60 Balconies is an exciting new project by a dynamic young architectural team. The apartments range from 31-sq-metre studios up to 103-sq-metre, three-bedroom apartments, all stylish, spacious and a wonderful alternative to hotels.

Another similarly excellent property is over in Chueca (p116).

Westin Palace LUXURY HOTEL €€€
(Map p88; ☎91 360 80 00; www.westinpalacemadrid.com; Plaza de las Cortes 7; d/ste from €200/470; ; Ⓜ Banco de España, Antón Martín) An old Madrid classic, this former palace of the Duque de Lerma opened as a hotel in 1911 and was Spain's second luxury hotel. Ever since it has looked out across Plaza de Neptuno at its rival, the Ritz, like a lover unjustly scorned. It may not have the world-famous cachet of the Ritz, but it's not called the Palace for nothing.

Salamanca

VP El Madroño BOUTIQUE HOTEL €€
(☎91 198 30 92; www.madrono-hotel.com; Calle del General Díaz Porlier 101; d/tr from €105/125; ; Ⓜ Diego de León) You're a long way from touristy Madrid out here, not far from the bullring, and therein lies part of this swish place's appeal. All of the rooms have been renovated, either in a vaguely classic style or with more contemporary designer flair. It also has family rooms and there's even a lovely garden out back.

Petit Palace Art Gallery HOTEL €€
(Map p104; ☎91 435 54 11; www.petitpalaceartgallerymadrid.com; Calle de Jorge Juan 17; d from €90; ; Ⓜ Serrano) Occupying a stately 19th-century Salamanca building, this landmark property of the Petit Palace chain is a lovely designer hotel that combines hi-tech facilities with an artistic aesthetic with loads of original works dotted around the public spaces and even in some of the rooms. Hydro-massage showers, laptops and exercise bikes in many rooms are just some of the extras, and the address is ideal for the best of Salamanca.

Villa Magna HOTEL €€€
(Map p104; ☎91 587 12 34; www.villamagna.es; Paseo de la Castellana 22; d €335-420, ste from €450; ; Ⓜ Rubén Darío) This is a very Salamanca address, infused as it is with elegance and impeccable service. The look is brighter than you might imagine with the use of Empire chairs, Bauhaus ideas and even Chinese screens. Rooms are studiously classic in look with supremely comfortable furnishings and plenty of space. No expense has been spared in the rooftop suites.

Malasaña & Chueca

★ **Hostal Main Street Madrid** HOSTAL €
(Map p78; ☎91 548 18 78; www.mainstreetmadrid.com; 5th fl, Gran Vía 50; r from €55; ; Ⓜ Callao, Santo Domingo) Excellent service is what travellers rave about here, but the rooms – modern and cool in soothing greys – are

also some of the best *hostal* rooms you'll find anywhere in central Madrid. It's an excellent package, and not surprisingly, they're often full, so book well in advance.

Hostal La Zona HOSTAL €
(Map p108; ☎91 521 99 04; www.hostallazona.com; 1st fl, Calle de Valverde 7; s €38-58, d €50-70, all incl breakfast; ❄📶; Ⓜ Gran Vía) Catering primarily to a gay clientele, the stylish Hostal La Zona has exposed brickwork, subtle colour shades and wooden pillars. We like a place where a sleep-in is encouraged – breakfast is served from 9am to noon, which is exactly the understanding Madrid's nightlife merits. Arnaldo and Vincent are friendly hosts.

Flat 5 Madrid HOSTAL €
(Map p108; ☎91 127 24 00; www.flat5madrid.com; 5th fl, Calle de San Bernardo 55; s/d with private bathroom €55/70, r with shared bathroom from €48; ❄📶; Ⓜ Noviciado) Unlike so many *hostales* in Madrid where the charm depends on a time-worn air, Flat 5 Madrid has a fresh, clean-line look with bright colours, flat-screen TVs and flower boxes on the window sills. Even the rooms that face onto a patio have partial views over the rooftops. If the rooms and bathrooms were a little bigger, we'd consider moving in.

Life Hotel HOTEL €
(Map p108; ☎91 531 42 96; www.hotellifemadrid.es; Calle de Pizarro 16; s/d from €42/58; ❄📶; Ⓜ Noviciado) If only all places to stay were this good. This place inhabits the shell of an historic Malasaña building, but the rooms are slick and contemporary with designer bathrooms. You're also just a few steps up the hill from Calle del Pez, one of Malasaña's most happening streets. It's an exceptionally good deal, even when prices head upwards.

Casa Chueca HOSTAL €
(Map p108; ☎91 523 81 27; www.casachueca.com; 2nd fl, Calle de San Bartolomé 4; s/d from €45/62; 📶; Ⓜ Gran Vía) If you don't mind lugging your bags up to the 2nd floor, Casa Chueca is outstanding. Rooms are modern, colourful and a cut above your average *hostal;* in keeping with the *barrio* that it calls home, Casa Chueca places a premium on style. Add casual, friendly service and you'd be hard-pressed to find a better price-to-quality ratio anywhere in central Madrid.

Hostal Don Juan HOSTAL €
(Map p108; ☎91 522 31 01; www.hostaldonjuan.net; 2nd fl, Plaza de Vázquez de Mella 1; s/d/tr €40/56/75; ❄📶; Ⓜ Gran Vía) Paying cheap rates for your room doesn't mean you can't be treated like a king. This elegant two-storey *hostal* is filled with original artworks and antique furniture that could grace a royal palace, although mostly it resides in the public areas. Rooms are large and simple but luminous; most have a street-facing balcony.

The location is good, close to where Chueca meets Gran Vía.

★60 Balconies Recoletos APARTMENT €€
(Map p104; ☎91 755 39 26; www.60balconies.com; Calle del Almirante 17; apt €132-212; ❄📶; Ⓜ Chueca) In a classy corner of Chueca, these architect-designed apartments, ranging from 45 sq metre up to 130 sq metre, are stylish and make you feel like you've found your own Madrid pad. They're a similar deal to their Atocha property (p115) and rank among the best apartment choices in town.

Only You Hotel BOUTIQUE HOTEL €€
(Map p108; ☎91 005 22 22; www.onlyyouhotels.com; Calle de Barquillo 21; d €200-280; ❄@📶; Ⓜ Chueca) This stunning boutique hotel makes perfect use of a 19th-century Chueca mansion. The look is classy and contemporary thanks to respected interior designer Lázaro Rosa-Violán. Nice touches include all-day à la carte breakfasts and a portable router that you can carry out into the city to stay connected.

Hotel Abalú BOUTIQUE HOTEL €€
(Map p108; ☎91 531 47 44; www.hotelabalu.com; Calle del Pez 19; d €75-120, ste from €150; ❄📶; Ⓜ Noviciado) Malasaña's very own boutique hotel is starting to age and the word on the street is that it's not what it was. We know what they mean but the rooms are still good, it's located on cool Calle del Pez and each room (some on the small side) has its own design drawn from the imagination of designer Luis Delgado.

Hotel Óscar BOUTIQUE HOTEL €€
(Map p108; ☎91 701 11 73; www.room-matehoteles.com; Plaza de Vázquez de Mella 12; d €90-195, ste from €150; ❄📶; Ⓜ Gran Vía) Hotel Óscar belongs to the highly original Room Mate chain of hotels. Designer rooms are stylish and sophisticated, some with floor-to-ceiling murals. The lighting is always cool, and the colour scheme has splashes of pinks, lime greens, oranges or more-minimalist black and white.

The Principal Madrid HOTEL €€€
(Map p88; ☎91 521 87 43; www.theprincipalmadridhotel.com; Calle Marqués de Valdeiglesias 1; r €210-360, ste from €460; ❄@📶; Ⓜ Sevilla) Just off the pretty end of Gran Vía and within sight of one of its more charming landmarks, the Edificio Metrópolis, the Principal is a fine, central choice. Some of the standard rooms are on the small side for a five-star hotel, but those with views towards Gran Vía are splendid. The pocket-wi-fi device is a nice touch.

Parque del Oeste & Northern Madrid

★ApartoSuites Jardines de Sabatini APARTMENT €€
(Map p78; ☎91 198 32 90; www.jardinesdesabatini.com; Cuesta de San Vicente 16; studio without/with views from €85/110, ste without/with views from €125/150; ❄📶; Ⓜ Plaza de España, Príncipe Pío) Modern, spacious studios and suites are only half the story at this terrific property just down the hill from Plaza de España. Definitely pay extra for a room with a view and the studios with a balcony and uninterrupted views over the lovely Jardines de Sabatini to the Palacio Real – simply brilliant. The Campo del Moro is just across the road.

★Hotel One Shot Luchana 22 HOTEL €€
(☎91 292 29 40; www.hoteloneshotluchana22.com; Calle de Luchana 22; r €105; ❄📶; Ⓜ Bilbao) Classy, contemporary rooms in an early-20th-century, neoclassical palace close to Plaza de Olavide in Chamberí make for a pleasant alternative to staying downtown. The wrap-around loft has abundant light and a modern four-poster bed.

★Hotel Orfila HOTEL €€€
(Map p104; ☎91 702 77 70; www.hotelorfila.com; Calle de Orfila 6; r from €225; P❄📶; Ⓜ Alonso Martínez) One of Madrid's best hotels, Hotel Orfila has all the luxuries of any five-star hotel – supremely comfortable rooms, for a start – but it's the personal service that elevates it into the upper echelon; regular guests get bathrobes embroidered with their own initials. An old-world elegance dominates the decor, and the quiet location and sheltered garden make it the perfect retreat at day's end.

★Hotel Silken Puerta América LUXURY HOTEL €€€
(☎91 744 54 00; www.hoteles-silken.com; Avenida de América 41; d/ste from €140/275; P❄📶; Ⓜ Cartagena) Given the location of their hotel (halfway between the city and the airport) the owners knew they had to do something special – to build a self-contained world so innovative and luxurious that you'd never want to leave. Their idea? Give 22 of architecture's most creative names (eg Zaha Hadid, Norman Foster, Ron Arad, David Chipperfield, Jean Nouvel) a floor each to design.

The result is an extravagant pastiche of styles, from zany montages of 1980s chic to bright-red bathrooms that feel like a movie star's dressing room. Even the bar ('a temple to the liturgy of pleasure'), restaurant, facade, gardens, public lighting and car park had their own architects. It's an extraordinary, astonishing place.

Eating

Madrid has transformed itself into one of Europe's culinary capitals, not least because the city has long been a magnet for people (and cuisines) from all over Spain. Travel from one Spanish village to the next and you'll quickly learn that each has its own speciality; travel to Madrid and you'll find them all.

Plaza Mayor & Royal Madrid

★Mercado de San Miguel TAPAS €
(Map p78; ☎91 542 49 36; www.mercadodesanmiguel.es; Plaza de San Miguel; tapas from €1.50; ⏲10am-midnight Sun-Wed, to 2am Thu-Sat; Ⓜ Sol) This is one of Madrid's oldest and most beautiful markets, within early-20th-century glass walls and an inviting space strewn with tables. You can order tapas and sometimes more substantial plates at most of the counter-bars, and everything here (from caviar to chocolate) is as tempting as the market is alive. Put simply, it's one of our favourite experiences in Madrid.

All the stalls are outstanding, but you could begin with the fine fishy *pintxos* (Basque tapas) atop mini toasts at **La Casa de Bacalao** (Stalls 16–17), follow it up with some *jamón* or other cured meats at **Carrasco Guijuelo** (Stall 18), cheeses at Stalls 20–21, all manner of pickled goodies at Stall 22, or the gourmet tapas of **Lhardy** (Stalls 61–62). There are also plenty of places to buy wine, Asturian cider and the like; at Stall 24, The Sherry Corner (p126) has sherry tastings with tapas.

★Gourmet Experience FOOD HALL €€
(Map p88; www.elcorteingles.es; 9th fl, Plaza del Callao 2; mains €8-20; ⏲10am-10pm; Ⓜ Callao) Ride the elevator up to the 9th floor of the

LOCAL KNOWLEDGE

WHAT'S COOKING IN MADRID?

Cocido a la madrileña (Madrid meat and-chickpea hotpot) Taberna La Bola, Lhardy (p120) or Malacatín

Cordero o cochinillo asado (roast lamb or suckling pig) Restaurante Sobrino de Botín

Sopa de ajo (garlic soup) Posada de la Villa

Callos a la madrileña (Madrid-style tripe) Taberna La Bola

Huevos rotos (potatoes cooked with eggs and *jamón*) Casa Lucio or Almendro 13 (p121)

El Corte Inglés department store for one of downtown Madrid's best eating experiences. The food is excellent, with everything from top-notch tapas or sushi to gourmet hamburgers, and the views fabulous, especially those that look over Plaza del Callao and down Gran Vía.

El Pato Mudo SPANISH €€

(Map p78; ☎91 559 48 40; elpatomudo@hotmail.es; Calle Costanilla de los Ángeles 8; mains €13-24; ⏲1-4pm & 8-11.30pm Wed-Sun; Ⓜ Ópera) El Pato Mudo isn't the most famous paella restaurant in Madrid, but it's known to locals for its variety of outstanding rice dishes at reasonable prices. Specialities include black rice with squid ink, soupy rice, authentic *paella valenciana* and shellfish paella. Served directly from the pan for two or more people, they go well with the local wines.

Taberna del Alabardero SPANISH €€

(Map p78; ☎91 547 25 77; www.grupolezama.es; Calle de Felipe V 6; bar raciones €6-26, restaurant mains €20-28; ⏲noon-1am; Ⓜ Ópera) This fine old Madrid *taberna* (tavern) is famous for its croquettes, fine *jamón, montaditos de jamón* (small rolls of cured ham) and *montaditos de bonito* (small rolls of cured tuna) in the bar, while out the back the more classic cuisine includes *rabo de toro estofado* (bull's tail, served with honey, cinnamon, mashed potato and pastry with herbs).

Taberna La Bola SPANISH €€

(Map p78; ☎91 547 69 30; www.labola.es; Calle de la Bola 5; mains €8-25; ⏲1.30-4.30pm & 8.30-11pm Mon-Sat, 1.30-4.30pm Sun, closed Aug; Ⓜ Santo Domingo) Going strong since 1870 and run by the sixth generation of the Verdasco family, Taberna La Bola is a much-loved bastion of traditional Madrid cuisine. If you're going to try *cocido a la madrileña* (meat-and-chickpea stew; €21) while in Madrid, this is a good place to do so. It's busy and noisy and very Madrid.

El Anciano Rey de los Vinos SPANISH €€

(Map p78; ☎91 559 53 32; www.elancianoreydelosvinos.es; Calle de Bailén 19; mains €9-20; ⏲8.30am-midnight Wed-Mon; Ⓜ Sol) With outdoor seating that gives you an unbeatable view of the cathedral, this bar has been serving its unique house wine – a sweet number similar to moscatel – since it opened in 1909. Food specialities include *cazuela del anciano* (shellfish stew featuring octopus and prawns) and *regalitos de toro* (crispy puff pastry stuffed with oxtail and red peppers).

★Restaurante Sobrino de Botín CASTILIAN €€€

(Map p78; ☎91 366 42 17; www.botin.es; Calle de los Cuchilleros 17; mains €18-27; ⏲1-4pm & 8pm-midnight; Ⓜ La Latina, Sol) It's not every day that you can eat in the oldest restaurant in the world (as recognised by the *Guinness Book of Records* – established in 1725). The secret of its staying power is fine *cochinillo asado* (roast suckling pig) and *cordero asado* (roast lamb) cooked in wood-fired ovens. Eating in the vaulted cellar is a treat.

Restaurante Sandó CONTEMPORARY SPANISH €€€

(Map p78; ☎91 547 99 11; www.restaurantesando.es; Calle de Isabel la Católica 2; mains €16-28, menú de degustación €49; ⏲1-4pm & 8-11pm Tue-Sat; Ⓜ Santo Domingo) Juan Mari Arzak, one of Spain's most famous chefs, has finally set up shop in Madrid just off Plaza de Santo Domingo. Bringing Basque innovation to bear upon local tradition, its cooking is assured with dishes like tuna chunks with ginger and hibiscus. If you can't decide, try the *menú de degustación* or head around the corner to the tapas bar.

La Latina & Lavapiés

La Latina is Madrid's best *barrio* for tapas, complemented by a fine selection of sit-down restaurants. If you're planning only one tapas crawl while in town, do it here in Calle de la Cava Baja and the surrounding streets.

Lavapiés is more eclectic and multicultural and, generally speaking, the further down the hill you go, the better it gets, especially along Calle de Argumosa.

Bar Melo's TAPAS €

(☎91 527 50 54; www.facebook.com/barmeloslavapies; Calle del Ave María 44; mains from €7.50; ⌚2.30pm-1.30am Tue-Sat, closed Aug; Ⓜ Lavapiés) There's no tradition of kebab shops for midnight attacks of the munchies, but there's always Bar Melo's. One of those Spanish bars that you'd normally walk past without a second glance, Bar Melo's is famous across the city for its *zapatillas* – great, spanking *bocadillos* (filled rolls) of *lacón* (cured shoulder of pork) and cheese.

Bar Santurce SPANISH €

(Map p82; ☎646 238303; www.barsanturce.com; Plaza General Vara del Rey 14; bocadillos/raciones from €2.50/4.50; ⌚noon-4pm Tue & Wed, noon-4pm & 7.30-10.30pm Thu-Sat, 9am-4pm Sun; Ⓜ La Latina) This basic bar is famous for its *sardinas a la plancha* (sardines cooked on the grill) and *pimientos de padrón* (fiery green peppers). It's wildly popular on Sundays during El Rastro market when it can be difficult to even get near the bar. The *media ración* (half serve) of six sardines for €2.50 is Madrid's best bargain.

★Taberna Matritum MODERN SPANISH €€

(Map p82; ☎91 365 82 37; www.tabernamatritum.es; Calle de la Cava Alta 17; mains €13-19.50; ⌚1.30-4pm & 8.30pm-midnight Wed-Sun, 8.30pm-midnight Mon & Tue; Ⓜ La Latina) This little gem is reason enough to detour from the more popular Calle de la Cava Baja next door. The seasonal menu encompasses terrific tapas, salads and generally creative cooking – try the Catalan sausage and prawn pie or the winter *calçots* (large spring onions), also from Catalonia. The wine list runs into the hundreds and it's sophisticated without being pretentious.

La Musa Latina MODERN SPANISH €€

(Map p82; ☎91 354 02 55; www.grupolamusa.com/restaurante-lamusalatina; Costanilla de San Andrés 1; tapas €3-7, mains €11-17; ⌚10am-1am Mon-Wed, to 1.30am Thu, to 2am Fri & Sat, to 1am Sun; Ⓜ La Latina) Laid-back La Musa Latina has an ever-popular dining area and food that's designed to bring a smile to your face. The outdoor tables are lovely when the weather is warm, while the downstairs bar in the former wine cellar, complete with table tennis and table football, is also charming. Like its sister restaurant in Malasaña, it serves creative tapas, including international adaptations.

Almacén de Vinos TAPAS €€

(Casa Gerardo; Map p82; ☎91 221 96 60; Calle de la Calatrava 21; tapas/raciones from €3/8.50; ⌚1-4pm & 8.30pm-midnight Sun-Thu, 1-5pm & 8.30pm-12.30am Fri & Sat; Ⓜ La Latina) It doesn't come much more traditional in La Latina than this tiled space with a marble bar and *tostas* (toasts; with *bacalao,* for example), *raciones* (such as *jamón ibérico* with wild mushrooms) and vermouth on tap. When busy, it has that unmistakeable buzz of a place beloved by locals whose attitude seems to be, 'Why change something this good?'.

Enotaberna del León de Oro SPANISH €€

(Map p82; ☎91 119 14 94; www.posadadelleondeoro.com; Calle de la Cava Baja 12; tapas from €6, mains €13-23; ⌚1-4pm & 8pm-midnight; Ⓜ La Latina) The stunning restoration work that brought to life the Posada del León de Oro (p114) also bequeathed to La Latina a fine bar-restaurant. The emphasis is on matching carefully chosen wines with creative dishes (such as baby squid with potato emulsion and rocket pesto) in a casual atmosphere. There are also plenty of gins to choose from. It's a winning combination.

Malacatín SPANISH €€

(Map p82; ☎91 365 52 41; www.malacatin.com; Calle de Ruda 5; mains €11-15; ⌚11am-5.30pm Mon-Wed & Sat, 11am-5.30pm & 8.15-11pm Thu & Fri, closed Aug; Ⓜ La Latina) If you want to see *madrileños* (residents of Madrid) enjoying their favourite local food, this is one of the best places to do so. The clamour of conversation bounces off the tiled walls of the cramped dining area adorned with bullfighting memorabilia. The speciality is as much *cocido* (meat-and-chickpea stew) as you can eat (€21).

★Casa Lucio SPANISH €€€

(Map p82; ☎91 365 32 52, 91 365 82 17; www.casalucio.es; Calle de la Cava Baja 35; mains €18-29; ⌚1-4pm & 8.30pm-midnight, closed Aug; Ⓜ La Latina) Casa Lucio is a Madrid classic and has been wowing *madrileños* with his light touch, quality ingredients and home-style local cooking since 1974, such as eggs (a Lucio speciality) and roasted meats in abundance. There's also *rabo de toro* (bull's tail) during the Fiestas de San Isidro Labrador and plenty of *rioja* (red wine) to wash away the mere thought of it.

Posada de la Villa SPANISH €€€

(Map p82; ☎91 366 18 80; www.posadadelavilla.com; Calle de la Cava Baja 9; mains €21-32.50; ⌚1-4pm & 8pm-midnight Mon-Sat, 1-4pm Sun, closed Aug; Ⓜ La Latina) This wonderfully restored 17th-century *posada* (inn) is something of a local landmark. The atmosphere is formal, the decoration sombre and traditional (heavy timber and brickwork), and the cuisine decidedly local – roast meats, *cocido* (which usually needs to be pre-ordered), *callos* (tripe) and *sopa de ajo* (garlic soup).

Sol, Santa Ana & Huertas

Casa Toni SPANISH €
(Map p88; ☎91 532 25 80; casatoni2@hotmail.com; Calle de la Cruz 14; mains €6-13; ⏲noon-4.30pm & 7pm-midnight; Ⓜ Sol) Locals flock to Casa Toni, one of Madrid's best old-school Spanish bars, for simple, honest cuisine fresh off the griddle. Specialities include cuttlefish, gazpacho and offal – the crispy pork ear is out of this world. While you're there, you can try one of the local Madrid wines. The prices are great and the old Madrid charm can't be beat.

Vinos González TAPAS, DELI €
(Map p88; ☎91 429 56 18; www.casagonzalez.es; Calle de León 12; tapas from €3.50, raciones €9-15; ⏲9.30am-midnight Mon-Thu, to 1am Fri & Sat, 11am-6pm Sun; Ⓜ Antón Martín) Ever dreamed of a deli where you could choose a tasty morsel and sit down and eat it right there? Well, the two are usually kept separate in Spain but here you can. On offer is a tempting array of local and international cheeses, cured meats and other typically Spanish delicacies. The tables are informal, cafe style and we recommend lingering.

La Finca de Susana SPANISH €
(Map p88; ☎91 429 76 78; www.grupandilana.com; Calle del Príncipe 10; mains €8-14; ⏲1-3.45pm & 8.30-11.30pm Sun-Wed, 1-3.45pm & 8.15pm-midnight Thu-Sat; 📶; Ⓜ Sevilla) It's difficult to find a better combination of price, quality cooking and classy atmosphere anywhere in Huertas. The softly lit dining area has a sophisticated vibe and the sometimes-innovative, sometimes-traditional food draws a hip young crowd. The duck confit with plums, turnips and couscous is a fine choice. No reservations.

★ **Casa Alberto** TAPAS €€
(Map p88; ☎91 429 93 56; www.casaalberto.es; Calle de las Huertas 18; tapas €3.25-10, raciones €7-16.50, mains €16-19; ⏲restaurant 1.30-4pm & 8pm-midnight Tue-Sat, 1.30-4pm Sun, bar noon-1.30am Tue-Sat, 12.30-4pm Sun, closed Sun Jul & Aug; Ⓜ Antón Martín) One of the most atmospheric old *tabernas* (taverns) of Madrid, Casa Alberto has been around since 1827 and occupies a building where Cervantes is said to have written one of his books. The secret to its staying power is vermouth on tap, excellent tapas at the bar and fine sit-down meals.

La Mucca de Prado SPANISH, INTERNATIONAL €€
(Map p88; ☎91 521 00 00; www.lamuccacompany.com/lamucca-de-prado; Calle del Prado 16; mains €9-16; ⏲1pm-1.30am Sun-Wed, to 2am Thu, to 2.30am Fri & Sat; Ⓜ Antón Martín) This wildly popular outpost of the similarly cool Malasaña La Mucca serves up terrific local dishes such as *jamón* (ham) platters, but the menu is mostly international with pizzas, steaks, burgers and salads, usually with a Spanish twist. The food is great, but there's also an irresistible buzz about this place that makes everything taste better and the night last longer.

Maceiras GALICIAN €€
(Map p88; ☎91 429 58 18; www.tabernamaceira.com; Calle de las Huertas 66; mains €6-14; ⏲1.15-4.15pm & 8pm-midnight Mon-Thu, 1.30-4.45pm & 8.30pm-1am Fri & Sat, 1.30-4.45pm & 8pm-midnight Sun; Ⓜ Antón Martín) Galician tapas (octopus, green peppers etc) never tasted so good as in this agreeably rustic bar down the bottom of the Huertas hill, especially when washed down with a crisp white Ribeiro. The simple wooden tables, loyal customers, Galician music playing in the background and handy location make it a fine place for before or after visiting the museums along the Paseo del Prado.

There's another **branch** (Map p88; www.tabernamaceira.com; Calle de Jesús 7; mains €6-14; ⏲1.15-4.15pm & 8.30pm-12.15am Mon-Fri, 1.30- 4.30pm & 8.30pm-1am Sat, 1.30-4.30pm & 8.30pm-midnight Sun; Ⓜ Antón Martín) around the corner.

★ **La Terraza del Casino** MODERN SPANISH €€€
(Map p88; ☎91 532 12 75; www.casinodemadrid.es; Calle de Alcalá 15; mains €44-56, set menus €79-185; ⏲1-4pm & 9pm-midnight Mon-Sat; Ⓜ Sevilla) Perched atop the lavish Casino de Madrid building, this temple of haute cuisine is the proud bearer of two Michelin stars and presided over by celebrity chef Paco Roncero. It's all about culinary experimentation, with a menu that changes as each new idea emerges from the laboratory and moves into the kitchen. The *menú de degustación* (€148) is a fabulous avalanche of tastes.

★ **Lhardy** SPANISH €€€
(Map p88; ☎91 521 33 85; www.lhardy.com; Carrera de San Jerónimo 8; mains €24-36; ⏲1-3.30pm & 8.30-11pm Mon-Sat, 1-3.30pm Sun, closed Aug;

TAPAS TOUR OF MADRID

La Latina & Lavapiés

Madrid's home of tapas is La Latina, especially along Calle de la Cava Baja and the surrounding streets. **Almendro 13** (Map p82; ☎91 365 42 52; www.almendro13.com; Calle del Almendro 13; mains €7-15; ⊙1-4pm & 7.30pm-midnight Sun-Thu, 1-5pm & 8pm-1am Fri & Sat; Ⓜ La Latina) is famous for quality rather than frilly elaborations, with cured meats, cheeses, tortillas and *huevos rotos* (literally 'broken eggs') the house specialities. Down on Calle de la Cava Baja, **Taberna Txakolina** (Map p82; ☎91 366 48 77; www.tabernatxacoli.com; Calle de la Cava Baja 26; tapas from €4; ⊙8pm-midnight Tue, 1-4pm & 8pm-midnight Wed-Sat, 1-4pm Sun; Ⓜ La Latina) does Basque 'high cuisine in miniature'; wash it all down with a *txacoli*, a sharp Basque white. **Casa Lucas** (Map p82; ☎91 365 08 04; www.casalucas.es; Calle de la Cava Baja 30; tapas/raciones from €5/12; ⊙1-3.30pm & 8pm-midnight Thu-Tue, 1-3.30pm Wed; Ⓜ La Latina) and **La Chata** (Map p82; ☎91 366 14 58; www.lachatacavabaja.com; Calle de la Cava Baja 24; mains €9-23, tapas from €3.70, set menu €18; ⊙1-4pm & 8.30pm-midnight Thu-Mon, 8.30pm-midnight Tue & Wed; Ⓜ La Latina) are also hugely popular. Not far away, **Juana La Loca** (Map p82; ☎91 366 55 00; www.juanalalocamadrid.com; Plaza de la Puerta de Moros 4; tapas from €4, mains €10-24; ⊙1.30-5.30pm Tue-Sun, 7pm-midnight Sat-Wed, to 1am Thu-Fri; Ⓜ La Latina) does a magnificent *tortilla de patatas* (potato and onion omelette), as does **Txirimiri** (Map p82; ☎91 364 11 96; www.txirimiri.es; Calle del Humilladero 6; tapas from €3; ⊙noon-4.30pm & 8.30pm-midnight; Ⓜ La Latina).

Plaza Mayor, Sol & Huertas

For *bacalao* (cod), **Casa Labra** (Map p88; ☎91 532 14 05; www.casalabra.es; Calle de Tetuán 11; tapas from €1; ⊙11.30am-3.30pm & 6-11pm; Ⓜ Sol) has been around since 1860 and was a favourite of the poet Federico García Lorca. However, many *madrileños* wouldn't eat *bacalao* anywhere except **Casa Revuelta** (Map p78; ☎91 366 33 32; Calle de Latoneros 3; tapas from €3; ⊙10.30am-4pm & 7-11pm Tue-Sat, 10.30am-4pm Sun, closed Aug; Ⓜ Sol, La Latina), clinched by the fact that the owner painstakingly extracts every fish bone in the morning.

In Huertas, **La Casa del Abuelo** (Map p88; ☎902 027334; www.lacasadelabuelo.es; Calle de la Victoria 12; raciones from €9; ⊙noon-midnight Sun-Thu, to 1am Fri & Sat; Ⓜ Sol) is famous for *gambas a la plancha* (grilled prawns) or *gambas al ajillo* (prawns sizzling in garlic on little ceramic plates) and a *chato* (small glass) of heavy, sweet El Abuelo red wine. For *patatas bravas* (fried potatoes lathered in a spicy tomato sauce), **Las Bravas** (Map p88; ☎91 522 85 81; www.lasbravas.com; Callejón de Álvarez Gato 3; raciones €4-13; ⊙12.30-4.30pm & 7.30pm-12.30am; Ⓜ Sol, Sevilla) is the place. Another good choice down the bottom of the Huertas hill is **Los Gatos** (Map p88; ☎91 429 30 67; Calle de Jesús 2; tapas from €3.75; ⊙11am-2am; Ⓜ Antón Martín) with eclectic decor and terrific canapés.

El Retiro, the Art Museums & Salamanca

Along the Paseo del Prado, there's only one choice for tapas and it's one of Madrid's best: Estado Puro (p122). In Salamanca, **Biotza** (Map p104; ☎91 781 03 13; Calle de Claudio Coello 27; pintxos €2.80-3.40, raciones from €6, set menus from €18; ⊙1-4.30pm & 8.30pm-midnight Mon-Sat; Ⓜ Serrano) offers creative Basque *pintxos* (tapas) in stylish surrounds.

Chueca

Chueca is another stellar tapas *barrio*. Don't miss Bocaito (p124), a purveyor of Andalucian jamón (ham) and seafood. Bodega de La Ardosa (p123) is extremely popular for its salmorejo (cold, tomato-based soup), croquetas, patatas bravas and tortilla de patatas, while Casa Julio (p122) is widely touted as the home of Madrid's best croquetas. Another brilliant choice is Baco y Beto (p123).

Ⓜ Sol, Sevilla) This Madrid landmark (since 1839) is an elegant treasure trove of takeaway gourmet tapas downstairs and six dining areas upstairs that are the upmarket preserve of traditional Madrid dishes with an occasional hint of French influence. House specialities include *cocido a la madrileña* (meat-and-chickpea stew), pheasant and wild duck in an orange perfume. The quality and service are unimpeachable.

El Retiro & the Art Museums

★Estado Puro TAPAS €€

(Map p92; 91 330 24 00; www.tapasenestadopuro.com; Plaza de Neptuno/Plaza de Cánovas del Castillo 4; tapas €4.50-12.50, mains €14-20; noon-midnight; M Banco de España, Atocha) A slick but casual tapas bar, Estado Puro serves up fantastic tapas, such as the *tortilla española siglo XXI* (21st-century Spanish omelette, served in a glass...), quail eggs in soy sauce or pig's trotters with cuttlefish noodles. The kitchen is overseen by Paco Roncero, head chef at La Terraza del Casino (p120), who learned his trade with master chef Ferran Adrià.

Palacio de Cibeles SPANISH €€€

(Map p92; 91 523 14 54; www.palaciodecibeles.com; 6th fl, Plaza de la Cibeles 1; mains €16-39, set menus €38.50-55; 1-4pm & 8pm-midnight; M Banco de España) High in the iconic Palacio de Comunicaciones on Plaza de la Cibeles, this much-loved restaurant by Adolfo Muñoz takes Spanish staples, gives them a twist from the Castilla-La Mancha region, and then riffs a little wherever the urge takes him. Dishes might include rice infused with saffron, vegetables and *manchego* cheese, or pig's trotters stuffed with onion and wild mushrooms.

Salamanca

★Astrolabius FUSION €€

(Map p104; 91 562 06 11; www.astrolabiusmadrid.com; Calle de Serrano 118; mains €10-25; 1-4pm & 8.30pm-midnight Tue-Sat, closed Aug; M Núñez de Balboa) This terrific family-run place in Salamanca's north has a simple philosophy – take grandmother's recipes and filter them through the imagination of the grandchildren. The result is a beguiling mix of flavours, such as scallops of the world in garlic, or the prawn croquettes. The atmosphere is edgy and modern, but casual in the best Madrid sense.

★Platea SPANISH €€

(Map p104; 91 577 00 25; www.plateamadrid.com; Calle de Goya 5-7; 12.30pm-12.30am Sun-Wed, to 2.30am Thu-Sat; M Serrano, Colón) The ornate Carlos III cinema opposite the Plaza de Colón has been artfully transformed into a dynamic culinary scene with more than a hint of burlesque. There are 12 restaurants, three gourmet food stores and cocktail bars.

Working with the original theatre-style layout, the multilevel seating has been used to array a series of restaurants that seem at once self-contained yet connected to the whole through the soaring open central space, with all of them in some way facing the stage area where cabaret-style or 1930s-era performances or live cooking shows provide a rather glamorous backdrop. It's where food court meets haute cuisine, a daring combination of lunch or dinner with the occasional floor show without the formality that usually infuses such places.

José Luis SPANISH €€

(Map p104; 91 563 09 58; www.joseluis.es; Calle de Serrano 89; tapas from €5; 8.30am-1am Mon-Fri, 9am-1am Sat, 12.30pm-1am Sun; M Gregorio Marañón) With numerous branches around Madrid, José Luis is famous for its fidelity to traditional Spanish recipes. It wins many people's vote for Madrid's best *tortilla de patatas* (Spanish potato omelette), but it's also good for *croquetas* and *ensaladilla rusa* (Russian salad). This outpost has a slightly stuffy, young-men-in-suits feel to it, which is, after all, *very* Salamanca.

Malasaña & Chueca

★Pez Tortilla TAPAS €

(Map p108; 653 919984; www.peztortilla.com; Calle del Pez 36; tapas from €4; noon-midnight Sun, 6.30pm-2am Mon-Wed, noon-2am Thu, noon-2.30am Fri & Sat; M Noviciado) Every time we come here, this place is full to bursting, which is not surprising given its philosophy of great tortilla (15 kinds!), splendid *croquetas* (croquettes) and craft beers (more than 70 varieties, with nine on tap). The *croquetas* with black squid ink or the tortilla with truffle brie and *jamón* (ham) are two stars among many.

★Casa Julio SPANISH €

(Map p108; 91 522 72 74; Calle de la Madera 37; 6/12 croquetas €6/12; 1-3.30pm & 6.30-11pm Mon-Sat Sep-Jul; M Tribunal) A citywide poll for the best *croquetas* in Madrid would see half of those polled voting for Casa Julio and the remainder not doing so only because they haven't been yet. They're that good that celebrities and mere mortals from all over Madrid come here to sample the traditional *jamón* (ham) variety or more creative versions such as spinach with gorgonzola.

Strangely, the place acquired a certain celebrity when U2 chose the bar for a photo shoot some years back.

★Bazaar MODERN SPANISH €

(Map p108; ☎91 523 39 05; www.restaurantbazaar.com; Calle de la Libertad 21; mains €7.50-13; ⏲1.15-4pm & 8.30-11.30pm Sun-Wed, 1.15-4pm & 8.15pm-midnight Thu-Sat; 📶; Ⓜ Chueca) Bazaar's popularity among the well-heeled Chueca set shows no sign of abating. Its pristine white interior design, with theatre-style lighting and wall-length windows, may draw a crowd that looks like it's stepped out of the pages of *¡Hola!* magazine, but the food is extremely well priced and innovative, and the atmosphere is casual.

Reservations are available only for dinner Sunday to Thursday. At all other times, get there early or be prepared to wait, regardless of whether you're famous or not. The cocktail list is long and prices start at just €5!

Bar Palentino TAPAS €

(Map p108; ☎91 532 30 58; Calle del Pez 8; bocadillos €2.50; ⏲7am-2pm Mon-Sat; Ⓜ Noviciado) Formica tables, not a single attention to decor detail, and yet... This ageless Malasaña bar is a reminder of an important lesson in eating Spanish style: don't be fooled by appearances. Wildly popular with young and old alike, Bar Palentino has an irresistible charm, thanks in large part to its owners María Dolores (who claims to be 'the house speciality') and Casto.

And the food? Simple traditional tapas and *bocadillos* (filled rolls) that have acquired city-wide fame, not least for their price.

Baco y Beto TAPAS €

(Map p108; ☎91 522 84 41; Calle de Pelayo 24; tapas from €4; ⏲8pm-1am Mon-Fri, 2-4.30pm & 8.30pm-1am Sat; Ⓜ Chueca) Some of the tastiest tapas in Madrid are what you'll find here. Tapas might include quail's eggs with *salmorejo cordobés* (cold, tomato-based soup from Córdoba), or *raciones* (larger tapas servings), such as aubergine with parmesan. The clientele is predominantly gay.

Bodega de la Ardosa TAPAS €

(Map p108; ☎91 521 49 79; www.laardosa.es; Calle de Colón 13; tapas & raciones €4-12; ⏲8.30am-2am Mon-Fri, 12.45pm-2.30am Sat & Sun; Ⓜ Tribunal) Going strong since 1892, the charming, wood-panelled bar of Bodega de la Ardosa is brimful with charm. To come here and not try the *salmorejo* (cold tomato soup made with bread, oil, garlic and vinegar), *croquetas* or *tortilla de patatas* (potato and onion omelette) would be a crime. On weekend nights there's scarcely room to move.

LOCAL KNOWLEDGE

BOCADILLO DE CALAMARES

One of the lesser-known culinary specialities of Madrid is a *bocadillo de calamares* (a small baguette-style roll filled to bursting with deep-fried calamari). You'll find them in many bars in the streets surrounding Plaza Mayor and neighbouring bars along Calle de los Botaderos off Plaza Mayor's southeastern corner. At around €2.90, they're the perfect street snack. **La Ideal** (Map p78; ☎91 365 72 78; Calle de Botoneras 4; bocadillos from €2.90; ⏲9am-11pm Sun-Thu, to midnight Fri & Sat; Ⓜ Sol) and **La Campana** (Map p78; ☎91 364 29 84; Calle de Botoneras 6; bocadillos from €2.90; ⏲9am-11pm Sun-Thu, to midnight Fri & Sat; Ⓜ Sol) are two spots to try them.

★Yakitoro by Chicote JAPANESE, SPANISH €€

(Map p88; ☎91 737 14 41; www.yakitoro.com; Calle de la Reina 41; tapas €3-8; ⏲1pm-midnight; Ⓜ Banco de España) Based around the idea of a Japanese tavern, driven by a spirit of innovation and a desire to combine the best in Spanish and Japanese flavours, Yakitoro is a hit. Apart from salads, it's all built around brochettes cooked over a wood fire, with wonderful combinations of vegetable, seafood and meat.

★La Carmencita SPANISH €€

(Map p108; ☎91 531 09 11; www.tabernalacarmencita.es; Calle de la Libertad 16; mains €13-27; ⏲9am-2am; Ⓜ Chueca) Around since 1854, La Carmencita is the bar where legendary poet Pablo Neruda was once a regular. The folk of La Carmencita have taken 75 of their favourite traditional Spanish recipes and brought them to the table, sometimes with a little updating but more often safe in the knowledge that nothing needs changing.

★Albur TAPAS €€

(Map p108; ☎91 594 27 33; www.restaurantealbur.com; Calle de Manuela Malasaña 15; mains €13-18; ⏲12.30-5pm & 7.30pm-midnight Mon-Thu, 12.30-5pm & 7.30pm-1.30am Fri, 1pm-1.30am Sat, 1pm-midnight Sun; 📶; Ⓜ Bilbao) One of Malasaña's best deals, this place has a wildly popular tapas bar and a classy but casual restaurant out the back. The restaurant waiters never seem to lose their cool, and their extremely well-priced rice dishes are the stars of the show, although in truth you could order anything here and leave well satisfied.

WORTH A TRIP

CASA JORGE

Arguably Madrid's best Catalan restaurant, classy **Casa Jorge** (914 16 92 44; www.casajorge.com; Calle de Cartagena 104; mains €16-22; 1.30-4pm & 9pm-midnight Mon-Thu, to 1am Fri & Sat, 1.30-4pm Sun; M Cartagena) serves up exquisite specialties from Spain's northwest, including *caracoles* (snails), perfectly executed rice dishes and, in season (roughly December to March or April), *calçots con salsa romescu* (big spring onions served with a tomato and red-pepper sauce); you eat the last of these with a bib, and they're extraordinarily delicious.

Celso y Manolo TAPAS, SPANISH €€
(Map p108; 91 531 80 79; www.celsoymanolo.es; Calle de la Libertad 1; raciones €7.50-12; 1-4.30pm & 8pm-2am; M Banco de España) One of Chueca's best bars, Celso y Manolo serves up *tostadas* for those looking to snack, oxtail for those looking for a touch of the traditional, and a host of dishes from Spain's north and northwest. There are also good wines, good coffee, even better cocktails and an artfully restored interior.

Bocaito TAPAS €€
(Map p108; 91 532 12 19; www.bocaito.com; Calle de la Libertad 4-6; tapas €2.50-8, mains €11-28; 1-4pm & 8.30pm-midnight Mon-Sat; M Chueca, Sevilla) Film-maker Pedro Almodóvar once described this traditional bar and restaurant as 'the best antidepressant'. Forget about the sit-down restaurant (though well regarded) and jam into the bar, shoulder-to-shoulder with the casual crowd, order a few Andalucian *raciones* off the menu and slosh them down with some gritty red or a *caña* (small glass of beer).

La Mucca de Pez TAPAS €€
(Map p108; 91 521 00 00; www.lamucca.es; Plaza Carlos Cambronero 4; mains €9-16; noon-1.30am Sun-Wed, 1pm-2am Thu, 1pm-2.30am Fri & Sat; M Callao) The only problem with this place is that it's such an agreeable spot to spend an afternoon it can be impossible to snaffle a table. An ample wine list complements the great salads, creative pizzas and a good mix of meat and seafood mains, and the atmosphere simply adds to the overall appeal.

Mercado de San Antón TAPAS €€
(Map p108; 91 330 07 30; www.mercadosananton.com; Calle de Augo Figueroa 24; tapas from €1.50, mains €5-20; 10am-midnight; M Chueca) Spain's fresh food markets make for an interesting alternative to bars and restaurants. Many have been transformed to meet all of your food needs at once. Downstairs is all about fresh produce, but upstairs there's all manner of appealing tapas varieties from Japan, the Canary Islands and other corners of the country/globe.

La Musa SPANISH, FUSION €€
(Map p108; 91 448 75 58; www.grupolamusa.com; Calle de Manuela Malasaña 18; tapas €3-7, mains €11-17; 9am-1am Mon-Thu, to 2am Fri, 1pm-2am Sat, 1pm-1am Sun; M San Bernardo) Snug, loud and unpretentious, La Musa is all about designer decor, lounge music and memorably fun food. The menu is divided into three types of tapas – Spanish, international and those from a wood-fired oven. Try the *degustación de tapas* (€30) for two.

★La Buena Vida SPANISH €€€
(Map p108; 91 531 31 49; www.restaurantelabuenavida.com; Calle del Conde de Xiquena 8; mains €25-28; 1-4pm & 9-11.30pm Tue-Thu, 1.30-4pm & 9pm-12.30am Fri & Sat; M Chueca, Colón) A cross between a Parisian bistro and an old-school upmarket Madrid restaurant, this prestigious Chueca place is popular with a well-heeled, knowledgable crowd. The menu is seasonal and leans towards classic Spanish tastes, although dishes like the red tuna sirloin with guacamole and sesame seeds suggest that the chefs are not averse to the odd playful interpretation. It's consistently one of Madrid's best.

★La Tasquita de Enfrente MODERN SPANISH €€€
(Map p108; 91 532 54 49; Calle de la Ballesta 6; mains €16-32, set menus €45-70; 1.30-4.30pm & 8.30pm-midnight Mon-Sat; M Gran Vía) It's difficult to overstate how popular this place is among people in the know in Madrid's food scene. The seasonal menu prepared by chef Juanjo López never ceases to surprise while also combining simple Spanish staples to stunning effect. The *menú de degustación* (tasting menu; €50) or *menú de Juanjo* (€65) would be our choice for first-timers. Reservations are essential.

Parque del Oeste & Northern Madrid

Bodega de la Ardosa TAPAS €

(☎91 446 58 94; Calle de Santa Engracia 70; raciones from €7.50; ⏰9am-3pm & 6-11.30pm Thu-Tue; Ⓜ Iglesia) Tucked away in a fairly modern corner of Chamberí, this fine relic has an extravagantly tiled facade complete with shrapnel holes dating back to the Spanish Civil War. For decades locals have been coming here for their morning tipple and some of the best traditional Spanish *patatas bravas* (fried potatoes with spicy tomato sauce) in town. It also has vermouth on tap.

Casa Mingo ASTURIAN €

(☎91 547 79 18; www.casamingo.es; Paseo de la Florida 34; raciones €2.70-11, pollo asado €11; ⏰11am-midnight; Ⓜ Príncipe Pío) Opened in 1888, Casa Mingo is a well known and vaguely cavernous Asturian cider house. Things are kept simple, focusing primarily on the signature dish of *pollo asado* (roast chicken, cut in quarters) accompanied by a bottle of cider. *Chorizo a la sidra* (chorizo cooked with cider), *queso cabrales* (blue cheese from Asturias) and a weekday lunch *cocido a la madrileña* (meat-and-chickpea stew) in winter are other favourites.

Ermita de San Antonio de la Florida is more or less next door.

★Mama Campo SPANISH €€

(☎91 447 41 38; www.mamacampo.es; Plaza de Olavide; mains €7-15; ⏰1.30-4pm & 8.30pm-midnight Tue-Sat, 1.30-4pm Sun; Ⓜ Bilbao, Iglesia, Quevedo) Mama Campo breaks the mould of sameness that unites the bars surrounding Plaza de Olavide. Positioning itself as an ecofriendly take on the Spanish *taberna* (tavern), it's gone for a winning white decor within and a fresh approach to Spanish staples, always with an emphasis on fresh, organic ingredients. It also has tables on one of our favourite squares.

★La Favorita SPANISH €€

(☎91 448 38 10; www.restaurantelafavorita.com; Calle de Covarrubias 25; mains €12-26, set menus €50-70; ⏰1.30-4pm & 9pm-midnight Mon-Fri, 9pm-midnight Sat; Ⓜ Alonso Martínez) Set in a delightful old mansion, La Favorita is famous for its opera arias throughout the night, sung by professional opera singers masquerading as waiters. The outdoor garden courtyard is delightful on a summer's evening, while the music and food (which leans towards the cuisine of the northeastern Spanish region of Navarra) are top drawer.

Costa Blanca Arrocería SPANISH €€

(☎91 448 58 32; Calle de Bravo Murillo 3; mains €11-23; ⏰1.30-4pm Mon, 1.30-4pm & 8.30-11.30pm Tue-Fri, 2-4pm & 8.30-11.30pm Sat & Sun; Ⓜ Quevedo) Even if you don't have plans to be in Chamberí, it's worth a trip across town to this bar-restaurant that offers outstanding rice dishes, including paella. The quality is high and prices are among the cheapest in town. Start with *almejas a la marinera* (baby clams) and follow it up with *paella de marisco* (seafood paella) for the full experience.

Sagaretxe TAPAS €€

(☎91 446 25 88; www.sagaretxe.com; Calle de Eloy Gonzalo 26; tapas €2.20, set menus €15.50-31; ⏰noon-5pm & 7pm-midnight; Ⓜ Iglesia) One of the best *pintxos* (Basque tapas) bars in Madrid, Sagaretxe takes the stress out of eating tapas, with around 20 varieties lined up along the bar (and more than 100 that can be prepared in the kitchen upon request). Simply point and any of the wonderful selection will be plated up for you.

Las Tortillas de Gabino SPANISH €€

(Map p104; ☎91 319 75 05; www.lastortillasdegabino.com; Calle de Rafael Calvo 20; tortillas €10.50-15.50, mains €14-22; ⏰1.30-4pm & 9-11.30pm Mon-Sat; Ⓜ Iglesia) It's a brave Spanish chef that fiddles with the iconic *tortilla de patatas* (potato omelette), but the results here are delicious. All manner of surprising combinations are available including tortilla with octopus. This place also gets rave reviews for its *croquetas*. The service is excellent and the bright yet classy dining area adds to the sense of a most agreeable eating experience.

★DiverXo MODERN SPANISH €€€

(☎91 570 07 66; www.diverxo.com; Calle de Padre Damián 23; set menus €195-250; ⏰2-3.30pm & 9-10.30pm Tue-Sat, closed three weeks in Aug; Ⓜ Cuzco) Madrid's only three-Michelin-starred restaurant, DiverXo in northern Madrid is one of Spain's most unusual culinary experiences. Chef David Muñoz is something of the *enfant terrible* of Spain's cooking scene. Still in his 30s, he favours what he has described as a 'brutal' approach to cooking – his team of chefs appear as you're mid bite to add surprising new ingredients.

The carefully choreographed experience centres on the short (2½-hour, seven-course) or long (four-hour, 11-course) menus, or the 'Wow' and 'Glutton Wow' menus, and is utterly unlike the more formal upmarket dining options elsewhere. The nondescript suburban setting and small premises (chefs sometimes end up putting the finishing touches to dishes in the hallway) only add to the whole street-smart atmosphere. Bookings up to six months in advance are required.

Drinking & Nightlife

Nights in the Spanish capital are the stuff of legend. They're invariably long and loud most nights of the week, rising to a deafening crescendo as the weekend nears.

Plaza Mayor & Royal Madrid

★The Sherry Corner WINE BAR
(Map p78; ☎68 1007700; www.sherry-corner.com; Stall 24, Mercado de San Miguel, Plaza de San Miguel; ⏲10am-9pm; Ⓜ Sol) The Sherry Corner, inside the Mercado de San Miguel, has found an excellent way to give a crash course in sherry. For €30, you get six small glasses of top-quality sherry to taste, each of which is matched to a different tapa. Guiding you through the process is an audioguide available in eight languages.

★Teatro Joy Eslava CLUB
(Joy Madrid; Map p78; ☎91 366 37 33; www.joy-eslava.com; Calle del Arenal 11; admission €12-15; ⏲11.30pm-6am; Ⓜ Sol) The only things guaranteed at this grand old Madrid dance club (housed in a 19th-century theatre) are a crowd and the fact that it'll be open (it claims to have operated every single day since 1981). The music and the crowd are a mixed bag, but queues are long and invariably include locals and tourists, and the occasional *famoso* (celebrity).

★Chocolatería de San Ginés CAFE
(Map p78; ☎91 365 65 46; www.chocolateriasangines.com; Pasadizo de San Ginés 5; ⏲24hr; Ⓜ Sol) One of the grand icons of the Madrid night, this *chocolate con churros* cafe sees a sprinkling of tourists throughout the day, but locals pack it out in their search for sustenance on their way home from a nightclub somewhere close to dawn. Only in Madrid...

Bodegas Ricla BAR
(Map p78; ☎91 365 20 69; Calle Cuchilleros 6; ⏲1-4pm & 7pm-midnight Wed-Sat & Mon, 1-4pm Sun; Ⓜ Tirso de Molina) Bodegas Ricla is so tiny you might be rubbing haunches with other customers as you sip your wine. For more than 100 years, it's been serving tasty authentic tapas and local vintages: red, white and pink wines, *cavas* and vermouth. Inside, little has changed in decades, with old-style terracotta barrels and pictures of bullfighters lining the walls.

Anticafé CAFE
(Map p78; www.anticafe.es; Calle de la Unión 2; ⏲5pm-2am Tue-Sun; Ⓜ Ópera) Bohemian kitsch at its best is the prevailing theme here and it runs right through the decor and regular cultural events (poetry readings and concerts). As such, it won't be to everyone's taste, but we think it adds some much-needed variety to the downtown drinking scene.

Cafe de Oriente CAFE
(Map p78; ☎91 541 39 74; Plaza de Oriente 2; ⏲8.30am-1.30am Mon-Thu, 9am-2.30am Fri & Sat, 9am-1.30am Sun; Ⓜ Ópera) The outdoor tables of this distinguished old cafe are among the most sought-after in central Madrid, providing as they do a front-row seat for the beautiful Plaza de Oriente, with the Palacio Real as a backdrop. The building itself was once part of a long-gone, 17th-century convent and the interior feels a little like a set out of Mitteleuropa.

Café del Real BAR
(Map p78; ☎91 547 21 24; Plaza de Isabel II 2; ⏲8am-1am Mon-Thu, to 2.30am Fri, 9am-2.30am Sat, 10am-11.30pm Sun; Ⓜ Ópera) A cafe and cocktail bar in equal parts, this intimate little place serves up creative coffees and a few cocktails (the mojitos are excellent) to the soundtrack of chill-out music. The best seats are upstairs, where the low ceilings, wooden beams and leather chairs make for a great place to pass an afternoon with friends.

La Latina & Lavapiés

★Taberna El Tempranillo WINE BAR
(Map p82; ☎91 364 15 32; Calle de la Cava Baja 38; ⏲1-4pm Mon, 1-4pm & 8pm-midnight Tue-Sun; Ⓜ La Latina) You could come here for the tapas, but we recommend Taberna El Tempranillo primarily for its wines, of which it has a selection that puts numerous Spanish bars to shame. It's not a late-night place, but it's always packed in the early evening and on Sunday after El Rastro. Many wines are sold by the glass.

★Delic BAR
(Map p82; ☎91 364 54 50; www.delic.es; Costanilla de San Andrés 14; ⏲11am-2am Sun & Tue-Thu, to

2.30am Fri & Sat; M La Latina) We could go on for hours about this long-standing cafe-bar, but we'll reduce it to its most basic elements: nursing an exceptionally good mojito or three on a warm summer's evening at Delic's outdoor tables on one of Madrid's prettiest plazas is one of life's great pleasures. Bliss.

Bocanó Specialty Coffee CAFE

(Map p82; 91 040 20 19; www.bocono.es; Calle de los Embajadores 3; coffee €1.60-3; 8.30am-8.30pm Mon-Thu, to 9pm Fri & Sat, 9.30am-8.30pm Sun; ; M La Latina) Close attention to every detail makes Bocanó unique – coffee is roasted on-site and fanatics have a choice of styles: espresso, AeroPress and Chemex, among others. Coffee is weighed before brewing and water is dosed out by the millilitre. The decor is minimal, with reclaimed wood and rough brick, the wi-fi is fast and the service is friendly.

El Eucalipto COCKTAIL BAR

(91 527 27 63; www.facebook.com/eeucalipto; Calle de Argumosa 4; 5pm-2am Sun-Thu, to 3am Fri & Sat; M Lavapiés) This fine little bar is devoted to all things Cuban – from the music to the clientele and the Caribbean cocktails (including nonalcoholic), it's a sexy, laid-back place. Not surprisingly, the mojitos are a cut above average, but the juices and daiquiris also have a loyal following.

El Bonanno WINE BAR

(Map p82; 91 366 68 86; www.elbonanno.com; Plaza del Humilladero 4; noon-2am; M La Latina) If much of Madrid's nightlife starts too late for your liking, Bonanno could be for you. It made its name as a cocktail bar, but many people also come here for the great wines. It's usually full of young professionals from early evening onwards. Be prepared to snuggle up close to those around you if you want a spot at the bar.

Café del Nuncio BAR

(Map p82; 91 366 08 53; www.cafedelnuncio.es; Calle de Segovia 9; 11am-1am; M La Latina) Café del Nuncio straggles down a laneway to Calle de Segovia. You can drink on one of several cosy levels inside or, better still in summer, enjoy the outdoor seating that one local reviewer likened to a slice of Rome. By day it's an old-world cafe with great coffee, but by night it's one of the best no-frills bars in the *barrio*.

Sol, Santa Ana & Huertas

★ La Venencia BAR

(Map p88; 91 429 73 13; Calle de Echegaray 7; 12.30-3.30pm & 7.30pm-1.30am; M Sol, Sevilla) La Venencia is a *barrio* classic, with *manzanilla* (chamomile-coloured sherry) from Sanlúcar and sherry from Jeréz poured straight from the dusty wooden barrels, accompanied by a small selection of tapas with an Andalucian bent. There's no music, no flashy decorations; here it's all about you, your *fino* (sherry) and your friends.

Salmón Gurú COCKTAIL BAR

(Map p88; 91 000 61 85; http://salmonguru.es; Calle de Echegaray 21; 5pm-2.30am Wed-Sun; M Antón Martín) When Sergi Arola's empire collapsed and the celebrated Le Cabrera cocktail bar went with it, Madrid lost one of its best cocktail maestros, Diego Cabrera. Thankfully, he's back with a wonderful multifaceted space where he serves up a masterful collection of drinks – work your way through his menu of 25 Cabrera *clasicos* to get started.

Tartân Roof LOUNGE

(La Azotea; Map p88; www.azoteadelcirculo.com; 7th fl, Calle Marqués de Casa Riera 2; admission €4; 9am-2am Mon-Thu, to 2.30am Fri, 11am-2.30am Sat & Sun) Order a cocktail, then lie down on the cushions and admire the vista from this fabulous rooftop terrace. It's a brilliant place to chill out, with the views at their best close to sunset.

El Imperfecto COCKTAIL BAR

(Map p88; Plaza de Matute 2; 5pm-2.30am Mon-Thu, 3pm-2.30am Fri & Sat; M Antón Martín) Its name notwithstanding, the 'Imperfect One' is our ideal Huertas bar, with occasional live jazz and a drinks menu as long as a saxophone, ranging from cocktails (€7, or two mojitos for €10) and spirits to milkshakes, teas and creative coffees. Its pina colada is one of the best we've tasted and the atmosphere is agreeably buzzy yet chilled.

Taberna La Dolores BAR

(Map p88; 91 429 22 43; Plaza de Jesús 4; 11am-1am; M Antón Martín) Old bottles and beer mugs line the shelves behind the bar at this Madrid institution (1908), known for its blue-and-white-tiled exterior and for a 30-something crowd that often includes the odd *famoso* (celebrity) or two. It claims to be 'the most famous bar in Madrid' – that's pushing it, but it's invariably full most nights of the week, so who are we to argue?

Taberna Alhambra BAR

(Map p88; ☎91 521 07 08; Calle de la Victoria 9; ⏰11am-1am Sun-Wed, to 2am Thu, to 2.30am Fri & Sat; Ⓜ Sol) There can be a certain sameness about the bars between Sol and Huertas, which is why this fine old *taberna* stands out. The striking facade and exquisite tile work of the interior are quite beautiful; however, this place is anything but stuffy and the feel is cool, casual and busy. It serves tapas and, later at night, there are some fine flamenco tunes.

La Terraza del Urban COCKTAIL BAR

(Map p88; ☎91 787 77 70; Carrera de San Jerónimo 34, Urban Hotel; ⏰noon-8pm Sun & Mon, to 3am Tue-Sat mid-May–Sep; Ⓜ Sevilla) A strong contender for best rooftop bar in Madrid, this indulgent terrace sits atop the five-star Urban Hotel and has five-star views with five-star prices – worth every euro. It's only open while the weather's warm.

In case you get vertigo, head downstairs to the similarly high-class **Glass Bar** (Map p88; Carrera de San Jerónimo 34, Hotel Urban; ⏰noon-3am; Ⓜ Sevilla).

Radio COCKTAIL BAR

(Map p88; ☎91 701 60 20; www.memadrid.com; 7th fl, Plaza de Santa Ana 14; ⏰7pm-2am Mon-Thu, 5pm-3am Fri, 1pm-3am Sat, 1pm-2am Sun; Ⓜ Antón Martín, Sol) High above the Plaza de Santa Ana, this sybaritic open-air cocktail bar has terrific views over Madrid's rooftops. It's a place for sophisticates, with chill-out areas strewn with cushions, DJs and a dress and door policy designed to sort out the classy from the wannabes.

El Retiro & the Art Museums

Teatro Kapital CLUB

(Map p92; ☎91 420 29 06; www.grupo-kapital.com; Calle de Atocha 125; admission from €17; ⏰midnight-6am Thu-Sat; Ⓜ Atocha) One of the most famous megaclubs in Madrid, this seven-storey venue has something for everyone, from cocktail bars and dance music to karaoke, salsa, hip hop, chilled spaces and an open-air rooftop. There's even a 'Kissing Room'. Door staff have their share of attitude and don't mind refusing entrance if you give them any lip.

It's such a big place that a cross-section of Madrid society (VIPs and the Real Madrid set love this place) hangs out here without ever getting in each other's way.

Salamanca

Gabana 1800 CLUB

(Map p104; ☎91 575 18 46; www.gabana.es; Calle Velázquez 6; admission €15; ⏰midnight-5.30am Wed-Sat; Ⓜ Retiro) With its upmarket crowd that invariably includes a few *famosos* (famous people), Gabana 1800 is very Salamanca. That this place has lasted the distance where others haven't owes much to the fabulous array of drinks, rotating cast of first-class DJs and fairly discerning door policy – dress to impress.

Almonte CLUB

(Map p104; ☎91 563 25 04; www.almontesalarocíera.com; Calle de Juan Bravo 35; ⏰11pm-5am Sun-Fri, 10pm-6am Sat; Ⓜ Núñez de Balboa, Diego de León) If flamenco has captured your soul, but you're keen to do more than watch, head to Almonte. Live acts kick off the night, paying homage to the flamenco roots of Almonte in Andalucía's deep south. The young and the beautiful who come here have *sevillanas* (a flamenco dance style) in their soul and in their feet.

Geographic Club BAR

(Map p104; ☎91 578 08 62; www.thegeographicclub.es; Calle de Alcalá 141; ⏰1pm-2am Sun-Thu, to 3am Fri & Sat; Ⓜ Goya) With its elaborate stained-glass windows, ethno-chic from all over the world and laid-back atmosphere, the Geographic Club is an excellent choice in Salamanca for an early-evening drink – try one of the 30-plus tropical cocktails. We like the table built around an old hot-air-balloon basket almost as much as the cavern-like pub downstairs.

Malasaña & Chueca

★**Museo Chicote** COCKTAIL BAR

(Map p88; ☎91 532 67 37; www.grupomercadodelareina.com/en/museo-chicote-en; Gran Vía 12; ⏰7pm-3am Mon-Thu, to 4am Fri & Sat, 4pm-1am Sun; Ⓜ Gran Vía) This place is a Madrid landmark, complete with its 1930s-era interior, and its founder is said to have invented more than 100 cocktails, which the likes of Ernest Hemingway, Ava Gardner, Grace Kelly, Sophia Loren and Frank Sinatra have all enjoyed at one time or another.

★**Café Belén** BAR

(Map p108; ☎91 308 27 47; www.elcafebelen.com; Calle de Belén 5; ⏰3.30pm-3am Tue-Thu, to 3.30am Fri & Sat, to midnight Sun; 📶; Ⓜ Chueca) Café

Belén is cool in all the right places – lounge and chill-out music, dim lighting, a great range of drinks (the mojitos are especially good) and a low-key crowd that's the height of casual sophistication. It's one of our preferred Chueca watering holes.

La Tape CRAFT BEER
(Map p108; ☎91 593 04 22; www.latape.com; Calle de San Bernardo 88; ⊙10am-2am; Ⓜ Bilbao, San Bernardo) Long before craft or artisan beers took hold in Madrid, La Tape was onto it. The menu has 22 Spanish and international beers, as well as a strong selection of gluten-free beers. With plenty on tap to choose from, it's a beer-lover's pleasure to come here.

Café Comercial CAFE
(Map p108; ☎91 088 25 25; www.cafecomercialmadrid.com; Glorieta de Bilbao 7; ⊙7.30am-midnight Mon-Fri, 8.30am-midnight Sat & Sun; 📶; Ⓜ Bilbao) The city's oldest cafe has a special place in the hearts of many *madrileños*. Open for more than a century, it's still pulsing with life. Any day of the week you can enjoy a coffee or some food at one of the old marble-topped tables and feel like you're part of Madrid's literary and cultural scene.

Nice to Meet You BAR
(Map p108; ☎638 908559; www.dearhotelmadrid.com/en/nice-to-meet-you; Gran Vía 80, 14th fl, Dear Hotel; ⊙7.30am-2am; Ⓜ Plaza de España) This rooftop bar occupying the top floor of Dear Hotel has a spectacular view of Plaza España and Malasaña. Come any time of day to sit down with a cocktail and enjoy the view, or try something to eat – food specialities include Mediterranean staples like cod and ox steak.

1862 Dry Bar COCKTAIL BAR
(Map p108; ☎609 531151; www.facebook.com/1862DryBar; Calle del Pez 27; ⊙3.30pm-2am Mon-Thu, to 2.30am Fri & Sat, to 10.30pm Sun; Ⓜ Noviciado) Great cocktails, muted early-20th-century decor and a refined air make this one of our favourite bars down Malasaña's southern end. Prices are reasonable, the cocktail list extensive and new cocktails appear every month.

Café-Restaurante El Espejo CAFE
(Map p104; ☎91 308 23 47; Paseo de los Recoletos 31; ⊙8am-midnight; Ⓜ Colón) Once a haunt of writers and intellectuals, this architectural gem blends Modernista and art-deco styles, and its interior could well overwhelm you with all the mirrors, chandeliers and bow-tied service of another era. The atmosphere is suitably quiet and refined, although our favourite corner is the elegant glass pavilion out on Paseo de los Recoletos.

Gran Café de Gijón CAFE
(Map p104; ☎91 521 54 25; www.cafegijon.com; Paseo de los Recoletos 21; ⊙7am-1.30am; Ⓜ Chueca, Banco de España) This graceful old cafe has been serving coffee and meals since 1888 and has long been favoured by Madrid's literati for a drink or a meal – *all* of Spain's great 20th-century literary figures came here for coffee and *tertulias* (literary and philosophical discussions). You'll find yourself among intellectuals, conservative Franco diehards and young *madrileños* looking for a quiet drink.

Irreale BAR
(Map p108; ☎91 172 28 02; www.facebook.com/irrealemadrid; Calle de Manuela Malasaña 20; ⊙6pm-1am Sun-Wed, to 2am Thu, 1pm-2.30am Fri & Sat; Ⓜ Bilbao) It's not that long ago that you entered any Madrid bar and ordered *una cerveza* (a beer). There was only one kind. But craft beers have now taken hold and Irreale has a particularly strong selection with a changing roster of around 10 beers on tap and dozens by the bottle. It's a great place to start your Malasaña night.

José Alfredo COCKTAIL BAR
(Map p78; ☎91 521 49 60; www.josealfredobar.com; Calle de Silva 22; cocktails from €9; ⊙7pm-3am Sun-Thu, to 3.30am Fri & Sat; Ⓜ Callao) This American-style cocktail bar just off Gran Vía is an institution. It plays indie music and does fabulous cocktails – try the 'Lazy Bitch' (rum, banana liqueur, cinnamon liqueur and lime juice) or the 'José Alfredo' (tequila, curaçao, grenadine, lime and pineapple and orange juice).

Kikekeller BAR
(Map p108; ☎91 522 87 67; www.kikekeller.com; Calle de la Corredera Baja de San Pablo 17; ⊙7pm-2.30am Thu-Sat; Ⓜ Callao) A small but growing trend of the Madrid night is that of *bares clandestinos* (clandestine bars). While it may sound vaguely illicit, it's all above board – shops by days morph effortlessly into cool bars after dark. Our favourite is Kikekeller, an avant-garde furniture and interior decoration shop where they can't even wait for the shop to close on Saturday before opening the bar.

It's one of the more original places to enjoy the Madrid night.

Fábrica Maravillas BREWERY

(Map p108; ☎91 521 87 53; www.fmaravillas.com; Calle de Valverde 29; ⏲6pm-midnight Mon-Wed, to 1am Thu, to 2am Fri, 12.30pm-2am Sat, 12.30pm-midnight Sun; Ⓜ Tribunal, Gran Vía) Spain has taken its time getting behind the worldwide trend of boutique and artisan beers, but it's finally starting to happen. The finest example of this in Madrid is Fábrica Maravillas, a microbrewery known for its 'Malasaña Ale'.

Tupperware BAR, CLUB

(Map p108; ☎91 446 42 04; www.tupperwareclub.com; Calle de la Corredera Alta de San Pablo 26; ⏲9pm-3am Mon-Wed, 8pm-3.30am Thu-Sat, 8pm-3am Sun; Ⓜ Tribunal) A Malasaña stalwart and prime candidate for the bar that best catches the enduring *rockero* (rocker) spirit of Malasaña, Tupperware draws a 30-something crowd, spins indie rock with a bit of soul and classics from the '60s and '70s, and generally revels in its kitsch (eyeballs stuck to the ceiling, and plastic TVs with action-figure dioramas lined up behind the bar).

By the way, locals pronounce it 'Tupper-warry'.

Café de Mahón CAFE

(Map p108; ☎91 532 47 56; www.facebook.com/cafedemahon; Plaza del Dos de Mayo 4; ⏲noon-1.30am Mon-Thu, to 3am Fri-Sun; Ⓜ Bilbao) If we had to choose our favourite slice of Malasaña life, this engaging little cafe, with outdoor tables that watch over Plaza del Dos de Mayo, would be a prime candidate. It's beloved by *famosos* (celebrities) as much as by the locals catching up for a quiet drink with friends. Official opening times notwithstanding, it has a habit of opening and closing whenever the whim takes it.

Antigua Casa Ángel Sierra TAVERNA

(Map p108; ☎91 531 01 26; http://tabernadeangelsierra.es; Calle de Gravina 11; ⏲noon-1am; Ⓜ Chueca) This historic old *taberna* (tavern) is the antithesis of modern Chueca chic – it has hardly changed since it opened in 1917. As Spaniards like to say, the beer on tap is very 'well poured' here and it also has vermouth on tap. It can get pretty lively weekend evenings when it not so much spills over onto the vibrant Plaza de Chueca as takes it over.

Moloko Sound Club BAR, CLUB

(Map p108; ☎626 529967; www.molokosoundclub.com; Calle de Quiñones 12; ⏲10.30pm-3.30am Wed-Sat; Ⓜ San Bernardo) With its walls plastered with old concert flyers and the odd art-house movie poster (eg *A Clockwork Orange*), Moloko remains an excellent middle-of-the-night option in the Conde Duque area of western Malasaña. The music – indie, rock, soul, garage and '60s – is consistently good, which is why people return here again and again.

Café Manuela CAFE

(Map p108; ☎91 531 70 37; www.facebook.com/CafeManuela; Calle de San Vicente Ferrer 29; ⏲4pm-2am Sun-Thu, to 2.30am Fri & Sat; Ⓜ Tribunal) Stumbling into this graciously restored throwback to the 1950s along one of Malasaña's grittier streets is akin to discovering hidden treasure. There's a luminous quality to it when you come in out of the night and, like so many Madrid cafes, it's a surprisingly multifaceted space, serving cocktails and delicious milkshakes as well as offering board games atop the marble tables.

Lolina Vintage Café CAFE

(Map p108; ☎91 523 58 59; www.lolinacafe.com; Calle del Espíritu Santo 9; ⏲10am-midnight Sun-Thu, to 2.30am Fri & Sat; Ⓜ Tribunal) Lolina Vintage Café seems to have captured the essence of the *barrio* in one small space, with its studied retro look (comfy old-style chairs and sofas, gilded mirrors and 1970s-era wallpaper). It's low-key, full from the first breakfast to closing, and it caters to every taste with salads and cocktails.

La Terraza de Arriba LOUNGE

(Splash Óscar; Map p108; Plaza de Vázquez de Mella 12; ⏲6.30pm-2.30am Wed & Thu, 4.30pm-2.30am Fri-Sun mid-May–mid-Sep; Ⓜ Gran Vía) One of Madrid's stunning rooftop terraces, this chilled space atop Hotel Óscar (p116), with gorgeous skyline views and a small swimming pool, has become something of a retreat among A-list celebrities.

Bar Cock COCKTAIL BAR

(Map p88; ☎91 532 28 26; www.barcock.com; Calle de la Reina 16; ⏲7pm-3am Sun-Thu, to 3.30am Fri & Sat; Ⓜ Gran Vía) With a name like this, Bar Cock could go either way, but it's definitely cock as in 'rooster'. The decor evokes an old gentlemen's club and the feeling is more elegant and classic than risqué. It's beloved by A-list celebrities and A-list wannabes, and a refined 30-something crowd who come here for the lively atmosphere and great cocktails.

On weekends all the tables seem to be reserved, so be prepared to hover on the fringes of fame.

La Vía Láctea BAR, CLUB

(Map p108; ☎91 446 75 81; www.facebook.com/lavialacteabar; Calle de Velarde 18; ⏰8pm-3am Sun-Thu, to 3.30am Fri & Sat; Ⓜ Tribunal) A living, breathing and delightfully grungy relic of *la movida madrileña* (the Madrid scene), La Vía Láctea remains a Malasaña favourite for a mixed, informal crowd who seems to live for the 1980s. The music ranges across rock, pop, garage, rockabilly and indie. There are plenty of drinks to choose from and by late Saturday night anything goes. Expect long queues to get in on weekends.

Del Diego COCKTAIL BAR

(Map p88; ☎91 523 31 06; www.deldiego.com; Calle de la Reina 12; ⏰7pm-3am Mon-Thu, to 3.30am Fri & Sat; Ⓜ Gran Vía) Del Diego is one of the city's most celebrated cocktail bars. The decor blends old-world cafe with New York style, and it's the sort of place where the music rarely drowns out the conversation. Even with around 75 cocktails to choose from, we'd still order the signature 'El Diego' (vodka, advocaat, apricot brandy and lime).

Parque del Oeste & Northern Madrid

La Violeta BAR

(☎667 058644; www.lavioletavermut.com; Calle Vallehermoso 62; ⏰7pm-1am Tue-Thu, 1-4.30pm & 7pm-2am Fri, 1pm-2am Sat, 1-5pm Sun; Ⓜ Canal) This breezy little Chamberí bar has many calling cards – among them, great music and a sense of being a real old-style Madrid neighbourhood bar. But we like it for its *vermut* (vermouth), one of the city's favourite drinks. Unusually, there are more than 20 different versions to try and staff are adept at pairing the perfect tapa (snack) with each variety.

La Vaquería Montañesa BAR

(Map p104; ☎911387106; www.lavaqueriamontanesa.es; Calle de Blanca de Navarra 8; ⏰1pm-1am Fri & Sat; Ⓜ Alonso Martínez) Inhabiting an old dairy and tucked away in a little-visited corner of Chamberí like some hidden Madrid treasure, La Vaquería Montañesa does terrific food but it's the vermouth, served in a martini glass, that really draws us back. The look here is whitewashed, classy and contemporary.

The Dash COCKTAIL BAR

(☎687 949064; www.facebook.com/thedashmadrid; Calle de Murillo 5; ⏰4pm-2am Tue-Thu, to 2.30am Fri & Sat, 1-11pm Sun; Ⓜ Iglesia) This neighbourhood cocktail bar with its big marble bar top evokes the classic cocktail bars of Madrid's past but it's a casual place with few pretensions. There's a terrific mix of cocktails with few surprises but all expertly mixed.

Real Café Bernabéu BAR

(☎91 458 36 67; www.realcafebernabeu.es; Gate 30, Estadio Santiago Bernabéu, Avenida de Concha Espina; ⏰10am-2am; Ⓜ Santiago Bernabéu) Overlooking one of the most famous football fields on earth, this trendy cocktail bar will appeal to those who live and breathe football or those who simply enjoy mixing with the beautiful people. Views of the stadium are exceptional, although it closes two hours before a game and doesn't open until an hour after. There's also a good restaurant.

☆ Entertainment

Madrid has a happening live-music scene that owes a lot to the city's role as the cultural capital of the Spanish-speaking world. There's flamenco, world-class jazz and a host of performers you may never have heard of but who may just be Spain's next big thing. For a dose of high culture, there's opera and *zarzuela* (Spanish mix of theatre, music and dance).

☆ Plaza Mayor & Royal Madrid

Las Tablas FLAMENCO

(Map p78; ☎91 542 05 20; www.lastablasmadrid.com; Plaza de España 9; admission incl drink from €29; ⏰shows 8pm & 10pm; Ⓜ Plaza de España) Las Tablas has a reputation for quality flamenco and reasonable prices; it's among the best choices in town. Most nights you'll see a classic flamenco show, with plenty of throaty singing and soul-baring dancing. Antonia Moya and Marisol Navarro, leading lights in the flamenco world, are regular performers here.

La Coquette Blues LIVE MUSIC

(Map p78; ☎91 530 80 95; Calle de las Hileras 14; ⏰8pm-3am Tue-Thu, to 3.30am Fri & Sat, 7pm-3am Sun; Ⓜ Ópera) Madrid's best blues bar has been around since the 1980s and its 8pm Sunday jam session is legendary. Live acts perform from Tuesday to Thursday at 10.30pm and the atmosphere is very cool at any time.

Torres Bermejas FLAMENCO

(Map p88; ☎91 532 33 22; www.torresbermejas.com; Calle de los Mesoneros Romanos 11; admission incl drink from €35; ⏰shows 7pm & 9pm; Ⓜ Callao) For decades this was the Madrid stage for

GAY & LESBIAN MADRID

Madrid is one of Europe's most gay-friendly cities. The heartbeat of gay Madrid is the inner-city *barrio* of Chueca, where Madrid didn't just come out of the closet, but ripped the doors off in the process. But even here the crowd is almost always mixed gay/straight. The best time of all to be in town if you're gay or lesbian is around the last Saturday in June, for Madrid's gay and lesbian pride march, Día del Orgullo de Gays, Lesbianas y Transexuales (p112). An excellent place to stay is Hostal La Zona (p116).

Librería Berkana (Map p108; ☎91 522 55 99; www.libreriaberkana.com; Calle de Hortaleza 62; ⏰10.30am-9pm Mon-Fri, 11.30am-9pm Sat, noon-2pm & 5-9pm Sun; Ⓜ Chueca) One of the most important gay and lesbian bookshops in Madrid, Librería Berkana stocks gay books, movies, magazines, music, clothing, and a host of free magazines for nightlife and other gay-focused activities in Madrid and around Spain.

Mamá Inés (Map p108; ☎91 523 23 33; www.mamaines.com; Calle de Hortaleza 22; ⏰9am-1.30am Sun-Thu, to 2.30am Fri & Sat; Ⓜ Chueca) A gay meeting place, this cafe-bar has a laid-back ambience by day and a romantic (never sleazy) air by night. You can get breakfast, yummy pastries and the word on where that night's hot spot will be. There's a steady stream of people coming and going throughout the day. The lights are turned down low as evening turns into night.

Café Acuarela (Map p108; ☎91 522 21 43; Calle de Gravina 10; ⏰11am-2am Sun-Thu, to 3am Fri & Sat; Ⓜ Chueca) A few steps up the hill from Plaza de Chueca, this longtime centrepiece of gay Madrid – a huge statue of a nude male angel guards the doorway – is an agreeable, dimly lit salon decorated with, among other things, religious icons. It's ideal for quiet conversation and catching the weekend buzz as people plan their forays into the more clamorous clubs in the vicinity.

Club 54 Studio (Map p108; ☎615 126807; www.studio54madrid.com; Calle de Barbieri 7; ⏰11am-3.30am Wed-Sun; Ⓜ Chueca) Modelled on the famous New York club Studio 54, this nightclub draws a predominantly gay crowd, but its target market is more upmarket than many in the *barrio*. Unlike other Madrid clubs where paid dancers up on stage try to get things moving, here they let the punters set the pace.

Why Not? (Map p108; ☎91 521 80 34; Calle de San Bartolomé 7; entrance €10; ⏰10.30pm-6am; Ⓜ Chueca) Underground, narrow and packed with bodies, gay-friendly Why Not? is the sort of place where nothing's left to the imagination (the gay and straight crowd who come here are pretty amorous) and it's full nearly every night of the week. Pop and Top 40 music are the standard, and the dancing crowd is mixed but all serious about having a good time.

We're not huge fans of the bouncers here, but once you get past them it's all good fun.

flamenco legend Camarón de la Isla, and after a drop in quality for a few years, it's once again a good place to see flamenco. The atmosphere is aided by the extravagantly tiled interior.

Café Berlin JAZZ

(Map p78; ☎91 559 74 29; www.berlincafe.es; Costanilla de los Ángeles 20; €5-20; ⏰9pm-3am Tue-Thu, to 5am Fri & Sat; Ⓜ Santo Domingo) El Berlín has been something of a Madrid jazz stalwart since the 1950s, although a makeover has brought flamenco (Wednesday is a flamenco jam session), R&B, soul, funk and fusion into the mix. Headline acts play at 11pm, although check the website as some can begin as early as 9pm.

Las Carboneras FLAMENCO

(Map p78; ☎91 542 86 77; www.tablaolascarboneras.com; Plaza del Conde de Miranda 1; show incl drink/meal €35/70; ⏰shows 8.30pm & 10.30pm Mon-Thu, 8.30pm & 11pm Fri & Sat; Ⓜ Ópera, Sol, La Latina) Like most of the *tablaos* (flamenco venues) around town, this place sees far more tourists than locals, but the quality is nonetheless excellent. It's not the place for gritty, soul-moving spontaneity, but it's still an excellent introduction and one of the few places that flamenco aficionados seem to have no complaints about.

Café de Chinitas FLAMENCO

(Map p78; ☎91 547 15 02; www.chinitas.com; Calle de Torija 7; admission incl drink/meal €36/55;

shows 8.15pm & 10.30pm Mon-Sat; M Santo Domingo) One of the most distinguished *tablaos* in Madrid, drawing in everyone from the Spanish royal family to Bill Clinton, Café de Chinitas has an elegant setting and top-notch performers. It may attract loads of tourists, but its authentic flamenco also gives it top marks. Reservations are highly recommended.

Teatro Real OPERA

(Map p78; 902 244848; www.teatro-real.com; Plaza de Oriente; M Ópera) After spending over €100 million on a long rebuilding project, the Teatro Real is as technologically advanced as any venue in Europe, and is the city's grandest stage for elaborate operas, ballets and classical music. The cheapest seats are so far away you'll need a telescope, although the sound quality is consistent throughout.

☆ La Latina & Lavapiés

★Casa Patas FLAMENCO

(Map p88; 91 369 04 96; www.casapatas.com; Calle de Cañizares 10; admission incl drink €38; shows 10.30pm Mon-Thu, 8pm & 10.30pm Fri & Sat; M Antón Martín, Tirso de Molina) One of the top flamenco stages in Madrid, this *tablao* always offers flawless quality that serves as a good introduction to the art. It's not the friendliest place in town, especially if you're only here for the show, and you're likely to be crammed in a little, but no one complains about the standard of the performances.

★Corral de la Morería FLAMENCO

(Map p82; 91 365 84 46; www.corraldelamoreria.com; Calle de la Morería 17; admission incl drink from €45; 7pm-12.15am, shows 8.30pm & 10.20pm; M Ópera) This is one of the most prestigious flamenco stages in Madrid, with 50 years of experience as a leading venue and top performers most nights. The stage area has a rustic feel, and tables are pushed up close. Set menus from €45 (additional to the admission fee).

ContraClub LIVE MUSIC

(Map p82; 91 365 55 45; www.contraclub.es; Calle de Bailén 16; entrance €3-15; 10pm-6am Wed-Sat; M La Latina) ContraClub is a crossover live music venue and nightclub, with an eclectic mix of live music (pop, rock, indie, singer-songwriter, blues etc). After the live acts (from 10pm), resident DJs serve up equally diverse beats (indie, pop, funk and soul) to make sure you don't move elsewhere.

☆ Sol, Santa Ana & Huertas

★Sala El Sol LIVE MUSIC

(Map p88; 91 532 64 90; www.elsolmad.com; Calle de los Jardines 3; admission incl drink €10, concert tickets €6-30; midnight-5.30am Tue-Sat Jul-Sep; M Gran Vía) Madrid institutions don't come any more beloved than the terrific Sala El Sol. It opened in 1979, just in time for *la movida madrileña* (the Madrid scene), and quickly established itself as a leading stage for all the icons of the era, such as Nacha Pop and Alaska y los Pegamoides.

★Villa Rosa FLAMENCO

(Map p88; 91 521 36 89; www.reservas.tablaoflamencovillarosa.com; Plaza de Santa Ana 15; admission incl drink adult/child €35/17; 11pm-6am Mon-Sat, shows 8.30pm & 10.45pm; M Sol) Villa Rosa has been going strong since 1914, and in that time it has seen many manifestations. It originally made its name as a flamenco venue and has recently returned to its roots with well-priced shows and meals that won't break the bank.

The extraordinary tiled facade (1928) is the work of Alfonso Romero, who was also responsible for the tile work in the Plaza de Toros – the facade is a tourist attraction in itself. This long-standing nightclub even appeared in the Pedro Almodóvar film *Tacones lejanos* (High Heels; 1991).

★Café Central JAZZ

(Map p88; 91 369 41 43; www.cafecentralmadrid.com; Plaza del Ángel 10; admission €12-18; 12.30pm-2.30am Mon-Thu, to 3.30am Fri, 11.30am-3.30am Sat, performances 9pm; M Antón Martín, Sol) In 2011 the respected jazz magazine *Down Beat* included this art-deco bar on the list of the world's best jazz clubs, the only place in Spain to earn the prestigious accolade (said by some to be the jazz equivalent of earning a Michelin star). With well over 1000 gigs under its belt, it rarely misses a beat.

Big international names like Chano Domínguez, Tal Farlow and Wynton Marsalis have all played here and you'll hear everything from Latin jazz and fusion to tango and classical jazz. Performers usually play here for a week and then move on, so getting tickets shouldn't be a problem, except on weekends. Shows start at 9pm and tickets go on sale from 6pm before the set starts. You can also reserve by phone.

WHAT'S ON IN MADRID?

EsMadrid Magazine (www.esmadrid.com) Monthly tourist-office listings.

Guía del Ocio (www.guiadelocio.com) Weekly magazine available for €1 at news kiosks.

In Madrid (www.in-madrid.com) Free monthly English-language publication.

Metropoli (www.elmundo.es/metropoli) *El Mundo* newspaper's Friday supplement magazine.

La Noche en Vivo (www.lanocheenvivo.com) Live music listings.

★Teatro de la Zarzuela THEATRE

(Map p88; ☎91 524 54 00; www.teatrodelazarzuela.mcu.es; Calle de Jovellanos 4; tickets €5-60; ⏲box office noon-6pm Mon-Fri, 3-6pm Sat & Sun; Ⓜ Banco de España, Sevilla) This theatre, built in 1856, is the premier place to see *zarzuela* (Spanish mix of theatre, music and dance). It also hosts a smattering of classical music and opera, as well as the cutting edge Compañía Nacional de Danza.

Costello Café & Niteclub LIVE MUSIC

(Map p88; ☎91 522 18 15; www.costelloclub.com; Calle del Caballero de Gracia 10; €8-20; ⏲8pm-2.30am Tue, to 3am Wed & Thu, to 3.30am Fri & Sat; Ⓜ Gran Vía) The very cool Costello Café & Niteclub weds smooth-as-silk ambience to an innovative mix of pop, rock and fusion in Warholesque surrounds. There's live music (pop and rock, often of the indie variety) at 9.30pm every night except Sunday and Monday, with resident and visiting DJs keeping you on your feet until closing time the rest of the week.

☆ Malasaña & Chueca

★Teatro Flamenco Madrid FLAMENCO

(Map p108; ☎91 159 20 05; www.teatroflamencomadrid.com; Calle del Pez 10; adult/student & senior/child €25/16/12; ⏲6.45pm & 8.15pm; Ⓜ Noviciado) This excellent new flamenco venue is a terrific deal. With a focus on quality flamenco (dance, song and guitar) rather than the more formal meal-and-floor-show package of the *tablaos* (choreographed flamenco shows), and with a mixed crowd of locals and tourists, this place generates a terrific atmosphere most nights for the hour-long show. Prices are also a notch below what you'll pay elsewhere.

Thundercat LIVE MUSIC

(Map p108; ☎654 511457; www.thundercatclub.com; Calle de Campoamor 11; ⏲10pm-6am Thu-Sat; Ⓜ Alonso Martínez) They keep it simple at Thundercat – it's rock, as classic as they can find it, with live gigs beginning after midnight and rolling on through the night. There's a fine jam session at 11.30pm Thursday.

El Junco Jazz Club JAZZ

(Map p108; ☎91 319 20 81; www.eljunco.com; Plaza de Santa Bárbara 10; €6-15; ⏲11pm-5.30am Tue-Thu, to 6am Fri & Sat; Ⓜ Alonso Martínez) El Junco has established itself on the Madrid nightlife scene by appealing as much to jazz aficionados as to clubbers. Its secret is high-quality live jazz gigs from Spain and around the world, followed by DJs spinning funk, soul, nu jazz, blues and innovative groove beats. There are also jam sessions at 11pm in jazz (Tuesday) and blues (Sunday).

The emphasis is on music from the American South and the crowd is classy and casual.

Café La Palma LIVE MUSIC, DANCE

(Map p108; ☎91 522 50 31; www.cafelapalma.com; Calle de la Palma 62; free-€15; ⏲5pm-3am Sun, Wed & Thu, to 3.30am Fri & Sat; Ⓜ Noviciado) It's amazing how much variety Café La Palma has packed into its labyrinth of rooms. Live shows featuring hot local bands are held at the back, while DJs mix it up at the front.

☆ Parque del Oeste & Northern Madrid

★Estadio Santiago Bernabéu FOOTBALL

(☎902 324324; www.realmadrid.com; Avenida de Concha Espina 1; tickets from €40; Ⓜ Santiago Bernabéu) Watching Real Madrid play is one of football's greatest experiences, but tickets are difficult to find. They can be purchased online, by phone or in person from the ticket office at Gate 42 on Av de Concha Espina; turn up early in the week before a scheduled game. Numerous online ticketing agencies also sell tickets. Otherwise, you'll need to take a risk with scalpers.

The football season runs from September (or the last weekend in August) until May, with a two-week break just before Christmas until early in the New Year.

Sala Clamores LIVE MUSIC

(☎91 445 79 38; www.clamores.es; Calle de Alburquerque 14; admission free-€15; ⏲6.30pm-2am Sun-Thu, to 5.30am Fri & Sat; Ⓜ Bilbao) Clamores is a one-time classic jazz cafe that has morphed into one of the most diverse live music stages in Madrid. Jazz is still a staple, but flamenco, blues, world music, singer-songwriters, pop and rock all make regular appearances. Live shows can begin as early as 7pm on weekends but sometimes really only get going after 1am.

Shopping

Our favourite aspect of shopping in Madrid is the city's small boutiques and quirky shops. Often run by the same families for generations, they counter the over commercialisation of mass-produced Spanish culture with everything from fashions to old-style ceramics to rope-soled espadrilles or gourmet Spanish food and wine.

Plaza Mayor & Royal Madrid

★Antigua Casa Talavera CERAMICS
(Map p78; 91 547 34 17; www.antiguacasatalavera.com; Calle de Isabel la Católica 2; 10am-1.30pm & 5-8pm Mon-Fri, 10am-1.30pm Sat; M Santo Domingo) The extraordinary tiled facade of this wonderful old shop conceals an Aladdin's cave of ceramics from all over Spain. This is not the mass-produced stuff aimed at a tourist market, but instead comes from the small family potters of Andalucía and Toledo, ranging from the decorative (tiles) to the useful (plates, jugs and other kitchen items). The elderly couple who run the place are delightful.

★El Arco Artesanía ARTS & CRAFTS
(Map p78; 91 365 26 80; www.artesaniaelarco.com; Plaza Mayor 9; 11am-10pm; M Sol, La Latina) This original shop in the southwestern corner of Plaza Mayor sells an outstanding array of homemade designer souvenirs, from stone, ceramic and glass work to jewellery and home fittings. The papier-mâché figures are gorgeous, but there's so much else here to turn your head. It sometimes closes earlier in the depths of winter.

Maty FLAMENCO
(Map p78; 91 531 32 91; www.maty.es; Calle del Maestro Victoria 2; 10am-1.45pm & 4.30-8pm Mon-Fri, 10am-2pm & 4.30-8pm Sat, 11am-2.30pm & 4.30-8pm 1st Sun of month; M Sol) Wandering around central Madrid, it's easy to imagine that flamenco outfits have been reduced to imitation dresses sold as souvenirs to tourists. That's why places like Maty matter. Here you'll find dresses, shoes and all the accessories that go with the genre, with sizes for children and adults. These are the real deal, with prices to match, but they make brilliant gifts.

Casa Hernanz SHOES
(Map p78; 91 366 54 50; www.alpargateriahernanz.com; Calle de Toledo 18; 9am-1.30pm & 4.30-8pm Mon-Fri, 10am-2pm Sat; M La Latina, Sol) Comfy, rope-soled *alpargatas* (espadrilles), Spain's traditional summer footwear, are worn by everyone from the king of Spain down. You can buy your own pair at this humble workshop, which has been hand-making the shoes for five generations; you can even get them made to order. Prices range from €6 to €40 and queues form whenever the weather starts to warm up.

Atlético de Madrid Store SPORTS & OUTDOORS
(Map p78; 902 260403; www.en.atleticodemadrid.com/shop; Gran Vía 47; 10am-9.30pm Mon-Thu, to 10pm Fri & Sat, 11am-8pm Sun; M Santo Domingo) Atlético de Madrid has something of a cult following in the city and has enjoyed considerable footballing success in recent years. Its downtown store has all the club's merchandise. In theory you can also buy tickets to games here, but most matches are sold out before you'll get a chance.

Así TOYS
(Map p78; 91 521 97 55; www.tiendas-asi.com; Calle del Arenal 20; 10am-8.30pm Mon-Sat, noon-3.30pm & 4.30-8pm Sun; M Ópera) Beautifully crafted baby dolls make a lovely gift or souvenir of your little one's visit to the city. These are the real deal, not mass-produced, and there are some fine baby's outfits to go with them.

La Madrileña FOOD
(Map p78; 91 522 34 36; www.fiambreslamadrilena.com; Calle del Arenal 18; 9.30am-2pm & 5.30-8.30pm Mon-Fri, 10am-2pm Sat; M Sol) La Madrileña has been serving its customers ham, cured meats and sausages since 1909. Its white sausages are perfect for the griddle, or you can try the *sobrasada* – a pâté made from ground pork and paprika. It's delectable spread on a piece of baguette. Other specialities are the *conservas* – high-quality, artisan fish, legumes and vegetables in tins or jars.

Sombrerería Medrano FASHION & ACCESSORIES
(Map p78; 91 366 42 34; www.sombrereriamedrano.com; Calle Imperial 12; 10am-2.30pm & 4.30-8pm Mon-Fri, 10am-2pm Sat; M Sol) They've been making hats at this place since 1832, and while concessions have been made to modern fashions, the look here is reassuringly a classic one. It's a marvellous old shop-workshop where the quality is unimpeachable. It does hats and gloves for men, women and children.

1

2

DANNY LEHMAN/GETTY IMAGES ©

1. Mercado de San Miguel (p117) **2.** El Rastro flea market (p82)
3. Flamenco dancers

Locals' Madrid

More than most other Spanish cities, Madrid can take time to get under your skin, but once it does it rewards your patience a thousand times over. A little local knowledge is the key.

A Very Madrid Sunday

Madrileños (residents of Madrid) like nothing better than Sunday morning at El Rastro flea market (p82), followed by tapas and vermouth around 1pm along Calle de la Cava Baja (p121) in La Latina. Then it's across town to the Parque del Buen Retiro (p93) where, east of the lake, crowds gather, drums start to beat and people begin to dance as the sun nears the horizon.

Food Icons

In this food-obsessed city you'll find countless treasures that capture the city's culinary essence. The Mercado de San Miguel (p117) epitomises the irresistible buzz that goes with eating here. Nearby Casa Revuelta (p121) is not much to look at but it's similarly adored by locals.

Informal Flamenco

Madrid has many outstanding flamenco stages but most are pretty formal affairs. While upstairs at **Candela** (☎91 467 33 82; www.candelaflamenco.com; Calle del Olmo 3; €10; ⏱10.30pm-late) fits this description, the downstairs bar is for true aficionados and it's a more spontaneous proposition. Sometimes it works, sometimes it doesn't, but therein lies the magic of flamenco.

Barrio Life

North of the centre, the locals reclaim their city. Plaza de Olavide (p107) is the heart and soul of Chamberí and offers an authentic slice of local life. It's not that there's much to see here: instead, the agreeable hum of Madrileños going about their daily life, watched from the outdoor tables that encircle the plaza, is a fascinating window on how locals experience Madrid.

Gourmet Experience FOOD & DRINKS

(Map p88; ☎91 379 80 00; www.elcorteingles.es; 9th fl, Plaza del Callao 9; ⏰10am-10pm Mon-Sat; Ⓜ Callao) On a winning perch high above Plaza del Callao and with stunning views down Gran Vía, this food court (p117) has a fabulous store for foodies looking for Spanish products, including cheeses, wines, cured meats and Spanish craft beers.

El Jardín del Convento FOOD

(Map p78; ☎91 541 22 99; www.eljardindelconvento.net; Calle del Cordón 1; ⏰11am-2.30pm & 5.30-8.30pm Tue-Sun; Ⓜ Ópera) In a quiet lane just south of Plaza de la Villa, this appealing little shop sells homemade sweets baked by nuns in abbeys, convents and monasteries all across Spain.

El Flamenco Vive FLAMENCO

(Map p78; ☎91 547 39 17; www.elflamencovive.es; Calle Conde de Lemos 7; ⏰10am-2pm & 5-8.30pm Mon-Fri, 10am-2pm Sat; Ⓜ Ópera) This temple to flamenco has it all, from guitars and songbooks to well-priced CDs, polka-dotted dancing costumes, shoes, colourful plastic jewellery and literature about flamenco. It's the sort of place that will appeal as much to curious first-timers as to serious students of the art. It also organises classes in flamenco guitar.

La Latina & Lavapiés

★Botería Julio Rodríguez ARTS & CRAFTS

(Map p82; ☎91 365 66 29; www.boteriajuliorodriguez.es; Calle del Águila 12; ⏰9.30am-2pm & 4.30-8pm Mon-Fri, 10am-1.30pm Sat; Ⓜ La Latina) One of the last makers of traditional Spanish wineskins left in Madrid, Botería Julio Rodríguez is like a window on a fast-disappearing world. They make a great gift and, as you'd expect, they're in a different league from the cheap wineskins found in souvenir shops across downtown Madrid.

★Helena Rohner JEWELLERY

(Map p82; ☎91 365 79 06; www.helenarohner.com.es; Calle del Almendro 4; ⏰9am-8.30pm Mon-Fri, noon-2.30pm & 3.30-8pm Sat, noon-3pm Sun; Ⓜ La Latina, Tirso de Molina) One of Europe's most creative jewellery designers, Helena Rohner has a spacious boutique in La Latina. Working with silver, stone, porcelain, wood and Murano glass, she makes inventive pieces that are a regular feature of Paris fashion shows. In her own words, she seeks to recreate 'the magic of Florence, the vitality of London and the luminosity of Madrid'.

El Rastro MARKET

(Map p82; Calle de la Ribera de Curtidores; ⏰8am-3pm Sun; Ⓜ La Latina, Puerta de Toledo, Tirso de Molina) Welcome to what is claimed to be Europe's largest flea market. Antiques are also a major drawcard with a concentration of stores at Nuevas Galerías and Galerías Piquer; most shops open 10am to 2pm and 5pm to 8pm Monday to Saturday and not all open during El Rastro.

Aceitunas Jiménez FOOD

(Map p82; ☎91 365 46 23; Plaza del General Vara del Rey 14; ⏰10.30am-2.30pm & 3.30-8pm Mon-Thu, 10.30am-2.30pm Fri & Sat, 10.30am-3pm Sun; Ⓜ La Latina) An institution on a Sunday stroll in El Rastro, this tiny shop serves up pickled olives in plastic cups and in all manner of varieties, as well as aubergines, garlic and anything else they've decided to soak in lashings of oil and/or vinegar.

De Piedra JEWELLERY

(Map p82; ☎91 365 96 20; www.depiedracreaciones.com; Calle de la Ruda 19; ⏰11am-2pm & 5-8.30pm Mon-Sat, noon-3pm Sun; Ⓜ La Latina) Necklaces, earrings, bracelets and home decorations made by a local design team fill this lovely showroom. Silver and semiprecious stones are the mainstays.

Sol, Santa Ana & Huertas

Casa de Diego FASHION & ACCESSORIES

(Map p88; ☎91 522 66 43; www.casadediego.com; Plaza de la Puerta del Sol 12; ⏰9.30am-8pm Mon-Sat; Ⓜ Sol) This classic shop has been around since 1858, making, selling and repairing Spanish fans, shawls, umbrellas and canes. Service is old style and occasionally grumpy, but the fans are works of antique art. There's another **branch** (Map p88; ☎91 531 02 23; www.casadediego.com; Calle del los Mesoneros Romanos 4; ⏰9.30am-1.30pm & 4.45-8pm Mon-Sat; Ⓜ Callao, Sol) nearby.

Licores Cabello WINE

(Map p88; ☎91 429 60 88; Calle de Echegaray 19; ⏰10am-3pm & 5.30-10pm Mon-Sat; Ⓜ Sevilla, Antón Martín) All wine shops should be like this one. This family-run corner shop really knows its wines and the interior has scarcely changed since 1913, with wooden shelves and even a faded ceiling fresco. There are fine wines in abundance (mostly Spanish, and a few foreign bottles), with some 500 wine labels on display or tucked away out the back.

The Corner Shop CLOTHING
(Map p88; ☎91 737 58 02; www.thecornershop.es; Calle de las Huertas 17; ⊙10.30am-9.30pm Mon-Fri, 11am-9.30pm Sat & Sun; M Antón Martín) This fine Huertas shop does a carefully curated collection of men's and women's fashions, with brand names like Scotch Soda, Blue Hole, Andy and Lucy and many others. Regardless of brands, it's always worth stopping by to check its casual street wear with a touch of style and a hint of the offbeat.

Justo Algaba GIFTS & SOUVENIRS
(Map p88; ☎91 523 37 17; www.justoalgaba.com; Calle de la Paz 4; ⊙10.30am-2pm & 5-8pm Mon-Fri, 10.30am-2pm Sat; M Sol) This is where Spain's *toreros* (bullfighters) come to have their *traje de luces* (suit of lights, the traditional bullfighting suit) made in all its intricate excess.

Tienda Real Madrid SPORTS & OUTDOORS
(Map p88; ☎91 755 45 38; www.realmadrid.com; Gran Vía 31; ⊙10am-9pm Mon-Sat, 11am-9pm Sun; M Gran Vía, Callao) The Real Madrid club shop sells replica shirts, posters, caps and just about everything else under the sun to which it could attach a club logo. In the centre of town there's a smaller **branch** (Tienda Real Madrid; Map p88; ☎91 521 79 50; www.realmadrid.com; Calle del Carmen 3; ⊙10am-9pm Mon-Sat, 11am-8pm Sun; M Sol) and, in the city's north, the stadium branch (p142).

Santarrufina RELIGIOUS
(Map p88; ☎91 522 23 83; www.santarrufina.com; Calle de la Paz 4; ⊙10am-2pm & 4.30-8pm Mon-Fri, 10am-2pm Sat; M Sol) This gilded outpost of Spanish Catholicism has to be seen to be believed. Churches, priests and monasteries are some of the patrons of this overwhelming three-storey shop full of everything from simple rosaries to imposing statues of saints and even a litter used to carry the Virgin in processions.

El Retiro & the Art Museums

Librería la Central BOOKS
(Map p92; ☎91 787 87 82; www.lacentral.com/museoreinasofia; Ronda de Atocha 2; ⊙10am-9pm Mon & Wed-Sat, to 2.30pm Sun; M Atocha) Part of the stunning extension to Centro de Arte Reina Sofía, La Central is perhaps Madrid's best gallery bookshop, with a range of posters, postcards and artistic stationery items as well as extensive sections on contemporary art, design, architecture and photography. Most, but by no means all, books are in Spanish.

Cuesta de Claudio Moyano Bookstalls BOOKS
(Map p92; Cuesta de Claudio Moyano; ⊙hours vary; M Atocha) Madrid's answer to the booksellers that line the Seine in Paris, these secondhand bookstalls are an enduring Madrid landmark. Most titles are in Spanish, but there's a handful of offerings in other languages. Opening hours vary from stall to stall, and some of the stalls close at lunchtime.

Salamanca

★**Agatha Ruiz de la Prada** FASHION & ACCESSORIES
(Map p104; ☎91 319 05 01; www.agatharuizdelaprada.com; Calle de Serrano 27; ⊙10am-8.30pm Mon-Sat; M Serrano) This boutique has to be seen to be believed, with pinks, yellows and oranges everywhere you turn. It's fun and exuberant, but not just for kids. It also has serious and highly original fashion. Agatha Ruiz de la Prada is one of the enduring icons of *la movida madrileña,* Madrid's 1980s outpouring of creativity.

Bombonerías Santa FOOD & DRINKS
(Map p104; ☎91 576 76 25; www.bombonerias-santa.com; Calle de Serrano 56; ⊙10am-2pm & 5-8.30pm Mon, 10am-8.30pm Tue-Sat, shorter hours Jul & Aug; M Serrano) If your style is as refined as your palate, the exquisite chocolates in this tiny shop will satisfy. The packaging is every bit as pretty as the *bombones* (chocolates) within, but they're not cheap – count on paying around €60 per kilo of chocolate.

Oriol Balaguer FOOD
(Map p104; ☎91 401 64 63; www.oriolbalaguer.com; Calle de José Ortega y Gasset 44; ⊙9am-8.30pm Mon-Fri, 10am-8.30pm Sat, 10am-2.30pm Sun; M Núñez de Balboa) Catalan pastry chef Oriol Balaguer has a formidable CV – he's worked in the kitchens of Ferran Adrià in Catalonia, won the prize for the World's Best Dessert (the 'Seven Textures of Chocolate') and his croissants once won the title of Spain's best. His chocolate boutique is presented like a small art gallery that is dedicated to exquisite chocolate collections and cakes.

Mantequería Bravo FOOD & DRINKS
(Map p104; ☎91 575 80 72; www.bravo1931.com; Calle de Ayala 24; ⊙9.30am-2.30pm & 5.30-8.30pm Mon-Fri, 9.30am-2.30pm Sat; M Serrano) Behind the attractive old facade lies a connoisseur's paradise, filled with local cheeses, sausages, wines and coffees. The products

here are great for a gift, but everything's so good that you won't want to share. Not that long ago, Mantequería Bravo won the prize for Madrid's best gourmet food shop or delicatessen.

Manolo Blahnik SHOES
(Map p104; ☎91 575 96 48; www.manoloblahnik.com; Calle de Serrano 58; ⏰10am-2pm & 4-8pm Mon-Sat; Ⓜ Serrano) Nothing to wear to the Oscars? Do what many Hollywood celebrities do and head for Manolo Blahnik. The showroom is exclusive and each shoe is displayed like a work of art.

Ekseption & Eks FASHION & ACCESSORIES
(Map p104; ☎91 361 97 76; www.ekseption.es; Calle de Velázquez 28; ⏰10.30am-2.30pm & 4.30-8.30pm Mon-Sat; Ⓜ Velázquez) This elegant showroom store consistently leads the way with the latest trends, spanning catwalk designs alongside a look that is more informal, though always sophisticated. The unifying theme is urban chic and its list of designer brands includes Balenciaga, Givenchy, Marc Jacobs and Dries van Noten.

Next door, Eks, which was being renovated when we visited, is the preserve of younger, more casual lines, including a fantastic selection of jeans.

Victoria Beckham was a regular customer here in her Madrid days; make of that what you will.

Camper SHOES
(Map p104; ☎91 578 25 60; www.camper.com; Calle de Serrano 24; ⏰10am-9pm Mon-Sat, noon-8pm Sun; Ⓜ Serrano) Spanish fashion is not all haute couture, and this world-famous cool and quirky shoe brand from Mallorca offers bowling-shoe chic with colourful, fun designs that are all about quality coupled with comfort. There are other outlets that are located throughout the city, including a **Malasaña shop** (Map p108; ☎91 531 23 47; www.camper.com; Calle de Fuencarral 42; ⏰10am-8pm Mon-Sat; Ⓜ Gran Vía, Tribunal); check the website for locations.

Purificación García FASHION & ACCESSORIES
(Map p104; ☎91 435 80 13; www.purificaciongarcia.com; Calle de Serrano 28; ⏰10am-8.30pm Mon-Sat; Ⓜ Serrano) Fashions may come and go but Puri consistently manages to keep ahead of the pack. Her signature style for men and women is elegant and mature designs that are just as at home in the workplace as at a wedding.

Malasaña & Chueca

Loewe FASHION & ACCESSORIES
(Map p88; ☎91 522 68 15; www.loewe.com; Gran Vía 8; ⏰10am-8.30pm Mon-Sat, 11am-8pm Sun; Ⓜ Gran Vía) Born in 1846 in Madrid, Loewe is arguably Spain's signature line in high-end fashion and its landmark store on Gran Vía is one of the most famous and elegant stores in the capital. Classy handbags and accessories are the mainstays. Prices can be jaw-droppingly high, but it's worth stopping by, even if you don't plan to buy.

There's another branch in **Salamanca** (Map p104; ☎91 426 35 88; www.loewe.com; Calle de Serrano 26 & 34; ⏰10am-8.30pm Mon-Sat; Ⓜ Serrano).

Patrimonio Comunal Olivarero FOOD
(Map p108; ☎91 308 05 05; www.pco.es; Calle de Mejía Lequerica 1; ⏰10am-2pm & 5-8pm Mon-Fri, 10am-2pm Sat Sep-Jun, 9am-3pm Mon-Sat Jul; Ⓜ Alonso Martínez) For picking up some of the country's olive-oil varieties (Spain is the world's largest producer), Patrimonio Comunal Olivarero is perfect. With examples of the extra-virgin variety from all over Spain, you could spend ages agonising over the choices. Staff know their oil and are happy to help out if you speak a little Spanish.

El Moderno HOMEWARES
(Map p108; ☎91 348 31 94; www.facebook.com/elmodernoconceptstore; Calle de la Corredera de San Pablo 19; ⏰11am-9pm Sun-Wed, to 10pm Thu-Sat; Ⓜ Callao, Gran Vía) This concept store down the Gran Vía end of Malasaña is the epitome of style, although it's less Malasaña retro than a slick new-Madrid look. Designer homewares, quirky gifts and shapely furnishings, all laid out in an open gallery space allow you to indulge your inner interior designer.

Xoan Viqueira FASHION & ACCESSORIES
(Map p108; ☎91 173 70 29; www.xoanviqueira.com; Calle de Gravina 22; ⏰11am-2pm & 5-8.30pm Mon-Fri, 11am-2pm Sat; Ⓜ Chueca) We love the playfulness of this designer Chueca store where screenprinting artist Xoan Viqueira throws his creativity at everything from *alpargatas* (traditional Spanish rope-soled shoes) to clothing and homewares. Bearded gay men are recurring motifs, but it's fun and mischeivous rather than in your face.

Sportivo CLOTHING
(Map p108; ☎91 542 56 61; www.sportivostore.com; Calle del Conde Duque 20; ⏰10am-9pm Mon-Sat, noon-4pm Sun; Ⓜ Plaza de España) It's rare

to find a Madrid store that focuses solely on men's fashions, but this place bucks the trend. Brands like Carven, YMC and Commune of Paris draw an appreciative crowd of metrosexuals, lumbersexuals and any fellow who appreciates style.

Monkey Garage FASHION & ACCESSORIES
(Map p108; ☎91 137 73 98; www.facebook.com/monkeygarage11; Calle de la Santa Brigida 11; ⌚noon-9.30pm Mon-Thu, 12.30-10pm Fri & Sat; Ⓜ Tribunal) Inhabiting an old mechanics workshop, this edgy, stylish shop sells clean-lined Scandivanian fashions, designer jewellery and modern artworks. It's a winning mix in an artfully converted space.

Flamingos Vintage Kilo VINTAGE
(Map p108; ☎649 877198; www.vintagekilo.com; Calle del Espíritu Santo 1; ⌚11am-9pm Mon-Sat; Ⓜ Tribunal) Flamingos sells vintage clothing for men and women, including a selection of old denim, cowboy boots, leather jackets, Hawaiian shirts and more. Some articles have a set price, while others are sold by the kilo. The first of its kind in Madrid, it's a great place to browse for the cool and unexpected from the '70s, '80s and '90s.

Malababa FASHION & ACCESSORIES
(Map p108; ☎91 203 59 51; www.malababa.com; Calle de Santa Teresa 5; ⌚10.30am-8.30pm Mon-Thu, to 9pm Fri & Sat; Ⓜ Alonso Martínez) This corner of Chueca is one of Madrid's happiest hunting grounds for the style-conscious shopper who favours individual boutiques with personality above larger stores. One such place, light-filled Malababa features classy Spanish-made accessories, including jewellery, handbags, shoes, purses and belts, all beautifully displayed.

Cacao Sampaka FOOD
(Map p108; ☎91 319 58 40; www.cacaosampaka.com; Calle de Orellana 4; ⌚10am-9pm Mon-Sat; Ⓜ Alonso Martínez) If you thought chocolate was about fruit 'n' nut, think again. This gourmet chocolate shop is a chocoholic's dream, with more combinations to go with humble cocoa than you ever imagined possible. There's also a cafe that's good for lunch.

Lurdes Bergada FASHION & ACCESSORIES
(Map p108; ☎91 531 99 58; www.lurdesbergada.es; Calle del Conde de Xiquena 8; ⌚10am-2.30pm & 4.30-8.30pm Mon-Sat; Ⓜ Chueca) Lurdes Bergada and Syngman Cucala, a mother-and-son designer team from Barcelona, offer classy and original men's and women's fashions using neutral colours and all-natural fibres. They've developed something of a cult following and it's difficult to leave without finding something that you just have to have. There's another branch in **Malasaña** (Map p108; ☎91 521 88 18; www.lurdesbergada.es; Calle de Fuencarral 70; ⌚10.30am-8.30pm Mon-Sat; Ⓜ Tribunal).

Poncelet FOOD
(Map p108; ☎91 308 02 21; www.poncelet.es; Calle de Argensola 27; ⌚10.30am-2.30pm & 5-8.30pm Mon-Thu, 10.30am-8.30pm Fri & Sat; Ⓜ Alonso Martínez) With 80 Spanish and 240 European cheese varieties, this fine cheese shop is the best of its kind in Madrid. The range is outstanding and the staff really know their cheese.

Reserva y Cata WINE
(Map p108; ☎91 319 04 01; www.reservaycata.com; Calle del Conde de Xiquena 13; ⌚11am-2pm & 5.30-8.30pm Mon-Fri, 11am-2pm Sat; Ⓜ Colón, Chueca) This old-style shop stocks an excellent range of local wines, and the knowledgable staff can help you pick out a great one for your next dinner party or a gift for a friend back home. It specialises in quality Spanish wines that you just don't find in El Corte Inglés department store. There's often a bottle open so you can try before you buy.

Snapo FASHION & ACCESSORIES
(Map p108; ☎91 017 16 72; www.snaposhoponline.com; Calle del Espíritu Santo 6; ⌚11am-2pm & 5-8.30pm Mon-Sat; Ⓜ Tribunal) Snapo is rebellious Malasaña to its core, thumbing its nose at the niceties of fashion respectability – hardly surprising given that one of its lines of clothing is called Fucking Bastardz Inc. It does jeans, caps and jackets, but its T-shirts are the Snapo trademark; there are even kids' T-shirts for *really* cool parents.

Down through the years, we've seen everything from a mocked-up cover of 'National Pornographic' to Pope John Paul II with fist raised and 'Vatican 666' emblazoned across the front. Need we say more?

Retro City CLOTHING
(Map p108; Calle de Corredera Alta de San Pablo 4; ⌚noon-2.30pm & 5.30-9pm Mon-Sat; Ⓜ Tribunal) Malasaña down to its Dr Martens, Retro City lives for the colourful '70s and '80s and proclaims its philosophy to be all about 'vintage for the masses'. Whereas other such stores in the *barrio* have gone for an angry, thumb-your-nose-at-society aesthetic, Retro City just looks back with nostalgia.

Parque del Oeste & Northern Madrid

Papelería Salazar BOOKS, STATIONERY
(Map p108; ☎91 446 18 48; www.papeleriasalazar.es; Calle de Luchana 7-9; ⏱9.30am-1.30pm & 4.30-8pm Mon-Fri, 10am-1.30pm Sat; Ⓜ Bilbao) Opened in 1905, Papelería Salazar is Madrid's oldest stationery store and is now run by the fourth generation of the Salazar family. It's a treasure trove that combines items of interest only to locals (old-style Spanish bookplates, First Communion invitations) with useful items like Faber-Castell pens and pencils, maps, notebooks and drawing supplies.

It's a priceless relic of the kind that is slowly disappearing in Madrid.

Relojería Santolaya ANTIQUES
(☎91 447 25 64; www.relojeriasantolaya.com; Calle Murillo 8; ⏱10am-1pm & 5-8pm Mon-Fri; Ⓜ Quevedo, Iglesia, Bilbao) Founded in 1867, this old clock repairer just off Plaza de Olavide is the official watch repairer to Spain's royalty and heritage properties. There's not much for sale here, but stop by the tiny shopfront and workshop to admire the dying art of timepiece repairs, with not a digital watch in sight.

Bazar Matey GIFTS & SOUVENIRS
(☎91 446 93 11; www.matey.com; Calle de la Santísima Trinidad 1; ⏱9.30am-1.30pm & 4.30-8pm Mon-Sat, closed Sat afternoons Jul & Aug; Ⓜ Iglesia, Quevedo) Bazar Matey is a wonderful store catering to collectors of model trains, aeroplanes and cars, and all sorts of accessories. The items here are the real deal, with near-perfect models of everything from old Renfe trains to obscure international airlines. Prices can be sky high, but that doesn't deter the legions of collectors who stream in from all over Madrid on Saturday.

Calzados Cantero SHOES
(☎91 447 07 35; Plaza de Olavide 12; ⏱9.45am-2pm & 4.45-8.30pm Mon-Fri, 9.45am-2pm Sat; Ⓜ Iglesia) A charming old-world shoe store, Calzados Cantero sells a range of shoes at rock-bottom prices. But it's most famous for its rope-soled *alpargatas* (espadrilles), which start from €8. This is a *barrio* classic, the sort of store to which parents bring their children as their own parents did a generation before.

Tienda Real Madrid SPORTS & OUTDOORS
(☎91 458 72 59; www.realmadrid.com; Gate 55, Estadio Santiago Bernabéu, Av de Concha Espina 1; ⏱10am-9pm Mon-Sat, 11am-7.30pm Sun; Ⓜ Santiago Bernabéu) The club shop of Real Madrid sells the full gamut of football memorabilia. From the shop window, you can see down onto the stadium itself.

Information

DANGERS & ANNOYANCES

Madrid is generally safe, but as in any large European city, keep an eye on your belongings and exercise common sense.

➡ El Rastro, around the Museo del Prado and the metro are favourite pickpocketing haunts, as are any areas where tourists congregate in large numbers.

➡ Avoid park areas (such as the Parque del Buen Retiro) after dark.

➡ Keep a close eye on your taxi's meter and try to keep track of the route to make sure you're not being taken for a ride.

EMERGENCY

To report thefts or other crime-related matters, your best bet is the **Servicio de Atención al Turista Extranjero** (Foreign Tourist Assistance Service; ☎91 548 85 37, 91 548 80 08; www.esmadrid.com/informacion-turistica/sate; Calle de Leganitos 19; ⏱9am-midnight; Ⓜ Plaza de España, Santo Domingo), which is housed in the central *comisaría* (police station) of the National Police. Here you'll find specially trained officers working alongside representatives from the Tourism Ministry. They can also assist in cancelling credit cards, as well as contacting your embassy or your family.

There's also a general number (902 102112; 24-hour English and Spanish, 8am to midnight other languages) for reporting crimes.

There's a **comisaría** (☎913 22 10 21; Calle de las Huertas 76; Ⓜ Antón Martín) down the bottom end of Huertas, near the Paseo del Prado.

Country Code	☎34
International access code	☎00
Ambulance	☎061
EU Standard Emergency Number	☎112
Fire Brigade (Bomberos)	☎080
Local Police (Policía Municipal)	☎092
Military Police (Guardia Civil) For traffic accidents.	☎062
Policía Nacional	☎091
Teléfono de la Víctima, hotline for victims of racial or sexual violence.	☎902 180995

INTERNET ACCESS

Most midrange and top-end hotels, as well as some cafes and restaurants, have wi-fi access. Otherwise, check out www.madridmemata.es/madrid-wifi for a reasonable list of the city's wi-fi hot spots.

Most of Madrid's internet cafes have fallen by the wayside. You'll find plenty of small *locutorios* (small shops selling phonecards and cheap phone calls) all over the city and many have a few computers out the back.

MEDICAL SERVICES

All foreigners have the same right as Spaniards to emergency medical treatment in a public hospital. EU citizens are entitled to the full range of health-care services in public hospitals free of charge, but you'll need to present your European Health Insurance Card (EHIC); enquire at your national health service before leaving home. Even if you have no insurance, you'll be treated in an emergency, with costs in the public system ranging from free to €150 for a basic consultation. Non-EU citizens have to pay for anything other than emergency treatment – one good reason among many to have a travel-insurance policy. If you have a specific health complaint, obtain the necessary information and referrals for treatment before leaving home.

Unidad Medica (Anglo American; ☎91 435 18 23, 24hr 916 56 90 57; www.unidadmedica.com; Calle del Conde de Aranda 1; ⌚9am-8pm Mon-Fri, 10am-1pm Sat Sep-Jul, 10am-5pm Mon-Fri, 10am-1pm Sat Aug; Ⓜ Retiro) A private clinic with a wide range of specialisations and where all doctors speak Spanish and English, with some also speaking French and German. Each consultation costs around €125.

Hospital General Gregorio Marañón (☎91 586 80 00; Calle del Doctor Esquerdo 46; Ⓜ Sáinz de Baranda, O'Donnell, Ibiza) One of the city's main (and more central) hospitals.

POST

Correos, the national postal service, is generally reliable, if a little slow at times. It has its **main post office** (Map p92; ☎91 523 06 94; www.correos.es; Paseo del Prado 1; ⌚8.30am-9.30pm Mon-Fri, to 2pm Sat; Ⓜ Banco de España) in the ornate Palacio de Comunicaciones on Plaza de la Cibeles.

Sellos (stamps) are sold at most *estancos* (tobacconists' shops, with *Tabacos* in yellow letters on a maroon background), as well as post offices.

A postcard or letter weighing up to 20g costs €1.25 from Spain to other European countries, and €1.35 to the rest of the world. For a full list of prices for *certificado* (certified) and *urgente* (express post), go to www.correos.es and click on 'Tarifas'.

Delivery times are erratic but ordinary mail to other Western European countries can take up to a week; to North America up to 10 days; and to Australia or New Zealand anywhere between one and three weeks.

TOURIST INFORMATION

Centro de Turismo de Madrid (☎010, 91 578 78 10; www.esmadrid.com; Plaza Mayor 27; ⌚9.30am-8.30pm; Ⓜ Sol) The Madrid government's Centro de Turismo is terrific. Housed in the Real Casa de la Panadería on the north side of the Plaza Mayor, it offers free downloads of the metro map to your mobile; staff are helpful.

Centro de Turismo Colón (Map p104; www.esmadrid.com; Plaza de Colón 1; ⌚9.30am-8.30pm; Ⓜ Colón) A small, subterranean tourist office, accessible via the underground stairs on the corner of Calle de Goya and the Paseo de la Castellana.

Punto de Información Turística Plaza de Callao (Map p88; www.esmadrid.com; Plaza de Callao; ⌚9.30am-8.30pm; Ⓜ Callao)

Punto de Información Turística CentroCentro (Map p92; ☎91 578 78 10; www.esmadrid.com; Plaza de la Cibeles 1; ⌚10am-8pm Tue-Sun; Ⓜ Banco de España)

Punto de Información Turística del Paseo del Prado (Map p92; ☎91 578 78 10; www.esmadrid.com; Plaza de Neptuno; ⌚9.30am-8.30pm; Ⓜ Atocha)

Punto de Información Turística Adolfo Suárez Madrid-Barajas T2 (www.esmadrid.com; between Salas 5 & 6; ⌚9am-8pm)

Punto de Información Turística Adolfo Suárez Madrid-Barajas T4 (www.esmadrid.com; Salas 10 & 11; ⌚9am-8pm)

ℹ Getting There & Away

AIR

Madrid's **Adolfo Suárez Madrid-Barajas airport** (☎902 404704; www.aena.es; Ⓜ Aeropuerto T1, T2 & T3, Aeropuerto T4) lies 15km northeast of the city, and it's Europe's sixth-busiest hub, with almost 50 million passengers passing through here every year.

Barajas has four terminals. Terminal 4 (T4) deals mainly with flights of Iberia and its partners, while the remainder leave from the conjoined T1, T2 and (rarely) T3. To match your airline with a terminal, visit the Adolfo Suárez Madrid-Barajas section of www.aena.es and click on 'Airlines'.

Although all airlines conduct check-in *(facturación)* at the airport's departure areas, some also allow check-in at the Nuevos Ministerios metro stop and transport interchange in Madrid itself – ask your airline.

There are car rental services, ATMs, money-exchange bureaus, pharmacies, tourist offices, left-luggage offices and parking services at T1, T2 and T4.

BUS

Estación Sur de Autobuses (☎91 468 42 00; Calle de Méndez Álvaro 83; M Méndez Álvaro), just south of the M30 ring road, is the city's principal bus station. It serves most destinations to the south and many in other parts of the country. Most bus companies have a ticket office here, even if their buses depart from elsewhere.

Northwest of the centre and connected to lines 1 and 3 of the metro, the subterranean **Intercambiador de Autobuses de Moncloa** (Plaza de la Moncloa; M Moncloa) sends buses out to the surrounding villages and satellite suburbs that lie north and west of the city. Major bus companies include:

ALSA (☎902 422242; www.alsa.es) One of the largest Spanish companies with many services throughout Spain. Most depart from Estación Sur with occasional services from T4 of Madrid's airport and other stations around town.

Avanzabus (☎902 020052; www.avanzabus.com) Services to Extremadura (eg Cáceres)

CAR & MOTORCYCLE

Madrid is surrounded by two main ring roads, the outermost M40 and the inner M30; there are also two partial ring roads, the M45 and the more distant M50. The R5 and R3 are part of a series of toll roads built to ease traffic jams. The big-name car-rental agencies have offices all over Madrid and offices at the airport, and some have branches at Atocha and Chamartín train stations.

TRAIN

Madrid is served by two main train stations. The bigger of the two is **Puerta de Atocha** (www.renfe.es; Av de la Ciudad de Barcelona; M Atocha Renfe), at the southern end of the city centre, while **Chamartín** (☎902 432343; Paseo de la Castellana; M Chamartín) lies in the north of the city. The bulk of trains for Spanish destinations depart from Atocha, especially those going south. International services arrive at and leave from Chamartín. For bookings, contact **Renfe** (p899).

High-speed Tren de Alta Velocidad Española (AVE) services connect Madrid with Albacete, Barcelona, Burgos, Cádiz, Córdoba, Cuenca, Huesca, León, Lerida, Málaga, Palencia, Salamanca, Santiago de Compostela, Seville, Valencia, Valladolid, Zamora and Zaragoza. In coming years, Madrid–Bilbao should also start up, and travel times to Galicia should fall. The same goes for Madrid–Granada and Madrid–Badajoz.

ℹ Getting Around

Madrid has an excellent public transport network. The most convenient way of getting around is via the metro, whose 13 lines criss-cross the city; no matter where you find yourself you're never far from a metro station. The bus network is equally extensive and operates under the same ticketing system, although the sheer number of routes (around 200!) makes it more difficult for first-time visitors to master. Taxis in Madrid are plentiful and relatively cheap by European standards.

TO/FROM THE AIRPORT

Bus

The **Exprés Aeropuerto** (Airport Express; www.emtmadrid.es; per person €5; ⏲24hr; 📶) runs between Puerta de Atocha train station and the airport. From 11.30pm until 6am, departures are from the Plaza de Cibeles, not the train station. Departures take place every 13 to 20 minutes from the station or at night-time every 35 minutes from Plaza de Cibeles.

METRO & BUS TICKETS

When travelling on Madrid's metro and bus services, you have three options when it comes to tickets, although only two really work for visitors.

Tarjeta Multi

As of 1 January 2018, nonresidents travelling on the city's public transport system require a Tarjeta Multi, a rechargeable card that, unlike the resident's version, is not tied to your identity (ie neither your name nor your photo appears on the card). They can be purchased at machines in all metro stations, *estancos* (tobacconists) and other authorised sales points.

Like London's Oyster Card, you top up your account at machines in all metro stations and *estancos*, and touch-on and touch-off every time you travel. Options include 10 rides (bus and metro) for €12.20 or a single-journey option for €1.50.

Tarjeta Turística

The handy Tarjeta Turística (Tourist Pass) allows for unlimited travel on public transport across the Comunidad de Madrid (Community of Madrid) for tourists. You'll need to present your passport or national identity card and tickets can be purchased at all metro stations. Passes are available for 1/2/3/5/7 days for €8.40/14.20/18.40/26.80/35.40.

Alternatively, from T1, T2 and T3 take bus 200 to/from the **Intercambiador de Avenida de América** (Ⓜ Av de América), the transport interchange on Avenida de América. A single ticket costs €4.50 including the €3 airport supplement. The first departures from the airport are at 5.10am (T1, T2 and T3). The last scheduled service from the airport is 11.30pm; buses leave every 12 to 20 minutes.

A free bus service connects all four airport terminals.

Metro

One of the easiest ways into town from the airport is line 8 of the metro to the Nuevos Ministerios transport interchange, which connects with lines 10 and 6 and the local overground *cercanías* (local trains serving suburbs and nearby towns). It operates from 6.05am to 1.30am. A single ticket costs €4.50 including the €3 airport supplement. If you're charging your public transport card with a 10-ride Metrobús ticket (€12.20), you'll need to top it up with the €3 supplement if you're travelling to/from the airport. The journey to Nuevos Ministerios takes around 15 minutes, around 25 minutes from T4.

Minibus

AeroCITY (☎ 91 747 75 70, 902 151654; www.aerocity.com; per person from €18, express service per minibus from €35; ⏱ 24hr) is a private minibus service that takes you door-to-door between central Madrid and the airport (T1 in front of Arrivals Gate 2, T2 between gates 5 and 6, and T4 arrivals hall). You can reserve a seat or the entire minibus; the latter operates like a taxi. Book by phone or online.

Taxi

A taxi to the centre (around 30 minutes, depending on traffic; 35 to 40 minutes from T4) costs a fixed €30 for anywhere inside the M30 motorway (which includes all of downtown Madrid). There's a minimum €20, even if you're only going to an airport hotel.

BICYCLE

Lots of people zip around town on *motos* (mopeds) and bike lanes are increasingly a part of the inner city's thoroughfares. Be aware, however, that the latter are relatively new and few drivers are accustomed to keeping an eye out for cyclists.

You can transport your bicycle on the metro all day on Saturday and Sunday, and at any time from Monday to Friday except 7.30am to 9.30am, 2pm to 4pm and 6pm to 8pm. You can also take your bike aboard *cercanías* (local trains to suburbs) at any time.

BUS

Buses operated by **Empresa Municipal de Transportes de Madrid** (EMT; ☎ 902 507850; www.emtmadrid.es) travel along most city routes regularly between about 6.30am and 11.30pm. Twenty-six night-bus *búhos* (owls) routes operate from 11.45pm to 5.30am, with all routes originating in Plaza de la Cibeles.

The **Intercambiador de Autobuses de Moncloa** has buses to many villages around the Comunidad de Madrid.

METRO

Madrid's modern metro (www.metromadrid.es), Europe's second largest, is a fast, efficient and safe way to navigate Madrid, and generally easier than getting to grips with bus routes. There are 11 colour-coded lines in central Madrid, in addition to the modern southern suburban MetroSur system, as well as lines heading east to the population centres of Pozuelo and Boadilla del Monte. Colour maps showing the metro system are available from any metro station or online. The metro operates from 6.05am to 1.30am.

TAXI

Daytime flagfall is, for example, €2.40 in Madrid, and up to €2.90 between 9pm and 7am, and on weekends and holidays. You then pay €1.05 to €1.20 per kilometre depending on the time of day. Several supplementary charges, usually posted inside the taxi, apply. These include: €5.50 to/from the airport (if you're not paying the fixed rate); €3 from taxi ranks at train and bus stations; €3 to/from the Parque Ferial Juan Carlos I; and €6.70 on New Year's Eve and Christmas Eve from 10pm to 6am. There's no charge for luggage.

Among the 24-hour taxi services are **Tele-Taxi** (☎ 91 371 21 31; www.tele-taxi.es; ⏱ 24hr) and **Radio-Teléfono Taxi** (☎ 91 547 82 00; www.radiotelefono-taxi.com; ⏱ 24hr).

A green light on the roof means the taxi is *libre* (available). Usually a sign like this is also placed in the lower passenger side of the windscreen.

Tipping taxi drivers is not common practice, though rounding fares up to the nearest euro or two doesn't hurt.

AROUND MADRID

It may be one of Spain's smallest *comunidades* by area, but there's still plenty to see in Madrid's hinterland. Both San Lorenzo de El Escorial and Aranjuez combine royal grandeur with great food while Alcalá de Henares is a surprise packet with stirring monuments, a real sense of history and night-time buzz. Chinchón has one of Spain's loveliest *plazas mayores* (town squares), while the Sierra de Guadarrama and Sierra Pobre offer quiet mountain back roads, forgotten villages, fine scenery and, in the case of the former, good winter skiing.

San Lorenzo de El Escorial

POP 18,038

The imposing palace and monastery complex of San Lorenzo de El Escorial is an impressive place, rising up from the foothills of the mountains that shelter Madrid from the north and west. The one-time royal getaway is now a prim little town overflowing with quaint shops, restaurants and hotels catering primarily to throngs of weekending *madrileños*. The cool air here has been drawing city dwellers since the complex was first ordered to be built by Felipe II in the 16th century. Most visitors come on a day trip from Madrid.

History

After Felipe II's decisive victory in the Battle of St Quentin against the French on St Lawrence's Day, 10 August 1557, he ordered the construction of the complex in the saint's name above the hamlet of El Escorial. Several villages were razed to make way for the huge monastery, royal palace and mausoleum for Felipe's parents, Carlos I and Isabel. It all flourished under the watchful eye of the architect Juan de Herrera, a towering figure of the Spanish Renaissance.

The palace-monastery became an important intellectual centre, with a burgeoning library and art collection, and even a laboratory where scientists could dabble in alchemy. Felipe II died here on 13 September 1598.

In1854 the monks belonging to the Hieronymite order, who had occupied the monastery from the beginning, were obliged to leave during one of the19th-century waves of confiscation of religious property by the Spanish state, only to be replaced 30 years later by Augustinians.

Sights

★Real Monasterio de San Lorenzo

MONASTERY, PALACE

(☎91 890 78 18; www.patrimonionacional.es; adult/concession €10/5, guide/audioguide €4/3, EU citizens free last 3 hours Wed & Thu; ⏲10am-8pm Apr-Sep, to 6pm Oct-Mar, closed Mon) This 16th-century complex and madrileños attracts its fair share of foreign tourists.

The monastery's main entrance is to the west. Above the gateway a statue of St Lawrence stands watch, holding a symbolic gridiron, the instrument of his martyrdom (he was roasted alive on one). From here you'll first enter the Patio de los Reyes (Patio of the Kings), which houses the statues of the six kings of Judah.

Directly ahead lies the sombre basilica. As you enter, look up at the unusual flat vaulting by the choir stalls. Once inside the church proper, turn left to view Benvenuto Cellini's white Carrara marble statue of Christ crucified (1576). The remainder of the ground floor contains various treasures, including some tapestries and an El Greco painting – impressive as it is, it's a far cry from El Greco's dream of decorating the whole complex. Then head downstairs to the northeastern corner of the complex.

You pass through the Museo de Arquitectura and the Museo de Pintura. The former tells (in Spanish) the story of how the complex was built, the latter contains a range of 16th- and 17th-century Italian, Spanish and Flemish art.

Head upstairs into a gallery around the eastern part of the complex known as the Palacio de Felipe II or Palacio de los Austrias. You'll then descend to the 17th-century Panteón de los Reyes (Crypt of the Kings), where almost all Spain's monarchs since Carlos I are interred. Backtracking a little, you'll find yourself in the Panteón de los Infantes (Crypt of the Princesses).

Stairs lead up from the Patio de los Evangelistas (Patio of the Gospels) to the Salas Capitulares (Chapter Houses) in the southeastern corner of the monastery. These bright, airy rooms, with richly frescoed ceilings, contain a minor treasure chest of works by El Greco, Titian, Tintoretto, José de Ribera and Hieronymus Bosch (known as El Bosco to Spaniards).

Just south of the monastery is the **Jardín de los Frailes** (Friars Garden; ⏲10am-8pm Apr-Sep, to 6pm Oct-Mar, closed Mon), which leads down to the town of El Escorial (and the train station), and contains the **Casita del Príncipe** (www.patrimonionacional.es; €5; ⏲10am-8pm Apr-Sep, to 6pm Oct-Mar, closed Mon), a neoclassical gem built in 1772 by Juan de Villanueva under Carlos III for his heir, Carlos IV.

Eating

La Cueva

SPANISH €€€

(☎91 890 15 16; www.mesonlacueva.com; Calle de San Antón 4; mains €19-33; ⏲1-4pm & 9-11pm) Just a block back from the monastery complex, La Cueva has been around since 1768 and it shows in the heavy wooden beams and hearty, traditional Castilian cooking – roasted meats and steaks are the mainstays, with a few fish dishes.

Montia SPANISH €€€
(☎91 133 69 88; www.montia.es; Calle de Calvario 4; set menus €45-65; ⏲1.30-3.30pm Sun & Tue-Thu, 1.30-3.30pm & 9-11pm Fri & Sat) There's a weekend waiting list here of over two months and we can see why – the tasting menus showcase creativity in abundance with a seasonal menu that could include wild boar meatballs or stout beer ice cream...

Restaurante Charolés MADRILEÑO €€€
(☎91 890 59 75; www.charolesrestaurante.com; Calle Floridablanca 24, San Lorenzo de El Escorial; mains €17-24, cocido per person €30; ⏲1-4pm & 9pm-midnight) One of the most popular destinations for *madrileños* heading for the hills, Charolés does grilled or roasted meats to perfection, and it's much loved for its *cocido* (chickpea-and-meat hotpot) which is perfect on a cold winter's day.

Information

Tourist Office (☎91 890 53 13; www.sanlorenzoturismo.org; Calle de Grimaldi 4, El Escorial; ⏲10am-2pm & 3-6pm Tue-Sat, 10am-2pm Sun) Right opposite the monastery complex.

Getting There & Away

San Lorenzo de El Escorial is 59km northwest of Madrid and it takes 40 minutes to drive there. Take the A6 highway to the M600, then follow the signs to El Escorial.

Every 15 minutes (every 30 minutes on weekends) buses 661 and 664 run to El Escorial (€3.35, one hour) from platform 30 at Madrid's Intercambiador de Autobuses de Moncloa.

Renfe (☎91 232 03 20; www.renfe.es) C8 *cercanías* (local trains) make the trip daily from Madrid's Atocha or Chamartín train stations to El Escorial (€1.50, one hour, frequent).

Aranjuez

POP 57,932

Aranjuez was founded as a royal pleasure retreat, away from the riff-raff of Madrid, and it remains an easy day trip to escape the rigours of city life. The palace is opulent, but the fresh air and ample gardens are what really stand out. With some terrific restaurants, Aranjuez is well worth making a day of it.

Sights

Palacio Real PALACE
(☎91 891 07 40; www.patrimonionacional.es; palace adult/concession €9/4, guide/audioguide €4/3, EU citizens last 3hr Wed & Thu free, gardens free; ⏲palace 10am-8pm Apr-Sep, to 6pm Oct-Mar, gardens 8am-9.30pm mid-Jun–mid-Aug, shorter hours mid-Aug–mid-Jun) The Royal Palace started as one of Felipe II's modest summer palaces but took on a life of its own as a succession of royals, inspired by the palace at Versailles in France, lavished money upon it. By the 18th century its 300-plus rooms had turned the palace into a sprawling, gracefully symmetrical complex filled with a cornucopia of ornamentation. Of all the rulers who spent time here, Carlos III and Isabel II left the greatest mark.

The obligatory guided tour (in Spanish) provides insight into the palace's art and history. And a stroll in the lush gardens takes you through a mix of local and exotic species, the product of seeds brought back by Spanish botanists and explorers from Spanish colonies all over the world. Within their shady perimeter, which stretches a few kilometres from the palace, you'll find the **Casa de Marinos**, which contains the **Museo de Falúas** (⏲10am-5.15pm Oct-Mar, to 6.15pm Apr-Sep), a museum of royal pleasure boats. The 18th-century neoclassical **Casa del Labrador** (☎91 891 03 05; €5; ⏲10am-8pm Apr-Sep, to 6pm Oct-Mar) is also worth a visit. Further away, towards Chinchón, is the **Jardín del Príncipe**, an extension of the massive gardens.

Eating

Casa Pablete TAPAS €€
(☎91 891 03 81; Calle de Stuart 108; tapas from €3, mains €12-22; ⏲1.30-4pm & 8.30-11pm Wed-Sun, 1.30-4pm Mon) Going strong since 1946, this casual tapas bar has a loyal following far beyond Aranjuez. Its *croquetas* (croquettes) are a major drawcard, as is the stuffed squid, and it's all about traditional cooking at its best without too many elaborations.

Carême SPANISH €€€
(☎91 892 64 86; www.caremejesusdelcerro.com; Avenida de Palacio 2; mains €16-25, set menu €55; ⏲1-4pm & 9pm-midnight Mon-Sat, 1-4pm Sun) Right across the road from the royal palace's gardens, Carême is the work of respected local chef Jesús del Cerro whose cooking is assured and faithful to Spanish traditions with a few twists along the way. Try the *solomillo con foie gras* (beef sirloin with foie gras).

★Casa José SPANISH €€€
(☎91 891 14 88; www.casajose.es; Calle de Abastos 32; mains €14-29, set menu €75; ⏲1.45-3.30pm & 9-11.30pm Tue-Sat, 1.45-3.30pm Sun Sep-Jul) The quietly elegant Casa José is packed on weekends with *madrileños* (people from Madrid)

DON'T MISS

THE STRAWBERRY TRAIN

You could take a normal train from Madrid to Aranjuez, but for romance it's hard to beat the **Tren de la Fresa** (Strawberry Train; ☎902 240202; www.museodelferrocarril.org/trendelafresa; return adult €23-30, child €9-15; ⏱9.50am Sat & Sun May-Oct). Begun in 1985 to commemorate the Madrid–Aranjuez route – Madrid's first and Spain's third rail line, which was inaugurated in the 1850s – the Strawberry Train is a throwback to the time when Spanish royalty would escape the summer heat and head for the royal palace at Aranjuez.

The journey begins at 9.50am on Saturday and Sunday between early May and late October when an antique Mikado 141F-2413 steam engine pulls out from Madrid's Museo del Ferrocarril, pulling behind it four passenger carriages that date from the early 20th century and have old-style front and back balconies. During the 50-minute journey, rail staff in period dress provide samples of local strawberries – one of the original train's purposes was to allow royalty to sample the summer strawberry crop from the Aranjuez orchards.

Upon arrival in Aranjuez, your ticket fare includes a guided tour of the Palacio Real, Museo de Falúas and other Aranjuez sights, not to mention more strawberry samplings. The train leaves Aranjuez for Madrid at 6.55pm for the return journey.

drawn by the beautifully prepared meats and local dishes with surprising innovations. It's pricey but worth every euro. Downstairs they serve innovative tapas, or head upstairs for more formal dining.

Information

Tourist Office (☎91 891 04 27; www.turismoenaranjuez.com; Plaza de San Antonio 9; ⏱10am-2pm & 4-6pm Tue-Sun) In the heart of town, a few hundred metres southwest of the Palacio Real.

Getting There & Away

By car from Madrid, take the N-IV south to the M-305, which leads to the city centre.

The **AISA** (☎90 2198788; www.aisa-grupo.com) bus company sends buses (route number 423) to Aranjuez from Madrid's Estación Sur (€4.20, 45 minutes) every 15 minutes or so.

From Madrid's Atocha station, C3 *cercanías* trains (€3.40, 45 minutes) leave every 15 or 20 minutes for Aranjuez.

Chinchón

POP 5294

Chinchón is just 45km from Madrid but worlds apart. Although it has grown beyond its village confines, visiting its antique heart is like stepping back into a charming, ramshackle past. It's worth an overnight stay to really soak it up, and lunch in one of the *méson* (tavern)-style restaurants around the plaza is another must.

Sights

The heart of town is its unique, almost circular **Plaza Mayor**, which is lined with tiered balconies – it wins our vote as one of the most evocative *plazas mayores* in Spain. In summer the plaza is converted into a bullring, and at Easter it's the stage for a Passion play.

Chinchón's historical monuments won't detain you long, but you should take a quick look at the 16th-century **Iglesia de la Asunción**, which rises above Plaza Mayor, and the late-16th-century Renaissance **Castillo de los Condes**, out of town to the south. The castle was abandoned in the 18th century and was last used as a liquor factory. Ask at the tourist office to find out if it's open.

Sleeping

Hostal Chinchón HOSTAL €
(☎91 893 53 98; www.hostalchinchon.com; Calle Grande 16; d/tr €55/70; ❄📶🏊) The public areas here are nicer than the smallish rooms, which are clean but worn around the edges. The highlight is the surprise rooftop pool overlooking Plaza Mayor.

Parador de Chinchón LUXURY HOTEL €€
(☎91 894 08 36; www.parador.es; Avenida Generalísimo 1; d from €125; ❄📶) The former Convento de Agustinos (Augustine Convent), Parador Nacional is one of the town's most important historical buildings and can't be beaten for luxury. It's worth stopping by for a meal or coffee (and a peek around) even if you don't stay here.

Eating

Chinchón is loaded with traditional-style restaurants dishing up *cordero asado* (roast lamb). But if you're after something a little lighter, there is nothing better than savouring a few tapas and drinks on sunny Plaza Mayor.

★Café de la Iberia SPANISH €€
(☎91 894 08 47; www.cafedelaiberia.com; Plaza Mayor 17; mains €14-26; ⏲12.30-4.30pm & 8-10.30pm) This is definitely our favourite of the *mesones* (home-style restaurants) on the Plaza Mayor. It offers wonderful food, including succulent roast lamb, served by attentive staff in an atmospheric dining area set around a light-filled internal courtyard (where Goya is said to have visited), or, if you can get a table, out on the balcony.

Mesón Cuevas del Vino SPANISH €€
(☎91 894 02 06; www.cuevasdelvino.com; Calle Benito Hortelano 13; mains €12-23; ⏲noon-4.30pm & 8-11pm Mon & Wed-Fri, noon-midnight Sat, noon-8pm Sun) From the huge goatskins filled with wine and the barrels covered in famous signatures, to the atmospheric caves underground, this is sure to be a memorable eating experience with delicious home-style cooking.

Information

Tourist Office (☎91 893 53 23; www.ciudad-chinchon.com; Plaza Mayor 6; ⏲10am-2pm & 4-6pm Tue-Sun) A small office with helpful staff.

Getting There & Away

Sitting 45km southeast of Madrid, Chinchón is easy to reach by car. Take the N-IV motorway and exit onto the M404, which leads to Chinchón.

La Veloz (☎91 409 76 02; www.samar.es/empresa/samar/laveloz; Avenida del Mediterráneo 49; Ⓜ Conde de Casal) has services (bus 337) to Chinchón (€3.35, 50 minutes, half-hourly). The buses leave from Avenida del Mediterráneo, 100m east of Plaza del Conde de Casal.

Alcalá de Henares

POP 195,907

Situated east of Madrid, Alcalá de Henares is full of surprises with historical sandstone buildings seemingly at every turn. Throw in some sunny squares and a university, and it's a terrific place to escape the capital for a few hours.

Sights

Museo Casa Natal de Miguel de Cervantes MUSEUM
(☎91 889 96 54; www.museocasanataldecervantes.org; Calle Mayor 48; ⏲10am-6pm Tue-Sun) FREE The town is dear to Spaniards because it's the birthplace of Miguel de Cervantes Saavedra. The site believed by many to be Cervantes' birthplace is re-created in this illuminating museum, which lies along the beautiful colonnaded Calle Mayor.

Universidad de Alcalá UNIVERSITY
(☎91 883 43 84; www.uah.es; guided tours €4; ⏲9am-9pm) FREE Founded in 1486 by Cardinal Cisneros, this is one of the country's principal seats of learning. A guided tour gives a peek into the Mudéjar chapel and the magnificent Paraninfo auditorium, where the King and Queen of Spain give out the Premio Cervantes literary award every year.

Sleeping & Eating

Parador de Alcalá de Henares HOTEL €€
(☎91 888 03 30; www.parador.es; Calle de los Colegios 8; r from €120; P❄📶) Unlike its wonderfully historic restaurant (p149) across the road, this luxury hotel is one of the newest *paradors* (luxurious state-owned hotels) in Spain and the look is classy and contemporary throughout.

Barataría TAPAS €€
(☎91 888 59 25; www.facebook.com/baratariala insula; Calle de los Cerrajeros 18; mains €15-28; ⏲noon-4pm & 8pm-midnight Mon-Tue & Thu-Sat, noon-4pm Sun) A wine bar, tapas bar and restaurant all rolled into one, Barataria is a fine place to eat whatever your mood. Grilled meats are the star of the show, with the ribs with honey in particular a local favourite.

★Hostería del Estudiante CASTILIAN €€
(Santo Tomás; ☎91 888 03 30; www.parador.es; Calle de los Colegios 3; set menus from €34; ⏲1.30-4pm & 8.30-11pm) Across the road from the *parador*, this charming restaurant has wonderful Castilian cooking and a classy ambience in a dining room decorated with artefacts from the city's illustrious history.

Information

Tourist Office (☎91 881 06 34; www.turismo alcala.es; Callejón de Santa María 1; ⏲10am-8pm) Free guided tours of the the Alcalá of Cervantes at 5.30pm Saturday and Sunday, as well as information on the town.

Getting There & Away

Alcalá de Henares is just 35km east of Madrid, heading towards Zaragoza along the A2.

There are regular bus departures (€2.99, about one hour, every five to 15 minutes) from Madrid's Intercambiador de Avenida de América.

Renfe (☎91 232 03 20; www.renfe.es) C2 and C7 *cercanías* trains (€2.65, 50 minutes) make the trip to Alcalá de Henares daily.

Sierra de Guadarrama

North of Madrid lies the Sierra de Guadarrama, a popular skiing destination and home to several charming towns. In **Manzanares El Real** you can explore the small 15th-century **Castillo de los Mendoza** (☎91 853 00 08; Manzanares El Real; admission incl guided tour €4; ⏰10am-5pm Tue-Fri, to 7.30pm Sat & Sun), a storybook castle with round towers at its corners and a Gothic interior patio.

Cercedilla is a popular base for hikers and mountain bikers. There are several marked trails, the main one known as the **Cuerda Larga** or **Cuerda Castellana**. This is a forest track that takes in 55 peaks between the Puerto de Somosierra in the north and Puerto de la Cruz Verde in the southwest.

Small ski resorts, such as **Valdesqui** (☎902 886446; www.valdesqui.es; Puerto de Cotos; lift tickets day/afternoon €40/24; ⏰9am-4pm) and **Navacerrada** (☎902 882328; www.puertonavacerrada.com; lift tickets €28-35; ⏰9.30am-5pm) welcome weekend skiers from the city.

Information

Centro de Información Valle de la Fuenfría (☎91 852 22 13; www.parquenacionalsierraguadarrama.es; Carretera de las Dehesas; ⏰9am-8pm Jul & Aug, 9am-4.30pm Mon-Fri, 9am-8pm Sat & Sun Jun & Sep, 9am-4.30pm Oct-May) Information centre located 2km outside Cercedilla on the M614.

Navacerrada Tourist Office (☎91 856 00 06; www.aytonavacerrada.org; Paseo de los Españoles; ⏰6-9pm Tue-Fri, 11am-2pm & 6-9pm Sat & Sun Jul & Aug, 11am-2pm & 4-7pm Sat & Sun Sep-May)

Getting There & Away

By car from Madrid, take the A-6 motorway to Cercedilla.

Bus 724 runs to Manzanares El Real from Plaza de Castilla in Madrid (€3.15, 45 minutes). From Madrid's Intercambiador de Autobuses de Moncloa, bus 691 heads to Navacerrada (€3.95, one hour) from platform 14 and bus 684 runs to Cercedilla (€3.95, one hour).

From Chamartín station you can get to Cercedilla (C2 *cercanías* line; €3.40, one hour 20 minutes, 15 daily) and Puerto de Navacerrada (C8B *cercanías* line; €6, two hours with train change in Cercedilla, four daily).

Buitrago & Sierra Pobre

Sleepy Sierra Pobre is a toned-down version of its more refined western neighbour, the Sierra de Guadarrama. Popular with hikers and others looking for nature without quite so many creature comforts or crowds, the 'Poor Sierra' has yet to develop the tourism industry of its neighbours.

Sights

Head first to Buitrago, the largest town in the area, where you can stroll along part of the old city walls. You can also take a peek into the 15th-century mudéjar and Romanesque Iglesia de Santa María del Castillo and into the small and unlikely **Picasso Museum** (☎91 868 00 56; www.madrid.org/museopicasso; Plaza de Picasso 1; ⏰11am-1.45pm & 4-6pm Tue-Fri, 10am-2pm & 4-7pm Sat, 10am-2pm Sun) FREE, which contains a few works that the artist gave to his barber, Eugenio Arias. Hamlets are scattered throughout the rest of the sierra; some, like Puebla de la Sierra and El Atazar, are the starting point for hill trails.

Eating

El Arco SPANISH €€€
(☎91 868 09 11; www.elarcodebuitrago.es; Calle del Arco 6, Villavieja del Lozoya; mains €17-36; ⏰1-4pm Fri-Sun mid-Sep–mid-Jun, 1-4pm & 8.30-10.30pm Tue-Sat, 1-4pm Sun mid-Jun–mid-Sep) The best restaurant in the region, El Arco is located in Villavieja del Lozoya, close to Buitrago, and is known for its fresh, creative cuisine based on local, seasonal ingredients and traditional northern Spanish dishes such as the classic Basque *bacalao al pil-pil* (salted cod and garlic in an olive-oil emulsion).

Information

Buitrago Tourist Office (☎91 868 16 15; Calle de Tahona 19; ⏰10am-noon & 4-6pm Tue-Fri, 10am-2pm & 4-7pm Sat, 10am-2pm Sun) Has limited information on the town.

Getting There & Away

By car from Madrid, take the N-I highway to Buitrago.

Buses (line 191) leave hourly from Madrid's Plaza de la Castilla to Buitrago (€5.25, 1½ hours).

Castilla y León

Includes ➡

Best Places to Eat

- ➡ Restaurante El Fogón Sefardí (p172)
- ➡ Restaurante Cocinandos (p193)
- ➡ La Cocina de Toño (p161)
- ➡ Cervecería Morito (p200)
- ➡ Restaurante Las Termas (p195)

Best Places to Stay

- ➡ Posada Real La Cartería (p185)
- ➡ Hostal de San Marcos (p192)
- ➡ Santa Cruz (p184)
- ➡ Don Gregorio (p161)
- ➡ Hotel Tres Coronas (p204)

Why Go?

If you're looking for a window on the Spanish soul, head to Castilla y León. This is Spain without the stereotypes: with vast plains, spectacular mountain peaks and evocative medieval towns and villages. Experience fabled cities like Salamanca, with its lively student population, and Segovia, famed for a fairy-tale fortress that inspired Disneyland's *Sleeping Beauty* castle. The multiturreted walls of Ávila have similar magical appeal, while the lofty cathedrals of León and Burgos are among Europe's most impressive. As with most of Spain, food here is an agreeable obsession, promising the country's best *jamón* (cured ham), roast lamb and suckling pig.

The region's story is equally told through its quiet back roads, half-timbered hamlets and isolated castles. From the scenic Sierra de Francia in the southwest to Covarrubias, Calatañazor and Medinaceli in the east, this is the hidden Spain most travellers don't know still exists.

When to Go

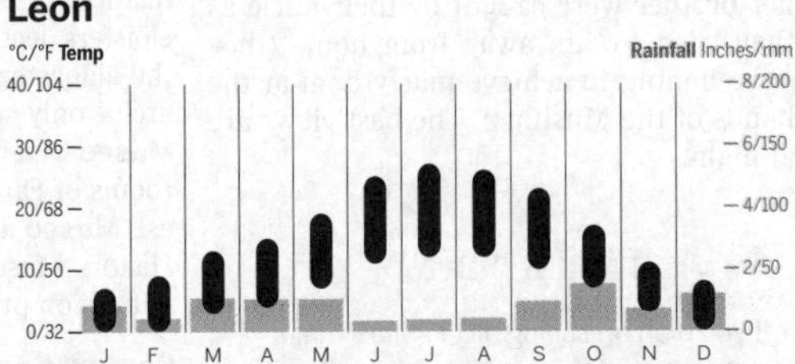

Mar & Apr Enjoy wild flowers in the countryside and soul-stirring Semana Santa processions.

Jun Get into holiday mode during annual fiesta time in Burgos, Soria and Segovia.

Sep & Oct Enjoy autumn colours, fewer tourists and (usually) mild, clear weather.

SOUTHWEST CASTILLA Y LEÓN

You could easily spend a week or more in southwestern Castilla y León, one of the region's most engaging corners. Salamanca, Ciudad Rodrigo and Ávila are three of the most appealing towns in central Spain, but the beautiful Sierra de Gredos and the time-worn villages of the Sierra de Francia and Sierra de Béjar promise fascinating breaks from city life.

Ávila

POP 58,083 / ELEV 1130M

Ávila's old city, surrounded by imposing city walls comprising eight monumental gates, 88 watchtowers and more than 2500 turrets, is one of the best-preserved medieval bastions in Spain. In winter, when an icy wind whistles in off the plains, the old city huddles behind the high stone walls as if seeking protection from the harsh Castilian climate. At night, when the walls are illuminated to magical effect, you'll wonder if you've stumbled into a fairy tale. It's a deeply religious city that for centuries has drawn pilgrims to the cult of Santa Teresa de Ávila, with its many churches, convents and high-walled palaces. As such, Ávila is the essence of Castilla and the epitome of old Spain.

Sights

★Los Cuatro Postes VIEWPOINT

Located northwest of the city, on the road to Salamanca, Los Cuatro Postes provides the best views of Ávila's walls. It also marks the place where Santa Teresa and her brother were caught by their uncle as they tried to run away from home (they were hoping to achieve martyrdom at the hands of the Muslims). The best views are at night.

> **VISITÁVILA CARD**
>
> If you plan on seeing all of Ávila's major sights, it may be worth buying the **Visitávila Card** (www.avilaturismo.com/en/organize-your-visit/visitavila-tourist-card; per person/family €13/25), which is valid for 48 hours and covers entrance fees to the main sights around town.

★Murallas WALLS

(www.muralladeavila.com; adult/child under 12yr €5/free; 10am-8pm Apr-Oct, to 6pm Nov-Mar;) Ávila's splendid 12th-century walls stretch for 2.5km atop the remains of earlier Roman and Muslim battlements and rank among the world's best-preserved medieval defensive perimeters. Two sections of the walls can be climbed – a 300m stretch that can be accessed from just inside the **Puerta del Alcázar**, and a longer (1300m) stretch from **Puerta de los Leales** that runs the length of the old city's northern perimeter.

★Catedral del Salvador CATHEDRAL

(920 21 16 41; Plaza de la Catedral; admission incl audioguide €5; 10am-7pm Mon-Fri, 10am-8pm Sat, noon-6.30pm Sun Apr-Sep, 10am-5pm Mon-Fri, 10am-6pm Sat, noon-5pm Sun Oct-Mar) Ávila's 12th-century cathedral is both a house of worship and an ingenious fortress: its stout granite apse forms the central bulwark in the historic city walls. The sombre, Gothic-style facade conceals a magnificent interior with an exquisite early-16th-century **altar frieze** showing the life of Jesus, plus Renaissance-era carved choir stalls. There is also a **museum** with an El Greco painting and a splendid silver monstrance by Juan de Arfe. (Push the buttons to illuminate the altar and the choir stalls.)

Monasterio de Santo Tomás MONASTERY, MUSEUM

(920 22 04 00; www.monasteriosantotomas.com; Plaza de Granada 1; €4; 10.30am-9pm Jul & Aug, 10.30am-2pm & 3.30-7.30pm Sep-Jun) Commissioned by the Reyes Católicos (Catholic Monarchs), Fernando and Isabel, and completed in 1492, this monastery is an exquisite example of Isabelline architecture, rich in historical resonance. Three interconnected cloisters lead to the church that contains the alabaster **tomb of Don Juan**, the monarchs' only son. There's also the impressive **Museo Oriental** (Oriental Museum), with 11 rooms of Far Eastern art, plus a more modest **Museo de Historia Natural** (Natural History Museum); both are included in the admission price.

Convento de Santa Teresa CHURCH, MUSEUM

(920 21 10 30; www.teresadejesus.com; Plaza de la Santa; church & relic room free, museum €2; 9.30am-1.30pm & 3.30-8pm Tue-Sun) Built in 1636 around the room where the saint was born in 1515, this is the epicentre of the cult

Castilla y León Highlights

❶ **Salamanca** (p157) Spending as long as you can amid the city's architectural elegance and energy.

❷ **León** (p189) Savouring the light in León's cathedral.

❸ **Santo Domingo de Silos** (p203) Being transported to medieval times listening to Gregorian chants.

❹ **Pedraza de la Sierra** (p174) Dining on *cordero asado* (roast lamb) in this gorgeous hilltop village.

❺ **Medinaceli** (p213) Escaping city life in a historic village.

❻ **Segovia** (p168) Finding yourself somewhere between ancient Rome and Disneyland.

❼ **Sierra de la Culebra** (p184) Looking for wolves close to Puebla de Sanabria.

❽ **Sierra de Francia** (p164) Exploring beautiful villages that time forgot.

❾ **Guijuelo** (p166) Going to the source to learn all about – and then taste – Spain's best *jamón*.

Ávila

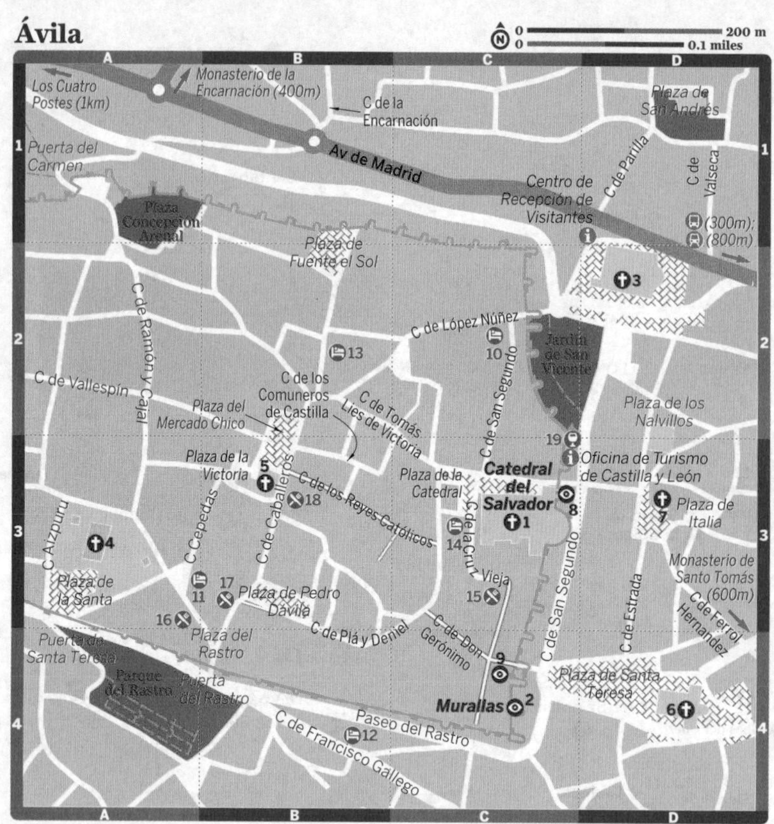

Ávila

Top Sights

1 Catedral del Salvador C3
2 Murallas C4

Sights

3 Basílica de San Vicente D2
4 Convento de Santa Teresa A3
5 Iglesia de San Juan Bautista B3
6 Iglesia de San Pedro D4
7 Iglesia de Santo Tomé El Viejo D3
8 Puerta de Los Leales C3
9 Puerta del Alcázar C4

Sleeping

10 Hostal Arco San Vicente C2
11 Hotel El Rastro A3
12 Hotel Las Leyendas B4
13 Hotel Palacio de Monjaraz B2
14 Hotel Palacio Valderrábanos C3

Eating

15 Hostería Las Cancelas C3
16 Mesón del Rastro A3
17 Posada de la Fruta B3
18 Soul Kitchen B3

Drinking & Nightlife

19 La Bodeguita de San Segundo C3

surrounding Teresa. There are three attractions in one here: the church, a relics room and a museum. Highlights include the gold-adorned **chapel** (built over the room where she was born), the baroque **altar** and the (macabre) **relic** of the saint's ring finger, complete with ring. Apparently Franco kept it at his bedside throughout his rule.

The elaborate chapel is lorded over by a baroque altar by Gregorio Fernández, which features a statue of the saint. There's also a basement museum dedicated to Santa Teresa, accessible from Calle Aizpuru.

Iglesia de Santo Tomé El Viejo CHURCH
(Plaza de Italia; admission incl Museo Provincial €1.20, Sat & Sun free; ⏲10am-2pm & 5-8pm Tue-Sat, 10am-2pm Sun Jul-Sep, 10am-2pm & 4-7pm Tue-Sat, 10am-2pm Sun Oct-Jun) This church dates from the 13th century, and it was from this pulpit that Santa Teresa was castigated most vehemently for her reforms. It has been restored to house mostly Roman foundation stones and a splendid **floor mosaic**.

Basílica de San Vicente CHURCH
(☎920 25 52 30; www.basilicasanvicente.es; Plaza de San Vicente; admission incl audio guide €2.30; ⏲10am-6.30pm Mon-Sat, 4-6pm Sun Apr-Oct, 10am-1.30pm & 4-6.30pm Mon-Sat, 4-6pm Sun Nov-Mar) This graceful church is a masterpiece of Romanesque simplicity: a series of largely Gothic modifications in sober granite contrasted with the warm sandstone of the Romanesque original. Work started in the 11th century, supposedly on the site where three martyrs – Vicente and his sisters, Sabina and Cristeta – were slaughtered by the Romans in the early 4th century. Their canopied **cenotaph** is an outstanding piece of Romanesque style, with nods to the Gothic.

Monasterio de la Encarnación MONASTERY
(☎920 21 12 12; Calle de la Encarnación; church free, museum €2; ⏲9.30am-1pm & 4-7pm Mon-Fri, 10am-1pm & 4-7pm Sat & Sun May-Sep, 9.30am-1.30pm & 3.30-6pm Mon-Fri, 10am-1pm & 4-6pm Sat & Sun Oct-Apr) North of the city walls, this unadorned Renaissance monastery is where Santa Teresa fully took on the monastic life and lived for 27 years. One of the three main rooms open to the public is where the saint is said to have had a vision of the baby Jesus. Also on display are relics, such as the piece of wood used by Teresa as a pillow (ouch!) and the chair upon which St John of the Cross made his confessions.

Iglesia de San Pedro CHURCH
(Plaza de Santa Teresa; €1.50; ⏲10am-noon & 5-8pm Easter–mid-Oct, 6-8pm Thu & Fri, 11am-noon, 1-2pm & 6-8pm Sat mid-Oct–Easter) One of the city's prettier churches, the light, sandstone exterior of the Iglesia de San Pedro (dating from the 12th or 13th centuries) is a pleasant complement to the granite austerity that reigns inside the city walls.

Iglesia de San Juan Bautista CHURCH
(Plaza de la Victoria; ⏲Mass 10am & 7.30pm Mon-Sat, noon Sun) FREE This quiet parish church dates from the 16th century and contains the font in which Santa Teresa was baptised on 4 April 1515. The church can be visited before and after Mass.

Festivals & Events

★Semana Santa RELIGIOUS
(Holy Week; ⏲Mar/Apr; 👪) Ávila is one of the best places in Castilla y León to watch the solemn processions of Easter. It all begins on Holy Thursday, though the most evocative event is the early morning (around 5am) Good Friday procession, which circles the city wall.

Fiesta de Santa Teresa CULTURAL
(⏲Oct; 👪) This annual festival, held during the second week of October, honours the city's patron saint with processions, concerts and fireworks.

Sleeping

★Hotel El Rastro HISTORIC HOTEL €
(☎920 35 22 25; www.elrastroavila.com; Calle Cepedas; s/d €38/60; ❄📶) This atmospheric hotel occupies a former 16th-century palace with original stone, exposed brickwork and a natural, earth-toned colour scheme exuding a calm, understated elegance. Each room has a different form, but most have high ceilings and plenty of space. Note that the owners also run a marginally cheaper *hostal* (budget hotel) of the same name around the corner.

Hostal Arco San Vicente HOSTAL €
(☎920 22 24 98; www.arcosanvicente.com; Calle de López Núñez 6; s/d incl breakfast €40/60; ❄📶) This gleaming *hostal* has small, blue-carpeted rooms with pale paintwork and wrought-iron bedheads. Rooms on the 2nd floor have attic windows and air-con; some on the 1st floor look out at the Puerta de San Vicente. The corner room 109 is particularly spacious and attractive.

★Hotel Palacio de Monjaraz HOTEL €€
(☎920 33 20 70; www.palaciodemonjaraz.com; Calle de Bracamonte 6; s €55-110, d €65-137; ❄📶) Stunning rooms in a wonderfully converted 16th-century Ávila townhouse make this one of our favourite places in town. The

rooms are large, have airy high ceilings and there's a quiet extravagance to the decor that changes from one room to the next. Some have Persian carpets and four-poster beds; others have exposed-brick walls and numerous original design features.

★Hotel Palacio Valderrábanos HISTORIC HOTEL €€
(☎920 21 10 23; www.hotelpalaciovalderrabanos.com; Plaza de la Catedral 9; r €55-115) A stone's throw from the door of the cathedral, this distinguished, converted 14th-century palace has a quiet elegance about it, with high ceilings, polished floorboards and reassuring tones. Some rooms even look out at the cathedral.

Hotel Las Leyendas HISTORIC HOTEL €€
(☎920 35 20 42; www.lasleyendas.es; Calle de Francisco Gallego 3; s €45-55, d €60-85;) Occupying the house of 16th-century Ávila nobility, this intimate hotel overflows with period touches wedded to modern amenities. Some rooms have views out across the plains, others look onto an internal garden. The decor varies between original wooden beams, exposed brick and stonework, and more modern rooms with walls washed in muted earth tones. Breakfast is a little sparse.

Eating

★Soul Kitchen CASTILIAN €€
(☎920 21 34 83; www.soulkitchen.es; Calle de Caballeros 13; mains €9-23; ⊙10am-midnight Mon-Fri, 11am-2am Sat, 11am-midnight Sun) This place has the kind of energy that can seem lacking elsewhere. The eclectic menu changes regularly and ranges from salads with dressings like chestnut and fig to hamburgers with cream of *setas* (oyster mushrooms). Lighter dishes include bruschetta with tasty toppings. Live music, poetry readings (and similar) happen in summer.

Mesón del Rastro CASTILIAN €€
(☎920 35 22 25; www.elrastroavila.com; Plaza del Rastro 1; mains €11-24; ⊙1-4pm & 9-11pm) The dark-wood-beamed interior announces immediately that this is a bastion of robust Castilian cooking, which it has been since 1881. Expect delicious mainstays such as *judías del barco de Ávila* (white beans, often with chorizo, in a thick sauce) and *cordero asado* (roast lamb), mercifully light salads and, regrettably, the occasional coach tour. The *menú de degustación*, priced for two people (€39), comes warmly recommended, but only if you're *really* hungry.

Hostería Las Cancelas CASTILIAN €€
(☎920 21 22 49; www.lascancelas.com; Calle de la Cruz Vieja 6; mains €15-24; ⊙1-4pm & 7.30-11pm) This courtyard restaurant occupies a delightful interior patio dating back to the 15th century. Renowned for being a mainstay of Ávila cuisine (steaks, roast lamb or suckling pig), traditional meals are prepared with a salutary attention to detail. Reservations are recommended for weekends and most evenings.

Posada de la Fruta CASTILIAN, INTERNATIONAL €€
(☎920 25 47 02; www.posadadelafruta.com; Plaza de Pedro Dávila 8; raciones €5-13, bar mains €8-11, restaurant mains €13-22, set menus €14-25; ⊙1-4pm & 7.30pm-midnight) Simple, tasty bar-style meals can be had in a light-filled, covered courtyard, while the traditional *comedor* (dining room) is typically all about hearty meat dishes offset by simple, fresh salads.

WHO WAS SANTA TERESA?

Teresa de Cepeda y Ahumada, probably the most important woman in the history of the Spanish Catholic Church (after the Virgin Mary of course...), was born in Ávila on 28 March 1515, one of 10 children of a merchant family. Raised by Augustinian nuns after her mother's death, she joined the Carmelite order at age 20. After her early, undistinguished years as a nun, she was shaken by a vision of hell in 1560, which crystallised her true vocation: she would reform the Carmelites.

In stark contrast to the opulence of the church in 16th-century Spain, her reforms called for the church to return to its roots, taking on the suffering and simple lifestyle of Jesus Christ. The Carmelites demanded the strictest of piety and even employed flagellation to atone for their sins. Not surprisingly, all this proved extremely unpopular with the mainstream Catholic Church.

With the help of many supporters, Teresa founded convents all over Spain and her writings proved enormously popular. She died in 1582 and was canonised by Pope Gregory XV in 1622.

Drinking & Nightlife

★La Bodeguita de San Segundo WINE BAR
(920 25 73 09; Calle de San Segundo 19; 11am-midnight Wed-Mon) Situated in the 16th-century Casa de la Misericordia, this superb wine bar is standing-room only most nights, though more tranquil in the quieter afternoon hours. Its wine list is renowned throughout Spain, with over a thousand wines to choose from and tapas-sized creative servings of cheeses and cured meats as the perfect accompaniment.

Information

Centro de Recepción de Visitantes (920 35 40 00, ext 370; www.avilaturismo.com; Avenida de Madrid 39; 9am-8pm Apr-Sep, to 5.15pm Oct-Mar) Municipal tourist office.

Oficina de Turismo de Castilla y León (920 21 13 87; www.turismocastillayleon.com; Casa de las Carnicerías, Calle de San Segundo 17; 9.30am-2pm & 5-8pm Mon-Sat, 9.30am-5pm Sun Jul–mid-Sep, 9.30am-2pm & 4-7pm Mon-Sat, 9.30am-5pm Sun mid-Sep–Jul)

Getting There & Away

Bus Frequent services run from the **bus station** (920 25 65 05; Avenida de Madrid 2) to Segovia (€6.80, one hour), Salamanca (€7.95, 1½ hours, five daily) and Madrid (€11, 1½ hours); a couple of daily buses also head for the main towns in the Sierra de Gredos.

Car & Motorcycle From Madrid the driving time is around one hour; the toll costs €9.35.

Train There are **Renfe** (902 240202; www.renfe.es) services to Madrid (from €12.25, 1¼ to two hours, up to 17 daily), Salamanca (from €12.25, 1¼ hours, eight daily) and León (from €21.90, three to four hours, five daily).

Getting Around

Bus Local bus 1 runs past the train station to Plaza de la Catedral.

Salamanca

POP 144,949

Whether floodlit by night or bathed in late-afternoon light, there's something magical about Salamanca. This is a city of rare beauty, awash with golden sandstone overlaid with ochre-tinted Latin inscriptions – an extraordinary virtuosity of plateresque and Renaissance styles. The monumental highlights are many and the exceptional Plaza Mayor (illuminated to stunning effect at night) is unforgettable. This is also Castilla's liveliest city, home to a massive Spanish and international student population that throngs the streets at night and provides the city with so much vitality.

DON'T MISS

CASTILLA Y LEÓN'S PRETTIEST VILLAGES

- Covarrubias (p202)
- Pedraza de la Sierra (p174)
- Medinaceli (p213)
- San Martín del Castañar (p164)
- Mogarraz (p164)
- Puebla de Sanabria (p185)
- La Alberca (p165)
- Calatañazor (p211)
- Yanguas (p212)
- Santo Domingo de Silos (p203)

Sights

★Plaza Mayor SQUARE
Built between 1729 and 1755, Salamanca's exceptional grand square is widely considered to be Spain's most beautiful central plaza. The square is particularly memorable at night when illuminated (until midnight) to magical effect. Designed by Alberto Churriguera, it's a remarkably harmonious and controlled baroque display. The medallions placed around the square bear the busts of famous figures.

After years of controversy, a bust of former dictator Franco was finally removed in June 2017.

Bullfights were held here well into the 19th century; the last ceremonial *corrida* (bullfight) took place in 1992.

★Universidad Civil HISTORIC BUILDING
(923 29 44 00, ext 1150; www.salamanca.es; Calle de los Libreros; adult/concession €10/5, audio guide €2; 10am-6.30pm Mon-Sat, 10am-1.30pm Sun) Founded initially as the Estudio General in 1218, the university reached the peak of its renown in the 15th and 16th centuries. The visual feast of the entrance facade is a tapestry in sandstone, bursting with images of mythical heroes, religious scenes and coats of arms. It's dominated by busts of Fernando and Isabel. Behind the facade, the highlight of an otherwise-modest collection

Salamanca

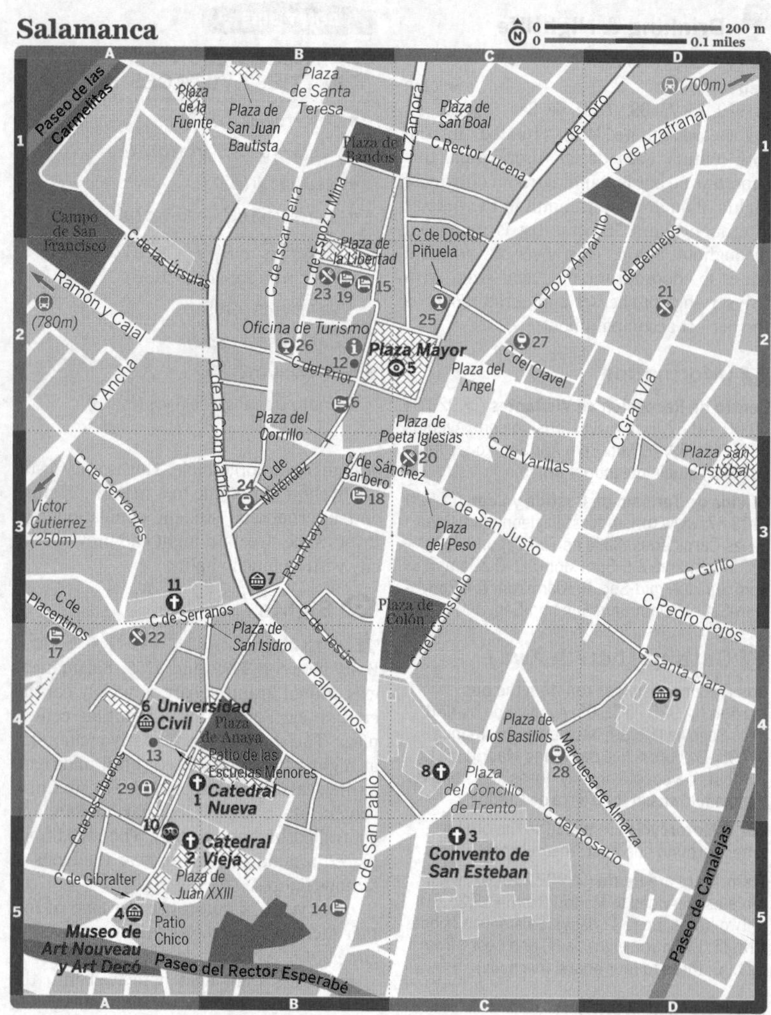

of rooms lies upstairs: the extraordinary **university library**, the oldest one in Europe.

★Catedral Nueva CATHEDRAL

(☎923 21 74 76; www.catedralsalamanca.org; Plaza de Anaya; adult/child incl audio guide & Catedral Vieja €4.75/3; ⊙10am-8pm Apr-Sep, 10am-6pm Oct-Mar) The tower of this late-Gothic cathedral lords over the city centre, its compelling Churrigueresque (an ornate style of baroque architecture) dome visible from almost every angle. The interior is similarly impressive, with elaborate choir stalls, main chapel and retrochoir, much of it courtesy of the prolific José Churriguera. The ceilings are also exceptional, along with the Renaissance doorways – particularly the **Puerta del Nacimiento** on the western face, which stands out as one of several miracles worked in the city's native sandstone.

★Catedral Vieja CATHEDRAL

(☎923 28 10 45; www.catedralsalamanca.org; Plaza de Anaya; adult/child incl audio guide & Catedral Nueva €4.75/3; ⊙10am-8pm Apr-Sep, 10am-6pm Oct-Mar) The Catedral Nueva's largely Romanesque predecessor, the Catedral Vieja, is adorned with an exquisite 15th-century

Salamanca

Top Sights
1 Catedral Nueva A4
2 Catedral Vieja A5
3 Convento de San Esteban C5
4 Museo de Art Nouveau y Art Decó A5
5 Plaza Mayor C2
6 Universidad Civil A4

Sights
7 Casa de las Conchas B3
8 Convento de las Dueñas C4
9 Convento de Santa Clara D4
10 Puerta de la Torre A5
11 Real Clerecía de San Marcos A3

Activities, Courses & Tours
12 Guided Tours B2
13 University of Salamanca A4

Sleeping
14 Don Gregorio B5
15 Hostal Concejo B2
16 Hostal Plaza Mayor B2
17 Microtel Placentinos A4
18 Rúa Hotel B3
19 Salamanca Suite Studios B2

Eating
20 El Pecado C3
21 La Cocina de Toño D2
22 Mandala Café A4
23 Zazu Bistro B2

Drinking & Nightlife
24 Café El Corrillo B3
25 Doctor C2
26 Garamond B2
27 Tío Vivo C2
28 Vinodiario C4

Shopping
29 Mercatus A4

altarpiece, one of the finest outside Italy. Its 53 panels depict scenes from the lives of Christ and Mary and are topped by a haunting representation of the Final Judgement. The cloister was largely ruined in an earthquake in 1755, but the **Capilla de Anaya** houses an extravagant alabaster sepulchre and one of Europe's oldest organs, a Mudéjar work of art from the 16th century.

★Convento de San Esteban CONVENT
(☎923 21 50 00; Plaza del Concilio de Trento; adult/concession/child €3.50/2.50/free; ⏲10am-1.15pm & 4-7.15pm) Just down the hill from the cathedral, the lordly Dominican Convento de San Esteban's church has an extraordinary altar-like facade, with the stoning of San Esteban (St Stephen) as its central motif. Inside is a well-presented museum dedicated to the Dominicans, a splendid Gothic-Renaissance cloister and an elaborate church built in the form of a Latin cross and adorned by an overwhelming 17th-century **altar** by José Churriguera.

★Museo de Art Nouveau y Art Decó MUSEUM
(Casa Lis; ☎923 12 14 25; www.museocasalis.org; Calle de Gibraltar; adult/child under 12yr €4/free, Thu morning free; ⏲11am-8pm Tue-Sun Apr-Oct plus 11am-8pm Mon Aug, 11am-2pm & 4-7pm Tue-Fri, 11am-8pm Sat & Sun Oct–Mar; 👪) Utterly unlike any other Salamanca museum, this stunning collection of sculpture, paintings and art deco and art nouveau pieces inhabits a beautiful, light-filled Modernista (Catalan art nouveau) house. There's abundant stained glass and exhibits that include Lalique glass, toys by Steiff (inventor of the teddy bear), Limoges porcelain, Fabergé watches, fabulous bronze and marble figurines and a vast collection of 19th-century children's dolls (some strangely macabre), which kids will love. There's also a cafe and an excellent gift shop.

Real Clerecía de San Marcos CHURCH, TOWER
(San Marcos; ☎923 27 71 00, 923 27 71 14; www.torresdelaclerecia.com; Calle de la Compañia; San Marcos €3, Scala Coeli €3.75, combined ticket €6; ⏲San Marcos 10.30am-12.45pm & 5-6.30pm Mon-Fri, 9am-3pm & 4-7pm Sat, 10am-2pm & 4-7pm Sun, Scala Coeli 10am-7.15pm) Visits to this colossal baroque church and the attached Catholic university are via obligatory **guided tours** (in Spanish), which run every 45 minutes. You can also climb the **Scala Coeli** (tower; €3.75, free 10am to 2pm Tuesday) – some 166 steps, including the bell tower – to enjoy superb panoramic views.

Puerta de la Torre VIEWPOINT
(Ieronimus; www.ieronimus.es; Plaza de Juan XXIII; €3.75; ⏲10am-7pm) For fine views over Salamanca, head to the tower at the southwestern corner of the Catedral Nueva's facade. From here, stairs lead up through the tower, past labyrinthine but well-presented exhibitions of cathedral memorabilia, then – a

DON'T MISS

FROG-SPOTTING

Arguably a lot more interesting than trainspotting (and you don't have to wear an anorak and drink tea from a thermos flask), a compulsory task facing all visitors to Salamanca is to search out the frog sculpted into the facade of the Universidad Civil (p157). Once pointed out, it's easily enough seen, but the uninitiated can spend considerable time searching. Why bother? Well, they say that those who detect it without help can be assured of good luck and even marriage within a year; some hopeful students believe they'll be guaranteed to ace their examinations. If you believe all this, stop reading now – spoilers ahead.

If you need help, look at the busts of Fernando and Isabel. From there, turn your gaze to the largest column on the extreme right. Slightly above the level of the busts is a series of skulls, atop the leftmost of which sits our little amphibious friend (or what's left of his eroded self).

real bonus – along the interior balconies of the sanctuaries of the Catedral Nueva and Catedral Vieja and out onto the exterior balconies.

Guided night tours take place at 8pm, 8.30pm and 10pm (per person €6).

Casa de las Conchas HISTORIC BUILDING
(House of Shells; ☎923 26 93 17; Calle de la Compañia 2; ⏲9am-9pm Mon-Fri, 9am-3pm & 4-7pm Sat, 10am-2pm & 4-7pm Sun) FREE One of the city's most endearing buildings, Casa de las Conchas is named after the 300 scallop shells clinging to its facade. The house's original owner, Dr Rodrigo Maldonado de Talavera, was a doctor at the court of Isabel and a member of the Order of Santiago, whose symbol is the shell. It now houses the public **library**, entered via a charming colonnaded courtyard with a central fountain and intricate stone tracery.

Convento de Santa Clara MUSEUM
(☎660 10 83 14; Calle Santa Clara 2; adult/senior/child €3/2/free; ⏲9.30am-12.45pm & 4.25-6.10pm Mon-Fri, 9.30am-2.10pm Sat & Sun) This much-modified convent started life as a Romanesque structure and now houses a small museum. You can admire the beautiful frescos and climb up some stairs to inspect the 14th- and 15th-century wooden Mudéjar ceiling at close quarters. You can visit only as part of a (Spanish-language) **guided tour**, which runs roughly every hour.

Convento de las Dueñas CONVENT
(☎923 21 54 42; Gran Vía; €2; ⏲10.30am-12.45pm & 4.30-7.15pm Mon-Sat) This Dominican convent is home to the city's most beautiful cloister, with some decidedly ghoulish carvings on the capitals.

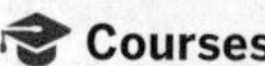

Courses

University of Salamanca LANGUAGE
(Cursos Internacionales, Universidad Civil; ☎923 29 44 18; www.cursosinternacionales.usal.es/es; Patio de las Escuelas Menores) Salamanca is one of the most popular places in Spain to study Spanish and the University of Salamanca is the most respected language school. Courses range from a three-hour daily course over three weeks (€565) to a 10-week course of five hours daily (€2035). Accommodation can be arranged.

Tours

Guided Tours WALKING
(☎622 52 46 90; visitasplaza@hotmail.es; tour per person €8-15; ⏲in Spanish 11am, 8pm & 8.30pm Mon-Fri, 8pm & 8.30pm Sat & Sun mid-Jul–Sep, 11am Mon-Fri Oct–mid-Jul, in English 11.30am Mon-Fri mid-Mar–Dec, 11am, 11.30am & 8pm Fri, 10.30am, 11.30am, 4.30pm, 5pm & 8pm Sat, 10.30am Sun Jan–mid-Mar) Two-hour guided tours run from the tourist office on Plaza Mayor. Although there are variations, daytime tours take in the main monumental highlights of Salamanca, while the summer nocturnal tour is all about local legends and curiosities. Buy your ticket in advance from the tourist office (p162).

Sleeping

Hostal Concejo HOSTAL €
(☎923 21 47 37; www.hconcejo.com; Plaza de la Libertad 1; s €28-50, d €37-70; P❄☎) A cut above the average *hostal*, the stylish Concejo has polished-wood floors, tasteful furnishings, light-filled rooms and a superb central location. Try to snag one of the corner rooms, such as number 104, which has a traditional, glassed-in balcony, complete with a table, chairs and people-watching views.

Hostal Plaza Mayor HOSTAL €
(☎923 26 20 20; www.hostalplazamayor.es; Plaza del Corrillo 20; s €32-45, d €35-70; ❄@☎) Near

Plaza Mayor, this friendly, family-owned *hostal* has simple but well-tended rooms washed in pale peach, with dark wood furniture and some with wooden beams. Three of the outside rooms have small balconies, which are pleasant for people watching but make it noisy for sleeping; interior rooms are far quieter.

★Salamanca Suite Studios APARTMENT **€€**
(☎923 27 24 65; www.salamancasuitestudios.com; Plaza de la Libertad 4; r €60-125;) This excellent place has smart and contemporary modern suites and apartments with kitchens; some have Nespresso coffee machines and all have bucketloads of style with their white-and-turquoise colour schemes. The location is lovely and central and the service is discreet but attentive. Ask for a plaza-facing room (*exterior*) – the double glazing works a treat.

★Microtel Placentinos BOUTIQUE HOTEL **€€**
(☎923 28 15 31; www.microtelplacentinos.com; Calle de Placentinos 9; s/d incl breakfast Sun-Thu €57/73, Fri & Sat €88/100;) One of Salamanca's most charming boutique hotels, Microtel Placentinos is tucked away on a quiet street and has rooms with exposed stone walls and wooden beams. The service is faultless, and the overall atmosphere one of intimacy and discretion. All rooms have a hydromassage shower or tub and there's an outside whirlpool spa (open summer only).

Rúa Hotel HOTEL **€€**
(☎923 27 22 72; www.hotelrua.com; Calle de Sánchez Barbero 11; s/d from €74/80;) The former apartments here have been converted to seriously spacious rooms with sofas and fridges. Light-wood floors, rag-rolled walls and arty prints set the tone. You can't get more central than this.

★Don Gregorio BOUTIQUE HOTEL **€€€**
(☎923 21 70 15; www.hoteldongregorio.com; Calle de San Pablo 80; r/ste incl breakfast from €165/280;) A palatial hotel with part of the city's Roman wall flanking the garden. Rooms are decorated in soothing cafe-con-leche shades with crisp white linens and extravagant extras, including private saunas, espresso machines, complimentary minibar, king-size beds and vast hydromassage tubs. Sumptuous antiques and medieval tapestries adorn the public areas.

Eating

Mandala Café MEDITERRANEAN **€**
(☎923 12 33 42; www.mandalasalamanca.com; Calle de Serranos 9-11; set menu €12.90; 8am-11pm;) Come here with an appetite, as cool and casual Mandala offers a three-course set menu (unusually available for lunch *and* dinner) with dishes like black rice with seafood, and vegetable lasagne. There are also 18 flavours of hot chocolate, 52 types of milkshake, 56 juice combinations and more teas than we could count.

★La Cocina de Toño TAPAS **€€**
(☎923 26 39 77; www.lacocinadetoño.es; Calle Gran Via 20; tapas from €2, menú €17-38, mains €18-23; noon-4.30pm & 8-11.30pm Tue-Sat, noon-4.30pm Sun;) This place owes its loyal following to its creative *pinchos* (tapas-like snacks) and half-servings of dishes such as escalope of foie gras with roast apple and passionfruit gelatin. The restaurant serves more traditional fare as befits the decor, but the bar is one of Salamanca's gastronomic stars. Slightly removed from the old city, it draws a predominantly Spanish crowd.

Zazu Bistro ITALIAN **€€**
(www.restaurantezazu.com; Plaza de la Libertad 8; mains €11-18; 2-4pm & 8.30pm-midnight) Enjoy a romantic intimate ambience and Italian-inspired dishes like asparagus, mint and cheese risotto or farfalle with tomato, bacon, vodka and parmesan. The culinary surprises extend to desserts, like that delectable British standard, sticky toffee pudding. Every dish is executed to perfection. Snag a table by the window overlooking this tranquil square.

El Pecado CONTEMPORARY SPANISH **€€**
(☎923 26 65 58; www.elpecadorestaurante.es; Plaza del Poeta Iglesias 12; mains €16-19, menú de degustación €25; 1.30-4pm & 8.30-11.30pm) A trendy place that regularly attracts Spanish celebrities and well-to-do locals, El Pecado (The Sin) has an intimate dining room and a quirky, creative menu. The hallmarks are fresh tastes, a lovely lack of pretension, intriguing combinations and dishes that regularly change according to what is fresh in the market that day. The *menú de degustación* is outstanding. Reservations recommended.

★Victor Gutierrez CONTEMPORARY SPANISH **€€€**
(☎923 26 29 73; www.restaurantevictorgutierrez.com; Calle de Empedrada 4; set menus €65-95;

1.30-4pm & 8.30-11.30pm Tue-Thu, 1.30-4pm & 9-11.30pm Fri & Sat, 2-4pm Sun;) This is still the best table in town. Chef Victor Gutierrez has a Michelin star and his place has a justifiably exclusive vibe, with an emphasis on innovative dishes with plenty of colourful drizzle. The choice of what to order is largely made for you with some excellent set menus that change regularly. Reservations essential.

Drinking & Nightlife

★Tío Vivo BAR
(923 215 768; www.tiovivosalamanca.com; Calle del Clavel 3-5; 3.30pm-late) Sip drinks by flickering candlelight to a background of '80s music, enjoying the whimsical decor of carousel horses and oddball antiquities. There's live music Tuesday to Thursday from midnight, sometimes with a €5 cover charge.

Doctor COCKTAIL BAR
(923 26 31 51; Calle del Doctor Piñuela 5; 4pm-late) Excellent cocktails, friendly bar staff and a cool crowd make for a fine mix just north of the Plaza Mayor. Apart from the creative list of cocktails, it has over 30 different kinds of gin to choose from and above-average tonic to go with it.

Café El Corrillo BAR
(923 27 19 17; www.cafecorrillo.com; Calle de Meléndez; 8.30am-3am) Great for a beer and tapas at any time, with live music (especially jazz or singer-songwriters) on Sunday and Thursday nights from 10pm; concerts sometimes take place on other nights. The *terraza* (terrace) out back is perfect on a warm summer's evening.

Vinodiario WINE BAR
(923 61 49 25; www.vinodiario.com; Plaza de los Basilios 1; 10am-1am Sun-Thu, to 1.30am Fri & Sat) Away from the crowds of the old-city centre, this quiet but classy neighbourhood wine bar is staffed by knowledgeable bar staff and loved by locals who, in summer, fill the outdoor tables for early-evening drinks. The tapas are good and wine by the glass starts from €2.50.

Garamond CLUB
(923 26 88 98; Calle del Prior 24; 9pm-late) A stalwart of Salamanca nightlife, with medieval-style decor. Garamond has music that's good to dance to without straying too far from the mainstream. No cover.

Shopping

★Mercatus GIFTS & SOUVENIRS
(923 29 46 48; www.mercatus.usal.es; Calle de Cardenal Pla y Deniel; 10am-8.15pm Mon-Sat, 10.15am-2pm Sun) The official shop of the University of Salamanca has a stunning range of stationery items, leather-bound books and other carefully selected reminders of your Salamanca visit.

Information

Oficina de Turismo (923 21 83 42; www.salamanca.es; Plaza Mayor 32; 9am-2pm & 4.30-8pm Mon-Fri, 10am-8pm Sat, 10am-2pm Sun Easter–mid-Oct, 9am-2pm & 4-6.30pm Mon-Fri, 10am-6.30pm Sat, 10am-2pm Sun mid-Oct–Easter) The municipal tourist office shares its space with the regional office on Plaza Mayor. An audio guide to city sights can be accessed on your smartphone from www.audioguiasalamanca.es.

Getting There & Away

The bus and train stations are a 10- and 15-minute walk, respectively, from Plaza Mayor.

Bus Buses include the following destinations: Madrid (regular/express €17/24.50, 2½ to three hours, hourly), Ávila (€7.95, 1½ hours, five daily), Segovia (€16, 2½ hours, four daily) and Valladolid (€9.20, 1½ hours, eight daily). There is a limited service to smaller towns with just one daily bus – except on Sunday – to La Alberca (€6, around 1½ hours), with stops in the villages of the Sierra de Francia, such as Mogarraz and San Martín del Castañar.

Train Regular departures to Madrid's Chamartín station (from €16, 1½ to four hours), Ávila (€12.25, 1¼ hour) and Valladolid (from €10.45, 1½ hours).

Ciudad Rodrigo

POP 12,896

Close to the Portuguese border and away from well-travelled tourist routes, sleepy Ciudad Rodrigo is one of the prettier towns in western Castilla y León. It's an easy day trip from Salamanca, 80km away, but staying overnight within the sanctuary of its walls enables you to better appreciate the town's medieval charm.

Sights

★Murallas WALLS
FREE There are numerous stairs leading up onto the crumbling ramparts of the city walls that encircle the old town and

which were built between the 12th and 15th centuries. You can follow their length for about 2.2km around the town and enjoy fabulous views over the surrounding plains.

★Catedral de Santa María CATHEDRAL

(www.catedralciudadrodrigo.com; Plaza de San Salvador 1; adult/concession €3/2.50, 4-6pm Sun free, tower €2; ⌚church & museum 11am-2pm Mon, 11am-2pm & 4-7pm Tue-Sat, noon-2pm & 4-6pm Sun) This elegant, weathered sandstone cathedral, begun in 1165, towers over the historic centre. Of particular interest are the **Puerta de las Cadenas**, with splendid Gothic reliefs of Old Testament figures; the elegant **Pórtico del Perdón**; and inside, the exquisite, carved-oak choir stalls. You can also climb the **tower** at 1.15pm on Saturday and Sunday; the views are Ciudad Rodrigo's best. Opening hours were in a state of flux at the time of writing so check with the tourist office.

★Plaza Mayor SQUARE

The long, sloping Plaza Mayor is a fine centrepiece for this beautiful town. At the top of the hill, the double-storey arches of the **Casa Consistorial** are stunning, but the plaza's prettiest building is the **Casa del Marqués de Cerralbo**, an early-16th-century townhouse with a wonderful facade. Sadly, cars are allowed to park around the perimeter, which diminishes the square's charm a bit.

Iglesia de San Pedro & San Isidro CHURCH

(Plaza de Cristobal de Castillo; ⌚before & after Mass) The fusion of 12th-century Romanesque-Mudéjar elements with later Gothic modifications makes this church worth seeking out. Don't miss the porticoes in the cloister. Discovered in 1994 during major restoration works, when they emerged from beneath later additions to the church's structure, the 12th-century reliefs of a Roman queen, Arab king and Catholic bishop reflect the various cultures of the region over the years.

Casa de los Vázquez HISTORIC BUILDING

(Correos; Calle de San Juan 12, Plaza Cristóbal Castillejo 16; ⌚8.30am-2.30pm Mon-Fri, 9.30am-1pm Sat) Even if you've nothing to post, the *correos* (post office) is worth stopping by to admire the magnificent *artesonado* (wooden Mudéjar ceiling), stained glass and medieval-style pictorial tiled friezes.

DON'T MISS

TOP TOWN SQUARES

- Salamanca (p157)
- Segovia (p169)
- La Alberca (p165)
- Pedraza de la Sierra (p174)
- Peñafiel (p205)
- Medinaceli (p213)

Museo del Orinal MUSEUM

(Chamber Pot Museum; ☎952 38 20 87; www.museodelorinal.es; Plaza Herrasti; adult/child under 10yr €2/free; ⌚11am-2pm & 4-7pm Mon-Sat, 11am-2pm Sun; 👪) Chamber pots, commodes, bed pans...Ciudad Rodrigo's Museo del Orinal may be located opposite the cathedral, but its theme is definitely more down to earth than sacred. This city is home to Spain's (possibly the world's) only museum dedicated to the not-so-humble chamber pot (or potty, as it is known in the UK). The private collection of former local resident José María del Arco comprises a staggering 1300 exhibits. Hailing from 27 countries, there are some truly historic pieces here.

Palacio de los Ávila y Tiedra HISTORIC BUILDING

(Plaza del Conde 3; ⌚9am-7pm Mon-Sat) FREE The 16th-century Palacio de los Ávila y Tiedra boasts one of the town's most engaging plateresque facades – it's the pick of a handful of fine examples that surround the Plaza del Conde. While most of the building is off limits, you can wander in to admire the pretty, compact courtyard surrounded by columns.

Tours

Guided Tours WALKING

(☎680 42 67 07; www.viveciudadrodrigo.com; day/night tours €6/7; ⌚noon, 4.30pm & 8pm Sat, noon Sun) Run by the tourist office (p164), two-hour walking tours by day take in the main monuments of Ciudad Rodrigo. The 90-minute Saturday-night version is all about local legends.

Festivals & Events

Carnaval CARNIVAL

(www.carnavaldeltoro.es; ⌚Feb; 👪) Celebrated with great enthusiasm in February. In addition to the outlandish fancy dress, you can witness (or join in) a colourful *encierro* (running of the bulls) and *capeas* (amateur bullfights).

Sleeping

★Hospedería Audiencia Real HISTORIC HOTEL €€

(☎923 49 84 98; www.audienciareal.com; Plaza Mayor 17; d €45-85; ❄📶) Right on Plaza Mayor, this fine 16th-century inn has been beautifully reformed and retains a tangible historic feel with lovely exposed stone walls. Some rooms have wrought-iron furniture and several sport narrow balconies overlooking the square; the very best has a private, glassed-in alcove containing a table for two, ideal for reading the morning newspaper.

★Parador Enrique II HISTORIC HOTEL €€

(☎923 46 01 50; www.parador.es; Plaza del Castillo 1; r €120-185; P❄@📶) Ciudad Rodrigo's premier address is a plushly renovated castle built into the town's western wall. Converted in 1931, it's the third-oldest *parador* in Spain. The views are good, the rooms brim with character and the restaurant is easily the best in town. The delightful terraced gardens out back overlook the Rio Agueda.

Eating

★Zascandil TAPAS €

(☎665 63 58 84; Correo Viejo 5; pinchos €3, tostas €5.50-8; ⏲1-4pm & 7.30-11pm) A fashionable spot with an art deco look to accompany the pretty-as-a-picture gastro tapas (such as sashimi and gourmet miniburgers). Organic veg come from the owner's *huerta* (market garden) and eco-wines are served. There's live music in summer.

El Sanatorio TAPAS €€

(☎923 46 10 54; Plaza Mayor 14; raciones & mains €5-16; ⏲11am-late) Dating from 1937, the interior here doubles as a fascinating social history of the town. The walls are papered floor to ceiling with B&W photos, mainly of the annual Carnaval and bullfights. The tapas and *raciones* are good: ask about the *farinato* (a rich, local pork sausage made with all manner of spices) – this version has a quail's egg inside.

★Parador Enrique II SPANISH €€€

(☎923 46 01 50; www.parador.es; Plaza del Castillo 1; mains €17.50-25, set menus from €26; ⏲1-4pm & 8-11.30pm) Ciudad Rodrigo's most celebrated restaurant, the rather formal Parador serves up some exquisite local cooking, but we recommend ordering one of the set menus to make sure you sample a range of tastes. Roasted meats are a recurring theme, and there's not much in the way of innovation – when the local specialities are this good, why mess with tradition?

Information

For online information on the town, check out www.turismociudadrodrigo.com.

Oficina de Turismo de Ciudad Rodrigo (☎923 49 84 00; www.aytociudadrodrigo.es; Plaza Mayor 27; ⏲10am-1.30pm & 4-7pm Sat & Sun Apr-Sep, hours vary Oct-May)

Oficina de Turismo de Castilla y León (☎673 57 37 98; www.turismocastillayleon.com; Plaza de Amayuelas 5; ⏲9am-2pm & 5-7pm Mon-Fri, 10am-2pm & 5-8pm Sat, 10am-2pm Sun)

Getting There & Away

From the **bus station** (☎923 46 10 36; Calle del Campo de Toledo) there are up to 13 daily services (fewer on weekends) to Salamanca (€6.80, one hour). For the Sierra de Francia, you'll need to go via Salamanca.

Sierra de Francia

Hidden away in a remote corner of southwestern Castilla y León and until recently secluded for centuries, this mountainous region with wooded hillsides and pretty stone-and-timber villages was once one of Spain's most godforsaken regions. Today it's among Castilla y León's best-kept secrets. Quiet mountain roads connect villages that you could easily spend days exploring. Here, the pace of life remains relatively untouched by the modern world.

Sights

The main tourist centre of the Sierra de Francia is **La Alberca**. Having your own car enables you to immerse yourself in quiet villages such as **Mogarraz**, east of La Alberca, which has some of the most evocative old houses in the region. It's also famous for its *embutidos* (cured meats), as well as the more recent novelty of over 300 portraits of past and present residents, painted by local artist Florencio Maíllo and on display outside the family homes. The history of this extraordinary project dates from the 1960s, when poverty was rife and many locals were seeking work, mainly in South America – they needed identity cards and it is this that inspired the portraits.

Miranda del Castañar, further east, is similarly intriguing, strung out along a narrow ridge. But **San Martín del Castañar** is the most enchanting, with half-timbered stone houses, flowers cascading from balconies, a bubbling stream and a small village bullring at the top of the town, next to the renovated castle with its historic cemetery (there is also an interpretation centre here). **Villanueva del Conde** is another lovely hamlet.

The main natural attraction of the region is the highest peak in the area, **Peña de Francia** (1732m). Topped by a monastery and reached by a sinuous 12km climb from close to La Alberca, it's a stunning place with views that extend east to the Sierra de Gredos, south into Extremadura and west towards Portugal.

Versos Microbodega WINERY
(☎923 20 81 31, 696 33 41 68; www.versosmicrobodega.com; Calle del Cementerio 3-13, San Martín del Castañar) This excellent little boutique winery produces some lovely reds and an intriguing white. With prior notice, it opens for tastings and for tours of the winery that dates back to 1846. It also has an excellent restaurant (*menú de degustación* €25).

Sleeping

Hostal Las Madras HOSTAL €
(☎627 45 52 90; www.gruposierrarural.es; Plaza Juan José Hidalgo Acera 21, Villanueva del Conde; d from €42; 📶) An excellent budget-value *hostal* in the pretty little village of Villanueva del Conde; the rooms have exposed brick walls. The restaurant is similarly excellent.

★**Abadía de San Martín** HOTEL €€
(☎923 43 73 50; www.abadiadesanmartin.com; Calle Paipérez 24, San Martín del Castañar; d €65-75, ste €75-95; 📶) Lovely, contemporary rooms in a converted old home in one of the Sierra de Francia's loveliest villages, along with a well-regarded restaurant – what more could you ask for?

Hotel Spa Villa de Mogarraz HOTEL €€
(☎923 41 81 80; www.hotelspamogarraz.com; Calle Miguel Ángel Maíllo 54, Mogarraz; r €48-130; ❄📶) At the pedestrian entrance to gorgeous Mogarraz, this artfully converted spa-hotel has amply sized rooms, some with wooden beams, others with exposed stone walls. We especially like the views down the cobblestone main street from room 125. There's also a good restaurant.

Information

There are no tourist offices in the Sierra de Francia. The tourist offices in Salamanca (p162) and Ciudad Rodrigo have limited information on the region.

Getting There & Away

Roads lead into the Sierra de Francia from Ciudad Rodrigo (SA220), Salamanca (CL512 and SA210) and Béjar (SA220). The only public transport here is one or two buses a day from Salamanca.

The drive south into Extremadura through the dreamy Valle de las Batuecas is spectacular. Just beyond La Alberca, a sweeping panorama of cascading lower mountain ranges opens up before you. The road corkscrews down into the valley before passing through beautiful terrain that has been praised by poets and the writer/academic Miguel de Unamuno. Time your visit for spring when purple heather and brilliant yellow rapeseed blanket the hillsides.

Getting Around

At least one daily bus from Salamanca passes through some Sierra de Francia villages from Monday to Saturday, but it's only of use to get to the region, rather than around it – you'll need your own wheels to properly explore the area.

La Alberca

POP 1125 / ELEV 1048M

La Alberca is one of the largest and most beautifully preserved of Sierra de Francia's villages; a historic and harmonious huddle of narrow alleys flanked by gloriously ramshackle houses built of stone, wood beams and plaster. Look for the date they were built (typically the late 18th century) carved into the door lintels.

Numerous stores sell local products such as *jamón*, as well as baskets and the inevitable tackier souvenirs. The centre is the pretty-as-a-postcard Plaza Mayor; there's a market here on Saturday mornings.

Sleeping

Hostal La Alberca HOSTAL €
(☎923 41 51 16; Plaza Padre Arsenio; s/d/tr €30/37/53; 📶) Housed above a restaurant in one of La Alberca's most evocative half-timbered buildings, this comfortable place has renovated rooms. Balconies overlook a small square at the entrance to the village.

★Hotel Doña Teresa HOTEL €€
(☎923 41 53 08; www.hoteldeteresa.com; Carretera de Mogarraz; s/d from €60/90; P❄📶) Lovely Doña Teresa is a perfect modern fit for the village's old-world charm. The large rooms combine character (wooden beams and exposed stone) with all the necessary mod cons; some open onto a garden. The owners also run a spa 1.5km away, with various treatments available at reduced rates for guests.

★Abadia de los Templarios HOTEL €€
(☎923 42 31 07; www.abadiadelostemplarios.com; Ctra SA201 (Salamanca–La Alberca) Km 76; d/ste/villas from €95/112/121; P❄📶🏊) Large rooms with wooden floors and wooden beams make this place an excellent choice. It's a large complex, close to the main entrance of town and on a pretty, leafy hillside, designed to recreate La Alberca's half-timbered architecture. There's also an on-site spa and swimming pool. Our only criticism is that it's often booked up by local tour groups.

Eating

Restaurante El Encuentro SPANISH €€
(☎923 41 53 10; www.restauranteelencuentro.es; Calle de Tablado 8; ⏲1-4pm & 8.30-11pm Thu-Tue) The consistently good reports from travellers made us sit up and take notice of this place. The decor is pretty average but the food is excellent from the *albóndigas de ternera* meatballs to the oxtail, pigs trotters and pheasant. Spaniards love this place for the authenticity of the cooking and no-nonsense but knowledgeable service. So do we.

Entrevinos SPANISH €€
(☎618 47 94 89; Calle de la Iglesia 37; mains €12-18; ⏲1-4pm & 8.30-11pm) La Alberca's most creative kitchen holds fast to the town's meat-eating obsession, but does a few riffs along the way, such as the sirloin medallions cooked in a sauce of red wine, raspberries and caviar. A more contemporary look to the dining area and young owners are a nice alternative to the dark, wood-panelled restaurants with grumpy waiters elsewhere.

Getting There & Away

Buses travel between La Alberca and Salamanca (€5.90, around one to 1½ hours) twice daily on weekdays and once a day on weekends.

Guijuelo

POP 5630

Guijuelo may not be Castilla y León's prettiest town (in fact, it's rather ugly), but locals couldn't care a jot because this place is one of Spain's culinary superstars. Many experts agree that Spain's best *jamón* comes from Guijuelo and the surrounding area, and there are few better places in Spain to draw near to this very Spanish, rather delicious obsession.

Sights

Museo de la Industria Chacinera MUSEUM
(Museo Guijuelo; ☎923 59 19 01; Calle Nueva 1; adult/child €2/1; ⏲10am-2pm Mon-Sat) Despite the rather functional name, this interactive museum is dedicated to *jamón* and nothing but. In the first room, videos demonstrate the production of *jamón* and the other *embutidos* (cured meats) for which Guijuelo is famous. The second room covers the special *cerdos ibéricos* (Iberian pigs) that form the centrepiece of this industry. The third and final room, which is not for the squeamish, is devoted to the ritual of *matanza* (the slaughter). Displays and videos are in Spanish only.

Tours

A handful of Guijuelo *jamón* producers offer guided visits of their factories, which is an excellent way to immerse yourself in the local obsession. There are no fixed times, so you'll need to ring or email ahead to find out when they have groups leaving. The tourist office also has a list of those offering tours, and can help in arranging your visit, though we recommend enquiring in advance – if you wait until you're in town, you may find that there are no tours that day.

★Alma de Ibérico FOOD & DRINK
(☎923 58 09 44; www.almadeiberico.com; Calle de Alfonso XIII 18; tour per person €20-30; ⏲shop 10am-7.30pm Mon-Fri, 10.30am-3.30pm Sat & Sun, tours noon Sat, other times by appointment) This local *jamón* producer offers 45-minute factory tours, where you'll be surrounded by thousands of hanging hams and get to eat a *jamón*-dominated meal at the end. Most explanations are in Spanish, but it's still a sensory marvel even if you don't understand them. Email in advance or stop by its Guijuelo shop to arrange your tour – reservations are essential.

Simón Martín FOOD & DRINK
(☎923 58 01 29; www.simonmartin.es; Calle de Filiberto Villalobos; tour per person €20-30; ⏰by appointment) This respected Guijuelo *jamón* producer offers one-hour guided visits of its factory, initiating you into the world of producing, drying, salting and everything else that goes into making *jamón*. Ring or email ahead to arrange a time.

Eating

★Alma de Ibérico JAMÓN €
(☎923 58 09 44; www.almadeiberico.com; Calle de Alfonso XIII 18; tapas from €3; ⏰10am-7.30pm Mon-Fri, 10.30am-3.30pm Sat & Sun) Part shop, part *jamón*-tasting centre, part small bar, this fine place combines many impulses in one. We especially like it for the opportunity to sample a range of cured meats, or a *ración* of its best *jamón* with a glass of fine local wine.

El Pernil Ibérico SPANISH €€
(☎923 58 14 02; Calle de Chinarral 6; tapas from €3.50, mains €12-24; ⏰9am-midnight) Spanish cooking – good and traditional – dominates here, alongside excellent *jamón* and a recommended *menú de degustación*. The tapas, too, are excellent – there's no better place to order a *ración* of Guijuelo's finest.

Shopping

Sabor Guijuelo FOOD
(☎923 58 12 87; Calle Fragua 2; ⏰10am-6.30pm) You could pick any of the shops around town selling *embutidos* (cured meats), but this excellent little place is just a stone's throw from the Plaza Mayor and the tourist office. Pick up a sliced, prepackaged *jamón ibérico de bellota en lonchas* (ham made from acorn-fed pigs) for around €10 and you'll quickly realise what all the fuss is about.

Information

Oficina de Turismo (☎923 58 04 72; www.guijuelo.es; Plaza Mayor 21; ⏰9am-3pm & 4-7pm Mon & Fri, 9am-3pm & 4-8pm Tue-Thu, 9am-2pm Sat) Signposted in the centre of town; it also has an office at the Museo de la Industria Chacinera. They have lists of which local jamón producers offer visits, and can help arrange guided tours. Check out also the useful online resource, www.saboraguijuelo.com.

Getting There & Away

Guijuelo lies just off the A66/E803, around 50km south of Salamanca, or 20km north of Béjar. A few buses each day pass through town towards Salamanca (€4.25, 30 minutes) or Béjar (€2.60, 15 minutes).

Sierra de Béjar

Between the Sierra de Francia and the Sierra de Gredos, the Sierra de Béjar is home to picturesque villages and rolling mountain scenery, normally snowcapped until well after Easter. It's an excellent region for outdoor activities, with signposted trails running off into the hills from numerous trailheads. While not far from Madrid, it's far enough not to get too overwhelmed by hikers on weekends.

Sights

The centre of the region is **Béjar**, with a partly walled, but somewhat neglected, old quarter straddling the western end of a high ridge. It's a dramatic sight if you're pulling into town from the A66.

Just east of the mountains is **El Barco de Ávila**, on the Río Tormes. It's lorded over by a proud, if ruined, castle.

The most scenic village in the region is tiny **Candelario** (population 934), a 5km detour from Béjar. Nudging against the steep foothills of the sierra, this charming village is dominated by mountain stone-and-whitewash buildings clustered closely together to protect against the harsh winter climate; note the wooden half-doors at the entrance to many homes, which are typical of the town. It's a popular summer resort and a great base for hiking.

Sleeping

★Casa de la Sal GUESTHOUSE €€
(☎923 41 30 51; www.casadelasal.com; Calle de la Fuente Perales 1, Candelario; r €75-90; 📶) Beautifully rustic and tastefully rough-hewn rooms with soothing pale colour schemes and attractive artworks make this friendly place an excellent Candelario base. The 'special' rooms have a sitting area.

Posada Puerta Grande GUESTHOUSE €€
(☎923 41 32 45; www.posadapuertagrande.com; Plaza del Humilladero 1, Candelario; r from €75; 📶) Exposed stone walls, wooden beams and tiled floors make for attractive rooms at the bottom of the hill that leads up into the old town. There's a restaurant and several other bar-restaurants nearby.

Information

Oficina de Turismo (☎923 41 30 11; Calle del Parque, Candelario; ⊙10.30am-2.30pm & 5-7pm Sat, 10.30am-2.30pm Sun) Close to the entrance of the old town at the bottom of the hill. You might find the doors open from 5pm to 7pm on Tuesday to Friday, when the local library (with which the tourist office shares premises) is open.

Getting There & Away

Béjar lies along the route between Salamanca (€6,50, 45 minutes) and Plasencia (€8, one hour), with several buses a day pulling into town off the motorway. Occasional services run to Candelario from Salamanca.

THE CENTRAL PLATEAU

There's something soul-stirring about the high *meseta* (plateau) with its seemingly endless horizon. But from the plains spring the delightful towns of the Castilian heartland – magical Segovia, energetic Valladolid, the Romanesque glories of Zamora and the exceptional cathedral of Palencia. Throw in some lovely mountain scenery in the Montaña Palentina, the chance to see wolves in the Sierra de la Culebra, and the beguiling village of Puebla de Sanabria, and you'll want to spend as much time in this region as you can.

Segovia

POP 52,257 / ELEV 1002M

Unesco World Heritage–listed Segovia has always had a whiff of legend about it, not least in the myths that the city was founded by Hercules or by the son of Noah. It may also have something to do with the fact that nowhere else in Spain is such a stunning monument to Roman grandeur (the soaring aqueduct) surviving in the heart of a vibrant modern city. Or maybe it's because art really has imitated life Segovia-style – Walt Disney is said to have modelled Sleeping Beauty's castle in California's Disneyland on Segovia's Alcázar. Whatever it is, the effect is stunning: a magical city of warm terracotta and sandstone hues set amid the rolling hills of Castilla, against the backdrop of the Sierra de Guadarrama.

Sights

★Acueducto LANDMARK

Segovia's most recognisable symbol is El Acueducto (Roman Aqueduct), an 894m-long engineering wonder that looks like an enormous comb plunged into Segovia. First raised here by the Romans in the 1st century

DON'T MISS

CASTILLA Y LEÓN'S BEST CASTLES

While Segovia's Disneyesque Alcázar and the wonderful fortified walls of Ávila (p152) may get all the attention, lonely hilltop castles are something of a regional speciality. Top choices include the following:

Coca (☎617 57 35 54; www.castillodecoca.com; Coca; guided tours €2.70; ⊙tours 10.30am-1pm & 4.30-6pm Mon-Fri, 11am-1pm & 4-6pm Sat & Sun) An all-brick, virtuoso piece of Gothic-Mudéjar architecture 50km northwest of Segovia.

Ponferrada (☎987 40 22 44; Avenida del Castillo; adult/concession €6/4, Wed free; ⊙9am-9pm daily early Jun-Sep, 10am-2pm & 4-6pm Oct-early Jun) A fortress-monastery west of León built by the Knights Templar in the 13th century.

Peñafiel (p205) One of the longest in Spain; now a wine museum.

Castillo de Gormaz (Fortaleza Califal de Gormaz; Gormaz; ⊙24hr) FREE A 10th-century, Muslim-era fortress with 21 towers; 14km south of El Burgo de Osma.

Castillo de Pedraza (p174) An unusually intact outer wall northeast of Segovia.

Turégano (☎634 46 02 15; €2; ⊙11am-2pm & 5-8pm Jul & Aug, hours vary rest of year) A unique 15th-century castle-church complex; 30km north of Segovia.

And if you prefer to track down a few of your own, why not try those in **San Felices de San Gallego** (north of Ciudad Rodrigo), **Ampudia** (southwest of Palencia), **Simancas** (southeast of Valladolid) or **Medina de Pomar** (northeast of Burgos). For these and other suggestions, pick up a copy of the booklet *turismo cultural* from any regional tourist office; it lists more than 100 castles across Castilla y León.

AD, the aqueduct was built with not a drop of mortar to hold more than 20,000 uneven granite blocks together. It's made up of 163 arches and, at its highest point in Plaza del Azoguejo, rises 28m high.

The aqueduct was originally part of a complex system of aqueducts and underground canals that brought water from the mountains more than 15km away. Its pristine condition is attributable to a major restoration project in the 1990s. For a different perspective, climb the stairs next to the aqueduct that begin behind the tourist office.

★Catedral CATHEDRAL

(☎921 46 22 05; www.turismodesegovia.com; Plaza Mayor; adult/concession €3/2, Sun morning free, tower tour €5; ⏲9am-9pm Mon-Sat, 1.15-9pm Sun Apr-Oct, 9.30am-5.30pm Mon-Sat, 1.15-5.30pm Sun Nov-Mar, tower tours 10.30pm & 12.30pm year-round, plus 4.30pm Apr-Oct, 4pm Nov-Mar) Started in 1525 on the site of a former chapel, Segovia's cathedral is a powerful expression of Gothic architecture that took almost 200 years to complete. The austere three-nave interior is anchored by an imposing choir stall and enlivened by 20-odd chapels, including the **Capilla del Cristo del Consuelo**, with its magnificent Romanesque doorway, and the **Capilla de la Piedad**, containing an important altarpiece by Juan de Juni. Join an hour-long guided tour to climb the tower for fabulous views.

★Alcázar CASTLE

(☎921 46 07 59; www.alcazardesegovia.com; Plaza de la Reina Victoria Eugenia; adult/concession/child under 6yr €5.50/5/free, tower €2.50, audio guides €3; ⏲10am-6.30pm Oct-Mar, to 7.30pm Apr-Sep; 👪) Rapunzel towers, turrets topped with slate witches' hats and a deep moat at its base make the Alcázar a prototype fairy-tale castle – so much so that its design inspired Walt Disney's vision of Sleeping Beauty's castle. Fortified since Roman days, the site takes its name from the Arabic *al-qasr* (fortress). It was rebuilt in the 13th and 14th centuries, but the whole lot burned down in 1862. What you see today is an evocative, over-the-top reconstruction of the original.

Highlights include the **Sala de las Piñas**, with its ceiling of 392 pineapple-shaped 'stalactites', and the **Sala de Reyes**, featuring a three-dimensional frieze of 52 sculptures of kings who fought during the Reconquista. The views from the summit of the Torre de Juan II, which was restored in 2016, are truly exceptional.

DON'T MISS

BEST VIEW OF TOWN

For *the* shot of Segovia for your computer wallpaper, head out of town due north (towards Cuéllar) for around 2km. The view of the city unfolds in all its movie-style magic, with the aqueduct taking a deserved star role.

Plaza Mayor SQUARE

The shady Plaza Mayor is the nerve centre of old Segovia, lined by an eclectic assortment of buildings, arcades and cafes and with an open pavilion in its centre. It's also the site of the *catedral* and the regional tourist office (p173).

Museo Gastronómico MUSEUM

(☎921 46 01 47; www.museogastronomicodesegovia.es; Calle de Daoiz 9; €1, with tasting €3; ⏲11am-3pm Mon-Fri, 11am-8pm Sat & Sun Apr–mid-Oct, 11am-3pm Mon-Fri, 11am-7pm Sat & Sun mid-Oct–Mar) This engaging little private museum takes you through the wonderful world of Spanish foods, with a focus on those from the Segovia region. There are sections on local cheeses, wines, cured meats, *ponche segoviano* and even a section on the local whisky, DYC. There are some good video displays (mostly in Spanish), though most sections of the museum have English summaries alongside the main text.

Centro Didáctico de la Judería MUSEUM

(☎921 46 23 96; www.juderia.tursimodesegovia.com; Calle de la Judería Vieja 12; €2, free Wed; ⏲10am-2pm Mon & Tue, 10am-2pm & 3-6pm Wed & Fri, 10am-1pm & 3-6pm Thu & Sat, 10am-1pm Sun, guided tours 1pm Thu, Sat & Sun) This interpretation centre and museum provides a fascinating history of the Jewish community in Segovia. It occupies the former 15th-century home of one of the community's most important members, Abraham Seneor. The adjacent **Iglesia de Corpus Cristi** occupies the site of Segovia's ancient synagogue.

Monasterio de Santa María del Parral MONASTERY

(☎921 43 12 98; Calle Del Marqués de Villena; by donation; ⏲11am & 5pm Wed-Sun) Ring the bell to see part of the cloister and church; the latter is a proud, flamboyant Gothic structure. The monks chant a Gregorian Mass at noon on Sundays, and at 1pm daily in summer.

Segovia

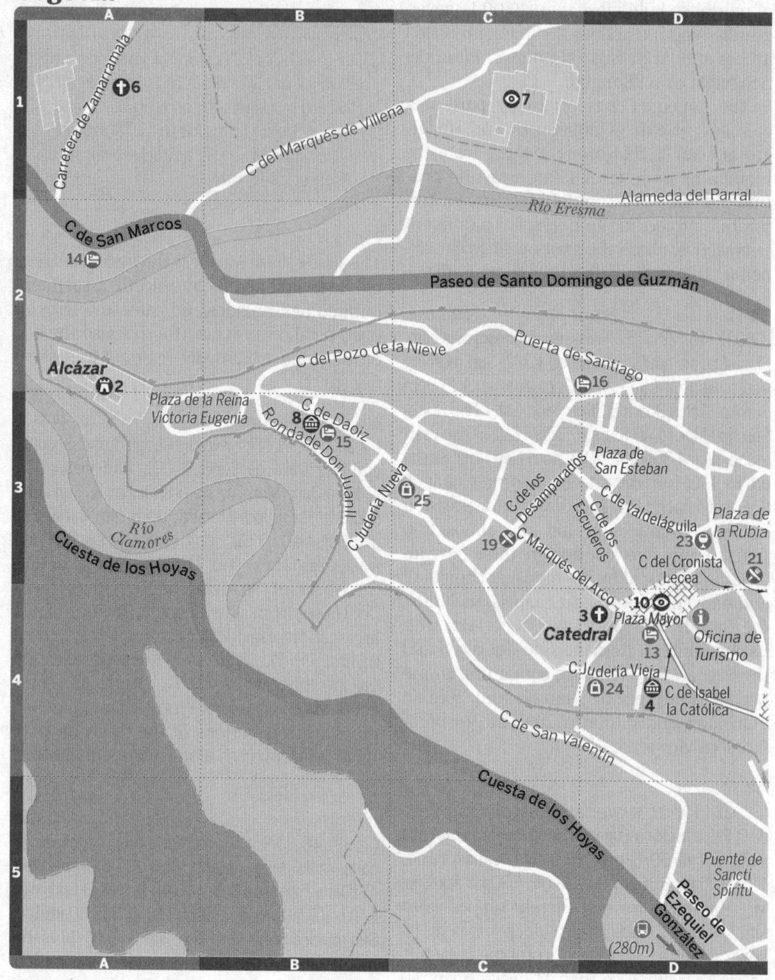

Iglesia de Vera Cruz
CHURCH

(921 43 14 75; Carretera de Zamarramala; €2; 10.30am-1.30pm & 4-7pm Tue-Sun Apr-Sep, 4-6pm Tue, 10.30am-1.30pm & 4-6pm Wed-Sun Oct-Mar) This 12-sided church is one of the best preserved of its kind in Europe. Built in the early 13th century by the Knights Templar and based on Jerusalem's Church of the Holy Sepulchre, it once housed a piece of the Vera Cruz (True Cross), which now rests in the nearby village church of Zamarramala (on view only at Easter). The curious two-storey chamber in the circular nave (the inner temple) is where the knights' secret rites took place.

Plaza de San Martín
SQUARE

This is one of the most captivating small plazas in Segovia. The square is presided over by a statue of Juan Bravo; the 14th-century **Torreón de Lozoya** (921 46 24 61; Plaza de San Martín 5; 5-9pm Tue-Fri, noon-2pm & 5-9pm Sat & Sun) FREE, a tower that now houses exhibitions; and the **Iglesia de San Martín** (before & after Mass), a Romanesque jewel with a Mudéjar tower and arched gallery.

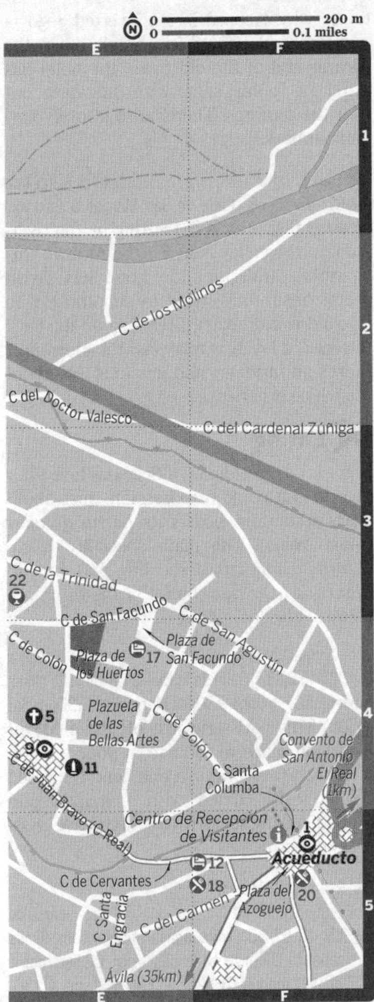

Segovia

Top Sights
1 Acueducto F5
2 Alcázar A2
3 Catedral D4

Sights
4 Centro Didáctico de la Judería D4
5 Iglesia de San Martín E4
6 Iglesia de Vera Cruz A1
7 Monasterio de Santa María del Parral C1
8 Museo Gastronómico B3
9 Plaza de San Martín E4
10 Plaza Mayor D4
11 Torreón de Lozoya E4

Sleeping
12 Häb Urban Hostel F5
13 Hospedería La Gran Casa Mudéjar D4
14 Hotel Alcázar A2
15 Hotel Don Felipe B3
16 Hotel Exe Casa de Los Linajes D2
17 Hotel Palacio San Facundo E4

Eating
18 Casa Duque F5
19 La Almuzara C3
Limón y Menta .... (see 13)
20 Mesón de Cándido F5
21 Mesón José María D3
Restaurante El Fogón Sefardí .... (see 13)

Drinking & Nightlife
22 Canavan's Theatre E3
23 La Tasquina D3

Shopping
24 Artesanía La Gárgola D4
25 Montón de Trigo Montón de Paja C3

Festivals & Events

Titirimundi International Puppet Festival THEATRE
(www.titirimundi.es; mid-May;) A week-long festival in mid-May that celebrates puppetry and puppet theatre with shows and street events throughout the city.

Fiestas de San Juan y San Pedro RELIGIOUS
(24-29 Jun;) On San Juan's day (29 June), a pilgrimage takes place to a hermitage outside town. Throughout the six days of festivities, there are parades, concerts and bullfights.

Sleeping

Hotel Exe Casa de Los Linajes HOTEL €
(921 41 48 10; www.exehotels.com; Calle del Doctor Valesco 9; r €44-78;) A recent makeover has made this excellent place even better. The rooms here are large and filled with character and contemporary style, with old-world charm filling the public areas. All rooms look out onto the hills; many also have cathedral and/or Alcázar views.

SWEET TREATS

If you are one of those people who scoffs all the marzipan off the Christmas cake, you will love Segovia's speciality: *ponche segoviano* (literally 'Segovian punch'). It's far removed from that insipid, low-alcohol drink you used to consume as a spotty teenager – this is a rich, lemon-infused sponge cake coated with marzipan and topped with icing sugar in a distinctive criss-cross pattern. A good place to indulge in your *ponche* passion is the patisserie Limón y Menta, just off Plaza Mayor.

Häb Urban Hostel HOSTAL €

(☎921 46 10 26; www.habhostel.com; Calle de Cervantes 16; r €50-80; ❄📶) This bright and welcoming *hostal* has doubles with private bathrooms rather than dorms with bunk beds, despite the name. It is modern and has a fine location just where the pedestrian street begins the climb up into the old town. Some rooms are on the small side, but the look is light and contemporary.

★Hotel Palacio San Facundo HISTORIC HOTEL €€

(☎921 46 30 61; www.hotelpalaciosanfacundo.com; Plaza San Facundo 4; s/d incl breakfast €95/130; ❄@📶) Segovia's hotels are proving adept at fusing stylishly appointed modern rooms with centuries-old architecture. This place is one of the best, with an attractive columned courtyard, a warm colour scheme, chic room decor and a central location. The breakfast buffet is more generous than most.

★Hospedería La Gran Casa Mudéjar HISTORIC HOTEL €€

(☎921 46 62 50; www.lacasamudejar.com; Calle de Isabel la Católica 8; r €55-105; ❄@📶) Spread over two buildings, this place has been magnificently renovated, blending genuine 15th-century Mudéjar carved wooden ceilings in some rooms with modern amenities. In the newer wing, top-floor rooms have fine mountain views out over the rooftops of Segovia's old Jewish quarter. Adding to the appeal is a small spa. The restaurant comes highly recommended.

Hotel Don Felipe HISTORIC HOTEL €€

(☎921 46 60 95; www.hoteldonfelipe.es; Calle de Daoiz 7; s €55-75, d €60-110) This place gets rave reviews from travellers and it's not difficult to see why. Housed in a converted Segovia mansion and one of few hotels down the Álcazar end of the old town, the hotel has attractive rooms, some with fine views out over the rooftops. There's also a lovely garden out back.

★Hotel Alcázar BOUTIQUE HOTEL €€€

(☎921 43 85 68; Calle de San Marcos 5; s/d incl breakfast €145/190; ❄📶) Sitting by the riverbank in the valley beneath the Alcázar, this charming, tranquil little hotel has lavish rooms beautifully styled to suit those who love old-world luxury. Breakfast on the back terrace is a lovely way to pass the morning – there's an intimacy and graciousness about the whole experience.

Eating

Segovianos (residents of Segovia) love their pigs to the point of obsession. Just about every restaurant boasts its *horno de asar* (roast ovens). The main speciality is *cochinillo asado* (roast suckling pig), but *judiones de la granja* (butter beans with pork chunks) also loom large.

Limón y Menta BAKERY €

(☎921 46 22 57; Calle de Isabel la Católica 2; cakes from €2.50; ⏲9am-9.30pm Mon-Fri, to 8.30pm Sat & Sun) This patisserie just off Plaza Mayor is a good place to indulge in your passion for *ponche segoviano*, a rich, lemon-infused sponge cake coated with marzipan and topped in icing sugar with a distinctive criss-cross pattern.

★Restaurante El Fogón Sefardí JEWISH €€

(☎921 46 62 50; www.lacasamudejar.com; Calle de Isabel la Católica 8; tapas from €2.50, mains €12-26, set menus €19-25; ⏲1.30-4.30pm & 7.30-11.30pm) Located within the Hospedería La Gran Casa Mudéjar, this is one of the most original places in town. Sephardic Jewish cuisine is served either on the intimate patio or in the splendid dining hall with original 15th-century Mudéjar flourishes. The theme in the bar is equally diverse. Stop here for a taste of the award-winning tapas. Reservations recommended.

★Mesón José María CASTILIAN €€

(☎921 46 11 11; www.restaurantejosemaria.com; Calle del Cronista Lecea 11; mains €14-26; ⏲restaurant 1-4pm & 8-11.30pm, bar 9am-1am Sun-Thu, 10am-2am Fri & Sat; 👪) Offers fine bar tapas and five dining rooms serving exquisite co-

chinillo asado and other local specialities – most of which, including the suckling pig, are displayed in the window. The bar is standing-room only at lunchtime.

La Almuzara ITALIAN €€
(☎921 46 06 22; Calle Marqués del Arco 3; mains €7-16; ⏰12.30-4pm & 8pm-midnight Wed-Sun, 8.30pm-midnight Tue;) If you're a vegetarian, you don't need to feel like an outcast in this resolutely carnivorous city. La Almuzara offers a dedicated vegetarian menu, as well as pizzas, pastas and 17 innovative salads. They're not too pious to scrimp on desserts either, with some decadent choices changing daily. The ambience is warm and artsy.

Mesón de Cándido GRILL €€
(☎921 42 81 03; www.mesondecandido.es; Plaza del Azoguejo 5; mains €12-26) Set in a delightful 18th-century building in the shadow of the aqueduct, Mesón de Cándido is famous for its *cochinillo asado* (roast suckling pig) and dishes such as pheasant. Reservations recommended.

★**Casa Duque** SPANISH €€€
(☎921 46 24 87; www.restauranteduque.es; Calle de Cervantes 12; mains €19.50-24, set menus €35-40; ⏰12.30-4.30pm & 8.30-11.30pm) *Cochinillo asado* (roast suckling pig) has been served at this atmospheric *mesón* (tavern) since the 1890s. For the uninitiated, try the *menú de degustación* (€40), which includes *cochinillo*. Downstairs is the informal *cueva* (cave), where you can get tapas (snacks) and full-bodied *cazuelas* (stews). Reservations recommended.

Drinking & Nightlife

Canavan's Theatre CLUB
(☎921 46 02 52; www.facebook.com/canavanstheatre/; Plaza de la Rubia; ⏰midnight-6.30am Thu-Sat) This is no cheesy disco – the decor is sumptuous with exquisite friezes, flocked wallpaper, chandeliers and an overall extravagant theatrical feel. It's over the top, just like a big night out should be.

La Tasquina WINE BAR
(☎921 46 39 14; Calle de Valdeláguila 3; ⏰9pm-late) This wine bar draws crowds large enough to spill out onto the pavement, nursing their good wines, *cavas* (sparkling wines) and cheeses.

Shopping

Montón de Trigo Montón de Paja ACCESSORIES, SOUVENIRS
(☎921 46 07 69; www.montondetrigomontondepaja.com; Plaza de la Merced 1; ⏰11.30am-2pm & 3.30-7.30pm Mon-Fri, 11am-2.30pm & 4-7.30pm Sat & Sun, longer hours in summer) With handcrafted handbags, jewellery, block-prints of Segovia and a host of other artsy, locally made items, this shop is ideal for creative gifts.

Artesanía La Gárgola ARTS & CRAFTS
(☎921 46 31 84; www.gargolart.com; Calle de la Judería Vieja 4; ⏰10am-8pm Mon-Sat Jul & Aug, 11.30am-2.30pm & 5-8pm Tue-Sat Sep-Jun) Check out these unusual, high-quality handmade crafts and souvenirs in ceramic, wood and textile.

Information

Centro de Recepción de Visitantes (☎921 46 67 21; www.turismodesegovia.com; Plaza del Azoguejo 1; ⏰10am-8pm Mon-Sat, to 7pm Sun Apr-Sep, 10am-6.30pm Mon-Sat, to 5pm Sun Oct-Mar) Segovia's main tourist office runs at least two guided tours of the city's monumental core daily (€10 to €17 per person), usually departing at 11am and 4pm (although check as this schedule can change). Reserve ahead.

Oficina de Turismo (☎921 46 60 70; www.segoviaturismo.es; Plaza Mayor 10; ⏰9.30am-2pm & 5-8pm Mon-Sat, 9.30am-5pm Sun Jul–mid-Sep, 9.30am-2pm & 4-7pm Mon-Sat, 9.30am-5pm Sun mid-Sep–Jun) Information on the wider region.

Getting There & Away

Bus The bus station is just off Paseo de Ezequiel González. **La Sepulvedana** (☎902 119699; www.lasepulvedana.es) buses run half-hourly to Segovia from Madrid's Paseo de la Florida bus stop (€7.89, 1½ hours). Buses also depart to Ávila (€6.80, one hour, eight daily) and Salamanca (€16, 2½ hours, four daily), among other destinations.

Car & Motorcycle Of the two main roads down to the AP6, which links Madrid and Galicia, the N603 is the prettier.

Train There are a couple of services by train operated by **Renfe** (☎902 240202; www.renfe.es): just three normal trains run daily from Madrid to Segovia (€8.25, two hours), leaving you at the main train station 2.5km from the aqueduct. The faster option is the high-speed Avant (€12.90, 28 minutes), which deposits you at the newer Segovia-Guiomar station, 5km from the aqueduct.

DON'T MISS

A SPANISH VERSAILLES

The magnificent, elaborate baroque gardens of **La Granja de San Ildefonso** (www.patrimonionacional.es; Sierra de Guadarrama; gardens free, Palacio Real adult/child €9/4, fountains €4, free for EU citizens 3-6pm Oct-Mar & 5-8pm Apr-Sep; ⌚10am-8pm Tue-Sun Apr-Sep, 10am-6pm Tue-Sun Oct-Mar; P 👪), famous for their 28 extravagant fountains depicting ancient myths, date from 1720, when French architects and gardeners, together with some Italian help, began laying them out. There's also a maze. The 300-room **Palacio Real**, once a favoured summer residence for Spanish royalty and restored after a fire in 1918, is similarly impressive; it includes the colourful **Museo de Tapices** (Tapestry Museum).

The palace was built for the Bourbon King Felipe V, who chose this site in the western foothills of the Sierra de Guadarrama to recreate in miniature his version of Versailles, the palace of his French grandfather, Louis XIV. If you time your visit for Wednesday, Saturday or Sunday at 5.30pm you can see the **fountains** in action.

Up to a dozen daily buses to La Granja depart regularly from Segovia's bus station (€2.20, 20 minutes).

Getting Around

Bus 9 does a circuit through the historic centre, bus 8 goes to Segovia train station and bus 11 goes to Segovia-Guiomar station. All services cost €1.30 and leave from just outside the aqueduct.

Around Segovia

Pedraza de la Sierra

POP 414

The captivating walled village of Pedraza de la Sierra, about 37km northeast of Segovia, is eerily quiet during the week; its considerable number of restaurants, bars and eclectic shops spring to life with the swarms of weekend visitors. It's a gorgeous place – one of the prettiest villages in this part of the country.

Sights

Plaza Mayor SQUARE

The evocative 14th-century Plaza Mayor is noteworthy for its ancient columned arcades. There are so many fine angles to get the perfect photo, but only one perfect time: the buildings turn the colour of honey an hour or two before sunset.

Castillo de Pedraza CASTLE

(Castillo de Ignazio Zuluaga; ☎607 66 16 18; Plaza del Castillo; adult/concession €6/4; ⌚10am-2pm & 5-8pm Wed-Sun mid-Apr–Oct, 11am-2pm & 4-7pm Wed-Sun Oct–mid-Apr) At the far (northwestern) end of town – go any further and you'll fall into the valley – stands the lonely Castillo de Pedraza, unusual for its intact outer wall. Begun in the 13th century, it sits atop far older fortifications.

Festivals & Events

Concierto de las Velas MUSIC

(☎921 50 99 60; www.pedraza.net/concierto-de-las-velas/; admission free, concerts €49-79; ⌚Jul) On the first and second Sunday in July, Pedraza hosts the atmospheric Concierto de las Velas and has done since 1993 – the electricity is shut down and live classical music is performed in a village lit only by candles. It's free to come here to see the town lit with candles – and is worth doing so – but the actual concerts cost extra.

Sleeping

★ **Hospedería de Santo Domingo** INN €€

(☎921 50 99 71; www.hospederiadesantodomingo.com; Calle Matadero 3; s €85-110, d €95-130, ste €110-155; ❄📶) This excellent *hospedería* (inn) has terrific rooms decked out in warm ochre and earth colours. Most have large terraces overlooking the low hills nearby, criss-crossed with drystone walls. Prices rise considerably on weekends.

El Hotel de la Villa HOTEL €€

(☎921 50 86 51; www.elhoteldelavilla.com; Calle de Calzada 5; s/d from €80/110; 📶) An astonishing breadth of rooms at this excellent place range from tiled floors, wooden beams and wrought-iron furnishings to frilly four-poster beds, floorboards and bright colours. Whichever one you choose, rest assured that the quality is high and the service excellent.

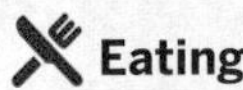

Eating

El Yantar de Pedraza SPANISH €€

(☎921 50 98 42; www.elyantardepedraza.com; Plaza Mayor; mains €12-23; ⏲1-4.30pm Wed-Sun) With a lovely setting overlooking Plaza Mayor from its upstairs balcony, El Yantar does near-perfect *cordero asado* (roast lamb) and *cochinillo* (roast suckling pig) and the many repeat customers tell us all we need to know about the quality. Its set menus are excellent value, but other menu highlights include the light salads, the home-made *croquetas* (croquettes) and local sheep's cheese.

El Soportal SPANISH €€

(☎921 50 98 26; www.restaurantesdepedraza.com; Plaza Mayor 3; mains €10-18, degustation menu from €30; ⏲1-4pm & 9-11.30pm Thu-Tue, 1-4pm Wed) Found behind the porticoes of a fine 16th-century Pedraza townhouse, El Soportal is one of Pedraza's most popular choices for *cordero asado* (roast lamb). Also popular is the bar, which stays open throughout the day (don't expect the restaurant to be open weeknights, despite official hours); a few small wooden tables sit out on the square. Bookings essential on weekends.

La Olma de Pedraza SPANISH €€

(☎921 50 99 81; www.laolma.com; Plaza del Álamo 1; mains €12-23; ⏲1.30-4pm Sun-Thu, 1.30-4pm & 9-11pm Fri & Sat) On a small square just west of Plaza Mayor, this lovely place feels every bit like the rural bastion of traditional cooking that it is, with warm service to match. Besides the usual, perfectly cooked roasted meats, try its *croquetas de setas* (wild mushroom croquettes); otherwise just let staff choose the dishes that play to its strengths.

Information

Oficina de Turismo (☎921 50 86 66; www.pedraza.info; Calle Real 3; ⏲4-7.30pm Tue, 11am-1.30pm & 3.30-7.30pm Mon-Fri, 11am-2pm & 3.30-8pm Sat & Sun) Runs Spanish-language **guided tours** (per person €3) of the town at 12.30pm and 5pm (daily except Mondays), if there are enough people.

Getting There & Away

Bus services to Pedraza are sporadic at best, with just a couple of weekly services from Segovia. Pedraza is just north of the N110.

Valladolid

POP 301,876

Valladolid is a lively provincial Spanish city and a convenient gateway to northern Spain. An attractive place with a very Spanish character, the city's appeal is in its striking monuments, the fine Plaza Mayor and some excellent museums. By night, Valladolid comes alive as its large student population overflows from the city's boisterous bars.

Sights

★Museo Nacional de Escultura MUSEUM

(☎983 25 03 75; www.mecd.gob.es/mnescultura/inicio.html; Calle de San Gregorio 2; adult/concession €3/1.50, Sun & 4-7.30pm Sat free; ⏲10am-2pm & 4-7.30pm Tue-Sat, 10am-2pm Sun) Spain's premier showcase of polychrome wood sculpture is housed in the former **Colegio de San Gregorio** (1496), a flamboyant Isabelline Gothic–style building where exhibition rooms line an exquisite, two-storey galleried courtyard. Works by Alonso de Berruguete, Juan de Juní and Gregorio Fernández are the star attractions. Don't miss Fernández' painfully realistic sculpture of the dead Christ in Room 15 or the choir stalls in Room 8. And don't forget to look up – some of the ceilings are extraordinary.

★Casa-Museo de Colón MUSEUM

(☎983 29 13 53; Calle de Colón; adult/child €2/free, Wed adult €1; ⏲10am-2pm & 5-8.30pm Tue-Sun; 👪) The Casa-Museo de Colón is a superb museum spread over four floors. It has interactive exhibits, as well as wonderful old maps that take you on a journey through Christopher Columbus' (Cristóbal Colón in Spanish) trips to the Americas. The top floor describes Valladolid in the days of the great explorer (who died here in 1506).

★Plaza de San Pablo SQUARE

This open square is dominated by the exquisite **Iglesia de San Pablo** (☎983 351 748; ⏲7.30am-1.30pm & 7-9.30pm Mon-Sat, 8am-2pm & 6-9.30pm Sun), which has one of northern Spain's most extraordinary church facades. Also here is the **Palacio de Pimentel** (⏲10am-2pm & 5-7pm Tue-Sat) FREE, the birthplace of Felipe II.

Catedral CATHEDRAL

(☎983 30 43 62; Calle Arribas 1; adult/concession €3/1.50; ⏲10am-1.30pm & 4.30-7pm Tue-Fri, 10am-2pm Sat, 11.45am-1.30pm Sun, tours every

Valladolid

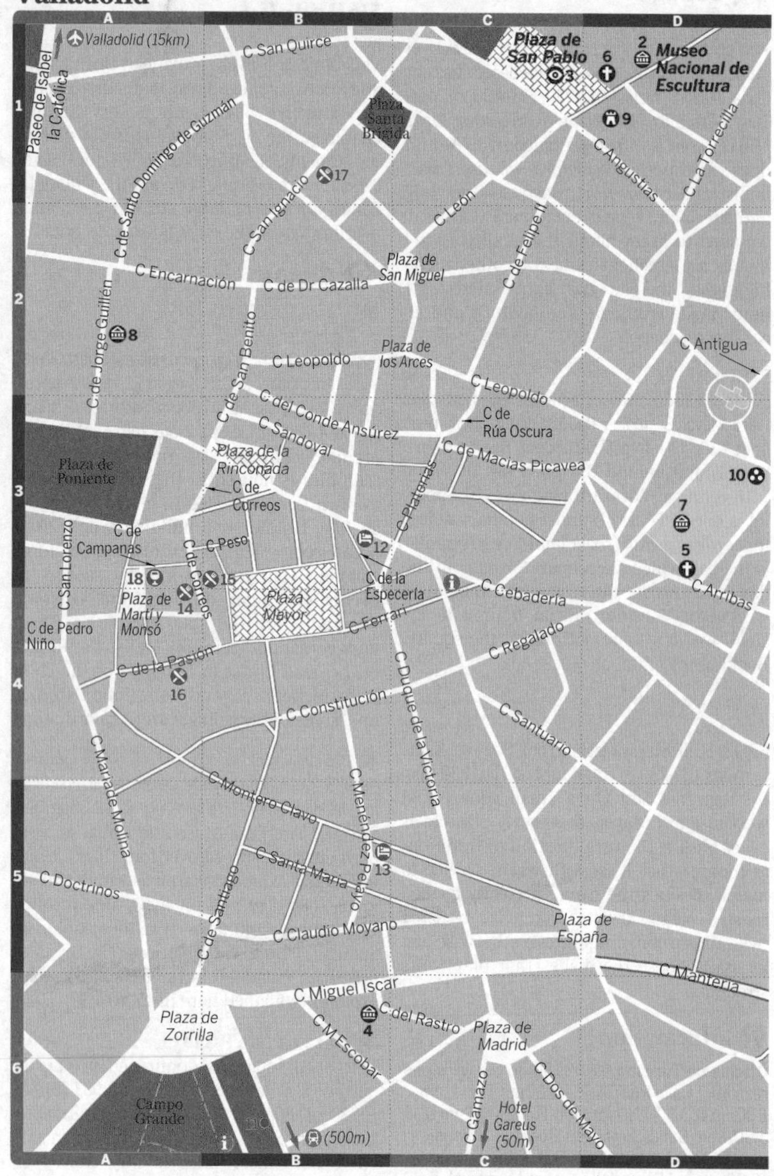

45min) Valladolid's 16th-century cathedral is not Castilla's finest, but it does have an extravagant altarpiece by Juan de Juní and a processional monstrance by Juan de Arfe in the attached **Museo Diocesano y Catedralicio** (Calle Arribas 1; adult/concession €3/1.50; ⌚10am-1.30pm & 4.30-7pm Tue-Fri, 10am-2pm Sat, 11.45am-1.30pm Sun). Guided tours (adult/concession €5/4) of the cathedral and bell tower last 45 minutes and the views are fabulous; combined with a guided visit to the museum (adult/concession €8/6) it takes two hours.

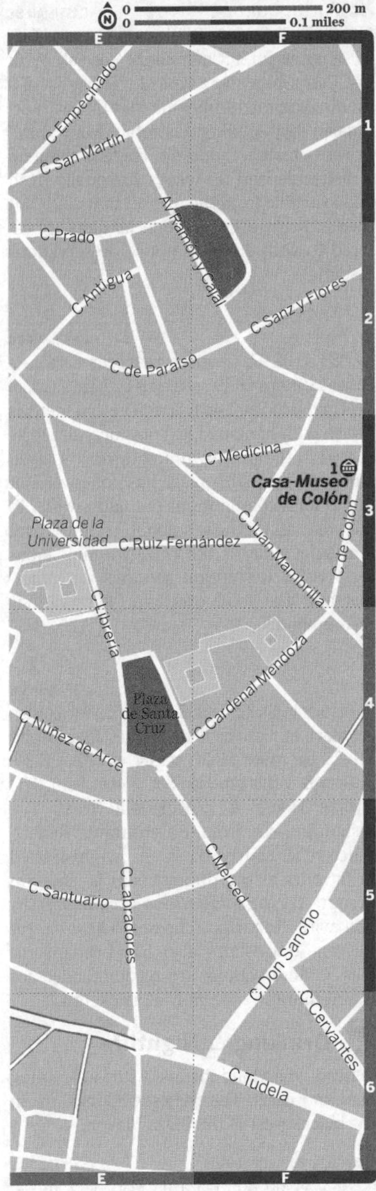

(You can visit the cathedral and museum on your own, but not the tower.)

The 13th-century **ruins of the Collegiate Church** (Calle del Arzobispo Gandásegui), atop which the cathedral was built, can be seen along the cathedral's northeastern perimeter.

Valladolid

Top Sights

Sights

Activities, Courses & Tours

Sleeping

Eating

Drinking & Nightlife

Casa de Cervantes MUSEUM

(983 30 88 10; www.mecd.gob.es/museocasacervantes; Calle del Rastro; adult/child under 12yr €3/free, Sun free; 9.30am-3pm Tue-Sat, 10am-3pm Sun) Cervantes was briefly imprisoned in Valladolid; his house is happily preserved behind a quiet little garden. You can purchase a combined adult ticket that also admits you to the Museo Nacional de Escultura (p175) for €5.

Museo Patio Herreriano GALLERY

(983 36 29 08; www.museopatioherreriano.org; Calle de Jorge Guillén 6; adult/child €3/2, Wed €1; 11am-2pm & 5-8pm Tue-Fri, 11am-8pm Sat, 11am-3pm Sun) FREE Dedicated to post-WWI Spanish art, this surprising museum contains works by Salvador Dalí, Joan Miró, Basque sculptor Eduardo Chillida, Jorge Oteiza, Antoni Tápies and Esteban Vicente, all arrayed around the cloisters of a former monastery.

Sleeping

★Hotel Mozart HOTEL €

(983 29 77 77; www.hotelmozart.net; Calle Menéndez Pelayo 7; s/d €58/69;) This is an extremely well-priced hotel, given the quality of its refurbished rooms and the

VALLADOLID CARD

A terrific way to save your euros, the **Valladolid Card** (www.valladolid.com/valladolid-card; adult/child €7/5) allows free access to a number of museums – including the Museo Nacional de Escultura, Casa-Museo de Colón, Museo Patio Herreriano and the Catedral and its museum – plus free travel on the **Bus Turístico de Valladolid** (983 33 03 59; www.auvasa.es/auv_busturistico.asp; Acera de Recoletos; adult/child €7/5; hourly 5-7pm Fri, noon-1pm & 5-7pm Sat & Sun Apr-Sep, hourly 5-6pm Fri, noon-1pm & 5-6pm Sat & Sun Oct-Mar) over a 24-hour period. The card can be purchased at either of the two tourist offices.

location. Here you'll find king-size beds, plush, earth-colour furnishings and fabrics, polished parquet floors, dazzling marble bathrooms and space enough for a comfortable armchair. The entrance has a whiff of grandeur about it as well – which contributes to the surprise of the budget-bracket price.

Hostal París HOSTAL €

(983 37 06 25; www.hostalparis.com; Calle de la Especería 2; s/d from €50/55;) One of the closest places to Plaza Mayor, Hostal París has clearly had the interior designers in. Washed in pale pastel colours with striking abstract art panels, good-size desks and flatscreen TVs, the rooms successfully combine comfort with a classy feel and budget prices.

★Hotel Gareus BOUTIQUE HOTEL €€

(983 21 43 33; www.hotelgareus.com; Calle de Colmenares 2; r from €75;) Polished floorboards, warm colours and creative lighting make these rooms some of the best in Valladolid. The service is similarly warm and welcoming and the place has a quiet sophistication. The location, just a 10-minute walk from the Plaza Mayor, is also excellent.

Eating

El Corcho TAPAS €

(Calle de Correos 2; tostas from €1.75, set menu €18; 1-4pm & 8-11.30pm) This spit-and-sawdust place, located on the city's top street for tapas bars, wins the prize of public opinion for its excellent selection of *tostas* (toasts) with tasty toppings.

★Martín Quiroga CASTILIAN €€

(605 78 71 17; Calle San Ignacio 17; mains €15-21; noon-4pm & 8pm-midnight Mon-Sat) With just four tables and a typical waiting list of a month, you might imagine that this extraordinarily high-quality gastrobar would have prices to match. It doesn't. There is no menu – dishes depend on what's seasonally fresh and available from the market that day – but there's plenty of choice. Special diets are catered to with advance notice. Reservations essential.

Los Zagales de Abadía CASTILIAN €€

(983 38 08 92; www.loszagales.com; Calle de la Pasión 13; mains €9-19, set menus €25-35; 1-4pm & 7-11pm Mon-Sat, 1-4pm Sun) The bar here is awash with hanging local produce, all represented in the prize-winning tapas displayed along the bar – this place has done well not just at local competitions but nationwide. To see what all the fuss is about, try the Menú Maridaje: nine of the prize-winning tapas for €34.95. Restaurant servings are generous and the food excellent. Reservations recommended.

El Caballo de Troya SPANISH €€

(Restaurante Santi; 983 33 93 55; www.restaurantesanti.es; Calle de Correos 1; restaurant mains €18-25, bar mains €8-22, set menu €25; 1.30-3.30pm & 9-11.30pm Mon-Sat, 2-4pm Sun) The 'Trojan Horse' is a Valladolid treat. The restaurant, set around a stunning, Renaissance-style courtyard, is as sophisticated in flavours as the dining room is classy in design – try the *solomillo con roquefort* (sirloin with Roquefort cheese). The *taberna* (tavern) downstairs also has brilliant *raciones*. Reservations are recommended for the restaurant, especially at weekends.

Drinking & Nightlife

Central Valladolid brims with welcoming bars and cafes. The richest pickings are in the blocks west of the Plaza Mayor.

Café de la Comedia COCKTAIL BAR

(983 34 00 80; Plaza de Martí y Monsó 4; 3.30pm-late) Decor here is suitably comedic, with Laurel and Hardy on the screen and Chaplin pics (and similar) decorating the walls. It's a reliable, popular choice that goes beyond fads and serves good cocktails and wines by the glass.

Information

Oficina de Turismo (983 21 93 10; www.info.valladolid.es; Acera de Recoletos; 9.30am-2pm & 5-8pm Mon-Sat, 9.30am-3pm Sun Jul–mid-Sep, 9.30am-2pm & 4-7pm Mon-Sat, 9.30am-3pm Sun mid-Sep–Jun)

Oficina de Turismo (983 33 08 93; www.info.valladolid.es; Plaza de Fuente Dorada; 11am-1.30pm & 5-7pm Tue-Sat, 11am-1.30pm Sun)

Getting There & Away

Air Ryanair (www.ryanair.com) and Vueling (www.vueling.com) have flights to Barcelona.

Train More than a dozen daily high-speed AVE train services connect Valladolid with Madrid (from €23.30, one hour); there are also slower services (three hours) for €19.30. Other regular trains run to León (from €16.40, 1¼ to two hours), Burgos (from €6.85, about 1½ hours) and Salamanca (from €8.35, 1½ hours).

Getting Around

Air Valladolid's **airport** (983 41 55 00; www.aena.es/es/aeropuerto-valladolid/index.html; Carretera Adanero-Gijón) is 10km northwest of the city centre. **Linecar** (www.linecar.es) has up to five daily bus services from Valladolid to the airport (one-way/return €3.50/5.50). A taxi between the airport and the city centre costs €23/25 by day/night.

Bus Local buses 2 and 10 pass the train and bus stations on their way to Plaza de España.

Around Valladolid

Medina de Rioseco

POP 4803

Medina de Rioseco is something of a faded jewel. This once-wealthy trading centre still has a tangible medieval feel, although, given the number of boarded-up frontages across town, it's sadly much poorer these days. Head for Calle Mayor, with its colonnaded arcades held up by ancient wooden columns; market stalls set up here on Wednesday mornings.

Sights

Iglesia de Santa María de Mediavilla CHURCH
(Calle de Santa María; guided tours €2; 11am-noon & 4-7pm Tue-Sun mid-Mar–Oct, shorter hours rest of year) This grandiose Isabelline Gothic work has three star-vaulted naves and the rightfully famous **Capilla de los Benavente** chapel. Anchored by an extravagant altarpiece by Juan de Juní and carved over eight years from 1543, it's sometimes referred to as the 'Sistine Chapel of Castilla' – it's certainly one of Spain's finest examples of Renaissance-era religious art. Tours in Spanish.

Museo de San Francisco CHURCH, MUSEUM
(983 70 00 20; www.museosanfrancisco.es; Paseo de San Francisco 1; adult/child €3/1; guided tours 11am-2pm & 5-8pm Tue-Sun May-Aug, 11am-2pm & 4-7pm Tue-Sun Sep-Apr) This 16th-century former convent has an extravagant *retablo* (altarpiece) by Fray Jacinto de Sierra, as well as a wide-ranging collection of sacred art. Tours in Spanish.

Museo de Semana Santa MUSEUM
(Calle de Lázaro Alonso; adult/concession/child €3.50/2.50/1; 11am-2pm & 5-8pm Tue-Sun mid-Jun–mid-Sep, shorter hours rest of year) Medina de Rioseco is famous for its Easter processions, but if you can't be here during Holy Week, this museum provides an insight into the ceremonial passion of Easter here. Like its sister museum in Zamora (p182), it's dedicated to *pasos* (floats carried in Semana Santa processions) and an extensive range of other Easter artefacts.

Sleeping & Eating

Vittoria Colonna HOTEL €
(983 72 50 87; www.hotelvittoriacolonna.es; Calle de San Juan 2B; s/d/ste €35/58/79;) This modern three-star hotel, with its raspberry-pink frontage, offers well-sized and well-appointed rooms a short walk from all of Medina de Rioseco's sights. Some rooms are nicer than others, but all have smart grey-and-white bathrooms.

Casa Manolo CASTILIAN €€
(676 28 98 45; Calle de Las Armas 4; mains €9-14; 8am-midnight Fri-Wed) The best of a clutch of restaurants on this side street in the historic centre. The courtyard provides a pleasant setting for enjoying reliably good, hearty Castilian dishes.

COMBINED TICKETS

If you plan on visiting all four of Medina de Rioseco's main sights, consider buying the combined ticket for €7/5 for adults/seniors. It can be purchased at any of the four sights and will save you €3.50. Note that between April and September this combined ticket can be purchased only at weekends.

Information

Oficina de Turismo (983 72 03 19; www.medinaderioseco.com; Paseo de San Francisco 1; 10am-2pm & 4-6pm Tue-Sat, 10am-2pm Sun) Alongside the Museo de San Francisco.

Getting There & Away

Up to eight daily buses run to León (€8.25, 1¼ hours); up to 10 go to Valladolid (€4, 30 minutes).

Tordesillas

POP 8905

Commanding a rise on the northern flank of Río Duero, this pretty little town has a historical significance that belies its size. Originally a Roman settlement, it later played a major role in world history in 1494, when Isabel and Fernando sat down here with Portugal to hammer out a treaty determining who got what in Latin America. Portugal got Brazil and much of the rest went to Spain. The museum dedicated to the moment and a stunning convent are the main reasons to come here.

Sights

Real Convento de Santa Clara CONVENT

(983 77 00 71; www.patrimonionacional.es; Calle de Alonso Castillo Solorzano 21; adult/child €6/free, EU citizens & residents 4-6.30pm Wed & Thu free; 10am-2pm & 4-6.30pm Tue-Sat, 10.30am-3pm Sun) Still home to a few Franciscan nuns living in near-total isolation, this Mudéjar-style convent dates from 1340, when it was begun as a palace for Alfonso XI. In 1494, the Treaty of Tordesillas was signed here. A 50-minute guided tour (in Spanish) takes in a wonderful Mudéjar patio left over from the palace, and the church with its stunning *techumbre* (roof). Other highlights include the Mudéjar door, Gothic arches, superb Arabic inscriptions and the Arab baths.

Museo del Tratado de Tordesillas MUSEUM

(983 77 10 67; Calle de Casas del Tratado; 10am-1.30pm & 5-7.30pm Tue-Sat, 10am-2pm Sun Jun-Sep, 10am-1.30pm & 4-6.30pm Tue-Sat, 10am-2pm Sun Oct-May) FREE Dedicated to the 1494 Treaty of Tordesillas, which divided the world into Spanish and Portuguese spheres of influence, the informative displays in this museum look at the world as it was before and after the treaty, with some fabulous old maps taking centre stage. There's also a multilingual video presentation.

Sleeping & Eating

Hostal San Antolín HOSTAL €

(983 79 67 71; www.hostalsanantolin.com; Calle San Antolín 8; s/d/tr €25/40/50;) Located near Plaza Mayor, this hostal's overall aesthetic is modern, with rooms painted in bright pastel tones. Its main focus is the attached restaurant (mains €12 to €20), with *raciones* downstairs in the bar, a pretty flower-decked inner patio and an elegant menu.

Parador de Tordesillas LUXURY HOTEL €€

(983 77 00 51; www.parador.es; Carretera de Salamanca 5; r from €75-169; P) Tordesillas' most sophisticated hotel is the low-rise, ochre-toned *parador*, surrounded by pine trees and just outside town. Some rooms have four-poster beds, all are large and many look out onto the tranquil gardens. There's also a cafe and an excellent restaurant that showcases local specialities.

Don Pancho SPANISH €€

(983 77 01 74; www.restaurantedonpancho.com; Plaza Mayor 10; mains €7-18; 1-4pm & 8.30pm-midnight) Don Pancho, with its tiled bar and home cooking – including meats roasted in a wood-fire oven – is the best sit-down restaurant in the old town centre.

Information

Oficina de Turismo (983 77 10 67; www.tordesillas.net; Calle de Casas del Tratado; 10am-1.30pm & 5-7.30pm Tue-Sat, 10am-2pm Sun Jun-Sep, 10am-1.30pm & 4-6.30pm Tue-Sat, 10am-2pm Sun Oct-Apr) Next to the Casas del Tratado, near the Iglesia de San Antolín.

Getting There & Away

From the **bus station** (983 77 00 72; Avenida de Valladolid), regular buses depart for Valladolid (€2.80, 30 minutes) and Zamora (€5.90, one hour).

Toro

POP 9115

With a name that couldn't be more Spanish and a stirring history that overshadows its present, Toro is your archetypal Castilian town. It was here that Fernando and Isabel cemented their primacy in Christian Spain at the Battle of Toro in 1476. The town sits on a rise high above the north bank of the Río

Duero and has a charming historic centre with half-timbered houses and Romanesque churches.

Sights

Colegiata Santa María La Mayor CHURCH
(Plaza de la Colegiata; church free, sacristy €4; 10.30am-2pm & 5-7.30pm Tue-Sun Apr-Oct, 10am-2pm & 4.30-6.30pm Tue-Sun Nov-Mar) This 12th-century church rises above the town and boasts the magnificent Romanesque-Gothic **Pórtico de la Majestad**. Treasures inside include the famous 15th-century painting *Virgen de la mosca* (Virgin of the Fly) in the sacristy; see if you can spot the fly on the virgin's robe. Entrance to the main sanctuary is free; an admission fee applies to the sacristy.

Monasterio Sancti Spiritus MONASTERY
(Calle del Canto 27; €4; 10.30am-2pm & 4-7.30pm Tue-Sun Apr-Sep, 10am-2pm & 4.30-6.30pm Tue-Sun Oct-Mar) Southwest of the town centre, this monastery features a fine Renaissance cloister and the striking alabaster tomb of Beatriz de Portugal, wife of Juan I.

Sleeping

Zaravencia HOTEL €
(980 69 49 98; www.hotelzaravencia.com; Plaza Mayor 17; s/d incl breakfast from €44/55;) Overlooking the lovely Plaza Mayor, this friendly place has a bar-restaurant downstairs and good-sized rooms, albeit with an anaemic decor of light-pine furniture and cream walls. Pay €10 more for a plaza view and balcony (it's worth it), although be aware that it can be noisy on weekends.

Hotel Juan II HOTEL €€
(980 69 03 00; www.hotelesentoro.es; Paseo del Espolón 1; s €50-70, d €52-85; P) Despite its modern red-brick exterior, the rooms here are charming, with warm terracotta-tiled floors, dark-wood furniture and large terraces. Request room 201 for its fabulous double-whammy vista of the Río Duero to one side and the Colegiata Santa María La Mayor to the other. The restaurant (mains €15 to €21), specialising in hearty meat dishes, is one of Toro's best.

Eating

La Esquina de Colas TAPAS €
(980 69 31 31; Plaza Mayor 24; tapas from €3; 11am-4pm & 8pm-midnight Thu-Tue) Artfully conceived tapas lined up along the bar (try the marinated sardines) and a full list of toasts topped with all manner of tasty morsels make this Toro's best place for tapas.

WORTH A TRIP

PAGOS DEL REY

This fine, state-of-the-art **wine museum** (980 69 67 63; www.pagosdelreymuseodelvino.com; Avenida de los Comuneros 90; guided/unguided incl wine-tasting €6/4; 11am-2pm & 4-8pm Tue-Sat, 11am-2pm Sun Apr-Oct, 11am-2pm & 4-7pm Tue-Sat, 11am-2pm Sun Nov & Dec, closed Tue Jan-Mar) is a welcome addition to Castilla y León's world of wine tourism, offering a fascinating insight into the Toro wine-producing area with plenty of opportunities to try (and buy) local wines. It's in Morales de Toro, 8km east of Toro.

★**Asador Castilla** SPANISH €€
(980 69 02 11; Plaza Bollos de Hito; mains €14-22; 1-4pm & 8.30pm-midnight Tue-Sun) Excellent service, roasted meats (the *cabrito* – roasted goat kid – is a speciality) and a pleasantly modern dining area make this a good choice. It's barely 50m from Plaza Mayor.

Information

Oficina de Turismo (980 69 47 47; www.turismotoro.com; Plaza Mayor 6; 10am-2pm & 4-7pm Tue-Sat, 10am-2pm Sun)

Getting There & Away

Regular buses operate to Valladolid (€5.25, one hour) and Zamora (€3.20, 30 minutes). There are two direct services to Salamanca (€6.50, 1½ hours) on weekdays.

Zamora

POP 63,217

First appearances can be deceiving: as with so many Spanish towns, your introduction to provincial Zamora is likely to be nondescript apartment blocks. But persevere, because the *casco historico* (old town) is hauntingly beautiful, with sumptuous medieval monuments that have earned Zamora the popular sobriquet, the 'Romanesque Museum'. It's a subdued encore to the monumental splendour of Salamanca and one of the best places to be during Semana Santa.

DON'T MISS

ZAMORA'S BEST VIEW

Zamora has numerous eye-catching vantage points, many of them from high in the old town – from the ramparts of the Castillo, or from the **Mirador del Troncoso** behind the Municipal Tourist Office, for example. But to see Zamora's old town in all its panoramic glory, head down from the old town to the riverbank and the pretty, multi-arched **Puente de Piedra**. Cross the bridge and walk southwest along the riverbank, past the small, sandy river beach, **Playa de los Pelambres**, to the modern **Puente de los Poetas**. Apart from being a lovely walk to get here, your reward is a fine view back towards the old town with the river in the foreground.

Sights

Catedral CATHEDRAL
(980 53 19 33; Plaza de la Catedral; adult/child €5/free; 10am-7pm Apr-Sep, 10am-2pm & 5-8pm Oct-Mar) Zamora's largely Romanesque cathedral features a square tower, an unusual, Byzantine-style dome surrounded by turrets, and the ornate **Puerta del Obispo**. The star attraction is the **Museo Catedralicio**, which features a collection of Flemish tapestries dating from the 15th century. Inside the 12th-century cathedral itself, the magnificent early-Renaissance choir stalls depict clerics, animals and a naughty encounter between a monk and a nun. Another major highlight is the **Capilla de San Ildefonso**, with its lovely Gothic frescos.

Castillo CASTLE
(Parque del Castillo; 10am-2pm & 7-10pm Tue-Sun Apr-Sep, 10am-2pm & 4-6.30pm Tue-Sun Oct-Mar;) FREE This fine, aesthetically restored castle of 11th-century origin is filled with local sculptures; you can also climb the tower and walk the ramparts. The surrounding park is a lovely place for a picnic.

Museo Etnográfico MUSEUM
(980 53 17 08; www.museo-etnografico.com; Plaza Viriato; adult/child €3/free; 10am-2pm & 5-8pm Tue-Sun) This excellent museum is a window onto the cultural history of Castilla y León, with everything from artefacts from everyday life down through the ages to sections on local legends and fiestas. It also has a dynamic calendar of temporary exhibitions, workshops and performances. Admission is free Tuesday through Thursday from 7pm to 8pm and Sunday from 5pm to 8pm.

Iglesia de la Magdalena CHURCH
(Rúa de los Francos; 10am-2pm & 5.30-8pm Tue-Sat, 10am-2pm Sun Apr-Sep, 10am-2pm & 4.30-7pm Tue-Sat, 10am-2pm Sun Oct-Mar) FREE The southern doorway of this church, set along the main thoroughfare through the old town, is considered the city's finest for its preponderance of floral motifs. The interior has the austere simplicity so typical of the Romanesque.

Iglesia de San Juan de Puerta Nueva CHURCH
(Plaza Mayor; 10am-2pm & 5.30-8pm Tue-Sat, 10am-2pm Sun Apr-Sep, 10am-2pm & 4.30-7pm Tue-Sat, 10am-2pm Sun Oct-Mar) FREE Iglesia de San Juan de Puerta Nueva provides a lovely Romanesque centrepiece for the central Plaza Mayor. Right outside, there's a fine statue of hooded Semana Santa penitents.

Iglesia de Santa María La Nueva CHURCH
(Calle de Carniceros; 10am-2pm & 5.30-8pm Tue-Sat, 10am-2pm Sun Apr-Sep, 10am-2pm & 4.30-7pm Tue-Sat, 10am-2pm Sun Oct-Mar) FREE This pretty church is actually a medieval replica of a 7th-century church destroyed by fire in 1158.

Museo de Semana Santa MUSEUM
(980 53 22 95; www.semanasantadezamora.com; Plaza de Santa María La Nueva; adult/child €4/2; 10am-2pm & 5-8pm Tue-Sat, 10am-2pm Sun) This museum will initiate you into the weird and wonderful rites of Easter, Spanish-style. It showcases the carved and painted *pasos* (figures) that are paraded around town during the colourful processions. The hooded models are eerily lifelike.

Tours

Zamora's tourist offices run two-hour guided tours around the old town at 11am daily from March to December. The **tours** (adult/child €8/free) leave from the Plaza de Viriato; the price *doesn't* include entrance to the cathedral. Ask also about **nocturnal guided tours** (from €8 to €12) which leave around 8pm or 9pm depending on the season. For those unable to walk, there's also a toy-like *tren turístico* (€2.50) that begins in the Plaza Mayor and does a circuit of the old town from April to September.

Festivals & Events

Semana Santa RELIGIOUS

(Holy Week; Mar or Apr) If you're in Spain during Holy Week (the week before Easter), make your way to Zamora, a town made famous for its elaborate celebrations. It's one of the most evocative places in the country to view the hooded processions. Watching the penitents weave their way through the historic streets, sometimes in near-total silence, is an experience you'll never forget.

Sleeping

★**Hostal Chiqui** HOSTAL €

(980 53 14 80; www.hostalchiqui.es; 2nd fl, Calle de Benavente 2; s/d from €35/45) This fine place is one of the best urban *hostales* in this part of Castilla y León, getting rave reviews and plenty of repeat visitors. Every room is different, but all are stylish and colourful, and the owners are switched on to what travellers need. All in all, it's outrageously good value.

NH Palacio del Duero HOTEL €€

(980 50 82 62; www.nh-hotels.com; Plaza de la Horta 1; r from €80; P ❄ @ ⓦ) In a superb position next to a lovely Romanesque church, the seemingly modern building has cleverly encompassed part of the former convent, as well as – somewhat bizarrely – a 1940s power station (the lofty brick chimney remains). As you'd expect from this excellent chain, the rooms here are stylishly furnished and the service is attentive.

Parador Condes de Alba y Aliste HISTORIC HOTEL €€€

(980 51 44 97; www.parador.es; Plaza Viriato 5; r €100-175; ❄ @ ⓦ ≋) Set in a sumptuous 15th-century palace, this is modern luxury with myriad period touches (mostly in the public areas). There's a swimming pool and – unlike many *paradores* – it's right in the heart of town. On the downside, there is very limited parking available (just eight places). The restaurant (set menu €35) is predictably *parador* quality.

Eating

De Picoteo TAPAS, SPANISH €

(980 03 21 55; Rúa los Notarios 3; tapas from €1.50, raciones €8-14; noon-4pm & 8pm-midnight Tue-Sun) Tucked away down a quiet back street in the old town, De Picoteo includes a fine *arroz a la zamorano* as part of its daily *menú del día* (€12), as well as some excellent and well-priced tapas and friendly service.

La Rua CASTILIAN €€

(980 53 40 24; Rúa de los Francos 21; mains €9-19; 1-4pm Sun-Fri, 1-4pm & 8.30-11.30pm Sat) Devoted to down-home Zamora cooking, this central place is a good place to try *arroz a la zamorana* (rice with pork and ham or chorizo), although you'll usually need two people ordering for staff to make it. It is sometimes closed on Tuesdays in winter.

El Rincón de Antonio CASTILIAN €€€

(980 53 53 70; www.elrincondeantonio.com; Rúa de los Francos 6; tapas from €1.90, mains €15-35, set menus €35.50-60; 1.30-4pm & 8.30-11.30pm Mon-Sat, 1.30-4.30pm Sun) A fine place offering tapas in the bar (including 17 different cheese *raciones* from the Zamora area), as well as sit-down meals in a classy dining area. There's a range of tasting menus in the restaurant, where dishes are classic with a contemporary twist – try, for example, the cockles with lime yoghurt, parsley mustard and dried tomatoes. Reservations recommended.

Shopping

Just west of Plaza Mayor, you'll find half a dozen gourmet food shops and delis selling cheeses, cured meats, wine and local pastries.

La Despensa FOOD

(699 56 91 52; Calle de Ramos Carrión 6; 10am-2.30pm & 5-9pm) Unlike other food shops in this stretch of street west of the Plaza Mayor, La Despensa is a delicatessen that focuses on *jamón* and other cured meats – if you're planning a picnic, make sure you take along some *jamón* from Guijuelo, available here.

La Buena Jera FOOD & DRINKS

(www.facebook.com/LaBuenaJera/; Calle de Ramos Carrión 12; 10am-2pm & 5-8.30pm) One of numerous gourmet food shops in this stretch of street, La Buena Jera has an excellent range of local cheeses and wines from Toro, as well as local pastries, honeys and other delicacies.

Information

Municipal Tourist Office (980 53 36 94; www.zamora-turismo.com; Plaza de Arias Gonzalo 6; 10am-2pm & 5-8pm Mon-Sat, 10am-2pm Sun Apr-Sep, 10am-2pm & 4-7.30pm Mon-Sat, 10am-2pm Sun Oct-Mar)

Regional Tourist Office (980 53 18 45; www.turismocastillayleon.com; Avenida Príncipe de Asturias 1; ⏰10am-2pm & 4.30-8.30pm Mar-Oct, 10am-2pm & 4-7pm Nov-Feb)

Provincial Tourist Office (☎980 53 64 95; Plaza Viriato; ⏰10am-2pm & 4.30-8.30pm Mar-Oct, 10am-2pm & 4-7pm Nov-Feb)

Getting There & Away

Bus Services operate almost hourly to/from Salamanca (from €5.30, one hour, five to 13 daily), with less frequent departures on weekends. Other regular services include those to León (€9.75, 1½ hours), Valladolid (€7.65, 1½ hours) and Burgos (€16.80, 4½ hours).

Train The fast-train line has reached Zamora, cutting travelling times to Madrid (from €15.30, 2¼ hours, four daily) considerably. Trains also head to Valladolid (€12.45, 1½ hours, one daily) and Puebla de Sanabria (from €9.25, 1¼ hours, four daily).

Around Zamora

Sierra de la Culebra

The Sierra de la Culebra, running along the Spanish–Portuguese border between Puebla de Sanabria and Zamora, consists of some lovely rolling hill country and pretty stone villages that rarely see foreign visitors. Best of all, this is the best place in Europe to see wolves in the wild.

Sights

★Centro de Lobo Ibérico de Castilla y León MUSEUM, ZOO
(☎608 05 34 15, 980 56 76 38; www.centrodellobo.es; Robledo; with/without guided tour €8/6; ⏰10am-2pm & 4-7.30pm Fri-Sun, Tue-Thu by appointment) This excellent interpretation centre devoted to the Iberian wolf opened in late 2015. Built in the form of a traditional, circular corral used by local farmers to protect their livestock from wolves, the centre has displays on legends surrounding wolves, their position in local culture and scientific studies of them. On the hill behind the main building, seven wolves inhabit three large enclosures, offering a good chance to take a photo if you missed seeing them in the wild.

Activities

Wild Wolf Experience WILDLIFE
(☎636 03 14 72; www.wildwolfexperience.com; five-night, four-day tour per person £995) Englishman John Hallowell runs excellent wolf-watching (and birdwatching) excursions in the Sierra de la Culebra; he's a knowledgable guide and puts together packages that begin and end at Madrid or Oviedo airports. He can also combine it with bear-watching in Asturias.

Zamora Natural WILDLIFE
(☎655 82 18 99; www.zamoranatural.com; per person €50) If you're keen to catch a glimpse of a wolf or two in the Sierra de la Culebra, contact Zamora Natural, which runs year-round excursions, including a dawn and sunset spent at a lookout overlooking areas commonly frequented by wolves. Sightings are not guaranteed, though; chances range between 20% and 40%, with the best months from October through to May or June.

Festivals & Events

Festival Territorio Lobo CULTURAL
(www.festivalterritoriolobo.com; Villardeciervos; ⏰early Aug) This fun festival features live music, great local food, presentations about the Iberian wolf and excursions into the sierra.

Sleeping

★Santa Cruz GUESTHOUSE €
(☎619 85 00 10; www.loscuerragos.com; Santa Cruz de los Cuérragos; per person full board €30; P 📶) Now here's something a little bit special. Fernando and Carmen have been largely responsible for bringing this charming stone village back to life. Their lovely rural home is beautifully restored and decorated with exposed stone walls, polished floorboards, comfortable beds and a general warmth – it's the sort of place where you'll want to stay longer than you planned. Cash only.

Hotel Remesal HOTEL €
(☎980 65 49 11; www.hotelruralremesal.com; Calle de Mediodía 25, Villardeciervos; s/d €38/55; P 📶) This excellent three-star hotel in Villadeciervos has 10 pretty rooms, all with exposed stone walls and excellent heating. It's on the main road through town and makes a convenient base for exploring the sierra, with numerous wolf-watching locales relatively nearby.

Eating

La Enredadera SPANISH €€
(☎980 59 31 21; Calle de Arriba 26, Ferreras de Arriba; mains €8-15, set lunch menu €13; ⏰1.30-4pm & 8.30-11.30pm Thu-Tue) What a find! In the otherwise-nondescript village of Ferreras de Arriba, close to some of the best wolf-watching

spots, La Enredadera looks for all the world like a cool urban cafe. The food is thoughtfully presented, the service is friendly and its specialities include *bacalao* (cod) or *carnes a la brasa* (grilled meats).

Hotel Remesal SPANISH €€
(☎980 65 49 11; www.hotelruralremesal.com; Calle de Mediodía 25, Villardeciervos; mains €8-17, set lunch menu weekdays/weekends €10/13; ⏰1-4pm & 8.30-11pm) Pass through this hotel's workaday bar and into the light-filled restaurant, where staff serve up hearty meat dishes and a generous lunchtime *menú del día*.

Getting There & Away

The N631, which connects Zamora with Puebla de Sanabria, runs parallel to the Sierra de la Culebra, with numerous side roads climbing up into the hills. Villardeciervos is the largest village in the region. Robledo, home to the Centro de Lobo interpretation centre, lies at the northwestern end of the range and is accessible from Puebla de Sanabria.

Puebla de Sanabria

POP 1460

Close to the Portuguese border, this captivating village is a tangle of medieval alleyways that unfold around a 15th-century castle and trickle down the hill. This is one of Spain's loveliest hamlets and it's well worth stopping overnight: the quiet cobblestone lanes make it feel like you've stepped back centuries.

Sights

Castillo CASTLE
(adult/child under 12yr €3/free; ⏰11am-2pm & 4-8pm; P 👪) Crowning the village's high point and dominating its skyline for kilometres around, the castle has some interesting displays on local history, flora and fauna; a slide show about the culture and history of the village; and a camera obscura. Kids will love the chance to try on the pieces of armour. The views from the ramparts are also superb.

Plaza Mayor SQUARE
At the top of the village, this striking town square is surrounded by some fine historical buildings. The 17th-century *ayuntamiento* (town hall) has a lovely arched facade and faces across the square to **Iglesia de Nuestra Señora del Azogue** (⏰noon-2pm & 4-6pm Fri, 11am-2pm & 4-7pm Sat & Sun), a pretty village church dating to the 12th century.

ONE OF SPAIN'S OLDEST CHURCHES

The lonely 7th-century **San Pedro de la Nave** (☎660 23 39 95, 696 29 24 00; Calle Larga, Campillo; ⏰10.30am-1.30pm & 5-8pm Tue-Sun Apr-Sep, 10am-1.30pm & 4.30-6.30pm Fri & Sat, 10am-1.30pm Sun Oct-Mar), about 24km northwest of Zamora, is a rare and outstanding example of Visigoth church architecture, with blended Celtic, Germanic and Byzantine elements. Of special note are the intricately sculpted capitals. The church was moved to its present site in Campillo in 1930, during the construction of the Esla reservoir, northwest of Zamora. To get there from Zamora, take the N122, then follow the signs to Campillo.

Sleeping

Hostal Carlos V HOSTAL €
(☎980 62 01 61; www.hostalcarlosv.es; Avenida Braganza 6; r from €50; ❄📶) The best budget deal here, the Carlos V has pleasant rooms, dazzling white bedding, extra fluffy towels, firm mattresses, rainforest shower heads and quality toiletries. There's a good cafe-restaurant here as well. It's at the bottom of the hill at the entrance to the old town.

★**Posada Real La Cartería** HISTORIC HOTEL €€
(☎980 62 03 12; www.lacarteria.com; Calle de Rúa 16; r from €90-155; ❄@📶) This stunning old inn is one of the best hotels in this part of the country. It blends modern comforts with all the old-world atmosphere of the village itself, featuring large, delightful rooms with exposed stone walls and wooden beams. The bathrooms have Jacuzzi tubs and there is even a small gym (as if walking around this hilly village wasn't exercise enough!).

La Hoja de Roble HISTORIC HOTEL €€
(☎980 62 01 90; www.lahojaderoble.com; Calle Constanilla 13; s/d from €65/75; ❄📶) Close to the bottom of the hill where you begin the climb up into the old town, this hotel is an outstanding choice. The building dates to the 17th century and the rooms have a real sense of history (exposed stone walls, original wooden beams) without ever being oppressive. There's also a wine bar and a good restaurant.

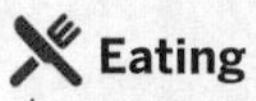

Eating

★Posada Real La Cartería CASTILIAN €€
(☎980 62 03 12; www.lacarteria.com; Calle de Rúa 16; mains €12-21; ⊙1-4pm & 9pm-midnight) The local obsession with wild mushrooms (*setas* and *boletus*) and *trucha* (trout) – caught in the river below the village – is alive and well here. Otherwise, it's an atmospheric choice in one of the village's most charming old buildings.

La Posada de Puebla de Sanabria CASTILIAN €€
(☎980 62 03 47; www.laposadadelavilla.com; Plaza Mayor 3; mains €10-16; ⊙1.30-4pm & 8.30-11pm Thu-Tue) This excellent restaurant right on Plaza Mayor has a white-tableclothed elegance and serves up local steaks and the wild mushrooms for which this region is famed. When the two are mixed, such as in the *tenera estofada con boletus*, a kind of hotpot of beef with wild mushrooms, the results are outstanding.

Information

Oficina de Turismo (☎980 62 07 34; www.turismosanabria.es; ⊙11am-2pm & 4-8pm) Inside the castle. At the height of summer, it sometimes stays open as late as 10pm, but don't count on it.

Getting There & Away

There are sporadic bus services to Puebla de Sanabria from Zamora (from €8.50, 1¼ hours).

Palencia

POP 79,137

Subdued Palencia boasts an immense Gothic cathedral, some pretty squares and a colonnaded main pedestrian street (Calle Mayor) flanked by shops and several other churches. It's an attractive town and one of the quieter provincial capitals. Most travellers come here on a day trip from Valladolid.

Sights

★Catedral CATHEDRAL
(☎979 70 13 47; www.catedraldepalencia.org; Calle Mayor Antigua 29; adult/child €5/1; ⊙10am-1.30pm & 4-7.30pm Mon-Fri, 10am-2pm & 4-7.30pm Sat, 4.30-8pm Sun May-Sep, 10am-1.30pm & 4-6pm Mon-Fri, 10am-1.30pm & 4-5.30pm Sat, 4-7pm Sun Oct-Mar) The sober exterior of this vast house of worship (one of the largest in Castilla) belies the extraordinary riches within – it's widely known as 'La Bella Desconocida' (Unknown Beauty). The **Puerta del Obispo** (Bishop's Door) is the highlight of the facade. Once inside, head for the **Capilla El Sagrario**: its ceiling-high altarpiece tells the story of Christ in dozens of exquisite panels. The stone screen behind the choir stalls is a masterpiece of bas-relief, attributed to Gil de Siloé.

Museo Diocesano MUSEUM
(☎979 70 69 13; Calle de Mayor Antigua; guided tours in Spanish €4; ⊙guided tours 10.30am, 11.30am, 12.30pm, 4.30pm, 5.30pm & 6.30pm Tue-Sun Jul-Sep, shorter hours rest of year) Within the 18th-century **Palacio Episcopal**, this museum showcases art from the Middle Ages through to the Renaissance. Pride of place goes to works by Pedro de Berruguete and an altarpiece starring the Virgin (attributed to Diego de Siloé).

Iglesia de San Miguel CHURCH
(☎979 74 07 69; Calle de Mayor Antigua; ⊙9.30am-1.30pm & 6.30-7.30pm Mon-Sat, 9.30am-1.30pm & 6.30-8pm Sun) FREE This church stands out for its tall Gothic tower with a castle-like turret. San Miguel's interior is unadorned and austerely beautiful. According to legend, El Cid was betrothed to his Doña Jimena here.

Sleeping

Eurostars Diana Palace BUSINESS HOTEL €
(☎979 01 80 50; www.eurostarsdianapalace.com; Avenida de Santander 12; s/d incl breakfast from €55/60; P❄📶) A comfortable, modern block of a hotel within walking distance of the town centre. The look is contemporary with a predominantly business clientele.

Hotel Colón 27 HOTEL €
(☎979 74 07 00; www.hotelcolon27.com; Calle de Colón 27; s €35-55, d €40-70; ❄📶) This two-star place is decent downtown value, with comfortable, if drab, carpeted rooms sporting light-pine furniture, good firm mattresses, green-tiled bathrooms and small flat-screen TVs.

Eating

Gloria Bendita CASTILIAN €€
(☎979 10 65 04; Calle de la Puebla 8; mains €14-26; ⊙1.30-4pm & 9pm-midnight Mon-Sat, 1.30-4pm Sun; 📶) Ignore the drab surroundings of modern apartment blocks and seek out this, one of Palencia's new breed of elegant restaurants serving sophisticated Castilian cuisine with a modern twist. Meat and fish dishes are the emphasis here, with classics

such as braised beef served with oyster mushrooms. There are just a handful of tables in an intimate space, so reservations are essential.

★Lucio Asador Gastrobar CASTILIAN €€€

(☎979 74 81 90; www.restaurantecasalucio.com; Calle de Don Sancho 2; mains €20-26, raciones €4.50-18; ⏰10am-midnight Mon-Sat, 10am-4pm Sun) This Palencia institution recently combined an *asador* (restaurant specialising in roasted meats) with a slick new gastrobar. Gone is the air of tradition, replaced by creativity bursting out of the kitchen. It still does the Castilian speciality of *cordero asado* (€39 for two) – exceptionally well – but it would be a shame to dine here and not try the creative tapas.

Information

Patronato de Turismo (☎979 70 65 23; www.turismocastillayleon.com; Calle Mayor 31; ⏰9.30am-2pm & 5-8pm Mon-Sat, 9.30am-5pm Sun Jul–mid-Sep, 9.30am-2pm & 4-7pm Mon-Sat, 9.30am-5pm Sun mid-Sep–Jun) Information about Palencia province and city, encompassing both the municipal and regional tourist offices.

Getting There & Away

Bus From the **bus station** (☎979 74 32 22; Carerra del Cementerio) there are regular services to Valladolid (€4.55, 45 minutes), Madrid (from €9.34, 3½ hours) and Aguilar de Campóo (€8.15, 1½ hours).

Train The AVE fast train now connects Palencia to Madrid (€16.30 to €33.10, 1½ to three hours) and León (from €11.75, 45 minutes). Other services include Burgos (from €7.35, 45 minutes) and Valladolid (from €4.25, 30 minutes).

Around Palencia

The area around Palencia is relatively small compared to other provincial capitals, but there are three small churches – one the oldest in Spain, the other two among the most beautiful of all Spain's rural churches – that are definitely worth visiting.

Sights

★Iglesia de Santa María La Blanca CHURCH

(☎979 88 08 54; Villalcázar de Sirga; €1.50; ⏰11am-2pm & 5-8pm daily Jun–mid-Sep, 10.30am-2pm & 4-6pm Sat & Sun mid-Sep–Apr) This extraordinary fortress-church, an important landmark along the Camino de Santiago, rises up from the Castilian plains between Frómista and Carrión de los Condes along the quiet P980. Begun in the 12th century and finished in the 14th, it spans both Romanesque and Gothic styles. Its soaring, elaborately carved portal is worth lingering over, while highlights inside include the royal tombs and an extravagant *retablo mayor* (altarpiece).

★Iglesia de San Martín CHURCH

(☎979 81 01 44; Avenida del Ejército Español, Frómista; adult/concession/child €1.50/1/free; ⏰9.30am-2pm & 4.30-8pm Apr-Sep, 10am-2pm & 3.30-6.30pm Oct-Mar) Dating from 1066 and restored in the early 20th century, this beautifully proportioned church is one of the loveliest Romanesque churches in rural Spain, adorned with a veritable menagerie of human and zoomorphic figures just below the eaves. The interior is a study in simplicity save for the column capitals, which are richly decorated.

There are two buses daily from Palencia (€3.50, 30 minutes), but most people visit en route between Palencia and the north.

Basílica de San Juan CHURCH

(☎628 72 08 85; Baños de Cerrato; €2, Wed free; ⏰10.30am-2pm & 4.50-8pm Tue-Sun Apr-Sep, 11am-2pm & 4-6pm Tue-Sun Oct-Mar) In Baños de Cerrato, close to the singularly unattractive rail junction of Venta de Baños,

WORTH A TRIP

IBERIA'S FINEST ROMAN VILLA

Okay, it's not Pompeii, but it is the most exciting and best preserved Roman villa on the Iberian Peninsula. Located seemingly in the middle of nowhere, the **Villa Romana La Olmeda** (☎979 14 20 03; www.villaromanalaolmeda.com; off CL615; adult/concession/child under 12yr €5/3/free, 3-6.30pm Tue free; ⏰10.30am-6.30pm Tue-Sun; 🅿👪) is surrounded by fertile plains and hidden behind an incongruous, futuristic-looking building. Step inside, however, to be transported back to the 4th century AD – once the villa of a wealthy aristocrat and landowner, the property spans some 1000 sq metres and contains some of the finest mosaics to be discovered in a private Roman villa anywhere in Europe.

WORTH A TRIP

THE ROMANESQUE CIRCUIT

There are no fewer than 55 Romanesque churches in the cool, hilly countryside surrounding Aguilar de Campóo; you could easily spend a day tracking them as you meander along quiet country trails.

At **Olleros de Pisuerga** there's a little church carved into rock; it's signposted as 'Ermita Rupestre'. Ask at Bar Feli on the main road through town for someone to open it up for you.

Further south, on a quiet back road, the Benedictine **Monasterio de Santa María de Mave** (620 13 70 55, 979 12 36 11; hours vary) has an interesting 13th-century Romanesque church, the only part of the complex open to visitors; ask at the cafe next door for the key. It's off the main highway around 8km south of Aguilar de Campóo. Nearby, the **Monasterio de San Andrés de Arroyo** (www.sanandresdearroyo.es; guided tours €5; tours 11am, noon, 12.30pm, 4pm, 5pm & 6pm, closed mid-Dec–mid-Mar & Easter) is an outstanding Romanesque gem – especially its cloister, which dates from the 13th century. Guided tours in Spanish run hourly.

lies Spain's oldest church, the 7th-century Basílica de San Juan. Built by the Visigoths in 661 and modified many times since, its stone-and-terracotta facade exudes a pleasing, austere simplicity and features a 14th-century alabaster statue of St John the Baptist.

Sleeping

★Hotel Monasterio Real San Zoilo HISTORIC HOTEL €€
(979 880 049; www.sanzoilo.com; Carrión de los Condes; s/d from €55/75; P) Inhabiting part of an 11th-century monastery, this fine place in Carrión de los Condes has charming rooms with wooden beams, exposed brickwork and ochre-painted walls. Some also surround the cloister and there's a good restaurant as well.

Information

Oficina de Turismo de Frómista (979 810 180; www.turismocastillayleon.com; Calle de Ingeniero Rivera; 10am-2pm & 4-7pm Mon-Fri, 10am-2pm Sat & Sun) Helpful tourist office.

Getting There & Away

You'll need your own wheels to explore most of the area. Although there are two daily buses to Frómista from Palencia, you may find yourself stranded when you want to move on.

Montaña Palentina

These hills in the far north of Castilla y León offer a beautiful preview of the Cordillera Cantábrica, which divides Castilla from Spain's northern Atlantic regions. The scenery around here is some of the prettiest in the region, with barely remembered Romanesque churches and quieter-than-quiet back roads, where you're more likely to be slowed by a tractor than annoyed by a tour bus.

Aguilar de Campóo

POP 6979

Aguilar de Campóo is a bustling town with some interesting monuments. Most importantly, it is a gateway for the stunning scenery and Romanesque churches of the Montaña Palentina, and it lets you break up the journey between Palencia and Santander.

Sights

Ermita de Santa Cecilia CHURCH
(979 18 14 24; Calle de Santa Cecilia; admission €1; 11am-2pm & 5-8pm Tue-Sun Apr-Sep, 11am-2pm & 4-6pm Tue-Sun Oct-Mar) Overlooking the town and providing its picturesque backdrop is a 12th-century *castillo* (castle) and the graceful Romanesque Ermita de Santa Cecilia, a pretty and humble little hermitage that acts as a prelude to the Romanesque gems nearby in the province.

Monasterio de Santa María la Real MONASTERY
(979 12 30 53; www.santamarialareal.org; Carretera de Cervera; adult/child €5/3; 10.30am-2pm & 4.30-8pm Jul-Sep, 4-7.30pm Tue-Fri, 10.30am-2pm & 4.30-7.30pm Sat & Sun Oct-Jun) Just outside town, on the highway to Cervera de Pisuerga, is the restored Romanesque Monasterio de Santa María la Real.

Its 13th-century Gothic cloister with delicate capitals is glorious. You can visit the church without a guide, but you'll need to join a tour to see the rest – check the website for times.

Sleeping & Eating

★Posada Santa María La Real HISTORIC HOTEL €€
(☎979 12 20 00; www.posadasantamarialareal.com/EN/hotel.html; Carretera de Cervera; s/d from €54/81; P ❄ 📶) Inhabiting part of the Romanesque monastery of the same name but with a contemporary makeover, this charming *posada* (rural home) is the most atmospheric place to stay in the region. Some rooms have stone walls, while others are split-level; all are decked out in wood. The restaurant offers medieval-themed dinners and several set menus (from €16).

Mesón Añejo SPANISH €€
(☎979 12 29 71; www.mesonanejo.wixsite.com/anejo; Calle Comercio 10; mains €12-18; ⏲1-3.30pm & 9-11.30pm Thu-Mon, 1-3.30pm Tue) In an attractive brick-and-wood-beam setting, Mesón Añejo is our pick of the restaurants in town with specialities including *carpaccio de solomillo relleno de foie* (sirloin carpaccio filled with foie gras) or *chuletón a la piedra* (steak cooked on hot stones). Local produce is a recurring theme.

Information

Oficina de Turismo (☎979 12 36 41; www.aguilardecampoo.com/turismo/; Paseo de la Cascajera 10; ⏲10am-1.45pm & 4-5.45pm Tue-Sat, 10am-1.45pm Sun)

Getting There & Away

Buses bound for Burgos, Palencia and Santander depart at least once daily. Up to five trains daily link Aguilar de Campóo with Palencia (from €8.85, one hour), but the station is 4km from town.

THE NORTHWEST

León

POP 126,192 / ELEV 837M

León is a wonderful city, combining stunning historical architecture with an irresistible energy. Its standout attraction is the cathedral, one of the most beautiful in Spain, but there's so much more to see and do here. By day you'll encounter a city with its roots firmly planted in the soil of northern Castilla, with its grand monuments, loyal Catholic heritage and a role as an important staging post along the Camino de Santiago. By night León is taken over by a deep-into-the-night soundtrack of revelry that floods the narrow streets and plazas of the picturesque old quarter, the Barrio Húmedo. It's a fabulous mix.

Sights

Set aside the best part of a day to make sure that you see all of León's attractions. Stop by the Municipal Tourist Office to pick up *Horarios de Museos y Monumentos de León* for a list of current opening hours.

The main pedestrian shopping street is Calle Ancha. Don't miss the fabulous **Farmacia Alonso Nuñez** (⏲9.30am-2pm & 4.30-8pm Mon-Fri, 9.30am-1.30pm Sat) at number 3. It dates from 1827 and, aside from the displays of anti-wrinkle creams and condoms, the sumptuous interior and ornate ceiling haven't changed a bit.

★Catedral CATHEDRAL
(☎987 87 57 70; www.catedraldeleon.org; Plaza de Regia; adult/concession/under 12yr €6/5/free, combined ticket with Claustro & Museo Catedralicio-Diocesano €9/8/free; ⏲9.30am-1.30pm & 4-8pm Mon-Fri, 9.30am-noon & 2-6pm Sat, 9.30-11am & 2-8pm Sun Jun-Sep, 9.30am-1.30pm & 4-7pm Mon-Sat, 9.30am-2pm Sun Oct-May) León's 13th-century cathedral, with its soaring towers, flying buttresses and breathtaking interior, is the city's spiritual heart. Whether spotlit by night or bathed in glorious northern sunshine, the cathedral, arguably Spain's premier Gothic masterpiece, exudes a glorious, almost luminous quality. The show-stopping facade has a radiant **rose window**, three richly sculpted doorways and two muscular towers. The main entrance is lorded over by a scene of the Last Supper, while an extraordinary gallery of *vidrieras* (stained-glass windows) awaits you inside.

French in inspiration and mainly executed from the 13th to the 16th centuries, the windows' kaleidoscope of coloured light is breathtaking. There seems to be more glass than brick here – 128 windows with a surface of 1800 sq metres in all – but mere numbers cannot convey the ethereal quality of light permeating this cathedral.

Other treasures include a silver urn by Enrique de Arfe on the altar, containing the

León

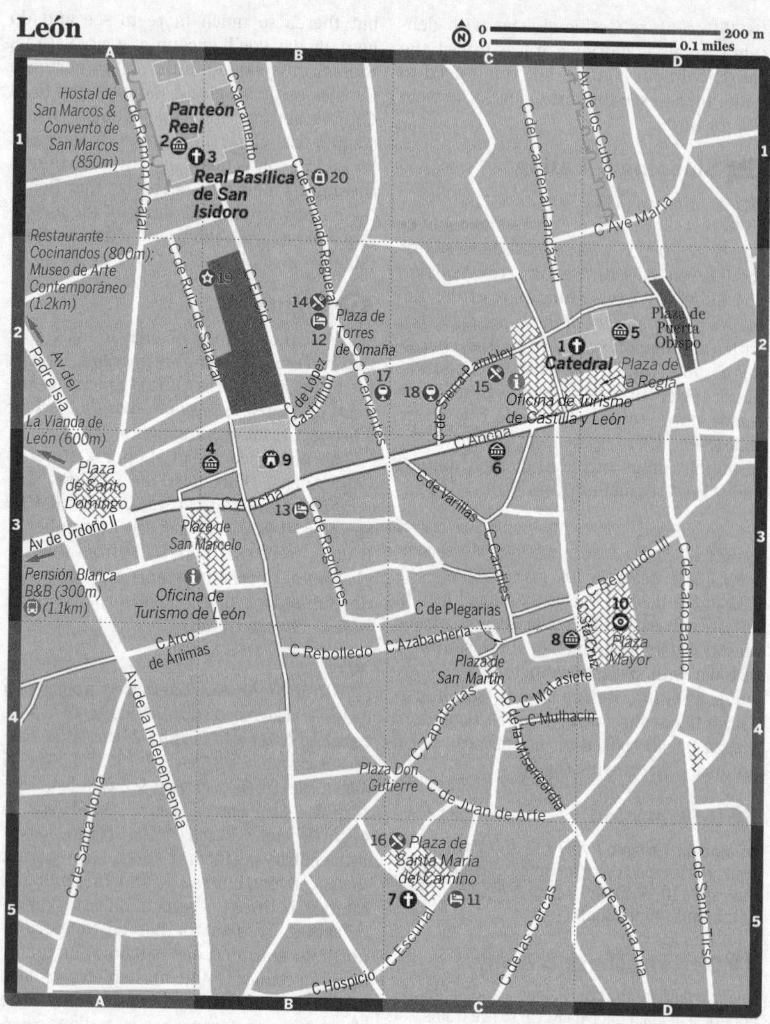

remains of San Froilán, León's patron saint. Also note the magnificent **choir stalls**.

Combine your time in the cathedral with a visit to the **Claustro & Museo Catedralicio-Diocesano** (Plaza de Regia; adult/concession/child under 12yr €5/4/free ⏲9.30am-1.30pm & 4-8pm Mon-Fri, 9.30am-noon & 2-6pm Sat, 9.30-11am & 2-8pm Sun Jun-Sep, 9.30am-1.30pm & 4-7pm Mon-Sat, 9.30am-2pm Sun Oct-May), just around the corner. In the peaceful, light-filled *claustro* (cloisters), 15th-century frescos provide a perfect complement to the main sanctuary, while the museum has an impressive collection encompassing works by Juní and Gaspar Becerra, alongside a precious assemblage of early Romanesque carved statues of the Virgin Mary.

★Museo de Arte Contemporáneo GALLERY

(Musac; ☎987 09 00 00; www.musac.es; Avenida de los Reyes Leóneses 24; adult/concession/child €3/2/1, 5-9pm Sun & 7-8pm Tue-Thu free; ⏲11am-2pm & 5-8pm Tue-Fri, 11am-3pm & 5-9pm Sat & Sun, guided tours 1pm & 6pm) León's showpiece Museo de Arte Contemporáneo has been acclaimed for the 37 shades of coloured glass that adorn the facade; they were gleaned

León

Top Sights
1 Catedral ... C2
2 Panteón Real ... A1
3 Real Basílica de San Isidoro ... A1

Sights
4 Casa Botines ... B3
5 Claustro & Museo Catedralicio-Diocesano ... D2
6 Farmacia Alonso Nuñez ... C3
7 Iglesia de Santa María del Mercado ... C5
8 Old Town Hall ... C4
9 Palacio de los Guzmanes ... B3
10 Plaza Mayor ... D3

Sleeping
11 Hospedería Monástica Pax ... C5
12 Hostal San Martín ... B2
13 La Posada Regia ... B3

Eating
14 La Trébede ... B2
15 Restaurante Zuloaga ... C2
16 Taberna La Piconera ... C5

Drinking & Nightlife
17 Camarote Madrid ... B2
18 Four Lions Brewery ... C2

Entertainment
19 La Lola ... B2

Shopping
20 El Escribano ... B1

from the pixelisation of a fragment of one of the stained-glass windows in León's cathedral. Within the museum is one of Spain's most dynamic artistic spaces. The airy galleries mostly display temporary exhibitions of cutting-edge Spanish and international photography, video installations and other similar forms; it also has a growing permanent collection. Concerts are held here regularly.

★Panteón Real HISTORIC BUILDING
(www.turismoleon.org; Plaza de San Isidoro; adult/child €5/free; 10am-2pm & 4-7pm Mon-Sat, 10am-2pm Sun) Attached to the Real Basílica de San Isidoro (p191), the stunning Panteón Real houses royal sarcophagi, which rest with quiet dignity beneath a canopy of some of the finest Romanesque frescos in Spain. Colourful motifs of biblical scenes drench the vaults and arches of this extraordinary hall, held aloft by marble columns with intricately carved capitals. The pantheon also houses a small **museum** where you can admire the shrine of San Isidoro, a mummified finger(!) of the saint and other treasures.

★Real Basílica de San Isidoro CHURCH
(987 87 61 61; Plaza de San Isidro; 7.30am-11pm) FREE Even older than León's cathedral, the Real Basílica de San Isidoro provides a stunning Romanesque counterpoint to the former's Gothic strains. Fernando I and Doña Sancha founded the church in 1063 to house the remains of the saint, as well as the remains of themselves and 21 other early Léonese and Castilian monarchs. Sadly, Napoleon's troops sacked San Isidoro in the early 19th century, but there's still plenty to catch the eye.

Convento de San Marcos CONVENT
(Plaza de San Marcos; 10am-2pm & 4-7pm Tue-Sat, 10am-2pm Sun) FREE You will have to check into the Hostal de San Marcos parador (p192) to appreciate most of this palatial former monastery, although the historic chapter house and magnificent cloister can be viewed by nonguests. The plateresque exterior is also superb, sectioned off by slender columns and decorated with delicate medallions and friezes that date from 1513. It's particularly lovely when floodlit at night.

Casa Botines HISTORIC BUILDING
(987 35 32 47; www.casabotines.es; Plaza de San Marcos 6; adult/child €5/free; 11am-2pm & 5-9pm Mon, Tue & Thu-Sat, 5-9pm Wed, 11am-2pm Sun) Antoni Gaudí's contribution to León's skyline is the castle-like, neo-Gothic Casa de Botines (1893) – though the zany architect of Barcelona fame seems to have been subdued by more sober León. A statue of Gaudí sits on a bench outside.

Palacio de los Guzmanes PALACE
(987 292 204; Plaza de San Marcelo 6; adult/child €2/1; 11am-5am Wed-Sun) León's recurring Renaissance theme finds expression in the splendid Palacio de los Guzmanes (1560), where the facade and patio stand out. The latter is accessible only by a free **guided tour**.

Plaza Mayor SQUARE

At the northeastern end of the old town is the beautiful and time-worn 17th-century Plaza Mayor. Sealed off on three sides by porticoes, this sleepy plaza is home to a bustling **produce market** on Wednesday and Saturday. On the west side of the square is the late 17th-century, baroque **old town hall**.

Iglesia de Santa María del Mercado CHURCH

(Plaza de Santa María del Camino; ⏲10am-1.30pm & 5-8pm Tue-Sun mid-Jun–mid-Sep, 11am-noon & 7-8pm Mon-Sat mid-Sep–mid-Jun) Down the hill, the careworn, stone Romanesque Iglesia de Santa María del Mercado looks out over a delightful square that feels like a cobblestone Castilian village plaza. Opening hours can vary but it's the exterior and the setting that most appeals.

Tours

Visitas Guiadas León TOUR

(☎688 94 14 03; www.visitasguiadasoficiales.com; free to €20; ⏲11am, 12.15pm, & 5.15pm Thu-Tue) These guided visits run for between an hour and three hours, and include a range of options, including (sometimes) an 8pm nocturnal tour. A donation based on your satisfaction is expected at the end of the free tour. Most tours start outside the cathedral entrance.

Festivals & Events

★Semana Santa RELIGIOUS

(Holy Week; ⏲Mar/Apr) León is an excellent place to see solemn Holy Week processions of hooded penitents, with the city's monuments as a stirring backdrop.

Fiestas de San Juan y San Pedro FIESTA

(⏲Jun; 👪) The city lets its hair down on the cusp of summer – from 21 to 30 June – with concerts, street stalls and general merriment.

Sleeping

Pensión Blanca B&B PENSION €

(☎987 25 19 91; www.pensionblanca.com; Calle de Villafranca 2; d/tr €45/60, s/d without bathroom €30/40; 📶) A cut above your average *pensión* and easily one of the best budget choices in León, Pensión Blanca has attractive, brightly coloured rooms in a good location about halfway between the bus/train stations and the cathedral; the latter is a 10-minute walk away, along the main shopping street.

Hostal San Martín HOSTAL €

(☎987 87 51 87; www.sanmartinhostales.es; 2nd fl, Plaza de Torres de Omaña 1; s/d €30/43, without bathroom €20/30; 📶) In a splendid central position occupying an 18th-century building, this is good old-fashioned budget value in the heart of town. The candy-coloured rooms are light and airy; all have small terraces. The spotless bathrooms have excellent water pressure and tubs, as well as showers, and there's a comfortable sitting area. The friendly owner can provide advice and a map.

★La Posada Regia HISTORIC HOTEL €€

(☎987 21 31 73; www.regialeon.com; Calle de Regidores 9-11; incl breakfast s €54-70, d €59-130; 📶) This place has the feel of a *casa rural* (village or farmstead accommodation) despite being in the city centre. The secret is a 14th-century building, magnificently restored (with wooden beams, exposed brick and understated antique furniture), with individually styled rooms and supremely comfortable beds and bathrooms. As with anywhere in the Barrio Húmedo, weekend nights can be noisy.

Hospedería Monástica Pax HOSTAL €€

(☎987 34 44 93; www.hospederiapax.com; Plaza de Santa María del Camino; r €51-80; ❄📶) Overlooking one of the loveliest squares in León, this excellent place inhabits a restored former monastery; the rooms are mostly spacious and stylishly appointed. Unless you're a really light sleeper, ask for a room overlooking the square.

★Hostal de San Marcos HISTORIC HOTEL €€€

(☎987 23 73 00; www.parador.es; Plaza de San Marcos 7; d incl breakfast from €110; P❄@📶) Despite the confusing *'hostal'* in the name, León's sumptuous *parador* is one of the finest hotels in Spain. With palatial rooms fit for royalty and filled with old-world luxury and decor, this is one of the Parador chain's flagship properties. As you'd expect, the service and attention to detail are faultless. It inhabits the landmark Convento de San Marcos (p191).

Eating

La Trébede TAPAS €

(☎637 25 91 97; Plaza de Torres de Omaña; tapas from €2.50, raciones from €7; ⏲noon-4pm & 8pm-midnight Mon-Sat) As good for tapas (try the croquettes) as for first drinks (wines by the glass start at €1.50), La Trébede is always full. The decor is eclectic – deer's antlers, historic wirelesses and the scales of justice – and the sign outside declaring 350km to Santiago may just prompt you to abandon the Camino and stay a little longer.

Taberna La Piconera TAPAS, SPANISH €€
(☎987 26 34 56; Plaza Santa María del Camino 2; tapas from €2.50, raciones €9-17, mains €15-18; ⏲1pm-midnight Tue-Sun) Excellent meat dishes are offered here, paired up nicely with fresh salads, but we like it for its setting on one of León's loveliest squares. Grab an outdoor table and linger either side of your meal as you nurse a wine and enjoy the view.

★**Restaurante Cocinandos** MODERN SPANISH €€€
(☎987 07 13 78; www.cocinandos.com; Calle de las Campanillas 1; set menu €43; ⏲1.45-3.30pm & 9.30-11pm Tue-Sat) The proud owner of León's only Michelin star, Cocinandos brings creative flair to the table with a menu that changes weekly with the seasons and market availability. The atmosphere is slightly formal so dress nicely and book in advance, but the young team puts diners at ease and the food is exceptional (in that zany new-Spanish-cuisine kind of way).

Drinking & Nightlife

★**Camarote Madrid** WINE BAR
(www.camarotemadrid.com; Calle de Cervantes 8; ⏲10am-4pm & 8pm-12.30am) With legs of ham displayed like some meaty Broadway chorus line, this popular bar is famed for its tapas – the little ceramic cup of *salmorejo* (a cold, tomato-based soup) is rightly famous. But the extensive wine list wins the day amid the buzz of a happy crowd swirling around the central bar.

Four Lions Brewery BAR
(☎619 89 19 02; www.fourlionsbrewery.com; Calle Sierra Pambley 6; ⏲1-5pm & 8pm-midnight Mon-Sat, 1pm-midnight Sun) We like this place for its boutique beers and agreeable atmosphere – it produces six beers of its own, including lagers, ales and a stout. The food gets decidedly mixed reviews.

Entertainment

La Lola LIVE MUSIC
(☎987 22 43 03; www.papaquijano.com; Calle de Ruiz de Salazar 22; ⏲9pm-5am Wed-Sat, live music from midnight Wed & Thu, from 1am Fri & Sat) Come here to listen to Papa Quijano, a legendary Latino-rock crooner who has recorded several CDs and accrued quite a fan base. He has run this atmospheric bar since the 1970s. Dimly lit and with a back alcove encompassing part of the Roman wall, it won't be to everyone's taste but it's a fascinating place.

Shopping

La Vianda de León FOOD
(☎987 24 03 70; www.laviandadeleon.com; Gran Vía de San Marcos 47; ⏲10.30am-3pm & 5.30-9pm Mon-Fri, 10am-3pm Sat) This is an excellent gourmet deli out in the newer part of town with everything from cheeses, wines and cured meats to local pastries.

El Escribano ARTS & CRAFTS
(☎987 07 32 22; www.elescribano.com; Calle de Fernando Regueral 6; ⏲11.30am-1.30pm & 6-8pm Mon-Fri) Some lovely etchings and reproductions of medieval art are among the many attractions of this classy shop.

Information

Oficina de Turismo de Castilla y León (☎987 23 70 82; www.turismocastillayleon.com; Plaza de la Regla 2; ⏲9.30am-2pm & 5-8pm Mon-Sat, 9.30am-5pm Sun Apr-Sep, 9.30am-2pm & 4-7pm Mon-Sat, 9.30am-5pm Sun Oct-Mar) Opposite the cathedral. Also has info on Castilla y León in general.

Oficina de Turismo de León (☎987 87 83 27; www.turismoleon.org; Plaza de San Marcelo 1; ⏲9am-8pm) Information on the city and surrounding region.

Getting There & Away

The train and bus stations lie on the western bank of Río Bernesga, off the western end of Avenida de Ordoño II.

Bus Services depart from the **bus station** (☎987 21 10 00; Paseo del Ingeniero Sáez de Miera) to Madrid (€24, 3½ hours, eight daily), Astorga (€3.95, one hour, 17 daily), Ponferrada (€9.25, two hours, up to 12 daily), Burgos (from €5.20, two hours, three daily) and Valladolid (€11.30, two hours, nine daily).

Car & Motorcycle Parking bays (€12 to €16 for 12 hours) can be found in the streets surrounding Plaza de Santo Domingo. Alternatively, look for free parking in the large open-air car park outside the Junta de Castilla y León; it's west of the centre, close to the Hostal San Marcos.

Train The AVE fast train network now reaches León, which has cut travel time considerably to/from Valladolid (from €16.40, 1¼ to two

WORTH A TRIP

MONASTERIO DE SAN MIGUEL DE ESCALADA

Rising from Castilla's northern plains, this beautifully simple **treasure** (€2; ⏲10am-2.30pm & 4.30-7.30pm Tue-Sun May-Oct, 10am-2.30pm Fri-Sun Mar & Apr, closed rest of year) was built in the 9th century by refugee monks from Córdoba atop the remains of a Visigoth church dedicated to the Archangel Michael. Although little trace of the latter remains, the church is notable for its Islamic-inspired horseshoe arches, rarely seen so far north in Spain. The graceful exterior and its portico are balanced by the impressive marble columns within. The entrance dates from the 11th century.

To get here, take the N601 southeast of León. After about 14km, take the small LE213 to the east; the church is 16km after the turn-off.

hours) and Madrid (from €27, 2¼ to five hours). Other non-AVE destinations include Burgos (from €9.90, two hours).

Getting Around

Drivers should note that León's central city underground car parks are privately owned and costlier than most (per hour €1.50) with, unusually, no reduction for overnight stays. You may want to consider a hotel with private parking instead.

Astorga

POP 11,264 / ELEV 870M

Perched on a hilltop on the frontier between the bleak plains of northern Castilla and the mountains that rise up to the west towards Galicia, Astorga is a fascinating small town with a wealth of attractions out of proportion to its size. In addition to its fine cathedral, the city boasts a Gaudí-designed palace, a smattering of Roman ruins and a personality dominated by the Camino de Santiago. Most enjoyable of all, perhaps, is the museum dedicated to chocolate.

Sights

Palacio Episcopal MUSEUM, ARCHITECTURE
(Museo de los Caminos; Calle de Los Sitios; adult/child €3/free; ⏲10am-2pm & 4-8pm Tue-Sat, 10am-2pm Sun Mar-Sep, 11am-2pm & 4-6pm Tue-Sat, 10am-2pm Sun Oct-Feb) Catalan architect Antoni Gaudí left his mark on Astorga in the fairy-tale turrets and frilly facade of the Palacio Episcopal. Built in the 19th century, it now houses the **Museo de los Caminos** (in the basement), an eclectic collection with Roman artefacts and coins; contemporary paintings (on the top floor); and medieval sculpture, Gothic tombs and silver crosses (on the ground and 1st floors). The highlight is the **chapel**, with its stunning murals and stained glass.

Museo del Chocolate MUSEUM
(☎987 61 62 20; www.museochocolateastorga.com; Avenida de la Estación 16; adult/child €2.50/free, incl Museo Romano adult/child €4/free; ⏲10.30am-2pm & 4.30-7pm Tue-Sat, 10.30am-2pm Sun; 👪) Proof that Astorga does not exist solely for the virtuous souls of the Camino comes in the form of this quirky private museum. Chocolate ruled Astorga's local economy in the 18th and 19th centuries; this eclectic collection of old machinery, colourful advertising and lithographs inhabits a lovely old mansion within walking distance of the centre. Best of all, you get a free chocolate sample at the end.

Catedral CATHEDRAL
(Plaza de la Catedral; incl museum & cloister €5; ⏲10am-8.30pm Mon-Sat, 10-11.15am & 1-8.30 Sun Apr-Oct, 10.30am-7pm Mon-Sat & 1-7 Sun Nov-Mar) The cathedral's striking plateresque southern facade is created from caramel-coloured sandstone with elaborate sculptural detail. Work began in 1471 and continued over three centuries, resulting in a mix of styles. The mainly Gothic interior has soaring ceilings and a superb 16th-century altarpiece by Gaspar Becerra. The attached **Museo Catedralicio** (☎987 61 58 20; incl Catedral & cloister €5; ⏲10am-2pm & 4-8pm Tue-Sat, 10am-2pm Sun Mar-Sep, 11am-2pm & 4-6pm Tue-Sat, 10am-2pm Sun Oct-Feb) features the usual religious art, documents and artefacts.

Museo Romano MUSEUM
(☎987 61 68 38; Plaza de San Bartolomé 2; adult/child €3/free, incl Museo del Chocolate adult/child €4/free; ⏲10am-2pm & 4.30-7pm Tue-Sun Jul-Sep, 10.30am-2pm & 4-6pm Tue-Sat, 10.30am-2pm Sun Oct-May; 👪) Housed in the Roman *ergástula* (slave prison), the Museo Romano has a modest selection of artefacts and an enjoyable big-screen slide show on Roman Astorga.

Tours

Ruta Romana WALKING

(☎987 61 69 37; rutaromana@ayuntamientodeastorga.com; per person €4, incl Museo Romano €5; ⏲11am & 5pm Tue-Sat, 11am Sun) This 1¾-hour guided tour of Astorga's Roman remains (some of which are accessible only as part of this tour) is an excellent way to really get under the skin of the town's Roman past. The tours are conducted in Spanish only but most of the sites have English information panels.

Festivals & Events

Festividad de Santa Marta RELIGIOUS

(⏲late Aug; 👪) The sacred and the profane mix seamlessly as Astorga celebrates its patron saint with fireworks and bullfights. Last week of August.

Sleeping

Hotel Vía de la Plata HOTEL €€

(☎987 61 90 00; www.hotelviadelaplata.es; Calle Padres Redentoristas 5; d/ste incl breakfast €80/100; ❄@📶) This spa hotel occupies a handsome former monastery just off Plaza España. Guests receive a considerable discount for the spa treatments, which include the deliciously decadent-sounding *chocoterapia* (chocolate therapy). The rooms are slick and modern, with fashionable mushroom-brown and cream decor, tubular lights and full-size tubs, as well as showers.

El Descanso de Wendy APARTMENT €€

(☎987 617 854; www.eldescansodewendy.com; Calle de Matadero Viejo 11; s/d from €64/90) At the western reaches of the old city but within easy walking distance of all the sights, El Descanso de Wendy has eclectic decor that ranges from the simple to the extravagant. Service is warm and friendly and travellers regularly sing its praises.

Hotel Astur Plaza HOTEL €€

(☎987 61 89 00; www.hotelasturplaza.es; Plaza de España 2; s/d/ste from €55/75/110; ❄@📶) Opt for one of the supremely comfortable rooms that face pretty Plaza de España – at weekends, however, you may want to forsake the view for a quieter room out the back. The suites have hydromassage tubs and there are three VIP rooms with 'super king-size' beds, but even the standard rooms here are good.

Eating

★Restaurante Las Termas CASTILIAN €€

(☎987 60 22 12; www.restaurantelastermas.com; Calle de Santiago Postas 1; mains €9.50-22; ⏲1-4pm Tue-Sun; 👪) This lunchtime restaurant is run by Santiago (a popular name in these parts), who, apart from being a charming host, oversees a menu renowned for the quality of its *cocido maragato* (€22) and *ensalada maragata* (salad of chickpeas and cod). It's one of those places where you're made to feel welcome from the minute you enter, and the food is unimpeachable.

COCIDO MARAGATO

The local speciality in Astorga and surrounding villages (although you also find it in León) is *cocido maragato*. Its constituent elements are indistinguishable from a normal *cocido*, beloved in Madrid and across the Castilian heartland – it's a stew or hotpot made of various meats (some say seven meats), potatoes, chickpeas and a noodle soup. What makes it different to *cocido* elsewhere is that in a *cocido maragato* the various elements are served in reverse: first the meats, then the vegetables, then the soup.

The origins behind the tradition are much disputed. Some say that it dates back to a time when those transporting goods to and from Las Médulas by donkey chose to eat the most solid foods first as they were easiest to eat when on the move. Another story claims that bandits were common in the area and if a meal had to be interrupted, at least those eating had their fill of meat. More prosaically, local farmworkers are said to have eaten their *cocido* in this way because out in the open air, the meat would be cold by the time they got to it if eaten like a normal *cocido*.

Whatever the reason, portions are huge, so one order usually feeds two. It's also really only considered a lunchtime dish (which is why most Astorga restaurants don't even bother opening in the evening). Two of the best places to try it are Restaurante Las Termas (p195) and Casa Maragata (p196). Bookings are essential on weekends.

WORTH A TRIP

LAS MÉDULAS

The ancient Roman goldmines at Las Médulas, about 20km southwest of Ponferrada, once served as the main source of gold for the entire Roman Empire – the final tally came to a remarkable 3 million kilograms. It's stunningly beautiful, especially at sunset – one of the more bizarre landscapes you'll see in Spain. The best views are from the Mirador de Orellán, while there are some terrific walks from the village of Las Médulas.

Las Médulas' otherworldly aspect is not a natural phenomenon: an army of slaves honeycombed the area with canals and tunnels (some over 40km long), through which they pumped water to break up the rock and free it from the precious metal.

To get here, take the N536 southwest of Ponferrada, then take signed turn-off in the village of Carucedo. On the outskirts of Carucedo, the road forks. The left fork leads to the pretty stone village of Orellán (2.8km on), which tumbles down into a valley, and then on to the car park for the Mirador de Orellán. From the car park it's a steep 750m climb up to the lookout, from where the views are breathtaking.

Returning to the fork, the right branch leads on to Las Médulas village (3km on). Park at the entrance to the village, then stop at at the **Aula Arqueológica** (☎987 42 28 48; www.ieb.org.es; adult/child €2/free; ⊙10am-1.30pm & 4-8pm Apr-Sep, 10am-2pm Sun-Fri, 10am-1.30pm & 3.30-7pm Sat Oct-Mar), an interpretation centre with interesting displays on the history of the mines (admission €2); it also has information on the walks that weave among chestnut trees to the caves, quarries and bizarre formations left behind by the miners. If you're feeling fit, a 5.1km trail climbs to the Mirador de Orellán (one way/return three/4½ hours) from here, but there are plenty of other shorter trails into the heart of Las Médulas. You can also enquire about horse riding in the area.

Las Médulas can get overwhelmed with visitors on weekends, but is much quieter during the week. Las Médulas village has a handful of restaurants and *casas rurales* in case you're tempted to linger.

Casa Maragata SPANISH €€
(☎987 61 88 80; www.casamaragata.com; Calle de Húsar Tiburcio 2; cocido per person €22; ⊙1.30-4pm Wed-Mon) One of the better (and hence more popular) restaurants serving *cocido maragato*. In fact, it doesn't serve much else. There's another branch across town you can head to if this one's full. It also does a gluten-free version.

Restaurante Serrano CONTEMPORARY SPANISH €€
(☎987 61 78 66; www.restauranteserrano.es; Calle de la Portería 2; mains €13-23; ⊙12.30-4pm & 8-11.30pm Tue-Sun) The menu at upmarket Restaurante Serrano has a subtle gourmet flourish, with fresh summery starters, innovative meat and fish mains and plenty of tempting desserts with chocolate. It also serves *cocido maragato* and other local dishes. Reservations recommended.

Shopping

Confitería Mantecadas Velasco FOOD
(☎987 61 59 35; www.mantecadasvelasco.com; Plaza Eduardo de Castro 1; ⊙10.30am-2pm & 4.30-7.30pm) The word among locals-in-the-know is that Confitería Mantecadas Velasco serves some of the best *mantecadas* and other pastries in Astorga. We've tried them and who are we to argue? It's an obligatory part of the Castilla y León foodie experience.

Information

Oficina de Turismo (☎987 61 82 22; www.turismocastillayleon.com; Glorieta Eduardo de Castro 5; ⊙10am-2pm & 4-8pm Apr-Sep, 10am-2pm & 4-6pm Oct-Mar) Opposite the Palacio Episcopal.

Getting There & Away

Regular bus services connect Astorga with León (€3.95, one hour, 17 daily) and Madrid (from €25, 4½ hours, three daily). The train station is inconveniently a couple of kilometres north of town.

Sahagún

POP 2645 / ELEV 807M

A modest, albeit quietly picturesque town today, Sahagún was once home to one of Spain's more powerful abbeys; it remains an important way station for pilgrims en route to Santiago.

Sights

Santuario de La Peregrina CONVENT
(987 78 10 15; off Avenida Fernando de Castro; €3; 10.30am-2pm & 4.30-8pm Tue-Sun Jul–mid-Sep, 11am-2pm & 4-6.30pm Wed-Sun, 4-6.30pm Tue mid-Sep–Jun) This 13th-century former convent has been stunningly restored, with glimpses of elaborate 13th-century frescos and 17th-century Mudéjar plasterwork (the latter is in the chapel to the right of the main nave). Contemporary artworks fill the spaces in between and a modern addition to the convent houses some excellent scale models of Sahagún's major monuments.

Iglesia de San Tirso CHURCH
(Plaza de San Tirso; 10am-2pm & 3-5.50pm Wed-Sat, 10am-2pm Sun) FREE The early-12th-century Iglesia de San Tirso, at the western entrance to town, is an important stop on the Camino de Santiago. It's known for its pure Romanesque design and Mudéjar bell tower laced with rounded arches.

Sleeping

La Bastide du Chemìn HOSTAL €
(987 78 11 83; www.labastideduchemin.es; Calle del Arco 66; s/d €28/40;) Opened in 2013, this small, cosy *hostal*, opposite the Albergue de Peregrinos (Hostel for Pilgrims), has pleasant rustic rooms with beamed ceilings.

San Facundo CASTILIAN €€
(987 78 02 76; Avenida de la Constitución 97-99; mains €14-26; 1-4pm & 8-11pm;) Part of the **Hostal La Codorniz** (www.hostallacodorniz.com; s/d €40/50, breakfast €4.50;), this traditional restaurant, which has an impressive carved Mudéjar ceiling, specialises in succulent roasted meats.

Information

Oficina de Turismo (987 78 21 17; www.sahagun.org; Calle del Arco 87; noon-2pm & 6-9pm Mon-Thu, 11am-2pm & 4-9pm Fri-Sun) Located within the Albergue de Peregrinos.

Getting There & Away

Trains run regularly throughout the day from León (from €5.75, 40 minutes) and Palencia (from €5.75, 35 minutes).

THE EAST

Burgos

POP 176,608 / ELEV 861M

The extraordinary Gothic cathedral of Burgos is one of Spain's glittering jewels of religious architecture – it looms large over the city and skyline. On the surface, conservative Burgos seems to embody all the stereotypes of a north-central Spanish town, with sombre grey-stone architecture, the fortifying cuisine of the high *meseta* (plateau) and a climate of extremes. But this is a city that rewards deeper exploration: below the surface lie good restaurants and, when the sun's shining, pretty streetscapes that extend far beyond the landmark cathedral. There's even a whiff of legend about the place: beneath the majestic spires of the cathedral lies the tomb of Burgos' favourite and most roguish son, El Cid.

Camino Francés in Castilla y León

Burgos

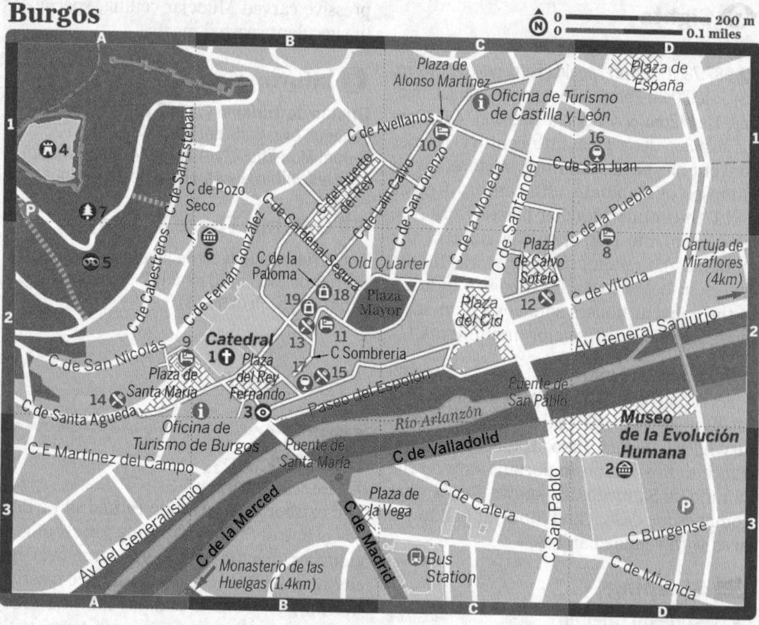

Burgos

Top Sights

1 Catedral B2
2 Museo de la Evolución Humana D3

Sights

3 Arco de Santa María B2
4 Castillo de Burgos A1
5 Mirador A2
6 Museo del Retablo B2
7 Parque de Castillo A1

Sleeping

8 Hotel Cuéntame La Puebla D2
9 Hotel Mesón del Cid A2
10 Hotel Norte y Londres C1
11 Rimbombín B2

Eating

12 Casa Ojeda C2
13 Cervecería Morito B2
14 El Huerto de Roque A2
15 Mari Castaña B2

Drinking & Nightlife

16 El Bosque Encantado D1
17 Vermutería Victoria B2

Shopping

18 Casa Quintanilla B2
19 Jorge Revilla B2

Sights

★Catedral CATHEDRAL

(☎947 20 47 12; www.catedraldeburgos.es; Plaza del Rey Fernando; adult/under 14yr incl audio guide €7/2, from 4.30pm Tue free; ⏲9.30am-7.30pm Apr-Sep, to 6.30pm Oct-Mar) This Unesco World Heritage–listed cathedral, once a former modest Romanesque church, is a masterpiece. Work began on a grander scale in 1221; remarkably, within 40 years most of the French Gothic structure had been completed. You can enter from Plaza de Santa María for free for access to the **Capilla del Santísimo Cristo**, with its much-revered 13th-century crucifix, and the **Capilla de Santa Tecla**, with its extraordinary ceiling. However, we recommend that you visit the cathedral in its entirety.

The cathedral's twin towers went up in the 15th century; each is 84m of richly decorated Gothic fantasy surrounded by a sea of similarly intricate spires. Probably the most impressive of the portals is the **Puerta del Sarmental**, the main entrance for visitors – although the honour could also go to the **Puerta de la Coronería**, on the northwestern side, which shows Christ surrounded by the evangelists.

Inside the main sanctuary, a host of other chapels showcase the diversity of the interior, from the light and airy **Capilla de la Presentación** to the **Capilla de la Concepción**, with its gilded, 15th-century altar, and the **Capilla de Santa Ana**, with its gorgeous *retablo* (altarpiece). The **Capilla del Condestable**, behind the main altar, bridges Gothic and plateresque styles; highlights here include three altars watched over by unusual star-shaped vaulting in the dome. The sculptures facing the entrance to the chapel are 15th- and 16th-century masterpieces of stone carving, portraying the Passion, death, resurrection and ascension of Christ.

The main altar is a typically overwhelming piece of gold-encrusted extravagance, while directly beneath the star-vaulted central dome lies the **tomb of El Cid**. With so much else to catch the eye, it's easy to miss the sublime main **dome**, high above the main sanctuary – it's a masterpiece of the plateresque, with a few Gothic flourishes. Another highlight is Diego de Siloé's magnificent **Escalera Dorada** (Gilded Stairway) on the cathedral's northwestern flank.

Also worth a look is the peaceful cloister, with its sculpted medieval tombs. Off the cloister is the **Capilla de Corpus Cristi**, where, high on the northwestern wall, hangs what legend calls the coffin of El Cid, although doubts remain as to its origins. The adjoining **Museo Catedralicio** has a wealth of oil paintings, tapestries and ornate chalices, while the lower cloister covers the history of the cathedral's development, with a scale model to help you take it all in.

★Museo de la Evolución Humana MUSEUM

(MEH; ☎902 02 42 46; www.museoevolucionhumana.com; Paseo Sierra de Atapuerca; adult/concession/child €6/4/free, 4.30-8pm Wed, 7-8pm Tue & Thu free; ⏲10am-2.30pm & 4.30-8pm Tue-Fri, 10am-8pm Sat & Sun) This exceptional museum just across the river from the old quarter is a marvellously told story of human evolution. The basement exhibitions on Atapuerca (p201), an archaeological site north of Burgos where a 2007 discovery of Europe's oldest human fossil remains was made, are stunning; the displays on Charles Darwin and the extraordinary 'Human Evolution' section in the centre of the ground floor are simply outstanding. Even if you've no prior interest in the subject, don't miss it.

Museo del Retablo MUSEUM

(Altar Museum; Calle de Pozo Seco; admission incl church €2, 5-8pm Tue free; ⏲10am-2pm & 5-8pm Tue-Sun) Just west of the cathedral, in the **Iglesia de San Esteban**, the Museo del Retablo has a display of some 18 altars dating from the 15th to 18th centuries.

Cartuja de Miraflores MONASTERY

(☎947 25 25 86; www.cartuja.org; by donation; ⏲10.15am-3pm & 4-6pm Mon-Sat, 11am-3pm & 4-6pm Sun) FREE Located in peaceful woodlands 4km east of the city centre, this monastery contains a trio of 15th-century masterworks by Gil de Siloé, the man responsible for so many of the more beautiful features in the Burgos cathedral. The walk to the monastery along Río Arlanzón takes about one hour. To get here, head north along Paseo de la Quinta (flanking the river), from where the monastery is clearly signposted.

Monasterio de las Huelgas MONASTERY

(☎947 20 16 30; www.monasteriodelashuelgas.org; Calle de Alfonso XIII; €6, 4-5.30pm Wed & Thu free; ⏲10am-1pm & 4-5.30pm Tue-Sat, 10.30am-2pm Sun) A 30-minute walk west of the city centre on the southern river bank, this monastery was once among the most prominent in Spain. Founded in 1187 by Eleanor of Aquitaine, daughter of Henry II of England and wife of Alfonso VIII of Castilla, it's still home to 35 Cistercian nuns. Entry is via one-hour guided tour only – unhelpfully, the timing of the tours is decided only at the beginning of each session, so it's worth ringing ahead.

Arco de Santa María GATE

(☎947 28 88 68; ⏲11am-1.50pm & 5-9pm Tue-Sat, 11am-1.50pm Sun) FREE The splendid Arco de Santa María was once the main gate to the old city and part of the 14th-century walls. It now hosts temporary exhibitions, but its real charm lies as a backdrop to the Puente de Santa María or Paseo de Espolón.

Castillo de Burgos CASTLE

(☎947 20 38 57; adult/child under 14yr €3.70/2.60; ⏲11am-6.30pm Sat & Sun; 👪) Crowning the leafy hilltop **Parque de Castillo** are the massive fortifications of the rebuilt Castillo de Burgos. Dating from the 9th century, the castle has witnessed a turbulent history, suffering a fire in 1736 and being blown up by Napoleon's troops in 1813. There's a small museum covering the town's history; some

ONLY IN SPAIN

Every year since 1620, the tiny village of Castrillo de Murcia (25km west of Burgos) has marked the feast of Corpus Cristi with the **Baby-Jumping Festival** (El Salto del Colacho; ⌚May/Jun). The village's babies are lined up on mattresses, while grown men leap over up to six supine (and somewhat bewildered) babies at a time. The ritual is thought to ward off the devil – but why jumping over babies? The villagers aren't telling. They do, however, assure us that no baby has been injured in the fiesta's recorded history.

of the original castle foundations are on view. Just south of the car park is a **mirador** with great views of the cathedral and across the city.

Tours

The Municipal Tourist Office runs (or sells tickets to) guided tours of the cathedral and other main monuments. Most leave around 11am and/or 5pm and cost from €5 to €8 per person.

Sleeping

★Rimbombín HOSTAL €
(☎947 26 12 00; www.rimbombin.com; Calle Sombrería 6; d/tr/apt from €60/70/110; ❄📶) Opened in 2013, this 'urban *hostal*' has an upbeat, contemporary feel – its slick white furnishings and decor are matched with light-pine beams and modular furniture. Three of the rooms have balconies overlooking the pedestrian street. Conveniently, it's in the heart of Burgos' compact tapas district. The apartment is excellent value for longer stays, with the same chic modern look and two bedrooms.

★Hotel Norte y Londres HISTORIC HOTEL €
(☎947 26 41 25; www.hotelnorteylondres.com; Plaza de Alonso Martínez 10; s/d from €38/40; P@📶) Set in a former 16th-century palace and decorated with understated period charm, this fine, family-run hotel promises spacious rooms with antique furnishings and polished wooden floors. All rooms have pretty balconies; those on the 4th floor are more modern. The bathrooms are exceptionally large and the service friendly and efficient.

Hotel Cuéntame La Puebla BOUTIQUE HOTEL €€
(☎947 25 09 00; www.hotelescuentame.com; Calle de la Puebla 20; d/tr from €48/65; ❄@📶) This boutique hotel adds a touch of style to the Burgos hotel scene. The rooms aren't huge and most don't have views but they're softly lit, beautifully designed and supremely comfortable. Extra perks include bikes and a pillow menu; on the downside, some readers have complained about the level of street noise.

Hotel Mesón del Cid HISTORIC HOTEL €€
(☎947 20 87 15; www.mesondelcid.es; Plaza de Santa María 8; d/ste from €60/115; P📶) Facing the cathedral, this hotel occupies a centuries-old building. Rooms have Regency-style burgundy-and-cream fabrics, aptly combined with dark-wood furnishings and terracotta tiles. Several have stunning front-row seats of the cathedral (for a supplement of €10).

Eating

★Cervecería Morito TAPAS €
(☎947 26 75 55; Calle de Diego Porcelos 1; tapas/raciones from €4/6; ⌚12.30-3.30pm & 7-11.30pm) Cervecería Morito is the undisputed king of Burgos tapas bars and as such it's always crowded. A typical order is *alpargata* (lashings of cured ham with bread, tomato and olive oil) or the *revueltos Capricho de Burgos* (scrambled eggs served with potatoes, blood sausage, red peppers, baby eels and mushrooms) – the latter is a meal in itself.

★El Huerto de Roque CASTILIAN €€
(☎947 27 87 93; www.facebook.com/ElHuertoDeRoque/; Calle de Santa Águeda 10; mains €11-15, set menu €16; ⌚restaurant 1-4pm Tue-Sat, gastrobar 9pm-12.30am Thu, 9pm-1.30am Fri & Sat; 🖉) Come here for an inexpensive lunch with plenty of choice. The emphasis is on the ecological, with a menu that changes with the seasons and according to what produce is fresh and good in the local market. The atmosphere throughout is boho-rustic, with original tiles, wooden furniture and edgy artwork. The adjacent gastropub reflects a similar cuisine, tapas-style.

Mari Castaña MODERN SPANISH €€
(☎947 20 61 55; www.facebook.com/maricastanaBU; Paseo del Espolón 10; mains €8-18; ⌚8.30am-11pm) This bright place takes some tired old culinary concepts and freshens them up with great success. The *plato combinado,*

that meat-and-three-veg warhorse, here retains the concept of a meal on one plate but is rethought with all fresh-market cooking. There's also breakfast, plates to share and some tempting set menus, including some that do wonderful things with mushrooms.

Casa Ojeda CASTILIAN €€
(☎947 20 90 52; www.grupojeda.com; Calle de Vitoria 5; mains €16-25, set menu €32; ⏰1-3.30pm & 8-11pm Mon-Sat, 1-4pm Sun) Dating from 1912, this Burgos institution, all sheathed in dark wood with stunning mullioned windows, is one of the best places in town to try *cordero asado* or *morcilla de Burgos*, but there are some surprising twists, such as the *solomillo* (sirloin) medallions with foie gras and essence of raspberry. The upstairs dining room has outstanding food and faultless service. Reservations recommended.

Drinking & Nightlife

★Vermutería Victoria BAR
(☎947 11 58 75; Plaza del Rey San Fernando 4; ⏰noon-4pm & 7.30-11pm) This wildly popular bar is a Burgos classic perfect for first drinks. That time-honoured Spanish tradition of a pre-meal *vermut* (vermouth, or martini) comes with a twist here – at 10pm nightly the entire crowd launches into song with Burgos' unofficial anthem. The vermouth is award-winning, smooth and, as Spaniards like to say, perfectly poured.

El Bosque Encantado BAR
(☎947 26 12 66; www.facebook.com/cafe.pub.elbosqueencantado.burgos/; Calle de San Juan 31; ⏰4.30pm-1am) 'The Enchanted Forest' revels in its kitsch decor and is good for early evening drinks. There are plenty of other bars in the vicinity to keep the night ticking over.

Shopping

Casa Quintanilla FOOD
(☎947 20 25 35; www.casaquintanilla.es; Calle de la Paloma 22; ⏰10am-2pm & 5-8.30pm Mon-Sat, 10am-2pm Sun) This is the pick of many stores around the town centre offering local produce that's ideal for a picnic or a gift for back home.

Jorge Revilla JEWELLERY
(☎947 274 040; www.jorgerevilla.com; Calle de la Paloma 29; ⏰10am-2pm & 5-8pm Mon-Fri, 10am-2pm Sat) Local Burgos jewellery designer Jorge Revilla is becoming a global name for his exquisite and sophisticated silver pieces.

ℹ Information

Oficina de Turismo de Burgos (☎947 28 88 74; www.aytoburgos.es/turismo; Plaza de Santa María; ⏰9am-8pm daily Jun-Sep, 9.30am-2pm & 4-7pm Mon-Sat, 9.30am-5pm Sun Oct-May) Pick up its 24-hour, 48-hour and 72-hour guides to Burgos. (These helpful itinerary suggestions can also be downloaded as PDFs from the website.)

Oficina de Turismo de Castilla y León (☎902 20 30 30; www.turismocastillayleon.com; Plaza de Alonso Martínez 7; ⏰9.30am-2pm & 4-7pm Mon-Sat, 9am-5pm Sun) For information on Castilla y León.

ℹ Getting There & Away

Bus The **bus station** (☎947 26 55 65; Calle de Miranda 4) is south of the river, in the newer part of town. Regular buses run to Madrid (from €12,25, three hours, up to 20 daily), Bilbao (€6.25 to €13.30, two hours, eight daily) and León (from €5.20, two hours, three daily).

Train The train station is a considerable hike northeast of the town centre; bus 2 (€1.30) connects the train station with Plaza de España. **Renfe** (☎947 20 91 31; www.renfe.com; Calle de la Moneda 21; ⏰9.30am-1.30pm & 5-8pm Mon-Fri, 9.30am-1.30pm Sat), the national rail network, has a convenient sales office in the centre of town. Destinations include Madrid (from €25.85, 2½ to 4½ hours, six daily), Bilbao (from €13.85, three hours, four daily), León (from €9.90, two hours, four daily) and Salamanca (from €14.40, 2½ hours, seven daily).

WORTH A TRIP

ATAPUERCA

The archeological site of **Atapuerca** (☎902 02 42 46; www.atapuerca.org; guided tours in Spanish €6; ⏰tours by appointment), around 15km west of Burgos, has long excited students of early human history. Archeologists made their greatest discovery here in July 2007 when they uncovered a jawbone and teeth of what is believed to be the oldest-known European: at 1.2 million years old, it's some 500,000 years older than any other remains discovered in Western Europe. Unesco World Heritage–listed and still under excavation, the site is open only to visitors with advance reservations.

Around Burgos

The hinterland of Burgos is one of the loveliest areas for exploring quiet Castilian villages. Two stand out – Covarrubias and Santo Domingo de Silos – but this region's quiet back roads have plenty of hidden treasures and churches in the most unexpected places.

Covarrubias

POP 578 / ELEV 975M

A breath away from the Middle Ages, picturesque Covarrubias is one of Castilla y León's hidden gems. Spread out along the shady banks of the Río Arlanza, its distinctive, arcaded half-timbered houses overlook intimate cobblestone squares.

A good time to be here is for the Mercado de la Cereza, a medieval market and cherry festival held on the second weekend of July.

Sights

★Colegiata de San Cosme y Damián CHURCH

(€2.50; guided tours 11am, noon, 1pm, 4.30pm & 5.30pm Mon & Wed-Sat, 1pm & 4.30pm Sun) This 15th-century Gothic church has the evocative atmosphere of a mini cathedral. Home to Spain's oldest still-functioning church organ, it has a gloriously ostentatious altar, fronted by several Roman stone tombs, plus that of Fernán González, the 10th-century founder of Castilla. Don't miss the graceful cloisters and the *sacristía* (sacristy) with its vibrant 15th-century paintings by Van Eyck and tryptic *Adoración de los Magos*. Entry is by guided visit only – check at the tourist office to make sure tours are running.

Festivals & Events

Mercado de la Cereza FOOD & DRINK

(www.covarrubias.es; Jul) A good time to be in Covarrubias is the second weekend of July, when the village hosts a medieval market and cherry festival.

Sleeping

Hotel Rural Princesa Kristina HOTEL €

(947 40 65 43; www.hotelprincesakristina.com; Calle de Fernan Gonzalez 5; s/d from €38/50;) Tucked away up a quiet side street that doesn't see much foot traffic, but right in the heart of the village, the Princesa Kristina has appealing rooms with wooden beams and window frames, splashes of colour and fresh flowers. It's outstanding value.

Hotel Rey Chindasvinto HOTEL €

(947 40 65 60; www.hotelreychindasvinto.com; Plaza del Rey Chindasvinto 5; s/d incl breakfast €36/55;) The best hotel in town, the Rey Chindasvinto has lovely, spacious rooms with wooden beams, exposed brickwork and a good restaurant. The owners are friendly but the service sometimes goes missing.

EL CID: THE HEROIC MERCENARY

Few names resonate through Spanish history quite like El Cid, the 11th-century soldier of fortune and adventurer whose story tells in microcosm of the tumultuous years when Spain was divided into Muslim and Christian zones. That El Cid became a romantic, idealised figure of history, known for his unswerving loyalty and superhuman strength, owes much to the 1961 film starring Charlton Heston and Sophia Loren. Reality, though, presents a different picture.

El Cid (from the Arabic *sidi* for 'chief' or 'lord') was born Rodrigo Díaz in Vivar, a hamlet about 10km north of Burgos, in 1043. After the death of Ferdinand I, he dabbled in the murky world of royal succession, which led to his banishment from Castilla in 1076. With few scruples, El Cid offered his services to a host of rulers, both Christian and Muslim. With each battle, he became ever more powerful and wealthy.

It's not known whether he suddenly developed a loyalty to the Christian kings or smelled the wind and saw that Spain's future would be Christian. Either way, when he heard that the Muslim armies had taken Valencia and expelled all the Christians, El Cid marched on the city, recaptured it and became its ruler in 1094 after a devastating siege. At the height of his power and reputation, the man also known as El Campeador (Champion) retired to spend the remainder of his days in Valencia, where he died in 1099. His remains were returned to Burgos, where he lies buried in the town's cathedral (p198).

Eating

Reastaurante Tiky CASTILIAN €€

(☎947 40 65 05; www.restaurantetiky.com; Plaza de Doña Urraca 9; mains €6-14, set menus €12-21; ⏰1-4pm & 9-11.30pm Fri-Wed) A good choice in the heart of town, Tiky does all the usual Castilian specialities – cured meats, roasted meats, stewed meats – but it also has a creative collection of set menus, as well as an informal bar (*raciones* from €5.25) with tables out on the square.

Restaurante de Galo CASTILIAN €€

(☎947 40 63 93; www.degalo.com; Calle Monseñor Vargas 10; mains €9-18, set menu €19; ⏰1.30-4pm Thu & Sun-Tue, 9-11pm Fri & Sat) This fine restaurant in the heart of Covarrubias is recommended for its robust traditional dishes, cooked in a wood-fired oven. You can sample the regional speciality of *cordero asado* (roast lamb). It also does a fine *olla podrida* (rotten pot), a medieval Castilian stew that includes red beans, ribs and blood sausage (it's much nicer than it sounds – terrific winter comfort food).

Information

Oficina de Turismo (☎947 40 64 61; www.ecovarrubias.com; Calle de Monseñor Vargas; ⏰10am-2pm & 5-8pm Mon-Fri, 10am-3pm & 5-8pm Sat & Sun Apr-Sep, 10am-2pm & 4-7pm Mon-Fri, 10am-3pm & 4-7pm Sat & Sun Oct-Mar) Located under the arches of the imposing northern gate, the tourist office runs guided tours at noon most weekends.

Getting There & Away

Two buses travel between Burgos and Covarrubias on weekdays, and one runs on Saturday (€4.10, one hour). There's free parking in the open area along the northwest edge of the old town.

Santo Domingo de Silos

POP 297

Nestled in the rolling hills south of Burgos, this tranquil, pretty stone village has an unusual claim to fame: monks from its monastery made the British pop charts in the mid-1990s with recordings of Gregorian chants. The monastery is one of the most famous in central Spain, known for its stunning cloister. The surroundings and general sense of calm make this a fine place to spend a day or two.

WORTH A TRIP

MONASTERIO DE SAN PEDRO DE ARLANZA

These haunting **ruins** (BU-905; adult/child €2/free; ⏰11am-1.55pm & 4-7.50pm Wed-Sun Apr-Sep, 10.30am-5pm Wed-Sun Oct-Mar) on a rise above the Río Arlanza show traces of both Gothic and Romanesque elements but the sense of elegant abandonment is what remains with you after a visit. Begun as a hermitage in the 10th century, it grew over the following centuries to become one of the most important monasteries in Castilla. It was abandoned in 1835, when the state decommissioned many churches and monasteries across the country. It's along the quiet BU-905 between Covarrubias and Hortigüela.

Sights

Abadía de Santo Domingo de Silos MONASTERY

(☎947 39 00 49; www.abadiadesilos.es; Calle de Santo Domingo 2; adult/child €3.50/free; ⏰10am-1pm & 4.30-6pm Tue-Sat, noon-1pm & 4-6pm Sun) The cloister and museum of this revered monastery is a two-storey treasure chest of some of Spain's most imaginative Romanesque art. The overall effect is spectacular, but the sculpted capitals are especially exquisite, with lions intermingled with floral and geometrical motifs. The guided tour covers the 17th-century **botica** (pharmacy) and a small **museum** containing religious artworks, Flemish tapestries and the odd medieval sarcophagus. Guided tours are in Spanish only; other visitors are usually allowed to wander more freely.

Basílica de San Sebastián CHURCH

(⏰6am-2pm & 4.30-10pm, vespers 6am, 7.30am, 9am, 1.45pm, 7pm & 9.30pm) Notable for its pleasingly unadorned Romanesque sanctuary dominated by a multidomed ceiling, this is where you can hear the monks chant vespers six times a day. The church was granted the coveted status of basilica by papal decree in 2000.

Sleeping & Eating

Hotel Santo Domingo de Silos HOTEL, HOSTAL €

(☎947 39 00 53; www.hotelsantodomingodesilos.com; Calle Santo Domingo 14; s €38-54, d €45-72, apt €75-125; P ❄ 📶 🏊) This place combines a simple *hostal* with a three-star hotel with large, comfortable rooms (some with spa bathtubs) right opposite the monastery. It also has several nearby apartments, a swimming pool and underground parking. There's a decent restaurant (mains €7 to €17) serving hearty but uninspiring food.

★ **Hotel Tres Coronas** HISTORIC HOTEL €€
(☎947 39 00 47; www.hoteltrescoronasdesilos.com; Plaza Mayor 6; incl breakfast s €58-80, d €75-105; P ❄ 📶) Set in a former 17th-century palace, this terrific hotel is brimming with character, with rooms of thick stone walls and old-world charm – including suits of armour and antique furnishings in the public spaces. The rooms at the front have lovely views over the square and rough-hewn stone walls.

Hotel Tres Coronas CASTILIAN €€
(☎947 390 047; www.hoteltrescoronasdesilos.com; Plaza Mayor 6; mains €10-21; ⏱1-4pm & 8-11pm) This atmospheric restaurant, which specialises in meats roasted in a wood-fire oven, is the village's best.

Information

Oficina de Turismo (☎947 39 00 70; www.turismocastillayleon.com; Calle de Cuatro Cantones 10; ⏱10am-1.30pm & 4-6pm Tue-Sun)

Getting There & Away

There is one daily bus (Monday to Saturday) from Burgos to Santo Domingo de Silos (€6.75, 1½ hours).

Ribera del Duero

The banks of the Río Duero are lined with poignant ruined castles amid pretty old towns such as El Burgo de Osma and Lerma. The river cuts through two dramatic networks of canyons, the Cañón del Río Lobos and the Hoz del Duratón. Add to this the Ribera del Duero wine-producing region, one of Spain's most respected, and you could easily spend the best part of a week exploring the area.

Lerma

POP 2652 / ELEV 827M

If you're travelling between Burgos and Madrid and finding the passing scenery none too eye-catching, you'll find Lerma rising up from the roadside to be a welcome diversion. An ancient settlement, Lerma hit the big time in the early 17th century, when Grand Duke Don Francisco de Rojas y Sandoval, a minister under Felipe II, launched an ambitious project to create another El Escorial. He failed, but the cobbled streets and delightful plazas of the historic quarter are an impressive legacy nonetheless.

Sights

Pass through the **Arco de la Cárcel** (Prison Gate), off the main road to Burgos, climbing up the long Calle del General Mola to the massive **Plaza Mayor**, which is fronted by the oversized **Palacio Ducal**, now a *parador* notable for its courtyards and 210 balconies. To the right of the square is the Dominican nuns' **Convento de San Blas**, which can be visited as part of a guided tour via the tourist office.

A short distance northwest of Plaza Mayor, a pretty passageway and viewpoint, **Mirador de los Arcos**, opens up over Río Arlanza. Its arches connect with the 17th-century **Convento de Santa Teresa**.

Sleeping

Posada La Hacienda de Mi Señor HISTORIC HOTEL €€
(☎947 17 70 52; www.lahaciendademisenor.com; Calle del Barco 6; s/d incl breakfast €48/70; ❄ @ 📶) This charming, quirky place near the top of the town (it's a couple of blocks down the hill from the square) is your best midrange bet, with enormous rooms in a renovated, historic building. The candyfloss colour scheme will start to grate if you stay too long; request room 205 for a more muted paint palette.

★ **Parador de Lerma** HISTORIC HOTEL €€€
(☎947 17 71 10; www.parador.es; Plaza Mayor 1; r €90-180; P ❄ @ 📶) Undoubtedly Lerma's most elegant place to stay, this *parador* occupies the renovated splendour of the old Palacio Ducal, but is devoid of the ostentatious decor (suits of armour etc) you find in some *paradors*. Even if you're not staying here, take a look at the graceful, cloistered inner patio. The rooms overflow with luxury and character; the service is impeccable.

Eating

You're in the heart of Castilian wood-fired-oven territory here. Plaza Mayor is encircled by high-quality restaurants with *cordero asado* on the menu (€40 for two is a good price to pay).

Asador Casa Brigante CASTILIAN €€

(☎947 17 05 94; www.casabrigante.com; Plaza Mayor 5; mains €14-23, roast lamb for two €40; ⏲1.30-4pm) Our favourite *asador* in town is the outstanding Asador Casa Brigante – you won't taste better roast lamb anywhere. Ask about its accommodation options nearby if you've eaten so much you're unable to move.

Information

Oficina de Turismo (☎947 17 70 02; www.citlerma.com; Calle de la Audiencia 6, Casa Consistorial; ⏲10am-2pm & 4-8pm daily Apr-Sep, 10am-2pm & 4-7pm Tue-Sun Oct-Mar) Offers 1¼-hour guided tours (€4) of the town and most of its monuments up to three times daily from April to September.

Getting There & Away

There are eight daily buses from Burgos (€4.20, 30 minutes), with only four on Saturday or Sunday. Some buses coming from Aranda de Duero or Madrid also pass through – but most will leave you down the hill with a long climb to the top.

Peñafiel

POP 5327

Peñafiel is the gateway to the Ribera del Duero wine region, which makes it a wonderful base for getting to know the region's celebrated wines. Watched over by a fabulous castle and wine museum, and with one of the region's celebrated town squares, it even has a few charms of its own.

Sights

★Plaza del Coso SQUARE

Get your camera lens poised for one of Spain's most unusual town squares. This rectangular, sandy-floored 15th-century 'square' was one of the first to be laid out for this purpose – it's considered one of the most important forerunners to the *plazas mayores* across Spain. It's still used for bullfights on ceremonial occasions, and it's watched over by distinctive, half-timbered facades, as well as the grande dame of the castle up on the hill.

★Castillo de Peñafiel CASTLE

(Museo Provincial del Vino; ☎983 88 11 99; Peñafiel; castle adult/child €3.30/free, incl museum €6.60/free; ⏲10.30am-2pm & 4-8pm Tue-Sun Apr-Sep, 10.30am-2pm & 4-6pm Tue-Sun Oct-Mar) Perched dramatically over Peñafiel, this castle houses the state-of-the-art **Museo Provincial del Vino**. A comprehensive story of the region's wines, this wonderful museum has interactive displays, dioramas and computer terminals. The rest of the castle, one of Spain's narrowest, can be visited on a (compulsory) 40-minute **guided tour**, which allows you to appreciate the castle's crenellated walls and towers (stretching over 200m, they're little more than 20m across). They were built and modified over 400 years, from the 10th century onward.

> **OFF THE BEATEN TRACK**
>
> **RELLO**
>
> Some 17km south of Berlanga de Duero, the hilltop stone village of Rello retains much of its medieval defensive wall and feels like the place time forgot. The views from the village's southern ledge are superb. There's at least one *casa rural* to stay in if you love peace and quiet.

Convento de Las Claras WINERY

(☎983 88 01 50; www.bodegasconventodelasclaras.com; Carretera Pesquera de Duero, Km 1.5; tour & tasting €12; ⏲tours hourly 10am-1pm Mon-Fri, 12.30pm Sat, 11.30am Sun) Offers excellent wine tours and tasting, close to Peñafiel. It is particularly proud of its reds; the 2012 rosé deserves a special mention.

Legaris WINERY

(☎983 87 80 88; www.legaris.es; Curiel de Duero; tasting & tour €12-25; ⏲tours 11am, 1pm & 4.30pm Mon-Fri, 11.30am & 1pm Sat & Sun) Just five minutes from Peñafiel, this winery offers excellent tours and has a wine bar in a striking building. Well-regarded reds are its hallmark, with a remarkable system of 20 different types of carefully chosen barrels for ageing the wine. Ring ahead to confirm tour times.

Matarromera WINERY

(☎983 10 71 00; www.bodegamatarromera.es; Valbuena de Duero; tasting & tour from €25; ⏲10am-2pm & 3-7pm Mon-Sat) One of the biggest of the Ribera del Duero wine producers, with a number of other wineries in the region. It produces excellent reds from the *tempranillo* grape that dominates in the Ribera de Duero region.

Protos WINERY

(☎983 87 80 11; www.bodegasprotos.com; Calle Bodegas Protos 24-28; tours €10; ⏲tours 10am, 11.30am, 1pm, 4.30pm & 6pm Tue-Fri, 10am, 11am, noon, 1pm, 4.30pm, 5.30pm & 6.30pm Sat & Sun) This state-of-the-art winery in the shadow of the castle wall produces one of Ribera del Duero's better-known wines. It produces both reds and whites that are commonly found in shops and restaurants all across the country.

Sleeping & Eating

Hotel Convento Las Claras HISTORIC HOTEL €€
(☎983 87 81 68; www.hotelconventolasclaras.com; Plaza de los Comuneros 1; r €83-133; P ❄ 📶 🏊) This cool, classy hotel – a former convent – is an unexpected find in little Peñafiel, with rooms that are quietly elegant. There's also a full spa available, with thermal baths and treatments. On-site is an excellent restaurant with, as you'd expect, a carefully chosen wine list. Lighter meals are available in the cafeteria.

Hotel Castillo de Curiel HISTORIC HOTEL €€
(☎983 88 04 01; www.castillodecuriel.com; Curiel de Duero; s/d/ste from €81/90/132; P 📶) Found just north of Peñafiel in the village of Curiel de Duero, this should be the hotel of choice for castle romantics. Occupying the oldest castle in the region (dating from the 9th century), the renovated hotel has lovely, antique-filled rooms, all with sweeping views. It also has a well-regarded restaurant.

Asados Alonso SPANISH €€
(☎983 88 08 34; www.facebook.com/restauranteasadosalonso/; Calle de Derecha al Coso 14; mains €14-21; ⏲1-4.30pm Sun & Tue-Thu, 1-4.30pm & 8.30-11.30pm Fri & Sat) Staff keep it simple at this *asador* of long standing, with roast spring lamb cooked in a wood-fired oven and served with salad – many a visitor's idea of bliss.

Shopping

Vinos Ojos Negros WINE
(☎983 88 00 68; www.vinosojosnegros.com; Plaza de San Miguel de Reoyo 1; ⏲9am-2pm & 5-8.30pm Mon-Fri, 9am-2.30pm & 4-8.30pm Sat) One of the better wine shops in town. It's not far from the river.

Ánagora WINE
(☎983 88 18 57; Calle Derecha al Coso 31; ⏲10.30am-2pm & 5-8pm Mon, Tue, Thu & Fri, 11am-2pm & 5-8pm Sat, 11am-2pm Sun) An excellent wine shop in the heart of the old town.

Information

Oficina de Turismo (☎983 88 15 26; www.turismopenafiel.com; Plaza del Coso 31-32; ⏲10.30am-2.30pm & 5-8pm Tue-Sun Apr-Sep, 10.30am-2pm & 4.30-7pm Tue-Sun Oct-Mar) Runs guided tours (€4) at 1.30pm Tuesday to Sunday. Has a list of wineries that you can visit; also on the website. Rents out bicycles (half-/full day €3/5).

Oficina de Turismo (Castillo de Peñafiel; ⏲11am-2.30pm & 5-8pm Sat & Sun Apr-Sep, 11.30am-2pm & 4.30-7pm Sat & Sun Oct-Mar) At the entrance to the castle.

Getting There & Away

Four or five buses a day run to Valladolid (€5.50, 45 minutes), 60km west of Peñafiel.

Sepúlveda

POP 1122 / ELEV 1313M

With its houses staggered along a ridge carved out by the gorge of Río Duratón, Sepúlveda is a favourite weekend escape for *madrileños* (Madrid residents) – especially for its famously good *cordero asado* and *cochinillo*. Wednesday is market day.

Sleeping & Eating

The warm, Tuscan-style tones of Sepúlveda's buildings fronting the central Plaza de España are an enviable setting for a hot Sunday roast. In fact, so sated are those who eat here that you'll be hard-pressed to find many places open in the evening for dinner.

Hospedería de los Templarios BOUTIQUE HOTEL €€
(☎921 54 00 89; www.hotelruralsepulveda.es; Plaza de España 19-20; r €70-95; 📶) This nicely restored hotel has delightful rooms that are furnished with antiques but exude an ambience that is far from old-fashioned, with stylish bathrooms, warm washes of colour on the walls and some edgy artwork. Small terraces afford superb views.

Fogón del Azogue CASTILIAN €€
(☎690 20 27 72; Calle de San Millán 6; mains €14-23; ⏲1.30-4pm & 9-11pm) One of Sepúlveda's best, Fogón del Azogue has built its culinary reputation around roasted meats in time-honoured Sepúlveda fashion, but around that it keeps things fresh with a menu that changes with the seasons.

Asador El Panadero CASTILIAN €€
(☎921 54 03 78; www.asadorelpanadero.es; Calle del Conde de Sepúlveda 4; mains €13-21, set menus €30-36) One of the more reliable choices around town for roast lamb and roast suckling pig. The usual warnings for Sepúlveda apply – book ahead on weekends or you'll go hungry.

Restaurante Figón Zute el Mayor CASTILIAN €€
(☎921 54 01 65; www.figondetinin.com; Calle de Lope Tablada 6; mains €11-25; ⏲1.30-4.30pm) A warmly recommended place, Figón Zute el Mayor is impossibly crowded on winter weekends, so be sure to reserve in advance. It's been around since 1850 – it's *that* good.

Information

Centro de Interpretación (☎921 54 05 86; www.miespacionatural.es; Calle del Conde de Sepúlveda 34; ⏲10am-6pm; 👪) This excellent centre offers an informative permanent exhibition about all aspects of the nearby Parque Natural del Hoz del Duratón, including its flora and fauna. It's housed in part of the Iglesia de Santiago.

Getting There & Away

At least two buses link Sepúlveda daily with Madrid (€8.75, two hours).

Parque Natural del Cañón del Río Lobos

Some 15km north of El Burgo de Osma, this park promises forbidding rockscapes and a magnificent, deep-river canyon, as well as abundant vultures and other birds of prey.

Sights

Ermita de San Bartolomé CHURCH
This fine, early-13th-century hermitage has a wonderfully lonely aspect and showcases a fusion of styles between late Romanesque and early Gothic, although only some of these are visible from the outside; the interior is rarely open, but it's the church in its setting that really makes visiting worthwhile. It's about 4km in from the road; take the signposted turn-off at the foot of the switchback road, drive to the car park then walk the final 1km.

Sleeping

Camping Cañón del Río Lobos CAMPGROUND €
(☎975 36 35 65; www.campingriolobos.es; sites per person/tent & car €5.50/13.50; ⏲Easter–mid-Sep; 📶🏊) This highly regarded campground is north of Ucero – if you're heading north along the switchback road that climbs up the canyon, you'll have some fine views back towards it. It's a lovely riverside site with a good restaurant and plenty of shade.

WORTH A TRIP

UXAMA

Just outside El Burgo de Osma lie the ruins of **Uxama** (⏲24hr) FREE, with layers of history sprinkled lightly across the hills. Originally a Celto-Iberian settlement, it became an important Roman town after falling under Roman control in 99 BC; it eventually fell to the Muslims in the 8th century. Low-lying remains of a former home and other fragments will make you wonder what else lies beneath the earth waiting to be excavated. Further into the site, the 9th-century Atalaya (watchtower) affords fabulous views over the surrounding countryside, especially northeast towards El Burgo de Osma and the Castillo de Osma.

A good dirt road runs through the site, which is signposted 3km west of El Burgo de Osma along the N122.

Posada Los Templarios GUESTHOUSE €€
(☎649 65 63 13; www.posadalostemplarios.com; Plaza de la Iglesia; s €48-55, d €62-80, ste €92-102; ❄📶) In Ucero, on the southern approach to the Parque Natural del Cañón del Río Lobos coming from El Burgo de Osma, you'll find this fine inn, which occupies a 17th-century home and has attractive rooms with stone walls, and a good restaurant.

Getting There & Away

There is no public transport to the park so you'll need your own wheels to get here. Access is via the SO920, which runs between El Burgo de Osma and San Leonardo de Yagüe.

El Burgo de Osma

POP 5005 / ELEV 943M

El Burgo de Osma is one of Castilla y León's most underrated medium-sized towns. Once important enough to host its own university, the town is still partially walled, has some elegant streetscapes and is dominated by a remarkable cathedral. It also stands in the heart of some fascinating country.

Sights

Catedral CATHEDRAL
(☎975 34 03 19; Plaza de San Pedro de Osma; adult/child €2.50/free; ⏲10.30am-1pm & 4-7.30pm Jul-Sep, 10.30am-1pm & 4-6pm Tue-Fri, 10.30am-1.30pm

& 4-7pm Sat Oct-Jun) Dating back to the 12th century, the cathedral's architecture evolved as a combination of the Gothic and, subsequently, baroque (notable in the weighty tower). The sanctuary is filled with art treasures, including the 16th-century main **altarpiece** and the **Beato de Osma**, a precious 11th-century codex (manuscript) displayed in the **Capilla Mayor**. Also of note are the light-flooded, circular **Capilla de Palafox**, a rare example of the neoclassical style in this region, and the beautiful **cloister** with original Romanesque traces.

Sleeping & Eating

★Hotel Il Virrey HOTEL €
(975 34 13 11; www.virreypalafox.com; Calle Mayor 2; r €50-60, ste €95-105;) This place has recently overhauled its decor. Now a curious mix of old Spanish charm and contemporary flair, public areas remain dominated by heavily gilded furniture, porcelain cherubs, dripping chandeliers and a sweeping staircase. Rates soar on weekends in February and March, when people flock here for the ritual slaughter *(matanza)* of pigs, after which diners indulge in all-you-can-eat feasts.

Mesón Marcelino SPANISH €€
(975 34 12 49; Calle Mayor 71; mains €12-32; 1-4.30pm & 8.30-11.30pm) A reliable choice along the main street, Mesón Marcelino feeds the passions of this unashamedly meat-loving town. It's all about *cordero* or *cochinillo asado* – roast lamb or suckling pig – with steaks and game meats as what passes for variety in El Burgo de Osma. Needless to say, the salads are an essential side order. It has a good tapas bar next door.

Information

Oficina de Turismo (975 36 01 16; www.sorianitelaimaginas.com; Plaza Mayor 9; 10am-2pm & 4-7pm Wed-Sun) Pick up a copy

OFF THE BEATEN TRACK

SIGHTS AROUND EL BURGO DE OSMA

About 8km southeast of Berlanga de Duero stands the **Ermita de San Baudelio** (€1; 10am-2pm & 4-8pm Wed-Sat, 10am-2pm Sun), the simple exterior of which conceals a remarkable 11th-century Mozarabic interior. A great pillar in the centre of the only nave opens up at the top like a palm tree to create delicate horseshoe arches. It's one of rural Castilla's most surprising finds.

With Celtiberian roots, **Yacimiento Arqueologico de Tiermes** (639 18 59 05; www.museodetiermes.es; admission free, guided visits adult/child €5/free; 10am-2pm & 4-8pm Tue-Sat, 10am-2pm Sun Apr-Sep, 10am-2pm & 4-6pm Tue-Sat, 10am-2pm Sun Oct-Mar) dates to the 1st century AD and is one of the most important Roman sites in Castilla y León. The pretty 12th-century Romanesque Iglesia de Nuestra Señora de Tiermes that watches over the site serves as testament to its use down through the millennia. Traces of the Roman town remain, including what's left of the houses, mosaic floors, forum and aqueduct, all make this a worthwhile excursion. It's 7km southeast of Montejo de Tiermes.

Castillo de Berlanga de Duero (Berlanga de Duero; 10am-2pm & 4-8pm) is lorded over by an extraordinary ruined castle made larger by the continuous ramparts at the base of its hill. The castle's oldest section dates from the 15th century, but most of the exterior was erected in the 16th century. The **tourist office** (975 34 34 33; www.berlangadeduero.es; Plaza de Nuestra Señora del Mercado 5, Berlanga de Duero; 10am-2pm & 4-8pm Sat & Sun), at the base of the castle next to the gate, runs free guided tours on weekends. If you want to visit and find the entrance closed, visit the town hall on Plaza Mayor to ask for the key.

When Fernando seized the Castillo de Gormaz (p168) from its Islamic defenders in 1059, one of his first acts in the following year was to construct the **Ermita de San Miguel de Gormaz** (975 34 09 02; Gormaz; €1.50; 11am-2pm & 5-8pm Sat, 11am-2pm Sun Jun–mid-Jul, hours vary mid-Jul–May), a small hermitage on the slopes below the castle. While it's not much to look at from the outside, the frescoes inside the main sanctuary are stunning, and one of the region's best-kept secrets. The church is just beyond the village of Gormaz, on the road up to the castle.

WORTH A TRIP

CARACENA

The quiet back roads south of El Burgo de Osma have always been known for their fine castles (at Gormaz and Berlanga de Duero) and remote and quietly beautiful villages (such as Rello). One tiny village that fits both profiles is Caracena, some 24km south of El Burgo de Osma along the SO-4123. This tiny village (population 16) climbs the slopes at the end of a long river valley, a beautiful collection of stone-and-terracotta houses. The town has two 12th-century Romanesque churches (the **Iglesia de San Pedro** is the more impressive of the two), as well as the **Ermita de La Virgen del Monte**, a simple baroque hermitage around 1km north of town and the scene of a small procession on the third Sunday in June. On a summit a few hundred metres above the village, the **Castillo de Caracena** seems to merge with the surrounding crags and is wonderfully atmospheric in the late afternoon – you'll need to walk a fair distance in either direction for the best views. The castle was built in the 12th century, but took on its current form with restoration works in the 15th century.

To get here, head south of El Burgo de Osma to La Rasa (5km), and then follow the signs for the final 19km.

of the excellent *Tierra del Burgo* brochure to guide your steps around town.

Getting There & Away

Buses link El Burgo with Soria (€4.20, 50 minutes, two daily, one on Sunday) and Valladolid (€11.25, two hours, three daily).

Parque Natural del Hoz del Duratón

A sizable chunk of land northwest of Sepúlveda has been constituted as a natural park, the centrepiece of which is the **Hoz del Duratón** (Duratón Gorge). The Parque Natural del Hoz del Duratón is a popular weekend excursion – some people take kayaks up to **Burgomillodo** to launch themselves down the waters of the canyon. To do likewise, contact **Situral** (☎656 904 303; www.situral.com; Sebúlcor).

A dirt track leads 5km west from the hamlet of Villaseca to the **Ermita de San Frutos**. In ruins now, the hermitage was founded in the 7th century by San Frutos and his siblings, San Valentín and Santa Engracia. They lie buried in a tiny chapel nearby. This is a magical place, overlooking one of the many serpentine bends in the gorge, with squadrons of buzzards and eagles soaring above.

There's an excellent Centro de Interpretación (p207) in Sepúlveda with an informative permanent exhibition about the park, including the flora and fauna.

Getting There & Away

There's no public transport to or from the park – you'll need your own wheels to explore it.

Soria

POP 39,171 / ELEV 1055M

Small-town Soria is one of Spain's smaller provincial capitals. Set on the Río Duero in the heart of backwoods Castilian countryside, it's a great place to escape 'tourist Spain', with an appealing and compact old centre and a sprinkling of stunning monuments across the town and down by the river. Plan on at least one full day to see all there is to see.

Sights

★Ermita de San Saturio HISTORIC BUILDING
(☎975 18 07 03; Paseo de San Saturio; ⏰10.30am-2pm & 4.30-8.30pm Tue-Sat, 10.30am-2pm Sun Jul & Aug, 10.30am-2pm & 4.30-7.30pm Tue-Sat, 10.30am-2pm Sun Apr-Jun, Sep & Oct,10.30am-2pm & 4.30-6.30pm Tue-Sat, 10.30am-2pm Sun Nov-Mar) FREE A lovely 2.3km riverside walk south from the Monasterio de San Juan de Duero will take you past the 13th-century church of the former Knights Templar, the **Monasterio de San Polo** (not open to the public) and on to the fascinating, baroque Ermita de San Saturio. This hermitage is one of Castilla y León's most beautifully sited structures, an octagonal building that perches high on the riverbank and over the cave where Soria's patron saint spent much of his life.

★Monasterio de San Juan de Duero RUINS
(☎975 23 02 18; Camino Monte de las Ánimas; €1, Sat & Sun free; ⏰10am-2pm & 4-8pm Tue-Sat, 10am-2pm Sun Jun-Sep, 10am-2pm & 4-7pm

ROMAN SORIA

The mainly Roman ruins of **Numancia** (☎975 25 22 48; www.numanciasoria.es; adult/concession/child under 13yr €5/3/free; ⏲10am-2pm & 4-8pm Tue-Sat, 10am-2pm Sun Jun-Sep, hours vary Oct-May) , just outside the village of Garray (8km north of Soria), are all that remains of a city that proved one of the most resistant to Roman rule. Finally Scipio, who had crushed Carthage, starved the city into submission in 134 BC. Under Roman rule, Numancia was an important stop on the road from Caesaraugustus (Zaragoza) to Astúrica Augusta (Astorga).

The **Villa Romana La Dehesa** (Magna Mater; ☎626 99 25 49; www.villaromanaladehesa.es; Las Cuevas de Soria; €2, audio guide €2; ⏲11am-8pm Tue-Sat, 11am-2.30pm Sun Jul-Sep, hours vary Oct-Jun) interpretation centre sits atop the site of an ancient Roman villa where stunning floor mosaics were found. The visit begins with a video presentation (in Spanish) of the villa's history, followed by a small museum of artefacts discovered at the site, before concluding with a walk along elevated walkways that overlook the remaining mosaics; the most spectacular mosaic now resides in Madrid's Museo Arqueológico (p105). The house, which was first unearthed in the 1930s, once covered 4000 sq metres.

Tue-Sat, 10am-2pm Feb-Jun & Oct, 10am-2pm & 4-6pm Tue-Sat, 10am-2pm Sun Nov-Jan) The most striking of Soria's sights, this wonderfully evocative and partially ruined cloister boasts exposed and gracefully interlaced arches, which artfully blend Mudéjar and Romanesque influences; no two capitals are the same. Inside the church, the carvings are worth a closer look for their intense iconography. It's located on the riverbank, down the hill from the historic centre.

Iglesia de Santo Domingo CHURCH
(☎975 21 12 39; Calle de Santo Tomé Hospicio; ⏲7am-9pm) FREE Soria's most beautiful church is the Romanesque Iglesia de Santo Domingo. Its small but exquisitely sculpted portal is something special, particularly at sunset when its reddish stone seems to be aglow.

Palacio de Los Condes Gomara HISTORIC BUILDING
(Calle de Aguirre) A block north of the Plaza Mayor is the majestic, sandstone 16th-century Palacio de los Condes Gomara. It can only be admired from the outside.

Museo Numantino MUSEUM
(Paseo del Espolón 8; €1, Sat & Sun free; ⏲10am-2pm & 5-8pm Tue-Sat, 10am-2pm Sun Jul-Sep, 10am-2pm & 4-7pm Tue-Sat, 10am-2pm Sun Oct-Jun) Archaeology buffs with a passable knowledge of Spanish should enjoy this well-organised museum dedicated to finds from ancient sites across the province of Soria, especially the Roman ruins of Numancia. It has everything from mammoth bones to ceramics and jewellery, accompanied by detailed explanations of the historical developments in various major Celtiberian and Roman settlements.

Festivals & Events

Fiestas de San Juan y de la Madre de Dios FIESTA
(www.sanjuaneando.com; ⏲Jun) Since the 13th century, the 12 *barrios* (districts) of Soria have celebrated this annual festival with considerable fervour. Held during the second half of June, and sometimes spilling over into July, the main festivities take place on Jueves (Thursday) La Saca, when each of the districts presents a bull to be fought the next day.

Sleeping

Hostería Solar de Tejada BOUTIQUE HOTEL €
(☎975 23 00 54; www.hosteriasolardetejada.es; Calle de Claustrilla 1; s/d €50/55; ❄📶) This handsome boutique hotel right along the historic quarter's pedestrianised zone has individually designed (albeit small) rooms with homey, brightly coloured decor. Several have balconies overlooking the bustling pedestrian street.

★**Parador de Soria** HOTEL €€
(☎975 24 08 00; www.parador.es; Calle de Fortún López, Parque del Castillo; r €65-155; ❄@📶) This modern parador occupies a fantastic perch high above the town – the rooms don't have a whole lot of character but they're supremely comfortable, service is exemplary and the views are splendid. The restaurant, too, is worth staying in for.

★Apolonia BOUTIQUE HOTEL €€
(☎975 23 90 56; www.hotelapoloniasoria.com; Puertas de Pro 5; s/d from €60/66;) This smart hotel has a contemporary urban feel with its charcoal, brown and cream colour scheme, abundance of glass, abstract artwork and, in four of the rooms, an interesting, if revealing, colour-lighting effect between the main room and the large walk-in shower – possibly best for romancing couples. The youthful management can arrange area excursions, such as truffle-hunting.

Eating

Crepería Lilot Du Ble Noir FRENCH €
(☎651 49 53 17; www.creperialilot.com; Calle Fueros de Soria 12; crêpes €6.60-12; ⏲1-4.30pm & 9pm-midnight) This appealing little French crepery adds some much-needed variety to Soria's culinary scene. Savoury versions include minced meat with camembert and mushrooms, or pork with rice noodles, teriyaki sauce and mango-pear chutney. It also has sweet crêpes and salads, and an English menu. Not surprisingly, it gets rave reviews from travellers and locals alike.

★Baluarte CASTILIAN €€
(☎975 21 36 58; www.baluarte.info; Calle de los Caballeros 14; mains €12-25, menú de degustación €48; ⏲1.30-4pm & 8.45-10.45pm Tue-Sat, 1.30-4pm Sun) Oscar Garcia is one of Spain's most exciting chefs and this venture in Soria appropriately showcases his culinary talents. Dishes are based on classic Castilian ingredients but treated with just enough foam and drizzle to ensure that they're both exciting and satisfying without being too pretentious. Seasonal set menus are particularly worth watching for. Reservations essential.

Fogón del Salvador CASTILIAN €€
(☎975 23 01 94; www.fogonsalvador.com; Plaza de El Salvador 1; mains €13-22; ⏲1.30-4pm & 9pm-midnight;) A Soria culinary stalwart and fronted by a popular bar, Fogón del Salvador has a wine list as long as your arm – literally – and a fabulous wood-fired oven churning out perfectly prepared meat-based dishes such as *cabrito al ajillo* (goat with garlic), as well as a variety of steaks in all their red-blooded glory.

Information

Oficina de Turismo (☎975 22 27 64; www.soria.es; Plaza Mariana Granados; ⏲10am-2pm & 4-7pm Tue-Sat, 10am-2pm Sun) Offers two-hour guided tours (€5) of the historic centre or the sights along the Río Duero on weekends, and more often in summer. Reserve in advance.

Oficina de Turismo (☎975 21 20 52; www.turismocastillayleon.com; Calle de Medinaceli 2; ⏲9.30am-2pm & 4-7pm Mon-Sat, 9.30am-5pm Sun) Information on both the town and the wider Castilla y León region.

Getting There & Away

Bus From the **bus station** (☎975 22 51 60; Avenida de Valladolid), a 15-minute walk west of the city centre, there are regular services to Burgos (€12.50, 2½ hours), Madrid (€16.80, 2½ hours) and Valladolid (€15.80, three hours), as well as main provincial towns.

Train The **train station** (☎912 320 320; www.renfe.com; Carretera de Madrid) is 2.5km southwest of the city centre. Trains connect Soria with Madrid (€22.15, three hours, three daily), but there are few other direct services.

Getting Around

In what must be the cheapest parking anywhere in any Spanish city, the underground **Aparcamiento Plaza del Olivo** (Plaza del Olivo; €2.95 per 24hr; ⏲24hr) in the city centre charges just €2.95 per 24 hours!

Around Soria

Calatañazor

POP 56 / ELEV 1071M

One of Castilla y León's most romantic tiny hilltop villages, Calatañazor is a charming detour. It's not visible from the highway (just 1km away) and has a crumbling medieval feel to it. Pass through the town gate and climb the crooked, cobbled lanes, wandering through narrow streets lined by ochre stone-and-adobe houses topped with red-tiled roofs and conical chimneys. Scenes from the movie *Doctor Zhivago* were shot here.

Sights

Castillo de Calatañazor RUINS
(⏲24hr) Towering above the village is the one-time Muslim fortress that gave Calatañazor its name (which comes from the Arabic Qala'at an-Nassur, literally 'The Vulture's Citadel'). Now in ruins, it has exceptional views from the walls and watchtowers, both down over the rooftops and north over a vast field called Valle de la Sangre (Valley of Blood).

OFF THE BEATEN TRACK

CHAORNA

In a corner of Castilla y León's far east, almost entirely surrounded by Castilla-La Mancha, little Chaorna is one of the region's best-kept secrets. Inhabiting the clefts and twists of a narrow canyon, the village is unlike any other in Castilla y León. Its largely well-preserved stone buildings are crowned by the **Iglesia de San Miguel** and and a **tower** that dates back to Islamic times. For the most dramatic views, get out and walk up to the top of the canyon for a vantage point looking down upon the village.

Chaorna is 9km south off the A2 – the turn-off is 15km northeast of Medinaceli.

Sleeping & Eating

El Mirador de Almanzor GUESTHOUSE €
(☎975 18 36 42; www.elmiradordealmanzor.com; Calle Puerta Vieja 4; r €55-65; 📶) This place at the upper end of the village, in a 15th-century, half-timbered home beneath the castle, is a fine Calatañazor choice. Rooms have exposed stone walls, wrought-iron furnishings and soft lighting.

★**Casa del Cura de Calatañazor** GUESTHOUSE €€
(☎975 18 36 42; www.posadarealcasadelcura.com; Calle Real 25; r €65-75; 📶) The most stylish rooms in Calatañazor are to be found here, around halfway up the hill on the main cobblestone thoroughfare through the village. Rooms have polished floorboards, chairs with zebra-skin upholstery and exposed wooden beams. The restaurant (mains from €13, *menú de degustación* €27) is also the best in the village. Enjoy the views down into the gorge.

Getting There & Away

There's no regular public transport to Calatañazor. If you're driving, the village lies around 1km north of the N122 – the well-signposted turn-off is about 29km west of Soria and about 27km northeast of El Burgo de Osma.

Sierra de Urbión & Laguna Negra

The Sierra de Urbión, northwest of Soria, is home to the beautiful Laguna Negra (Black Lake), a small glacial lake resembling a black mirror at the base of brooding rock walls amid partially wooded hills.

Located 18km north of the village of **Vinuesa**, the lake is reached by a scenic, winding and sometimes bumpy road. It ends at a car park, where there's a small **information office** (⏲10am-2pm & 4-6.30pm Jun-Oct). It's a further 2km uphill to the lake, either on foot or via shuttle bus (return €1.50, departing half-hourly from 10am to 2pm and 4pm to 6.30pm June to October), which leaves you 300m short of the lake.

A steep trail leads from the lake up to the **Laguna de Urbión** in La Rioja or to the summit of the **Pico de Urbión**, above the village of Duruelo de la Sierra, and on to a series of other tiny glacial lakes.

Getting There & Away

There's no public transport to this area; you'll need your own vehicle to get here.

Yanguas

POP 104

The tiny village of Yanguas, close to where Castilla y León climbs into La Rioja, is one of the loveliest villages of Soria's beautiful Tierras Altas (High Country). Yanguas is hemmed in by canyons and hills on all sides and its beautiful, stone-built architecture and cobblestone lanes, accessed beneath a medieval stone arch, are utterly charming.

Sleeping

Los Cerezos de Yanguas GUESTHOUSE €
(☎975 39 15 36; www.loscerezosdeyanguas.com; Paseo San Sebastián 6; s/d €48/58, 2-bedroom apt €130; P❄📶) Close to the entrance of town, this family-run *casa rural* occupies a typical stone-built Yanguas building. Rooms have an oldish style, with wooden bedheads and tiled or parquetry floors, but they're comfy enough. The home-cooked food is reason enough to stay here.

El Rimero de la Quintina GUESTHOUSE €
(☎625 48 58 74; www.elrimerodelaquintina.net; Calle de la Iglesia 4; d/tr €55/75; ❄📶) At the top of the village just off Plaza de la Constitución, this fine *casa rural* has attractive rooms with wooden beams, tiled floors and pastel colours, not to mention a lovely garden out back.

Getting There & Away

There is no regular public transport to Yanguas, which lies 47km northwest of Soria along the SO615.

South of Soria

Medinaceli

POP 741 / ELEV 1210M

One of Castilla y León's most beautiful *pueblos* (villages), Medinaceli lies draped along a high, windswept ridge just off the A2 motorway. Its mix of Roman ruins, cobblestone laneways and terrific places to stay and eat make an excellent base for exploring this beautiful corner of Castilla y León.

Far down the hill below the old town, modern Medinaceli, along a slip road just north of the A2 motorway, is the contemporary equivalent of a one-horse town.

Sights

Medinaceli's charm consists of rambling through silent cobblestone lanes and being surrounded by delightful stone houses redolent of the noble families who lived here after the town fell to the Reconquista in 1124. Roman ruins also lie dotted around the village.

★Plaza Mayor SQUARE

The partly colonnaded Plaza Mayor is a lovely centrepiece to the village and one of Castilla y León's prettiest. The oldest remaining building is the 16th-century **Alhónidga**, which is the only building on the square with two-storey colonnades.

Arco Romano RUINS

Watching over the entrance to the town and visible on the approach, Medinaceli's 1st-century-AD Arco Romano (Roman triumphal arch) is one of the best preserved in Spain. It's also the only one in the country to boast three intact arches.

Puerta Árabe GATE

Although modified down through the centuries, this gate on the west side of the village first served as one of four entrances to the settlement in Roman times and was an important gate during the era of Muslim occupation. It's a lovely corner, where narrow Medinaceli byways open out onto sweeping views of the rolling Castilian countryside.

Palacio Ducal PALACE

(Palacio del Duque de Medinaceli; ☎975 32 64 98; Plaza Mayor; €2; ⏲10am-2pm & 4-7pm Thu-Mon) This largely 17th-century palace overlooks the Plaza Mayor, and hosts regular high-quality exhibitions of contemporary art in rooms arrayed around the stunning two-storey Renaissance courtyard. In one of the rooms is a 2nd-century **Roman mosaic** and information panels on the mosaics that have been found around Medinaceli. The building's facade is the work of Juan Gómez de Mora, who designed Madrid's Plaza Mayor.

Colegiata de Santa María CHURCH

(Plaza de la Iglesia; by donation; ⏲11am-2pm & 4-8pm Tue-Sun Jul & Aug, 11am-2pm & 4-6pm Sat & Sun Sep-Nov & Easter-Jun, closed Dec-Easter) This moderately interesting Gothic church was built in 1561 on the site of what may have been a synagogue or mosque. The 17th-century late-Gothic tower is visible from across the town, while the highlights of the interior are the 18th-century Cristo de Medinaceli (Christ of Medinaceli) and Romanesque crypt. Opening hours can be unreliable.

Festivals & Events

Festival Ópera Medinaceli MUSIC

(☎913 08 46 35; ⏲Jul-Aug) In the last week of July and the first couple of weeks in August,

WORTH A TRIP

SANTA MARÍA DE LA HUERTA

This wonderful Cistercian **monastery** (☎975 327 002; www.monasteriohuerta.org; €3; ⏲10am-1pm & 4-6pm Mon-Sat, 10-11.15am & 4-6pm Sun) was founded in 1162, expropriated in 1835, then restored to the order in 1930; 20 Cistercians are now in residence. Before entering the monastery, note the church's impressive 12th-century facade, with its magnificent rose window. Inside the monastery, the **Claustro de los Caballeros** is the more beautiful of the two cloisters. Off it is the spare yet gorgeous *refectorio* (dining hall); built in the 13th century, it's notable for the absence of columns to support its vault.

Medinaceli's Palacio Ducal (p213) hosts fine operatic performances.

Festival Internacional de Música MUSIC
(http://festivalmusicamedinaceli.blogspot.com.es) On Saturdays and/or Sundays in July, the Colegiata de Santa María (p213) hosts mostly classical concerts by international performers.

Sleeping

★Medina Salim BOUTIQUE HOTEL €€
(975 32 69 74; www.hotelmedinasalim.com; Calle Barranco 15; s/d incl breakfast from €60/80; P ❄ 🛜) A welcoming boutique hotel which sports large, airy rooms with fridges and terraces that overlook either the sweeping valley or medieval cobblestones out front. Decor is contemporary and light, with pale woodwork and excellent bathrooms. Perks include a small spa and a delightful breakfast room that overlooks part of the original Roman wall, where staff serve Medinaceli's best breakfast.

Hostal Rural Bavieca BOUTIQUE HOTEL €€
(975 32 61 06; www.bavieca.net; Calle del Campo de San Nicolás 6; s/d from €40/58; P ❄ 🛜) The bold colours and style of the rooms here may not be to everyone's taste, but this is unmistakably a boutique hotel offering high-quality rooms and ambience to match. There's a good **restaurant** (mains €12 to €25) on site.

La Ceramica HOTEL €€
(975 32 63 81; Calle de Santa Isabel 2; s/d/tr incl breakfast €45/65/89, d incl breakfast & dinner €88; Feb–mid-Dec; 🛜) Located in the centre of the historic quarter, the rooms here are intimate and comfortable, with a strong dose of rustic charm. The attic room 22 is lovely, and the CR2 apartment, which sleeps four, feels just like home. There's sometimes a two-night minimum stay.

Eating

Medinaceli has three good restaurants. From October onwards, opening hours for dinner can be unreliable – we stayed on a Tuesday in October and not a single restaurant opened for dinner in the old town; we had to drive down the hill to the new town.

Asador de la Villa El Granero CASTILIAN €€
(975 32 61 89; www.asadorelgranero.es; Calle de Yedra 10; mains €13-21; 1.30-4pm & 9-11pm May-Sep, hours vary Oct-Apr) This well-signposted place, with a shop selling local food products at the front, is thought by many to be Medinaceli's best restaurant. The *setas de campo* (wild mushrooms) are something of a local speciality, though unsurprisingly, grilled and roasted meats dominate this bastion of hearty Castilian cooking. Book ahead on summer weekends and don't expect them to open for dinner on winter weeknights.

La Bavieca SPANISH €€
(975 32 61 06; www.bavieca.net; Calle del Campo de San Nicolás 6; mains €12-22, set menus from €17; 1-4pm & 9-11pm Thu-Tue May-Sep, hours vary Oct-Apr) One of Medinaceli's more creative kitchens, La Bavieca does traditional specialities like lamb chops, but also a lovely pork-sirloin hamburger. For starters, why not try the quail eggs with truffles and wild mushrooms in a brandy and duck sauce? Service is attentive and the dining area classy. There's also a good wine list.

La Ceramica SPANISH €€
(975 32 63 81; Calle de Santa Isabel 2; mains €9-19, set menus €16-25; 1-3.30pm & 9-11pm, closed mid-Dec–Jan) An intimate yet informal dining experience, La Ceramica serves excellent local specialities such as *migas del pastor* (shepherd's breadcrumbs) or *ensalada de codorniz* (quail salad), as well as the usual meats.

Information

Oficina de Turismo (975 32 63 47; www.medinaceli.es; Calle del Campo de San Nicolás; 10am-2pm & 4-7pm Wed-Sun) At the entrance to town, just around the corner from the arch.

Getting There & Away

ALSA (www.alsa.es; Plaza del Ayuntamiento) runs up to four daily buses to/from Soria (€5.50, 45 minutes) or three daily to/from Madrid (€10.70, 1¾ hours) from outside the *ayuntamiento* in the new town. There's no transport between the old and new towns, and it's a long, steep hike.

Toledo & Castilla-La Mancha

Includes ➡

Best Places to Eat

- ➡ Raff San Pedro (p242)
- ➡ Cenador de las Monjas (p244)
- ➡ Alfileritos 24 (p225)
- ➡ Calle Mayor (p245)
- ➡ El Bodegón (p242)

Best Places to Stay

- ➡ Casa Rural Tia Pilar (p231)
- ➡ Antiguo Palacio de Atienza (p247)
- ➡ Posada de San José (p241)
- ➡ Casa de Cisneros (p222)
- ➡ Hotel Albamanjón (p236)

Why Go?

Castilla-La Mancha is one of Spain's least-populated regions. Located on a windswept fertile plateau, the landscape is richly patterned, with undulating plains of rich henna-coloured earth, neatly striped and stippled with olive groves and grape vines, stretching to a horizon you never seem to reach. This is the land where Cervantes set the fictional journeys of Don Quijote with quixotic reminders everywhere: from the solitary windmills to the abundant (mostly ruined) castles.

The area's best-known city is glorious Toledo, Spain's spiritual capital, while Cuenca is another wondrous place, seemingly about to topple off its eagle's-eyrie perch high above a gorge.

On a more sensory level, this is where saffron is grown and also the capital of Spain's unrivalled Manchego cheese. The latter makes the perfect accompaniment to the local wines – La Mancha grows more vines than any other region worldwide.

When to Go

Toledo

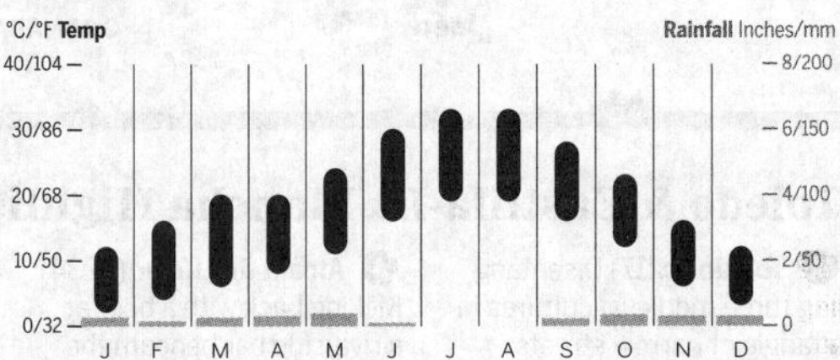

Mar & Apr See Cuenca's spine-tingling and atmospheric Semana Santa parades.

Apr & May Enjoy the countryside's colourful dazzle of wildflowers against a lush green landscape.

Sep & Oct Hike across Castilla-La Mancha's natural parks and picturesque villages.

Toledo & Castilla-La Mancha Highlights

❶ **Toledo** (p217) Disentangling three medieval cultures in a tangle of narrow streets.

❷ **Atienza** (p246) Hiking into the hilltop town of Atienza on a southern branch of the Camino de Santiago.

❸ **Consuegra** (p228) Taking *the* Don Quijote shot of the windmills of Consuegra.

❹ **Alcalá del Júcar** (p234) Kicking back with a beer at a riverside bar beneath the cascade of houses and a castle.

❺ **Cuenca** (p238) Visiting the extraordinary hanging houses and rambling medieval core of Cuenca.

❻ **Almagro** (p230) Marvelling at the handsome plaza and historic theatre in this enticing town.

❼ **Oropesa** (p228) Being king or queen of the castle by staying in a *parador*.

❽ **Sigüenza** (p244) Checking out the evocative medieval historic centre in the under-appreciated town of Sigüenza.

TOLEDO

POP 85,593 / ELEV 655M

Toledo is truly one of Spain's most magnificent cities. Dramatically sited atop a gorge overlooking the Río Tajo, it was known as the 'city of three cultures' in the Middle Ages, a place where – legend has it – Christian, Muslim and Jewish communities peacefully coexisted. Unsurprisingly, rediscovering the vestiges of this unique cultural synthesis remains modern Toledo's most compelling attraction. Horseshoe-arched mosques, Sephardic synagogues and one of Spain's finest Gothic cathedrals cram into its dense historical core. But the layers go much deeper. Further sleuthing will reveal Visigothic and Roman roots. Toledo's other forte is art, in particular the haunting canvases of El Greco, the influential, impossible-to-classify painter with whom the city is synonymous. Though it's justifiably popular with day trippers, try to stay overnight to really appreciate the city in all its haunting glory.

Sights

★Catedral de Toledo CATHEDRAL

(925 22 22 41; www.catedralprimada.es; Plaza del Ayuntamiento; adult/child €12.50/free, incl Museo de Textiles y Orfebrería admission; 10am-6pm Mon-Sat, 2-6pm Sun) Toledo's illustrious main church ranks among the top 10 cathedrals in Spain. An impressive example of medieval Gothic architecture, its enormous interior is full of the classic characteristics of the style, rose windows, flying buttresses, ribbed vaults and pointed arches among them. The cathedral's sacristy is a veritable art gallery of old masters, with works by Velázquez, Goya and – of course – El Greco.

From the earliest days of the Visigothic occupation, the current site of the cathedral has been a centre of worship. During Muslim rule, it contained Toledo's central mosque, converted into a church in 1085, but ultimately destroyed 140 years later. Dating from the 1220s and essentially a Gothic structure, the cathedral was rebuilt from scratch in a melting pot of styles, including Mudéjar and Renaissance. The Visigothic influence continues today in the unique celebration of the Mozarabic Rite, a 6th-century liturgy that was allowed to endure after Cardinal Cisneros put its legitimacy to the test by burning missals in a fire of faith; they survived more or less intact. The rite is celebrated in the Capilla Mozarabe at 9am Monday to Saturday, and at 9.45am on Sunday.

The high altar sits in the extravagant **Capilla Mayor**, the masterpiece of which is the *retablo* (altarpiece), with painted wooden sculptures depicting scenes from the lives of Christ and the Virgin Mary; it's flanked by royal tombs. The oldest of the cathedral's magnificent stained-glass pieces is the rose window above the Puerta del Reloj. Behind the main altar lies a mesmerising piece of 18th-century Churrigueresque (lavish baroque ornamentation), the **Transparente**, which is illuminated by a light well carved into the dome above.

In the centre of things, the *coro* (choir stall) is a feast of sculpture and carved wooden stalls. The 15th-century lower tier depicts the various stages of the conquest of Granada.

The *tesoro,* however, deals in treasure of the glittery kind. It's dominated by the extraordinary **Custodia de Arfe**: with 18kg of pure gold and 183kg of silver, this 16th-century processional monstrance bristles with some 260 statuettes. Its big day out is the Feast of Corpus Christi, when it is paraded around Toledo's streets.

Other noteworthy features include the sober cloister, off which is the 14th-century **Capilla de San Blas**, with Gothic tombs and stunning frescoes; the gilded **Capilla de Reyes Nuevos**; and the *sala capitular* (chapter house), with its remarkable 500-year-old *artesonado* (wooden Mudéjar ceiling) and portraits of all the archbishops of Toledo.

The highlight of all, however, is the *sacristía* (sacristy), which contains a gallery with paintings by masters such as El Greco, Zurbarán, Caravaggio, Titian, Raphael and Velázquez. It can be difficult to appreciate the packed-together, poorly lit artworks, but it's a stunning assemblage in a small space. In an adjacent chamber, don't miss the spectacular Moorish standard captured in the Battle of Salado in 1340.

An extra €3 gets you entrance to the upper level of the cloister, and the bell tower, which offers wonderful views over the centre of historic Toledo.

★Alcázar FORTRESS

(Museo del Ejército; 925 22 30 38; Calle Alféreces Provisionales; adult/child €5/free, Sun free; 10am-5pm Thu-Tue) At the highest point in the city looms the foreboding Alcázar. Rebuilt under Franco, it has been reopened as a vast military museum. The usual displays of uniforms and medals are here, but the

Toledo

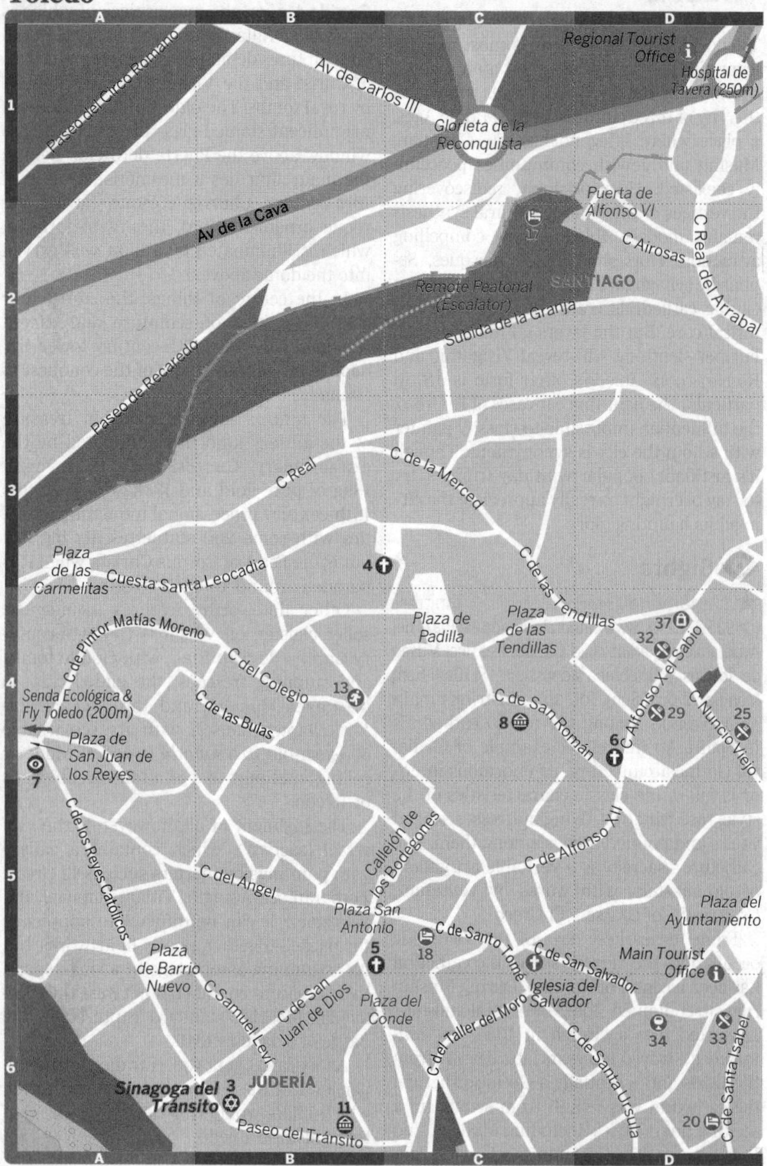

best part is the exhaustive historical section, with an in-depth examination of the nation's history in Spanish and English. The exhibition is epic in scale but like a well-run marathon, it's worth the physical (and mental) investment.

Abd ar-Rahman III raised an *al-qasr* (fortress) here in the 10th century, which was thereafter altered by the Christians. Alonso Covarrubias rebuilt it as a royal residence for Carlos I, but the court moved to Madrid and the fortress eventually became a

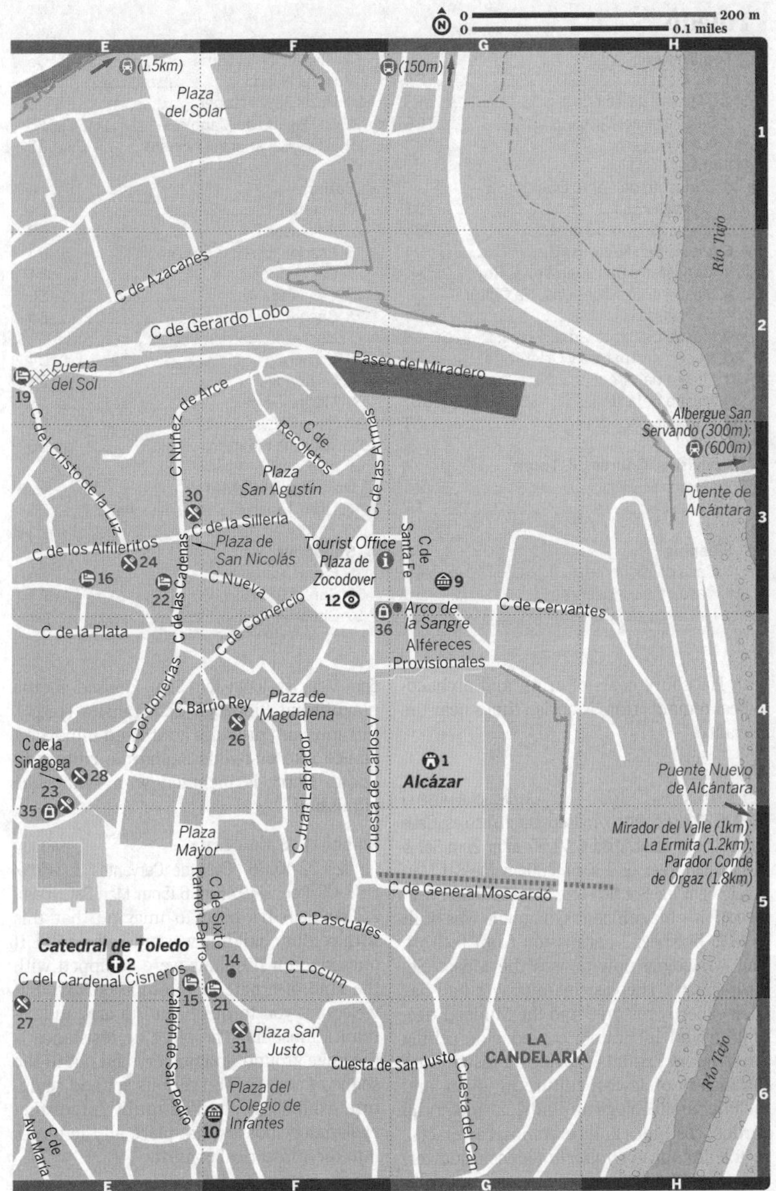

military academy. The Alcázar was heavily damaged during the siege of the garrison by loyalist militias at the start of the civil war in 1936. The soldiers' dogged resistance, and the famous refusal of their commander, Moscardó, to give it up in exchange for his son's life, made the Alcázar a powerful nationalist symbol.

The most macabre sight at the Alcazár is the recreation of Moscardó's office wrecked with bullet holes; other highlights include the monumental central patio decorated

Toledo

with Habsburg coats of arms, and archaeological remains from Moorish times near the entrance.

★ Sinagoga del Tránsito SYNAGOGUE, MUSEUM

(☎925 22 36 65; http://museosefardi.mcu.es; Calle Samuel Leví; adult/child €3/1.50, after 2pm Sat & all day Sun free; ⏲9.30am-7.30pm Tue-Sat Mar-Oct, to 6pm Tue-Sat Nov-Feb, 10am-3pm Sun year-round) This magnificent synagogue was built in 1355 by special permission from Pedro I. The synagogue now houses the Museo Sefardí (p220). The vast main prayer hall has been expertly restored and the Mudéjar decoration and intricately carved pine ceiling are striking. Exhibits provide an insight into the history of Jewish culture in Spain, and include archaeological finds, a memorial garden, costumes and ceremonial artefacts.

Toledo's former *judería* (Jewish quarter) was once home to 10 synagogues and comprised some 10% of the walled city's area. After the expulsion of the Jews from Spain in 1492, the synagogue was variously used as a priory, hermitage and military barracks.

Museo Sefardí MUSEUM

(☎925 22 36 65; http://museosefardi.mcu.es; Sinagoga del Tránsito, Calle Samuel Leví; ⏲9.30am-6pm Mon-Sat, 10am-3pm Sun) Housed in the magnificent Sinagoga del Tránsito (p220), this museum provides a rare and important glance into erstwhile Sephardic culture in Spain. Entry is included with synagogue admission.

Museo de Santa Cruz MUSEUM

(☎925 22 10 36; Calle de Cervantes 3; adult/child €5/free; ⏲9.45am-6.15pm Mon-Sat, 10am-2.30pm Sun) It's hard to imagine that this 16th-century building was once a hospital. If only modern hospitals were equipped with the kind of ornate plateresque portico that welcomes you to this beautiful arts and ceramics museum. The pièce de résistance is the huge ground-floor gallery laid out in the shape of a cross. The various art and sculpture exhibits are backed up by interesting explanatory boards that place all the pieces into their historical context.

Museo del Greco MUSEUM, GALLERY

(☎925 22 44 05; www.mecd.gob.es/mgreco; Paseo del Tránsito; adult/child €3/1.50, from 2pm Sat & all day Sun free; ⏲9.30am-7.30pm Tue-Sat Mar-Oct, to 6pm Nov-Feb, 10am-3pm Sun) In the early 20th century, an aristocrat bought what he thought was El Greco's house and did a meritorious job of returning it to period style.

He was wrong – El Greco never lived here – but the museum remains. As well as the house itself, there are fascinating excavated cellars from a Jewish-quarter palace and a good selection of paintings, including a Zurbarán, a set of the apostles by El Greco and works by his son and followers.

Museo de Textiles y Orfebrería MUSEUM
(Tapestry Museum; ☎925 22 22 41; Plaza del Colegio de Infantes 11; admission €2, incl in cathedral admission; ⏲10am-6pm) Opened in 2014 in the former 17th-century college for choirboys, there are some magnificent tapestries here dating as far back as the 15th century. The majority cover religious themes with the largest measuring around 10m in length. The tapestries have an annual airing on Corpus Christi when they hang outside the cathedral (despite the obvious ill effects from the elements). The museum's lower ground floor has an interesting exhibit about the college, complete with audiovisuals and evocative taped choral music.

Mirador del Valle VIEWPOINT
(Carretera Circunvalación) To get the ultimate photo of Toledo you need to cross the Río Tajo and climb the road on the other side to this strategic viewpoint. You can either walk up from the Puente Nuevo de Alcántara or catch the Trainvision (p227) from Plaza de Zocodover which makes a stop here during its 30-minute scenic journey. The view is not dissimilar to the one depicted by El Greco in his famous landscape, *Vista de Toledo* (1596–1600).

Museo de los Concilios y la Cultura Visigoda MUSEUM
(☎925 22 78 72; Calle de San Román; adult/child €1/free; ⏲10am-2.30pm & 4-6.30pm Tue-Sat, 10am-2pm Sun) Sometimes dismissively called the 'Invisigoths' due to their foggy medieval legacy, the Visigoths inhabit a little-known chapter of Spanish history sandwiched in between the Romans and Moors. Information about them is often difficult to procure until you come to Toledo, their de-facto capital in the 6th and 7th centuries. The era's history can be partially relived at this modest, but important, museum set in the shadowy 13th-century San Román church.

Iglesia del Salvador CHURCH
(☎925 25 60 98; Plaza del Salvador; admission €2.80; ⏲10am-6.45pm Sat-Thu, 10am-2.45 & 4-6.45pm Fri) This little-visited but hugely interesting church exposes multiple historical layers in true Toledan fashion. Until 1159, it was a mosque; before that, a Visigothic church. One of its most fascinating artefacts is a richly engraved Visigothic pillar scavenged by later builders to hold up the roof.

Iglesia de Santo Tomé CHURCH
(☎925 25 60 98; www.santotome.org; Plaza del Conde; adult/child €2.80/free; ⏲10am-6.45pm mid-Mar–mid-Oct, 10am-5.45pm mid-Oct–mid-Mar) Iglesia de Santo Tomé contains El Greco's most famous masterpiece *El entierro del conde de Orgaz* (The Burial of the Count of Orgaz), which is accessed by a separate entrance on Plaza del Conde. When the count was buried in 1322, Sts Augustine and Stephen supposedly descended from heaven to attend the funeral. El Greco's work depicts the event, complete with miracle guests including himself, his son and Cervantes.

Activities

★Senda Ecológica WALKING
This remarkably varied walking path tracks the Río Tajo through a steep-sided gorge where you'll feel as if you've left the city far behind (although urban life reverberates only metres above you). It stretches between the Azarquiel and San Martín bridges and includes some relatively wild stretches where a wooden walkway has been stapled to the rock face.

TOP TOLEDO VIEWS

For superb city views, head over the Puente de Alcántara to the other side of Río Tajo and follow the road that rises to your right (there's a pavement!), where the vista becomes more marvellous with every step. If you're staying overnight, along this road is the **Parador de Toledo**, which has superlative views, as does the restaurant La Ermita (p226), which has a short, quality menu of elaborate Spanish cuisine.

In the town centre, you can also climb the towers at the **Iglesia San Ildefonso** (Iglesia de los Jesuitas; ☎925 25 15 07; Plaza Juan de Mariana 1; adult/child €2.80/free; ⏲10am-6.45pm Apr-Sep, to 5.45pm Oct-Mar) for up-close views of the cathedral and Alcázar.

Fly Toledo ADVENTURE SPORTS
(☎693 464845; www.flytoledo.com; Puente de San Martin 2; €10; ⏰10.30am-6.30pm) Heavy museum legs sometimes need to relieve themselves and this bracing high-wire act that catapults vertigo-shunners across the Río Tajo gorge via the longest urban *tirolina* (zipline) in Europe might just do the trick. The ride begins and ends close to the San Martín bridge on the western side of town.

Medina Mudéjar HAMMAM
(☎925 22 93 14; www.medinamudejar.com; Calle Santa Eulalia 1; €27, incl massage €45; ⏰10am-10pm Mon-Fri, to 11pm Sat, to 8pm Sun) Luxuriate in the self-pampering surrounds of this relaxing hammam with its warm ochre walls, arches, exposed stone, and brick vaulted ceilings. Hot, warm and cold baths, steam baths and options for various massages make for a relaxing respite from sightseeing. Moroccan tea is served as an ideal relaxing finale.

Tours

Various companies offer guided (and usually themed) walking tours around the town. Themes include Three Cultures (Muslim, Christian and Jewish) and El Greco. There are also night tours based around local legends.

Rutas de Toledo WALKING
(☎630 709338; www.rutasdetoledo.es; Calle de Sixto Ramón Parro 9; per person €6-20; ⏰10.30am-2pm & 5.30-8pm) A good mix of standard tours (El Greco, Sephardic Jewish culture) with more creative night tours, including some which are more theatrical with actors in traditional dress.

Festivals & Events

Corpus Christi RELIGIOUS
This is one of the finest Corpus Christi celebrations in Spain, taking place on the Thursday 60 days after Easter Sunday. Several days of festivities reach a crescendo with a procession featuring the massive Custodia de Arfe.

Sleeping

Oasis Backpackers Hostel HOSTEL €
(☎925 22 76 50; www.hostelsoasis.com; Calle de las Cadenas 5; dm €18, d €34-44; @📶) One of four Oasis hostels in Spain, this hostel sparkles with what have become the chain's glowing hallmarks: laid-back but refreshingly well-organised service and an atmosphere that is fun without ever being loud or obnoxious. There are private rooms if you're not up for a dorm-share, and lots of free information on city attractions.

Hotel Santa Isabel HOTEL €
(☎925 25 31 20; www.hotelsantaisabeltoledo.es; Calle de Santa Isabel 24; s/d €40/50; 📶) Providing a safe, economical base to stay in Toledo, the Santa Isabel is clean, central and friendly. It's encased in an old noble house with simple rooms set around two courtyards. Several have cathedral views, along with the charming rooftop terrace, accessed by a spiral staircase. The on-site cafeteria offers a simple breakfast (at a small extra cost).

Albergue San Servando HOSTEL €
(☎925 22 45 58; www.reaj.com; Subida del Castillo; dm €15-18; ❄@📶🏊) Occupying digs normally reserved for *paradores* (luxurious state-owned hotels) is this unusual youth hostel encased in a 14th-century castle – built by the Knights Templar, no less. Dorms have either two single beds or two double bunks, and there's a cafeteria serving meals as well as a summer pool. If you're not an HI member, you'll need to buy a card here.

★**Hacienda del Cardenal** HISTORIC HOTEL €€
(☎925 22 49 00; www.haciendadelcardenal.com; Paseo de Recaredo 24; r incl breakfast €90-135; ❄📶🏊) This wonderful 18th-century former cardinal's mansion has pale ochre-coloured walls, Moorish-inspired arches and stately columns. Some rooms are grand, others are more simply furnished, but all come with dark furniture, plush fabrics and parquet floors. Several overlook the glorious terraced gardens. Underground parking is available nearby (€15 per day).

★**Casa de Cisneros** BOUTIQUE HOTEL €€
(☎925 22 88 28; www.hospederiacasadecisneros.com; 12 Calle del Cardenal Cisneros; s/d €40/66; ❄📶) Across from the cathedral, this seductive hotel is built on the site of an 11th-century Islamic palace, which can be best appreciated by visiting their basement restaurant. In comparison, this building is a 16th-century youngster, with pretty stone-and-wood beamed rooms and exceptionally voguish bathrooms. A rooftop terrace offers stunning views of the cathedral and beyond. Excellent value.

Hostal Santo Tomé HOSTAL €€
(☎925 22 17 12; www.hostalsantotome.com; Calle de Santo Tomé 13; s/d €55/72; P❄📶) Located

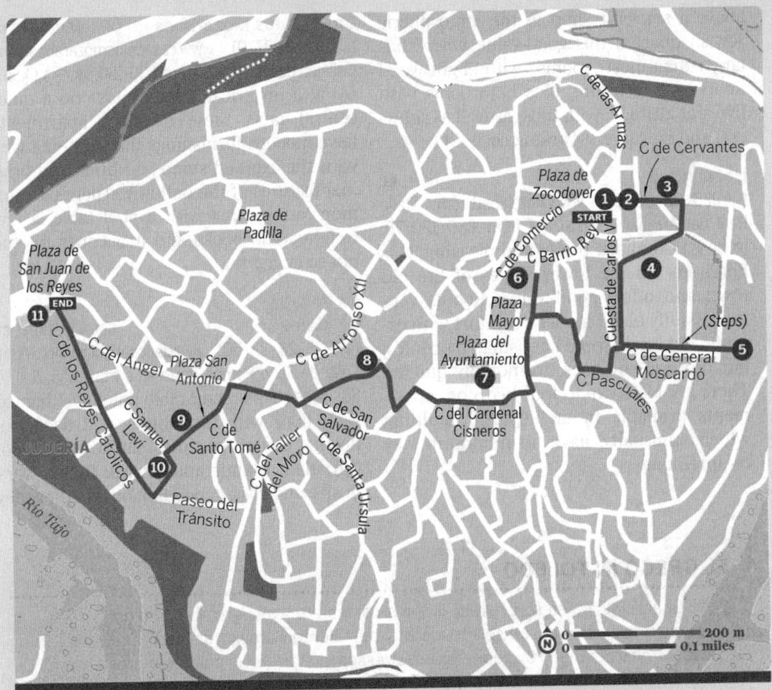

Walking Tour
A Stroll through History

START PLAZA DE ZOCODOVER
END MONASTERIO SAN JUAN DE LOS REYES
LENGTH 2KM, 1½–2½ HOURS

Start off in central ❶ **Plaza de Zocodover** (p225), for centuries the city's marketplace and scene for bullfights and Inquisition-led burnings at the stake, then pass through the ❷ **Arco de la Sangre** on the eastern side of the square to admire the facade of the ❸ **Museo de Santa Cruz** (p220). Up the hill to the south is Toledo's signature ❹ **Alcázar** (p217), beyond which there are some fine ❺ **views over the Río Tajo**; follow Cuesta de Carlos V along the west wall of the Alcázar and then turn left to walk down Calle de General Moscardó. As the Alcázar's commanding position and sweeping views attest, Toledo was perfectly sited for medieval defences.

Follow the spires down the hill to the west, passing the remnants of a the ❻ **Mezquita de las Tornerías** before reaching the ❼ **Catedral de Toledo** (p217), the spiritual home of Catholic Spain. Twist your way northwest to the ❽ **Centro Cultural San Marcos**. Housed in the 17th-century San Marcos church, its original domed roof, complete with ceiling frescoes, creates an evocative gallery space for temporary art exhibitions.

Down the hill you enter the heart of Toledo's old Jewish quarter. Admire the swords in the shops along ❾ **Calle de San Juan de Dios** and head past the ❿ **Sinagoga del Tránsito** (p220) to admire further clifftop views over the river. The synagogue takes on a special poignancy if you continue along Calle de los Reyes Católicos to the splendid ⓫ **Monasterio San Juan de los Reyes**. Spain's Catholic rulers hoped this church would represent the ultimate triumph of their religion over others. This is a fine spot to end your walk, but you could drop down from here to the riverside pathway that will take you on a half-circuit of the old town back to near your starting point (an additional 2km).

above a souvenir shop in the atmospheric Jewish quarter, this good-value *hostal* has larger-than-most rooms with light-wood floors and furniture, plus bathrooms with five-star attitude, with tubs (as well as showers) and hairdryers. Parking costs €12.

Hotel Abad HOTEL €€
(☎925 28 35 00; www.hotelabad.com; Calle Real del Arrabal 1; r/ste/apt from €80/120/75; P ❄ 📶) Compact, pretty and pleasing, this hotel sits on the lower slopes of the old town and offers good value. Rooms very successfully blend modern comfort with exposed old brick; some have small balconies, but those at the back are notably quieter. There are also two- to four-bedroom apartments available in an adjacent building which, unusually, have no minimum stay requirement.

Casa de los Mozárabes APARTMENT €€
(☎925 21 17 01; www.casadelosmozarabes.com; Callejón de Menores 10; apt €90-150; ❄ 📶) Occupying a historical Toledo house on a quiet central lane, these excellent apartments have modern furnishings that combine well with the exposed stone and brick and original features of the building. There's a common lounge area with a pool table, a few weights, and books and magazines for the not so energetic.

La Posada de Manolo BOUTIQUE HOTEL €€
(☎925 28 22 50; www.laposadademanolo.com; Calle de Sixto Ramón Parro 8; s from €55, d €77-88; ❄ 📶) This memorable hotel has themed each floor with furnishings and decor reflecting one of the three cultures of Toledo: Christian, Islamic and Jewish. Rooms vary in size and cost, depending on whether they

EL GRECO IN TOLEDO

Of all Spain's old masters, El Greco is the most instantly recognisable. You don't need a degree in art history to be able to identify the talented Greek's distinctive religious canvases characterised by gaunt figures dressed in stark, vivid colours. Spread liberally around the museums and churches of Toledo, they practically jump out at you.

Born Doménikos Theotokópoulos on Crete in 1541, El Greco will always be intrinsically linked with Toledo, where he arrived as a bolshie 36-year-old in 1577. Never one to court popularity, the artist had already sparked controversy during a tempestuous apprenticeship in Italy where he had criticised the work of Michelangelo. His arrival in Spain proved to be equally thorny. Hindered by a thinly veiled arrogance and adhering to what were unconventional painting methods for the time (though 'revolutionary' by modern yardsticks), El Greco failed in his early attempts to ingratiate himself to the court of King Philip II. Gravitating instead to Toledo, he found an improbable artistic refuge where he worked to refine his style and establish his reputation.

Despite earning a degree of respectability during his lifetime, El Greco was largely ignored in the years following his death. Indeed, his prophetic work wasn't seriously reappraised until the early 20th century, when he was embraced by artists such as Picasso whose murky 'blue period' echoed the melancholy of some of El Greco's early compositions.

Outside Madrid's Museo del Prado, Toledo protects El Greco's greatest work. The Iglesia de Santo Tomé (p221) contains his magnum opus *El entierro del conde de Orgaz* (The Burial of the Count of Orgaz), depicting the count's burial in 1322. Look out for El Greco himself and Cervantes among the guests. The nearby Museo del Greco (p220) also has a solid collection of El Greco's works.

One of the oldest convents in Toledo, the 11th-century **Convento de Santo Domingo El Antiguo** (☎925 22 29 30; Plaza de Santo Domingo el Antiguo; adult/child €2.50/free; ⌚11am-1.30pm & 4-7pm Mon-Sat, 4-7pm Sun) includes some of El Greco's early commissions, other copies and signed contracts of the artist. Visible through a hole in the floor is the crypt and wooden coffin of the painter himself.

Other spots in Toledo where you can contemplate El Greco's works include the Museo de Santa Cruz (p220), the *sacristía* (sacristy) in the cathedral (p217) and the **Hospital de Tavera** (☎925 22 04 51; Calle Duque de Lerma 2; courtyard & chapel €4, full ticket €6; ⌚10am-2.30pm & 3-6.30pm Mon-Sat, 10am-2.30pm Sun)

are interior or exterior, and some have balconies. There are stunning views of the old town and cathedral from the terrace, where breakfast is served, weather permitting.

★Parador Conde de Orgaz HOTEL €€€
(☎925 22 18 50; www.parador.es; Cerro del Emperador; r €115-215; P ❄ 🛜 🏊) High above the southern bank of Río Tajo, Toledo's low-rise *parador* (luxurious state-owned hotel) has a classy interior and sublime-at-sunset city views. The *parador* is well signposted: turn right just after crossing the bridge northeast of the old centre. You'll need a car or be prepared to pay for a taxi (around €8).

Eating

Madre Tierra VEGETARIAN €
(☎925 22 35 71; www.restaurantemadretierra.com; Bajada de la Tripería 2; mains €9-12; ⏲1-4pm & 8-11pm Wed-Mon; 🛜 ✎) In this haven for *jamón* and game, vegetarians can go hungry in Toledo. This excellent vegetarian restaurant has a menu that ranges from tofu and seitan choices to more mainstream pizzas and pastas. The salads are imaginative and generous and the soups have a real wow factor. Find it tucked down a side alley, behind the southeastern corner of the cathedral.

Bar Ludeña SPANISH €
(☎925 22 33 84; Plaza de Magdalena 10; mains €8-12; ⏲10.30am-4.30pm & 8-11.30pm) Despite its central location close to Toledo's main tourist thoroughfare, Ludeña retains a wholesome local image courtesy of the flock of regulars who – despite the tourist infiltration – still frequent it. Join them as they prop up the bar with a *caña* (beer) and a plate of the Toledano speciality, *carcamusa* (pork and vegetable stew). Alternatively, grab a pew on the delightful shady terrace.

Palacios SPANISH €
(☎925 22 34 97; Calle Alfonso X el Sabio 3; tapas €2, set menus from €7.50; ⏲7am-10.30pm) Spain's no-fuss, old-school taverns can sometimes be hit or miss in the food stakes, but Palacios edges into the 'hit' category, courtesy of its super-economical *menú del día* – a basic, but tasty three-course meal (with bread and a drink). It's also an excellent place for early morning churros, as well as tapas, with carafe-loads of local atmosphere.

★Alfileritos 24 MODERN SPANISH €€
(☎925 23 96 25; www.alfileritos24.com; Calle de los Alfileritos 24; mains €19-20, bar food €4.50-12; ⏲9.30am-midnight Sun-Thu, to 1am Fri & Sat) The 14th-century surroundings of columns, beams and barrel-vault ceilings are cleverly coupled with modern artwork and bright dining rooms in an atrium space spread over four floors. The menu demonstrates an innovative flourish in the kitchen, with dishes such as green rice with quail or loins of venison with baked-in-the-bag reineta (pippin) apple.

La Abadía CASTILIAN, TAPAS €€
(☎925 25 11 40; www.abadiatoledo.com; Plaza de San Nicolás 3; raciones €7-15; ⏲bar 8am-midnight, restaurant 1-4pm & 8.30pm-midnight) In a former 16th-century palace, this atmospheric bar and restaurant has arches, niches and coloured bottles lined up as decoration, spread throughout a warren of brick-and-stone-clad rooms. The menu includes lightweight dishes and tapas, but the three-course 'Menú de Montes de Toledo' (€20) is a fabulous collection of tastes from the nearby mountains, including partridge, wild mushrooms and almonds (as is the scrumptious marzipan-cum-cheesecake dessert).

Asador Palencia de Lara GRILL €€
(☎925 25 67 46; www.asadorpalenciadelara.es; Calle Nuncio Viejo 6; tapas €2.50, mains €17-20; ⏲1-4pm & 8.30-11.30pm Mon-Sat, 1-4pm Sun, closed Jul & Aug) This smart place has a modern dining room set in a covered patio and specialises in grilled meats. Eschew the overpriced starters and start your meal in the small, vaguely corporate-feeling bar area, which turns out a delicious series of inexpensive tapas, then head through for the meat-based mains. Everything goes down well with a glass of house red.

DON'T MISS

MARZIPAN

Not a marzipan fan? Think again. You probably won't have tasted it so good anywhere else. Toledo is famed for this wonderful almond-based confectionery (*mazapán* in Spanish), which every shop seems to sell. The Santo Tomé marzipan brand is highly regarded and there are several outlets in town, including one on **Plaza de Zocodover** (☎925 22 11 68; www.mazapan.com; Plaza de Zocodover 7; ⏲9am-10pm). Even the local nuns get in on the marzipan act; most of the convents sell the sweets.

Taberna El Botero SPANISH €€

(☎925 22 90 88; www.tabernabotero.com; Calle de la Ciudad 5; raciones €9-17; ⏰noon-4pm & 8pm-midnight Wed-Sun, noon-4pm Mon & Tue) Handy for the cathedral, this atmospheric bar and restaurant offers up elaborately presented dishes based on traditional Spanish ingredients such as octopus, cod and game. It also does expertly prepared cocktails and mixed drinks; ask master bartender, Javier, for his recommendations.

Kumera MODERN SPANISH €€

(☎925 25 75 53; www.restaurantekumera.com; Calle Alfonso X El Sabio 2; mains €16-20, set menu €30; ⏰8am-2.30am Mon-Fri, 11am-2.30am Sat & Sun) This place serves up innovative takes on local dishes such as *cochinillo* (suckling pig), *rabo de toro* (bull's tail) or *lomo de venado* (venison with chestnut gnocchi and red berries), alongside other creatively conceived dishes. Those with foie gras as the centrepiece are especially memorable. Sit on the terrace within confessional distance of the picturesque Iglesia de San Ildefonso.

★Adolfo MODERN EUROPEAN €€€

(☎925 22 73 21; www.adolforestaurante.com; Callejón Hombre de Palo 7; mains €25-28, set menu €76; ⏰1-4pm & 8pm-midnight Mon-Sat, 1-4pm Sun) Toledo doffs its hat to fine dining at this temple of good food and market freshness. Run by notable La Mancha–born chef Adolfo Muñoz, the restaurant has been around for over 25 years, and in that time has morphed into one of Spain's best gourmet establishments. Partridge is the speciality.

The restaurant is also known for its extensive wine cellar within which lurk over 32,000 bottles.

Casa Aurelio SPANISH €€€

(☎925 22 41 05; www.casa-aurelio.com; Calle de la Sinagoga 6; mains €19-22, set menu €33; ⏰1-4.30pm & 8-11.30pm Tue-Sat, 1-4.30pm Mon; 📶) Purporting to be Toledo's oldest restaurant, Casa Aurelio has been around since 1953 and still ranks among the best of Toledo's traditional eateries. Game and grilled meat dishes are the pride of the place as evidenced by the cabinet of meat cuts and stuffed partridges by the door. There's another **branch** (☎925 21 36 18; www.casa-aurelio.com; Plaza del Ayuntamiento; mains €10-16, set menu €18; ⏰9.30am-6pm Mon, Wed & Sun, 10.30am-6pm & 8pm-midnight Fri & Sat) near the cathedral.

Hostal del Cardenal SPANISH €€€

(☎925 22 49 00; www.hostaldelcardenal.com; Paseo de Recaredo 24; mains €18-25; ⏰1-4pm & 8-11pm) This hotel restaurant enjoys one of Toledo's most magical locations for dining alfresco: it's tucked into a private garden entered via its own gate in the city walls. The food is classic Spanish, with roast meats – suckling pig and lamb are the best dishes on show here – to the fore. It's a bit touristy, but the location is unforgettable on a balmy summer's night.

La Ermita SPANISH €€€

(☎925 25 31 93; www.laermitarestaurante.com; Carretera de Circunvalación; mains €18-22, degustation menu €48; ⏰1.30-4pm & 8.45-11pm) Location. Location. Location. La Ermita sits across the Río Tajo gorge from the city, meaning you'll have the tangled medieval core of Toledo winking back at you as you peruse its reassuringly brief menu of beautifully presented Spanish cuisine. The menu changes regularly but you can expect to see wild boar, salmon and suckling pig prepared with innovative culinary skill.

Vegetarians are graciously catered to.

Drinking & Nightlife

★Libro Taberna El Internacional BAR, CAFE

(☎925 67 27 65; www.facebook.com/librotabernatoledo; Calle de la Ciudad 15; ⏰8pm-1.30am Tue-Thu, noon-1.30am Fri & Sat, noon-4pm Sun) If you think Toledo is more touristy than trendy, you clearly haven't found your way into the cool confines of El Internacional, a proud purveyor of slow food, spray-painted tables, overflowing bookcases, rescued 1970s armchairs and, of course, beards.

Shopping

Simón ARTS & CRAFTS

(☎925 22 21 32; Plaza de San Vicente 1; ⏰10am-4pm & 4.30-7.30pm) Since 1963, this small slightly shabby shop has specialised in *damasquinados* (damascene), the art of

STAIRWAY TO HEAVEN

The **remonte peatonal** (Puerta de Alfonso VI; ⏰7am-11pm Mon-Fri, 8am-2am Sat, 8am-10pm Sun) – a series of escalators – starting near the Puerta de Alfonso VI and ending near the Monasterio de Santo Domingo El Antiguo, is a good way to avoid the steep uphill climb to reach the historic quarter of town.

decorating steel with threads of gold and silver. It is one of just a handful of places that sells the genuine handmade pieces; the majority of what you see in Toledo these days is machine made.

Casa Cuartero FOOD, DRINK
(☎925 22 26 14; www.casacuartero.com; Calle Hombre de Palo 5; ⏲10am-2pm & 5-8pm Mon-Fri, 10am-3pm & 4-8pm Sat) Just north of the cathedral, this fabulous food shop (here since 1920) sells marzipan, cured meats, wines, cheeses and all manner of local delicacies from around Castilla-La Mancha. It's ideal for gifts to take home or to stock up for a picnic.

Information

Main Tourist Office (☎925 25 40 30; www.toledo-turismo.com; Plaza Consistorio 1; ⏲10am-6pm) Within sight of the cathedral. There are also offices in **Plaza de Zocodover** (☎925 25 40 30; www.toledo-turismo.com; Plaza de Zocodover; ⏲10am-7pm) and the **train station** (☎925 25 40 30; www.toledo-turismo.com; Estación de Renfe, Paseo de la Rosa; ⏲9.30am-3pm).

Regional Tourist Office (☎925 22 08 43; www.turismocastillalamancha.es; Puerta de Bisagra; ⏲10am-2pm & 3-7pm Mon-Fri, 10am-3pm & 4-6pm Sat, 10am-3pm Sun) Has a wealth of information about the region. Located north of the old town.

Getting There & Away

To get to most major destinations, you'll need to backtrack to Madrid.

From the pretty **train station** (☎902 240202; www.renfe.es; Paseo de la Rosa), high-speed Alta Velocidad Española (AVE) trains run every hour or so to Madrid (€13, 30 minutes).

From Toledo's **bus station** (☎925 21 58 50; www.alsa.es; Bajada Castilla La Mancha), buses depart for Madrid's Plaza Elíptica (from €5.50, one to 1¾ hours) roughly every half-hour; some are direct, some via villages. There are also daily services to Cuenca (€15, 3¼ hours).

Getting Around

Buses (€1.50) run between Plaza de Zocodover and the bus station (bus 5) and train station (buses 61 and 62).

The **Trainvision** (☎625 301890; Plaza de Zocodover; adult/child €5.50/2.60; ⏲10am-8.30pm Mon-Thu, to 9pm Fri & Sun, to 10pm Sat) trolley bus runs around the main monuments and up to the Mirador del Valle. It leaves from Plaza Zocodover every 30 minutes.

Driving in the old town is a nightmare. There are several underground car parks throughout the area. Zones blocked off by bollards can be accessed if you have a hotel reservation.

TALAVERA DE LA REINA

POP 88,565

Talavera de la Reina, long famous worldwide for its ceramics, has a laid-back appeal. Talavera is strikingly located, surrounded by mountains, and divided by the Río Tajo. Three bridges, one of which dates from Roman times and has been aesthetically restored, connect the two sides of the city. Historically, the city is famed for being the site of the Battle of Talavera against Napoleon's army in 1809, when the Duke of Wellington successfully expelled the French army from the city.

Sights

Basílica de Nuestra Señora del Prado BASILICA
(Jardines del Prado) Talavera's main church is sometimes dubbed the 'Sistine Chapel of ceramics' for its intricate tilework, which showcases the city's finest *azulejos* (tiles), many of them painted with religious themes. It sits amid elegant gardens right next to Talavera's bullring, where an infamous *corrida* (bullfight) saw Spain's most famous bullfighter, 'Joselito El Gallo' fatally gored in May 1920. A statue of the fallen idol decorates the gardens outside.

Shopping

Cerámica San Agustín CERAMICS
(☎925 80 89 16; www.ceramicasanagustin.es; Calle de la Puerta del Río 9; ⏲9am-2pm & 4-8.30pm Mon-Fri, 9am-2pm Sat) This bright, family-run ceramics shop is very close to the tourist office and is useful if you don't want to carry your shopping bag to the outlets on the western side of town. It has all the classic Talavera designs.

Information

Tourist Office (☎925 82 63 22; www.talavera.org; Ronda del Cañillo 22; ⏲9.30am-2pm & 5-7pm Mon-Fri, 10am-2pm Sat & Sun) Doubles as a gallery displaying – you guessed it – ceramics. It's located next to the old Roman bridge.

Getting There & Away

The bus station is in the town centre. Regular buses between Madrid and Badajoz stop in

Talavera de la Reina. **Autocares Toletum** (www.autocarestoletum.es; Avenida de Toledo) runs buses to Toledo (from €7.15, 1½ hours) roughly hourly. There is also a regular train service to Madrid (from €12, 1½ hours, seven daily) from the main train station on Paseo de la Estación to the north of the centre.

Oropesa

POP 2850

The village of Oropesa, 34km west of Talavera de la Reina and enticingly visible south from the N5 motorway, is dominated by – and famous for – its turreted 14th-century castle that looks north across the plains towards the Sierra de Gredos. Parts of the old town walls survive and the village has a handful of noble mansions and a couple of Renaissance churches that are worth checking out, as well a small main square flanked by bars and restaurants.

Sights

Castillo de Oropesa CASTLE

(925 45 00 06; Calle Castillo; adult/child €3/1.50; 10am-2pm & 4-6pm Tue-Sun) This sturdy 14th-century castle built on older roots looks north across the plains to the mighty Sierra de Gredos. There are five towers, four of which can be climbed to access the ramparts and really appreciate the stunning views; not suitable for anyone with mobility issues, however. Part of the castle is now a parador hotel, but it can be visited separately.

Sleeping

La Hostería de Oropesa HOTEL €

(925 43 08 75; Paseo Escolar 5; s/d €50/65; P ❄) La Hostería, just below Oropesa's castle, has pretty, individually decorated rooms with beamed ceilings and a popular restaurant with tables spilling out into a flower-festooned courtyard. Excellent value but the rooms do differ considerably so if possible check them out in advance.

Parador de Oropesa HISTORIC HOTEL €€

(925 43 00 00; www.parador.es; Plaza Palacio 1; r €75-145; P ❄) Attached to Oropesa's hilltop castle is a 14th-century palace housing Spain's second-oldest *parador,* which has managed to retain a heady historical feel without the 'overheritaging' that typifies many Spanish *paradores*. Rooms are large and luxurious, with heavy brocade curtains and antiques.

Getting There & Away

Buses travel from Talavera de la Reina to Oropesa (€4, 40 minutes) three or four times daily.

SOUTH CASTILLA–LA MANCHA

This is the terrain that typifies La Mancha for many people: the flat, often featureless plains of Spain's high inland *meseta* (plateau) stretching to the horizon, punctuated by the occasional farmhouse or emblematic windmill. The southeast, however, is surprisingly verdant and lush with rivers, natural parks and some of the prettiest villages in the province.

Consuegra

POP 10,668

If you choose just one place to go windmill-spotting in Castilla–La Mancha, make it Consuegra.

Sights

Castillo de Consuegra CASTLE

(925 47 57 31; Cerro Calderico; adult/child €4/free; 10am-1.30pm & 4.30-6.30pm Mon-Fri, 10.30am-1.30pm & 4.30-6.30pm Sat & Sun Jun-Sep, shorter hours Oct-May; P) This is *the* place for the novice windmill spotter, where you can get that classic shot of up to a dozen *molinos de vientos* (windmills) flanking Consuegra's 12th-century castle, an atmospheric perch that remains under renovation with aesthetically restored rooms melding with untouched ruins. There are lots of stairs and narrow passages so it could be physically challenging for some.

Molino Rucio WINDMILL

(925 09 53 39; www.elmolinoquefunciona.es; Carretera del Castillo; admission €2; 9am-6.30pm) Of the 12 windmills that line a grassy ridge either side of Consuegra's castle, *Rucio* is the only one in full working order. Inside there are displays on local saffron-farming, details of the mill's internal machinery, and samples of some of the flour it grinds. Your entrance ticket includes a drink from the small shop downstairs.

Sleeping

La Vida de Antes HOTEL €€

(925 48 06 09; www.lavidadeantes.com; Calle de Colón 2; s/d €55/75; P ❄ @) The best

digs in Consuegra are encased in a noble old house with tiled floors, antique furnishings and a pretty patio that evokes a bygone era. The duplex rooms are particularly cosy and there's interesting art exhibited throughout the building. Recent changes include a downstairs restaurant serving traditional local specialties in a pretty open courtyard (open for dinner only).

Eating

El Alfar SPANISH €€
(☎925 48 18 07; www.restaurantealfar.com; Calle de Valderribas; mains €16-23; ⏲1-5pm & 8pm-late Fri-Sun, 1-5pm Mon; 📶) Concentrating on exquisitely prepared La Mancha specialities, Consuegra's most ambitious restaurant is also something of a museum, inhabiting an old ceramics workshop that was built over the ruins of the town's ancient Roman circus. Ruined columns and capitals mingle with a profusion of pots, plants and trees in the expansive courtyard, while the decor indoors is equally museum-worthy.

It's easy to forget you're in a restaurant – until the food arrives. The three-course tasting menu includes dishes like partridge salad, *migas* (breadcrumbs, often cooked with chorizo and served with grapes) and a plethora of local wines (from the world's largest wine-growing region, no less). Reservations are recommended.

Information

Tourist Office (☎925 47 57 31; www.consuegra.es; Ronda Molinos 29; ⏲9am-6pm, to 7pm Jun-Sep) Located in the Bolero windmill (they all have names), the first you come to as the road winds up from the town. You can climb the steps here and see the original windmill machinery. There's another tourist office next to the bus station.

Getting There & Away

There are regular weekday buses (three on weekends) running between Consuegra and Toledo (€5.50, one hour) and up to seven buses daily to Madrid (€10.60, two hours). There's also a daily connection (€4.75, one hour) to Ciudad Real.

Campo de Criptana

POP 14,600

One of the most popular stops on the Don Quijote route, Campo de Criptana is crowned by 10 windmills visible from kilometres around. Revered contemporary film-maker Pedro Almodóvar was born here, but left for Madrid in his teens. The town is pleasant, if unexceptional.

Sights

Windmill Ticket Office WINDMILL
(www.campodecriptana.es; visits per mill €2; ⏲10am-2pm & 4.30-7pm Tue-Sat) Poyatos, one of the 10 windmills on the northern edge of town, acts as a ticket office for visits to three other mills. Guided tours are also available.

Museo Eloy Teno MUSEUM
(☎926 56 22 31; www.campodecriptana.es; Calle Rocinante 39; adult/child €2/free; ⏲10am-2pm & 6-9pm Tue-Sat Jun-Sep, 10am-2pm & 4-6.30pm Oct-May; 👪) This small family-friendly museum in the tourist office displays local artisan products, models of windmills and clever art – often Don Quijote–themed – made out of recycled metal.

Sleeping

Casa Rural del Bachiller CASA RURAL €€
(☎926 55 01 04; www.lacasadelbachiller.es; Calle Bachiller Sansón Carrasco 26; r €95; 📶) An unexpected hideout. Enjoy a veritable Quijote experience staying in this aesthetically reformed historic house with its heady views of the windmills and original caves (the former main living spaces in the house). Rooms have a timeless classic feel and are restfully decorated to ensure a tranquil stay; guests are treated to complimentary wine from the region (which helps).

Eating

Cueva La Martina SPANISH €€
(☎926 56 14 76; www.cuevalamartina.com; Calle Rocinante 13; mains €8-15; ⏲1.30-4pm Mon, 1.30-4pm & 8.30pm-midnight Tue-Sun; Ⓟ) The best place to eat is atmospheric Cueva La Martina, opposite the windmills. The cave-like dining area is dug into the rock, and there's a breezy upstairs terrace with views over town. Dishes to try include the super simple *asadillo manchego* (a slow-roasted vegetable casserole dominated by red peppers) or the richer Burgos-style black pudding.

It's popular with coach tours so get here early to snag a table.

Information

Tourist Office (Calle Rocinante 39; ⏲10am-7pm Mon-Sat, to 2pm Sun) Located in a

WORTH A TRIP

PALACIO DE LA SERNA

A 20-minute drive south of the uninteresting provincial capital of Ciudad Real in the sleepy village of Ballesteros de Calatrava, this superb **hotel** (☎926 84 22 08; www.hotelpalaciodelaserna.com; Calle Cervantes 18, Ballesteros de Calatrava; r €90-140, ste €180-220; P ❄ 📶 ≋ 🐾) feels a world away. Set around a courtyard, it combines rural comfort with appealing design; the owner's evocative modern sculptures feature heavily. Rooms are slick and modern with lots of mirrors, spot lighting, bright colours and edgy contemporary paintings.

There's also a spa, complete with flotation tank (€30 per session), and a good on-site restaurant.

low-rise building opposite the Inca Garcilaso windmill. It shares the space with Museo Eloy Teno (p229).

ℹ Getting There & Away

There are trains to Madrid's main Atocha station (€17, 1½ hours, four daily) from the town's Estación de Tren located on Calle Agustín de la Fuente, south of the centre.

Campo de Criptana is linked to Ciudad Real (€9, 1¼ hours) by two buses Monday to Friday and one on Saturday.

Almagro

POP 9100

The theatre and pickled aubergines are Almagro's improbable bedfellows. Almagro is to the theatre what Seville is to flamenco, the spiritual home of the art – at least in Spain – courtesy of its 'golden age' playhouse (Spain's oldest) and all-encompassing theatre museum. Not that you have to be a thespian to appreciate the place. The diminutive town, which gained importance during the Reconquista, might have been designed with 21st-century tourists in mind. Everything of note is a short, traffic-free stroll from its cobbled nexus, Plaza Mayor.

Sights

Corral de Comedias HISTORIC BUILDING

(☎926 88 24 58; www.corraldecomedias.com; Plaza Mayor 18; adult/child incl English audio guide €4/free; ⏲10am-2pm & 5-8pm Mon-Fri, to 6pm Sat, 10am-12.45pm & 5-8pm Sun Apr-Sep, shorter hours rest of the year) Opening onto the plaza is the oldest theatre in Spain. The 17th-century Corral de Comedias is an evocative tribute to the golden age of Spanish theatre, with rows of wooden balconies facing the original stage, complete with dressing rooms. Once daily (twice on Saturday) visits become 'theatrised' with costumed actors replacing the audio guide: this costs €3 more. It's still used for performances on Saturday evenings from the end of March to the end of October; buy tickets via the website.

The history of the theatre is intriguing. It was founded in 1628 by a wealthy priest, but, after a century of performances, was closed during the cultural clampdowns of King Philip V. After that, the theatre was pretty much forgotten until a local inn-owner found a deck of old playing cards in the 1950s. Subsequent excavations on the site in Plaza Mayor led to the rediscovery of the theatre, which reopened for performances in 1954. The 18th-century playing cards are now on show in the town's Museo Nacional de Teatro. Hours vary in winter and during festivals.

Museo Nacional de Teatro MUSEUM

(☎926 26 10 14; http://museoteatro.mcu.es; Calle Gran Maestre 2; adult/child €3/free; ⏲10am-2pm & 4-6.30pm Tue-Fri, from 10.30am Sat, 10.30am-2pm Sun) Thespian or not, you could spend hours in Almagro's illustrious museum just sifting through the highlights. Theatrical musings include a hand-painted set of playing cards from 1729 found in the nearby Corral de Comedias, a deftly sculpted model of Mérida's Roman theatre, costumes and props relating to *zarzuela* (Spanish mix of theatre, music and dance) and – anchoring it all – a handsome 13th-century courtyard.

Tours

Visitas Guiadas a Almagro WALKING

(☎609 79 36 54; www.almagrovisitasguiadas.com; Plaza Mayor 41; per person €12) Aside from the standard two-hour Almagro walking tour, it also offers out-of-town tours to Calatrava la Nueva, Parque Nacional Tablas de Daimiel and Lagunas de Ruidera.

Festivals & Events

Festival Internacional de Teatro Clásico THEATRE

(www.festivaldealmagro.com; Corral de Comedias; ⏲Jul) In July the Corral de Comedias holds a month-long international theatre festival, attracting world-class theatre companies performing, primarily, classical plays.

Sleeping

La Posada de Almagro GUESTHOUSE €
(☎926 88 22 44; www.laposadadealmagro.com; Calle Gran Maestre 5; s/d €44/60; ❄📶) A short hop from the Plaza Mayor, this fine inn has simple, tidy rooms with wrought-iron bedheads, thoughtfully decorated walls and tiled bathrooms. Bring earplugs if you're here on a weekend as the noise from the restaurant can be loud and long.

★**Casa Rural Tía Pilar** GUESTHOUSE €€
(☎926 88 27 24; www.tiapilar.com; Calle de los Carrascos 1; s/d €40/70; P❄📶≋) This beautiful 18th-century house is a delight with four patios, a lovely common room (with a fancy coffee machine) and a small but elegant swimming pool. Rooms are decorated with antiques and are well heated and/or air-conditioned for an old house. The owners live on-site to provide warm but discreet service. Excellent value.

La Casa del Rector HOTEL €€
(☎926 26 12 59; www.lacasadelrector.com; Calle Pedro de Oviedo 8; s/d €85/100; ❄@📶≋) A three-way marriage between modern rooms, 'design' rooms and traditional historical rooms, the Rector is, in a word, magnificent. It's difficult to imagine what taste isn't being catered for in its lush interior set around three courtyards with elegant fountains, retro antiques (sewing machines!) and a streamlined cafe.

Design rooms have wood-floor showers, coffee machines and electric window blinds. Modern rooms are a little more beige and mainstream. Traditional rooms retain many of the building's original features such as wood beams and heavy tiled floors. To top it all off, there's an on-site spa.

Retiro del Maestre HOTEL €€
(☎926 26 11 85; www.retirodelmaestre.com; Calle de San Bartolomé 5; s €60-80, d €75-100; P❄📶) Enjoy cosseted treatment and style without the hurly-burly of a big hotel. Rooms here are spacious and washed in warm yellow and blue; go for one on the upper floor with a private balcony. The location, a five-minute walk from the Plaza Mayor, couldn't be better. The higher prices are for the superior rooms with king-size beds, Jacuzzis and other perks.

Eating

El Patio de Ezequiel SPANISH €€
(☎926 09 72 03; Calle de San Agustín 4; mains €10-14; ⏰noon-midnight; 📶) The most romantic setting in town for a meal or drink with tables set in a softly lit patio, complete with trickling fountain. The menu includes several excellent salads with smoked fish, partridge or sardines, plus egg-based dishes, grilled meats and fish. Portions are vast.

DON'T MISS

CASTILLO DE CALATRAVA

This magnificent **castle-monastery** (☎926 850 371; www.castillodecalatrava.com; Ctra de Calzada de Calatrava Km 2.3, Calzada de Calatrava; adult/child €4/free; ⏰11am-2pm & 5.30-8.30pm Tue-Fri, 10am-2pm & 5.30-8.30pm Sat, 10am-2pm & 5-9pm Sun Apr-Sep, shorter hours rest of the year; P) looms high in the sky some 6km south of the town of Calzada de Calatrava and 30km south of Almagro, from where it once controlled the path into the Sierra Morena and Andalucía. A steep cobbled road takes you to the top, where you can alternate gazing at expansive views with exploring this extraordinary castle-cum monastery in closer detail. Highlights include the vast basilica and the chapter hall with its coffins and segment from an original mural.

The complex was once headquarters for the Calatrava Knights, Spain's oldest military order, founded in 1158 to challenge Moorish power in Iberia. Their original base was Calatrava La Vieja, located 60km to the north, a castle twice snatched audaciously from the Moors. As the Christians pushed further into Moorish territory following Alfonso VIII's victory in the Battle of Las Navas de Tolosa in 1212, the Calatrava Knights commissioned this newer citadel in 1217 built using the labour of prisoners caught in the battle.

You can explore the castle on your own or opt for a guided tour (in Spanish), which is included in the price.

In Search of Don Quijote

Few literary landscapes have come to define an actual terrain quite like the La Mancha portrayed in Miguel de Cervantes' *El ingenioso hidalgo Don Quijote de la Mancha,* better known in Spain as *El Quijote*.

The Man from La Mancha

In a village in La Mancha whose name I cannot recall, there lived long ago a country gentleman...

Thus begins the novel and thus it was that the village where our picaresque hero began his journey had always remained a mystery. That was, at least, until 10 eminent Spanish academics marked the 400th anniversary of the book's publication in 1605 by carefully following the clues left by Cervantes. Their conclusion? That Villanueva de los Infantes (population 5243) in Castilla-La Mancha's far south was Don Quijote's starting point. These days, the town is otherwise most memorable for its ochre-hued Plaza Mayor, surrounded by wood-and-stone balconies and watched over by the 15th-century Iglesia de San Andrés. If you're staying overnight, look no further than La Morada de Juan de Vargas (p237).

Staying for the Knight

There is little consensus as to where Don Quijote went next, and there are as many *rutas de Don Quijote* (Don Quixote routes) as there are La Mancha towns eager to claim an impeccable Cervantes pedigree. In fact, few towns are actually mentioned by name in the book.

One that does appear is the now-unremarkable town of Puerto Lápice, southeast of Toledo. It was here that Don

TATYANA VYC / SHUTTERSTOCK ©

2

PANORAMIC IMAGES / GETTY IMAGES ©

1. Windmills, Campo de Criptana (p229) **2.** Plaza Mayor and Iglesia de San Andrés, Villanueva de los Infantes (p237) **3.** Don Quijote and Sancho Panza statues by Pedro Requejo outside Museo Casa Natal de Miguel de Cervantes in Alcalá de Henares (p149)

3

DANILOVSKI / SHUTTERSTOCK ©

Quijote stayed in an inn that he mistook for a castle and, after keeping watch over it all night, convinced the innkeeper to knight him. El Toboso, northeast of Alcázar de San Juan, also appears in the book as the home of Dulcinea, the platonic love of Quijote. Nowadays you'll find in El Toboso the 16th-century Casa-Museo de Dulcinea (p236), as well as the obligatory Don Quijote statue and a library with more than 300 editions of the book in various languages.

Windmills

Don Quijote may have spent much of his quest tilting at windmills *(molinos de viento)*, but nowhere is the exact location of these 'monstrous giants', against whom honourable battles must be fought, revealed. The finest windmills are arguably the nine of Consuegra (p228), strung out along a ridge line that rises from the pancake-flat plains, and clearly visible from far away. Mota del Cuervo, northeast of Alcázar de San Juan, also has some seven candidates, but Campo de Criptana (p229) is Consuegra's main rival. Only 10 of Campo de Criptana's original 32 windmills remain, but they sit dramatically above the town. Local legend also maintains that Cervantes was baptised in the town's Iglesia de Santa Maria.

Restaurante Abrasador CASTILIAN €€

(☎926 88 26 56; www.abrasador.es; Calle San Agustín 18; tostas €2, mains €12-25, set menus from €28; ⏰11.30am-4pm & 8.30-11pm) Thoughtfully prepared cooking including perfectly grilled meats dominates the restaurant out the back. Snaffle the table next to the open fire in winter if you can. Out the front, you'll find some of the most creative tapas in Almagro – the famed local aubergine features prominently and it's our pick of the orders, whatever guise it's in.

Information

Tourist Office (☎926 86 07 17; www.ciudad-almagro.com; Calle Ejido de Calatrava; ⏰10am-2pm & 5-8pm Tue-Fri, 10am-2pm & 5-7pm Sat, 10am-2pm Sun) This well-stocked tourist office next to the small bus station has helpful English-speaking staff. Afternoon opening and closing is one hour earlier from November to March.

Getting There & Away

Buses run to Ciudad Real (€4, 30 minutes, up to five daily Monday to Saturday).

Parque Nacional Tablas de Daimiel

Forty kilometres northeast of Ciudad Real, this small wetland national park is great for birdwatching. From the visitor centre, which has an exhibition on the fragile local ecosystem, three trails lead out along the lake shore and over boardwalks. From these, and the various observation hides – bring binoculars – you can see an astonishing variety of wildlife, including ducks, geese, kingfishers, flamingos, herons and other waders, tortoises and otters. Early morning and late afternoon are the best times to visit.

Information

National Park Visitor Centre (Centro de Visitantes Parque Nacional de Daimiel; ☎926 69 31 18; www.lastablasdedaimiel.com; Carretera a las Tablas de Daimiel; ⏰9am-8pm; 📶) This visitor centre signposted near the centre of the park has a small exhibition about the flora and fauna of the Parque Nacional Tablas de Daimiel. It can also supply maps for suggested itineraries.

Getting There & Away

The park is 10km northwest of the town of Daimiel, which is linked by regular buses to Ciudad Real. From Daimiel you'll need your own wheels.

Alcalá del Júcar

POP 1300

Northeast of Albacete, the deep, tree-filled gorge of Río Júcar makes for a stunning detour. About halfway along the CM3201, the crag-clinging town of Alcalá del Júcar comes into view as you descend via hairpin turns. Its landmark castle, dating mostly from the 15th century, towers over the houses (many in caves) that spill down the steep bank of the river gorge. At the foot of the town there's a medieval bridge with Roman origins and a leafy meeting-and-greeting plaza. It's a good destination for young kids, with a large, traffic-free area, and safe paddling in a bend of the river.

Sights

Cuevas del Diablo CAVE

(☎967 47 31 02; www.cuevasdeldiablo.com; Calle San Lorenzo 7; admission €3; ⏰9am-9pm Mon-Fri, 10am-9pm Sat & Sun) A vast cave complex with tunnels and a private collection of eccentric and historical artefacts and farming tools. A complimentary drink is included in the price. Owner Juan José Martínez García is easy to spot around town thanks to his flamboyant Dalí-style moustache.

Castillo de Alcalá de Júcar CASTLE

(☎967 47 30 90; Calle Laberinto 10; adult/child €2.50/1.50; ⏰11am-2pm & 5-8pm May-Sep, 11am-2pm & 3-6pm Oct-Apr) Alcalá del Júcar's landmark castle with its pentagonal main tower is of Almohad origin, but what you see today dates mostly from the 15th century. There are year-round temporary exhibitions mainly concentrated on art and antiquities – and great views from the ramparts.

Tours

Avenjúcar ADVENTURE

(☎967 47 41 34; www.avenjucar.com; Avenida Constitución; 👪) Adventure activities in the Alcalá de Júcar area including wet and dry canyoning and river experiences. Some trips run for two or three days with a night (or two) in rural accommodation.

Sleeping

Hostal Rambla HOSTAL €

(☎967 47 40 64; www.hostalrambla.es; Paseo de los Robles 2; s/d €50/55; ❄📶) One of several well-priced hotels in Alcalá, Hostal Rambla is by the Roman bridge. Rooms are compact and bland, but it's friendly and well located, and there's a pleasant restaurant with a large terrace, specialising in chargrilled meats served with green peppers and potatoes.

Eating

Fogones el Chato SPANISH €€

(☎622 035696; Calle Canal 16; mains €10-12, set menu €15; ⏲noon-4pm & 8-11pm Thu-Mon, noon-4pm Tue) The sun-dappled terrace here is a place to linger, flanked by vegetable allotments (yes, expect organic fresh produce in the dishes), near the river. The uncomplicated menu concentrates on traditional dishes prepared with panache. The menu of the day is excellent value.

Information

Tourist Office (☎967 47 30 90; www.turismo castillalamancha.com; Paseo de los Robles 1; ⏲10am-2pm Sat & Sun) The small tourist office has a wealth of information about *casas rurales* (farmstead accommodation), cave accommodation and activities, including maps showing local walking trails. If it is closed the ticket office-cum-souvenir shop at the castle can also provide information and a town map.

Getting There & Away

There is one daily bus on weekdays only between Albacete and Alcalá (€6.50, 1½ hours). It's run by Emisalba (www.emisalba.com).

Belmonte

POP 2010

Situated about 17km northeast of Mota del Cuervo and partially enclosed by fortified walls, small tranquil Belmonte is most notable for its story-book castle, the Castillo de Belmonte. The small town is enclosed by 15th-century walls with three original gateways still standing. It is well worth a stroll with other sights including a handsome Gothic church and a 17th-century former Jesuit monastery, now housing law courts and the post office.

Sights

Castillo de Belmonte CASTLE

(☎967 81 00 40; www.castillodebelmonte.com; Calle Eugenia de Montijo; adult/child incl audio guide €9/5; ⏲10am-2pm & 4-7pm Tue-Sun Jun-Sep, 10am-2pm & 3.30-6.30pm Oct–mid-Feb, 10am-2pm & 4-7pm mid-Feb–May; P) This is how castles *should* look, with turrets, largely intact walls and a commanding position over the plains of La Mancha from the ramparts. Visitors are well catered for with an elevator between the ground and 1st floor and a small cafe. The castle was once home to France's Empress Eugénie after her husband, Napoleon III, lost the French throne in 1871 and rooms have been grandly furnished in 19th-century style. The former dungeons are now home to a small armory.

Sleeping

Palacio Buenavista Hospedería BOUTIQUE HOTEL €€

(☎967 18 75 80; www.palaciobuenavista.es; Calle José Antonio González 2; s/d/ste incl breakfast €50/80/100; P❄📶) Palacio Buenavista Hospedería is a classy boutique hotel set in a 16th-century palace next to the Colegiata. Stylish rooms are positioned around a balconied central patio with historic columns; request a room with a castle view, if possible. There's an excellent restaurant and a pretty outside terrace where the buffet breakfast is served (weather permitting).

Information

Tourist Office (☎967 17 07 41; www.turismo castillalamancha.es; Estación de Autobuses, Avenida Luis Pinedo Alarcón; ⏲10am-2pm & 5-8pm) Can provide information on the village and surrounds and also assist with accommodation.

Getting There & Away

There are daily buses to Belmonte from Cuenca (€7, 1¼ hours) and Madrid (€12, 2½ hours).

El Toboso

POP 1887

If you're on the trail of Don Quijote, it's practically obligatory to stop in the small village of El Toboso, home of the Knight Errant's fictional sweetheart and one of the few places mentioned definitively by name in the book. So strong is the Quijote legend here that it is said that Bonaparte's troops refused to torch the place during the Peninsula War in the early 19th century.

El Toboso has two decent Quijote-themed museums and a wonderful statue of the Don kneeling gallantly before La Dulcinea in the pretty main square. Surrounded by vineyards, it also sports some good bodegas and a couple of homey restaurants.

Sights

Museo Cervantino MUSEUM

(925 19 74 56; Calle de Daoíz y Velarde 3; adult/child €2/1; 10am-2pm & 4-8pm Tue-Sun) This museum of over 300 books all with the same title (you've guessed it – *Don Quijote*) is more interesting than it sounds. Included among its well laid-out exhibits are copies of the Cervantes classic in braille and multiple languages, including Basque. There are also signed copies by notable personalities; look out for Nelson Mandela and – more chillingly – Adolf Hitler.

In an upstairs room, two short films (with English subtitles) relate the story of Don Quijote and how it relates to the La Mancha landscape.

Casa-Museo de Dulcinea MUSEUM

(925 19 72 88; Calle Don Quijote 1; adult/child €3/1.50; 9.45am-1.45pm & 3-6.15pm Tue-Sat, 10am-2pm Sun) Since she was a fictional heroine and largely a figment of Don Quijote's imagination, this museum is obviously not the *real* house of the famous Dulcinea del Toboso. Rather it once belonged to Ana Martínez Zarco de Morales, a women known to Cervantes who may have acted as a model for Dulcinea. Its aim is to evoke the spirit of Don Quijote and the book by displaying artefacts typical of the era.

Various rooms on two floors are set around a suitably bucolic patio where chickens roam. Look out for the distinctive blue and white Talavera ceramics in the kitchen.

Bodega Campos de Dulcinea WINERY

(925 56 81 63; www.camposdedulcinea.es; Calle Garay 1; tours €6; 9am-7pm Mon-Fri, 10am-2pm Sat; P) One of the longest standing wineries in town, the appropriately named Campos de Dulcinea has won numerous awards over the years; the *tempranillo* is a good constant bet if you want to make a purchase. Note, however, that tours of the bodega, along with wine tasting (with cheese), must be made in advance by phone or via the online contact form.

Eating

Mesón La Noria de Dulcinea SPANISH €€

(925 56 81 92; www.mesonlanoriatoboso.com; Calle Don Quijote; mains €12-20; noon-4pm & 8-11pm) Looking like the kind of inn Don Quijote might have frequented can't be a bad thing in El Toboso. There are no surprises in the cooking at Noria, which is 100% Manchegan. Expect excellent renditions of *migas*, roast lamb and partridge. The open courtyard looks like it has sprung straight from Cervantes' imagination.

They also rent rooms in the village.

Information

Tourist Office (925 56 82 26; www.eltoboso.es; Calle de Daoíz y Velarde; 10am-2pm & 4-7pm Tue-Sun) Has a handy town map with listed sights. Located on the western edge of town.

Getting There & Away

There's one daily bus to Toledo (€10, 2¼ hours) from Monday to Saturday run by Samar (www.samar.es).

Parque Natural de las Lagunas de Ruidera

This ribbon of 15 small lakes is surrounded by lush parkland, campgrounds, picnic areas, and discreetly situated restaurants and hotels. Turn off along the lakeshore in the town of Ruidera; along this road there are several places hiring pedalos, canoes and bikes, or offering horseriding to explore the area.

Sleeping

Camping Los Batanes CAMPGROUND €

(926 69 90 20; www.losbatanes.com; Laguna Redondilla; sites incl 2 people, tent & car €18-35, bungalows €55-130; P) This leafy campsite overlooks Laguna Redondilla, one of the larger lakes here, and has excellent facilities with a small supermarket, restaurant, cafe and children's playground, as well as two pools set amid pretty landscaped gardens. During the summer months there's an entertainment program for children. Rates vary considerably according to the season.

★**Hotel Albamanjón** HOTEL €€€

(926 69 90 48; www.albamanjon.net; Calle Extramuros 16, Laguna de San Pedro; d €120-195; P) A great place to stay right on the shores of Laguna de San Pedro, 10km southeast of Ruidera. Running up the hill behind the main building, these attractive suites are all separate from each other and have a private terrace with lake views, wood fires for winter, and most have a Jacuzzi.

Getting There & Away

There's one daily bus (Monday to Saturday) linking Albacete and Ruidera (€9, 1½ hours). You really need your own transport to explore the park.

Sierra de Alcaraz

Stretching across the southern strip of Albacete province, the cool, green peaks of the Sierra de Alcaraz offer a great escape from the dusty plains around Albacete. The gateway to the region, sleepy hilltop Alcaraz, has a lovely renaissance Plaza Mayor and a lattice of narrow cobbled streets. The most scenic countryside is to be found along the CM412, particularly between Puerto de las Crucetas (elevation 1300m) and Elche de la Sierra. And then there's the spectacular Nacimiento del Río Mundo.

Sights

Nacimiento del Río Mundo WATERFALL
(Source of the River Mundo; CM3204; 10am-dusk; P) Take a photo of yourself standing in front of the Nacimiento del Río Mundo, send it to the folks back home and they will think that you have sidestepped to Niagara Falls for the day. To get to these amazing waterfalls, follow the signs just before Riópar for around 8km on the CM3204 – past the amusing pictorial 'beware of the *anfibios* (amphibians)' signs – until you reach the entrance and car park.

It's a short walk through the forest of mainly coniferous trees to the bottom of the falls, where the water splashes and courses via several rock pools. There are two miradors: the first is at the base of the falls with neck-craning views of the dramatic waterfall above; it's a steep climb to the second mirador, but worth the effort. At some 800m above sea level, the water emerges from the rocks just above the platform, almost close enough to touch, in a dramatic drop of some 24m (spraying you liberally en route). The falls are surrounded by dense forest stretching to a rocky horizon – all those sceptics who say La Mancha is flat and boring should definitely visit these falls.

Sleeping

Mirador Sierra de Alcaraz HOTEL €
(967 38 00 17; www.alcarazmirador.com; Calle Granada 1, Alcaraz; d €48-70;) In the centre of Alcaraz, this handsome, mainly 16th-century building houses the Mirador Sierra de Alcaraz, with its central Moorish courtyard dating, incredibly, from the 9th century. The rooms have beamed ceilings, carved wooden bedheads and heavy period-style curtains and furnishings. All have good views and there is easy parking on the street outside.

Las Salegas del Maguillo HOTEL €€
(660 24 96 92; www.lassalegasdelmaguillo.es; Carretera Riópar-Siles Km11; d €90, 4-/6-person apt €150/210; P) High up in the hills above the road 11km west of Riópar, beyond the Nacimiento del Río Mundo turn-off, this place consists of a collection of handsome stone buildings set amid the woods. Some of the villas have fireplaces and there is an outdoor swimming pool. It's rustic, tranquil and comfortable.

Eating

Restaurante Alfonso VIII GRILL €€
(067 38 04 14; Calle Padre Pareja 1, Alcaraz; mains €10-15; 9am-midnight Tue-Sun) Just off the town's stunning Plaza Mayor, this time-tested favourite restaurant is housed in a handsome Renaissance-era building. The cuisine is strictly traditional with an

WORTH A TRIP

VILLANUEVA DE LOS INFANTES

Villanueva de los Infantes is an attractive and busy provincial town notable for its baroque and Renaissance architecture. It's also rumoured to be the starting point of Don Quijote's La Mancha wanderings. A highlight is its Plaza Mayor, with ochre-coloured buildings, wood-and-stone balconies, and lively bars and restaurants. On the square stands the 15th-century Iglesia de San Andrés, where 16th-century poet Francisco de Quevedo is buried. A prime location in the historic centre, just off the main square, makes **La Morada de Juan de Vargas** (926 36 17 69; www.lamoradadevargas.com; Calle Cervantes 3; d €60-70;) the best of the town's several appealing rural hotel options. The decor is full of unique, arty touches and the hosts are exceptionally warm and inviting.

Buses run to Ciudad Real (€9, two hours) three times daily from Monday to Friday and once on Saturday.

emphasis on grilled meats (you can see the various cuts in a display cabinet at the entrance), served with slow-fried potatoes, rather than chips. Reservations are recommended at weekends.

Getting There & Away

There are a couple of daily buses from Alcaraz to Albacete (€6.50, 1½ hours).

NORTHEAST CASTILLA-LA MANCHA

This region has a rich hinterland of craggy mountains and lush green valleys studded by unspoilt, pretty villages. It is also home to some of the country's most enchanting *pueblos* and towns, including the provincial capital of Cuenca with its splendid medieval old town and refreshing lack of tourists.

Cuenca

POP 55,102

A World Heritage Site, Cuenca is one of Spain's most memorable cities, its old centre a stage set of evocative medieval buildings, many painted in bright colours, stacked on a steep promontory at the meeting of two deep river gorges. Narrow meandering streets separate tall houses with wooden balconies that literally jut out over the sheer cliffs. Yet, despite its age and Unesco listing, Cuenca has somewhat ironically established itself as a vortex of abstract modern art. Two of its most iconic buildings – including one of the famed *casas colgadas* (hanging houses) – have transformed their interiors into modern galleries. It's a theme continued in many of the town's hotels, museums and restaurants.

Like many Spanish cities, the surrounding new town is bland and modern, so keep the blinkers on during the approach – up the hill lies another world.

Sights

★Casas Colgadas HISTORIC BUILDING

(Calle Canónigos) The most striking element of medieval Cuenca, the *casas colgadas* jut out precariously over the steep defile of Río Huécar. Dating from the 14th century, the houses, with their layers of wooden balconies, seem to emerge from the rock as if an extension of the cliffs. The best views of the *casas colgadas* is from the Puente de San Pablo footbridge. Today the houses host – somewhat improbably – an abstract art museum founded in the 1960s.

★Museo de Arte Abstracto Español MUSEUM

(Museum of Abstract Art; ☎969 21 29 83; www.march.es/arte/cuenca; Calle Canónigos; adult/child €3/free; ⏰11am-2pm & 4-6pm Tue-Fri, 11am-2pm & 4-8pm Sat, 11am-2.30pm Sun) From the outside, they look as if they've been sawn off from some high-altitude Tibetan temple, but, from the inside, Cuenca's famous *casas colgadas* have been transformed into a suite of airy, clean-lined galleries displaying some of central Spain's finest abstract art. You can spend hours in here trying to decipher blurry Fernando Zóbel's (the museum's founder), bright and direct José Guerrero's or the highly individual works of Catalan Antoni Tàpies.

★Museo de la Semana Santa MUSEUM

(☎969 22 19 56; Calle Andrés de Cabrera 13; adult/child €3/free; ⏰11am-2pm & 4.30-7.30pm Thu-Sat, 11am-2pm Sun, closed Aug) This museum is the next best thing to experiencing one of Spain's most spine-tingling Semana Santa parades firsthand. Spread over two floors, the hugely accomplished audiovisual show moves from room to room showing the processions by local brotherhoods against a background of sombre music. Afterwards you are allowed to wander around at leisure, admiring the costumes, crosses and religious iconography.

Catedral de Cuenca CATHEDRAL

(☎969 22 46 26; Plaza Mayor; adult/child €4.80/free, incl Museo Diocesano adult/child €8/free; ⏰10am-7.30pm) Lured in by the impressive old-looking facade (it was actually cleverly rebuilt in neo-Gothic style in 1902), Cuneca's cathedral is well worth a visit. It was built on the site of the main mosque after the city's reconquest by Alfonso VIII in 1177. Highlights include the magnificent Renaissance doorway leading to the cloisters and the chapter house *artesonado* (wooden) ceiling painted in pastel colours. The striking abstract stained-glass windows were added in the 20th century.

Túneles de Alfonso VIII TUNNEL

(Calle Alfonso VIII; guided tour €3.50, minimum 4 people; ⏰hours vary) A mole hill of tunnels lies under Cuenca's old town. Over time

LOCAL KNOWLEDGE

ABSTRACT CUENCA

One of the latent joys of this historical city that hangs surreally above two dramatic gorges is the way it has managed to incorporate avant-gardism into its crusty historic core.

Cuenca's penchant for abstract art can be traced back to the 1950s, when a loose collection of locally based artists formed what became known as the 'Cuenca School'. Notable in the group was Fernando Zóbel, a Spanish-Filipino painter and art collector who got together with Cuenca-born engineer-turned-artist Gustavo Torner in 1966 to open the **Museo de Arte Abstracto** inside the town's famous hanging houses. It was an inspired choice. Encased in a historical medieval residence, beautifully laid-out exhibits made use of reconfigured minimalist rooms. The museum prospered and others followed. In 1998 Sigüenza-born artist and poet Antonio Pérez opened up an eponymous **foundation** in an old Carmelite monastery and stuffed it with works from Warhol to Antoni Tàpies. Seven years later, Torner founded his own museum, **Espacio Torner**, in Cuenca's San Pedro convent (the museum is currently on extended hiatus due to funding issues).

But the abstractness extends beyond traditional museums. The brilliant yellow and orange stained glass in Cuenca's 12th-century **cathedral** was fashioned by Torner in the early 1990s to create a whimsical hybrid, while, further down the hill in the new town, the concrete and glass **Museo de Paleontología**, with its cube-like display halls, pays more than a passing nod to avant-gardism. You'll even spot abstract influences in the decor of some of Cuenca's hotels and restaurants, the arty interiors of which often belie their medieval outer shells.

they have served multiple purposes as aqueducts, crypts and, most recently, air-raid shelters during the civil war. The tunnels have been restored and fitted with walkways, lighting and explanatory boards. Tours are guided only (in Spanish) and must be booked through the main tourist office (p243).

Cerro del Socorro HILL

(Cerro del Socorro) This hill across the Río Huécar gorge from Cuenca's old town is crowned by a giant statue of Christ, which is illuminated at night. A 3km trail marked by the 14 Stations of the Cross follows a zigzag route to the top. It starts just behind the Parador de Cuenca.

Fundación Antonio Pérez GALLERY

(☎969 23 06 19; www.fundacionantonioperez.es; Ronda de Julián Romero 20; adult/child €2/free; ⏲11am-2pm & 5-8pm) This huge modern-art gallery in the labyrinthine ex–Convento de las Carmelitas is a typical Cuenca synthesis of old and new. Stuffed with exhibits that may perplex, inspire and (possibly) amuse, it is large, but crammed. Antonio Saura is well represented, as are plenty of other 1950s and '60s-era artists. Included in the collection are two works by renowned American pop artist Andy Warhol.

Mirador Barrio del Castillo VIEWPOINT

(Calle Larga) Climb to the top of the old town for this fine viewpoint over Cuenca and its plunging gorges. You can also catch bus number 2 from the new town which stops close by.

Museo de Paleontología MUSEUM

(☎969 27 17 00; Río Gritos 5; adult/child €3/1.50, Wed afternoon & Sun free; ⏲10am-2.30pm & 4.30-7pm Tue-Sat; 10am-2.30pm Sun; 👪) Cuenca's former Ars Nature has been transformed into a streamlined palaeontology museum anchored by its appropriately kid-friendly dinosaur exhibition ('Tierra de Dinosaurios'). Spacious modern galleries are decorated with locally found fossils, skeletons and skulls, plus mock-ups of enormous Jurassic reptiles. There are some fun audiovisual exhibits and the landscaped grounds are home to more prehistoric giants that kids can pose beside for that ultimate photo op for show-and-tell back home.

Museo de Cuenca MUSEUM

(☎969 21 30 69; Calle Obispo Valero 12; adult/child €3/free, Wed afternoon & weekends free; ⏲10am-2pm & 4-7pm Tue-Sat, 10am-2pm Sun) The city's history museum is comprehensive, but heavily weighted towards the pre-medieval age. The story kicks off in the Bronze Age, but the real scoop is Sala 7, stuffed with original

Cuenca

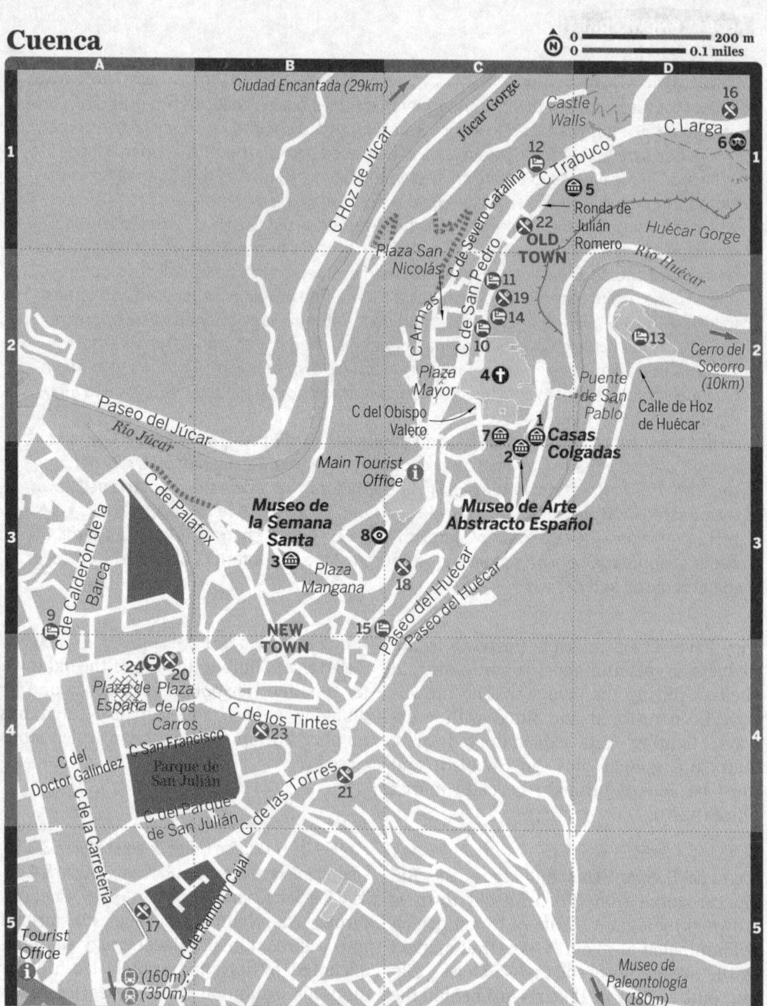

Roman statues (including Emperor Augustus), plus columns and pediments plucked from the nearby archaeological sites at Segóbriga and Valeria. Post-Renaissance history gets only a light dusting.

Festivals & Events

Semana Santa RELIGIOUS

(www.juntacofradiascuenca.es; Easter) Cuenca's Holy Week celebrations are renowned throughout Spain for the eerie, silent processions through the streets of the old town. There's even a town museum (p238) dedicated to the annual event.

Sleeping

★ Posada Huécar HOTEL €

(969 21 42 01; www.posadahuecar.com; Paseo del Huécar 3; s/d €35/48; P ❄) Feel luxurious on a tight budget. Located squarely between the old and new towns, this attractive hotel has spacious rooms with river views, rustic furnishings and bathrooms with tubs, as well as showers and excellent water pressure. Packaged breakfast pastries and coffee are included in the price. There are bicycles to rent (€20 for one day). There is generally free parking available across the street.

Cuenca

Top Sights

1 Casas Colgadas C2
2 Museo de Arte Abstracto Español C3
3 Museo de la Semana Santa B3

Sights

4 Catedral de Cuenca C2
5 Fundación Antonio Pérez D1
6 Mirador Barrio del Castillo D1
7 Museo de Cuenca C2
8 Túneles de Alfonso VIII C3

Sleeping

9 CH Victoria Alojamientos A3
10 Convento del Giraldo C2
11 Hostal San Pedro C2
12 Hostal Tabanqueta C1
13 Parador de Cuenca D2
14 Posada de San José C2
15 Posada Huécar B3

Eating

16 Asador María Morena D1
17 El Bodegón A5
18 El Secreto C3
19 Figón del Huécar C2
20 La Bodeguilla de Basilio A4
21 Posada de San Julián B4
22 Raff San Pedro C1
23 Romera Bistrót B4

Drinking & Nightlife

24 La Tasca del Arte A4

Hostal Tabanqueta HOSTAL €

(969 21 40 76; www.hostaltabanqueta.com; Calle Trabuco 13; d €45, apt €50-100; P ❄ 📶) Up the hill from Plaza Mayor, this friendly spot has free parking nearby and top-of-the-town views. The accommodation is excellent, with heating, stylish tiled bathrooms, attractive artwork and hotel-standard amenities such as toiletries, an espresso machine and hospitality tray with pastries. The owners also rent out a number of apartments nearby.

★ **Posada de San José** HISTORIC HOTEL €€

(969 21 13 00; www.posadasanjose.com; Ronda de Julián Romero 4; s/d €60/85, d with view €97, s/d with shared bathroom €32/45; ❄ @ 📶) Owned by Antonio and his Canadian wife Jennifer, this 17th-century former choir school retains an extraordinary monastic charm with its labyrinth of rooms, eclectic artwork, uneven floors and original tiles. All rooms are different; cheaper ones are in former priests' cells and share bathrooms, while more costly doubles combine homey comfort with old-world charm. Several have balconies with dramatic views of the gorge. There's a reputable restaurant on the ground floor.

Convento del Giraldo HISTORIC HOTEL €€

(969 23 27 00; www.hotelconventodelgiraldo.com; Calle de San Pedro 12; d/ste €66/125; ❄ @ 📶) Just above the cathedral, this conversion of a 17th-century convent wins points for location and style, though there aren't too many original features left. Nevertheless, the attractive rooms feature dark wooden furniture and big bathrooms, and many sport great views. You can find good discounts online.

CH Victoria Alojamientos HOTEL €€

(620 782937; www.grupochvictoria.es; Calle Mateo Miguel Ayllón 2; s €25-45, d €50-80; P 📶) Blurring the lines between *hostal* and hotel, the rooms at this excellent place offer every comfort, with stylish decoration, modern bathrooms, firm mattresses and plenty of thoughtful extras. There's no reception, so you'll need to book in advance and arrange to pick up the key.

Hostal San Pedro HOSTAL €€

(628 407601, 969 23 45 43; www.hostalsanpedro.es; Calle de San Pedro 34; s/d €40/70; 📶) In this excellently priced and positioned *hostal,* rooms have butter-coloured paintwork, traditional tiles, wrought-iron bedheads and rustic wood furniture and shutters; the bathrooms are large and modern. The owners run the restaurant Mangana on Plaza Mayor, so you can enquire there or call ahead.

Parador de Cuenca HISTORIC HOTEL €€€

(969 23 23 20; www.parador.es; Calle de Hoz de Huécar; s/d €100/175; P ❄ 📶 🏊) This majestic former convent commands possibly the best views in town of the *casas colgadas* that are suspended on the opposite side of the gorge. The revamped rooms have a luxury corporate feel, while the public areas, including an old cloister, are headily historic with giant tapestries and antiques.

Eating

★El Bodegón SPANISH €

(969 21 40 29; Cerrillo de San Roque A1; mains €7-10, set menu €10; 1-4pm & 8.30-11.30pm Tue-Sun;) No frills, great value, lightning-fast service. Up a narrow lane in the new town, this sociable bar could turn out to be the Castilla-La Mancha eating experience that lingers longest in your memory. It's the perfect place to enjoy a long, slow lunch. Try the excellent-value *menú del día*.

Posada de San Julián SPANISH €

(969 21 17 04; Calle de las Torres 1; mains €7-12, set menu €11; noon-3pm & 7-10pm Tue-Sat, noon-3pm Sun) Just down the hill from the historic centre, revel in 16th-century surroundings with lofty ceilings, original columns and creaking floors. It's family run (get here early and you will see grandpa peeling potatoes), and the cuisine may not be art-on-a-plate but it's tasty, filling and excellent value with huge portions and market-fresh produce.

Asador María Morena SPANISH €€

(969 23 88 25; www.asadormariamorena.com; Calle Larga 31; mains €17-20; 1-4pm & 8-11pm) A good all-round restaurant located at the top of the old town with panoramic views over the river gorge, this place will satisfy both romantic diners and those seeking a more casual evening meal. Everything from the black paella (with squid ink) to homey *patatas a lo pobre* (potatoes with onions, garlic and peppers) are enhanced with a deft artistic touch.

El Secreto SPANISH €€

(678 611301; www.elsecretocuenca.com; Calle de Alfonso VIII 81; mains €10-17; 11am-4.30pm Mon & Tue, 11am-4.30pm & 8pm-midnight Thu-Sun;) El Secreto isn't much of a secret. Exuberant decor featuring painted beams and tiled murals coupled with a friendly, laid-back attitude means this place stays pretty busy. There's a good selection of pastas, salads and meat dishes, including an unorthodox venison burger, all of which can be savoured in the back dining room (with vistas) or the painfully thin front bar.

La Bodeguilla de Basilio TAPAS €€

(969 23 52 74; Calle Fray Luis de León 3; raciones €10-13; 1-4pm & 8-11pm Tue-Sat, 1-4pm Sun) Arrive here with an appetite, as you're presented with a complimentary plate of tapas when you order a drink, and not just a slice of dried-up cheese – typical freebies are a combo of quail eggs and fried potatoes or a bowl of *caldo* (meat-based broth). *Zarajos* (barbecued lamb served on a skewer), a traditional Cuenca dish, is also a speciality here. This is one of the most popular tapas bars in the new town so get here early to grab a pew.

Understandably, it gets packed out, so head to the restaurant at the back for specials such as *patatas a lo pobre* or lamb chops. The walls are covered with fascinating clutter, ranging from old pics of Cuenca to farming tools.

★Raff San Pedro MODERN SPANISH €€€

(969 69 08 55; www.raffsanpedro.es; Ronda de Julian Romero; mains €18-25, set menus €27-36; 1-4pm & 8.30-11pm Tue-Sat, 1-4pm Sun;) Tucked down a narrow pedestrian street near the cathedral, Raff's innovative culinary convictions run deep with lively fresh flavours and combinations like tomatoes stuffed with scallop cerviche and stuffed gnocchi made with yams. The set menus are an excellent way to taste a variety of contemporary-style dishes, although there is nothing nouvelle about the generous portion size.

★Romera Bistrót INTERNATIONAL €€€

(626 087832; www.romerabistrot.com; Calle de los Tintes 19; mains €18-25; noon-3pm & 8-11pm Mon-Sat;) Bikes, truffles, sashimi... sound interesting so far? Romero is one of Cuenca's new breed of contemporary restaurants with a short menu that's all over the map: salmon sashimi, black spaghetti and a foie-gras royale. Everything is executed perfectly in a 10-table, light-filled space that carries the air of a Parisian bistro. To add to the atmosphere (and perhaps the sustainability) there are bike motifs – including (sometimes) bike-shaped pasta.

★Figón del Huécar SPANISH €€€

(969 24 00 62; www.figondelhuecar.es; Ronda de Julián Romero 6; mains €13-25, set menus €26-36; 1.30-3.30pm & 9-10.30pm Tue-Sat, 1.30-3.30pm Sun;) With a romantic terrace offering spectacular views, Figón del Huécar is a highlight of old-town eating. Roast suckling pig, lamb stuffed with wild asparagus, and a host of Castilian specialities are presented and served with panache. The house used to be the home of Spanish singer José Luis Perales.

Drinking & Nightlife

La Tasca del Arte BAR

(☎969 16 01 95; www.la-tasca-del-arte.es; Calle Fray Luis de León 9; ⏰1pm-2am) Head to the *tasca* (tapas bar) here to enjoy live flamenco in an intimate atmosphere where tapas and drinks are also served, including an impressive number of imported and craft beers. Performances take place from 9pm Thursday to Saturday but space is limited so get here early to grab a table. The restaurant also receives rave reviews from readers.

Information

Main Tourist Office (☎969 24 10 51; http://turismo.cuenca.es; Calle de Alfonso VIII 2; ⏰10am-2pm & 4.30-7.30pm Mon-Fri, 10am-8pm Sat & Sun) Book here for tours of the medieval Túneles de Alfonso VIII that honeycomb the old town.

Tourist Office (☎969 23 58 15; http://turismo.cuenca.es; Avenida de la República Argentina 4; ⏰10am-2pm & 5-8pm Mon-Sat, 10am-2pm Sun) Cuenca's second, slightly smaller tourist office is in the new town. It's open somewhat reduced hours on weekends in winter.

Getting There & Away

Cuenca has two train stations. Fast AVE trains (serving Valencia and Madrid) use the modern **Estación de Cuenca-Fernando Zóbel** (☎912 43 23 43; www.renfe.com; Avenida Cerro de la Estrella; ⏰6.45am-10.30pm), 6km southwest of town. Bus 12 (€1.25, every 30 minutes) links it with the town centre.

The regional train station **Estación de Cuenca** (☎912 32 03 20; www.renfe.com; Calle Mariano Catalina 10; ⏰ticket office 8.30am-9.15pm) is located in the new part of town, southwest of Calle de Fermín Caballero and across from the bus station.

Numerous daily trains run to Madrid, ranging from slow *regionales* (trains operating within one region, usually stopping all stations; €15, three hours) to swift AVEs (€35, 55 minutes). The other way, to Valencia, is a similar deal (€16 to €38).

There are up to nine buses daily to Madrid (€15, 2¼ hours) and regular services to other cities in Castilla-La Mancha including Toledo (€14.50, 3¼ hours) and Albacete (€12, 2¾ hours).

Getting Around

Local buses 1 and 2 do the circuit from the new town to Plaza Mayor (€1.20, every 30 minutes), stopping outside the Estación de Cuenca-Fernando Zóbel. There's a large free car park on Calle Larga above the arch at the top of the old town.

WORTH A TRIP

SERRANÍA DE CUENCA

Head out from Cuenca 30km via the CM2105 to the extraordinary **Ciudad Encantada** (Carretera CM2104, Km 19; adult/child €5/free; ⏰10am-sunset; 🅿), where limestone rocks have been eroded into fantastical shapes by nature. The CM2105 continues north via the picturesque village of **Uña**, the crystal-clear waters of **Embalse del Tobar** and past the **Reserva Natural de El Hosquillo**, a protected park where reintroduced brown bears roam wild.

You can return to Cuenca via the CM210, a quiet rural route that passes several traditional villages like **Priego**, a lovely valley town that dates from Roman times. If you're heading on to Sigüenza, track northeast from Beteta to **Molina de Aragón**, a pretty town utterly dominated by one of Spain's most spectacular castles.

Pastrana

POP 1054

Pastrana should not be missed. It's an unspoilt place with twisting cobbled streets flanked by honey-coloured stone buildings, with small family-owned shops, good restaurants and atmospheric bars with tables on the cobblestones. It is famous for a notorious 16th-century court scandal as well as being home to some magnificent Flemish tapestries.

Sights

The heart and soul of the town is the **Plaza de la Hora**, a large square framed by acacias and fronted by the sturdy **Palacio Ducal**. It's in Pastrana that the one-eyed princess of Éboli, Ana Mendoza de la Cerda, was confined in 1581 for having a love affair with the Spanish king Felipe II's secretary. You can see the caged window of her 'cell', where she died 10 years later, and join a tour on Saturday at 11.30am (Spanish only; €6) run from the tourist office (p244).

Iglesia de Nuestra Señora de la Asunción & Museo Parroquial MUSEUM

(Colegiata; ☎949 37 00 27; www.museoparroquialdetapicesdepastrana.com; Calle Mayor; adult/child €5/free; ⏲11.30am-2pm & 4.30-7pm Tue-Fri, 1-2pm & 4.30-7pm Sun) Walk from the Plaza de la Hora along Calle Mayor and you'll soon reach the massive Iglesia de Nuestra Señora de la Asunción. Inside, the interesting little Museo Parroquial contains the jewels of the princess of Éboli, some exquisite 15th-century Flemish tapestries and even an El Greco.

Parque Arqueológico de Recópolis ARCHAEOLOGICAL SITE

(Roman ruins; ☎949 37 68 98; www.recopolis.com; Carretera de Almoguera, Zorita de los Canes; adult/child €5/2.50; ⏲10am-6pm Wed-Sun; P) Recópolis, a fascinating archaeological site, is a rarity. It was one of possibly only four cities that were built during the Visigothic era in Western Europe. Founded by King Leovigildo in AD 578, it was originally conceived as a rival to Constantinople (the dream soon faded). The site is equipped with an interpretive centre that offers guided tours around the ruins, which lie 13km south of Pastrana, signposted off the Tarancón road (turn right just after passing the nuclear power plant).

Sleeping

Hotel Palaterna HOTEL €

(☎949 37 01 27; www.hotelpalaterna.com; Plaza de los Cuatro Caños 4; r/ste €65/95; ❄📶) Hotel Palaterna is a pleasant, modern hotel overlooking a small square complete with bubbling fountain. Rooms are painted in cool colours with pretty fabrics and light wood furniture.

Eating

★**Cenador de las Monjas** SPANISH €€

(☎949 37 01 01; www.cenadordelasmonjas.es; Calle de las Monjas; mains €12-20, set menus €35-40; ⏲2-4pm & 9-11pm Fri & Sat, 2-4pm Sun; P) The dining room in the old 16th-century San José monastery offers beautifully prepared Spanish food that is anything but austere. Sit under a wood-beamed ceiling, overlooked by oil paintings of severe-looking nobility and indulge in venison meatballs or tuna with a honey glaze. Abiding by monastic tradition, most of the vegetables are grown here.

Information

Tourist Office (☎949 37 06 72; www.pastrana.org; Plaza de la Hora 5; ⏲10am-2pm & 4-7pm Mon-Fri, 10am-2pm & 4-8pm Sat, 10am-2pm Sun)

Getting There & Away

Pastrana is 42km south of the regional capital of Guadalajara along the CM200. If travelling by public transport from either Madrid or Cuenca, you'll need to take a bus or train to Guadalajara, from where there's a daily bus run by Guadalbus (www.guadalbus.com) to/from Pastrana (€6, 1¼ hours).

Sigüenza

POP 4335

Sleepy, historical and filled with the ghosts of a turbulent past, Sigüenza is well worth a detour. The town is built on a low hill cradled by Río Henares and boasts a castle, a cathedral and several excellent restaurants set among twisting lanes of medieval buildings. Start your ambling at the beautiful 16th-century Plaza Mayor. It's a popular day trip from Madrid.

Sights

★**Catedral de Santa María de Sigüenza** CATHEDRAL

(☎619 362715; www.lacatedraldesiguenza.com; Plaza del Obispo Don Bernardo; ⏲9.30am-2pm & 4-8pm Tue-Sat, noon-5.30pm Sun) Rising up from the heart of the old town is the city's centrepiece – the cathedral. Begun as a Romanesque structure in 1130, work continued for four centuries as the church was expanded and adorned. The largely Gothic result is laced with elements of other styles, from plateresque through to Renaissance to Mudéjar. The church was heavily damaged during the civil war (note the pockmarks from bullets and shells in the bell tower), but was subsequently rebuilt.

The dark interior has a broodingly ancient feel and some fine stained glass, plus an impressive 15th-century altarpiece. To enter the chapels, sacristy and Gothic cloister, you'll need to join a Spanish-language guided tour (per person €7; noon, 1pm, 4.30pm and 5.30pm Tuesday to Sunday). A highlight of the tour is the **Capilla Mayor**, home of the reclining marble statue of Don Martín Vázquez de Arce (the statue is named *El Doncel*), who died fighting the Muslims in the final stages of the Reconquista.

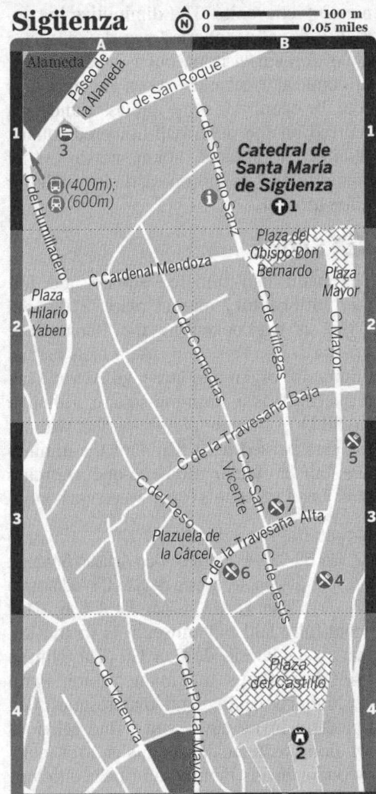

Particularly beautiful is the **Sacristía de las Cabezas**, with a ceiling adorned with hundreds of heads sculpted by Covarrubias. The **Capilla del Espíritu Santo's doorway** combines plateresque, Mudéjar and Gothic styles; inside is a remarkable dome and an *Anunciación* by El Greco.

Castillo de Sigüenza CASTLE
(www.parador.es; Plaza del Castillo; P) Calle Mayor heads south up the hill from the cathedral to a magnificent-looking castle, which was originally built by the Romans and was, in turn, a Moorish *alcázar* (fortress), royal palace, asylum and army barracks. Virtually destroyed during the Spanish Civil War, it was subsequently rebuilt under Franco as a *parador*.

Non-guests are welcome to wander in and use the cafeteria and other general areas, which overlook a beautiful courtyard.

Sigüenza

Top Sights
1 Catedral de Santa María de Sigüenza B1

Sights
2 Castillo de Sigüenza B4

Sleeping
3 El Doncel A1
Parador de Sigüenza .... (see 2)

Eating
4 Bodega Sigüenza B3
5 Calle Mayor B3
6 Gurugú de la Plazuela B3
7 Nöla B3

Sleeping

★El Doncel HOTEL €€
(949 39 00 01; www.eldoncel.com; Paseo de la Alameda 3; d €60-70;) With earthy colours, exposed stone, spot lighting, fridges (for the *cava*), and marshmallow-soft duvets and pillows, this place is aimed squarely at couples on a romantic weekend away from Madrid. It's comfortable and attractive, and there's an excellent restaurant. Prices drop substantially midweek.

Parador de Sigüenza HISTORIC HOTEL €€€
(949 39 01 00; www.parador.es; Plaza del Castillo; d €110-185; P) Sigüenza's luxurious *parador* is set in the castle, which dates back to the 12th century and overlooks the town. The magnificent courtyard is a wonderful place to pass the time. The rooms have period furnishings and castle-style windows, so they can be on the dark side; ask for one with a balcony to make the most of the natural light and views.

Eating

★Calle Mayor SPANISH €€
(949 39 17 48; www.restaurantecallemayor.com; Calle Mayor 21; mains €12-18; 1-3.30pm & 8.30-11pm) A standout meal stop between the cathedral and castle, be sure to order the simple starter of tomatoes which are grown in the owner's backyard. Mains here tend to be traditional with local roasted meats, such as goat and lamb, as well as more elaborate creations like artichokes stuffed with prawns. The service is gracious and English is spoken.

Bodega Sigüenza SPANISH €€

(☎949 39 32 46; www.bodegasiguenza.es; Calle Mayor 41; mains €12-14, set menu €27; ⏱1.30-4pm & 8.30-11pm Thu-Sun) Offers a limited menu of traditional Castilla-La Mancha recipes in a small but pleasantly intimate space near the castle. A speciality is *callos* (tripe), but they also serve more familiar (for some) mains, like burgers with sundried tomatoes and creamy Manchego cheese.

Gurugú de la Plazuela TAPAS €€

(☎949 39 01 34; www.gurugudelaplazuela.com; Plazuela de la Cárcel; mushroom dishes €16-19; ⏱12.30-4pm & 8-11pm Thu-Sat, 12.30-4pm Sun) Overlooking the small, atmospheric Plazuela de la Cárcel, the speciality of this historical tavern is mushrooms – lots of them – with some 16 varieties on the menu, prepared all sorts of ways. Other choices include a nice line in game dishes. It holds regular art and photography exhibitions in the traditionally tiled dining space.

Nöla MODERN SPANISH €€€

(☎949 39 32 46; www.nolarestaurante.es; Calle Arcedianos 20; mains €15-32, set menu €26; ⏱1.30-3.30pm & 8.30-10.30pm Thu-Sat, 1.30-3.30pm Sun; 📶) Nöla is located in a grand Gothic Mudéjar mansion so is a place to linger. The menu stirs up traditional cuisine in the most delightful and innovative ways with dishes like *salmorejo* (tomato and bread purée) with spider crab and fresh bean sprouts and roasted lamb with hazelnuts.

Information

Tourist Office (☎949 34 70 07; www.turismocastillalamancha.es; Calle de Serrano Sanz 9; ⏱10am-2pm & 4-6pm Mon-Thu & Sat, 10am-2pm & 4-8pm Fri, 10am-2pm Sun) Just down the hill from the cathedral. Opens and closes an hour later in the afternoon in summer.

Getting There & Away

Regional trains go to Madrid's Chamartín station (€12 to €14, 1½ to 1¾ hours, five daily) via Guadalajara; some go on to Soria in the other direction.

Atienza

POP 444

Standing amid the ruins of Atienza's blustery castle and looking out at the arid plains and low hills that couldn't be anywhere but Spain is one of Castilla-La Mancha best memory souvenirs. The diminutive but romantically atmospheric town doesn't get a lot of foreign visitors, but is a great place to come at weekends (when its museums actually open!) for some aimless wandering centred on the main half-timbered square. Atienza is situated 30km northwest of Sigüenza and its hilltop castle is visible for miles around.

Sights

The main half-timbered square and former 16th-century market place, **Plaza del Trigo**, is overlooked by the Renaissance **Iglesia San Juan Bautista**, which has an impressive organ and lavish gilt *retablo* (altarpiece). It is a stunning square, although would be even more picture-perfect without the cars parked here. Three of the diminutive but muscular Romanesque churches hold small museums (open weekends only).

Museo de San Gil MUSEUM

(☎949 39 99 04; Plaza de Don Agustín González Martínez Sacerdote, Iglesia de San Gil; admission €2; ⏱11.30am-2pm & 4-7pm Sat & Sun) This beautifully laid out museum is in the Romanesque Iglesia de San Gil. The church itself is perhaps the main 'exhibit' with its Mudéjar ceiling and plateresque door. Lined up in its naves you'll find religious art along with small sections on archaeology (arrowheads mainly) and palaeontology (fossils).

Castillo Roquero CASTLE

(Camino de San Salvador; ⏱sunrise-sunset; 👪) FREE Now that's what you call a castle! Looking like a natural extension of the crag upon which it sits, Atienza's romantically dishevelled *castillo* has Roman, Visigothic and Moorish antecedents. It was finally wrested from the Moors by Christian king Alfonso VI in 1085 and is now a windy ruin enjoying fabulous views over the surrounding *meseta* (plains).

Sleeping

Hostal El Mirador HOSTAL €

(☎949 39 90 38; www.elmiradordeatienza.com; Calle Barruelo; s/d €30/45; P❄📶) El Mirador, with spotless rooms that are a steal at this price, is a budget option in a modern whitewashed building offering great panoramic views over the fields below. The excellent restaurant shares the vistas and serves creative dishes, as well as the standard *cordero* (lamb) and *cabrito* (kid).

OFF THE BEATEN TRACK

CAMINO TO ATIENZA

Buses serving the hilltop-hugging town of Atienza are a little thin on the ground; but, for those with strong legs, there's a viable alternative. You can walk to the town on a little-trekked southern branch of the Camino de Santiago through a quintessential Castillan landscape of arid hills punctuated by half-forgotten, semiabandoned villages.

A well-signposted 32km section of the route connects the two historic towns of Sigüenza and Atienza, passing through the pinprick but atmospheric villages of Palazuelos, Olmeda de Jadraque and Riofrío del Llano.

To get started, exit Sigüenza via Calle Santa Bárbara, passing a football field and crossing a railway line. Then, take the unpaved, vehicle-width track uphill and follow the purple and yellow 'Camino' signs decorated with the famous scarab symbol. The well-marked path is good year-round (weather permitting), but, whichever season you hike, take plenty of food and water. The villages along the way offer little in the way of refreshment.

★Antiguo Palacio de Atienza HISTORIC HOTEL €€
(949 39 91 80; www.palaciodeatienza.com; Plaza de Agustín González 1; d €55-85;) Want to stay in a palace skilfully updated with well-chosen artworks, comfortable beds and exposed beams fine enough to satisfy the expectations of modern-day princes and princesses (and tourists)? The variation in price relates to the size of the room and whether there's a hot tub in the stylish little bathrooms. Balconies overlook the lawns and pool, and there's a good restaurant.

La Casa de San Gil CASA RURAL €€
(626 165544; www.lacasadesangil.com; Plaza de Don Agustín González Martínez Sacerdote 1; r €70-80;) This traditional 18th-century stone cottage is located in the shadow of the Iglesia de San Gil and has been aesthetically restored by its *madrileño* (residents of Madrid) owners. Each of the five rooms is different but all are soothingly decorated with earth colours and rustic charm. There's a sitting room with fireplace and pretty small garden.

Information

Tourist Office (949 39 90 01; www.atienza.es; Calle Héctor Vázquez 2; 11am-2pm & 4-7pm Mon-Fri, 11am-2pm Sat & Sun) Contains a small museum displaying local costumes and paraphernalia relating to the town's customs and festivals.

Getting There & Away

Buses are scant. A couple leave early in the morning, bound for Madrid (€12, 2¾ hours) and Sigüenza (€4, 45 minutes).

Alarcón

POP 160

One hundred kilometres or so south of Cuenca is the seductive medieval village of Alarcón. Flanked on three sides by the Río Júcar forming a natural moat, the approach is via a narrow road winding through three medieval defensive arches. The most famous sight here is the triangular-based Islamic castle, dating from the 8th century and captured by the Moors in 1184 after a nine-month siege. It is now a *parador* – one of Spain's smallest. The surrounding countryside is stunning and popular for hiking.

Sleeping & Eating

★Parador de Alarcón HISTORIC HOTEL €€€
(Marqués de Villena; 969 33 03 15; www.parador.es; Avenida Amigos de los Castillos 3; d from €195;) Parador de Alarcón is one of the grand castle *paradores* found throughout the country, so you might as well go the whole hog and reserve a room with a four-poster bed and a chaise longue. Regal it might be, but this is actually one of Spain's smallest *paradores* with just 24 rooms. Historic, but intimate.

La Cabaña de Alarcón SPANISH €€
(969 33 03 73; www.restaurantelacabanadealarcon.es; Álvaro de Lara 21; mains €12-16, set menu €18; 1-4pm & 8.30-11pm Mon-Sat, 1-4pm Sun;) The best restaurant in town is La Cabaña de Alarcón, with its picture windows, dark-pink paintwork, contemporary artwork and well-executed local dishes with an emphasis on game and grilled meats.

Information

Tourist Office (969 33 03 01; Calle Posadas 6; 10am-2pm Tue-Sat) Stop here for a map of walks around the village and beyond. If it's closed, there are detailed signboards with maps nearby.

Getting There & Away

There's one daily bus to Cuenca (€4.50, 1½ hours) run by Rubiocar (www.rubiocar.com). There's a large free car park at the foot of the village.

Imón

POP 40

This tiny gem of a hamlet, located 16km northwest of Sigüenza, has a surprising amount on offer, including sophisticated places to stay and eat (for weekending *madrileños*), a spa complex affiliated with the Salinas de Imón, and excellent walking and birdwatching potential.

Sights

Don't miss the **salt-extraction pans** a short stroll away along the Sigüenza road; with the crumbling buildings around them as a backdrop, there are some great photo opportunities here. The pans were abandoned in 1996.

For an easy walk, follow Don Quijote's path at the end of the main street (Calle Cervantes), heading north. The 4.5km pleasant stroll through fields leads to a 15th-century castle, **La Riba de Santiuste**, perched high on a rock above the semi-abandoned village of the same name. The castle is partly in ruins and is fascinating to explore.

Imón is also at the heart of the migratory destination for a large number of bird species, including the black stork, golden eagle and black-winged kite.

Sleeping

La Botica BOUTIQUE HOTEL €€
(949 39 74 15; www.laboticahotelrural.com; Calle Cervantes 40; d €70-80;) La Botica is a former chemist with six romantic rooms – nay, 'suites' – that come equipped with Jacuzzis; some also have balconies and fireplaces. There's an outdoor pool, salubrious terrace and a restaurant where they serve excellent breakfasts and dinners. There's even a little museum honouring the building's previous incarnation.

Salinas de Imón HISTORIC HOTEL €€
(949 39 73 11; www.salinasdeimon.com; Calle Real 49; d €95-145, ste €195;) Salinas de Imón is housed in a mid-17th-century stone building. It has 13 rooms, restored with sensitive integrity, that retain a sense of history. Luxurious bathrooms and a secluded, lovely garden with lawns, a bower and a pool add appeal. There's also an affiliated spa offering massages and other therapies.

Getting There & Away

Imón is 16km northwest of Sigüenza along the CM110. Public transport is effectively nonexistent.

Barcelona

POP 1,621,090

Includes ➡

Best Places to Eat

➡ Disfrutar (p311)
➡ Kaiku (p308)
➡ Tickets (p316)
➡ Tapas 24 (p308)
➡ La Cova Fumada (p307)
➡ Restaurant 7 Portes (p308)

Best Places to Stay

➡ Casa Gràcia (p300)
➡ Casa Camper (p297)
➡ Cotton House (p300)
➡ Serras Hotel (p296)
➡ DO Reial (p297)

Why Go?

Barcelona is a mix of sunny Mediterranean charm and European urban style, where dedicated hedonists and culture vultures feel equally at home. From Gothic to Gaudí, the city bursts with art and architecture; Catalan cooking is among the country's best; summer sun seekers fill the beaches in and beyond the city; and the bars and clubs heave year round.

From its origins as a middle-ranking Roman town, of which vestiges can be seen today, Barcelona became a medieval trade juggernaut. Its old centre holds one of the greatest concentrations of Gothic architecture in Europe. Beyond this are some of the world's more bizarre buildings, surreal spectacles capped by Antoni Gaudí's Sagrada Família. Barcelona has been breaking ground in art, architecture and style since the late 19th century, from Picasso and Miró to today's modern wonders.

When to Go

Barcelona

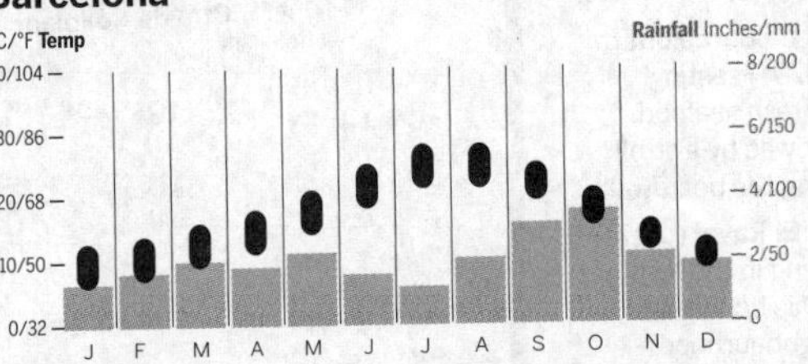

May Plaça del Fòrum rocks during Primavera Sound, four days of pop and rock concerts.

Jun Sónar, Europe's biggest celebration of electronic music, is a long weekend of concerts.

Sep Festes de la Mercè is Barcelona's end-of-summer finale and biggest party.

Barcelona Highlights

❶ **La Sagrada Família** (p274) Marvelling at Antoni Gaudí's still unfolding Modernista masterpiece.

❷ **Barri Gòtic** (p255) Strolling the narrow medieval lanes of Barcelona's enchanting old quarter.

❸ **Palau de la Música Catalana** (p265) Seeing a concert in one of Europe's most extravagant concert halls.

❹ **Camp Nou** (p327) Joining the riotous carnival at an FC Barça match in this hallowed stadium.

❺ **Park Güell** (p283) Drinking in the views from Gaudí's fabulous creation.

❻ **L'Eixample** (p273) Dining and drinking amid the architecturally rich streetscape.

❼ **Museu Picasso** (p268) Discovering Pablo's early masterpieces inside this atmospheric museum.

❽ **La Barceloneta** (p270) Feasting on fresh seafood, followed by a stroll along the boardwalk.

❾ **El Raval** (p317) Taking in the nightlife of this bohemian neighbourhood.

❿ **Montjuïc** (p288) Exploring this hilltop bastion of Romanesque art, a brooding fort, Miró and beautiful gardens.

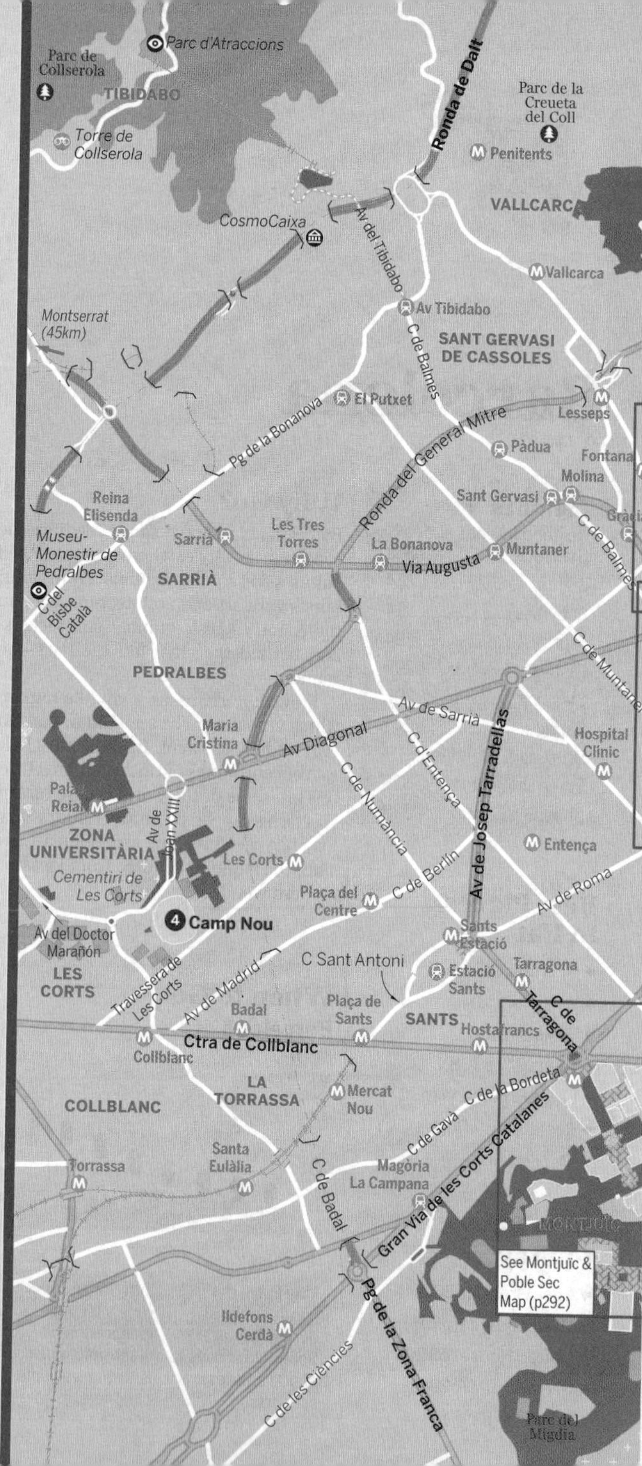

EL GUINARDÓ
Turó de la Rovira
Túnel de la Rovira
Park Güell
5
EL CARMEL
Gaudí Experience
Travessera de Dalt
Alfons X
Recinte Modernista de Sant Pau
Guinardó
C de Sant Antoni Maria Claret
Camp de l'Arpa
CAMP DE L'ARPA
Sagrera
Av Meridiana
C de Felip II
Navas
C de las Navas Tolosa
C d'Aragó
Rambla de Prim
Sant Martí
Bac de Roda
Gran Via de les Corts Catalanes
C de Pere IV
EL CLOT
Clot
LA VERNEDA
SANT MARTÍ
C de Bac de Roda
Sant Pau/ Dos de Maig
Encants
Travessera de Gràcia
C de Pi i Margall
Joanic
C de Còrsega
Sagrada Família
C de Padilla
C d'Aragó
Av Diagonal
See Gràcia Map (p286)
1 La Sagrada Família
C de Sardenya
Glòries
Museu Can Framis
Poblenou
Pg de Sant Joan
GRÀCIA
Verdaguer
Av Diagonal
Monumental
Gran Via de les Corts Catalanes
Museu de la Música
Av Meridiana
C dels Almogàvers
C de Pallars
Llacuna
EL POBLENOU
Pg de Calvell
See L'Eixample Map (p278)
Estació del Nord
Cementiri de l'Est
L'Eixample
6
Pg de Gràcia
Marina
Bogatell
Platja de Bogatell
Arc de Triomf
EL FORT PIENC
C de la Marina
VILA OLÍMPICA
Ronda del Litoral
Av del Litoral
L'EIXAMPLE
Ronda de Sant Pere
Palau de la Música Catalana
3
Pg de Pujades
Platja de la Nova Icària
C d'Aragó
See La Ribera Map (p266)
Pg de Picasso
Port Olímpic
Universitat
See Barri Gòtic, La Rambla & El Raval Map (p256)
Museu Picasso 7
C del Comte d'Urgell
Urgell
Ronda de Sant Antoni
Barri Gòtic
2
Via Laietana
Platja de la Barceloneta
El Raval
9
LA BARCELONETA
CIUTAT VELLA
8 La Barceloneta
Platja de Sant Sebastià
Rocafort
La Rambla
Pg de Colom
SANT ANTONI
Platja de Sant Miquel
Av del Paral·lel
POBLE SEC
Marina
See La Barceloneta Map (p272)
PORT VELL
Port Vell
MEDITERRANEAN SEA
Montjuïc 10
Ronda del Litoral
Cementiri del Sud-Oest
Sitges (38km)
0 1 km
0 0.5 mile

Neighbourhoods at a Glance

❶ La Rambla & Barri Gòtic (p255)

La Rambla, Barcelona's most famous pedestrian strip, is always a hive of activity, with buskers and peddlers, tourists and con artists (watch out!) mingling amid the crowds gracing the sunlit cafes and shops on the boulevard. The adjoining Barri Gòtic is packed with historical treasures – relics of ancient Rome, 14th-century Gothic churches and atmospheric cobblestone lanes lined with shops, bars and restaurants.

❷ El Raval (p264)

The once down-and-out district of El Raval is still seedy in parts, though it has seen remarkable rejuvenation in recent years, with the addition of cutting-edge museums and cultural centres, including the Richard Meier–designed Museu d'Art Contemporani de Barcelona. Other highlights not to be missed include El Raval's bohemian nightlife and the sprawling culinary delights of Mercat de la Boqueria.

❸ La Ribera (p265)

This medieval quarter has a little of everything, from high-end shopping to some of Barcelona's liveliest tapas bars. Key sights include the superb Museu Picasso, the awe-inspiring Gothic Basílica de Santa Maria del Mar and the artfully sculpted Modernista concert hall of Palau de la Música Catalana. For a bit of fresh air,

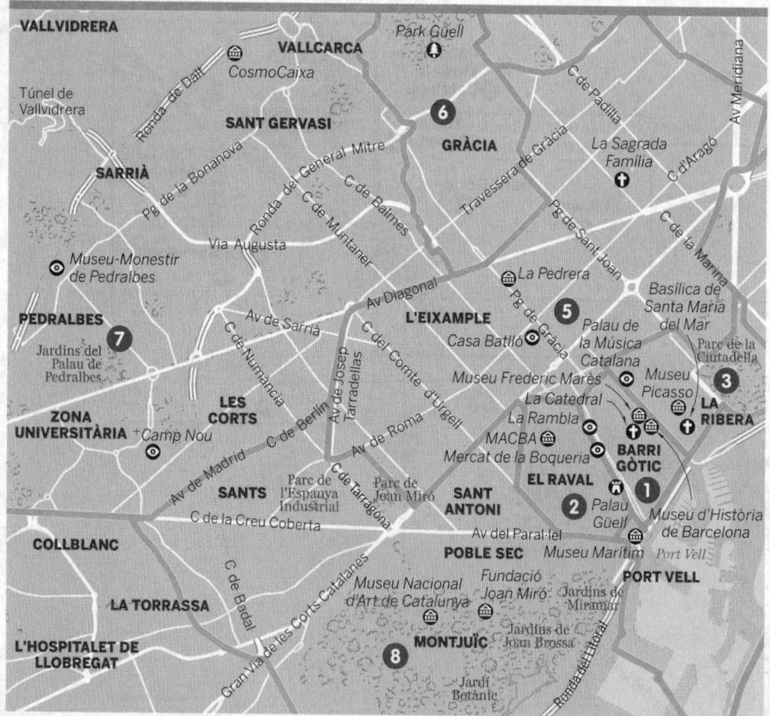

locals head to the leafy gardens of Parc de la Ciutadella.

❹ Barceloneta & the Waterfront (p270)

Since the late 20th century, Barcelona's formerly industrial waterfront has experienced a dramatic transformation, with sparkling beaches and seaside bars and restaurants, elegant sculptures, a 4.5km-long boardwalk, ultramodern high-rises and yacht-filled marinas. The gateway to the Mediterranean is the gridlike neighbourhood of Barceloneta, an old-fashioned fishing quarter full of traditional seafood restaurants.

❺ La Sagrada Família & L'Eixample (p273)

The elegant, if traffic-filled, district of L'Eixample (pronounced 'lay-sham-pluh') is a showcase for Modernista architecture, including Gaudí's unfinished masterpiece, La Sagrada Família. L'Eixample also has a celebrated dining scene, along with high-end boutiques and wildly diverse nightlife: university party spots, gilded cocktail lounges and the buzzing gay club scene of 'Gaixample' are all part of the mix.

❻ Gràcia & Park Güell (p283)

Gràcia was an independent town until the 1890s, and its narrow lanes and picturesque plazas still have a village-like feel. Well-worn cafes and bars, vintage shops and a smattering of multicultural eateries make it a magnet to a young, hip, largely international crowd. On a hill to the north lies one of Gaudí's most captivating works, the outdoor Modernista storybook of Park Güell.

❼ Camp Nou, Pedralbes & La Zona Alta (p286)

Some of Barcelona's most sacred sights are situated within the huge expanse stretching northwest beyond L'Eixample. One is the peaceful medieval monastery of Pedralbes; another is the great shrine to Catalan football, Camp Nou. Other reasons to venture here include an amusement park and great views atop Tibidabo, the wooded trails of Parc de Collserola, and a whizz-bang, kid-friendly science museum.

❽ Montjuïc, Poble Sec & Sant Antoni (p288)

The hillside overlooking the port has some of the city's finest art collections: Museu Nacional d'Art de Catalunya (MNAC), Fundació Joan Miró and CaixaForum. Other galleries, gardens and an imposing castle form part of the scenery. Just below Montjuïc lie the lively tapas bars and eateries of Poble Sec, while the up-and-coming neighbourhood of Sant Antoni draws the young and hip.

History

It is thought that Barcelona may have been founded by the Carthaginians in about 230 BC, taking the surname of Hamilcar Barca, Hannibal's father. Roman Barcelona (known as Barcino) covered an area within today's Barri Gòtic and was overshadowed by Tarraco (Tarragona), 90km to the southwest. In the wake of Muslim occupation and then Frankish domination, Guifré el Pilós (Wilfred the Hairy) founded the house of the Comtes de Barcelona (Counts of Barcelona) in AD 878. In 1137 Count Ramon Berenguer IV married Petronilla, heiress of Aragón, creating a joint state and setting the scene for Catalonia's golden age. Jaume I (1213–76) wrenched the Balearic Islands and Valencia from the Muslims in the 1230s to '40s. Jaume I's son Pere II followed with Sicily in 1282. The accession of the Aragonese noble Fernando to the throne in 1479 augured ill for Barcelona, and his marriage to Queen Isabel of Castilla more still. Catalonia effectively became a subordinate part of the Castilian state. After the War of the Spanish Succession (1702–13), Barcelona fell to the Bourbon king, Felipe V, in September 1714.

Modernisme, Anarchy & Civil War

The 19th century brought economic resurgence. Wine, cotton, cork and iron industries developed, as did urban working-class poverty and unrest. To ease the crush, Barcelona's medieval walls were demolished in 1854, and in 1869 work began on L'Eixample, an extension of the city beyond Plaça de Catalunya. The flourishing bourgeoisie paid for lavish buildings, many of them in the eclectic Modernisme style, whose leading exponent was Antoni Gaudí. In 1937, a year into the Spanish Civil War, the Catalan communist party (PSUC; Partit Socialista Unificat de Catalunya) took control of the city after fratricidal street battles against anarchists and Trotskyists. George Orwell recorded the events in his classic *Homage to Catalonia*. Barcelona fell to Franco in 1939 and there followed a long period of repression.

From Franco to the Present

Under Franco, Barcelona received a flood of immigrants, chiefly from Andalucía. Some 750,000 people came to Barcelona in the '50s and '60s, and almost as many to the rest of Catalonia. Many lived in appalling conditions. Three years after Franco's death in 1975, a new Spanish constitution created the autonomous community of Catalonia (Catalunya in Catalan; Cataluña in Castilian), with Barcelona as its capital. The 1992 Olympic Games put Barcelona on the map. Under the visionary leadership of popular Catalan Socialist mayor Pasqual Maragall, a burst of public works brought new life to Montjuïc and the once shabby waterfront.

Flush with success after the Olympics makeover, Barcelona continued the revitalisation of formerly run-down neighbourhoods. El Raval, still dodgy in parts, has seen a host of building projects, from the opening of Richard Meier's cutting-edge MACBA in 1995 to the Filmoteca de Catalunya in 2012.

Further west, the once derelict industrial district of Poble Nou has been reinvented as 22@ (pronounced 'vint-i-dos arroba'), a 200-hectare zone that's a centre for technology and design. Innovative companies and futuristic architecture (such as the Museu del Disseny) continue to reshape the urban landscape of this ever-evolving city.

Separatism on the Rise

The economic crisis that erupted in 2007 has largely shifted the conversation to the realm of economic recovery. Soaring unemployment and painful austerity measures – not to mention Catalonia's heavy tax burden – have led to anger and resentment towards Madrid, and fuelled the drive towards independence.

The fervour to secede has only grown in the last few years. Recent polls and the regional elections held at the end of 2017 indicate that about half of Catalans support the region becoming a new European state. At the time of writing, however, Madrid had imposed direct rule as a result of Catalan leader Carles Puigdemont's declaration of independence, which Spanish judges ruled was in clear violation of the Spanish constitution, and – at the beginning of 2018 – several Catalan politicians found themselves in jail on charges of sedition and rebellion.

Sights

In the Barri Gòtic and La Ribera you'll find the bulk of the city's ancient and medieval splendours. Along with El Raval, on the other side of La Rambla, and Port Vell, where old Barcelona meets the sea, this is the core of the city's life, both by day and by night. Top attractions here include the Museu d'Història de Barcelona, La Catedral and the Museu Picasso. L'Eixample is where the Modernistas went to town. Attractions here are more spread out, but Passeig de Gràcia is a concentrated showcase for some of their most outlandish work.

Other areas of interest include the beaches and seafood restaurants of the working-class district of La Barceloneta. Montjuïc, with its gardens, museums, art galleries and Olympic Games sites, forms a microcosm on its own. Not to be missed are the Museu Nacional d'Art de Catalunya and the Fundació Joan Miró.

Gaudí's Park Güell is just beyond the area of Gràcia, whose narrow streets and squares set the scene for much lively nightlife. Further out, you'll find the amusement park and church of high-up Tibidabo, the wooded hills of Parc de Collserola, FC Barcelona's Camp Nou football stadium and the peaceful haven of the Museu-Monestir de Pedralbes.

La Rambla & Barri Gòtic

The Barri Gòtic is flanked by mile-long La Rambla to the south-east and the Via Laietana to the north-west. At its heart is the vast, Gothic cathedral, while some of the city's best museums, such as the Museu d'Història de Barcelona and the Museu

BARCELONA IN...

One Day

On day one, spend the morning exploring the narrow medieval lanes of the Barri Gòtic. Have a peek inside **La Catedral** (p258) – not missing its geese-filled cloister – and stroll through the picturesque squares of **Plaça de Sant Josep Oriol** and **Plaça Reial** (p264). Discover Barcelona's ancient roots in the fascinating **Museu d'Història de Barcelona** (p258). Before lunch, have a wander down La Rambla to take in the passing people parade.

In the afternoon, wander over to La Ribera, which is packed with architectural treasures. Have a look inside the majestic **Basílica de Santa Maria del Mar** (p265). At the **Museu Picasso** (p268), beautifully set inside conjoined medieval mansions, you can spend a few hours taking in the early works of one of the great artists of the 20th century.

Before having a late dinner (as is the custom in Spain), catch a show inside the **Palau de la Música Catalana** (p265), one of the great Modernista masterpieces of Barcelona. Afterwards end the night with tropically infused libations at candlelit **Rubí** (p320).

Two Days

On day two start with a morning visit to **La Sagrada Família** (p274), Gaudí's wondrous work in progress. It's worth paying a little extra for a guided tour (or audioguide) for a deeper understanding of Barcelona's most famous sight.

After lunch, explore more of the great Modernista buildings by taking a stroll down L'Eixample's **Passeig de Gràcia**. Have a look at one of Gaudí's house museums – either **Casa Batlló** (p273) or **La Pedrera** (p280) – further up the street.

In the evening catch a football match at **Camp Nou** (p327), the home of the top-ranked FC Barcelona. Amid the roar of the crowds, prepare for a serious adrenaline rush, especially if Barça is playing arch-rival Real Madrid.

Three Days

On your third day in Barcelona it's time to take in the lovely Mediterranean. Start the morning with a stroll, jog or a bike ride along the waterfront. Beach-facing restaurants and cafes provide refreshment along the way.

Stroll through Barceloneta, stopping for a peek inside the Mercat de la Barceloneta and for pastries at **Baluard** (p306). Afterwards visit the **Museu d'Història de Catalunya** (p271) and peel back the centuries on an interactive journey into Catalan history.

At night catch a live band inside the Gothic quarter. **Harlem Jazz Club** (p326) and **Jamboree** (p325) are good bets for jazz and world music. If you still have energy, check out a few bars more off the beaten track, like **L'Ascensor** (p317), a cosy drinking den with nicely mixed cocktails and a more grown-up crowd than other parts of Barri Gòtic.

Barri Gòtic, La Rambla & El Raval

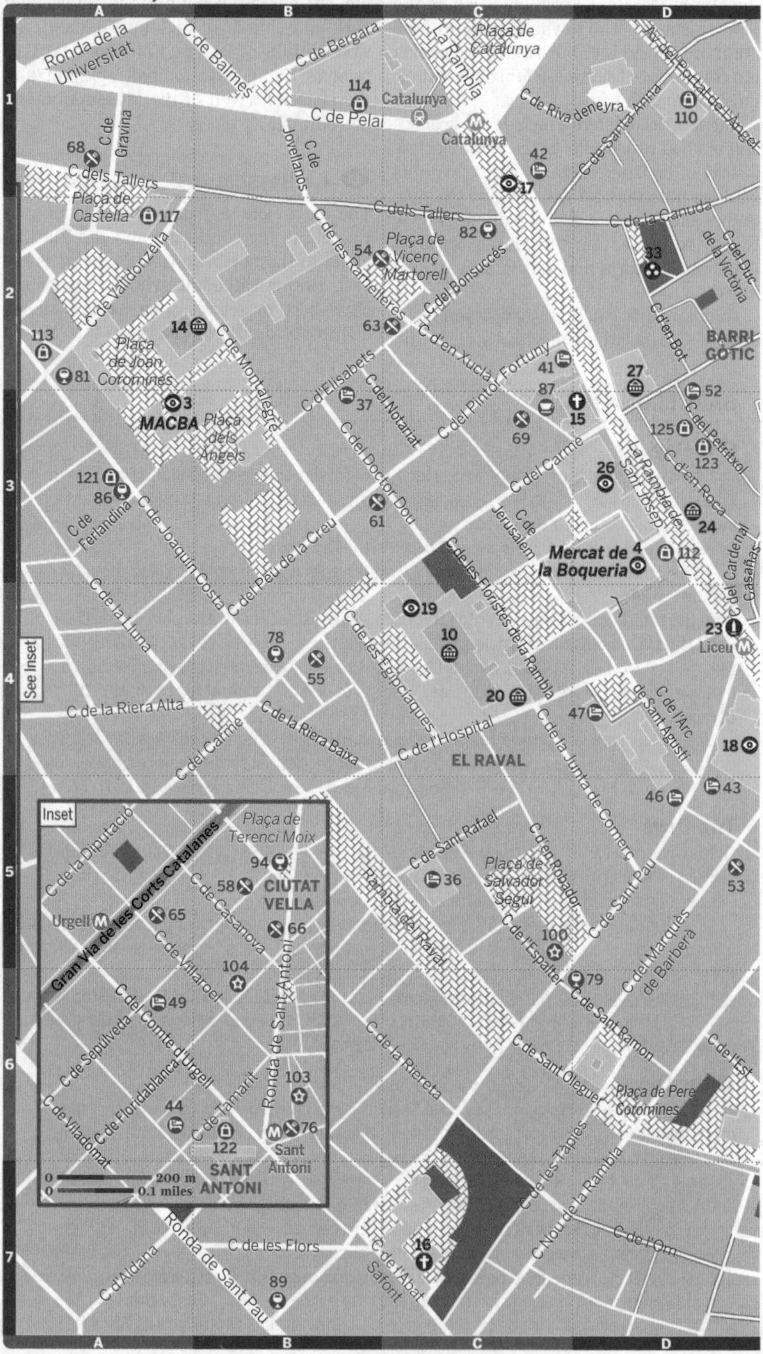

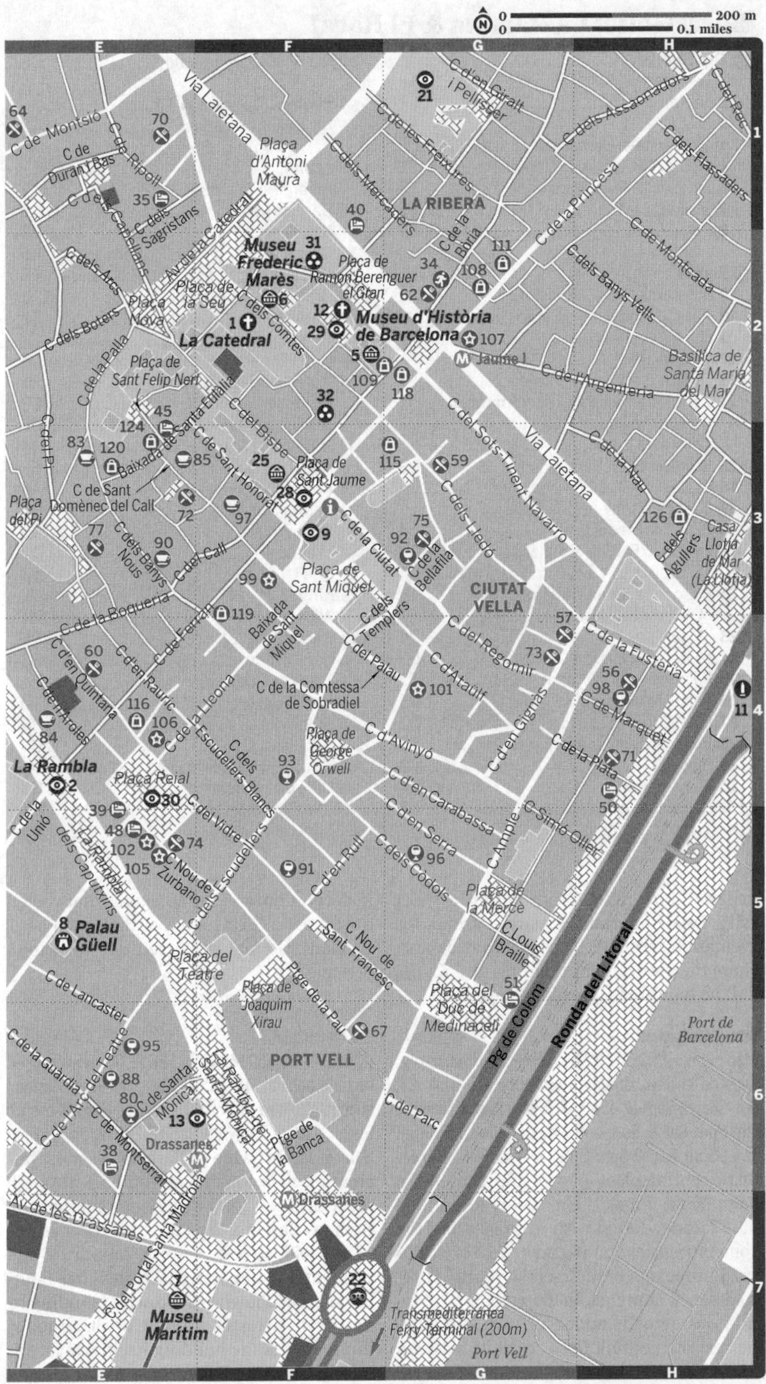

0 200 m
0 0.1 miles
La Ribera
Ciutat Vella
Port Vell
Museu Frederic Marès
La Catedral
Museu d'Història de Barcelona
La Rambla
Palau Güell
Museu Marítim
Plaça d'Antoni Maura
Plaça de Ramon Berenguer el Gran
Plaça de la Seu
Plaça Nova
Plaça de Sant Felip Neri
Plaça de Sant Jaume
Plaça del Pi
Plaça de Sant Miquel
Plaça de George Orwell
Plaça Reial
Plaça del Teatre
Plaça de Joaquim Xirau
Plaça de la Mercè
Plaça del Duc de Medinaceli
Via Laietana
Ronda del Litoral
Pg de Colom
La Rambla de Santa Mònica
Av de les Drassanes
Jaume I
Drassanes
Basílica de Santa Maria del Mar
Casa Llotja de Mar (La Llotja)
Port de Barcelona
Port Vell
Transmediterránea Ferry Terminal (200m)

Barri Gòtic, La Rambla & El Raval

Frederic Marès (p265), are within a short walk. Two important squares, useful for orientation, are the Plaça de Sant Jaume, where the government buildings are found, and the handsome, arcaded Plaça Reial.

★La Catedral CATHEDRAL

(Map p256; ☎93 342 82 62; www.catedralbcn.org; Plaça de la Seu; donation entrance €7, choir €3, roof €3; ⏲8am-12.45pm & 5.45-7.30pm Mon-Fri, 8am-8pm Sat & Sun, entry by donation 1-5.30pm Mon,1-5pm Sat, 2-5pm Sun; Ⓜ Jaume I) Barcelona's central place of worship presents a magnificent image. The richly decorated main facade, dotted with gargoyles and the stone intricacies you would expect of northern European Gothic, sets it quite apart from other churches in Barcelona. The facade was actually added in 1870, although the rest of the building was built between 1298 and 1460. The other facades are sparse in decoration, and the octagonal, flat-roofed towers are a clear reminder that, even here, Catalan Gothic architectural principles prevailed.

★Museu d'Història de Barcelona MUSEUM

(MUHBA; Map p256; ☎93 256 21 00; www.museuhistoria.bcn.cat; Plaça del Rei; adult/concession/child €7/5/free, 3-8pm Sun & 1st Sun of month free; ⏲10am-7pm Tue-Sat, to 2pm Mon, to 8pm Sun; Ⓜ Jaume I) One of Barcelona's most fascinating museums takes you back through the centuries to the very foundations of Roman Barcino. You'll stroll over ruins of the old streets, sewers, laundries and wine- and fish-making factories that flourished here following the town's founding by Emperor Augustus around 10 BC. Equally impressive is the building itself, which was once part of the Palau Reial Major (Grand

62 Cat Bar G2
63 Elisabets C2
64 Els Quatre Gats E1
65 Escribà A5
66 Fàbrica Moritz B5
67 Federal F6
68 Flax & Kale A1
69 Gats C3
70 Koy Shunka E1
71 La Plata H4
72 La Vinateria del Call E3
73 Milk G4
74 Ocaña E5
75 Pla G3
76 Sésamo B6
77 Taller de Tapas E3

Drinking & Nightlife
78 33|45 B4
79 Bar Marsella D6
80 Bar Pastís E6
81 Betty Ford's A2
82 Boadas C2
83 Caelum E3
84 Cafè de l'Òpera E4
85 Čaj Chai E3
86 Casa Almirall A3
87 Granja M Viader C3
88 Kentucky E6
89 La Confitería B7
90 La Granja E3
91 La Macarena F5
92 L'Ascensor G3
93 Marula Café F4
94 Metro B5
95 Moog E6
96 Polaroid G5
97 Salterio F3
98 Sor Rita H4

Entertainment
99 El Paraigua F3
100 Filmoteca de Catalunya C5
Gran Teatre del Liceu (see 18)
101 Harlem Jazz Club G4
102 Jamboree E5
103 Jazz Sí Club B6
104 Renoir Floridablanca B6
105 Sala Tarantos E5
106 Sidecar Factory Club E4
107 Tablao Nervión G2

Shopping
108 Arlequí Màscares G2
109 Cereria Subirà G2
110 El Corte Inglés D1
111 El Rei de la Màgia G2
112 Escribà D3
113 Fantastik A2
114 FNAC B1
115 Formatgeria La Seu G3
116 Herboristeria del Rei E4
117 Holala! Plaza A2
118 La Colmena G2
119 La Manual Alpargatera F3
120 L'Arca E3
121 Les Topettes A3
122 Mercat de Sant Antoni B6
123 Petritxol Xocoa D3
124 Sabater Hermanos E3
125 Torrons Vicens D3
126 Vila Viniteca H3

Royal Palace) on Plaça del Rei, among the key locations of medieval princely power in Barcelona.

Gran Teatre del Liceu ARCHITECTURE

(Map p256; ☎93 485 99 00; www.liceubarcelona.cat; La Rambla 51-59; tours adult/concession/child under 7yr 45min €9/7.50/free, 25min €6/5/free; ⏰45min tours hourly 2-6pm Mon-Fri, from 9.30am Sat, 25min tours 1.30pm Mon-Sat; Ⓜ Liceu) If you can't catch a night at the opera, you can still have a look around one of Europe's greatest opera houses, known to locals as the Liceu. Smaller than Milan's La Scala but bigger than Venice's La Fenice, it can seat up to 2300 people in its grand auditorium.

Plaça del Rei SQUARE

(King's Square; Map p256; Ⓜ Jaume I) Plaça del Rei is a picturesque plaza where Fernando and Isabel are thought to have received Columbus following his first New World voyage. It is the courtyard of the former Palau Reial Major. The palace today houses a superb history museum, with significant Roman ruins underground.

Palau de la Generalitat HISTORIC BUILDING

(Map p256; http://presidencia.gencat.cat; Plaça de Sant Jaume; ⏰2nd & 4th weekend of month; Ⓜ Jaume I) Founded in the early 15th century, the Palau de la Generalitat is open on limited occasions only (one-hour guided tours on the second and fourth weekends of the month, plus open-door days). The most impressive of the ceremonial halls is the Saló de Sant Jordi (Hall of St George), named after the region's patron saint. To see inside, book on the website.

TAKASHI IMAGES / SHUTTERSTOCK ©

TOP SIGHT
LA RAMBLA

Barcelona's most famous street is both a tourist magnet and a window into Catalan culture, with cultural centres, theatres and intriguing architecture. The middle of La Rambla is a broad pedestrian boulevard – a stroll here is pure sensory overload, with souvenir hawkers, buskers, pavement artists, mimes and living statues all part of the ever-changing street scene.

History

La Rambla takes its name from a seasonal stream (*ramla* in Arabic) that once ran here. From the early Middle Ages, it was better known as the Cagalell (Stream of Shit) and lay outside the city walls until the 14th century. Monastic buildings were then built and, subsequently, mansions of the well-to-do from the 16th to the early 19th centuries. Unofficially La Rambla is divided into five sections, which explains why many know it as Las Ramblas.

DON'T MISS

- Palau de la Virreina
- Centre d'Art Santa Mònica
- Església de Betlem
- Palau Moja
- Mosaïc de Miró

PRACTICALITIES

- Map p256
- M Catalunya, Liceu, Drassanes

La Rambla de Canaletes

The section of La Rambla north of Plaça de Catalunya is named after the **Font de Canaletes**, an inconspicuous turn-of-the-20th-century drinking fountain, the water of which supposedly emerges from what were once known as the springs of Canaletes. It used to be said that a proper *barcelonin* was one who 'drank the waters of Les Canaletes'. Nowadays people claim that anyone who drinks from the fountain will return to Barcelona, which is not such a bad prospect. Delirious football fans gather here to celebrate whenever the main home side, FC Barcelona, wins a cup or the league premiership.

La Rambla dels Estudis

La Rambla dels Estudis, from Carrer de la Canuda running south to Carrer de la Portaferrissa, was formerly home to a twittering bird market, which closed in 2010 after 150 years in operation. Just north of Carrer del Carme, the **Església de Betlem** (☎93 318 38 23; www.mdbetlem.net; Carrer d'en Xuclà 2; ⏱8.30am-1.30pm & 6-9pm; Ⓜ Liceu) was constructed in baroque style for the Jesuits in the late 17th and early 18th centuries to replace an earlier church destroyed by fire in 1671. Fire was a bit of a theme for this site: the church was once considered the most splendid of Barcelona's few baroque offerings, but leftist arsonists torched it in 1936.

Looming over the eastern side of La Rambla, **Palau Moja** (☎93 316 27 40; https://palaumoja.com; Carrer de Portaferrissa 1; ⏱10am-9pm, cafe 9.30am-midnight Mon-Fri, 11am-midnight Sat & Sun; Ⓜ Liceu) FREE is a neoclassical building dating from the second half of the 18th century. Its clean, classical lines are best appreciated from across the other side of the street. It mostly houses government offices, but access is now an option thanks to a large gift shop and cafe.

La Rambla de Sant Josep

From Carrer de la Portaferrissa to Plaça de la Boqueria, what is officially called La Rambla de Sant Josep is lined with flower stalls, which give it the alternative name La Rambla de les Flors. This stretch also contains the bawdy **Museu de l'Eròtica** (Erotica Museum; Map p256; ☎93 318 98 65; www.erotica-museum.com; €10; ⏱10am-midnight; Ⓜ Liceu).

The Palau de la Virreina (p264) is a grand 18th-century rococo mansion (with some neoclassical elements) that now houses the **Centre de la Imatge** (☎93 316 10 00; www.ajuntament.barcelona.cat/lavirreina; Palau de la Virreina; ⏱noon-8pm Tue-Sun; Ⓜ Liceu) FREE, which has rotating photography exhibits.

Just south of the Palau, in El Raval, is the Mercat de la Boqueria (p264), one of the best-stocked and most colourful produce markets in Europe. At Plaça de la Boqueria, just north of Liceu metro station, you can walk all over a Miró – the colourful mosaic (p270) in the pavement, with one tile signed by the artist.

La Rambla dels Caputxins

La Rambla dels Caputxins, named after a former monastery, runs from Plaça de la Boqueria to Carrer dels Escudellers. On the western side of La Rambla is the Gran Teatre del Liceu (p259); to the southeast is the entrance to the palm-shaded Plaça Reial (p264).

La Rambla de Santa Mònica

The final stretch of La Rambla widens out to approach the Mirador de Colom (p272) overlooking Port Vell. La Rambla here is named after the Convent de Santa Mònica, which once stood on the western flank of the street and has since been converted into the **Centre d'Art Santa Mònica**, a cultural centre that mostly exhibits modern multimedia installations.

CIVIL WAR

Many writers and journalists headed to Barcelona during the Spanish Civil War, including British author George Orwell, who vividly described La Rambla gripped by revolutionary fervour in the early days of the war in his book *Homage to Catalonia*.

A block east from the Rambla dels Estudis, along Carrer de la Canuda, is the Plaça de la Vila de Madrid, which has a sunken garden where Roman tombs lie exposed in what was once the Via Sepulcral Romana.

TOP TIPS

La Rambla is at its best first thing in the morning, before the cruise ships disgorge their passengers. Do keep an eye on your belongings and wear backpacks on your front. Pickpockets find easy pickings along this stretch.

The best spot for breakfast – or coffee at any tie of day – is the Café de l'Opera (La Rambla 74).

La Rambla

A TIMELINE

Look beyond the human statues and tourist-swarmed restaurants, and you'll find a fascinating piece of Barcelona history dating back many centuries.

13th century A serpentine seasonal stream (called *ramla* in Arabic) runs outside the city walls. As Barcelona grows, the stream will eventually become an open sewer until it's later paved over.

1500–1800 During this early period, La Rambla was dotted with convents and monasteries, including the baroque ❶ **Església de Betlem**, completed in the early 1700s.

1835 The city erupts in anticlericism, with riots and the burning of convents. Along La Rambla, many religious assets are destroyed or seized by the state. This paves the way for new developments, including the ❷ **Mercat de la Boqueria** in 1840, the ❸ **Gran Teatre**

Teatre Poliorama
Built in 1894 as the seat of the Royal Academy of Sciences and Arts, it later served as a cinema, and a strategic lookout for one communist faction during the Spanish Civil War.

KIEVVICTOR/SHUTTERSTOCK ©

Església de Betlem
Dedicated to the Holy Family, this is the last standing of the many churches once lining La Rambla. Its once sumptuous interior was gutted during the Spanish Civil War.

Mercat de la Boqueria
The official name of Barcelona's most photogenic market is El Mercat de Sant Josep, which references the convent of St Josep that once stood here.

ALE ARGENTIERI/SHUTTERSTOCK ©

TONO BALAGUER/SHUTTERSTOCK ©

Gran Teatre del Liceu
Although badly damaged by fire in 1994, this gorgeous opera house was restored and reborn in 1999, and remains one of Europe's finest theatres.

del Liceu in 1847 and ❹ **Plaça Reial** in 1848.

1883 Architect Josep Vilaseca refurbishes the ❺ **Casa Bruno Cuadros**. As Modernisme is sweeping across the city, Vilaseca creates an eclectic work using stained glass, wrought iron, Egyptian imagery and Japanese prints.

1888 Barcelona hosts the Universal Exhibition. The city sees massive urban renewal projects, with the first electric lights coming to La Rambla, and the building of the ❻ **Mirador de Colom**.

1936–39 La Rambla becomes the site of bloody street fighting during the Spanish Civil War. British journalist and author George Orwell, who spends three days holed up in the ❼ **Teatre Poliorama** during street battles, later describes the tumultuous days in his excellent book, *Homage to Catalonia*.

2017 A horrific terrorist attack saw a van driving into pedestrians, killing 14 and injuring scores of others.

Temple d'August RUINS

(Map p256; ☎93 256 21 22; www.muhba.cat; Carrer del Paradis 10; ⏰10am-7pm Tue-Sat, to 8pm Sun, to 2pm Mon; Ⓜ Jaume I) FREE Opposite the southeast end of La Catedral, narrow Carrer del Paradis leads towards Plaça de Sant Jaume. Inside No 10, an intriguing building with Gothic and baroque touches, are four columns and the architrave of Barcelona's main Roman temple, dedicated to Caesar Augustus and built to worship his imperial highness in the 1st century AD.

Plaça Reial SQUARE

(Map p256; Ⓜ Liceu) One of the most photogenic squares in Barcelona, and certainly its liveliest. Numerous restaurants, bars and nightspots lie beneath the arcades of 19th-century neoclassical buildings, with a buzz of activity at all hours.

Ajuntament ARCHITECTURE

(Casa de la Ciutat; Map p256; ☎93 402 70 00; www.bcn.cat; Plaça de Sant Jaume; ⏰10.30am-1.30pm Sun; Ⓜ Jaume I) FREE The Ajuntament, otherwise known as the Casa de la Ciutat, has been the seat of power for centuries. The Consell de Cent (the city's ruling council) first sat here in the 14th century, but the building has lamentably undergone many changes over the centuries, and only the original, now disused, entrance on Carrer de la Ciutat retains its Gothic ornament.

Plaça de Sant Jaume SQUARE

(Map p256; Ⓜ Liceu, Jaume I) In the 2000 or so years since the Romans settled here, the area around this often-remodelled square, which started life as the forum, has been the focus of Barcelona's civic life. This is still the central staging area for Barcelona's traditional festivals. Facing each other across the square are the Palau de la Generalitat (p259), seat of Catalonia's regional government, on the north side and the Ajuntament to the south.

Palau de la Virreina ARCHITECTURE

(Map p256; La Rambla 99; Ⓜ Liceu) The Palau de la Virreina is a grand 18th-century rococo mansion (with some neoclassical elements) housing an arts/entertainment information and ticket office run by the Ajuntament. Built by Manuel d'Amat i de Junyent, the corrupt captain general of Chile (a Spanish colony that included the Peruvian silver mines of Potosí), it is a rare example of such a post-baroque building in Barcelona.

El Raval

★MACBA ARTS CENTRE

(Museu d'Art Contemporani de Barcelona; Map p256; ☎93 412 08 10; www.macba.cat; Plaça dels Àngels 1; adult/concession/child under 14yr €10/8/free; ⏰11am-7.30pm Mon & Wed-Fri, 10am-9pm Sat, 10am-3pm Sun & holidays; Ⓜ Universitat) Designed by Richard Meier and opened in 1995, MACBA has become the city's foremost contemporary art centre, with captivating exhibitions for the serious art lover. The permanent collection is on the ground floor and dedicates itself to Spanish and Catalan art from the second half of the 20th century, with works by Antoni Tàpies, Joan Brossa and Miquel Barceló, among others, though international artists, such as Paul Klee, Bruce Nauman and John Cage, are also represented.

ROMAN REMAINS

From Plaça del Rei it's worth taking a detour northeast to see the two best surviving stretches of Barcelona's **Roman walls** (Map p256; Ⓜ Jaume I), which once boasted 78 towers (as much a matter of prestige as of defence). One wall is on the southern side of Plaça Ramon de Berenguer Gran, with the **Capella Reial de Santa Àgata** (Map p256; MUHBA, Plaça del Rei; ⏰10am-7pm Tue-Sat, to 2pm Mon, to 8pm Sun; Ⓜ Jaume I) atop. The square itself is dominated by a statue of count-king Ramon de Berenguer Gran done by Josep Llimona in 1880. The other wall is a little further south, by the northern end of Carrer del Sots-Tinent Navarro. The Romans built and reinforced these walls in the 3rd and 4th centuries AD, after the first attacks by Germanic tribes from the north.

Along Carrer de la Canuda, a block east of the top end of La Rambla, is a sunken garden where a series of **Roman tombs** (Map p256; ☎93 256 21 22; www.muhba.cat; Plaça de la Vila de Madrid; adult/concession/child €2/1.50/free; ⏰11am-2pm Tue & Thu, to 7pm Sat & Sun; Ⓜ Catalunya) lies exposed. A smallish display in Spanish and Catalan by the tombs explores burial and funerary rites and customs. A few bits of pottery (including a burial amphora with the skeleton of a three-year-old Roman child) accompany the display.

★Mercat de la Boqueria MARKET

(Map p256; ☎93 318 20 17; www.boqueria.info; La Rambla 91; ⏰8am-8.30pm Mon-Sat; Ⓜ Liceu) Mercat de la Boqueria is possibly La Rambla's most interesting building, not so much for its Modernista-influenced design (it was actually built over a long period, from 1840 to 1914, on the site of the former St Joseph Monastery), but for the action of the food market within.

★Palau Güell PALACE

(Map p256; ☎93 472 57 71; www.palauguell.cat; Carrer Nou de la Rambla 3-5; adult/concession/child under 10yr incl audioguide €12/9/free, 1st Sun of month free; ⏰10am-8pm Tue-Sun Apr-Oct, to 5.30pm Nov-Mar; Ⓜ Drassanes) Palau Güell is a magnificent example of the early days of Gaudí's fevered architectural imagination. The extraordinary neo-Gothic mansion, one of the few major buildings of that era raised in Ciutat Vella, gives an insight into its maker's prodigious genius.

Església de Sant Pau del Camp CHURCH

(Map p256; ☎93 441 00 01; Carrer de Sant Pau 101; adult/concession/child under 14yr €3/2/free; ⏰10am-1.30pm & 4-7.30pm Mon-Sat; Ⓜ Paral·lel) The best example of Romanesque architecture in the city is the dainty little cloister of this church. Set in a dusty garden, the 12th-century church also boasts some Visigothic sculptural detail on the main entrance.

Antic Hospital de la Santa Creu HISTORIC BUILDING

(Former Hospital of the Holy Cross; Map p256; www.barcelonaturisme.com; Carrer de l'Hospital 56; ⏰9am-10pm; Ⓜ Liceu) FREE Behind La Boqueria stands the Antic Hospital de la Santa Creu, which was once the city's main hospital. Founded in 1401, it functioned until the 1930s, and was considered one of the best in Europe in its medieval heyday – it is famously the place where Antoni Gaudí died in 1926. Today it houses the **Biblioteca de Catalunya** and the **Institut d'Estudis Catalans** (Institute for Catalan Studies; Map p256; ☎93 270 16 20; www.iec.cat; Carrer del Carme 47; ⏰8am-8pm Mon-Fri Sep-Jul; Ⓜ Liceu). The hospital's 15th-century former chapel, **La Capella** (Map p256; ☎93 256 20 44; www.bcn.cat/lacapella; ⏰noon-8pm Tue-Sat, 11am-2pm Sun & holidays; Ⓜ Liceu) FREE, shows temporary exhibitions.

Centre de Cultura Contemporània de Barcelona GALLERY

(CCCB; Map p256; ☎93 306 41 00; www.cccb.org; Carrer de Montalegre 5; adult/concession/child under 12yr for 1 exhibition €6/4/free, 2 exhibitions €8/6/free, Sun 3-8pm free; ⏰11am-8pm Tue-Sun; Ⓜ Universitat) A complex of auditoriums, exhibition spaces and conference halls opened here in 1994 in what had been an 18th-century hospice, the Casa de la Caritat. The courtyard, with a vast glass wall on one side, is spectacular. With 4500 sq metres of exhibition space in four separate areas, the centre hosts a constantly changing program of exhibitions, film cycles and other events.

DON'T MISS

MUSEU FREDERIC MARÈS

The **Museu Frederic Marès** (Map p256; ☎93 256 35 00; www.museumares.bcn.cat; Plaça de Sant Iu 5; adult/concession/child €4.20/2.40/free, 3-8pm Sun & 1st Sun of month free; ⏰10am-7pm Tue-Sat, 11am-8pm Sun; Ⓜ Jaume I) is a wild collection of historical curios, set in a vast medieval complex, once part of the royal palace of the counts of Barcelona. A rather worn coat of arms on the wall indicates that it was also, for a while, the seat of the Spanish Inquisition in Barcelona. Frederic Marès i Deulovol (1893–1991) was a rich sculptor, traveller and obsessive collector, and displays of religious art and vast varieties of antiques *objets* litter the museum.

La Ribera

★Palau de la Música Catalana ARCHITECTURE

(Map p278; ☎93 295 72 00; www.palaumusica.cat; Carrer de Palau de la Música 4-6; adult/concession/child under 10yr €18/15/free; ⏰guided tours 10am-3.30pm, to 6pm Easter, Jul & Aug; Ⓜ Urquinaona) This concert hall is a high point of Barcelona's Modernista architecture, a symphony in tile, brick, sculpted stone and stained glass. Built by Domènech i Montaner between 1905 and 1908 for the Orfeo Català musical society, it was conceived as a temple for the Catalan Renaixença (Renaissance).

★Basílica de Santa Maria del Mar CHURCH

(Map p266; ☎93 310 23 90; www.santamariadelmarbarcelona.org; Plaça de Santa Maria del Mar; €8 1-5pm, incl guided tour; ⏰9am-8.30pm Mon-Sat, 10am-8pm Sun; Ⓜ Jaume I) At the southwest end of Passeig del Born stands the apse of Barcelona's finest Catalan Gothic church, Santa Maria

La Ribera

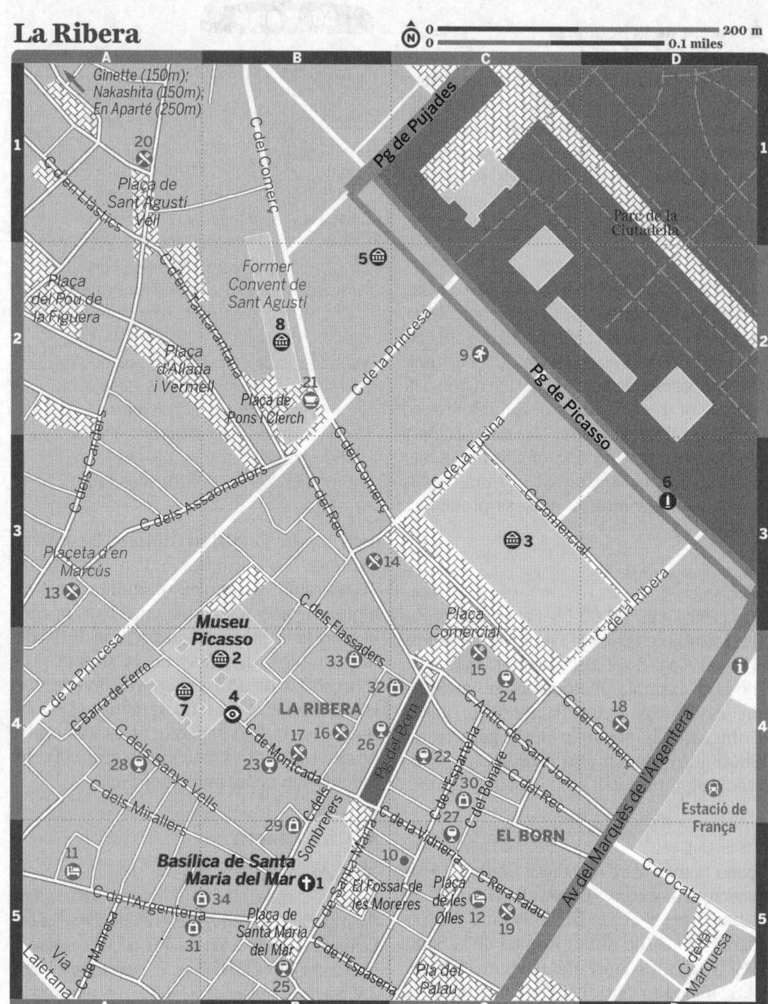

del Mar (Our Lady of the Sea). Constructed in the 14th century with record-breaking alacrity for the time (it took just 54 years), the church is remarkable for its architectural harmony and simplicity.

Carrer de Montcada STREET

(Map p266; Ⓜ Jaume I) An early example of town planning, this medieval high street was driven towards the sea from the road that in the 12th century led northeast from the city walls. It was the city's most coveted address for the merchant classes. The great mansions that remain today mostly date from the 14th and 15th centuries.

Museu de Cultures del Món MUSEUM

(Map p266; ☎93 256 23 00; http://museucultures mon.bcn.cat; Carrer de Montcada 12; adult/concession/under 16yr €5/3.50/free, temporary exhibition €2.20/1.50/free, 3-8pm Sun & 1st Sun of month free; ⏲10am-7pm Tue-Sat, to 8pm Sun; Ⓜ Jaume I) The Palau Nadal and the Palau Marquès de Llió, which once housed the Museu Barbier-Mueller and the Museu Tèxtil respectively, reopened in 2015 to the public as the site of the new Museum of World Cultures. Exhibits from private and public collections, including many from the Museu Etnològic on Montjuïc, take the visitor on a trip through

La Ribera

the ancient cultures of Africa, Asia, the Americas and Oceania. There's a combined ticket with the Museu Egipci (p281) and Museu Etnològic (p289) for €12.

Mercat de Santa Caterina MARKET

(Map p256; 93 319 57 40; www.mercatsantacaterina.com; Avinguda de Francesc Cambó 16; 7.30am-3.30pm Mon, Wed & Sat, to 8.30pm Tue, Thu & Fri, closed afternoons Jul & Aug; M Jaume I) Come shopping for your tomatoes at this extraordinary-looking produce market, designed by Enric Miralles and Benedetta Tagliabue to replace its 19th-century predecessor. Finished in 2005, it is distinguished by its kaleidoscopic and undulating roof, held up above the bustling produce stands, restaurants, cafes and bars by twisting slender branches of what look like grey steel trees.

Fundació Foto Colectania GALLERY

(Map p266; 93 217 16 26; www.colectania.es; Passeig de Picasso 14; adult/concession/child under 14yr €4/3/free, free 1st Sun of month; 11am-8pm Mon-Sat, 11am-3pm Sun; M Arc de Triomf, Jaume I) Photography lovers should swing by here to see the latest exhibition from this nonprofit foundation, which showcases thought-provoking works from across the globe. In 2016 the foundation moved from its base in Gràcia to this 500-sq-metre space in El Born. The exhibits may come from the foundation's extensive 3000-piece collection of Spanish and Portuguese photographers from the 1950s onwards, but more likely will be temporary exhibitions.

Parc de la Ciutadella PARK

(Map p272; Passeig de Picasso; 8am-9pm May-Sep, to 7pm Oct-Apr; ; M Arc de Triomf) Come for a stroll, a picnic, a boat ride on the lake or to inspect Catalonia's parliament, but don't miss a visit to this, the most central green lung in the city. Parc de la Ciutadella is perfect for winding down.

Born Centre de Cultura i Memòria HISTORIC BUILDING

(Map p266; 93 256 68 51; http://elbornculturaimemoria.barcelona.cat; Plaça Comercial 12; centre free, exhibition spaces adult/concession/child under 16yr €4.40/3/free; 10am-8pm Tue-Sun Mar-Oct, 10am-7pm Tue-Sat, to 8pm Sun Nov-Feb; M Jaume I) Launched in 2013, as part of the events held for the tercentenary of the Catalan defeat in the War of the Spanish Succession, this cultural space is housed in the **former Mercat del Born**, a handsome 19th-century structure of slatted iron and brick. Excavation in 2001 unearthed remains of whole streets flattened to make way for the much-hated *ciutadella* (citadel) – these are now on show on the exposed subterranean level.

MARCO RUBINO / SHUTTERSTOCK ©

TOP SIGHT
MUSEU PICASSO

The setting alone, in five contiguous medieval stone mansions, makes the Museu Picasso unique. The permanent collection is housed in Palau Aguilar, Palau del Baró de Castellet and Palau Meca, all dating from the 14th century. The 18th-century Casa Mauri, built over medieval remains (even some Roman leftovers have been identified), and the adjacent 14th-century Palau Finestres accommodate temporary exhibitions.

History of the Museum

Allegedly it was Picasso himself who proposed the museum's creation to his friend and personal secretary Jaume Sabartés, a Barcelona native, in 1960. Three years later, the 'Sabartés Collection' was opened, since a museum bearing Picasso's name would have been met with censorship – Picasso's opposition to the Franco regime was well known. The Museu Picasso we see today opened in 1983. It originally held only Sabartés' personal collection of Picasso's art and a handful of works hanging at the Barcelona Museum of Art, but the collection gradually expanded with donations from Salvador Dalí and Sebastià Junyer i Vidal, among others, though most artworks were bequeathed by Picasso himself. His widow, Jacqueline Roque, also donated 41 ceramic pieces and the *Woman with Bonnet* painting after Picasso's death.

Sabartés' contribution and years of service are honoured with an entire room devoted to him, including Picasso's famous Blue Period portrait of him wearing a ruff.

DON'T MISS

- *Retrato de la tía Pepa* (Portrait of Aunt Pepa)
- *Ciència i caritat* (Science and Charity)
- *Terrats de Barcelona* (Roofs of Barcelona)
- *El foll* (The Madman)
- *Las meninas* (The Ladies-in-Waiting)

PRACTICALITIES

- Map p266
- www.museupicasso.bcn.cat
- Carrer de Montcada 15-23
- adult/concession/child under 16yr all collections €14/7.50/free, permanent collection €11/7/free, temporary exhibitions varies, 6-9.30pm Thu & 1st Sun of month free
- 9am-7pm Tue-Sun, to 9.30pm Thu
- M Jaume I

The Collection

The collection concentrates on the artist's formative years in Barcelona and elsewhere in Spain, yet there is enough material from subsequent periods to give you a thorough impression of the man's versatility and genius. Above all, you come away feeling that Picasso was the true original, always one step ahead of himself (let alone anyone else) in his search for new forms of expression. The collection includes more than 3500 artworks, largely pre-1904, which is apt considering the artist spent his formative creative years in Barcelona.

It is important, however, not to expect a parade of his well-known works, or even works representative of his best-known periods. What makes this collection truly impressive – and unique among the many Picasso museums around the world – is the way in which it displays his extraordinary talent at such a young age. Faced with the technical virtuosity of a painting such as *Ciència i caritat* (Science and Charity), for example, it is almost inconceivable that such a work could have been created by the hands of a 15-year-old. Some of his self-portraits and the portraits of his parents, which date from 1896, are also evidence of his precocious talent.

Las Meninas Through the Prism of Picasso

From 1954 to 1962 Picasso was obsessed with the idea of researching and 'rediscovering' the greats, in particular Velázquez. In 1957 he created a series of renditions of the Velázquez masterpiece *Las meninas* (The Ladies-in-Waiting), now displayed in rooms 12–14. It is as though Picasso has looked at the original Velázquez painting through a prism reflecting all the styles he had worked through until then, creating his own masterpiece in the process. This is a wonderful opportunity to see *Las meninas* in its entirety in this beautiful space.

Ceramics

What is also special about the Museu Picasso is its showcasing of his work in lesser-known media. The last rooms contain engravings and some 40 ceramic pieces completed throughout the latter years of his unceasingly creative life. You'll see plates and bowls decorated with simple, single-line drawings of fish, owls and other animal shapes, typical of Picasso's daubing on clay.

GETTING AROUND THE COLLECTION

The permanent collection is housed in Palau Aguilar, Palau del Baró de Castellet and Palau Meca. Casa Mauri and the adjacent 14th-century Palau Finestres accommodate temporary exhibitions.

At €15, the 'Carnet del Museu Picasso' annual pass is barely more expensive than a day pass and allows multiple entries. There is a special desk for this, separate from the general ticket desk.

TAKE A BREAK

Euskal Etxea (p304), also on the Carrer de Montcada, is one of the best pintxo bars in town.

ART ON THE STREETS

Barcelona hosts an array of street sculpture, from Miró's 1983 **Dona i Ocell** (Map p292; Carrer de Tarragona; M Tarragona) (Woman and Bird), in the park dedicated to the artist, to **Peix** (Map p272; Carrer de Ramon Trias Fargas 2; M Ciutadella Villa Olímpica) (Fish), Frank Gehry's shimmering, bronze-coloured headless fish facing Port Olímpic. Halfway along La Rambla, at Plaça de la Boqueria, you can walk all over Miró's **mosaic** (Map p256; Plaça de la Boqueria; M Liceu).

Picasso left an open-air mark with his design on the facade of the Col·legi d'Arquitectes de Catalunya opposite La Catedral in the Barri Gòtic. Other works include the **Barcelona Head** (Map p256; Passeig de Colom; M Barceloneta) by Roy Lichtenstein at the Port Vell end of Via Laietana and Fernando Botero's rotund *El Gat* on Rambla del Raval.

Wander down to the Barceloneta seaside for a gander at Rebecca Horn's 1992 tribute to the old shacks that used to line the waterfront. The precarious stack is called **Homenatge a la Barceloneta** (Map p272; Passeig Marítim; M Barceloneta) (Tribute to La Barceloneta). A little further south is the 2003 **Homenatge a la Natació** (Homage to the Swimmers; Map p272; Plaça del Mar; M Barceloneta), a complex metallic rendition of swimmers and divers in the water by Alfredo Lanz.

Heading a little further back in time, in 1983 Antoni Tàpies constructed **Homenatge a Picasso** (Map p266; Passeig de Picasso; M Arc de Triomf, Jaume I) (Tribute to Picasso) on Passeig de Picasso; it's essentially a glass cube set in a pond and filled with, well, junk. Antoni Llena's *David i Goliat* (David and Goliath), a massive sculpture of tubular and sheet iron, in the Parc de les Cascades near Port Olímpic's two skyscrapers, looks like an untidy kite inspired by Halloween. Beyond this Avinguda d'Icària is lined by architect Enric Miralles' so-called *Pergoles* – bizarre, twisted metal contraptions.

Museu de la Xocolata MUSEUM

(Map p266; ☎93 268 78 78; www.museuxocolata.cat; Carrer del Comerç 36; adult/concession/child under 7yr €6/5/free; ⊙10am-7pm Mon-Sat, 10am-3pm Sun; ♿; M Arc de Triomf) Chocoholics have a hard time containing themselves in this museum dedicated to the fundamental foodstuff – particularly when faced with tempting displays of cocoa-based treats in the cafe at the exit. The displays trace the origins of chocolate, its arrival in Europe, and the many myths and images associated with it. Among the informative stuff and machinery used in the production of chocolate are large chocolate models of emblematic buildings such as La Sagrada Família, along with various characters, local and international.

Zoo de Barcelona ZOO

(Map p272; ☎902 457545; www.zoobarcelona.cat; Parc de la Ciutadella; adult/concession/child under 3yr €20/12/free; ⊙10am-5.30pm Nov-Mar, 10am-7pm Apr, May, Sep & Oct, 10am-8pm Jun-Aug; ♿; M Barceloneta) The zoo is a great day out for kids, with 7500 critters that range from geckos to gorillas, lions and elephants – there are more than 400 species, plus picnic areas dotted all around and a wonderful adventure playground. There are pony rides, a petting zoo and a minitrain meandering through the grounds. Thanks to recent advances in legislation prohibiting the use of animals for performances (including circuses and bullfighting) the zoo called time on its dolphin shows in late 2015.

Barceloneta & the Waterfront

On the approach to **Port Olímpic** (Map p272; Moll de Mestral; M Ciutadella Vila Olímpica) from Barceloneta, the giant copper-like *Peix* (Fish) sculpture by Frank Gehry glitters in the sunlight. Port Olímpic was built for the 1992 Olympic sailing events and is now a somewhat touristy marina surrounded by bars and restaurants. From the marina, a string of popular beaches (p282) stretches along the coast northeast to the modern somewhat soulless **El Fòrum** (M El Maresme Fòrum) district, which has lots of space for summer concerts and funfairs. Strollers, cyclists and skaters parade on the broad beachside boulevard (dotted with seafood restaurants), while sunbathers soak up the rays on warm summer days.

★Museu Marítim MUSEUM
(Map p256; ☎93 342 99 20; www.mmb.cat; Avinguda de les Drassanes; adult/child €10/5, free from 3pm Sun; ⊙10am-8pm; Ⓜ Drassanes) The city's maritime museum occupies Gothic shipyards – a remarkable relic from Barcelona's days as the seat of a seafaring empire. Highlights include a full-scale 1970s replica of Don Juan of Austria's 16th-century flagship, fishing vessels, antique navigation charts and dioramas of the Barcelona waterfront.

Museu Can Framis MUSEUM
(☎93 320 87 36; www.fundaciovilacasas.com; Carrer de Roc Boronat 116-126; adult/child €5/2; ⊙11am-6pm Tue-Sat, to 2pm Sun; Ⓜ Glòries, Llacuna) Set in an 18th-century former textile factory, this contemporary museum is a showcase for Catalan painting from the 1960s onwards. The galleries display some 300 works, arranged in thought-provoking ways – with evocative paintings by different artists (sometimes working in different time periods) creating fascinating intersections and collisions.

L'Aquàrium AQUARIUM
(Map p272; ☎93 221 74 74; www.aquariumbcn.com; Moll d'Espanya; adult/child €20/15, dive €300, Sleeping with Sharks €90; ⊙10am-9.30pm Jul & Aug, shorter hours Sep-Jun; Ⓜ Drassanes) It's hard not to shudder at the sight of a shark gliding above you, displaying its toothy, wide-mouthed grin. But this, the 80m shark tunnel, is the highlight of one of Europe's largest aquariums. It has the world's best Mediterranean collection and plenty of colourful fish from as far off as the Red Sea, the Caribbean and the Great Barrier Reef. All up, some 11,000 creatures (including a dozen sharks) of 450 species reside here. Tickets are €2 cheaper online.

Museu d'Història de Catalunya MUSEUM
(Museum of the History of Catalonia; Map p272; ☎93 225 47 00; www.mhcat.cat; Plaça de Pau Vila 3; adult/child €4.50/3.50, last Tue of the month Oct-Jun free; ⊙10am-7pm Tue & Thu-Sat, to 8pm Wed, to 2.30pm Sun; Ⓜ Barceloneta) Inside the **Palau de Mar** (Map p272; Plaça de Pau Vila; Ⓜ Barceloneta), this worthwhile museum takes you from the Stone Age through to the early 1980s. It's a busy hotchpotch of dioramas, artefacts, videos, models, documents and interactive bits: all up, an entertaining exploration of 2000 years of Catalan history. Signage is in Catalan and Spanish.

Museu del Disseny de Barcelona MUSEUM
(☎93 256 68 00; www.museudeldisseny.cat; Plaça de les Glòries Catalanes 37; permanent/temporary exhibition adult €6/4.50, child €4/3, combination ticket adult/child €8/5.50, free from 3pm Sun & 1st Sun of the month; ⊙10am-8pm Tue-Sun; Ⓜ Glòries) Barcelona's design museum lies inside a monolithic contemporary building with geometric facades and a rather brutalist appearance that's nicknamed *la grapadora* (the stapler) by locals. Inside, it houses a dazzling collection of ceramics, decorative arts and textiles, and is a must for anyone interested in the design world.

Museu Blau MUSEUM
(Blue Museum; ☎93 256 60 02; www.museuciencies.cat; Edifici Fòrum, Parc del Fòrum; adult/child €6/free, free from 3pm Sun & 1st Sun of month; ⊙10am-7pm Tue-Sat, to 8pm Sun Mar-Sep, to 6pm Tue-Fri, to 7pm Sat, to 8pm Sun Oct-Feb; Ⓜ El Maresme Fòrum) Set inside the futuristic Edifici Fòrum, the Museu Blau takes visitors on a journey across the natural world. Multimedia and interactive exhibits explore topics like the history of evolution, the earth's

ℹ DISCOUNTS

Possession of a **Bus Turístic** (p294) ticket entitles you to discounts at some museums.

Articket (www.articketbcn.org) gives admission to six sites for €30 and is valid for six months. You can pick up the ticket at the tourist offices at Plaça de Catalunya, Plaça de Sant Jaume and Estació Sants train station and at the museums themselves. The six sights are the Museu Picasso, the Museu Nacional d'Art de Catalunya, the Museu d'Art Contemporani de Barcelona, the Fundació Antoni Tàpies, the Centre de Cultura Contemporània de Barcelona and the Fundació Joan Miró.

Arqueoticket is for those with an interest in archaeology and ancient history. The ticket (€14.50) is available from participating museums and tourist offices and grants free admission to the following: Museu d'Arqueologia de Catalunya, Museu Egipci, Museu d'Història de Barcelona, Born Centre de Cultura i Memòria.

La Barceloneta

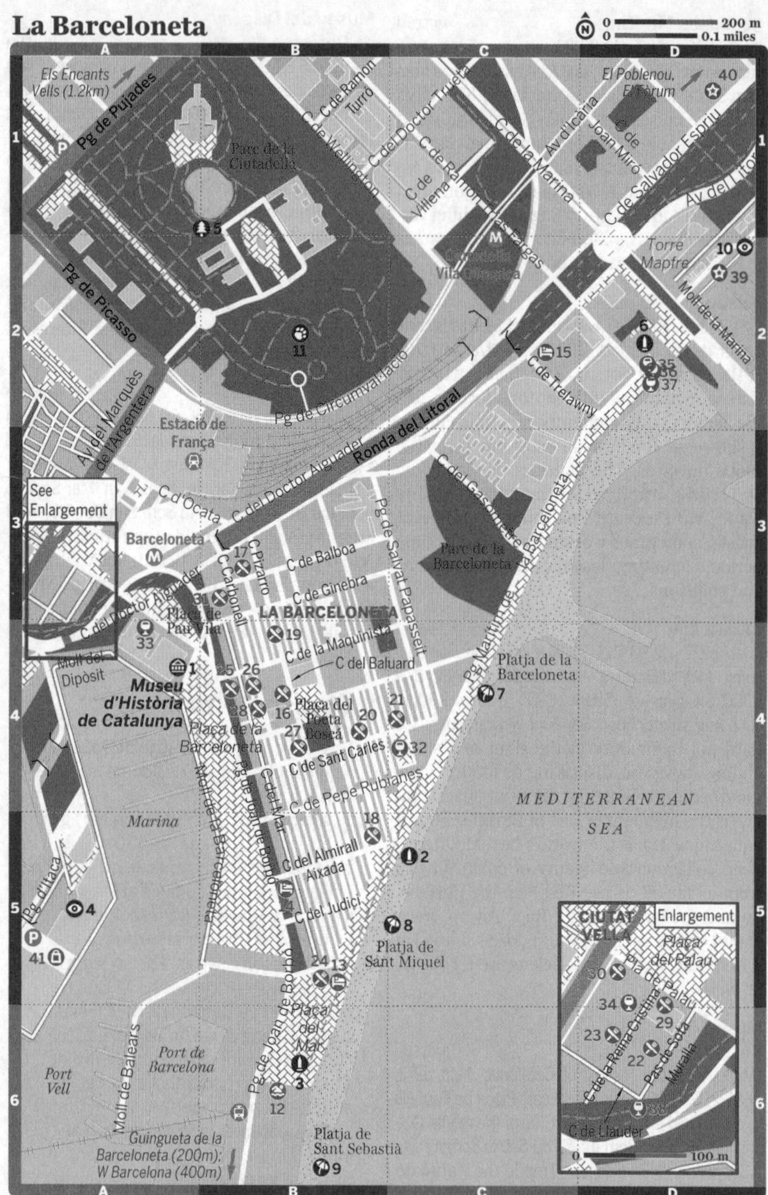

formation and the great scientists who have helped shaped human knowledge. There are also specimens from the animal, plant and mineral kingdoms – plus dinosaur skeletons – all rather dramatically set amid the sprawling 9000 sq metres of exhibition space.

Mirador de Colom VIEWPOINT

(Columbus Monument; Map p256; ☎93 285 38 32; www.barcelonaturisme.com; Plaça del Portal de la Pau; adult/child €6/4; ⌚8.30am-8.30pm; Ⓜ Drassanes) High above the swirl of traffic on the roundabout below, Columbus keeps per-

La Barceloneta

manent watch, pointing vaguely out to the Mediterranean from this Corinthian-style iron column built for the 1888 Universal Exhibition. Zip up 60m in a lift for bird's-eye views back up La Rambla and across Barcelona's ports.

It was in Barcelona that Columbus allegedly gave the delighted Catholic monarchs a report of his first explorations in the Americas after his voyage in 1492. In the 19th century, it was popularly believed here that Columbus was one of Barcelona's most illustrious sons. Some historians still make that claim.

Cementiri del Poblenou CEMETERY
(Poblenou Cemetery; ☎93 225 16 61; www.cbsa.cat; Av d'Icària; ⏰8am-6pm; Ⓜ Llacuna) FREE Located just inland from Platja de Bogatell near Carrer del Taulat, this cemetery dates from 1773. The cemetery was positioned outside the then city limits for health reasons; its central monument commemorates the victims of a yellow-fever epidemic that swept across Barcelona in 1821. It is full of bombastic family memorials, but an altogether disquieting touch is the sculpture *El petó de la mort* (The Kiss of Death), in which a winged skeleton kisses a young kneeling lifeless body.

Museu de la Música MUSEUM
(☎93 256 36 50; www.museumusica.bcn.cat; Carrer de Lepant 150; adult/child €6/4.50, free from 3pm Sun; ⏰10am-6pm Tue, Wed & Fri, to 9pm Thu, to 7pm Sat & Sun; Ⓜ Monumental) Some 500 instruments (less than a third of those held) are on show in this museum, housed on the 2nd floor of the administration building in **L'Auditori** (☎93 247 93 00; www.auditori.cat; Carrer de Lepant 150; tickets free-€59; ⏰box office 5-9pm Tue-Fri, 10am-1pm & 5-9pm Sat; Ⓜ Marina), the city's main classical-music concert hall.

La Sagrada Família & L'Eixample

L'Eixample's biggest sightseeing draws are its Modernista buildings, particularly the four that line the Passeig de Gràcia – La Pedrera, Casa Amatller, Casa Batlló and Casa Lleó Morera. Up in the north of the neighbourhood (best reached by the metro or cab) is where you'll find La Sagrada Família and the Recinte Modernista de Sant Pau.

★Casa Batlló ARCHITECTURE
(Map p278; ☎93 216 03 06; www.casabatllo.es; Passeig de Gràcia 43; adult/child €28/free;

TOP SIGHT
LA SAGRADA FAMÍLIA

If you have time for only one sightseeing outing, this should be it. La Sagrada Família inspires awe by its sheer verticality, and, in the manner of the medieval cathedrals it emulates, it's still under construction: work began in 1882 and is hoped (although by no means expected) to be finished in 2026, a century after the architect's death.

A Holy Mission

The Temple Expiatori de la Sagrada Família was Antoni Gaudí's all-consuming obsession and he saw its completion as his holy mission. He devised a building with a central tower 170m high above the transept (representing Christ) and another 17 of 100m or more. The 12 along the three facades represent the Apostles, while the remaining five represent the Virgin Mary and the four evangelists. With his characteristic dislike for straight lines (there were none in nature, he said), Gaudí gave his towers swelling outlines inspired by the peaks of the holy mountain Montserrat outside Barcelona, and encrusted them with a tangle of sculpture.

At Gaudí's death, only the crypt, the apse walls, one portal and one tower had been finished. In 1936 anarchists burned and smashed the interior, including plans and models. Opponents of the continuation of the project claim that the computer models based on what little of Gaudí's plans survived have led to the creation of a monster that has little to do with the original. It is a debate that appears to have little hope of resolution.

The Interior & the Apse

The roof is held up by a forest of extraordinary angled pillars. As the pillars soar towards the ceiling, they sprout a web of supporting branches, creating the effect of a forest canopy.

DON'T MISS

- The apse, pillars and stained glass
- Nativity Facade
- Passion Facade (pictured)
- Museu Gaudí

PRACTICALITIES

- 93 208 04 14
- www.sagradafamilia.org
- Carrer de Mallorca 401
- adult/child €15/free
- 9am-8pm Apr-Sep, to 7pm Mar & Oct, to 6pm Nov-Feb
- M Sagrada Família

Sunlight pours through carefully placed window as though through the branches of a thick forest. The pillars are of four different types of stone, from the soft Montjuïc stone pillars along the lateral aisles through to granite, dark grey basalt and finally burgundy-tinged Iranian porphyry for the key columns at the intersection of the nave and transept. The stained glass, divided in shades of red, blue, green and ochre, creates a hypnotic, magical atmosphere when the sun hits the windows.

Nativity Facade

The Nativity Facade is the artistic pinnacle of the building, mostly created under Gaudí's personal supervision. You can climb high up inside some of the four towers by a combination of lifts and narrow spiral staircases – a vertiginous experience. Three sections of the portal represent, from left to right, Hope, Charity and Faith. Among the forest of sculpture on the Charity portal you can see, low down, the manger surrounded by an ox, an ass, the shepherds and kings, and angel musicians. To the right of the facade is the Claustre del Roser, a Gothic-style mini-cloister tacked on to the outside of the church. Once inside, look back to the intricately decorated entrance. On the lower right-hand side you'll notice the sculpture of a reptilian devil handing a terrorist a bomb. Bombings in Barcelona were frequent in the decades prior to the civil war.

Passion Facade

The southwest Passion Facade, on the theme of Christ's last days and death, has four towers and a large, sculpture-bedecked portal. The sculptor, Josep Subirachs, worked on its decoration from 1986 to 2006, somewhat controversially. He did not attempt to imitate Gaudí, instead producing angular images of his own. The main series of sculptures are in an S-shaped sequence, starting with the Last Supper at the bottom left and ending with Christ's burial at the top right.

Glory Facade

The Glory Facade will, like the others, be crowned by four towers – the total of 12 representing the Twelve Apostles. Inside will be the narthex, a kind of foyer made up of 16 'lanterns', a series of hyperboloid forms topped by cones. Further decoration will make the whole building a microcosmic symbol of the Christian church, with Christ represented by a massive 170m central tower above the transept, and the five remaining planned towers symbolising the Virgin Mary and the four evangelists.

A HIDDEN PORTRAIT

Careful observation of the Passion Facade will reveal a special tribute from sculptor Josep Subirachs to Gaudí. The central sculptural group (below Christ crucified) shows, from right to left, Christ bearing his cross, Veronica displaying the cloth with Christ's bloody image, a pair of soldiers and, watching it all, a man called the evangelist. Subirachs used a rare photo of Gaudí, taken a couple of years before his death, as the model for the evangelist's face.

Unfinished it may be, but La Sagrada Família attracts over 4.5 million visitors a year and is the most visited monument in Spain. Pope Benedict XVI consecrated it as a minor basilica in a ceremony in November 2010.

MUSEU GAUDÍ

Open at the same times as the church, the Museu Gaudí, below ground level, includes interesting material on Gaudí's life and other works, as well as models and photos of La Sagrada Família.

La Sagrada Família

A TIMELINE

1882 Construction begins on a neo-Gothic church designed by Francisco de Paula del Villar y Lozano.

1883 Antoni Gaudí takes over as chief architect and plans a far more ambitious church to hold 13,000 faithful.

1926 Gaudí dies; work continues under Domènec Sugrañes i Gras. Much of the **apse** ❶ and **Nativity Facade** ❷ is complete.

1930 Bell towers ❸ of the Nativity Facade completed.

1936 Construction interrupted by Spanish Civil War; anarchists destroy Gaudí's plans.

1939–40 Architect Francesc de Paula Quintana i Vidal restores the crypt and meticulously reassembles many of Gaudí's lost models, some of which can be seen in the **museum** ❹.

1976 Passion Facade ❺ completed.

1986–2006 Sculptor Josep Subirachs adds sculptural details to the Passion Facade including the panels telling the story of Christ's last days, amid much criticism for employing a style far removed from what was thought typical of Gaudí.

2000 Central nave vault ❻ completed.

2010 Church completely roofed over; Pope Benedict XVI consecrates the church; work begins on a high-speed rail tunnel that will pass beneath the church's **Glory Facade** ❼.

2020s–40s Projected completion date.

TOP TIPS

➡ The best light through the stained-glass windows of the Passion Facade bursts into the heart of the church in the late afternoon.

➡ Visit at opening time on weekdays to avoid the worst of the crowds.

➡ Head up the Nativity Facade bell towers for the views, as long queues generally await at the Passion Facade towers.

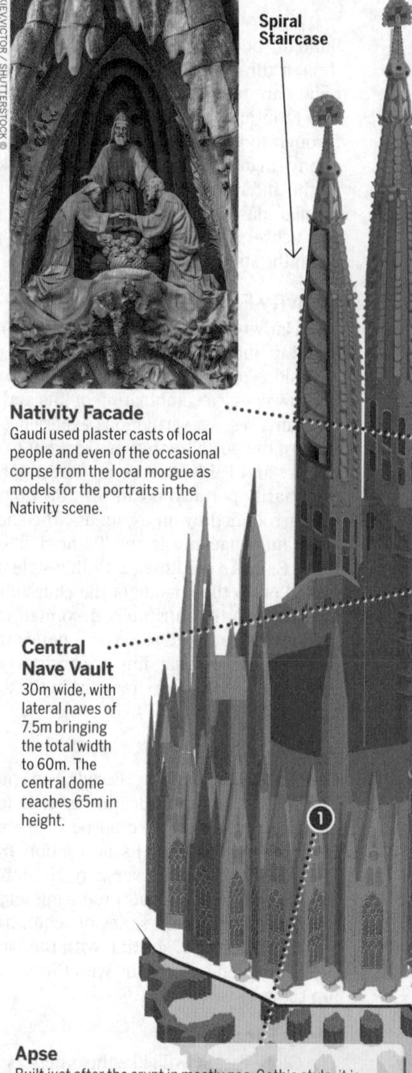

Nativity Facade
Gaudí used plaster casts of local people and even of the occasional corpse from the local morgue as models for the portraits in the Nativity scene.

Central Nave Vault
30m wide, with lateral naves of 7.5m bringing the total width to 60m. The central dome reaches 65m in height.

Apse
Built just after the crypt in mostly neo-Gothic style, it is capped by pinnacles that show a hint of the genius that Gaudí would later deploy in the rest of the church.

Bell Towers
The towers of the three facades will represent the Twelve Apostles. Eight are completed. Lifts whisk visitors up one tower of the Nativity and Passion Facades (the latter gets longer queues) for fine views.
NIKADA / GETTY IMAGES ©
Completed Church
Along with the Glory Facade and its four towers, six other towers remain to be completed. They will represent the four evangelists, the Virgin Mary and, soaring above them all over the transept, a 170m colossus symbolising Christ.
Glory Facade
This will be the most fanciful facade of all, with a narthex boasting 16 hyperboloid lanterns topped by cones that will look something like an organ made of melting ice cream.
Museu Gaudí
Jammed with old photos, drawings and restored plaster models that bring Gaudí's ambitions to life, the museum also houses an extraordinarily complex plumb-line device he used to calculate his constructions.
Escoles de Gaudí
Crypt
The first completed part of the church, the crypt is in largely neo-Gothic style and lies under the transept. Gaudí's burial place here can be seen from the Museu Gaudí.
FOTOKON / SHUTTERSTOCK ©
Passion Facade
See the story of Christ's last days from Last Supper to burial in an S-shaped sequence from bottom to top of the facade. Check out the cryptogram in which the numbers always add up to 33, Christ's age at his death.
YURY DMITRIENKO / SHUTTERSTOCK ©
2
3
4
5
6
7

L'Eixample

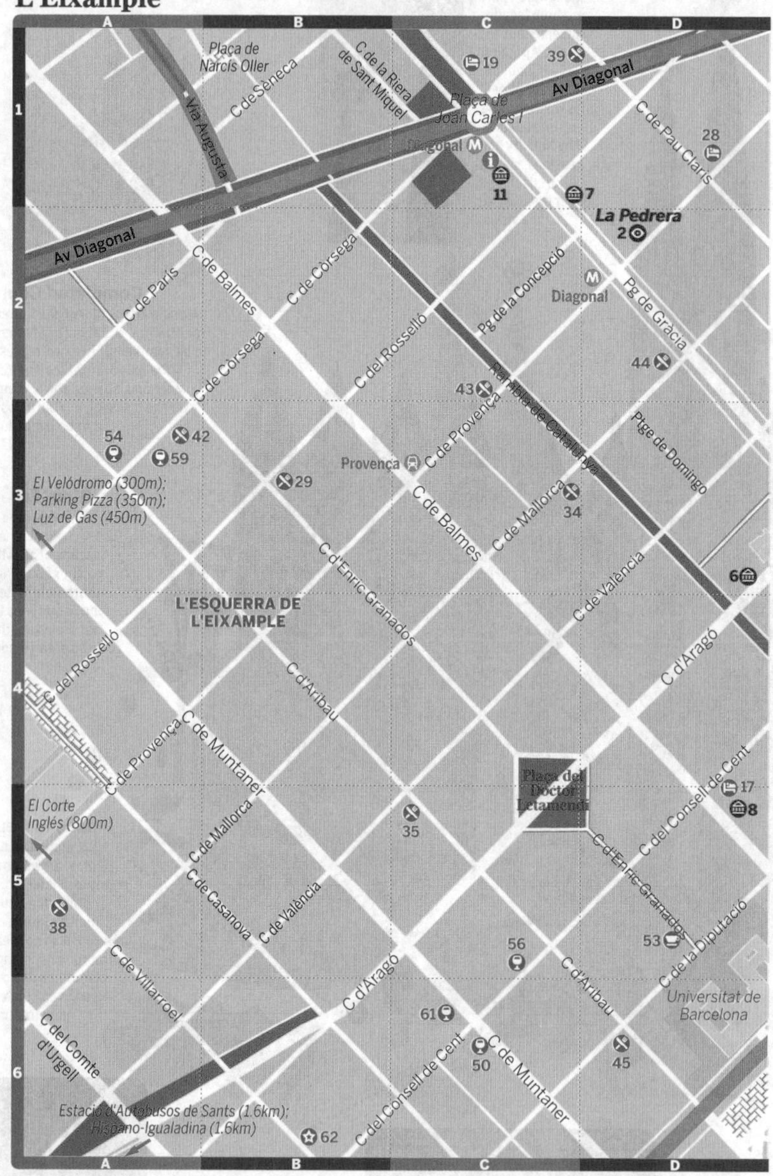

⌚9am-9pm, last admission 8pm; Ⓜ Passeig de Gràcia) One of the strangest residential buildings in Europe, this is Gaudí at his hallucinatory best. The facade, sprinkled with bits of blue, mauve and green tiles and studded with wave-shaped window frames and balconies, rises to an uneven blue-tiled roof with a solitary tower.

It is one of the three houses on the block between Carrer del Consell de Cent and Carrer d'Aragó that gave it the playful name **Illa de la Discòrdia** (Spanish: Manzana de la

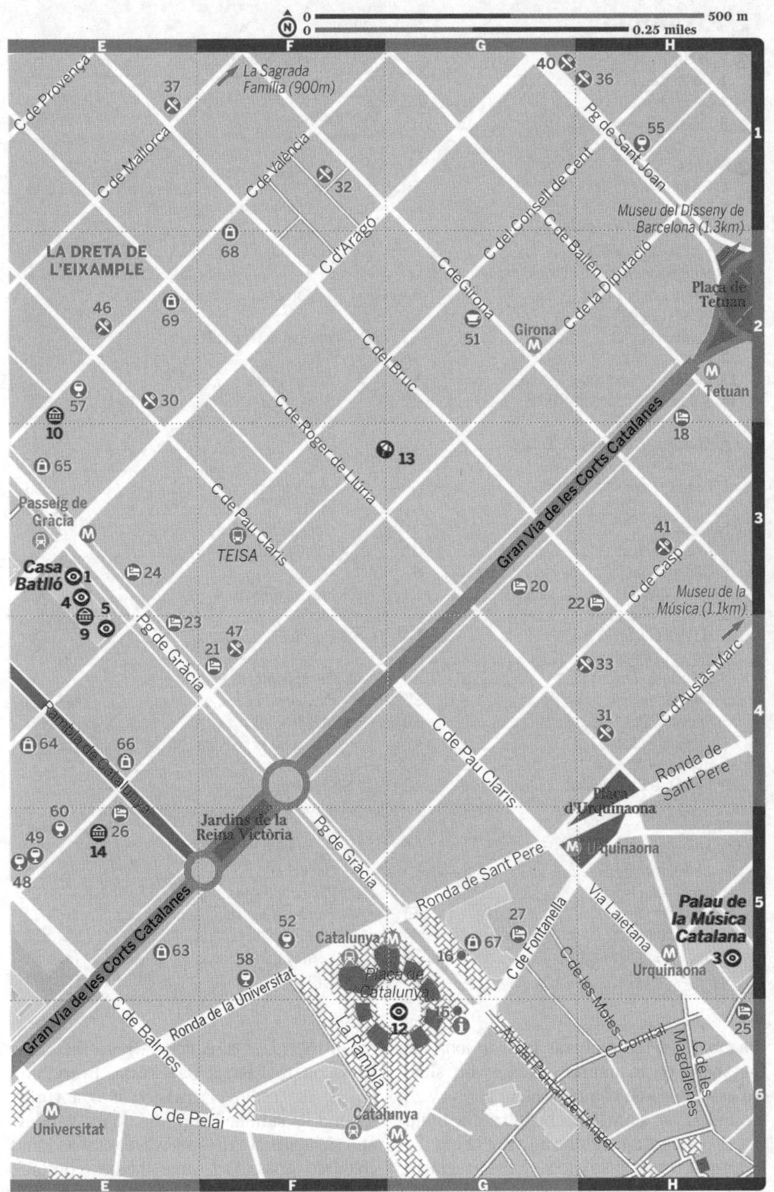

Discordia), meaning 'Apple (Block) of Discord'. The others are Puig i Cadafalch's Casa Amatller (p281) and Domènech i Montaner's Casa Lleó Morera (p282). They were all renovated between 1898 and 1906 and show how eclectic a 'style' Modernisme was.

Locals know Casa Batlló variously as the *casa dels ossos* (house of bones) or *casa del drac* (house of the dragon). It's easy enough to see why. The balconies look like the bony jaws of some strange beast and the roof represents Sant Jordi (St George) and the

L'Eixample

Top Sights

1 Casa Batlló........E3
2 La Pedrera........D2
3 Palau de la Música Catalana........H5

Sights

4 Casa Amatller........E3
5 Casa Lleó Morera........E4
6 Fundació Antoni Tàpies........D3
7 Fundació Suñol........C1
8 Museu del Modernisme Barcelona........D5
9 Museu del Perfum........E4
10 Museu Egipci........E2
11 Palau Robert........C1
12 Plaça de Catalunya........G6
13 Platja de l'Eixample........F3
14 Sala Fundación MAPFRE........E5

Activities, Courses & Tours

15 Barcelona Walking Tours........G6
16 Catalunya Bus Turístic........G5

Sleeping

17 Anakena House........D5
18 Casa Bonay........H2
19 Casa Gràcia........C1
20 Cotton House........G3
21 Hostal Oliva........F4
22 Hotel Constanza........H3
23 Mandarin Oriental........E4
24 Margot House........E3
25 Pensió 2000........H6
26 Praktik Rambla........E5
27 Room Mate Pau........G5
28 The One Barcelona........D1

Eating

29 Auto Rosellon........B3
30 Cafe Emma........E2
31 Casa Alfonso........H4
32 Casa Amalia........F1
33 Casa Calvet........H4
34 Cerveseria Catalana........C3
35 Charlot Cafè........C5
36 Chicha Limoná........H1
37 De Tapa Madre........E1
38 Disfrutar........A5
39 Entrepanes Díaz........C1
40 Granja Petitbo........G1
41 Hawker 45........H3
42 Koyuki........A3
43 La Bodegueta Provença........C2
44 Lasarte........D2
45 Mont Bar........D6
46 Mr Kao........E2
47 Tapas 24........F4

Drinking & Nightlife

48 Aire........E5
49 Arena Classic........E5
50 BierCaB........C6
51 Cafè del Centre........G2
52 City Hall........F5
53 Cosmo........D5
54 Dry Martini........A3
55 El Viti........H1
56 Garage Beer Co........C5
57 Les Gens Que J'Aime........E2
58 Milano........F5
59 Monkey Factory........A3
60 Monvínic........E5
61 Punto BCN........C6

Entertainment

City Hall........(see 52)
62 Méliès Cinemes........B6
Palau de la Música Catalana........(see 3)

Shopping

63 Altaïr........E5
64 Cacao Sampaka........E4
65 Casa Del Llibre........E3
66 Dr Bloom........E4
67 El Corte Inglés........G5
68 Flores Navarro........F2
69 Joan Múrria........E2
Loewe........(see 5)
Regia........(see 9)

dragon. Even the roof was built to look like the shape of an animal's back, with shiny scales – the 'spine' changes colour as you walk around. If you stare long enough at the building, it seems almost to be a living being. Before going inside, take a look at the pavement. Each paving piece carries stylised images of an octopus and a starfish, designs that Gaudí originally cooked up for Casa Batlló.

When Gaudí was commissioned to refashion this building, he went to town inside and out. The internal light wells shimmer with tiles of deep-sea blue. Gaudí eschewed the straight line, and so the staircase wafts you up to the 1st (main) floor, where the salon looks on to Passeig de Gràcia. Everything swirls: the ceiling is twisted into a vortex around its sunlike lamp; the doors, window and skylights are dreamy waves of wood and coloured glass. The same themes continue in the other rooms and covered terrace. The attic is characterised by Gaudí trademark hyperboloid arches. Twisting, tiled chimney pots add a surreal touch to the roof.

★**La Pedrera** ARCHITECTURE

(Casa Milà; Map p278; ☎902 202138; www.lapedrera.com; Passeig de Gràcia 92; adult/child €25/15; ⏰9am-8.30pm Mar-Oct, 9am-6.30pm Nov-Feb;

Ⓜ Diagonal) This madcap Gaudí masterpiece was built in 1905–10 as a combined apartment and office block. Formally called Casa Milà, after the businessman who commissioned it, it is better known as La Pedrera (the Quarry) because of its uneven grey stone facade, which ripples around the corner of Carrer de Provença.

Recinte Modernista de Sant Pau ARCHITECTURE

(☎ 93 553 78 01; www.santpaubarcelona.org; Carrer de Sant Antoni Maria Claret 167; adult/child €13/free; ⏲ 9.30am-6.30pm Mon-Sat, to 2.30pm Sun Apr-Oct, 9.30am-4.30pm Mon-Sat, to 2.30pm Sun Nov-Mar; Ⓜ Sant Pau/Dos de Maig) Domènech i Montaner outdid himself as architect and philanthropist with the Modernista Hospital de la Santa Creu i de Sant Pau, renamed the 'Recinte Modernista' in 2014. It was long considered one of the city's most important hospitals but was repurposed, its various spaces becoming cultural centres, offices and something of a monument. The complex, including 16 pavilions – together with the Palau de la Música Catalana (p265), a joint Unesco World Heritage Site – is lavishly decorated and each pavilion is unique.

Casa Amatller ARCHITECTURE

(Map p278; ☎ 93 461 74 60; www.amatller.org; Passeig de Gràcia 41; adult/child 1hr guided tour €17/8.50, 40min multimedia tour €14/7, with 20min chocolate tasting €17/10; ⏲ 11am-6pm; Ⓜ Passeig de Gràcia) One of Puig i Cadafalch's most striking flights of Modernista fantasy, Casa Amatller combines Gothic window frames with a stepped gable borrowed from Dutch urban architecture. But the busts and reliefs of dragons, knights and other characters dripping off the main facade are pure caprice.

The pillared foyer and staircase lit by stained glass are like the inside of some romantic castle. The building was renovated in 1900 for the chocolate baron and philanthropist Antoni Amatller (1851–1910).

Fundació Antoni Tàpies GALLERY

(Map p278; ☎ 93 487 03 15; www.fundaciotapies.org; Carrer d'Aragó 255; adult/child €7/5.60; ⏲ 10am-7pm Tue-Sun; Ⓜ Passeig de Gràcia) The Fundació Antoni Tàpies is both a pioneering Modernista building (completed in 1885) and the major collection of leading 20th-century Catalan artist Antoni Tàpies. Tàpies died in February 2012, aged 88; known for his esoteric work, he left behind a powerful range of paintings and a foundation intended to promote contemporary artists. Admission includes an audioguide.

Museu Egipci MUSEUM

(Map p278; ☎ 93 488 01 88; www.museuegipci.com; Carrer de València 284; adult/child €11/5; ⏲ 10am-8pm Mon-Sat, to 2pm Sun mid-Jun–early Oct & Dec, 10am-2pm & 4-8pm Mon-Fri, 10am-8pm Sat, 10am-2pm Sun Jan–mid-Jun & early Oct-Nov; Ⓜ Passeig de Gràcia) Hotel magnate Jordi Clos has spent much of his life collecting ancient Egyptian artefacts, brought together in this private museum. It's divided into different thematic areas (the pharaoh, religion, funerary practices, mummification, crafts etc) and boasts an interesting variety of exhibits.

Sala Fundación MAPFRE GALLERY

(Map p278; ☎ 93 401 26 03; www.fundacionmapfre.org; Carrer de la Diputació 250; adult/child €3/free, Mon free; ⏲ 2-8pm Mon, 10am-8pm Tue-Sat, 11am-7pm Sun; Ⓜ Passeig de Gràcia) Formerly the Fundación Francisco Godia, this stunning, carefully restored Modernista residence was taken over in 2015 by the charitable cultural arm of Spanish insurance giants MAPFRE as a space for art and photography exhibitions. Housed in the Casa Garriga i Nogués, it is a stunning, carefully restored Modernista residence originally built for a rich banking family by Enric Sagnier in 1902–05.

Casa de les Punxes ARCHITECTURE

(Casa Terrades; Map p286; ☎ 93 016 01 28; www.casadelespunxes.com; Avinguda Diagonal 420; adult/child audiogude tour €12.50/11.25, guided tour €20/17; ⏲ 9am-8pm; Ⓜ Diagonal) Puig i Cadafalch's Casa Terrades, completed in 1905, is better known as the Casa de les Punxes (House of Spikes) because of its pointed turrets. Resembling a medieval castle, the former apartment block is the only fully detached building in L'Eixample, and was declared a national monument in 1976. Since 2017 it has been open to the public. Visits take in its stained-glass bay windows, handsome iron staircase, and rooftop. Guided tours in English lasting one hour depart at 4pm.

Museu del Modernisme Barcelona MUSEUM

(Map p278; ☎ 93 272 28 96; www.mmbcn.cat; Carrer de Balmes 48; adult/child €10/5; ⏲ 10.30am-7pm Tue-Sat, to 2pm Sun; Ⓜ Passeig de Gràcia) Housed in a Modernista building, this museum's ground floor seems like a big Modernista furniture showroom. Several items by Antoni Gaudí, including chairs from Casa Batlló and a mirror from Casa Calvet,

BEST BEACHES

Barcelona has miles of golden shoreline. Some of its best beaches are:

Platja de la Barceloneta (Map p272; http://lameva.barcelona.cat; M Barceloneta) Just east of its namesake neighbourhood, Barceloneta's golden-sand beach is beloved by sunseekers, and has ample eating and drinking options just inland when you need a bit of refreshment.

Platja de Sant Miquel (Map p272; http://lameva.barcelona.cat; M Barceloneta) Taking its name from the 18th-century church in nearby Barceloneta, this stretch of sand fills with beachgoers when warm days arrive. Given its proximity to the old city, the crowds are thicker here than at beaches further out.

Platja de Sant Sebastià (Map p272; http://lameva.barcelona.cat; M Barceloneta) On the edge of Barceloneta, this is a handy beach for a bit of sun and surf action when you need a quick break from the old city.

El Poblenou Platges (http://lameva.barcelona.cat; M Ciutadella Vila Olímpica, Llacuna, Poblenou, Selva de Mar) A series of broad, sandy beaches stretches northeast from the Port Olímpic marina. They are largely artificial, but that doesn't deter the millions of sunseekers and swimmers from descending in summer.

are supplemented by a host of items by his lesser-known contemporaries, including some typically whimsical, mock medieval pieces by Puig i Cadafalch.

Casa Lleó Morera ARCHITECTURE

(Map p278; Passeig de Gràcia 35; M Passeig de Gràcia) Domènech i Montaner's 1905 contribution to the Illa de la Discòrdia, with Modernista carving outside and a bright, tiled lobby in which floral motifs predominate, is perhaps the least odd-looking of the three main buildings on the block. Luxury fashion store **Loewe** (Map p278; 93 216 04 00; www.loewe.com; Passeig de Gràcia 35; 10am-8.30pm Mon-Sat; M Passeig de Gràcia) is located here.

Palau Robert GALLERY

(Map p278; 93 238 80 91; http://palaurobert.gencat.cat; Passeig de Gràcia 107; 9am-8pm Mon-Sat, to 2.30pm Sun; M Diagonal) FREE Catalonia's regional tourist office (p334) also serves as an exhibition space, mostly for shows with Catalan themes. In summer, concerts are occasionally held in the peaceful gardens at the back of the 1903-completed building, or in its main hall.

Fundació Suñol GALLERY

(Map p278; 93 496 10 32; www.fundaciosunol.org; Passeig de Gràcia 98; adult/child €4/free; 11am-2pm & 4-8pm Mon-Fri, 4-8pm Sat; M Diagonal) Rotating exhibitions of portions of this private collection of mostly 20th-century art (some 1200 works in total) offer anything from Man Ray's photography to sculptures by Alberto Giacometti. Over two floors, you are most likely to run into Spanish artists – anyone from Picasso to Jaume Plensa – along with a sprinkling of international artists.

Museu del Perfum MUSEUM

(Map p278; 93 216 01 21; www.museudelperfum.com; Passeig de Gràcia 39; adult/child €5/free; 10.30am-8pm Mon-Fri, 11am-2pm Sat; M Passeig de Gràcia) At the back of the **Regia perfume store** (Map p278; 93 216 01 21; www.regia.es; Passeig de Gràcia 39; 9.30am-8.30pm Mon-Fri, 10.30am-8.30pm Sat; M Passeig de Gràcia), this museum contains oddities from ancient Egyptian and Roman scent receptacles (the latter mostly from the 1st to 3rd centuries AD) to classic eau de cologne bottles – all in all, some 5000 bottles of infinite shapes, sizes and histories. Other items include ancient bronze Etruscan tweezers and little early-19th-century potpourri bowls made of fine Sèvres porcelain. Also on show are old catalogues and advertising posters.

Platja de l'Eixample BEACH

(Map p278; 93 423 43 50; Carrer de Roger de Llúria 56; €1.55; 10am-8pm late Jun–Sep; M Girona) In a hidden garden inside a typical Eixample block is an old water tower and an urban 'beach', the Platja de l'Eixample. In reality, this is a knee-height swimming pool (60cm at its deepest) surrounded by sand. It's perfect for little ones, with lifeguards on hand.

Plaça de Catalunya SQUARE

(Map p278; M Catalunya) At the intersection of the old city and L'Eixample, Plaça de Catalunya is the city's central transport hub, both for buses and trains, and a convenient meeting point. A large square with some impressive fountains and elegant statuary, it is ringed with four lanes of traffic and thus is not really a place to linger.

Gràcia & Park Güell

★Park Güell PARK

(☎93 409 18 31; www.parkguell.cat; Carrer d'Olot 7; adult/child €8/5.60; ⏲8am-9.30pm May-Aug, to 8.30pm Apr, Sep & Oct, to 6.30pm Nov-Mar; 🚌24, 92, Ⓜ Lesseps, Vallcarca) North of Gràcia, Unesco-listed Park Güell is where Gaudí turned his hand to landscape gardening. It's a strange, enchanting place where his passion for natural forms really took flight and the artificial almost seems more natural than the natural.

The park is extremely popular, receiving an estimated four million visitors a year. Access is limited to a certain number of people every half-hour, and it's wise to book ahead online (you'll also save a euro on the admission fee).

Park Güell was created in 1900, when Count Eusebi Güell bought a tree-covered hillside (then outside Barcelona) and hired Gaudí to create a miniature city of houses for the wealthy in landscaped grounds. The project was a commercial flop and was abandoned in 1914 – but not before Gaudí had created 3km of roads and walks, steps, a plaza and two gatehouses in his inimitable manner. In 1922 the city bought the estate for use as a public park.

Just inside the main entrance on Carrer d'Olot, immediately recognisable by the two Hansel-and-Gretel gatehouses, is the park's **Centre d'Interpretaciò**, in the Pavelló de Consergeria, which is a typically curvaceous former porter's home that hosts a display on Gaudí's building methods and the history of the park. There are superb views from the top floor.

The steps up from the entrance, guarded by a mosaic dragon/lizard (a copy of which you can buy in many downtown souvenir shops), lead to the **Sala Hipóstila** (aka the Doric Temple). This is a forest of 86 stone columns, some of which lean like mighty trees bent by the weight of time, originally intended as a market. To the left curves a gallery whose twisted stonework columns and roof give the effect of a cloister beneath tree roots – a motif repeated in several places in the park. On top of the Sala Hipóstila is a broad open space whose centrepiece is the **Banc de Trencadís**, a tiled bench curving sinuously around its perimeter and designed by one of Gaudí's closest colleagues, architect Josep Maria Jujol (1879–1949). With Gaudí, however, there is always more than meets the eye. This giant platform was designed as a kind of catchment area for rainwater washing down the hillside. The water is filtered through a layer of stone and sand, and it drains down through the columns to an underground cistern.

The spired house over to the right is the **Casa-Museu Gaudí** (☎93 219 38 11; www.casamuseugaudi.org; Park Güell, Carretera del Carmel 23a; adult/child €5.50/free; ⏲9am-8pm Apr-Sep, 10am-6pm Oct-Mar; 🚌24, 92, 116, Ⓜ Lesseps), where Gaudí lived for most of his last 20 years (1906–26). It contains furniture by him (including items that were once at home in La Pedrera, Casa Batlló and Casa Calvet) and other memorabilia. The house was built in 1904 by Francesc Berenguer i Mestres as a prototype for the 60 or so houses that were originally planned here.

Much of the park is still wooded, but it's laced with pathways. The best views are from the cross-topped **Turó del Calvari** in the southwest corner.

One-hour guided tours in multiple languages including English take place year-round and cost €7 (plus park admission); prebook online.

The walk from metro stop Lesseps is signposted. From the Vallcarca stop, it is marginally shorter and the uphill trek is eased by escalators. Buses 24 and 92 drop you at an entrance near the top of the park.

Casa Vicens MUSEUM

(☎93 348 42 58; www.casavicens.org; Carrer de les Carolines 18-24; adult/child €16/14, guided tour per person additional €3; ⏲10am-8pm, last tour 7.30pm; Ⓜ Fontana) A Unesco-listed masterpiece, Casa Vicens was first opened regularly to the public in 2017. The angular, turreted 1885-completed private house created for stock and currency broker Manuel Vicens i Montaner was Gaudí's inaugural commission, when the architect was aged just 30. Tucked away west of Gràcia's main drag, the richly detailed facade is awash with ceramic colour and shape. You're free to wander through at your own pace but 30-minute guided tours (available in English) bring the building to life.

Gaudí Experience MUSEUM

(☎93 285 44 40; www.gaudiexperiencia.com; Carrer de Larrard 41; adult/child €9/7.50; ⏲10.30am-7pm Apr-Sep, to 5pm Oct-Mar; Ⓜ Lesseps) The Gaudí

1

The Genius of Gaudí

The name Gaudí has become a byword for Barcelona and, through his unique architectural wonders, one of the principal magnets for visitors to the city.

A Catholic & a Catalan

Born in Reus and initially trained in metalwork, Antoni Gaudí i Cornet (1852–1926) personifies, and largely transcends, the Modernisme movement that brought a thunderclap of innovative greatness to turn-of-the-century Barcelona. Gaudí was a devout Catholic and Catalan nationalist, and his creations were a conscious expression of Catalan identity and, in some cases, great piety.

The Masterworks

Gaudí devoted much of the latter part of his life to what remains Barcelona's call sign: the unfinished Sagrada Família. His inspiration in the first instance was Gothic, but he also sought to emulate the harmony he observed in nature, eschewing the straight line and favouring curvaceous forms.

He used complex string models weighted with plumb lines to make his calculations. You can see examples in the upstairs mini-museum in La Pedrera.

The architect's work evokes sinuous movement often with a dreamlike or surreal quality. The private apartment house Casa Batlló is a fine example in which all appears as a riot of the unnaturally natural – or the naturally unnatural. Not only are straight lines eliminated, but the lines between real

1. Park Güell **2.** Nativity Facade, La Sagrada Família

and unreal, sober and dream-drunk, good sense and play are all blurred. Depending on how you look at the facade, you might see St George defeating a dragon, or a series of fleshless sea monsters straining out of the wall.

He seems to have particularly enjoyed himself with rooftops. At La Pedrera and Palau Güell, in particular, he created all sorts of fantastical, multicoloured tile figures as chimney pots looking like anything from *Alice in Wonderland* mushrooms to *Star Wars* imperial troopers.

Saint Gaudí?

Much like his work in progress, La Sagrada Família, Gaudí's story is far from over. In March 2000 the Vatican decided to examine the case for canonising him, and pilgrims already stop by the crypt to pay homage to him. One of the key sculptors at work on the church, the Japanese Etsuro Sotoo, converted to Catholicism because of his passion for Gaudí.

GREATEST HITS

- La Sagrada Família (p274), a symphony of religious devotion.
- La Pedrera (p280), dubbed 'the Quarry' because of its flowing facade.
- Casa Batlló (p273), a fairy-tale dragon.
- Park Güell (p283), a park full of Modernista twists.
- Palau Güell (p265), one of Gaudí's earliest commissions.

Gràcia

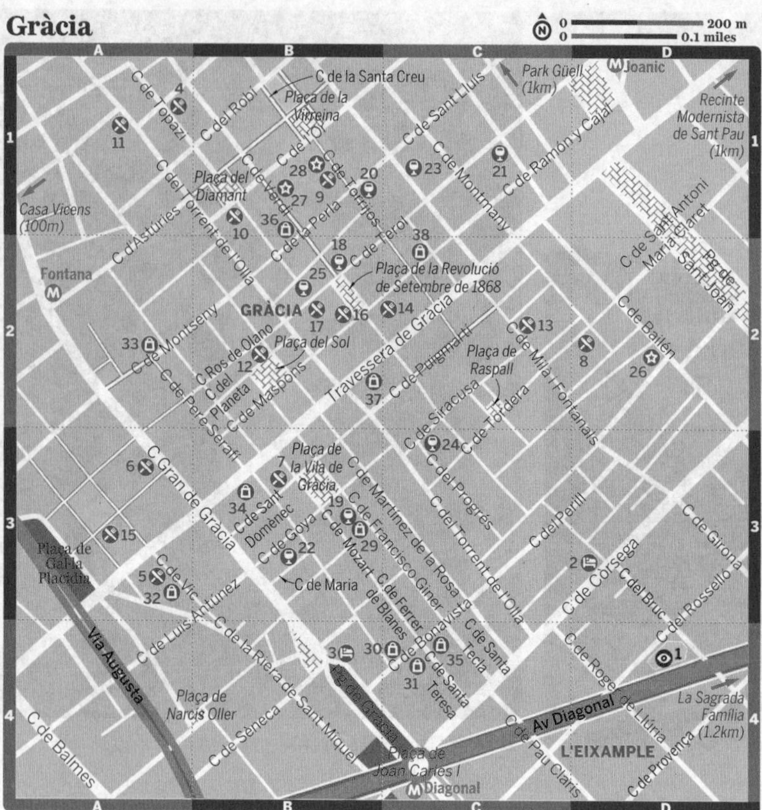

Experience is a fun-filled Disney-style look at the life and work of Barcelona's favourite son, just a stone's throw from Park Güell. There are models of his buildings and whizz-bang interactive exhibits and touchscreens, but the highlight is the stomach-churning 4D presentation in its tiny screening room. Not recommended for the frail or children aged under six years.

Camp Nou, Pedralbes & La Zona Alta

★Camp Nou Experience MUSEUM
(902 189900; www.fcbarcelona.com; Gate 9, Avinguda de Joan XXIII; adult/child €25/20; 9.30am-7.30pm Apr-Sep, 10am-6.30pm Mon-Sat, to 2.30pm Sun Oct-Mar; M Palau Reial) A pilgrimage site for football fans from around the world, Camp Nou (p327) is a must for FC Barcelona fans. On this self-guided tour, you'll get an in-depth look at the club, starting with a museum filled with multimedia exhibits, trophies and historical displays, followed by a tour of the stadium. Set aside about 2½ hours all up.

★Museu-Monestir de Pedralbes MONASTERY
(93 256 34 34; http://monestirpedralbes.bcn.cat; Baixada del Monestir 9; adult/child €5/free, after 3pm Sun free; 10am-5pm Tue-Fri, to 7pm Sat, to 8pm Sun Apr-Sep, 10am-2pm Tue-Fri, to 5pm Sat & Sun Oct-Mar; 63, 68, 75, 78, H4, FGC Reina Elisenda) Founded in 1326, this convent was first opened to the public in 1983 and is now a museum of monastic life (the few remaining nuns have moved into neighbouring buildings). It stands at the top of Avinguda de Pedralbes in a residential area that was countryside until the 20th century, and which remains a divinely quiet corner of Barcelona.

Gràcia

Sights
1 Casa de les Punxes ... D4

Sleeping
2 Generator Hostel ... D3
3 Hotel Casa Fuster ... B4

Eating
4 .IT ... A1
5 Bar Bodega Quimet ... A3
6 Botafumeiro ... A3
7 Café Godot ... B3
8 Cal Boter ... D2
9 Cantina Machito ... B1
10 Casa Portuguesa ... B1
11 Chivuo's ... A1
12 Envalira ... B2
13 Himali ... C2
14 La Nena ... C2
15 La Pubilla ... A3
16 Pepa Tomate ... B2
17 Taverna La Llesca ... B2

Drinking & Nightlife
18 Bar Canigó ... B2
19 Bobby Gin ... B3
20 Chatelet ... B1
21 La Vermuteria del Tano ... C1
22 Musical Maria ... B3
23 Rabipelao ... C1
24 Raïm ... C3
25 Viblioteca ... B2

Entertainment
26 Cine Texas ... D2
27 Verdi ... B1
28 Verdi Park ... B1

Shopping
29 Amalia Vermell ... B3
30 Be ... C4
31 Bodega Bonavista ... C4
32 Colmillo de Morsa ... A3
33 Hibernian ... A2
34 Lady Loquita ... B3
35 Mushi Mushi ... C4
36 Picnic ... B1
37 Tintin Shop ... B2
38 Vinil Vintage ... C2

★CosmoCaixa MUSEUM
(Museu de la Ciència; 93 212 60 50; www.cosmocaixa.com; Carrer d'Isaac Newton 26; adult/child €4/free, guided tours from €2, planetarium €4; 10am-8pm Tue-Sun; 60, 196) Kids (and kids at heart) are fascinated by displays at this science museum. The single greatest highlight is the re-creation of over 1 sq km of flooded **Amazon** rainforest (Bosc Inundat). More than 100 species of Amazon flora and fauna (including anacondas, colourful poisonous frogs, and caimans) prosper in this unique, living diorama in which you can even experience a tropical downpour.

Tibidabo MOUNTAIN
Framing the north end of the city, the forest-covered mountain of Tibidabo, which tops out at 512m, is the highest peak in Serra de Collserola. Aside from the superb views from the top, the highlights of Tibidabo include the 8000-hectare Parc de Collserola (p288), an old-fashioned amusement park (p287), a **telecommunications tower** (93 406 93 54; www.torredecollserola.com; Carretera de Vallvidrera al Tibidabo; adult/child €5.60/3.30; hours vary, closed Jan-Feb; 111, Funicular de Vallvidrera) with viewing platform, and a looming **church** (Basilica of the Sacred Heart of Jesus; 93 417 56 86; www.templotibidabo.es; Plaça de Tibidabo; lift €3.50; 11am-7pm; T2A, Funicular del Tibidabo) FREE that's visible from many parts of the city.

Parc d'Atraccions AMUSEMENT PARK
(93 211 79 42; www.tibidabo.cat; Plaça de Tibidabo 3-4; adult/child €28.50/10.30; closed Jan & Feb; T2A, Funicular del Tibidabo) The reason most *barcelonins* come up to Tibidabo is for some thrills at this funfair, close to the top funicular station. Here you'll find whirling high-speed rides and high-tech 4D cinema, as well as old-fashioned amusements including an old steam train and the Museu d'Autòmats, with automated puppets dating as far back as 1880. Check the website for seasonal opening times.

Jardins del Laberint d'Horta GARDENS
(93 413 24 00; http://lameva.barcelona.cat; Passeig del Castanyers 1; adult/child €2.23/1.42, free Wed & Sun; 10am-8pm Apr-Oct, to 7pm Dec-Mar; M Mundet) Laid out in the late 18th century by Antoni Desvalls, Marquès d'Alfarràs i de Llupià, this carefully manicured park remained a private family idyll until the 1970s, when it was opened to the public. The *laberint* ('labyrinth' in Catalan) refers to the central maze; other paths take you past a pleasant artificial lake, waterfalls, a

neoclassical pavilion and a false cemetery. The last is inspired by 19th-century romanticism, characterised by an obsession with a swooning vision of death.

Parc de la Creueta del Coll PARK
(Passeig de la Mare de Déu del Coll 77; 10am-9pm Apr-Oct, to 7pm Nov-Mar; 92, 129, N5, M Penitents) A favourite with families, this refreshing public park has a meandering, splashing lake pool, along with swings, showers and a snack bar. Only the pool closes outside summer. The park is set inside a deep crater left by long years of stone quarrying, with an enormous concrete sculpture, *Elogio del agua* (In Praise of Water) by Eduardo Chillida, suspended on one side.

Enter from Carrer Mare de Déu del Coll, a 1km walk east from the Penitents metro station.

Bellesguard ARCHITECTURE
(93 250 40 93; www.bellesguardgaudi.com; Carrer de Bellesguard 16; adult/child €9/free; 10am-3pm Tue-Sun; FGC Avinguda Tibidabo) This Gaudí masterpiece was rescued from obscurity and opened to the public in 2013. Built between 1900 and 1909, this private residence (still owned by the original Guilera family) has a castle-like appearance with crenellated walls of stone and brick, narrow stained-glass windows, elaborate ironwork and a soaring turret mounted by a Gaudían cross. It's a fascinating work that combines both Gothic and Modernista elements.

Parc de Collserola PARK
(93 280 35 52; www.parcnaturalcollserola.cat; Carretera de l'Església 92; Centre d'Informació 9.30am-3pm, Can Coll 9.30am-2.30pm Sun & holidays, closed late Jun-early Sep; FGC Baixador de Vallvidrera, Funicular de Vallvidrera) *Barcelonins* needing an escape from the city without heading far seek out this extensive, 80-sq-km park in the hills. It's a great place to hike and bike, and has plenty of cafes and snack bars. Pick up a map from one of the information centres (such as the Carretera de l'Església 92 location, close to the Baixador de Vallvidrera FGC train station).

Montjuïc, Poble Sec & Sant Antoni

With its splendid museums, galleries and gardens, the challenge here is planning: there's far too much to see in one day, and distances can be great.

★Museu Nacional d'Art de Catalunya MUSEUM
(MNAC; Map p292; 93 622 03 76; www.museunacional.cat; Mirador del Palau Nacional; adult/child €12/free, after 3pm Sat & 1st Sun of month free, rooftop viewpoint only €2; 10am-8pm Tue-Sat, to 3pm Sun May-Sep, to 6pm Tue-Sat Oct-Apr; 55, M Espanya) From across the city, the bombastic neobaroque silhouette of the Palau Nacional can be seen on the slopes of Montjuïc. Built for the 1929 World Exhibition and restored in 2005, it houses a vast collection of mostly Catalan art spanning the early Middle Ages to the early 20th century. The high point is the collection of extraordinary Romanesque frescoes.

★Fundació Joan Miró MUSEUM
(Map p292; 93 443 94 70; www.fmirobcn.org; Parc de Montjuïc; adult/child €12/free; 10am-8pm Tue, Wed, Fri & Sat, to 9pm Thu, to 3pm Sun; 55, 150, Paral·lel) Joan Miró, the city's best-known 20th-century artistic progeny, bequeathed this art foundation to his hometown in 1971. Its light-filled buildings, designed by close friend and architect Josep Lluís Sert (who also built Miró's Mallorca studios), are crammed with seminal works, from Miró's earliest timid sketches to paintings from his last years.

Telefèric de Montjuïc CABLE CAR
(Map p292; 93 328 90 03; www.telefericdemontjuic.cat; Avinguda de Miramar 30; adult/child one way €8.20/6.50; 10am-9pm Jun-Sep, 10am-7pm Mar-May & Oct, 10am-6pm Nov-Feb; 55, 150) From Estació Parc Montjuïc, this cable car carries you to the Castell de Montjuïc via the mirador (lookout point).

Teleférico del Puerto CABLE CAR
(Map p292; 93 430 47 16; www.telefericodebarcelona.com; Avinguda de Miramar; one way/return €11/16.50; 10.30am-8pm Jun–mid-Sep, 10.30am-7pm Mar-May & mid-Sep–Oct, 11am-5.30pm Nov-Feb; 150) The quickest way from the beach to the mountain is via the cable car that runs between Torre de Sant Sebastiá in Barceloneta and the Miramar stop on Montjuïc. From Estació Parc Montjuïc, the separate Telefèric de Montjuïc cable car carries you to the Castell de Montjuïc via the mirador (lookout point).

Museu d'Arqueologia de Catalunya MUSEUM
(MAC; Map p292; 93 423 21 49; www.mac.cat; Passeig de Santa Madrona 39-41; adult/child €5.50/free; 9.30am-7pm Tue-Sat, 10am-2.30pm Sun;

55, Poble Sec) This archaeology museum, housed in what was the Graphic Arts Palace during the 1929 World Exhibition, covers Catalonia and cultures from elsewhere in Spain. Items range from copies of pre-Neanderthal skulls to lovely Carthaginian necklaces and jewel-studded Visigothic crosses.

MUHBA Refugi 307 HISTORIC SITE

(Map p292; 93 256 21 22; http://ajuntament.barcelona.cat/museuhistoria; Carrer Nou de la Rambla 175; adult/child incl tour €3.40/free; tours in English 10.30am Sun; Paral·lel) Part of the Museu d'Història de Barcelona (MUHBA), this shelter dates back to the days of the Spanish Civil War. Barcelona was the city most heavily bombed from the air during the war and had more than 1300 air-raid shelters. Local citizens started digging this one under a fold of Montjuïc in March 1937. Compulsory tours are conducted in English at 10.30am, Spanish at 11.30am and Catalan at 12.30pm on Sundays. Reserve ahead as places are limited.

Font Màgica FOUNTAIN

(Map p292; 93 316 10 00; Avinguda de la Reina Maria Cristina; every 30min 7.30-10.30pm Wed-Sun Jun-Sep, 9-10pm Thu-Sat Apr, May & Oct, 8-9pm Thu-Sat Nov-early Jan & mid-Feb–Mar; Espanya) FREE A huge fountain that crowns the long sweep of the Avinguda de la Reina Maria Cristina to the grand facade of the Palau Nacional, Font Màgica is a unique performance in which the water can look like seething fireworks or a mystical cauldron of colour.

Castell de Montjuïc FORTRESS

(Map p292; 93 256 44 45; http://ajuntament.barcelona.cat/castelldemontjuic; Carretera de Montjuïc 66; adult/child €5/3, after 3pm Sun & 1st Sun of month free; 10am-8pm Apr-Oct, to 6pm Nov-Mar; 150, Telefèric de Montjuïc, Castell de Montjuïc) This forbidding *castell* (castle or fort) dominates the southeastern heights of Montjuïc and enjoys commanding views over the Mediterranean. It dates, in its present form, from the late 17th and 18th centuries. For most of its dark history, it has been used to watch over the city and as a political prison and killing ground.

Poble Espanyol CULTURAL CENTRE

(Map p292; www.poble-espanyol.com; Avinguda de Francesc Ferrer i Guàrdia 13; adult/child €14/7; 9am-8pm Mon, to midnight Tue-Thu & Sun, to 3am Fri, to 4am Sat; 13, 23, 150, Espanya) Welcome to Spain! All of it! This 'Spanish Village' is an intriguing scrapbook of Spanish architecture built for the Spanish crafts section of the 1929 World Exhibition. You can meander from Andalucía to the Balearic Islands in the space of a couple of hours, visiting surprisingly good copies of Spain's characteristic structures. The 117 buildings include 17 restaurants, cafes and bars, and 20 craft shops and workshops (for glass artists and other artisans), as well as souvenir stores.

CaixaForum GALLERY

(Map p292; 93 476 86 00; www.caixaforum.es; Avinguda de Francesc Ferrer i Guàrdia 6-8; adult/child €4/free, 1st Sun of month free; 10am-8pm; Espanya) The Caixa building society prides itself on its involvement in (and ownership of) art, in particular all that is contemporary. Its premier art expo space in Barcelona hosts part of the bank's extensive collection from around the globe. The setting is a completely renovated former factory, the Fàbrica Casaramona, an outstanding Modernista brick structure designed by Puig i Cadafalch. From 1940 to 1993 it housed the First Squadron of the police cavalry unit – 120 horses in all.

Museu Etnològic MUSEUM

(Map p292; 93 424 68 07; http://ajuntament.barcelona.cat/museuetnologic; Passeig de Santa Madrona 16-22; adult/child €5/free, 4-8pm Sun & 1st Sun of month free; 10am-7pm Tue-Sat, to 8pm Sun; 55) Barcelona's ethnology museum presents an intriguing permanent collection that delves into the rich heritage of Catalonia. Exhibits cover origin myths, religious festivals, folklore, and the blending of the sacred and the secular (along those lines, don't miss the Nativity scene with that quirky Catalan character *el caganer*, aka 'the crapper').

Jardí Botànic GARDENS

(Map p292; www.museuciencies.cat; Carrer del Doctor Font i Quer 2; adult/child €3.50/free, after 3pm Sun & 1st Sun of month free; 10am-7pm Apr-Sep, to 5pm Oct-Mar; 55, 150) This botanical garden is dedicated to Mediterranean flora and has a collection of some 40,000 plants and 1500 species, including many that thrive in areas with a climate similar to that of the Mediterranean, such as the Canary Islands, North Africa, Australia, California, Chile and South Africa.

Estadi Olímpic Lluís Companys STADIUM

(Map p292; 93 426 20 89; www.estadiolimpic.cat; Passeig Olímpic 15-17; 8am-8pm May-Sep, 10am-6pm Oct-Apr; 13, 150) FREE The Estadi Olímpic was the main stadium of Barcelona's Olympic Games. If you saw the Olympics on TV, the 60,000-capacity stadium

Montjuïc

A ONE-DAY ITINERARY

Montjuïc, perhaps once the site of pre-Roman settlements, is today a hilltop green lung looking over city and sea. Interspersed across varied gardens are major art collections, a fortress, an Olympic stadium and more. A solid one-day itinerary can take in the key spots.

Alight at Espanya metro stop and make for ❶ **CaixaForum**, always host to three or four free top-class exhibitions. The nearby ❷ **Pavelló Mies van der Rohe** is an intriguing study in 1920s futurist housing by one of the 20th century's greatest architects. Uphill, the Romanesque art collection in the ❸ **Museu Nacional d'Art de Catalunya** is a must, and its restaurant is a pleasant lunch stop. Escalators lead further up the hill towards the ❹ **Estadi Olímpic**, scene of the 1992 Olympic Games. The road leads east to the ❺ **Fundació Joan Miró**, a shrine to the master surrealist's creativity. Contemplate ancient relics in the ❻ **Museu d'Arqueologia de Catalunya**, then have a break in the peaceful ❼ **Jardins de Mossèn Cinto Verdaguer**, the prettiest on the hill, before taking the cable car to the ❽ **Castell de Montjuïc**. If you pick the right day, you can round off with the gorgeously kitsch ❾ **La Font Màgica** sound and light show, followed by drinks and dancing in an open-air nightspot in ❿ **Poble Espanyol**.

TOP TIPS

➡ Ride the Transbordador Aeri from Barceloneta for a bird's eye approach to Montjuïc. Or take the Teleféric de Montjuïc cable car to the Castell for more aerial views.

➡ The Castell de Montjuïc features outdoor summer cinema and concerts (see http://salamontjuic.org).

➡ Bursting with colour and serenity, the Jardins de Mossèn Cinto Verdaguer are exquisitely laid out with bulbs, especially tulips, and aquatic flowers.

CaixaForum
This former factory and barracks designed by Josep Puig i Cadafalch is an outstanding work of Modernista architecture; like a Lego fantasy in brick.

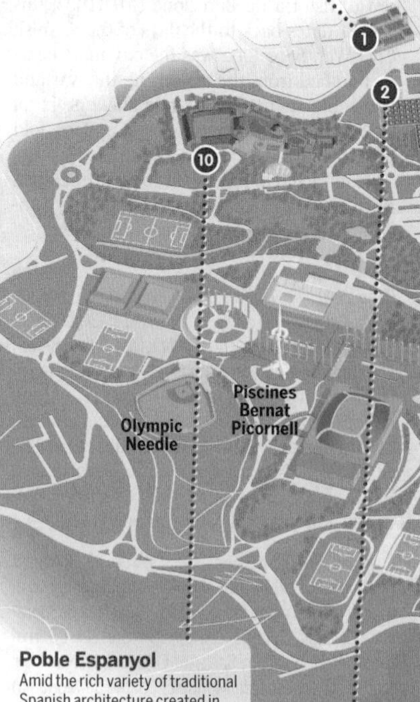

Poble Espanyol
Amid the rich variety of traditional Spanish architecture created in replica for the 1929 Barcelona World Exhibition, browse the art on show in the Fundació Fran Daurel.

Pavelló Mies van der Rohe
Admire the inventiveness of the great German architect Ludwig Mies van der Rohe in this recreation of his avant garde German pavillion for the 1929 World Exhibition.

La Font Màgica
Take a summer evening to behold the Magic Fountain come to life in a unique 15-minute sound and light performance, when the water glows like a cauldron of colour.

Museu Nacional d'Art de Catalunya
Make a beeline for the Romanesque art selection and the 12th-century polychrome image of Christ in majesty, which was recovered from the apse of a country chapel in northwest Catalonia.

9
3
6
Museu Etnològic
Teatre Grec
5
7
Museu Olímpic i de l'Esport
4
Estadi Olímpic
Jardí Botànic
8

Museu d'Arqueologia de Catalunya
This archaeology museum, housed in what was the Graphic Arts palace during the 1929 World Exhibition, covers Catalonia and cultures from elsewhere in Spain. Items range from copies of pre-Neanderthal skulls to lovely Carthaginian necklaces and jewel-studded Visigothic crosses.

Jardins de Mossèn Cinto Verdaguer

Castell de Montjuïc
Enjoy the sweeping views of the sea and city from atop this 17th-century fortress, once a political prison and long a symbol of oppression.

Fundació Joan Miró
Take in some of Joan Miró's giant canvases, and discover little-known works from his early years in the Sala Joan Prats and Sala Pilar Juncosa.

Montjuïc & Poble Sec

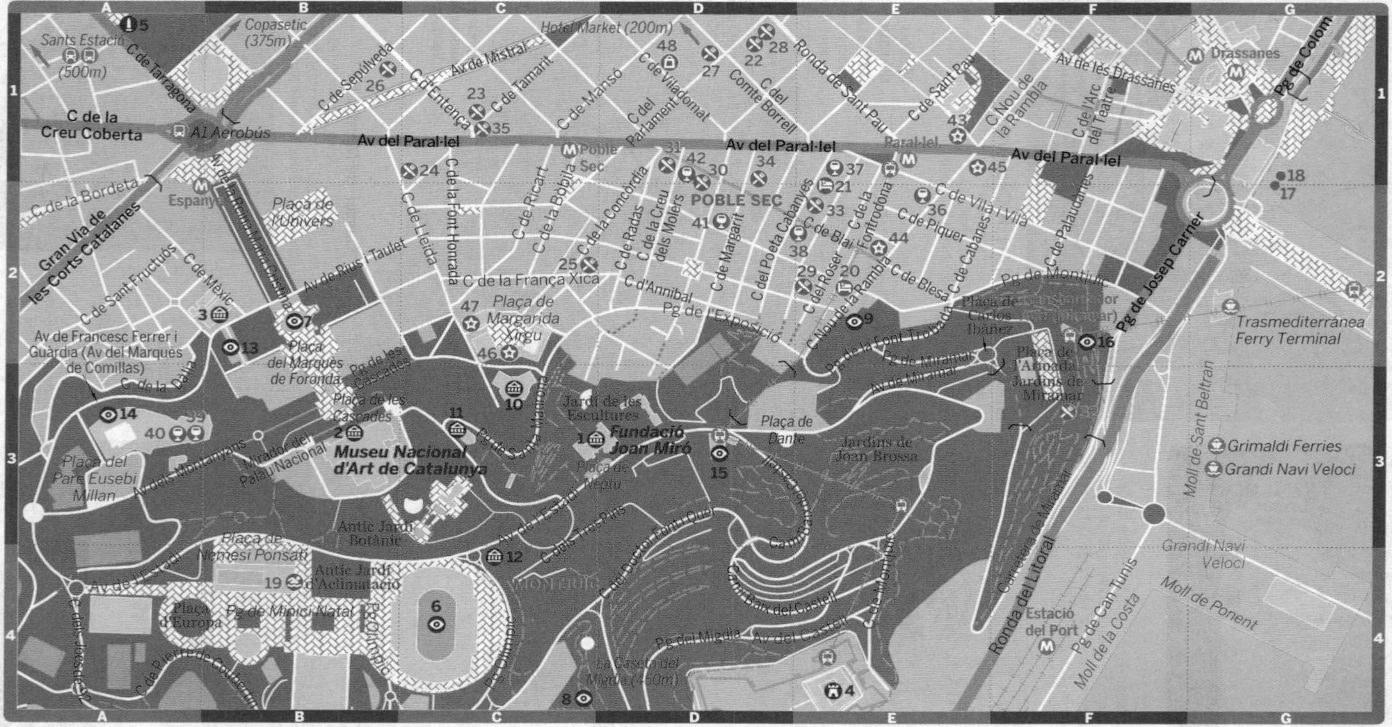

Montjuïc & Poble Sec

Top Sights
1 Fundació Joan Miró C3
2 Museu Nacional d'Art de Catalunya B3

Sights
3 CaixaForum B2
4 Castell de Montjuïc E4
5 Dona i Ocell A1
6 Estadi Olímpic Lluís Companys C4
7 Font Màgica B2
8 Jardí Botànic C4
9 MUHBA Refugi 307 E2
10 Museu d'Arqueologia de Catalunya C3
11 Museu Etnològic C3
12 Museu Olímpic i de l'Esport C4
13 Pavelló Mies van der Rohe B2
14 Poble Espanyol A3
15 Telefèric de Montjuïc D3
16 Teleférico del Puerto F2

Activities, Courses & Tours
17 Las Golondrinas G2
18 Orsom G1
19 Piscines Bernat Picornell B4

Sleeping
20 Hotel Brummell E2
21 Sant Jordi Mambo Tango E2

Eating
22 Agust Gastrobar D1
23 Bodega 1900 C1
24 Casa de Tapas Cañota C1
25 Casa Xica C2
26 Enigma B1
27 Federal D1
28 Horchateria Sirvent D1
29 Lascar 74 E2
30 Malamén D1
31 Mano Rota D1
32 Martínez F3
33 Quimet i Quimet E2
34 Spice D1
35 Tickets C1

Drinking & Nightlife
36 Abirradero E2
37 El Rouge E1
38 La Cambicha E2
39 La Terrrazza A3
40 Pervert Club @ The One A3
41 Redrum D2
42 Tinta Roja D1

Entertainment
43 BARTS E1
44 Gran Bodega Saltó E2
45 Sala Apolo E1
46 Teatre Lliure C2
47 Teatre Mercat De Les Flors C2

Shopping
48 Popcorn Store D1

may seem surprisingly small. So might the Olympic flame holder into which an archer spectacularly fired a flaming arrow during the opening ceremony. The stadium was opened in 1929 and restored for the 1992 Olympics.

Cementiri del Sud-Oest CEMETERY

(Cementiri Nou; 93 484 19 99; www.cbsa.cat; Carrer de la Mare de Déu de Port 56-58; 8am-6pm; 21, 107) FREE On the hill to the south of the Anella Olímpica, this huge 1883-opened cemetery stretches down the southern slopes, combining elaborate architect-designed tombs for rich families and small niches for the rest. It includes the graves of numerous Catalan artists and politicians, and, at the southern entrance, the Col·lecció de Carrosses Fúnebres (p294) hearse collection. On Sundays and public holidays only, bus 107 goes right through the cemetery. From Monday to Saturday, take bus 21 to the main gates.

Museu Olímpic i de l'Esport MUSEUM

(Map p292; 93 292 53 79; www.museuolimpicbcn.cat; Avinguda de l'Estadi 60; adult/child €5.80/free; 10am-8pm Tue-Sat, to 2.30pm Sun Apr-Sep, 10am-6pm Tue-Sat, to 2.30pm Sun Oct-Mar; 55, 150) The Museu Olímpic i de l'Esport is an information-packed interactive sporting museum. After picking up tickets, you wander down a ramp that snakes below ground level and is lined with multimedia displays on the history of sport and the Olympic Games, starting with the ancients.

Pavelló Mies van der Rohe ARCHITECTURE

(Map p292; 93 215 10 11; www.miesbcn.com; Avinguda de Francesc Ferrer i Guàrdia 7; adult/child €5/free; 10am-8pm Mar-Oct, 10am-6pm Nov-Feb; M Espanya) The Pavelló Mies van der Rohe is a work of artful simplicity that is emblematic of the Modernisme movement. The structure has been the subject of many studies and interpretations, and it has inspired several generations of architects. That said, unless you're an avid architecture fan, there isn't much to see inside beyond what you can glean from the building's exterior.

Col·lecció de Carrosses Fúnebres MUSEUM

(☎93 484 19 99; www.cbsa.cat; Carrer de la Mare de Déu de Port 56-58; ⊙10am-2pm Sat & Sun; 🚌21, 107) FREE If late-18th-century to mid-20th-century hearses capture your imagination, then this collection at the Cementiri del Sud-Oest (p293) is probably the city's weirdest sight, a place to contemplate the pomp and circumstance of people's last earthly ride. The funeral company claims it is the biggest museum of its kind in the world.

Activities

Base Nautica Municipal WATER SPORTS

(☎93 221 04 32; www.basenautica.org; Avinguda de Litoral; 2hr lessons from €40, equipment hire per hour from €20, wetsuit hire per day €10; ⊙10am-7pm; M Poblenou) Just back from Platja de la Mar Bella, at Base Nautica Municipal you can learn the basics of kayaking, windsurfing, catamaran sailing or stand-up paddleboarding. You can also hire equipment here. Prices for lessons are cheaper in groups of two or more. Longer courses, running from eight to 12 hours over several days, are also available.

Aire De Barcelona SPA

(Map p266; ☎93 295 57 43; www.airedebarcelona.com; Passeig de Picasso 22; thermal baths & aromatherapy Mon-Thu €36, Fri-Sun €39; ⊙9am-11pm Sun-Thu, to midnight Fri & Sat; M Arc de Triomf) With low lighting and relaxing perfumes wafting around you, this basement spa could be the perfect way to end a day. Hot, warm and cold baths, steam baths and options for various massages, including on a slab of hot marble, make for a delicious hour or so. Book ahead and bring a swimming costume.

Club Natació Atlètic-Barcelona SWIMMING

(Map p272; ☎93 221 00 10; www.cnab.cat; Plaça del Mar; day pass adult/child €12.55/7.15; ⊙7am-11pm Mon-Fri, to 10pm Sat, to 8pm Sun; 🚌V15, 39, 59, 64, M Barceloneta) Operating since 1907, this athletic club has one indoor and two outdoor pools. Of the latter, one is heated for lap swimming in winter. Admission includes use of the gym, spa and private beach access.

Piscines Bernat Picornell SWIMMING

(Map p292; ☎93 423 40 41; www.picornell.cat; Avinguda de l'Estadi 30-38; adult/child €11.90/7.30, nudist hours €6.55/4.70; ⊙6.45am-midnight Mon-Fri, 7am-9pm Sat, 7.30am-4pm Sun; 🚌13, 150) Admission to Barcelona's official Olympic pool on Montjuïc also includes use of the complex's fitness room, sauna, Jacuzzi, steam bath and track. On Saturday nights, between 9pm and 11pm, the pool (with access to sauna and steam bath) is open only to nudists. On Sundays between October and May the indoor pool also opens for nudists only from 4.15pm to 6pm.

My Beautiful Parking CYCLING

(Map p256; ☎93 510 8724; www.mybeautifulparking.com; Carrer de la Bòria 17; bike hire per 2hr/24hr €5/14; ⊙10.30am-8pm Mon-Sat, also Sun Apr-Sep; M Jaume I) Friendly shop with three types of bikes – foldable, 'track' or 'city' – to rent, from €5 for two hours.

Tours

Bus Turístic BUS

(☎93 298 70 00; www.barcelonabusturistic.cat; adult/child 1 day €29/16, 2 days €39/16; ⊙9am-8pm) This hop-on, hop-off service covers three circuits (44 stops) linking virtually

TRAVEL WITH CHILDREN

Barcelona is great for older kids and teens – the Mediterranean attitude means they are included in many seemingly adult activities, like eating late meals at bars or restaurants. Babies will love the welcoming Mediterranean culture, and toddlers will be showered with attention.

Babysitting Get a babysitter at Tender Loving Canguros (https://tlcanguros.wordpress.com) or **5 Serveis** (☎93 412 56 76; www.5serveis.com; Carrer de Pelai 50; M Catalunya).

Supplies Nappies (diapers), dummies, creams and formula can be bought at any of the city's many pharmacies. Nappies are cheaper in supermarkets.

Metro Barcelona's metro is accessible and great for families with pushchairs. Be mindful of pickpockets.

Accessibility The Ciutat Vella, with its unpredictable traffic and cobbled streets, is less buggy-friendly than the rest of Barcelona.

all the major tourist sights. Tourist offices, TMB transport authority offices and many hotels have leaflets explaining the system. Each of the two main circuits takes approximately two hours. The third circuit, from Port Olímpic to El Fòrum, runs from April to September and is less interesting.

Possession of a Bus Turístic ticket entitles you to discounts to some museums.

Barcelona Walking Tours WALKING
(Map p278; ☎93 285 38 34; www.barcelonaturisme.com; Plaça de Catalunya 17; Ⓜ Catalunya) The **Oficina d'Informació de Turisme de Barcelona** (Map p278; ☎93 285 38 34; www.barcelonaturisme.com; Plaça de Catalunya 17-S, underground; ⌚8.30am-9pm; Ⓜ Catalunya) organises several one-hour guided walking tours (available in English) exploring the Barri Gòtic (adult/child €16/free), Picasso's footsteps (€22/7) and Modernisme (€16/free). A two-hour gourmet food tour (€22/7) includes tastings. Various street-art walking and cycling tours (from €17) also take place. There is a 10% discount on all tours if you book online.

Devour Barcelona TOURS
(☎695 111832; www.devourbarcelonafoodtours.com; tours €49-99) Knowledgeable guides lead food tours around Gràcia, the Old City and Barceloneta that mix gastronomy with history. The various tastings and spots visited are especially focused on small, local producers and family-run joints. Most tours last three to four hours.

My Favourite Things TOURS
(☎637 265405; www.myft.net; tours from €26) Offers tours (with no more than 10 participants) based on numerous themes: street art, shopping, culinary tours, movies, musical journeys and forgotten neighbourhoods are among the offerings. Other activities include flamenco and salsa classes, cooking workshops, and bicycle rides in and out of Barcelona. Some of the more unusual activities cost more and times vary.

Bike Tours Barcelona CYCLING
(Map p266; ☎93 268 21 05; www.biketoursbarcelona.com; Carrer de l'Esparteria 3; per person €25; ⌚10am-7pm; Ⓜ Jaume I) One of numerous operators offering daily three-hour tours of the Barri Gòtic, waterfront, La Sagrada Família and other Gaudí landmarks. Tours depart from the tourist office on Plaça de Sant Jaume; check the website for departure times, and for details of vineyard tours. Bike rental is also available, from €5 per hour.

Festivals & Events

Festes de Santa Eulàlia CULTURAL
(http://lameva.barcelona.cat/santaeulalia; ⌚Feb) Around 12 February this big winter fest celebrates Barcelona's first patron saint with a week of cultural events, including parades of *gegants* (giants), open-air art installations, theatre, *correfocs* (fire runs) and *castells* (human castles).

Dia de Sant Jordi CULTURAL
(⌚23 Apr) This is the day of Catalonia's patron saint (George) and also the Day of the Book: lovers and friends give one another books and roses, publishers launch new titles. La Rambla, Plaça de Sant Jaume and other central city streets and squares are filled with book and flower stalls.

Primavera Sound MUSIC
(www.primaverasound.com; ⌚May-Jun) For three days in late May or early June, the Parc del Fòrum becomes the centre stage for a phenomenal range of international bands and DJs.

Sónar MUSIC
(www.sonar.es; ⌚Jun) Usually in mid-June, Sónar is Barcelona's massive celebration of electronic music, with DJs, exhibitions, sound labs, record fairs and urban art. Locations change each year.

La Revetlla de Sant Joan CULTURAL
(Nit de Sant Joan, Verbenas de Sant Joan; http://santjoan.bcn.cat; ⌚Jun) On 23 June locals hit the streets or hold parties at home to celebrate the Revetlla de Sant Joan (St John's Night), which involves drinking, dancing, bonfires and fireworks.

Pride Barcelona LGBT
(www.pridebarcelona.org; ⌚late Jun-early Jul) The Barcelona gay-pride festival is a week of celebrations held in late June or early July with a crammed program of culture and concerts, along with the massive gay-pride march on Sunday.

Festa Major de Gràcia CULTURAL
(www.festamajordegracia.org; ⌚Aug) Locals compete for the most elaborately decorated street in this popular week-long Gràcia festival held around 15 August. The fest also features free outdoor concerts, street fairs and other events.

Festes de la Mercè CULTURAL
(www.bcn.cat/merce; ⌚Sep) The city's biggest party involves four days of concerts, dancing,

castells (human castles), a fireworks display synchronised with the Montjuïc fountains, dances of giants on the Saturday, and *correfocs* – a parade of fireworks-spitting monsters and demons who run with the crowd – on the Sunday. Held around 24 September.

Reis/Reyes CULTURAL
(6 Jan) Epifanía (Epiphany) on 6 January is also known as the Dia dels Reis Mags/Día de los Reyes Magos (Three Kings' Day). The night before, children delight in the Cavalcada dels Reis Mags (Parade of the Three Kings), a colourful parade of floats and music during which tons of sweets are thrown into the crowd of eager kids (and not a few adults).

Sleeping

La Rambla & Barri Gòtic

Alberg Hostel Itaca HOSTEL €
(Map p256; 93 301 97 51; www.itacahostel.com; Carrer de Ripoll 21; dm €15-27, d without bathroom €76; M Jaume I) A bright, quiet hostel near the cathedral, Itaca has spacious dorms (sleeping six to 10 people) with parquet floors and spring colours, as well as two doubles. There's a lively vibe, and the hostel organises activities (pub crawls, flamenco concerts, free daily walking tours), making it a good option for solo travellers.

Kabul HOSTEL €
(Map p256; 93 318 51 90; www.kabul.es; Plaça Reial 17; dm from €11; M Liceu) The dorm rooms are small and cramped, the service is brusque, and if you're a light sleeper you can forget about falling asleep before 4am. But for partiers, centrally located Kabul is a top choice. It's easy to meet other travellers, with its nightly activities (pub crawls, club nights) and lively common areas (including a lounge with pool table, and a roof terrace).

Hotel Continental HOTEL €€
(Map p256; 93 301 25 70; www.hotelcontinental.com; La Rambla 138; s/d from €110/116; M Catalunya) In 1937 George Orwell stayed here on his return from the front during the Spanish Civil War, when Barcelona was tense with factional strife. The Continental's rooms are worn and rather spartan, but have romantic touches like ceiling fans, brass bedsteads and frilly bedclothes. An extra €20 yields a room with a small balcony overlooking La Rambla, and there is a free 24-hour buffet.

Vrabac B&B €€
(Map p256; 663 494029; https://vrabacguesthouse.wordpress.com; Carrer de la Portaferrissa 14; s/d incl breakfast €65/85; M Liceu) In a central location just off La Rambla, Vrabac is set in a beautifully restored heritage building complete with original decorative ceilings, exposed sandstone walls and large oil paintings. Rooms vary in size and features – the best have elegant ceramic tile floors, private bathrooms and sizeable balconies. The cheapest are small and basic, lack a bathroom and are not recommended. Cash only.

Soho House BOUTIQUE HOTEL €€€
(Map p256; 93 220 46 00; www.sohohousebarcelona.com; Plaça del Duc de Medinaceli 4; r from €300; M Drassanes) An elegant outpost of the famous London member's club, with luxuriously appointed rooms, an exclusive bar peopled with celebs, and a rooftop pool with incredible views out to sea. Cecconi's, the Italian restaurant on the ground floor, is worth a visit in its own right.

Serras Hotel BOUTIQUE HOTEL €€€
(Map p256; 93 169 18 68; www.hoteltheserras-barcelona.com; Passeig de Colom 9; r from €266; M Barceloneta) A fresh and funky five-star that has every comfort – including a rooftop bar with a small dipping pool and a terrific view over the port – but never feels stuffy. Rooms at the front are brighter and have a better view (from the bathtub, in some cases) but rooms at the side are spared the traffic noise.

Hotel Neri DESIGN HOTEL €€€
(Map p256; 93 304 06 55; www.hotelneri.com; Carrer de Sant Sever 5; d €362; M Liceu) This tranquil hotel occupies a beautifully adapted, centuries-old building backing onto Plaça de Sant Felip Neri. The sandstone walls and timber furnishings lend a sense of history, while the rooms feature cutting-edge technology, including plasma-screen TVs and infrared lights in the stone-clad designer bathrooms. Choose from a menu of sheets and pillows, and sun yourself on the roof deck.

Hotel 1898 LUXURY HOTEL €€€
(Map p256; 93 552 95 52; www.hotel1898.com; La Rambla 109; d €189-221; M Liceu) The former Compañía de Tabacos Filipinas (Philippines Tobacco Company) building has been resurrected as a luxury hotel, complete with an idyllic rooftop bar and pool. Some rooms are smallish, but deluxe rooms and suites have their own terraces. All combine modern

comfort and elegance, with hardwood floors and tasteful furniture.

DO Reial BOUTIQUE HOTEL €€€

(Map p256; ☎93 481 36 66; www.hoteldoreial.com; Plaça Reial 1; s/d incl breakfast from €288/360; ; M Liceu) Overlooking the magnificent plaza for which it is named, this 18-room property has handsomely designed rooms with beamed ceilings, hardwood floors and all-important soundproofing. The service is excellent and the facilities extensive, with a roof terrace (bar in summer), dipping pool, solarium and spa. Its excellent market-to-table restaurants draw in visiting foodies.

El Raval

Hotel Peninsular HOTEL €

(Map p256; ☎93 302 31 38; www.hotelpeninsular.net; Carrer de Sant Pau 34; s/d €53/80; ; M Liceu) An oasis on the edge of the slightly dicey Barri Xino, this former convent (which was connected by tunnel to the Església de Sant Agustí) has a plant-draped atrium extending its height and most of its length. The 60 rooms are simple, with tiled floors and whitewash, but spacious and well kept. There are some great bargains to be had during quiet periods.

★**Barceló Raval** DESIGN HOTEL €€

(Map p256; ☎93 320 14 90; www.barceloraval.com; Rambla del Raval 17-21; r from €144; ; M Liceu) Part of the city's plans to pull the El Raval district up by the bootstraps, this cylindrical designer hotel tower makes a 21st-century splash. The rooftop terrace offers fabulous views and the B-Lounge bar-restaurant is a lively joint for meals and cocktails. Rooms have slick aesthetics (white with lime green or ruby red splashes of colour), Nespresso machines and iPod docks.

Chic & Basic Ramblas DESIGN HOTEL €€

(Map p256; ☎93 302 71 11; www.chicandbasicramblashotel.com; Passatge Gutenberg 7; r €156-208; ; M Drassanes) The latest in the Chic & Basic chain is the most riotous to date, with quirky and colourful interiors that hit you from the second you walk in and see a vintage Seat 600 car in the foyer. Note that the name is misleading – the hotel is a couple of blocks into El Raval.

The rooms themselves are solid blocks of colour and each loosely pays homage to an aspect of Barcelona life in the 1960s. All have balconies and very basic kitchens.

Hotel Sant Agustí HOTEL €€

(Map p256; ☎93 318 16 58; www.hotelsa.com; Plaça de Sant Agustí 3; r €115-152; ; M Liceu) This former 18th-century monastery opened as a hotel in 1840, making it the city's oldest. The location is perfect – a quick stroll off La Rambla on a curious square. Rooms sparkle, and are mostly spacious and light filled. Consider the attic room with sloping ceiling and view of the rooftops.

Casa Camper DESIGN HOTEL €€€

(Map p256; ☎93 342 62 80; www.casacamper.com; Carrer d'Elisabets 11; s/d €277/297; ; M Catalunya) The massive foyer looks like a contemporary art museum, but the rooms, decorated in red, black and white, are the real surprise. Most have a sleeping and bathroom area, where you can contemplate the hanging gardens outside your window, with a separate, private sitting room with balcony, TV and hammock located across the corridor.

If you prefer more privacy, the city-view rooms integrate the sleeping and living areas. Get to the rooftop for sweeping cityscapes.

Hotel España HOTEL €€€

(Map p256; ☎93 550 00 00; www.hotelespanya.com; Carrer de Sant Pau 9-11; r €261-282; ; M Liceu) Known for its wonderful Modernista interiors in the dining rooms and bar, in which architect Domènech i Montaner, sculptor Eusebi Arnau and painter Ramon Casas had a hand, this hotel offers plush, contemporary rooms in a building that still manages to ooze a little history. There's a plunge pool and sun deck on the roof, along with a bar.

The ground-floor restaurant, La Fonda, serves good-value Catalan dishes.

La Ribera

Pensió 2000 PENSION €

(Map p278; ☎93 310 74 66; www.pensio2000.com; Carrer de Sant Pere més Alt 6; d €70-80; ; M Urquinaona) This 1st-floor, family-run place is opposite the anything-but-simple Palau de la Música Catalana. Seven reasonably spacious doubles have mosaic-tiled floors, and all have private bathrooms. You can eat your breakfast in the little courtyard.

Pensión Francia PENSION €

(Map p266; ☎93 319 03 76; www.milisa.com/P.Francia; Carrer de Rera Palau 4; d €90; ; M Barceloneta) The homey smell of laundry pervades this quaint little *pensión* in a great location close to the shore, the Parc de la Ciutadella and the nightlife of El Born. The 11 simple rooms are kept spick and span, with nothing much in the way of frills. Rooms with balconies benefit from plenty of natural light but little noise.

Hotel Banys Orientals BOUTIQUE HOTEL €€
(Map p266; ☎93 268 84 60; www.hotelbanysorientals.com; Carrer de l'Argenteria 37; s/d €72/120; ; Jaume I) Book well ahead to get into this magnetically popular designer haunt. Cool blues and aquamarines combine with dark-hued floors to lend this clean-lined boutique hotel a quiet charm. All rooms, on the small side, look onto the street or back lanes. There are more spacious suites in two other nearby buildings.

Grand Hotel Central DESIGN HOTEL €€€
(Map p256; ☎93 295 79 00; www.grandhotelcentral.com; Via Laietana 30; d €218; P; Jaume I) With supersoundproofed rooms no smaller than 21 sq metres, this design hotel, complete with rooftop infinity pool, is one of the standout hotel offerings along Via Laietana. Rooms are decorated in style, with high ceilings, muted colours (beiges, browns and creams), dark wooden floors and subtle lighting.

Barceloneta & the Waterfront

Equity Point Sea Hostel HOSTEL €
(Map p272; ☎93 231 20 45; www.equity-point.com; Plaça del Mar 1-4; dm €20-34; @; V15, 39, Barceloneta) This busy backpackers hostel is perched near the sea in a rather ugly high-rise. Rooms are basic, cramped and noisy (bring earplugs), but you won't find a room closer to the beach. A self-catering kitchen helps keep costs down. Note that no alcohol is allowed.

Bed & Beach GUESTHOUSE €€
(☎630 528156; www.bedandbeachbarcelona.com; Pasaje General Bassols 26; d €75-130, s/d without bathroom €40/70; ; Bogatell) Just 200m west of the beach on a quiet narrow street, this eight-room guesthouse has clean and comfortable rooms of varying styles. Some lack natural light, while others are bright, with simple modern furnishings and in-room kitchens. There's also a shared kitchen for self-caterers. The rooftop terrace is a fabulous spot for an afternoon drink.

Slippers are provided for the no-shoes-indoors policy.

Poblenou Bed & Breakfast GUESTHOUSE €€
(☎93 221 26 01; www.hostalpoblenou.com; Carrer del Taulat 30; s/d from €55/88; @; Llacuna) Just back from the beach and mere steps from the restaurant-lined Rambla del Poblenou, this 1930s house, with high ceilings and beautifully tiled floors, has six appealing rooms named for Spanish artists. Some of its uniquely decorated rooms have little balconies, and all have a fresh feel, light colours and comfortable beds. Minimum stay two nights from May to November.

Hotel 54 HOTEL €€
(Map p272; ☎93 225 00 54; www.hotel54barceloneta.es; Passeig de Joan de Borbó 54; s/d from €135/155; @; Barceloneta) Hotel 54 is all about location. Modern rooms, with dark tile floors and designer bathrooms, are sought after for the marina and sunset views. Other rooms look out over Barceloneta's lanes. You can also sit on the roof terrace and enjoy the panorama over the city and harbour.

Pullman Barcelona Skipper Hotel HOTEL €€€
(Map p272; ☎93 221 65 65; www.pullmanhotels.com; Avinguda del Litoral 10; d/ste from €212/475; P@; Ciutadella Vila Olímpica) Mesmerising views of Frank Gehry's shimmering Peix (p270) sculpture unfold from the rooftop infinity pool at this five-star hotel and from some of the 241 rooms, which are decorated in sleek timbers (some open to terraces). There's a second swimming pool at the base of the winged towers in the courtyard. Family-friendly facilities include interconnecting rooms, cots and babysitting services.

W Barcelona HOTEL €€€
(☎93 295 28 00; www.w-barcelona.com; Plaça de la Rosa del Vents 1; d/ste from €314/554; P@; V15, 39, Barceloneta) Designed by Barcelona-born architect Ricardo Bofill and opened in 2009, this glinting, spinnaker-shaped glass tower is a coastal landmark. Inside are 473 rooms and 67 suites that epitomise contemporary chic. Guests can flit between the gym, infinity pool (with an adjacent cocktail bar) and spa as well as the gourmet restaurant by star chef Carles Abellán.

La Sagrada Família & L'Eixample

Urbany Barcelona HOSTEL €
(☎93 245 84 14; www.urbanyhostels.com; Avinguda Meridiana 97; dm/s/tw from €29.50/118/126; @; Clot, Encants) Near El Poblenou, this massive 400-bed hostel is a good place

to meet other travellers, with its own bar and airy lounge set amid graffiti-esque artwork, plus a large terrace with views of Jean Nouvel's glowing Torre Glòries. Single and twin rooms have en suite bathrooms and small fridges. Self-caterers can cook up a storm in the kitchen.

Guests also have access to a pool and gym nearby.

★Praktik Rambla BOUTIQUE HOTEL €€
(Map p278; ☎93 343 66 90; www.hotelpraktikrambla.com; Rambla de Catalunya 27; s/d/tr from €119/140/165; ❄📶; M Passeig de Gràcia) This Modernista gem hides a gorgeous little boutique number. While the high ceilings and most of the original tile floors have been maintained, the 43 rooms have bold ceramics, spot lighting and contemporary art. There's a chilled reading area and deck-style lounge terrace. The handy location on a tree-lined boulevard is another plus.

This is Praktik's flagship; its other hotels in the same neighbourhood are the Praktik Bakery (with an in-house bakery), Praktik Garden (filled with plants) and Praktik Vinoteca (themed around wine).

Hotel Constanza BOUTIQUE HOTEL €€
(Map p278; ☎93 270 19 10; www.hotelconstanza.com; Carrer del Bruc 33; s/d/f from €85/135/190; ❄📶; M Urquinaona) This 46-room beauty has stolen the hearts of many a visitor to Barcelona. Design elements abound and little details like flowers in the bathroom add charm. Strewn with white sofas, the roof terrace is a stylish spot to relax while looking over L'Eixample's rooftops. Street-facing rooms have balconies.

Family rooms come with fold-out couches; baby cots are available. Several rooms are equipped for wheelchairs.

Anakena House HOTEL €€
(Map p278; ☎93 467 36 15; www.anakenahouse.com; Carrer del Consell de Cent 276; d from €157; ❄📶; M Passeig de Gràcia) The 1st floor of this Modernista building designed by Catalan architect Enric Sagnier i Villavecchia has been transformed into an intimate, elegant hotel. Its eight rooms have olive tones, antique furniture and designer lighting. All but one, which overlooks the courtyard, have street views.

Casa Bonay HOTEL €€
(Map p278; ☎93 545 80 70; www.casabonay.com; Gran Via de les Corts Catalanes 700; d/f from €150/234; ❄📶; M Tetuan) Hip Casa Bonay has sparingly decorated, stylishly tiled rooms, some with glassed-in balconies and others with terraces and outdoor showers. A bar opens on the roof terrace in summer. The hotel's unique selling point is the range of 'guest' shops, bars and restaurants it houses downstairs. These include a specialist coffee bar, a Vietnamese barbecue and a juice bar.

Room Mate Pau HOTEL €€
(Map p278; ☎93 343 63 00; www.room-matehotels.com; Carrer de Fontanella 7; d/ste from €192/252; ❄📶; M Catalunya) Just off Plaça de Catalunya, Room Mate Pau sits somewhere between an upscale hostel and boutique hotel. Its 66 rooms are cleverly configured with designer furnishings, good mattresses and USB-connected TVs. The striking interior terrace with a bar and vertical garden wall draws a young, hip crowd. Higher-priced rooms and suites come with terraces.

In the same neighbourhood are four other, equally striking Room Mate hotels: Anna, Emma, Carla and Gerard.

Hostal Oliva HOSTAL €€
(Map p278; ☎93 488 01 62; www.hostaloliva.com; Passeig de Gràcia 32; s/d from €79/89, without bathroom from €64/74; ❄@📶; M Passeig de Gràcia) A picturesque antique lift wheezes its way up to this 4th-floor *hostal*, a terrific, reliable cheapie in one of the city's most expensive neighbourhoods. Some of the single rooms can barely fit a bed but the doubles are big enough, and light and airy (some with tiled floors, others with parquet).

Avoid room 5, which is next to the entrance and night buzzer.

★The One Barcelona DESIGN HOTEL €€€
(Map p278; ☎93 214 20 70; www.hotelstheone.com; Carrer de Provença 277; d/ste from €230/330; M Diagonal) Opened in 2017, this stunning five-star property has 89 light-filled rooms including 25 suites. Works by Chilean artist Fernando Prats are displayed in rooms and public areas. A panoramic terrace (open May to October), with a bar, restaurant and plunge pool, and a spa with an indoor pool, Finnish sauna and 24-hour gym are just some of the up-to-the-minute amenities.

Margot House BOUTIQUE HOTEL €€€
(Map p278; ☎93 272 00 76; www.margothouse.es; Passeig de Gràcia 46; d/ste from €202/310; ❄@📶; M Passeig de Gràcia) Halfway up Passeig de Gràcia, this elegant boutique hotel with nine rooms (including five suites) is

perfect for those who want to be in the thick of it but still need peace, complete with a large, quiet book-filled sitting room with an honesty bar. Splash out for the front rooms, with more natural light. Rates include a fabulous gourmet buffet breakfast.

Cotton House HOTEL €€€

(Map p278; 93 450 50 45; www.hotelcottonhouse.com; Gran Via de les Corts Catalanes 670; d/tr/ste from €240/340/490; ; M Urquinaona) This splendid luxury hotel occupies the former headquarters of the Cottonmakers' Guild, something which is alluded to throughout, from the huge sprays of cotton bolls in the lobby to the room names (damask, taffeta etc). There's even a space off the library where you can select fabric and have a shirt custom made.

Mandarin Oriental DESIGN HOTEL €€€

(Map p278; 93 151 88 88; www.mandarinoriental.com/barcelona; Passeig de Gràcia 38-40; d/ste from €625/1350; P; M Passeig de Gràcia) At this imposing former bank, the 98 rooms have a contemporary designer style with straight lines, lots of white and muted colours. Many of the standard rooms (no smaller than 32 sq metres) have deep bathtubs, and all overlook either Passeig de Gràcia or an interior sculpted garden. Amenities include a spa with lap pool, fitness area and Michelin-starred restaurant.

Gràcia & Park Güell

★Casa Gràcia HOSTEL €

(Map p278; 93 174 05 28; www.casagraciabcn.com; Passeig de Gràcia 116; dm/s/d/tr/apt from €31/106/120/147/194; @; M Diagonal) A hostel with a difference, the hip Casa Gràcia has raised the bar for budget accommodation. Enticing common spaces include a terrace, library nook and artistically decorated lounge as well as a fully equipped self-catering kitchen – not to mention a restaurant and DJ-fuelled bar. Dorms aside, there are private rooms and apartments with their own terraces.

All are decorated in crisp white with bursts of colour. Casa Gràcia hosts a wide range of activities and events: cocktail-making workshops, yoga classes, wine tastings and screenings of foreign films (and FC Barcelona games) on the big-screen TV.

Generator Hostel HOSTEL €

(Map p286; 93 220 03 77; www.generatorhostels.com; Carrer de Còrsega 373; dm/d/q/penthouse from €20/109/186/329; M Diagonal) Part of the design-forward Generator brand, this stylish hostel has much to recommend it, including a quirky bar made from reclaimed lumber and recycled elevator parts and festooned with an explosion of paper lanterns. The rooms themselves are quite simple if adequately equipped – unless you opt for the penthouse room with a terrace offering panoramic views over the city.

★Hotel Casa Fuster HISTORIC HOTEL €€€

(Map p286; 93 255 30 00; www.hotelcasafuster.com; Passeig de Gràcia 132; d/ste from €287/396; P@; M Diagonal) This sumptuous Modernista mansion, built in 1908–11, is one of Barcelona's most luxurious hotels. Standard rooms are plush, if small. Period features have been restored at considerable cost and complemented by hydromassage tubs, plasma TVs and king-size beds. The rooftop terrace (with pool) offers spectacular views.

Camp Nou, Pedralbes & La Zona Alta

Alberg Mare de Déu de Montserrat HOSTEL €

(93 210 51 51; www.xanascat.cat; Passeig de la Mare de Déu del Coll 41-51; dm €24; P; 87, M Vallcarca) The main building of this 197-bed hostel is a magnificent former mansion with a Mudéjar-style lobby. Rooms sleep from six to 12 and the common areas are extensive and relaxed, though due to the thick walls, wi-fi can be hit-and-miss. It's 4km north of Barcelona's city centre, 100m uphill northeast from the Móra d'Ebre–Sant Eudald bus stop.

Anita's Bed & Breakfast B&B €€

(670 064258; www.anitasbarcelona.com; Carrer d'August Font 24; d incl breakfast from €95; @; 124) Spectacular views of the city and the Mediterranean beyond extend from the three rooms at this hillside B&B. Rooms are generously sized, with sitting areas and en suite bathrooms. The continental buffet breakfast (included in the rate) can be taken on the communal terrace, which also has sweeping vistas.

Fairmont Rey Juan Carlos I LUXURY HOTEL €€€

(93 364 40 40; www.fairmont.com/barcelona; Avinguda Diagonal 661-671; d/ste from €229/389; P@; M Zona Universitària) Like an ultramodern lighthouse at this southwest gateway to the city, the glass towers of this luxury megahotel hold more than 400 spacious rooms, most with stunning views. Extensive gardens, once part of the farmhouse

that stood here until well into the 20th century, surround the hotel. Facilities include two outdoor pools, a lake, a fitness club and five restaurants.

If you can drag yourself away, the nearby metro can take you to central Barcelona in around 20 minutes.

Montjuïc, Poble Sec & Sant Antoni

Pars Tailor's Hostel HOSTEL €

(Map p256; ☎93 250 56 84; www.parshostels.com; Carrer de Sepúlveda 146; dm €25-33; ; Ⓜ Urgell) Decorated like a mid-20th-century tailor's shop, with rooms themed around different fabrics, this popular hostel's common areas have old sewing machines, lovingly framed brassieres and vintage fixtures. You can shoot a round on the old billiards table, hang out in the comfy lounge, cook a meal in the well-equipped kitchen, or join one of the activities on offer.

The hostel organises day trips and pub crawls, hires bikes, arranges cooking classes (such as paella making), and holds evening gatherings over tapas and drinks. Friendly staff have good local insight into Barcelona.

Sant Jordi Mambo Tango HOSTEL €

(Map p292; ☎93 442 51 64; www.hostelmambotango.com; Carrer del Poeta Cabanyes 23; dm/d from €33/104, d with shared bathroom from €74; ; Ⓜ Paral·lel) A fun, international hang-out, the Mambo Tango has basic dorms (sleeping four to nine) and a welcoming, somewhat chaotic atmosphere. The beds are a touch on the hard side, and light sleepers should bring earplugs. With pub crawls and other nightly activities, it's a good place to meet other travellers.

★**Hotel Brummell** BOUTIQUE HOTEL €€

(Map p292; ☎93 125 86 22; www.hotelbrummell.com; Carrer Nou de la Rambla 174; d from €160; ; Ⓜ Paral·lel) Stylish Brummell has been turning heads since its 2015 opening. It's a thoughtfully designed hotel with a creative soul and great atmosphere. The 20 bright rooms have a minimalist design, and the best of the bunch have sizeable terraces with views and even outdoor soaking tubs. The cheapest (the 'poolside classic' rooms) feel a little tight.

Rooms are only a small part of Brummell's appeal. There's a great on-site restaurant/cafe, Brummell Kitchen (its weekend brunch is an event), a terrace with a small dip pool, and kind-hearted staff who are happy to share insight into Barcelona's lesser-known gems. Don't miss the vending machines in the corridor with bottles of wine and gourmet snacks, or the free yoga and exercise classes.

Hotel Market BOUTIQUE HOTEL €€

(Map p256; ☎93 325 12 05; www.hotelmarketbarcelona.com; Carrer del Comte Borrell 68; d/ste from €158/186; ; Ⓜ Sant Antoni) Attractively located in a renovated building along a narrow lane north of the grand old Sant Antoni market, this chic spot has 68 black-and-white-toned rooms with wide-plank floors, oversized armoires, bold art prints and nicely designed bathrooms (stone basins, rain showers). Some rooms have tiny (two-seat) balconies; suites come with terraces.

There's a first-rate restaurant and bar on the main floor, with outdoor seating on the lane. Room rates plummet outside high season.

Eating

Barcelona has a celebrated food scene fuelled by a combination of world-class chefs, imaginative recipes and magnificent ingredients fresh from farms and the sea. Catalan culinary masterminds like Ferran and Albert Adrià, and Carles Abellán have become international icons, reinventing the world of haute cuisine, while classic old-world Catalan recipes continue to earn accolades in dining rooms and tapas bars across the city.

La Rambla & Barri Gòtic

Federal CAFE €

(Map p256; ☎93 280 81 71; www.federalcafe.es; Passatge de la Pau 11; mains €7-10; ⏲9am-11pm Mon-Thu, to 11.30pm Fri & Sat, 9am-5pm Sun; ; Ⓜ Drassanes) Don't be intimidated by the industrial chic, the sea of open MacBooks or the stack of design mags – this branch of the Poble Sec Federal mothership is incredibly welcoming, with healthy, hearty and good-value food. Choose a salad and a topping (poached eggs, strips of chicken) or a yellow curry, say, and follow it up with a moist slab of carrot cake.

La Plata TAPAS €

(Map p256; ☎93 315 10 09; www.barlaplata.com; Carrer de la Mercè 28; tapas €2.50-5; ⏲9am-3.30pm & 6.30-11.30pm Mon-Sat; Ⓜ Jaume I) Tucked away on a narrow lane near the waterfront, La Plata is a humble but well-loved bodega that serves just three plates: *pescadito frito* (small fried fish), *butifarra* (sausage) and tomato salad. Add in the drinkable, affordable wines (per glass €1.20) and you have the makings of a fine predinner tapas spot.

Milk INTERNATIONAL €

(Map p256; 93 268 09 22; www.milkbarcelona.com; Carrer d'en Gignàs 21; mains €9-12; 9am-2am Thu-Mon, to 3am Fri & Sat; ; Jaume I) Also known to many as an enticing cocktail spot, Irish-run Milk's key role for Barcelona night owls is providing morning-after brunches (served till 4.30pm). Avoid direct sunlight and tuck into pancakes, eggs Benedict and other hangover dishes in a cosy lounge-like setting complete with ornate wallpaper, framed prints on the wall and cushion-lined seating. The musical selection is also notable.

Benedict BRUNCH €

(Map p256; 93 250 75 11; www.benedictbcn.com; Carrer d'en Gignás 23; mains €10-11; 9am-4pm Mon, 9am-4pm & 7pm-2am Tue-Fri, 9am-2.30am Sat & Sun; ; Jaume I) As the name suggests, brunch is the main event at friendly little Benedict, with eggs prepared every which way and an option for the full English fry-up. There's also a list of handmade burgers and club sandwiches, and in the evening various tapas are served, along with onion rings, deep-fried brie, chicken wings and other American favourites.

Taller de Tapas CATALAN €

(Map p256; 93 301 80 20; www.tallerdetapas.com; Plaça de Sant Josep Oriol 9; mains €7-10; noon-1am May-Sep, noon-midnight Oct-Apr; ; Liceu) A well-placed spot with outdoor seating on Plaça de Sant Josep Oriol, with a long list of tapas and more substantial bites.

★La Vinateria del Call SPANISH €€

(Map p256; 93 302 60 92; www.lavinateriadelcall.com; Carrer de Sant Domènec del Call 9; raciones €7-12; 7.30pm-1am; ; Jaume I) In a magical setting in the former Jewish quarter, this tiny jewel-box of a restaurant serves up tasty Iberian dishes including Galician octopus, cider-cooked chorizo and the Catalan *escalivada* (roasted peppers, aubergine and onions) with anchovies. Portions are small and made for sharing, and there's a good and affordable selection of wines.

★Cafè de l'Acadèmia CATALAN €€

(Map p256; 93 319 82 53; Carrer dels Lledó 1; mains €15-20; 1-3.30pm & 8-11pm Mon-Fri; ; Jaume I) Expect a mix of traditional Catalan dishes with the occasional creative twist. At lunchtime, local city hall workers pounce on the *menú del día* (€15.75). In the evening it is rather more romantic, as low lighting emphasises the intimacy of the beamed ceiling and stone walls. On warm days you can also dine in the pretty square at the front.

Belmonte TAPAS €€

(Map p256; 93 310 76 84; Carrer de la Mercè 29; tapas €4-10, mains €13-14; 8pm-midnight Tue-Fri, 1-3.30pm & 8pm-midnight Sat Jul-Oct, 7.30pm-midnight Tue-Thu, 1-3.30pm & 7.30pm-midnight Fri & Sat Oct-Jun; ; Jaume I) This tiny tapas joint in the southern reaches of Barri Gòtic whips up beautifully prepared small plates – including an excellent *truita* (tortilla), rich *patatons a la sal* (salted new potatoes with *romesco* sauce) and tender *carpaccio de pop* (octopus carpaccio). Wash it down with the homemade *vermut* (vermouth).

Ocaña INTERNATIONAL €€

(Map p256; 93 676 48 14; www.ocana.cat; Plaça Reial 13; mains €9.50-16; noon-2am Sun-Thu, to 2.30am Fri & Sat; ; Liceu) A flamboyant but elegantly designed space of high ceilings, chandeliers and plush furnishings, Ocaña blends late-night carousing with serious eating. The Spanish and Catalan dishes are given a creative and successful twist, and are now complemented on Thursday, Friday and Saturday nights by a superb selection of Mexican dishes.

You can still have a cocktail at Moorish-inspired Apotheke downstairs, or out on the Plaça Reial terrace, but it's a shame to pass up on the culinary offering.

Can Culleretes CATALAN €€

(Map p256; 93 317 30 22; www.culleretes.com; Carrer d'en Quintana 5; mains €10-18; 1.30-3.45pm & 8-10.45pm Tue-Sat, 1.30-3.45pm Sun; ; Liceu) Founded in 1786, Barcelona's oldest restaurant is still going strong, with tourists and locals flocking here to enjoy its rambling interior, old-fashioned tile-filled decor and enormous helpings of traditional Catalan food, including fresh seafood and sticky stews. From Tuesday to Friday there is a fixed lunch menu for €14.50.

Pla FUSION €€

(Map p256; 93 412 65 52; www.restaurantpla.cat; Carrer de la Bellafila 5; mains €17-23; 1.30-5.30pm & 7-11.30pm Sun-Thu, to midnight Fri & Sat; ; Jaume I) One of Gòtic's long-standing favourites, Pla is a stylish, romantically lit medieval dining room where the cooks churn out such temptations as oxtail braised in red wine, seared tuna with oven-roasted peppers, and polenta with seasonal mushrooms.

Koy Shunka JAPANESE €€€

(Map p256; ☎93 412 79 39; www.koyshunka.com; Carrer de Copons 7; tasting menu €89-132; ⏲1.30-3pm & 8.30-11pm Tue-Sat, 1.30-3pm Sun; Ⓜ Urquinaona) Down a narrow lane north of the cathedral, Koy Shunka opens a portal to exquisite dishes from the East – mouth-watering sushi, sashimi, seared Wagyu beef and flavour-rich seaweed salads are served alongside inventive cooked fusion dishes such as steamed clams with sake or tempura of scallops and king prawns with Japanese mushrooms. Don't miss the house speciality of tender *toro* (tuna belly).

Most diners sit at the large wraparound counter, where you can watch the culinary wizardry in action. Set multicourse menus are pricey but well worth it for those seeking a truly extraordinary dining experience.

Els Quatre Gats CATALAN €€€

(Map p256; ☎93 302 41 40; www.4gats.com; Carrer de Montsió 3; mains €23-29; ⏲1-4pm & 7pm-1am; Ⓜ Urquinaona) Once the lair of Barcelona's Modernista artists, Els Quatre Gats is a stunning example of the movement, inside and out, with its colourful tiles, geometric brickwork and wooden fittings. The restaurant is not quite as thrilling as its setting, though you can just have a coffee and a croissant in the cafe (open from 9am to 1am) at the front.

El Raval

Sésamo VEGETARIAN €

(Map p256; ☎93 441 64 11; Carrer de Sant Antoni Abat 52; mains €9-13; ⏲7pm-midnight Tue-Sun; 📶🥕; Ⓜ Sant Antoni) Widely held to be the best veggie restaurant in the city (admittedly not as great an accolade as it might be elsewhere), Sésamo is a cosy, fun place. The menu is mainly tapas, and most people go for the seven-course tapas menu (€25, wine included), but there are a few more substantial dishes. Nice touches include the home-baked bread and cakes.

Bar Muy Buenas CATALAN €

(Map p256; ☎93 807 28 57; Carrer del Carme 63; mains €9-13; ⏲1-3.30pm & 8-11pm Sun-Thu, 1-4pm & 8-11.30pm Fri & Sat; Ⓜ Liceu) After a couple of years in the doldrums, the Modernista classic Muy Buenas, which has been a bar since 1924, is back on its feet and under new ownership. Its stunning and sinuous century-old woodwork has been meticulously restored, as have its etched-glass windows and marble bar. These days it's more restaurant than bar, though the cocktails are impressive.

Though the kitchen (which turns out traditional Catalan dishes) is only open during the listed hours, Muy Buenas is open all day, until 2am (later on Friday and Saturday nights). From Monday to Friday it offers a two-course *menú del día* for €13.

Caravelle INTERNATIONAL €

(Map p256; ☎93 317 98 92; www.caravelle.es; Carrer del Pintor Fortuny 31; mains €10-13; ⏲9.30am-5pm Mon, 9.30am-midnight Tue-Thu, 10am-1am Fri & Sat, 10am-5pm Sun; Ⓜ Liceu) A bright little joint, beloved of the hipster element of El Raval and anyone with a discerning palate. It dishes up tacos as you've never tasted them (cod, lime aioli and radish, and pulled pork with roast corn and avocado), a superior steak sandwich on homemade brioche with pickled celeriac, and all manner of soul food.

Drinks are every bit as inventive – try the homemade ginger beer or grapefruit soda.

Bar Kasparo CAFE €

(Map p256; ☎93 302 20 72; www.kasparo.es; Plaça de Vicenç Martorell 4; mains €7-11; ⏲9am-11pm Tue-Sat, to midnight Jun-Sep; 📶; Ⓜ Catalunya) This friendly outdoor cafe, which overlooks a traffic-free square with a playground, is a favourite with the neighbourhood parents and serves juices, tapas and salads, as well as more substantial dishes from around the globe.

Elisabets CATALAN €

(Map p256; ☎93 317 58 26; Carrer d'Elisabets 2-4; mains €8-10; ⏲7.30am-11.30pm Mon-Thu & Sat, to 1.30am Fri Sep-Jul; Ⓜ Catalunya) A great old neighbourhood restaurant, its walls dotted with old radio sets, Elisabets is known for its unpretentious, good-value cooking. The *menú del día* (€12) changes daily, but if you prefer *a la carta,* try the *ragú de jabalí* (wild boar stew) and finish with *mel i mató* (Catalan dessert made from cheese and honey).

★Bar Pinotxo TAPAS €€

(Map p256; ☎93 317 17 31; www.pinotxobar.com; Mercat de la Boqueria; mains €9-17; ⏲7am-4pm Mon-Sat; Ⓜ Liceu) Bar Pinotxo is arguably La Boqueria's, and even Barcelona's, best tapas bar. The ever-charming owner, Juanito, might serve up chickpeas with pine nuts and raisins, a soft mix of potato and spinach sprinkled with salt, soft baby squid with cannellini beans, or a quivering cube of caramel-sweet pork belly.

Gats FUSION €€

(Map p256; 93 144 00 44; www.encompaniadelobos.com; Carrer d'en Xuclà 7; mains €9-19; noon-midnight; ; Liceu) A relatively recent addition to the *barri,* Gats has been an instant hit, and its terrace is constantly full. A deliciously fresh spread of dishes ranges from baba ganoush to Thai green curry, but there's plenty here that's local – try the 'mountain paella' with sausage, or the smoked sardines with honey and truffle. The kitchen is open all day.

Flax & Kale VEGETARIAN €€

(Map p256; 93 317 56 64; www.teresacarles.com; Carrer dels Tallers 74; mains €13-18; 9.30am-11.30pm Mon-Fri, from 10am Sat & Sun; ; Universitat) A far cry from the veggie restaurants of old, Flax & Kale marks a new approach (for Barcelona, at least) that declares that going meat-free does not mean giving up on choice, creativity or style. There are gluten-free and vegan options, and dishes include tacos with guacamole, aubergine and sour cashew cream, or Penang red curry.

Bar Cañete TAPAS €€

(Map p256; 93 270 34 58; www.barcanete.com; Carrer de la Unió 17; tapas from €4.50; 1pm-midnight Mon-Sat; ; Liceu) Part of a trend in creating upmarket versions of traditional bars with food to match. A long, narrow dining room holds an open kitchen along which runs a wooden bar, where diners sit – from here, they can point at what they want or order from a long list of classic tapas and *platillos* (plates for sharing).

Many of the choices (such as the mussels with a citric dressing) have a modern twist.

La Ribera

Paradiso/Pastrami Bar SMOKERY, COCKTAIL BAR €

(Map p266; 639 310671; www.rooftopsmokehouse.com; Carrer de Rera Palau 4; mains €7-9; 7pm-2am Mon-Thu, to 3am Fri & Sat; ; Barceloneta) A kind of Narnia-in-reverse, Paradiso is fronted with a snowy-white space, not much bigger than a wardrobe, with pastrami sandwiches, pulled pork and other home-cured delights. But this is only the portal – pull open the huge wooden fridge door, and step through into a glam, sexy speakeasy of a cocktail bar guaranteed to raise the most world-weary of eyebrows.

Euskal Etxea TAPAS €

(Map p266; 93 310 21 85; www.euskaletxeataberna.com; Placeta de Montcada 1; tapas €2.10; 10am-12.30am Sun-Thu, to 1am Fri & Sat; ; Jaume I) Barcelona has plenty of Basque and pseudo-Basque tapas bars, but this is the real deal. It captures the feel of San Sebastián better than many of its newer competitors. Choose your *pintxos* (Basque tapas piled on slices of bread), sip *txakoli* (Basque white wine), and keep the toothpicks so the staff can count them up and work out your bill.

Koku Kitchen Buns ASIAN €

(Map p266; 93 269 65 36; www.kokukitchen.es; Carrer del Comerç 29; mains €9-11; 1-4pm & 7.30-11.30pm; ; Barceloneta) Steamed buns stuffed with beef or pork with coriander, peanuts, pickled fennel and a sake sauce are the big draw here, but the starters, sides and even the excellent home-made lemonade are also worthy of note, as is the list of inventive cocktails. A great-value lunch *menú del día* is €13.

Cat Bar VEGAN €

(Map p256; www.catbarcat.com; Carrer de la Bòria 17; mains €6-9; 1-10pm Thu-Mon; ; Jaume I) This tiny little joint squeezes in a vegan kitchen, a great selection of local artisanal beers and a smattering of live music. The food mostly centres on a list of different burgers, plus a gluten-free dish of the day, tapas and hummus. The beers change regularly, but there is always one wheat, one porter, one gluten-free and an IPA.

Bormuth TAPAS €

(Map p266; 93 310 21 86; Carrer del Rec 31; tapas €4-10; noon-1.30am Sun-Thu, to 2.30am Fri & Sat; ; Jaume I) Bormuth has tapped into the vogue for old-school tapas with modern-day service and decor, and serves all the old favourites – *patatas bravas* (potatoes in a spicy tomato sauce), *ensaladilla* (Russian salad) and tortilla – along with some less predictable and superbly prepared numbers (try the chargrilled red pepper with black pudding).

The split-level dining room is never less than animated, but there's a more peaceful space with a single long table if you can assemble a group.

En Aparté FRENCH €

(93 269 13 35; www.enaparte.es; Carrer de Lluís el Piadós 2; mains €8-13; 10am-1am Mon-Thu, to 2am Fri & Sat, to 12.30am Sun; ; Arc de Triomf) A great low-key place for good-quality French food, just off the quiet Plaça de Sant Pere. The restaurant is small but spacious, with sewing-machine tables and vintage de-

tails, and floor-to-ceiling windows that bring in some wonderful early-afternoon sunlight.

The lunch menu (€13) is excellent, offering a salad (such as beetroot, apple and walnut), and a quiche or another dish, such as stuffed peppers with a potato gratin. Brunch – including French toast, eggs Benedict and muesli with yoghurt – is served on weekends.

★Casa Delfín CATALAN €€

(Map p266; ☎93 319 50 88; www.facebook.com/Casa-Delfin-326525620764565/; Passeig del Born 36; mains €10-17; ⏰8am-midnight Sun-Thu, to 1am Fri & Sat; 📶; Ⓜ Jaume I) One of Barcelona's culinary delights, Casa Delfín is everything you dream of when you think of Catalan (and Mediterranean) cooking. Start with the tangy and sweet *calçots* (spring onions; February and March only) or salt-strewn *Padrón* peppers, moving on to grilled sardines speckled with parsley, then tackle the meaty monkfish roasted in white wine and garlic.

Or tease some mussels and clams out of their shells while crunching on the Catalan *coca* flatbread – done here to perfection and smeared with tomatoes and olive oil. For the finale, choose the Eton Mess (the English owner Kate's only tribute to her homeland) – a long glass of mashed-up cream, meringue and berries.

Nakashita JAPANESE €€

(☎93 295 53 78; www.nakashitabcn.com; Carrer del Rec Comtal 15; mains €12-22; ⏰1.30-4pm & 8.30pm-midnight Mon-Sun; 📶; Ⓜ Arc de Triomf) Brazil's particular immigration story means it has a tradition of superb Japanese food, and the Brazilian chef at Nakashita is no slouch, turning out excellent sashimi, maki rolls, softshell crab and *kakiage* (a mix of tempura). One of the best Japanese restaurants in the city, with just a handful of tables – book if you can.

Bar del Pla TAPAS €€

(Map p266; ☎93 268 30 03; www.bardelpla.cat; Carrer de Montcada 2; mains €12-16; ⏰noon-11pm Mon-Thu, to midnight Fri & Sat; 📶; Ⓜ Jaume I) A bright and occasionally rowdy place, with glorious Catalan tiling, a vaulted ceiling and bottles of wine lining the walls. At first glance, the tapas at informal Bar del Pla are traditionally Spanish, but the riffs on a theme display an assured touch. Try the ham croquettes, Wagyu burger, T-bone steak or marinated salmon, yoghurt and mustard.

Ginette FRENCH €€

(☎93 280 95 03; www.ginette.es; Carrer del Rec Comtal 12; mains €16-18; ⏰8.30am-2am Tue-Sun Sep-Jun, 6pm-2am Mon-Sat Jul & Aug; Ⓜ Arc de Triomf) Opened in 2017, with a Parisian chef at the helm, Ginette blends Scandinavian and Barcelona chic in its decor, but the menu has an overwhelmingly Gallic feel, with dishes such as cod *meunière* with hazelnuts or duck *magret* with orange. There are also tapas – and even these include a *croque monsieur* with Comté cheese.

El Chigre TAPAS €€

(Map p266; ☎93 782 63 30; http://elchigre1769.com; Carrer dels Sombrerers 7; mains €10-17; ⏰noon-11.45pm, from 1pm Mon-Fri Nov-Mar; Ⓜ Jaume I) Styling itself as part Asturian cider house and part Catalan *vermuteria* (bar specialising in vermouth, served on ice with a slice of orange and a green olive), El Chigre brings sophisticated versions of classic dishes from both regions to its menu. Try the superb tomato and tuna salad with tomato *gelée,* or the puffed corn *tortos* with lamb stew.

Santagustina TAPAS €€

(Map p266; ☎93 315 79 04; www.santagustina.com; Plaça Sant Agustí Vell 9; mains €9-14; ⏰noon-1am Sun-Thu, to 3am Fri & Sat; 📶; Ⓜ Arc de Triomf) This tapas bar-restaurant has tables outside on a charming little plaza. Invoking a slightly wicked ecclesiastical theme, with menus sectioned into 'Blessed Tapas', 'Divine Tapas', 'Immaculate Tapas' and 'Temptations', it serves up well-executed Spanish and Catalan food – oxtail stew, 'Granny's meatballs', grilled octopus etc – in small portions designed for sharing. Service could be a little more attentive.

Barceloneta & the Waterfront

El 58 TAPAS €

(Le cinquante huit; Rambla del Poblenou 58; tapas €3.50-12; ⏰1.30-11pm Tue-Sat, to 4pm Sun; Ⓜ Llacuna) This French-Catalan place serves imaginative, beautifully prepared tapas dishes: codfish balls with romesco sauce, scallop ceviche, *tartiflette* (cheese, ham and potato casserole), salmon tartare. Solo diners can take a seat at the marble-topped front bar. The back dining room with its exposed brick walls, industrial light fixtures and local artworks is a lively place to linger over a long meal.

L'Òstia TAPAS

(Map p272; ☎93 221 47 58; www.facebook.com/barceloneta; Plaça de la Barceloneta 1; tapas €2.50-8, mains €11-19; ⏰10am-11.45pm; 📶; Ⓜ Barceloneta)

On a charming hidden square, this neighbourhood bar opens to a terrace facing Barceloneta's beautiful baroque church Església de Sant Miquel del Port. Tapas reflect the area's heritage but also come with fusion twists like Szechuan pepper-dusted sardines or Spanish omelette with duck and truffles. Wines are primarily Catalan; the sangría is some of the best around.

A heated marquee sets up on the terrace in winter.

La Bodega La Peninsular TAPAS €
(Map p272; ☎93 221 40 89; www.tabernaycafetin.es; Carrer del Mar 29; tapas €3.50-9; ⊙11.30am-midnight; Ⓜ Barceloneta) Wine barrels double as tables at this traditional bodega, where over three dozen different tapas dishes pair with Catalan vintages and house-made vermouth. Adhering to the Slow Food ethos, ingredients are organic, seasonal and locally sourced; try the *mojama* (salt-cured, air-dried tuna) or renowned spicy *bombas* (meat and potato croquettes) topped with tangy aioli. It's standing room only most nights.

Timesburg Poblenou BURGERS €
(www.timesburg.com; Carrer de Pujades 168; burgers €6-13; ⊙1-4.30pm & 8.30pm-midnight; 📶; Ⓜ Poblenou) Barcelona success story Timesburg has several locations including this cavernous mezzanine space in El Poblenou. Burger buns are stamped with its logo; its 16 different varieties include La Massimo (beef, parmesan, sun-dried tomato, sunflower seeds and red onion) and Balear (Mallorca sausage, Mahón cheese, capers and honey mayo). Hand-cut fries are twice-fried in olive oil.

Més De Vi TAPAS €
(☎93 007 91 51; www.mesdvi.cat; Carrer de Marià Aguiló 123; tapas €8-13; ⊙7-11pm Mon, 1-4pm & 7-11pm Tue-Sat; Ⓜ Poblenou) At this buzzing wine bar, Catalan wines are accompanied by tapas dishes that are inventive and delicious: courgette pesto and burrata salad, red tuna pickled with Peruvian yellow chilli, smoked mackerel with aubergine caviar and lamb neck with mashed baked turnip. Brick walls, hardwood floors, timber tables and studded Chesterfield sofas give it a cosy ambience.

Cal Cuc ASIAN €
(☎93 000 28 37; www.mosquitotapas.com/calcuc; Carrer del Taulat 109; tapas €4-8; ⊙6pm-midnight Mon-Thu, 1pm-1am Fri-Sun; 🖉; Ⓜ Poblenou) At this sleek spot, Asian street-food-inspired tapas such as Chinese-inspired bang bang aubergine (in spicy sauce), *gyoza* (Japanese pan-fried dumplings), kimchi (Korean fermented cabbage), tofu *larb* (Laotian marinated tofu) and *takoyaki* (Japanese battered octopus) pair with craft beers from local brewers including BeerCat, Guineu and Les Clandestines.

Filferro TAPAS €
(Map p272; ☎93 221 98 36; Carrer de Sant Carles 29; tapas €5-8, mains €7-12; ⊙10am-1am; 📶🖉; Ⓜ Barceloneta) One of the few spots in Barceloneta where the focus isn't on seafood, Filferro has a loyal following for its good-value tapas, *bocadillos* (filled rolls), salads and pasta. It has a warmly lit and eclectically furnished interior, or you can dine at an outdoor table on the square (popular with families, with a playground just a few steps away).

Aguaribay VEGETARIAN €
(☎93 300 37 90; www.aguaribay-bcn.com; Carrer del Taulat 95; mains €7-13; ⊙1-4pm Mon-Wed, 1-4pm & 8.30-11pm Thu-Sat, 1-4.30pm Sun; 🖉; Ⓜ Llacuna) Polished Aguaribay serves a small well-executed à la carte menu by night: miso and smoked tofu meatballs, soba noodles with shiitake mushrooms, and seasonal vegetables with rich black rice, along with craft beers and biodynamic wines. At lunchtime, stop in for the prix-fixe lunch specials, which change daily. All ingredients are organic; vegan and gluten-free options abound.

Guingueta de la Barceloneta SPANISH €
(www.carlesabellan.com; Platja de la Barceloneta; dishes €6-16; ⊙9am-midnight Mar-Nov; Ⓜ Barceloneta) Part of Carles Abellán's gastronomic empire, this open-sided beachside spot serves salads, sandwiches (including a Spanish omelette sandwich) and tapas (such as cod croquettes, marinated anchovies, and cockles with tomato salsa), accompanied by freshly squeezed juices, individual twists on classic cocktails (Napoleon Sour, Cubano Loco) and sparkling sea views.

Baluard Barceloneta BAKERY €
(Map p272; Carrer del Baluard 38; items €1-3.50; ⊙8am-9pm Mon-Sat; Ⓜ Barceloneta) Baluard has one of the best ranges of freshly baked breads in the city, along with filled baguettes that are perfect for beach picnics. It also bakes a range of tempting pastries, such as *xuiuixo* (deep-fried custard-filled pastries from Girona) and *bunyols* (doughnut-shaped pastries stuffed with cheese or jam), and tarts such as fig or wild berries.

El Ben Plantat INTERNATIONAL €

(Map p272; ☎93 624 38 32; Carrer de Sant Carles 21; tapas €5-10, lunch specials €9; ⊗1-4pm & 8.30-11.30pm Wed-Mon; ✎; Ⓜ Barceloneta) A welcome find in seafood-centric Barceloneta, El Ben Plantat serves a varied menu of small plates, with excellent vegetarian choices (hummus, guacamole and chips, tofu pâté, stuffed marinated mushrooms). On weekdays you'll also find good value multicourse lunch specials – mussels with potatoes, homemade falafel, sausage with ratatouille, vegetable croquettes.

La Cova Fumada TAPAS €

(Map p272; ☎93 221 40 61; Carrer del Baluard 56; tapas €4-12; ⊗9am-3.15pm Mon-Wed, 9am-3.15pm & 6-8.15pm Thu & Fri, 9am-1pm Sat; Ⓜ Barceloneta) There's no sign and the setting is decidedly downmarket, but this tiny, buzzing family-run tapas spot always packs in a crowd. The secret? Mouthwatering *pulpo* (octopus), calamari, sardines, *bombas* (meat and potato croquettes served with aioli) and grilled *carxofes* (artichokes) cooked in the open kitchen. Everything is amazingly fresh.

Bitácora TAPAS €

(Map p272; ☎93 319 11 10; Carrer de Balboa 1; tapas €4-12.50; ⊗9am-2.30am Mon-Fri, from 10am Sat & Sun; Ⓜ Barceloneta) Bitácora is a neighbourhood favourite for its simple but congenial ambience and well-priced tapas plates, which come in ample portions. There's also a small hidden terrace at the back. Top picks: *ceviche de pescado* (fish ceviche), *chipirones* (baby squid) and *gambas a la plancha* (grilled prawns). Cash only, no cards.

There's a second location in **El Poblenou** (☎93 277 87 12; www.facebook.com/bitacorapoblenou; Plaça de la Unió 24; tapas €2-8, one/two/three course lunch €5/7/10; ⊗9am-1am; Ⓜ Poblenou).

Can Maño SEAFOOD €

(Map p272; Carrer del Baluard 12; mains €7-15; ⊗8-11pm Mon, 8.30am-4pm & 8-11pm Tue-Fri, 8.30am-4pm Sat; Ⓜ Barceloneta) It may look like a dive, but you'll need to be prepared to wait before being squeezed in at a packed table for a raucous night of *raciones* (full-plate-size tapas serving) over a bottle of cloudy white *turbio* (Galician wine) at this family-run stalwart. The seafood is abundant, with first-rate squid, prawns and fish served at rock-bottom prices.

Vaso de Oro TAPAS €

(Map p272; ☎93 319 30 98; www.vasodeoro.com; Carrer de Balboa 6; tapas €4-12; ⊗11am-midnight; Ⓜ Barceloneta) Always packed with diners, this narrow bar gathers a high-spirited crowd who come for fantastic tapas. Wisecracking, white-jacketed waiters serve plates of grilled *gambes* (prawns), *foie a la plancha* (grilled liver pâté) or *solomillo* (sirloin) chunks. Want something a little different to drink? Ask for a *flauta cincuenta* – half lager and half dark beer.

El Tío Ché CAFE €

(www.eltioche.es; Rambla del Poblenou 44; dishes €2-6; ⊗10am-10pm Sun-Thu, to 1am Fri & Sat; Ⓜ Poblenou) First opened back in 1912 (in El Born), this local icon is famed for its *horchata,* a sweet and refreshing if mildly grainy drink made of tigernut milk. Some love it, others less so, though you can also opt for other homemade beverages along with sandwiches and ice cream.

★Isla Tortuga TAPAS €€

(Map p272; ☎93 198 40 74; www.encompaniadelobos.com/en/isla-tortuga; Carrer de Llauder 1; tapas €3-9.50, mains €11-18; ⊗noon-midnight; 📶; Ⓜ Barceloneta) Stripped timbers, bare bricks and a namesake *tortuga* (turtle) above the bar create a stylised castaway feel in this chic space. Seasonally changing menus incorporate over 20 contemporary tapas dishes (eg vodka-steamed clams, stingray with black butter, grilled octopus with Kalamata tapenade, kimchi-stuffed Padrón peppers) along with tacos (Peking duck, crackling prawn, marinated rib) and several varieties of paella.

★Can Recasens CATALAN €€

(☎93 300 81 23; www.facebook.com/canrecasens; Rambla del Poblenou 102; mains €8-21; ⊗8.30am-1.30pm & 5-11.45pm Mon, to 1am Tue-Thu, to 3am Fri, 9am-1pm & 9pm-3am Sat, 9pm-1am Sun; Ⓜ Poblenou) One of El Poblenou's most romantic settings, Can Recasens hides a warren of warmly lit rooms full of oil paintings, flickering candles, fairy lights and baskets of fruit. The food is outstanding, with a mix of salads, smoked meats, fondues, and open sandwiches topped with delicacies like wild mushrooms and Brie, *escalivada* (grilled vegetables) and Gruyère, and spicy chorizo.

There's live jazz every second Wednesday.

Green Spot VEGETARIAN €€

(Map p272; ☎93 802 55 65; www.encompaniadelobos.com/en/the-green-spot; Carrer de la Reina Cristina 12; mains €10-15; ⊗12.30pm-midnight Mon-Fri, from 1pm Sat & Sun; ✎; Ⓜ Barceloneta) Purple carrot salad with papaya and feta, aubergine and courgette tacos, buckwheat and spinach *spätzle* (hand-rolled egg noodles), sweet potato gnocchi with black truffle, and hemp pizza with cashew cheese and asparagus are among the inventive vegetarian, vegan and gluten-free dishes presented in a stylish, minimalist dining room with vaulted ceilings. Live flamenco plays on Tuesday evenings.

Kaiku SEAFOOD **€€**

(Map p272; 93 221 90 82; www.restaurantkaiku.cat; Plaça del Mar 1; mains €13-19; 1-3.30pm & 7-10.30pm Tue-Sat, 1-3.30pm Sun; M Barceloneta) Overlooking the waterfront at the south end of Barceloneta, Kaiku incorporates ingredients from the nearby fish market in dishes such as crayfish with mint, swordfish carpaccio with avocado and sun-dried tomatoes, chilli-smeared tuna with green apples and mushrooms, and rice dishes for two.

★Oaxaca MEXICAN **€€€**

(Map p272; 93 018 06 59; www.oaxacacuinamexicana.com; Pla de Palau 19; mains €22-32; 1-4pm & 8pm-midnight; ; M Barceloneta) Chef Joan Bagur trained in Mexico for a decade under traditional cooks, and has his own garden of Mexican plants, which supplies ingredients for culinary creations like *coyoacán* (roast corn with chilli ash) and *cochinita pibil* (slow-roasted pork tacos). Hefty tables are made from Mexican hardwoods and original Mexican art lines the walls; there's alfresco seating under the cloisters.

Bagur's neighbouring bar, La Mezcalería d'Oaxaca, is guarded by a carved wooden *calaca* (Day of the Dead skeleton) and serves over 200 varieties of mezcal in a striking space with cowhide-covered chairs, taxidermied birds and silent Mexican black-and-white films screening on one wall.

★La Barra de Carles Abellán SEAFOOD **€€€**

(Map p272; 93 760 51 29; www.carlesabellan.com/mis-restaurantes/la-barra; Passeig Joan de Borbó 19; tapas €5-8.50, mains €24-36; 1.30-4pm & 8-11pm; M Barceloneta) Catalan chef Carles Abellán's stunning glass-encased, glossy-tiled restaurant celebrates seafood in tapas such as pickled octopus, mini anchovy omelettes and fried oyster with salmon roe. Even more show-stopping are the mains: grilled razor clams with *ponzu* citrus sauce, squid filled with spicy poached egg yolk, stir-fried sea cucumber, and lush lobster paella with smoked prawns.

Video screens let diners watch the kitchen staff in action downstairs. Most seats are at long, communal counter-style tables, making it great for solo diners.

Restaurant 7 Portes SEAFOOD **€€€**

(Map p272; 93 319 30 33; www.7portes.com; Passeig d'Isabel II 14; mains €19-32; 1pm-1am; ; M Barceloneta) Founded in 1836 as a cafe and converted into a restaurant in 1929, 7 Portes has a grand setting beneath the cloisters, and exudes an old-world atmosphere with its wood panelling, tiles, mirrors and plaques naming luminaries – such as Orson Welles – who have passed through. Paella is the speciality, or try the *gran plat de marisc* ('big plate of seafood').

Els Pescadors SEAFOOD **€€€**

(93 225 20 18; www.elspescadors.com; Plaça de Prim 1; mains €18-42; 1-3.45pm & 8-11.30pm; ; M Poblenou) On a picturesque square lined with low houses and long-established South American *bella ombre* trees, this quaint family restaurant continues to serve some of the city's best grilled fish and seafood-and-rice dishes. There are three dining areas inside: two are quite modern, while the main room preserves its old tavern flavour. On warm nights, try for a table outside.

Can Majó SEAFOOD **€€€**

(Map p272; 93 221 54 55; www.canmajo.es; Carrer del Almirall Aixada 23; mains €15-36; 1-4pm & 8-11.30pm Tue-Sat, 1-4pm Sun; M Barceloneta) On a square across from the beachside promenade, with outdoor tables and heat lamps in winter, Can Majó has a long and steady reputation for fine seafood, particularly its rice dishes and bountiful *suquets* (fish stews). The bouillabaisse of fish and seafood is succulent.

La Sagrada Família & L'Eixample

★Tapas 24 TAPAS **€**

(Map p278; 93 488 09 77; www.carlesabellan.com; Carrer de la Diputació 269; tapas €2.20-12; 9am-midnight; ; M Passeig de Gràcia) Hotshot chef Carles Abellán runs this basement tapas haven known for its gourmet versions of old faves. Highlights include the *bikini* (toasted ham and cheese sandwich – here the ham is cured and the truffle makes all the difference) and zesty *boquerones al limón* (lemon-marinated anchovies). You can't book but it's worth the wait.

For dessert, choose *xocolata amb pa, sal i oli* (delicious balls of chocolate in olive oil with a touch of salt and wafer).

Hawker 45 ASIAN €

(Map p278; ☎93 763 83 15; Carrer de Casp 45; mains €8.50-16; ⏰1-4pm & 8-11pm Mon-Fri, 12.30-4pm & 8-11.30pm Sat, 12.30-4pm Sun; Ⓜ Tetuan) Taking its cues from an Asian hawkers market, this aromatic spot sizzles up street-food dishes such as spicy Malaysian squid laksa, Indonesian lamb satay, Korean Kalbi pork ribs with rice cakes, Thai crying tiger beef salad and Singaporean green mango sambal with steamed crab. Its six-course tasting menu (€35) is best paired with craft beers (€42) or Asian-inspired cocktails (€60).

Dine at the long, red bar overlooking the open kitchen or head out the back to the cavernous postindustrial dining space with bare beams and ventilation pipes.

Copasetic CAFE €

(☎93 532 76 66; www.copaseticbarcelona.com; Carrer de la Diputació 55; mains €6-13.50; ⏰10.30am-midnight Tue & Wed, to 1am Thu, to 2am Fri & Sat, to 5.30pm Sun; 📶🖉; Ⓜ Rocafort) Decked out with retro furniture, Copasetic has a fun, friendly vibe. The menu holds plenty for everyone, whether your thing is eggs Benedict, wild-berry tartlets or a fat, juicy burger. There are lots of vegetarian, gluten-free and organic options, and superb (and reasonably priced) weekend brunches. Lunch *menús* (Tuesday to Friday) cost between €9.50 and €12.

Charlot Cafè CAFE €

(Map p278; ☎93 451 15 65; Carrer d'Aribau 67; dishes €6.50-13.50; ⏰kitchen 8.30am-10pm Mon-Fri, 7am-10pm Sat, bar to 3am Fri & Sat; 📶🖉; Ⓡ FGC Provença) Movie stills and posters, from *Breakfast at Tiffany's* to *Pulp Fiction,* line the walls at Charlot. Get a morning kick-start with a truffled *tortilla española* (Spanish omelette) or eggs baked in Iberian ham, or drop by for lunch (sautéed quinoa salad; burgers with hand-cut fries) or dinner (duck with blackberry sauce). Craft beers and cocktails are all-day-long options.

Cantina Mexicana MEXICAN €

(☎93 667 66 68; www.cantinalamexicana.es; Carrer de València 427; mains €7-13; ⏰1pm-midnight; 🖉; Ⓜ Sagrada Família) Just far enough from La Sagrada Família to dodge the crowds, this simply decorated spot serves authentic Mexican fare, including over 20 different corn or flour tacos (such as sautéed shrimp and beans), *cochinita pibil* (traditional slow-roasted pork seasoned with annatto seeds) and four styles of ceviche. Vegetarian options include a delicious pumpkin-flower quesadilla.

Granja Petitbo MEDITERRANEAN €

(Map p278; ☎93 265 65 03; www.granjapetitbo.com; Passeig de Sant Joan 82; sandwiches €4-8, mains €8-12; ⏰9am-11pm Mon-Wed, 9am-11.30pm Thu & Fri, 10am-11.30pm Sat, 10am-5pm Sun; 📶; Ⓜ Girona) High ceilings, battered leather armchairs and dramatic flower arrangements set the tone in this sunny little corner cafe, beloved of local hipsters and young families. As well as an all-day parade of homemade cakes, freshly squeezed juices and superior coffee, there are burgers, salads and pastas, along with a brunch menu on weekends.

Koyuki JAPANESE €

(Map p278; ☎93 237 84 90; http://koyuki.eltenedor.rest; Carrer de Còrsega 242; mains €8-12; ⏰1-3.30pm & 8-11pm Tue-Sun; Ⓡ FGC Provença) This unassuming basement Japanese diner is one of those rough-edged diamonds. Order from the menu complete with pictures courtesy of the Japanese owner – you won't be disappointed. The variety of *sashimi moriawase* is generous and constantly fresh. The tempura udon is a particularly hearty noodle option with breaded shrimp.

★ **Auto Rosellon** INTERNATIONAL €€

(Map p278; ☎93 853 93 20; www.autorosellon.com; Carrer de Rosselló 182; mains €12-18; ⏰8am-1am Mon-Wed, 8am-2am Thu & Fri, 9am-2am Sat, 9am-midnight Sun; 📶🖉; Ⓡ FGC Provença) 🍃 With cornflower-blue paintwork and all its fresh produce on display, Auto Rosellon utilises mostly organic ingredients sourced from small producers and its own garden in dishes like eggs Benedict, salmon tartare with avocado, ricotta gnocchi with confit tomatoes and thyme, and slow-roasted pork tacos. Homemade juices and rose lemonade are exceptional; there are also great cocktails and craft beers.

Mr Kao DIM SUM €€

(Map p278; ☎93 445 25 88; www.misterkao.com; Carrer de València 271; dim sum €2.80-4, mains €11-28; ⏰12.30-3.30pm & 8.30-11.30pm Tue-Sat, 12.30-3.30pm Sun; Ⓜ Passeig de Gràcia) Within the grand Hotel Claris, this elegant Shanghai-style dim sum restaurant serves top-flight dumplings. They're not cheap, but every bite is a joy; the *jiao zi* with pig's trotters are especially good, as are the *siu mai* with langoustines and trout roe. More substantial dishes include Peking duck and noodles with wild mushrooms, poached egg and truffles.

Entrepanes Díaz SANDWICHES €€
(Map p278; 93 415 75 82; Carrer de Pau Claris 189; sandwiches €6-10, tapas €3-10; 1pm-midnight; Diagonal) Gourmet sandwiches, from roast beef to suckling pig or crispy squid with squid-ink aioli, are the highlight at this sparkling old-style bar, along with sharing plates of Spanish specialities such as sea urchins and prawn fritters or blood-sausage croquettes. The policy of only hiring experienced waiters over 50 lends a certain gravitas to the operation and some especially charming service.

Black-and-white photos of Barcelona line the walls.

Parking Pizza PIZZA €€
(93 633 96 45; www.parkingpizza.com; Carrer de Londres 98; pizza €9.50-14.50; 1-4pm & 8-11pm Mon-Sat, 1-4pm Sun; FGC Provença) In this garage-style space, you might well have to share a long unvarnished wooden table, squeezed in on a cardboard box stool. The wood-fired pizzas more than make up for any forced intimacy, however, as do the starters, which include a creamy burrata *'stracciatella'* and a superb red quinoa salad with guacamole and a poached egg.

Chicha Limoná MEDITERRANEAN €€
(Map p278; 93 277 64 03; www.chichalimona.com; Passeig de Sant Joan 80; mains €12-17; 9.30am-1am Tue-Thu, to 2am Fri & Sat, to 5pm Sun; ; Tetuan) Passeig de Sant Joan is a hipster hot spot, and bright, bustling Chicha Limoná has provided them with somewhere great to eat. Steak tartare with yuzu dressing, rabbit tacos, yoghurt-marinated salmon and tequila, mango and chilli sorbet are among the oft-changing dishes (set menu €13.90), along with steaming pizza.

Cerveseria Catalana TAPAS €€
(Map p278; 93 216 03 68; Carrer de Mallorca 236; tapas €3-14; 9am-1.30am; FGC Provença) The 'Catalan Brewery' is perfect at all hours: for a morning coffee and croissant, or sangria, *montaditos* (canapés) and tapas at lunch or dinner. You can sit at the bar, on the pavement terrace or in the restaurant at the back. The variety of hot tapas, salads and other snacks draws a well-dressed crowd. No reservations.

Cafe Emma BISTRO €€
(Map p278; 93 215 12 16; www.cafe-emma.com; Carrer de Pau Claris 142; mains €14-25.50; 8am-10.30pm Mon-Fri, 9am-10.30pm Sat & Sun; ; Passeig de Gràcia) French-inspired Cafe Emma combines local and international influences, though wines are sourced solely from France. It's a superb bet for all-day dining on its terrace, in its dining room or at its bar. Tartines (open sandwiches), such as goat cheese, beetroot and roast beef, are excellent. Don't miss the freshly shucked oysters with a crisp glass of white in season.

La Bodegueta Provença TAPAS €€
(Map p278; 93 215 17 25; www.provenca.labodegueta.cat; Carrer de Provença 233; tapas €6-15, mains €9.50-16; 7am-1.45am Mon-Fri, 8am-1.45am Sat, 1pm-12.45am Sun; ; FGC Provença) The 'Little Wine Cellar' offers classic tapas presented with a touch of class, from *calamares a la andaluza* (lightly battered squid rings) to *cecina* (dried cured veal meat). The house speciality is *ous estrellats* (literally 'smashed eggs') – a mix of scrambled egg white, egg yolk, potato and ingredients ranging from foie gras to *morcilla* (black pudding).

El Velódromo TAPAS, MEDITERRANEAN €€
(93 430 60 22; www.moritz.com; Carrer de Muntaner 213; tapas €2.50-10.50, mains €9.50-24; kitchen 1pm-1am, bar 24hr; ; Hospital Clínic) The restoration of this history-steeped literary tavern by Barcelona brewer Moritz brought back a wonderfully atmospheric establishment. Stop in for an aperitif and tapas or more substantial dishes such as salmon with caramelised cabbage or veal meatballs with fresh tomato and mozzarella. The spectacular high-ceilinged space retains many of its original art deco fittings.

Casa Alfonso SPANISH €€
(Map p278; 93 301 97 83; www.casaalfonso.com; Carrer de Roger de Llúria 6; tapas & sandwiches €4-15, mains €13-23; 8am-1am Mon-Fri, 1pm-1am Sat; ; Urquinaona) In business since 1934, Casa Alfonso is perfect for a morning coffee or a tapas stop at the long marble bar. Wood-panelled and festooned with old photos, posters and swinging hams, it attracts a faithful local clientele at all hours for its *flautas* (thin baguettes with a choice of fillings), hams, cheeses, hot dishes and homemade desserts.

There are also more substantial dishes, mostly involving grilled meat. Consider rounding off with an *alfonsito* (miniature Irish coffee).

Casa Amalia CATALAN €€
(Map p278; 93 458 94 58; www.casamaliabcn.com; Passatge del Mercat 4-6; mains €9-20; 1-3.30pm & 9-10.30pm Tue-Sat, 1-3.30pm Sun; Girona) This very local split-level restaurant is

popular for its hearty Catalan cooking that uses fresh produce from the busy market next door. On Thursdays during winter it offers the mountain classic, *escudella* (Catalan stew). Otherwise, try light variations on local cuisine like the *bacallà al allioli de poma* (cod in apple-based aioli sauce). The three-course *menú del día* is a bargain at €15.50.

De Tapa Madre CATALAN €€
(Map p278; ☎93 459 31 34; www.detapamadre.com; Carrer de Mallorca 301; tapas €4-7.50, mains €14-25.50; ⏰11.30am-midnight; Ⓜ Verdaguer) A lively atmosphere greets you from the moment you swing open the door. A few tiny tables line the window (there's also terrace seating out front), but head upstairs for more space in the gallery, which hovers above the array of tapas on the bar below. The *arròs amb llamàntol* (a hearty rice dish with lobster) is delicious.

★Lasarte MODERN EUROPEAN €€€
(Map p278; ☎93 445 32 42; www.restaurantlasarte.com; Carrer de Mallorca 259; mains €52-58; ⏰1.30-3.30pm & 8.30-10.30pm Tue-Sat, closed 1st 3 weeks Aug; Ⓜ Diagonal) One of the preeminent restaurants in Barcelona – and the city's first to gain three Michelin stars – Lasarte is overseen by lauded chef Martín Berasategui. From Duroc pig's trotters with quince to squid tartare with kaffir consommé, this is seriously sophisticated stuff, served in an ultra-contemporary dining room by waiting staff who could put the most overawed diners at ease.

★Disfrutar MODERN EUROPEAN €€€
(Map p278; ☎93 348 68 96; www.en.disfrutarbarcelona.com; Carrer de Villarroel 163; tasting menus €120-185; ⏰1-2.45pm & 8-9.45pm Tue-Sat; Ⓜ Hospital Clínic) Disfrutar ('Enjoy' in Catalan) is among the city's finest restaurants, with two Michelin stars. Run by alumni of Ferran Adrià's game-changing (now closed) El Bulli restaurant, nothing is as it seems, such as black and green olives that are actually chocolate ganache with orange-blossom water.

★Mont Bar BISTRO €€€
(Map p278; ☎93 323 95 90; www.montbar.com; Carrer de la Diputació 220; tapas €2-13, mains €12.50-26.50; ⏰noon-3.30pm & 7pm-midnight; Ⓜ Universitat) Named for the owner's Val d'Aran hometown, Mont Bar is a stylish wine-bar-style space with black-and-white floors, forest-green banquette and bottle-lined walls offers next-level cooking. Exquisite tapas (pig's trotters with baby shrimp; plankton meringue with sea anemone and Mascarpone) precede 'small plate' mains (tuna belly with pine-nut emulsion) and showstopping desserts (sheep's milk ice cream with blackcurrant liqueur sauce). Reservations essential.

Casa Calvet CATALAN €€€
(Map p278; ☎93 412 40 12; www.casacalvet.es; Carrer de Casp 48; mains €27-35; ⏰1-3.30pm & 8-10.30pm Mon-Sat; Ⓜ Urquinaona) An early Gaudí masterpiece loaded with his trademark curvy features houses a swish restaurant (just to the right of the building's main entrance). Dress up and ask for an intimate *taula cabina* (wooden booth). You could opt for scallop- and prawn-stuffed artichokes, partridge and chestnut casserole or veal with duck-liver sauce.

Gràcia & Park Güell

Chivuo's BURGERS €
(Map p286; ☎93 218 51 34; www.chivuos.com; Carrer del Torrent de l'Olla 175; burgers €7-9; ⏰1-5pm & 7pm-midnight Mon-Sat; Ⓜ Fontana) Burgers and craft beers make a fine pair at this buzzing den. A mostly local crowd comes for huge burgers (served rare unless you specify otherwise) with house-made sauces – best ordered with fluffy, golden-fried *fritas* (chips). Mostly Catalan and Spanish brews, including excellent offerings from Barcelona-based Edge Brewing, Catalan Brewery, Napar and Garage Beer, rotate on the eight taps.

.IT ITALIAN €
(Map p286; ☎93 461 92 71; Carrer del Topazi 26; mains €6.50-12; ⏰9.30am-midnight Mon-Fri, noon-4pm & 7pm-midnight Sat, closed Aug; 📶🌿; Ⓜ Fontana) Pizza bases at .IT ('Italian Tradition') are made from Caputo flour and fermented for 48 hours before being baked in a 400°C wood-fired oven. Just some of the classic topping combinations include Veneto (gorgonzola, mozzarella, radicchio and walnuts) and Abbruzzo (fresh tomato, scamorza cheese, pistachio mortadella and basil). Huge, fresh salads are a meal in themselves; pastas change daily.

Casa Portuguesa BAKERY €
(Map p286; ☎93 021 88 03; www.acasaportuguesa.com; Carrer de l'Or 8; dishes €2-8; ⏰10.30am-9pm; Ⓜ Fontana) Overlooking Plaça del Diamant, Casa Portuguesa is a delightful bakery and purveyor of delicacies. The *pasteis de belém* (Portuguese-style custard tarts) are magnificent, and you'll also find fruit tarts, daily

changing organic salads, good coffee and Portuguese wines. For a kick, have a shot of *ginjinha* (cherry brandy).

Bar Bodega Quimet TAPAS €

(Map p286; ☎93 218 41 89; Carrer de Vic 23; tapas €3-11.50; ⏰10am-11.30pm Mon-Fri, noon-11.30pm Sat & Sun; Ⓜ Fontana) A remnant from a bygone age, Bar Bodega Quimet is a delightfully atmospheric bar, with old bottles lining the walls, marble tables and a burnished wooden bar. The list of tapas and seafood is almost exhaustive, while another house speciality is *torrades* – huge slabs of toasted white bread topped with cured meats, fresh anchovies and sardines.

La Pubilla CATALAN €

(Map p286; ☎93 218 29 94; Plaça de la Llibertat 23; mains €8-13.50; ⏰8.30am-5pm Mon, to midnight Tue-Sat; Ⓜ Fontana) Hidden away by the Mercat de la Llibertat, La Pubilla specialises in hearty *'esmorzars de forquilla'* ('fork breakfasts') beloved by market workers and nearby residents. There's also a daily three-course *menú del día* for €16, which includes Catalan dishes such as baked cod, or roast pork cheek with chickpeas. Arrive early for a chance of a table.

La Nena CAFE €

(Map p286; ☎93 285 14 76; www.facebook.com/chocolaterialanena; Carrer de Ramon i Cajal 36; dishes €2-4.50; ⏰8.30am-10.30pm Mon-Fri, 9am-10.30pm Sat & Sun; 👪; Ⓜ Fontana) At this delightfully chaotic space, indulge in cups of *suïssos* (rich hot chocolate) served with a plate of heavy homemade whipped cream and *melindros* (spongy sweet biscuits), desserts and a few savoury dishes (including crêpes). The place is strewn with books, and you can play with the board games on the shelves.

Himali NEPALI €

(Map p286; ☎93 285 15 68; www.restaurantehimalibcn.com; Carrer de Milà i Fontanals 60; mains €7.50-13; ⏰noon-11.30pm; Ⓜ Joanic) Strung with Nepalese prayer flags, this simple spot serves dishes such as lamb curry, mixed grills with rice and naan, and lamb and vegetable *momo* (dumplings).

Pepa Tomate TAPAS €€

(Map p286; ☎93 210 46 98; www.pepatomategrup.com; Plaça de la Revolució de Setembre de 1868 17; sharing plates €7-17; ⏰8pm-midnight Mon, from 9am Tue-Fri, from 10am Sat, from 11am Sun; 👪; Ⓜ Fontana) This casual tapas spot on Plaça de la Revolució de Setembre de 1868 is popular at all hours of the day. Fresh produce takes front and centre on the wide-ranging menu in dishes like fried green tomatoes, Andalucian baby squid, tandoori lamb tacos, Iberian pork or mushroom, croquettes, and carrot gazpacho in summer.

Café Godot INTERNATIONAL €€

(Map p286; ☎93 368 20 36; www.cafegodot.com; Carrer de Sant Domènec 19; mains €10-18.50; ⏰10am-1am Mon-Fri, 11am-2am Sat & Sun; Ⓜ Fontana) A stylish space of exposed brick, timber and tiles, opening to a garden out back, Godot is a relaxing place with an extensive menu, ranging from white-wine-steamed mussels and scallops with Thai-style green curry to duck confit with lentils and spinach. Brunch is an American-style affair with eggs, crispy bacon and fluffy pancakes.

Cantina Machito MEXICAN €€

(Map p286; ☎93 217 34 14; Carrer de Torrijos 47; mains €9.50-16.50; ⏰1-4pm & 7pm-1am; Ⓜ Fontana, Joanic) On a leafy street, colourful Machito – adorned with Frida Kahlo images – gets busy with locals, and the outside tables are a great place to eat and drink until late. Start with a *michelada* (spicy beer cocktail) before dining on Mexican delights like quesadillas, tacos and enchiladas. Refreshing iced waters are flavoured with honey and lime or mint and fruit.

La Panxa del Bisbe TAPAS €€

(☎93 213 70 49; Carrer del Torrent de les Flors 158; tapas €8.50-15, tasting menus €28-36; ⏰1.30-3.30pm & 8.30pm-midnight Tue-Sat; Ⓜ Joanic) With low lighting and an artfully minimalist interior, the 'Bishop's Belly' serves creative tapas that earn high praise from the mostly local crowd. Feast on prawn-stuffed courgette flowers, grilled octopus with green chilli and watermelon, and slow-roasted lamb with mint couscous. Top off the meal with a bottle of wine such as an Albariño white from Galicia (by-the-glass options are more limited).

Cal Boter CATALAN €€

(Map p286; ☎93 458 84 62; www.restaurantcalboter.com; Carrer de Tordera 62; mains €8-15; ⏰1-4pm & 9pm-midnight Tue-Sat, 1-4pm Sun & Mon; Ⓜ Joanic) Families and high-spirited groups of pals are drawn to this classic restaurant for *cargols a la llauna* (snails sautéed in a tin), *filet de bou amb salsa de foie* (a thick clump of tender beef drowned in an orange and foie gras sauce), and other Catalan specialities.

Envalira CATALAN €€
(Map p286; ☎93 218 58 13; Plaça del Sol 13; mains €13-21; ⊙1.30-4pm & 9pm-midnight Tue-Sat, 1.30-5pm Sun; Ⓜ Fontana) You might not notice the modest entrance to this Gràcia relic, where serious waiters deliver all sorts of seafood and rice dishes to your table, from *arròs a la milanesa* (savoury rice with chicken, pork and a light cheese gratin) to a *bullit de lluç* (slice of white hake boiled with herb-laced rice and a handful of clams).

Taverna La Llesca CATALAN €€
(Map p286; ☎93 285 02 46; www.tavernalallesca.com; Carrer de Terol 6; mains €10-18; ⊙1.30-4pm & 8.30pm-midnight; Ⓜ Fontana) Barrels of vermouth overhang the bar at this old-school tavern, which dishes up hearty portions of meat. Wash it down with a Spanish red.

Can Travi Nou CATALAN €€€
(☎93 428 03 01; www.gruptravi.com; Carrer de Jorge Manrique 8; mains €15.50-30; ⊙1-4pm & 8-11pm; Ⓜ Montbau) Dining areas stretch out across two floors of this expansive 18th-century mansion. The warm colours, grandfather clock and rustic air make for a magical setting for dining on Catalan specialities like slow-roasted pork and lamb, and seafood casseroles. Reserve ahead.

Botafumeiro SEAFOOD €€€
(Map p286; ☎93 218 42 30; www.botafumeiro.es; Carrer Gran de Gràcia 81; mains €22-59; ⊙noon-1am; Ⓜ Fontana) This temple of Galician shellfish has long been a magnet for VIPs visiting Barcelona. You can bring the price down by sharing a few *medias raciones* (large tapas plates) to taste a range of marine offerings followed by mains like spider crab pie, squid ink paella or grilled spiny lobster.

It's a good place to try *percebes*, the strangely twisted goose barnacles harvested along Galicia's north Atlantic coast, which many Spaniards consider the ultimate seafood delicacy.

Camp Nou, Pedralbes & La Zona Alta

La Fermata de Sarrià PIZZA €
(☎93 315 84 02; www.lafermata.es; Carrer Major de Sarrià 2-4; pizza per kg €14-28; ⊙12.30-4pm & 7.30-11pm; 🚌66,130, 🚆FGC Sarrià) Rectangular pizza slices are sold *al taglio* (by weight) at this little pizzeria run by a Rome-trained chef, and come in an array of classic and Catalonian-inspired toppings (150 varieties altogether, though not at the same time). It's perfect for picking up takeaway, but there's also a counter with stool seating and a handful of tables on the pavement.

Mitja Vida TAPAS €
(www.morrofi.cat; Carrer de Brusi 39; tapas €3-7; ⊙6-11pm Mon-Thu, noon-4pm & 6-11pm Fri & Sat, noon-4pm Sun, closed Aug; 🚆FGC Sant Gervasi) A young, fun, mostly local crowd gathers around the stainless-steel tapas bar of tiny Mitja Vida. It's a jovial eating and drinking spot, with good-sized portions of anchovies, calamari, smoked herring, cheeses and *mojama* (salt-cured tuna). The drink of choice is house-made vermouth.

Santamasa CATALAN €
(☎93 676 35 74; www.santamasarestaurant.com; Carrer Major de Sarrià 97; dishes €6.50-13; ⊙8am-midnight Mon-Fri, 9am-midnight Sat & Sun; 🚆FGC Reina Elisenda) Next door to Sarrià's pretty 18th-century church Sant Vicenç de Sarrià, Santamasa is an enticing spot for a light meal at any time of day. The menu here is wide-ranging, with a mix of creatively topped *pizzetes* (small pizzas), salads, open-faced sandwiches, fondue, burgers, quesadillas and good sharing appetisers like hummus and guacamole.

★**Acontraluz** MEDITERRANEAN €€
(☎93 203 06 58; www.acontraluz.com; Carrer del Milanesat 19; mains €15-27; ⊙1.30-4pm & 8.30pm-midnight Mon-Sat, 1.30-4pm Sun; 🚆FGC Les Tres Torres) The most magical place to dine at this romantic restaurant is in the bougainvillea-draped, tree-filled garden, reached by an arbour. Olive-crusted monkfish with caramelised fennel, black paella with squid and clams, and suckling pig with fig jam are all outstanding choices. Don't miss the rum-soaked carrot cake with cardamom ice cream for dessert.

★**Aspic** CAFE, DELI €€
(☎93 200 04 35; www.aspic.es; Avinguda de Pau Casals 24; dishes €9-19.50; ⊙cafe 11am-1.30pm & 6-8.30pm Tue-Sat, 11am-4pm Sun, deli 9am-8pm Tue-Sat, to 4pm Sun, bar to midnight Tue-Sat, to 4pm Sun; 📶✍; 🚋T1, T2, T3 Francesc Macià) Luxury ingredients (smoked salmon, premium charcuterie and cheeses, high-grade olive oils and carefully chosen Spanish wines) are utilised at the flagship cafe of this Barcelona caterer in stunning dishes like local carrelet fish with cockle foam and broccoli purée. The attached deli is perfect for picking up items for a gourmet picnic in nearby Jardins del Poeta Eduard Marquina.

Bangkok Cafe THAI €€

(☎93 339 32 69; Carrer d'Evarist Arnús 65; mains €10-14; ⏰8-11pm Mon-Wed, 1-3.45pm & 8-11pm Thu-Sun; Ⓜ Plaça del Centre) If you're craving Thai cuisine, it's well worth making the trip out to Bangkok Cafe, which serves up spicy green papaya salad, *tam yam kung* (spicy prawn soup), crispy prawns with plum sauce, red curries and other standouts, with more spice than you'll find in most Catalan eateries.

It's a small, buzzing place with an open kitchen, photos of the Thai royals, blackboard specials and an oversized chandelier. Enter from the side lane.

El Asador de Aranda SPANISH €€

(☎93 417 01 15; www.asadordearanda.net; Avinguda del Tibidabo 31; tapas €6-16.50, mains €15-22.50; ⏰1-4.30pm & 8-11.30pm; 📶; 🚊FGC Avinguda Tibidabo) Set in a striking Modernista building, complete with stained-glass windows, Moorish-style brick arches and elaborate ceilings, El Asador de Aranda's most popular seats are on the landscaped terrace. You'll find a fine assortment of tapas plates for sharing, though the speciality is the meat (roast lamb, spare ribs, beef), prepared in a wood-fired oven.

★**La Balsa** MEDITERRANEAN €€€

(☎93 211 50 48; www.labalsarestaurant.com; Carrer de la Infanta Isabel 4; mains €20-28; ⏰1.30-3.30pm & 8.30-10.30pm Tue-Sat, 1.30-3.30pm Sun; 📶; 🚊FGC Avinguda Tibidabo) With its grand ceiling and the scented gardens that surround the main terrace dining area, La Balsa is one of the city's premier dining addresses. The seasonally changing menu is a mix of traditional Catalan and creative expression (suckling pig with melon; cod confit with prune compote). Lounge over a cocktail at the bar before being directed to your table.

★**Via Veneto** GASTRONOMY €€€

(☎93 200 72 44; www.viaveneto.es; Carrer de Ganduxer 10; mains €28-52.50; ⏰1-4pm & 8-11.45pm Mon-Fri, 8-11.45pm Sat, closed Aug; 🚊FGC La Bonanova) Dalí was a regular in this high-society restaurant after it opened in 1967, and you can still dine at his favourite table today. The oval mirrors, orange-rose tablecloths, leather chairs and fine cutlery set the stage for intricate dishes such as smoked oysters with minced black bread and red mullet with chargrilled onion leaves.

Can Cortada CATALAN €€€

(☎93 427 23 15; www.cancortada.com; Avinguda de l'Estatut de Catalunya; mains €21.50-29; ⏰1-4pm & 8-11pm; Ⓜ Mundet) The setting and the hearty welcome make this 11th-century estate (complete with the remains of a defensive tower) worth the excursion. Grilled meats dominate, though you'll also find seasonal dishes like artichokes fired up on the grill and *calçots* (spring onions) in winter. Try for a table in the former cellars or on the garden terrace.

Montjuïc, Poble Sec & Sant Antoni

Spice CAFE €

(Map p292; ☎93 624 33 59; www.spicecafe.es; Carrer de Margarit 13; dishes €3.50-5; ⏰4-9pm Tue-Thu, 11am-9pm Fri-Sun; 📶; Ⓜ Poble Sec) Run by friendly English-speaking staff, Spice is a delightful cafe that's earned a following for its delicious homemade desserts, such as ricotta and cinnamon cheesecake or a gluten-free orange and cardamom loaf. Along with excellent coffees, there are loose-leaf teas and homemade sodas.

Federal CAFE €

(Map p292; ☎93 187 36 07; www.federalcafe.es; Carrer del Parlament 39; mains €9-12; ⏰8am-11pm Mon-Thu, 8am-1am Fri, 9am-1am Sat, 9am-5.30pm Sun; 📶🖋; Ⓜ Sant Antoni) On a stretch that now teems with cafes, Australian-run Federal was the trailbazer, with its good coffee (including a decent flat white) and superb brunches. Later in the day, healthy, tasty options span snacks (prawn toast, polenta chips with gorgonzola) to larger dishes like veggie burgers or grilled salmon with soba noodles. Head to the small, breezy roof terrace.

Escribà PASTRIES €

(Map p256; ☎93 454 75 35; www.escriba.es; Gran Via de les Corts Catalanes 546; pastries €2-6.50; ⏰8.30am-8.30pm; Ⓜ Urgell) Antoni Escribà carries forward a family tradition (since 1906) of melting *barcelonins'* hearts with remarkable pastries and chocolate creations. Seasonal treats include the Easter *bunyols de xocolata* (little round pastry balls filled with chocolate cream). Escribà has another branch (p328) in a Modernista setting at La Rambla.

Horchateria Sirvent ICE CREAM €

(Map p292; ☎93 441 27 20; www.turronessirvent.com; Carrer del Parlament 56; ice cream €1.60-3, horchata €2.20-3.90; ⏰9am-10pm; Ⓜ Sant Antoni) Along with ice cream, *granissat* (iced fruit crush) and *turrón* (nougat), this old-school parlour has served *barcelonins'* favourite source of *orxata/horchata* (tiger-nut drink) since 1926 – the best you'll try without having to catch the train down to this drink's spiritual home, Valencia. You can get it by the glass or take it away.

★Agust Gastrobar BISTRO €€
(Map p292; ☎93 162 67 33; www.agustbarcelona.com; Carrer del Parlament 54; mains €12.50-24; ⏲kitchen 7pm-midnight Mon-Thu, 2pm-midnight Fri-Sun, bar to 2am; Ⓜ Poble Sec) Set up by two French chefs (one of whom trained under Gordon Ramsay), Agust occupies a fabulous mezzanine space with timber beams, exposed brick and textured metro tiles. Baby scallops with seaweed butter and prawn-stuffed avocado cannelloni are savoury standouts; desserts include the extraordinary 'el cactus' (chocolate-crumble soil, mojito mousse and prickly pear sorbet) served in a terracotta flower pot.

★Quimet i Quimet TAPAS €€
(Map p292; ☎93 442 31 42; Carrer del Poeta Cabanyes 25; tapas €4-10, montaditos €2.80-4; ⏲noon-4pm & 7-10.30pm Mon-Fri, noon-4pm Sat, closed Aug; Ⓜ Paral·lel) Quimet i Quimet is a family-run business passed down from generation to generation. There's barely space to swing a *calamar* (squid) in this bottle-lined, standing-room-only place, but it is a treat for the palate, with *montaditos* (tapas on a slice of bread) made to order.

Mano Rota BISTRO €€
(Map p292; ☎93 164 80 41; www.manorota.com; Carrer de la Creu dels Molers 4; mains €15-22; ⏲8-11.30pm Mon, 1-3.30pm & 8-11.30pm Tue-Sat, 1-3.30pm Sun; Ⓜ Poble Sec) Exposed brick, aluminium pipes, industrial light fittings and recycled timbers create a hip, contemporary setting for inspired bistro cooking at Mano Rota (which literally translates as 'broken hand', but is actually a Spanish idiom for consummate skill). Asian, South American and Mediterranean flavours combine in dishes such as crispy squid with yuzu aioli or dorade (bream) with pak choy pesto.

Lascar 74 PERUVIAN €€
(Map p292; ☎93 017 98 72; www.lascar.es; Carrer del Roser 74; mains €12-15; ⏲7-11.30pm Mon-Thu, 2-5pm & 7pm-11.30pm Fri-Sun; Ⓜ Paral·lel) At this self-styled 'ceviche and pisco bar', oyster shooters with leche de tigre (the traditional ceviche marinade) are served alongside exquisite Peruvian ceviches as well as renditions from Thailand, Japan and Mexico. Pisco sours are the real deal, frothy egg white and all.

Malamén CATALAN €€
(Map p292; ☎93 252 77 63; www.malamen.es; Carrer de Blai 53; mains €12-24; ⏲8pm-midnight Tue-Sun; Ⓜ Poble Sec) Carrer de Blai is lined with bars and restaurants, but Malamén towers above most for its elegant art-deco-inspired design, immaculate service and gourmet versions of Catalan classics. Its shortish menu offers confit tuna, dill and caper salad, juicy steak with creamed mushrooms and blue-cheese croquettes, and the wine list is equally concise.

Bodega 1900 TAPAS €€
(Map p292; ☎93 325 26 59; www.bodega1900.com; Carrer de Tamarit 91; tapas €6-15; ⏲1pm-10.30pm Tue-Sat, closed Aug; Ⓜ Poble Sec) Bodega 1900 mimics an old-school tapas and vermouth bar, but don't be fooled: this venture from the world-famous Adrià brothers creates gastronomic tapas such as 'spherified' reconstructed olives, or its *mollete de calamars,* probably the best squid sandwich in the world, hot from the pan and served with chipotle mayonnaise, kimchi and lemon zest.

Casa Xica FUSION €€
(Map p292; ☎93 600 58 58; Carrer de la França Xica 20; sharing plates €5-15; ⏲8.30-11pm Mon, 1.30-11pm Tue-Sat; Ⓜ Poble Sec) On the parlour floor of an old house, Casa Xica is a casual but artfully designed space where elements of the Far East are fused with fresh Catalan ingredients (owners Marc and Raquel lived and travelled in Asia).

Casa de Tapas Cañota TAPAS €€
(Map p292; ☎93 325 91 71; www.casadetapas.com; Carrer de Lleida 7; tapas €5-14; ⏲1-4pm & 7.30pm-midnight Tue-Sat, 1-4pm Sun; Ⓜ Poble Sec) Between Poble Sec and Plaça d'Espanya, this friendly, unfussy option serves affordable, nicely turned out tapas plates. Seafood is the speciality, with rich razor clams, garlic-fried prawns and tender octopus. Wash it down with a refreshing bottle of *albariño* (a Galician white).

Fàbrica Moritz GASTROPUB €€
(Map p256; ☎93 426 00 50; www.moritz.com; Ronda de Sant Antoni 41; sandwiches €6.50-11, mains €8-19.50; ⏲9am-3am; Ⓜ Sant Antoni) In a building redesigned by architect Jean Nouvel, with a menu created by chef Jordi Vilà of Michelin-starred Alkímia (p317) (also on the premises), this restaurant at the Moritz brewery offers pan-European gastropub fare such as gourmet sandwiches, *moules-frites* (mussels

and fries), steak tartare, whole roast chicken, fish and chips, frankfurters with sauerkraut and *flammkuchen* (Alsatian-style pizza).

Bodega Sepúlveda CATALAN €€
(Map p256; ☎93 323 59 44; www.bodegasepulveda.net; Carrer de Sepúlveda 173; mains €11-21; ⊙1.30-4.30pm & 8pm-1am Mon-Fri, 8pm-1am Sat; Ⓜ Universitat) This venerable tavern has been in business since 1952. The dizzying range of dishes mixes traditional (Catalan faves like *cap i pota* – stew made with bits of the calf you don't want to think about) with more surprising options like *carpaccio de calabacín con bacalao y parmesán* (thin courgette slices draped in cod and Parmesan).

★Enigma GASTRONOMY €€€
(Map p292; ☎616 696322; www.enigmaconcept.es; Carrer de Sepúlveda 38-40; tasting menu €220; ⊙1-4pm & 4.30-10.30pm Tue-Fri, noon-5.30pm & 6-10.30pm Sat; Ⓜ Espanya) Resembling a 3D art installation, this conceptual offering from the famed Adrià brothers is a 40-course tour de force of cutting-edge gastronomy across six different dining spaces. A meal takes 3½ hours all up and includes customised cocktail pairings (you can order additional drinks). There's a minimum of two diners; reserve months in advance. A €100 deposit is required upon booking.

★Tickets TAPAS, GASTRONOMY €€€
(Map p292; ☎93 292 42 50; www.ticketsbar.es; Avinguda del Paral·lel 164; tapas €3-26; ⊙7-11.30pm Tue-Fri, 1-3.30pm & 7-11.30pm Sat, closed Aug; Ⓜ Paral·lel) A flamboyant affair playing with circus images and theatre lights, this is one of the sizzling tickets in the restaurant world, a Michelin-starred tapas bar opened by Ferran Adrià, of the legendary (since closed) El Bulli, and his brother Albert. Bookings are only taken online two months in advance, but you can try calling for last-minute cancellations.

BEST CAFÉS IN THE BARRI GÒTIC

Some of Barcelona's most atmospheric cafes lie hidden in the old cobbled lanes of Barri Gòtic. Our favourite spots for a pick-me-up include:

Salterio (Map p256; ☎93 302 50 28; Carrer de Sant Domènec del Call 4; ⊙noon-1am; 📶; Ⓜ Jaume I) A wonderfully photogenic candlelit spot tucked down a tiny lane in El Call, Salterio serves Turkish coffee, authentic mint teas and snacks amid stone walls, incense and ambient Middle Eastern music. If hunger strikes, try the sardo (grilled flat-bread covered with pesto, cheese or other toppings).

Čaj Chai (Map p256; ☎93 301 95 92; www.cajchai.com; Carrer de Sant Domènec del Call 12; ⊙10.30am-10pm; Ⓜ Jaume I) Inspired by Prague's bohemian tearooms, this bright and buzzing cafe in the heart of the old Jewish quarter is a tea connoisseur's paradise. Čaj Chai stocks around 200 teas from China, India, Korea, Japan, Nepal, Morocco and beyond. It's a much-loved local haunt.

Caelum (Map p256; ☎93 302 69 93; Carrer de la Palla 8; ⊙10am-8.30pm Mon-Fri, to 9pm Sat & Sun; 📶; Ⓜ Liceu) Centuries of heavenly gastronomic tradition from across Spain are concentrated in this exquisite medieval space in the heart of the city. The upstairs cafe is a dainty setting for decadent cakes and pastries, while descending into the underground chamber with its stone walls and flickering candles is like stepping into the Middle Ages.

Cafè de l'Òpera (Map p256; ☎93 317 75 85; www.cafeoperabcn.com; La Rambla 74; ⊙8am-2am; 📶; Ⓜ Liceu) Opposite the Gran Teatre del Liceu is La Rambla's most traditional cafe. Operating since 1929 and still popular with opera-goers, it is pleasant enough for an early evening libation or, in the morning, coffee and croissants. Head upstairs for a seat overlooking the busy boulevard, and try the house speciality, the cafè de l'Òpera (coffee with chocolate mousse).

La Granja (Map p256; ☎93 302 69 75; Carrer dels Banys Nous 4; ⊙9am-9pm; 📶; Ⓜ Jaume I) This long-running cafe serves up thick, rich cups of chocolate, in varying formats, but it doesn't make its own churros. Buy them a few doors down at Xurreria and bring them here for the perfect combo of churros dipped in chocolate. Also worth a look is the section of Roman wall visible at the back.

Martínez SPANISH €€€

(Map p292; ☎93 106 60 52; www.martinezbarcelona.com; Carretera de Miramar 38; mains €21.50-32; ⊙1-11pm; 🚌21, 🚡Teleférico del Puerto) With a fabulous panorama over the city and port, Martínez is a standout among the lacklustre dining options atop Montjuïc. On warm days, head to the outdoor terrace for its signature rice and paella dishes (€38 to €62 for two). There are also oysters, calamari, fresh market fish and other seafood hits, plus *jamón* and grilled meat dishes.

Alkímia CATALAN €€€

(Map p256; ☎93 207 61 15; www.alkimia.cat; Ronda de Sant Antoni 41; mains €22-42; ⊙1.30-3.30pm & 8-10.30pm Mon-Fri; MUniversitat) Inside the Fàbrica Moritz (p315) brewery, culinary alchemist Jordi Vilà creates refined Catalan dishes with a twist (oyster-stuffed courgette flowers; roast royal hare with beetroot; candied lemon soufflé with pickled plum ice cream) that have earned him a Michelin star. Set menus range from €98 to €155.

Drinking & Nightlife

La Rambla & Barri Gòtic

L'Ascensor COCKTAIL BAR

(Map p256; ☎93 318 53 47; Carrer de la Bellafila 3; ⊙6pm-2.30am Mon-Thu, to 3am Fri-Sun; 📶; MJaume I) Named after the lift (elevator) doors that serve as the front door, this elegant drinking den with its vaulted brick ceilings, vintage mirrors and marble-topped bar gathers a faithful crowd that comes for old-fashioned cocktails and lively conversation against a soundtrack of up-tempo jazz and funk.

Sor Rita BAR

(Map p256; ☎93 176 62 66; www.sorritabar.es; Carrer de la Mercè 27; ⊙7pm-2.30am Sun-Thu, to 3am Fri & Sat; 📶; MJaume I) A lover of all things kitsch, Sor Rita is pure eye candy, from its leopard-print wallpaper to its high-heel-festooned ceiling and deliciously irreverent decorations inspired by the films of Almodóvar. It's a fun and festive scene, with special-event nights including tarot readings on Mondays, all-you-can-eat snack buffets (€7) on Tuesdays and karaoke on Thursdays.

Polaroid BAR

(Map p256; ☎93 186 66 69; www.polaroidbar.es; Carrer dels Còdols 29; ⊙7.30pm-2.30am Sun-Thu, to 3am Fri & Sat; 📶; MDrassanes) For a dash of 1980s nostalgia, Polaroid is a blast from the past, with its wall-mounted VHS tapes, old film posters, comic-book-covered tables, action-figure displays and other kitschy decor. Not surprisingly, it draws a fun, unpretentious crowd who come for cheap *cañas* (draught beer), mojitos and free popcorn.

Marula Café BAR

(Map p256; ☎93 318 76 90; www.marulacafe.com; Carrer dels Escudellers 49; cover up to €10; ⊙11pm-5am Mon-Thu & Sun, 11.30pm-6am Fri, 9.30pm-6am Sat; MLiceu) A fantastic find in the heart of the Barri Gòtic, Marula will transport you to the 1970s and the best in funk and soul. James Brown fans will think they've died and gone to heaven. It's not, however, a mono-thematic place: DJs slip in other tunes, from breakbeat to house. Samba and other Brazilian dance sounds also penetrate here.

La Macarena CLUB

(Map p256; ☎93 301 30 64; www.macarenaclub.com; Carrer Nou de Sant Francesc 5; cover €5-10; ⊙midnight-5am Sun-Thu, to 6am Fri & Sat; MDrassanes) You won't believe this was once a tile-lined Andalucian flamenco musos' bar. Now it is a dark dance space, of the kind where it is possible to sit at the bar, meet people around you and then stand up for a bit of a shake to the DJ's electro and house offerings, all within about five square metres.

Boadas COCKTAIL BAR

(Map p256; ☎93 318 95 92; www.boadascocktails.com; Carrer dels Tallers 1; ⊙noon-2am Mon-Thu, to 3am Fri & Sat; MCatalunya) One of the city's oldest cocktail bars, Boadas is famed for its daiquiris. Bow-tied waiters have been serving up unique, drinkable creations since Miguel Boadas opened it in 1933 – in fact Miró and Hemingway both drank here. Miguel was born in Havana, where he was the first barman at the immortal La Floridita.

El Raval

Bars and clubs have been opening up along the shadowy sidestreets of El Raval for the last two decades, and despite its vestigial edginess, this is a great place to go out. You'll find super-trendy places alongside great old taverns that still thrive – there are joints that have been the hangouts of the city's bohemia since Picasso's time. The lower end of El Raval has a history of insalubriousness and the area around Carrer de Sant Pau retains its seedy feel: drug dealers, pickpockets and prostitutes mingle with

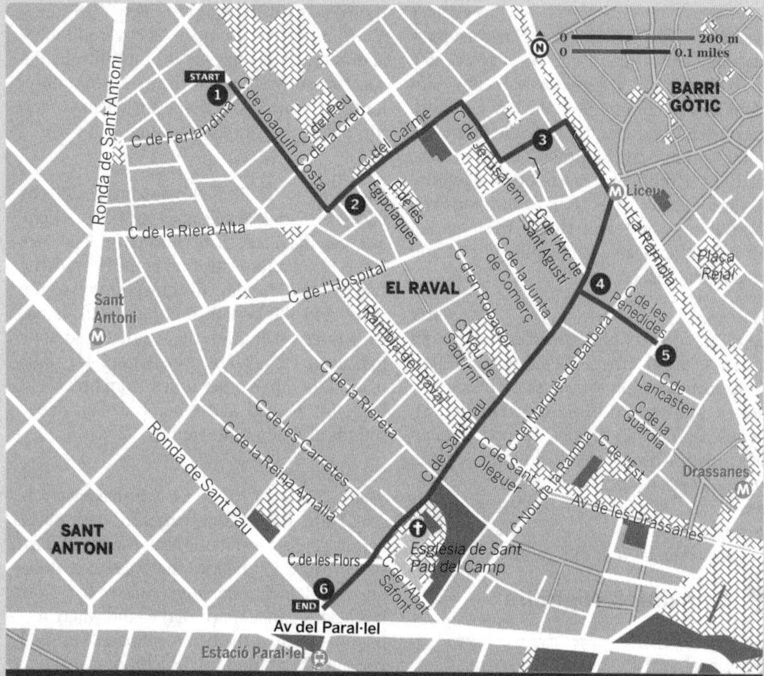

City Walk
Modernista Wining & Dining in El Raval

START CASA ALMIRALL
END LA CONFITERÍA
LENGTH 2KM; ONE HOUR

Long run by the Almirall family that opened it in the mid-19th century, the corner tavern **1 Casa Almirall** (p319) on Carrer de Joaquín Costa preserves much of its Modernista decor, especially in the picture windows opening on to the street, and the counter and display cabinet.

You'll recognise similarly sinuous curves as you enter the **2 Bar Muy Buenas** (p303) on Carrer del Carme. Opened as a milk bar in the late 19th century, it retains much of its original decoration. It's a welcoming, cosy place for lunch or a drink.

The **3 Mercat de la Boqueria** (p264), with half a dozen or so unassuming places to eat, dates back to the 13th century, but it wasn't until 1840 that it was officially inaugurated on this site. In 1914 it was capped with a metal roof and given its charming, wrought-iron, Modernista entrance sign, which is inset with colourful stained glass.

The **4 Hotel España** (p297) is known above all for its dining rooms, part of the 1903 design by Domènech i Montaner. The Sala Arnau (Arnau Room) features an alabaster fireplace designed by Eusebi Arnau. Moderately priced traditional Catalan fare is served.

While wandering around El Raval you should not miss **5 Palau Güell** (p265), one of Gaudí's earlier big commissions. Not designed in his conventional Modernista style, it nonetheless has unmistakeable Gaudí touches, such as the smashed tile chimneys on the rooftop terrace. If passing by at night while doing a round of the bars, make a note to return here by day.

On Carrer de Sant Pau, walk south past the Romanesque church to **6 La Confitería** (p319), once a barber's shop and then a long-time confectioner's. It was lovingly restored for its reconversion into a bar in 1998. Most of the elements in the front section, including facade, bar counter and cabinets, are the real deal. The back room has been completely renovated more recently, but the style is sympathetic.

nocturnal hedonists. Keep your wits about you if walking around here late at night.

★ La Confitería BAR

(Map p256; 93 140 54 35; Carrer de Sant Pau 128; 7pm-2.30am Mon-Thu, 6pm-3am Fri & Sat, 5pm-2.30am Sun; ; Paral·lel) This is a trip into the 19th century. Until the 1980s it was a confectioner's shop, and although the original cabinets are now lined with booze, the look of the place barely changed with its conversion. A recent refurb of the back room is similarly sympathetic, and the vibe these days is lively cocktail bar.

Later in the evening, it fills with those falling out of the nearby BARTS (p327) and Sala Apolo (p328) concert halls.

Bar Pastís BAR

(Map p256; www.barpastis.es; Carrer de Santa Mònica 4; 8pm-2am Tue-Thu & Sun, to 3am Fri & Sat; ; Drassanes) A French cabaret theme (with lots of Piaf on the stereo) pervades this tiny, cluttered classic, which has been going, on and off, since the end of WWII. You'll need to be in before 9pm to have any hope of sitting or getting near the bar. On some nights it features live acts, usually performing French *chanson*.

Bar Marsella BAR

(Map p256; 93 442 72 63; Carrer de Sant Pau 65; 10pm-2.30am Mon-Thu, to 3am Fri & Sat; Liceu) Bar Marsella has been in business since 1820, and has served the likes of Hemingway, who was known to slump here over an *absenta* (absinthe). The bar still specialises in absinthe, a drink to be treated with respect.

Granja M Viader CAFE

(Map p256; 93 318 34 86; www.granjaviader.cat; Carrer d'en Xuclà 6; 9am-1pm & 5-9pm Mon-Sat; Liceu) For more than a century, people have been coming here for hot chocolate with whipped cream (ask for a *suís*) ladled out in this classically Catalan milk bar. In 1931, the Viader clan invented Cacaolat, a bottled chocolate milk drink, with iconic label design. The interior here is delightfully old-fashioned and the atmosphere always lively.

Casa Almirall BAR

(Map p256; 93 318 95 92; www.casaalmirall.com; Carrer de Joaquín Costa 33; 5.30pm-2am Mon-Wed, noon-2.30am Thu-Sat, noon-12.30am Sun; ; Universitat) In business since the 1860s, this unchanged corner bar is dark and intriguing, with Modernista decor and a mixed clientele. There are some great original pieces in here, such as the marble counter, and the cast-iron statue of the muse of the Universal Exposition, held in Barcelona in 1888.

33|45 BAR

(Map p256; 93 187 41 38; www.3345.struments.com; Carrer de Joaquín Costa 4; 1pm-2am Sun-Mon, to 3am Fri & Sat; ; Universitat) A super-trendy bar on a street that's not short of them, this place has excellent mojitos, a fashionable crowd and a frequently changing exhibition of art on the walls. There are DJs most nights, along with plenty of sofas and armchairs for a post-dancing slump.

Moog CLUB

(Map p256; 93 319 17 89; www.masimas.com/moog; Carrer de l'Arc del Teatre 3; entry €5-10; midnight-5am Sun-Thu, to 6am Fri & Sat; Drassanes) This fun and minuscule club is a standing favourite with the downtown crowd. In the main dance area DJs dish out house, techno and electro, while upstairs you can groove to a nice blend of indie and occasional classic-pop throwbacks.

Betty Ford's BAR

(Map p256; 93 304 13 68; Carrer de Joaquín Costa 56; 1pm-2.30am Tue-Sat, from 5pm Sun & Mon; ; Universitat) This enticing corner bar is one of several good stops along the student-jammed run of Carrer de Joaquín Costa. It puts together some nice cocktails and the place fills with an even mix of locals and foreigners, generally aged not much over 30. There's a decent line in burgers and soups, too.

Kentucky BAR

(Map p256; Carrer de l'Arc del Teatre 11; 10pm-4am Wed-Sat; Drassanes) Once a haunt of visiting US Navy boys, this exercise in Americana kitsch is the perfect way to finish an evening – if you can squeeze in. All sorts of odd bods from the *barri* and beyond gather here. An institution in the wee hours, Kentucky often stays open (unofficially) until dawn.

La Ribera

Guzzo COCKTAIL BAR

(Map p266; 93 667 00 36; www.guzzoclub.es; Plaça Comercial 10; 6pm-2.30am Mon-Thu, to 3am Fri & Sat, noon-3am Sun; ; Jaume I) This swish but relaxed cocktail bar is run by much-loved Barcelona DJ Fred Guzzo, who is often to be found at the decks, spinning his delicious selection of funk, soul and rare groove. You'll also find frequent live-music acts of consistently decent quality, and a funky atmosphere at almost any time of day.

La Vinya del Senyor WINE BAR

(Map p266; ☎93 310 33 79; Plaça de Santa Maria del Mar 5; ⊙noon-1am Mon-Thu, to 2am Fri & Sat, to midnight Sun; 📶; Ⓜ Jaume I) Relax on the *terraza*, which lies in the shadow of the Basílica de Santa Maria del Mar, or crowd inside at the tiny bar. The wine list is as long as *War and Peace* and there's a table upstairs for those who opt to sample the wine away from the madding crowd.

Bar del Convent CAFE

(Map p266; ☎93 256 50 17; www.bardelconvent.com; Plaça de l'Acadèmia; ⊙10am-9pm Tue-Sat; 👪; Ⓜ Arc de Triomf) Alongside the Gothic arches of what remains of the Sant Agusti convent's cloister is this pleasant cafe-bar – particularly good for people with children. Kids often play football in the cloister grounds, and there are children's books and toys in the cafe itself. You can also enter at Carrer del Comerç 36 through James Turrell's light sculpture.

Rubí BAR

(Map p266; ☎647 737707; Carrer dels Banys Vells 6; ⊙7.30pm-2.30am Sun-Thu, to 3am Fri & Sat; 📶; Ⓜ Jaume I) With its boudoir lighting and cheap mojitos, Rubí is where the Born's cognoscenti head for a nightcap – or several. It's a narrow, cosy space – push through to the back where you might just get one of the coveted tables, with superior bar food, from Vietnamese rolls to more traditional selections of cheese and ham.

El Born Bar BAR

(Map p266; ☎93 319 53 33; www.elbornbar.com; Passeig del Born 26; ⊙10am-2am Mon-Thu, to 3am Fri & Sat, noon-2.30am Sun; 📶; Ⓜ Jaume I) Moss-green paintwork, marble tables and a chequered black-and-white tiled floor create a timeless look for this popular little cafe-bar. A spiral wrought-iron staircase leads to a quieter room upstairs (the twisting steps mean that there is no table service and hot drinks can't be carried upstairs).

El Xampanyet WINE BAR

(Map p266; ☎93 319 70 03; Carrer de Montcada 22; ⊙noon-3.30pm & 7-11.15pm Tue-Sat, noon-3.30pm Sun; 📶; Ⓜ Jaume I) Nothing has changed for decades in this, one of the city's best-known *cava* (wine) bars. Plant yourself at the bar or seek out a table against the decoratively tiled walls for a glass or three of the cheap house *cava* and an assortment of tapas, such as the tangy *boquerones en vinagre* (fresh anchovies in vinegar).

Miramelindo BAR

(Map p266; ☎93 310 37 27; www.barmiramelindobcn.com; Passeig del Born 15; ⊙8pm-2.30am Mon-Thu, to 3.30am Fri & Sat, 7pm-2.30am Sun; 📶; Ⓜ Jaume I) A spacious tavern in a Gothic building, this remains a classic on Passeig del Born for mixed drinks, while soft jazz and soul sounds float overhead. Try for a comfy seat at a table towards the back before it fills to bursting. A couple of similarly barn-sized places sit on this side of the *passeig*.

Mudanzas BAR

(Map p266; ☎93 319 11 37; Carrer de la Vidrieria 15; ⊙8am-2.30am Mon-Fri, 10am-2.30am Sat & Sun; 📶; Ⓜ Jaume I) This was one of the first bars to get things into gear in El Born and it still attracts a faithful crowd. With its chequered floor and marble-topped tables, it's an attractive, lively place for a beer and perhaps a sandwich or a tapa. It also has a nice line in rum and malt whisky.

Barceloneta & the Waterfront

★Perikete WINE BAR

(Map p272; www.gruporeini.net/perikete; Carrer de Llauder 6; ⊙11am-1am; Ⓜ Barceloneta) Since opening in 2017, this fabulous wine bar has been jam-packed with locals. Hams hang from the ceilings, barrels of vermouth sit above the bar and wine bottles cram every available shelf space – over 200 varieties are available by the glass or bottle, accompanied by 50-plus tapas dishes. In the evening, the action spills into the street.

BlackLab MICROBREWERY

(Map p272; ☎93 221 83 60; www.blacklab.es; Plaça de Pau Vila 1; ⊙noon-1.30am; Ⓜ Barceloneta) Barcelona's first brewhouse opened back in 2014 inside the historic Palau de Mar (p271). Its taps feature 18 house-made brews, including saisons, double IPAs and dry stouts, and the brewmasters constantly experiment with new flavours, such as a sour Berliner Weisse with fiery jalapeño. One-hour tours (5pm Sundays; €12) offer a behind-the-scenes look at the brewers in action plus four samples.

Absenta BAR

(Map p272; ☎93 221 36 38; www.absenta.bar; Carrer de Sant Carles 36; ⊙6pm-2am Mon-Thu, 11am-3am Fri & Sat, 6pm-1am Sun; Ⓜ Barceloneta) Decorated with old paintings, vintage lamps and curious sculptures (including a dangling butterfly woman), this whimsical drinking den specialises in absinthe, with over 20 varieties available. (Go easy, though: an alcohol content of 50% to 90% provides a kick!) It also has a house-made vermouth, if you're not a fan of the green fairy.

Can Paixano WINE BAR

(Map p272; ☎93 310 08 39; www.canpaixano.com; Carrer de la Reina Cristina 7; ⏰9am-10.30pm Mon-Sat; Ⓜ Barceloneta) This lofty *cava* bar (also called La Xampanyeria) has long been run on a winning formula. The standard tipple is bubbly rosé in elegant little glasses, combined with bite-sized *bocadillos* (filled rolls) and tapas. Note that this place is usually packed to the rafters, and elbowing your way to the bar can be a titanic struggle.

Madame George LOUNGE

(www.madamegeorgebar.com; Carrer de Pujades 179; ⏰6pm-2am Mon-Thu, to 3am Fri & Sat, to 12.30am Sun; Ⓜ Poblenou) A theatrical (veering towards campy) elegance marks the interior of this small, chandelier-lit lounge just off the Rambla del Poblenou. Deft bartenders stir well-balanced cocktails like a Lychee-tini (vanilla-infused vodka, fresh lychees, lychee liqueur and lemon juice) in vintage glassware, while a DJ spins vinyl (mainly soul and funk) in the corner.

Balius COCKTAIL BAR

(☎93 315 86 50; www.baliusbar.com; Carrer de Pujades 196; ⏰6pm-2am Tue & Wed, 5pm-3am Thu-Sat, to 1am Sun; Ⓜ Poblenou) There's an old-fashioned jauntiness to this vintage cocktail den in El Poblenou. Staff pour a mix of classic libations as well as vermouths, and there's a small tapas menu until 10.30pm. Stop by on Sundays to catch live jazz, starting around 7.30pm.

Guingueta del Bogatell BAR

(Platja del Bogatell; ⏰9am-10.30pm May-Sep; Ⓜ Llacuna) At this summertime spot, you can dig your feet in the sand and enjoy a cold brew, cocktail or fruity glass of sangría while watching the lapping waves.

Catwalk CLUB

(Map p272; ☎93 224 07 40; www.clubcatwalk.net; Carrer de Ramon Trias Fargas 2-4; cover €15-20; ⏰11.30pm-6am; Ⓜ Ciutadella Vila Olímpica) One of the largest nightclubs in the Port Olímpic area, beachside Catwalk has a capacity of 1000 over two floors. A well-dressed crowd piles in for good house music, occasionally mellowed down with electro, R&B, hip-hop and funk. The chill-out zone, with comfy lounges, is upstairs from the dance floor. Entry is usually free before 1am. Check the schedule online.

Opium CLUB

(Map p272; ☎93 225 91 00; www.opiumbarcelona.com; Passeig Marítim de la Barceloneta 34; cover €10-20; ⏰club 10pm-5am Sun-Thu, to 6am Fri & Sat, restaurant from noon; Ⓜ Ciutadella Vila Olímpica) This seaside dance place has a spacious dance floor that only begins to fill from about 3am and is best in summer, when you can spill onto a terrace overlooking the beach.

CDLC LOUNGE

(Carpe Diem Lounge Club; Map p272; ☎93 224 04 70; www.cdlcbarcelona.com; Passeig Marítim de la Barceloneta 32; ⏰noon-5am; Ⓜ Ciutadella Vila Olímpica) Ideal for a slow warm-up before heading to the nearby clubs, Carpe Diem Lounge Club has Asian-inspired decor and opens onto the beach. Its Asian-fusion food (sushi et al) is quite good, but pricey; alternatively wait until about midnight, when the tables are rolled up and the DJs and dancers take full control.

La Sagrada Família & L'Eixample

★Monvínic WINE BAR

(Map p278; ☎93 272 61 87; www.monvinic.com; Carrer de la Diputació 249; ⏰1-11pm Tue-Fri, 7-11pm Mon & Sat; Ⓜ Passeig de Gràcia) At this rhapsody to wine, the digital wine list details more than 3000 international varieties searchable by origin, year or grape. Some 50 selections are available by the glass; you can, of course, order by the bottle too. There is an emphasis on affordability, but if you want to splash out, there are fantastic vintage options.

★Milano COCKTAIL BAR

(Map p278; ☎93 112 71 50; www.camparimilano.com; Ronda de la Universitat 35; ⏰noon-3am; Ⓜ Catalunya) Completely invisible from street level, this gem of hidden Barcelona nightlife is a subterranean old-school cocktail bar with velvet banquettes and glass-fronted cabinets, presided over by white-jacketed waiters. Live music (Cuban, jazz, blues, flamenco and swing) plays nightly; a DJ takes over after 11pm. Fantastic cocktails include the Picasso (tequila, honey, absinthe and lemon) and six different Bloody Marys.

★Les Gens Que J'Aime BAR

(Map p278; ☎93 215 68 79; www.lesgensquejaime.com; Carrer de València 286; ⊙6pm-2.30am Sun-Thu, 7pm-3am Fri & Sat; Ⓜ Passeig de Gràcia) Atmospheric and intimate, this basement relic of the 1960s follows a deceptively simple formula: chilled jazz music in the background, minimal lighting from an assortment of flea-market lamps and a cosy, cramped scattering of red-velvet-backed lounges around tiny dark tables.

BierCaB CRAFT BEER

(Map p278; ☎644 689045; www.biercab.com; Carrer de Muntaner 55; ⊙bar noon-midnight Mon-Thu, noon-2am Fri & Sat, 5pm-midnight Sun, shop 3.30pm-10pm Mon-Sat; ; Ⓜ Universitat) Beneath an artistic ceiling installation resembling a forest of giant matchsticks, this brilliant craft-beer bar has 30 brews from around the world rotating on its taps. Burgers to accompany them are made from Wagyu beef and named for Barcelona neighbourhoods. Pop into its adjacent shop for another 500 bottled varieties kept cold in fridges.

Monkey Factory COCKTAIL BAR

(Map p278; ☎93 681 78 93; Carrer de Còrsega 234; ⊙6.30pm-2am Tue & Wed, to 3am Thu-Sat; FGC Provença) DJs spin on weekends at this high-spirited venue but it's positively hopping from early on most nights. 'Funky monkey' (triple sec, gin, lime and egg white), 'chimpa sour' (cardamom-infused pisco sour) and 'chita' (passionfruit purée, vodka, cinnamon syrup and ginger) are among the inventive cocktails mixed up behind the neon-green-lit bar.

Garage Beer Co CRAFT BEER

(Map p278; ☎93 528 59 89; www.garagebeer.co; Carrer del Consell de Cent 261; ⊙5pm-midnight Mon-Thu, 5pm-2.30am Fri, noon-3am Sat, 2pm-midnight Sun; Ⓜ Universitat) One of the first of the slew of craft-beer bars to pop up in Barcelona, Garage brews its own in a space at the bar, and offers around 10 different styles at a time. The eponymous Garage (a delicate session IPA) and Slinger (a more robust IPA) are always present on the board.

Dry Martini BAR

(Map p278; ☎93 217 50 80; www.drymartiniorg.com; Carrer d'Aribau 162-166; ⊙1pm-2.30am Mon-Fri, 6.30pm-2.30am Sat & Sun; FGC Provença) Waiters make expert cocktail suggestions, but the house drink, taken at the bar or on one of the plush green banquettes, is always a good bet. The gin and tonic comes in an enormous mug-sized glass – one will take you most of the night.

El Viti BAR

(Map p278; ☎93 633 83 36; www.elviti.com; Passeig de Sant Joan 62; ⊙noon-midnight Sun-Thu, to 1am Fri & Sat; ; Ⓜ Tetuan) Along the hip Passeig de Sant Joan, El Viti checks all the boxes – high ceilings, brick walls both bare and glazed, black-clad staff and a barrel of artisanal vermouth on the bar. It also serves a good line in tapas.

City Hall CLUB

(Map p278; ☎93 238 07 22; www.cityhallbarcelona.com; Rambla de Catalunya 2-4; cover from €10; ⊙10pm-6am Mon, 12.30am-6am Tue-Sun; Ⓜ Catalunya) A long corridor leads to the dance floor of this venerable and popular club, located in a former theatre. Music styles, from house and other electric sounds to funk, change nightly; check the agenda online. The cover charge includes a drink.

Cosmo CAFE

(Map p278; ☎93 105 79 92; www.galeriacosmo.com; Carrer d'Enric Granados 3; ⊙10am-10pm; Ⓜ Universitat) Set on a pedestrian strip just behind the university, this groovy cafe-gallery has a bicycle hanging from the high, white walls, bright splashy murals and gaily painted ventilation pipes, and even makes a feature of its fire hose. Along with fresh juices, hot chocolate, teas, pastries and snacks, it serves beer and wine.

Cafè del Centre CAFE

(Map p278; ☎93 488 11 01; Carrer de Girona 69; ⊙9am-11pm Mon-Fri, 11am-11pm Sat; ; Ⓜ Girona) Step back into the 19th century in this cafe that's been in business since 1873. The mahogany bar extends down the right side as you enter, fronted by marble-topped tables and wooden chairs. It exudes an almost melancholy air by day but gets busy at night, when live jazz piano plays. It stocks 50 beers and 15 loose-leaf teas.

Gràcia & Park Güell

★Bobby Gin COCKTAIL BAR

(Map p286; ☎93 368 18 92; www.bobbygin.com; Carrer de Francisco Giner 47; ⊙4pm-2am Sun-Wed, to 2.30am Thu, to 3am Fri & Sat; Ⓜ Diagonal) With over 60 varieties, this whitewashed stone-walled bar is a haven for gin lovers. Try an infusion-based concoction (rose-tea-infused Hendrick's with strawberries and lime; tangerine-infused Tanqueray 10 with agave nectar and bitter chamomile) or a cocktail like the Santa Maria (chardonnay, milk-thistle syrup, thyme, sage and lemon). Fusion tapas choices include G&T-cured salmon.

Shrimp coated in green puffed rice and beef and shiitake wontons are other great options.

★Rabipelao COCKTAIL BAR

(Map p286; ☎93 182 50 35; www.elrabipelao.com; Carrer del Torrent d'En Vidalet 22; ⊙7pm-1.30am Sun-Thu, to 3am Fri & Sat, 1-4.30pm Sun; M Joanic) An anchor of Gràcia's nightlife, Rabipelao is a celebratory space with a shiny disco ball and DJs spinning salsa beats. A silent film plays in one corner beyond the red velvety wallpaper-covered walls and there's a richly hued mural above the bar. Tropical cocktails like mojitos and caipirinhas pair with South American snacks such as *arepas* (meat-filled cornbread patties) and ceviche.

Tables spread across the covered patio at the back. There's occasional live music.

La Vermuteria del Tano BAR

(Map p286; ☎93 213 10 58; Carrer Joan Blanques 17; ⊙9am-9pm Mon-Fri, noon-4pm Sat & Sun; M Joanic) Scarcely changed in decades, with barrels on the walls, old fridges with wooden doors, vintage clocks and marble-topped tables, this vermouth bar is a local gathering point. Its house-speciality Peruchi is served traditionally with a glass of carbonated water. Tapas is also traditional, with most dishes utilising ingredients from tins (anchovies, smoked clams, cockles and pickled octopus).

Chatelet COCKTAIL BAR

(Map p286; ☎93 284 95 90; Carrer de Torrijos 54; ⊙6pm-2.30am Mon-Fri, from noon Sat & Sun; M Joanic) A popular meeting point in the 'hood, Chatelet has big windows for watching the passing people parade, and a buzzing art-filled interior that sees a wide cross-section of Gràcia society. Blues and old-school American soul plays in the background. The cocktails are excellent, and the drink prices fair (with discounts before 10pm).

Viblioteca WINE BAR

(Map p286; ☎93 284 42 02; www.viblioteca.com; Carrer de Vallfogona 12; ⊙7pm-midnight; M Fontana) A glass cabinet piled high with ripe cheese (over 50 varieties) entices you into this small, white, cleverly designed contemporary space. The real speciality at Viblioteca, however, is wine, and you can choose from 150 mostly local labels, many of them available by the glass.

Bar Canigó BAR

(Map p286; ☎93 213 30 49; www.barcanigo.com; Carrer de Verdi 2; ⊙10am-2am Mon-Thu, 10am-3am Fri, 8pm-3am Sat; M Fontana) Now run by the third generation of owners, this corner bar overlooking Plaça de la Revolució de Setembre de 1868 is an animated spot to sip on a house vermouth or an Estrella beer around rickety old marble-top tables, as people have done here since 1922.

Earlier in the day, it's a great spot for a coffee.

Musical Maria BAR

(Map p286; ☎93 501 04 60; Carrer de Maria 5; ⊙9pm-2.30am Sun-Thu, to 3am Fri & Sat; 📶; M Diagonal) Even the music hasn't changed since this place got going in the late 1970s. Those longing for rock 'n' roll crowd into this animated bar, listen to old hits and knock back beers. Out the back there's a pool table and the bar serves pretty much all the variants of the local Estrella Damm brew.

Raïm BAR

(Map p286; Carrer del Progrés 48; ⊙8pm-2am Tue-Thu, to 3am Fri & Sat; M Diagonal) The walls in Raïm are alive with black-and-white photos of Cubans and Cuba. Weathered old wooden chairs of another epoch huddle around marble tables, while grand old wood-framed mirrors hang from the walls. It draws a friendly, garrulous crowd who pile in for first-rate mojitos and an excellent selection of rum.

🍷 Camp Nou, Pedralbes & La Zona Alta

El Maravillas COCKTAIL BAR

(☎93 360 73 78; www.elmaravillas.cat; Plaça de la Concòrdia 15; ⊙noon-midnight Mon & Tue, to 1am Wed, to 2am Thu, to 3am Fri-Sun; M Maria Cristina, 🚊T1, T2, T3 Numància) Overlooking the peaceful Plaça de la Concòrdia, El Maravillas feels like a secret hideaway – especially if you've just arrived from the crowded lanes of the *Ciutat Vella* (Old City). The glittering bar has just a few tables, plus outdoor seating on the square in warm weather. Creative cocktails, good Spanish red wines and easy-drinking vermouths are the drinks of choice.

Dō Bar BAR

(☎93 209 18 88; www.do-bcn.com; Carrer de Santaló 30; ⊙7pm-midnight Tue-Thu, 8pm-1am Fri & Sat; 📶; 🚆FGC Muntaner) This neighbourhood charmer has a warm and inviting interior, where locals gather at wooden tables to enjoy excellent gin and tonics, wines by the glass, craft beer and satisfying small plates (anchovies, mussels, tacos, charcuterie). On warm nights, arrive early for one of the terrace tables out the front. Enter via Carrer de l'Avenir.

Mirablau BAR

(☎93 418 58 79; www.mirablaubcn.com; Plaça del Doctor Andreu; ⊙11am-3.30am Mon-Wed, 11am-4.30am Thu, 10am-5am Fri-Sat, 10am-2.30am Sun; 🚌196, 🚆FGC Avinguda Tibidabo) Gaze out over the entire city from this privileged balcony restaurant at the base of the Funicular del Tibidabo. The bar is renowned for its gin selection, with 30 different varieties. Wander downstairs to join the folk in the tiny dance space, which opens at 11.30pm. In summer you can step out onto the even smaller terrace for a breather.

Bikini CLUB

(☎93 322 08 00; www.bikinibcn.com; Avinguda Diagonal 547; cover from €12; ⊙midnight-6am Thu-Sat; 🚌6, 7, 33, 34, 63, 67, L51, L57, 🚊T1, T2, T3 L'Illa) This old star of the Barcelona nightlife scene has been keeping the beat since 1953. Every possible kind of music gets a run, from Latin and Brazilian beats to 1980s disco, depending on the night and the space you choose.

Montjuïc, Poble Sec & Sant Antoni

★Abirradero BREWERY

(Map p292; ☎93 461 94 46; www.abirradero.com; Carrer Vila i Vilà 77; ⊙5pm-1am Mon-Thu, noon-2am Fri & Sat, noon-1am Sun; 📶; Ⓜ Paral·lel) Barcelona is spoilt for choice with craft breweries, and this bright, buzzing space has 20 of its own beers rotating on the taps, including IPAral·lel (a double IPA), Excuse Me While I Kiss My Stout, and Tripel du Poble Sec. Tapas, sharing boards and burgers are standouts from the kitchen. You'll occasionally catch live jazz and blues here.

★La Caseta del Migdia BAR

(☎617 956572; www.lacaseta.org; Mirador del Migdia; ⊙8pm-1am Wed-Fri, noon-1am Sat & Sun Apr-Sep, noon-sunset Sat & Sun Oct-Mar; 🚌150) The effort of getting to what is, for all intents and purposes, a simple *chiringuito* (makeshift cafe-bar) is worth it. Gaze out to sea over a beer or coffee by day. As sunset approaches the atmosphere changes, as reggae, samba and funk wafts out over the hillside. Drinks aside, you can also order food fired up on the outdoor grills.

GAY & LESBIAN BARCELONA

Barcelona has a vibrant gay and lesbian scene, with a fine array of restaurants, bars and clubs in the district known as the 'Gaixample' (a portmanteau of Gay and L'Eixample), an area about five to six blocks southwest of Passeig de Gràcia around Carrer del Consell de Cent.

Aire (Sala Diana; Map p278; ☎93 487 83 42; www.grupoarena.com; Carrer de la Diputació 233; cover Fri/Sat €5/6; ⊙11pm-2.30am Thu-Sat; Ⓜ Passeig de Gràcia) At this popular lesbian hang-out, the dance floor is spacious and there's usually a DJ in command of the tunes, which veer from hits of the '80s and '90s to Latin and techno. As a rule, only male friends of the girls are allowed entry, although in practice the crowd tends to be fairly mixed.

Arena Classic (Map p278; ☎93 487 83 42; www.grupoarena.com; Carrer de la Diputació 233; cover Fri/Sat €6/12; ⊙2.30am-6am Fri & Sat; Ⓜ Passeig de Gràcia) Spinning mostly techno, Arena Classic attracts an upbeat, energetic gay crowd. Entry includes a drink.

Metro (Map p256; ☎93 323 52 27; www.metrodiscobcn.com; Carrer de Sepúlveda 185; cover before/after 2am from €8/20; ⊙12.15am-5.30am Sun-Thu, to 6.45am Fri & Sat; Ⓜ Universitat) Metro attracts a fun-loving gay crowd with its two dance floors, three bars and very dark room. Keep an eye out for shows and parties, which can range from parades of models to bingo nights (on Thursday nights, with sometimes-interesting prizes), plus the occasional striptease.

Punto BCN (Map p278; ☎93 451 91 52; www.grupoarena.com; Carrer de Muntaner 65; ⊙6pm-2.30am Sun-Thu, to 3am Fri & Sat; Ⓜ Universitat) It's an oldie but a goody. A big bar over two levels with a slightly older crowd, this place fills to bursting on Friday and Saturday nights with its blend of Spanish pop and dance. It's a friendly early stop on a gay night out, and you can shoot a round of pool here.

La Terrrazza CLUB

(Map p292; ☎687 969825; www.laterrrazza.com; Avinguda de Francesc Ferrer i Guàrdia; cover from €15; ⏲midnight-6.30am Thu-Sat May-Sep; 🚌13, 23, 150, Ⓜ Espanya) Come summer, La Terrrazza attracts squadrons of beautiful people, locals and foreigners alike, for a full-on night of music (mainly house, techno and electronica) and cocktails partly under the stars inside the Poble Espanyol (p289) complex.

El Rouge BAR

(Map p292; ☎666 251556; Carrer del Poeta Cabanyes 21; ⏲9pm-2am Thu, 10pm-3am Fri & Sat, 11am-2am Sun; 📶; Ⓜ Poble Sec) Decadence is the word that springs to mind in this bordello-red lounge-cocktail bar, with acid jazz, drum and bass and other sounds drifting along in the background. The walls are covered in heavy-framed paintings, dim lamps and mirrors, and no two chairs are alike. You can sometimes catch DJs, risqué poetry soirées, cabaret shows or even nights of tango dancing.

Pervert Club @ The One GAY

(Map p292; ☎93 453 05 10; http://pervert-club.negocio.site; Avinguda Francesc Ferrer i Guàrdia 13; cover from €18; ⏲midnight-6am Sat; 🚌13, 23, 150, Ⓜ Espanya) This weekly fest takes place at The One club in Poble Espanyol (p289). Electronic music dominates and, in spite of the 6am finish, for many this is only the start of the 'evening'. Expect loads of tanned and buff gym bunnies – and plenty of topless eye candy.

La Cambicha BAR

(Map p292; ☎93 187 25 13; Carrer del Poeta Cabanyes 43; ⏲6pm-2am Mon-Wed, 1pm-2am Thu-Sun; Ⓜ Paral·lel) This shoebox-sized bar feels a bit like a lost cabin in the woods with its newspaper-covered walls, lanterns and old sporting photos. Once you've wedged yourself alongside a tiny table, you can join the young soul- and blues-loving crowd over inexpensive empanadas and vermouth. Bands also occasionally play.

Redrum BAR

(Map p292; ☎670 269126; Carrer de Margarit 36; ⏲6pm-1am Mon-Thu, 6pm-2am Fri, 2pm-2am Sat, 6pm-12.30am Sun; Ⓜ Poble Sec) Redrum's craft brews and cocktails are complemented by Mexican street food (including excellent tacos and ceviche). It has a brightly coloured interior and friendly service. Happy hour runs from 6pm to 8pm.

Tinta Roja BAR

(Map p292; ☎93 443 32 43; www.tintaroja.cat; Carrer de la Creu dels Molers 17; ⏲8.30pm-12.30am Wed, to 2am Thu, to 3am Fri & Sat, closed Aug; Ⓜ Poble Sec) A succession of nooks and crannies, dotted with flea-market finds and dimly lit in violets, reds and yellows, makes Tinta Roja an intimate spot for a craft beer, cocktail or glass of Argentinean wine – and the occasional show in the back, featuring anything from actors to acrobats.

☆ Entertainment

☆ La Rambla & Barri Gòtic

Gran Teatre del Liceu THEATRE, LIVE MUSIC

(Map p256; ☎93 485 99 00; www.liceubarcelona.cat; La Rambla 51-59; ⏲box office 9.30am-7.30pm Mon-Fri, to 5.30pm Sat & Sun; Ⓜ Liceu) Barcelona's grand old opera house, restored after a fire in 1994, is one of the most technologically advanced theatres in the world. To take a seat in the grand auditorium, returned to all its 19th-century glory but with the very latest in acoustics, is to be transported to another age.

Tickets can cost anything from €10 for a cheap seat behind a pillar to €200 for a well-positioned night at the opera.

El Paraigua LIVE MUSIC

(Map p256; ☎93 302 11 31; www.elparaigua.com; Carrer del Pas de l'Ensenyança 2; ⏲noon-2am Sun-Wed, to 1am Thu, to 3am Fri & Sat; Ⓜ Liceu) FREE A tiny chocolate box of dark tinted Modernisme, the 'Umbrella' has been serving up drinks since the 1960s. The turn-of-the-20th-century decor was transferred here from a shop knocked down elsewhere in the district and cobbled back together to create this cosy locale.

Sidecar Factory Club LIVE MUSIC

(Map p256; ☎93 302 15 86; www.sidecarfactoryclub.com; Plaça Reial 7; ⏲7pm-5am Mon-Thu, to 6am Fri & Sat; Ⓜ Liceu) Descend into the red-tinged, brick-vaulted bowels for live music most nights. Just about anything goes here, from UK indie through to country punk, but rock and pop lead the way. Most shows start around 10pm and DJs take over at 12.30am. Upstairs at ground level you can get food (until midnight) or a few drinks (until 3am).

Jamboree LIVE MUSIC

(Map p256; ☎93 319 17 89; www.masimas.com/jamboree; Plaça Reial 17; tickets €5-20; ⏲8pm-6am; Ⓜ Liceu) For over half a century, Jamboree has been bringing joy to the jivers of Barcelona, with high-calibre acts featuring jazz trios, blues, Afrobeats, Latin and big-band sounds. Two concerts are held most nights (at 8pm and 10pm), after which Jamboree morphs into a DJ-spinning club at midnight. WTF jam sessions are held Mondays (entrance a mere €5).

Harlem Jazz Club JAZZ
(Map p256; ☎93 310 07 55; www.harlemjazzclub.es; Carrer de la Comtessa de Sobradiel 8; tickets €7-10; ⊙8pm-3am Sun & Tue-Thu, to 5am Fri & Sat; Ⓜ Liceu) This narrow, old-city dive is one of the best spots in town for jazz, as well as funk, Latin, blues and gypsy jazz. It attracts a mixed crowd that maintains a respectful silence during the acts. Most concerts start around 10pm. Get in early if you want a seat in front of the stage.

Sala Tarantos FLAMENCO
(Map p256; ☎93 304 12 10; www.masimas.com/tarantos; Plaça Reial 17; tickets €15; ⊙shows 7.30pm, 8.30pm & 9.30pm Oct-Jun, plus 10.30pm Jul-Sep; Ⓜ Liceu) Since 1963, this basement locale has been the stage for up-and-coming flamenco groups performing in Barcelona. These days Tarantos has become a mostly tourist-centric affair, with half-hour shows held three times a night. Still, it's a good introduction to flamenco, and not a bad setting for a drink.

☆ El Raval

★Filmoteca de Catalunya CINEMA
(Map p256; ☎93 567 10 70; www.filmoteca.cat; Plaça de Salvador Seguí 1-9; adult/concession €4/3; ⊙screenings 5-10pm, ticket office 10am-3pm & 4-9.30pm Tue-Sun; Ⓜ Liceu) The Filmoteca de Catalunya – Catalonia's national cinema – sits in a modern 6000-sq-metre building in the midst of the most louche part of El Raval. The films shown are a superior mix of classics and more recent releases, with frequent themed cycles. A 10-session pass is an amazingly cheap €20.

Jazz Sí Club LIVE MUSIC
(Map p256; ☎93 329 00 20; www.tallerdemusics.com/en/jazzsi-club; Carrer de Requesens 2; entry incl drink €6-10; ⊙8.30-11pm Tue-Sat, 6.30-10pm Sun; Ⓜ Sant Antoni) A cramped little bar run by the Taller de Músics (Musicians' Workshop) serves as the stage for a varied program of jazz jams through to some good flamenco (Friday and Saturday nights). Thursday night is Cuban night, Tuesday and Sunday are rock, and the rest are devoted to jazz and/or blues sessions. Concerts start around 9pm but the jam sessions can get going earlier.

☆ La Ribera

★Palau de la Música Catalana CLASSICAL MUSIC
(Map p278; ☎93 295 72 00; www.palaumusica.cat; Carrer de Palau de la Música 4-6; tickets from €18; ⊙box office 9.30am-9pm Mon-Sat, 10am-3pm Sun; Ⓜ Urquinaona) A feast for the eyes, this Modernista confection is also the city's most traditional venue for classical and choral music, although it has a wide-ranging program, including flamenco, pop and – particularly – jazz. Just being here for a performance is an experience. In the foyer, its tiled pillars all a-glitter, you can sip a pre-concert tipple.

Tablao Nervión DANCE
(Map p256; ☎93 315 21 03; www.restaurantenervion.com; Carrer de la Princesa 2; show incl 1 drink €18, show & set dinner €30; ⊙shows 8-10pm Wed-Sun; Ⓜ Jaume I) For admittedly tourist-oriented flamenco, this unassuming bar (shows take place in the basement) is cheaper than most, and has good offerings. Check the website for further details.

☆ Barceloneta & the Waterfront

Sala Monasterio LIVE MUSIC
(Map p272; ☎616 287197; www.facebook.com/sala.monasterio; Moll de Mestral 30; tickets vary; ⊙10pm-5am Sun-Thu, to 6am Fri & Sat; Ⓜ Ciutadella Vila Olímpica) Overlooking the bobbing masts and slender palm trees of Port Olímpic, this pocket-sized music spot stages an eclectic line-up of live bands, including jazz, *forró* (music from northeastern Brazil), blues jams and rock.

Razzmatazz LIVE MUSIC
(☎93 320 82 00; www.salarazzmatazz.com; Carrer de Pamplona 88; tickets from €17; ⊙9pm-4am; Ⓜ Bogatell) Bands from far and wide occasionally create scenes of near hysteria in this, one of the city's classic live-music and clubbing venues. Bands can appear throughout the week (check the website), with different start times. On weekends live music later gives way to club sounds.

Yelmo Cines Icària CINEMA
(Map p272; ☎902 220922; www.yelmocines.es; Carrer de Salvador Espriu 61; tickets adult/child €9.90/7.30; Ⓜ Ciutadella Vila Olímpica) This vast cinema complex shows films in the original language on 15 screens, making for plenty

of choice. Aside from the screens, you'll find several cheerful places to eat, bars and the like to keep you occupied before and after the movies.

☆ La Sagrada Família & L'Eixample

City Hall LIVE MUSIC
(Map p278; ☎93 238 07 22; www.cityhallbarcelona.com; Rambla de Catalunya 2-4; Ⓜ Catalunya) Also home to a nightclub (p322), this former theatre is also the perfect size and shape for live music, holding a crowd of around 500. The acoustics are great and the layout means everyone gets a good view of the stage.

Méliès Cinemes CINEMA
(Map p278; ☎93 451 00 51; www.meliescinemes.com; Carrer de Villarroel 102; tickets €4-7; Ⓜ Urgell) A cosy cinema with two screens, the Méliès specialises in the best of recent releases from Hollywood and Europe.

☆ Gràcia & Park Güell

Cine Texas CINEMA
(Map p286; ☎93 348 77 48; www.cinemestexas.cat; Carrer de Bailèn 205; Ⓜ Joanic) All films at this contemporary four-screen cinema are shown in their original languages (with subtitles in Catalan). Genres span art house through to Hollywood blockbusters. Catalan-language films are subtitled in English.

Verdi Park CINEMA
(Map p286; ☎93 238 79 90; www.cines-verdi.com; Carrer de Torrijos 49; Ⓜ Fontana) Verdi Park is a perennially popular art-house cinema with four screens. Most films are shown in their original language.

Verdi CINEMA
(Map p286; ☎93 238 79 90; www.cines-verdi.com; Carrer de Verdi 32; Ⓜ Fontana) In the heart of Gràcia, this five-screen cinema shows art-house and blockbuster films in their original language as well as films in Catalan and Spanish. It's handy to lots of local eateries and bars for pre- and post-film enjoyment.

☆ Camp Nou, Pedralbes & La Zona Alta

Camp Nou FOOTBALL
(☎902 189900; www.fcbarcelona.com; Carrer d'Arístides Maillol; Ⓜ Palau Reial) The massive stadium of Camp Nou ('New Field' in Catalan) is home to the legendary Futbol Club Barcelona. Attending a game amid the roar of the crowds is an unforgettable experience; the season runs from September to May. Alternatively, get a taste of all the excitement at the interactive Camp Nou Experience (p286), which includes a tour of the stadium.

ⓘ SEEING AN FC BARÇA MATCH

Tickets to FC Barcelona matches are available at Camp Nou, online (through FC Barcelona's official website), and through various city locations. Tourist offices sell them – the **main office** (p295) at Plaça de Catalunya is a centrally located option – as do FC Botiga stores. Tickets can cost anything from €39 to upwards of €250, depending on the seat and match. On match day the ticket windows (at **gates 9** (Gate 9, Avinguda de Joan XXIII; ⏱10am-6pm Mon-Sat, to 2.15pm Sun, 9.15am–kick-off match days; Ⓜ Palau Reial) and 15) open from 9.15am until kick off. Tickets for matches with Real Madrid sell out years in advance.

If you attend a game, go early so you'll have ample time to find your seat (this stadium is massive) and soak up the atmosphere.

You will almost definitely find scalpers lurking near the ticket windows. They are often club members and can sometimes get you in at a significant reduction. Don't pay until you are safely seated.

Luz de Gas LIVE MUSIC
(☎93 209 77 11; www.luzdegas.com; Carrer de Muntaner 246; ⏱midnight-6am Thu-Sat; 🚌6, 7, 27, 32, 33, 34, H8, 🚊T1, T2, T3 Francesc Macià) Several nights a week this club, set in a grand former theatre, stages concerts ranging through rock, soul, salsa, jazz and pop. Concerts typically kick off around 1am; from about 2am, the place turns into a club that attracts a well-dressed crowd with varying musical tastes, depending on the night. Check the website for the latest schedule.

☆ Montjuïc, Poble Sec & Sant Antoni

BARTS CONCERT VENUE
(Barcelona Arts on Stage; Map p292; ☎93 324 84 92; www.barts.cat; Avinguda del Paral·lel 62; Ⓜ Paral·lel) BARTS has a solid reputation

for its innovative line-up of urban dance troupes, electro swing, psychedelic pop and other eclectic fare. Its smart design combines a comfortable midsized auditorium with excellent acoustics. Hours and ticket prices vary; check the agenda online.

Gran Bodega Saltó LIVE MUSIC
(Map p292; 93 441 37 09; www.bodegasalto.net; Carrer de Blesa 36; 7pm-2am Mon-Thu, noon-3am Fri & Sat, noon-midnight Sun; M Paral·lel) The ranks of barrels give away the bar's history as a traditional bodega. Now, after a little home-made psychedelic redecoration with odd lamps, figurines and old Chinese beer ads, it's a magnet for an eclectic barfly crowd. The crowd is mixed and friendly, and gets pretty animated on nights when there's live music.

Sala Apolo LIVE MUSIC
(Map p292; 93 441 40 01; www.sala-apolo.com; Carrer Nou de la Rambla 113; club from €15, concerts vary; concerts from 8pm, club from midnight; M Paral·lel) This is a fine old theatre, where red velvet dominates and you feel as though you're in a movie-set dancehall scene. 'Nasty Mondays' and 'Crappy Tuesdays' are aimed at a diehard, never-stop-dancing crowd. Club entry includes a drink. Earlier in the evening, concerts generally take place here and in 'La 2', a smaller auditorium downstairs.

Tastes are as eclectic as possible, from local bands and burlesque shows to big-name international acts.

Teatre Mercat De Les Flors DANCE
(Map p292; 93 256 26 00; www.mercatflors.cat; Carrer de Lleida 59; box office 11am-2pm & 4-7pm Mon-Fri, plus 1hr before show; 55) Next door to the **Teatre Lliure** (Map p292; 93 289 27 70; www.teatrelliure.com; Plaça de Margarida Xirgu 1; box office 9am-8pm, plus 2hr before performance; 55), and together with it known as the Ciutat de Teatre (Theatre City), this spacious modern stage is Barcelona's top venue for local and international contemporary dance acts.

Renoir Floridablanca CINEMA
(Map p256; 91 542 27 02; www.cinesrenoir.com; Carrer de Floridablanca 135; M Sant Antoni) With seven screens, this cinema shows a mix of quality art-house flicks and blockbusters in their original language (with Spanish subtitles). It's handily located just beyond El Raval, so you'll find no shortage of post-film entertainment options nearby.

Shopping

La Rambla & Barri Gòtic

Torrons Vicens FOOD
(Map p256; 93 304 37 36; www.vicens.com; Carrer del Petritxol 15; 10am-8.30pm Mon-Sat, 11am-8pm Sun; M Liceu) You can find the *turrón* (nougat) treat year-round at Torrons Vicens, which has been selling its signature sweets since 1775.

Sabater Hermanos COSMETICS
(Map p256; 93 301 98 32; www.sabaterhermanos.es; Plaça de Sant Felip Neri 1; 10.30am-9pm; M Jaume I) This fragrant little shop sells handcrafted soaps of all sizes. Varieties such as fig, cinnamon, grapefruit and chocolate smell good enough to eat, while sandalwood, magnolia, mint, cedar and jasmine add spice to any sink or bathtub.

Formatgeria La Seu FOOD
(Map p256; 93 412 65 48; www.formatgerialaseu.com; Carrer de la Dagueria 16; 10am-2pm & 5-8pm Tue-Sat Sep-Jul; M Jaume I) Dedicated to artisan cheeses from all across Spain, this small shop is run by the oh-so-knowledgeable Katherine McLaughlin and is the antithesis of mass production – it sells only the best from small-scale farmers and the stock changes regularly. Wine and cheese tastings in the cosy room at the back are fun.

Escribà FOOD & DRINKS
(Map p256; 93 301 60 27; www.escriba.es; La Rambla 83; 9am-9.30pm; ; M Liceu) Chocolates, dainty pastries and mouth-watering cakes can be nibbled behind the Modernista mosaic facade here or taken away for private, guilt-ridden consumption. This Barcelona favourite is owned by the Escribà family, a name synonymous with sinfully good sweet things. More than that, it adds a touch of authenticity to La Rambla.

El Corte Inglés DEPARTMENT STORE
(Map p256; 93 306 38 00; www.elcorteingles.es; Av del Portal de l'Àngel 19-21; 9.30am-9pm Mon-Sat Oct-May, 9.30am-10.15pm Jun-Sep; M Catalunya) A secondary branch of Spain's only remaining department store, selling electronics, fashion, stationery and sports gear.

L'Arca VINTAGE, CLOTHING
(Map p256; 93 302 15 98; www.larca.es; Carrer dels Banys Nous 20; 11am-2pm & 4.30-8.30pm Mon-Sat; M Liceu) Step inside this enchanting shop for a glimpse of beautifully crafted

apparel from the past, including 18th-century embroidered silk vests, elaborate silk kimonos, and wedding dresses and shawls from the 1920s. Thanks to its incredible collection, it has provided clothing for films including *Titanic, Talk to Her* and *Perfume: The Story of a Murderer*.

Herboristeria del Rei COSMETICS
(Map p256; ☎93 318 05 12; www.herboristeriadelrei.com; Carrer del Vidre 1; ⊙2.30-8.30pm Tue-Thu, 10.30am-8.30pm Fri & Sat; Ⓜ Liceu) Once patronised by Queen Isabel II, this timeless corner store flogs all sorts of weird and wonderful herbs, spices and medicinal plants. It's been doing so since 1823 and the decor has barely changed since the 1860s – some of the products have, however, and nowadays you'll find anything from fragrant soaps to massage oil.

Film director Tom Tykwer shot some scenes from *Perfume: The Story of a Murderer* here.

Cereria Subirà HOMEWARES
(Map p256; ☎93 315 26 06; http://cereriasubira.net; Calle de la Llibreteria 7; ⊙9.30am-1.30pm & 4-8pm Mon-Thu, 9.30am-8pm Fri, 10am-8pm Sat; Ⓜ Jaume I) Even if you're not interested in myriad mounds of colourful wax, pop in just so you've been to the oldest shop in Barcelona. Cereria Subirà has been churning out candles since 1761 and at this address since the 19th century; the interior has a beautifully baroque quality, with a picturesque *Gone With the Wind*–style staircase.

La Colmena FOOD
(Map p256; ☎93 315 13 56; www.pastisserialacolmena.com; Plaça de l'Angel 12; ⊙9am-9pm; Ⓜ Jaume I) A pastry shop selling many delicacies including pine-nut-encrusted *panellets* (sweet almond cakes), flavoured meringues and feather-light *ensaïmadas* (soft, sweet buns topped with powdered sugar) from Mallorca.

La Manual Alpargatera SHOES
(Map p256; ☎93 301 01 72; www.lamanualalpargatera.es; Carrer d'Avinyó 7; ⊙9.30am-1.30pm & 4.30-8pm Mon-Fri, from 10am Sat; Ⓜ Liceu) Clients from Salvador Dalí to Jean Paul Gaultier have ordered a pair of *espadrilles* (rope-soled canvas shoes) from this famous store. The shop was founded just after the Spanish Civil War, though the roots of the simple shoe design date back hundreds of years and originated in the Catalan Pyrenees.

Petritxol Xocoa FOOD
(Map p256; ☎93 301 82 91; www.xocoa-bcn.com; Carrer del Petritxol 11-13; ⊙9.30am-9pm; Ⓜ Liceu) Tucked along 'chocolate street' Carrer del Petritxol, this den of dental devilry displays ranks and ranks of original bars in stunning designs, chocolates stuffed with sweet stuff, gooey pastries and more. It has various other branches scattered about town.

El Raval

★Les Topettes COSMETICS
(Map p256; ☎93 500 55 64; www.lestopettes.com; Carrer de Joaquín Costa 33; ⊙11am-2pm & 4-9pm Tue-Sat, 4-9pm Mon; Ⓜ Universitat) It's a sign of the times that such a chic little temple to soap and perfume can exist in El Raval. The items in Les Topettes' collection have been picked for their designs as much as for the products themselves, and you'll find gorgeously packaged scents, candles and unguents from Diptyque, Cowshed and L'Artisan Parfumeur, among others.

Fantastik ARTS & CRAFTS
(Map p256; ☎93 301 30 68; www.fantastik.es; Carrer de Joaquín Costa 62; ⊙11am-2pm & 4-8.30pm Mon-Fri, 11am-3pm & 4-9pm Sat; Ⓜ Universitat) Over 400 products, including a Mexican skull rattle, robot moon explorer from China and recycled plastic zebras from South Africa, are to be found in this colourful shop, which sources its items from Mexico, India, Bulgaria, Russia, Senegal and 20 other countries. It's a perfect place to buy all the things you don't need but can't live without.

Holala! Plaza FASHION & ACCESSORIES
(Map p256; www.holala-ibiza.com; Plaça de Castella 2; ⊙11am-9pm Mon-Sat; Ⓜ Universitat) Backing on to Carrer de Valldonzella, where it boasts an exhibition space (Gallery) for temporary art displays, this Ibiza import is inspired by that island's long-established (and somewhat commercialised) hippie tradition. Vintage clothes are the name of the game, along with an eclectic program of exhibitions and activities.

La Ribera

El Rei de la Màgia MAGIC
(Map p256; ☎93 319 39 20; www.elreydelamagia.com; Carrer de la Princesa 11; ⊙10.30am-2pm & 4-7.30pm Mon-Sat; Ⓜ Jaume I) For more than 100 years, the owners have been keeping locals both astounded and amused. Should you decide to stay in Barcelona and make a living

as a magician, this is the place to buy levitation brooms, glasses of disappearing milk and decks of magic cards.

Vila Viniteca WINE

(Map p256; ☎93 777 70 17; www.vilaviniteca.es; Carrer dels Agullers 7; ⏲8.30am-8.30pm Mon-Sat; Ⓜ Jaume I) One of the best wine stores in Barcelona (and there are a few…), Vila Viniteca has been searching out the best local and imported wines since 1932. On a couple of November evenings it organises what has become an almost riotous wine-tasting event in Carrer dels Agullers and surrounding lanes, at which cellars from around Spain present their young new wines.

Casa Gispert FOOD

(Map p266; ☎93 319 75 35; www.casagispert.com; Carrer dels Sombrerers 23; ⏲10am-8.30pm Mon-Sat; Ⓜ Jaume I) The wonderful, atmospheric and wood-fronted Casa Gispert has been toasting nuts and selling all manner of dried fruit since 1851. Pots and jars piled high on the shelves contain an unending variety of crunchy titbits: some roasted, some honeyed, all of them moreish. Your order is shouted over to the till, along with the price, in a display of old-world accounting.

El Magnífico COFFEE

(Map p266; ☎93 319 60 81; www.cafeselmagnifico.com; Carrer de l'Argenteria 64; ⏲9.30am-8pm Mon-Sat; Ⓜ Jaume I) All sorts of coffee has been roasted here since the early 20th century. The variety of coffee (and tea) available is remarkable – and the aromas hit you as you walk in. Across the road, the same people run the exquisite tea shop **Sans i Sans** (Map p266; ☎93 310 25 18; www.sansisans.com; Carrer de l'Argenteria 59; ⏲10am-8pm Mon-Sat; Ⓜ Jaume I).

Coquette FASHION & ACCESSORIES

(Map p266; ☎93 310 35 35; www.coquettebcn.com; Carrer de Bonaire 5; ⏲11am-3pm & 5-9pm Mon-Fri, 11.30am-9pm Sat; Ⓜ Barceloneta) Elegant women's store with designers from around the globe, but particularly Spain.

Loisaida CLOTHING, ANTIQUES

(Map p266; ☎93 295 54 92; www.loisaidabcn.com; Carrer dels Flassaders 42; ⏲11am-9pm Mon-Sat, 11am-2pm & 4-8pm Sun; Ⓜ Jaume I) A sight in its own right, housed in the former coach house and stables for the Royal Mint, Loisaida (from the Spanglish for 'Lower East Side') is a deceptively large emporium of colourful, retro and somewhat preppy clothing for men and women, costume jewellery, music from the 1940s and '50s and some covetable antiques. One space is devoted entirely to denim.

Arlequí Màscares ARTS & CRAFTS

(Map p256; ☎93 268 27 52; www.arlequimask.com; Carrer de la Princesa 7; ⏲11.30am-8pm Mon, 10.30am-8pm Tue-Fri, 11am-8pm Sat, 11.30am-7pm Sun; Ⓜ Jaume I) A wonderful little oasis of originality, this shop specialises in masks for costume and decoration. Some of the pieces are superb, while stock also includes a beautiful range of decorative boxes in Catalan themes, and some old-style marionettes.

Hofmann Pastisseria FOOD

(Map p266; ☎93 268 82 21; www.hofmann-bcn.com; Carrer dels Flassaders 44; ⏲9am-2pm & 3.30-8pm Mon-Sat, 9am-2.30pm Sun; Ⓜ Barceloneta) With its painted wooden cabinets, this bite-sized gourmet patisserie, linked to the prestigious Hofmann cooking school, has an air of timelessness. Choose between jars of delicious chocolates, the renowned croissants (in various flavours) and more dangerous pastries, or an array of cakes and other sweet treats.

Barceloneta & the Waterfront

Vernita CHILDREN'S CLOTHING

(☎625 092341; www.facebook/vernitastudioshop; Carrer del Joncar 27; ⏲10am-1.30pm & 5-8pm Tue-Fri, 10am-2pm & 5-8pm Sat; Ⓜ Poblenou) Three mothers, Neli, Laura and Nacha, design and hand-stitch children's clothing and accessories such as animal-print cushions, bags, kids' jewellery, bow ties, towels (including adorable dinosaur designs) and washable nappies as well as soft cuddly toys at this light, bright studio-boutique. During the evenings, they also offer sewing lessons and origami workshops for kids (English available).

Ultra-Local Records MUSIC

(☎661 017638; www.ultralocalrecords.com; Carrer de Pujades 113; ⏲4-8.30pm Mon-Fri, 11am-8.30pm Sat; Ⓜ Llacuna) Along a fairly empty stretch of El Poblenou, this small, well-curated shop sells mostly used records (plus some re-releases and albums by current indie rock darlings) from Catalan, Spanish, French, American and British artists. Vinyl aside, you'll find a smaller CD selection, plus zines and a few other curiosities. There's a €1 bargain bin in front of the store.

Bestiari BOOKS, HANDICRAFTS

(Map p272; www.bestiari.net; Plaça de Pau Vila 3; ⏲10am-7pm Tue & Thu-Sat, to 8pm Wed, to 2.30pm

Sun; Ⓜ Barceloneta) On the ground floor of the Museu d'Història de Catalunya (p271), this well-stocked shop sells books in English, Catalan and Spanish for all ages, along with Catalan-themed gift ideas: CDs, T-shirts, umbrellas, messenger bags, chess sets, mugs and toys (along the lines of the build-your-own Gothic or Gaudí structures).

Els Encants Vells MARKET

(Fira de Bellcaire; ☎ 93 246 30 30; www.encantsbcn.com; Plaça de les Glòries Catalanes; ⏲ 9am-8pm Mon, Wed, Fri & Sat; Ⓜ Glòries) In a gleaming open-sided complex near Plaça de les Glòries Catalanes, the 'Old Charms' flea market is the biggest of its kind in Barcelona. Over 500 vendors ply their wares beneath massive mirror-like panels. It's all here, from antique furniture through to secondhand clothes. There's a lot of junk, but you'll occasionally stumble across a *ganga* (bargain).

Maremàgnum MALL

(Map p272; ☎ 93 225 81 00; www.maremagnum.es; Moll d'Espanya 5; ⏲ 10am-10pm; Ⓜ Drassanes) Created out of largely abandoned docks, this buzzing shopping centre, with its 19 places to eat, bars and cinemas, is home to 59 shops including youthful Spanish chain Mango, and eye-catching fashions from Barcelona-based Desigual. Football fans will be drawn to the paraphernalia at FC Botiga. It's particularly popular on Sundays when most other stores in the city remain shuttered.

La Sagrada Família & L'Eixample

★ Joan Múrria FOOD & DRINKS

(Map p278; ☎ 93 215 57 89; www.murria.cat; Carrer de Roger de Llúria 85; ⏲ 10am-8.30pm Tue-Fri, 10am-2pm & 5-8.30pm Sat; Ⓜ Girona) Ramon Casas designed the 1898 Modernista shopfront advertisements featured at this culinary temple of speciality food goods from around Catalonia and beyond. Artisan cheeses, Iberian hams, caviar, canned delicacies, smoked fish, *cavas* and wines, coffee and loose-leaf teas are among the treats in store.

★ Flores Navarro FLOWERS

(Map p278; ☎ 93 457 40 99; www.floristeriasnavarro.com; Carrer de València 320; ⏲ 24hr; Ⓜ Girona) You never know when you might need flowers, and this florist never closes. Established in 1960, it's a vast space (or couple of spaces, in fact), and worth a visit just for the bank of colour and wonderful fragrance.

Cacao Sampaka FOOD

(Map p278; ☎ 93 272 08 33; www.cacaosampaka.com; Carrer del Consell de Cent 292; ⏲ 9am-9pm Mon-Sat; Ⓜ Passeig de Gràcia) Chocoholics will be convinced they have died and passed on to a better place. Load up in the shop or head for the bar out the back where you can have a classic *xocolata* (hot chocolate) and munch on exquisite chocolate cakes, tarts, ice cream, sweets and sandwiches. The bonbons make particularly good presents.

Altaïr BOOKS

(Map p278; ☎ 93 342 71 71; www.altair.es; Gran Via de les Corts Catalanes 616; ⏲ 10am-8.30pm Mon-Sat; 📶; Ⓜ Catalunya) Enter a wonderland of travel in this extensive bookshop, which has enough guidebooks, maps, travel literature and other books to induce a severe case of itchy feet. It has a travellers noticeboard and, downstairs, a cafe.

Dr Bloom FASHION & ACCESSORIES

(Map p278; ☎ 93 292 23 27; www.drbloom.es; Rambla de Catalunya 30; ⏲ 10am-9pm Mon-Sat; Ⓜ Passeig de Gràcia) A new collection comes out every month at Dr Bloom, so the stock is constantly rotating. Designed and made in Barcelona, the fashion label's dresses, tops, shawls and more have an emphasis on bright colours and bold prints no matter the season.

El Corte Inglés DEPARTMENT STORE

(Map p278; ☎ 93 306 38 00; www.elcorteingles.es; Plaça de Catalunya 23; ⏲ 9.30am-9pm Mon-Sat; Ⓜ Catalunya) Spain's only remaining department-store chain stocks everything you'd expect, from computers to cushions and high fashion to homewares. Fabulous city views extend from the top-floor restaurant. Nearby branches include one at **Avinguda Diagonal 471-473** (☎ 93 493 48 00; www.elcorteingles.es; Avinguda Diagonal 471-473; ⏲ 9.30am-9pm Mon-Sat; Ⓜ Hospital Clínic).

Casa Del Llibre BOOKS

(Map p278; ☎ 902 026407; www.casadellibro.com; Passeig de Gràcia 62; ⏲ 9am-9.30pm Mon-Sat, 11am-9.30pm Sun; Ⓜ Passeig de Gràcia) With branches throughout Spain, the 'Home of the Book' is a well-stocked general bookshop with sections devoted to literature in English, French and other languages, as well as a good number of guidebooks.

FNAC ELECTRONICS, BOOKS

(Map p256; ☎ 902 100632; www.fnac.es; El Triangle, Plaça de Catalunya 4; ⏲ 9.30am-9pm Mon-Sat;

Ⓜ Catalunya) FNAC, the French electronics, book and music emporium, has a couple of branches around town, but this is the biggest.

Gràcia & Park Güell

★Colmillo de Morsa FASHION & ACCESSORIES
(Map p286; ☎645 206365; www.facebook.com/colmillodemorsa; Carrer de Vic 15-17; ⏱4.30-8.30pm Mon, 11am-2.30pm & 4.30-8.30pm Tue-Sat; Ⓡ FGC Gràcia) Design team Javier Blanco and Elisabet Vallecillo have made waves at Madrid's Cibeles Fashion Week and Paris' fashion fair Who's Next, and showcase their Barcelona-made women's fashion here at their flagship boutique. They've also opened the floor to promote other young, up-and-coming local labels. The light-filled space also hosts art, graphic design and photography exhibitions and fashion shows.

Hibernian BOOKS
(Map p286; ☎93 217 47 96; www.hibernian-books.com; Carrer de Montseny 17; ⏱4-8.30pm Mon, 11am-8.30pm Tue-Sat; Ⓜ Fontana) Barcelona's biggest secondhand English bookshop stocks thousands of titles covering all sorts of subjects, from cookery to children's classics. There's a smaller collection of new books in English too.

Amalia Vermell JEWELLERY
(Map p286; ☎655 754008; www.amaliavermell.com; Carrer de Francisco Giner 49; ⏱11am-2pm & 5-9pm Mon-Sat; Ⓜ Diagonal) Striking geometric jewellery made from high-quality materials such as sterling silver is handcrafted by Amalia Vermell here in her atelier. Browse for pendants and necklaces, bracelets and rings, or sign up for a jewellery-making course (from €65 for two hours; English available).

Vinil Vintage MUSIC
(Map p286; ☎93 192 39 99; Carrer de Ramón y Cajal 45-47; ⏱10.30am-2pm & 5-8.30pm Tue-Sat; Ⓜ Joanic) Crate diggers will love rummaging through the vinyl collection here. There's a huge range of rock, pop and jazz, including plenty of Spanish music. It also sells turntables and speakers.

Lady Loquita CLOTHING
(Map p286; ☎93 217 82 92; www.ladyloquita.com; Travessera de Gràcia 126; ⏱11am-2pm & 5-8.30pm Mon-Sat; Ⓜ Fontana) At this hip little shop you can browse through light, locally made summer dresses by Tiralahilacha, evening wear by Japamala and handmade jewellery by local design label Klimbim. There are also whimsical odds and ends: dinner plates with dog-people portraits and digital prints on wood by About Paola.

Tintin Shop GIFTS & SOUVENIRS
(Map p286; ☎93 289 25 24; www.tintinshopbcn.com; Travessera de Gràcia 176; ⏱10.30am-2.30pm & 5-8.30pm Mon-Fri, 11am-2.30pm Sat; Ⓜ Fontana) Fans of the Belgian boy wonder should make a beeline to this Gràcia store, where you'll find Tintin T-shirts, posters, action figures, book bags, wristwatches, pencil cases, and even a soft, irresistible Milou (Tintin's wire fox terrier, known as Snowy in English) – plus, of course, the books that made him famous (with titles in Catalan, Spanish and French).

Picnic CLOTHING
(Map p286; ☎93 016 69 53; www.picnicstore.es; Carrer de Verdi 17; ⏱11am-9pm Mon-Fri, 11am-3pm & 4-9pm Sat; Ⓜ Fontana) This tiny, beautifully curated boutique has many temptations: stylish sneakers by Meyba (a Barcelona brand), striped jerseys from Basque label Loreak Mendian and boldly patterned Mödernaked backpacks. Other finds include animal-print ceramics for the home, small-scale art prints and fashion mags.

Be GIFTS & SOUVENIRS
(Map p286; ☎93 218 89 49; www.bethestore.com; Carrer de Bonavista 7; ⏱10.30am-9pm Mon-Sat; Ⓜ Diagonal) Be is a fun place to browse for accessories and gift ideas. You'll find rugged vintage-looking satchels, leather handbags, stylish (and reflective) Happy Socks, portable record players, sneakers (Vans, Pumas, old-school Nikes) and gadgets (including richly hued Pantone micro speakers and Polaroid digital cameras).

Bodega Bonavista WINE
(Map p286; ☎93 218 81 99; Carrer de Bonavista 10; ⏱10am-2.30pm & 5-9pm Mon-Fri, noon-3pm & 6-9pm Sat, noon-3pm Sun; Ⓜ Fontana) An excellent little neighbourhood bodega, Bonavista endeavours to seek out great wines at reasonable prices. The stock is mostly from Catalonia and elsewhere in Spain, but there's also a well-chosen selection from France. The Bonavista also acts as a deli, and there are some especially good cheeses. You can sample wines by the glass, along with cheeses and charcuterie, at one of the in-store tables.

Mushi Mushi FASHION & ACCESSORIES
(Map p286; ☎93 292 29 74; www.mushimushicollection.com; Carrer de Bonavista 12; ⏰11am-3pm & 4.30-8.30pm Mon-Sat; Ⓜ Diagonal) A gorgeous little fashion boutique in an area that's not short of them, Mushi Mushi specialises in quirky but elegant women's fashion and accessories. It stocks small labels such as Des Petits Hauts, Sessùn and Orion London, as well as jewellery by Adriana Llorens. The collection changes frequently, so a return visit can pay off.

Camp Nou, Pedralbes & La Zona Alta

Normandie CHILDREN'S CLOTHING
(☎93 209 14 11; www.normandiebaby.com; Plaça de Sant Gregori Taumaturg; ⏰10.30am-2.30pm & 4.30-8.30pm Mon-Sat; 🚆FGC La Bonanova) Set up by Barcelona-born, Paris-trained designer Graziella Antón de Vez in 2000, this fashion label for babies and children aged up to six years utilises all-natural materials such as angora, cotton, cashmere and wool. Adorable outfits are inspired by France's Normandy region, with vintage- and retro-style lines.

Ukka FASHION & ACCESSORIES
(☎661 919710; Carrer de Laforja 122; ⏰10.30am-2pm & 5-8.30pm Mon-Fri, 11am-2pm & 5.30-8.30pm Sat; 🚆FGC Muntaner) Ukka makes its bohemian-inspired women's fashion and accessories (including scarves, hats and some eye-catching jewellery) at its Barcelona factory and sells them exclusively in this chic little terracotta-floored boutique.

Labperfum COSMETICS
(☎93 298 95 12; www.labperfum.com; Carrer de Santaló 45; ⏰10am-2.30pm & 5-8.30pm Mon-Sat; 🚆FGC Muntaner) This tiny shop looks like an old apothecary, with its shelves lined with pretty glass bottles of extraordinary fragrances (for men and women) made in-house and beautifully packaged. Scents diverge from run-of-the-mill Obsession, with varieties like tobacco, black orchid and leather. You can also buy scented candles, soaps and creams.

L'Illa Diagonal MALL
(☎93 444 00 00; www.lilla.com; Avinguda Diagonal 557; ⏰9.30am-9pm Mon-Sat; Ⓜ Maria Cristina) One of Barcelona's best malls, this is a fine place to while away a few hours (or days), with high-end shops and a mesmerising spread of eateries.

Montjuïc, Poble Sec & Sant Antoni

Popcorn Store FASHION & ACCESSORIES
(Map p292; Carrer Viladomat 30-32; ⏰11am-3pm & 4.30-8.30pm Mon-Sat) Cutting-edge Barcelona labels for women at this 2017-opened boutique include Sister Dew, with asymmetrical tops, jackets, dresses and more, and Ester Gueroa, with bold prints and lace. Men will find stylish shirts, trousers and belts from Italian and other European designers.

10000 Records MUSIC
(☎93 292 77 76; www.10000records.es; Carrer de Floridablanca 70; ⏰5-8pm Mon, 10am-2pm & 5-8pm Tue-Fri, 10am-2pm Sat; Ⓜ Poble Sec) As its name suggests, this record shop overflows with vintage and new vinyl in all genres but especially rock, pop, metal and jazz. You'll also unearth retro radios, cassettes and music books.

Mercat de Sant Antoni MARKET
(Map p256; ☎93 426 35 21; www.mercatdesantantoni.com; Carrer de Comte d'Urgell 1; ⏰7am-2.30pm & 5-8.30pm Mon-Thu, 7am-8.30pm Fri & Sat; Ⓜ Sant Antoni) Just beyond the western edge of El Raval is Mercat de Sant Antoni, a glorious old iron-and-brick building constructed between 1872 and 1882. The second-hand book market takes place alongside on Sunday mornings.

The market recently underwent a nine-year renovation and reopened in 2018 with 250 stalls.

Information

EMERGENCY & USEFUL NUMBERS

Ambulance	☎061
EU standard emergency number	☎112
Country code	☎34
International access code	☎00
Tourist police	☎93 256 24 30

MEDICAL SERVICES

➡ All foreigners have the same right as Spaniards to emergency medical treatment in public hospitals. EU citizens are entitled to the full range of health-care services in public hospitals, but must present a European Health Insurance Card (enquire at your national health service) and may have to pay upfront.

➡ Non-EU citizens have to pay for anything other than emergency treatment. Most travel-insurance policies include medical cover.

➡ For minor health problems you can try any *farmàcia* (pharmacy), where pharmaceuticals tend to be sold more freely without prescription than in places such as the USA, Australia or the UK.

➡ If your country has a consulate in Barcelona, its staff should be able to refer you to doctors who speak your language.

MONEY

Barcelona abounds with banks, many of which have ATMs. ATMs are in plentiful supply around Plaça de Catalunya, and along Via Laietana and La Rambla. Most ATMs allow you to use international debit or credit cards to withdraw money in euros. There is usually a charge (around 1.5% to 2%) on ATM cash withdrawals when abroad.

You can change cash or travellers cheques in most major currencies without problems at virtually any bank or *bureau de change* (usually indicated by the word *canvi/cambio*).

The foreign-exchange offices that you see along La Rambla and elsewhere are open for longer hours than banks, but they generally offer poorer rates. Also, keep a sharp eye open for commissions at *bureaux de change*.

POST

Correos is Spain's national postal service. Barcelona's main post office is a lovely fresco-filled building just opposite the northeast end of Port Vell at Plaça d'Antonio López. Another handy post office branch lies just off Passeig de Gràcia at Carrer d'Aragó 282. Many other branches tend to open between 8.30am and 2.30pm Monday to Friday and from 9.30am to 1pm on Saturday.

Segells/sellos (stamps) are sold at most *estancs* (tobacconists' shops) and at post offices throughout the city.

TOURIST INFORMATION

Several tourist offices operate in Barcelona. A couple of general information telephone numbers worth bearing in mind are 010 and 012. The first is for Barcelona and the other is for all Catalonia (run by the Generalitat). You sometimes strike English speakers, although for the most part operators are Catalan/Spanish bilingual. In addition to tourist offices, information booths operate at Estació del Nord bus station and at Portal de la Pau, at the foot of the Mirador de Colom at the port end of La Rambla. Others set up at various points in the city centre in summer.

Plaça de Catalunya (p295)

Plaça Sant Jaume (Map p256; ☎93 285 38 34; www.barcelonaturisme.com; Plaça Catalunya 17; ⏲8.30am-8.30pm; Ⓜ Catalunya)

Estació Sants (☎93 285 38 34; www.barcelonaturisme.com; Barcelona Sants; ⏲8.30am-8.30pm; Ⓡ Sants Estació)

El Prat Airport (www.barcelonaturisme.com; ⏲8.30am-8.30pm)

Palau Robert Regional Tourist Office (Map p278; ☎93 238 80 91; www.palaurobert.gencat.cat; Passeig de Gràcia 107; ⏲10am-8pm Mon-Sat, to 2.30pm Sun; Ⓜ Diagonal) Offers a host of material on Catalonia, audiovisual resources, a bookshop and a branch of Turisme Juvenil de Catalunya (for youth travel).

ℹ Getting There & Away

AIR

Barcelona's **El Prat airport** (☎902 404704; www.aena.es) lies 17km southwest of Plaça de Catalunya at El Prat de Llobregat. The airport has two main terminal buildings: the T1 terminal and the older T2, itself divided into three terminal areas (A, B and C).

Arrivals In T1, the main arrivals area is on the 1st floor (with separate areas for EU Schengen Area arrivals, non-EU international arrivals and the Barcelona–Madrid corridor).

Departures In T1, boarding gates are on the 1st and 3rd floors.

Tourist Information The main **tourist office** (p334) is on the ground floor of Terminal 2B. Others on the ground floor of Terminal 2A and in Terminal 1 operate the same hours.

BOAT

It is possible to travel between Barcelona and the Balearic Islands and Italy by ferry, though it is rarely the cheaper option.

Passenger and vehicular ferries operated by **Trasmediterránea** (☎902 454645; www.trasmediterranea.es; Ⓜ Drassanes) to/from the Balearic Islands dock around the Moll de Barcelona wharf in Port Vell. Information and tickets are available at the terminal buildings along Moll de Sant Bertran, on Moll de Barcelona and from travel agents.

Fares vary enormously according to season, how far in advance you book and whether or not you want a cabin. Fares for a Butaca Turista (seat) from Barcelona to any of the islands typically start around €60. Cabins for up to four people are also available on overnight standard ferries.

Grandi Navi Veloci (Map p292; www.gnv.it; Ronda del Port; Ⓜ Drassanes) runs high-speed, luxury ferries three (sometimes more) days a week between Genoa and Barcelona. The journey takes 18 hours. Ticket prices vary wildly depending on season and how far in advance you purchase them. They start at about €80 one way for an airline-style seat in summer, and can be bought online or at Trasmediterránea ticket windows. The same company runs a similar number of ferries between Barcelona and Tangier, Morocco (voyage time about 26 hours).

Grimaldi Ferries (Map p292; www.grimaldi-lines.com; Ronda del Port; Ⓜ Drassanes) operates similar services from Barcelona to Civitavecchia (near Rome, 20½ hours, six to seven times a week), Livorno (Tuscany, 19½ hours, three times a week) and Porto Torres (northwest Sardinia, 12 hours, daily).

BUS

Long-distance buses leave from **Estació del Nord** (☎93 706 53 66; www.barcelonanord.cat; Carrer d'Ali Bei 80; Ⓜ Arc de Triomf). A plethora of companies service different parts of Spain; many come under the umbrella of **Alsa** (☎902 422242; www.alsa.es). For other companies, ask at the bus station. There are frequent services to Madrid, Valencia and Zaragoza (20 or more a day) and several daily departures to distant destinations such as Burgos, Santiago de Compostela and Seville.

Eurolines (www.eurolines.es), in conjunction with local carriers all over Europe, is the main international carrier. Its website provides links to national operators; it runs services across Europe and to Morocco from Estació del Nord, and from **Estació d'Autobusos de Sants** (☎902 432343; www.adif.es; Carrer de Viriat; Ⓜ Sants Estació), next to Estació Sants Barcelona.

Much of the Pyrenees and the entire Costa Brava are served only by buses, as train services are limited to important railheads such as Girona, Figueres, Lleida, Ripoll and Puigcerdà.

Various bus companies operate across the region. Most operate from Estació del Nord, but **Hispano-Igualadina** (☎93 339 79 29; www.igualadina.com; Carrer de Viriat; Ⓜ Sants Estació) and **TEISA** (Map p278; ☎93 215 35 66; www.teisa-bus.com; Carrer de Pau Claris 117; Ⓜ Passeig de Gràcia) do not.

Hispano-Igualadina buses depart from Estació Sants, which is also Barcelona's main train station. TEISA buses depart from a stop on Carrer de Pau Claris in L'Eixample.

TRAIN

Train is the most convenient overland option for reaching Barcelona from major Spanish centres like Madrid and Valencia. It can be a long haul from other parts of Europe – budget flights frequently offer a saving in time and money. The main train station in Barcelona is **Estació de Sants** (⊙8am-8pm; Ⓜ Sants Estació). Frequent high-speed Tren de Alta Velocidad Española (AVE) trains between Madrid and Barcelona run daily in each direction, several of them in under three hours.

Most long-distance (largo recorrido or Grandes Líneas) trains have 1st and 2nd classes (known as preferente and turista). After the AVE, Euromed and several other similarly modern trains, the most common long-distance trains are the slower, all-stops Talgos. A trenhotel is a sleeping-car train with up to three classes: turista (seats or couchettes), preferente (sleeping car) and gran clase (for those who prefer to sleep in sheer luxury!).

WARNING: WATCH YOUR BELONGINGS

- Violent crime is rare in Barcelona, but petty crime (bag-snatching, pickpocketing) is a major problem.
- You're at your most vulnerable when dragging around luggage to or from your hotel; make sure you know your route before arriving.
- Be mindful of your belongings, particularly in crowded areas.
- Avoid walking around El Raval and the southern end of La Rambla late at night.
- Don't wander down empty city streets at night. When in doubt, take a taxi.
- Take nothing of value to the beach and don't leave anything unattended.

A network of *rodalies/cercanías* serves towns around Barcelona (and the airport). Contact **Renfe** (☎91 232 03 20; www.renfe.es).

Getting Around

Barcelona has abundant options for getting around town. The excellent metro can get you most places, with buses and trams filling in the gaps. Taxis are the best option late at night.

TO/FROM THE AIRPORT

The A1 **Aerobús** (Map p292; ☎902 100104; www.aerobusbcn.com; Plaça d'Espanya; one way/return €5.90/10.20; ⊙5.05am-12.35am) runs from Terminal 1 to Plaça de Catalunya (30 to 40 minutes depending on traffic) via Plaça d'Espanya, Gran Via de les Corts Catalanes (corner of Carrer del Comte d'Urgell) and Plaça de la Universitat every five to 10 minutes from 6.10am to 1.05am. Departures from Plaça de Catalunya are from 5.30am to 12.30am and stop at the corner of Carrer de Sepúlveda and Carrer del Comte d'Urgell, and at Plaça d'Espanya. The A2 Aerobús from Terminal 2 (stops outside terminal areas A, B and C) runs from 6am to 1am with a frequency of between 10 and 20 minutes and follows the same route as the A1 Aerobús.

Slower local buses (such as the No 46 to/from Plaça d'Espanya and two night buses, the N17 and N18, to/from Plaça de Catalunya) also serve Terminals 1 and 2. Metro L9 connects with the airport (special tickets are €4.60) but is slow and only really convenient if you are staying in the north of the city.

A taxi between either terminal and the city centre – about a half-hour ride depending on traffic – costs around €25. Fares and charges are posted inside the passenger side of the taxi; make sure the meter is used.

Train operator **Renfe** (p335) runs the R2 Nord line every half-hour from Terminal 2 (from 5.42am to 11.38pm) via several stops to Barcelona's main train station, Estació Sants, and Passeig de Gràcia in central Barcelona, after which it heads northwest out of the city. The first service from Passeig de Gràcia leaves at 5.08am and the last at 11.07pm, and about five minutes later from Estació Sants. The trip between the airport and Passeig de Gràcia takes 25 minutes. A one-way ticket costs €2.50.

CAR & MOTORCYCLE

With the convenience of public transport and the high price of parking in the city, it's unwise to drive in Barcelona. However, if you're planning a road trip outside the city, a car is handy.

Avis, Europcar, National/Atesa and Hertz have desks at El Prat airport, Estació Sants and Estació del Nord. Rental outlets in Barcelona include the following:

Avis (☎902 110275; www.avis.com; Carrer de Còrsega 293-295; ⏲8am-9pm Mon-Fri, to 5pm Sat, to 1pm Sun; Ⓜ Diagonal)

Cooltra (☎93 221 40 70; www.cooltra.com; Via Laietana 6; scooter hire per day €28-35; ⏲10am-8pm; Ⓜ Barceloneta) Rents out scooters and organises scooter tours.

Europcar (☎93 302 05 43; www.europcar.es; Gran Via de les Corts Catalanes 680; ⏲8am-2pm & 3.30-7.30pm Mon-Fri, 9am-2pm Sat; Ⓜ Girona)

Hertz (☎902 998707; www.hertz.com; Carrer de Viriat 45; ⏲7am-10pm Mon-Fri, to 9pm Sat & Sun; Ⓜ Sants Estació)

MondoRent (☎93 295 32 68; www.mondorent.com; Passeig de Joan de Borbó 80-84; scooter rental per day from €35; ⏲10am-8pm; Ⓜ Barceloneta) Rents out scooters as well as electric bikes.

Enterprise (☎93 323 07 01; www.enterprise.es; Carrer de Muntaner 45; ⏲8am-8pm Mon-Fri, 9am-1pm Sat; Ⓜ Universitat)

PUBLIC TRANSPORT

Bus

Buses run along most city routes every few minutes from between 5am and 6.30am to around 10pm and 11pm. Many routes pass through Plaça de Catalunya and/or Plaça de la Universitat. After 11pm a reduced network of yellow *nitbusos* (night buses) runs until 3am or 5am. All *nitbus* routes pass through Plaça de Catalunya and most run every 30 to 45 minutes.

Metro & FGC

The easy-to-use metro system has 11 numbered and colour-coded lines. It runs from 5am to midnight Sunday to Thursday and holidays, from 5am to 2am on Friday and days immediately preceding holidays, and 24 hours on Saturday.

Suburban trains run by the **Ferrocarrils de la Generalitat de Catalunya** (FGC; ☎012; www.fgc.net) include a couple of useful city lines. All lines heading north from Plaça de Catalunya stop at Carrer de Provença and Gràcia. One of these lines (L7) goes to Tibidabo and another (L6 to Reina Elisenda) has a stop near the Monestir de Pedralbes. Most trains from Plaça de Catalunya continue beyond Barcelona to Sant Cugat, Sabadell and Terrassa. Other FGC lines head west from Plaça d'Espanya, including one for Manresa that is handy for the trip to Montserrat.

Depending on the line, these trains run from about 5am (with only one or two services before 6am) to 11pm or midnight Sunday to Thursday, and from 5am to about 1am on Friday and Saturday.

Tickets & Passes

The metro, FGC trains, *rodalies/cercanías* (Renfe-run local trains) and buses come under a combined system. Single-ride tickets on all standard transport within Zone 1 cost €2.15.

Targetes are multitrip transport tickets. They are sold at all city-centre metro stations. The prices given here are for travel in Zone 1. Children under four years of age travel free. Options include the following:

➡ Targeta T-10 (€10.20) – 10 rides (each valid for 1¼ hours) on the metro, buses, FGC trains and *rodalies*. You can change between metro, FGC, *rodalies* and buses, and users can share the same *targeta*.

➡ Targeta T-DIA (€8.60) – unlimited travel on all transport for one day.

➡ Two-/three-/four-/five-day tickets (€15/22/28.50/35) – unlimited travel on all transport except the Aerobús; buy them at metro stations and tourist offices.

➡ T-Mes (€54) – 30 days' unlimited use of all public transport.

➡ Targeta T-50/30 (€43.50) – 50 trips within 30 days, valid on all transport.

➡ T-Trimestre (€145.30) – 90 days' unlimited use of all public transport.

TAXIS

Taxis charge €2.10 flag fall plus meter charges of €1.10 per kilometre (€1.30 from 8pm to 8am and all day on weekends). A further €3.10 is added for all trips to/from the airport, and €1 for luggage bigger than 55cm × 35cm × 35cm. The trip from Estació Sants to Plaça de Catalunya, about 3km, costs about €11.

Taxi Amic (☎93 420 80 88; www.taxi-amic-adaptat.com) is a special taxi service for people with disabilities or difficult situations (such as transport of big objects). Book at least 24 hours in advance if possible.

Catalonia

Includes ➡

Best Places to Stay

- Mil Estrelles (p355)
- Parador de Cardona (p387)
- Set Terres (p375)
- Palau dels Alemanys (p353)

Best Places to Eat

- El Celler de Can Roca (p354)
- Les Cols (p367)
- Cal Ton (p393)
- El Jardinet (p385)
- Can Ventura (p375)

Why Go?

With its own language and unique local customs, Catalonia feels distinct from the rest of Spain, and, beyond Barcelona, its four provinces unveil an astounding wealth of natural splendour. Pyrenean peaks loom above meadows and glittering lakes, plains are pock-marked with volcanic cones, rocky coves border sandy beaches and wind-blown capes give way to serene seaside paths and fertile vineyards.

The Costa Brava's shores are its biggest lure, though travellers will also uncover medieval architecture, Jewish history and culinary wizardry in Girona, and Dalí's gloriously surreal 'theatre-museum' in Figueres. Sitges, on the Costa Daurada, fizzes with summer fun and Modernista mansions.

North, where the Pyrenees rise to 3000m, hiking trails weave between hushed valleys and outstanding Romanesque churches and monasteries crown lonely villages. Spinning back in time, the Roman ruins of Tarragona and Empúries rank among Spain's most impressive, while entirely different landscapes await amid the Delta de l'Ebre's shimmering wetlands.

When to Go

Tarragona

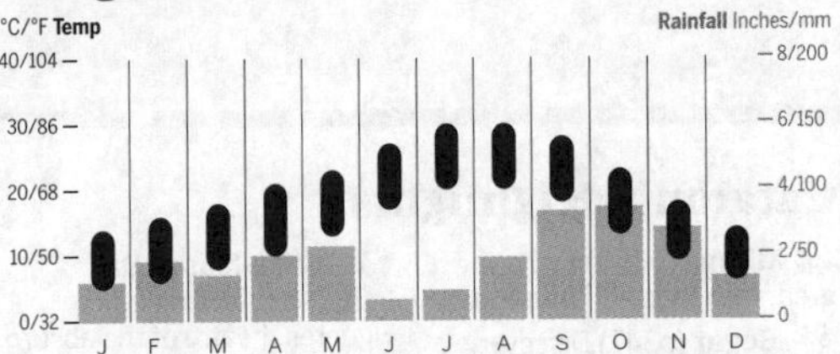

May The Costa Brava's beaches and trails are free from crowds (though the water is chilly).

Sep Perfect hiking in the Catalan Pyrenees, aflame in autumnal colours; quiet returns to the coast.

Dec–Feb Ski season in the winter-clothed Pyrenees.

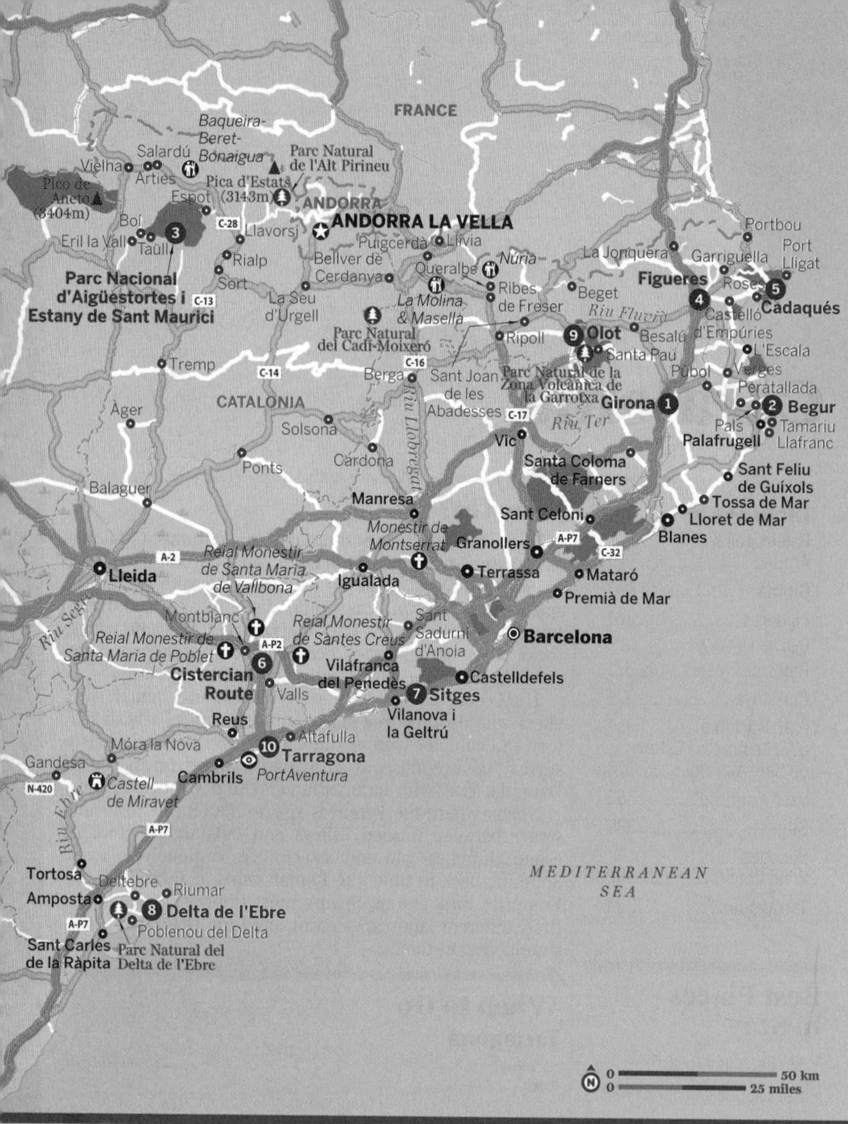

Catalonia Highlights

1. **Girona** (p350) Exploring great laneways and museums.
2. **Begur** (p347) Discovering secret coves.
3. **Parc Nacional d'Aigüestortes i Estany de Sant Maurici** (p378) Conquering high-altitude lakeside trails in Catalonia's sole national park.
4. **Teatre-Museu Dalí** (p362) Unravelling Dalí's Figueres theatre of the absurd.
5. **Cadaqués** (p359) Wandering seaside trails to Dalí's home and Cap de Creus.
6. **Cistercian Route** (p398) Admiring stately monasteries on a hilly drive.
7. **Sitges** (p389) Partying hard in this gay-friendly town.
8. **Delta de l'Ebre** (p399) Watching flocks of flamingos.
9. **Olot** (p366) Feeling a rumble beneath your feet in volcano-carved hills.
10. **Tarragona** (p394) Marvelling at Roman ruins in this lively city.

COSTA BRAVA

Stretching north from Barcelona to the Spanish–French border, the Costa Brava ('rugged coast') is undoubtedly the most beautiful of Spain's three main holiday coasts. Though there's plenty of tourism development, this wonderfully scenic region of Catalonia also unveils unspoiled coves, spectacular seascapes, wind-battered headlands, coast-hugging hiking paths, charming seaside towns with outstanding restaurants, and some of Spain's finest diving around the protected Illes Medes.

Delightful stone villages and the majestic Romanesque monastery of Sant Pere de Rodes nestle in the hilly backcountry, cloaked in the south in brilliant-green umbrella pine. Inland, wander northern Catalonia's biggest city, Girona, home to a moodily atmospheric, strikingly well-preserved medieval centre and one of the world's top restaurants. Neighbouring Figueres is famed for its bizarre Teatre-Museu Dalí, foremost of a series of sites associated with eccentric surrealist artist Salvador Dalí, who fell, like many others, for the wild natural beauty of seaside Cadaqués.

Tossa de Mar

POP 5050

Tossa de Mar curves around a boat-speckled bay, guarded by a headland crowned with impressive defensive medieval walls and towers. Tourism has bolted a larger, modern extension onto this picturesque village of crooked, narrow streets, though its old town and clifftop views retain their beauty.

Tossa was one of the first places on the Costa Brava to attract foreign visitors: a small colony of artists and writers gravitated towards what Russian-French painter Marc Chagall dubbed 'Blue Paradise' in the 1930s. It was made famous by Ava Gardner in the 1951 film *Pandora and the Flying Dutchman*; you'll find a statue of the silver-screen queen along the path towards the lighthouse.

In July and August it's hard to reach the water's edge without tripping over oily limbs. Outside high season, many attractions and amenities limit hours or close entirely.

Sights

The deep-ochre fairy-tale walls and towers on pine-dotted **Mont Guardí**, the headland at the southern end of Tossa's main beach, were built between the 12th and 14th centuries. They encircle the **Vila Vella** (old town), which reached peak splendour in the 15th century; it's now crammed with steep cobbled streets and whitewashed houses garlanded with flowers. A 1917 **lighthouse** (Passeig de Vila Vella, Mont Guardí; €1.50; ⌚10am-2pm & 4-8pm daily Jul & Aug, 10am-4pm Tue-Sun Sep-Jun) crowns Mont Guardí.

Sleeping & Eating

Manà Manà HOSTEL €

(☎972 34 25 49; www.manamanahostel.com; Carrer Sant Telm 9; dm €20-26, d €58-92; ⌚Easter-Oct; 📶) A colourful, sociable hostel just two minutes' walk from the beach, Manà Manà sleeps budgeteers in four- or six-bed dorms (including a female-only dorm) with individual lockers, shared bathrooms and lively decor. Facilities include a kitchen, self-service laundry and rooftop terrace where communal meals happen. The hostel organises walking tours and other activities, so it's great for solo travellers.

Cap d'Or HOTEL €€

(☎972 34 00 81; www.hotelcapdor.com; Passeig del Mar 1; incl breakfast s €79-85, d €119-135, q €172-195; ⌚Easter–mid-Oct; ❄📶) Get wrapped up in Tossa's history at this family-run spot right below the old-town walls. The 10 rooms are lovingly decorated in an array of pastels, each with vintage-feel pictures and cutesy marine miscellany; the best look straight onto the beach. There's a cheery all-day cafe-restaurant serving seafood, salads, omelettes and snacks (€7 to €12) overlooking the sand.

La Cuina de Can Simón CATALAN €€€

(☎972 34 12 69; http://restaurantcansimon.com; Carrer del Portal 24; mains €28-35, tasting menus €68-135; ⌚1-3.30pm & 8-10.30pm, closed Mon Apr-Jul & Sep, closed Sun night, Mon & Tue Oct-Mar) This is the standout of a slew of restaurants hugging the old wall along Carrer del Portal. Within an 18th-century fisherman's stone house, Michelin-starred La Cuina de Can Simón credits its innovative dishes to a dual heritage: the owners' grandparents were a fisherman and an artist. Flavoursome seasonal fusions include meunière sole with Iberian ham, or prawns in *cava* (sparkling wine).

Information

Oficina de Turisme de Tossa de Mar (☎972 34 01 08; www.infotossa.com; Avinguda del Pelegrí 25; ⌚9am-9pm Mon-Sat, 10am-2pm & 5-8pm Sun Jun-Sep, 10am-2pm & 4-7pm Mon-Sat, 10am-2pm Sun Oct-May, closed Sun Nov-Apr) Next to Tossa's bus station.

Getting There & Away

From Tossa's **bus station** (Plaça de les Nacions Sense Estat), **Sarfa** (www.sarfa.com) runs bus services to and from Barcelona's Estació del Nord (€12.15, 1¼ hours, five to 15 daily) and airport (€14.25, two hours, two to 11 daily), plus Girona airport from mid-June to October (€10, 55 minutes, two daily).

Palafrugell & Around

Halfway up the coast from Barcelona to the French border begins one of the most beautiful stretches of the Costa Brava. The town of Palafrugell, 4km inland, is the main access point for a cluster of enticing beach spots. Calella de Palafrugell, Llafranc and Tamariu, one-time fishing villages squeezed into gorgeous small bays, are three of the Costa Brava's most charming, low-key resorts.

Begur, 7km northeast of Palafrugell, is a handsomely conserved, castle-topped village with a cluster of less-developed beaches nearby. Inland, seek out tiny Pals and the fabulous cobbled village of Peratallada.

Palafrugell

POP 21,050

Palafrugell, 4km west of the coast, is the main transport, shopping and services hub for the exquisite stretch of Costa Brava extending north from Calella de Palafrugell to Begur. But this inland town is more than just a way station en route to the beach. There are artistic and cultural treasures to uncover in Plaça Can Mario, plus one of the region's most striking Gothic churches.

Sant Martí de Palafrugell CHURCH
(Plaça de l'Església; ⌚hours vary) The incomplete multipointed turret of this fine Gothic construction extends skywards like a crown above central Palafrugell. Old documents state that a church has stood here since the 11th century, but what you see of the stately edifice dates to the 17th and 18th centuries.

Information

Oficina de Turisme Palafrugell (☎972 30 02 28; www.visitpalafrugell.cat; Avinguda de la Generalitat 33; ⌚10am-8pm Mon-Sat Jul & Aug, 10am-1pm & 4-7pm Mon-Sat Easter-Jun & Sep–mid-Oct, 10am-5pm Mon-Fri, 10am-1pm & 4-7pm Sat mid-Oct–Easter, 9.30am-1.30pm Sun year-round) Just off the C31 on the southwest edge of town.

Getting There & Away

From the **bus station** (Carrer de Lluís Companys), **Sarfa** (www.sarfa.com) connects Palafrugell with Barcelona (€18.50, 2¼ hours, six to seven daily) and Girona (€6.50, one to 1½ hours, 10 to 21 daily). Buses also run to Calella de Palafrugell, Llafranc and Tamariu (summer only) on the coast.

Calella de Palafrugell

POP 670

The whitewashed buildings of Calella, the southernmost of Palafrugell's seaside crown jewels, cluster Aegean-style around a bay of rocky points and small, pretty beaches, with a few fishing boats hauled up on the sand. Though deservedly well known for its beauteous bay, Calella has resisted the temptation to sprawl, and maintains its agreeably tucked-away feel, despite being merrily packed with visitors in summer.

Sights & Activities

From Calella, you can stroll along dreamy **coastal footpaths** – including the long-distance GR92 and Camí de Ronda – northeast to Llafranc (30 minutes, 1.5km), Tamariu (two to three hours, around 6km) and beyond, or south to Platja del Golfet, near Cap Roig (1.5km, 40 minutes).

THE CAMÍ DE RONDA

The 230km-long stretch of cliffs, coves, rocky promontories and pine groves that make up the signposted **Camí de Ronda** (also known as the Costa Brava Way) extends from Blanes in Catalonia to Collioure in France. Unsurprisingly, it offers some of the finest walks in Catalonia, from gentle rambles to high-octane scrambles. If you fancy tackling the whole thing, it's a demanding hike of around 10 days. The trail mostly follows the established GR92, but includes a number of coastal deviations.

Some of the most popular stretches link Calella de Palafrugell, Llafranc (p346), Tamariu (p346) and the Begur area. Another choice route is Cadaqués (p359) to the **Far Cap de Creus** (p361) lighthouse, a relatively easy walk (8km; 2½ hours) that passes Port Lligat and several isolated beaches.

Costa Brava

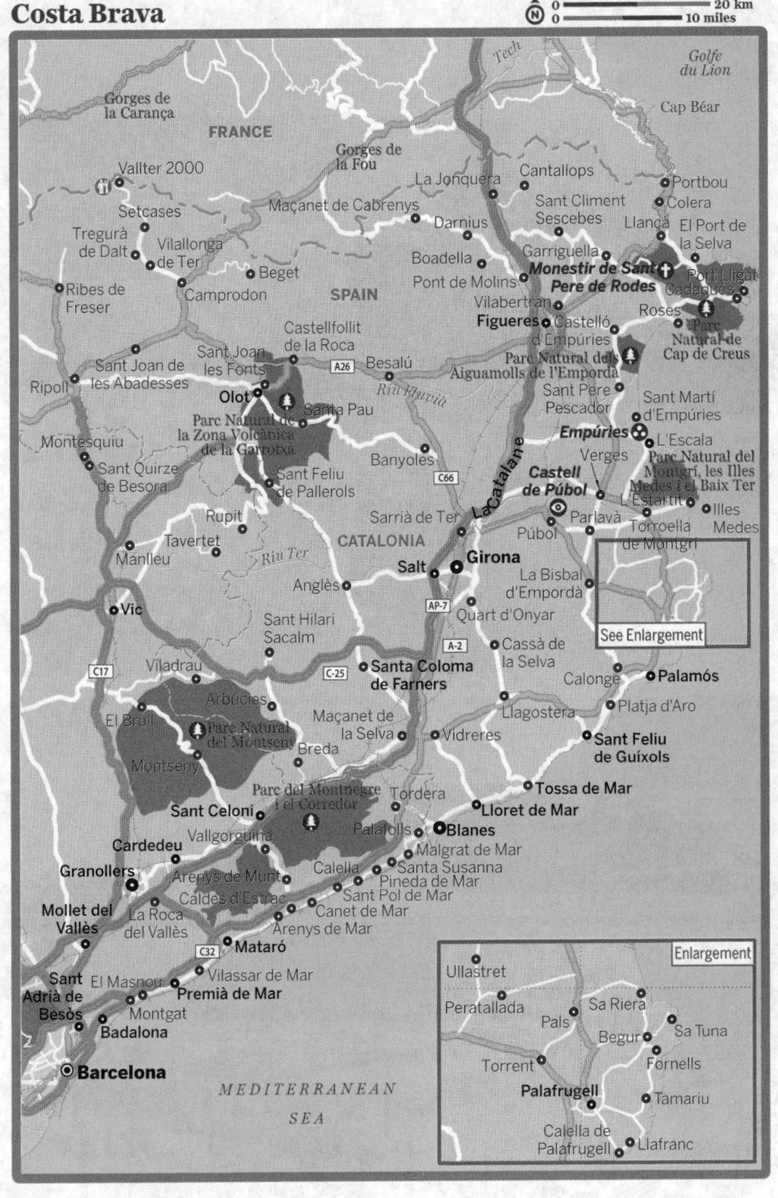

Jardins de Cap Roig GARDENS

(Cap Roig; adult/child €7/free; ⏲10am-8pm Apr-Sep, to 6pm Oct-Mar, weekends only Jan & Feb) Atop Cap Roig, 2km southwest of central Calella, these beautiful botanical gardens contain approximately 1000 floral species, set around the early-20th-century castle-palace of Nikolai Voevodsky – a tsarist colonel with expensive tastes, who fell out of grace in his homeland after the Russian revolution.

1

2

SILVIA GREGORIO ESCOBAR / SHUTTERSTOCK ©

1. Praia As Catedrais, near Ribadeo 2. Playa de la Concha, San Sebastián 3. La Isleta del Moro, Cabo de Gata

3

Spain's Best Beaches

Spaniards argue for hours about which is their district's finest beach, so picking favourites from 5000km of coastline is a controversial, albeit mighty pleasurable, task. The Mediterranean's gentle strands and pretty coves contrast with the rougher beauty of the Atlantic coasts.

Illas Cíes (p591) A protected archipelago off Galicia, with beaches so stunning you'll gasp in disbelief.

Aiguablava/Fornells (p347) Neighbouring Costa Brava coves near Begur, so divine that we couldn't choose between them.

Cabo de Gata (p790) A series of stunning beaches, all distinct, on this memorable peninsula in Almería province.

Playa del Silencio (p539) Backed by a natural rock amphitheatre, this Asturian jewel between Cudillero and Luarca is hard to beat.

Playa de la Concha (p463) A scallop-shaped stretch of sand in the heart of San Sebastián, and possibly Europe's finest city beach.

Praia As Catedrais (p582) The unearthly rock formations at this Galician strand near Ribadeo are such a drawcard that daily numbers are limited.

CATALONIA & SPAIN

Like many European nations, the kingdom of Spain was cobbled together by a series of conquests and dynastic alliances from what were once separate states. Though the last of these was over 500 years ago, people in the peninsula still tend to identify more strongly with their ancestral village or local region – the *patria chica* ('small fatherland') – than with the nation as a whole. There are separatist movements in parts of the peninsula, but especially in the Basque Country and Catalonia.

Away from Barcelona and the Costa Brava, Catalonia feels as if you've entered a separate country. Little Spanish is spoken and the red-and-yellow flag of the region flutters from the balconies. The widespread feeling, as expressed by an often-encountered piece of graffiti, is that 'Catalonia is not Spain'.

The genesis of Catalonia began when the Franks, under Charlemagne, pushed back the Moors in the 8th and 9th centuries. The Catalan golden age came in the early 12th century when Ramon Berenguer III, who already controlled Catalonia and parts of southern France, launched the region's first seagoing fleet. In 1137 his successor, Ramon Berenguer IV, was betrothed to the one-year-old heiress to the Aragonese throne, thereby giving Catalonia sufficient power to expand its empire out into the Mediterranean but joining it to another crown. Modern Spain was effectively created when Fernando became king of Aragón in 1479, having already married Isabel, Queen of Castile.

Catalonia resented its new subordinate status but could do little to overturn it. After backing the losing side in the War of Spanish Succession (1702–14), Barcelona rose up against the Spanish crown, whose armies besieged the city from March 1713 until 11 September 1714. The victorious Felipe V abolished Catalan privileges, banned writing and teaching in Catalan, and farmed out Catalonia's colonies to other European powers.

Trade again flourished from Barcelona in the centuries that followed, and by the late 19th and early 20th centuries there were growing calls for greater self-governance. However, after the Spanish Civil War ended in 1939, pro-republic Catalonia was treated harshly by victorious General Franco. Reprisals and purges resulted in the shootings of at least 35,000 people. The use of Catalan in public was banned and all street and town names were changed into Spanish, which became the only permitted language in schools and the media. Self-government was returned after Franco's death in 1975, though the sense of grievance remains.

Recent decades have seen Catalan culture flourish, reflected in the reemergence of traditional festivals and dances, the prevalence of Catalan flags and the near-universal use of Catalan in public. For Catalans, their language is the key to their identity.

The issue of independence from Spain has been at the forefront of Catalan politics for years, and it took on greater importance and urgency following Spain's economic crisis beginning in 2008. In September 2015, the pro-independence coalition Junts pel Sí ('Together for Yes'), led by Carles Puigdemont, won over 39% of votes in Catalan parliamentary elections. With the support of the far-left, pro-independence Candidatura d'Unitat Popular (CUP), Junts pel Sí formed a government, promising to hold a referendum on Catalan independence.

Sleeping & Eating

Hotel Mediterrani HOTEL **€€€**

(☎972 61 45 00; www.hotelmediterrani.com; Carrer de Lladó 55; incl breakfast s €99-150, d €99-245; ⏲Apr-Oct; P❄📶) Fresh, boutique-ified rooms decked out in serene creams, many with exquisite views of a sliver of sand and the aquamarine sea, make this long-standing and welcoming family-run hotel at the southwest end of town very hard to beat. Best are the top-floor boudoirs with private sun decks.

Tragamar SEAFOOD, INTERNATIONAL **€€**

(☎972 62 43 36; www.tragamar.com; Platja del Canadell; mains €12-22; ⏲noon-11pm Jul & Aug, closed 1 day weekly Easter-Jun & Sep–mid-Oct, closed mid-Oct–Easter; ✎) Barely a metre off the beach, with tables gazing out on the bay, this is the Calella branch of Barcelona's hugely successful Tragaluz restaurant empire. The menu trots around the globe, contrasting Catalan favourites and Costa Brava seafood with Asian- and Mediterranean-inspired bites like salt-crusted edamame, tuna *tataki* with guacamole and tasty salads.

The central Spanish government in Madrid, under Prime Minister Mariano Rajoy of the Partido Popular (PP; People's Party), said that such a referendum would be illegal. The Catalan government went ahead and declared it was going to hold one on 1 October 2017. The Spanish government sent in the Policía Nacional (Spain's national police) to try to prevent the referendum taking place, resulting in some scenes of violence at polling stations, with, the Catalan government said, over 800 people injured. According to the Catalan government, of the 43% of potential voters who took part in the referendum, 90% voted for independence. Spain's constitutional court had declared the referendum illegal before it took place.

Large crowds, especially in Barcelona, protested against the Spanish police action and the Spanish government's attempt to stop the referendum. In the following days, however, a wave of support for Spanish national unity swept through much of the rest of the country and even Catalonia itself, including an anti-independence demonstration of 350,000 people in Barcelona. Before the referendum, some opinion polls had come up with the finding that only about 40% to 45% of the Catalan population supported independence.

On 27 October, after a period of shadow boxing between Madrid and Barcelona in which hopes for a compromise came to nothing, the Catalan parliament voted for independence, and the national parliament in Madrid invoked Article 155 of the Spanish constitution (never used before), which allows it to rescind the autonomy of regions in extreme circumstances, bringing them under direct rule from Madrid. This meant the dismissal of Puigdemont, the dissolution of the Catalan parliament, and the announcement of new regional elections in Catalonia for 21 December 2017.

Not long after, Spain's attorney-general charged Puigdemont and 13 of his ministers with rebellion and sedition, which carry maximum sentences of 30 years and 15 years respectively. But by then Puigdemont and four ministers had disappeared to Brussels, and, at the time of writing, remain there, adamant that they will not return to Spain unless they are guaranteed a fair trial.

In the 21 December election, Catalonia's separatist parties won 70 of the 135 parliamentary seats, giving them the possibility of forming the new Catalan government. The exiled Puigdemont was the favourite for the new Catalan presidency, but in March 2018 he abandoned his bid to return to office; Puigdemont backed as president Jordi Sànchez, also of his Junts per Catalunya party (which was newly formed for the December election). At the time of writing, Spain's Supreme Court refuses to allow Sànchez to be released for an investiture ceremony (Sànchez has been in police custody on charges of sedition since October 2017), while Puigdemont is highly likely to be arrested upon returning to Spain.

The overall situation remains uncertain, though the Catalan independence movement shows no signs of slowing down. Some Catalans feel their taxes subsidise the rest of the nation, and the tough economic times resulting from the 2008 economic crisis have exacerbated this feeling. But the very fact that Catalonia is such a valuable asset makes the central government very unwilling to let it go.

Information

Oficina de Turisme Calella de Palafrugell (☎ 972 61 44 75; www.visitpalafrugell.cat; Carrer de les Voltes 4; ⌚10am-1pm & 5-8pm Jul & Aug, 10am-1pm & 5-8pm Mon-Sat, 10am-1pm Sun Jun & Sep, open weekends only Apr & May) Seasonal office just back from the beachfront.

Getting There & Away

Sarfa/Moventis (www.sarfa.com; www.moventis.es) buses link Calella with Palafrugell (€1.70, 15 minutes, three to 19 daily), plus Tamariu and Llafranc.

Llafranc

POP 280

Barely 2km northeast of Calella de Palafrugell, and now merging with it along the roads set back from the rocky coast between them, upmarket Llafranc has a small aquamarine bay and a gorgeous long stretch of golden sand, cupped on either side by craggy pine-dotted outcrops and coastline. July and August bring sun-seeking crowds, but otherwise it's a peaceful, beautiful spot.

Sights & Activities

The long-distance GR92 and Camí de Ronda (p340) link Llafranc with nearby coastal villages, including Tamariu (1½ hours, about 4.5km) and Calella de Palafrugell (30 minutes, 1.5km), allowing for short, spectacular walks. There are plenty of easy walks doable in beach sandals; the tourist office (p346) has details. Kayaking, SUP (stand-up paddle-boarding) and SUP yoga are other popular activities.

★Cap de Sant Sebastià — VIEWPOINT

The magical promontory framing the eastern end of Llafranc offers fabulous views in both directions and out to sea. It hosts an 1857 **lighthouse** (with a summer lounge bar), plus a 15th-century **watchtower** and an 18th-century chapel now incorporated into an upmarket hotel. Also here are the ruins of a pre-Roman Iberian **settlement** (with multilingual explanatory panels). It's a 1.2km (20-minute) walk up from central Llafranc: follow the steps from the harbour. You can continue north to Tamariu (4km, about an hour).

Sleeping & Eating

Terralet — HOTEL €€

(☎972 30 64 54; www.terraletllafranc.com; Carrer de Carudo 12-14; d €95-125, tr €135-155, q €135-175; ⌚Mar-Oct; 📶) Freshly launched at research time, turquoise-accented Terralet is just a stumble north from the beach. Immaculate, stripped-back white-and-aqua rooms come in a range of shapes and sizes, from tasteful twins to family pads with lounge, all simply yet stylishly furnished. There's a pleasant downstairs cafe-bar, and rooftop yoga and meditation are offered.

Hotel El Far — HOTEL €€€

(☎972 30 16 39; www.hotelelfar.com; Cap de Sant Sebastià; r incl breakfast €200-300; ⌚mid-Feb–mid-Jan; P ❄ 📶) At romantic El Far – a happy marriage between secluded clifftop luxury and delectable local seafood – each plush, maritime-feel room has its own balcony, most affording superb sea vistas. The restaurant turns out fresh seafood and rice dishes (mains €17 to €27), including good *fideuà* (seafood and noodle dish), while the surrounding pathway has panoramic views of Llafranc's glowing coast, a steep 1.2km (20-minute) walk away.

Casamar — CATALAN €€€

(☎972 30 01 04; www.hotelcasamar.net; Carrer del Nero 3; mains €21-30, set menus €48-73; ⌚1.30-3.30pm & 8.30-11pm Tue-Sun Apr-Dec, closed Sun evening Sep-Dec & Apr-Jun) Fabulously located on a headland overlooking Llafranc's bay and harbour, this top-notch Michelin-starred restaurant serves classy seafood and artful mains concocted with creatively selected ingredients, in a refreshingly friendly atmosphere. For sunny days, there's a lovely pine-fringed terrace. Stairs lead up from the western end of the beach.

It's also a popular **hotel** (☎972 30 01 04; www.hotelcasamar.net; Carrer del Nero 3; r incl breakfast €120-145; ⌚Apr-Dec; ❄📶), with 20 cosy, contemporary, all-white rooms, most sporting balconies and sea vistas.

Information

Oficina de Turisme de Llafranc (☎972 30 50 08; www.visitpalafrugell.cat; Passeig de Cípsela; ⌚10am-1pm & 5-8pm Jul & Aug, 10am-1pm & 5-8pm Mon-Sat, 10am-1pm Sun Jun & Sep–mid-Oct, weekends only Apr & May) Seasonal kiosk at the western end of the beach.

Getting There & Away

Sarfa/Moventis (www.sarfa.com; www.moventis.es) buses serve Llafranc from Palafrugell (€1.70, 20 minutes, three to 20 daily), as well as Tamariu and Calella de Palafrugell.

Tamariu

POP 130

Four kilometres north from Llafranc, tiny, quiet Tamariu fronts a fabulous, crescent-shaped cove infused with the scent of pine and fringed by pretty whitewashed houses. This beach has some of the most translucent waters on Spain's Mediterranean coast.

Lovely **coastal walks** start from Tamariu, mostly along the long-distance GR92 and Camí de Ronda (p340); the most popular walk is south to Llafranc via Cap de Sant Sebastià (1½ hours, about 4.5km). It's also easy to find kayaking and SUP outlets.

Sleeping & Eating

Hotel Tamariu — HOTEL €€

(☎972 62 00 31; www.tamariu.com; Passeig del Mar 2; incl breakfast s €84-102, d €96-168; ⌚late Feb-early Nov; ❄📶) A former fishermen's tavern, the jolly Hotel Tamariu has been family-run for four generations. It has spacious rooms in nautical turquoises and whites, some with a balcony offering vine-draped views of this little beach town. The owners also rent two- to three-bedroom apartments nearby.

The beach-facing restaurant, **El Clot dels Mussols** (☎972 62 00 31; www.tamariu.com; Passeig del Mar 2; mains €16-23; ⏲1-10.30pm mid-Jun–mid-Sep, 1-3.30pm & 7-10.30pm mid-Sep–Nov & late Feb–mid-Jun), is popular for its seafood and set menus (€25 to €30).

Information

Oficina de Turisme de Tamariu (☎972 62 01 93; www.visitpalafrugell.cat; Carrer de la Riera; ⏲10am-1pm & 5-8pm Jul & Aug, 10am-1pm & 5-8pm Mon-Sat, 10am-1pm Sun Jun & Sep) Summer-only information point.

Getting There & Away

Sarfa/Moventis (www.sarfa.com; www.moventis.es) buses connect Tamariu with Palafrugell (€1.70, 15 minutes, three to 12 daily) from mid-May to mid-October only.

Begur & Around

POP 1240

Crowned by an 11th-century castle, with exquisite coast glistening in its surrounds, Begur is one of the most beautiful and sought-after spots along the Costa Brava. This fairy-tale town, 8km northeast of Palafrugell, has a tempting array of restaurants, beach-chic boutiques, soothing heritage and boutique hotels, and Modernista mansions that add splashes of colour among the stone streets of its medieval centre. And if that weren't enough, a series of scenic winding roads spiral down to dreamy little coves hemmed in by pines, like Aiguablava, Fornells, Sa Tuna, Sa Riera and Aiguafreda.

Sights & Activities

There are some lovely **walking trails** around Begur, including to several attractive beaches and an 11.5km hike south to Tamariu (five hours) along the GR92.

The tourist office (p348) has leaflets for self-guided historical walking tours.

Castell de Begur CASTLE

(Pujada al Castell; ⏲24hr) FREE There is little to explore aside from the ragged ruins of this medieval castle, still in much the same state as when it was wrecked by Spanish troops to impede the advance of Napoleon's army in 1810. A steep, signposted 1km walk leads from central Begur to the ramparts (25 minutes), with breathtaking views over hills rolling towards the Mediterranean.

Església de Sant Pere CHURCH

(Plaça de l'Església; ⏲hours vary) Begur's stocky sandstone church presides over lively Plaça de la Vila. Much of the building dates to the 17th century, though a church has stood on this spot since 1199.

DON'T MISS

TREASURED BEACHES AROUND BEGUR

With tiny coves framed by pine trees and subtropical flowers, and lapped by crystalline water, the sublime coastline around Begur is home to some of Spain's most gorgeous beaches. Thanks to their small size and difficult access, many remain largely undeveloped.

From mid-June to mid-September, **Sarfa** (www.sarfa.com) runs *bus platges* (€1) services to Sa Tuna, Sa Riera, Fornells and Aiguablava from Begur's Plaça de Forgas.

Cala d'Aiguafreda (Cala d'Aiguafreda) Around 4.5km northeast of Begur you'll find this tiny, divine rocky cove, where trails fringed by pine trees stretch around a headland. It's more a picturesque place for a stroll than a sunbathing spot.

Platja Fonda (Fornells) From just northeast of Fornells' car park (4km south of Begur), stone stairs lead down to signposted Platja Fonda, a slate-grey pebbly beach that lures sunbathers (though it can be choppy). A path signed 'Fornells' branches off just before the steps to reach a stunning stony outcrop with a natural pool, where cerulean waves smash against rocks.

Cala de Sa Tuna (Sa Tuna) The finely pebbled beach of Sa Tuna sits in a small cove 3km east of Begur, fringed by now-remodelled fishers' houses. There are restaurants and parking, though the water can be a little unsettled, and this scenic stretch of coast is backed by an old stone watchtower. You can walk to Sa Tuna along a 2.3km path from Begur.

Sleeping & Eating

Sa Barraca B&B €€
(☎972 62 33 60; www.sabarraca.com; Carrer Begur–Aiguablava (GIV6532); r €67-85; P ❄ 📶) This exceptionally welcoming, good-value B&B sits hidden up high on a pine-covered hillside, 3km south of Begur en route to Aiguablava beach, unveiling some of the finest coastal views around. It's expertly run by charming hosts who prepare fresh breakfasts, and there are just seven homey, spacious rooms, all with wide-open terraces.

★ **Cluc Hotel** BOUTIQUE HOTEL €€€
(☎972 62 48 59; www.cluc.cat; Carrer del Metge Pi 8; r incl breakfast €99-171; ❄ 📶) One of old-town Begur's chicest, yet friendliest, hotels unfolds across this ravishing, revamped 1800 *casa d'indians* (house built by a returned colonist). The 12 rooms are on the small side, but decorated in elegant vintage style with restored furniture and tile-covered floors. Expect an honesty bar, a library and home-made breakfasts on a charming terrace. No kids under 12.

Sa Rascassa HOSTAL €€€
(☎972 62 28 45; www.hostalsarascassa.com; Cala d'Aiguafreda; s/d incl breakfast €128/160; ⏱Mar-Nov; ❄ 📶 🐾) It's a choice of five rooms at this glammed-up and efficiently operated *hostal* tucked away in pine-shaded Cala d'Aiguafreda, 4.5km northeast of Begur. Dove greys and cosy creams speckle the tasteful, unfussy rooms, all with garden views. There's ample outdoor lounging space, plus an honesty bar and a summer *xiringuito* (beach bar), and you can't beat the secluded location.

In the candlelit garden, the fantastic contemporary-Catalan **restaurant** (☎972 62 28 45; www.hostalsarascassa.com; Cala d'Aiguafreda; mains €13-21; ⏱1.30-3.30pm & 8.30-11pm Mar-Nov, closed Tue Sep-Nov & Apr-Jun, evenings only Mar; 📶) delights palettes with daily fresh seafood, grilled meats, crunchy salads, creamy rices and more.

Aiguaclara HERITAGE HOTEL €€€
(☎972 62 29 05; www.hotelaiguaclara.com; Carrer Santa Teresa 3; ⏱mid-Feb–mid-Dec; ❄ 📶) Filled with both historical charm and boutique flavour, romantic Aiguaclara is set within a pink-washed mid-19th-century *casa d'indians*. Original soaring ceilings and antique tiles mingle with contemporary art, retro styling, pops of colour and gleaming modern bathrooms in the 10 airy, uncluttered rooms. Great breakfasts start the day, while a cocktail lounge and excellent **restaurant** (mains €12-19; ⏱7.30-10.30pm Mon-Sat Jul & Aug, 7.30-10.30pm Tue-Sat Sep–mid-Dec & mid-Feb–Jun) occupy the fairy-lit garden.

Information

Oficina de Turisme de Begur (☎972 62 45 20; www.visitbegur.com; Avinguda del Onze de Setembre 5; ⏱9am-9pm Mon-Fri, 10am-9pm Sat & Sun Jul-Sep, to 8pm Oct & Jun, 9am-3pm Mon-Fri Nov-May, hours vary) Helpful office with information on Begur's sights, walks and beaches.

Getting There & Away

Sarfa (www.sarfa.com) buses run to Barcelona's Estació del Nord (€19.50, two to 2½ hours, two to seven daily), many via Palafrugell (€1.70, 15

WHAT'S COOKING IN CATALONIA?

Cuina Catalana rivals Basque cuisine as Spain's best, drawing ingredients from *mar i muntanya* (sea and mountain). Its essence lies in quality local ingredients and sauces for meat and fish. There are five main sauces: *sofregit*, of fried onion, tomato and garlic; *samfaina*, *sofregit* plus red pepper and aubergine or courgette; *picada*, based on ground almonds, usually with garlic, parsley, pine nuts or hazelnuts, and sometimes breadcrumbs; *allioli*, garlic pounded with olive oil and egg yolk to make a mayonnaise; and *romesco*, an almond, tomato, olive oil, garlic and vinegar sauce.

Enjoy top-notch seafood all along the Costa Brava, served grilled or in *fideuà* (a noodle-based paella). Down south, don't miss duck with rice in the Delta de l'Ebre.

Inland, cheeses, cured meats and root vegetables reign supreme. *Llonganissa* sausage, a speciality of Vic, is one must-try delicacy. *Calçots*, a type of long spring onion, are delicious as a starter with *romesco* sauce and in season in late winter/early spring. The La Garrotxa region is famous for its earthy *cuina volcànica* (volcanic cuisine).

Otherwise, Catalans seem to live on *pa amb tomàquet*, bread rubbed with tomato, olive oil and garlic.

DON'T MISS

DALÍ'S CASTELL DE PÚBOL

If you're intrigued by artist Salvador Dalí, the **Castell de Púbol** (www.salvador-dali.org; Plaça de Gala Dalí, Púbol; adult/concession €8/6; ⏲10am-7.15pm mid-Jun–mid-Sep, 10am-5.15pm Tue-Sun mid-Mar–mid-Jun & mid-Sep–Oct, 10am-4.15pm Tue-Sun Nov-early Jan) is an essential piece of the puzzle. Between Girona and Palafrugell (22km northwest of the latter, south off the C66), this 14th-century castle was Dalí's gift to his wife and muse Gala, who is buried here. The Gothic-Renaissance building, with creeper-covered walls, spiral stone staircases and a shady garden, was decorated to Gala's taste, though there are surrealist touches like a grimacing anglerfish fountain and a pouting-lips sofa.

The life of Gala Dalí is fascinating in its own right, due to her entanglement with several pivotal figures in the first half of the 20th century. Gala married French poet Paul Éluard in 1917, had a two-year affair with pioneer of Dadaism Max Ernst, and then met Dalí in 1929. With Dalí's approval she continued to take lovers, though their loyalty to each other remained fierce. Russian-born Gala was as admired for her elegance as much as she was feared for her imposing manners.

In 1969 Dalí finally found the ideal residence to turn into Gala's refuge. At the age of 76, Gala preferred to flit in and out of Dalí's decadent lifestyle. Dalí was only permitted to visit the castle with advance written permission, a restriction that held considerable erotic charge for the artist.

To get here, catch a bus to Cruilla de la Pera from Girona (€3, 40 minutes, 10 to 19 daily) or Palafrugell (€3.05, 25 minutes, seven to 13 daily), and alight at the stop on the C66 then walk 2km south to the castle. Alternatively, take a train from Girona to Flaça (€3.30, 15 minutes, at least 15 daily), then taxi the last 5km.

minutes, four to 16 daily), and to Girona (€8.35, 1¼ hours, one daily weekdays).

Pals

POP 1040

About 7km northwest of shimmering Begur, halfway to popular Peratallada, sits the gorgeous walled town of Pals. Although most of its historical buildings can only be admired from outside, simply wandering the uneven cobbled lanes and peeking into the many medieval corners makes a visit worthwhile.

Sights

The **tourist office** (☎972 63 73 80; www.visitpals.com; Plaça Major; ⏲10am-2.30pm & 5-8pm Apr-Sep, 10am-5pm Oct-Mar) provides detailed booklets (Catalan, Spanish and English) for self-guided walking tours of Pals' old town.

Torre de les Hores TOWER

(Clock Tower; Carrer de la Torre) Pals' main monument is the 15m-high Romanesque Torre de les Hores, originally part of a castle; its 16th-century bell still rings today.

Getting There & Away

Sarfa (www.sarfa.com) buses run from Pals to Barcelona's Estació del Nord (€20, 2½ hours, three daily) and airport (€22, 3¼ hours, two daily), plus Begur (€1.70, 10 minutes, four to six daily), Palafrugell (€1.70, 25 minutes, four to six daily) and Girona (€6.70, one hour, daily on weekdays).

Peratallada

POP 130

As soon as you set foot in heart-stoppingly pretty Peratallada, 15km northwest of Begur, it's obvious why this fortified medieval town is beloved by Barcelona day trippers, French tourists and everyone else. Pale archways, cobbled squares and sandstone houses strung with ivy conjure an air of fairy-tale romance, though most of the historic buildings can only be gazed at from the outside. Peratallada's many visitors are well catered for by handicraft and clothing shops that beckon from laneways winding between crumbling walls and an 11th-century castle.

Església de Sant Esteve CHURCH

(Plaça de l'Església; ⏲hours vary) This graceful late-Romanesque church stands just outside Peratallada's historic centre, on the north edge of town.

El Cau del Papibou HOTEL €€

(☎972 63 47 16; http://hotelelcaudelpapibou.com; Carrer Major 10; r €110-130; ⏲Jan-Nov, closed Mon & Tue Oct-Mar; 📶) Stylish, colour-themed rooms with beamed ceilings, distressed-wood decor and rustic views fill this friendly, characterful hideaway in a 12th-century building in the heart of Peratallada. Downstairs, the restaurant serves creative, local-inspired tapas (€3.80) at benches in an ivy-draped alley.

La Riera CATALAN **€€**
(☎972 63 41 42; www.lariera.es; Plaça de les Voltes 3; mains €13-20; ⏰1-3.30pm & 8-10.30pm Mar-Jan) Opening onto a flower-filled terrace, this sophisticated yet friendly eatery within a 15th-century old-town building simmers up an excellent range of rice dishes, from simple seafood paella to *arròs de llamàntol* (lobster rice), as well as earthy roasted meats such as entrecôte in mushroom sauce and grilled duck.

It's also an esteemed *hostal* (double including breakfast €80).

Getting There & Away

Weekday **Sarfa** (www.sarfa.com) buses serve Peratallada from Palafrugell (€4, 35 to 55 minutes, two daily), Begur (€2.50, 20 to 40 minutes, two daily) and Girona (€6, 55 minutes, one daily).

Girona

POP 94,300

Northern Catalonia's largest city, Girona is a jewellery box of museums, galleries and Gothic churches, strung around a web of cobbled lanes and medieval walls. Reflections of Modernista mansions shimmer in the Riu Onyar, which separates the walkable historic centre on its eastern bank from the gleaming commercial centre on the west.

The Roman town of Gerunda lay on the Via Augusta from Gades (now Cádiz) to the Pyrenees. Taken from the Muslims by the Franks in the late 8th century, Girona became the capital of one of Catalonia's most important counties, falling under the sway of Barcelona in the late 9th century. Girona's wealth in medieval times produced many fine Romanesque and Gothic buildings that have survived repeated attacks, while a Jewish community flourished here until its expulsion in 1492.

With Catalonia's most diverse nightlife and dining scene outside Barcelona, Girona makes a delicious distraction from the coast.

Sights

Girona's exquisitely preserved **Call** (Jewish Quarter) – a labyrinth of low-slung stone arches and slender cobbled streets – flourished around narrow Carrer de la Força for six centuries, until relentless Christian persecution forced the Jews out of Spain.

★Catedral de Girona CATHEDRAL
(www.catedraldegirona.org; Plaça de la Catedral; adult/student incl Basílica de Sant Feliu €7/5; ⏰10am-7.30pm Jul & Aug, to 6.30pm Apr-Jun, Sep & Oct, to 5.30pm Nov-Mar) Towering over a flight of 86 steps rising from Plaça de la Catedral, Girona's imposing cathedral is far more ancient than its billowing baroque facade suggests. Built over an old Roman forum, parts of its foundations date from the 5th century. Today, 14th-century Gothic styling (added over an 11th-century Romanesque church) dominates, though a beautiful, double-columned Romanesque **cloister** dates from the 12th century. With the world's second-widest Gothic nave, it's a formidable sight to explore, but audio guides are provided.

Highlights include the richly carved fantastical beasts and biblical scenes in the cloister's southern gallery, and a 14th-century silver altarpiece, studded with gemstones. Also seek out the bishop's throne and the **museum**, which holds the masterly Romanesque *Tapís de la creació (Tapestry of the Creation)*. There is also a Mozarabic illuminated Beatus manuscript, dating from 975. The facade and belltower weren't completed until the 18th century.

★Museu d'Història dels Jueus MUSEUM
(www.girona.cat/call; Carrer de la Força 8; adult/child €4/free; ⏰10am-8pm Mon-Sat, 10am-2pm Sun Jul & Aug, 10am-2pm Mon & Sun, 10am-6pm Tue-Sat Sep-Jun) Until 1492, Girona was home to Catalonia's second-most important medieval Jewish community (p351), after Barcelona, and one of the country's finest Jewish quarters. This excellent museum takes pride in Girona's Jewish heritage, without shying away from less salubrious aspects such as Inquisition persecution and forced conversions. You also see a rare 11th-century *miqvé* (ritual bath) and a 13th-century Jewish house.

Museu d'Art de Girona GALLERY
(www.museuart.com; Pujada de la Catedral 12; admission €4.50, incl Catedral and Basílica de Sant Feliu €10; ⏰10am-7pm Tue-Sat May-Sep, to 6pm Oct-Apr, 10am-2pm Sun year-round) Next to the cathedral, in the 12th- to 16th-century Palau Episcopal, this art gallery impresses with the scale and variety of its collection. Around 8500 pieces of art, mostly from this region, fill its displays, which range from Romanesque wood-

carvings and murals to paintings of the city by 20th-century Polish-French artist Mela Mutter, early-20th-century sculptures by influential Catalan architect Rafael Masó i Valentí, and works by leading Modernista artist Santiago Rusiñol.

Basílica de Sant Feliu BASILICA
(Plaça de Sant Feliu; adult/student incl Catedral €7/5; ⌚10am-5.30pm Mon-Sat, 1-5.30pm Sun) Just downhill from the cathedral stands Girona's second great church, with its landmark truncated bell tower. The nave is majestic with Gothic ribbed vaulting, while St Narcissus, the city's patron, is venerated in an enormous marble-and-jasper, late-baroque side chapel. To the right of the chapel is the saint's Gothic, 1328 sepulchre (which previously held his remains), displaying his reclining form and scenes from his life including the conversion of women, martyrdom and expelling of an evil genie. Audio guides included.

Banys Àrabs RUINS
(www.banysarabs.org; Carrer de Ferran el Catòlic; adult/child €2/1; ⌚10am-7pm Mon-Sat, to 2pm Sun Mar-Oct, 10am-2pm Nov-Feb) Although modelled on earlier Islamic and Roman bathhouses, the Banys Àrabs are a finely preserved, 12th-century Christian affair in Romanesque style (restored in the 13th century). The baths contain an *apodyterium* (changing room), with a small octagonal pool framed by slender pillars, followed by a *frigidarium* and *tepidarium* (with respectively cold and warm water) and a *caldarium* (a kind of sauna) heated by an underfloor furnace.

Passeig Arqueològic WALLS
(Passeig de la Muralla; Carrer de Ferran el Catòlic; ⌚dawn-dusk) FREE A walk along Girona's majestic medieval walls is a wonderful way to soak up the city landscape. There are several access points; the most popular is opposite the Banys Àrabs (at the north end of the old town), where steps lead up into heavenly gardens where town and plants merge into one organic masterpiece. The southernmost part of the wall ends near Plaça de Catalunya, and the Torre de Sant Domènec is a fantastic lookout point.

Monestir de Sant Pere de Galligants MONASTERY
(www.mac.cat; Carrer de Santa Llúcia; adult/child incl Museu d'Arqueologia de Catalunya–Girona €4.50/3.50; ⌚10am-6pm Tue-Sat Oct-Apr, 10am-7pm Tue-Sat May-Sep, 10am-2pm Sun year-round) This beautiful 11th- and 12th-century Romanesque Benedectine monastery has a sublime bell tower and a splendid cloister featuring otherworldly animals and mythical creatures on the 60 capitals of its double columns; there are some great ones in the church too.

Spread across the monastery is the **Museu d'Arqueologia de Catalunya–Girona**

GIRONA'S JEWS

The first records of a Jewish presence in Girona date to the 9th century and, by its 13th-century heyday, Girona's Jewish community was the second-largest in Catalonia (behind Barcelona). Jewish inhabitants lived, generally speaking, peacefully alongside their Christian neighbours, gaining in prosperity and contributing to fields as diverse as astronomy, mathematics and medicine.

Nevertheless, the Jewish communities came under Christian attack, especially in the 12th and 13th centuries. Girona's Call – a maze of slim alleys, surrounded by a stone wall – went from refuge to ghetto as Jews were gradually confined to their tiny corner of the town and banned from living beyond its western limits. Especially stomach-churning were the 'Disputes', rigged debates intended to ridicule pillars of the Jewish community against the supposedly superior logic of Christians. The spin of the day reported that these debates led to mass conversions, but it's likelier that Jews converted out of pressure and fear. Slander against Jews became increasingly grotesque, with tales of murdered Christian infants.

Things came to a head during a riot in 1391, when a mob broke into the Call, massacring 40 residents. Since the Jews were still under the king's protection, troops were sent in and the survivors confined to the Galligants Tower for 17 weeks (allegedly for their own safety), only to find their houses destroyed upon returning. Many converted to Christianity during the 15th century. In 1492, those who remained unconverted were expelled from Spain, ending a story that had been over 500 years in the making.

Girona

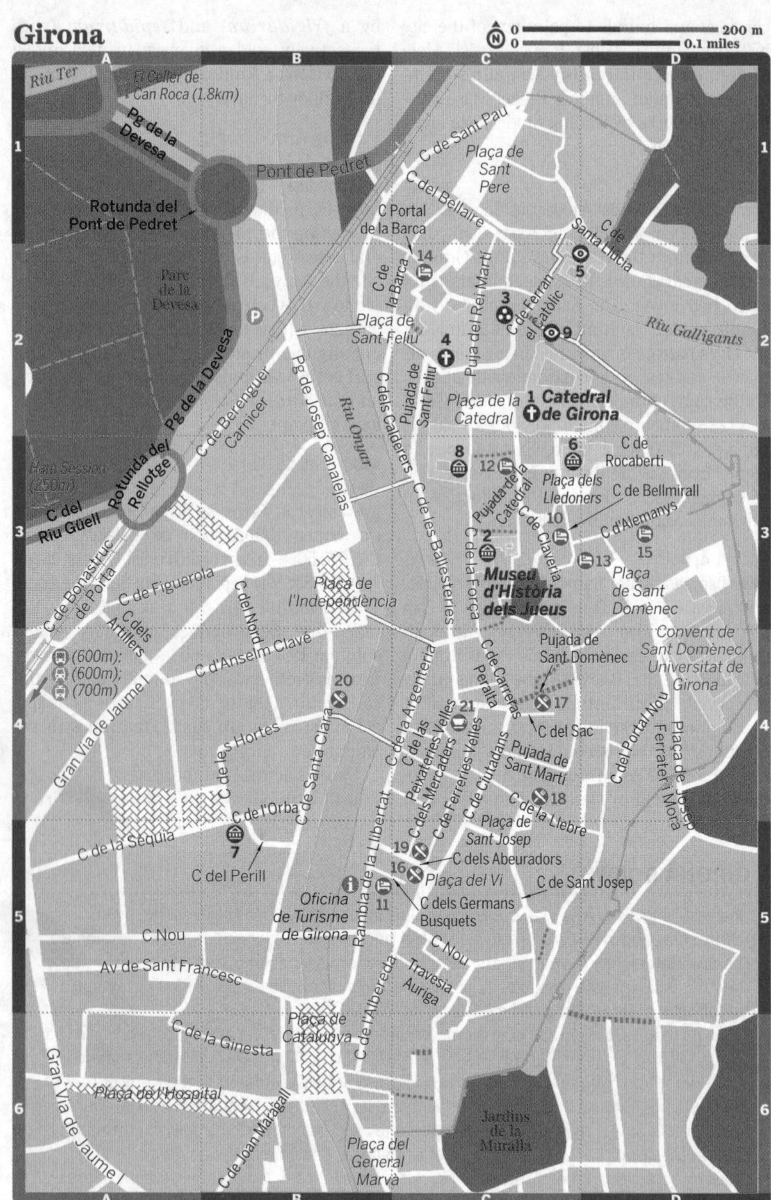

(www.mac.cat; Carrer de Santa Llúcia 8; incl Monestir de Sant Pere de Galligants adult/child €4.50/3.50; ⏲10am-6pm Tue-Sat Oct-Apr, 10am-7pm Tue-Sat May-Sep, 10am-2pm Sun year round), exhibiting artefacts dating from prehistoric to medieval times.

Museu d'Història de Girona MUSEUM

(www.girona.cat/museuhistoria; Carrer de la Força 27; adult/student/child €4/2/free; ⏲10.30am-5.30pm Tue-Sat Oct-Apr, 10.30am-6.30pm Tue-Sat May-Sep, 10.30am-1.30pm Sun year-round) Eighteenth-century cloisters lend an appro-

Girona

Top Sights
1 Catedral de Girona C2
2 Museu d'Història dels Jueus C3

Sights
3 Banys Àrabs C2
4 Basílica de Sant Feliu C2
5 Monestir de Sant Pere de Galligants D2
Museu d'Arqueologia de Catalunya–Girona .... (see 5)
6 Museu d'Art de Girona C3
7 Museu del Cinema B5
8 Museu d'Història de Girona C3
9 Passeig Arqueològic C2

Sleeping
10 Bellmiral C3
11 Bells Oficis B5
12 Casa Cúndaro C3
13 Hotel Històric D3
14 Hotel Llegendes de Girona Catedral C2
15 Palau dels Alemanys D3

Eating
16 B12 .... C5
17 Café Le Bistrot C4
18 La Fábrica C4
19 Nu C5
20 Rocambolesc B4

Drinking & Nightlife
21 Espresso Mafia C4

priately antique feel to this journey from Roman Girona to medieval times to the present day. The museum's highlights include an exhibition illuminating the 3rd- to 4th-century Can Pau Birol mosaic, which depicts a lively circus scene with charioteers, and an explanation of the 1808 to 1809 siege of Girona by Napoleonic troops. Many pieces on display are copies rather than originals. Spanish-, English- and French-language booklets help with the Catalan-only display labels.

Sleeping

Girona's most atmospheric accommodation choices are hidden away in the old town. Don't rule out the west bank of the river, Girona's commercial side: there are some quality hotels within walking distance of the top sights.

★Bells Oficis B&B €€
(☎972 22 81 70; www.bellsoficis.com; Carrer dels Germans Busquets 2; r incl breakfast €42-93; ❄📶) A lovingly restored 19th-century apartment towards the south end of the old town, Bells Oficis makes a stylish, ultra-welcoming base. It's the former home of Catalan artist Jaume Busquets i Mollera, and retains period details in the five very different rooms (one of which is a teeny two-bunk pad). Three rooms share a bathroom; one en-suite room has no bathroom door.

Casa Cúndaro GUESTHOUSE €€
(☎972 22 35 83; www.casacundaro.com; Pujada de la Catedral 7; d €59-79, q & apt €99; ❄📶) The understated exterior of this medieval Jewish house hides five characterful rooms and four self-catering apartments (for two to five people), all mixing original open-stone walls and antique doors with modern comfort. It's right next to the cathedral – a boon or a bane, depending on whether you enjoy the sound of church bells. Reserve well in advance.

The owners also run the more upmarket **Hotel Històric** (☎972 22 35 83; www.hotelhistoric.com; Carrer de Bellmirall 4A; r €90-170; ❄📶), just down the street.

Bellmiral PENSION €€
(☎972 20 40 09; http://bellmirall.eu; Carrer de Bellmiral 3; incl breakfast s €49-66, d €83-88; 📶) An inviting rustic-feel guesthouse hidden up high in Girona's historic core, Bellmiral unravels across a centuries-old stone house artily decorated with paintings and bright accents of colour. The seven rooms, five of which have old-town views, are a tad more modern than you'd expect, with exposed-stone walls.

★Palau dels Alemanys HERITAGE HOTEL €€€
(☎618 536852; www.allotjamentsingular.com; Carrer dels Alemanys 10; r incl breakfast €150-250) A stay at this intimate historical boutique beauty of an old-town hotel revolves around three exquisite 'suites' (mini-apartments with kitchenettes), under the watch of a keen young owner. Original architectural features, like Gothic arches and 18th-century stone walls, mingle with vintage furniture and chic contemporary styling. Breakfasts are brought to your door, and a chunk of Roman-era wall graces the courtyard.

GIRONAMUSEUS CARD

The excellent **Gironamuseus** card (www.gironamuseus.cat) covers six Girona museums: the Museu d'Història dels Jueus (p350), Museu d'Art de Girona (p350), Museu d'Història de Girona (p352), Museu d'Arqueologia de Catalunya–Girona (p351), Museu del Cinema and Casa Masó. You pay the full entrance fee at the first museum you visit and then get a 50% discount at the remainder. It's valid for six months.

Hotel Llegendes de Girona Catedral HOTEL €€€
(972 22 09 05; www.llegendeshotel.com; Carrer Portal de la Barca 4; r €137-329; P ❄) Each of the 15 rooms within this restored 18th-century building has been styled according to a different Catalan legend or theme. It's a pleasing fusion of ancient and modern, with comfortable beds, rain showers and complimentary *cava*. Some rooms have cathedral views. Book ahead for one of the three decadent, couples-oriented 'Eros' suites, boasting buttock-shaped chairs and tantric-sex sofas (with handy instruction manuals).

Eating

★La Fábrica CAFE €
(http://lafabrica.cc; Carrer de la Llebre 3; dishes €3-8; 9am-3pm;) Girona's culinary talents morph into top-quality coffee and Catalan-inspired brunchy favourites made using local ingredients at this German-Canadian-owned cycle-themed cafe. Pillowy artisan *torrades* (toasts) – perhaps topped with avocado, feta and peppers – arrive on wooden sliders, washed down with expertly poured brews made with beans sourced from ecoconscious suppliers.

Rocambolesc ICE CREAM €
(972 41 66 67; www.rocambolesc.com; Carrer de Santa Clara 50; ice cream €2.90-4.50; 11am-10pm Sun-Thu, to midnight Fri & Sat) Savour some of Spain's most lip-smackingly delicious ice cream at Rocambolesc, part of the world-famous El Celler de Can Roca culinary clan. Candy-striped decor sets the magical scene for creatively cool concoctions like baked-apple ice cream or mandarin sorbet sprinkled with passionfruit flakes.

B12 VEGAN, VEGETARIAN €
(972 01 32 02; Plaça del Vi 11; 3-course set menu €12.50; 11am-10pm Mon-Wed, 11am-midnight Thu & Fri, closed Sat & Sun;) Poised under stone arches, low-key B12 throws organic vegan and vegetarian produce together into light, fresh and totally delicious plant-fuelled cooking. You might find yourself digging into cashew-cream pasta, veggie burgers, spicy falafel or tofu salad. Lunch is a three-course set menu. Evenings are devoted to tapas and the other house speciality – craft beer.

Nu FUSION €€
(972 22 52 30; www.nurestaurant.cat; Carrer dels Abeuradors 4; mains €14-20; 8.15-10.30pm Mon, 1.15-3.30pm & 8.15-10.30pm Tue-Sat;) Sleek and confident, this beautiful, contemporary old-town spot has innovative, top-notch plates prepared in view by a friendly team. Catalan-Asian flavour fusions keep things exciting: sample red-tuna sashimi with soy, beef tenderloin in Iberian-ham sauce, or squid-ink rice with poached egg. Considering the high level of culinary quality, it's excellent value.

Café Le Bistrot CATALAN, FRENCH €€
(972 21 88 03; www.lebistrot.cat; Pujada de Sant Domènec 4; mains €7.50-14; noon-4pm & 7-11pm) Walls are draped in jasmine and tables spill out onto stairs climbing to a 17th-century church at what might just be Girona's most romantically set restaurant. The classic bistro-style menu twins French and Catalan cuisine, with crêpes, pastas, meaty mains, '*pagès*' pizzas and a rainbow of salads served alongside local cheeses. Inside, it's all check-print tiles and an old-world feel.

★El Celler de Can Roca CATALAN €€€
(972 22 21 57; www.cellercanroca.com; Carrer Can Sunyer 48; degustation menus €180-205; 12.30-2pm Tue, 12.30-2pm & 8-9.30pm Wed-Sat, closed late Dec–mid-Jan & 10 days late Aug) Ever-changing avant-garde takes on Catalan dishes have catapulted El Celler de Can Roca to global fame. Holding three Michelin stars, it was named the best restaurant in the world in 2015 by The World's 50 Best. Each year brings new innovations, from molecular gastronomy to multi-sensory food-art interplay to sci-fi dessert trolleys, all with mama's home cooking as the core inspiration.

Run by the three Girona-born Roca brothers, El Celler is set in a refurbished country house, 2km northwest of central Girona. Book online 11 months in advance or join the standby list.

Drinking & Nightlife

Espresso Mafia COFFEE

(www.espressomafia.cc; Carrer de la Cort Reial 5; ⊙9am-7pm Mon-Thu, to 8pm Fri & Sat, 10am-4pm Sun; 📶) With stripped-back white-on-white decor and (nonsmoking) tables below moody stone arches, Espresso Mafia is your go-to caffeine-shot spot on Girona's growing coffee scene. From smooth espresso and art-adorned latte to good old *café amb llet* (coffee with milk), coffee creations here are based on sustainably sourced beans, and best enjoyed with a nice slab of homemade cake.

Ham Session WINE BAR

(☎682 189023; http://donjamon.cat; Carrer del Riu Güell 18; ⊙9.30pm-2am Fri & Sat) Wine, late nights and uncompromisingly good Ibérico ham: together at last. Nocturnal grazers will find heaven at this gourmet-focused wine bar, which pairs fine wines with a seemingly endless buffet of local cheeses and freshly carved ham. Book ahead to assure your spot at seats that are surrounding the wine barrels.

Information

Oficina de Turisme de Girona (☎972 22 65 75; www.girona.cat/turisme; Rambla de la Llibertat 1; ⊙9am-8pm Mon-Fri, 9am-2pm & 4-8pm Sat Apr-Oct, 9am-7pm Mon-Fri, 9am-2pm & 3-7pm Sat Nov-Mar, 9am-2pm Sun year-round) Helpful, multilingual office by the river.

Getting There & Away

AIR

The **Aeroport de Girona–Costa Brava** (www.aena.es), a Ryanair hub, is 13km southwest of central Girona.

BUS

TEISA (www.teisa-bus.com) runs from Girona to Besalú (€4.70, 40 minutes to one hour, eight to 16 daily) and Olot (€7.45, one to 1½ hours, eight to 16 daily). **Sarfa** (www.sarfa.com) serves Cadaqués (€11, 1¾ hours, one to two weekdays, plus weekends in summer) and other coastal destinations. The **bus station** (☎972 21 23 19; Plaça d'Espanya) is next to the train station, 1km southwest of the old town.

CAR & MOTORCYCLE

The experience of parking in Girona is alluded to in the *Book of Revelations* (probably). Underground car parks are demonically expensive (often €35 a day), while free places are snapped up quickly. There's some free parking around Carrer Josep Morató i Grau, just south of the historic centre, plus free parking galore off the Carrer de Sant Gregori roundabout near El Celler de Can Roca, a 3km (30-minute) walk northwest of the centre.

TRAIN

Girona is on the train line between Barcelona (€10 to €31, 40 minutes to 1¼ hours, at least half-hourly), Figueres (€4.10 to €6.90, 30 to 40 minutes, at least half-hourly) and Portbou, on the French border (€6.15 to €8.25, one hour, 11 to 15 daily). There are several through trains to France and beyond.

Getting Around

TO/FROM THE AIRPORT

Sagalés (www.sagales.com) connects the airport to Girona's bus/train station (€2.75, 25 minutes, hourly) and Barcelona's Estació del Nord (return €25, 1¼ hours). Other direct bus services run to various Costa Brava destinations, including Tossa de Mar (€12, 55 minutes, two daily).

Taxis (☎972 22 23 23) to central Girona cost around €25 during the day and €35 at night.

WORTH A TRIP

SLEEP UNDER THE STARS

Stargazers and lovers will adore **Mil Estrelles** (☎972 59 67 07; www.milestrelles.com; La Bastida, Borgonyà; d €112-236; P❄📶), a unique, owner-designed country hideaway, 16km north of Girona. Fabulously combining old stone and modern plastic, it offers three lovably rustic rooms in a noble 18th-century farmhouse, as well as fun, stylish boudoirs (some with bath tubs) in clear plastic bubbles scattered around the garden, perfect for spotting constellations from the comfort of your double bed.

It's all designed for couples, with eco credentials in mind; there are no bathroom doors and facilities include a floatarium, sauna and hot tub, along with massages. Dinners are available, often delivered to your room.

It's 1.5km northwest of Pont-Xetmar (which is on the C66) and well signposted.

L'Estartit & the Illes Medes

L'Estartit, an 18km drive southeast of L'Escala and 6km east of Torroella de Montgrí, has a long, wide beach of fine sand and a flashy St Tropez vibe along its palm-lined promenade. But it's the fantastic diving that pulls travellers to this pretty stretch of Catalonia's coast. The protected Illes Medes, a spectacular group of rocky islets barely 1km offshore, are home to some of the most abundant marine life in coastal Spain.

Sights & Activities

Kiosks by the harbour, at the northern end of L'Estartit beach, offer diving classes, snorkelling trips and glass-bottomed boat excursions (€20 for a 90-minute cruise) to the Illes Medes. You can also head out on two-hour kayaking (€15) or SUP (€25) jaunts to the islands. Guided two-hour SUP and kayak excursions cost €30.

L'Estartit gets busy with divers between April and October. If you're a qualified diver, a two-hour trip usually costs €35 per person, while full gear rental costs €25 a day. If you're a novice, there are introductory dives for around €65, or full, five-day PADI Open Water Dive courses for around €400. A reliable, long-standing operator is **Les Illes** (972 75 12 39; www.hotellesilles.com; Carrer de les Illes 55, L'Estartit; single dive incl equipment from €50; Apr-Oct). Two-hour snorkelling trips cost €30/25 per adult/child.

★Illes Medes DIVE SITE, ISLAND
(972 75 17 01; www.gencat.cat/parcs/illes_medes; L'Estartit) The allure of the Illes Medes, seven islets off L'Estartit beach, lies in their range of depths (down to 50m), kaleidoscopic marine life, and underwater cavities and tunnels. Since being gazetted as a *reserva natural submarina* in 1983, this archipelago has seen marine species thrive, making it Spain's most popular destination for snorkellers and divers. As of 2010, the islets form part of the protected 80-sq-km **Parc Natural del Montgrí, les Illes Medes i el Baix Ter**.

Sleeping

★Les Medes CAMPGROUND €
(972 75 18 05; www.campinglesmedes.com; Paratge Camp de l'Arbre, L'Estartit; sites €17-34, adult €7.45-9.30, child €4.10-6.30; P) Spread across leafy grounds 2km southwest of L'Estartit and 1km from the seaside, this friendly, year-round operation is one of Catalonia's best campgrounds. It has a sauna, two pools (one heated), bike rental, laundry facilities, a dive school and even massage service. There are also smart, modern two- to four-person bungalows (double €87 to €96).

Hotel Les Illes HOTEL €€
(972 75 12 39; www.hotellesilles.com; Carrer de les Illes 55, L'Estartit; incl breakfast s €53-84, d €106-136, tr €159-198; mid-Mar–mid-Nov;) With its excellent diving centre (p356), this bright, white, family-friendly divers' hangout just behind the harbour is a top pick if you want to venture beneath the waves. Rooms sleep up to four guests and are functional though unremarkable; some have sea-view balconies.

Information

Oficina de Turisme de l'Estartit (972 75 19 10; www.visitestartit.com; Passeig Marítim, L'Estartit; 9am-9pm Jul & Aug, 9.30am-2pm & 4-8pm Jun & Sep, 9am-1pm & 4-7pm Mon-Fri, 10am-2pm & 4-7pm Sat & Sun May, 9am-1pm & 3-6pm Mon-Fri, 10am-2pm Sun Oct, Mar & Apr, 9am-5pm Mon-Fri, 10am-2pm Sat & Sun Nov-Feb) Has lists of L'Estartit's scuba-diving and other activity outfits.

Getting There & Away

Ampsa (www.ampsa.org) buses link L'Estartit with Torroella de Montgrí (€1.70, 10 minutes, nine to 19 daily) and Girona (€6, 1¼ hours, six to 12 daily). **Sarfa** (www.sarfa.com) buses run to Barcelona's Estació del Nord (€22, 2¼ hours, four daily) and airport (€24, three hours, three to four daily).

L'Escala

POP 9870

At the southern end of the 16km Golf de Roses, sprawling L'Escala is a resort town with a difference. Yes, summer brings sun-worshippers to amble along its seafront, lick ice cream on sandy beaches and clink glasses of wine. But merry L'Escala is also the access point to the magnificent Greco-Roman site Empúries, on the north edge of this bustling town behind a near-virgin beach facing the Mediterranean.

★Empúries ARCHAEOLOGICAL SITE
(972 77 02 08; www.mac.cat; Carrer Puig i Cadafalch; adult/child €5.50/free; 10am-8pm Jun-Sep, to 6pm Oct–mid-Nov & mid-Feb–May, to 5pm & closed Mon mid-Nov–mid-Feb) The evocative seaside archaeological site of Empúries, 1.5km northwest of central L'Escala, im-

merses you in a strategic Greek, and later Roman, trading port. A lively audio guide commentary (included in the price) unravels the history of the **Greek town** in the lower part of the site, before leading up to the **Roman town**, with its reconstructed 1st-century-BC forum. The **museum** exhibits the top finds, including a marble statue of Asclepius, Greek god of medicine, dating to the 2nd century BC.

Traders from Phocaea set up shop here in the 6th century BC at what is now the charming village of Sant Martí d'Empúries, then an island. Soon afterwards they founded a mainland colony, Emporion (Market), which remained an important trading centre and conduit of Greek culture to the Iberians for centuries.

In 218 BC Roman legions clanked ashore to cut off Hannibal's supply lines in the Second Punic War. Around 195 BC they set up a military camp and by 100 BC had added a town. A century later the Roman town had merged with the Greek one. Later, an early Christian basilica and a cemetery stood on the site of the Greek town, before the whole place disappeared under the sands for a millennium until its excavation in the 20th century.

Points of interest in the Greek ruins include the thick southern **defensive walls**, the site of the **Asklepieion** (shrine to the god of medicine) with a copy of his statue, and the **agora** (town square), with remnants of the early Christian **basilica** (4th to 7th centuries AD) and the Greek **stoa** (market complex) beside it.

The larger Roman town includes palatial **Domus 1**, source of many of the finest mosaics (displayed April to October only, for conservation purposes), and the newly excavated **Roman baths**. Outside the walls are the remains of an oval **amphitheatre**, dating to the 1st century BC.

Hostal Spa Empúries HOTEL €€€
(972 77 02 07; www.hostalempuries.com; Platja del Portitxol; r €150-300; P ❄ ☎) This stylish hotel next to the Greco-Roman ruins fronts a sandy splash of beach. Breezy neutral-toned rooms have mosaic bathrooms inspired by the ruins; some boast sea views. Those in the newer 'spa' wing, with rain showers and enormous beds, are particularly comfortable. The two restaurants (mains €17 to €27) specialise in creative Mediterranean and seafood dishes using local produce.

★La Gruta FUSION €€€
(972 77 62 11; www.restaurantlagruta.com; Carrer de la Casa Gran 1; 2-/3-course menu from €27/32; 12.30-3pm & 8-10.30pm Mon-Sat, closed Mon lunch Jul-Sep, closed Mon Oct-Dec & Apr-Jun) A fusion of French and Spanish flavours, spiced with occasional Asian flair, impresses diners at this innovative restaurant overlooking a tiny beach in central L'Escala. Highlights include beef *tataki* with aubergine caviar, truffled *oeuf cocotte* (French-style baked egg), and courgette tossed with saffron, mussels and prawns, plus a rainbow of home-cooked desserts.

Information

Oficina de Turisme (972 77 06 03; www.visitlescala.com; Plaça de les Escoles 1; 9am-8.30pm Mon-Sat, 9am-1pm Sun Jun-Sep, 9am-1pm & 4-7pm Mon-Fri, 10am-1pm & 4-7pm Sat, 10am-1pm Sun Oct-May) Beside L'Escala's bus stop.

Getting There & Away

Sarfa (www.sarfa.com) has daily buses to/from Barcelona's Estació del Nord (€22, three hours, three daily), Girona (€6.40, one hour, two to five daily) and Figueres (€4.95, one hour, six daily). Arriving in L'Escala, buses stop on Plaça de les Escoles, outside the tourist office.

Castelló d'Empúries

POP 3840

This handsome town once presided over Empúries, a medieval Catalan county that maintained a large degree of independence up to the 14th century. Modern Castelló d'Empúries retains the imperious aura and historical feel of a former capital, along with remnants of its once-thriving medieval Jewish community. These days its cobbled lanes are trodden less by counts and more by affable locals and the odd tourist.

The town also makes a superb base for outdoors lovers. The nearby Parc Natural dels Aiguamolls de l'Empordà is popular for birdwatching and has a number of easy hikes and biking trails, while wind-blown (but otherwise pretty peaceful) beaches lie just 6km east.

Sights

Pick up a leaflet from the **tourist office** (972 15 62 33; www.castelloempuriabrava.com; Plaça dels Homes; 10am-2pm & 4-8pm Jul & Aug, 10am-2pm & 4-7pm Mon-Sat, 10am-2pm Sun

WORTH A TRIP

SANT MARTÍ D'EMPÚRIES

Tiny walled **Sant Martí d'Empúries**, 1km north of **L'Escala's ruins of Empúries** (p356), impresses with its glorious shores, gold-tinged lanes and medieval history. Until 1079 it was the seat of Empúries county before its vulnerability to pirate attacks prompted a power shift. These days it makes a wonderful excursion from L'Escala (4km south) or Castelló d'Empúries (p357), 16km north. Sandy beaches extend just beyond its historical centre. The main square, flanked by a broad 16th-century sandstone church, is packed with more than its fair share of excellent restaurants.

Sep, Oct & Mar-Jun, 10am-4pm Mon-Thu, 10am-2pm & 4-6pm Fri & Sat, 10am-2pm Sun Nov-Feb) for a self-guided tour of Castelló d'Empúries' Jewish quarter.

Parc Natural dels Aiguamolls de l'Empordà PARK

(☎972 45 42 22; www.gencat.cat/parcs/aiguamolls_emporda; GIV6216 Sant Pere Pescador–Castelló d'Empúries Km 4.2; parking motorbike or car €5, van €10; ⊙El Cortalet information centre 9am-6.30pm Easter-Sep, 9am-4pm Oct-Easter) The remnants of the mighty marshes that once covered the whole coastal plain here are preserved in this 47-sq-km natural park, a key site for migrating birds, just south of Castelló d'Empúries. The March to May and August to October migration seasons bring big increases in the numbers of wading birds. Keen twitchers may glimpse flamingos, purple herons, glossy ibis, spoonbills, rare black storks and more of the 329 species that pass through (82 of which nest here).

There are enough birds to make a visit worthwhile at any time of year. The park's **El Cortalet** information centre (signposted) is 1km east off the GIV6216 Sant Pere Pescador–Castelló d'Empúries road, halfway between the two towns.

The centre has wildlife information, maps of trails and two on-site lookout points, hires binoculars (€2.50), and is the trailhead for several walking and biking paths.

Basílica de Santa María BASILICA

(Plaça Mossèn Cinto Verdaguer; adult/child €2.50/free; ⊙9am-9pm Jul–mid-Sep, 10am-2pm & 4-6pm mid-Sep–Jun) This broad church seizes attention with its Romanesque tower, intricately carved portal, and a delicate sculpture on its tympanum (above the main entrance) of the Virgin Mary clasping Jesus while the three Magi look on admiringly. A church was first consecrated here in 1064, but today's imposing Catalan Gothic structure dates from the 13th to 15th centuries. Within, check out the 15th-century alabaster main altarpiece and a 14th-century baptismal font used to convert Jews to Christianity.

Sleeping & Eating

Hostal Casa Clara HOSTAL €€

(☎972 25 02 15; www.hostalcasaclara.com; Plaça de les Monges; s/d incl breakfast €65/85; ⊙Mar-Dec; P ❄ ≋) Genial service and cosy rooms make this colourful *hostal* a splendid mid-range option in the heart of old-town Castelló d'Empúries. All eight spacious rooms feature natural light, comfortable beds, bottled water and individual colour schemes. There's a pleasant lounge with books, board games and birdwatching information, and the restaurant serves flavoursome, seasonal Catalan fare (three-course set menu €18 to €25).

Hotel de la Moneda HOTEL €€€

(☎972 15 86 02; www.hoteldelamoneda.com; Plaça de la Moneda 8-10; r incl breakfast €99-240; ⊙Mar-Nov; P ❄ ≋ ≈) An enticing couples' retreat, Hotel de la Moneda inhabits a plush 18th-century mansion full of low-slung medieval archways, intimate old-world atmosphere, and 11 rooms awash in bright primary colours, some with Andalucian-tiled bathrooms sporting hot tubs. There's a small swimming pool, along with romantic touches like *cava* on arrival and slippers to pad around the enormous rooms. Leave the kids at home.

Les Voltes CATALAN €€

(☎972 25 08 12; www.lesvoltesrestaurant.net; Placa dels Homes 4; tapas €2-6, mains €10-18; ⊙12.30-3.30pm & 7.30-10.30pm Fri-Wed) As pleasant for a *tinto de verano* (red wine and soda) as for a full-blown feast of grilled entrecôte, Les Voltes spreads from a cavernous stone-walled interior onto atmospheric, central Placa dels Homes. Service is cheery, tablecloths are white, and the outdoor terrace is casual enough for tapas and *entrepans* (filled rolls).

Getting There & Away

Sarfa (www.sarfa.com) runs buses to Figueres (€1.70, 15 minutes, eight to 29 daily), Cadaqués (€4.20, 45 minutes, six to 13 daily) and Barcelona's Estació del Nord (€21, two hours, one to four daily).

Cadaqués

POP 2700

Cadaqués gleams above the cobalt-blue waters of a rocky bay on Catalonia's most easterly outcrop. This easygoing whitewashed village owes its allure in part to its windswept pebble beaches, meandering lanes, pretty harbour and the wilds of nearby Cap de Creus, but it's Salvador Dalí who truly gave Cadaqués its sparkle.

The surrealist artist spent family holidays here during his youth, and lived much of his later life at nearby Port Lligat, where the Dalís' otherworldly seaside home stands. Thanks to Dalí and other luminaries, such as his friend Federico García Lorca, Cadaqués pulled in a celebrity crowd, and still does.

Summer in Cadaqués is *very* busy, so advance bookings can make or break a trip. September is often less crowded, while tourist amenities begin to slumber from mid-October. There can also be sea storms at this time of year, bringing autumn breaks to an abrupt and soggy halt.

Sights & Activities

★Casa Museu Dalí HOUSE, MUSEUM

(☎972 25 10 15; www.salvador-dali.org; Port Lligat; adult/child under 8yr €11/free; ⏲9.30am-9pm mid-Jun–mid-Sep, 10.30am-6pm mid-Sep–Jan & mid-Feb–mid-Jun, closed mid-Jan–mid-Feb, closed Mon Nov–mid-Mar) Overlooking a peaceful cove in Port Lligat, a tiny fishing settlement 1km northeast of Cadaqués, this magnificent seaside complex was the residence and sanctuary of Salvador Dalí, who lived here with his wife Gala from 1930 to 1982. The splendid whitewashed structure is a mishmash of cottages and sunny terraces, linked by narrow labyrinthine corridors and containing an assortment of offbeat furnishings. Access is by semi-guided eight-person tour; it's essential to book well ahead, by phone or online.

The cottage was originally a mere fisherman's hut, but was steadily altered and enlarged by the Dalís. Every corner reveals a new and wondrous folly or objet d'art: a bejewelled taxidermied polar bear, stuffed swans (something of an obsession for Dalí) perched on bookshelves, and the echoing, womb-like **Oval Room**. The artist's **workshop**, containing two unfinished original works, is especially interesting. Meanwhile, **Dalí's bedroom** still has a suspended mirror, positioned to ensure he was the first person to see the sunrise each morning. The **dressing room**, decorated by Gala, is covered in photos of the couple with high-profile acquaintances including Picasso, Coco Chanel and even Franco. Post-tour, you're free to explore the olive-tree-strewn grounds (dotted with giant white eggs) and pale-aqua pool (with its hot-pink lip-shaped bench) independently.

Museu de Cadaqués MUSEUM

(☎972 25 88 77; Carrer de Narcís Monturiol 15; ⏲approx Easter-Oct) Salvador Dalí often features strongly in the temporary exhibitions displayed here, as do his contemporaries also connected to Cadaqués, such as Picasso. Enquire at the tourist office (p361) for current opening times.

Beaches

Cadaqués' main beach and others along the surrounding coast are small and pebbly, but their picturesqueness and beautiful blue waters more than make up for that. Overlooking **Platja Llané**, south of the town centre, is Dalí's parents' holiday home. All the beaches around here experience strong winds.

Sleeping

★Tramuntana Hotel BOUTIQUE HOTEL €€

(☎972 25 92 70; www.hotel-tramuntana-cadaques.com; Carrer de la Torre 9; r incl breakfast €125; ⏲Mar-Sep; P❄📶) A traditional whitewashed facade conceals 11 chic, soft-grey-on-white rooms with balconies at this fabulous little boutique bolthole pocketed away in the old town. It's expertly run and personally designed in minimalist contemporary style by a knowledgeable local couple. Thoughtful touches include a pine-fringed terrace, a luminous lounge, an honesty bar, and lovingly prepared breakfasts featuring the owners' own olive oil.

Hotel Tarongeta HOTEL €€

(☎972 25 82 89; hoteltarongeta@telefonica.net; Paratge Tarongeta; r €90-180; ⏲Easter-Nov; P❄📶) A gleaming, welcoming two-star hotel with free parking, perfectly positioned for drivers on the northern fringe of town. The corridors feel a tad impersonal, but that's soon forgotten thanks to smart,

DON'T MISS

MONESTIR DE SANT PERE DE RODES

Views of distant Pyrenean peaks and the deep-blue Mediterranean combine with a spectacular piece of Romanesque architecture at **Monestir de Sant Pere de Rodes** (☎972 19 42 38; http://monuments.mhcat.cat/conjunt_monumental_de_sant_pere_de_rodes; GIP6041; adult/child €4.50/free; ⏰10am-7.30pm Tue-Sun Jun-Sep, to 5pm Oct-May), a hillside monastery, 500m up in the hills 7km southwest of El Port de la Selva (which is 13km northwest of Cadaqués). Founded in the 9th century, it became the most powerful monastery in the county of Empúries. The great triple-naved, barrel-vaulted basilica is flanked by the square 12th-century Torre de Sant Miquel bell tower and a two-level cloister dating from the 11th and 20th centuries.

Also here is an **info centre** (p361) for the Cap de Creus natural park. Approaching from El Port de la Selva, stop in the signposted car park, a 10-minute walk from the monastery.

modern rooms adorned with floral or nautical themes, bathrooms that sparkle, and, for some, private balconies. Newer suites and 'romantic' rooms feature fun touches like four-poster beds.

Hostal Vehí HOSTAL €€
(☎972 25 84 70; www.hostalvehi.com; Carrer de l'Església 6; s/d €40/85; ⏰Mar-Oct; ❄📶) In the heart of the old town, this warm family-run guesthouse has carefully designed, impeccably kept rooms with homey touches such as floral duvets, wood furnishings and natural light. Superior doubles are vast, with views over Cadaqués' coral-coloured rooftops. Cars can't access this part of town, but it's the best midrange deal around. Book way ahead for July and August.

L'Horta d'en Rahola BOUTIQUE HOTEL €€€
(☎972 25 10 49; www.hortacadaques.com; Carrer Sa Tarongeta 1; r €140-205; ⏰mid-Mar–Nov; P❄📶🏊) By the roundabout on the north edge of Cadaqués, this characterful conversion of an 18th-century family-owned farmhouse is adults-only and has a gorgeous fruit-and-vegetable garden and turquoise pool. The nine contemporary rooms, all different, are light and bright with a maritime feel. Personal service is excellent and you're made to feel very welcome.

Eating & Drinking

Mut CATALAN, INTERNATIONAL €
(www.facebook.com/Mutcadaques; Plaça Doctor Pont 12; tapas €5-7, mains €8-12; ⏰9am-late Easter-Sep, weekends only Oct, hours vary; 🍸) With its cluster of terrace tables gazing out on Port Doguer, fashionable Mut serves an exciting, innovative menu that dances the world, from chorizo in cider to chilli-infused vegetable curry and lentil-duck-and-mango salad. There are also tapas such as hummus and *patatas mojo picón* (potatoes in spicy sauce). Or just swing by for vermouth and cocktails.

Lua FUSION €€
(☎972 15 94 52; www.facebook.com/lua.cdqs; Carrer Santa Maria 1; dishes €8-16; ⏰noon-4pm & 8pm-midnight May-Sep, closed Wed Oct-Apr, may close Jan-Mar; 🍸) A yellow door sets the jazzy tone for tasty, creative Mediterranean-Asian 'soul food' at this laid-back bar-restaurant with beer-barrel tables and benches on an old-town alley. This spot is perfect for vegetarians; try a Veggie Venus bowl of black rice, hummus and babaganoush, or lighter bites like cheese platters, original ceramic-bowl salads, and *pa amb tomàquet* (bread with tomato and olive oil).

Compartir FUSION €€€
(☎972 25 84 82; www.compartircadaques.com; Riera Sant Vicenç; mains €20-26; ⏰1-3.30pm & 8-10.30pm, closed Mon Jul & Aug, closed Mon & Tue Oct, Nov, Apr & May, closed Mon & Sun Nov-Mar) Headed up by a trio of elBulli alumni, this terrace restaurant revolves around innovative, gourmet sharing plates (*'compartir'* means 'to share'), yet retains a (comparatively) laid-back feel. The always-evolving menu fuses traditional Catalan flavours into contemporary delights like Thai-style turbot or marinated sardines with raspberry, beetroot and pistachios. The setting is a 300-year-old house, and bookings are essential.

Es Baluard SEAFOOD €€€
(☎972 25 81 83; www.esbaluard-cadaques.net; Carrer de la Riba Nemesi Llorens; mains €17-27; ⏰1-3.30pm & 8.30-11pm Mar-Sep) There may be roe-deer carpaccio and salt-sprinkled grilled asparagus on the menu, but the family behind

Es Baluard clearly worships at the throne of Poseidon. Seafood dishes such as Cadaqués anchovies, spider-crab rice and *suquet de peix* (local fish stew) fill the menu. There's also a formidable selection of desserts including syrup-soaked figs and cream-cheese ice cream with orange marmalade.

Bar Boia BAR, CAFE
(http://boianit.com; Passeig de Cadaqués; ⌚8.30am-3am Jun-Sep, 9am-10pm Oct-May; 📶) Frequented by arty types and intellectuals since 1946, this sand-side *xiringuito* (beach bar) has been voguishly reimagined as a fantastic high-profile cocktail bar. Expertly crafted liquid fusions (€9.50 to €12) – plankton-and-sea-fennel G&T, *cava*-loaded 'Gala Dalí' – come courtesy of award-winning, elBulli-trained mixologist Manel Vehí. The cafe/tapas terrace opens early; the Boia Nit *coctelería* springs to life on summer nights.

Information

Oficina de Turisme (☎972 25 83 15; www.visitcadaques.org; Carrer del Cotxe 2; ⌚9am-9pm Mon-Sat, 10am-1pm & 5-8pm Sun Jul–mid-Sep, 9am-1pm & 3-6pm Mon-Sat, 10am-1pm Sun mid-Sep–Jun, closed Sun Oct-Mar)

Getting There & Away

Sarfa (www.sarfa.com) buses connect Cadaqués to Barcelona's Estació del Nord (€25, 2¾ hours, two to five daily) and airport (€27, 3½ hours, one to two daily), plus Figueres (€5.50, one hour, four to seven daily) and Girona (€11, 1¾ hours, one to two weekdays, plus weekends in summer) via Castelló d'Empúries (€4.20, 45 minutes, six to 13 daily).

Cap de Creus

Declared a nature reserve in 1998, Cap de Creus is the easternmost point of the Spanish mainland, and a place of sublime, rugged beauty, battered by the merciless *tramuntana* wind. With a steep, rocky coastline indented by coves of turquoise water, it's an especially magical spot to be at dawn or sunset.

The odd-shaped rocks, barren plateaux and deserted shorelines that fill Salvador Dalí's famous paintings were not just a product of his fertile imagination: this is the landscape that inspired the great surrealist artist.

The cape is reached by a lonely, 8km-long road that winds its way northeast from Cadaqués through the moonscapes, or via a gorgeous 8km hike from Cadaqués (2½ hours).

Sights & Activities

The Cap de Creus peninsula is much loved for the walking trails along its craggy cliffs; pick up route maps at the information centre or Cadaqués' tourist office. **Itinerari 17**, from the Paratge de Tudela car park to Cala Culop (4km return), weaves past the huge Roca Cavallera, which morphed into the subject of Dalí's painting *The Great Masturbator*.

Far Cap de Creus LIGHTHOUSE
The lighthouse glinting from the top of the cape dates to 1853.

Eating

Bar Restaurant Cap de Creus CATALAN, INDIAN **€€**
(☎972 19 90 05; www.facebook.com/pg/restaurante.capdecreus; mains €10-15; ⌚9.30am-8pm Sun-Thu, to midnight Fri & Sat Nov-Apr, 9.30am-midnight daily May-Oct, hours vary) Perched atop the cape, this all-day restaurant caters to exhausted hikers and beach-goers with an unexpected combination of Catalan and Indian food. The latter makes an agreeably aromatic change from Cadaqués' endless seafood grills; try a fragrant lamb curry or a veggie samosa. Coastal panoramas from the breezy terrace are exquisite and there's often live music.

Information

Espai Cap de Creus (http://parcsnaturals.gencat.cat/ca/cap-creus; ⌚10am-2pm & 3-7pm Jul–mid-Sep, 10am-3pm May, Jun & 2nd half Sep) The park's main information centre, with walking route maps and displays about local fauna and flora, inside the cape's lighthouse.

Centre d'Informació del Parc Natural (☎972 19 31 91; http://parcsnaturals.gencat.cat/ca/cap-creus; Palau de l'Abat, Monestir de Sant Pere de Rodes, GIP6041; ⌚10am-2pm & 3-6pm Jul-Sep, 10am-3pm Oct-Jun) At the Monestir de Sant Pere de Rodes, 30km west of Cap de Creus.

Figueres

POP 45,100

Fourteen kilometres inland from Catalonia's glistening Golf de Roses lies Figueres, birthplace of Salvador Dalí and now home to the artist's flamboyant theatre-museum. Although Dalí's career took him to Madrid, Barcelona, Paris and the USA, Figueres remained close to his heart. In the 1960s and '70s he created the extraordinary Teatre-Museu Dalí – a monument to surrealism and a legacy that outshines any other Spanish artist, in terms of both popularity and sheer flamboyance. Whatever your feelings about this complex, egocentric man, this museum is worth every euro and minute you can spare.

Beyond its star attraction, busy Figueres is a lively place with a couple of interesting museums, some good restaurants, pleasant shopping streets around Carrer de Peralada, and a grand 18th-century fortress. It's well worth staying to see the town breathe after Dalí day-trippers board their buses at sundown.

Sights

★Teatre-Museu Dalí MUSEUM

(www.salvador-dali.org; Plaça de Gala i Salvador Dalí 5; adult/child under 9yr €14/free; ⌚9am-8pm Jul-Sep, 10.30am-6pm Oct-Jun, closed Mon Oct-May, also open 10pm-1am Aug) The first name that pops into your head when you lay eyes on this red castle-like building, topped with giant eggs and stylised Oscar-like statues and studded with plaster-covered croissants, is Salvador Dalí. An entirely appropriate final resting place for the master of surrealism, it has assured his immortality. Exhibits range from enormous, impossible-to-miss installations – like *Taxi Plujós* (Rainy Taxi), an early Cadillac surmounted by statues – to the more discreet, including a tiny, mysterious room with a mirrored flamingo.

'Theatre-museum' is an apt label for this trip through the incredibly fertile imagination of one of the great showmen of the 20th century. Between 1961 and 1974, Dalí converted Figueres' former municipal theatre, destroyed by a fire in 1939 at the end of the civil war, into the Teatre-Museu Dalí. It's full of illusions, tricks and the utterly unexpected, and contains a substantial portion of Dalí's life's work, though you won't find his most famous pieces here (they're scattered around the world).

VISITING THE TEATRE-MUSEU DALÍ

The **Teatre-Museu Dalí** (p362) is Spain's most-visited museum outside Madrid (over 1.1 million visitors in 2016), so it's worth double-checking opening hours (it's closed on Mondays from October to May) and reserving tickets online in advance. In August the museum opens at night from 10pm to 1am (admission €15, bookings essential). Arrive early to avoid long queues.

Even outside, the building aims to surprise, from its entrance watched over by medieval suits of armour balancing baguettes on their heads, to bizarre sculptures outside the entrance on Plaça de Gala i Salvador Dalí, to the pink walls along Pujada al Castell and Carrer Canigó. The **Torre Galatea**, added in 1983, is where Dalí spent his final years.

Opening the show is *Taxi Plujós*; put a coin in the slot and water washes all over the occupant of the car. The **Sala de Peixateries** (Fishmongers' Hall) holds a collection of Dalí oils, including the famous *Autoretrat Tou amb Tall de Bacon Fregit* (Soft Self-Portrait with Fried Bacon) and *Retrat de Picasso* (Portrait of Picasso). Beneath the former stage of the theatre is the crypt with Dalí's plain **tomb**.

After you've seen the more notorious pieces, such as climbing the stairs in the famous **Mae West Room**, see if you can track down a turtle with a gold coin balanced on its back, peepholes into a green-lit room where a mirrored flamingo stands amid fake plants, and Dalí's heavenly reimagining of the Sistine Chapel in the **Palau del Vent** (Palace of the Wind Room).

Gala, Dalí's wife and lifelong muse, is seen throughout – from the *Gala Nua Mirant el Mar Mediterrani* (Gala Nude Looking at the Mediterranean Sea) on the 2nd level, which also appears to be a portrait of Abraham Lincoln from afar (best seen from outside the Mae West room), to the classic *Leda Atòmica* (Atomic Leda).

A separate entrance (same ticket and opening times) leads into **Dalí Joies**, a collection of 37 Dalí-designed, New-York-made jewels dating between 1941 and 1970. Each piece, ranging from the disconcerting *Ull del Temps* (Eye of Time) to the *Elefant de l'Espai* (Space Elephant) and the *Cor Reial* (Royal Heart), is unique.

Castell de Sant Ferran FORT

(www.lesfortalesescatalanes.info; Pujada del Castell; adult/child €3.50/free; ⌚10am-8pm Jul–mid-Sep, 10.30am-6pm mid-Sep–Oct & Apr-Jun, 10.30am-3pm Nov-Mar) Figueres' sturdy 18th-century fortress commands the surrounding plains from a low hill 1km northwest of the centre. The complex is a wonder of military engineering: it sprawls over 32 hectares, with the capacity for 6000 men to march within its walls and snooze in military barracks. Admission fees include clanking audio guides (nearly as old as the castle).

SALVADOR DALÍ

One of the 20th century's most recognisable icons, Salvador Dalí (1904–89) could have had the term 'larger-than-life' invented for him. He then would probably have decorated it with pink pineapples.

Born in Figueres, Dalí turned his hand to everything from film-making to painting to architecture to literature to jewellery-making. His surrealist trajectory through the often-serious landscape of 20th-century Spain brought him into contact and collaboration with figures such as Pablo Picasso, Luís Buñuel, Federico García Lorca and (controversially) Franco. A raft of foreign celebrities flocked to be seen in his extravagant company.

Self-consciously eccentric and a constant source of memorable soundbites, Dalí was nevertheless in some ways a conservative figure and devout Catholic. A 1929 visit to Cadaqués by French poet Paul Éluard and his Russian wife, Gala, caused an earthquake in Dalí's life: he ran off to Paris with Gala (who became his lifelong obsession and, later, his wife) and joined the surrealist movement. His long relationship with Gala provided the stable foundation that his whirligig life revolved around.

The celebrity, the extraordinarily prolific output and, let's face it, the comedy moustache tend to pull focus from the fact that Dalí was an artist of the highest calibre. In his paintings, Dalí's surrealism is often far more profound than it seems at first glance. The floppy clocks of his most famous work, *The Persistence of Memory*, are interpreted by some as a reference to the flexibility of time proposed by Einstein. His *Christ of St John of the Cross* combines expert composition, symbol-laden Renaissance-style imagery and a nostalgic, almost elegiac view of the Catalan coast that he so loved.

Northeastern Catalonia's so-called **Dalí Triangle** (which received a staggering 1.4 million visitors in 2016) encompasses the spectacularly out-of-this-world **Teatre-Museu Dalí** in Figueres, the artist's eclectic home at Port Lligat's **Casa Museu Dalí** (p359) near Cadaqués, and the conversely less flamboyant **Castell de Púbol** (p349), northeast of Girona.

Museu de l'Empordà MUSEUM
(www.museuemporda.org; La Rambla 2; adult/child €4/free; ⌚11am-8pm Tue-Sat May-Oct, 11am-7pm Tue-Sat Nov-Apr, 11am-2pm Sun year-round) Extending over four floors, the local museum time travels from ancient amphorae to 7th-century sculptures to rotating installations of contemporary art. The region's culture and history are presented in a fragmented way, but it's an enjoyable journey. The 17th-century religious art is especially worthy of attention. Don't miss a colour-bursting 1962 *Sant Narcís* by Dalí.

Sleeping & Eating

Hostel Figueres HOSTEL €
(☎630 680575; www.hostelfigueres.com; Carrer dels Tints 22; dm/d €21/42; ❄📶) Energetic and fresh-faced, this hostel is exactly the backpacker hideaway Figueres needs. The four-, six- and eight-person dorms are modern, airy and spotless, with fans and personal lockers. The three air-conditioned doubles share bathrooms, while the fully-equipped three-bedroom apartment (from €65) suits groups. Staff fizz with recommendations, and the hostel provides a kitchen, terrace, lounge and towel hire (€1).

Hotel Duran HOTEL €€
(☎972 50 12 50; www.hotelduran.com; Carrer de Lasauca 5; s/d €80/95; P❄📶) For absolute immersion in the Dalí legend, stay at this mid-19th-century hotel, where the artist and his wife often made appearances. There's a fitting blend of old-style elegance with contemporary design, surrealist touches, and photos of Dalí with the former hotel manager, whose descendants now proudly run the place. Rooms are bright, modern and good value. Breakfast costs €10, parking €15.

The glittering **restaurant** (☎972 50 12 50; www.hotelduran.com; Carrer Lasauca 5; mains €16-25; ⌚12.45-4pm & 8.30-11pm), meanwhile, has all the opulence of a royal banquet hall, with smooth service, a tasting menu (€49) and lightly creative Catalan fare.

El Motel CATALAN €€€
(☎972 50 05 62; www.hotelemporda.com; Hotel Empordà, Avinguda Salvador Dalí 170; mains €13-30; ⌚12.45-3.45pm & 8.30-10.30pm; P📶) Jaume Subirós, the chef and owner of this smart roadside hotel-restaurant 1km north

of Figueres' centre, is a seminal figure of the transition from traditional Catalan home cooking to the polished, innovative affair it is today. Local, seasonal ingredients star on the menu, which may feature highlights like salted Roses shrimp, ricotta-and-parmesan-stuffed courgette flowers, and rice with Cap de Creus lobster.

There are also appealing, classic rooms for sleeping off the gastronomic indulgence (double €65 to €105, suite €110 to €145).

Information

Oficina de Turisme Figueres (972 50 31 55; http://visitfigueres.cat; Plaça de l'Escorxador 2; 9am-8pm Mon-Sat, 10am-3pm Sun Jul-Sep, 9.30am-2pm & 4-6pm Tue-Sat, 10am-2pm Mon & Sun Oct-Jun)

Getting There & Away

Sarfa (www.sarfa.com) buses serve Cadaqués (€5.50, one hour, four to seven daily) via Castelló d'Empúries (€1.70, 15 minutes, 13 to 25 daily) from Figueres' **bus station** (Plaça de l'Estació 7).

Figueres train station, 800m southeast of the centre, has half-hourly trains to/from Girona (€4.10 to €5.45, 30 minutes) and Barcelona (€12 to €16, 1¾ to 2½ hours), plus hourly trains to/from Portbou (€3.40, 30 minutes) on the French border. High-speed trains to Girona, Barcelona and into France depart from Figueres-Vilafant station, 1.5km west of central Figueres.

WORTH A TRIP

CENTRE DE REPRODUCCIÓ DE TORTUGUES DE L'ALBERA

This long-running little **wildlife sanctuary** (972 55 22 45; www.tortugues.cat; Garriguella; adult/child €6/4.50; 10am-6pm Jul–mid-Sep, 10am-1pm mid-Mar–Jun & mid-Sep–Oct, closed Nov–mid-Mar) is a haven for Hermann's tortoises, and a force for educating people about these threatened little armoured tanks of the Pyrenees. There's an introductory film (Catalan, Spanish, English, French or German) explaining menaces to the region's tortoises, but the biggest thrill is a stroll around the boardwalk outside, to peep at the 140 tortoises ambling among rocks and flower beds. The well-signposted sanctuary is just north of Garriguella, a teeny town 13km north-east of Figueres.

Besalú

POP 2400

The delightfully well-preserved medieval town of Besalú looms into sight with its elegant, show-stopping 11th-century Pont Fortificat (Fortified Bridge) spanning the Riu Fluvià, and leading into the coiled maze of cobbled narrow streets that make up its historic core. Following a succession of Roman, Visigothic and Muslim rulers, during the 10th and 11th centuries Besalú was the capital of an independent county that stretched as far west as Cerdanya before it came under Barcelona's control in 1111. Today Besalú is a favourite day-trip destination from Girona (35km south) and the Olot area (20km west), with a steady stream of visitors roaming the ramparts and exploring its Jewish history.

Sights & Activities

Guided walking tours of Besalú's old town are offered by the tourist office (p365) and **Ars Didàctica** (607 453531; www.arsdidactica.com; Carrer Major 2; 30min/1hr tour €3/4.80; tours daily mid-Jun–mid-Sep, weekends only mid-Sep–mid-Jun).

★Pont Fortificat BRIDGE

(Carrer del Pont) Besalú's fortified stone bridge is so old, it strains memory. The first records of the bridge date to 1075, though periodic modifications have bolstered its defensive structure. It was bombed in 1939 during the Spanish Civil War and repaired soon after. Today this exquisite pale sandstone bridge, with its two turreted gates and heavy portcullis, is an arresting vantage point for the loveliest views of medieval Besalú.

Jewish Square RUINS

(Baixada de Miqvé; guided tours €2.25-4.80) Besalú's thriving Jewish community fled the town in 1436 after relentless Christian persecution. It left behind a 12th-century riverside *miqvé* (ritual bath), a rare survivor of its kind in Spain, which was rediscovered in 1964. It sits inside a vaulted stone chamber, around which remnants of the 13th-century **synagogue** were unearthed in 2005. Access to the *miqvé* is by guided tour with the tourist office (p365) or Ars Didàctica, but you can see the square and ruin exterior independently.

Monestir de Sant Pere MONASTERY

(Plaça Prat de Sant Pere; by donation; hours vary) This Romanesque monastery dates from the

WORTH A TRIP

MUSEU MEMORIAL DE L'EXILI

Anyone familiar with Picasso's *Guernica* has an insight into the horror of civilian suffering during the Spanish Civil War. This thought-provoking **museum** (www.museuexili.cat; Carrer Major 43-47, La Jonquera; adult/child €4/free; ⏲10am-8pm Tue-Sat Jun-Sep, 10am-6pm Tue-Sat Oct-May, 10am-2pm Sun year-round) traces the experiences of Catalonian people exiled and persecuted during this era. It's aptly located in La Jonquera, 20km north of Figueres, close to the Spain–France border where many Spaniards fled following the Republican defeat in 1939. It explains the build-up to the civil war through photographs, audio guides (Catalan, Spanish, English or French), and haunting art installations.

11th century and has an unusual ambulatory (walkway) with floral-motif capitals behind the altar.

Sleeping & Eating

3 Arcs HOTEL €€
(☎972 59 16 78; www.hotel3arcs.com; Carrer de Ganganell 15; s/d/tr incl breakfast €81/89/103; ❄📶) As the name suggests, you'll know this place by the slender stone archways adjoining a fine, refurbished old-town building. Its 12 simple rooms are compact and modern, management is friendly, and there's a pleasant downstairs cafe.

Casa Marcial HOTEL €€
(☎608 029427; www.casa-marcial.com; Carrer del Comte Tallaferro 15; incl breakfast s €85-90, d €110-139; ❄📶🏊) Partly set within a revamped turn-of-the-20th-century mansion, Casa Marcial makes an attractive old-town choice for its cordial service, small pool and 12 smart, uncluttered, contemporary rooms. Some rooms boast balconies and all have plenty of light; the five spacious 'suites', including a family-sized option, come with tea/coffee kits. A grassy garden wraps around a 12th-century church to reach the pool.

Amb els 5 Sentits CATALAN €€
(☎633 633390; www.facebook.com/ambels5sentitsbesalu; Carrer Abat Zafont 8; degustation menus €15-19; ⏲1-3.30pm Mon-Thu & Sun, 1-3.30pm & 9-10.30pm Fri & Sat) Seasonal, local ingredients fuel fun, imaginative, elegantly prepared degustation menus at this intimate, stone-walled, bodega-like eatery. Over five or six artful courses (often involving a rice dish), enjoy the likes of duck-and-chickpea paella, L'Escala anchovies, red-tuna tartare with mandarin, or *coca* (pastry) topped with Mallorcan sausage and Garrotxa cheese. Bookings recommended.

Pont Vell CATALAN €€
(☎972 59 10 27; www.restaurantpontvell.com; Carrer Pont Vell 24; mains €15-24; ⏲1-3.30pm Mon, 1-3.30pm & 8.30-10.30pm Wed-Sun Jul & Aug, 1-3.30pm Mon & Sun, 1-3.30pm & 8.30-10.30pm Wed-Sat Sep-Jun, closed late Dec-late Jan) The views to the old bridge (after which the restaurant is named) are enough to tempt you into this converted 18th-century building, even without considering the superb wide-ranging menu full of locally sourced delights, such as home-made terrines, Girona entrecôte in Cabrales-cheese sauce, and mushroom-stuffed squid in its own ink.

Information

Oficina de Turisme (☎972 59 12 40; www.besalu.cat; Carrer del Pont 1; ⏲10am-2pm & 4-7pm) On the eastern side of the bridge, across from the centre; runs 30-minute to one-hour walking tours (€2.25 to €4.60).

Getting There & Away

Teisa (www.teisa-bus.com) buses serve Barcelona (€15, two hours, four daily), Olot (€3.90, 40 minutes, 12 to 25 daily), Figueres (€4, 30 minutes, three daily) and Girona (€4.70, 40 minutes to one hour, eight to 16 daily).

THE CATALAN PYRENEES

Catalonia's Pyrenees are much more than an all-season adventure playground, and, beyond the major resorts, conceal a raw natural beauty that invites discovery. Certainly, the Val d'Aran draws winter skiers and snowboarders (with resorts ranging from red-carpet to family-focused), while summer and autumn lure hikers to the jewel-like lakes and valleys of the Parc Nacional d'Aigüestortes i Estany de Sant Maurici, the low-lying countryside of Cerdanya, and the climbing terrain of the Serra del Cadí.

But there's also Catalan heritage to be uncovered amid the majestic scenery, plunging valleys and snow-dusted peaks. Thousand-year-old monasteries slumber in these mountains – including some of Spain's outstanding Romanesque architecture – meaning Pyrenean hikes are as likely to pass ruined churches as valley panoramas.

Meanwhile, taste buds yearning for more than hiking fodder will find full satisfaction in the rich volcanic gastronomy of Olot and the Parc Natural de la Zona Volcànica de la Garrotxa.

Olot

POP 24,580 / ELEV 443M

If you perceive a rumbling sensation during your travels in Olot, it might be more than your appetite lusting after the rich local *cuina volcànica*. This bustling town is the regional capital of La Garrotxa, a lush landscape of cone-shaped hills chiselled by more extreme geological activity up to 700,000 years ago, now protected as Catalonia's Parc Natural de la Zona Volcànica de la Garrotxa. The park completely surrounds Olot, making the town an excellent base for volcanic explorations.

Olot sprawls over a large area with broad, tree-lined boulevards, but the medieval centre is agreeably walkable, with a handful of museums, grand Modernista buildings, exceptional restaurants and a lively Monday market, and well worth a stop in its own right.

Sights & Activities

Pick up a self-guided walking-tour leaflet of Olot's **Modernista architecture** (which includes Lluís Domènech i Montaner's 1916 floral-patterned Casa Solà Morales) at the tourist office (p367).

Four hills of volcanic origin stand sentry on the fringes of Olot. You can follow a 2km (45-minute) trail up the **Volcà del Montsacopa**, north of the centre.

Museu dels Volcans MUSEUM
(https://museus.olot.cat; Parc Nou, Avinguda de Santa Coloma; adult/child €3/1.50; ⏲10am-2pm

OUT & ABOUT IN CATALONIA'S PYRENEES

The Catalan Pyrenees provide magnificent walking. You can undertake strolls of a few hours, or embark on day walks that can be strung together into treks of several days. Nearly all can be done without camping gear, with nights spent in delightful villages or *refugis* (no-frills mountain shelters).

Most of the *refugis* are run by two mountain clubs, the **Federació d'Entitats Excursionistes de Catalunya** (FEEC; www.feec.cat) and the **Centre Excursionista de Catalunya** (CEC; www.cec.cat), which also provide info on trails. A night in a *refugi* costs €18 to €20 with breakfast. Moderately priced meals (around €15 to €20) are sometimes available in high season. It's worth booking ahead online or by phone to ensure your place (in summer, *refugis* fill up fast, and, in shoulder season, many are closed). **La Central de Refugis** (p380) is the handy booking portal.

The coast-to-coast **GR11 long-distance trail** traverses the entire Pyrenees from Cap de Creus on the Costa Brava to Hondarribia on the Bay of Biscay. Other hiking highlights include hardy trails between glittering high-altitude lakes in the Parc Nacional d'Aigüestortes i Estany de Sant Maurici (p378) and gentle rambles across the lush volcanic landscapes of the Parc Natural de la Zona Volcànica de la Garrotxa (p367).

The season for walking in the high Pyrenees is late June to early October, with quieter September providing the best all-round conditions. Always be prepared for fast-changing weather, no matter when you're visiting.

Local advice from tourist offices, park rangers, mountain *refugis* and other walkers is invaluable. Dedicated hiking maps are essential; **Editorial Alpina** (www.editorialalpina.com) produces some of the best.

There's boundless scope for **climbing**; Pedraforca in the Serra del Cadí (p376) offers some of the most exciting ascents. The ever-growing selection of other Pyrenees adventure activities includes whitewater rafting, kayaking, canyoning, *vie ferrate*, biking and more, for all of which the Pallars Sobirà (p377) region and the Val d'Aran (p382) are favourites. Skiing, of course, is the other speciality, with the richest pickings on the Val d'Aran's **Baqueira-Beret-Bonaigua** (p384) slopes.

& 3-6pm Tue-Sat, 10am-2pm Sun) In the middle of verdant Parc Nou (a botanical garden of Olot-area flora), this schoolroom-like museum has detailed displays on volcanoes, tremors, types of eruptions, Catalonia's volcanic history and La Garrotxa's geology. The intriguing audiovisual includes a knee-trembling earthquake simulator. There's a scenic cafe attached.

Sleeping & Eating

Alberg Torre Malagrida HOSTEL €
(☎972 26 42 00; www.xanascat.cat; Passeig de Barcelona 15; dm under/over 30yr €13/15;) With tile-floored corridors and stone lions guarding the entrance to a marble-columned early-20th-century Modernista building, surrounded by gardens, it's hard to believe that this is a youth hostel (HI). The unadorned, locker-equipped dorms – for two, three, six, eight or 10 – are comfortable without living up to the grandeur of the exterior. Meals and bike hire available.

Can Blanc CASA RURAL €€
(☎972 27 60 20; www.canblanc.es; Paratges de la Deu; s/d incl breakfast €67/110; P) Surrounded by leafy parkland on the southeastern edge of Olot, this secluded dusty-pink country house is a charm. Colourful, simple, modern-rustic rooms come in a range of shapes and sizes. The gardens and small pool will put a smile on your face, and a great breakfast is thrown in.

La Deu CATALAN €€
(☎972 26 10 04; www.ladeu.es; Carretera La Deu; mains €10-23; 1-4pm & 8.30-10.30pm Mon-Sat, 1-4pm Sun; P) Down a tree-lined road with a volcanic stone fountain bubbling away in its terrace dining area, family-run La Deu has been perfecting its filling *cuina volcànica* since 1885. Service is charmingly efficient, and there's huge culinary variety, including slow-cooked lamb, pork with sweet chestnuts, oven-baked hake, asparagus 'cake' lashed with basil oil, and the house spin on classic *patates d'Olot*.

★**Les Cols** CATALAN €€€
(☎972 26 92 09; www.lescols.com; Carretera de la Canya; degustation menu €95, incl wine €150; 1-3.30pm & 8.30-10.30pm Wed-Sat, 1-3.30pm Sun) Set in a converted 19th-century *masia* (country house), 2km northeast of central Olot, Les Cols is the queen of La Garrotxa's fabulous restaurants. The interior has an avant-garde edge, with glass walls and glittery-gold decor. Two-Michelin-starred chef Fina Puigdevall's dishes are powered by local products and prepared with a silken touch, from Olot sausage and pork ribs to charcoal-tempura beans.

LOCAL KNOWLEDGE

VOLCANIC CUISINE

In Olot and around, since 1994, a dedicated group of chefs has been proudly carrying on the *cuina volcànica* tradition, which stems from the area's exceptionally fertile volcanic soil. Traditional ingredients include black radishes, wild mushrooms, Santa Pau beans, Montserrat tomatoes, *ratafia* (liquor with aromatic herbs, sometimes flavoured with walnut) and *piumoc* (dry pork sausage), though some of the final creations are deliciously contemporary. Find out more at www.cuinavolcanica.cat.

Information

Casal dels Volcans (☎972 26 60 12; http://parcsnaturals.gencat.cat/ca/garrotxa; Parc Nou, Avinguda de Santa Coloma; 10am-2pm Tue-Sun) Official advice about the Parc Natural de la Zona Volcànica de la Garrotxa.

Oficina de Turisme d'Olot (☎972 26 01 41; www.turismeolot.cat; Carrer Doctor Fàbregas 6; 10am-2pm & 3-7pm Mon-Sat, 10am-2pm Sun) Slick, modern info office with multilingual staff, maps and park walking details.

Getting There & Away

TEISA (www.teisa-bus.com) runs buses between Olot's **bus station** (Carrer de Tomàs de Lorenzana) and Girona (€7.25 to €8.50, one to 1½ hours, eight to 30 daily), some via Besalú (€3.90, 40 minutes, 12 to 25 daily), and to/from Barcelona (€16 to €19, 1½ to 2½ hours, nine to 11 daily).

Parc Natural de la Zona Volcànica de la Garrotxa

The green-clad volcanic-origin hills surrounding Olot make up the 150-sq-km Parc Natural de la Zona Volcànica de la Garrotxa (http://parcsnaturals.gencat.cat/garrotxa). Volcanic eruptions began here about 350,000 years ago, but the last one was 11,500 years ago. As the African and Eurasian tectonic plates nudge ever closer (at a rate of 2cm per year), the occasional mild earthquake still sends a shiver across La Garrotxa, and more than 100 small earthquakes set Catalonia

Hiking in the Pyrenees

The Pyrenees aren't Europe's highest mountains, but they are certainly among its most formidable. The craggy behemoths stretch from the Bay of Biscay to the Mediterranean like a giant wall, with barely a low-level pass to break them. Spectacular for many reasons, not least the abundance of powerful waterfalls, they act like a siren's call for hikers.

The GR11

Anyone who hikes in the Spanish Pyrenees will get on to first-name terms with Gran Recorrido 11 (GR11), the long-distance footpath that runs along the range's entire Spanish flank from Hondarribia on the Bay of Biscay to Cap de Creus on the Costa Brava. Approximately 820km long and with a cumulative elevation gain equivalent to five Mt Everests, it takes around 45 days even without rest days. Many people elect to walk it in a series of shorter hops. Well-frequented sections run along Aragón's Valle de Ordesa and past Catalonia's Estany de Sant Maurici.

Hiking Bases

You don't have to embark on a marathon march to enjoy the best of the Spanish Pyrenees. There are countless superb day walks and these can often be strung together into routes of several days with the aid of village accommodation, mountain *refugios* (refuges), or a tent. The two national parks, Ordesa y Monte Perdido (p425) in Aragón and Aigüestortes i Estany de Sant Maurici (p378) in Catalonia, have particularly high concentrations of spectacular trails. Wonderful full-day outings in the former park include the high-level Faja de Pelay path (to an exuberant waterfall) and the Balcón de Pineta route to a superb lookout point. Fit walkers can

GLENN NEVIS / SHUTTERSTOCK ©

DANIMART / 500PX ©

MICHAL SZYMANSKI / SHUTTERSTOCK ©

1. Valle de Ordesa in the Parque Nacional de Ordesa y Monte Perdido, Aragón (p425) **2.** Climbers in the Catalan Pyrenees (p365) **3.** Hikers walking the GR11 (p50), Catalonia

cross the Aigüestortes park in one day along the Sant Maurici–Boí traverse, a 22km sequence of lakes, waterfalls, verdant valleys, rocky peaks and inspiring vistas. You'll need several days to complete the 55km **Carros de Foc** (www.carrosdefoc.com) circuit that links all nine of the park's *refugios*.

Other fine hiking bases with good accommodation and easy access to good trail networks include Hecho (p418) and Benasque (p430) in Aragón, and Olot (p366) in Catalonia, which has good, family-friendly walking terrain.

Practicalities

June to October are generally the best months for hiking. There may be snow on passes and high valleys until mid-June or from October, and the weather is never predictable, so walkers should always be prepared for extreme conditions. However, since this is Europe (rather than Alaska), you're never too far from a mountain village with basic shops, bars and accommodation.

Up in the mountains are a variety of *refugios* (*refugis* in Catalan) – some staffed and serving meals, others providing shelter only. At holiday times staffed *refugios* often fill up, so book ahead. For *refugio* bookings in Aragón, visit www.alberguesyrefugiosdearagon.com. For *refugis* in Catalonia, see the **Federació d'Entitats Excursionistes da Catalunya** (FEEC; www.feec.cat) and the **Centre Excursionista de Catalunya** (CEC; http://cec.cat).

Editorial Alpina (www.editorialalpina.com) and **Prames** (www.prames.com) produce excellent maps for walkers. The definitive English-language guide to the GR11 is the excellent *The GR11 Trail* by Brian Johnson (2014).

trembling each year (most are barely perceptible). La Garrotxa's volcanoes, however, have long snoozed under a blanket of meadows and oak forests.

The park has around 40 volcanic cones, up to 160m high and 1.5km wide. Together with the lush vegetation (resulting from fertile soils and a damp climate), these create a landscape of unique verdant beauty. The park's most interesting area lies between Olot and the pretty village of Santa Pau, 10km southeast.

Sights

Santa Pau VILLAGE

(GI524, Santa Pau) With its tangle of slender cobbled lanes leading past flower-filled corners and pottery workshops to the attractive colonnaded Plaça Major, medieval Santa Pau is arguably La Garrotxa's most ravishing village. A 13th-century castle looms over the main square.

Castellfollit de la Roca VILLAGE

(GI522, Castellfollit de la Roca) Aside from the hills, one of La Garrotxa's most remarkable geological sights is the town of Castellfollit de la Roca (10km northeast of Olot), teetering on the edge of a blackened basalt cliff face made up of two superposed lava flows. The best views are from the road beneath town, near Hostal Mont-Rock.

Monestir de Sant Joan les Fonts MONASTERY

(www.turismesantjoanlesfonts.com; Sant Joan les Fonts; noon-2pm Sat & Sun) FREE Dating to the 12th century, this broad Romanesque riverside monastery is squirrelled away at the northern end of Sant Joan les Fonts, 6km northeast of Olot. Note the distinctive bulge, stone bell tower and pink-tinged local stone.

Activities

There are 28 hiking routes within the natural park, most of which are clearly signposted. Olot's Casal dels Volcans (p367) and tourist office (p367) provide maps, information and advice.

A number of easy walking trails lead directly from the **car parks** near Olot and Santa Pau to the volcanic cones. The basalt lava flows near **Sant Joan les Fonts** are an especially stunning place to walk; routes are signposted from the town's tourist office. One of the park's most popular hikes is up to the crater of the **Volcà de Santa Margarida**, where there's a Romanesque chapel; the 2km trail begins from a signposted car park 3km west of Santa Pau on the GI524.

Sleeping

Camping Ecològic Lava CAMPGROUND €

(972 68 03 58; www.campinglava.com; Carretera Olot-Santa Pau (GI524), Km 7; car & tent/adult/child €17/8/7;) Wrapped in greenery 6km southeast of Olot, this animated year-round campground inside La Garrotxa's *parc natural* has solid amenities, including laundry facilities and hot showers, plus ample outdoor space, a pool (summer only), a restaurant and easy access to hiking trails and horse riding. There are also bungalows for four to 10 people (quad €90).

Cal Sastre BOUTIQUE HOTEL €€

(972 68 00 95; www.calsastre.com; Plaça dels Balls, Santa Pau; d €120-160;) Hidden across two exquisitely revamped 15th-century houses, behind medieval arches, Cal Sastre's eight rooms have an air of updated old-world glamour, with gold-patterned bedheads and claw-foot baths set against sparkling modern bathrooms. It's right opposite the castle in the heart of pretty little Sant Pau, attached to the family restaurant.

Mas La Ferreria BOUTIQUE HOTEL €€€

(972 29 13 45; www.hotelmaslaferreria.com; Santa Margarida de Bianya; r incl breakfast €155-200;) A sparkling blend of historical charm, contemporary flair and personal service makes a boutique bijou of this stylishly converted 14th-century country house, 8km northwest of Olot. Six individually designed rooms (some with terraces, or four-poster beds) skilfully show off the building's original architecture, between calming colours and exposed-stone walls. The tiny saltwater pool overlooks La Garrotxa's volcanic wilds.

Getting There & Away

TEISA (www.teisa-bus.com) runs buses from La Garrotxa's main hub Olot to Girona (€7.25 to €8.50, one to 1½ hours, eight to 30 daily), some via Besalú (€3.90, 40 minutes, 12 to 25 daily), and Barcelona (€16 to €19, 1½ to 2½ hours, nine to 11 daily).

Getting Around

La Garrotxa is best explored by car or bicycle, as public transport around the region is light.

TEISA (www.teisa-bus.com) runs buses from Olot to Castellfollit de la Roca (€1.70, 15 minutes, six to 23 daily) via Sant Joan de les Fonts (€1.70, 10 minutes).

Ripoll

POP 9270 / ELEV 691M

With an especially impressive monastery at its heart, and another 10km northeast in tiny Sant Joan de les Abadesses (p372), otherwise unremarkable Ripoll is a worthy stopover for admirers of Romanesque art.

Ripoll can claim, with some justice, to be the birthplace of Catalonia. In the 9th century it was the power base from which local strongman Guifré el Pilós (Wilfred the Hairy) succeeded in uniting several counties of the Frankish March along the southern side of the Pyrenees. Guifré went on to become the first in a line of hereditary counts of Barcelona. To encourage repopulation of the Pyrenean valleys, he founded (and now lies buried in) the Monestir de Santa Maria, medieval Catalonia's most powerful monastery.

Ripoll is well-positioned for rambling the vertiginous hiking and skiing terrain of the Vall de Núria, extending from 13km north, or the dormant volcanoes of La Garrotxa, 30km east.

★Monestir de Santa Maria MONASTERY
(www.monestirderipoll.cat; Plaça de l'Abat Oliba; adult/child €5.50/2.75; ⌚10am-2pm & 4-7pm Apr-Sep, 10am-1.30pm & 3.30-6pm Mon-Sat, 10am-2pm Sun Oct-Mar) Consecrated in AD 888, Ripoll's monastery was Catalonia's spiritual and cultural heart from the mid-10th to mid-11th century. The five-naved **basilica** was adorned in about 1100 with a stone portal that ranks among Spain's most splendid Romanesque art; its well-restored interior contains admirable floor mosaics, a multi-language display on the Bibles of Ripoll (rare illustrated manuscripts created between 1008 and 1020), plus the **tomb of Guifré el Pilós**, who founded the monastery.

La Trobada HOTEL €€
(☎972 70 23 53; www.latrobadahotel.com; Passeig del Compositor Honorat Vilamanyà 4; s €42-47, d €70-100, tr €88-98; P📶) Clean, simple and with polite, eager-to-please staff, La Trobada is Ripoll's most comfortable accommodation choice, on the east edge of town. Rooms are plain but well maintained, many offering glimpses of the Monestir de Santa Maria; those in the front building are most stylish. The restaurant serves simple Catalan fare, specialising in *carnes a la piedra* (hot-rock-cooked meats).

ℹ Information

Oficina de Turisme de Ripoll (☎972 70 23 51; www.ripoll.cat/turisme; Plaça del Abat Oliba; ⌚10am-2pm & 4-7pm Mon-Sat Apr-Sep, 10am-1.30pm & 3.3-6pm Mon-Sat Oct-Mar, 10am-2pm Sun year-round) Next to the Monestir de Santa Maria, with an interpretation centre on the history of the town and monastery.

ℹ Getting There & Away

Daily *rodalies* (local) trains (line R3) run to/from Barcelona (€9, two hours, 11 to 17 daily) via Vic (€6.15, 40 minutes). North from Ripoll, trains reach Ribes de Freser (€2.50, 20 minutes, eight daily) and Puigcerdà (€5, one hour, six to seven daily).

Vall de Núria & Ribes de Freser

A trio of little towns populates the Vall de Ribes and Vall de Núria, southeast of Cerdanya and north of Ripoll. Here, pine forests, plummeting dales and spectacular rugged hills huddle between the Serra Cavallera and Serra de Montgrony, rippling north to the Capçaleres del Ter i del Freser mountains.

Sheltered within the Vall de Ribes is small, well-equipped **Ribes de Freser**, 13km north of Ripoll. Six kilometres further north lies the charming stone village of **Queralbs** (1180m), home to a 10th-century church with a beautiful Romanesque portico. Beyond, accessible only by *cremallera* (rack railway), are **Núria** (1960m) and its lofty valley. Núria holds the revered Santuari de la Mare de Déu, though in winter it draws as many winter-sports devotees as pilgrims. A trip to Núria by *cremallera* is worth it for the views alone as the train rattles past lichen-wrapped rubble, miniature waterfalls, patches of forest, and gaping valleys.

👁 Sights & Activities

In winter, Núria transforms into a small-scale **ski resort** (☎972 73 20 20; www.valldenuria.cat/hivern; Núria; day pass incl train adult/child €30/23; ⌚Dec-Mar; 👪), while summer months lure energetic hikers.

The Vall de Núria has some lovely marked **hiking trails**; Nùria's tourist office (p373) provides maps (€4). One of the best and most popular routes is the **Camí Vell**, which leads through the gorge from Núria to Queralbs (8km, two to three hours); allow double the time if making the ascent.

WORTH A TRIP

SANT JOAN DE LES ABADESSES

Who gallops through the hills on stormy nights around **Sant Joan de les Abadesses** (10km northeast of Ripoll on the N260 towards Olot) on a horse engulfed in flames and accompanied by ravenous black dogs? If you believe the legends, it's the cursed Count Arnau, whose association with the Romanesque **Monestir de Sant Joan de les Abadesses** (www.monestirsantjoanabadesses.cat; Plaça de l'Abadia; adult/child €3/free; ⏲10am-7pm Jul & Aug, 10am-2pm & 4-7pm May, Jun & Sep, 10am-2pm & 4-6pm Oct, Mar & Apr, 10am-2pm Mon-Fri, 10am-2pm & 4-6pm Sat & Sun Nov-Feb) has bequeathed it a heritage of brooding fairy-tales alongside its centuries of spiritual activity. The monastery, founded in AD 887 by Guifré el Pilós, is notable for both its architectural treasures and the legend.

In the same building as Sant Joan's **tourist office** (☎972 72 05 99; www.santjoandelesabadesses.cat; Plaça de l'Abadia 9; ⏲10am-2pm & 4-7pm Mon-Sat, 10am-2pm Sun), the monastery's 14th-century **Palau de l'Abadia** houses a fascinating **audiovisual exhibition** (€2.50) tracing the source of the Count Arnau legend.

If you fancy stopping overnight in Sant Joan, **Hotelet de St Joan** (☎872 59 96 99; www.hoteletdestjoan.com; Carrer del Mestre Josep Maria Andreu 3; r €75-95; ❄📶) is a smartly minimalist, industrial-chic boutique find with good breakfasts (€8) and 10 rooms in calming greys.

TEISA (www.teisa-bus.com) operates buses at least hourly on weekdays and two-hourly at weekends to/from Ripoll (€2.20, 20 minutes).

From Núria, you can also cap several 2700m to 2900m peaks on the main Pyrenees ridge in about 2½ to four hours' walking (around 4km to 9km each one way). The most popular is **Puigmal** (2909m).

★Santuari de la Mare de Déu CHURCH

(www.valldenuria.cat; Núria; ⏲8am-6pm) FREE The region's high point (literally and figuratively) is Núria's strangely austere 1911 sanctuary, which sits incongruously in a building (now a hotel) that emits an unfortunate boarding-school vibe. A gold-trimmed pastel-painted passageway leads to its upper level, housing the **Mare de Déu de Núria** above the altar. Mary, with a regal expression, sits in star-spangled robes, clasping a grown-up Jesus. The icon is in 12th-century Romanesque style, despite believers insisting that Sant Gil sculpted it in AD 700.

The sanctuary's austere feel initially underwhelms, after all those valley panoramas and brooding mountains on the journey to Núria. Nonetheless, the views, icon and accompanying folklore make this a worthy trip.

Sleeping & Eating

Alberg Pic de l'Àliga HOSTEL €

(☎972 73 20 48; www.xanascat.cat; Núria; dm under/over 30yr incl breakfast €21/25; ⏲Dec-Oct) Fancy a cheap sleep 2120m above sea level? This youth hostel in a spacious lodge is perched at the top of the *telecabina* (cable car) whizzing up from Núria. Dorms sleep three to 18 people and it has a cafe, board games and a common room for mingling with other travellers. Check the website for seasonal closures.

★Hotel Els Caçadors HOTEL €€

(☎972 72 70 77; www.hotelsderibes.com; Carrer de Balandrau 24-26, Ribes de Freser; s/d from €70/88; ⏲Dec-Oct; ❄📶) Family-run since 1920, this local institution has 37 spacious rooms in three grades. 'Bronze' is decked with warm beige tones and wood fittings, while 'silver' ramps up the comfort with skylights, balconies or hydromassage baths; romantic 'gold' rooms and suites are most luxurious. There's a top-floor lounge plus a terrace with a mountain-view hot tub.

The popular **restaurant** (☎972 72 70 06; www.hotelsderibes.com; Carrer de Balandrau 24-26, Ribes de Freser; mains €14-19; ⏲8-10.30am, 1-3.45pm & 8.30-10pm Mon-Sat, 8-10.30am & 1-3.45pm Sun Dec-Oct) dishes up excellent Catalan food, such as squid cannelloni or baked hake with prawns, and three-course weekday lunch menus (€17).

Hostal les Roquetes HOSTAL €€

(☎972 72 73 69; www.hostalroquetes.com; Carretera de Ribes 5, Queralbs; s €38, d €68-78; P📶) This comforting stone guesthouse sits just above the train station in Queralbs, perfect for walking or day trips up to Núria via the *cremallera*. Rooms are sizeable, simple and spotless, some with a balcony and inspiring mountain views. The good-value restaurant emphasises hearty hiking fuel like *botifarra* (Catalan sausage), giant *entrepans* (filled rolls), and goat's cheese salads (three-course menu €12).

Information

Oficina de Turisme de Núria (☎972 73 20 20; www.valldenuria.com; Núria; ⏰9am-2pm & 3-4.45pm Mon-Fri, 9.15am-5.45pm Sat & Sun) Next to Núria's Santuari.

Oficina de Turisme de Ribes de Freser (☎972 72 77 28; www.vallderibes.cat; Carretera de Bruguera 2, Ribes de Freser; ⏰10am-2pm & 4-6pm Tue-Thu, 10am-2pm & 4-7pm Fri & Sat, 10am-2pm Sun) At the southern entrance to town.

Getting There & Away

There are two train stations in Ribes de Freser, both on the *cremallera* line to Núria (which isn't reachable by car).

Ribes-Enllaç, at the south end of town, has *rodalies* trains to Barcelona (€10, two to 2½ hours, seven daily) and Ripoll (€2.50, 20 minutes, eight daily).

The central Ribes-Vila is a *cremallera* stop between Ribes-Enllaç and Queralbs. **Cremallera** (www.valldenuria.cat; Ribes de Freser-Núria return adult/child €25/15) trains run from Ribes de Freser to Núria (35 to 40 minutes) via Queralbs (15 to 20 minutes) every 50 minutes between 7.50am and 6.20pm in high season, operating a reduced schedule during low season. There are car parks at Ribes-Vila and Queralbs if you're day-tripping to Núria via *cremallera*; they can be crammed in high season.

Cerdanya

Picturesque Cerdanya, along with French Cerdagne across the border, occupies a low-lying green basin between the higher reaches of the Pyrenees to its east and west. Although Cerdanya and Cerdagne, once a single Catalan county, were divided by the Treaty of the Pyrenees in 1659, Catalan is spoken on both sides of the border and Spain flows seamlessly into France. Hikers and mountain-bikers converge on Puigcerdà, the region's main town, and pretty nearby Llívia in summer, while winter sees skiers and snowboarders hit the slopes of La Molina and Masella. Cerdanya also makes an excellent jumping-off point to ramble and rock climb the Serra del Cadí (p376) to the southwest.

Puigcerdà

POP 6800 / ELEV 1202M

Barely 2km south of France, Puigcerdà (puh-cher-*da*) dates back to the 12th century – not that you'd know it, since most of its historical buildings were obliterated during the civil war. Prior to that it was a favourite summer hangout for the Catalan bourgeoisie in the 19th century. Today, the town is essentially a way station, but it's a jolly one, with good shops and restaurants, a friendly buzz and a pretty lake, used as a base by skiers during the winter season and teeming with hikers

LOCAL KNOWLEDGE

DRAGONS, GIANTS & BIG-HEADS

Fire and fireworks play a big part in many Spanish festivals, but Catalonia adds its own special twist with the *correfoc* (fire-running), in which devil and dragon figures run through the streets spitting fireworks at the crowds.

Correfocs often happen during the *festa major*, a town or village's main annual festival, usually in July or August. Parts of the *festa major* fun are the *sardana* (Catalonia's national folk circle dance) and *gegants*, splendidly attired 5m-high giants that parade through the streets or dance in the squares. Almost every Catalonian town and village has its own pair of *gegants* (usually male-and-female duos), often up to six pairs. They're accompanied by grotesque 'dwarfs' (*capgrossos*, or 'big-heads').

On **La Nit de Sant Joan** (23 June), Catalonia burns big bonfires in a combined midsummer and St John's Eve celebration, and fireworks explode all night. Catalonia's supreme fire festival is **La Patum de Berga** (www.lapatum.cat), held 30km west of Ripoll in Berga. An evening of dancing and firework-spitting angels, devils, mule-like monsters, dwarfs, giants and men covered in grass culminates in a mass frenzy of fire and smoke on Corpus Christi (the Thursday 60 days after Easter Sunday).

in summer. A dozen Spanish, Andorran and French ski resorts lie within 45km.

Sights

Església de Santa Maria TOWER
(Plaça Santa Maria; tower adult/child €1.50/free; 9.30am-1pm & 4.30-7pm Mon-Fri, 10.15am-1pm & 5-7.30pm Sat, 10.15am-1pm Sun) Though only the tower of the 17th-century Església de Santa Maria still stands, this stocky Romanesque structure dominates bustling Plaça Santa Maria. Steps within allow you to climb the tower.

Sleeping & Eating

Sant Marc CASA RURAL €€
(972 88 00 07; www.santmarc.es; Camí de Sant Marc 34; s/d incl breakfast €70/100;) Sprawling tree-lined grounds and plush beds greet you at this welcoming rural hideaway, 2km south of Puigcerdà's centre. Spacious wood-floored rooms are elegantly styled in soothing creams, and there's horse riding plus a lovely pool and plenty of outdoor space. Delicious fresh breakfasts come courtesy of the stone-walled restaurant, which specialises in winning dishes fuelled by local meats and cheeses.

Hotel Parada Puigcerdà BOUTIQUE HOTEL €€
(972 14 03 00; www.hotelparadapuigcerda.com; Plaça de l'Estaciò; s/d €63/79;) Who knew railway stops could have so much style? Hidden within Puigcerdà's 20th-century red-brick train station, this boutique pick preserves the attractive original architecture, combining it with thoroughly up-to-date interiors. The 28 crisp, stripped-back rooms are washed in moody greys and cool whites; top-floor rooms have slanted wood-beamed ceilings. Sassy features include a hot tub and, for some, in-room showers.

La Caixeta TAPAS, INTERNATIONAL €
(619 202174; www.facebook.com/caixetabistro; Carrer Querol 22; dishes €5-14; 7.30pm-2am Tue-Fri, noon-4pm & 7.30pm-2am Sat & Sun;) All wood-block walls, mismatched furniture and arty decor, this buzzy cafe-bistro-bar criss-crosses the Spanish-French border with its beautifully presented creative tapas, from camembert, homemade guacamole and quiche of the day to salads, mini-burgers, *torrades* (topped toasts) and Catalan charcuterie. It also does cupcakes, cocktails and generous glasses of French wine.

TapaNyam CATALAN, TAPAS €€
(972 88 23 60; http://tapanyam.es; Plaça de l'Alguer 2; tapas €4.50-13; 8am-midnight Wed-Sun) Pair crisp Catalan wines with equally invigorating views at this friendly restaurant. Terrace diners can enjoy panoramas of Puigcerdà's slate rooftops and green meadows stretching to the Pyrenees while feasting on local favourites like *trinxat* (potato and cabbage with a pork garnish), grilled snails and Girona entrecôte in green-pepper sauce, or tapas of mussels, octopus and mountain cheeses.

Information

Oficina de Turisme de la Cerdanya (972 14 06 65; N260; 9am-1pm & 3.30-7pm Mon-Sat, 10am-1pm Sun) On the main road, 1km southwest of the centre.

Oficina de Turisme de Puigcerdà (972 88 05 42; Plaça Santa Maria; 9.30am-1.30pm & 4.30-7.30pm Mon-Fri, 10am-1.30pm & 5-8pm Sat, 10am-1.30pm Sun) Within a historical tower in central Puigcerdà.

Getting There & Away

ALSA (www.alsa.es) buses run to/from Barcelona (€20, 3¼ hours, one or two daily) and La Seu d'Urgell (€6.90, one hour, four to six daily), stopping at **Plaça de l'Estació**, next to the train station just southwest of central Puigcerdà, as well as Plaça Barcelona.

Rodalies trains link Puigcerdà with Barcelona (€12, three hours, six daily) via Ribes de Freser (45 minutes), Ripoll (one hour) and Vic (1¾ hours). Four continue across the border to Latour-de-Carol (Catalan: Lo Tor de Querol), where you can connect to the French network.

From Barcelona, the C16 approaches Puigcerdà through the Túnel del Cadí (€11). Puigcerdà is also reachable via the picturesque N260 from Ribes de Freser, to the southeast. The main crossing into France is at Bourg-Madame, 1km east of central Puigcerdà.

Llívia

POP 1400 / ELEV 1224M

Glance carefully at your map of the Spain-France border. Just 6km northeast of Puigcerdà, amid verdant meadows and little French villages, is Llívia, a tiny slate-roofed bastion of Catalonia beyond the main border between France and Spain. Under the 1659 Treaty of the Pyrenees, Spain ceded 33 villages to France, but Llívia was a *vila* (town), so, together with the 13 sq km of its municipality, it remained a Spanish possession. Much more than just a cartographical oddity, this small town has a gorgeous medieval centre, a couple of worthwhile hotels and more excellent restaurants than you'd expect for its size. Most visitors arrive to hike the hills during summer or access winter ski resorts in the Spanish and French Pyrenees.

Sights

Llívia's few sights lie in its tiny medieval nucleus at the top (east end) of town.

Castell de Llívia CASTLE
(24hr) FREE Though little more than walls remain of Llívia's ruined hilltop castle, it's worth the hefty 15-minute climb for the fabulously beautiful wraparound views across the French countryside. Restoration works have unearthed parts of the fortress dating as far back as the 9th century.

Església de Mare de Déu dels Àngels CHURCH
(hours vary) Llívia's 16th-century, late-Gothic church is encircled by three defensive towers and contains a Romanesque baptismal font.

Museu Municipal MUSEUM
(Carrer dels Forns 10; adult/child €3.50/1; 10am-8pm mid-Jul–Aug, 10am-2pm & 4-6pm Tue-Fri, 11am-2pm & 4-8pm Sat & Sun Sep–mid-Jul) Proudly occupying what's alleged to be Europe's oldest pharmacy (dating to 1415, it operated until 1926), this multi-language, multimedia museum explores the region's history from Paleolithic times to modern day.

Sleeping & Eating

★Set Terres BOUTIQUE HOTEL €€
(972 89 64 99; www.setterres.com; Carrer Puigcerdà 8; r incl breakfast €90-170;) A keen husband-and-wife team has transformed the stables of the 1772 family home into an exquisite boutique hideaway. There are just seven rooms, each different, designed with pared-back yet homey country-chic style, incorporating open-stone walls, crisp white decor and, for three top-floor rooms, sloping ceilings. It's a special, romantic place, with breakfast a lovingly prepared local-produce buffet.

★Can Ventura CATALAN, FUSION €€
(972 89 61 78; www.canventura.com; Plaça Major 1; mains €14-20; 1.30-3.30pm & 8-10.30pm, closed Sun dinner, Mon & Thu approx Sep-Jun) Skilfully updated Catalan cuisine pulls diners to this excellent modern-rustic restaurant set inside a 1791 building. Traditional Catalan flavours take pride of place, like grilled octopus, slow-cooked lamb and smoky *trinxat* (dish with potato, cabbage and pork), but you'll also find hints of Asian fusion and whispers of French flair. Desserts like silky yoghurt mousse with berries, or steamy gluten-free chocolate fondant, make an irresistible finish.

Information

Oficina de Turisme (972 89 63 13; www.llivia.org; Carrer dels Forns 10; 10am-8pm mid-Jul–Aug, 10am-2pm & 4-6pm Tue-Fri, 11am-2pm & 4-8pm Sat & Sun Sep–mid-Jul) Inside the Museu Municipal.

Getting There & Away

ALSA (www.alsa.es) buses run from Puigcerdà to Llívia (€1.70, 20 minutes, four to eight daily).

La Molina & Masella

The twin ski resorts of La Molina and Masella lie either side of **Tosa d'Alp** (2537m), 15km south of Puigcerdà, linked by the Alp 2500 lift. The site provides a combined total of 141km of runs of all grades, at altitudes of 1600m to over 2500m. Rental equipment and ski schools are available at both resorts, with La Molina a better choice for beginners. Lift passes cover the whole area.

La Molina is Spain's oldest ski resort, with its origins in the 1940s; in summer, it caters to activity lovers with its mountain-bike park, quad-biking, canyoning, open-air yoga and more.

Sleeping & Eating

Hotel Adserà HOTEL €€
(972 89 20 01; www.hoteladsera.com; Carrer Pere Adserà, La Molina; s/d/tr/q incl breakfast €78/130/162/195; Dec-Easter & Jul–mid-Sep; P) Unlike many of the region's resorts, this homey hotel in a stone building offers a personal touch and a dash of historical charm. Just 2.5km below the slopes, it's an excellent choice for families with its rotating daily kids' activities, plus a games room, garden, pool and restaurant. Rooms are plain, old-fashioned and perfectly comfy, and staff are full of tips.

Getting There & Away

In ski season, there's a weekend-only bus between La Molina's *telecabina* (cable car) and Llívia (1¼ hours) via Puigcerdà (one hour), departing Llívia at 7.40am and returning at 2.30pm. There are also half-hourly or hourly buses between La

OFF THE BEATEN TRACK

SERRA DEL CADÍ

The spectacular **Serra del Cadí** comprises a string of charming stone villages and rugged mountains that offer excellent walking for those suitably equipped and experienced. **Pedraforca** ('Stone Pitchfork'; 2506m) is the most legendary peak in the range, offering the most challenging rock-climbing in Catalonia. The main Cadí range is part of the 410-sq-km **Parc Natural Cadí-Moixeró** (http://parcsnaturals.gencat.cat/ca/cadi), and hosts a number of staffed *refugis* in the park for serious multiday hikes.

The villages used as jumping-off points for exploring the area are strung along the picturesque B400 and C563, between the C16 to Puigcerdà and the C14 to La Seu d'Urgell. These include **Saldes** (a popular hiking base in the shadow of Pedraforca), **Gósol** (topped by a ruined 11th-century castle), **Josa de Cadí** and **Tuixent**. The best information points are Bagà's **Centre del Parc Natural del Cadí-Moixeró** (☎938 24 41 51; http://parcsnaturals.gencat.cat/cadi; Carrer de la Vinya 1, Bagà; ⊙9am-1pm & 4-7pm Mon-Sat, 9am-1pm Sun Jul-Sep, 8am-3pm Mon-Thu, 8am-3pm & 4-6.30pm Fri, 9am-1pm & 4-8.30pm Sat, 9am-1pm Sun Oct-Jun) and Saldes' **tourist office** (☎938 25 80 05; www.elbergueda.cat; Saldes; ⊙9am-2pm Tue, 9am-2pm & 4-7pm Wed-Sun), both on the eastern side of the Serra. The valley makes an exquisite drive: a longer, super-scenic route between Puigcerdà and La Seu d'Urgell.

Molina town and the slopes (€2), connecting with *rodalies* trains from Puigcerdà (20 minutes, six daily).

La Seu d'Urgell

POP 10,930 / ELEV 691M

The lively valley town of La Seu d'Urgell (la *se*-u dur-*zhey*) is Spain's gateway to Andorra (p378), 10km north. La Seu has an attractive medieval centre full of arcaded stone streets, watched over by a beautiful Romanesque cathedral. When the Franks evicted the Muslims from this part of the Pyrenees in the early 9th century, they made La Seu a bishopric and capital of the counts of Urgell; it remains an important market and cathedral town.

Sights

★Catedral de Santa Maria & Museu Diocesà CATHEDRAL

(Plaça dels Oms; adult/child €4/free; ⊙10am-1.30pm & 4-7pm Mon-Sat Jun-Sep, 10am-1.30pm & 4-6pm Mon-Sat Oct-May) Dominating La Seu d'Urgell's old town is the 12th-century, pale sandstone Santa Maria cathedral – one of Catalonia's outstanding Romanesque buildings. Its neat cloister, with three original galleries, is rich in characterful carved capitals depicting mythical beasts and grimacing gargoyles. The superb **museum** within exhibits a wealth of Romanesque frescoes from various churches, and one of just 25 famous **medieval illustrated Beatus manuscripts** still in existence.

Next to the cloister is the 11th-century Romanesque **Església de Sant Miquel**, rougher-hewn and pleasantly unembellished; its 13th-century murals now live in Barcelona's Museu Nacional d'Art de Catalunya (p288).

Sleeping & Eating

Groc Rooms APARTMENT, GUESTHOUSE €€

(☎644 966034; Carrer Major 59; d €65-77, tr €85-135, q €143; P 📶) Vintage mirrors, antique fireplaces and original-period tiled floors meet colourful, contemporary styling at these four 'boutique apartments' in a gorgeously revamped old-town house. The massive kitchen-equipped Loft apartment sleeps four to eight, while others are more like cosy-chic rooms; the Suite features an in-room bath tub. Helpful staff meet you on arrival.

Parador de La Seu d'Urgell HERITAGE HOTEL €€

(☎973 35 20 00; www.parador.es; Carrer de Sant Domènec 6; r €75-125; P 📶 🏊) While not as palatial as some of Spain's other *paradores*, this pleasing hotel has plain, modern rooms surrounding an elegant Renaissance cloister, which now hosts a cafe-bar between stone archways. Corridors are illuminated in colour at night, there's a good restaurant (three-course menu €29) and indoor pool, and you're just down the street from La Seu d'Urgell's cathedral.

PKtus CATALAN €€

(☎973 35 08 46; Carrer de la Creu 14; dishes €10-16; ⊙1-3.30pm & 8.30-10.30pm Tue-Sat; 📶) Modern, minuscule and friendly, PKtus concentrates on a limited menu of delicious deli produce, with great cheeses, patés, croquettes, cured ham and a few well-prepared hot dishes like fondues and burgers, alongside quality wines. Local ingredients are the focus and quality is sky-high.

Les Tres Portes CATALAN **€€**
(973 35 56 58; restaurantlestresportes@gmail.com; Avinguda Joan Garriga i Massó 7; mains €10-20; 1.30-3.30pm & 8.30-10.30pm Mon-Sat, 1.30-3.30pm Sun) Delight in fresh seasonal flavours, small tasting plates of Andalucian squid, *patatas bravas* (potatoes in a spicy tomato sauce), Galician octopus and *percebes* (goose barnacles), or a hearty range of Catalan favourites like grilled rabbit. The warm restaurant interior is cheerfully decorated, while the tranquil garden is perfect for summer dining. There's also a three-course set menu (€19).

Information

Turisme La Seu (973 35 15 11; www.turismeseu.com; Carrer Major 8; 10am-2pm & 4-7pm Mon-Sat, 10am-1pm Sun, closed Sun approx Oct-Mar) Helpful office across the street from the cathedral offering maps for historical walks and displays on local history.

Getting There & Away

The **bus station** (Carrer Mont) is on the northern edge of the old town. **ALSA** (www.alsa.es) runs buses to Barcelona (€28, three to 3½ hours, eight to nine daily), Puigcerdá (€6.90, one hour, four to six daily) and Lleida (€19, 2¼ hours, three to seven daily).

Pallars Sobirà

The Riu Noguera Pallaresa tumbles south from the heights of the Val d'Aran, with the pristine scenery of the Pallars Sobirà area extending from both sides. West of the river lies the majestic **Parc Nacional Aigüestortes i Estany de Sant Maurici**; to its east, the vast 698-sq-km **Parc Natural de l'Alt Pirineu** (http://parcsnaturals.gencat.cat/ca/alt-pirineu), sprinkled with lonely Romanesque churches among which weave hiking trails.

The river itself draws whitewater rafters and other adventure-sports enthusiasts to the small towns along its banks, principally (from north to south) **Llavorsí**, **Rialp** and **Sort**. Each of these towns is well-equipped with accommodation, cafes and restaurants, though outside the March-to-October season things are very quiet.

Activities

Beyond whitewater rafting, this valley packs in an astounding range of summer adventure activities, including kayaking, canyoning, stand-up paddleboarding, horse riding, rock-climbing, canoeing and guided hikes, plus wintertime skiing higher up. There are good independent hikes in the Parc Natural de l'Alt Pirineu; tourist offices in **Llavorsí** (Carrer de la Riba, Llavorsí; 9am-3pm Mon-Fri, 9.30am-5.30pm Sat, 9am-2pm Sun) and Sort (p378) provide details.

The Riu Noguera Pallaresa's grade IV drops attract a constant stream of whitewater fans between mid-March and mid-October. Conditions are best in May and June, when the snow melts off the surrounding mountains.

The finest stretch is the 12km from Llavorsí to Rialp, on which standard two-hour raft outings cost €40 to €45 per person. Longer rides to Sort and beyond cost more. Sort is the jumping-off point for the river's tougher grade IV rapids. There's usually a four-person minimum, but outfitters can combine smaller groups. Llavorsí has several reliable rafting operators, including **Roc Roi** (973 62 20 35; www.rocroi.com; Plaça Biuse 8, Llavorsí; 2hr rafting from €45; mid-Mar–mid-Oct) and **Rafting Llavorsí** (973 62 21 58; http://raftingllavorsi.cat; Carrer Vilanova, Llavorsí; 2hr rafting €41; approx Mar-Sep); in Sort, **LA Rafting Company** (973 62 14 62; www.laraftingcompany.com; Plaça Caterina Albert 2, Sort; 2hr rafting €45-50; mid-Mar–mid-Oct) is a popular choice.

Sleeping & Eating

Hostal Noguera HOSTAL **€**
(973 62 20 12; www.hostalnoguera.info; Carretera Vall d'Aran, Llavorsí; s/d incl breakfast €36/68; Mar-Dec; P) This stone building on the southern edge of town has 15 pleasant rooms, nine with balconies overlooking the rushing river. The three wood-beamed top-floor rooms have a dash more charm, while the downstairs restaurant serves filling local specialities like grilled meats and fried eggs swimming in ratatouille.

Hotel Pessets SPA HOTEL **€€**
(973 62 00 00; www.hotelpessets.com; Avinguda de la Diputació 3, Sort; d incl breakfast from €101;) At this wellness-focused hotel, lodgings range from unfussy neutral-toned doubles to smart suites with naturalist prints and

WORTH A TRIP

ANDORRA

If you're on the lookout for outstanding hiking or skiing, fancy stocking up on duty-free booze, smokes, cosmetics or electronics, or just want to say you've been to another country, then the curious nation of **Andorra** (population 78,260), 10km north of La Seu d'Urgell, is worth a spin across the border. At only 468 sq km, it's one of Europe's smallest countries. Though it has its own democratic parliament, the nominal heads of state are two co-princes: the bishop of Urgell in Spain, and the French president. Catalan is the official language, though Spanish, French and, due to a large immigrant workforce, Portuguese are widely spoken. Beyond the duty-free shops, busy capital **Andorra la Vella** has a couple of intriguing sights, most notably the small, cobbled **Barri Antic** and its 16th-century **Casa de la Vall**, until 2011 home to the Consell General d'Andorra.

Hourly (less on Sunday) **Montmantell** (www.montmantell.com) buses link La Seu d'Urgell with Andorra la Vella (€3.10, 45 minutes). If driving, fuel up in Andorra; it's significantly cheaper. There's rarely any passport control, but you may be stopped by customs on the way back into Spain, so don't go over the duty-free limit. Although Andorra isn't part of the EU, it uses the euro.

wood-panelled ceilings. The highlights are the spa area complete with pool, a private outdoor lounge area with mountain views, and a seasonal open-air pool.

Information

Oficina de Turisme del Pallars Sobirà (☎973 62 10 02; http://turisme.pallarssobira.cat; Camí de la Cabanera, Sort; ⏰9am-3pm & 4-7pm Mon-Sat, 9am-3pm Sun late Jun–mid-Sep, 10am-2pm Mon-Thu & Sun, 10am-2pm & 4-7pm Fri & Sat mid-Sep–early Jun) The area's main tourist office, crammed with maps and walking info supplied by multilingual staff. Also has displays on local history and culture.

Getting There & Away

ALSA (www.alsa.es) runs buses to Llavorsí via Sort and Rialp from Barcelona (€36, one daily, five hours) and Lleida (€12, one to two daily, three hours). On-demand transport runs between La Seu d'Urgell and Sort (€4, 11.15am and 7.30pm, one hour) with **Viatges Matí** (☎689 495777); book a day ahead.

Parc Nacional d'Aigüestortes i Estany de Sant Maurici & Around

Catalonia's only national park extends 20km east to west, and just 9km north to south. But the rugged mountain terrain within this small area sparkles with over 200 lakes and countless streams and waterfalls, combined with pine and fir forests, and open bush and grassland, decked with springtime wildflowers or fringed with scarlet autumn leaves.

Created by glacial action over two million years, the park comprises two east–west valleys at 1600m to 2000m altitudes framed by jagged 2600m to 2900m peaks of granite and slate.

The national park lies at the core of a wider wilderness area. The outer limit, the *zona periférica*, includes some magnificent high country north and south.

The main approaches are **Espot**, 4km east of the park and 8km from **Estany de Sant Maurici**, and the **Vall de Boí**, to the west. July and (especially) August are peak hiking season, but quieter September and October appeal more.

Private vehicles cannot enter the park. Wild camping is not allowed, nor are swimming or other 'aquatic activities' in lakes and rivers. The best map of the park is produced by **Editorial Alpina** (www.editorialalpina.com).

Getting Around

The closest you can drive to the eastern side of the park is a car park 4km west of Espot; on the west side, it's a car park 3km north of Boí.

There are 4WD-taxi services between Espot and Estany de Sant Maurici (€5.25 each way) – with services available to some higher lakes and refuges – and between Boí and Aigüestortes (€5.25 each way), saving you, respectively, an 8km and 10km walk. Services run from outside the park information offices in **Espot** (p381) and **Boí** (p381) (9am to 7pm July to September, less frequent outside summer and in bad weather).

From mid-June to September, **ALSA** (www.alsa.es) buses run twice daily (in each direction) between Espot and Taüll (€12, 2½ hours), via Boí and Erill la Vall, enabling hikers to walk across the park and return by bus the same/next day.

Espot

POP 300 / ELEV 1300M

Scenic little Espot is the main eastern gateway for the Parc Nacional d'Aigüestortes i Estany de Sant Maurici; the park begins 4km west of town. Espot makes an excellent, well-equipped base, with plenty of hotels, restaurants and charming stone buildings, while its mountain views will have you keen to lace up your hiking boots.

Sleeping & Eating

Camping Voraparc CAMPGROUND €

(☎973 62 41 08; www.voraparc.com; Prat del Vedat; tent/car/adult €6/6/6, glamping tent €58-90; ⏲Easter–mid-Oct; P ᯤ ≋) This shady riverside campground, 1.5km northwest of town, is Espot's best. It has a cafe-bar, games room, play area, minimarket and pleasant swimming pool. If you don't have your own tent, there are some already set up, including three glamping ones. There are also three cosy glamping huts for two (€68 to €82) or four (€87 to €112).

★ **Roca Blanca** HOTEL €€

(☎973 62 41 56; www.hotelrocablanca.com; Carrer Església; incl breakfast d €80-90, ste €120-125; P ᯤ) From the 16 gleaming, impressively spacious rooms with modern bathrooms to the polished lounge with fireplace, this cheerful hotel is one of the region's most welcoming and inviting. Contemporary art adorns the walls, service is attentive and personal, and breakfast is a feast. Extra touches include a gym, sauna and gorgeous garden – plus a dopey resident St Bernard called Homer Simpson.

Cafè & Bistro È Bo CATALAN, FRENCH €€

(Plaça Doctor Benavent 3; dishes €6-15; ⏲9am-10pm Aug, 10.30am-10pm Sep-Jul; ✎) With tables

Parc Nacional d'Aigüestortes i Estany de Sant Maurici

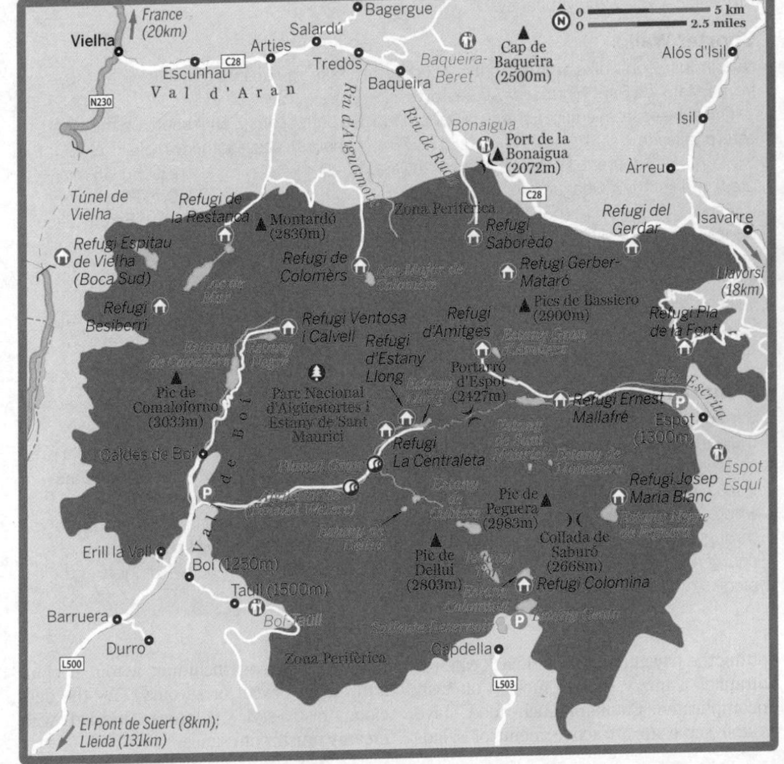

WALKING: PARC NACIONAL D'AIGÜESTORTES I ESTANY DE SANT MAURICI

The park is criss-crossed by walking paths, ranging from well marked to unmarked; hear expert advice at the **Casa del Parc** in either **Espot** or **Boí**. There are also downloadable walking routes on Spain's official national parks website (www.mapama.gob.es/es/red-parques-nacionales), often in Spanish only.

East–West Traverse

It's perfectly possible to walk right across the park in one day. The full **Espot–Boí** (or vice versa) walk is about 30km and takes about 9½ hours plus stops, but you can shorten this by using 4WD-taxis to/from Estany de Sant Maurici or Aigüestortes (4km southwest of Estany Llong) or both. **Espot** (1300m) to **Estany de Sant Maurici** (1950m) is 8km (two hours). A path then climbs to the **Portarró d'Espot pass** (2427m; around two hours), where there are spectacular views over both of the park's main valleys. From the pass you descend to **Estany Llong** (1985m; about 3½ hours from Estany de Sant Maurici) and **Aigüestortes** (1820m; 4½ hours from Estany de Sant Maurici). Then it's 3.5km to the park entrance, 4km to the L500 and 2.5km south to **Boí** (1250m) – a total of around three hours. It's best to walk the route east to west, and start with a 4WD-taxi (€5.25) from Espot to Estany de Sant Maurici to avoid the initial 8km uphill: this way you end up 700m lower than you started. Wear suitable clothing for a high-mountain trek.

Carros de Foc

The **Carros de Foc** (www.carrosdefoc.com) – a circular 55km trek linking nine of the park's *refugis* – incorporates the best of the national park's glorious mountainscapes, at altitudes between 1885m and 2395m. You spend five to seven nights in the park, starting from whichever *refugi* you fancy.

Shorter Walks

Numerous good walks of three to five hours return take you up into majestic side valleys from Estany de Sant Maurici or Aigüestortes.

From the eastern end of Estany de Sant Maurici, a path heads 2.5km south up the Monestero valley to **Estany de Monestero** (2171m; 1½ hours), passing the two peaks of **Els Encantats**. Another trail climbs 3km northwest via **Estany de Ratera** (2190m; 45 minutes) and Estany d'Obagues de Ratera to **Estany Gran d'Amitges** (2350m; 1¾ hours).

Espot's **4WD-taxis** (p381) run to several points further into the park than Estany de Sant Maurici, enabling walks beginning from Estany Gran d'Amitges, Estany de Ratera and Estany Negre (in the park's Peguera valley).

On the west side, from **Planell Gran** (1850m), 1km northeast up the Sant Nicolau valley from Aigüestortes, a path climbs 2.5km southeast to **Estany de Dellui** (2370m). You can descend to **Estany Llong** (1985m); it's about 5.5km, or four hours, total from Aigüestortes to Estany Llong.

Mountain-Refuge Accommodation

Serious walkers are catered for by a dozen *refugis* (mountain refuges) in and around the park. Most have large dorms with bunk beds (bring your own sleeping bag or sheet), and tend to be staffed over Easter and from early or mid-June to September, plus some weeks in the first half of the year for skiers. At other times, several leave a section open where you can stay overnight. Check details and book ahead (crucial in summer) online through **La Central de Refugis** (☎973 64 16 81; www.lacentralderefugis.com). Most charge €20 to €25 per person (including breakfast), and provide lunches, dinners and picnics (sometimes also for day-hikers passing through).

dotting the pavement, this laid-back cafe-restaurant is a buzzy spot to fuel up on tasty, uncomplicated Catalan-French food. Lively staff serve an attractive menu of salads, fondues, burgers (including a tofu option) and crepes (sweet or savoury). Try the delicious 'bistro-style' potatoes, drizzled with creamy mushroom sauce.

Information

Casa del Parc d'Espot (973 62 40 36; www.gencat.cat/parcs/aiguestortes; Carrer de Sant Maurici 5; 9am-2pm & 3.30-5.45pm, closed Sun afternoon Sep-Jun) Maps, hiking tips, transport advice, weather forecasts and more from Espot's national park office.

Getting There & Away

ALSA (www.alsa.es) buses from Barcelona (€39, five hours, daily) and Lleida (€13, three hours, one to two daily) to Esterri d'Áneu stop at the Espot turn-off on the C13. From there, it's a 7km uphill walk west to Espot along the LV5004.

Getting Around

Visit the Parc Nacional d'Aigüestortes i Estany de Sant Maurici with a little help from a fleet of **4WDs** (973 62 41 05; www.taxisespot.com; Carrer de Sant Maurici; 1-way Espot–Estany de Sant Maurici adult/child €5.25/3.25; 9am-7pm) offering fixed-rate trips to various drop-off points within the park. Usually you have to wait until there are at least four people and operating hours depend on weather conditions.

Boí

POP 220 / ELEV 1250M

The delightful valley location of petite Boí, 3km northwest of Taüll, draws hikers and winter-sports lovers, while its church bell tower is one of the jewels of the Vall de Boí's Catalan Romanesque architecture.

Sant Joan de Boí CHURCH

(www.centreromanic.com; Plaça del Treio, Boí; €2; 10am-2pm & 4-7pm Sep-Jun, to 8pm Jul & Aug) Boí's 11th-century church gives the village an air of romance with its angular five-storey stone bell tower, which was restored after a major fire in the 13th century and can now be climbed (all 75 steps of it). The wall paintings that brighten the interior are copies of Romanesque originals, preserved in Barcelona's Museu Nacional d'Art de Catalunya (p288).

Santa Eulàlia d'Erill la Vall CHURCH

(Erill la Vall; €2; 10am-2pm & 4-7pm Sep-Jun, to 8pm Jul & Aug) The slender six-storey, 12th-century tower of Santa Eulàlia d'Erill la Vall, once used for communications and valley surveillance, is thought to be the most elegant in the area. The church interior is decorated by copies of seven Romanesque poplar-wood sculptures depicting the Descent from the Cross; the originals are split between Barcelona's Museu Nacional d'Art de Catalunya (p288) and Vic's Museu Episcopal (p385).

Erill la Vall is a 2.5km walk or drive west of Boí.

Hotel-Hostal Pey HOTEL, HOSTAL €€

(973 69 60 36; www.hotelpey.com; Plaça del Treio 3; incl breakfast d €72-98, tr €100, q €120;) This mellow, popular two-part hotel in the heart of teeny Boí features comfy, home-style rooms and a decent restaurant (mains €9 to €14), plus ski storage, staff brimming with local advice and a lovely shop crammed with handmade Pyrenean soaps and Catalan wines. The smartest, most contemporary rooms live in the hotel half. Book ahead.

Information

Casa del Parc de Boí (973 69 61 89; Carrer de les Graieres 2; 9am-2pm & 3.30-5.45pm, closed Sun afternoon Sep-Jun) Pick up trekking and winter-sports information.

Getting There & Away

ALSA (www.alsa) buses from Barcelona (€31, four to five hours, four to six daily) and Lleida (€10, two to 2¼ hours, six to 10 daily) to Vielha stop year-round at El Pont de Suert, 19km southwest of Boí. From here, there may be irregular services to Boí.

Getting Around

Nine-person **taxis** (973 69 63 14; www.taxisvalldeboi.com; Plaça del Treio 3, Boí; 1-way Boí–Estany de Sant Maurici adult/child €5.25/3.25; 9am-7pm) spin between Boí and Aigüestortes (€5.25), 10km northeast in the Parc Nacional d'Aigüestortes i Estany de Sant Maurici; operating hours vary with the weather.

Taüll

POP 250 / ELEV 1500M

Three kilometres southeast (uphill) from Boí, Taüll is by far the most picturesque place to stay on the west side of the Parc Nacional d'Aigüestortes i Estany de Sant Maurici. It's also home to two outstanding, Unesco-listed Catalan Romanesque churches.

Sights

★**Sant Climent de Taüll** CHURCH

(www.centreromanic.com; Taüll; €5; 10am-2pm & 4-7pm Sep-Jun, to 8pm Jul & Aug) On Taüll's fringes, this 12th-century Romanesque church is a gem not only for its elegant, simple lines and slender six-storey bell tower (which you can climb), but also for the art that once graced its interior. The central apse contains a copy of a famous 1123 mural that now resides in

DON'T MISS

CATALAN ROMANESQUE CHURCHES IN THE VALL DE BOÍ

On the west side of the Parc Nacional d'Aigüestortes i Estany de Sant Maurici, the **Vall de Boí** is dotted with some of Catalonia's finest Romanesque churches – elegant, unadorned stone structures sitting in the crisp alpine air. Together, these 11th- to 14th-century constructions were declared a Unesco World Heritage site in 2000.

Some of the loveliest churches are in **Boí** (p381), **Taüll** (p381) and **Erill la Vall** (p381); other finds are **Sant Feliu** in Barruera and **La Nativitat** in Durro. Explore their history, book guided tours and pick up combined tickets (three churches €7) at Erill la Vall's **Centre del Romànic de la Vall de Boí** (973 69 67 15; www.centreromanic.com; Carrer del Batalló 5, Erill la Vall; €2; 9am-2pm & 5-7pm Apr-Dec).

Barcelona's Museu Nacional d'Art de Catalunya (p288); at its centre is a Pantocrator, whose rich Mozarabic-influenced colours and expressive but superhuman features have become an emblem of Catalan Romanesque art.

Santa Maria de Taüll CHURCH
(www.centreromanic.com; Taüll; 10am-7pm Sep-Jun, to 8pm Jul & Aug) FREE Up in Taüll's old centre, at the northwestern end of town, the 12th-century Romanesque Santa Maria church is crowned by a five-storey tower. As with many churches in the Vall de Boí, its original artwork has been whisked away to Barcelona.

Sleeping & Eating

★ Alberg Taüll HOSTEL €
(645 750600; www.alberguetaull.com; Avinguda Feixanes 5-7, Taüll; dm/d/ste incl breakfast €28/45/100; P) This is everything a hostel should be: stylish rooms for two to seven guests feature large beds with orthopaedic mattresses, the suite has a hot tub, there's underfloor heating for crisp mornings, and the lounge includes a large park map for planning hikes. Families are welcome and you'll get great walking advice. Sheets and a towel cost €4.50. Cheaper midweek.

Hotel Santa Maria Relax BOUTIQUE HOTEL €€
(973 69 62 50; www.taull.com; Plaça Cap del Riu 3, Taüll; r incl breakfast €80-110; possibly closed Nov; P) A grand stone archway leads into the hushed courtyard of this cosy country haven with a rose-draped balcony and friendly hosts. The four rooms and three apartments are tastefully furnished with antiques and a sprinkle of boutique style, while the ancient building is all stonework with a timber-and-slate roof. Sunbeds and a hot tub with mountain views adorn the garden.

Sedona INTERNATIONAL €
(973 69 62 54; Les Feixes 2, Taüll; mains €8.50-13; 1-4pm & 8-11pm;) *Torrades* (topped toasts), salads, mixed tapas, Tex-Mex (quesadillas, nachos) and flavoursome veggie-friendly delights like wok-fried vegetable rice and asparagus with caramelised goat's cheese unleash a parade of world flavours at this après-ski hangout.

Getting There & Away

Year-round **ALSA** (www.alsa.es) buses from Barcelona (€31, four to five hours, four to six daily) and Lleida (€10, two to 2¼ hours, six to 10 daily) stop at El Pont de Suert, from where irregular local buses reach Taüll.

Val d'Aran

Catalonia's northernmost region, famous for its plunging valleys, stone-and-slate villages, Romanesque churches and snowy peaks huddled up against the French border, is an adventure playground. The Baqueira-Beret-Bonaigua pistes and Arties' luxe hotels lure the winter-sports jet set, while charming villages like Salardú enchant hikers with views of cloud-scraping mountains. Walkers can head over the mountains in any direction, notably southward to the Parc Nacional d'Aigüestortes i Estany de Sant Maurici.

The Val d'Aran was inaccessible until the 1948 completion of a 5km tunnel connecting its main town, Vielha, to the rest of Spain. Thanks in part to its geography, the native language is not Catalan but Aranese *(Aranés)*, a dialect of Occitan or the *langue d'oc*, the old Romance language of southern France.

Vielha

POP 3490 / ELEV 974M

A sprawl of stone-and-slate houses, outdoor-gear shops and holiday apartments make up hectic Vielha, 'capital' of the Val d'Aran. The tiny town centre, anchored by the distinctive spire of the Gothic Sant Miquèu church, is packed with rustic restaurants, especially along the gushing Riu Garona. While Vielha doesn't have the charisma of the Val d'Aran's smaller towns, its shops, supermarkets, lively dining scene and varied accommodation make it a popular base for hiking, skiing and other adventures around the valley. It's best to have your own wheels: the Vall de Boí's hiking terrain is 20km south, while the Baqueira-Beret-Bonaigua ski pistes lie 15km east.

Sleeping & Eating

★Hotel El Ciervo BOUTIQUE HOTEL €€
(☎973 64 01 65; www.hotelelciervo.net; Plaça de Sant Orenç 3; s/d incl breakfast €45/70; ⊙mid-Dec–Easter & mid-Jun–mid-Oct;) Super-central, family-owned and exceptionally welcoming, El Ciervo is a real departure from the mundane ski-town norm. With a facade covered in paintings of forest creatures and a delightfully cosy interior crammed with florals, pastels, check-prints and other decorative touches, it feels like a Pyrenean fairy tale. Each lovely room is different, and breakfast spreads are fantastic. Excellent value.

Parador de Vielha HOTEL €€
(☎973 64 01 00; www.parador.es; Carretera del Túnel; r €80-130; ⊙early Dec–mid-Oct; P) Looming above town, Vielha's sprawling (roadside) *parador* makes a supremely comfortable place to lay your head after a hard day's hiking or skiing. Earthy creams and warm pastels dress the 118 smart rooms, scattered around a family-friendly complex that also features a pool, restaurant, garden and spa. Splash out on a 'superior' room, with balcony and valley or mountain views.

Woolloomooloo INTERNATIONAL €
(☎654 788327; rennyhut@hotmail.com; Carrèr Major 8; dishes €5-12; ⊙3pm-2am Thu-Tue) Quite the Vielha-centre surprise, purple-walled, Australian-Italian owned Woolloomooloo whips up a globetrotting rustic-modern menu of (mostly) Catalan, Italian and Aussie bites served at tree-trunk tables. From grilled prawns, *patatas bravas* (potatoes in spicy tomato sauce) and spinach-mushroom croquettes to Aussie-style patties and home-made-falafel salad coated in tzatziki, it's all brilliantly tasty.

Era Móla CATALAN, FRENCH €€
(Restaurant Gustavo i María José; ☎973 64 24 19; www.facebook.com/eramolavielha; Carrèr de Marrèc 14; mains €15-20; ⊙8-11pm Mon-Fri, 1-3.30pm & 8-11pm Sat & Sun) One of the top restaurants in town, Era Móla is known for its carefully prepared local cooking with a heavy French hand, plated up inside a handsome stone building hidden down an alley in central Vielha. Savour the *solomillo de cerdo al Calvados* (pork fillet bathed in calvados), and one of the artistically arranged desserts.

Information

Oficina d'Informació Turística Val d'Aran
(☎973 64 01 10; www.visitvaldaran.com; Carrèr de Sarriulèra 10; ⊙10am-1.30pm & 4-8pm, closed Sun mid-Sep–Dec) Near Vielha's Sant Miquèu church.

Getting There & Away

From Vielha's **bus stop** (Carretera N230) on the northwest edge of town, **ALSA** (www.alsa.es) serves Barcelona (€35, five to six hours, five to seven daily) and Lleida (€14, 2¾ hours, eight to 10 daily), and runs east up the valley to Baqueira (€1.10, 10 to 15 times daily) via Arties (€1.10, 10 minutes) and Salardú (€1.10, 15 minutes).

Most travellers explore the Val d'Aran by driving, though parking can be a problem. There's a massive free car park at the southeast end of town, a two-minute walk from the centre.

The N230 from Lleida and El Pont de Suert reaches the Val d'Aran through the 5km Túnel de Vielha. From the Pallars Sobirà region, the C28 tracks northwest across the Port de la Bonaigua pass (2072m) into the upper Aran valley, meeting the N230 at Vielha.

Arties

POP 400 / ELEV 1143M

The fetching village of Arties sits astride the confluence of the Rius Garona and Valarties, 7km east of Vielha. Its proximity to the upmarket Baqueira-Beret-Bonaigua ski area (6km east) has allowed upmarket hotels to flourish. Arties snoozes outside peak summer and winter seasons, but remains a pretty stop year-round, with geraniums overflowing from the balconies of its handsome houses.

Sights & Activities

Església de Santa Maria CHURCH
(⊙hours vary) This 12th- to 13th-century Romanesque church, with its three-storey belfry and triple apse, stands proudly in the midst of Arties' flower-festooned houses.

WORTH A TRIP

TOP SKIING: BAQUEIRA-BERET-BONAIGUA

Catalonia's premier **ski resort** (www.baqueira.es; day pass adult/child €51/34; ⏲ late Nov-early Apr) is formed by Baqueira, 3km east of Salardú; **Beret**, 8km north of Baqueira; and **Bonaigua**, at the top of the 2072m pass of the same name (9km southeast of Baqueira). These gleaming slopes lure an upmarket crowd (the Spanish royals are regulars) and lodgings tend to be luxe. A quality lift system gives access to pistes totalling 156km (larger than any other Spanish resort), between 1500m and 2510m.

ALSA (www.alsa.es) buses reach Baqueira from Vielha (€1.10, 25 minutes, 10 to 15 daily), via Arties (€1.10, 10 minutes) and Salardú (€1.10, five minutes).

Banys d'Arties THERMAL BATHS

(C28 Km 28; 1hr session adult/child €3/free; ⏲ 10.30am-2.30pm & 4.30-8pm Tue-Sun Jul & Aug, 10am-5pm Tue-Sun Sep-Jun, hours vary) Soothe those all-hiked-out limbs with an open-air soak in these two thermal pools (one adults-only). From the west end of Arties, follow a path west for 700m; if driving, take the 1.4km dirt track signposted off the C28 at Garòs, 2.5km west of Arties.

Sleeping & Eating

Casa Irene SPA HOTEL €€

(☎973 64 43 64; www.hotelcasairene.com; Carrer Major 22; r €75-150; ⏲ Dec-Easter & Jul-Sep; P ❄ 📶 ≋) Expect exposed wooden beams, marble bathrooms and colourful throws on king-sized beds at this 22-room property. The lounge nails the rustic-chic balance, rooms are huge and stylish, some suites have hydromassage baths, and the two attic-like duplexes are perfect for families. On-site muscle soothers range from hammam to sauna and hot tub. The upmarket restaurant (mains €24 to €28) serves updated Catalan favourites.

Urtau CATALAN, BASQUE €

(www.facebook.com/urtau; Plaça Urtau 12; tapas €4.50-11; ⏲ 8am-midnight) Overlooking Arties' main square, this self-styled mountain tavern is forever popular for its grilled meats, hearty breakfasts (bacon omelettes, ham-and-cheese scrambles) and Val d'Aran cheese platters. But the real culinary stars are the 70-odd varieties of *pintxos* (Basque tapas) that take over the bar from noon.

Getting There & Away

ALSA (www.alsa.es) buses reach Arties from Vielha (€1.10, 20 minutes, 10 to 15 daily).

Salardú

POP 500 / ELEV 1267M

Glamorous Arties lies 3km to its west, chic ski area Baqueira looms 3km east, yet pint-sized Salardú retains its own rugged, outdoorsy ambience, welcoming hikers with its decent budget and midrange digs. The even dinkier, flower-filled village of **Bagergue**, 2km northeast, is a tranquil spot for solitary treks and glorious mountain views.

Església de Sant Andrèu CHURCH

(Plaça Pica; ⏲ 10am-2pm & 4-7pm) FREE Within the remarkably colourful frescoed walls of this 12th- and 13th-century church, gaze upon the haunting Romanesque form of the Crist de Salardú. This gaunt wooden sculpture of Jesus on the cross dates to the 13th century, while the Renaissance frescoes lay hidden until the 20th century. Sant Andrèu's sturdy bell tower was a castle keep until 1649, though only the church and some ruined castle walls remain today.

Refugi Rosta HOSTEL €

(☎973 64 53 08; www.refugirosta.com; Plaça Major 3; dm/d incl breakfast €27/73; P 📶) Pyrenean mountain *refugis* are special, convivial places, and this creaky old building (going strong since 1858!) is one of the most characterful. There are no luxuries, but there's plenty of good cheer. Dormitories, with typical side-by-side sleeping, are comfortable enough. Bring a sleeping bag or hire sheets and towels. The restaurant serves hearty set menus.

Hotel Seixes HOTEL €€

(☎973 64 54 06; www.hotelseixes.com; Bagergue; s/d/tr/q €55/80/115/150; ⏲ Dec-Mar & Jun-Oct; P 📶) This efficiently run hikers' favourite is perched within tinkling distance of the pealing bell of Sant Feliu church in tiny Bagergue, 2km northeast of Salardú. Its 17 rooms are comfortable though simple, sleeping one to five people, and the location will appeal to nature lovers and seclusion seekers. Ask staff for tips on local hikes.

Getting There & Away

ALSA (www.alsa.es) buses reach Salardú from Vielha (€1.10, 15 minutes, 10 to 15 daily).

CENTRAL CATALONIA

Vic

POP 42,640

This feisty Catalonian town, 70km north of Barcelona, en route to the Pyrenees, combines dreamy medieval architecture with youthful energy. Remarkably restored Roman ruins, jazzy Modernista houses and an 11th-century Romanesque bridge add to a spirited mix of architectural styles dotted across the old quarter's meandering streets, which branch off smouldering Plaça Major and its ochre and brick-red mansions. Despite its resolutely Catalan political outlook, the town is very multicultural, with a large student population.

A day trip from Barcelona is enough to take in Vic's superb cathedral and museum, plus a restaurant or two, though a longer stay allows time to get lost amid the street art and medieval alleyways.

Sights

★Catedral de Sant Pere CATHEDRAL

(Plaça de la Catedral; adult/child €3/free; ⏲10am-1pm & 4-7pm) Centuries of styles clash in Vic's exquisite cathedral. Most of the neoclassical exterior dates to the 18th century, but the seven-storey Romanesque bell tower is one of few remnants from the 11th century. Within, the Stations of the Cross are animated in bold World War II–era frescoes by Josep Maria Sert, while Corinthian columns glow gold in the darkness. Entrance to the cathedral is free; admission applies to the 14th-century Gothic cloisters, 11th-century crypt and Pere Oller's impressive altarpiece.

★Museu Episcopal GALLERY

(www.museuepiscopalvic.com; Plaça Bisbe Oliba 3; adult/child over 10 €7/3.50; ⏲10am-7pm Tue-Sat Apr-Sep, 10am-1pm & 3-6pm Tue-Fri, 10am-7pm Sat Oct-Mar, 10am-2pm Sun year-round) This museum holds a marvellous collection of Romanesque and Gothic art, second only to Barcelona's Museu Nacional d'Art de Catalunya. The Romanesque collection contains strikingly gory images, including saints being beheaded or tortured, along with a fine 12th-century woodcarved Descent from the Cross group from the Pyrenees' Vall de Boí. The Gothic collection displays works by such key figures as Lluís Borrassà and Jaume Huguet, plus the beautiful original 1420s doors to Vic cathedral's altarpiece, designed by Pere Oller.

Plaça Major SQUARE

Vic's Plaça Major, the largest square in Catalonia, has a pleasing medley of medieval, baroque and Modernista architecture. A crop of cafes spill onto the square. It's also the site of the town's twice-weekly **market** (Tuesday and Saturday mornings).

Temple Romà ROMAN SITE

(Plaça de la Pietat; ⏲11am-1pm & 6-8pm Tue-Sat, 6-8pm Sun) FREE This 1st-century Roman temple, painstakingly restored during the 19th and 20th centuries, is framed by the walls of an 11th-century castle.

Sleeping & Eating

Seminari Allotjaments GUESTHOUSE €€

(☎938 86 15 55; www.seminarivic.cat; Ronda Francesc Camprodón 2; incl breakfast s €49-64, d €72-75, tr €93, q €124; P ❄ 📶) Everything functions like clockwork at this pleasingly contemporary guesthouse within a former seminary, 600m north of Vic's Plaça Major. Spotless, rooms are decorated in primary colours and spread across a cavernous complex surrounding a grassy courtyard. It also houses university residences, so there's a student atmosphere, but expect helpful staff, on-site parking (€6), 24-hour reception and a restaurant.

★El Jardinet CATALAN €€

(☎938 86 28 77; www.eljardinetdevic.com; Carrer de Corretgers 8; mains €15-23; ⏲1-3.30pm & 8.30-11pm Tue-Sat, 1-3.30pm Sun; 📶) This always-packed, warm-hearted restaurant has been perfecting Catalan cuisine since 1980, making it one of the best choices in town. There's a good selection, including duck with figs and strawberries, prawn-and-ham salads draped in brie, and artistically presented desserts. Diners can choose between the minimalist interior or outdoor space, and there's a good €28 three-course set menu.

Information

Oficina de Turisme (☎938 86 20 91; www.victurisme.cat; Plaça del Pes; ⏲10am-2pm & 4-8pm Mon-Fri, 10am-2pm & 4-7pm Sat, 10.30am-1.30pm Sun) Just off Plaça Major, within the town hall, this office has friendly, multilingual staff who provide audio guides (€2) and maps for exploring Vic, plus exhibits on Catalan culture.

Getting There & Away

Regular *rodalies* trains (line R3) run to/from Barcelona (€6.15, one to 1½ hours); the train station is 500m west of Plaça Major.

Montserrat

ELEV 720M

Montserrat, 50km northwest of Barcelona, is at the heart of Catalan identity for its mountain, monastery and natural park weaving among distinctive rock formations. Montserrat mountain is instantly recognisable, sculpted over millennia by wind and frost. Its turrets of rock, a coarse conglomerate of limestone and eroded fragments, extend like gnarled fingers from its 1236m-high bulk. More than halfway up the mountain lies the Benedictine Monestir de Montserrat, home to La Moreneta ('Little Brown One', or 'Black Virgin'), one of Spain's most revered icons. Extending from this sacred spot is the **Parc Natural de la Muntanya de Montserrat**, superlative hiking terrain where brooks tumble into ravines and lookout points deliver panoramas of rocky pillars.

Montserrat (often used interchangeably for the monastery and mountain) is a hugely popular day trip from Barcelona. The monastery throngs with visitors, but serenity can still be found on the walking trails or by staying overnight.

Sights

★Monestir de Montserrat MONASTERY
(www.abadiamontserrat.net) Catalonia's most renowned monastery was established in 1025 to commemorate local shepherds' visions of the Virgin Mary, accompanied by celestial light and a chorus of holy music. Today, a community of 55 monks lives here. The monastery complex encompasses two blocks: on one side, the basilica and monastery buildings, and on the other, tourist and pilgrim facilities. Admirable monastery architecture lining the main **Plaça de Santa Maria** includes elegant 15th-century cloisters and a gleaming late-19th-century facade depicting St George and St Benedict in relief.

➡ Cambril de la Mare de Déu
(⏲8-10.30am & noon-6.30pm, plus 7.30-8pm Jul–mid-Sep) Signs to the right of the entrance to Montserrat's main basilica lead into the intimate Cambril de la Mare de Déu, where you can pay homage to the famous **La Moreneta** ('Little Brown One', or 'Black Virgin'), a revered 12th-century Romanesque wood-carved statue of the Virgin Mary with Jesus seated on her knee (and Catalonia's official patroness since 1881).

➡ Basílica
(www.abadiamontserrat.net; ⏲7.30-10.30am & noon-8pm) FREE With marbled floors and art nouveau–style frescoes visible between graceful archways, the open courtyard fronting Montserrat's basilica immediately sets an impressive tone. The basilica itself, consecrated in 1592, has a brick facade featuring carvings of Christ and the 12 Apostles, dating to the early 20th century. Beyond its heavy doors, the interior glitters with white marble and gold in a blend of Renaissance and Catalan Gothic styles.

Museu de Montserrat MUSEUM
(www.museudemontserrat.com; Plaça de Santa Maria; adult/child €7/4, incl Espai (space) audiovisual €10/6; ⏲10am-5.45pm Mon-Fri, 10am-6.45pm Sat & Sun) This museum has excellent displays, ranging from an archeological section with an Egyptian mummy to Gothic altarpieces to fine canvases by Caravaggio, El Greco, Picasso and several Impressionists (Monet, Degas), as well as a comprehensive collection of 20th-century Catalan art, and some fantastic Orthodox icons.

Activities

Beyond the touristic hubbub surrounding Montserrat's monastery and basilica, there's tranquillity to be found in the web of walking trails across the mountain. The tourist office has basic maps.

Take the 10-minute **Funicular de Sant Joan** (www.cremallerademontserrat.cat; one-way/return €8.10/13; ⏲every 12-20min 10am-4.50pm Nov-Mar, to 5.50pm Sep, Oct, Apr & May, to 6.50pm Jul–mid-Sep, closed 3 weeks Jan) for the first 250m uphill from the monastery; alternatively, it's a 45-minute walk along the road between the funicular's lower and upper stations. From the top, it's a 20-minute stroll (signposted) to the **Ermita de Sant Joan**, with fine westward views.

More exciting is the signposted 7.5km (2½-hour) loop walk from the Funicular de Sant Joan's upper station, northwest to Montserrat's highest peak, **Sant Jeroni** (1236m), then back. The walk takes you across the upper part of the mountain, with a close-up experience of some of the rock pillars.

Entertainment

Escolania de Montserrat LIVE MUSIC
(www.escolania.cat; ⏲performances 1pm Mon-Thu, 11am Sun, 6.45pm Sun-Thu) The clear voices of one of Europe's oldest boys' choirs have echoed

through the basilica since the 14th century. The choir performs briefly on most days (except school holidays), singing *Virolai*, written by Catalonia's national poet Jacint Verdaguer, and *Salve Regina*. The 50 *escolanets*, aged between nine and 14, go to boarding school in Montserrat and must endure a two-year selection process to join the choir.

Information

Oficina de Turisme (938 77 77 77; www.montserratvisita.com; 9am-8pm Easter-Sep, to 5.45pm Oct-Easter) At the entrance to the monastery, with information on walking trails.

Getting There & Away

The R5 line trains operated by **FGC** (www.fgc.net) run half-hourly to hourly to/from Barcelona's Plaça d'Espanya station (one hour). Services start at 5.16am, but take the 8.36am train to connect with the first **AERI cable car** (938 35 00 05; www.aeridemontserrat.com; one-way/return €7/10; every 15 min 9.40am-7pm, reduced hours Nov-Feb, closed mid-late Jan) to the monastery from the Montserrat Aeri stop.

Alternatively, take the R5 to the next stop (Monistrol de Montserrat), from where **cremallera trains** (902 31 20 20; www.cremallerademontserrat.com; one-way/return €6/10; every 20-40min 8.48am-6.15pm mid-Sep–Jun, to 8.15pm Easter & Jul–mid-Sep) run up to the monastery (20 minutes) every 20 to 40 minutes. There are various train/*cremallera* combo tickets available.

By car, take the C16 northwest from Barcelona, then the C58 northwest shortly beyond Terrassa, followed by the C55 south to Monistrol de Montserrat. You can leave your vehicle at the free car park and take the *cremallera* up to the top, or drive up and park (cars €6.50).

Cardona

POP 3590

Long before arrival, you spy in the distance the outline of an impregnable 11th-century fortress towering above Cardona, 30km northwest of Manresa. Once ruled by the self-styled 'Lords of Salt', who brought Cardona wealth by mining the Muntanya de Sal (Mountain of Salt), today the castle lures tourists to admire its stocky watchtowers and Romanesque church. Aside from this standout attraction, Cardona is a sleepy place, best experienced as an atmospheric day trip or stopover between Barcelona and the Pyrenees – unless, that is, you're staying at the sumptuous *parador* that now inhabits the castle.

★Castell de Cardona CASTLE
(10am-1pm & 3-7pm Jun-Sep, 10am-1pm & 3-5pm Tue-Sun Oct-May) FREE Visible long before entering Cardona, this hilltop fortress broods above the modern town. From this strategic position, centuries of noblemen have kept a watchful eye over Cardona's Muntanya de Sal (Salt Mountain), the white gold that gave Cardona its wealth. The ramparts have panoramic views of the vast Lleida plain; the loftiest vantage point is the 11th-century **Torre de la Minyona**. You're free to wander the castle, but sights within the complex have admission charges.

A fortress has stood on this spot since the 3rd century BC, but the castle reached its zenith under the Lords of Cardona, who arrived in the 11th century and built the palace buildings and the elegant Romanesque **Colegiata de Sant Vicenç** (Castell de Cardona; adult/child €3.50/2.50; tours 10.30am, 11.30am, 12.30pm, 3.30pm & 4.30pm, plus 6pm Oct-May). Through 11 centuries of history, the Castell de Cardona has been never conquered.

★Parador de Cardona HISTORIC HOTEL €€
(938 69 12 75; www.parador.es; Castell de Cardona; r €88-155; P) Rooms occupy an adjoining modern building, but that doesn't dim the magic of sleeping like a lord at this *parador* within Cardona's medieval castle. Lodgings are spacious and comfortable, in old-world style, many with exceptional views. Common areas are resplendent with antique furnishings and displays of historical finery. The highlight is breakfasting under Gothic arches in a converted monks' refectory.

★La Volta del Rector CATALAN €€
(938 69 16 37; http://lavoltadelrector.cat; Carrer de les Flors 4; mains €12-16; 8am-5pm Tue-Thu & Sun, 8am-midnight Fri & Sat;) Twelfth-century stone walls mix with wild violet decor at La Volta del Rector, in the heart of medieval Cardona. The atmosphere is rustic, romantic and fashionable all at once, while dishes – from grills and wild game to the house special: mountain potatoes with free-range fried eggs and/or chorizo – are whipped up with flair. The region's best wines are expertly recommended by staff.

Information

Oficina de Turisme (938 69 27 98; http://cardonaturisme.cat; Avinguda del Rastrillo; 10am-2pm & 4-8pm Mon-Sat & 10am-2pm Sun Apr-Oct, 10am-2pm Mon-Fri & Sun & 10am-2pm & 4-7pm Sat Nov-Mar) At the top of the old town, next to the path leading up to the castle (where there's another tiny information office).

Getting There & Away

ALSA (www.alsa.es) buses reach Cardona from Barcelona (€13, 1¾ hours, two to four daily) and Manresa (€4.40, 35 minutes to one hour, hourly Monday to Friday, three daily at weekends). The bus stop is just north of the tourist office on Avinguda del Rastrillo.

Lleida

POP 131,520

Lleida's battle-torn history has faded into memory, replaced by today's pacey, workaday city. During the 14th and 15th centuries, arid, inland Lleida was a centre of economic activity, fed in part by Jewish and Muslim communities. Culture and art flourished, thanks to surrounding monasteries, and a university was founded in 1300. Relics of the holy cloth and thorns made Lleida's cathedral a revered stopping point on the Camino de Santiago (the Camí de Sant Jaume in Catalonia) pilgrimage route towards Santiago de Compostela.

Battle lines were drawn here across Catalonia's history, with Lleida nearly always backing the losing side. The old town was destroyed during the War of the Spanish Succession, only for the conquerors' replacement settlement to be sacked by the French in 1812.

The fortress-cathedral crowning the city, La Seu Vella, evokes Lleida's former grandeur, while a smattering of museums and Modernista buildings offer other reasons to visit.

Sights

Grab a trail map of Lleida's prettiest old-town buildings at the tourist office; the elegant 15th-century **Antic Hospital de Santa Maria** and the 20th-century **Casa Magí Llorenç**, with its colourful Modernista ceiling frescoes, are worth a peep.

★La Seu Vella CATHEDRAL
(www.turoseuvella.cat; adult/child €5/free, incl Castell del Rei €7/free; 10am-7.30pm Tue-Sat May-Sep, 10am-1.30pm & 3-5.30pm Tue-Fri, 10am-5.30pm Sat Oct-Apr, 10am-3pm Sun year-round) Lleida's 'old cathedral', enclosed within a later fortress complex, towers above the city from its commanding hilltop location. Work began on the cathedral in 1203, though today it's a masterpiece of bold Romanesque forms complemented by Gothic vaults and elaborate tracery. The octagonal 60m-high **bell tower**, crowned with Gothic flourishes, rises in the southwest corner of the 14th-century Gothic **cloister**, a forest of slender columns with expansive Lleida views. Climb the tower's 238 steps for the finest panoramas.

Església de Sant Llorenç CHURCH
(Plaça Sant Josep; 9.30am-12.30pm & 5-8pm Mon-Fri, 10am-1.30pm & 5-8pm Sat & Sun, hours vary) FREE This well-refurbished, triple-naved 12th-century Romanesque church is worth admiring for its elegant octagonal bell tower and the gargoyles leaping from its eaves.

Museu de Lleida MUSEUM
(www.museudelleida.cat; Carrer del Sant Crist 1; adult/child €5/2.50; 10am-2pm & 5-7pm Tue-Thu & Sat Jun-Sep, 10am-2pm & 4-6pm Tue-Thu & Sat Oct-May, 10am-2pm Fri & Sun year-round) This brilliant, expansive museum brings together artefacts reaching back to the Stone Age, through Roman remains, Visigothic relics and medieval art into the 19th century. Highlights include the atmospherically lit collection of medieval religious sculptures, the containers of the oldest-known beer in the Iberian peninsula, and the delicate 1st- to 4th-century mosaics from the Roman El Romeral villa, a patchwork of peacock feathers and leaves. Labels are in Catalan, but English- and Spanish-language booklets are provided.

Sleeping & Eating

Parador de Lleida HISTORIC HOTEL €€
(973 00 48 66; www.parador.es; Carrer del Cavallers 15; r €80-103; P ❄ 📶) Unveiled in 2017, Lleida's *parador* makes a characterful, welcome addition to the city's otherwise uninspiring accommodation scene. Smartly contemporary rooms, styled in creams, beiges and warm woods, rise up around the elegant, curtain-draped cloister of the converted 17th-century Convent del Roser. The upscale restaurant occupies the chapel, and you're right in the heart of Lleida's historic centre.

Macao FUSION, JAPANESE €€
(973 04 63 08; www.facebook.com/macaolleida; Carrer del Camp de Mart 27; mains €9-15; 1-4pm & 8.30-11.30pm Tue-Fri, 1.30-3pm & 8.30pm-midnight Sat & Sun; 📶 ✎) A triumphant marriage of Japanese, Catalan and Mediterranean flavours transforms into beautifully presented contemporary plates at this stylish, popular restaurant with an updated maritime feel, 500m west of La Seu Vella. Snack on salt-sprinkled edamame while you pick from

an ultra-tempting range of stir fries, sashimi, *tataki*, *uramaki* and *niguiri*, all from the open-plan kitchen.

L'estel de la Mercè CATALAN, FUSION €€€
(☎973 28 80 08; www.lesteldelamerce.com; Carrer Cardenal Cisneros 30; mains €19-25; ⊙1-3.30pm & 8.30-11.30pm Wed-Sat, 1-3.30pm Tue & Sun) About 1km southwest of central Lleida, this sleek fine-dining place creates fusion dishes using fresh seasonal produce. Feast on the likes of rabbit with veg and snails (a Lleida speciality), Asian-inspired fish dishes such as tuna with ginger-infused *ajo blanco* (white gazpacho soup), and strawberries flambéed in pepper.

Information

Turisme de Lleida (☎973 70 03 19; www.turismedelleida.cat; Carrer Major 31; ⊙10am-2pm & 4-7pm Mon-Sat, 10am-1.30pm Sun) On the main pedestrian street, providing maps and local tips.

Oficina de Turisme (☎973 23 84 46; La Seu Vella; ⊙10am-7.30pm Tue-Sat, 10am-3pm Sun May-Sep, 10am-1.30pm & 3-5.30pm Tue-Fri, 10am-5.30pm Sat & 10am-3pm Sun Oct-Apr) Within the cathedral complex; covers Lleida and beyond.

Getting There & Away

From Lleida's central **bus station** (off Avinguda de Blondel), just southwest of the old town, **ALSA** (www.alsa.es) serves Zaragoza (€11, 1¾ to 2½ hours, two to three daily), Barcelona Nord (€21, 2¼ hours, 10 to 14 daily), El Prat airport (€22, 2¾ to 3¼ hours, two to four daily), Vielha (€14, 2¾ hours, eight to 10 daily) and La Seu d'Urgell (€19, 2¼ hours, three to seven daily).

Regular trains reach Lleida from Barcelona (€23 to €52, one hour), some proceeding to Madrid (€73 to €100, two hours, 10 daily) via Zaragoza (€15 to €33, 40 minutes to 1¼ hours).

COSTA DAURADA & AROUND

Sitges

POP 25,880

Just 35km southwest of Barcelona, Sitges sizzles with beach life, late-night clubs and an enviable festival calendar. Sitges has been a resort town since the 19th century, and was a key location for the Modernisme movement, which paved the way for the likes of Picasso. These days it's Spain's most famous gay holiday destination. In July and August, Sitges cranks up the volume to become one big beach party, while Carnaval (p390) unbridles the town's hedonistic side. But despite the bacchanalian nightlife, Sitges remains a classy destination: its array of galleries and museums belie its small size, there's a good choice of upmarket restaurants in its historic centre (which is lined with chic boutiques), and the October **film festival** (Festival Internacional de Cinema Fantàstic de Catalunya; www.sitgesfilmfestival.com; ⊙Oct) draws culture fiends from miles around. The town is quieter during the off season, but you can still get a feel for it.

Sights

The most beautiful part of Sitges is the headland area, where noble Modernista palaces and mansions strike poses around the pretty Església de Sant Bartomeu i Santa Tecla, with the sparkling-blue Mediterranean as a backdrop.

★**Museu del Cau Ferrat** MUSEUM
(www.museusdesitges.cat; Carrer de Fonollar; incl Museu Maricel del Mar adult/child €10/free; ⊙10am-8pm Tue-Sun Jul-Sep, to 7pm Apr-Jun & Oct, to 5pm Nov-Mar) Built in the 1890s as a house-studio by Catalan artist Santiago Rusiñol, a pioneer of the Modernisme movement, this seaside mansion is crammed with his own art and that of his contemporaries (including his friend Picasso), as well as his extensive private collection of ancient relics and antiques. The visual feast is piled high, from Grecian urns and a 15th-century baptismal font to 18th-century tilework that glitters all the way to the floral-painted wood-beamed ceiling.

Information is in Spanish and Catalan only, but there are info placards with some detail also in English and French. Attached is the **Museu Maricel del Mar** (www.museusdesitges.cat; Carrer de Fonollar; incl Museu del Cau Ferrat adult/child €10/free; ⊙10am-8pm Tue-Sun Jul-Sep, to 7pm Apr-Jun & Oct, to 5pm Nov-Mar).

Església de Sant Bartomeu i Santa Tecla CHURCH
(Plaça de l'Ajuntament; ⊙Mass 7.30pm Mon-Fri, 8pm Sat, 9am, 11am, 12.30pm & 7.30pm Sun, hours vary) Sitges' most striking landmark is this 17th-century parish church, sitting proudly on a rocky outcrop lapped by the sea, which separates the 2km-long main beach to the southwest from the smaller sandy strands to the northeast.

Beaches

Dotted with *xiringuitos* (beach bars), Sitges' main beach is divided into nine sections by a series of breakwaters and flanked by the attractive seafront Passeig Marítim. The most central are lively **La Fragata**, just below Sant Bartomeu church, and **La Ribera**, immediately west. About 500m southwest of the centre, **L'Estanyol** has summer *xiringuitos* with sunbeds; 1.5km further southwest, **Les Anquines** and **Terramar** have paddleboat rental. Northeast of the centre lie easy-access **Sant Sebastià**, sheltered **Balmins** (favoured by nudists; 1km northeast of town) and brown-sand **Aiguadolç** (500m further east). **Bassa Rodona**, immediately west of the centre, is Sitges' famous unofficial 'gay beach'.

Festivals & Events

Carnaval CARNIVAL
(www.carnavaldesitges.com; Feb/Mar) Carnaval in Sitges is a week-long booze-soaked riot, complete with masked balls and capped by extravagant gay parades held on the Sunday and Tuesday, featuring flamboyantly dressed drag queens, giant sound systems and an all-night party with bars staying open until dawn. Dates change yearly; check online.

Sleeping

Utopia Beach House HOSTEL €
(938 11 11 36; www.utopiasitges.com; Carrer Socias 22; dm €20-32, d €50-99;) A short walk from the beach, 1.5km west of central Sitges, this bubbly hostel has pastel-painted four-, six- or 10-person dorms (lockers and towels provided), and double rooms with private bathrooms and, for some, big balconies. There's a cheerful cafe-bar amid leafy gardens that often hosts live music, plus laundry facilities (€3), a communal kitchen and a colourful lounge with mini-library.

Babalu Sitges Beach Hostel HOSTEL €€
(938 94 62 74; www.sitgesbeachhostel.com; Calle Anselm Clavé 9; dm €30-40, d €80-110;) A breezy modern hostel near the beach, 1km west of the centre. Comfortable locker-equipped dorms for four, six, eight or 14 people (with private bathroom) are pricey, but you get plenty for your euro, with cheap meals, bike hire, a sociable lounge and plenty of outdoor terrace space on offer.

Parrots Hotel HOTEL €€
(938 94 13 50; www.parrotshotel.com; Calle de Joan Tarrida 16; incl breakfast s €109, d €120-160; Feb-Oct;) It's hard to miss this bright-blue gay-friendly hotel. Courteous staff usher you towards thoroughly modern rooms done out in crisp whites and royal blues, most with balconies or terraces with sun lounges. It's right in the heart of the Sitges action and there's a sauna to get steamy in.

Hotel Platjador HOTEL €€€
(938 94 50 54; www.hotelsitges.com; Passeig de la Ribera 35; s €110-160, d €137-200;) This welcoming seafront hotel has fabulous colourful, modern rooms (many with balconies) featuring enormous plush beds and pillow menus. Enjoy the cool blue pool and rooftop bar overlooking the sea. It's superb value off-season, when rates drop by up to 50%.

The team also runs the popular **Hotel Galeón** (938 94 06 12; www.hotelsitges.com; Carrer de Sant Francesc 46-48; incl breakfast s €80-123, d €123-160;), with plain but smart, comfy rooms and a pool surrounded by greenery.

Eating

★**El Cable** TAPAS €
(938 94 87 61; www.facebook.com/elcablebarsitges; Carrer de Barcelona 1; tapas €2-6; 7-11.30pm Mon-Fri, 12-3.30pm & 7-11.30pm Sat & Sun) Always packed, down-to-earth El Cable might just be Sitges' most loved tapas bar, rolling out classics like *patatas bravas* (often branded the best in town) alongside divine, inventive bite-sized creations. Try the veggie-stuffed puff-pastry '*saquito*' or the award-winning mushroom-filled squid with risotto and almond praline. Wash it all down with fine organic Penedès wines, rustled up by welcoming waiters.

Nem FUSION €€
(938 94 93 32; www.nemsitges.com; Carrer de l'Illa de Cuba 9; tapas €4.50-7; 7.30-11pm Tue-Fri, 1.30-3.30pm & 7.30-11pm Sat & Sun, closed Sun approx Nov-Apr;) At this packed-out fusion tapas spot, Spanish and Asian flavours collide in short, often-changing menus of deliciously creative concoctions that might include sea-bream sashimi, citrusy *patatas bravas* and baked beetroot with cottage cheese. Dine in a semi-open space at cosy corner tables or perched at the bar. Sitges-brewed craft beer and original desserts, like lemon-and-basil white-chocolate cream, round things off.

Lady Green VEGETARIAN, VEGAN €€
(931 71 59 14; www.facebook.com/ladygreensitges; Carrer de Sant Pau 11; 2-/3-course set menu €15/20; 7-10pm Mon, 1-4pm & 7-10pm Tue, Wed

Sitges

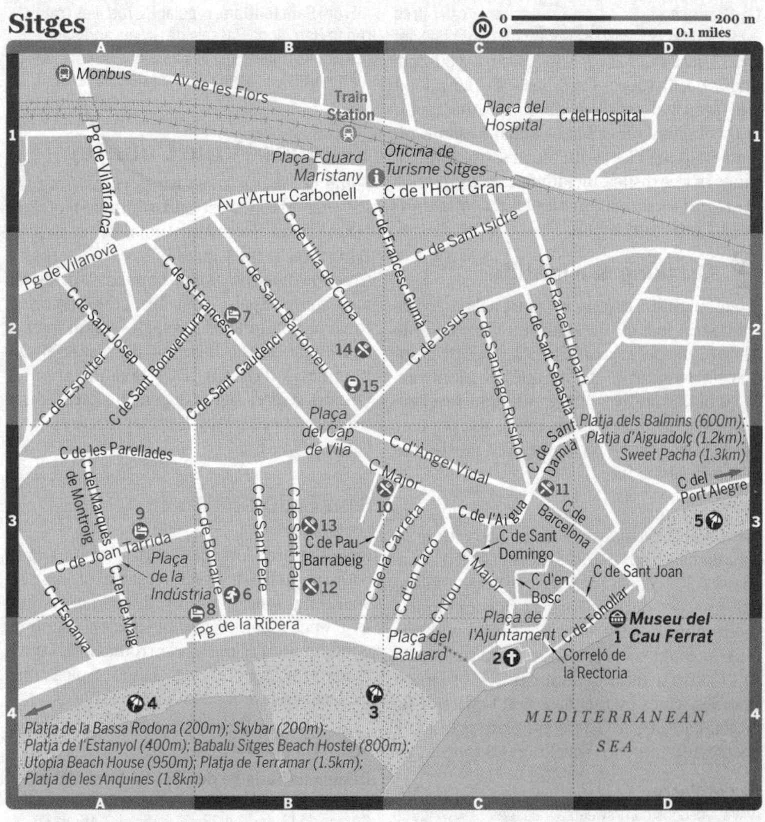

Sitges

Top Sights
1 Museu del Cau Ferrat D4

Sights
2 Església de Sant Bartomeu i Santa Tecla C4
Museu Maricel del Mar .... (see 1)
3 Platja de la Fragata B4
4 Platja de la Ribera A4
5 Platja de Sant Sebastià D3

Activities, Courses & Tours
6 Sitges SUP B3

Sleeping
7 Hotel Galeón B2
8 Hotel Platjador B3
9 Parrots Hotel A3

Eating
10 33 Sitges C3
11 El Cable C3
12 La Salseta B3
13 Lady Green B3
14 Nem B2

Drinking & Nightlife
15 La Sitgetana B2

& Sun, 1-4pm & 7-11pm Thu-Sat, closed Mon & Tue approx Nov-May;) Zesty Mexican platters, veggie burgers, falafel with quinoa tabouli, and delectable American-style vegan cheesecake: vegetarian Lady Green will satisfy even the most demanding taste buds with its imaginative meat-free dishes, bold flavours and wonderful desserts. There are also vegan and gluten-free choices, plus invigorating fresh juices and smoothies.

La Salseta CATALAN €€
(☎938 11 04 19; www.lasalseta.com; Carrer de Sant Pau 35; mains €10-20; ⊙1.30-3.30pm & 8.30-11pm Wed-Sat, 1.30-3.30pm Tue & Sun) Slow food and seasonal produce dominate the menu at this homey yet elegant Catalan restaurant, with crisp pig's feet with blood sausage and a range of rice dishes, including creamy *arròs a la sitgetana*, among the highlights of a thoroughly satisfying menu.

 Drinking & Nightlife

Sitges' nightlife centres on one packed pedestrian strip just off the seafront: Carrer 1er de Maig (Calle del Pecado; Sin St), Plaça de la Indústria and Carrer del Marquès de Montroig. Most bars shut by 3.30am. All-night revellers head to clubs just outside town; the popular ones change name regularly. Boat parties are also part of the fun.

La Sitgetana CRAFT BEER
(www.facebook.com/lasitgetanacraftbeer; Carrer de Sant Bartomeu 10; ⊙6.30-11.30pm Mon-Fri, noon-3pm & 6.30-11.30pm Sat & Sun;) Spy the on-site brewery out the back at this ambitious, modern-minimalist craft-beer pub, with six taps devoted to artisan brews (pints €4.90 to €6). Try a Tecla Centennial IPA, or sip on Penedès wines by the glass and bottles of La Sitgetana Pale Ale. There are platters of ham, cheese and more for snacking (€3 to €9).

Sweet Pacha CLUB
(www.facebook.com/sweetpachasitges; Avinguda Port d'Aiguadolç 9; cover incl 2 drinks €20; ⊙midnight-5.30am Fri & Sat) Follow the sounds of sultry R & B and hypnotic house towards this cocktail-fuelled club, just back from Aiguadolç marina (a 20-minute walk east from Sitges centre). For quieter nights, there's also a seafood restaurant. Check online for events and look out for posters in the old town.

Information

Oficina de Turisme Sitges (☎938 94 42 51; www.sitgestur.cat; Plaça Eduard Maristany 2; ⊙10am-2pm & 4-8pm Mon-Sat mid-Jun–mid-Oct, 10am-2pm & 4-6.30pm Mon-Sat mid-Oct–mid-Jun, 10am-2pm Sun year-round) By the train station.

Getting There & Away

Monbus (www.monbus.cat) runs to Barcelona (€4, 50 minutes, every 15 to 50 minutes) and Barcelona airport (€7, 25 minutes, half-hourly to hourly) from Passeig de Vilafranca, stopping along Passeig de Vilanova.

From 5am to 10pm, regular R2 *rodalies* trains run to Barcelona Passeig de Gràcia and Sants (€4.10, 45 minutes). For Barcelona airport (€4.10, 40 minutes), change at El Prat de Llobregat.

Penedès Wine Country

Some of Spain's finest wines come from the Penedès plains west and southwest of Barcelona. Sant Sadurní d'Anoia, 35km west of Barcelona, is the capital of *cava*, a sparkling, Champagne-style wine popular worldwide and across Spain. The attractive historical town of Vilafranca del Penedès, 12km further southwest, is the heart of the Penedès Denominació d'Origen (DO; Denomination of Origin) region (www.dopenedes.cat), which produces noteworthy light whites and some very tasty reds.

Sant Sadurní d'Anoia

POP 12,310

One hundred or so wineries around Sant Sadurní make it Spain's centre of *cava*, a sparkling wine made by the same method as French Champagne. Beyond the popping corks in Sant Sadurní's surrounds, the town is a sleepy place, though it has a pleasingly rich calendar of food and wine festivals.

Information

Oficina de Turisme de Sant Sadurní d'Anoia (☎938 91 03 25; www.turismesantsadurni.cat; Carrer de l'Hospital 23; ⊙9.15am-2.45pm & 4-6.30pm Tue-Fri, 10am-2pm & 4.30-7pm Sat, 10am-2pm Sun) Books winery tours, provides maps and houses Sant Sadurní's interactive *cava* interpretation centre.

Getting There & Away

Rodalies trains run from Barcelona Sants to Sant Sadurní (€4.10, 40 minutes, half-hourly).

Vilafranca del Penedès

POP 39,000

To experience Penedès wine country without attaching yourself to a long guided tour or having to drive (a burden for anyone sipping greedily), base yourself in Vilafranca. Livelier than nearby Sant Sadurní, the town sprawls, but its centre is dotted with uplifting medieval and Modernista architecture and enjoys a selection of truly excellent restaurants with equally impressive wine lists. Vineyard excursions are easy to organise from here.

Pick up pamphlets at the tourist office for a self-guided tour of Vilafranca's medieval and Modernista architecture.

El Convent CATALAN, TAPAS €€

(☎931 69 43 84; www.facebook.com/elconvent1850; Carrer de la Fruita 12; dishes €8-19; ⏰7pm-midnight Tue-Fri, 9am-3.30pm & 8pm-midnight Sat) This warren-like, modern-rustic tavern delivers well-executed Catalan specials such as Pyrenean entrecôte, wild-salmon carpaccio, goat's-cheese salad and a selection of fondues for two, along with tempting platters of cheese, hummus or cold meats. It's friendly, low-key and very popular.

★Cal Ton CATALAN €€€

(☎938 90 37 41; www.restaurantcalton.com; Carrer Casal 8; mains €16-27, tasting menus €26-50; ⏰1-3.30pm Tue & Sun, 1-3.30pm & 8.30-10.30pm Wed-Sat; 📶) An evening of gastronomic wonder awaits at Cal Ton, going strong since 1982. From feather-light potato-and-prawn ravioli to cuttlefish rice and sirloin with truffle sauce, meals at this crisp modern restaurant exhaust superlatives. The unpretentious yet knowledgeable service ensures the perfect local wine to complement any dish. Don't miss the quivering chocolate fondant with passion-fruit ice cream.

WINE TASTING IN PENEDÈS

The Penedès region's more enthusiastic bodegas will unravel their wine-making history and unique architecture, show you how *cava* and/or other wines are made, and finish off with a glass or two. Tours generally last 1½ hours and advance booking is essential. Most run in Catalan, Spanish or English; other languages may be available. Browse www.dopenedes.es and www.enoturismepenedes.cat for more wine-tourism options.

If you're intent on serious wine sampling, **Catalunya Bus Turístic** (Map p278; ☎932 85 38 32; www.catalunyabusturistic.cat; Plaça de Catalunya; ⏰9am-8pm Jun-Sep, to 7pm Oct-May; Ⓜ Catalunya) conducts day tours from Barcelona (€66 to €73).

Codorníu (☎938 91 33 42; www.visitascodorniu.com; Avinguda de Jaume Codorníu, Sant Sadurní d'Anoia; adult/child €12/8; ⏰tours 10am-5pm Mon-Fri, to 1pm Sat & Sun) There is no more glorious spot to sip *cava* than the vaulted interior of Codorníu's palatial Modernista headquarters, designed by Catalan architect Josep Puig i Cadafalch, just beyond the northeast edge of Sant Sadurní d'Anoia. Codorníu's wine-making activities are documented back to the 16th century. Josep Raventós was the first to create sparkling Spanish wine by the Champagne method in 1872, while his son Manuel is credited with bringing this winemaker into the big time during the late 19th century.

Ninety-minute tours run in Catalan, Spanish, English and French; check schedules and book ahead online.

Freixenet (☎938 91 70 96; www.freixenet.es; Carrer de Joan Sala 2, Sant Sadurní d'Anoia; adult/child €12/8.50; ⏰tours 9am-4.30pm Mon-Sat, to 1pm Sun) The biggest *cava*-producing company, easily accessible right next to Sant Sadurní's train station. Book ahead for 1½-hour visits (in Catalan, Spanish, English, French, German or Japanese) that include a tour of its 1920s cellar, a spin around the property on the tourist train and samples of Freixenet *cava*. If you don't join a tour, you can still sample top fizz and platters of ham and nibbles in the atmospheric tasting room or taste by the glass on the lovely terrace.

Torres (☎938 17 73 30; www.torres.es; Pacs del Penedès; tours adult/child from €9/6.50; ⏰9.15am-4pm Mon-Sat, to noon Sun) Just 3km northwest of Vilafranca on the BP2121, this is the area's premier winemaker, with a family winemaking tradition dating from the 17th century and a strong emphasis on organic production and renewable energy. Torres revolutionised Spanish winemaking in the 1960s by introducing temperature-controlled, stainless-steel technology and French grape varieties, and now produces reds, whites and sparkling wines of all qualities.

Jean León (☎938 17 76 90; www.jeanleon.com; Chatêau Leon, Torrelavit; adult/child €10.25/free; ⏰9am-6pm Mon-Fri, 9am-1pm Sat & Sun) Since 1963, this winery has been using cabernet sauvignon and other French varietals to create high-quality wines. Ninety-minute visits (in Catalan, Spanish or English) to the wonderfully scenic vineyard include a tasting of three wines and must be booked in advance.

Information

Oficina de Turisme de Vilafranca del Penedès (938 18 12 54; www.turismevilafranca.com; Carrer Hermenegild Clascar 2; 3-6pm Mon, 9.30am-1.30pm & 3-6pm Tue-Sat, 10am-1pm Sun)

Getting There & Away

Rodalies trains run frequently from Barcelona Sants to Vilafranca (€4.90, 50 minutes).

Tarragona

POP 63,600

In this effervescent port city, Roman history collides with beaches, bars and a food scene that perfumes the air with freshly grilled seafood. The biggest lure is the wealth of ruins in Spain's second-most important Roman site, including a mosaic-packed museum and a seaside amphitheatre. A roll-call of fantastic places to eat gives you good reason to linger in the knot of lanes in the attractive medieval centre, flanked by a towering cathedral with Romanesque and Gothic flourishes.

Tarragona is also a gateway to the Costa Daurada's sparkling beaches and the feast of Modernisme architecture in nearby Reus (p400).

History

Tarragona was occupied by the Romans, who called it Tarraco, in 218 BC; prior to that, the area was first settled by Iberians, followed by Carthaginians. In 27 BC, Augustus made Tarraco the capital of his new Tarraconensis province (roughly three-quarters of modern Spain) and stayed until 25 BC, directing campaigns.

> **MUSEU D'HISTÒRIA DE TARRAGONA**
>
> The **Museu d'Història de Tarragona** (MHT; www.tarragona.cat/patrimoni/museu-historia; adult/child per site €3.30/free, all sites €7.40/free; sites 9am-9pm Tue-Sat, 9am-3pm Sun Easter-Sep, 9am-7pm Tue-Sat, 9am-3pm Sun Oct-Easter) consists of various Unesco World Heritage Roman sites, as well as some other historic buildings around town. A combined ticket covers the Pretori i Circ Romans, Amfiteatre Romà, Passeig Arqueològic Muralles and Fòrum de la Colònia. Get exploring!

During its Roman heyday, Tarragona was home to over 200,000 people, and, though abandoned when the Muslims arrived in AD 714, the city was reborn as the seat of a Christian archbishopric in the 11th century.

Sights & Activities

Several private operators run guided tours of Tarragona's old town; the tourist office (p397) has a list. A good choice is efficient, long-running **Itinere** (977 23 96 57; www.facebook.com/ItinereTarragona; Baixada del Roser 8; 2hr tour €90), whose multilingual guides lead in-depth two- or three-hour walks.

★Catedral de Tarragona CATHEDRAL
(www.catedraldetarragona.com; Plaça de la Seu; adult/child €5/3; 10am-8pm Mon-Sat mid-Jun–mid-Sep, 10am-7pm Mon-Sat mid-Mar–mid-Jun & mid-Sep–Oct, 10am-5pm Mon-Fri, 10am-7pm Sat Nov–mid-Mar) Crowning the town, Tarragona's cathedral incorporates both Romanesque and Gothic features, as typified by the main facade. The flower-filled cloister has Gothic vaulting and Romanesque carved capitals, one of which shows rats conducting a cat's funeral…until the cat comes back to life! Chambers off the cloister display the remains of a Roman temple (found in 2015) and the **Museu Diocesà**, its collection extending from Roman hairpins to 13th- and 14th-century polychrome Virgin woodcarvings. Don't miss the east nave's 14th-century frescoes.

★Museu Nacional Arqueològic de Tarragona MUSEUM
(www.mnat.cat; Plaça del Rei 5; adult/child €4.50/free; 9.30am-6pm Tue-Sat Oct-May, to 8.30pm Jun-Sep, 10am-2pm Sun year-round) This excellent museum does justice to the cultural and material wealth of Roman Tarraco. The mosaic collection traces changing trends from simple black-and-white designs to complex full-colour creations; highlights include the fine 2nd- or 3rd-century *Mosaic de la Medusa* and the large, almost complete 3rd-century *Mosaic dels Peixos de la Pineda*, showing fish and sea creatures. Explanations are in Catalan and Spanish, but there are English-language booklets across the galleries.

Amfiteatre Romà RUINS
(Parc de l'Amfiteatre; adult/child €3.30/free; 9am-9pm Tue-Sat, 9am-3pm Sun Easter-Sep, 9am-7pm Tue-Sat, 9am-3pm Sun Oct-Easter) Near the beach is Tarragona's well-preserved amphitheatre, dating from the 2nd century AD, where gladiators fought each other or wild animals. In its

arena are the remains of a 6th-century Visigothic church and a 12th-century Romanesque church, both built to commemorate the martyrdom of the Christian bishop Fructuosus and two deacons, believed to have been burnt alive here in AD 259.

Aqüeducte de les Ferreres BRIDGE
(Pont del Diable; ⏲24hr; P) FREE This magnificent aqueduct sits in a tangle of dusty pathways and glades 4km north of central Tarragona, just off the AP7 (near where it intersects with the N240). It is a fine stretch of two-tiered aqueduct (217m long and 27m high), which you can totter across. Buses 5 and 85 (€1.50, every 30 minutes) to Sant Salvador from Plaça Imperial de Tarraco stop nearby; you can walk 4.6km back to the city along the river (about 90 minutes).

Pretori i Circ Romans RUINS
(Plaça del Rei; adult/child €3.30/free; ⏲9am-9pm Tue-Sat, 9am-3pm Sun Easter-Sep, 9am-7pm Tue-Sat, 9am-3pm Sun Oct-Easter) This sizeable complex with two separate entrances includes part of the vaults of Tarragona's well-preserved, late-1st-century **Roman circus**, where chariot races were once held, as well as the Plaça del Rei's **Pretori tower** (climb it for 360° city views) and part of the **provincial forum**, the political heart of Roman Tarraconensis province. The circus, over 300m long and accommodating 30,000 spectators, stretched from here to beyond Plaça de la Font to the west.

Passeig Arqueològic Muralles WALLS
(Avinguda de Catalunya; adult/child €3.30/free; ⏲9am-9pm Tue-Sat, 9am-3pm Sun Easter-Sep, 9am-7pm Tue-Sat, 9am-3pm Sun Oct-Easter) A peaceful walk takes you around the inland part of the old town's perimeter between two lines of city walls. The inner walls are mainly Roman and date back to the 3rd century BC, while the outer ones were put up by the British in 1709 during the War of the Spanish Succession. The earliest stretches are a mighty 4m thick. There's a helpful interpretation centre (Catalan, Spanish and English).

Sleeping

Tarragona Hostel HOSTEL €
(☎877 05 58 96; www.tarragonahostel.com; Carrer de la Unió 26; dm €14-25, tr €50-60; Wi-Fi) All the backpacker essentials are well executed at this friendly central hostel with chirpy staff, a leafy patio, a comfy common room, a shared kitchen and laundry facilities. Choose from two eight-bed dorms and a more modern four-bed dorm (all with air-con and personal lockers), or a private fan-cooled triple room.

LOCAL KNOWLEDGE

CATALONIA'S HUMAN CASTLES

Among Catalonia's strangest spectacles are *castells*, or human 'castles'. This sport originated in the 18th century in Valls, 20km north of Tarragona, but has since spread to other parts of the region. Teams of *castellers* clamber onto each other's shoulders, then a daredevil child scrambes up the side of this human tower to perch at the top before the whole structure gracefully disassembles itself; towers up to nine levels high are built. For the most spectacular *castells*, swing by Tarragona's **Festival de Santa Tecla** (⏲mid-Sep).

Hotel Plaça de la Font HOTEL €€
(☎977 24 61 34; www.hotelpdelafont.com; Plaça de la Font 26; s/d/tr €63/78/98; air-con, Wi-Fi) Comfortable modern rooms, individually decorated with photos of local monuments, make this cheerful, convenient hotel one of Tarragona's most attractive options. Rooms at the front have tiny balconies and are well soundproofed from the sociable murmur on bustling Plaça de la Font below. With tables right on the square, the cafe is perfect for light breakfasts.

Gran Claustre BOUTIQUE HOTEL €€
(☎977 65 15 57; www.granclaustre.com; Carrer del Cup 2, Altafulla; s €77-133, d €90-157; P air-con, Wi-Fi, pool) For an upmarket stay, seek out this soothing, floral-scented hideaway overlooking the 17th-century castle in Altafulla's attractive old town, 11km northeast of Tarragona. Minimalist style dominates the elegant rooms, but those with the most colour, character and historical feel occupy the original 18th-century building, where there's a pool between stone walls. Other perks: a spa, hot tub and smart restaurant.

Hotel Sant Jordi HOTEL €€
(☎977 20 75 15; www.hotelsantjordi.info; Avinguda Vía Augusta 185; r €68-80; ⏲mid-Jan–mid-Dec; P air-con, Wi-Fi) The reception decor screams 1970s, but this popular hotel, 2.5km northeast of central Tarragona by appealing Platja de la Savinosa, has spotless, comfortable rooms with balconies and sea views. The old-world atmosphere and courteous service make it far cosier than it appears at first glance.

Tarragona

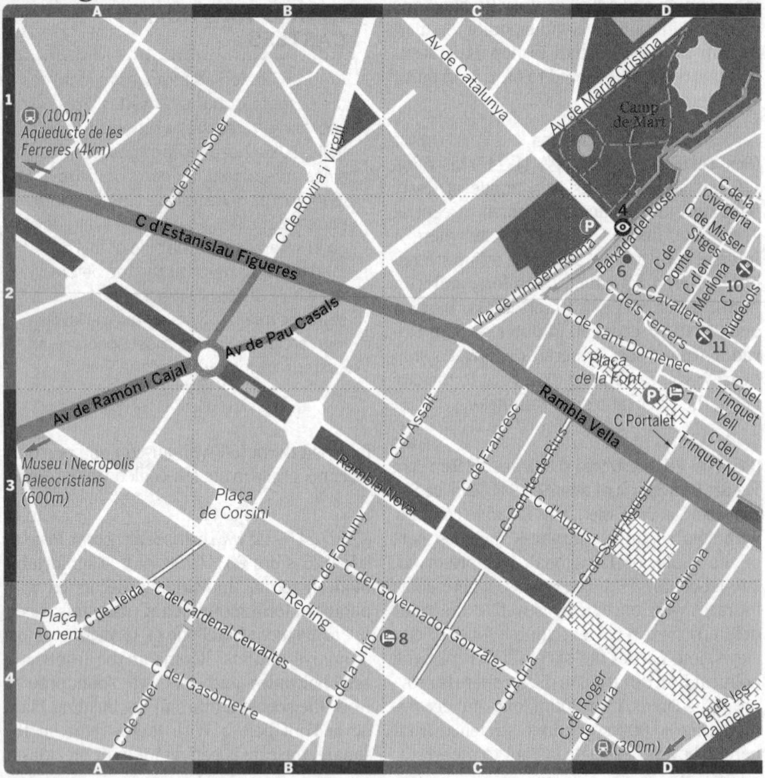

Tarragona

Top Sights

1 Catedral de Tarragona........E2
2 Museu Nacional Arqueològic de Tarragona........E3

Sights

3 Amfiteatre Romà........E4
4 Passeig Arqueològic Muralles........D2
5 Pretori i Circ Romans........E3

Activities, Courses & Tours

6 Itinere........D2

Sleeping

7 Hotel Plaça de la Font........D3
8 Tarragona Hostel........C4

Eating

9 AQ........E1
10 Arcs Restaurant........D2
11 Degvsta........D2
12 El Vergel........E2
13 Korxo........E2

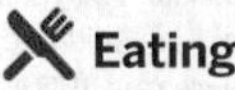

Eating

El Vergel VEGAN €€

(877 06 48 50; www.elvergeltarragona.com; Carrer Major 13; 3-course set menu €15-18; 1-11pm;) This fabulous, fashionable vegan spot turns out creative plant-based deliciousness in two- or three-course menus, between whitewashed walls offset by mint-green shutters, patterned tiles and original artwork. Menus change often: feast on the likes of tofu stew, all-veg pizza, mushroom risotto, cauliflower croquettes or ginger-infused coconut soup, rounded off with cold-pressed juices, homemade vermouth and organic wines.

Degvsta FUSION, CATALAN €€
(☎977 25 24 28; www.degvsta.com; Carrer Cavallers 6; mains €15-19; ⏲1.30-4pm Mon, 1.30-4pm & 9-10.30pm Tue-Sat) Beyond a stylish lounge/bar hides this rustic-chic restaurant styled in cool creams, adorned with a claw-foot bath tub (!) and specialising in deliciously inventive contemporary Catalan cuisine. Dishes delivered with flair might be avocado gazpacho, citrus-infused sea bass, fancied-up *pa amb tomàquet* or sheep's-cheese salad with zingy strawberry vinaigrette. People pack in for the three-course weekday lunch *menú* (€16).

AQ MEDITERRANEAN, FUSION €€
(☎977 21 59 54; www.aq-restaurant.com; Carrer de les Coques 7; mains €11-24; ⏲1.30-3.30pm & 8.30-11pm) The crisp interior design of this palm-patterned restaurant promises fine dining and AQ amply delivers, with its impeccably crafted, playfully executed fusion dishes taking inspiration from Catalan, Italian and Asian cuisines. Treat your taste buds to squid-ink croquettes, chunky strips of *patatas bravas*, grilled Wagyu steak, cod-and-aubergine teriyaki or wok-fried mussels.

Arcs Restaurant CATALAN €€€
(☎977 21 80 40; www.restaurantarcs.com; Carrer de Misser Sitges 13; mains €17-22; ⏲1-4pm & 8.30-11pm Tue-Sat) Inside a medieval cavern decorated with bright contemporary art and original Gothic arches, dine on Catalan dishes that follow the seasons (some traditional, others updated). Sample duck with hazelnut-and-vermouth sauce, salmon *tataki* with wasabi ice cream, or the always-excellent catch of the day.

Information

Tarragona Turisme (☎977 25 07 95; www.tarragonaturisme.es; Carrer Major 39; ⏲10am-8pm late Jun-Sep, 10am-2pm & 3-5pm Mon-Fri, 10am-2pm & 3-7pm Sat, 10am-2pm Sun Oct-late Jun)

Getting There & Away

AIR

Eleven kilometres northwest of Tarragona, **Reus airport** (www.aena.es; off C14, Reus) has flights to London, Dublin, Manchester, Brussels, Eindhoven and Frankfurt–Hahn among others, mostly with Ryanair.

BUS

The **bus station** (Plaça Imperial Tarraco) is 1.5km west of the old town along Rambla Nova. **ALSA** (www.alsa.es) destinations include Barcelona Nord (€8.70, 1½ hours, seven daily) and Valencia (€22, three to 4½ hours, six daily). **Hispano Igualadina** (www.igualadina.com) serves Lleida (€6, 1¼ to 1¾ hours, one to five daily).

CAR & MOTORCYCLE

There's a central underground car park (€5.50 per day) just off Via de l'Imperi Romà, on the west edge of the old town.

TRAIN

Tarragona has two train stations (www.renfe.com). The **local train station** (Tarragona) is a 10-minute walk south of the old town near the beach, with services to/from Barcelona (€8.05 to €21, one to 1½ hours, every 10 to 30 minutes) and Valencia (€17 to €27, two to four hours, 15 to 17 daily).

The second, out-of-town train station, **Camp de Tarragona**, lies 10km north of the centre (a 20-minute taxi ride). There are frequent high-speed trains to Barcelona (€12 to €32, 35 minutes) and Lleida (€14 to €26, 30 minutes).

DON'T MISS

THE CISTERCIAN ROUTE

The **Cistercian Route** (Ruta del Cister; www.larutadelcister.info) weaves among the mountainous territory between Tarragona and Lleida, linking a trio of spectacular monasteries that feature some of Catalonia's most ancient and beautiful religious architecture: **Santa Maria de Poblet**, **Santes Creus** and **Santa Maria de Vallbona**. Driving the route is a great way to explore the hilly scenery of inland Catalonia's Conca de Barberà winemaking region, while the long-distance GR175 walking trail links the three monasteries in a 104km loop.

Tackling all three monasteries is possible as a single-day drive from Lleida or, more conveniently, Tarragona, but it requires careful timing: two of the three monasteries only allow access by irregular guided tours. Start early, aiming to reach the first monastery by its 10am opening time. A combined ticket (€12; valid for a year) gives access to all three monasteries.

If returning to urban bustle feels like hard work, **Fèlix Hotel** (☎977 60 90 90; http://felixhotel.net; Carretera N240, Km 17, Valls; s/d €54/62; P ❄ 🏊) is a convenient, well-equipped roadside guesthouse just south of Valls, 17km north of Tarragona.

Reial Monestir de Santes Creus (☎977 63 83 29; www.larutadelcister.info; Plaça de Jaume el Just, Santes Creus; adult/senior & student €4.50/3.50; ⊙10am-6.30pm Jun-Sep, 10am-5pm Oct-May) On approaching this majestic monastery, an atmosphere of awe descends in broad Plaça de Sant Bernat Calbó: its mix of architectural styles spans seven centuries, including an ornamental 18th-century fountain. Behind the monastery's Romanesque-Gothic facade lie a 14th-century Gothic sandstone cloister (note the carved elephant and monkey on the 12th-century lavabo), a 12th-century chapter house whose ceiling ripples with rib-shaped vaults, a church begun in the 12th century, and royal apartments for the *comtes-reis* (count-kings; rulers of the joint state of Catalonia and Aragón).

The church is a lofty Gothic structure in the French tradition, with a couple of royal tombs; the north side of the transept has rare examples of Cistercian stained glass dating to the 13th century. Cistercian monks arrived here in 1160; from then on the monastery developed as a major centre of learning and a launch pad for the repopulation of the surrounding territory. Audiovisual presentations (Catalan, Spanish, English and more) give background info. The monastery is 15km northeast of Valls and well signposted.

Reial Monestir de Santa Maria de Poblet (☎977 87 12 01; www.poblet.cat; Plaça Corona d'Aragó 11, Poblet; adult/student €7.50/4.50; ⊙10am-12.30pm & 3-5.55pm Mon-Sat, 10.30am-12.25pm & 3-5.25pm Sun) The largest monastery of the Cistercian Route, Unesco-listed Santa Maria de Poblet was founded by monks from southern France in 1150, and rose rapidly to become Catalonia's most powerful monastery. Today, 28 monks live here. Highlights include the mostly Gothic, herb-scented main cloister and the sculptural treasures of the 12th-century church's Panteó Reial (Royal Pantheon); the raised alabaster sarcophagi contain such greats as Jaume I (conqueror of Mallorca and Valencia) and Pere III. Entry is by semi-guided tour (Catalan and Spanish), every 30 minutes. The monastery is well signposted 3.5km southwest of L'Espluga de Francolí, just off the N240 8.5km northwest of Montblanc. Its long lunchtime closure means it's best visited early.

Reial Monestir de Santa Maria de Vallbona (☎973 33 02 66; www.monestirvallbona.cat; Carrer Major, Vallbona de les Monges; adult/child €4/1; ⊙10.30am-1.30pm & 4.30-6.30pm Tue-Sat, noon-1.30pm & 4.30-6.45pm Sun Mar-Oct, 10.30am-1.30pm & 4.30-5.30pm Tue-Sat, noon-1.30pm & 4.30-5.30pm Sun Nov-Feb) Eight *monges* (nuns) still live at this 12th-century institution, the only women's monastery along the Cistercian Route. Years of restoration have cleared up most of the extensive civil-war damage, revealing a hushed cloister spanning the 12th to 16th centuries. Queen Violant of Hungary, a formidable political influencer and queen consort to Jaume I of Aragón, is entombed in the Romanesque-Gothic church (note the bilingual plaque in Catalan and Hungarian). Visits are by hourly 40-minute guided tour (Spanish or Catalan). The monastery is 25km north of Montblanc, 11km northwest of the C14 along the LP2335.

Getting Around

TO/FROM THE AIRPORT

Buses (timed for flights) run to/from Tarragona **bus station** (p397) (20 minutes, €4, three to five daily) as well as to/from Barcelona (1¾ hours, €15, one daily).

Priorat & Montsant Wine Regions

Rambling across softly sloping vine-wrapped hills, 40km west of Tarragona, Catalonia's Priorat region famously produces some of Spain's most prestigious (and most expensive) wines under the Priorat Denominació d'Origen Qualificada (DOQ; www.doqpriorat.org). It's one of just two Spanish winemaking areas awarded this coveted categorisation (the other is Rioja), and specialises in robust reds, mostly from *cariñena* (carignan) and *garnatxa* (grenache) grapes. Priorat's wine country is almost completely encircled by the undulating vineyards of the Montsant Denominació d'Origen (www.domontsant.com) territory, also known for its full-bodied reds from the same grapes, as well as its unique kosher wines.

Falset, just north of the N420, is the region's main town, and its liveliest, best-equipped base. Alternatively, make for charming hilltop **Gratallops** (10km northwest of Falset), home to several of Priorat's most high-profile wineries.

Clos Mogador WINERY
(☎977 83 91 71; http://closmogador.com; Camí Manyetes, Gratallops; tours €30; ⊙hours vary) A five-minute walk southwest of Gratallops, this is one of Priorat's outstanding wineries, founded in 1979 by pioneering French winemaker René Barbier. It's the creator of two aromatic reds, mostly from *cariñena* and *garnatxa* grapes, plus a fine white (*garnatxa blanca* and *macabeu*). In-depth three-hour tours involve a vehicle jaunt across vineyards followed by a tasting of the three wines.

Catedral del Vi WINERY
(Cooperativa Falset-Marça; ☎696 545254; www.etim.cat; Carrer Miquel Barceló 1, Falset; tours €10; ⊙11am-7pm, tours noon Sat & Sun Apr-Dec) Combining Modernista and Noucentista styles, this majestic medieval-inspired winery with a dramatic vaulted interior dates from 1919 and was designed by Gaudí's architectural disciple Cèsar Martinell. It's still a working bodega, producing full-bodied Montsant reds and the odd white, rosé and vermouth. Visitors can pop in for free low-key tastings, or for theatrical weekend tours. Guided tours may also be available; call or email ahead.

Lotus Priorat BOUTIQUE HOTEL **€€**
(☎977 83 10 45; www.lotuspriorat.com; Carrer de Baix 33, Falset; r incl breakfast €75-78) Skilfully run by three brothers, this fabulous rustic-chic boutique find is tucked away in a stylishly revamped 18th-century townhouse in Falset's centre. The 11 bold-coloured rooms are fun, cosy and contemporary, with open-stone walls, wood-beamed ceilings, tree-trunk bedside tables and antique doors as bedheads. Many have balconies, while some are apartment-style with kitchenettes.

The excellent on-site **bar-restaurant** (☎977 83 10 45; www.lotuspriorat.com; Carrer de Baix 33, Falset; dishes €7-12; ⊙7pm-late Mon & Tue, 9am-3pm & 7pm-late Wed-Sun) serves imaginative Catalan-international bites infused with local ingredients, on a view-laden terrace.

Information

Oficina de Turisme del Priorat (☎977 83 10 23; www.turismepriorat.org; Plaça de la Quartera 1, Falset; ⊙10am-2pm Tue-Sat, 11am-2pm Sun)

Getting There & Away

Hispano Igualadina (www.igualadina.com) runs two daily buses Monday to Friday between Falset and Tarragona (50 minutes).

From Marçà-Falset station, 2.5km southwest of Falset, five to six daily trains run to/from Tarragona (€5.60, 50 minutes) and Barcelona Sants (€11.95, two hours). Buses run seven to eight times daily between the train station and Falset.

Delta de l'Ebre

Laced by waterways that melt into the Balearic Sea, the Delta de l'Ebre, a 20km-long bulge of silt-formed land near Catalonia's southern border, comes as an unexpected highlight of the region. Flamingos and ibis strut in reed-fringed lagoons, dune-backed beaches are lashed by the wind, and marshes reflect sunsets like mirrors. This is the final flourish of Spain's most voluminous river, which meanders over 900km southeast from Fontibre in Cantabria. Exploring this remote rural landscape, with its whitewashed farmhouses marooned between electric-green rice paddies, lingers in the memory.

Seventy-eight sq kms of this wild, exposed place is the **Parc Natural del Delta** de l'Ebre**, northern Spain's most important waterbird habitat, with 330 bird species. Migration season (October and November) sees bird populations peak, but birds are also numerous in winter and spring. The park's flat expanse of waterside trails is ideal for cyclists and ramblers, and watersports abound.

Scruffy, sprawling **Deltebre** sits at the centre of the delta, but smaller villages like **Riumar**, at the delta's easternmost point, or **Poblenou del Delta**, in the south of the delta area, are more appealing bases.

Sights

Ecomuseu MUSEUM

(www.facebook.com/PNDeltaEbre; Carrer de Dr Martí Buera 22, Deltebre; €2; 10am-2pm & 3-6pm Mon-Sat Sep-Jun, 10am-2pm & 4-7pm Mon-Sat Jul & Aug, 10am-2pm Sun year-round) This engaging open-air museum shines a light on the delta's ecosystems and traditional trades, especially fishing and rice cultivation. The garden's pathways and wooden boardwalks weave past local flora, birdlife, fishers' tools and even a *llagut*, an early 20th-century boat used to haul around 350 sacks of rice at once. There's also an aquarium offering a glimpse of the freshwater denizens of the delta.

WORTH A TRIP

REUS' GAUDÍ CENTRE

Visionary Catalan architect Antoni Gaudí was born in Reus, 14km northwest of Tarragona, in 1852, and is celebrated at the **Gaudí Centre** (www.gaudicentre.cat; Plaça del Mercadal 3, Reus; adult/child €9/5; 10am-8pm Mon-Sat Jun-Sep, 10am-2pm & 4-7pm Mon-Sat Oct-May, 10am-2pm Sun year-round). Though there are no Gaudí buildings here, he was inspired by many of his home town's historical structures. The superb Gaudí Centre gives a thorough introduction to the man and his global influence through engaging multilingual and audiovisual displays. The inspiration Gaudí found in nature, along with his thoughtfulness, are portrayed alongside touchable scale models of his designs.

The museum doubles up as the tourist office; pick up a map to guide you around Reus' notable Modernista buildings. Regular trains connect Reus with Tarragona (€2.85, 15 minutes).

Activities

Birdwatching

Grab some binoculars and flock to **L'Encanyissada** and **La Tancada** lagoons and **Punta de la Banya**, all in the south of the delta. As of 2017, around 2700 pairs of greater flamingos nest at the lagoons and the Punta; the delta is one of only a handful of places in Europe where they reproduce.

L'Encanyissada has five free-access observation points and La Tancada two; others around the park are marked on maps provided by the Centre d'Informació (p401). Punta de la Banya, connected to the mainland by a narrow 5km sand spit with a dirt road, is mostly off limits, but you can go as far as a lookout point on its east side. Birdwatching is at its best during early mornings and dusk.

Boat Trips

Creuers Olmos (645 927110, 977 07 70 22; Passeig Reinosa, Deltebre; adult/child €11/7) and **Creuers Delta de l'Ebre** (977 48 01 28; https://creuersdeltaebre.com; Carretera Final Goles de l'Ebre, Riumar; adult/child €8.75/6.75) run boat trips (45 minutes to 1½ hours) to the mouths of the Ebro and the delta's tip. The frequency and timings of departures depend on the season, but each company usually offers at least two daily and up to seven or eight in high season. The large size of the boats spooks birdlife so bring binoculars if you want to spy a distant ibis.

Cycling

Cycling is an excellent way to explore the delta, with routes ranging from 7km to 43km; the Centre d'Informació (p401) provides maps and there are downloadable multilanguage guides on http://parcsnaturals.gencat.cat. Bicycles can be rented at Deltebre, Riumar and Poblenou del Delta (€10 per day).

Sleeping & Eating

Mas del Tancat CASA RURAL €

(656 901014; masdeltancat@gmail.com; Camí dels Panissos, Amposta; s/d €43/55; P) A converted farmhouse poised between rice fields, Mas del Tancat is a friendly, tranquil escape with just five rooms sporting iron bedsteads and soothing colour schemes. Farm animals wander the grounds, a peaceful pool beckons, and homemade dinners (€15) and breakfasts (€6) are available. From Amposta, take the TV3405 3km east; then it's 1km south and signposted.

★Hostal Cling 43 B&B €€
(☎659 335577; www.hostalcling43.com; Avinguda Colom 43, Deltebre; s €40-45, d €65-80, tr €90-100; ❄📶) Hidden away in a converted townhouse, this boutique-ified B&B is a fabulous find for its cosy-stylish rooms, warm welcome and brilliant local-produce breakfasts. Gorgeous hand-painted murals of local birds complement open-brick walls, wood-beamed ceilings and splashes of colour in the six all-different doubles.

★Masia Tinet CASA RURAL €€
(☎977 48 93 89; www.masiatinet.com; Barrio Lepanto 13, Deltebre; d incl breakfast €72-80; P❄📶) The six rooms at this cushy, family-run guesthouse are elegant but rustic, with wooden beams, high ceilings and bare-brick or cheery-coloured walls. There's a garden with deck chairs and a small pool, so you can watch the sun set over marshlands speckled with birdlife. Breakfasts are a banquet of homemade preserves and fresh produce, and service has a personal touch.

★Mas Prades CATALAN €€
(☎977 05 90 84; www.masdeprades.cat; Carretera T340, Km 8, Deltebre; mains €15-22; ⌚1.30-4pm & 8.30-10.30pm, weekends only Nov-Mar; 📶) Gourmets travel all the way from Barcelona to this attractively revamped country house to sample its fantastic delta cuisine. The three-course €20 lunch menu makes a lip-smacking introduction to local delicacies, while à la carte options range from baby squid, grilled sole and tender mussels roasted in garlic butter to the classic delta rice with wild duck.

★Casa Nuri SEAFOOD €€
(☎977 48 01 28; www.restaurantnuri.com; Carretera Final Goles de l'Ebre, Riumar; mains €13-25; ⌚9am-10pm, closed early Jan) Locals fill this bubbly riverfront restaurant, thanks to its long-standing reputation for superb local cuisine such as razor clams, rice with squid ink, oven-baked sea bass, duck with orange sauce, and paella in all shapes and sizes.

ℹ Information

Centre d'Informació (☎977 48 96 79, 977 48 90 11; http://parcsnaturals.gencat.cat; Carrer de Dr Martí Buera 22, Deltebre; ⌚10am-2pm & 3-6pm Mon-Sat Sep-Jun, 10am-2pm & 4-7pm Mon-Sat Jul & Aug, 10am-2pm Sun year-round) In the same complex as Deltebre's Ecomuseu; pick up maps and cycle route brochures.

Casa de Fusta (☎977 26 10 22; http://parcsnaturals.gencat.cat; Partida Cuixota, Poblenou del Delta; ⌚10am-2pm & 3-6pm Mon-Sat Sep-Jun, 10am-2pm & 4-7pm Mon-Sat Jul & Aug, 10am-2pm Sun year round)

WORTH A TRIP

CASTELL DE MIRAVET

Southern Catalonia's finest **castle** (Miravet; adult/child €3.50/2.50; ⌚10am-7.30pm Tue-Sun Jun-Sep, to 5pm Mar-May & Oct–mid-Dec, to 3.30pm mid-Dec–Feb) was built in the 11th century by the Moors, conquered by the Christians in the 1150s before being given to the Templars, and later taken by Nationalist forces during the civil war. It's a formidable stronghold, with incredibly solid walls, towering above a pretty village that cascades down the banks of the Ebro. Miravet is 8km southwest of the N420, 70km west of Tarragona. A path meanders down from beside the castle entrance to the riverside at old Miravet, from where you get the best views.

ℹ Getting There & Away

Weekday **Hife** (www.hife.es) buses connect Tortosa with Deltebre (€3.90, 50 minutes, seven daily) and Poblenou del Delta (€5.15, one hour, two daily). Buses also head to delta towns Amposta and Sant Carles de la Ràpita from Tarragona (€12 to €14, one to two hours, four to eight daily) and Tortosa (€2.25 to €2.70, 20 to 45 minutes, every 30 to 90 minutes).

ℹ Getting Around

If you don't reach the Delta de l'Ebre with your own wheels, consider renting a bike: the area has extremely limited public transport.

Tortosa

POP 24,100

With a neck-straining castle, otherworldly sculpture garden and architectural gems spanning Gothic to Modernista styles, arid Tortosa is experiencing a quiet tourism renaissance. It's a sleepy, slightly scruffy town, 70km southwest of Tarragona, but one that's slowly becoming increasingly popular for cultural weekend breaks.

Tortosa was a battleground between medieval Christian and Moorish Spain. More recently, it was on the front line between Nationalists and Republicans during the civil war (suffering a staggering 86 air raids between 1937 and 1938) and the site of an epic battle, which destroyed much of its medieval centre and cost over 35,000 lives. Tortosa is also suffused with Jewish history that dates back to the 6th century.

Sights

Catedral de Santa Maria CATHEDRAL
(Carrer Portal del Palau; adult/child €4/3; 10am-2pm & 4-7pm Tue-Sat, 11am-2pm Sun) Built between 1347 and the mid-18th century on the site of a Romanesque predecessor, this Gothic cathedral seizes attention with its many turrets, gargoyles jutting from every eave, and austere adjoining 13th-century cloister.

Museu de Tortosa MUSEUM
(977 51 01 44; www.museudetortosa.cat; Rambla Felip Pedrell 3; adult/child €3/free; 10am-1.30pm & 5-8pm Tue-Sat May-Sep, 10am-1.30pm & 4-7pm Tue-Sat Oct-Apr, 11am-1.30pm Sun year-round) Within a splendid blue Modernista building, decorated with white checkerboard designs, lies Tortosa's modern, minimalist town museum. The 1908 building is worth ogling: formerly a city slaughterhouse, its design has delicate Moorish elements. Within, the museum does a great job of contextualising the area's history, from traces of early Iberian settlement to Roman rule, Moorish times and the devastation of the Spanish Civil War. Pick up an audio guide (€1).

Castell de la Suda CASTLE, RUIN
(24hr) FREE Looming high above the old town, Tortosa's 10th-century fortress is a maze of unfinished stairways, trails to nowhere, and spectacular lofty views, now mostly occupied by the luxurious Parador de Tortosa. Next to the entrance to the *parador* lies a small Islamic cemetery dating to the 10th to 12th centuries.

Sleeping & Eating

Parador de Tortosa HISTORIC HOTEL €€
(977 44 44 50; www.parador.es; Castell de la Suda; r €85-130; P) Tortosa's formidable fortress encloses a *parador*, allowing you to repose in medieval surroundings overlooking vertiginous views of the town. Expect cosy old-world rooms, a smart restaurant, a hill-top pool, and a plush lounge bar with terrace.

Xampu Xampany TAPAS €€
(977 50 13 41; www.xampu-xampany.com; Rambla de Catalunya 41; tapas €3-13; 11.30am-5pm & 7pm-late Mon-Fri, 11.30am-4pm & 7pm-late Sat;) This buzzing bar-restaurant on Tortosa's west bank serves up regional favourites alongside inventive tapas, allowing you to snack on ham, sheep's cheese and tomato-slathered bread just as easily as on hummus platters or prawn-and-veg ravioli. Alternatively, fill up on the menu of well-presented Catalan classics, enjoyed with local wines.

Information

Oficina de Turisme de les Terres de l'Ebre
(977 44 96 48; www.tortosaturisme.cat; Rambla Felip Pedrell 3; 10am-1.30pm & 4.30-7.30pm Mon-Sat May-Sep, 10am-1.30pm & 3.30-6.30pm Mon-Sat Oct-Apr, 10am-1.30pm Sun year-round) Attached to the Museu de Tortosa; also covers the Delta de l'Ebre area.

Getting There & Away

Hife (www.hife.es) buses link Tortosa with Tarragona (€12, one to 1¾ hours, four to nine daily), plus several towns in the Delta de l'Ebre area.

Trains reach Tortosa from Tarragona (€8.05, one to 1½ hours, nine or 10 daily) and Valencia (€13.35 to €15.30, 2½ to three hours, three or four daily).

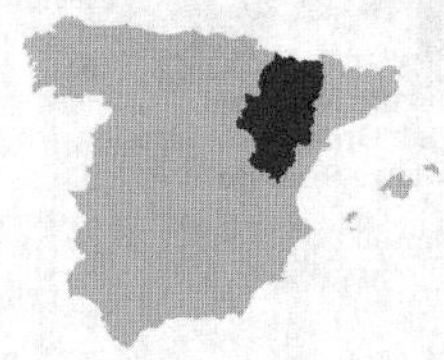

Aragón

Includes ➡

Best Places to Eat

- ➡ Casa Pardina (p436)
- ➡ Restaurante Callizo (p430)
- ➡ La Tasca de Ana (p423)
- ➡ Restaurante Gaby (p419)
- ➡ La Torre del Salvador (p441)

Best Places to Stay

- ➡ Hotel Barosse (p423)
- ➡ La Casa del Tío Americano (p443)
- ➡ Hotel Los Siete Reyes (p429)
- ➡ Parador de Sos del Rey Católico (p417)
- ➡ Hotel Sauce (p408)

Why Go?

Probably Spain's most underrated region, Aragón offers riches wherever you travel, from the crusader-like castles and Romanesque churches of the north to the outstanding Mudéjar architecture of Teruel in the south. The regional capital, Zaragoza, is a major Spanish city of ebullient nightlife and absorbing culture (not least the work of local artistic genius Francisco de Goya), while dozens of picturesque medieval villages dot the serrated landscape, from pink-hued Albarracín to stone-clothed Sos del Rey Católico. But above all, what sets Aragón apart is the majesty of the central Pyrenees along its northern fringe. This is the highest and, for many, most beautiful section of the mighty mountain range – a rare delight for the eyes and a massive natural adventure playground with not only Spain's finest hiking and climbing but also much of its best skiing, canyoning, rafting and paragliding.

When to Go

Zaragoza

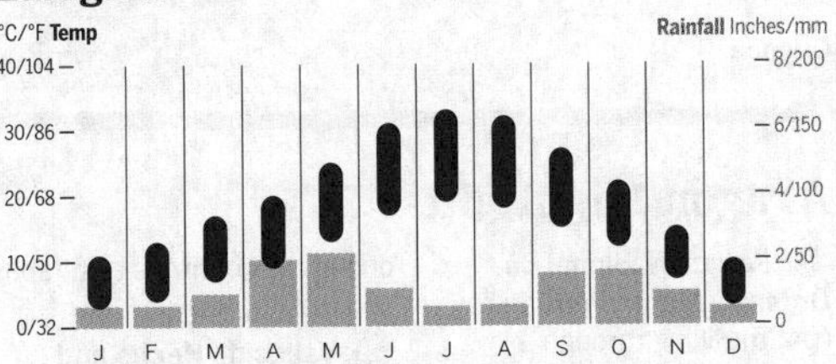

May–Jun & Sep–Oct Best temperatures for enjoying Zaragoza and the rest of lowland Aragón.

Jun–Oct The best months for hiking in the spectacular Aragón Pyrenees.

Oct Zaragoza's Fiestas del Pilar combine the sacred with the city's famed love of revelry.

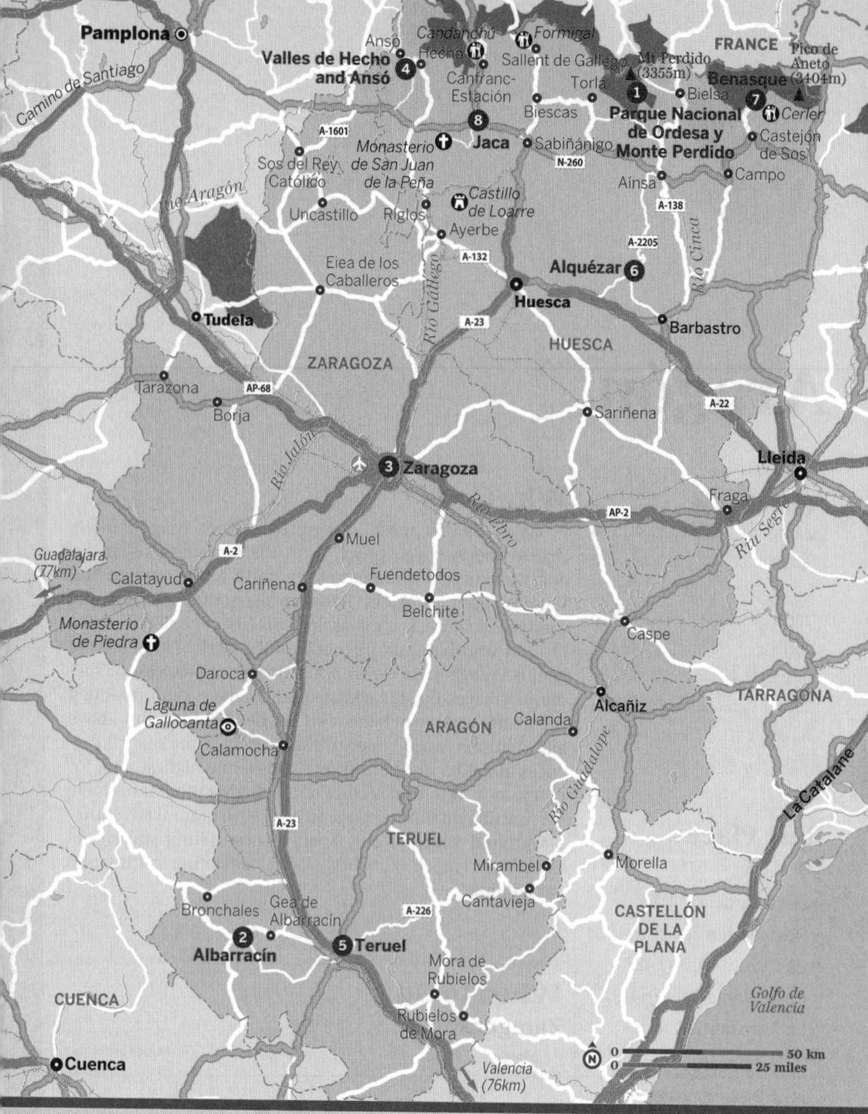

Aragón Highlights

❶ **Parque Nacional de Ordesa y Monte Perdido** (p425) Hiking through spectacular mountainscapes in the Pyrenees.

❷ **Albarracín** (p442) Exploring this village's pink-hued houses and medieval history.

❸ **Zaragoza** (p405) Discovering monuments and one of the country's best tapas and bar scenes.

❹ **Valles de Hecho and Ansó** (p418) Meandering through Pyrenean valleys of forests and ancient villages.

❺ **Teruel** (p438) Admiring the superb Mudéjar architecture and fine eating in the provincial capital.

❻ **Alquézar** (p433) Plunging down canyons and rambling along quaint village streets.

❼ **Benasque** (p430) Getting outdoorsy around this stone village, the gateway to the Pyrenees' highest peaks.

❽ **Jaca** (p422) Enjoying some top tapas bars in this lively Pyrenees gateway town.

History

Aragón came into existence as a tiny Christian bridgehead on the southern flank of the Pyrenees after the Muslim invasion of the Iberian Peninsula in the 8th century. Over the following centuries it grew into one of the strongest kingdoms on the peninsula as it expanded southward and then, in 1137, was united by royal betrothal with the neighbouring county of Barcelona (the combined kingdom-county is known as the Crown of Aragón). It was the marriage of the future Aragonese king Fernando II to his powerful Castilian counterpart Isabel in 1469 that effectively gave birth to modern Spain as we know it.

ZARAGOZA

POP 661,000 / ELEV 200M

The ethereal image of the multi-domed Basílica del Pilar reflected in the Río Ebro is a potent symbol of Zaragoza, one of Spain's most underrated regional capitals. There's plenty more fine architecture here too, including a turreted castle with an interior like a mini-Alhambra, and some very creatively displayed underground Roman remains, but Zaragoza's appeal goes well beyond its monuments. Spain's fifth-largest city (and home to more than half of Aragón's 1.3 million residents), it has one the best tapas and bar scenes in the country and is well stocked with the epoch-defining art of local lad Francisco de Goya, the genius painter who was born a short horse ride away in 1746.

The historic centre (between the Río Ebro, Calle del Coso and Avenida César Augusto) is refreshingly almost traffic-free, including the vast, 400m-long Plaza del Pilar alongside the famous basilica.

History

The Romans founded Caesaraugusta (from which 'Zaragoza' is derived) in 14 BC. As many as 25,000 people migrated to the city whose river traffic brought the known world to the banks of Río Ebro. The city prospered for almost three centuries, but its subsequent decline was confirmed in AD 472 when the city fell to the Visigoths. In Islamic times, Zaragoza was capital of the Upper March, one of Al-Andalus' frontier territories. In 1118, it fell to Alfonso I, ruler of the expanding Christian kingdom of Aragón, and immediately became Aragón's capital. In the centuries that followed, Zaragoza grew into one of inland Spain's most important economic and cultural hubs and a city popular with Catholic pilgrims. It is now Spain's fifth-largest city and, since the 2008 Expo, has greatly improved its modern infrastructure.

Sights

★Basílica de Nuestra Señora del Pilar CHURCH

(www.basilicadelpilar.es; Plaza del Pilar; 6.45am-8.30pm Mon-Sat, 6.45am-9.30pm Sun) Brace yourself for this great baroque cavern of Catholicism. The faithful believe that here on 2 January AD 40, the Virgin Mary appeared to Santiago (St James the Apostle) atop a *pilar* (pillar) of jasper, and left the pillar behind as testimony of her visit. A chapel was built around the pillar, followed by a series of ever more grandiose churches, culminating in the enormous basilica.

A **lift** (Torre; adult/child €3/free; 10am-2pm & 4-8pm Apr-Oct, to 6pm Nov-Mar) whisks you most of the way up the basilica's northwest tower from where you climb to a superb viewpoint over the domes and city.

Originally designed in 1681 by local architect Felipe Sánchez y Herrera, the basilica was greatly modified in the 18th century by the royal architect Ventura Rodríguez, who added the ultra-baroque **Santa Capilla** at the east end (housing the legendary pillar), and the flurry of 10 colourfully tiled mini-domes that surround the main dome on the roof.

FOLLOW THE GOYA TRAIL

Francisco José de Goya y Lucientes, better known simply as Goya, was born in Aragón and his work can be seen all over his native region.

- Museo Goya – Colección Ibercaja (p407), Zaragoza
- Casa Natal de Goya (p412), Fuendetodos
- Museo del Grabado de Goya (p412), Fuendetodos
- Museo de Zaragoza (p408), Zaragoza
- Museo de Huesca (p414), Huesca
- Basílica de Nuestra Señora del Pilar, Zaragoza

Zaragoza

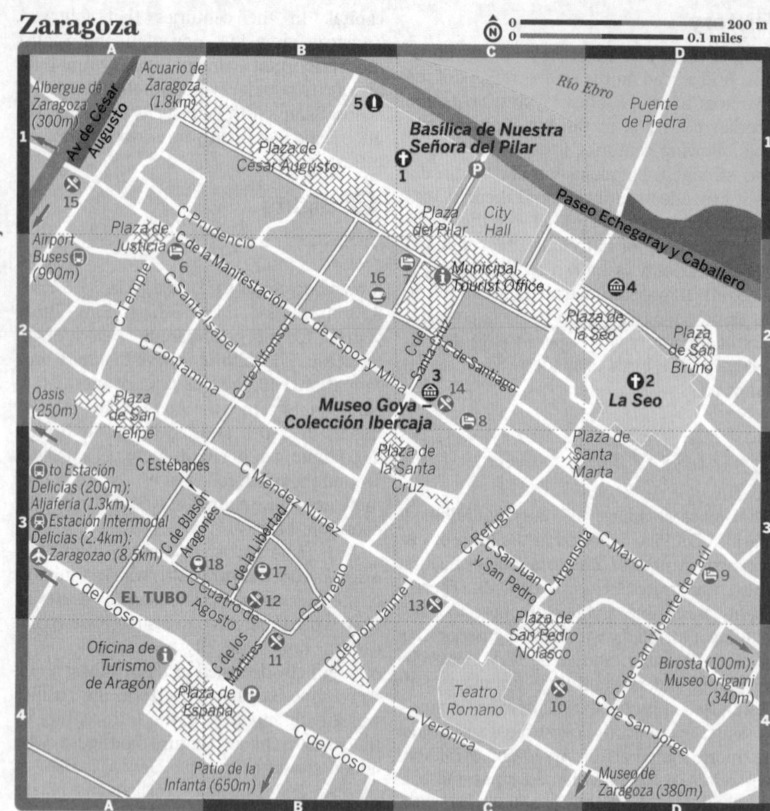

The famous **pillar** is topped by a 15th-century Gothic sculpture of the Virgin and child, and is concealed inside an elaborate silver casing which is itself usually three-quarters hidden by the long mantle in which the Virgin image is dressed (except on the 2nd, 12th and 20th of each month). A tiny oval-shaped portion of the pillar is exposed in the passage on the chapel's outer west side and a steady stream of people line up to brush lips with its polished and cracked cheek, which even popes have air-kissed. Parents also line up from 1.30pm to 2pm and 6.30pm to 7.30pm to have their babies blessed next to the Virgin. More than the architecture, these sacred symbols, and the devotion they inspire, are what make this church special.

Hung from the northeast column of the Santa Capilla are two shells that were lobbed at the church during the civil war. They failed to explode. A miracle, said the faithful; typical Czech munitions, said the more cynical.

The basilica's finest artwork is the 16th-century alabaster **retablo mayor** (main altarpiece) by Damián Forment, facing west in the middle of the basilica. There are also two Goyas: *La Adoración del Nombre del Dios,* on the ceiling of the *coreto* (small choir) at the church's far east end, is an early classical piece from 1772; vastly different is *Regina Martirum* painted above the north aisle in 1780 (in the third cupola from the east). With its blurry impressionistic figures, it was hugely controversial at the time.

★La Seo CATHEDRAL

(Catedral de San Salvador; ☎976 29 12 31; www.zaragozaturismo.es; Plaza de la Seo; adult/senior/child €4/3/free; ⏲10am-6.30pm & 7.45-9pm Mon-Thu, 10am-6.30pm Fri, 10am-noon, 3-6.30pm & 7.45-9pm Sat & Sun mid-Jun–mid-Oct, 10am-2pm & 4-6.30pm mid-Oct–mid-Jun) Dominating

Zaragoza

Top Sights
1 Basílica de Nuestra Señora del Pilar ... C1
2 La Seo ... D2
3 Museo Goya – Colección Ibercaja ... C2

Sights
4 Alma Mater Museum ... D2
5 Lift ... B1
Museo de Tapices ... (see 2)

Sleeping
6 Catalonia El Pilar ... A2
7 Hotel Pilar Plaza ... C2
8 Hotel Sauce ... C2
9 The Bridge ... D3

Eating
10 Café Nolasco ... C4
11 Casa Lac ... B4
12 El Limpia ... B3
13 La Clandestina Café ... C3
14 Los Xarmientos ... C2
15 Mercado Central ... A1

Drinking & Nightlife
16 Café Botánico ... B2
17 Libertad 6.8 ... B3
18 Rock & Blues Café ... A3

the eastern end of Plaza del Pilar, La Seo is Zaragoza's finest work of Christian architecture, built between the 12th and 17th centuries and displaying a fabulous spread of styles from Romanesque to baroque. It stands on the site of Islamic Zaragoza's main mosque (which itself stood upon the temple of the Roman forum). The admission price includes La Seo's **Museo de Tapices** (open same hours as the cathedral), a collection of Flemish and French tapestries considered the best of its kind in the world.

The cathedral's northeast external wall is a Mudéjar masterpiece, deploying classic brickwork and colourful ceramic decoration in complex geometric patterns. Inside, beautiful fan vaulting adorns the ceiling while the chapels, framed by encrusted stonework, ring the changes from the eerie solemnity of the **Capilla de San Marcos** to the golden baroque baldachin of the **Capilla del Santo Cristo**. The exquisite 15th-century alabaster **high altarpiece** is well worth scrutiny too.

Alma Mater Museum MUSEUM
(☎976 39 94 88; www.almamatermuseum.com; Plaza de la Seo 5; €3; ⏲10am-8pm Tue-Sat, 10am-2pm Sun) Church museums can sometimes be boring emporiums of anonymous sacred art, but not this one. Slick multimedia exhibits set an arty tone, which is continued as you navigate through a skilfully laid-out trajectory that takes in the older elements of the building (a former royal and episcopal palace), learning about Roman forums, the venerated Virgen del Pilar and Aragonese history (especially church history). The top floor is a Renaissance feast with paintings by the two local Franciscos: Goya and Bayeu.

★Museo Goya – Colección Ibercaja MUSEUM
(☎976 39 73 87; http://museogoya.ibercaja.es; Calle de Espoz y Mina 23; adult/senior & child €4/free, audio guide or tablet €2; ⏲10am-8pm Mon-Sat, 10am-2pm Sun Apr-Oct, 10am-2pm & 4pm-8pm Mon-Sat, 10am-2pm Sun Nov-Mar) Apart from Madrid's Museo del Prado, this exceedingly well-laid-out museum contains arguably the best exposé of the work of one of Spain's most revered artists. Each of the three floors has a different focus, the 2nd floor being the one that exhibits Goya's own work. Four complete sets of his prints are included, most notably the ground-breaking, sometimes grotesque *Desastres de la Guerra* (Disasters of War), a bitter attack on the cruelty and folly of war.

★Aljafería PALACE
(☎976 28 96 83; www.cortesaragon.es; Calle de los Diputados; adult/student & senior/child €5/1/free, Sun free; ⏲10am-2pm & 4.30-8pm Apr-Oct, 10am-2pm & 4-6.30pm Nov-Mar) The Aljafería is Spain's finest Islamic-era edifice outside Andalucía. Built as a fortified palace for Zaragoza's Islamic rulers in the 11th century, it underwent various alterations after 1118 when Zaragoza passed into Christian hands. In the 1490s the Reyes Católicos (Catholic Monarchs), Fernando and Isabel, tacked on their own palace. From the 1590s the Aljafería was developed into more of a fortress than a palace. Twentieth-century restorations brought it back to life, and Aragón's regional parliament has been housed here since 1987.

Inside the main gate, cross the rather dull introductory courtyard into the **Patio de Santa Isabel**, once the central courtyard of the Islamic palace. Here you encounter the delicate interwoven arches typical of the

RESERVATIONS

Aragón has a full sweep of accommodation from boutique B&Bs and luxury *paradores* to hostels, campgrounds, mountain refuges, *hostales* (budget hotels), tourist apartments and *casas rurales* (rural houses with rooms for tourists). In the Pyrenees, you'll generally find some accommodation in or around even the smallest villages.

Reservations are advisable for all kinds of accommodation in July and August and during other major holiday periods such as Semana Santa and local festivals. Some mountain refuges get booked up three months ahead for these times: for reservations see www.alberguesyrefugiosdearagon.com.

geometric mastery of Islamic architecture. Opening off the stunning northern portico is a small, octagonal **oratorio** (prayer room) with a superb horseshoe-arched doorway leading into its *mihrab* (prayer niche indicating the direction of Mecca). The finely chiselled floral motifs, Arabic inscriptions from the Quran and a pleasingly simple cupola are fine examples of Islamic art.

Moving upstairs, you pass through rooms of the **Palacio Cristiano Medieval**, created mostly by Aragonese monarchs in the 14th century, followed by the **Palacio de los Reyes Católicos** (Catholic Monarchs' Palace) which, as though by way of riposte to the Islamic finery beneath it, contains some exquisite Mudéjar coffered ceilings, especially in the lavish **Salón del Trono** (Throne Room).

Spanish-language tours take place several times a day, and there are two daily tours each in English and French in July and August. The palace is often closed Thursday, Friday morning or Sunday afternoon in non-peak times.

Museo Origami MUSEUM

(876 03 45 69; www.emoz.es; Centro de Historias, Plaza San Agustín 2; adult/student & senior €3/2; 10am-2pm & 5-9pm Tue-Sat, 10am-2.30pm Sun;) This museum devoted to the art of folding paper has six galleries of permanent and temporary exhibitions of a staggeringly high standard. It attracts worldwide interest from origami aficionados. If you're not very familiar with the art, you will probably be amazed by what you see.

Museo de Zaragoza MUSEUM

(www.museodezaragoza.es; Plaza de los Sitios 6; 10am-2pm & 5-8pm Tue-Sat, 10am-2pm Sun) FREE Devoted to archaeology and fine arts, the city museum displays artefacts from prehistoric to Islamic times, with some exceptional mosaics from Roman Caesaraugusta. The upper floor contains 19 paintings by Goya and more than two dozen of his prints. It's 400m south of the Teatro Romano.

Festivals & Events

★Fiestas del Pilar RELIGIOUS

(Oct) Zaragoza's biggest event is a week of full-on celebrations (religious and otherwise). Festivities peak on 12 October, the Día de Nuestra Señora del Pilar, when a veritable mountain of flowers is piled up around the Virgin's image from the basilica, brought out on to Plaza del Pilar, by hundreds of thousands of devotees, many in colourful regional or national dress.

Sleeping

★Hotel Sauce HOTEL €

(976 20 50 50; www.hotelsauce.com; Calle de Espoz y Mina 33; s €43-49, d €46-70;) This stylish small hotel with a great central location is a superb option not just for its fresh, cheerful, contemporary rooms with tasteful watercolours, but also for its outstandingly friendly and helpful staff, pleasant 24-hour cafe serving excellent breakfasts, cakes and cocktails – and not least for its prices, which are very reasonable given everything that the hotel provides.

The Bridge HOSTAL €

(627 307932; www.thebridgerooms.es; Calle de San Vicente de Paul 30; s €36-45, d €38-60;) New in 2017, the Bridge has a friendly, hostel-like atmosphere, though at research time all rooms were private (a small dorm and a kitchen were due to be added). The dozen or so rooms have pleasing, bright, practical but stylish design, tea/coffee makers, minibars, and individual welcome messages. The cheaper doubles share toilets but have their own shower and washbasin.

Albergue de Zaragoza HOSTEL €

(976 28 20 43; http://behostels.com; Calle Predicadores 70; incl breakfast dm €16-18, d/tr with shared bathroom €35/45;) This large, popular hostel offers the choice of neat, clean, small private rooms or mixed dorms for four to 10 people with metal bunks. All share clean bathrooms. The special feature here is the

brick-vaulted basement, known as La Bóveda, where varied live music (with a bar) happens a couple of times a week.

Hotel Pilar Plaza HOTEL €€

(☎976 39 42 50; www.hotelpilarplaza.es; Plaza del Pilar 11; s €57-72, d €60-75, breakfast €9;) The Goya museum might be around the corner, but this basilica-facing hotel prefers to exhibit edgier art by the likes of Banksy (a copy of his *Girl with a Balloon* decorates the staircase). The 50 rooms are stylish, comfy, shiny and almost boutique-ish in whites, blacks and greys, with a few more ornate touch such as chandeliers.

Catalonia El Pilar HOTEL €€

(☎976 20 58 58; www.hoteles-catalonia.com; Calle de la Manifestación 16; s/d from €72/78, breakfast €14;) Ten out of 10 for the facade, a handsome Modernista construction that has been artfully renovated to house this eminently comfortable contemporary hotel. Inside, rooms are spacious and decorated in restful, muted earth tones with elegant marble-clad bathrooms. Some of the beds are king-size.

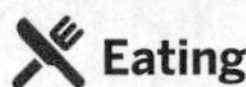

Eating

Head to the quadrangle of lanes known as El Tubo, north of Plaza de España, for one of Spain's richest gatherings of tapas bars. This is a quintessential Zaragoza experience and a bubbling scene any night of the year. Just wander round and see what takes your fancy: many bar staff speak English and/or French.

Café Nolasco CAFE €

(www.facebook.com/cafenolasco; Calle San Jorge 18; breakfast items & cakes €2.50-4.50, set menus Mon-Fri €11, Sat €15; ⏲8.30am-11pm Mon-Thu, 8.30am-2.30am Fri, 10.30am-2.30am Sat, 10.30am-11pm Sun;) This stylish, clean-lined spot, overlooking a pretty old-town plaza and with a wall of plants in the front room, fulfils many roles – it's great for breakfasts, tasty lunches, evening drinks in a club/lounge atmosphere, and coffee and wi-fi with tempting cakes any time of day!

Birosta VEGETARIAN €

(www.birosta.com; Calle Universidad 3; dishes €5-9; ⏲11am-11pm Tue-Sat Sep-Jul, from 6.30pm Aug;) Birosta is an excellent, cooperatively run vegetarian restaurant-cafe-bar with, like

CAESARAUGUSTA – A CITY UNDERGROUND

Underneath modern Zaragoza's streets lies a parallel universe little known to unversed outsiders. It tells the story of Caesaraugusta, the Roman city founded in 14 BC that flourished as one of Hispania's most illustrious and strategically important colonies.

Left to rot as medieval Zaragoza grew up around it, Caesaraugusta lay buried and forgotten for more than 1500 years. Not until the 1980s and 90s were its crumbled remnants resuscitated – and given new life in a brilliant quartet of museums. Hidden in four subterranean exhibition spaces are the **Museo del Foro de Caesaraugusta** (☎976 72 12 21; www.zaragozaturismo.es; Plaza de la Seo 2; adult/student/senior & child €3/2/free; ⏲10am-2pm & 5-9pm Tue-Sat, 10am-2.30pm Sun), the excavated substructures of the Roman city's forum; the **Museo del Puerto Fluvial** (Plaza de San Bruno 8; adult/student/senior & child €3/2/free; ⏲10am-2pm & 5-9pm Tue-Sat, 10am-2.30pm Sun), erstwhile river port installations; the **Museo de las Termas Públicas** (Roman Baths; Calle San Juan y San Pedro 3-7; adult/student/senior & child €3/2/free; ⏲10am-2pm & 5-9pm Tue-Sat, 10am-2.30pm Sun), public baths; and – best of all – the **Museo del Teatro de Caesaraugusta** (☎976 72 60 75; www.zaragozaturismo.es; Calle de San Jorge 12; adult/student/senior & child €4/3/free; ⏲10am-2pm & 5-9pm Tue-Sat, 10am-2.30pm Sun), showcasing a 6000-seat theatre that was one of the largest in Hispania.

While the ruins might be, well, 'ruins' compared to better preserved Roman sites in Mérida and Tarragona, the genius of Zaragoza's museums lies in their layout and creative extras. Well-curated exhibition chambers combine mock-ups of how things used to look with clever multimedia exhibits. The pièce de résistance is the Roman theatre, protected by a huge polycarbonate roof and perhaps best viewed through panoramic windows from its adjacent museum.

A joint ticket is available for all four museums (adult/student/child €7/5/free) and is a fantastic investment. Situated in close proximity to each other, the museums can all easily be visited in the same day.

WHAT'S COOKING IN ARAGÓN?

The kitchens and tables of Aragón are dominated by meat, which may come in inventive combination with other ingredients in numerous gastro establishments, or in good old-fashioned grilled, roast or stewed form in more traditional restaurants.

The region's cold, harsh winds create the ideal conditions for curing *jamón* (ham), a top tapa here; some of the best comes from the Teruel area, which has its own DO (Denominación de Origen; quality-certified producing region). Hearty *ternasco* (suckling lamb) is generally served roasted or as ribs with potatoes – a good place to try it is **Los Xarmientos** in Zaragoza.

Aragón's local cheeses, 130 varieties of them, should be tried wherever you go – those of Albarracín, Tronchón and Benasque are among the most highly rated.

With France just up the road, it's no surprise, perhaps, that *caracoles* (snails) are another Aragonese speciality. Try them!

The Aragonese love their baked goods too: anywhere from Zaragoza northwards, look out for *trenza de Almudévar*, a long, bread-like cake made from flour, egg yolks, butter, almonds, walnuts and raisins, with its strands woven together like plaits *(trenzas)*.

Vegetarians should seek out *alubias pochas* (a tasty white-bean stew with peppers, tomatoes and onion) – one place you'll find it is **La Cocina del Principal** (p418) in Sos del Rey Católico. Plant-based eaters might be tempted to base their entire holiday at **Posada Magoría** (p420), a rare vegan guesthouse, in the Pyrenees village of Ansó.

most of the Magdalena *barrio* (neighbourhood) in which it's situated, an alternative, animal-rights, ecological vibe. Lunch is served in the neat, green-and-white dining room from 1.30pm to 4pm, and dinner from 8.30pm. Dishes range from pizza, moussaka or dolmades to rice, tofu and pasta offerings, all well prepared and presented.

El Limpia TAPAS €

(Calle Cuatro de Agosto 17; raciones €5-16; noon-4pm & 8pm-midnight Wed-Sun) A tightly squeezed hubbub of a bar where you place your order then wait for the barman's bellow to tell you it's ready. The *papapico* (minced pork and potatoes in a spicy *mojo picón* sauce) is celebrated, but there's plenty more on offer including wild-mushroom risotto, *tablas* (boards) of ham and/or cheese, or *tostadas* (topped toast slices) of wild-boar pâté.

Los Xarmientos ARAGONESE €€

(976 29 90 48; www.facebook.com/xarmientos; Calle de Espoz y Mina 25; mains €12-16, set menus €15-27; 1.30-4pm & 8.30-11.30pm Wed-Sat, 1.30-4pm Tue & Sun) Aragonese meat dishes are a speciality at this artfully designed restaurant. It styles itself as a *parrilla*, meaning the dishes are cooked on a barbecue-style grill. It's a fine place to sample the local *ternasco* (lamb), Aragon's most emblematic dish, accompanied by a good Somontano wine and perhaps preceded by a spinach and goat's-cheese salad…or even some snails?

Casa Lac TAPAS €€

(976 39 61 96; www.restaurantecasalac.es; Calle de los Mártires 12; mains €16-27, tapas €1.50-7, set menus €30-41; 1-4pm & 8pm-midnight Mon-Sat, 1-4pm Sun) The grande dame of Zaragoza dining, Casa Lac opened in 1825 and is reputedly Spain's oldest licensed restaurant. The cuisine today is tastily contemporary whether you go for 'gastro-tapas', a set menu or à la carte. The ground-floor bar is smart but relatively casual; an elegant staircase leads to the more formal upstairs dining room.

La Clandestina Café CAFE €€

(876 28 11 65; Calle San Jorge 4; brunch €15, light dishes €6-15; 10am-midnight Tue-Fri, from 11am Sat & Sun;) There's an eye-catching huge pair of red lips painted on one white brick wall, but this place is as much about gastronomy as style, particularly in the brunch (11.30am to 3.30pm, includes a glass of *cava*) and coffee-and-cake departments. It's a popular cocktail spot too – and the cold-pressed juices (including an orange-lime-lemon-ginger combo) are divine on a hot day.

Drinking & Entertainment

After the tapas bars close around midnight, late-night and music bars come into their own. There's a good scattering of these in the historic centre. You can find live music somewhere almost any night except perhaps in quieter July and August. Pick up the free what's-on guide *Go!* (www.laguiago.com).

Café Botánico CAFE

(Calle de Santiago 5; ⌚9am-10.30pm Sun-Wed, 9am-11.30pm Thu, 9am-3am Fri & Sat; 📶) Café Botánico combines a florist with a greenery-decked cafe serving great coffee, teas, *tostadas* (toast slices with various toppings), cocktails and some truly delicious cakes. Thanks in part to its central location, it is perennially popular.

Rock & Blues Café BAR

(Calle Cuatro de Agosto 5-7; ⌚4pm-2am) Rock 'n' roll paraphernalia, paying homage to the likes of Jimi Hendrix and the Beatles, set the tone for the music and style of this long-standing favourite. There's live pop, rock or blues most Thursdays, Fridays and Sundays around 9.30pm. It's a popular and atmospheric spot.

Oasis CLUB

(☎976 43 95 34; www.salaoasis.es; Calle de Boggiero 28; cover from €6; ⌚midnight-6am Fri & Sat) A few streets west of the old centre, Oasis began life long ago as a variety theatre. It's currently going strong as a club and is a top place to carry on partying after the bars quieten down around 3am or 4am. It also hosts occasional live concerts and theme parties.

Libertad 6.8 BAR

(www.facebook.com/libertad.terraza; Calle de la Libertad 6-8; ⌚8pm-1am Tue-Thu, 1pm-2am Fri & Sat, 1-6pm Sun & Mon) A fashionable, half-open-air space situated in El Tubo serving 20 types of gin and plenty of other cocktails. The bar also offers meals.

ℹ Information

Municipal Tourist Office (☎976 20 12 00; www.zaragozaturismo.es; Plaza del Pilar; ⌚10am-8pm; 📶) Has branch offices around town, including at the train station.

Oficina de Turismo de Aragón (☎976 28 21 81; www.turismodearagon.com; Plaza de España 1; ⌚9.30am-2.30pm & 4.30-7.30pm) Helpful place with plenty of brochures covering all of Aragón.

ℹ Getting There & Away

Trains and buses share the futuristic **Estación Intermodal Delicias** (Avenida de Navarra 80), 3km west of the city centre.

AIR

Zaragoza Airport (☎976 71 23 00; www.zaragoza-airport.com), 10km west of the city, has Ryanair (www.ryanair.com) flights to/from London (Stansted), Brussels (Charleroi), Milan (Bergamo) and Paris (Beauvais, March to October).

BUS

Dozens of bus lines fan out across Aragón and Spain from the **bus station** (☎976 70 05 99; www.estacion-zaragoza.es) in the Estación Intermodal Delicias.

Alosa (☎974 21 07 00; www.avanzabus.com) Runs 14 or more daily buses to Huesca (€7.80, 1¼ hours) and six or more to Jaca (€16, 2½ hours).

ALSA (☎902 422242; www.alsa.es) Buses to/from Madrid (from €16, three to four hours, 19 or more daily) and Barcelona (from €16, 3¾ hours, 16 or more daily).

Autobuses Jiménez (www.autobusesjimenez.com) Four or more daily buses to Teruel (€11, 2¼ hours).

Conda (www.conda.es) Eight or nine daily buses to Pamplona (€16, two to 2½ hours).

WORTH A TRIP

THE CIVIL WAR RUINS OF BELCHITE

The haunting remains of Belchite village, 45km southeast of Zaragoza, which was reduced to ruins in a fierce civil war battle in 1937, were left unreconstructed after the war. The **Pueblo Viejo de Belchite** (Belchite Old Village; Belchite; tour €6) ruins are now fenced off but popular guided tours (in Spanish, with English, French and German audio guides available) are given two or three times daily by the **Belchite tourist office** (☎976 83 07 71; http://belchite.es; Calle Becú, Pueblo Nuevo de Belchite; ⌚10am-1pm & 3-6pm Sep-Jun, 10am-2pm & 4-7pm Jul & Aug), next to the church in Belchite's new village nearby. At any time you can view the ruins from outside the fence.

The battle of Belchite in August 1937 saw the Republicans drive out the Nationalists from the village, with thousands killed. The Nationalists later retook Belchite (and won the war). They ordered that the village be left in its ruined state and had a new village built by Republican prisoners next door. The ruins include four churches from the 18th century or earlier (two of them attached to convents and one of which little remains except its Mudéjar clock tower).

TRAIN

Renfe (☎91 232 03 20; www.renfe.com) runs trains all over Spain from the **Estación Intermodal Delicias** (Avenida de Navarra 80). Around 20 daily high-speed AVE services whizz to Madrid (€21 to €55, 1½ hours) and Barcelona (€23 to €60, 1¾ hours). Further direct AVE services head to Seville (€59 to €68, 3¾ hours, two or three daily) and Huesca (€9 to €15, 45 minutes, one or two daily). Some slower, mostly cheaper trains also serve Barcelona, Madrid and Huesca. Two or three Huesca trains continue to Jaca (€15, 3¼ hours) and Canfranc-Estación (€16, four hours) in the Pyrenees. Four daily trains run to Teruel (€15 to €20, 2½ hours).

Getting Around

BUS

Bus 501 (☎902 30 60 65) runs between Paseo María Agustín 7 and the airport (€1.85, 45 minutes) via Delicias station every half-hour (hourly on Sunday).

Bus 34 (€1.35) runs from the Estación Intermodal Delicias to Avenida César Augusto near the **Mercado Central** (Central Market; Avenida de César Augusto; ⏲9am-2pm & 5-8pm Mon-Fri, 9am-2pm Sat). To return to the station, catch it westbound on **Calle Conde Aranda** about 100m west of César Augusto.

BICYCLE

Zaragoza is flat and has a good network of bike lanes and streets with speed limits of 30kph. You can rent bikes at **La Ciclería** (☎876 16 73 56; http://lacicleria.com; Calle Gavín 6; per 2/4/8/24/48hr €6/8/12/15/22; ⏲9am-2pm & 5-10pm Mon-Fri, 10am-10pm Sat, 10am-5pm Sun Sep-Jul, 10am-2pm & 5-9pm Mon-Sat, 10am-8pm Sun Aug) and **Bicicletas La Pomada** (Zaragoza en Bici; ☎876 03 62 69; www.lapomadabikestore.com; Calle Manifestación 17; per 2/5/12hr €5/6/15 Mon-Fri, €5/6/18 Sat; ⏲9am-2pm & 4.30-8.30pm Mon-Fri, 10am-2pm Sat).

CENTRAL ARAGÓN

Central Aragón is dominated by the flat valley of the Río Ebro, which meanders across the region west to east. Outside Zaragoza, the main settlements of interest lie to the west (principally Tarazona) and south. Most of the towns here fell to the Christian armies later than those in the north, meaning you'll spot a heavier sprinkling of Mudéjar architecture. This is also Goya country: he was born in the village of Fuendetodos (45km south of Zaragoza), where you can visit his birthplace and a museum with collections of his prints.

Fuendetodos

POP 125

Casa Natal de Goya MUSEUM

(www.fundacionfuendetodosgoya.org; Plaza de Goya; incl Museo del Grabado de Goya adult/student & senior/child €3/2/free; ⏲11am-2pm & 4-7pm Tue-Sun) This humble birthplace of Goya was owned by his family until the early 20th century, when it was purchased by the Basque painter Ignacio Zuloaga. Destroyed during the civil war, the house was subsequently restored with furniture and exhibits relating to Goya's life and times.

Inside, you can view the austere 18th-century kitchen, the room where Goya was born in 1746, and a large wall display illustrating his family tree.

In a house located next door, the Sala Zuloaga (admission is included in the ticket price) has temporary exhibitions of mainly graphic art.

Museo del Grabado de Goya MUSEUM

(www.fundacionfuendetodosgoya.org; Calle Zuloaga 3; incl Casa Natal de Goya adult/student & senior/child €3/2/free; ⏲11am-2pm & 4-7pm Tue-Sun) Situated just one hundred metres along the street from Goya's birthplace, this museum contains an important collection of the artist's engravings. There are four series, including the famously satirical *Los Caprichos* and the bullfighting-themed *La Tauromaquia*.

Getting There & Away

One or two buses daily head to Fuendetodos (€6.75, one hour) from Zaragoza.

Tarazona

POP 10,330 / ELEV 480M

A pleasant stop or detour between Zaragoza and the Basque Country or Castilla y León, Tarazona rewards the curious with an intriguing earth-toned labyrinth of an old town (that has a medieval Jewish quarter in its midst) situated above the little Río Queiles, a large and fascinating Gothic and Mudéjar cathedral, and the bizarre Cipotegato festival, when a brave local dressed as a harlequin gets pelted with tomatoes by boisterous crowds every August.

Sights

★Catedral Santa María de la Huerta CATHEDRAL
(www.catedraldetarazona.es; Plaza de la Seo; adult/student & senior/child €4/3/free; ⏲11am-2pm & 4-7pm Tue-Sat, to 6pm Sun Apr-Sep, 11am-2pm & 4-6pm Wed-Fri, to 7pm Sat, to 2pm Sun Oct-Mar) This magnificent cathedral dates from the 13th century but was much modified in later centuries. It reopened in 2011 after 30 years of restoration work (still ongoing), which has uncovered previously hidden treasures. The cathedral's French-Gothic origins are evident in the vaulting and pointed arches of the nave; Mudéjar influences permeate the intricate masonry of the tower and dome; Renaissance artwork adorns the Capilla Mayor; and the baldachin over the exterior main portal is a flight of baroque fancy.

Ayuntamiento ARCHITECTURE
(Town Hall; Plaza de España) The town hall's 16th-century facade is a storybook of sculpture. The larger carvings depict mythical beings (you'll spot Hercules on the left). Running along the full 35m length is a frieze of hundreds of miniature mounted and walking figures, showing the parade for the papal coronation of Spanish King Carlos I as Holy Roman Emperor in Bologna in 1530.

Palacio Episcopal PALACE
(Bishop's Palace; Plaza Palacio; adult/child €1.50/free; ⏲11.30am-2.30pm & 4.30-7.30pm Tue-Sat, 11.30am-2.30pm & 4.30-6.30pm Sun Apr-Sep, 11.30am-2.30pm Wed-Fri & Sun, 11.30am-2.30pm & 4.30-7.30pm Sat Oct-Mar) FREE On the site of a Muslim citadel and, subsequently, the residence of several Aragonese kings, the imposing Bishop's Palace was completed in the mid-16th century after well over a century of construction.

The exterior has a striking series of perfectly proportioned arches, while highlights within include a pretty Renaissance patio, an outstanding series of 16th-century episcopal portraits and a magnificent Mudéjar coffered ceiling (two more Mudéjar ceilings are missing – purchased by William Randolph Hearst for his California 'castle' in the early 20th century).

Judería AREA
Tarazona has one of Spain's best preserved Jewish quarters, overlooked by the *casas colgadas* (hanging houses) of Calle Conde, which jut out over the streets below. While there are no monuments to visit as such, you can take an informed stroll around the Judería with the aid of a map from the tourist office and/or explanatory boards *in situ*.

More than 70 Jewish families lived here from the 12th to the 15th centuries, in a tight web of streets around Calle Judería and Rúa Alta de Bécquer.

Festivals & Events

Cipotegato CULTURAL
(⏲27 Aug) In a country known for its bizarre festivals, Tarazona's Cipotegato takes the weirdness to a new level. The star of the show is a hapless harlequin dressed in red, green and yellow, who emerges from Ayuntamiento at noon on 27 August and runs through the streets while getting pelted with tomatoes by practically everyone in town.

Sleeping & Eating

Hostal Santa Águeda HOSTAL €
(☎976 64 00 54; www.santaagueda.com; Calle Visconti 26; incl breakfast s €41-50, d €54-63; ❄📶) Just off Plaza San Francisco, this 200-year-old home has attractive old-style rooms with wooden beams and a cheery decor. The little breakfast room and the lobby are a glorious

WORTH A TRIP

THE DIY FRESCO

The small town of Borja, 23km southeast of Tarazona, attracted worldwide attention in 2012 after an 81-year-old amateur artist botched the restoration of a 20th-century religious painting called *Ecce Homo* in a nearby church. The result (subsequently dubbed 'potato Jesus') went viral on the internet and, ironically, has brought the area a welcome boom in tourism. Visitors still flock to view the painting, which has been reproduced on advertising banners and copied by pop artists. Potato Jesus aside, the 15th-century shrine where the painting resides, **Santuario de la Misericordia** (La Muela Alta de Borja; €2; ⏲11am-2pm & 4.30-8pm Apr-Sep, 10.30am-1.30pm & 3.30-7pm Oct-Mar), is located on a pleasant hillside perch 6km northwest of Borja. While there you can look into the adjoining **El Caserón**, a 16th-century hostel for visitors to the shrine, and pick up an *Ecce Homo* T-shirt or jigsaw – or even a bottle of *Ecce Homo* wine (DO Campo de Borja).

shrine to local girl Raquel Meller, Aragón's queen of popular song during the early 20th century. You'll hear her crooning over your croissants.

Hotel Condes de Visconti HOTEL €€
(☎976 64 49 08; www.condesdevisconti.com; Calle Visconti 15; r €59-69, ste €79-110;) Beautiful rooms, mostly with colourful individual decor, plus a preserved Renaissance patio, make this 16th-century former palace a fine stopover. It also has a cafe and good old-fashioned service. Breakfast costs €5.50.

Saboya 21 ARAGONESE €€
(☎976 64 24 90; www.restaurantesaboya21.com; Calle Marrodán 34; mains €14-20; ⊙1-4pm Sun-Thu, 1-4pm & 9.30-11pm Fri & Sat;) Talented chef José Tazueco whips up a selection of culinary treats that zap traditional ingredients with a creative flair. Expect artistically presented dishes such as duck breast with liquorice or endives with smoked salmon, kefir and dill. It's perched above the busy Cafetería Amadeo I. Reservations recommended.

Information

Tourist Office (☎976 64 00 74; www.tarazona.es; Plaza San Francisco 1; tours €5-8; ⊙9.30am-2.30pm & 4-7pm Apr-Sep, 9.30am-2pm & 4-7pm Mon-Sat, 10am-6pm Sun Oct-Mar) Offers guided tours of the historic centre and main monuments, in Spanish, on Saturdays and Sundays.

Getting There & Away

Five or more **Therpasa** (☎976 30 00 45; www.therpasa.es) buses run daily to/from Zaragoza (€7.90, 1½ hours) and Soria (€5.90, 1¼ hours).

THE ARAGÓN PYRENEES

As you leave behind central Aragón's parched flatlands, a hint of green tinges the landscape and there's a growing anticipation of very big mountains somewhere up ahead. The Aragonese Pyrenees reach well over the 3000m mark and, together with their counterparts on the French side, form the heart of the range, with much of its most magnificent scenery. Viewed from the south, their crenellated ridges fill the northern horizon wherever you turn. The verdant river valleys are dotted with charming old stone-built villages, and the whole region forms a giant adventure playground to which Spaniards, and French neighbours – but surprisingly few other foreigners – flock not only for the wonderful walking but also for a host of other exciting activities from climbing and skiing to white-water rafting and canyoning.

Huesca

POP 51,450 / ELEV 465M

The hard-working provincial capital of Huesca doesn't delay most travellers too long, but while here you can blow the dust off Spain's oldest grocery store, visit a multifarious museum juxtaposing Goya prints with a medieval royal palace, and take an eye-opening lesson in Gothic and Romanesque architecture courtesy of two outstanding churches.

Sights

★**Iglesia de San Pedro El Viejo** CHURCH
(www.sanpedroelviejo.com; Plaza de San Pedro; adult/child €2.50/1.50; ⊙10am-1.30pm & 4.30-6pm Mon-Sat, 11am-12.15pm & 1-2pm Sun) The church of San Pedro is one of the oldest and most important Romanesque structures in Spain, dating from the early 12th century. It's particularly notable for its hexagonal tower, its open cloister adorned with 38 beautifully carved Romanesque capitals (in some cases 19th-century copies), and the mausoleum containing the tombs of two Aragonese kings (and brothers), Alfonso 1 (r 1104–34) and Ramiro II (r 1134–37).

Catedral de Santa María CATHEDRAL
(www.museo.diocesisdehuesca.org; Plaza de la Catedral; adult/senior & student/child €4/2/free; ⊙10.30am-2pm & 4-7pm Mon-Sat) This Gothic cathedral is one of Aragón's great surprises. The richly carved main portal dates from 1300, the attached **Museo Diocesano** contains some extraordinary frescos and painted altarpieces, and the stately interior features a superb, 16th-century alabaster *retablo* (altarpiece) by Damián Forment showing scenes from Christ's crucifixion. To round off your visit, climb the 180 steps of the **bell tower** for 360-degree views all the way to the Pyrenees.

Museo de Huesca MUSEUM
(Plaza Universidad 1; ⊙10am-2pm & 5-8pm Tue-Sat, 10am-2pm Sun) FREE The city museum with its pretty courtyard contains a well-displayed collection covering the archaeology of Huesca province, and progressing on to early modern art, including eight works by Goya. The museum also incorporates a 12th-century Aragonese royal palace, one

chamber of which (now with suitably spooky sound-effects) is believed to have been the scene of a gruesome episode known as La Campana de Huesca (Bell of Huesca), in which King Ramiro II had 13 uncooperative nobles decapitated.

Sleeping & Eating

La Posada de la Luna BOUTIQUE HOTEL €
(974 24 17 38; www.posadadelaluna.com; Calle Joaquín Costa 10; s €46-51, d €46-60;) This attractive little eight-room hotel achieves a whimsical contemporary yet historical effect, juxtaposing century-old floor tiles and antique-style murals with designer bathrooms and hydromassage showers, in rooms themed on different celestial bodies. It's a comfortable place with a degree of charm, although some rooms are on the small side.

Hostal Joaquín Costa HOSTAL €
(Hostal Un Punto Chic; 974 24 17 74; www.hostaljoaquincosta.com; Calle Joaquín Costa 20; s €37-51, d €42-66;) The well-kept rooms are of the white-and-black minimalist school, in some cases enlivened by pleasing murals and/or encouraging inscriptions (eg Kipling's *If*, in Spanish, engraved on the glass shower wall). Bathrooms are good and modern; rooms are smallish or medium-sized; and it's a convenient and comfy place to stay.

★**Tatau Bistro** TAPAS €€
(974 04 20 78; www.tatau.es; Calle Azara; dishes €5-25; 1-3.30pm & 8-10.45pm Tue-Sat;) This hugely popular central gastro-bar has a unique style with besuited staff, 1950s-inspired decor with framed pin-ups and posters, and tapas-bar-style seating at a few tables or along the bar. The seasonally changing menu of very tasty offerings ranges from the small and relatively simple (meat croquettes) to the more ambitious likes of duck with pears and liquorice or octopus-and-aubergine cannelloni.

El Origen ARAGONESE €€
(974 22 97 45; Plaza del Justicia 4; set menus €17-40; 1.15-3.30pm & 9-11pm Mon, Tue & Thu-Sat, 1.15-3.30pm Sun) Ignore the inauspicious setting on this somewhat drab modern square as this restaurant is an oasis of elegance and fine dining, with set menus that vary from traditional Aragonese to more innovative and contemporary. Sustainable produce is used as far as possible. Reservations recommended.

Information

Tourist Office (974 29 21 70; www.huescaturismo.com; Plaza López Allué 1; 9am-2pm & 4-8pm) Excellent office providing information on all of Aragón; it runs tours of Huesca's historic centre (adult/senior and student/child €5/2.50/free) daily from July until mid-September, and on weekends at other times.

Getting There & Away

BUS

From the **Estación Intermodal** (Calle Gil Cávez 10), **Alosa** (974 21 07 00; www.avanzabus.com) runs buses to/from Zaragoza (€7.80, 1¼ hours, 14 or more daily), Jaca (€7.80, 1¼ hours, six daily), Barbastro (€4.60, 50 minutes, six or more daily), Barcelona (€17, four hours, five daily) and Benasque (€13, 2¾ hours, once on Sunday, twice other days).

TRAIN

Six to eight trains a day run to/from Zaragoza: one or two are high-speed AVE services (from €7.85, 40 minutes), continuing to/from Madrid (from €22, 2¼ hours); the rest are regional trains (€7.15, one to 1¼ hours). There are two or three regional trains to/from Jaca (€8.25, 2¼ hours) and Canfranc-Estación (€11, 2¾ hours).

WORTH A TRIP

THE CASTILLO DE LOARRE

The agricultural village of Loarre, 30km northwest of Huesca, is famous for one reason – the **Castillo de Loarre** (www.castillodeloarre.es; adult/senior or student/child €4.50/4/3; 10am-8pm Jun-Sep, 10am-7pm Mar-May & Oct, 11am-5.30pm Tue-Sun Nov-Feb), a multi-towered Reconquista-era castle looming on the hillside a 5km drive (or 2km uphill walk) above the village.

The 11th-century fortress, reminiscent of a crusader castle, was raised by Sancho III of Navarra and expanded by Sancho Ramírez of Aragón. There's plenty to see, including a Romanesque chapel and crypt, and you can climb to the upper levels of the two main towers.

If you want to stay, there's a hotel in a 16th-century building on the village's central square, and a popular campground halfway between village and castle.

One or two Alosa buses link Loarre with Huesca (€3.05, 40 minutes) Monday to Friday. Timings don't enable a one-day return trip from Huesca, however.

Riglos & Around

POP (RIGLOS) 80 / ELEV (RIGLOS) 650M

Little Riglos, 43km northwest of Huesca, sits at the foot of **Los Mallos de Riglos**, a set of awe-inspiring rock towers that dwarf the village and wouldn't look out of place in the Grand Canyon. Los Mallos are a popular challenge for serious rock climbers – and popular too with large numbers of huge griffon vultures.

For those who prefer to keep their feet on non-vertical terrain, a circular walk of about 2½ hours, the **Camino del Cielo**, takes you around the top side of Los Mallos from Riglos.

The village of **Murillo de Gállego** on the A132, 2.5km southwest of Riglos across the Río Gállego (10km by road or a 45-minute walk), is a busy centre for rafting and kayaking beneath the gaze of Los Mallos. Several companies offer half-day trips (per person from €40) from March to September.

There are several *casas rurales* (rural houses adapted for tourist accommodation) and *hostales* in both villages, plus a year-round climbers' hostel in Riglos.

Riglos is on the Zaragoza–Canfranc rail line, between Huesca (€3.65, one hour) and Jaca (€5.45, 1¼ hours), with one northbound train in the morning and one southbound in the late afternoon. A car offers far more flexibility in these parts.

Centro de Interpretación de Aves Arcaz BIRDWATCHING
(☎974 56 19 10; www.vultouris.net; Riglos; adult/child €2/1; ⏲10am-2pm & 3-7.30pm Wed-Sun Jun-Sep, 10am-2pm & 4-6pm Sat & Sun Apr-May & Oct) A 1km walk or drive south of Riglos, this centre has good displays and information on the vultures of the Pyrenees region, and a great observation deck for viewing Los Mallos' large colony of huge griffon vultures.

Sos del Rey Católico

POP 500 / ELEV 625M

If King Fernando II of Aragon were reincarnated in the 21st century, he'd probably still recognise his modest birthplace in Sos del Rey Católico. Take away the motor vehicles and summer tourist crowds, and outwardly not a huge amount has changed in this small, tightly packed hilltop village since 1452 when the future husband of Isabel of Castile and king of a united Spain was born in the Sada palace. Legend has it that Fernando's mother travelled 14km on horseback from Sangüesa in Navarra while already in labour, purely to ensure her son was born Aragonese.

Royalty aside, Sos is a fine place to soak up the feel of an old Aragonese village. When you've finished having historical hallucinations in its labyrinthine streets, you can investigate the network of mossy walking paths that dissolve into the surrounding countryside.

Sights

Casa Palacio de Sada HISTORIC BUILDING
(Plaza de la Hispanidad; adult/child €2.90/1.90; ⏲10am-1pm & 4-7pm Mon-Fri, 10am-2pm & 4-7pm Sat & Sun, closed Mon Sep-Jun) Fernando II of Aragón was born in this building in 1452. It's an impressive mansion – more so now than in Fernando's time, following a major expansion around 1600 and restoration in the 20th century. The rooms contain Spanish-language information panels on Fernando's highly eventful and historically significant life, plus a few models. Also here is the **Capilla de San Martín de Tours** where an audiovisual on Sos's history and the chapel's own 14th-century Gothic murals is shown.

Iglesia de San Esteban CHURCH
(€1; ⏲10am-1pm & 3.30-5.30pm Mon-Sat, 10am-noon Sun) This Romanesque-Gothic church, with a weathered Romanesque portal, has a deliciously gloomy crypt decorated with medieval frescos.

Castillo de la Peña Feliciano CASTLE
The 12th-century keep and some of the walls are all that still stand of the castle that once guarded the frontier between the two Christian kingdoms of Aragón and Navarra. Climb up for views over the village roofs and the countryside in all directions.

Sleeping

Hostal Las Coronas HOSTAL €
(☎948 88 84 08; www.hostallascoronas.com; Calle Pons Sorolla 2; s/d incl breakfast €40/60; ❄📶) Run by friendly Fernando, this *hostal* has modest, rustic rooms. Try for No 3 with its spa shower and balcony overlooking Sos' hauntingly hemmed-in plaza. The popular ground-floor bar serves tapas, *bocadillos* (€3.50 to €6), *raciones* (€3 to €22), *platos combinados* (€12.50 to €18.50) and your included breakfast to a refreshing classical soundtrack.

★Parador de Sos del Rey Católico HOTEL €€

(☎948 88 80 11; www.parador.es; Calle Arquitecto Sainz de Vicuña 1; r €64-156; ⊙mid-Feb–Dec; P❄📶) Though not a historic building (it was erected in the 1970s), Sos's *parador* is well in harmony with the town's architecture and provides all the expected *parador* services and comforts. You can hole up with a book, sink sangrías on the restaurant terrace, or just lie back and enjoy the views from your suitably regal bedroom. There's an excellent restaurant (set menus €30 to €38) serving a changing menu of regional specialities.

Ruta del Tiempo BOUTIQUE HOTEL €€

(☎948 88 82 95; www.rutadeltiempo.es; Plaza de la Villa; incl breakfast s €50, d €70-110; ❄📶) Evocatively located under the arches of the central plaza, rooms on the 1st floor are themed around three Aragonese kings connected with Sos, while the four 2nd-floor rooms have decorations dedicated to four different continents. They're all good, but spacious 'Asia' and 'Africa' are the best.

El Peirón BOUTIQUE HOTEL €€

(☎948 88 82 83; www.elpeiron.com; Calle Fernando el Católico 24; s from €75, d €85-140; ⊙Mar-Dec; ❄📶) Family-run El Peirón is an appealing mix of thick stone walls, wrought iron, period decor (including some original 16th- and 17th-century doors and furnishings), contemporary art, colour feature walls and ample bathrooms. It has 14 rooms, including two suites set in one of the old town gates, the Puerta de Zaragoza.

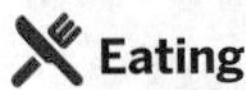

Eating

Landa Terraza SPANISH €€

(Calle Fernando el Católico 37; dishes €5.50-8.50, set menus €13; ⊙9am-midnight) Straightforward food at very good prices, served with good humour, packs in the punters to this smallish bar and its bright open-air terrace. You could enjoy a *ración* or *media ración* of eggs and ham, or the *longaniza* sausage served with *setas* (wild mushrooms), or opt for a quick *bocadillo* or the good-value *menú del día.*

ACTIVE ADVENTURES IN THE PYRENEES

With its wild and varied terrain, Aragón is Spain's natural adventure playground. The high point, literally, is the breathtaking Aragonese Pyrenees, arguably the wildest and most stunning section of the Pyrenees either side of the Spanish–French border. There are plenty of chances to get up close and personal with the peaks and passes, with rock climbing (including a growing number of vie ferrate), mountain trails and snowy slopes promising year-round scope for adrenaline-charged outdoor activities.

Serious hikers can also embark on all or parts of the famous coast-to-coast GR11 long-distance trail, while folk who prefer a more gentle Sunday-morning-style stroll can head for the foothills in places such as the awe-inspiring Parque Nacional de Ordesa y Monte Perdido with its waterfalls, crystal streams and limestone cliffs and canyons. Water-sports fans can take the plunge with white-water rafting, kayaking and canoeing on the Gállego and Ésera rivers; and canyon lovers can slide, jump and abseil down gorges around Alquézar and elsewhere. Paragliders can take to the air around Castejón de Sos, while Aínsa is the perfect base for mountain biking. After your exertions, picturesque stone villages throughout the region ensure that R&R (and refreshments) are never too far away.

Montaña Segura (www.montanasegura.com) has a great deal of useful info about walks and climbs in Aragón's mountains. Much of it is only in Spanish, but the 'Folletos' (Leaflets) section has information on walking routes in English and French, too.

Birdwatching

This is one of the best regions in Europe for raptors, and birdwatchers flock here to catch a glimpse of red and black kites; Egyptian, griffon, and threatened lammergeier vultures; and, among the highest peaks, that majestic king of all birds: the golden eagle. Even non-enthusiasts will be thrilled by vulture-viewing at the Garganta de Escuaín (p426) or the Centro de Interpretación de Aves Arcaz at Riglos.

Turismo de Aragón, the regional tourism body, has detailed information on 16 *rutas ornitológicas* spread all over Aragón (www.turismodearagon.com/es/naturaleza.html). Tourist offices around the region will also help, and birders can also check www.birdingpirineos.com (for northwest Aragón) and www.aragonbirding.com.

La Cocina del Principal ARAGONESE €€

(☎948 88 83 48; www.lacocinadelprincipal.es; Calle Fernando el Católico 13; mains €17-26; ⏰1.30-3.30pm & 8.30-10.30pm Tue-Sat Mar-Nov, by reservation Dec-Feb) Generally hailed as the best food in town, this place wins plaudits for its roast *ternasco* (suckling lamb), barbecued beef tenderloin and pigs' trotters. It's set down steps that seem to be leading to a basement cellar but reveal a stone-walled dining room with a panoramic terrace outside, enhanced by some interesting art.

Information

Tourist Office (☎948 88 85 24; www.oficinaturismososdelreycatolico.com; Plaza Hispanidad; tours adult/child €4.40/1.90, incl Palacio de Sada €6.40/2.90; ⏰10am-1pm & 4-7pm Mon-Fri, 10am-2pm & 4-7pm Sat & Sun, closed Mon Sep-Jun) Housed in the Palacio de Sada, the tourist office runs two or three Spanish-language guided tours of the village daily.

Getting There & Away

An **Autobuses Cinco Villas** (☎976 66 09 80; www.autobusescincovillas.com) bus leaves Sos for Zaragoza (€11, 2½ hours) at 7am Monday to Friday, returning at 5pm.

Valles de Hecho & Ansó

These enchanting parallel valleys, tucked away in Aragón's far northwest corner, run up through dense mixed woodlands, punctuated by a few ancient stone-built villages, between crags of increasing height and drama, where raptors circle high above, to end at the main Pyrenean ridge along the French border. Flowing south from these mountains, the Río Aragón Subordán and, a few kilometres to its west, the Río Veral have carved out the Hecho (Echo) and Ansó valleys. Little known to non-Spaniards, the valleys and their surrounding mountains are a paradise for walkers, with rivers, lakes, gorges and waterfalls, as well as spectacular mountain scenery and plentiful accommodation. The upper parts of the valleys are part of the 270-sq-km Parque Natural de los Valles Occidentales.

Activities

There are endless walking options here on well-marked trails among gorgeous scenery – everything from one-hour strolls to long-day peak ascents or multi-day hiking tours. Weather is never predictable, but June to October are generally the best months for hiking. The top goals for peak baggers are Bisaurín (2670m), Castiello d'Acher (2384m) and Meseta d'os Tres Rais (Mesa de los Tres Reyes; 2448m), each a round-trip hike of seven hours or more (1200m to 1300m of ascent and descent) from the nearest roadhead.

The 1:25,000 map *Valles Occidentales Ansó-Echo*, published by Prames, is excellent.

Local tourist offices have some printed route information, and there are route descriptions and data in Spanish, with maps, at www.rutasvalledehecho.com, www.montanasegura.com and http://senderosturisticos.turismodearagon.com.

Getting There & Around

The good A176 road heads up to Hecho and Ansó villages (13km apart) from Puente la Reina on the N240. Lesser but adequate roads head up the valleys, paved as far as Selva da Oza in the Valle de Hecho and Zuriza in the Valle de Ansó.

A bus to Hecho (€3.50, 1¼ hours), continuing to Siresa and Ansó, leaves Jaca bus station at 6.20pm Monday to Thursday and Saturday (7.40pm Friday, and Monday to Saturday in July and August; no bus Sundays). It starts back from Ansó at 6.30am Monday to Saturday, stopping in Siresa at 6.50am and Hecho at 7am.

Hecho

POP 590 / ELEV 820M

There probably isn't a more pleasant spot from which to launch sorties into the Pyrenees than humble Hecho (Echo), an attractive warren of solid stone houses with steep roofs, tall chimneys and flower-decked balconies.

Museo de Arte Contemporáneo SCULPTURE

(www.valledehecho.es; Carretera de Oza) FREE Thanks to an international art symposium held here annually from 1975 to 1984, Hecho is endowed with a large collection of contemporary sculpture and painting from that epoch. More than 40 sculptures, mostly in stone, stand behind the tourist office building and elsewhere around the village. Inside the tourist office (and viewable when the office is open) is a collection of 26 paintings and nine wooden sculptures.

Val d'Echo Activa ADVENTURE SPORTS

(☎974 37 54 21; www.valdechoactiva.com; Carretera de Oza 2; half-day per person €40-45) This Hecho-based firm offers exciting canyoning in the Boca del Infierno gorge, and vie ferrate (climbing routes equipped with steel steps, ladders and cables) in the Selva de Oza and elsewhere (minimum three or four people).

Casa Blasquico HOSTAL €

(974 37 50 07; www.casablasquico.es; Plaza La Fuente 1; d €55-60, tr €75; Mar-Dec;) The best place to stay in town, family-run Casa Blasquico has just seven rooms, so it's a good idea to book ahead. With its flower boxes, gables, floral-pattern textiles and woody decor, it might have been plucked straight out of the Swiss Alps.

★ **Restaurante Gaby** ARAGONESE €€

(974 37 50 07; www.casablasquico.es; Plaza La Fuente 1; mains €12-19; 1.30-3.30pm & 8.30-10pm, Mar-Dec;) The restaurant in Casa Blasquico is a delightful place to eat, with an intimate wood-beamed dining room plus a small outside terrace overlooking a cobbled plaza. It offers uncomplicated mountain fare with top-class ingredients expertly prepared: the wild mushroom crêpes, duck confit and beef entrecôte are all great choices. There's an extensive wine list too. Reservations highly advisable.

Restaurante Canteré SPANISH €€

(974 37 52 14; www.cantere.es; Calle Aire 1; mains €14-23, set menus €21; 1.30-3.30pm & 8.30-10.30pm Jul-Sep, 1.30-1.30pm Thu-Tue Oct-Jun) First-class creative preparation of classic ingredients and welcoming service in a bright, contemporary-style dining room are the secrets of success here. The four-course *menú* is too tempting to overlook: the numerous options might include carrot soup with coconut foam, beef entrecôte, or hake with mushrooms *au gratin* – and you can try every starter and dessert on offer if you like!

Information

Tourist Office (974 37 55 05, town hall 974 37 50 02; www.valledehecho.es; Carretera de Oza; 10am-1.30pm & 5.30-8pm Jul–mid-Sep, 10am-1.30pm & 4.30-7pm Sat & Sun mid-Sep–Jun)

Siresa

POP 125 / ELEV 870M

The tiny and captivating village of Siresa, a couple of kilometres north of Hecho, is where medieval Christian Aragón got its start in life.

Iglesia de San Pedro CHURCH

(€2; 11am-1pm & 5-8pm Jul-Sep, Sat & Sun only Oct-Jun) This thick-walled church, Siresa's centrepiece, was founded in the 9th century as part of a monastery that was, in its early years, the hub of the nascent County of Aragón. It was rebuilt in Romanesque style in the 11th century, and restored in the 13th century and more recently in the 1990s. Artworks inside include a wonderful Gothic crucifixion sculpture in polychromed wood, discovered during the 1990s restoration.

Hotel Usón HOTEL €

(974 37 53 58; www.hoteluson.com; Carretera Selva de Oza, Km 7; s €40-50, d €50-70, apt €75-85; Mar-Oct;) Cosy rooms in peaceful, wonderfully scenic surroundings are what you'll find here, 5km north of Siresa on the road to the Selva de Oza. A good base for walkers and birdwatchers, the Usón has a restaurant serving decent home-style meals (breakfast/dinner €7/17), and the superb Pirineos Bier craft beer is brewed right here on the spot.

Hotel Castillo d'Acher HOTEL €

(974 37 53 13; www.castillodacher.com; Plaza Mayor; s/d/tr/q €35/55/65/75;) This stone-built hotel has pleasant rooms, pine-furnished and relatively modern. The owners also offer holiday apartments in the village for weekend or longer stays. The in-house restaurant does a hearty *menú del día* (set menu) for €15.

Selva de Oza

The top end of the Valle de Hecho is particularly beautiful; the increasingly rutted road runs parallel to the Río Aragón Subordán as it bubbles its way through thick woodlands. Around 7km beyond Siresa, the road squeezes through the **Boca del Infierno** (Hell's Mouth), emerging about 3km further on in the particularly dense and beautiful forests of the Selva de Oza. From here the road continues another 3km, unpaved, to the junction of valleys and paths known as **A Mina**.

Day hikes starting from A Mina include the trails up to **Puerto del Palo** pass on the French border, following the course of a Roman road across the Pyrenees (about five hours round trip; 750m ascent and descent); to the mountain lake **Ibón d'Acherito** (four to five hours round trip; 660m ascent and descent); and to **Ibón d'Estanés** lake via **Aguas Tuertas** meadows. For this last you can drive 4.5km east from A Mina to shorten the walk to about 3½ hours each way (600m ascent and descent).

An easier, shorter hike of around 3½ hours (520m of ascent and descent) is the circuit round Boca del Infierno gorge in the Hecho valley from Puen de Santana bridge, which includes another stretch of the same Roman road.

SKIING ARAGÓN

Aragón is one of Spain's premier skiing destinations, with the season in the Pyrenees running from December to mid-April. The following are the major ski stations:

Candanchú (974 37 31 94; www.candanchu.com;) About 30km north of Jaca (a possible base), Candanchú offers some 60km of varied pistes and a nice alpine village feel. A favourite with families as well as experts, it's one of Spain's less expensive ski stations.

Astún (974 37 30 88; www.astun.com) The Pyrenees' newest resort, purpose-built (and rather ugly) Astún is 3km from Candanchú, with which it shares ski passes and a shuttle service. It has 40km of pistes, for a wide range of standards.

Panticosa (974 48 72 48; www.formigal-panticosa.com;) The smallest of Aragón's five Pyrenees resorts, and an antidote to the bigger Formigal nearby, village-based Panticosa has mostly red and blue pistes.

Formigal (974 49 00 00; www.formigal-panticosa.com) High in the Valle de Tena north of Sabiñánigo, Formigal is Aragón's largest ski resort, with 137km of varied pistes in four different valleys. It has good modern facilities and a relatively lively après-ski scene.

Cerler (974 55 10 12; www.cerler.com) This well-equipped resort is closely connected with the town of Benasque and thus enjoys tons of eating, sleeping and après-ski options. Especially good for intermediate and beginner skiers, it has 81km of pistes.

Bosque de Oza ADVENTURE SPORTS
(974 37 54 21; http://bosquedeoza.com; adult/child €18/16; 11am-7pm Jun-Aug, Sat & Sun only Mar-May, Sep & Oct;) Great for kids, this activity park among the Selva de Oza trees comprises eight circuits of ziplines, aerial climbing/crawling nets, ropeways, walkways and Tibetan bridges – a good two to three hours' fun.

Camping Selva de Oza CAMPGROUND €
(974 56 55 15; http://camping-selvadeoza.com; adult/tent/car €6/6/5.50, s/d/tr/q incl breakfast from €35/60/95/110;) Reopened and revamped in 2017 after being closed for more than 20 years, this campground has a lovely riverside site, a good car-free tent area under the trees, a restaurant, a bar and seven decent pine-panelled rooms with well-sprung beds.

Ansó

POP 410 / ELEV 840M

Ansó's grid of narrow streets, lined by neatly trimmed stone houses, sits above the east bank of the Río Veral, surrounded in all directions by beautiful mountain and forest vistas. The two focal points for your wanderings are the compact main square, Plaza Domingo Miral, and the surprisingly large 16th-century Iglesia de San Pedro.

Posada Magoría CASA RURAL €
(974 37 00 49; http://posadamagoria.com; Calle Milagros 32; d €55-60;) Just below the church, delightful Posada Magoría is crammed with vintage character and lovingly kept by a family with lots of local knowledge. The kitchen cooks up excellent vegan meals (dinner €10 to €16, breakfast €6), largely sourced from their own organic garden, and served at a long communal table. There's good organic wine to go with dinner too.

Hostal Kimboa HOSTAL €
(650 987837; www.hostalkimboa.com; Paseo Chapitel 24; s/d incl breakfast €45/55, incl half-board Jul & Aug €50/85; Semana Santa-Oct;) A welcoming family-owned *hostal* towards the top of the village, with pleasant pine-furnished rooms above a good restaurant specialising in traditional grilled meats (*menús* €15 to €35), plus a popular bar with outside terrace.

Maiberal ARAGONESE €
(974 37 01 74; www.restaurantemaiberal.es; Calle Arrigo 1; mains €8-14, set menus €17-27; 11am-4.30pm & 7-10.30pm Mon-Fri, 10am-10.30pm Sat-Sun mid-Jun–Jul & Sep, 10am-10.30pm Aug, 11am-4.30pm & 7-10.30pm Fri, 10am-10.30pm Sat-Sun Oct–mid-Jun) A friendly, authentic place serving delicious dishes like vegetable-stuffed lamb, tagliatelle with courgette, shrimp and mushroom sauce, or stewed venison in a raspberry-and-wine sauce. There are also delectable tapas (€1.20), *tostas* (toasts with toppings), burgers, salads and *huevos rotos* (broken fried eggs) with sausage or ham.

Information

Tourist Office (974 37 02 25; www.turismoanso.es; Plaza Domingo Miral; 10am-1pm & 5-8pm Jul & Aug, Sat & Sun only May, Jun & Sep)

Valle de Zuriza

Beyond the Foz Veral gorge, situated 11km north of Ansó village, the Ansó valley widens out into what's called the Valle de Zuriza, a beautiful area of pastures, woodlands and rivers, where a few minor roads and some fine walking trails, including the GR11, meet.

From Camping Zuriza it's a fine walk of about three hours each way up to the **Cuello Petraficha** pass and back, with about 750m of ascent and descent. The serrated ridge of the Sierra d'Alano is your companion to the south much of the way. A bit more demanding is the ascent of **Achar d'Alano** (2078m; about seven hours round trip; 845m of ascent and descent). You can cut half an hour each way off both these routes by driving the unpaved road as far as A Taxera.

An unpaved road running past Camping Zuriza heads 5km north to the **Refugio de Linza**, one of the refuges of the Senda de Camille circuit and also the starting point for the ascent of **Meseta d'os Tres Rais** (Mesa de los Tres Reyes; 2448m), about seven hours round trip with ascent and descent of 1275m.

Camping Zuriza CAMPGROUND €
(620 879572; www.campingzuriza.es; adult/tent/car €5/5/5, d shared/private bathroom €45/55, bungalow for 2-4 persons €75; Semana Santa-early Oct; P) Parts of the site are quite tightly packed but it offers a range of accommodation options, a simple restaurant, a food shop and superb surroundings at the heart of the valley.

Santa Cruz de la Serós

POP 150 / ELEV 780M

Santa Cruz de la Serós is a pretty, stone-built village spread around the 11th-century Romanesque Iglesia de Santa María, which was originally part of Aragón's earliest convent. The village, 4km south of the N240 west of Jaca, is primarily visited as a gateway to what is, arguably, Aragón's most fascinating monastery – the Monasterio de San Juan de la Peña.

Sights

★Monasterio de San Juan de la Peña MONASTERY
(Old Monastery; www.monasteriosanjuan.com; Monasterio Viejo/incl 1 centre/incl 2 centres adult €7/8.50/12, child €4.50/5/7; 10am-2pm & 3.30-7pm Mar-May, Sep & Oct, 10am-2pm & 3-8pm Jun-Aug, 10am-2pm Sun-Fri, 10am-5pm Sat Nov-Feb; P) The two monasteries of San Juan de la Peña sit high on the rocky Sierra de la Peña above Santa Cruz de la Serós village. A fire in 1675 led the monks to abandon the original 10th-century **Monasterio Viejo** and build a new one, the **Monasterio Nuevo**, higher up the hill. Abandoned by the mid-19th century, these historic monasteries have since been rehabilitated and merit a visit by anyone interested in old architecture and sculpture, history, scenery or wildlife.

The road from Santa Cruz winds 7km up to the Monasterio Viejo, tucked protectively under an overhanging lip of rock at a bend in the road. One of the most important monasteries of medieval Aragón, it contains the tombs of Aragón's first three kings – Ramiro I (1036–64), Sancho Ramírez (1064–94) and Pedro I (1094–1104) – and two churches (the lower one a rare Mozarabic–Romanesque hybrid, the upper one pure Romanesque). But its greatest highlight is the **Romanesque cloister**, with marvellous carved 12th- and 13th-century capitals depicting stories from Genesis and the life of Christ.

The Monasterio Nuevo is a larger, two-towered, brick complex 1.5km further up the road. It hosts the sizable Centro de Interpretación del Monasterio, built over the archaeological remains of ruined parts of the monastery, which has Spanish-language panels on the history of the monasteries and the kingdom of Aragón, as well as a glass floor through which you look down on somewhat cheesy life-sized models of monks and scenes of monastic life. Also here is the Centro de Interpretación del Reino de Aragón in the reconstructed main monastery church, playing a 40-minute audiovisual show about early Aragonese history.

Tickets for both the monasteries are sold at the Monasterio Nuevo and, during the summer (June to August), this is where you'll have to park. A bus shuttles down to the Monasterio Viejo and back every few minutes. Ticket prices depend on how many of the interpretation centres you wish to visit.

Viewpoints & Vultures

From the **Balcón del Pirineo**, a 400m walk north of the Monasterio Nuevo, you have superb vistas of the Pyrenees spread across the horizon and, with luck, some of the local vultures gliding the thermals in front of you.

To find out more about the vultures and the area's natural features, visit the **Centro de Interpretación San Juan de la Peña y Monte Oroel** (974 36 14 76; 10am-2pm & 3-6pm Tue-Sun Jul & Aug, Sat & Sun Apr-Jun & Sep-Nov), next to the Monasterio Nuevo.

Sleeping & Eating

Hostal Santa Cruz HOSTAL €
(974 36 19 75; www.santacruzdelaseros.com; Calle Ordana; s/d/tr incl breakfast €40/60/80;) Beside the church in Santa Cruz de la Serós, this is a beautiful place with friendly service and eight charming rooms, four with balconies overlooking the church. It has a bar where you can get a *bocadillo,* and a restaurant (closed Monday except August) serving meaty dishes such as wild boar ragout and a good *menú del día* (€14).

It closes for a few weeks per year; check the website.

Getting There & Away

There's no public transport to the monastery or even into Santa Cruz de la Serós. For walkers, a stiff 4km marked path leads up from Santa Cruz to the Monasterio Viejo. With an ascent of 350m, it takes about 1½ hours.

Jaca

POP 12,000 / ELEV 820M

A gateway to the western valleys of the Aragonese Pyrenees, Jaca has a compact and attractive old town, dotted with remnants of its past as the 11th-century capital of the nascent Aragón kingdom and a strongpoint in Spain's 16th-century lines of defence against possible French invasion.

Summer tourism in July and August, and après-ski funsters on winter weekends, keep a lively atmosphere going well into the night.

Sights

Catedral de San Pedro CATHEDRAL
(Plaza de la Catedral; 11am-1.30pm & 4.15-8pm) Jaca's 11th-century cathedral is a formidable building, its imposing exterior typical of the sturdy stone architecture of northern Aragón. It was once more gracefully French Romanesque in style, but Gothic and Renaissance additions and alterations in the 15th and 16th centuries bequeathed a hybrid look. The interior retains some fine features, in particular the northwest-corner chapel dedicated to Santa Orosia, the city's patron saint, whose martyrdom is depicted in a series of mysterious murals.

★Museo Diocesano MUSEUM
(www.diocesisdejaca.org; Plaza de la Catedral; adult/senior & student/child €6/4.50/3; 10am-2pm & 4-8.30pm Jul & Aug, 10am-1.30pm & 4-7pm Mon-Sat, 10am-1.30pm Sun Sep-Jun) Jaca's excellent Museo Diocesano (set in rooms surrounding the cathedral cloister and accessed from inside the cathedral) is a kind of mini equivalent of Barcelona's Museu Nacional d'Art de Catalunya. Its speciality is a collection of Romanesque and Gothic art rescued from Jaca diocese churches, and the highlight is a recreation of the church in Bagüés village whose late-11th-century murals amount to one of the finest sets of European Romanesque painting.

Ciudadela FORTRESS
(Citadel; www.ciudadeladejaca.es; Avenida del Primer Viernes de Mayo; adult/senior & student/child €6/5/4, incl Museo de Miniaturas Militares €10/8/5; 10.30am-2.30pm & 4.30-8.30pm Jul-Sep, 11am-2pm & 4-7pm Tue-Sun Oct & Dec-May) Jaca's large, star-shaped citadel, built in the 1590s to defend against a possible French invasion, is one of only two extant pentagonal fortresses in Europe. Visits are by 40-minute guided tour (in Spanish, with information sheets in other languages), hourly during the opening hours.

Museo de Miniaturas Militares MUSEUM
(Museum of Military Miniatures; www.museominiaturasjaca.es; Avenida del Primer Viernes de Mayo, Ciudadela; adult/senior & student/child €6/5/4; 10.30am-2.30pm & 4.30-8.30pm Jul-Sep, 11am-2pm & 4-7pm Tue-Sun Oct & Dec-May) The thought of a model soldier museum might not sound particularly enticing to anyone over the age of 10, but think again. The 3D battle scenes displayed in these interconnecting rooms inside the Ciudadela offer a pictorial history lesson, from neolithic spear-throwers to Franco's fascist tanks.

Festivals & Events

Festival Folklórico de los Pirineos MUSIC, DANCE
(www.festivaljaca.es; Jul/Aug) This folklore festival, held in late July or early August in odd-numbered years, provides a week of local, national and international music, dance and crafts, in several organised venues and on the streets.

Sleeping

Hostal París HOSTAL €
(974 36 10 20; www.hostalparisjaca.com; Plaza de San Pedro 5; s/d with shared bathroom €32/42;) Close to the cathedral, this friendly, central option has high ceilings, creaky, wooden floorboards, spotless, ample-sized rooms and smart, shared bathrooms. Many rooms overlook the square. A minimal breakfast (€3) is available.

Hotel Jaqués HOTEL €€
(974 35 64 24; www.hoteljaques.com; Calle Unión Jaquesa 4; s €40-50, d €60-70;) A solid midrange choice with a faint Regency air to its decor, smart modern bathrooms and a good cafe. It also runs several spick-and-span, recently opened apartment rooms, around the corner in Calle Obispo, at similar prices.

★**Hotel Barosse** BOUTIQUE HOTEL €€€
(974 36 05 82; www.barosse.com; Calle Estiras 4, Barós; incl breakfast s €110-159, d €138-199;) In the quiet hamlet of Barós, 2km south of Jaca, Hotel Barosse has five individually styled rooms with lovely attention to detail, from exposed stone walls and splashes of colour to fine bathroom packages of goodies. A cosy sitting and reading room, pretty garden, spa, honesty bar and fine Pyrenees views all help make this a delightful base for exploring the region.

The owners, José and Gustavo, are wonderful hosts, and prepare terrific dinners (€26 to €28) on request. It's adults only.

Eating

★**La Tasca de Ana** TAPAS €
(Calle de Ramiro I 3; tapas €1.80-3.50, raciones €2.50-14; 12.30-3.30pm & 7.30pm-midnight Jul-Sep, 7-11.30pm Mon-Fri, 12.30-3.30pm & 7-11.30pm Sat & Sun Oct-Jun;) One of Aragón's best tapas bars – hence the crowds – La Tasca has tempting options lined up along the bar, more choices cooked to order and a well-priced list of local wines. Check out its *tapas mas solicitados* (most popular orders) listed on the blackboard. Top contenders include the *tostada* (toast) topped with goat's cheese, *trigueros* (asparagus) and a hard-boiled egg.

★**La Terapia** TAPAS, ARGENTINE €
(649 088874; Calle Mayor 31; tapas & raciones €3-12, mains €8-24; noon-4pm & 7pm-midnight Tue-Sun) Lively Terapia offers varied options for different appetites – traditional tapas or *raciones* of croquettes, ham, sausages or seafood, a variety of salads, fried fish, Argentine meat grills – but arguably the stars of the show are the scrumptious *empanadas* (Argentine pastry pies) with fillings like ham, cheese, tomato and basil, or *setas* (wild mushrooms) with tangy Cabrales cheese.

Restaurante Asador Biarritz ARAGONESE €€
(974 36 16 32; www.restaurantebiarritz.com; Avenida Primer Viernes de Mayo 12; mains €16-28, set menus €15-55; 1-4pm & 8-11pm Thu-Tue) The Biarritz is frequently *completo* (full) with happy eaters enjoying its classic Aragonese cuisine specialising in good grilled meats and fish, its range of set menus at different prices, and its setting on Jaca's leafy main avenue, with a big outdoor section. Reservations advisable.

Information

Tourist Office (974 36 00 98; www.jaca.es; Plaza de San Pedro 11-13; 9am-9pm Mon-Sat, 9am-3pm Sun Jul & Aug, 9am-1.30pm & 4.30-7.30pm Mon-Sat Sep-Jun)

Getting There & Away

From the central **bus station** (974 35 50 60; Plaza Biscós), six or more Alosa (www.avanzabus.com) buses go daily to Huesca (€7.80, 1¼ hours) and Zaragoza (€16, 2½ hours). La Burundesa (www.laburundesa.com) runs one or two daily services to Pamplona (€7.80, 1¾ hours).

Twice-daily trains go south to Huesca (€8.25, two hours) and Zaragoza (€15, 3¼ hours) and north to Canfranc-Estación (€2.80, 35 minutes).

Valle del Aragón

Aragón takes its name from the Río Aragón which runs south from the Pyrenees towards Jaca before veering west to Navarra. The river lent its name to the small Christian county born here in the 8th century AD, and as the county grew into a powerful kingdom it carried the name with it. Today the N330 road runs north up the Valle del Aragón between impressive mountains from Jaca, heading for 1640m-high Puerto de Somport pass on the French border.

Apart from being a route to France's Vallée d'Aspe (with the 8.6km-long Somport tunnel now providing an alternative to the pass), the Valle del Aragón is home to the extraordinary Canfranc train station and the Astún and Candanchú ski resorts (p420), and offers plenty of scenic walks.

There are beautiful summer day walks in side valleys including the Valle de Izas east of Canfranc-Estación; the tourist office has information. Walking right up to the Collado de Izas pass and back is an undertaking of about seven hours with 1000m of ascent and descent, but there are numerous shorter options. (And you can drive the first 2km up an unpaved road as far as the Fuerte de Coll de Ladrones, an abandoned fort.)

Estación Internacional de Canfranc ARCHITECTURE

(Canfranc International Station; Canfranc-Estación) The magnificent Modernista structure of Canfranc station stands as a monument to a trans-Pyrenean railway that has lain idle for nearly 50 years. With its 250m-long main building, the station opened in 1928, housing customs and immigration on the then-new line between Zaragoza and Pau (in France). It saw plenty of traffic until 1970, when a bridge collapsed on the French side, never (as yet) to be repaired – although the two governments are now discussing reopening the line.

Railway nuts and lovers of decaying grandeur will enjoy the 40-minute guided tours (€4) given by **Canfranc tourist office** (☎974 37 31 41; www.canfranc.es; Plaza del Ayuntamiento, Canfranc-Estación; ⊙9am-8pm Jul & Aug, 4.30-7.30pm Tue, 9am-1.30pm & 4.30-7.30pm Wed-Sat, 9am-1.30pm Sun Sep-Jun), which are the only way of getting inside the now sadly dilapidated grand edifice. The tours – in Spanish, with English and French translation available via free audio guide – go at various times daily (except Monday from September to June): check the tourist office website for schedules. Reservations are essential.

ℹ Getting There & Away

The Mancomunidad Alto Valle del Aragón (www.mavaragon.es) runs five daily buses from Jaca bus station to Astún (€2.90, 35 minutes) and back, calling at Canfranc-Estación (€2.05, 20 minutes), Candanchú and the Puerto de Somport.

Two daily trains run to Canfranc-Estación from Zaragoza (€16, four hours) via Huesca (€11, 2¾ hours) and Jaca (€2.80, 35 minutes), and back.

FRANCE

French Nouvelle-Aquitaine regional buses (http://car.aquitaine.fr) run at least four times daily from Canfranc-Estación to Bedous in the Vallée d'Aspe, France (€6.40, one hour), and back, connecting at Bedous with trains to/from Oloron Sainte Marie and Pau. A combined bus-and-train ticket from Canfranc to Pau (2¼ hours) costs €16.

Valle de Tena

The Valle de Tena, watered by the Río Gállego, runs north into the mountains from the town of Sabiñánigo, with the A136 road reaching the Puerto del Portalet pass (1794m), gateway to France's Vallée d'Ossau.

The upper Valle de Tena is home to two ski resorts (p420): Panticosa (small) and Formigal (large, with installations strung up the mountainsides for most of the 6km to the Portalet border). Between the two resorts stands the pretty, and much older, stone-built village of Sallent de Gállego, a good base for hikes. From Panticosa an 8km road winds up through the Garganta del Escalar gorge to the recently modernised Baños de Panticosa hot-springs resort.

Resort Balneario de Panticosa SPA

(☎974 48 71 61; www.panticosa.com; Baños de Panticosa; 30min adult/child €36/12; ⊙noon-8pm Jun-Oct & Christmas-Semana Santa; 👪) There has been a bathhouse here since the 1690s, although 'taking the waters' didn't become truly popular until the mid-19th century. Today the Balneario is a luxurious, recently remodelled spa resort, with two four-star hotels and several restaurants. You don't have to be staying here to enjoy the facilities, and all sorts of circuits, massages, treatments and packages are offered. The main *zona de aguas* (waters zone) includes five different pools, a sauna, Turkish bath, ice igloo, solarium and more.

Respomuso Hike WALKING

A fine day hike, avoiding terrain cluttered with ski installations, follows the well-named Río Aguas Limpias (Clean Waters River) up from Sallent de Gállego to the **Embalse de Respomuso**, a picturesque reservoir at 2200m, surrounded by high peaks. The walk, part of the GR11 long-distance trail, is 12km up from Sallent (about 3½ hours, with 900m of ascent), and 12km back.

You can make it less demanding by driving up to the Asador La Sarra restaurant at the far end of Embalse de la Sarra, which saves about 3.5km and one hour in each direction.

If you'd rather stay up in the mountains, there's dorm accommodation at the **Refugio de Respomuso** (☎974 33 75 56; www.alberguesyrefugiosdearagon.com; Embalse de Respomuso; dm adult/child €17/9, breakfast €6, lunch or dinner €16; ⊙mid-Mar–mid-Dec), though this can be full in busy seasons.

Pirineos Sur CULTURAL
(www.pirineos-sur.es; ⊙Jul) Sallent de Gállego and nearby Lanuza village host this terrific world-music festival, with nightly concerts through the second half of July. Recent editions have featured artists such as flamenco stars Diego El Cigala and Duquende, Puerto Rican rapper Residente and west African musicians Youssou N'Dour and Toumani Diabaté.

Hotel Balaitus HOTEL €
(☎974 48 80 59; http://hotelbalaitus.com; Calle Francia 18, Sallent de Gállego; s €39-52, d €52-76; 📶) An 18th-century building in the centre of Sallent village, the Balaitus has a lot of history and creaking wooden floors to go with it. Rooms are mostly quite prettily decorated, if not large, and there's a cheerful lounge-bar serving *platos combinados, bocadillos* and salads, plus a walled front garden that's great for summer evenings.

Getting There & Away

From Jaca, one or two daily buses wind over to Panticosa village (€5.35, one hour), Sallent de Gállego (€6.25, 1¼ hours) and Formigal (€6.75, 1½ hours). There is also bus service to these villages from Zaragoza and Huesca by Alosa (www.avanzabus.com).

Parque Nacional de Ordesa y Monte Perdido

This is where the Spanish Pyrenees really take your breath away. The park extends south from a dragon's back of limestone peaks along the French border: a southeastward spur from this includes Monte Perdido (3355m), the third-highest peak in the Pyrenees. Deep valleys slice down from the high ground. Most were carved by glaciers and at their heads lie bowl-like glacial *circos* (cirques) backed by spectacular curtain walls of rock. Chief among the valleys are Ordesa (west), Añisclo (south), Escuaín (southeast) and Pineta (east).

The wonderful scenery of plunging canyons, towering cliffs, thick forests, rivers, waterfalls, snow peaks, mountain lakes and high-level glaciers makes this arguably *the* place to head for if you can manage only one destination in the Spanish Pyrenees.

Activities

The Parque Nacional de Ordesa y Monte Perdido is fantastic walking country.

The best weather and walking conditions are generally from mid-June to early September. Lower-level routes are practicable for longer, but once there's snow on the ground, easy paths become difficult and harder ones become dangerous.

It's always advisable to carry a good map such as Editorial Alpina's *Parque Nacional de Ordesa y Monte Perdido* (1:25,000). Park information offices give out diagrams of the park's four sectors (Ordesa, Añisclo, Escuaín and Pineta) with walking route descriptions, and will give further information verbally (most staff speak English and/or other languages as well as Spanish).

★**Cola de Caballo** WALKING
This very popular route heads 8km (with 500m ascent) along the Valle de Ordesa from Pradera de Ordesa, between soaring cliffs and passing numerous waterfalls, to the Circo de Soaso, a rock amphitheatre decorated by the Cola de Caballo (Horsetail) waterfall, where Monte Perdido towers far above. Return the way you came. The 16km round trip takes about 5½ hours plus stops.

★**Faja de Pelay** WALKING
An initially more demanding but more spectacular variation on the standard Cola de Caballo walk. From Pradera de Ordesa you zigzag up the Senda de los Cazadores (Hunters' Path), gaining 600m altitude in a remorseless 1½ hours. Then it's gently downhill almost the whole rest of the way, beginning with a spectacular high-level path leading to the Cola de Caballo waterfall.

From the waterfall, return to Pradera along the main valley path. Total time is about 6½ hours plus stops.

Refugio de Góriz & Monte Perdido WALKING
Fit walkers can climb the Circo de Soaso above the Cola de Caballo by a series of steep switchbacks to reach the Refugio de Góriz (p427) in 1½ to two hours. The refuge is the usual starting point for ascents of many high peaks including Monte Perdido, and is one of the great crossroads of the Pyrenees.

Be warned, Monte Perdido is a serious undertaking: most of the year the route from

Parque Nacional de Ordesa y Monte Perdido

the refuge is completely or partly covered in snow and requires mountaineering skills, crampons and ice axes. Even when snow-free (roughly mid-July to some time in September in a typical year), it's still a very demanding hike requiring fitness and mountain-hiking experience. You ascend from 2200m to 3355m, with a long, very steep section over loose stones – from Góriz, it's approximately four hours up and three hours back down, and you should start early.

Cañón de Añisclo WALKING

This gaping wound in the earth's fabric is 500m deep in parts. A trail up the canyon from Puente de San Úrbez bridge, beside the HU631, leads in about 2½ hours (450m ascent) to La Ripareta, where the Barranco de la Pardina joins the Río Bellós, and in a further two hours (300m more ascent) to another confluence below the powerful Fuen Blanca waterfall.

★Balcón de Pineta WALKING

This challenging but exhilarating day hike (about seven hours round trip) begins at the car park near the west end of the Pineta valley and ascends 1300m (getting steadily steeper as you go) to the Balcón. This barren, vaguely plateau-like area far above the treeline provides fantastic panoramas back along the valley and also close-up views of the glacier-laden north side of Monte Perdido.

Miradores de Revilla BIRDWATCHING

Thanks to a feeding site established nearby by conservationists, there are high chances of seeing the rare lammergeier (bearded vulture), as well as Egyptian and griffon vultures and golden eagles, from the Miradores de Revilla observation points, which are reached by an easy 1.25km path from Revilla village, 12km by a winding paved road off the A138.

Sleeping

There's just one overnight mountain refuge, Refugio de Góriz, within the park, but there is plenty of accommodation – campgrounds, walkers' refuges, hostels, *hostales*, holiday apartments, *casas rurales*, hotels – in towns, villages and the countryside surrounding the park including in Torla, Broto, Aínsa, Escalona, Bielsa and the Valle de Bujaruelo. Some accommodation closes down from about November to March.

Refugio de Góriz HOSTEL €
(974 34 12 01; www.goriz.es; dm €17) One of the Spanish Pyrenees' star refuges sits in the shadow of Monte Perdido, for which it acts as an unofficial base camp. It sits at the crossroads of an enviable network of paths. The 72 bunks are fully occupied throughout July and August and on June and September weekends, so reserve ahead for those times.

The quickest hike in (about four hours) is from Pradera de Ordesa via the Circo de Soaso. Camping is permitted outside between sunset and sunrise only. Open and staffed year-round, the refuge has an all-day bar, and offers picnic lunches as well as serving breakfast (€6) and dinner (€17).

Information

The national park's main information offices (opening hours can vary):

Bielsa (974 50 10 43; Casa Larraga, Plaza Mayor, Bielsa; 8am-3pm & 4.15-7pm Easter-Oct, 8am-3pm Mon-Fri, 9am-2pm & 3.15-6pm Nov-Easter)

Centro de Visitantes de Torla (974 48 64 72; Avenida Ordesa, Torla; 9am-2pm & 4.15-7pm Easter-Oct, 8am-3pm Mon-Fri, 9am-2pm & 3.15-6pm Sat & Sun Nov-Easter)

Centro de Visitantes de Tella (Calle La Iglesia, Tella; 9am-2pm & 4.15-7pm Easter-Oct, 9am-2pm & 3.15-6pm Sat & Sun Nov-Easter)

Escalona (974 50 51 31; Calle Mayor, Escalona; 8am-3pm & 4.15-7pm Easter-Oct, 8am-3pm Mon-Fri, 9am-2pm & 3.15-6pm Sat & Sun Nov-Easter)

Escuaín (9am-2pm & 3-7pm)

Getting There & Away

The main jumping-off points for the park are the village of **Torla** in the west, with easy access to the Valle de Ordesa; the small town of **Aínsa**, southeast of the park, from which you can drive to the Añisclo and Escuaín sectors; and **Bielsa** village in the east, at the mouth of the Pineta valley, 34km north up the A138 from Aínsa. All three places can be reached by bus.

From **Torla** it's an 8km drive or walk to **Pradera de Ordesa**, starting point of several fine walks in the Valle de Ordesa. Private vehicles may not go beyond Pradera de Ordesa at any time and are banned from the Valle de Ordesa completely during Easter week, July, August and early September. During these periods a shuttle bus (one way/return adult €3/4.50, child free) runs between Torla's **Centro de Visitantes** and Pradera de Ordesa. A maximum of 1800 people are allowed in the Ordesa sector of the park at any one time.

From **Escalona**, 11km north of Aínsa on the A138, a minor paved road, the HU631, heads northwest across to **Sarvisé**, 7km south of Torla. This road crosses the park's southern tip, with a narrow, sinuous section winding up the dramatic Bellos valley and giving access to walks in the spectacular Añisclo canyon (the upper reaches of the Bellos valley). During Easter week, July, August and early September, a one-way system is enforced on part of the road, with only northwestward traffic allowed on the 13km stretch between Puyarruego and the Buerba turn-off. Southeastward traffic uses the roughly parallel, more southerly road through Buerba.

Torla

POP 220 / ELEV 1040M

The pre-eminent gateway to the Parque Nacional de Ordesa y Monte Perdido, Torla is a lovely alpine-style village of slate-roofed stone houses. The setting is delightful, with the village houses clustered above Río Ara and the national park's mountains forming an awe-inspiring backdrop. It gets overrun by tourists in July and August.

Activities

Guías de Torla ADVENTURE SPORTS
(974 48 64 22; www.guiasdetorla.com; Calle Francia; half-day canyoning per person from €46) The Ordesa-Monte Perdido national park and its surroundings are rich in adventure opportunities, including canyoning, with many exhilarating jumping-sliding-abseiling routes down the area's gorges. Guías de Torla is a well-established professional company offering a variety of guided canyoning trips from Easter to October, for all skill levels.

Sleeping

Edelweiss Hotel HOTEL €
(974 48 61 73; www.edelweisshotelordesa.es; Avenida Ordesa 1; s/d incl breakfast €44/60; Easter–mid-Nov; P) Rooms here may lack decorative flair, but they're perfectly comfy and many of them have panoramic terraces or balconies. Staff are notably welcoming and

helpful, prices are good, the breakfast is ample, and it's conveniently located beside the road to Ordesa with a reasonable amount of (free) parking.

Hotel Villa de Torla HOTEL €
(974 48 61 56; www.hotelvilladetorla.com; Plaza Aragón 1; s €45-50, d €58-75, tr €85-95;) The rooms here are tidy – some are stylish in whites and creams with patterned wallpaper, others have floral bedspreads and look a little old-fashioned. An undoubted highlight is the swimming pool, from where there are lovely views. A generous buffet breakfast (€6) is available.

Hotel Villa Russell HOTEL €€
(974 48 67 70; www.hotelvillarussell.com; Calle Francia; incl breakfast s €63, d €88-99, q €165; Easter-Nov;) Villa Russell has rooms that won't win a style contest, but they're enormous and come with sofas, microwaves and hydromassage showers. There is also a similarly well-kitted-out family apartment on the top floor. Room rates rise about €25 in August. On-site parking (€8.80) is available.

Eating

La Brecha ARAGONESE €
(974 48 62 21; www.lucienbriet.com; Calle Francia; set menus €16; 1.30-3.30pm & 8-10.30pm Semana Santa & Jun-Nov;) Home-style local dishes like roast lamb with breaded potatoes, veal escalope and *longaniza* sausages are the speciality of this bustling upstairs restaurant. The *menú* includes wine but do give the homemade *pacharán* (sloe liqueur, said to help with digestion) a try.

Café Mondarruego SPANISH €
(Calle Francia 44; dishes €6.50-12; 8am-11pm) Doing the simple things well, this friendly cafe-restaurant-bar serves up just what most hungry hikers are looking for – filling, well-prepared food at good prices. Generous *platos combinados* based around the likes of pork chops or chicken escalope are the mainstay, but there are also good salads and burgers, and *raciones* such as ham croquettes or chicken brochette.

Restaurante El Duende ARAGONESE €€
(974 48 60 32; www.restauranteelduende.com; Calle de la Iglesia; mains €13-26, set menus €22-32; 1.30-3.30pm & 8-10.30pm Feb-Dec;) Encased in a 19th-century building made from local stone, Duende (Elf) is the finest dining in town, serving top-class grilled meats and creative desserts. Tables are in high demand so reserve ahead.

Information

The village has a couple of ATMs, and shops selling outdoor equipment, food and maps.

Getting There & Away

Alosa (902 21 07 00; www.avanzabus.com) operates one or two daily buses to/from Sabiñánigo (€4.25, one hour) with bus and rail connections to/from Jaca and Zaragoza. There are one or two daily services to/from Aínsa (€4.35, one hour) and, from July to October, Barbastro (€10, two hours)

Valle de Bujaruelo

North of Torla and just outside the western boundary of the Parque Nacional de Ordesa y Monte Perdido, the pretty Valle de Bujaruelo has scenery rivalling parts of the national park, and is another excellent walking area.

Private vehicles can drive as far as San Nicolás de Bujaruelo, 10km north of Torla. It's also perfectly feasible to hike in from Torla, following the GR11 trail north from the Puente de los Navarros.

Many good day walks start from San Nicolás de Bujaruelo, including easy options into the **Valle de Otal** (west) and **Valle de Ordiso** (northwest) or a slightly harder circuit of about six hours combining the two. The beautiful mountain lake **Ibón de Bernatuara** is about 3½ hours north from San Nicolás (with an ascent of 975m), and 2½ hours back down.

Eastward, it's a climb of 4.5km (about 3½ hours, with 950m ascent) from San Nicolás to the **Puerto de Bujaruelo** pass on the French border, and three hours back down – or you continue in to France – either down to Gavarnie village in about three hours or over to the Refuge des Sarradets (about 1½ hours).

Camping Valle de Bujaruelo CAMPGROUND €
(974 48 63 48; www.campingvalledebujaruelo.com; per adult/tent/car €4.90/5/5, d/tr/q with shared bathroom €30/45/58, bungalow €80-105; Apr-Oct;) This campground, 7km north from Torla, has a lovely setting and well-maintained facilities. As well as good shady tent sites, there are wooden bungalows for up to four people with kitchen and bathroom, and *'refugio'* rooms for two to five. Plus a decent restaurant and a shop.

Aínsa

POP 1640 / ELEV 560M

A masterpiece hewn from uneven stone, the beautiful medieval hilltop village of Aínsa is one of Aragón's gems, albeit one that's half-swamped by tourism in high summer. From its perch, you'll have commanding panoramas of the mountains, particularly the great rock bastion of La Peña Montañesa. The modern part of Aínsa, down below, is spread around a busy crossroads and two rivers flowing down from the Pyrenees: the Ara and Cinca.

Sights

★Plaza Mayor PLAZA

Old Aínsa's broad, cobbled main plaza, 80m long and lined by handsome stone arcades and houses, is one of Spain's loveliest. It was created as a market place and fairground back in the 12th and 13th centuries and the architecture has changed little since then – even if the buzz today comes from the tables and sunshades of the plaza's numerous restaurants instead of medieval market stalls.

Castillo CASTLE

FREE The castle off the northwest end of Plaza Mayor mostly dates from the 16th and 17th centuries, though the Torre del Homenaje (keep) is from the 11th century; there are good views from the walls.

The castle's two surviving towers house moderately interesting museums: the **Eco Museo** (974 50 05 97; www.quebrantahuesos.org; Castillo; €4; 11am-2pm & 4-8pm May-Oct, 11am-2pm Mon, Thu & Fri, 11am-2pm & 4-7pm Sat & Sun Mar, Apr, Nov & Dec) on Pyrenean fauna in the Torre del Homenaje; and the **Espacio del Geoparque de Sobrarbe** (www.geoparquepirineos.com; Castillo; 9.30am-2pm & 4.30-7pm) FREE with displays on the region's intriguing geology.

Iglesia de Santa María CHURCH

(tower €1; 7.30am-8pm Jul-Sep, 4-8pm Oct-Jun) Aínsa's main church bears all the hallmarks of unadulterated Romanesque. Few embellishments mark its thick, bare walls, which date from the 11th century. Don't leave without exploring the beautiful little crypt and funny little trapezoid cloister, and climbing the bell tower.

Sleeping

Some cute, olde-worlde lodgings are to be found on and around Plaza Mayor, but most accommodation is down in the newer part of town.

Albergue Mora de Nuei HOSTEL €

(974 51 06 14; www.alberguemoradenuei.com; Calle del Portal de Abajo 2; dm/d €20/55; Feb-Dec;) At the lower end of the old town, this fine place is one of Aragón's best hostels. The colourful rooms and dorms – for two, four or 10 – all have their own bathrooms. There's good, inexpensive food and 40 craft beers served in the bar (which has a pleasant terrace) and a regular calendar of live music and other events.

★Hotel Los Siete Reyes BOUTIQUE HOTEL €€

(974 50 06 81; www.lossietereyes.com; Plaza Mayor; r €90-120;) Tucked under an arcade on Aínsa's ancient main square and exhibiting a style perhaps best described as historical-boutique, the Siete Reyes offers

AÍNSA, ADVENTURE CAPITAL

With the Pyrenees and all their subsidiary ranges and valleys on its doorstep, Aínsa is a natural centre for all kinds of adventure activities including mountain biking, canyoning, vie ferrate, rafting and kayaking, with trips offered by several companies.

The valleys, hills, canyons and mountains of the Sobrarbe district around Aínsa are a mountain-biking paradise, with some 500km of off-road tracks, many of them waymarked for bikers. The **Zona Zero project** (http://bttpirineo.com) provides masses of information for mountain bikers and brings together bike-friendly accommodation, repair shops, guides and bike-transport services. You can rent enduro mountain bikes (per half-/full day €40/60), with discounts for multiday hires, at **T-T Aventura** (974 51 00 24; www.ttaventura.com; Avenida Pirenaica 10; office 9am-2pm & 4-9pm).

InterSport (Avenida Sobrarbe 4; 9am-9pm Mon-Sat, 9am-2pm & 4-9pm Sun) sells most things you could need for outdoor activities, from boots to backpacks, helmets and sleeping mats. It's good on maps, too.

six rooms fit for kings (and queens). Modern art hangs on old stone walls and mood lighting shines from ceilings crossed by wooden beams.

Hotel Sánchez HOTEL €€
(☎974 50 00 14; www.hotelsanchez.com; Avenida Sobrarbe 10; s €41-71, d €51-105, ste €84-140; P ❄ 📶) This popular, well-run place in the lower part of town offers tidy medium-size 'classic' rooms in yellow, white and light pine, and a newer 'design zone' of spacious, comfortable suites and apartments with contemporary features from silver-and-grey colour schemes to graduated lighting to different wood finishes. Shower pressure is superb.

Eating options are bright and excellent, too. The classy restaurant specialises in fish and meat BBQ grills, while the busy cafeteria runs from tempting *pinchos* displayed on the bar to salads, pizzas and *platos combinados* (most between €6 and €9).

Casa de San Martín HISTORIC HOTEL €€€
(☎974 50 31 05; www.casadesanmartin.com; San Martín de la Solana; s/d from €132/165; ⏲Mar-Jan; P ❄ 📶) A stunning rural retreat with spectacular panoramas over a deserted valley, this tall, stone, 18th-century house has been beautifully renovated and the rooms are temples to good taste, without being overdone. Meals (set menus €25) are exceptional. To find it, head 16km west from Aínsa on the N260, then 5km up an unpaved road from the 'San Martín de la Solana' sign.

Eating

L'Alfil TAPAS €
(Travesera de la Iglesia; raciones €6.50-10; ⏲11am-4pm & 7pm-midnight May-Oct, shorter hours Nov-Apr) This pretty little cafe-bar, with floral accompaniment to its outside tables, is in a side street opposite the church. Its *raciones* are more creative than you'll find elsewhere, from casseroles of wild mushrooms, venison or snails to duck pâté and cured wild boar. It's also a good spot to the try the locally celebrated sausage *longaniza de Graus*.

Bodegón de Mallacán ARAGONESE €€
(☎974 50 09 77; Plaza Mayor 6; mains €17-21; ⏲9am-4.30pm & 7-11pm) You won't want to wave *adiós* to Aragón without tasting the slow-roasted local lamb, known as *ternasco*, and Bodegón de Mallacán on Aínsa's ancient plaza is a fine place to try it. Duck, wild boar, beef, partridge, frogs' legs and venison pâté are other classics you can enjoy here.

★Restaurante Callizo CONTEMPORARY SPANISH €€€
(☎974 50 03 85; www.restaurantecallizo.es; Plaza Mayor; set menus adult/child €50/25; ⏲12.45-3pm & 8.45-10pm Wed-Mon) Callizo succeeds in marrying Aragonese tradition with modern gastronomic theatre and the result is not just a meal but a true eating experience. Dishes include Río Cinca trout, partridge and veal tournedos, all in imaginative preparations. It's essential to reserve (possible on the website) and to arrive on time!

Information

Municipal Tourist Office (☎974 50 07 67; www.villadeainsa.com; Avenida Ordesa 5; ⏲10am-2pm & 4-7.30pm) In the new town down the hill.

Oficina Comarcal de Turismo (District Tourist Office; ☎974 50 05 12; www.turismosobrarbe.com; Torre Nordeste, Plaza del Castillo 1; ⏲9.30am-1.30pm & 4.30-7pm) Inside the Castillo.

Getting There & Away

Alosa (☎902 21 07 00; www.avanzabus.com) runs one or two daily buses to/from Barbastro (€5.85, one hour) and Torla (€4.35, one hour). For Huesca, Zaragoza or Barcelona, change at Barbastro.

Autocares Bergua (☎974 50 06 01; www.autocaresbergua.com) heads to/from Bielsa (€5, one hour) once daily in July and August, and on Monday, Wednesday and Friday in other months.

The bus stop is at the south end of the Río Ara bridge.

Benasque

POP 1535 / ELEV 1150M

Aragón's northeastern corner is crammed with the highest and arguably the shapeliest peaks in the Pyrenees, and the likeable little town of Benasque is a perfectly sited gateway to the high valleys. Even in high summer, these epic mountains are fringed with ice. Much of the region is protected as the Parque Natural Posets-Maladeta.

Benasque's neat, alpine-style, stone-and-slate architecture appears fairly modern, but the town goes back a long way: its church has Romanesque origins and the Palacio de los Condes de Ribagorza on Calle Mayor dates from the 16th century.

Activities

The Benasque region is a true adventure playground. As well as hiking and climbing in the valleys and mountains, there's good skiing at Cerler (p420), a few kilometres northeast of town; paragliding at **Castejón de Sos**, 14km south; and rafting at **Campo**, 33km south. Several agencies in Benasque can organise all these activities for you.

The region offers walkers almost limitless options, especially in the upper Benasque valley (p432) and its side valleys. The best season is from about May to October. Depending on snow cover, low-level routes may be practicable for longer, and higher-level ones for shorter periods.

Compañía de Guías Valle de Benasque ADVENTURE SPORTS
(974 55 16 90; www.guiasbenasque.com; Avenida de Francia, Edificio Els Ibons; office 10am-2pm & 4.30-8.30pm) This company has more than 20 years' experience and offers a vast range of activities and courses for both summer and winter, including hiking, climbing, canyoning and ski touring. It also rents all the necessary kit for these activities.

Sleeping

Hotel Avenida HOTEL €
(974 55 11 26; www.hotelavenidabenasque.es; Avenida de los Tilos 14; incl breakfast s €39-46, d €62-74;) Rooms are small but clean in this centrally located, typical ski-lodge-type hotel with a woody decor, gabled roof and helpful staff. It has a restaurant, plus triple and quadruple room options for families and/or groups.

★Hotel Aneto HOTEL €€
(974 55 10 61; www.hotelesvalero.com; Avenida de Francia 4; s/d incl breakfast from €73/106; Jun–mid-Sep & Christmas-Easter;) The streamlined, super-modern Aneto is a cut above your cosy ski lodge with a wide selection of rooms, from the snazzy to the positively luxurious. Bonuses include a small indoor pool, a great lobby bar and filling breakfasts.

Hotel Vallibierna HOTEL €€
(974 55 17 23; www.hotelvallibiernabenasque.com; Paseo Campalets; s/d incl breakfast €50/75;) Set a little away from the central hubbub, this former private home is a peaceful retreat with wood beams, stone or colourfully painted walls, and a few hunting trophies, redolent with the scent of pines from the tall trees in its garden. With good breakfasts and free parking, it's an excellent find.

Rates rise in the first three weeks of August. The hotel closes in November and for a few weeks after Easter.

Eating

El Veedor de Viandas SPANISH €€
(www.elveedordeviandas.com; Avenida Los Tilos 6; tapas €1.80, mains €8-13; noon-3.30pm & 6-11pm Thu-Tue;) A welcoming informal space combining a gourmet deli, wine shop, tapas bar and restaurant. Tapas and *tostadas* have innovative toppings such as *solomillo* (tenderloin) with red pepper and cheese, or duck breast with red berries. Plus there are salads, carpaccios, egg-based dishes, belly-filling *cazuelitas* (mini-stews) and excellent cakes too!

Mesón de Benás ARAGONESE, BRASSERIE €€
(692 189033; Calle Mayor 47; mains €7-20, set menus €15-22; 1-4pm & 8-11pm) A very good and popular stone-walled restaurant with river views from its upstairs room, specialising in home-style mountain fare with an emphasis on barbecued meats and good-value set menus.

WHITE WATER, BLUE SKIES

On the Río Ésera 33km south of Benasque, Campo village is one of the Pyrenees' top rafting centres (best from April to June). Operators are dotted along the N260 road through Campo: a good choice is **Sin Fronteras** (974 55 01 77; www.sinfronterasadventure.com; Carretera Benasque 1, Campo; half-day rafting €35-45; 10am-7pm Easter-Sep;), by the roundabout at the south end of town, which offers a slew of summer activities including canoeing, and canyoning in the nearby Aigüeta de Barbaruéns canyon, as well as rafting – all with child-friendly route options..

Fourteen kilometres south of Benasque, Castejón de Sos, with its Liri take-off point at 2300m, is one of Spain's top paragliding centres. It's flyable year-round. Several paragliding schools and shops are dotted along the main street. Tandem flights of 20 to 30 minutes cost around €70.

PLAN D'AIGUALLUT WALKS

Surely one of the world's most perfect picnic spots, the Plan d'Aiguallut is a broad grassy meadow under the gaze of the Pyrenees' highest peak, Aneto, with half a dozen meandering mountain streams uniting to tumble over its lip as the powerful Cascada d'Aiguallut waterfall. Fortunately the 45-minute walk required to reach this beautiful spot from La Besurta is sufficient to save it from getting overrun.

Numerous variations and extensions of the walk enable a great full day's outing on clear, generally well-signed paths. En route from La Besurta you can detour up to the **Refugio de la Renclusa** (974 34 46 46; www.alberguesyrefugiosdearagon.com; dm €17, breakfast €6, lunch or dinner €16), then approach the Plan d'Aiguallut via the little Collado de Renclusa pass (1½ hours one way). From the Plan, it's a 2.5km walk east (one hour one way, with 200m ascent) up to **Ibón de Coll de Toro lake**; or you can head south-southeast up the lovely Barrancs valley, below Aneto's east flank, to **Ibón de Barrancs lake** (2km one way, about 1½ hours, with 300m ascent) or even the **Collado de Salenques pass** (4km, about three hours, 750m of ascent).

Restaurante El Fogaril ARAGONESE €€
(974 55 16 12; Calle Mayor 5; mains €14-26, set menus €24; 1-4pm & 8.30-11pm;) Part of the popular Hotel Ciria, El Fogaril serves outstanding Aragonese mountain fare. Specialities include wood-oven-roasted meats, game such as venison, partridge and wild boar, and typical local stews with beans and other bases.

It also offers *bocadillos* (baguette-like sandwiches), salads and generous *platos combinados* (combined plates, priced €10 to €18) if you're peckish between main meals or after something that is relatively light and quick.

Shopping

Barrabés SPORTS & OUTDOORS
(www.barrabes.com; Avenida de Francia; 10am-2pm & 5-9pm) This really is the one-stop sports store in town, selling equipment and sportswear for just about every activity you can think of. It also carries a good range of guides and maps, and has an online shopping option.

Information

Tourist Office (974 55 12 89; www.turismobenasque.com; Calle San Pedro; 9.30am-1pm & 4.30-7.45pm daily Jul-Sep, Tue-Sat Oct-Jun)

Getting There & Away

Alosa (www.avanzabus.com) runs two buses daily (one on Sunday) to/from Huesca (€13, 2¾ hours) via Castejón de Sos, Campo and Barbastro.

Upper Benasque Valley & the Maladeta Massif

Northeast of Benasque, the A139 continues up the valley of the Río Ésera (known as the Valle de Benasque) for 13km to a dead end 1.5km short of the mountain ridgeline that forms the French border. The side valleys off this upper Benasque valley provide the area's most spectacular scenery and best walks and climbs. Just before the A139's end, a 6km unpaved road forks east, following the upper Ésera past the Hospital de Benasque hotel to a parking area at La Besurta, the starting point for several good routes. The Maladeta massif – a line of high, glacier-fringed peaks culminating in Aneto (3404m), the Pyrenees' highest summit – rises to the south of La Besurta. West of the A139 rises the Pyrenees' second-highest peak, Posets (3375m).

Activities

Information on walking routes, including maps, is available at Benasque tourist office and at the starting point of the summer bus service at Vado del Hospital. Editorial Alpina's map *Parque Natural Posets Maladeta* (1:25,000) is a very good investment.

Ibón d'Escarpinosa Walk WALKING
One of the best day hikes on the Valle de Benasque's west side, this route leads up the verdant Estós valley to two mountain lakes, the tiny Ibonet de Batisielles and the slightly bigger Ibón d'Escarpinosa, with a backdrop of jagged high peaks. It's 6km each way, with

700m ascent and descent (about five hours round trip plus stops).

To start, head 3km up the A139 from Benasque then go left up the signposted Valle d'Estós road for 700m, to a parking area where the signed trail starts. For the first 3km or so you're following the GR11 on its route to the Refugio de Estós.

Sleeping

Hospital de Benasque HOTEL €€
(974 55 20 12; www.llanosdelhospital.com; Llanos del Hospital; d incl breakfast €60-128; Dec-Oct; P) In the Ésera valley's beautiful upper reaches, 2km off the A139 towards La Besurta, this 55-room mountain lodge borders on the luxurious. 'Special' rooms are newer and larger, with a cosier, more old-fashioned feel than the Standards, but all are good and comfortable. The hotel has a spa, bar and restaurant and is also a cross-country-skiing centre.

Getting There & Away

From about mid-September to the end of June, you can drive as far as La Besurta; there's no public transport. From July to mid-September, private vehicles (unless going to the Hospital de Benasque) must be parked at Vado del Hospital, 1.5km off the A319 along the La Besurta road. From here a shuttle bus (one way/return €2.80/5) runs the remaining 4.5km to La Besurta and back. A few times a day the bus starts its run in Benasque (one way/return €7.90/12, 45 minutes). Benasque **tourist office** has schedules.

Alquézar

POP 226 / ELEV 610M

Like so many Aragonese villages, Alquézar jumps out at you unexpectedly. You'll barely guess its magnificence until you're virtually inside its tight labyrinth of streets above the steep cliffs of the plunging Río Vero gorge. Beauty aside, Alquézar is Spain's capital of canyoning, with several companies offering to take you jumping, sliding and abseiling down the numerous dramatic canyons carved into the surrounding Sierra de Guara, a sparsely populated limestone massif in the Pyrenees foothills.

Sights

Colegiata de Santa María MONASTERY, CASTLE
(€3; 11am-1.30pm & 4.30-7.30 Mar-Dec, Sat & Sun only Jan & Feb) Alquézar is crowned by this large castle-monastery. Originally built as an *alcázar* (fortress) by the Moors in the 9th century, it was subsequently conquered and replaced by a fortified Augustinian monastery in 1099. Some of the columns in its delicate cloister are crowned by carved capitals depicting animals, flowers and grapes as well as biblical scenes, and the cloister walls are covered with captivating murals. On the upper level is a museum of sacred art.

Activities

Canyoning runs from about April to October, but the main season for easy and medium-level adventures is mid-June to mid-September. Small-group prices are typically €45 to €50 per person, with around four hours' actual canyon descent. The fee covers gear, guide and insurance, but not transport (you need your own vehicle or a taxi for nearly all routes).

Guías Boira ADVENTURE SPORTS
(974 31 89 74; www.guiasboira.com; Paseo San Hipólito) Guías Boira is a specialist in Pyrenean peak ascents as well as canyoning, vie ferrate and rafting. Offers two-day packages with two canyons or one canyon and either rafting, climbing or a via ferrata (per person from €90).

Vertientes ADVENTURE SPORTS
(974 31 83 54; www.vertientesaventura.com; Paseo San Hipólito) Offers canyoning (per person €46 to €52), a half-day of abseiling *(rápel)*, via ferrata (per person €39 to €48) or climbing (per person €58 to €68).

Sleeping

Albergue Rural de Guara HOSTEL €
(974 31 83 96; www.albergueruraldeguara.com; Calle Pilaseras; dm/d €16/48;) This cheerfully run hostel is perched up above the village with fine views of the surrounds. There are cosy double rooms as well as bunk dorms for six or eight. All have their own bathroom. Staff can arrange picnic lunches (€8). Breakfast costs €5.50.

Hotel Maribel BOUTIQUE HOTEL €€
(974 31 89 79; www.hotelmaribel.es; Barrio Arrabal; d incl breakfast €120-150; P) This boutique hotel has plenty of charm and, while the decor won't be to everyone's taste (very tasteful contemporary art is interspersed with dashes of kitsch), the nine rooms are supremely comfortable (all with a Jacuzzi, for example). If there's no-one at reception, try the nearby Restaurante Casa Gervasio.

1

2

1. Aínsa **2.** Albarracín **3.** Sos del Rey Católico

Villages of Aragón

Aragon's small villages are, perhaps, the region's most surprising revelation, all of them unique but many sharing a similarly exotic time-stood-still atmosphere. Their settings – against a backdrop of Pyrenean peaks or hidden amid isolated southern canyons – are equally beguiling.

Albarracín (p442)

After several weeks of dissecting Aragon's prettiest rural settlements, quite a few travellers are happy to award the Oscar to Albarracín. Something about its winding lanes of warped, pink-hued houses, agreeably ruined medieval watchtowers, lovingly resuscitated monuments and craggy backdrop just seems to click.

Aínsa (p429)

Stick a perfect grey stone village on a rocky eminence with the snow-doused peaks of the Pyrenees lined up in the distance. Add arguably Spain's loveliest medieval plaza, an unadulterated Romanesque church and streets that haven't changed much since Christians and Moors crossed swords. Call it Aínsa.

Alquézar (p433)

Activity centres are rarely this historic. Beneath the adrenaline-hungry exterior of Spain's canyoning capital lies a tranquil sandy-hued village eerily redolent of a Tuscan hill town.

Sos del Rey Católico (p416)

Uniformly cobblestoned streets, the whiff of erstwhile Aragonese kings and wonderfully preserved old stone mansions make Sos a memorable stop en route to or from the Pyrenees.

Ansó (p418)

A warren of narrow streets lined by neatly trimmed stone houses, surrounded in all directions by beautiful mountain and forest vistas, Ansó is the perfect gateway to one of the most magical and remote Aragón Pyrenees valleys. Hecho, just a few kilometres away, is almost as quaint.

Hotel Villa de Alquézar HOTEL €€

(☎974 31 84 16; www.villadealquezar.com; Calle Pedro Arenal Cavero 12; incl breakfast s €68-84, d €75-125; ⏰Feb–mid-Dec; P❄📶≋) This is a lovely larger hotel with plenty of style in its 34 airy rooms; there are period touches throughout, and the 12m swimming pool is a distinct plus in the summer heat. The most expensive (top floor) rooms are large and have wonderful covered balconies – perfect for watching the sun set over town with a glass of Somontano wine.

Eating

L'Artica CAFE €

(☎974 31 88 69; www.panaderialartica.com; Calle Iglesia 1; pizza €10-16, light dishes €5-11; ⏰8am-6pm Mon-Fri, 8am-7pm Sat & Sun; 📶) Split over two floors, with terraces hanging over the village's spectacular gorge, L'Artica is decked out bistro-style with creamy furniture and cabinets displaying musical instruments. The downstairs is more cafe-like, the upstairs more restaurant-ish, but both are lovely perches, offering the same good fare from *tostadas* (toast slices with toppings), egg dishes and salads to burgers and biscuity pizzas.

★**Casa Pardina** ARAGONESE €€

(☎660 399472; www.casapardina.com; Calle Medio; set menus €29-38; ⏰1.30-3.30pm & 8.30-10.30pm Apr-Oct, Sat & Sun only Nov-Mar) A very special restaurant where the food exudes contemporary creativity and the setting is all soothing stonework, twinkling chandeliers and views that could have sprung from the pages of *National Geographic*. The menu is subtle yet classy with dishes including oxtail with chestnuts, and stewed venison with dates and honey. Reservations recommended.

Information

Tourist Office (☎974 31 89 40; www.alquezar.org; Paseo San Hipólito; ⏰9.30am-2pm & 4-7.30pm Fri-Tue Sep-May, daily Jun-Aug) Runs Spanish-language village tours (€4) twice daily and offers audio guides (€6) in Spanish, French, Dutch and German.

Getting There & Away

One bus to Barbastro (€2.75, 40 minutes) departs from Alquézar Monday to Friday at 7.30am during school terms and 9.25am in school holidays, starting back from Barbastro at 2.30pm year-round.

Somontano Wine Region

Somontano is Aragón's most prestigious wine-growing region. Centred on the town of **Barbastro**, the Somontano DO (Denominación de Origen) has more than 30 wineries producing reds, whites and rosés from 15 different local and other grape varieties. Nearly all the wineries are in the countryside outside the town, which isn't a particularly pretty place, although the older part around the late-Gothic cathedral and the Paseo del Coso boulevard is pleasant enough. More charming Alquézar, 26km northwest of Barbastro, can also be used as a base for winery visits.

Barbastro's **tourist office** (☎974 30 83 50; http://turismosomontano.es; Avenida de la Merced 64, Barbastro; ⏰10am-2pm & 4-7.30pm Tue-Sat) and its website, as well as the websites for the Ruta del Vino Somontano (www.rutadelvinosomontano.com) and DO Somontano (http://dosomontano.com), have plenty of information on the various wineries that can be visited for sales, tours and/or tastings. For anything more than a call at a winery's shop, you should ring ahead to arrange a time – the tourist office will help you do this if you turn up in person. Three wineries – Viñas del Vero, its neighbour **Bodegas Pirineos** on the A1232 road towards Alquézar, and **Bodegas Otto Bestué**, 8km north of Barbastro on the A138 towards Aínsa – offer free tastings in their shops.

Viñas del Vero WINE

(☎974 30 22 16; www.vinasdelvero.es; Carretera Naval, Km 3.7; ⏰10am-2pm & 4-7pm Mon-Fri, 10am-2pm Sat) Aragón's best-known winery has handsome premises 3km out of Barbastro on the A1232 towards Alquézar, and offers free tastings in its spacious shop where you can inspect its full range of wines, priced from €5 to €68-plus for the top-of-the-line Blecua.

Winery tours (by reservation) start at €7 per person for a 1¾-hour visit including tasting of three wines.

Hotel San Ramón BOUTIQUE HOTEL €€

(☎974 31 28 25; www.hotelsanramonsomontano.com; Calle Academia Cerbuna 2; incl breakfast s €75, d €90-125, ste from €144; P❄📶) Centrally located near the cathedral, the San Ramón is easily the best lodging in town – a handsome, century-old, Modernista building transformed a few years ago with 18 stylish, comfortable rooms all equipped with hydromassage showers or Jacuzzis. It also has a spa, a bar and one of Barbastro's best restaurants.

Getting There & Away

Barbastro's **bus station** (Plaza Aragón 2) is centrally located and has several daily bus services that run to/from Huesca (€4.60, 50 minutes), Zaragoza (€12, two to 2½ hours), Lleida (€6.25, 1½ hours) and Barcelona (€14, three to 3½ hours), plus one or two to/from Aínsa (€5.85, one hour).

SOUTHERN ARAGÓN

Daroca

POP 2070 / ELEV 775M

The old walled town of Daroca is the meeting point of two different Aragóns: the Romanesque north and the Mudéjar south. This cultural transition is etched into the town's buildings, which at times mix distinct Romanesque and Mudéjar elements, like sedimentary rock, on the same building.

Ringed by a circuit of evocatively crumbling medieval walls, Daroca once sported 114 towers, though only a handful of them remain. Since many of its old buildings are only viewable from the outside, it's best to enjoy Daroca as a kind of giant alfresco museum.

Sights

Basílica de Santa María de los Sagrados Corporales CHURCH

(Plaza de España; ⏲11am-1pm & 5.30-7pm Tue-Sun Oct-May, 11am-1pm & 6.30-8pm Tue-Sun Jun-Sep) Pretty Plaza de España is dominated by this ornate Romanesque-Gothic-Mudéjar-Renaissance church, which boasts a lavish interior and organ. Some original medieval blue paint remains on the *Last Judgement* sculpture of the 14th/15th-century Gothic Puerta del Perdón at the west end. Overall, Santa María is one of Daroca's most appealing (and unexpected) gems.

Castillo Mayor CASTLE

FREE The hilltop castle on the north side of Daroca is not visible from the town below, but the hike up to it is well worthwhile for the evocatively ruined state of its buildings and the nearby city walls, and the town panoramas from the edge of the hill. Founded as a Muslim fort in the 8th century, the castle went through numerous sieges, battles and rebuildings and was in use as late as the 19th-century Carlist Wars.

Iglesia de San Miguel CHURCH

(Plaza de San Miguel) Up in northwest corner of town, this 12th-century church is an austerely beautiful masterpiece of Romanesque architecture, but its greatest treasures are the colourful, 14th-century Gothic murals in the apse. The church is kept closed, but you can go inside on guided tours run by the tourist office.

Iglesia de San Juan CHURCH

(Plaza de San Juan) Not generally open to the public, but no matter...what makes this church important (and interesting) is the delineation of its architecture. On the semicircular apse, you can clearly see the line where the builders switched from Romanesque grey stone to terracotta brick and finished building the church in a Mudéjar style. The switch came in the middle of the 13th century, making this one of the earliest examples of Mudéjar architecture in Aragón.

Tours

Guided Walks WALKING

The tourist office offers a few worthwhile guided walks. The special advantage of the 1¾-hour **Ruta Monumental** (per person €5, 11am and 4.30 or 6pm daily Tuesday to Sunday) is that it takes you into the otherwise closed Iglesia de San Miguel and the Puerta Baja city gate.

Sleeping & Eating

La Posada del Almudí HERITAGE HOTEL €

(☎976 80 06 06; www.posadadelalmudi.es; Calle Grajera 7; incl breakfast s €45, d €65-80; ❄@📶) This lovely old place exudes charm. The rooms in the main building, a 16th-century palace, have been lovingly restored, with wooden floors and the original beams, while across the street are more contemporary rooms, with stylish black-and-white decor and parquet floors. All rooms are a good size.

The restaurant (set menu €12.50) offers good local cuisine and has a delightful terrace in a walled garden. The hotel's bar bursts into life once a week: Saturday lunchtime, when it serves glorious fresh tapas.

Hotel Cien Balcones HOTEL €€

(☎976 54 50 71; www.cienbalcones.com; Calle Mayor 88; incl breakfast s €56, d €72-90; P❄📶) This contemporary, family-run hotel has large, designer rooms, modern bathrooms and bold colour schemes throughout. There's an excellent restaurant (mains €9 to €20, set menus €14 to €20) and a cafe that serves up *raciones, bocadillos* and pizza, with seating in the attractive central courtyard.

Information

Tourist Office (☎976 80 01 29; http://turismo.comarcadedaroca.com; Calle Mayor 44; ⏲10am-2pm & 4-8pm) Come here for the essential town maps marked with self-guided walking tours.

Getting There & Away

Buses stop outside Mesón Félix bar (Calle Mayor 106), except from mid-June to mid-September, when they stop at the Puerta Baja gate, 70m down the street. Buses run to Zaragoza (€6.80, two hours) at 8am and 4.30pm Monday to Friday, and 6pm Saturday and Sunday. For Teruel (€6.80, two hours), there are two daily buses Sunday to Friday, and one at 11.35am Saturday.

Laguna de Gallocanta

ELEV 993M

Some 20km southwest of Daroca, this is Spain's largest natural lake, with an area of about 15 sq km (though it can almost dry up in summer). It's a winter home or migration stopover for huge numbers of cranes, as well as many other waterfowl – more than 260 bird species have been recorded here. The cranes start to arrive in mid-October and fly off back to their Scandinavian breeding grounds in late February or March. Numbers at the lake usually peak in December, at around 25,000 to 30,000 – though on 28 February 2013, an amazing 135,600 cranes were counted here.

The lake is circled by more than 30km of mostly unpaved roads, which pass a series of hides and observation points, and can be driven in normal vehicles except after heavy rain. Take binoculars.

There are two interpretation centres: the bright modern **Centro de Interpretación Laguna de Gallocanta** (☎976 80 30 69; www.facebook.com/oficinaturismo.gallocanta; adult/child €2/1; ⏲9am-1.30pm & 3.30-6.30pm Oct-Mar, shorter hours rest of year; P) in Gallocanta village near the north end of the lake, and an older, smaller **centre** (☎978 73 40 31; Carretera A1507, Km 18; ⏲10am-2pm & 4-7pm Tue-Sun Nov & Feb, weekends only Mar-Oct, Dec & Jan; P) FREE on the Tornos-Bello road the near the lake's south end.

Allucant HOSTAL, HOSTEL €
(☎976 80 31 37; www.allucant.com; Calle San Vicente, Gallocanta; dm €13, d €30-60; P ᯤ) Birders will feel right at home at this simple but well-run base in Gallocanta village. Rooms (some with shared bathrooms) and dorms are bright and colourful, with bird and flower photos, and there's a good library, plus a bright dining room (breakfast/lunch/dinner €4.50/9/12) and a bar. Picnic lunches (€7) and binocular rental (€3) can be arranged.

Getting There & Away

You really need your own wheels to explore the lake properly. The daily Agreda bus from Daroca to Molina de Aragón (departing 4.30pm Monday to Friday, 2.55pm Saturday and Sunday) stops at the Gallocanta turn-off (Empalme de Gallocanta) on the A211, 3.5km north of Gallocanta village (€1.45, 20 minutes). Return services leave the Empalme at 7.30am weekdays and 5.30pm Saturday and Sunday.

Teruel

POP 33,000 / ELEV 928M

The town of Teruel is synonymous with Mudéjar architecture. Nowhere else, with the possible exception of Seville, is this glamorous amalgamation of Islamic craft and Christian taste in such evidence. Its hallmarks – patterns of terracotta bricks and glazed tiles, ornate wooden ceilings – are crafted skilfully into the town's towers and churches, four of which are Unesco-listed.

Teruel is Spain's smallest provincial capital, but a surprisingly bustling and lively place, with some good restaurants. A Moorish fort existed here from the 10th century onwards, but the city itself was founded in 1171 by a conquering Christian king, Alfonso II. In subsequent centuries, Teruel floundered as a forgotten outpost in Aragón's isolated southern highlands. Its most famous historical moment was also its most tragic. The battle of Teruel in the bitter winter of 1937–38 was one of the bloodiest in the Spanish Civil War, claiming an estimated 140,000 casualties.

Sights

★**Fundación Amantes** MUSEUM, CHURCH
(www.amantesdeteruel.es; Calle Matías Abad 3; complete visit adult/child, student & senior €9/7; ⏲10am-2pm & 4-8pm) Teruel's most popular and interesting attraction pulls out the stops on the city's famous legend of the lovers *(amantes)* Isabel de Segura and Juan Diego Martínez de Marcilla. The lovers' mausoleum sits in a side chapel of the Mudéjar Iglesia de San Pedro and there are various ticket op-

Teruel

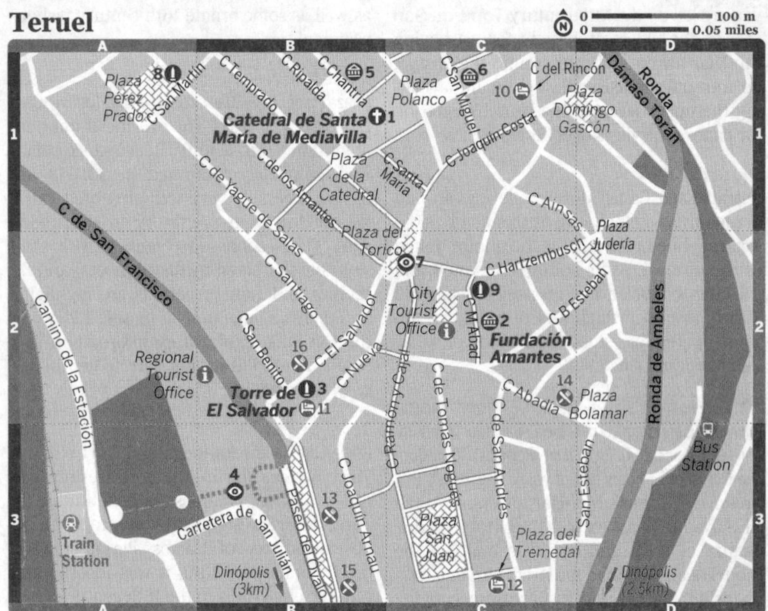

Teruel

Top Sights

1	Catedral de Santa María de Mediavilla	B1
2	Fundación Amantes	C2
3	Torre de El Salvador	B2

Sights

	Iglesia de San Pedro	(see 9)
4	La Escalinata	B3
5	Museo de Arte Sacro	B1
6	Museo de Teruel	C1
7	Plaza del Torico	C2
8	Torre de San Martín	A1
9	Torre de San Pedro	C2

Sleeping

10	Fonda del Tozal	C1
11	Hotel El Mudayyan	B2
12	Hotel Teruel Plaza	C3

Eating

13	Bar Gregory	B3
14	La Barrica – Calle Abadía	C2
15	La Barrica – Paseo del Óvalo	B3
16	La Torre del Salvador	B2

tions for different parts of the complex, but the complete visit to the mausoleum, church, cloister, tower and *ándito* (exterior walkway) is well worth it.

The complete visits are guided, in Spanish only, but English and French audio guides are available and the only parts where you have to follow the guide are the tower and *ándito.* You begin with an audiovisual display on the history of the Amantes and Teruel, then move into exhibition rooms that include the Mausoleo de los Amantes itself, where the lovers' remains are entombed beneath modern alabaster effigies sculpted by Juan de Ávalos, with their hands almost (but not quite) touching. You'll learn not just the story of the lovers' lives, but also about the bizarre treatment of their mummified bodies since their deaths.

From the mausoleum you progress into the 14th-century **Iglesia de San Pedro** (Calle Matías Abad), which is Teruel's only Mudéjar church (as opposed to tower) – though the predominant impression is made by its colourful murals and gold-starred ceiling by Salvador Gisbert, fruit of a Modernista renovation around 1900. The cloister and adjoining garden comprise act three. For a final flourish you are led up the 13th-century **Torre de San Pedro**, the oldest of Teruel's four surviving Mudéjar towers, and then round the *ándito*, an unusual arched walkway circumnavigating the upper levels of the church's exterior, for panoramic views over Teruel.

Plaza del Torico PLAZA
(Plaza de Carlos Castel) Most wanderings around Teruel arrive before long at this gently sloping, cafe-lined plaza that is the unquestioned centre of town. At its bottom end you'll find the city's symbol, a tiny bronze bull called El Torico, just 35cm high and of unknown authorship, that has stood here on top of its far taller pedestal since 1865.

★**Torre de El Salvador** TOWER, MUSEUM
(www.teruelmudejar.com; Calle El Salvador 7; adult/child & senior €2.50/2; ⌚11am-2pm & 4.30-7.30pm Feb-Oct, shorter hours rest of year) The most impressive of Teruel's Mudéjar towers, 40m-tall El Salvador is an early-14th-century extravaganza of brick and ceramics built on the model of an Almohad minaret, with one tower inside another and a staircase occupying the space between. You can climb up to the bell chamber at the top, with its two levels of elegantly arched windows providing Teruel's best city panoramas. On the way up you'll find interesting exhibits on Mudéjar art and architecture and old Teruel.

★**Catedral de Santa María de Mediavilla** CATHEDRAL
(Plaza de la Catedral; incl Museo de Arte Sacro adult/child €3/2; ⌚11am-2pm & 4-8pm Apr-Oct, to 7pm Nov-Mar) The outside of Teruel's cathedral is a rich example of the Mudéjar imagination at work with its kaleidoscopic brickwork and colourful ceramic tiles, notably on the superb 13th-century bell tower. Inside, the astounding (and neck-craning) Mudéjar ceiling *(techumbre)* is covered with paintings that add up to a medieval cosmography – from musical instruments and hunting scenes to coats of arms and Christ's crucifixion. Independent visitors can join groups for a close-up inspection of the ceiling if there's one going up.

Museo de Arte Sacro MUSEUM
(Museo Diocesano; ☎978 61 99 50; Plaza Francés de Aranda 3; incl Catedral de Santa María de Mediavilla adult/child €3/2; ⌚10am-2pm & 4-8pm Mon-Sat Apr-Oct, to 7pm Nov-Mar) Adjacent to the cathedral, the Museo de Arte Sacro is housed in the stately Palacio Episcopal and has two floors of outstanding religious paintings and sculptures dating from the 12th to 18th centuries, as well as some ornate 16th-century bishops' vestments.

Museo de Teruel MUSEUM
(Plaza Polanco; ⌚10am-2pm & 4-7pm Tue-Fri, 10am-2pm Sat & Sun) FREE The provincial museum, housed in a 16th-century Renaissance palace, was completely renovated in 2011–13 and has six floors of very well-presented exhibits ranging from prehistory to the middle ages. The sections on ceramics (with some superbly preserved medieval pieces) and the Iberian and Roman periods are highlights, and there's a huge Roman mosaic laid out on the top floor. Explanatory information is in Spanish only, but it's not hard to get the gist of what's what.

Torre de San Martín TOWER
(Calle San Martín) Although you can't climb it, Torre de San Martín, the northwestern gate of the old city, is almost as beautiful as the Torre de El Salvador, and you can get an unobstructed view of it across Plaza Pérez Prado. Completed in 1316, it was incorporated into the city's walls in the 16th century.

Festivals & Events

Fiestas del Ángel FERIA
(www.vaquillas.es; ⌚Jul) Popularly known as La Vaquilla, the weeklong Fiestas del Ángel revolve around 10 July, the Día de San Cristóbal (St Christopher's Day), which commemorates Teruel's founding.

Lots of music, celebratory crowds, colourful costumes and a running of four roped bulls around the city on the Monday are essential ingredients of the fiesta.

Sleeping

Fonda del Tozal INN €
(☎649 103411; Calle del Rincón 5; d €38-45; 📶) Dating from the 16th century and one of the oldest inns in Spain, Tozal has a considerable variety of rooms, but all have a real sense of the past with beams, solid furniture and ancient floor tiles. And, while not deluxe, they're perfectly comfortable. In some rooms, paintwork has been stripped back to reveal the original faintly patterned plasterwork beneath.

The cavernous wood-beamed tavern in the inn's former stables is classic old-school Spain, where commentary from the latest Barça game competes with the clack of dominoes, and all manner of ancient bric-a-brac hang from the walls and ceiling.

★ **Hotel El Mudayyan** BOUTIQUE HOTEL €€
(978 62 30 42; www.elmudayyan.com; Calle Nueva 18; s €39-99, d €59-99;) The recently expanded Mudayyan is unique. Modern, clean, comfortable rooms and friendly, efficient staff are a given, but pushing the boat out further are the fantastic buffet breakfasts, including bacon and eggs and homemade pastries (per person €5.90), and a secret 16th-century tunnel to the priest's house of the church next door (staff give free tours at 10am).

Hotel Teruel Plaza HOTEL €€
(978 60 88 17; www.hotelteruelplaza.com; Plaza del Tremedal 3; s €40, d €50-150;) This welcoming and recently renovated hotel provides 18 spacious rooms with sofas or armchairs and neon-style spot lighting in vivid colours. The smart bathrooms are done out in blue and ochre tiling. The hotel has a ground-floor cafe-restaurant with amusing prints and a basement breakfast room with – a very nice touch for families – a kids' play room adjoining. Breakfast costs €6.

Eating

La Barrica – Paseo del Óvalo ARAGONESE €
(Paseo del Óvalo 10; raciones €7-12; 9am-4pm & 8.30pm-midnight Tue-Sat, 9am-4pm Sun) A recently opened new venture by a top Teruel tapas bar of the **same name** (Calle Abadía 5; tapas €2-3; 9.30am-3.30pm & 8-11pm Mon-Fri, noon-3.30pm & 8-11pm Sat, noon-3.30pm Sun, closed Tue Sep-May, Sun Jun-Aug), Barrica takes a refreshingly adventurous approach to classic ingredients, with offerings like grilled octopus with asparagus and romesco sauce, or a salad of spinach, brie, ham and dried fruits. The indoor space is clean-lined and uncluttered, and they have plenty of outdoor tables.

★ **La Torre del Salvador** ARAGONESE €€
(978 60 52 63; Calle El Salvador; mains €12-19; noon-4pm Tue, Wed & Sun, noon-4pm & 9-11pm Thu-Sat;) This smart restaurant raises the stakes with subtle *nueva cocina aragonesa* dishes riffing on traditional themes – the likes of duck in a sauce of red fruits and *pacharán* (sloe liqueur), ham knuckle roasted in white wine, or monkfish-and-prawn fishballs in saffron sauce. It's very popular and not very big, so reserving or arriving early is advisable.

Bar Gregory ARAGONESE €€
(Paseo del Óvalo 6; mains €7-14; 8am-midnight) Speedy, helpful service and a long list of well executed, ample-sized dishes, plus plenty of outdoor tables for enjoying the balmier seasons, are the ingredients of Gregory's long-running success. Salads, egg dishes and plenty of seafood complement the meatier options – which include your chance to try pig's ears, snouts or trotters as well more familiar cuts of ham, pork and lamb.

ARAGONESE MUDÉJAR – THE ULTIMATE IN CHRISTIAN-ISLAMIC FUSION

Many Spanish buildings are hybrids, but few cityscapes can equal the dynamic Christian-Islamic hybridisation of Teruel, Spain's capital of Mudéjar.

Mudéjar is an architectural style unique to Spain that arose out of the peculiar history of the Reconquista, which saw towns and villages fall from Muslim back into Christian hands between the mid-8th century and 1492. Skilled Muslim architects and artisans living in the newly conquered lands were employed by the Christians to create their new buildings, applying Islamic building and decorative techniques to basic Christian models.

Different nuances of Mudéjar can been seen over much of Spain, but the style reached its apex between the 13th and 16th centuries in a triangle of land between Teruel, Zaragoza and Tarazona. The inspiration probably came from Zaragoza's Aljafería (p407), a Moorish palace that had been taken over and fortified by Christian king Alfonso I in 1118.

Aragonese Mudéjar borrowed from both Romanesque and Gothic, but used terracotta brick rather than grey stone as its main building material. In Teruel a quartet of bell-cum-lookout towers is adorned with arches and decorated with glazed tiles in geometric patterns. The impression is not a million miles from the Almohad minarets of Morocco.

Mudéjar had died out by the 17th century, but it re-emerged briefly in Teruel in the early 20th century, reinvigorated by Gaudí-inspired Modernistas such as Pau Monguió (who also designed many of Teruel's art-nouveau buildings). The decorative portico on the cathedral and the sweeping Escalinata, a grand staircase connecting Paseo del Óvalo to the railway station, both date from this period.

Information

City Tourist Office (978 62 41 05; www.turismo.teruel.es; Plaza de los Amantes 6; 10am-2pm & 4-8pm Sep-Jul, 10am-8pm Aug) Ask here for English/French/Spanish audio guides (€2) to the old city, and pick up the leaflet *Teruel Ruta Europea del Modernismo,* which maps out 17 early-20th-century modernist and art-nouveau buildings around town

Getting There & Away

BUS

Destinations served from Teruel's **bus station** (978 61 07 89; www.estacionteruel.es; Ronda de Ambeles) include Barcelona (€32, 5¼ hours, one daily), Cuenca (€12, 2¼ hours, one daily), Daroca (€6.80, 1¾ hours, one to three daily), Madrid (€22, 3½ to 4½ hours, two to four daily), Valencia (€11, two hours, four or five daily) and Zaragoza (€11, 2¼ to three hours, four to six daily).

TRAIN

Teruel is on the railway between Zaragoza (€15 to €20, 2½ hours) and Valencia (€13 to €18, 2¾ hours), with three or four trains in each direction daily. The station is at the foot of the Escalinata.

Albarracín

POP 940 / ELEV 1150M

The pink-hued medieval houses of Albarracín are like nowhere else in Spain. So authentic are the twisting streets with their wooden balconies that one half expects Don Quixote and Sancho Panza to appear from around a blind corner. You can argue all day about Spain's prettiest village, but Albarracín, with its fortifications, churches and houses on a rocky promontory carved out by the Río Guadalaviar, is definitely a contender. Its medieval history as an independent mini-state, and the story of its resurrection from near-abandonment over the past 60 years, add to the fascination. The town is 38km west of Teruel and worth a stay of a night or two.

The pink colour, by the way, comes from the unusual hue of the local gypsum, an important construction material hereabouts.

History

The Banu Razin clan of Berbers took control of the Albarracín area in the 10th century and ruled as an independent Muslim dynasty from 1013 to 1104. The tiny statelet passed into Christian hands in 1170 but remained effectively independent until subsumed into Aragón in 1284. Christian Albarracín had its own bishop and cathedral, and prospered from livestock herding until the 17th century, but by the mid-20th century it had declined into a state of semi-ruin. Restoration efforts began and have continued to this day.

Sights

Many of Albarracín's sights are managed by the **Fundación Santa María de Albarracín** (978 70 40 35; http://fundacionsantamariadealbarracin.com; Calle Catedral; 10am-2pm & 4-6.30pm) and the cathedral and castle can only be entered on their (Spanish only) guided visits. Head to their information centre in the old bishop's stables to plan your visit. Opening hours and tour frequencies vary with the seasons – generally more in July and August, fewer in winter. The Fundación's website gives current schedules.

★Catedral del Salvador CATHEDRAL
(tours €3.50; tours 10.30am, noon & 4.30pm, closed Sun afternoon Sep-Jun) After two decades of painstaking restoration, Albarracín's 16th-century cathedral has been returned to the splendour it enjoyed in the 18th century, by which time baroque modifications had altered its original Gothic and Renaissance lines. You can visit on a guided tour with the Fundación Santa María de Albarracín – in Spanish only, but worthwhile even if your understanding is minimal. Highlights include frescos and a 16th-century altarpiece in local pine, devoted to the life of St Peter.

Museo Diocesano MUSEUM
(Calle Catedral; €2.50; 10.30am-2pm & 4.30-6.30pm, closed Sun afternoon Sep-Jun) The 18th-century Bishop's Palace, adjoining the cathedral, houses this collection of religious art, which is a cut well above your average church museum. The six huge tapestries depicting the biblical story of Gideon stand out, as does an Italian salt- or incense-holder of rock crystal and gems, in the shape of a fish.

Museo de Albarracín MUSEUM
(Calle San Juan; €2.50; 10.30am-1pm & 4.30-5.30pm, closed Sun afternoon Sep-Jun) In the town's old hospital, this museum explains Albarracín's fascinating history in absorbing detail in Spanish. Displays include numerous finds from the archaeological digs in the castle, which have contributed in a big way to the understanding of the town's history.

Castle CASTLE
(Castillo; tours €2.50) Crowning the old village, Albarracín's castle was founded in the 9th century and abandoned by the 17th.

Apart from its perimeter wall and 12 towers, everything you see – including the remains of the residence of the 11th-century Banu Razin Muslim rulers – has been excavated over the past decade or so from what had become animal pasture. Visits are by Spanish-language tour starting at the Museo de Albarracín.

Muralla WALLS

Albarracín's highest point, the **Torre del Andador** (Walkway Tower), dates from the 10th century, when it was built as a defensive outpost at a time when the Muslim town was still huddled around the castle. The walls that climb so picturesquely up to the tower were added in the 11th century as the town expanded. The reward for *your* climb up to it is a panorama over the town and the unique topography that made its location so strategic.

Sleeping

Posada del Adarve HERITAGE HOTEL €

(978 70 03 04; www.posadadeladarve.com; Calle Portal de Molina 23; s €35, d €50-75; @) Set in a tower of the medieval walls, this prettily restored hotel has five beautifully decorated, if small, rooms and friendly service.

★La Casa del Tío Americano BOUTIQUE HOTEL €€

(978 71 01 25; www.lacasadeltioamericano.com; Calle Los Palacios 9; s/d incl breakfast €80/100;) A wonderful small hotel, 'The House of the American Uncle' proffers brightly painted rooms, some with exposed stone walls, and friendly, impeccable service. The views of the village from the breakfast terrace (and from the galleried rooms 2 and 3) are magnificent. A welcoming bottle of champagne is a lovely touch, and the generous breakfast features local cheeses, honey and ham.

Casa de Santiago HERITAGE HOTEL €€

(978 70 03 16; www.casadesantiago.es; Subida a las Torres 11; s €48-54, d €64-95;) A beautiful place with prettily decorated rooms including exposed wood and tiled floors, with charming service to go with it, the Casa lies in the heart of the old town a few steps up from Plaza Mayor. You step off the street into an immediate comfort zone. It has its own restaurant and three sitting rooms. Breakfast costs €6.

La Casona del Ajimez HERITAGE HOTEL €€

(978 71 03 21; www.casonadelajimez.com; Calle de San Juan 2; s/d €60/76;) Like other lovingly restored Albarracín small hotels, this 18th-century house has warm and charming decor (with interesting botanical drawings), and fine views from some rooms – and nowhere else has a grassy, terraced garden right below the castle walls! Breakfast costs €5.

Eating

Some places open and close pretty randomly outside the high seasons, which are essentially Semana Santa, July to mid-September and holiday weekends.

★La Despensa ARAGONESE €

(Calle del Chorro 18; dishes €3.50-8; 7.30-11pm Mon & Wed-Fri, 12.30-11pm Sat & Sun;) FREE It's a delight to come across this tiny, friendly corner bar if you're looking for something tasty to eat that's not a full sit-down meal. The specialities are varieties of *embutidos* (cured meats and sausages) and cheeses, available as tapas, *raciones* (larger plates), *bocadillos* (long, filled bread rolls) or *tostas* (on toast).

★Tiempo de Ensueño CONTEMPORARY SPANISH €€

(978 70 60 70; www.tiempodeensuenyo.com; Calle Los Palacios 1B; mains €19-20, menús €39-45; 1.30-3.30pm Mon & Wed, 1.30-3.30pm & 8.30-10.30pm Thu-Sun) This high-class restaurant has a sleek, light-filled dining room, attentive but discreet service, and changing menus of innovative food that you'll remember. The venison was the tenderest we've ever had, the *jamón* starter an enormous platter, and the beetroot soufflé and apple cream divine.

Rincón del Chorro ARAGONESE €€

(978 71 01 12; http://rincondelchorro.es; Calle del Chorro 5; mains €11-20, tasting menu €23; 1-4pm & 8-11pm Wed-Sun, 1-4pm Mon, Fri-Sun only Dec-Jun) Traditional local dishes from Albarracín are the stars at this long-established favourite, including roast lamb, suckling kid *(cabrito lechal)*, and truffles and wild mushrooms at certain times of year. There are good tapas and *raciones* (larger plates) in the downstairs bar too, and a sophisticated (for Albarracín) drinks menu that includes 25 types of gin.

Information

Tourist Office (978 71 02 62; www.turismo sierradealbarracin.es; Calle San Antonio 2; 10am-2pm & 4-8pm Mon-Sat, to 7pm Sun) Beside the main road just before you reach the old town coming from Teruel.

Getting There & Away

A bus to Teruel (€4.50, 45 minutes) leaves Albarracín at 8.55am Monday to Saturday, starting back from Teruel bus station at 2.10pm.

Basque Country, Navarra & La Rioja

POP POP 3.8 MILLION

Includes ➡

Best Places to Eat

- ➡ La Viña del Ensanche (p455)
- ➡ Arzak (p470)
- ➡ Bar Borda Berri (p471)
- ➡ Mesón Arropain (p462)
- ➡ Restaurante Amelibia (p504)
- ➡ Bar Gaucho (p487)

Best Places to Stay

- ➡ Hotel Marqués de Riscal (p502)
- ➡ Hotel Zubieta (p461)
- ➡ Miró Hotel (p453)
- ➡ Palacio Guendulain (p486)
- ➡ La Casa de los Arquillos (p481)
- ➡ Hotel Maria Cristina (p469)

Why Go?

The jade hills and drizzle-filled skies of this pocket of Spain are quite a contrast to the popular image of the country. The Basques, the people who inhabit this corner, also consider themselves different. They claim to be the oldest Europeans and to speak the original European language. Whether or not this is actually the case remains unproven, but what is beyond doubt is that they live in a land of exceptional beauty and diversity. There are mountains watched over by almost forgotten gods, cultural museums and art galleries, street parties a million people strong and, arguably, the best food in Spain.

Leave the rugged north behind and feel the temperature rise as you hit the open, classically Spanish plains south of Pamplona. Here you enter the world of Navarra and La Rioja. It's a region awash with glorious wine, sunburst colours, dreamy landscapes, medieval monasteries and enticing wine towns.

When to Go

Bilbao

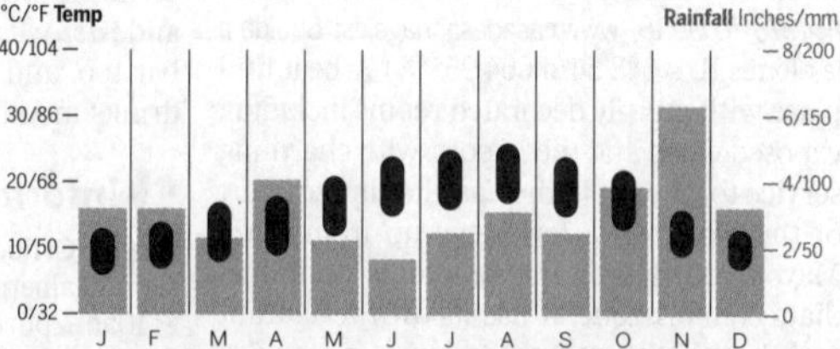

May Spring brings crowds, and a bustling modern art scene, in the museums and galleries of Bilbao.

Jul–Sep San Sebastián at its best and, unless you're skiing, the best time to visit the Pyrenees.

Sep Harvest festivals bring revelry and free-flowing wine to the villages of La Rioja.

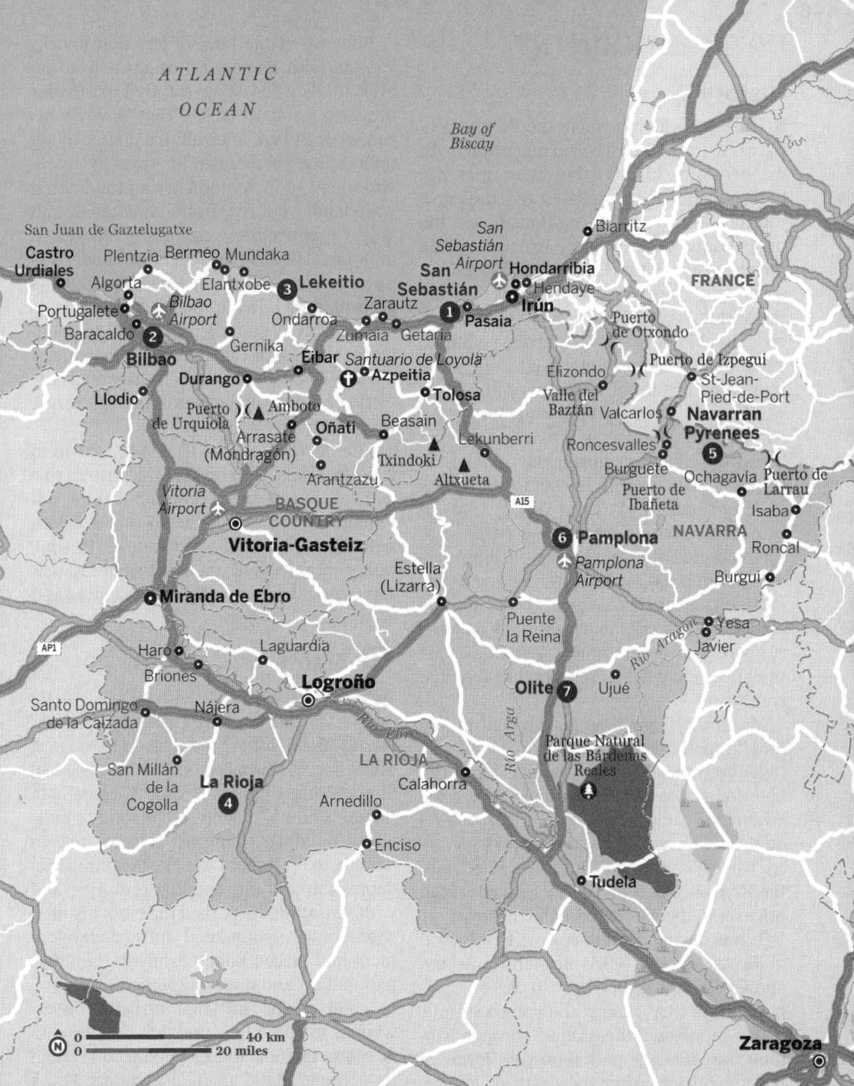

Bilbao, Basque Country & La Rioja Highlights

❶ **San Sebastián** (p463) Playing on a perfect beach, gorging on fabulous cuisine and exploring the cobblestone lanes at this stylish seaside city.

❷ **Bilbao** (p446) Finding artistic inspiration at the Guggenheim, one of Europe's great architectural treasures.

❸ **Lekeitio** (p461) Strolling at low tide out to a scenic island just off shore of this picture-perfect village.

❹ **La Rioja** (p501) Learning the secrets of a good drop in the vineyards and museums of La Rioja.

❺ **Navarran Pyrenees** (p488) Climbing slopes haunted by witches in this magnificent mountain region.

❻ **Pamplona** (p483) Following in the steps of Hemingway, while joining in the revelry of Sanfermines.

❼ **Olite** (p492) Stepping into a fairy tale amid the turrets and spires of the old walled quarter.

BASQUE COUNTRY

History

No one quite knows where the Basque people came from (they have no migration myth in their oral history), but their presence here is believed to predate even the earliest known migrations. The Romans left the hilly Basque Country more or less to itself, but the expansionist Castilian crown gained sovereignty over Basque territories during the Middle Ages (1000–1450), although with considerable difficulty; Navarra constituted a separate kingdom until 1512. Even when they came within the Castilian orbit, Navarra and the three other Basque provinces (Guipúzcoa, Vizcaya and Álava) extracted broad autonomy arrangements, known as the *fueros* (the ancient laws of the Basques).

After the Second Carlist War in 1876, all provinces except Navarra were stripped of their coveted *fueros*, thereby fuelling nascent Basque nationalism. Yet, although the Partido Nacionalista Vasco (PNV; Basque Nationalist Party) was established in 1894, support was never uniform as all Basque provinces included a considerable Castilian contingent.

When the Republican government in Madrid proposed the possibility of home rule (self-government) to the Basques in 1936, both Guipúzcoa and Vizcaya took up the offer. When the Spanish Civil War erupted, conservative rural Navarra and Álava supported Franco, while Vizcaya and Guipúzcoa sided with the Republicans, a decision they paid a high price for in the four decades that followed.

It was during the Franco days that Euskadi Ta Askatasuna (ETA; Basque Homeland and Freedom) was first born. It was originally set up to fight against the Franco regime, which suppressed the Basques through banning the language and almost all forms of Basque culture. After the death of Franco, ETA called for nothing less than total independence and continued its bloody fight against the Spanish government until, in October 2011, the group announced a 'definitive cessation of its armed activity'.

Bilbao

POP 345,200

Staggering architecture, a venerable dining scene and stunning landscapes just outside the city centre: Bilbao is one of the great treasures of the Basque Country.

Bilbao isn't the kind of city that knocks you out with its physical beauty – head on over to San Sebastián for that particular pleasure – but it's a city that slowly wins you over. Bilbao, after all, has had a tough upbringing. Surrounded for years by an environment of heavy industry and industrial wastelands, its riverfront landscapes and quirky architecture were hardly recognised or appreciated by travellers on their way to more pleasant destinations. But Bilbao's graft paid off when a few wise investments left it with a shimmering titanium landmark, the Museo Guggenheim Bilbao – and a horde of art world types from around the world started coming to see what all the fuss was about.

The *Botxo* (Hole), as it's fondly known to its inhabitants, has now matured into its role of major European art centre. But at heart it remains a hard-working town, and one with real character. It's this down-to-earth soul, rather than its plethora of art galleries, that is the real attraction of the vital, exciting and cultured city of Bilbao.

Sights

★Museo Guggenheim Bilbao GALLERY

(☎944 35 90 16; www.guggenheim-bilbao.es; Avenida Abandoibarra 2; adult/student/child from €16/9/free; ⏲10am-8pm, closed Mon Sep-Jun) Shimmering titanium Museo Guggenheim Bilbao is one of modern architecture's most iconic buildings. It played a major role in helping to lift Bilbao out of its postindustrial depression and into the 21st century – and with sensation. It sparked the city's inspired regeneration, stimulated further development and placed Bilbao firmly in the international art and tourism spotlight.

Some might say that structure overwhelms function here and that the museum is more famous for its architecture than its content. But Canadian architect Frank Gehry's inspired use of flowing canopies, cliffs, promontories, ship shapes, towers and flying fins is irresistible.

Gehry designed the museum with historical and geographical contexts in mind. The site was an industrial wasteland, part of Bilbao's wretched and decaying warehouse district on the banks of the Ría del Nervión. The city's historical industries of shipbuilding and fishing reflected Gehry's own interests, not least his engagement with industrial materials in previous works. The gleaming titanium tiles that sheathe most of the building like giant herring scales are said to have been inspired by the architect's childhood fascination with fish.

Other artists have added their touch as well. Lying between the glass buttresses of the central atrium and the Ría del Nervión is a simple pool of water that emits a mist installation by Fujiko Nakaya. Near the riverbank is Louise Bourgeois' *Maman*, a skeletal spider-like canopy said to symbolise a protective embrace. In the open area west of the museum, the child-favourite fountain sculpture randomly fires off jets of water. Jeff Koons' kitsch whimsy *Puppy*, a 12m-tall highland terrier made up of thousands of begonias, is on the city side of the museum. Bilbao has hung on to 'El Poop', who was supposed to be a passing attraction as part of a world tour. *Bilbaínos* will tell you that El Poop came first – and then they had to build a kennel behind it.

Heading inside, the interior is purposefully vast. The cathedral-like atrium is more than 45m high, with light pouring in through the glass cliffs. Permanent exhibitions fill the ground floor and include Richard Serra's massive maze-like sculptures in weathered steel and Jenny Holzer's 9 LED columns of ever-flowing phrases and text fragments (in English, Spanish and Basque) that reach for the skies.

For many people, it is the temporary shows – from retrospectives of the groundbreaking contemporary video artist Bill Viola to wide-ranging exhibitions that explore fin de siècle Paris – that are the main attraction. Excellent self-guided audio tours in various languages are free with admission and there is also a special children's audio guide.

Free guided tours in Spanish take place at 12.30pm and 5pm; sign up half an hour before at the information desk. Tours can be conducted in other languages but you must ask at the information desk beforehand. Groups are limited to 20 (and there needs to be a minimum of eight), so get there early. It's also possible to organise private group tours in Spanish, English, French and German, among others, by prior arrangement. The museum is equipped with specially adapted magnetic loop PDA video guides for those with hearing impairments.

Entry queues can be horrendous, with wet summer days and Easter almost guaranteeing you a wait of over an hour. The museum is wheelchair accessible.

★Museo de Bellas Artes GALLERY

(☎944 39 60 60; www.museobilbao.com; Plaza del Museo 2; adult/student/child €9/7/free, free 10am-3pm Wed & 3-8pm Sun; ⏰10am-8pm Wed-Mon) The Museo de Bellas Artes houses a compelling collection that includes everything from Gothic sculptures to 20th-century pop art. There are three main subcollections: classical art, with works by Murillo, Zurbarán, El Greco, Goya and van Dyck; contemporary art, featuring works by Gauguin, Francis Bacon and Anthony Caro; and Basque art, with works of the great sculptors Jorge Oteiza and Eduardo Chillida, and strong paintings by the likes of Ignacio Zuloaga and Juan de Echevarría.

Casco Viejo OLD TOWN

The compact Casco Viejo, Bilbao's atmospheric old quarter, is full of charming streets, boisterous bars and plenty of quirky and independent shops. At the heart

CITY TOURS

There are a number of different city tours available. Some are general-interest tours, others focus on specific aspects of the city such as architecture or food. The following are recommended.

Bilbao Tourist Office (p458) Organises 1½-hour walking tours covering either the old town or the architecture in the newer parts of town. At busy times tours can run with more frequency.

Bilboats (☎946 42 41 57; www.bilboats.com; Plaza Pío Baroja; adult/child from €13/9) Runs boat cruises along the Nervión several times a day.

Bilbao Greeters (www.bilbaogreeters.com; donation suggested) One of the more original, and interesting, ways to see the city and get to know a local is through the Bilbao Greeters organisation. Essentially a local person gives you a tour of the city showing you their favourite sights, places to hang out and, of course, *pintxo* (Basque tapas) bars. You need to reserve through the website at least a fortnight in advance.

Bilbao

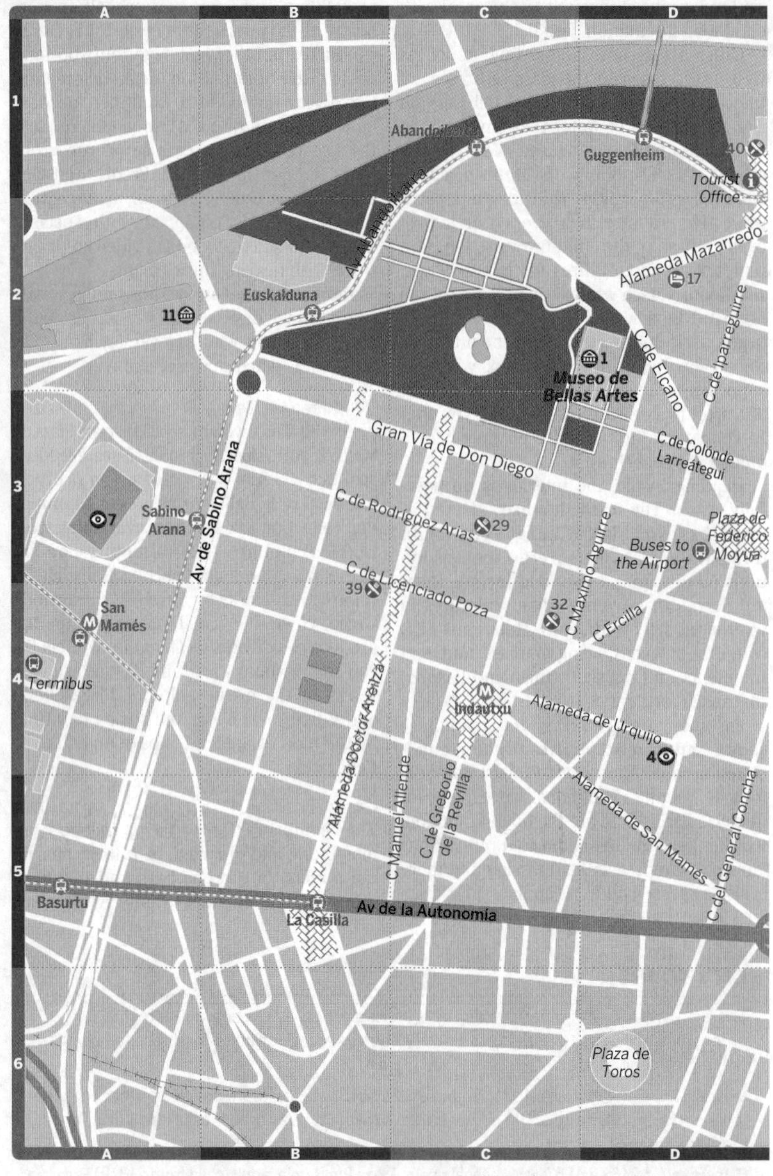

of the Casco are Bilbao's original seven streets, **Las Siete Calles**, which date from the 1400s.

The 14th-century Gothic **Catedral de Santiago** (www.bilbaoturismo.net; Plaza de Santiago; adult/student €5/3.50; ⏲10am-2pm & 4-8pm Mon-Sat) has a splendid Renaissance portico and pretty little cloister. Further north, the 19th-century arcaded **Plaza Nueva** (Plaza Barria) is a rewarding *pintxo* haunt. There's a small Sunday-morning **flea market** here, which is full of secondhand book and

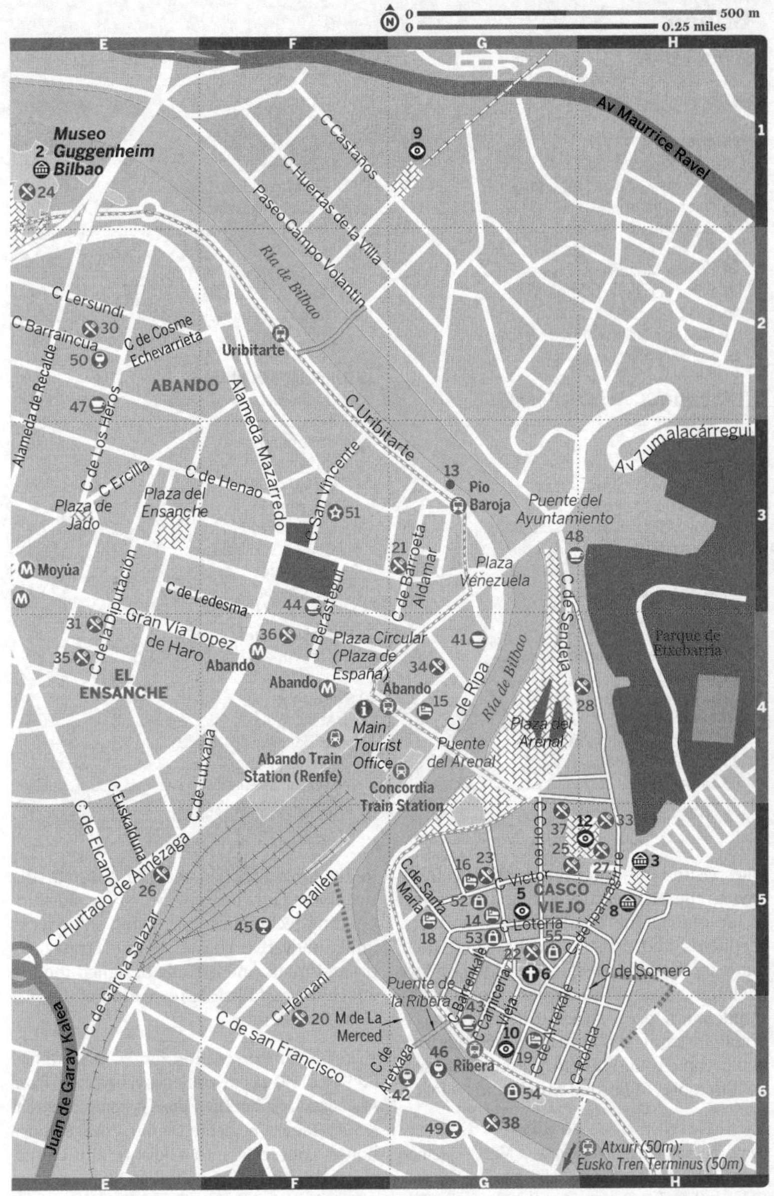

record stalls. Street performers and waiters with trays piled high weave in between. The market is much more subdued in winter. A sweeter-smelling **flower market** takes place on Sunday mornings in the nearby **Plaza del Arenal**.

Euskal Museoa MUSEUM

(Museo Vasco; ☎944 15 54 23; www.euskal-museoa.eus; Plaza Miguel Unamuno 4; adult/child €3/free, Thu free; ⏰10am-7pm Mon & Wed-Fri, 10am-1.30pm & 4-7pm Sat, 10am-2pm Sun) One of Spain's best museums devoted to Basque culture

Bilbao

Top Sights
1 Museo de Bellas Artes ... D2
2 Museo Guggenheim Bilbao ... E1

Sights
3 Arkeologi Museo ... H5
4 Azkuna Zentroa (Alhóndiga) ... D4
5 Casco Viejo ... G5
6 Catedral de Santiago ... G5
7 Estadio San Mamés ... A3
8 Euskal Museoa ... H5
9 Funicular de Artxanda ... G1
10 Las Siete Calles ... G6
11 Museo Marítimo Ría de Bilbao ... A2
12 Plaza Nueva ... H5

Activities, Courses & Tours
13 Bilboats ... G3

Sleeping
14 Casual Bilbao Gurea ... G5
15 Hostal Begoña ... G4
16 Hotel Bilbao Jardines ... G5
17 Miró Hotel ... D2
18 Pensión Iturrienea Ostatua ... G5
19 Quartier Bilbao ... G6

Eating
20 Agape Restaurante ... F6
21 Basquery ... G3
22 Baster ... G5
23 Berton ... G5
24 Bistró Guggenheim Bilbao ... E1
25 Café-Bar Bilbao ... G5
26 Casa Rufo ... E5
27 Casa Victor Montes ... H5
28 Claudio: La Feria del Jamón ... H4
29 Colombo ... C3
30 Coppola ... E2
31 El Globo ... E4
32 El Puertito ... C4
33 Gure Toki ... H5
34 La Camelia ... G4
35 La Viña del Ensanche ... E4
36 Ledesma No 5 ... F4
37 Los Fueros ... G5
38 Mina Restaurante ... G6
39 Mugi ... B4
40 Nerua Guggenheim Bilbao ... D1
Sorginzulo ... (see 33)

Drinking & Nightlife
41 Baobab ... G4
42 Bihotz ... G6
43 Bohemian Lane ... G6
44 Café Iruña ... F3
45 El Balcón de la Lola ... F5
46 Marzana 16 ... G6
47 Mr Marvelous ... E2
48 Opila ... G3
49 Peso Neto ... G6
50 Residence ... E2

Entertainment
51 Kafe Antzokia ... F3

Shopping
52 Ätakontu ... G5
La Bendita ... (see 6)
53 Malmö ... G5
54 Mercado de la Ribera ... G6
55 Nukak Bilbao ... G5

takes visitors on a journey from Paleolithic days to the 21st century, giving an overview of life among the boat builders, mariners, shepherds and artists who have left their mark on modern Basque identity. Displays of clothing, looms, fishing nets, model boats, woodcutters' axes, sheep bells and navigational instruments illustrate everyday life, while iconic round funerary stones help segue into topics of Basque rituals and beliefs.

Museo Marítimo Ría de Bilbao MUSEUM
(www.museomaritimobilbao.org; Muelle Ramón de la Sota 1; adult/child €6/3.50, free Tue Sep-Jun; 10am-8pm Tue-Sun, to 6pm Oct-Mar;) This interactive maritime museum, appropriately situated down on the waterfront, uses bright and well-designed displays to bring the watery depths of Bilbao and Basque maritime history to life. Start off by watching the 10-minute video which gives an overview of Bilbao history from the 1300s to the present, then wander through the two floors of displays, which show old shipbuilding techniques, harrowing shipwrecks (and innovative coastal rescue strategies), pirate threats and artfully designed models – including a full-scale recreation of the 1511 Consulate Barge.

Azkuna Zentroa (Alhóndiga) ARCHITECTURE
(944 01 40 14; www.azkunazentroa.com; Plaza Alhóndiga 4; 7am-11pm Mon-Fri, from 8.30am Sat & Sun) Take a neglected wine storage warehouse, convert it into a leisure and cultural centre, add a bit of Bilbao style and the result is the Azkuna Zentroa (Alhóndiga). Designed by renowned architect Philippe Starck, it now houses a cinema, an art gallery, a rooftop swimming pool with a glass bottom, a public media centre, cafes and restaurants. The ground floor is notable for its 43 tubby columns, each constructed with a unique design.

Parque de Doña Casilda de Iturrizar PARK

(Paseo de José Anselmo Clavé) Floating on waves of peace and quiet just beyond the Museo de Bellas Artes is another work of fine art – the Parque de Doña Casilda de Iturrizar. The centrepiece of this elegant green space, which was completed in 1920, is the small pond filled with ducks and swans.

Arkeologi Museo MUSEUM

(Calzadas de Mallona 2; adult/student/child €3/1.50/free, Fri free; ⌚10am-2pm & 4-7.30pm Tue-Sat) This two-storey museum takes you deep into the past, beginning with fossils found in the Sierra de Atapuerca a mere 430,000(!) years ago. On the second floor, along the romp through the ages, you'll see models of early fortified villages, Celtiberian carvings, and statues and fragments from the Roman period; descend into the Visigothic times and the ensuing Middle Ages. Stones for catapults, a 10th-century trephined skull and jewellery from the 1200s are other curiosities.

Zubizuri BRIDGE

The most striking of the modern bridges that span the Ría del Nervión, the Zubizuri (Basque for 'White Bridge') has become an iconic feature of Bilbao's cityscape since its completion in 1997. Designed by Spanish architect Santiago Calatrava, it has a curved walkway suspended under a flowing white arch to which it's attached by a series of steel spokes.

Estadio San Mamés STADIUM

(www.athletic-club.eus; Calle de Licenciado Poza) Bilbao's modern football stadium, home of local team Athletic Bilbao, overlooks the river to the east of the city centre. It's within easy walking distance of the San Mamés metro station. There's a good cafe and tapas bar in the stadium.

Funicular de Artxanda FUNICULAR

(Plaza Funicular; adult/child €0.95/0.31; ⌚8.15am-10pm Sun, 7.15am-11pm Mon-Sat Jun-Sep, to 10pm Oct-May) Bilbao is a city hemmed in by hills and mountains, resting in a tight valley. For a breathtaking view over the city and the wild Basque mountains beyond, take a trip on the funicular railway that has creaked and moaned its way up the steep slope to the summit of Artxanda for nearly a century.

Festivals & Events

Aste Nagusia CULTURAL

(⌚Aug) Bilbao's grandest fiesta begins on the first Saturday after 15 August. It has a full program of cultural events over nine days and features music and dancing, Basque rural sports (like chopping wood and lifting heavy stones), parades of giants and nightly fireworks.

Noche Blanca CULTURAL

(⌚Jun) For one night in June, the streets, bridges and plazas of Bilbao become a living art piece, with colourful light installations and audiovisual exhibitions. It usually happens on a Saturday night from about 8.30pm to 2am.

Carnaval CARNIVAL

(⌚Feb or Mar) Carnaval is celebrated with vigour in Bilbao, and features parades with floats and costumes, concerts, processions, dances and lots of hands-on children's activities. The revelry runs for about six days, kicking off on the Thursday before Ash Wednesday and ending on Shrove Tuesday, with the ceremonial burning of the sardine. Casco Viejo is the place to be.

Bilbao BBK Live MUSIC

(www.bilbaobbklive.com; 3-day pass from €80; ⌚Jul) Bilbao's biggest musical event is Bilbao BBK Live, which draws top artists from around the globe, including the likes of

WORTH A TRIP

PUENTE COLGANTE

Designed by Alberto Palacio, a disciple of Gustave Eiffel, the Unesco World Heritage–listed **Puente Colgante** (Vizcaya Bridge; www.puente-colgante.com; per person €0.40, walkway €8, with audio guide €10; ⌚walkway 10am-7pm Nov-Mar, to 8pm Apr-Oct; Ⓜ Areeta, Portugalete) – also known as the Vizcaya or Bizkaia Bridge – was the world's first transporter bridge, opening in 1883. The bridge, which links the towns of Getxo and Portugalete (part of greater Bilbao), consists of a suspended platform that sends cars and passengers gliding silently over the Ría del Nervión.

You can take a lift up to the superstructure at 46m and walk across for some great, though decidedly breezy, views.

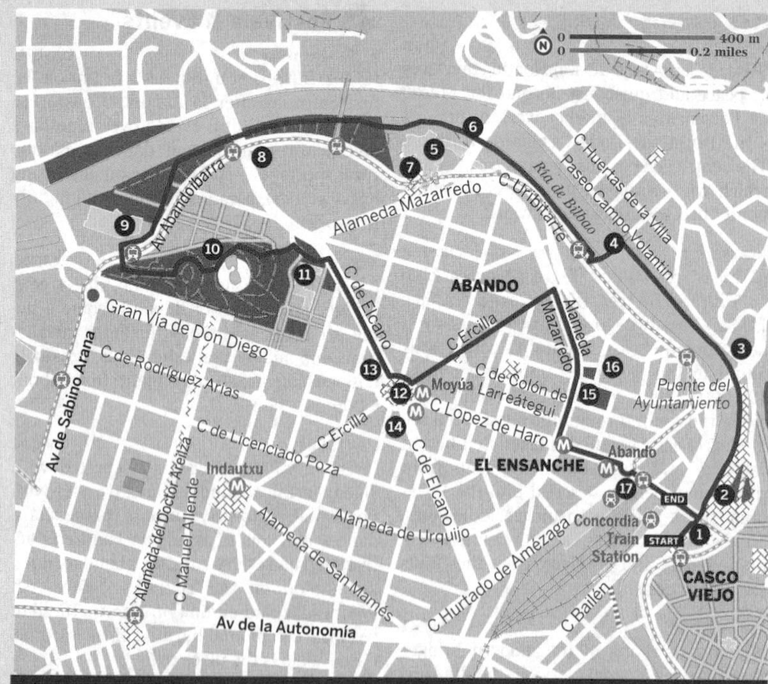

City Walk
Architecture and River Views

START TEATRO ARRIAGA
END TEATRO ARRIAGA
LENGTH 4KM; THREE HOURS

One of the pleasures of a visit to Bilbao is just walking around admiring its crazy mix of architectural styles and the riverside walkways.

Start at the 1 **Teatro Arriaga** (p457), on the edge of the Casco Viejo, which was built in 1890. Follow the river through the 2 **Plaza del Arenal** and pass by the grand 3 **ayuntamiento** (town hall), dating from the late 19th century. Continue upriver along the Paseo Campo Volantín, which is lined with buildings covering a range of styles. Cross over the 4 **Puente Zubizuri**; this wave-like bridge was designed by Santiago Calatrava and is the most striking bridge in the city.

Arriving on the other side of the river turn right and carry on up the waterfront towards the most famous building in the city, the 5 **Museo Guggenheim Bilbao** (p446). It's hard to unhinge your eyes from the museum, but do be sure to check out the spider-like 6 **Maman** and 7 **Puppy**, the sweetest-smelling dog you ever did see.

Continue walking along the river past numerous sculptures. On your left is the 8 **Iberdrola tower**, a 165m glass office block, the tallest building in the region. Eventually you arrive at the modern 9 **Euskalduna Palace** (p457). Turn left and enjoy the stroll through the 10 **Parque de Doña Casilda de Iturrizar** (p451), pass by the 11 **Museo de Bellas Artes** (p447) and head down Calle de Elcano to 12 **Plaza de Federico Moyúa**, which marks the centre of the new town. This square is lined by impressive buildings including, on your right, the early-20th-century Flemish-style 13 **Palacio de Chávarri** and, opposite, the oh-so-grand 14 **Hotel Carlton** (p453). Turn down Calle Ercilla, then right down Alameda Mazarredo until you come to the 15 **Jardines Albia**, overlooked by the 16th-century church 16 **Iglesia San Vicente Mátir**. Cut down to Calle Lopez de Haro and, passing the art-nouveau facade of the 17 **FEVE train station**, cross the Puente del Arenal to arrive back at the start of the walk.

Depeche Mode, Brian Wilson, Two Door Cinema Club, Die Antwoord, Naranja – who all performed in 2017. It takes place over three days (typically early to mid-July) in Parque Kobetamendi, a hillside park located about 2km west of the centre.

Sleeping

Quartier Bilbao HOSTEL €
(☎944 97 88 00; www.quartierbilbao.com; Calle Artekale 15; dm/d with shared bathroom from €18/55;) In a great location in the old town, this new hostel has much to recommend it including modern, well-maintained facilities and helpful staff. It's spread over several floors of a six-storey building, and the attractive common areas are good places to meet other travellers.

Hostal Begoña GUESTHOUSE €
(☎944 23 01 34; www.hostalbegona.com; Calle de la Amistad 2; s/d from €60/75; P) Friendly Begoña has small but cosy guest rooms decorated with modern artwork, wrought-iron beds, and colourful tiled bathrooms. The cosy common areas have plenty of books and information about local culture and attractions. It's a great place to meet other travellers, too.

Pensión Iturrienea Ostatua BOUTIQUE HOTEL €€
(☎944 16 15 00; www.iturrieneaostatua.com; Calle de Santa María 14; s/d €85/95;) One of Bilbao's more eccentric hotels, Pensión Iturrienea Ostatua has a unique look: part farmyard and part old-fashioned toy shop, it mixes floral wallpaper and brightly painted railings with black and white–tiled floors. It sounds unusual, but the aesthetic works – located on one of the charming pedestrian streets in the historic centre, it's a travellers' favourite.

Casual Bilbao Gurea PENSION €€
(☎944 16 32 99; www.casualhoteles.com; Calle de Bidebarrieta 14; s/d €90/100;) The family-run Gurea has arty, modern rooms with wooden floors, good natural light and exceptionally friendly staff. It's set on the third and fourth floors of a building in the old town, with great dining options just steps from the entrance.

Hotel Bilbao Jardines BOUTIQUE HOTEL €€
(☎944 79 42 10; www.hotelbilbaojardines.com; Calle Jardines 9; s/d/tr/q €60/85/95/125;) Though this hotel has a faintly institutional look from the outside, and the green-hued interior decor is somewhat dated, it's a good-value place to stay in the Casco Viejo (Old Town). Its guest rooms are comfortable and guests can borrow bicycles for free.

Miró Hotel DESIGN HOTEL €€€
(☎946 61 18 80; www.mirohotelbilbao.com; Alameda Mazarredo 77; d from €234; @) This hip hotel, facing the Museo Guggenheim Bilbao, is the passion project of fashion designer Antonio Miró. It's filled with modern photography and art, quirky books, and minimalist decor – a perfect fit with art-minded Bilbao.

Hotel Carlton HISTORIC HOTEL €€€
(☎944 16 22 00; www.hotelcarlton.es; Plaza de Federico Moyúa 2; d €145-315; P@) Style, class and sophistication: at Hotel Carlton, sitting proudly in a prominent position on Plaza Federico Moyúa, it's old-fashioned glamour with a retro twist all the way. The grand building, constructed in French Empire style between 1919 and 1926, was the work of Bilbao architect Manuel María Smith.

Eating

Basquery INTERNATIONAL €
(☎944 07 27 12; www.basquery.com; Ibañez de Bilbao 8; mains €10-13; 8am-10pm Mon-Thu, to 11pm Fri & Sat, 9am-4.30pm Sun) The folks behind the celebrated restaurant Bascook opened this more vibrant spot down the block in 2017, and it quickly earned many fans. The industrial, multiroom space is equal parts cafe, bakery, microbrewery and dining destination, with a line-up of pulled-pork or pastrami sandwiches, vegan burgers, plus charcuterie and appetisers that go nicely with the in-house IPA, golden ale and session stout.

El Puertito SEAFOOD €
(☎944 02 62 54; Calle de Licenciado Poza 22, cnr Calle Maestro García Rivero; oysters €2-4.50; 10am-10pm) On warm summer evenings, wine-sipping crowds congregate at this small bar to enjoy an oyster or six. Aficionados can choose from a chalked-up menu of French and Galician oysters, while amateurs can simply ask the knowledgeable, English-speaking staff for their recommendations.

Baster PINTXOS €
(https://basterbilbao.com; Calle Correo 22; pintxos €2.50-7; 10am-10pm Tue-Thu, to 11pm Fri & Sat, to 5pm Sun;) A relaxed and popular bar, Baster serves a range of outstanding

THE ART OF EATING PINTXOS

Just rolling the word *pintxo* (peen-cho) around your tongue defines the essence of this cheerful, cheeky little slice of Basque cuisine. The perfect *pintxo* should have exquisite taste, texture and appearance and should be savoured in two elegant bites. The Basque version of a tapa, the *pintxo* transcends the commonplace by the sheer panache of its culinary campiness.

Many *pintxos* are bedded on small pieces of bread or on tiny half baguettes, upon which towering creations are constructed. Some bars specialise in seafood, with much use of marinated anchovies, prawns and strips of squid, all topped with anything from chopped crab to pâté. Others deal in pepper or mushroom delicacies, or simply offer a mix of everything. And the choice isn't normally limited to what's on the bar top in front of you: many of the best *pintxos* are the hot ones you need to order. These are normally chalked up on a blackboard on the wall somewhere.

Locals prefer to just have one or two *pintxos* in each bar before moving on to the next place. When it comes to ordering, tell the barman what you want first and never just help yourself to a *pintxo* off the counter.

pintxos, including octopus skewers with potato, mini-quiches, housemade croquettes and delectable *jamón*. All goes nicely with a glass of refreshing *txakoli* (local white wine). It gets very busy at weekend lunchtimes when bar-hoppers crowd its pavement tables and bright, modern interior.

★Casa Rufo BASQUE €€

(☎944 43 21 72; www.casarufo.com; Hurtado de Amézaga 5; mains €16-20; ⏲1.30-3.30pm & 8.30-10.30pm Mon-Sat) Tucked in back of a small deli and wine shop, Casa Rufo feels something like a hidden dining spot – albeit one that's terrible at keeping secrets (reserve ahead). Amid shelves packed with top-quality wines, diners tuck into delectable Navarran asparagus and mushrooms with foie, followed by rich oxtail stew, chargrilled steak and flavour-packed *chipirones en su tinta* (baby squid in ink).

Colombo INTERNATIONAL €€

(☎944 39 22 45; http://colombobilbao.com; Calle de Rodríguez Arias 32; mains €11-19; ⏲1-4pm & 8-11pm;) Colombo has effortless style with its big booths, vintage fixtures, oversized windows and upbeat grooves playing overhead. The food is no afterthought, however, with a globally inspired menu that features wild mushroom risotto with black truffle oil and asparagus, charcoal-grilled pork ribs and king prawns in tempura – plus some great appetisers.

La Camelia VEGAN €€

(Calle Villarías 3; mains €6-13; ⏲1-10pm;) On a mostly pedestrian lane near the bridge to the old town, La Camelia serves up excellent vegan fare, including hijiki salad, quinoa tabbouleh, tofu or seitan sandwiches and six varieties of vegetarian maki (rice and vegetables rolled in seaweed).

Agape Restaurante BASQUE €€

(☎944 16 05 06; www.restauranteagape.com; Calle de Hernani 13; menú del día €13, menús €22-36; ⏲1-4pm Mon & Tue, 1-4pm & 9-11pm Wed-Sat;) With a solid reputation among locals for good-value meals that don't sacrifice quality, this is a highly recommended place for a slice of real Bilbao culinary life. Think sea bass served over shrimp and leek risotto, lamb confit with roasted aubergines and stir-fried vegetables with almond and sesame pesto – all served in a stylish but rustic setting.

Los Fueros BASQUE €€

(☎944 15 30 47; www.losfueros.com; Calle Fueros 6; tapas €5-6, mains €12-19; ⏲noon-4pm & 8-11pm Wed-Sun) Seafood stars at this backstreet bar-restaurant near Plaza Nueva, appearing in time-honoured crowd-pleasers like grilled prawns, fresh fish of the day or codfish-stuffed peppers. The bar is smarter than many Old Town places, decked out in contemporary mosaic tiling and cool Mediterranean blues.

Coppola ITALIAN €€

(☎944 24 94 63; Calle Barraincúa 6; mains €13-16; ⏲1-4pm & 8-11pm;) Widely hailed as Bilbao's best Italian restaurant, Coppola serves excellent thin-crust pizza, which you can top with a dizzying variety of ingredients. Other hits include juicy caprese salad, vegetarian risotto and pasta with mushrooms and truffle cream. Coppola also has friendly staff and occasional live music, plus fair prices. Reserve ahead.

★Mina Restaurante BASQUE €€€
(☎944 79 59 38; www.restaurantemina.es; Muelle Marzana; tasting menu €74-110; ⏲2-3.30pm Wed-Sun & 9-10.30pm Wed-Sat) Offering unexpected sophistication and fine dining in an otherwise fairly down-at-the-heels neighbourhood, this riverside restaurant has some critics calling it Bilbao's best. Expect serious culinary creativity: think along the lines of spider crab with passion fruit, aubergine confit with prawns or bone-marrow cake with seasonal mushrooms – followed perhaps by saffron crème brûlée.

Nerua Guggenheim Bilbao BASQUE €€€
(☎944 00 04 30; www.neruaguggenheimbilbao.com; Avenida Abandoibarra 2; lunch/dinner menu from €80/110; ⏲1-3pm Tue-Sun & 8.30-10pm Wed-Sat) The Museo Guggenheim Bilbao's modernist, white, and very minimalist restaurant is under the direction of Michelin-starred chef Josean Alija (a disciple of Ferran Adrià). Needless to say, the *nueva cocina vasca* (Basque nouvelle cuisine) is breathtaking, with 9- and 18-course meals that you'll be remembering (and perhaps paying for) long after you return home.

Reservations are essential. If the gourmet restaurant is a bit much, try the Guggenheim's **Bistró** (☎944 23 93 33; www.bistroguggenheimbilbao.com; Ave Abandoibarra 2; 2-/3-course menu

BEST PINTXO BARS IN BILBAO

Although Bilbao lacks San Sebastián's stellar reputation for *pintxos* (Basque tapas), prices are generally slightly lower here (all charge from around €2.50 per *pintxo*) and the quality is about the same. There are literally hundreds of *pintxo* bars throughout Bilbao, but the Plaza Nueva on the edge of the Casco Viejo offers especially rich pickings, as do Calle de Perro and Calle Jardines. Some of the city's standouts, in no particular order:

Gure Toki (Plaza Nueva 12; pintxos from €2.50; ⏲10am-11.30pm Mon-Sat, to 4pm Sun) With a subtle but simple line in creative *pintxos* including some made with ostrich.

Café-Bar Bilbao (Plaza Nueva 6; pintxos from €2.50; ⏲7am-11pm Mon-Fri, 9am-11.30pm Sat, 10am-3pm Sun) Cool blue southern tile work and warm northern atmosphere.

Casa Victor Montes As well known for its *pintxos* as for its full meals.

Sorginzulo (Plaza Nueva 12; pintxos from €2.50; ⏲10am-midnight) A matchbox-sized bar with an exemplary spread of *pintxos*. The house special is calamari but it's only served on weekends.

Berton (www.berton.eus; Calle Jardines; pintxos from €2.10; ⏲8.30am-11pm Wed-Mon) Here you can watch informative films on the crafting of the same superb *pintxos* that you're munching on.

Claudio: La Feria del Jamón (Calle Iparragirre 9-18; pintxos from €2.50; ⏲10am-2pm & 5-9pm Mon-Fri, 10am-2pm Sat) A creaky old place full of ancient furnishings. As you'll guess from the name and the dozens of legs of ham hanging from the ceiling, it's all about those tasty ungulates.

La Viña del Ensanche (☎944 15 56 15; www.lavinadelensanche.com; Calle de la Diputación 10; small plates €5-15, menú €30; ⏲8.30am-11pm Mon-Fri, noon-1am Sat) Hundreds of bottles of wine line the walls of this outstanding *pintxos* bar. And when we say outstanding, we mean that it could well be the best place to eat *pintxos* in the city.

El Globo (www.barelglobo.com; Calle de la Diputación 8; pintxos from €2.50; ⏲8am-11pm Mon-Fri, 11am-midnight Sat) This is an unassuming but popular bar with favourites such as *txangurro gratinado* (spider crab).

Mugi (www.mugiardotxoko.es; Calle de Licenciado Poza 55; pintxos from €2.50; ⏲9am-midnight Mon-Sat) Widely regarded *pintxo* bar. It can get so busy that you might have to stand outside.

Ledesma No 5 (www.ledesma5.com; Calle de Ledesma 5; pintxos from €3.75; ⏲10am-10pm Mon-Sat) An unmissable spot among the outdoor eateries on pedestrianised Ledesma.

BILBAO CAFES

Bilbao has some appealing cafes in which to enjoy a bit of drinkable latte art and a sweet snack. Styles range from fusty and old fashioned to modern and flash. Here's our pick of the crop.

Café Iruña (www.cafeirunabilbao.net; Calle de Colón de Larreátegui 13; ⌚7am-1am Mon-Fri, 10am-1am Sat & Sun) Moorish style and a century of gossip are the defining characteristics of this grande old dame. It's the perfect place to indulge in a bit of people watching and it works just as well for breakfast or afternoon coffee, lunch or an evening drink. Don't miss the delicious *pinchos morunos* (spicy kebabs).

Bohemian Lane (www.bohemianlanebilbao.com; Calle Carnicería Vieja 3; ⌚10am-8.30pm Mon-Fri, 10am-2.30pm & 4.30-8.30pm Sat) An inviting coffeehouse that also whips up decadent cakes, cookies and other sweets that are 100% vegan. It's a laid-back spot for coffees, tea and fresh juices, with a light, arty design that invites leisurely chatter.

Mr Marvelous (Calle de los Heros; ⌚9am-10pm Mon-Fri, 10am-11pm Sat, 11am-6pm Sun; 📶) While the name is slightly ridiculous, this stylish cafe, bar and eatery does hit all the right notes with its good (and inexpensive) wines, steamy coffees and satisfying *pintxos* (don't overlook the excellent tortillas). It's also quite a handsome space, with eye-catching tile floors and exposed brick walls strung with a changing array of artwork.

Baobab (www.baobabteteria.com; Calle Principe 1; ⌚5-11pm Mon, 11am-11pm Tue-Thu, noon-2am Fri & Sat, noon-10pm Sun) When the rains arrive, Baobab is a fine place to retreat. This bar-teahouse has a warm, welcoming ambience, tasty snacks and an excellent array of teas, infusions, beer, wine, vermouth and other liquid refreshments. Artwork by local artists cover the walls, and there's a regular line-up of acoustic jam sessions, poetry readings and special dinners featuring Senegalese cooking.

Opila (Calle de Sendeja 4; ⌚8am-10pm Mon-Fri, from 10am Sat & Sun) It's worth strolling up to this patisserie and cafe for a caffeinated pick-me-up coupled with a delectable treat or two (pastries from €1.50) baked in house. The interior is set with art deco furnishings and glass display cabinets, while the upstairs tables are a fine spot to settle in with a creamy Portuguese-style tart with a view over the lane and estuary beyond.

from €22/30; ⌚1.30-3.30pm Tue-Sun & 8-10.30pm Thu-Sat Sep-Jun, daily Jul & Aug).

Casa Victor Montes BASQUE €€€
(☎944 15 70 67; www.victormontes.com; Plaza Nueva 8; mains €19-27, pintxos from €2.50; ⌚10.30am-11pm Mon-Thu, to midnight Fri & Sun) Part bar, part shop, part restaurant and total work of art, the Victor Montes is quite touristy, but locals also appreciate its over-the-top decoration, good food and the 1000 or so bottles of wine. If you're stopping by for a full meal, book in advance and savour the house special, *bacalao* (salted cod).

Drinking & Nightlife

Peso Neto BAR
(www.pesoneto.es; Calle San Francisco 1; ⌚11am-1am) For a friendly, laid-back drinking scene – with great food to boot – this bohemian south-bank spot is hard to top. The interior is awash with Mason-jar light fixtures, strings of faerie lights, and curious papier-maché heads on the walls, plus old-school funk playing overhead. Stop in for well-crafted cocktails, Paulaner on draft and no shortage of culinary temptations.

Bihotz BAR
(Calle de Aretxaga 6; ⌚3-10pm Tue-Fri, from 11am Sat & Sun) This unabashedly hipster joint draws lovers of craft beer to its cosy, eclectically adorned interior of mismatched furniture and artfully hung bicycle parts with an alternative soundtrack playing overhead. A friendly crowd and tasty snacks (hummus, veggie sandwiches, cake) – plus outstanding coffees – add to the appeal.

Residence BAR
(www.facebook.com/residencecafe; Calle Barraincua 1; ⌚4pm-1am Sun-Thu, to 3am Fri & Sat) A great little bar that hosts acoustic jam sessions throughout the month, including Irish folk, blues and roots. Even when there's nothing on, it's a fine spot for a well-made

cocktail and a chat with the friendly bar staff. Whiskey lovers take note: Residence stocks more than 200 varieties.

Marzana 16 BAR

(Muelle Marzana 16; 4-11pm Mon-Fri, from noon Sat & Sun) Overlooking the Nervión, Marzana is a hip little spot that draws a festive and bohemian crowd, who come for evening drinks and people watching. The inside of the old-fashioned bar is tiny, so on warm nights, most people take their drinks on the patio and steps above the estuary.

El Balcón de la Lola CLUB

(Calle Bailén 10; €12; 11.45pm-6.15am Thu & Fri, 2-3.30pm & 11.45pm-6.15am Sat, noon-4.30pm Sun) One of Bilbao's most popular mixed gay/straight clubs, this is the place to end the night if you want to keep the party rolling till daybreak. It has industrial decor and packs in dance lovers on weekend. Located under the railway lines, it doesn't get going until late.

Entertainment

★Kafe Antzokia LIVE MUSIC

(944 24 46 25; www.kafeantzokia.com; Calle San Vicente 2) This is the vibrant heart of contemporary Basque Bilbao, featuring international rock, blues and reggae, as well as the cream of Basque rock-pop. Weekend concerts run from 10pm to 1am, followed by DJs until 5am. During the day it's a cafe, restaurant and cultural centre all rolled into one and hosts frequent exciting events.

Euskalduna Palace LIVE MUSIC

(944 03 50 00; www.euskalduna.net; Avenida Abandoibarra 4) About 600m downriver from the Museo Guggenheim Bilbao is this modernist gem, built on the riverbank in a style that echoes the great shipbuilding works of the 19th century. The Euskalduna is home to the Bilbao Symphony Orchestra and the Basque Symphony Orchestra, and hosts a wide array of events.

Teatro Arriaga THEATRE

(944 79 20 36; www.teatroarriaga.com; Plaza Arriaga) The baroque facade of this venue commands the open spaces of El Arenal between the Casco Viejo and the river. It stages theatrical performances and classical music concerts.

Shopping

Malmö ARTS & CRAFTS

(www.facebook.com/malmogallery; Calle Torre 7; 11am-2pm & 5-8pm Mon-Fri, 11am-2pm Sat) Named after the city in Sweden, Malmö specialises in beautiful Scandinavian design with products you won't find elsewhere. Check out handsome Ölend backpacks, animal prints on wood by Ferm Living and colourful enamel mugs by Öm Design. There's much to discover in this friendly shop, with an ever-changing assortment of housewares, artwork, toys and even some clothing.

Ätakontu CLOTHING

(www.atakontu.es; Calle Jardines 8; 11am-2pm & 5-8.30pm Mon-Sat) A pair of Bilbao textile artists created this small shop, which is making waves across the Basque Country. Graphic T-shirts are the speciality – and feature whimsical and art-naïf designs (the dinosaur head is an icon); all are manufactured locally, made with organic cotton and come in unisex sizes. And with limited production runs, you won't see these elsewhere.

Mercado de la Ribera MARKET

(www.mercadodelaribera.net; Calle de la RIbera; 8am-2.30pm Mon & Sat, 8am-2pm & 5-8pm Tue-Fri) Overlooking the river, the Mercado de la Ribera is an expansive food market that draws many of the city's top chefs for their morning selection of fresh produce. If you're not up for a picnic, don't miss the *pintxo* counters upstairs (open till 10pm), which offer an excellent spread – plus seating indoors and out.

La Bendita FOOD & DRINKS

(www.labenditabilbao.com; Carrera de Santiago 1; 10.30am-2pm & 4.30-8.30pm Mon-Sat, noon-2.30pm & 6.30-8.30pm Sun) Next to the cathedral, this is Bilbao's smallest shop, but one well worth seeking out for its unique gourmet delicacies sourced almost exclusively from the Basque Country. You'll find chocolates, foie gras, anchovies, olive oils, pâté, and drinks worth checking your suitcase for, including *patxaran* (a sloe-berry liqueur) and *txakoli* (local white wine).

Nukak Bilbao FASHION & ACCESSORIES

(www.facebook.com/nukakbilbao; Calle Correo 25; 11am-2.30pm & 5-8.30pm Mon-Sat) Street fashion goes green at this hip little store where everything is made from recycled

BARIK CARD

You can save money by purchasing a Barik card for €3 at metro vending machines, topping it up with credit (from €5) and using it on the metro, tram and bus lines. One card can be used for multiple people, and the card pays for itself after five uses. Single passes can also be purchased from metro machines.

materials. You'll find colourful messenger bags made from old advertising banners, sleek backpacks made of truck tires, eye-catching belts made from former firefighter hoses and bicycle inner tubes reconfigured into wallets. The designs are bright and bold – and make fine conversation pieces as well.

Information

Bilbao's friendly tourist-office staffers are extremely helpful, well informed and, above all, enthusiastic about their city. At all offices ask for the free bimonthly *Guía Bilbao*, with its entertainment listings plus tips on restaurants, bars and nightlife.

At the newly opened, state-of-the-art **main tourist office** (944 79 57 60; www.bilbaoturismo.net; Plaza Circular 1; 9am-9pm;) there's free wi-fi access, a bank of touch-screen information computers and, best of all, some humans to help answer questions (take a number). There are also branches at the **airport** (944 03 14 44; www.bilbaoturismo.net; Bilbao Airport; 9am-9pm) and the **Museo Guggenheim Bilbao** (www.bilbaoturismo.net; Alameda Mazarredo 66; 10am-7pm Jul-Aug, to 3pm Sun Sep-Jun).

Getting There & Away

AIR

Bilbao's **airport** (BIO; 902 404 704; www.aena.es; Loiu;) is in Loiu, near Sondika, 12km northeast of the city. A number of European flag carriers serve the city. Of the budget airlines, **EasyJet** (www.easyjet.com) and **Vueling** (www.vueling.com) cover the widest range of destinations.

BUS

Bilbao's main bus station, **Termibus** (944 39 50 77; www.termibus.es; Gurtubay 1, San Mamés), is west of the centre. There are regular services to the following destinations:

DESTINATION	FARE (€)	DURATION (HR)
Barcelona	36-52	7-8½
Biarritz (France)	12-20	3
Logroño	10-14	2¾
Madrid	32-43	4½-5½
Oñati	7	1¼
Pamplona	15	2-2½
San Sebastián	7-12	1¼
Santander	7-15	1¼
Vitoria	9	1½

Bizkaibus travels to destinations throughout the rural Basque Country, including coastal communities such as Mundaka and Gernika (€2.50). Euskotren buses serve Lekeitio (€6.65).

If you're heading directly to San Sebastián after arriving in Bilbao airport, there's a direct bus service from the airport departing hourly from 6.45am to 11.45pm (€17, 1¼ hours).

TRAIN

The **Abando train station** (902 43 23 43; Plaza Circular 2) is just across the river from Plaza Arriaga and the Casco Viejo. There are frequent train services to the following destinations:

DESTINATION	FARE (€)	DURATION (HR)
Barcelona	from 27	6¾
Burgos	from 12	3
Madrid	from 27	5-7
Valladolid	from 21	4

Nearby is the **Concordia train station** (Calle Bailén 2), with its handsome art-nouveau facade of wrought iron and tiles. It is used by **Renfe Feve** (www.renfe.com/viajeros/feve), part of Spain's national Renfe line, which has trains running west into Cantabria. There are three slow daily trains to Santander (from €9, three hours) where you can change for stations in Asturias.

The **Atxuri train station** (944 01 99 00; Calle Atxuri 6) is just upriver from Casco Viejo. From here, **Eusko Tren/Ferrocarril Vasco** (www.euskotren.es) operates services every half-hour to the following:

DESTINATION	FARE (€)	DURATION (HR)
Bermeo	3.40	1½
Gernika	3.40	1
Mundaka	3.40	1½

Getting Around

TO/FROM THE AIRPORT

Airport The **airport bus** (Bizkaibus A3247; €1.50) departs from a stand on the extreme right as you leave arrivals. It runs through the northwestern section of the city, passing the Museo Guggenheim Bilbao, stopping at Plaza de Federico Moyúa and terminating at the Termibus (bus station). It runs from the airport every 20 minutes in summer and every 30 minutes in winter from 6.20am to midnight. There is also a direct hourly bus from the airport to San Sebastián (€17, 1¼ hours). It runs from 7.45am to 11.45pm. Taxis from the airport to the Casco Viejo cost about €25 to €35 depending on traffic.

METRO

There are metro stations at all the main focal points of El Ensanche and at Casco Viejo. Tickets cost €1.60 to €1.90 (€0.90 to €1.20 with a Barik card), depending on distance travelled. The metro runs to the north coast from a number of stations on both sides of the river and makes it easy to get to the beaches closest to Bilbao.

TRAM

Bilbao's Eusko Tren tramline is a boon to locals and visitors alike. It runs to and fro between Basurtu, in the southwest of the city, and the Atxuri train station. Stops include the Termibus station, the Museo Guggenheim Bilbao and Teatro Arriaga by the Casco Viejo. Tickets cost €1.50 (€0.73 with a Barik card) and need to be validated in the machine next to the ticket dispenser before boarding.

Around Bilbao

Gernika

POP 16,900

A name synonymous with the brutality of the Spanish Civil War, Gernika (Guernica in Spanish), suffered a devastating bombing raid that levelled the city in 1937. That harrowing April day left a deep mark on the city's identity. Following the war, Gernika was quickly reconstructed, and although it lost its historic buildings, the narrow lanes of the centre are today brimming with life. You'll find some excellent museums that deal with the bombing as well as the indestructibility of Basque culture through the ages. This is also a great unsung destination for *pintxos*, and well worth a day's exploring.

Sights

Museo de la Paz de Gernika MUSEUM
(Gernika Peace Museum; ☎946 27 02 13; www.museodelapaz.org; Plaza Foru 1; adult/child €5/3, free Sun; ⊙10am-7pm Tue-Sat, 10am-2pm Sun Mar-Sep, 10am-2pm & 4-6pm Tue-Sat, 10am-2pm Sun Oct-Feb, closed Jan) Gernika's seminal experience is a visit to the peace museum, where audiovisual displays calmly reveal the horror of war, both in the Basque Country and around the world. Aside from creating a moving portrait of the events that transpired on the April day, the museum grapples with the topic of peace and reconciliation with illuminating insights by the Dalai Lama, Adolfo Pérez Esquivel and others.

Museo de Euskal Herría MUSEUM
(☎946 25 54 51; Allende Salazar 5; adult/child €3.50/1.75; ⊙10am-2pm & 4-7pm Tue-Sat, 10.30am-2.30pm Sun) Housed in the beautiful 18th-century Palacio de Montefuerte, this museum contains a comprehensive exhibition on Basque history, with fine old maps, engravings and a range of other documents and portraits. The top two floors are the most interesting and explore rich cultural traditions, with exhibits on dance, folklore, mythology and sports.

Parque de los Pueblos de Europa PARK
(Allende Salazar) The Parque de los Pueblos de Europa contains a typically curvaceous **sculpture** by Henry Moore and a monumental work by renowned Basque sculptor Eduardo Chillida. The park leads to the attractive **Casa de Juntas**, where the provincial government has met since 1979. Nearby is the **Tree of Gernika**, under which the Basque parliament met from medieval times to 1876.

Cuevas de Santimamiñe CAVE
(☎944 65 16 57; www.santimamiñe.com; adult/child €5/3; ⊙10am-5.30pm mid-Apr–mid-Oct, 10am-1pm Tue-Sun mid-Oct–mid-Apr) The walls of this cave system, a short way northeast of Gernika, are decorated with around fifty different Neolithic paintings depicting bison, horses, rhinos and the like. In order to protect these delicate artworks, only reproductions are on display.

Tours take place on the hour and last 90 minutes. Call ahead to reserve an English-speaking guide.

THE BOMBING OF GERNIKA

The reasons Franco wished to destroy Gernika are pretty clear. The Spanish Civil War was raging and World War II was looming on the horizon. Franco's Nationalist troops were advancing across Spain, but the Basques, who had their own autonomous regional government consisting of supporters of the Left and Basque nationalists, stood opposed to Franco and Gernika was the final town between the Nationalists and the capture of Bilbao. What's harder to understand is why Hitler got involved, but it's generally thought that the Nazis wanted to test the concept of 'terror bombing' on civilian targets. So when Franco asked Hitler for some help, he was only too happy to oblige.

On the morning of 26 April 1937, planes that were from Hitler's Condor Legion flew backwards and forwards over the town demonstrating their newfound concept of saturation bombing. In the space of a few hours, the town was destroyed and many people were left dead or injured. Exactly how many people were killed remains hard to quantify, with figures ranging from a couple of hundred to well over one thousand. The Museo de la Paz de Gernika (p459) claims that around 250 civilians were killed and several hundred injured. What makes the bombings even more shocking is that it wasn't the first time this had happened. Just days earlier, the nearby town of Durango suffered a similar fate, but that time the world had simply not believed what it was being told.

Aside from blocking the path to Bilbao, Gernika may also have been targeted by Franco because of its symbolic value to the Basques. It's the ancient seat of Basque democracy and the site at which the Basque parliament met beneath the branches of a sacred oak tree from medieval times until 1876. Today the original oak is nothing but a stump, but the Tree of Gernika lives on in the form of a young oak tree.

The tragedy of Gernika gained international resonance with Picasso's iconic painting *Guernica*, which has come to symbolise the violence of the 20th century. A copy of the painting now hangs in the entrance hall of the UN headquarters in New York, while the original hangs in the Centro de Arte Reina Sofía in Madrid. In Gernika, you can find a full-size copy made in ceramic tiles on a wall on Calle Pedro Elejalde near the Museo de la Paz de Gernika.

Eating

There are plenty of bars in Gernika serving good *pintxos*, particularly situated along Calle Pablo Picasso and intersecting streets. Ask at the tourist office about the Ruta del Pintxo, a €9.90 pass (and map) that gives you eight *pintxos* in total from any of 17 listed bars.

Auzokoa PINTXOS €

(Calle Pablo Picasso 5; pintxos from €2; noon-3.30pm & 7-10.30pm) Set on the restaurant-lined lane in the heart of Gernika, Auzokoa whips up some of the best *pintxos* in town.

Information

The friendly multilingual **tourist office** (946 25 58 92; www.gernika-lumo.org; Artekalea 8; 10am-2pm & 4-7pm Mon-Sat, 10am-2pm Sun Apr-Oct, 10am-2pm & 4-6pm Mon-Fri, 10am-2pm Sat & Sun Nov-Mar) doles out info on Gernika and nearby attractions.

Getting There & Away

Genika is an easy day trip from Bilbao by ET/FV train from Atxuri train station (€3.40, one hour). Trains run every half-hour; buses also make the journey.

Central Basque Coast

The coastline that lies between Bilbao and San Sebastián is set with spectacular seascapes, with cove after cove of sun-dappled waves and verdant fields suddenly ending where cliffs plunge into the sea. While some people stop for a day or two along the way, you could easily make a week of it, basking on lovely beaches, taking memorable walks along the craggy coastline and delving into the history of the place – this means everything from 110-million-year-old rock formations to a futuristic museum that is devoted to couture.

Mundaka

POP 1880

Universally regarded as the home of the best left-hand wave in Europe, Mundaka is a name of legend for surfers across the world. The wave breaks on a perfectly tapering sandbar formed by the outflow of the Río Urdaibai and, on a good day, offers heavy, barrelling lefts that can reel off for hundreds of metres. Fantastic for experienced surfers, Mundaka is generally not a place for novices to take to the waves.

Despite all the focus being on the waves, Mundaka remains a resolutely Basque port with a pretty main square and harbour area.

Sights

Playa de Laida BEACH

The lovely golden sands of Laida Beach make a fine setting for a fun day out from Mundaka. The scenic 1km-long beach is located just across the estuary and reached by regular ferry service operated by **Urdai Ferry** (☎622 222919; http://urdaiferry.com; Muelle de Txorrokopunta; return trip €4; ⏱10am-8pm Jun-Sep, 10am-8pm Sat, Sun & holidays Oct-May). Where the water meets the shore, the surface bottom is fairly shallow, making it a fine place for children. Further out, you'll find good breaks for surfing.

Sleeping & Eating

Hotel Atalaya HOTEL €€

(☎946 17 70 00; www.atalayahotel.es; Kalea Itxaropena 1; s/d €100/130; P) This grand hotel is in a lovely old building located near the waterfront and has attractively furnished rooms, many with terraces facing the sea. The kind, English-speaking staff and great location make this a top choice (reserve well ahead).

El Puerto CAFE €

(www.hotelelpuerto.com; Portu 1; small plates €6-12; ⏱11am-10pm) The shady terrace at Hotel El Puerto, a stately blue-and-white building that is facing the harbour, is a good place to stop for a coffee, a glass of wine, or a bite to eat.

Information

Pick up info on the area from the small **tourist office** (☎946 17 72 01; www.mundaka.org; Kepa Deuna; ⏱10.30am-1.30pm & 4-7pm Tue-Sat, 11am-2pm Sun) near the harbour.

Getting There & Away

Buses and ET/FV trains between Bilbao and Bermeo (€3.20, one hour) stop here. You can also catch a Bizkaibus bus from Bilbao (€2.50, one hour).

Lekeitio

POP 7200

Bustling Lekeitio is gorgeous. The attractive old core is centred on the unnaturally large and slightly out-of-place late-Gothic Basílica de Santa María de la Asunción and a busy harbour lined by multicoloured, half-timbered old buildings – some of which house fine seafood restaurants and *pintxo* bars. But for most visitors, it's the two beaches that are the main draw. The one just east of the river, with a small rocky mound of an island offshore, is one of the finest beaches in the Basque Country. In many ways the town is like a miniature version of San Sebastián, but for the moment at least, Lekeitio remains a fairly low-key and predominantly Spanish and French holiday town.

Sights

Isla de San Nicolás ISLAND

One of the great attractions of Lekeitio is the rocky island, known in Basque as Garraitz, sitting just offshore of the main beach (Playa Isuntza). When the tides are low, a paved path appears, allowing visitors to stroll straight out to the island, and take a 200m trail to the top for a fine view over the seaside. Be mindful of the tides, so you don't have to swim back! The tourist office (p462) posts tidal charts.

Sleeping & Eating

★**Hotel Zubieta** BOUTIQUE HOTEL €€

(☎946 84 30 30; www.hotelzubieta.com; Atea; s/d from €95/110; P) A gorgeous and romantic boutique hotel, 10 minutes' walk from the centre of town, which is filled with memories of upper-class 18th-century life. It sits within beautiful flower gardens and is surrounded by spring-blossoming cherry trees.

Hotel Metrokua HOTEL €€

(☎946 84 49 80; www.metrokua.com; Playa de Karraspio; s/d €96/120;) Overlooking Karraspio beach, the welcoming Metrokua has nine small, but light-filled rooms with wood floors and mini-fridges. The best rooms open onto a shared terrace facing the wave-kissed shoreline below. It's about 1.3km (a 20-minute walk) to the centre of town.

WORTH A TRIP

SAN JUAN DE GAZTELUGATXE

On the road between the small towns of Bakio and Bermeo is one of the most photographed features of the Basque coast: the small island of **San Juan de Gaztelugatxe**. Attached to the mainland by a short causeway, this rocky isle is topped by a **hermitage** (⏲11am-6pm Tue-Sat, 11am-3pm Sun Jul & Aug). The island is named after St John the Baptist who local tradition holds visited the island. *Game of Thrones* fans will recognise the setting, which was featured in season 7.

Taberna Bar Lumentza PINTXOS €
(www.lumentza.com; Buenaventura Zapirain 3; pintxos €2-5; ⏲noon-3.30pm & 7-10.30pm Tue-Sun) A big hit with the locals, this no-fuss *pintxos* bar is tucked away in the side streets. Try the octopus cooked on the *plancha* (grill), some savoury codfish *pil-pil* (an emulsion of garlic and olive oil) or top-notch anchovies. All go well with a glass of wine or two.

★Mesón Arropain SEAFOOD €€€
(☎946 84 03 13; Iñigo Artieta Etorbidea 5; mains €20-25, fish per kg €48-62; ⏲1.30-3.30pm & 8.30-10.30pm) About 1km south of the centre, this attractive but easygoing restaurant serves up some of the best seafood for miles around. The chef lets the high-quality products speak for themselves in simple but beautifully prepared dishes. Start off with savoury clams and a tomato and guacamole salad and move on to grilled turbot, sea bream or monkfish. Good wine selection.

Information

Stop by the **tourist office** (☎946 84 40 17; Plaza Independencia; ⏲10am-2pm & 4-8pm) on the main square for info on self-guided tours of the old town.

Getting There & Away

Bizkaibus bus A3512 (€3.30, 1½ hours) leave hourly from Bilbao's Termibus. Slower buses go via Gernika and Elantxobe (two hours). Buses also run four to five times daily from Lekeitio to San Sebastián (€6.85, 1½ hours).

Drivers take note: finding a parking space can be challenging in the summer. If the car parks at the entrance to town are full, you'll find spaces on the road out to the lighthouse (Faro de Santa Catalina).

Getaria

POP 2,820

The attractive medieval fishing settlement of Getaria is a world away from nearby cosmopolitan San Sebastián and is a much better place to get a feel for coastal Basque culture. The old village tilts gently downhill to a baby-sized harbour and a short but very pleasant beach, almost totally sheltered from all but the heaviest Atlantic swells. Its safe bathing makes it an ideal family beach.

At the end of the harbour is a forested island known as El Ratón (the Mouse) – though any resemblance to a rodent is only visible after several strong drinks. Perhaps it was this giant mouse that first encouraged the town's most famous son, the sailor Juan Sebastián Elcano, to take to the ocean. His adventures eventually led him to become the first man to sail around the world, after the captain of his ship, Magellan, died halfway through the endeavour.

Sights

★Cristóbal Balenciaga Museoa MUSEUM
(☎943 00 88 40; www.cristobalbalenciagamuseoa.com; adult/student €10/7; ⏲10am-8pm Jul & Aug, 10am-7pm Tue-Sun Mar-Jun & Sep-Oct, 10am-3pm Tue-Sun Nov-Feb) Although Getaria is mainly about sun, sand and seafood, don't miss a visit to the Cristóbal Balenciaga Museoa. Local boy Cristóbal became a giant in the fashion world in the 1950s and '60s, and this impressive museum showcases some of his best works.

Sleeping & Eating

Hotel Itxas-Gain HOTEL €€
(☎943 14 10 35; www.hotelitxasgain.com; St San Roque 1, Getaria; s €50, d €70-125; P 📶) A short walk from two beaches, the Hotel Itxas-Gain is a great deal with a mixture of room types: some have little balconies and hydromassage baths that overlook the seafront. Weather permitting, breakfast (€6) is served in the peaceful gardens.

Pensión Getariano GUESTHOUSE €€
(☎943 14 05 67; www.pensiongetariano.es; Calle Herrerieta 3, Getaria; s €40-75, d €55-95; P 📶) This is a charming, mellow yellow building with flower-filled balconies and comfortable rooms. It's on the edge of the main road through town, in a great location within a few steps of the old cobblestone centre.

Txoko Getaria SEAFOOD €€

(☎943 14 05 39; http://txokogetaria.com; Calle Katrapona 5; mains €17-21, grilled fish per kilo €40-70; ⏲12.30-4pm & 7.30-11.30pm) Overlooking the seaside, this breezy spot has earned many fans for its fresh sea bream, turbot and flounder – fired up on the grill out front. Fish aside, the seafood rices (particularly the aioli black rice with calamari) are outstanding. Call ahead to reserve an outdoor table.

Getting There & Away

Buses run regularly to Getaria (€2.45, one hour) from San Sebastián's bus station. In Getaria, the buses stop on the main road, outside the tourist office, on the edge of the historic quarter and within easy walking distance of the port (downhill) and the Balenciaga museum (uphill).

San Sebastián

POP 186,100

Framed by golden beaches and lush hillsides, San Sebastián has undeniable allure, from its venerable dining scene to its grand architecture and packed cultural calendar. It's a city filled with people who love to indulge – and with Michelin stars apparently falling from the heavens onto its restaurants, not to mention *pintxo* (tapas) culture almost unmatched anywhere else in Spain, San Sebastián frequently tops lists of the world's best places to eat.

Just as good as the food is the summertime fun in the sun. For its setting, form and attitude, Playa de la Concha is the equal of any city beach in Europe. Then there's Playa de la Zurriola, with its surfers and sultry beach-goers. As the sun falls on another sweltering summer's day, you'll sit back with a drink and an artistic *pintxo* and realise that, yes, you too have fallen under the city's captivating spell.

San Sebastián has four main centres of action. The lively Parte Vieja (old town) lies across the neck of Monte Urgull, the bay's eastern headland, and is where the most popular *pintxo* bars and its least expensive guesthouses are to be found. South of the Parte Vieja is the commercial and shopping district, the Área Romántica, its handsome grid of late-19th-century buildings extending from behind Playa de la Concha to the banks of Río Urumea. On the east side of the river is the district of Gros, a pleasant and increasingly hip enclave that, with its relaxed ambience and the surfing beach, makes a cheerful alternative to more tourist-centric west side of the river.

Sights

★Playa de la Concha BEACH

(Paseo de la Concha) Fulfilling almost every idea of how a perfect city beach should be formed, Playa de la Concha (and its westerly extension, Playa de Ondarreta), is easily among the best city beaches in Europe. Throughout the long summer months a fiesta atmosphere prevails, with thousands of tanned and toned bodies spread across the sands. The swimming is almost always safe.

★Aquarium AQUARIUM

(www.aquariumss.com; Plaza Carlos Blasco de Imaz 1; adult/child €13/6.50; ⏲10am-9pm Jul & Aug, 10am-8pm Mon-Fri, 10am-9pm Sat & Sun Easter-Jun & Sep, 10am-7pm Mon-Fri, to 8pm Sat & Sun Oct-Easter) Fear for your life as huge sharks bear down behind glass panes, or gaze in disbelief at tripped-out fluoro jellyfish. The highlights of a visit to the city's excellent aquarium are the cinema-screen-sized deep-ocean and coral-reef exhibits and the long tunnel, around which swim monsters of the deep. The aquarium also contains a maritime museum section. Allow at least 1½ hours for a visit.

★Parque de Cristina Enea PARK

(www.cristinaenea.eus/es/inicio; Paseo Duque de Mandas; ⏲8am-9pm May-Sep, 9am-7pm Oct-Apr) Created by the Duke of Mandas in honour of his wife, the Parque de Cristina Enea is a favourite escape for locals. This formal park, the most attractive in the city, contains ornamental plants, ducks and peacocks, and open lawns. Its wooded paths make for a scenic stroll, past towering red sequoias and a magnificent Lebanese cedar.

San Telmo Museoa MUSEUM

(☎943 48 15 80; www.santelmomuseoa.com; Plaza Zuloaga 1; adult/student/child €6/3/free; ⏲10am-8pm Tue-Sun) One of the best museums in the Basque Country, the San Telmo Museoa has a thought-provoking collection that explores Basque history and culture in all its complexity. Exhibitions are spread between a restored convent dating back to the 16th century and a cutting-edge newer wing that blends into its plant-lined backdrop of Mount Urgull. The collection ranges from historical artifacts to bold fusions of contemporary art. San Telmo also stages some outstanding temporary exhibitions.

San Sebastián

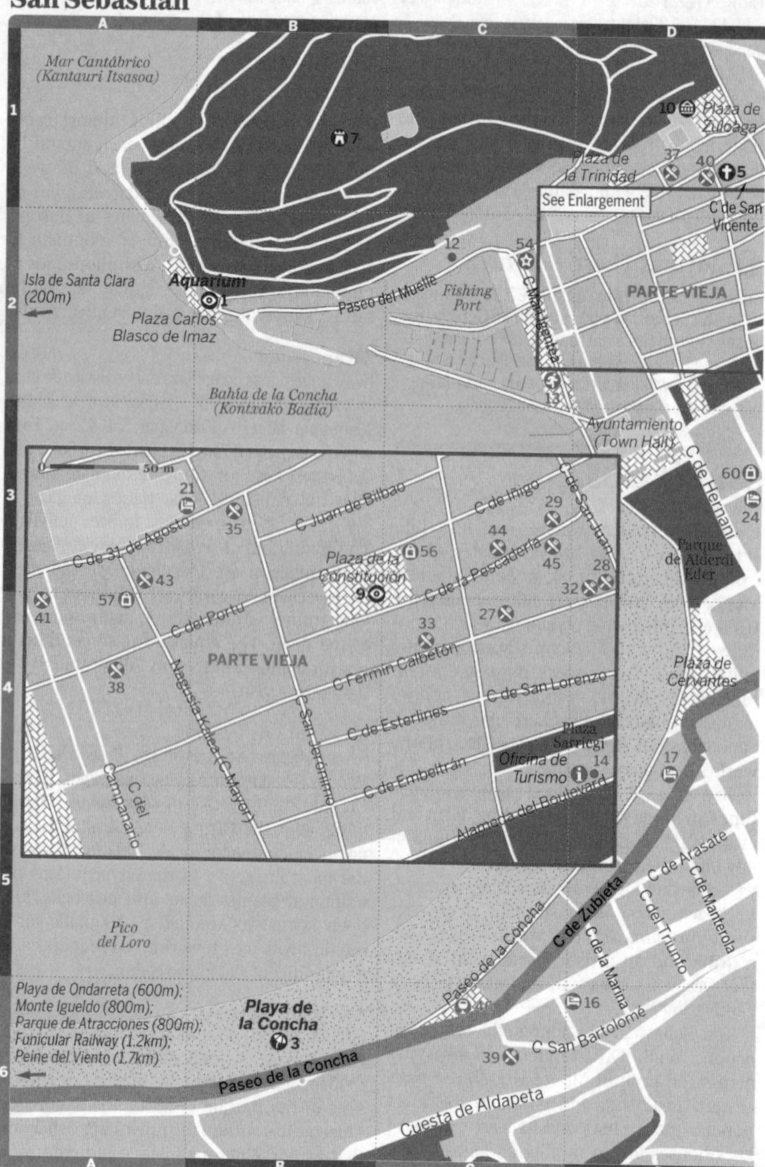

Isla de Santa Clara ISLAND

Located about 700m from Playa de la Concha, this island is accessible by **boats** (943 00 04 50; www.motorasdelaisla.com; Lasta Plaza; normal boat €4, glass-bottom boat €6.50; 10am-8pm Jun-Sep) that run every half-hour from the fishing port in the summer. At low tide the island gains its own tiny beach and you can climb its forested paths to a small lighthouse. There are also picnic tables and a simple cafe.

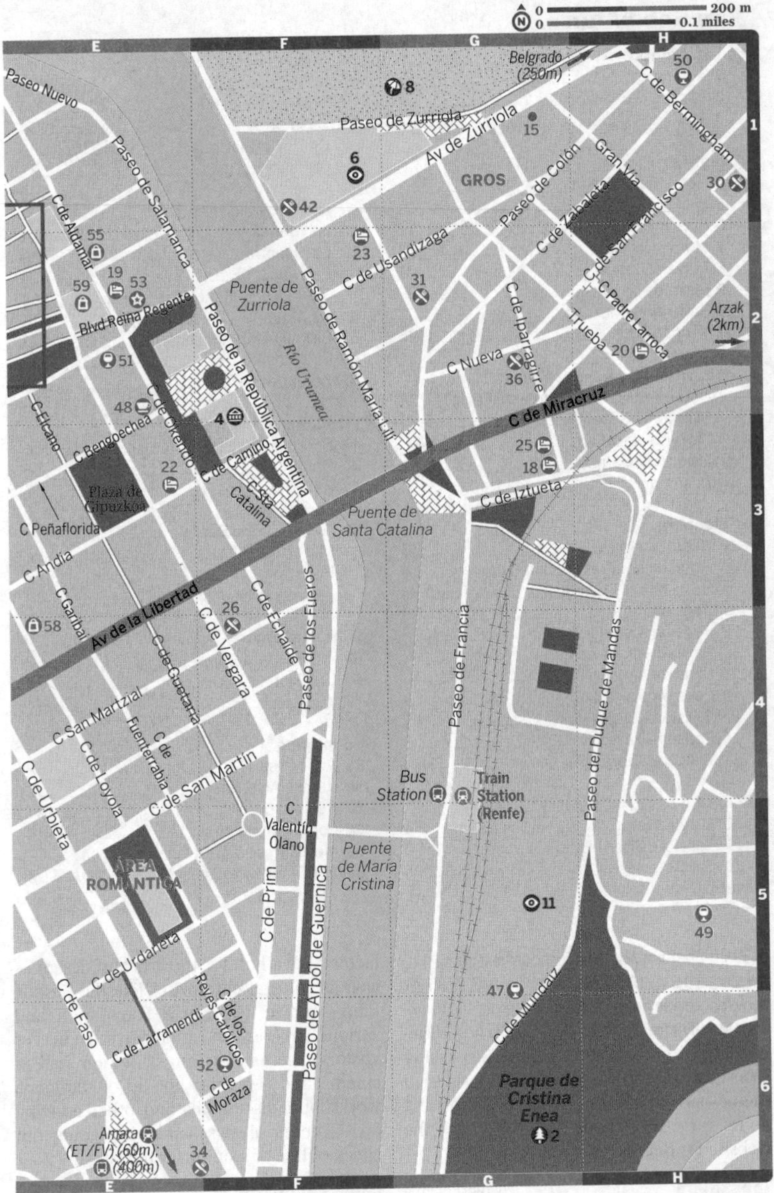

Monte Igueldo VIEWPOINT

(www.monteigueldo.es; ⏲10am-9pm Mon-Fri, to 10pm Sat & Sun Jul & Aug, 10am-7pm Mon-Fri, to 8pm Sat & Sun Jun & Sep; shorter hours rest of year) The views from the summit of Monte Igueldo, just west of town, will make you feel like a circling hawk staring down over the vast panorama of the Bahía de la Concha and the surrounding coastline and mountains. The best way to get there is via the old-world **funicular railway** (www.monteigueldo.es; Plaza del Funicular; return adult/child €3.15/2.35;

San Sebastián

Top Sights
1 Aquarium ... B2
2 Parque de Cristina Enea ... G6
3 Playa de la Concha ... B6

Sights
4 Hotel Maria Cristina ... F2
5 Iglesia de San Vicente ... D1
6 Kursaal ... F1
7 Monte Urgull ... B1
8 Playa de Zurriola ... G1
9 Plaza de la Constitución ... B3
10 San Telmo Museoa ... D1
11 Tabakalera ... G5

Activities, Courses & Tours
12 Catamarán Ciudad San Sebastián ... C2
Mimo San Sebastián ... (see 4)
13 Motoras de la Isla ... C2
14 Pintxos of San Sebastián ... D4
15 Pukas Surf Eskola ... G1

Sleeping
16 Hostal Alemana ... D6
17 Hotel de Londres y de Inglaterra ... D4
Hotel Maria Cristina ... (see 4)
18 Pensión Aida ... G3
19 Pensión Aldamar ... E2
20 Pensión Altair ... H2
21 Pensión Amaiur ... A3
22 Pensión Joakina ... E3
23 Pensión Kursaal ... F2
24 Pensión Peñaflorida ... D3
25 Welcome Gros ... G3

Eating
26 Antonio Bar ... F4
27 Bar Borda Berri ... C4
28 Bar Goiz-Argi ... D3
29 Bar Nestor ... C3
30 Bergara Bar ... H1
31 Bodega Donostiarra ... G2
32 Bodegón Alejandro ... D3
33 Casa Urola ... C4
34 Chutney Gastrobar ... E6
35 Gandarias ... B3
36 Gerald's Bar ... G2
37 La Cuchara de San Telmo ... D1
38 La Fábrica ... A4
39 La Madame ... C6
40 La Viña ... D1
41 Restaurante Kokotxa ... A4
42 Restaurante Ni Neu ... F1
43 Sirimiri Atari Akademy ... A3
44 Txepetxa ... C3
45 Zeruko ... C3

Drinking & Nightlife
46 Bataplan Disco ... C6
47 Dabadaba ... G5
48 Koh Tao ... E2
49 Le Bukowski ... H5
50 Mala Gissona Beer House ... H1
51 Museo del Whisky ... E2
52 Pub Drop ... F6
Terraza Ni Neu ... (see 42)

Entertainment
53 Altxerri Jazz Bar ... E2
54 Etxekalte ... C2
Kursaal ... (see 6)

Shopping
55 Aitor Lasa ... E2
56 Alboka Artesanía ... C3
57 Kukuxumusu ... A4
58 Loreak Mendian ... E4
59 Mercado de la Bretxa ... E2
60 Perfumería Benegas ... D3

10am-9pm Jun-Aug, shorter hours rest of year) to the **Parque de Atracciones** (943 21 35 25; www.monteigueldo.es; Paseo de Igeldo; 10am-9pm Mon-Fri, to 10pm Sat & Sun Jul & Aug, 10am-7pm Mon-Fri, to 8pm Sat & Sun Jun & Sep; shorter hours rest of year), a small, old-fashioned theme park at the top of the hill. Opening hours vary throughout the year; check the website for details.

Tabakalera CULTURAL CENTRE
(International Centre for Contemporary Culture; 943 11 88 55; www.tabakalera.eu; Andre Zigarrogileak Plaza 1; noon-8pm Tue-Thu, to 9pm Fri, 10am-9pm Sat, 10am-8pm Sun) One of San Sebastian's most celebrated new attractions is this sun-drenched cultural space set in a beautifully reconfigured 90-year-old tobacco factory. It's a hub for the arts and design as well as cultural enterprises like the Basque Film Archive, the Kutxa Foundation and various galleries and innovative firms. For visitors, there's also an exhibition hall, a cinema and a regular line-up of seminars, workshops, discussions and other edifying fare. There's always something going on; check online or stop by for the latest.

Peine del Viento SCULPTURE
A symbol of the city, the *Peine del Viento* (Wind Comb) sculpture, which lies at the far western end of the Bahía de la Concha, below Monte Igueldo, is the work of the famous Basque sculptor Eduardo Chillida and architect Luis Peña Ganchegui. The artwork is made of giant iron shapes anchored

by pink granite and is spread across three nearby sites. Its powerful but mysterious forms look all the more striking against the wave-battered coastline.

Playa de Zurriola BEACH

Stretching in front of Gros, from the Kursaal to Monte Ulía, 'Zurri', as it's known locally, has some excellent waves and draws surfers from near and far. Conditions are generally too rough for swimming, but it's a fine place to hang out and take in the local scene – which means volleyball, football and of course people watching.

Monte Urgull CASTLE

You can walk to the summit of Monte Urgull, topped by the low castle walls of the Castillo de la Mota and a grand statue of Christ, by taking a path from Plaza de Zuloaga or from behind the aquarium. The views are breathtaking and the shady parkland on the way up is a peaceful retreat from the city.

Iglesia de San Vicente CHURCH

(Calle de San Vicente 3; ⏲9am-1pm & 5-8pm) Lording it over the Parte Vieja, this striking church is thought to be the oldest building in San Sebastián. Its origins date to the 12th century, but it was rebuilt in its current Gothic form in the early 1500s. The towering facade gives onto an echoing vaulted interior, featuring an elaborate gold altarpiece and a 19th-century French organ. Also impressive are the stained-glass rose windows.

Plaza de la Constitución PLAZA

One of the most attractive city squares in the Basque Country, the Plaza de la Constitución sits at the heart of the old town. The square dates from 1813 but sits on the site of an older square. It was once used as a bullring; the balconies of the fringing houses were rented to spectators.

Kursaal NOTABLE BUILDING

(☎943 00 30 00; www.kursaal.eus; Zurriola Hiribidea 1) Designed by Rafael Moneo, the Kursaal is one of the city's most beloved and noteworthy buildings. Consisting of two cubes made of translucent glass, the structure, which serves as San Sebastián's cultural and conference centre, was designed to represent two beached rocks. A lively array of musical and cultural events is held here year-round.

Activities & Tours

Mimo San Sebastián FOOD

(☎943 42 11 43; http://sansebastian.mimofood.com; Calle Camino 1; ⏲9am-8pm Mon-Fri, 9am-1pm & 4-8pm Sat & Sun) The highly recommended Mimo San Sebastián runs an array of *pintxo* tasting tours (from €95) and cookery courses (from €165) in and around the city, as well as wine tastings (from €60). The cooking courses happen across the street at the **Hotel Maria Cristina** (☎943 43 76 00; www.hotel-mariacristina.com/en; Paseo de la República Argentina 4), where there's also a shop selling an array of high-quality local food and drink products.

Pintxos of San Sebastián TOURS

(☎943 48 1166; www.sansebastianturismo.com/en/offers/other; tours €22; ⏲11.30am Wed & Sat May & Jun; Tue, Thu & Sat Jul; Fri & Sat Sep) The tourist office runs a two-hour tour (in English; French tours are available on request) of some of the city's *pintxo* haunts. Tours are also held with less frequency outside high season – contact the tourist office for dates. The meeting point is outside the main tourist office (p473) on the edge of the old town.

Catamarán Ciudad San Sebastián BOATING

(☎607 201155; www.ciudadsansebastian.com; Paseo del Muelle 14; adult/child €10/6; ⏲noon-8pm Jul-Aug, shorter hours Sep-Jun) Boat tours of the bay and out onto the open ocean on a motorised catamaran run hourly (except at 3pm) in the summer. The scenic 40-minute trip takes in a fine view of Isla de Santa Clara, the Peine del Viento sculpture and Playa de Zurriola, among other locales.

Pukas Surf Eskola SURFING

(☎943 32 00 68; www.pukassurf.com; Avenida de Zurriola 24; ⏲10am-2pm & 4-8pm Mon-Sat, 9am-2.30pm Sun) Playa de Zurriola, with its generally reliable waves, can be a good place for learners to come to grips with surfing – though be mindful of those heavy swell days (in winter mostly). Aspiring surfers should drop by Pukas, where lessons and board and wetsuit hire are available. Prices vary depending on group size and lesson length, but start at €64 for a weekend course comprising a 1½-hour lesson each day.

Festivals & Events

Semana Grande SUMMER FESTIVAL

(https://astenagusia.donostiakultura.eus; ⏲mid-Aug) Semana Grande, or Aste Nagusia in

Basque, is the big summer festival and features an action-packed line-up of street parties, concerts and fireworks, plus rural sports, an ambitious swim race (from Getaria to San Sebastián), children's activities and parades with giants and big heads. To see the city at its liveliest, the Semana Grande is hard to top.

San Sebastián International Film Festival FILM
(www.sansebastianfestival.com; Sep) The world-renowned, two-week film festival has been an annual fixture in the second half of September since the 1950s. It usually features an excellent line-up of films from Europe, the USA and Latin America, with a few big premieres.

Heineken Jazzaldia MUSIC
(www.heinekenjazzaldia.com; Jul) This long-running music festival has been around for more than 50 years, and features world-class performers playing jazz and world music at over a dozen stages around town. The event runs for five to six days, typically in late July, with many free shows. The 1800-seat **Kursaal** (943 00 30 00; www.kursaal.eus; Zurriola Hiribidea 1) stages some of the bigger acts.

Día de San Sebastián FIESTA
(20 Jan) The city celebrates its patron saint (St Sebastian of course) with fervour. The big event is the Tamborrada, when thousands of drummers wearing 19th-century military dress parade through the city. The fest runs for exactly 24 hours from midnight to midnight (late evening of the 19th to late evening of the 20th) and ends at the Plaza de la Constitución.

Carnaval CARNIVAL
(Feb or Mar) Carnaval (dates change) is a big event in San Sebastián, and features parades with wild costumes and live music on the streets. It runs for six days, from the Thursday before Ash Wednesday to Shrove Tuesday, though the biggest events happen on the weekend. Nearby Tolosa also has a famed Carnaval celebration.

Sleeping

Pensión Altair PENSIÓN €
(943 29 31 33; www.pension-altair.com; Calle Padre Larroca 3; s/d €75/110;) This *pensión* is in a beautifully restored town house, with unusual church-worthy arched windows and modern, minimalist rooms that are a world away from the fusty decor of the old-town *pensiones*. Interior rooms lack the grandiose windows but are much larger.

Welcome Gros HOTEL €€
(943 32 69 54; www.welcomegros.com; Calle Iparragirre Kalea 3; s/d/ste from €85/130/150;) An excellent base in one of San Sebastián's most charming neighbourhoods, Welcome Gros is set in an elegant seven-storey building and has attractive rooms – though rather on the compact side. For more space and style, book one of the seven sunny suites, with nicely framed artwork and small kitchen units.

Pensión Aida PENSION €€
(943 32 78 00; www.pensionesconencanto.com; Calle de Iztueta 9; s/d €75/99;) The owners of this excellent *pensión* must have read the rule book on what makes a good hotel and followed it precisely. The nine rooms are bright and bold, full of exposed stone, and the communal area, with soft sofas and plenty of information, is a nice extra.

Pensión Kursaal BOUTIQUE HOTEL €€
(943 29 26 66; www.pensionkursaal.com; Calle Peña y Goñi 2; d from €75;) The Kursaal has a great location a one-minute walk to the beach and just up the road from some excellent eateries. Although rooms are small, the big windows and attractive paint job (with touches of artwork in the rooms) make this a top-value choice in Gros.

Pensión Joakina GUESTHOUSE €€
(656 301790; www.pensionjoakina.com; Calle de Camino 4; r with/without bathroom from €90/75;) Around the corner from the Plaza de Gipuzkoa, the family-run Pensión Joakina lays out the welcome mat for visitors with bright, spotless guest rooms set with wood floors and splashes of colour, plus tiny balconies over the lane. Rooms are on the small side, but still an excellent value for the money.

Pensión Peñaflorida GUESTHOUSE €€
(943 43 53 31; http://pensionpeñaflorida.es; Calle Peñaflorida 1; s/d €95/125;) In a great location near both the beach and the old town, the Pensión Peñaflorida impresses with its attractive design and welcoming staff. Each of 10 rooms has style with light woods and greys, nice lighting and excellent modern bathrooms. Some of the rooms are rather small, though the decorative balconies (some with beach views) keep things from feeling too cramped.

Hostal Alemana BOUTIQUE HOTEL €€
(943 46 25 44; www.hostalalemana.com; Calle de San Martín 53; r €80-150;) With a great location just a sandy footstep from the beach, this smart hotel has small rooms done in muted colour schemes with black-and-white photos adding a dash of style to the otherwise minimalist ensemble. The belle époque exterior only adds to the appeal.

Pensión Amaiur BOUTIQUE HOTEL €€
(943 42 96 54; www.pensionamaiur.com; Calle de 31 de Agosto 44; d with/without bathroom from €75/60;) A top-notch guesthouse in a prime old-town location, Amaiur has bright floral wallpapers and bathrooms tiled in Andalucian blue and white. The best rooms are those that overlook the main street, where you can sit on a little balcony and be completely enveloped in blushing red flowers. Some rooms share bathrooms. Guest kitchen and free snacks add to the value.

Pensión Aldamar HOTEL €€
(943 43 01 43; www.pensionaldamar.com; Calle Aldamar 2; d from €130;) This friendly *pensión* offers superb modern rooms with white decor and stone walls, some of which have little balconies from which to watch the theatre of street life below. It's a big step up in quality from many of the other old-town *pensiones*.

Hotel Maria Cristina HISTORIC HOTEL €€€
(943 43 76 00; www.hotel-mariacristina.com; Paseo de la República Argentina 4; d from €576;) Audrey Hepburn stayed here – as did Coco Chanel, Alfred Hitchcock and Mick Jagger, to name a few. The palatial Maria Cristina, now a member of the Starwood Collection, dominates the riverfront skyline at sunset. Glamorous and impeccably maintained, with huge and luxurious rooms, it's still a favourite with royalty and Hollywood stars.

Hotel de Londres y de Inglaterra HISTORIC HOTEL €€€
(943 44 07 70; www.hlondres.com; Calle de Zubieta 2; d €370;) Sitting pretty on the beachfront, Hotel de Londres y de Inglaterra (Hotel of London and England) is as proper as it sounds. Queen Isabel II set the tone for this hotel well over a century ago, and things have stayed pretty regal ever since. The place exudes elegance; some rooms have stunning views over Playa de la Concha.

LOCAL KNOWLEDGE

SAGÜÉS SUNSETS

San Sebastián's location ensures it has endless places from which to admire the setting summer sun, but for the best sunset of all head to the Sagüés neighbourhood at the far eastern end of Playa de Zurriola. Just east of Sagüés, Monte Ulía is another top sunset spot (and departure point for a scenic but hilly 7.6km walk to Pasajes).

Eating

With 18 Michelin stars, San Sebastián stands atop a pedestal as one of the culinary capitals of the planet. As if that alone weren't enough, the city is overflowing with bars – almost all of which have bar tops weighed down under a mountain of *pintxos* that almost every Spaniard will tell you are the best in country.

Sirimiri Atari Akademy PINTXOS €
(943 44 03 14; www.sirimirigastroleku.com; Calle de Mayor 18; pintxos €2.50-5; 6.30pm-1am Mon & Wed-Fri, 12.30-5pm & 6.30pm-1am Sat & Sun) A bit smarter than many of the bars in the Parte Vieja, this contemporary joint dishes up a modern, jazzy vibe, artful *pintxos* and skilfully shaken cocktails. It can get very busy, so you may be tempted to sneak out and munch on the steps of the nearby basilica. Next door is its more traditional sister outfit, Atari.

Chutney Gastrobar FUSION €
(943 35 89 39; www.facebook.com/arifyalex; Calle de Egaña 8; pintxos from €2.50; 12.30-3pm & 7-10pm Tue-Sat;) When a French bartender and an English cook with Pakistani-Saudi roots teamed up, they created one of the most innovative *pintxos* spots in town. This stylish den of culinary alchemy has a menu of spicy spinach and potato Bombay wraps, smoked sardines with grated tomatoes, blue sheep's milk cheese with red onion marmalade and mini-vegetable tagines.

Belgrado CAFE €
(Avenida de Navarra 2; mains €8-13; 9am-11pm Sun-Thu, to 1.30am Fri & Sat;) Just across from Zurriola beach, Belgrado is a cafe, deli and boutique all rolled into one. You can munch on freshly made pastries, burgers or delicious cheese-centric sandwiches, recharge over drinks (beer, wine, teas), or

browse the small but well-curated selection of artisanal soaps, wines and apparel.

★La Fábrica BASQUE €€
(☎943 43 21 10; www.restaurantelafabrica.es; Calle del Puerto 17; mains €15-20, menús from €29; ⏲1-4pm & 7.30-11.30pm Mon-Fri, 1-3.30pm & 8-11.30pm Sat & Sun) The red-brick interior walls and white tablecloths lend an air of class to this restaurant, whose modern takes on Basque classics have been making waves with San Sebastián locals in recent years. La Fábrica only works with multicourse *menús,* which means you'll get to sample various delicacies like wild mushroom ravioli with foie gras cream or venison in red wine sauce.

Bar Nestor BASQUE €€
(☎943 42 48 73; Calle de la Pescadería 11; small plates €5-14, steak per kilo around €40; ⏲1-3pm & 8-11pm Tue-Sat, 1-3pm Sun) It would be very easy to overlook this dated-looking bar, but for those in the know this place has exceptional steaks, best when enjoyed alongside grilled green peppers. It's very popular and there's very little space, so get there when it opens to ensure you get a table.

La Viña PINTXOS €€
(☎943 42 74 95; www.lavinarestaurante.com; Calle de 31 de Agosto 3; pintxos from €2, mains €14-24; ⏲10.30am-5pm & 6.30pm-midnight Tue-Sun) The bar of this traditional spot displays a wonderful array of fishy *pintxos* and delectable snacks, but the real highlight is the cheesecake (€5). Prepared daily according to a special recipe and left to stand on shelves over the bar, it's creamy and flavoursome, ideal for a midmorning snack, afternoon dessert or really any time. One slice is rich enough for two.

Bergara Bar PINTXOS €€
(www.pinchosbergara.es; General Artetxe 8; pintxos from €2.50; ⏲10am-3pm & 6-11pm) The Bergara Bar is one of the most highly regarded *pintxo* bars in Gros and has a mouthwatering array of delights piled onto the bar counter, as well as others chalked up onto the board. You can't go wrong, whether you opt for rich foie gras with mango jam, plump grilled mushrooms or mini portions of *fideuá* (noodles with seafood).

Gerald's Bar FUSION €€
(☎943 08 30 01; http://geraldsbar.eu; Calle Iparragirre 13; mains €12-20; ⏲1-4pm & 7pm-midnight Tue-Sun) Melbourne-based restaurateur Gerald Diffey fell so hard for San Sebastián that he decided to open a second Gerald's in the city – never mind that the first is 17,000km away. Rather than *pintxos,* here you'll find uncommon delicacies like tabbouleh with cucumber and feta, duck curry, jerk chicken with pineapple and other dishes not found elsewhere in town.

La Madame FUSION €€
(☎943 44 42 69; www.lamadamesansebastian.com; Calle San Bortolomé 35; mains €14-20; ⏲6pm-1am Mon & Wed-Fri, noon-5pm & 8pm-1am Sat & Sun) For a break from *pintxos* and classic Basque cooking, search out this modern New York–style setup a block back from the beach. A restaurant-cum-lounge bar, it specialises in innovative fusion fare – think Moroccan spiced lamb or rock shrimp tempura with seaweed salad – and creative cocktails. Brunch is served at the weekend and regular DJ sets ensure an atmosphere.

Arzak BASQUE €€€
(☎943 27 84 65; www.arzak.info; Avenida Alcalde Jose Elósegui 273; tasting menu €210; ⏲1.30-3.15pm & 9-10.30pm Tue-Sat, closed mid-Jun–early Jul) With three shining Michelin stars, acclaimed chef Juan Mari Arzak is king when it comes to *nueva cocina vasca* and his restaurant is considered one of the best in the world. Arzak is now assisted by his daughter Elena, and they never cease to innovate. Reservations, well in advance, are obligatory.

The restaurant is located 2.5km east of San Sebastián.

Restaurante Kokotxa MODERN SPANISH €€€
(☎943 42 19 04; www.restaurantekokotxa.com; Calle del Campanario 11; mains €27-35, menús €65-90; ⏲1.30-3.30pm & 8.30-10.45pm Tue-Sat) This Michelin-star restaurant is hidden away down an overlooked alley in the old town, but the food rewards those who search. Most people opt for the *menú de mercado* (€65) and enjoy the flavours of the traders from the busy city market. It's closed from mid-February through March and two weeks in late October.

Bodegón Alejandro SEAFOOD €€€
(☎943 42 71 58; www.bodegonalejandro.com; Calle de Fermín Calbetón 4; menú del día from €16, mains €21-32; ⏲1-3.30pm & 8-10.30pm Jun–mid-Oct, 1-3.30pm Tue & Sun, 1-3.30pm & 8-10.30pm Wed-Sat mid-Oct–May) This handsome cellar restaurant, tucked down the steps off a pedestrian-packed street, earns rave reviews for its small but brilliant menu.The changing menu has treats as succulent as the spider

BEST PINTXO BARS IN SAN SEBASTIÁN

Enter any bar in town, and the counter is sure to be groaning under the weight of a small mountain of tiny plates of culinary art. A few great places to begin the great culinary journey:

La Cuchara de San Telmo (043 44 16 55; www.lacucharadesantelmo.com; Calle de 31 de Agosto 28; pintxos from €2.50; 7.30-11pm Tue, 12.30-3.30pm & 7.30-11pm Wed-Sun) This bustling, always packed bar offers miniature *nueva cocina vasca* (Basque nouvelle cuisine) from a supremely creative kitchen. Unlike many San Sebastián bars, this one doesn't have any *pintxos* (Basque tapas) laid out on the bar top; instead you must order from the blackboard menu behind the counter.

Bar Borda Berri (943 43 03 42; Calle Fermín Calbetón 12; pintxos from €2.50; 12.30-3.30pm & 7.30-11pm Tue-Sat, 12.30-3.30pm Sun) The uber-popular Bar Borda Berri is a *pintxos* (Basque tapas) bar that really lives up to the hype. Amid mustard-coloured walls hung with old photos and strands of garlic, hungry diners crowd in for house specials like braised veal cheeks in wine, mushroom and *idiazabal* (a sheep cheese) risotto, and the decadent octopus.

Gandarias (943 42 63 62; www.restaurantegandarias.com; Calle 31 Agosto 23; pintxos from €2.50; noon-3.30pm & 7-11pm) An obligatory destination for anyone interested in San Sebastián's foodie hot spots, Gandarias has a sterling reputation for its artfully prepared *pintxos*. You'll find all the classics on hand, with house specials like seared foie with red currants, Joselito Iberian ham, scrumptious *solomillo* (tenderloin) sandwiches and delicious crab pie.

Txepetxa (943 42 22 27; www.bartxepetxa.com; Calle Pescadería 5; pintxos from €2.50; 7-11pm Tue, noon-3pm & 7-11pm Wed-Sun) The humble *antxoa* (anchovy) is elevated to royal status at this wood-panelled old-fashioned local favourite. You can order it a dozen different ways topped with everything from sea urchin roe to black olive paté. Not to be missed for seafood fans.

Zeruko (www.barzeruko.com; Calle Pescadería 10; pintxos from €3; 1-4pm Tue-Sun & 7.30-11.30pm Tue-Sat) A fun and festive eatery, Zeruko has garnered its share of awards and earns rave reviews for its creative high-quality *pintxos*. It's famous for its smoked cod, served with its own mini-grill (and a side of puréed asparagus), though it's hard to go wrong with foie gras and fig, grilled scallops, creamy sea urchins and countless other hits.

Bodega Donostiarra (943 01 13 80; www.bodegadonostiarra.com; Calle de Peña y Goñi 13; pintxos from €2.50, mains from €11; 9.30am-4pm & 7-11pm Mon-Thu, to midnight Fri & Sat) The stone walls, potted plants and window ornaments give this place a real old-fashioned French bistro look, though the crowds can be so thick that you might not even notice during prime time. The draw? Some of the best *pintxos* this side of the Urumea.

Casa Urola (943 44 13 71; www.casaurolajatetxea.es; Calle Fermin Calbetón 20; pintxos from €2.50, mains €22-31; noon-3.30pm & 7-11.30pm Wed-Mon) Founded in 1956, Casa Urola has been wowing more than three generations of diners. Join the lunch and evening crowds over perfectly turned out *pintxos* like grilled white asparagus, foie with pear compote, and mushroom and Idiazabal cheese tart.

Bar Goiz-Argi (Calle de Fermín Calbetón 4; pintxos from €2.70; 11am-3.30pm & 6.30-11.30pm Wed-Sun, 11am-3.30pm Mon) *Brochetas de gambas* (prawn skewers) are the house speciality. Sounds simple, but no one in town grills them up to such tender perfection. Other hits: fried green peppers drizzled with sea salt and the *mari juli* (salmon and anchovy on toast).

Antonio Bar (www.antoniobar.com; Calle de Vergara 3; pintxos from €2.50; 7.30am-4pm & 7-11.30pm Mon-Sat) One of the top *pintxos* bars in the new town, Bar Antonio packs them in for house specials like prawn ravioli; the peppers are also worth fawning over. It's a small place that from the outside looks more like the sort of cafe you'd get in a train station waiting room.

crab salad with fennel cream, crispy-skin hake with a zesty lemon vinaigrette or juicy dry-aged beef with garlic sauce.

Drinking & Nightlife

Mala Gissona Beer House CRAFT BEER
(☎943 04 56 15; Calle Zabaleta 53; ⊙5-11.30pm Mon, 1pm-11.30pm Tue-Thu, to 1.30am Fri & Sat, noon-12.30am Sun) A much welcome addition to Gros, this craft-beer bar has the long wooden bar, industrial fixtures and inviting front terrace that show off Mala Gissona's design smarts. Which makes a suitable backdrop to the quality brews on draft (12 in all) – some of which come from the namesake brewery in Oiartzun.

Koh Tao CAFE
(Calle Bengoechea 2; ⊙7.30am-10pm Mon-Thu, to 2am Fri, 9am-2am Sat, 9am-10pm Sun) An enticing, friendly cafe on the edge of the Parte Vieja. Good at any time of the day, it's a laid-back place with mismatched vintage furniture, comfy armchairs and good tunes – the ideal spot to check your email over a coffee or kick back with an early evening drink.

Terraza Ni Neu BAR
(☎943 00 31 62; www.restaurantenineu.com; Ave de Zurriola 1; ⊙10am-8pm Tue, Wed & Sun, to 11pm Thu-Sat) The terrace cafe attached to **Restaurante Ni Neu** (☎943 00 31 62; www.restaurantenineu.com; Avenida de Zurriola 1; mains €14-30; ⊙1-3.30pm Tue, Wed & Sun, 1-3.30pm & 8.30-10.30pm Thu-Sat) is a fine place to nurse a drink and enjoy some satisfying *raciones* (such as fried calamari, tuna tartar or mussels). Fine views over the waterfront draw the afternoon crowd.

Dabadaba BAR
(☎943 26 58 26; www.dabadabass.com; Calle de Mundaiz 8; ⊙5-11pm Sun-Wed, to 1am Thu, to 4am Fri & Sat) Everyone's favourite indie venue, Dabadaba is a fine spot to escape the old-town crowds, with a laid-back ambiance, good craft brews and an inviting terrace on warm nights. On weekends, it's a great place to catch some live music or DJs, with a line-up of rock, pop, afrobeat and other eclectic sounds.

Pub Drop PUB
(Calle de los Reyes Católicos 18; ⊙4pm-midnight Mon-Thu, to 4am Fri, noon-4am Sat, noon-midnight Sun) One of a number of haunts on a popular drinking strip near the cathedral, this shabby-hip bar is the place to get to grips with the local beer. There are up to 50 craft ales on offer, including 19 on draft. Try one of the strong hoppy brews from the aptly named Basque Brewing Project.

Le Bukowski CLUB
(www.facebook.com/lebukowski; Calle Egia; ⊙11am-11pm Mon-Wed, to 2am Thu, to 4am Fri, 7pm-4am Sat, 7pm-midnight Sun; 📶) A long-running nightspot south of Gros, Le Bukowski has an eclectic musical line-up with DJs spinning a wide range of sounds – funk, hip hop, soul, rock. Live bands take the stage most nights. It's located in the up-and-coming district of Egia.

Museo del Whisky BAR
(www.museodelwhisky.com; Alameda Boulevard 5; ⊙3.30pm-3.30am) Appropriately named, this piano bar is full of bottles of Scotland's finest (3400 bottles to be exact) as well as a museum's worth of whisky-related knick-knacks – old bottles, tacky mugs and glasses, and a nice, dusty atmosphere.

Bataplan Disco CLUB
(☎943 47 36 01; www.bataplandisco.com; Paseo de la Concha; ⊙club 1am-7am Thu-Sat, terrace 2pm-2.30am Jun-Sep) San Sebastián's top club, a classic disco housed in a grand seafront complex, sets the stage for memorable beach-side partying. The club action kicks in late, but in summer you can warm up with a drink or two on the street-level terrace. Note that door selection can be arbitrary and groups of men might have trouble getting in.

Entertainment

Altxerri Jazz Bar LIVE MUSIC
(www.altxerri.eu; Blvd Reina Regente 2; ⊙4pm-3am) This jazz-and-blues temple has regular live gigs by local and international artists. Jamming sessions take over on nights with no gig; there's also an in-house art gallery.

Etxekalte JAZZ
(www.facebook.com/etxekaltejazzclub; Calle Mari Igentea 11; ⊙6pm-4am Tue-Thu & Sun, 6pm-5am Fri & Sat) A late-night haunt near the harbour, which moves to dance music and grooves to jazz. There's a guest DJ most weeks.

Shopping

Alboka Artesanía ARTS & CRAFTS
(www.albokaartesania.com; Plaza de la Constitución; ⊙10.30am-1.30pm & 4-8pm Mon-Fri, 10.30am-1.30pm Sat) On one of the old town's prettiest plazas, this lovely store is packed with crafts and objects made in the Basque

Country. You'll find ceramics, tea towels, marionettes, picture frames, T-shirts, jai alai balls and of course those iconic oversized berets.

Loreak Mendian CLOTHING
(www.loreakmendian.com; Calle de Hernani 27; ⏲10.30am-8pm Mon-Sat) The San Sebastián branch of Basque brand Loreak Mendian specialises in affordable style for men and women, selling everything from T-shirts and hoodies to dresses and lightweight sweaters. There's a hair salon on the lower level if you need a trim.

Perfumería Benegas COSMETICS
(Calle de Garibai 12; ⏲10am-1.15pm & 4-8pm Mon-Sat) A historic perfume shop stocking leading international brands and in-house creations such as Ssirimiri, which uses Donostia as its inspiration – the rains, sunshine and sea breezes all packaged in one lovely box (featuring iconic imagery of the city no less). You'll also find make-up and gents' grooming products.

Kukuxumusu CLOTHING
(Nagusía Kalea 15; ⏲10.30am-2.30pm & 4.30-9pm Mon-Sat, 11am-3pm & 4.30-8pm Sun) The funkiest and best-known Basque clothing label has a whole wardrobe of original T-shirts, featuring its humorous bulls, sheep and wolves in various guises. Kukuxumusu also stocks bags, iPhone covers and other gear.

Aitor Lasa FOOD
(www.aitorlasa.com; Calle de Aldamar 12; ⏲8.30am-2pm & 5-8pm Mon-Fri, 8.30am-2.30pm Sat) This high-quality deli is the place to stock up on ingredients for a gourmet picnic you'll never forget. It specialises in a heavenly array of cheeses, mushrooms and seasonal products.

Mercado de la Bretxa MARKET
(Alameda del Boulevard; ⏲8am-9pm Mon-Sat) On the east side of the Parte Vieja, Mercado de la Bretxa is where every chef in the old town comes to get the freshest produce. It's a good place to stock up on picnic supplies and a worthwhile sight in its own right.

ℹ Information

The friendly **Oficina de Turismo** (☎943 48 11 66; www.sansebastianturismo.com; Alameda del Boulevard 8; ⏲9am-8pm Mon-Sat, 10am-7pm Sun Jul-Sep, 9am-7pm Mon-Sat, 10am-2pm Sun Oct-May) offers comprehensive information on the city and the Basque Country in general.

ℹ Getting There & Away

AIR

The city's airport, **Aeropuerto de San Sebastián** (EAS; ☎902 404704; www.aena.es), is 22km out of town, near Hondarribia. There are regular flights to Madrid and Barcelona and occasional charters to other major European cities. Biarritz, just over the border in France, is served by Ryanair and EasyJet, among various other budget airlines, and is generally much cheaper to fly into.

BUS

San Sebastián's sparkling new **bus station** (Estación Donostia Geltokia; www.estaciondonostia.com; Paseo Federico García Lorca 1) is 1km southeast of the Parte Vieja, on the east side of the river, and just across from the Renfe train station. All the bus companies have offices and ticket booths in the station, which lies underground.

There are daily bus services to the following:

DESTINATION	FARE (€)	DURATION (HR)
Biarritz (France)	from 6.75	1¼
Bilbao	from 7	1¼
Bilbao airport	17.10	1¼
Madrid	from 37	5-6
Pamplona	from 8	1
Vitoria	12	1½

TRAIN

The main **Renfe train station** (Paseo de Francia) is just across Río Urumea, on a line linking Paris to Madrid. There are several services daily to Madrid (from €29, 5½ hours) and two to Barcelona (from €39, six hours).

For France you must first go to the Spanish/French border town of Irún (or sometimes trains go as far as Hendaye; from €2.25, 27 minutes), which is also served by Eusko Tren/Ferrocarril Vasco (www.euskotren.es), and change there. Trains depart every half-hour from **Amara train station** (Easo Plaza 9), about 1km south of the city centre, and also stop in Pasajes (from €1.70, 12 minutes) and Irún/Hendaye (€2.45, 25 minutes). Another ET/FV railway line heads west to Bilbao via Zarautz, Zumaia and Durango, but it's painfully slow, so the bus is usually a better plan.

ℹ Getting Around

DBus (www.dbus.eus) is the city's public bus network. The standard fare is €1.70 (€2.10 at night), payable to the bus driver.

Buses run roughly from 7.30am to 10.30pm. After that, more limited night bus services continue until about 4am. One of the most useful routes is bus 16, which connects the city centre with Monte Igueldo.

Basque Culture

The Basques are different. They have inhabited their corner of Spain and France seemingly forever. While many aspects of their unique culture are hidden from prying eyes, the following are visible to any visitor.

Pelota

The national sport of the Basque country is *pelota basque,* and every village in the region has its own court – normally backing up against the village church. Pelota can be played in several different ways: bare-handed, with small wooden rackets, or with a long hand-basket called a *chistera,* with which the player can throw the ball at speeds of up to 300km/h. It's possible to see pelota matches throughout the region during summer.

Lauburu

The most visible symbol of Basque culture is *lauburu,* the Basque cross. The meaning of this symbol is lost – some say it represents the four old regions of the Basque Country, others that it represents spirit, life, consciousness and form – but today many regard it as a symbol of prosperity, hence its appearance in modern jewellery and above house doors. It is also used to signify life and death, and is found on old headstones.

Traditional Basque Games

Basque sports aren't just limited to pelota: there's also log cutting, stone lifting, bale tossing and tug of war. Most stemmed from the day-to-day activities of the region's farmers and fisherfolk.

LONGJON / SHUTTERSTOCK ©

RICARDO HERNANDEZ / SHUTTERSTOCK ©

1. Traditional red-and-white dress at Sanfermines (p486)
2. A game of *pelota basque* **3.** *Lauburu* (the Basque cross)

TERESA EGUIDAZU URRUTICOECHEA / GETTY IMAGES ©

Although technology has replaced the need to use most of these skills on a daily basis, the sports are kept alive at numerous fiestas.

Bulls & Fiestas

No other Basque festival is as famous as Sanfermines (p486), with its legendary *encierro* (running of the bulls) in Pamplona. The original purpose of the *encierro* was to transfer bulls from the corrals where they would have spent the night to the bullring where they would fight. Sometime in the 14th century someone worked out that the quickest and 'easiest' way to do this was to chase the bulls out of the corrals and into the ring. It was only a small step from that to the full-blown carnage of Pamplona's Sanfermines.

Traditional Dress

Basque festivals are a good way to see traditional Basque dress and dance. It's said that there are around 400 different Basque dances, many of which have their own special kind of dress.

Basque Language

Victor Hugo described the Basque language as a 'country', and it would be a rare Basque who'd disagree with him. The language, known as *euskara,* is the oldest in Europe and has no known connection to any Indo-European languages. Suppressed by Franco, Basque was subsequently recognised as one of Spain's official languages, and it has become the language of choice among a growing number of young Basques.

Around San Sebastián

Pasajes

POP 16,200

Pasajes (Basque: Pasaia), where the river Oiartzun meets the Atlantic, has multiple personalities. It is both a massive industrial port (the largest in the province of Guipúzcoa) and a sleepy village with quaint medieval houses hunkering over the waterfront. In fact, Pasajes is made up of four distinct districts, though it's Pasai Donibane and Pasai San Pedro that have all the charm. These two villages face each other on opposite sides of the river, and are sprinkled with sights that pay homage to the region's maritime history.

Pasai Donibane on the east bank is the more appealing of the two, with several attractive squares and some notable seafood restaurants. A frequent speedboat ferry connects the two towns. Dining aside, highlights include the spectacular entrance to the port, through a keyhole-like split in the cliff face – even more impressive when a huge container ship passes through it.

Sights & Activities

Albaola Foundation MUSEUM

(943 39 24 26; www.albaola.com; Ondartxo Ibilbida 1, Pasai San Pedro; adult/child €7/5; 10am-2pm & 3-7pm Tue-Sun Easter-Sep, to 6pm Oct-Easter) This terrific museum charts the history of Pasajes' whaling industry. At the centre of the story is the *San Juan*, a galleon that sunk off the coast of Newfoundland in 1565. Models and explanatory panels describe the ship and illustrate how a team of Canadian underwater archaeologists discovered its wreck in 1978. The highlight, though, is the life-size replica of the ship that they are building using the same techniques and materials that were used to build the original.

Casa Museo Victor Hugo MUSEUM

(943 34 15 56; Calle Donibane 63, Pasai Donibane; 9am-2pm & 4-7pm Jul & Aug, 10am-2pm & 4-6pm Tue-Sat Sep-Jun) FREE French author Victor Hugo spent the summer of 1843 in Pasajes, lodging at this typical 17th-century waterfront house and working on his travelogue *En Voyage, Alpes et Pyrénées*. Sadly, his eldest daughter died in September, and he didn't write the book he intended. The second floor retains a smattering of period furniture and various prints and first editions, plus audio commentary on Hugo's robust diet (peas, nectarines, oysters, cider and a glass of Malaga for breakfast).

Faro de la Plata LIGHTHOUSE

It's quite a climb from Pasai San Pedro, but the views from around the lighthouse (closed to the public) are worth the effort. This is especially so when a large cargo ship slips through the cliff walls that form the entrance to the narrow but perfect port of Pasajes. The 2km walk takes about 30 minutes.

Coastal Path HIKING

The nicest way of getting between San Sebastián and Pasajes is to walk along the coastal path that wends its way over the cliffs between the two towns. There are lovely sea views, unusual cliff formations and, halfway along, a hidden beach that tempts when it's hot. Ask at San Sebastián tourist office (p473) for route information. The 7.6km trek takes 2½ to 3 hours.

Eating

Ziaboga Bistrot SEAFOOD €€

(943 51 03 95; www.ziabogabistrot.com; Calle Donibane 91, Pasai Donibane; mains €18-21, tapas €4-16, menús €20-50; 1-4pm & 8-11pm) Pasajes is full of excellent seafood restaurants, but Ziaboga Bistrot is one of the best. And with a weekday lunch *menú* of just €20, it's also very good value. Outside of meal times, there's also tapas on hand (from 11am to 11pm).

Casa Cámara SEAFOOD €€€

(943 52 36 99; www.casacamara.com; Calle San Juan 79; mains €18-36; 1.30-4pm & 8.30-11pm Tue-Sun) Managed by the same family for generations, Casa Cámara is built half on stilts over the Bay of Pasajes. The bulk of the menu is seafood based and the cooking is assured and traditional. The lobsters live in a cage lowered down through a hole in the middle of the dining area straight into the sea.

Information

In Pasai Donibane, the **tourist office** (943 34 15 56; Calle Donibane 63; 9am-2pm & 4-7pm Jul & Aug, 10am-2pm & 4-6pm Tue-Sat Sep-Jun) has info on walks and other attractions in the area.

Getting There & Away

Pasajes is practically a suburb of San Sebastián; numerous buses (€1.70, 25 minutes) ply the route between them. If you're driving, it's easier to park in Pasai San Pedro than in Pasai Donibane.

For a much more enjoyable way of getting here, though, you can walk over the cliffs from San Sebastián. The walk takes about 2½ to three hours and passes through patches of forest and past the occasional idyllic beach and strange rock formations covered in seabirds; it then descends to Pasajes, which you reach by taking the small ferry boat across the inlet.

Getting Around

Once in Pasajes, you'll want to use the tiny **ferry** (one-way €0.70; ⏲6.30am-11pm Mon-Thu, 6.30am-midnight Fri, 7am-midnight Sat, 7.45am-11pm Sun) for the speedy crossing between Pasai San Pedro and Pasai Donibane.

Hondarribia

POP 16,950

Picturesque Hondarribia (Castilian: Fuenterrabía), staring across the estuary to France, has a heavy Gallic fragrance, a charming Casco Antiguo (old city) and a buzzing beach scene.

You enter the Casco through an archway at the top of Calle San Compostela to reach the pretty Plaza de Gipuzkoa. Head straight on to Calle San Nicolás and go left to reach the bigger Plaza de Armas and the Gothic **Iglesia de Santa María de la Asunción** (Calle Mayor).

For La Marina, head the other way from the archway. This is Hondarribia's most picturesque quarter. Its main street, Calle San Pedro, is flanked by typical fishermen's houses, with facades painted bright green or blue and wooden balconies gaily decorated with flower boxes.

The beach is about 1km from the town. Lined by bars and restaurants, it's not the prettiest stretch of coastline, but it does offer some of the calmest waters in the entire region.

Sights

Casco Histórico AREA

Hondarribia's walled historic centre, much of which dates to the 15th and 16th centuries, is an atmospheric grid of graceful plazas, cobbled lanes, and fetching buildings adorned with wood-carved eaves and wrought-iron balconies. The focal square is **Plaza de Armas**, where you'll find the local tourist office (p478), but prettier still is picture-perfect **Plaza de Gipuzkoa**.

Monte Jaizkibel MOUNTAIN

Monte Jaizkibel is a giant slab of rock sitting at 547m that acts as a defensive wall, protecting the inland towns and fields from the angry, invading ocean. A very strenuous walking trail (about 8km from Hondarribia) and a car-taxing road wend their way up the mountain to a ruined fortress and spectacular views. From here you can walk all the way to Pasajes (another 9km).

Castillo de Carlos V CASTLE

(Plaza de Armas 14) Today it's a government-run hotel (p477), but for over a thousand years this castle hosted knights and kings. Its position atop the old town hill gave it a commanding view over the strategic Bidasoa estuary, which has long marked the Spain–France border. Poke your head into the reception lobby to admire the medieval decor.

Hendaye BEACH

(France) Just across the river from Hondarribia lies the pretty French town of Hendaye. The main reason to come, apart from nibbling on perfectly flaky croissants, is Hendaye's 3km-long-stretch of lovely beach, which is a short stroll from the ferry dock. A regular ferry (p478) connects the two towns, though lines can be long in the summer.

Sleeping

Hotel San Nikolás HOTEL €€

(☎943 64 42 78; www.hotelsannikolas.es; Plaza de Armas 6; s €83, d €109-127; 📶) Located inside a charming old building on the main plaza, in the heart of Hondarribia's historic centre, this small hotel is an enjoyable spot to stay for a night or two.

Parador de Hondarribia HISTORIC HOTEL €€€

(☎943 64 55 00; www.parador.es; Plaza de Armas 14; d from €288; P ❄ @ 📶) It's not every day that the opportunity to sleep in a thousand-year-old fortress guarding the boundaries of Spain arises. This sumptuous offering from the Parador chain has modern guest rooms with hard-wood floors and stone walls, many with sea views. But the place to be at sunset is one of the castle's courtyards or terraces, glass of wine in hand.

Eating

★Gastroteka Danontzat BASQUE €€

(☎943 64 65 97; Calle Denda 6; small plates €7-17; ⏰noon-4pm & 8pm-midnight Wed-Mon) Gastroteka Danontzat has a fun, creative approach to dining, serving beautifully prepared market-fresh fare with a dash of whimsy. Start off with smoked sardines, anchovies or crab pudding, before moving on to tender tuna sashimi, squid with potato confit or Jamaican-style chicken wings. Small servings mean you can try a lot of flavours.

La Hermandad de Pescadores SEAFOOD €€

(☎943 64 27 38; http://hermandaddepescadores.com; Calle Zuloaga 12; mains €18-22; ⏰1-3.30pm Tue-Sun & 8-10pm Tue & Thu-Sat) Locals in the know travel from San Sebastián to eat at this historic Hondarribia restaurant. Housed in a traditional white-and-blue cottage, it serves an array of seafood classics but is best known for its *sopa de pescado* (fish soup), said by some to be the best in the area.

Gran Sol BASQUE €€

(☎943 64 27 01; www.bargransol.com; Calle San Pedro 65; pintxos €2.20-4.20; ⏰12.30-3.30pm & 8.30-10.30pm Tue-Sun) Gran Sol is one of Hondarribia's best-known eateries. Creative *pintxos*, such as pan-fried foie gras with caramelised onions, are served in the woody bar, while next door equally innovative fare is dished up in the adjoining restaurant (menus from €35).

Arroka Berri BASQUE €€

(☎943 64 27 12; www.arrokaberri.com; Calle Higer Bidea 6; mains €18-26; ⏰1-3.30pm & 8-11pm Thu-Sun) As with many trend-setting Basque restaurants, Arroka Berri takes high-quality local produce and refines old-fashioned recipes with a dash of invention. Highlights include oxtail-stuffed peppers, filet of hake loin with mussels and crispy vegetables, and sirloin with Idiazabal cheese sauce.

WORTH A TRIP

SANTUARIO DE ARANTZAZU

About 10km south of Oñati, the **Santuario de Arantzazu** (☎943 78 09 51; www.arantzazu.org; Barrio de Arantzazu 8; ⏰9am-8pm) is a busy Christian pilgrimage site that's a fabulous conflation of piety and avant-garde art. The sanctuary was built in the 1960s on the site where, in 1468, a shepherd found a statue of the Virgin under a hawthorn bush. The sanctuary's design is based on this.

The overwhelming impression is one of mystery and abstract artistry, with halls guarded by 14 chiselled apostles and one cloakless virgin standing over the prone figure of Christ – all comprising one monumental work created by the great Basque sculptor Jorge Oteiza. Descend into the crypt for a look at the powerful murals by Néstor Basterretxea.

Information

On the main square in the walled old town, the **tourist office** (☎943 64 36 77; www.hondarribia.org; Plaza de Armas 9; ⏰9.30am-7.30pm Jul–mid-Sep, 10am-6pm Mon-Sat & 10am-2pm Sun mid-Sep–Jun) has handy info on nearby attractions.

Getting There & Away

Buses run every half-hour or so to San Sebastián (€2.45, 35 minutes); catch them from Sabin Arana a short walk east of the old town.

To cross over to France, take the **Hendaye-Hondarribia Ferry** (www.transfermuga.eu; one-way €1.90; ⏰10.15am-1am Jul–mid-Sep, to 7pm Apr-Jun & mid-Sep–Oct, to 6pm Nov-Mar), which departs approximately every 15 minutes. Find the ferry a few streets over from Calle San Pedro in La Marina.

Oñati

POP 11,400

With a flurry of magnificent architecture and a number of interesting sites scattered through the surrounding green hills, the small and resolutely Basque town of Oñati is a great place to get to know the rural Basque heartland. Many visitors pass through on their way to or from the nearby Santuario de Arantzazu.

Sights

Iglesia de San Miguel CHURCH

(☎943 78 34 53; Avenida de Unibertsitate 2; ⏰hours vary) This late-Gothic confection has a cloister built over the river and a 17th-century crypt where the Counts of Guevara are buried. The church faces onto the main square, Foruen Enparantza, dominated by the eye-catching baroque *ayuntamiento* (town hall). Contact the tourist office for guided tours.

Monastery of Bidaurreta — MONASTERY

(☎943 78 34 53; Kalea Lazarraga; ⏲hours vary) Founded in 1510, this monastery contains a beautiful baroque altarpiece. It's at the opposite end of town from the tourist office and Iglesia de San Miguel. As a still functioning cloistered convent for the Poor Clares, it's rarely open to the public; though the tourist office sometimes arranges tours.

Universidad de Sancti Spiritus — HISTORIC BUILDING

(Avenida de la Universidad 8) Oñati's number-one attraction is the Renaissance treasure of the Universidad de Sancti Spiritus. Built in the 16th century, it was the first university in the Basque Country and, until its closure in 1902, alumni here were schooled in philosophy, law and medicine. The Mudéjar courtyard is worth a look.

Sleeping

Oñati doesn't get a lot of tourists staying overnight. But the countryside around town is awash in *casas rurales* – ask at the tourist office for a list.

Torre Zumeltzegi — HOTEL €€

(☎943 54 00 00; www.hoteltorrezumeltzegi.com; Calle Torre Zumeltzegi 11; s/d from €87/123; ❄📶) On a hillside a few minutes' (uphill) walk from the centre, this restored 13th-century property offers lodging in a fortified mansion. Its 12 unique rooms have beamed ceilings and stone walls, with windows that afford pretty views over the town. The peaceful terrace is a great spot to unwind after a day spent exploring.

Zumeltzegi also has one of Oñati's best restaurants (mains €16 to €20).

Information

The **tourist office** (☎943 78 34 53; www.oñatiturismo.eus; Calle San Juan 14; ⏲9.30am-2pm & 3.30-7pm Jun-Sep, 10am-2pm & 4-6pm Tue-Sun Oct-Apr) is just west of Iglesia de San Miguel, by the river. In July (weekends) and August (daily) the office runs guided tours in Spanish at 1pm to the Universidad de Sancti Spiritus and the Iglesia de San Miguel. English tours are also sometimes offered, though you'll need to contact them at least 24 hours in advance.

Getting There & Away

PESA buses serve Oñati from many destinations in the Basque Country, including Bilbao (€6.85, 60 to 75 minutes, three daily).

Vitoria-Gasteiz

POP 245,000 / ELEV 512M

Vitoria-Gasteiz – often shortened to simply Vitoria – has a habit of falling off the radar, yet it's actually the capital of not just the southern Basque province of Álava (Basque: Araba) but also the entire Basque Country. Maybe it was given this honour precisely because it is so forgotten, but if that's the case, prepare for a pleasant surprise. With an art gallery whose contents frequently surpass those of the more famous Bilbao galleries, a delightful old quarter, dozens of great *pintxo* bars and restaurants, a large student contingent and a friendly local population, you have the makings of a lovely city.

Sights

★Catedral de Santa María — CATHEDRAL

(☎945 25 51 35; www.catedralvitoria.eus; Plaza Santa María; tours €8.50-10.50; ⏲10am-1pm & 4-7pm) At the summit of the old town and dominating its skyline is the medieval Catedral de Santa María. Although the church has been undergoing a lengthy restoration project for many years, it is open for guided visits, which provide a fascinating glimpse of the many layers of history hidden inside this 13th-century masterpiece.

The recommended cathedral & tower tour (€10.50) shows you the evolution of building techniques over the centuries, taking you through underground chambers and up to the rooftop where you'll have a view over the city. The tour ends with a magnificent 3D projection along the walls, showing just how colourful these churches were in centuries past (not the cold grey stone of common belief). Hard hats provided. Call ahead or book a tour online. English-language tours are offered at least once a day.

★Artium — MUSEUM

(☎945 20 90 00; www.artium.org; Calle de Francia 24; adult/child €5/free, by donation Wed & last weekend of month; ⏲11am-2pm & 5-8pm Tue-Fri, 11am-8pm Sat & Sun; 👪) Vitoria's palace of modern art may not have much in the way of grand architecture, but it stages some of the most daring and thought-provoking exhibitions in the Basque Country. Art lovers shouldn't miss this temple to the avant-garde.

Anillo Verde — PARK

Ringing the city is the Anillo Verde (Green Belt), the pride of Vitoria. A series of interconnecting parks, ponds and marshes

Vitoria-Gasteiz

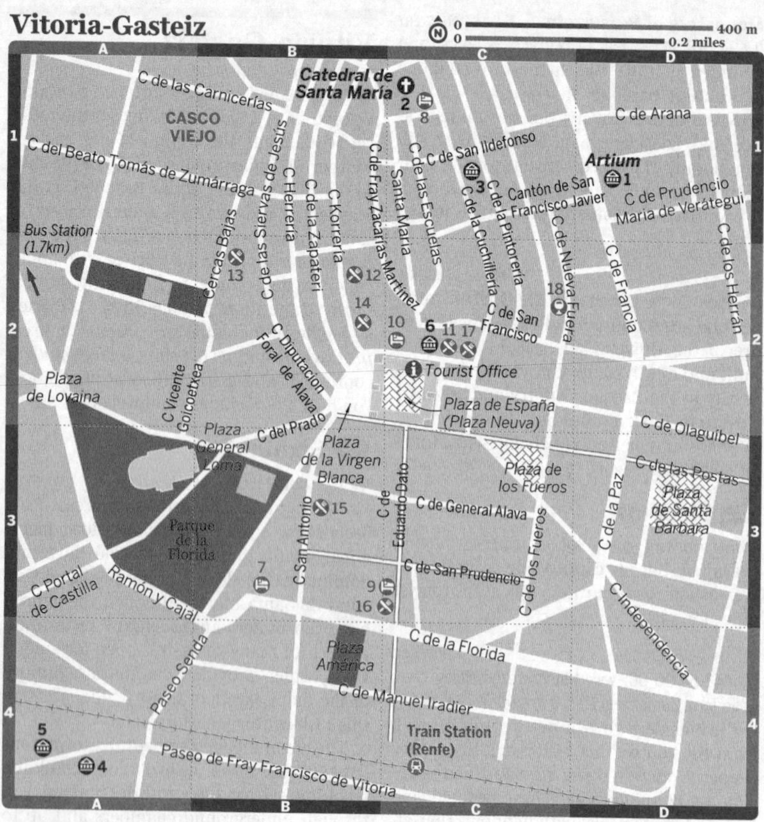

Vitoria-Gasteiz

Top Sights
1 Artium D1
2 Catedral de Santa María C1

Sights
3 Bibat C1
4 Museo de Armería A4
5 Museo de Bellas Artes A4
Museo Fournier de Naipes .... (see 3)
6 Paseo de los Arquillos C2

Sleeping
7 Abba Jazz Hotel B3
8 Albergue de la Catedral C1
9 Hotel Dato C3
10 La Casa de los Arquillos C2

Eating
11 Asador Matxete C2
12 Bar El Tabanko B2
13 El Clarete B2
14 La Malquerida B2
15 PerretxiCo B3
16 Saburdi C3
17 Toloño C2

Drinking & Nightlife
18 La Cassette Vitoria C2

linked to one another by cycle paths, this 31km loop is one of the reasons Vitoria was named the European Green Capital in 2012. The most important of these green areas is the Parque de Salburúa (Salburúa Park). Several outfitters rent bicycles; Capital Bikes (p483) also runs guided bike tours (from €20 to €30).

Bibat MUSEUM
(☎945 20 90 00; Calle de la Cuchillería 54; ⏲10am-2pm & 4-6.30pm Tue-Fri, 10am-2pm Sat,

11am-2pm Sun) FREE The **Museo de Arqueología** and the **Museo Fournier de Naipes** (Calle de la Cuchillería 54; adult/student/child €3/1/free; 10am-2pm & 4-6.30pm Tue-Fri, 10am-2pm Sat, 11am-2pm Sun) are combined into one museum known as Bibat. The Museo de Arqueología has interactive displays that bring the dim and distant past to life. The eccentric Museo Fournier de Naipes has an impressive collection of historic presses and playing cards, including some of the oldest European decks.

Museo de Bellas Artes GALLERY
(Paseo de Fray Francisco 8; 10am-2pm & 4-6.30pm Tue-Fri, 10am-2pm & 5-8pm Sat, 11am-2pm Sun) FREE Housed in an exquisite neo-Renaissance building, the absorbing Museo de Bellas Artes has Basque paintings and sculpture from the 18th and 19th centuries. The works of local son Fernando de Amaríca are on display and reflect an engaging romanticism that manages to mix drama with great warmth of colour and composition.

Paseo de los Arquillos HISTORIC BUILDING
The Paseo de los Arquillos is a gorgeous neoclassical covered arcade that serves as the border between the old and new towns. It was built between 1787 and 1802.

Museo de Armería MUSEUM
(Paseo de Fray Francisco 3; 10am-2pm & 4-6.30pm Tue-Fri, 10am-2pm Sat, 11am-2pm Sun) FREE On a peaceful, tree-lined boulevard southwest of the centre, this low-lit armaments museum showcases weapons used over the centuries, from Bronze Age spearheads to 19th-century muskets. The global collection includes African weaponry, some beautifully designed 17th-century samurai costumes and a shiny suit of armour on an equally well-protected horse.

Festivals & Events

Fiestas de la Virgen Blanca CITY FESTIVAL
(4-9 Aug) The calm, sophisticated Vitoria goes a bit wild during the boisterous Fiestas de la Virgen Blanca. Fireworks, bullfights, concerts and street dancing are preceded by the symbolic descent of Celedón, a beret-wearing, umbrella-holding Basque effigy that flies down on strings from the Iglesia de San Miguel into the plaza below.

Jazz Festival MUSIC
(www.jazzvitoria.com; mid-Jul) One of the city's biggest summertime festivals is this popular five-day music festival, which features some great bands from across the globe. Aside from concerts held in venues like the Teatro Principal, there's also *jazz en la calle*, with free outdoor shows around town.

Azkena Rock Festival MUSIC
(www.azkenarockfestival.com; 3rd weekend of Jun) This annual rock festival features musical headliners from Spain and abroad, plus audiovisual events and outdoor cinema.

Sleeping

Albergue de la Catedral HOSTEL €
(945 27 59 55; www.alberguecatedral.com; Calle de la Cuchillería 87; dm €18-24, d €50;) This appealing 17-room hostel is virtually built into the walls of the cathedral. The clean, unadorned rooms are given a dash of character thanks to the exposed wooden roof beams. Aside from the dorms (which sleep from four to eight), there are several simple private rooms, including a couple of top-floor chambers under the roof.

Hotel Dato HOTEL €
(945 14 72 30; www.hoteldato.com; Calle de Eduardo Dato 28; s/d from €40/60;) In a central location, the Hotel Dato is packed with antiques and artwork. Its 14 rooms are all uniquely designed, dotted with oil paintings or art deco flourishes – though some of the grandest works (including paintings by Utrillo) are in the common areas. Six rooms also have small balconies over the street.

La Casa de los Arquillos B&B €€
(945 15 12 59; www.lacasadelosarquillos.com; Paseo Los Arquillos 1; r €120;) Housed inside a beautiful old building in a prime location above the main square, this immaculate guesthouse has eight attractive rooms set with light, high-end fabrics and attractive furnishings (including a sofa bed, mini kitchens and a small breakfast nook). Some rooms have the original stone walls, while the upstairs rooms have skylights. Five rooms have balconies.

Abba Jazz Hotel HOTEL €€
(945 10 13 46; www.abbahotels.com; Calle de la Florida 7; s/d €76/85;) This confident little hotel has small, searing-white rooms adorned with black-and-white pictures of piano keys, trumpets and other suitably jazzy instruments. Room sizes vary, so ask to see a few before committing. It's located on the edge of the lovely Parque de la Florida.

THE PAINTED CITY

Strolling through the winding lanes of Vitoria-Gasteiz's old quarter is at times pure sensory overload – thanks to its surprising collection of murals soaring high above the streetscape. Beginning in 2007, two artists transformed one of the city's blank walls into one massive painting called *The Thread of Time*, a fabric-like work bursting with colour. And so was born the Itinerario Muralístico Vitoria-Gasteiz (IMVG), a movement that would use the blank walls around town as canvases to create a kaleidoscopic open-air gallery at the epicentre of Vitoria.

Over the next six years, Verónica y Christina Werckmeister, the artists behind the first painting, were joined by other artists from around the globe who added their own vibrant touch to Vitoria. Today more than a dozen murals lie scattered around the centre. Many of the works reference Vitoria's history, with folkloric costumes, medieval minstrels and Basque legends all featured in vibrant colour.

While you can explore the murals on your own, artists from **IMVG** (☎633 184457; www.muralismopublico.com; guided tours €7) lead fascinating 90-minute guided tours in English, French and other languages. Get in touch with them to set up an excursion.

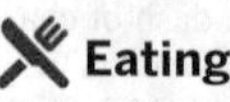

Eating

Internationally Vitoria might not have the same culinary cachet as San Sebastián, but among in-the-know Spaniards this is a city with serious culinary pedigree. How serious? Well, in 2014 it was awarded the title of *Capital Nacional de la Gastronomía* (National Gastronomic Capital) on account of its stellar array of *pintxo* bars and highly creative chefs.

Saburdi PINTXOS €
(Calle Eduardo Dato 32; pintxos from €2.50; ⌚8am-midnight Mon-Sat, from 11am Sun) One of the best, if somewhat underrated, *pintxos* spots in town, Saburdi serves up gourmet creations featuring high-end ingredients. Nibble on creamy codfish-stuffed peppers, Iberian ham topped with egg, tuna with roasted peppers and other morsels of heavenly perfection. The interior is sleek and modern, with a few outdoor tables for enjoying fine sunny days.

Toloño PINTXOS €
(Calle de San Francisco 3; pintxos from €3; ⌚9am-midnight Mon-Thu, to 4am Fri & Sat, 10.30am-3.30pm Sun) This bar has won awards for its creative *pintxos;* the house specials often involve creative takes on local mushrooms. It's a large bar, so there's normally somewhere to sit down, plus a small outdoor space that's a charming spot to people-watch.

Bar El Tabanko PINTXOS €
(www.eltabanko.com; Calle de la Korrería 46; pintxos from €2.50; ⌚7-11.30pm Tue-Thu, 1.30-4pm & 7-11pm Fri & Sat, 12.30-4.30pm Sun) Taking its cue, in terms of both decoration and food, from the steamy southern region of Andalucía, this is an ever-busy, ever-reliable *pintxo* bar. Come early to grab a seat out front and watch the city stroll past.

La Malquerida PINTXOS €
(http://lamalqueridavitoria.com; Calle de la Correría 10; pintxos from €3; ⌚10am-4pm & 6.30pm-midnight Mon-Fri, 10am-1am Sat & Sun) A fantastic *pintxo* bar hidden away under the shadows of the church spires. Many locals consider it the best in town.

PerretxiCo PINTXOS €€
(☎945 13 72 21; http://perretxico.es; Calle San Antonio 3; pintxos from €2, mains €11-13; ⌚10am-midnight) This award-winning eatery packs in the crowds with its perfect, creative bites like mini-servings of mushroom risotto, grilled foie with apples and pine nuts, or codfish tempura. For something more substantial, book a table in the back and linger over roasted turbot with mushrooms or beef cheeks in red wine sauce.

Asador Matxete STEAK €€
(☎945 13 18 21; www.matxete.com; Plaza de Matxete 4-5; mains €15-22; ⌚1-3.45pm & 8.30-11pm Tue-Sat, noon-3.45pm Sun) There are two types of *asador* (restaurants specialising in barbecued meat): smoky old farmhouse-like places that haven't changed in decades, and sleek new urban remakes. This one falls into the second category and it fires up grilled steaks and whole fish served up with flair. It's delightfully situated on a quiet old town plaza and has a lovely summer terrace.

El Clarete BASQUE €€€
(945 26 38 74; Calle Cercas Bajas 18; lunch/dinner menu €22/55; 1.30-3.30pm Mon-Sat & 9-11pm Thu-Sat, closed Aug) Foodies flock to this outpost of culinary creativity, one of Vitoria's best restaurants. The menu changes based on seasonal produce, and might feature seafood risotto, foie with rich port wine sauce or roast lamb, though the chef can accommodate dietary restrictions. It's a small intimate space with stone walls and considerate service, plus an impressive wine cellar.

Drinking & Nightlife

There's a strong politico-arty vibe in the Casco Viejo, where a lively student cadre keeps things swerving with creative street posters and action. The main action is at Calle de la Cuchillería/Aiztogile and neighbouring Cantón de San Francísco Javier, both of which are packed with busy bars that attract a wide range of age groups. There's a heavy Basque nationalist atmosphere in some bars.

La Cassette Vitoria BAR
(www.lacassettevitoria.com/home/english; Calle Nueva Fuera 7; 6-11pm Sun, Wed & Thu, to 4am Fri & Sat) A fun and festive spot that draws all ages and creeds with its outstanding mojitos and gin and tonics poured by friendly bar staff. Things get lively on weekends, with DJs spinning highly danceable grooves from the '70s, '80s and '90s.

Information

The **tourist office** (945 16 15 98; www.vitoria-gasteiz.org/turismo; Plaza de España 1; 10am-8pm Jul-Sep, 10am-7pm Mon-Sat, 11am-2pm Sun Oct-Jun) is in the central square of the old town. It can organise fascinating guided tours of the numerous giant wall murals of the city, and tours out to the extensive green spaces and birdwatching sites that fringe the city.

Getting There & Away

There are car parks by the train station, by the Artium, and just east of the cathedral.

Vitoria's **bus station** (www.vitoria-gasteiz.org; Plaza de Euskaltzaindia) has regular services to the following:

DESTINATION	FARE (€)	DURATION (HR)
Barcelona	from 32	7
Bilbao	6.30	1¼
Madrid	27	4½
Pamplona	from 8	1¾
San Sebastián	from 7	1¼

Trains go to the following:

DESTINATION	FARE (€)	DURATION (HR)	FREQUENCY (DAILY)
Barcelona	from 44	5	1
Madrid	from 42	4-6	5
Pamplona	from 6	1	5
San Sebastián	from 13	1¾	up to 10

Getting Around

Vitoria-Gasteiz is a bike-friendly city; to hire one, get in touch with **Capital Bikes** (691 112292; www.capitalbikes.es; Casa de la Dehesa de Olárizu; bike per hour/day €5/13, electric bike per hour/day €8/30; 10am-3pm Tue-Fri, 9am-2pm & 4.30-8.30pm Sat & Sun), who will deliver a bike to you.

NAVARRA

Several Spains intersect in Navarra (Nafarroa in Basque). The soft greens and bracing climate of the Navarran Pyrenees lie like a cool compress across the sun-struck brow of the south, which is all stark plains, cereal crops and vineyards, sliced by high sierras with cockscombs of raw limestone. Navarra is also pilgrim territory: for centuries the faithful have used the pass at Roncesvalles to cross from France on their way to Santiago de Compostela.

Navarra was historically the heartland of the Basques, but dynastic struggles and trimming due to reactionary politics, including Francoism, have left it a semi-autonomous province, with the north being Basque by nature and the south leaning towards Castilian Spain.

The Navarran capital, Pamplona, tends to grab the headlines with its world-famous running of the bulls, but the region's real charm is in its spectacularly diverse landscapes and its picturesque small towns and villages.

Pamplona

POP 201,300 / ELEV 456M

Senses are heightened in Pamplona (Basque: Iruña), capital of the fiercely independent Kingdom of Navarra and home to one of Spain's most famous and wildest festivals. Yet even when the bulls aren't thundering down the cobblestones through the centre of town, Pamplona makes a fascinating place

Pamplona

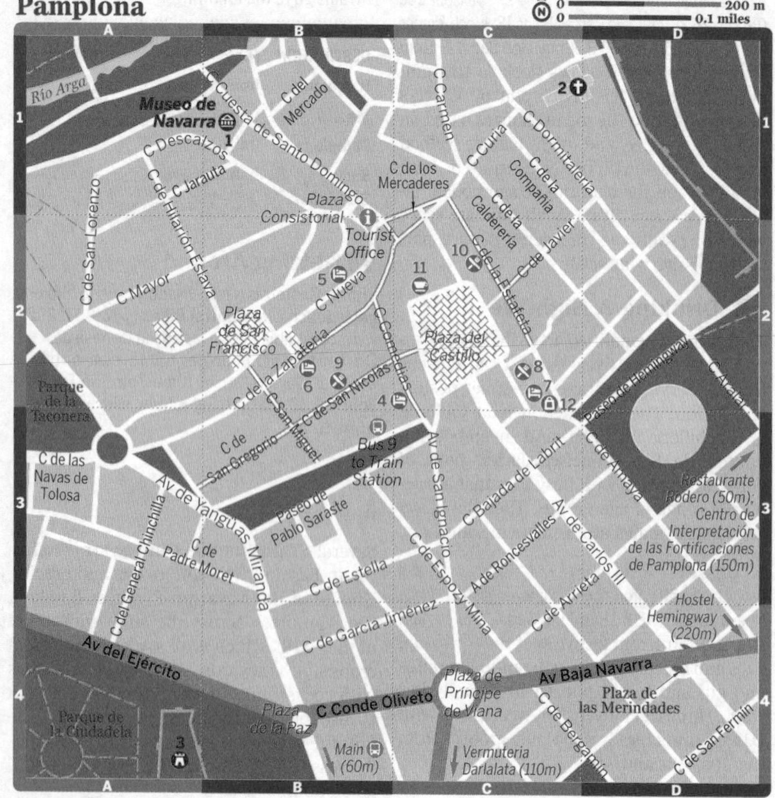

Pamplona

Top Sights
1 Museo de Navarra ... B1

Sights
2 Catedral de Santa María ... C1
3 Ciudadela ... A4

Sleeping
4 Hostal Arriazu ... C2
5 Hotel Maisonnave ... B2
6 Palacio Guendulain ... B2
7 Sercotel Europa ... C2

Eating
8 Bar Gaucho ... C2
9 Baserri ... B2
10 La Cocina De Alex Múgica ... C2

Drinking & Nightlife
11 Café Iruña ... C2

Shopping
12 Kukuxumusu ... C2

to explore. With its grand cathedral, archaeological treasures and 16th-century fortifications, there's much history hidden in these atmospheric medieval lanes. And with its lush parks and picturesque city centre full of vibrant eating and drinking spots, it's easy to see why so many – Hemingway included – have fallen under Pamplona's spell. The village also sees its fair share of pilgrims arriving on foot along the Camino de Santiago, a tradition that dates back many centuries.

Sights

★Museo de Navarra MUSEUM

(☎848 42 89 26; www.cfnavarra.es/cultura/museo; Calle Cuesta de Santo Domingo 47; adult/student/child €2/1/free, free Sat afternoon & Sun; ⏲9.30am-2pm & 5-7pm Tue-Sat, 11am-2pm Sun) Housed in a former medieval hospital, this superb museum has an eclectic collection of archaeological finds (including a number of fantastic Roman mosaics unearthed mainly in southern Navarra), as well as a selection of art, including Goya's *Marqués de San Adrián*. Labelling is in Spanish only, but foreign translation leaflets are available.

Catedral de Santa María CATHEDRAL

(www.catedraldepamplona.com; Calle Dormitalería; adult/child €5/3; ⏲10.30am-7pm Mon-Sat Apr-Sep, to 5pm Oct-Mar) Pamplona's main cathedral stands on a rise just inside the city ramparts amid a dark thicket of narrow streets. The cathedral is a late-medieval Gothic gem spoiled only by its rather dull neoclassical facade, an 18th-century appendage. The vast interior reveals some fine artefacts, including a silver-plated Virgin and the splendid 15th-century tomb of Carlos III of Navarra and his wife Doña Leonor. The real joy is the Gothic **cloister**, where there is marvellous delicacy in the stonework.

Ciudadela FORTRESS

(Avenida del Ejército; ⏲8am-9.30pm Mon-Sat, from 9am Sun) FREE The walls and bulwarks of the grand fortified citadel, the star-shaped Ciudadela, were built between 1571 and 1645 under the direction of King Felipe II. They're considered one of the best examples of military architecture from the Spanish Renaissance. The former moats and bastions have become a setting for artists to display their works in the evenings from 6.30pm to 9pm, and on weekends from noon to 2pm.

Centro de Interpretación de las Fortificaciones de Pamplona MUSEUM

(Interpretation Center of the Fortifications of Pamplona; ☎948 21 15 54; www.murallasdepamplona.com; cnr Calles Arrieta & Aralar; adult/child €3/1.50; ⏲11am-2pm & 5-7pm Tue-Sun Apr-Oct, 10am-2pm & 4-6pm Nov-Mar) If these walls could talk. This excellent interpretation centre, located in the Fortín de San Bartolomé, explains the design and function of Pamplona's original fortifications, whose construction dates from the 16th century. It's still considered one of the best preserved bastions in Europe. Among the many curiosities in the museum: centuries-old graffiti, most likely created by guardsmen.

Sleeping

Outside of Sanfermines, you'll find a wide selection of enticing lodging options within the old centre. During the big festival, hotels raise their rates mercilessly – all quadruple their normal rack rates and many increase them fivefold – and it can be nearly impossible to get a room without reserving between six months and a year in advance.

Hostel Hemingway HOSTEL €

(☎948 98 38 84; www.hostelhemingway.com; Calle Amaya 26; dm €17-20, s/d from €35/42; @📶) This well-run hostel, located a few minutes' walk from the old town, was renovated in 2013. Clean and friendly, with a lounge where you can meet other travellers (or browse books, listen to music, put on a film), it's a great budget pick. There's also a communal kitchen.

Hostal Arriazu HOTEL €

(☎948 21 02 02; www.hostalarriazu.com; Calle Comedias 14; r €54-84; 📶) Falling somewhere between a budget *pensión* and a midrange hotel, this good-value option is located in a former theatre. The 14 rooms are pleasingly old-fashioned, though the en suite bathrooms are perfectly modern. There's also a pretty courtyard and an appealing lounge area.

Hotel Maisonnave HOTEL €€

(☎948 22 26 00; www.hotelmaisonnave.es; Calle Nueva 20; d from €99; ❄📶) In an excellent location near the centre of the old town, Hotel Maisonnave has friendly service and modern, attractively designed wood-floored rooms with all the creature comforts (including a small fitness centre, a sauna and a good restaurant). Book a superior room or a suite for views over the rooftops and church steeples of the historic quarter.

Sercotel Europa HOTEL €€

(☎948 22 18 00; www.hoteleuropapamplona.com; Espoz y Mina 11; s/d from €80/95; 📶) Though the building is better known for its restaurant, the sleek Europa – part of the quality Sercotel chain – also features several floors of modern hotel rooms. Note that the most economical accommodations are tiny and windowless, but the location is tough to beat.

THE RUNNING OF THE BULLS

Liberated, obsessive or plain mad is how you might describe aficionados (and there are many) who regularly take part in Pamplona's Sanfermines (Fiesta de San Fermín), a nonstop cacophony of music, dance, fireworks and processions – and the small matter of running alongside a handful of agitated, horn-tossing *toros* (bulls) – that takes place from 6 to 14 July each year.

The bullrun is said to have originally developed way back in the 14th century as a way of herding bulls into market, with the seller running alongside the bulls to speed up their movement into the marketplace. In later times the same technique was used to transport bulls from the corrals to the bullring, and essentially that is still the case today. *El encierro*, the running of the bulls from their corrals to the bullring for the afternoon bullfight, takes place in Pamplona every morning during Sanfermines. Six bulls are let loose from the Coralillos de Santo Domingo to charge across the square of the same name. They continue up the street, veering onto Calle de los Mercaderes from Plaza Consistorial, then sweep right onto Calle de la Estafeta for the final charge to the ring. Devotees, known as *mozos* (the brave or foolish, depending on your point of view), race madly with the bulls, aiming to keep close – but not too close. The total course is some 825m long and lasts little more than three minutes.

Participants enter the course before 7.30am from Plaza de Santo Domingo. At 8am two rockets are fired: the first announces that the bulls have been released from the corrals; the second lets participants know they're all out and running. The first danger point is where Calle de los Mercaderes leads into Calle de la Estafeta. Here many of the bulls skid into the barriers because of their headlong speed on the turn. They can become isolated from the herd and are then always dangerous. A very treacherous stretch comes towards the end, where Calle de la Estafeta slopes down into the final turn to Plaza de Toros. A third rocket goes off when all the bulls have made it to the ring and a final one when they have been rounded up in the stalls.

Those who prefer to be spectators rather than action men (and we use the word 'men' on purpose here as, technically, women are forbidden from running, although an increasing number are doing it anyway) bag their spot along the route early. A space doesn't mean an uninterrupted view because a second 'security' fence stands between the spectators and runners, blocking much of the view (only police, medical staff and other authorised people can enter the space between the two fences). Some people rent a space on one of the house balconies overlooking the course. Others watch the runners and bulls race out of the entrance tunnel and into the bullring by buying a ticket for a seat in the ring. Whatever the vantage point, it's all over in a few blurred seconds.

Each evening a traditional bullfight is held. Sanfermines winds up at midnight on 14 July with a candlelit procession, known as the Pobre de Mí (Poor Me), which starts from Plaza Consistorial.

Concern has grown about the high numbers of people taking part in recent *encierros*. Since records began in 1924, 16 people have died during Pamplona's bullrun. Many of those who run are full of bravado (and/or drink) and have little idea of what they're doing. The number of injuries differs from year to year, but serious injuries are common (usually due to goring, but also from pile-ups of participants) and deaths are not unheard of. On top of the dangers to runners, the bulls themselves are all destined to die in the bullring and that aspect of the running, as well as the stress of the run itself and the possibility of the bulls slipping and injuring themselves in the stampede, have led to animal welfare groups condemning the spectacle as a cruel tradition.

★**Palacio Guendulain** HISTORIC HOTEL **€€€** (☎948 22 55 22; www.palacioguendulain.com; Calle de la Zapatería 53; d from €160; P❄🛜) Inside the converted former home of the viceroy of New Granada, this sumptuous hotel offers Pamplona's most atmospheric overnights. On arrival, you're greeted by a museum-piece 17th-century carriage and a collection of classic cars being guarded by the viceroy's private chapel. The rooms contain *Princess and the Pea*–soft beds, enormous showers and regal armchairs.

Eating

★Bar Gaucho PINTXOS €
(www.cafebargaucho.com; Espoz y Mina 7; pintxos €2-4; ⏱8am-3pm & 6.30-11pm) This bustling bar serves multi-award-winning *pintxos* that, despite some serious competition, many a local will tell you are the finest in the city.

La Cocina De Alex Múgica PINTXOS €
(☎948 51 01 25; www.alexmugica.com; Estafeta 24; pintxos from €2; ⏱1-5pm Tue-Sun & 7-11pm Tue-Sat) Go early to score a place at this much-loved *pintxos* institution. Culinary whiz kid Alex Múgica has a devoted local following for his mix of traditional and cutting-edge combinations, including some delicious *anchoas con txangurro* (anchovies with spider crab) served in a sardine tin.

Baserri BASQUE €€
(☎948 22 20 21; www.restaurantebaserri.com; Calle de San Nicolás 32; tasting menu €25-40, pintxos from €2; ⏱pintxos bar noon-11.30pm Tue-Sun, restaurant 1.30-3.30pm & 8.30-10.30pm Tue-Sun) This place, one of many bars, restaurants, and cafés on busy Calle San Nicolás, has won numerous awards for its *pintxos*. Highlights include ceviche, potatoes with red curry, and jamon croquettes.

Restaurante Rodero SPANISH €€€
(☎948 22 80 35; http://restauranterodero.com; Calle Emilio Arrieta 3; menus €65-78, mains €26-32; ⏱1.30-3.30pm Mon-Sat & 9-11pm Wed-Sat) For a memorable meal, book a table at this Michelin-starred, family-run restaurant just east of the bullring. Celebrated chef Koldo Rodero uses the finest Navarran ingredients to create imaginative dishes that dazzle the senses. Friendly service and an elegant dining room add to the charm.

Drinking & Nightlife

Café Iruña CAFE
(www.cafeiruna.com; Plaza del Castillo 44; ⏱8am-midnight Mon-Thu, from 9am Fri-Sun) Opened on the eve of Sanfermines in 1888, Café Iruña's dominant position, powerful sense of history and belle époque decor make this by far the most famous watering hole in the city. In addition to a long list of wine and spirits, it also has a good range of *pintxos* and light meals.

Hemingway was a regular here – indeed, he helped immortalise the place in his novel *The Sun Also Rises*.

Vermutería Darlalata BAR
(www.facebook.com/vermuteriadarlalata; Calle Navarro Villoslada 14; ⏱11am-11pm Sun-Thu, to 2am Fri & Sat) Just off the beaten path, this delightful little corner bar has obvious charm with its vintage decor, friendly barkeeps and delicious spread of *pintxos*. The real draw though is the collection of vermouths, with more than 80 varieties on hand. It's a jovial, but easygoing space, welcome to all, that draws a fine cross-section of Pamplona society.

Shopping

Kukuxumusu CLOTHING
(www.kukuxumusu.com; Estafeta 76; ⏱10am-2pm & 5-8pm Mon-Sat) With shops all around the Basque Country, this long-running clothing company was born right here in Pamplona during a the San Fermín festival in 1989. Here you'll find Kukuxumusu's iconic T-shirts that feature whimsical images of cartoon bulls in various poses. You'll also find bags, wallets, mugs, magnets, stickers and other gear.

Information

The extremely well-organised **tourist information office** (☎948 42 07 00; www.turismo.navarra.es; Plaza Consistorial; ⏱10am-2pm & 3-7pm Mon-Sat, 10am-2pm Sun mid-Sep–mid-Jun, 9am-2pm & 3-8pm daily mid-Jun–mid-Sep), just opposite the statue of the bulls in the new town, has plenty of information about the city and Navarra. There are a couple of summer-only tourist info booths scattered throughout the city.

Getting There & Away

AIR

Pamplona's **airport** (☎902 40 47 04; www.aena.es; 📶), about 7km south of the city, has regular flights to Madrid and Barcelona. Bus 16 travels every 15 minutes or so between the bus station in the city to the suburb of Noáin (20 minutes) from where it's about an 800m walk to the airport. A taxi costs €15 to €20.

BUS

From the **main bus station** (☎902 02 36 51; www.estaciondeautobusesdepamplona.com; Ave de Yanguas y Miranda 2), which is cleverly concealed underground near La Ciudadela, buses leave for most towns throughout Navarra. Service is restricted on Sunday.

Regular bus services travel to the following places:

DESTINATION	FARE (€)	DURATION (HR)
Bilbao	15	2-2½
Logroño	10	2
San Sebastián	8	1-1½
Vitoria	9	1¼-2

Regional destinations include the following:

DESTINATION	FARE (€)	DURATION (HR)	FREQUENCY
Estella	5.25	1	10 daily
Olite	3.75	¾	16 daily

TRAIN

Pamplona's train station is linked to the city centre by **bus 9** from Paseo de Sarasate every 15 minutes. Buy tickets online or at the station.

Note that it's much quicker to take the bus to San Sebastián. Trains run to/from the following:

DESTINATION	FARE (€)	DURATION (HR)	FREQUENCY
Madrid	42-66	3	4 daily
San Sebastián	16-22	2	2 daily
Tudela	9-18	1	5 daily
Vitoria	7-12	1	4 daily

Navarran Pyrenees

Awash in greens and often concealed in mists, the rolling hills, ribboned cliffs, clammy forests and snow-plastered mountains that make up the Navarran Pyrenees are a playground for outdoor enthusiasts and pilgrims on the Camino de Santiago. Despite being firmly Basque in history, culture and outlook, there is something of a different feeling to the tiny towns and villages that hug these slopes. Perhaps it's their proximity to France, but in general they seem somehow more prim and proper than many of the lowland towns. This only adds to the charm of exploring what are, without doubt, some of the most delightful and least exploited mountains in western Europe.

Valle del Baztán

This is rural Basque Country at its most typical, a landscape of splotchy reds and greens. Minor roads take you in and out of charming little villages, such as **Arraioz**, known for the fortified Casa Jaureguizar; and **Ziga**, with its 16th-century church. Just beyond Irurita on the N121B is the valley's biggest town, **Elizondo**, a good base for exploring the area.

Beyond Elizondo, the NA2600 road meanders dreamily amid picturesque farms, villages and hills before climbing sharply to the French border pass of **Puerto de Izpegui**, where the world becomes a spectacular collision of crags, peaks and valleys. At the pass, you can stop for a short, sharp hike up to the top of **Mt Izpegui**.

The N121B continues northwards to the Puerto de Otxondo and the border crossing into France at Dantxarinea. Just before the border, a minor road veers west to the almost overly pretty village of **Zugarramurdi**.

Sights

La Cueva de Zugarramurdi CAVE
(www.turismozugarramurdi.com; Zugarramurdi; adult/child €4/2; ⏲11am-7.30pm Jul-Sep, to 6pm Oct-Jun) According to the Inquisition, these caves (also known as Cuevas de Las Brujas, or Caves of the Witches) were once the scene of evil debauchery. True to form, inquisitors tortured and burned scores of alleged witches here. The caves are a short walk west of the village centre of Zugarramurdi.

Museo de las Brujas MUSEUM
(www.turismozugarramurdi.com; Calle Beitikokarrika 22, Zugarramurdi; adult/child €4.50/2; ⏲11am-7.30pm Tue-Sun mid-Jul–mid-Sep, 11am-6pm Wed-Sun mid-Sep–mid-Jul) Playing on the flying-broomstick theme of La Cueva de Zugarramurdi, this museum is a fascinating dip into the mysterious cauldron of witchcraft in the Pyrenees. The museum is near the centre of the village of Zugarramurdi.

Sleeping

Hostal Trinquete Antxitónea HOSTAL €€
(☎948 58 18 07; www.antxitonea.com; Braulío Iríarte 16, Elizondo; d/tr from €66/91; 📶) This well-run *hostal* has plain rooms with flower-bedecked balconies, some with river views. The attached restaurant (mains €11 to €16) is worth a stop.

Getting There & Away

Most travellers drive here. Zugarramurdi is located about 80km north of Pamplona via N121A.

Burguete

POP 240

A steady stream of pilgrims on the Camino de Santiago pass through this quaint 12th-century town. The main road runs tightly between neat, whitewashed houses with bare cornerstones at Burguete (Basque: Auritz), lending a more sober French air to things. Despite lacking the history, it actually makes a better night's halt than nearby Roncesvalles.

Sleeping

Hostal Burguete GUESTHOUSE €

(948 76 00 05; www.hotelburguete.com; San Nicolás 71; s/d/tr €44/59/79;) On the main street in peaceful Burguete, this pleasant inn has 20 simple rooms with wood furnishings and rustic touches. Hemingway fans should try to book room 23, where Hemingway allegedly wrote much of *The Sun Also Rises* during one of his many stays in the area.

Camping Urrobi CAMPGROUND €

(948 76 02 00; www.campingurrobi.com; campsite incl 2 adults & car €30, bungalow for up to 3 people €74, dm from €12; Apr-Oct;) Campers will be happy at this riverside campsite a few kilometres south of town. It also has a hostel and bungalows.

Hotel Rural Loizu HOTEL €€

(948 76 00 08; www.loizu.com; Calle de San Nicolás 13; s/d from €63/87; Apr-Dec;) In the sleepy village of Burguete, this is a pleasant country hotel whose upper rooms have attractive beams and exposed stone walls, plus fine views over the countryside. Downstairs, there's a good restaurant (mains €12 to €20).

Getting There & Away

Most visitors arrive by car or on foot, but there's also regular bus service to Pamplona (€5.50, one hour).

Roncesvalles

POP 30

History hangs heavily in the air of Roncesvalles (Basque: Orreaga). Legend has it that it was here that the armies of Charlemagne were defeated and Roland, commander of Charlemagne's rearguard, was killed by Basque tribes in 778. This event is celebrated in the epic 11th-century poem *Chanson de Roland* (Song of Roland) and is still talked about by today's Basques. In addition to violence and bloodshed, though, Roncesvalles has long been a key point on the road to Santiago de Compostela, and today Camino pilgrims continue to give thanks at the famous monastery for a successful crossing of the Pyrenees, one of the hardest parts of the Camino de Santiago.

The main event here is the **monastery complex** (948 79 04 80; www.roncesvalles.es; guided tours adult/child €5/2.50; 10am-2pm & 3.30-7pm Apr-Oct, 10am-2pm & 3-6pm Nov & Mar, 10.30am-2.30pm Thu-Tue Dec & Feb), which contains a number of different buildings of interest.

Sights

Real Colegiata de Santa María CHURCH

(948 79 04 80; 9am-8.30pm) FREE The 13th-century Gothic Real Colegiata de Santa María, a good example of Navarran Gothic architecture, contains a much-revered, silver-covered statue of the Virgin beneath a modernist-looking canopy worthy of Frank Gehry.

Sleeping

Casa de Beneficiados HOTEL €€

(948 76 01 05; www.casadebeneficiados.com; Orreaga-Roncesvalles; s/d/tr €80/90/115, apt

OFF THE BEATEN TRACK

SIERRA DE ARALAR

One of Navarra's many natural parks, the scenic Sierra de Aralar offers pleasant walking and dramatic drives. There's not much to **Lekunberri**, the area's main town, except a gaggle of solid Basque farmhouses in the old quarter and an ever-growing estate of soulless modern housing beyond.

For most, the main reason for visiting Lekunberri is to travel the bendy back road NA1510, which leads southwest through a tasty tapestry of mixed deciduous and evergreen forests to culminate (after 21km) at the **Santuario de San Miguel de Aralar** (www.aralarkosanmigel.info; Monte Aralar; 10am-2pm & 4-6pm) FREE.

The **tourist office** (948 50 72 04; www.plazaola.org; Plazaola 21, Lekunberri; 10am-2pm Tue-Sun) here is very helpful and can advise on the numerous fantastic walks the area offers.

€90-150; ⏲mid-Mar–Dec; 📶) In a former life this was an 18th-century monks' residence. Today it has attractive rooms, some with fine views over the countryside, and the atmospheric common areas make fine places to unwind after a day's hike. You can also dine at the good-value restaurant on site, hire bicycles or arrange horse-riding trips.

ℹ Getting There & Away

Many travellers arrive on foot or by car, but you can also get to Roncesvalles by bus from Pamplona (€5, one hour); these run twice a day from July through September, and once a day the rest of the year.

In the summer, four daily buses connect Roncesvalles with St-Jean-Pied-de-Port (€5, 40 minutes).

Ochagavía

POP 540

This charming Pyrenean town lying astride narrow Río Zatoya sets itself quite apart from the villages further south. Grey stone, slate and cobblestones dominate the old centre, which straddles a bubbling stream crossed by a pleasant medieval bridge. The town's sober dignity is reinforced by the looming presence of the **Iglesia de San Juan Evangelista**.

Sleeping & Eating

Hostal Casa Sario HOTEL €

(☎948 89 01 87; www.casasario.com; Llana 11, Jaurrieta; s/d/tr €47/65/80; 📶) This sweet little rural hotel, in the heart of the village of Jaurrieta (about 8km southwest of Ochaga-

THE CAMINO IN NAVARRA & LA RIOJA

At the gates of Spain, Navarra is the first Spanish leg of the journey to Santiago de Compostela for walkers on the Camino Francés route. The opening section, which crosses over the Pyrenees, is also one of the most spectacular parts of the entire Camino.

Roncesvalles to Pamplona

From the Puerto de Ibañeta, the Camino dramatically enters Spain and drops down to Roncesvalles (p489). Dominated by its great, imposing abbey, Roncesvalles admirably sets the tone for this extraordinary route. Inside the heavily restored 13th-century Gothic church, you'll find the first statue of Santiago dressed as a pilgrim (with scallop shells and staff).

Pamplona (p483) became an official stop along the Camino in the 11th century, cementing its prosperity. Just inside the cathedral's bland neoclassical facade are the pure, soaring lines of the 14th-century Gothic interior.

Pamplona to Logroño & Beyond

Heading west out of Pamplona via Zariquiegui and the Sierra del Perdón, pilgrims reach Puente la Reina (p494), where the Camino Aragonés, coming from the east, joins up with the Camino Francés.

Estella (p495), the next stop, contains exceptional monumental Romanesque architecture: the outstanding portal of the Iglesia de San Miguel; the cloister of the Iglesia de San Pedro de la Rúa; and the Palacio de los Reyes de Navarra.

Outside Estella, evergreen oaks and vineyards fill undulating landscapes until a long, barren stretch leads through the sleepy towns of Los Arcos, Sansol and Torres del Río. In hillside Torres you'll find another remarkably intact eight-sided Romanesque chapel, the Iglesia del Santo Sepulcro.

The great Río Ebro marks the entrance to Logroño (p497) and explains its wealth and size. The dour Gothic Iglesia de Santiago houses a large Renaissance altarpiece depicting unusual scenes from the saint's life, including run-ins with the wicked necromancer Hermogenes.

Nájera literally grew out of the town's red cliff wall when King Ramiro discovered a miraculous statue of the Virgin in one of the cliff's caves in the 11th century.

Santo Domingo de la Calzada (p500) is one of the road's most captivating places. It is named for its energetic 11th-century founder, Santo Domingo, who cleared forests, built roadways, a bridge, a pilgrim's hospice and a church, and performed many wondrous miracles depicted masterfully in Hispano-Flemish paintings in the cathedral.

Camino Francés in Navarra & La Rioja

0 — 40 km
0 — 20 miles

vía), has six simple wood-floored rooms and a busy bar-restaurant downstairs.

Hotel Rural Auñamendi HOTEL €€

(☎948 89 01 89; www.hotelruralaunamendi.com; Urrutià 23; d/tr €80/105; 📶) After extensive renovations in 2014, this lovely hotel in peaceful Ochagavía is a top pick for its 11 bright, spacious rooms, comfortable public spaces, and coffee bar with outdoor terrace seating.

The restaurant is a reliable spot for a meal or some *pintxos*.

Asador Sideria Kixkia BASQUE €€

(☎646 387407; www.kixkia.com; Urrutia 59; menús €25-33; ⏰1-3.30pm & 9-11pm; 🐾) There are plenty of places to eat in the area, but it's hard to beat the earthy, rural atmosphere and filling mountain food of the Asador Sideria Kixkia at the northern end of the village.

ℹ Getting There & Away

There's one daily ALSA bus departing Ochagavía for Pamplona at 9am (€9.15, 1½ hours), returning from Pamplona at 3pm. There's no service on Sundays.

To reach France, take the NA140 northeast from Ochagavía into the Sierra de Abodi and cross at the Puerto de Larrau (1585m), a majestically bleak pass.

Valle del Roncal

Navarra's most spectacular mountain area is around Roncal, and this easternmost valley, made up of seven villages, is an alternative route for leaving or entering the Navarran Pyrenees.

BURGUI

POP 220

The gateway to this part of the Pyrenees is Burgui – an enchanting huddle of stone houses built beside a clear, gushing stream (the Río Esca) bursting with frogs and fish and crossed via a humpbacked Roman bridge.

Burgui isn't well served by public transport. The village is roughly a one-hour drive east of Pamplona via A21.

Hostal El Almadiero HOSTAL €€

(☎948 47 70 86; www.almadiero.com; Plaza Padre Tomás de Burgui 1; d from €65; ❄📶) In the heart of the village, this pleasant *hostal rural* has bright, cosy rooms with 19th-century charm and a first-rate restaurant on site.

RONCAL

POP 210

The largest centre along this road, though still firmly a village, Roncal is a place of cobblestone alleyways that twist and turn between dark stone houses and meander down to a river full of trout.

ISABA

POP 440

Lording it over the other villages in the valley, lofty Isaba, lying above the confluence of Ríos Belagua and Uztárroz, is another popular base for walkers and skiers. Heading north out of town towards the French border, the scenery becomes ever more spectacular. The road starts off confined between mountain peaks before suddenly opening out into high Alpine pastures with a backdrop of the most majestic mountains in the western Pyrenees. Approaching the French border the road corkscrews up and up to the pass of Roncalia, where you'll find a small ski resort. Beyond is France and another, larger ski resort, Pierre St Martin. There are signed walking trails on both sides of the border.

Stop by the **tourist office** (☎948 89 32 51; www.vallederoncal.es; Barrio Izargentea 28; ⏰10am-1.30pm & 5-8pm Mon-Sat, 10am-1.30pm mid-Jul–mid-Sep, Sat & Sun only mid-Sep–mid-Jul) in the village centre for info on nearby walks and other activities.

Most travellers arrive here in their own cars, but you could also take a La Tafallesa bus from Pamplona to nearby Uztárroz (€10, two hours) and then hire a taxi into Isaba (from €15, 15 minutes).

Onki Xin GUESTHOUSE €
(☎618 317837; http://onkixin.com; Barrio Izarjentea 25; d €55, apt €110-140; 📶) In a traditional house in the village centre, Onki Zin offers nine attractive rooms with beamed ceilings, antique furnishings and fine views. For a bit more space, book one of Onki Xin's spacious 2- or 3-bedroom apartments just around the corner. The kind English-speaking owners have a wealth of information on exploring the region.

Hostal Lola HOTEL €€
(☎948 89 30 12; www.hostal-lola.com; Mendigatxa 17; d €75; 📶) This family-run place hidden down a narrow side alley offers probably the best value for money and has rooms loaded with desks, sofas and big beds. There's a nice flower-hemmed terrace and a decent restaurant (*menú del día* €15).

Ezkaurre Restaurant BASQUE €€
(☎657 621467; www.restauranteezkaurre.es; Garagardoya 14; menú del día €18; ⏰1-3.30pm & 7.30-9.30pm) This humble-looking eatery serves up beautifully prepared recipes that feature market-fresh ingredients. Oven-baked trout, beef cheeks with truffled potatoes and risotto with mushroom and bacon are recent highlights.

Southern Navarra

Take the A15 south of Pamplona and you only have to drive for 15 minutes before you enter an entirely new world. Within the space of just a few kilometres, the deep greens that you have grown to love in the Basque regions and northern Navarra vanish, replaced with a lighter and more Mediterranean ochre. As the sunlight becomes more dazzling (and more common!), the shark's-teeth hills of the north flatten into tranquil lowland plains, while the wet forests become scorched vineyards and olive groves, and even the people change – they're more gregarious and, as the graffiti suggests, sometimes fiercely anti-Basque. Awaiting travellers in this region are several medieval villages that look straight out of a fairy tale, plus the unlikely desert-like landscape of the Bárdenas Reales, Navarra's very own badlands.

Olite

POP 3890 / ELEV 365M

The turrets and spires of Olite are filled with stories of kings and queens, brave knights and beautiful princesses – it's as if it has burst off the pages of a fairy tale. Though it might seem a little hard to believe today, this quiet village was once the home of the royal families of Navarra, and the walled old quarter is crowded with their memories.

Founded by the Romans (parts of the town wall date back to Roman times), Olite first attracted the attention of royalty in 1276. However, it didn't really take off until it caught the fancy of King Carlos III (Carlos the Noble) in the 15th century, when he embarked on a series of daring building projects.

Sights

Palacio Real CASTLE
(Castillo de Olite; www.guiartenavarra.com; Plaza Carlos III; adult/child €3.50/2; ⏰10am-8pm Jul-Aug, 10am-7pm Mon-Fri, 10am-8pm Sat & Sun May-Jun & Sep, shorter hours Oct-Apr) It's Carlos III that we must thank for the exceptional Palacio Real, which towers over the village. Back in Carlos' day (early 15th century), the inhabitants of the castle included not just royalty but also lions and other exotic pets, as well as Babylon-inspired hanging gardens. Today, the restored castle makes a wonderfully atmospheric place to wander. To help bring the past come alive, take a guided tour, or explore at your own pace with a handy audioguide (€2).

You can clamber up scenic watchtowers, wander through once richly gilded halls, and stroll the ramparts, all while imagining the jousts, bullfights and even pelota games held back in medieval times. Integrated into the castle is the **Iglesia de Santa María la Real**, which has a superbly detailed Gothic portal.

Laguna de Pitillas LAKE

FREE The lakes and marshes that make up the Laguna de Pitillas are one of the top birding sites in Navarra. Now a protected Ramsar wetland site of international importance, the Laguna de Pitillas provides a home for around 160 permanent and migratory species, including marsh harriers, great bitterns and even ospreys.

Museo de la Viña y el Vino de Navarra MUSEUM

(www.guiartenavarra.com; Plaza de los Teobaldos 10; adult/child €3.50/2; 10am-2pm & 4-7pm Mon-Sat, 10am-2pm Sun Mar-Oct, shorter hours Nov-Feb) Don't miss this museum, which takes visitors on a fascinating journey through wine and wine culture. Over three floors, English signage and interactive displays reveal the grape in all its complexity, from the soils and grape varieties found in Navarra to old-fashioned harvesting techniques. There's also a case of scents (animal, spices, wood, etc) where you can breathe in a few common elements found in many wines.

Sleeping & Eating

★Parador de Olite HISTORIC HOTEL €€

(948 74 00 00; www.parador.es; Plaza de los Teobaldos 2; r from €135;) The most spectacular lodging option in town is set in a wing of Olite's restored medieval castle (though some rooms are in a newer extension). Part of the Parador chain and a national monument, this photogenic hotel, with its heavy wood furniture and gilt-framed prints (some also have balconies with views over the countryside), has plenty of atmosphere.There's a superb restaurant as well.

Hotel el Juglar BOUTIQUE HOTEL €€

(948 74 18 55; www.merindaddeolitehoteles.com; Rúa Romana 39; s/d/ste €100/115/155;) Hotel El Juglar has top-notch service and handsomely appointed rooms set in stone-walled mansion 10 minutes' walk (800m) northwest of the village centre. The nine rooms here are all slightly different from one another (some have big round Jacuzzi baths, others balconies), though all have elegant furnishings. The pool is rather enticing on a hot summer day.

Hotel Merindad de Olite HISTORIC HOTEL €€

(948 74 07 35; www.merindaddeolitehoteles.com; Rúa de la Judería 11; s €58-68, d €68-84, ste €104;) Built almost into the old town walls, this charming place has small but comfortable rooms and masses of medieval style. Reserve well ahead because it fills quickly.

Information

Olite has a friendly and helpful **tourist office** (948 74 17 03; Plaza de los Teobaldos 10; 10am-2pm & 4-7pm Mon-Sat, 10am-2pm Sun), in the same building as the wine museum.

Getting There & Away

Up to 16 buses a day run between Olite and Pamplona (€3.75, 45 minutes). The bus from Pamplona drops passengers near the entrance to the walled city. Heading back to the city, catch the bus outside Olite's historic area, at the bus shelters on the road to Pamplona.

Ujué

POP 180

Balancing atop a hill criss-crossed with terraced fields, the tiny village of Ujué, some 18km east of Olite and overlooking the plains of southern Navarra, is a perfect example of a fortified medieval village. Today the almost immaculately preserved township is sleepy and pretty, with steep, narrow streets tumbling down the hillside.

The village plays host to a fascinating *romería* (pilgrimage) on the first Sunday after St Mark's Day (25 April), when hundreds of people walk through the night from Tudela to celebrate Mass in the village church.

Iglesia-Fortaleza de Santa María de Ujué CHURCH

(San Isidro 8; admission by donation; 10am-6.30pm Apr-Oct, to 5.30pm Nov-Mar) Standing at the highest point in the village, this church of mixed Romanesque-Gothic style has a commanding presence over the valley. Aside from magnificent views from its outer walkways, the church contains a rare statue of the Black Virgin, which is said to have been discovered by a shepherd who was led to the statue by a dove. In addition to the Virgin, the church also contains the heart of Carlos II.

Pastas Urrutia BAKERY €€
(☎948 73 92 57; www.pastasurrutia.com; San Isidro 41; menú del dia €15-18; ⏲bakery 10am-6pm Thu-Tue, restaurant 1.30-3.30pm Thu-Tue) This bakery just north of the village centre also serves up delicious, three-course lunch specials, which includes Urrutia's famous house-made bread as well as wine. Expect dishes like oven-baked cod, beef cheeks or eggs with truffles in season (December to February).

Getting There & Away

Most travellers arrive by car. If you're taking the bus from Pamplona, you'll make a connection in Tafalla or Olite, both roughly 20km east of the village.

Parque Natural de las Bárdenas Reales

In a region largely dominated by wet mountain slopes, the last thing you'd expect to find is a sunburnt desert. The Bárdenas Reales are badlands, the dramatic landscape shaped by the forces of water, wind, and erosion.

There are hiking and cycling trails through the park, though many are only vaguely signposted. Given the heat, lack of shade and big distances involved, most people come to drive the park's 34km-long loop road.

Sights

Parque Natural de las Bárdenas Reales NATURE RESERVE
(☎948 83 03 08; www.bardenasreales.es; ⏲8am-dusk) FREE Established as a natural park in 1999 and as a UN Biosphere Reserve in 2000, the Bárdenas Reales is a desiccated landscape of blank tabletop hills, open gravel plains and snakelike gorges covering over 410 sq km of southeastern Navarra. As well as spectacular scenery, the park plays host to numerous birds and animals, including the great bustard, golden eagles, Egyptian and griffon vultures, numerous reptiles, mountain cats and wild boar.

A visitor centre gives out information on park highlights.

Sleeping

Cuevas Rurales Bardenas BUNGALOW €€€
(☎661 846757; www.bardeneras.com; Palomares 23, Valtierra; ⏲apt from €150; ❄📶) In the small town of Valtierra, you can overnight it inside a cave – albeit one with wi-fi, modern bathrooms, a full kitchen and cheerful furnishings. Nine dwellings carved into the hillside sleep from two to eight, making it a fine choice for families and bigger groups. A two- to four-night minimum stay required.

Hotel Aire de Bardenas BOUTIQUE HOTEL €€€
(☎948 11 66 66; www.airedebardenas.com; Carretera de Ejea, Km 1, Tudela; d €225-292, ste €418; P❄📶🏊) In a barren landscape well off the beaten path, you'll find humble shipping crates transformed into a stylish boutique hotel. All rooms have luxurious amenities; some also have exterior bathtubs or patios with views over an expanse of semi-desert. There's great service, a swimming pool, and a superb in-house restaurant (mains €15 to €25).

Getting There & Away

There's no public transport to the park; drive or take a bus or train to nearby Tudela.

Puente la Reina

POP 2810 / ELEV 421M

The chief calling card of Puente la Reina (Basque: Gares), 22km southwest of Pamplona on the A12, is the spectacular six-arched **medieval bridge** that dominates the western end of town, but Puente la Reina rewards on many other levels. A key stop on the Camino de Santiago, the town's pretty streets throng with the ghosts of a multitude of pilgrims. Their first stop here was at the late-Romanesque **Iglesia del Crucifijo**, erected by the Knights Templars and still containing one of the finest Gothic crucifixes in existence. And just a short way out of town is one of the prettiest chapels along the whole Camino. Throw into this mix some fine places to stay and, in the nearby countryside, a ruined Roman city, and the result is a fine place to be based for a day or so.

Sights

Santa María de Eunate CHURCH
(www.santamariadeeunate.es; Carretera de Campanas; €1; ⏲10.30am-1.30pm Tue-Fri, 11am-1.30pm & 4.30-6.30pm Sat & Sun, Apr-Jun, Sep & Oct, 10.30am-1.30pm & 5-6.30pm Wed-Mon Jul & Aug) Surrounded by cornfields and brushed by wild flowers, the near-perfect octagonal

Romanesque chapel of Santa María de Eunate is one of the most picturesque chapels along the whole Camino. Dating from around the 12th century its origins – and the reason why it's located in the middle of nowhere – are something of a mystery. The chapel is 2km southeast of Muruzábal, which is itself 5km northeast of Puente la Reina.

Sleeping & Eating

Hotel Rural El Cerco BOUTIQUE HOTEL €€
(948 34 12 69; www.elcerco.es; Calle de Rodrigo Ximénez de Rada 36; s/d €50/75;) At the eastern end of the old quarter, this hotel is one of the most charming places to stay in town. It's housed in an antique building, smartly transformed into a stylish, small boutique hotel with exposed stone walls and wooden roof beams.

Casa Martija CAFE
(www.facebook.com/casamartija; Calle Mayor 104; 8am-2pm & 4.30-9pm) On a cobblestone lane, a short stroll from the bridge, Casa Martija is a charming deli and cafe that serves up coffees, wines and pastries, with well-placed tables out front. It's also a fine spot for assembling picnic fare from the cheeses, breads, olive oils and other gourmet goodies on hand.

Getting There & Away

Frequent buses (€5.25, one hour) run between Pamplona's bus station and Estella; they all stop along the main road in the village of Puente la Reina.

Estella

POP 13,700 / ELEV 483M

Estella (Basque: Lizarra) was known as 'La Bella' in medieval times because of the splendour of its monuments and buildings, and though the city has lost some of its beauty to modern suburbs, its historic centre is still thoroughly charming. During the 11th century, Estella became the main reception point for the growing flood of pilgrims along the Camino de Santiago. Today most visitors are continuing that same plodding tradition.

Sights

Iglesia de San Pedro de la Rúa CHURCH
(948 55 00 70; 10am-1.30pm & 6-7pm Mon-Sat, 10am-12.30pm Sun, shorter hours Nov-Mar) FREE This 12th-century church is the most important monument in Estella. Its cloisters are a fine example of Romanesque sculptural work.

Museo Gustavo de Maeztu PALACE
(www.museogustavodemaeztu.com; Calle San Nicolás 1, Palacio de los Reyes; 9.30am-1.30pm & 4-7pm Tue-Sat May-Sep, 9.30am-1.30pm Tue-Sat Oct-Apr) FREE Adjacent to the tourist office is the **Palacio de los Reyes**, a rare example of Romanesque civil construction. It houses a museum with an intriguing collection of paintings by Gustavo de Maeztu y Whitney (1887–1947), who was of Cuban-English parentage but emphatically Basque in upbringing and identity. Landscapes, portraits and full-bodied nudes reflect Maeztu's engaging sensual romanticism.

WORTH A TRIP

MONASTIC WANDERS

The countryside around Estella is littered with monasteries. One of the best is the **Monasterio de Irache** (off Carretera NA-1110, Ayegui; 10am-1.15pm & 4-6pm Wed-Sun, mid-Jan–mid-Nov) FREE, 3km southwest of Estella, near Ayegui. This ancient Benedictine monastery has a lovely 16th-century plateresque cloister and its **Puerta Especiosa** is decorated with delicate sculptures. Those unimpressed by beauty dedicated to God may find the **Fuente de Vino** (Fountain of Wine) enough to make them a believer. It's behind the **Bodegas Irache** (948 55 19 32; www.irache.com; Monasterio de Irache, off Carretera NA-1110, Ayegui; 10am-2pm & 4-7pm weekends, to 6pm in winter), a well-known local wine producer (just in front of the church), and yes, it really is a free-flowing wine fountain, though you'll have to get there early since only 100 litres are released per day.

About 10km north of Estella, near Abárzuza, is the **Monasterio de Iranzu** (off Carretera NA-7135, Abárzuza; €3; 10am-2pm & 4-6pm). Originally founded way back in the 11th century, but recently restored, this sand-coloured monastery with beautiful cloisters is so calm and tranquil that it could inspire religious meditation in Lucifer himself.

Los Llanos PARK

(Paseo los Llanos) This lush park just south of the centre makes a pleasant escape from medieval monuments. The trickling Río Ega forms the southern boundary of the greenery, and there's a snack bar near the riverbank where you can unwind with a drink and gaze at the cliffs edging up beyond the river.

Festivals & Events

Semana Medieval CULTURAL

(mid-Jul) For one week in mid-July, Estella hosts its exuberant medieval fair, complete with costumed performers, jousts, street theatre, falconry displays, special markets and much merriment.

Sleeping & Eating

Hotel Tximista DESIGN HOTEL €€

(948 55 58 70; www.sanvirilahoteles.com/en/hotel-tximista; Zaldu 15; s/d/ste €87/97/120; P ❄) About 1km north of the centre, this striking modern hotel, built into and out of an old watermill, mixes rusty old industrial cogs and wheels from the mill with poppy-red artwork. Rooms are comfortable, although some suffer from road noise, and there's a nice garden overlooking the gurgling river.

Hospedería Chapitel HOTEL €€

(948 55 10 90; www.hospederiachapitel.com; Chapitel 1; s/d from €80/105; P) In a great location in Estella's historic centre, Hospedería Chapitel has comfortable rooms with wood floors, beamed ceilings and small balconies – some with views of the cathedral. Despite the central location, it's quite peaceful inside.

Casanellas Taller Gastronómico FUSION €€

(638 912838; www.tallergastronomico.es; Espoz y Mina 3; mains €16-20, tasting menu weekday/weekend €35/45; 1.30-3.30pm Tue-Sat) A purveyor of slow cooking, this elegant restaurant uses local products with global touches to create beautifully executed recipes. The market-fresh menu features dishes like duck with pineapple and red curry, lamb with rosemary, and a perfectly cooked turbot.

Getting There & Away

Buses leave from the **bus station** (Plaza Coronación) for Pamplona (€5.25, one hour, 10 daily Monday to Friday, six daily Saturday and Sunday).

Javier

POP 110 / ELEV 448M

Tiny Javier (Xavier), 11km northeast of Sangüesa, is a quiet rural village set in gentle green countryside. It's utterly dominated by a childhood-fantasy castle that is so perfectly preserved you half expect the drawbridge to come crashing down and a knight in armour to gallop out on a white steed. As well as being an inspiration for fairytale dreams, this is also the birthplace of the patron saint of Navarra, San Francisco Xavier, who was born in the village in 1506. Xavier spent much of his life travelling, preaching, teaching and healing in Asia. Today his body lies in a miraculous state of preservation in a cathedral in Goa, India.

Sights

Castillo de Javier CASTLE

(948 88 40 24; Plaza del Santo, Javier; €2.75; 10am-6.30pm Mar-Oct, to 4pm Nov-Feb) This tenth-century castle, strategically located on the border between the kingdoms of Navarra y Aragón, is Javier's main attraction. Inside, there's a small museum dedicated to the life of San Francisco Xavier, the patron saint of Navarra, who was born in the village in 1506.

Sleeping

Hotel Xabier HOTEL €

(948 88 40 06; www.hotelxabier.com; Paseo de la Abadía 2, Javier; s/d/tr €47/56/71; P) If you want to sleep near the castle, stay at the red-brick, ivy-clad Hotel Xabier. You can peer out of your window on a moonlit night and look for ghosts flitting around the castle keep. There's a good restaurant here (*menú del día* €20).

Getting There & Away

Most travellers come here by car. Several daily buses serve Sangüesa from Pamplona's bus station; Javier is a short taxi ride away. Tafallesa buses also go directly to Javier, usually once a day, from Pamplona's bus station.

LA RIOJA

Get out the *copas* (glasses) for La Rioja and some of the best red wines produced in the country. Wine goes well with the region's ochre earth and vast blue skies, which seem far more Mediterranean than the Basque greens further north. In fact, it's hard not to feel as if you're in a different country altogether. The bulk of the vineyards line Río Ebro around the town of Haro, but some also extend into neighbouring Navarra and the Basque province of Álava. This diverse region offers more than just the pleasures of the grape, though, and a few days here can see you mixing it up in lively towns and quiet pilgrim churches, and even hunting for the remains of giant reptiles.

Logroño

POP 151,000

Logroño is a stately wine-country town with a heart of tree-studded squares, narrow streets and hidden corners. There are few monuments here, but perhaps more importantly to some, a great selection of *pintxos* (Basque tapas) bars. In fact, Logroño is quickly gaining a culinary reputation to rival anywhere in Spain.

Sights

★Museo de la Rioja MUSEUM

(☎941 29 12 59; www.museodelarioja.es; Plaza San Agustín 23; ⊙10am-2pm & 4-9pm Tue-Sat, 10am-2pm Sun) FREE This superb museum in the centre of Logroño takes you on a wild romp through Riojan history and culture in both Spanish and English. Highlights include mystifying Celtiberian stone carvings from the 5th century BC, beautiful jewellery and statuary displays from the Roman period, colourful altarpieces from Medieval times, as well as lush portraits and landscape paintings from the 19th century.

Catedral de Santa María de la Redonda CATHEDRAL

(Calle de Portales; ⊙8.30am-1pm & 6-8.45pm Mon-Sat, 8.30am-2pm & 6-8.45pm Sun) The Catedral de Santa María de la Redonda sits on the site of a 12th-century oratory, and was built in varying styles between the 15th and 18th centuries. The eye-catching towers (known as the *gemelas* or twins) and splendid altarpiece are fine examples of the Rioja baroque manner. Don't miss the small exquisite painting depicting Christ on the Cross attributed to Michelangelo. It's behind the main altar and can be illuminated by placing a coin in the box.

Iglesia de San Bartolomé CHURCH

(Calle de Rodríguez Paterna; ⊙11.30am-1.15pm) The impressive main entrance of Logroño's oldest church (built between the 12th and 13th centuries) has a splendid portico of deeply receding borders and an expressive collection of statuary.

Activities

Rioja Trek WINE

(☎941 58 73 54; www.riojatrek.com; Calle Francisco de Quevedo 12) Based 3km east of the centre, Rioja Trek offers a wide range of winery tours, wine tastings and hikes along some of La Rioja's fabulous mountain trails. One of the highlights is a three-hour excursion (per person €28) where you play wine grower for a day, visiting a traditional vineyard and bodega and even doing some wine-making yourself.

The same people also run tapas tours around Logroño, two-hour wine-tasting courses and activities for families with children.

Festivals & Events

Fiesta de San Mateo CULTURAL

(⊙Sep) Logroño's week-long Fiesta de San Mateo starts on the Saturday before 21 September and doubles as a harvest festival, during which all of La Rioja comes to town to watch the grape-crushing ceremonies in the Espolón and to drink ample quantities of wine.

Actual CULTURAL

(www.actualfestival.com; ⊙Jan) A program of cultural, musical and artistic events held in the first week of January.

Feast of San Bernabé FEAST DAY

(⊙11 Jun) The Feast of San Bernabé commemorates the French siege of Logroño in 1521 with food and wine tasting, traditional concerts, fireworks and a re-enactment of the medieval battle.

Sleeping

Hostal La Numantina PENSION €

(☎941 25 14 11; www.hostalnumantina.com; Calle de Sagasta 4; s/d/tr from €35/56/70; 📶) This budget-minded outfit has comfortable and homey rooms, some with large bathtubs and tiny balconies with views over the street below. Unfortunately, street noise is an issue, so light sleepers are better off with an interior room. There's a communal space downstairs with cosy sofas and good maps of the Logroño and the surrounding area.

Logroño

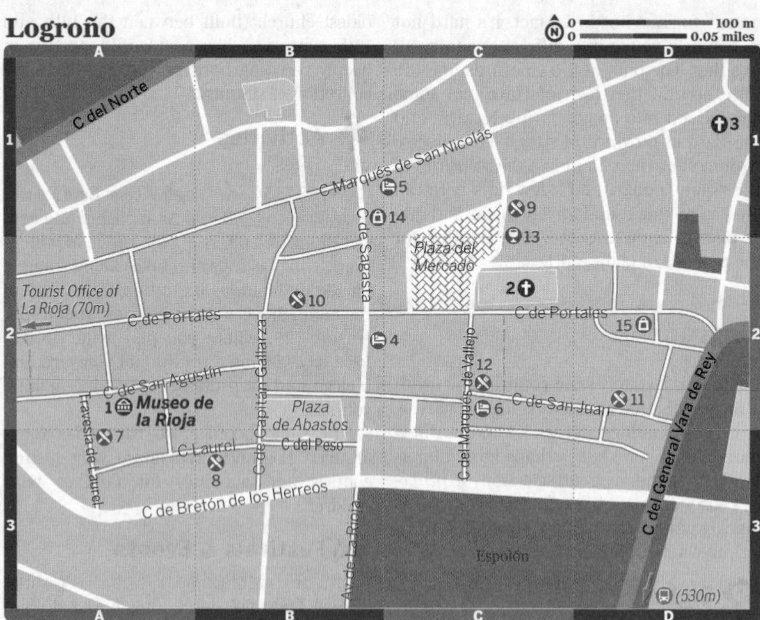

Logroño

Top Sights

1 Museo de la Rioja.....A2

Sights

2 Catedral de Santa María de la Redonda.....C2
3 Iglesia de San Bartolomé.....D1

Sleeping

4 Hostal La Numantina.....B2
5 Hotel Calle Mayor.....C1
6 Hotel Marqués de Vallejo.....C2

Eating

7 Bar Soriano.....A3
8 Bar Torrecilla.....B3
9 Camino Vegano.....C1
10 La Cocina de Ramón.....B2
11 Tastavin.....D2
12 Umm.....C2

Drinking & Nightlife

13 Odeón Mercado Craft Beer.....C1

Shopping

14 Félix Barbero Botas Rioja.....B1
15 La Luci Delicatessen.....D2

Hotel Calle Mayor BOUTIQUE HOTEL €€€
(☎941 23 23 68; www.hotelcallemayor.com; Calle Marqués de San Nicolás 71; d from €110; P ❄ @ ☎) Set in a restored 16th-century building, this classy hotel is *the* place to stay in Logroño. It has large, comfortable rooms bathed in light, with attractive flooring, modular furniture and modern bathrooms.

Hotel Marqués de Vallejo DESIGN HOTEL €€€
(☎941 24 83 33; www.hotelmarquesdevallejo.com; Calle del Marqués de Vallejo 8; d from €126; P ❄ ☎) With a lobby full of driftwood sculptures, beach pebbles and bold artwork on the walls, the Marqués de Vallejo aims to set itself apart from the Logroño's more traditional options. The rooms themselves are quite comfortable, though lacking the artful touches of the lobby.

Eating

Tastavin PINTXOS €
(Calle San Juan 25; pintxos from €2.50; ⏱8-11pm Tue, 1-4pm & 8-11pm Wed-Sun) A stylish, modern eatery on *pintxos*-lined San Juan, Tastavin whips up some of the tastiest morsels in town, including smoked trout, fried artichokes, tuna tataki and braised ox tail. The wines are outstanding.

Umm PINTXOS €
(www.ummfoodanddrink.com; Calle San Juan 1; pintxos from €2.50; ⏱1-4pm & 8-11pm Tue-Sun) It's hard not to be pulled inside to this

sleek contemporary space on a bustling culinary corner. One look at the spread of heavenly, rather elaborate bites and you won't be able to resist. Grilled foie, pastrami with kimchi, codfish with cream sauce and seaweed, and pulled pork are among the many hits.

Camino Vegano VEGETARIAN €
(941 48 37 33; Plaza del Mercado 25; mains €9-12, lunch menu €12.50; 1-3.30pm Sun-Tue, 1-3.30pm & 8.30-11pm Wed-Sat) Take a break from animal products at this handsome vegan eatery on the main plaza. Friendly English-speaking staff serve up delicious comfort fare like mushroom and vegan béchamel croquettes, veggie lasagna, fajitas with stir-fried vegetables and barbecue seitan ribs with coleslaw.

Bar Torrecilla PINTXOS €
(Calle Laurel 15; pintxos from €2; 1-4pm & 8-11pm Wed-Sun) The best *pintxos* in town? You be the judge. Go for the melt-in-your-mouth foie gras or the mini-burgers, or anything else that strikes your fancy, at this modern bar on buzzing Calle del Laurel.

Bar Soriano TAPAS €
(Travesía de Laurel 2; pintxos from €2; 11.45am-3pm & 7-11.45pm Thu-Tue) This bar has been serving up the same delicious mushroom tapa, topped with a shrimp, for more than 40 years.

La Cocina de Ramón SPANISH €€€
(941 28 98 08; www.lacocinaderamon.es; Calle de Portales 30; menús €28-55, mains €16-25; 1.30-4pm & 8.30-11pm Tue-Sat, 1.30-4pm Sun) It looks unassuming from the outside, but Ramón's mixture of high-quality, locally grown market-fresh produce and tried-and-tested family recipes has earned him a lot of fans. The fine cooking is matched by the top service, and Ramón likes to come and explain the dishes to each and every guest.

Drinking & Nightlife

Odeón Mercado Craft Beer BAR
(Plaza del Mercado 27; 6.30pm-3.30am Wed-Fri, from 4.30pm Sat & Sun) Brew lovers from far and wide descend on this laid-back bar on the plaza. You'll find some 20 different craft beers on tap, with a fine selection of quaffs from the Basque Country, Catalonia and beyond. There's live music from time to time.

Shopping

La Luci Delicatessen FOOD & DRINKS
(941 44 18 54; Calle Portales 3; 10.30am-2pm & 5.30-9pm Tue-Sun) Browse for gourmet gift ideas at this charming little store that's stocked with wines, cheeses, olive oils, craft beers, vermouth and handsomely boxed biscuits in carousel tins.

Félix Barbero Botas Rioja ARTS & CRAFTS
(http://botasrioja.artesaniadelarioja.org; Calle de Sagasta 8; 9am-1.30pm & 4-8pm Mon-Sat) Maintaining a dying craft, Félix Barbero handmakes the classic Spanish animal skin wine carriers in which farmers carried their daily rations of wine while working in the fields. The price for a quality one-litre wine carrier starts around €20.

Information

Near the west end of the historic centre, the **tourist office** (941 29 12 60; www.lariojaturismo.com; Calle de Portales 50; 9am-8pm Mon-Fri, 10am-8pm Sat, 10am-2pm Sun Jul-Sep, 9am-2pm & 4-7pm Mon-Fri, 10am-2pm & 5-7pm Sat, 10am-2pm Sun Oct-Jun) can provide lots of information on both the city and La Rioja in general.

Getting There & Away

If you arrive at the train or **bus station** (941 23 59 83; Avenida de España 1), first head up Avenida de España and then Calle del General Vara de Rey until you reach the Espolón, a large, park-like square lavished with plane trees (and with an underground car park). The Casco Viejo starts just to the north.

Buses go to the following:

DESTINATION	FARE (€)	DURATION
Bilbao	15	2hr
Haro	6.05	40 minutes
Pamplona	10	2hr
Santo Domingo de la Calzada	3.50	45 minutes
Vitoria	10	2¼hr

By train, Logroño is regularly connected to the following:

DESTINATION	FARE (€)	DURATION
Bilbao	from 16	2½hr
Burgos	from 14	2hr
Madrid	from 31	3½hr
Zaragoza	from 15	2hr

San Millán de Cogolla

POP 290 / ELEV 733M

About 16km southwest of Nájera, the hamlet of San Millán de Cogolla, home to only a few hundred people, is set in a lush valley. Like Nájera, San Millán de Cogolla has a long and fascinating Jewish history that dates back to the 10th century AD. But most people come here to see two remarkable monasteries that helped give birth to the Castilian language. On account of their linguistic heritage and artistic beauty, they have been recognised by Unesco as World Heritage sites.

Sights

Monasterio de Yuso MONASTERY

(☎941 37 30 49; www.monasteriodesanmillan.com; San Millán de la Cogolla; adult/child €7/3; ⏲10am-1.30pm & 4-6.30pm Tue-Sun Apr-Sep, to 5.30pm Oct-Mar) The Monasterio de Yuso, sometimes called El Escorial de La Rioja, contains numerous treasures in its museum. You can only visit as part of a guided tour (in Spanish only; non-Spanish speakers will be given an information sheet in English and French). Tours last 50 minutes and run every half-hour or so. In August it's also open on Mondays.

Monasterio de Suso MONASTERY

(☎941 37 30 82; www.monasteriodesanmillan.com/suso; San Millán de la Cogolla; €4; ⏲9.30am-1.30pm & 3.30-6.30pm Tue-Sun Apr-Sep, to 5.30pm Oct-Mar) Built above the caves where San Millán once lived, the Monasterio de Suso was consecrated in the 10th century. It's believed that in the 13th century a monk named Gonzalo de Berceo wrote the first Castilian words here. It can only be visited on a guided tour. Tickets must be bought in advance and include a short bus ride up to the monastery.

Getting There & Away

Most travellers drive here. The village is located about an hour's drive west of La Rioja via A12.

Santo Domingo de la Calzada

POP 6370 / ELEV 640M

Santo Domingo is small-town Spain at its very best. A large number of the inhabitants continue to live in the partially walled old quarter, a labyrinth of medieval streets where the past is alive and the sense of community is strong. It's the kind of place where you can be certain that the baker knows all his customers by name and that everyone will turn up for María's christening. Santiago-bound pilgrims have long been a part of the fabric of this town, and that tradition continues to this day, with most visitors being foot-weary pilgrims. All this helps to make Santo Domingo one of the most enjoyable places in La Rioja.

Sights

Catedral de Santo Domingo de la Calzada CATHEDRAL

(☎941 34 00 33; www.catedralsantodomingo.es; Plaza del Santo 4; adult/student/child €5/3/free; ⏲9am-8pm Mon-Fri, 9am-7pm Sat, 9am-noon & 2-8pm Sun Apr-Oct, shorter hours Nov-Mar) The monumental cathedral and its attached museum glitter with the gold that attests to the great wealth the Camino has bestowed on otherwise backwater towns. An audio guide to the cathedral and its treasures is €1. Guided tours, including a nighttime tour, are also available.

The cathedral's most eccentric feature is the white rooster and hen that forage in a glass-fronted cage opposite the entrance to the crypt (look up!). Their presence celebrates a long-standing legend, the Miracle of the Rooster, which tells of a young man who was unfairly executed only to recover miraculously, while the broiled cock and hen on the plate of his judge suddenly leapt up and chickened off, fully fledged.

Sleeping & Eating

Hostal Rey Pedro I HOTEL €

(☎941 34 11 60; www.hostalpedroprimero.es; Calle San Roque 9; s/d from €45/56; 📶) This carefully renovated town house, which has terracotta-coloured rooms with wooden roof beams and entirely modern bathrooms, is a terrific deal.

Parador de Santo Domingo de la Calzada HISTORIC HOTEL €€

(☎941 34 03 00; www.parador.es; Plaza del Santo 3; r from €135; 🅿📶) The Parador Santo Domingo is the antithesis of the town's general air of piety. Occupying a 12th-century former hospital opposite the cathedral, this palatial hotel offers anything but a frugal medieval-like existence. The in-house restaurant is reliably good.

Parador Santo Domingo Bernado de Fresneda HOTEL €€
(☎941 34 11 50; www.parador.es; Plaza de San Francisco 1, Ave Juan Carlos I; d from €90; P 📶) Just on the edge of the old town, the Parador Santo Domingo Bernado de Fresneda occupies a former convent and pilgrim hostel. With its divine beds and opulent rooms, it's now a pretty luxurious place to stay.

Los Caballeros SPANISH €€
(☎941 342 789; http://restaurantelos caballeros.com; Calle Mayor 58; mains €18-23; ⏰1-4pm & 7.30-11pm Mon-Sat, 1-4pm Sun) In a classy dining room set with exposed brick, wood-beamed ceiling and stained glass details, Los Caballeros serves up flavourful suckling pig, smoked sardines and codfish dishes, among other classic Navarran fare. Reserve ahead.

ℹ Getting There & Away

Frequent buses run to Nájera (€2.60, thirty minutes) and onward to Logroño. The bus stop, where you'll find posted bus schedules, is located on Plaza San Jerónimo Hermosilla, just off Avenida Juan Carlos I (also known as Calle San Roque), and across the street from the historic centre.

La Rioja Wine Region

La Rioja wine rolls on and off the tongue with ease, by name as well as by taste. All wine fanciers know the famous wines of La Rioja, where the vine has been cultivated since Roman times. The region is classic vine country and vineyards cover the hinterland of Río Ebro. On the river's north bank, the region is part of the Basque Country and is known as La Rioja Alavesa.

Haro

POP 11,300 / ELEV 426M

Despite its fame in the wine world, there's not much of a heady bouquet to Haro, the capital of La Rioja's wine-producing region. But the town has a cheerful pace and its compact old quarter, leading off Plaza de la Paz, has some intriguing alleyways with bars and wine shops aplenty.

There are plenty of wine bodegas in the vicinity of the town, some of which are open to visitors (almost always with advance reservation). The tourist office keeps a full list.

Activities

Bodegas Muga WINE
(☎941 30 60 60; www.bodegasmuga.com; Barrio de la Estación; winery tour from €15; ⏰Mon-Sat by reservation) Just after the railway bridge on the way out of town, this bodega is particularly receptive and gives daily guided tours (except Sunday) and tastings in Spanish. Book ahead to join a tour.

Festivals & Events

Batalla del Vino WINE
(Wine Battle; www.batalladelvino.com; ⏰29 Jun) The otherwise mild-mannered citizens of Haro go temporarily berserk during the Batalla del Vino, squirting and chucking wine all over each other in the name of San Juan, San Felices and San Pedro. Plenty of it goes down the right way, too.

Sleeping & Eating

Hotel Arrope HOTEL €€
(☎941 30 40 25; www.hotelarrope.com; Calle Virgen de la Vega 31; s/d from €70/80; ❄📶) This town-centre hotel has a young-and-cool attitude, which is quite unexpected in conservative Haro. The attractive rooms feature bold colours, shiny parquet floors and (in some) pretty balconies overlooking the courtyard.

The attached bar-cafe, with a large terrace, is a very pleasant place for a glass of wine and some small plates.

Hotel Los Agustinos HISTORIC HOTEL €€
(☎941 31 13 08; www.hotellosagustinos.com; San Agustín 2; s/d from €99/131; P❄📶) History hangs in the air of this stately hotel, set in a 14th-century convent. Rooms could use an update, but the stunning covered courtyard is a wonderful place to linger over a glass of wine. The hotel's restaurant (mains €16 to €22) is also highly excellent.

El Rincón del Noble SPANISH €€
(☎941 31 29 32; www.elrincondelnoble.net; Martinez Lacuesta 11; mains €16-20; ⏰1-4pm daily & 9-11pm Fri & Sat) Although Haro isn't much of a foodie town, this easygoing dining room earns high marks for its simple but thoughtfully prepared classic fare. Tender oxtail in Rioja wine sauce, steaming oven-baked bass, and sizzling duck breast with caramelised apples are a few standout dishes.

EXPERIENCE THE WEALTH OF THE GRAPE

The humble grape has created great wealth for some of the villages around La Rioja. Proof of this are some of the extravagant bodegas and hotels that have sprung up in recent years in what otherwise appear to be backwater farming communities.

Before hitting the wine road, it's helpful to learn a few basics: wine categories in La Rioja are termed Young, Crianza, Reserva and Gran Reserva. Young wines are in their first or second year and are inevitably a touch 'fresh'. Crianzas must have matured into their third year and have spent at least one year in the cask, followed by a few months resting in the bottle. Reservas pay homage to the best vintages and must mature for at least three full years in cask and bottle, with at least one year in the cask. Gran Reservas depend on the very best vintages and are matured for at least two years in the cask followed by three years in the bottle. These are the 'velvet' wines.

When the owner of the Bodegas Marqués de Riscal, in the village of Elciego, decided he wanted to create something special, he didn't hold back. The result is the spectacular Frank Gehry–designed **Hotel Marqués de Riscal** (945 18 08 80; www.hotel-marquesderiscal.com; Calle Torrea 1, Elciego; r from €344; P ❄ ⓦ). Costing around €85 million, the building is a flamboyant wave of multicoloured titanium sheets that stands in utter contrast to the village behind. Although casual visitors are not welcome at the hotel, you can join one of the bodega's **wine tours** (Vinos de los Herederos del Marqués de Riscal; 945 18 08 88; www.marquesderiscal.com; Hotel Marqués de Riscal, Calle Torrea 1, Elciego; tours €12; tours 10.30am-1pm & 4-6pm) – there's at least one English language tour a day, but it's best to book in advance. You won't get inside the building, but you will get to see its exterior from some distance. A much closer look can be obtained by reserving a table at one of the two superb in-house restaurants: the Michelin-approved **Restaurante Marqués de Riscal** (945 18 08 80; www.restaurantemarquesderiscal.com; Hotel Marqués de Riscal, Calle Torrea 1, Elciego; 14-/21-course menu €110/140) or the **1860 Tradición** (945 18 08 80; www.hotel-marquesderiscal.com/restaurante-1860-tradicion; Hotel Marqués de Riscal, Calle Torrea 1, Elciego; mains €22-34; 1.30-3.30pm & 8-10.15pm). For the most intimate look at the building, you'll need to reserve a room for the night, but be prepared to part with some serious cash!

Just a couple of kilometres to the north of Laguardia is the **Bodegas Ysios** (902 239 773; www.ysios.com; Camino de la Hoya; tours €12; tours 11am, 1pm & 4pm Mon-Fri, 11am & 1pm Sat & Sun). Designed by Santiago Calatrava as a 'temple dedicated to wine', its wave-like roof, made of aluminium and cedar wood, matches the flow of the rocky mountains behind it. It looks its best at night when pools of light flow out of it. Daily tours of the bodega are an excellent introduction to wine production. Reserve ahead.

There are several other, somewhat less confronting, wine cellars around Laguardia that can be visited, often with advance notice only – contact the tourist office (p504) in Laguardia for details. **Bodegas Palacio** (945 60 01 51; www.bodegaspalacio.com; Carretera de Elciego; tours €5; tours 1pm, other times by appointment) is only 1km from Laguardia on the Elciego road; reservations are again a good idea. The same bodega also runs excellent wine courses. There's also a hotel attached to the complex, but compared to options in Laguardia, it lacks character.

Also just outside Laguardia is the **Centro Temático del Vino Villa Lucía** (945 60 00 32; www.villa-lucia.com; Carretera de Logroño; tours €12; 9am-2pm & 4-8pm Tue-Sat, 9am-2pm Sun), a wine museum and shop selling high-quality wine from a variety of small, local producers. Museum visits are by guided tour only and finish with a 4D film and wine tasting.

Information

Just off the main plaza, the **tourist office** (941 30 35 80; www.haroturismo.org; Plaza de la Paz 1; 10am-2pm Mon, 10am-2pm & 4-7pm Tue-Sun mid-Jun–Sep, 10am-2pm Sun & Tue-Thu, 10am-2pm & 4-7pm Fri & Sat Oct–mid-Jun) provides useful info on the area's many wineries.

Getting There & Away

Regular trains connect Haro with Logroño (from €6, 40 minutes).

Buses additionally serve Logroño, Nájera, Vitoria, Bilbao, Santo Domingo de la Calzada and Laguardia. The **bus station** (Calle Castilla), which has a small indoor space with a cafe, is located around five blocks south of the historic centre. Walk along Avenida de la Rioja to get there.

Briones

POP 810 / ELEV 501M

One man's dream has put the small, obscenely quaint village of Briones firmly on the Spanish wine and tourism map. The sunset-gold village crawls gently up a hillside and offers commanding views over the surrounding vine-carpeted plains. Here you'll find the fantastic Vivanco (p503). Over several floors and numerous rooms, you will learn all about the history and culture of wine and the various processes that go into its production. View the world's largest collection of corkscrews, then sample a few varietals at the winery.

Sights

Vivanco MUSEUM
(Museo de la Cultura del Vino; ☎941 32 23 23; www.vivancoculturadevino.es; Carretera Nacional, Km 232; guided visit with wine tasting €18-25; ⊙10am-6pm Tue-Fri & Sun, 10am-8pm Sat) A must for wine lovers. Tour the winery before or after a visit to the excellent **Museo de la Cultura del Vino** (Museum of the Culture of Wine), where you'll learn all about the history and culture of wine and the various processes that go into its production. All of this is done through interesting displays brought to life with the latest in technology. The treasures on display include Picasso-designed wine jugs, Roman and Byzantine mosaics, and wine-inspired religious artifacts.

Sleeping

Los Calaos de Briones HOTEL €
(☎941 32 21 31; www.loscalaosdebriones.com; San Juan 13; d from €65) Rest your wine-heavy head at this lovely hotel. Some rooms have suitably romantic four-poster beds. The attached restaurant, in an old wine cellar, is stuffed with excellent locally inspired cuisine (mains €11 to €16).

Getting There & Away

Briones is located between Haro and Logroño. Autobuses Jiménez runs frequent buses from Logroño to Briones (€3.95, 50 minutes), continuing onward to Haro. In Briones, the bus stops on the edge of town, just off the highway.

Laguardia

POP 1480 / ELEV 557M

It's easy to spin back the wheels of time in the medieval fortress town of Laguardia, or the 'Guard of Navarra' as it was once appropriately known, sitting proudly on its rocky hilltop. The walled old quarter, which makes up most of the town, is virtually traffic-free and is a sheer joy to wander around. As well as offering memories of long-lost yesterdays, the town further entices visitors with its wine-producing present and striking scenery.

Sights

Bodega El Fabulista WINERY
(☎945 62 11 92; Plaza San Juan; tours €7; ⊙11.30am-1pm & 5.30-7pm) You can tour the medieval cellars of this traditional winery, which is located right in Laguardia. The tour finishes with a tasting of two of the bodega's wines. Reserve ahead for a one-hour English-language tour.

Bodegas Casa Primicia WINERY
(☎945 621 266; www.bodegascasaprimicia.com/en/visits-and-lunches; tours €9; ⊙tours 11am, 1pm & 5.30pm Tue-Sun) About 600m north of the historic centre, you'll find the oldest winery in Laguardia. On a 75-minute tour through this atmospheric 16th-century building, knowledgeable guides will give you an overview of the winemaking process and the rich heritage of Rioja wines, with a tasting at the end. It's essential to reserve ahead.

Torre Abacial TOWER
(Calle Mayor 52; €2; ⊙10.30am-2.30pm & 3.30-7.30pm) For a splendid view over town and the vineyards beyond, climb the 100-plus steps of the 'Abbot's Tower' – so named as it was once part of a monastery. Parts of the structure date back to the 12th century.

Iglesia de Santa María de los Reyes CHURCH
(☎945 60 08 45; Travesía Mayor 1; tours €3; ⊙guided tours 11.15am, 1.15pm, 5.30pm & 6.30pm Jun-Sep) The impressive Iglesia de Santa María de los Reyes has a breathtaking late-14th-century Gothic doorway, adorned with beautiful sculptures of the disciples and other motifs. If the church doors are locked, pop down to the tourist office where you can get a key. Otherwise, guided tours (in Spanish) run throughout the day in summer.

Sleeping

Posada Mayor de Migueloa HISTORIC HOTEL €€
(945 600 187; www.mayordemigueloa.com; Calle Mayor 20; s/d incl breakfast €112/124;) Set in a converted 17th-century building, this mansion-hotel has seven atmospheric rooms that evoke a bygone age with old stone walls, low beamed ceilings and touches of polished antique furnishings to complete the look. Be sure to pay a visit to the hotel's wine cellar. The on-site restaurant is also top notch (mains from €21).

Castillo el Collado HISTORIC HOTEL €€€
(945 62 12 00; www.hotelcollado.com; Paseo el Collado 1; d/ste €138/193;) Like a fairy-tale castle with its crenellated tower, coat of arms and pretty flower gardens, the Castillo el Collado is an utterly charming place to stay. The 10 rooms all have unique flourishes, from elaborately moulded ceilings to richly painted walls and antique bed frames.

Also onsite and open to the public is a great restaurant and a relaxing terrace cafe overlooking the old walls of Laguardia.

Hospedería de los Parajes HISTORIC HOTEL €€€
(945 62 11 30; www.hospederiadelosparajes.com; Calle Mayor 46-48; r from €150;) Extraordinarily plush rooms that combine a bit of today with a dollop of yesteryear. The 18 rooms have polished wood floors, touches of artwork and original ceilings. The beds are quite comfortable, the showers have rustic stone floors and the service is professional.

Hotel Viura DESIGN HOTEL €€€
(945 60 90 00; www.hotelviura.com; Calle Mayor, Villabuena de Álava; d from €209;) A modern architectural landmark in wine country, the Hotel Viura appears to be, on first glance, a collection of metallic, multi-coloured boxes piled haphazardly on the hillside. On closer investigation, its a sleek designer hotel that stands in whimsical contrast to the traditional village of Villabuena de Álava. Service and amenities are top-rate; it's a unique place to stay.

The hotel is located 12km east of Laguardia.

Eating

★ **Restaurante Amelibia** SPANISH €€
(945 62 12 07; www.restauranteamelibia.com; Barbacana 14; mains €16-22; 1-3.30pm Wed-Sun & 9-10.30pm Fri & Sat) This classy restaurant is one of Laguardia's highlights: gaze out the windows at a view over the scorched plains and distant mountain ridges while dining on sublime traditional cuisine. Think oxtail and wild mushrooms in red wine sauce with seasonal vegetables, or baked sea bass with pumpkin cream and truffle oil.

Castillo el Collado Restaurant SPANISH €€
(www.hotelcollado.com; Paseo El Collado 1; menus from €30) There's an old-world feeling to the place, and classic Riojan dishes like roasted suckling pig. There's also an English-language menu, and, naturally, a great wine selection.

Information

On the main road in the heart of town, the **tourist office** (945 60 08 45; www.laguardia-alava.com; Calle Mayor 52; 10am-2pm & 4-7pm) has a list of local bodegas that can be visited.

Getting There & Away

Eight or nine daily buses leave Logroño for Vitoria (€8, 1½ hours), stopping in Laguardia (€3, 25 to 30 minutes) on the way. There's no bus station: buses stop at the covered shelters along the main road that runs through town, near the lookout point.

Cantabria & Asturias

Includes ➡

Best Places to Eat

- ➡ Real Balneario de Salinas (p539)
- ➡ Tierra Astur (p529)
- ➡ La Huertona (p536)
- ➡ Bar Javi (p514)
- ➡ Agua Salada (p511)
- ➡ Arbidel (p536)

Best Places to Stay

- ➡ Hotel Torre de Villademoros (p541)
- ➡ La Casa del Puente (p515)
- ➡ Posada del Valle (p548)
- ➡ Hotel del Oso (p556)
- ➡ 3 Cabos (p541)
- ➡ Palacio de Flórez-Estrada (p545)

Why Go?

You can traverse either of these two regions from north to south in little more than an hour – but don't. Cantabria and Asturias reward those who linger. The stunning coastline is a sequence of sheer cliffs, beautiful beaches and small fishing ports. Behind it, gorgeously green river valleys dotted with stone-built villages rise to the 2000m-plus mountain wall of the Cordillera Cantábrica, which reaches majestic heights in the Picos de Europa. The beauty is endless and ever-changing.

Cantabria's and Asturias' fertile landscapes also ensure that you'll eat and drink well: on offer are quality meat, local cheeses and Asturias' renowned cider, along with abundant local seafood. Meanwhile, travellers with a feel for history will be in their element: early humans painted some of the world's most magnificent prehistoric art at Altamira and elsewhere, and it was at Covadonga that the seed of the Spanish nation first sprouted 1300 years ago.

When to Go

Oviedo

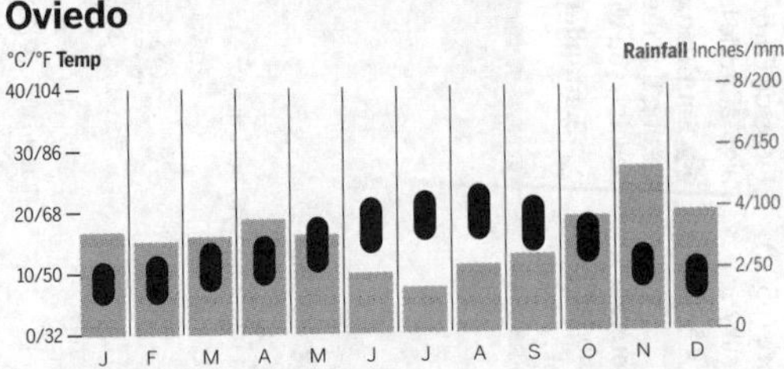

May, Jun & Sep The best times to visit: higher temperatures, lower prices, fewer crowds.

Jul Santander's Semana Grande brings the summer fun.

Oct Celebrate the apple harvest in Asturias' heavily laden orchards and bustling *sidrerías*.

Cantabria & Asturias Highlights

1 Playa de Oyambre (p522) Hitting the exquisite silky sands lining Cantabria's west coast.

2 Lagos de Covadonga (p550) Wandering among the Picos de Europa's twinkling high-altitude lakes.

3 Santillana del Mar (p519) Letting this medieval beauty bewitch you with its charms.

4 Santander (p507) Getting lost in the tapas and surf scenes of this lively capital.

5 Cueva de Tito Bustillo (p536) Admiring exquisite cave art in seaside Ribadesella.

6 Oviedo (p526) Delighting in the grace of Oviedo's cathedral and pre-Romanesque buildings and hitting *el bulevar de la sidra*, the heart of the Spanish cider scene.

7 Garganta del Cares (p552) Walking the length of Spain's most famous gorge.

8 Playa de Torimbia (p538) Bathing at this secluded strand of golden sand.

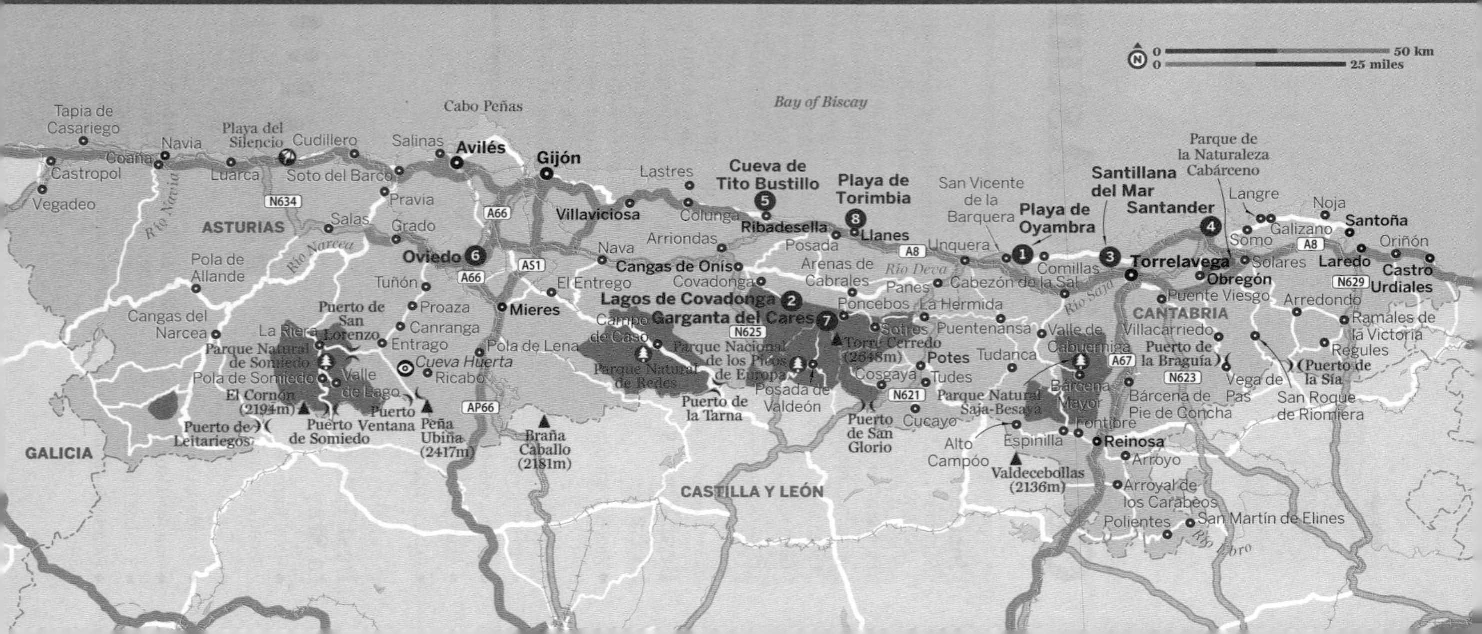

0 — 50 km
0 — 25 miles
Bay of Biscay
Cabo Peñas
ASTURIAS
CANTABRIA
GALICIA
CASTILLA Y LEÓN
Tapia de Casariego
Castropol
Vegadeo
Navia
Coaña
Playa del Silencio
Luarca
Cudillero
Soto del Barco
Salinas
Avilés
Gijón
Pravia
Salas
Grado
Oviedo
Villaviciosa
Lastres
Colunga
Ribadesella
Llanes
Posada
Nava
Arriondas
Cangas de Onís
Covadonga
Lagos de Covadonga
Garganta del Cares
Mieres
El Entrego
Pola de Lena
Pola de Allande
Cangas del Narcea
Tuñón
Proaza
Canranga
Entrago
Cueva Huerta
Ricabo
Puerto de San Lorenzo
La Riera
Parque Natural de Somiedo
Pola de Somiedo
Valle de Lago
El Cornón (2194m)
Puerto de Leitariegos
Puerto Ventana
Puerto de Somiedo
Peña Ubiña (2417m)
Braña Caballo (2181m)
Campo de Caso
Parque Natural de Redes
Puerto de la Tarna
Parque Nacional de los Picos de Europa
Posada de Valdeón
Torre Cerredo (2648m)
Sotres
Poncebos
Arenas de Cabrales
Panes
Río Deva
La Hermida
Potes
Cosgaya
Tudes
Cucayo
Puerto de San Glorio
Puentenansa
Tudanca
Parque Natural Saja-Besaya
Alto Campóo
Espinilla
Valdecebollas (2136m)
Valle de Cabuérniga
Bárcena Mayor
Fontibre
Reinosa
Arroyo
Arroyal de los Carabeos
Polientes
San Martín de Elines
Río Ebro
San Vicente de la Barquera
Unquera
Playa de Oyambra
Comillas
Cabezón de la Sal
Río Saja
Santillana del Mar
Torrelavega
Santander
Puente Viesgo
Villacarriedo
Puerto de la Braguía
Bárcena de Pie de Concha
Vega de Pas
San Roque de Riomiera
Parque de la Naturaleza Cabárceno
Langre
Somo
Galizano
Solares
Obregón
Noja
Santoña
Laredo
Oriñón
Castro Urdiales
Arredondo
Ramales de la Victoria
Regules
Puerto de la Sía
Río Navia
Río Narcea
N634
A66
AS1
N625
AP66
A8
N621
A67
N623
N629

CANTABRIA

For modern travellers, Cantabria offers a bit of everything. Verdant headlands and wild, cliff-backed beaches dominate the 150km-long coastline, interspersed with colourful fishing ports and sandy coves perfect for a summer day by the seaside (unreliable weather permitting). Just inland lie Cantabria's strikingly green mountains – sliced up by deep, multi-branched valleys connected by steep passes and culminating in the spectacular Picos de Europa. These interior landscapes, sprinkled with sleepy villages, prove a feast for the eyes, whether you're driving the country roads or walking the trails.

Lively capital Santander provides a slice of urban life, with buzzing beaches and bodegas. Santillana del Mar and Comillas entice with their medieval and Modernista trappings; and the prehistoric art of Altamira, El Castillo and Covalanas caves is some of the oldest and finest in the world. With so much variety, you could easily spend your entire vacation here.

Santander

POP 171,951

The belle-époque elegance of El Sardinero aside, modern Santander is not the most beautiful of cities. A huge fire raged through the centre back in 1941, leaving little that's old or quaint. Still, Cantabria's capital is an engaging place, making the most of its setting along the northern side of the handsome Bahía de Santander, and the city's forward-facing outlook is epitomised in the striking modernist Centro Botín, which opened on the waterfront in mid-2017.

Santander is a lively spot to spend a night or two, with fine urban beaches, busy shopping streets, a heaving bar and restaurant scene, plenty of surf, and some intriguing cultural attractions. It's a popular summer holiday resort for Spaniards.

Sights

★Centro Botín ARTS CENTRE

(☎942 22 60 72; www.centrobotin.org; Jardines de Pereda; galleries €8; ⊙10am-9pm Tue-Sun Jun-Sep, to 8pm Oct-May) Santander's newest and splashiest landmark, this ambitious waterfront arts and cultural centre opened to great fanfare in June 2017. Designed by Italian architect Renzo Piano, the distinctly modernist building encompasses 2500 sq metres of gallery space on two floors, along with futuristic upper-level viewing platforms that jut dramatically out over the Bahía de Santander. The welcoming ground-floor **cafe** (☎942 04 71 50; www.centrobotin.org/el-muelle; Centro Botín; lunch menus €13-21; ⊙cafe 9.30am-8pm Sun, Tue & Wed, to midnight Thu-Sat, lunch 1-4pm Tue-Fri, dinner 9-11pm Thu-Sat) has quickly become one of the city's social hubs, as has the surrounding plaza, where everyone from skateboarders to seniors congregates.

There's an admission fee for the 1st- and 2nd-floor galleries, which display rotating exhibits of international contemporary art. Access to the rest of the building is free of charge.

★Museo de Prehistoria y Arqueología de Cantabria MUSEUM

(☎942 20 99 22; www.museosdecantabria.es; Calle de Bailén; adult/child €5/2, Sun afternoon free; ⊙10am-2pm & 5-8pm Tue-Sun Jun-Sep, 10am-2pm & 5-7:30pm Tue-Sun Oct-May) Santander's excellent, elegant prehistory and archaeology museum showcases Cantabria's immense archaeological wealth, with explanatory matter in French, English and Spanish. The detailed, interactive multimedia displays range from early hominid remains to giant stelae (stone disks) carved by the pre-Roman Cantabrians, a replica Roman patio, prehistoric cave art and the medieval Spanish kingdoms of Asturias and León.

★Península de la Magdalena PARK

(⊙8am-9pm) At the eastern tip of the bay, this sprawling parkland is perfect for a stroll and popular with picnickers. Kids will enjoy the resident seals and penguins, the replica Spanish galleons, and the little train that choo-choos around the headland (adult/child €2.45/1.45). The views of nearby beaches across the crashing sea are sensational.

Palacio de la Magdalena PALACE

(☎942 20 30 84; www.palaciomagdalena.com; Península de la Magdalena; tours €3; ⊙tours hourly 11am-1pm & 4-6pm Mon-Fri, hourly 10am-noon Sat & Sun, weekends only mid-Jun–mid-Sep) The eclectically styled, English-inspired palace crowning the Península de la Magdalena was built between 1908 and 1912 as a gift from the city to the royal family, who used it every summer until 1930. Detailed 45-minute guided tours (in Spanish) lead you past oak floors, bronze chandeliers, surprisingly simple bedrooms, a carved chestnut-wood staircase and the king's former study.

Santander

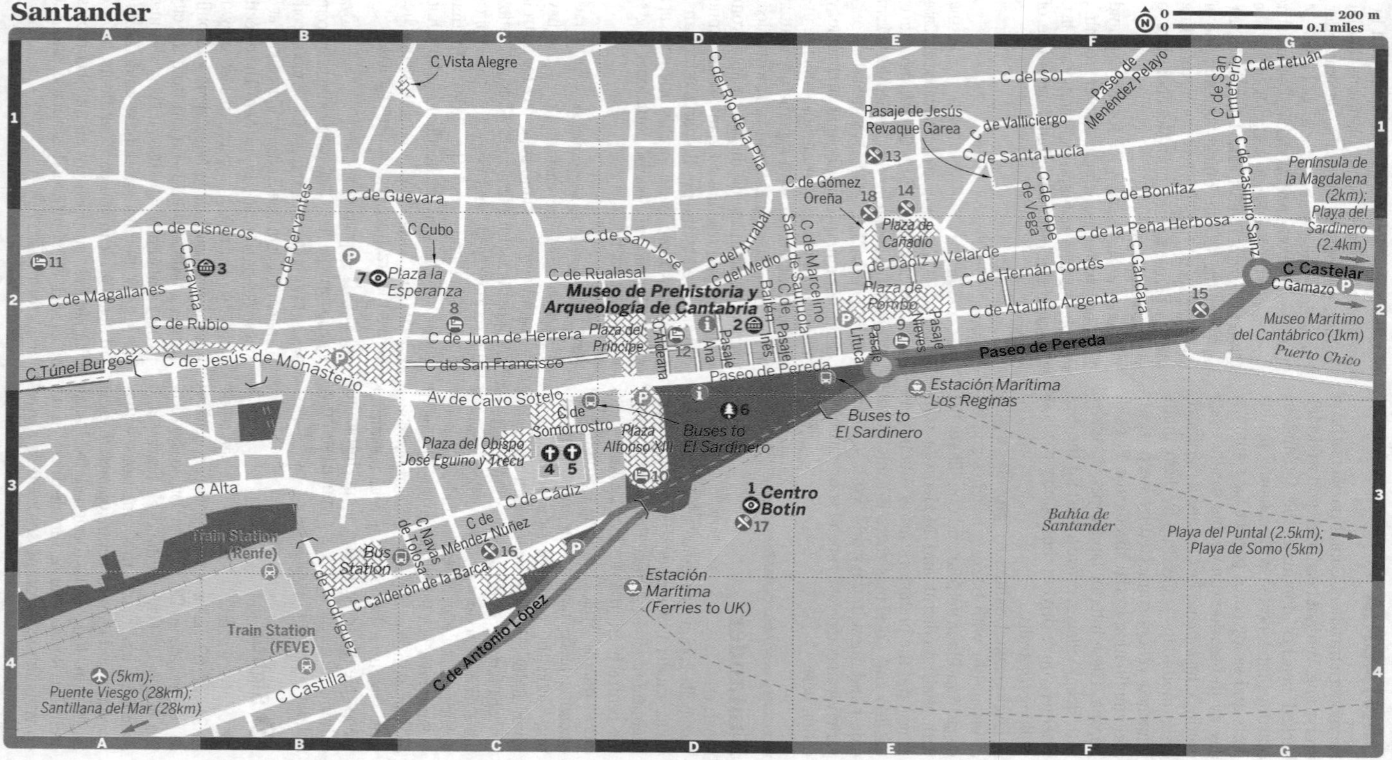

0 200 m
0 0.1 miles

C Vista Alegre
C del Sol
C de Tetuán
C de San Emeterio
Paseo de Menéndez Pelayo
Pasaje de Jesús Revaque Garea
C de Valliciergo
C de Santa Lucía
C de Casimiro Sainz
C del Río de la Pila
Península de la Magdalena (2km); Playa del Sardinero (2.4km)
C de Gómez Oreña
C de Guevara
C Cubo
C de Cisneros
C de Cervantes
C de San José
C de Lope de Vega
C de Bonifaz
Plaza de Cañadío
C de la Peña Herbosa
C del Arrabal
C del Medio
C de Marcelino Sanz de Sautuola
C de Daóiz y Velarde
C de Hernán Cortés
C Gándara
C Castelar
C Gamazo
C Gravina
Plaza la Esperanza
C de Rualasal
Museo de Prehistoria y Arqueología de Cantabria
C de Bailén
Plaza de Pombo
C de Ataúlfo Argenta
C de Magallanes
C de Rubio
C de Juan de Herrera
Plaza del Príncipe
C Aldeana
Pasaje Ana
Pasaje Inés
Pasaje Lituca
Pasaje Nieves
Paseo de Pereda
Museo Marítimo del Cantábrico (1km)
Puerto Chico
C Túnel Burgos
C de Jesús de Monasterio
C de San Francisco
Estación Marítima Los Reginas
Av de Calvo Sotelo
C de Somorrostro
Buses to El Sardinero
Plaza Alfonso XIII
Buses to El Sardinero
Plaza del Obispo José Eguino y Trecu
C Alta
C de Cádiz
Centro Botín
Bahía de Santander
C de Méndez Núñez
C Navas de Tolosa
Bus Station
Playa del Puntal (2.5km); Playa de Somo (5km)
Train Station (Renfe)
C de Rodríguez
C Calderón de la Barca
Estación Marítima (Ferries to UK)
Train Station (FEVE)
C de Antonio López
C Castilla
(5km); Puente Viesgo (28km); Santillana del Mar (28km)

Santander

Top Sights

Sights

Sleeping

Eating

Visits are limited to weekends only in summer, when the palace hosts the **Universidad Internacional Menéndez Pelayo** (www.uimp.es), a global get-together for specialists in all sorts of disciplines.

Jardines & Paseo de Pereda PARK, PROMENADE

(Pereda's Gardens; Paseo de Pereda) The pretty, recently refurbished Jardines de Pereda are named after 19th-century Cantabrian writer José María de Pereda. Scenes of mountain life described in the author's seminal work, *Escenas Montañesas,* are sculpted here in bronze and stone.

The bayside promenade fronting these gardens continues east to **Puerto Chico** (Little Port), a marina. Half the city strolls or jogs here on summer (and, often, winter) evenings. Both Paseo de Pereda and Calle Castelar, opposite the Puerto Chico, are lined with grand buildings flaunting typical glassed-in balconies.

Mercado La Esperanza MARKET

(Plaza La Esperanza; 8am-2pm & 5-7.30pm Mon-Fri, 8am-2pm Sat) Housed in a 19th-century cast-iron structure behind Santander's city hall, this bustling market offers an authentic slice of local life. Shoppers throng two levels of stalls laden with seafood, meat, cheese, fruit and *orujo* (firewater from Cantabria's Liébana Valley).

Catedral de la Asunción CATHEDRAL

(942 22 60 24; Plaza del Obispo José Eguino y Trecu; by donation; 8am-1pm & 4-8pm Jun-Sep, 8am-1pm & 5-8pm Oct-May) Santander's serene cathedral is composed of two Gothic churches, one above the other. The 14th-century **upper church**, off which is a 15th-century cloister, was extensively rebuilt after a 1941 fire, and contains the **tomb of Marcelino Menéndez Pelayo** (942 23 44 93; Calle de Rubio 6; 10.30am-1pm & 5.30-8pm Mon-Fri, 10.30am-1pm Sat) FREE, a celebrated local scholar. Directly below lies the 13th-century **Iglesia del Santísimo Cristo** (Iglesia Vieja; 942 21 15 63; Calle de Somorrostro; 8am-1pm & 4-8pm Jun-Sep, 8am-1pm & 5-8pm Oct-May), where you can view relics of Santander's patron saints and catch glimpses of ancient Roman foundations through the glass floors.

Beaches

Playa del Sardinero BEACH

El Sardinero's 1.5km-long strand of gorgeous golden sand faces the open sea, north of the Península de la Magdalena. It's backed by some of Santander's most expensive real estate, including emblematic early-20th-century creations such as the **Gran Casino**. Surfers emerge in force along Sardinero when the waves are right, mainly in autumn and winter, when they can reach 1.5m. Buses 1 and 2 (€1.30) run east to Sardinero from the Jardines de Pereda in the centre.

Playa del Puntal BEACH

A 2km-long finger of sand jutting out across the bay towards Santander, roughly opposite the Península de la Magdalena, Playa del Puntal is idyllic on calm days (but beware the currents). A couple of popular *chiringuitos* (beach bars) open up here over summer. Weather permitting, passenger ferries (€4 return) sail over about every 30 minutes from 10.30am to 7.30pm, May to October, from the Estación Marítima Los Reginas (p512).

Playa de Somo BEACH

Across the bay from Santander, and just beyond Playa del Puntal (p509), Playa de Somo is a beautiful, gold-tinged beach with (usually) pretty good surf. A year-round ferry (one way/return €2.70/4.85, 30 minutes) runs to Somo from the Estación Marítima Los Reginas (p512) every 30 or 60 minutes, from 8.30am to 7.30pm.

WORTH A TRIP

BEACHES AROUND SANTANDER

Playas de Langre (Langre; P) The two gorgeously wild golden beaches of Langre are backed by cliffs topped with rolling green fields, and often have surfable waves. Most beach-goers head for **Langre La Grande**, although the smaller, adjacent **Langre La Pequeña** is more protected. It's a 30km drive east of Santander: round the bay to Somo, then head east on the CA141 for 4km, then 2km north to Langre; the beaches (signposted) are another 500m northeast.

Playa de Valdearenas (Playa de Liencres; Liencres; P) Protected by the pine-filled **Parque Natural de las Dunas de Liencres**, this exquisite 3km-long, gold-tinged beach has a delightful natural feel and is hugely popular with surfers and beach-lovers alike. It's a 16km drive west of Santander. Take the A67 west for 11km, then the CA231 north for 4km; it's signposted.

Courses

Escuela de Surf Sardinero SURFING
(☎942 27 03 01; www.escueladesurfsardinero.com; Balneario de la Primera Playa del Sardinero; 2hr group class per person incl board, wetsuit & transport €35, board/wetsuit hire per day €25/12; ⊙Mar-Nov) Perfectly placed in the middle of Playa del Sardinero, this well-organised surf school and shop offers surfing classes run in Spanish, English and French. Depending on the day's conditions, sessions might run in Liencres, 10km west.

Escuela Cántabra de Surf SURFING
(☎609 482823, 942 51 06 15; www.escuelacantabradesurf.com; Calle Isla de Mouro 12, Somo; board & wetsuit hire per day €20, 2hr group class per person incl board & wetsuit €30; ⊙10.30am-8pm Mon-Sun mid-Mar–mid-Nov, weekends only rest of year) Based in Somo, across the bay from central Santander, this well-established surf school has been leading surf-lovers into the waves for 25 years, with classes run in English, Spanish or Italian and a range of surf camps and courses. Also does SUP (stand-up paddleboard) group sessions (two hours €50).

Festivals & Events

Festival Internacional de Santander MUSIC
(FIS; www.festivalsantander.com; ⊙Aug) Santander's sweeping summer musical season covers everything from opera, piano and jazz to ballet.

Semana Grande FIESTA
(www.semanagrandesantander.com; ⊙Jul) Santander's big summer fiesta runs for 10 days of fun around 25 July.

Sleeping

Hostel Santander HOSTEL €
(☎942 22 39 86; www.hostelsantander.es; Paseo de Pereda 15; dm incl breakfast €24-29; ❄📶) This excellent, modern, central hostel is built into an old townhouse fronting the Paseo de Pereda. Elephant-stamped cushions adorn the airy communal lounge, with tables, TV and sea views from its glassed-in balcony. The three dorms – simple, clean and fresh, with lockers – sleep six to nine; the back one overlooks the Plaza de Pombo.

Hostal La Mexicana HOSTAL €
(☎942 22 23 54; www.hostallamexicana.com; Calle de Juan de Herrera 3; s €41-50, d €57-65; 📶) A welcoming, well-kept and well-run 38-room *hostal* (budget hotel) on a mostly traffic-free shopping street in central Santander. Rooms have a solid old-fashioned style full of florals, but they are perfectly comfy. There are interconnecting rooms for families. Breakfast (€3) is available.

★**Los Balcones del Arte** APARTMENT €€
(☎942 03 65 47; www.losbalconesdelarte.com; Plaza del Príncipe 2, 5th fl; 1-bedroom apt €80-140, 2-bedroom apt €125-190; P📶) Four stunning contemporary-design apartments grace the top floor of this beautifully renovated, super-central building, right beside the Plaza Porticada. Each is impeccably designed in its own elegant character, with antique furniture, fun fabrics, splashes of bold detail and fully kitted-out kitchens. Shimmery-blue snakeskin wallpaper decorates one-bedroom 'Argenta'; four-person 'Puerto' features leopard-print cushions, a gold-themed bedroom and a sea-view balcony. Minimum five nights from July to mid-September; two nights at other times.

Le Petit Boutique Hotel BOUTIQUE HOTEL €€
(☎942 07 57 68; www.lepetithotelsantander.com; Avenida de los Castros 10; d incl breakfast €65-168; ❄📶) Seven smart, individually styled rooms make attractive (if slightly snug) lodgings at this ultramodern boutique hotel near Playa del Sardinero. Each room is inspired by a different international location, with thematic touches including teak furniture ('Bali') and urban-panorama wallpaper ('New York'); chic creams dominate the pretty 'Paris' suite. All have warm, tasteful decor, plus cushy beds and spotless, hairdryer-equipped bathrooms.

Jardín Secreto BOUTIQUE HOTEL €€
(☎942 07 07 14; www.jardinsecretosantander.com; Calle de Cisneros 37; r €55-80; 📶) Named for its little back garden, this is a charming, six-room world of its own, spread across a 200-year-old house near the city centre. It's run by an on-the-ball brother-and-sister team, and designed by their mother in a stylish, contemporary blend of silvers, greys and pastels with exposed stone, brick and wood. Top-floor rooms 3 and 4 have tiny garden-facing terraces.

Hotel Bahía HOTEL €€€
(☎942 20 50 00; www.hotelbahiasantander.com; Calle de Cádiz 22; r €80-194; P❄📶) Central Santander's top hotel, opposite the UK ferry port, is hard to beat for location and amenities. Large, comfortable rooms are done up in sparkly silvers and creams, with elegant, minimalist style and rich floor carpets. Some have sea views; others overlook the cathedral. Cosy kids' bunks are a nice touch for family rooms, and service is professional and friendly.

Eating

★Casa Lita TAPAS €
(☎942 36 48 30; www.casalita.es; Paseo de Pereda 37; pinchos €2.60; ⏱noon-midnight Tue-Sun) Pack into 'the house of *pinchos*' (snacks) amid crowds of stylish *santanderinos* and brick walls plastered with early-20th-century Santander posters. You'll be lucky to score a table. Classic Iberian ham and local cheese *raciones* put in an appearance, while inventive contemporary creations, such as miniburgers and pumpkin-and-leek quiche, keep flavours exciting. There are even a few Cantabrian artisanal beers.

★Agua Salada FUSION €€
(☎942 04 93 87; www.facebook.com/aguasaladasantander; Calle San Simón 2; lunch menu €14, mains €11-18; ⏱1-4pm Mon, 1-4pm & 8pm-midnight Wed-Sun) A labour of love for owners Carlos García and Pilar Montiel, this intimate corner bistro serves superb, reasonably priced market-fresh cuisine that walks the line between traditional and innovative. Indulge in a superb tuna tartare with English-mustard ice cream, grilled pork shoulder with homemade peach-ginger chutney, or wok-sautéed vegies with extra-virgin olive oil. The weekday lunch menu offers fantastic value.

★La Conveniente TAPAS €€
(☎942 21 28 87; Calle de Gómez Oreña 9; raciones & tablas €7-20; ⏱7pm-midnight Mon-Sat) This cavernous bodega has soaring stone walls, wooden pillars and more wine bottles than you've ever seen in one place. Squeeze into the tram-like front enclosure, line up for the vast dining room or just snack at the bar. The food is straightforward – *tablas* (platters) of cheese, *embutidos* (sausages), ham, pâtés – with generous servings. Arrive by 8.30pm for a table.

El Machi SEAFOOD, BREAKFAST €€
(El Machichaco; ☎942 21 87 22; www.elmachi.es; Calle de Calderón de la Barca 9; mains €16-30; ⏱8am-midnight Mon-Fri, from 9am Sat & Sun) A welcoming, good-value seafood spot convenient to all transport terminals and the city centre. Go for tapas such as the Santander speciality *rabas* (deep-fried squid), their prize-winning seafood tortilla stuffed with *pulpo a la gallega* (Galician-style paprika-sprinkled octopus) or heartier choices such as seafood *arroces* (rices) and baked fish of the day. Also good for breakfast (even bacon and eggs).

Cañadío CANTABRIAN €€€
(☎942 31 41 49; www.restaurantecanadio.com; Calle de Gómez Oreña 15; raciones €9-18, mains €18-25; ⏱1-4pm & 9pm-midnight Mon-Sat; 📶) A tastefully contemporary spot with art on the red walls, comfy booths and timber floors, Cañadío offers top-notch creative cooking with local inspiration. Hake is prepared in a variety of styles, the deep-fried goat's-cheese salad is delicious and there's usually a traditional Cantabrian special. Or you can join the crowds in the front bar for very tempting *pinchos* (snacks).

Drinking & Nightlife

Plaza de Cañadío and Calles de Daoíz y Velarde and Hernán Cortés have plenty of popular *bares de copas* (bars), where you can chat over beer, cocktails, spirits and wine. Calle de Santa Lucía, Calle del Sol and, in particular, the upper half of Calle del Río de la Pila teem with more bohemian bars. Paseo de Pereda and its eastward continuation, Calle Castelar, are dotted with cafes.

Information

Oficina de Turismo de Cantabria (942 31 07 08; www.turismodecantabria.com; Calle de Hernán Cortés 4; 9am-9pm) Inside the Mercado del Este.

Oficina de Turismo Municipal (942 20 30 00; www.santanderspain.info; Jardines de Pereda; 9am-9pm mid-Jun–mid-Sep, 9am-7pm Mon-Fri, 10am-7pm Sat, 10am-2pm Sun rest of year) A summer branch operates at **El Sardinero** (942 20 30 09; Primera Playa del Sardinero; 10am-9pm Jul–mid-Sep, 10am-9pm Sat & Sun Easter-Jun & late Sep).

Getting There & Away

AIR

Santander's **Aeropuerto Seve Ballesteros** (942 20 21 00; www.aena.es; Avenida de Parayas) is 5km south of town, at Parayas. Half-hourly buses run to/from Santander's bus station (€2.90, 10 minutes) between 6.30am and 11pm daily, leaving the airport on the hour and 30 minutes past the hour, and leaving downtown at 15 and 45 minutes past the hour.

Airlines and destinations:

Iberia (www.iberia.com) Flies to Madrid.

Ryanair (www.ryanair.com) Flies to Barcelona, Berlin (Schönefeld), Brussels (Charleroi), Budapest, Dublin, Dusseldorf, Edinburgh, London (Stansted), Málaga, Marrakesh, Milan (Bergamo), Rome (Ciampino), Tenerife, Valencia.

Vueling (www.vueling.com) Flies to Barcelona.

BOAT

Brittany Ferries (www.brittany-ferries.co.uk) runs three car ferry services each week, including one no-frills service, from Portsmouth, UK (24 to 32 hours), and one from Plymouth, UK (20 hours), to **Estación Marítima** in downtown Santander. Fares vary considerably. A standard return trip for two adults and a car, with two-berth interior cabins, booked in February, costs around UK£800 for travel in July or August, or UK£500 in October, from either UK port. Taking the no-frills Portsmouth ferry, a similar deal (also with two-berth interior cabins), costs approximately UK£600 for July and UK£400 for October.

In 2018, Brittany Ferries announced a twice-weekly service from Cork, Ireland, to Santander.

BUS

ALSA (902 42 22 42; www.alsa.es) is the major company operating from Santander's **bus station** (942 21 19 95; Calle Navas de Tolosa).

DESTINATION	FARE (€)	TIME (HR)	MIN FREQUENCY (DAILY)
Bilbao	6.65	1¼-1¾	16
Madrid	32-39	5-6¼	6
Oviedo	13-28	2¼-3¼	13
San Sebastián	13-30	2½-3	11

TRAIN

There are two train stations, beside each other on Calle de Rodríguez: **FEVE** (Renfe Ancho Métrico; 912 32 03 20; www.renfe.com/viajeros/feve) serves destinations along Spain's northern coast, while **Renfe** (912 32 03 20; www.renfe.com) runs to destinations to the south.

Bilbao (€8.90, three hours, three FEVE trains daily)

Madrid (€26 to €52, four to six hours, three to five long-distance Renfe trains daily) Via Reinosa, Palencia and Valladolid.

Oviedo (€16.35, five hours, two FEVE trains daily) Via San Vicente de la Barquera, Llanes, Ribadesella and Arriondas.

Getting Around

BOAT

Regular ferries depart from the **Estación Marítima Los Reginas** (942 21 67 53; www.losreginas.com; Paseo Marítimo), linking central Santander with the beaches of **El Puntal** (one way/return €2.80/4.10) and **Somo** (one way/return €2.80/4.95) on the opposite side of the bay.

BUS

Central Santander is easy to explore on foot, but urban buses 1 and 2 are handy for getting to/from El Sardinero (€1.30); they stop on **Avenida de Calvo Sotelo** near the main post office, and at the **Jardines de Pereda**.

Around Santander

There are several worthwhile attractions around Santander, all within easy reach of the city: beautiful surf-mad beaches (p510), one of Spain's finest wildlife parks and, in the sleepy little town of Puente Viesgo, some of the world's oldest prehistoric cave art.

Parque de la Naturaleza Cabárceno ZOO (902 21 01 12; www.parquedecabarceno.com; Obregón; adult/child €30/17; 9.30am-6pm Mar-

WORTH A TRIP

CUEVAS DE MONTE CASTILLO

Of these four Unesco World Heritage–listed **caves** (☎942 59 84 25; http://cuevas.culturadecantabria.com/el-castillo-2; Puente Viesgo; adult/child per cave €3/1.50; ⏲10.30am-2.30pm & 3.30-7.30pm Tue-Sun mid-Jun–mid-Sep, reduced hours & closed Tue rest of year; P) 27km southwest of Santander, two – **El Castillo** and **Las Monedas** – are open for 45-minute guided visits (in Spanish). Booking ahead is highly recommended, especially for the more spectacular El Castillo, which contains Europe's most ancient cave art. As you explore 500m into the cave, you'll see art almost as breathtaking as that of Cantabria's famous **Cueva de Altamira** (p521) – and unlike at Altamira, this is the genuine article, not a replica.

Discovered in 1903, the 275 paintings and engravings of deer, bison, horses, goats, aurochs, handprints, mysterious symbols and a mammoth (very rare) found within El Castillo date from around 39,000 to 11,000 BC. A red symbol here, believed to be 40,800 years old, is the oldest known cave art in Europe. El Castillo also has some exquisite cathedral-like rock formations. Las Monedas contains less art (black animal outlines, from around 10,000 BC), but has an astounding labyrinth of shimmering stalactites and stalagmites.

Five to eight daily buses run from Santander to Puente Viesgo (€2.30, 35 minutes); from here, it's a 2km uphill walk or taxi ride to the cave. With your own wheels, the cave's parking lot is 40 minutes from Santander.

Oct, 10am-5pm Mon-Fri, to 6pm Sat & Sun Nov-Feb; P) This open-air zoo 17km south of Santander is a curious but successful experiment: a free-range home on the site of former open-cut mines for everything from rhinos, wallabies, gorillas, dromedaries and lynxes to endangered Cantabrian brown bears. You'll need a car and about three hours to tour its 14km of roadways. Alternatively, enjoy 6km worth of aerial perspectives from the park's two brand-new *telecabinas* (cable cars).

From Santander, take the N623 towards Burgos, then the S30 southeast, following signs to Cabárceno.

Eastern Cantabria

The 95km stretch of coast between Santander and Bilbao (in the Basque Country) offers citizens of both cities several seaside escapes. While the towns are less attractive than those on Cantabria's western coast, some of the beaches are divine. Inland, a sea of green awaits in the Valles Pasiegos and the Alto Asón district of southeastern Cantabria.

Santoña

POP 11,004

The laid-back fishing port of Santoña, 42km east of Santander, is famed for its anchovies, which are bottled or tinned here with olive oil to preserve them. North of town lies the beautiful Playa de Berria.

Sights & Activities

Playa de Berria BEACH

Head 2.5km north along the CA141 to Playa de Berria, a magnificent sweep of blonde sand and crashing surf on the open sea, linked to Santoña by frequent buses (€1.45, five minutes).

Parque Cultural Monte Buciero HIKING

(www.santona.es/turismo/monte-buciero-0) The Parque Cultural Monte Buciero occupies the hilly headland rising northeast of Santoña. Explore by heading off on one of five hiking paths, including the relatively easy 12km **Sendero de Faros y Acantilados** (four hours), which loops around past lighthouses, cliffs and forts.

Sleeping

Hotel Juan de la Cosa HOTEL €€

(☎942 66 12 38; www.hoteljuandelacosa.com; Playa de Berria 14; s €65-98, d €70-138, q €104-185; ⏲Easter-Oct; P❄📶🏊) Hotel Juan de la Cosa may be in an unsympathetic-looking building, but about two-thirds of its spacious, blue-hued, maritime-inspired rooms have full-on beach views. It also offers a good restaurant with a seafood emphasis and plain, self-catering apartments designed for families.

Information

Oficina de Turismo de Santoña (☎942 66 00 66; www.turismosantona.es; Calle Santander 5;

(⏲10am-2pm & 5-8pm mid-Jun–Aug, 9am-4pm Mon-Fri, 10am-2pm Sat Sep–mid-Jun) A summer information booth also opens on the seafront promenade from mid-June to August.

Getting There & Away

BOAT

From March to November, **Excursiones Marítimas** (☎637 584164; www.excursionesmaritimas.com; ⏲9am-9pm mid-Jul–mid-Sep, 9am-7pm Mon-Fri, to 8pm Sat & Sun Mar–mid-Jul & mid-Sep–Nov) runs a shuttle ferry from Santoña across the estuary to the northwestern end of Laredo beach (one way/return €2/3.50). From June to September, they also offer one-hour bay cruises with commentary several times daily, stopping off in central Laredo and at the picturesque Faro del Caballo lighthouse (return €10).

BUS

ALSA (p512) and **Autobuses Palomera** (☎942 88 06 11; www.autobusespalomera.com) serve Santoña's **bus station** (Calle Marinos de Santoña). Sixteen buses run between Santoña and Santander (€4.25, one hour) Monday to Friday, with 10 on Saturday and eight on Sunday. There are also seven to 13 buses daily to Laredo (€1.80, 30 minutes), from where there are services to Castro Urdiales.

Castro Urdiales & Around

POP 31,817

Just 31km west of Bilbao (the Basque Country) and 26km east of Laredo, Castro Urdiales is a lively, attractive seafront town with a pretty harbour, a tangle of narrow lanes making up its medieval core and a dramatically Gothic church perched above. The town played an important part as one of the Cuatro Villas de la Costa, a group of four major medieval ports that were united in 1779 as Cantabria province (the others were Santander, Laredo and San Vicente de la Barquera).

Off the A8 motorway en route between Laredo and Castro Urdiales, you'll find Playas de Oriñón and Sonabia, two golden beaches that are well worth a stop. Both are accessed by the same minor road; Sonabia (not signposted) is 1.7km beyond Oriñón.

Sights

Iglesia de Santa María de la Asunción — CHURCH

(⏲10am-1pm & 4-6pm Mon-Sat) The haughty Gothic jumble that is the Iglesia de Santa María de la Asunción stands out spectacularly above Castro Urdiales' harbour. It was built in 1208, but additions continued until almost the 20th century. The church shares its little headland with the ruins of what was, for centuries, the town's defensive bastion, now supporting a lighthouse, and a much-reworked, one-arched medieval bridge.

Playa de Sonabia — BEACH

(Sonabia) About 14km east of Laredo, small, wild Playa de Sonabia is tucked into a rock-lined inlet beneath high crags, above which rare griffon vultures circle the sky. Drive through tiny Sonabia village and turn left directly after the church; you'll have to park up above the beach and walk down. It is accessed by the same minor road used to reach Playa de Oriñón.

There are a couple of seasonal bar-restaurants by the car park above Playa de Sonabia.

Playa de Oriñón — BEACH

(Oriñón) This broad sandy strip, just off the A8 16km west of Castro Urdiales, is set deep behind protective headlands, making the water calm and *comparatively* warm. The settlement here consists of ugly holiday flats and caravan parks. An up-and-down 10km **walking trail** links Oriñón with Laredo via Playa de Sonabia and the even more isolated **Playa de San Julián**.

Sleeping & Eating

Ardigales 11 — BOUTIQUE HOTEL €€

(☎942 78 16 16; www.pensionardigales11.com; Calle de Ardigales 11; s €48-56, d €68-88, q €98-120; ❄📶) Behind a solid stone exterior, on old-town Castro's main bar street, hides this somewhat futuristic hotel, with 11 slick modern rooms decked out in tasteful blacks, whites and greys. Downstairs, soft neon lights brighten up the cosy lounge area, complete with its own bar.

★Bar Javi — TAPAS €

(☎942 78 35 30; www.barjavi.com; Ardigales 42; pinchos €2.50-3; ⏲11.30am-4.30pm & 6.30pm-midnight) *¡Advertencia!* The warning on the napkins at this sweet local tapas bar says it all: 'We take no responsibility for addiction to our *pintxos*'. Indeed, with daily specials ranging from delicately fried baby-squid croquettes to smoked turbot or codfish with braised mushrooms – all accompanied by reasonably priced glasses of top-quality wine – it's hard not to get hooked.

Information

Oficina de Turismo (☎942 87 15 12; www.turismocastrourdiales.net; Parque Amestoy;

WORTH A TRIP

CANTABRIA'S EASTERN VALLEYS

Rich in unspoilt rural splendour, the little-visited valleys of eastern Cantabria are ripe for exploration. The following route could be taken after a visit to the **Cuevas de Monte Castillo** (p513) in Puente Viesgo, 25km south of Santander. Check weather conditions before setting off.

From El Soto, just off the N623 shortly south of Puente Viesgo, take the CA270 and CA142 southeast to Selaya. From here, signs lead to family-run **Quesería La Jarradilla** (☎652 779660, 942 59 03 42; www.quesoslajarradilla.com; Barcenilla 246, Tezanos de Villacarriedo; ⏲tours noon Sat, shop 11am-2pm & 4.30-6.30pm Mon-Sat, 11am-2pm Sun), where you can taste, purchase and find out all about the soft, young cheeses of the **Valles Pasiegos** (the Pas, Pisueña and Miera valleys; www.vallespasiegos.org), one of Cantabria's most traditional rural areas.

Continue south along the CA262 towards **Vega de Pas**, the 'capital' of the Valles Pasiegos; the views from the 720m **Puerto de la Braguía** pass are stunning. From Vega de Pas, head southeast on the CA631 into Castilla y León (where it becomes the BU570), before turning north again near Las Nieves. Follow the BU571 up over the 1240m **Puerto de la Sía** pass towards Arredondo, on the CA265, in Cantabria's southeastern **Alto Asón district** (www.citason.com). The road is full of switchbacks, has a couple of mountain passes and takes you past the 50m waterfall that constitutes the **Nacimiento (Source) del Río Asón**. Alternatively, fork right at the junction just beyond the Puerto de la Sía pass to visit the **Centro de Interpretación Collados del Asón** (☎619 892634, 942 67 73 71; www.facebook.com/colladosdelason; Barrio Lavín, La Gándara; ⏲10am-3.30pm Wed-Fri, to 6pm Sat & Sun), which offers information on the area's activities and has a marvellous lookout point high above the Río Gándara's valley.

Alto Asón claims more than half of Cantabria's 9000 known caves. You can go east from Arredondo or northeast from the visitors centre to **Ramales de la Victoria**, a valley town with two outstanding caves which you can visit. The **Cueva de Cullalvera** (☎942 59 84 25; http://cuevas.culturadecantabria.com/cullalvera-2; Ramales de la Victoria; adult/child €3/1.50; ⏲10.30am-2.30pm & 3.30-7.30pm Tue-Sun mid-Jun–mid-Sep, reduced hours mid-Sep–mid-Jun) is an impressively vast cavity with some signs of prehistoric art. The slim **Cueva de Covalanas** (☎942 59 84 25; http://cuevas.culturadecantabria.com/covalanas-2; adult/child €3/1.50; ⏲10.30am-2.30pm & 3.30-7.30pm Tue-Sun mid-Jun–mid-Sep, reduced hours mid-Sep–mid-Jun), 3km up the N629 south from Ramales, then 650m up a footpath, is on the Unesco World Heritage List for its stunning depictions of deer and other animals – which date to around 20,000 BC – rendered in an unusual dot-painting technique. Guided visits to either cave last 45 minutes; book ahead.

In a tranquil, shady spot beside the Río Gándara in Regules, 10km southwest of Ramales, stands **La Casa del Puente** (☎942 63 90 20, 645 820418; www.lacasadelpuente.es; Regulesabajo 3, Regules; r incl breakfast €86-154; P 📶), a beautifully restored *casa de indianos* (mansion built by a returned emigrant from Latin America or the Caribbean). Rooms follow a cosy, multicoloured, modern-rustic style, with exposed stonework, floral fabrics and, for some, a private spa. Top-floor rooms are attic-style, with sloping wood-beamed ceilings. You can enjoy good Cantabrian cooking in the glassed-in restaurant, and owner Emilio is a font of local knowledge.

South of Ramales the N629 climbs to the panoramic 920m **Alto de los Tornos** lookout, before continuing towards Burgos in Castilla y León.

⏲9am-9pm Jul–mid-Sep, 9.30am-2pm & 4-7pm mid-Sep–Jun) On the seafront.

ℹ Getting There & Away

ALSA (p512) runs at least eight buses daily to Santander (€6.40, one hour) via Laredo from Castro's **bus station** (☎942 86 71 45; Calle Leonardo Rucabado 42).

IRB Castro (☎942 86 70 26; www.bilbao-castro.es) buses to Bilbao (€2.75, 45 minutes) leave half-hourly from 6am to 10pm (hourly on Sunday), making various stops including at **Calle La Ronda 52**, half a block from the seafront.

There's no public transport to Playas de Oriñón and Sonabia, so you'll need your own wheels.

Laredo

POP 11,347

Laredo, 46km east of Santander, is a ridiculously popular Spanish beach resort. Its sandy, 5km-long Playa de Salvé, across the bay from Santoña, is backed by ugly 20th-century building blocks. But at the eastern end of town, the evocative cobbled streets of the old Puebla Vieja slope down dramatically from La Atalaya hill, packed with busy bars and restaurants.

Sights

Fuerte del Rastrillar FORTRESS
(10am-10pm) The dwindling remains of this 16th-century fortress crown La Atalaya hill above the Puebla Vieja, accessed by a steep but quick 500m track. From the **Mirador de la Caracola** here, you'll enjoy sensational views of Laredo's beach, the green-cloaked mountains behind and across the waves to Santoña.

Túnel de Laredo TUNNEL
(10am-10pm) Built in 1885, this cavernous 220m tunnel at the eastern end of town leads under La Atalaya hill to a rugged seafront lookout point. It was originally designed to reach a now destroyed port, but came in handy as a refuge during the Spanish Civil War.

Iglesia de Santa María CHURCH
(942 84 03 17; Calle Santa María; €1; 10am-1pm & 4-7pm Mon-Fri, 10am-1pm Sat) A Spanish national monument since 1931, the impressive 13th-century Iglesia de Santa María sits at the top of the Puebla Vieja, housing a beautiful 15th-century Flemish *retablo* (altarpiece).

Eating

Somera FUSION €€
(942 60 30 19; www.divinocanalla.com; Rua Mayor 17; mains €12-20; noon-5pm & 8pm-1am Tue-Sun Jul–mid-Sep, 8pm-midnight Thu, 1-4pm & 8pm-midnight Fri-Sun rest of year) Run by an ambitious, attentive young team, Somera specialises in highly creative Cantabrian-Asian fusion cooking full of local ingredients. Delicate starters include fried-egg and sushi-rice *pinchos* (snacks) and enormous crispy salads (such as king prawns, fruit and apple ice cream). Mains take a hearty turn with gourmet burgers and tuna tartare, and the one-mouthful *bombón* chocolate desserts top things off perfectly.

Information

Oficina de Turismo (942 61 10 96; www.laredoturismo.es; Alameda Miramar; 9am-9pm Jul–mid-Sep, 9.30am-2pm & 4-7pm mid-Sep–Jun) At the eastern end of town.

Getting There & Away

BUS

ALSA (p512) runs at least 17 buses daily between Laredo and Santander (€4.25, 40 minutes) and Bilbao (€3.60, 50 minutes) from the **bus station** (Calle Reconquista de Sevilla 1). There are also at least 15 buses daily to Castro Urdiales (€2.15, 20 to 40 minutes).

BOAT

From March to November, **Excursiones Marítimas** (p514) offers regular boat crossings to Santoña (one way/return €2/3.50) from the northwestern end of Laredo's beach. The same company also runs sightseeing cruises from central Laredo to Santoña several times daily (return €10) from June to September.

Southern Cantabria

Fine panoramas of high peaks and deep river valleys flanked by patchwork quilts of green await the traveller venturing into the Cantabrian interior. Every imaginable shade of green seems to have been employed to set this stage, strewn with warm stone villages and held together by a network of narrow country roads. The area's major town is Reinosa.

Reinosa & Around

POP 9331 / ELEV 851M

Southern Cantabria's main town, 70km south of Santander, is itself an unexceptional place, but Reinosa has plenty of curiosities nearby, including the remains of Cantabria's most important Roman settlement, an impressive collection of rock-cut and Romanesque churches, and the source of one of Spain's mightiest rivers, the Río Ebro.

Sights

Nacimiento del Río Ebro SPRING
(Fontibre; P) Spain's most voluminous river, the Río Ebro, starts life at this serene tree-shaded spring 5km northwest of Reinosa. It's a stunning, peaceful spot, with deep-turquoise water, a tiny shrine and a few ducks splashing around. From here, the Ebro meanders 930km southeast via Logroño (La

OFF THE BEATEN TRACK

TOURING THE EBRO'S ROCK-CUT CHURCHES

Spain's most voluminous river, the Ebro, rises at Fontibre (5km northwest of Reinosa), fills the Embalse del Ebro reservoir to the east, then meanders south and east into Castilla y León. Its course is strung with some fascinating, picturesque stops. You can follow it on the GR99 long-distance footpath or on minor roads out of Reinosa.

From Reinosa, head east along the CA730 – visiting Roman **Julióbriga** (p517) en route, if you fancy – to Arroyo, where you turn south on the CA735 and follow signs to the **Santuario de Montesclaros** (942 77 05 50; Carretera CA741, Montesclaros; hours vary; P), a monastery with a fascinating pre-Romanesque crypt and a fine site overlooking the Ebro valley. From here, follow the CA741 southwest to Arroyal de los Carabeos (via the **Mirador del Cañon**, a fantastic viewpoint across to the monastery), then head south on the CA272 to a roundabout where it meets the CA273. Nine kilometres west on the CA273 is the remarkable **Iglesia Rupestre de Santa María de Valverde** (Santa María de Valverde; €1; 11am-6pm Tue-Sun Jul–mid-Sep, Mass 1pm Sun year-round). This beautiful, multiarched church, hewn from the living rock, is the most impressive of several *iglesias rupestres* (rock-cut churches) in this area, dating from probably the 7th to 10th centuries, the early days of Christianity in the region. Beside the church, the **Centro de Interpretación del Rupestre** (942 77 61 46; Santa María de Valverde; adult/child €2/free; 10am-2pm & 4-7pm Tue-Sun Jul–mid-Sep, reduced hours rest of year; P) tells the story of the area's curious rock-church phenomenon through photos, maps, video and multimedia – well worth a visit, even if you don't understand Spanish, and full of useful information. From here, head back east to La Puente del Valle, where you can cross the river to the collection of anthropomorphic tombs at **Ermita de San Pantaleón**, then continue east to Campo de Ebro, where the tiny, rock-cut **Ermita de Santa Eulalia** is hidden behind a 17th-century church just off the main road. Just 3km further east lies **Polientes**, the area's biggest village, which has a bank, petrol station (self-service; credit cards only) and a few places to stay, of which the pick is **Posada El Cuartelillo Viejo** (942 77 61 51, 619 918281; www.elcuartelilloviejo.com; Carretera General 31, Polientes; incl breakfast s €34-37, d €60-70; Apr-Oct;), in the centre of town.

East of Polientes, along the CA275, you'll find the finest of the area's other rock-cut churches. First comes a little rock-cut roadside church in **Cadalso**, then the dramatic two-level church at **Arroyuelos**. Across the Ebro from Arroyuelos, **San Martín de Elines** is well worth a detour for its exquisite Romanesque church. Finally, the small but wonderfully sited **El Tobazo** cave-church is part of a small group of caves towards the top of the Ebro gorge east of Arroyuelos. To find it, cross the bridge into Villaescusa del Ebro, 2.5km east of Arroyuelos, park your vehicle, and set off on foot, following a pretty track along the river's south bank. A few hundred metres further on, a signposted trail for El Tobazo branches off to the right; from here you have a 700m uphill walk. A beautiful waterfall (appearing as a moss-covered, cave-pocked cliff after prolonged dry weather) comes into view about halfway up, with the cave-church just above it to the right.

Except for Santa María from July through mid-September, all these churches are usually locked (though they're striking from the outside too). You'll need to contact the helpful **Oficina de Turismo de Valderredible** (942 77 61 46; www.valderredible.es; Avenida de Cantabria, Polientes; 10am-2pm Tue-Sun) in advance to arrange visits.

From Villaescusa del Ebro, the CA275 continues along the Ebro gorge to Orbaneja del Castillo in Castilla y León.

Rioja) and Zaragoza (Aragón) to meet the Mediterranean.

Colegiata de San Pedro CHURCH

(942 75 02 24; Cervatos; €2; 11am-1.30pm & 4-7.30pm) The 12th-century Colegiata de San Pedro in Cervatos, 5km south of Reinosa, is one of Cantabria's finest Romanesque churches, with rare erotic carvings on its corbels. If you're keen on seeing the interior, call ahead to confirm current hours.

Julióbriga RUINS

(942 59 84 25; http://centros.culturadecantabria.com; Retortillo; adult/child €3/1.50; 10.30am-2.30pm & 3.30-7.30pm Tue-Sun mid-Jun–mid-Sep,

reduced hours mid-Sep–mid-Jun; P) The remains of Julióbriga, Cantabria's most significant Roman town, lie 5km east of Reinosa. Julióbriga peaked in the 1st and 2nd centuries, and was abandoned in the 3rd century. Guided visits (45 minutes, in Spanish), which start at 40 minutes past the hour, lead you through the **Museo Domus**, a full-scale recreation of a Roman house. You're free to explore the rest of the site, including its 12th-century **Romanesque church**, independently.

Sleeping & Eating

Reinosa's city centre offers half a dozen sleeping options. For a more peaceful and verdant village setting, head to Fontibre, 5km to the west.

Posada Fontibre INN €€
(942 77 96 55; www.posadafontibre.com; El Molino 23, Fontibre; s €52-59, d €69-84;) A tranquil haven in the heart of Fontibre village, this old stone *posada* offers six well-kept rooms and a pleasant grassy yard just steps from the source of the Río Ebro. Decor is rustic, with beamed ceilings, stone walls, colourful rugs and chequer-tiled bathrooms. The adjacent riverside park is a delightful place to stroll.

La Cabaña CANTABRIAN €€
(942 75 08 37, 637 798731; Calle de Juan José Ruano 4, Reinosa; mains €10-20, set menu €13.50; 1.30-4pm Mon, 1.30-4pm & 9-11pm Wed-Sun;) A Madrid-trained chef heads

NORTHERN WAYS: THE OTHER CAMINOS DE SANTIAGO

Around 65% of Camino de Santiago pilgrims reach Santiago de Compostela via the traditional Camino Francés, which marches 783km west across Castilla y León from Roncesvalles in the Pyrenees. In recent years, however, walkers looking for less beaten paths have set their sights on Spain's northernmost reaches, where several other *caminos* wind through un-tramped country to the final spectacle of Santiago de Compostela and its glorious cathedral in Galicia.

Traversing the Basque Country, Cantabria and Asturias, these northern *caminos* reveal exquisite, green-cloaked landscapes unseen by the approximately 181,000 pilgrims, who, in 2017, reached the pilgrimage office in Santiago having made their way along the Camino Francés. In 2015, four northern ways joined the Camino Francés in its Unesco World Heritage status.

Camino de la Costa (Camino del Norte) The main Camino de la Costa – now chosen by around 6% of pilgrims – starts at Irún on the Spanish-French border, near San Sebastián. This wilder 815km route hugs Spain's jagged northern coastline as it travels west, taking in San Sebastián, Bilbao, Santander and Asturias' east coast, before splitting in two just before it reaches Oviedo. One branch heads southwest to Oviedo, but the Costa path continues along Asturias' west coast via Gijón, Avilés and Luarca, then turns inland at Ribadeo (Galicia) to meet the Camino Francés just before landing in Santiago.

Camino Primitivo This beautifully rustic trail officially begins in Oviedo – long an important pilgrimage spot for the holy relics hidden inside its multispired cathedral, which include the Santo Sudario, a cloth that allegedly covered Christ's face. The 321km path ventures on to Lugo (Galicia) and, in its final stretches, links up with the Camino Francés. The Primitivo is said to be Spain's most ancient *camino:* after the 9th-century discovery of St James' remains, Oviedo-based King Alfonso II of Asturias set off for Santiago in AD 829. In 2016, 4% of *camino* pilgrims – around 12,000 hikers – followed in his royal footsteps.

Camino Lebaniego This route travels from either Santander or San Vicente de la Barquera on the Cantabrian coast to the Monasterio de Santo Toribio de Liébana in the foothills of the Picos de Europa – a 120km walk from Santander. Though the Lebaniego isn't technically a Camino de Santiago, the monastery contains a relic believed to be the largest surviving chunk of Christ's cross, making it a major pilgrimage destination, and, like Santiago's cathedral, offers pilgrims the possibility of plenary indulgence (the removal of punishment for all sins) in jubilee years (the next will be 2023).

Camino del Interior Vasco-Riojano The least-used trail tracks 200km southwest from Irún to meet the Camino Francés in Castilla y León.

this friendly eatery specialising in fun, local-inspired concoctions that manage to be inventive without turning excessively modern. Lovingly created dishes focus on meat grills, huge salads and delicious home-made pastas (a rare find in these parts). The ravioli is a four-cheese extravaganza, with pungent Picos de Europa cheeses, while mushrooms arrive battered in local Orzales bread.

Information

Oficina de Turismo (942 75 52 15; www.surdecantabria.es; Avenida del Puente de Carlos III 23; 9.30am-2.30pm & 4-7pm Mon-Fri, 9.30am-2.30pm Sat)

Getting There & Away

BUS

At least six daily **ALSA** (p512) buses run between Reinosa's **bus station** (942 75 40 67; Avenida de Castilla) and Santander (€6.50, 1½ hours). Two daily buses head south to Palencia (€6.80, two hours), Valladolid (€9.25, 2¾ hours), Salamanca (€15.25, 4¼ hours) and Madrid (€30, five hours).

TRAIN

Five daily **Renfe** (p512) trains run between Reinosa and Santander (from €8.10, 1¼ hours). A few daily trains go south to Palencia, Valladolid, Salamanca and Madrid.

Getting Around

The best (and usually only) way to visit the main sights in the area is with your own vehicle.

Western Cantabria

Cantabria's most exquisite (and most popular) villages are strung like pearls across the green-cloaked coastline west of Santander. First comes medieval beauty Santillana del Mar, with the prehistoric wonders of the Cueva de Altamira close by; then Comillas and its unexpected Modernista architecture; and, finally, handsome San Vicente de la Barquera, with its pretty port.

Heading inland, a whole new world opens up in the off-the-beaten-track valleys of western Cantabria. Here, tucked in among lush green mountains, you'll find beautiful stone villages such as Barcena Mayor and Tudanca, where you can get a feel for rural Cantabria's history and cultural traditions.

Santillana del Mar

POP 4154

They say Santillana is the town of the three lies: not holy *(santi)*, flat *(llana)* or by the sea *(del mar)*. This medieval jewel is in such a perfect state of preservation, with its bright cobbled streets, flower-filled balconies and huddle of tanned stone and brick buildings – it's a film set, surely? Well, no. People still live here, passing their grand precious houses down from generation to generation. In summer, the streets get busy with curious visitors.

Strict town-planning rules were first introduced back in 1575, and today they include the stipulation that only residents or guests in hotels with garages may bring vehicles into the old heart of town. Other hotel guests may drive to unload luggage and must then return to the car park at the town entrance.

Santillana is a *bijou* in its own right, but also makes the obvious base for visiting nearby Altamira (p520).

Sights

Colegiata de Santa Juliana CHURCH

(Plaza del Abad Francisco Navarro; adult/child €3/free; 10am-1.30pm & 4-7.30pm, closed Mon Oct-Jun) A stroll along Santillana's cobbled main street, past solemn 15th- to 18th-century nobles' houses, leads to this beautiful 12th-century Romanesque ex-monastery. The big drawcard is the **cloister**, a formidable storehouse of Romanesque handiwork, with the capitals of its columns finely carved into a huge variety of figures. The monastery originally grew up around the relics of Santa Juliana (her name was later modified to become Santillana), a 3rd-century Christian martyr from Turkey whose sepulchre stands in the centre of the church.

Sleeping

Posada de la Abadía GUESTHOUSE €

(942 84 03 04; www.posadadelabadia.com; Calle de Revolgo 26; s €48-65, d €55-75; P) A small, friendly, family-run hotel set in a revamped 19th-century Cantabrian-style house, 200m south of the main road. The 10 pretty, spotless and perfectly comfy rooms all have bathtubs, and they do decent breakfasts (included in room rates).

★ **Casa del Organista** HOTEL €€
(☎942 84 03 52; www.casadelorganista.com; Calle de Los Hornos 4; s €66-79, d €82-96; ⊙closed 1st half Jan; P ☜) The 14 rooms at this elegant 18th-century house, once home to the Colegiata de Santa Juliana's organist, are particularly attractive, with plush rugs, antique furniture and plenty of exposed oak beams and stonework. Some have balconies looking towards the *colegiata* or across red-tiled roofs. Expect a warm welcome and excellent breakfasts (€6.50).

There are several similarly styled places up this street.

★ **Casa del Marqués** HISTORIC HOTEL €€€
(☎942 81 88 88; www.hotelcasadelmarques.com; Calle del Cantón 24; r €99-199; ⊙early Mar–early Dec; P ✻ ☜) Feel like the lord or lady of the manor in this 15th-century Gothic mansion, once home to the Marqués de Santillana. Exposed timber beams, thick stone walls and cool terracotta floors contribute to the atmosphere of the 15 sumptuous rooms (all different, some surprisingly modern). Three 1st-floor chambers overlook gorgeous gardens, where you can sip an afternoon tea or gin and tonic.

The owners are proud of their 700-year-old banister, made from a single tree. On-site parking (a rare commodity in Santillana) is available for €11 per day.

Parador de Santillana Gil Blas HISTORIC HOTEL €€€
(☎942 81 80 00, 942 02 80 28; www.parador.es; Plaza Ramón Pelayo 11; r €135-205; ☜) Sleep in an exquisitely preserved, centuries-old nobles' home gazing out across Santillana's cobbled main plaza. The 28 rooms – comfy, stylish and well equipped, yet full of historical character – tick your classic *parador* boxes, and service is superb. There are oodles of lavish tucked-away lounges to get lost in, complemented by an elegant walled garden where you can breakfast in summer.

Eating

La Villa CANTABRIAN €€
(☎942 81 83 64; www.lavillarestaurante.es; Calle La Gándara; menú €16.50; ⊙1-4pm & 8-11pm) La Villa's three-course lunch or dinner menu, including a full bottle of wine, offers great value for touristy Santillana. Settle into the stone-walled garden courtyard and sample northern Spanish classics such as *cocido montañes* (Cantabrian stew with meat and beans) or veal entrecôte with Cabrales cheese from the Picos de Europa village of Sotres, followed by excellent rice pudding for dessert.

Restaurante Gran Duque CANTABRIAN €€
(☎942 84 03 86; www.granduque.com; Calle del Escultor Jesús Otero 7; mains €15-20; ⊙1-3.30pm & 8-10.30pm year-round, closed Sun dinner & Mon lunch Sep-Jun) High-quality local fare is served in this stone house with noble trappings and decorative touches such as exposed brick and beams. There's a reasonable balance of surf and turf options, including *mariscadas* for two (seafood feasts; from €50) and a decent *menú del día* (€19), available for lunch and dinner.

Information

Oficina Regional de Turismo (☎942 81 82 51, 942 81 88 12; Calle del Escultor Jesús Otero; ⊙9am-9pm Jul–mid-Sep, 9.30am-2pm & 4-7pm mid-Sep–Jun)

Getting There & Away

Autobuses La Cantábrica (☎942 72 08 22; www.lacantabrica.net) runs three or more daily buses from Santander to Santillana (€2.65, 40 minutes), continuing to Comillas (€1.50, 20 minutes from Santillana) and San Vicente de la Barquera (€2.20, 40 minutes from Santillana). Buses stop by **Campo del Revolgo**, just south of the main road.

Altamira

Spain's finest prehistoric art, the wonderful paintings of bison, horses, deer and other animals in the **Cueva de Altamira**, 2.5km southwest of Santillana del Mar, was discovered in 1879 by Cantabrian historian and scientist Marcelino Sanz de Sautuola and his eight-year-old daughter María Justina. By 2002, Altamira had attracted so many visitors that the cave was closed to prevent deterioration of the art, but a replica cave in the museum here now enables everyone to appreciate the inspired, 13,000- to 35,000-year-old paintings. These magical carbon-and-ochre illustrations are particularly special for depicting completely coloured-in beasts, rather than animal outlines (as in other Cantabrian caves).

Since 2014 the Altamira authorities have begun allowing five lucky visitors, randomly selected by lottery, to enter the real Altamira cave each Friday morning. People entering the museum before 10.30am on Friday will be offered an application form if interested; the drawing takes place at 10.40am.

WORTH A TRIP

TOURING CANTABRIA'S WESTERN VALLEYS

Generally ignored by holidaymakers, who focus on the Picos de Europa further west, the western Cantabrian valleys of the Río Saja and, next west, the Río Nansa, make a soft contrast to the craggy majesty of the Picos, and are a delight to explore.

A beautiful drive, starting from the eastern side of the Picos de Europa, is along the CA282, which snakes up high and eastwards from La Hermida on the Río Deva. The village of **Puentenansa** forms a crossroads. Fifteen kilometres north on the CA181 (turn east at Rábago and climb 7km) is **El Soplao** (☎902 82 02 82; www.elsoplao.es; adult/reduced €12/9.50; ⊙10am-9pm Aug, to 7pm Jul, 10am-2pm & 3-6pm Apr-Jun, Sep & Oct, 10am-2pm & 3-5pm Nov-Mar, closed Mon Oct-Jun; P), a 20km stretch of caves full of stalactites and stalagmites, and, until 1979, a lead and zinc mine.

The CA281 south from Puentenansa follows the Río Nansa upstream. Along the way, a 2km detour east leads to the attractive hamlet of Tudanca, dominated by the **Casona de Tudanca** (☎942 59 84 25; www.museosdecantabria.es; Tudanca; adult/child €3/1.50, Sun free; ⊙11.30am-2.30pm & 3.30-7.30pm Wed-Sun mid-Jun–mid-Sep, reduced hours rest of year), a brilliantly white, 18th-century rural mansion. The house, filled with centuries-old furniture, was built by an *indiano* (returned emigrant made rich in the Americas, in this case Peru). It also contains the 18,000-volume library of writer José María de Cossío, to whom it belonged in the 20th century. Guided visits last 45 minutes.

The CA281 eventually meets the CL627, on which you can head south to Cervera de Pisuerga in Castilla y León or turn northwest back to the Picos.

Alternatively, heading east from Puentenansa on the CA182 takes you through **Carmona**, with fine stone mansions best viewed from the lookout point high above. When you reach the village of Valle de Cabuérniga and the Río Saja, track south on the CA280. The gorgeous, popular hamlet of **Bárcena Mayor**, 9.5km east off the CA280 along the CA871, is one of Cantabria's oldest villages. It has a few *casas rurales* (village lodgings) and wonderfully atmospheric *mesones* (taverns), such as **La Jontana** (☎942 74 12 11; www.lajontana.es; Calle La Larga, Bárcena Mayor; mains €9-16, menú del dia €12; ⊙10am-late Wed-Mon; 👪) – perfect for trying the region's beloved *cocido montañés*, served in huge sharing pots. It's also a good base for walks in the dense beech forests, valleys and hills of the surrounding **Parque Natural Saja-Besaya**. The **Centro de Interpretación Parque Natural Saja-Besaya** (☎608 065846; Carretera CA280, Km 13, Saja, Los Tojos; ⊙10am-7pm Jul & Aug, 10am-7pm Tue-Sun Sep, reduced hours Oct-Jun), 6km south of the Bárcena Mayor turn-off on the CA280, offers maps, info and guided hikes.

From the Centro, the road winds past fantastic views all the way to Reinosa, in southern Cantabria, via the beautifully positioned **Balcón de la Cardosa** lookout and the 1260m **Puerto de Palombera**, with its roaming horses.

Sights

★Museo de Altamira MUSEUM

(☎942 81 80 05; http://museodealtamira.mcu.es; Avenida Marcelino Sanz de Sautuola, Santillana del Mar; adult/child €3/free, Sun & from 2pm Sat free; ⊙9.30am-8pm Tue-Sat May-Oct, to 6pm Tue-Sat Nov-Apr, to 3pm Sun & holidays year-round; P 👪) The museum's highlight is the **Neocueva**, a dazzling, full-sized re-creation of the real Cueva de Altamira's most interesting chamber, the **Sala de Polícromos** (Polychrome Hall), which is covered in exquisite, 15,000-year-old ochre-and-black bison paintings created using the natural rock relief. Other excellent English- and Spanish-language displays cover prehistoric humanity and cave art worldwide, from Altamira to Australia. The museum is incredibly popular (288,000 visitors in 2017), so it's best to reserve tickets ahead, especially for Easter, July, August and September.

Sleeping

The most obvious base for exploring Altamira is beautiful, cobbled Santillana del Mar, 2.5km northeast, which has an excellent array of accommodation mostly set inside grand historical homes.

Getting There & Away

ALSA (p512) runs four daily buses from Santillana del Mar to Altamira (€1.50, five minutes); schedules change seasonally. Otherwise, those without vehicles must walk (30 minutes via a paved path) or take a taxi (€5) to Altamira from Santillana, 2.5km northeast.

Comillas & Around

POP 2195

Sixteen kilometres west of Santillana through verdant countryside, Comillas is set across hilltops crowned by some of the most original and beautiful buildings in Cantabria. For these, the town is indebted to the first Marqués de Comillas (1817–83), who was born here as plain Antonio López, made a fortune in Cuba as a tobacco planter, shipowner, banker and slave trader, and then returned to commission leading Catalan Modernista architects to jazz up his hometown in the late 19th century. This, in turn, prompted the construction of other quirky mansions in Comillas. Adding to the town's charms are a lovely golden beach, a tiny fishing port and a pleasant, cobbled old centre.

Sights

★Palacio de Sobrellano HISTORIC BUILDING
(☎942 72 03 39; http://centros.culturadecantabria.com; Barrio de Sobrellano; adult/child €3/1.50, grounds free; ⌚9.45am-2.30pm & 3.30-6.30pm Tue-Sun Apr-Oct, to 7.30pm mid-Jun–mid-Sep, reduced hours Nov-Mar) In hillside parkland stands the Marqués de Comillas' fabulous neo-Gothic palace. With this 1888 building, Modernista architect Joan Martorell truly managed to out-Gothic real Gothic. On the 25-minute guided tour (in Spanish), you'll see the grand lounge, featuring ornate wood-carved fireplaces with Gaudí-designed dragons; the elaborate dining room with its gold-wood *artesonado* (ceiling of interlaced beams with decorative insertions); beautiful stained-glass windows and vibrant original murals detailing the marquis' story. Martorell also designed the marquis' majestic **family tomb** (adult/child €3/1.50), next door.

★Capricho de Gaudí ARCHITECTURE
(☎942 72 03 65; www.elcaprichodegaudi.com; Barrio de Sobrellano; adult/child €5/2.50; ⌚10.30am-9pm Jul-Sep, to 8pm Mar-Jun & Oct, to 5.30pm Nov-Feb, closed 1 week Jan) Antoni Gaudí left few reminders of his genius beyond Catalonia, but of them the 1885 Capricho de Gaudí is easily the most flamboyant. This brick building, one of Gaudí's earliest works and originally a summer playpad for the Marqués de Comillas' sister-in-law's brother, is striped all over the outside with ceramic bands of alternating sunflowers and green leaves. The elegant interior is comparatively restrained, with quirky touches including *artesonado* ceilings (interlaced beams with decorative insertions), stained-glass windows and slim spiral staircases.

★Playa de Oyambre BEACH
(P) The 2km-long, soft-blonde Playa de Oyambre, 5km west of Comillas, is a sandy dream protected by the Parque Natural Oyambre. It has some surfable waves, a couple of year-round campgrounds and a dash of intriguing history as the emergency landing spot of the first ever USA–Spain flight, in 1929.

Fuente de los Tres Caños FOUNTAIN
(Calle de Joaquín del Piélago) In the heart of town, this elaborate triple-tiered fountain and lamp post was created in 1899 by Modernista Lluís Domènech i Montaner and decorated with intricate floral motifs.

Antigua Universidad Pontificia ARCHITECTURE
(☎630 256767; Calle de Manuel Noriega; adult/child €3.50/free, car €2; ⌚10am-1pm & 5-8pm Jun-Sep, 10am-1pm Oct-May; P) Modernista architects Joan Martorell, Cristóbal Cascante and Lluís Domènech i Montaner all had a hand in this complex 1892 former seminary, with Domènech i Montaner contributing its medieval flavour. It's now an international Spanish language and culture study centre, the **Centro Universitario CIESE-Comillas** (☎942 71 55 00; www.fundacioncomillas.es; group lessons per 1/2/3/4 weeks from €225/430/620/800). Visits to its elaborate interiors and patios are guided in Spanish; from June to September, the 6pm tour is in English. Access to just the grounds is free (unless you take a car in).

Sleeping & Eating

Posada Los Trastolillos INN €€
(☎942 72 22 12; www.lostrastolillos.com; Barrio Ceceño, El Tejo; d €90-120, ste €120-150; wifi) At this peaceful rural retreat between Comillas and Playa del Oyambre, 10 guest rooms, including three spacious suites, are complemented by a sunny breakfast room, a comfy *salón* with wood stove, and a library and game room with cute wicker chairs for kids. Outside is a field full of cows, with distant vistas of hills, rocky headlands and the ocean.

Hotel Marina de Campíos BOUTIQUE HOTEL €€
(☎942 72 27 54, 607 441647; www.marinadecampios.com; Calle del General Piélagos 12; s €75-105, d €90-160; ⏱daily Jun-Sep, Sat & Sun Oct-May; ❄📶) This bright-red, 19th-century house a few steps from Comillas' central plaza has been revamped into a classy contemporary hotel with 19 boldly styled rooms, most sporting curtained beds, patterned walls and the names of famous operas. Out the back, there's a lovely inner patio, with a piano bar and snack spot opening onto it. Breakfast costs €5. Outside summer the hotel opens only some weekends; check ahead.

Restaurante Gurea CANTABRIAN, BASQUE €
(☎942 72 24 46; Calle Ignacio Fernández de Castro 11; mains €9-15; ⏱1-3.45pm & 8.15-11pm, closed Tue dinner & Wed) This friendly, elegant restaurant and social bar, hidden in a small street a few blocks east of the town centre, dishes up Basque-Cantabrian fare and can throw together excellent salads and *raciones*. You'll find a variety of fixed-price menus, from the weekday lunch menu (€14.50) to the *menú especial* (€24, lunch or dinner) to 'dinner for two' (€50).

Information

Oficina de Turismo (☎942 72 25 91; www.comillas.es; Plaza de Joaquín del Piélago 1; ⏱9am-9pm Jul–mid-Sep, 9am-2pm & 4-6pm Mon-Sat, 9am-3pm Sun mid-Sep–Jun) Just off the main plaza.

Getting There & Away

Autobuses La Cantábrica (p520) runs three to four daily buses between Comillas and Santander (€4, one hour), via Santillana del Mar. The main **bus stop** (Calle del Marqués de Comillas) is just west of the town centre.

San Vicente de la Barquera & Around

POP 4173

The fishing port of San Vicente de la Barquera, the final town on the western Cantabrian coast before you enter Asturias, sits handsomely on a point of land between two long inlets, backed by dramatic Picos de Europa mountainscapes. Together with Santander, Laredo and Castro Urdiales, it was one of the Cuatro Villas de la Costa, a federation of four dominant medieval ports that was converted into the province of Cantabria in 1779. The long sandy beaches east of town make it a busy summer spot.

Sights

Playas El Rosal & de Merón BEACH
Along the coast east of town, these two beautiful beaches are basically one broad, 4km-long golden strand. Merón gets some surf, while El Rosal enjoys the prettiest San Vicente views around from its western end. Heed the warning flags: red means don't swim, yellow means take care.

Iglesia de Nuestra Señora de los Ángeles CHURCH
(☎942 84 03 17; Calle Alta; adult/child €1.50/free; ⏱10am-2pm & 4-8pm Tue-Sun Jul–mid-Sep, reduced hours rest of year) The outstanding monument in San Vicente's old town is the Iglesia de Nuestra Señora de los Ángeles, commissioned by Alfonso VIII in 1210. Although Gothic, it sports a pair of impressive Romanesque doorways. Inside, the eerily lifelike statue of 16th-century Inquisitor Antonio del Corro (reclining on one elbow, reading) is deemed one of the best pieces of Renaissance funerary art in Spain. Behind the church, there are lovely views of the Río del Escudo estuary backed by mountains.

Castillo del Rey CASTLE
(Calle Padre Antonio; adult/child €2/1; ⏱10.30am-2pm & 4.30-8pm Jul & Aug, reduced hours Mar-Jun & Sep-Dec, closed Jan & Feb) San Vicente's 13th-century medieval castle, one of Cantabria's best preserved, tops the old part of town. Sights inside the castle are limited, and exhibits are Spanish-only, but on a clear day the views of the Picos de Europa, the Ría de San Vicente, the Atlantic Ocean and the town itself are spectacular.

Courses

Escuela de Surf Costa Norte SURFING
(☎609 282963; www.escueladesurfcostanorte.com; Avenida Francisco Giner de los Ríos 20; surfboard/wetsuit hire per hr €10/5, 2hr group class per person €30) Based just back from San Vicente's Playas El Rosal and de Merón, on the eastern side of the estuary, this popular surf school offers group classes (board and wetsuit included) and three- to seven-day surf camps of varied levels, along with surfboard and wetsuit hire and SUP (stand-up paddleboarding) sessions (€30).

Sleeping & Eating

Hotel Luzón HOTEL €€
(☎942 71 00 50; www.hotelluzon.net; Avenida Miramar 1; s/d/tr/q €45/70/95/115; ⏱closed Jan; 📶)

Surprises of the North

The small northern regions of Cantabria and Asturias are a delightful discovery. Green valleys stretch down from snow-topped peaks to beautiful beaches. Locals drink cider and eat fantastic seafood and cheese, and the region's fascinating history begins with some of the world's most outstanding cave art.

Spectacular Peaks

Rising majestically only 15km inland, the Picos de Europa mark the greatest, most dramatic heights of the Cordillera Cantábrica, with enough awe-inspiring mountainscapes to make them arguably the finest hill-walking country in Spain. You can ramble past high-level lakes, peer over kilometre-high precipices or traverse the magnificent Garganta del Cares gorge (p552).

Legendary Cider Bars

In a region that rolls out 80% of Spanish cider, Asturias' boisterous, fabulously fun *sidrerías* (cider bars) are a way of local life. There's no greater pleasure than knocking back a fizzing *culín* (cider shot), expertly poured from high above into a low-held glass (p532).

Ancient Cave Art

Humanity's first accomplished art was painted, drawn and engraved on the walls of European caves by Stone Age hunter-gatherers between about 39,000 and 10,000 BC, and reached some of its greatest artistic genius at the World Heritage-listed caves of Altamira (p521), Monte Castillo (p513) and Covalanas in Cantabria.

Glorious Beaches

Wild, rugged and unspoilt, the hundreds of secluded sandy stretches and mysterious coves that line the 550km-long Cantabrian and Asturian coast are some of Spain's most beautiful and breathtaking beaches, and when the waves are up, the region's surf scene comes alive.

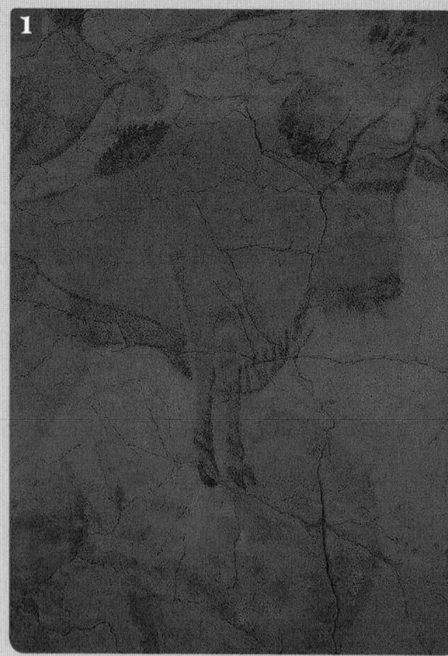

1. Museo de Altamira (p521) **2.** Praia As Catedrais (p582), Galicia **3.** Garganta del Cares, Central Picos (p552)

2

KSL/SHUTTERSTOCK ©

This centrally positioned two-star hotel occupies a stately, century-old stone townhouse, which still possesses an air of older times with its high ceilings, long corridors, ornate staircases and quiet drawing rooms. All 36 rooms are plain and simple, but most are spacious. Ask for a front room with broad views over town and water.

Boga-Boga SEAFOOD €€
(☎942 71 01 50; www.restaurantebogaboga.es; Plaza José Antonio 9; mains €11-24; ⏲1-4pm & 8-11pm year-round, closed Mon dinner & Tue Sep-Jun) Despite its less than stunning exterior, this popular seafood spot has a warm, maritime feel, its walls decked with Spanish warship insignia. Try the Boga-Boga hake, cooked in a clay pot with oil and garlic, the *marmita de bogavante* (seafood stew with European lobster) or unusual northern sea creatures such as *centollo* (spider crab) or *cabracho* (scorpion fish).

Information

Oficina Municipal de Turismo (☎942 71 07 97; www.sanvicentedelabarquera.es; Avenida del Generalísimo 20; ⏲10am-2pm & 4-8pm Jul & Aug, 9.30am-2pm & 5-8pm Sep, reduced hours rest of year)

Getting There & Away

BUS

San Vicente's **bus station** (☎942 71 08 33; Avenida Miramar), next to the Puente de la Maza, is served by **ALSA** (p512), **Autobuses Palomera** (p514) and **Autobuses La Cantábrica** (p520).

DESTINATION	FARE (€)	TIME (HR)	FREQUENCY
Gijón	10.90	2½	4 daily
Oviedo	9.10	2	5 daily, some via Llanes, Ribadesella & Arriondas
Potes	3.80	1¼	2 daily
Santander	5.15	1¼	6 daily, some via Comillas & Santillana del Mar

TRAIN

San Vicente's **train station** is at La Acebosa, 2km south of town. Two **FEVE** (p512) trains stop here daily on their way between Santander (€5.15, 1½ hours) and Oviedo (€11.15, 3½ hours).

ASTURIAS

'Ser español es un orgullo', the saying goes, *'ser asturiano es un título.'* 'If being Spanish is a matter of pride, to be Asturian is a mark of nobility.' Asturias, the sole patch of Spain never conquered by the Muslims is, some claim, the real Spain: the rest is simply *tierra de reconquista* (reconquered land).

This gorgeously green northern region has many similarities with Cantabria, its eastern neighbour. The jagged coast is wildly dramatic, strung with colourful fishing ports, such as Ribadesella and Cudillero, and more than 200 beaches. Inland, the mountains (including much of the Picos de Europa) soar high, the valleys run deep and the villages are delightfully rustic. For architecture lovers, Asturias is the land of the pre-Romanesque, most strikingly expressed in early medieval survivors such as the exquisite Iglesia de San Salvador de Valdediós or in the Unesco World Heritage monuments of Oviedo, Asturias' cultured capital.

Oviedo

POP 220,301 / ELEV 232M

The compact but characterful and historic *casco antiguo* (old town) of Asturias' civilised capital is agreeably offset by elegant parks and busy, modern shopping streets to its west and north. Oviedo is a fun, sophisticated city, with a stash of intriguing sights, some excellent restaurants and a lively student population. Out on the periphery, the hum and heave of factories is a strong reminder that Oviedo is a major producer of textiles, weapons and food.

Sights

★**Catedral de San Salvador** CATHEDRAL
(☎985 21 96 42; www.catedraldeoviedo.com; Plaza de Alfonso II; adult/senior/student/child €7/6/5/free; ⏲10am-8pm Jun-Aug, 10am-7pm Sep, 10am-1pm & 4-6pm Mar-May & Oct, 10am-6pm Nov-Feb, closed Sun year-round) Spanning nearly a millennium of architectural styles, Oviedo's stunning cathedral complex is the city's spiritual and artistic centrepiece. While the majority of the structure was built in Gothic and baroque styles between the 13th and 18th centuries, its origins and greatest interest lie in the 9th-century

Oviedo

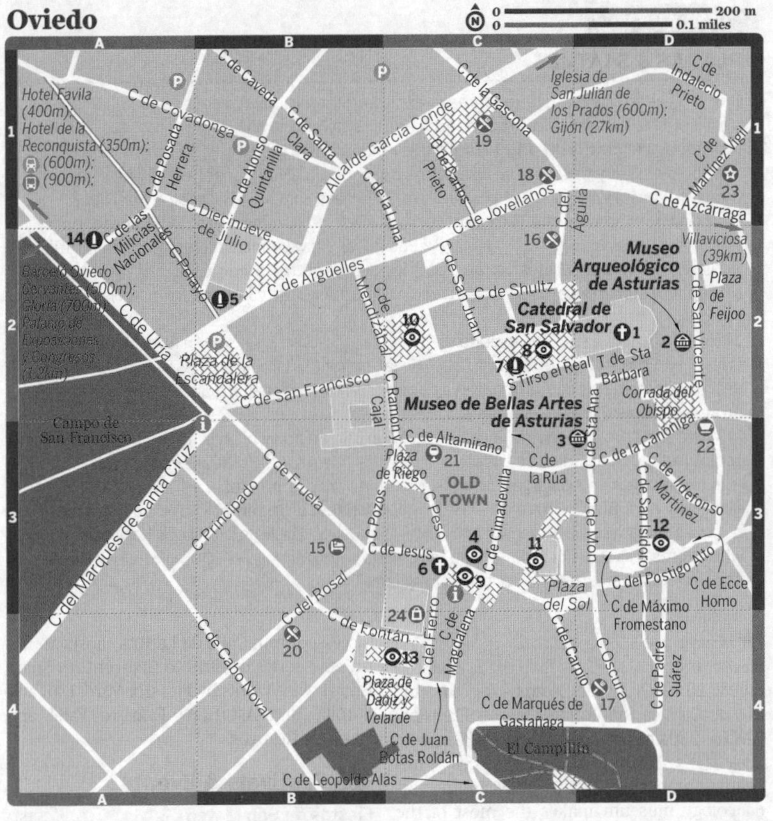

Oviedo

Top Sights
1 Catedral de San Salvador D2
2 Museo Arqueológico de Asturias D2
3 Museo de Bellas Artes de Asturias D3

Sights
4 Ayuntamiento C3
5 Culis Monumentalibus B2
6 Iglesia de San Isidoro C3
7 La Regenta Statue C2
8 Plaza de Alfonso II C2
9 Plaza de la Constitución C3
10 Plaza de Porlier C2
11 Plaza de Trascorrales C3
12 Plaza del Paraguas D3
13 Plaza Fontán C4
14 Woody Allen Statue A2

Sleeping
15 Hotel Fruela B3

Eating
16 Mar de Llanes C2
17 Sidrería El Fartuquín D4
18 Tierra Astur C1
19 Tierra Astur Parrilla C1
20 Veintiséis Grados B4

Drinking & Nightlife
21 La Leyenda del Gallo C3
22 Per Se D3

Entertainment
23 Ca Beleño D1

Shopping
24 Mercado El Fontán C4

Cámara Santa, a pre-Romanesque chapel built by Alfonso II to house exquisite holy relics. Enshrined in 1998 as a Unesco World Heritage site, the chapel now contains several key symbols of medieval Spanish Christianity.

DON'T MISS

PLAZAS & STATUES

One of Oviedo's greatest pleasures is exploring the old town's corners. The **Plaza de Alfonso II**, home of the cathedral, and the neighbouring **Plaza de Porlier** are fronted by elegant 17th- and 18th-century mansions. The **Plaza de la Constitución** occupies a barely perceptible rise at the heart of old Oviedo, capped at one end by the 16th-century **Iglesia de San Isidoro** (Mass 8pm Mon-Fri, noon & 8pm Sat & Sun) and bordered by the 17th-century **ayuntamiento** (Town Hall). Just south, past the colourful **Mercado El Fontán** (985 20 43 94; www.mercadofontan.es; Plaza 19 de Octubre; 8am-8pm Mon-Fri, to 3pm Sat) food market, the arcaded **Plaza Fontán** has a couple of *sidrerías* and passages leading in under pretty houses from surrounding streets.

Other attractive squares include the **Plaza de Trascorrales**, with its milkmaid statue, and the **Plaza del Paraguas**. The latter got its name from its inverted-umbrella design, which once accommodated an open-air market; today a giant concrete umbrella protects people from the elements.

Wandering around central Oviedo, you'll run into an array of striking, modern, open-air sculptures, such as Eduardo Úrculo's **Culis Monumentalibus** (Calle Pelayo), a pair of legs topped by a pair of large buttocks; Mauro Álvarez Fernández' **La Regenta** (Plaza de Alfonso II), a tribute to Leopoldo Alas' Oviedo-inspired, 19th-century novel *La Regenta*, outside the cathedral; and a **statue of Woody Allen** (Calle de las Milicias Nacionales), who expressed a particular affection for Oviedo when filming his 2008 film *Vicky Cristina Barcelona* here, describing it as 'a fairy tale'.

★Museo Arqueológico de Asturias MUSEUM

(985 20 89 77; www.museoarqueologicodeasturias.com; Calle de San Vicente 3-5; 9.30am-8pm Wed-Fri, 9.30am-2pm & 5-8pm Sat, 9.30am-3pm Sun) FREE Partly within a restored 16th-century monastery, Asturias' fascinating archaeology museum makes the most of the region's archaeological riches through video and informative artefact displays. Subject matter ranges from prehistoric cave art to *castro* (pre-Roman fortified village) culture, Roman times and the medieval Kingdom of Asturias. On the top floor, keep an eye out for relics from Oviedo's unique pre-Romanesque buildings (p530) and limestone-carved heads of medieval nobles. Explanatory details are in Spanish only, but staff will lend you an English or French guide booklet.

★Museo de Bellas Artes de Asturias MUSEUM

(985 21 30 61; www.museobbaa.com; Calle de Santa Ana 1; 10.30am-2pm & 4-8pm Tue-Sat, 10.30am-2.30pm Sun Jul & Aug, reduced hours rest of year) FREE Oviedo's Fine Arts Museum, housed in two of the city's finest palaces, has a large, rewarding and growing collection, featuring paintings by Spanish and European greats such as Goya, Zurbarán, El Greco, Ribera, Titian and Brueghel the Elder. The museum's sparkling-white 2015 **Ampliación** (accessed from Calle de La Rúa) hosts an impressive series of 19th- to 21st-century Spanish art, with works by Picasso, Miró, Dalí and Sorolla, and Asturians Evaristo Valle and Darío de Regoyos.

Festivals & Events

Fiestas de San Mateo FIESTA

(late Sep) Oviedo's biggest fiesta is that of San Mateo, celebrated in the third week of September and peaking on 21 September. For nine days, the city's plazas and concert halls buzz with live music, theatre, fireworks and a wide-ranging line-up of kids' events.

Sleeping

Hotel Favila HOTEL €

(985 25 38 77; www.hotelfavila.es; Calle Uria 37; s €32-45, d €40-59) It's certainly not the Ritz, but this little hotel has two big things going for it: dirt-cheap prices and an ultra-convenient location a stone's throw from Oviedo's train station. Rooms are perfectly passable, with dependable wi-fi, and there's a cafe-restaurant downstairs where you can grab breakfast in the morning.

★Barceló Oviedo Cervantes HOTEL €€

(985 25 50 00; www.barcelo.com; Calle de Cervantes 13; r €75-170, ste from €260) Comprising a revamped century-old mansion and two modern smoked-glass wings, the

Barceló is just two blocks northwest of the central Campo de San Francisco. Impeccably contemporary style runs right through it, from the reception's suspended mirrored orbs and the shiny, club-like lobby bar to the 72 spacious, luxurious rooms, with their chain curtains, masses of mirrors and glass-partitioned bathrooms.

Hotel Fruela HOTEL €€

(☎985 20 81 20; www.hotelfruela.com; Calle de Fruela 3; s €57-110, d €79-140; P❄️📶) With an attractive contemporary style, original art, professional yet friendly service and a cosy, almost intimate feel, the 28-room Fruela is easily the top midrange option in central Oviedo. Behind its gorgeously maintained late-19th-century facade, business-oriented rooms are bright and welcoming, with desks, dangling lamps and plenty of plugs for gadgets. Breakfast and tapas are available in the ground-floor cafe-restaurant.

Hotel de la Reconquista HISTORIC HOTEL €€€

(☎985 24 11 00; www.eurostarshoteldelareconquista.com; Calle de Gil de Jaz 16; r €130-190, ste €240-480; P❄️@📶) Oviedo's swishest lodgings, two blocks northwest of the Campo de San Francisco, was once an 18th-century hospice. The 142 rooms, in all shapes and sizes, frame two patios and are perfectly balanced between tradition and comfort, with timber furniture, tumbling curtains and floor-to-ceiling windows. Spanish royalty and other luminaries hang out here during the annual Príncesa de Asturias prizes jamboree.

Eating

Veintiséis Grados CAFE €

(☎985 73 83 31; www.facebook.com/veintiseisgrados; Calle del Rosal 13; breakfasts €2.10-4.50, mains €8-12; ⏰8am-11pm Mon-Thu, to midnight Fri, 9am-midnight Sat, 9am-5pm Sun; 📶) Insanely popular at all times of day, this cosy modern-rustic cafe and bakery with a semi-open patio-style entrance and murals on the walls is a particularly good bet for breakfast, coffees, pastries and sandwiches or even brunch. People type away on laptops and there's a fun city-life buzz.

★Tierra Astur SIDRERÍA, ASTURIAN €€

(☎985 20 25 02; www.tierra-astur.com; Calle de la Gascona 1; mains €9-33, menús €11-28; ⏰1-4.30pm & 8pm-midnight; 📶) A particularly atmospheric *sidrería*-restaurant famous for its prize-winning cider and ridiculously good-value *menú del día* (€10.80, lunch Monday to Friday). People queue for tables, settle for tapas at the bar or just buy traditional products for home. Try enormous salads, Asturian *cachopo* (stuffed breaded veal), giant grilled-veg platters, *tortos* (fried maize cakes) with a million toppings, or local cheese *raciones*.

For longer hours and excellent grilled meats, head one block down the street to their sister restaurant, **Tierra Astur Parrilla** (☎984 84 66 24; www.tierra-astur.com/parrilla; Calle Gascona 9; mains €13-33; ⏰1pm-1am).

★Gloria ASTURIAN €€

(☎984 83 42 43; www.estasengloria.com; Calle de Cervantes 24; tapas €4.50-6, raciones €12-18; ⏰12.30-6pm & 8.30pm-1am Mon-Sat, 12.30-6pm Sun; 📶) Two-Michelin-starred Asturian chef Nacho Manzano brings his culinary genius to Oviedo with this elegant *casa de comidas* (food house). Exquisitely prepared traditional dishes come as tapas, *medias raciones* or *raciones,* and there's a €20 weekday lunch menu. Lounge at the bar, or dine among suited professionals in the sultry, black-clad dining room with candlelit tables and leather booths. Bookings recommended.

Sidrería El Fartuquín SIDRERÍA, ASTURIAN €€

(☎985 22 99 71; www.restauranteelfartuquin.es; Calle del Carpio 19; mains €11.50-22, menús €10-16; ⏰1-4pm & 8pm-midnight Mon-Sat) The Fartuquín's busy little dining room offers an excellent range of well-priced Asturian meat, fish and seafood, plus a great-value set menu (€10), including wine, available at lunchtime Monday to Friday. There's a fancier €16 *menú* for Saturday lunch. *Ovetenses* (people from Oviedo) pack into the front bar for evening tapas.

Mar de Llanes SEAFOOD €€€

(☎984 29 22 84; www.mardellanes.es; Calle Águila 11; mains €22-25; ⏰1.15-3.30pm & 8.15-11.45pm Tue-Sun) All of the seafood served at this friendly, family-run eatery is freshly caught by the owners in Llanes. Appetizers of *rabas* (fried squid) and main courses of perfectly grilled *merluza* (hake) or *salmonete* (red mullet) come accompanied by sautéed vegetables, potatoes, crusty bread and superb olive oil in a simple, unpretentious dining room with sturdy wood tables and white linen tablecloths.

Drinking & Entertainment

For *sidrerías* head to Calle de la Gascona. On weekends, the old town's narrow pedestrian streets are packed with party-goers. The

DON'T MISS

PRE-ROMANESQUE OVIEDO

Largely cut off from the rest of Christian Europe by the Muslim invasion, the tough and tiny kingdom that emerged in 8th-century Asturias gave rise to a unique style of art and architecture known as pre-Romanesque.

The 15 buildings (six of which constitute a World Heritage site) that survive from the two centuries of the Asturian kingdom are mostly churches; they take some inspiration from Roman, Visigothic and possibly Carolingian French buildings, but have no real siblings. They are typified by straight-line profiles, semicircular Roman-style arches, and a triple-naved plan for the churches. In many cases the bases and capitals of columns, with their Corinthian or floral motifs, were simply cannibalised from earlier structures. The use of lattice windows as a design effect owes something to developments in Muslim Spain.

Some of the best of the genre are found in and near Oviedo, including the cathedral's **Cámara Santa** (p526). The **Iglesia de San Julián de los Prados** (Iglesia de Santuyano; ☎687 052826, 607 353999; Calle de Selgas 1; adult/child €2/0.50; ⏲10am-1pm Mon, 9.30am-1pm & 4-6pm Tue-Fri, 9.30am-12.30pm & 4-6pm Sat Jul-Sep, reduced hours rest of year), 1km northeast of the town centre, just above the A66, is the largest remaining pre-Romanesque church, and one of the oldest, built in the early 9th century under Alfonso II. It's flanked by two porches – another Asturian touch – and the inside is covered with wonderfully preserved geometric, floral and other frescos.

On the slopes of Monte Naranco, 3.5km northwest of central Oviedo, the tall, narrow **Palacio de Santa María del Naranco** (☎638 260163; Monte Naranco; adult/child incl Iglesia de San Miguel de Lillo €3/2, Mon free; ⏲9.30am-1pm & 3.30-7pm Tue-Sat, 9.30am-1pm Sun & Mon Apr-Sep, 10am-2.30pm Tue-Sat, 10am-12.30pm Sun & Mon Oct-Mar) and the restored **Iglesia de San Miguel de Lillo** (Iglesia de San Miguel de Lliño; ☎638 260163; Monte Naranco; adult/child incl Palacio de Santa María del Naranco €3/2, Mon free; ⏲9.30am-1pm & 3.30-7pm Tue-Sat, 9.30am-1pm Sun & Mon Apr-Sep, 10am-2.30pm Tue-Sat, 10am-12.30pm Sun & Mon Oct-Mar) were built by Ramiro I (842–50), and mark an advance in Asturian art. An outstanding decorative feature of the beautifully proportioned two-floor Santa María (probably originally a royal hunting lodge) is the *sogueado*, the sculptural motif imitating rope used in its columns. Some of its 32 medallions are copies of ancient Iranian motifs, known here through Roman contact. Of the original San Miguel, only one-third remains (the rest collapsed centuries ago), but what's left has a singularly pleasing form. In particular, note the one-stone lattice windows.

Just below, the **Centro de Interpretación del Prerrománico** (☎902 30 66 00, 985 18 58 60; www.prerromanicoasturiano.es; Monte Naranco; ⏲10am-2pm & 3.30-7.30pm Jul & Aug, 10am-1.30pm & 3.30-6pm Wed-Sun Feb-Jun & Sep-Dec, closed Jan; P) FREE has informative displays in English, Spanish and French. To get here, take bus A2 (€1.20), hourly from around 9.30am to 8.30pm, northwest from the Uría Norte stop at the northern end of Calle de Uría near the train station; bus A1 runs back down. By car, park 300m below Santa María and walk up.

From these two churches, you can hike, bike or drive the final 3km up to the **Monumento al Sagrado Corazón** (Monte Naranco; P), a 30m-high, 1981 stone sculpture of Christ, adorned with Asturias' Cruz de la Victoria (Cross of Victory), which crowns Monte Naranco. The views are sensational, with Oviedo sprawling below between often snow-topped peaks and the Bay of Biscay twinkling to the north.

Visits to San Julián, Santa María and San Miguel are guided (in Spanish), except on Monday when visits are without a guide.

main axis is Calle de Mon, with wall-to-wall bars, and its extension Calle Oscura, as well as adjacent Calles del Carpio and Postigo Alto and Plaza del Sol. Weekdays, old-town bars generally open until 1am and can be quiet. On Friday and Saturday, they're busy until at least 3am.

★**La Leyenda del Gallo** COCKTAIL BAR, CLUB

(☎984 84 06 84; www.facebook.com/laleyendadelgallo; Calle de Altamirano 9; ⏲1-4pm & 8pm-2.30am Tue, to 3.30am Wed & Thu, to 5.30am Fri & Sat) A keen young team has transformed this old-town house into Oviedo's hottest party spot. Inside, it's all mosaic floors, low lights and stone walls. Try one of the divine, expertly mixed, original cocktails – perhaps a gin-based basil-bramble sling. Book well ahead to taste inventive Spanish-international dishes (€10 to €19). At midnight, tables disappear and the place morphs into party mode.

Per Se CAFE, BAR

(Calle de la Canóniga 18; ⌚5pm-1am Sun & Mon, to 2.30am Tue & Wed, to 3.30am Thu, to 5.30am Fri & Sat; 🐾) This wonderfully comfy, cave-like cafe-bar is crammed with fairy lights, chunky mirrors, open-stone walls, tropical-print cushions and rattan lounge chairs. Kick back over coffee, homemade cakes or cocktails served in artsy jars. The vibe is friendly, mellow and (partly) studenty. There are regular swing-dance classes and poetry events.

Ca Beleño LIVE MUSIC

(www.facebook.com/cabeleno; Calle de Martínez Vigil 4; ⌚4.30pm-1am Sun-Wed, to 3.30am Thu-Sat) Oviedo's first craft-beer bar has five home-brews on tap and is also a well-established venue for Celtic music, whether of Asturian, Galician or Irish extraction. Live jams get going at around 10pm Thursday.

ℹ Information

Oficina de Turismo de Asturias (☎902 30 02 02, 984 49 35 60; www.turismoasturias.es; Plaza de la Constitución 4; ⌚9am-7pm Jun-Sep, 9am-6pm Mon-Fri, 10am-6pm Sat & Sun Oct-May) Covers all of Asturias.

Oficina de Turismo El Escorialín (☎985 22 75 86; oficina.turismo@oviedo.es; Calle del Marqués de Santa Cruz; ⌚10.30am-6pm) Oviedo's municipal tourist office, at the Campo de San Francisco.

ℹ Getting There & Away

AIR

The **Aeropuerto de Asturias** (☎902 40 47 04; www.aena.es; Santiago del Monte) is 47km north-west of Oviedo and 40km west of Gijón. Direct hourly buses leave Oviedo's bus station for the airport (€8, 40 minutes) from 7am to 8pm, plus 9.30pm, returning hourly from 7am to 7pm, plus 8.30pm, 10pm and 11.20pm.

Airlines and destinations include the following:

Air Europa (www.aireuropa.com) Mallorca and Tenerife.

EasyJet (www.easyjet.com) Geneva and London (Stansted).

Iberia (www.iberia.com) London (Heathrow) and Madrid.

Volotea (www.volotea.com) Ibiza, Málaga, Seville, Valencia and Munich.

Vueling Airlines (www.vueling.com) Barcelona and London (Gatwick).

BUS

ALSA (☎902 42 22 42; www.alsa.es) is the major company operating from Oviedo's **bus station** (☎985 96 96 96; www.estaciondeautobusesdeoviedo.com; Calle de Pepe Cosmen), 700m north of the central Campo de San Francisco.

DESTINATION	FARE (€)	TIME	FREQUENCY
Avilés	2.55	30min-1hr	every 15-30min, 6.30am-11pm
Cangas de Onís	7	1½hr	7-13 daily
Gijón	2.45	30min	every 10-30min, 6.30am-10.30pm
Llanes	10.75	1¼-2¾hr	10-11 daily
Madrid	34-59	5-7hr	12-13 daily
Ribadesella	8.05	1¼-2hr	6-8 daily
Santander	13-29	2¼-3hr	9-12 daily
Santiago de Compostela	30-43	4½-6¾hr	3-4 daily

TRAIN

Oviedo's one **train station** (☎912 43 23 43; Avenida de Santander; 📶) serves both train companies: **Renfe** (☎912 32 03 20; www.renfe.com), for destinations to the south, and **FEVE** (Renfe Ancho Métrico; ☎912 32 03 20; www.renfe.com/viajeros/feve), on the upper floor, for destinations along Spain's north coast.

Cudillero (€3.30, 1¼ hours, three direct FEVE trains daily)

Gijón (€3.30, 35 minutes, half-hourly or hourly Renfe *cercanías* 6.25am to 10pm)

León (€10 to €20, two to 2¾ hours, five to six Renfe trains daily)

Llanes (€8.55, 2¾ hours, three to four FEVE trains daily) Via Arriondas (€5.15, 1¾ hours) and Ribadesella (€6.65, 2¼ hours).

Luarca (€7.40, 2½ hours, two FEVE trains daily) Continuing into Galicia as far as Ferrol (€24.10, 7¼ hours).

Madrid (€33 to €55, 4¼ to 7¼ hours, six to eight Renfe trains daily)

Santander (€16.35, five hours, two FEVE trains daily) Via Arriondas, Llanes and Ribadesella.

ℹ Getting Around

Bus A2 (€1.20) runs up to the Monte Naranco monuments from the northern end of Calle Uría, near the train station; bus A1 runs back into town. **Transportes Unidos de Asturias** (www.tua.es) is a handy source for Oviedo's urban buses.

Gijón

POP 272,365

Bigger, grittier and gutsier than Oviedo, seaside Gijón (khi-*hon)* – Asturias' largest city – produces iron, steel and chemicals, and is the main loading terminal for Asturian coal. But Gijón has emerged like a phoenix from its industrial roots, having given itself a thorough face-lift with pedestrianised streets, parks, seafront walks, cultural attractions and lively eating, drinking and shopping scenes. It's a surprisingly engaging city, and a party and beach hot spot too, with endless summer entertainment. Though it's no quaint Asturian fishing port, Gijón sure knows how to live.

Gijón's ancient core is concentrated on the headland known as Cimadevilla, the old fishermen's quarter. The harmonious, porticoed Plaza Mayor marks the southern end of this promontory. To the west stretch the Puerto Deportivo (marina) and the broad golden Playa de Poniente. South lies the busy, 19th- to 20th-century city centre, bounded on its eastern side by Playa de San Lorenzo.

Sights

Plaza de Jovellanos SQUARE

An enticing web of narrow lanes and small squares wraps itself around the landward side of Cimadevilla, though the area was significantly damaged during the civil war. The Plaza de Jovellanos is dominated by the home of Gijón's most celebrated scion, the 18th-century Enlightenment politician Gaspar Melchor de Jovellanos, now the **Museo Casa Natal de Jovellanos** (☎985 18 51 52; http://museos.gijon.es; ⏲9.30am-2pm & 5-7.30pm Tue-Fri, from 10am Sat & Sun) FREE. A section of Gijón's **Roman walls** has been reconstructed stretching west from the plaza.

Festivals & Events

Fiesta de la Sidra Natural FOOD & DRINK

(Natural Cider Festival; ⏲Aug) Gijón's cider festival includes brewery tours, free tastings and an annual attempt on the world record number of people simultaneously pouring cider (9403 people in 2017). It takes place on Playa de Poniente during the fourth weekend in August.

LOCAL KNOWLEDGE

THE ART OF CIDER-DRINKING

Asturian cider is served *escanciada:* poured from a bottle held high overhead into a glass held low, which gives it some fizz. Don't worry, you don't have to do this yourself – bar staff will flaunt their own skills by not even looking at the glass or bottle as they pour, probably chatting to somebody else over their shoulder at the same time. A shot of cider, about one-fifth of a glass, is known as a *culete* or *culín;* immediately knock it back in one go (leaving a tiny bit in the glass), before the fizz dissipates.

Every Asturian town has plenty of *sidrerías* (cider bars) but the epicentre of the scene is Oviedo's El bulevar de la sidra (p529), lined with a dozen jam-packed *sidrerías*.

Asturias churns out 80% of Spanish cider: anything up to 45 million litres a year, depending on the apple harvest. About 95% of this is consumed in Asturias itself. Apples are reaped in autumn and crushed to a pulp (about three-quarters of which winds up as apple juice). The cider is fermented in *pipes* (barrels) kept in *llagares* (the places where the cider is made) over winter. It takes about 800kg of apples to fill a 450L *pipa*, which makes 600 bottles. Traditionally, the *pipes* were transported to *chigres* (cider taverns) and drinkers would be served direct from the *pipa*. The *chigre* is dying out, though, and most cider now comes in bottles in *sidrerías*.

Since 2002, a Denominación de Origen Protegida (DOP) Sidra de Asturias has been established for 21 Asturian ciders, which meet particular technical and quality standards and make exclusive use of indigenous Asturian apple varieties, such as Raxao and Xuanina – but this is certainly not to say that non-DOP ciders cannot be as good.

The main cider-producing region is east of Oviedo, centred on Gijón, Nava, Villaviciosa and Siero. Find out more at **Comarca de la Sidra** (www.lacomarcadelasidra.com) and **Consejo Regulador Sidra de Asturias** (www.sidradeasturias.es).

Semana Grande SUMMER FESTIVAL
(Aug) Gijón's biggest fiesta spans the first two weekends of August and the week between them, with concerts, dance sessions, fireworks and plenty of partying across the city's plazas, streets and beaches.

Sleeping & Eating

Hotel Central HOTEL €€
(985 09 86 51; www.hotelcentralasturias.com; Plaza del Humedal 4; s €49-59, d €52-79;) The warm, family-run Central may feel a little dated here and there, but it's by far one of Gijón's most characterful hotels, tucked away in its own fluffy-cushioned world 900m south of Cimadevilla, near the bus station. There are nine smallish but homey rooms, in a fuss-free, white-and-cream boutique style. Breakfast (€6) is served in the snug lounge.

Hotel Asturias HOTEL €€
(985 35 06 00; www.hotelasturiasgijon.es; Plaza Mayor 11; r €74-154;) The welcoming Asturias offers plain but spacious and comfy rooms in a super-central location, overlooking Cimadevilla's main square. 'Classic' rooms have a minimalist, old style and, for corner chambers, sea and plaza glimpses from glassed-in galleries. Less characterful 'modern' rooms are better equipped, with hydromassage baths or showers.

Restaurante Ciudadela ASTURIAN €€
(985 34 77 32; www.restauranteciudadela.com; Calle de Capua 7; tapas €7-15, mains & raciones €11-22; 12.30-4pm & 8pm-midnight Tue-Sat, 12.30-4pm Sun) Like most Gijón eateries, Ciudadela has a front tapas bar backed by a dining room, but here they're combined with a unique, cave-like basement recreating a Castilian bodega of yesteryear. Carefully concocted dishes encompass the best of Asturian cuisine, from daily €10 *pucheros* (casseroles/stews) to salads and *tortos* (maize cakes) to excellent seafood and meats. There's even a low-calorie selection.

La Galana ASTURIAN €€
(985 17 24 29; www.restauranteasturianolagalana.es; Plaza Mayor 10; mains & raciones €16-25; 1.30-4pm & 8pm-midnight;) The front bar is a boisterous *sidrería* for snacking on tapas (€8 to €18) accompanied by free-flowing cider. For a smarter dining experience, head to the spacious back room with mural-covered ceilings. Fish – like wild sea bass or *pixín* (anglerfish) with clams – is the strong suit. There are also excellent vegetarian dishes, including giant veg-tempura platters and beautifully prepared salads.

Casa Gerardo ASTURIAN €€€
(985 88 77 97; www.restaurantecasagerardo.es; Carretera AS19, Km 9, Prendes; mains €19-39, set menus €66-115; 1-3.45pm Tue-Sun, plus 9-10.45pm Fri & Sat; P) About 12km west of Gijón, this stone-fronted modern-rustic house has been serving top-quality local cooking since 1882. Five generations of the Morán family have refined their art to the point of snagging a Michelin star. The *fabada,* fish and shellfish are famously delectable. To best sample the Morán blend of tradition and innovation, go for one of the set menus.

Drinking & Nightlife

Hit the *sidrerías* (cider bars) in Cimadevilla, along Cuesta del Cholo (Tránsito de las Ballenas) and around town. Further up in Cimadevilla a student scene flourishes around Plaza Corrada. South of Cimadevilla, lively bars abound near Playa de San Lorenzo, along *la ruta de los vinos* (Calles del Buen Suceso, Santa Rosa and Begoña), and on Calles Rodríguez San Pedro and Marqués de San Esteban, parallel to Playa de Poniente.

Toma3 CAFE
(984 04 70 61; www.facebook.com/toma3gijon; Calle del Marqués de Casa Valdés 27; 11am-11pm Mon-Wed, to 1am Thu, to 3am Fri, noon-3am Sat, noon-11pm Sun;) With cushy velvet sofas and contemporary art on its whitewashed walls, this delightfully cosy, family-friendly coffee lounge and bookshop makes the perfect peaceful spot to linger over your *café con leche* or, later on, Spanish wines and the odd artisanal beer. A dynamic calendar of art shows, cooking demos, DJ nights and live music keep things hopping round the clock.

Varsovia COCKTAIL BAR
(984 19 68 42; www.varsoviagijon.com; Calle de Cabrales 18; 4pm-2am Sun-Thu, to 3am Fri & Sat) Bottles tower up to the ceiling at this sensational, split-level, open-stone-walled cocktail bar opposite the waterfront. Soak up the Playa de San Lorenzo scene through huge arched windows while sipping ambitious liquid creations such as the rum-based 'Purple' (made with violet liqueur), or perhaps a more conventional watermelon martini.

Information

The main tourist office, **Gijón Turismo** (☎985 34 17 71; www.gijon.info; Espigón Central de Fomento; ⏰10am-8pm May-Oct, 10am-2.30pm & 4.30-7.30pm Nov-Apr), on a Puerto Deportivo pier, is very helpful. There is also a **summer information booth** (Playa de San Lorenzo; ⏰May-Sep).

Getting There & Away

BUS

ALSA (p531) buses fan out across Asturias and beyond from the **bus station** (Calle de Magnus Blikstad).

DESTINATION	FARE (€)	TIME	FREQUENCY
Aeropuerto de Asturias	8	45min	hourly 6am-8pm & 9.30pm
Oviedo	2.45	30min-1hr	every 10-20min, 6.30am-10.30pm
Ribadesella	6.85	1½hr	7-10 daily
Santander	14.45	2¾-3½hr	12-15 daily

TRAIN

All **Renfe** (p531) and **FEVE** (p531) trains depart from the **Estación Sanz Crespo** (Calle Sanz Crespo), 1.5km west of the city centre. Destinations include Cudillero (€3.30, 1¾ hours, five to 10 direct FEVE trains daily) and Oviedo (€3.30, 35 minutes, two to three Renfe *cercanías* hourly 6am to 11.30pm).

Change at Pravia or Oviedo for most other FEVE destinations. Renfe also has several daily trains to León (€14 to €23, 2½ hours) and Madrid (€40 to €56, five hours).

East Coast Asturias

Mostly Spanish holidaymakers seek out a summer spot on the beaches and coves along the Asturian coast east of Gijón, backed by the Picos de Europa, which rise only 15km inland.

Villaviciosa & Around

POP 6386

About 27km east of Gijón, Villaviciosa rivals Nava as Asturias' cider capital. Apart from the Romanesque **Iglesia de Santa María**, its pretty little town centre is mostly a child of the 18th century.

Sights

Playa de Rodiles BEACH

(P) The beautiful, broad golden sands of 1km-long Playa de Rodiles, backed by pines and eucalyptus trees, front the sea at the mouth of the Ría de Villaviciosa, 11km north of Villaviciosa. Surfers might catch a wave here in late summer. Take the N632 northeast from Villaviciosa, then bear left on the VV6 through Selorio and follow signs to the beach.

Iglesia de San Salvador de Valdediós CHURCH

(☎670 242372; www.hospederiavaldedios.es; Valdediós; adult/child €4/1.50; ⏰11am-1.30pm & 4.30-7pm Tue-Sun Apr-Sep, 11am-1.30pm Tue-Sun Oct-Mar) The area surrounding Villaviciosa is sprinkled with ancient churches. Don't miss this beautifully preserved, triple-naved church, built in AD 893 as part of a palace complex for Alfonso III in the old Kingdom of Asturias' unique pre-Romanesque (p530) style. It's 9km southwest of Villaviciosa, well signposted off the AS267 to Pola de Siero.

Museo del Jurásico de Asturias MUSEUM

(MUJA; ☎902 30 66 00; www.museojurasicoasturias.com; Rasa de San Telmo, Colunga; adult/senior & child €7.24/4.70, Wed free; ⏰10.30am-8pm Jul & Aug, 10am-2.30pm & 3.30-6pm Wed-Fri, 10.30am-2.30pm & 4-7pm Sat & Sun Feb-Jun & Sep-Dec, closed Jan; P) Dotted with Jurassic-era fossils, the Asturian coastline between Gijón and Ribadesella is known as *La costa de la los dinosaurios* (the Dinosaur Coast). Asturias' popular claw-shaped Jurassic museum, 18km east of Villaviciosa and 24km west of Ribadesella, takes you through 4.5 billion years of prehistory, with dinosaur footprints, fossils and bones and 20 giant dinosaur replicas – the pair of mating tyrannosaurus is more than 12m high. Kids will love the dinosaur-themed playground.

Tours

El Gaitero BREWERY

(☎985 89 01 00; www.sidraelgaitero.com; La Espuncia, Villaviciosa; ⏰10am-12.45pm & 4-5.45pm Mon-Fri, 10am-12.45pm Sat mid-May–mid-Sep, 10am-12.30pm & 4-6.30pm Thu-Sun mid-Sep–mid-May) FREE For the full-blown cider experience, take a free tour of the long-standing El Gaitero cider-brewing bodegas, 2km northeast of central Villaviciosa on the N632. Set up in 1890, El Gaitero now produces up to

LOCAL KNOWLEDGE

WHAT'S COOKING IN ASTURIAS?

Fabada asturiana No dish better represents Asturias' taste for simplicity than the humble *fabada*, a hearty bean dish jazzed up with meat and sausage. For a taste of this classic favourite, head to Casa Cobrana (p546) in Parque Natural de Somiedo.

Ultra-tangy blue cheeses from the Picos de Europa King of Asturian cheeses is the powerful – but surprisingly moreish – blueish-green *queso de Cabrales*, made from untreated cow's milk, or a blend of cow's, goat's and sheep's milk, and matured in mountain caves. It often pops up in meat sauces or is poured on top of potatoes *(patatas al Cabrales)*. To sample local cheeses, order a *tabla de quesos* (platter of cheeses) at any sophisticated city eatery.

Seafood There is a wealth of fresh seafood in Asturias, while inland rivers provide trout, salmon and eels. You can go with good old, top-quality traditional fish preparations or explore a world of 'new-concept' seafood at the Real Balneario de Salinas (p539), near Avilés.

Cachopo This Asturian speciality of breaded veal stuffed with ham, cheese and vegetables is a carnivore's dream. Dig in at Tierra Astur (p529) in Oviedo.

27 million bottles of cider a year. One-hour guided visits (in Spanish) include a free tasting session and the detailed museum. Advance bookings recommended.

Sleeping & Eating

★La Casona de Amandi HISTORIC HOTEL €€
(☎985 89 34 11; www.lacasonadeamandi.com; Calle de San Juan 6, Amandi; s €65-90, d €85-130, all incl breakfast; P 📶) A warm welcome awaits at this exquisite 19th-century farmhouse surrounded by tranquil gardens, the most attractive lodgings in the Villaviciosa area. Wonderfully comfy rooms, all of which ooze their own character and vary in size, contain antique beds, plenty of pillows, hand-painted furnishings and organic soaps, and floors are original chestnut. Dinner available on request. It's located 1.5km south of Villaviciosa.

La Cacharrería ASTURIAN €€
(☎984 84 69 83; www.lacacharreriavillaviciosa.com; Calle del Agua 16, Villaviciosa; mains €12-18; ⏲12.30-4pm & 8-11pm Wed, Thu & Sun, to midnight Fri & Sat) Chequered floors and exuberantly colourful table settings set a festive mood at this recently opened eatery in Villaviciosa's town centre. Sample a smorgasbord of tasty small plates, from *tortos* (maize cakes) topped with blood sausage and candied mango, to fried codfish with lime-wasabi mayonnaise, to steak with wild mushrooms – and save room for cheesecake at dessert time!

Information

Oficina de Turismo de Villaviciosa (☎985 89 17 59; www.turismovillaviciosa.es; Calle Agua 29, Villaviciosa; ⏲10.30am-2pm & 4-7.30pm Wed-Sun Apr-Sep, 10.30am-2pm & 4-7.30pm Tue-Sat Oct-Mar) Inside the 16th-century Casa de los Hevia.

Getting There & Away

Villaviciosa's **bus station** (Calle Ramón Rivero Solares, Villaviciosa) is a few blocks northwest of the centre. **ALSA** (p531) has seven or more buses daily to Oviedo (€4.30, 30 minutes to one hour) and Ribadesella (€3.90, 35 minutes to one hour), and 13 or more to Gijón (€3, 25 minutes to one hour).

Ribadesella & Around

POP 2796 (RIBADESELLA)

Split in two by the Río Sella's estuary, Ribadesella is a low-key fishing town and lively beach resort. Its two halves are joined by the long, low Sella bridge. The western part (where most hotels are) has an expansive golden beach, Playa de Santa Marina, while the older part of town and fishing harbour are on the eastern side. Between Ribadesella and Llanes, 28km east along the coast, more than 20 sandy beaches and pretty coves await discovery.

Unless you've booked far ahead, it's best to stay away from Ribadesella on the first weekend of August, when the whole place goes mad for the Descenso Internacional del Sella canoeing festival.

Sights

★Cueva de Tito Bustillo CAVE

(☎985 18 58 60, reservations 902 30 66 00; www.centrotitobustillo.com; Avenida de Tito Bustillo; incl Centro de Arte Rupestre adult/senior, student & child €7.34/5.30, Wed free; ⏲10.15am-5pm Wed-Sun Mar-Oct; P) To admire some of Spain's finest cave art, including superb horse paintings probably done around 15,000 to 10,000 BC, visit this World Heritage–listed cave, 300m south of the western end of the Sella bridge. Daily visitor numbers are limited, so online or phone reservations are essential. Even if you miss the cave itself, the modern **Centro de Arte Rupestre Tito Bustillo** (adult/reduced €5.30/3.16, Wed free; ⏲10am-7pm Wed-Sun Jul & Aug, 10am-2.30pm & 3.30-6pm Wed-Fri, 10am-2.30pm & 4-7pm Sat & Sun Feb-Jun & Sep-Dec, closed Jan; P), 200m south, is well worth a visit for its displays, video and replicas.

Festivals & Events

Descenso Internacional del Sella CANOEING

(www.descensodelsella.com; ⏲Aug) The Río Sella is at its busiest on the first Saturday after 2 August, when hundreds of professional paddlers (followed by many more fun paddlers) head downriver to Ribadesella from Arriondas in the Descenso Internacional del Sella, an international kayaking and canoeing event that kicked off in 1930.

Sleeping & Eating

The lively waterfront *sidrerías* on the eastern side of the Río Sella are a good bet for seafood. Ribadesella also has some excellent top-end restaurants.

Villa Rosario HISTORIC HOTEL €€€

(☎985 86 00 90; www.hotelvillarosario.com; Calle de Dionisio Ruisánchez 3-6; r €89-275; ⏲Mar-mid-Jan; P ❄ @ 📶) Set inside a century-old *casa de indianos* (the house was built by a returned colonist), this luxurious, history-filled hotel overlooks Playa de Santa Marina. Interiors are tastefully styled with marble floors, rich-toned carpets and an original cherry-wood staircase, while white-on-white rooms are fashionably contemporary and minimalist. The Villa Rosario II block out back is cheaper but utterly lacking in historic character.

★Arbidel ASTURIAN €€€

(☎985 86 14 40; www.arbidel.com; Calle Oscura 1; mains €26-32, set menus €50-80; ⏲1.30-4pm & 8.30-11pm Tue-Fri, 1.30-4pm Mon & Sat, closed Jan) Much-loved, Michelin-starred Arbidel is famous for chef Jaime Uz's reinvention of classic Asturian flavours and ingredients with a distinctly modern flair – at non-exorbitant prices (relatively speaking). Exquisitely prepped, locally inspired delights might feature green-apple gazpacho, baked *pixín* (anglerfish) with squid noodles or a giant beef chop for two, but the good-value *degustación* menus are the way to go.

★La Huertona ASTURIAN €€€

(☎985 86 05 53; www.restaurantelahuertona.com; Carretera de la Piconera; mains €20-29, tasting menu €50; ⏲1.30-4pm Wed-Mon, 9-11.30pm Thu-Sun; P) Beautifully prepared, high-quality contemporary meat and seafood creations, complemented by an excellent selection of Spanish wines, mean top-notch dining at this airy, elegant restaurant with sprawling views across fields and gardens. Waiters in smart-white deliver red-hot sharing plates of sizzling meats that you cook yourself. Ask about the fresh, locally sourced fish-of-the-day offerings. It's 2km south from Playa de Santa Marina.

Information

Oficina de Turismo de Ribadesella (☎985 86 00 38; www.ribadesella.es; Paseo Princesa Letizia; ⏲10am-2pm & 4-8pm Jul & Aug, 10am-2pm & 4-6.30pm Tue-Sat, 11am-2pm Sun Sep-Jun) At the eastern end of the Sella bridge.

Getting There & Away

BUS

ALSA (p531) buses depart from the **bus station** (Avenida del Palacio Valdés), 300m south of the Sella bridge, east of the river.

DESTINATION	FARE (€)	TIME	FREQUENCY (DAILY)
Gijón	6.85	1½-1¾hr	6
Llanes	2.75	40min	7
Oviedo	8.05	1-1¾hr	6
Santander	8.05	1½-2½hr	2

TRAIN

Three or four **FEVE** (p531) trains run daily to/from Oviedo (€6.65, 2¼ hours), Arriondas (€1.85, 30 minutes) and Llanes (€2.55, 35 minutes), and two to/from Santander (€9.65, 2¾ hours).

Llanes & Around

POP 13,759 (LLANES)

Inhabited since ancient times, Llanes was for a long time an independent-minded town and whaling port with its own charter, awarded by Alfonso IX of León in 1206. Today, with a small medieval centre, a bustling harbour and some sensational beaches within easy reach, it's one of northern Spain's more popular holiday destinations. While not particularly exciting in itself, it makes a handy base for the Asturias coast, with the Picos de Europa also close at hand.

Sights

Bufones de Arenillas LANDMARK

(Puertas de Vidiago) The Bufones de Arenillas is a dozen geyser-style jets of seawater, which are pumped up through holes in the earth by the pressure of the tides – with heavy seas, some jets can spurt a spectacular 20m high (it's dangerous to get too close). When seas are calm, you'll just hear air and water whooshing eerily through the tunnels below.

From Puertas de Vidiago (6km east of Llanes) on the N634, signs lead you past the church 2km (along a bumpy track) to the Bufones.

Cueva del Pindal CAVE

(608 175284; www.artepaleoliticoenasturias.com; Pimiango; adult/reduced €3.13/1.62, Wed free; tours 10.30am, noon & 1.30pm Wed-Sun, plus 3.30pm Jul & Aug) The World Heritage–listed Cueva del Pindal, 2km northeast of Pimiango, contains 31 Palaeolithic paintings and engravings of animals, mostly in ochre, including bison, horses and rare depictions of a mammoth and a fish. It's not in the same league as Cantabria's Altamira (p521) or Ribadesella's Tito Bustillo (p536) caves, but it was the first prehistoric cave art discovered in Asturias. With its setting among wooded sea cliffs, close to a 16th-century chapel, ruined Romanesque monastery and interpretation centre, it's an appealing visit.

Cave visits must be booked by phone at least one day ahead; the maximum group size is 20, and children under seven are not allowed. It's signposted off the N634, 21km east of Llanes. En route, you'll pass a spectacular **coastal lookout**, about 1km before the cave.

Sleeping & Eating

Plenty of lively *marisquerías* (seafood eateries) and *sidrerías* line Calles Mayor and Manuel Cué, so finding a place to tuck into sea critters and wash them down with cascades of cider will be no problem here.

★**Cae a Claveles** DESIGN HOTEL €€

(985 92 59 81, 658 110774; www.caeaclaveles.com; La Pereda; s €95-120, d €100-140; P) Absolutely not what you'd expect in countryside Asturias, this exquisitely contemporary five-room design pad with a chic urban feel is built to resemble a little hill. The slim, curvy, low-rise structure doubles as its warm artist-owner's home studio: her creations adorn the walls. Alluring, airy doubles channel cool minimalism, splashed with rich colours and flooded with light through floor-to-ceiling windows.

There's plenty of outdoor space for lounging against a beautiful mountain backdrop, plus bar service. It's 4km south of Llanes.

★**La Posada de Babel** DESIGN HOTEL €€

(985 40 25 25; www.laposadadebabel.com; La Pereda; s €75-90, d €99-128, ste €135-170; mid-Mar–mid-Dec; P) About 4km south of Llanes, this unique spot combines striking modern architecture and bold design with sprawling lawns and a relaxed yet civilised vibe, all inspired by its owners' extended travels through Asia. The 12 different rooms occupy four contrasting buildings, including one in a typical Asturian *hórreo* (grain store) on stone stilts.

The kitchen (breakfast €7.50, dinner €28) puts an emphasis on market-fresh and organic food.

El Bálamu SEAFOOD €€€

(985 41 36 06; www.facebook.com/elbalamu; Barrio Valles; tapas €4-14, mains €19-29; 1-4pm & 8.30-11.30pm, closed Wed) From outside, this unassuming portside spot resembles a cavernous gray warehouse, but climb the stairs to find Llanes' best seafood eatery, where fish comes straight from the boat to your plate. Snack on *rabas* (fried squid) and *gambas al ajillo* (garlic shrimp) at the bar, or reserve ahead for a table under the sleek slanted windows overlooking the harbour.

Information

Oficina de Turismo (985 40 01 64; www.llanes.es; Calle Marqués de Canillejas, Antigua Lonja; 10am-2pm & 5-9pm mid-Jun–mid-Sep, 10am-2pm & 4-6.30pm Mon-Sat, 10am-2pm Sun mid-Sep–mid-Jun) The tourist office can tell you about plenty of good walking routes in the area, including the 5000km E9 coastal path that passes through here on its journey from Portugal to Russia.

WORTH A TRIP

BEACHES AROUND LLANES

More than 20 sandy stretches and concealed coves lie scattered along the dramatic coastline between Llanes and Ribadesella, 28km west.

Playa de Torimbia (Niembro) This beautiful, gold-blonde crescent bounded by rocky headlands and a bowl of green hills, 9km west of Llanes, is truly spectacular. It's also a particularly popular nudist beach. Turn off the AS263 at Posada to reach Niembro (2km), from where it's a further 2km to the beach; it's well signposted through Niembro's narrow streets. You have to walk the last kilometre or so, which keeps the crowds down.

Playa de Toranda (Niembro) About 8km west of Llanes, Playa de Toranda is a beach dramatically backed by fields and a forested headland. To get here, turn off the AS263 at Posada and head 2km northwest to Niembro; the beach is 500m beyond Niembro and well signed.

Playa de Gulpiyuri (Naves) More a sight than a sunbathing spot, this magical, 50m-long hidden cove framed by cliffs and greenery is one of Spain's most famous inland beaches. It doesn't front the sea, but you can hear waves sloshing through underwater tunnels to reach its gold-toned sands. To get here, turn north off the AS263 or A8 at the eastern end of Naves – the beach is 500m north, with the final 300m on foot.

You can also walk here from Playa de San Antolín, 1.5km southeast.

Playa de la Ballota (Andrín) A particularly attractive 350m-long beach 4.5km east of Llanes, hemmed in by green cliffs and signposted down a dirt track from the LLN2 Cué–Andrín road.

Getting There & Away

BUS

ALSA (p531) operates from the **bus station** (☎985 40 24 85; Calle Bolera).

DESTINATION	FARE (€)	TIME	FREQUENCY (DAILY)
Arriondas	4.55	30-60min	5-7
Gijón	8.75	2hr	4-5
Oviedo	10.75	1¼-2¼hr	11-12
Ribadesella	2.75	20-40min	7-11
San Vicente de la Barquera	2.25	30min	4-7
Santander	5.95	1½-2hr	4-8

TRAIN

Three or four **FEVE** (p531) trains arrive daily from Oviedo (€8.55, 2¾ hours), Arriondas (€4, 65 minutes) and Ribadesella (€2.55, 40 minutes), two of them continuing on to Santander (€7.80, 2¼ hours).

West Coast Asturias

The cliffs of Cabo Peñas, 20km northwest of Gijón, mark the start of the western half of Asturias' coast, which includes its most northerly and highest (almost 100m) points. The industrial steel-producing town of Avilés is a world away from the peaceful, colourful fishing ports of Cudillero and Luarca, to its west. Further west, you'll reach Galicia. Gorgeous sandy stretches and towering cliffs dot this entire coastline.

Avilés

POP 75,744

Avilés, 29km west of Gijón and 34km north of Oviedo, is an old estuary port and steel-making town. The historic core's elegant colonnaded streets and its central Plaza de España, fronted by two fine 17th-century buildings, make for a lovely stroll, and there are some good, authentic Asturian restaurants to enjoy in town. While you're here, you might catch one of the occasional innovative, independent Spanish and global music, theatre, cinema or art events at the Centro Cultural Internacional Oscar Niemeyer.

Sights

Centro Cultural Internacional Oscar Niemeyer CULTURAL CENTRE

(Centro Niemeyer; ☎984 83 50 31; www.niemeyercenter.org; Avenida del Zinc; tours adult/child €3/2; ⏲tours 5pm Wed-Fri, 12.30pm & 5pm Sat & Sun Sep-Jun, 12.30pm & 5pm daily Jul & Aug) This multifaceted international cultural centre, founded in 2011 on once-industrial land just east across the river from the city centre, was designed by Brazilian architect Oscar Niemeyer as a gift to Asturias, and as a cultural nexus between the Iberian Peninsula and Latin America. The bold-white complex now hosts a range of independent avant-garde theatre, music, cinema, literature and art shows. Informative one-hour **guided tours** (in Spanish) take in the auditorium and dome, detailing Niemeyer's work both here and elsewhere.

Sleeping & Eating

Hotel Don Pedro HOTEL €€
(☎627 561723, 985 51 22 88; www.hdonpedro.com; Calle de La Fruta 22; s €50-70, d €65-80, tr €75-90;) Just off the central Plaza de España, Hotel Don Pedro has attractive, comfy rooms with exposed stone or brick, velvet sofas, rich colour schemes and rugs on wooden floors.

Casa Tataguyo ASTURIAN €€
(☎985 56 48 15; www.tataguyo.com; Plaza del Carbayedo 6; mains €12-22; ⊙1-4pm & 8pm-late) Tucked into a busy, restaurant-lined plaza, Tataguyo has being going strong since the 1840s. Feast on delectable classic meat- and fish-focused Asturian fare, including frills-free *cocidos* (stews) and *lechazo al horno* (roast lamb), or keep it light with platters of cold meats and cheeses and piled-high salads. The high-quality, three-course lunchtime *menú* (€16, including wine) is popular.

★**Real Balneario de Salinas** ASTURIAN, SEAFOOD €€€
(☎985 51 86 13; www.realbalneario.com; Avenida de Juan Sitges 3, Salinas; mains €25-36, menús €50-154; ⊙1-3.30pm & 8-11.30pm Tue-Sat, 1-3.30pm Sun, closed mid-Jan–mid-Feb) Serious food lovers: head to the seaside suburb of Real Balneario de Salinas, 5.5km northwest of central Avilés. Opened as a beachside bathing centre by King Alfonso XIII in 1916, today it's a top seafood restaurant. Choose from traditional or creative 'new concept' dishes, plus some very tempting desserts. Lobster is a current favourite; the long-standing speciality is champagne sea bass.

Information

Oficina de Turismo (☎985 54 43 25; www.avilescomarca.info; Calle de Ruiz Gómez 21; ⊙10am-8pm Jul–mid-Sep, 10am-2pm & 4.30-6.30pm Mon-Fri, 10.30am-2.30pm Sat & Sun mid-Sep–Jun) Just off the main Plaza de España.

Getting There & Away

BUS

From the **bus station** (Avenida Telares), 800m north of the central Plaza de España, **ALSA** (p531) buses run frequently to Oviedo (€2.55, 30 to 60 minutes, at least 37 buses daily) and Gijón (€2.40, 30 minutes, at least 27 buses daily).

TRAIN

From the **train station** (Avenida Telares), 700m north of the Plaza de España, trains head to Gijón (€1.95, 40 minutes, at least 31 times daily), some with connections for Oviedo (€3.30, 1½ to two hours).

Cudillero

POP 1355

Cudillero, 60km northwest of Oviedo, is the most picturesque fishing village on the Asturian coast – and it knows it. The houses, painted in a rainbow of pastels, cascade down to a tiny port on a narrow inlet. Despite its touristy feel, Cudillero is reasonably relaxed and makes an appealing stop, even in mid-August when every room in town is taken. The surrounding coastline is a dramatic sequence of sheer cliffs and fine beaches.

Sights

Playa del Silencio BEACH
(Castañeras) This is one of Spain's most beautiful beaches: a long, silver-sandy cove backed by a natural rock amphitheatre. It isn't particularly good for swimming due to underwater rocks, but it's a stunning spot for a stroll and, weather permitting, some sun-soaking. It's 15km west of Cudillero: take the A8 west, then exit 441 for Santa Marina, and head west on the N632 to Castañeras, from where the beach is signposted. The last 500m down is on foot.

Playa de Aguilar BEACH
(Muros de Nalón; P) The nearest beach to Cudillero is the fine, sandy Playa de Aguilar, which is 5km east on the AS317 from El Pito to Muros de Nalón. Immediately east and accessed by a short path from the joint car park lies tiny, cliff-framed **Playa de Xiró**.

Mirador de La Garita-Atalaya VIEWPOINT
A tangle of narrow, sloping, twisting streets threads up to this battered lookout point perched high above the harbour. Up top, riveting views extend across Cudillero's rooftops, past the boats bobbing in the port and out to the open Atlantic. It's a spectacular spot to watch the sunset.

Sleeping & Eating

La Casona de Pío HOTEL €€
(☎985 59 15 12; www.lacasonadepio.com; Calle del Ríofrío 3; s €59-73, d €73-98; ⊙closed mid-Jan–mid-Feb;) Pocketed away right behind the port is this charming, rustic-style hotel in a 200-year-old stone building, featuring 11 very comfortable rooms with hydromassage baths, earth-toned decor and, in some cases, timber terraces festooned with flowers. It serves a terrific breakfast (€7.70) full of home-made goodies.

Hotel Casa Prendes HOTEL €€
(☎985 59 15 00; www.hotelcasaprendes.com; Calle San José 4; r €65-85, 2-person apt €65-100, 4-person apt €90-130;) A brilliantly maintained two-star in a bright blue townhouse just back from Cudillero's harbour, Casa Prendes offers nine comfy, stone-walled rooms with colourful curtains and flower-print bedspreads, attentive service and a small private breakfast cafe. The friendly owners also rent seven apartments nearby.

El Faro SEAFOOD €€
(☎985 59 15 32; Calle del Ríofrío 4; mains €14-22; ⊙noon-4pm & 8pm-midnight Thu-Tue) Though it doesn't enjoy sea views, this smart, attractive eatery is tucked one street back from the port. Stone, timber, colourful artwork and cool cream decor create a welcoming atmosphere for digging into fish of the day, *merluza* (hake) in a variety of styles, fish-filled salads, *parrilladas de marisco* (mixed grilled shellfish) or *arroz caldoso* (seafood and rice stew).

Information

Oficina de Turismo de Cudillero (☎tourist office 985 59 13 77, town hall 985 59 00 03; www.turismocudillero.com; Puerto del Oeste; ⊙10am-2pm & 4-7.30pm Jul & Aug, shorter hours rest of year) By the port. On low-season weekdays, it operates from the *ayuntamiento* (town hall), just behind the port.

Getting There & Away

BUS

From the **bus stop** (Calle Juan Antonio Bravo), at the top of the hill 800m from the port, three or more daily **ALSA** (p531) buses go to Gijón (€5.55, 1¼ to 1½ hours) via Avilés (€3.20, 50 minutes), where you can connect for Oviedo.

CAR

The only place to park is at the port, in front of the tourist office.

TRAIN

The **train station** (Camin de la Estación) for **FEVE** (p531) services is 2km inland from the port: trains to Gijón (€3.30, 1½ to two hours) run about hourly until 6pm (fewer on weekends); for Oviedo (€3.30, 1½ to 2¼ hours) you usually change at Pravia.

Luarca & Around

POP 5013

Marginally less scenic than its rival coastal town Cudillero, Luarca has a similar setting in a deep valley running down to an expansive harbour full of colourful fishing boats. It's a handy base for some good nearby beaches and the last major Asturian stop before you enter Galicia to the west.

Sights

Mirador de la Atalaya VIEWPOINT
(P) Find your way up to Luarca's Atalaya lookout, with its small church, surprisingly elaborate cemetery and dramatic coastal vistas, above the port's northeastern end. Luarca's mariners' guild met for centuries at the nearby **Mesa de Mareantes**, where the town's history is now told in colourful tiles.

Ermita de la Regalina CHAPEL, VIEWPOINT
(Cadavedo) Spectacularly positioned on a grassy headland fringed by jagged cliffs, sandy beaches and crashing seas, this delicate little blue-and-white chapel 16km east of Luarca is absolutely worth finding for the sensational views alone. A couple of typical stilted Asturian *hórreos* (grain stores) complete the panorama. From Luarca, head 13km east on the A8; take exit 451 for Cadavedo and follow signs to Playa de Cadavedo, then Ermita de la Regalina.

Cabo Busto AREA
(Busto) Twelve kilometres east of Luarca, wind-lashed Cabo Busto gives you an idea of the Asturian coast's wildness as waves crash onto its rocky cliffs below a 19th-century lighthouse. The coastal views are fantastic.

To get here, turn off the A8 about 9km east of Luarca and follow a well-signposted series of back roads 4km north to Cabo Busto.

Castro de Coaña ARCHAEOLOGICAL SITE
(☎985 97 84 01; www.castrosdeasturias.es; Coaña; adult/reduced €3.20/1.60, Wed free; ⊙10.30am-5.30pm Wed-Sun Apr-Sep, to 3.30pm Oct-Mar; P) The small town of Coaña lies 4km inland from the port of Navia, 19km west of Luarca. Two kilometres south, the hillside Castro de

Coaña is one of northern Spain's best-preserved Celtic settlements, dating back to the 4th century BC and well worth visiting. From the visitors centre, where you'll find Spanish-language exhibits on local Celtic history, a walking path leads to Coaña's well-preserved collection of stone foundations, evocatively perched on a green hillside with sweeping views.

Playa de Barayo BEACH

(Barayo; P) Part of a protected nature reserve, Playa de Barayo is a good sandy beach in a pretty bay at the mouth of a river winding through wetlands and dunes. Turn off the N634 11km west of central Luarca onto the NV2 towards Puerto de Vega; after 800m turn right towards Vigo (1.5km) and follow signs. From the car park, the beach is accessible by a well-marked, 30-minute hike.

Playa de Cueva BEACH

(Cueva; P) Soft, 600m-long Playa de Cueva, 7km east of Luarca on the old N634 coast road, is one of the district's top beaches, with cliffs, caves, a river and occasional decent surf. It's signposted.

Sleeping & Eating

★Hotel Torre de Villademoros CASA RURAL €€

(☎985 64 52 64; www.torrevillademoros.com; Villademoros, Cadavedo, Valdés; s €63-87, d €88-132, ste €286;) The crowning glory of this gorgeous country retreat, 17km east of Luarca, is its eponymous medieval tower, recently converted into a luxurious three-level suite. Just as appealing are the hotel's 10 beautifully appointed rooms; the spacious, relaxing common areas; and the good on-site restaurant. Out back, trails lead through the surrounding fields to dramatic coastal bluffs.

★3 Cabos HOTEL €€

(☎985 92 42 52; www.hotelrural3cabos.com; Carretera de El Vallín, Km 4; incl breakfast d €105-125, tr €135-155; mid-Feb–Dec; P@) A beautiful contemporary conversion of a 120-year-old farmhouse, 3 Cabos enjoys fabulous panoramas from its elevated inland site. Its six exquisitely designed, well-equipped rooms feature open-stone walls, comfy beds and spacious bathrooms. Best are the top-floor, sea-facing, attic-design rooms, with original timber beams.

El Barómetro SEAFOOD €€

(☎985 47 06 62; Paseo del Muelle 5; mains €8.50-19; 1-4.30pm & 8.30-11pm) Ask Luarca locals to recommend the best seafood in town, and they'll point you to this portside eatery with its vintage barometer embedded in the wall out front. Specialities include *arroz con bogavante* (rice with fresh local lobster) and *calamares en su tinta* (squid cooked in their own ink). Its lunchtime *menú especial* (€14) is especially popular. Book ahead.

Information

Oficina Municipal de Turismo de Luarca
(☎985 64 00 83; www.turismoluarca.com; Plaza Alfonso X; 10.30am-1.45pm & 4-7.15pm, shorter hours in winter)

Getting There & Away

BUS

From Luarca's **bus station** (Calle García Prieto), 150m east of Plaza Alfonso X in the heart of town, at least four daily **ALSA** (p531) buses run east to Oviedo (€9.90, 1¼ to 1¾ hours) and west to Ribadeo (€6.95, 1¾ hours) in Galicia.

TRAIN

The **FEVE** (p531) train station is 800m south of the town centre. Two trains run daily east to Cudillero (€3.60, 1¼ hours) and Oviedo (€7.40, 2¾ hours), and west to Ribadeo (€4.75, 1½ hours) and as far as Ferrol (€16.35, 4¾ hours) in Galicia.

Inland Western Asturias

There's some gorgeous country in southwest Asturias. Even just driving through on alternative routes into Castilla y León can be rewarding, such as the AS228 via the 1587m **Puerto Ventana**, the AS227 via the beautiful 1486m **Puerto de Somiedo** or the AS213 via the 1525m **Puerto de Leitariegos** – all scenic mountain roads crossing dramatic passes.

Most people head off biking along the popular Senda del Oso cycling and hiking path, where you stand a good chance of spotting four Cantabrian brown bears in a hillside enclosure. Further west, the green-covered valleys of the Parque Natural de Somiedo, a Unesco-listed biosphere reserve, lie well off the beaten track.

Senda del Oso

The Senda del Oso (Path of the Bear) is a popular cycling and walking track along the course of a former mine railway, southwest of Oviedo. The most popular stretch runs 20km between the villages of Tuñón and Entrago. With easy gradients, it runs through increasingly spectacular valley scenery into

Wild Spain

Spain is one of Europe's best destinations for watching wildlife. Most of the excitement surrounds three species – the Iberian lynx, the Iberian wolf and the brown bear – but birdwatchers also rave about the twitching possibilities in Spain. Other opportunities include whale-watching off the south coast, especially from Tarifa, and Europe's only primates, the Barbary macaques, in Gibraltar.

Iberian Lynx

The beautiful *lince ibérico* (Iberian lynx), one of the most endangered wild cat species on Earth, once inhabited large areas of the peninsula, but numbers fell below 100 at the beginning of the 21st century. A captive-breeding program and the reintroduction of captive-bred lynx into the wild have seen the wild population reach an estimated 320 individuals, with a further 150 in captivity.

The two remaining lynx populations are in Andalucía: the Parque Nacional de Doñana (with around 80 lynxes); and the Sierra Morena (nearly 250) spread across the Guadalmellato (northeast of Córdoba), Guarrizas (northeast of Linares) and Andújar-Cardeña (north of Andújar) regions.

Iberian Wolf

Spain's population of *lobo ibérico* (Iberian wolf) has been stable at between 2000 and 2500 for a few years now, up from a low of around 500 in 1970. Though officially protected, wolves are still considered an enemy by many country people and the hunting of wolves is still permitted in some areas. The species is found in small populations across the north, including

ALFREDO GARCIA/SHUTTERSTOCK ©

IVAN VIEITO GARCIA/SHUTTERSTOCK ©

APPLE2499/SHUTTERSTOCK ©

1. *Lobo ibérico* (Iberian wolf) **2.** *Oso pardo* (brown bear) **3.** *Lince ibérico* (Iberian lynx)

the Picos de Europa. But Europe's densest and most easily accessible wild wolf population is in the Sierra de la Culebra, close to Zamora. Riaño, close to León, is another possibility.

Brown Bear

The charismatic *oso pardo* (brown bear) inhabits the Cordillera Cantábrica (in Cantabria, Asturias and northern Castilla y León) with a further, tiny population in the Pyrenees – close to 250 bears survive, spread across the two populations. The last known native Pyrenean bear died in October 2010. The current population, which is on the rise thanks to intensive conservation measures, is entirely made up of introduced bears from Slovenia and their offspring.

The best place to see brown bears in the wild is the Parque Natural de Somiedo in southwestern Asturias. There is also a small chance of seeing bears in the Picos de Europa. A bear enclosure and breeding facility at Senda del Oso, also in Asturias, is a good chance to get a little closer.

Tour Operators

In addition to numerous local operators, the following outfits run recommended wildlife-watching tours:

Iberian Wildlife (www.iberianwildlife.com)

Julian Sykes Wildlife Holidays (www.juliansykeswildlife.com)

Nature Trek (www.naturetrek.co.uk)

Wild Wolf Experience (www.wildwolfexperience.com)

Wildwatching Spain (www.wildwatchingspain.com)

THERE'S A BEAR IN THERE

The wild mountain area of southwest Asturias and northwestern Castilla y León, including the Parque Natural de Somiedo, is the main stronghold of Spain's biggest animal, the brown bear *(oso pardo)*. Bear numbers in the Cordillera Cantábrica have climbed to more than 250, from as low as 70 in the mid-1990s, including a smaller population of around 40 in a separate easterly area straddling southeast Asturias, southwest Cantabria and northern Castilla y León. Killing bears has been illegal in Spain since 1973, but only since the 1990s have concerted plans for bear recovery been carried out. Experts are heartened by the fact there has been at least one recent case of interbreeding between the western and eastern groups.

This lumbering beast can reach 300kg and live 25 to 30 years, and has traditionally been disliked by farmers – despite being almost entirely vegetarian. Public support has played a big part in its recent recovery in the Cordillera Cantábrica, which owes a lot to the celebrated bears of Asturias' Senda del Oso (p541), southwest of Oviedo. Experts warn that the bear population is not yet completely out of the woods – illegal snares set for wild boar and poisoned bait put out for wolves continue to pose serious threats, as do forest fires, new roads and ski stations, which reduce the bears' habitat and mobility. Poaching has also claimed the lives of at least two bears in the last few years.

You can see bears in semi-liberty at the **Cercado Osero** on the Senda del Oso. The **Fundación Oso Pardo** (www.fundacionosopardo.org) is Spain's major resource and advocate for brown bears and its Centro de Interpretación 'Somiedo y El Oso', in Pola de Somiedo, is a good place to brush up on bear facts.

deep, narrow canyons, with several bridges and more than 30 tunnels. It also offers the high probability of seeing Cantabrian brown bears in a large enclosure at Cercado Osero (which is probably as close as you'll ever get to them), and it's a fun outing with (or without) the kids.

More recently opened branch tracks, south from Entrago to Cueva Huerta, and southeast from Caranga to Ricabo in the Valle de Quirós, have increased the total rideable track to 48km.

Sights

★Cercado Osero WILDLIFE RESERVE

(☎985 96 30 60; www.osodeasturias.es) About 5.5km south of Tuñón (or a 1.1km walk south from the Área Recreativa Buyera, where cars can park), the Senda del Oso cycling and hiking path reaches the Cercado Osero, a 40,000-sq-metre hillside compound that's home to three female Cantabrian brown bears: Paca, Tola and Molina. The two older bears, Paca and Tola, were orphaned as cubs by a hunter in 1989. Since 2008, they've lived in a second 7000-sq-metre enclosure just below the path at the same spot.

Parque de la Prehistoria MUSEUM

(☎902 30 66 00, 985 18 58 60; www.parquedelaprehistoria.es; San Salvador de Alesga; adult/reduced €6.12/3.57; ⏲10.30am-8pm Jul & Aug, 10.30am-2.30pm & 4-6pm Wed-Sun Feb-Jun & Sep-Dec, closed Jan; P) Four kilometres south of Entrago, this park-museum is well worth a visit for its excellent introduction to Spanish and European cave art. It includes replicas of Asturias' World Heritage–listed Tito Bustillo (p536) and Candamo caves and France's Niaux cave, along with a good museum-gallery that explains much of the what, when, who, how and why of Europe's Palaeolithic cave-art phenomenon.

Adjacent to the museum, visitors can observe modern-day descendants of prehistoric horses, cows and bison grazing peacefully in their enclosures.

Casa del Oso MUSEUM

(☎985 96 30 60; www.osodeasturias.es; Proaza; ⏲10am-2pm & 4-6pm) FREE Proaza's Casa del Oso is the headquarters of the Fundación Oso de Asturias, which runs the Paca-Tola bear conservation project, and has exhibits on Spanish brown bears. It also doubles up as the tourist office, offering info on the Senda del Oso and other local activities.

Activities

Numerous trailside outfitters hire out bikes (€9 to €22) for day trips on the Senda del Oso. Some offer the option of a one-way downhill ride from Entrago to Tuñon, with van transport back to Entrago.

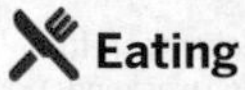

Eating

★ L'Esbardu ASTURIAN €€

(☎985 76 11 52; www.lesbardu.es; Calle El Puente, Proaza; mains €8.50-20; ⏲2-4pm Wed-Sun, plus 8.30-11pm Fri & Sat;) Break your bike ride at this wonderfully rustic, stone-walled, wood-beamed eatery in Proaza. Diners crowd around tables draped in red-and-white checked tablecloths for skillets of comfort food (potatoes, eggs, sausages, ham and peppers), bean stews, and wild game specialities including venison, goat and wild boar. There's also an extensive vegetarian menu.

Information

Regional tourist information is available in the **Casa del Oso**, at the north end of Proaza.

Getting There & Away

Pullmans Llaneza (☎985 46 58 78; www.pullmansllaneza.com) runs three or four daily buses from Oviedo bus station to Tuñón (€2, 30 minutes), Proaza (€2, 45 minutes) and Entrago (€2.50, one hour), terminating at San Martín, 1km beyond Entrago and 3km before the Parque de la Prehistoria.

Parque Natural de Somiedo

If you fancy exploring beautiful mountain country that few foreigners reach, head for this 291-sq-km, Unesco-listed biosphere reserve on the northern flank of the Cordillera Cantábrica. Composed chiefly of five valleys descending from the Cordillera's 2000m-plus heights, the park combines thick woodlands, rocky mountains and high pastures dotted with *brañas* (groups of now largely abandoned *cabanas de teito* – thatched herders' shelters). It's also a key stronghold of Spain's bear population.

The main population centre is plain **Pola de Somiedo** (70km southwest of Oviedo), which has a bank, an ATM, a supermarket, a petrol station and the park's Centro de Interpretación del Parque Natural de Somiedo (p546). **Valle de Lago**, reached by a wonderful 8km drive southeast of Pola de Somiedo that winds and climbs to about 1300m, is another base, with good walking.

Sights

Centro de Interpretación 'Somiedo y El Oso' MUSEUM

(☎942 23 49 00, 985 76 34 06; www.fundacionosopardo.org; Calle Flórez Estrada, Pola de Somiedo; adult/child €3/1; ⏲11am-2pm & 5-9pm mid-Jun–mid-Sep, 11am-2pm & 4-7pm Sat & Sun late Apr–mid-Jun & mid-Sep–Oct) Run by the Fundación Oso Pardo, this exposition is a good place to brush up on facts about Northern Spain's brown bears, with informative displays and videos (in Spanish) that include details about the species' continuous battle for survival.

Activities

One of Somiedo's best (and most popular) walking areas is the **Valle de Lago**, whose upper reaches contain glacial lakes and high summer pastures. Here the **Ruta de Valle de Lago** (6km, around 2½ hours one way) trail leads to Asturias' most expansive lake. You must leave vehicles in Valle de Lago village.

Other good walks include the **La Peral–Villar de Vildas** route in the upper Pigüeña valley (13km, around five hours one way), which passes one of the largest and best-preserved *brañas,* La Pornacal; and the challenging ascent of **El Cornón** (2194m), the park's highest peak (14km, around nine hours return).

Heading east from Somiedo towards the Senda del Oso, you'll find more good hiking opportunities at the **Puerto de San Lorenzo**, a 1347m pass where the the road crosses the **Camín Real de la Mesa** (GR101), an ancient track linking Astorga (Castilla y León) with the Asturian coast.

Alto Aragón HIKING

(☎616 452337; www.altoaragon.co.uk) Experienced British guide Richard Cash leads occasional hiking tours in the Parque Natural de Somiedo, with an emphasis on local botany, wildlife, birds and butterflies. Weeklong tours run for about €1000 per person, and include quality accommodation, guide services, ground transport and meals. His company also offers nature-oriented tours elsewhere in Spain, from the Pyrenees to Doñana National Park.

Sleeping & Eating

★ Palacio de Flórez-Estrada HISTORIC HOTEL €€

(☎616 170018, 985 76 37 09; www.florezestrada.com; Pola de Somiedo; s €60-70, d €80-90, apt €70-80, ste €90-110; ⏲rooms Apr-Oct, apt year-round; P) A gorgeous, old-world riverside mansion in sprawling gardens just off the road to Valle de Lago, on the eastern side of Pola de Somiedo. Cosy rooms occupy a 15th-century tower, simple meals are served and the owner hosts various cultural events and yoga retreats. The four two-person apartments, inside revamped stables on the same pretty site.

Auriz APARTMENT €€
(☎619 320001; www.auriz.es; Calle Álvaro Florez Estrada 8, Pola de Somiedo; 2-/4-/6-person apt €90/125/160; ⏰closed mid-Jan–early Feb; P 📶 🐾) Six excellent, modern, two-floor, three-bedroom apartments have kitchens and wood-burning stoves, all bursting with colour, beside a trout stream. They're just off the road to Valle de Lago, on the eastern side of Pola de Somiedo.

Casa Cobrana ASTURIAN €€
(☎687 483388, 985 76 37 48; Valle del Lago; mains €11-20; ⏰8.30am-10.30pm Thu-Tue Jun-Sep, closed Tue dinner) For traditional Asturian mountain cuisine, you can't beat this simple restaurant in Valle del Lago's village centre. Classics such as *fabada asturiana* and *cachopo de setas al Cabrales* (veal stuffed with wild mushrooms and Cabrales cheese) are served at sturdy wood tables, while football matches play on the big-screen TV. Order ahead for delicacies such as *cabrito guisado* (stewed kid goat).

ℹ Information

Centro de Interpretación del Parque Natural de Somiedo (☎985 76 37 58; www.parquenaturalsomiedo.es; Pola de Somiedo; ⏰10am-2pm & 4-8pm Mon-Sat, to 6pm Sun Jun-Sep, shorter hours Oct-May) Has ample free information on the park and its walking trails.

ℹ Getting There & Away

BUS

An **ALSA** (p531) bus departs Oviedo bus station for Pola de Somiedo (€8.65, two hours) at 5pm Monday to Friday and 10am on weekends, returning from Pola at 6.45am (5.30pm on weekends).

CAR

With your own wheels, you can approach Somiedo from the Senda del Oso area by the spectacular AS265 west from San Martín to La Riera, via the Puerto de San Lorenzo pass (1347m, often snowed under in winter).

ℹ PICOS WEBSITES

El Anillo de Picos (www.elanillodepicos.com) Useful for mountain *refugios* (walkers' huts).

Incatur Picos de Europa (www.picosdeeuropa.com) For the Asturian Picos.

Liébana y Picos de Europa (www.liebanaypicosdeeuropa.com) For the eastern Picos.

Organismo Autónomo Parques Nacionales (www.mapama.gob.es/en/red-parques-nacionales) Spain's official national parks site.

PICOS DE EUROPA

The jagged, deeply fissured Picos de Europa straddle southeast Asturias, southwest Cantabria and northern Castilla y León, offering some of Spain's finest walking country – and some of Europe's most spectacular mountain scenery.

The Picos comprise three majestic massifs: the eastern Macizo Ándara, with a summit of 2444m; the western Macizo El Cornión, rising to 2596m; and the particularly rocky Macizo Central (or Macizo de los Urrieles), reaching 2648m. The 671-sq-km **Parque Nacional de los Picos de Europa** covers all three massifs. At the park's higher elevations, open meadows filled with grazing cattle are backed by a wild landscape of sparkling lakes and imposing limestone peaks; down below, sheer rock faces plunge into a series of stunning river gorges.

Virtually deserted in winter, the area bursts with visitors in August. July is not far behind. June and September are quieter and just as likely to be sunny as August.

ℹ Information

MAPS

The best maps of the Picos, sold in shops in Cangas de Onís, Potes and elsewhere for €5 to €6 each, are Adrados Ediciones' *Picos de Europa* (1:80,000), *Picos de Europa Macizos Central y Oriental* (1:25,000) and *Picos de Europa Macizo Occidental* (1:25,000).

TOURIST INFORMATION

The national park has three main information centres.

Centro de Información Casa Dago (p549) For the Western Picos; in Cangas de Onís. Offers Picos-wide hiking and access info.

Centro de Visitantes Sotama (p555) For the Eastern Picos; on the N621 in Tama, 2km north of Potes. Provides hiking details and excellent exhibitions on Picos geology, rivers and wildlife.

Oficina de Información Posada de Valdeón (☎987 74 05 49; www.valdeon.org; El Ferial, Posada de Valdeón; ⏰8am-3pm Mon-Fri

Picos de Europa

year-round, 9am-2pm & 4-6.30pm Sat & Sun Jul-Sep) For the Southern Picos. Hours can vary considerably.

Other information points are open at strategic places around the national park from 1 July to 15 September and during other major national holidays. Local tourist offices provide information, too.

Getting There & Around

CAR & BUS

The main access towns for the Picos are Cangas de Onís in the northwest, Arenas de Cabrales in the central north, Potes in the southeast and Posada de Valdeón in the south. Paved roads lead from Cangas southeast up to Covadonga and the Lagos de Covadonga; from Arenas south up to Poncebos then east up to Sotres and Tresviso; from Potes west to Fuente Dé; and from Posada de Valdeón north to Caín (this one's extremely narrow in parts).

The four main access towns have fair to good bus connections with other places in Cantabria, Asturias and Castilla y León, but only a few bus services (mostly in summer) will get you into the hills from the access towns.

TAXI

As well as regular taxis that stick to the better roads, such as the cooperative **Taxitur** (p550) in Cangas de Onís, there are 4WD taxi services that can manage some of the mountain tracks. Several of these offer 4WD day trips in the Picos, typically for €50 per person.

Western Picos

Approaching the Picos from the Asturian (western) side, the Macizo Occidental (El Cornión) unfolds in a series of gorgeous high-altitude lakes, green-on-green pastures and bald-rock panoramas. Plain Cangas de Onís is the area's main base, with a host of outdoor activities, while unassuming Arriondas, 8km to the northwest, is the starting point for kayak and canoe rides down the Río Sella. About 10km southeast of Cangas lies holy Covadonga, famous as the first spot in Spain where the Muslims were defeated. From Covadonga, a twisting mountain road straggles up to the beautiful (and incredibly popular) Lagos de Covadonga, where several fine hiking trails begin.

Arriondas

ELEV 85M

The ordinary little town of Arriondas, 8km northwest of Cangas de Onís, is the base for hugely popular and fun kayak and canoe trips down the pretty Río Sella to various end points between Toraño and Llovio (7km to 16km, 1½ to four hours).

Arriondas is mayhem on the first Saturday after 2 August, when tens of thousands of people converge for the Descenso Internacional del Sella (p536), an international kayaking and canoeing event that sees hundreds of serious paddlers starting off downriver to Ribadesella at noon, followed by many more fun paddlers later on.

Activities

Local agencies can hire out a kayak, paddle, life jacket and waterproof container for the Río Sella trip, show you how to paddle and bring you back to Arriondas at the end. This stretch of the Sella has a few entertaining minor rapids, but it isn't a serious white-water affair, and anyone from about eight years old can enjoy the outing. The standard charge, including a picnic lunch, is €25/15 per adult/child. Starting time is normally between 11am to 1pm. Bring a change of clothes.

Agencies in Cangas de Onís and nearby coastal towns offer much the same deal, including return transport to Arriondas.

Sleeping & Eating

★Posada del Valle HOTEL €€

(☎985 84 11 57; www.posadadelvalle.com; Collía; s €62-68, d €77-94; ⊙Apr-Oct; P 📶) This remarkable, English-run spot, in a beautiful valley 3km north of Arriondas, is not only a charming 12-room rural retreat and a wonderful walking base, but also a multifaceted sustainable-living experience. Design and decor emphasise local art and artistry, and all rooms have valley views.

About 35% of the food served comes fresh from the hotel's organic farm (managed partly for wildflower conservation). Breakfasts (€9) and four-course dinners (€26; nonguests by pre-booking only) always include a vegetarian option.

Self-guided walking information is provided for the Picos de Europa and Asturias coast, as well as the local area. Also on offer are various **courses and workshops**, including organic cooking, Spanish conversation and felt-making. It's just past Collía village, on the AS342.

★Casa Marcial GASTRONOMY €€€

(☎985 84 09 91; www.casamarcial.com; Calle La Salgar, La Salgar; menús €98-148; ⊙1-3pm & 9-11pm Tue-Sat, 1-3pm Sun) Hidden in gorgeous countryside north of Arriondas is this double-Michelin-starred restaurant in Asturian chef Nacho Manzano's childhood home. Even the 'short' menús here are 12-course extravaganzas, showcasing local seafood (mussels, hake, clams, red mullet, limpets stewed in cider) and Manzano's trademark renderings of regional classics such as *fabada asturiana* (white-bean stew) and *arroz con pitu* (slow-cooked chicken and rice).

El Corral del Indianu ASTURIAN €€€

(☎985 84 10 72; www.elcorraldelindianu.com; Avenida de Europa 14; mains €28-39; ⊙1.30-4pm Fri-Wed, 9-11pm Fri, Sat, Mon & Tue) Putting a gourmet spin on traditional Asturian cooking, this Michelin-starred favourite is Arriondas' most original dining spot. If you don't fancy the highly creative and extensive tasting *menús* (€60 to €89), go for modernised Asturian *fabada* (bean, meat and sausage stew) or *tortos de maíz* (maize cakes) and guacamole, followed by baked hake in cider sauce with toasted onions.

Getting There & Away

BUS

From Oviedo, **ALSA** (☎902 42 22 42; www.alsa.es) runs at least seven buses daily to Arriondas (€6.25, 1¼ hours), continuing from there on to Cangas de Onís (€1.50, 15 minutes). There are also five or more daily ALSA buses to Arriondas from Llanes (€4.55, 30 minutes to one hour) and three or more from Ribadesella (€1.80, 25 minutes), on the eastern Asturian coast.

TRAIN

Arriondas is on the FEVE railway line between Oviedo, Ribadesella, Llanes and Santander, with up to four train services running in each direction daily.

Cangas de Onís

POP 6368 / ELEV 84M

The largely modern and rather unremarkable Asturian town of Cangas de Onís, 30km west of Arenas de Cabrales, was (briefly) the first capital of the medieval Kingdom of Asturias. Today it's the major launchpad for excursions into the western Picos. In August especially, Cangas bursts with trekkers, campers and holidaymakers. Nonetheless, it's a decent, friendly base, with more than enough facilities and plenty of opportunities for adventure activities nearby.

Sights

Puente Romano BRIDGE

Arching like a cat in fright, the so-called 'Roman Bridge' that spans the Río Sella was actually built in the 13th century, but is no less beautiful for its mistaken identity. From it hangs a 1939 copy of the Cruz de la Victoria, the symbol of Asturias that resides in Oviedo's cathedral.

Capilla de Santa Cruz CHAPEL

(Avenida Contranquil; adult/child €2/free; ⏲10am-2pm & 4-7pm Mon-Sat Jul & Aug, mornings only Sep-Jun) This tiny chapel was built in the mid-20th century to replace its 8th-century predecessor (erected by Pelayo's son Favila), which was destroyed during the Spanish Civil War. The 1940s rebuilders discovered that the mound the chapel sits on was an artificial one containing a 5000-year-old megalithic tomb; it's now visible beneath the chapel's floor. Visits are semi-guided in Spanish, English or French; enquire at the tourist office (p549).

Sleeping & Eating

For typical *sidrerías* – cider houses serving Asturian specialities such as *fabada asturiana* (bean, sausage and meat stew) and *cachopo* (stuffed breaded veal) – head to Calles de Constantino González and Ángel Tarano, between Avenida de Covadonga and Cangas' second river, the Río Güeña. There are plenty more eating options on and around central Calle San Pelayo.

Hotel Nochendi HOTEL €€

(☎985 84 95 13; www.elmolin.com/nochendi; Avenida Constantino González 4; r €65-110; ⏲Mar-Oct; wifi) Spread across one sparkling floor of a modern apartment block beside the Río Güeña, the Nochendi is a lovely surprise and an easy place to feel at home. The 12 spacious, spotless, bright rooms feature comfy beds, spot lighting, all-white decor and a touch of modern art, and most have river views.

Parador de Cangas de Onís HISTORIC HOTEL €€€

(☎985 84 94 02; www.parador.es; Villanueva de Cangas; r €140-180; P ❄ wifi) Cangas' *parador* (luxurious state-owned hotel) overlooks the Río Sella, 3km northwest of town. The main building, with 11 gorgeously characterful rooms, was originally a monastery, built between the 12th and 18th centuries on the site of early Asturian king Favila's palace. Rooms have a comfortable, classical style; some are former monks' cells (though suitably upgraded!). There's a smart on-site **restaurant** (mains €19-25, menús €26-57; ⏲8-11am, 1.30-4pm & 8.30-11pm).

La Sifonería ASTURIAN €€

(☎985 84 90 55; www.lasifoneria.net; Calle San Pelayo 28; dishes €9-20; ⏲noon-4pm & 8pm-midnight Wed-Mon) Crammed with ancient cider-making siphons, blue-and-white-tiled walls and photos of the friendly cider-pouring owners, this wonderfully down-to-earth tapas spot is perfect for tucking into uncomplicated Asturian cooking at good prices. Try Cabrales cheese croquettes, *tortos* (maize cakes) and a variety of *revueltos* (scrambled-egg dishes) or heartier classics such as *cachopo*. There's just a handful of bench-style tables.

★El Molín de la Pedrera ASTURIAN €€€

(☎985 84 91 09; www.elmolin.com; Calle Río Güeña 2; mains €17-26; ⏲noon-4.30pm & 8.30-11.30pm Thu-Mon, noon-4.30pm Tue) This good-value, stone-and-brick-walled, family-run eatery wins with both its traditional Asturian dishes – such as *fabada*, *tortos de maíz* and local cheese platters – as well as more creative efforts such as filo parcels with Cabrales cheese and hazelnuts, and delicious homemade desserts. Excellent meat dishes, welcoming service and good wines complete a top dining experience.

Shopping

Quesos Aquilino FOOD & DRINKS

(☎985 94 71 06; www.quesosaquilino.com; Calle Ángel Tárano 1; ⏲9am-10pm) Cangas abounds in shops selling Asturian food and drink specialities. This place, in business since 1865, is packed floor-to-ceiling with one of the region's best selections of local cheeses, meats, ciders, marmalades and liqueurs.

Information

Centro de Información Casa Dago (☎985 84 86 14; Avenida de Covadonga 43; ⏲8am-2.30pm Mon-Fri, 9am-2pm & 4-7pm Sat & Sun) Offers Picos hiking info and free guided walks from July to September (bookings recommended).

Oficina de Turismo (☎985 84 80 05; www.cangasdeonis.es; Avenida de Covadonga 1; ⏲9am-9pm Jul–mid-Sep, 10am-2pm & 4-7pm Mon-Sat, 10am-2pm Sun mid-Sep–Jun)

Getting There & Away

ALSA runs at least seven daily buses from Oviedo to Cangas (€7, 1½ to two hours) and back, all stopping in Arriondas en route. Cangas' bus station is in the Barrio La Pedrera on the northern side of the Río Güeña, linked by a footbridge to the town centre.

Taxis stick to the better roads and are a good alternative to the buses. **Taxitur** (☎985 84 87 97) offers service in Cangas.

Covadonga

POP 54 / ELEV 260M

Though Covadonga, 10km southeast of Cangas de Onís, is also a spectacular spot with a striking 19th-century basilica tucked between soaring mountains, its importance lies in what it represents.

Somewhere hereabouts, in approximately AD 722, the Muslims suffered their first defeat in Spain, at the hands of the Visigothic nobleman (and, later, Asturian king) Pelayo – an event considered to mark the beginning of the 800-year Reconquista. According to legend, before the battle the Virgin appeared to Pelayo's warriors in a hillside cave here. Covadonga is still an object of pilgrimage today.

Sights

Santa Cueva CAVE

(9am-7pm) FREE In this cave, now with a chapel installed, the Virgin supposedly appeared to Pelayo's warriors before their AD 722 victory over the Muslims. Weekends and summers see long queues of the faithful and curious lining up to enter. The cave's two tombs are claimed to be those of Pelayo himself, his daughter Hermesinda and her husband Alfonso I.

Basílica de Covadonga CHURCH

(9am-7pm) Covadonga's original wooden church burnt down in 1777 and landslides destroyed much of the settlement in the 19th century. The main church, the Basílica de Covadonga, is a neo-Romanesque affair built between 1877 and 1901.

Getting There & Away

Three or more **ALSA** (p548) buses daily run from Cangas de Onís to Covadonga (€1.50, 15 minutes). From late July to mid-September, a shuttle bus (€1.50) operates to Covadonga from four car parks (per vehicle €2) in Cangas de Onís (beside the bus station).

Lagos de Covadonga

Don't let summer crowds deter you from continuing 12km uphill past Covadonga to these two beautiful little lakes, set against jaunty (often snow-topped) peaks. Most day trippers don't get past patting a few cows' noses and snapping photos near the lakes, so walking here is as delightful as anywhere else in the Picos.

Lago de Enol is the first lake you'll reach, with the main car park and an info point just beyond it (downhill). It's linked to **Lago de la Ercina**, 1km away, not only by the paved road but also by a footpath (part of the PRPNPE2) via the Centro de Visitantes Pedro Pidal (p551), which has displays on Picos flora and fauna.

En route, about 8km uphill from Covadonga, the **Mirador de la Reina** is worth a stop for its dramatic panoramas across hills to the Bay of Biscay.

Activities

The Lagos de Covadonga are the starting point for several fine walks.

A marked loop walk, the **Ruta de los Lagos** (PRPNPE2; 5.7km, about 2½ hours), takes in the two lakes, the Centro de Visitantes Pedro Pidal (p551) and an old mine, the Minas de Buferrera. About 400m southwest of Lago de Enol, the route passes the **Refugio Vega de Enol** (Casa de Pastores; ☎630 451475; www.facebook.com/refugioenol; Lago de Enol; dm €15; year-round;), whose 16 bunks are the nearest accommodation to the lakes. It has a hot shower, serves good food (mains €8 to €15) and is reachable by vehicle.

Two other relatively easy trails from the lakes will take you slightly further afield. The PRPNPE4 leads 7.6km southeast from Lago de la Ercina, with an ascent of 610m, to the **Vega de Ario**, where the **Refugio Vega de Ario** (Refugio Marqués de Villaviciosa; ☎656 843095, 984 09 20 00; www.refugiovegadeario.es; dm adult/child €15/8; Easter & Jun-Oct) has 40 bunks and meal service. The reward for about three hours' effort in getting there is magnificent views across the Garganta del Cares to the Picos' Macizo Central.

The PRPNPE5 leads you roughly south from Lago de Enol to the 59-bed **Refugio de Vegarredonda** (☎985 92 29 52, 626 343366; www.vegarredondaremis.com; dm adult/child €15/8; Mar-Nov) at 1410m, with meal service, and on to the **Mirador de Ordiales**, a lookout point over a 1km sheer drop into the Valle de Angón. It's a 10km (about a 3½-hour) walk each way – relatively easy along a mule track as far as the *refugio,* then a little more challenging on up to the mirador. Track conditions permitting, drivers can save about 40 minutes by driving as far as the Pandecarmen car park, 2km south of Lago de Enol.

Information

Centro de Visitantes Pedro Pidal (985 84 86 14; www.parquenacionalpicoseuropa.es; 10am-6pm Easter & mid-Jun–mid-Oct) Between the two Lagos de Covadonga, with displays on Picos wildlife, plus some hiking info.

Getting There & Away

BUS

From July to mid-September, and on occasional holiday weekends throughout the year, a shuttle bus (day ticket adult/child €8/3.50) operates to the Lagos de Covadonga from four car parks (parking per vehicle €2) beside the bus station in Cangas de Onís, as well as along the road between there and Covadonga.

CAR

To avoid traffic chaos from July to mid-September and during some other major holidays, private vehicles cannot drive up from Covadonga to the Lagos de Covadonga from about 8.30am to 8pm. They can, however, drive up to the lakes before 8.30am or after 8pm, and can then drive down at any time.

TAXI

A regular taxi costs €30 one way from Cangas de Onís to the Lagos de Covadonga, €48 round trip with one hour's waiting time at the lakes, or €60 round trip with an hour at the lakes and 30 minutes in Covadonga. From July to mid-September and during some other major holidays, **Taxitur** (p550) operates a round-trip service (per adult/child €11/5) in eight-passenger vehicles.

Central Picos

The star attraction of the Picos' central massif is the gorge that divides it from the western Macizo El Cornión. The popular Garganta del Cares (Cares Gorge) trail running through it gets busy in summer, but the walk is always an exhilarating experience. This part of the Picos, however, also has plenty of less heavily tramped paths and climbing challenges. Arenas de Cabrales, on the AS114 between Cangas de Onís and Panes, is a popular base, but Poncebos, Sotres, Bulnes and Caín also offer facilities.

Arenas de Cabrales

POP 782 / ELEV 135M

Arenas de Cabrales (also Las Arenas) lies at the confluence of the bubbling Ríos Cares and Casaño, 30km east of Cangas de Onís. The busy main road is lined with hotels, restaurants and bars, and just off it is a little tangle of quiet squares and back lanes. Arenas is a popular base for walking the spectacular Garganta del Cares gorge.

Sights

Cueva-Exposición Cabrales MUSEUM

(985 84 67 02; www.fundacioncabrales.com; Carretera AS264; adult/child €4.50/3; tours hourly 10.15am-1.15pm & 4.15-7.15pm Apr-Sep, to 6.15pm Oct-Mar) Learn all about and sample the fine smelly Cabrales cheese at Arenas' Cueva-Exposición Cabrales, a cheese-cave museum 500m south of the centre on the Poncebos road. Guided visits (45 minutes) are in Spanish and, occasionally, English.

Activities

Arenas is a good access point for the popular Garganta del Cares walk (p552), which begins 6km south at Poncebos. Cheese-making tours are also a hit here; check with the local tourist office (p552) and the one in Cangas de Onís (p549) to find out which makers welcome visitors.

Sleeping & Eating

La Portiella del Llosu CASA RURAL €

(984 11 24 34, 646 866780; www.llosu.es; Pandiello; r incl breakfast €65;) Set against magnificent valley and Picos panoramas in peaceful Pandiello, 10km northwest of Arenas, this is a delightfully rustic restoration of a 17th-century home. The five warm-coloured rooms (with views) come furnished with antiques and family heirlooms, such as hand-painted cupboards and ceramic sinks, all spruced up by the hospitable owners. Breakfasts are homemade.

It's 2km from the Pandiello turn-off just east of Ortiguero.

Hotel Rural El Torrejón HOTEL €

(985 84 64 28; www.hotelruraleltorrejon.com; Calle del Torrejón; r incl breakfast €50-65; mid-Jan–mid-Dec;) This friendly, family-run country house welcomes weary travellers with flower-filled balconies, gorgeous gardens, original colour schemes and tastefully decorated rooms in a cosy rural style. It's good value and the setting is idyllic: beside the Río Casaño towards the eastern end of Arenas.

Restaurante Cares ASTURIAN **€€**

(☎985 84 66 28; Calle Mayor; mains €8.75-24, menús €15; ⏰1-3.30pm & 8-11.30pm Jul–mid-Sep, 1-3.30pm Tue-Thu & Sun, 1-3.30pm & 8-11.30pm Fri & Sat mid-Sep–Jun;) On the main road, beside the Poncebos junction, Cares is one of the best-value restaurants for miles. It does well-priced lunch and dinner *menús*, including a vegetarian *menú* (a rare breed in northern Spain), plus *platos combinados* (meat/eggs with chips and veg), kids' meals, à la carte fish and meats, and a choice of hearty Asturian *cachopo* (stuffed breaded veal).

Information

Oficina de Turismo (☎985 84 64 84; www.cabrales.es/turismo; Calle Mayor; ⏰10am-2pm & 4-8pm Tue-Sat, 10am-2pm Sun Easter & Jun–mid-Sep) In the middle of town, opposite the Poncebos road junction.

Getting There & Away

Two or more daily **ALSA** (☎902 42 22 42; www.alsa.es) buses run from Cangas de Onís to Arenas (€2.95, 40 minutes) and back. Two buses daily, Monday to Friday only, link Arenas with Llanes (€3.40, 55 minutes, or €6.45, 2¼ hours). Buses stop next to the **tourist office**, in the middle of town at the junction of the Poncebos road.

Garganta del Cares

Traversed by the Río Cares, the magnificent 1km-deep, 10km-long Garganta del Cares gorge separates the Picos' western massif from its central sibling. This dramatic limestone canyon extends between Poncebos, 6km south of Arenas de Cabrales in Asturias, and Caín in Castilla y León. People flock here year-round, but especially in summer, to walk the insanely popular Ruta del Cares, carved high into and through the rugged walls of the gorge between the two villages.

Activities

★Ruta del Cares WALKING

(Garganta del Cares Walk; PRPNPE3) You can walk Spain's favourite trail, the 10km Ruta del Cares, in either direction, but head from north (Poncebos) to south (Caín) to save its finest stretches for last. The beginning involves a steady climb in the gorge's wide, mostly bare, early stages. From the top end of Poncebos, follow the 'Ruta del Cares' sign pointing uphill 700m along the road. After 3km, you'll reach some abandoned houses. A little further and you're over the highest point of the walk.

Getting There & Away

From about mid-July to early September, **ALSA** runs two or three morning buses from Cangas de Onís to Caín (€8, two hours), starting back from Caín to Cangas in early or mid-afternoon; and two or three afternoon/early-evening buses from Cangas to Poncebos (€4.50, 45 minutes) via Arenas de Cabrales, and back. These schedules enable you to take a bus from Cangas to Caín, walk the Garganta del Cares north from Caín to Poncebos, and get a bus back from Poncebos to Cangas, all in one day.

There is a similar service from León via Posada de Valdeón to Caín in the morning and back from Poncebos to Posada de Valdeón and León in the afternoon (€20 round trip).

A number of agencies in Picos towns will transport you to either end of the walk and pick you up at the other end. At extra cost, some will add on 4WD tours into the Picos.

Bulnes

POP 35 / ELEV 647M

The rust-roofed hamlet of Bulnes, inaccessible by road, sits high up a side valley off the Cares gorge, south of Poncebos. You can reach it by a quite strenuous, 5km uphill walk (about two hours) from Poncebos or aboard the Funicular de Bulnes, a tunnel railway that climbs steeply for more than 2km inside the mountain from its lower station just below Poncebos. At the top of this thrill-inducing ride, tiny Bulnes sits in a pretty, secluded valley surrounded on all sides by towering rocky peaks.

You can also approach Bulnes from the east by walking about 2.5km (1¼ hours) down from the Collado de Pandébano.

Bulnes is divided into two parts: the upper Barrio del Castillo and the lower La Villa. All amenities are in La Villa.

Activities

Roadless Bulnes sits on some good walking routes for those who don't mind plenty of up and down.

The PRPNPE19 trail comes up from **Poncebos** in a relatively strenuous 5km, with an ascent of about 500m (about two hours), then continues even more demandingly 4km southward with an ascent of more than 1100m, often on stony slopes, up to the **Refugio Vega de Urriello** (☎650 780381, 638 278041, 984 09 09 81; www.refugiodeurriellu.com; dm adult/child €15/8, breakfast €5, lunch or dinner €15; ⏰year-round), beneath the mighty **El Naranjo de Bulnes**.

You can also head 2.5km east uphill from Bulnes to the **Collado de Pandébano** pass, where the PRPNPE21 provides an easier (though not easy) approach to the Refugio Vega de Urriello. From the Collado, you can also descend 4km eastward to Sotres in about one hour.

Sleeping & Eating

La Casa del Chiflón CASA RURAL €
(985 84 59 43; www.lacasadelchiflon.com; La Villa; s/d incl breakfast €45/60; Easter & Jun–mid-Oct;) An attractive, stone-walled *casa rural* (village accommodation) with six snug rooms, efficient management and a riverside restaurant (La Casa del Puente) in the lower half of Bulnes.

Getting There & Away

The **Funicular de Bulnes** (985 84 68 00; one way/return adult €17.61/22.16, child €4.32/6.71; 10am-8pm Easter & Jun–mid-Sep, 10am-12.30pm & 2-6pm rest of year) makes the seven-minute trip between Poncebos and Bulnes every half-hour in both directions.

Sotres

POP 113 / ELEV 1045M

A side road twists and turns 11km from Poncebos up to little Sotres, the highest village in the Picos and the starting point for a number of good walks.

Activities

A popular walking route goes east to the village of **Tresviso** and on down to Urdón, on the Potes–Panes road. As far as Tresviso (10km) it's a paved road, but the final 7km is a dramatic walking trail, the **Ruta Urdón-Tresviso** (PRPNPE30), snaking 850m down to the Desfiladero de la Hermida gorge. Doing this in the upward direction, starting from Urdón, is also popular.

Many walkers head west from Sotres to the **Collado de Pandébano** pass (1212m), a 4km walk (one to 1½ hours) on the far side of the Duje valley. At Pandébano the 2519m rock finger called **El Naranjo de Bulnes** (Pico Urriello) comes into view – an emblem of the Picos de Europa and a classic challenge for climbers. Few walkers can resist the temptation to get even closer to El Naranjo. From Pandébano, it's 5km (about three hours), with 700m of ascent, up the PRPNPE21 trail to the **Vega de Urriello** (1953m), at the foot of the mountain. Here the 96-bunk Refugio Vega de Urriello is attended year-round (weather permitting), with meal service. Otherwise, you can descend 2.5km (about one hour) west from Pandébano to Bulnes.

You can also walk south from Sotres along 4WD tracks to the Hotel Áliva (p555) or Espinama in the southeast of the national park.

Sleeping & Eating

Hotel Peña Castil HOTEL €
(hotel 985 94 50 80, restaurant 985 94 50 49; www.hotelpenacastil.com; CA1; s/d incl breakfast €40/60; closed Jan or Feb;) Friendly Hotel Peña Castil has 10 smallish but impeccably characterful rooms spread across a renovated stone house with graciously tiled floors, half-stone walls and, in some cases, little balconies – plus its own bar-restaurant.

Getting There & Away

The only ways to reach Sotres are to drive up the winding, 11km paved road from Poncebos; to walk (from Urdón, Tresviso, Bulnes or elsewhere); or to approach from the south (Hotel Áliva or Espinama) on a 4WD trip. A taxi from Arenas de Cabrales costs about €20.

Eastern Picos

The AS114 east from Cangas de Onís and Arenas de Cabrales in Asturias meets the N621, running south from the coast, at the humdrum town of Panes. South of Panes, the N621 follows the Río Deva upstream through the impressive **Desfiladero de la Hermida** gorge. After crossing into Cantabria at Urdón, 2km north of the hamlet of **La Hermida**, continue 18km south to **Potes**, the major base and activity hub for the eastern Picos. About 23km west of Potes lies **Fuente Dé**, with its cable car providing the main Picos access point in this area.

Potes & the Liébana Valley

POP 1360 / ELEV 291M

Potes is a hugely popular staging post on the southeastern edge of the Picos, with the Macizo Ándara rising close at hand. It's overrun in peak periods but still lively and delightful in its cobbled old town, and is effectively the 'capital' of Liébana, a beautifully verdant and historic valley area lying between the Picos and the main spine of the Cordillera Cantábrica.

Sights

The heart of Potes is a cluster of bridges, towers and charming backstreets restored in traditional slate, wood and red tile after the considerable damage done during the civil war. The Centro de Visitantes Sotama (p555), 2km north of Potes, has excellent displays on Picos de Europa wildlife, history and geology, as well as on the medieval monk Beato de Liébana and Romanesque architecture.

Monasterio de Santo Toribio de Liébana MONASTERY
(☎942 73 05 50; www.santotoribiodeliebana.org; CA885, Camaleño; ⏲10am-1pm & 4-7pm May-Sep, to 6pm Oct-Apr; P) FREE Christian refugees, fleeing from Muslim-occupied Spain to Liébana in the 8th century, brought with them the **Lígnum Crucis**, purportedly the single biggest chunk of Christ's cross and featuring the hole made by the nail that passed through Christ's left hand. The Santo Toribio Monastery, 3km west of Potes, has housed this holy relic ever since. The monastery is also famous for having been the home of 8th-century medieval monk and theologian Beato de Liébana, celebrated across Europe for his *Commentary on the Apocalypse*.

Iglesia de Santa María de Lebeña CHURCH
(Lebeña; adult/child €1.50/1; ⏲10am-1.30pm & 4-7.30pm Tue-Sun Jun-Sep, to 6pm Oct-May; P) Nine kilometres northeast of Potes, the fascinating Iglesia de Santa María de Lebeña dates back to the 9th or 10th century. The horseshoe arches are a telltale sign of its Mozarabic style – rare this far north in Spain. The floral motifs on its columns are Visigothic, while below the main 18th-century *retablo* (altarpiece) stands a Celtic stone engraving. The yew tree outside (reduced to a sad stump by a storm in 2007) was planted a thousand years ago.

Activities

The Potes area provides good access to Fuente Dé. Potes is the main base for all eastern Picos activities, with several agencies offering a host of options, from mountain biking and horse riding to climbing, canyoning and tandem paragliding. You can also take tours to see how cheese and orujo (a potent local liquor) are made.

Quesería Alles FOOD & DRINK
(☎942 73 35 13; www.quesopicon.es; Calle Mayor 6, Bejes; ⏲10am-1pm & 4-7pm) FREE If you're keen on Cantabria's super-pungent blue Picón cheese, head 20km north of Potes to tiny **Bejes** (582m; signposted off the N621), where you can tour and taste at one of the region's most successful *queserías* (cheese makers). Detailed Spanish-language tours take in the cheese-making process and facilities and, if you enquire ahead, possibly the local cheese-maturing cave, too.

Sleeping & Eating

★**Posada de Cucayo** HOTEL €
(☎942 73 62 46; www.laposadadecucayo.com; Cucayo; d incl breakfast €56-73; ⏲mid-Feb–mid-Jan; P 📶) This brilliant little family-run hotel sits at more than 900m high, a lovely 12km drive up from La Vega de Liébana. All around are scarred mountain peaks and green fields below. Eleven of the 12 spacious, tasteful rooms enjoy sweeping views. There's also a good-value **restaurant** (mains

POTES FIREWATER

The potent liquor *orujo*, made from leftover grape pressings, is drunk throughout northern Spain and is something of a Potes speciality. People here like to drink it as an after-dinner aperitif as part of a herbal tea called *té de roca* or *té de puerto*. Plenty of shops around town sell *orujo*, including varieties flavoured with honey, fruits and herbs, and most will offer you tastings if you're thinking of buying.

Potes' fun-filled **Fiesta del Orujo** (www.fiestadelorujo.es) kicks off on the second weekend in November, and involves practically every bar in town setting up a stall selling *orujo* shots for a few cents, the proceeds of which go to charity.

Several Potes-area *orujo*-makers have recently swung open their doors to visitors. About 5km northwest of Potes, **El Coterón** (☎942 73 08 76; www.elcoteron.com; Argüébanes; ⏲tours 10.30am & 4pm Mon-Fri, noon & 4pm Sat & Sun) FREE is a small family-run *orujo* distillery offering informative tours (sometimes in English) of their facilities and, of course, the chance to taste and purchase products at the source. Visit in October or November to witness the apples being picked and pressed. Bookings recommended.

€8-15; ⏲2-3.30pm & 9-10pm mid-Feb–mid-Jan; 📶) 🍃 featuring produce from the farm next door.

★Posada San Pelayo HOTEL €€

(☎942 73 32 10; www.posadasanpelayo.com; San Pelayo; s €50-60, d €65-80; P📶🏊) About 5km west of Potes, Posada San Pelayo is a beautiful, welcoming, family-run rural hotel of recent construction in traditional country style. Spacious modern-rustic rooms, many with timber terraces, are decorated in cheerful, earthy colours; there are plenty of cosy common areas, a winter fire and a gorgeous garden and pool with exquisite mountain views. Breakfast (€6.50) is good.

La Casa de las Chimeneas APARTMENT €€

(☎942 73 63 00, 648 531594; www.lacasadelaschimeneas.es; Plaza Mayor, Tudes; 1-bedroom apt €83-116, 2-bedroom apt €127-170; P📶🏊) In a pretty hillside hamlet stands this old farmstead converted into eight exquisitely comfy, well-equipped and characterful apartments, most on two or three levels. Each apartment follows its own theme, detailed by beautifully intricate and hand-painted medieval-inspired murals. Enjoy the curved infinity pool, games room, fabulous Picos panoramas and light bites at their equally original **Taberna del Inglés** (raciones & mains €4.50-15; ⏲9am-9.30pm year-round, Fri-Sun only Nov-Apr).

Asador Llorente CANTABRIAN €€

(☎942 73 81 65; Calle de San Roque 1, Potes; mains €10-19; ⏲1-4pm & 8.30-11pm Wed-Mon) For super-generous helpings of fresh, high-quality local food, head upstairs to this warm, wood-beamed loft-like space with Picos photos and a tiny trickling fountain. Carnivores should try the Liébana speciality *cocido lebaniego* (a filling stew of chickpeas, potato, greens, chorizo, black pudding, bacon and beef) or tuck into a half-kilogram *chuletón* (giant beef chop). Crisp salads are also tasty.

ℹ Information

Centro de Visitantes Sotama (☎942 73 81 09; N621, Tama; ⏲9am-7pm Jul-Sep, to 6pm Oct-Jun) Info on Picos hiking routes; about 2km north of Potes.

Oficina de Turismo (☎942 73 07 87; turismopotes@yahoo.es; Plaza de la Independencia, Potes; ⏲10am-2pm & 4-8pm Jun–mid-Sep, to 7pm mid-Sep–May) In the deconsecrated 14th-century, rustic Gothic Iglesia de San Vicente.

ℹ Getting There & Away

From Santander, **Autobuses Palomera** (☎942 88 06 11; www.autobusespalomera.com) travels via San Vicente de la Barquera, Panes, Urdón and Lebeña to Potes (€8.30, 2½ hours), and back again, one to three times daily.

Fuente Dé & Southeastern Picos

POP 9 (FUENTE DÉ) / ELEV 1078M

Tiny Fuente Dé village is situated dramatically at the foot of the stark southern wall of the Picos' Macizo Central, comprising just two hotels and a campground huddled around the ridiculously popular Teleférico de Fuente Dé. At the top of this cable car, walkers and climbers can make their way deeper into the central massif. The winding CA185 from Potes to Fuente Dé is a beautiful 23km trip.

Sights

★Teleférico de Fuente Dé CABLE CAR

(☎942 73 66 10; www.cantur.com; Fuente Dé; adult/child return €17/6, one way €11/4; ⏲9am-8pm Easter & Jul–mid-Sep, 10am-6pm mid-Sep–Jun, closed 2nd half Jan; P) In less than four minutes, this spine-tingling cable car whisks visitors 753m up to the top of the sheer southern wall of the Picos' central massif (1823m), from where hikers and climbers can venture further in. Cable cars depart continually throughout the day, weather permitting. You can check online for updates, but it's better to phone. During high season (especially August) you can wait over an hour for a seat, in both directions. There are cafes at either end.

Mogrovejo VILLAGE

One of Cantabria's most picturesque villages, tiny Mogrovejo (population 44) hugs a hillside 10km west of Potes and 15km east of Fuente Dé. It's well worth a wander, especially in early morning or late afternoon, when its medieval watchtower, 16th-century houses and 17th-century church are vividly illuminated against the town's stunning Picos de Europa backdrop.

Activities

There are some fantastic walks starting from the top of the Teleférico de Fuente Dé (p555). Fuente Dé's hotels also offer 4WD trips into the mountains (around €100).

It's an easy 3.5km, one-hour walk from the top of the Teleférico de Fuente Dé (p555) to the **Hotel Áliva** (☎942 73 09 99; www.cantur.com; s/d/tr €50/80/95; ⏲mid-Jun–mid-Oct), where you'll find refreshments. From the hotel, two 4WD tracks descend into the valley that separates the central massif from its eastern cousin. One heads north to **Sotres** via Vegas de Sotres (about 9km or two hours' walking). The other winds 7km south down to **Espinama** on the CA185 (about 2½ hours' walking). The PRPNPE24, popular for its contrasting landscapes of stark limestone peaks and lush alpine pastures, starts off along the Hotel Áliva–Espinama track, then branches off about halfway down to return to Fuente Dé (11km, about 3¼ hours from the hotel).

Other possibilities for the suitably prepared include making your way across the massif to **El Naranjo de Bulnes** (Pico Urriello; the Picos' emblem) or climbing **Peña Vieja** (2613m). These require proper equipment and mountaineering experience – Peña Vieja has claimed more lives than any other mountain in the Picos. Less challenging is the PRPNPE23, a route of 5.5km northwest from the Teleférico de Fuente Dé, passing below Peña Vieja to the **Collado de Horcados Rojos** pass, which opens up spectacular panoramas (including El Naranjo de Bulnes) with an ascent of 500m. Allow about 4½ hours return.

There are also some relatively gentle valley walking trails starting from villages on or not far from the CA185, such as **Brez** (5km north of Camaleño), Mogrovejo (p555) and Espinama.

Sleeping & Eating

Fuente Dé has a campground and two hotels, including an ugly *parador*. The 23km-long CA185 between Potes and Fuente Dé is dotted with attractive rural hotels, *hostales* (budget hotels) and campgrounds. There are particularly good options in Espinama and Cosgaya, 3.5km and 10km southeast of Fuente Dé respectively.

Puente Deva HOSTAL €
(942 73 66 58; www.hostalpuentedeva.com; Espinama; s/d/tr incl breakfast €36/49/64;) With 16 simple, tidy and charmingly rustic rooms – most overlook the river – the friendly Puente Deva is a solid no-frills choice. It's just off the CA185, 3.5km southeast of Fuente Dé.

★ **Hotel del Oso** HOTEL €€
(942 73 30 18; www.hoteldeloso.com; Cosgaya; s €63-71, d €78-89; Feb-Dec; P) This venerable hotel comprises majestic twin stone houses facing each other across the Río Deva and the road. Spacious, rustic-style rooms with timber floors and floral decor are very inviting, and there's a lovely pool. The **restaurant** (mains €15-25, menú €21; 1-3.45pm & 8.30-10.30pm Feb-Dec; P) is one of the area's finest, with top-quality meat, stews and desserts (breakfast is offered for €11). It's 13km southwest of Potes or 10km southeast of Fuente Dé.

Hotel Rebeco HOTEL €€
(942 73 66 00; www.hotelrebeco.com; Fuente Dé; d €70, incl breakfast/half-board/full board €82/109/137; closed Jan, variable; P) Many of the 30 rooms in this handsome, warm stone lodge have mountain views, and 11 include loft levels that are perfect for kids. You can't help but admire owner Conchi Cuesta's tapestries. It has a good, reasonably priced **restaurant** (942 73 66 01; www.hotelrebeco.com; Fuente Dé; mains €10-20; 1-10.30pm Feb-Dec;) and a roaring winter fire, and organises 4WD outings into the Picos (around €100, maximum six people).

Vicente Campo CANTABRIAN €€
(942 73 66 58; Espinama; mains €10-21; 1-5pm & 8-11pm) In the heart of tiny Espinama, this roadside eatery serves up honest Cantabrian fare that makes ample use of the family's own livestock. Dishes range from *estofado de añojo al vino tinto* (veal stewed in red wine) to *cabrito al horno* (roast goatling) to grilled steaks with local Tresviso cheese sauce.

Getting There & Away

From July to mid-September **Autobuses Palomera** (p555) runs a bus service once or twice daily between Potes and Fuente Dé (€2, 30 minutes). A taxi from Potes to Fuente Dé costs about €25.

Santiago de Compostela & Galicia

Includes ➡

Best Places to Eat

- ➡ Quinta de San Amaro (p584)
- ➡ O Curro da Parra (p566)
- ➡ Abastos 2.0 (p566)
- ➡ Adega O Bebedeiro (p575)

Best Places to Stay

- ➡ Quinta de San Amaro (p584)
- ➡ Hotel Herbeira (p579)
- ➡ Hotel Costa Vella (p564)
- ➡ Casa de Trillo (p572)
- ➡ Parador Hostal dos Reis Católicos (p565)

Why Go?

Galicia, a unique region with its own language and distinctive culture, is home to Santiago de Compostela, the destination of more than quarter of a million souls who travel each year along the Camino de Santiago pilgrim trails. Santiago is one of Spain's most beautiful and magical cities, an exceptionally good reason for any traveller to make their way to Spain's northwestern corner.

But Galicia is much more than Santiago. The wild coastline is frayed up and down its 1200km length by majestic *rías* (coastal inlets), and strung with cliffs, beaches, islands and fishing ports – which bring in arguably the best seafood in Europe. Inland is a labyrinth of deep-green valleys, speckled with stone villages, medieval monasteries and age-old vineyards. And as you travel you'll repeatedly run into reminders of Galicia's unique cultural identity: the sound of bagpipes, the wayside *cruceiros* (carved-stone crosses), the *castro* fort-villages of Galicians' Celtic ancestors.

When to Go

Santiago de Compostela

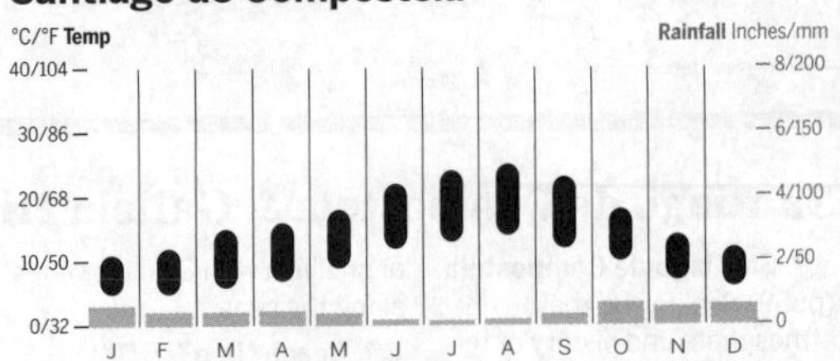

Jun & Sep No peak-season crowds or prices but (hopefully) reasonable weather.

Jul & Aug Your best chances of sunny weather are now.

24 Jul Spectacular fireworks launch Santiago de Compostela's celebration of the Día de Santiago.

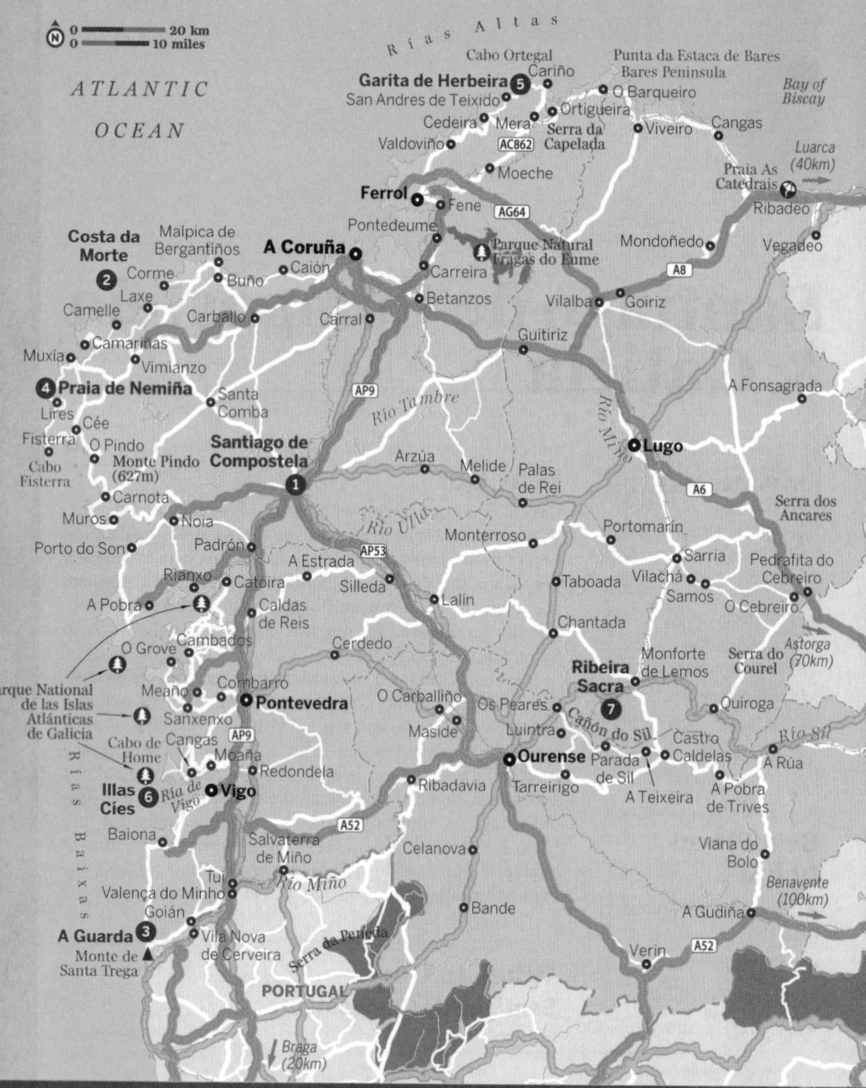

Santiago de Compostela & Galicia Highlights

❶ **Santiago de Compostela** (p559) Soaking up the atmosphere and history of this beautiful and fascinating city.

❷ **Costa da Morte** (p568) Exploring the capes and lighthouses north of Cabo Fisterra, Spain's 'Land's End'.

❸ **Seafood and wine** (p593) Feasting on fresh fish, octopus or shellfish with Galician wines along the coast.

❹ **Beach time** (p571) Chilling in the cold water under the hot sun, admiring the lovely scenery and maybe even surfing at Praia de Nemiña.

❺ **Cliffs and capes of the Riás Altas** (p580) Standing atop Europe's highest ocean cliffs at the Garita de Herbeira.

❻ **Illas Cíes** (p591) Sailing out to the beaches and walking trails of these spectacular, traffic-free islands.

❼ **Ribeira Sacra** (p598) Meandering around the wineries and dramatic canyons of the 'Holy Riverbank'.

History

Early Galicians built numerous dolmens (megalithic tombs) and Iron Age *castros* (protected settlements of circular stone huts). Many of these monuments have been excavated and can be visited today. The *castro*-builders are widely reckoned to have been Celts. The Romans pacified the region in the 1st century BC, founding cities including Lucus Augusti (Lugo).

A Germanic tribe, the Suevi, settled in Galicia in AD 409, founding the Kingdom of Galicia, which endured, in name at least, until 1834. Though medieval Galicia was absorbed into León and then Castilla, it did enjoy brief independent spells in the 10th and 11th centuries, with northern Portugal closely tied to it in this period.

The supposed grave of Santiago Apóstol (St James the Apostle), discovered in about the 820s at what became Santiago de Compostela, grew into a rallying symbol for the Christian Reconquista of Spain, and pilgrims from all over Europe began trekking to Santiago, which grew into a key centre of Christendom.

The Rexurdimento, an awakening of Galician identity, surfaced late in the 19th century. In the 19th and 20th centuries, hundreds of thousands of impoverished Galicians departed on transatlantic ships in search of better lives in Latin America.

Things looked up after democracy returned to Spain in the 1970s. Galicia today is an important fishing, shipbuilding and agricultural region, with more ports than any other region of the EU.

SANTIAGO DE COMPOSTELA

POP 79,800

The final stop on the epic Camino de Santiago pilgrimage trail, Santiago is a unique city imbued with the aura of a millennium's worth of journeys. Long-gone centuries live on in its arcaded streets and magnificent stone architecture, of which the famous cathedral is the jewel in the crown.

Today some 300,000 Camino pilgrims and many thousands of others venture here each year, giving Santiago a greater international dimension than ever. Yet this is also the capital of the Spanish autonomous region of Galicia, with a strong local character – a place where the skirl of bagpipes wafts across plazas and the countless restaurants and bars specialise in fine Galician seafood and local wines.

It's hard not to be both wowed and charmed by this city. Even the precipitation has its upside: Santiago is, many feel, at its most beautiful when the stone streets are glistening in the rain.

The biggest numbers of people hit the city in July and August, but Santiago has a festive atmosphere throughout the warmer half of the year. For fewer crowds, May, June and September are good months to come.

History

The faithful believe that Santiago Apóstol (St James the Apostle, one of Christ's closest disciples) preached in Galicia and, after his execution in Palestine, was brought back by stone boat and buried here. The tomb was supposedly rediscovered circa AD 820 by a religious hermit, Pelayo, following a guiding star (hence, it's thought, the name Compostela – from the Latin *campus stellae,* field of the star). Asturian king Alfonso II had a church erected above the holy remains, pilgrims began flocking to it, Alfonso III replaced it with a bigger church in the 890s, and by the 11th century the pilgrimage along the Camino de Santiago was a major European phenomenon, bringing a flood of funds into the city. The building of the magnificent cathedral we see today began in 1075, and Bishop Diego Xelmírez obtained archbishopric status for Santiago in 1100 and added numerous other churches in the 12th century. The following centuries, however, were marked by squabbling between rival nobles, and Santiago gradually slipped into the background.

Only since the 1980s, as capital of the autonomous region of Galicia and a rediscovered tourist and pilgrimage destination, has the city been revitalised.

Sights

The magnificent cathedral and Praza do Obradoiro are the natural starting points and focus for exploring Santiago. The Old Town in which they sit – a roughly oval-shaped area bounded by the line of the medieval city walls – is where almost everything of interest is found. Its stone-paved streets are a delight to wander, with plenty of cafes, bars and restaurants to drop into as you go.

Praza de Galicia marks the boundary between the Old Town and the Ensanche (Extension), the 20th-century shopping and residential area to its south.

Santiago de Compostela

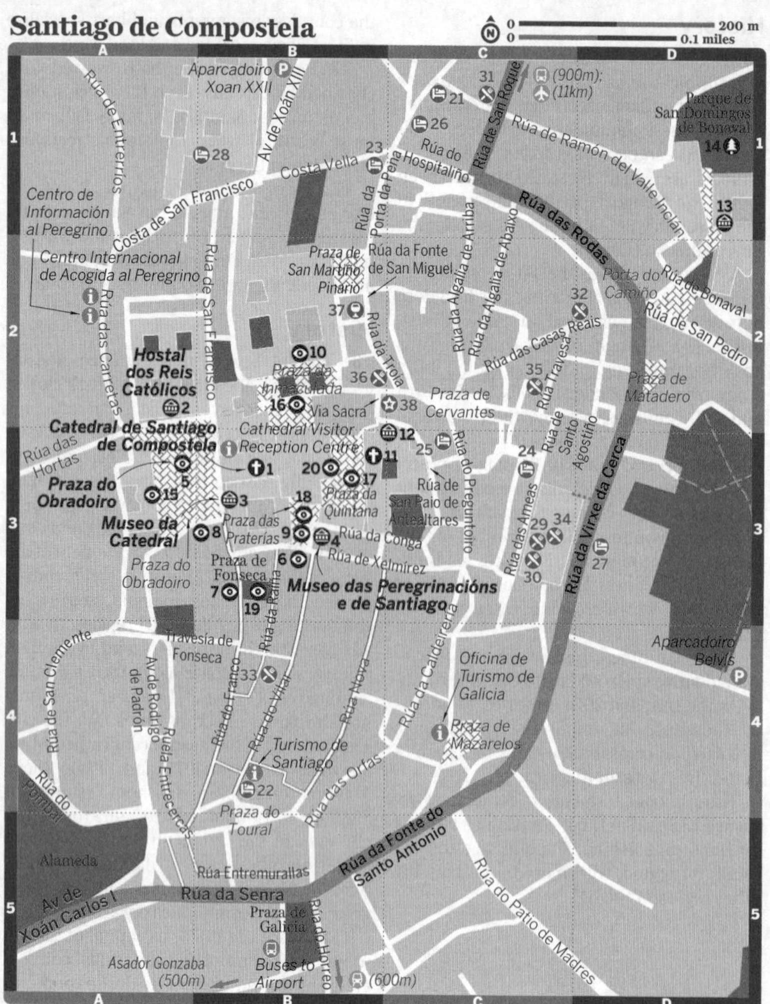

★Catedral de Santiago de Compostela CATHEDRAL

(http://catedraldesantiago.es; Praza do Obradoiro; ⏲7am-8.30pm) The grand heart of Santiago, the cathedral soars above the city in a splendid jumble of spires and sculpture. Built piecemeal over several centuries, its beauty is a mix of the original Romanesque structure (constructed between 1075 and 1211) and later Gothic and baroque flourishes. The tomb of Santiago beneath the main altar is a magnet for all who come here. The cathedral's artistic high point is the Pórtico de la Gloria inside the west entrance, featuring 200 masterly Romanesque sculptures.

Over the centuries the cathedral has suffered considerable wear and tear from water seepage, settlement and humidity. Restoration works in recent years meant that much of the main facade facing Praza do Obradoiro, and the Pórtico de la Gloria inside that facade, were covered in scaffolding. It was expected that work on the facade, and hopefully the Pórtico de la Gloria, would be completed in 2018, meaning that people would again be able to get a close look at the Pórtico de la Gloria. Works on

Santiago de Compostela

Top Sights
1 Catedral de Santiago de Compostela ... B3
2 Hostal dos Reis Católicos ... A2
3 Museo da Catedral ... B3
4 Museo das Peregrinacións e de Santiago ... B3
5 Praza do Obradoiro ... A3

Sights
6 Casa do Cabido ... B3
7 Colexio de Fonseca ... B3
8 Colexio de San Xerome ... B3
9 Fuente de los Caballos ... B3
10 Mosteiro de San Martiño Pinario ... B2
11 Mosteiro de San Paio de Antealtares ... B3
12 Museo de Arte Sacra ... C3
13 Museo do Pobo Galego ... D1
14 Parque de San Domingos de Bonaval ... D1
15 Pazo de Raxoi ... A3
16 Praza da Inmaculada ... B2
17 Praza da Quintana ... B3
18 Praza das Praterías ... B3
19 Praza de Fonseca ... B3
20 Puerta Santa ... B3

Sleeping
21 Altaïr Hotel ... C1
22 Hostal Suso ... B4
23 Hotel Costa Vella ... B1
24 Hotel Pazo de Altamira ... C3
25 Last Stamp ... C3
26 Moure Hotel ... C1
27 O Xardín de Julia ... D3
Parador Hostal dos Reis Católicos ... (see 2)
28 San Francisco Hotel Monumento ... B1

Eating
29 Abastos 2.0 ... C3
Café de Altamira ... (see 24)
Café-Jardín Costa Vella ... (see 23)
30 Cocina María ... C3
31 La Bodeguilla de San Roque ... C1
32 La Flor ... D2
33 María Castaña ... B4
Mariscomanía ... (see 34)
34 Mercado de Abastos ... C3
35 O Curro da Parra ... C2
36 O Filandón ... B2

Drinking & Nightlife
37 Pub Atlántico ... B2

Entertainment
38 Casa das Crechas ... C2

other parts of the cathedral are expected to continue until 2020.

The cathedral has a traditional Latin-cross layout and three naves, separated by majestic lines of Romanesque arches. The lavish baroque western facade facing Praza do Obradoiro was erected in the 18th century, replacing the weather-damaged Romanesque one. The only facade that still conserves its original Romanesque structure is the southern one from Praza das Praterías, which now serves as the main visitor entrance.

The artistically unparalleled **Pórtico de la Gloria** (Galician: Porta da Gloria) stands just inside the western facade. The Pórtico features 200 Romanesque sculptures by Maestro Mateo, who was placed in charge of the cathedral-building program in the late 12th century. These detailed, inspired and remarkably lifelike sculptures add up to a comprehensive review of major figures from the Bible, with the Old Testament and its prophets on the north side, the New Testament and Apostles on the south, and glory and resurrection depicted in the central archway.

The main figure in the central archway is a throned, resurrected Christ, surrounded by the four evangelists plus angels and symbols of Jesus' passion. In an arc above are the 24 musicians said in Revelations to sit around the heavenly throne. Below Christ's feet is Santiago, and below him Hercules (holding open the mouths of two lions). Visitors arriving in the cathedral traditionally said a brief prayer while placing their fingers in five holes above Hercules' head, created by the repetition of this very act by millions of faithful over the centuries. On the other side of the central pillar is a sculpture of Maestro Mateo. For centuries, tradition called for visitors to bump heads with the maestro to acquire some of his genius. These countless knocks led to Mateo's notably flat nose, and both he and Hercules were blocked off behind metal barriers even before the Pórtico acquired its scaffold covering in 2013.

Among the Old Testament prophets, the very bright smile on Daniel's face is, according to one legend, caused by the tightly dressed figure of Queen Esther on the pillar opposite

EXPLORING AROUND THE CATHEDRAL

The cathedral is surrounded by handsome plazas that invite you to wander through them.

The grand square in front of the cathedral's west facade earned its name, **Praza do Obradoiro** (Workshop Sq), from the stonemasons' workshops set up here while the cathedral was being built. It's free of both traffic and cafes, and has a unique, magical atmosphere.

Stretching across the northern end of the *praza,* the Renaissance-style **Hostal dos Reis Católicos** (981 58 22 00; www.parador.es; adult/child €3/free, Mon free; noon-2pm & 4-7pm Sun-Fri) was built in the early 16th century by order of the Catholic Monarchs, Isabel and Fernando, as a recuperation centre for exhausted pilgrims. Today it's a *parador* (luxurious state-owned hotel) and shelters well-heeled travellers instead, but its four courtyards and some other areas are open to visitors: the self-guided tour, with leaflet and more than 40 information panels, is well worthwhile.

Along the western side of the *praza* stretches the elegant 18th-century **Pazo de Raxoi**, now Santiago's city hall. At the south end stands the **Colegio de San Xerome** (hr vary Mon-Fri), a former college for the poor that is now the rectorate of Santiago University. This 17th-century building has a 15th-century Romanesque/Gothic portal that was transferred from the college's previous site.

South of the cathedral, stop in cafe-lined **Praza de Fonseca** to look into the **Colexio de Fonseca** (cloister 9am-9pm Mon-Fri, exhibitions 11am-2pm & 5-8.30pm Tue-Sat, 11am-2pm Sun) with its beautiful Renaissance courtyard; this was the original seat of Santiago's university (founded in 1495) and now houses the university's main library. Its Gothic chapel and Salón Artesonado, either side of the entrance, house assorted temporary exhibitions.

Praza das Praterías (Silversmiths' Sq) is marked by an elegant 1825 fountain, the **Fuente de los Caballos** (Fountain of the Horses), a popular photo op, with the cathedral's Romanesque south portal at the top of the steps. Curiously, the baroque **Casa do Cabido** (10am-2pm & 5-8pm Sat, 11am-2pm Sun), on the lower side of the square, is no more than a 3m-deep facade, erected in the 1750s to embellish the plaza.

Broad **Praza da Quintana** opens up outside the cathedral's eastern end. The cathedral's **Puerta Santa** here is opened only in holy years (next in 2021): it's flanked by 24 Romanesque sculptures of biblical figures that were once part of the cathedral's original stone choir, created by Maestro Mateo and his team in the late 12th century.

The plaza's east side is lined by the long, stark wall of the **Mosteiro de San Paio de Antealtares**, founded in the 9th century for the monks who looked after Santiago's relics (now a convent). Its **Museo de Arte Sacra** (Vía Sacra 5; €1.50; 10.30am-1.30pm & 4-7pm Mon-Sat, 4-7pm Sun), accessed through the convent church at the top of the plaza steps, contains the original altar raised over those relics.

On the cathedral's north side, the **Praza da Inmaculada** is where most pilgrims arriving in Santiago first set eyes on the cathedral. Opposite looms the huge, austerely baroque **Mosteiro de San Martiño Pinario**, now a seminary.

him. Legend also has it that Esther's stone breasts were originally much larger, but were filed down on orders of a disapproving bishop – to which townspeople responded by inventing Galicia's cone-shaped *tetilla* (nipple) cheese in Esther's honour.

Towards the east end of the cathedral, the fantastically elaborate, Churrigueresque **Altar Mayor** (High Altar) rises up from the central crossing where the transepts intersect the nave. From the right side of the ambulatory (walkway) that runs round behind the Altar Mayor, a small staircase leads up to a statue of Santiago that has watched over the cathedral since its consecration in 1211. The faithful queue up here to kiss or embrace the statue. From the statue you emerge on the left side, then descend some steps into the **Cripta Apostólica**, where we are assured Santiago's remains lie, inside a large 19th-century silver casket. Behind the Altar Mayor is the **Puerta Santa** (Holy Door), which opens onto Praza da

Quintana and is cracked open only in holy years (next in 2021).

Mass is usually celebrated at the High Altar at noon and 7.30pm daily, and at 10am and 6pm on Saturday and Sunday, and at 1.15pm on Sunday. Touristic visits are discouraged during Mass.

Restoration work on the eastern part of the cathedral may mean some restrictions on access to the statue of Santiago and Cripta Apostólica, and on the number of Masses held in the cathedral and the number of people who can attend them, until 2020.

For wonderful views of the cathedral's interior from its upper storeys, and of the city from the cathedral roof, take a cathedral rooftop tour.

★Museo da Catedral MUSEUM

(Colección Permanente; http://catedraldesantiago.es; Praza do Obradoiro; adult/reduced/child €6/4/free; ⏲9am-8pm Apr-Oct, 10am-8pm Nov-Mar) The Cathedral Museum spreads over four floors and incorporates the cathedral's large 16th-century Gothic/plateresque cloister. You'll see a sizeable section of Maestro Mateo's original carved-stone choir (destroyed in 1604 but pieced back together in 1999), an impressive collection of religious art (including the *botafumeiros*, the cathedral's famous giant censers, in the 2nd-floor library), the lavishly decorated 18th-century *sala capitular* (chapter house), a room of tapestries woven from designs by Goya, and, off the cloister, the Panteón de Reyes, with tombs of kings of medieval León.

★Museo das Peregrinacións e de Santiago MUSEUM

(http://museoperegrinacions.xunta.gal; Praza das Praterías; adult/pilgrim & student/senior & child €2.40/1.20/free; ⏲9.30am-8.30pm Tue-Fri, 11am-7.30pm Sat, 10.15am-2.45pm Sun) The brightly displayed Museum of Pilgrimages & Santiago gives fascinating insights into the phenomenon of Santiago (man, city and pilgrimage) down the centuries. Much of the explanatory material is in English as well as Spanish and Galician. There are also great close-up views of some of the cathedral's towers from the 3rd-floor windows. Free entry on Sunday and from 2.30pm Saturday.

Mosteiro de San Martiño Pinario MONASTERY

(http://espacioculturalsmpinario.com; Praza da Inmaculada; adult/student, pilgrim & senior €3/2; ⏲10.30am-6.30pm or later, closed 2-4pm May-Jun) This huge baroque monastery looming over Praza da Inmaculada is now a seminary, and its central sections, including the grand cloister, aren't open to visitors – but its enormous church, with spectacular decoration, is open as part of a museum that's well worth a visit (enter from the plaza's upper end). The church's centrepiece is its incredibly ornate main altarpiece, encrusted with carved saints, cherubim, flowers, plants, horses and bishops. The walnut choir stalls behind this also merit close inspection.

Museo do Pobo Galego MUSEUM

(Museum of the Galician People; www.museodopobo.gal; Campo de San Domingos de Bonaval; adult/senior & student/child €3/1/free, Sun free; ⏲10.30am-2pm & 4-7.30pm Tue-Sat, 11am-2pm Sun) This museum in a former convent is a fascinating window into traditional Galician ways of life that still persist in some rural areas. Displays range over music, agriculture, architecture, fishing and more, with exhibits including fishing boats, bagpipes, costumes and antique printing presses. The upper floors are accessed by an extraordinary triple spiral staircase designed by Domingo de Andrade around 1700. Behind the museum, the **Parque de San Domingos de Bonaval** (Campo de San Domingos de Bonaval; ⏲8am-11pm Apr-Sep, 8am-8pm Oct-Mar) is a lovely, tranquil retreat from the Santiago bustle.

☞ Tours

★Cathedral Rooftop Tour TOURS

(☎881 55 79 45; http://catedraldesantiago.es; adult/reduced/child €12/10/free, combined ticket with Museo da Catedral €15/12/free; ⏲tours hourly 10am-1pm & 4-7pm; 👪) For unforgettable bird's-eye views of the cathedral interior from its upper storeys, and of the city from the cathedral roof, take the rooftop tour, which starts in the visitor reception centre (p567). The tours are popular, so book beforehand, either at the visitor reception centre for same-day visits, or on the cathedral website up to several weeks ahead. Tours are given in Spanish, but some guides also speak some English.

The guides provide a good insight into Santiago's and the cathedral's history. From late October through March, the last tour is at 5pm.

Festivals & Events

Fiestas del Apóstol Santiago CULTURAL, RELIGIOUS
(Fiestas of the Apostle St James; ⌚Jul) Two weeks of music, parades and other festivities surround the Día de Santiago (Feast of St James; 25 July), which is simultaneously Galicia's 'national' day. Celebrations peak in a truly spectacular lasers-and-fireworks display, the Fuegos del Apóstol, on Praza do Obradoiro on the night of 24 July.

Sleeping

From hostels for pilgrims and backpackers to chic boutique lodgings and historic luxury hotels, Santiago has hundreds of places to stay at all price levels. Even so, the best-value and most central places can fill up weeks ahead in summer, especially July and August.

★ **Hostal Suso** HOSTAL €
(☎981 58 66 11; www.hostalsuso.com; Rúa do Vilar 65; r €48-65; ❄@📶) Stacked above a convenient cafe (with excellent-value breakfasts), the friendly, family-run 14-room Suso received a full makeover in 2016 and boasts immaculate, thoughtfully designed rooms in appealing greys and whites, with up-to-date bathrooms and firm beds. It's very good for the price. Everything is thoroughly soundproofed, too – the street outside is traffic-free but can get quite celebratory in summer.

O Xardín de Julia HOTEL €
(☎626 004591; www.oxardindejulia.com; Rúa da Virxe da Cerca 20; r €45-90; ⌚closed Jan & Feb; ❄📶) Opened in 2016, 'Julia's Garden' is a delightful little 10-room option on the edge of the Old Town. Everything is bright and clean-lined, with plenty of wood and stone but without unnecessary clutter. The icing on the cake is the lovely strip of garden, with a camellia tree, overlooked from the *galerías* of some rooms.

Last Stamp HOSTEL €
(El Último Sello; ☎981 56 35 25; www.thelaststamp.es; Rúa Preguntoiro 10; dm €15-20; ⌚closed late Dec–late Feb; @📶) A purpose-designed hostel, the Last Stamp occupies a 300-year-old, five-storey house (with lift) in the heart of the Old Town. The cleverly designed dorms (all mixed) feature semi-private modules with ultra-solid bunks, electrical plugs, good mattresses and individual reading lights. Some rooms enjoy cathedral views. Bathrooms and kitchen are big, and Camino-themed murals add a bit of fun.

★ **Hotel Costa Vella** BOUTIQUE HOTEL €€
(☎981 56 95 30; www.costavella.com; Rúa da Porta da Pena 17; s €50-60, d €55-97; ❄@📶) Tranquil, thoughtfully designed rooms (some with typically Galician *galerías* – glassed-in balconies), a friendly welcome, super-helpful management and staff, and a lovely garden cafe (p565) make this family-run hotel a wonderful option. It's set in an old stone house just a 400m stroll from the cathedral; the €6 breakfast is substantial.

★ **Altaïr Hotel** BOUTIQUE HOTEL €€
(☎981 554 712; http://altairhotel.net; Rúa dos Loureiros 12; s €60-85, d €75-120; ⌚closed Jan; ❄📶) The Altaïr combines traditional stone walls and solid oak floors with cosy comfort, attentive staff, soft furnishings and splashes of contemporary design. The breakfast (€8.50) is a gourmet affair, and the super-colourful Carlos Sansegundo canvas hung in the bar-breakfast area is a masterstroke! There are some great city views from the rooms.

★ **Moure Hotel** DESIGN HOTEL €€
(☎981 58 36 37; www.mourehotel.com; Rúa dos Loureiros 6; d incl breakfast €65-110; ⌚closed Jan; ❄@📶) An award-winning conversion of a 19th-century building, the Moure will please anyone who likes a bit of contemporary adventure in their hotel design. It's comfortable, friendly and practical, with spacious bathrooms and good beds, as well as being stylishly minimalist in whites, greys and splashes of bright lime green, with sections of exposed stone wall. A good breakfast is included.

Hotel Pazo de Altamira BOUTIQUE HOTEL €€
(☎981 55 85 42; www.pazodealtamira.com; Rúa Altamira 18; r €70-120; ⌚closed Jan & Feb; ❄@📶🐾) A sturdy stone house just steps from the bustling Mercado de Abastos, the Altamira provides 16 stylish, bright, white rooms with real wood floors, comfy beds, marble-lined bathrooms and, in superior rooms, *galerías*. Breakfast costs €10 to €12. Reception is helpful with Santiago tips, and the hotel is also home to the good **Café de Altamira** (Rúa das Ameas 9; mains €9-18, lunch menú Mon-Fri €14; ⌚1.30-3.45pm & 8.30-11.15pm, closed Sun night & Wed Nov-Mar; 📶).

★Parador Hostal dos Reis Católicos HISTORIC HOTEL €€€
(☎981 58 22 00; www.parador.es; Praza do Obradoiro 1; incl breakfast s €146-226, d €167-392; P❄@📶) Opened in 1509 as a pilgrims' hostel, and with a claim as the world's oldest hotel, this palatial *parador* occupies a wonderful building that is one of Santiago's major monuments in its own right. Even standard rooms are grand, if a little old-fashioned, with wooden floors, original art and good-size bathrooms with big glass showers. Some have four-poster beds.

★San Francisco Hotel Monumento HISTORIC HOTEL €€€
(☎981 58 16 34; www.sanfranciscohm.com; Campillo San Francisco 3; incl breakfast s €110-138, d €154-334; P❄@📶🏊) The three cloister-courtyards and low-lit hallways with their stone doorways recall the hotel's former life as a Franciscan monastery. But the modern, spacious rooms are all about contemporary comfort, and there's a great indoor pool as well as a huge grassy garden, a cafe, a monastery-style restaurant and very spacious common areas. Room rates include parking.

Eating

Central Santiago is packed with eateries and there are good options for most palates and budgets, from cheap *menú del día* places (see www.santiagomenus.es) to gastronomic fusion. Busy Rúa do Franco is almost end-to-end restaurants and bars, but the most enticing options are scattered elsewhere.

Don't leave without trying a *tarta de Santiago,* the city's famed almond cake.

★Café-Jardin Costa Vella CAFE €
(www.costavella.com; Rúa da Porta da Pena 17; breakfast €2.70-4.50; ⏰8am-11pm; 📶) The garden cafe of Hotel Costa Vella (p564) is the most delightful spot for breakfast (or a drink later in the day), with its fountain, a scattering of statuary and beautiful flowering fruit trees. And if the weather takes a Santiago-esque rainy turn, you can still enjoy it from the glass pavilion or the *galería.*

★Mercado de Abastos MARKET €
(www.mercadodeabastosdesantiago.com; Rúa das Ameas 5-8; ⏰8am-3pm Mon-Sat) 🍃 Santiago's food market is a fascinating, always lively scene, very clean, with masses of fresh produce from the seas and countryside attractively displayed at 300-odd stalls. Stock up on *tetilla* cheese, cured meats, sausage, fruit, *empanada* (pastry pie) or the tasty take-away dishes of **Cocina María** (Posto C61, Mercado de Abastos; items €1.30-14; ⏰9.30am-3pm Mon-Sat) for a picnic.

Numerous bars and cafes line the street outside, and there are several more within the market itself, including a wine bar in the central alley. You can buy seafood or meat and have it cooked up on the spot for €5 per person at hugely popular **Marisco-manía** (Posto 81, Mercado de Abastos; ⏰9am-3pm Tue-Sat), though they don't do octopus or fish. The eastern side of the market is reserved for villagers and stallholders selling the produce of their orchards or vegetable gardens.

La Flor FUSION €
(Rúa das Casas Reais 25; dishes €7-10; ⏰noon-12.30am Mon-Sat, 4pm-midnight Sun, kitchen 1.30-3.30pm & 8-11.30pm; 📶🖊) La Flor is a buzzy bar for drinks (with free tapas) and good music – but it's also a place to enjoy an eclectic range of creative, not-too-heavy dishes from chicken *fajitas* to rocket and goat's-cheese salad, or homemade burgers to pita bread stuffed with veg sticks and wasabi – all amid a uniquely random melange of art, *objets* and hanging lamps.

O Filandón TAPAS, RACIONES €
(Rúa Acibechería 6; medias raciones €10-12; ⏰1-4pm & 8pm-1am, to 2am Fri & Sat) Squeeze past the cheese-shop counter into the thin, cellar-like bar area behind, where you'll receive exceedingly generous free *pinchos* (snacks) with drinks, and can order *empanadas* or plates of ham, sausage, cured meats, cheese, peppers or anchovies. Thousands of notes and words of wisdom scribbled by past clients are pinned to the walls, and a welcoming log fire burns on chilly winter evenings.

> **GALEGO**
>
> Most Galicians speak both Spanish (Castilian) and the separate Galician language (*galego* or, in Castilian, *gallego*). Galician is close to Portuguese (which developed out of Galician in the late Middle Ages), and slightly less close to Castilian. We use the place names you're most likely to encounter during your travels. By and large, these are Galician.

★O Curro da Parra GALICIAN, FUSION €€
(www.ocurrodaparra.com; Rúa do Curro da Parra 7; mains €15-23, starters & half-raciones €5-15; 1.30-3.30pm & 8.30-11.30pm Tue-Sun;) With a neat little stone-walled dining room upstairs and a narrow food-and-wine bar below, busy Curro da Parra serves thoughtfully created, market-fresh fare, changing weekly. Everything is delicious; typical offerings might include line-caught hake with cockles and green beans or beef tenderloin with shiitake mushrooms. The 2010 cheesecake has been a favourite ever since they opened.

On weekday lunchtimes there's an excellent €13 *menú mercado* (market menu). On busy summer evenings they have two dinner sittings, at 8.30pm and 10.30pm.

★Abastos 2.0 GALICIAN €€
(654 015937; www.abastoscompostela.com; Rúa das Ameas; dishes €6-13, menú from €30; noon-3.30pm & 8.30-11pm Mon-Sat) This highly original, popular marketside eatery offers new dishes concocted daily from the market's offerings, with an emphasis on seafood. Inside is one long 12-seat table where they serve a daily changing menu for €30-plus: reservations highly advisable! Outside are a few tables (not reservable) where they serve small to medium-size individual dishes. Almost everything in both sections is delicious.

María Castaña GALICIAN €€
(Rúa da Raiña 19; raciones €6-22; noon-3.30pm & 7.30-11.30pm) A solid central choice for many varieties of seafood, cheese or ham boards, salads, scrambled-egg dishes and a few meaty options. The *pulpo á feira* is tops. There's a long bar area, and two stone-walled rooms with tables as you go further in.

La Bodeguilla de San Roque SPANISH €€
(981 56 43 79; www.labodeguilla.gal; Rúa de San Roque 13; raciones & mains €5-18; 9am-12.30am Mon-Fri, 10.30am-4pm & 7pm-12.30am Sat & Sun) An amiable two-storey restaurant and wine bar just northeast of the Old Town, the Bodeguilla serves an eclectic range of appetising dishes, from vegetarian salads to casseroles of prawn, wild mushroom and seaweed, Galician beef sirloin in port, or plates of cheeses, sausages or ham.

Drinking & Entertainment

On summer evenings every streetside nook in the Old Town is filled with people relaxing over tapas and drinks. The liveliest bar area lies east of the cathedral. Santiago's large student population comes out in full force around midnight, Thursday to Saturday. Later, people gravitate towards clubs along Rúas da República Arxentina and Nova de Abaixo, in the Ensanche.

Pub Atlántico BAR
(981 57 21 52; Rúa da Fonte de San Miguel 9; 5.30pm-3am, shorter hours in winter) This buzzing bar pulls in an artsy crowd of 20- and 30-somethings, with excellent gin and tonics and cocktails, and a great soundtrack ranging from Cajun blues to Spanish indie.

★Casa das Crechas LIVE MUSIC
(www.facebook.com/casadascrechas; Vía Sacra 3; 6pm-3am;) There's no better place for Celtic and other live music. Head to

TOP FIVE FOOD EXPERIENCES

Mercado de Abastos (p565) Santiago de Compostela's fascinating food market is piled with fine produce displaying the bounty of Galicia's seas and countryside, and there are lively eateries and bars right on the spot.

Albariño and seafood at Cambados (p585) Galicia's best-known white wine is the perfect pairing to a plate of scallops, cockles, mussels or freshly caught fish in the taverns of albariño's 'capital', Cambados.

Pulpo á feira (p575) Galicia's iconic octopus dish: tender slices of tentacle with olive oil and paprika, even better when accompanied by cachelos (sliced boiled potatoes). Delicious at A Coruña's Pulpeira de Melide and great almost everywhere.

Tapas in Lugo (p601) The tapas zones of A Coruña, Ourense and Pontevedra run close, but Lugo wins our tapas accolade for the animated atmosphere and the fact that almost every door is a bar; and because they give you two tasty tapas free with every drink.

Fish and shellfish at A Guarda (p593) The harbourfront of this small fishing port at Galicia's southwest tip is lined with restaurants preparing the local catch for customers' palates. Wander along and take your pick.

the tightly packed downstairs bar at about 10.30pm most Wednesdays from September to mid-June for terrific Galician folk sessions with the Banda das Crechas (cover €1). There's usually live jazz, folk or flamenco a couple of other nights a week too, and DJ sessions on Friday and Saturday.

Information

Cathedral Visitor Reception Centre (881 55 79 45; http://catedraldesantiago.es; Praza do Obradoiro; 9am-8pm Apr-Oct, 10am-8pm Nov-Mar) You can buy tickets for the Museo da Catedral and cathedral rooftop tours here, and this is also the starting point for the rooftop tours. As of early 2018, owing to restoration work on the cathedral's Obradoiro facade, the reception centre was located in the Pazo de Xelmírez on the cathedral's north side. When the facade works finish the reception centre may move back to its previous location in the crypt beneath the steps of the Obradoiro facade.

Centro Internacional de Acogida al Peregrino (Pilgrim's Reception Office; 981 56 88 46; http://oficinadelperegrino.com; Rúa das Carretas 33; 8am-8pm Easter-Oct, 10am-7pm Nov-Easter) People who have covered at least the last 100km of a Camino de Santiago on foot or horseback, or the last 200km by bicycle, for religious or spiritual reasons or with an 'attitude of search', can obtain their 'Compostella' certificate to prove it here. The website has a good deal of useful info for pilgrims.

Oficina de Turismo de Galicia (881 86 63 97; www.turismo.gal; Praza de Mazarelos 15; 10am-5pm Mon-Sat, 10am-2.30pm Sun) The scoop on all things Galicia.

Turismo de Santiago (981 55 51 29; www.santiagoturismo.com; Rúa do Vilar 63; 9am-9pm Apr-Oct, 9am-7pm Mon-Fri, 9am-2pm & 4-7pm Sat & Sun Nov-Mar) The very efficient city tourist office. Its website is a multilingual mine of information.

Getting There & Away

AIR

Santiago's busy **Lavacolla airport** (902 404 704; www.aena.es) is 11km east of the city. Direct flights (some only operating during variable summer months) include the following:

Air Europa (www.aireuropa.com) Ibiza, Menorca, Palma de Mallorca, Seville

Aer Lingus (www.aerlingus.com) Dublin

EasyJet (www.easyjet.com) Basel-Mulhouse, Geneva, London (Gatwick), Milan (Malpensa)

Iberia (www.iberia.com) Barcelona, Bilbao, Madrid

BRING YOUR UMBRELLA

Swept by one rainy front after another from the Atlantic, Galicia has, overall, twice as much rain as the Spanish national average. Galicians have more than 100 words to describe different nuances of precipitation, from *babuxa* (a species of drizzle) to *xistra* (a type of shower) to *treboada* (a thunderstorm). June to August are the least rainy months. If you haven't brought an umbrella, don't panic – you're never far from an umbrella shop in any Galician town: just ask for the nearest *paragüería* (par-ag-wer-ee-ah).

Lufthansa (www.lufthansa.com) Frankfurt, Munich

Ryanair (www.ryanair.com) Alicante, Barcelona, Frankfurt (Hahn), London (Stansted), Madrid, Málaga, Milan (Bergamo), Palma de Mallorca, Seville, Valencia

Swiss (www.swiss.com) Zurich

Vueling Airlines (www.vueling.com) Alicante, Amsterdam, Barcelona, Brussels, Ibiza, London (Gatwick), Málaga, Palma de Mallorca, Paris (Charles de Gaulle), Rome (Fiumicino), Zurich

BUS

The **bus station** (981 54 24 16; Praza de Camilo Díaz Baliño;) is about a 20-minute walk northeast of the city centre. **Monbus** (982 29 29 00; www.monbus.es) runs to many places in Galicia; Empresa Freire (www.empresafreire.com) and **ALSA** (902 422242; www.alsa.es) operate to Lugo; ALSA serves destinations outside Galicia.

DESTINATION	FARE (€)	DURATION (HR)	FREQUENCY (DAILY)
A Coruña	6	1-1½	13
Cambados	5.60	1½	2
Ferrol	10	1½	5
Fisterra	13	2-3	4
León	30	6	1
Lugo	9-13	1½-2¾	10
Madrid	20-67	8½-10	3
Muxía	8	1½	2
Ourense	12	2	4
Oviedo	30	5¼-6¾	2
Pontevedra	5.85	1-1½	11
Porto (Portugal)	27-34	4¼	1
Santander	43-50	8-10	2

TRAIN

The **train station** (www.renfe.com; Rúa do Hórreo) is about a 15-minute walk south from the Old Town. All trains are run by **Renfe** (☎91 232 03 20; www.renfe.com), which has a **ticket office** (Rúa das Carretas 29; ⊙3-7.30pm Mon, 9.30am-2pm & 3-7.30pm Tue-Fri, 9.30am-2pm Sat) on the edge of the Old Town as well as at the station. There is high-speed service to A Coruña and Ourense.

DESTINATION	FARE (€)	DURATION	MINIMUM FREQUENCY (DAILY)
A Coruña	6.10-16	30-40min	19
Madrid	17-56	5¼hr	2
Ourense	6-20	35-45min	9
Pontevedra	6.10-7.35	35min-1hr	15
Vigo	9.25-11	50min-1½hr	15

Getting Around

TO/FROM THE AIRPORT

Empresa Freire (www.empresafreire.com) runs buses (€3, 45 minutes) to Lavacolla airport from **Praza de Galicia** half-hourly from 6am to midnight, via the train and bus stations. Returning buses leave the airport every half-hour from 7am to 1am. Taxis charge around €21.

CAR

Private vehicles are barred from the Old Town. Underground car parks around its fringes generally charge about €16 per 24 hours. Cheaper are **Aparcadoiro Xoan XXIII** (Avenida de Xoan XXIII; per 24hr €11; ⊙24hr) and the open-air **Aparcadoiro Belvís** (Rúa das Trompas; per 24hr €7.50; ⊙24hr). These two also offer seven-day deals for €30 from about June to September. Many Old Town lodgings offer small discounts on the underground car parks for their guests.

COSTA DA MORTE

Rocky headlands, winding inlets, small fishing towns, plunging cliffs, wide sweeping bays and many a remote, sandy beach – this is the eerily beautiful 'Coast of Death', the most westerly outpost of mainland Spain, where mysteries and legends abound. One of the most enchanting parts of Galicia, this remote, thinly populated and, for the most part, unspoilt shore runs from Muros, at the mouth of the Ría de Muros y Noia, round to Caión, just before A Coruña. Inland, narrow lanes weave through woodlands between tiny stone hamlets clustered around ancient churches in the folds of undulating hills. The treacherous coast has seen a lot of shipwrecks, and the idyllic landscape can undergo a rapid transformation when ocean mists blow in. Then it's time to settle into a local bar for some of the top-class local seafood and good Galician wines.

PIPERS & FIDDLERS

Galician folk music has much in common with Celtic traditions in Brittany, Ireland and Scotland, and the haunting sounds of the *gaita* (bagpipe), violin, *bombo* (a big drum), flutes and the extraordinary *zanfona* (a vaguely accordion-like combined wind and string instrument) provide the soundtrack to many moments here.

The most sure-fire spot for hearing a Galician piper is the passageway between Praza do Obradoiro and Praza da Inmaculada in Santiago de Compostela, a day-long haunt of local folk buskers. The best place to catch a live group on a regular basis is Santiago's Casa das Crechas (p566). Several Celtic music festivals liven up the summer months. The biggest and best is the four-day **Festival Ortigueira** (www.festivaldeortigueira.com; ⊙Jul) at Ortigueira in the Rías Altas in mid-July, which attracts bands and musicians from several countries and tens of thousands of music lovers. Other annual festivals well worth seeking out include the **Festival Intercéltico do Morrazo** (⊙Jul/Aug) in Moaña (Ría de Vigo) on a weekend in July or August, and the **Festa da Carballeira** (www.festadacarballeira.com; ⊙Aug), on the first Saturday of August at Zas (Costa da Morte).

Leading *gaiteros* (bagpipers) and other folkies are popular heroes in Galicia. If you fancy tuning into this soulful, quintessentially Galician cultural scene, look for gigs by piper and multi-instrumentalist Carlos Núñez, pipers Xosé Manuel Budiño or Susana Seivane, violinist Begoña Riobó, piper and singer Mercedes Peón, singer Uxía, harpist and *zanfona*- and bouzouki-player Roi Casal, or groups Luar Na Lubre or Milladoiro.

Fisterra & Around

POP 2800 (FISTERRA)

The fishing port of Fisterra (Castilian: Finisterre) has a picturesque harbour, fine views across the Ría de Corcubión, and some beautiful beaches within a few kilometres, but the main reason throngs of people head here is to continue out to Cabo Fisterra. This beautiful, windswept cape is the western edge of Spain, at least in popular imagination (the real westernmost point is Cabo Touriñán, 20km north) and the end point of an ever more popular extension of the Camino de Santiago (90km from Santiago de Compostela)

Fisterra and its cape get busier by the year with Camino travellers and tourists drawn to this oddly magnetic corner of Spain.

Sights

★Cabo Fisterra AREA

(Cabo Finisterre; P) Panoramic Cabo Fisterra is a 3.5km drive or walk south of Fisterra town. It's crowned by a lighthouse, the Faro de Fisterra. Camino de Santiago pilgrims ending their journeys here ritually burn smelly socks, T-shirts and the like on the rocks just past the lighthouse. Many people come for sunset but it's a magnificent spot at any time (except when shrouded in fog or rain). The former lighthouse-keepers' residence is now a comfortable hotel, with a good cafe-bar and restaurant.

On the way out from Fisterra you pass the 12th-century **Igrexa de Santa María das Areas**. Some 600m past the church, a track signed 'Conxunto de San Guillermo' heads up the hill to the right to **Monte de San Guillermo**, which was once a site of pagan fertility rites. This provides a longer (by 2km to 3km), more challenging, but even more scenic alternative walking route to the cape: separate tracks on the upper part of the hill lead to the faint, excavated remains of an old hermitage, the **Ermida de San Guillermo** (or Guillerme), and the **Pedras Santas**. The latter are rocks where, as late as the 18th century, childless couples would come to try to improve their chances of conception.

A taxi to the cape from town costs €5 one way.

Praia da Mar de Fora BEACH

The spectacular beach Praia da Mar de Fora, over on the ocean (western) side of the Fisterra Peninsula, is reachable via an 800m walk from the top of the town. The scenery is glorious, but with strong winds and waves, the beach is not safe for swimming.

Sleeping

Albergue Cabo da Vila HOSTEL €

(981 74 04 54; www.alberguecabodavila.com; Avenida A Coruña 13; dm/s/d/q €12/25/30/48; mid-Mar–mid-Nov; @) Cabo da Vila is an especially welcoming hostel, with multilingual owners and 10 private rooms (with shared bathrooms) as well as the big 24-bunk dorm with good solid metal bunks and big lockers. Sheets and towel (included) are cotton, and the hostel has a kitchen, laundry facilities (€3/4 for washing/drying), an ample indoor sitting area and a small rear garden area. Breakfast €4.

★Hotel Mar da Ardora DESIGN HOTEL €€

(667 641304; www.hotelmardaardora.com; Rúa Atalaia 15; incl breakfast s €77-99, d €85-110; closed mid-Dec–Jan; P@) This delightful little family-run hotel sits at the top of town, with fantastic westward ocean views from the big windows and terraces of its six rooms. Everything is in impeccably contemporary but comfortable style, from the cubist architecture to the soothing white, grey, and silver colour schemes. Downstairs is an excellent spa and gym with solar-heated pool and Turkish bath.

Hotel Rústico Spa Finisterrae HOTEL €€

(981 71 22 11; www.hotelspafinisterrae.com; Lugar da Insua 128; s €39-79, d €49-129; closed Jan & Feb; P) The Finisterrae provides spacious, bright rooms with brass beds, fresh white linen and stone-walled charm. A characterful converted farmhouse, it's 700m up from the harbour, with panoramic views and a garden. Good breakfasts and dinners (€29; order ahead) are available.

O Semáforo de Fisterra BOUTIQUE HOTEL €€

(981 11 02 10; www.hotelsemaforodefisterra.com; Cabo Fisterra; r incl breakfast €99-270;) Possibly Spain's most spectacularly located hotel, the former lighthouse-keepers' residence next to the Faro de Fisterra is now a very comfortable five-room lodging with bright, up-to-date rooms. The **restaurant** (dishes €9-22; 1-4pm & 8-10.30pm) and cafe specialise in traditional Galician dishes, which are mostly prepared from locally bought fish and seafood. Needless to say, the views (when not obscured by rain or fog) are unbeatable.

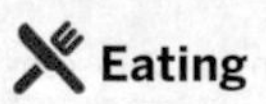

Eating

O Pirata SEAFOOD €

(Paseo de Calafigueira; raciones €7-12; ⏲11am-5pm Feb-May & Sep-Nov, 11am-11pm Jun-Aug, closed Mon & Dec-Jan) With just half a dozen tables but a nice view over the harbour and a short but sweet menu, O Pirata serves up the freshest of fish and seafood at good prices. Try one of its 'portions' of mixed fish and/or seafood (€15 to €20).

Mesón A Cantina GALICIAN €

(Paseo de Calafiguera 1; raciones & mains €6-15; ⏲10am-1am, kitchen 1-4pm & 8-11.30pm; 📶) Multitasking as a hang-out for fishermen, pilgrims, tourists and everyone else, A Cantina is a great, lively option for *bocadillos* (long-bread sandwiches), octopus, squid, fish, *caldeirada* (fish stew), big salads, meat main dishes, and good Estrella de Galicia beer.

O' Fragón GALICIAN €€

(☎981 74 04 29; www.ofragon.es; San Martiño de Arriba 22; mains €14-20; ⏲1.15-3.45pm & 8.15-10.45pm) Several degrees more gastronomically refined than anywhere else in the district, O' Fragón serves beautifully prepared, market-based, mainly fish and seafood dishes in a stylish dining room with picture windows. Service is expertly attentive and the vistas across the wide Ría de Corcubión and the minimalist pine-clad design add to the experience.

O' Fragón is located in a hillside hamlet 2km north of town. Heading north out of Fisterra, turn off the main road at Hotel Arenal and go 1km uphill. The restaurant is below the road and not particularly obvious to spot: look for its small three-car parking area, from which a zig-zag path leads down to the building.

Information

Oficina Municipal de Turismo (☎981 74 07 81; www.concellofisterra.com; Rúa Real 2; ⏲1-9pm) Helpful office inside the municipal pilgrims' hostel, 50m uphill from the main harbour car park.

Getting There & Away

Monbus (www.monbus.es) runs four to six daily buses to/from Santiago de Compostela (€13, two to three hours) via Cée, O Pindo, Carnota and Muros. Monbus can get you from Fisterra to Muxía with a transfer at Cée (Monday to Friday only; the 9.45am and 11.45am buses from Fisterra have the best connections). **Arriva** (www.

CAMIÑO DOS FAROS

There's no better way to experience the essence of the Costa da Morte than to walk along its dramatic coastline. Thanks to what was originally just a small local group of friends, who set out in 2012 to find a route as close to the shore as possible, there is now a 200km footpath, the Camiño dos Faros (Way of the Lighthouses; www.caminodos-faros.com/en), running all the way from Malpica de Bergantiños, about 40km west of A Coruña, to Cabo Fisterra in the southwest.

The route is divided into eight one-day stages of between 18km and 32km, and is a continuous succession of spectacular vistas, as long sweeping beaches, plunging cliffs, high capes and picturesque fishing villages follow one after another. It is, however, not a Sunday stroll in the park, or even much like a Camino de Santiago, but more like mountain hiking by the sea. There is a lot of up and down, the terrain is sometimes rough and the path narrow, and the route passes close to cliffs. Approach it with a sense of adventure, strong footwear with good grip, and appropriate care and caution where necessary. If you're not happy with where you're heading, retrace your steps.

The website is a mine of helpful detailed information, and it's a good idea to download the Wikiloc tracks to consult as you walk.

The trail as originally created was marked and signalled only in the Malpica-to-Fisterra direction, with little green arrows and paint markers which are occasionally easy to miss. It is being upgraded into an officially recognised GR (Gran Recorrido) route, meaning, among other things, improved trail quality and better route marking – in both directions. Until that's completed, don't try to walk it in the Fisterra-to-Malpica direction.

The website has good information on places to stay and eat along the way, but there isn't always a great selection at the end of every stage. Many people enjoy the Camiño dos Faros in day walks covering single stages, using taxis to get back to their starting point if necessary.

arriva.gal) runs five daily buses (fewer Saturday and Sunday) to/from A Coruña (€15, 2¼ hours).

Lires & Around

POP 150 (LIRES)

The pretty and peaceful village of Lires sits just inland from the coast, above the little Ría de Lires. By road it's about 13km north of Fisterra and 20km south of Muxía. For walkers it's conveniently about halfway between Fisterra and Muxía on both the 29km route of the Camino de Santiago and the 51km route of the Camiño dos Faros. With two rivers meeting here, amid typically green, wooded Costa da Morte countryside, plus some wonderful beaches nearby, it's a fine spot to linger even if you're not walking any *camino*.

Sights

Praia de Nemiña BEACH

The beautiful, 1.5km sandy curve of the Praia de Nemiña, stretching north from the mouth of the Ría de Lires, attracts surfers in numbers from roughly April to November and has a couple of surf schools. The *ría* mouth can be crossed at low tide in summer, but otherwise it's a walk of about 2.5km (or a roundabout drive of 9km) from Lires village to the beach.

Praia do Rostro BEACH

(P) One of Galicia's most spectacular beaches, Praia do Rostro is a broad 2km stretch of unbroken sand beginning about 4km south of Lires. It's a particularly magnificent sight from the headlands at either end, with the Atlantic surf pouring in from the open ocean. Unfortunately it's not good for swimming (even if you wanted to brave its very cold waters) but it's a wonderful walk.

Sleeping

As Eiras HOTEL, HOSTEL €

(981 74 81 80; http://ruralaseiras.com; Lires; dm €12, s €35-45, d €45-65; P @ wi-fi) A great stop whether you're walking a *camino* or vehicle-touring, As Eiras has both a budget hostel (with solid bunks in four- to nine-person dorms) and a hotel section with good-sized rooms in pinks and greys, sporting comfy beds and hydromassage showers (the best have sea-view terraces). It's in the middle of Lires and also has a good cafe-restaurant.

Casa Fontequeiroso HOTEL €€

(617 490851; www.casafontequeiroso.com; Hotel Rural Fontequeiroso, Lugar de Queiroso; d incl breakfast €75 Jul-Sep, €65 Oct-Jun; P wi-fi) Just 2km above Praia de Nemiña surf beach (and the Camiño dos Faros), and 2.5km from the Camino de Santiago, this restored, century-old stone house in the minuscule hamlet of Queiroso is a lovely and welcoming place to stay. Delicious meals are based around traditional Galician country recipes with local, often organic ingredients.

Muxía & Around

POP 1540 (MUXÍA)

The stone-built fishing village of Muxía, on the south side of the Ría de Camariñas, is a beloved pilgrimage spot thanks to the belief that the Virgin Mary appeared to Santiago (St James) while he was preaching here.

Sights

Santuario da Virxe da Barca CHURCH

(Mass noon & 7pm Sun year-round, 7pm Mon-Sat Jun-Oct; P) This 18th-century church on the rocky seashore at the north end of town marks the spot where (legend attests) the Virgin Mary arrived in a stone boat and appeared to Santiago (St James) while he was preaching here.

★Cabo Touriñán NATURAL FEATURE

(P) The picturesque rocky Cabo Touriñán, 17km southwest of Muxía and marked by one the area's many lighthouses, is great for a breezy walk. The northwest corner of the cape, Punta de Sualba, is the westernmost point of peninsular Spain (longitude 9º18'), and Touriñán is also the place where, from 21 March to 25 April and from 13 August to 22 September, the sun sets later than anywhere else on mainland Europe.

Sleeping & Eating

★Bela Muxía HOSTEL €

(687 798222; www.belamuxia.com; Rúa da Encarnación 30, Muxía; dm €12-15, d €40-50; closed Jan or Feb; @ wi-fi) Very comfortable and stylish, this designer hostel features bright, hotel-standard private rooms with bathroom, as well as spacious dorms with good mattresses, reading lights and electrical plugs for each bunk, big lockers and plenty of showers and toilets. Common areas, including the

kitchen and dining area, are spacious and well designed, and there are great panoramas from the upper floors.

Albergue Arribada HOSTEL €
(☎981 74 25 16; www.arribadaalbergue.com; Rúa José María del Río 30, Muxía; dm €12, s/d/tr €40/50/67; @ 🛜) This well-designed, welcoming modern hostel opened in 2015, and features two enormous private rooms with private bathrooms, four 10-person dorms, and good bathroom, kitchen and laundry facilities. They even have a saltwater foot bath to soothe sore feet!

★**Casa de Trillo** HOTEL €€
(☎634 759557; www.casadetrillo.com; Santa Mariña; incl breakfast s €48-73, d €60-92, apt for 2 people €80-95; ⏲closed late Dec–Jan; P @ 🛜) Deep in the Galician countryside at Santa Mariña, about 8km south of Muxía (well signposted along the country lanes), this charming 16th-century manor house has history, cosy rooms, a nice bright dining room overlooking the lovely gardens, and home-grown food. It's a marvellous base for exploring the area or just relaxing, and the hospitable owners can answer your every question.

Restaurante A Marina GALICIAN €
(Avenida A Marina 30, Muxía; raciones & mains €6-14; ⏲8am-11pm; 🛜) A busy, friendly place with outside tables facing the harbour across the road, A Marina does hearty breakfasts for those setting out on (or winding down from) long walks. Later in the day there's reliably good octopus (*á feira* or *flambé*) and other seafood favourites, salads, grilled sole, *raxo* (chunks of spicy marinated pork) and scrambled or fried egg dishes.

ℹ Getting There & Away

Hefe SL (www.grupoferrin.com) runs two daily buses between Muxía and Santiago de Compostela (€8, 1½ hours). **Arriva** (www.arriva.gal) operates a bus from Muxía to Camariñas and A Coruña (€13, two hours) at 6am Monday to Friday and 6.10pm on Sunday, and from A Coruña to Muxía at 3pm Monday to Saturday.

Camariñas to Camelle: the Ruta do Litoral

POP 2500 (CAMARIÑAS)

The fishing village of Camariñas, wrapped around its colourful harbour, is known for its delicate traditional lacework, which can be viewed at several specialist shops and the **Museo do Encaixe** (Lace Museum; Praza Insuela, Camariñas; €2; ⏲11am-2pm & 4-7pm Tue-Sat, to 6pm Sun).

The rugged coast between Camariñas and Camelle, to the northeast, is one of the most beautiful stretches of the Costa da Morte, and you can drive, ride or walk it along the 24km **Ruta do Litoral** (part paved, part potholed dirt/gravel). It's 5km northwest from Camariñas to the **Cabo Vilán lighthouse** (with a cafe and an exhibition on shipwrecks and lighthouses) then a further 19km east to Camelle. The route winds past secluded beaches, across windswept hillsides and past weathered rock formations, and there are several places to stop along the way. **Praias da Pedrosa, da Balea and da Reira** are a picturesque set of short sandy strands divided by groups of boulders a couple of kilometres east of Cabo Vilán; then there's the **Ceminterio dos Ingleses** (English Cemetery; Areal de Trece), the sad burial ground from an 1890 shipwreck that took the lives of 172 British naval cadets.

If you want to stick even closer to the shoreline than the Ruta do Litoral does,

CAMINOS OF THE MUXÍA–FISTERRA REGION

Muxía is the destination of increasingly popular pilgrim trails from Santiago de Compostela and Fisterra. The Camino de Santiago, coming from Santiago de Compostela, divides just after Hospital village (60km from Santiago), with one branch heading 27km northwest to Muxía and the other going 30km southwest to Cabo Fisterra. Completing the triangle, a 29km route links Muxía with Fisterra.

The Camino de Santiago follows a pretty, well-marked route between Muxía and Fisterra, through woodlands and green countryside. A different kind of trail from Muxía to Fisterra, the Camiño dos Faros (p570), sticks close to the spectacular coast and covers a more demanding and adventurous 51km route, visiting dramatic capes such as Cabo Touriñán (p571) and spectacular beaches including Praia de Nemiña (p571) and Praia do Rostro (p571).

you can walk the fifth stage of the Camiño dos Faros (p570), westbound from Arou to Camariñas.

For further information on Camariñas area walking routes, see www.turismocamarinas.net.

Camelle village has no outstanding charm, but it does have two touching mementoes of 'Man' (Manfred Gnädinger), an eccentric long-time German resident who died in 2002: the **Museo Xardín de Man**, his quirky sculpture garden beside the pier, and the **Museo Man de Camelle** (981 71 02 24; www.mandecamelle.com; Rúa do Muelle 9; adult/child €1/free; 11am-2pm & 5-8pm Tue-Sun mid-Jun–mid-Sep, 11am-2pm & 5-7pm Sat & Sun mid-Sep–mid-Jun; P), back along the waterfront.

Praia de Traba is a lovely 4km walk east along the coast from Camelle.

Sleeping

★Lugar do Cotariño CASA RURAL **€€**
(639 638634; www.docotarino.com; Camariñas; d incl breakfast €75-120; P @) A labour of love for its owners, this beautifully reconstructed 400-year-old farmstead sits in verdant countryside 1km out of Camariñas. The seven rooms are homey and pretty in perfect country style, the two 'specials' in the main house being especially large and appealing. The lovely garden includes two ancient stone *hórreos*.

Getting There & Away

Arriva (www.arriva.gal) runs buses to A Coruña (€12, 1½ hours) at 6.30am Monday to Friday and at 6.40pm on Sundays. From A Coruña to Camariñas, there is direct service only on Sundays (departing at 3.30pm); other days you have to go to Cée and change.

Laxe & Around

POP 1800 (LAXE)

A sweeping bay beach runs right along the waterfront of the fishing port of Laxe, and the 15th-century Gothic church of **Santa María da Atalaia** stands guard over the harbour. Laxe's **tourist office** (981 70 69 65; www.concellodelaxe.com/turismo; Avenida Cesáreo Pondal 26; 9am-3pm Mon-Fri) and its website (in Spanish and Galician) have information on walks in the area, including a 4.6km round trip to the **lighthouse** at the tip of the Insua promontory, north of town (route PRG70), and the 8km (each way) coastal walk west to **Praia de Traba** via the surf beach Praia de Soesto (PRG114).

For a fascinating archaeological outing, drive 7km east on the AC429 to As Grelas, then 2.4km south on the AC430 to find the turn-off for the Castro A Cidá de Borneiro, a pre-Roman castro amid thick woodlands. One kilometre further along the AC430, turn right along the DP1404 for 1km to the **Dolmen de Dombate** (Dombate; 9am-2pm & 3-9pm Jul-Sep, to 8pm Oct-Jun, free guided tours every 30min 10am-1.30pm & 4-6.30pm daily Jul-Sep, Fri-Sun Oct-Jun; P) FREE, a large, well-preserved prehistoric tomb dubbed the 'megalithic cathedral of Galicia' and now, since 2011, encased in a protective pavilion.

Getting There & Away

Laxe is linked to A Coruña by one or more daily direct Arriva buses (€9 to €10, 1¼ to two hours). There are further services with a change at Carballo.

RÍAS ALTAS

In few places do land and sea meet in such abrupt beauty. The untamed beaches, towering cliffs and powerful waves of the Rías Altas (Galicia's north coast from A Coruña eastward) are certainly more dramatic than the landscapes of the Rías Baixas. They're also less touristed and less populated, making an ideal destination for travellers yearning to get off the heavily beaten path. Add in the allure of cultured, maritime A Coruña, medieval towns including Betanzos and Pontedeume, several lively little fishing ports and the backdrop of a green, farmhouse-studded countryside, and you're in for a travel treat.

A Coruña

POP 213,400

A Coruña (Castilian: La Coruña) is a port city and beachy hot spot; a cultural hub and a busy commercial centre; a historic city and a proud modern metropolis with a fine food scene and buzzing nightlife – all in all, an intriguing place to discover that is too often overlooked by travellers.

The city occupies a particularly contorted corner of the Galician coast. The centre sits on an isthmus straddled by the port on its southeast side and the main ocean beaches on the northwest. An irregularly shaped peninsula extends 2km north out to the Torre de

A Coruña

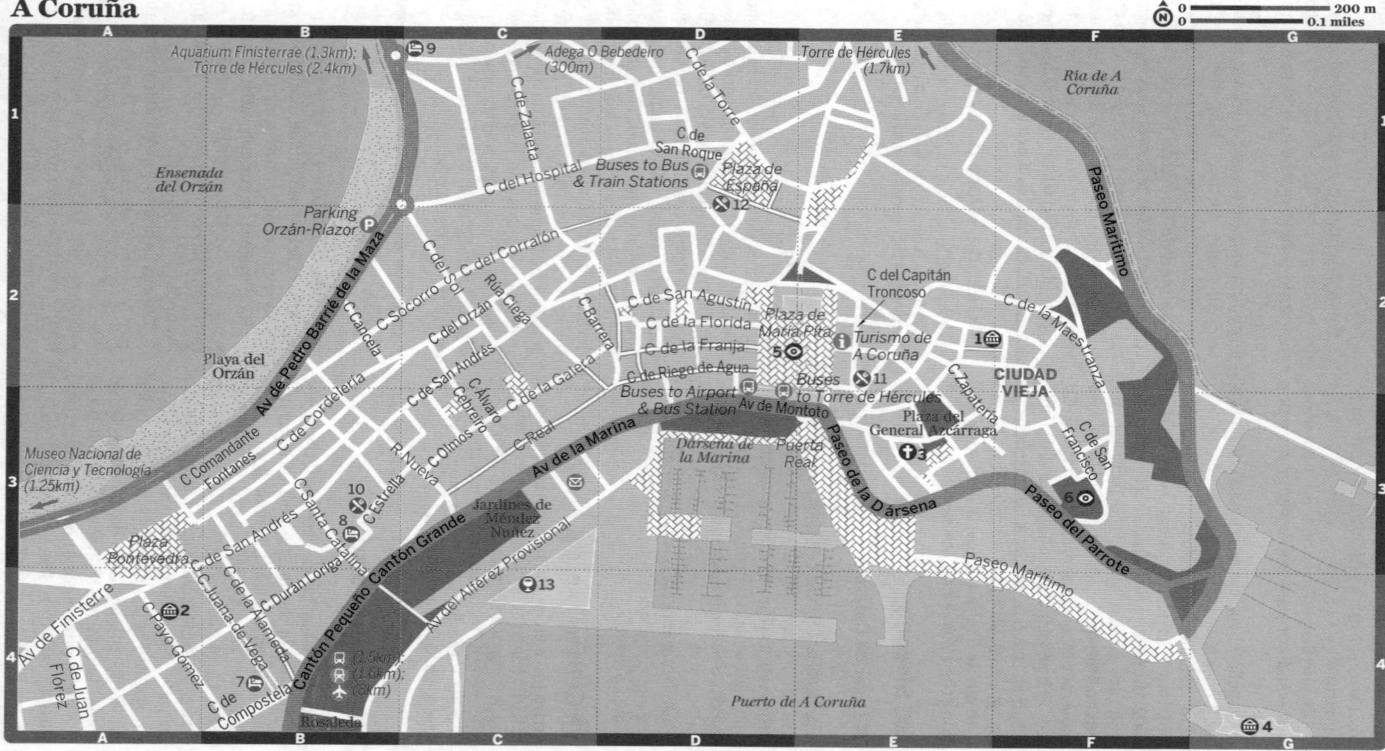

0 200 m
0 0.1 miles
Aquarium Finisterrae (1.3km); Torre de Hércules (2.4km)
Adega O Bebedeiro (300m)
Torre de Hércules (1.7km)
Ría de A Coruña
Ensenada del Orzán
Parking Orzán-Riazor
Playa del Orzán
Museo Nacional de Ciencia y Tecnología (1.25km)
Av de Pedro Barrié de la Maza
C de Zalaeta
C de la Torre
C de San Roque
C del Hospital
Buses to Bus & Train Stations
Plaza de España
C del Sol
C del Corralón
C Socorro
Rúa Ciega
C del Orzán
C Cancela
C de Cordelería
C de San Andrés
C Álvaro Cebreiro
C de la Galera
C Barrera
C de San Agustín
C de la Florida
C de la Franja
C de Riego de Agua
Plaza de María Pita
Turismo de A Coruña
C del Capitán Troncoso
Buses to Airport & Bus Station
Buses to Torre de Hércules
Av de Montoto
C de la Maestranza
CIUDAD VIEJA
C Zapatería
Plaza del General Azcárraga
C de San Francisco
Paseo Marítimo
Paseo del Parrote
Paseo de la Dársena
Dársena de la Marina
Puerta Real
C Comandante Fontanes
R Nueva
C Olmos
C Real
Av de la Marina
C Estrella
C Santa Catalina
Jardines de Méndez Núñez
Plaza Pontevedra
C Durán Loriga
C de la Alameda
C Juana de Vega
C Payo Gómez
Cantón Pequeño
Cantón Grande
Av del Alférez Provisional
C de Compostela
Av de Finisterre
C de Juan Flórez
(1.5km); (1.6km); (8km)
Rosaleda
Puerto de A Coruña

A Coruña

Sights
1 Casa Museo María Pita E2
2 Casa Museo Picasso A4
3 Iglesia de Santiago E3
4 Museo Arqueológico e Histórico G4
5 Plaza de María Pita D2
6 Xardín de San Carlos F3

Sleeping
7 Blue Coruña Hotel B4
8 Lois B3
9 Meliá María Pita C1

Eating
10 A Taberna de Cunqueiro B3
11 Pablo Gallego E2
12 Pulpeira de Melide D1

Drinking & Nightlife
13 Los Cantones Village C4

Hércules, a World Heritage–listed Roman lighthouse. The Paseo Marítimo, a wonderful 13km walkway and bike path, runs all the way from the port, around the peninsula, along the ocean beaches and on out to the west.

Sights

★Torre de Hércules LIGHTHOUSE

(www.torredeherculesacoruna.com; Avenida Doctor Vázquez Iglesias; adult/senior & child €3/1.50, Mon free; 10am-9pm Jun-Sep, 10am-6pm Oct-May; P) The World Heritage–listed Tower of Hercules sits near the windy northern tip of the city. Legend attributes its construction to one of the labours of Hercules, but it was actually the Romans who originally built this lighthouse in the 1st century AD – a beacon on what was then the furthest edge of the civilised world. Climb the 234 steps for great panoramas of the city and coast. Buses 3 and 5 run here from **Puerta Real** near Plaza de María Pita.

★Aquarium Finisterrae AQUARIUM

(981 18 98 42; www.mc2coruna.org/aquarium; Paseo Marítimo 34; adult/senior & child €10/4; 10am-8pm Jul & Aug, shorter hours rest of year; P) Kids love the seal colony and the underwater Nautilus room (surrounded by sharks and 50 other fish species) at this excellent aquarium on the city's northern headland. The focus is on the marine life of Galicia's coasts and the Atlantic.

★Museo Nacional de Ciencia y Tecnología MUSEUM

(www.muncyt.es; Plaza del Museo Nacional 1; 11am-8pm Tue-Sat, 11am-3pm Sun Jul–mid-Sep, 10am-5pm Tue-Fri, 11am-7pm Sat, 11am-3pm Sun mid-Sep–Jun;) FREE Not just for techies, A Coruña's National Science and Technology Museum will engage everybody. You'll see the first computer used in Spain (a monstrous IBM 650 from 1959), and the entire front section of a Boeing 747. Perhaps most fascinating is the room displaying innovations from every year of the 20th century – a 1965 SEAT 600 (the tiny car that 'got Spain motoring'), a Sony PlayStation (1994), a 1946 state-of-the-art pencil sharpener and much more.

Casa Museo Picasso MUSEUM

(Calle Payo Gómez 14, 2º; 11am-1pm & 6-8pm Tue-Sat, noon-2pm Sun) FREE Pablo Picasso lived in this large apartment from the age of nine to 13 (1891–95), while his father taught art at the Instituto da Guarda school on nearby Plaza de Pontevedra. The apartment still has the same layout, and is kitted out with period furniture and copies of the many paintings and drawings that Picasso did while here, testament to his precocious talent. Enthusiastic attendants make visits all the more interesting. Ring the bell to enter.

Ciudad Vieja AREA

Shady plazas, charming old churches, hilly cobbled lanes and a scattering of cafes and bars fill A Coruña's compact original nucleus, at the southern tip of the northern promontory. Start from stately **Plaza de María Pita** and make your way through the labyrinth to the 16th-century Castillo de San Antón, the fort guarding the entrance to the port, which now houses the **Museo Arqueológico e Histórico** (981 18 98 50; Paseo Marítimo; adult/senior & child €2/1, Sat free; 10am-9pm Tue-Sat, 10am-3pm Sun Jul & Aug, 10am-7.30pm Tue-Sat, 10am-2.30pm Sun Sep-Jun).

Interesting stops en route include the **Iglesia de Santiago** (Calle de Santiago); the **Casa Museo María Pita** (Calle Herrerías 28; 11am-1.30pm & 6-8pm Tue-Sat, noon-2pm Sun) FREE, home of a local heroine who inspired the defeat of an English invasion force in 1589; and the **Xardín de San Carlos** (Calle de San Francisco; approx sunrise-sunset), where English general Sir John Moore, who died fighting in alliance with the Spanish in 1809, lies buried.

Sleeping

Lois HOTEL €
(☎ 981 21 22 69; www.loisestrella.com; Calle Estrella 40; s €46, d €58-78; ❄ 📶) The Lois is a class above other budget hotels with its comfy and stylish rooms in contemporary greys and whites, up-to-date bathrooms, and its own stone-walled restaurant (breakfast €8). The few singles are a squeeze but the seven doubles are a good size; they all have their own *galerías* (glassed-in balconies).

Blue Coruña Hotel HOTEL €€
(☎ 881 88 85 55; www.hotelbluecoruna.com; Calle Juana de Vega 7; s €73-110, d €81-125; ❄ 📶) Contemporary-style Blue has every room themed to a different world city, with a unique mural. Everything is bright, comfortable and convenient, with up-to-date fittings like touch-on, touch-off lamps, and good bathrooms with rainhead showers, and nonsteam and magnifying mirrors. Singles are on the small side, but doubles are b-i-g. Breakfast €11.

Meliá María Pita HOTEL €€
(☎ 981 20 50 00; http://melia.com; Avenida Pedro Barrié de la Maza 3; incl breakfast s €87-166, d €100-180; P ❄ @ 📶) This classy 180-room hotel boasts a big, glittery lobby, good eating options including an excellent buffet breakfast, plenty of private parking, and spacious rooms in attractive grey, silver and white. Its biggest plus, though, is the location just across the street from Playa del Orzán and the glorious beach views from the upper floors, with floor-to-ceiling windows.

Eating

For tapas, *raciones*, wine and cheap lunch menus, hit the streets west of Plaza de María Pita – Calles de la Franja, Barrera, Galera, Olmos and Estrella. Moving westward along these lanes the vibe mutates from old-style *mesones* (eating houses) and *tabernas* (taverns) to contemporary tapas bars.

Restaurants for more substantial sit-down meals are dotted all around the central areas.

★ **Adega O Bebedeiro** GALICIAN €€
(☎ 981 21 06 09; www.adegaobebedeiro.com; Calle de Ángel Rebollo 34; mains €16-25; ⏲ 1.30-4pm & 8pm-midnight Tue-Sat, 1.30-4pm Sun) It's on a humble street on the northern headland and doesn't look like much from outside, but the inside is rustically neat with a conversation-inspiring assortment of Galician bric-a-brac. The food is classic home-style cooking with some inventive touches, such as scallop-stuffed sea bass in puff pastry, or Galician beef entrecôte with goat's cheese, all in generous quantities. Packed on weekends.

A Taberna de Cunqueiro GALICIAN, TAPAS €€
(www.atabernadecunqueiro.com; Calle Estrella 22; raciones & mains €9-21; ⏲ noon-4pm & 7pm-midnight; 📶) One of a string of busy, indoor-outdoor bar-restaurants along narrow Calle Estrella, the Cunqueiro is frequently the busiest and liveliest of them all, attracting a totally mixed crowd with its free tapas and well-prepared typical Galician seafood and meat dishes at reasonable prices.

Pulpeira de Melide SEAFOOD €€
(Plaza de España 16; raciones €8-18; ⏲ 12.30-4pm & 7.30pm-midnight Tue-Sun) Frequently packed, this informal bar-restaurant is one of the very best places to enjoy that quintessential Galician favourite, *pulpo á feira* (tender octopus slices with paprika and olive oil, €11 per *ración*), perfectly complemented by an order of *cachelos* (boiled potatoes, €2.40). There's a daily selection of other market-fresh seafood if you fancy something different.

Pablo Gallego GALICIAN €€€
(☎ 981 20 88 88; www.pablogallego.com; Calle del Capitán Troncoso 4; mains €18-25; ⏲ 1-4pm & 9pm-midnight Mon-Sat, 1-4pm Sun) This fine little restaurant prepares artful 21st-century dishes with traditional Galician market ingredients. Try sardines with guacamole and spicy Mexican *pico de gallo* relish, or entrecôte steak in gorgonzola and sweet Pêdro Ximénez wine, or maybe opt for the fish or shellfish of the day.

Drinking & Nightlife

A Coruña buzzes with taverns, bars and clubs. Before midnight, head to Plaza de María Pita for low-key drinks or navigate the taverns and tapas bars to its west. From Thursday to Saturday, dozens of bars in the streets behind Playa del Orzán party on until 3am or 4am, and the harbour-view clubs in **Los Cantones Village** (Avenida del Alférez Provisional; ⏲ midnight-5am Thu-Sat, from 10pm for live music) go on longer.

Information

Turismo de A Coruña (981 92 30 93; www.turismocoruna.com; Plaza de María Pita 6; 9am-8.30pm Mon-Fri, 10am-2pm & 4-8pm Sat, 10am-7pm Sun, shorter hr Nov-Jan) Very helpful and professional main city tourist office, with information in several languages.

Getting There & Away

AIR

From **A Coruña airport** (Aeropuerto de Alvedro; 981 18 72 00; www.aena.es), 8km south of the city centre, Iberia (www.iberia.com) and Air Europa (www.aireuropa.com) both fly several times daily to Madrid; Vueling Airlines (www.vueling.com) flies daily to London (Heathrow) and Barcelona (three flights daily), and a few times weekly to Seville and Valencia; and TAP Portugal (www.flytap.com) flies to Lisbon four times weekly.

BUS

From the **bus station** (981 18 43 35; www.coruna.gal/estacionautobuses; Calle de Caballeros 21), 2km south of the city centre, Monbus heads south to Santiago de Compostela (€6, one to 1½ hours, 12 or more daily) and beyond. **Arriva** (981 33 00 46, 981 31 12 13; www.arriva.gal) serves the Costa da Morte, Ferrol, the Rías Altas, Lugo and Ourense; and ALSA heads to Madrid and destinations in Asturias, Cantabria, the Basque Country and Castilla y León.

TRAIN

The **train station** (Plaza de San Cristóbal) is 2km south of the city centre. Direct services:

DESTINATION	FARE (€)	DURATION	FREQUENCY (DAILY)
Ferrol	6.10-15.40	1¼hr	5-6
León	25-44	5-6hr	1-4
Lugo	10-15	1½-2hr	3-5
Madrid	35-58	5½-11hr	1-3
Pontevedra	14-16	1-1½hr	12-14
Santiago de Compostela	6.10-16	30-40min	19-26

Trains to the Rías Altas, Asturias, Cantabria and the Basque Country start from Ferrol and are operated by FEVE (www.renfe.com/viajeros/feve).

Getting Around

Blue 'Aeropuerto' buses (€1.50, 30 minutes) run every half-hour (hourly on Saturdays and Sundays) from about 7.15am to 9.45pm between the airport and **Puerta Real** in the city centre.

Local bus 5 runs from the train station to Puerta Real in the city centre, and back to the station from **Plaza de España**. Buses 1, 1A and 4 run from the bus station to the city centre; returning, take bus 1 or 1A from Puerta Real or bus 4 from Plaza de España. Rides cost €1.30.

The least exorbitantly priced central car park is **Parking Orzán-Riazor** (Avenida de Pedro Barrié de la Maza; per 24hr €20; 24hr), which stretches for 1.3km below the beachfront road Avenida de Pedro Barrié de la Maza, with several entrances.

Betanzos

POP 10,200

Once a thriving estuary port rivalling A Coruña, Betanzos is renowned for its welcoming taverns with local wines and good food, and has a well-preserved medieval Old Town that harmoniously combines galleried houses, old-fashioned shops and some monumental architecture.

Take Rúa Castro up from the central plaza into the **Old Town**, where handsome Praza da Constitución is flanked by a couple of appealing cafes along with the Romanesque/Gothic **Igrexa de Santiago**, whose main portico was inspired by Santiago de Compostela's Pórtico de la Gloria. A short stroll northeast, two beautiful Gothic churches, **Santa María do Azougue** and **San Francisco** (Rúa San Francisco; €2; 10-30am-1.30pm & 4.30-7pm, to 6pm Sun), stand almost side by side opposite the municipal market. San Francisco is full of particularly fine carved-stone tombs.

Sleeping

Hotel Garelos HOTEL €€

(981 77 59 30; www.hotelgarelos.com; Calle Alfonso IX 8; incl breakfast s €55-60, d €66-82; P) Hotel Garelos, 150m from Praza dos Irmáns Garcia Naviera, has spick-and-span rooms with comfy beds, parquet floors, good bathrooms and original watercolours, and the buffet breakfast is good and generous.

O Pote GALICIAN €€

(www.mesonopote.com; Travesía do Progreso 9; raciones €9-18; 1.30-3.45pm & 8.30-11pm, closed Sun night & Tue;) One of several inviting taverns on two narrow streets descending from the central plaza, O Pote does a classic *tortilla de Betanzos* (the town's particularly gooey version of the standard Spanish potato omelette), plus well-prepared octopus and other seafood options.

Getting There & Away

Arriva (p577) buses head to/from A Coruña (€2.20, 40 minutes) about every half-hour Monday to Friday (6.30am to 9.30pm) and hourly at weekends (7am to 8pm). Four or more Arriva buses head to Pontedeume (€2.50, 30 minutes) and a few to Ferrol and Viveiro. All buses stop in Praza dos Irmáns García Naveira.

Betanzos Cidade station is northwest of the town centre, across the Río Mendo. At least three trains go daily to/from A Coruña (€4, 40 minutes) and at least five to Pontedeume (€2.25, 15 minutes) and Ferrol (€4, 40 minutes).

Pontedeume

POP 4500

Climbing a hillside above the Eume estuary, where fishing boats bob, Pontedeume's Old Town is an appealing combination of handsome galleried houses, cobbled lanes and occasional open plazas, liberally sprinkled with taverns and tapas bars. Several parallel narrow streets climb up from the main road, the central one being the porticoed Rúa Real.

The stout, 18m-high Torreón dos Andrade (Avenida Torreón; interpretation centre adult/child €2/1; ⏱11am-1.30pm & 5-7pm, to 8.30pm mid-Jun–mid-Sep) was erected in the late 14th century, probably by Fernán Pérez de Andrade 'O Boo' (The Good), who fought on the winning side in wars among Castilian royalty and as a reward was made lord of a sizeable chunk of northern Galicia by King Enrique II. The tower contains a worthwhile interpretation centre on the Andrade family, who went on to dominate this area for two centuries, and also houses the local **tourist office** (☎981 43 02 70; www.pontedeume.gal; ⏱11am-1.30pm & 5-7pm, to 8.30pm mid-Jun–mid-Sep).

Buses and trains between A Coruña, Betanzos and Ferrol stop here.

There are a few adequate *hostales* in town but the area's most enticing sleeping options are rural hotels (p578).

Parque Natural Fragas do Eume

East of Pontedeume, the valley of the Río Eume is home to Europe's best-preserved Atlantic coastal forest, with beautiful deciduous woodlands and rare relict ferns. The 91-sq-km Parque Natural Fragas do Eume (http://parquesnaturais.xunta.gal/es/fragas-do-eume) has a helpful visitors centre, the **Centro de Interpretación** (☎981 43 25 28; Carretera DP6902; ⏱10am-2pm Tue-Sun year-round, afternoon hr vary with seaason), 6km from Pontedeume on the DP6902 Caaveiro road. From here a paved road and an off-road path (the Camiño dos Encomendeiros) lead along the thickly forested valley to the beautifully sited old **Mosteiro de Caaveiro** (⏱tours hourly 11.15am-2.15pm & 4-6pm daily mid-Jun–mid-Sep, Fri-Sun mid-Sep–Dec) FREE, 8km further east.

With time and a vehicle it's well worth venturing to the park's further reaches. In Monfero, a few kilometres outside the park's southern boundary, you'll find a grander monastery, the **Mosteiro de Monfero** (Carretera DP5003; ⏱11am-2pm & 4-6.30pm Tue-Sun mid-Jun–mid-Sep, 3-6.30pm Fri, 11am-2pm & 4-6.30pm Sat & Sun rest of year; P) FREE, with another **visitors centre** (☎881 06 39 92; Carretera DP5003; ⏱10am-6pm Tue-Sun mid-Mar–mid-Sep, shorter hr mid-Sep–mid-Mar) nearby. A few kilometres east from here you can access several well-marked walking trails within the park – particularly scenic is the 6.5km **Camiño dos Cerqueiros** loop above the Encoro do Eume reservoir.

Sleeping

★Casa do Castelo de Andrade HOTEL €€

(☎981 43 38 39; www.casteloandrade.com; Lugar Castelo de Andrade; r €105-130; ⏱closed mid-Oct–Mar; P📶) This enchanting rural hotel sits in the hills 7km southeast of Pontedeume. It's a pretty stone farmhouse in enormous grounds, with spacious common areas and 10 immaculate, olde-worlde-style rooms, all unique. The owner is a mine of helpful information about the area. Rates drop outside of summer. Breakfast €11.

Getting There & Around

Over Easter and from mid-June to the end of September, the last 6.5km of the road to the Mosteiro de Caaveiro is closed to cars, but is covered by a free bus service. Another easy option during these periods is to hire one of **Tour e-bike's** (☎660 428637; www.tour-ebike.com; rental per 1/1½/2hr/day €8/12/16/25; 👪) electric bicycles at La Alameda, the point from which the road is closed, 1km past the Centro de Interpretación.

Cedeira & Around

POP 4600 (CEDEIRA)

The coast north of the naval port of Ferrol is studded with small maritime towns and pretty beaches. The fishing port and low-key resort of Cedeira, tucked into a sheltered *ría* (coastal inlet), makes a very good base for exploring the Rías Altas.

Ferrol itself is a transport hub (among other things, it's the western terminus of the FEVE railway along the coast to the Basque Country), but has little to detain you.

Sights & Activities

Cedeira's cute, tiny old town sits on the west bank of the little Río Condomiñas, while **Praia da Magdalena** fronts the modern, eastern side of town. Around the headland to the south (a 7km drive) is the much more appealing **Praia de Vilarrube**, a long, sandy beach with shallow waters between two river mouths, in a protected area of dunes and wetlands.

Praia de Pantín SURFING

() This beach 12km southwest of Cedeira has a great right-hander for surfers. Over six days in late August or early September, it hosts the **Pantín Classic** (www.pantinclassic.com; Aug/Sep), a qualifying event in the World Surf League. Several surf schools operate here from about late June to early September, charging around €30 per two-hour class or €110 for a course of five two-hour classes.

Punta Sarridal Walk WALKING

For a nice stroll of an hour or two, walk along Cedeira's waterfront to the fishing port, climb up beside the 18th-century Castelo da Concepción above it, and walk out to Punta Sarridal, overlooking the mouth of the Ría de Cedeira. The rocky coast around here produces rich harvests of *percebes* (goose barnacles).

Sleeping

Cedeira has a fair supply of *hostales* and small hotels, but two places in Cordobelas, just off the main road 1km south of Cedeira, stand out.

Casa Cordobelas HOTEL €

(981 48 06 07; www.cordobelas.com; Cordobelas; s €44-55, d €55-72, 1-bedroom apt €61-83, 2-bedroom apt €83-110; closed mid-Dec–mid-Jan;) A charming stone-built property run by a friendly family, Casa Cordobelas comprises four century-old, village houses converted into one, with seven comfortable, spacious, rustic-style rooms, and a lovely garden. Breakfast €7.70.

★**Hotel Herbeira** DESIGN HOTEL €€

(981 49 21 67; www.hotelherbeira.com; Cordobelas; s €60-105, d €70-125; closed 22 Dec-12 Jan;) As sleek as Galicia gets, this welcoming, family-run hotel offers 16 large, contemporary rooms with glassed-in galleries, well-equipped bathrooms and stunning views over the *ría* – a perfect combination of design, comfort and practicality. There's a beautiful pool at the front and a bright, spacious cafe and sitting area for the good breakfasts (€4 to €8).

Eating

With its own *ría* and small fishing fleet, Cedeira is a great place to enjoy fresh Galician seafood. It's specially famous for its *percebes* (goose barnacles), a much-prized (and high-priced) delicacy.

A Taberna do Jojó SEAFOOD €€

(cnr Rúas Ezequiel López & Ferrol; raciones €8-17; 11am-4pm & 8-11pm Tue-Sat) For seafood as it should be done – top ingredients prepared with minimal fuss – head to this popular bar-restaurant and order some *berberechos/almejas/calamares a la plancha* (hotplate-grilled cockles/clams/squid), or *mejillones al vapor* (steamed mussels), or *pulpo á feira* (octopus slices in olive oil and paprika) or *percebes* (goose barnacles). Perfect with a glass of albariño.

Information

Tourist Office (981 48 21 87; http://turismo.cedeira.gal; Avenida Castelao 18; 9am-9pm Mon-Fri, 10am-2pm Sat, 11.30am-1.30pm Sun Jun-Sep, shorter hours rest of year) A helpful place on the main road in the new part of town.

Getting There & Away

By bus from the south, you'll need to get to Ferrol, then take a Monbus bus from Praza de Galicia to Cedeira (€1.50, one hour, four daily Monday to Friday, two daily Saturday and Sunday). Cedeira's bus station is on Rúa Deportes, just off Avenida Castelao, 700m southeast of the Río Condomiñas.

Cabo Ortegal & Around

The wild, rugged coastline for which the Rías Altas is famous begins in earnest above

LOCAL KNOWLEDGE

GALICIA SEAFOOD TIPS

Galician seafood is plentiful and fresh and may well be the best you have ever tasted. Almost every restaurant and bar has lots of it on the menu. Shellfish fans will delight over the variety of *ameixas* (clams), *mexillons* (mussels), *vieiras* (scallops), *zamburiñas* (small scallops), *berberechos* (cockles) and *navajas* (razor clams). But Galicia's ultimate crustacean delicacy is the much-prized *percebes* (goose barnacles), which bear a disconcerting resemblance to fingernails or claws: to eat them you hold the 'claw' end, twist off the other end and eat the soft, succulent bit inside!

Other delicacies include various crabs, from little *nécoras* and *santiaguiños* to huge *centollos* (spider crabs) and the enormous *buey del mar* ('ox of the sea'), and the *bogavante* or *lubrigante* (European lobster), with two enormous claws.

Shellfish in restaurants is often priced by weight: around 250g per person usually makes a fairly large serving. Simple steaming or hotplate-grilling (a la plancha) is almost always the best way to prepare shellfish, maybe with a dash of olive oil, garlic or herbs to enhance the natural flavour.

While mussels, oysters and some fish are farmed, most crabs are caught wild. Look for *salvaje* (wild) or *del pincho* (line-caught) on menus to identify nonfarmed fish.

Cedeira. If you have your own transport, Galicia's northwestern corner is a spectacular place to explore, with vertigo-inducing cliffs, stunning oceanscapes, lush forests and horses roaming free over the hills.

Sights & Activities

San Andrés de Teixido VILLAGE

Busloads of tourists and pilgrims descend on the holy hamlet of San Andrés de Teixido, renowned for its sanctuary of relics of St Andrew, in a beautiful fold of the coastal hills a 12km drive north from Cedeira. You can sample the area's famed *percebes* at several cafes here. A spectacular 5km stretch of the **Ruta dos Peiraos path** runs along the clifftops from Chao do Monte lookout, 4km up the road towards Cedeira (or a steep 1km walk).

★Garita de Herbeira VIEWPOINT

(P) From San Andrés de Teixido the DP2205 winds up and across the Serra da Capelada towards Cariño for incredible views. Six kilometres from San Andrés is the must-see Garita de Herbeira, a naval lookout post built in 1805, 615m above sea level and the best place to be awed by southern Europe's highest ocean cliffs.

★Cabo Ortegal VIEWPOINT

(P) Four kilometres north of the workaday fishing town of Cariño looms the mother of Spanish capes, Cabo Ortegal, where the Atlantic Ocean meets the Bay of Biscay. Great stone shafts drop sheer into the ocean from such a height that the waves crashing on the rocks below seem pitifully benign. **Os Tres Aguillóns**, three jagged rocky islets, provide a home to hundreds of marine birds, and with binoculars you might spot dolphins or whales.

On the road from Cariño, you can stop at the first mirador (Miradoiro Gabeira) to take the well-marked clifftop trail to the little **Ermida de San Xiao do Trebo** chapel (1.6km). The path traverses a forest, crosses the Río Soutullo and affords grand views. From the chapel you can rejoin the road and continue 1.5km to Cabo Ortegal.

Sleeping & Eating

A Miranda HOTEL €€

(☎654 341150; www.hotelamiranda.com; Lugar do Barral; r incl breakfast €80-110; ⊙Mar-Oct; P 📶) Five of the six uncluttered, comfortable rooms at this contemporary-style small hotel have balconies looking out over the Ría de Ortigueira. Breakfast is healthy and generous, there's a good bright lounge, and dinners are available. It's 6.5km south of Cariño on the DP6121, then 200m up a side road (signposted).

Muiño das Cañotas HOTEL €€

(☎698 138588; www.muinodascanotas.es; A Ortigueira 10; r incl breakfast €60-90; P 📶) Charming Muiño das Cañotas, in a pretty little valley just off the DP6121, 2km south of Cariño, has five country-style wood-and-stone rooms in a converted 14th-century watermill. It's signposted from the DP6121.

Chiringuito de San Xiao GALICIAN €€
(☎690 309968; Lugar San Xiao do Trebo; raciones €6-15; ⊙noon-11.30pm Tue-Sun, shorter hours Nov-Feb) You'll be hard-pressed to find a better eating spot in the area than this friendly little wood-beamed bar. The panoramic dining room and terrace overlook the ocean from the Cariño–Ortegal road, 1.5km before the cape. There's all manner of good Galician seafood, but their real specialities are fish and meat grilled over open coals, and *caldeiradas* (fish or seafood stews).

Getting There & Away

Arriva (☎981 31 12 13; www.arriva.gal) runs three buses each way, Monday to Friday only, between Cariño and Mera (20 minutes, €1.40), 10km south. Some of these services connect at Mera with Arriva buses along the AC862 between Ferrol and Viveiro. From Cedeira, the 1pm (Monday to Friday) Arriva bus to Mera (€1.95) connects with the 1.30pm Mera–Cariño bus.

Bares Peninsula

The Bares Peninsula is a marvellously scenic spur of land jutting north into the Bay of Biscay, with walking trails, beaches and a few delightfully low-key spots to stay over.

The road along the peninsula leaves the AC862 road at **O Barqueiro**, a classic fishing village where slate-roofed, white houses cascade down to the port. For an even quieter base, push north to tiny **Porto de Bares**, on a lovely half-moon of sand lapped by the *ría's* waters.

Take a walk to the panoramic **Punta da Estaca de Bares** at the end of the peninsula, Spain's most northerly point, and, a few kilometres southwest, enjoy the vistas from the bench known as the 'Best Bank of the World' (p581), overlooking the spectacular **Acantilados de Loiba** cliffs and little-known beaches such as **Praia do Picón** (P).

★'Best Bank of the World' VIEWPOINT
(P) West along the Loiba clifftops from Praia do Picón, two benches after 200m and 400m afford magnificent panoramas along the jagged coast all the way from the Punta da Estaca de Bares to Cabo Ortegal. The second bench has acquired celebrity status under the curious English name 'Best Bank of the World', thanks to a confusion about the Spanish word *banco*, meaning both bench and bank. You may have to queue behind squads of selfie-stick-wielders to actually sit on it.

Sleeping & Eating

Hospedaxe Porto Mar HOSTAL €
(☎981 41 40 23; www.portomar.eu; Calle Feliciano Armada, Porto de Bares; s/d €35/45;) The only accommodation in Porto de Bares itself has 17 smallish but clean and cosy rooms, half of which are sea-facing. The amiable owners also run one of the three seafood-focused eateries near the beach, **O Centro** (Porto de Bares; raciones €7-20; ⊙9.30am-midnight, from 8.30am Jul-Sep).

Semáforo de Bares HOTEL €€
(☎981 417 147, 699 943584; www.hotelsemaforodebares.com; s €56-66, d €80-150, ste €180-200; ⊙closed 2nd half Feb & 2nd half Oct; P) For a treat, book a room in this maritime-signalling station turned contemporary hotel, whose five rooms (the best are quite indulgent) sit 3km above Porto de Bares village on a panoramic hilltop. Breakfast (€8) and dinner (€18 to €30) are available for guests.

It also has a convenient cafe-bar open to the public.

La Marina SEAFOOD €€
(www.lamarinabares.es; Porto de Bares; mains €8-30; ⊙10am-midnight) With a panoramic dining room overlooking Porto de Bares' beach, La Marina does great seafood paellas as well as a host of other maritime and terrestrial fare, from fried eggs with chips to Galician beef, *percebes* or grilled fish.

Getting There & Away

A few daily FEVE trains and Arriva buses, on Ferrol–Viveiro routes, serve O Barqueiro.

Viveiro

POP 7400

This town at the mouth of the Río Landro has a well-preserved historic quarter of stone buildings and stone-paved streets (several of them pedestrian-only), where outward appearances haven't changed a

TOP FIVE BREATHTAKING VIEWS

- Garita de Herbeira (p580)
- Best Bank of the World (p581)
- Ruta Monte Faro (p591)
- Monte de Santa Trega (p593)
- Cabo Fisterra (p569)

great deal since Viveiro was rebuilt after a 1540 fire. A 500m-long, 15th-century bridge, the **Puente de la Misericordia**, still carries traffic across the *ría* in front of the old town.

Viveiro is famous for its elaborate **Semana Santa** (www.semanasantaviveiro.com; ⌚Mar/Apr) celebrations, when the town fills with processions and decorations. On a completely different note is the summer **Resurrection Fest** (Resu; www.resurrectionfest.es; ⌚Jul), which brings in up to 90,000 fans for four days of heavy metal and punk music.

Sights

Check out the Gothic **Igrexa de Santiago-San Francisco** (Rúa de Cervantes; ⌚11.30am-1.30pm & 6.30-8pm) and the 12th-century Romanesque **Igrexa de Santa María do Campo** (Rúa de Felipe Prieto; ⌚7.30am-8.30pm Mon-Sat, 11am-noon Sun). The 4km drive up to the **Mirador San Roque** rewards with expansive panoramas. There are several good beaches on the Ría de Viveiro within a few kilometres of town.

Playa de Area is a fine, 1.2km-long stretch of sand with a semi-built-up backdrop, 5km northeast by the LU862. Five kilometres beyond – by the LUP2610 winding through woodlands or the well-signposted Camino Natural da Ruta do Cantábrico walking trail – is the lovely, less-frequented **Praia de Esteiro**, with waves that are good for beginner (and sometimes more experienced) surfers.

Sleeping & Eating

Viveiro Urban Hotel HOTEL €€
(☎982 56 21 01; www.urbanviveiro.es; Avenida Navia Castrillón 2; s €66-100, d €88-180; P ❄ ☎) A black glass cube overlooking the *ría* 400m south of the Puente de la Misericordia, the Urban, opened in 2017, is a big advance on Viveiro's other in-town hotels. Rooms are large, bright and very comfortable, with big mirrors, spot lighting and excellent bathrooms. And you can satisfy your stomach without leaving the premises thanks to its good catering options.

Hotel Ego HOTEL €€
(☎982 56 09 87; www.hotelego.es; Playa de Area; s €77-110, d €100-165, ste €165-275; P ❄ ☎ ≋) The classy, contemporary-style Hotel Ego is 5km north of Viveiro on the Ribadeo road, overlooking Playa de Area. Most of its 45 ample rooms have sea views and balconies, and the adjacent **Restaurante Nito** (mains €12-35; ⌚1.30-4pm & 8pm-midnight), under the same ownership, is one of the area's best eateries.

Getting There & Away

A few Arriva buses fan out to Lugo and along the Rías Altas as far as A Coruña and Ribadeo. The bus station is on the waterfront street Avenida Ramón Canosa, just north of the Old Town.

FEVE trains between Ferrol and Oviedo stop here.

Ribadeo

POP 6860

This lively port town on the Ría de Ribadeo, which separates Galicia from Asturias, is a sun-seeker magnet in summer. The Old Town between the central Praza de España and the harbour is an attractive mix of handsome old galleried and stone houses. For a beach you'll have to head out of town, but Praia As Catedrais (p582), 10km west, is one of Spain's most spectacular strands.

An excellent, well-marked walking and cycling trail, the Camino Natural de la Ruta del Cantábrico, runs west for more than 150km along the coast from Ribadeo. The first 3km, from Ribadeo's central Praza de España to the Illa Pancha lighthouse, make a nice *ría*-side leg stretch. From Illa Pancha, the route continues 17km along a beautiful length of coast to Praia As Catedrais, via the tiny fishing village of Rinlo, which has some good seafood eateries and several other beaches en route.

★**Praia As Catedrais** BEACH
(Cathedrals Beach; P 👪) You won't be disappointed with Praia As Catedrais, 10km west of Ribadeo by road. This spectacular 1.5km sandy stretch is strung with awesome Gothic-looking rock towers, and arches and chambers carved out by aeons of sea-water action. Avoid the hour or two either side of high tide when the whole beach is under water. Such is the beach's popularity that during Semana Santa, July, August and September, permits are required for beach access (they're free and easily obtained in Ribadeo).

Sleeping & Eating

Hotel Rolle HOTEL €€
(☎982 12 06 70; www.hotelrolle.com; Rúa de Ingeniero Schulz 6; r incl breakfast €60-98; ❄ @ ☎) Just two blocks from Praza de España, the Rolle has spacious, attractive rooms in a rustically modern style, with up-to-date bathrooms and plenty of exposed stone and wood. The owner is happy to tell you about things to see and do in the area.

Casona de Lazúrtegui HERITAGE HOTEL **€€**
(☎982 12 00 97; www.hotelcasona.com; Rúa Julio Lazúrtegui 26-28; d €50-92; ⊙Mar–mid-Dec; P❄@☎) It's a little bit away from the centre of things, 500m northwest of Praza de España, but this is a beautifully modernised early-20th-century townhouse, with immaculate, very comfortable, contemporary rooms and welcoming, helpful staff.

La Botellería FUSION **€€**
(https://labotelleriaribadeo.es; Rúa de San Francisco 24; mains €9-18; ⊙noon-4pm & 8pm-midnight, closed Mon & Thu lunch; ☎) Head to this convivial bar, or its pretty white-tabled dining room, for good wine and original, varied and very tasty dishes including tuna tartare with guacamole and mango sauce, or banana-and-chorizo croquettes with mint sauce. It's just 100m off Praza de España.

ℹ Information

Tourist Office (☎982 12 86 89; http://turismo.ribadeo.gal; Praza de España; ⊙10am-2pm & 4-7pm, closed Sun & Mon Oct-Jun) Conveniently located on the main square.

ℹ Getting There & Away

At least four daily buses head to Luarca and Oviedo in Asturias. For Viveiro there are eight daily buses Monday to Friday, but only two on Saturday and Sunday. There's daily service to Lugo, A Coruña and Santiago de Compostela. The bus station is on Avenida Rosalía de Castro, about 500m north of Praza de España.

Multistop FEVE trains operate across Asturias to/from Oviedo (€12, four hours, two daily) and across Galicia to/from Ferrol (€11, three hours, four daily).

RÍAS BAIXAS

Long, wide beaches and relatively calm (if cold) waters have made the Rías Baixas (Castilian: Rías Bajas) Galicia's most popular holiday destination. The Rías de Muros y Noia, de Arousa, de Pontevedra and de Vigo – Galicia's four longest *rías* (coastal inlets) – boast way more towns, villages, hotels and restaurants than other stretches of the Galician coast, which obscures some of their natural beauty. Still, the mix of pretty villages, sandy beaches and good eating options, especially the wonderful seafood, keep most people happy. Throw in lovely old Pontevedra, the big-city feel of lively Vigo, the quaint albariño wine capital Cambados and trips to offshore

islands including the magnificent Illas Cíes, and you have a tempting travel cocktail.

There's a vast array of accommodation of all types for all budgets, but it's still a great idea to reserve ahead for the second half of July or August. At other times room prices often dip dramatically.

Ría de Arousa

Cambados

POP 7000

The capital of the albariño wine country, the pretty little *ría*-side town of Cambados makes an excellent base for touring the Rías Baixas. Its old streets are lined by stone architecture dotted with inviting taverns and eateries. Cambados is actually a fusion of three medieval villages – Fefiñáns at the north end of town (centred on beautiful, broad Praza de Fefiñáns), Cambados proper in the middle, and the fishing quarter Santo Tomé in the south.

Sights

You can visit and taste at 10 different wineries in the Cambados municipality (in the town and up to 6km outside – see www.cambadosenoturismo.com) and more than 20 others within about 12km (see www.rutadelvinoriasbaixas.com). The best-known wineries are outside town, but there are two small and interesting ones on broad Praza de Fefiñáns at the northern end of town. Cambados' **tourist office** (986 52 07 86; www.cambados.es; Edificio Exposalnés, Paseo da Calzada; 10am-2pm & 5-8pm Jun-Sep, 10am-2pm Tue-Fri & Sun, 10.30am-2pm & 4.30-7.30pm Sat Oct-May) has details on all visitable wineries. It's always advisable to call ahead before making a trip out to a winery to check that someone will be available for visitors.

★Gil Armada HISTORIC BUILDING, WINERY
(660 078252; http://bodegagilarmada.com; Praza de Fefiñáns; tours €7-15; tours noon, 1pm, 6pm, 7pm Jun-Sep, 12.30pm & 5.30pm Oct-May, closed Sun afternoon) Gil Armada is a small family-run winery housed in the handsome 17th-century Pazo de Fefiñáns. A variety of absorbing guided tours are offered: the basic one-hour version covers the main rooms of the historic house (with some fascinating antiques and art), its distillery and its vast gardens with 150-year-old vines and an ancient woodland. The more expensive options (up to two hours) include wine-tasting and a visit to the panoramic tower. It's advisable to call ahead between June and September.

Bodegas del Palacio de Fefiñanes WINERY
(986 54 22 04; www.fefinanes.com; Praza de Fefiñáns; visit €3, incl tasting 1/2 wines €6/10, minimum per group €30/40; 10am-1pm & 4-7pm Mon-Fri, closed Jan) This small establishment, one of two wineries in the handsome, 17th-century Pazo de Fefiñáns, produces some quality, garlanded albariño wines that you can buy for €12 upwards. Guides speak fluent English.

Igrexa de Santa Mariña Dozo CHURCH
(Rúa do Castro; 24hr) FREE This ruined 15th-century church, beside the wine museum, is now roofless but still has its four semicircular roof arches intact, and is surrounded by a well-kept cemetery with elaborate graves – all particularly picturesque when floodlit after dark.

Martín Códax WINERY
(986 52 60 40; www.martincodax.com; Rúa Burgáns 91, Vilariño; tours incl tasting of 1/2/3/4 wines €3/5/10/15, incl vineyard & tasting of 3/4 wines €15/25; tours 11am, noon, 1pm, 5.30pm & 7pm Mon-Fri, 11am, noon & 1pm Sat Jun-Sep, shorter hours rest of year; P) Galicia's best-known winery, a 2.5km drive east of Cambados, offers a variety of tours from 45 minutes to three hours, including tasting of up to four wines. Some include vineyard visits. It's essential to call ahead.

Festivals & Events

Festa do Albariño WINE
(http://fiestadelalbarino.com; Aug) Concerts, fireworks, exhibitions and the awarding of prizes for the year's best wines accompany the consumption of huge quantities of wine and tapas during the Festa do Albariño, on the first Sunday of August and the four preceding days.

Sleeping

Hotel O Lagar HOTEL €
(986 52 08 07; www.hotelolagar.com; Rúa Pontevedra 14; s €40, d €50-60; P) A fine budget choice, Hotel O Lagar has 16 well-sized, sparkling clean rooms, all with bath-tubs, and its own bar-cafe serving good, inexpensive *raciones*. Try for rooms 107, 108, 207 or 208, which look out on a pretty little plaza and church.

★Quinta de San Amaro BOUTIQUE HOTEL €€
(986 74 89 38; www.quintadesanamaro.com; Rúa San Amaro 6, Meaño; incl breakfast s €95-130, d €110-190; P) A dream base for enjoying the Rías Baixas, unique Quinta de San Amaro sits surrounded by vineyards 12km south of Cambados. A converted and extended farmhouse with an inspired design combining traditional and contemporary elements, it unites 14 different rooms with a similar variety of common spaces, including a panoramic pool and (top-class) restaurant, and lovely gardens with a solarium in a converted *hórreo*!

Guests are invited on free visits to a local winery (with tasting), service is first-class (many staff speak English), and an important part of the magic is the panoramic **restaurant** (986 74 89 38; mains €14-20; 1.30-4pm & 8.30-11.30pm, closed Mon-Thu mid-Oct–Mar), one of the area's very best, serving delicious updates on traditional

Galician cuisine (it's open to all; reservations recommended). Groups of four or more can do cooking classes – Galician, Mexican, Japanese – in a lovely big kitchen for €50 per person, including a full lunch or dinner based on what you've prepared.

Pazo A Capitana HOTEL €€
(☎986 52 05 13, 679 282259; www.pazoacapitana.com; Rúa Sabugueiro 46; incl breakfast s €59-70, d €80-100; ⊙closed mid-Dec–Jan; P ❄ 🛜) This 17th-century country house on the edge of town is a lovely sleeping option, with stately rooms, expansive gardens and an on-site winery with four century-old stone presses.

Hotel Real Ribadomar BOUTIQUE HOTEL €€
(Hotel Real Cambados; ☎986 52 44 04; http://hotelrealcambados.com; Rúa Real 8; s €55-90, d €70-125; ❄ 🛜) A charmingly renovated central townhouse with pretty rooms combining exposed stone and wallpaper, fresh white linen on soft beds, gleaming bathrooms and homey touches, including ribbon-wrapped towels and baskets of potpourri.

Eating

Seafood is top of the bill here (scallops are a particular Cambados speciality) and there are endless varieties of albariño to complement it. Pedestrian-friendly Rúas Príncipe and Real, the main streets of the Fefiñáns part of town, have plenty of eateries that mostly serve up decent food at decent prices; there are more options in lanes leading off them.

Restaurante Ribadomar GALICIAN €€
(www.ribadomar.es; Rúa Valle Inclán 17; mains €13-18, menús €24-30; ⊙1.30-4pm & 9-11pm, closed Sun-Thu evenings Oct-Jun) For something more upscale than taverns, you can get a great Galician meal at family-run Restaurante Ribadomar, with dishes such as sole with scallops or *chuletón de ternera* (giant beef chop), in a relatively formal setting with original paintings and sculptures.

Getting There & Away

The bus station is on Avenida de Galicia, roughly in the middle of town, 600m south of Praza de Fefiñáns. Monbus runs to/from Santiago de Compostela (€5.60, 1½ hours) at least twice daily and to/from O Grove (€1.55, 30 minutes) at least three times. Autocares Cuiña (www.autocarescuina.com) runs to/from Pontevedra (€3.15, one hour) at least three times daily.

WORTH A TRIP

CASTRO DE BAROÑA

The Ría de Muros y Noia, the most northerly of the four main Rías Baixas, is home to a couple of lively old towns, Muros and Noia, and some good beaches on the south shore, where you'll also find Galicia's most spectacularly sited prehistoric settlement, the **Castro de Baroña** (⊙24hr) FREE. The *castro* sits poised majestically on a wind-blasted headland overlooking the Atlantic waves, 4km southwest of Porto do Son. Park near Cafe-Bar Castro and take the rocky 600m path down to the ruins. Clearly the exposed location was chosen for its defensive qualities: a moat and two stone walls protect its access across a small isthmus. Inside are the excavated bases of about 20 round stone buildings. The settlement was abandoned in the 1st century AD.

Pontevedra

POP 62,000

Pontevedra is an inviting, small riverside city that combines history, culture and style into a lively base for exploring the Rías Baixas. The interlocking lanes and plazas of the compact Old Town are abuzz with shops, markets, cafes and tapas bars.

Back in the 16th century, Pontevedra was Galicia's biggest city and an important port. Columbus' flagship, the *Santa María,* was built here, and indeed some locals are convinced that Columbus himself was not Genoese as is commonly believed, but was really a Pontevedra nobleman called Pedro Madruga, who for obscure reasons faked his own death and took on a new identity.

Sights

An excellent museum and some unusual old churches are well worth devoting time to, but really it's the Old Town as a whole that is Pontevedra's star turn. It's a pleasure just to wander round its narrow, mainly pedestrianised streets linking more than a dozen plazas. **Praza da Leña** is a particularly quaint nook.

Museo de Pontevedra MUSEUM
(☎986 80 41 00; www.museo.depo.es) Pontevedra's eclectic museum is scattered over five city-centre buildings. At research time, two

Pontevedra

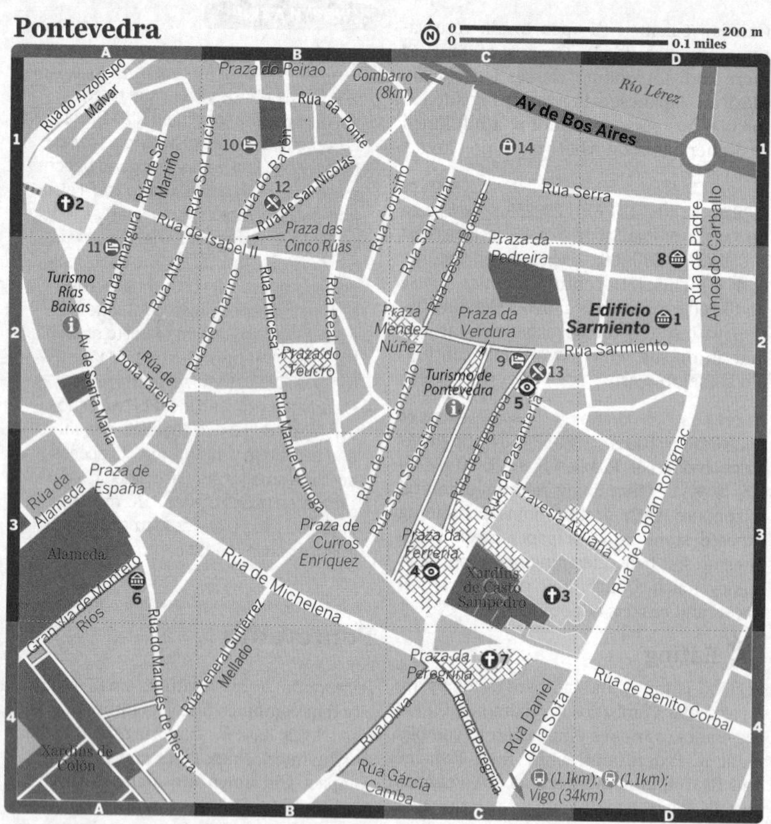

Pontevedra

Top Sights
1 Edificio Sarmiento D2

Sights
2 Basílica de Santa María a Maior A1
3 Igrexa de San Francisco C3
4 Praza da Ferrería C3
5 Praza da Leña C2
6 Ruínas de San Domingos A3
7 Santuario da Virxe Peregrina C4
8 Sexto Edificio D2

Sleeping
9 Hotel Rúas C2
10 Parador Casa del Barón B1
11 Slow City Hostel A2

Eating
12 Casa Fidel O Pulpeiro B1
13 Loaira Xantar C2
Restaurante Rúas .... (see 9)

Shopping
14 Mercado Municipal C1

were closed for restoration, though the newest and most interesting sections were open: the recently built **Sexto Edificio** (Rúa de Padre Amoedo; ⏲10am-9pm Tue-Sat, 11am-2pm Sun) FREE and the adjoining **Edificio Sarmiento** (Rúa Sarmiento; ⏲10am-9pm Tue-Sat, 11am-2pm Sun) FREE in a renovated 18th-century Jesuit college, plus the **Ruínas de San Domingos** (Gran Vía de Montero Ríos; ⏲10am-2pm & 4-8.30pm Tue-Sat, 11am-2pm Sun May-Sep, to 7.30pm Tue-Sat Mar, Apr & Oct, closed Nov-Feb) FREE, a ruined 14th-century church housing an intriguing collection of heraldic shields, sepulchres and other medieval carvings.

The Edificio Sarmiento houses an absorbing collection ranging over Galician

Sargadelos ceramics, modern art (including one work each by Picasso, Miró and Dalí), and prehistoric Galician gold jewellery, petroglyphs and carvings. The Sexto Edificio has three floors of Galician and Spanish art from the 14th to 20th centuries – some interesting exhibits, though you won't find any really big names.

Basílica de Santa María a Maior CHURCH
(Praza de Alonso de Fonseca; ⏲10am-1.30pm & 5-9pm, except during Mass) Pontevedra's most impressive church is a beautiful, mainly late-Gothic affair, with some plateresque and Portuguese Manueline influences, built by Pontevedra's sailors' guild in the 16th century. Busts of Christopher Columbus and Hernán Cortés flank the rosette window on the elaborate western facade, a plateresque work by the Flemish Cornelis de Holanda and the Portuguese João Nobre.

Praza da Ferrería SQUARE
Praza da Ferrería has the best selection of cafes in town and is a hub of Pontevedra social life. It's overlooked by the **Igrexa de San Francisco** (⏲7.30am-12.45pm & 5.30-6.45pm), said to have been founded in the 13th century by St Francis of Assisi when on pilgrimage to Santiago (the main portico remains from the original church). Just off the plaza, you can't miss the distinctive curved facade of the **Santuario da Virxe Peregrina** (Praza da Peregrina; ⏲9am-2pm & 4-9pm), an 18th-century caprice with a distinctly Portuguese flavour.

Sleeping

Hotel Rúas HOTEL €
(☎986 84 64 16; www.hotelruas.net; Rúa de Figueroa 35; s €34-44, d €44-62; ❄@📶) The rooms are pleasant, with shiny wooden floors, unfussy furnishings and large, sparkling bathrooms (though some showers are small), and some have nice plaza views – excellent value for this absolutely central Old Town location. Reception is amiable and the hotel has both a good restaurant and a cafe that is one of the town's most popular breakfast spots.

Slow City Hostel HOSTEL €
(☎631 062896; www.slowcityhostelpontevedra.com; Rúa da Amargura 5; dm/d €17.50/40; ⏲closed Nov; 📶) Run by a welcoming, well-travelled local couple, Slow City has one spacious dorm with six solid and comfy bunks, and two spotless, all-white private doubles. With an excellent Old Town location, a good kitchen and free tea, coffee and fruit, it's a great option for budget travellers, whether following the Camino Portugués or not.

Parador Casa del Barón HISTORIC HOTEL €€
(☎986 85 58 00; www.parador.es; Rúa do Barón 19; d €80-163; P❄📶) This elegant, refurbished 16th-century palace is equipped throughout with antique-style furniture and historical art, and has a lovely little garden beside the cafe and restaurant terrace. Rooms vary in size and those facing the street may get late-night noise from weekend partiers.

Eating

Casa Fidel O Pulpeiro SEAFOOD €
(Rúa de San Nicolás 7; raciones €6-14; ⏲11am-3pm & 7pm-midnight Thu-Tue) For more than 50 years, Fidel's has been serving up perfectly done *pulpo á feira*, Galicia's quintessential octopus dish of tender tentacle slices with paprika and olive oil (ask for some *cachelos*, sliced boiled potatoes, to accompany it). But this simple, spotless eatery with pine tables and white paper tablecloths also offers plenty of shellfish, *empanadas* and omelettes if you fancy something different.

Restaurante Rúas GALICIAN €€
(Rúa de Figueroa 35; mains €12-20; ⏲11am-4pm & 8pm-midnight) A reliable option for tasty and satisfying meat, fish, seafood, salads and egg dishes, served without pretension. They have tables out under the Praza da Leña arches as well an upstairs dining room.

Loaira Xantar GALICIAN €€
(Praza da Leña 2; raciones €6-14; ⏲1.30-4pm & 8.30-11.30pm, closed Sun evening; 📶) With tables out on the lovely little plaza and in the upstairs dining room, this is a fine spot for excellent Galician specialities with a creative touch, such as prawn-and-vegetable tempura or spider-crab croquettes. Local pork and fish, tempting desserts, and good Galician wines too. Portions are medium-sized.

Information

Turismo de Pontevedra (☎986 09 08 90; www.visit-pontevedra.gal; Praza da Verdura; ⏲9.30am-2pm & 4.30-8.30pm Mon-Sat, 10am-2pm Sun Jun-Oct, shorter hr rest of year) The helpful city tourist office has a convenient central location.

Turismo Rías Baixas (☎886 21 17 00; http://turismoriasbaixas.com; Praza de Santa María; ⏲9am-9pm Mon-Fri, 10am-2.30pm & 4.30-9pm Sat & Sun mid-Jun–mid-Sep, shorter hr rest of year) Information on all of Pontevedra province.

PRAIA A LANZADA

The O Grove–Sanxenxo area, at the end of the peninsula separating the Rías de Arousa and Pontevedra, is Galicia's biggest magnet for Spanish summer beach tourism. The towns are not pretty, but there are certainly some fine, if far from deserted, beaches.

Dune-backed **Praia A Lanzada** (P) sweeps a spectacular 2.3km along the west side of the low-lying isthmus leading to O Grove. It's Galicia's most splendid stretch of sand, and enticingly natural, but not exactly deserted, as the mammoth car parks attest.

Getting There & Away

The **bus station** (☎986 85 24 08; www.autobusespontevedra.com; Rúa da Estación) is about 1.5km southeast of the Old Town. Monbus goes at least 18 times daily to Vigo (€2.50, 30 minutes) and 14 or more times to Santiago de Compostela (€5.85, one hour). Buses also run to Sanxenxo, O Grove, Cambados, Padrón, Bueu, Tui, Ourense and Lugo.

Pontevedra's **train station** (Rúa Eduardo Pondal), across the roundabout from the bus station, has roughly hourly services, from 7am or 8am to 10pm or 11pm, to Santiago de Compostela (€6.10 to €7.35, 35 minutes to one hour), A Coruña (€14 to €16, one to 1¾ hours) and Vigo (€3.20 to €3.65, 15 to 30 minutes).

Ría de Pontevedra

The small, old city of Pontevedra sits at the head of the *ría* and is one of the Rías Baixas' most appealing destinations. The shores of the *ría* are quite built up until you get towards their outer ends where you'll find some decent beaches. On the north shore, the Sanxenxo area, together with O Grove a little further north, forms Galicia's busiest summer beach tourism zone.

Combarro

POP 1270

Near Pontevedra on the *ría's* north shore, Combarro has a particularly quaint old quarter that is worth a meal stop on your way through. A jumble of *hórreos* (traditional stone grain stores on stilts) stands right on the waterside, with a smattering of waterside restaurants, and behind them is a web of crooked lanes (some of them hewn directly out of the rock bed) dotted with *cruceiros* (stone crucifixes; a traditional Galician art form). It can, however, get extremely busy in high summer.

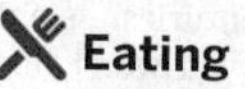

Eating

Bodega O Bocoi SEAFOOD €€

(☎986 77 11 42; Rúa do Mar 20; dishes €8-18, rice dishes for 2 €35-45) You won't beat O Bocoi for perfectly prepared fresh seafood – the octopus, shellfish a la plancha (hotplate-grilled) and fried fish are all delicious, but you're unlikely to be disappointed with anything you order. And they do large, fresh salads too.

There's a choice between sitting in the tavern section with two little stone-walled rooms, or the bright, check-cloth dining room with picture windows looking out on the *ría*.

Illa de Ons

POP 67

In summer you can get away from urban civilisation by hopping on a boat to vehicle-free Illa de Ons at the mouth of the Ría de Pontevedra. Part of the Parque Nacional de las Islas Atlánticas de Galicia, the island is 5.6km long with one tiny village, several sandy beaches, cliffs, ruins, four walking trails (circuits of between 1km and 8km) and rich bird life. You're unlikely, however, to find it empty: up to 1800 visitors are allowed on the island at any one time. May, June and September are the most tranquil.

Camping Isla de Ons TENTED CAMP €

(☎986 44 16 78; www.campingisladeons.com; site for own tent €7, rentals standard tent for 2/4/6 €30/60/90, superior tent €70/100/120, sleeping bag or mat €5) This campground, reopened in 2016 after a revamp, is at Chan de Pólvora, about 600m west from the boat jetty. It accommodates over 200 people, and has tents and sleeping equipment to rent, including a glamping option of 'superior' tents with beds and bedding on a wooden platform. There's also a cafeteria. Reserve ahead.

Casa Acuña HOSTAL €€

(☎986 44 16 78; www.isladeons.net; d incl breakfast €65-90, apt for 2 €90-110, apt for 4 €120-160) You can stay in bright rooms or apartments at Casa Acuña in Ons village. It has 20 rooms and six apartments: reservations strongly advised. The restaurant here serves prize-winning *pulpo á feira*.

Getting There & Away

Three companies, Cruceros Rías Baixas (www.crucerosriasbaixas.com), Naviera Mar de Ons (www.mardeons.com) and Nabia Naviera (www.piratasdenabia.com), sail to Ons from Sanxenxo and Portonovo on the north side of the Ría de Pontevedra, and Bueu on the south side of the *ría*, during the summer season. There are weekend sailings from Sanxenxo and/or Portonovo from early to late June, then daily sailings until about late September (up to about 12 a day in July and August). The trip takes 45 minutes one way; return fares are €12 to €14 for adults and €6 or €7 for children. From Bueu there are sailings during Semana Santa, on weekends in May and daily from June to about late September.

Ría de Vigo

The far end of the *ría's* north shore is one of the least populated and most scenic parts of the Rías Baixas. The peaceful village of Hío draws visitors for a look at Galicia's most famous *cruceiro* (carved-stone wayside cross; a traditional Galician art form), the **Cruceiro de Hío** (P).

Several sandy beaches are within easy reach of Hío, including 800m-long **Praia Areabrava**, 3km north.

★Cabo de Home AREA

(P) From the hamlet of Donón, 4km west of Hío, the windswept, rocky cape Cabo de Home stretches 2.5km south. The cape is strung with walking trails and a few driveable tracks, and has three lighthouses, a couple of beaches and great views of the Illas Cíes. The partly excavated and wonderfully panoramic Iron Age *castro* **Berobriga** sits atop Monte Facho nearby, about a 20-minute uphill walk (part of the way runs along a *castro*-era stone-paved track).

Sleeping

Hotel Doade HOTEL €€

(986 32 83 02; www.hoteldoade.com; Rúa Baixada a Rioesteiro, Hío; d incl breakfast €55-77; closed Nov; P) Friendly, sparkling clean Doade has eight cosy, spacious rooms with fresh white linen and wood ceilings, and a good **restaurant** (mains €10-28, menú €10-20; 1-4.30pm & 8.30-11.30pm Tue-Sun, closed Nov) focusing on *ría*-fresh seafood, with oven-baked fish a speciality.

Vigo

POP 293,000

Depending on where you point your lens, Vigo is either a historic and cultured city or

GALICIAN WINES

There's no better accompaniment to Galician food than Galician wines, which have a character all their own. Best known are the fruity whites from the albariño grape, which constitute more than 90% of the wine produced in the Rías Baixas Denominación de Origen (DO), located near Galicia's southwestern coast and along the lower Río Miño. Albariño's surge in popularity in the last couple of decades has, to some palates, yielded some wines that are *too* sweet and fruity. A good traditional albariño should have the aroma of a green apple and a slightly sour taste.

Encouraged by albariño's success, vintners elsewhere in Galicia are innovating, expanding and producing ever better wines. Many of the best reds come from the native mencía grape, and winemakers are reviving other Galician grapes that almost disappeared in the 19th-century phylloxera plague – among them the white godello and the red brancellao and merenzao. Galicians often order wine just by naming the grape: *'un mencía'* or *'un albariño'*...

Galicia's other DOs include:

Ribeiro From the Ribadavia area in southern Galicia, Ribeiro produces some very good whites, mostly from the treixadura grape.

Ribeira Sacra In the southeast, yielding rich reds from mencía grapes, some of them grown on the amazingly steep hillsides above the Río Sil.

Monterrei In the warmest, driest part of southeast Galicia, bordering Portugal, Monterrei produces both reds and whites: look for Crego e Monaguillo's very drinkable mencía reds and fruity godello whites.

Valdeorras This southeastern region bordering Castilla y León produces, among others, godello whites and mencía and brancellao reds.

a gritty industrial port. Home to Europe's largest fishing fleet, this is an axis of commerce in northern Spain. Yet its central areas are very walkable and full of intriguing nooks, and it's the main gateway to the beautiful Illas Cíes. Above all, Vigo is a welcoming and confident city whose citizens really know how to enjoy life, especially after dark in the many buzzing tapas bars, restaurants and clubs.

The Casco Vello (Old Town) climbs uphill from the cruise-ship port; the heart of the modern city spreads east from here, with the parklike Praza de Compostela a welcome green space in its midst.

Sights

At the heart of the intriguingly jumbled lanes of the **Casco Vello** is elegant **Praza da Constitución**, a perfect spot for a drink. Head down **Rúa dos Cesteiros**, with its quaint wicker shops, and you'll reach the Old Town's main church, the **Concatedral de Santa María** (Praza da Igrexa; 6-8pm Mon-Sat). Just below here is Rúa Pescadería (p590), famed for its oyster shuckers.

Parque do Castro PARK
() Head directly south (and uphill) from the Old Town for a wander in this verdant park with nearly 100 camellia trees. It's a magnificent place to be when the sun is dropping into the ocean behind the Illas Cíes! You can look at the partly reconstructed **Castro de Vigo** (986 81 02 60; Parque do Castro;) FREE dating back to the 3rd century BC, and poke around the hilltop **Castelo do Castro**, which formed part of Vigo's defences, built under Felipe IV in the 17th century.

Museo de Arte Contemporánea de Vigo MUSEUM
(Marco; www.marcovigo.com; Rúa do Príncipe 54; 11am-2.30pm & 5-9pm Tue-Sat, 11am-2.30pm Sun) FREE Vigo is something of a modern art centre, with several museums and galleries to prove it. The Contemporary Art Museum is the number-one venue for thought-provoking exhibitions ranging from painting and sculpture to fashion and design.

Praia de Samil BEACH
() A long swath of sandy beaches stretches southwest of the city. Best is 1.2km-long Praia de Samil, beginning about 5km from the city centre. It's backed by a long promenade and has great views of the Illas Cíes. Several buses run from the city centre.

Sleeping

Hotel Compostela HOTEL €
(986 22 82 27; www.hcompostela.com; Rúa García Olloqui 5; s €44-82, d €48-82;) Solidly comfy, spotlessly clean and reasonably spacious rooms make this efficient hotel near Praza de Compostela a sound choice. The cafe is handy for breakfast.

Hotel América HOTEL €€
(986 43 89 22; http://hotelamerica-vigo.com; Rúa de Pablo Morillo 6; incl breakfast s €70-110, d €85-120;) The América gets a big thumbs-up for its well-equipped, spacious rooms with tasteful modern art and elegantly muted colour schemes; its friendly, efficient staff; and its quiet sidestreet location near the waterfront. Nearly all the 47 rooms are exterior-facing, and the breakfast is a large and excellent buffet, served on the roof terrace in summer.

★**Gran Hotel Nagari** LUXURY HOTEL €€€
(986 21 11 11; www.granhotelnagari.com; Praza de Compostela 21; d €105-230, incl buffet breakfast & spa €140-275;) Luxurious Nagari has a welcome personal feel to its high-class contemporary design and service. Beautiful rooms in silver, gold, white, grey and dark wood boast remote-controlled colour lighting, giant-headed showers (also colour-changing), high-tech coffee makers and big-screen smart TVs, and there's a heated rooftop spa pool with fabulous views, plus a ground-floor restaurant and wine bar.

Eating

Good restaurants, tapas bars and cafes are scattered all over the central area, and beyond. The narrow lanes of the Old Town, especially around Praza da Constitución, and the Praza de Compostela area all have plenty of options.

Rúa Pescadería SEAFOOD €
(Rúa das Ostras; oysters per dozen €12-15) Short Rúa Pescadería, in the lower part of the Old Town, is jammed with people tucking into fresh seafood. From about 10am until 4pm (sometimes shorter hours in winter) you can buy oysters from the *ostreras* (shuckers) here, and sit down to eat them with a drink at one of the restaurants. Oysters and albariño wine are a traditional Vigo Sunday-morning hangover cure.

Othilio Bar GALICIAN €€
(986 19 00 17; Rúa Luis Taboada 9; mains €10-19, lunch menú Mon-Fri €12.50; 1.30-3.30pm &

WORTH A TRIP

ILLAS CÍES

The Illas Cíes, three spectacularly beautiful islands that are home to some of Galicia's most splendid beaches, are a 45-minute (14km) ferry ride from Vigo. This small archipelago forms a 6km breakwater that protects the Ría de Vigo from the Atlantic's fury and is the main jewel of the **Parque Nacional de las Islas Atlánticas de Galicia** (Atlantic Islands of Galicia National Park; www.iatlanticas.es) .

The Cíes are perfect for lolling on sandy beaches, such as the 1km-long, lagoon-backed crescent of **Praia das Rodas**, or nudist Praia das Figueiras. The islands are also great for walking and exploring: trails such as the 7.4km-loop **Ruta Monte Faro** lead to some spectacular high lookouts. While the eastern coasts are relatively gentle, the western sides drop away dramatically in sheer cliffs.

The islands are vehicle-free and their nature pristine, but you won't be alone. Up to 3000 visitors are allowed at one time and this limit is often reached in July and August.

To stay overnight on the islands you must camp at **Camping Islas Cíes** (986 438 358; www.campingislascies.com; adult/child/tent €8.90/6.70/8.90, 2/4-person tent & bed rental per night €52/79; Semana Santa, late May–late Sep). The campground has a restaurant and supermarket, and a capacity of 800 people – it often fills up in August. There's a two-night minimum stay if you're renting one of their tents.

Reservations can be made online or at the **camping office** (986 43 83 58; Estación Marítima de Ría, Vigo; 8.30am-1.30pm & 3.30-7.30pm). If you book online, you must show a printout of your reservation at the camping office in Vigo (if you are sailing from there), or when you board the ferry in Cangas or Bueu.

Getting There & Away

Public boats to the Cíes (round trip adult/child €18.50/6 in July and August, €16/free at other times) normally sail during Semana Santa (Easter week), on weekends and holidays in May, daily from June to late September, and on the first two weekends of October. Vigo is the main port of departure, but there are also sailings from Cangas and Baiona. At least four companies operate these routes. Reservations (always advisable) can normally be made online or by phone (with a credit card) or at the ports of departure.

Naviera Mar de Ons (986 22 52 72; www.mardeons.es) runs at least four daily trips (10 in July and August) from Vigo's **Estación Marítima de Ría** (Ferry Port; Rúa Cánovas del Castillo 3), four or more from Cangas, and four or more from Baiona; **Nabia Naviera** (986 32 00 48; www.piratasdenabia.com) makes up to five trips a day from Vigo, three or four from Cangas and four (July to mid-September) from Baiona; **Cruceros Rías Baixas** (678 491922; http://crucerosriasbaixas.com) runs three daily trips from Vigo, from July to mid-September; and **Tours Rías Baixas** (680 733990; www.toursriasbaixas.com) has four sailings (July and August only) from Baiona.

8-11.30pm Mon-Fri, noon-4pm & 8pm-midnight Sat) Friendly service by a busy team complements the expertly prepared fish, meat and shellfish (and desserts) here. It's contemporary Galician fare – steak tartare, steamed hake with coconut milk – and the clean-lined design (light wood furnishings and stone walls) add to the experience. And it's very popular, so try to book ahead, or get there early.

Follas Novas GALICIAN €€
(986 22 93 06; Rúa de Serafín Avendaño 10; mains €12-19; 1-3.45pm & 8-11.45pm Mon-Sat) It's well worth venturing about 400m east of Praza de Compostela for the top-class fare at this small, unpretentious restaurant, but it's advisable to reserve as it fills up super-fast. Attentive, friendly service complements the excellent preparations of quality fresh ingredients.

For a starter try some grilled shellfish or octopus or the *saquitos rellenos* (a mix of pork tenderloin, leeks and mushrooms in a sort of pancake bag) and follow up with any of the perfectly done fish or *ternera* (beef) options.

Drinking & Entertainment

For early evening drinks, the bars around Praza da Constitución in the Old Town and Praza de Compostela are enticing. From around 11pm the action shifts east to the music bars and pubs along Rúa de Areal and Rúa de Rosalía de Castro.

The Churruca district about 1km southeast of the Old Town is the epicentre of Vigo's student and alternative nightlife and here you'll find two of northern Spain's top small-scale clubs for live rock and indie: **La Iguana Club** (www.facebook.com/laiguanaclub; Rúa de Churruca 14; ⊙midnight-5am Tue-Sat, opens earlier for live gigs) and **La Fábrica de Chocolate Club** (http://fabricadechocolateclub.com; Rúa Rogelio Abalde 22; ⊙midnight-4.30am Thu-Sat, from 10pm for live gigs), both hosting two or three gigs weekly.

Information

Oficina de Turismo de Vigo (986 22 47 57; www.turismodevigo.org; Estación Marítima de Ría, Rúa Cánovas del Castillo 3; ⊙10am-5pm) Helpful tourist office in the ferry terminal.

Getting There & Away

AIR

Vigo's **Peinador airport** (986 26 82 00; www.aena.es), 9km east of the city centre, has direct flights to/from Madrid (Iberia and Air Europa), Barcelona (Vueling and Ryanair), Bilbao (Iberia), Málaga (Air Europa), and Bologna, Italy (Ryanair), plus seasonal Ryanair flights to/from Edinburgh, Dublin, Milan (Bergamo) and Bologna.

BUS

The **bus station** (986 37 34 11; Avenida de Madrid 57) is 2km southeast of the Old Town. **Monbus** (www.monbus.es) makes several trips daily to all main Galician cities, including Pontevedra (€2.50, 30 minutes to one hour), Santiago de Compostela (€8, 1½ hours) and Ourense (€6.55, 1½ hours). **ATSA** (www.automovilesdetuy.es) serves Baiona, A Guarda and Tui. **Avanza** (www.avanzabus.com) runs to/from Madrid (€41 to €44, 7¼ to nine hours) at least four times daily. **Autna** (www.autna.com) runs at least twice daily to/from Porto (Portugal; €12, 2½ hours), with connections there for Lisbon.

TRAIN

Vigo has two stations. High-speed trains (10 or more daily) to/from Pontevedra (€3.65, 15 minutes), Santiago de Compostela (€11, 50 minutes to one hour) and A Coruña (€18, 1½ hours) use **Vigo-Urzáiz station** (Praza da Estación), 1km southeast of the Old Town. **Vigo-Guixar station** (Rúa Areal), 1km east of the Old Town, has five or more slower, slightly cheaper trains to the same cities, plus trains to Ourense (€12 to €23, 1½ to two hours, eight or more daily), Porto (Portugal, €15, 2½ hours, two daily) and other destinations including Ribadavia, Tui, Valença (Portugal), A Coruña, León and Madrid.

Getting Around

Vitrasa (986 29 16 00; www.vitrasa.es) runs city buses (€1.33 per ride). Bus 9A runs between the central Rúa Policarpo Sanz and the airport. The bus station and Vigo-Guixar train station are linked to the city centre by bus C2 (to/from Porta do Sol). Bus 4C runs between the bus station and Rúa Policarpo Sanz.

SOUTHWEST GALICIA

Galicia's southwest corner is home to three towns that all make enjoyable stops on a circuit of the region or a journey to or from Portugal – the pretty fishing town A Guarda, the riverside cathedral town Tui, and the historic port and resort Baiona. The first two, set on the Río Miño which divides Galicia from Portugal, are particularly inviting.

Baiona

POP 2780

(Castilian: Bayona) is a popular resort with its own little place in history: the shining moment came on 1 March 1493, when one of Columbus' small fleet, the *Pinta*, stopped in for supplies, bearing the remarkable news that the explorer had made it to the Indies (in fact, the West Indies). Then an important trading port, Baiona was later eclipsed by Vigo – but there's still a hefty reminder of its former importance in the shape of the stout defensive walls, towers and gun batteries of Monte Boi promontory jutting out from the town's waterfront.

A tangle of inviting lanes, with a handful of 16th- and 17th-century houses and chapels, makes up Baiona's **casco histórico** (historic centre), behind the harbourfront road, Rúa Elduayen. Four kilometres east of town is the magnificent sweep of **Praia América** at Nigrán.

Fortaleza de Monterreal FORTRESS
(pedestrian/car €1/5 late-Jun–mid-Sep, rest of year free; ⊙10am-10pm Jul & Aug, 10am-7pm Sep-Jun; P) You can't miss the pine-covered promontory **Monte Boi**, dominated by the walls of the Fortaleza de Monterreal. The fortress was erected between the 11th and 17th centuries and its impregnable 3km circle of walls still stands, though there's not much that's old left inside it these days. An enticing 40-minute walking trail loops round the promontory's rocky shoreline, which is broken up by a few small beaches.

Within the precinct today is a luxurious hotel, the **Parador de Baiona** (☎986 35 50 00; www.parador.es; Monterreal; incl breakfast s €111-280, d €127-339; P ❄ 📶 🏊) – have a drink on its cafe terrace, with fabulous views across the bay.

Information

Get maps and more at the helpful **tourist office** (☎986 68 70 67; www.turismodebaiona.com; Paseo da Ribeira; ⌚10am-2pm & 4-9pm mid-May–mid-Sep, shorter hr rest of year) on the approach to the Monte Boi promontory.

Getting There & Away

ATSA (www.automovilesdetuy.es) buses run to and from Vigo (€2.55, 45 minutes) every 30 or 60 minutes until 9pm. Just a couple a day go south to A Guarda (€3.25, 45 minutes). Catch buses at stops on the harbourfront road, Rúa Elduayen.

A Guarda

POP 6050

A fishing port just north of where the Río Miño spills into the Atlantic, A Guarda (Castilian: La Guardia) has a pretty harbour, some excellent seafood restaurants, a lovely hotel in an old convent and a cute if small *casco antiguo* (Old Town) of stone buildings centred on Praza do Reló. But its prize attraction is the hill Monte de Santa Trega (p593), rising just outside of town. You can drive or walk up to its magnificently panoramic summit. Another fine walking path runs 3km south from A Guarda's harbour along the coast to the heads of the Miño. The Camino Portugués de la Costa, a variant of the Camino Portugués pilgrim route to Santiago de Compostela, comes through here, and all in all A Guarda is a bit of an unsung gem and an enjoyable place to hang out for a day or two.

Sights

★Monte de Santa Trega HILL

(adult/child in vehicle Tue-Sun Feb-Dec €1/0.50, Mon & Jan free; P 👪) A Guarda's unique draw is the beautiful Monte de Santa Trega, whose 341m summit is a 4km drive or 2km uphill walk (the PRG122) from town. On the way up, stop to poke around the partly restored Iron Age Castro de Santa Trega. At the top, you'll find a 16th-century chapel, an interesting small **archaeological museum** (⌚9am-9pm Jul & Aug, 10am-8pm Apr-Jun & Sep, 10am-7pm Mar & Oct, 11am-5pm 2nd half Feb & Nov-Dec; P) FREE on *castro* culture, a couple of cafes and souvenir stalls – and truly magnificent panoramas up the Miño, across to Portugal and out over the Atlantic.

Castelo de Santa Cruz FORT

(Avenida de Santo Domingo de Guzmán; ⌚10am-9pm Apr-Sep, 10am-6pm Oct-Mar; P 👪) FREE This fort with four arrowhead-shaped corner bastions makes an interesting visit. It was built to defend A Guarda against the Portuguese in the 17th century.

Sleeping & Eating

A Guarda is famed for its seafood, especially *arroz con bogavante* (rice with European lobster). A dozen seafood eateries line up facing the fishing harbour.

★Hotel Convento de San Benito HISTORIC HOTEL **€€**

(☎986 61 11 66; www.hotelsanbenito.es; Praza de San Bieito; s €48-61, d €51-99; ⌚closed mid-Dec–early Jan; P ❄ 📶) A real treat, Hotel Convento de San Benito is housed in a 16th-century convent down near the harbour. Its 33 elegant rooms are romantic, individually decorated, comfortable and very well kept, and the whole place is like a mini-museum with fascinating antiques, paintings, sculptures, books and manuscripts at every turn.

The €7.50 breakfast is a great way to start the day, and the decanter of port placed in the main lounge for guests is a very nice way to end it!

Casa Chupa Ovos SEAFOOD **€€**

(☎986 61 10 15; Rúa La Roda 24; mains & raciones €7-19; ⌚1.45-4pm & 8.30-11.30pm Thu-Tue) It's up a flight of steps from the harbourfront street Rúa do Porto, and it doesn't have a sea view, but Chupa Ovos is a deservedly firm favourite with locals and visitors alike for its perfectly prepared fresh seafood, friendly and prompt service, bright atmosphere and good wines.

Getting There & Away

ATSA (www.automovilesdetuy.es) buses run to/from Vigo (€6.05, 80 minutes) every 30 or 60 minutes until 7pm (fewer on weekends). Most go via Tui, but two or three daily go via Baiona. Buses stop on the main street through the town centre, Avenida de Galicia.

A **ferry** (☎986 61 15 26, Portugal 258 092 564; www.cm-caminha.pt; car/motorcycle/bicycle incl driver or rider €3/2/1, vehicle or foot passenger €1; hourly 10.30am-1.30pm & 3.30-8.15pm Tue-Fri, from 11.30am Sat & Sun) crosses the Miño from Camposancos, 2km south of A Guarda, to Caminha, Portugal. Schedules may vary because of tides or seasonally. A Guarda's **tourist office** (986 61 45 46; www.turismoaguarda.es; Praza do Reló; 9am-2pm Mon-Fri) has current schedules on its website. The nearest bridge is 13km upstream, near Goián.

Tui

POP 6125

Sitting above the broad Río Miño 25m inland, the border town of Tui (Castilian: Tuy) draws Portuguese and Spanish day trippers with its lively bar scene, tightly packed medieval centre and magnificent cathedral. It's well worth strolling round the Old Town and down to the Paseo Fluvial, a riverside path that heads 1km down the Miño. At the southwest end of town the 19th-century **Puente Internacional** (International Bridge), with two levels (railway above, road below), crosses the Miño to Portugal's equally appealing Valença.

Sights

★Catedral de Santa Maria CATHEDRAL
(www.catedraldetui.com; adult/senior/student/child €4/3.50/3/free; 10.45am-8pm Jul–mid-Sep, 10.45am-2pm & 4-7pm mid-Sep–Jun) The highlight of the Old Town is the fortress-like Catedral de Santa Maria, which reigns over Praza de San Fernando. Begun in the 12th century, it reflects a stoic Romanesque style in most of its construction, although the ornate main portal is reckoned the earliest work of Gothic sculpture on the Iberian Peninsula. Standard admission includes a multilingual audio guide and covers the lovely Gothic cloister as well as the main nave and chapels.

Sleeping & Eating

Ideas Peregrinas HOSTEL €
(986 07 63 30; www.ideas-peregrinas.com; Rúa Porta da Pía 1; dm €13-15, r €35-55;) Clean and welcoming, this family-run hostel in the heart of the Old Town is a boon for hikers on the Camino Portugués and anyone else. White paint and light wood predominate, and there's a choice between private rooms (some with private bathroom) or four-person dorms with solid wooden bunks. The same people also run a very pleasant **cafe** (items €3-11; 7am-10pm;) downstairs.

Hotel A Torre do Xudeu HISTORIC HOTEL €€
(986 60 35 35; www.atorredoxudeu.es; Rúa Tide 3; r incl breakfast €60-75; closed mid-Dec–Feb; P) A lovely 1746 mansion with thick stone walls and a pretty garden, the atmospheric 'Jew's Tower' has just six beautiful rooms in a fairly formal style, with large bathrooms. Several rooms look across the Río Miño to Portugal. The free parking is very welcome.

O Novo Cabalo Furado GALICIAN €€
(Praza do Concello; mains €11-23, seafood starters €6-15, menú del día €14; 1-3.30pm & 8.30-11pm, closed Sun Jul-Sep) A couple of doors from the cathedral, this popular restaurant is very strong on fish, shellfish and heaping plates of lamb chops. It's a separate business from the nearby Novo Cabalo Furado *hostal*.

Information

Oficina Municipal de Turismo (677 418405; www.concellotui.org; Praza de San Fernando; 8am-9pm Apr-Sep, shorter hr Oct-Mar) Helpful office in front of the cathedral.

Getting There & Away

ATSA (www.automovilesdetuy.es) buses to Vigo (€3.30, 40 minutes) and A Guarda (€3.25, 40 minutes), both every 30 or 60 minutes until about 7.45pm (fewer services on weekends), stop on Paseo de Calvo Sotelo in front of Hostal Generosa. There are also two daily trains each to Vigo (€4, 45 minutes) and Valença (Portugal; €2.15, 10 minutes) from Tui station, 1km north of the centre.

EASTERN GALICIA

Though often overshadowed by Galicia's glorious coastline and the better-known attractions of Santiago de Compostela, eastern Galicia is a treasure trove of enticing provincial cities, lovely landscapes, wine-growing regions and old-fashioned rural enclaves – perfect territory for travellers who like digging out their own gems.

Ourense

POP 98,900

Galicia's unsung but beguiling third-largest city has an appealingly labyrinthine historic quarter, a lively tapas scene and unusual riverside thermal baths. Ourense (Castilian: Orense) first came into its own as a trading centre in the 11th century. The broad Río Miño runs east–west across the city, crossed by several bridges, including the elegant, stone-built, part-Roman, part-medieval Ponte Vella (Old Bridge) and the soaring concrete-and-metal Ponte do Milenio (Millennium Bridge) that opened in 2001. The central area, including the compact Old Town, rises south of the river.

Sights

The Old Town unfolds around the 12th-century Catedral de San Martiño, in a maze of narrow streets and small plazas that are a pleasure to wander. Among the stone-flagged streets, stone-faced buildings and stone arcades, with almost no vehicular traffic, you may have to remind yourself you're in the 21st century. The largest square is sloping **Praza Maior**, rimmed by old stone buildings with cafes under the arcades and the classical-faced **Casa do Concello** (City Hall) at its foot.

Catedral de San Martiño CATHEDRAL
(www.catedralourense.com; Rúa de Juan de Austria; incl audio guide adult/child/student/pilgrim/senior €5/2/3/3.50/4.50; 11.30am-2.30pm&4-6.30pm Mon-Sat, 1-3pm & 4-6.30pm Sun) FREE The artistic highlight of Ourense's Romanesque-Gothic cathedral, built mainly in the 12th and 13th centuries, is the gilded Santo Cristo chapel, inside the northern entrance. At the west end is the Pórtico do Paraíso, a less inspired but colourfully painted Gothic copy of Santiago de Compostela's Pórtico de la Gloria.

Sleeping

Grelo Hostel HOSTEL €
(988 61 45 64; www.grelohostel.com; Rúa Pena Trevinca 40; dm incl breakfast pilgrim/other €15/17; closed 10 Dec-10 Jan;) About half the guests at this good, friendly hostel are Camino de Santiago pilgrims on the Camino Mozárabe routes, which start in Andalucía – but it's open to everyone and has 24-hour access (no curfew or early-morning kick-out time). The three 10- to 12-person dorms have good metal bunks, with duvets, cotton sheets and towels included in rates.

Hotel Novo Cándido HOTEL €
(988 98 91 25; www.hotelnovocandido.com; Rúa San Miguel 14; s/d €40/55;) New in 2017, this is a step up from other similarly priced central options. The 14 pleasant, bright rooms have discreet lighting, wood floors and panelling, big mirrors and rectangular white washbasins. Some bathrooms are equipped with glassed-in showers; others have bath-tubs. There's a lively cafe-bar on the ground floor.

Eating

Ir de tapeo (going for tapas) is a way of life in Ourense, and streets near the cathedral including Fornos, Paz, Lepanto, Viriato, San Miguel and Praza do Ferro brim with taverns where having to push your way to the bar is

OURENSE'S THERMAL POOLS

Ourense's original *raison d'être* was its hot springs and today the city's attractively modernised thermal pools (http://termalismo.ourense.es) enable everyone to take a therapeutic dip, even in winter. Along a nicely landscaped 4km stretch of the north bank of the Miño are four sets of free open-air pools and two privately run sets of partly indoor pools.

You can walk to any of the pools, but another option is the **Tren das Termas minitrain** (www.urbanosdeourense.es; one way €0.85; hourly 10am-1pm & 4-8pm, reduced frequency Oct-May), which runs to all the riverbank pools from Praza Maior. Take swimming gear, a towel and flip-flops (thongs), and remember that the waters are hot (around 40°C) and mineral-laden, so don't stay in them longer than about 10 minutes without a break.

One of the closest groups of privately run pools to the city centre (a 20- to 30-minute walk) is the Japanese-style, part-outdoor, part-indoor **Estación Termal de A Chavasqueira** (www.termaschavasqueira.com; Rúa Feira Nova; €4; 9am-11.30pm or later Tue-Sun), with four warm pools and one cold one, plus two saunas, massage service and a cafe.

The thermal pools of **Termas de A Chavasqueira** (10am-7pm or 8pm) , right on the riverbank, are the closest to the city centre of Ourense's free, open-air, riverside pools. You can walk there in 20 to 30 minutes from the Old Town.

The four relatively large (up to 15m long) pools of **Termas de Muiño da Vega** (10am-7 or 8pm) are the most enticing of Ourense's free open-air thermal pools, sitting in a pleasantly green spot beside the Miño about 5km northwest of the city centre.

a sign of quality. Tapas start at €1.20 and are washed down with a glass of local wine.

Casa do Pulpo GALICIAN €
(Rúa de Juan de Austria; raciones €5-12; noon-4pm & 8pm-midnight;) Facing the cathedral wall across a narrow street, this local favourite doesn't just do perfect *pulpo* (octopus) but also other tasty Galician items such as *zamburiñas* (small scallops), *xoubas* (pilchards) and *raxo* (spicy pork chunks), plus combination bites including anchovies with cheese or *solomillo* (tenderloin) with cheese, bacon and red pepper.

Sybaris 2.0 SPANISH €€
(Rúa Santo Domingo 15, entrance Rúa Cardenal Quiroga 22; dishes €8-16, lunch menú €12; 11am-8pm Mon, 11am-11.30pm Tue-Fri, noon-11.30pm Sat) Sybaris is not just a restaurant with a contemporary twist on Spanish fare, but also a well-stocked wine shop and Galicia-specialist deli (cheeses and hams, of course, but also lampreys in oil, crab pâté and sea-urchin caviar). The frequently changing menu might include partridge-and-artichoke risotto or Iberian pork tenderloin in port with glazed apple and chestnuts.

Entertainment

Café Latino JAZZ, BLUES
(www.cafelatino.es; Rúa Coronel Ceano 7; 7.30am-3am Mon-Sat, 8.30am-2am Sun;) Classy Café Latino has a fabulous corner stage that hosts jazz gigs most Thursdays, starting around 10pm or 11pm, and a jazz festival in May. It's been serving up jazz for three decades and is a good breakfast spot too.

THE ULTIMATE OCTOPUS FEAST

Most Galicians agree that the best *pulpo á feira* (Galicia's signature octopus dish) is cooked far from the sea in the inland town of O Carballiño, 30km northwest of Ourense. Tens of thousands of people pile into O Carballiño on the second Sunday of August for the **Festa do Pulpo de O Carballiño** (www.festadopulpodocarballino.es; 2nd Sun in Aug).

Cooks here invented the recipe in the Middle Ages, when the local monastery received copious supplies of octopus from tenants on its coastal properties.

Information

Oficina Municipal de Turismo (988 36 60 64; www.turismodeourense.gal; Calle Isabel La Católica 2; 9am-2pm & 4-8pm Mon-Fri, 11am-2pm Sat & Sun) A very helpful place beneath the Xardinillos Padre Feijóo park, just off pedestrianised Rúa do Paseo.

Getting There & Away

BUS

From Ourense's **bus station** (988 21 60 27; Carretera de Vigo 1), 2km northwest of the centre, **Monbus** (p567) runs to Santiago (€9, 1¾ hours, four or more daily), Vigo (€6.55, 1½ hours, four or more daily), Pontevedra (€7.10, 1½ hours, one or more daily) and Lugo (€6.05, 1¾ hours, two or more daily). **Arriva** (p577) heads to A Coruña (€19 to €22, 2¼ to three hours, three or four daily). **Avanza** (www.avanzabus.com) journeys to Madrid (€34 to €39, six to seven hours, five daily).

TRAIN

The **train station** (Avenida de Marín) is 500m north of the Río Miño. **Renfe** (p568) runs to Santiago (€10 to €20, 40 minutes to 1¾ hours, 10 daily), Vigo (€12 to €24, 1¾ to 2½ hours, 10 or more daily), León (€15 to €35, 3¾ to 4½ hours, five daily) and elsewhere.

Getting Around

Local buses 1, 3, 6A and others (€0.85) run between the train station and the central Parque de San Lázaro. Buses 6A, 6B and 12 connect the bus station with Parque San Lázaro.

Ribadavia & the Ribeiro Wine Region

POP 3130 (RIBADAVIA)

The headquarters of the Ribeiro wine Denominación de Origen (DO), which produces some of Galicia's best whites, Ribadavia sits beside the Río Avia 30km west of Ourense, among green, rolling hills strewn with vineyards and old stone villages (the Avia valley north of town is particularly charming). The town's little historic centre is an enticing maze of narrow streets lined with heavy stone arcades and broken up by diminutive plazas; within this, in medieval times, was Galicia's largest Jewish quarter, centred on Rúa Merelles Caulla.

Sights & Activities

More than 20 wineries in the area are open for visits. Most require a phone call in advance: the best strategy is to talk to the staff at Ribadavia's tourist office, who really know their wineries and can help arrange visits. For further information, check www.rutadelvinoribeiro.com and www.ribeiro.wine.

Museo Sefardí MUSEUM
(Centro de Información Xudía de Galicia; Praza Maior 7; adult/child incl Castelo dos Sarmento & audio guide €3.50/free; 9.30am-2.30pm & 5-8pm Mon-Sat, 10.30am-2.30pm Sun Jun-Sep, shorter hours rest of year) Above the tourist office on the lovely main square, this centre has exhibits on the Jews of Galicia since their expulsion from Spain in 1492.

Castelo dos Sarmento CASTLE
(Castelo dos Condes; Rúa Progreso; adult/child incl Museo Sefardí & audio guide €3.50/free; 9.30am-2.30pm & 5-8pm Mon-Sat, 10.30am-2.30pm Sun Jun-Sep, shorter hours rest of year) The large, chiefly 15th-century castle of the Counts of Ribadavia is one of Galicia's biggest medieval castles and contains a medieval necropolis within its bare stone precinct, which is brought alive by the audio guide (available in English). Tickets are sold at the tourist office.

Bodega Viña Meín WINERY
(676 358763; www.vinamein.com; Lugar de Meín, San Clodio; daily by reservation; P) FREE This medium-size winery adjoining the Viña Meín country hotel produces more than 100,000 bottles annually of good reds and whites, from indigenous Galician grapes grown on 16 hectares of vineyards around the Avia valley. It has a lovely bright modern tasting room for you to sample its vintages.

Paseo Fluvial WALKING
Relax with a stroll along this riverside path beside the Ríos Avia and Miño. You can access it by steps down from Praza Buxán, next to Praza Madalena in Ribadavia's Judería (old Jewish quarter): it's 600m to the Avia's confluence with the much bigger Miño, then 1.8km along the Miño to the path's end.

If you're up for a longer stretch of the legs, Ribadavia's tourist office can tell you about several longer marked walking trails in and around the Avia valley.

Festivals & Events

Feira do Viño do Ribeiro WINE
(http://feiravinoribeiro.com; May) Ribadavia parties on the first weekend in May with this big wine festival.

Sleeping & Eating

Lodgings in town are limited but there are some wonderful rural hotels in the area, especially in the beautiful Avia valley to the north.

★**Casal de Armán** HOTEL €€
(699 060464; www.casaldearman.net; O Cotiño, San Andrés; r incl breakfast €75-90; P) You can kill several birds with one stone at this dignified country house set among vineyards and lovely Avia valley countryside. The six cosy rooms feature plenty of exposed stone and toiletries made from grape extract! Also here are a top-class restaurant (p598) (reservations essential at weekends), and a top Ribeiro **winery** (638 043335; incl tasting €7; visits by reservation Tue-Sun Nov-Aug; P) with free visits for restaurant or hotel guests.

It's 6km northeast of Ribadavia.

Pazo de Esposende HOTEL €€
(696 378670; http://pazoesposende.es; Carretera OU211, Esposende; r incl breakfast €50-85; P) Fully modernised under new ownership in 2017, this 16th-century mansion in the Avia valley, a few kilometres north of Ribadavia, boasts appealingly comfortable and up-to-date rooms with subtle lighting and full-wall murals of local scenes, but retains its thick stone walls, handsome, pillared courtyard, and charming views over the village and countryside. The welcome is friendly and the breakfast filling.

Viña Meín CASA RURAL €€
(617 326385; www.vinamein.com; Lugar de Meín, San Clodio; d incl breakfast €66; P) Viña Meín, in a beautiful part of the Avia valley about 10km north of Ribadavia, is a delightful six-room, old-stone, country guesthouse, with a medium-sized on-site winery producing good whites and reds from indigenous Galician grapes. All in all, a fine base for visiting the region.

O Birrán Gastrobar GALICIAN €
(Praza da Madalena 8; mains €6.50-13; noon-3.30pm & 8-11pm Tue-Sun) Set in a medieval house in the old Judería (Jewish quarter), O Birrán cooks up some very tasty plates from classic Galician ingredients – good choices include the *pulpo con tetilla* (octopus with cheese) and the *tortilla abierta* (omelette with greens, cheese, bacon and wild mushrooms).

★ **Sábrego** GALICIAN €€

(☎988 49 18 09; www.sabrego.es; Casal de Armán, O Cotiño, San Andrés; mains €17-19; ⏲1.15-3.45pm & 8.45-11.15pm Tue-Sun, closed evenings Tue-Thu & Sun mid-Oct–mid-Jun; Ⓟ) The rustic-chic restaurant at the lovely country hotel Casal de Armán serves a seasonally changing array of excellent, chiefly Galician fare with some creative twists. Standouts include the lamb shoulder with *cachelos* (boiled potatoes) and spinach, the red tuna with cream of San Simón cheese, and the octopus dim sum. Reservations essential for weekends.

ℹ Information

Tourist Office (☎988 47 12 75; http://ribadaviaturismo.weebly.com; Praza Maior 7; ⏲9.30am-2.30pm & 5-8pm Mon-Sat, 10.30am-2.30pm Sun Jun-Sep, shorter hr Oct-May) Very helpful office in an old mansion of the Counts of Ribadavia on the lovely main square.

ℹ Getting There & Away

At least two buses and two trains run daily to Ourense and Vigo from stations in the east of town, just across the Río Avia.

Ribeira Sacra

Northeast of Ourense, along the Ríos Sil and Miño, unfold the natural beauty and unique cultural heritage of the Ribeira Sacra (Sacred Riverbank), so called for the many medieval monasteries founded here after early Christian hermits and monks were drawn to this remote area. Amid the beautiful and sometimes severe scenery – particularly dramatic along the Cañón do Sil (Sil Canyon) – the area offers good walking and mountain-bike trails, winery visits (Ribeira Sacra is one of Galicia's five wine DOs) and boat trips along the rivers.

The area is poorly served by public transport, but it makes for a marvellous driving trip. A good route is to head from Ourense to Monforte de Lemos via the Mosteiro de San Pedro de Rocas, Mosteiro de Santo Estevo, Parada de Sil and Castro Caldelas. Try to give yourself at least two days to make the most of what the area has to offer.

ℹ Information

The website Ribeira Sacra (www.ribeirasacra.org) is a very useful resource with, among other things, detailed information on the area's wineries and more than 20 walking routes (with maps). There are tourist information offices in many villages but their opening times are often limited: the best information office for the area overall is in the **Centro do Viño da Ribeira Sacra** (☎982 10 53 03; www.centrovino-ribeirasacra.com; Rúa Comercio 6; tour incl glass of wine €2.50; ⏲10am-2pm & 5-9pm Tue-Sun Jul-Sep, 10am-2pm & 4.30-8pm Tue-Sun Oct-Jun) in Monforte de Lemos.

ℹ Getting There & Around

Monforte de Lemos has reasonable bus or train connections with Ourense, Lugo and other Galician cities. Villages on the south side of the Cañón do Sil have limited bus service, Monday to Friday only, to/from Ourense; there's also a Monday-to-Friday service between Castro Caldelas and Monforte de Lemos.

Luintra & Around

POP 410 (LUINTRA) / ELEV 640M (LUINTRA)

Two of the Ribeira Sacra's most impressive and contrasting monasteries stand a few kilometres either side of the village of Luintra, about 25km northeast of Ourense. They make a fine pair of first stops if you're starting out on a Ribeira Sacra tour from Ourense.

Sights

★ **Mosteiro de San Pedro de Rocas** MONASTERY

(☎661 508243; www.centrointerpretacionribeirasacra.com; ⏲10.30am-1.45pm & 4-7.45pm daily Apr-Sep, 10.30am-1.45pm & 4-6pm Tue-Sun Oct-Mar; Ⓟ) FREE Founded in AD 573, this enchanting mini-monastery stands hidden among dense woods 11km south of Luintra. It contains three cave chapels, originally carved out of the rock as retreats for early hermits, plus a number of rock-cut graves from the 10th century onwards. The adjacent interpretation centre has interesting displays on the Ribeira Sacra. You can also take a lovely walk from here along the Camiño Real (PRG4), a 9km circuit trail looping through this picturesque area.

To drive direct from Ourense, take the OU536 east as far as Tarreirigo. Here, 500m past the Km 15 post, turn left on to the OU0509 and follow signs along minor roads for 4km through the forests to the monastery. Afterwards you can continue north to Luintra on the OU0509.

★ **Mosteiro de Santo Estevo** MONASTERY

(Monasterio de San Esteban; ⏲closed Jan–mid-Feb; Ⓟ) FREE The enormous Mosteiro de Santo Estevo, on the side of the steep, thickly wooded valley above the Río Sil, dates from the 12th century and has three magnificent cloisters (one Romanesque-Gothic, two Renaissance), a Romanesque-Gothic church and an 18th-century baroque facade. It's now a luxurious **parador hotel** (☎988 01 01 10; www.parador.es; Santo Estevo; s/d incl breakfast from €108/126; ⊙closed Jan–mid-Feb; P ❄ wifi), but everyone is free to wander round the main monuments and eat in the cafe or restaurant.

Sleeping

A Casa da Eira CASA RURAL €
(☎696 749493; www.acasadaeira.com; Lugar Alberguería 31, Cerreda; s/d €45/55, apt for 2/4 €90/136; P wifi) A Casa da Eira provides ample, comfortably modernised rooms in an old granite-and-timber farmhouse in a tiny hamlet 300m off the OU0508, 11.5km east of Luintra. The welcoming hosts are full of helpful information on the numerous walks and other things to do in the area, and serve up big breakfasts (€5.50) with homemade jams from their orchard (but no other meals).

Parada de Sil & Around

POP 190 (PARADA DE SIL) / ELEV 660M (PARADA DE SIL)

The village of Parada de Sil sits on the plateau high above the Cañón do Sil, 22km east of Luintra. From the village, separate roads lead 1km to the spectacular **Balcóns de Madrid** viewpoint over the canyon and 4km down to the lovely **Mosteiro de Santa Cristina de Ribas de Sil** (interior €1; ⊙exterior 24hr, interior 11am-2pm & 4-6pm Tue-Sun; P), with its 12th-century Romanesque church, hidden among trees above the canyon. Part of the PRG98 walking trail heads down to the monastery and back up to the viewpoint in a loop of about 10km from the village.

★**Ruta Cañón do Río Mao** WALKING
(PRG177) This excellent trail starts at the Albergue A Fábrica da Luz (p599), 11km east of Parada de Sil. You can shorten the full 16km circuit to an enjoyable 5km loop (about 2½ hours) by descending the pretty Mao canyon (initially on a boardwalk) to Barxacova village, then climbing 1.5km past vineyards to San Lourenzo village, then descending back to A Fábrica.

At San Lourenzo take a 500m (each way) detour to the interesting medieval necropolis of San Vítor.

The full, relatively demanding 16km circuit, with a total altitude gain of over 600m, continues south from San Lourenzo to the upland villages of A Miranda and Forcas and the medieval bridge at Conceliños before heading back north down the Mao canyon/valley to San Lourenzo and A Fábrica da Luz.

Sleeping

Reitoral de Chandrexa CASA RURAL €
(☎605 867622, 988 20 80 99; www.chandrexa.com; Chandrexa; d €48-56; ⊙closed mid-Dec–Jan; P wifi) A charming little guesthouse occupying the former curate's house next to Santa María de Chandrexa church, and serving excellent organic breakfasts (€5.50) and dinners (€12 to €15), with many ingredients from its own garden. The three comfy rooms have stone walls, wood floors and ceilings, and good bathrooms, and there's a cosy farmhouse-style dining-cum-sitting room.

Albergue A Fábrica da Luz HOSTEL €
(☎988 98 49 90; http://afabricadaluz.com; OU0605 Km 5.7; dm/d incl breakfast €17/34; ⊙daily Jun-Sep, Sat, Sun & holidays mid-Mar–May & Oct–mid-Dec; P wifi) Housed in a converted small hydroelectric station in the beautiful leafy canyon of the Río Mao (a tributary of the Río Sil), this is a well-run place. The two 14-bunk dorms and two double rooms (sharing bathrooms) are clean and well kept, and good, inexpensive food is available. It's 11km east of Parada de Sil along the OU0605.

The Ruta Cañón do Río Mao walking trail (p599) starts right here with an 850m-long boardwalk, the Pasarela do Río Mao, heading down the canyon. The hostel has kayaks to rent (€10 per hour) on the river at the foot of the canyon, 1km away, and also functions as the Centro BTT Ribeira Sacra (Ribeira Sacra Mountain Bike Centre), with bikes to rent (€15 per day including helmet) and plentiful information on good routes.

Castro Caldelas & Around

POP 610 (CASTRO CALDELAS) / ELEV 780M (CASTRO CALDELAS)

The hilltop village of Castro Caldelas, with its cobbled streets and old stone houses with Galician *galerías* and well-tended flower boxes, is a good spot to spend the night. Explore the old quarter at the top of the village, crowned by a panoramic 14th-century **castle** (adult/child €2/free; ⊙10am-2pm & 4-7pm; P). It's located 52km east of Ourense.

From Castro Caldelas, the OU903 winds 10km northward down to the Sil Canyon, crosses the river on the Ponte do Sil bridge, then becomes the LU903 as it climbs across almost vertical vineyards en route towards

Monforte de Lemos. Interesting wineries to visit on this route include Ponte da Boga, **Adega Algueira** (982 41 02 99; www.adegaalgueira.com; Doade; tour incl tasting in Spanish/English €5/7; tours in English noon, Spanish 1pm; P) and **Regina Viarum** (619 009777; http://reginaviarum.es; Doade; tour incl tasting €1-5; 10.30am-2.30pm & 4.30-8pm daily Jun-Sep, 10.30am-2pm & 4-7pm Thu-Sun Oct-May; P) – these last two are both at Doade, a few kilometres up the hill on the north side of the canyon.

From the Ponte do Sil, you can take river cruises on the 16-passenger **Brandán** (982 41 02 99; www.adegaalgueira.com; adult/child €15/7; 11am, 12.30pm, 5pm & 6.30pm Thu-Tue Mar-Nov) or larger boats operated by the **Diputación de Lugo** (982 26 01 96; Embarcadoiro de Doade; adult/senior & child €9/5; 11.30am & 4 or 4.30pm daily Jun-Sep, Wed-Sun Oct-Nov & Apr-May, also 7pm daily Jun–mid-Sep).

There are four small hotels in the quaint old part of Castro Caldelas.

★Ponte da Boga WINERY

(988 20 33 06; www.pontedaboga.es; Carretera OU903, Km 21.8, O Couto, San Paio; 45min tour incl 7 wine tastings €5; 10am-2pm & 4-10pm Easter-Oct, 10am-1.30pm & 3-7pm Nov-Easter; P) FREE One of the most interesting wineries in the Castro Caldelas area, Ponte da Boga dates back to 1898 and is one of a growing number of wineries that are reviving autochthonous Galician grape varieties. Some of its wines are among Ribeira Sacra's best, and you get to taste seven of them on the standard tour. It's located 6km down the OU903 from Castro Caldelas towards the Sil Canyon.

Sleeping

Hotel Casa de Caldelas HOTEL €

(988 20 31 97; www.hotelcasadecaldelas.com; Praza do Prado 5, Castro Caldelas; incl breakfast s €35-40, d €45-55;) Snug, up-to-date rooms in a handsome 18th-century stone house on the village's main square make this small, welcoming hotel a great choice. Bathrooms are small but have good contemporary fittings.

Monforte de Lemos

POP 16,335 / ELEV 300M

This crossroads town is neither as compact nor as pristine as other stops in the region, but it has a historic heart and it's well worth making your way north of the centre up the hill, **Monte de San Vicente**. Here the 17th-century Monasterio de San Vicente is occupied by a *parador* hotel whose courtyard, cafe and restaurant are open to all, and you can visit the **Torre da Homenaxe** (€1.50; 11am-1.45pm & 4-6.30pm or later Tue-Sun; P), the last vestige of the Counts of Lemos' medieval castle. You can drive up Monte de San Vicente, but it's interesting to walk up past medieval walls and houses from Praza de España in the town centre. Follow Rúas Zapaterías, Pescaderías and Falagueira then head up the 'Castillo' path a few metres inside the Porta Nova gate.

At **Pazo Molinos de Antero** (676 573563; www.pazomolinosdeantero.com; Carretera de Malvarón; r €55-65, d €105-115; P) the old stables of an 18th-century manor house on the east side of town have been converted into cosy, modern rooms and self-catering apartments. Added to the attractions of staying here – which include a warm welcome, good large bathrooms, a sitting room with free coffee and tea, and a grassy garden – are guided tours of the house, which is still in the hands of its original family.

Lugo

POP 90,000

The grand Roman walls encircling old Lugo are considered the best preserved of their kind in the world and are the number-one reason visitors land here. Within the fortress is a beautifully preserved web of streets and squares, most of them traffic-free and ideal for strolling, with plenty of interesting things to see (nearly all free) and a terrific tapas-bar scene. Lucus Augusti was a major town of Roman Gallaecia and modern Lugo is a quiet but engaging city, with a good number of other Roman remains besides the walls.

Sights

★Roman Walls WALLS

(24hr;) FREE The path running right round the top of the World Heritage–listed Roman walls is to Lugo what a maritime promenade is to a seaside resort: a place to jog, take an evening stroll, see and be seen. The walls, erected in the 3rd century AD, make a 2.2km loop around the Old Town, rise 15m high and are studded with 85 stout towers. They failed, however, to save Lugo from being taken by the Suevi in 460 and the Muslims three centuries later.

Until well into the 19th century, tolls were charged to bring goods into the walled city, and its gates were closed at night.

The **Centro de Interpretación de la Muralla** (Praza do Campo 11; ⌚11am-1.30pm & 5-7.30pm Mon-Wed, 11am-7.30pm Thu-Sat, 11am-6pm Sun mid-Jun–mid-Oct, 11am-2pm & 4-6pm Mon-Wed, 11am-6pm Thu-Sun mid-Oct–mid-Jun) FREE, a block north of Lugo's cathedral, gives interesting background on the Roman walls, with videos and free audio guides, all available in English.

Catedral de Santa María CATHEDRAL
(☎982 23 10 38; Praza Pio XII; ⌚8.25am-8.45pm) The cathedral, inspired by Santiago de Compostela's, was begun in 1129, though work continued for centuries, yielding an aesthetic mix of styles ranging from Romanesque (as in the transepts) to neoclassical (the main facade). It's a serene building that merits a close look. The superb gilded main altarpiece, carved with scenes from the life of Christ by Cornelis de Holanda in the 1530s, now stands in two parts in the two transepts.

Behind the ultra-baroque high altar (which is surrounded by very colourful stained-glass windows), an ultra-baroque chapel houses the beautiful Gothic image of Nosa Señora dos Ollos Grandes (Our Lady of the Big Eyes), in polychromed alabaster. Outside, just above the north doorway, the sculpture of Christ in majesty is a masterpiece of Spanish Romanesque stone carving.

Museo Provincial MUSEUM
(http://redemuseisticalugo.org; Praza da Soidade; ⌚9am-9pm Mon-Fri, 10.30am-2pm & 4.30-8pm Sat, 11am-2pm Sun) FREE Lugo's main museum includes parts of the Gothic Convento de San Francisco and is one of Galicia's best and biggest museums. The well-displayed exhibits range from pre-Roman gold jewellery and Roman mosaics to Galician Sargadelos ceramics and a large collection of 19th- and 20th-century Galician art.

Casa dos Mosaicos ARCHAEOLOGICAL SITE
(Rúa de Doutor Castro 20-22; ⌚11am-1.30pm & 4-7.30pm Tue-Sat, 11am-2pm Sun mid-Jun–mid-Oct, 11.30am-1.30pm & 5-7pm Thu-Sat, 11.30am-1.30pm Sun mid-Oct–mid-Jun) FREE These remains of a Roman mansion sit beneath an Old Town street, with some beautiful, wonderfully preserved mosaics and murals.

Festivals & Events

Arde Lucus FIESTA
(www.ardelucus.com; ⌚Jun;) Around half a million people pack into Lugo over three days in June (sometimes running into the first days of July), as the city returns to its Roman roots with this festival featuring chariot races, gladiator fights, a whole lot of Roman costume and plenty more.

Sleeping

Hotel Méndez Núñez HOTEL €
(☎982 23 07 11; www.hotelmendeznunez.com; Rúa da Raíña 1; r €50-135;) The 69-room Méndez Núñez offers bright, spacious quarters with good beds, gleaming bathrooms and parquet floors. With a great Old Town location and parking nearby for €6, it's a good deal when rates are in the €50 to €65 range, as they often are. The wi-fi signal can be feeble on some floors.

Hotel España HOTEL €
(☎982 81 60 62; hotelespanalugo@hotmail.com; Rúa Vilalba 2 Bis; s/d €25/35;) With a cheerful

Camino Francés in Galicia

CAMINOS DE SANTIAGO IN GALICIA

All of the Caminos de Santiago converge in Galicia, their shared goal. About 63% of pilgrims reach Santiago de Compostela by the **Camino Francés**, which starts in the Pyrenees. This route enters Galicia at O Cebreiro in the hills bordering Castilla y León, then heads west for the final 154km across welcome green countryside to Santiago de Compostela. But growing numbers of pilgrims also reach Santiago by the Camino Portugués (entering Galicia from Portugal at Tui or A Guarda), Camino del Norte (along the coast from the Basque Country through Cantabria and Asturias), Vía de la Plata (from Andalucía), Camino Primitivo (from Oviedo via Lugo) and Camino Inglés (from A Coruña or Ferrol).

Tiny **O Cebreiro**, 1300m high, marks the top of the Camino Francés' longest, hardest climb. About half the buildings here are bar-restaurants (many offering cheap set menus) or *pensiones* or pilgrims' hostels: among them are dotted several *pallozas* (circular, thatched dwellings of a type known in rural Galicia since pre-Roman times, where families shared living space with their livestock). The nicest accommodation is the five wood-beamed, stone-walled rooms in the main building of **Hotel Cebreiro** (982 36 71 82; www.hotelcebreiro.com; O Cebreiro; s/d €40/50;); reservations advised.

In Triacastela, 19km downhill from O Cebreiro, the *camino* divides, with both paths reuniting later in Sarria. The longer (25km) southern route passes through **Samos**, a village built around the very fine Benedictine **Mosteiro de Samos** (982 54 60 46; www.abadiadesamos.com; tours €4; tours hourly 9.30am-12.30pm & 4.30-6.30pm Mon-Sat, 12.45pm & hourly 4.30-6.30pm Sun May-Oct, hourly 10am-noon, 4.30pm & 5.30pm Mon & Wed-Sat, 12.45pm, 4.30pm & 5.30pm Sun Nov-Apr; P). This monastery has two beautiful big cloisters – one Gothic, with distinctly unmonastic Greek nymphs adorning its fountain; the other neoclassical and filled with roses. Samos has plenty of inexpensive lodgings, but another good option is the welcoming **Casa de Díaz** (982 54 70 70; www.casadediaz.com; Vilachá; r €35-50, breakfast €6.30; closed approx Nov-Mar; P @), an 18th-century farmhouse turned rural hotel at Vilachá, 3.5km west. It has 12 comfy rooms in olde-worlde style.

People undertaking just the last 100km of the *camino* usually start 12km west of Samos at **Sarria** (114km from Santiago). From here the *camino* winds through village after village, across forests and fields, then descends steeply to Portomarín, above the Río Miño. After a tough 25km stretch to Palas de Rei, the next 15km to Melide follows some lovely rural lanes. From Melide, 53km remain through woodlands, villages, countryside and, at the end, city streets. The *camino* approaches central Santiago along Rúa de San Pedro and arrives in Praza da Inmaculada on the northern side of the cathedral. Most pilgrims take a few more steps down through an archway to emerge on magnificent Praza do Obradoiro, before the cathedral's famous western facade.

If you're touring Galicia rather than *camino*-ing it, the 30km from O Cebreiro to Samos make a marvellous side trip. Drivers entering Galicia along the A6 from Astorga can turn off into Pedrafita do Cebreiro, then follow the LU633 4km south up to O Cebreiro. The road from there to Samos winds down through green countryside with great long-distance views, frequently criss-crossing the *camino*.

reception and cheerful decorative touches in the rooms such as tangerine walls or bird murals, the España is a good deal for its prices. Seven of the 17 rooms look out at the Roman walls across the street. Breakfast costs €2.50.

Orbán e Sangro BOUTIQUE HOTEL **€€€**
(Hotel Pazo de Orbán; 982 24 02 17; www.pazodeorban.es; Travesía do Miño 6; d €110-220, incl breakfast €132-253; P) The 12 rooms of this welcoming hotel, in an 18th-century mansion just inside the Roman walls, are regal, with rich linen, antique furnishings, designer bathrooms and (in 10 rooms) huge 2.15m beds. The hotel serves a great 'ecological' breakfast, is full of intriguing antiques and classical art, and has its own tavern in a highly original early-20th-century style.

Eating

The Old Town, especially Rúa da Cruz, Rúa Nova and Praza do Campo, north of the cathedral, is liberally endowed with inviting bar-restaurants serving both tapas and main dishes. Many offer two free tapas with each drink: one selected by the bar, the other chosen by you from a list recited verbally (usually at high speed!) by bar staff.

Las Cinco Vigas TAPAS **€**
(Rúa da Cruz 9; raciones €4-12; ⏲9am-midnight Wed-Mon) Always one of the busiest tapas bars, with a totally mixed crowd enjoying exceptionally good free tapas, including a great *terneira al vino tinto* (veal in red wine). Items are also available as *raciones* (full plate servings) if you want more than a couple of mouthfuls.

Restaurante Paprica GALICIAN **€€€**
(www.paprica.es; Rúa das Nóreas 10; mains €19-29; ⏲1.30-3.45pm & 8.30-10.45pm, closed Mon night & Sun Jun-Sep, Sun night & Mon Oct-May) The talented young team here creates satisfying original dishes based on time-honoured Galician ingredients of fresh fish, shellfish, vegetables and quality meat – a contemporary experience enhanced by the clean-lined, unfussy decor. You can eat light in the bar or sit down to a la carte meals or a set menu. Everything is delicious, including the desserts!

Mesón de Alberto GALICIAN **€€€**
(☎982 22 83 10; www.mesondealberto.com; Rúa da Cruz 4; mains €13-30; ⏲1-4pm Sun & Mon, 1-4pm & 8.30-11.30pm Wed-Sat) The classiest place in the tapas zone, Alberto serves good, traditionally prepared meat, fish and shellfish with a few inventive touches – meals in the main dining room upstairs; tapas on the ground floor. The €15 tapas tasting menu (three dishes and wine) is a fair bet.

ℹ Information

Oficina Municipal de Turismo (☎982 25 16 58; http://lugo.gal; Praza do Campo 11; ⏲11am-1.30pm & 5-7.30pm Mon-Wed, 11am-7.30pm Thu-Sat, 11am-6pm Sun mid-Jun–mid-Oct, shorter hr rest of year) Helpful office in the Centro de Interpretación de la Muralla.

ℹ Getting There & Away

From the **bus station** (☎982 22 39 85; Praza da Constitución), just outside the southern walls, **Empresa Freire** (www.empresafreire.com) runs to Santiago de Compostela (€9.45, two hours, six or more daily), and **Arriva** (p577) heads to A Coruña (€9.15, 1¼ to two hours, five or more daily). Other services head to Monforte de Lemos, Ourense, Pontevedra, Viveiro, Ribadeo, León, Madrid, Asturias and beyond.

Renfe (p568) trains head at least three times daily to A Coruña (€10 to €12, 1¾ hours) and Monforte de Lemos (€6 to €16, one hour), and once or more daily to Madrid (€28 to €53, seven to 9½ hours).

Extremadura

Includes ➡

Best Places to Eat

- ➡ Atrio (p609)
- ➡ Restaurante La Meancera (p620)
- ➡ La Rebotica (p628)
- ➡ La Cacharrería (p609)
- ➡ Villa Xarahiz (p618)

Best Places to Stay

- ➡ Atrio (p609)
- ➡ El Jardín del Convento (p620)
- ➡ La Flor de Al-Andalus (p625)
- ➡ Eurostars Palacio de Santa Marta (p614)
- ➡ Hospedería del Real Monasterio (p615)

Why Go?

Exploring Extremadura is a journey into the heart of old Spain, from the country's finest Roman ruins to mysterious medieval cities and time-worn villages. Mérida, Cáceres and Trujillo rank among Spain's most beautifully preserved historical settlements. *Extremeño* hamlets have a timeless charm, from the remote northern hills to sacred eastern Guadalupe and seductive Zafra on the cusp of Andalucía in the south.

Few foreign travellers make it this far. Spaniards, however, know Extremadura as a place to sample some of inland Spain's best food: roasted meats, the pungent, creamy Torta del Casar cheese and the finest Monesterio *jamón* (ham).

This is a region of broad blue skies and vast swathes of sparsely populated land with isolated farmhouses and crumbling hilltop castles. Wooded sierras rise along the northern, eastern and southern fringes, while the raptor-rich Parque Nacional de Monfragüe is Extremadura's most dramatic corner.

When to Go

Caceres

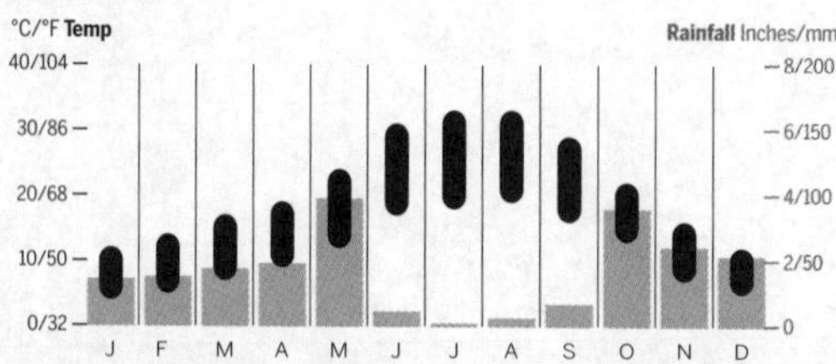

Mar–Apr The Valle del Jerte becomes a spectacular white sea of cherry blossom.

Jul–Aug Mérida's 2000-year-old Roman theatre hosts the Festival Internacional de Teatro Clásico.

Sep–Oct Prime time to visit: fewer tourists and good weather, without the intense summer heat.

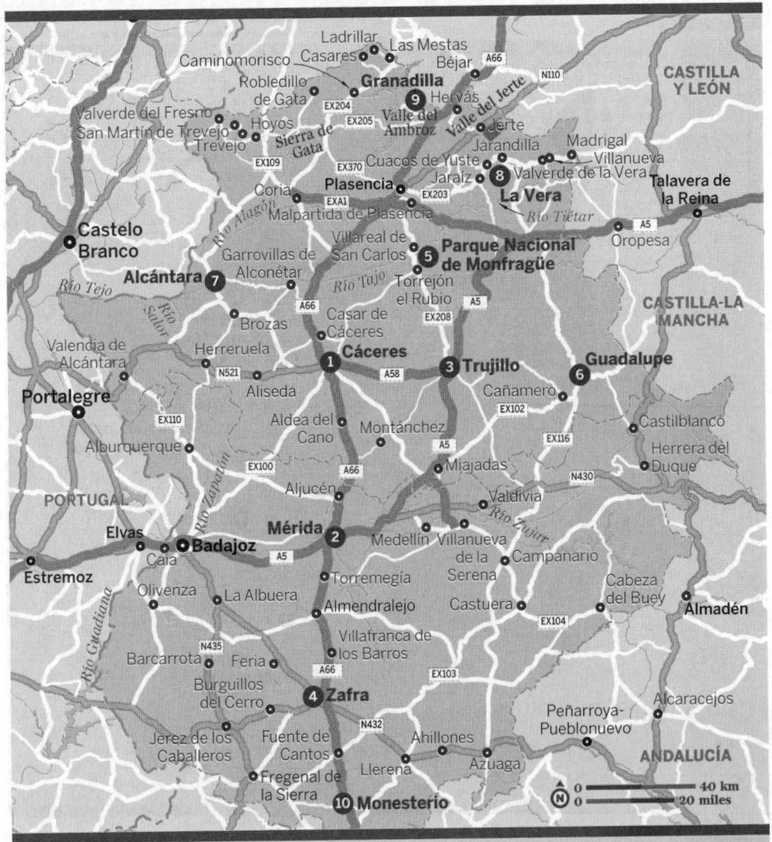

Extremadura Highlights

1. **Cáceres** (p605) Wandering the Ciudad Monumental's cobbled streets and packed-out tapas bars.
2. **Mérida** (p622) Clambering over Spain's finest Roman ruins.
3. **Trujillo** (p611) Travelling to the medieval hometown of some of Latin America's most infamous conquistadors.
4. **Zafra** (p627) Feasting on tapas beneath the Plaza Grande's palms, then sleeping in a castle.
5. **Parque Nacional de Monfragüe** (p621) Spotting majestic birds of prey high above the Tajo.
6. **Guadalupe** (p615) Admiring art and architecture at Guadalupe's extraordinary monastery.
7. **Alcántara** (p610) Checking out the mighty, impressive Roman bridge over the Tajo.
8. **La Vera** (p618) Exploring half-timbered villages and rushing rivers, then marvelling at the cherry blossom of the adjacent Valle del Jerte.
9. **Granadilla** (p619) Pacing the quiet lanes of this restored historic museum village.
10. **Monesterio** (p629) Learning all about Spain's favourite food at the Museo del Jamón, and then tasting it.

Cáceres

POP 95,814

Welcome to one of Spain's most beautiful cities. While the suburbs of Cáceres are largely unremarkable in the manner of so many Spanish cities, the Ciudad Monumental (Monumental City) at its core is truly extraordinary. Narrow cobbled streets twist and climb among ancient stone walls lined

Cáceres

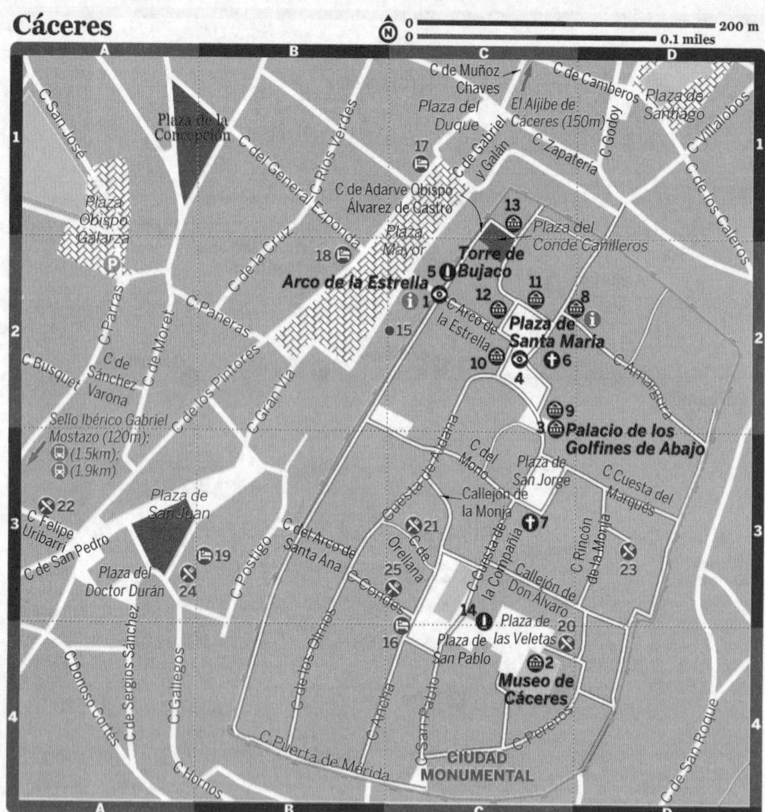

with palaces, mansions, arches and churches, while the skyline is decorated with turrets, spires, gargoyles and enormous storks' nests. Protected by defensive walls, it has survived almost intact from its 16th-century period of splendour. At dusk or after dark, when the crowds have gone, you'll feel like you've stepped back into the Middle Ages.

Stretching at its feet, the lively, arcaded Plaza Mayor is one of Spain's most beautiful public squares.

Sights

Plaza de Santa María & Around

Most visitors approach the stunning Ciudad Monumental from the Plaza Mayor, passing under the 18th-century **Arco de la Estrella** (Calle Arco de la Estrella) onto the **Plaza de Santa María**. Notable facades on the Plaza de Santa María include the **Palacio Episcopal** (Bishop's Palace; Plaza de Santa María), the **Palacio de Mayoralgo** (Plaza de Santa María) and the **Palacio de Ovando** (Plaza de Santa María), all in 16th-century Renaissance style.

As you wander further into the Ciudad Monumental to the southeast, you'll pass the Renaissance-style **Palacio de la Diputación** (Plaza de Santa María).

★Torre de Bujaco TOWER

(927 24 67 89; Plaza Mayor; adult/child €2.50/free; 10am-2pm & 5.30-8.30pm Tue-Sun May-Sep, 10am-2pm & 4.30-7.30pm Tue-Sun Oct-Apr) As you head up the steps to the Ciudad Monumental from the Plaza Mayor, turn left to climb the 12th-century, 25m-high Torre de Bujaco, home to an interpretative display on Cáceres' history. Up on the rooftop there's a fabulous stork's-eye view over the Plaza Mayor. From here, you can also walk across the top of the 18th-century Arco de la Estrella.

Cáceres

Concatedral de Santa María CATHEDRAL
(Plaza de Santa María; adult/senior/student/child €4/3.50/3/free; 10am-9pm Mon-Sat, 10am-12.30pm & 2-7pm Sun May-Sep, hours vary Oct-Apr) This 15th-century Gothic cathedral creates an impressive opening scene for the Ciudad Monumental. Inside, you'll find a magnificent carved 16th-century cedar altarpiece, fine noble tombs and chapels, and a small ecclesiastical museum. Beautiful colourful murals (including dragons) adorn the vaulted ceiling above the altarpiece. Climb the bell tower for old-town views.

Palacio de Carvajal HISTORIC BUILDING
(927 25 55 97; Calle Amargura 1; 8am-8.45pm Mon-Fri, 10am-1.45pm & 5-7.45pm Sat, 10am-1.45pm Sun) FREE Just off the northeastern corner of the main Plaza de Santa María stands this late-15th-century mansion. The building was abandoned after fires tore through in the 19th century. Now restored, it houses a modern display on the province's attractions and the helpful regional tourist office (p610).

Palacio Toledo-Moctezuma HISTORIC BUILDING
(Plaza del Conde Canilleros) Just north of the Plaza de Santa María lies the domed 16th-century Palacio Toledo-Moctezuma, once home to Isabel Moctezuma, daughter of the Aztec emperor Moctezuma II, who was brought to Cáceres as a conquistador's bride. The palace now contains the municipal archives.

Iglesia de San Francisco Javier CHURCH
(Iglesia de la Preciosa Sangre; Plaza de San Jorge; adult/child €1/free; 10am-2pm & 5-8pm Apr-Sep, 10am-2pm & 4.30-7.30pm Oct-Mar) An 18th-century Jesuit church with a baroque facade that rises above the Plaza de San Jorge. You can climb its towers for glorious old-town views, obscured a little by the netting.

Plaza de San Mateo & Around

★**Palacio de los Golfines de Abajo** HISTORIC BUILDING
(927 21 80 51; www.palaciogolfinesdeabajo.com; Plaza de los Golfines; tours adult/child €2.50/free; tours hourly 10am-1pm & 5-7pm Tue-Sat, 10am-1pm Sun May-Sep, 10am-1pm & 4.30-6.30pm Tue-Sat, 10am-1pm Sun Oct-Apr) The sumptuous home of Cáceres' prominent Golfín family has been beautifully restored. Built piecemeal between the 14th and 20th centuries, it's crammed with historical treasures: original 17th-century tapestries and armoury murals, a 19th-century bust of Alfonso XII, a signed 1485 troops request from the Reyes Católicos (Catholic Monarchs) to their Golfín stewards. But it's the detailed, theatrical tours (Spanish, English, French or Portuguese), through four richly decorated lounges, an extravagant chapel and a fascinating documents room, that make it a standout.

★**Museo de Cáceres** MUSEUM
(927 01 08 77; www.museodecaceres.gobex.es; Plaza de las Veletas; EU citizens/other free/€1.20; 9am-3pm & 5-8.30pm Tue-Sat, 10.15am-2.30pm

EXTREMADURA'S TOP FOOD & WINE EXPERIENCES

- Tracking down one of Spain's most celebrated cheeses, the Torta del Casar, in Casar de Cáceres' Museo del Queso (p610).
- Visiting the Museo del Jamón (p629) and sampling the region's best *jamón* in Monesterio.
- Glamming up for one of Spain's most sought-after fine-dining experiences at Atrio (p609) in Cáceres.
- Going food shopping for an Extremaduran picnic in Zafra at Iberllota (p629), **Joaquín Luna** (☎ 924 55 05 37; www.joaquinluna.com; Plaza de España 10; ⏲10am-2pm & 5.30-8.30pm Mon-Fri, 10am-1.30pm Sat) and La Cava del Queso (p629).
- Sampling the robust reds of the Ribera de Guadiana wine-producing region, at Bodegas Medina (p627), Palacio Quemado (p627) and Bodegas Ruíz Torres (p615).
- Enjoying the best in Spanish cheeses in Trujillo's late-April Feria del Queso (p613), or year-round at Zafra's **Quesería La Bendita** (☎ 615 266265; Plaza Chica 14; tapa/ración from €4/11; ⏲12.30-3.30pm & 7.30pm-midnight Tue-Sat, 12.30-4pm Sun).

Sun Apr-Sep, 9am-3pm & 4-7.30pm Tue-Sat, 10.15am-2.30pm Sun Oct-Mar) The excellent Museo de Cáceres, spread across 12 buildings in a 16th-century mansion built over an evocative 12th-century *aljibe* (cistern), is the only surviving element of Cáceres' Moorish castle. The impressive archaeological section includes an elegant stone boar dated to the 4th to 2nd centuries BC, while the equally appealing fine-arts display (behind the main museum; open only in the mornings) showcases works by such greats as Picasso, Miró, Tàpies and El Greco. It's one of Spain's most underrated collections.

Torre de las Cigüeñas TOWER
(Tower of the Storks; Plaza de San Pablo) Sandwiched between the Plaza de San Mateo and the Plaza de las Veletas, at the top of the old town, this is the only Cáceres tower to retain its battlements: the rest were lopped off in the late 15th century under orders from Isabel la Católica.

Activities

El Aljibe de Cáceres HAMMAM
(☎ 927 22 32 56; www.elaljibedecaceres.com; Calle de Peña 5; from €20; ⏲10am-2pm & 6-10pm Tue-Sun) This luxurious re-creation of the Moorish-style bath experience combines soothing architecture and a range of treatments. The basic thermal bath pass includes aromatherapy and herbal tea, but you can also throw in a range of massages (bath and massage from €20).

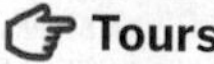

Tours

★ **Cuentatrovas de Cordel** WALKING
(☎ 666 836332, 667 776205; www.cuentatrovas.com; adult from €7, child over/under 10yr €5/free) Guides and other actors dress up in period costume and take you on a tour with a difference through the Ciudad Monumental. It's fun, informative (for Spanish speakers) and very much recommended. Times vary, with after-dark tours the speciality, departing from the Arco de la Estrella.

Asociación de Guías Turísticos WALKING
(Tourist Guides Association; ☎ 927 21 72 37; Plaza Mayor 2; tour adult/child €6/free) These guides lead 1½- to two-hour Spanish-language tours taking in the highlights of the Ciudad Monumental at 11am, 12.30pm and 6pm (5pm October to April) Monday to Saturday and 11am and 12.30pm Sunday. Tours start from the office on the Plaza Mayor. Minimum 10 people, but you can (usually) join an existing group.

Festivals & Events

Fiesta de San Jorge LOCAL FIESTA
(⏲22-23 Apr) Cáceres celebrates the Fiesta de San Jorge, in honour of its patron saint, with shows, fireworks, competitions, a re-creation of a Christian-Moorish battle and a giant dragon on the Plaza Mayor.

Womad MUSIC

(World of Music, Arts & Dance; www.womad.org; ⏱May) For three fiesta-fuelled days in mid-May, Cáceres stages a long-running edition of Womad, with international bands playing in the old city's squares.

Sleeping

Hotel La Boheme HOTEL €

(☎674 014060; www.hotellaboheme.com; Plaza Mayor; s/d/ste €45/60/80; ❄📶) At the lower, northern end of Plaza Mayor, Hotel La Boheme has large rooms with a wonderfully whimsical air to them. The rooms have plenty of colour and character but they're never overdone and the terrace suite is a particularly good choice; rooms overlooking the plaza have plenty of light but can also be noisy.

★Hotel Soho Boutique Casa Don Fernando BOUTIQUE HOTEL €€

(☎927 62 71 76, 927 21 42 79; www.casadonfernando.com; Plaza Mayor 30; s/d from €55/65; P❄📶) Cáceres' smartest midrange choice sits on Plaza Mayor right opposite the Arco de la Estrella. Boutique-style rooms, spread over four floors, are tastefully modern, with gleaming bathrooms through glass doors. Pricier 'superiors' enjoy the best plaza views (though weekend nights can be noisy), and attic-style top-floor rooms are good for families. Service hits that perfect professional-yet-friendly note.

NH Collection Palacio de Oquendo HISTORIC HOTEL €€

(☎927 21 58 00; www.nh-collection.com; Plaza de San Juan 11; r from €95; ❄📶) Classy, spacious cream-coated rooms, complete with coffee kits, chunky mattresses, soothing lighting and stylish modern bathrooms, await within this beautifully revamped 16th-century palace. Best are the balcony rooms with views across the Plaza de San Juan. Step into on-site **Tapería Yuste** (tapas €4.85, raciones €9-19, set menus €21.50-30; ⏱1-4pm & 8pm-midnight) for deliciously inventive tapas.

★Atrio BOUTIQUE HOTEL €€€

(☎927 24 29 28; www.restauranteatrio.com; Plaza de San Mateo 1; d €270-500; P❄📶🏊) Impeccably sleek modern styling, sultry white-on-white rooms and some serious pieces of original contemporary art dominate this fabulous fusion of five-star boutique hotel and one of Spain's most garlanded restaurants. The old-town location is exquisite, with panoramic Cáceres views from the orange tree–lined rooftop pools and terrace. Throw in top-notch personal service and it's obvious why Atrio is considered Extremadura's finest hotel.

Eating

Los Siete Jardines CAFE €

(☎927 21 73 36; www.lossietejardines.es; Calle Rincón de la Monja 9; snacks & light meals from €5; ⏱4pm-late Mon-Fri, noon-late Sat & Sun) Lost in the old-town maze, Los Siete Jardines triples as contemporary art gallery, cultural hub and bohemian-feel cafe. Order a coffee and one of their snacks or light meals in the back garden, with Cáceres' monuments towering around, or soak up the scene through floor-to-ceiling windows from the brick-and-stone-clad interior.

★La Cacharrería TAPAS €€

(☎927 03 07 23; lacacharreria@live.com; Calle de Orellana 1; tapas €5, raciones €10-18; ⏱restaurant 12.30-4pm & 8.30-midnight Thu-Mon, cafe 4pm-1.30am Thu-Sat, 4-11pm Sun; 🌱) Local flavours and ingredients combine in exquisite, international-inspired concoctions at this packed-out, minimalist-design tapas bar tucked into an old-town house. *Solomillo* (tenderloin) in Torta del Casar cheese arrives in martini glasses. Delicious guacamole, hummus, falafel and 'salsiki' are a godsend for vegetarians. No advance reservations: get here by 1.45pm or 8.30pm.

★Atrio CONTEMPORARY SPANISH €€€

(☎927 24 29 28; www.restauranteatrio.com; Plaza de San Mateo 1; menús from €135; ⏱2-4pm & 8.30-11.30pm; 🌱) With a stunning location in the heart of old-town Cáceres, this is Extremadura's top restaurant. Chic contemporary design and service that's both formal and friendly back up the wonderful, inventive culinary creations. The focus is on local produce of the highest quality, via a 12- to 13-course degustation menu. Vegetarian and gluten-free menus available with advance notice. Bookings essential.

Torre de Sande FUSION, SPANISH €€€

(☎927 21 11 47; www.castillodelaarguijuela.com; Calle Condes 3; mains €19-26, set menus €28-40; ⏱1.30-4pm Tue & Sun, 1.30-4pm & 8.30pm-midnight Wed-Sat; 🌱) Sit in the pretty courtyard and dine on roast suckling pig or goat kid, or on ambitious seasonal dishes such as seafood-filled *merluza* (hake) or tomato and basil soup with goat's cheese and figs at this elegant gourmet restaurant in the heart of the Ciudad Monumental. For something more modest, stop for drinks and tapas at the busy interconnecting *tapería* (tapas bar).

Information

Oficina de Turismo (927 11 12 22, 674 301332; www.turismoextremadura.com; Plaza Mayor; 10am-2pm & 5.30-8.30pm Jun-Sep, 10am-2pm & 4.30-7.30pm Oct-May) On Plaza Mayor, focusing on the city and wider Extremadura attractions.

Oficina de Turismo (927 25 55 97; www.turismocaceres.org; Palacio Carvajal, Calle Amargura 1; 8am-8.45pm Mon-Fri, 10am-1.45pm & 5-7.45pm Sat, 10am-1.45pm Sun) Inside the Palacio de Carvajal.

Getting There & Away

BUS

The **bus station** (927 23 25 50; www.estacionautobuses.es; Calle Túnez 1; 6.30am-10.30pm) is 2km southwest of the old town.

DESTINATION	FARE (€)	TIME	FREQUENCY
Badajoz	6.30	1¼hr	3-6 daily
Madrid (normal/ express)	23/30	4½/ 3¾hr	5/2 daily
Mérida	6.50	1hr	2-3 daily
Plasencia	5.90	50min	1-4 daily
Trujillo	3.65	45min	5-6 daily

TRAIN

From the train station, 2.5km southwest of the old town, trains run to/from Madrid (€28 to €33, 3¾ hours to 4¼ hours, five daily), Mérida (€6.10 to €7.35, one hour, six daily) and Plasencia (€5.20 to €6.05, one hour, four daily).

Casar de Cáceres

POP 4604

Cheese lovers rejoice! Extremadura may be well known for its *jamón*, but its smooth Torta del Casar cheese is equally celebrated in Spanish culinary circles. Casar de Cáceres, 12km north of Cáceres and well signposted off the N630 to/from Plasencia, is where this regional treasure was born and is still produced – it's an easy short, foodie excursion from Cáceres.

Sights

Museo del Queso MUSEUM

(927 290081; Calle Barrionuevo Bajo 7; 10am-2pm Tue-Sat) FREE This small museum is dedicated to Extremadura's beloved Torta del Casar, a pungent, creamy cheese that's aged for 40 days and eaten most often as a spread on *tostas* (topped toast), but also pops up with a steak or, nowadays, in creative modern concoctions. Most of the exhibits are Spanish-only, but it's still worth exploring even if you don't speak the language.

Getting There & Away

If you don't have your own wheels, eight buses run daily Monday to Friday (two on Saturday) between Casar de Cáceres and Cáceres bus station (€2.10, 20 minutes).

Alcántara

POP 1518

Alcántara is Arabic for 'the Bridge', and sure enough, below this remote Extremaduran town, a spectacular Roman bridge extends across the Río Tajo. The town itself retains old walls, a ruined castle of Moorish origin, several imposing mansions and churches, and the enormous Renaissance Convento de San Benito. It all adds up to one of inland Spain's most rewarding (and least-known) detours.

Sights

For a partial view of the Puente Romano from above, walk 100m west from the Iglesia de Santa María de Almocóvar down Calle de Carnicería, then continue along the pedestrian-only stone path that leads downhill for around 250m to a mirador (tower).

There's an even better **mirador**, power lines notwithstanding, that takes in both the town and Puente Romano in one sweep. To get there, drive across the Puente Romano along the EX207 in the direction of Portugal. After just over 1km, take the turn-off signposted 'Embalse' and the (now-closed) campground; the lookout is 400m along this road on your right.

Puente Romano BRIDGE

On the northwest side of Alcántara, a magnificent 2nd-century Roman bridge – 204m long, 61m high, with six arches and much reinforced over the centuries – spans the Río Tajo below a huge dam retaining

WORTH A TRIP

MALPARTIDA DE CÁCERES & LOS BARRUECOS

The pretty whitewashed town of **Malpartida de Cáceres** (www.malpartidadecaceres.es), southwest of Cáceres, is reason enough to detour off the N521 on your way to/from Mérida or Valencia de Alcántara. From May to September in particular, the Plaza de los Paraguas is given shade cover by more than a thousand brightly coloured raised umbrellas. Malpartida de Cáceres is also a good base for exploring boat trips and other activities around the Río Tajo. But arguably the region's greatest attraction is the **Monumento Natural Los Barruecos**, a stirring world of beautiful boulders piled high along the shores of pretty natural lakes and with important (and picturesque) breeding colonies for white storks. The cinematic beauty of the landscapes here also caught the eye of producers of *Game of Thrones* – the epic battle scenes in episodes four and five of Season Seven were filmed here.

the Embalse de Alcántara (Alcántara Resevoir). The restorations may have dulled the bridge's obvious antiquity but it's still a stirring sight. From the bridge, a beautiful 20km walking circuit follows the river then loops up into the hills via a village and a prehistoric menhir (standing stone).

Conventual de San Benito CONVENT
(927 39 00 81; Calle Regimiento de Argel; tours hourly 10.15am-1.15pm & 5-7pm Mon-Fri, 11.15am-1.15pm & 5-7pm Sat, 11.15am-1.15pm Sun Apr-Oct, hours vary Nov-Mar) FREE What a surprise this is out in the Extremadura backblocks! Built in the 16th century to house the Orden de Alcántara, an order of Reconquista knights – part monks, part soldiers – who ruled much of western Extremadura as a kind of private fiefdom, this grand Renaissance convent was abandoned in the 19th century. The highlights of the restored monastery include the Gothic cloister and the perfectly proportioned three-tier loggia. Admission is by free guided visit (ring the bell if the door is shut).

Sleeping

Hospedería Conventual de Alcántara HISTORIC HOTEL €€
(927 390638; www.hospederiasdeextremadura.es; Carretera del Poblado Iberdrola; r incl breakfast from €75;) On the eastern edge of town, this comfortable and stylish modern hotel enjoys a marvellous setting in a 15th-century monastery-turned-flour factory. It offers bright, lime-green rooms bursting with colour. The restaurant serves up Extremaduran specialties such as pheasant and all manner of dishes that include wild mushrooms and the pungent creamy Torta del Casar cheese.

Shopping

Artesanía Pepi FOOD
(605 929657, 927 39 09 38; Calle Arco de la Concepción 3; 10am-2pm & 5-8pm) This wonderful old pastry shop sells the much-loved local pastry, known as *mormentera*, which is filled with honey and almonds and has strong links to Arab and Sephardic recipes from the region's past. Opening hours vary – ask at the tourist office if you find it closed.

Information

Oficina de Turismo de Alcántara (927 39 08 63; www.alcantara.es; Avenida de Mérida 21; 10am-2pm & 4.30-6.30pm Mon-Fri, 10.30am-2.30pm Sat & Sun)

Getting There & Away

Mirat (927 23 33 54; www.mirat-transportes.es) runs four buses Monday to Friday to/from Cáceres (€6.80, 1½ hours), but none on weekends.

Trujillo

POP 9436

Whether bathed in the warm light of a summer sunset or shrouded in winter mists, Trujillo can feel truly magical. The town's historic core is one of the best-preserved medieval towns in Spain. Beginning in the Plaza Mayor, its splendour extends up the hillside into a labyrinth of mansions, leafy courtyards, fruit gardens, quiet plazas, churches and convents enclosed within 900m of walls circling the upper town. It all dates to the 16th century, when Trujillo's favourite sons returned home from the Americas as wealthy conquistadors, and what they bequeathed to their home town lives on in a most beautiful way.

A SINGULAR SWIMMING HOLE

Hotel swimming pools are one thing. Swimming in an ancient Roman quarry is another altogether. It was at the **Cantera de Alcántara** that the stones were quarried by the Romans to build the Puente Romano. In the two millennia since, this *deep* hole has filled with water and is a wonderful place to swim, surrounded by the towering rock walls cut in steps above the water, and complete with its own little sand beach.

To get here, drive across the Puente Romano along the EX207 in the direction of Portugal. After just over 1km, take the turn-off signposted as 'Embalse' and the (now-closed) campsite. Continue for 2.7km after leaving the EX207. The Cantera is on your left, with an entrance just where the paved road ends.

Sights

★Plaza Mayor SQUARE

Trujillo's main square is is one of Spain's most spectacular plazas, surrounded by baroque and Renaissance stone buildings sporting intricately carved facades, topped with a skyline of towers, turrets, cupolas, crenellations and nesting storks.

A large, bronze equestrian **statue** (Plaza Mayor) of the conquistador Francisco Pizarro by American sculptor Charles Rumsey dominates the plaza. But all is not as it seems. Apparently Rumsey originally sculpted it as a statue of Hernán Cortés to present to Mexico, but Mexico, which takes a dim view of Cortés, declined it, so it was given to Trujillo as Pizarro instead.

On the south side of the plaza, carved images of Pizarro and his lover Inés Yupanqui (sister of the Inca emperor Atahualpa) adorn the corner of the 16th-century **Palacio de la Conquista** (Plaza Mayor). To the right is their daughter Francisca Pizarro Yupanqui with her husband (and uncle), Hernando Pizarro. The mansion was built in the 1560s for Hernando and Francisca after Hernando (the only Pizarro brother not to die a bloody death in Peru) emerged from 20 years in jail for murder. Higher up, a bas-relief carving shows the Pizarro family shield (two bears and a pine tree), the walls of Cuzco (in present-day Peru) and Pizarro's ships.

Off the plaza's northeastern corner lies the 16th-century **Palacio de los Duques de San Carlos** (Palacio de los Carvajal Vargas; Plaza Mayor), with its sober classical patio, grand granite staircase and distinctive brick chimneys built in Mudéjar style (though some say they represent New World cultures conquered by Spain). Nowadays it's a convent for the Jerónimo order.

Also looming over the plaza is the 16th-century **Iglesia de San Martín** (Plaza Mayor; adult/child €1.50/free; ⏲10am-2pm & 5-8pm Apr-Sep, 10am-2pm & 4-7pm Oct-Mar), with delicate Gothic ceiling tracery in its single nave, striking stained-glass windows, a 1724 altarpiece and a grand 18th-century organ. Climb up to the choir loft (right as you enter) for the best view.

★Castillo de Trujillo CASTLE

(adult/child €1.50/free; ⏲10am-2pm & 5-8pm Apr-Sep, 10am-2pm & 4-7pm Oct-Mar) Occupying the town's 600m-high summit, Trujillo's castle is of 10th-century Islamic origin (note the horseshoe arch just inside the entrance) and was later strengthened by the Christians. Patrol the battlements for magnificent sweeping views (sunset views are exquisite), visit the derelict *aljibe* (cistern) and climb to the hermitage of Our Lady of the Victory, Trujillo's patron. A 50-céntimo coin makes her spin around in her alcove; you can also spot her above the entrance gate as you approach.

★Iglesia de Santa María la Mayor CHURCH

(Plaza de Santa María; adult/child €2/free; ⏲10.30am-2pm & 4.30-7.30pm) This 13th-century church is a stunner. It has a mainly Gothic nave and two towers that you can climb for fabulous views across Trujillo, the castle and the sprawling countryside. The church's magnificent altarpiece includes 25 brilliantly coloured 15th-century paintings by Spanish artist Fernando Gallego in the Hispano-Flemish style, depicting scenes from the lives of Mary and Christ. The 124-step Torre Julia is a Romanesque stunner, while the 106-step Torre Nueva has some interesting architectural notes on the first landing.

Centro de Visitantes Los Descubridores MUSEUM

(Cuesta de la Sangre; adult/child €1.50/free; ⏲10am-2pm & 5-8pm Apr-Sep, 10am-2pm & 4-7pm Oct-Mar) Opened in July 2016, this museum inhabits the 17th-century Iglesia de la

Preciosa Sangre de Cristo with a high-tech display on Spain's conquest of the Americas and the larger-than-life Trujillo heroes who very often led the way. Displays include the role of religion, a timeline of conquest and Trujillos around the world. Surprisingly, the Americas' indigenous population is barely mentioned, save for a wooden bust of Atahualpa – it's as if they didn't exist.

Casa-Museo de Pizarro MUSEUM
(Calle del Convento de las Jerónimas; adult/child €1.50/free; ⏲10am-2pm & 5-8pm Apr-Sep, 10am-2pm & 4-7pm Oct-Mar) High in the upper old town (and signposted from the Puerta de Santiago), this small museum occupies a 15th-century home believed to have belonged to the Pizarro family. It includes period furniture, various knick-knacks from the Pizarro boys' conquests, a handy Pizarro family tree and, upstairs, historical displays (in Spanish and, in parts, English) detailing Spanish conquests in the Americas.

Tours

Informative, fast-paced two-hour guided tours of Trujillo (in Spanish) leave from the tourist office (p614) daily at 11am and 5.30pm (4.30pm from October to March). Tickets cost €7.50 (kids free) and take in the Castillo de Trujillo, Iglesia de Santa María la Mayor, Casa-Museo de Pizarro, Iglesia de Santiago, Aljibe Hispano-Musulmán (otherwise off limits) and Plaza Mayor. Tickets also entitle you to free entry into the Iglesia de San Martín, Centro de Visitantes Los Descubridores and the Torre del Alfiler. Tours may run in other languages with advance bookings.

Festivals & Events

Feria del Queso FOOD & DRINK
(www.feriadelquesotrujillo.es; ⏲late Apr–early May) Cheese makers from all over Spain (and beyond) converge on the Plaza Mayor for Trujillo's pungent cheese fair.

Fiestas de Trujillo LOCAL FIESTA
(⏲late Aug–early Sep) The town springs to life with music, theatre and plenty of partying for the annual Fiestas de Trujillo.

Sleeping

★**El Mirador de las Monjas** HOTEL €
(☎927 65 92 23; www.elmiradordelasmonjas.com; Plaza de Santiago 4; r with/without breakfast €65/55; ❄) High in the old town, this super-friendly six-room *hostería* (small hotel) has bright, spotless, modern rooms decorated in a minimalist-chic style with lots of creams and whites and gorgeous, gleaming bathrooms. Upstairs rooms with sloping ceilings and pretty vistas are slightly better than those below, but all are outrageously good value and there's a quality **restaurant** (☎927 65 92 23; www.elmiradordelasmonjas.com; mains €10-22, set menu €20; ⏲1-3.30pm & 8-10pm Easter-Aug, 1-3.30pm & 8-10pm Fri & Sat, 1-3.30pm Mon, Thu & Sun Sep, Oct & Mar, closed Nov-Feb; 📶) attached.

★**Posada Dos Orillas** HISTORIC HOTEL €
(☎927 65 90 79; www.dosorillas.com; Calle de Cambrones 6; d €50-70; 📶) In a fantastic old-town corner, this tastefully renovated 15th-century mansion is full of character. The 13 comfy rooms replicate Spanish colonial taste and are named for countries containing towns called Trujillo. Twin-room

WHAT'S COOKING IN EXTREMADURA?

- *Migas extremeñas* (breadcrumbs fried with garlic, peppers and pork) at Mesón La Troya (p614) or with honey at Tabula Calda (p626).
- *Caldereta de cabrito* (stewed kid) at Villa Xarahiz (p618).
- *Cochinillo asado* (roast suckling pig) at **La Tahona** (☎620 389991; www.asadorlatahonadecaceres.com; Calle Felipe Uribarri 4; tapas from €4.50, raciones €12-22, mains €18-28, set menus €15-35; ⏲1-4pm & 8-11pm).
- Torta del Casar (a strong, creamy cheese served on toast), at many places, including **Fusiona Gastrobar** (☎924 10 29 36; Calle de José Ramón Mélida, 14; tapas from €4.50; ⏲noon-midnight Tue-Sun; 📶) or **Alma del Sabor** (☎927 22 76 82; www.restaurantealmadelsabor.com; Plaza de las Veletas 4; tapas €5.50, mains €12.50-22, set menu €17.50; ⏲noon-3.30pm & 7.30-11.30pm) 🌿.
- *Jamón ibérico* (Iberian ham), anywhere, but especially the bars of Monesterio (p629); the mountain hamlet of Montánchez is also known for its first-rate *jamón*.

'Extremadura' has glimpses of Santa María church from its bathroom. Nights are deliciously quiet, while personal service from the welcoming owners couldn't be better. Rooms cost €10 more on weekends.

★ **Eurostars Palacio de Santa Marta** HOTEL €€
(☎927 65 91 90; www.eurostarshotels.com; Calle de los Ballesteros 6; d standard/premium from €60/90; P ❄ 📶 🏊) Just above Plaza Mayor, the refurbished 16th-century Santa Marta Palace combines slick, wood-floored chambers with beautiful original features such as exposed stone walls and high ceilings. There's a summer-only pool with views across Trujillo's rooftops. For prime vistas over the square, book a superior or premium room. Spacious room 208, with its little pillared balcony, is stunning. Outstanding breakfasts, too.

Parador de Trujillo HISTORIC HOTEL €€
(☎927 32 13 50; www.parador.es; Calle Santa Beatriz de Silva 1; r €75-160; P ❄ @ 📶 🏊) Given Trujillo's delightful overdose of hotels in historic buildings, it's no surprise that this *parador* (luxury state-owned hotel) occupies a former 16th-century convent. Large terracotta-tiled rooms with understated historical touches branch off two evocative orange-and-olive-tree-dotted cloisters. Breakfast is served in a restored chapel and there's a summer pool. It's in the old town's winding backstreets, 350m east of the Plaza Mayor.

✕ Eating

Mesón La Troya SPANISH €
(☎927 32 13 64; www.mesonlatroya.com; Plaza Mayor 10; mains €7-22, set menus €16-25; ⏲1-4pm & 8-11pm; 👪) Famous across Spain for its copious servings of no-frills *comida casera* (home-style cooking), Troya enjoys a prime location on Trujillo's main square. The food is decent, but it's more about quantity. At lunchtime, you'll be directed to one of several dining areas, where plates of tortilla, chorizo and lettuce-and-tomato salad materialise before you've even ordered your three-course *menú*. Weekend queues stretch out the door.

★ **El 7 de Sillerías** SPANISH €€
(☎927 32 18 56; www.el7desillerias.com; Calle Sillerías 7; raciones €9-22, mains €10-24; ⏲noon-late Wed-Mon; 📶 🖉) With a friendly local buzz, snug wood-beamed interior and elegantly presented traditional fare, this cafe-bar-restaurant just southeast off the Plaza Mayor is the pick of Trujillo's eateries. Tasty menu choices include Extremaduran *jamón*/cheese boards, plenty of Iberian pork and huge *parrilladas de verduras* (grilled vegetable platters). The cafe-bar area dishes out *raciones* (large plate servings), *bocadillos* (filled rolls) and *tostas* (topped toast).

Restaurante Corral del Rey SPANISH €€
(☎927 32 30 71; www.corraldelreytrujillo.com; Plazuela Corral del Rey 2; mains €12-28, set menus €25-36; ⏲1.30-4pm & 9-11.30pm Mon-Sat Apr-Sep, 1.30-4pm & 8.30-11pm Oct-Apr, closed Wed & Sun night Oct-Apr) Pocketed into a Plaza Mayor corner, this classically smart restaurant has four intimate dining rooms – choose the subterranean vaulted brick dining room for atmosphere. Excellent set menus are the way to go, or choose from a tempting range of grills, roasts, fish and soups. One speciality is *bacalao Corral del Rey* (grilled cod in courgette and roasted garlic sauce).

ℹ Information

Oficina de Turismo (☎927 32 26 77; www.turismotrujillo.com; Plaza Mayor; ⏲10am-2pm & 5-8pm Apr-Sep, 10am-2pm & 4-7pm Oct-Mar) Right on the Plaza Mayor.

ℹ Getting There & Away

The **bus station** (☎927 32 12 02; Avenida de Extremadura) is 1km south of the Plaza Mayor.

DESTINATION	FARE (€)	TIME	FREQUENCY
Badajoz (normal/ express)	12/21	2/1¾hr	4/4 daily
Cáceres	3.65	45min	5-6 daily
Madrid (normal/ express)	19/31	3½/ 2¾hr	10/3 daily
Lisbon (normal/ express)	30/34	4¼/4hr	2/1

ℹ Getting Around

Note that parking is (in theory) only allowed in the parking spots of the Plaza Mayor for 30 minutes between 10am and 8pm from Monday to Friday. For unlimited street parking, head north of the Plaza Mayor along Calle de García de Paredes and Avenida de la Coronación.

The building is an architectural delight, crammed with historical riches.

Guadalupe

POP 1999

Centred on its palatial monastery, a treasure trove of art, architecture and history, the sparkling white village of Guadalupe is a hugely popular pilgrimage centre. It's also a worthy destination in its own right, a bright jewel set in the green crown of the surrounding ranges and ridges of the Sierra de Villuercas (part of the Geoparque Villuercas, Ibores y Jara). These hushed hills offer plenty of good walks, through thick woods of chestnut, oak and cork meshed with olive groves and vineyards.

Sights

★Real Monasterio de Santa María de Guadalupe MONASTERY

(☎927 36 70 00; www.monasterioguadalupe.com; Plaza de Santa María de Guadalupe; church free, monastery by guided tour adult/child €5/2.50; ⌚church 9am-7.30pm, monastery 9.30am-1pm & 3.30-6pm) Guadalupe's renowned, Unesco World Heritage–listed monastery is located, according to legend, on the spot where, in the early 14th century, a shepherd received a vision of the Virgin Mary. A sumptuous church-monastery was built on the site, drawing pilgrims from across the world ever since. Now cared for by nine Franciscan monks, it remains one of Spain's most important pilgrimage sites, especially for South American and Filipino Catholics. The building is an architectural delight, crammed with historical riches.

Bodegas Ruíz Torres WINERY

(☎927 36 90 21; www.ruiztorres.com; Carretera EX116, Km 33; ⌚10am-2pm & 5-8pm) Around 6km south of Guadalupe, close to the Puerta Llano, this well-regarded winery produces whites, reds and *cavas* (sparkling wine), and occupies a lovely perch overlooking the hills. It offers a comprehensive hour-long tour of its operations and the winemaking process, with a chance to taste and buy at the end. It's just south of the pass, along the road to/from Navalvillar de Pela.

Festivals & Events

Fiesta de la Virgen de Guadalupe RELIGIOUS

(⌚6-8 Sep) Guadalupe honours its beloved Virgen de Guadalupe with an intricate ceremony that sees the Virgin's image removed from its usual *camarín* (chamber), dressed in special jewels and temporarily displayed to the public. A statue is paraded around on the evening of the 6th and again on the 8th (which also happens to be Extremadura's regional feast day).

Sleeping

★Hospedería del Real Monasterio HISTORIC HOTEL €€

(☎927 36 70 00; www.hotelhospederiamonasterioguadalupe.com; Plaza de Juan Carlos I; s €55-62, d/tr €75/103; ⌚closed mid-Jan–mid-Feb; P ❄ ☜)

OUR LADY OF GUADALUPE

Few shrines in Spain incite quite so much fervour as **Our Lady of Guadalupe** (Virgen de Guadalupe). The story begins back in the 8th century AD, when priests fleeing the Muslim assault on Seville in 712 buried a statue of the Virgin Mary high in the mountains above the Río Guadalupe. Devotees claim that the statue was carved by Luke the Evangelist. Six centuries after it was buried, in the 14th century, the Virgin appeared to a local shepherd named Gil Cordero who was looking for a lost animal. According to Cordero, the Virgin told him to bring priests to the exact site where he had seen the vision and for them to dig. Upon doing so, the priests found the statue lost centuries before. A shrine was built over the site, and it grew into the lavish monastery you see today over the centuries that followed.

The first pilgrims began arriving in 1326, and 14 years later King Alfonso XI built a Hieronymite monastery on the site after claiming that the Virgin's intercession was responsible for his victory over the Muslim armies at the Battle of Río Salado. In 1492, the Reyes Católicos, Isabel and Fernando, signed the official documents authorising the first voyage of Christopher Columbus (Cristobel Colón) to the Americas and Columbus came here to give thanks after his successful journey. On 12 October 1928, Pope Pius XI carried out what is known as a canonical coronation using the diamond-and-sapphire-encrusted crown that can be seen on the guided tour of the monastery.

OFF THE BEATEN TRACK

GARROVILLAS DE ALCONÉTAR

If you're driving between Alcántara and Cáceres or Plasencia, make time for a stop in little Garrovillas de Alconétar. This otherwise unremarkable town is distinguished by a truly remarkable **Plaza Mayor**, surrounded by arched porticoes and two-storey buildings dating back as far as the 15th century – it's one of the most beautiful in Extremadura.

Hospedería Puente de Alconétar (927 30 94 25; www.hospederiasdeextremadura.es/hotel/hospederia-puente-de-alconetar; Plaza de la Constitución 18; s/d €67/75;) is one of the few places to stay in town. Right on the historic Plaza de la Constitución, the four-star hotel inhabits a restored 15th-century palace. Rooms are modern and attractively clean-lined, though some in the older wing have lovely feature walls in stone or brick that add a real sense of character.

Garrovillas de Alconétar lies along the EX302, 10km west of the N630. It's a 40km drive east from Alcántara or 47km north from Cáceres. Public transport amounts to the occasional bus from Cáceres.

Centred on the Real Monasterio's beautiful Gothic cloister (now housing a bar and cafe), this old-fashioned hotel lets you live it up in a national monument without paying *parador*-style prices. High-ceilinged rooms are darkish and venerable but comfortable and full of character. There's a sumptuous flower-filled patio just off the lobby, plus a good restaurant, and the whole place is thick with history.

Parador de Guadalupe HISTORIC HOTEL €€
(927 36 70 75; www.parador.es; Calle Marqués de la Romana 12; r €95-145;) Guadalupe's *parador* occupies a converted 15th-century hospital and 16th-century religious school opposite the monastery. Spacious rooms are tastefully decorated and the cobbled courtyard is delightful, with its central fountain, lemon and orange trees and surrounding cloister-like colonnade with arches. There's a gorgeous summer-only pool, along with a smart (if slightly overpriced) restaurant.

Eating

Hospedería del Real Monasterio SPANISH €€
(927 36 70 00; www.hotelhospederiamonasterioguadalupe.com; Plaza de Juan Carlos I; raciones €6-21, mains €11-24; 1-3pm & 9-10.30pm, closed mid-Jan–mid-Feb;) Dine grandly under the arches of the magnificent Gothic cloister or in the lavish dining hall, rich with 17th-century timber furnishings and antique ceramics. There's a competent range of both meat and fish dishes and classic *raciones*, and most of the desserts are homemade. Three-course *menús* (€15 to €18) keep things simple.

Parador de Guadalupe EXTREMADURAN €€€
(927 36 70 75; www.parador.es; Calle Marqués de la Romana 12; mains €17-28, set menu €23-35; 1.30-4pm & 8.30-11pm) Set inside a reworked 15th-century hospital, the *parador*'s smart restaurant serves refined Extremaduran fare by changing seasonal menu. The *menú tradicional de Guadalupe* is especially good. In summer, sit outside in the orange tree–dotted courtyard, its pretty fountain tinkling away in the background.

Information

Oficina de Turismo de Guadalupe (675 286987, 927 15 41 28; www.oficinadeturismoguadalupe.blogspot.co.uk; Plaza de Santa María de Guadalupe; 10am-2pm & 4-6pm) On the main square, opposite the monastery.

Getting There & Away

Buses stop on Avenida Conde de Barcelona, near the town hall, 200m south of the Plaza de Santa María de Guadalupe. **Mirat** (927 23 33 54; www.mirat-transportes.es) runs two services Monday to Friday (one on Sunday) to/from Cáceres (€13, 2½ hours) via Trujillo. **Samar** (902 25 70 25; www.samar.es) has one to two daily buses to/from Madrid (€18, four hours).

Plasencia

POP 40,663

This pleasant, bustling town is the natural hub of northern Extremadura. Rising above a bend of the Río Jerte, it retains long sections of its defensive walls, though they're tricky to spot once you're actually in town. The attractive old quarter of narrow streets, Romanesque churches, stately stone palaces and buzzing tapas bars is worth exploring.

Plasencia is also a good base for forays into the nearby La Vera, Jerte and Ambroz valleys.

Sights

Catedral de Plasencia CATHEDRAL

(927 42 44 06; www.catedraldeplasencia.org; Plaza de la Catedral; €4; 11am-2pm & 5-8pm Tue-Sun Apr-Sep, 11am-2pm & 4-7pm Tue-Sun Oct-Mar) Plasencia's magnificent cathedral is two-in-one. The 16th-century **Catedral Nueva** is a Gothic-Renaissance blend with a handsome plateresque facade, a soaring 17th-century *retablo* (altarpiece) and intricate walnut-carved choir stalls featuring seats dedicated to the Reyes Católicos (Catholic Monarchs). Within the Romanesque **Catedral Vieja** are 13th-century cloisters surrounding a fountain and lemon trees. The octagonal **Capilla de San Pablo** has a dramatic 1569 Caravaggio painting of John the Baptist, a religious museum and, out the front, the arched Romanesque doorway.

Plaza Mayor SQUARE

Plasencia life flows through the lively, arcaded Plaza Mayor: meeting place of 10 streets, home to plenty of bar-restaurants and scene of a Tuesday farmers market since the 12th century. The jaunty figure striking the hour atop the Gothic **town hall** is El Abuelo Mayorga, a 1970s replica of the 13th-century original and the unofficial symbol of the town. The town hall also sports a Carlos I coat of arms.

Sleeping & Eating

★**Palacio Carvajal Girón** HISTORIC HOTEL €€

(927 42 63 26; www.palaciocarvajalgiron.com; Plaza Ansano 1; r €97-177; P) An impressive conversion job has transformed this formerly ruined palace in the heart of the old town into a chic address. Rooms have modern fittings, fresh white decor, plus original features, including fireplaces. The top-floor attic-style standard rooms have sloping ceilings and in-room concrete baths or showers, while the swish 1st-floor suite has an XXL bathroom with original tilework.

Parador de Plasencia HISTORIC HOTEL €€€

(927 42 58 70; www.parador.es; Plaza de San Vicente Ferrer; r €85-175; P) One of Extremadura's finest, Plasencia's *parador* is a classic – oozing the atmosphere and austerity of its 15th-century convent roots, with massive stone columns, soaring ceilings and a traditional Renaissance cloister. The 66 rooms are far from monastic, luxuriously furnished with rugs, rich fabrics, wood-carved bedheads, red-velvet curtains and varnished terracotta floors. The on-site bar occupies an old bodega.

Succo CONTEMPORARY SPANISH €€

(927 41 29 32; www.restaurantesucco.es; Calle Vidrieras 7; mains €10-19; 9am-late Mon-Sat, to 4pm Sun;) In the heart of Plasencia's eating area, just off the Plaza Mayor, this urban-chic tapas bar plates up delectable inventive tapas and *raciones*, delicately presented at tall white tables or in the bamboo-dotted dining room. The *huevos rotos* (smashed eggs) with *jamón* and *patatas panaderas* (potatoes with tomato and onion) gets a big thumbs up, as does the friendly service.

Casa Juan EXTREMADURAN €€

(655 585 146, 927 42 40 42; www.restaurantecasajuan.com; Calle de las Arenillas 2; mains €15-18; 1.30-4pm & 8.30-11pm, closed Jan;) Tucked down a quiet old-town lane, welcoming Casa Juan does well-prepared *extremeño* meat dishes (such as roast suckling pig) plus some tasty vegetarian and gluten-free bites. Start with locally made olive oil and bread, then try the homemade Torta del Casar gratin or the expertly hung local *retinto* beef. Fairly priced wines from around Spain seal an excellent deal.

Information

Oficina de Turismo (927 42 38 43; www.plasencia.es; Calle de Santa Clara 4; 8am-3pm & 4-7pm Mon-Fri, 10am-2pm & 4-7pm Sat & Sun) Information on Plasencia and northern Extremadura.

Getting There & Away

BUS

The **bus station** (927 41 45 50; Calle de Tornavacas 2) is 1km east of the Plaza Mayor. Destinations include Cáceres (€6, 50 minutes, one to four daily), Madrid (€18 to €23, 3½ hours, two to three daily) and Salamanca (€11, 1½ to 2¼ hours, seven to eight daily). Buses also serve smaller destinations around northern Extremadura.

TRAIN

The train station is off Avenida de España (the Cáceres road), 1km southwest of town. Trains depart up to four times daily from Plasencia for Madrid (€24 to €28, 2¾ hours), Cáceres (€5.20 to €6.05, one hour) and Mérida (€13 to €15, two hours).

La Vera

Surrounded by the Sierras de Tormantos and Gredos, with mountains often still capped with snow as late as May, Extremadura's fertile La Vera region produces raspberries, asparagus and, above all, *pimentón* (paprika), sold in charming old-fashioned tins and with a distinctive smoky flavour. Typical, too, are half-timbered houses leaning at odd angles, their overhanging upper storeys supported by timber or stone pillars. With its gurgling streams and easily manageable roads, La Vera makes a great driving tour from Plasencia.

Sights

★Monasterio de Yuste MONASTERY
(☎902 04 44 54; www.patrimonionacional.es; Carretera de Yuste, Cuacos de Yuste; adult/child €7/4, audio guide/guide €3/4, admission free for EU citizens and residents last three hours Wed & Thu; ⏲10am-8pm Apr-Sep, 10am-6pm Oct-Mar; P) In a lovely shady setting 1.5km northwest of Cuacos de Yuste, this monastery is where Carlos I of Spain (Charles I; also known as Carlos V of Austria) came in 1557 to prepare for death after abdicating his emperorship over much of Western and Central Europe. It's a soulful, evocative place amid the forested hills, and a tranquil counterpoint to the grandeur of so many formerly royal buildings elsewhere in Spain.

Festivals & Events

Los Empalaos RELIGIOUS
(Valverde de la Vera; ⏲Mar/Apr) At midnight on Good Friday eve, Valverde hosts one of Spain's most bizarre religious festivities, Los Empalaos ('the Impaled'). Penitent locals strap their arms to a beam, their near-naked bodies wrapped tight with 60m-long cords from waist to fingertips. Barefoot, veiled, with two swords strapped to their backs and wearing crowns of thorns, these 'walking crucifixes' follow a painful Way of the Cross.

Sleeping

★Parador de Jarandilla HISTORIC HOTEL €€
(☎927 56 01 17; www.parador.es; Avenida de García Prieto 1, Jarandilla de la Vera; r €85-115; P ❄ ☜ ≋) Be king of the castle at this 15th-century castle-turned-hotel with a warm, welcoming feel. Carlos I stayed here for a few months while waiting for his monastery digs to be completed. Within the stout walls and turrets lie period-furnished rooms that are wonderfully comfy without being ostentatiously grand, plus a classic courtyard where you can dine royally from the restaurant menu.

La Vera de Yuste CASA RURAL €€
(☎927 17 22 89; Calle Teodoro Perianes 17, Cuacos de Yuste; s/d incl breakfast €55/75; ❄) This beauty is set in two typical 18th-century village houses near Cuacos de Yuste's Plaza Mayor. The wood-beamed rooms have chunky rustic furniture and the garden is a delight, surrounded by rose bushes with a small courtyard and vegetable patch.

Eating

★Villa Xarahiz SPANISH €€
(☎927 66 51 50; www.villaxarahiz.com; Carretera EX203, Km 32.8, Jaraíz de la Vera; mains €14-22; ⏲1.30-3.45pm & 9-10.45pm Tue-Sat, 1.30-3.45pm Sun; ☜ 👪) Offering spectacular sierra views from the terrace and the upmarket wood-beamed dining room, this hotel restaurant 1km north of Jaraíz is one of La Vera's best bets for Spanish wines and smart regional pan-Spanish food, featuring local peppers, Torta del Casar cheese, Extremaduran *jamón* and stewed kid, among other quality Extremadura produce. The €12 weekday lunch *menú* is a hit.

Parador de Jarandilla SPANISH €€
(☎927 56 01 17; www.parador.es; Avenida de García Prieto 1, Jarandilla de la Vera; mains €18-22; ⏲1.30-4pm & 8.30-11pm; P ☜ 🖉) Dine in regal style on elegant Extremaduran dishes and fine Spanish wines inside the chunky walls of Jarandilla's 15th-century castle, where you can sit outside in the romantic palm-studded courtyard. Signature dishes include *migas extremeñas* (Extremaduran breadcrumbs) or *caldereta de cabra* (goat stew), but always check out what set menus are on offer.

Information

Oficina de Turismo de Jarandilla de la Vera (☎927 56 04 60; www.jarandilla.com; Avenida Soledad Vega Ortiz, Jarandilla de la Vera; ⏲10am-2pm & 4.30-7.30pm Tue-Sat, 10am-2pm Sun) The most useful of a number of tourist offices dotted around La Vera.

Oficina de Turismo de Villanueva de la Vera (☎639 068544; www.villanuevadelavera.es; Avenida de la Vera, Villanueva de la Vera; ⏲9am-3pm Wed & Thu, 9am-5pm Fri-Sun) On the main road through Villanueva de la Vera.

EXPLORING LA VERA'S VILLAGES

Head first to prettily positioned **Pasarón**, with its fine 16th-century palace of the Condes de Osorno. Next east is **Jaraíz**, *pimentón* HQ and a good spot for a feed. Tracking north-east, **Cuacos de Yuste** is rich in typical half-timbered houses and lovely plazas, with an evocative royal monastery (p618) nearby. Further east, **Jarandilla** is one of La Vera's most appealing stops. Its castle-like church was built by the Templars and features an ancient font brought from the Holy Land, while its 15th-century castle once housed Carlos I. After Jarandilla, explore **Valverde**,home of the Easter ritual of **Los Empalaos** (p618), with its 15th-century church and pretty Plaza de España lined with timber balconies. Head on up the valley to **Madrigal** and its majestic **Roman bridge** (Puente de Alardos; Madrigal de la Vera). Double back to **Garganta La Olla**, a picturesque, steeply pitched village with overhanging balconies on the main street and centuries-old inscriptions above the doors. From here, it's a spectacular twisting drive over the 1269m **Puerto de Piornal** pass (Piornal is famous for its *jamón*) and down into the cherry-growing Valle del Jerte.

Getting There & Away

BUS

Mirat (927 23 33 54; www.mirat-transportes.es) runs three buses Monday to Friday from Plasencia to Jarandilla (€6.40, one hour) via Jaraíz (€4.25, 50 minutes) and lower La Vera villages, and one on Sunday. Some continue further up the valley. There's also one daily bus Monday to Friday and Sunday between Cáceres and Jarandilla (€16.50, 2¼ hours).

CAR

Self-drivers can cross north into the Valle del Jerte from La Vera via the winding CC17 over the 1269m Puerto de Piornal.

Valle del Ambroz

This broad valley northwest of the Valle del Jerte and northeast of Plasencia is split by the Vía de la Plata and the A66 motorway. It has a friendly feel and some intriguing sights, most notably the ghost village of Granadilla, the ruined Roman city of Cáparra and lively Hervás, with its beautifully preserved Jewish Quarter.

Sights

★Granadilla VILLAGE

(927 01 49 75; Carretera CC168; 10am-1.30pm & 4-8pm Tue-Sun Apr-Oct, 10am-1.30pm & 4-6pm Tue-Sun Nov-Mar; P) FREE About 25km west of Hervás, the ghost village of Granadilla is a beguiling reminder of how Extremadura's villages must have looked before modernisation. Founded by the Moors in the 9th century but abandoned in the 1960s when the nearby dam was built, Granadilla's traditional architecture has been painstakingly restored since the 1980s as part of a government educational project. Enter through the narrow **Puerta de Villa**, overlooked by the sturdy 15th-century **castle**, which you can climb for brilliant panoramas.

Yacimiento Romano de Cáparra ARCHAEOLOGICAL SITE

(927 19 94 85; Carretera CC13.3; 10am-2pm & 5-8pm Tue-Sat, 10am-2pm Sun Jun-Sep, 10am-2pm & 4-7pm Tue-Sat, 10am-2pm Sun Oct-May; P) FREE Unearthed in 1929, the fascinating, substantial remains of the once-splendid Roman city of Cáparra mostly date to around the 1st century. Initially favoured for its strategic location on the Vía de la Plata, the city fell into decay in the 4th century and was eventually deserted. Wander the 14-hectare site to spot its crumbled walls, gates, forum, thermal baths and amphitheatre. Most impressive of all is the wonderfully preserved, late-1st-century **Arco de Cáparra**, a four-arch granite gateway.

Information

Oficina de Turismo de Hervás (p620)

Getting There & Away

One Cevesa (p621) bus runs daily Monday to Friday between Hervás and Plasencia (€3.30, one hour), continuing to Cáceres (€8.45, 2¼ hours). From Hervás, there are also three daily buses up the valley to Baños de Montemayor (€1.15, 10 minutes).

Hervás

POP 4120

Hervás, 45km northeast of Plasencia, is a lively and handsome town with a picturesque old quarter and some excellent restaurants. It makes a great base for exploring the Valle del Ambroz and even northern Extremadura as a whole.

OFF THE BEATEN TRACK

LAS HURDES

Quiet mountain roads connect Las Hurdes with the Sierra de Francia in Castilla y León.

A worthwhile loop could begin in **Las Mestas**, home to the handsome 17th-century stone **Iglesia de Nuestra Señora del Carmen**. From here a pretty, serpentine road climbs up through the **Valle de Las Batuecas** to La Alberca (20km) in Castilla y León. If you stay in Extremadura, continue on to picturesque **Ladrillar**, which tumbles down a steep ridge, then on to tiny **Riomalo de Arriba**, home to Las Hurdes' best collection of original stone-and-slate homes; just three inhabitants lived here at last count. The road then climbs steeply to the **Mirador de las Carrascas**, with vast views down the two main valleys of Las Hurdes. Continue on to **Casares de Las Hurdes**, with its tangle of narrow thoroughfares and its church which, unusually, has a freestanding clocktower separate from the main building. Continue your descent to lively **Nuñomoral**, then take the quiet 9km detour to **El Gasco**, home to some traditional Las Hurdes houses and **Restaurante La Meancera** (☎927 03 53 68, 674 18 97 92; www.facebook.com/RestauranteCafeteriaMeancera/; mains €14-18, set menus €20-30; ⏲1-4pm & 8-11pm), one of Extremadura's best restaurants. Around 1km before reaching El Gasco (or on the return journey as you'll need to return to Nuñomoral), stop at the **Mirador de El Gasco**, for fine views down into the river valley with a striking double oxbow defining the stream's path through it.

Sights

Barrio Judío AREA

Hervás houses Extremadura's best surviving *barrio judío* (Jewish quarter), whose narrow streets extend down to the river. This neighbourhood thrived until the 1492 expulsion of the Jews, when most families fled to Portugal. Seek out, in particular, Calles Rabilero and Sinagoga.

Sleeping

★El Jardín del Convento HOTEL €€

(☎660 452292, 927 48 11 61; www.eljardindelconvento.com; Plaza del Convento 22; r €50-85, cottage €100-115; ❄📶) Bordering the Jewish quarter, this is one of Extremadura's most fabulous hotels. The gorgeous garden – all roses, vegetables and tranquil seating – makes for rural yet stylish relaxation. All-different rooms are full of character, with wooden floors, open-stone walls, elegant period furniture and, for some, a big wooden balcony. Breakfast (€7.50) is a dream of homemade jams, cakes and other local treats.

Hospedería Valle de Ambroz HISTORIC HOTEL €€

(☎927 47 48 28; www.hospederiasdeextremadura.es; Plaza del Hospital; r from €75; P❄📶🏊) Inhabiting a 17th-century convent at the southern edge of the old town, this fine, four-star *hospedería* has a gorgeous courtyard, vaguely old-world rooms and an excellent restaurant (set menus €15 to €37) serving dishes such as cod with pumpkin, apple and a beetroot aioli or zucchini ravioli with goat's cheese.

Eating

La Bodeguita SPANISH €

(☎676 782828; Calle Relator González 2; raciones €4-8; ⏲noon-4pm & 8-11pm Wed-Mon) Beautiful traditional dishes make busy little La Bodeguita an excellent choice for a fuss-free feed in a no-frills setting. Grilled prawns, chorizo tortilla, *pulpo a la gallega* (Galician-style octopus) and light fresh salads await you – after, of course, your complimentary tapa. It's a simple, bubbly spot amid a cluster of old-quarter houses.

★Nardi EXTREMADURAN €€

(☎927 48 13 23; www.restaurantenardi.com; Calle Braulio Navas 19; raciones €9-15, mains €14-22; ⏲1.30-4pm & 8.30-11pm Wed-Mon; 🌿👪) Nardi impresses with rich, classic dishes given a contemporary zing, served in a warm, elegant dining room with wood beams, yellow walls and rustic art. Extremaduran meats, such as *solomillo ibérico de bellota* (Iberian pork tenderloin), are the focus, but it has excellent vegetarian options too, including salads, pumpkin soup and stir-fried boletus (mushrooms) with truffle foam, plus a kids' menu.

Information

Oficina de Turismo de Hervás (☎927 47 36 18; www.turismodehervas.com; Calle Braulio Navas 6; ⏲10am-2pm & 4.30-7pm Tue-Sun Sep-May, 10am-2pm & 5-8pm Tue-Sun Oct-Apr) Good info on Hervás and the Valle del Ambroz.

Getting There & Away

Cevesa (☎902 39 31 32; www.cevesa.es) runs one bus daily Monday to Friday between Hervás and Plasencia (€3.30, one hour), continuing to Cáceres (€8.45, 2¼ hours).

Parque Nacional de Monfragüe

Spain's 14th national park is a dramatic, hilly 180-sq-km paradise for birdwatchers (and other nature lovers). Straddling the Tajo valley, it's home to spectacular colonies of raptors and more than 75% of Spain's protected species. Among some 175 feathered varieties are around 300 pairs of black vultures (the largest concentration of Europe's biggest bird of prey) and populations of two other rare large birds: the Spanish imperial eagle (12 pairs) and the black stork (30 pairs). Deer, otters, genets, badgers, rabbits, foxes and wild boar are other inhabitants.

The best time to visit is between March and October, since many bird species winter in Africa.

The pretty hamlet of **Villareal de San Carlos**, from where most hiking trails leave, is the most convenient base. There are also amenities in **Torrejón el Rubio**, on the south side of the park.

Sights

★Mirador Salto del Gitano VIEWPOINT
(P) Arguably the most spectacular spot in the national park is the Mirador Salto del Gitano. From this lookout point, 5km south of Villareal along the EX208, there are stunning views across the Río Tajo gorge to the Peña Falcón crag, home to a colony of circling griffon vultures. The 8km 'Ruta Roja' walk between Villareal and the Castillo de Monfragüe passes through here.

★Castillo de Monfragüe CASTLE
The hilltop Castillo de Monfragüe, a ruined 9th-century Islamic fort, has sweeping 360° views across the park, with birds swooshing by above and below. It's signposted up a steep winding road off the EX208, 8km south of Villareal de San Carlos. The castle can also be reached via an attractive 8km, 1½-hour walk from Villareal, along the so-called Ruta Roja (Red Route).

Centro de Interpretación del Arte Rupestre de Monfragüe MUSEUM
(☎927 45 52 92; www.centrosurmonfrague.com/centro-arte-rupestre-monfrague/; Paseo de la Carrera, Torrejón el Rubio; ⊙10am-2pm & 4-7pm Wed & Thu, 10am-2pm & 4-8pm Fri & Sat, 10am-2pm Sun) This excellent new installation serves as an interpretation centre for the rock art found in the Parque Nacional de Monfragüe, close to the Castillo. The centre explains the historical context in which these neolithic artworks were created, explains how they were painted and otherwise does an excellent job of explaining these mysterious representations on remote rock walls.

Tours

Monfragüe Vivo BIRDWATCHING, ADVENTURE SPORTS
(☎927 45 94 75, 620 941778; www.monfraguevivo.com) Birdwatching tours and a variety of park activities, including walking, kayaking and jeep trips, with local guides.

EN-RUTA Rutas por Monfragüe BIRDWATCHING
(☎927 40 41 13, 605 898154; www.rutaspormonfrague.com) A range of birdwatching, walking and jeep excursions into the park.

Iberian Nature BIRDWATCHING
(☎676 784221; www.iberian-nature.com) Local birdwatching experts offering guided hikes (from €35 per person) and courses.

Birding Extremadura BIRDWATCHING
(☎927 31 93 49; www.birdingextremadura.com) Birdwatching trips run by British ornithologist Martin Kelsey.

Sleeping & Eating

★Casa Rural El Recuerdo CASA RURAL €€
(☎609 684719, 927 31 93 49; www.casaruralelrecuerdo.com; Calle Aguaperal 8, Pago de San Clemente; s/d incl breakfast €59/70; P🛜🏊) Birdwatchers won't want to miss this lovely six-room *casa rural* just 12km southeast of Trujillo. It's run by expert birdwatchers, Martin and Claudia, who also run Birding Extremadura (p621). Each room is different, but they're nicely turned out and inhabit a former winery, with olive groves in abundance. There's also a dinner-only restaurant (€20) in the wine cellar.

WORTH A TRIP

EL MEANDRO DEL MELERO

One of Extremadura's most beautiful geographical features, **El Meandro del Melero** is where the Río Alagon does an extraordinary loop, forming a near-perfect oxbow formation around a forested, teardrop-shaped island. It's at its best when the river is at full capacity, but even during a recent drought with little water it was still spectacular. The best views are from the Mirador de La Antigua.

To get here, take the EX204 (known as the SA225 on the Castilla y León side) to Riomalo de Abajo. On the Extremadura side of the bridge, take the road (Calle Escuelas) that runs south along the river. The road twists up into the hills for 1.5km, where the paved road ends. To continue, you'll either need to drive the rough dirt track – it's OK for 2WD vehicles if you drive carefully, but it's treacherous after rains – or, better, walk the remaining 1.6km to the lookout. The Meandro itself lies within Castilla y León, but the lookout is in Extremadura.

★**Hospedería Parque de Monfragüe** HOTEL €€
(☎927 45 52 78; www.hospederiasdeextremadura.es; Carretera EX208, Km 39, Torrejón el Rubio; d incl breakfast €75-125; P ❄ @ 🛜 ≋) 🍃 This tranquil four-star hotel, 1km north of Torrejón el Rubio, looks out across the plains to the national park and is partly run on solar power and bioenergy. Freshly revamped dark-turquoise and varnished-wood rooms come with desks, squeaky floors and tile-covered bathrooms. Duplexes are good for families, and there's a decent restaurant.

Paraíso de los Sentidos EXTREMADURAN €€
(☎927 45 52 78; www.hospederiasdeextremadura.es; Hospedería Parque de Monfragüe, Carretera EX208, Km 39, Torrejón el Rubio; mains €15-22, set menu €15-28; ⏲1.30-4pm & 8.30-11pm) A classy hotel restaurant that does a decent job of refined Extremaduran dishes in a bright peaceful setting. It's 1km north of Torrejón el Rubio on the EX208.

ℹ Information

Centro de Visitantes (☎927 19 91 34; Villareal de San Carlos; ⏲9.30am-7.30pm daily Jul-Sep, 9.30am-6pm Mon-Fri, 9am-6pm Sat & Sun Oct-Jun) The park's main information centre advises on hikes and birdwatching spots. It also organises free two-hour guided hikes at 9am on Friday, Saturday and Sunday (minimum three people; phone ahead).

Centro de Interpretación del Parque Nacional de Monfragüe (Villareal de San Carlos; ⏲9.30am-7.30pm Jul-Sep, 9.30am-6pm Oct-Jun, from 9am Sat & Sun year-round) With displays on local history, fauna and flora, this is the perfect introduction to the park.

Monfragüe Bird Center (☎927 19 95 79; www.centrosurmonfrague.com; Monfragüe Centro de Visitantes Sur, Torrejón el Rubio; ⏲10am-2pm Tue-Sat, 4-6pm Wed & Thu, 4-7pm Fri & Sat, hours vary) Maps and advice on birdwatching spots, plus Spanish-language displays on local birds, migration patterns and, next door, Monfragüe's prehistoric cave art.

Oficina de Turismo de Torrejón el Rubio (☎927 45 52 92; www.torrejonelrubio.com; Calle Madroño 1, Torrejón el Rubio; ⏲10am-2pm & 4.30-7.30pm Wed-Sun) On the main road; helpful for hiking, birdwatching and other park activities.

ℹ Getting There & Away

Public transport through the park is limited. **Emiz** (☎607 514078, 927 24 72 21; www.emiz.es) runs one bus daily Monday to Friday in each direction between Plasencia and Torrejón el Rubio (€4.40, 45 minutes), stopping in Villareal de San Carlos. There's also one bus on Monday and Friday between Torrejón el Rubio and Trujillo (45 minutes).

Mérida

POP 58,174

Mérida, capital of Extremadura, was once also capital of the Roman province of Lusitania (as Emerita Augusta, founded 25 BC). and is still home to the most impressive and extensive Roman ruins in all Spain. The ruins lie sprinkled around town, often appearing in the most unlikely corners, and one can only wonder what still lies buried beneath the lively, modern city.

Centred on the site of modern Mérida, Emerita Augusta was founded by Emperor Augustus as a colony for veterans of Rome's campaigns in Cantabria; the Roman name translates roughly as 'bachelors' or 'discharged soldiers' from the army of Augustus. The city's location also served the strategic purpose of protecting a nearby pass and the bridge over the Río Guadiana. The city prospered and became the capital of the Roman province of Lusitania and one of the empire's most important cultural and political centres, with a population of 40,000 in its heyday. After the fall of the Western Roman Empire, the city became the Visigoth capital of Hispania in the 6th century and its monuments remained largely intact. The city later passed into Muslim hands in the 8th century and has been Christian since 1230. During Napoleon's 19th-century invasion of Spain, many of Mérida's monuments were destroyed.

Sights

★Teatro Romano RUINS

(Paseo Álvarez Sáez de Buruaga; adult/child incl Anfiteatro €12/6, combined 6-site ticket adult/concession/child €15/7.50/free; 9am-9pm Apr-Sep, 9.30am-6.30pm Oct-Mar) Mérida's most spectacular Roman monument, and the only one to once again fulfil its original function – by hosting performances during the Festival Internacional de Teatro Clásico (p625) in summer – the Teatro Romano is the city's indisputable highlight. It was built around 15 BC to seat 6000 spectators. The adjoining (slightly less-dazzling) **Anfiteatro** (Paseo Álvarez Sáez de Buruaga; adult/child incl Teatro Romano €12/6, combined six-site ticket adult/concession/child €15/7.50/free; 9am-9pm Apr-Sep, 9am-6.30pm Oct-Mar) opened in 8 BC for gladiatorial contests and held 14,000; the gladiator-versus-lion fresco in the Museo Nacional de Arte Romano was taken from here.

★Puente Romano BRIDGE

Don't miss the extraordinarily powerful spectacle of the Puente Romano spanning the Río Guadiana. At 792m in length with 60 granite arches, it's one of the longest bridges built by the Romans. It was constructed in 25 BC when Emerita Augusta (modern-day Mérida) was founded, and then partly restored in the 17th century. The 20th-century **Puente Lusitania**, a sleek suspension bridge designed by Santiago Calatrava, mirrors it to the northwest. The best Roman bridge views are from the Alcazaba's southwestern ramparts.

★Museo Nacional de Arte Romano MUSEUM

(924 31 16 90; www.museoarteromano.mcu.es; Calle de José Ramón Mélida; adult/child €3/free, after 2pm Sat & all day Sun free; 9.30am-8pm Tue-Sat, 10am-3pm Sun Apr-Sep, 9.30am-6.30pm Tue-Sat, 10am-3pm Sun Oct-Mar) Even if you visit only a handful of Mérida's sights, make sure one of them is this fabulous museum, which has a superb three-floor collection of statues, busts, mosaics, frescoes, coins, pottery and other Roman artefacts, all beautifully displayed alongside information panels in Spanish and English. Designed by Navarran architect Rafael Moneo, the soaring arched brick structure makes a stunning home for the collection, its walls hung with some of the largest, most beautiful mosaics.

★Alcazaba FORTRESS

(Calle Graciano; adult/child €6/3, combined 6-site ticket adult/concession/child €15/7.50/free; 9am-9pm Apr-Sep, 9am-6.30pm Oct-Mar) This large Islamic fort was built in the mid-9th century on a site already occupied by the Romans and Visigoths, probably becoming the first ever *alcazaba* in Al-Andalus. In the middle of the sprawling complex, its pretty goldfish-populated *aljibe* (cistern) reuses Visigothic marble, flower motifs and stone slabs, while the ramparts look out over the Puente Romano and the Río Guadiana. The 15th-century monastery in the northeast corner now serves as regional government offices.

Circo Romano RUINS

(Avenida Juan Carlos I; adult/child €6/3, combined 6-site ticket adult/concession/child €15/7.50/free; 9am-9pm Apr-Sep, 9am-6.30pm Oct-Mar) The 1st-century Circo Romano could accommodate 30,000 spectators. Discovered in the 16th century, its remains represent the only surviving hippodrome of its kind in Spain. In the attached interpretive centre you can read

COMBINED TICKET

Admission to most of Mérida's Roman sites is via a combined ticket (€15 for adults, €7.50 for students and pensioners, free for children under 12). It covers admission to the Teatro Romano and Anfiteatro, Casa del Anfiteatro (if/when it reopens), Los Columbarios, Casa del Mitreo, Alcazaba, Circo Romano, Cripta de Santa Eulalia and the Zona Arqueológica de Morería. The Museo Nacional de Arte Romano is not included. The ticket allows you one entry to each sight, has no time limit and can be bought at any of the sights except the Zona Arqueológica de Morería.

Mérida

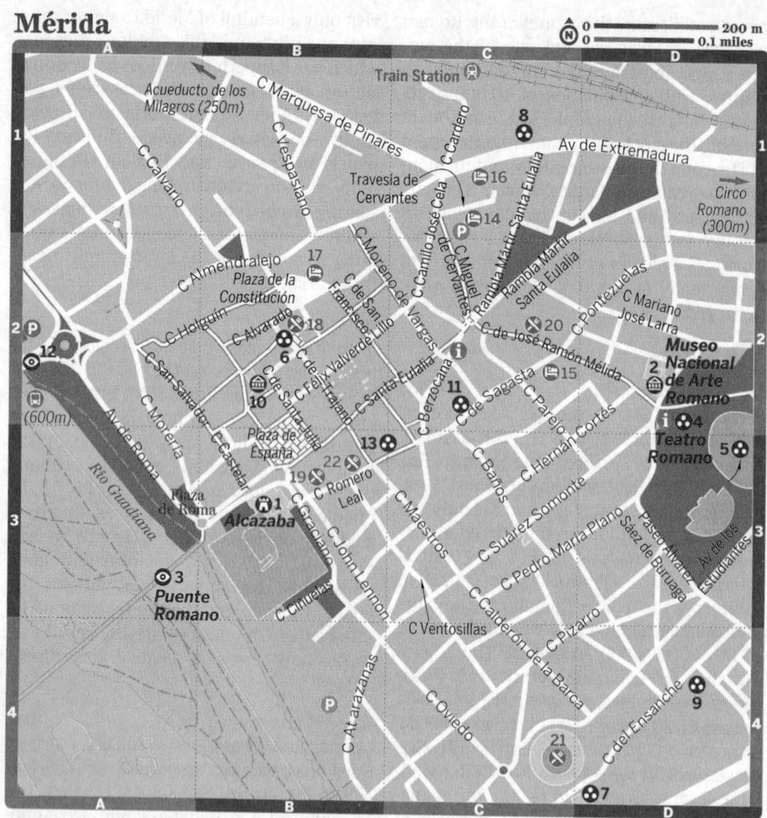

Mérida

Top Sights

1 Alcazaba B3
2 Museo Nacional de Arte Romano D2
3 Puente Romano A3
4 Teatro Romano D2

Sights

5 Anfiteatro D3
6 Arco de Trajano B2
7 Casa del Mitreo D4
8 Cripta de Santa Eulalia C1
9 Los Columbarios D4
10 Museo de Arte Visigodo B2
11 Pórtico del Foro C2
12 Puente Lusitania A2
13 Templo de Diana C3

Sleeping

14 Capitolio C1
15 Hostal Emeritae C2
16 La Flor de Al-Andalus C1
17 Parador de Mérida B2

Eating

18 A de Arco B2
19 El Trasiego B3
20 Fusiona Gastrobar C2
21 Mercado Gastronómico San Albín C4
22 Tábula Calda B3

(in Spanish) all about Diocles, a champion *auriga* (horse and chariot racer) who served his apprenticeship in Mérida before going on to the big league in Rome.

Cripta de Santa Eulalia RUIN, CHURCH

(Avenida de Extremadura; adult/child €6/3, combined 6-site ticket adult/concession/child €15/7.50/free; ⏲9am-9pm Apr-Sep, 9am-6pm Oct-Mar) This basilica was built in the 5th century in honour of Mérida's patron saint, who is said to have been martyred in the 4th century. It was then reconstructed in the 13th century. The modern-day church is closed to the public, but, beside it, a museum and excavated areas allow you to identify Roman houses, a 4th-century Christian cemetery and the original 5th-century church.

Acueducto de los Milagros RUINS
(Calle Marquesa de Pinares) Built between the 1st century BC and the 3rd century, the 830m-long Acueducto de los Milagros once supplied Roman Mérida with water from the dam at Lago Proserpina, 6km north of town. It's now highly favoured by nesting storks.

Casa del Mitreo RUINS
(Calle de Oviedo; adult/child €6/3, combined 6-site ticket adult/concession/child €15/7.50/free; ⏲9am-9pm Apr-Sep, 9am-6.30pm Oct-Mar) Beside Mérida's Plaza de Toros, the Casa del Mitreo is a late-1st- or 2nd-century Roman house with a well-preserved fresco and several intricate mosaics. Among the mosaics you'll find the partial but beautiful remains of the 3rd-century *mosaico cosmológico* (with its bright colours and allegories about the creation of the world), which was damaged by a fire. The Casa del Mitreo is connected by footpath to the adjacent **Los Columbarios** (Calle del Ensanche; adult/child €6/3, combined 6-site ticket adult/concession/child €15/7.50/free; ⏲9am-9pm Apr-Sep, 9am-6.30pm Oct-Mar) Roman funeral site.

Templo de Diana RUINS
(Calle de Sagasta) Inaccurately named, for it's now known to have been dedicated to the Imperial cult, this 1st-century-BC temple stood in the municipal forum, where the city government was based. Parts of the temple were later incorporated into a 16th-century mansion built within it. The forum's restored **Pórtico del Foro** (Calle de Sagasta) is 100m northeast up Calle de Sagasta.

Arco de Trajano RUINS
(Calle de Trajano) This imposing 15m-high granite archway isn't known to have anything to do with Roman emperor Trajan, but it was situated on one of Mérida's main Roman streets and, in its original marble-covered form, may have served as an entrance to a sacred area.

Museo de Arte Visigodo MUSEUM
(Calle de Santa Julia; ⏲9.30am-8pm Apr-Sep, 9.30am-6.30pm Tue-Sat, 10am-3pm Sun Oct-Mar) FREE Many of the Visigothic objects unearthed in Mérida are exhibited in this archaeological museum, set inside a 16th-century church-convent just off the Plaza de España. It's a fascinating (Spanish-language) insight into a little-known period of Spanish history. In a little side room, there's a stone-carved Moorish inscription dating the Alcazaba's 835 foundation.

Festivals & Events

Festival Internacional de Teatro Clásico THEATRE
(www.festivaldemerida.es; €15-45; ⏲Jul-Aug) This prestigious summer festival, held at Mérida's Roman theatre and amphitheatre, features Greek and more recent drama classics, plus music, photography and dance. It starts at 10.45pm most nights.

Sleeping

★La Flor de Al-Andalus HOSTAL €
(☎924 31 33 56; www.hostallaflordeal-andalus.com; Avenida de Extremadura 6; s €33-50, d €45-90; ❄📶) If only all *hostales* were such good value. A self-appointed 'boutique *hostal*', La Flor de Al-Andalus has 18 comfy, colourful rooms beautifully decorated in Andalucian style (with elegant tiles, elaborate mirrors and hanging lanterns), plus friendly service and a convenient location within walking distance of Mérida's main sights. Try to avoid ground-floor rooms by reception.

Capitolio APARTMENT €
(☎924 30 31 63; www.capitolio.es; Travesía de Cervantes 2; s/d/ste from €50/60/130; P❄📶) These gorgeously styled modern mini-apartments in a handy central location have equipped kitchens, plus plenty of space, light and sparkle. The individual colour schemes alternate between elegantly sober and minimalist and luxuriantly colourful, with full-wall flower photographs, asymmetric bedheads or slogan-covered pillows. Whichever version you choose, it's excellent value.

★Hostal Emeritae HOSTAL €€
(☎924 30 31 83; www.hostalemeritae.com; Calle de Sagasta 40; s €30-40, d €42-70, tr €56-70; P❄📶) This fabulous place opened in 2015 and has a relaxed feel enhanced by cosy, contemporary rooms drenched in fresh whites and creams. Top-floor 'superior doubles', with soft-toned art and private balconies, are worth that little extra, and there's a tasteful purple-and-grey-themed communal patio.

Parador de Mérida HISTORIC HOTEL €€€
(Parador Vía de la Plata; ☎924 31 38 00; www.parador.es; Plaza de la Constitución 3; r €85-215; P❄📶🏊) You'll be sleeping on the site of a Roman temple in what was once an 18th-century convent, though this isn't Extremadura's finest *parador*. The lounge is a former chapel, which then served as both hospital and prison. The gardens' assembled hunks of Roman, Visigothic and Mudéjar artefacts whizz you through Mérida's architectural history.

Eating

★Mercado Gastronómico San Albín TAPAS €
(☎647 591261; www.facebook.com/MercadoGastronomicoSanAlbin/; Plaza de Toros, Calle Oviedo; tapas €4-10; ⏱noon-4pm & 9pm-midnight) The halls of Mérida's red-washed 20th-century bullring have been transformed into a busy tapas-style hangout. In each alcove, individual stalls deliver their own specialities, with everything from *jamón* and croquettes to cocktails and cakes making an appearance. Mix and match and and sit wherever you like. It's a wonderful alternative to the formal atmosphere of the sit-down restaurants.

★El Trasiego CONTEMPORARY SPANISH €€
(☎924 48 50 66; Calle Romero Leal 3; tapas €4-7, raciones €9-19, mains €9-15; ⏱1-4.30pm & 8.30-11.30pm; 📝) Relatively fresh on Mérida's culinary scene, popular El Trasiego mixes rustic-chic decor with a fun contemporary atmosphere and exquisite creative dishes infused with local ingredients. Waiters deliver bread in metallic buckets; breadboard menus put a modern spin on classic Spanish cooking. Tuck into huge portions of creamy pasta, mushroom risotto and feta salad, plus gourmet tapas, seafood-focused treats and excellent Spanish wines.

★Tábula Calda SPANISH €€
(☎924 30 49 50; www.tabulacalda.com; Calle Romero Leal 11; mains €12-19, set menu €13-25; ⏱1-4.30pm & 8pm-midnight) 🌿 This inviting yellow-washed space, filled with tilework and greenery, serves well-priced, quality meals encompassing Spain's favourite staples. Everything either comes from its garden or is sourced from within 100km of the kitchen. Before your food arrives, you'll enjoy a complimentary tapa, house salad (orange, sugar and olive oil, reflecting the family's Jewish roots) and olives. Manuel is a welcoming host.

A de Arco SPANISH €€
(☎924 30 13 15; www.adearco.com; Calle Trajano 8; mains €8-19; ⏱1-4pm & 8pm-midnight) In the shadow of Mérida's prettiest monumental Roman arch, this appealing place serves up a range of *extremeño* and wider Spanish dishes in a lovely setting – try the *queso con trufa* (cheese with truffles). It's the sort of place where you'll want to stay for a drink after your meal.

Information

Oficina de Turismo (☎924 38 01 91; www.turismomerida.org; Calle Santa Eulalia 64; ⏱9am-7.30pm Mon-Wed, 9.30am-2pm & 5-8pm Thu-Sun Apr-Sep, 9am-7.30pm Mon-Wed, 9.30am-2pm & 4.30-7.30pm Thu-Sun Oct-Mar) At the top (northeastern) end of the main shopping street.

Oficina de Turismo (Teatro Romano) (☎924 33 07 22; www.turismomerida.org; Paseo Álvarez Sáez de Buruaga; ⏱9am-7.30pm Apr-Sep, 9am-6.30pm Oct-Mar) Next to the Roman theatre.

Getting There & Away

TRAIN

From the station, just off Avenida de Extremadura, trains run to Madrid (€31 to €47, 4½ to 7½ hours, six or seven daily), Cáceres (€6.10 to €7.35, one hour, four to five daily), Seville (€21, 3¾ hours, one daily) and Zafra (€6.10 to €7.35, 45 minutes, one to three daily).

BUS

Buses depart from the **bus station** (☎924 37 14 04; Avenida de la Libertad), across the river via the Puente Lusitania.

DESTINATION	FARE (€)	TIME	FREQUENCY
Badajoz	6	50min	3-7 daily
Cáceres	6.50	1hr	2-3 daily
Lisbon (normal/express)	26/29	4/3hr	1/1 daily
Madrid (normal/express)	26/39	5/4hr	4/4 daily
Seville	15	2¾hr	5 daily
Zafra	5.75	1¼hr	5-10 daily

Olivenza

POP 12,032

Pretty, intriguing Olivenza, 27km southwest of Badajoz, clings to its Portuguese heritage

– it has only been Spanish since 1801. The town's cobbled ancient core is distinctive for its whitewashed houses, impressive churches and castle, typical turreted defensive walls and taste for beautiful blue-and-white ceramic tilework, which you'll spot immediately on street signs.

Sights

Castillo de Olivenza CASTLE
(☎924 49 02 22; Plaza Santa María del Castillo; adult/child €2.50/free; ⏲10.30am-2pm & 5-8pm Tue-Fri, 10am-2.15pm Sun May-Sep, hours vary Oct-Apr) Smack-bang in the old-town centre stands Olivenza's majestic 14th-century castle, dominated by the 36m-high **Torre del Homenaje**. Make your way to the roof for exquisite panoramas over the town and surrounding countryside. Tickets also include the detailed **Museo Etnográfico Extremeño** (www.museodeolivenza.com; adult/child €2.50/free; ⏲10.30am-2pm & 5-8pm Tue-Sat, 10am-2.15pm Sun May-Sep, 10.30am-2pm & 4-7pm Tue-Sat, 11am-2.15pm Sun Oct-Apr).

Sleeping & Eating

Hotel Heredero HOTEL €
(☎924 49 08 35; www.hotelheredero.net; Carretera de Badajoz, Km 23.7; s/d incl breakfast €40/70; P ❄ 📶) The charmless modern exterior of this place just north of the old town means that the handsome, old-style rooms come as something of a surprise. The wood furnishings give it a touch of old-world style, although the effect is muted rather than over-the-top.

Casa Maila EXTREMADURAN, TAPAS €€
(☎924 49 15 05; Calle Colón 3; tapas €3.50-5, mains €12-19; ⏲noon-midnight Tue-Sun, to 4pm Mon) Refreshingly down to earth, friendly Casa Maila is excellent for both delicious tapas and *raciones* and more elaborate, mostly meaty, mains, on the edge of bubbly Plaza de España.

Information

Oficina de Turismo (☎924 49 01 51; www.olivenzavirtual.com; Plaza Santa María del Castillo 15; ⏲9.30am-2pm & 5-7pm Tue-Sat, 10am-2pm Sun May-Sep, 9.30am-2pm & 4-6pm Tue-Sat, 10am-2pm Sun Oct-Apr) On the old town's main plaza in the Convento San Juan de Dios.

Getting There & Away

From the **bus station** (☎924 49 05 31; Calle Avelino Palma Brioa), there are buses to/from Badajoz (€2.20, 25 minutes) almost hourly Monday to Friday and twice on Saturday.

Zafra

POP 16,855

Looking for all the world like an Andalucian *pueblo blanco* (white village), gleaming-white Zafra is a serene, attractive stop along the A66 between Seville and Mérida. Affectionately labelled *'Sevilla la chica'* ('the little Seville') for its similarities with Andalucía's capital, Zafra was originally a Muslim settlement. Its narrow streets are lined with baroque churches, old-fashioned shops, glassed-in balconies and traditional houses decorated with overflowing bougainvillea and hot-pink splashes of geraniums. The newer part of town isn't all that enthralling, but Zafra's historic core is a beauty.

Sights

Zafra's 15th-century **castle**, a blend of Gothic, Mudéjar and Renaissance architecture, is now the luxurious Parador de Zafra (p628), which dominates the town. The **Plaza Grande** and the adjoining **Plaza Chica**, both beautifully arcaded and bordered by tapas bars, are the places to soak up Zafra life. The southwestern end of Plaza Grande, with its palm trees and centuries-old homes, is one of Extremadura's prettiest. Guarding the western entry point to the old town is the **Puerta de Jerez**, part of Zafra's 15th-century wall.

★**Palacio Quemado** WINERY
(☎924 12 00 82; www.palacioquemado.com; Carretera Almendralejo-Palomas Km 6.9, Alange; ⏲10am-3pm Mon-Fri May-Sep, 10am-6pm Mon-Fri Oct-Apr, other times by appointment) One of the stars of Extremadura's Ribera del Guadiana wine-producing region, Palacio Quemado produces excellent reds and runs guided tours (including one by tractor), wine tasting and wine-tasting courses. It also has cellar-door sales. It's east off the A66 northeast of Zafra and you'll need to ring ahead to make an appointment and to ask for directions.

Bodegas Medina WINERY
(☎924 57 50 60; www.bodegasmedina.net; Carretera de Córdoba (N432); tour without/with tasting €6/12; ⏲8.30am-2pm & 4-7pm Mon-Fri, 10am-1pm Sat) Extremadura's only wine DO (Denominación de Origen) is Ribera del Guadiana.

Just east of town, you can tour and taste on 45- to 90-minute visits at one of the DO's most prominent southern wineries, Bodegas Medina, which produces reds, whites, rosés and *cava*. Bookings recommended.

Convento de Santa Clara CONVENT
(☎924 55 14 87; www.museozafra.es; Calle Sevilla 30; ⏰10am-2pm Tue-Sun mid-Jun–mid-Oct, 11am-2pm & 5-7pm Tue-Sat, 11am-2pm Sun mid-Oct–mid-Jun) FREE Tucked away off Zafra's main shopping street, this imposing 15th-century Mudéjar convent was originally designed as a holy resting place for the powerful local Feria dynasty. It's still a working convent with cloistered nuns. Visitors can, however, explore the detailed on-site museum, with its interesting (Spanish-language) insights into the sisters' lives and Zafra's history. Visits include the gilded chapel, where Jane Dormer, lady-in-waiting to Mary I of England and wife of the first Duque de Feria, is buried.

Iglesia de la Candelaria CHURCH
(Calle Tetuán; ⏰11am-2pm & 6-7pm Tue-Thu, 11am-2pm Fri, 11am-2pm & 5-7pm Sat) FREE This 16th-century church is worth a look for its fine altarpieces, featuring works by Francisco de Zurbarán.

Sleeping

★Hotel Plaza Grande HOTEL €
(☎924 56 31 63; www.hotelplazagrande.es; Calle Pasteleros 2; incl breakfast s €31-38, d €50; P ❄ 📶) Right on the Plaza Grande, this friendly, sparkling gem of a hotel is an excellent deal. Elegant modern-rustic decor accentuates terracotta with cream paintwork, exposed brick, floral prints and soft pastels. Go for room 108, with its corner balconies overlooking the plaza; room 208 is the same but with windows instead of balconies. The lively downstairs **cafe-restaurant** (☎924 56 31 63; www.hotelplazagrande.es; Calle Pasteleros 2; tapas €4.50-7, raciones €9-18, mains €14-21; ⏰12.30pm-midnight; 📶) is reliably good.

Hotel Huerta Honda HOTEL €€
(☎924 55 41 00; www.hotelhuertahonda.com; Calle de López Asme 30; s/d/superior/ste €55/65/85/120; P ❄ 📶 🏊) Whichever room type you go for, the rich-orange-and-yellow Huerta Honda is a classy choice, with top-notch service. Standards and superiors are comfy, contemporary and tastefully styled in browns and beiges. 'Gran Clase' rooms are sumptuous suites with neo-Moorish decor, woodcarved ceilings, four-poster beds, tiled bathrooms and antiques. Ask for a room overlooking the bougainvillea-draped courtyard and Zafra's castle.

Parador de Zafra HISTORIC HOTEL €€
(☎924 55 45 40; www.parador.es; Plaza Corazón de María 7; r €80-125, ste €120-195; P ❄ 📶 🏊) They say a person's home is their castle: at this gorgeously restored 15th-century fortress, it's the reverse. Beyond the exquisite marble-pillared Renaissance patio, airy rooms come richly decorated with burgundy-coloured fabrics and antiques. Ivy and turrets surround the secluded pool, and the **restaurant** (☎924 55 45 40; www.parador.es; Plaza Corazón de María 7; mains €12-22, set menu €23-35; ⏰1.30-4pm & 8.30-11pm mid-Dec–Oct) is excellent. Guests can climb up to the battlements for Zafra's finest views.

Eating

★La Casabar TAPAS €
(☎924 55 39 72; www.lacasabar.es; Avenida Campo del Rosario 2; tapas €2.50-4, raciones €5-8; ⏰8.30pm-1am Wed-Thu, 7pm-2.30am Fri, 1.30pm-2.30am Sat, 1.30pm-11pm Sun Jul & Aug, 8.30pm-1am Thu, 1.30pm-2.30am Fri & Sat, 1.30pm-11pm Sun Sep-Jun; 📶) A fun, friendly bar-restaurant that morphs into a popular late-night drinks spot, this fine choice is tucked into a restored 15th-century house on the west edge of the old town. Exposed-brick arches, open-stone walls and tiled floors dominate the modern-rustic interior. Food focuses on meat-heavy *extremeño* tapas and *raciones* given a light contemporary twist, plus tasty salads, *tostas* (topped toast) and *revueltos* (scrambles).

★La Rebotica SPANISH €€
(☎924 55 42 89; www.lareboticazafra.com; Calle Boticas 12; mains €16-21; ⏰1.30-4pm & 8.30pm-midnight Tue-Sat, 1.30-4pm Sun; 📶) This refined restaurant in the heart of Zafra's old town delivers with its traditional meaty menu (note the innovative twists) and subtly sophisticated setting among wall mirrors and leather chairs. Dine on elegantly prepared *rabo de toro* (oxtail) and different pork dishes, plus a few seafood or vegie options; finish with outstanding desserts such as chocolate mousse with strawberry sorbet. Reservations recommended.

WORTH A TRIP

MONESTERIO

Since the completion of the A66 motorway, many bypassed towns have disappeared into quiet obscurity, but not Monesterio: this is one of Spain's (and certainly Extremadura's) most celebrated sources of *jamón* (ham). The chance to learn more about this Spanish culinary icon and, even better, to sample it in one of the town's numerous bars, is reason enough to take the motorway exit.

Occupying pride of place at the southern end of Monesterio, the excellent **Museo del Jamón** (924 51 67 37; www.museodeljamondemonesterio.com; Paseo de Extremadura 314; 9.30am-2pm & 5.30-8pm Mon-Sat, 10am-2pm Sun; P) is arguably the best of its kind in Spain. Displays, interactive exhibits and videos starring local ham producers (all in Spanish) take visitors through the process of *jamón* production, from types of Iberian pigs and their ideal habitats to the *matanza* (killing of the pigs) and the curing process. English-language audio guides provided.

Los Templarios (924 51 61 88; www.lostemplariosmonesterio.com; Calle de los Templarios 20; mains €13-15; 10am-midnight) has been around since 1980 and the secret of its longevity is simple – the *jamón* and other pork or steak dishes are first rate and well priced, supplemented with a few fish dishes. It has even freshened up the dining area.

Getting There & Away

Three to seven buses operated by **Leda** (www.leda.es) run daily between Monesterio and Zafra (€3.56, 40 minutes).

Shopping

La Cava del Queso CHEESE
(924 55 36 95; www.facebook.com/lacavadelquesozafra/; Calle de Huelva 32; 11am-3pm Wed, 11am-3pm & 7-10pm Thu & Fri, 11am-3pm & 7.30-10pm Sat, noon-3pm & 7.30-10pm Sun) This enticing cheese shop is like a one-stop introduction to Extremadura's and Spain's cheeses, with a focus on little-known local cheeses. There are plenty of opportunities to try before you buy.

Iberllota FOOD
(924 55 59 95; www.iberllota.com; Calle de López Asme 36; 10am-2pm & 5-8pm Mon-Sat, 10am-2pm Sun) Specialising in the finest cured meats, cheeses and some *extremeño* wines, Iberllota is perfect for picnic treats and local-flavour gifts. Tuck into *jamón*-stuffed *pulguitas* (mini-*bocadillos*, or filled rolls; €1) while you're here.

Information

Oficina de Turismo (Turismo Zafra; 924 55 10 36; www.visitazafra.com; Plaza de España; 10am-2pm & 5.30-7.30pm Mon-Fri, 10am-2pm Sat & Sun Jun-Sep, 10am-2pm & 4.30-6.30pm Mon-Fri, 10am-2pm Sat & Sun Oct-May) In Plaza España off the southern edge of the old town.

Getting There & Away

BUS

Zafra's **bus station** (924 55 39 07; Carretera Badajoz-Granada 4) is 1km northeast of the old town. Destinations include Badajoz (€6.95, 1¼ hours, five to seven daily), Cáceres (€10.75, 1¾ to 2¼ hours, six daily), Mérida (€5.75, 1¼ hours, five to 10 daily) and Seville (€12.90, 1¾ hours, four to six daily).

TRAIN

Destinations from Zafra by train include Mérida (from €6.10, 45 minutes, three daily), Cáceres (from €9.50, two hours, three daily) and Seville (€15.30, three hours, one daily)

Around Zafra

From Zafra, roads head southwest into northern Huelva province (Andalucía) through the rolling Sierra de Aracena and southeast into the Parque Natural Sierra Norte de Sevilla (Andalucía).

Quiet **Burguillos del Cerro**, 19km southwest of Zafra, is overlooked by a 15th-century **castle** atop a grassy hill.

Fregenal de la Sierra, 40km southwest of Zafra, appeals with its churches, noble homes, bullring and 13th-century castle, **Castillo Templario** (Calle El Rollo 1, Frenegal de la Sierra; 10am-2.45pm & 6-8pm Jul & Aug, 10am-2.45pm & 5-7pm Sep-Jun) FREE. The (much reworked) 13th-century **Iglesia de Santa María** (Plaza de la Constitución, Frenegal de la Sierra) FREE is attached to the castle. It's mainly intriguing for its 18th-century baroque altarpieces.

Walled, hilly and handsome **Jerez de los Caballeros**, 42km southwest of Zafra, was a cradle of conquistadors. Attractions here include the 13th-century **Templars' castle** (Plaza del Ayuntamiento, Jerez de los Caballeros; 8am-10pm) FREE, plus several stunning churches, three with towers emulating Seville's Giralda. The 15th-century **Iglesia de San Miguel** (Plaza del Padre Ruíz, Jerez de los Caballeros; 12.15-2.30pm) FREE dominates the main plaza.

About 19km northwest of Zafra, little **Feria** rose to fame in the 14th century as home of the formidable local Feria dynasty. With its sensational hilltop perch, the refurbished 15th-century **castle** (685 147292; Feria; adult/child €5/2.50; 11.30am-1.30pm & 5.30-8.30pm mid-Mar–mid-Sep, 11am-2pm & 4-6pm mid-Sep–mid-Mar) is a regional highlight.

Information

Oficina de Turismo de Frenegal de la Sierra (924 70 00 00; Calle El Rollo 1, Frenegal de la Sierra; 10am-2.45pm & 6-8.15pm Jul & Aug, 10am-2.45pm & 5-7.15pm Sep-Jun)

Oficina de Turismo de Jerez de los Caballeros (924 73 03 72; www.jerezcaballeros.es; Plaza de San Agustín 1, Jerez de los Caballeros; 10am-2.30pm & 4.30-6.30pm Mon-Sat, 10am-2pm Sun)

Getting There & Away

From Zafra, buses run once daily Monday to Friday to/from Fregenal de la Sierra (€3.45, 50 minutes) and Jerez de los Caballeros (€3.70, 45 minutes to one hour), via Burguillos (€2.15, 20 minutes). For Feria, it's your own wheels or nothing.

Badajoz

POP 149,946

Close to the Portuguese border, Badajoz has a handful of good museums and a hilltop Alcazaba. Otherwise it's a scruffy, sprawling, industrial city that's hardly Extremadura's prettiest or most interesting. Even so, persist through the dispiriting outskirts to the historic centre and you'll find it's worth a few hours if you're in the area.

Sights

★Alcazaba FORTRESS

(24hr; P) FREE Badajoz' majestic 12th-century, 8-hectare Alcazaba, the largest in Spain, lords over the city above the Plaza Alta. Guarding all is the **Torre de Espantaperros** (by guided tour 10.30am 1st Sat of month) FREE (Scare-Dogs Tower), symbol of Badajoz, constructed by the Moors and topped by a 16th-century Mudéjar bell tower wrapped around an older original. Within the fort, a refurbished Renaissance palace houses the **Museo Arqueológico Provincial** (924 00 19 08; www.museoarqueologicobadajoz.gobex.es; Plaza José Álvarez y Sáenz de Buruaga, Alcazaba; 9am-3pm Tue-Sat, 10am-3pm Sun) FREE, crammed with artefacts from prehistoric to Roman, Islamic and medieval Christian periods.

Plaza Alta SQUARE

At the top of the old town, beneath the walls of the Alcazaba, is the unusual Plaza Alta, dating to 1681, framed on its east side by the strikingly bold, deep-red-and-white, Moorish-inspired Casas Coloradas.

Museo Extremeño e Iberoamericano de Arte Contemporáneo GALLERY

(MEIAC; 924 01 30 60; www.meiac.es; Calle del Museo 2; 9.30am-1.30pm & 5-7pm Tue-Sat, 9.30am-1.30pm Sun) FREE Badajoz' pride and joy, this commanding, circular modern building dedicated to Spanish, Portuguese and Latin American contemporary art showcases a wide-ranging collection of avant-garde painting, sculpture and photography. It's 800m south of the central Plaza de España.

Museo de Bellas Artes GALLERY

(924 21 24 69; www.dip-badajoz.es/cultura/museo; Calle del Duque de San Germán 3; 10am-2pm Tue-Sun year-round, 6-8pm Tue-Fri Jun-Aug, 5-7pm Tue-Fri Sep-May) FREE This excellent fine-arts gallery displays works by Zurbarán, Morales, Goya, Picasso and Dalí, plus particularly striking pieces by Badajoz-born artists Felipe Checa (19th century) and Antonio Juez Nieto (20th century).

Activities

Baraka HAMMAM

(924 25 08 26; www.barakalasoledad.com; Calle Virgen de la Soledad 14; 90min session per person €23-70; sessions noon, 5.30pm & 7.30pm Tue-Thu, noon, 6pm, 8pm & 10pm Fri & Sat) A beau-

tiful take on the hot-warm-and-cold Moorish-style baths with dazzling architecture, soothing beats, mint tea and a range of massages (hot stone, anti-stress) and beauty treatments (facials, scrubs). Book ahead.

Festivals & Events

Carnaval CARNIVAL
(www.carnavalbadajoz.es; Feb) Badajoz' colour-bursting Carnaval celebrations and street parties have been kicking on since (at least) the 19th century and are among Spain's most elaborate and popular.

Sleeping

Hotel San Marcos HOTEL €
(924 22 95 18; www.hotelsanmarcos.es; Calle Meléndez Valdés 53; s €32-55, d €38-60;) Polished service and excellent facilities make this superfriendly, vanilla-scented city-centre hotel top value. Rooms are a good size, with plenty of light, plus fridges, safes and, for some, balconies. Bathrooms are sleek and modern; many feature hydromassage showers.

NH Gran Hotel Casino Extremadura HOTEL €€
(924 28 44 02; www.nh-hotels.com; Avenida Adolfo Díaz Ambrona 11; r €60-125;) Several of Badajoz' classiest hotel picks are just across the Río Guadiana, a short walk west of the old town. This swish, sprawling complex sports modern, elegant, business-style rooms decked out in smart dark woods, with desks and in-room espresso machines. It offers an on-site spa and gym, plus a friendly yet professional welcome.

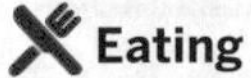

Eating

Papabuey GRILL, SPANISH €€
(924 18 15 93; www.papabuey.com; Calle Vicente Barrantes 5; mains €8-16; 2-4.30pm & 8.30-11pm Thu-Sun, 1-4pm Tue & Wed) Succulent meats grilled to perfection are the key to astounding success at this busy little *asador* (restaurant specialising in roasted meats), just off Plaza de España. Carnivores will drool over the meat-packed menu, featuring specialities such as *chuletón de buey* (giant beef chop) and classic *extremeño cochinillo asado* (roast suckling pig). The three-course weekday lunchtime *menú* (€15) gets you started.

La Casona Alta TAPAS €€
(924 24 73 95; Plaza Alta; tapas €2-5, mains €8-16; 8.30am-late Mon-Fri, noon-late Sat & Sun) With chairs on Badajoz' coolest square and a buzzy bar area with barrel tables, La Casona Alta lets you choose from a healthy menu of standard *raciones* or more substantial Moroccan-influenced dishes.There's a decent-value €11 to €13 *menú del día* (daily set menu).

Information

Oficina Municipal de Turismo (924 22 49 81; www.turismobadajoz.es; Paseo de San Juan; 10am-2pm & 5.30-8pm Mon-Sat, 10am-2pm Sun Jul-Sep, 10am-2pm & 5-7.30pm Mon-Sat, 10am-2pm Sun Oct-Jun) Just off the central Plaza de España.

Oficina de Turismo Casas Mudéjares (924 29 13 69; www.turismobadajoz.es; Plaza de San José 18; 10am-2pm & 5-7.30pm Mon-Fri, 10am-2pm Sat) Right below the Alcazaba.

Getting There & Away

BUS

Buses leave from the **bus station** (924 25 86 61; Calle José Rebollo López), 1.5km south of the main Plaza de España.

DESTINATION	FARE (€)	TIME	FREQUENCY
Cáceres	6.30	1¼hr	3-6 daily
Lisbon (normal/ express)	24/27	2½/ 2hr	2/1 daily
Madrid (normal/ express)	31/43	5¾/ 4¾hr	5/4 daily
Mérida	6	50min	3-7 daily
Seville	18	3½hr	2-4 daily
Zafra	6.95	1¼hr	5-7 daily

Seville & Andalucía's Hill Towns

Includes ➡

Best Places to Eat

- ➡ Bar-Restaurante Eslava (p655)
- ➡ Almocábar (p696)
- ➡ Casa Pepe de la Judería (p715)
- ➡ Jesus Carrión (p669)
- ➡ El Jardín del Califa (p698)

Best Places to Stay

- ➡ Hotel Casa 1800 (p652)
- ➡ Aire de Ronda (p696)
- ➡ La Casa del Califa (p698)
- ➡ Casa Olea (p717)
- ➡ Hotel Convento Aracena (p668)

Why Go?

With its distinctive Mudéjar architecture, hilltop *pueblos blancos* (white towns) and fiery flamenco traditions, western Andalucía encapsulates much of the spirit and beauty of Spain's sun-baked south. Its charismatic capital, Seville, is one of Spain's hottest destinations right now and few visitors are left untouched by its elegant palaces, teeming tapas bars and infectious passions. For a change of pace, venture south to Cádiz province where a string of precarious white towns mark what was once the border between Christian Spain and Moorish Al-Andalus. Andalucía's Moorish history has had an enduring impact on the region and everywhere you go you'll find remnants of its Islamic past, most spectacularly in the form of Córdoba's Mezquita.

Nature lovers are also well served in these parts with everything from bird-rich wetlands in Parque Nacional de Doñana to windswept beaches at Tarifa and pockets of unspoiled wilderness criss-crossed by walking trails.

When to Go

Seville

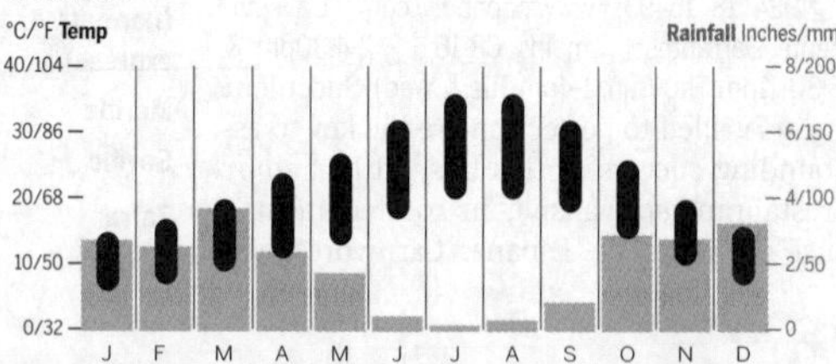

Mar–Apr Sombre Semana Santa processions are followed by exuberant spring fairs.

May–Jun Warm, sunny weather, excellent hiking, and yet more colourful festivals.

Sep–Oct Ideal period for hiking and beach going without the crowds.

SEVILLE

POP 690,570

Some cities blast you away, others slowly win you over. Seville disarms and seduces you. Its historic centre, lorded over by a colossal Gothic cathedral, is an intoxicating mix of resplendent Mudéjar palaces, baroque churches and winding medieval lanes. Flamenco clubs keep the intimacy and intensity of this centuries-old tradition alive whilst aristocratic mansions recall the city's past as a showcase Moorish capital and, later, a 16th-century metropolis rich on the back of New World trade.

But while history reverberates all around, Seville is as much about the here and now as the past. It's about eating tapas in a crowded bar or seeing out the end of the day over a drink on a buzzing plaza. The *sevillanos* have long since mastered the art of celebrating and the city's great annual festivals, notably the Semana Santa and Feria de Abril, are among Spain's most heartfelt.

History

According to legend Seville was founded by the Greek demigod Hercules. More plausibly, it probably started life as an Iberian town before growing to become an important Roman port (Hispalis). But it was under a succession of Islamic rulers that the city really came into its own. It enjoyed a heyday in the late 11th century as a major cultural centre under the Abbadid dynasty, and then again in the 12th century when the Almohads took control and built, among other things, a great mosque where the cathedral now stands. Almohad power dwindled after the disastrous defeat of Las Navas de Tolosa in 1212, and in 1248, the city fell to Castilla's King Fernando III (*El Santo*; the Saint).

Some 240-odd years later, the discovery of the Americas paved the way for another golden era. In 1503 the city was awarded an official monopoly on Spanish trade with the new-found continent. The riches poured in and Seville blossomed into one of the world's largest, richest and most cosmopolitan cities.

But it was not to last. A plague in 1649 killed half the city's population, and as the 17th century wore on, the Río Guadalquivir became more silted and difficult to navigate. In 1717 the Casa de la Contratación (Contracting House), the government office controlling commerce with the Americas, was transferred to Cádiz. The city went into decline.

The beginnings of industry in the mid-19th century saw a spate of major building projects. Notably, the first bridge across the Guadalquivir, the Puente de Triana (or Puente de Isabel II), was built in 1852, and in 1869 the old Almohad walls were knocked to let the city expand. The city's hosting of the 1929 Exposición Iberoamericana led to further building projects.

The Spanish Civil War saw the city fall to the Nationalists in 1936 shortly after the outbreak of hostilities, despiteresistance in working-class areas (which brought savage reprisals). More recently, Seville has undergone something of a roller-coaster ride. It was made capital of the autonomous Andalucía region in 1982, and in 1992 it hosted Expo's world fair. By the early 2000s, its economy was on the up thanks to a mix of tourism, commerce, technology and industry. But then the 2008 financial crisis struck and despite the continuation of projects such as the Metropol Parasol, the economy tanked, reaching rock bottom in 2012. Recent years have seen growth returning to the Spanish economy but unemployment, particularly youth unemployment, remains a worrying issue.

SEVILLE IN TWO DAYS

Start by exploring the charming lanes of the Barrio de Santa Cruz. Once you've got your bearings, head to the **Real Alcázar** (p637), Seville's fabled palace complex. Enjoy the spectacular Mudéjar decor, cooling patios and entrancing gardens. Next, lunch on refined tapas at nearby **Mamarracha** (p654). In the afternoon, strike north via **Calle Sierpes** (p647) to the **Metropol Parasol** (p643), Seville's massive wooden sunshade known locally as *las setas* (the mushrooms). Get the lift to the top and bask in expansive views over the city's rooftops. See the day out amid the bars and eateries of the Alameda de Hércules.

Kick off day two at the **cathedral** (p636). Savour the art treasures in the colossal interior and ascend its celebrated bell tower, the **Giralda** (p636). Then, work your way through the Arenal district and over the river to Triana. Learn about the neighbourhood's traditional ceramics industry at the **Centro Cerámica Triana** (p648). After lunch at **Casa Cuesta** (p655), cross the river and make your way to the **Parque de María Luisa** (p648) for some downtime amongst the trees. Take in **Plaza de España** (p648) before finishing the day with a flamenco show at the **Casa de la Guitarra** (p656).

Seville & Andalucía's Hill Towns Highlights

❶ **Seville** (p633)
Exploring Andalucía's most beguiling city with its fabulous monuments, creative tapas bars and passionate spirit.

❷ **Jerez de la Frontera** (p681)
Unravelling a fashionable world of flamenco, horses, sherry and bodegas.

❸ **Córdoba** (p704) Discovering the marvellous Mezquita and much more in this fascinatingly historic but also buzzing contemporary city.

❹ **Zuheros** (p717)
Taking in this charming white village with a craggy canyon backdrop, good walks and a perfectly perched castle.

❺ **Sanlúcar de Barrameda** (p679)
Tucking into fresh-from-the-ocean fish along Bajo de Guía and venturing into the Parque Nacional de Doñana.

❻ **Tarifa** (p700)
Soaking up the kitesurfing, windsurfing and beach-lazing scene, with Morocco looming in the background.

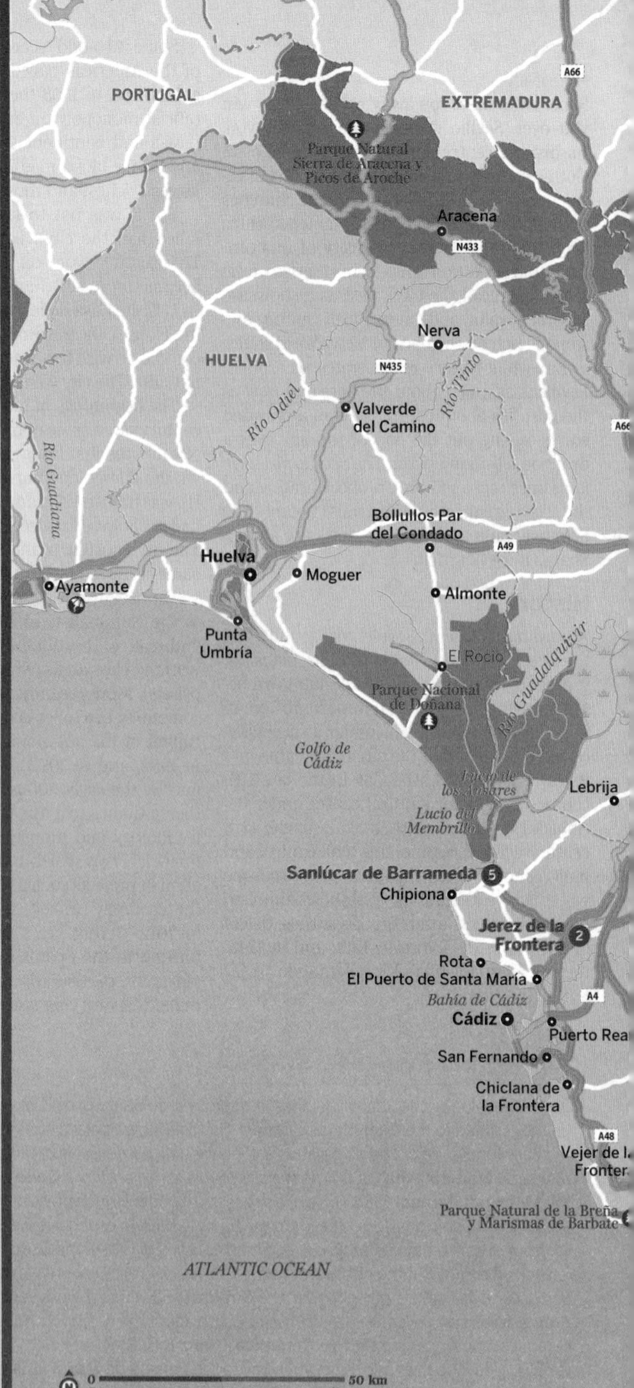

Peñarroya-
Pueblonuevo
Río Guadiato
CÓRDOBA
Montoro
Cazalla de
la Sierra
Parque Natural
Sierra Norte
Parque Natural
Sierra de
Hornachuelos
Córdoba
3
Medina
Azahara
A4
Constantina
A431
Río Huéznar
SEVILLE
Palma
del Río
A4
Lora del Río
Baena
Pradollano
Río Corbones
Écija
N331
Carmona
Aguilar de
la Frontera
Zuheros
4
A4
Parque Natural
Sierras Subbéticas
1
Seville
Alcalá de Guadaira
Puente
Genil
Lucena
Dos
Hermanas
A92
Marchena
Arahal
Río Guadaira
Osuna
A92
Utrera
Los Palacios
y Villafranca
Morón de la
Frontera
A92
AP4
Antequera
A384
Olvera
Embalse del Conde
del Guadalhorce
Villamartín
A384
MÁLAGA
Zahara de
la Sierra
Setenil de
las Bodegas
Arcos de la
Frontera
Embalse de
Bornos
A45
Álora
Grazalema
Vélez
Málaga
A382
Ronda
Parque Natural
Sierra de Grazalema
Cártama
A7
Ubrique
A397
Parque Natural
Sierra de las
Nieves
Málaga
Torre
del Mar
Coín
A374
Río Guadiaro
CÁDIZ
Mijas
Río Genal
Marbella
Fuengirola
Medina
Sidonia
A381
Jimena de
la Frontera
San Pedro
de Alcántara
Playa La Luna
Estepona
A7
Embalse de
Barbate
Costa del Sol
Parque Natural
Los Alcornocales
Barbate
La Línea de
la Concepción
A7
Mediterranean
Sea
Algeciras
Gibraltar
Bahía
de Algeciras
6
Tarifa
Strait of
Gibraltar
MOROCCO
Ceuta (Spain)

Sights

Catedral de Sevilla & Around

★Catedral de Sevilla & Giralda CATHEDRAL

(Map p644; ☎954 21 49 71; www.catedraldesevilla.es; Plaza del Triunfo; adult/child €9/free, rooftop tours €15; ⏰11am-3.30pm Mon, to 5pm Tue-Sat, 2.30-6pm Sun) Seville's immense cathedral is awe-inspiring in its scale and majesty. The world's largest Gothic cathedral, it was built between 1434 and 1517 over the remains of what had previously been the city's main mosque. Highlights include the Giralda, the mighty bell tower, which incorporates the mosque's original minaret, the monumental tomb of Christopher Columbus, and the Capilla Mayor with an astonishing gold altarpiece.

The history of the cathedral goes back to the 15th century but the history of Christian worship on the site dates to the mid-13th century. In 1248, the Castilian King Fernando III captured Seville from its Almohad rulers and transformed their great 12th-century mosque into a church. Some 153 years later, in 1401, the city's ecclesiastical authorities decided to replace the former mosque, which had been damaged by an earthquake in 1356, with a spectacular new cathedral: 'Let's construct a church so large future generations will think we were mad', they quipped (or so legend has it).

The result is the staggering cathedral you see today, officially known as the Catedral de Santa María de la Sede. It's one of the world's largest churches and a veritable treasure trove of art with notable works by Zurbarán, Murillo, Goya and others.

> **CATHEDRAL TICKETS TIP**
>
> To avoid queueing for tickets at the cathedral, you have two choices: you can either book through the cathedral's Spanish-language website or you can buy tickets at the Iglesia Colegial del Divino Salvador (p647). There are rarely queues at this church, which sells combined tickets covering admission to the church, the cathedral and the Giralda.

➡ Exterior

From close up, the bulky exterior of the cathedral with its Gothic embellishments gives hints of the treasures within. Pause to look at the **Puerta del Perdón** (now the cathedral's exit) on Calle Alemanes. It's one of the few remaining elements from the original mosque.

➡ Sala del Pabellón

Selected treasures from the cathedral's art collection are exhibited in this room, the first after the ticket office. Much of what's displayed here, as elsewhere in the cathedral, is the work of masters from Seville's 17th-century Golden Age.

➡ Tomb of Christopher Columbus

Once inside the cathedral proper, head right and you'll see the tomb of Christopher Columbus (the Sepulcro de Cristóbal Colón) in front of the **Puerta del Príncipe** (Door of the Prince). The monument supposedly contains the remains of the great explorer, but debate continues as to whether the bones are actually his.

Columbus' remains were moved many times after his death (in 1506 in Valladolid, northern Spain), and there are those who claim his real bones lie in Santo Domingo. Certainly his bones spent time in the Dominican Republic after they were shipped to Spanish-controlled Hispaniola from their original resting place, the Monasterio de la Cartuja (p649), in 1537. However, they were later sent to Havana and returned to Seville in 1898.

DNA testing in 2006 proved a match between the bones supposed to be Columbus' and bones known to be from his brother Diego. And while that didn't conclusively solve the mystery, it strongly suggested that the great man really is interred in the tomb that bears his name.

➡ Sacristía de los Cálices

To the right of Columbus' tomb are a series of rooms containing some of the cathedral's greatest masterpieces. First up is the Sacristy of the Chalices, where Francisco de Goya's painting of the Sevillan martyrs, *Santas Justa y Rufina* (1817), hangs above the altar.

➡ Sacristía Mayor

Next along is this large room with a finely carved stone cupola, created between 1528 and 1547: the arch over its portal has carvings of 16th-century foods. Pedro de Campaña's

1547 *El Descendimiento* (Descent from the Cross), above the central altar at the southern end, and Francisco de Zurbarán's *Santa Teresa*, to its right, are two of the cathedral's most precious paintings. Also look out for the *Custodia de Juan de Arfe*, a huge 475kg silver monstrance made in the 1580s by Renaissance metalsmith Juan de Arfe.

➡ Sala Capitular

The circular chapter house, also called the Cabildo, features a stunning carved dome and a Murillo masterpiece, *La inmaculada*, set high above the archbishop's throne. The room was built between 1558 and 1592 as a venue for meetings of the cathedral hierarchy.

➡ Capilla Mayor

Even in a church as spectacular as this, the Capilla Mayor (Main Chapel) stands out with its astonishing Gothic retable, reckoned to be the world's largest altarpiece. Begun by Flemish sculptor Pieter Dancart in 1482 and finished by others in 1564, this sea of gilt and polychromed wood holds more than 1000 carved biblical figures. At the centre of the lowest level is a tiny 13th-century silver-plated cedar image of the *Virgen de la Sede* (Virgin of the See), patron of the cathedral.

West of the Capilla is the Choir into which is incorporated a vast organ.

➡ Southern & Northern Chapels

The chapels along the southern and northern sides of the cathedral hold yet more artistic treasures. Of particular note is the Capilla de San Antonio, at the western end of the northern aisle, housing Murillo's humongous 1656 depiction of the vision of St Anthony of Padua. The painting was victim of a daring art heist in 1874.

➡ Giralda

In the northeastern corner of the cathedral you'll find the entry to the Giralda. The climb to the top involves walking up 35 ramps, built so that the guards could ride up on horseback, and a small flight of stairs at the top. Your reward is sensational rooftop views.

The decorative brick tower, which tops out at 104m, was the minaret of the mosque, constructed between 1184 and 1198 at the height of Almohad power. Its proportions, delicate brick-pattern decoration and colour, which changes with the light, make it perhaps Spain's most perfect Islamic building. The topmost parts – from bell level up – were added in the 16th century, when Spanish Christians were busy 'improving on' surviving Islamic buildings. At the very top is *El Giraldillo*, a 16th-century bronze weathervane representing 'faith', that has become a symbol of Seville.

➡ Patio de los Naranjos

Outside the cathedral's northern side, this patio was originally the mosque's main courtyard. It's planted with 66 *naranjos* (orange trees), and has a small Visigothic fountain in the centre. Look out for a stuffed crocodile hanging over the courtyard's doorway – it's a replica of a gift the Sultan of Egypt gave Alfonso X in around 1260.

★Real Alcázar PALACE

(Map p644; ☎954 50 23 24; www.alcazarsevilla.org; Plaza del Triunfo; adult/child €9.50/free; ⌚9.30am-7pm Apr-Sep, to 5pm Oct-Mar) A magnificent marriage of Christian and Mudéjar architecture, Seville's Unesco-listed palace complex is a breathtaking spectacle. The site, which was originally developed as a fort in 913, has been revamped many times over the 11 centuries of its existence, most spectacularly in the 14th century when King Pedro added the sumptuous Palacio de Don Pedro, still today the Alcázar's crown jewel. More recently, the Alcázar featured as a location for the *Game of Thrones* TV series.

The Alcázar started life in the 10th century as a fort for the Cordoban governors of Seville but it was in the 11th century that it got its first major rebuild. Under the city's Abbadid rulers, the original fort was enlarged and a palace known as Al-Muwarak (the Blessed) was built in what's now the western part of the complex. Subsequently, the 12th-century Almohad rulers added another palace east of this, around what's now the Patio del Crucero. The Christian king Fernando III moved into the Alcázar when he captured Seville in 1248, and several later monarchs used it as their main residence. Fernando's son Alfonso X replaced much of the Almohad palace with a Gothic one and then, between 1364 and 1366, Pedro I created his stunning namesake palace.

Seville Cathedral

THE HIGHLIGHTS TOUR

In 1402 the inspired architects of Seville set out on one of the most grandiose building projects in medieval history. Their aim was to shock and amaze future generations with the size and magnificence of the building. It took until 1506 to complete the project, but 500 years later Seville Cathedral is still the largest Gothic cathedral in the world.

To avoid getting lost, orient yourself by the main highlights. Directly inside the southern (main) entrance is the grand ❶ **Tomb of Columbus**. Turn right here and head into the southeastern corner to uncover some major art treasures: a Goya in the Sacristía de los Cálices, a Zurbarán in the ❷ **Sacristía Mayor**, and Murillo's shining *La inmaculada* in the Sala Capitular. Skirt the cathedral's eastern wall past the often closed ❸ **Capilla Real**, home to some important royal tombs. By now it's impossible to avoid the lure of the ❹ **Capilla Mayor** with its fantastical altarpiece. Hidden over in the northwest corner is the ❺ **Capilla de San Antonio** with a legendary Murillo. That huge doorway nearby is the rarely opened ❻ **Puerta de la Asunción**. Make for the ❼ **Giralda** next, stealing admiring looks at the high, vaulted ceiling on the way. After looking down on the cathedral's immense footprint, descend and depart via the ❽ **Patio de los Naranjos**.

TOP TIPS

➡ Don't try to visit the Alcázar and cathedral on the same day. There is far too much to take in.

➡ Take time to admire the cathedral from the outside. It's particularly stunning at night from the Plaza Virgen de los Reyes, and from across the river in Triana.

➡ Skip the line by booking tickets online or buying them at the Iglesia Colegial del Divino Salvador on Plaza del Salvador.

TRABANTOS / SHUTTERSTOCK ©

Capilla de San Antonio
One of 80 interior chapels, you'll need to hunt down this little gem notable for housing Murillo's 1656 painting, *The Vision of St Anthony*. The work was pillaged by thieves in 1874 but later restored.

Patio de los Naranjos
Inhale the perfume of 60 Sevillan orange trees in a cool patio bordered by fortress-like walls – a surviving remnant of the original 12th-century mosque. Exit is gained via the horseshoe-shaped Puerta del Perdón.

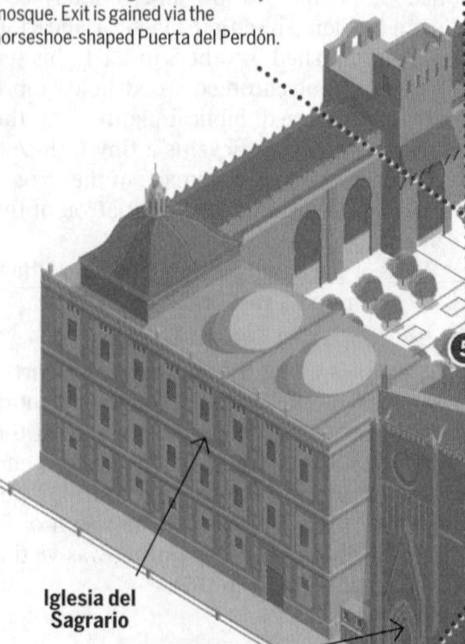

Puerta de la Asunción
Located on the western side of the cathedral and also known as the Puerta Mayor, these huge, rarely opened doors are pushed back during Semana Santa to allow solemn processions of Catholic *hermandades* (brotherhoods) to pass through.

DMITRY SHAKIN / GETTY IMAGES ©

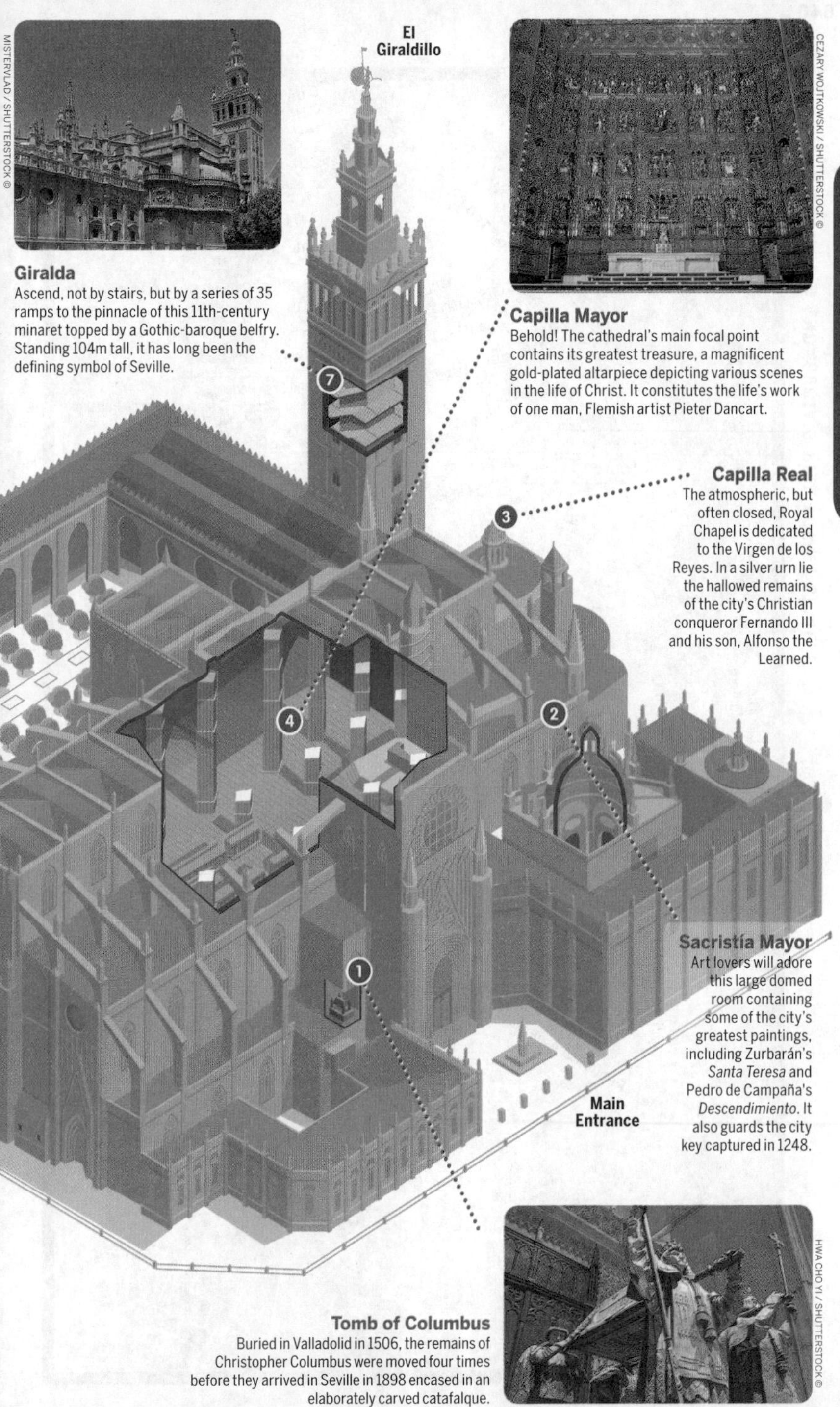

MISTERVLAD / SHUTTERSTOCK ©
El
Giraldillo
CEZARY WOJTKOWSKI / SHUTTERSTOCK ©
Giralda
Ascend, not by stairs, but by a series of 35 ramps to the pinnacle of this 11th-century minaret topped by a Gothic-baroque belfry. Standing 104m tall, it has long been the defining symbol of Seville.
Capilla Mayor
Behold! The cathedral's main focal point contains its greatest treasure, a magnificent gold-plated altarpiece depicting various scenes in the life of Christ. It constitutes the life's work of one man, Flemish artist Pieter Dancart.
7
Capilla Real
The atmospheric, but often closed, Royal Chapel is dedicated to the Virgen de los Reyes. In a silver urn lie the hallowed remains of the city's Christian conqueror Fernando III and his son, Alfonso the Learned.
3
4
2
Sacristía Mayor
Art lovers will adore this large domed room containing some of the city's greatest paintings, including Zurbarán's *Santa Teresa* and Pedro de Campaña's *Descendimiento*. It also guards the city key captured in 1248.
1
Main
Entrance
HWA CHO YI / SHUTTERSTOCK ©
Tomb of Columbus
Buried in Valladolid in 1506, the remains of Christopher Columbus were moved four times before they arrived in Seville in 1898 encased in an elaborately carved catafalque.

Seville

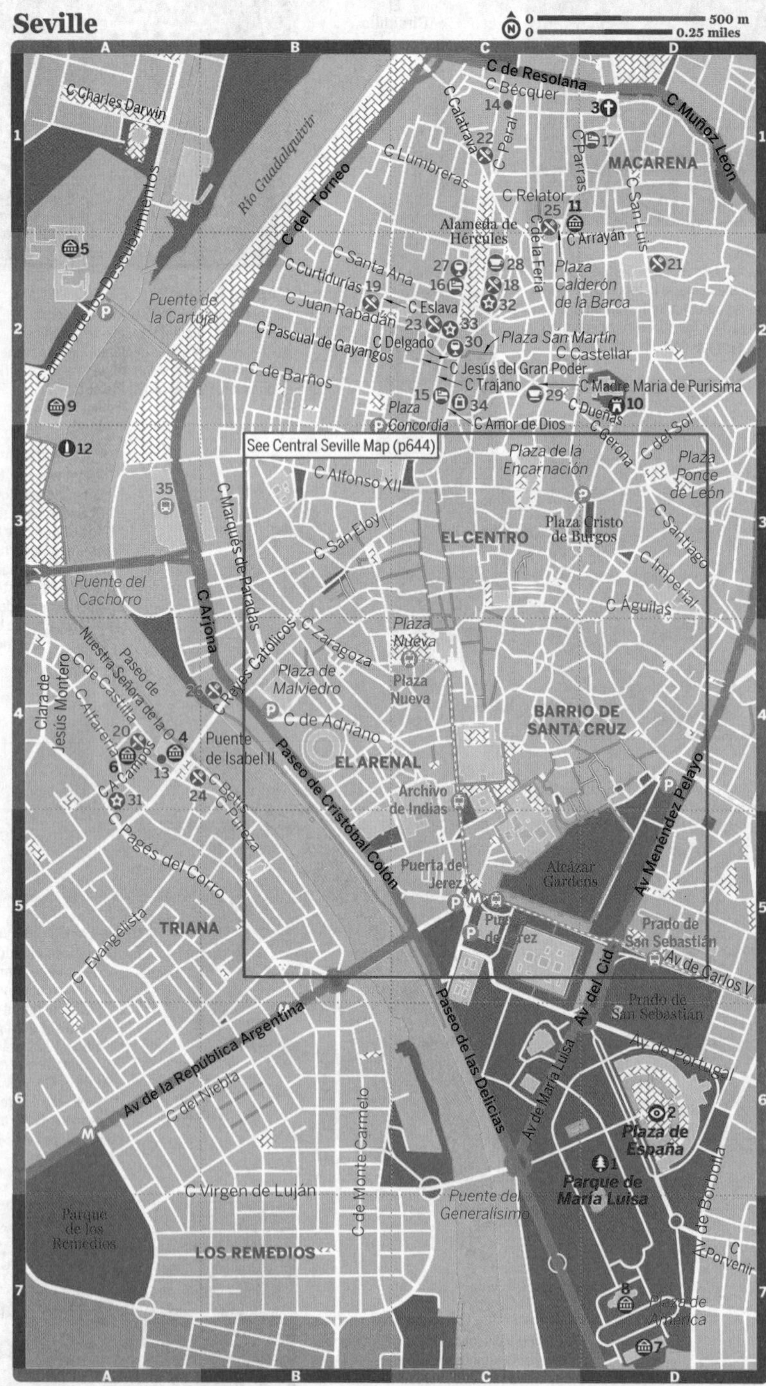

0 500 m
0 0.25 miles
C de Resolana
C Bécquer
C Muñoz León
C Calatrava
C Peral
C Parras
MACARENA
C Lumbreras
C Relator
C San Luis
Alameda de Hércules
C de la Feria
C Arrayán
Río Guadalquivir
C del Torneo
Camino de los Descubrimientos
C Charles Darwin
C Santa Ana
C Curtidurías
Plaza Calderón de la Barca
C Juan Rabadán
C Eslava
Puente de la Cartuja
C Pascual de Gayangos
C Delgado
Plaza San Martín
C Castellar
C Jesús del Gran Poder
C de Baños
C Trajano
C Madre Maria de Purisima
C Dueñas
Plaza Concordia
C Amor de Dios
C Gerona
C del Sol
See Central Seville Map (p644)
Plaza de la Encarnación
Plaza Ponce de León
C Alfonso XII
C Marqués de Paradas
C San Eloy
EL CENTRO
Plaza Cristo de Burgos
C Santiago
C Imperial
Puente del Cachorro
C Arjona
C Águilas
Plaza Nueva
C Zaragoza
C Reyes Católicos
Plaza de Malviedro
Paseo de Nuestra Señora de la O
C de Castilla
Clara de Jesús Montero
C Alfarería
C de Adriano
BARRIO DE SANTA CRUZ
Puente de Isabel II
EL ARENAL
C Campos
C Betis
C Pureza
Paseo de Cristóbal Colón
Archivo de Indias
Av Menéndez Pelayo
C Pagés del Corro
Puerta de Jerez
Alcázar Gardens
TRIANA
C Evangelista
Prado de San Sebastián
Av de Carlos V
Av del Cid
Paseo de las Delicias
Av de la República Argentina
Av de María Luisa
Av de Portugal
C del Niebla
C de Monte Carmelo
Plaza de España
Parque de María Luisa
C Virgen de Luján
Puente del Generalísimo
Av de Borbolla
Parque de los Remedios
LOS REMEDIOS
C Porvenir
Plaza de América

Seville

Top Sights
1 Parque de María Luisa ... D6
2 Plaza de España ... D6

Sights
3 Basílica de La Macarena ... D1
4 Castillo de San Jorge ... A4
5 Centro Andaluz de Arte Contemporáneo ... A2
6 Centro Cerámica Triana ... A4
7 Museo Arqueológico ... D7
8 Museo de Artes y Costumbres Populares ... D7
9 Pabellón de la Navegación ... A2
10 Palacio de Las Dueñas ... D2
11 Palacio de los Marqueses de la Algaba ... C1
12 Torre Schindler ... A3

Activities, Courses & Tours
13 Taller Andaluz de Cocina ... A4
14 Taller Flamenco ... C1

Sleeping
Corner House ... (see 27)
15 Hotel Boutique Doña Lola ... C2
16 Hotel Sacristía de Santa Ana ... C2
17 Hotel San Gil ... D1

Eating
18 Arte y Sabor ... C2
19 Bar-Restaurante Eslava ... B2
20 Casa Cuesta ... A4
21 conTenedor ... D2
22 Dúo Tapas ... C1
23 La Azotea ... C2
24 Manu Jara Dulcería ... A4
25 Mercado de Feria ... C1
26 Mercado Lonja del Barranco ... B4

Drinking & Nightlife
27 Corner House Roof Terrace Bar ... C2
28 El Viajero Sedentario ... C2
29 Gallo Rojo ... C2
30 Maquila ... C2

Entertainment
31 Casa Anselma ... A4
32 Fun Club ... C2
33 Naima Café Jazz ... C2

Shopping
Cerámica Triana ... (see 6)
34 Tarico ... C2

Transport
ALSA ... (see 35)
Damas ... (see 35)
35 Estación de Autobuses Plaza de Armas ... A3
Eurolines ... (see 35)

Patio del León

Entry to the complex is through the **Puerta del León** (Lion Gate) on Plaza del Triunfo. Passing through the gateway, which is flanked by crenellated walls, you come to the Patio del León (Lion Patio), which was the garrison yard of the original Al-Muwarak palace. Off to the left before the arches is the **Sala de la Justicia** (Hall of Justice), with beautiful Mudéjar plasterwork and an *artesonado* (ceiling of interlaced beams with decorative insertions). This room was built in the 1340s by the Christian King Alfonso XI, who disported here with one of his mistresses, Leonor de Guzmán, reputedly the most beautiful woman in Spain. It leads to the pretty **Patio del Yeso**, part of the 12th-century Almohad palace reconstructed in the 19th century.

Patio de la Montería

Dominated by the facade of the Palacio de Don Pedro, the Patio de la Monteria owes its name (The Hunting Courtyard) to the fact that hunters would meet here before hunts with King Pedro. Rooms on the western side of the square were part of the **Casa de la Contratación** (Contracting House), founded in 1503 to control trade with Spain's American colonies. The **Salón del Almirante** (Admiral's Hall) houses 19th- and 20th-century paintings showing historical events and personages associated with Seville. The room off its northern end has an international collection of beautiful, elaborate fans. The **Sala de Audiencias** (Chapter House) is hung with tapestry representations of the shields of Spanish admirals and Alejo Fernández' celebrated 1530s painting *Virgen de los mareantes* (Madonna of the Seafarers).

Cuarto Real Alto

The Alcázar is still a royal palace. In 1995 it hosted the wedding feast of Infanta Elena, daughter of King Juan Carlos I, after her marriage in Seville's cathedral. The **Cuarto Real Alto** (Upper Royal Quarters), the rooms used by the Spanish royal family on their visits to Seville, are open for guided tours (€4.50; half hourly 10am to 1.30pm; booking required). Highlights of the tours, which are conducted in either Spanish or English, include the 14th-century **Salón de**

Audiencias, still the monarch's reception room, and Pedro I's bedroom, with marvellous Mudéjar tiles and plasterwork.

➡ Palacio de Don Pedro

This palace, also known as the Palacio Mudéjar, is Seville's single most stunning architectural feature.

King Pedro, though at odds with many of his fellow Christians, had a long-standing alliance with the Muslim emir of Granada, Mohammed V, the man responsible for much of the decoration at the Alhambra. So when Pedro decided to build a new palace in the Alcázar in 1364, Mohammed sent many of his top craftsmen. These were joined by others from Seville and Toledo. Their work, drawing on the Islamic traditions of the Almohads and caliphal Córdoba, is a unique synthesis of Iberian Islamic art.

Inscriptions on the palace's facade encapsulate the collaborative nature of the enterprise. While one, in Spanish, announces that the building's creator was the 'highest, noblest and most powerful conqueror Don Pedro, by God's grace King of Castilla and León', another proclaims repeatedly in Arabic that 'there is no conqueror but Allah'.

At the heart of the palace is the sublime **Patio de las Doncellas** (Patio of the Maidens), surrounded by beautiful arches, plasterwork and tiling. The sunken garden in the centre was uncovered by archaeologists in 2004 from beneath a 16th-century marble covering.

To the north of the patio, the **Alcoba Real** (Royal Quarters) feature stunningly beautiful ceilings and wonderful plaster- and tilework. Its rear room was probably the monarch's summer bedroom.

Continuing on brings you to the covered **Patio de las Muñecas** (Patio of the Dolls), the heart of the palace's private quarters, featuring delicate Granada-style decoration; indeed, plasterwork was actually brought here from the Alhambra in the 19th century, when the mezzanine and top gallery were added for Queen Isabel II. The **Cuarto del Príncipe** (Prince's Suite), to its north, has an elaborate gold ceiling intended to recreate a starlit night sky.

The most spectacular room in the Palacio, and indeed the whole Alcázar, is the **Salón de Embajadores** (Hall of Ambassadors), south of the Patio de las Muñecas. This was originally Pedro I's throne room, although the fabulous wooden dome of multiple star patterns, symbolising the universe, was added later in 1427. The dome's shape gives the room its alternative name, Sala de la Media Naranja (Hall of the Half Orange).

On the western side of the Salón, the beautiful **Arco de Pavones**, named after its peacock motifs, leads onto the **Salón del Techo de Felipe II**, with a Renaissance ceiling (1589–91) and beyond, to the **Jardín del Príncipe** (Prince's Garden).

➡ Palacio Gótico

Reached via a staircase at the southeastern corner of the Patio de las Doncellas is Alfonso X's much remodelled 13th-century Gothic palace. Interest here is centred on the **Salones de Carlos V**, named after the 16th-century Spanish King Carlos I who was also the Holy Roman Emperor Charles V, and the **Salone de los Tapices**, a huge vaulted hall with a series of vast tapestries.

➡ Patio del Crucero

Beyond the Salone de los Tapices, the Patio del Crucero was originally the upper storey of a patio from the 12th-century Almohad palace. Initially it consisted only of raised walkways along its four sides and two cross-walkways that met in the middle. Below grew orange trees, whose fruit could be plucked at hand height by the lucky folk strolling along the walkways. The patio's lower level was built over in the 18th century after it suffered earthquake damage.

➡ Gardens & Exit

On the other side of the Salone de los Tapices are the Alcázar's gardens. Formal gardens with pools and fountains sit closest to the palace. From one, the **Jardín de la Danza** (Garden of the Dance), a passage runs beneath the Salones de Carlos V to the photogenic **Baños de Doña María de Padilla** (María de Padilla Baths). These are the vaults beneath the Patio del Crucero – originally the patio's lower level – with a grotto that replaced the patio's original pool.

The gardens' most arresting feature is the **Galeria de Grutesco**, a raised gallery with porticoes fashioned in the 16th century out of an old Muslim-era wall. There is also a fun hedge maze, which will delight children. The gardens to the east, beyond a long wall, are 20th-century creations, but no less heavenly for it.

Archivo de Indias MUSEUM

(Map p644; ☎954 50 05 28; Calle Santo Tomás; ⏲9.30am-5pm Mon-Sat, 10am-2pm Sun) FREE

Occupying a former merchant's exchange on the western side of Plaza del Triunfo, the Archivo de Indias provides a fascinating insight into Spain's colonial history. The archive, established in 1785 to house documents and maps relating to Spain's American empire, is vast, boasting 7km of shelves, 43,000 documents, and 80 million pages dating from 1492 to the end of the empire in the 19th century. Most documents are filed away but you can examine some fascinating letters and hand-drawn maps.

Barrio de Santa Cruz

Seville's medieval *judería* (Jewish quarter), east of the cathedral and Real Alcázar, is today a tangle of atmospheric, winding streets and lovely plant-decked plazas perfumed with orange blossom. Among its most characteristic plazas is Plaza de Santa Cruz, which gives the *barrio* (district) its name, and the wonderfully romantic Plaza de Doña Elvira.

★Hospital de los Venerables Sacerdotes MUSEUM

(Map p644; ☎954 56 26 96; www.focus.abengoa.es; Plaza de los Venerables 8; adult/child €8/4, 1st Thu of month to 2pm free; ⏲10am-2pm Thu-Sat summer, to 6pm Thu-Sat rest of year) This gem of a museum, housed in a former hospice for ageing priests, is one of Seville's most rewarding. The artistic highlight is the Focus-Abengoa Foundation's collection of 17th-century paintings in the Centro Velázquez. It's not a big collection but each work is a masterpiece of its genre – highlights include Diego Velázquez' *Santa Rufina*, his *Inmaculada Concepción*, and a sharply vivid portrait of *Santa Catalina* by Bartolomé Murillo.

Elsewhere, you can admire the Hospital's ornately decorated chapel and delightful patio – a classic composition of porticoes, ceramic tiles and orange trees arranged around a sunken fountain.

Casa de Salinas HISTORIC BUILDING

(Map p644; ☎618 254498; www.casadesalinas.com; Calle Mateos Gago 39; guided tour €6; ⏲10am-6pm Mon-Fri mid-Oct–mid-Jun, to 2pm Mon-Fri mid-Jun–mid-Oct) If you've already seen the Alcázar, check out this little-known microversion nearby in Santa Cruz, with no queues. Like Casa de Pilatos, Palacio de Lebrija and Palacio de Las Dueñas, it's privately owned, with the family still occupying the mansion (the redoubtable nonagenarian chatelaine with three of her 12 sons). You'll see 16th-century patios with stunning Mudéjar plasterwork arches and a Roman mosaic of Bacchanalian shenanigans, original ceramic tiles, and the family's winter and summer drawing rooms with exquisite painted wooden ceilings.

Centro de Interpretación Judería de Sevilla MUSEUM

(Map p644; ☎954 04 70 89; www.juderiadesevilla.es; Calle Ximénez de Enciso 22; adult/reduced €6.50/5; ⏲11am-7pm) Dedicated to Seville's Jewish history, this small, poignant museum occupies an old Sephardic house in the higgledy-piggledy Santa Cruz district, the one-time Jewish neighbourhood that never recovered from a brutal pogrom and massacre in 1391. The events of the pogrom and other historical happenings are catalogued inside, along with a few surviving mementos including documents, costumes and books.

El Centro

As the name suggests, this is Seville's central district, and the densely packed zone of narrow streets and squares north and east of Plaza Nueva, centred on Calles Sierpes and Tetuán/Velázquez, is the heart of Seville's shopping world, as well as home to some excellent bars and restaurants.

★Metropol Parasol LANDMARK

(Map p644; ☎606 635214; www.metropolsevilla.com; Plaza de la Encarnación; €3; ⏲10am-10.30pm Sun-Thu, to 11pm Fri & Sat) Since opening in 2011, the opinion-dividing Metropol Parasol, known locally as *las setas* (the mushrooms), has become something of a city icon. Designed as a giant sunshade by German architect Jürgen Mayer-Hermann, it's said to be the world's largest wooden structure, and it's certainly a formidable sight with its 30m-high mushroom-like pillars and undulating honeycombed roof. Lifts run up from the basement to the top where you can enjoy killer city views from a winding walkway.

Palacio de Las Dueñas PALACE

(Map p640; ☎954 21 48 28; www.lasduenas.es; Calle Dueñas 5; adult/child €8/€6; ⏲10am-8pm Apr-Oct, to 6pm Nov-Mar) This 15th-century palace was the favourite home of the world's most titled noble, the late Duchess de Alba, who owned mansions, castles and estates all over Spain. Marvel at the pretty lemon-tree-filled garden, gorgeous arcaded courtyard, paintings and

Central Seville

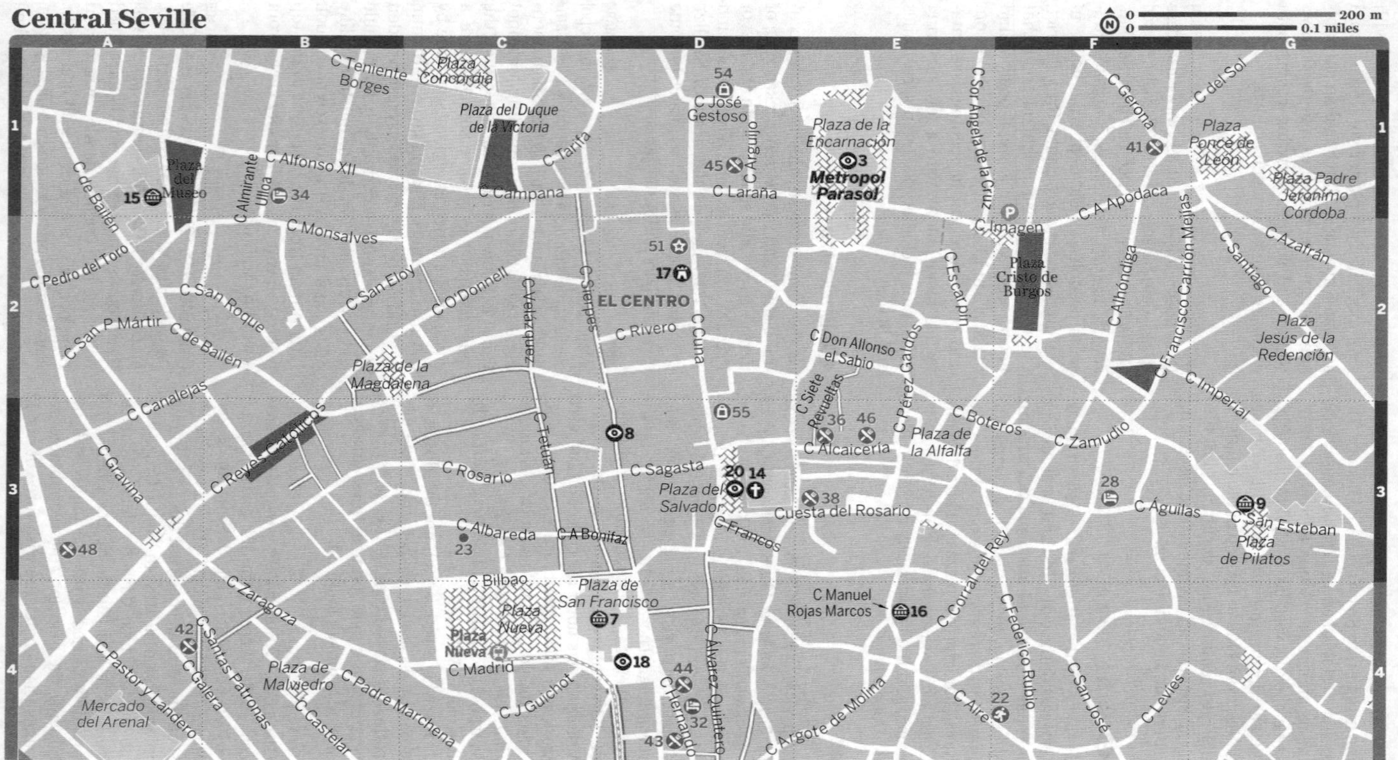

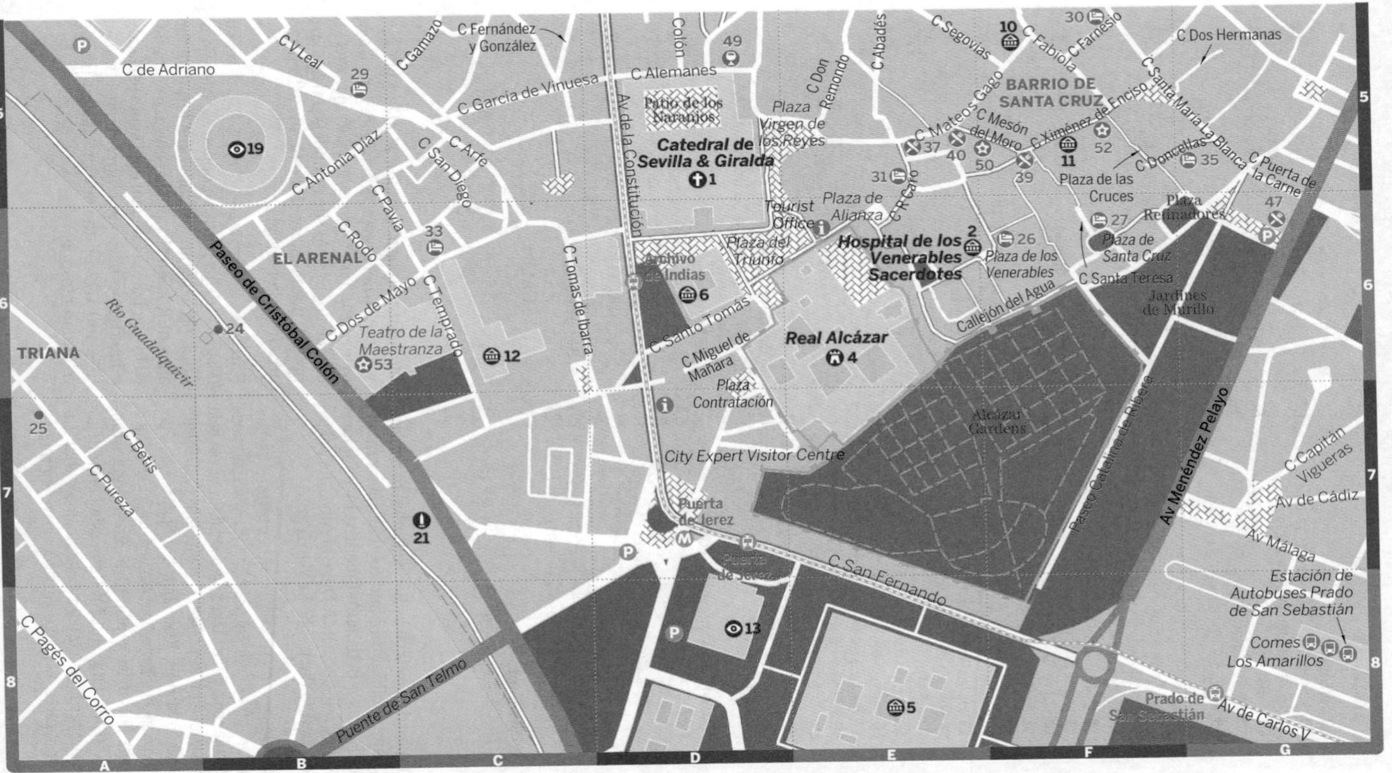

BARRIO DE SANTA CRUZ
EL ARENAL
TRIANA
Catedral de Sevilla & Giralda
Patio de los Naranjos
Real Alcázar
Hospital de los Venerables Sacerdotes
Archivo de Indias
Alcázar Gardens
Jardines de Murillo
Teatro de la Maestranza
Tourist Office
City Expert Visitor Centre
Puerta de Jerez
Estación de Autobuses Prado de San Sebastián
Comes
Los Amarillos
Prado de San Sebastián
Río Guadalquivir
Paseo de Cristóbal Colón
Av de la Constitución
Av Menéndez Pelayo
Paseo Catalina de Ribera
C San Fernando
Puente de San Telmo
Av de Carlos V
Av de Cádiz
Av Málaga
C Capitán Vigueras
C Santa María La Blanca
C Puerta de la Carne
C Dos Hermanas
C Doncellas
Plaza Refinadores
Plaza de las Cruces
Plaza de Santa Cruz
C Santa Teresa
Plaza de los Venerables
Callejón del Agua
C Ximénez de Enciso
C Farnesio
C Fabiola
C Mesón del Moro
C Mateos Gago
C Segovias
C Abadés
C R Caro
C Don Remondo
Plaza Virgen de los Reyes
Plaza de Alianza
Plaza del Triunfo
C Santo Tomás
C Miguel de Mañara
Plaza Contratación
Colón
C Alemanes
C Fernández y González
C García de Vinuesa
C Tomas de Ibarra
C Arfe
C San Diego
C Gamazo
C Pavia
C Temprado
C Rodo
C Dos de Mayo
C Antonia Díaz
C V Leal
C de Adriano
C Betis
C Pureza
C Pagés del Corro

Central Seville

tapestries, as well as her collection of Semana Santa, bullfighting and football memorabilia (she was a Betis fan). Inherited by her eldest son, Carlos, the 18th Duke of Alba, the palace opened to the public in March 2016.

Palacio de la Condesa de Lebrija PALACE

(Map p644; ☎954 22 78 02; www.palaciodelebrija.com; Calle Cuna 8; ground fl €6, whole bldg €9, ground fl free 10am & 11am Mon; ⊙10.30am-7.30pm Mon-Fri, 10am-2pm & 4-6pm Sat, to 2pm Sun Sep-Jun, 10am-3pm Mon-Fri, to 2pm Sat Jul & Aug) This aristocratic 16th-century mansion, set around a beautiful Renaissance-Mudéjar courtyard, boasts an eclectic look that incorporates a range of decorative elements, including Roman mosaics, Mudéjar plasterwork and Renaissance masonry. Its former owner, the late Countess of Lebrija, was an archaeologist, and she remodelled the house in 1914, filling many of the rooms with treasures from her travels.

Plaza del Salvador SQUARE

(Map p644) This plaza, a popular early evening drinking hangout, was once the forum of the ancient Roman city of Hispalis. It's dominated by the Iglesia Colegial del Divino Salvador, a handsome baroque church built between 1674 and 1712 on the site of Muslim Ishbiliya's main mosque.

Iglesia Colegial del Divino Salvador CHURCH

(Map p644; www.iglesiadelsalvador.es; Plaza del Salvador; admission €4, incl cathedral & Giralda €9; ⏲11am-6pm Mon-Sat, 3-7.30pm Sun Sep-Jun, 10.30am-5.30pm Mon-Sat, 3-7pm Sun Jul & Aug) Overlooking Plaza Salvador, this baroque church was built between 1674 and 1712 on the site of Muslim Ishbiliya's main mosque. The tiered red-brick facade is actually Mannerist in style, while the interior reveals a rich display of carving and gilding. At sunset, light seeping in through the stained-glass windows plays on the carvings to enhance their surreal beauty.

Casa de Pilatos HISTORIC BUILDING

(Map p644; ☎954 22 52 98; www.fundacionmedinaceli.org; Plaza de Pilatos; ground fl €8, whole house €10; ⏲9am-7pm Apr-Oct, to 6pm Nov-Mar) The haunting Casa de Pilatos, which is still occupied by the ducal Medinaceli family, is one of the city's most glorious mansions. Originally dating to the late 15th century, it incorporates a wonderful mixture of Mudéjar, Gothic and Renaissance decor, with some beautiful tilework and *artesonados*. The overall effect is like a mini-Alcázar.

Museo del Baile Flamenco MUSEUM

(Map p644; ☎954 34 03 11; www.museoflamenco.com; Calle Manuel Rojas Marcos 3; adult/reduced €10/8; ⏲10am-7pm) The brainchild of *sevillana* flamenco dancer Cristina Hoyos, this museum makes a noble effort to showcase the mysterious art with sketches, paintings and photos of erstwhile (and contemporary) flamenco greats, as well as a collection of dresses and shawls. Even better than the displays are the fantastic nightly performances (7pm and 8.45pm; €20) staged in the on-site courtyard.

Plaza de San Francisco SQUARE

(Map p644) Plaza de San Francisco has been Seville's main public square since the 16th century. Forming its western flank is the city's historic city hall, the **Ayuntamiento** (Casa Consistorial; Map p644; www.visitasayto.sevilla.org; Plaza de San Francisco; guided tour Mon-Thu €4, Sat free; ⏲tours 7pm & 8pm Mon-Thu, 10am Sat), whose southeastern walls boast some lovely Renaissance carvings from the 1520–30s.

Calle Sierpes STREET

(Map p644) Pedestrianised Calle Sierpes, heading north from Plaza de San Francisco, and the parallel Calle Tetuán/Velázquez form the heart of Seville's main shopping district. Lined with chain stores, family-run shops, the occasional independent boutique, and frozen drinks outlets, they're busiest between 6pm and 9pm.

Museo de Bellas Artes MUSEUM

(Fine Arts Museum; Map p644; ☎955 54 29 42; www.museodebellasartesdesevilla.es; Plaza del Museo 9; EU citizens/other free/€1.50; ⏲9am-8pm Tue-Sat, to 3pm Sun mid-Sep–mid-Jun, 9am-3pm Tue-Sun mid-Jun–mid-Sep) Housed in the beautiful former Convento de la Merced, Seville's Fine Arts Museum provides an elegant showcase for a comprehensive collection of Spanish and Sevillan paintings and sculptures. Works date from the 15th to 20th centuries, but the onus is very much on brooding religious paintings from the city's 17th-century *Siglo de Oro* (Golden Age).

El Arenal & Triana

Hugging the Río Guadalquivir to the west of Santa Cruz, the compact El Arenal district boasts plenty of lively bars and the city's historic bullring. In times past, this was where colonising *caballeros* (gentlemen) made rich on New World gold stalked the streets, watched over by Spanish galleons offloading their American booty.

Over the river on the west bank of the Guadalquivir is the legendary *barrio* of Triana. This atmospheric quarter, famous for its ceramic tiles, was once home to many of Seville's most quintessential bullfighting and flamenco characters and it still hosts some of its most evocative sights.

Plaza de Toros de la Real Maestranza BULLRING, MUSEUM

(Map p644; ☎954 22 45 77; www.realmaestranza.com; Paseo de Cristóbal Colón 12; tours adult/child €8/3; ⏲half hourly 9.30am-9pm, to 3pm bullfight days) In the world of bullfighting, Seville's bullring is the Old Trafford and Camp Nou. In other words, if you're selected to fight here, you've made it. In addition to being regarded as a building of almost religious significance to fans, it's also the oldest ring in Spain (building began in 1758) and it was here, along with the bullring in Ronda, that bullfighting on foot began in the 18th century. A visit here is a way to learn about this deep-rooted tradition without witnessing a bullfight.

Hospital de la Caridad MUSEUM
(Map p644; ☎954 22 32 32; www.santa-caridad.es; Calle Temprado 3; €5; ⏰10.30am-7.30pm Mon-Sat, 10.30am-1pm & 2.30-7.30pm Sun) The Hospital de la Caridad, a large sturdy building one block east of the river, was established in the late 17th century as a hospice for the poor and elderly. It was founded by Miguel de Mañara, by legend a notorious libertine who supposedly changed his ways after seeing a vision of his own funeral procession.

The Hospital's headline act is its gilded chapel, decorated with works by several Golden Age painters and sculptors, most notably Murillo and Roldán.

Torre del Oro TOWER, MUSEUM
(Map p644; Paseo de Cristóbal Colón; adult/reduced €3/1.50, Mon free; ⏰9.30am-6.45pm Mon-Fri, 10.30am-6.45pm Sat & Sun) One of Seville's signature landmarks, this 13th-century riverside watchtower was the last great building constructed by the Muslims in the city. Part of a larger defensive complex, it supposedly had gilded tiles, hence its name, 'Tower of Gold', although some dispute this, claiming the name is a reference to the fact that conquistadors returning from Mexico and Peru used the tower to store booty they'd siphoned off colonial coffers. Today, it hosts a small maritime museum and a rooftop viewing platform.

Castillo de San Jorge MUSEUM
(Map p640; ☎954 33 22 40; Plaza del Altozano; ⏰11am-5.30pm Tue-Sat, 10am-2.30pm Sun) FREE Adjacent to the Isabel II bridge in Triana, the Castillo de San Jorge is steeped in notoriety for it was here that the infamous Spanish Inquisition had its headquarters from 1481 to 1785. When the Inquisition fires were finally doused in the early 19th century, the castle was destroyed and a market built over the top. Its foundations were rediscovered in 1990, and what's left of the castle today houses a museum charting the Inquisition's activities and life in the *castillo*.

Centro Cerámica Triana MUSEUM
(Map p640; ☎954 34 15 82; Calle Antillano Campos 14; €2.10; ⏰11am-5.30pm Tue-Sat, 10am-2.30pm Sun) Opened in 2014, this smart Triana museum is an attempt to rekindle the flames that once lit the kilns of the neighbourhood's erstwhile ceramic industry. It cleverly mixes the methodology and history of ceramic production with the wider history of Triana and its people.

South of the Centre

South of Santa Cruz and El Centro, the city opens out into expansive parks and broad boulevards that in recent years have been reclaimed by trams, bikes and strollers. The chief attraction here is the Parque de María Luisa, the city's main park, and the extravagant Plaza de España.

★**Parque de María Luisa** PARK
(Map p640; ⏰8am-10pm Sep-Jun, to midnight Jul & Aug; 👪🐾) A delightful oasis of green, the extensive Parque de María Luisa is a lovely place to escape the noise of the city, with duck ponds, snoozing *sevillanos* and shady paths snaking under the trees.

If you'd rather continue your cultural exploration than commune with the flowers, the park contains several notable drawcards. Chief among them is Plaza de España. A vast, brick-and-tile confection, it features fountains, mini-canals, and a series of tile pictures depicting historical scenes. You can hire row boats to pootle around the canals for €6 (for 35 minutes).

In the south of the park, the **Museo Arqueológico** (Map p640; ☎955 12 06 32; Plaza de América, Parque de María Luisa; EU citizens/other free/€1.50; ⏰9am-8pm Tue-Sat, to 3pm Sun mid-Sep–mid-Jun, 9am-3pm Tue-Sun mid-Jun–mid-Sep) boasts some wonderful Roman sculptures, mosaics and statues – many gathered from the nearby site of Itálica.

Opposite is the **Museo de Artes y Costumbres Populares** (Map p640; ☎955 54 29 51; Plaza de América 3, Parque de María Luisa; EU citizens/other free/€1.50; ⏰9am-8pm Tue-Sat, to 3pm Sun mid-Sep–mid-Jun, 9am-3pm Tue-Sun mid-Jun–mid-Sep), dedicated to local customs, costumes and traditions.

The park is a great place for children to let off steam and families to bond over a bike ride – four-person quad bikes are available to hire for €12 per half-hour.

★**Plaza de España** SQUARE
(Map p640; Avenida de Portugal, Parque de María Luisa) This bombastic plaza in the Parque de María Luisa was the most grandiose of the building projects completed for the 1929 Exposición Iberoamericana. A huge brick-and-tile confection, it's all very over the top, but it's undeniably impressive with its fountains, mini-canals and Venetian-style bridges. A series of gaudy tile pictures depict maps and historical scenes from each Spanish province.

Antigua Fábrica de Tabacos HISTORIC BUILDING
(Map p644; ☎954 55 10 00; Calle San Fernando; ⊙8am-9pm Mon-Fri, to 2pm Sat, free tours 11am Mon-Thu) FREE Now home to the University of Seville, this massive former tobacco factory – workplace of Bizet's fictional heroine, Carmen – was built in the 18th century and is said to be the second-largest building in Spain after the El Escorial monastery complex northwest of Madrid.

You can wander in at will or partake in a free tour at 11am Monday to Thursday. Meet in the main lobby.

Hotel Alfonso XIII LANDMARK
(Map p644; Calle San Fernando 2) As much a local landmark as an accommodation option, this striking, only-in-Seville hotel – conceived as the most luxurious in Europe when it was built in 1928 – was constructed in tandem with Plaza de España for the 1929 world fair. Ring-fenced by towering palm trees, it sports a classic neo-Mudéjar look complete with glazed tiles and terracotta bricks.

North of the Centre

To the north of El Centro, the Alameda de Hércules area is one of the city's coolest and most vibrant districts, crammed with trendy bars, chic shops and popular eateries. Facing it across the river is the Isla de la Cartuja, site of a historic monastery and the 1992 Expo.

Palacio de los Marqueses de la Algaba HISTORIC BUILDING, MUSEUM
(Map p640; ☎955 47 20 97; Plaza Calderón de la Barca; ⊙10am-2pm & 6-9pm Mon-Fri, to 2pm Sat Apr-Oct, 10am-2pm & 5-8pm Mon-Fri, to 2pm Sat Nov-Mar) FREE One of Seville's classic Mudéjar-style palaces, complete with lovely central courtyard, this historic mansion houses the Centro de la Interpretación Mudéjar, a small museum showcasing Mudéjar relics from the 12th to the 20th centuries. Though the collection gets a little lost in the wonderfully restored mansion, the captions (in Spanish and English) do a good job of explaining the nuances of the complex Mudéjar style.

Basílica de La Macarena BASILICA
(Map p640; ☎954 90 18 00; Calle Bécquer 1; basilica/museum free/€5; ⊙9am-2.30pm & 6-9.30pm Mon-Sat, 9am-2pm & 6-9pm Sun) This mustard-yellow basilica is home to Seville's most revered religious treasure, the *Virgen de la Esperanza Macarena* (Macarena Virgin of Hope), popularly known as the Macarena. This magnificent statue, a star of the city's fervent Semana Santa (Holy Week) celebrations, stands in splendour behind the main altarpiece, adorned with a golden crown, lavish vestments and five diamond-and-emerald brooches donated by the famous 20th-century matador Joselito El Gallo.

Centro Andaluz de Arte Contemporáneo MUSEUM
(Map p640; ☎955 03 70 70; www.caac.es; Camino de los Descubrimientos; temporary exhibition €1.80, complete visit €3, 7-9pm Tue-Fri & all day Sat free; ⊙11am-9pm Tue-Sat, 10am-3.30pm Sun) This historic but offbeat site was once a monastery, then a ceramics factory, and is today the Centro Andaluz de Arte Contemporáneo, Seville's shrine to modern art with temporary exhibitions set alongside some truly bizarre permanent pieces. You can't miss *Alicia*, by Cristina Lucas, a massive head and arm poking through two old monastery windows that was supposedly inspired by *Alice in Wonderland*, though you could be forgiven for walking obliviously past Pedro Mora's *Bus Stop*, which looks exactly like...well, a bus stop.

Pabellón de la Navegación MUSEUM
(Map p640; ☎954 04 31 11; www.pabellondelanavegacion.es; Camino de los Descubrimientos 2; adult/child €4.90/3.50; ⊙11am-8.30pm Tue-Sat, to 3pm Sun Sep-Jun, 10am-3.30pm daily Jul & Aug; 👪) This boxy concrete-and-glass pavilion on the banks of the Río Guadalquivir revived a previous navigation museum that had been here from the 1992 Expo until 1999. Its permanent collection is split into four parts – navigation, mariners, shipboard life and historical views of Seville – and although its exhibits are interactive and kid-friendly, they might be a little underwhelming for an adult. The ticket includes a ride up the adjacent **Torre Schindler** (Map p640).

Note that only temporary exhibitions are open on Mondays in July and August.

LOCAL KNOWLEDGE

CYCLING IN SEVILLE

Since the inauguration of the **Sevici** (☎900 900722; www.sevici.es) bike-sharing scheme in 2007, cycling in Seville has taken off in a big way. The scheme has been a major success and it remains one of the largest of its kind in Europe with 2500 bikes and 250 docking stations.

Most of Sevici's users are locals, but visitors can use bikes by getting a seven-day subscription for €13.33 (plus a €150 returnable deposit). To register, go to a Sevici docking station and follow the on-screen instructions. Seville has 130km of bike lanes (all painted green and equipped with their own traffic signals) and the first 30 minutes of usage are free. Beyond that, it's €1.03 for the first hour and €2.04 an hour thereafter.

Alternatively, a number of operators offer bike tours, including Pancho Tours (p650), whose 2½-hour rides cost €25.

Activities

Aire Baños Árabes HAMMAM

(Map p644; ☎955 01 00 24; www.beaire.com; Calle Aire 15; bath/bath with massage from €33/49; ⊙10am-10pm Sun-Thu, to midnight Fri & Sat) These smart, Arabic-style baths win prizes for tranquil atmosphere, historic setting (in the Barrio de Santa Cruz) and Moroccan *riad*-style decor. Various bath and massage packages are available – see the website for details – for which it's always best to book a day or so in advance.

Courses

Seville is a great city in which to learn a new skill. Many overseas visitors take a Spanish-language course and there are dozens of schools offering lessons. Alternatively, you could release your inner performer at one of the city's flamenco and dance schools or brush up on Spanish cuisine on a cookery course.

Taller Andaluz de Cocina COOKING

(Map p640; ☎672 162621; www.tallerandaluzdecocina.com; Mercado de Triana, Plaza del Altozano; courses €35-55) Located in Triana market, this cooking school offers a range of hands-on courses covering classic Spanish cuisine and tapas as well as tastings and guided market tours. Check the website for further details.

Taller Flamenco DANCING, LANGUAGE

(Map p640; ☎954 56 42 34; www.tallerflamenco.com; Calle Peral 49) Offers flamenco dance courses, singing and guitar lessons, and language classes with the possibility of being taught in groups or on a one-to-one basis. A one-week semi-intensive language course costs €102; for a one-week flamenco course for beginners reckon on €259.

CLIC LANGUAGE

(International House; Map p644; ☎954 50 21 31; www.clic.es; Calle Albareda 19) A well-established language centre headquartered in a pleasant house with a good social scene and adjacent bookshop. Courses are available for children, adults and seniors with prices starting at €190 for a week-long course of 20 lessons. Accommodation can also be arranged.

Fundación Cristina Heeren de Arte Flamenco DANCING

(Map p644; ☎954 21 70 58; www.flamencoheeren.com; Calle Pureza 76; workshops €60-80) Seville's best-known flamenco school offers a range of courses and workshops in singing, dancing and guitar playing. Reckon on €60 to €80 for a 90-minute workshop; €2000 for an intensive summer course.

Tours

★**Pancho Tours** TOURS

(☎664 642904; www.panchotours.com) FREE Runs excellent free tours, although you're welcome to tip the hard-working guide who'll furnish you with an encyclopedia's worth of anecdotes, stories, myths and theories about Seville's fascinating past. Tours kick off daily, normally at 11am – check the website for exact details. Pancho also offers bike tours (€25), skip-the-line cathedral and Alcázar visits (€15,) and nightlife tours (€10 to €15).

Mimo Sevilla FOOD

(Map p644; ☎854 55 68 00; www.sevilla.mimofood.com/en; Calle San Fernando 2; tours €60-285) This professional set-up, based at the Hotel Alfonso XIII (p649), offers wine tastings, cooking classes, tapas tours and day trips, including to the sherry city of Jerez. Bank on

€95 for a three-hour tapas tour, €60 for two hours of wine tasting. The shop has excellent gourmet products such as extra-virgin olive oil, squid ink and dehydrated caviar.

Past View TOURS
(Map p644; ☎954 32 66 46; www.pastview.es; Plaza de la Encarnación; tours €15; ⏲10.30am Tue-Sun, 8pm Wed, Fri & Sat Jun-Sep, 11am Tue-Sun, 4.30pm Wed, Fri & Sat Oct-May;) This ingenious augmented-reality video tour takes you on a guided walk using 3D video glasses that recreate scenes from the past in the actual locations they happened. The ticket office and starting point is in the Metropol Parasol (p643) and the two-hour walk (with a guide) proceeds through Seville's main sights to the Torre del Oro (p648).

Cruceros Torre del Oro CRUISE
(Map p644; ☎954 56 16 92; www.crucerostorredeloro.com; adult/child €16/free; ⏲11am-10pm May-Sep, to 7pm Oct-Apr;) One-hour river cruises run every half hour from 11am, departing from the river bank by the Torre del Oro (p648). Last departure ranges from 7pm in winter to 10pm in summer.

Festivals & Events

Semana Santa RELIGIOUS
(www.semana-santa.org; ⏲Mar/Apr) Seville's Holy Week celebrations are legendary. Every day from Palm Sunday to Easter Sunday, large, life-size *pasos* (sculptural representations of events from Christ's Passion) are solemnly carried from the city's churches to the cathedral, accompanied by processions of marching *nazarenos* (penitents).

Adding to the sombre atmosphere are the white robes and sinister conical hats the penitents wear – a look that was incongruously copied by America's Ku Klux Klan.

The processions, which culminate in the *madrugada* (early hours) of Good Friday, are organised by more than 50 different *hermandades* or *cofradías* (brotherhoods, some of which include women).

Schedules are widely available during Semana Santa, or on the Semana Santa website. Arrive near the cathedral in the early evening for the best views.

Feria de Abril FERIA
(www.turismosevilla.org; ⏲Apr) The largest and most colourful of all Andalucía's *ferias* (fairs), Seville's week-long spring fair is held in the second half of the month (sometimes edging into May) on El Real de la Feria, in the Los Remedios area west of the Río Guadalquivir.

For six nights, *sevillanos* dress up in elaborate finery, parade around in horse-drawn carriages, eat, drink and dance till dawn.

Bienal de Flamenco DANCE
(www.labienal.com; ⏲Sep) The big names of the flamenco world descend on Seville for this major flamenco festival. Held in September in even-numbered years, it features a comprehensive program of events including performances, exhibitions and workshops.

Sleeping

There's a good selection of hotels, hostels and *pensiones* in the three most atmospheric areas: Barrio de Santa Cruz (walkable from Prado de San Sebastián bus station), El Arenal and El Centro (both nearer Plaza de Armas bus station).

Expect high season rates March to June and in September and October. Rates also skyrocket during Semana Santa and the Feria de Abril, for which you'll have to book well in advance.

Cathedral Area

EME Catedral Hotel DESIGN HOTEL $$$
(Map p644; ☎954 56 00 00; www.emecatedralhotel.com; Calle de los Alemanes 27; d €180-411, ste €274-609;) Marrying contemporary design with a fabulous location and stunning close-ups of Seville's mammoth Gothic cathedral, the EME impresses on all fronts. The hotel occupies the shell of 14 fine old Sevillan houses, offering 60 slick modern rooms, the best with cathedral views, and fine facilities including a rooftop bar, pool, wellness centre and several restaurants.

Barrio de Santa Cruz

Casual Sevilla Don Juan Tenorio HOTEL $$
(Map p644; ☎955 54 44 16; www.casualhoteles.com/hoteles-sevilla/casual-don-juan-tenorio; Plaza de los Venerables 5; d €77-155;) At this cheerful hotel, in the heart of Barrio Santa Cruz, each room is themed after a character from *Don Juan Tenorio*, with quirky lights and stone-effect wall coverings. Although it's only two-star, the hotel has excellent wi-fi, hydromassage showers and wall-mounted TVs; the genius mobile-phone pack features router, battery charger and selfie stick to loan.

Hostal Plaza Santa Cruz HOTEL $$

(Map p644; 954 22 88 08; www.hostalplazasantacruz.com; Calle Santa Teresa 15; d €40-95;) Offering decent value and a lovely location in the Barrio de Santa Cruz, this modest outfit has rooms spread over several sites. Those in the main hotel, just off Plaza Santa Cruz, are unflashy with laminated parquet floors and the occasional blast of colourful wallpaper, whilst those in its nearby apartments are slightly more upmarket with tiles, artworks and heavy wooden furniture.

★Hotel Amadeus BOUTIQUE HOTEL $$$

(Map p644; 954 50 14 43; www.hotelamadeussevilla.com; Calle Farnesio 6; d €92-185, tr €121-325, q €180-355;) A musical oasis in the heart of the old *judería* (Jewish quarter) district, this elegant hotel exudes a sense of calm with its ceramic-tiled lobby, white walls, period furniture and artfully displayed musical instruments. Rooms, named after composers, are equally stylish and there's a small panoramic terrace offering views over to the Giralda.

Un Patio en Santa Cruz HOTEL $$$

(Map p644; 807 31 70 70; www.patiosantacruz.com; Calle Doncellas 15; s €55-185, d €70-200;) Feeling more like a gallery than a hotel, this place has stark white walls hung with bright works of art and lofty pot plants. The summery rooms, complete with parquet and dashes of purple, are good looking and comfortable, staff are friendly, and there's a cool rooftop terrace with Moroccan-mosaic tables.

★Hotel Casa 1800 LUXURY HOTEL $$$

(Map p644; 954 56 18 00; www.hotelcasa1800sevilla.com; Calle Rodrigo Caro 6; d €120-650;) A short hop from the cathedral in the heart of Santa Cruz, this stately *casa* (house) is positively regal. Setting the tone is the elegant, old-school decor – wooden ceilings, chandeliers, parquet floors, and plenty of gilt – but everything about the place charms, from the helpful staff to the rooftop terrace and complimentary afternoon tea.

El Centro

Oasis Backpackers' Hostel HOSTEL $

(Map p644; 955 26 26 96; www.oasissevilla.com; Calle Almirante Ulloa 1; dm €13-40, d €45-150;) A veritable oasis in the busy city-centre district, this welcoming hostel is set in a palatial 19th-century mansion. There are various sleeping options ranging from mixed 14-person dorms to doubles with en-suite bathrooms, and excellent facilities, including a cafe-bar, kitchen and rooftop deck with a small pool. Breakfast, not included in most rates, is available for €3.50.

★Hotel Casa de Colón BOUTIQUE HOTEL $$

(Map p644; 955 11 78 28; www.hotelcasadecolon.com; Calle Hernando Colón 3; d €65-180;) This small, family-owned hotel stands out for its superbly central location between the cathedral and city hall; warm, friendly service; and quirky architectural and decorative features: white cast-iron pillars in the bright patio, cobalt-blue stained-glass in the neo-Mudéjar windows. Some rooms have exposed-brick walls and side views of the cathedral; top-floor *aticos* have private terraces. Continental breakfast is available for €8.

Hotel Abanico HOTEL $$

(Map p644; 954 21 32 07; www.hotelabanico.com; Calle Águilas 17; s €47-95, d €47-125;) From the beautiful, vaulted lobby to the distinctive tilework, wrought-iron balconies and radiant religious art, this welcoming hotel has Seville written all over it. Rooms are simple affairs with pronounced colours and modest, old-school furniture.

Hotel Boutique Doña Lola BOUTIQUE HOTEL $$

(Map p640; 954 91 52 75; www.donalolasevilla.com; Calle Amor de Dios 19; s €36-63, d €40-135;) Ensconced in an ordinary-looking tenement in El Centro, gay-friendly Doña Lola is a little haven of modernity and well positioned for sorties pretty much everywhere. From the lobby, complete with a coloured chequered floor, stairs lead to guest rooms which, although small, are modern and surgically clean.

El Arenal & Triana

★La Banda HOSTEL $

(Map p644; 955 22 81 18; www.labandahostel.com; Calle Dos de Mayo 16; dm €18-38;) Run by a young, energetic crew, this Arenal hostel ticks all the boxes. Its mixed dorms are clean and tidily furnished, communal areas are relaxed and inviting, and best of all, it has a great rooftop bar. Evening meals are available at 9pm and a weekly program of events ensures there's always something going on.

Hotel Adriano HOTEL $$

(Map p644; 954 29 38 00; www.adrianohotel.com; Calle de Adriano 12; s €70-80, d €80-150;

(P ❄ ☎) In the Arenal neighbourhood near the bullring, the three-star Adriano scores across the board with friendly staff, traditional, individually styled rooms and a lovely coffee shop, Pompeia, on the ground floor. Garage parking is available for €18 per day.

North of the Centre

Corner House HOTEL $$
(Map p640; ☎954 91 32 62; www.thecornerhousesevilla.com; Alameda de Hércules 31; d €45-100; ❄ ☎) Opened in 2016, this friendly newcomer sits well with the buzzing bars and cafes on the Alameda de Hércules. Modern in look and upbeat in vibe, it offers sun-filled rooms with minimal, low-key decor and wet-room style bathrooms. To eat and drink, there's a ground-floor restaurant, El Disparate, and, up top, a chilled rooftop bar (p656).

Hotel San Gil HOTEL $$
(Map p640; ☎954 90 68 11; www.hotelsangil.com; Calle Parras 28; d €65-180; ❄ ☎ ≋) Shoehorned at the northern end of the Macarena neighbourhood, San Gil's slightly out-of-the-way location is balanced by its proximity to the nightlife of the Alameda de Hércules. Behind the mustard-yellow colonial facade, an ostentatiously tiled lobby fronts plain but modern rooms with large beds and ample space.

Hotel Sacristía de Santa Ana BOUTIQUE HOTEL $$$
(Map p640; ☎954 91 57 22; www.hotelsacristia.com; Alameda de Hércules 22; d €95-250; ❄ ☎) This delightful hotel, superbly positioned for the buzzing bars and eateries on the Alameda de Hércules, makes a fabulous first impression. On entering you're greeted by a splendid red-tiled courtyard centred on a small fountain and overlooked by carved wooden balustrades. Up from here, hallways lead to old-fashioned rooms furnished with arty bedsteads, beamed ceilings and cascading showers.

Eating

It's not hard to eat well in Seville. The city is brimming with bars, cafes, restaurants and markets ranging from centuries-old watering holes serving traditional tapas to hip gourmet joints cooking up innovative contemporary dishes. Bar hotspots include the Barrio de Santa Cruz, the streets around Plaza de la Alfalfa and the Alameda de Hércules. Note that some restaurants close for part of August.

Barrio de Santa Cruz

Bodega Santa Cruz TAPAS $
(Map p644; ☎954 21 86 18; Calle Rodrigo Caro 1; tapas €2; ⏰8am-midnight) This is as old-school as it gets, a perennially busy bar staffed by gruff waiters and frequented by locals and visitors alike. Its fiercely traditional tapas are best enjoyed alfresco with a cold beer as you watch the passing armies of Santa Cruz tourists traipse past.

Vinería San Telmo TAPAS $$
(Map p644; ☎954 41 06 00; www.vineriasantelmo.com; Paseo Catalina de Ribera 4; tapas €2.90-5.80, medias raciones €6.90-14.20; ⏰10.30am-4.30pm & 8-11.30pm) San Telmo's own brand of innovative tapas has proved a hit with diners, and tables in the salmon-orange and brick interior are a prized commodity. Bag one, for which you'll either have to wait or book, and you'll be sitting down to the likes of crispy bread-crumbed prawns with soy mayonnaise or foie gras with vanilla oil and caramelised peanuts.

Casa Tomate TAPAS $$
(Map p644; ☎954 22 04 21; Calle Mateos Gago 24; tapas €3-4.50, raciones €8.50-17; ⏰noon-midnight) Hams swing from ceiling hooks, old posters are etched with art-nouveau and art-deco designs, and outdoor blackboards relay what's cooking in the kitchen of Casa Tomate. It's a touristy spot, but don't let that put you off what is a fine tapas bar serving the likes of fried aubergine sticks sweetened with honey and succulent grilled calamari with pesto.

Café Bar Las Teresas TAPAS $$
(Map p644; ☎954 21 30 69; www.lasteresas.es; Calle Santa Teresa 2; tapas €3.50, mains €8-14; ⏰10am-1am) The hanging hams look as ancient as the bar itself, a sinuous wraparound affair with a cheerfully cluttered interior and wonky wooden tables outside. Not surprisingly, the menu is highly traditional, featuring staples such as fried *bacalao* (salted cod) and hearty *salchichón ibérico* (sausage).

El Centro

Bolas ICE CREAM $
(Map p644; ☎954 22 74 11; www.bolasheladosartesanos.com; Cuesta del Rosario 1; €2.50-4.40; ⏰1pm-midnight) If you're wilting in the

summer heat, or even if you're not, an ice cream from Bolas makes for a refreshing treat. Choose from a selection of classic fruit flavours or opt for something more exotic – perhaps La Medina, a sorbet of orange, ginger and cinnamon, or the strange sounding goat's cheese and quince jelly.

Sal Gorda ANDALUCIAN **$**

(Map p644; ☎955 38 59 72; www.facebook.com/SalGordaSevilla; Calle Alcaicería de la Loza 23; tapas €2.50-8.50; ⊙1-4.30pm & 8-11.30pm Wed-Mon) Incongruously located in an old shoe shop – you sit in the plate glass window – this tiny, low-key place serves innovative takes on Andalucian dishes – strawberry gazpacho with pistachios, and a first-class version of the ubiquitous tuna *tataki*. Chicken kimchi is a firm favourite, and the wine list features good local whites such as El Mirlo Blanco from Constantina.

El Rinconcillo TAPAS **$**

(Map p644; ☎954 22 31 83; www.elrinconcillo.es; Calle Gerona 40; tapas €2.20-3.50, raciones €5.50-13; ⊙1pm-1.30am) The blueprint for centuries' worth of imitators, this is the oldest bar in Seville – and some say, Spain – dating to 1670. Over the years, it's become pretty touristy, but it's managed to retain a gnarled sense of authenticity and its woody, tiled interior sets a memorable backdrop for classic tapas.

★Mamarracha TAPAS **$$**

(Map p644; ☎955 12 39 11; www.mamarracha.es; Calle Hernando Colón 1-3; tapas €2.20-8, mains €6.50-16; ⊙1.30pm-midnight) Ideal for a lunch after a morning visit to the cathedral, this is a fine example of the modern tapas bars that Seville so excels at. Its interior is a handsome mix of blond wood, bare cement surfaces and exposed ducts, whilst its menu reveals some adventurous combos, including a terrific foie gras and orange dish.

★La Azotea FUSION, ANDALUCIAN **$$**

(Map p640; ☎955 11 67 48; www.laazoteasevilla.com; Calle Conde de Barajas 13; tapas €3.75-6.50, raciones €11-19; ⊙1.30-4.30pm & 8.30pm-midnight Tue-Sat) Fashionable and much recommended by locals, Azotea is one of Seville's stable of modern eateries with culinary ambitions. Its pearl-grey Scandi-inspired interior sets the scene for artfully plated tapas and contemporary creations such as tomato, *burrata* and lemon sorbet salad. Note there are three other branches across town, including one near the cathedral at Calle Mateos Gago 8.

Bar Europa TAPAS **$$**

(Map p644; ☎954 21 79 08; Calle Siete Revueltas 35; tapas €3.50-4.80, media raciones €6.50-15; ⊙8.30am-4.30pm & 7.30pm-12.30am) An old-school bar with a classic tiled interior and a few alfresco tables, Bar Europa has been knocking out tapas since 1925. Notwithstanding, it isn't afraid to experiment and it serves some excellent modern creations such as grilled mackerel with a strawberry and radish tartar and sweet nut bread with foie gras, mushrooms and crunchy ham.

laCava.bar TAPAS **$$**

(Map p644; ☎954 53 16 52; www.lacava.bar; Calle Hernando Colón 12; tapas €3.50-12; ⊙12.30pm-midnight Sun-Thu, to 1am Fri & Sat) Original tapas, a relaxed, unpretentious atmosphere and a prime central location, laCava is one of the better options in the city's touristy centre. It gets very busy at lunchtime but bag a perch and you'll be rewarded with a choice of classic tapas staples and more creative efforts such as strawberry gazpacho and herbed fish ceviche.

Perro Viejo FUSION **$$**

(Map p644; ☎955 44 00 30; www.equipompuntor.com/perro-viejo; Calle Arguijo 3; tapas €4, mains €9-19; ⊙1.30-4.30pm & 8pm-midnight) Fusing the lively buzz of a Seville tapas bar with an upbeat New York loft vibe, this three-storey emporium has well-priced Asian and Andalucian dishes, plus decent local craft beer and wine. Pork dumplings, marinaded sardines and ceviche are among the perennial crowd pleasers. Perfectly placed on a quiet side street for post-shopping lunch, complete with a sun-soaker's outdoor terrace.

El Arenal & Triana

★La Brunilda TAPAS **$**

(Map p644; ☎954 22 04 81; www.labrunildatapas.com; Calle Galera 5; tapas €3.20-7.50; ⊙1-4pm & 8.30-11.30pm Tue-Sat, 1-4pm Sun) A regular fixture on lists of Seville's best tapas joints, this backstreet Arenal bar is at the forefront of the city's new wave of gourmet eateries. The look is modern casual with big blue doors, brick arches and plain wooden tables and the food is imaginative and good looking. The word is out, though, so arrive promptly or expect to queue.

★Manu Jara Dulcería PASTRIES $
(Map p640; ☎675 873674; Calle Pureza 5; pastries €1.15-2.80; ⏰10am-3pm daily & 6-9.30pm Mon-Fri, 4-9.30pm Sat) Tradition, history, flamenco – forget all that. The real reason to cross the river to Triana is to visit this exquisite patisserie and stock up on heavenly cakes. These mini-masterpieces are laid out in ceremonial splendour in the traditional wood and tiled interior, just demanding to be eaten. Try the creamy *milohajas* (mille-feuille, aka vanilla slice) with chantilly cream.

Mercado Lonja del Barranco INTERNATIONAL $
(Map p640; www.mercadodelbarranco.com; Calle Arjona; snacks from €2; ⏰10am-midnight Sun-Thu, to 2am Fri & Sat) A food court in a handsome glass-and-wrought-iron pavilion near the Isabel II bridge, with stalls serving everything from seafood salads and avocado wraps to tortillas, cakes and craft beer. Browse through, load up and then tuck in at one of the shared tables. Out back, you can enjoy cocktails and soothing riverside breezes.

Casa Cuesta TAPAS $
(Map p640; ☎954 33 33 35; www.casacuesta.net; Calle de Castilla 1; tapas €3, medias raciones €7.50-10; ⏰8am-12.30am Mon-Fri, 9am-12.30am Sat, 12.30pm-12.30am Sun) Plate-glass windows look out onto a crowded Triana plaza, mirrors artfully reflect bullfighting and flamenco memorabilia, and gleaming beer pumps fur nish a wooden bar shielding bottles that look older than most of the clientele. In keeping with its looks, the food is traditional with a good selection of tapas, rice dishes, and meat and fish *raciones*.

Zoko ANDALUCIAN $$
(Map p644; ☎954 96 31 49; www.facebook.com/zokosevilla; Calle Marqués de Paradas 55; tapas from €4.50; ⏰1-4pm & 8pm-midnight) The fishing town of Zahara de los Atunes on the Cádiz coast is famed for its superb sustainably caught bluefin tuna *(atun de almadraba)* – this is the Seville outpost of one of its top restaurants, Zokarra. As well as the tenderest tuna, which comes in tacos, *tataki* and empanadas, the prawn satay has a bite unusual in spice-averse Spain.

North of the Centre

Mercado de Feria MARKET $
(Lonja de Feria; Map p640; www.lonjadeferia.com; Plaza Calderón de la Barca; tapas €3, mains €8; ⏰1pm-midnight Mon-Sat, to 6pm Sun) For a casual, great-value meal in atmospheric surrounds, head up to this Macarena market, said to be the oldest in Seville. Tapas and mountainous mains, mostly fresh seafood but not exclusively so, are dished out in a cool, white food hall set around a large central island. To order, buy a ticket then hand it in to one of the cheerful ladies skilfully working the counters.

Dúo Tapas TAPAS $
(Map p640; ☎955 23 85 72; Calle Calatrava 10; tapas €3-4.50, medias raciones €8-12; ⏰12.30-4.30pm & 8.30pm-midnight) Missed by the masses who rarely wander north from the Alameda de Hércules, Duo Tapas is a casual, 'new school' tapas bar. But, what it lacks in *azulejo* (tiles) and illustrious past patrons, it makes up for with inventive tapas with an Asian twist such as noodles with veggies and shrimp spring rolls.

★conTenedor ANDALUCIAN $$
(Map p640; ☎954 91 63 33; www.restaurantecontenedor.com; Calle San Luis 50; mains €9-21; ⏰1.30-4pm & 8.30-11.30pm Mon-Thu, 1.30-4.30pm & 8.30pm-midnight Fri-Sun, closed Aug) This slow-food restaurant in the boho Macarena district prides itself on using local, organic produce. The atmosphere is arty and relaxed, with an open kitchen, mismatched furniture and colourful contemporary paintings by co-owner Ricardo. Try the duck rice, justly famous for its perfect taste and texture, or the venison *tataki* with chard, mushrooms and sweet potato.

★Bar-Restaurante Eslava FUSION, ANDALUCIAN $$
(Map p640; ☎954 90 65 68; www.espacioeslava.com; Calle Eslava 3; tapas €2.90-4.20, restaurant mains €15-22; ⏰bar 1-4.30pm & 7.30-11.30pm Tue-Sat, 1.30-4.30pm Sun, restaurant 1.30-4pm & 9-11.30pm Tue-Sat, 1.30-4pm Sun) A hit with locals and savvy visitors, much-lauded Eslava shirks the traditional tilework and bullfighting posters of tapas-bar lore in favour of a simple blue space and a menu of creative contemporary dishes. Standouts include slow-cooked egg served on a mushroom cake, and memorable pork ribs in a honey and rosemary glaze. Expect crowds and a buzzing atmosphere.

Next door, the smarter restaurant shares the same kitchen.

Arte y Sabor TAPAS $$
(Map p640; ☎954 37 28 97; www.arteysabor.es; Alameda de Hércules 85; tapas €2.90-4.50,

raciones €7.50-14; ⊙1pm-midnight; ☑) People-watching and eating go hand in hand at this casual eatery on the Alameda de Hércules. Grab a table – though you'll need to come early – and go vegetarian with classic North African–inspired dishes such as tabbouleh and felafel or stick to traditional Spanish staples such as pork loin with *serrano* ham.

Drinking & Nightlife

Cafes and bars are a fundamental part of Sevillan life and you'll have no trouble finding somewhere to drink. Popular areas abound, including Calle Betis in Triana, Plaza de Salvador, Barrio de Santa Cruz, and the Alameda de Hércules, host to a lively scene and the city's gay nightlife. In summer, dozens of *terrazas de verano* (open-air bars) pop up on the river's banks.

★El Viajero Sedentario CAFE
(Map p640; ☎677 535512; www.elviajeroseden tario.jimdo.com; Alameda de Hércules 77; ⊙9am-2pm & 6pm-2am) With its bright murals, shady courtyard and tiny book-stacked interior, this boho book cafe is a lovely place to hang out. From breakfast to the early hours people stop by, and it's not uncommon to find people dancing to low-key jazz tunes on sultry summer nights.

Gallo Rojo CAFE, BAR
(Map p640; ☎628 056489; http://gallorojo.es; Calle Madre Maria de Purisima 9; ⊙5pm-midnight Tue-Thu & Sun, to 2am Fri-Sat) A bar, cafe, gallery, co-working space and cultural centre, Gallo Rojo is a lively yet laid-back spot near Calle Feria which has events every night, from concerts to poetry readings. Settle into a vintage leather sofa and try the house craft beers, Zurda golden ale and Pallaksch IPA; more Sevillan brews are on offer, plus homemade cakes and empanadas.

Maquila MICROBREWERY
(Map p640; ☎955 18 23 20; www.maquilabar.com; Calle Delgado 4; ⊙1-4.30pm & 8pm-midnight Tue-Sun) Craft beer is big in Seville, so why not try a microbrewery? The six different beers on tap here change monthly – three in-house Son beers, which might include fruity numbers made from pineapple and coconut, or blackberry, plus guest brews from the US and Europe. To accompany them there are decent tapas, including crunchy, smoky *patatas bravas* (roasted potatoes in a spicy tomato sauce).

Rooftop Bar EME Catedral ROOFTOP BAR
(Map p644; www.emecatedralhotel.com; Calle de los Alemanes 27; ⊙noon-1am Sun-Thu, to 2am Fri & Sat) Enjoy spectacular cathedral close-ups and classic cocktails (€14) at the chic roof terrace bar of the five-star EME Catedral Hotel (p651). To experience it at its most glamorous stop by on Friday or Saturday night when DJs spin tunes to the elegant crowd.

Corner House Roof Terrace Bar ROOFTOP BAR
(Map p640; ☎954 91 32 62; www.thecornerhouse sevilla.com; Alameda de Hércules 31; ⊙5.30pm-1am Wed-Sun winter, from 8.30pm summer) With its wooden decking, handmade tables and grandstand views over the vibrant, tree-lined plaza below, the laid-back rooftop terrace at the Corner House (p653) is a top spot to kick back and enjoy a cool evening drink.

☆ Entertainment

★Casa de la Memoria FLAMENCO
(Map p644; ☎954 56 06 70; www.casadela memoria.es; Calle Cuna 6; adult/child €18/10; ⊙10.30am-10.30pm, shows 6pm & 9pm) Housed in the old stables of the Palacio de la Condesa de Lebrija (p646), this cultural centre stages authentic, highly charged flamenco shows. On nightly, they are perennially popular and as space is limited, you'll need to reserve tickets a day or so in advance by calling or visiting the venue.

Naima Café Jazz JAZZ
(Map p640; ☎653 753976; Calle Trajano 47; ⊙8pm-3am) Popular, laid-back and mellow, this bar is an evergreen favourite for live jazz and blues, staged most nights. Drinks are reasonably priced and its tiny interior – you could easily find yourself squeezed in next to the drummer with a hi-hat crashing inches from your nose – ensures a humming vibe.

Teatro de la Maestranza CONCERT VENUE
(Map p644; ☎954 22 33 44; www.teatrodela maestranza.es; Paseo de Cristóbal Colón 22; concerts €8-20, opera €46-125) Home to Seville's Royal Symphony Orchestra, this modern theatre, inaugurated in 1991, stages a rich program of classical music concerts, opera and ballet by top Spanish and international performers. Check the website for upcoming dates.

Casa de la Guitarra FLAMENCO
(Map p644; ☎954 22 40 93; www.flamencoen sevilla.com; Calle Mesón del Moro 12; adult/child

€17/10; ⏲shows 7.30pm & 9pm) This is a tiny flamenco-only venue in Santa Cruz (no food or drinks served). Its two evening shows are intimate affairs with three on-stage performers and the audience squeezed into a small seating area flanked by display cases full of guitars. To guarantee a place, it's best to book ahead.

La Casa del Flamenco FLAMENCO
(Map p644; ☎954 50 05 95; www.lacasadelflamencosevilla.com; Calle Ximénez de Enciso 28; adult/child €18/10; ⏲shows 7pm autumn & winter, 8.30pm spring & summer) This beautiful patio in an old Sephardic Jewish mansion in Santa Cruz is home to La Casa del Flamenco. Shows, performed on a stage hemmed in by seating on three sides, are mesmerising.

Casa Anselma FLAMENCO
(Map p640; Calle Pagés del Corro 49; ⏲11.45pm-late Mon-Sat) True, the music is often more folkloric than flamenco, but this characterful Triana spot is the antithesis of a touristy flamenco *tablao*, with cheek-to-jowl crowds, zero amplification and spontaneous outbreaks of dancing. Beware: there's no sign of life until the doors open at around 11.45pm.

Fun Club LIVE MUSIC
(Map p640; ☎636 669023; www.funclubsevilla.com; Alameda de Hércules 86; €5-12; ⏲midnight-late Thu-Sat, from 9.30pm concert nights) Positively ancient by nightlife standards, the mythical Fun Club has been entertaining the nocturnal Alameda de Hércules crowd since the late 1980s. It still packs them in, hosting club nights and regular gigs – indie, rock, hip-hop.

Shopping

Seville's main shopping district is centred on Calles Sierpes, Velázquez/Tetuán and Cuna, north of Plaza Nueva. For a more alternative choice of shops, head for 'Soho Benita', the area around Calle Pérez Galdós and Calle Regina; also Calles Amor de Dios near the Alameda de Hércules.

Over the river, Triana is the place to shop for ceramic ware.

Libelula Shop CLOTHING
(Map p644; ☎954 22 28 19; www.libelulashop.com; Calle Cuna 45-49; ⏲10am-9pm Mon-Sat) A large fashion emporium spread over two floors and several houses, Libelula offers clothing and accessories for men, women and children. From kids pyjamas to fringed manta shawls, fine knits to sparkly tops, over 20 different designers cover all styles and tastes. The layout makes it inviting to browse, with rails suspended by ropes, and traditional light-filled courtyards.

Tarico FOOD & DRINKS
(Map p640; ☎954 02 68 03; www.facebook.com/TiendaTarico; Calle Amor de Dios 14; ⏲10am-2.30pm & 6.30-10pm) A pleasant, light-filled space near the Alameda, packed with (mostly Andalucian) craft beer, wine, cheese, olive oil, cold meats, pâté, honey and other foods made by small producers. Look out for goat's milk cheese from Huelva; award-winning Supremo extra-virgin olive oil from Jaén; and a kit for cooking rice with goose, complete with meat preserve and stock.

Caotica BOOKS
(Map p644; ☎955 54 19 66; www.facebook.com/espaciocaotica; Calle José Gestoso 8; ⏲10am-2pm & 5-9pm Mon-Sat) Downstairs in this multilevel bookstore you can have a coffee, fresh juice, or healthy breakfast of yoghurt with muesli and fruit; upstairs are endless shelves of tomes, from literary and popular novels, to comics, travel, art and architecture titles. The children's section has a gallery above a wooden tree, so they're up in their own world. Also quirky gifts.

Cerámica Triana CERAMICS
(Map p640; ☎954 33 21 79; Calle San Jorge 31; ⏲10am-9pm Mon-Fri, to 8pm Sat, 11am-6pm Sun) Seville specialises in distinctive *azulejos* (ceramic tiles) and they are best seen in the Triana neighbourhood, the historic hub of the city's ceramic industry. Cerámica Triana (previously called Cerámica Santa Ana) has been around for more than 50 years and its tiled shopfront is famous locally. Inside, you can browse shelves laden with decorative crockery, tiles, signs, crucifixes and figurines.

Information

Tourist information is readily available at official tourist offices throughout the city.

Airport Tourist Office (☎954 78 20 35; www.andalucia.org; Seville Airport; ⏲9am-7.30pm Mon-Fri, 9.30am-3pm Sat & Sun)

Tourist Office (Map p644; ☎954 21 00 05; www.turismosevilla.org; Plaza del Triunfo 1; ⏲9am-7.30pm Mon-Fri, 9.30am-7.30pm Sat & Sun)

Train Station Tourist Office (☎954 78 20 02; www.andalucia.org; Estación Santa Justa; ⏲9am-7.30pm)

There are also private City Expert offices providing information and booking services in

WORTH A TRIP

ITÁLICA

Some 9km northwest of Seville, the small town of Santiponce is home to Andalucía's most thrilling Roman site.

The evocative ruins of ancient **Itálica** (☎600 141767; www.museosdeandalucia.es; Avenida de Extremadura 2; EU/non-EU citizens free/€1.50; ⏲9am-9pm Tue-Sat, 8am-3pm Sun Apr-Jun, 9am-3pm Tue-Sun Jul–mid-Sep, 9am-6pm Tue-Sat, to 3pm Sun mid-Sep–Mar; P) are impressive and wonderfully maintained. Broad paved streets lead to the remains of houses set around beautiful mosaic patios and, best of all, a stunning 20,000-seat **amphitheatre**, one of the largest ever built.

Founded in 206 BC and later the birthplace of emperors Trajan and Hadrian (he who built the wall across northern England), Itálica enjoyed a golden age in the 2nd century AD, when many of its finest buildings were constructed.

To get to the site, bus M172 runs from Seville's Plaza de Armas station to Santiponce (€1.55, 25 minutes, at least half hourly), making its final stop at the site's entrance.

the **centre** (Map p644; ☎673 289848; www.cityexpert.es; Avenida de la Constitución 21B; ⏲9.30am-8pm) and at the **train station** (www.cityexpert.es; Estación Santa Justa; ⏲9.30am-6pm Mon-Sat, to 2.30pm Sun).

Tourist staff generally speak English.

ℹ Getting There & Away

AIR

Seville Airport (Aeropuerto de Sevilla; ☎902 404704; www.aena.es; A4, Km 532), 7km east of the city, has flights to/from Spanish cities and destinations across Europe including London, Paris, Amsterdam, Dublin, Frankfurt and Rome.

It's served by international airlines such as Ryanair, EasyJet and Vueling Airlines.

BUS

Estación de Autobuses Plaza de Armas (Map p640; ☎955 03 86 65; www.autobusesplazadearmas.es; Avenida del Cristo de la Expiración) Seville's main bus station. From here, **ALSA** (Map p640; ☎902 422242; www.alsa.es) buses serve Málaga (€18.50 to €23.50, 2¾ hours, seven daily), Granada (€23 to €29, three hours, eight daily), Córdoba (€12, two hours, seven daily) and Almería (€37 to €45, 5½ to 8½ hours, three daily). **Damas** (Map p640; ☎902 114492; www.damas-sa.es) runs buses to Huelva province and **Eurolines** (Map p640; ☎902 405040; www.eurolines.es) has international services to Germany, Belgium, France and beyond.

Estación de Autobuses Prado de San Sebastián (Map p644; Plaza San Sebastián) Has services to smaller towns in western Andalucía. Operators include **Los Amarillos** (Map p644; ☎902 210317; http://losamarillos.autobusing.com), which serves towns in the provinces of Sevilla, Cádiz and parts of Málaga, and **Comes** (Map p644; ☎956 29 11 68; www.tgcomes.es), which runs to various regional destinations including Cádiz and some of the harder-to-reach *pueblos blancos* (white towns) in Cádiz province.

TRAIN

Seville's principal train station, **Estación Santa Justa** (Avenida Kansas City), is 1.5km northeast of the centre.

High-speed AVE trains go to/from Madrid (€60, 2½ to 3¼ hours, 14 daily) and Córdoba (from €21, 45 minutes to 1¼ hours, 25 daily). Slower trains head to Cádiz (€16 to €23, 1¾ hours, 13 daily), Huelva (€12, 1½ hours, four daily), Granada (€30, 3½ hours, four daily) and Málaga (€24 to €44, two to 2½ hours, 10 daily).

ℹ Getting Around

Central Seville is relatively compact and is best explored on foot. Getting around by bike (p650) is also an option – the city is flat and bike lanes are ubiquitous. Driving is not recommended in the city centre.

Public transport comprises buses, trams and a metro. Buses are the most useful for getting around the main visitor areas.

TO/FROM THE AIRPORT

The **EA Bus** (☎955 010010; www.tussam.es; one way/return €4/6) (€4) connects the airport to the city centre, running to/from Plaza de Armas bus station via Santa Justa train station, Prado de San Sebastián bus station and the Torre del Oro.

Departures from the airport are every 20 to 30 minutes between 5.20am and 12.45am; from Plaza Armas between 4.30am and midnight. Note that services are reduced slightly on Sundays, very early in the morning and late in the evening.

Taxis charge set fares: €22 (daytime Monday to Friday); €25 (weekends and night-time Monday to Friday); €31 (night-time Easter and the Feria de Abril). There's a €0.49 surcharge for each bag over 10kg.

BUS

Buses run from around 6am to 11.30pm.

Useful routes include:

C1 and C2 External route around the centre.

C3 and C4 Internal route around the centre.

C5 Runs through the centre.

Tickets can be bought on buses, at stations and at kiosks next to stops. A standard ticket is €1.40 but a range of passes are also available, including one/three-day passes for €5/10.

CAR & MOTORCYCLE

Driving in Seville is generally not worth the hassle. Traffic restrictions are in force and the small streets of the historic centre are not car friendly. Parking can be hard to find.

For car hire, there's **Avis** (902 110283; www.avis.com; Estación Santa Justa; 8am-midnight) or **Enterprise** (954 41 26 40; www.enterprise.es; 7.30am-11pm) at Santa Justa train station, and all the normal brands at the airport.

TRAM

Operated by **Tussam** (955 01 00 10; www.tussam.es), Seville's tram service has a single line. T1 runs between Plaza Nueva and San Bernado via Avenida de la Constitución, Puerta de Jerez and San Sebastián.

The standard ticket is €1.40 but a range of passes is available if you're likely to use it a lot.

SEVILLA PROVINCE

Just outside Seville, the wonderfully preserved ruins of Itálica make for one of southern Spain's most remarkable Roman sites. To the east, the vast, shimmering plains of La Campiña are punctuated by a string of handsome towns, most notably Carmona and Écija.

Carmona

POP 28,595

Rising above a sea of golden, sun-baked plains 35km east of Seville, Carmona is a delight. Its hilltop old town sparkles with noble palaces, majestic Mudéjar churches and two Moorish forts; nearby, a haunting Roman necropolis recalls its ancient past.

The strategically sited town flourished under the Romans, who laid out a street plan that survives to this day: Via Augusta, running from Rome to Cádiz, entered Carmona by the eastern Puerta de Córdoba and left by the western Puerta de Sevilla. The Muslims subsequently built a strong defensive wall but in 1247 the town fell to Fernando III. Later, Mudéjar and Christian artisans constructed grand churches, convents and mansions.

Sights

★Necrópolis Romana ROMAN SITE

(Roman cemetery; 600 143632; www.museosdeandalucia.es; Avenida de Jorge Bonsor 9; EU/non-EU citizens free/€1; 9am-6pm Tue-Sat, to 3pm Sun Apr–mid-Jun, 9am-3pm Tue-Sun mid-Jun–mid-Sep, 9am-6pm Tue-Sat, to 3pm Sun mid-Sep–Mar) This ancient Roman necropolis, on the southwestern edge of town, is considered one of the most important of its kind in Andalucía. Hundreds of tombs, some elaborate and many-chambered, were hewn into the rock in the 1st and 2nd centuries AD. Most of the inhabitants were cremated: in the tombs are wall niches for the box-like stone urns. You can enter the huge **Tumba de Servilia**, the tomb of a family of Hispano-Roman VIPs, and climb down into several others.

Alcázar de la Puerta de Sevilla FORTRESS

(Plaza de Blas Infante; adult/child €2/1, free Mon; 9am-3pm Mon-Fri, 10am-3pm Sat & Sun summer, 10am-6pm Mon-Sat, to 3pm Sun winter) Carmona's signature fortress is a formidable sight. Set atop the Puerta de Sevilla, the imposing main gate of the old town, it had already been standing for five centuries when the Romans reinforced it and built a temple on top. The Muslim Almohads added an *aljibe* (cistern) to the upper patio, which remains a hawklike perch from which to admire the typically Andalucian tableau of white cubes and soaring spires.

Prioral de Santa María de la Asunción CHURCH

(954 19 14 82; Plaza Marqués de las Torres; €3; 9.30am-2pm & 6.30-8pm Tue-Fri, 7-8.30pm Sat, 10am-noon & 7-8.30pm Sun summer, 9.30am-2pm & 5.30-6.30pm Tue-Fri, 9.30am-2pm Sat winter) This splendid church was built mainly in the 15th and 16th centuries on the site of Carmona's former mosque. The Patio de los Naranjos, through which you enter, has a **Visigothic calendar** carved into one of its pillars. The interior, capped by high Gothic vaults, is centred on an **altar** detailed to an almost perverse degree with 20 panels

of biblical scenes framed by gilt-scrolled columns.

Sleeping

Hostal Comercio HOSTAL $
(☎954 14 00 18; hostalcomercio@hotmail.com; Calle Torre del Oro 56; s €35, d €40-50, tr €70, q €90; ❄📶) A warm welcome awaits at this long-standing, family-run *hostal* just inside the Puerta de Sevilla. Its 14 rooms, set around a plant-filled patio with Mudéjar-style arches, are modest and simply furnished with brick floors and heavy wood furniture.

★El Rincón de las Descalzas BOUTIQUE HOTEL $$
(☎954 19 11 72; www.elrincondelasdescalzas.com; Calle de las Descalzas 1; incl breakfast s €52-62, d €64-112, ste €134-175; ❄📶) Elegantly sited in a revamped 18th-century townhouse, this rambling hotel offers 13 colourful rooms and a picturesque, orange-hued patio. Each room is different, and some are better than others, but all sport a refined period look with carved-wood beds, exposed brick and sandstone, timber arches and the occasional fireplace.

Posada San Fernando BOUTIQUE HOTEL $$
(☎954 14 14 08, 666 907788; www.posadasanfernando.es; Plaza de San Fernando 6; s/d/tr €55/65/100; ❄📶) This excellent-value hotel enjoys a prime location on Carmona's main square. It's a cosy affair with characterful and tastefully designed rooms ensconced in a 16th-century building. Expect antique furnishings, hand-painted bathroom tiles and, in some rooms, balconies overlooking the palm-lined plaza.

Eating

Cervecería San Fernando ANDALUCIAN $$
(☎661 654960; Plaza de San Fernando 18; tapas €2.50, mains €10-17; ⏲noon-5pm & 8pm-midnight Tue-Sun) With ringside seating on Carmona's vibrant central square, friendly service and fine food, Cerveceria San Fernando hits all the right notes. The menu, which lists tapas and *raciones,* covers multiple bases, with everything from fried fish to scrambled eggs and steaks. Particularly good is the artichoke capped by *jamón* (ham) and a sweet-wine reduction.

Molino de la Romera ANDALUCIAN $$
(☎954 14 20 00; www.molinodelaromera.es; Calle Sor Ángela de la Cruz 8; tapas €2.50-4, mains €11-20; ⏲1-4pm & 8.30pm-midnight Mon-Sat) Housed in a cosy, 15th-century olive-oil mill with a terrace and wonderful views across the *vega* (valley), this popular restaurant serves hearty, well-prepped meals with a splash of contemporary flair. For a taste of traditional Carmona cuisine, there's *alboronías* (a kind of ratatouille); for something more international try the fig and burrata salad.

Information

Tourist Office (☎954 19 09 55; www.turismo.carmona.org; Alcázar de la Puerta de Sevilla; ⏲9am-3pm Mon-Fri, 10am-3pm Sat & Sun) Helpful office housed in the Alcázar de la Puerta de Sevilla.

Getting There & Away

Casal (☎954 99 92 90; www.autocarescasal.com) runs buses to Seville (€2.80, one hour, at least seven daily) from the **stop** on Paseo del Estatuto.

ALSA (☎902 42 22 42; www.alsa.es) has three daily buses to Córdoba (€9.70, 1½ hours) via Écija (€4.70, 35 minutes) leaving from a **stop** near the Puerta de Sevilla.

Écija

POP 40,270

Écija, the least known of the Campiña towns, is something of an underrated star. Many travellers overlook it, perhaps put off by its reputation as *la sartén de Andalucía* (the frying pan of Andalucía) – in July and August temperatures can reach a suffocating 45°C. But avoid high summer and you'll find it a fascinating town rich in architectural and historic interest.

Its compact centre is riddled with Gothic-Mudéjar palaces, churches and baroque towers – hence a second nickname, *la ciudad de las torres* (the city of towers) – whilst Roman ruins tell of its past as a wealthy Iberian centre. Then known as Colonia Augusta Firma Astigi, it flourished in the 1st and 2nd centuries supplying olive oil to markets across the Roman Empire.

Sights

★Museo Histórico Municipal MUSEUM
(☎954 83 04 31; http://museo.ecija.es; Plaza de la Constitución 1; ⏲10am-1.30pm & 4.30-6.30pm Tue-Fri, 10am-2pm & 5.30-8pm Sat, 10am-3pm Sun) FREE Écija's history museum, housed in the 18th-century **Palacio de Benamejí**, is an

authentic gem. It has rooms dedicated to the area's prehistory and protohistory, but its chief drawcard is its fabulous collection of local Roman finds. These include a graceful sculpture of a wounded Amazon (a legendary female warrior) and a series of stunningly preserved mosaics, mostly unearthed in and around the town. A particular highlight is the *Mosaico del Triunfo de Baco* depicting the 'birth' of wine.

Palacio de Peñaflor PALACE
(Calle Emilio Castelar 26) The huge, 18th-century 'Palace of the Long Balconies', 300m east of Plaza de España, is Écija's most iconic image. The palace's interior is off limits, but you can still admire its curved facade complete with ornate, columned portal, wrought-iron balconies and traces of flamboyant frescoes.

Sleeping & Eating

Hotel Palacio de los Granados HISTORIC HOTEL $$
(955 90 53 44; www.palaciogranados.com; Calle Emilio Castelar 42; d/ste incl breakfast €99/145;) This charming palace, sections of which date to the 15th century, has been lovingly restored by its architect owner. The rooms, which are all slightly different, have a stately look with wood-beamed ceilings, Mudéjar arches, 18th-century floors and even the occasional fireplace. Adding to the romance is a tiny courtyard where pomegranate trees grow over a tiny plunge pool.

★**Ágora** TAPAS $
(955 31 70 77; Calle Barquete 38A; tapas €1.50-2.50, raciones €9.50-12.50; 11am-4pm Mon, to 11pm Wed & Thu, to midnight Fri, noon-midnight Sat, noon-11pm Sun) This friendly tapas joint run by a young, energetic crew is one of Écija's favourite bars. Its outdoor tables, overlooked by a gnarled olive tree, are much sought after – particularly at weekends, when crowds of locals pour in to dine on decadently seasoned scrambled eggs and slow-cooked pork cheeks in wine sauce.

Information

Tourist Office (955 90 29 33; www.turismoecija.com; Calle Elvira 1; 10am-2pm & 4.30-6.30pm Mon-Sat, 10am-2pm Sun) Helpful, English-speaking staff.

Getting There & Away

Écija is 53km east of Carmona on the A4 between Córdoba and Seville.

From the **bus station** (Avenida del Genil; 7am-10.30pm), **ALSA** (902 42 22 42; www.alsa.es) buses connect with Carmona (€4.70, 35 minutes, three daily), Córdoba (€5, one hour, six daily) and Seville (€7.30, 1¼ hours, at least four daily).

HUELVA PROVINCE

Huelva province, Andalucía's most westerly, end-of-the-line destination, packs in a mix of historical intrigue, natural beauty and sun worship, but still remains largely off the

ÉCIJA'S TOWERS

Nicknamed *la ciudad de las torres* (the city of towers) Écija is famous for its spire-studded skyline. A series of baroque towers rises above the town's rooftops, most dating to the late 18th century, when many churches were rebuilt following a devastating earthquake in 1755.

One of the town's finest towers belongs to the **Iglesia de Santa María** (Plaza de Santa María; 9.30am-1.30pm & 5.30-8.30pm Mon-Fri, 9.30am-1.30pm & 5-30-7.45pm Sat, 10am-1pm Sun), an 18th-century church just off Plaza de España. A few blocks to the northeast, the striking baroque belfry of the **Iglesia de San Juan** (Plaza de San Juan; tower €2; 10.30am-1.30pm & 4.30-7.30pm Tue-Sat, 10.30am-1.30pm Sun) is the only tower in town you can actually climb. Nearby, the Gothic-Mudéjar **Iglesia de San Pablo y Santo Domingo** (Plaza de Santo Domingo; 6.30-7.30pm Tue-Fri, 7-8pm Sat, 11.30am-12.30pm & 7-8pm Sun) features an 18th-century brick tower.

Fronting a pretty plaza in the north of the old town, the **Parroquia Mayor de Santa Cruz** (Plazuela de Nuestra Señora del Valle; €1; 9am-1pm & 5-9pm Mon-Sat, 9am-1pm & 6-10pm Sun summer, 10am-1pm & 4-8pm Mon-Sat, 10am-1pm & 6-8pm Sun winter) was once Écija's principal mosque and still has traces of Islamic features and some Arabic inscriptions. Beyond the roofless atrium, which retains a series of impressive Gothic arches from the original 13th-century church, the interior is crammed with sacred paraphernalia and baroque silverwork.

beaten track for foreign visitors. Here you'll find sleepy mountain villages, relics from Columbus' voyages of discovery, endless stretches of untainted coastline and Spain's most beloved national park. Foodies will enjoy the province's prized pork products while festival goers can join the pilgrims at the boisterous Romería del Rocío festival.

Huelva

POP 147,000

The capital of Huelva province is a modern, unpretentious industrial port set between the Odiel and Tinto estuaries. Despite its unpromising approaches and slightly grimy feel, central Huelva is a lively enough place, and the city's people – called *choqueros* because of their supposed preference for the locally abundant *chocos* (cuttlefish) – are noted for their warmth.

Sights

Muelle-Embarcadero de Mineral de Río Tinto HISTORIC SITE

An odd legacy of the area's mining history, this impressive iron pier curves out into the Odiel estuary 500m south of the port. It was designed for the Rio Tinto company in the 1870s by British engineer George Barclay Bruce. Equipped with boardwalks on upper and lower levels, it makes for a delightful stroll or jog to admire the harbour and ships. It's 1km southwest of Plaza de las Monjas.

Museo de Huelva MUSEUM

(959 65 04 24; www.museosdeandalucia.es; Alameda Sundheim 13; EU non-citizens/citizens €1.50/free; 9am-3pm Tue-Sun mid-Jun–mid-Sep; 9am-8pm Tue-Sat, 9am-3pm Sun rest of year) FREE This wide-ranging museum is stuffed with history and art. The permanent ground-floor exhibition concentrates on Huelva province's impressive archaeological pedigree, with interesting items culled from its Roman and mining history; upstairs houses a collection of Spanish painting spanning seven centuries. Don't miss the stunning ancient Roman *noria* (waterwheel), the best preserved of its kind anywhere in the world.

Festivals & Events

Fiestas Colombinas CULTURAL

(late Jul/early Aug) Huelva celebrates Columbus' departure for the Americas (3 August 1492) with this six-day festival of music, dance, cultural events and bullfighting.

Sleeping

Senator Huelva Hotel BUSINESS HOTEL $

(959 28 55 00; www.senatorhuelvahotel.com; Avenida Pablo Rada 10; r from €60;) Catering to the business set, this impeccably maintained hotel is definitely your best bet in Huelva. Bright-red banisters draped in greenery liven up the lobby, and staff are charmingly efficient. All 162 rooms are smartly outfitted with dark-wood desks and crisp white sheets, and Huelva's central square is only a five-minute walk away.

Albergue Inturjoven Huelva HOSTEL $

(959 65 00 10; www.inturjoven.com/albergues/huelva; Avenida Marchena Colombo 14; dm/d incl breakfast €22/44; @; 6) A good, modern youth hostel, with 53 rooms around a pleasant bright courtyard. Rooms have two to six beds, and private bathrooms; towel and bike rentals are available. It's 2km north of the bus station: city bus 6 from the station stops just around the corner from the hostel, on Calle JS Elcano.

Eating

Ciquitrake TAPAS $

(956 25 69 58; www.ciquitrake.com; Calle Rascón 21; tapas €2.70-8, raciones €7.50-14; 8.30am-midnight Mon-Fri, from 10am Sat;) 'To know how to eat is to know how to live' is the motto of this innovative tapas maker, which specialises in novel variations on *choquero* mainstays, attractively presented in cool minimalist surroundings (with a glossary of Huelva slang as wallpaper). Perennial favourites include *albóndigas de choco* (cuttlefish balls) and *salmorejo*.

★**Azabache** TAPAS $$

(959 25 75 28; www.restauranteazabache.com; Calle Vázquez López 22; raciones €7-18; 8.30am-midnight Mon-Fri, to 4pm Sat) After a taste of traditional Huelva? Squeeze into this narrow tiled tapas bar where busy, helpful waiters are quick to deliver cheese and *jamón* (ham) platters, scrambled *gurumelos* (local wild mushrooms), fried *chocos* (cuttlefish) and fresh fish specials. Beyond the front bar area is a more formal restaurant serving a rather pricey set menu (€36 including wine, dessert and coffee).

Information

Regional Tourist Office (959 25 74 67; www.turismohuelva.org; Calle Jesús Nazareno 21; 9am-7.30pm Mon-Fri, 9.30am-3pm Sat & Sun) Helpful for the whole province.

Tourist Office (☎959 54 18 17; Plaza de las Monjas; ⏲10am-2pm Mon-Sat, plus 5-8pm Mon-Fri)

Getting There & Away

Most buses from the **bus station** (Calle Doctor Rubio) are operated by **Damas** (☎902 11 44 92; www.damas-sa.es; Calle Doctor Rubio). Destinations include Almonte (for El Rocío, €4, 1¼ hours), Aracena (€10.85, 2½ to three hours), La Rábida (€1.65, 20 minutes), Moguer (€1.65, 45 minutes), Palos de la Frontera (€1.65, 30 minutes), Seville (€8.65, 1¼ to two hours) and Faro, Portugal (€16, 2½ hours). Frequency is reduced on Saturday, Sunday and public holidays.

From Huelva's **train station** (Avenida de Italia), just south of the centre, **Renfe** (☎912 43 23 43; www.renfe.com; Avenida de Italia) runs three services to Seville (€12.25, 1½ hours) and one direct high-speed ALVIA train to Córdoba (€38, 1¾ hours) and Madrid (€38 to €73, 3¾ hours) daily.

Lugares Colombinos

The 'Columbian Sites' are the three townships of La Rábida, Palos de la Frontera and Moguer, along the eastern bank of the Tinto estuary. All three played a key role in Columbus' preparation for his journey of discovery and can be visited in a fun day trip from Huelva, Doñana or Huelva's eastern coast. As the countless greenhouses suggest, this is Spain's main strawberry-growing region (Huelva province produces 90% of Spain's crop).

Getting There & Away

At least 11 daily buses leave Huelva for La Rábida (€1.65, 25 minutes) and Palos de la Frontera (€1.65, 30 minutes); half continue to Moguer (€1.65, 45 minutes). The same buses allow easy transport connections between the three towns.

La Rábida

POP 500

Sights

Monasterio de la Rábida MONASTERY
(☎959 35 04 11; www.monasteriodelarabida.com; Paraje de la Rábida; adult/student €3.50/3; ⏲10am-1pm & 4-7pm Tue-Sat, from 10.45am Sun; P) In the pretty, peaceful village of La Rábida, don't miss this 14th- and 15th-century Franciscan monastery, visited several times by Columbus before his great voyage of discovery. Highlights include a chapel with a 13th-century alabaster Virgin before which Columbus prayed, and a fresco-lined Mudéjar cloister, one of the few parts of the original structure to survive the 1755 earthquake.

Muelle de las Carabelas HISTORIC SITE
(Wharf of the Caravels; €3.60; ⏲10am-9pm Tue-Sun mid-Jun–mid-Sep; 9.30am-7.30pm Tue-Sun rest of year; P) On the waterfront below the Monasterio de la Rábida is this pseudo 15th-century quayside, where you can board life-size replicas of the *Niña,* the *Pinta* and the *Santa María* – the three ships used by Columbus in his initial trans-Atlantic expedition. A single ticket grants access to all three ships and the attached museum, which features excellent bilingual (English-Spanish) displays tracing the history of Columbus' voyages. Here you can see instruments of navigation and get a glimpse of the indigenous experience at the time of the Spaniards' arrival.

Palos de la Frontera

POP 5300

It was from the port of Palos de la Frontera that Columbus and his merry band set sail into the unknown. The town provided the explorer with two of his ships, two captains (Martín Alonso Pinzón and Vicente Yáñez Pinzón) and more than half his crew.

Sights

Iglesia de San Jorge CHURCH
(Calle Fray Juan Pérez; ⏲variable) Towards the northern end of Calle Colón is this 15th-century Gothic-Mudéjar church, where Columbus and his sailors took Communion before embarking on their great expedition. Water for their ships came from La Fontanilla well nearby.

Casa Museo Martín Alonso Pinzón MUSEUM
(☎959 10 00 41; Calle Colón 24; adult/concession €1/0.50; ⏲10am-2pm & 5-8.30pm Mon-Fri) The former home of the Pinzón brothers (captains of the *Niña* and the *Pinta*) now houses a permanent exhibition on Palos' crucial contribution to Columbus' famous first expedition.

Eating

El Bodegón ANDALUCIAN $$
(☎959 53 11 05; Calle Rábida 46; mains €12-25; ⏲noon-4pm & 8.30-11.30pm Wed-Mon) This atmospheric brick-floored grotto of a restaurant specialises in meat, fish and vegetables cooked to perfection over an oak-fired grill.

Moguer

POP 14,300

The sleepy whitewashed town of Moguer, 8km northeast of Palos de la Frontera on the A494, is where Columbus' ship, the *Niña,* was built.

It also has a historical claim to fame as the home town of Nobel Prize-winning poet Juan Ramón Jiménez.

Sights

Monasterio de Santa Clara MONASTERY

(☎959 37 01 07; www.monasteriodesantaclara.com; Plaza de las Monjas; guided tours adult/concession €3.50/2.50, free Sun; ⏲tours 10.30am, 11.30am, 12.30pm, 5.30pm & 6.30pm Tue-Sat, 10.30am & 11.30am Sun) Columbus spent a night of vigil and prayer at this grand 14th-century monastery upon returning from his first voyage in March 1493. Highlights of the 45-minute guided visit include a lovely Mudéjar cloister, a 14th-century kitchen, the whitewashed Claustro de las Madres, illuminated manuscripts and a one-of-a-kind 14th-century Nasrid choir stall bearing images of Alhambra-inspired lions, columns and Arabic capitals.

Casa Museo Zenobia y Juan Ramón Jiménez HISTORIC BUILDING

(☎959 37 21 48; www.fundacion-jrj.es/servicios/visita-a-la-casa-museo; Calle Juan Ramón Jiménez 10; adult/concession €3.50/2.50; ⏲10am-2pm & 4-8pm Tue-Fri, 10am-2.30pm Sat & Sun mid-Jun–mid-Sep; 10.15am-1pm Tue-Sun & 5.15-7pm Tue-Sat rest of year) The lovingly maintained former home of renowned poet Juan Ramón Jiménez and his writer wife, Zenobia Camprubí Aymar, is open for both guided and independent visits, encompassing the poet's private library and several upstairs rooms filled with original period furniture.

All exhibits are in Spanish.

Eating

Mesón El Lobito ANDALUCIAN $$

(☎959 37 06 60; www.mesonellobito.com; Calle Rábida 31; mains €7-16; ⏲noon-4pm & 8.30pm-midnight) About 300m southwest of the central Plaza del Cabildo, Mesón El Lobito dishes up huge, good-value clay platters of traditional country fare in a cavernous bodega; grilled meats and fish are cooked over an open log fire.

Information

Tourist Office (☎959 37 18 98; Calle Andalucía 17, Teatro Municipal Felipe Godínez; ⏲10am-2pm & 5-7pm Tue-Sat) The excellent tourist office is inside the Teatro Municipal.

Parque Nacional de Doñana

The World Heritage–listed Parque Nacional de Doñana is a place of haunting natural beauty and exotic horizons, where flocks of flamingos tinge the evening skies pink above one of Europe's most extensive wetlands (the Guadalquivir delta), huge herds of deer and boar flit through *coto* (woodlands), and the elusive Iberian lynx battles for survival. Here, in the largest roadless region in Western Europe, and Spain's most celebrated national park, you can experience nature at her most raw and powerful.

The 542-sq-km national park extends 30km along or close to the Atlantic coast and up to 25km inland. Much of the perimeter is bordered by the separate **Parque Natural de Doñana**, under less strict protection, which forms a 538-sq-km buffer for the national park.

Access to the park's interior is restricted, although anyone can walk or cycle along the 28km Atlantic beach between Matalascañas and the mouth of the Río Guadalquivir (which can be crossed by boat from Sanlúcar de Barrameda in Cádiz province), as long as they do not stray inland.

Activities

Sendero Charco de la Boca WALKING

At the Centro de Visitantes La Rocina (p665), the Sendero Charco de la Boca is a 3.5km return walk along a stream, then through a range of habitats, passing four birdwatching hides.

Sendero Lagunas del Acebuche WALKING

From the Centro de Visitantes El Acebuche (p665), the two Senderos del Acebuche (Acebuche Paths; 1.5km and 3.5km round trip) lead to birdwatching hides overlooking nearby lagoons (though these can get quite dry).

Information

The park has seven information points. The most important four for visitors accessing the park from Huelva province are as follows:

NATIONAL PARK TOURS

To enter the park from the western side you'll need to join a guided jeep tour. These generally last about four hours and involve rides in eight- to 30-passenger all-terrain vehicles. Bookings can be made directly with various accredited agencies, including **Doñana Nature** (959 44 21 60, 630 978216; www.donana-nature.com; Calle Moguer 10; tours per person €28), **Cooperativa Marismas del Rocío** (959 43 04 32, 648 762914; www.donanavisitas.es; Centro de Visitantes El Acebuche; tours €30) and **Doñana Reservas** (629 060545, 959 44 24 74; www.donanareservas.com; Avenida de la Canaliega; tours per person €28). Especially in the larger vehicles, the experience can feel a bit theme park–like, but guides have plenty of in-depth information to share.

During spring, summer and holidays, book as far ahead as possible, but otherwise a week or less is usually sufficient notice. Bring binoculars (if you like), drinking water and mosquito repellent (except in winter). English-, German- and French-speaking guides are normally available if you ask in advance.

Centro de Visitantes La Rocina (959 43 95 69; A483; 9am-3pm & 4-7pm) Beside the A483, 1km south of El Rocío.

Centro de Visitantes El Acebrón (671 593138; 9am-3pm & 4-7pm) Located 6km along a minor paved road west from the Centro de Visitantes La Rocina.

Centro de Visitantes El Acebuche (959 43 96 29; 8am-3pm & 4-9pm May–mid-Sep, to 7pm mid-Sep–Mar, to 8pm Apr) Twelve kilometres south of El Rocío on the A483, then 1.6km west, El Acebuche is the national park's main visitor centre.

Centro de Visitantes José Antonio Valverde (671 564145; 10am-8pm Apr-Sep, to 7pm Mar & Oct, to 6pm Nov-Feb) On the eastern edge of the park. The easiest way to reach it is by authorised tour from El Rocío; the alternative is to drive yourself on rough roads from Villamanrique de la Condesa or La Puebla del Río to the northeast.

Getting There & Away

You cannot enter the national park in your own vehicle, though you can drive to the four main visitor centres. **Damas** (www.damas-sa.es) runs eight to 10 buses daily between El Rocío and Matalascañas, which stop at the El Acebuche turn-off on the A483 on request. Some tour companies will pick you up from Matalascañas with advance notice.

El Rocío

POP 1340

El Rocío, the most significant town in the vicinity of the Parque Nacional de Doñana, surprises first-timers. Its sand-covered streets are lined with colourful single-storey houses with sweeping verandahs, left empty half the time. But this is no ghost town: these are the well-tended properties of 115 *hermandades* (brotherhoods), whose pilgrims converge on the town every Pentecost (Whitsunday) weekend for the Romería del Rocío (p666), Spain's largest religious festival.

Beyond its uniquely exotic ambience, El Rocío impresses with its striking setting in front of luminous Doñana *marismas* (wetlands), where herds of deer drink at dawn and, at certain times of year, pink flocks of flamingos gather in massive numbers.

Whether it's the play of light on the marshes, an old woman praying to the Virgin at the Ermita, or someone passing by in a flamenco dress, there's always something to catch the eye on El Rocío's dusky, sand-blown streets.

Sights

Ermita del Rocío CHURCH

(Calle Ermita; 8am-9pm Apr-Sep; to 7pm Oct-Mar) A striking splash of white at the heart of the town, the Ermita del Rocío was built in its present form in 1964. This is the permanent home of the celebrated Nuestra Señora del Rocío (Our Lady of El Rocío), a small wooden image of the Virgin dressed in long, jewelled robes, which normally stands above the main altar.

Activities

The marshlands in front of El Rocío, which have water most of the year, offer some of the best bird- and beast-watching in the entire Doñana region. Deer and horses graze in the shallows and you may be lucky enough to spot a big pink cloud of flamingos wheeling through the sky. Pack a pair of binoculars and stroll the waterfront promenade.

DON'T MISS

SPAIN'S GREATEST RELIGIOUS PILGRIMAGE: ROMERÍA DEL ROCÍO

Every Pentecost (Whitsunday) weekend, seven weeks after Easter, El Rocío transforms from a quiet backwater into an explosive mess of noise, colour and passion. This is the culmination of Spain's biggest religious pilgrimage, the **Romería del Rocío**, which draws up to a million joyous pilgrims.

The focus of all this revelry is the tiny image of Nuestra Señora del Rocío (Our Lady of El Rocío), which was found in a marshland tree by a hunter from Almonte village back in the 13th century. When he stopped for a rest on the way home, the Virgin magically returned to the tree. Before long, a chapel was built on the site of the tree (El Rocío) and pilgrims started arriving.

Solemn is the last word you'd apply to this quintessentially Andalucian event. Participants dress in their finest Andalucian costume and sing, drink, dance, laugh and romance their way to El Rocío. Most belong to the 115 *hermandades* (brotherhoods) who arrive from towns all across southern Spain on foot, horseback and in colourfully decorated covered wagons.

The weekend reaches an ecstatic climax in the very early hours of Monday. Members of the Almonte *hermandad*, which claims the Virgin as its own, barge into the church and bear her out on a float. Violent struggles ensue as others battle for the honour of carrying La Paloma Blanca (the White Dove). The crush and chaos are immense, but somehow the Virgin is carried round to each of the *hermandad* buildings before finally being returned to the church in the afternoon. Upcoming dates: 9 June 2019, 31 May 2020 and 23 May 2021.

In recent years, Spaniards' rising concern for animal rights, spearheaded by animal-welfare political party PACMA (https://pacma.es), has drawn attention to mistreatment and neglect of animals, particularly horses and mules, during the Romería del Rocío festivities, and, despite the presence of voluntary veterinary services, 10 horses and one ox died during the 2017 romería.

Francisco Bernis Birdwatching Centre BIRDWATCHING
(☎959 44 23 72; www.seo.org; Paseo Marismeño; ⏰9am-2pm & 4-6pm Tue-Sun) FREE About 700m east of the Ermita along the waterfront, this birdwatching facility backs on to the marshes. Flamingos, glossy ibis, spoonbills and more can be observed through the rear windows or from the observation deck with high-power binoculars (free). Experts here can help you identify species and inform you about visiting migratory birds and where to see them.

Doñana a Caballo HORSE RIDING
(☎674 219568; www.donanaacaballo.com; Avenida de la Canaliega; per 1/2hr €20/30, half day €50) Guided horse rides for all levels through the Coto del Rey woodlands east of El Rocío.

Sleeping & Eating

Hotel Toruño HOTEL $$
(☎959 44 23 23; www.toruno.es; Plaza Acebuchal 22; s €35-59, d €50-80, all incl breakfast; P❄📶) About 350m east of the Ermita, this brilliantly white villa stands right by the *marismas* (wetlands), where you can spot flamingos going through their morning beauty routine. Inside, tile murals continue the wildlife theme – from otters to ibises – even in the showers! Interior rooms are rather bland and uninspiring, especially on the ground floor; request one overlooking the marshes if available.

Hotel La Malvasía HOTEL $$
(☎959 44 27 13; www.hotellamalvasia.com; Calle Sanlúcar 38; s €100-110, d €110-150, ste €160-190; ❄📶) This idyllic hotel occupies a grand *casa señorial* (manor house) overlooking the marshes at the eastern end of town. Rooms have character: rustic tiled floors, vintage El Rocío photos and floral-patterned iron bedsteads. The top-floor sun terrace makes a spectacular bird-viewing perch, as does the suite, with its front-facing views of the lagoon.

★Restaurante Toruño ANDALUCIAN $$
(☎959 44 24 22; www.toruno.es; Plaza Acebuchal; mains €13-25; ⏰1-4pm & 8-11pm; 🖉) With its traditional Andalucian atmosphere, authentically good food and huge portions, this is El Rocío's one must-try restaurant.

A highlight on the menu is the free-range *mostrenca* calf, unique to Doñana; for non-carnivores, the huge *parrillada* (grilled assortment) of vegetables is fantastic. Dine in front of the restaurant by the 1000-year-old *acebuche* (olive) tree or out back overlooking the wetlands.

Information

Tourist Office (☎959 44 23 50; www.almonte.es/es; Calle Muñoz Pavón; ⏲9.30am-2pm) Inside the town hall.

Getting There & Away

Damas (www.damas-sa.es) buses run from Seville's Plaza de Armas to El Rocío (€6.30, 1½ hours, two daily), continuing to Matalascañas (€1.30, 25 minutes). From Huelva, take a Damas bus to Almonte (€4, 1¼ hours, one to four daily), then another to El Rocío (€1.30, 20 minutes, eight daily).

Minas de Riotinto

POP 3260 / ELEV 420M

Tucked away on the southern fringe of Huelva's Sierra Morena is one of the world's oldest mining districts; King Solomon of Jerusalem is said to have mined gold here for his famous temple, and the Romans were digging up silver by the 4th century BC. The mines were then left largely untouched until the British Rio Tinto company made this one of the world's key copper-mining centres in the 1870s (leading, incidentally, to the foundation of Spain's first football club). The mines were sold back to Spain in 1954, and the miners clocked off for the last time in 2001. Nowadays it's a fascinating place to explore, with a superb museum, and opportunities to visit the old mines and ride the mine railway.

The Río Tinto itself rises a few kilometres northeast of town, its name ('red river') stemming from the deep red-brown hue of its iron- and copper-infused waters.

Sights

Peña de Hierro MINE

(☎959 59 00 25; www.parquemineroderiotinto.es; adult/child €8/7; ⏲10.30am-3pm & 4-7pm) These are old copper and sulphur mines 3km north of Nerva (6km east of Minas de Riotinto). Here you see the source of the Río Tinto and a 65m-deep opencast mine, and are taken into a 200m-long underground mine gallery. There are three guaranteed daily visits but schedules vary, so it's essential to book ahead through the Museo Minero (by phone or online).

Museo Minero MUSEUM

(☎959 59 00 25; www.parquemineroderiotinto.es; Plaza Ernest Lluch; adult/child €5/4; ⏲10.30am-3pm & 4-7pm; P) Riotinto's mining museum is a figurative goldmine for devotees of industrial archaeology. Displays take you through the area's unique history from the megalithic tombs of the 3rd millennium BC to the Roman and British colonial eras, then the 1888 *año de los tiros* (year of the gunshots) upheaval and finally the closure of the mines in 2001. The tour includes an elaborate 200m-long recreation of a Roman mine.

Tours

Ferrocarril Turístico-Minero RAIL

(☎959 59 00 25; www.parquemineroderiotinto.es; adult/child €11/10; ⏲1.30pm & 5.30pm mid-Jul–mid-Sep, 1.30pm mid-Sep–mid-Jul, closed Mon-Fri Nov–mid-Feb) A fun way to see the area (especially with children) is to ride the old mining train, running 22km (round trip) through the surreal landscape in restored early 20th-century carriages. The train parallels the river for the entire journey, so you can appreciate its constantly shifting hues. It's mandatory to book ahead, either at the town's museum or the railway station.

Trips along the rust-red Río Tinto start at the old railway repair workshops 4km east of Minas de Riotinto off the road to Nerva. Commentary is in Spanish (with English-language handouts).

Getting There & Away

Damas (www.damas-sa.es) runs three to five daily buses between Minas de Riotinto and Huelva (€6.85, 1¾ hours).

Aracena & Around

POP 6700 / ELEV 730M

Sparkling white in its mountain bowl, the thriving old market town of Aracena is an appealingly lively place that's wrapped like a ribbon around a medieval church and ruined castle.

Sights

★**Gruta de las Maravillas** CAVE

(Cave of Marvels; ☎663 937876; www.aracena.es/es/municipio/gruta; Calle Pozo de la Nieve; tours adult/child €9/6.50; ⏲10am-1.30pm & 3-6pm) Beneath the town's castle hill is a web of caves

LOCAL KNOWLEDGE

JAMONES EÍRIZ JABUGO

For a first-hand understanding of Denominación de Origen Calificada (DOC) Iberian ham production, nothing beats the two- to three-hour tours offered by award-winning, fourth-generation, family-run **Jamones Eíriz Jabugo** (www.rutadeljamondejabugo.com; Calle Pablo Bejarano 43, Corteconcepción; per person incl tasting €39.50). After an hour mingling with acorn-crazed pigs in their little patch of paradise under the oak trees, decamp to the maze of salting and curing chambers, where you'll witness hundreds of dangling hams developing their prized flavour.

Finish with a tasting of multiple meat products (ham, *lomito, salchicha* and chorizo). All tours must be booked in advance, and can be offered in English or other languages upon request. It's about a 6km drive northeast of Aracena.

and tunnels carved from the karstic topography. An extraordinary 1.2km, 50-minute loop takes you through 12 chambers and past six underground lakes, all beautifully illuminated and filled with weird and wonderful rock formations, which provided a backdrop for the film *Journey to the Center of the Earth*.

Museo del Jamón MUSEUM
(Gran Vía; adult/child €3.50/2.50; ⌚10.45am-2.30pm & 3.45-6.30pm) The *jamón* for which the sierra is famed gets due recognition in this modern museum. You'll learn why the acorn-fed Iberian pig gives such succulent meat, about the importance of the native pastures in which they are reared, and about traditional and contemporary methods of slaughter and curing. Displays are in Spanish, with free audio guides available in four other languages. Afterwards, the museum shop invites visitors to 'pig' out with a free tasting of local *bellota* ham.

Plaza Alta SQUARE
Originally Aracena's central square, this gently sloping plaza near the top of town is home to an attractive 15th-century town hall, backed by the imposing castle and church on the hilltop just above.

Castillo CASTLE
(Cerro del Castillo; guided tour adult/child €2.50/1) Dramatically dominating the town are the tumbling, hilltop ruins of the *castillo,* built by the kingdoms of Portugal and Castilla in the 12th century atop the ruins of an earlier Islamic settlement. Directly adjacent is the Gothic-Mudéjar **Iglesia Prioral de Nuestra Señora del Mayor Dolor** (Plazoleta Virgen del Mayor Dolor; ⌚10am-5pm, to 7.30pm Jul & Aug). Both are reached via a steep lane from Plaza Alta; guided tours grant access to the castle's interior, though it's honestly more impressive from the outside.

Activities

Linares de la Sierra Walk HIKING
This sublime and fairly gentle 5km, two-hour ramble takes you down a verdant valley to beautifully sleepy Linares de la Sierra. The signposted path (PRA48) is easy to find off the HU8105 on the southwestern edge of Aracena, 500m beyond the municipal swimming pool.

Sleeping

★**Hotel Convento Aracena** HISTORIC HOTEL $$
(☎959 12 68 99; www.hotelconventoaracena.es; Calle Jesús y María 19; d €98-149, ste €173-234; P❄📶🏊) Glossy, modern rooms contrast with flourishes of original Andalucian baroque architecture at this thoughtfully converted 17th-century convent, Aracena town's finest lodging. Enjoy the on-site spa, sierra cuisine and year-round saltwater pool, with gorgeous village views and summer bar. Room 9 is fabulously set in the church dome (though be forewarned that it's windowless, save for the skylight in the cupola).

Finca Valbono HOTEL $$
(☎959 12 77 11; www.fincavalbono.com; Carretera Aracena-Carboneras, Km 1; d €55-70, 2-person apt €65-80, 4-person apt €100-120; P❄📶🏊) Just 1km northeast of Aracena, this lovingly run farmhouse immersed in greenery offers a splendid mix of country charm and convenient location. It has 20 *casitas* (cottages) set up with log fires, kitchenettes and supplementary sofa beds (perfect for groups or families), plus six rustic rooms. Other standout features include a lovely pool, friendly staff and an on-site **riding school** (☎959 12 77 11; Finca Valbono, Carretera Aracena-Carboneras Km 1; 2hr rides per person €30).

Eating

★**Rincón de Juan** TAPAS $
(Avenida de Portugal 3; tapas €2-3, raciones €7-10; ⌚7.30am-4pm & 6.30pm-midnight Mon-Sat) It's

standing room only at this wedge-shaped, stone-walled corner bar, indisputably the top tapas spot in town. Iberian ham is the star attraction and forms the basis for a variety of *montaditos* (small stuffed rolls) and *rebanadas* (sliced loaves for several people). The local goat's cheese is always a good bet.

★ Jesús Carrión TAPAS **$$**
(☎959 46 31 88; www.jesuscarrionrestaurante.com; Calle Pozo de la Nieve 35; tapas €6.50-13, mains €12-25; ⏲1.15-4pm Wed-Sun, 8.15-11pm Thu-Sat;) Devoted chef Jesús heads up the creative kitchen at this wonderful family-run restaurant, which is causing quite the stir with its lovingly prepared, contemporary twists on traditional Aracena dishes. Try the Iberian ham carpaccio or the local boletus-mushroom risotto. Homemade breads come straight from the oven and salads are deliciously fresh – not a tinned vegetable in sight!

Information

Centro de Visitantes Cabildo Viejo (☎959 12 95 53; Plaza Alta; ⏲9.30am-2.30pm, opening days vary) Gives out hiking information and maps, and has an exhibit on the Parque Natural Sierra de Aracena y Picos de Aroche.

Tourist Office (☎663 937877; www.aracena.es; Calle Pozo de la Nieve; ⏲10am-2pm & 4-6pm) Opposite the Gruta de las Maravillas; sells a good walking map.

Getting There & Away

The **bus station** (Calle José Andrés Vázquez) is 700m southeast of Plaza del Marqués de Aracena. **Damas** (www.damas-sa.es) runs one morning and two afternoon buses (one on Sunday) from Seville (€7.40, 1¼ hours), continuing to Cortegana via Alájar or Jabugo. From Huelva, there are two afternoon departures Monday to Friday, and one on weekends (€10.85, 2½ to three hours). There's also a local service between Aracena and Cortegana via Linares de la Sierra, Alájar and Almonaster la Real.

CÁDIZ PROVINCE

If you had to pick just one region to attempt to explain Andalucía in its full, complex beauty, it'd probably be Cádiz province. Lying in wait across Spain's southernmost province are craggy mountains, oceans of olive trees, thrillingly sited white towns, fortified sherry, festivals galore, flamenco in its purest incarnation, the font of Andalucian horse culture, and a dreamy blonde-sand coastline, the uncommercial Costa de la Luz.

Packed in among all this condensed culture are two extensive natural parks, covering an unbroken tract of land from Olvera in the north to Algeciras in the south. The same line once marked the everchanging frontier between Christian Spain and Moorish Granada, and that ancient border remains dotted with castle-topped, whitewashed towns, many with a 'de la Frontera' suffix that testifies to their volatile history.

Cádiz

POP 118,920

You could write several weighty tomes about Cádiz and still fall short of nailing its essence. Cádiz is generally considered to be the oldest continuously inhabited settlement in Europe, founded as Gadir by the Phoenicians in about 1100 BC. Now well into its fourth millennium, the ancient centre, surrounded almost entirely by water, is a romantic jumble of sinuous streets where Atlantic waves crash against eroded sea walls, cheerful taverns fry up fresh fish and salty beaches teem with sun-worshippers.

Spain's first liberal constitution (La Pepa) was signed here in 1812, while the city's distinctive urban model provided an identikit for fortified Spanish colonial cities in the Americas.

Enamoured return visitors talk fondly of Cádiz' seafood, sands and intriguing monuments and museums. More importantly, they gush happily about the *gaditanos*, an upfront, sociable bunch whose crazy Carnaval is an exercise in ironic humour and whose upbeat *alegrías* (flamenco songs) warm your heart.

Sights

To understand Cádiz, first you need to befriend its *barrios* (districts). The old city is split into classic quarters: the Barrio del Pópulo, home of the cathedral, and nexus of the once prosperous medieval settlement; Barrio de Santa María, the old Roma and flamenco quarter; Barrio de la Viña, a former vineyard that became the city's main fishing quarter and Carnaval epicentre; and Barrio del Mentidero (said to take its name from the many rumours spread on its streets), centred on Plaza de San Antonio in the northwest.

Cádiz

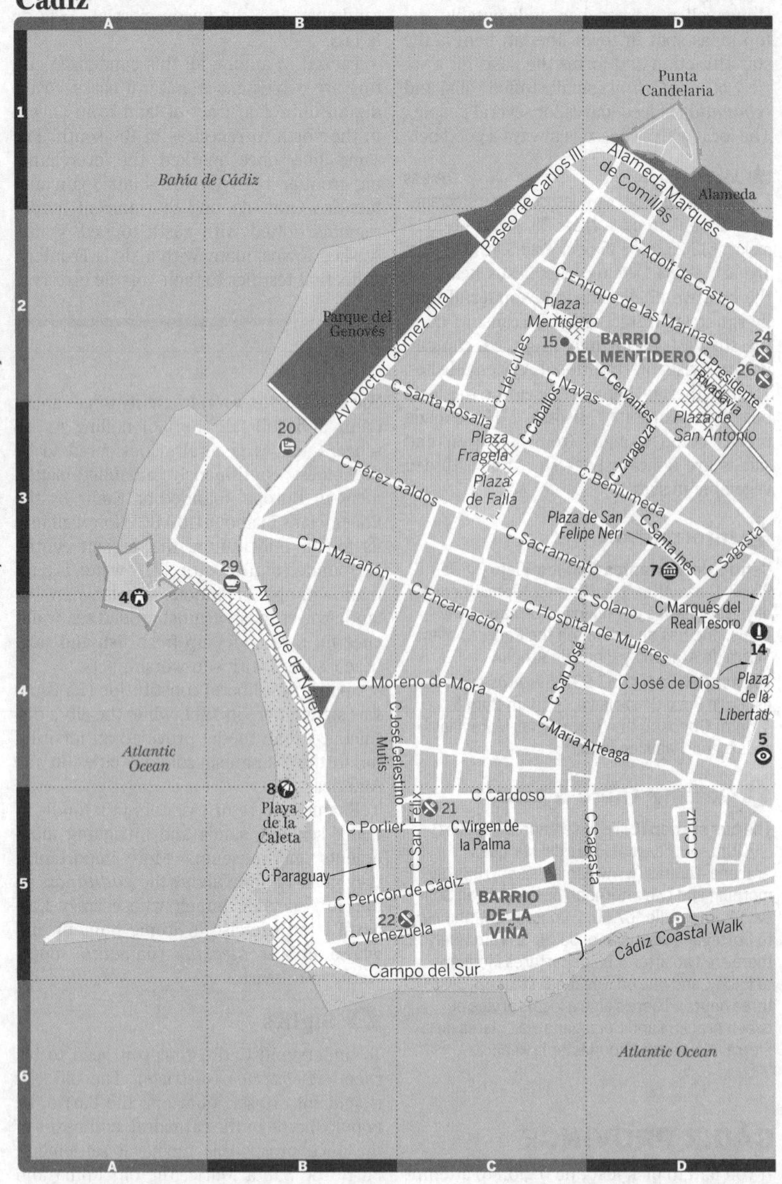

★Catedral de Cádiz CATHEDRAL

(☎608 090424; www.catedraldecadiz.com; Plaza de la Catedral; incl Museo Catedralicio & Torre del Reloj adult/child €5/free; ⊙10am-9pm Jul & Aug, to 8pm Apr-Jun & Sep, to 7pm Oct-Mar) Cádiz' beautiful yellow-domed cathedral is an impressively proportioned baroque-neoclassical construction, best appreciated from seafront Campo del Sur in the evening sun. Though commissioned in 1716, the project wasn't finished until 1838, by which time neoclassical elements (the dome, tow-

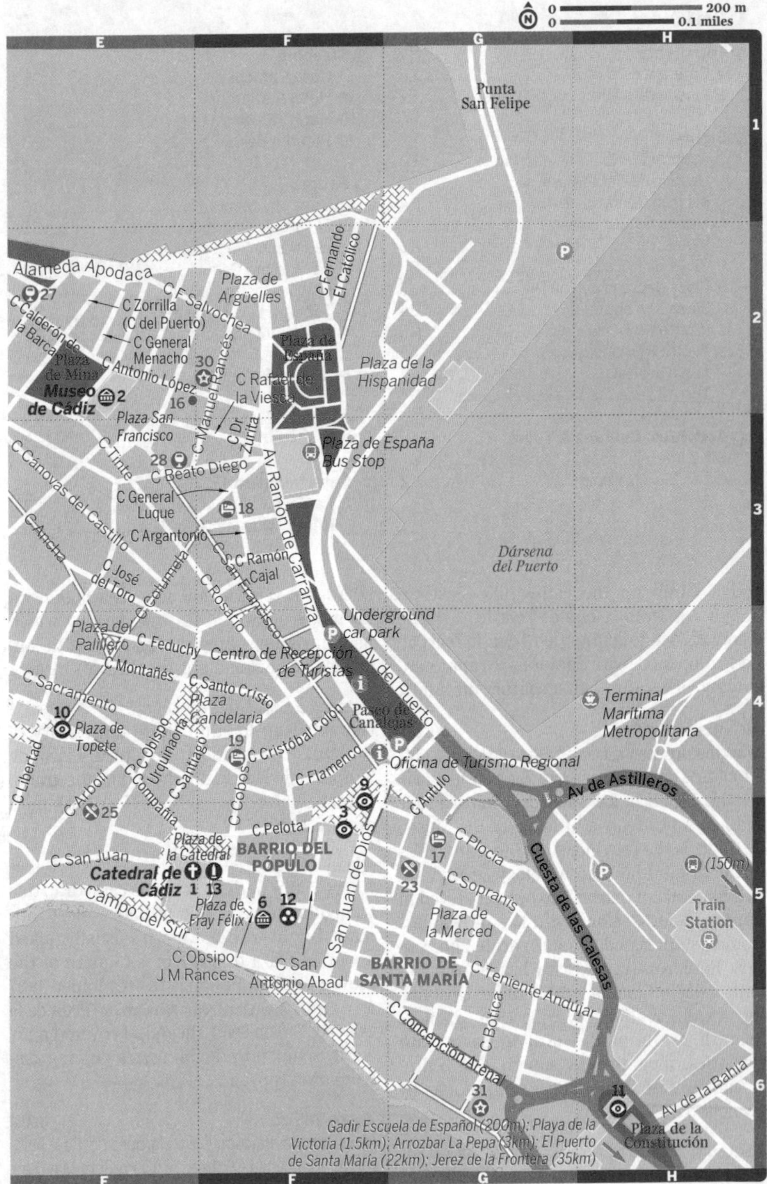

ers and main facade) had diluted architect Vicente Acero's original baroque plan. Highlights within are the intricate wood-carved choir and, in the crypt below, the tomb of renowned 20th-century *gaditano* composer Manuel de Falla.

Tickets include audio guides, the religious treasures of the **Museo Catedralicio** (www.catedraldecadiz.com; Plaza de Fray Félix; incl Catedral de Cádiz & Torre del Reloj adult/child €5/free; ⌚10am-4.30pm Mon-Sat Jul & Aug, to 3.30pm Apr-Jun & Sep, to 3pm Oct-Mar), just east,

Cádiz

Top Sights

1 Catedral de Cádiz E5
2 Museo de Cádiz E2

Sights

3 Ayuntamiento F5
4 Castillo de Santa Catalina A4
5 Mercado Central de Abastos D4
6 Museo Catedralicio F5
7 Museo de las Cortes de Cádiz D3
8 Playa de la Caleta B5
9 Plaza de San Juan de Dios F5
10 Plaza de Topete E4
11 Puerta de Tierra H6
12 Teatro Romano F5
13 Torre del Reloj F5
14 Torre Tavira D4

Activities, Courses & Tours

15 K2 Internacional C2
16 Las Bicis Naranjas E2

Sleeping

17 Casa Caracol G5
18 Hotel Argantonio F3
19 Hotel Patagonia Sur F4
20 Parador de Cádiz B3

Eating

21 Casa Manteca C5
22 El Faro de Cádiz C5
23 La Esquina de Sopranis G5
24 La Marmita Centro D2
Rincón Gastronómico .... (see 5)
25 Taberna La Sorpresa E5
26 Ultramar&nos D2

Drinking & Nightlife

27 La Colonial E2
28 Nahu Centro E3
29 Quilla B3

Entertainment

30 La Cava F2
31 Peña Flamenca La Perla G6

and a climb up the cathedral's (eastern) **Torre del Reloj** (Torre de Levante; 10am-10pm Jul & Aug, to 8pm Apr-Jun & Sep, to 7pm Oct-Mar), reopened with fabulous wraparound old-city views after half a century off limits.

★Museo de Cádiz MUSEUM

(www.museosdeandalucia.es; Plaza de Mina; €1.50, EU citizens free; 9am-3pm Tue-Sun mid-Jun–mid-Sep, 9am-8pm Tue-Sat, to 3pm Sun mid-Sep–mid-Jun) Admittedly a little dusty, the Museo de Cádiz is the province's top museum. Stars of the ground-floor archaeology section are two Phoenician marble sarcophagi carved in human likeness, along with lots of headless Roman statues and a giant marble 2nd-century Emperor Trajan (with head) from Bolonia's Baelo Claudia (p703) ruins. Upstairs, the excellent fine-art collection displays Spanish art from the 18th to early 20th centuries, including 18 superb 17th-century canvases of saints, angels and monks by Francisco de Zurbarán.

Teatro Romano ARCHAEOLOGICAL SITE

(Calle Mesón 12; 11am-5pm Mon-Sat, 10am-2pm Sun Apr-Sep, 10am-4.30pm Mon-Sat, to 2pm Sun Oct-Mar, closed 1st Mon of month) FREE On the seaward edge of the Barrio del Pópulo is Cádiz' Roman theatre, dating from the late 1st century BC and, originally, with space for 10,000 spectators. The theatre is undergoing renovation works (due for completion in 2020), but you can still access parts of it via its modern **interpretation centre**, which has intriguing English- and Spanish-language displays detailing the theatre's history.

Plaza de San Juan de Dios SQUARE

Glammed up for the 200th anniversary of the 1812 constitution, cafe-lined Plaza de San Juan de Dios is dominated by the grand, neoclassical **ayuntamiento** (Town Hall), built around 1800.

Plaza de Topete SQUARE

About 250m northwest of the cathedral, this triangular plaza is one of Cádiz' most intimate. Bright with flowers, it's usually talked about as Plaza de las Flores (Square of the Flowers). Right beside is the revamped 1837 **Mercado Central de Abastos** (Plaza de la Libertad; 9am-3pm), the oldest covered market in Spain, now doubling as a buzzing gastromarket (p674).

Torre Tavira TOWER

(www.torretavira.com; Calle Marqués del Real Tesoro 10; adult/child €6/free; 10am-8pm May-Sep, to 6pm Oct-Apr) Northwest of Plaza de Topete, the 18th-century Torre Tavira is the highest point in town, opening up dramatic panoramas of Cádiz, and has a camera obscura that projects live, moving images of the city onto a screen (sessions every 20 to 30 minutes).

Museo de las Cortes de Cádiz MUSEUM
(Calle Santa Inés 9; 9am-6pm Tue-Fri, to 2pm Sat & Sun) FREE The remodelled Museo de las Cortes de Cádiz travels through the city's 18th- to 20th-century history, and is full of memorabilia associated with the revolutionary 1812 Cádiz parliament. The highlight? A huge, marvellously detailed model of 18th-century Cádiz, made in mahogany, silver and ivory by Alfonso Ximénez between 1777 and 1779.

Playa de la Caleta BEACH
Hugging the western side of the Barrio de la Viña, this small, popular city beach catches the eye with its mock-Moorish, oriental-inspired Modernista *balneario* (bathhouse). It's flanked by two forts: the **Castillo de San Sebastián** (Paseo Fernando Quiñones; 9.30am-5pm) FREE, for centuries a military installation, and the star-shaped **Castillo de Santa Catalina** (956 22 63 33; Calle Antonio Burgos, Playa de la Caleta; 11am-8.30pm Mar-Oct, to 7.30pm Nov-Feb) FREE, built after the 1596 Anglo-Dutch sacking of the city and with a 1683 chapel.

Mimicking Ursula Andress in *Dr. No,* Halle Berry famously strode out of the sea here in an orange bikini in the 2002 James Bond film *Die Another Day.*

Puerta de Tierra GATE
(Plaza de la Constitución; 9.30am-1.30pm & 3.30-6.30pm Tue-Sat) FREE The imposing 18th-century 'Land Gate' guards the southeastern (and only land) entry to Cádiz' old town. You can wander the upper fortifications and defence tower, where Spanish- and English-language panels detail visible sights and the evolution of Cádiz' complex fortification system.

Playa de la Victoria BEACH
Often overshadowed by the city's historical riches, Cádiz' beaches are Copacabana-like in their size, feel and beauty. This fine, wide strip of Atlantic sand, with summer beach bars, starts 1km south of the Puerta de Tierra and stretches 4km back along the peninsula.

Take bus 1 (Plaza España-Cortadura) from **Plaza de España** or bus 7 (Hospital Mora-Ingeniero La Cierva) from Playa de la Caleta or Campo del Sur to Playa de la Victoria (€1.10), or walk/jog along the promenade from the Barrio de Santa María.

Courses

K2 Internacional LANGUAGE
(956 21 26 46; www.k2internacional.com; Plaza Mentidero 19) Based in the Barrio del Mentidero, this old-city school offers special courses for long-term students and people over 50 years old, as well as regular classes. An intensive one-week course costs €175. It also organises city tours, accommodation, and flamenco, cooking and even surf courses.

Gadir Escuela de Español LANGUAGE
(956 26 05 57; http://gadir.net; Calle Pérgolas 5) About 300m southeast of the Puerta de Tierra, this long-established school has a wide range of classes in small, specialised groups. Sample rates are €170 for a week-long intensive course.

Tours

Las Bicis Naranjas CYCLING
(956 22 97 25; https://lasbicisnaranjas.com; Calle Antonio López 5; bike hire per hour/day €4/15, 3hr tours €30; 10am-9pm) Bike hire and a range of multi-language bike trips around Cádiz, from basic three-hour city jaunts (€30) to four-hour bike-and-tapas trails (€45) and four-hour photography tours (€60).

Sleeping

Casa Caracol HOSTEL $
(956 26 11 66; www.casacaracolcadiz.com; Calle Suárez de Salazar 4; incl breakfast dm €22-28, d €43-55, with shared bathroom €40-50;) Mellow Casa Caracol is Cádiz' original old-town backpacker hostel. Cheery as only Cádiz can be, it has colourful, contemporary, locker-equipped dorms for four, six or seven, a sociable communal kitchen, and a roof terrace with hammocks, along with three private doubles (one a duplex-style affair with bathroom). Other perks include home-cooked dinners, yoga, and bike and surfboard rental. No lift.

Hotel Patagonia Sur HOTEL $$
(856 17 46 47; www.hotelpatagoniasur.es; Calle Cobos 11; s €86-113, d €89-155;) This glossy Argentine-run gem offers clean-lined modernity and efficient yet friendly management just steps from the cathedral. The 16 rooms, all with tea-and-coffee sets, are smart, bright, fresh and snug. Bonuses include a glass-fronted cafe and sun-filled 5th-floor attic rooms with cathedral views and sun loungers on private terraces.

Hotel Argantonio HOTEL **$$**
(956 21 16 40; www.hotelargantonio.com; Calle Argantonio 3; incl breakfast s €80-90, d €100-155;) Rambling across an 18th-century home, this stylishly charming hotel in Cádiz' old quarter sparkles with its hand-painted, wood-carved doors, colourfully tiled floors adorning bedrooms, bathrooms and corridors, and intricate Moorish-style arch and fountain in the lobby. The 1st floor is Mudéjar, the 2nd 'colonial romantic', the 3rd a mix. There's a tucked-away roof-terrace lounge, plus a cafe and good breakfasts.

★**Parador de Cádiz** LUXURY HOTEL **$$$**
(956 22 69 05; www.parador.es; Avenida Duque de Nájera 9; incl breakfast d €183-268, ste €200-400;) Bold, beautiful and right beside Playa de la Caleta, the so-called Parador Atlántico contrasts with Andalucía's other *paradores* (luxurious state-owned hotels) in that it's super modern and built from scratch. Sultry reds, ocean blues and bright turquoises throw character into the sleek, contemporary rooms with balcony and floor-to-ceiling windows. Soak in four sea-view swimming pools, or seek out the spa.

Eating

Just as the air in Jerez is thick with sherry, Cádiz smells unforgettably of fresh fish. Calle Virgen de la Palma, in the Barrio de la Viña, is the city's go-to fresh-seafood street. Calles Plocia and Sopranis, off Plaza de San Juan de Dios, are upmarket eat streets. There are good options off Plaza de Mina in the Barrio del Mentidero.

★**Casa Manteca** TAPAS **$**
(956 21 36 03; www.facebook.com/tabernamanteca; Calle Corralón de los Carros 66; tapas €2.50; noon-4pm & 8.30pm-12.30am, may close Sun & Mon evenings Nov-Mar) The hub of the Barrio de la Viña's Carnaval fun, with every inch of its walls covered in flamenco, bullfighting and Carnaval paraphernalia, always-busy Casa Manteca is full of old tapas favourites. Ask the chatty waiters for a tapa of mussels or *chicharrones* (pressed pork dressed with a squeeze of lemon), and it'll fly across the bar on waxed paper.

Rincón Gastronómico TAPAS **$**
(Mercado Central de Abastos, Plaza de la Libertad; tapas €2-8; 9am-4pm Mon, 9am-3.30pm & 7pm-midnight Tue-Fri, 9am-4pm & 8pm-1am Sat;) Cádiz' neoclassical market is the setting for this ultra-buzzy gastromarket, where globe-roaming stalls get packed with lunching *gaditanos*. Sample gloriously simple specialities like *patatas aliñadas*, mountain cheeses and platters of Ibérico ham; pick your fresh fish and have it grilled before your eyes; venture into a plant-based world of vegan tortilla (convincingly delicious!); or hit the sushi stand.

Taberna La Sorpresa TAPAS **$**
(956 22 12 32; www.tabernalasorpresa.com; Calle Arbolí 4; tapas €2.50-5.50; 11.30am-4.30pm & 8.30-11.30pm Tue-Sat, 11.30am-4.30pm Sun) Wood barrels of Pedro Ximénez, *manzanilla* (chamomile-coloured sherry) and *oloroso* (sweet, dark sherry) stack up behind the bar at this buzzy, down-to-earth 1956 tavern, thoughtfully revamped keeping Cádiz' old-school vibe alive. Tapas focus on *almadraba* tuna, but there are plenty of other tasty bites, such as mussels, *chicharrones* and Iberian *bellota* ham, along with other Cádiz-province wines and vermouth on tap.

Pay at the tiny local-products shop on the way out.

La Marmita Centro TAPAS, FUSION **$$**
(956 21 52 27; www.grupolamarmita.com; Calle Buenos Aires 5-7; tapas €4.50-10, 5-course set menu €25; 1.30-3pm & 8.30-11.30pm;) Courtesy of Cádiz' popular La Marmita Group, this sleekly minimalist old-city spot thrills diners with its wonderfully imaginative, exquisitely presented Andalucian-international tapas. Border-crossing dishes put the focus on local produce, such as Cádiz burgers with *payoyo* cheese or *cucuruchos* (cones) of avocado and red *almadraba* tuna. Veggie-friendly delights include Vietnamese rolls stuffed with avocado, basil and cashew pesto.

You can book for the smart back restaurant, which serves excellent-value, five-course degustation menus (€25), but not the tapas bar.

Ultramar&nos ANDALUCIAN, FUSION **$$**
(856 07 69 46; www.ultramarynos.com; Calle Enrique de las Marinas 2; dishes €6-15; 1.30-4pm & 8.30-11pm;) Busy with travellers and *gaditanos* alike, this expertly reimagined former grocer's shop (*ultramarinos*) oozes stripped-back contemporary styling with its recycled materials and long blue-tiled bar. Putting a twist on Cádiz favourites, its inventive seasonal cooking revolves around local produce, showcasing a drool-worthy menu of lime-dressed *chicharrones*, zesty vegetable curry, tuna-sashimi salad and king-prawn skewers.

LOCAL KNOWLEDGE

CÁDIZ CARNAVAL

No other Spanish city celebrates **Carnaval** (www.turismo.cadiz.es; ⌚Feb) with as much spirit, dedication and humour as Cádiz. Here it becomes a 10-day singing, dancing and drinking fancy-dress street party spanning two February weekends. The fun, fuelled by huge amounts of alcohol, is irresistible.

Costumed groups of up to 45 people, called *murgas*, tour the city on foot or on floats and tractors, dancing, drinking, singing satirical ditties or performing sketches. The biggest hits are the 12-person *chirigotas* with their scathing humour, irony and double meanings, often directed at politicians. Most of their famed verbal wit will be lost on all but fluent Spanish speakers.

This being carefree Cádiz, in addition to the 300 or so officially recognised *murgas* (who are judged by a panel in the Gran Teatro Falla), there are also plenty of ilegales – any singing group that fancies taking to the streets.

The heart of Carnaval, where you'll stumble across some of the liveliest and most drunken scenes, is the working-class Barrio de la Viña, between the Mercado Central de Abastos and Playa de la Caleta, and along Calle Ancha and around Plaza de Topete, where *ilegales* tend to congregate.

Typically, the first weekend sees the mass arrival of nonlocal party goers, while the second weekend is when the *gaditanos* (people from Cádiz) really come out to play. Surprisingly, things can be quiet midweek.

If you plan to sleep in Cádiz during Carnaval, book accommodation months ahead.

La Esquina de Sopranis TAPAS **$$**

(☎956 26 58 42; www.sopranis.es; Calle Sopranis 5; tapas €2-5; ⌚1-4pm & 8.45-11.30pm Tue-Sat, 1-4pm Sun, daily Jul & Aug; ✎) One of those bubbly, contemporary tapas places you'll never want to leave, Sopranis blends casual and sophisticated to perfection. The food is equally enticing. Local, seasonal ingredients are thrown together in beautifully presented creative combos, like miniburgers, portobello-mushroom carpaccio or falafel with yoghurt sauce, alongside a few classics (*patatas aliñadas*, fried fish). Top pick: the melt-in-the-mouth cheeses.

El Faro de Cádiz TAPAS, SEAFOOD **$$$**

(☎956 21 10 68; www.elfarodecadiz.com; Calle San Félix 15; tapas €2.70-3.50, mains €17-24; ⌚1-4pm & 8.30-11.30pm) Ask any *gaditano* for their favourite Cádiz tapas bar and there's a high chance they'll choose El Faro. Seafood, particularly the *tortillitas de camarones* (shrimp fritters), is why people come here, though the *rabo de toro* (oxtail) and *patatas aliñadas* (potato salad) have their devotees. El Faro's upmarket restaurant, decorated with pretty ceramics, gets mixed reviews.

Drinking & Nightlife

The Plaza de Mina–Plaza San Francisco–Plaza de España triangle is the centre of the old city's late-night bar scene, especially Calle Beato Diego; things get going around midnight, but it can be quiet early in the week. More bars are scattered around the Barrio del Pópulo, east of the cathedral. Punta San Felipe (La Punta), on the northern side of the harbour, has a string of drinks/dance bars packed with a youngish crowd from about 3am to 6am Thursday to Saturday.

Cádiz' other nocturnal haunt, especially in summer, is down along Playa de la Victoria and the Paseo Marítimo, on and around Calle Muñoz Arenillas near the Hotel Playa Victoria (2.5km southeast of the Puerta de Tierra).

La Colonial COCKTAIL BAR

(www.facebook.com/lacolonialalameda; Calle Buenos Aires 20; ⌚8pm-2am) This chic cocktail bar sits at the northern edge of old Cádiz, dressed in neon lighting, and with sea-view tables around a gurgling, palm-fringed fountain on the promenade opposite. Mixologists whip up a world of original cocktails (€7), or go for *manzanilla, oloroso* and (pricier) extra-aged sherries from the renowned Bodegas Tradición (p681) in Jerez. Hours can vary.

Nahu Centro BAR

(www.facebook.com/NahuCentro; Calle Beato Diego 8; ⌚8pm-3am Tue-Thu, 6pm-4am Fri & Sat; 📶) Stylish student-oriented cocktail bar with mood lighting, Moroccan lamps and chill-out sofas. At its best when you're perched at the bar, G&T in hand, but good for coffee and wi-fi too. Regular DJ sessions; check the Facebook page.

Quilla CAFE, BAR
(www.quilla.es; Playa de la Caleta; 11am-midnight Sun-Thu, to 2am Fri & Sat;) A bookish cafe-bar encased in what appears to be the rusty hulk of an old ship overlooking Playa de la Caleta, with coffee, pastries, tapas, wine, art exhibitions, gratis sunsets and lightly modernised Andalucian dishes (burgers, salads, *tostas*, grilled fish; €7 to €12). Opening hours spill over in summer.

☆ Entertainment

Cádiz helped invent flamenco and subtly nurtured the talent of Andalucía's finest classical composer, Manuel de Falla, and this weighty musical legacy is ingrained in the city's entertainment scene.

★**Peña Flamenca La Perla** FLAMENCO
(956 25 91 01; www.laperladecadiz.es; Calle Carlos Ollero) Paint-peeled, sea-splashed La Perla, set romantically next to the crashing Atlantic surf off Calle Concepción Arenal in the Barrio de Santa María, hosts flamenco at 10pm most Fridays, more often in spring and summer, for an audience full of aficionados. It's an unforgettable experience.

La Cava FLAMENCO
(956 21 18 66; www.flamencolacava.com; Calle Antonio López 16; €22) Cádiz' main *tablao* (choreographed flamenco show) happens in a rustically bedecked tavern on Tuesday, Thursday and Saturday at 9.30pm. Schedules are reduced November to February.

Information

Centro de Recepción de Turistas (956 24 10 01; www.turismo.cadiz.es; Paseo de Canalejas; 9am-7pm Mon-Fri, to 5pm Sat & Sun Jul-Sep, 8.30am-6.30pm Mon-Fri, 9am-5pm Sat & Sun Oct-Jun) Near the bus and train stations.

Oficina de Turismo Regional (956 20 31 91; www.andalucia.org; Avenida Ramón de Carranza; 9am-7.15pm Mon-Fri, 10am-2.45pm Sat & Sun)

Getting There & Away

BOAT

From Cádiz' **Terminal Marítima Metropolitana** (Muelle Reina Victoria), 17 to 19 daily CMTBC (p676) catamarans head to El Puerto de Santa María (€2.70, 30 minutes).

BUS

All out-of-town buses leave from Cádiz' new **bus station** (Avenida de Astilleros), inaugurated in late 2017, on the eastern side of the train station (at the southeastern end of the old city). Most buses are operated by **Comes** (902 64 64 28; www.tgcomes.es) or **Los Amarillos** (902 21 03 17; http://losamarillos.autobusing.com). The **Consorcio de Transportes Bahía de Cádiz** (CMTBC; 955 03 86 65; www.cmtbc.es) runs to/from **Jerez airport** (p687).

DESTINATION	COST (€)	DURATION	FREQUENCY
Arcos de la Frontera	7.30	1-1½hr	3-8 daily
El Puerto de Santa María	2.70	45min	every 30-60min
Granada	34	5¼hr	4 daily
Jerez de la Frontera	3.80	50min	2-7 daily
Jerez de la Frontera airport	3.80	1½hr	1-2 daily
Málaga	28	4½hr	4 daily
Ronda	16	3¼hr	1-2 daily
Sanlúcar de Barrameda	5	1hr	5-10 daily
Seville	13	1¾hr	9-10 daily
Tarifa	10	1¼-1¾hr	8 daily
La Barca de Vejer (for Vejer de la Frontera)	5.85	1-1½hr	9-11 daily

CAR & MOTORCYCLE

The AP4 motorway from Seville to Puerto Real on the eastern side of the Bahía de Cádiz carries a €7.20 toll.

TRAIN

From the train station, next to the bus station on the southeastern edge of the old town, trains go to El Puerto de Santa María (€4.05 to €5.05, 25 to 35 minutes, 28 to 38 daily), Jerez de la Frontera (€4.05 to €6.05, 45 minutes, 33 to 42 daily) and Seville (€16 to €22, 1¾ hours, 12 to 15 daily). Three or four daily high-speed ALVIA trains go to Madrid (€68 to €74, 4½ hours).

El Puerto de Santa María

POP 43,890

When you're surrounded by such cultural luminaries as Cádiz, Jerez de la Frontera and Seville, it's easy to overlook the small print; such is the fate of El Puerto de Santa María, despite its collection of well-known icons. Osborne sherry, with its famous bull logo (a highly recognisable symbol of Spain), was founded and retains its headquarters here, as do half a dozen other sherry bodegas. With its abundance of sandy blonde beaches, tempting cuisine, sherry wineries and smattering of architectural heirlooms, El Puerto can seem like southern Andalucía in microcosm. It's an easy day trip from Cádiz or Jerez.

Sights

★Bodegas Osborne WINERY
(956 86 91 00; www.bodegas-osborne.com; Calle los Moros 7; tours from €14, tastings €8-30) Creator of the legendary black-bull logo still exhibited on life-size billboards all over Spain (now without the name), Osborne is El Puerto's best-known sherry winery. It was set up by an Englishman, Thomas Osborne Mann, in 1772. It remains one of Spain's oldest companies run continuously by the same family.

The gorgeous whitewashed bodega leads tours with tastings at noon in Spanish, 10am in English and 11am in German. Book ahead.

From June to mid-September there's an additional 7.30pm Spanish tour.

Bodegas Gutiérrez Colosía WINERY
(956 85 28 52; www.gutierrezcolosia.com; Avenida de la Bajamar 40; tours €10) No bookings are needed for tours of this intimate, family-run, 1830-founded sherry bodega, right beside the catamaran dock. Visits end with a six-wine tasting, which can include tapas and flamenco on request. Visits run at 11.15am in English and 12.30pm in Spanish Monday to Friday, and at 1pm in both languages on Saturday; additional evening tours happen July to September.

Castillo de San Marcos CASTLE
(627 569335; servicios.turisticos@caballero.es; Plaza Alfonso X El Sabio; adult/child €8/4, Tue free; tours hourly 11.30am-1.30pm Tue, 10.30am-1.30pm Wed-Sat, closed Wed & Fri Nov-Apr) Heavily restored in the 20th century, El Puerto's fine castle was constructed over an Islamic mosque by Alfonso X El Sabio after he took the town in 1260. The old mosque inside, now converted into a church, is the highlight. Wednesday-to-Saturday visits end with a five-sherry tasting (the castle is owned by Bodegas Caballero). All 11.30am sessions are in English; Tuesday tours require bookings.

Fundación Rafael Alberti MUSEUM
(956 85 07 11; www.rafaelalberti.es; Calle Santo Domingo 25; adult/child €4/2; 10am-2pm Tue-Fri, 11am-2pm Sat & Sun) Two blocks inland from Plaza Alfonso X El Sabio, this foundation has interesting, well-displayed exhibits on Rafael Alberti (1902–99), one of Spain's great Generation of '27 poets, in what was his childhood home. Free English, French or Spanish audio guides.

Plaza Real de Toros NOTABLE BUILDING
(956 86 11 88; www.visitasplazarealelpuerto.com; Plaza Elías Ahuja; €3, tours €6; 10am-2pm & 6-9pm Mon-Fri, 10am-2pm Sat & Sun Jun-Sep, 4-7pm Mon-Fri Oct-May) Four blocks southwest of Plaza de España is El Puerto's grand Plaza de Toros, built in 1880 with room for 15,000 spectators and still one of Andalucía's most important bullrings. Entry is from Calle Valdés. Touring a bullring is not the same as watching a bullfight; if you're happy to support a bullring in this way (which many travellers may not be), it could be a way of learning about this deep-rooted Spanish tradition without actually attending a bullfight.

Festivals & Events

Feria de Primavera y Fiestas del Vino Fino WINE
(Spring Fair; Apr-May) Around 200,000 half-bottles of *fino* (dry, straw-coloured sherry) are drunk during this six-day fiesta.

Festividad Virgen del Carmen RELIGIOUS
(16 Jul) Fisherfolk Andalucía-wide pay homage to their patron at this festival; El Puerto parades the Virgin's image along the Río Guadalete.

Sleeping

El Baobab Hostel HOSTEL $
(956 54 21 23; www.baobabhostel.com; Calle Pagador 37; dm €20-35, d €40-80; mid-Feb–mid-Oct;) In a converted 18th-century building near the bullring, this 10-room hostel is El Puerto's best budget choice, with a homey, friendly feel, simple interiors, and communal kitchen and courtyard. There are private doubles, while fan-cooled, locker-equipped dorms sleep four to eight; half have private bathrooms. Renovations were under way at research time: all rooms should have air-con and bathrooms from 2018.

Casa de Huéspedes Santa María GUESTHOUSE $$
(956 85 36 31; www.casadehuespedessantamaria.com; Calle Pedro Muñoz Seca 38; d €58-70,

with shared bathroom €47-55, tr €66-75;) Exposed-stone walls, tile-covered floors and flamingo-stamped cushions create a retro-chic feel at this homey, welcoming, low-key guesthouse. The 10 rooms (two with shared bathroom) are dotted around a peaceful patio within a stylishly renovated 19th-century house. Thoughtful touches include a tea/coffee stand, a communal kitchen, beach towels and umbrellas, and breakfasts featuring homebaked cakes.

Eating

El Puerto is famous for its outstanding seafood and tapas bars. Look along central Calles Luna and Misericordia, Calle Ribera del Marisco to the north, Avenidas de la Bajamar and Aramburu de Mora to the south, and Calle La Placilla near Plaza de España.

At the other end of the spectrum, El Puerto also hosts Andalucía's first ever three-Michelin-starred restaurant, Aponiente.

Romerijo SEAFOOD $

(956 54 12 54; www.romerijo.com; Ribera del Marisco 1; seafood per 250g from €5, raciones €4-15; noon-11.30pm) A huge, always-busy El Puerto institution, Romerijo has been going strong since 1952 and has three sections: one boiling seafood, another (opposite) frying it, and the third a *cervecería* (beer bar). Buy seafood by the quarter-kilo in paper cones.

La Taberna del Chef del Mar TAPAS, SEAFOOD $$

(956 11 20 93; Calle Puerto Escondido 6; tapas & raciones €5-17; 1.30-4.30pm & 8.30pm-midnight Mon-Sat, 1.30-4.30pm Sun Apr-Oct) Decked with dangling fish carvings and splashes of vibrant colour, this fashionable tavern provides a tapas-sized taste of the cutting-edge seafood-mad cuisine concocted by top Spanish chef Angel León, of El Puerto's three-Michelin-starred Aponiente (p678) fame. Expertly plated-up bites, mostly designed for sharing, range from octopus brochettes and red-tuna *bao* buns to creamy plankton rice and seafood *ajo blanco*.

Mesón del Asador SPANISH, BARBECUE $$

(956 54 03 27; Calle Misericordia 2; tapas €2-4, mains €9-20; 1-4pm & 8.15pm-midnight) It's a measure of El Puerto's gastronomic nous that, in such a seafood-oriented town, there's a meat restaurant that could compete with any Buenos Aires steakhouse. The power of the Mesón's delivery is in its deceptively simple chicken brochettes, two-person *parrilladas* (grilled-meat mixes), and chargrilled beef and pork sizzling away on mini-barbecues brought to your table.

★ Aponiente SEAFOOD, FUSION $$$

(956 85 18 70; www.aponiente.com; Molino de Mareas El Caño, Calle Francisco Cossi Ochoa; 21-course menu €205; 1-1.30pm & 8-8.30pm Tue-Sat early Mar-early Dec, plus Mon Jul & Aug) Audacious is the word for the bold experimentation of leading Spanish chef Angel León, whose seafood-biased *nueva cocina* has won a cavalcade of awards, transforming Aponiente into Andalucía's first triple-Michelin-starred restaurant. Occupying a design-led 19th-century tide mill, Aponiente splits opinion in traditional El Puerto. Some snort at its pretension, others salivate at the thought of its uber-imaginative 21-course tasting menus.

El Faro del Puerto ANDALUCIAN, SEAFOOD $$$

(956 87 09 52; www.elfarodelpuerto.com; Carretera de Fuentebravía, Km 0.5; tapas €5-15, mains €18-27; 1.30-4.30pm & 8.30-11pm Mon-Sat, 1.30-4.30pm Sun;) El Faro is worth hunting down for its traditional-with-a-hint-of-innovation take on local seafood, excellent Spanish wine list, and classically smart, multi-room setting inside an old *casa señorial* (manor house). The *almadraba* tuna tartare is a highlight. The bar/tapas menu has some exciting vegetarian and gluten-free choices. It's on the roundabout at the northwestern end of Calle Valdés.

Drinking & Nightlife

Bodega Obregón BAR

(956 85 63 29; Calle Zarza 51; 9am-2pm & 6-11pm Mon-Fri, 9am-late Sat, 10am-2pm Sun) Think sherry is just a drink for grandmas? Come and have your illusions blown to pieces at this family-run, spit-and-sawdust-style bar where its own sweet stuff is siphoned from woody barrels. The home-cooked Saturday-lunch *guisos* (stews) are a local favourite.

Entertainment

Peña Flamenca Tomás El Nitri FLAMENCO

(956 54 32 37; Calle Diego Niño 1) This good, honest *peña* (small private club), with the air of a foot-stomping, 19th-century flamenco bar, showcases some truly amazing guitarists, singers and dancers in a lively space full of regulars. Shows are usually on Saturday nights; call or ask at the tourist office.

Information

Oficina de Turismo (956 48 37 15; www.turismoelpuerto.com; Plaza de Alfonso X El Sabio 9; 9am-2.50pm & 5-8pm Mon-Sat, 9am-2pm & 6-8pm Sun Jun-Oct, closed Sun afternoon Nov-May) In the 16th-century Palacio de Aranibar, which has a Tuscan-pillared patio.

Getting There & Away

BOAT

The **catamaran** (www.cmtbc.es; 6.45am-9.10pm Mon-Fri, 9am-2pm & 3.30-9.25pm Sat & Sun) leaves for Cádiz (€2.70, 30 minutes) up to 18 times daily Monday to Friday, and up to 16 times at weekends, from in front of the Hotel Santa María.

BUS

El Puerto has two bus stops. CMTBC (p676) buses to Cádiz (€2.70, 45 minutes, every 30 to 60 minutes), Jerez de la Frontera (€1.65, 20 minutes, two to eight daily) and Sanlúcar de Barrameda (€1.95, 25 minutes, five to 11 daily) go from the **bus stop** (Plaza Elías Ahuja) outside the bullring. **Comes** (902 64 64 28; www.tgcomes.es) buses to Seville (€10, 1½ hours, one or two daily) go from outside the train station.

TRAIN

From the train station at the northeastern end of town, frequent trains go to/from Jerez de la Frontera (€2.70, eight minutes), Cádiz (€5.05, 35 minutes) and Seville (€14, 1¼ hours).

Sanlúcar de Barrameda

POP 46,100

Sanlúcar is one of those lesser-known Andalucian towns that pleasantly surprise. Firstly, there's the gastronomy: Sanlúcar cooks up some of the region's best seafood on a hallowed waterside strip called Bajo de Guía. Secondly, Sanlúcar's unique location at the northern tip of the esteemed Sherry Triangle enables its earthy bodegas, nestled in the somnolent, monument-strewn old town, to produce the much-admired one-of-a-kind *manzanilla* (dry, chamomile-coloured Sanlúcar-made sherry). Thirdly, plonked at the mouth of the Río Guadalquivir estuary, Sanlúcar provides a quieter, less touristed entry point into the ethereal Parque Nacional de Doñana (p664) than the more popular western access points in Huelva province.

As if that weren't enough, the town harbours a proud nautical history. Both Christopher Columbus, on his third sojourn, and Portuguese mariner Ferdinand Magellan struck out from here on their voyages of discovery.

Sights

★Bodegas Barbadillo — WINERY

(956 38 55 21; www.barbadillo.com; Calle Sevilla 6; tours €10; tours noon & 1pm Tue-Sun, in English 11am Tue-Sun, open Mon Jul & Aug, closed Sun Nov-Mar) With its bodega founded in 1821, Barbadillo was the first family to bottle Sanlúcar's famous *manzanilla* and also produces one of Spain's most popular *vinos*. Bodega tours end with a four-wine tasting. This 19th-century building also houses the eye-opening **Museo de la Manzanilla** (10am-3pm) FREE, which traces the 200-year history of *manzanilla*.

Castillo de Santiago — CASTLE

(956 92 35 00; www.castillodesantiago.com; Plaza del Castillo 1; adult/child €7/5; 10.15am-3pm & 6.15-9pm Mon & Tue, 10.15am-7.30pm Wed, 10.15am-9pm Thu-Sun approx May-Oct, 10am-3pm & 5-7pm Mon-Sat, 10am-3pm Sun approx Nov-Apr) Surrounded by Barbadillo bodegas, Sanlúcar's restored 15th-century castle has sprawling views across the Guadalquivir delta from its hexagonal Torre del Homenaje (keep), and displays military uniforms and weapons. According to legend, Isabel la Católica first saw the sea from here. Opening hours vary seasonally.

Iglesia de Nuestra Señora de la O — CHURCH

(Plaza de la Paz; suggested donation €2; 11am-1.15pm, Mass 8pm Mon, Wed & Thu, noon & 8pm Sun) Fronting the old town's Calle Caballeros, this medieval church stands out among Sanlúcar's many others for its elaborate 1360s Gothic-Mudéjar portal and its rich interior embellishment, particularly the Mudéjar *artesonado* (ceiling of interlaced beams). The bell tower was built reusing a tower from the Moorish *alcázar* (fortress) that once stood here.

Palacio de los Guzmán — PALACE

(956 36 01 61; www.fcmedinasidonia.com; Plaza Condes de Niebla 1; tours €5; tours noon Wed & Thu, 11.30am & noon Sun) Just off Calle Caballeros, this rambling palace was the home of the Duques de Medina Sidonia, the aristocratic family that once owned more of Spain than anyone else. The mostly 17th-century house, of 12th-century origin, bursts with antiques, and paintings by Goya, Zurbarán and other Spanish greats.

Palacio de Orleans y Borbón PALACE
(cnr Calles Cuesta de Belén & Caballeros; 10am-1.30pm Mon-Fri) FREE At the top of Calle Cuesta de Belén you'll spot this beautiful neo-Mudéjar old-town palace, built as a 19th-century summer home for the aristocratic Montpensier family. Washed in horizontal red and yellow stripes, it's now Sanlúcar's town hall; you can only visit the gardens.

Tours

Sanlúcar is a good base for exploring the Parque Nacional de Doñana (p664), which glistens just across the Río Guadalquivir.

Trips are run by the licensed **Visitas Doñana** (956 36 38 13; www.visitasdonana.com; Centro de Visitantes Fábrica de Hielo, Bajo de Guía; 9am-7pm). Your first option is a 2½-hour boat/jeep combination (€35), which goes 30km through the park's dunes, marshlands and pine forests in 21-person 4WD vehicles. There are two trips in the morning and two in the afternoon March to September, and one daily trip November to February. The second (less interesting) option is a three-hour hop-on, hop-off ferry tour with a little walking (adult/child €17/9), which runs with the same frequency. Book at the Centro de Visitantes Fábrica de Hielo (p681).

Viajes Doñana (956 36 25 40; http://viajesdonana.es; Calle San Juan 20; 10am-2pm & 5-8.30pm Mon-Fri, 10.30am-2pm Sat) agency books the same trips, as well as 3½-hour tours (adult/child €40/24) into the park.

Festivals & Events

Feria de la Manzanilla WINE
(late May/early Jun) A big *manzanilla*-fuelled fair kicks off Sanlúcar's summer.

Carreras de Caballos SPORTS
(www.carrerassanlucar.es; Aug) Two horse-race meetings held almost every year since 1845, on the beaches beside the Guadalquivir estuary.

Sleeping

★**Hostal Alcoba** BOUTIQUE HOTEL $$
(956 38 31 09; www.hotelalcoba.com; Calle Alcoba 26; s €65-80, d €73-90; P) The stylish 14-room Alcoba, with a slick contemporary courtyard complete with loungers, hammock and lap pool, looks like something that architect Frank Lloyd Wright might have conceived. Skilfully put together (and run), it's a genius white-on-white creation that's wonderfully homey, functional and central (just off the northeastern end of Calle Ancha), all at once. Breakfast (€7) is a good buffet.

La Casa BOUTIQUE HOTEL $$
(617 575913; www.lacasasanlucar.com; Calle Ancha 84; r €50-90) A friendly young team manages this gorgeously fresh boutique guesthouse. Done up in blues, whites, pinks and turquoises, the eight rooms are loosely inspired by Doñana national park, blending traditional charm (19th-century shutters, marble-effect floors) with contemporary style (see-through showers, geometric lamps, rectangular sinks). Breakfasts feature organic Huelva jams, fresh orange juice and other local goodies.

Hotel Barrameda HOTEL $$
(956 38 58 78; www.hotelbarrameda.com; Calle Ancha 10; r €80-116; mid-Feb–mid-Dec;) This gleaming, 40-room hotel overlooks the tapas-bar fun on Plaza del Cabildo, and makes an excellent, central choice for its sparkling modern rooms, wood-and-cream decor, ground-floor interior patio, marble floors and efficient service. Among the 12 superior rooms, all with little terraces, four have hot tubs.

Eating

Strung out along **Bajo de Guía**, 1km northeast of central Sanlúcar, is one of Andalucía's most famous eating strips, once a fishing village and now a haven of high-quality seafood restaurants that revel in their simplicity. The undisputed speciality is *arroz caldoso a la marinera* (seafood rice); the local *langostinos* (king prawns) are another favourite. Plaza del Cabildo is another food hot spot.

★**Casa Balbino** TAPAS, SEAFOOD $
(956 36 05 13; http://casabalbino.es; Plaza del Cabildo 14; tapas €2-3; noon-5pm & 8pm-midnight, closed first 3 weeks Nov) It doesn't matter when you arrive, Casa Balbino is always overflowing with people, drawn in by its fantastic seafood tapas. Whether you're perched at the bar, tucked into a corner or lucky enough to score an outdoor plaza table, you'll have to elbow your way through and shout your order to a waiter, who'll yell back and provide your dish.

Taberna Argüeso ANDALUCIAN, SUSHI $$
(956 36 07 87; http://tabernaargüeso.com; Calle Mar 2; dishes €6-16; 1-3.30pm & 8.30pm-

midnight Tue-Sat, 1-3.30pm Sun, sushi from 9.30pm Thu-Sat) With its beamed ceiling and tiled floors, Taberna Argüeso feels like an old-time tapas bar but, out the back, it morphs into a smart glassed-in sushi bar and Andalucian-Japanese fusion restaurant. *Nigiri, maki* and sashimi are crafted using red *almadraba* tuna; experimental dishes feature Sanlúcar king prawns and *manzanilla*. Or keep it local with tapas like *patatas aliñadas.*

Poma SEAFOOD **$$**

(☎956 36 51 53; www.restaurantepoma.com; Bajo de Guía 6; mains €12-20; ⌚1-4.30pm & 8pm-midnight) You could kick a football on Bajo de Guía and guarantee it'd land on a decent plate of fish, but you should probably aim for Poma, where the *frito variado* (€15) arrives loaded with lightly fried species plucked out of the nearby sea and river. Seafood stews, grilled fish and *arroz a la marinera* for two are also popular.

Information

Centro de Visitantes Fábrica de Hielo (☎956 38 65 77; Bajo de Guía; ⌚9am-8pm Apr-Sep, to 7pm Oct-Mar)

Oficina de Información Turística (☎956 36 61 10; www.sanlucarturismo.com; Avenida Calzada Duquesa Isabel; ⌚10am-2pm & 5-7pm Mon-Sat, 10am-2pm Sun)

Getting There & Away

From Sanlúcar's **bus station** (Avenida de la Estación), **Los Amarillos** (☎902 21 03 17; http://losamarillos.autobusing.com) goes hourly to/from El Puerto de Santa María (€2.15, 30 minutes), Cádiz (€5.10, one hour) and Seville (€8.77, two hours), less frequently at weekends. **Autocares Valenzuela** (p687) has hourly buses to/from Jerez de la Frontera (€1.95, 40 minutes), fewer at weekends.

Jerez de la Frontera

POP 191,550

Stand down, all other claimants. Jerez, as most savvy Hispanophiles know, *is* Andalucía. It just doesn't broadcast it in the way that Seville and Granada do. Jerez is the capital of Andalucian horse culture, stop one on the famed Sherry Triangle and – cue protestations from Cádiz and Seville – the cradle of Spanish flamenco. The *bulería* (flamenco songs), Jerez' jokey, tongue-in-cheek antidote to Seville's tragic *soleá,* was first concocted in the legendary Roma *barrios* of Santiago and San Miguel. But Jerez is also a vibrant modern Andalucian city, where fashion brands live in old palaces and stylishly outfitted businesspeople sit down to distinctly contemporary cuisine between glasses of *fino* at bubbly *tabancos* (simple taverns serving sherry).

If you really want to unveil the eternal riddle that is Andalucía, start with Jerez.

Sights

Scattered across town, often tucked behind other buildings, Jerez' understated sights creep up on you. It can take a day or two to bond with the city. But once you're bitten, it's like *duende* (flamenco spirit) – there's no turning back.

Jerez (the word even means 'sherry') has around 20 sherry bodegas. Most require bookings for visits, but a few offer tours where you can just turn up. The tourist office has details.

★Bodegas Tradición WINERY, GALLERY

(☎956 16 86 28; www.bodegastradicion.com; Plaza Cordobeses 3; tours €25; ⌚9am-5pm Mon-Fri Jul & Aug, reduced hours Sep-Jun) An intriguing, evocative bodega, not only for its extra-aged sherries (at least 20, mostly 30 years old) but also because it houses the **Colección Joaquín Rivero**, a private Spanish art collection that includes important works by Goya, Velázquez, El Greco and Zurbarán. Tours (in English, Spanish or German) require bookings, and are worth splashing out on.

Catedral de San Salvador CATHEDRAL

(Plaza de la Encarnación; adult/child €5/2.50, 10.30am-12.30pm Sun & 7-9pm Mon free; ⌚10am-6.30pm Mon-Sat) Echoes of Seville colour Jerez' dramatic cathedral, a surprisingly harmonious mix of baroque, neoclassical and Gothic styles. Standout features are its broad flying buttresses and intricately carved stone ceilings. Behind the main altar, a series of rooms and chapels shows off the cathedral's collection of silverware, religious garments and art (including works by Zurbarán and Pacheco). Across the square, the bell tower is 15th-century Gothic-Mudéjar on its lower half and 17th century at the top.

Alcázar FORTRESS

(☎956 14 99 55; Alameda Vieja; excl/incl camera obscura €5/7; ⌚9.30am-5.30pm Mon-Fri, 9.30am-2.30pm Sat & Sun Jul–mid-Sep, 9.30am-2.30pm daily mid-Sep–Jun) Jerez' muscular yet elegant 11th- or 12th-century fortress is one

Jerez de la Frontera

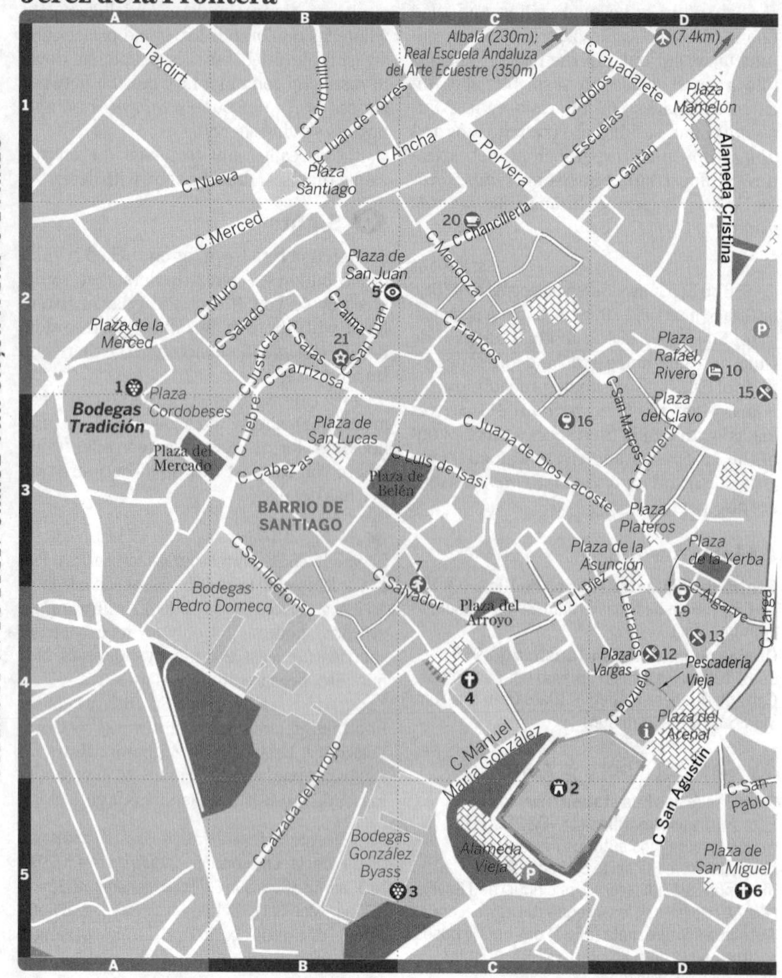

of Andalucía's best-preserved Almohad-era relics. It's notable for its octagonal tower, a classic example of Almohad defensive forts, reached through Islamic-style **gardens**, past a 12th-century **mosque-turned-chapel** and the 17th- and18th-century baroque **Palacio Villavicencio**. Fortress hours vary.

You enter the Alcázar via the **Patio de Armas**. On the left is the beautiful *mezquita* (mosque), transformed into a chapel by Alfonso X in 1264, though retaining its fountain and horseshoe arches; it's the only remaining one of 18 mosques that once stood in Jerez. On the right, the Palacio Villavicencio, built over the Almohad palace ruins, displays artwork but is best known for its bird's-eye views of Jerez; the camera obscura inside its tower provides a picturesque panorama of the city.

Beyond the Patio de Armas, the peaceful gardens recreate the ambience of Islamic times with geometric flower beds and tinkling fountains. The well-preserved, domed Almohad Baños Árabes (Arabic Baths), with their star-shaped shafts of light, are particularly worth a look.

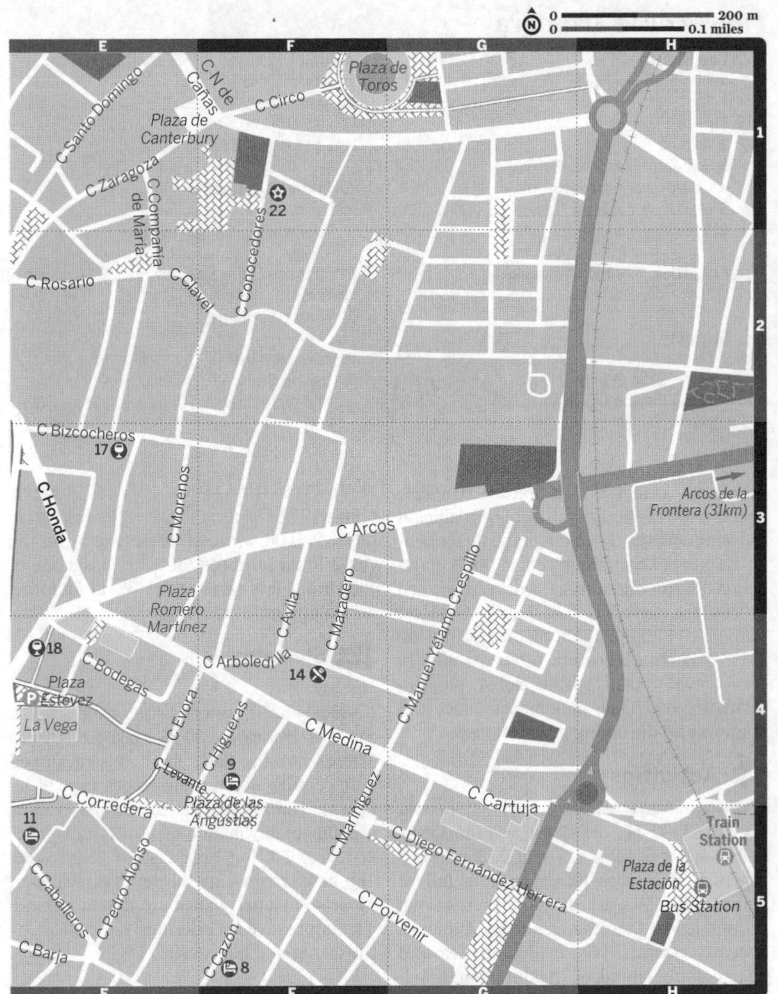

Iglesia de San Miguel CHURCH
(Plaza de San Miguel; adult/child €2/free; 9.30am-1.30pm Mon-Fri) Built between the 15th and 18th centuries, this beautiful church is a blend of Gothic, Renaissance and baroque architecture. Its three-tiered, elaborately carved baroque bell tower is topped by a colourful tile-patterned roof.

Bodegas González-Byass WINERY
(Bodegas Tío Pepe; 956 35 70 16; www.bodegastiopepe.com; Calle Manuel María González 12; tours from €15; tours hourly noon-6pm Mon-Sat, noon-2pm Sun) Home to the famous Tío Pepe brand, González-Byass is one of Jerez' biggest sherry houses, handily located just west of the Alcázar. Three to five daily tours run in Spanish, three to four in English and two to three in German. Basic visits include a two-wine tasting; others have tapas and extra sherries. You can book online, but it isn't essential.

Centro Andaluz de Flamenco ARTS CENTRE
(Andalucian Flamenco Centre; 956 90 21 34, 956 34 92 65; www.centroandaluzdeflamenco.es; Plaza de San Juan 1; 9am-2pm Mon-Fri) FREE At once architecturally intriguing – note the

Jerez de la Frontera

Top Sights
1 Bodegas Tradición ... A2

Sights
2 Alcázar ... C5
3 Bodegas González-Byass ... C5
4 Catedral de San Salvador ... C4
5 Centro Andaluz de Flamenco ... B2
6 Iglesia de San Miguel ... D5

Activities, Courses & Tours
7 Hammam Andalusí ... C3

Sleeping
8 Hostal Fenix ... F5
9 Hotel Casa Grande ... F4
10 Hotel Palacio Garvey ... D2
11 Nuevo Hotel ... E5

Eating
12 A Mar ... D4
13 Albores ... D4
14 La Carboná ... F4
15 La Moderna ... D2

Drinking & Nightlife
16 Damajuana ... C3
17 Tabanco El Guitarrón de San Pedro ... E3
18 Tabanco El Pasaje ... E4
19 Tabanco Plateros ... D4
20 Tetería La Jaima ... C2

Entertainment
21 Centro Cultural Flamenco Don Antonio Chacón ... B2
22 Puro Arte ... F1

entrance's original 15th-century Mudéjar *artesonado* and the intricate Andalucian baroque courtyard – and a fantastic flamenco resource, this unique centre holds thousands of print and musical works. Flamenco videos are screened half hourly between 9am and 1.30pm. Staff members provide lists of flamenco-hosting *tabancos* and 19 local *peñas* (small private clubs), plus information on classes in flamenco dance and singing, and upcoming performances.

Activities

Hammam Andalusí HAMMAM
(☎956 34 90 66; www.hammamandalusi.com; Calle Salvador 6; baths €25, with 15/30min massage €35/55; ⊙10am-10pm) Jerez is full of echoes of its Moorish past, but there's none more magical than the Hammam Andalusí. Incense, essential oils, fresh mint tea and the soothing sound of trickling water welcome you through the door, then you enjoy three turquoise pools (tepid, hot and cold). You can even throw in a massage. Numbers are limited, so book ahead.

Festivals & Events

Festival de Jerez DANCE, MUSIC
(www.facebook.com/FestivalDeJerez; ⊙late Feb-early Mar) Jerez' biggest flamenco celebration.

Feria del Caballo FAIR
(⊙late Apr-early May) Jerez' week-long horse fair is one of Andalucía's grandest festivals, with music and dance, and equestrian competitions and parades.

Motorcycle Grand Prix SPORTS
(⊙May) The **Circuito de Jerez** (Racing Circuit; ☎956 15 11 00; www.circuitodejerez.com), on the A382 10km northeast of town, hosts one of the Grand Prix races of the World Motorcycle Championship.

Sleeping

Hostal Fenix HOSTAL $
(☎956 34 52 91; www.hostalfenix.com; Calle Cazón 7; incl breakfast s €30-35, d €35-40;) There's nothing flash about this revamped 19th-century home – and that's part of its charm. The 14 characterful, unfussy rooms are impeccably maintained by friendly owners, who'll bring breakfast to your room. Top-floor rooms are bigger and brighter. Moorish-inspired patios are dotted around. The impressive art adorning the walls is by the owner and her cousin.

Nuevo Hotel HOTEL $
(☎956 33 16 00; www.nuevohotel.com; Calle Caballeros 23; s €25-30, d €40-60;) One of the sweetest family-run hotels in Andalucía, the Nuevo is an ancient home filled with comfortable, simple rooms. But the star is spectacular room 208, replete with Moorish-style stucco work and blue-and-white tiling creeping up the walls; you'll wake thinking you've taken up residence in the Alhambra. Breakfast (€5) is available.

Hotel Casa Grande HOTEL $$
(☎956 34 50 70; www.hotelcasagrande.eu; Plaza de las Angustias 3; r/ste €100/165; P) This brilliant hotel lives within a beautifully

restored 1920s mansion. The 15 smartly classic rooms are set over three floors around a light-flooded patio, where local-produce breakfasts (€12) are served, or beside the fantastic roof terrace with views across Jerez' rooftops. All is overseen by the congenial Monika Schroeder, a mine of information about Jerez.

Hotel Palacio Garvey HOTEL **$$**
(956 32 67 00; www.hotelpalaciogarvey.com; Calle Tornería 24; incl breakfast s €65-70, d €77-99, ste €105-110; P ❄) Jerez' nominal posh hotel is a gorgeous 19th-century neoclassical palace conversion, with part of the ancient city wall visible from the lift. The public areas sport leopard prints, African-themed paintings and low-slung tables, while bold colours, luxurious leather furniture, tiled bathrooms and mirrored Moroccan-inspired bowls feature in the 16 individually decorated rooms.

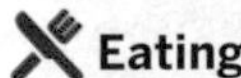

Eating

La Moderna TAPAS, ANDALUCIAN **$**
(956 32 13 79; Calle Larga 67; tapas €1.80; 7am-late) As popular for breakfast *tostadas* as for lunchtime tapas (cod-stuffed peppers, *patatas aliñadas, riñones al Jerez* – Jerez kidneys), La Moderna's marble-topped tables are busy all day long. Beyond its hot-red doors, it's built into the city's Islamic-era walls, which you can see out the back.

★Albores ANDALUCIAN, FUSION **$$**
(956 32 02 66; www.restaurantealbores.com; Calle Consistorio 12; tapas €2.50-4.50, mains €8-18; 8am-midnight Mon-Sat, noon-midnight Sun) Pitching itself among age-old city-centre favourites, Albores brings a sophisticated, contemporary edge to local flavours with its original tapas and mains combos. If there's one overall highlight it's probably the fish, though the artfully presented goats'-cheese *tosta* (open sandwich on toasted bread) is just as delectable. One of Jerez' top breakfast spots.

The Albores team is also behind stylish, seafood-starring Jerez restaurant **A Mar** (956 32 29 15; www.a-marrestaurante.com; Calle Latorre 8; mains €11-22; noon-4.30pm & 8pm-midnight Tue-Sat year-round, noon-5pm Sun Oct-May, 8pm-midnight Sun Jun-Sep), where fresh fish of the day is served *a la plancha* (grilled), paired with an impressive menu of sherries and other Cádiz wines.

DON'T MISS

JEREZ' TABANCOS

Sprinkled across the city centre, Jerez' famous old *tabancos* are, essentially, simple taverns serving sherry from the barrel. Most date from the early 20th century and, although *tabanco* comes from the fusion of *tabaco* (tobacco) and *estanco* (tobacco shop), the focus is indisputably the local plonk (ie sherry). In danger of dying out just a few years ago, Jerez' *tabancos* have sprung back to life as fashionable modern-day hangouts, reinvigorated by keen new ownership and frequented by crowds of stylish young *jerezanos* as much as old-timers. Several stage regular flamenco (though you're just as likely to catch an impromptu performance) and some now offer sherry tastings. All are fantastic, cheap, down-to-earth places to get a real feel for Jerez – *fino* in hand.

The tourist office (p687) hands out information on the official **Ruta de los Tabancos de Jerez** (www.facebook.com/rutadelostabancosdejerez), though there are plenty of other places, too. Suddenly, every other bar is calling itself a *tabanco*! We recommend the following for the real deal:

Tabanco El Pasaje (956 33 33 59; www.tabancoelpasaje.com; Calle Santa María 8; 11am-4pm & 8pm-midnight, shows 2pm & 10pm;) Born back in 1925, Jerez' oldest *tabanco* serves up sherry with tapas (€2 to €3) and twice-daily flamenco sessions.

Tabanco El Guitarrón de San Pedro (www.facebook.com/guitarrondesanpedro; Calle Bizcocheros 16; noon-4pm & 8pm-midnight Mon-Sat, shows 10pm Thu-Sat) Hosts regular flamenco dancing (Thursday) and singing (Friday and Saturday) to go with its sherries and local-style tapas (€2 to €4).

Tabanco Plateros (956 10 44 58; www.facebook.com/tabanco.plateros; Calle Algarve 35; noon-4pm & 8pm-midnight) Join the crowds spilling out from this lively drinking house for a glass of *fino*, *oloroso* or *amontillado* glugged alongside ingeniously simple tapas (€2 to €3).

DON'T MISS

JEREZ' FLAMENCO SCENE

Jerez' moniker as the 'cradle of flamenco' is regularly challenged by aficionados in Cádiz and Seville, but the claim has merit. This comparatively untouristed city harbours not just one but *two* Roma quarters, Santiago and San Miguel, which have produced numerous renowned artists, including Roma singers Manuel Torre and Antonio Chacón. Like its rival cities, Jerez has concocted its own flamenco *palo* (musical form), the intensely popular *bulería*, a fast, rhythmic musical style with the same *compás* (accented beat) as the *soleá*.

Begin your explorations at the Centro Andaluz de Flamenco (p683), Spain's only bona fide flamenco library, where you can pick up information on *peñas* (small private clubs), *tabancos*, performances, and singing, dance and guitar lessons. From here, stroll down Calle Francos past a couple of legendary flamenco bars where singers and dancers still congregate. North of the Centro Andaluz de Flamenco, in the Santiago quarter, you'll find dozens of flamenco *peñas* (clubs) known for their accessibility and intimacy; entry is normally free if you buy a drink. The *peña* scene is particularly lively during the February flamenco festival (p684). Jerez' revitalised tabancos (p685) (taverns that serve sherry from the barrel) are also fantastic for flamenco:

Centro Cultural Flamenco Don Antonio Chacón (☎605 858371; www.facebook.com/DAChaconFlamencoJerez; Calle Salas 2) One of the best *peñas* in town (and hence Andalucía), the Chacón often stages top-notch flamenco performers. For upcoming events, check the Facebook page.

Puro Arte (☎647 743832; www.puroarteflamencojerez.com; Calle Conocedores 28; €30, with tapas/dinner €39/50) Jerez' main *tablao* (choreographed flamenco show) stages popular local-artist performances at 10pm daily. Advance bookings essential.

Damajuana (www.facebook.com/damajuanajerez; Calle Francos 18; ⏲8pm-3am Sun-Thu, to 4am Fri & Sat Jul-Sep, 8pm-3am Tue-Thu, 4pm-3am Fri-Sun Oct-Jun) One of two historic bars on Calle Francos, with varied live music, tapas (€2 to €5.50) and a fun *movida flamenca* (flamenco scene).

★La Carboná ANDALUCIAN **$$**
(☎956 34 74 75; www.lacarbona.com; Calle San Francisco de Paula 2; mains €15-22; ⏲12.30-4.30pm & 8pm-12.30am Wed-Mon) This cavernous, imaginative restaurant occupies an exquisite old bodega set around a suspended fireplace that's oh-so-cosy in winter. Delicately presented specialities, often infused with sherry, include grilled meats, fresh fish, boletus rice jazzed up with razor clams or red *almadraba* tuna tartare with egg-yolk-and-*amontillado* (dry sherry) emulsion, plus outstanding local wines. Or go all-in with sherry-pairing menus (€45).

Albalá ANDALUCIAN, FUSION **$$**
(☎956 34 64 88; www.restaurantealbala.com; cnr Calle Divina Pastora & Avenida Duque de Abrantes; tapas €2-4, mains €8-15; ⏲noon-4pm & 8.30pm-midnight; 📶) Slide into blonde-wood booths amid minimalist oriental-inspired decor for chef Israel Ramos' beautifully creative contemporary meat, fish and veg dishes fuelled by typical Andalucian ingredients. House specials include *rabo de toro* (oxtail) croquettes and *almadraba* red tuna with Thai-style salad, plus deliciously crispy chunky asparagus tempura dipped in soy aioli. It's 1km north of Plaza del Arenal.

🍷 Drinking & Nightlife

Tucked away on the narrow streets north of Plaza del Arenal are a few wine, beer and *copas* (drinks) bars, while, northeast of the centre, Plaza de Canterbury has a couple of pubs popular with a 20-something crowd. Jerez' tabancos (p685) are busy drinking spots.

Tetería La Jaima TEAHOUSE
(Calle Chancillería 10; ⏲4-11.30pm Tue-Thu, to 2am Fri & Sat, to 9pm Sun & Mon mid-Sep–mid-Jun; 📶) Recline with a fruity, aromatic brew (chilled versions available) in the cavernous depths of this atmospherically dark tearoom, decked out with breezy curtains and Moroccan lanterns. If you're hungry, try some hummus, a stuffed pitta bread or a vegetable tagine (dishes €4 to €10).

Information

Oficina de Turismo (956 33 88 74; www.turismojerez.com; Plaza del Arenal; 9am-3pm & 5-6.30pm Mon-Fri, 9.30am-2.30pm Sat & Sun)

Getting There & Away

AIR

Jerez airport (956 15 00 00; www.aena.es; Carretera A4), the only one serving Cádiz province, is 10km northeast of town on the A4.

BUS

The **bus station** (956 14 99 90; Plaza de la Estación) is 1.3km southeast of the centre, served by CMTBC (p676), **Comes** (902 64 64 28; www.tgcomes.es), **Los Amarillos** (902 21 03 17; http://losamarillos.autobusing.com) and **Autocares Valenzuela** (956 34 10 63; www.grupovalenzuela.com).

DESTINATION	COST (€)	DURATION	FREQUENCY
Arcos de la Frontera	1.95-3.09	30-40min	18-29 daily
Cádiz	3.75	1hr	3-9 daily
El Puerto de Santa María	1.65	20min	2-8 daily
Ronda	13	2¼hr	1-2 daily
Sanlúcar de Barrameda	1.95	40min	7-14 daily
Seville	8.85	1¼hr	5-7 daily

TRAIN

Jerez' train station is beside the bus station.

DESTINATION	COST (€)	DURATION	FREQUENCY
Cádiz	4.05-6.05	35-45min	29-42 daily
Córdoba	21-37	1¾-3hr	12 daily
El Puerto de Santa María	2.70	8min	29-45 daily
Seville	11	1¼hr	13-16 daily

Getting Around

TO/FROM THE AIRPORT

Eight to 10 daily trains run between the airport and Jerez (€2.45, seven minutes), El Puerto de Santa María (€3.65, 15 minutes) and Cádiz (€6.05, 45 minutes).

Local airport buses run three times on weekdays and once daily Saturday and Sunday to Jerez (€1.10, 30 minutes), once on weekdays to El Puerto de Santa María (€1.65, 50 minutes) and once daily to Cádiz (€3.80, 1½ hours).

Taxis to/from the airport cost €15.

Arcos de la Frontera

POP 22,350

Everything you've ever dreamed a *pueblo blanco* (white town) could be miraculously materialises in Arcos de la Frontera (33km east of Jerez): a thrilling strategic clifftop location, a swanky *parador,* a volatile frontier history and a soporific old town full of mystery, with whitewashed arches soaring above a web of slender, twisting alleys. The odd tour bus and foreign-owned guesthouse do little to dampen the drama.

For a brief period during the 11th century, Arcos was an independent Berber-ruled *taifa* (small kingdom). In 1255 it was claimed by Christian king Alfonso X El Sabio for Seville and it remained literally *de la frontera* (on the frontier) until the fall of Granada in 1492.

Sights

Basílica Menor de Santa María de la Asunción BASILICA

(Plaza del Cabildo; €2, incl Iglesia de San Pedro €3; 10am-12.45pm & 4-6.45pm Mon-Fri, 10am-1.30pm Sat Mar–mid-Dec) This Gothic-baroque creation is one of Andalucía's more beautiful, intriguing small churches, built over several centuries on the site of a mosque. Check out the ornate gold-leaf altarpiece (a miniature of that in Seville's cathedral) carved between 1580 and 1608, the striking painting of San Cristóbal (St Christopher), the restored 14th-century Gothic-Mudéjar mural, the ornate woodcarved 18th-century choir and the lovely Isabelline ceiling tracery. The original bell tower was toppled by the 1755 Lisbon earthquake; its neoclassical replacement remains incomplete.

Plaza del Cabildo SQUARE

Lined with fine ancient buildings, Plaza del Cabildo is the heart of Arcos' old town, its vertiginous **mirador** affording exquisite panoramas over the Río Guadalete. The Moorish-origin **Castillo de los Duques**, rebuilt in the 14th and 15th centuries, is closed to the public, but its outer walls frame classic Arcos views. On the square's eastern side, the Parador de Arcos de la Frontera (p688) is a reconstruction of a grand 16th-century magistrate's house; pop in for coffee.

Iglesia de San Pedro CHURCH

(Calle San Pedro 4; €2, incl Basílica Menor de Santa María de la Asunción €3; 10am-12.45pm & 4-6.45pm Mon-Fri, 10am-1.30pm Sat) Containing a 16th-century main altarpiece said to be the oldest in Cádiz province, this Gothic-baroque confection sports what is perhaps one of Andalucía's most magnificent small-church interiors, behind an 18th-century facade, and may have been constructed atop an Almohad-era fortress.

Festivals & Events

Semana Santa RELIGIOUS
(Mar/Apr) Dramatic Semana Santa processions see hooded penitents inching through Arcos' narrow streets.

Velada de la Virgen de las Nieves MUSIC, DANCE
(early Aug) Begun in 1961, this festival includes a top-class flamenco night in Plaza del Cabildo.

Feria de San Miguel FAIR
(late Sep) Arcos celebrates its patron saint with a colourful four- or five-day fair.

Sleeping

Casa Campana GUESTHOUSE $
(600 284928; www.casacampana.com; Calle Núñez de Prado 4; r/apt €54/78;) One of several charming guesthouses in old Arcos, Casa Campana has two cosy doubles and a massive five-person apartment with kitchenette that's filled with character, in a house dating back 600 years. The intimate, flower-filled patio is dotted with sun loungers and the rooftop terrace flooded with views. It's expertly run by knowledgeable owners, who supply excellent old-town walking-tour leaflets.

★ **La Casa Grande** HERITAGE HOTEL $$
(956 70 39 30; www.lacasagrande.net; Calle Maldonado 10; r €90-118, ste €120-135; closed 6-31 Jan;) This gorgeous, rambling, cliff-side mansion dating to 1729 once belonged to the great flamenco dancer Antonio Ruiz Soler. With each of the seven rooms done in different but tasteful modern-rustic design (most with divine views), it feels more arty home than hotel. Great breakfasts (€10), a well-stocked library, a rooftop terrace, and on-demand massage and yoga complete the perfect package.

Parador de Arcos de la Frontera HERITAGE HOTEL $$
(956 70 05 00; www.parador.es; Plaza del Cabildo; r €85-150;) A rebuilt 16th-century magistrate's residence that combines typical *parador* luxury with a splendid setting and the best views in town. Eight of the 24 classic-style rooms have balconies opening onto sweeping cliff-top panoramas; most others look out on Plaza del Cabildo. With its gorgeous terrace, the elegant **restaurant** (mains €13-22; 8-11am, noon-4pm & 8.30-11pm) offers a smart menu rooted in local specialities. Best deals online.

Eating

★ **Taberna Jóvenes Flamencos** ANDALUCIAN, TAPAS $
(657 133552; www.facebook.com/pg/taberna.jovenezflamencos; Calle Deán Espinosa 11; tapas €2.50-3.50; noon-midnight Thu-Tue, closed 1 week Oct;) You've got to hand it to this cheerful, popular place, which successfully opened amid the recession. Along with wonderful flamenco/bullfighting decor, tiled floors and hand-painted hot-red tables, it has an enticing menu of meat, fish, vegetarian, scramble and stew tapas and *raciones,* including aubergines and grilled goat's cheese drizzled with local honey. Service is impeccable. Music and dance break out regularly.

Babel MOROCCAN, FUSION $
(671 138256; www.restaurantebabel.es; Calle Corredera 11; dishes €5-12; 1-4pm & 7.30-11.30pm Mon-Sat, evenings only Jul–mid-Sep;) Arcos' Moroccan-fusion restaurant has tasteful decor (red-washed walls, cushy booths and ornate stools shipped in from Casablanca) and some equally tasty dishes. Choose from perfectly spiced tagines and couscous, zingy hummus, chicken-and-almond *pastela* (a stuffed pastry), or the full Arabic tea treatment with silver pots and sweet pastries. It's a cosy, friendly place. Hours vary.

Information

Oficina de Turismo (956 70 22 64; http://turismoarcos.com; Calle Cuesta de Belén 5; 9.30am-2pm & 3-7.30pm Mon-Sat, 10am-2pm Sun) The tourist office doubles as an interpretation centre with history exhibits and a model of present-day Arcos.

Getting There & Away

Buses from Arcos' **bus station** (Calle Los Alcaldes) in the new town (down to the west of the old town), off Avenida Miguel Mancheño, are operated by **Los Amarillos** (902 21 03 17; http://losamarillos.autobusing.com), **Comes** (902 64 64 28; www.tgcomes.es) and/or the Consorcio de Transportes Bahía de

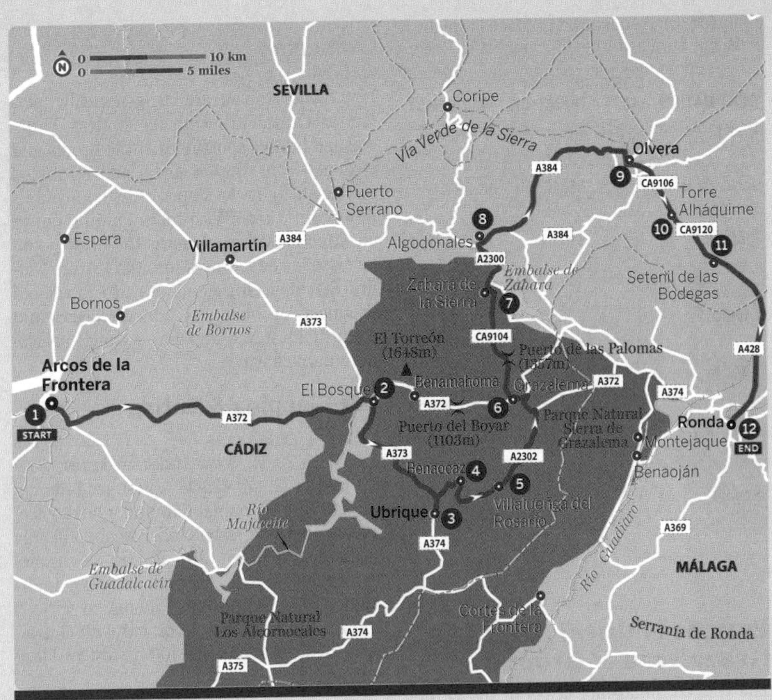

Driving Tour
White Towns

START ARCOS DE LA FRONTERA
END RONDA
LENGTH 147KM; TWO DAYS

Rev up in dramatic ❶ **Arcos de la Frontera** (p687), a Roman-turned-Moorish-turned-Christian citadel perched atop a sheer-sided sandstone ridge. Head 32km east along the A372 to ❷ **El Bosque**, the western gateway to Cádiz province's Parque Natural Sierra de Grazalema. The A373 takes you 13km south round to leather-making ❸ **Ubrique**, close to the borders of the Grazalema and Alcornocales natural parks. Mountains rise quickly as you drive 7km up the A2302 to tiny ❹ **Benaocaz**, where several Grazalema park hikes start/finish, then another 7km on to equally diminutive ❺ **Villaluenga del Rosario** with its artisanal-cheese museum. Plying the craggy eastern face of the sierra and then taking the A372 west brings you to ❻ **Grazalema** (p690), a red-roofed park-activity nexus also famous for its blanket making and honey. Count the switchbacks on the steep CA9104 as you climb to the view-splayed 1357m Puerto de las Palomas and, beyond, quintessential white town ❼ **Zahara de la Sierra** (p691), with its huddle of houses spread around the skirts of a castle-topped crag above a glassy reservoir at the foot of the Grazalema mountains. The A2300 threads 10km north to ❽ **Algodonales**, a white town on the edge of the natural park known for its guitar-making workshop and hang-gliding/paragliding obsession. Take the A384 19km northeast from here past the Peñón de Zaframagón to reach ❾ **Olvera** (p691), visible for miles around thanks to its Moorish castle but also known for its olive oil and Vía Verde cycling/hiking path. Following the CA9106 southeast, you'll pass the little-known white town of ❿ **Torre Alháquime**. From here, the CA9120 winds 11km southeast towards the border with Málaga province and ⓫ **Setenil de las Bodegas** (p693), a village instantly recognisable for its cave houses. Once used for storing wine, today they offer a shady antidote to the summer heat plus some good tapas bars. From Setenil, head 17km south and wrap up in beautiful gorge-top ⓬ **Ronda** (p693) in Málaga province.

Cádiz (p676). Frequency is reduced at weekends. For Seville, it's best to connect in Jerez.

DESTINATION	COST (€)	DURATION	FREQUENCY
Cádiz	5.73-7.30	1hr	5-10 daily
Jerez de la Frontera	1.95-3.09	30-40min	18-29 daily
Málaga	18	3¾hr	7.40am & 3.45pm Mon-Fri
Olvera	8	1¾hr	2.35pm Mon-Fri
Ronda	10	2hr	12.20pm & 3.20pm Mon-Fri, 10.20am Sat & Sun
Seville	9	2hr	9am & 4pm daily

Parque Natural Sierra de Grazalema & Around

The rugged, pillar-like peaks of the Parque Natural Sierra de Grazalema rise abruptly from the plains northeast of Cádiz, revealing sheer gorges, rare firs, wild orchids and the province's highest summits, against a beautifully green backdrop at altitudes of 260m to 1648m. This is the wettest part of Spain – stand aside, Galicia and Cantabria, Grazalema village logs an average 2200mm annually. It's gorgeous walking country (best months: May, June, September and October). For the more intrepid, adventure activities abound.

The 534-sq-km park, named Spain's first Unesco Biosphere Reserve in 1977, extends into northwestern Málaga province, where it includes the Cueva de la Pileta.

Activities

Hiking, caving, canyoning, kayaking, rock climbing, cycling, birdwatching, horse riding, paragliding, vie ferrate – this beautiful protected area crams it all in. For the more technical stuff, go with a guide; Zahara's **Zahara Catur** (☎657 926394, 656 986009; www.zaharacatur.com) and Grazalema-based **Horizon** (☎655 934565, 956 13 23 63; www.horizonaventura.com; Calle Las Piedras 1; ⏰10am-2pm & 5-8pm Mon-Sat) are respected adventure-activity outfits.

Grazalema

POP 1635 / ELEV 825M

Few white towns are as generically perfect as Grazalema, with its spotless whitewashed houses sporting rust-tiled roofs and wrought-iron window bars, and sprinkled on the steep, rocky slopes of its eponymous mountain range. With hikes fanning out in all directions, Grazalema is the most popular base for adventures into the Parque Natural Sierra de Grazalema. It's also an age-old producer of blankets, honey, cheese and meat-filled stews, and has its own special mountain charm.

Sleeping & Eating

Casa de las Piedras HOTEL **$**

(☎956 13 20 14; www.casadelaspiedras.es; Calle Las Piedras 32; s/d €35/48, with shared bathroom €15/28; ❄📶) Mountain air and a homey feel go together like Isabel and Fernando at this rustic-design hotel with a snug downstairs lounge and masses of park activities information. The simple, cosy rooms, in various shapes and sizes, are decorated with Grazalema-made blankets. It's 100m west of Plaza de España.

La Maroma TAPAS, ANDALUCIAN **$$**

(☎617 543756; www.facebook.com/gastrobarlamaroma; Calle Santa Clara; tapas €2-6, mains €6-16; ⏰noon-5pm & 7.30-11pm; 📶) The cooking is significantly more fun and inventive than the rustic check-cloth, beamed-ceiling, bull-festival-inspired decor suggests at this cosy gastrobar, run by a young family team. Creative local-inspired tapas and *raciones* throw mountain ingredients into tasty bites like mushrooms in honey-and-thyme sauce, *huevos rotos* (fried eggs with potatoes), topped *tostas* (open toasted sandwiches) or *payoyo*-cheese salad with Grazalema-honey dressing.

Information

Oficina de Turismo (☎956 13 20 52; www.grazalema.es; Plaza de los Asomaderos; ⏰9am-3pm Tue-Sun Jun-Sep, 10am-2pm & 3-5.30pm Tue-Sun Oct-May) Excellent Parque Natural Sierra de Grazalema walking information, plus last-minute, same-day hiking permits (in person only). Probably the province's most helpful tourist office.

Getting There & Away

Los Amarillos (☎902 21 03 17; http://losamarillos.autobusing.com) runs two daily buses to/from Ronda (€2.85, one hour); two daily to/

DON'T MISS

HIKING IN THE SIERRA DE GRAZALEMA

The Sierra de Grazalema is criss-crossed by 20 beautiful official marked trails. Four of the best – the **Garganta Verde**, **El Pinsapar**, **Llanos del Rabel** and **El Torreón** (16 Oct-May) paths – enter restricted areas and require (free) permits from the **Centro de Visitantes El Bosque** (956 70 97 33; cvelbosque.amaya@juntadeandalucia.es; Calle Federico García Lorca 1, El Bosque; 10am-2pm, closed Mon Jun-Sep). Ideally, book a month or two ahead. The center will email permits on request with minimum five days' notice; communication may be in English, but permits are in Spanish only. Additional (leftover) permits are sometimes available on the day; you can ask ahead by phone or email, but you'll have to collect them at the Centro or Grazalema's tourist office (p690) on the day. Some trails are fully or partly off limits from 1 June to 15 October due to fire risk.

The Centro de Visitantes El Bosque, Grazalema's tourist office and the unofficial Punto de Información Zahara de la Sierra have maps outlining the main walking possibilities. There's downloadable Spanish- and English-language hiking information with maps online at www.ventanadelvisitante.es.

from Ubrique (€2.32, 30 to 40 minutes) via Benaocaz (€1.61, 20 to 30 minutes); and one to two daily Monday to Friday to/from El Bosque (€1.45, 30 minutes), where you can change for Arcos de la Frontera.

Zahara de la Sierra

POP 1250 / ELEV 550M

Rugged Zahara, strung around a vertiginous crag at the foot of the Grazalema mountains, overlooking the glittering turquoise Embalse de Zahara, hums with Moorish mystery. For over 150 years in the 14th and 15th centuries, it stood on the old medieval frontier facing off against Christian Olvera, clearly visible in the distance. These days Zahara ticks all the classic white-town boxes and, with vistas framed by tall palms and hot-pink bougainvillea, its streets invite exploration. It's also a great base for hiking the **Garganta Verde**, so it's popular. Visit during the afternoon siesta, however, and you can still hear a pin drop.

The precipitous CA9104 road over the ultra-steep 1357m Puerto de las Palomas (Doves' Pass) links Zahara with Grazalema (17km south) and is a spectacular drive full of white-knuckle switchbacks.

Sights

Zahara village centres on Calle San Juan; towards its western end stands the 20th-century **Capilla de San Juan de Letrán** (Calle San Juan; 11am-1.30pm), with a Moorish-origin clock tower, while at its eastern end is the pastel-pink, 18th-century baroque **Iglesia de Santa María de Mesa** (Plaza del Rey; admission by donation; 11am-1.30pm & 3.30-5.15pm).

Sleeping

Al Lago BOUTIQUE HOTEL **$$**
(956 12 30 32; www.al-lago.es; Calle Félix Rodríguez de la Fuente; incl breakfast s €72-82, d €90-120, f €110-125; mid-Feb–mid-Nov;) Understated rustic-chic elegance runs through the six colourfully contemporary, individually styled rooms created by designer-owner Mona at this gorgeous, British-American-run boutique hotel looking out on Zahara's reservoir. All rooms feature private balconies with lake views, the two superiors have bath tubs, and there's a little terrace alcove for lounging.

Downstairs, in the excellent **restaurant** (mains €12-17; 1-4pm & 8-11pm mid-Feb–mid-Nov, closed Wed approx mid-Feb–May & Oct–mid-Nov;), chef Stefan crafts seasonal, local produce into contemporary-Andalucian bites and tasting menus that are accompanied by Ronda-area and other Spanish wines.

Information

Punto de Información Zahara de la Sierra (956 12 31 14; Plaza del Rey 3; 10am-2pm Tue-Sun) Info on Zahara and the Parque Natural Sierra de Grazalema from a private agency.

Getting There & Away

Comes (902 64 64 28; www.tgcomes.es) runs two daily buses to/from Ronda (€4.55, one hour) Monday to Friday.

Olvera

POP 8060 / ELEV 643M

Dramatically topped by a Moorish-era castle, Olvera (27km northeast of Zahara de la

DON'T MISS

VÍA VERDE DE LA SIERRA

The 36km **Vía Verde de la Sierra** (www.fundacionviaverdedelasierra.com) between Olvera and Puerto Serrano (to the west) is regularly touted as the finest of Spain's *vías verdes*, greenways that have transformed old railway lines into traffic-free thoroughfares for bikers, hikers and horse riders. Aside from the wild, rugged scenery, this route is notable for four spectacular viaducts, 30 tunnels and three old stations transformed into hotel-restaurants. The train line itself was never actually completed: it was constructed in the late 1920s as part of the abortive Jerez–Almargen railway, but the Spanish Civil War put a stop to construction works. The line was restored in the early 2000s.

The Hotel Estación Vía Verde de la Sierra, 1km north of Olvera, is the route's official eastern starting point. Here, **Sesca** (☎657 987432, 687 676462; www.sesca.es; Calle Pasadera 4; half-/full-day bike hire €9/12; ⊙9am-2pm & 4-6pm) rents bicycles from €12 per day, and you can check out the **Centro de Interpretación Vía Verde de la Sierra** (www.fundacionviaverdedelasierra.es; Calle Pasadera 4; adult/child €2/1; ⊙9.30am-4.30pm Thu-Mon). Bike hire is also available at Coripe and Puerto Serrano stations (daily October to May, weekends only June to September). Other services include the **Patrulla Verde** (☎638 280184; ⊙8am-3.30pm Sat & Sun Jun-Sep, 9am-5pm Sat & Sun Oct-May), a staff of on-the-road bike experts.

A highlight of the Vía Verde is the **Peñón de Zaframagón**, a distinctive crag that's a prime breeding ground for griffon vultures. The **Centro de Interpretación y Observatorio Ornitológico** (☎956 13 63 72; www.fundacionviaverdedelasierra.es; Antigua Estación de Zaframagón; adult/child €2/1; ⊙9.30am-5.30pm), in the former Zaframagón station building 16km west of Olvera, allows close-up observations by means of a high-definition camera placed up on the crag.

The Vía Verde de la Sierra can be traversed in either direction and, if you're going only one way, there are taxis to bring you back to your starting point (bikes included); enquire at the route's information centres.

Sierra) beckons from miles away across olive-covered country. Reconquered by Alfonso XI in 1327, this relatively untouristed town was a bandit refuge until the mid-19th century. Most people now come to Olvera to walk or cycle the Vía Verde de la Sierra, but, as a white town par excellence, it's also renowned for its olive oil, two striking churches and roller-coaster history, which probably started with the Romans.

Sights

Castillo Árabe CASTLE

(Plaza de la Iglesia; incl La Cilla adult/child €2/1; ⊙10.30am-2pm & 4-8pm Tue-Sun Jun-Sep, 10.30am-2pm & 4-6pm Tue-Sun Oct-May) Perched on a crag high atop town is Olvera's late-12th-century Arabic castle, which later formed part of Nasrid Granada's defensive systems. Clamber up to the tower, with ever-more-exquisite town and country views opening up as you go.

Iglesia Parroquial Nuestra Señora de la Encarnación CHURCH

(Plaza de la Iglesia; €2; ⊙11am-1pm Tue-Sun) Built over a Gothic-Mudéjar predecessor, Olvera's neoclassical top-of-the-town church was commissioned by the Duques de Osuna and completed in the 1840s.

Sleeping & Eating

Hotel Estación Vía Verde de la Sierra HOTEL $

(☎644 747029; www.hotelviaverdedelasierra.es; Calle Pasadera 4; s/d/tr €45/55/65, 2-/6-person apt €90/110; ⊙Tue-Sun; P ❄ 🛜 ≋) This unique hotel 1km north of Olvera is the official start of the Vía Verde de la Sierra, Spain's finest *vía verde*. Accommodation is in seven smartly updated rooms for one to four people tucked into the converted station, or in train-wagon-inspired 'apartments' with kitchens, sleeping up to six. Other facilities include bike hire, a restaurant and a salt-water pool.

Taberna Juanito Gómez TAPAS $

(☎956 13 01 60; Calle Bellavista; tapas €2-3; ⊙1.30-4.30pm & 8.30-11.30pm Mon-Sat) A simple little place that does tasty, decent-value tapas and *montaditos* (bite-sized filled rolls) taking in all your usual favourites: garlic prawns, grilled mushrooms, Manchego cheese and Iberian ham.

Information

Oficina de Turismo (956 12 08 16; www.olvera.es; Plaza de la Iglesia; 10.30am-2pm & 4-8pm Tue-Sun Jun-Sep, 10.30am-2pm & 4-6pm Tue-Sun Oct-May)

Getting There & Away

Los Amarillos (902 21 03 17; http://losamarillos.autobusing.com) runs one daily bus to/from Jerez de la Frontera (€9.11, 2½ hours) and Ronda (€5.40, 1½ hours) and one to two daily to/from Málaga (€12, two hours). **Comes** (902 64 64 28; www.tgcomes.es) has one daily bus Monday to Friday to/from Cádiz (€15, three hours).

Ronda

POP 34,400 / ELEV 744M

Built astride a huge gash in the mountains carved out by the Río Guadalevín, Ronda is a brawny town with a dramatic history littered with outlaws, bandits, guerrilla warriors and rebels. Its spectacular location atop El Tajo gorge and its status as the largest of Andalucía's white towns have made it hugely popular with tourists – particularly notable when you consider its relatively modest size. Modern bullfighting was practically invented here in the late 18th century, and the town's fame was spread further by its close association with American Europhiles Ernest Hemingway (a lover of bullfighting) and Orson Welles (whose ashes are buried in the town).

South of the gorge, Ronda's old town largely dates from Islamic times, when it was an important cultural centre filled with mosques and palaces. Further north, the grid-shaped 'new' town is perched atop steep cliffs, with parks and promenades looking regally over the surrounding mountains.

Sights

La Ciudad, the historic old town on the southern side of El Tajo gorge, is an atmospheric area for a stroll, with its evocative, still-tangible history, Renaissance mansions and wealth of museums. The newer town, where you'll be deposited if you arrive by bus or train, harbours the emblematic bullring, the leafy Alameda del Tajo gardens and armies of visitors. Three bridges crossing the gorge connect the old town with the new.

Plaza de Toros NOTABLE BUILDING

(Calle Virgen de la Paz; €7, incl audio guide €8.50; 10am-8pm) In existence for more than 200 years, the Plaza de Toros is one of Spain's oldest bullrings and the site of some of the most important events in bullfighting history. A visit is a way of learning about this deep-rooted Spanish tradition without actually attending a bullfight.

The on-site Museo Taurino is crammed with memorabilia such as blood-spattered costumes worn by 1990s star Jesulín de Ubrique. It also includes artwork by Picasso and photos of famous fans such as Orson Welles and Ernest Hemingway.

WORTH A TRIP

SETENIL DE LAS BODEGAS

While most white towns sought protection atop lofty crags, the people of Setenil de las Bodegas (14km southeast of Olvera) did the opposite and burrowed into the dark caves beneath the steep cliffs of the Río Trejo. Clearly, the strategy worked: it took the Christian armies a 15-day siege to dislodge the Moors from their well-defended positions in 1484. Many of the town's original cave-houses remain, some converted into bars and restaurants, and Setenil is now an increasingly popular day trip from the Ronda and Grazalema areas.

The **tourist office** (635 365147, 616 553384; www.setenil.com; Calle Villa 2; 10am-2pm Tue-Sun) is near the top of the town in the 16th-century Casa Consistorial (which exhibits a rare wooden Mudéjar ceiling) and runs guided walks around Setenil. Above is the 12th-century **castle** (Calle Villa; 10.30am-2pm & 5-8pm Mon-Fri, 10.30am-7pm Sat & Sun), captured by the Christians just eight years before the fall of Granada; you can climb the 13th-century tower.

Setenil has some great tapas bars that make ideal pit stops while you study its unique urban framework – try the **Restaurante Casa Palmero** (956 13 43 60; www.facebook.com/RestauranteCasaPalmero; Plaza de Andalucía 4; mains €8-19; 1am-late Fri-Wed;).

Ronda

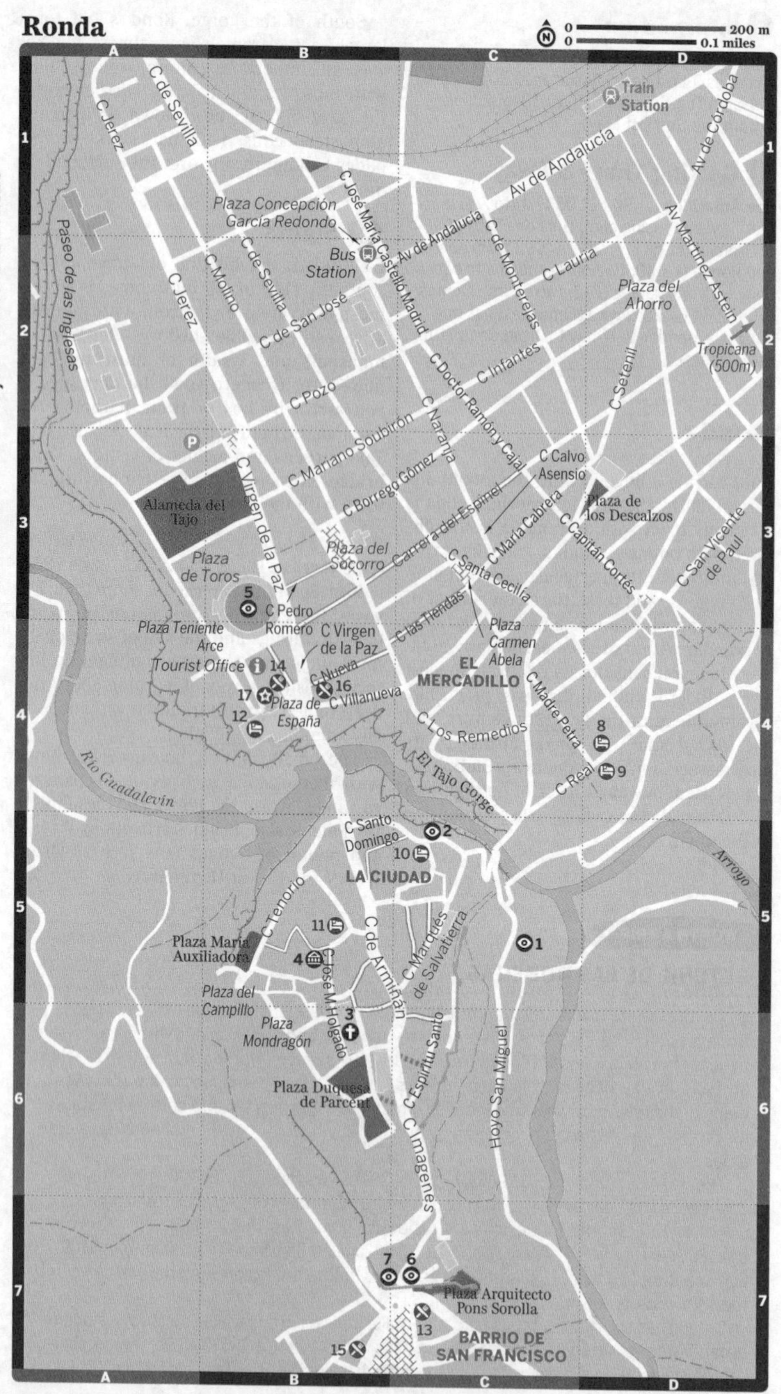

0 200 m
0 0.1 miles
Train Station
Av de Córdoba
Av de Andalucía
C de Sevilla
C Jerez
Paseo de las Inglesas
Plaza Concepción García Redondo
C José María Castelló Madrid
Bus Station
C Molino
C de Montereelas
C Lauria
Av Martínez Astein
Plaza del Ahorro
C de San José
Tropicana (500m)
C Infantes
C Setenil
C Pozo
C Doctor Ramón y Cajal
C Naranja
C Mariano Soubirón
C Borrego Gómez
C Calvo Asensio
Alameda del Tajo
C Virgen de la Paz
Plaza de los Descalzos
Carrera del Espinel
C María Cabrera
C Capitán Cortés
C San Vicente de Paúl
Plaza del Socorro
Plaza de Toros
C Santa Cecilia
C Pedro Romero
Plaza Teniente Arce
C Virgen de la Paz
C las Tiendas
Plaza Carmen Abela
Tourist Office
C Nueva
EL MERCADILLO
C Villanueva
Plaza de España
C Madre Petra
C Los Remedios
Río Guadalevín
El Tajo Gorge
C Real
C Santo Domingo
LA CIUDAD
Arroyo
C Tenorio
C de Armiñán
C Marqués de Salvatierra
Plaza María Auxiliadora
C José M Holgado
Plaza del Campillo
Plaza Mondragón
C Espíritu Santo
Hoyo San Miguel
Plaza Duquesa de Parcent
C Imágenes
Plaza Arquitecto Pons Sorolla
BARRIO DE SAN FRANCISCO

Ronda

Casa del Rey Moro GARDENS
(House of the Moorish King; Calle Santo Domingo 17; adult/child €5/3; ⏲10am-7pm) Several landscaped terraces give access to La Mina, an Islamic stairway of more than 300 steps cut into the rock all the way down to the river at the bottom of the gorge. These steps enabled Ronda to maintain water supplies when it was under attack. It was also the point where Christian troops forced entry in 1485. The steps are not well lit and are steep and wet in places. Take care.

The landscaped terraces were the work of French landscape architect Jean-Claude Forestier in 1912. Forestier was also responsible for Seville's Parque de María Luisa (p648).

Museo Joaquín Peinado GALLERY
(☎952 87 15 85; www.museojoaquinpeinado.com; Plaza del Gigante; €4; ⏲10am-5pm Mon-Fri, to 3pm Sat) Native Ronda artist Joaquín Peinado was an amigo and contemporary of Picasso's, a fact reflected in his work, with its strong abstract lines, flirtations with cubism and seeming obsession with female nudes. It's all on show in a most typical Andalucian gallery: a historic building that's been fitted with a plush minimalist interior.

Iglesia de Santa María La Mayor CHURCH
(Calle José M Holgado; adult/child €4.50/2; ⏲10am-7pm Mon-Sat, 10am-12.30pm & 2-6pm Sun) The city's original mosque metamorphosed into this elegant church. Just inside the entrance is an arch covered with Arabic inscriptions that was part of the mosque's *mihrab* (prayer niche indicating the direction of Mecca). The church has been declared a national monument, and its interior is an orgy of decorative styles and ornamentation. A huge central cedar choir stall divides the church into two sections: aristocrats to the front, everyone else at the back.

Baños Árabes HISTORIC SITE
(Arab Baths; Hoyo San Miguel; €3.50, Mon free; ⏲10am-7pm Mon-Fri, to 3pm Sat & Sun) Enjoy the pleasant walk here from the centre of town. Backing onto Ronda's river, these 13th- and 14th-century Arab baths are in good condition, with horseshoe arches, columns and clearly designated divisions between the hot and cold thermal areas. They're some of the best-preserved Arab baths in Andalucía. A short video and several explanatory boards help shed some light on their history.

Puerta de Almocábar GATE
The old town is surrounded by massive fortress walls pierced by two ancient gates: the Islamic Puerta de Almocábar, which in the 13th century was the main gateway to the castle, and the 16th-century **Puerta de Carlos V**. Inside, the Islamic layout remains intact, but the maze of narrow streets now takes its character from the Renaissance mansions of powerful families whose predecessors accompanied Fernando el Católico in the taking of the city in 1485.

Festivals & Events

Ronda Guitar Festival MUSIC
(www.rondaguitarfestival.com; ⏲Jun) Introduced in 2016 and based at the relatively new Ronda Guitar House, this five-day affair celebrates that most emblematic of Spanish instruments. Concerts, conferences, wine tasting and a guitar maker's exhibition characterise proceedings, which encompass far more than flamenco.

Sleeping

★Aire de Ronda BOUTIQUE HOTEL $$
(952 16 12 74; www.airederonda.com; Calle Real 25; r from €125; P) Located in a particularly tranquil part of town, this hotel is one of those old-on-the-outside, super-modern-on-the-inside places that Spain does so well. Smart minimalist rooms come in punchy black and white, and fabulous bathrooms have shimmering silver- or gold-coloured mosaic tiles, walk-in showers and, in one romantic couples' room, a glass partition separating the shower from the bedroom.

★Hotel San Gabriel HOTEL $$
(952 19 03 92; www.hotelsangabriel.com; Calle José M Holgado 19; s/d incl breakfast €72/130;) This heavyweight historic hotel is filled with antiques and faded photographs that offer an insight into Ronda's history – bullfighting, celebrities and all. Ferns hang down the huge mahogany staircase, and there's a billiard room, a cosy living room stacked with books, and a DVD-screening room with 10 velvet-covered seats rescued from Ronda's theatre.

★Enfrente Arte HOTEL $$
(952 87 90 88; www.enfrentearte.com; Calle Real 40; r incl breakfast from €99; @) If you hate off-the-rack, middle-of-the-road hotels, you'll love this place. The first hint of its personality greets you at the reception desk: the front of a sawn-in-half Spanish SEAT car. And that's before you've even got to the cosmically colourful rooms, which are as comfortable as they're quirky. Rates include all drinks, to which you help yourself, and a sumptuous buffet breakfast.

Hotel Ronda BOUTIQUE HOTEL $$
(952 87 22 32; www.hotelronda.net; Ruedo Doña Elvira; s/d €53/70;) With its geranium-filled window boxes and whitewashed *pueblo* exterior, Hotel Ronda offers relatively simple (for Ronda) contemporary rooms painted in vivid colours and accentuated by punchy original abstracts. Several rooms overlook the beautiful Mina gardens across the way. It's a bargain for the price.

Parador de Ronda HOTEL $$$
(952 87 75 00; www.parador.es; Plaza de España; r €134-150; P@) Acres of shining marble and deep-cushioned furniture give this modern *parador* a certain appeal, but really it's all about the views. The terrace is a wonderful place to drink in the sight of the gaping gorge with your coffee or wine, especially at night.

Eating

Typical Ronda food is hearty mountain fare, with an emphasis on stews (called *cocido, estofado* or *cazuela*), *trucha* (trout), *rabo de toro* (oxtail stew) and game such as *conejo* (rabbit), *perdiz* (partridge) and *codorniz* (quail).

Casa María ANDALUCIAN $
(951 08 36 63; Plaza Ruedo Alameda 27; menú €20; noon-3.30pm & 7.30-10.30pm Thu-Tue;) Walk straight through Ronda's old town and out of the Carlos V gate (p695) and the crowds mysteriously melt away, leaving just you and a few locals propping up the bar at Casa María. Lap it up. Set menus include dishes featuring the likes of steak, scallops, salmon, cod and asparagus.

Tragatá TAPAS $
(952 87 72 09; www.tragata.com; Calle Nueva 4; tapas €2-3; 1.15-3.45pm & 8-11pm;) A small outpost for Ronda's new gourmet guru, Benito Gómez, who runs the nearby Bardal (p697), Tragatá allows you to sample some of the same *cocina alta* (haute cuisine) at a fraction of the price. Get ready for an eruption of flavours in an interesting menu of small bites, such as cod sandwiches and (believe it or not) pig's ear.

Tropicana ANDALUCIAN $$
(952 87 89 85; cnr Avenida Málaga & Calle Acinipo; mains €12-20; 12.30-3.30pm & 7.30-10pm Wed-Sun) A little off the trail in Ronda's new town, the Tropicana has nonetheless garnered a strong reputation for its certified-organic food, served in a small but handsome restaurant with the feel of a modern bistro.

★Almocábar ANDALUCIAN $$$
(952 87 59 77; Calle Ruedo Alameda 5; tapas €2, mains €15-30; 12.30-4.30pm & 8-11pm Wed-Mon) Tapas here include *montaditos* (small pieces of bread) topped with delicacies like duck breast and chorizo. Mains are available in the elegant dining room, where meat dominates – rabbit, partridge, lamb and beef cooked on a hot stone at your table. There's a bodega upstairs, and wine tastings and dinner can be arranged for a minimum of eight people (approximately €50 per person).

Bardal GASTRONOMY $$$

(☎951 48 98 28; Aparicio 1; tasting menu €60-77; ⏱1-3.30pm & 8-10.30pm Tue-Sat, 1-3.30pm Sun) The once famed Tragabuches restaurant has been replaced by the equally ambitious Bardal (with some staff crossover), where you'll need to reserve ahead in order to enjoy the astounding 15- to 20-course menu, a whistle-stop tour through oyster stew, yellow-tomato gazpacho, frozen apple water, monkfish foie gras and other such uncommon dishes. Hold onto your hat – and fork.

☆ Entertainment

El Quinqué LIVE PERFORMANCE

(☎633 778181; www.elquinqueronda.com; Paseo de Blas Infante; tickets €8-15; ⏱shows 2pm & 8.30pm Tue-Sun) For a traditional flamenco show employing a three-pronged attack of voice, guitar and dance, come to El Quinqué. Entry prices are very reasonable for the short 40-minute lunchtime shows. Evening shows are double the length. Food and drink are available at the on-site bar-restaurant.

ℹ Information

Tourist Office (www.turismoderonda.es; Paseo de Blas Infante; ⏱10am-6pm Mon-Fri, to 7pm Sat, to 2.30pm Sun) Helpful staff with a wealth of information on the town and region.

ℹ Getting There & Away

BUS

From the town's **bus station** (Plaza Concepción García Redondo 2), **Comes** (☎956 29 11 68; www.tgcomes.es) runs services to Arcos de la Frontera (€9.50, two hours, one to two daily), Jerez de la Frontera (€13, three hours, one to three daily) and Cádiz (€18, two hours, one to three daily). **Los Amarillos** (☎902 21 03 17; www.samar.es) goes to Seville via Algodonales and Grazalema. **Portillo** (☎952 87 22 62; www.portillo.avanzabus.com) has four daily buses to Málaga (€12.25, 2¾ hours) and five to Marbella (€6.50, 1¼ hours).

TRAIN

Ronda's **train station** (☎952 87 16 73; www.renfe.com; Avenida de Andalucía) is on the line between Bobadilla and Algeciras. Trains run to Algeciras (€30, 1½ hours, five daily) via Gaucín and Jimena de la Frontera. This train ride is one of Spain's finest and worth taking just for the views. Other trains depart for Málaga (€10, two hours, one daily), Madrid (€69, four hours, three daily) and Granada (€20, three hours, three daily). For Seville, change at Bobadilla or Antequera-Santa Ana.

It's less than 1km from the train station to most accommodation. A taxi will cost around €7.

Southern Costa de la Luz

The Costa de la Luz is a world of flat-capped farmers, grazing bulls and furtive slugs of dry sherry with lunchtime tapas. Throw in beautiful blonde, windswept beaches, a buzzing surfing/kitesurfing scene and a string of spectacularly located white towns, and you're unequivocally in Andalucía. Spaniards, well aware of this, flock to places like Tarifa and Los Caños de Meca in July and August. It's by no means a secret, but the stunning Costa de la Luz remains the same old laid-back beachy hangout it's always been, admittedly with a little upmarket flair creeping in around Vejer de la Frontera.

Vejer de la Frontera

POP 9260

Vejer – the jaw drops, the eyes blink, the eloquent adjectives dry up. Looming moodily atop a rocky hill above the busy N340, 50km south of Cádiz, this serene, compact white town is something very special. Yes, there's a labyrinth of twisting old-town streets plus some serendipitous viewpoints, a ruined castle, a surprisingly elaborate culinary scene, a smattering of exquisitely dreamy hotels and a tangible Moorish influence. But Vejer has something else: an air of magic and mystery, an imperceptible touch of *duende* (spirit).

◉ Sights

Plaza de España SQUARE

With its elaborate 20th-century, Seville-tiled fountain and perfectly white town hall, Vejer's palm-studded, cafe-filled Plaza de España is a favourite, much-photographed hangout. There's a small lookout above its western side (accessible from Calle de Sancho IV El Bravo).

Walls WALLS

Enclosing the 40,000-sq-metre old town, Vejer's imposing 15th-century walls are particularly visible between the Arco de la Puerta Cerrada (of 11th- or 12th-century origin) and the 15th-century Arco de la Segur, two of the four original gateways to survive. The area around the Arco de la Segur and Calle Judería was, in the 15th century, the *judería* (Jewish quarter). Start with the 10th- or 11th-century Puerta de Sancho IV (another surviving gateway) next to Plaza de España and work round.

Castillo CASTLE
(Calle del Castillo; ⌚10am-2pm & 5-9pm approx May-Sep, 10am-2pm & 4-8pm approx Oct-Apr) FREE Vejer's much-reworked castle, once home of the Duques de Medina Sidonia, dates from the 10th or 11th century. It isn't astoundingly impressive, but you can wander through the Moorish entrance arch and climb the hibiscus-fringed ramparts for fantastic views across town and down to the white-sand coastline.

Courses

★Annie B's Spanish Kitchen COOKING
(☎620 560649; www.anniebspain.com; Calle Viñas 11; 1-day course €165) This is your chance to master the art of Andalucian cooking with top-notch local expertise. Annie's popular day classes (Andalucian, Moroccan or seafood focused) end with lunch by the pool or on the roof terrace at her gorgeous old-town house. She also offers six-day Spanish Culinary Classics courses, plus tapas, food and sherry tours of Vejer, Cádiz, Jerez and more.

La Janda LANGUAGE
(☎956 44 70 60; http://lajanda.org; Avenida San Miguel 19; per 20hr week €190) Who wouldn't want to study Spanish in Vejer, with its winding streets, authentic bars and mysterious feel? La Janda's small-group courses emphasise cultural immersion, incorporating everything from flamenco, yoga, horse riding, tapas crawls and cooking classes to Almodóvar movie nights.

Sleeping

★La Casa del Califa BOUTIQUE HOTEL $$
(☎956 44 77 30; www.califavejer.com; Plaza de España 16; incl breakfast s €92-145, d €106-155, ste €175-230; P❄📶) Rambling over several floors of labyrinthine corridors, this gorgeous hotel oozes style and character, and inhabits a building with its roots in the 10th century. Rooms are wonderfully soothing, with Morocco-chic decor; the top-floor 'Africa' suite is divine. Special 'emir' service (€45) brings flowers, pastries and *cava* (sparkling wine). Breakfast is a delicious spread in the fabulous Moroccan–Middle Eastern restaurant.

★Casa Shelly BOUTIQUE HOTEL $$
(☎639 118831; www.casashelly.com; Calle Eduardo Shelly 6; r €105-140; ⌚Mar-Nov; ❄📶) All understated elegance and homey Andalucian cosiness, Casa Shelly feels as though it's wandered out of the pages of an old-meets-new interior-design magazine and into the thick of Vejer's old town. Beyond a calming reception lounge and fountain-bathed patio, it has seven exquisitely designed rooms adorned with antique-style tiles, wood-beamed ceilings, shuttered windows and fresh decor in pinks, blues and whites.

La Fonda Antigua BOUTIQUE HOTEL $$
(☎625 372616; www.chicsleepinvejer.com; Calle San Filmo 14; r incl breakfast €90-150; ❄📶) A *jerezano* couple with an eye for contemporary-chic interiors runs this boutiquey adults-only bolt-hole on the fringes of Vejer's old town. In the seven individually styled rooms, antique doors morph into bedheads, mismatched vintage tiles dot polished-concrete floors and include glass-walled showers and, for room 6, a claw-foot tub. The rooftop chill-out terrace opens up sprawling old-town vistas.

★V... BOUTIQUE HOTEL $$$
(☎956 45 17 57; www.hotelv-vejer.com; Calle Rosario 11-13; r €219-329; ❄📶) V... (that's V for Vejer, and, yes, the three dots are part of the name) is one of Andalucía's most exquisite creations. It's a brilliantly run 12-room hotel where fashionable, contemporary design (luxurious open-plan bathrooms with huge tubs and giant mirrors) mixes with antique artefacts (pre-Columbus doors). On the vista-laden rooftop there's a tiny pool and a bubbling hot tub.

Eating

Mercado de Abastos ANDALUCIAN, INTERNATIONAL $
(Calle San Francisco; dishes €2-8; ⌚noon-4pm & 7pm-midnight) Glammed up with modern gastrobar design, Vejer's Mercado de San Francisco has morphed into a buzzy foodie hot spot. Grab a *vino* and choose between classic favourites and bold contemporary creations at its wonderfully varied tapas stalls: Iberian ham *raciones, tortilla de patatas* (potato omelette), fried fish in paper cups or hugely popular sushi.

★El Jardín del Califa MOROCCAN, FUSION $$
(☎956 45 17 06; www.califavejer.com; Plaza de España 16; mains €12-18; ⌚1.30-4pm & 8-11.30pm; 🌶) The sizzling atmosphere matches the cooking at this exotically beautiful restaurant, also a hotel and *tetería* (teahouse). It's hidden in a cavernous house where even finding the bathroom is a full-on

adventure. The Moroccan-Middle Eastern menu – tagines, couscous, hummus, falafel – is crammed with Maghreb flavours (saffron, figs, almonds). Book ahead, whether that's for the palm-sprinkled garden or the moody interior.

With tables on Plaza de España, **Califa Exprés** (www.califavejer.com; Plaza de España 16; dishes €4-6; ⏱12.30-4pm & 7.30-11.30pm, may close Dec-Mar;) offers a taste of the Califa magic in a simpler setting.

★Corredera 55 ANDALUCIAN, MEDITERRANEAN **$$**
(☎956 45 18 48; www.califavejer.com; Calle de la Corredera 55; mains €10-19; ⏱noon-11pm;) This fresh-faced veggie-friendly eatery delivers elegant, inventive cooking packed with local flavours and ingredients. Menus change with the seasons. Try chilled, lemon-infused grilled courgette and goat's-cheese parcels, cauliflower fritters with honey-yoghurt dressing, or *cava*-baked prawn-stuffed fish of the day. Perch at street-side tables (complete with winter blankets!) or eat in the cosily stylish dining room amid Vejer paintings.

☆ Entertainment

Peña Cultural Flamenca 'Aguilar de Vejer' FLAMENCO
(☎606 171732, 956 45 07 89; Calle Rosario 29) Part of Vejer's magic is its small-town flamenco scene, best observed in this atmospheric bar and performance space founded in 1989. Free shows usually happen on Saturday at 9.30pm; book in for dinner (mains €12 to €23) or swing by for drinks and tapas (€6). The tourist office has schedules.

ℹ Information

Oficina Municipal de Turismo (☎956 45 17 36; www.turismovejer.es; Avenida Los Remedios 2; ⏱10am-2.30pm & 4.30-9pm Mon-Fri, 10am-2pm & 4.30-9pm Sat, 10am-2pm Sun, reduced hours mid-Oct–Apr) About 500m below the town centre, beside the bus stop and a big, free car park.

ℹ Getting There & Away

From Avenida Los Remedios, **Comes** (☎902 64 64 28; www.tgcomes.es) runs buses to Cádiz, Barbate, Zahara de los Atunes, Jerez de la Frontera and Seville. More buses stop at La Barca de Vejer, on the N340 at the bottom of the hill; from here, it's a steep 20-minute walk or €6 taxi ride up to town.

DESTINATION	COST (€)	DURATION	FREQUENCY
Algeciras	7.20	1¼hr	10 daily
Barbate	1.40	15min	4 daily
Cádiz	5.70	1¼hr	3-4 daily
Jerez de la Frontera	7.80	1½hr	1 daily Mon-Fri
La Línea (for Gibraltar)	9.10	1¾hr	4 daily
Málaga	22	3¼hr	2 daily
Seville	16	2¼hr	4 daily
Seville (from Avenida Los Remedios)	17	3hr	1 daily Mon-Fri
Tarifa	4.49	40min	8 daily
Zahara de los Atunes	2.50	25min	2-3 daily

Los Caños de Meca

POP 120

Little laid-back Los Caños de Meca, 16km southwest of Vejer, straggles along a series of spectacular open white-sand beaches that will leave you wondering why Marbella even exists. Once a hippie haven, Caños still attracts beach lovers of all kinds and nations – especially in summer – with its alternative, hedonistic scene and nudist beaches, as well as kite-surfing, windsurfing and board-surfing opportunities.

◉ Sights & Activities

Caños' **main beach** is straight in front of Avenida de Trafalgar's junction with the A2233 to Barbate. Nudists head to its eastern end for more secluded coves, including **Playa de las Cortinas**, and to **Playa del Faro** beside Cabo de Trafalgar. Broad, blonde **Playa de Zahora** extends northwest from Los Caños.

★Parque Natural de la Breña y Marismas del Barbate NATURE RESERVE
(www.ventanadelvisitante.es) This 50-sq-km coastal park protects important marshes, cliffs and pine forest from Costa del Sol–type development. Its main entry point is a 7.2km (two-hour) walking trail, the **Sendero del Acantilado**, between Los Caños de Meca and Barbate, along cliff tops that rival Cabo de Gata in their beauty.

Cabo de Trafalgar LIGHTHOUSE
At the western end of Los Caños de Meca, a side road (often half-covered in sand) leads out to an 1860 lighthouse on a low spit of land. This is the famous Cabo de Trafalgar, off which Spanish naval power was swiftly terminated by a British fleet under Admiral Nelson in 1805.

Escuela de Surf 9 Pies SURFING, YOGA
(☎620 104241; www.escueladesurf9pies.com; Avenida de la Playa, El Palmar; board & wetsuit rental per 2/4hr €12/18, 2hr group class €28) Professional surf school offering board hire and surf classes for all levels, plus yoga sessions (€10) and SUP (stand-up paddleboard) rental (€15 for two hours), towards the northern end of El Palmar beach.

Sleeping & Eating

Casas Karen HOTEL $$
(☎649 780834, 956 43 70 67; www.casaskaren.com; Camino del Monte 6; d €85-135, q €155-195; P) This eccentric, easygoing Dutch-owned hideaway has characterful, rustic rooms and apartments across a flower-covered, pine-sprinkled plot. Options range from a converted farmhouse to thatched *chozas* (traditional huts) and two modern, split-level 'studios'. Decor is casual Andalucian-Moroccan, full of throws, hammocks and colour. It's 1km northeast of Caños' Cabo de Trafalgar turn-off.

Las Dunas CAFE $
(☎956 43 72 03; www.barlasdunas.es; Carretera del Cabo de Trafalgar; dishes €4-12; ⊙9am-midnight Sep-Jun, to 3am Jul & Aug;) Say *hola* to the ultimate relaxation spot, where kitesurfers kick back between white-knuckle sorties launched from the beach outside. Bob Marley tunes, great *bocadillos* (filled rolls), fresh juices, *platos combinados*, a warming winter fire, and a laid-back, beach-shack feel.

Getting There & Away

Comes (☎902 64 64 28; www.tgcomes.es) has two daily weekday buses from Los Caños de Meca to Cádiz (€6.30, 1½ hours) via El Palmar (€2, 15 minutes). Additional summer services may run to Cádiz and Seville.

Tarifa

POP 13,680

Tarifa's southern-tip-of-Spain location, where the Mediterranean and the Atlantic meet, gives it a different climate and character to the rest of Andalucía. Stiff Atlantic winds draw in surfers, windsurfers and kitesurfers who, in turn, lend this ancient yet deceptively small settlement a refreshingly laid-back international vibe. Tarifa is the last stop in Spain before Morocco, and it's also a taste of things to come. With its winding whitewashed streets and tangible North African feel, the walled windswept old town could easily pass for Chefchaouen or Essaouira. It's no secret, however, and, in August especially, Tarifa gets packed (but that's half the fun).

Tarifa may be as old as Phoenician Cádiz and was definitely a Roman settlement. It takes its name from Tarif ibn Malik, who led a Muslim raid in AD 710, the year before the main Islamic invasion of the peninsula.

Sights

Tarifa's narrow old-town streets, mostly of Islamic origin, hint at Morocco. Wander through the fortified Mudéjar **Puerta de Jerez**, built after the Reconquista, then pop into the lively **Mercado de Abastos** (Calle Colón; ⊙8.30am-2pm Tue-Sat) before winding your way past the whitewashed, 18th-century baroque-neoclassical **Iglesia de San Francisco de Asís** (Calle Santísima Trinidad; ⊙10am-1pm & 6.15-8.15pm Mon-Sat, 9.15-11am Sun) to the mainly 16th-century **Iglesia de San Mateo** (Calle Sancho IV El Bravo; ⊙8.45am-1pm Mon, 8.45am-1pm & 6-8pm Tue-Sat, 10am-1pm & 7-8.30pm Sun). Head south along Calle Coronel Moscardó, then up Calle Aljaranda; the **Miramar** (Calle Amargura) (atop part of the castle walls) has spectacular views across to Africa and 851m Jebel Musa, one of the 'Pillars of Hercules' (Gibraltar is the other).

Castillo de Guzmán CASTLE
(Calle Guzmán El Bueno; adult/child €4/free; ⊙11am-2.30pm & 5-7.30pm Mon-Sat approx Mar-Sep, 11am-2.30pm & 4-6.30pm Mon-Sat approx Oct-Feb, 11am-4pm Sun year-round) Though built in 960 on the orders of Cordoban caliph Abd ar-Rahman III, this restored fortress is named after Reconquista hero Guzmán El Bueno. In 1294, when threatened with the death of his captured son unless he surrendered the castle to Merenid attackers from Morocco, El Bueno threw down his own dagger for his son's execution. Guzmán's descendants later became the Duques de Medina Sidonia, one of Spain's most powerful families. Above the interior entrance, note the 10th-century castle-foundation inscription.

DON'T MISS

TARIFA BEACH BLISS

Jazzed up by the colourful kites and sails of kitesurfers and windsurfers whizzing across turquoise waves, the exquisite bleach-blonde beaches that stretch northwest from Tarifa along the N340 are some of Andalucía's (and Spain's) most beautiful. In summer they fill up with sun-kissed beach lovers and chill-out bars, though the relentless winds can be a hassle. If you tire of lazing on the sand, kitesurfing, windsurfing and horse riding await.

Playa Chica On the isthmus leading out to Isla de las Palomas at the southernmost tip of Tarifa town, tiny Playa Chica is more sheltered than other local beaches.

Playa de los Lances This broad snow-white sandy beach stretches for 7km northwest from Tarifa. The low dunes behind it are a *paraje natural* (protected natural area); you can hike across them on the 1.5km Sendero de los Lances, signposted towards the northwestern end of Calle Batalla del Salado.

Playa de Valdevaqueros Sprawling between 7km and 10km northwest of Tarifa, to the great white dune at Punta Paloma, Valdevaqueros is one of Tarifa's most popular kite-surfing beaches, blessed with dusty alabaster-hued sand and aqua waters.

Punta Paloma One of Andalucía's most fabulous beaches, Punta Paloma, 10km northwest of Tarifa, is famous for its huge blonde sand dune. At its far western end, you can lather yourself up in a natural mudbath.

Activities

Horse Riding

Aventura Ecuestre HORSE RIDING
(☎956 23 66 32, 626 480019; www.aventuraecuestre.com; Hotel Dos Mares, Carretera N340, Km 79.5) Well-organised, multilingual equestrian outfit running one-hour rides along Playa de los Lances (€30), four-hour hacks across the Punta Paloma dunes (€80) and four-hour forays into the Parque Natural Los Alcornocales (€80), plus kids' pony rides (€15 for 30 minutes) and private courses (five days €300). It's 5km northwest of Tarifa.

Molino El Mastral HORSE RIDING
(☎646 964279; www.mastral.com; Carretera Santuario Virgen de la Luz; per hour €30) This excellent horse-riding establishment, 5km northwest of Tarifa, offers excursions into the hilly countryside. It's signposted off the CA9210 (off the N340).

Whale Watching

The waters off Tarifa are one of the best places in Europe to see whales and dolphins as they swim between the Atlantic and the Mediterranean from April to October; sightings of some kind are almost guaranteed during these months. In addition to striped and bottlenose dolphins, long-finned pilot whales, orcas (killer whales) and sperm whales, you may also spot endangered fin whales and common dolphins. Sperm whales swim the Strait of Gibraltar from April to August; the best months for orcas are July and August. Find out more at Tarifa's **Centro de Interpretación de Cetáceos** (www.facebook.com/CICAMTARIFA; Avenida Fuerzas Armadas 17; ⏲Mar-Oct) FREE.

FIRMM WHALE WATCHING
(☎956 62 70 08; www.firmm.org; Calle Pedro Cortés 4; 2hr tours adult/child €30/20; ⏲10am-7pm Easter-Oct) Among Tarifa's dozens of whale-watching outfits, not-for-profit FIRMM is a good option. Its primary purpose is to study the whales and record data, and this gives rise to environmentally sensitive two- or three-hour tours and week-long whale-watching courses.

Kitesurfing & Windsurfing

Tarifa's legendary winds have turned the town into one of Europe's premier windsurfing and kitesurfing destinations. The most popular strip is along the coast between Tarifa and Punta Paloma, 10km northwest. Over 30 places offer equipment hire and classes, from beginner to expert level. The best months are May, June and September, but bear in mind that the choppy seas aren't always beginners' territory. Some schools also offer SUP sessions.

ION Club WINDSURFING, KITESURFING
(☎956 68 90 98; www.ion-club.net; Hurricane Hotel, Carretera N340, Km 78; 2hr group kitesurfing/windsurfing class €80/60; ⏲Easter-Dec) Recommended group/private windsurfing and kitesurfing classes (beginner, intermediate

or advanced level), equipment rental (€90 per day) and paddle-boarding (€25 per hour), 7km northwest of Tarifa. Spanish, English, French, Italian and German spoken. Also at **Valdevaqueros** (☎619 340913; www.ion-club.net; Carretera N340, Km 76, Playa de Valdevaqueros; 2hr group kitesurfing/windsurfing class €80/60; Easter-Dec), 10km northwest of town.

Gisela Pulido Pro Center KITESURFING
(☎608 577711; www.giselapulidoprocenter.com; Calle Mar Adriático 22; 3hr group courses per person €70) World champion Gisela Pulido's highly rated kitesurfing school offers year-round group/private courses, including six-hour 'baptisms' (€135) and nine-hour 'complete' courses (€199), in Spanish, French, English and German. Also rents kitesurfing gear (€70 per day).

Spin Out WINDSURFING, KITESURFING
(☎956 23 63 52; www.tarifaspinout.com; Carretera N340, Km 75.5, Playa de Valdevaqueros; 90min windsurfing class per person €59, board & sail rental per hour €30; 10.30am-7pm Apr-Oct) Daily windsurfing classes and five-day courses for beginners, kids and experts, from a switched-on, multilingual team, 11km northwest of town. There's also a kitesurfing school.

Festivals & Events

Feria de la Virgen de la Luz FAIR
(1st week Sep) Tarifa's town fair, honouring its patron, mixes religious processions, handsome horses and your typical Spanish fiesta.

Sleeping

★Hostal África HOSTAL $
(☎956 68 02 20; www.hostalafrica.com; Calle María Antonia Toledo 12; s €40-55, d €55-80, tr €80-110; Mar-Nov;) This mellow, revamped 19th-century house within Tarifa's old town is one of the Costa de la Luz' (and Cádiz province's) best *hostales* (budget hotels). Full of potted plants and sky-blue-and-white arches, it's run by hospitable, on-the-ball owners, and the 13 all-different rooms (including one triple) sparkle with bright colours. Enjoy the lovely roof terrace, with its loungey cabana and Africa views.

Sulok Hostel HOSTEL $
(☎603 567229; http://suloktarifa.com; Calle Sancho IV El Bravo 23; dm €20-40; may close Dec-Feb;) This contemporary hostel, accessed through a Tarifa-chic old-town boutique, is a welcoming, reliable budget choice. There are three spotless dorms sleeping six, eight or 10 people, plus separate bathrooms for men and women; each capsule-style bunk bed comes with two plugs, a light, a locker and a curtain for privacy.

Hotel Misiana BOUTIQUE HOTEL $$
(☎956 62 70 83; www.misiana.com; Calle Sancho IV El Bravo 16; s €105-120, d €125-155, ste €235-310;) The Misiana's penthouse suite, with private roof terrace engulfed in wrap-around Morocco views, is one of Tarifa's top-choice rooms. But the doubles are lovely, too, with their stylish whiteness, pale greys, driftwood-chic decor, sea-life paintings and desks with tea/coffee sets. Light sleepers might prefer a quieter room at the back. It's predictably popular; book ahead.

Breakfast (€10) is served in the lively streetside cafe-bar.

Hotel Convento Tarifa HOTEL $$
(☎956 68 33 75; www.hotelconventotarifa.es; Calle Batalla del Salado 14; d €90-160, tr €113-195;) White, bright and pastels are the themes at this efficient hotel built around the ruined walls of an ancient convent just outside the old town. Expect power showers, huge mirrors and vases of flowers in the modern, tranquil-toned rooms.

★Riad BOUTIQUE HOTEL $$$
(☎856 92 98 80; www.theriadtarifa.com; Calle Comendador 10; r incl breakfast €140-210) This seductive hotel is an exquisitely converted 17th-century townhouse. Opening through a polished-concrete lobby punctuated by an ornamental fountain/pool, it's dressed with original architecture: exposed-stone walls, antique doors, red-brick arches and a frescoed facade. The 10 intimate rooms are pocketed away off the patio, styled with *tadelakt* (waterproof plaster) walls, bold reds and blues, and chic Andalucía-meets-Morocco design.

Eating

★Café Azul CAFE, BREAKFAST $
(www.facebook.com/cafeazultarifa; Calle Batalla del Salado 8; breakfasts €2-8; 9am-3pm;) This long-established Italian-run place with eye-catching blue-and-white Moroccan-inspired decor whips up the best breakfasts in Tarifa, if not Andalucía. You'll want to eat everything. The fresh fruit salad with muesli, yoghurt and coconut, and the fruit-

WORTH A TRIP

BAELO CLAUDIA

The ruined town of **Baelo Claudia** (956 10 67 96; www.museosdeandalucia.es; €1.50, EU citizens free; 9am-3pm Tue-Sun mid-Jun–mid-Sep, 9am-8pm Tue-Sat, to 3pm Sun Apr–mid-Jun, 9am-6pm Tue-Sat, to 3pm Sun mid-Sep–Mar) is one of Andalucía's most important Roman archaeological sites. These majestic beachside ruins – with fine views across to Morocco – include the substantial remains of a theatre, a paved forum, thermal baths, a market, a marble statue and the columns of a basilica, and the workshops that turned out the products that made Baelo Claudia famous in the Roman world: salted fish and *garum* (spicy seasoning made from leftover fish parts). There's a good museum.

Baelo Claudia particularly flourished during the reign of Emperor Claudius (AD 41–54), but it declined after an earthquake in the 2nd century. In 2017, the site celebrated a century since it was first excavated.

The site is near the village of Bolonia, signposted off the N340 15km northwest of Tarifa. In July and August, three weekday Horizonte Sur (p704) buses run between Bolonia and Tarifa (€2.50, 30 to 40 minutes). Otherwise it's your own wheels.

and-yoghurt-stuffed crêpe are works of art. It also serves good coffee, smoothies, juices, *bocadillos* (filled rolls) and cooked breakfasts, with delicious gluten-free and vegan options.

Tarifa Eco Center VEGETARIAN $
(956 92 74 56; www.tarifaecocenter.com; Calle San Sebastián 6; mains €8.50-12.50; 9.30am-11.30pm;) This relaxed terrace restaurant, co-working space and cocktail/juice bar pulls out all the stops with its ultra-enticing, organic vegetarian and vegan cooking. Wholemeal wood-oven pizzas with a rainbow of plant-based toppings are the speciality, or pick from wholesome bites like vegetable curry, soy burgers, pasta specials or 'Verdísima' green salads, many artfully presented in mini paella pans.

El Francés TAPAS $
(Calle Sancho IV El Bravo 21; tapas €2.50-4.80; 12.30pm-midnight Fri-Tue;) Squeeze into the standing-room-only bar or battle for your terrace table at always-rammed El Francés, which gives Andalucian classics a subtle twist. Tarifa's favourite tapas bar is a buzzing place, serving *patatas bravas* and *tortillitas de camarones* (shrimp fritters) alongside mini chicken-veg couscous or prawn curry. No reservations; pop in on the day to secure a table (dinner from 6.30pm only).

La Oca da Sergio ITALIAN $$
(956 68 12 49, 615 686571; Calle General Copons 6; mains €8.50-19; 1-4pm & 8pm-midnight daily Jun-Oct & Dec, 8pm-midnight Mon & Wed-Fri, 1-4pm & 8pm-midnight Sat & Sun Jan-May) Italians rule the Tarifa food scene. Amiable Sergio roams the tables Italian style, armed with loaded plates and amusing stories, and presides over genuine home-country cooking at this forever popular restaurant tucked behind the Iglesia de San Mateo (p700). Look forward to *caprese* salads, homemade pasta (try the truffle pappardelle), wood-oven thin-crust pizzas, cappuccinos and after-dinner *limoncello*.

Mandrágora MOROCCAN, ANDALUCIAN $$
(956 68 12 91; www.mandragoratarifa.com; Calle Independencia 3; mains €11-18; 6.30pm-midnight Mon-Sat Easter-Oct;) On a quiet street behind the Iglesia de San Mateo (p700), this intimate palm-dotted spot serves Andalucian–Moroccan–Middle Eastern food and does so terrifically well. It's hard to know where to start, but tempting choices include falafel and hummus, lamb with plums and almonds, Moroccan vegetable couscous and chicken or monkfish tagine.

Drinking & Nightlife

With all the surfers, kitesurfers and beachgoers breezing through, Tarifa has a busy bar scene (especially in summer), plus a few late-night clubs. The after-dark fun centres on the old town's narrow Calles Cervantes, San Francisco and Santísima Trinidad. Summer *chiringuitos* (snack bars) get going with music/DJs on Playa de los Lances and the beaches northwest of town, particularly around sunset.

Tumbao LOUNGE, BAR
(www.facebook.com/tumbaotarifa; Carretera N340, Km 76, Playa de Valdevaqueros; 5pm-midnight Easter-Sep) The ultimate Tarifa-cool beach

hangout, Tumbao serves up cocktails, *tinto de verano* (cold, wine-based drink similar to sangria) loungey sunset beats on a grassy, beanbag-strewn patch overlooking the kitesurfing action on Playa de Valdevaqueros, 10km northwest of town. The kitchen delivers burgers, salads, nachos, grilled *chuletones* (giant beef chops) and other tasty bites, mostly sizzled up on the open barbecue (mains €7 to €15).

Tangana BAR
(☎956 68 51 32; www.tarifaweb.com/tangana; Carretera N340, Km 75.5, Playa de Valdevaqueros; ⏰10am-9pm Easter-Oct; 📶) This mellow beach bar is set around a boho-chic boutique and two chill-out lounges, one with deckchairs looking out across the beach, 11km northwest of Tarifa. Turquoise-washed bench-style tables set a lazy-life scene for sipping mojitos and caipirinhas (€6), balanced out by *bocadillos* (filled rolls), burgers, pastas, paella and build-your-own salad bowls (dishes €5 to €12).

Bear House BAR
(www.facebook.com/bearhousetarifa; Calle Sancho IV El Bravo 26; ⏰4pm-2am Sun-Thu, to 3am Fri & Sat) This neon-lit *bar de copas* (drinks bar) has low, cushioned chill-out sofas, good mojitos and other cocktails, a lengthy happy hour, and football on the big screen (but no bears). Hours vary.

ℹ Information

Oficina de Turismo (☎956 68 09 93; Paseo de la Alameda; ⏰10am-1.30pm & 4-6pm Mon-Fri, 10am-1.30pm Sat & Sun)

ℹ Getting There & Away

BOAT

FRS (☎956 68 18 30; www.frs.es; Avenida de Andalucía 16; adult/child/car/motorcycle 1 way €41/15/136/33) runs one-hour ferries up to eight times daily between Tarifa and Tangier (Morocco). **Inter Shipping** (☎956 68 47 29; www.intershipping.es; Recinto Portuario, Local 4; adult/child/car/motorcycle 1 way €38/14/100/24) offers up to seven daily one-hour ferries to Tangier. All passengers need a passport.

BUS

Comes (☎902 64 64 28; www.tgcomes.es) operates from the **bus station** (☎956 68 40 38; Calle Batalla del Salado) beside the petrol station at the northwestern end of town. In July and August, **Horizonte Sur** (☎699 427644; http://horizontesur.es) runs 11 to 14 daily buses Monday to Saturday from here to Punta Paloma via Tarifa's beaches.

DESTINATION	COST (€)	DURATION	FREQUENCY
Algeciras	2.45	30min	13-25 daily
Cádiz	9.83	1½hr	6 daily
El Puerto de Santa María	10	2hr	2 daily
Jerez de la Frontera	11	2½hr	12 daily
La Barca de Vejer (for Vejer de la Frontera)	4.49	40min	7 daily
La Línea (for Gibraltar)	4.45	1hr	6 daily
Málaga	17	2¾hr	3 daily
Marbella	11	1¾hr	3 daily
Seville	20	3hr	4 daily

CÓRDOBA PROVINCE

Once the dazzling beacon of Al-Andalus, the historic city of Córdoba is the main magnet of its namesake province. But there's plenty of less-trampled territory to explore outside the provincial capital. To the north rises the Sierra Morena, a rolling upcountry expanse of remote villages, ruined castles and protected forests. To the south, olive trees and grapevines carpet the rippling terrain, yielding some of Spain's best oils and wines.

Córdoba

POP 294,300 / ELEV 130M

One building alone is reason enough to put Córdoba high on your itinerary: the mesmerising multiarched Mezquita. One of the world's greatest Islamic buildings, the Mezquita is a symbol of the worldly, sophisticated culture that flourished here more than a millennium ago when Córdoba was capital of Islamic Spain and western Europe's biggest, most cultured city. But today's Córdoba is much more than the Mezquita. With a lot to see and do, some charming accommodation, and excellent restaurants and bars, it merits far more than the fleeting visit many travellers give it. Córdoba's real charms unfold as you explore the winding, stone-paved lanes of the medieval city to the west, north and east of the gaudy touristic area immediately around the Mezquita.

Andalucía's major river, the Guadalquivir, flows just below the Mezquita, and the riverfront streets are home to a band of lively restaurants and bars making the most of the view. The life of the modern city, meanwhile, focuses just to the north of the historic centre, around Plaza de las Tendillas, where you'll find a more local feel with some excellent bars and restaurants.

Córdoba bursts into life from mid-April to mid-June, when it stages most of its major fiestas. At this time of year the skies are blue, the temperatures are perfect and the city's many trees, gardens and courtyards drip with foliage and blooms. September and October are also excellent weatherwise, but July and August sizzle.

History

The Roman settlement of Corduba was established in the 3rd century BC as a provisioning point for Roman troops. In about 25 BC Emperor Augustus made the city capital of Baetica, one of the three Roman provinces on the Iberian Peninsula, ushering in an era of prosperity and cultural ascendancy that saw Córdoba produce the famous writers Seneca and Lucan. The Roman bridge over the Guadalquivir and the temple on Calle Claudio Marcelo are the most visible remains of this important Roman city, most of whose traces now lie a metre or two below ground. By the 3rd century, when Christianity reached Córdoba, the Roman city was already in decline. It fell to Islamic invaders in AD 711.

The city took centre stage in 756 when Abd ar-Rahman I set himself up here as the emir of Al-Andalus (the Muslim-controlled parts of the Iberian Peninsula), founding the Umayyad dynasty, which more or less unified Al-Andalus for two and a half centuries. Abd ar-Rahman I founded the great Mezquita in 785. The city's, and Al-Andalus', heyday came under Abd ar-Rahman III (r 912–61). Spurred by rivalry with the Fatimid dynasty in North Africa, he named himself caliph (the title of the Muslim successors of Mohammed) in 929, ushering in the era of the Córdoba caliphate.

Córdoba was by now the biggest city in western Europe, with a flourishing economy based on agriculture and skilled artisan products, and a population somewhere around 250,000. The city shone with hundreds of dazzling mosques, public baths, patios, gardens and fountains. This was the famed 'city of the three cultures', where Muslims, Jews and Christians coexisted peaceably and Abd ar-Rahman III's court was frequented by scholars from all three communities. Córdoba's university, library and observatories made it a centre of learning whose influence was still being felt in Christian Europe many centuries later.

Towards the end of the 10th century, Al-Mansur (Almanzor), a ruthless general whose northward raids terrified Christian Spain, took the reins of power from the caliphs. But after the death of Al-Mansur's son Abd al-Malik in 1008, the caliphate descended into anarchy. Berber troops terrorised and looted the city and, in 1031, Umayyad rule ended. Córdoba became a minor part of the Seville *taifa* (small kingdom) in 1069, and has been overshadowed by Seville ever since.

Twelfth-century Córdoba did nevertheless produce the two most celebrated scholars of Al-Andalus – the Muslim Averroës (1126–98) and the Jewish Maimonides (1135–1204), men of multifarious talents most remembered for their efforts to reconcile religious faith with Aristotelian reason. After Córdoba was taken by Castilla's Fernando III in 1236, it declined into a provincial city and its fortunes only looked up with the arrival of industry in the late 19th century. Christian Córdoba did, however, give birth to one of the greatest Spanish poets, Luis de Góngora (1561–1627), still much remembered in the city.

Sights

★Mezquita MOSQUE, CATHEDRAL

(Mosque; ☎957 47 05 12; www.mezquita-catedraldecordoba.es; Calle Cardenal Herrero; adult/child €10/5, 8.30-9.30am Mon-Sat free; ⏲8.30-9.30am & 10am-7pm Mon-Sat, 8.30-11.30am & 3-7pm Sun Mar-Oct, 8.30-9.30am & 10am-6pm Mon-Sat, 8.30-11.30am & 3-6pm Sun Nov-Feb) It's impossible to overemphasise the beauty of Córdoba's great mosque, with its remarkably serene (despite tourist crowds) and spacious interior. One of the world's greatest works of Islamic architecture, the Mezquita hints, with all its lustrous decoration, at a refined age when Muslims, Jews and Christians lived side by side and enriched their city with a heady interaction of diverse, vibrant cultures.

Arab chronicles recount how Abd ar-Rahman I purchased half of the Visigothic church of San Vicente for the Muslim

Córdoba

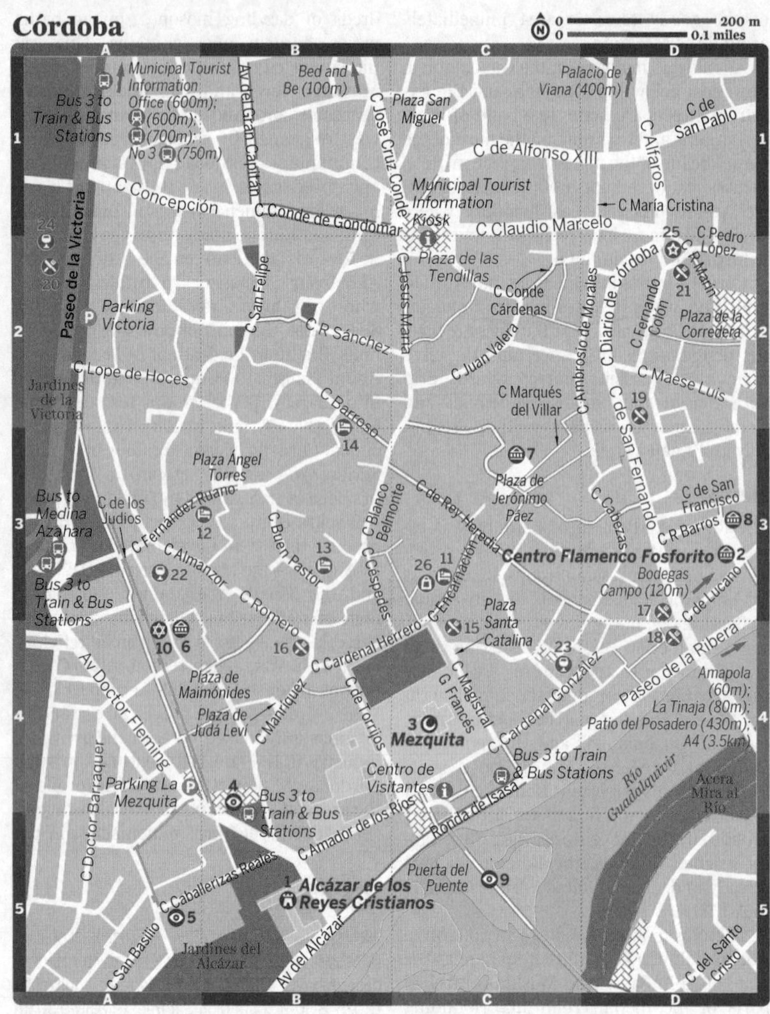

community's Friday prayers, and then, in AD 784, bought the other half on which to erect a new mosque. Three later extensions nearly quintupled the size of Abd ar-Rahman I's mosque and brought it to the form you see today – with one major alteration: a Christian cathedral plonked right in the middle of the mosque in the 16th century (hence the often-used description 'Mezquita-Catedral').

Mass is celebrated in the central cathedral at 9.30am Monday to Saturday, and at noon and 1.30pm Sundays.

➡ Patio de los Naranjos

This lovely courtyard, with its orange, palm and cypress trees and fountains, forms the entrance to the Mezquita. It was the site of ritual ablutions before prayer in the mosque. Its most impressive entrance is the Puerta del Perdón, a 14th-century Mudéjar archway next to the bell tower. The Mezquita's ticket office is just inside here.

➡ Bell Tower (Torre Campanario)

You can climb the 54m-high bell tower for fine panoramas and an interesting bird's-eye angle on the main Mezquita building. Up to 20 people are allowed up the tower every

Córdoba

Top Sights
1 Alcázar de los Reyes Cristianos B5
2 Centro Flamenco Fosforito D3
3 Mezquita C4

Sights
4 Baños del Alcázar Califal B4
5 Caballerizas Reales A5
6 Casa de Sefarad A4
7 Museo Arqueológico C3
8 Museo Julio Romero de Torres D3
9 Puente Romano C5
10 Sinagoga A4

Sleeping
11 Balcón de Córdoba C3
12 Hospedería Alma Andalusí B3
13 Hospedería del Atalia B3
14 Option Be Hostel B2

Eating
15 Bar Santos C4
16 Casa Pepe de la Judería B4
17 Garum 2.1 .... D3
18 La Bicicleta D4
19 La Boca D2
20 Mercado Victoria A2
21 Taberna Salinas D2

Drinking & Nightlife
22 Bodega Guzmán A3
23 El Barón C4
24 Sojo Mercado A2

Entertainment
25 Jazz Café D2

Shopping
26 Meryan C3

half hour from 9.30am to 1.30pm and 4pm to 6.30pm (to 5.30pm November to February; no afternoon visits in July or August). Tickets (€2) are sold on the inner side of the Puerta del Perdón, next to the tower: they often sell out well ahead of visit times, so it's a good idea to buy them early in the day. Originally built by Abd ar-Rahman III in 951–52 as the Mezquita's minaret, the tower was encased in a strengthened outer shell and heightened by the Christians in the 16th and 17th centuries. You can still see some caliphal vaults and arches inside.

The original minaret would have looked something like the Giralda in Seville, which was practically a copy. Córdoba's minaret influenced all minarets built thereafter throughout the western Islamic world.

➡ The Mezquita's Interior

The Mezquita's architectural uniqueness and importance lies in the fact that, structurally speaking, it was a revolutionary building for its time. Earlier major Islamic buildings such as the Dome of the Rock in Jerusalem and the Great Mosque in Damascus placed an emphasis on verticality, but the Mezquita was intended as a democratically horizontal and simple space, where the spirit could be free to roam and communicate easily with God – a kind of glorious refinement of the original simple Islamic prayer space (usually the open yard of a desert home).

Men prayed side by side on the *argamasa*, a floor made of compact, reddish slaked lime and sand. A flat roof, decorated with gold and multicoloured motifs, was supported by striped arches suggestive of a forest of date palms. The arches rested on, eventually, 1293 columns (of which 856 remain today). Useful leaflets in several languages are available free just inside the door by which visitors enter.

Abd ar-Rahman I's initial prayer hall – the area immediately inside today's visitor entrance – was divided into 11 'naves' by lines of arches striped in red brick and white stone. The columns of these arches were a mishmash of material collected from the earlier church on the site, Córdoba's Roman buildings and places as far away as Constantinople. To raise the ceiling high enough to create a sense of openness, inventive builders came up with the idea of a two-tier construction, using taller columns as a base and planting shorter ones on top.

Later enlargements of the mosque, southward by Abd ar-Rahman II in the 9th century and Al-Hakim II in the 960s, and eastward by Al-Mansur in the 970s, extended it to an area of nearly 14,400 sq metres, making it one of the biggest mosques in the world. The arcades' simplicity and number give a sense of endlessness to the Mezquita.

The final Mezquita had 19 doors along its north side, filling it with light and yielding a sense of openness. Nowadays, nearly all these doorways are closed off, dampening the vibrant effect of the red-and-white double arches. Christian additions to the building, such as the solid mass of the cathedral in the centre and the 50 or so chapels

Mezquita

TIMELINE

6th century AD Foundation of a Christian church, the Basilica of San Vicente, on the site of the present Mezquita.

786-87 Salvaging Visigothic and Roman ruins, Emir Abd ar-Rahman I replaces the church with a *mezquita* (mosque).

833-48 Mosque enlarged by Abd ar-Rahman II.

951-2 A new minaret is built by Abd ar-Rahman III.

962-71 Mosque enlarged, and superb new ❶ **mihrab** added, by Al-Hakim II.

991-4 Mosque enlarged for the last time by Al-Mansur, who also enlarged the courtyard (now the ❷ **Patio de los Naranjos**), bringing the whole complex to its current dimensions.

1236 Mosque converted into a Christian church after Córdoba is recaptured by Fernando III of Castilla.

1271 Instead of destroying the mosque, the Christians modify it, creating the ❸ **Capilla de Villaviciosa** and ❹ **Capilla Real**.

1523 Work on a Gothic/Renaissance-style cathedral inside the Mezquita begins, with permission of Carlos I. Legend has it that on seeing the result the king lamented that something unique in the world had been destroyed.

1593-1664 The 10th-century minaret is reinforced and rebuilt as a Renaissance-baroque ❺ **belltower**.

2004 Spanish Muslims petition to be able to worship in the Mezquita again. The Vatican doesn't consent.

TOP TIPS

➡ The Patio de los Naranjos can be enjoyed free of charge at any time.

➡ Entry to the main Mezquita building is offered free every morning, except Sunday, between 8.30am and 9.30am.

➡ Group visits are prohibited before 10am, meaning the building is quieter and more atmospheric in the early morning.

The Mihrab
Everything leads to the mosque's greatest treasure – the beautiful prayer niche, in the wall facing Mecca, that was added in the 10th century. Cast your eyes over the gold mosaic cubes crafted by sculptors imported from Byzantium.

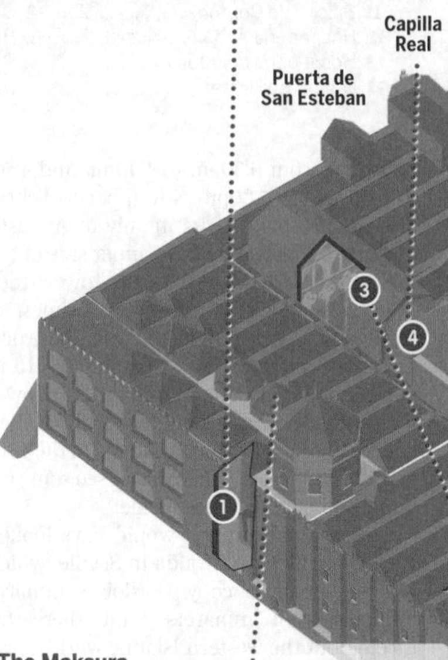

The Maksura
Guiding you towards the mihrab, the *maksura* was the former royal enclosure where the caliphs and their retinues prayed. Its lavish, elaborate arches were designed to draw the eye of worshippers towards the mihrab and Mecca.

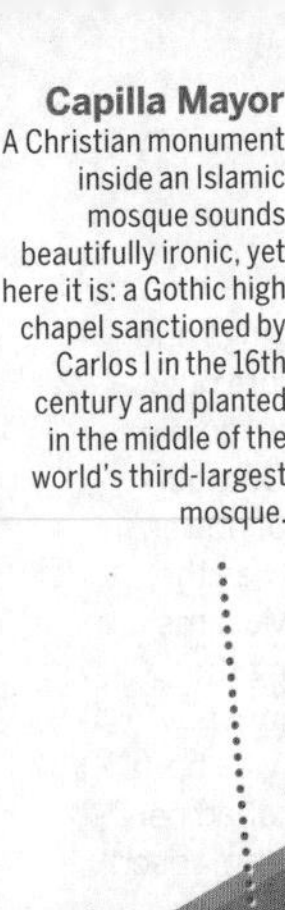

Capilla Mayor

A Christian monument inside an Islamic mosque sounds beautifully ironic, yet here it is: a Gothic high chapel sanctioned by Carlos I in the 16th century and planted in the middle of the world's third-largest mosque.

Belltower

Reopened to visitors in 2014 after a 24-year restoration, the 54m-tall belltower has the best views in the city. It was built in the 17th century around and above the remains of the Mezquita's 10th-century minaret.

5

BILL PERRY/SHUTTERSTOCK ©

The Mezquita Arches

No, you're not hallucinating. The Mezquita's most defining characteristic is its unique terracotta-and-white striped arches that are supported by 856 pillars salvaged from Roman and other ruins. Glimpsed through the dull light they're at once spooky and striking.

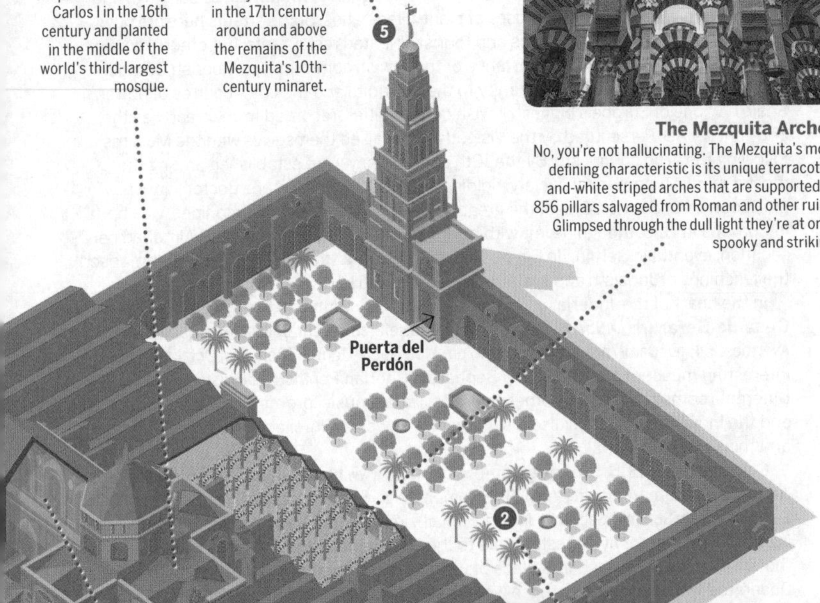

Puerta del Perdón

2

Patio de los Naranjos

Abandon architectural preconceptions all ye who enter here. The ablutions area of the former mosque is a shady courtyard embellished with orange trees that acts as the Mezquita's main entry point.

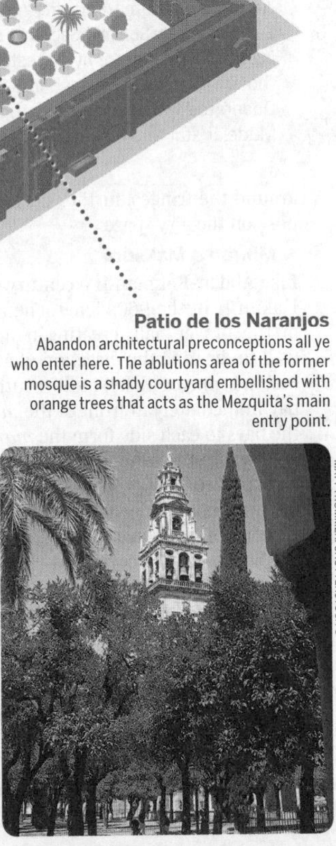

MATT TROMMER/SHUTTERSTOCK ©

JAMES'S TRAVEL AND PHOTOS/SHUTTERSTOCK ©

Capilla de Villaviciosa

Sift through the building's numerous chapels till you find this gem, an early Christian modification which fused existing Moorish features with Gothic arches and pillars. It served as the Capilla Mayor until 1607.

The Cathedral Choir

Few ignore the impressive *coro* (choir), built in the 16th and 17th centuries. Once you've admired the skilfully carved mahogany choir stalls depicting scenes from the Bible, look up at the impressive baroque ceiling.

DON'T MISS

CÓRDOBA'S JEWISH QUARTER

The Judería, Córdoba's old Jewish quarter, west and northwest of the Mezquita, is part of the old city's labyrinth of narrow streets and small squares, whitewashed buildings and wrought-iron gates allowing glimpses of plant-filled patios. Some streets here are now choked with gaudy souvenir shops and tourist-oriented restaurants, but others remain quiet and unblemished. The importance of the Jewish community in Moorish Córdoba is illustrated by the Judería's proximity to the Mezquita and the city's centres of power. Spain had one of Europe's biggest Jewish communities, recorded from as early as the 2nd century AD. Persecuted by the Visigoths, they allied themselves with the Muslims following the Arab conquests. By the 10th century they were established among the most dynamic members of society, holding posts as administrators, doctors, jurists, philosophers and poets. One of the greatest Jewish theologians, Maimonides, was born in Córdoba in 1135, though he left with his family at an early age to escape Almohad persecution, eventually settling in Egypt. His magnum opus, the *Mishne Torah*, summarised the teachings of Judaism and systematised all Jewish law.

In the heart of the Judería, and once connected by tunnel to the synagogue, the **Casa de Sefarad** (957 42 14 04; www.casadesefarad.es; cnr Calles de los Judíos & Averroes; €4; 10am-7pm Jul-Sep, 11am-7pm Mon-Sat & 11am-2.30pm Sun Oct-Jun) is an interesting museum devoted to the Sephardic (Iberian Peninsula Jewish) tradition. Different rooms cover food, domestic crafts, ritual, music, prominent Jews of Córdoba and the Inquisition. There's also a section on the women intellectuals (poets, artists and thinkers) of Al-Andalus.

Constructed in 1315, **Sinagoga** (957 74 90 15; www.turismodecordoba.org; Calle de los Judíos 20; EU citizen/other free/€0.30; 9am-3pm Tue-Sun mid-Jun–mid-Sep, 9am-8pm Tue-Sat & 9am-3pm Sun mid-Sep–mid-Jun) is a small, probably private or family synagogue that is one of the best-surviving testaments to the Jewish presence in medieval Andalucía, though it hasn't been used as a place of worship since the expulsion of Jews in 1492. Decorated with extravagant stucco work that includes Hebrew inscriptions and intricate Mudéjar star and plant patterns, it has an upper gallery reserved for women.

around the fringes, further enclose and impose on the airy space.

➡ Mihrab & Maksura

Like Abd ar-Rahman II a century earlier, Al-Hakim II in the 960s lengthened the naves of the prayer hall, creating a new *qiblah* wall (indicating the direction of Mecca) and *mihrab* (prayer niche) at the south end. The bay immediately in front of the *mihrab* and the bays to each side form the *maksura,* the area where the caliphs and courtiers would have prayed. The *mihrab* and *maksura* are the most beautifully and intricately decorated parts of the whole mosque.

The greatest glory of Al-Hakim II's extension was the portal of the *mihrab* – a crescent arch with a rectangular surround known as an *alfiz*. For the portal's decoration, Al-Hakim asked the emperor of Byzantium, Nicephoras II Phocas, to send him a mosaicist capable of imitating the superb mosaics of the Great Mosque of Damascus, one of the great 8th-century Syrian Umayyad buildings. The Christian emperor sent the Muslim caliph not only a mosaicist but also a gift of 1600kg of gold mosaic cubes. Shaped into flower motifs and inscriptions from the Quran, this gold is what gives the *mihrab* portal its magical glitter. Inside the *mihrab*, a single block of white marble sculpted into the shape of a scallop shell, a symbol of the Quran, forms the dome that amplified the voice of the imam (the person who leads Islamic worship services) throughout the mosque.

The arches of the *maksura* are the mosque's most intricate and sophisticated, forming a forest of interwoven horseshoe shapes. Equally attractive are the *maksura*'s skylit domes, decorated with star-patterned stone vaulting. Each dome is held up by four interlocking pairs of parallel ribs, a highly advanced technique for 10th-century Europe.

➡ Cathedral

Following the Christian conquest of Córdoba in 1236, the Mezquita was used as a cathedral but remained largely unaltered for nearly three centuries. But in the 16th century King Carlos I gave the cathedral authorities permission to rip out the centre of the Mezquita in order to construct a new Capilla Mayor (main altar area) and *coro* (choir).

Legend has it that when the king saw the result he was horrified, exclaiming that the builders had destroyed something unique in the world. The cathedral took nearly 250 years to complete (1523–1766) and thus exhibits a range of architectural fashions, from plateresque and late Renaissance to extravagant Spanish baroque. Among the later features are the Capilla Mayor's rich 17th-century jasper and red-marble retable (altar screen), and the fine mahogany stalls in the choir, carved in the 18th century by Pedro Duque Cornejo.

➡ Night Visits

A one-hour sound-and-light show (www.elalmadecordoba.com), in nine languages via audio guides, is presented in the Mezquita twice nightly except Sundays from March to October, and on Friday and Saturday from November to February. Tickets are €18 (senior or student €9).

★ Alcázar de los Reyes Cristianos FORTRESS

(Fortress of the Christian Monarchs; ☎957 42 01 51; www.alcazardelosreyescristianos.cordoba.es; Campo Santo de Los Mártires; adult/student/child €4.50/2.25/free; ⏲8.30am-3pm Tue-Sat & to 2.30pm Sun mid-Jun–mid-Sep, 8.30am-8.45pm Tue-Fri, to 4.30pm Sat & to 2.30pm Sun mid-Sep–mid-Jun; 👪) Built under Castilian rule in the 13th and 14th centuries on the remains of a Moorish predecessor, this fort-cum-palace was where the Catholic Monarchs, Fernando and Isabel, made their first acquaintance with Columbus in 1486. One hall displays some remarkable Roman mosaics, dug up from Plaza de la Corredera in the 1950s. The Alcázar's terraced gardens – full of fish ponds, fountains, orange trees and flowers – are a delight to stroll around.

At 9pm (except Mondays) there's a popular multimedia show featuring lights, flamenco music and dancing fountains called **Noches Mágicas en el Alcázar** (Magic Nights in the Alcázar; adult/child €6.50/free). While here, it's also interesting to visit the nearby **Baños del Alcázar Califal** (☎608 158893; www.banosdelalcazarcalifal.cordoba.es; Campo Santo de los Mártires; adult/student/child €2.50/1.50/free, free from noon Thu; ⏲8.30am-8.45pm Tue-Fri, to 4.30pm Sat & to 2.30pm Sun mid-Sep–mid-Jun, 8.30am-3pm Tue-Sat & to 2.30pm Sun mid-Jun–mid-Sep), the impressive 10th-century bathhouse of the Moorish Alcázar.

Caballerizas Reales STABLES

(Royal Stables; ☎957 49 78 43; www.cordobaecuestre.com; Calle Caballerizas Reales 1; adult/child training €5/1, show €15/10; ⏲10am-1.30pm Sun & Mon, 10am-1.30pm & 4-8pm Tue, 10am-1.30pm & 5-8pm Wed-Sat, show 9pm Wed-Sat) These elegant stables were built on orders of King Felipe II in 1570 as a centre for developing the tall Spanish thoroughbred warhorse *(caballo andaluz)*. The centre still breeds these fine horses (47 are here today) and trains horses and riders in equestrian disciplines. You can watch training during the daily opening times from Tuesday to Sunday (from 11am in the mornings), or attend the one-hour show which impressively combines horse and rider skills with flamenco dance and music!

Puente Romano BRIDGE

Spanning the Río Guadalquivir just below the Mezquita, the handsome, 16-arched Roman bridge formed part of the ancient Via Augusta, which ran from Girona in Catalonia to Cádiz. Rebuilt several times down the centuries, it's now traffic-free and makes for a lovely stroll. With the aid of CGI, it not long ago featured as the Long Bridge of Volantis in *Game of Thrones*.

★ Centro Flamenco Fosforito MUSEUM

(Posada del Potro; ☎957 47 68 29; www.centroflamencofosforito.cordoba.es; Plaza del Potro; ⏲8.30am-3pm Tue-Sun mid-Jun–mid-Sep, 8.30am-7.30pm Tue-Fri, 8.30am-2.30pm Sat & Sun mid-Sep–mid-Jun) FREE Possibly the best flamenco museum in Andalucía, the Fosforito centre has exhibits, film and information panels in English and Spanish telling you the history of the guitar and all the flamenco greats. Touch-screen videos demonstrate the important techniques of flamenco song, guitar, dance and percussion – you can test your skill at beating out the *compás* (rhythm) of different *palos* (song forms). Regular free live flamenco performances are held here, too, often at noon on Sundays (listed on the website).

The museum benefits from a fantastic location inside the Posada del Potro, a legendary inn that played a part in *Don Quijote*, where Cervantes described it as a 'den of thieves'. The famous square it stands on, once a horse market, features a lovely 16th-century stone fountain topped by a rearing *potro* (colt).

★Palacio de Viana MUSEUM
(www.palaciodeviana.com; Plaza de Don Gome 2; whole house/patios €8/5; ⏲10am-7pm Tue-Sat & to 3pm Sun Sep-Jun, 9am-3pm Tue-Sun Jul & Aug) A stunning Renaissance palace with 12 beautiful, plant-filled patios, the Viana Palace is a particular delight to visit in spring. Occupied by the aristocratic Marqueses de Viana until 1980, the large building is packed with art and antiques. You can just walk round the lovely patios and garden with a self-guiding leaflet, or take a guided tour of the rooms as well. It's an 800m walk northeast from Plaza de las Tendillas.

Museo Julio Romero de Torres GALLERY
(Plaza del Potro 1; adult/student/child €4.50/2.25/free; ⏲8.30am-3pm Tue-Sat & 8.30am-2.30pm Sun mid-Jun–mid-Sep, 8.30am-8.45pm Tue-Fri, 8.30am-4.30pm Sat & 8.30am-2.30pm Sun mid-Sep–mid-Jun) A former hospital houses this popular museum devoted to much-loved local painter Julio Romero de Torres (1874–1930), who is famed for his paintings expressing his admiration of Andalucian female beauty. He was also much inspired by flamenco and bullfighting.

Museo Arqueológico MUSEUM
(☎957 35 55 17; www.museosdeandalucia.es; Plaza de Jerónimo Páez 7; EU citizen/other free/€1.50; ⏲9am-8pm Tue-Sat & 9am-3pm Sun mid-Sep–mid-Jun, 9am-3pm Tue-Sun mid-Jun–mid-Sep) The well-displayed Archaeological Museum traces Córdoba's many changes in size, appearance and lifestyle from pre-Roman to early Reconquista times, with some fine sculpture, an impressive coin collection, and interesting exhibits on domestic life and religion, with explanations in English and Spanish. In the basement, you can walk through the excavated remains of the city's Roman theatre.

Festivals & Events

Fiesta de los Patios de Córdoba FIESTA
(http://patios.cordoba.es; ⏲May) This 'best patio' competition sees 50 or more of Córdoba's beautiful private courtyards open for public viewing till 10pm nightly for two weeks, starting in early May, when the patios are at their prettiest. A concurrent cultural program stages flamenco and other concerts in some of the city's grandest patios and plazas.

★Noche Blanca del Flamenco MUSIC
(http://nocheblancadelflamenco.cordoba.es; ⏲Jun) An all-night fest of top-notch flamenco by leading song, guitar and dance artists of the genre, in picturesque venues around the city such as the Mezquita's Patio de los Naranjos and Plaza del Potro. All performances are free. On a Saturday night around 20 June.

Festival de la Guitarra de Córdoba MUSIC
(www.guitarracordoba.org; ⏲early Jul) A two-week celebration of the guitar, with performances of classical, flamenco, rock, blues and more by top Spanish and international names in Córdoba's theatres.

Sleeping

★Bed and Be HOSTEL $
(☎661 420733; www.bedandbe.com; Calle José Cruz Conde 22; incl breakfast dm €17-35, s €30-50, d €49-80; ❄📶) An exceptional hostel option 300m north of Plaza de las Tendillas. Staff are clued up about what's on in Córdoba, and there's a social event every evening – often a drink on the roof followed by a bar or tapas tour. The shared-bathroom private rooms and four- or eight-bunk dorms are all super clean and as gleaming white as a *pueblo blanco*.

Option Be Hostel HOSTEL $
(☎661 420733; www.facebook.com/optionbecordoba; Calle Leiva Aguilar 1; incl breakfast dm €18-45, d €44-99; ❄📶🏊) Option Be is a small, attractive, welcoming, contemporary-design hostel in a quiet old-city street, with a delightful roof terrace and plunge pool. It has just two private rooms (with private bathrooms) and two dorms, plus a bright ground-floor kitchen and neat central patio-lounge area. It's run by the same team as the excellent Bed and Be, and guests can share Bed and Be's nightly social activities.

Hospedería Alma Andalusí HOTEL $
(☎957 20 04 25; www.almaandalusi.com; Calle Fernández Ruano 5; r €38-70; ❄📶) This small hotel in a quiet section of the Judería has been brilliantly converted from an ancient structure into a stylish, modern establishment, while rates have been kept sensible. Rooms are small but attractive, with blue-and-white colour schemes, thoughtfully

WORTH A TRIP

MEDINA AZAHARA

Eight kilometres west of Córdoba stands what's left of **Medina Azahara** (Madinat al-Zahra; ☎957 10 49 33; www.museosdeandalucia.es; Carretera Palma del Río Km 5.5; EU citizen/other free/€1.50; ⏰9am-7pm Tue-Sat Apr–mid-Jun, to 3pm mid-Jun–mid-Sep, to 6pm mid-Sep–Mar, 9am-3pm Sun year-round; P), the sumptuous palace-city built by Caliph Abd ar-Rahman III in the 10th century. The complex spills down a hillside, with the caliph's palace (the area you visit today) on the highest levels overlooking what were gardens and open fields. The residential areas (still unexcavated) were set away to each side. A fascinating modern museum has been installed below the site.

Legend has it that Abd ar-Rahman III built Medina Azahara for his favourite wife, Az-Zahra. Dismayed by her homesickness and yearnings for the snowy mountains of Syria, he surrounded his new city with almond and cherry trees, replacing snowflakes with fluffy white blossoms. More realistically, it was probably Abd ar-Rahman's declaration of his caliphate in 929 that spurred him to construct, as caliphs were wont to do, a new capital. Building started in 940 and chroniclers record some staggering statistics: 10,000 labourers set 6000 stone blocks a day, with outer walls stretching 1518m east to west and 745m north to south.

It is almost inconceivable to think that such a city, built over 35 years, was to last only a few more before the usurper Al-Mansur transferred government to a new palace complex of his own in 981. Then, between 1010 and 1013, Medina Azahara was wrecked by Berber soldiers. During succeeding centuries its ruins were plundered repeatedly for building materials.

From the museum, where you arrive and get tickets for the site (and where you must park if coming in your own vehicle), a shuttle bus (*lanzadera*; adult/child & senior €2.10/1.50 return) takes you 2km up to the top of the site. The visitors' route then leads down through the city's original northern gate. Highlights of the visitable area are the grand, arched **Edificio Basilical Superior**, which housed the main state admin offices, and the **Casa de Yafar**, believed to have been residence of the caliph's prime minister. The crown jewel of the site, the royal reception hall known as the **Salón de Abd ar-Rahman III** (or Salón Rico), has been closed for restoration since 2009 (with no expected completion date at the time of research). This hall has exquisitely carved stucco work and is said to have been decorated with gold and silver tiles, arches of ivory and ebony, and walls of multicoloured marble.

The museum takes you through the history of Medina Azahara, with sections on its planning and construction, its inhabitants and its eventual downfall – all illustrated with beautifully displayed pieces from the site and interactive displays, and complemented by flawless English translations.

Drivers should leave Córdoba westward along Avenida de Medina Azahara. This feeds into the A431 road, with the turn-off to Medina Azahara signposted after 6km.

A bus to Medina Azahara (adult/child €9/5 return including the shuttle from museum to site and back) leaves from a stop on Glorieta Cruz Roja near Córdoba's Puerta de Almodóvar at 10.15am and 11am Tuesday to Sunday, plus 2.45pm Tuesday to Saturday from mid-September to mid-June. You can get tickets on the bus, or in advance at tourist offices. Buying in advance is sensible for weekends and public holidays. The bus starts back from Medina Azahara 3¼ hours after it leaves Córdoba.

chosen furnishings, appealing large photos of Córdoba's sights and polished-wood or traditional-tile floors – all making for a comfortable base.

★Patio del Posadero BOUTIQUE HOTEL $$
(☎957 94 17 33; www.patiodelposadero.com; Call Mucho Trigo 21; r incl breakfast €95-170; ❄📶🏊) A 15th-century building in a quiet lane 1km east of the Mezquita has been superbly converted into a welcoming boutique hideaway combining comfort and unique contemporary design with that old-Córdoba Moorish style. At its centre is a charming cobble-floored, brick-arched patio, with steps leading up to a lovely upper deck with plunge pool, where the first-class homemade breakfasts are served.

★Viento10 BOUTIQUE HOTEL **$$**

(☎957 76 49 60; www.hotelviento10.es; Calle Ronquillo Briceño 10; s €84-147, d €100-172; ❄📶) An inspired conversion of a 15th-century hospital building, Viento10 has just eight relaxing, comfortable rooms, in a beautiful, bright, clean-lined style that harmonises perfectly with the ancient stone pillars of its courtyard. A strong sense of light suffuses the property, not least on the roof terrace with its loungers and views over tiled rooftops to the Mezquita.

Hospedería del Atalia BOUTIQUE HOTEL **$$**

(☎957 49 66 59; www.hospederiadelatalia.com; Calle Buen Pastor 19; r €50-200; ❄📶) Entered from a quiet patio in the Judería, the Atalia sports elegant, owner-designed rooms in burgundies, russets and olive greens. Good breakfasts with a wide choice are €6, and there's a big, sunny roof terrace with chairs, tables and a Mezquita view.

★Balcón de Córdoba BOUTIQUE HOTEL **$$$**

(☎957 49 84 78; www.balcondecordoba.com; Calle Encarnación 8; incl breakfast s €160-320, d €170-400; ❄📶) Offering top-end boutique luxury a stone's throw from the Mezquita, the 10-room Balcón is a riveting place with a charming patio, slick rooms and ancient stone relics dotted around as if it were a wing of the nearby archaeological museum. Service doesn't miss a beat and the rooms have tasteful, soothing, contemporary decor with a little art but no clutter.

Eating

Córdoba's signature dish is *salmorejo*, a delicious, thick, chilled soup of blended tomatoes, garlic, bread, lemon, vinegar and olive oil, sprinkled with hard-boiled egg and strips of ham. Along with *rabo de toro* (oxtail stew), it appears on every menu. There's traditional meaty and fishy Andalucian fare aplenty here, but also a good sprinkling of more contemporary eateries putting successful fresh twists on Spanish ingredients. Don't miss the sweet local Montilla-Moriles wine.

★Mercado Victoria FOOD HALL **$**

(http://mercadovictoria.com; Paseo de la Victoria; items €2-19; ⏲10am-midnight Sun-Thu, 10am-2pm Fri & Sat) The Mercado Victoria is, yes, a food court – but an unusually classy one, with almost everything, from Argentine empanadas and Mexican burritos to sushi and classic Spanish seafood and grilled meats, prepared fresh before your eyes. The setting is special too – a 19th-century wrought-iron-and-glass pavilion in the Victoria gardens just west of the old city.

★La Bicicleta CAFE **$**

(☎666 544690; Calle Cardenal González 1; light dishes €4-13; ⏲noon-1am, from 6pm Mon-Thu Jul-Aug; 📶✍) 🍃 This friendly, informal spot welcomes one and all with an array of drinks – from long, cool multi-fruit juices whizzed up on the spot to cocktails, beer and wine – and tasty light dishes such as hummus, avocado-and-ham toasts and delicious fresh-daily cakes.

La Tinaja ANDALUCIAN **$**

(☎957 04 79 98; http://latinajadecordoba.com; Paseo de la Ribera 12; raciones €8-18; ⏲1.30-5pm & 7.30pm-1.30am) The food at some river-facing restaurants doesn't live up to the location, but La Tinaja serves reliably good and thoughtful preparations from classic Spanish ingredients, and its terrace is the most romantic of all when candlelit after dark. You might go for the seafood-stuffed leeks, spinach-and-hake ravioli, or the grilled pork with pumpkin hummus. Portions aren't for giant appetites.

Taberna Salinas ANDALUCIAN **$**

(☎957 48 01 35; www.tabernasalinas.com; Calle Tundidores 3; raciones €8-9; ⏲12.30-4pm & 8-11.30pm Mon-Sat, closed Aug) A historic bar-restaurant (since 1879), with a patio and several rooms, Salinas is adorned in classic Córdoba fashion with tiles, wine barrels, art and photos of bullfighter Manolete. It's popular with tourists (and offers a five-language menu), but it retains a traditional atmosphere and the waiters are very helpful. Not least, the food is very good, from the orange-and-cod salad to the pork loin in hazelnut sauce.

Bar Santos TAPAS **$**

(Calle Magistral González Francés 3; tapas €2-5; ⏲10am-midnight) This legendary little bar across the street from the Mezquita serves the best *tortilla de patata* (potato omelette) in town – and don't the *cordobeses* know it. Thick wedges (€2.30) are deftly cut from giant wheels of the stuff and customarily served with plastic forks on paper plates to eat outside under the Mezquita's walls. Plenty of other tapas are on offer too. Don't miss it.

★Casa Pepe de la Judería ANDALUCIAN $$
(☎957 20 07 44; http://restaurantecasapepedelajuderia.com; Calle Romero 1; raciones €10-26; ⏰1-4pm & 7.30-11pm; 📶) Thoughtfully prepared classic Andalucian fare, on a sunny roof terrace or in rooms adorned with traditional and contemporary Cordoban art, keeps Pepe's (first opened in 1920) high in the popularity charts. Dishes range from good *salmorejo* (a cold tomato-based soup), gazpacho, *flamenquín* (breaded pork loin wrapped with slices of ham) and salads to turbot meunière or lamb shoulder with apple purée. Service remains attentive and friendly even when it's packed out.

★Bodegas Campos ANDALUCIAN $$
(☎957 49 75 00; www.bodegascampos.com; Calle de Lineros 32; mains €14-24; ⏰1.30-4.30pm & 8.30-11.30pm Mon-Sat, 1.30-4.30pm Sun) This atmospheric warren of rooms and patios is a Córdoba classic, popular with *cordobeses* and their visitors alike. The restaurant and more informal *taberna* (tavern) serve up delicious dishes putting a slight creative twist on traditional Andalucian fare – the likes of cod-and-cuttlefish ravioli or pork tenderloin in grape sauce. Campos also produces its own house Montilla.

Garum 2.1 ANDALUCIAN $$
(☎957 48 76 73; Calle de San Fernando 122; tapas €3-9, raciones €8-18; ⏰noon-midnight) Garum serves up traditional meaty, fishy and veggie ingredients in creative, tasty concoctions. We recommend the *presa ibérica con patatas al pelotón* (Iberian pork with a juicy potato-onion-capsicum combination). Service is helpful and friendly.

La Boca FUSION $$
(☎957 47 61 40; www.facebook.com/restaurante.laboca; Calle de San Fernando 39; dishes €6-15; ⏰noon-4pm & 8pm-midnight Wed-Mon; 📶) If oxtail tacos, red-tuna *tataki,* or a salad of duck-prosciutto and mango in walnut vinaigrette sound appetising, you'll like La Boca. This inventive eatery serves up global variations in half a dozen appealingly arty, rustic-style *'taberna'* rooms or in its marginally more formal restaurant section. It's very well done, though portions are not large. Reservations advisable at weekends.

🍷 Drinking & Nightlife

El Barón BAR
(Plaza de Abades 4; ⏰12.30pm-midnight) Set on a traffic-free, orange tree–shaded plaza in the old city, the outside tables at this unassuming local bar are a lovely place for quiet nocturnal drinks. It has Montilla and other wines, *cava*, craft and other beers, and some good snacks including a very tempting chocolate cake.

Sojo Mercado BAR, LOUNGE
(http://sojomercado.com; Mercado Victoria, Paseo de la Victoria; ⏰1pm-2am Sun-Thu, to 3am Fri & Sat) Occupying a corner of the Mercado Victoria gastro-market and a roof terrace above, this fashionable spot gets very lively at weekends, with the 20- and 30-something crowd already starting to dance to the pop/electronic/Latin soundtrack by mid-afternoon on Saturdays.

Bodega Guzmán WINE BAR
(Calle de los Judíos 7; ⏰noon-4pm & 8.30-11.30pm Fri-Wed) This atmospheric, somewhat cavern-like Judería drinking spot, frequented by both locals and tourists, is bedecked with bullfighting memorabilia and dispenses Montilla wine from three giant barrels behind the bar: don't leave without trying some *amargoso* (bitter).

Amapola BAR
(www.facebook.com/amapolabarcordoba; Paseo de la Ribera 9; ⏰4pm-2.30am or later, from noon Fri-Sun) The artiest bar in the riverside area, with elaborate cocktails and a great terrace looking down to the river. Often DJs or live music on Friday and/or Saturday nights.

☆ Entertainment

Córdoba has a pretty good live music scene, with several venues regularly hosting flamenco, jazz, rock or blues. The Centro Flamenco Fosforito (p711) is one place staging regular flamenco events and is a good place to ask about what else is coming up.

Jazz Café LIVE MUSIC
(www.facebook.com/jazzcafecordoba; Calle Rodríguez Marín; ⏰6pm-3am or 4am; 📶) An enticing music den decked with musical paraphernalia, Jazz Café stages blues jams on Thursdays and jazz jams on Tuesdays (both from 10pm), plus other live acts. It rocks on until the wee hours; on Fridays and Saturdays you'll often find DJs spinning EDM.

🛍 Shopping

Córdoba's time-honoured craft specialities are colourful embossed leather *(cuero repujado),* silver jewellery and some attractive pottery. The embossed leather is also known as *guadamecí* (if it's sheepskin) or *cordobán* (goatskin). Calles Cardenal González and Manríquez have some of the classier craft shops.

Meryan ARTS & CRAFTS
(957 47 59 02; www.meryancor.com; Calleja de las Flores 2; 9am-8pm Mon-Fri, 9.30am-2.30pm Sat) This shop has a particularly good range of embossed leather goods: wallets, bags, boxes, notebooks, leather-covered wooden chests and even copies of Picasso paintings.

Information

Córdoba (www.cordobaturismo.es) Tourist information for Córdoba province.

Centro de Visitantes (Visitors Centre; 902 201774; www.turismodecordoba.org; Plaza del Triunfo; 9am-7pm Mon-Fri, 9.30am-2.15pm Sat & Sun) The main tourist information centre, with an exhibit on Córdoba's history, and some Roman and Visigothic remains downstairs.

Municipal Tourist Information Kiosk (902 201774; www.turismodecordoba.org; Plaza de las Tendillas; 9am-2pm)

Municipal Tourist Information Office (902 201774; www.turismodecordoba.org; train station; 9am-2pm & 4.30-7pm) In the station's main entry hall.

Getting There & Away

TRAIN

Córdoba's modern **train station** (91 232 03 20; www.renfe.com; Plaza de las Tres Culturas), 1.2km northwest of Plaza de las Tendillas, is served both by fast AVE services and by some slower regional trains.

DESTINATION	COST (€)	DURATION	FREQUENCY (DAILY)
Andújar	8-16	50min	5
Antequera (Santa Ana)	14-34	30-40min	12-16
Granada			service due to restart 2018
Jaén	15	1¾hr	4
Madrid	33-63	1¾-2hr	24-33
Málaga	20-42	1hr	14-18
Seville	14-30	45-80min	27-39

Getting Around

BUS

Bus 3 (957 76 46 76; www.aucorsa.es) (€1.30, every 14 to 20 minutes), from Avenida Vía Augusta (the street between the train and bus stations), runs down Calle Diario de Córdoba and Calle de San Fernando, east of the Mezquita. For the return trip, catch it on **Ronda de Isasa** near the Puente Romano, or from **Campo Santo de los Mártires**, **Glorieta Cruz Roja** or **Paseo de la Victoria**.

CAR

Córdoba's one-way system is nightmarish, and cars are banned from the historic centre unless they are going to unload, load or park at hotels, most of which are reasonably well signposted as you approach. There is free, unmetered parking south of the river across the Puente de Mira-

BUSES FROM CÓRDOBA

The **bus station** (957 40 40 40; www.estacionautobusescordoba.es; Avenida Vía Augusta) is located behind the train station, 1.3km northwest of Plaza de las Tendillas.

Alsa (902 422242; www.alsa.es)

Autocares Carrera (957 50 16 32; www.autocarescarrera.es)

Autocares San Sebastián (957 42 90 30; www.autocaressansebastian.es)

Grupo Sepulvedana (902 119699; www.sepulvedana.es)

Socibus (902 229292; http://socibus.es)

DESTINATION	BUS COMPANY	COST (€)	DURATION (HR)	FREQUENCY (DAILY)
Baeza	Alsa	12	2¼	2
Granada	Alsa	15	2¾-4	7
Jaén	Grupo Sepulvedana	11	2	5-6
Madrid	Socibus	17-23	5	8
Málaga	Alsa	12	3	4
Seville	Alsa	12	2	7
Úbeda	Alsa	12	2½	4

WORTH A TRIP

CASA OLEA

Set in its own little olive grove 12km north of Priego, the British-owned country house **Casa Olea** (☎696 748209; www.casaolea.com; Carretera CO7204, near El Cañuelo; s/d incl breakfast €107/121; P ❄ 📶 🏊) has a beautifully spacious and relaxed feel. It makes a delightful rural retreat and base for exploring the region, with easy access to walks in the Sierras Subbéticas, mountain bikes to rent (€15 per day), and Córdoba and Granada both within 1½ hours' drive.

There's a lovely pool, and excellent dinners (two/three courses €20/25) are available five nights a week. Your hosts are full of information and tips on where to go and what to do. No children under seven.

flores, and a mixture of free and metered parking on **Paseo de la Victoria**, **Avenida Doctor Fleming** (Avenida Doctor Fleming) and streets to their west. Metered zones (with blue lines along the street) are free of charge from 2pm to 5pm and 9pm to 9am, and from 2pm Saturday to 9am Monday.

Parque Natural Sierras Subbéticas

This 320-sq-km park in the southeast of Córdoba province encompasses a set of craggy, emerald-green limestone hills pocked with caves, springs and streams, with some charmingly appealing old villages and small towns set round its periphery. It makes for lovely exploring and good hiking among valleys, canyons and high peaks (the highest is 1570m La Tiñosa). Most visitors base themselves in or near picturesque Zuheros or Priego de Córdoba. The ideal months for walking are April, May, September and October.

The park's visitor centre, the **Centro de Visitantes Santa Rita** (☎957 50 69 86; Carretera A339, Km 11.2; ⏰9am-2pm Wed-Fri & 9am-2pm & 6-8pm Sat & Sun May-Jun, 9am-2pm Fri-Sun Jul-Aug, 9am-2pm Wed-Sun Sep, 9am-2pm Wed-Fri & 9am-2pm & 4-6pm Sat & Sun Oct-Apr), is on the Cabra–Priego de Córdoba road.

Zuheros

POP 660 / ELEV 640M

On the northern edge of the Parque Natural Sierras Subbéticas, Zuheros sits in a supremely picturesque location, its tangle of white streets and crag-top castle crouching in the lee of towering hills with olive groves stretching away below as far as the eye can see. Approached by twisting roads up from the A318, the village has a delightfully relaxed atmosphere.

Sights

Castillo de Zuheros CASTLE
(Plaza de la Paz; admission or tour incl Museo Arqueológico adult/child €2/1.25; ⏰10am-2pm & 5-7pm Tue-Fri, tours 11am, 12.30pm, 2pm, 5pm & 6.30pm Sat, Sun & holidays, all afternoon times 1hr earlier Oct-Mar) Set on a picturesque pinnacle, Zuheros' castle is of 9th-century Moorish origin, but most of what survives is Christian construction from the 13th and 14th centuries, with remains of a 16th-century Renaissance palace attached. It's small but panoramic, with fine views from the top. Visits on weekends and holidays are guided; other days, visits are unguided. Tickets are sold at, and include, the little **Museo Arqueológico** (Archaeological Museum; ☎957 69 45 45; Plaza de la Paz; adult/child incl Castillo €2/1.25; ⏰10am-2pm Tue-Sun year-round, 5-7pm Tue-Fri Apr-Sep, 4-6pm Tue-Fri Oct-Mar), just across the square, which also doubles as Zuheros' tourist office (p718).

Cueva de los Murciélagos CAVE
(Cave of the Bats; ☎957 69 45 45; adult/child €6/5; ⏰guided tours 12.30pm & 5.30pm Tue-Fri, 11am, 12.30pm, 2pm, 5pm & 6.30pm Sat & Sun, afternoon tours 1hr earlier Oct-Mar; P) Carved out of the limestone massif 4km above Zuheros is this extraordinary cave. From the vast hall at the start of the tour, it's a 415m loop walk (with 700 steps) through a series of corridors filled with fantastic rock formations and traces of Neolithic rock paintings showing abstract figures of goats. Visits are by guided tour only: reserve by phoning or emailing Zuheros' tourist office (p718) between 10am and 1.30pm Tuesday to Friday.

Sleeping & Eating

★**Hotel Zuhayra** HOTEL $
(☎957 69 46 93; www.zercahoteles.com; Calle Mirador 10; incl breakfast s €42-48, d €52-60;

DON'T MISS

VÍA VERDE DEL ACEITE

The area's easiest and best marked path is the **Vía Verde del Aceite** (www.viasverdes.com;) , a disused railway converted to a cycling and walking track, which you can see snaking across the countryside below Zuheros. It runs 128km across Córdoba and Jaén provinces from Camporreal near Puente Genil to Jaén city, skirting the western and northern fringes of the Parque Natural Sierras Subbéticas.

With gentle gradients and utilising old bridges, tunnels and viaducts, the greenway makes for a fun outing for travellers of all ages. There are cafes and bike-hire outlets in old station buildings along the route, and informative map-boards – it's impossible to get lost! The section in Córdoba province is also still known by its old name, Vía Verde de la Subbética.

Subbética Bike's Friends (691 843532, 672 605088; www.subbeticabikesfriends.com; bikes per half-day/day €9/12, baby seats per day €2; 10am-6pm Sat & Sun;) at Doña Mencía station, 4km west down the hill from Zuheros, rents a range of different bikes, including children's, and can normally provide them any day of the week if you call ahead.

) A short distance below Zuheros' castle, this hotel has breathtaking views of the countryside from every one of its unfussily comfortable rooms, and is an excellent base for exploring the area. The friendly proprietors, the Ábalos brothers (who speak English), offer masses of information about things to see and do.

There is also a first-class **restaurant** (mains & raciones €7-18, medias raciones €4-7.50; 1-4pm & 8.30-11pm;).

Mesón Atalaya ANDALUCIAN $$
(957 69 45 28; Calle Santo 58; mains €7-19; 1-4pm & 9-11pm Tue-Sun) This family-run establishment at the east end of the village does excellent local fare, with plenty of lamb, pork, ham, *potajes* and *cazuelas* (types of stew), local cheese and homemade desserts. There are two nice, plant-filled patios inside. It's pretty popular and fills up at weekends.

Information

Tourist Office (957 69 45 45; http://turismodelasubbetica.es/zuheros; Plaza de la Paz 1; 10am-2pm Tue-Sun year-round, 5-7pm Tue-Fri Apr-Sep, 4-6pm Tue-Fri Oct-Mar) Zuheros' helpful tourist office shares premises with the archaeological museum. Come here for tickets or guided visits to the castle.

Getting There & Away

Buses depart from Mesón Atalaya.

Autocares Carrera (p716) Two to four daily buses to/from Córdoba (€6.45, 1¾ hours).

Autocares Valenzuela (956 70 26 09; www.grupovalenzuela.com) Two or more to/from Seville (€17, 3¾ hours).

Granada & South Coast Andalucía

Includes ➡

Best Places to Eat

- ➡ El Mesón de Cervantes (p757)
- ➡ El Bar de Fede (p738)
- ➡ La Fábula Restaurante (p738)
- ➡ Palacio de Gallego (p778)
- ➡ 4 Nudos (p791)

Best Places to Stay

- ➡ Claude (p763)
- ➡ Santa Isabel La Real (p735)
- ➡ Hotel Real de Poqueira (p746)
- ➡ MC San José (p791)
- ➡ Hostal El Olívar (p793)

Why Go?

From high-rise coastal developments to white mountain villages seemingly forgotten by time, Andalucía's southeastern corner is a compelling package of holiday fun, high culture and stunning, often unexpected, natural beauty.

In the heart of the area, Granada thrills with its Arab-infused street life and spectacular Alhambra palace, while to the south, vibrant Málaga continues to reinvent itself as a hub of contemporary culture. Nearby, summer holidaymakers flock to the brazen beach resorts that line the Costa del Sol.

But away from the cities and holiday mayhem, there's a quieter, less frenzied side to the region. The imposing peaks of the Sierra Nevada are within striking distance of Granada and, with their rustic white villages and thrilling hiking trails, offer superb touring. Further afield, the Cabo de Gata promontory is a world apart with its haunting semi-desert terrain, blissfully undeveloped coastline and gorgeous beaches.

When to Go

Granada

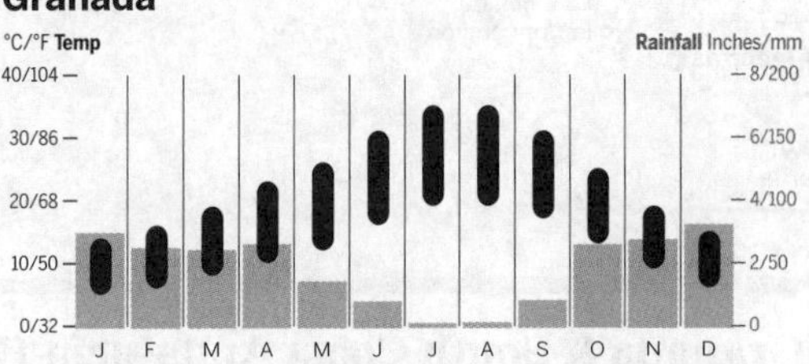

Mar & Apr Festivals and Easter processions draw crowds and high-season prices.

May & Jun A busy, sunny period, ideal for touring, hiking and exploring.

Nov–Feb Winter means fewer tourists, bargain prices and skiing in the Sierra Nevada.

Granada & South Coast Andalucía Highlights

1. **Alhambra** (p722) Basking in the awe-inspiring majesty of Spain's most spectacular monument, a masterpiece of exquisite Islamic architecture and horticultural landscaping.

2. **Parque Natural de Cabo de Gata-Níjar** (p790) Hopping around the heavenly beaches and plunging cliffs of Andalucía's southeastern coastline.

3. **Málaga** (p751) Taking a trip from Picasso to modern graffiti in Spain's ever-evolving art-city extraordinaire.

4. **Gibraltar** (p769) Climbing the Mediterranean Steps

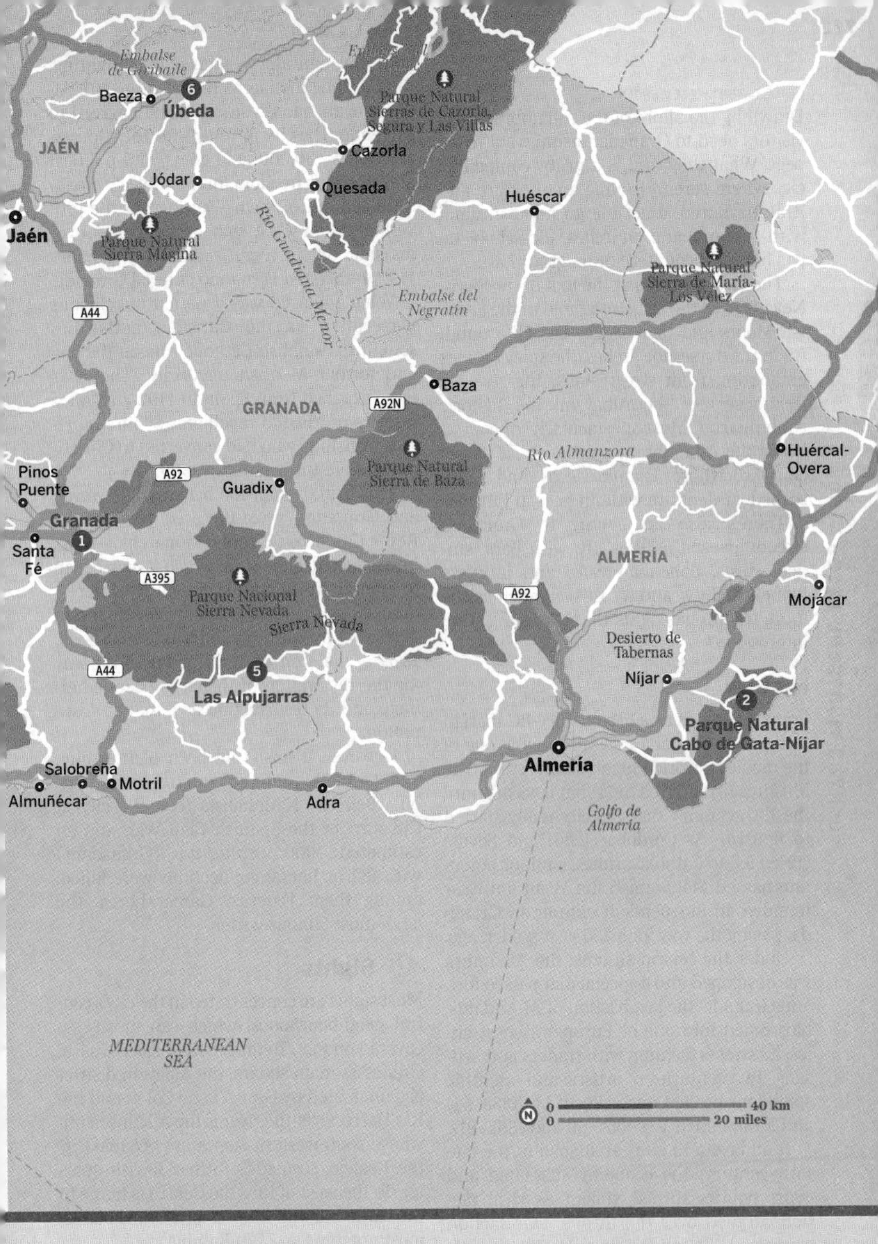

in Gibraltar and gazing out at Africa, the jaws of the Mediterranean and huge flocks of gliding seabirds.

❺ **Las Alpujarras** (p743) Hiking through the white villages and vertiginous canyons of the Sierra Nevada's southern slopes.

❻ **Úbeda** (p779) Indulging the senses on inspired architecture and cuisine.

GRANADA

POP 234,758 / ELEV 680M

Drawn by the allure of the Alhambra, many visitors head to Granada unsure what to expect. What they find is a gritty, compelling city where serene Islamic architecture and Arab-flavoured street life go hand in hand with monumental churches, old-school tapas bars and counterculture graffiti art.

The city, sprawled at the foot of the Sierra Nevada, was the last stronghold of the Spanish Moors and their legacy lies all around: it's in the horseshoe arches, the spicy aromas emanating from street stalls, the *teterías* (teahouses) of the Albayzín, the historic Arab quarter. Most spectacularly, of course, it's in the Alhambra, an astonishing palace complex whose Islamic decor and landscaped gardens are without peer in Europe.

There's also an energy to Granada's streets, packed as they are with bars, student dives, bohemian cafes and intimate flamenco clubs, and it's this as much as the more traditional sights that leaves a lasting impression.

History

From its origins as a 5th-century-BC Iberian settlement, Granada grew to become one of the medieval world's great Islamic cities. The Muslims first arrived in 711 but it wasn't until the 13th century that the city really started to flourish. As Córdoba (1236) and Seville (1248) fell to Catholic armies, a minor potentate named Mohammed ibn Yusuf ibn Nasr founded an independent emirate in Granada, paving the way for a 250-year golden age.

Under the Nasrid sultans, the Alhambra was developed into a spectacular palace-fort, and Granada, the last bastion of Al-Andalus, blossomed into one of Europe's richest cities, its streets teeming with traders and artisans. Two centuries of artistic and scientific splendour peaked under Yusuf I (r 1333–54) and Mohammed V (r 1354–59 and 1362–91).

It all began to go pear-shaped in the late 15th century: the economy stagnated and court politics turned violent as rival factions argued over the throne. One faction supported the emir Abu al-Hasan and his Christian concubine, Zoraya, while another backed Boabdil (Abu Abdullah), Abu al-Hasan's son by his wife Aixa – even though Boabdil was still just a child. In 1482 civil war broke out and, following Abu al-Hasan's death in 1485, Boabdil won control of the city. It proved a pyrrhic victory, though, and with the emirate weakened by infighting, the Catholic monarchs pounced in 1491. After an eight-month siege, Boabdil agreed to surrender the city in return for the Alpujarras valleys, 30,000 gold coins, and political and religious freedom for his subjects. Boabdil hiked out of town – letting out the proverbial 'Moor's last sigh' as he looked over his shoulder in regret – and on 2 January 1492, Isabel and Fernando entered Granada.

What followed was a period of religious persecution as the Christian authorities sought to establish Catholic rule on the city and former Moorish territories. The Jews were expelled from Spain in 1492 and, after a series of Muslim rebellions, Spain's *moriscos* (Muslims who had converted to Christianity) were thrown out in 1609.

This brutal expulsion backfired, however, and Granada – once the prize jewel of the Reyes Católicos (Catholic Monarchs) – sank into a deep decline from which it only began to emerge in the mid-19th century. Interest aroused by the Romantic movement, and in particular by Washington Irving's 1832 book, *Tales of the Alhambra,* helped pave the way for the restoration of the city's Islamic heritage and its resurrection as a tourist destination.

However, it hasn't all been plain sailing and Granada suffered another dark period when the Nationalists took the city at the start of the Spanish Civil War, and an estimated 4000 *granadinos* (Granadans) with left or liberal connections were killed, among them Federico García Lorca, the city's most famous writer.

Sights

Most sights are concentrated in the city's central neighbourhoods, which can mostly be covered on foot. To the north of Plaza Nueva, Granada's main square, the Albayzín district is demarcated by Gran Vía de Colón and the Río Darro. Over the river is the Alhambra hill whose southwestern slopes are occupied by the Realejo, Granada's former Jewish quarter. To the west of this, the Centro is home to the cathedral and a series of vibrant plazas, most notably Plaza Bib-Rambla.

Alhambra & Realejo

★Alhambra ISLAMIC PALACE

(☎958 02 79 71, tickets 858 95 36 16; http://alhambra-patronato.es; adult/12-15yr/under 12yr €14/8/free, Generalife & Alcazaba adult/under 12yr €7/free;

(⏲8.30am-8pm Apr–mid-Oct, to 6pm mid-Oct–Mar, night visits 10-11.30pm Tue-Sat Apr–mid-Oct, 8-9.30pm Fri & Sat mid-Oct–Mar) The Alhambra is Granada's – and Europe's – love letter to Moorish culture. Set against a backdrop of brooding Sierra Nevada peaks, this fortified palace complex started life as a walled citadel before going on to become the opulent seat of Granada's Nasrid emirs. Their showpiece palaces, the 14th-century Palacios Nazaríes, are among the finest Islamic buildings in Europe and, together with the gorgeous Generalife gardens, form the Alhambra's great headline act.

As one of Spain's most high-profile attractions, the Alhambra can draw up to 6000 daily visitors. Tickets sell out quickly so to avoid disappointment it pays to book ahead, either online or by phone. Note that when you buy a ticket you'll be given a time to enter the Palacios Nazaríes, admission to which is strictly controlled. For more information, see Alhambra Practicalities (p727).

The origins of the Alhambra, whose name derives from the Arabic *al-qala'a al-hamra* (the Red Castle), are mired in mystery. The first references to construction in the area appear in the 9th century but it's thought that buildings may already have been standing since Roman times. In its current form, it largely dates to the 13th and 14th centuries when Granada's Nasrid rulers transformed it into a fortified palace complex. Following the 1492 Reconquista (Christian reconquest), its mosque was replaced by a church and the Habsburg emperor Charles V had a wing of palaces demolished to make space for the huge Renaissance building that still today bears his name. Later, in the early 19th century, French Napoleonic forces destroyed part of the palace and attempted to blow up the entire site. Restoration work began in the mid-1800s and continues to this day.

➡ Palacio de Carlos V

From the entrance pavilion (p727), a signposted path leads into the core of the complex, passing a couple of notable religious buildings. The first is the Convento de San Francisco (p732), now the Parador de Granada (p734) hotel, where the bodies of Isabel and Fernando were laid to rest while their tombs were being built in the Capilla Real (p732). A short walk further on brings you to the **Iglesia de Santa María de la Alhambra** (⏲10am-1pm Tue-Sun & 4-6pm Tue-Sat), a 16th-century church on the site of the Alhambra's original mosque.

Beyond the church, the **Palacio de Carlos V** clashes spectacularly with the style of its surroundings. The hulking palace, begun in 1527 by the Toledo architect Pedro Machuca, features a monumental facade and a two-tiered circular courtyard ringed by 32 columns. This circle inside a square is the only Spanish example of a Renaissance ground plan symbolising the unity of heaven and earth.

Inside the palace are two museums: the **Museo de la Alhambra** (☎958 02 79 00; ⏲8.30am-8pm Wed-Sat, to 2.30pm Sun & Tue Apr–mid-Oct, 8.30am-6pm Wed-Sat, to 2.30pm Sun & Tue mid-Oct–Mar) FREE, which showcases an absorbing collection of Islamic artefacts, including the door from the Sala de Dos Hermanas; and the **Museo de Bellas Artes** (Fine Arts Museum; ☎958 56 35 08; EU citizens/other free/€1.50; ⏲9am-3pm Tue-Sat mid-Jun–mid-Sep, to 8pm Apr–mid-Jun & mid-Sep–mid-Oct, to 6pm Jan-Mar & mid-Oct–Dec, 9am-3pm Sun year-round), home to a collection of 15th- to 20th-century artworks.

➡ Alcazaba

Occupying the western tip of the Alhambra are the martial remnants of the **Alcazaba** (with Alhambra adult/12-15yr/under 12yr €14/8/free, Generalife & Alcazaba adult/under 12yr €7/free), the site's original 13th-century citadel. The **Torre de la Vela** (Watchtower; adult/12-15yr/under 12yr €14/8/free, Generalife & Alcazaba adult/under 12yr €7/free) is famous as the tower where the cross and banners of the Reconquista were raised in January 1492. A winding staircase leads to the top where you can enjoy sweeping views over Granada's rooftops.

➡ Palacios Nazaríes

The Alhambra's stunning centrepiece, the palace complex known as the **Palacios Nazaríes** (Nasrid Palaces), was originally divided into three sections: the Mexuar, a chamber for administrative and public business; the Palacio de Comares, the emir's official and private residence; and the Palacio de los Leones, a private area for the royal family and harem.

Entrance is through the **Mexuar**, a 14th-century hall where the council of ministers would sit and the emir would adjudicate citizens' appeals. Two centuries later, it was converted into a chapel, with a prayer room at the far end. Look up here and elsewhere

Alhambra

A TIMELINE

900 The first reference to *al-qala'a al-hamra* (the Red Castle) atop Granada's Sabika Hill.

1237 Founder of the Nasrid dynasty, Mohammed I, moves his court to Granada. Threatened by belligerent Christian armies he builds a new defensive fort, the **1 Alcazaba**.

1302–09 Designed as a summer palace-cum-country estate for Granada's foppish rulers, the bucolic **2 Generalife** is begun by Mohammed III.

1333–54 Yusuf I initiates the construction of the **3 Palacios Nazaríes**, still considered the highpoint of Islamic culture in Europe.

1350–60 Up goes the **4 Palacio de Comares**, taking Nasrid lavishness to a whole new level.

1362–91 The second coming of Mohammed V ushers in even greater architectural brilliance, exemplified by the construction of the **5 Patio de los Leones**.

1527 The Christians add the **6 Palacio de Carlos V**. Inspired Renaissance palace or incongruous crime against Moorish art? You decide.

1829 The languishing, half-forgotten Alhambra is 'rediscovered' by American writer Washington Irving during a protracted sleepover.

1954 The Generalife gardens are extended southwards to accommodate an outdoor theatre.

TOP TIPS

- Reserve tickets either by phoning ☎858 95 36 16 or online http://alhambra-patronato.es.
- http://alhambra-patronato.es. You can visit the general areas of the palace free of charge any time by entering through the Puerta de la Justicia.
- Two fine hotels are housed on the grounds if you wish to stay over: Parador de Granada (pricey) and Hotel América (more economical).

Sala de la Barca
Throw your head back in the anteroom to the Comares Palace, where the gilded ceiling is shaped like an upturned boat. Destroyed by fire in the 1890s, it has been painstakingly restored.

Palacio de Carlos V
It's easy to miss the stylistic merits of this Renaissance palace, added in 1527. Check out the ground-floor Museo de la Alhambra for artefacts directly related to the palace's history.

Alcazaba
Find time to explore the towers of the original citadel, the most important of which – the Torre de la Vela – takes you, via a winding staircase, to the Alhambra's best viewpoint.

TAKASHI IMAGES / SHUTTERSTOCK ©

Palacio de Comares
The neck-ache continues in the largest room in the Comares Palace, renowned for its rich geometric ceiling. A negotiating room for the emirs, the Salón de los Embajadores is a masterpiece of Moorish design.

JOSE IGNACIO SOTO / SHUTTERSTOCK ©

Patio de los Arrayanes
If only you could linger longer beside the rows of *arrayanes* (myrtle bushes) that border this calming rectangular pool. Shaded porticos with seven harmonious arches invite further contemplation.

Salón de los Embajadores

4

Baños Reales

Washington Irving Apartments

Sala de Dos Hermanas
Focus on the *dos hermanas* – two marble slabs either side of the fountain – before enjoying the intricate cupola embellished with 5000 tiny moulded stalactites. Poetic calligraphy decorates the walls.

Patio de los Arrayanes

Patio de la Lindaraja

Sala de los Reyes

Palacio del Partal

Jardines del Partal

Sala de los Abencerrajes

Generalife
A coda to most people's visits, the 'architect's garden' is no afterthought. While Nasrid in origin, the horticulture is relatively new: the pools and arcades were added in the early 20th century.

SKANDARAMANA / SHUTTERSTOCK ©

Patio de los Leones
Count the 12 lions sculpted from marble, holding up a gurgling fountain. Then pan back and take in the delicate columns and arches built to signify an Islamic vision of paradise.

FOTOGRAFIECOR.NL / SHUTTERSTOCK©

to appreciate the geometrically carved wood ceilings.

From the Mexuar, you pass into the **Patio del Cuarto Dorado**, a courtyard where the emirs gave audiences, with the **Cuarto Dorado** (Golden Room) on the left. Opposite the Cuarto Dorado is the entrance to the **Palacio de Comares** through a beautiful facade of glazed tiles, stucco and carved wood. A dogleg corridor (a common strategy in Islamic architecture to keep interior rooms private) leads through to the **Patio de los Arrayanes** (Court of the Myrtles). This elegant patio, named after the myrtle hedges around its rectangular pool, is the central space of the palace that was built in the mid-14th century as Emir Yusuf I's official residence.

The southern end of the patio is overshadowed by the walls of the Palacio de Carlos V. To the north, in the 45m-high **Torre de Comares** (Comares Tower), the **Sala de la Barca** (Hall of the Blessing) leads into the **Salón de los Embajadores** (Chamber of the Ambassadors), where the emirs would have conducted negotiations with Christian emissaries. The room's marvellous domed marquetry ceiling contains more than 8000 cedar pieces in an intricate star pattern representing the seven heavens of Islam.

The Patio de los Arrayanes leads into the **Palacio de los Leones** (Palace of the Lions), built in the second half of the 14th century under Muhammad V. The palace rooms branch off the **Patio de los Leones** (Lion Courtyard), centred on an 11th-century fountain channelling water through the mouths of 12 marble lions. The courtyard layout, using the proportions of the golden ratio, demonstrates the complexity of Islamic geometric design – the 124 slender columns that support the ornamented pavilions are placed in such a way that they are symmetrical on numerous axes.

Of the four halls around the patio, the southern **Sala de los Abencerrajes** is the most impressive. Boasting a mesmerising octagonal stalactite ceiling, this is the legendary site of the murders of the noble Abencerraj family, whose leader, the story goes, dared to dally with Zoraya, Abu al-Hasan's favourite concubine. The rusty stains in the fountain are said to be the victims' indelible blood.

At the eastern end of the patio is the **Sala de los Reyes** (Hall of the Kings) with a leather-lined ceiling painted by 14th-century Christian artists. The hall's name comes from the painting on the central alcove, thought to depict 10 Nasrid emirs.

On the patio's northern side is the richly decorated **Sala de Dos Hermanas** (Hall of Two Sisters), probably named after the slabs of white marble flanking its fountain. It features a dizzying *muqarnas* (honeycomb vaulted) dome with a central star and 5000 tiny cells, reminiscent of the constellations. This may have been the room of the emir's favourite paramour. The carved wood screens in the upper level enabled women (and perhaps others involved in palace intrigue) to peer down from hallways above without being seen. At its far end, the tile-trimmed **Mirador de Daraxa** (Daraxa lookout) was a lovely place for palace denizens to look onto the garden below.

From the Sala de Dos Hermanas, a passageway leads through the **Estancias del Emperador** (Emperor's Chambers), built for Carlos I in the 1520s, and later used by the American author Washington Irving. From here descend to the **Patio de la Reya** (Patio of the Grille) and the **Patio de la Lindaraja**, where, in the southwest corner you can peer into the bathhouse lit by star-shaped skylights.

You eventually emerge into the **Jardines del Partal**, an area of terraced gardens laid out at the beginning of the 20th century. Here a reflecting pool stands in front of the **Palacio del Partal**, a small porticoed building with its own tower (the Torre de las Damas) dating to the early 14th century. Leave the Partal gardens by a gate facing the Palacio de Carlos V, or continue along a path to the Generalife.

➡ Generalife

The Generalife, the sultans' gorgeous summer estate, dates to the 14th century. A soothing ensemble of pathways, patios, pools, fountains, trees and, in season, flowers of every imaginable hue, it takes its name from the Arabic *jinan al-'arif,* meaning 'the overseer's gardens'.

A string of elegant rectangular plots, the **Jardines Nuevos**, leads up to the whitewashed **Palacio del Generalife** (adult/12-15yr/under 12yr €14/8/free, Generalife & Alcazaba adult/under 12yr €7/free), the emirs' summer palace. The courtyards here are particularly graceful – in the second one, the **Patio del Ciprés de la Sultana**, the trunk of a 700-year-old cypress tree suggests what delicate shade would once have graced

ALHAMBRA PRACTICALITIES

The Alhambra is Spain's most visited tourist attraction, drawing almost 2.5 million visitors a year. To ease your visit, it pays to book ahead and know the ropes.

Tickets

Some parts of the Alhambra can be visited free of charge, but for the main areas, you'll need a ticket. There are several types:

General (€14) Covers all areas.

Gardens (€7) Gives entry to all areas except the Palacios Nazaríes.

Night Visit Palacios Nazaríes (€8) For year-round night visits to the Nasrid Palaces.

Night Visit Gardens & Generalife (€5) Available from April to May and September to mid-October.

Dobla de Oro (€11.65 to €19.65) Covers admission to the Alhambra and several sites in the Albayzín neighbourhood.

How to Buy a Ticket

You can buy tickets from two hours to three months in advance, online or by phone (☎858 95 36 16; https://tickets.alhambra-patronato.es), or at the Alhambra ticket office. Depending on the number of tickets reserved in advance, a limited number of same-day tickets are available at the ticket office. These sell out quickly, so get in early.

If you've booked a ticket, you can either print it yourself or pick it up at the ticket office at the Alhambra Entrance Pavilion (p722) or the Corral del Carbón (p732) where there's a ticket machine.

All children's tickets must be collected at the Alhambra ticket office as you'll need to prove your kids' ages – take their ID documents or passports.

All tickets are named and non-transferable.

Admission to the Alhambra is covered by the Granada Card (p733).

On-Site Facilities

Audio guides are available for €6.

No outside food is allowed, but there's a cafe-bar at the Parador de Granada (p737) and a kiosk in front of the Alcazaba. You'll also find vending machines by the ticket office and in a services pavilion by the Puerta del Vino.

Strollers and prams are not permitted in the Palacios Nazaríes. You can leave them at the services pavilion.

Getting There

By foot, walk up the Cuesta de Gomérez from Plaza Nueva through the woods to the **Puerta de la Justicia** (☎958 02 79 71; http://alhambra-patronato.es; ⏰8.30am-8pm Apr–mid-Oct, to 6pm mid-Oct–Mar, night visits 10-11.30pm Tue-Sat Apr–mid-Oct, 8-9.30pm Fri & Sat mid-Oct–Mar) FREE. Enter here if you already have your ticket, otherwise continue to the ticket office.

Bus C3 runs to the ticket office from a **bus stop** (Plaza Isabel a Católica; €1.20) just off Plaza Isabel la Católica.

the area. Beyond the courtyard, a staircase known as the **Escalera del Agua** is a delightful work of landscape engineering with water channels running down the shaded steps.

Casa-Museo Manuel de Falla MUSEUM
(☎958 22 21 88; www.museomanueldefalla.com; Paseo de los Mártires; adult/reduced €3/1; ⏰10am-5pm Tue-Sat, to 3pm Sun) Arguably Spain's greatest classical composer and an artistic friend of Lorca, Manuel de Falla (1876–1946) was born in Cádiz, but spent the key years of his life in Granada until the Civil War forced him into exile. You can learn all about the man at this attractive *carmen* (traditional house with garden) where he lived and composed, and which has been preserved pretty much as he left it. Ring the bell to get in.

Granada

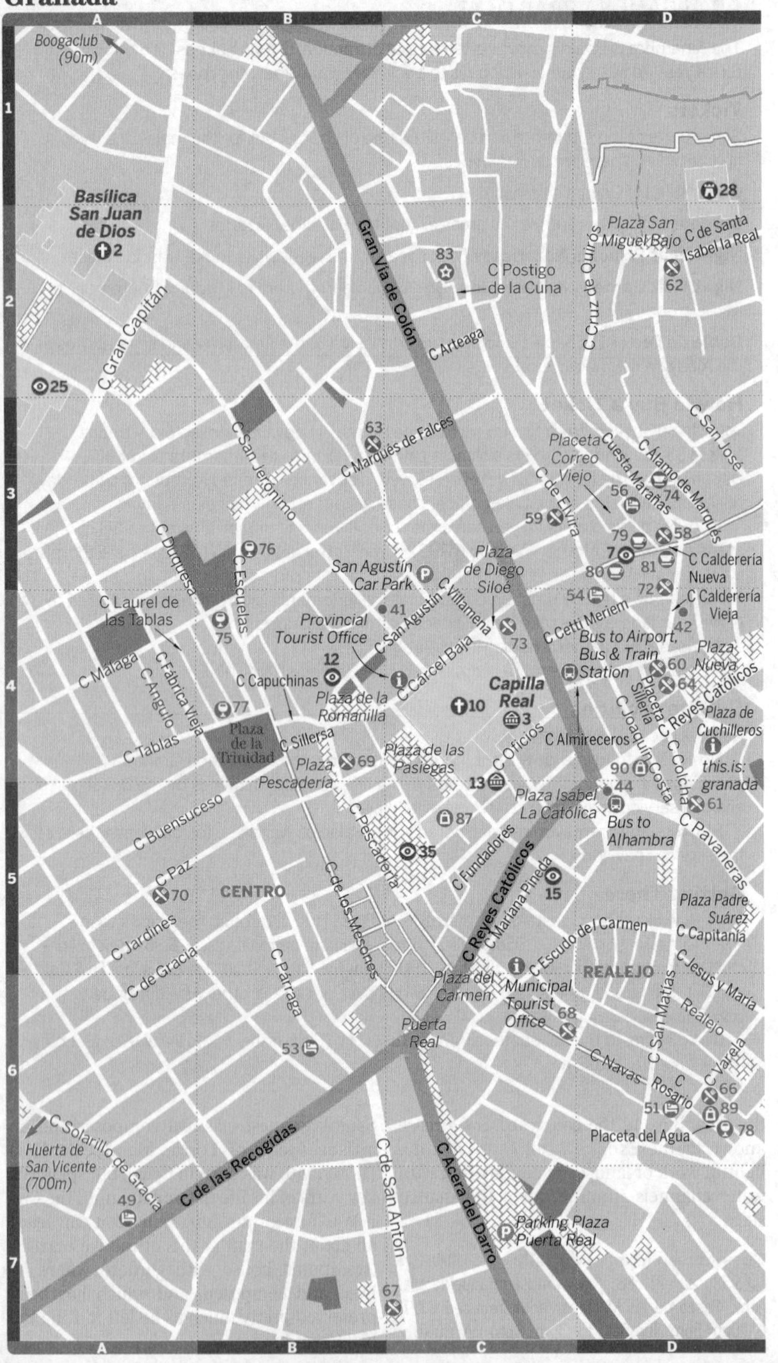

Boogaclub (90m)
Basílica San Juan de Dios
2
25
C Gran Capitán
Gran Vía de Colón
83
C Postigo de la Cuna
C Arteaga
C Cruz de Quirós
Plaza San Miguel Bajo
C de Santa Isabel la Real
28
62
C San José
63
C Marqués de Falces
C San Jerónimo
Placeta Correo Viejo
Cuesta Marañas
C Álamo de Marqués
C de Elvira
56
74
59
79
58
7
81
C Calderería Nueva
C Duquesa
76
C Escuelas
San Agustín Car Park
Plaza de Diego Siloé
80
54
72
C Calderería Vieja
C Villamena
C Laurel de las Tablas
41
C San Agustín
42
75
Provincial Tourist Office
73
C Cetti Meriem
Bus to Airport, Bus & Train Station
Plaza Nueva
60
64
C Málaga
C Fábrica Vieja
C Angulo
C Capuchinas
12
C Cárcel Baja
Capilla Real
Plaza de la Romanilla
10
3
Placeta Sillería
C Reyes Católicos
Plaza de Cuchilleros
77
C Joaquín Costa
C Tablas
Plaza de la Trinidad
C Sillersa
C Oficios
C Almireceros
this.is: granada
Plaza Pescadería
69
Plaza de las Pasiegas
13
90
C Colcha
44
Plaza Isabel La Católica
61
C Buensuceso
C Pescadería
87
Bus to Alhambra
C Pavaneras
35
C Fundadores
C Reyes Católicos
15
C Paz
C Mariana Pineda
70
CENTRO
C de los Mesones
Plaza Padre Suárez
C Capitanía
C Escudo del Carmen
C Jardines
C Párraga
C de Gracia
Plaza del Carmen
Municipal Tourist Office
REALEJO
C Jesús y María
C San Matías
Realejo
68
Puerta Real
53
C Navas
C Varela
C Rosario
66
51
89
C Solarillo de Gracia
Huerta de San Vicente (700m)
Placeta del Agua
78
C de las Recogidas
C de San Antón
C Acera del Darro
49
Parking Plaza Puerta Real
67
CENTRO

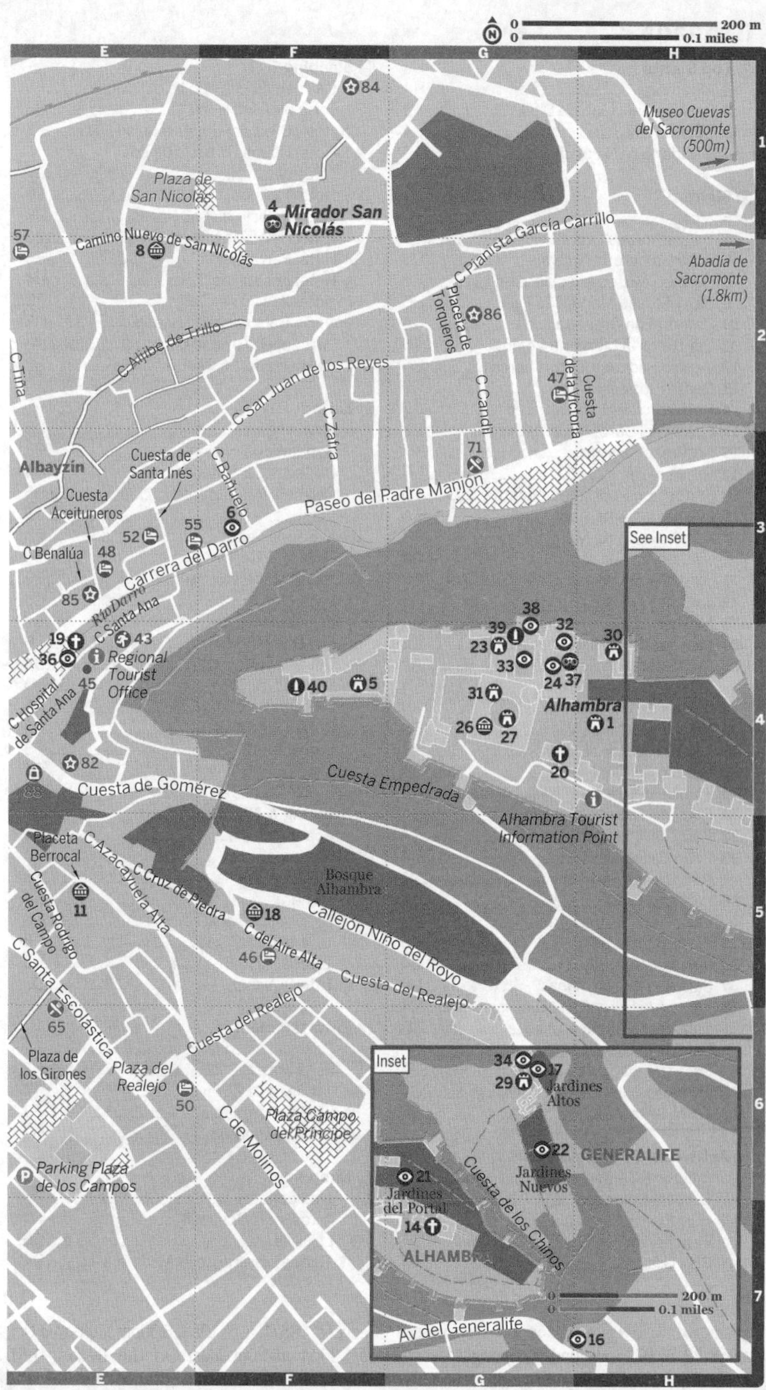

0 200 m
0 0.1 miles
Museo Cuevas del Sacromonte (500m)
Abadía de Sacromonte (1.8km)
84
Plaza de San Nicolás
4 Mirador San Nicolás
57
8
Camino Nuevo de San Nicolás
C Pianista García Carrillo
Placeta de Torqueros
86
C Aljibe de Trillo
C Tiña
C San Juan de los Reyes
47
Cuesta de la Victoria
C Candil
C Zafra
71
Albayzín
Cuesta de Santa Inés
C Bañuelo
Cuesta Aceituneros
Paseo del Padre Manjón
6
55
52
C Benalúa
48
Carrera del Darro
85
Río Darro
C Santa Ana
43
19
36
Regional Tourist Office
45
See Inset
38
39
32
30
23
33
24
37
40
5
31
Alhambra
1
C Hospital de Santa Ana
26
27
82
20
Cuesta de Gomérez
Cuesta Empedrada
Alhambra Tourist Information Point
Placeta Berrocal
C Azacayuela Alta
C Cruz de Piedra
Bosque Alhambra
Cuesta Rodrigo del Campo
11
18
Callejón Niño del Royo
C del Aire Alta
46
C Santa Escolástica
Cuesta del Realejo
Cuesta del Realejo
65
Plaza de los Girones
Plaza del Realejo
50
C de Molinos
Plaza Campo del Príncipe
Parking Plaza de los Campos
Inset
34
17
29
Jardines Altos
22
GENERALIFE
Jardines Nuevos
Cuesta de los Chinos
21
Jardines del Portal
14
ALHAMBRA
0 200 m
0 0.1 miles
Av del Generalife
16

Granada

Top Sights
1 Alhambra ... H4
2 Basílica San Juan de Dios ... A2
3 Capilla Real ... C4
4 Mirador San Nicolás ... F1

Sights
5 Alcazaba ... F4
6 Baños Árabes El Bañuelo ... F3
7 Calle Calderería Nueva ... D3
8 Carmen Museo Max Moreau ... E2
9 Casa-Museo Manuel de Falla ... H6
10 Catedral de Granada ... C4
11 Centro de la Memoria Sefardí ... E5
12 Centro Federico García Lorca ... B4
13 Centro José Guerrero ... C5
14 Convento de San Francisco ... G7
15 Corral del Carbón ... C5
16 Entrance Pavilion ... H7
17 Escalera del Agua ... G6
18 Fundación Rodríguez-Acosta ... F5
19 Iglesia de Santa Ana ... E4
20 Iglesia de Santa María de la Alhambra ... G4
21 Jardines del Partal ... G6
22 Jardines Nuevos ... G6
23 Mexuar ... G4
24 Mirador de Daraxa ... G4
25 Monasterio de San Jerónimo ... A2
Museo de Bellas Artes ... (see 31)
26 Museo de la Alhambra ... G4
27 Palacio de Carlos V ... G4
28 Palacio de Dar-al-Horra ... D1
29 Palacio del Generalife ... G6
30 Palacio del Partal ... H4
31 Palacios Nazaríes ... G4
32 Patio de la Lindaraja ... G4
33 Patio de los Arrayanes ... G4
Patio de los Leones ... (see 24)
34 Patio del Ciprés de la Sultana ... G6
Patio del Cuarto Dorado ... (see 23)
35 Plaza Bib-Rambla ... C5
36 Plaza de Santa Ana ... E4
37 Sala de Dos Hermanas ... G4
38 Sala de la Barca ... G4
Sala de los Abencerrajes ... (see 24)
Sala de los Reyes ... (see 24)
Salón de los Embajadores ... (see 38)
39 Torre de Comares ... G4
40 Torre de la Vela ... F4

Activities, Courses & Tours
41 Cicerone Cultura y Ocio ... B4
42 Escuela Delengua ... D4
43 Hammam Al Ándalus ... E4
44 Pancho Tours ... D5
45 Play Granada ... E4

Sleeping
46 Carmen de la Alcubilla del Caracol ... F5
47 Casa Morisca Hotel ... G2
48 Hotel Casa del Capitel Nazarí ... E3
49 Hotel Hospes Palacio de Los Patos ... A7
50 Hotel Molinos ... E6
51 Hotel Palacio de Los Navas ... D6
52 Hotel Palacio de Santa Inés ... E3
53 Hotel Párragasiete ... B6
54 Hotel Posada del Toro ... D4
55 Hotel Zawán del Darro ... E3
56 Oasis Backpackers' Hostel ... D3
Parador de Granada ... (see 14)
57 Santa Isabel La Real ... E2

Eating
58 Arrayanes ... D3
59 Babel World Fusion ... C3
60 Bodegas Castañeda ... D4
61 Carmela Restaurante ... D5
62 El Ají ... D2
63 El Bar de Fede ... B3
64 Greens & Berries ... D4
65 Hicuri Art Restaurant ... E6
66 La Botillería ... D6
67 La Fábula Restaurante ... C7
68 Los Diamantes ... C6
69 Oliver ... B4
Parador de Granada ... (see 14)
70 Poë ... A5
71 Ruta del Azafrán ... G3
72 Samarkanda ... D3
73 Siloé Café & Grill ... C4

Drinking & Nightlife
74 Abaco Té ... D3
75 Botánico ... B4
76 El Bar de Eric ... B3
77 Mundra ... B4
78 Taberna La Tana ... D6
79 Tetería Dar Ziryab ... D3
80 Tetería Kasbah ... D3
81 Tetería Nazarí ... D3

Entertainment
82 Casa del Arte Flamenco ... E4
83 Eshavira ... C2
84 Jardines de Zoraya ... F1
85 Le Chien Andalou ... E3
86 Peña La Platería ... G2

Shopping
87 Alcaicería ... C5
88 Artesanías González ... E4
89 La Oliva ... D6
90 Tienda Librería de la Alhambra ... D4

Fundación Rodríguez-Acosta MUSEUM
(958 22 74 97; www.fundacionrodriguezacosta.com; Callejón Niño del Royo 8; guided tour adult/reduced €5/4; 10am-6.30pm Apr–mid-Oct, to 4.30pm mid-Oct–Mar) On the Realejo hill, the so-called 'Carmen Blanco' houses the

Rodríguez-Acosta foundation in a building built by the Granada-born modernist artist, José María Rodríguez-Acosta, in 1914. It's an unusual and whimsical place that borrows from several architectural genres including art deco, Nasrid, Greek and baroque. The one-hour guided tour includes a walk through the house's subterranean tunnels, and entry to a well-curated museum containing works by Francisco Pacheco, Alonso Cano and Francisco de Zurbarán.

Centro de la Memoria Sefardí MUSEUM
(☎610 060255; Placeta Berrocal 5; guided tour €5; ⏲10am-2pm Sun-Fri year-round, plus 5-8.30pm summer, 4-8pm winter) Since being expelled en masse in 1492, there are very few Sephardic Jews left living in Granada. But this didn't stop one enterprising couple from opening a museum to their memory in 2013, the year the Spanish government began offering Spanish citizenship to any Sephardic Jew who could prove their Iberian ancestry. The museum is tiny, but the selected artefacts make excellent props to the passionate and fascinating historical portrayal related by its owners.

Plaza Nueva & Around

Plaza de Santa Ana SQUARE
Plaza Nueva extends northeast into Plaza de Santa Ana, overlooked by the **Iglesia de Santa Ana** (Plaza Santa Ana; admission €1.50; ⏲10.30am-1.30pm Tue-Fri) and its distinctive bell tower.

A short walk along the riverside Carrera del Darro brings you to the Baños Árabes El Bañuelo.

Baños Árabes El Bañuelo BATHHOUSE
(Carrera del Darro 31; ⏲9am-2.30pm & 5-8.30pm summer, 10am-5pm winter) FREE Located by the river on Carrera del Darro is this well-preserved, 11th-century Islamic bathhouse. Its bare brick rooms feature columns, capitals and marble-tiled floors.

Albayzín

The Albayzín, Granada's old Muslim quarter, is sprawled over a hill facing the Alhambra. Ideal for aimless wandering – you'll almost certainly get lost at some point – it's a fascinating district of steep cobblestone streets, *teterías* (teahouses) and whitewashed *cármenes* (mansions with walled gardens, from the Arabic *karm* for garden).

★Mirador San Nicolás VIEWPOINT
(Plaza de San Nicolás) This is the place for those classic sunset shots of the Alhambra sprawled along a wooded hilltop with the dark Sierra Nevada mountains looming in the background. It's a well-known spot, accessible via Callejón de San Cecilio, so expect crowds of camera-toting tourists, students and buskers. It's also a haunt of pickpockets and bag-snatchers, so keep your wits about you as you enjoy the views.

Carmen Museo Max Moreau MUSEUM
(☎958 29 33 10; Camino Nuevo de San Nicolás 12; ⏲10.30am-1.30pm & 6-8pm Tue-Sat) FREE Most of the Albayzín's *cármenes* are true to their original concept – quiet, private houses with high walls that hide beautiful terraced gardens. But you can get a rare (and free) glimpse of one of these secret domains at the former home of Belgium-born portrait painter and composer Max Moreau. His attractive house has been made into a museum displaying his former living quarters and work space, along with a gallery showcasing his best portraits.

Palacio de Dar-al-Horra PALACE
(Callejón de las Monjas; €5, Sun free; ⏲9am-2.15pm & 5-8.15pm mid-Mar–mid-Oct, 10am-5pm mid-Oct–mid-Mar) Up in the Albayzín – down a short lane off Callejón del Gallo – this 15th-century Nasrid palace was home to the mother of Boabdil, Granada's last Muslim ruler. It's surprisingly intimate, with rooms set around a central courtyard and fabulous views over the surrounding neighbourhood and over to the Alhambra (p722).

Calle Calderería Nueva STREET
Linking the upper and lower parts of the Albayzín, Calle Calderería Nueva is a narrow street famous for its *teterías* (teahouses). It's also a good place to shop for slippers, hookahs, jewellery and North African pottery from an eclectic cache of shops redolent of a Moroccan souk.

Centro

Catedral de Granada CATHEDRAL
(☎958 22 29 59; www.catedraldegranada.com; Plaza de las Pasiegas; adult/reduced €5/3.50; ⏲10am-6.30pm Mon-Sat, 3-6pm Sun) From street level it's difficult to appreciate the immensity of Granada's cavernous cathedral. It's too boxed in by other buildings to stand out, but it's nonetheless a monumental work of architecture. Built atop the city's

LOCAL KNOWLEDGE

GRANADA'S STREET ART

While the UK has Banksy, Granada has El Niño de las Pinturas (real name Raúl Ruíz), a street artist whose creative graffiti has become a defining symbol of the city. Larger-than-life, lucid and thought-provoking, El Niño's murals, many of which are in the Realejo neighbourhood, often juxtapose vivid close-ups of human faces with short poetic stanzas written in highly stylised lettering. Over the last two decades, El Niño has become a famous underground personality in Granada and has sometimes been known to give live painting demonstrations at the university. Although he risks criticism and occasional fines for his work, most *granadinos* agree that his street art brings creative colour and a contemporary edge to their ancient city.

former mosque, it was originally intended to be Gothic in appearance, but over the two centuries of its construction (1523–1704) it underwent major modifications. Most notably, architect Diego de Siloé changed its layout to a Renaissance style, and Alonso Cano added a magnificent 17th-century baroque facade.

Cano was also responsible for two wooden busts of Adam and Eve on the altar in the Capilla Mayor (main chapel). The cathedral's interior is vast with a series of 20 huge white piers rising from a black-and-white tiled floor to a ceiling capped by a 30m-high dome.

★Capilla Real HISTORIC BUILDING

(Royal Chapel; ☎958 22 78 48; www.capillarealgranada.com; Calle Oficios; adult/student/child €5/3.50/free; ⏲10.15am-6.30pm Mon-Sat, 11am-6.30pm Sun) The Royal Chapel is the last resting place of Spain's Reyes Católicos (Catholic Monarchs), Isabel I de Castilla (1451–1504) and Fernando II de Aragón (1452–1516), who commissioned the elaborate Isabelline-Gothic-style mausoleum that was to house them. It wasn't completed until 1517, hence their interment in the Alhambra's **Convento de San Francisco** (www.parador.es; Calle Real de la Alhambra) until 1521.

Their monumental marble tombs (and those of their heirs) lie in the chancel behind a gilded wrought-iron screen, created by Bartolomé de Jaén in 1520.

However, the tombs are just for show as the monarchs actually lie in simple lead coffins in the crypt beneath the chancel. Also there are the coffins of Isabel and Fernando's unfortunate daughter, Juana the Mad; her husband, Philip of Flanders; and Miguel, Prince of Asturias, who died as a boy.

The sacristy contains a small but impressive museum, with Fernando's sword and Isabel's sceptre, silver crown and personal art collection, which is mainly Flemish but also includes Botticelli's *Prayer in the Garden of Olives*. Felipe de Vigarni's two early-16th-century statues of the Catholic Monarchs at prayer are also here.

Plaza Bib-Rambla PLAZA

A picturesque, pedestrian-only square ringed by 19th-century townhouses, lime trees, kiosks and cafes. Ornamental lampposts stand around the plaza's baroque centrepiece, a 17th-century fountain whose rather underwhelming statue of Neptune stands atop an obelisk-like structure, itself balanced on a disk supported by grotesque figures, the so-called *gigantones*.

Corral del Carbón COURTYARD

(Calle Mariana Pineda; ⏲9am-8pm) Just east of Calle Reyes Católicos, an elaborate horseshoe arch leads through to the 14th-century Corral del Carbón, a cobbled courtyard surrounded by two-storeys of brick galleries. Initially, this was a Nasrid-era corn exchange, but in subsequent centuries it was used as an inn for coal dealers (hence its modern name, Coal Yard) and later as a theatre.

Centro José Guerrero GALLERY

(☎958 22 01 09; www.centroguerrero.org; Calle Oficios 8; ⏲10.30am-2pm Tue-Sun & 4.30-9pm Tue-Sat) FREE An exhibition space and gallery named after the Granada-born abstract painter (1914–91) who went to live in the US. Exhibitions are temporary and with a modernist bent, though the gallery keeps a roomful of Guerrero's characteristically vibrant works in a permanent collection.

Outside the Centre

★Basílica San Juan de Dios BASILICA

(www.sjdgranada.es; Calle San Juan de Dios 19; €4; ⏲10am-1.30pm Mon-Sat, 4-6.45pm Sun) Head to this historic basilica, built between 1737 and 1759, for a blinding display of opulent baroque decor. Barely a square inch of its interior lacks embellishment, most of it in gleaming gold and silver. Frescos by Diego Sánchez Sarabia and the Neapolitan painter Corrado Giaquinto adorn the ceilings and side chapels, while up above, the basilica's dome soars to a height of 50m. The highlight, however, is the extraordinary gold altarpiece in the Capilla Mayor (main chapel).

Once you've taken in the head-spinning details, search out a staff member to accompany you up the stairs behind the altar to where St John of God's remains are set deep in a niche surrounded by gold, gold and yet more gold.

Monasterio de San Jerónimo MONASTERY
(☎958 27 93 37; Calle Rector López Argüeta 9; €4; ⊙10am-1.30pm & 4-7.30pm) This 16th-century monastery, complete with cloisters and a lavishly decorated interior, is one of Granada's most stunning Catholic buildings. The church, a mix of late Gothic and Renaissance styling, boasts a profusion of painted sculptures and vivid colours, most spectacularly on the apse's immense eight-level gilt retable.

Gonzalo Fernández de Córdoba, the Reyes Católicos' (Catholic Monarchs') military man known as *El Gran Capitán*, is entombed in the church, at the foot of the steps, and figures of him and his wife stand on either side of the retable.

Monasterio de la Cartuja MONASTERY
(☎958 16 19 32; Paseo de la Cartuja; €5; ⊙10am-8pm) Built between the 16th and 18th centuries by the Carthusian monks themselves, this monastery features an imposing sandstone exterior and some incredibly lavish baroque decor. A highlight is the *sagrario* (sanctuary) behind the main altar in the church, a dizzying ensemble of coloured marble, columns and sculpture capped by a beautiful frescoed cupola.

To get to the monastery, take bus LAC or N7 from the city centre.

Also in the church, to the left of the main altar, the *sacristía* (sacristy) offers another blast of late-baroque effusion with its 'wedding-cake' stucco and brown-and-white Lanjarón marble. The *sacristía's* cabinets, veneered and inlaid with mahogany, ebony, ivory, shell and silver during the 18th century, represent a high point of Granada's marquetry art.

San Bruno, founder of the Carthusian order, can be seen everywhere; a few of his bones are embedded in the gilt and mirrored altar.

Activities

Hammam Al Ándalus HAMMAM
(☎902 33 33 34; www.granada.hammamalandalus.com; Calle Santa Ana 16; bath/bath & massage €30/45; ⊙10am-midnight) With three pools of different temperatures, plus a steam room and the option of skin-scrubbing massages, this is the best of Granada's Arab-style baths. Its dim, tiled rooms are suitably sybaritic and relaxing. Reservations required.

Courses

Escuela Delengua LANGUAGE
(☎958 20 45 35; www.delengua.es; Calle Calderería Vieja 20; individual lessons €36, 2-week course €260) With a massive student population, Granada is an ideal place to learn Spanish. This school in the heart of the Albayzín runs a range of courses, as well as offering individual lessons and loads of extracurricular

GRANADA CARD

This city pass comes in two forms, both available for pre-purchase or to buy in Granada:

Granada Card Básica (€37) Valid for three days, it provides admission to 10 monuments, including the Alhambra, Catedral, and Capilla Real, and covers five trips on local city buses.

Granada Card Plus (€40) Valid for five days, it covers admission to the same monuments as the basic card plus nine trips on local buses and a single tour on a tourist train.

Kids passes (€10.50) Available for children aged between three and 11. These must be associated with a regular adult card and there's a maximum of three passes per adult.

Further details, along with online booking, are available at www.granadatur.com or by phoning 858 88 09 90. Note that when you buy a pass you have to specify a start date as admission to parts of the Alhambra are regulated and require you to visit at a set time.

activities, including guided tours and tapas nights. It can also arrange accommodation.

Tours

Play Granada CULTURAL
(958 16 36 84; www.playgranada.com; Calle Santa Ana 2; tours from €20) On foot, by electric bike, on a Segway – this outfit offers a choice of tours, taking in the city and its historic quarters, as well as packages for the Alhambra (p722). Reckon on €20 for a two-hour 8km Segway ride, and from €60 for a guided tour of the Alhambra.

Pancho Tours WALKING
(664 64 29 04; www.panchotours.com) FREE The guys in orange T-shirts lead excellent free tours of the city. The walks, which depart daily at 10.30am from Plaza Isabella la Católica, last around 2½ hours. Also available are tours of the Albayzín and Sacromonte (€13 per person) and skip-the-line entry to the Alhambra (p722) combined with an Albayzín tour (€134). Book online.

Cicerone Cultura y Ocio WALKING
(958 56 18 10; www.ciceronegranada.com; Calle San Jerónimo 10) Offers a range of individual and group walking tours, as well as thematic itineraries and excursions out of the city to Las Alpujarras and the Costa Tropical. Reckon on €18 to join a two-hour city walk.

Festivals & Events

Semana Santa RELIGIOUS
(Holy Week) The two most striking events in Granada's Easter week are Los Gitanos (Wednesday), when members of the *fraternidad* (brotherhood) parade to the **Abadía de Sacromonte** (€4; 10am-1pm Mon-Sat, 11am-1pm Sun & 5-7.30pm daily summer, 4-6pm winter), lit by bonfires, and El Silencio (Thursday), when the street lights are turned off for a silent candlelit march.

Feria del Corpus Christi RELIGIOUS
(Corpus Christi Fair; May/Jun) The most spectacular of Andalucía's Corpus Christi celebrations, this is Granada's big annual party. Held approximately 60 days after Easter, it involves a week of bullfighting, dancing, street parades and processions. Events are held across town and in fairgrounds near the bus station.

Bullfighting has deep cultural roots in Andalucía but there is opposition to it and visitors may wish to avoid the fights, held in the Plaza de Toros north of the city centre.

Festival Internacional de Música y Danza MUSIC
(www.granadafestival.org; Jun & Jul) For three weeks in June and July, first-class classical and modern performances are staged at the Alhambra and other historic sites.

Sleeping

Granada has plenty of hotels and hostels, many in the compact area around the cathedral. Some of the prettiest lodgings are in the Albayzín district, though these might call for some hill-walking, and many aren't accessible by taxi. The few hotels near the Alhambra are scenic but a hassle for sightseeing elsewhere. Rates are highest in spring and autumn, spiking over Easter.

Alhambra & Realejo

Carmen de la Alcubilla del Caracol HISTORIC HOTEL €€
(958 21 55 51; www.alcubilladelcaracol.com; Calle del Aire Alta 12; r €100-180; closed mid-Jul–Aug;) This much-sought-after small hotel inhabits a traditional whitewashed *carmen* (house dating to the Moorish period) on the slopes of the Alhambra. It feels more like a B&B than a hotel with its elegant homey interiors and seven quietly refined rooms washed in pale pastel colours. Outside, you can bask in fabulous views from the spectacular terraced garden.

Hotel Molinos HOTEL €€
(958 22 73 67; www.hotelmolinos.es; Calle Molinos 12; s €35-53, d €39-85;) Don't let the 'narrowest hotel in the world' moniker put you off – and yes, it actually is, with a certificate from *Guinness World Records* to prove it – there's plenty of breathing space in Molinos' attractively fashioned rooms. Situated at the foot of the Realejo, it's an economical central option.

Hotel Palacio de Los Navas HISTORIC HOTEL €€
(958 21 57 60; www.hotelpalaciodelosnavas.com; Calle Navas 1; s €65-130, d €70-165;) This 16th-century building, set around a classic columned patio, has attractive rooms with lots of cool creams, wrought-iron headsteads and terracotta-tiled floors. Location-wise, it's well placed for tapas action on Calle Navas, one of Granada's quintessential bar streets.

Parador de Granada HISTORIC HOTEL €€€
(958 22 14 40; www.parador.es; Calle Real de la Alhambra; r €220-436; P @) Few hotels can

LOCAL KNOWLEDGE

SACROMONTE

Sacromonte, Granada's historic *gitano* (Roma) neighbourhood, sits northeast of the Albayzín (p731). Renowned for its flamenco traditions, it draws tourists to nightclubs and aficionados to music schools yet still feels like the fringes of the city. This despite the fact that some of the caves dug out of the hillside date back to the 14th century.

The area, centred on the Camino del Sacromonte, is good for an idle stroll, yielding some great views, particularly from the Vereda de Enmedio, which overlooks the Alhambra (p722) and Albayzín. For some local insight, stop off at the **Museo Cuevas del Sacromonte** (☎958 21 51 20; www.sacromontegranada.com; Barranco de los Negros; €5; ⏲10am-8pm mid-Mar–mid-Oct, to 6pm mid-Oct–mid-Mar) where you can see what a traditional cave home once looked like. The diligent can then press on to the Abadía de Sacromonte (p734) at the top of the hill, to explore some catacombs and underground cave chapels.

Note that it's not considered safe for lone women to wander around the uninhabited parts of the area, day or night.

claim a more impressive setting than this luxury *parador* (state-run-hotel), housed in a 15th-century convent in the Alhambra (p722). Book here if you're looking for romance or want to revel in the history of its surrounds. Reserve ahead; it's mega-popular – obviously.

Near Plaza Nueva

Hotel Palacio de Santa Inés HOTEL €€
(☎958 22 23 62; www.palaciosantaines.es; Cuesta de Santa Inés 9; d €85-125; ❄📶) A Moorish-era house, extended in the 16th and 17th centuries, with a fetching double patio around which rooms, some with Alhambra views, are arranged on three levels. The interior resembles a coaching inn, its decor a mix of burnt sienna tiles, old timber beams and heavy furniture.

Hotel Zawán del Darro HISTORIC HOTEL €€
(☎958 21 57 30; http://hotelzawandeldarro.com; Carrera del Darro 23; s €50-70, d €65-99; ❄@📶) In the buzzy riverside area of the Albayzín, this pleasant three-star occupies a tastefully restored 16th-century mansion. Expect stone floors, wood-beams and 13 characterful rooms, the best of which have Alhambra (p722) views. There are plenty of eating and drinking options nearby, hence a bit of evening noise.

Albayzín

Oasis Backpackers' Hostel HOSTEL €
(☎958 21 58 48; https://hostelsoasis.com/granada-hostels/oasis-granada; Placeta Correo Viejo 3; dm €11-23; ❄@📶🏊) Budget digs in a bohemian quarter, the friendly Oasis is seconds away from the *teterías* (teahouses) and bars on Calle Elvira. The first in what is now a chain of Oasis hostels, it has beds in six- to 10-person dorms, both mixed and women only, and a long list of facilities including a fully equipped kitchen and rooftop terrace.

Hotel Posada del Toro HOTEL €
(☎958 22 73 33; www.posadadeltoro.com; Calle de Elvira 25; s/d/ste from €45/49/71; ❄📶) A lovely little hotel in the lively Albayzín quarter. Bullfighting posters line a small passageway that leads to the main body of the hotel where tasteful rooms are decked out with parquet floors, Alhambra-style stucco and rustic furniture. Rates are a bargain considering its central location.

Hotel Casa del Capitel Nazarí HISTORIC HOTEL €€
(☎958 21 52 60; www.hotelcasacapitel.com; Cuesta Aceituneros 6; s €52-100, d €65-125; ❄@📶) Another slice of Albayzín magic in a Renaissance palace that's as much architectural history lesson as midrange hotel. The sound of trickling water follows you through the columned courtyard to traditional, low-ceilinged rooms clad in tiles, bricks and heavy wood. It scores for its location too, just off Plaza Nueva.

★**Santa Isabel La Real** BOUTIQUE HOTEL €€€
(☎958 29 46 58; www.hotelsantaisabellareal.com; Calle de Santa Isabel La Real 19; r €119-199; ❄@📶) Up in hilltop Albayzín, this welcoming small hotel occupies a whitewashed 16th-century building. Many original architectural

features endure, including marble columns and flagged stone floors, while a fireplace and sofa add a homey touch in the communal area. The guest rooms, which are set around a central patio, are individually decorated with embroidered pictures and hand-woven rugs.

Go for room 11 if you can, for its Alhambra views.

★Casa Morisca Hotel HISTORIC HOTEL €€€
(☎958 22 11 00; www.hotelcasamorisca.com; Cuesta de la Victoria 9; d €129-175, ste €231; ❄📶) Live like a Nasrid emir in this late-15th-century mansion in the historic Albayzín quarter. Atmosphere and history are laid on thick in the form of timber-beamed ceilings, brick columns and an enchanting tiled courtyard. Rooms, the best of which have Alhambra views, are attractive and simply furnished.

Centro

Hotel Párragasiete HOTEL €€
(☎958 26 42 27; www.hotelparragasiete.com; Calle Párraga 7; s €36-65, d €48-150; ❄📶) With its blond-wood floors, severe furniture and clean modern lines, this smart hotel seems more Scandinavia than southern Spain. However, Granada appears in the form of wall sketches of local monuments and a sleek downstairs bar-restaurant called Vitola – ideal for breakfast or tapas.

Hotel Hospes Palacio de Los Patos LUXURY HOTEL €€€
(☎958 53 57 90; www.hospes.com/en/granada-palacio_patos; Solarillo de Gracia 1; d €140-420, ste €344-1456; P❄📶🏊) Housed in a palatial 19th-century building, this is one of Granada's top hotels. Its sharply designed minimalist rooms, all in clean whites and pearl greys, are spread over the original building and a contemporary new wing. To relax, drinks are served in a delightful Arabian garden or you can sign up for a massage in the spa.

Eating

Eating out in Granada is largely about the joys of tapas and traditional Andalucian fare. The city boasts a good mix of restaurants and batteries of bars and cafes, many catering to locals as much as tourists and out-of-towners. It also excels in Moroccan cuisine with a number of authentic places in the Albayzín quarter.

FEDERICO GARCÍA LORCA

Spain's greatest poet and playwright, Federico García Lorca (1898–1936), epitomised many of Andalucía's potent hallmarks – passion, ambiguity, exuberance and innovation. Born in Fuente Vaqueros, a village 17km west of Granada, he won international acclaim in 1928 with *El romancero gitano* (Gypsy Ballads), a collection of verses on Roma themes, full of startling metaphors yet crafted with the simplicity of flamenco song. Between 1933 and 1936 he wrote the three tragic plays for which he's best known: *Bodas de sangre* (Blood Wedding), *Yerma* (Barren) and *La casa de Bernarda Alba* (The House of Bernarda Alba) – brooding, dramatic works dealing with themes of entrapment and liberation.

Lorca was killed at the start of the Civil War in August 1936. Although the whereabouts of his remains has proven elusive, it's generally held he was executed by military authorities loyal to Franco for his perceived left-wing political views and his homosexuality.

Lorca's summer house, the **Huerta de San Vicente** (☎958 25 84 66; www.huertadesanvicente.com; Calle Virgen Blanca; €3, Wed free; ⊙9.30am-5pm Tue-Sun mid-Sep–May, 9am-2pm Tue-Sun Jun–mid-Sep), is now a museum in the city's southern suburbs. Back in the centre, the **Centro Federico García Lorca** (☎958 27 40 62; www.centrofedericogarcialorca.es; Plaza de la Romanilla; ⊙11am-2pm & 5-8pm Tue-Sat, 11am-2pm Sun) FREE houses the Lorca foundation and provides a modern setting for exhibitions and cultural events.

In Fuente Vaqueros, the **Museo Casa Natal Federico García Lorca** (☎958 51 64 53; www.patronatogarcialorca.org; Calle Poeta Federico García Lorca 4; €1.80; ⊙guided visits hourly 10am-1pm Tue-Sat year-round & 4-5pm Oct-Mar, 5-6pm Apr-Jun & Sep) displays photos, posters and costumes for the writer's plays. Hourly **Ureña** (☎953 22 01 71) buses serve the village (€1.70, 20 minutes) from Avenida de Andaluces near the bus station in Granada.

Alhambra & Realejo

Hicuri Art Restaurant VEGAN €

(☎858 98 74 73; www.restaurantehicuriartvegan.com; Plaza de los Girones 3; mains €7.50-10, menú del día €13.80; ⏰11am-11pm Mon-Fri, noon-11pm Sat, to 4.30pm Jul & Aug; ✍) Granada's leading graffiti artist, El Niño de las Pinturas, has been let loose inside Hicuri, creating a psychedelic backdrop to the vegan food served at this friendly, laid-back restaurant. Zingy salads, tofu, and curried seitan provide welcome alternatives to the traditional meat dishes that dominate so many city menus.

La Botillería SPANISH €€

(☎958 22 49 28; www.labotilleriagranada.es; Calle Varela 10; mains €10.90-18; ⏰12.30pm-1am Wed-Sun) Since opening in 2013, La Botillería has established a fine local reputation thanks to its elegantly presented food and thoughtful wine list. It's smart in a modern, casual way, with a bar area for tapas and a back restaurant where you can dine on starters of Cantabrian anchovies and creative mains such as *milhoja de presa ibérica* (millefeuille with pork and avocado).

Los Diamantes TAPAS, SEAFOOD €€

(www.barlosdiamantes.com; Calle Navas 26; raciones €10-14; ⏰12.30-4.30pm & 8.30pm-midnight) A Granada institution, this scruffy old-school joint is one of the best eateries on bar-lined Calle Navas. Always busy, it's generally standing room only but the seafood – the first tapas comes free with your drink – is excellent and there's usually a wonderful sociable vibe.

There's a second, smarter branch on Plaza Nueva.

Carmela Restaurante SPANISH €€

(☎958 22 57 94; www.restaurantecarmela.com; Calle Colcha 13; tapas €7, mains €7.50-16.90; ⏰8am-midnight, kitchen noon-midnight) Traditional tapas updated for the 21st century are the star turn at this smart all-day cafe-restaurant at the jaws of the Realejo quarter. Bag a table in the cool brick-lined interior or on the outdoor terrace and bite into croquettes with black pudding and caramelised onion, or tuna *tataki* with soy reduction.

Parador de Granada INTERNATIONAL €€€

(☎958 22 14 40; Calle Real de la Alhambra; mains €16-26; ⏰1-4pm & 8-10.30pm) As much as the food – mainly contemporary Andalucian – a meal at the Parador de Granada (p734) hotel restaurant is all about its unique Alhambra setting. The terrace, which it shares with the hotel's all-day bar-cafe, is a magical spot for a formal dinner or a post-sightseeing snack. The location does, however, bump up the prices a fair bit.

Near Plaza Nueva

Bodegas Castañeda TAPAS €

(☎958 21 54 64; Calle Almireceros 1; tapas €2-5; ⏰11.30am-4.30pm & 7.30pm-1.30am) Eating becomes a contact sport at this traditional tapas bar where crowds of hungry punters jostle for food under hanging hams. Don't expect any experimentation nonsense here, just classic tapas (and *raciones*) served lightning-fast with booze poured from big wall-mounted casks.

Greens & Berries FAST FOOD €

(Plaza Nueva 1; snacks from €2.50; ⏰9am-10pm; ✍) Fast food, Granada style. This hole-in-the-wall joint is ideal for a quick pit stop, serving a range of toasties, wraps, *bocadillos* (filled baguettes), salads and fresh smoothies made with juicy, sun-kissed fruit. Benches on the plaza provide the seating.

Ruta del Azafrán INTERNATIONAL €€

(☎958 22 68 82; www.rutadelazafran.es; Paseo del Padre Manjón 1; mains €17-21; ⏰1-11.30pm) At this hit riverside restaurant, modern design goes hand in hand with Alhambra (p722) views and an eclectic menu of international dishes. Moroccan starters pave the way for Asian-inspired tuna creations and hearty Andalucian staples such as pork cheeks slow-cooked in red wine.

Albayzín

Babel World Fusion TAPAS €

(☎958 22 78 96; Calle de Elvira 41; beer & tapas €2, mains from €6.50; ⏰12.30-4.30pm & 6pm-2am; ✍) A laid-back eatery loved by foreign students, Babel stands out from its more traditional neighbours on the bar-lined Calle de Elvira. It takes an international approach to the tapas concept, cooking up falafels, Mexican fajitas and Thai noodles alongside more regular Andalucian creations.

Arrayanes MOROCCAN €€

(☎619 076862, 958 22 33 53; www.rest-arrayanes.com; Cuesta Marañas 4; mains €9-16; ⏰1.30-4.30pm & 7.30-11.30pm Wed-Mon; ✍) The Albayzín quarter is the place to sample Moroccan food, and this well-known restaurant has a reputation as one of the

LOCAL KNOWLEDGE

FREE TAPAS

Granada is one of the last bastions of the highly civilised practice of serving a free tapas with every drink. Place your drink order at the bar and, hey presto, a plate will magically appear with a generous portion of something delicious-looking on it. Order another drink and another plate will materialise. The process is repeated with every round you buy. As many bars serve only small glasses of beer (*cañas* measure just 250ml) it's just about possible to fill up on free tapas over the course of an evening without getting totally legless. Indeed, some people 'crawl' from bar to bar getting a drink and free tapas in each place. Packed shoulder-to-shoulder with tapas institutions, Calle de Elvira and Calle Navas are good places to start.

neighbourhood's best. Ceramic tiles, ornate lattice-work arches and crimson seats set the stage for classic North African staples such as *bisara* soup, made with split beans, rich, fruity tagine casseroles, and flaky *pastelas* (stuffed pastries). Note that alcohol isn't served.

El Ají SPANISH €€

(☎958 29 29 30; Plaza San Miguel Bajo 9; mains €12-20; ⊙1-11pm) With alfresco seating on a charming hilltop plaza in the Albayzín, this cosy neighbourhood restaurant offers a warm welcome and a something-for-everyone menu. There are pastas if you fancy Italian, delicious chargrilled steaks, and inventive fish dishes such as prawns with tequila and honey, or cod in lime sauce.

Samarkanda LEBANESE €€

(Calle Calderería Vieja 3; mains €8-12; ⊙1-4.30pm & 7.30-11.30pm Thu-Tue; ✎) Despite the rather tired decor, this friendly family-run Lebanese restaurant is a sound choice, cooking up a menu of traditional mainstays in the backstreets of the Albayzín. Kick off with hummus and *mutabal* (aubergine and tahini-based dip) before digging into a bowl of *kafta* (ground beef baked and served with potatoes and a sesame sauce).

Centro

Poë TAPAS €

(www.barpoe.com; cnr Calles Paz & Verónica de la Magdalena; tapas €1.50, raciones €5; ⊙8pm-12.30am) Friendly Poë offers an inviting multicultural vibe and international favourites such as Brazilian *feijoada* (black bean and pork stew) and spicy-hot Thai chicken. It doesn't look much from the outside, but like Dr Who's Tardis, it's a whole different world once you walk through the door.

★El Bar de Fede INTERNATIONAL €€

(☎958 28 88 14; Calle Marqués de Falces 1; raciones €7.50-16; ⊙9am-2am Mon-Thu, to 3am Fri & Sat, 11am-2am Sun) The 'Fede' in the name is hometown poet Federico García Lorca, whose free spirit seems to hang over this hip, gay-friendly bar. It's a good-looking spot with patterned wallpaper and high tables set around a ceramic-tiled island, and the food is a joy. Standouts include chicken pâté served with orange sauce and heavenly melt-in-your mouth grilled squid.

Siloé Café & Grill INTERNATIONAL €€

(☎958 22 07 52; http://siloebarygrill.com; Plaza de Diego Siloé; mains €10-20; ⊙10am-11pm) Tucked in behind the cathedral, the Siloé is something of a Jack of all trades, as good for a relaxed coffee as for a full-blown lunch or dinner. In summer, its pleasant outdoor terrace is the place to be, while in the cooler months diners take to the modern interior to enjoy the likes of burgers and barbecued wings.

Oliver SEAFOOD €€

(☎958 26 22 00; www.restauranteoliver.com; Plaza Pescadería 12; mains €12-22; ⊙12.30-3.30pm & 8-11.30pm Mon-Sat) One of the best of the seafood bar-restaurants that throng Plaza Pescadería in central Granada. Well-dressed office folk pack in alongside street-sweepers to devour *raciones* of garlicky shrimps and fried treats at the mobbed bar, while families and tourists dine in comfort at the calmer outside tables.

★La Fábula Restaurante GASTRONOMY €€€

(☎958 25 01 50; www.restaurantelafabula.com; Calle de San Antón 28; mains €24-28, tasting menus €75-90; ⊙1-4pm & 8.30-11pm Tue-Sat) It's hard to avoid the pun, Fábula is pretty fabulous. A formal fine-dining restaurant set in the refined confines of the Hotel Villa Oniria, it's the domain of chef Ismael Delgado López whose artfully composed plates of contemporary Spanish cuisine are sure to impress. Be sure to book.

Drinking & Nightlife

From old-school tapas bars to historic cafes, traditional wine bars and Arabian Nights teahouses, Granada is well stocked with drinking options. Hotspots include the rather scruffy Calle de Elvira, the Río Darro at the base of the Albayzín, Calle Navas, and the area to the north of Plaza de Trinidad where you'll find several cool, hipster-leaning bars.

Taberna La Tana WINE BAR

(☎958 22 52 48; Placeta del Agua 3; ⏲12.30-4pm & 8.30pm-midnight) With bottles stacked to the rafters, hanging strings of garlic, and a small wood-and-brick interior, friendly La Tana is a model wine bar. It specialises in Spanish wines, which it backs up with some beautifully paired tapas. Ask the bartender about the 'wines of the month' and state your preference – a *suave* (smooth) red, or something more *fuerte* (strong).

El Bar de Eric BAR

(☎958 27 63 01; Calle Escuelas 8; ⏲10am-2am Mon-Thu, to 3am Fri, 1.30pm-3am Sat, 1am-2am Sun) Strewn with old gig posters and framed photos of musical heroes, from Debbie Harry to Jim Morrison, this laid-back bar is the creation of Spanish drummer Eric Jiménez of band Los Planetas. Get into the swing with some fusion tapas and a jar of sangria.

Botánico BAR

(☎958 27 15 98; www.botanicocafe.es; Calle Málaga 3; ⏲1pm-1am Mon-Thu, to 2am Fri & Sat, to 6pm Sun) Dudes with designer beards, students finishing off their Lorca dissertations, and bohemians with arty inclinations hang out at Botánico, a casual eatery by day, a cafe at *merienda* time (5pm to 7pm), and a buzzing bar come the evening.

Mundra BAR

(Plaza de la Trinidad; ⏲8.30pm-2am Mon-Thu, to 3am Fri & Sat) One of the best bars on leafy Plaza de Trinidad, Mundra has something of a new-age feel with its exposed brick walls, Buddha statues and chill-out sounds. There are outdoor tables, great for people-watching,

LOCAL KNOWLEDGE

GRANADA'S TEAHOUSES

Granada's *teterías* (teahouses) have proliferated in recent years, but there's still something invitingly exotic about their dark atmospheric interiors, stuffed with lace veils, stucco and low cushioned seats. Most offer a long list of aromatic teas and infusions, along with a selection of sticky Arabic sweets. Many still permit their customers to puff on *cachimbas* (hookah pipes).

Calle Caldererría Nueva in the Albayzín is Granada's most celebrated '*tetería* street'.

Abaco Té (☎958 22 19 35; Calle Álamo de Marqués 5; ⏲3-9.30pm Mon-Thu, 1.30-11.30pm Fri-Sun) Abaco's Arabian minimalist interior is a soothing spot to bask in Alhambra views from a comfy-ish floor mat. You can choose from an encyclopaedic list of teas and medicinal infusions or keep it fruity with a fresh juice or shake. Excellent cakes and a small menu of mainly vegetarian snacks will fend off the munchies.

Tetería Nazarí (Calle Caldererría Nueva 13; ⏲2pm-midnight) The best of the teahouses on this touristy stretch of the Albayzín. Plonk yourself on a stool at a small elaborately painted table and choose from the decent selection of teas, perhaps a mint and cinnamon infusion accompanied by a sweet, honey-based pastry.

Tetería Dar Ziryab (☎655 446775; Calle Caldererría Nueva 11; ⏲1pm-1am) Duck into the dimly lit interior, adorned with tiling, cushioned benches and typical Moorish latticework arches, to puff on a *cachimba* (hookah pipe) and drink herb tea from ornately decorated glasses.

Tetería Kasbah (Calle Caldererría Nueva 4; ⏲noon-1am) Wispy curtains, amazing stuccoed arches and low lighting set the scene for a relaxed tea break – service can be slow – in Calle Caldererría Nueva's largest and busiest *tetería*. A full food menu is also available.

and a decent choice of tapas and platters to share.

Boogaclub CLUB
(www.boogaclub.com; Calle Santa Barbara 3; 2am-6am Mon-Wed, 11pm-6am Thu & Sun, to 7am Fri & Sat) A historic club, good for full-on dance sessions. Chill to soulful house, funk and electro then kick off to international DJs spinning rock, soul, Latin and reggae. Also hosts jam sessions and regular gigs. Check the website for upcoming events.

Entertainment

Jardines de Zoraya FLAMENCO
(958 20 62 66; www.jardinesdezoraya.com; Calle Panaderos 32; ticket €20, dinner from €29; shows 8pm & 10.30pm) Hosted in a restaurant in the Albayzín district, the Jardines de Zoraya appears, on first impression, to be a touristy *tablao* (choreographed flamenco show). But reasonable entry prices, talented performers and a highly atmospheric patio make it a worthwhile stop for any aficionado.

Casa del Arte Flamenco FLAMENCO
(958 56 57 67; www.casadelarteflamenco.com; Cuesta de Gomérez 11; tickets €18; shows 7.30pm & 9pm) A small flamenco venue that is neither a *tablao* nor a *peña* (private club), but something in between. The performers are invariably top-notch, managing to conjure a highly charged mood in the intimate space.

Le Chien Andalou FLAMENCO
(717 709100; www.lechienandalou.com; Carrera del Darro 7; tickets €10-12; shows 7.30pm, 9.30pm & 11.30pm) Small cavernous bar that was once a cistern, but now hosts three nightly flamenco shows for half the price of the bigger places. Performances can be hit or miss, but at this price, it's probably worth the gamble.

Peña La Platería FLAMENCO
(958 21 06 50; www.laplateria.org.es; Placeta de Toqueros 7) Peña La Platería claims to be Spain's oldest flamenco club, founded in 1949. Unlike other more private clubs, it regularly opens its doors to non-members for performances on Thursday nights at 10pm. Tapas and drinks are available. Reservations recommended.

Eshavira JAZZ, FLAMENCO
(958 29 08 29; https://eshaviraclub.wordpress.com; Calle Postigo de la Cuna 2; €6-15; 10pm-4am) Just off Calle Azacayas, this is one of Granada's historic jazz and flamenco haunts, staging a regular program of gigs, jam sessions and flamenco performances – check its website for upcoming dates. It's a late-starter though, and events rarely kick off much before 11pm with the partying continuing throughout the night.

Shopping

Many shops in Granada play on the city's Moorish heritage to sell a range of colourful exotica ranging from bags of spices to curly-toed slippers and handmade leather bags. A local craft speciality to look out for is *taracea* (marquetry) – the best work has shell, silver or mother-of-pearl inlay, applied to boxes, tables, chess sets and more.

La Oliva FOOD & DRINKS
(958 22 57 54; Calle Rosario 9; 11am-2.30pm Mon-Sat & 7-10pm Mon-Fri) By day, La Oliva is a small food shop, stocking a selection of fine Spanish wines, olive oils and gourmet treats. By night, the tables come out and owner Francisco welcomes a few guests – bookings necessary – to dine on his €38.50 tasting menu.

Tienda Librería de la Alhambra BOOKS
(958 22 78 46; www.alhambratienda.es; Calle Reyes Católicos 40; 9.30am-8.30pm) This is a fabulous shop for Alhambra aficionados, with a great collection of books dedicated to the monument, its art and history. You'll find everything from simple guidebooks to glossy coffee-table tomes on Islamic art, as well as a selection of quality gifts, including hand-painted fans, stationery and stunning photographic prints, which you select from a vast digital library.

Alcaicería GIFTS & SOUVENIRS
(Calle Alcaicería; 10am-9pm) Laden with everything from leather satchels and Moroccan-style slippers to gaudy ceramic wares, cheap jewellery, scarves and Swiss Army knives, the brazen stalls on this narrow street are all that remain of what was once Granada's great bazaar. Try to get in early before the coach parties arrive.

Artesanías González ARTS & CRAFTS
(Cuesta de Gomérez 12; 11am-8.30pm) Specialising in the art of marquetry since 1920, this artisan shop is a great place to pick up a memento or small gift. There's a good selection

of handcrafted inlaid boxes, as well as coasters, chess sets and beautiful backgammon boards.

Information

Information is available at various offices in town:

Alhambra Tourist Information Point (958 02 79 71; www.granadatur.com; Calle Real de la Alhambra Granada, Alhambra; 8.30am-8.30pm) Up in the Alhambra.

Municipal Tourist Office (958 24 82 80; www.granadatur.com; Plaza del Carmen 9; 9am-8pm Mon-Sat, to 2pm Sun) The official city tourist office.

Provincial Tourist Office (958 24 71 28; www.turgranada.es; Cárcel Baja 3; 9am-8pm Mon-Fri, 10am-7pm Sat, 10am-3pm Sun) Information on Granada province.

Regional Tourist Office (958 57 52 02; www.andalucia.org; Calle Santa Ana 2; 9am-7.30pm Mon-Fri, 9.30am-3pm Sat & Sun) For information on the whole Andalucía region.

this.is:granada (958 21 02 39; www.thisisgranada.com; Plaza de Cuchilleros; 9.30am-2pm & 4-7pm Mon-Sat, to 6pm Sun) An agency selling tickets for flamenco shows, city tours and buses.

Getting There & Away

AIR

Granada Airport (Aeropuerto Federico García Lorca; 902 40 47 04; www.aena.es) is 17km west of the city, near the A92. Direct flights connect with Madrid, Barcelona, Bilbao, Palma de Mallorca, and, outside Spain, London, Manchester and Milan. It's served by international airlines such as easyJet, Vueling, Iberia and British Airways.

Alsa (902 42 22 42; www.alsa.es) bus 245 runs to the city centre (€2.90, 40 minutes) at 6am and then at least hourly between 9.15am and 11.30pm. It stops at various points, including Gran Vía de Colón near the cathedral. Get tickets on-board. A taxi to the bus station will cost around €20 to €24.

BUS

Granada's **bus station** (958 18 54 80; Avenida Juan Pablo II; 6.30am-1.30am) is 3km northwest of the city centre. To get into the centre, take city bus SN1 for the **Gran Vía de Colón** (Gran Vía de Colón).

Alsa (902 42 22 42; www.alsa.es) runs buses in the province and across the region, and has a night bus direct to Madrid's Barajas airport (€47.85, 6¼ hours).

DESTINATION	COST (€)	DURATION (HR)	FREQUENCY (DAILY)
Almuñécar	8.34	1¼-2	9
Córdoba	15	2¼-4	8
Guadix	5.50	1	14
Jaén	8.87	1¼	15
Lanjarón	4.27	1-1½	9
Málaga	10.25-13.70	1¾	17
Seville	23-29	3	8

CAR

Granada is at the junction of the A44 and the A92. The Alhambra has easy car access from the A395 spur.

TRAIN

The **train station** (958 27 12 72; Avenida de Andaluces) is 1.5km northwest of the centre. For the centre, walk straight ahead to Avenida de la Constitución and turn right to pick up bus SN1 to Gran Vía de Colón.

DESTINATION	COST (€)	DURATION (HR)	FREQUENCY (DAILY)
Almería	20.10	2½	4
Madrid	27.65-39	4	5
Barcelona	40-59	7¾	2
Córdoba	23.10-36.50	2¼-3	7
Algeciras	30	4¼-5	3
Seville	30.15	3¼	4

Getting Around

BUS

One-way tickets, which can be bought on buses (cash only), cost €1.40.

Useful bus lines:

C1 From Plaza Nueva up to the Albayzín.

C2 From Plaza Nueva up to Sacramonte.

C3 From Plaza Isabel II to the Alhambra via the Realejo quarter.

SN1 Connects the bus and train stations with Via Gran Vía de Colón in the centre.

CAR

Driving in central Granada – in common with most large Andalucian cities – can be frustrating and should be avoided if possible. Park your car on the outskirts and use public transport; there are plenty of options. If you have to drive, there are several central car parks: **Parking La Alhambra** (information 902 44 12 21; Paseo de la Sabika;

per hr/day €2.70/18.40; ⌚24hr), **Parking San Agustín** (Calle San Agustín; per hr/day €1.70/25; ⌚24hr) and **Parking Plaza de los Campos** (Plaza de los Campos 4; per hr/day €1.95/19.50; ⌚8am-1am Mon-Sat, 8.30am-11pm Sun).

TAXI

Taxis congregate in Plaza Nueva and at the train and bus stations.

To call a taxi, contact **Tele-Radio Taxi Granada** (☎958 28 00 00; www.granadataxi.com).

GRANADA PROVINCE

Rising above Granada are the mighty peaks of the Sierra Nevada. Snowcapped for about half the year, the mountains' vertiginous slopes offer wonderful skiing and terrific hiking in the warmer months. The southern side of the range shelters Las Alpujarras, a verdant area riven by valleys and massive canyons speckled with white villages replete with traditional flat-roofed Berber houses.

To the southwest, the province's coastline, the relatively low-key Costa Tropical, boasts a number of popular beach resorts nestled amid its coves and plunging cliffs.

DON'T MISS

SKIING THE SIERRA NEVADA

Some 33km from Granada, the modern village of Pradollano (2100m) is home to **Sierra Nevada Ski** (☎902 70 80 90; www.sierranevada.es; Pradollano; one-day ski pass adult €36.50-48, child €24-35; 👪), Europe's most southerly ski resort. The well-equipped resort, which is very popular with day trippers from Granada, caters to all levels with some 125 marked pistes ranging from tough black descents to mild green runs and cross-country routes. There's also a dedicated snowboard area, a family slope and kids' snow park, and night skiing on Thursdays and Saturdays.

In summer, skiing gives way to mountain biking in the **Sierra Nevada Bike Park** (http://sierranevadabikepark.com; Pradollano; one-day pass €21; ⌚lifts 9.45am-6pm), which has eight routes covering a total of 37km.

In winter **Tocina** (☎958 46 50 22; www.autocarestocina.es) operates three daily buses (four on the weekend) to Pradollano from Granada's bus station (€5, one hour). Outside the ski season there's just one daily bus (9am from Granada, 5pm from the ski station).

Sierra Nevada

Providing Granada's dramatic backdrop, the Sierra Nevada range extends about 75km from west to east. Its wild snowcapped peaks boast the highest point in mainland Spain (Mulhacén, 3479m) and Europe's most southerly ski resort at Pradollano. The lower southern reaches, peppered with picturesque white villages, are collectively known as Las Alpujarras.

Some 859 sq km are encompassed by the Parque Nacional Sierra Nevada. Spain's largest national park, this protected area is home to 2100 of Spain's 7000 plant species, including unique types of crocus, narcissus, thistle, clover, poppy and gentian, as well as Andalucía's largest ibex population. Bordering the national park at lower altitudes is the Parque Natural Sierra Nevada.

From July to early September, the higher mountains offer wonderful multi-day trekking and day hikes. Outside of this period, there's a risk of inclement weather, but the lower Alpujarras are always welcoming, with most snow melted by May.

ℹ Information

Centro de Visitantes El Dornajo (☎958 34 06 25; A395, Km 23; ⌚10am-5pm Wed-Sun) Information centre for the Sierra Nevada; on the A395 about 23km from Granada.

ℹ Getting There & Away

From Granada, the main approach road to the Sierra Nevada is the A395. Pick this up on the southeast edge of town.

Mulhacén & Veleta

The Sierra Nevada's two highest peaks are Veleta (3395m) and Mulhacén which, at 3479m, is the highest mountain in mainland Spain. Both are on the western end of the range, and both can be summitted from a national park post at **Hoya de la Mora** (2512m) on the mountains' northern flank. The post, accessible by road from

WORTH A TRIP

GUADIX

Guadix (gwah-deeks), a lively provincial town near the foothills of the Sierra Nevada, is best known for its cave houses, many of which are still occupied by local townsfolk. The cave district, **Barrio de las Cuevas**, is a weird, almost other-worldly place on the southern fringes of town where some 2000 dwellings are said to lie burrowed into the rocky terrain. For a grandstand view of the area, head up to the signposted **Mirador Padre Poveda**.

In the town centre, Guadix's flamboyant **cathedral** (☎958 66 51 08; Paseo de la Catedral; adult/reduced €5/3.50; ⏱10.30am-2pm & 4-6pm Mon-Sat Oct-May, 4.30-6.30pm Mon-Sat Apr-May, 5-7.30pm Mon-Sat Jun-Sep, 10.30am-2.30pm Sun year-round & 5-7.30pm Sun Jun-Sep) is an imposing sight and the old quarter an attractive place for a wander with its own distinctive architecture, much of it rendered in warm sandstone.

To overnight, the **Hotel GIT Abentofail** (☎958 66 92 81; www.hotelabentofail.com; Calle Abentofail; s €40-63, d €48-73; ❄📶) offers elegant boutique accommodation in the heart of the old town.

Regular buses serve Guadix from Granada (€5.50, one hour, up to 12 daily), Almería (€9.37, two hours, three daily) and Málaga (€18, three to 3½ hours, four daily). There are also daily trains from Granada and Almería.

Granada and the Pradollano ski resort, sits by the entrance to a mountain pass that runs over to the Alpujarran village of Capileira on the southern side. However, the top road is closed to private vehicles and the mountains' upper reaches can only be accessed by a national park shuttle bus that's operational between late June and October (snow permitting).

Activities

To climb Mulhacén and Veleta from the north, take the **shuttle bus** (☎671 564407; one way/return €6/10; ⏱8am-6pm Jun-Oct) from the Albergue Universitario at **Hoya de la Mora**. This drops you at the Posiciones del Veleta (3100m), from where it's a 4km trek (1½ hours) to the top of Veleta or 14km (four to five hours) to the summit of Mulhacén.

To tackle Mulhacén from the south side, take the summer shuttle bus from **Capileira** to the **Mirador de Trevélez**, from where it's around a three-hour hike to the summit (6km, 800m ascent).

To make the trip into an overnight excursion, you can bunk down at the **Refugio Poqueira** (☎958 34 33 49; www.refugiopoqueira.com; per person €17.50), which sits at 2500m below the southwestern face of Mulhacén. The loop to Mulhacén from the Mirador de Trevélez incorporating the *refugio* takes six to seven hours. Book in advance.

It's always best to phone ahead and check availability on the shuttle buses.

The routes described here are suitable for walkers of good to moderate fitness. Always check on weather forecasts beforehand and be prepared for changing conditions and possible high winds. A good source of information is http://sierranevadaguides.co.uk/information-about-the-sierra-nevada.

Las Alpujarras

Las Alpujarras is a 70km stretch of valleys and deep gorges on the southern flank of the Sierra Nevada. A mix of rocky, arid slopes, woods, and terraced farmlands made fertile by melted snow water, it's best known for its picturesque white villages. These cling to the verdant hillsides, their Berber-style flat-roofed houses recalling the area's past as a refuge for Moors escaping the Christian conquest of Granada. These days, the villages host a mixed population of locals and expats, while towns in the lower reaches simmer with spiritual seekers, long-term travellers and rat-race dropouts. Well-trod footpaths criss-cross the hills, linking the villages and offering superlative hiking.

Getting There & Away

The main western approach road to Las Alpujarras is the A348, which exits the A44 about 34km south of Granada.

Alsa (☎902 42 22 42; www.alsa.es) operates daily buses from Granada to the towns and villages of Las Alpujarras.

Western Sierra Nevada & Las Alpujarras

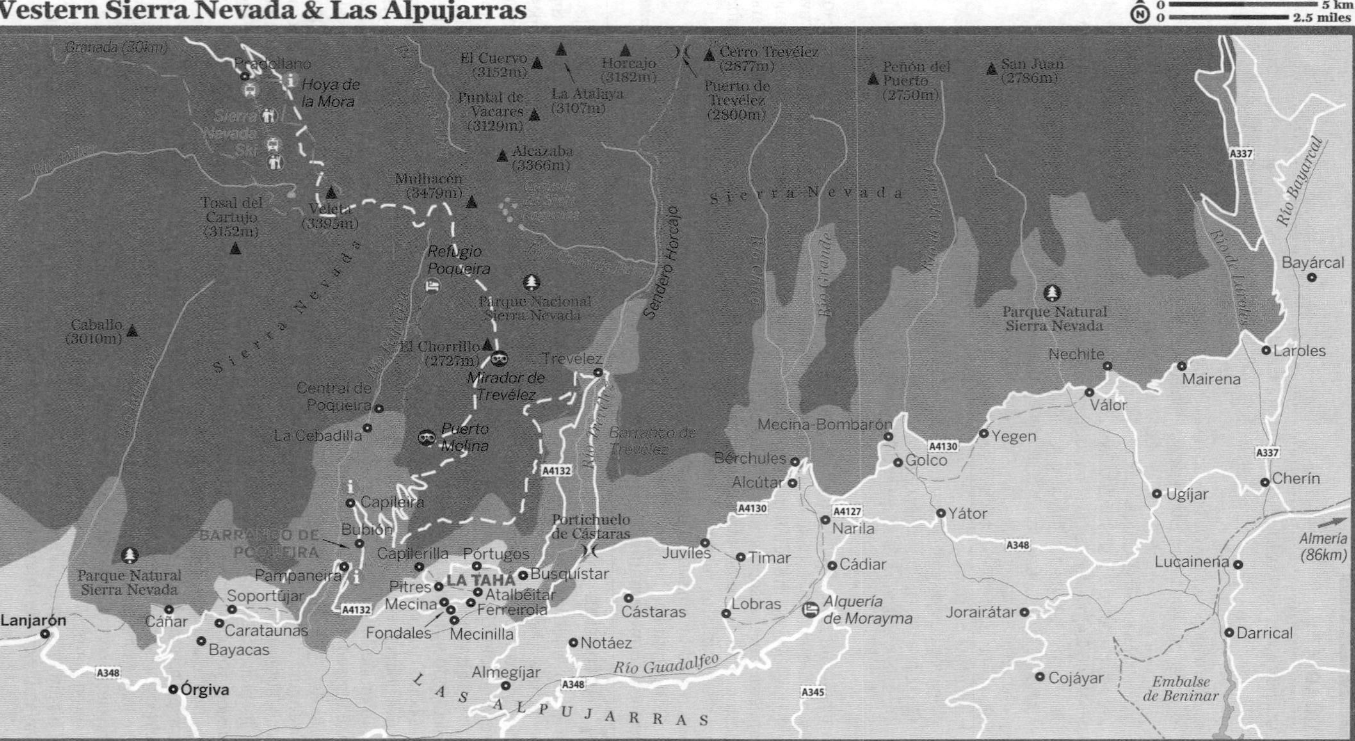

Lanjarón

POP 3587

A popular day-trip destination, Lanjarón is the main gateway to the western Alpujarras. An attractive, leafy mountain town, it's best known for its therapeutic spa waters, which have long been a major source of local income and still today draw coach-loads of visitors. It also profits from its pure spring water, which is bottled and sold across Spain, and its air-cured *jamón serrano* (ham) which enjoys pride of place on many local menus.

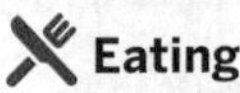

Activities

Balneario de Lanjarón SPA

(☎958 77 04 54; www.balneariodelanjaron.com; Avenida de Madrid 2; baths from €18) Lanjarón's thermal waters have been a major draw to the town for centuries. To test their medicinal properties, this spa – now part of a four-star hotel complex – offers a range of bathing options, massages and beauty treatments.

Caballo Blanco Trekking Centre HORSE RIDING

(☎627 794891; www.caballoblancotrekking.com; 2/4hr rides €40/70, full-day plus picnic €95) Located just east of Lanjarón, this well-established outfit offers horse-riding lessons and treks into the surrounding hills and mountains. English, Spanish, German and a little French are spoken. Book in advance.

Eating

El Arca de Noé SPANISH €€

(☎958 77 00 27; Avenida de la Alpujarra 38; mains €6-18; ⊙10am-3pm daily, plus 6.30-10.30pm Mon-Sat) The orderly rows of hanging hams and shelves laden with wine bottles, conserves and marinated goodies give the game away. This deli-eatery is the place to sample the celebrated local *jamón,* as well as a smorgasbord of regional delicacies: spicy sausages, goat's cheese, pâtés and tomato salads.

Getting There & Away

Alsa (☎902 42 22 42; www.alsa.es) buses serve Lanjarón from Granada (€4.27, one to 1½ hours, up to nine daily) and Málaga (€12.66, 3¼ hours, one daily Monday to Saturday).

Órgiva

The main town of the western Alpujarras, Órgiva is a bit scruffier and considerably larger than neighbouring villages. A hippy scene has long been fertile here – the alternative lifestyle community of Benéficio is nearby and its inhabitants regularly come into town to sell their wares or busk at the Thursday market. British visitors might recognise the town from Chris Stewart's best-selling book, *Driving over Lemons.*

Sleeping & Eating

Casa Rural Jazmín CASA RURAL €€

(☎958 78 47 95; www.casaruraljazmin.com; Calle Ladera de la Ermita; d €53-70; P❄🛜🏊) A warm welcome awaits at this peaceful sanctuary in the upper part of town. It's a cosy set-up with four homey guest rooms, each decorated in a different style and some larger than others. Outside, there's a bountiful garden where breakfast is served in summer and you can splash around in a pool.

Tetería Baraka INTERNATIONAL €€

(☎958 78 58 94; www.teteria-baraka.com; Calle Estación 12; mains €10-15; ⊙10am-11pm Mon-Wed,

OFF THE BEATEN TRACK

VÁLOR'S MOROS Y CRISTIANOS

Now a typical Alpujarras village, Válor has an important history. It was the birthplace of Aben Humeya, a *morisco* (converted Muslim) who led a 1568 rebellion against Felipe II's repressive policies banning Arabic names, dress and even language. Two years of guerrilla mountain warfare ended only after Don Juan de Austria, Felipe's half-brother, was brought in to quash the insurrection and Aben Humeya was assassinated by his cousin Aben Aboo. To recreate the historical clash, Válor musters a large *Moros y Cristianos* (Moors and Christians) **festival** (⊙12-15 Sep), with colourfully costumed 'armies' battling it out.

Two daily **Alsa** (☎902 42 22 42; www.alsa.es) buses serve the village from Granada (€10.23, 3½ hours) via Lanjarón, Órgiva, Cádiar and Bérchules.

BARRANCO DE POQUEIRA

The Barranco de Poqueira (Poqueira Gorge) is home to three of Las Alpujarras' most celebrated, and most visited, villages: Pampaneira, Bubión and Capileira, respectively 14km, 18.5km and 20km northeast of Órgiva. Seen from a distance they resemble flecks of white paint flicked Jackson Pollock–style on the vertiginous green landscape. Up close, they're textbook models of the steeply stacked white villages for which the Alpujarras are so famous.

The valley is also known for its handicrafts and you'll find plenty of shops selling leather goods, woven rugs and tilework.

For more active pursuits, hiking trails link the villages and most are perfectly doable in a day. For further information on walking in the area, ask at the **Servicio de Interpretación de Altos Cumbres** (☎671 564406; picapileira@oapn.mma.es; Carretera de Sierra Nevada; ⏲10am-2pm & 5-8pm) in Capileira.

Three daily **Alsa** (☎902 42 22 42; www.alsa.es) buses serve the villages from Granada.

Pampaneira

Estrella de las Nieves (☎958 76 39 81; www.estrelladelasnieves.com; Calle Huertos 21; s/d/ste €50/75/100; P ≋) This dazzling white complex at the top of the village offers elegant, understated modern rooms with terraces overlooking the rooftops and surrounding mountains. It also has pleasant gardens and the twin perks of a pool and car park (€5 per day).

Bodega El Lagar (☎673 636394; Calle Silencio; raciones €10; ⏲11am-5pm & 8pm-midnight daily) Hidden on a winding side street behind Plaza de la Libertad, this tiny bodega is one of the village's best eateries. Decked out in classic rustic fashion – picture rough white walls adorned with farm tools and wicker baskets – it cooks up huge helpings of reassuring farmhouse food, including wonderful chargrilled steaks.

Bubión

Casa Alpujarreña (Calle Real; €1.80; ⏲11am-2pm Sun, Mon, Wed & Thu, 11am-2pm & 5-7pm Fri, Sat & holidays) Located in the lower village beside the church, this folk museum occupies a typical mountain house, giving a glimpse of bygone Alpujarran life through its display of household utensils, farming tools and traditional furnishings.

Estación 4 (☎651 831363; Calle Estación 4; mains €9-15; ⏲7-11pm Mon, Tue, Thu & Fri, 1-4pm & 7-11pm Sat & Sun) Wind your way down from the main road to find this lovely, rustic restaurant. Its snug dining room is a charming spot to dig into classic local staples such as air-cured *jamón serrano*, pastas and Moroccan-inspired lamb dishes.

Capileira

Hotel Real de Poqueira (☎958 76 39 02; www.hotelpoqueira.com; Doctor Castillas 11; s €40-50, d €60-70; ≋) Occupying a typical old house opposite Capileira's lily-white church, this terrific three-star is one of several village hostelries run by the same family. But with its modern, boutique-like rooms, designer bathrooms and small swimming pool, this is the pick of the crop.

Taberna Restaurante La Tapa (☎618 30 70 30; Calle Cubo 6; mains €9-18; ⏲noon-4pm & 8pm-midnight;) Las Alpujarras is a culinary micro-region with its own distinct flavours and, at La Tapa, they're skilfully melded with the area's Moorish past in dishes such as wild boar casserole and vegetable couscous. The restaurant, which is snugly ensconced in a classic whitewashed house, is tiny, so book ahead if you want to guarantee a table.

El Corral del Castaño (Plaza del Calvario 16; mains €8-21; ⏲1-4pm & 7.30-10pm Thu-Tue) Enjoy a lovely setting on a quaint plaza and excellent food at this welcoming village restaurant. Take your pick from the extensive selection of traditional Alpujarran classics or opt for something more inventive such as skewered chicken with citrus fruit and ginger. Alternatively, go Italian with a pizza or focaccia.

Fri & Sat, 9am-11pm Thu, 11am-11pm Sun) A much-loved local haunt, especially on Thursdays when the market crowds flock here from mid-morning. Its laid-back vibe comes with an eclectic menu featuring Moroccan tagines, couscous, *shawarmas,* wraps and natural juices. You'll find it above the municipal car park in the upper part of town.

Shopping

Tara FASHION & ACCESSORIES

(Avenida González Robles 19; 10am-2pm & 5.30-8pm Mon-Sat) In keeping with Órgiva's hippy spirit, Tara can sort out your ethnic wardrobe with a choice of subcontinental-styled clothes, drapes, bags and jewellery. You can also pick up joss sticks in a range of exotic aromas.

Getting There & Away

Órgiva is well served by **Alsa** (902 42 22 42; www.alsa.es) buses with up to nine weekday services from Granada (€5.11, 1½ to 1¾ hours), and six daily on Saturdays and Sundays.

La Tahá

In La Tahá, the valley east of the Barranco de Poqueira, life slows and the number of tourists drops noticeably. The area, still known by the Arabic term for the administrative districts into which the Islamic caliphate divided the Alpujarras, consists of Pitres and its outlying villages – Mecina Fondales, Capilerilla, Mecinilla, Ferreirola and Atalbéitar – in the valley below.

Ancient paths (marked with signposts labelled 'Sendero Local Pitres–Ferreirola') link the hamlets, wending their way through woods and orchards, while the tinkle of running water provides the soundtrack. About 15 minutes' walk below Mecina Fondales, an old Moorish-era bridge spans the deep gorge of the Río Trevélez.

Eating

L'Atelier VEGETARIAN €€

(958 85 75 01; www.facebook.com/latelierveg restaurant; Calle Alberca 21, Mecina Fondales; mains €10-14; 1-4pm & 7-10pm;) Set in a traditional house in the hamlet of Mecina Fondales, this tiny, candlelit restaurant flies in the face of the local love for meat and presents an array of globetrotting vegetarian and vegan dishes (tabbouleh, Moroccan tagine, miso soup). It's always best to book ahead, particularly in winter. Michel, the owner, will also organise vegetarian cooking courses on request.

It also has a couple of **rooms** (d/q €50/56;).

Getting There & Away

Pitres, the largest centre in La Tahá, is on the main A4132 road and is served by three daily **Alsa** (902 42 22 42; www.alsa.es) buses from Granada (€6.79, 2¾ hours). For the other villages you'll need your own transport.

Trevélez

POP 776

To gastronomes, Trevélez is celebrated for its *jamón serrano,* one of Spain's finest cured hams, which matures perfectly in the village's rarefied mountain air. To hikers it's the gateway to a cobweb of high mountain trails, including one of the main routes up Mulhacén, mainland Spain's highest peak. To statisticians it's the second-highest village in Spain after Valdelinares in Aragón.

Sited at 1486m on the almost treeless slopes of the Barranco de Trevélez, the village is divided into two sections: the *alto* (high) part, which is older, more labyrinthine, and commands the best views; and the *bajo* (low) part, which has the bulk of the tourist facilities.

Sleeping & Eating

Hotel La Fragua II HOTEL €

(958 85 86 26; www.hotellafragua.com; Calle Posadas; d/tr/q €62/78/85;) La Fragua is something of a mini-chain with two hotels – this and the more modest **Hotel La Fragua I** (Calle San Antonio 4; s/d/tr/q €38/50/65/70;) – and a cosy **restaurant** (Calle San Antonio; mains €8-14; 12.30-4pm & 8-10.30pm;). La Fragua II sports a smart alpine look with a white-and-stone exterior adorned with potted flowers, and spacious, sun-filled rooms. Outside, you can revel in mountain views as you laze in the pool.

Mesón Joaquín ANDALUCIAN €€

(958 85 85 14; http://jamonestrevelez.com; Carretera Laujar Órgiva, Km 22; mains €8-20; 12.30-4.30pm) Starters of thinly sliced *jamón,* vermicelli soup with ham and eggs, and trout capped by ham. No prizes for spotting the star ingredient at this casual restaurant by the village's southern entrance. As if to reinforce the point, scores of cured hams hang from the ceiling in the ceramic-tiled interior.

Legacy of the Moors

Between 711 and 1492, Andalucía spent nearly eight centuries under North African influence and reminders flicker on every street, from the palatial Alhambra to the tearooms and bathhouses of Córdoba and Málaga.

Teterías

Andalucía's caffeine lovers hang around in exotic *teterías*, Moorish-style tearooms that carry a whiff of Marrakech or even Cairo in their ornate interiors. Calle Caldería Nueva in Granada's Albayzín is where the best stash is hidden, but they have proliferated in recent years; now even Torremolinos has one! Look out for dimly lit, cushion-filled, fit-for-a-sultan cafes where pots of herbal tea accompanied by plates of Arabic sweets arrive at your table on a silver salver.

Andalucian Bathhouses

Sitting somewhere between a Western spa and a Moroccan hammam, Andalucía's bathhouses retain enough old-fashioned elegance to satisfy a latter-day emir with a penchant for Moorish-era opulence. You can recline in candlelit subterranean bliss sipping mint tea, and experience the same kind of bathing ritual – successive immersions in cold, tepid and hot bathwater – as the Moors did. Seville, Granada, Almería, Córdoba and Málaga all have excellent Arabic-style bathhouses, with massages also available.

Architecture

The Alhambra was undoubtedly the pinnacle of Moorish architectural achievement in Andalucía, but there are many other buildings in the region that draw inspiration from the rulers of

1. Geometric tile pattern, Alhambra (p722)
2. Casa de Yafar at the Medina Azahara archaeological site (p713), Andalucía
3. The interior of a *tetería* (Moorish-style tearoom), Granada (p739)

Al-Andalus. Sometimes the influences are obvious. At others, hybrid buildings constructed in Mudéjar or neo-Moorish styles hint at former Nasrid glories: an ornate wooden ceiling, geometric tile patterns, or an eruption of stucco. Granada is the first stop for Moorish relics, closely followed by Málaga, Córdoba, Almería, Seville and Las Alpujarras.

Cuisine

Spain's cuisine, particularly in Andalucía, draws heavily upon the food of North Africa where sweet spicy meat and starchy couscous are melded with Mediterranean ingredients. The Moors introduced many key ingredients into Spanish cooking: saffron, used in paella; almonds, used in Spanish desserts; and aubergines, present in the popular Andalucian tapa, *berenjenas con miel de caña* (aubergines with molasses). If you'd prefer the real thing, there are plenty of pure Moroccan restaurants in Andalucía, especially in Granada and Tarifa.

MOORISH HIGHLIGHTS

Granada Alhambra (p722), Albayzín (p731)

Córdoba Mezquita (p705), Madina Azahara (p713)

Seville Giralda (p637), Torre del Oro (p648)

Málaga Alcazaba (p754), Castillo de Gibralfaro (p754)

Almería Alcazaba (p785)

Las Alpujarras Berber-style houses in the village of Capileira (p746)

Shopping

Jamones Cano González FOOD
(☎958 85 86 32; www.jamonescanogonzalez.com; Calle Pista del Barrio Medio 18; ⏰10am-2pm & 5-7pm Mon-Fri, 11am-2pm & 4-8pm Sat, 11am-2pm Sun) Load up on Trevélez's celebrated ham at this small shop bursting with ham, cured meats and other local gourmet treats.

Getting There & Away

Three daily **Alsa** (☎902 42 22 42; www.alsa.es) buses make the long climb up to Trevélez from Granada (€7.96, 3¼ hours).

By car, the village is easily accessible via the A4132.

Costa Tropical

There's a hint of Italy's Amalfi Coast about the Costa Tropical, Granada province's 80km coastline. Named after its subtropical microclimate, it's far less developed than the Costa del Sol to the east and often dramatically beautiful, with dun-brown mountains cascading into the sea and whitewashed villages nestled into coves and bays. The main resorts of Almuñécar and Salobreña are popular summer destinations with long beaches, hilltop castles and handsome historic centres.

Almuñécar & La Herradura

POP 27,397

The main resort town on the Costa Tropical, Almuñécar heaves in summer as crowds of Spanish holidaymakers and northern European sun-seekers flock to its long pebble beaches and palm-fringed esplanade. Back from the seafront, it's not an obviously attractive place, but look beyond the dreary high-rises and you'll discover a picturesque *casco antiguo* (historic town centre) with narrow lanes, bar-flanked plazas and a striking hilltop castle.

Some 7km to the west, the neighbouring village of La Herradura maintains a more castaway feel, catering to a younger crowd of windsurfers and water-sports fans.

Sights

Peñón del Santo VIEWPOINT
(⏰7am-midnight May-Sep, to 10pm Oct-Apr) A rocky outcrop crowned by a large crucifix, the Peñón del Santo commands sweeping views of the town's seafront. To the west, the Playa de San Cristóbal is the best of Almuñécar's beaches, a strip of grey pebbles that catches the sun well into the evening. On the other side, Playa Puerta del Mar is the main eastern beach, backed by high-rise tower blocks.

Castillo de San Miguel CASTLE
(☎958 83 86 23; Explanada del Castillo; adult/child €2.35/1.60; ⏰10am-1.30pm & 6.30-9pm Tue-Sat Jul–mid-Sep, 10am-1.30pm & 5.30-7.30pm Tue-Sat Apr-Jun & mid-Sep–Oct, 10am-1.30pm & 4-6.30pm Tue-Sat Nov-Mar, 10am-1pm Sun year-round) Crowning the town, Almuñécar's impressive hilltop castle was built over Islamic and Roman fortifications by the conquering Christians in the 16th century. The hot, circuitous climb up to the entrance rewards with excellent views and an informative little museum. Don't forget to check out the skeleton in the dungeon: it's a reproduction of human remains discovered here.

Festivals & Events

Jazz en la Costa MUSIC
(www.jazzgranada.es; ⏰Jul) The biggest jazz festival on the Andalucian coast sees nightly performances by Spanish and international musicians in the **Parque Botánico El Majuelo** (Avenida de Europa, Almuñécar; ⏰8am-10pm) FREE.

Sleeping & Eating

Hotel Casablanca HOTEL €€
(☎958 63 55 75; www.hotelcasablancaalmunecar.com; Plaza de San Cristóbal 4; s €35-86, d €42-96; ❄📶) Convenient for both the beach and Almuñécar's lively centre, the Hotel Casablanca sports a distinctive Al-Andalus look and offers handsomely decorated rooms, some with sea views. For breakfast, available for about €7, or a relaxed afternoon drink, there's a ground-floor bar with tables outside on the plaza.

★ **Los Geráneos** ANDALUCIAN €€
(☎958 63 40 20; Placeta de la Rosa 4, Almuñécar; menú del día €15; ⏰1-5pm & 7.30-11pm Mon-Sat) With tables on a sunny cobbled plaza or beneath a low wood-beamed ceiling in the rustic interior, Los Geráneos makes a good first impression. Things only get better when the food arrives: zingy salads, fresh grilled fish tasting magically of the sea, and sweet, ripe melons. And all for €15 – magnificent.

WORTH A TRIP

WATER SPORTS IN LA HERRADURA

If you're craving a more remote beach scene than Almuñécar, or more activity, head 7km west to the small, horseshoe-shaped bay at La Herradura, where a younger crowd of windsurfers and water-sports enthusiasts congregate. On the beach, **Windsurf La Herradura** (958 64 01 43; www.windsurflaherradura.com; Paseo Andrés Segovia 34, La Herradura; windsurf rent/lesson €20/30; school 10.30am-8pm Easter-Oct, shop 10.30am-2pm & 5.30-8.30pm year-round) is a good point of reference, providing equipment rental, courses and lessons.

The waters around La Herradura offer good diving, with a varied seabed of seagrass, sand and rock flecked with caves, crevices and passages. To see for yourself, **Buceo La Herradura** (958 82 70 83; www.buceolaherradura.com; Puerto Marina del Este; dive plus equipment €48; 10.30am-4.30pm Mon, Wed-Fri, 9.30am-4.30pm Sat & Sun) is a reliable dive outfit, operating out of the marina at Punta de la Mona between Almuñécar and La Herradura.

La Ventura ANDALUCIAN **€€**
(958 88 23 78; Calle Alta del Mar 18; lunch menu €10, tasting menu €29.90; 1-4pm & 8-11.30pm Wed-Sun) A bit of a flamenco secret in Almuñécar and all the better for it, Ventura is best visited on Thursday, Friday or Sunday evenings when music and dance inflame the intimate atmosphere, providing a memorable accompaniment to solidly traditional Andalucian fare.

Information

Information Kiosk (958 61 60 70; Paseo del Altillo; 10am-1pm & 6.30-9pm Jul–mid-Sep) Just back from the seafront. Shorter hours in winter.

La Herradura Tourist Office (958 61 86 36; Centro Civico La Herradura; 10am-1pm & 5.45-8.15pm Tue-Sun Jul–mid-Sep) Can provide information on La Herradura and environs. Shorter hours in winter.

Main Tourist Office (958 63 11 25; www.turismoalmunecar.es; Avenida Europa; 10am-1pm & 6.30-9pm Jul–mid-Sep) A block back from the seafront, in the pink neo-Moorish Palacete de la Najarra. Shorter hours in winter.

Getting There & Away

Almuñécar Bus Station (958 63 01 40; Avenida Juan Carlos I 1) is north of the town centre. **Alsa** (902 42 22 42; www.alsa.es) services run to/from Granada (€8.34, 1½ hours, up to 12 daily), Málaga (€7.43, 1¾ to two hours, up to eight daily) and Almería (€11.80, 3½ hours, five daily).

There are also buses to La Herradura (€1.16, 15 minutes, up to 17 daily) and Órgiva (€4.68, 1¼ hours, one daily).

MÁLAGA PROVINCE

After decades of being pointedly ignored, particularly by tourists to the coastal resorts, hip, revitalised Málaga is now the Andalucian city everyone is talking about. Its 30-odd museums and edgy urban art scene are well matched by contemporary-chic dining choices, a stash of new boutique hotels and a shopping street voted one of the most stylish in Spain. Málaga is at its most vibrant during the annual feria, when the party atmosphere is infused with flamenco, *fino* (dry, straw-coloured sherry) and carafe-loads of fiesta spirit.

Each region of the province has equally fascinating diversity, from the mythical mountains of La Axarquía to the tourist-driven razzle-dazzle of the Costa del Sol. Inland are the *pueblos blancos* (white towns) and the under-appreciated, elegant old town of Antequera, with its nearby archaeological site and fabulous *porra antequera* (thick local soup).

Málaga

POP 569,000

If you think the Costa del Sol is soulless, you clearly haven't been to Málaga. Loaded with history and brimming with a youthful vigour that proudly acknowledges its multilayered past, the city that gave the world Picasso has transformed itself in spectacular fashion in the last decade, with half a dozen new art galleries, a radically rethought port area and a nascent art district called Soho. Not that Málaga was ever lacking in energy: the Spanish-to-the-core bar scene could put bags under the eyes of an insomniac

Málaga

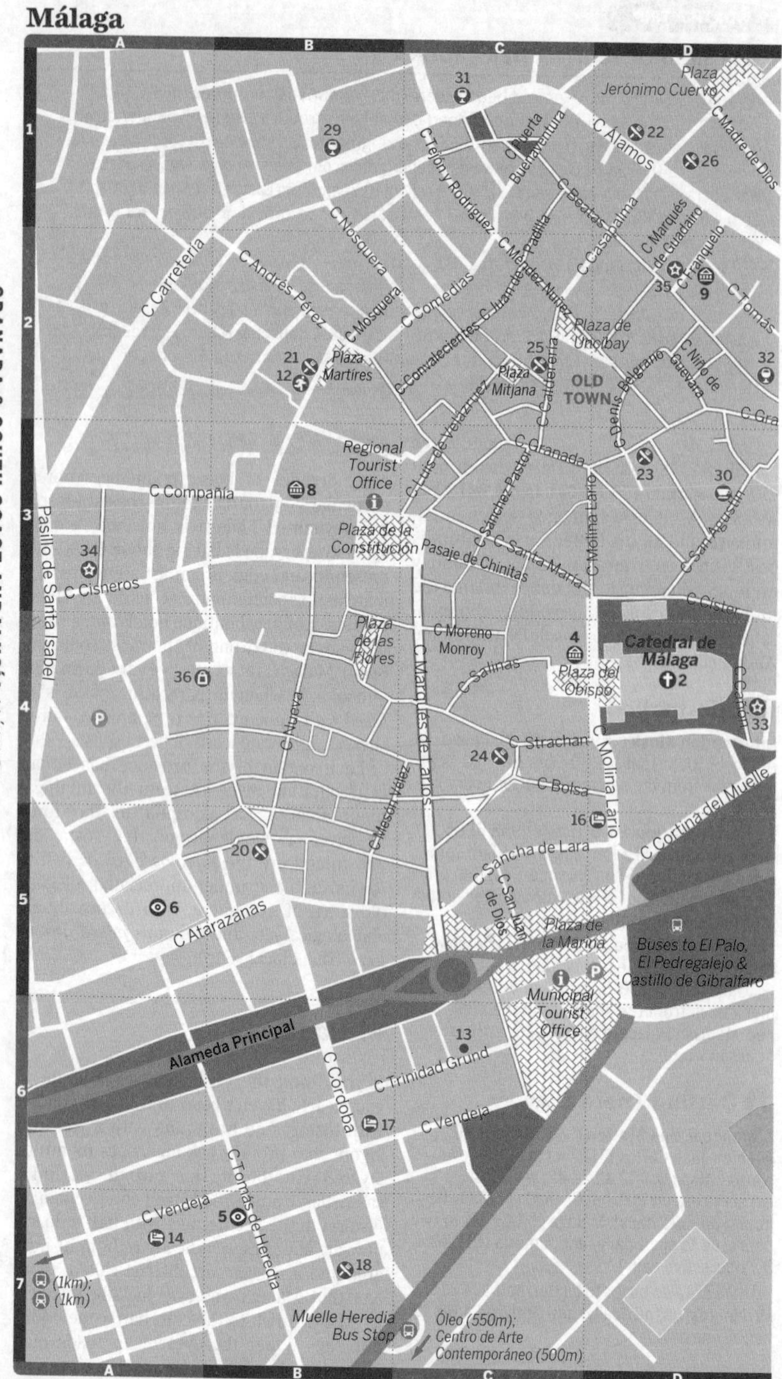

GRANADA & SOUTH COAST ANDALUCÍA MÁLAGA

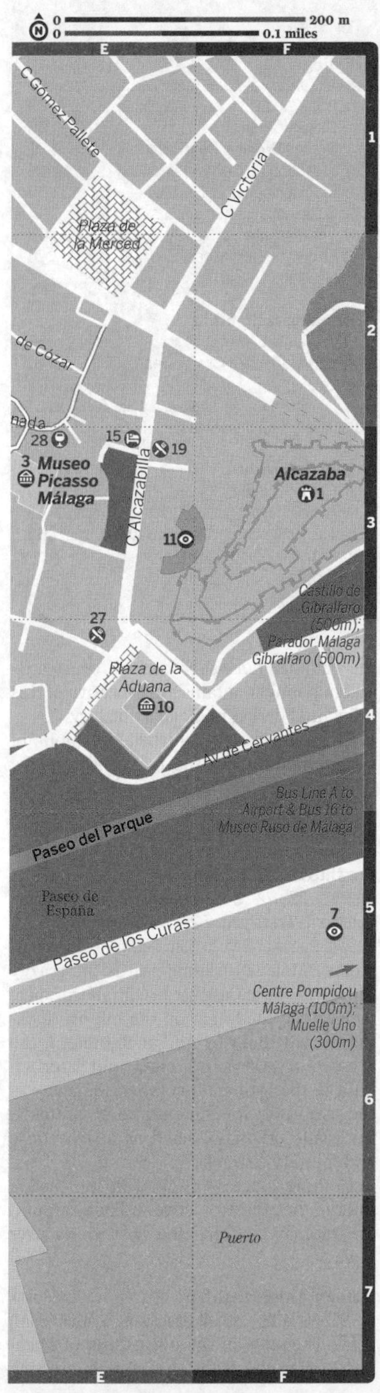

madrileño, while the food culture encompasses both Michelin stars and tastefully tatty fish shacks.

Come here for tapas washed down with sweet local wine, and stay in a creative boutique hotel sandwiched between a Roman amphitheatre, a Moorish fortress and the polychromatic Pompidou Centre, while you reflect on how eloquently Málaga has reinvented itself for the 21st century. Look out, Seville.

Sights

★Museo Picasso Málaga MUSEUM

(☎952 12 76 00; www.museopicassomalaga.org; Calle San Agustín 8; €7, incl temporary exhibition €10; ⊙10am-8pm Jul & Aug, to 7pm Mar-Jun, Sep & Oct, to 6pm Nov-Feb) This unmissable museum in the city of Picasso's birth provides a solid overview of the great master and his work, although, surprisingly, it only came to fruition in 2003 after more than 50 years of planning. The 200-plus works in the collection were donated and loaned to the museum by Christine Ruiz-Picasso (wife of Paul, Picasso's eldest son) and Bernard Ruiz-Picasso (Picasso's grandson) and catalogue the artist's sparkling career with a few notable gaps (the 'blue' and 'rose' periods are largely missing).

Nonetheless, numerous gems adorn the gallery's lily-white walls. Highlights include a painting of Picasso's sister Lola undertaken when the artist was only 13; sculptures made from clay, plaster and sheet metal; numerous sketches; a quick journey through cubism; and some interesting late works when Picasso developed an obsession with musketeers. The museum, which is housed in the 16th-century Buenavista Palace, has a excellent cafe and holds revolving temporary exhibitions.

★Catedral de Málaga CATHEDRAL

(☎952 21 59 17; www.malagacatedral.com; Calle Molina Lario; cathedral & Ars Málaga €6, incl roof €10; ⊙10am-9pm Mon-Fri, to 6.30pm Sat, 2-6.30pm Sun Apr-Oct, closes 6.30pm daily Nov-Mar) Málaga's elaborate cathedral was started in the 16th century on the site of the former mosque. Of the mosque, only the **Patio de los Naranjos** survives, a small courtyard of fragrant orange trees.

Inside, the fabulous domed ceiling soars 40m into the air, while the vast colonnaded nave houses an enormous cedar-wood choir. Aisles give access to 15 chapels with

Málaga

gorgeous 18th-century retables and religious art. It's worth taking the guided tour up to the *cubiertas* (roof) to enjoy panoramic city views.

Building the cathedral was an epic project that took some 200 years. Such was the project's cost that by 1782 it was decided that work would stop. One of the two bell towers was left incomplete, hence the cathedral's well-worn nickname, La Manquita (The One-Armed Lady). The ticket price includes use of an audio guide as well as entry to the **Ars Málaga** (www.arsmalaga.es; Plaza del Obispo; €4, incl cathedral €6; 10am-9pm Mon-Fri, to 6.30pm Sat, 2-6.30pm Sun Apr-Oct, closes 6.30pm daily Nov-Mar) museum of religious art and African artefacts in the Bishop's House opposite.

★Alcazaba CASTLE

(630 932987; www.malagaturismo.com; Calle Alcazabilla; €2.20, incl Castillo de Gibralfaro €3.55; 9.30am-8pm Tue-Sun) No time to visit Granada's Alhambra? Then Málaga's Alcazaba can provide a taster. The entrance is next to the Roman amphitheatre, from where a meandering path climbs amid lush greenery: crimson bougainvillea, lofty palms, fragrant jasmine bushes and rows of orange trees. Extensively restored, this palace-fortress dates from the 11th-century Moorish period; the caliphal horseshoe arches, courtyards and bubbling fountains are evocative of this influential period in Málaga's history.

There are various unlabelled exhibits of Islamic pottery, but the main joys are the building itself, the gardens and the views. The dreamy **Patio de la Alberca** is especially redolent of the Alhambra.

Castillo de Gibralfaro CASTLE

(952 22 72 30; www.malagaturismo.com; Camino de Gibralfaro; €2.20, incl Alcazaba €3.55; 9am-9pm Apr-Sep, to 6pm Oct-Mar) One remnant of Málaga's Islamic past is the craggy ramparts of the Castillo de Gibralfaro, spectacularly located high on the hill overlooking the city. Built by Abd ar-Rahman I, the 8th-century Córdoban emir, and later rebuilt in the 14th century when Málaga was the main port for the emirate of Granada, the castle originally acted as a lighthouse and military barracks.

Nothing much is original in the castle's interior, but the protective walkway around the ramparts affords the best views over Málaga.

Roman Amphitheatre LANDMARK

(951 50 11 15; Calle Alcazabilla 8; 10am-8pm) FREE The story of the unearthing of Málaga's Roman theatre is almost as interesting

as the theatre itself. Dating from the time of Augustus (1st century AD), it was rediscovered in 1951 by workers building the foundations for a new Casa de Cultura. Today the theatre sits fully exposed beneath the walls of the Alcazaba. A small interpretive centre next door outlines its history and displays a few artefacts shovelled from its crusty foundations.

Museo de Málaga MUSEUM
(☎951 29 40 51; Plaza de la Aduana; ⏲9am-3pm Tue-Sun mid-Jun–mid-Sep, to 8pm Tue-Sun mid-Sep–mid-Jun) FREE Reopened in Málaga's neoclassical Palacio de Aduana in December 2016 following a full renovation, this museum houses art and archaeological collections. The 1st-floor fine-arts collection, kept in storage for nearly two decades, consists primarily of 19th-century Andalucian landscape and genre paintings, plus more modern work from the 'Generation of '27'. The extensive archaeological collection, bequeathed to the city by the noble Loring-Heredia family, ranges from Neolithic shards uncovered in the nearby Cueva de Nerja (p768) to a headless statue of a Roman noblewoman.

Museo de Arte Flamenco MUSEUM
(☎952 22 13 80; www.museoflamencojuanbreva.com; Calle Franquelo 4; donation €1; ⏲10am-2pm Mon-Sat) Fabulously laid out over two floors in the HQ of Málaga's oldest and most prestigious *peña* (private flamenco club), this collection of fans, costumes, posters and other flamenco paraphernalia is testament to the city's illustrious flamenco scene.

Museo Carmen Thyssen MUSEUM
(www.carmenthyssenmalaga.org; Calle Compañía 10; €6, incl temporary exhibition €9; ⏲10am-8pm Tue-Sun) Located in an aesthetically renovated 16th-century palace in the heart of the city's former Moorish quarter, this extensive collection concentrates on 19th-century Spanish and Andalucian art by painters such as Joaquín Sorolla y Bastida and Ignacio Zuloaga.

MAUS AREA
(Málaga Arte Urbano en el Soho; www.mausmalaga.com) The antithesis of Málaga's prestigious world-class art museums is refreshingly down-to-earth MAUS, a grassroots movement born out of an influx of street artists to the area. The result is a total transformation of the formerly rundown district between the city centre and the port – now called Soho, the district has edgy contemporary murals several stories high, as well as arty cafes, ethnic restaurants and street markets.

Centro de Arte Contemporáneo MUSEUM
(Contemporary Art Museum; www.cacmalaga.org; Calle Alemania; ⏲9am-2pm & 5-9pm Tue-Sun) FREE The contemporary-art museum is housed in a skilfully converted 1930s wholesale market on the river estuary. The bizarre triangular floor plan of the building has been retained, with its cubist lines and shapes brilliantly showcasing the modern art on display. Painted entirely white, windows and all, the museum hosts temporary shows featuring the work of well-known contemporary artists and has an obvious Spanish bias. It's usually filled with plenty of spectacularly weird exhibits.

Centre Pompidou Málaga MUSEUM
(☎951 92 62 00; www.centrepompidou.es; Pasaje Doctor Carrillo Casaux, Muelle Uno; €7, incl temporary exhibition €9; ⏲9.30am-8pm Wed-Mon) Opened in 2015 in the port, this offshoot of Paris' Pompidou Centre is housed in a low-slung modern building crowned by a playful multicoloured cube. The permanent exhibition includes the extraordinary *Ghost,* by Kader Attia, depicting rows of Muslim women bowed in prayer and created from domestic aluminium foil, plus works by such modern masters as Frida Kahlo, Francis Bacon and Antoni Tàpies. There are also audiovisual installations, talking 'heads' and temporary exhibitions.

Muelle Uno PORT
(P) The city's long-beleaguered port area underwent a radical rethink in 2013 and was redesigned to cater to the increase in cruise-ship passengers to the city. Wide quayside walkways now embellish Muelle 1 and Muelle 2, which are lined by palm trees and backed by shops, restaurants, bars and a small kid-focused aquarium, the **Museo Alborania** (☎951 60 01 08; www.museoalborania.com; Palmeral de las Sopresas, Muelle 2; adult/child €7/5; ⏲11am-2pm & 5-8pm Jul-10 Sep, 10.30am-2pm & 4.30-6.30pm 11 Sep-Jun; 👪).

Activities

Hammam Al-Andalus HAMAM
(☎952 21 50 18; www.hammamalandalus.com; Plaza de los Mártires 5; baths €30; ⏲10am-midnight) These Moorish-style baths provide

malagueños with a luxurious marble-clad setting in which to enjoy the same relaxation benefits as those offered by similar facilities in Granada and Córdoba. Massages are also available.

Tours

★Málaga Bike Tours CYCLING

(☎606 978513; www.malagabiketours.eu; Calle Trinidad Grund 1; tours €25; ⏲10am-8pm Apr-Sep, to 7pm Oct-Mar;) One of the best tours in town and certainly the best on two wheels. Málaga Bike Tours was a pioneer in city cycling when it was set up a decade ago. Its perennially popular excursions, including the classic **City Bike Tour**, are available in at least five languages, with kids' seats on offer if you're bringing the family.

Daily tours leave from outside the municipal tourist office in Plaza de la Marina at 10am. Reservations are required. Book at least 24 hours ahead.

Alternatively, you can rent your own bike from €5 for four hours.

Festivals & Events

Semana Santa HOLY WEEK

Each night from Palm Sunday to Good Friday, six or seven *cofradías* (brotherhoods) bear holy images for several hours through the city, watched by large crowds.

Feria de Málaga FAIR

(⏲mid-Aug) Málaga's nine-day feria, launched by a huge fireworks display, is the most ebullient of Andalucía's summer fairs. It resembles an exuberant Rio-style street party, with plenty of flamenco and *fino* (dry and straw-coloured sherry); head for the city centre to be in the thick of it.

At night, festivities switch to large fairgrounds and nightly rock and flamenco shows at Cortijo de Torres, 3km southwest of the city centre; special buses run from all over the city.

Sleeping

Hotels have been another beneficiary of Málaga's 21st-century renaissance. Boutique apartments, rooftop swimming pools, funky hostels and throwback Moorish guesthouses are here in abundance.

★Dulces Dreams HOSTEL €

(☎951 35 78 69; www.dulcesdreamshostel.com; Plaza de los Mártires 6; r incl breakfast €45-60;) Managed by an enthusiastic young team, the rooms at Dulces (sweet) Dreams are, appropriately, named after desserts; 'Cupcake' is a good choice, with a terrace overlooking the imposing red-brick church across the way. This is an older building, so there's no lift and the rooms vary in size, but they're bright and whimsically decorated, using recycled materials as much as possible.

Feel Málaga Hostel HOSTEL €

(☎952 22 28 32; www.feelhostels.com; Calle Vendeja 25; d €45, with shared bathroom €35, dm from €16; @) Located within a suitcase trundle of the city-centre train station, the accommodation here is clean and well equipped,

ARTISTIC REVIVAL

Befitting Picasso's birthplace, Málaga has an art collection to rival those of Seville and Granada, particularly in the field of modern art, where galleries and workshops continue to push the envelope. It wasn't always thus.

Little more than 15 years ago, Málaga's art scene was patchy and understated. The first big coup came in 2003, when, after 50 years of on-off discussion, the city finally got around to honouring its most famous son with the opening of the Museo Picasso Málaga (p753). More galleries followed, some focusing on notable *malagueños* such as Jorge Rando and Félix Revello de Toro, others – such as the Museo Carmen Thyssen (p755), which shines a light on *costumbrismo* (Spanish folk art) – taking in a broader sweep of Spanish painting. Then, in 2015, Málaga earned the right to be called a truly international art city when it opened offshoot galleries of St Petersburg's prestigious Russian State Museum and Paris' Pompidou Centre. Around the same time, edgy street artists put forward the idea of MAUS (p755), an urban-renewal project that has fostered a free creative space in the Soho neighbourhood for street and graffiti artists.

The finishing touches to this colourful canvas were added in December 2016: after 20 years in the dark, Málaga's 2000-piece-strong fine-arts collection was reinstated in the city's beautifully restored old customs house (p755) down by the port.

with a choice of doubles and shared rooms. The downstairs communal area has a colourful seaside look, with striped deck chairs and mini football; bathrooms sport classy mosaic tiles; and the top-floor kitchen has all the essentials for whipping up a decent meal.

★Hotel Boutique Teatro Romano BOUTIQUE HOTEL €€
(☎951 20 44 38; www.hotelteatroromano.com; Calle Alcazabilla 7; r €117-130; ❄📶) One in a new wave of plush new boutique offerings in Málaga, this place overlooks the Roman theatre (p754) and has chocolate-brown corridors leading to sparkling white rooms so clean they look as if they've never been used. The whole place is modern, well managed, and studded with interesting design accents. The healthy breakfasts in the bright on-site cafe are a bonus.

★Molina Lario HOTEL €€
(☎952 06 20 02; www.hotelmolinalario.com; Calle Molina Lario 20-22; r €125-137; ❄📶🏊) Perfect for romancing couples, this hotel has a sophisticated, contemporary feel, with spacious rooms decorated in a cool palette of earthy colours. There are crisp white linens, marshmallow-soft pillows and tasteful paintings, plus a fabulous rooftop terrace and pool with views to the sea. Situated within confessional distance of the catedral (p753).

Soho Málaga Boutique Hotel BOUTIQUE HOTEL €€
(☎952 22 40 79; https://sohomalaga.sohohoteles.com; Calle Córdoba 5; r €86-118; ❄📶) The renaissance of the Soho neighbourhood is reflected vividly in hotels like this one, which has added slick new rooms to a handsome 19th-century building. Enjoy plush bathrooms and bedside espresso machines alongside older features such as large French windows and cast-iron balconies. Huge photo prints of Málaga are hung in each room, and there's a great little cafe downstairs.

Parador Málaga Gibralfaro HISTORIC HOTEL €€€
(☎952 22 19 02; www.parador.es; Castillo de Gibralfaro; r incl breakfast €130-155; P❄📶🏊) Perched next to Málaga's Moorish castle (p754) on the pine-forested Gibralfaro, the city's stone-built *parador* (luxurious state-owned hotel) hums with a sultan-like essence. Like most Spanish *paradores*, the kick is more in the setting and facilities than the rooms, which are modern and business-like. Most have spectacular views from their terraces.

You can dine at the excellent terrace restaurant, even if you're not a hotel guest.

Eating

Málaga has a staggering number of tapas bars and restaurants, particularly around the historic centre (more than 400 at last count), so finding a place to eat poses no problem.

Dulces Dreams Cafeteria CAFE €
(Plaza de los Mártires 6; breakfast €5-7; ⏲8am-10pm) Located in an intimate traffic-free square, one of Málaga's great breakfast spots offers muesli, fruit juice, coffee, and tomato on toast. You might throw all your health commitments aside when you come back for an afternoon *merienda* – it's hard to go past the cake case.

Casa Aranda CAFE €
(www.casa-aranda.net; Calle Herrería del Rey; churro €0.45; ⏲8am-3pm Mon-Sat; 👪) Casa Aranda is in a narrow alleyway next to the market and, since 1932, has been *the* place in town to enjoy chocolate and churros (tubular-shaped doughnuts). The cafe has taken over the whole street, with several outlets overseen by an army of mainly elderly, white-shirted waiters who welcome everyone like an old friend (and most are).

Tapeo de Cervantes TAPAS €
(www.eltapeodecervantes.com; Calle Cárcer 8; media raciones €4.50-8, raciones €9-16; ⏲1.30-3.30pm & 7.30-11.30pm Tue-Sat, 7.30-11.30pm Sun) The original Cervantes bar-restaurant (there are now four) is a little more boisterous and crowded than the Mesón around the corner, although the menu is almost identical – ie the best in the city.

★El Mesón de Cervantes TAPAS, ARGENTINE €€
(☎952 21 62 74; www.elmesondecervantes.com; Calle Álamos 11; media raciones €4.50-8, raciones €9-16; ⏲7pm-midnight Wed-Mon) Cervantes started as a humble tapas bar run by expat Argentine Gabriel Spatz but has now expanded into four bar-restaurants (each with a slightly different bent), all within a block of each other. This one is the HQ, where pretty much everything on the menu is a show-stopper – lamb stew with couscous, pumpkin and mushroom risotto, and, boy, the grilled octopus!

LOCAL KNOWLEDGE

TAPAS TRAIL

The pleasures of Málaga are essentially undemanding, easy to arrange and cheap. One of the best is a slow crawl around the city's numerous tapas bars and old bodegas (cellars).

La Tranca Drinking in this slim, always busy bar is a physical contact sport, with small tapas plates passed over people's heads.

El Piyayo (952 22 90 57; Calle Granada 36; raciones €6-11; 12.30pm-midnight) A popular, traditionally tiled bar and restaurant famed for its *pescaitos fritos* (fried fish) and typical local tapas, including wedges of crumbly Manchego cheese, the ideal accompaniment to a glass of hearty Rioja wine.

Uvedoble Taberna (www.uvedobletaberna.com; Calle Císter 15; tapas €2.70; 12.30-4pm & 8pm-midnight Mon-Sat;) If you're seeking something a little more contemporary, head to this popular spot with its innovative take on traditional tapas.

Pepa y Pepe (615 656984; Calle Calderería 9; tapas €1.30-2, raciones €3.60-5.50; 12.30-4.30pm & 7.30pm-12.30am) A snug tapas bar that brims with young diners enjoying tapas such as *calamares fritos* (battered squid) and fried green peppers.

Gorki (952 22 70 00; www.grupogorki.com; Calle Strachan 6; mains €10-13; noon-4pm & 8pm-midnight) A tastefully decorated tapas bar for enjoying sophisticated small bites such as mini burgers and sweetbreads encased in light, flaky pastry.

★Óleo FUSION €€

(952 21 90 62; www.oleorestaurante.es; Edificio CAC, Calle Alemania; mains €16-22; 1.15-4.30pm & 8.30pm-midnight Wed-Sat, 1.15-4.30pm Tue & Sun;) Located at the city's contemporary-art museum (p755) with white-on-white minimalist decor, Óleo provides diners with the unusual choice of Mediterranean or Asian food, with some subtle combinations such as duck breast with a side of seaweed with hoisin, as well as more purist Asian and gourmet palate-ticklers such as candied roasted piglet.

Batik MODERN SPANISH €€

(952 22 10 45; www.batikmalaga.com; Calle Alcazabilla 12; mains €9-16; 12.30-4pm & 8pm-midnight;) With Málaga's Alcazaba (p754) posing like the Alhambra in the background, this classy but not-too-posh restaurant (you can opt for stools rather than chairs) is where *malagueños* come to impress a date. The food is about taste and arty presentation rather than quantity, but it packs a punch: octopus with puréed squash and green *mole* is among the whimsical creations.

Al Yamal MOROCCAN €€

(Calle Blasco de Garay 7; mains €13-16; noon-3pm & 7-11pm Mon-Sat) Moroccan restaurants aren't as ubiquitous in Málaga as they are in Granada, but, in the heart of the now trendy Soho district, this family-run place serves the authentic stuff, including tagines, couscous, hummus and *kefta* (meatballs). The street profile looks unpromising, but the tiny dining room has six cosy booths decorated with vivid Moroccan fabrics and a trickling fountain.

El Balneario de los Baños del Carmen SEAFOOD €€

(www.elbalneariomalaga.com; Calle Bolivia 40, La Malagueta; mains €8-18; 8.30am-1am Sun-Thu, to 2.30am Fri & Sat; P) El Balneario is a wonderful place to sit outside on a balmy evening and share a plate of prawns or grilled sardines, along with some long, cold beverages. Built in 1918 to cater to Málaga's bourgeoisie, it's rekindling its past as one of the city's most celebrated venues for socialising.

Drinking & Nightlife

The international brigade has yet to cotton on to the fact that Málaga has one of the raciest nightlife scenes in Spain (and that's saying something). The city might not be as big as Madrid, but it's just as fun. The pedestrianised old town is the main hive, especially around Plaza de la Constitución and Plaza de la Merced.

★La Tetería TEAHOUSE

(www.la-teteria.com; Calle San Agustín 9; speciality teas €2.50; 9am-midnight Mon-Sat) There are numerous *teterías* in Málaga, but only one *La* Tetería. While it's less Moorish than some of its more atmospheric brethren, it still sells a wide selection of fruity teas, backed by a range of rich cakes. Along with the cafe's location next to the Museo Picasso Málaga (p753), this ensures that the place is usually close to full.

La Tranca BAR
(www.latranca.es; Calle Carretería 93; 12.30pm-2am Mon-Sat, to 4pm Sun) You'll have to elbow your way through the melee to get served in La Tranca, a slim, old-fashioned bar with a rock-band-like following where discarded napkins litter the floor, obscure vinyl sleeves decorate the walls and loud outbursts of song aren't unusual.

La Madriguera Craft Beer CRAFT BEER
(951 71 62 11; Calle Carretería 73; noon-4pm & 6pm-1am Mon-Thu, noon-3am Sat & Sun) Craft beer barely registered in Spain a few years ago, but the 'Rabbit Hole', as its name translates, is riding a new wave with daily listings of a dozen ever-changing craft beers and an equal number of more permanent light bites to soak them up. A wall chart honours the feats of punters past – 11 pints appears to be the record.

Bodegas El Pimpi BAR
(www.elpimpi.com; Calle Granada 62; noon-2am Mon-Fri, to 3am Sat & Sun;) This rambling bar is an institution in this town. The interior encompasses a warren of rooms, and there's a courtyard and open terrace overlooking the Roman amphitheatre (p754). Walls are decorated with historic feria posters and photos of visitors past, while the enormous barrels are signed by more well-known passers-by, including Tony Blair and Antonio Banderas. Tapas and meals are also available.

Los Patios de Beatas WINE BAR
(952 21 03 50; www.lospatiosdebeatas.com; Calle Beatas 43; 1-5pm & 8pm-midnight Mon-Sat, 1-6pm Sun;) Two 18th-century mansions have metamorphosed into this sumptuous space where you can sample fine wines from a selection reputed to be the most extensive in town. Stained-glass windows and beautiful resin tables inset with mosaics and shells add to the overall art-infused atmosphere. Innovative tapas and *raciones* (full-plate servings) are also on offer.

☆ Entertainment

★ Kelipe FLAMENCO
(692 829885; www.kelipe.net; Muro de Puerta Nueva 10; €25; shows 9.30pm Thu-Sat) There are many flamenco clubs springing up all over Andalucía, but few are as soul-stirring as Kelipe. Not only are the musicianship and dancing of the highest calibre, but the talented performers create an intimate feel and a genuine connection with the audience.

Tablao Flamenco Los Amayas FLAMENCO
(686 936804; www.flamencomalagacentro.com; Calle Beatas 21; €25; shows 7pm & 9pm) An agreeable performance space on the 1st floor of a slightly faded Málaga mansion with plenty of grandiose touches sets the tone for some raucous music and dance provided by a long-standing flamenco family hailing from Granada.

Clarence Jazz Club LIVE MUSIC
(951 91 80 87; www.clarencejazzclub.com; Calle Cañón 5; 8pm-2am Wed & Thu, 4pm-4am Fri & Sat) American-style jazz club across from the cathedral with some quality concerts and some freer jams, usually on Sunday. It's advisable to reserve a table at weekends. Prices vary, but €5 is the average.

Shopping

The chic, marble-clad Calle Marqués de Larios is increasingly home to designer stores and boutiques. In the surrounding streets are family-owned small shops in handsomely restored old buildings, selling everything from flamenco dresses to local sweet Málaga wine. Don't miss the fabulous daily **Mercado Atarazanas** (Calle Atarazanas; market 8am-3pm Mon-Sat; P).

La Recova ARTS & CRAFTS
(www.larecova.es; Pasaje Nuestra Señora de los Dolores de San Juan; 9.30am-1.30pm & 5-8pm Mon-Thu, 9.30am-8pm Fri, 10am-2pm Sat) Seek out this intriguing Aladdin's cave of an art, crafts and antique shop selling traditional *sevillana* tiles, handmade jewellery, antique irons, textiles and much more. It also has a small local bar tucked into the corner, handy for enjoying a beer between browsing.

Information

Municipal Tourist Office (951 92 60 20; www.malagaturismo.com; Plaza de la Marina; 9am-8pm Mar-Sep, to 6pm Oct-Feb) Offers a range of city maps and booklets. It also operates information kiosks at the Alcazaba entrance (Calle Alcazabilla), at the main train station (Explanada de la Estación), on Plaza de la Merced and on the eastern beaches (El Palo and La Malagueta).

Regional Tourist Office (Plaza de la Constitución 7; ⌚9.30am-7.30pm Mon-Fri, 10am-7pm Sat, 10am-2pm Sun) Located in a noble 18th-century former Jesuit college with year-round art exhibitions, this small tourist office carries a range of information on all of Málaga province, including maps of the regional cities.

Getting There & Away

AIR

Málaga airport (AGP; ☎952 04 88 38; www.aena.es), the main international gateway to Andalucía, is 9km southwest of the city centre. It is a major hub in southern Spain, serving top global carriers as well as budget airlines

BUS

The **bus station** (☎952 35 00 61; www.estabus.emtsam.es; Paseo de los Tilos) is 1km southwest of the city centre and has links to all major cities in Spain. The main bus lines are **Alsa** (☎952 34 17 38; www.alsa.es) and **Portillo** (☎91 272 28 32; www.avanzabus.com).

Buses to the Costa del Sol (east and west) also usually stop at the more central **Muelle Heredia bus stop**.

Destinations include the following; note that the prices listed are the minimum quoted for the route.

DESTINATION	COST (€)	DURATION (HR)	FREQUENCY (DAILY)
Almería	19	4¾	8
Cádiz	27	4	3
Córdoba	12	3-4	4
Granada	12	2	18
Jaén	20	3¼	4
Madrid airport	45	10	5
Seville	19	2¾	6

TRAIN

Málaga María Zambrano Train Station (☎902 43 23 43; www.renfe.com; Explanada de la Estación; ⌚5am-12.45am) is near the bus station, 15 minutes' walk from the city centre. Destinations include Córdoba (€27.50, one hour, 18 daily), Seville (€24, 2¾ hours, 11 daily) and Madrid (€80, 2½ hours, 17 daily). Note that for Córdoba and Seville the daily schedule includes fast AVE trains at roughly double the cost.

Getting Around

TO/FROM THE AIRPORT

Bus line A to the city centre (€3, 20 minutes) leaves from outside the arrivals hall every 20 minutes, from 7am to midnight. The bus to the airport leaves from the eastern end of Paseo del Parque, and from outside the bus and train stations, about every half-hour from 6.30am to 11.30pm.

Trains run every 20 minutes from 6.50am to 11.54pm to María Zambrano station, and Málaga-Centro station beside the Río Guadalmedina. Departures from the city to the airport are every 20 minutes from 5.30am to 11.30pm.

A taxi to the city centre costs between €20 and €25.

BUS

Useful buses around town (€1.35 for all trips around the centre) include bus 16 to the **Museo Ruso de Málaga**, bus 34 to **El Pedregalejo and El Palo**, and bus 35 to Castillo de Gibralfaro, all departing from points on Paseo del Parque.

Costa del Sol

Regularly derided but perennially popular, Spain's famous 'sun coast' is a chameleonic agglomeration of end-to-end resort towns that were once (hard to believe) mere fishing villages. Development in the last 60 years has been far-reaching and not always subtle, throwing up a disjointed muddle of *urbanizaciones*, each with its own niche. Torremolinos is a popular gay resort, Benalmádena plugs theme parks and aquariums, Fuengirola draws families and water-sport lovers, Marbella is loudly rich and partial to big yachts and golf, while Estepona maintains a semblance of its former Spanish self. Take your pick.

Torremolinos & Benalmádena

POP 136,000

Once a small coastal village dotted with *torres* (towers) and *molinos* (watermills), 'Terrible Torre' became a byword for tacky package holidays in the 1970s, when it welcomed tourism on an industrial scale and morphed into a magnet for lager-swilling Brits whose command of Spanish rarely got beyond the words '*dos cervezas, por favor*'. But times, they are a-changing. Torre has grown up and widened its reach. These days the town attracts a far wider cross-section of people, including trendy clubbers, beach-loving families, gay visitors and, yes, even some Spanish tourists. Waiting for them is an insomniac nightlife, 7km of unsullied sand and a huge array of hotels, most of which subscribe to an architectural style best described as 'disastrous'.

Benalmádena, Torre's western twin, is more of the same with a couple of added quirks: a large marina designed as a kind of homage to Gaudí and a giant Buddhist stupa.

Sights

Casa de los Navajas HISTORIC BUILDING
(Calle del Bajondillo, Torremolinos; 11am-2pm & 6-8pm) FREE Impossible to miss in the concrete jungle of Torremolinos is this neo-Mudéjar beauty, a mini palace that formerly belonged to a local sugar baron, António Navajas. Originally constructed in 1925 in a style not dissimilar to that of Seville's Plaza de España, the house was renovated in 2014 and subsequently opened to the public. While there's no specific museum here, the terraced gardens, detailed architecture and sweeping views from the upstairs balconies are all impressive.

La Carihuela BEACH
(Torremolinos) La Carihuela, Torremolinos' most western beach, stretching from a small rocky outcrop (La Punta) to Benalmádena, is a former fishing district and one of the few parts of town that hasn't suffered rampant over-development. The beachside promenade is lined with low-rise shops, bars and restaurants, and is one of the most popular destinations for *malagueños* to enjoy fresh seafood at weekends.

Buddhist Stupa MUSEUM, MONUMENT
(Benalmádena Pueblo; 10am-2pm & 3.30-6.30pm Tue-Sat, 10am-7.30pm Sun; P) FREE The largest Buddhist stupa in Europe is in Benalmádena Pueblo. It rises up, majestically out of place, on the outskirts of the village, surrounded by new housing and with sweeping coastal views. The lofty interior is lined with exquisitely executed devotional paintings.

Activities

Tivoli World AMUSEMENT PARK
(www.tivolicostadelsol.com; Avenida de Tivoli, Benalmádena; €8, Supertivolino ticket €15; 6pm-1am summer;) The oldest and largest amusement park in Málaga province, with various rides and slides, as well as daily dance, flamenco and children's events. Consider the good-value 'Supertivolino' ticket, which covers admission and unlimited access to some 35 rides.

Sleeping & Eating

★ **Hostal Guadalupe** HOSTAL €€
(952 38 19 37; www.hostalguadalupe.com; Calle del Peligro 15, Torremolinos; s €57-63, d €66-87, 3/4/5-person apt €118/144/171;) At the bottom of the staircases that lead down to Torre's main beach is this nugget of old Spain that sits like a wonderful anachronism amid the concrete jungle. Enter through a delightful tiled tavern and ascend to plain but comfortable rooms, several with terraces overlooking the sea. There's also a couple of apartments with kitchen facilities for longer stays.

★ **El Gato Lounge** SEAFOOD €
(951 25 15 09; www.elgatolounge.com; Paseo Marítimo 1; mains €5-10; 10am-late) Gato Lounge tries to be a little different from the other places on the beach, so you won't find the default sardines here. The menu leans towards international dishes with a bit of Asian flair: Thai fish cakes and Japanese carpaccio. The relaxing beach-facing interior has a luxuriant allure, and the cocktails and highly attentive staff mean most people linger.

La Zoca SEAFOOD €€
(95 238 59 25; www.restaurantelazoca.es; Calle Bulto 61, La Carihuela; mains €15-20; 12.30-5pm & 7.30pm-midnight;) Families, take note: this seaside restaurant has a playground across the promenade. The emphasis here is on seafood such as *gambas pil-pil* (prawns in a spicy oil-based sauce) and rice-based dishes (with five to choose from). The place gets packed with rowdy Spanish families on Sunday, so that's not the time for an intimate *tête a deux*.

Information

The main **tourist office** (951 95 43 79; https://turismotorremolinos.es; Plaza de Andalucía, Torremolinos; 9.30am-6pm) is in the town centre. There are additional tourist kiosks at **Playa Bajondillo** (Playa Bajondillo; 10am-2pm) and **La Carihuela** (Playa Carihuela; 10am-2pm).

Getting There & Away

BUS

Portillo (91 272 28 32; www.avanzabus.com) runs services to Málaga (€2.50, 25 minutes, 14 daily), Marbella (€5.90, 1¼ hours, 24 daily) and Ronda (€13, 2½ hours, six daily).

TRAIN

Trains run on the Renfe *cercanías* line to **Torremolinos** (Avenida Palma de Mallorca 53) and **Arroyo de la Miel-Benalmádena** (Avenida de la Estación 3) every 20 minutes from Málaga (€2.05, 18 minutes) from 5.30am to 10.30pm, continuing on to the final stop, Fuengirola (€2.05, 22 minutes).

Fuengirola

POP 77,500

Fuengirola is a crowded beach town decorated with utilitarian apartment buildings, but, despite half a century of rampant development, it retains a few redeeming qualities. Check out the beach – all 7km of it – adorned with a 10th-century Moorish castle. The town also has a large foreign-resident population, many of whom arrived in the '60s – and stayed (yes, there are a few grey ponytails around).

Sights

Bioparc ZOO

(952 66 63 01; www.bioparcfuengirola.es; Avenida Camilo José Cela; adult/child €20/15; 10am-sunset; P) This zoo has spacious enclosures and treats its animals very well. It runs conservation and breeding programs as well as educational activities. The grounds also have a bat cave, a reptile enclosure, cafes and a large gift shop.

Eating

★ Arte y Cocina MEDITERRANEAN €€

(952 47 54 41; Calle Cervantes 15; mains €11-20; 7.30-11.30pm Tue-Sun;) The Italian-inflected food here is as fresh as the decor. Expect handmade pasta, and arty renditions of rabbit ravioli and creamy prawn-and-courgette risotto.

Information

Tourist Office (952 46 74 57; Paseo Jesús Santos Rein; 9.30am-6pm Mon-Fri, 10am-2pm Sat & Sun;) Has a wealth of information on the town.

Getting There & Away

BUS

Portillo (91 272 28 32; www.avanzabus.com) runs bus services to Málaga (€4.25, 50 minutes, 15 daily), Estepona (€6.70, 1¾ hours, 10 daily) and Marbella (€4.25, 30 minutes, four daily). Fuengirola's **bus station** is half a block from the train station.

TRAIN

Trains (Avenida Jesús Santos Rein) on the Renfe *cercanías* line run every 20 minutes to Málaga (€3.60, 45 minutes) from 6.20am to 12.40am, with stops including the airport and Torremolinos.

Marbella

POP 140,750

The Costa del Sol's bastion of bling is, like most towns along this stretch of coast, a two-sided coin. Standing centre stage in the tourist showroom is the 'Golden Mile', a conspicuously extravagant collection of star-studded clubs, shiny restaurants and expensive hotels stretching as far as Puerto Banús, the flashiest marina on the coast, where black-tinted Mercs slide along a quay populated by luxury yachts.

But Marbella has other, less ostentatious attractions. Its natural setting is magnificent, sheltered by the beautiful Sierra Blanca mountains, while its surprisingly attractive *casco antiguo* (old town) is replete with narrow lanes and well-tended flower boxes.

Long before Marbella starting luring golfers, zillionaires and retired Latin American dictators, it was home to Phoenicians, Visigoths, Romans and Moors. One of the joys of a visit to the modern city is trying to root out their legacy.

Sights

Plaza de los Naranjos SQUARE

At the heart of Marbella's *casco antiguo* (old town) is the extremely pretty Plaza de los Naranjos, dating back to 1485, with tropical plants, palms, orange trees and, inevitably, overpriced bars.

Museo Ralli MUSEUM

(www.museoralli.cl; Urbanización Coral Beach; 10am-3pm Tue-Sat) FREE This superb private art museum exhibits paintings by primarily Latin American and European artists in bright, well-lit galleries. Part of a nonprofit foundation with four other museums (in Chile, Uruguay and Israel), it has exhibits including sculptures by Henry Moore and Salvador Dalí, vibrant contemporary paintings by Argentinian surrealist Alicia Carletti and Cuban Wilfredo Lam, plus works by Joan Miró, Marc Chagall and Giorgio de Chirico.

The museum is 6km west of central Marbella near Puerto Banús.

Museo del Grabado Español MUSEUM
(Calle Hospital Bazán; €3; 9am-7.30pm Tue-Fri, to 2pm Sat & Mon) This small art museum in the old town includes works by some of the great masters, including Pablo Picasso, Joan Miró and Salvador Dalí, among the work of other, primarily Spanish, painters.

Sleeping

Hotel San Cristóbal HOTEL €€
(952 86 20 44; www.hotelsancristobal.com; Avenida Ramón y Cajal 3; s/d incl breakfast €60/85;) Not the most 'Marbella' (ie flashy) of Marbella's hotels, the well-located San Cristóbal dates back to the 1960s. However, regular revamps have kept the place looking solidly contemporary: rooms sport tasteful pale-grey and cream decor and smart navy fabrics. Most rooms have balconies.

★**Claude** BOUTIQUE HOTEL €€€
(952 90 08 40; www.hotelclaudemarbella.com; Calle San Francisco 5; d/ste €265/330;) The former summer home of Napoleon III's wife has updated its regal decor to create a hotel fit for a 21st-century empress. Situated in the quieter upper part of town, the Claude's arched courtyards and shapely pillars successfully marry contemporary flourishes with the mansion's original architecture, while claw-foot bath tubs and crystal chandeliers add to the classic historical feel.

Eating

Garum INTERNATIONAL €€
(952 858 858; www.garummarbella.com; Paseo Marítimo; mains €9-18; 11am-11.30pm;) Finnish owned and set in a dreamy location right on the 'Golden Mile' across from the beach, Garum has a menu that'll especially please those seeking a little gourmet variety. Expect dishes ranging from smoked-cheese soup to Moroccan chicken samosas and red-lentil falafal.

★**Farm** SPANISH €€€
(952 82 25 57; www.thefarm-marbella.com; Plaza Altamirano 2; 3-course set menus €24-32; noon-11pm;) First, it's not a farm but rather an exceptionally pretty restaurant in Marbella's old town consisting of a patio, a terrace and a dining room furnished with modern 'chill-out' flourishes. The food's all farm fresh and there's a brilliant selection of set menus showcasing organic ingredients, including vegetarian and kids' options. Cheap? Not particularly (this is Marbella). Worth it? Absolutely.

Bonus: there are flamenco shows for diners most Tuesdays, Thursdays and Saturdays at 8pm and 10pm.

Drinking & Nightlife

For the most spirited bars and nightlife, head to Puerto Banús, 7km west of Marbella. In town, the best area is around the small Puerto Deportivo. There are also some beach clubs open only in summer.

Information

Tourist Office (www.marbellaexclusive.com; Plaza de los Naranjos; 9am-8pm Mon-Fri, 10am-2pm Sat) Has plenty of leaflets and a good town map.

Getting There & Away

The **bus station** (952 823 409; Avenida del Trapiche) is 1.5km north of the old town just off the A7 *autovía*.

Portillo (91 272 28 32; www.avanzabus.com) runs buses to Fuengirola (€4.25, 30 minutes, four daily), Estepona (€4.30, one hour, hourly), Málaga (€7.25, 45 minutes, half-hourly) and Ronda (€7.50, 1½ hours, nine daily).

Estepona

POP 66,500

Estepona was one of the first resorts to attract foreign residents and tourists some 45 years ago and, despite the surrounding development, the centre of the town still has a cosy, old-fashioned feel. There's good reason for that: Estepona's roots date back to the 4th century. Centuries later, during the Moorish era, the town was an important and prosperous centre due to its strategic proximity to the Strait of Gibraltar.

Estepona is steadily extending its promenade to Marbella; at its heart is the pleasant Playa de la Rada beach. The Puerto Deportivo is the focal point of the town's nightlife, especially at weekends, and is also excellent for water sports.

Sleeping & Eating

Hotel Boutique Casa Veracruz BOUTIQUE HOTEL €€
(951 46 64 70; www.hotelboutiquecasaveracruz.com; Calle Veracruz 22; d/ste €85/125;) The 'boutique' label barely does this place justice. With its diminutive courtyard, trickling fountain, stately paintings

and stylish antique furniture, it's like a little slice of historic Seville dispatched to the Costa del Sol – and all yours for a very economical sum. Extra touches include Nespresso machines, ample continental breakfasts, and complimentary tea, coffee and sweets available all day.

La Escollera SEAFOOD €
(Puerto Pesquero; mains €8-11; ⌚1-4.30pm & 8-11.30pm Tue-Sat, 1-4.30pm Sun) Locals in the know arrive at this port-located eatery in shoals to dine on arguably the freshest and best seafood in town. The atmosphere is no-frills basic, with plastic tables and paper cloths. But when the fish tastes this good and the beer is this cold, who cares?

Venta García EUROPEAN €€
(☎952 89 41 91; Carretera de Casares, Km 7; mains €12-18; ⌚noon-10pm Tue-Sat, to 5pm Sun; P) Venta Garcia specialises in superbly presented and conceived dishes using local produce, and the countryside views are similarly sublime. There's an emphasis on meat like venison (served with a red fruit sauce) and pork: the Montes de Málaga dish executes a local take on pork served with peppers, fried egg and chips. The word is out, though: reserve at weekends.

It's on the road to Casares, around 7km from the centre of Estepona.

Information

Tourist Office (www.estepona.es; Plaza de las Flores; ⌚9am-8pm Mon-Fri, 10am-2pm Sat & Sun) Located on a historical square, this office has brochures and a decent map of town.

Getting There & Away

Portillo (☎91 272 28 32; www.avanzabus.com) buses run more than a dozen times a day to Marbella (€4.30, one hour) and Málaga (€9.90, two hours).

Mijas

POP 77,750 / ELEV 428M

The story of Mijas encapsulates the story of the Costa del Sol. Originally a humble village, it's now the richest town in the province. Since finding favour with discerning bohemian artists and writers in the 1950s and '60s, Mijas has sprawled across the surrounding hills and down to the coast, yet it's managed to retain the throwback charm of the original *pueblo* (village).

Sights

Virgen de la Peña HISTORIC SITE
(Avenida Virgen de la Peña) If you walk past the *ayuntamiento* (town hall), you will reach this gorgeous grotto where the Virgin is said to have appeared to two children who were led here by a dove in 1586. Within the clifftop cave is a flower-adorned altar in front of an image of the Virgin, plus some religious chalices and pennants in glass cases. It's a poignant spot despite the barrage of visitors.

Centro de Arte Contemporáneo de Mijas MUSEUM
(CAC; www.cacmijas.info; Calle Málaga 28; adult/child €3/free; ⌚10am-6pm Tue-Sun) This art museum houses an extraordinary exhibition of Picasso ceramics (the second-largest collection in the world), plus some exquisite Dalí bronze figurines, glassware and bas-relief. There are also temporary exhibitions. Note that, despite the name, this museum is not affiliated with Málaga's CAC museum.

Sleeping

★TRH Mijas HOTEL €€
(☎952 48 58 00; www.trhhoteles.com; Plaza de la Constitución; s/d €65/85; P) The spectacularly sited TRH offers possibly the best views on the Costa del Sol from its long terrace bar, where the evocative decor recalls the art-deco era with a bit of old empire thrown in. Then there are the orange-tree patio, on-site spa, lovely outdoor pool, head-turning paintings and vintage motorbikes on display in the lobby.

Getting There & Away

The quickest way to get to Mijas is to take the half-hourly M122 bus from Fuengirola bus station (€1.55, 15 minutes). There are also four daily **Portillo** (☎91 272 28 32; www.avanzabus.com) buses to/from Málaga (€2.30, one hour).

The Interior

The mountainous interior of Málaga province is an area of raw beauty and romantic white villages sprinkled across craggy landscapes. Beyond the mountains, the verdant countryside opens out into a wide chequerboard of floodplains. It's a far cry from the tourist-clogged coast.

Ardales & El Chorro

Fifty kilometres northwest of Málaga, the Río Guadalhorce carves its way through the awesome **Garganta del Chorro** (El Chorro gorge). Also called the Desfiladero de los Gaitanes, the gorge is about 4km long, as much as 400m deep and sometimes just 10m wide. Its sheer walls, and other rock faces nearby, are a magnet for rock climbers, with hundreds of bolted climbs snaking their way up the limestone cliffs.

While Ardales (population 2700) is the main town in the area, most people use the hamlet of El Chorro, with its train station, hiking trails and decent hotel, as a base. Lying 6km west is the serene **Embalse del Conde del Guadalhorce**, a huge reservoir that dominates the landscape and is noted for its carp fishing. This is also the starting point for the legendary and recently revitalised Caminito del Rey path. The whole area is protected in a natural park.

Activities

★El Caminito del Rey HIKING

(www.caminitodelrey.info; €10; ⏲10am-5pm Tue-Sun Apr-Oct, to 3pm Tue-Sun Nov-Mar) The Caminito del Rey (King's Path) – so named because Alfonso XIII walked along it when he opened the Guadalhorce hydroelectric dam in 1921 – consists of a 2.9km boardwalk that hangs 100m above the Río Guadalhorce and snakes around the cliffs, affording breathtaking views at every turn. Required walks to/from the northern and southern access points make the total hiking distance 7.7km.

The *caminito* had fallen into severe disrepair by the late 1990s, and it became known as the most dangerous pathway in the world; it officially closed in 2000 (though some daredevils still attempted it). Following an extensive €5.5 million restoration, it reopened in March 2015 and is now safe and open to anyone with a reasonable head for heights.

The boardwalk is constructed with wooden slats; in some sections the old crumbling path can be spied just below. The walk can only be done in one direction (north-south), and it's highly advisable to book a timeslot online. Buses (€1.55, 20 minutes) leave on the half-hour from El Chorro train station to the starting point, where there's a couple of restaurants. From here you must walk 2.7km to the northern access point of the *caminito*, where you'll show your ticket and be given a mandatory helmet to wear. At the end of the *caminito* there's another 2.1km to walk from the southern access point back to El Chorro. Allow about four hours for the walk, as the views are made for savouring.

Getting There & Away

The most convenient entry point is El Chorro with its railway station. Trains to Málaga (€4.85, 42 minutes) run two or three times daily. There are also connections north to Ronda.

A half-hourly shuttle bus (€1.55, 20 minutes) runs between the train station and the starting point of the Caminito del Rey (p765).

If you're driving, you can park at either end and use the bus to make your connection.

Antequera

POP 41,000 / ELEV 577M

Known as the crossroads of Andalucía, Antequera sees plenty of travellers pass through but few lingering visitors. But those who choose not to stop are missing out. The town's foundations are substantial: two Bronze Age burial mounds guard its northern approach and Moorish fables haunt its grand Alcazaba. The undoubted highlight here, though, is the opulent Spanish-baroque style that gives the town its character and that the civic authorities have worked hard to restore and maintain. There's also an astonishing number of churches – more than 30, many with wonderfully ornate interiors. It's little wonder that Antequera is often referred to as the 'Florence of Andalucía'.

Sights

★Antequera Dolmens Site ARCHAEOLOGICAL SITE

(⏲9am-6pm Tue-Sat, to 3pm Sun) FREE Antequera's two earth-covered burial mounds – the **Dolmen de Menga** and the **Dolmen de Viera** – were built out of megalithic stones by Bronze Age people around 2500 BC. When they were rediscovered in 1903, they were found to be harbouring the remains of several hundred bodies. Considered to be some of the finest Neolithic monuments in Europe, they were named a Unesco World Heritage site in 2016.

Alcazaba FORTRESS

(adult/child incl Colegiata de Santa María la Mayor €6/3; ⏲10am-7pm Mon-Sat, 10.30am-3pm Sun)

Favoured by the Granada emirs of Islamic times, Antequera's hilltop Moorish fortress has a fascinating history and covers a massive 62,000 sq metres. The main approach to the hilltop is from Plaza de San Sebastián, up the stepped Cuesta de San Judas and then through an impressive archway, the **Arco de los Gigantes**, built in 1585 and formerly bearing huge sculptures of Hercules. All that's left today are the Roman inscriptions on the stones.

Colegiata de Santa María la Mayor CHURCH
(Plaza Santa María; adult/child incl Alcazaba €6/3; 10am-7pm) Just below the Alcazaba is the large 16th-century Colegiata de Santa María la Mayor. This church-college played an important part in Andalucía's 16th-century humanist movement, and flaunts a beautiful Renaissance facade, lovely fluted stone columns inside and a Mudéjar *artesonado* (a ceiling of interlaced beams with decorative insertions). It also plays host to some excellent musical events and exhibitions.

Dolmen del Romeral ARCHAEOLOGICAL SITE
(Cerro Romeral; 9am-6pm Tue-Sat, to 3pm Sun) FREE This megalithic burial site was constructed around 1800 BC and features much use of small stones for its walls. To get here, continue 2.5km past the town's other two, more ancient dolmens through an industrial estate, then turn left following 'Córdoba, Seville' signs. After 500m, turn left at a roundabout and follow 'Dolmen del Romeral' signs for 200m.

Museo Conventual de las Descalzas MUSEUM
(Plaza de las Descalzas; compulsory guided tour €3.30; 10am-2pm & 5-7.30pm Tue-Sat, 9am-12.30pm Sun) This museum, in the 17th-century convent of the Carmelitas Descalzas (barefoot Carmelites), approximately 150m east of the town's **Museo Municipal** (Museo Municipal; Plaza del Coso Viejo; compulsory guided tour €3; 10am-2pm & 4.30-6.30pm Tue-Fri, 9.30am-2pm & 4.30-6.30pm Sat, 9am-12.30pm Sun), displays highlights of Antequera's rich religious-art heritage. Outstanding works include a painting by Lucas Giordano of St Teresa of Ávila (the 16th-century founder of the Carmelitas Descalzas), a bust of the Dolorosa by Pedro de Mena and a *Virgen de Belén* sculpture by La Roldana.

Festivals & Events

Semana Santa RELIGIOUS
(Holy Week; Mar) One of the most traditional celebrations in Andalucía; items from the town's treasure trove are used in the religious processions.

Sleeping

Hotel Coso Viejo HOTEL €
(952 70 50 45; www.hotelcosoviejo.es; Calle Encarnación 9; s/d incl breakfast €45/55;) This converted 17th-century neoclassical palace is right in the heart of Antequera, opposite Plaza Coso Viejo and the town museum (p766). The simply furnished rooms are set around a handsome patio with a fountain, and there's an excellent tapas bar and restaurant next door.

Parador de Antequera HISTORIC HOTEL €€
(952 84 02 61; www.parador.es; Paseo García del Olmo; s/d incl breakfast €85-120;) This *parador* is in a quiet area of parkland north of the bullring and near the bus station. It's comfortably furnished and set in pleasant gardens with wonderful views, especially at sunset.

Eating

Welcome to a bastion of traditional cooking. Antequera specialities include *porra antequerana* (a thick and delicious garlicky soup that's similar to gazpacho), *bienmesabe* (literally 'tastes good to me'; a sponge dessert) and *angelorum* (a dessert incorporating meringue, sponge and egg yolk). Antequera also does a fine breakfast *mollete* (soft bread roll), served with a choice of fillings.

Baraka TAPAS €
(951 21 50 88; Plaza de las Descalzas; tapas €2-4; 8am-2am Wed-Sat & Mon, 10am-2am Sun) Sombreros off to the brave staff at Baraka, who cross a busy road, trays loaded, risking life and limb to serve punters sitting in a little park opposite. Like all good Antequera restaurants, Baraka doesn't stray far from excellent local nosh (*porra antequerana* calls loudly), although it does a nice side line in *pintxos* (Basque tapas) and serves heavenly bread.

★Arte de Cozina ANDALUCIAN €€
(www.artedecozina.com; Calle Calzada 27-29; mains €14-17, tapas €2.50; 1-11pm) It's hard not to notice the surrounding agricultural lands as you approach Antequera, and this

WORTH A TRIP

PARAJE NATURAL TORCAL DE ANTEQUERA

South of Antequera are the weird and wonderful rock formations of the Paraje Natural Torcal de Antequera. This 12-sq-km area of gnarled, serrated and pillared limestone formed as a sea bed 150 million years ago and now rises to 1336m (El Torcal). Not surprisingly, this other-worldly landscape fanned by fresh mountain breezes was declared a Unesco World Heritage site (along with Antequera's dolmens (p765)) in 2016.

There are three marked walking trails that you can do unguided. The 1.5km **Ruta Verde** (Green Route) and the 3km **Ruta Amarilla** (Yellow Route) both start and end at the **Centro de Visitantes** (✆952 24 33 24; www.torcaldeantequera.com; ⏲10am-7pm Apr-Oct, to 5pm Nov-Mar) and take in the full sweep of rocky surrealism. Be prepared for plenty of rock-hopping. The 3.7km **Ruta Naranja** (Orange Route) runs between the upper and lower car parks, tracking below the road. Gentler options are the miradors (lookouts) near the Centro de Visitantes, about 500m down the road.

There's no public transport to El Torcal. If you're travelling by car, leave central Antequera along Calle Picadero, which soon joins the Zalea road. After 1km or so you'll see signs on the left to Villanueva de la Concepción. Take this road and, after 12km (before entering Villanueva), turn right and head 3.75km uphill to the information centre.

fascinating little hotel-restaurant combo is where you get to taste what they produce. Slavishly true to traditional dishes, it plugs little-known Antequeran specialities such as gazpacho made with green asparagus or *porra* with oranges, plus meat dishes that include *lomo de orza* (preserved pork loin).

ℹ Information

Municipal Tourist Office (✆952 70 25 05; www.antequera.es; Plaza de San Sebastián 7; ⏲9.30am-7pm Mon-Sat, 10am-2pm Sun) A helpful tourist office with information about the town and region.

ℹ Getting There & Away

BUS

The **bus station** (Paseo García del Olmo) is 1km north of the centre. **Alsa** (✆952 34 17 38; www.alsa.es) runs buses to Seville (€14, 2½ hours, five daily), Granada (€9, 1½ hours, five daily), Córdoba (€11, two hours 40 minutes, one daily), Almería (€23, six hours, one daily) and Málaga (€6, one hour, five daily).

Buses run between Antequera and Fuente de Piedra village (€2.50, 30 minutes, two daily).

TRAIN

Antequera has two train stations. **Antequera-Ciudad train station** (www.renfe.com; Avenida de la Estación) is 1.5km north of the town centre. At research time, bus transfers were being offered to Seville, Granada and Almería while work was being done on a new high-speed train line.

The **Antequera-Santa Ana Train Station**, 18km northwest of the town, has high-speed AVE trains to and from Málaga (€26, 30 minutes, 12 daily), Córdoba (€33, 30 minutes, 15 daily) and Madrid (€75, 2½ hours, 12 daily), as well as services to Granada and Seville via Córdoba.

A bus runs roughly three times a day from the Santa Ana station into Antequera (€5), or you can take a taxi (from €25).

East of Málaga

The coast east of Málaga, sometimes described as the Costa del Sol Oriental, is less developed than the coast to the west. The suburban sprawl of Málaga extends through a series of unmemorable and unremarkable seaside towns that pass in a concrete high-rise blur before culminating in more attractive Nerja.

The area's main redeeming feature is the rugged region of La Axarquía, which is just as stunning as Granada's Las Alpujarras yet, as well as being even more difficult to pronounce (think of taking a chopper to one of those infuriating Scandinavian flatpack stores: 'axe-ikea'), is hardly known. It's full of great walks.

Nerja

POP 21,200

Nerja, 56km east of Málaga with the Sierra Almijara rising behind it, has succeeded in rebuffing developers, allowing its centre to retain a low-rise village charm despite the proliferation of souvenir shops and the large number of visitors it sees. At its heart is the perennially beautiful Balcón de Europa, a palm-lined promontory built on the foundations of an old fort that offers panoramic views of the cobalt-blue sea flanked by honey-coloured coves.

The town is increasingly popular with package holidaymakers and 'residential tourists', which has pushed it far beyond its old confines. There's significant urbanisation, especially to the east. The holiday atmosphere, and seawater contamination, can be overwhelming from July to September, but the place is more *tranquilo* the rest of the year.

Sights

★Cueva de Nerja CAVE
(www.cuevadenerja.es; adult/child €10/6, incl Museo de Nerja €12, incl train btwn caves & museum €15; ⊙unguided visit 10am-1pm & 4-5.30pm Sep-Jun, 10am-6pm Jul & Aug, guided visit 1-2pm & 5.30-6.30pm Sep-Jun, 11am-noon & 6.30-7.30pm Jul & Aug) It's hard to imagine the surreal world that lies beneath the mountain foothills 4km east of Nerja, and it's even harder to believe that these vast caverns weren't discovered until five local *chicos* (young men) who had gone out looking for bats stumbled across an opening in 1959. Hollowed out by water around five million years ago and once inhabited by Stone Age hunters, this theatrical wonderland of extraordinary rock formations, subtle shifting colours, and stalactites and stalagmites evokes a submerged cathedral.

Balcón de Europa VIEWPOINT
Located in the heart of town, the fabulous *balcón* juts out like a natural pier, forming a beautiful palm-lined terrace with panoramic views of the sea. The only downside is that it's perennially crowded.

Playa Burriana BEACH
(P) This is Nerja's longest and best beach, with plenty of towel space on the sand. You can walk here via the bleached white Calle Carabeo, continuing down the steps to the beach and along to Burriana. The beach is backed by a line of *merenderos* (open-sided restaurants). You can rent kayaks or paddleboards here for €5.50 per hour.

Sleeping

★Hotel Carabeo HOTEL €€
(☎952 52 54 44; www.hotelcarabeo.com; Calle Carabeo 34; d/ste incl breakfast from €90/190; ⊙Apr-Oct; ❄@☜≋) Full of stylish antiques and wonderful paintings, this small, family-run seafront hotel is set above manicured terraced gardens. There's also a good **restaurant** (mains €16-25; ⊙1-3pm & 7-11pm Tue-Sun Mar-Nov; ☜) and the pool is on a terrace overlooking the sea. The building is an old schoolhouse and is located on one of the prettiest pedestrian streets in town, festooned with pink bougainvillea.

Hotel Balcón de Europa HOTEL €€
(☎952 52 08 00; www.hotelbalconeuropa.com; Paseo Balcón de Europa 1; s/d €82/115; ≋) This terraced hotel sticks out on a small promontory like a boat departing for Africa. Outside it's usually mayhem (this is Nerja's popular tourist playground), but inside the mood is surprisingly tranquil, with private room balconies overlooking a snug section of beach lapped by the translucent Mediterranean. A pool, sauna, piano bar and restaurant with a view all add value.

Eating

★Chiringuito de Ayo SEAFOOD €
(www.ayonerja.com; Playa Burriana; mains €9-13; ⊙9am-midnight; P) The menu is listed in nine languages, but the only word you need to understand at beachside Ayo is 'paella'. They cook the rice dish every day in a huge pan atop an open wood-burning fire right next to the sand. A plateful is yours for €7.50.

La Piqueta TAPAS €
(Calle Pintada 8; tapas €2, raciones €4.50-6; ⊙10am-midnight Mon-Sat) There are two very good reasons why this is the most popular tapas bar in town: first, the house wine is excellent; second, you get a free tapas with every drink in a tradition that's more Granada than Málaga province. On the menu are sturdy classics such as tripe and *huevos estrellados* (literally, smashed eggs) prepared with ham, garlic, potatoes and peppers.

Information

Tourist Office (www.nerja.org; Calle Carmen; ⊙10am-2pm & 6-10pm Mon-Fri, 10am-1pm Sat & Sun) Has plenty of useful leaflets.

Getting There & Away

Alsa (☎952 52 15 04; www.alsa.es) runs regular buses to/from Málaga (€4.50, one hour, 23 daily), Marbella (€11, 2¼ hours, one daily) and Antequera (€9, 2¼ hours, two daily). There are also buses to Almería and Granada.

WORTH A TRIP

COMARES

Comares sits like a snowdrift atop its lofty hill. The adventure really is in getting there: you see it for kilometre after kilometre, before a final twist in an endlessly winding road lands you below the hanging garden of its cliff. From a little car park you can climb steep, winding steps to the village. Look for ceramic footprints underfoot and simply follow them through a web of narrow, twisting lanes past the **Iglesia de la Encarnación** and eventually to the ruins of Comares' **castle** and a remarkable summit **cemetery**.

The village has a history of rebellion, having been a stronghold of Omar ibn Hafsun, but today there is a tangible sense of contented isolation, enjoyed by locals and many newcomers. Visitors are often of the adventurous variety. The village has established itself as a nexus for climbing and hiking excursions and has what is reputedly Andalucía's longest **zip line** (1/2 rides €15/20).

Bus M-360 leaves Málaga bus station (p760) for Comares at 6pm and starts back at 7am the next morning (one way €3.20, 1½ hours). There's no service on Sunday.

There's no bus station, just a ticket office and **bus stop** on the main roundabout on Carretera N340.

Cómpeta

POP 3700

This instantly attractive village, with its panoramic views, steep, winding streets and central bar-lined plaza overlooking a 16th-century church, has long attracted a large, mixed, foreign population. This has contributed to an active cultural scene, and Cómpeta is home to one or two above-*pueblo*-average restaurants serving contemporary cuisine. The village also has a couple of charity shops (rare in Spain) and a big following among organised walking groups. Not surprisingly, Cómpeta is a good base for hiking and similar adrenalin-fuelled activities.

Getting There & Away

Loymer runs three daily buses from Málaga to Cómpeta (€4.50, 1½ hours), stopping in Torre del Mar.

La Axarquía

The Axarquía region is riven by deep valleys lined with terraces and irrigation channels that date to Islamic times – nearly all the villages dotted around the olive-, almond- and vine-planted hillsides were founded in this era. The wild inaccessible landscapes, especially around the Sierra de Tejeda, made it a stronghold of *bandoleros* who roamed the mountains without fear or favour. Nowadays, its chief attractions include fantastic scenery; pretty white villages; strong, sweet wine made from sun-dried grapes; and good walking in spring and autumn.

The 'capital' of La Axarquía, **Vélez Málaga**, 4km north of Torre del Mar, is a busy but unspectacular town, although its restored hilltop castle is worth a look.

Some of the most dramatic La Axarquía scenery is up around the highest villages of **Alfarnate** (925m) and **Alfarnatejo** (858m), with towering, rugged crags such as Tajo de Gomer and Tajo de Doña Ana rising to their south.

Information

You can pick up information on La Axarquía at the tourist offices in Málaga (p759), Nerja (p768), Torre del Mar or **Cómpeta** (952 55 36 85; Avenida de la Constitución; 10am-3pm Mon-Sat, to 2pm Sun). Prospective walkers should ask for the leaflet on walks in the Parque Natural Sierras de Tejeda, Almijara y Alhama. Good maps for walkers are *Mapa topográfico de Sierra Tejeda* and *Mapa topográfico de Sierra Almijara* by Miguel Ángel Torres Delgado, both at 1:25,000. You can also follow the links at www.axarquia.es for walks in the region.

GIBRALTAR

POP 32,700

Red pillar boxes, fish-and-chip shops and creaky 1970s seaside hotels: Gibraltar – as British writer Laurie Lee once commented – is a piece of Portsmouth sliced off and towed 500 miles south. 'The Rock' overstates its Britishness, a bonus for pub-grub and afternoon-tea lovers, but a confusing double-take for modern Brits who thought

Gibraltar

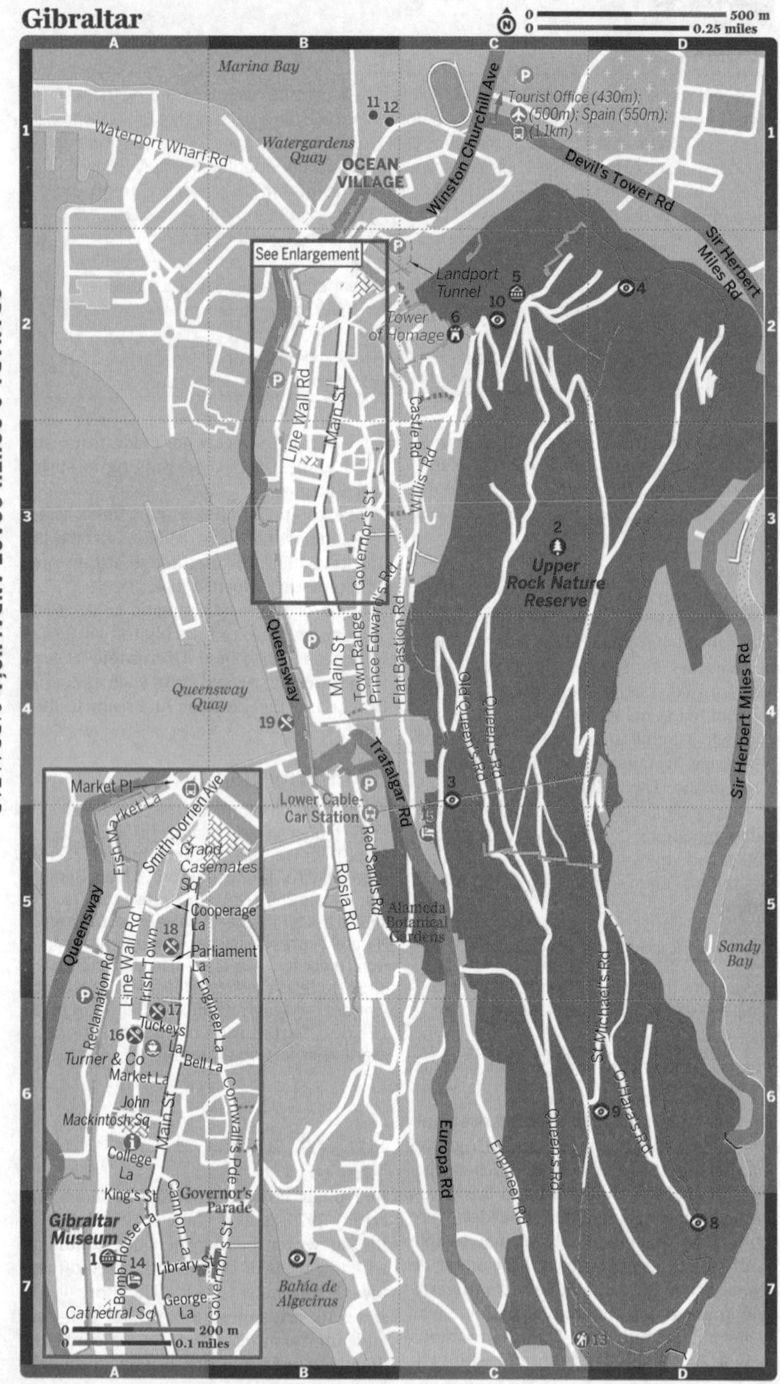

0 500 m
0 0.25 miles
Marina Bay
Waterport Wharf Rd
Watergardens Quay
OCEAN VILLAGE
Winston Churchill Ave
Tourist Office (430m); (500m); Spain (550m); (1.1km)
Devil's Tower Rd
Sir Herbert Miles Rd
See Enlargement
Landport Tunnel
Tower of Homage
Line Wall Rd
Main St
Castle Rd
Willis' Rd
Governor's St
Prince Edward's Rd
Upper Rock Nature Reserve
Queensway
Town Range
Flat Bastion Rd
Old Queen's Rd
Queen's Rd
Sir Herbert Miles Rd
Queensway Quay
Trafalgar Rd
Lower Cable-Car Station
Red Sands Rd
Rosia Rd
Alameda Botanical Gardens
Sandy Bay
St Michael's Rd
O'Hara's Rd
Europa Rd
Engineer Rd
Queen's Rd
Bahía de Algeciras
Market Pl
Fish Market La
Smith Dorrien Ave
Grand Casemates Sq
Cooperage La
Parliament La
Queensway
Line Wall Rd
Irish Town
Reclamation Rd
Engineer La
Tuckeys La
Bell La
Turner & Co
Market La
Cornwall's Pde
John Mackintosh Sq
Main St
College La
King's St
Cannon La
Governor's Parade
Gibraltar Museum
Bomb House La
Library St
Governor's St
George La
Cathedral Sq
0 200 m
0 0.1 miles

Gibraltar Town

Top Sights
1 Gibraltar Museum ... A7
2 Upper Rock Nature Reserve ... C3

Sights
3 Apes' Den ... C4
4 Great Siege Tunnels ... D2
5 Military Heritage Centre ... C2
6 Moorish Castle ... C2
7 Nelson's Anchorage ... B7
8 O'Hara's Battery ... D7
9 St Michael's Cave ... D6
10 WWII Tunnels ... C2

Activities, Courses & Tours
11 Dolphin Adventure ... B1
12 Dolphin Safari ... B1
13 Mediterranean Steps ... C7

Sleeping
14 Bristol Hotel ... A7
15 Rock Hotel ... C5

Eating
16 Clipper ... A6
17 Sacarello's ... A6
18 Star Bar ... A5
19 The Lounge ... B4

the days of Lord Nelson memorabilia were long gone. Poised strategically at the jaws of Europe and Africa, Gibraltar, with its Palladian architecture and camera-hogging Barbary macaques, makes an interesting break from the white towns of bordering Cádiz province (Andalucía, Spain). Playing an admirable supporting role is the swashbuckling local history; the Rock has been British longer than the United States has been American.

This towering 5km-long limestone ridge rises to 426m, with cliffs on its northern and eastern sides. Gibraltarians speak English, Spanish and a curiously accented, sing-song mix of the two, swapping mid-sentence. Signs are in English.

History

Both the Phoenicians and the ancient Greeks left traces here, but Gibraltar really entered the history books in AD 711 when Tariq ibn Ziyad, the Muslim governor of Tangier, made it the initial bridgehead for the Islamic invasion of the Iberian Peninsula, landing with an army of 10,000 men. The name Gibraltar derives from Jebel Tariq (Tariq's Mountain).

The Almohad Muslims founded a town here in 1159 and were usurped by the Castilians in 1462. In 1704 an Anglo-Dutch fleet captured Gibraltar during the War of the Spanish Succession. Spain ceded the Rock to Britain by the 1713 Treaty of Utrecht, but it didn't give up military attempts to regain it until the failure of the Great Siege of 1779–83; Spain has wanted it back ever since.

In 1969, Francisco Franco (infuriated by a referendum in which Gibraltarians voted by 12,138 to 44 to remain under British sovereignty) closed the Spain–Gibraltar border. The same year a new constitution committed Britain to respecting Gibraltarians' wishes over sovereignty, and gave Gibraltar domestic self-government and its own parliament, the House of Assembly (now the Gibraltar Parliament). In 1985, just before Spain joined the European Community (now the EU), the border was reopened after 16 long years.

Gibraltarians believe in their right to self-determination and, in a 2002 vote, resoundingly rejected the idea of joint British-Spanish sovereignty. The thorny issue of the Rock's long-term future still raises its head, with debates sparked by conflict over who controls its surrounding waters and, more recently, the still-unclear effects of the UK's decision to leave the EU.

Sights

Most Gibraltar sojourns start in Grand Casemates Sq, accessible through Landport Tunnel (at one time the only land entry through Gibraltar's walls), then continue along Main St, a slice of the British high street under the Mediterranean sun.

★Upper Rock Nature Reserve NATURE RESERVE
(adult/child incl attractions £10/5, vehicle £2, pedestrian excl attractions 50p, combined ticket with cable car adult/child £22/14; 9.30am-6.45pm Apr-Sep, 9am-5.45pm Oct-Mar) The Rock is one of the most dramatic landforms in southern Europe. Most of its upper sections (but not the main lookouts) fall within the Upper Rock Nature Reserve. Entry tickets include admission to **St Michael's Cave** (St Michael's Rd), the **Apes' Den**, the **Great Siege Tunnels**, the **Moorish Castle** (Tower of Homage; Willis' Rd), the **Military Heritage Centre** (crn Willis' & Queen's Rds) and Nelson's Anchorage (p772). The upper Rock is home to 600 plant species and is

COMBO TICKETS

The best way to explore the Rock is to whizz up on the **cable car** (Lower Cable-Car Station; Red Sands Rd; adult one way/return £13/15, child one way/return £6/6, adult/child one way incl nature reserve £22/14; 9.30am-7.45pm Apr-Oct, to 5.15pm Nov-Mar) to the **top cable-car station**, then stop off at all the Upper Rock Nature Reserve (p771) sights on your way down. You can get special cable car–nature reserve one-way combo tickets for this (adult/child £22/14). Note that the lower cable-car station stops selling these about two hours before the reserve closes. For the Apes' Den (p771), hop out at the middle station (closed Apr-Oct).

Combined dolphin-watching and cable-car (p773) tickets (adult/child £30/16) are also available through dolphin-watching companies.

the perfect vantage point for watching bird migration between Europe and Africa.

About 1km (15 minutes' walk) south down St Michael's Rd from the top cable-car station, O'Hara's Rd leads left up to **O'Hara's Battery** (9.2 Gun; O'Hara's Rd; adult/child £3/2; 10am-5pm Mon-Fri), a gun emplacement on the Rock's summit (not included in nature-reserve tickets). Slightly further down is the extraordinary St Michael's Cave, a spectacular natural grotto full of stalagmites and stalactites. People once thought the cave was a possible subterranean link with Africa. Today, apart from attracting tourists in droves, it's used for concerts, plays and even fashion shows. For a more extensive look (including a glimpse of the cave's underground lake), take the three-hour guided **Lower St Michael's Cave Tour** (£10); the tourist office (p773) can recommend guides; no children under 10.

A 1.5km (30-minute) walk north (downhill) from the top cable-car station, the Military Heritage Centre occupies the 18th-century Princess Caroline's Battery. From here one road leads down to Princess Royal Battery – more gun emplacements – while another heads 300m up to the Great Siege Tunnels, a complex defence system hewn out of the Rock by the British during the siege of 1779–83 to provide gun emplacements. The **WWII tunnels** (20071649; Willis' Rd, Hay's Level; tours £8, incl Upper Rock Nature Reserve & attractions £18; 10am-4pm Mon-Sat), where the Allied invasion of North Africa was planned, can also be visited, but you'll need to book ahead; you must have a nature-reserve ticket to access the tunnels, but they aren't actually included in that ticket. Even combined, the Great Siege and WWII tunnels constitute only a tiny proportion of the Rock's more than 50km of tunnels, most of which remain off-limits to visitors.

Gibraltar's Moorish Castle was rebuilt in 1333 after being retaken from the Spanish; it's on the way down to town from Princess Caroline's Battery.

★Gibraltar Museum MUSEUM
(20074289; www.gibmuseum.gi; 18-20 Bomb House Lane; adult/child £2/1; 10am-6pm Mon-Fri, to 2pm Sat) Gibraltar's swashbuckling history quickly unfolds in this fine museum, which comprises a labyrinth of rooms and exhibits ranging from prehistoric and Phoenician Gibraltar to the infamous Great Siege (1779–83). Don't miss the well-preserved 14th-century Islamic baths, and a 7th-century-BC Egyptian mummy found in the bay in the 1800s.

Nelson's Anchorage LANDMARK
(100-Tonne Gun; Rosia Rd; £1, incl Upper Rock Nature Reserve & attractions adult/child £10/5; 9.30am-6.15pm Apr-Sep, 9am-5.45pm Oct-Mar) At the southwestern end of town, Nelson's Anchorage pinpoints the site where Nelson's body was brought ashore from the HMS *Victory* after the Battle of Trafalgar – preserved in a rum barrel, so legend says. A 100-tonne, British-made Victorian supergun (1870) commemorates the spot.

Activities

★Mediterranean Steps HIKING
Not the most well-known attraction in Gibraltar, but surely the most spectacular, this narrow, ancient path with steep steps – many hewn into the limestone – starts at the nature reserve's southern entrance at Jews' Gate and traverses the southern end of Gibraltar before steeply climbing the crag on the eastern escarpment. It emerges on the ridge near O'Hara's Battery.

Sleeping

Bristol Hotel HOTEL €€
(20076800; www.bristolhotel.gi; 10 Cathedral Sq; s £69-74, d £86-93, tr £99-105;)

Where else can you stay in a retro 1970s hotel that isn't even trying to be retro? The dated but decent-enough Bristol has creaking floorboards, red patterned carpets, a walled garden and a small swimming pool, though staff aren't particularly helpful. Breakfast is available (£6). It's just off Main St.

Rock Hotel HOTEL €€€
(☎20073000; www.rockhotelgibraltar.com; 3 Europa Rd; incl breakfast r £120-150, ste £145-240; P ❄ 📶 ≋) As famous as the local monkeys, Gibraltar's grand old dame is looking fab and rejuvenated after a massive makeover. There are 86 elegant yet cosy, creamy, wood-floored rooms with fresh flowers, tea/coffee kits, sea views and, for some, private balconies. Tick off gym, pool, welcome drink, writing desks, bathrobes, a sparkling cafe-bar, winter Sunday roasts (£25) and summer poolside barbecues.

Eating

Goodbye tapas, hello fish and chips. Gibraltar's food is unashamedly British – and pretty pricey by Andalucian standards. The staples are pub grub, beer, sandwiches, chips and stodgy desserts, though a few international flavours can be found at Queensway Quay, Marina Bay and Ocean Village. There's a cluster of good restaurants on Fish Market Lane, just outside Grand Casemates Sq.

Clipper PUB FOOD €
(78B Irish Town; mains £5-9; ⌚9am-10pm Mon-Fri, 10am-4pm Sat, 10am-10pm Sun; 📶) Ask five...10...20 people in Gibraltar for their favourite pub and, chances are, they'll choose the Clipper. Looking sparklingly modern nowadays, the Clipper does real pub grub in traditionally large portions. British faves include jacket potatoes, chicken tikka masala, cheesy chips, Sunday roasts and that essential all-day breakfast (£5.95).

Star Bar PUB FOOD €€
(www.starbargibraltar.com; 12 Parliament Lane; dishes £5-14; ⌚8am-11pm Mon-Sat, 10am-10pm Sun) The Rock's oldest bar (if house advertising is to be believed) has a vaguely Mediterranean-influenced pub menu that even features evening tapas like *patatas bravas* (potatoes in spicy tomato sauce) and Manchego cheese. Squeeze inside for wraps, burgers, pies, salads, rib-eye steak, butternut-squash-and-goat's-cheese pasta and, of course, fish and chips.

Sacarello's INTERNATIONAL, CAFE €€
(☎20070625; www.sacarellosgibraltar.com; 57 Irish Town; mains £8-15; ⌚8.30am-7.30pm Mon-Fri, 9am-3pm Sat; 📶🖉) A jack of all trades and master of...well...some, Sacarello's offers a great range of vegetarian cooking (pastas, quiches) alongside pub-style dishes in an old multilevel coffee warehouse. There's a good coffee list, plus lots of cakes, a salad bar and daily specials. From 3.30pm to 7.30pm you can linger over cream tea (£6.20).

The Lounge INTERNATIONAL €€€
(☎20061118; 17A & B Ragged Staff Wharf, Queensway Quay; mains £14-19; ⌚noon-4pm & 6-10pm Mon-Sat, noon-4pm Sun) This popular, stylish waterside gastrobar and lounge, just south of the town centre, serves a globetrotting, fresh-produce menu of salads, pastas, risottos, sandwiches, meats, and fish and chips, along with creative, seasonal specials. Starters like gin-cured salmon with beetroot are followed by, say, beer-battered cod or rib-eye steak with chimichurri sauce, all overlooking Queensway Quay's megayachts.

Information

Tourist Office (☎20045000; www.visitgibraltar.gi; Heritage Bldg, 13 John Mackintosh Sq; ⌚9am-4.30pm Mon-Fri, 9.30am-3.30pm Sat, 10am-1pm Sun)

Tourist Office (☎20050762; www.visitgibraltar.gi; Customs Bldg, Winston Churchill Ave; ⌚9am-4.30pm Mon-Fri)

DOLPHIN WATCHING

The Bahía de Algeciras has a sizeable year-round population of dolphins (striped, bottlenose and short-beaked common) and a Gibraltar highlight is spotting them. **Dolphin Adventure** (☎20050650; www.dolphin.gi; 9 The Square, Marina Bay; adult/child £25/13) and **Dolphin Safari** (Blue Boat; ☎20 071914; www.dolphinsafari.gi; 6 The Square, Marina Bay; adult/child £25/15) run excellent dolphin-watching trips of one to 1½ hours. Most of the year each usually has two to three daily excursions. Dolphin Adventure also does summer whale-watching trips in the Strait of Gibraltar (adult/child £40/30). Advance bookings essential.

September to November are the best months for seeing dolphins, while March and April have the least sightings.

Getting There & Away

AIR

Gibraltar's well-connected **airport** (☎20 012345; www.gibraltarairport.gi) is at the northern end of the Rock, next to the Spanish border.

British Airways (www.britishairways.com) To/from London (Heathrow).

EasyJet (www.easyjet.com) To/from London (Gatwick), Bristol and Manchester.

Royal Air Maroc (www.royalairmaroc.com) To/from Casablanca and Tangier.

BOAT

FRS (www.frs.es) sails from Gibraltar to Tangier Med (Morocco; adult/child one way £39/26, 1½ hours) every other Friday at 7pm (at research time there were indications that this route may be discontinued). **Turner & Co** (☎20078305; www.turnershipping.com; 67 Irish Town; ⏲9am-4pm Mon-Fri) books tickets.

BUS

No buses go directly to Gibraltar, but the **bus station** (Avenida de Europa) in La Línea de la Concepción (Spain) is only 400m north of the border. From here, there are regular buses to/from Algeciras, Cádiz, Málaga, Seville and Tarifa.

CAR & MOTORCYCLE

Long vehicle queues at the border and congested streets in Gibraltar make it far less time-consuming to park in La Línea and walk south across the frontier (1.5km to Casemates Sq). To take a car into Gibraltar (free), you need an insurance certificate, a registration document, a nationality plate and a driving licence. Gibraltar drives on the right.

In Gibraltar, there are car parks on Line Wall Rd, Reclamation Rd and Devil's Tower Rd (50p per 30 minutes). La Línea has some street parking, but it's easier and safer to use the underground car parks (€21 per 24 hours) just north of Avenida Príncipe de Asturias.

Getting Around

Bus 5 runs between town and the border every 10 to 20 minutes. Bus 2 serves Europa Point, bus 3 the southern town; buses 4 and 8 go to Catalan Bay. All these buses stop at **Market Pl** (Market Pl), immediately northwest of Grand Casemates Sq. Tickets cost £1.50, or £2.25 for a day pass. Check schedules at www.gibraltarbuscompany.gi/site.

JAÉN PROVINCE

For anyone who loves culture, nature, history or good food, this relatively little-visited province turns out to be one magical combination. Endless lines of pale-green olive trees – producing one-sixth of all the world's olive oil – carpet much of the landscape. Castle-crowned hills are a reminder that this was once a frontier zone between Christians and Muslims, while the gorgeous Renaissance architecture of Unesco World Heritage towns Úbeda and Baeza showcases the wealth amassed by the Reconquista nobility.

Beyond the towns and olive groves, Jaén has wonderful mountain country. The Parque Natural Sierras de Cazorla, Segura y Las Villas, Spain's biggest protected area, is a highlight of Andalucía for nature lovers, with rugged mountains, deep green valleys, prolific wildlife and dramatically perched villages – and good lodgings, roads and trails to help you make the most of it.

Jaén

POP 111,000 / ELEV 575M

Set amid vast olive groves, upon which its precarious economy depends, Jaén is somewhat overshadowed by the beauty of nearby Úbeda and Baeza, and is often passed over by visitors to the province. But once you make it into town you will discover a charming, if mildly dilapidated, historic centre with hidden neighbourhoods, excellent tapas bars and a grandiose cathedral.

Muslim Yayyan was a significant city before its conquest by Castilla in 1246. For 2½ centuries Christian Jaén remained important thanks to its strategic location near the border with Nasrid Granada – until the Muslims were finally driven out of Granada in 1492. Jaén then sank into a decline with many of its people emigrating to the Spanish colonies – hence the existence of other Jaéns in Peru and the Philippines.

Sights

★Catedral de la Asunción CATHEDRAL

(Plaza de Santa María; adult incl audio guide €5, child/senior €1.50/2; ⏲10am-2pm & 4-8pm Mon-Fri, 10am-2pm & 4-7pm Sat, 10am-noon & 4-7pm Sun) Jaén's massive cathedral still dwarfs the rest of the city, especially when seen from the hilltop eyrie of Cerro de Santa Catalina. Its construction lasted from 1540 to 1724, replacing a crumbling Gothic cathedral which itself had stood on the site of a mosque. Its perceived perfection of design – by Andrés de Vandelvira, the master architect of Úbeda and Baeza, and his father Pedro – made Jaén

Cathedral a model for many of the great churches of Latin America.

The facade on Plaza de Santa María, completed in the 18th century, owes more to the baroque tradition than to the Renaissance, thanks to its host of statuary by Seville's Pedro Roldán. But the predominant aesthetic is Renaissance – particularly evident in its huge, round arches and clusters of Corinthian columns. A great circular dome rises over the crossing before the main altar. From the sacristy antechamber, south of the crossing, a 57-step staircase leads up to corridors along the cathedral's south and west sides yielding impressive views down into the cathedral.

★Castillo de Santa Catalina CASTLE

(Cerro de Santa Catalina; adult/senior, student & child €3.50/1.50, 3-6pm Wed free; 10am-6pm Mon-Sat, to 3pm Sun; P) High above the city, atop cliff-girt Cerro de Santa Catalina, this fortress's near-impregnable position is what made Jaén important during the Muslim and early Reconquista centuries. At the end of the ridge stands a large cross, on the spot where Fernando III had a cross planted after Jaén finally surrendered to him in 1246; the views are magnificent.

Palacio de Villardompardo BATHHOUSE, MUSEUM

(Centro Cultural Baños Árabes; www.bañosarabesjaen.es; Plaza de Santa Luisa de Marillac; 9am-10pm Tue-Sat, to 3pm Sun) FREE This Renaissance palace houses one of the most intriguing collections of historical, archaeological and artistic exhibits found under one roof in Andalucía: the beautiful 11th-century **Baños Árabes**, one of the largest surviving Islamic-era bathhouses in Spain; the **Museo de Artes y Costumbres Populares**, with extensive, diverse exhibits showcasing the life of pre-industrial Jaén province; and the **Museo Internacional de Arte Naïf** with a large collection of colourful and witty Naïve art.

Sleeping

Hotel Xauen HOTEL €

(953 24 07 89; www.hotelxauenjaen.com; Plaza del Deán Mazas 3; incl breakfast s €52-56, d €56-82;) The Xauen has a superb location in the centre of town. Communal areas are decorated with large colourful photos on a random range of themes, while the rooms are a study in brown and moderately sized, but comfy and well cared for. The rooftop sun terrace has stunning cathedral views. Parking nearby is €11.

★Parador Castillo de Santa Catalina LUXURY HOTEL €€

(953 23 00 00; www.parador.es; Cerro de Santa Catalina; r €100-180; P) Next to the castle high on the Cerro de Santa Catalina, Jaén's *parador* has an incomparable setting and theatrically vaulted halls. Rooms are luxuriously dignified with plush furnishings, some with four-poster beds. There is also an excellent restaurant and a bar with panoramic terrace seating.

Eating

There aren't many fancy restaurants in Jaén, but one of Andalucía's best tapas zones is here, north of the cathedral, along and between Calles Maestra and Cerón. There are plenty of bars to choose from, but in the wafer-thin alleys that run between the two streets, you'll find a couple of particularly cherished establishments that have been going strong for well over a century.

El Gorrión ANDALUCIAN €

(Calle Arco del Consuelo 7; tapas from €2, raciones €8-18; 1.30-4pm Tue-Sun & 8.30pm-12.30am Fri & Sat) Lazy jazz plays in the background, old newspaper cuttings and lopsided paintings hang from the walls, and it feels as though local punters have been propping up the bar ever since 1888 (when it opened). But all ages from near and far drop in to sample the atmosphere, the local wine and food offerings such as pepper sausage and seafood-stuffed artichokes.

Taberna La Manchega ANDALUCIAN €

(Calle Bernardo López 12; bocadillos €2-2.50, platos combinados & raciones €6-12; 10am-5pm & 8pm-1am Wed-Mon) La Manchega has been in action since the 1880s; apart from enjoying the *bocadillos* (long bread rolls with fillings including five types of *tortilla*) and *raciones* (full plates of tapas items) such as *chorizo de ciervo* (venison chorizo), *conejo al ajillo* (rabbit in garlic) and *solomillo* (pork tenderloin), you can drink wine and practise your Spanish with the old-time barmen.

★Casa Antonio SPANISH €€€

(953 27 02 62; www.casantonio.es; Calle Fermín Palma 3; mains €19-24; 1-4pm & 8.30-11.30pm Tue-Sat, 1-4pm Sun, closed Aug) This elegant little restaurant, in an unpromising street off Parque de la Victoria, prepares top-class Spanish

fare rooted in local favourites, such as partridge in escabeche (an oil-vinegar-wine marinade), lamb chops or roast shoulder of goat kid. There's also excellent seafood. Nothing over-complicated, just top ingredients expertly prepared. Service is polished and attentive.

Information

Oficina de Turismo (953 19 04 55; www.turjaen.org; Calle Maestra 8; 9am-7.30pm Mon-Fri, 10am-3pm & 5-7pm Sat, to 3pm Sun) Combined city and regional tourist office with helpful multilingual staff.

Getting There & Away

BUS

Alsa (902 422242; www.alsa.es), **Grupo Sepulvedana** (902 119699; www.lasepulvedana.es) and **Autocares Samar** (902 257025; www.samar.es) run services from the **bus station** (953 23 23 00; www.epassa.es/autobus; Plaza de la Libertad).

DESTINATION	COMPANY	COST (€)	DURATION (HR)	FREQUENCY (DAILY)
Baeza	Alsa	4.50	1	10-16
Cazorla	Alsa	9.25	2½	3
Córdoba	Sepulvedana	11	2	6-9
Granada	Alsa	8.90	1¼	11-14
Madrid	Samar	20	4-5	3-4
Málaga	Alsa	20-24	2¾-4½	4
Úbeda	Alsa	5.40	1-1¾	10-17

TRAIN

Jaén's **train station** (www.renfe.com; Plaza Jaén por la Paz) has four trains a day to Cádiz (€38, five hours) via Córdoba (€15, 1¾ hours) and Seville (€28, three hours), and four to Madrid (€35, 3¾ hours).

Baeza

POP 15,400 / ELEV 760M

The World Heritage–listed twin towns of Baeza (ba-*eh*-thah) and Úbeda, 9km apart, scupper any notion that there is little of architectural interest in Andalucía apart from Moorish buildings. These two remote country towns guard a treasure trove of superb Christian Renaissance buildings from a time when a few local families managed to amass huge fortunes and spent large parts of them beautifying their home towns. Baeza, the smaller of the two, can be visited in a day trip from Úbeda, though it has some good accommodation of its own. Here a handful of wealthy, fractious families, rich from grain-growing and cloth and leather production, left a marvellous catalogue of perfectly preserved Renaissance churches and civic buildings.

Baeza was one of the first Andalucian towns to fall to the Christians (in 1227), and little is left today of the Muslim town of Bayyasa after so many centuries of Castilian influence.

Sights

Baeza's main sights mostly cluster in the narrow streets south of the central Plaza de España and the broad Paseo de la Constitución (once Baeza's marketplace and bullring).

★Oleícola San Francisco WORKSHOP
(953 76 34 15; www.oleoturismojaen.com; Calle Pedro Pérez, Begíjar; 1½hr tours €5; tours 11am & 5pm) These fascinating tours of a working oil mill near Baeza will teach you all you could want to know about the process of turning olives into oil, how the best oil is made and what distinguishes extra virgin from the rest. At the end you get to taste a few varieties, and you'll probably emerge laden with a bottle or two of San Francisco's high-quality product.

★Catedral de Baeza CATHEDRAL
(Plaza de Santa María; adult/child €4/1.50; 11am-2pm & 4-7pm Mon-Fri, 10am-7pm Sat, to 6pm Sun) As was the case in much of Andalucía, the Reconquista destroyed Baeza's mosque and in its place built a cathedral. This was the first step towards the town's transformation into a Castilian gem. The cathedral is a stylistic melange, though the predominant style is 16th-century Renaissance, visible in the facade on Plaza de Santa María and in the basic design of the three-nave interior (by Andrés de Vandelvira).

★Palacio de Jabalquinto PALACE
(Plaza de Santa Cruz; 9am-2pm Mon-Fri, 10am-2pm & 4-8pm Sat-Sun) FREE Baeza's most flamboyant palace was probably built in the late 15th century for a member of the noble Benavides clan. Its chief glory is the spectacular facade in decorative Isabelline Gothic style, with a strange array of naked humans clambering along the moulding over the

doorway; above is a line of shields topped by helmets topped by mythical birds and beasts. The patio has a two-tier Renaissance arcade with marble columns, an elegant fountain, and a magnificent carved baroque stairway.

Plaza del Pópulo SQUARE
(Plaza de los Leones) This handsome square is surrounded by elegant 16th-century buildings. The central **Fuente de los Leones** (Fountain of the Lions) is made of carvings from the Ibero-Roman village of Cástulo and is topped by a statue reputed to represent Imilce, a local princess who became one of the wives of the famous Carthaginian general Hannibal.

Antigua Universidad HISTORIC BUILDING
(Old University; Calle del Beato Juan de Ávila; ⏲10am-2pm & 4-7pm) FREE Baeza's historic university was founded in 1538. It became a font of progressive ideas that generally conflicted with Baeza's conservative dominant families, often causing scuffles between the highbrows and the well-heeled. Since 1875 the building has housed a secondary school. The main patio, with elegant Renaissance arches, is open to visitors, as is the preserved early-20th-century classroom of the famed poet Antonio Machado, who taught French here from 1912 to 1919.

Festivals & Events

Semana Santa RELIGIOUS
(www.semanasantabaeza.com; ⏲Mar/Apr) Baeza's Easter processions are solemn, grand and rooted very deep in the town's traditions. Evenings from Palm Sunday to Good Friday.

Feria FERIA
(⏲mid-Aug) The summer fair starts with a big Carnaval-style procession of *gigantones* (papier-mâché giants) and other colourful figures, and continues with five days of fireworks, a huge funfair, concerts and bullfights.

Sleeping

Hostal Aznaitín HOSTAL €€
(☎953 74 07 88; www.hostalaznaitin.com; Calle Cabreros 2; incl breakfast s €50-75, d €60-85; ❄📶🏊) Welcoming, bright Aznaitín is a far cry from the dreary *hostales* of old. Rooms are stylish and well sized, with good mattresses and large, appealing photos of Baeza sights. Reception has plenty of information and ideas on what to see and do in and around Baeza.

Hotel Puerta de la Luna HERITAGE HOTEL €€
(☎953 74 70 19; www.hotelpuertadelaluna.com; Calle Canónigo Melgares Raya 7; s €70-130, d €70-139; P❄@📶🏊) There is no doubt where Baeza's Renaissance-era nobility would stay if they were to return today. This luxurious hotel in a 17th-century mansion sports orange trees and a pool in its elegant patio, and beautifully furnished salons with welcoming fireplaces. The spacious rooms are enhanced by classical furnishings and art, and good big bathrooms. Buffet breakfast costs €15.

Eating

Paseo de la Constitución and Plaza de España are lined with bar-cafe-restaurants that are great for watching local life, but most of the best finds are tucked away in the narrow old-town streets. As throughout the province, you'll get a free tapas with drinks in almost every bar.

Bar Pacos SPANISH €
(Calle de Santa Catalina; tapas & medias raciones €4.50-12; ⏲1.30-4pm & 8.30pm-midnight) Frequently thronged with locals and visitors, Pacos prepares a big array of well-presented, creative taste experiences – mostly larger than your average tapas. The crêpes (with fillings such as pork and fried egg) are one speciality, but there are dozens of other tempting choices such as spinach with prawns, or beef tartare with an apple sauce.

WORTH A TRIP

FORTALEZA DE LA MOTA

From a distance the **Fortaleza de la Mota** (www.tuhistoria.org; Alcalá la Real; adult/child €6/3; ⏲10.30am-7.30pm Apr–mid-Oct, 10am-5.30pm mid-Oct–Mar; P👪) looks more like a city than a mere fort, with its high church tower and doughty keep rising above the surrounding walls. And in a sense that's what it was, for back in the Middle Ages this fortified hill now looming over the town of Alcalá la Real was Alcalá la Real. It's a marvellous stop if you're heading along the Granada–Córdoba road across southwestern Jaén province, and well worth a detour even if you're not.

WORTH A TRIP

PARQUE NATURAL SIERRA DE ANDÚJAR

This large (748 sq km) natural park north of Andújar town has the biggest expanses of natural vegetation in the Sierra Morena as well as plenty of bull-breeding ranches. It's an exciting destination for wildlife-spotters, with numerous large mammals and birds found here including five emblematic endangered species: the Iberian lynx, wolf, black vulture, black stork and Spanish imperial eagle. The Iberian lynx population is the largest in the world, with around 200 lynxes here and in the neighbouring Parque Natural Sierra de Cardeña y Montoro (Córdoba province). There are also 25 breeding pairs of Spanish imperial eagle in the Andújar park (one-tenth of the total population of this mighty bird, found only in the Iberian Peninsula).

Staff at the park visitors centre, the **Centro de Visitantes Viñas de Peñallana** (953 53 96 28; Carretera A6177, Km 13; 10am-2pm Thu, 10am-2pm & 3-6pm Fri-Sun, closed afternoons mid-Jun–mid-Sep, closed Thu Jul & Aug), 13km north of Andújar town, can tell you the best areas for wildlife sightings, though you also need luck on your side. The best months for spotting lynxes are December and January, the mating season. Local guiding outfits can take you on to private land where sighting prospects are often higher: they include **Iberus Birding&Nature** (680 468098; www.iberusmedioambiente.com; Centro de Visitantes Viñas de Peñallana, Carretera A6177, Km 13), **IberianLynxLand** (636 984515, English 626 700525; www.iberianlynxland.com) and **Turismo Verde** (628 709410; www.lasierradeandujar.com). A full-day outing costs around €150/250 for two/four people.

On a hilltop in the heart of the park stands the **Santuario de la Virgen de la Cabeza** (Carretera A6177, Km 31, Cerro del Cabezo; P), a chapel that is the focus of one of Spain's biggest and most emotive religious events, the **Romería de la Virgen de la Cabeza**, on the last weekend in April.

A great base for wildlife watchers, hotel **La Caracola** (640 758273; www.lacaracolahotelrural.com; Carretera A6177, Km 13.8; s/d incl breakfast €40/60; P) sits among woodlands and offers bright, contemporary rooms, comfortable common areas and good meals (lunch or dinner €15). They'll serve breakfast as early as you like, or make you a picnic. It's 1.4km off the A6177: the signed turn off is 800m north of the park visitors centre.

Andújar town is served by several daily trains and buses from Jaén and Córdoba, and by buses from Baeza and Úbeda. There are buses to the sanctuary on Saturday and Sunday.

★**Palacio de Gallego** SPANISH €€
(667 760184; www.palaciodegallego.com; Calle de Santa Catalina 5; mains €15-30; 8pm-midnight Wed, 1-4pm & 8pm-midnight Thu-Mon) In the atmospheric setting of a 16th-century house, with tables on the delightful patio as well as in an old wood-beamed dining room, the Gallego serves up superb meat and fish dishes, barbecued and otherwise. There's a list of well over 100 Spanish wines, and you won't come across many starters better than their goat's cheese, orange and walnut salad.

Drinking & Nightlife

★**Café Teatro Central** BAR
(www.facebook.com/cafeteatrocentral; Calle Barreras 19; 4pm-3am;) The most original and consistent nightspot in the province, with fascinatingly eclectic decor and determined support for live music, the Central fills up around midnight Thursday to Saturday with an arty-indie crowd from other towns as well as Baeza. Live acts play to enthusiastic crowds amid the Buddha statues, historic instruments and coloured lighting every Thursday and most Fridays from October to June.

Shopping

La Casa del Aceite FOOD
(www.casadelaceite.com; Paseo de la Constitución 9; 10am-2pm & 5-8.30pm Mon-Sat, 10am-2pm & 4-6pm Sun) Sells a big range of quality olive oil, plus other intriguing local products such as wild-boar or partridge pâté, olives and olive-based cosmetics.

Information

Tourist Office (953 77 99 82; www.andalucia.org; Plaza del Pópulo; 9am-7.30pm Mon-Fri, 9.30am-3pm Sat & Sun) Housed in the 16th-century Casa del Pópulo.

Getting There & Away

BUS

Alsa (902 422242; www.alsa.es) runs services from the **bus station** (953 74 04 68; Avenida Alcalde Puche Pardo), 900m northeast of Plaza de España.

DESTINATION	COST (€)	DURATION	FREQUENCY (DAILY)
Cazorla	4.85	1¼-1½hr	3
Córdoba	11.50	2½hr	2
Granada	13	2½hr	7-9
Jaén	4.50	45min-1hr	7-14
Úbeda	1.15	15min	12-19

TRAIN

The nearest station is Linares-Baeza (www.renfe.com), 13km northwest of town, with a few daily trains to Almería, Córdoba, Jaén, Madrid and Seville. An **Alsa** (902 422242; www.alsa.es) bus leaves Baeza bus station for the train station (€2.70, one hour) at 5.30pm, and two come back, at 7.10am and 3.45pm. There are more buses from Úbeda. A **taxi** costs €24.

Úbeda

POP 33,600 / ELEV 760M

Beautiful Renaissance buildings grace almost every street and plaza in the *casco antiguo* (old quarter) of World Heritage–listed Úbeda (*oo*-be-dah). Charming hotels in several historic mansions, and some top-class restaurants and tapas bars, make a stay here an all-round delight.

Úbeda's aristocratic lions jockeyed successfully for influence at the Habsburg court in the 16th century. Francisco de los Cobos y Molina became state secretary to King Carlos I, and his nephew Juan Vázquez de Molina succeeded him in the job and kept it under Felipe II.

High office exposed these men to the Renaissance aesthetic just then reaching Spain from Italy. Much of the wealth that they and a flourishing agriculture generated was invested in some of Spain's purest examples of Renaissance architecture. As a result, Úbeda (like its little sister Baeza) is one of the few places in Andalucía boasting stunning architecture that was *not* built by the Moors.

Sights

Plaza Vázquez de Molina PLAZA

The lovely Plaza Vázquez de Molina is the monumental heart of Úbeda's old town and the perfect place to start exploring. An early case of Andalucian urban redevelopment, the plaza took on its present aspect in the 16th century when Úbeda's nobility decided to demolish existing buildings to make way for an assemblage of grand Renaissance buildings befitting their wealth and importance.

★Sacra Capilla de El Salvador CHAPEL

(Sacred Chapel of the Saviour; www.fundacionmedinaceli.org; Plaza Vázquez de Molina; adult/child incl audio guide €5/2.50; 9.30am-2.30pm & 4.30-7.30pm Mon-Sat, 11.30am-3pm Sun, plus 4-6pm Sun Oct-Apr) This famous chapel, built between 1536 and 1559, is the flagship of Úbeda Renaissance architecture. Commissioned by Francisco de los Cobos y Molina as his family's funerary chapel, it presents a marked contrast between the relatively sober proportions of the interior (by Diego de Siloé, architect of Granada's cathedral) and the more decorative western facade. The facade, a pre-eminent example of plateresque style, was designed by Andrés de Vandelvira, one of Siloé's stonemasons, who took over the project in 1540.

★Sinagoga del Agua HISTORIC BUILDING

(953 75 81 50; www.sinagogadelagua.com; Calle Roque Rojas 2; tours adult/child €4.50/3.50; tours every 45min 10.30am-1.30pm & 5-7.15pm, 5.45-8pm Jul & Aug) The medieval Sinagoga del Agua was discovered in 2006 by a refreshingly ethical property developer who intended to build apartments here, only to discover that every swing of the pickaxe revealed some tantalising piece of an archaeological puzzle. The result is this sensitive re-creation of a centuries-old synagogue and rabbi's house, using original masonry whenever possible. Features include the women's gallery, a bodega with giant storage vessels, and a *miqvé* ritual bath.

★Palacio de Vázquez de Molina HISTORIC BUILDING

(Plaza Vázquez de Molina; 8am-8pm Mon-Fri, 10am-2pm & 5-7.30pm Sat & Sun) FREE Úbeda's *ayuntamiento* (town hall) is undoubtedly one of, if not the, most beautiful town halls in Spain. It was built by Vandelvira in about 1562 as a mansion for Juan Vázquez de Molina, whose coat of arms surmounts the doorway. The perfectly proportioned, deeply Italian-influenced facade is divided into three tiers by slender cornices, with the sculpted caryatids on the top level continuing the lines of the Corinthian and Ionic pilasters on the lower tiers.

Casa Museo Andalusí MUSEUM

(953 75 40 14; Calle Narváez 11; €4; 11am-2pm & 5.30-8pm) This fascinating private museum comprises a 16th-century house that was inhabited by *conversos* (Jews who converted to Christianity) and a huge, diverse collection of antiques assembled by owner Paco Castro. The informal guided tours make it all come alive. The first hint that this is somewhere special is the original 16th-century heavy carved door. Ring the bell if it's closed.

Centro de Interpretación Olivar y Aceite VISITOR CENTRE

(www.centrodeolivaryaceite.com; Corredera de San Fernando 32; adult/child €3.50/free; 10am-1pm & 6-9pm Tue-Sat, to 1pm Sun Jun-Sep, 11am-2pm & 5-8pm Tue-Sat, to 2pm Sun Oct-May) Úbeda's olive-oil interpretation centre explains all about the area's olive-oil history, and how the oil gets from the tree to your table, with the help of models, mill equipment and videos in English and Spanish. You get the chance to taste different oils, and to buy from a broad selection.

Sleeping

Hotel El Postigo HOTEL €

(953 79 55 00; www.hotelelpostigo.com; Calle Postigo 5; s/d Sun-Thu €51/56, Fri & Sat €73/78;) A smallish modern hotel on a quiet street, El Postigo provides spacious, comfy rooms in red, black and white. Staff are welcoming, and there's a pleasant courtyard as well as a large sitting room with Spotify music, and a log fire in winter. Breakfast €6.50 per person.

★**Las Casas del Cónsul** HERITAGE HOTEL €€

(953 79 54 30; www.lascasasdelconsul.es; Plaza del Carmen 1; d Sun-Thu €65-70, Fri & Sat €80-90;) An attractive Renaissance mansion conversion, the welcoming 'Consul's Houses' has elegant, predominantly white rooms with old-time touches, and spacious common areas centred on a two-storey pillared patio, but what sets it apart from similar hotels is the fabulous panoramic terrace (with pool) gazing over the olive groves to the distant mountains of Cazorla.

★**Afán de Rivera** HERITAGE HOTEL €€

(953 79 19 87; www.hotelafanderivera.com; Calle Afán de Rivera 4; s/d/tr incl breakfast Sun-Thu €45/69/89, Fri & Sat €52/108/130;) This superb small hotel lies inside one of Úbeda's oldest buildings, predating the Renaissance. Expertly run by the amiable Jorge, it has beautifully historic common areas, and comfortable rooms that offer far more than is usual at these prices: shaving kits, fancy shampoos and tastefully eclectic decor combining the traditional and the contemporary.

Breakfast is a locally sourced feast that makes staying here even more of a pleasure.

Parador de Úbeda HISTORIC HOTEL €€€

(Parador Condestable Dávalos; 953 75 03 45; www.parador.es; Plaza Vázquez de Molina; r €95-200;) One of Spain's original *paradors* (opened in 1930) and an inspiration for many that were to follow, this plush hotel occupies a historic monument, the **Palacio del Deán Ortega**, on the wonderful Plaza Vázquez Molina. It has been comfortably modernised in period style and the rooms and common areas are appropriately luxurious. Breakfast costs €17.

The best rooms have their own little garden patios.

Eating

Úbeda is the culinary hotspot of Jaén province; its talented *andaluz*-fusion chefs are one reason why Spaniards flock here for weekend breaks.

★**Cantina La Estación** ANDALUCIAN €€

(687 777230; www.facebook.com/cantinalaestacion; Cuesta Rodadera 1; mains €17-21; 1-4pm & 8pm-midnight Thu-Mon, 1-4pm Tue;) The charming originality here starts with the design – three rooms with railway themes (the main dining room being the deluxe carriage). It continues with the seasonal array of inspired fusion dishes, such as wild boar in red-wine sauce, or octopus with garlic chips and paprika. Do sample an anchovy or two with the 'false olive' of cheese as an aperitif.

★**Misa de 12** ANDALUCIAN €€

(www.misade12.com; Plaza 1º de Mayo 7; raciones €10-24; 1-4pm & 8.30pm-midnight Wed-Sun) From the tiny cooking station in this little corner bar, a succession of truly succulent platters magically emerges – slices of *presa ibérica* (a tender cut of Iberian pork) grilled to perfection, juicy fillets of *bacalao* (cod), or *revuelto de pulpo y gambas* (eggs scrambled with octopus and shrimp).

Llámame Lola ANDALUCIAN €€
(Calle Baja del Salvador 5; mains & raciones €9-15; 12.30pm-midnight;) With an inviting location under the trees near the Sacra Capilla de El Salvador, Lola serves up good, creative *andaluz* fare with less fanfare than some other places and at slightly lower prices. The *solomillo ibérico* (pork tenderloin), the octopus and the *revueltos* (scrambled-egg dishes) are all very tasty.

They do more vegetarian dishes than most Úbeda eateries, including hummus and various salads.

Zeitúm ANDALUCIAN, FUSION €€
(www.zeitum.com; Calle San Juan de la Cruz 10; mains €10-16, menú €25; 1-4pm & 8.30-11.30pm Tue-Sat, 1-4pm Sun) Zeitúm is housed in a headily historic 14th-century building, where staff will show you the original well, and the stonework and beams bearing Jewish symbols. Olive-oil tastings (selected oils to soak into bread) are a feature here, along with top-class preparation of a diverse, frequently changing menu – the likes of venison and tuna sashimi, trout tartare, or pork tenderloin in wild-mushroom sauce.

Restaurante Antique ANDALUCIAN €€
(953 75 76 18; www.restauranteantique.com; Calle Real 25; mains €15-20, raciones €9-19; noon-4pm & 8pm-midnight) Antique is not at all 'antique', but puts a contemporary, high-quality twist on traditional raw materials – try its vegetable wok with partridge and rice noodles, or the mini-brochette of seafood marinated in soy, olive oil and spiced yoghurt. Decor is fittingly simple but stylish.

Shopping

Calles Real and Juan Montilla in the old town are dotted with shops selling local crafts and products such as oils, wines, olives and honey. The main high-street-style shopping streets are Calles Mesones and Obispo Cobos, between Plaza de Andalucía and the Hospital de Santiago.

Alfarería Tito CERAMICS
(Plaza del Ayuntamiento 12; 9am-2pm & 4-8pm) Juan Tito's distinctive style veers away from the classic green glaze, with intricate patterns and bright colours, especially blue. His large old-town showroom/workshop displays and sells a big range of very covetable wares. You're looking at €30 or more for a decorative plate; the dazzling designs and artisanship are well worth it.

Information

Oficina de Turismo (953 75 04 40; www.turismodeubeda.com; Plaza de Andalucía 5; 9am-7.30pm Mon-Fri, 9.30am-3pm & 5-7.30pm Sat, 9.30am-3pm Sun) Helpful place on the edge of the old town.

Getting There & Away

BUS

Alsa (902 422242; www.alsa.es) runs services from the **bus station** (953 79 51 88; Calle San José 6), which is in the new part of town, 700m west of Plaza de Andalucía.

DESTINATION	COST (€)	DURATION	FREQUENCY (DAILY)
Baeza	1.15	15min	11-17
Cazorla	4.25	1hr	3-5
Córdoba	12.20	2½hr	4
Granada	13	2¼-3hr	6-10
Jaén	5.40	1-1¼hr	9-15

TRAIN

The nearest station is **Linares–Baeza** (www.renfe.com), 21km northwest, which you can reach on four daily buses (€2.10, 30 minutes).

DESTINATION	COST (€)	DURATION	FREQUENCY (DAILY)
Almería	20-28	3¼hr	3
Córdoba	14-20	1¾hr	1
Jaén	6	45min	3-4
Madrid	21-33	3-4hr	5-7
Seville	20-29	3hr	1

Cazorla

POP 7265 / ELEV 800M

This picturesque, bustling white town sits beneath towering crags just where the Sierra de Cazorla rises up from a rolling sea of olive trees, 45km east of Úbeda. It makes the perfect launching pad for exploring the beautiful Parque Natural Sierras de Cazorla, Segura y Las Villas, which begins dramatically among the cliffs of Peña de los Halcones (Falcon Crag) directly above the town.

Sights

The heart of town is **Plaza de la Corredera**, with busy bars and the elegant *ayuntamiento* and clock tower looking down from the southeast corner. Canyonlike streets lead south to the **Balcón de Zabaleta**. This little mirador is like a sudden window in a blank wall, with stunning views up to the Castillo de la Yedra and beyond. From here another narrow street leads down to Cazorla's most picturesque square, **Plaza de Santa María**.

★Castillo de la Yedra CASTLE

(Museo del Alto Guadalquivir; EU citizen/other free/€1.50; 9am-3pm Tue-Sun mid-Jun–mid-Sep, 9am-8pm Tue-Sat, to 3pm Sun mid-Sep–mid-Jun) Cazorla's dramatic Castle of the Ivy, a 700m walk above Plaza de Santa María, has great views and is home to the interesting Museum of the Upper Guadalquivir, whose diverse collections include traditional agricultural and kitchen utensils, religious art, models of an old olive mill, and a small chapel featuring a life-size Romanesque-Byzantine crucifixion sculpture.

Activities

There are some great walks straight out of Cazorla town – all uphill to start with, but your reward is beautiful forest paths and fabulous panoramas of cliffs, crags and circling vultures. Agencies here offer a host of other activities locally, including canyoning in the *parque natural* and an exciting via ferrata for climbers at the neighbouring village of La Iruela.

Via Ferrata La Mocha CLIMBING

(La Iruela) This high-adrenaline challenge is a set of steel ladders, steps, cables and chains fixed into the precipitous rocky cone, La Mocha, above La Iruela village just outside Cazorla. Established in 2016, it ascends 130m and includes a 'Tibetan bridge' – a set of horizontal cables strung across a precipice. **Tierraventura** (953 71 00 73; www.aventuracazorla.com; Carretera A319, Km 16.5, La Iruela; 10am-2pm & 5-8pm Mon-Sat) offers guided climbs (€36 per person, about three hours).

Tours

Turisnat WILDLIFE WATCHING

(953 72 13 51; www.turisnat.es; Calle Martínez Falero 11; half-day tours per person €30-39; office 10am-2pm & 5-8pm Mon-Sat, to 2pm Sun) This highly experienced agency is a good option for 4WD trips along the forest tracks of the *parque natural*, with an emphasis on wildlife-spotting. English- or French-speaking guides are available at no extra cost.

Sleeping

Hotel Guadalquivir HOTEL €

(953 72 02 68; www.hguadalquivir.com; Calle Nueva 6; s/d incl breakfast €43/57;) Welcoming, family-run Guadalquivir has well-kept, comfy, ample rooms with pine furniture, though no memorable views. It's well run, just a few steps from the central Plaza Corredera, and serves up a decent breakfast. It all equals straightforward, no-fuss, good value for money.

Casa Rural Plaza de Santa María CASA RURAL €€

(953 72 20 87; www.plazadesantamaria.com; Callejón Plaza Santa María 5; incl breakfast s €39-44, d €55-77;) This multilevel house is set round a lovely garden-patio with a fish pond. Its terraces and a couple of the rooms enjoy superb views over Plaza de Santa María, Cazorla's castle and the mountains beyond. The attractive rooms are all different, in yellows, oranges and blues, with a variety of folksy styles.

Eating

Bar Las Vegas TAPAS €

(Plaza de la Corredera; tapas €1, raciones €4-12; 10am-4pm & 8pm-midnight Tue-Sat, 10am-4pm Sun) It's tiny but it's the best of Cazorla's central bars, with barrel tables outside (and it gets packed inside when the weather's poor). They do great tapas including one called *gloria bendita* (blessed glory – scrambled eggs with prawns and capsicum), as well as *raciones* of local favourites such as cheese, ham, venison and *lomo de orza* (spiced pork).

Mesón Leandro SPANISH €€

(www.mesonleandro.com; Calle Hoz 3; mains €9-19; 1.30-4pm & 8.30-11pm Wed-Mon) Leandro is a step up in class from most other Cazorla eateries – professional but still friendly service in a bright dining room with lazy music, and only one set of antlers on the wall. The broad menu of nicely presented dishes ranges from partridge-and-pheasant pâté to *fettuccine a la marinera* (seafood fettuccine) and a terrific *solomillo de ciervo* (venison tenderloin).

La Cueva de Juan Pedro ANDALUCIAN €€
(Plaza de Santa María; raciones & mains €8-20, menú €13; noon-10pm;) The ancient, wood-beamed bar has antlers and boar heads protruding from the walls, and there's a dining room adjoining, plus outdoor tables on the plaza just below. It's a place for no-frills traditional Cazorla fare including meaty grills (lamb, pork, rabbit, wild boar, venison), trout and *rin-rán* (a mix of salted cod, potato and dried red peppers).

Information

Oficina Municipal de Turismo (953 71 01 02; www.cazorla.es/turismo; Plaza de Santa María; 10am-1pm & 4-8pm Tue-Sun Apr-Oct, to 7pm Nov-Mar) Inside the remains of Santa María church, with some information on the natural park as well as the town.

Punto de Información Cazorla (953 72 13 51; Calle Martínez Falero 11; 10am-2pm & 5-8pm Mon-Sat, 10am-2pm Sun) Good for information on the *parque natural* as well as the town and surrounds.

Getting There & Away

Alsa (www.alsa.es) runs three to five daily buses to Úbeda (€4.25, one hour), Baeza (€4.85, 1¼ hours), Jaén (€9.25, two to 2½ hours) and Granada (€17.60, 3¾ hours). The bus stop is on Calle Hilario Marco, 500m north of Plaza de la Corredera via Plaza de la Constitución.

Parque Natural Sierras de Cazorla, Segura y Las Villas

One of the biggest drawcards in Jaén province – and, for nature lovers, in all of Andalucía – is the mountainous, lushly wooded Parque Natural Sierras de Cazorla, Segura y Las Villas. This is the largest protected area in Spain – 2099 sq km of craggy mountain ranges, deep, green river valleys, canyons, waterfalls, remote hilltop castles and abundant wildlife, threaded by well-marked walking trails and forest roads, with a snaking, 20km-long reservoir, the Embalse del Tranco, in its midst. The abrupt geography, with altitudes varying from 460m up to 2107m at the summit of Cerro Empanadas, makes for dramatic changes in the landscape. The Río Guadalquivir, Andalucía's longest river, rises in the south of the park, and flows northwards into the Embalse del Tranco, before heading west across Andalucía to the Atlantic Ocean.

The best times to visit the park are spring and autumn, when the vegetation is at its most colourful and temperatures are pleasant. The park is hugely popular with Spanish tourists and attracts several hundred thousand visitors each year. Peak periods are Semana Santa, July, August, and weekends from April to October.

Getting There & Away

Cazorla town is the nearest you can get by bus to the southern part of the park. For the northern part, a Transportes Sierra Segura bus to Segura de la Sierra (€2.60, 45 minutes) leaves **Puente de Génave bus station** (953 43 53 17; Puente de Génave), just off the N322, at 12.15pm Monday to Friday. The return service departs Segura at 7.30am Monday to Friday.

Getting Around

Exploring the park is far easier if you have a vehicle. The network of paved and unpaved roads and footpaths reaches some remote areas and offers plenty of scope for panoramic day walks or drives. If you don't have a vehicle, you have the option of guided walks, 4WD excursions and wildlife-spotting trips with agencies based in Cazorla (p782) and elsewhere. Bus services are effectively nonexistent.

Hornos

POP 410 / ELEV 867M

Like better-known Segura de la Sierra, little Hornos is fabulously located – atop a crag backed by a sweep of mountains, with marvellous views over the shimmering Embalse del Tranco and the lush, green countryside, richly patterned with olive, pine and almond trees and the occasional tossed dice of a farmhouse.

The castle on the crag was built by Christians in the mid-13th century, probably on the site of an earlier Muslim fortification. Don't expect colour-coordinated geraniums, souvenir shops or a tourist office: Hornos' charms lie in exploring the narrow, winding streets and wondering at the view from several strategically placed miradors.

Sights

Iglesia de la Asunción CHURCH
(Plaza de la Rueda) The early-16th-century Iglesia de la Asunción has the oldest, albeit crumbling, plateresque portal in the province, plus a vibrant and colourful *retablo*

DON'T MISS

RÍO BOROSA WALK

The most popular walk in the Cazorla natural park, **Río Borosa Walk**, follows the crystal-clear Río Borosa upstream to its source through scenery that progresses from the pretty to the majestic, via a gorge, two tunnels and a mountain lake. The walk is about 11km each way, with an ascent of about 600m, and takes about seven hours there and back.

To reach the start, turn east off the A319 at the 'Sendero Río Borosa' sign opposite the **Centro de Visitantes Torre del Vinagre** (953 72 13 51; Ctra A319 Km 48; 10am-2pm & 4-7pm, 5-8pm Jul–mid-Sep, 4-6pm Nov-Mar, closed Mon Nov-Mar), and go 1.7km. The first section of the walk criss-crosses the tumbling, beautiful river on a couple of bridges. After just over 3km, where the main track starts climbing to the left, take a path forking right (with a rickety 'Cerrada de Elías' sign at research time). This leads through a lovely 1.5km section where the valley narrows to a gorge, the **Cerrada de Elías**, where the path becomes a wooden walkway. You re-emerge on the dirt road and continue 4km to the **Central Eléctrica**, a small hydroelectric station.

Past the power station, the path crosses a footbridge, after which a 'Nacimiento Aguas Negras, Laguna Valdeazores' sign directs you on and upward. The path winds its way up the valley, through increasingly dramatic scenery and getting gradually steeper. After about an hour, you enter the first of two tunnels cut through the rock for water flowing to the power station. It takes about five minutes to walk the narrow path through the first tunnel (the path is separated from the watercourse by a metal handrail), then there's a short section in the open air before a second tunnel, which takes about one minute to get through. You emerge just below the dam of the **Embalse de los Órganos** (Laguna de Aguas Negras), a small reservoir surrounded by forested hills. Take the leftward path at the dam and in five minutes you reach the **Nacimiento de Aguas Negras**, where the Río Borosa begins life welling out from under a rock. Enjoy your picnic beneath the spreading boughs of a large tree here, then head back down the way you came.

Due to its popularity, it's preferable to do this walk on a weekday! Do carry a water bottle: all the trackside springs are good and drinkable but the last is at the Central Eléctrica. A torch is comforting, if not absolutely essential, for the tunnels.

(altarpiece) with nine painted panels dating from 1589.

Sleeping & Eating

Hornos has a handful of tourist apartments, *hostales* and *pensiones* if you fancy staying.

At least three of Hornos' *hostales* have restaurants attached – serving straightforward but hearty sierra fare.

Getting There & Away

To get to Hornos, take the A319 12km north of the Tranco dam to a T-junction; from here the A317 winds 4km up to Hornos village.

Segura de la Sierra

POP 250 / ELEV 1145M

One of Andalucía's most picturesque villages, Segura de la Sierra perches on a steep hill crowned by a Reconquista castle. The village takes some of its character from its five Moorish centuries before the Knights of Santiago captured it in 1214, after which it became part of the Christian front line against the Almohads and then the Granada emirate.

As you drive up into the village, the Puerta Nueva, one of four gates of Islamic Saqura, marks the entrance to the old part of Segura. Signs to the Castillo lead you round to a junction on the northern side by the little walled bullring. Turn left here for the castle itself.

Sights

★Castillo de Segura CASTLE

(627 877919; adult/child & senior €4/3, audio guide €2.50; 10.30am-2pm & 5-8.45pm Jul & Aug, approx 11am-2pm & 4.30-7.45pm Wed-Sun Mar-Jun & Sep-Dec, closed Wed Apr-May;) This lofty castle dates from Moorish times but was rebuilt after the Christian conquest in the 13th century. Abandoned in the 17th century, it was restored in the 1960s and has now become a 'frontier territory ' interpretation centre. The ticket office is also Segura's main tourist information point.

Sleeping & Eating

La Mesa Segureña APARTMENT €
(☎953 48 21 01; Calle Cruz de Montoria; incl breakfast 2-person apt €45-55, 4-person apt €80;) Seven cosy apartments just below Segura castle, with great views, a touch of bright art, cast-iron trimmings, fireplaces and minikitchens.

Mirador de Peñalta ANDALUCIAN €€
(☎953 48 20 71; Calle San Vicente 29; mains €5-18; ⏲1.30-4pm & 8-10pm Tue-Sun;) On the street entering Segura from below, this place caters to hungry travellers with a meaty menu that includes steaks, lamb chops and pork, as well as smoked trout and some sierra specialities such as *ajo atao* (a belly-filling fry-up of potatoes, garlic and eggs).

Getting There & Away

Several country roads meet here: the main approach is from the A317 between Cortijos Nuevos and La Puerta de Segura.

ALMERÍA PROVINCE

Boasting silent mountain valleys, sublime beaches and vast tracts of semi-desert scrubland, Almería province is an area of haunting natural beauty. Despite this, and despite enjoying 3000 hours of annual sunshine, it remains relatively unknown outside of Spain. Its obvious drawcard is its glorious coastline, most notably the thrilling beaches of the Parque Natural de Cabo de Gata-Níjar, and the lively, good-time resort of Mojácar. But venture inland, and you'll discover plenty to explore in its sparsely populated and often other-worldly hinterland. Tour the spaghetti-western badlands of the Desierto de Tabernas and discover underground treasures in the Sorbas caves. Further north, the wooded peaks of Los Vélez provide a majestic backdrop for mountain walking. After so much nature, the port city of Almería offers a welcome blast of urban energy with its impressive monuments, handsome centre and buzzing tapas bars.

Almería

POP 165,180

An energetic port city with an illustrious past, Almería is one of Andalucía's emerging destinations. Until fairly recently the city was generally overlooked by travellers, but recent efforts to spruce it up are beginning to pay dividends. It boasts a handsome centre, punctuated by palm-fringed plazas and old churches, several interesting museums and a plethora of fantastic tapas bars. Best of all – and reason alone for a visit – is its spectacular Moorish Alcazaba (fortress).

Sights

Almería's top sights are the Alcazaba and the cathedral, both of which can be explored in a morning, but there are plenty of interesting additional distractions in the city's meandering streets. Orientate yourself from Paseo de Almería, the city's main drag, which runs north–south through the historic centre.

★**Alcazaba** FORTRESS
(☎950 80 10 08; Calle Almanzor; ⏲9am-8pm Tue-Sat Apr–mid-Jun, to 3pm Tue-Sat mid-Jun–mid-Sep, to 6pm Tue-Sat mid-Sep–Mar, to 3pm Sun year-round) FREE A looming fortification with great curtain-like walls rising from the cliffs, Almerìa's Alcazaba was founded in the mid-10th century and went on to become one of the most powerful Moorish fortresses in Spain. It's survived in good shape and while it lacks the intricate decoration of Granada's Alhambra, it's still a magnificent sight. Allow about 1½ hours to explore everything. Pick up a guide leaflet at the kiosk inside the four-arch entrance gate.

The Alcazaba is divided into three distinct *recintos* (compounds). The lowest, the **Primer Recinto**, was residential, with houses, streets, wells, baths and other necessities – now replaced by lush gardens and water channels. From the battlements, you can look over the city's huddled rooftops and down to the **Muralla de Jayrán**, a fortified wall built in the 11th century to defend the outlying northern and eastern parts of the city.

Further up in the **Segundo Recinto** you'll find the ruins of the Muslim rulers' palace, built by the *taifa* ruler Almotacín (r 1051–91), under whom medieval Almería reached its peak, as well as a chapel, the **Ermita de San Juan**, that was originally a mosque. The highest section, the **Tercer Recinto**, is a castle added by the Catholic Monarchs.

★**Catedral de la Encarnación** CATHEDRAL
(☎950 23 48 48; www.catedralalmeria.com; Plaza de la Catedral 8, entrance Calle Velázquez; €5, 8.30-9am Mon-Sat & 10.30-11.30am Sun free; ⏲10am-

LOCAL KNOWLEDGE

THE OLD MEDINA

Sprawled at the foot of the Alcazaba (p785), the maze-like Almedina is one of Almería's most atmospheric neighbourhoods. This was the area occupied by the original Almería – a walled medina (city), bounded by the Alcazaba to the north, the sea to the south, and what are now Calle de la Reina and Avenida del Mar to the east and west. At its heart was the city's main mosque – whose *mihrab* (a prayer niche indicating the direction of Mecca) survives inside the **Iglesia de San Juan** (Calle General Luque; open for Mass 8pm Apr-Sep, 7pm Oct-Mar, closed Tue & Fri) FREE – with the commercial area of markets and warehouses spread around it. Calle de la Almedina still traces the line of the old main street running diagonally across the medina.

An excellent place for refreshment is Tetería Almedina (p787), a friendly tea-house-restaurant. Also worth seeking out is the **Plaza de Pavía market** (9am-2pm Mon-Sat), at its liveliest on Saturdays, with stalls selling everything from cheap shoes to churros (delicious, fat, tubular doughnuts).

7pm Mon-Fri, 10am-2.30pm & 3.30-7pm Sat, 1.30-7pm Sun Apr-Jun, 10am-8.30pm Mon-Fri, 10am-2.30pm & 3.30-7pm Sat, 1.30-7pm Sun Jul-Sep, shorter hours Oct-Dec) Almería's formidable, six-towered cathedral, begun in 1525, was conceived both as a place of worship and a refuge for the population from frequent pirate raids from North Africa. It was originally Gothic-Renaissance in style, but baroque and neoclassical features were added in the 18th century. The Gothic interior, entered through a fine neoclassical cloister, is an impressive spectacle with its sinuous, ribbed ceiling, 16th-century walnut choir stalls and monumental Capilla Mayor (Chancel).

Museo de la Guitarra MUSEUM
(950 27 43 58; Ronda del Beato Diego Ventaja; adult/reduced €3/2; 10.30am-1.30pm Tue-Sun & 6-9pm Fri & Sat Jun-Sep, 10am-1pm Tue-Sun, 5-8pm Fri & Sat Oct-May) It's worth establishing two important facts before you enter this absorbing museum. First: the word 'guitar' is derived from the Andalucian-Arabic word *qitara*, hinting at its Spanish roots. Second: all modern acoustic guitars owe a huge debt to Almerían guitar-maker Antonio de Torres (1817–92), to whom this museum is dedicated. The museum itself details the history of the guitar and pays homage to Torres' part in it.

Museo de Almería MUSEUM
(Museo Arqueológico; 950 17 55 10; www.museosdeandalucia.es; Calle Azorín; 9am-3pm Tue-Sun & 6-9.30pm Wed-Sat mid-Jun–mid-Sep, 9am-8pm Tue-Sat, 9am-3pm Sun mid-Sep–mid-Jun) FREE Almería's excellent archaeology museum, housed in a spacious modern building, focuses on two local prehistoric cultures – Los Millares (3200–2250 BC; probably the Iberian Peninsula's first metalworking culture), and El Argar (2250–1550 BC), which ushered in the Bronze Age. Artefacts from these important sites are well displayed and accompanied by informative explanatory panels in English and Spanish.

Refugios de la Guerra Civil HISTORIC SITE
(Civil War Shelters; 950 26 86 96; Plaza de Manuel Pérez García; adult/reduced €3/2; tours 10am, 11.30am, 12.30pm, 6pm & 7.30pm Jun-Sep, 10.30am & noon Tue-Sun, plus 5pm & 6.30pm Fri & Sat Oct-May) During the civil war, Almería was the Republicans' last holdout in Andalucía, and was repeatedly and mercilessly bombed. The attacks prompted a group of engineers to design and build the Refugios, a 4.5km-long network of concrete shelters under the city. Visits – by 1¼-hour guided tour, in Spanish only – take you through 1km of the tunnels, including the recreated operating theatre and store rooms.

Sleeping

Hotel Nuevo Torreluz HOTEL €
(950 23 43 99; www.torreluz.com; Plaza de las Flores 10; r €55-70; P) A polished four-star enjoying a superb location on a small square in the historic centre. Carpeted corridors lead to smallish but comfortable rooms sporting parquet floors and modern pearl-grey colours. The hotel also runs a trio of cafes and restaurants around the square. Parking is available for €11.90.

★Plaza Vieja Hotel & Lounge BOUTIQUE HOTEL €€
(950 28 20 96; www.airehotelalmeria.com; Plaza de la Constitución 5; d €69-150, ste €119-175;)

Part of the plush **Hammam Aire de Almería** (☎950 28 20 95; 1½hr session €27 Mon-Thu, €29 Fri-Sun; ⏲10am-10pm), this elegant hideaway is perfectly situated on beautiful Plaza de la Constitución, just steps from some of the city's top tapas bars. Its slick, contemporarily attired rooms come with high ceilings, polished wood floors and vast photo-walls of local sights such as the Cabo de Gata.

Hotel Catedral BOUTIQUE HOTEL €€
(☎950 27 81 78; www.hotelcatedral.net; Plaza de la Catedral 8; r €90-150; ❄📶) Boasting a prime location overlooking the cathedral, this debonair four-star occupies a handsome 1850s building. Inside, the decor slickly marries the old and the new, combining clean contemporary lines with Gothic arches and an *artesonado* (coffered) ceiling in the restaurant. Rooms are large and high-ceilinged, and the roof terrace offers heady cathedral views.

Eating

Almería is a great place to eat well. The city is awash with restaurants and tapas bars, ranging from old-school bodegas to trendy modern hang-outs. Frequented as much by locals as out-of-towners and tourists, many are squeezed into the tight-knit area between Plaza de la Constitución and Paseo de Almería.

★**Tetería Almedina** MOROCCAN €€
(☎629 277827; www.teteriaalmedina.com; Calle Paz 2, off Calle de la Almedina; mains €10-15,

LOCAL KNOWLEDGE

TAPAS TOUR

The area between Paseo de Almería and Plaza de la Constitución is packed with busy and atmospheric tapas bars. Many maintain the civilised tradition of serving a free tapas with your drink. As a rule, portions are generous, and for the hungry – or to share – almost everywhere offers *raciones* and *medias raciones* (full- and half-sized plates of tapas items).

Casa Puga (www.barcasapuga.es; Calle Jovellanos 7; tapas from €1.70, raciones €8-15; ⏲noon-4pm & 8.15pm-midnight Mon-Sat) Dating to 1870, this is one of Almería's oldest and best-known tapas bars. Its small interior, a cluttered space of hanging hams, yellowing wall pictures and wine bottles, gets very animated as locals and visitors squeeze in to snack on classic, old-school tapas.

Nuestra Tierra (Calle Jovellanos 16; tapas €2.80-5; ⏲7.30am-noon Mon, to midnight Tue-Thu, to 1am Fri, 8.30am-1am Sat, noon-midnight Sun) Head to this good-looking modern eatery on bar-heavy Calle Jovellanos for creative tapas made with seasonal Andalucian ingredients. Showstoppers include garlic lamb with potatoes and octopus grilled to buttery softness.

El Quinto Toro (☎950 23 91 35; Calle Juan Leal 6; tapas from €1.50, raciones €8-15; ⏲noon-5pm Mon-Sat & 8pm-midnight Mon-Fri) Keep it traditional at this old-school bar near the central market. Don't expect culinary fireworks, just tried-and-tested staples such as *chorizo ibérico* (spicy sausage) and *albóndigas* (meatballs) in wine sauce.

La Mala (Calle Real 69; tortillas €8-12, raciones €6-22; ⏲1-5pm & 8.30pm-1.30am) A favourite local hang-out, this buzzing corner bar fills quickly on weekend evenings. With its boho decor and young crowd, it's a great spot to try a genuine Spanish *tortilla* (omelette), here prepared with everything from tuna to prawns and chilli.

Entrefinos (☎950 25 56 25; www.entrefinos.es; Calle Padre Alfonso Torres 8; tapas €3.50, fixed-price menus €35-50; ⏲1-4pm & 8pm-midnight Mon-Sat) Dressed like a woody wine bar with a timber-beamed ceiling, barrel-top tables and blackboard menus, this ever-popular eatery offers a menu of timeless tapas, such as grilled mushrooms and fried anchovies.

Taberna Postigo (Calle Guzmán; tapas €2.50-3; ⏲11am-5pm & 7pm-midnight Tue, Wed & Sun, to 1am Thu-Sat) Laid-back, friendly and often very busy, this tavern is tucked away in a leafy corner off Paseo de Almería. Grab an outdoor table and dig into crowd-pleasing tapas *a la brasa* (grilled over hot coals), including a flavoursome bacon with *pimientos* (peppers). No credit cards.

fixed-price menus €17-30; ⏱1-11pm Tue-Sun; ☑) For a break from tapas, this welcoming little tearoom-restaurant is the answer. Hidden away in a backstreet below the Alcazaba, it serves a reassuring menu of home-style Moroccan staples – think tagines, tabbouleh, couscous and lightly spiced legume soups. To drink, a herbed tea or infusion is the way to go.

The restaurant is run by a local group dedicated to revitalising the old town, with its many Moroccan immigrants, and reviving the culture of Al-Andalus.

El Asador SPANISH €€€
(☎950 23 45 45; www.elasadoralmeria.com; Calle Fructuoso Pérez 14; mains €18-25; ⏱1.30-4.30pm Mon-Sat & 8.30pm-midnight Tue-Sat) Formal and elegantly furnished, El Asador is smarter than most of its tapas-bar neighbours. Tall-backed chairs and starched table settings set the tone for high-end Spanish cuisine that features foie-gras starters and succulent barbecued steaks.

Casa Joaquín SEAFOOD €€€
(☎950 26 43 59; Calle Real 111; raciones €12-36; ⏱1.30-4.30pm & 9-11.30pm Mon-Fri, to 3.30pm Sat) Fresh seafood is the star of this historic Almería bodega, classically attired with hanging hams and rustic clutter. What's on offer depends on the day's catch but regular crowd-pleasers include juicy *gambas rojas* (red prawns) cooked a la plancha (grilled on a hotplate), and fried *calamares* (squid).

Drinking & Nightlife

La Cueva PUB
(☎950 08 25 21; www.lacueva-almeria.com; Calle Canónigo Molina Alonso 23; ⏱4pm-4am) Craft beer goes hand-in-hand with jam sessions and live music at this laid-back pub. The subdued lighting and walls plastered with posters and concert flyers create an intimate vibe for everything from blues and rock to punk, rap and heavy metal. Gigs are either free or cost around €3 to €5.

Bar Hotel Catedral BAR
(Plaza de la Catedral 8; ⏱7.30am-11pm) Almería's cathedral provides the atmospheric backdrop to leisurely drinks at the slick in-house bar of the Hotel Catedral (p787). Sit out on the plaza or head inside to the bar's elegant interior, decked out with giant blackboards and sharp, minimalist furniture.

Entertainment

MadChester LIVE MUSIC
(☎661 696930; www.facebook.com/madchesterclub; Parque Nicolás Salmerón 9; cover €8-16; ⏱11pm-late Fri & Sat, 6-11pm Sun) This club venue hosts Spanish and international DJs and regular gigs by bands playing indie, rock and electronica.

Clasijazz JAZZ
(www.clasijazz.com; Calle Maestro Serrano 9; nonmembers €2-25) Located in a bland shopping centre, Clasijazz is a thriving music club that stages four or five weekly gigs – ranging from jam sessions to jazz, big band and classical concerts – in a clean, contemporary space. Check the website for upcoming events.

Peña El Taranto FLAMENCO
(☎950 23 50 57; www.eltaranto.com; Calle Tenor Iribarne 20) This is Almería's top flamenco club, where local guitar star Tomatito has been known to stroke the strings. Housed in a series of medieval cisterns, it hosts exhibitions, runs courses and puts on occasional recitals and performances.

Information

Oficina Municipal de Turismo (☎950 21 05 38; www.turismodealmeria.org; Plaza de la Constitución; ⏱10am-2pm & 6-8pm Jul & Aug, 9am-3pm Mon-Fri, 10am-2pm Sat & Sun Sep-Jun) Helpful English-speaking staff can provide maps and city information.

Regional Tourist Office (☎950 17 52 20; www.andalucia.org; Parque de Nicolás Salmerón; ⏱9am-7.30pm Mon-Wed, to 3pm Thu & Fri, 9.30am-3pm Sat & Sun) Can provide information and printed material on the entire Andalucía region.

Getting There & Around

AIR

Almería's small **airport** (☎902 40 47 04; www.aena.es) is 9km east of the city centre.

EasyJet (☎902 59 99 00; www.easyjet.com), **Ryanair** (☎902 05 12 92; www.ryanair.com) and **Thomas Cook Airlines** (☎950 21 39 78; www.thomascookairlines.com) fly direct to/from various English airports (Ryanair also flies from Dublin and Brussels); **Iberia** (☎901 11 13 42; www.iberia.com) and **Vueling** (☎902 80 80 22; www.vueling.com) serve Spanish destinations.

Surbus (www.surbus.com) city bus 30 (€1.05, 35 minutes) runs from the airport to the city centre, stopping at the main **Estación**

Intermodal (☎950 17 36 02; Plaza de la Estación 6), among other places. Services run at least hourly, and often half-hourly, between about 7.15am and 11.20pm (finishing earlier on Sundays).

BOAT

Acciona Trasmediterránea (☎902 454645; www.trasmediterranea.es) sails from the **passenger port** (☎950 23 60 33; www.apalmeria.com) to the Moroccan ports of Nador (€62, six hours) and Melilla (€35, eight hours) at least once daily, and to the Algerian cities of Orán (€81, nine hours) and Ghazaouet (€81, nine hours) at least once weekly.

BUS

Buses and trains share the Estación Intermodal just east of the centre. **Bus Bam** (☎902 22 72 72; www.busbam.com) runs up to six daily buses (one on Sunday) to/from Madrid (€23, 6¾ hours). Most other intercity services are operated by **ALSA** (☎902 42 22 42; www.alsa.es).

DESTINATION	COST (€)	DURATION (HR)	FREQUENCY (DAILY)
Córdoba	29	5	1
Granada	14-17.50	2-4¼	8
Guadix	9.50	2	2
Jaén	19.50	4-5	3
Málaga	19-22	2½-5½	7
Murcia	14	2¾-4½	7
Seville	37	5½-8½	4

TRAIN

From the **Estación Intermodal**, there are direct trains to Granada (€20, 2½ hours, four daily), Seville (€41, 5¾ hours, four daily) and Madrid (€33 to €83, 6½ hours, three daily).

Desierto de Tabernas

Travel 30km north of Almería and you enter another world. The Desierto de Tabernas (Tabernas Desert) is a strange and haunting place, a vast, sun-baked scrubland of shimmering, dun-coloured hills scattered with tufts of tussocky brush. In the 1960s the area was used as a film location for Sergio Leone's famous spaghetti westerns (*A Fistful of Dollars; For a Few Dollars More; The Good, the Bad and the Ugly;* and *Once Upon a Time in the West*), and still today filmmakers come to shoot within its rugged badlands. Many of its 'Western' sets have now been incorporated into Wild West theme parks, which make for a fun family day out.

The main town in the area is Tabernas, on the N340A road.

Sights

Fort Bravo AMUSEMENT PARK

(Texas Hollywood; ☎902 07 08 14; www.fortbravooficial.com; Carretera N340A, Km 468; adult/child €19.40/10; ⏲9am-7.30pm; P 👪) Situated in the desert outside Tabernas, this popular Wild West theme park has a certain dusty charm with its movie sets – which are still used for filming – and daily cowboy and can-can shows. There's a pool (in summer only), buggy rides and horse treks; plus you can stay overnight in a log cabin. The park is 1km off the N340A, signposted 31km from Almería.

Oasys Mini Hollywood AMUSEMENT PARK

(☎902 53 35 32; www.oasysparquetematico.com; Carretera N340A, Km 464; adult/child €22.50/12.50; ⏲10am-7.30pm Jun & Sep, to 9pm Jul & Aug, to 6pm Oct-May, closed Mon-Fri Nov-Mar; P 👪) This, the best-known and most expensive of Tabernas' Wild West parks, provides good family entertainment. The set itself is in decent condition, and the well-kept zoo has some 800 animals, including lions, giraffes, tigers and hippos. Children usually enjoy the 20-minute shoot-outs, while adults may prefer the clichéd can-can show (or at least the beer) in the saloon. There

WORTH A TRIP

CUEVAS DE SORBAS

The rare and spectacular **Cuevas de Sorbas** (☎950 36 47 04; www.cuevasdesorbas.com; basic tour adult/child €15/10.50; ⏲tours 10am-1pm year-round & 3-7pm summer, 4-6pm spring, 4-5pm winter & autumn; P 👪), 2km east of Sorbas, are part of a vast network of underground galleries and tunnels. Guided visits lead through the labyrinthine underworld, revealing glittering gypsum crystals, tranquil ponds, stalactites, stalagmites and dark, mysterious tunnels. The basic tour, suitable for everyone from children to seniors, lasts about 1½ hours. Tours need to be reserved at least one day ahead; English- and German-speaking guides are available

are also two summer pools, restaurants and cafes. Take sunscreen and a hat: there's little shade.

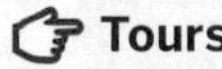

Tours

Malcaminos TOURS
(☎652 022582; www.malcaminos.com; Avenida de las Angustias, Tabernas) A local outfit running excellent tours of Tabernas' cinematic landscape. The guides are enthusiastic and knowledgeable about the area – not just its filmic geography but also its history and geology. Packages include a two-hour 4WD tour (per adult/child €30/18.50) of the area's movie locations.

Parque Natural de Cabo de Gata-Níjar

Extending southeast of Almería, the **Parque Natural de Cabo de Gata-Níjar** (www.degata.com/en) boasts some of Spain's flawless and least crowded beaches. The park, which stretches from Retamar in the west up to Agua Amarga in the east, encompasses 340 sq km of dramatic cliff-bound coastline and stark semi-desert terrain punctuated by remote white villages and isolated farmsteads. Adding to the often eerie atmosphere are the abandoned mines and bizarre rock formations that litter the landscape.

There is plenty to do in the area besides enjoying the beaches and walking: diving, snorkelling, kayaking, sailing, cycling, horse riding, and 4WD and boat tours are all popular. A host of operators offers these activities from the coastal villages during Easter and from July to September, though only a few carry on year-round.

The park's main hub is **San José**, a popular resort on the east coast.

Sights

Faro de Cabo de Gata LIGHTHOUSE
(P) Marking the southwest point of the promontory, this photogenic lighthouse commands stirring views of a jagged volcanic reef known as the **Arrecife de las Sirenas** (Reef of the Mermaids), after the monk seals that used to lounge here.

From the site, a side road runs 3km up to the **Torre Vigía Vela Blanca**, an 18th-century watchtower boasting even more coastal vistas.

Mirador de la Amatista VIEWPOINT
(P) On the main road between La Isleta del Moro and Rodalquilar, this high viewpoint commands breathtaking views of the vertiginous, unspoilt coastline. From here the road snakes down into the basin of the Rodalquilar valley.

Gold Mines RUINS
(P) Set amid the Martian red-rock terrain at the top of the village, the skeletal remains of Rodalquilar's gold mines are an eerie sight. The complex, which was fully operational as recently as the mid-20th century, lies abandoned – and you're free to explore its former crushing towers and decantation tanks.

Jardín Botánico El Albardinal GARDENS
(☎971 56 12 26; Calle Fundición; ⊙9am-2pm Tue-Fri, 10am-2pm & 4-6pm Sat & Sun; P) FREE Rodalquilar's extensive botanical gardens showcase the vegetation of Andalucía's arid southeast. It's well planned, with every plant, tree and shrub identified. There's also a charming *huerta* (vegetable garden), complete with jam recipes and a scarecrow.

Tours

El Cabo a Fondo BOATING
(☎637 449170; www.elcaboafondo.es; 1½hr tour adult/child €25/20) Some of the most spectacular views of the Cabo de Gata coast are from the sea – a perspective you'll get on Cabo a Fondo's outings, which start from La Isleta del Moro, Las Negras or La Fabriquilla. Tours run up to seven times daily and are offered year-round, weather permitting (minimum numbers may be needed in low season). Reservations required.

Sleeping

El Jardín de los Sueños CASA RURAL €€
(☎669 184118, 950 38 98 43; www.eljardindelossuenos.es; Calle Los Gorriones; incl breakfast d €76-98, ste €96-140; P ❄ 📶 ≋) Just outside Rodalquilar, signposted off the main road, this year-round retreat is ideal for getting away from it all. The main farmhouse is surrounded by a beautiful garden of dry-climate plants and fruit trees, some of which contribute to the substantial breakfasts. Inside, the rooms are notable for bright colours, original art, private terraces and the absence of TVs.

La Posada de Paco HOTEL €€
(☎950 38 00 10; www.laposadadepaco.com; Avenida de San José 12; d €61-150; ⊙closed

Cabo de Gata

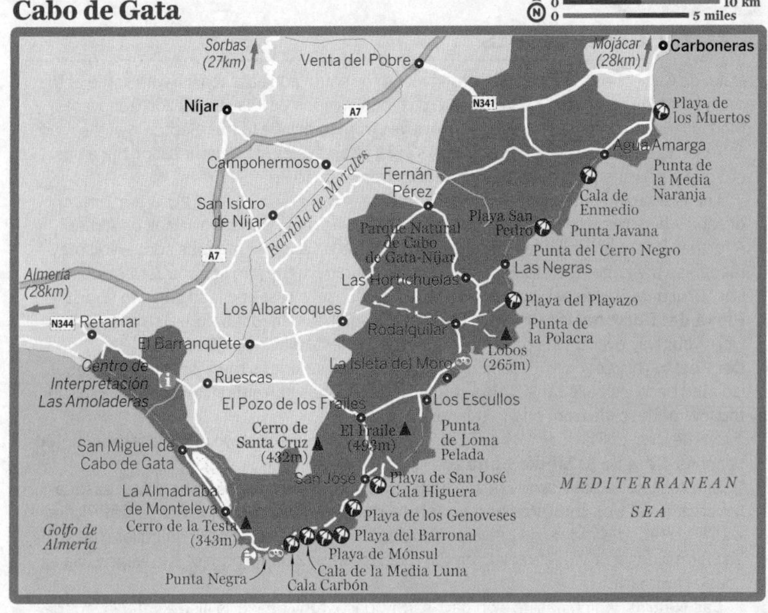

Nov-Feb; P ❄ ☎ ≋) With a convenient central location, gleaming tiled rooms and a sunny, summery feel, Paco's scores across the board. Rooms, which come in various sizes and colours, have their own terraces, some of which offer sea views, and there's a decent range of facilities including a spa, gym, breakfast cafe and pool.

Hotel Senderos HOTEL €€
(☎950 13 80 87; www.hotelsenderos.com; Calle Pueblecico 1; s €59-105, d €79-135; ❄ ☎ ≋) Like everywhere in Agua Amarga, the Senderos hides its charms behind a cool white exterior. Inside it reveals spacious, light-filled rooms with polished marble floors and big, firm beds. There's public parking just outside and the beach is about two minutes' walk away.

★MC San José BOUTIQUE HOTEL €€€
(☎950 61 11 11; www.hotelesmcsanjose.com; Calle El Faro 2; r incl breakfast €92-220; ⏲closed Nov-Feb; P ❄ ☎ ≋) The MC offers the best of both worlds – warm family hospitality and a chic, designer look. Inside, it's all sharp modern furniture, cool whites and slate-greys, while outside the plant-lined terrace and small pool are ideal for basking in the sun.

★MiKasa BOUTIQUE HOTEL €€€
(☎950 13 80 73; www.mikasasuites.com; Carretera Carboneras 20; d incl breakfast €130-240; P ❄ ☎ ≋) MiKasa is an enchanting romantic retreat. A few blocks back from the beach (but still within easy walking distance), it's a lovely villa set up with charming, individually styled rooms, two pools, a spa and a beach bar. Room rates drop considerably outside August.

Eating

★4 Nudos SEAFOOD €€
(☎620 938160; Club Náutico, Puerto Deportivo; mains €15-20; ⏲9am-5pm & 7.30pm-midnight Tue-Sun) Of San José's various seafood restaurants, the 'Four Knots' is the star performer. Aptly housed in the Club Náutico at the marina, it serves classic Spanish dishes – paella included – alongside more innovative creations such as baby-prawn ceviche and tuna marinated in soy sauce, ginger and rosemary. Reservations advised except at the quietest times.

La Gallineta MEDITERRANEAN €€
(☎950 38 05 01; El Pozo de los Frailes; mains €11-27; ⏲1.30-3.30pm & 9-11pm, closed dinner Sun & Mon) An elegant restaurant in the village

DON'T MISS

CABO DE GATA BEACHES

Cabo de Gata's best beaches are strung along the south and east coasts, with some of the most beautiful southwest of San José. A dirt road signposted 'Playas' and/or 'Genoveses/Mónsul' runs to them from San José. However, from mid-June to mid-September, the road is closed to cars once the beach car parks (€5) fill up, typically by about 10am, but a bus (€1 one way) runs from town every half hour from 9am to 9pm.

The first beach outside of San José is **Playa de los Genoveses** (P), a 1km stretch of sand where the Genoese navy landed in 1147 to help the Christian attack on Almería. A further 2.5km on, pristine **Playa de Mónsul** (P) is another glorious spot – you may recognise the large free-standing rock on the sand from the film *Indiana Jones and the Last Crusade*. Tracks behind the large dune at Mónsul's east end lead down to nudist **Playa del Barronal** (600m from the road). If you bear left just before Barronal, and work your way over a little pass just left of the highest hillock, you'll come to **El Lance del Perro**. This beach, with striking basalt rock formations, is the first of four gorgeous, isolated beaches called the **Calas del Barronal**. Tides permitting, you can walk round the foot of the cliffs from one to the next.

A little west of Playa de Mónsul, paths lead from the road to two other less-frequented beaches, **Cala de la Media Luna** and **Cala Carbón**.

San José has a busy sandy beach of its own, and to the northeast there are reasonable beaches at **Los Escullos** and **La Isleta del Moro**. Much finer is **Playa del Playazo** (P), a broad, sandy strip between two headlands 3.5km east of Rodalquilar (the last 2km along a drivable track from the main road) or 2.5km south of Las Negras via a coastal footpath.

Las Negras, which has its own part-sandy, part-stony beach, is also a gateway to the fabulous **Playa San Pedro**, 3km to the northeast. Set between dramatic headlands and home to a small New Age settlement, this fabled beach can be reached only on foot or by boat (€12 return) from Las Negras.

Further up the coast, the small resort of **Agua Amarga** is fronted by a popular sandy beach. A short but steep 1.5km trek to the southwest leads to **Cala de Enmedio**, a pretty, secluded beach enclosed between eroded rocks.

of El Pozo do los Frailes, 4km north of San José, La Gallineta is a hit with city escapees who make the drive out for its innovative, outward-looking cuisine. Menu highlights include ravioli stuffed with foie gras and carpaccio of red prawns.

Casa Miguel SPANISH **€€**
(☎950 38 03 29; www.restaurantecasamiguel.es; Avenida de San José 43-45; mains €10-20; ⏰1-4.30pm & 7.30-11.30pm Tue-Sun) Service and food are reliably good at this long-standing San José favourite, one of several places with outdoor seating on the main drag. There's plenty to choose from on the extensive menu but you'll rarely go wrong ordering the grilled fish of the day.

★**Restaurante La Villa** MEDITERRANEAN **€€€**
(☎950 13 80 90; Carretera Carboneras 18; mains €15-25; ⏰8pm-midnight Jun-Sep, closed Mon & Tue Oct-Dec & Mar-May, closed Jan & Feb) La Villa is a sophisticated Agua Amarga restaurant with a romantically lit dining room and an elegant outdoor terrace. Dishes are original and artfully presented, ranging from Tex-Mex starters to steak tartare and gourmet black-Angus burgers. Reservations advised.

Information

Centro de Información (☎950 38 02 99; www.cabodegata-nijar.com; Avenida San José 27; ⏰10am-2pm & 5.30-8.30pm Apr-Oct, to 2pm Nov-Mar) Park information centre in San José.

Centro de Interpretación Las Amoladeras (☎950 16 04 35; Carretera Retamar-Pujaire, Km 7; ⏰10am-2pm Wed-Sun) The park's main visitor centre, 2km west of Ruescas on the main road from Almería.

Getting There & Away

ALSA (☎902 42 22 42; www.alsa.es) runs at least six daily buses from Almería's Estación Intermodal to San Miguel de Cabo de Gata (€2.90, one hour), and one to Las Negras

(€2.90, 1¼ hours) and Rodalquilar (€2.90, 1½ hours).

Autocares Bernardo (☎950 25 04 22; www.autocaresbernardo.com) operates buses from Almería to San José (€2.90, 1¼ hours, two to four daily).

Mojácar

POP 6490

Both a massively popular beach resort and a charming hill town, Mojácar is divided into two quite separate parts. Mojácar Pueblo is the attractive historic centre, a picturesque jumble of white-cube houses daubed down an inland hilltop. Some 3km away on the coast, Mojácar Playa is its young offspring, a modern low-rise resort fronting a 7km-long sandy beach.

As recently as the 1960s, Mojácar was decaying and almost abandoned. But a savvy mayor managed to resurrect its fortunes by luring artists and travellers to the area with offers of free land – which brought a distinct bohemian air that endures to this day.

Sights

The main sight is Mojácar's hilltop *pueblo,* with its whitewashed houses, charming plazas, bars and cafes. Beach lovers should head down to Mojácar Playa, which boasts 7km of mainly sandy beach. To reach the *pueblo* from the *playa* turn inland at the roundabout by the Parque Comercial, a large shopping centre towards the north end of the beach. Regular buses also connect the two.

Mirador del Castillo VIEWPOINT

(Plaza Mirador del Castillo, Mojácar Pueblo) Perched on the highest point in town – originally the site of a castle and now home to the hotel **El Mirador del Castillo** (☎694 454768; www.elmiradordelcastillo.com; r €68-145, ste €136-145; Easter-Oct;) – this hilltop mirador (viewpoint) looks down to the sea and over a hazy brown-green landscape studded with white buildings and stark volcanic cones just like the one Mojácar occupies.

Casa La Canana HOUSE

(☎950 16 44 20; Calle Esteve 6, Mojácar Pueblo; €2.50; 10.30am-2pm & 5.30-10pm Tue-Sat, 11am-3pm Sun) This recently opened house-museum recreates the dwelling of a well-to-do villager from the first half of the 20th century. The layout of the furniture, some of which is original to the house, reflects the interior decor of the period, while information panels, tools and model animals illustrate the household habits of the time.

Fuente Pública FOUNTAIN

(Public Fountain; Calle La Fuente, Mojácar Pueblo) Hidden near the foot of the hilltop *pueblo,* this historic fountain is a village landmark. Locals and visitors come to fill containers with the water that pours out of 13 spouts into marble troughs and tinkles along a courtyard below colourful plants. A plaque states that in 1488 this was where the envoy of the Reyes Católicos (the Catholic Monarchs Fernando and Isabel) met Mojácar's last Moorish mayor, Alavez, to negotiate the village's surrender.

Sleeping

★Hostal Arco Plaza HOSTAL €

(☎950 47 27 77, 647 846 275; www.hostalarcoplaza.es; Calle Aire 1, Mojácar Pueblo; d €39-45, tr €45-50;) Right in the heart of the action, this friendly, good-value *hostal* has attractive sky-blue rooms with wrought-iron beds and terracotta-tiled floors. The best have private balconies overlooking Plaza Nueva, though you can enjoy the same views from the communal rooftop terrace. The plaza can be noisy in the evening but generally quietens after midnight.

★Hostal El Olivar HOSTAL €€

(☎950 47 20 02, 672 019767; www.hostalelolivar.es; Calle Estación Nueva 11, Mojácar Pueblo; incl breakfast s €44-59, d €54-89;) A stylish retreat in Mojácar's historic centre, the welcoming Olivar has eight pearl-grey rooms furnished in a cool, modern style. Some overlook a plaza, others the mountains behind the *pueblo.* Breakfast is generous and you can take it on the panoramic roof terrace when the weather is decent.

Eating

★Tito's INTERNATIONAL €€

(☎950 61 50 30; Paseo del Mediterráneo 2, Mojácar Playa; mains €9.50-16; 10am-9pm Apr-Oct, to midnight late Jun–Aug;) Picture the ideal beachside bar and chances are it would look something like Tito's, a cane-canopied hangout set amid palm trees on the southern promenade. It's a wonderfully laid-back spot to sate your thirst on fresh-fruit cocktails and enjoy international, fusion-leaning food.

Arlequino FUSION €€
(☎950 47 80 37; Plaza de las Flores, Mojácar Pueblo; mains €10-20; ⊙1-4pm Wed-Sun & 7pm-2am daily) The Arlequino's studiedly mismatched bohemian decor and panoramic rooftop terrace pair well with the fusion Middle Eastern cuisine it serves. Vegetable samosas pave the way for mains such as lightly herbed lamb, elegantly presented on a slate-grey plate, and satisfyingly rich desserts.

ℹ Information

Oficina Municipal de Turismo (☎950 61 50 25; www.mojacar.es; Plaza Frontón, Mojácar Pueblo; ⊙9.30am-2pm & 5-8pm Mon-Fri, 10am-2pm & 5-8pm Sat, 10am-2pm Sun) Up in Mojàcar's hilltop *pueblo*.

Tourist Information Point (www.mojacar.es; Playa Villazar, Mojácar Playa; ⊙10am-2pm daily & 5-8pm Mon-Sat) Down on the beach in front of the Parque Comercial (shopping centre).

ℹ Getting There & Away

Intercity buses stop at various spots around the Parque Comercial roundabout in Mojácar Playa and on **Avenida de Andalucía** in Mojácar Pueblo.

ALSA (☎902 42 22 42; www.alsa.es) runs buses to/from Almería (€7.67, 1¼ to 1¾ hours, two to four daily) and Murcia (€9.18, 2½ to three hours, three daily). Buy tickets at **Mojácar Tour** (☎950 47 57 57; Centro Comercial Montemar, Avenida de Andalucía, Mojácar Playa; ⊙10am-1.30pm & 5.30-8pm), a travel agency at the Parque Comercial in Mojácar Playa.

A local bus (€1.20) runs a circuit from Mojácar Pueblo along the full length of the beach and back again, roughly every half-hour from 9.15am to 11.35pm June to September, and until 9.15pm from October to May.

Valencia & Murcia

Includes ➜

Best Places to Eat

- ➜ Quique Dacosta (p828)
- ➜ El Portal (p826)
- ➜ El Granaino (p833)
- ➜ El Pasaje de Zabalburu (p837)
- ➜ La Pequeña Taberna (p837)
- ➜ Magoga (p840)

Best Places to Stay

- ➜ Bajo el Cejo (p846)
- ➜ Cases Noves (p831)
- ➜ Caro Hotel (p806)
- ➜ Hotel Mayarí (p841)
- ➜ Mont Sant (p818)

Why Go?

The home of one of Spain's most famous exports, paella, is a marvellous stretch of coast offering fine beaches, truly wonderful eating and fabulous festivals. Addictive Valencia city's sophisticated cultural scene and stunning architecture make it wonderful.

Throughout this sun-bathed coastal pleasure-ground, a wealth of festivals awaits you, whether you fancy top-notch rock music at Benicàssim, hooded processions and friendly rivalry at Lorca's Semana Santa, re-enactments of Reconquista battles in the numerous Moros y Cristianos festivals or one of the world's biggest food fights at La Tomatina.

While some coastal resorts – hello Benidorm! – are notoriously overdeveloped, there are plenty that aren't, with towns such as Dénia and Xàbia managing to conserve great charm. The ancient port of Cartagena has a magnificent array of Roman and Carthaginian ruins, while Murcia is a buzzy regional capital with pleasant parks and a cracking eating scene.

When to Go

Valencia City

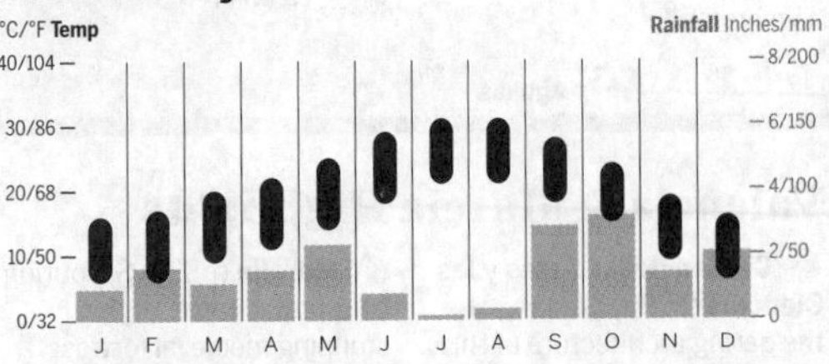

Jan Warm temperatures make this a tempting winter getaway; very low accommodation prices.

Mar–Apr Las Fallas, Valencia's wild spring festival, brings two million visitors to town.

Oct The sea is still swimmable, and there's decent weather but far fewer people.

Valencia & Murcia Highlights

❶ **Ciudad de las Artes y las Ciencias** (p799) Gasping at the daring architecture of this complex of Valencia buildings.

❷ **Russafa** (p806) Living it up in this popular *barrio's* tapas, cafe and bar scene.

❸ **La Tomatina** (p816) Painting the town red at this famous tomato fight in Buñol.

❹ **Morella** (p822) Savouring your first glimpse of this stunning medieval fortress town from afar.

❺ **Murcia** (p835) Strolling the pretty centre of this seriously underrated city for a dose of history and getting right into the great eating scene.

❻ **Cartagena** (p838) Exploring the fascinating Roman and Carthaginian sites and other layers of history of this intriguing port city.

❼ **Lorca** (p842) Enjoying the noble beauty of the old town and its castle, and investigating the traditions of Semana Santa celebrations.

VALENCIA

POP 790,200

Spain's third-largest city is a magnificent place, content for Madrid and Barcelona to grab the headlines while it gets on with being a wonderfully liveable city with thriving cultural, eating and nightlife scenes. Never afraid to innovate, Valencia diverted its flood-prone river to the outskirts and converted the former riverbed into a glorious green ribbon of park winding right through the city. On it are the strikingly futuristic buildings of the Ciudad de las Artes y las Ciencias, designed by local boy Santiago Calatrava. Other brilliant contemporary buildings grace the city, which also has a fistful of fabulous Modernista buildings, great museums, a long stretch of beach and a large, characterful old quarter. Valencia, surrounded by its *huerta,* a fertile zone of market gardens, is famous as the home of rice dishes such as paella, but its buzzy dining scene offers plenty more besides; it's a superb spot for eating.

History

Pensioned-off Roman legionaries founded 'Valentia' on the banks of Río Turia in 138 BC, but the first city was destroyed by Pompey in 75 BC during the Sertorian War.

The Moors made Valencia an agricultural and industrial centre, establishing ceramics, paper, silk and leather industries and extending the network of irrigation canals in the rich agricultural hinterland.

Muslim rule was briefly interrupted in AD 1094 by the triumphant rampage of the legendary Castilian knight El Cid. Much later the Christian forces of Jaime I definitively retook the city in 1238 after a siege. The city finally surrendered and tens of thousands of Muslims were displaced.

Valencia's golden age was the 15th and early 16th centuries, when the city was one of the Mediterranean's strongest trading centres. New World discoveries led to a Spanish pivot towards the Atlantic and began the preeminence of Seville as a trading city and the decline of Valencia. Economic hardship led to the Germanías revolt of 1519–22 of the guilds against the crown and aristocracy. The lean centuries were relieved in the 19th century by industrialisation and the development of a lucrative citrus trade to northern Europe.

Valencia was the capital of republican Spain during part of the Spanish Civil War after the government abandoned Madrid, fearing it was about to fall to the Nationalists. In the traumatic final days of the war, the city surrendered and a period of repression ensued. Severe floods in 1949 and 1957 led to the Río Turia being diverted away from the centre of the city.

Sights

North Ciutat Vella

★Catedral de Valencia CATHEDRAL
(Map p804; ☎963 91 81 27; www.catedraldevalencia.es; Plaza de la Virgen; adult/child incl audio guide €7/5.50; ⏰10am-6.30pm Mon-Sat, 2-6.30pm Sun Jun-Sep, to 5.30pm Oct-May, closed Sun Nov-Feb) Valencia's cathedral was built over a mosque after the 1238 reconquest. Its low, wide, brick-vaulted triple nave is mostly Gothic, with neoclassical side chapels. Highlights are its museum, rich Italianate frescoes above the altarpiece, a pair of Goyas in the **Capilla de San Francisco de Borja**, and…ta-da…in the flamboyant Gothic **Capilla del Santo Cáliz**, what's claimed to be the **Holy Grail** from which Christ sipped during the Last Supper. It's a Roman-era agate cup, later modified, so at least the date is right.

Various relics and a beautiful transitional altarpiece in the **Capilla de San Dionisio** are other noteworthy features.

Left of the main portal is the entrance to the bell tower, **El Miguelete** (Map p804; adult/child €2/1; ⏰10am-7pm Mon-Fri, to 7.30pm Sat, 10am-12.10pm & 2-7.30pm Sun). Climb the 207 steps of its spiral staircase for terrific 360-degree views.

As done for more than a thousand years, the Tribunal de las Aguas (Water Court) meets every Thursday exactly at noon outside the cathedral's Puerta de los Apóstoles. Here, Europe's oldest legal institution settles local farmers' irrigation disputes in Valenciano, the regional language.

Museo Catedralicio Diocesano MUSEUM
(Map p804; ☎963 91 81 27; www.catedraldevalencia.es; Catedral de Valencia; incl in cathedral entry; ⏰10am-6.30pm Mon-Sat, 2-6.30pm Sun Jun-Sep, 10am-5.30pm Mon-Sat, 10am-2pm Sun Oct-May, closed Sun Nov-Feb) Newly reopened, this cathedral museum is a good-looking blend of the modern and venerable. There are some excellent religious paintings here; it's intriguing to see the huge evolution in style in just one generation between the Renaissance paintings of Vicente Macip and those of his son, the great Juan de Juanes. The highlights, though, are

the wonderful 14th-century carved apostles, precursors of those that flank the cathedral's main door. In the basement you can view Roman and medieval remains.

★Mercado Central MARKET

(Map p804; ☎963 82 91 00; www.mercadocentralvalencia.es; Plaza del Mercado; ⏰7.30am-3pm Mon-Sat) Valencia's vast Modernista covered market, constructed in 1928, is a swirl of smells, movement and colour. Spectacular seafood counters display cephalopods galore and numerous fish species, meat stalls groan under the weight of sausages and giant steaks, while the fruit and vegetables, many produced locally in Valencia's *huerta* (area of market gardens), are of special quality. A tapas bar lets you sip a wine and enjoy the atmosphere.

★La Lonja HISTORIC BUILDING

(Map p804; ☎962 08 41 53; www.valencia.es; Calle de la Lonja; adult/child €2/1, Sun free; ⏰10am-7pm Mon-Sat, to 2pm Sun) This splendid building, a Unesco World Heritage site, was originally Valencia's silk and commodity exchange, built in the late 15th century when the city was booming. It's one of Spain's finest examples of a civil Gothic building. Two main structures flank a citrus-studded courtyard: the magnificent Sala de Contratación, a cathedral of commerce with soaring twisted pillars, and the Consulado del Mar, where a maritime tribunal sat. The top floor boasts a stunning coffered ceiling brought here from another building.

★Iglesia de San Nicolás CHURCH

(Map p804; ☎963 91 33 17; www.sannicolasvalencia.com; Calle Caballeros 35; €5; ⏰10.30am-7pm Tue-Fri, 11am-6.30pm Sat, 1-7pm Sun Oct-Jun, 10.30am-9pm Tue-Fri, 10.30am-7.30pm Sat, 11.30am-9pm Sun Jul-Sep) Recently reopened to the public after a magnificent restoration, this single-naved church down a passageway is a striking sight. Over the original Gothic vaulting, the ceiling is a painted baroque riot, with enough cherubs for a serious documentary on childhood obesity. The altarpiece is in similar style, with corkscrew (solomonic) columns framing the twin saints who share the church: San Nicolás saving boys from the pickling tub, and San Pedro Mártir with a cutlass in his head.

La Almoina RUINS

(Map p804; ☎963 08 41 73; www.valencia.es; Plaza Décimo Junio Bruto; adult/child €2/1, Sun free; ⏰10am-7pm Mon-Sat, to 2pm Sun) Beneath the square just east of Valencia's cathedral, the archaeological remains of the kernel of Roman, Visigoth and Islamic Valencia shimmer through a water-covered glass canopy. Head downstairs for an impressively excavated, atmospheric melange of Roman baths, forum buildings and a factory, as well as bits of the Moorish *alcázar* (fortress) and a royal cemetery. Later remains come from a building erected on this square as a hospital for the poor. Get the audio guide: it's tough to interpret otherwise.

South Ciutat Vella

★Museo del Patriarca GALLERY, CHURCH

(Colegio de San Juan; Map p804; ☎692 491769; www.patriarcavalencia.es; Calle de la Nave 1; admission €4, guided visits €5-7; ⏰11am-1.30pm daily, also often 5-7pm Mon-Fri) This seminary was founded in the late 16th century by San Juan de Ribera, a towering Counter-Reformation figure who wielded enormous spiritual and temporal power in Spain and beyond. With an impressive if austere Renaissance courtyard-cloister, its main attraction is a small but excellent religious-art museum. Caravaggio, El Greco and local boys José de Ribera and Juan de Juanes are represented. Most surprising is the manuscript that Thomas More was writing while awaiting his execution in the Tower of London.

★Museo Nacional de Cerámica MUSEUM

(Map p804; ☎963 08 54 29; www.mecd.gob.es/mnescultura; Calle del Poeta Querol 2; adult/child €3/free, Sat afternoon & Sun free; ⏰10am-2pm & 4-8pm Tue-Sat, 10am-2pm Sun) Inside a striking palace this ceramics museum celebrates an important local industry. Downstairs (which also features a decadent hand-painted 1753 carriage) you can learn about the history of ceramics from baroque to modern, with great information that's albeit sometimes a little difficult to relate to the pottery on display. Upstairs, historical ceramics are cleverly dotted with modern works, but the sumptuous, over-the-top interiors, ornate stucco, chinoiserie, damask panels and elaborate upholstery pull plenty of focus. It's an outrageous rococo extravaganza.

Museo de la Seda MUSEUM

(Colegio del Arte Mayor de la Seda; Map p804; ☎697 155299; www.museodelasedavalencia.com; Calle del Hospital 7; adult/child €6/4.50; ⏰10am-2pm & 4-7pm Tue-Fri, 10am-7.30pm Sat, 10am-3pm Sun mid-Sep–mid-Jun, 10am-2.30pm & 5-7.30pm

DON'T MISS

CIUDAD DE LAS ARTES Y LAS CIENCIAS

Ciudad de las Artes y las Ciencias (City of Arts & Sciences; Map p800; ☎961 97 46 86; www.cac.es; Avenida del Profesor López Piñero;) This aesthetically stunning complex occupies a massive 350,000-sq-metre swath of the old Turia riverbed. It's occupied by a series of spectacular buildings that are mostly the work of world-famous, locally born architect Santiago Calatrava. The principal buildings are a majestic opera house, a science museum, a 3D cinema and an aquarium. Calatrava is a controversial figure for many Valencians, who complain about the expense and various design flaws. Nevertheless, if your taxes weren't involved, it's awe-inspiring and pleasingly family-oriented. The promenades and pools around the buildings make for pleasant strolling and you can hire bikes, paddleboards and various other contraptions to enjoy them.

Palau de les Arts Reina Sofía (Map p800; ☎tours 672 062523; www.lesarts.com; Avenida del Professor López Piñero 1; guided visit adult/child €10.60/8.10; guided visits 10.45am, noon & 1.30pm daily, plus 3.45pm & 5pm Mon-Sat) Brooding over the riverbed like a giant beetle, its shell shimmering with translucent mosaic tiles, this ultramodern arts complex, grafted onto the Ciudad de las Artes y las Ciencias, has four auditoriums and enticing levels of plants poking out from under the ceramic exoskeleton. Outside of performance times, you can't enter except by guided visits. These run in Spanish, but there's usually an English summary provided.

Museo de las Ciencias Príncipe Felipe (Map p800; ☎961 97 47 86; www.cac.es; Ciudad de las Artes y las Ciencias; adult/child €8/6.20, with Hemisfèric €12.60/9.60; 10am-6pm or 7pm mid-Sep–Jun, 10am-9pm Jul–mid-Sep;) This interactive science museum, stretching like a giant whale skeleton within the Ciudad de las Artes y las Ciencias, has plenty of touchy-feely things for children, and machines and displays for all ages. It has some excellent sections, with that elusive concept of learning for fun never closer. Each section has a pamphlet in English summarising its contents.

Oceanogràfic (Map p800; ☎960 47 06 47; www.oceanografic.org; Camino de las Moreras; adult/child €29.10/21.85, audio guide €3.70, combined ticket with Hemisfèric & Museo de las Ciencias Príncipe Felipe €37.40/28.40; 10am-6pm Sun-Fri, 10am-8pm Sat mid-Sep–mid-Jun, 10am-8pm mid-Jun–mid-Jul & early Sep, 10am-midnight mid-Jul–Aug;) Spain's most famous aquarium is the southernmost building of the Ciudad de las Artes y las Ciencias. It's an impressive display, divided into a series of climate zones, reached overground or underground from the central hub building. The sharks, complete with tunnel, are an obvious favourite, while a series of beautiful tanks present species from temperate, Mediterranean, Red Sea and tropical waters. Less happily, the aquarium also keeps captive dolphins and belugas – research suggests this is detrimental to their welfare.

Hemisfèric (Map p800; ☎961 97 46 86; www.cac.es; sessions adult/child €8.80/6.85, with Museo de las Ciencias Príncipe Felipe €12.60/9.60; from 10am) The unblinking heavy-lidded eye of the Hemisfèric is at once planetarium, IMAX cinema and laser show. Sessions are roughly hourly, with a break at lunchtime, and multilingual soundtracks are available. It's definitely worth booking ahead in summer, as it has limited capacity and often fills up.

Tue-Fri, 10am-7.30pm Sat, 10am-3pm Sun mid-Jun–mid-Sep) This visually elegant modern museum makes the most of its lovely location in the 15th-century (with baroque additions) palace that was the seat of the silkmakers' guild. Silk was a major Valencian industry, and the compact, manageable display takes you through the process from caterpillars to velvet-sleeved courtiers. There are some lovely restored rooms upstairs, with the highlight being a fabulous rococo tiled floor depicting the fame of silk, here in woman's form, across four continents represented by geographically relevant beasts.

Barrio del Carmen

The northwest corner of the old town is Valencia's oldest quarter, offering bohemian local character and several good museums. El Carme is fertile ground for eating and drinking, with a profusion of little bars and restaurants to track down in its narrow, confusing medieval street plan.

Valencia City

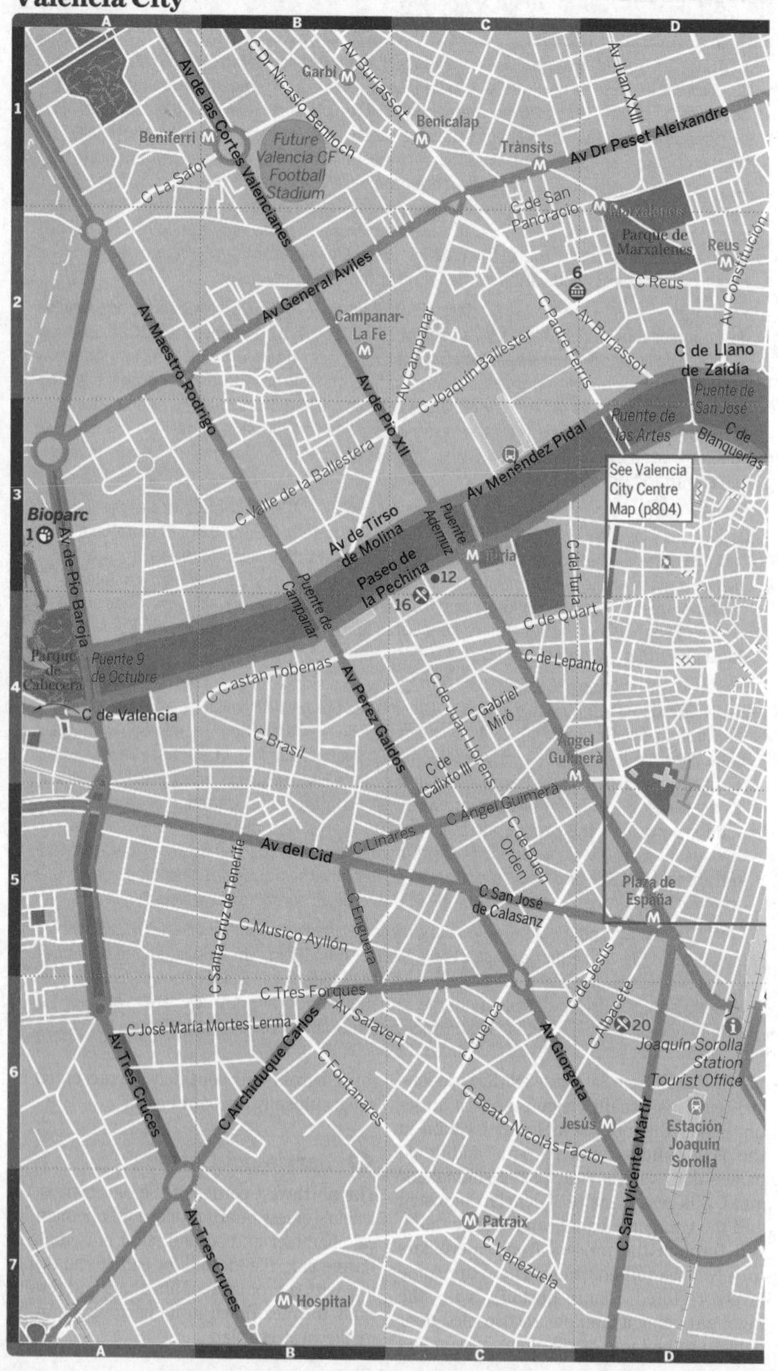

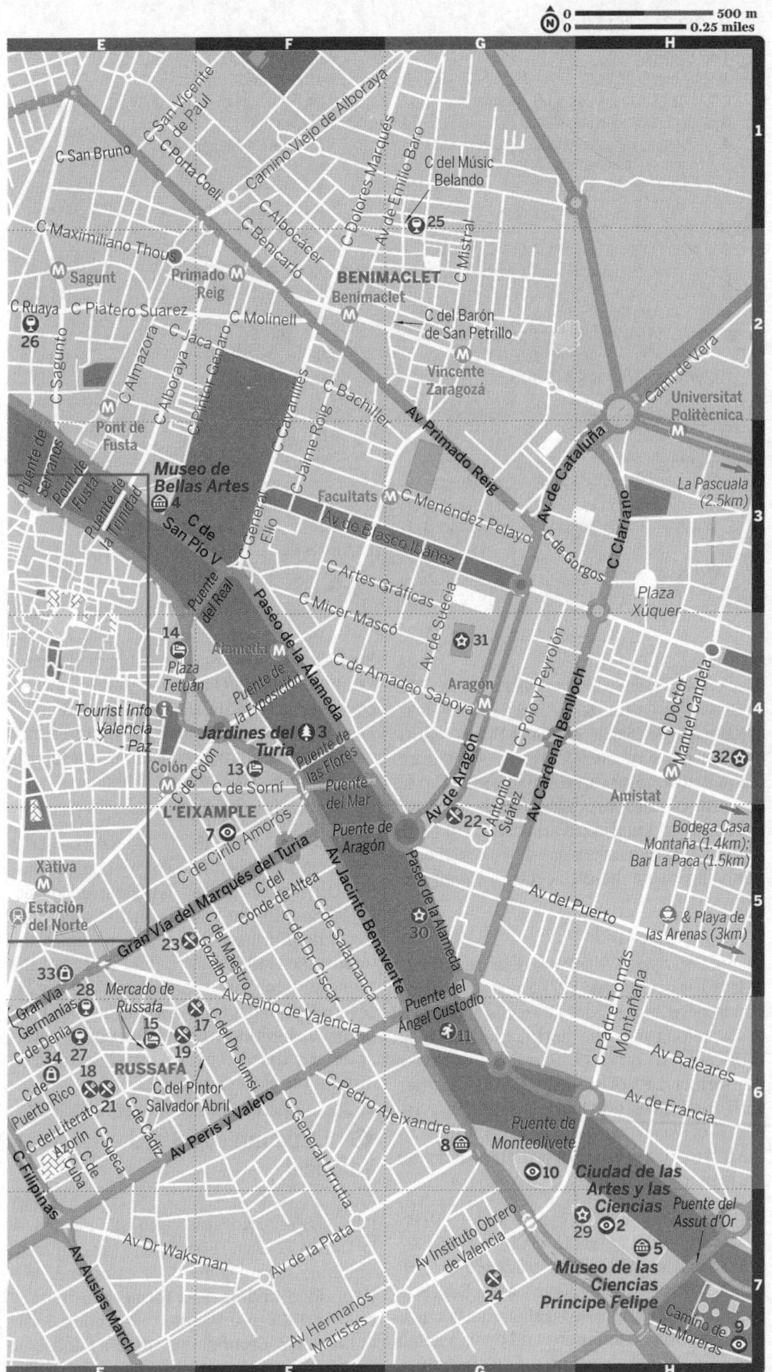

0 500 m
0 0.25 miles
C San Vicente de Paul
C San Bruno
C Porta Coeli
Camino Viejo de Alboraya
C Dolores Marqués
Av de Emilio Baro
C del Músic Belando
25
C Maximiliano Thous
C Albocácer
C Benicarló
C Mistral
Sagunt
Primado Reig
BENIMACLET
Benimaclet
C Ruaya
C Piatero Suarez
C Molinell
C del Barón de San Petrillo
26
C Jaca
C Almazora
C Alboraya
C Pintor Genaro
C Sagunto
Vincente Zaragozá
Camí de Vera
Universitat Politècnica
C Bachiller
C Cavanilles
C Jaime Roig
Av Primado Reig
Pont de Fusta
Puente de Serranos
Pont de Fusta
Puente de la Trinidad
Museo de Bellas Artes
4
C de San Pio V
C General Elio
Facultats
C Menéndez Pelayo
Av de Blasco Ibáñez
Av de Cataluña
La Pascuala (2.5km)
C Clariano
C de Gorgos
C Artes Gráficas
Puente del Real
Paseo de la Alameda
C Micer Mascó
Av de Suecia
Plaza Xúquer
14
Plaza Tetuán
Alameda
31
Puente de la Exposición
C de Amadeo Saboya
Aragón
C Polo y Peyrolón
Tourist Info Valencia - Paz
Jardines del Turia
3
Puente de las Flores
C Doctor Manuel Candela
Av de Aragón
C Antonio Suárez
Av Cardenal Benlloch
32
Colón
C de Colón
13
C de Sorní
Puente del Mar
Amistat
L'EIXAMPLE
7
C de Cirilo Amorós
Puente de Aragón
22
Bodega Casa Montaña (1.4km); Bar La Paca (1.5km)
Xàtiva
Gran Via del Marqués del Turia
C del Conde de Altea
Av Jacinto Benavente
Paseo de la Alameda
Av del Puerto
Estación del Norte
C del Maestro Gozalbo
C del Dr Císcar
C de Salamanca
30
& Playa de las Arenas (3km)
23
33
Gran Via Germanías
28
Mercado de Russafa
Av Reino de Valencia
Puente del Ángel Custodio
C Padre Tomás Montañana
C de Denia
15
17
C del Dr Sumsi
11
Av Baleares
34
27
19
18
RUSSAFA
C del Pintor Salvador Abril
C de Puerto Rico
21
C de Cádiz
Av Peris y Valero
C Pedro Aleixandre
Av de Francia
C del Literato Azorín
C Sueca
C de Cuba
C General Urrutia
8
Puente de Monteolivete
10
Ciudad de las Artes y las Ciencias
C Filipinas
29
2
Puente del Assut d'Or
5
Av Dr Waksman
Av de la Plata
Av Instituto Obrero de Valencia
Museo de las Ciencias Príncipe Felipe
Av Ausiàs March
24
Av Hermanos Maristas
Camino de las Moreras
9

Valencia City

★Torres de Quart GATE
(Map p804; ☎618 803907; www.valencia.es; Calle de Guillem de Castro; adult/child €2/1, Sun free; ⏰10am-7pm Tue-Sat, to 2pm Sun) Spain's most magnificent city gate is quite a sight from the new town. You can clamber to the top of the 15th-century structure, which faces towards Madrid and the setting sun. Up high, notice the pockmarks caused by French cannonballs during the 19th-century Napoleonic invasion.

Torres de Serranos GATE
(Map p804; ☎963 91 90 70; www.valencia.es; Plaza de los Fueros; adult/child €2/1, Sun free; ⏰10am-7pm Mon-Sat, to 2pm Sun) Once the main exit to Barcelona and the north, the imposing 14th-century Torres de Serranos overlooks the former bed of the Río Turia. Together with the Torres de Quart, it is all that remains of Valencia's old city walls. Climb to the top for a great overview of the Barrio del Carmen and riverbed.

Institut Valencià d'Art Modern GALLERY
(IVAM; Map p804; ☎963 17 66 00; www.ivam.es; Calle de Guillem de Castro 118; adult/child €6/3, Fri night & Sun free; ⏰11am-7.30pm Tue-Thu, Sat & Sun, to 9pm Fri) This impressive gallery hosts excellent temporary exhibitions and owns a small but impressive collection of 20th-century Spanish art. The most reliably permanent exhibition on display is the Julio González collection. This Catalan sculptor (1876–1942) lived in Paris and produced exquisite work with iron that influenced later artists such as David Smith and Eduardo Chillida.

Centro del Carmen CULTURAL CENTRE
(Map p804; ☎963 15 20 24; www.consorciomuseos.gva.es; Calle del Museo 2; ⏰11am-7pm Tue-Sun Oct–mid-Jun, to 9pm Tue-Sun mid-Jun–Sep) FREE Behind the church on the landmark Plaza del Carmen, this centre occupies the handsome Gothic cloister and rooms of the monastery that once backed it. It's in a fairly severe Cistercian style and devoted to temporary exhibitions; there are usually several on at a time. It's worth a visit for a stroll around the cloister alone.

L'Eixample & Southern Valencia

Mercado de Colón MARKET
(Map p800; www.mercadocolon.es; Calle de Cirilo Amorós; ⏰7am-1.30am) This magnificent building, now colonised by cafes and boutique food outlets, was formerly a market, built in 1916 to serve the rising bourgeoisie of the new L'Eixample suburb. Its handsome metal skeleton is garnished with Modernista

flourishes to create a stunning ensemble. It's a good place to try *horchata* (a sugary drink made from tiger nuts) and Sundays are nice, with free noon concerts.

Museo Fallero MUSEUM
(Map p800; ☎963 52 54 78; www.valencia.es; Plaza Monteolivete 4; adult/child €2/free, Sun free; ⏰10am-7pm Mon-Sat, to 2pm Sun) Each Fallas festival (p807), just one of the thousands of *ninots*, the figurines that pose at the base of each *falla* (huge statues of papier mâché and polystyrene), is saved from the flames by popular vote. Those reprieved over the years are displayed here. It's fascinating to see their evolution over time, and to see the comical, grotesque, sometimes moving figures up close.

Northern & Eastern Valencia

★Jardines del Turia PARK
(Map p800; 👪) Stretching the length of Río Turia's former course, this 9km-long lung of green is a fabulous mix of playing fields, cycling, jogging and walking paths, lawns and playgrounds. As it curves around the eastern part of the city, it's also a pleasant way of getting around. See Lilliputian kids scrambling over a magnificent, ever-patient **Gulliver** (Map p800; ⏰10am-8pm Sep-Jun, 10am-2pm & 5-9pm Jul & Aug; 🚌19, 95) south of the Palau de la Música.

★Museo de Bellas Artes GALLERY
(San Pío V; Map p800; ☎963 87 03 00; www.museobellasartesvalencia.gva.es; Calle de San Pío V 9; ⏰10am-8pm Tue-Sun) FREE Bright and spacious, this gallery ranks among Spain's best. Highlights include a collection of magnificent late-medieval altarpieces, and works by several Spanish masters, including some great Goya portraits, a haunting Velázquez self-portrait, an El Greco *John the Baptist* and works by Murillos, Riberas and the Ribaltas, father and son. Downstairs, an excellent series of rooms focuses on the great, versatile Valencian painter Joaquín Sorolla (1863–1923), who, at his best, seemed to capture the spirit of an age through sensitive portraiture.

Western Valencia

★Bioparc ZOO
(Map p800; ☎902 250340; www.bioparcvalencia.es; Avenida Pío Baroja 3; adult/child €24/18; ⏰10am-dusk; 👪) 🌿 This zoo devoted solely to African animals has an educational and conservationist remit and an unusual approach. Though, as always, the confinement of creatures such as gorillas in limited spaces raises mixed feelings, the innovative landscaping is certainly a thrill. The absence of obvious fences makes it seem that animals roam free as you wander from savannah to equatorial landscapes. Aardvarks, leopards and hippos draw crowds, but most magical is Madagascar, where large-eyed lemurs gambol around your feet among waterfalls and grass.

Estación del Norte NOTABLE BUILDING
(Map p804; Calle de Xàtiva; ⏰5.30am-midnight) Trains first chugged into this richly adorned Modernista terminal in 1917. Its main foyer is decorated with ceramic mosaics and murals – and mosaic 'bon voyage' wishes in major European languages. There's a riot of oranges and greenery outside and the wooden ticket booths inside are especially lovely. Don't miss the ceramic paintings by Gregorio Muñoz Dueñas in a room to your right.

Valencia's Beaches

Valencia's town beaches are 3km from the centre. Playa de las Arenas runs north into Playa de la Malvarrosa and Playa de la Patacona, forming a wide strip of sand some 4km long. It's bordered by the Paseo Marítimo promenade and a string of restaurants and cafes. The marina and port area, refurbished for the 2007 Americas Cup, is south of here and backed by the intriguing and increasingly trendy fishing district of El Cabanyal, which makes for excellent exploration.

Activities & Courses

Valencia Bikes CYCLING
(Map p800; ☎650 621436; www.valenciabikes.com; Paseo de la Pechina 32; ⏰9.30am-8pm) This well-established set-up runs daily three-hour guided bicycle tours in various languages, with guaranteed departures (€25 including rental and snack). It also hires out quality bikes from here and two other locations.

Escuela de Arroces y Paella Valenciana COOKING
(Map p804; ☎961 04 35 40; www.escueladearrocesypaellas.com; Calle Obispo Don Jerónimo 8; €50-75) Once you know how, cooking paella isn't nearly as intimidating as you might think. So this social, fun and friendly course might be just the thing. Start with a visit to the market, then learn to make a typical rice dish in a restaurant kitchen. Then sit down to eat it, with plenty of wine to wash it down.

Valencia City Centre

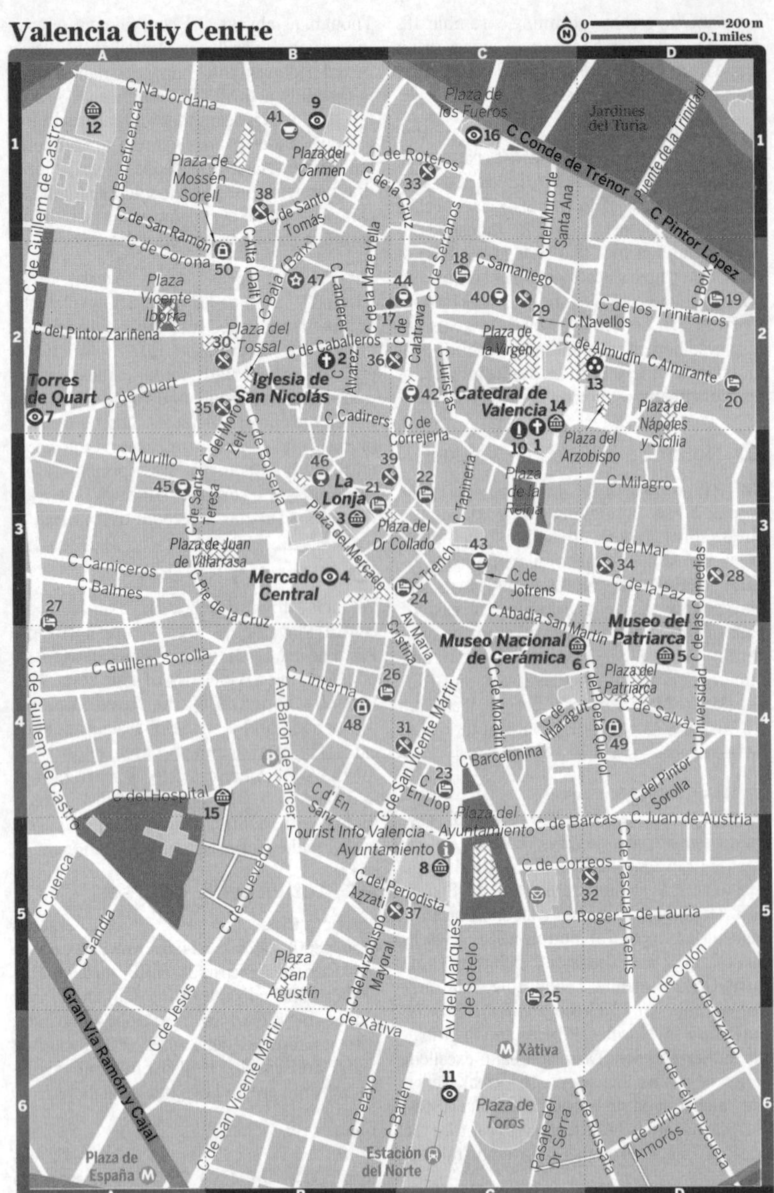

Sleeping

North Ciutat Vella

Home Youth Hostel HOSTEL €
(Map p804; ☎963 91 62 29; www.homeyouthhostel.com; Calle de la Lonja 4; dm €24-27, d €59-67; ❄@📶) Offering location, facilities and plenty more, this hostel sits right opposite the Lonja, a few steps from the central market. The rooms have happy retro decor, proper beds with decent sheets, and a minimum number of room-mates. Kitchen, film library and cheery staff make this a top

Valencia City Centre

Top Sights
1 Catedral de Valencia C2
2 Iglesia de San Nicolás B2
3 La Lonja B3
4 Mercado Central B3
5 Museo del Patriarca D4
6 Museo Nacional de Cerámica C4
7 Torres de Quart A2

Sights
8 Ayuntamiento C5
9 Centro del Carmen B1
10 El Miguelete C2
11 Estación del Norte C6
12 Institut Valencià d'Art Modern A1
13 La Almoina D2
14 Museo Catedralicio Diocesano C2
15 Museo de la Seda B4
Palacio del Marqués de Dos Aguas .... (see 6)
16 Torres de Serranos C1

Activities, Courses & Tours
17 Escuela de Arroces y Paella Valenciana B2

Sleeping
18 Ad Hoc Carmen C2
19 Ad Hoc Monumental D2
20 Caro Hotel D2
21 Home Youth Hostel B3
22 Hostal Antigua Morellana C3
23 Hostal Venecia C4
24 Hotel Plaza del Mercado C3
25 Hotel Sorolla Centro C5
26 One Shot Mercat 09 .... B4
27 Quart Youth Hostel A3

Eating
28 Cinnamon D3
29 Delicat C2
30 El Celler del Tossal B2
31 El Encuentro C4
32 El Poblet D5
33 El Tap C1
34 Entrevins D3
35 La Pilareta B2
36 La Salvaora C2
L'Ostrería del Carme .... (see 50)
37 Navarro C5
38 Refugio B1
39 Tasca Ángel B3
Vuelve Carolina .... (see 32)

Drinking & Nightlife
40 Café de las Horas C2
41 Café Museu B1
42 Café Negrito C2
43 Horchatería de Santa Catalina C3
44 L'Ermità C2
45 Radio City A3
46 Tyris on Tap B3

Entertainment
47 Jimmy Glass B2

Shopping
48 Cestería El Globo B4
49 Lladró D4
50 Mercado de Mossén Sorell B2

budget spot. Dorms are substantially cheaper outside high season.

Purple Nest HOSTEL €
(Map p800; ☎963 53 25 61; www.nesthostelsvalencia.com; Plaza de Tetuán 5; dm €17-24, d €65-79; ❄@📶) Well equipped and with plenty of events to help your Valencian social life along, this makes a pleasing base. There's a bar, kitchen and deck, and spacious, colourful rooms sleeping four to 10. If you value space, it's worth upgrading to the four-bed dorms. Breakfast is available for €3 extra.

★**Hostal Antigua Morellana** HOSTAL €€
(Map p804; ☎963 91 57 73; www.hostalam.com; Calle En Bou 2; s/d €55/65; ❄@📶) This friendly, family-run, 18-room spot occupies a renovated 18th-century *posada* (where wealthier merchants bringing produce to market would spend the night) and has cosy, good-sized rooms, many with balconies. It's kept shipshape by the house-proud owners and there are loads of great features, including memory-foam mattresses, handsome fabrics and lounge with coffee. Higher floors have more natural light. Great value.

Ad Hoc Carmen HOTEL €€
(Map p804; ☎960 45 45 45; www.adhochoteles.com; Calle Samaniego 20; s/d/q €54/84/134; @📶) Strategically placed for sorties to the centre's historic buildings or the bars and restaurants of Barrio del Carmen, this hotel offers a variety of handsome modern rooms with clean lines and whitewashed wood. Many chambers are duplexes, offering good sleeping solutions for families, groups or squabbling couples. No breakfast or parking available. Good value.

Ad Hoc Monumental HOTEL €€
(Map p804; ☎963 91 91 40; www.adhochoteles.com; Calle Boix 4; s/d from €71/83; ❄📶) Friendly Ad Hoc offers comfort and charm deep within the old quarter and also runs a splendid small restaurant. The late-19th-century building has been restored to its former

DON'T MISS

RUSSAFA

The new town's most captivating corner, the district of **Russafa** (p809) may be comparatively compact but it packs a weighty punch. A downmarket *barrio* turned trendy, its collection of quirky galleries and vintage shops keep people entertained by day, while by night it becomes the city's best zone for eating and cafe-bar nightlife – a buzzing hub of quality tapas, modish vermouth bars, literary cafes and innovative cultural offerings. It's a district with its own very distinctive feel and an essential Valencian evening experience, particularly at weekends.

splendour with great sensitivity, revealing original ceilings, mellow brickwork and solid wooden beams. Superior rooms on the top floor have a great private balcony terrace, where you can breakfast.

Hotel Plaza del Mercado APARTMENT €€
(Map p804; ☎963 15 33 67; www.myrhotelplaza mercado.com; Plaza del Mercado 45; r €134-179; P❄@☎) Smart rooms in modish shades of grey have decent kitchens at this super-central location. Right opposite the market, it boasts a spa complex, a buzzy cafe-restaurant area and – one of the few in this area – a car park. Many of the rooms can sleep up to two kids, making it a fine choice for families.

★**Caro Hotel** HOTEL €€€
(Map p804; ☎963 05 90 00; www.carohotel.com; Calle Almirante 14; r €160-330; P❄☎) Housed in a sumptuous 19th-century mansion, this hotel sits atop two millennia of Valencian history, with restoration revealing a hefty hunk of the Arab wall, Roman column bases and Gothic arches. Each room is furnished in soothing dark shades, with a great king-sized bed and varnished cement floors. Bathrooms are tops. For special occasions, reserve the 1st-floor grand suite, once the ballroom.

South Ciutat Vella

Quart Youth Hostel HOSTEL €
(Map p804; ☎963 27 01 01; www.quarthostel.com; Calle Guillem de Castro 64; dm €12-24, d with shared bathroom from €42; ❄@☎) Handsome and contemporary, this hostel places itself firmly in the flashpacker class with facilities that include a gym, quality beds and an upbeat urban vibe. The dorms are great, with step access to the bunks and plenty of privacy. Breakfast is a steal at €2 and staff are motivated and helpful. Bring a padlock for the lockers.

★**Hotel Sorolla Centro** HOTEL €€
(Map p804; ☎963 52 33 92; www.hotelsorollac entro.com; Calle Convento Santa Clara 5; s/d €77/99; ❄☎) Neat and contemporary but without any flashy design gimmicks, this hotel offers very solid value for comfortable, well-thought-out modern rooms with powerful showers and lots of facilities. Staff are extremely helpful and the location, on a pedestrian street close to the main square, is fab.

Hostal Venecia HOSTAL €€
(Map p804; ☎963 52 42 67; www.hotelvenecia.com; Plaza del Ayuntamiento 3; r €97-147; ❄@☎) Right on Valencia's main square, this sumptuous building's functional interior doesn't give many hints of the noble exterior, but it offers compact modern rooms, many with small balcony. Rates vary substantially; it's a good deal if you pay around €80. Despite the *hostal* name, facilities are those of a midrange hotel. Strong points are friendly service and its prime location.

★**One Shot Mercat 09** BOUTIQUE HOTEL €€€
(Map p804; ☎963 11 00 11; www.hoteloneshot mercat09.com; Calle Músic Peydró 9; r €100-180; ❄☎≋) Opened in 2017, this handsome hotel occupies a strategic corner in an area of quiet lanes near the market. With just 22 rooms, it's a personal, intimate place with art exhibitions in the lobby and a lovely rooftop pool. The four room types basically vary by size and outlook; the executive- and junior-suite categories face the street. There's an excellent restaurant.

L'Eixample & Russafa

★**Russafa Youth Hostel** HOSTEL €
(Map p800; ☎963 31 31 40; www.russafayouth hostel.com; Carrer del Padre Perera 5; dm €18-20, s with shared bathroom €30, d with shared bathroom €40-54; @☎) You'll feel at home in this super-welcoming, cute hostel set over various floors of a venerable building in the heart of vibrant Russafa. It's all beds, rather than bunks, and with a maximum of three to a room, there's no crowding. Sweet rooms and spotless bathrooms make for an easy stay.

★**Hospes Palau de la Mar** HOTEL €€€
(Map p800; ☎963 16 28 84; www.hospes.com; Avenida Navarro Reverter 14; r €170-255; P❄@☎≋) Created by the merging of two elegant

19th-century mansions, this boutique hotel, all black, white, soft fuscous and beige, is cool and contemporary. There's a sizeable interior garden courtyard, a sauna, spa and plunge pool. Rooms are comfortable without the wow factor and staff are extremely courteous.

Eating

Valencia is surrounded by its *huerta*, a fertile coastal agricultural plain that supplies it with excellent fruit and vegetables.

You're seriously spoiled for choice when it comes to the numerous restaurants. Less tapas-hopping is done in Valencia than in the rest of Spain. Locals tend to sit down at bar or table to eat a meal of various tapas portions.

North Ciutat Vella

Tasca Ángel TAPAS €

(Map p804; ☎963 91 78 35; Calle de la Purísima 1; sardines €4; ⌚10.30am-3pm & 7.30-11.30pm Mon-Sat, 11.30am-3pm Sun) This no-frills place has been in business for 70 years and is famous for its fishy tapas, but in particular grilled sardines, which are delicious. Order them with a cold beer or white wine and find inner peace.

La Pilareta TAPAS €

(Bar Pilar; Map p804; ☎963 91 04 97; www.barlapilareta.es; Calle del Moro Zeit 13; mussels €7.10; ⌚noon-midnight) Earthy, century-old and barely changed, La Pilareta is great for hearty tapas and *clóchinas* (small, juicy local mussels), available between May and August. For the rest of the year it serves *mejillones* (mussels), altogether fatter if less tasty. A platterful comes in a spicy broth that you scoop up with a spare shell. It's got atmosphere in spades.

★La Salvaora SPANISH €€

(Map p804; ☎963 92 14 84; www.lasalvaora.com; Calle de Calatrava 19; mains €13-19; ⌚1.30-3.30pm Wed, 1.30-3.30pm & 8.30pm-midnight Thu-Mon Sep-May, 8.30pm-midnight daily Jun-Aug) Refined, elegant but not expensive, this intimate spot is decorated with black-and-white portraits of flamenco stars. At first glance, the menu of Spanish favourites – think beef cheek, bull tail, ham, croquettes – looks familiar, but modern presentation and exquisite quality soon prove this is no ordinary *tasca*. Exceptional value for this standard; the tapas degustation menu is a steal.

★Cinnamon FUSION €€

(Map p804; ☎963 15 48 90; Calle de las Comedias 5; dishes €9-16; ⌚1.30-4pm Mon, 1.30-4pm & 8.30-11pm Tue-Sat; 📶📝) This intimate space is so tiny, you wonder how it prepares anything more elaborate than a fried egg. But wonders emerge from the open kitchen, with dishes bursting with taste and freshness. Creative plates include the crunchy house salad, a fab daily special and good options for vegetarians. A very worthwhile eating experience, if there's room.

Delicat TAPAS €€

(Map p804; ☎963 92 33 57; Calle Conde Almodóvar 4; dishes €8-18; ⌚1.45-3.30pm & 8.45-11.30pm Tue-Sat, 1.45-3.30pm Sun; 📶) At this particularly

LAS FALLAS

The exuberant, anarchic swirl of **Las Fallas de San José** (www.fallas.com; ⌚Mar) – fireworks, music, festive bonfires and all-night partying – is a must if you're visiting Spain in mid-March. The *fallas* themselves are huge sculptures of papier mâché on wood built by teams of local artists.

Each neighbourhood sponsors its own *falla*, and when the town wakes after the *plantà* (overnight construction of the *fallas*) on the morning of 16 March, more than 350 have sprung up. Reaching up to 15m in height, with the most expensive costing hundreds of thousands of euros, these grotesque, colourful effigies satirise celebrities, current affairs and local customs. They range from comical to moving. It's a custom that grew through the 19th and 20th centuries.

Around-the-clock festivities include street parties, paella-cooking competitions, parades, open-air concerts, bullfights and free fireworks displays. Valencia considers itself the pyrotechnic capital of the world and each day at 2pm from 1 to 19 March, a *mascletà* (more than five minutes of deafening thumps and explosions) shakes the window panes of Plaza del Ayuntamiento.

After midnight on the final day, each *falla* goes up in flames – backed by yet more fireworks. A popular vote spares the most-cherished *ninot* (figure), which gets housed for posterity in the Museo Fallero (p803).

friendly, intimate option, the open kitchen offers an unbeatable-value set menu of samplers for lunch (€14.50) and delicious tapas choices for dinner. There's a range of influences at play. The decor isn't lavish but the food is memorable. It's best to book ahead as the small space fills fast.

★Entrevins SPANISH €€€
(Map p804; ☎963 33 35 23; www.entrevins.es; Calle de la Paz 7; mains €19-23; ⊙1.30-3.45pm & 8.30-11.30pm Tue-Sat) With a quiet, restrained elegance, this upstairs restaurant makes a lovely lunchtime retreat from the bustle of the street and is handy for several nearby sights. Grab a window table to watch the passers-by below and enjoy the seriously tasty food. The lunchtime set menu (€20, weekdays only) is top value for this quality and includes two shared starters.

South Ciutat Vella

★Navarro VALENCIAN €€
(Map p804; ☎963 52 96 23; www.restaurantenavarro.com; Calle del Arzobispo Mayoral 5; rices €14-17, set menu €22; ⊙1.30-4pm Mon-Fri, 1.30-4pm & 8.30-11pm Sat; 📶) A byword in the city for decades for its quality rice dishes, Navarro is run by the grandkids of the original founders and it offers plenty of choice, outdoor seating and a set menu, including one of the rices as a main.

El Encuentro SPANISH €€
(Map p804; ☎963 94 36 12; www.restauranteelencuentro.es; Calle de San Vicente Mártir 28; mains €9-18; ⊙1.30-4.30pm & 8.30pm-12.30am Mon-Sat; 📶) There's a very likeable old-fashioned feel about this place, which offers stalwart Spanish cuisine at fair prices. Expect plenty of stew-type dishes such as beans and chorizo; the meat and fish plates are also reliable. Browse the wines on your way in so you don't have to get up again. The pleasant summer terrace is set back from the street.

Vuelve Carolina MEDITERRANEAN €€
(Map p804; ☎963 21 86 86; www.vuelvecarolina.com; Calle de Correos 8; dishes €10-20; ⊙1.30-4.30pm & 8.30-11.30pm Mon-Sat; 📶) Overseen from a distance by noted chef Quique Dacosta, this upbeat bar-restaurant offers style – those clothes-horse bar stools could be more comfy though – and an inspiring selection of tapas and fuller plates. These range from exquisite Japanese-influenced creations to tacos, rices and more. Service is solicitous, and watching the open kitchen under the benevolent gaze of cardboard deer heads is always entertaining.

★El Poblet GASTRONOMY €€€
(Map p804; ☎961 11 11 06; www.elpobletrestaurante.com; Calle de Correos 8; degustation menus €85-120, mains €25-35; ⊙1.30-3.30pm Tue, 1.30-3.30pm & 8.30-10.30pm Mon & Wed-Sat; 📶) This upstairs restaurant, overseen by famed Quique Dacosta and with Luis Valls as chef, offers elegance and fine gastronomic dining at prices that are very competitive for this quality. Modern French and Spanish influences combine to create sumptuous degustation menus. Some of the imaginative presentation has to be seen to be believed, and staff are genuinely welcoming and helpful.

Barrio del Carmen

★L'Ostrería del Carme SEAFOOD €
(Map p804; ☎629 145026; www.laostreriadelcarmen.com; Plaza de Mossén Sorell; oysters €2-4; ⊙11am-3pm Mon-Sat, plus 5-8.30pm Thu & Fri) This little stall inside the **Mossén Sorell market** (⊙7.30am-3pm Mon-Sat, plus 5-8.30pm Thu & Fri except in Aug) is a cordial spot and a fabulous snack stop. It has oysters of excellent quality from Valencia and elsewhere; sit down and let them shuck you a few, washed down with some white wine.

★El Tap TAPAS, VALENCIAN €€
(Map p804; ☎963 91 26 27; www.facebook.com/restauranteeltapvalencia; Calle de Roteros 9; mains €10-18; ⊙1.30-4pm & 7.30-11.30pm Tue-Sat, 1.30-4pm Sun; 📶) Tap is one of Barrio del Carmen's rich selection of small, characterful restaurants and is genuinely welcoming. The food is market-based and originally and delightfully prepared. Dishes with local tomatoes are a standout, and there's a carefully chosen list of both wines and boutique beers. Excellent value.

Refugio FUSION €€
(Map p804; ☎690 617018; www.refugiorestaurante.com; Calle Alta 42; mains €14-22, set menu €13-16; ⊙2-4pm & 9-11.30pm; 📶) Named for the civil-war hideout opposite and simply decorated in whitewashed brick, Refugio preserves some of the Carmen *barrio's* former revolutionary spirit. Excellent Med-fusion cuisine is presented in lunchtime menus of surprising quality: there are some stellar plates on show, though the veggie options aren't always quite as flavoursome. Evening dining is high quality and innovative.

LOCAL KNOWLEDGE

RICE DISHES OF VALENCIA

Valencia is the home of rice dishes, which go far beyond what the rest of the world thinks of as paella. For Valencians, rice is exclusively a lunchtime dish, though a few places do prepare it at dinnertime for the tourist trade.

On weekends, heading to the beach, into the *huerta* or to Albufera villages such as Pinedo or El Palmar to eat rice dishes is a local tradition, but Valencians also love to get together at someone's house and cook up a rice dish themselves.

There's a whole world of rices in Valencia. Paella is a dry rice, with the liquid evaporated. Rices served with broth are known as *caldoso* (soupy) or *meloso*, which are wet. Rices reflect the seasons, with winter and summer ingredients making their way into the dish depending on the month. Almost any ingredient can find its way into one, including all types of vegetables, fish, seafood and meat.

Paellas are typical of the Valencian coast. Meat paellas normally have chicken and rabbit, with green beans and other vegetables in summer, or perhaps fava beans and artichokes in winter.

Fish rices tend to be served more liquid, with calamari or cuttlefish supplying the flavour and prawns or langoustines for decoration. If you add prawns to a meat paella, it's a paella *mixta*. *Arroz negro* (black rice) is another typical coastal rice that's made with squid ink and fish stock.

Fideuà is similar to paella, but made with fine pasta. Fresh rockfish are used to make a fish stock. The dish is faster to cook, as the noodles are done faster than rice.

Popular seafood-based winter rices include a cauliflower and salt-cod paella.

In the interior, rices tend to be heavier. In Alcoy and Xàtiva, rices are baked in the oven and might have pork, sausage, beans and black pudding. In Alicante's interior one typical rice has snails, rabbit and chickpeas, while around Orihuela *arroz con costra* (crusty rice) is made in the oven with a crust of beaten egg on top.

El Celler del Tossal VALENCIAN €€
(Map p804; ☎963 91 59 13; www.elcellerdeltossal.com; Calle de Quart 2; mains €16-24; ⊙2-4pm Sun-Wed, 2-4pm & 9-11pm Thu-Sat) One of the Carmen's best lunchtime *menú* options (€20) is backed up by excellent à la carte dinners, including a couple of quality rice dishes. It's an intimate, elegant, two-level spot that takes its food seriously, combining quality ingredients with flair and the odd flourish. It's all delicious.

Russafa

Russafa (p806) is Valencia's best place for an evening meal, with a staggering variety of options in a small area. Most lean towards modern, fusion cuisine or international specialities. It gets very busy at weekends, when the buzz is intoxicating.

Copenhagen VEGETARIAN €
(Map p800; ☎963 28 99 28; www.grupocopenhagen.com; Calle del Literato Azorín 8; dishes €8-12; ⊙1.30-4pm & 8.30-11.30pm Thu-Mon, 1.30-4pm Tue & Wed; 📶✎) Bright and vibrant, the buzz from this popular vegetarian restaurant seems to spread a contagion of good cheer all along the street. It does a very toothsome soy burger as well as top homemade pasta, but the truth is it's all pretty tasty.

★**Dos Estaciones** SPANISH €€
(Map p800; ☎963 03 46 70; www.2estaciones.com; Calle del Pintor Salvador Abril 28; mains €17-23, degustation menus €35-48; ⊙1.30-4pm & 8.30-11pm Tue-Sat) Two talented chefs oversee this small restaurant, which consists of a line of small tables and a bar counter behind which the food is cooked in limited space. Despite this, some extraordinary creations are produced at a very reasonable price; freshness and innovation are guaranteed.

El Rodamón de Russafa FUSION, TAPAS €€
(Map p800; ☎963 21 80 14; www.elrodamon.com; Calle Sueca 47; tapas €6-12; ⊙7.30pm-midnight Mon & Tue, 2-4pm & 7.30pm-midnight Wed-Sun, evenings only Jul–mid-Sep; 📶) The deal here is that they've picked their favourite dishes encountered around the world and made a Valencian tapas plate from them, so you can pick from a whole range of eclectic morsels from several nations, including Spain. It's modern and buzzy, with excellent staff, and the quality is very high. There are several dozen wines available by the glass.

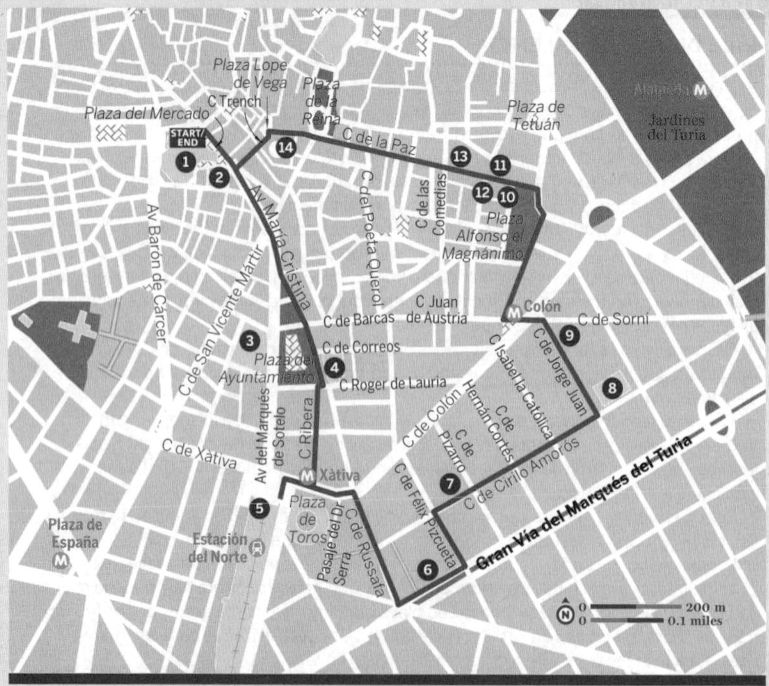

Walking Tour
Modernisme Meander

START MERCADO CENTRAL
FINISH MERCADO CENTRAL
LENGTH 3.25KM; 1½ HOURS

This walk takes in Valencia's main Modernista buildings. After sniffing around **1 Mercado Central** (p798), take in the stucco facade, with neo-Gothic pilasters above allegories of Valencia's fertility, of **2 Calle Ramilletes 1**. Follow Avenida María Cristina to Plaza del Ayuntamiento, site of the sober **3 town hall** and resplendent **4 central post office**, a lighter neoclassical affair with 1920s flourishes. Drop in and look up to savour its magnificent leaded-glass dome.

At the end of Calle Ribera, detour to **5 Estación del Norte** (p803), with its cute original Modernista booking area of dark wood, and adjacent hall with elaborate tile work. Take Calle de Russafa, then turn left for **6 Casa Ortega** (Gran Vía 9), with its ornate floral decoration and balcony, supported by a pair of handsome caryatids. Go left along Calle de Félix Pizcueta, then take the first right onto Calle de Cirilo Amorós. From here, lift your gaze above the modern, ground-floor shops to appreciate each building's original structure. Pause by **7 Casa Ferrer** (No 29), garlanded with stucco roses and ceramic tiling. Continue northwards to **8 Mercado de Colón** (p802), a chic spot for a drink stop, then head northwest to **9 Casa del Dragón** (Calle de Jorge Juan 3), named for its dragon motifs.

Cross Calle de Colón, turn right along Calle Poeta Quintana and pass the mounted statue of a haughty King Jaime I to join Calle de la Paz. Back in the 19th century, **10 Hotel Vincci Palace** was Valencia's finest. Both it and **11 No 31**, opposite, have elaborate, decorated miradors (corner balconies), while **12 Red Nest Hostel** (No 36) has delicate, leafy iron railings. Opposite, on the corner of Calle de las Comedias, **13 Nos 21 and 23** have characteristically magnificent window and balcony work, and a columned mirador.

At the end of Calle de la Paz, continue straight, maybe calling in for an *horchata* at **14 Horchatería de Santa Catalina** (p813). Then at Plaza Lope de Vega, turn left into Calle Trench to return to the Mercado Central.

Canalla Bistro FUSION **€€**
(Map p800; ☎963 74 05 09; www.canallabistro.com; Calle del Maestro José Serrano 5; mains €10-17; ⏱1.30-3.30pm & 8.30-11.30pm; 📶) Chic but commodious, with an interior featuring packing crates, cartoon chickens and other decorative quirks, this is where top Valencian chef Ricard Camarena (p811) can be a little more light-hearted. Sensationally presented dishes draw their inspiration from street food from around the world. Creative, fun and delicious.

L'Eixample & Southern Valencia

★La Gallineta SPANISH **€€**
(Map p800; ☎963 36 36 64; www.lagallineta.es; Calle del Conde de Altea 7; mains €10-19; ⏱8am-6pm Mon-Thu, to midnight Fri & Sat) This welcoming contemporary space has a short, quality menu of dishes inspired by what's fresh and good at the moment: the power of the market at work. It's intimate and luminous; a large portrait of the fish from which it takes its name holds centre stage. Lunches are great value and breakfast *tostadas* are a fine way to start the day.

★Sólo del Mar SEAFOOD **€€**
(Map p800; ☎963 74 40 45; www.solodelmar.com; Calle Poeta Josep Cervera i Grifol 12, off Avenida Instituto Obrero de Valencia; dishes €7-14; ⏱noon-4pm Tue-Thu & Sun, noon-4pm & 8pm-midnight Fri & Sat, closed Aug, open Thu night & closed Sun Jul & Sep) A great lunch option when visiting the Ciudad de las Artes y las Ciencias, this innovative place in a residential complex is a fishmonger that doubles as a restaurant and tapas bar at mealtimes. The seafood is of excellent quality, simply and deliciously prepared at very fair prices. There's no menu; go with the recommendations of the helpful boss.

Northern & Eastern Valencia

★Gran Azul VALENCIAN **€€€**
(Map p800; ☎961 47 45 23; www.granazulrestaurante.com; Avenida de Aragón 12; mains €17-23; ⏱1.30-6pm & 8.30pm-1am Tue-Sat, 1-6.30pm Sun; 📶) Spacious and stylish, this main-road spot is a temple to excellent dining. Things are focused on rice dishes and the grill, with premium quality steaks from mature cows as well as superb fresh fish simply done and garnished with flair. For a starter, try the *molletes* – mini burgers with fillings such as steak tartare or bull's tail.

Ricard Camarena GASTRONOMY **€€€**
(Map p800; ☎963 35 54 18; www.ricardcamarenarestaurant.com; Bombas Gens, Avenida de Burjassot 54; degustation menu €98-150; ⏱1.30-3.30pm & 8.30-10.30pm Tue-Sat; 📶) Valencia's most highly rated current chef showcases the range of his abilities here, in a new location in the Bombas Gens **factory-turned-art-centre** (☎963 46 38 56; www.bombasgens.com; Avenida de Burjassot 54; ⏱5-9pm Wed, 11am-2pm & 5-9pm Thu & Fri, 11am-9pm Sat, noon-9pm Sun) FREE. A range of tasting menus focuses on the Valencian ideal of fresh market produce, presented here in innovative ways that bring out exceptional and subtle flavours. There's a weekday lunchtime set menu for €55.

Western Valencia

★Bar Ricardo TAPAS **€€**
(Map p800; ☎963 22 69 49; www.barricardo.es; Calle de Doctor Zamenhof 16; mains €10-18; ⏱8am-midnight Tue-Sat) Ice-cold beer – one of the best *cañas* in Valencia – and a fabulous array of tapas and other dishes characterise this gloriously traditional place with its old-style mezzanine and pleasant terrace. Snails, top-quality seafood and many other delights await you. The kitchen is open all day, so it's a good spot for eating outside of normal Spanish hours.

El Pederniz SPANISH **€€**
(Map p800; ☎963 32 41 06; www.elpederniz.com; Pasaje de Ventura Feliú 20; mains €11-22; ⏱10.30am-4.30pm & 8.30-11pm Mon & Wed-Sat, 10.30am-4.30pm Tue; 📶) A warm, genuine welcome and lots of enthusiasm give a great first impression at this comfortably decorated restaurant in a nondescript area a short hop from the fast-train station. Delicious seafood and game dishes make for a reliably excellent experience. It's a good one for a leisurely lunch before catching a train, but worth seeking out in any case.

Valencia's Beaches

Bar La Paca TAPAS **€**
(☎637 860528; Calle del Rosario 30; tapas €3-8; ⏱1pm-1am) Cosy and buzzing, this bar has an eclectic crowd and an upbeat atmosphere. Visually striking with its chessboard tiles and deep reds, it does simple, tasty tapas (including vegetarian options) and craft beers at fair prices. It's the sort of place where you wish you lived upstairs.

★**Bodega Casa Montaña** TAPAS €€
(963 67 23 14; www.emilianobodega.com; Calle de José Benlliure 69; tapas €4-14; 1-4pm & 8-11.30pm Mon-Fri, 12.30-4pm & 8-11.30pm Sat, 12.30-4pm Sun) One of Valencia's most characterful spots, with venerable barrels and an older-era atmosphere, this place has been around since 1836. There's a superb, changing selection of wines and a long list of exquisite tapas, including many seafood conserves. We fell in love with the smoked eel, but it's all great.

Drinking & Nightlife

North Ciutat Vella

★**Café Negrito** BAR
(Map p804; 963 91 42 33; Plaza del Negrito; 3pm-3.30am;) Something of a local legend, Negrito has had a bit of a facelift in recent years and boasts a rather handsome interior. It hasn't changed its character though, with an intellectual, socially aware, left-wing clientele dominating and art exhibitions often focused on sustainable development or NGOs. The large terrace is a top spot to while away an evening.

★**Radio City** CLUB
(Map p804; 963 91 41 51; www.radiocityvalencia.es; Calle de Santa Teresa 19; 11pm-4am) Almost as much mini-cultural-centre as club, Radio City, which gets packed from around 1am, pulls in the punters with activities such as language exchange, and DJs or live music every night. There's everything from flamenco (Tuesday) to reggae and funk, and the crowd is eclectic and engaged.

Tyris on Tap MICROBREWERY
(Map p804; 961 13 28 73; www.cervezatyris.com; Calle Taula de Canvis 6; 6pm-1am or 1.30am Tue-Sun;) White-painted industrial brick, long-drop pendant lights and no-frills decor lend an air of warehouse chic to this bar. It's an outlet for a local microbrewery, and 10 taps issue some pretty tasty craft beers. There's one of our favourite central terraces out front to enjoy it, and some simple bar food such as nachos to soak it up.

Café de las Horas BAR
(Map p804; 963 91 73 36; www.cafedelashoras.com; Calle Conde Almodóvar 1; 10am-2am Mon-Fri, 11am-2am Sat & Sun, from 4pm Aug;) Offers high baroque, tapestries, music of all genres, candelabras, bouquets of fresh flowers and a long list of exotic cocktails. It does themed Sunday brunches (11am to 4pm). Service could improve, but it's always an intriguing place to stop, whether for a coffee or a *copa* (mixed drink).

Barrio del Carmen

L'Ermità BAR
(Map p804; 963 91 67 59; www.facebook.com/lermitacafe; Calle Obispo Don Jerónimo 4; 7pm-1.30am Wed-Sat) On a very central backstreet, this is a top option for a drink with decent music, regular cultural events, a friendly crowd of regulars and cordial staff. The quirky interior is comfortably cosy, but the streetside tables are prime territory on a warm night.

Café Museu CAFE
(Map p804; 960 72 50 47; Calle del Museo 7; 9am-11pm Tue-Thu, to 1.30am Fri, 11am-1.30am Sat, 11am-11pm Sun;) A real forum for bohemian souls in the Carmen district, this grungy, edgy spot has an impressive cultural program, including English/Spanish conversation sessions, regular live music, theatre and more. The terrace is a popular place to knock back a few beers.

Northern & Eastern Valencia

★**Chico Ostra** BAR
(Map p800; 960 71 99 44; www.chicoostra.com; Calle del Músico Belando 15; 6pm-midnight Sun-Thu, to 1.30am Fri & Sat;) This lovable cafe-bar in Benimaclet is our favourite in the *barrio*. With a grotto-like entrance giving way to a cool white interior, it does a range of tasty snacks (€2 to €9), peddles second-hand clothes and books and has a great series of cultural happenings.

Deseo 54 GAY & LESBIAN
(Map p800; 697 699166; www.deseo54.com; Calle de la Pepita 13; 1.30-7.30am Fri & Sat night;) It's mostly the young and beautiful at this upmarket and famous *discoteca*, which plays quality electronic music to a largely, but by no means exclusively, LGBT crowd. Admission prices vary depending on night and DJ, but you can buy cheaper advance tickets on the website.

Russafa

★**La Fustería** BAR
(Map p800; 633 100428; www.lafusteriaruzafa.com; Calle de Cádiz 28; 7-11.30pm Mon-Thu, to

2.30am Fri & Sat;) This former carpentry workshop is now a likeable jumbled bar and restaurant with mismatched furniture and exposed brick walls. It's a great venue for an after-dinner drink, with an amiable mix of folk, and regular events – flamenco when we were last there – out the back.

Slaughterhouse BAR

(Map p800; 963 28 77 55; Calle de Denia 22; 6pm-1.30am;) Once a butcher's shop (hence its title, also inspired by the Kurt Vonnegut novel with a similar name), Slaughterhouse abounds in books (even in the toilets) – new, old, for sale and simply for browsing. There's a limited menu of burgers, salads and cheeses, with every dish (€7 to €10) having a 1970s literary or pop-culture reference.

Entertainment

★Jimmy Glass LIVE MUSIC

(Map p804; www.jimmyglassjazz.net; Calle Baja 28; 8pm-2.30am Mon-Thu, 9pm-3.30am Fri & Sat;) Atmospheric Jimmy Glass is just what a jazz bar should be, with dim lighting and high-octane cocktails. It has four live performances a week, many of them free, and also runs an annual jazz festival in October/November that attracts some top musicians. At other times it plays tracks from the owner's vast CD collection. Tapas are available Thursday to Saturday.

★Valencia Club de Fútbol FOOTBALL

(Estadio de Mestalla; Map p800; 963 37 26 26; www.valenciacf.com; Avenida de Aragón) The city's principal team, and a major player in Spanish football, with famously demanding fans. A move to a new ground in the city's northwest has been stalled for several years, so for now it's still at Mestalla, an atmospheric, steeply tiered ground close to the centre. You can buy tickets a few weeks in advance through the website.

Wah Wah LIVE MUSIC

(Map p800; www.wahwahclub.es; Calle Campoamor 52; 10.30pm-3am Thu-Sat;) For many, Wah Wah remains Valencia's hottest venue for live music, especially for underground and international indie, though classic Spanish garage and rock also get a good airing. Check the website; tickets are sometimes cheaper if purchased in advance.

Palau de la Música PERFORMING ARTS

(Map p800; 902 010284; www.palaudevalencia.com; Paseo de la Alameda 30) Perched over the dry riverbed, this is an attractive venue hosting mainly classical-music recitals; it's the home base of Valencia's principal orchestra. That long glass tube looks good, but it can get pretty hot under there on a summer day.

Shopping

★Madame Mim VINTAGE, CLOTHING

(Map p800; 963 25 59 41; www.facebook.com/madame.mim.shop; Calle de Puerto Rico 30; 11am-2.30pm & 5.30-9.30pm Tue, Thu & Fri, 11am-2.30pm & 6-10pm Sat) Many Valencians would say this is the city's best vintage shop, and we're always intrigued by what it has in stock. As well as clothes, there's a quirky line of interesting objects that's always worth a peek.

★Cestería El Globo ARTS & CRAFTS

(Map p804; 963 52 64 15; www.facebook.com/cesteriaelglobo; Calle del Músico Peydró 16; 9.45am-1.30pm & 4.30-8pm Mon-Fri, 10am-2pm & 5-8.15pm Sat) In business since 1856, this charming shop features piles of traditional wickerwork – how about a basket for your bicycle? – plus rocking horses and other solid wooden toys.

Abanicos Carbonell ARTS & CRAFTS

(Map p800; 963 41 53 95; www.abanicoscarbonell.com; Calle de Castellón 21; 9.30am-1.30pm & 4-8pm Mon-Fri) This historic fan-maker, in business since 1810, offers hand-painted manual cooling units ranging from a very reasonable €10 for the basic but pretty ones,

HORCHATA

A summer delight across Spain, *horchata (orxata)*, a Valencian speciality, is an opaque sugary drink made from pressed *chufas* (tiger nuts: despite the name, it's a small tuber), into which you dip a large finger-shaped bun called – no sniggering – a *fartón*. A traditional place to sample *horchata* in the heart of town is **Horchatería de Santa Catalina** (Map p804; 963 91 23 79; www.horchateriasantacatalina.com; Plaza de Santa Catalina 6; 8.15am-9.30pm;), while the **Mercado de Colón** (Map p800; www.mercadodecolon.es; Calle de Cirilo Amorós; 7am-1.30am;) has several choices. Head out on a tour with **Horta Viva** (691 093721; www.hortaviva.net) if you want to understand more about *chufas* and the *horchata*-making process.

BIKING VALENCIA

Cycling is a great way to get around: the riverbed park gives you easy access to most of the city and there's now an excellent network of bike lanes. There are numerous hire places, and most accommodation can organise a hire bike. **Valenbisi** (www.valenbisi.es) is the city-bike scheme – sign up for a week-long contract (€13.30) at machines at the bike racks or online.

to works by famous fan painters that run to thousands of euros. It's been run by the same family for five generations.

Lladró CERAMICS

(Map p804; ☎963 51 16 25; www.lladro.com; Calle del Poeta Querol 9; ⊙10am-8pm Mon-Sat) More than 50 years ago, three Lladró brothers produced the first of their famed porcelain sculptures. Nowadays, their factory on the city's northern outskirts employs hundreds of people, and exports its figurines worldwide. Its retail outlet is deliberately sited on the city's smartest street. In what is almost a mini-museum, you can browse among and purchase its winsome figurines.

Information

The city's tourism website is www.visitvalencia.com. There is a tourist office at the airport and three around the city:

Ayuntamiento Tourist Office (Map p804; ☎963 52 49 08; Plaza del Ayuntamiento 1; ⊙9am-6.50pm Mon-Sat, 10am-1.50pm Sun) In the town hall.

Joaquín Sorolla Station Tourist Office (Map p800; ☎963 80 36 23; Valencia Joaquín Sorolla; ⊙10am-5.50pm Mon-Fri, to 2.50pm Sat & Sun) At the fast train station.

Paz Tourist Office (Map p800; ☎963 98 64 22; Calle de la Paz 48; ⊙9am-6.50pm Mon-Sat, 10am-1.50pm Sun; 📶)

Getting There & Away

AIR

Valencia's **airport** (VLC; ☎902 404 704; www.aena.es) is 10km west of the city centre along the A3, towards Madrid. Flights, including many budget routes, serve major European destinations, including London, Paris and Berlin.

BOAT

Trasmediterránea (p817) and Baleària (p828) operate car and passenger ferries to Ibiza and Mallorca. Less frequent ferries go to Menorca and Algeria.

BUS

Valencia's **bus station** (Map p800; ☎963 46 62 66; Avenida Menéndez Pidal) is beside the riverbed. Bus 8 connects it to Plaza del Ayuntamiento.

Avanza (www.avanzabus.com) operates hourly bus services to/from Madrid (€30 to €36, four to 4½ hours).

ALSA (www.alsa.es) has up to 10 daily buses to/from Barcelona (€29 to €36, four to five hours) and more than 10 to Alicante (€21 to €25, 2½ to 5¾ hours), most via Benidorm.

TRAIN

All fast trains now use the **Valencia Joaquín Sorolla station** (www.adif.es; Calle San Vicente Mártir 171), 800m south of the old town. It's meant to be temporary, but looks like sticking around for a long time.

It's linked with nearby **Estación del Norte** (p803), 500m away, by free shuttle bus. Estación del Norte has slow trains to Gandia, Alicante and Madrid, as well as local *cercanía* lines.

Though there are some departures from Estación del Norte, *cercanía* lines to the west leave from **Valencia San Isidro/Sant Isidre** in the west of the city.

Major destinations include the following:

DESTINATION	FARE (€)	TIME (HR)	FREQUENCY (DAILY)
Alicante	17-30	1½-2	12
Barcelona	29-45	3¼-5¾	14
Madrid	27-73	1¾-7	18

Getting Around

Valencia has an integrated bus, tram and metro network. Tourist offices sell the **Valencia Tourist Card** (☎900 701818; www.valenciatouristcard.com; 24/48/72hr €15/20/25), entitling you to free urban travel and various other discounts and freebies.

PUBLIC TRANSPORT

Most buses run until about 10pm, with various night services continuing until around 1am. One-/two-/three-day travel cards valid for the bus, metro and tram cost €4/6.70/9.70.

The tram is a pleasant way to get to the beach and port. Pick it up at Pont de Fusta or where it intersects with the metro at Benimaclet.

Metro (www.metrovalencia.es) lines cross town and serve the outer suburbs. The closest stations to the city centre are Ángel Guimerá, Xàtiva, Colón and Pont de Fusta.

VALENCIA PROVINCE

La Albufera

About 15km south of Valencia, La Albufera is a huge freshwater lagoon separated from the sea by a narrow strip of pine-forested sand dunes. It's legendary for the rice that is grown here. It's also an important dune and wetland ecosystem and much of the area is covered by the **Parque Natural de la Albufera** (www.parquealbufera.com) FREE. The zone is great for birdwatching.

The most interesting Albufera communities are **El Palmar**, right on the lagoon, and **El Saler**, which has a beach backed by piney dunes and a lagoon side. **Pinedo**, just across the river mouth from Valencia, is another popular destination for its beach and rice dishes.

Sunsets can be spectacular here. You can take a boat trip from El Palmar or El Saler out on the lagoon, joining the local fisherfolk, who use flat-bottomed boats and nets to harvest fish and eels from the shallow waters.

Bus 25 runs from central Valencia to El Saler and El Palmar every 20 minutes or so. Buses 14 and 15 serve Pinedo. These services are all part of the urban Valencia system. Some other El Saler services are run by Autocares Herca.

Bike lanes run from Valencia right down to El Saler, making this a great way to explore the area.

Sagunto

POP 64,400

The port town of Sagunto (Valenciano: Sagunt), 25km north of Valencia, primarily offers spectacular panoramas of the coast and a sea of orange groves from its vast but ruinous hilltop castle complex. It's an easy half-day excursion from Valencia.

Sights

★Castillo de Sagunto CASTLE

(☎962 61 71 67; www.aytosagunto.es; ⏲10am-6pm or 8pm Tue-Sat, 10am-2pm Sun) FREE Sagunto's castle is majestically located, with stone walls girdling a twin hilltop for almost 1km. Its seven rambling, mostly ruinous sections each speak of a different period in Sagunto's history. The fortress could do with a bit of care and is currently best for a stroll among the ruins, appreciating the magnificent vistas along the coast, rather than gaining a detailed understanding of its long, long history. Don't expect interpretative panels, but the downloadable Tour Sagunto app has audio-guide content.

Its fabulous history began with a thriving Iberian community (called – infelicitously, with hindsight – Arse) that traded with Greeks and Phoenicians. In 219 BC Hannibal besieged and destroyed the town, sparking the Second Punic War between Carthage and Rome. Rome won, named the town Saguntum and set about rebuilding it. The Moors gave the castle its current form; it was later embellished by the Christians and fought hard over in the Peninsular War.

The entrance is on the eastern hilltop, where the Roman town was located. Around the excavated ruins of the forum you can see the stairs and foundations of a Republican temple – a column capital and some stone lettering remains. This area is the Plaza de Armas that formed the heart of the medieval castle. From here, the Puerta de Almenara leads to the fortified eastern compound.

The western hilltop was the site of the original Iberian city, but what you can see here is mostly later fortifications from the 18th and 19th centuries, with one particularly sturdy bastion the most impressive sight. Views are stirring.

Between the two hilltops, the **Museo de Epigrafía** is a collection of engraved stones found on the site. There are Latin funerary and honorary inscriptions, some column capitals and a few stones inscribed in Hebrew from the medieval era. There's some quite interesting information on Roman customs, but it's only in Spanish and Valenciano.

Below the castle you can visit the **Roman theatre**. An overzealous restoration has resulted in a gigantic stage building and marble seating no doubt great for staging performances, but devoid of any historical atmosphere.

Information

Tourist Office (☎962 65 58 59; www.sagunto.es/turismo; Plaza Cronista Chabret; ⏲10am-2.30pm & 4.30-7.30pm Mon-Fri, 9am-2.30pm & 4.30-6.30pm Sat & Sun Apr-Oct, 9.30am-2.30pm & 4-6.30pm Mon-Fri, 9am-2pm Sat & Sun Nov-Mar) A 15-minute walk from the train station. In summer an additional office operates down by the beach.

DON'T MISS

LA TOMATINA

Held in Buñol, 40km west of Valencia, **La Tomatina** (www.latomatina.info; tickets €10; late Aug) is a key summer event:

The last Wednesday in August marks Spain's messiest festival. La Tomatina is a tomato-throwing bonanza attracting more than 20,000 visitors to a town of just 9000 inhabitants. At 11am, more than 100 tonnes of squishy tomatoes are tipped from trucks to the waiting crowd. For one hour, everyone joins in a cheerful, anarchic tomato battle.

After being pounded with pulp, expect to be sluiced down with hoses by the local fire brigade.

Participation costs €10 through the official website, though there are numerous tour operators offering tickets and packages from Valencia, Alicante and elsewhere. There are cloakroom facilities on-site, as you aren't allowed to take bags or cameras into the festival area. Bring a set of fresh clothes to change into afterwards. In the Tomatina itself, some people choose a pair of goggles to protect their eyes. Flip-flops don't work very well; you're better off with shoes but don't expect them to be clean again.

If you're buying a package, try to opt out of the 'paella and sangría' add-ons, as these are readily available for less on the street in Buñol. While most visitors just come in from Valencia for the event, it can be worthwhile staying over the night before and after. La Tomatina is one element of the locals' main fiesta and there's plenty of atmosphere, as well as concerts, across a whole week.

On the Saturday before the Tomatina, there's a children's version, which is free to enter, and is for four- to 14-year-olds.

Getting There & Away

The best option from Valencia to Sagunto is taking the *cercanía* train on lines C5 and C6 (one way €3.70, 30 minutes, regular departures).

Gandia

POP 74,800

The pleasant, spacious town of Gandia (Spanish: Gandía), once home to a branch of the Borja dynasty (more familiar as the infamous Borgias), is a prosperous commercial centre with a lively atmosphere. The other side of the coin is the fun-in-the-sun beach town, 6km away. The adjacent port area has a new ferry connection to the Balearics.

Sights

★Palacio Ducal dels Borja PALACE

(962 87 14 65; www.palauducal.com; Calle Duc Alfons el Vell 1; adult/child €6/4, audio guide €2; 10am-1.30pm & 3-6.30pm Mon-Sat, 10am-1.30pm Sun Nov-Mar, 10am-1.30pm & 4-7.30pm Mon-Sat, 10am-1.30pm Sun Apr-Oct) Gandia's magnificent palace was built in the early 1300s and was for centuries the home of the Borja dukes of Gandia, who included the Jesuit saint Francis Borgia. Though much remodelled in the 19th century, the building preserves some original detail. The fine Salón de las Coronas is one of several sumptuous spaces, while the highlight is the Galería Dorada, a suite of decorated rooms culminating in a tiled floor depicting the world composed of the four elements.

Look out, too, for the low oratory with marvellous wooden floor and grisaille paintings on the walls. Beautiful tile work and ceilings are present throughout. Guided tours (in Spanish, with an English leaflet) leave a few times a day and cost €1 more.

Eating

★Telero VALENCIAN €€

(962 86 73 18; www.telero.es; Calle Sant Ponç 7; mains €13-19; 1.30-3.30pm & 8.30-11.30pm Tue-Sat) Tucked away but worth seeking out, this intimate restaurant focuses on quality ingredients. Admire the cosy, exposed-brick dining area in the traditional house, then listen to what is available off-menu and choose a meal based on top-quality vegetables and fish sourced locally.

Information

Playa de Gandia Tourist Office (962 84 24 07; www.visitgandia.com; Paseo de Neptuno; 9.30am-2pm & 3.30-6.30pm Mon-Fri, 9.30am-1.30pm Sat & Sun mid-Sep–Jun,

9.30am-8.30pm Mon-Sat, to 1.30pm Sun Jul–mid-Sep) At the beach.

Town Tourist Office (☎962 87 77 88; www.visitgandia.com; Avenida Marqués de Campo; ⊙9.30am-1.30pm & 3.30-7.30pm Mon-Fri, 9.30am-1.30pm Sat mid-Sep–Jun, 9.30am-2.30pm & 4-8pm Mon-Fri, 9.30am-1.30pm Sat Jul–mid-Sep) Opposite the bus and train station.

Getting There & Away

Cercanía trains run between Gandia and Valencia (€5.80, one hour) every 30 minutes (hourly on weekends). The combined bus and train station is opposite the town tourist office; there's also a stop near the beach.

ALSA runs regular buses to Dénia (€3.60, 30 minutes) and other coastal towns.

Trasmediterránea (☎902 454645; www.trasmediterranea.es) runs fast ferries to Ibiza Sant Antoni (passenger/car €82/119, two hours, one or more daily) and, in summer, to Formentera (passenger/car €60/120, four hours, one weekly).

Getting Around

Stopping beside the town tourist office, La Marina Gandiense buses run to Playa de Gandia every 20 minutes.

Requena

Requena, 65km west of Valencia, grew rich from silk, though today it's primarily wine and livestock country, producing robust reds (try the local bobal grape), *cavas* (sparkling wines), rich sausages and spicy meats. From its heart rears La Villa, the medieval nucleus, with its twisting streets and blind alleys. It's great to explore – atmospheric without being dolled up for tourism. Check out the 15th-century guard tower at its entrance, the lovely Gothic facades, small museums and the narrow lanes of the one-time Jewish quarter.

Two venues for wine lovers are **Museo del Vino** (☎962 30 32 81; Carrer Somera 13; adult/child €2/1.50; ⊙noon-2pm Wed-Fri, noon-2pm & 5-7pm Sat), a wine museum within the handsome 15th-century Palacio del Cid, and **Ferevin** (☎962 30 57 06; www.ferevin.com; Cuesta de las Carnicerías; ⊙11am-2pm & 4-7pm Mon-Fri, 11am-2.30pm & 4-7pm Sat, 11am-2.30pm Sun), a showroom for local wine producers. There's a wine festival at the end of August. A useful website is www.rutavino.com.

There are regular buses (€5.47, one hour) and *cercanías* (€5.80, 1½ hours) to/from Valencia. Pricier fast trains use a different station, 6km from town.

Xàtiva

POP 29,000

Xàtiva (Spanish: Játiva) makes an easy and rewarding 50km day trip from Valencia, or a stop on the way north or south. It has an intriguing historic quarter and a mighty castle strung along the crest of the Serra Vernissa, with the town snuggled at its base.

The Moors established Europe's first paper-manufacturing plant in Xàtiva, which is also famous as the birthplace of the Borgia Popes Calixtus III and Alexander VI, as well as the painter José de Ribera. The glory days ended in 1707 when Felipe V's troops torched most of the town.

Sights

The old town lies south and uphill from the Alameda. Ask at the tourist office for its English brochure, *Xàtiva: Monumental Town*. There are several noble buildings in the town, which merit an extended stroll. Look out for the handsome facade of the Renaissance hospital opposite the main church and the historic pharmacy nearby.

★Castillo de Xàtiva CASTLE
(☎962 27 42 74; www.xativaturismo.com; adult/child €2.40/1.20; ⊙10am-6pm Tue-Sun Nov-Mar, to 7pm Tue-Sun Apr-Oct) Xàtiva's castle, which clasps to the summit of a double-peaked hill overlooking the old town, is arguably the most evocative and interesting in the Valencia region. Behind its crumbling battlements you'll find flower gardens (bring a picnic), tumbledown turrets, towers and other buildings (some used in the 20th century and hence much changed), such as dungeons and a pretty Gothic chapel. The walk up to the castle is a long one, but the views are sensational.

If you think it's big today, imagine what it must have looked like 300 years ago at full size. Sadly, it was badly damaged by an earthquake in 1748 and never really recovered.

Before the current incarnation, the castle hill was always a fortified vantage point thanks to its crucial strategic position, and was important in the wars between Rome and Carthage, as well as in the Roman strife of the 1st century BC.

On the way up, the 18th-century **Ermita de Sant Josep** is on your left, and to the right is the lovely Romanesque **Iglesia de Sant Feliu** (1269), Xàtiva's oldest church. You'll also pass by the very battered remains of part of the old **Muslim town**. A tourist train zips up the hill a couple of times a day from the tourist office (€4.20).

Various signposted walks cover the castle hill and environs.

Sleeping & Eating

★Mont Sant HOTEL €€
(☎962 27 50 81; www.mont-sant.com; Subida al Castillo; incl breakfast s €104-137, d €112-144; ⊙Feb-Dec; P ❄ 🛜 🏊) Enthusiastic management makes for a wonderful stay at this enchanting place, set amid city walls, the ruins of a convent and palm and citrus gardens between the old town and castle. It feels way out in the countryside rather than just a few minutes' walk from town. Stay in the beautifully adapted main building or in a spacious, modern, wood-faced cabin.

All have balcony/terrace spaces and there's a suite with private pool. The restaurant serves upmarket gourmet fare and packages including meals are available. Don't leave without seeing the amazing medieval cistern.

La Picaeta de Carmeta VALENCIAN €€
(☎619 511971; Plaça de Mercat 19; mains €13-18; ⊙1.30-4pm Tue-Thu & Sun, 1.30-4pm & 8.30pm-midnight Fri & Sat) At one end of an attractive old-town square (a promising destination for drinks and tapas), this is a fine restaurant, with cool, sober decor of exposed brick and well-selected art. There's a selection of meaty rices, as well as simply cooked fish and tastily creative salads. It's all delicious, and there are some fine wines to accompany your meal.

Information

Tourist Office (☎962 27 33 46; www.xativaturismo.com; Alameda Jaime I 50; ⊙10am-5pm Tue-Thu, to 6pm Fri, 10.15am-2pm Sat & Sun) On the Alameda, Xàtiva's shady main avenue.

Getting There & Away

Frequent *cercanía* trains on line C2 connect Xàtiva with Valencia (€4.35, 45 minutes, half-hourly), and most Valencia–Madrid trains also stop here, though these are more expensive. You can also reach Alicante by train (€13 to €17, 1¼ hours, seven daily) from here.

CASTELLÓN PROVINCE

Castellón

POP 171,000

Castellón de la Plana (Valenciano: Castelló) is a provincial capital that's off the tourist radar. Though not over-endowed with sights, it's a pleasant place with good-value accommodation and a lively eating scene in its centre. Four kilometres from the centre, the Grao district is centred on the fishing port, and just north of here are the city's beaches.

Sleeping & Eating

Tryp Castellón Center BUSINESS HOTEL €€
(☎965 34 27 77; www.melia.com; Ronda del Millars; r €52-74; P ❄ 🛜) As Castellón sees comparatively few tourists, its hotel offering is reduced to chain business spots dotted around the edge of the central district. This is the lobest of them, with very spacious rooms, gleaming new parquet and a bit of an effort to make it feel more personal. Prices for this standard are great.

★Bodega La Guindilla TAPAS €€
(☎964 22 88 94; www.grupolaguindilla.com; Calle Asarau 2; mains €13-17; ⊙1-4pm & 7pm-1am Mon-Sat) Sit around barrels, grab an outdoor table or head downstairs to the dining room at this bright corner spot, an expansion of its crowded Calle Barracas tapas bar. There's a seafood focus, but everything is delicious and superbly presented. Expect cuttlefish on slates, creamy cod balls and wonderful daily specials: suckling-pig gyozas and fried sea anemone when we last dropped by.

Information

Tourist Office (☎965 35 86 88; www.castellonturismo.com; Plaza de la Hierba; ⊙10am-6pm Mon-Fri, to 2pm Sat) In the centre of things, by the cathedral. There's another office in the port area.

Getting There & Away

AIR

A famous white elephant of the Spanish building boom – one year there were more landings on Mars than here – Castellón's **airport** (☎964 57 86 00; www.aeropuerto-castellon.com; Carretera CV13, Benlloch), 33km north of town, now has some budget flights to Britain and several Eastern European countries. There are some bus and minibus services to Castellón (€12, one hour) and other coastal destinations run by

Autos Mediterráneo that must be pre-booked online.

BUS & TRAIN

Castellón is a regional bus hub, with services throughout the province run mostly by **Autos Mediterráneo** (☎964 22 00 54; www.autosmediterraneo.com). Buses run five or more times a day to Valencia (€6.35, 1¼ hours).

Castellón is the northern terminus of the C6 *cercanías* local train line that runs between here and Valencia (€5.80, one to 1½ hours, half-hourly).

Very frequent faster trains (€6 to €20, 45 minutes to one hour) run to Valencia on the standard train network. There are also frequent services to Barcelona (€24 to €40, 2½ to four hours) via Tarragona.

Benicàssim

POP 18,000

Likeable Benicàssim stretches for 6km along the coast. It has been a popular resort since the 19th century, when wealthy Valencian families built summer residences here. It's still a place more characterised by local than foreign tourism, with plenty of Valenciano spoken on the streets. It's also famous for its huge summer music festival.

Sights

Desierto de les Palmes NATURE RESERVE

The twisting, climbing CV147 leads, after about 6km, to this occasionally misty inland range – cooler than the coast – with a Carmelite monastery and first-class **restaurant** (☎964 30 09 47; CV147, Km 9; mains €13-22; ⌚9.30am-5.30pm Wed-Mon Mar-Dec, to midnight Jun-early Sep) at its heart. Nowadays it's a nature reserve and far from being a desert (for the monks that meant a place for mystic withdrawal), it's green area perfect for outdoor activities. From **Monte Bartolo** (728m), its highest point, there are staggering views. The tourist office hands out an excellent booklet listing a range of different hill walks.

Activities

Aquarama WATER PARK

(☎902 998711; www.aquarama.net; N340, Km 987; adult/child/small child day ticket €26/19/15.50; ⌚11am-7pm mid-Jun–early Sep; 🚸) This vast water park is just southwest of town, off the N340. There's a reasonable discount for booking online.

Festivals & Events

★ **Festival Internacional de Benicàssim** MUSIC

(FIB; www.fiberfib.com; ⌚mid-Jul) Fans gather by the tens of thousands for this annual four-day bash, one of Europe's major outdoor music festivals. Top acts in recent years have included some classic names, but the majority are up-to-the-minute acts popular with the predominantly 20-something crowd. Late-afternoon starts mean you can spend the day on the beach.

Sleeping & Eating

★ **Hotel Voramar** HOTEL €€

(☎964 30 01 50; www.voramar.net; Paseo Pilar Coloma 1; s/d incl breakfast €105/130, with sea view €145/170; P❄📶) Venerable (same family for four generations) and bloodied in battle (it was a hospital in the Spanish Civil War), this place has character and is spectacularly located at the beach's northeastern end. The rooms with balconies (and hammock) have utterly magnificent sea views and sounds. The first-class restaurant also has great perspectives. It hires bikes and kayaks (free for guests).

El Charquito TAPAS €€

(☎964 30 27 04; Calle Santo Tomás 3; mains €8-14; ⌚6pm-1.30am Mon-Sat) Draw a Spanish bar from muscle memory and this is what you get: hanging hams, strings of garlic and peppers, orderly family frenzy behind the counter, seafood gleaming on ice and a cosy conviviality. The food is very tasty, the people are sound, the price is right. A Benicàssim classic.

Information

Tourist Office (☎964 30 01 02; http://turismo.benicassim.es; Calle Santo Tomás 74; ⌚9am-2pm & 4-7pm Mon-Fri, 10.30am-1.30pm & 4-7pm Sat, 10.30am-1.30pm Sun Oct-May, 9am-2pm & 5-8pm Mon-Fri, 10.30am-1.30pm & 5-8pm Sat & Sun Jun-Sep) Inland, in the centre of town. There's an additional summer office on the beach.

Getting There & Away

There are nine daily trains from Benicàssim to Valencia (€7.15 to €13.10, one to 1½ hours), and services north to Tortosa, Tarragona and Barcelona. Buses run every 15 minutes to Castellón, from where there are more connections.

Peñíscola

POP 7400

Peñíscola's old town, all cobbled streets and whitewashed houses, huddles within stone walls that protect the rocky promontory jutting into the sea. It's pretty as a postcard, and just as commercial, with ranks of souvenir and ceramics shops. By contrast, the high-rises sprouting northwards along the coast are mostly leaden and charmless. But the Paseo Marítimo promenade makes for pleasant walking, and the beach, which extends as far as neighbouring Benicarló, is superb, sandy and more than 5km in length. Peñíscola is quiet in low season, but there's enough on to not make it spooky – and you'll have the old town to yourself.

Sights

Castillo de Peñíscola CASTLE
(964 48 00 21; www.dipcas.es; Calle Castillo; adult/9-16yr €5/3.50; 10.30am-5.30pm mid-Oct–Easter, 9.30am-9.30pm Easter–mid-Oct) The rambling 14th-century castle was built by the Knights Templar on Arab foundations and later became home to Pedro de Luna ('Papa Luna', the deposed Pope Benedict XIII). There are various exhibits relating to the history of the castle and town, as well as a former cannon outpost converted into a garden with special views.

Sleeping & Eating

Pensión Chiki PENSION €
(605 280295; www.restaurantechiki.es; Calle Mayor 3-5; d €55-70;) Right in the old town, this place has seven spotless, modern rooms with views and a genuine welcome. The nearby church chimes tinnily from 8am. It's homey, cosy and the price is right. From March to October it has an attractive restaurant with a great-value three-course *menú*. The friendly owner isn't always here, so ring ahead.

Hotel La Mar BOUTIQUE HOTEL €€€
(964 48 00 57; www.hotelboutiquelamar.com; Calle Porteta 16; r €220-260;) With a lovely old-town waterside location, looking down the sweep of beach and bay, this refined, modern hotel offers excellent comfort, a fine restaurant and a warm welcome. Rooms are sleek and modern, with some looking up to the old town, others over the sea. The sublime roof terrace has wraparound vistas. Prices plunge outside high summer. No children.

La Taverneta de Sant Roc SPANISH €€
(964 48 21 70; Calle San Roque 15; mains €11-18; 11am-4pm & 7pm-midnight) In the touristy heart of Peñíscola, you fear the worst from the throng of places with photos of food out on the street. But this is a real exception: a generous, kindly spot intent on its customers leaving full and happy. There's an excellent range of fare, from great croquettes to well-cooked seafood and decent steaks.

Information

Main Tourist Office (964 48 02 08; www.peniscola.es; Paseo Marítimo; 10am-8pm mid-Jun–mid-Sep, 10am-7pm Apr–mid-Jun & mid-Sep–mid-Oct, 9.30am-5.30pm Mon-Sat, 10am-2pm Sun mid-Oct–Mar) At the southern end of Paseo Marítimo. Pick up town information; you can also grab it from the website.

Getting There & Away

Buses run at least half-hourly between Peñíscola, Benicarló and Vinaròs, from where you can connect to Valencia or Castellón. From July to mid-September there's an hourly run to Peñíscola/Benicarló train station, 7km from town.

El Maestrazgo

Straddling northwestern Valencia and southeast Aragón, El Maestrazgo (Valenciano: El Maestrat) is a mountainous land, a world away from the coastal strip. Here spectacular ancient *pueblos* (villages) huddle on rocky outcrops and ridges. The Maestrazgo is great, wild, on-your-own trekking territory.

Blazing your own trails across the Maestrazgo on foot, bike or by car is most appealing. There are numerous lonely landscapes and lovely villages to discover.

Getting There & Around

There are limited bus services from Castellón to the major Maestrazgo towns. Smaller villages have few or no services and in general the region is best explored with your own vehicle.

Sant Mateu

POP 2000 / ELEV 325M

Not as picturesque from a distance as the hilltop villages further into the region, Sant Mateu, once capital of the Maestrazgo, has a lovely town centre nonetheless, framed around a pretty plaza. The solid mansions and elaborate facades recall the town's more illustrious past and former wool-based wealth.

Sights

Ermita de la Mare de Déu dels Àngels CHURCH
(☎605 382935; ⏲11am-7pm) Follow signs from the Plaza Mayor to this loveable chapel perched on a rocky hillside, a 2.5km drive, or somewhat shorter walk, away. It was a monastery until the Spanish Civil War and preserves a baroque chapel with a typical regional tiled floor and a cherub-infested altarpiece. The views are great, and there's an excellent restaurant (p821). Midweek opening is a little unreliable; you can phone to arrange a visit.

Iglesia Arciprestal CHURCH
(http://turismosantmateu.es/iglesia-arciprestal; Calle Santo Domingo 6; adult/youth/child €1.50/1.20/free; ⏲10am-2pm & 4-7pm daily Jun-Sep, daily guided visits only Oct-May) Just off the plaza, this Gothic village church has a Romanesque portal and a fine interior. The frescoed neo-classical side chapel has a macabre reliquary with a skeleton apparently dressed for a local Moorish and Christian fiesta. Guided tours, optional in summer and the only way to enter at other times, include the sacristy and a small museum with jewellery, processional crosses and two pieces of the true cross. The church interior is visible through a glass screen any time.

Museo de Valltorta MUSEUM
(☎964 33 60 10; www.ceice.gva.es; Pla de l'Om, Tirig; ⏲9.30am-2pm & 4-7pm or 5-8pm Tue-Sun) FREE An informative museum, 2km from Tirig, itself 10km southwest of Sant Mateu. It presents a detailed overview of prehistoric art and El Maestrazgo's World Heritage ensemble of rock paintings (info in various languages available). There's a reproduction of the most interesting piece – a hunting scene. From here, free guided walks to the painting sites leave a few times daily.

Sleeping

L'hostal de Cabrit HOTEL €€
(☎964 41 66 21; www.hostaldecabrit.com; Plaza Mare de Déu de la Font 19; s/d/ste incl breakfast €45/75/115; ❄📶) Decent value is had at this good-looking spot on a central square. Rooms vary in size but are cute, equipped with safe and fridge, and commodious. The suite has a king-sized bed and an in-room shower. Prices drop substantially midweek and in winter. The stone-faced cafe-restaurant does a nice line in rices and other plates (mains €12 to €16).

LOCAL WALKS

Radiating from the village are signed circular walking trails of between 2½ and five hours that lead through the surrounding hills. Ask for the free tourist-office pamphlet *Senderos de Sant Mateu* (in Spanish). The website (http://turismosantmateu.es) also has details (not in English at time of research, but understandable: look for 'Senderismo').

Eating

★Farga VALENCIAN €€
(☎663 909586; fargarestaurant@gmail.com; Ermita de la Mare de Déu dels Àngels; set menus €25-35; ⏲noon-4pm Wed-Sun, plus Tue May-Oct, call for dinner opening) This quality restaurant at a former monastery (p821) perched on a hill 2.5km from town offers sublime views of the surrounding plain from its terrace, and a characterful vaulted interior space. It's run by a friendly young couple who offer delicious, sophisticated cuisine. They'll usually open for dinner bookings, so call ahead.

La Perdi SPANISH €€
(☎964 41 60 82; www.laperdi.es; Calle de Historiador Betí 9; mains €8-15; ⏲1-4pm & 7.30-11pm) Our favourite place for a traditional meal in the centre of Sant Mateu, the Perdi has been run for generations by the same family. A couple of set menus and solid à la carte options showcase warming regional cuisine in a pleasantly rustic ambience.

Information

Tourist Office (☎964 41 66 58; http://turismosantmateu.es; Calle de Historiador Betí 13; ⏲10am-2pm Mon, 10am-2pm & 4-6pm Tue-Sun) Very helpful. Just off the main square in a sturdy palace.

Getting There & Away

Autos Mediterráneo buses (p819) link Sant Mateu with the following destinations:

DESTINATION	FARE (€)	TIME	FREQUENCY
Castellón	5.20	1½hr	3 Mon-Fri, 2 Sat
Morella	3.40	45min	2 Mon-Fri, 2 Sat
Vinaròs	2.70	1hr	4 Mon-Fri

OFF THE BEATEN TRACK

EXPLORING THE MAESTRAZGO

If you have time, it's worth exploring away from the major villages and seeking out some smaller ones. **Ares**, 30km south of Morella, is one of the most spectacular, hanging over a cliff. Around 13km from here, **Vilafranca** (del Cid) has a museum – the excellent **Museo de la Pedra en Sec** (☎964 44 14 32; www.ajuntamentdevilafranca.es; Calle de la Iglesia, Villafranca del Cid; adult/child €2/1.50; ⏲10am-1.30pm & 4-7pm Fri & Sat, 10.30am-1.30pm Sun) – that explores its dry-stone-wall tradition. If there's no one there, ask in the tourist office opposite. And don't miss some stunning spots just over the border in Teruel province: Cantavieja and Mirambel are two of the prettiest villages.

Morella

POP 2500 / ELEV 984M

Bitingly cold in winter and refreshingly cool in summer, striking Morella is the Valencian Maestrazgo's principal settlement. This outstanding example of a medieval fortress town, breathtaking at first glimpse, is perched on a hilltop, crowned by a castle and girdled by an intact rampart wall more than 2km long. It's the ancient capital of Els Ports, the 'Mountain Passes', a rugged region offering some outstanding scenic drives and strenuous cycling excursions, plus excellent possibilities for walkers.

Sights

Castillo de Morella CASTLE

(adult/child €3.50/2.50; ⏲11am-5pm Oct-Apr, to 7pm May-Sep) Though badly knocked about, Morella's castle well merits the long wiggly ascent to savour breathtaking views of the town and surrounding countryside. Built by the Moors, it was regularly remodelled and saw action in the Napoleonic and Carlist wars of the 19th century. Carlists took it in 1838 by climbing up through the long-drop toilet. At its base is the bare church and cloister of the **Convento de San Francisco**, by which you enter.

Torres de San Miguel GATE

(Plaza San Miguel; €1.50; ⏲10am-1pm & 4-6pm Tue-Sun) The twin towers of this imposing city gateway are a good place to begin your exploration of the town. With a solid octagonal form, they were first built in the 14th century. There's a small exhibition inside and appealing views.

Basílica de Santa María la Mayor CHURCH

(☎964 16 03 79; Plaza Arciprestal; adult/child €2.50/2; ⏲10am-2pm & 3-6pm or 7pm Mon-Sat, 12.15-6pm Sun) This imposing Gothic basilica has two elaborately sculpted doorways on its southern facade. A richly carved polychrome stone staircase leads to the elaborate overhead choir, while cherubs clamber and peek all over the gilded altarpiece. There's a museum that houses the church's treasures and some religious art.

Sleeping & Eating

Hotel Cardenal Ram HOTEL €€

(☎964 16 00 46; www.hotelcardenalram.com; Cuesta Suñer 1; s €62, d €82-112; P ❄ 📶) Bang in the heart of old Morella, this noble Renaissance palace has been completely refurbished and offers a tantalising blend of historical feel and modern amenities. Half the rooms have splendid views (and cost a little more); those without are generally very spacious. There's also a handsome restaurant and midweek discounts.

Hotel del Pastor HOTEL €€

(☎964 16 10 16; www.hoteldelpastor.com; Carrer San Julián 12; s/d incl breakfast €56/74; P ❄ 📶) This central hotel is an excellent deal, with delightful service and pleasingly old-fashioned rooms – some with vistas – spread over four floors (there's no lift but that's the hotel's only downside). Rooms are traditionally furnished and come in warm ochre colours with plenty of polished wood. Bathrooms have marble washstands, bath-tubs and large mirrors.

★**Daluan** SPANISH €€

(☎964 16 00 71; www.daluan.es; Carreró de la Presó 6; mains €13-20, degustation menu €42; ⏲1-3.30pm Thu-Tue, plus 9-10.30pm Fri & Sat, closed Jan) Daluan is run by Avelino Ramón, a cookery teacher by trade, and his wife Jovita: a very friendly team! Its small upstairs interior is satisfyingly contemporary and its terrace, filling a quiet alley, is equally relaxing. Expect friendly service and a hugely creative menu that changes regularly with the seasons. A backstreet gem and very well priced for this standard.

Information

Tourist Office (964 17 30 32; www.morellaturistica.com; Plaza San Miguel 3; 10am-2pm & 4-7pm Mon-Sat, 10am-2pm Sun Apr–mid-Oct, 10am-2pm & 4-6pm Tue-Sat, 10am-2pm Sun mid-Oct–Mar) Just inside the imposing San Miguel towers and entrance gate to the old town.

Getting There & Away

Morella is best reached via Castellón, which has good train connections.

Two daily weekday buses (€9.70, 2¼ hours) and one Saturday service with Autos Mediterráneo (p819) run to/from Castellón's train station. There are also weekday buses to Vinaròs on the coast and Alcañiz in Teruel province.

If coming by car, the easiest way is to ignore the first town entrance to Puerta San Mateo, and continue on the main road to the top of town and the Puerta San Miguel entrance, where there's a council car park just outside the gates.

ALICANTE PROVINCE

Alicante

POP 330,500

Of all Spain's mainland provincial capitals, Alicante (Valenciano: Alacant) is the most influenced by tourism, thanks to the nearby airport and resorts. Nevertheless it is a dynamic, attractive Spanish city with a castle, old quarter and long waterfront. The eating scene is exciting and the nightlife is absolutely legendary, whether you're chugging pints with the stag parties at 7pm or twirling on the dance floor with the locals seven hours later. On a weekend night it's impossibly busy and buzzy year-round.

Sights

★Museo de Arte Contemporáneo de Alicante GALLERY

(MACA; www.maca-alicante.es; Plaza Santa María 3; 10am-8pm Tue-Sat, from 11am summer, 10am-2pm Sun) FREE This splendid museum, inside the 17th-century Casa de la Asegurada, has an excellent collection of 20th-century Spanish art, including works by Dalí, Miró, Chillida, Sempere, Tàpies and Picasso. The pieces on display rotate regularly, as the collection is a sizeable one. The foundation of the collection was a donation by noted abstract artist Eusebio Sempere, an Alicante native who has a section to himself.

★Museo Arqueológico de Alicante MUSEUM

(MARQ; 965 14 90 00; www.marqalicante.com; Plaza Dr Gómez Ulla; adult/child €3/1.50; 10am-7pm Tue-Fri, 10am-8.30pm Sat, 10am-2pm Sun mid-Sep–mid-Jun, 10am-2pm & 6-10pm Tue-Sat, 10am-2pm Sun mid-Jun–mid-Sep) This museum has a strong collection of ceramics and Iberian art. Exhibits are displayed to give the visitor a very visual, high-tech experience, and it's all beautifully presented. There are also high-quality temporary exhibitions.

Museo Volvo Ocean Race MUSEUM

(965 13 80 80; http://museovolvooceanrace.esatur.com; Muelle de Levante; 5-8pm Mon, 10am-2pm & 5-8pm Tue-Fri, 10am-2pm Sat Sep-Jun, 6-9pm Mon, 11am-2pm & 6-9pm Tue-Fri, 11am-2pm Sat Jul & Aug) FREE On the pier, this museum brings to life the gruelling conditions of the round-the-world Volvo Ocean Race with a simulator, videos, photos and a display of the gear taken on-board. One of the participating yachts is also here for you to have a look at: fancy jumping aboard for 10 months?

Castillo de Santa Bárbara CASTLE

(965 92 77 15; www.castillodesantabarbara.com; Calle Vázquez de Mella; 10am-10pm Apr-Sep, to 8pm Oct-Mar) FREE There are sweeping views over the city from the ramparts of this large 16th-century castle, which houses a **museum** (MUSA; 965 15 29 69; 10am-2.30pm & 4-8pm) FREE recounting the history of the city and contains a couple of chambers with temporary exhibitions. It's a sweaty walk up the hill to the castle, but there's a **lift** (up/down €2.70/free; 10am-7.40pm, last lift up 7.20pm) that rises through the bowels of the mountain to the summit. To return, it's a pleasant stroll down through **Parque de la Ereta**.

Tours

Kon Tiki BOATING

(686 994538; www.cruceroskontiki.com; Puerto Deportivo; return €19; Tue, Thu, Sat & Sun Mar-Dec) Makes the 45-minute boat trip to the popular island of Tabarca, giving you about 4½ hours there. It leaves Alicante at 11pm, departing from the island at 4.30pm. There are additional departures from late June to late September.

Alicante

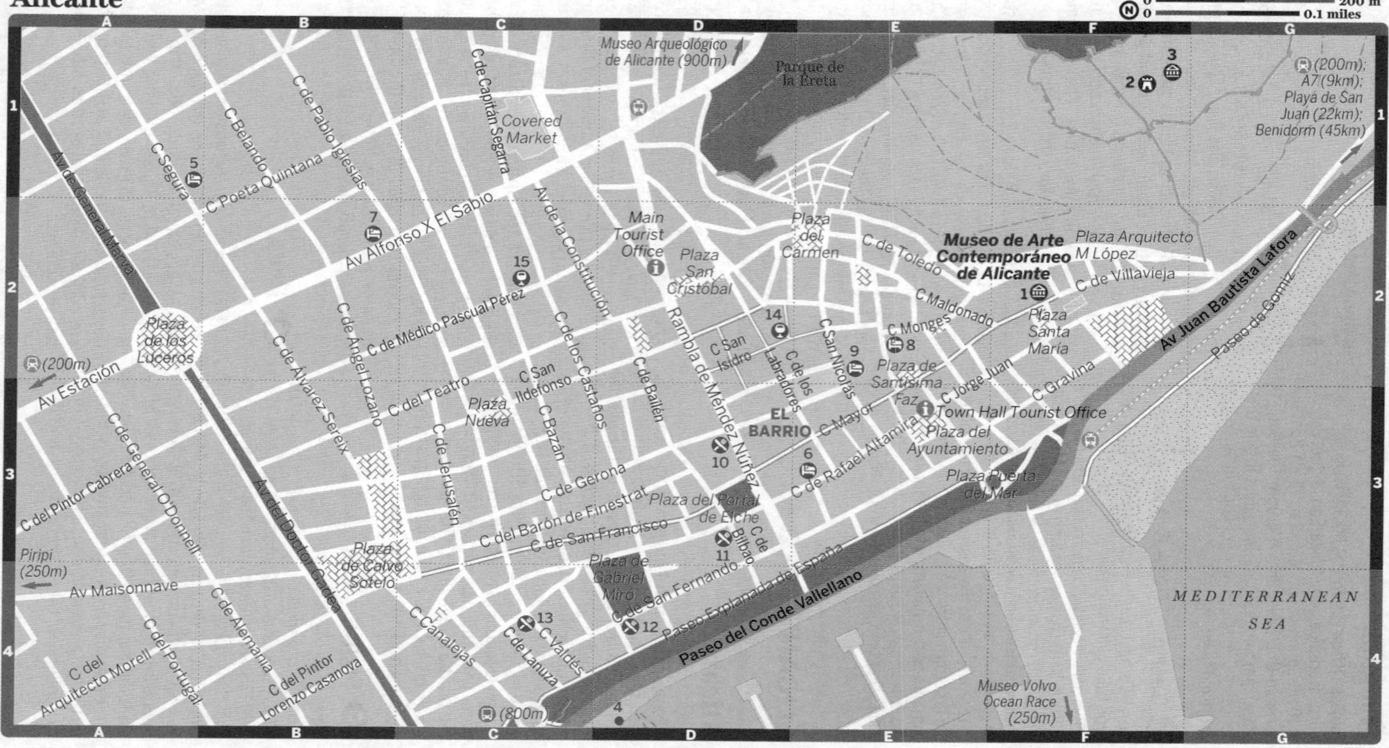
0 200 m
0 0.1 miles
Museo Arqueológico de Alicante (900m)
Parque de la Ereta
(200m); A7 (9km); Playa de San Juan (22km); Benidorm (45km)
Covered Market
C de Capitán Segarra
C de Pablo Iglesias
C Belando
C Segura
C Poeta Quintana
Av de General Marva
Av Alfonso X El Sabio
Av de la Constitución
Main Tourist Office
Plaza San Cristóbal
Plaza del Carmen
C de Toledo
Museo de Arte Contemporáneo de Alicante
Plaza Arquitecto M López
C de Villavieja
C Maldonado
Plaza Santa María
C Monges
Av Juan Bautista Lafora
Paseo de Gomiz
C de Médico Pascual Pérez
Plaza de los Luceros
(200m)
Av Estación
C de Ángel Lozano
C de Álvarez Sereix
C del Teatro
C San Ildefonso
Plaza Nueva
C de los Castaños
C de Bailén
Rambla de Méndez Núñez
C San Isidro
C de los Labradores
C San Nicolás
Plaza de Santísima Faz
C Jorge Juan
C Gravina
Town Hall Tourist Office
EL BARRIO
C Mayor
C de Rafael Altamira
Plaza del Ayuntamiento
Plaza Puerta del Mar
C Bazán
C de Jerusalén
C de Gerona
C del Barón de Finestrat
C de San Francisco
Plaza del Portal de Elche
C de Bilbao
Plaza de Gabriel Miró
C de San Fernando
Paseo Explanada de España
Paseo del Conde Vallellano
C del Pintor Cabrera
C de General O'Donnell
Av del Doctor Gadea
Plaza de Calvo Sotelo
Piripi (250m)
Av Maisonnave
C de Alemania
C del Portugal
C del Arquitecto Morell
C del Pintor Lorenzo Casanova
C Canalejas
C de Lanuza
C Valdés
(800m)
MEDITERRANEAN SEA
Museo Volvo Ocean Race (250m)

Alicante

Top Sights

1 Museo de Arte Contemporáneo de Alicante F2

Sights

2 Castillo de Santa Bárbara F1
3 Museo de la Ciudad de Alicante F1

Activities, Courses & Tours

4 Kon Tiki D4

Sleeping

5 Guest House A1
6 Hotel Hospes Amérigo E3
7 La City Hotel Mercado B2
8 Les Monges Palace E2
9 Pensión San Nicolás E2

Eating

10 Cervecería Sento D3
11 El Portal D3
12 La Barra de César Anca D4
13 OneOne C4

Drinking & Nightlife

14 El Coscorrón D2
15 Söda Bar C2

Festivals & Events

★Hogueras de San Juan FIESTA

(Fiesta de Sant Joan; www.hogueras.es; 20-24 Jun) Alicante's major festival is on the night of 24 June, when midsummer bonfires are lit. In a celebration reminiscent of Valencia's Las Fallas (p807), satirical effigies *(ninots)* go up in smoke all over town. This act, known as the *cremà,* is the culmination of several days of parades and partying, which begins when the effigies appear overnight on 20 June.

Sleeping

Guest House HOSTAL €

(650 718353; www.guesthousealicante.com; Calle Segura 20; s/d/apt €40/60/90; P) Here's a magnificent budget choice. Each of the eight large, tastefully decorated rooms differs: some have exposed stone walls and others are painted in pale green, daffodil yellow or deep-sea blue. All come with a safe, full-sized fridge and free beverage-making facilities. There are also a couple of well-equipped apartments. Ring ahead as it's not always staffed.

Pensión San Nicolás PENSION €

(965 21 70 39; www.alicantesanicolas.com; Calle San Nicolás 14; s/d with private bathroom €30/45, d with shared bathroom €40;) This small, well-located, family-run guesthouse is beautifully kept, with spotless rooms decorated cheerfully with bright colours and wall-mounted photos. All rooms come with tea- and coffee-making facilities, and some have tiny bathrooms. One room has its own kitchen. It's on one of the quieter central streets, but there's still plenty of weekend noise. It's great as a partying base.

Les Monges Palace BOUTIQUE HOTEL €€

(965 21 50 46; www.lesmonges.es; Calle San Agustín 4; s €61-80, d €75-90; P@) This agreeably quirky place in the nightlife zone is a treasure with winding corridors, tiles, mosaics and antique furniture. Each room is individually decorated – some are considerably more spacious than others – with plenty of character; some are in a more modern wing. The rooftop terrace bar is great and reception couldn't be more welcoming.

La City Hotel Mercado HOTEL €€

(965 98 01 53; www.lacityhotelmercado.com; Avenida Alfonso X El Sabio 26; s/d €65/95; @) With bright, minimalist lines and an airy feel, this friendly small hotel is well placed on the main boulevard. Rooms are a decent size with fridge and desk, and bathrooms come with powerful showers. Breakfast is available on-site and prices are fair. Basically it's a three-star that ticks all the boxes except parking, but there are stations nearby.

Hotel Hospes Amérigo HOTEL €€€

(965 14 65 70; www.hospes.es; Calle de Rafael Altamira 7; r €229-298; P@) Within an old Dominican convent, this commodious five-star choice harmoniously blends traditional and ultramodern. Enjoy the views from the small rooftop pool, or build up a sweat in the fitness area...if you can tear yourself away from the comfort of your smartly designed room. There are very few parking spaces, so make sure you pre-book one.

Eating

Where's the tapas zone? Virtually the whole centre: wherever it seems all the action is, you can be sure there's even more going on in another node a couple of streets further on. Great scenes.

Unusually for Spain, lots of restaurants and tapas bars have all-day opening. A number of gourmet ice-cream parlours cool things down around town.

★Cervecería Sento TAPAS €
(www.somossento.com; Calle Teniente Coronel Chápuli 1; tapas €2-10; 8am-midnight) Top-notch *montaditos* (little rolls) and inventive grilled tapas (try the turrón and pork 'Chupachups') are the reason to squeeze into this brilliant little bar. Watching the cheeky, nonstop staff in action is quite an experience too: they make every visit intriguing. It has a bigger branch nearby, but this one has the atmosphere.

OneOne BISTRO €€
(965 20 63 99; Calle Valdés 9; mains €12-20; noon-5pm & 9pm-midnight Tue-Sat, closed mid-Aug–mid-Sep) It's easier if you speak a little Spanish at this wonderfully eccentric place with its faithful following of regulars, but your ebullient host will make sure you get the best anyway. It's a true bistro, with the walls scarcely visible for Parisian-style photos and posters, and there's no menu. Just listen carefully as Bartolomé intones. Characterful and memorable.

La Barra de César Anca SPANISH €€
(965 20 15 80; www.grupocesaranca.com; Calle Ojeda 1; dishes €3-20; 8am-4pm Mon, 8am-4pm & 8-11.30pm Tue-Fri, noon-4pm & 8pm-midnight Sat, noon-4pm Sun;) Upmarket and buzzy, this is a fun place to sit at the bar and try some high-class gastro creations using plenty of excellent fish and showcasing fine presentation. There's always something new on the go. There's sit-down restaurant seating too, but the bar is more fun. It's also a popular spot for a mid-morning coffee and bite.

★El Portal SPANISH €€€
(965 14 32 69; www.elportaltaberna.com; Calle Bilbao 2; mains €18-30; 1pm-1.30am;) Excellent in every way, this plush corner spot sports deliberately OTT decor that changes biannually but is always interesting. Grab a table or squeeze up at the bar to enjoy some of this part of Spain's finest produce. Plump Dénia prawns, excellent tuna, fresh fish, mouthwatering ham; it's a feast for the palate. Excellent wines are available by the glass.

It's not cheap but the quality is sky-high. The atmosphere is smart but relaxed with a DJ responding to the mood as plates of seafood make way for gin and tonics in the mid-afternoon and later at night.

Piripi VALENCIAN €€€
(965 22 79 40; www.noumanolin.com; Avenida Oscar Esplá 30; mains €12-30; 1-4.15pm & 8.15pm-12.15am;) This quality restaurant is strong on rice, seafood and fish, which arrives fresh daily from the wholesale markets of Dénia and Santa Pola. There's a huge variety of tapas and a *valenciano* speciality that changes daily. It's a short walk west of the centre or downhill from the train station.

Drinking & Nightlife

Alicante's nightlife is an impressive thing to behold. Wet your night-time whistle in the wall-to-wall weekend bars of the old quarter (known as El Barrio) around Catedral de San Nicolás. Alternatively, head for the sea. Paseo del Puerto, tranquil by day, is a double-decker line of casino, restaurants, bars and nightclubs. Calle Castaños is worth a wander for a quieter, all-week scene.

★El Coscorrón BAR
(965 21 27 27; Calle Tarifa 5; 9pm-3.30am) Mind your head – actually, it's more like bend double – as you enter this intriguing cellar bar, presciently named 'bump on the head'. Once inside enjoy the cosy atmosphere with mellow soundtrack, friendly regulars and walls plastered with graffiti and notes. The mojitos (€4) are served out of a mint-filled teapot on the bar and are great.

Söda Bar BAR
(639 918836; www.facebook.com/sodabar; Calle de Médico Pascual Pérez 8; 7pm-2am Fri, 5pm-2.30am Sat;) For quality drinks and well-curated sounds in a welcoming, relaxed but stylish atmosphere, head out of the mayhem of the Barrio to this place, with a friendly local crowd and hipster tendencies. Regular events include DJs, literary readings and dance classes.

Information

Main Tourist Office (965 20 00 00; www.alicanteturismo.com; Rambla de Méndez Núñez 41; 10am-6pm Mon-Fri, to 2pm Sat) There are also branches near the **town hall** (965 14 92 19; Plaza del Ayuntamiento 1; 10am-2pm & 4-7pm Mon-Sat, 10am-2pm Sun Sep-May, 10am-2pm & 5-8pm daily Jun-Aug) and at the **train station** (965 12 56 33; Avenida de Salamanca; 10am-2pm & 4-7pm Mon-Sat, 10am-2pm Sun Sep-May, 10am-2pm & 5-8pm daily Jun-Aug), beach and airport.

Getting There & Away

AIR

Alicante's **airport** (☎902 404704; www.aena.es; L'Altet), gateway to the Costa Blanca, is around 12km southwest of the city centre. It's served by budget airlines, charters and scheduled flights from all over Europe.

BUS

From the **bus station** (Avenida de Salamanca), destinations include Murcia (€6 to €7.50, one to two hours, 11 to 17 daily) and Valencia (€21, 2½ to 5¾ hours, 18 to 21 daily).

TRAIN

Mainline destinations from the principal train station include the following. For Murcia, there are also very regular *cercanía* trains (€5.75, 1¼ hours) via Elche and Orihuela.

DESTINATION	COST (€)	TIME (HR)	FREQUENCY (DAILY)
Barcelona	53	4¾-5¾	8
Madrid	66	from 2¼	11
Murcia	10-18	1¼	5
Valencia	17-30	1½-2	12

TRAM

The coastal tram/light-rail service is a handy option; see the TRAM (www.tramalicante.es) website. Scenic Line 1 heads to Benidorm with a connection to Dénia. Catch it from beside the covered market.

Dénia

POP 41,500

A major passenger port for the fairly nearby Balearic Islands, Dénia (Spanish: Denia) is a cheery place that lives for more than just tourism. The old town snuggles up against a small hill mounted by a tumbledown castle, and the town's streets buzz with life and top foodie choices. The beaches of La Marina, to its northwest, are good and sandy, while southeastwards the fretted coastline of Les Rotes and beyond offers less-frequented rocky coves. With its excellent selection of hotels and restaurants, and mix of local and tourist life, Dénia is perhaps the Costa Blanca's most appealing base.

Sights

Castillo de Dénia CASTLE

(☎966 42 06 56; www.denia.net/castillo-de-denia; Calle San Francisco; adult/child €3/1; ⏲10am-6pm or later, to 12.30am Jul & Aug) From Plaza de la Constitución steps lead up to the ruins of Dénia's castle, from where there's a great overview of the town and coast. The castle grounds contain the **Museo Arqueològic de Dénia**, a collection of potsherds illustrating the town's long history. The closing time changes according to the time of year; check the website for exact times.

Sleeping

★**Hotel Chamarel** BOUTIQUE HOTEL €€

(☎966 43 50 07; www.hotelchamarel.com; Calle Cavallers 13; d/ste incl breakfast €102/120; P❄☎) This delightful hotel, tastefully furnished in period style, occupies a lovably attractive, 19th-century bourgeois mansion. Rooms surround a tranquil patio and are all different, with space and lots of character. Bathrooms artfully combine modern fittings with venerable floor tiles. The internal salon with marble-topped bar is equally relaxing. The whole place is a capacious gallery for the artist-owner's paintings.

Hotel Nou Romá BOUTIQUE HOTEL €€

(☎966 43 28 43; www.hotelnouroma.com; Calle Nou 28; incl breakfast s €78, d €90-144; P❄☎) Perfectly located for excursions to the Calle Loreto eating strip, this hotel is on a quietish backstreet but very central. Staff are really excellent, and the spacious rooms with their bright-tiled bathrooms are a delight. The on-site restaurant is worthwhile and the overall package very impressive. Lots of thoughtful details add that extra something to your stay.

Hostal L'Anfora HOSTAL €€

(☎966 43 01 01; www.hostallanfora.com; Esplanada de Cervantes 8; s/d €55/72; ❄☎) The genial boss here is rightly proud of this top *hostal* on the waterfront strip. Rooms are compact but new in feel, with colourful bedcovers, faultless bathrooms and not a speck of dust or dirt. Outside of high summer, prices are very fair: it's a budget gem. Rooms with a sea view cost a few euros more.

★**El Raset** HOTEL €€€

(☎965 78 65 64; www.hotelelraset.com; Calle Bellavista 1; s/d incl breakfast €130/157; P❄@☎) This modern designer hotel, set in a handsome four-square old building, overlooks the port with just 20 spotlit rooms, colourful bedspreads and art on the walls. There's a buzzy vibe and very friendly service. A row of house restaurants alongside gives you eating options on the doorstep. Prices drop off sharply either side of August.

Eating

Bar Bus SEAFOOD €

(☎965 78 11 37; Plaza del Archiduque Carlos 4; dishes €4-10; ⏰noon-10pm; 📶) Bars beside bus stations aren't normally recommended for their culinary qualities, but this vivacious corner spot breaks the mould. As well as being a spot where people drop a quick coffee before jumping aboard the 12.10, it's also a place to try simple, quality seafood selected daily from the market. Oysters, cuttlefish and other delights are reliably excellent.

El Baret de Miquel Ruiz TAPAS €€

(☎WhatsApp only 673 740595; www.miquelruizcuiner.com; Carrer Historiador Palau 1; tapas €4-16; ⏰1.30-3.30pm & 8-10.30pm Tue-Sat) This is a real find for gastronomes. The chef had a Michelin-starred restaurant but chose to reject the pretension of that world in favour of a more normal existence. Delicious, exquisitely presented morsels of traditionally influenced dishes using market produce are taste sensations in the simple, retro-casual vibe of the front room of an old house. Book months ahead.

Els Tomassets TAPAS €€

(☎966 43 25 60; www.tascaelstomassets.com; Calle Loreto 35; mains €7-15; ⏰9am-midnight; 📶) Informal and vibrant, with an open kitchen, this spot turns out delicious fare. In winter, chargrilled artichokes *(alcachofas a la brasa)* are a delight, while the acquired, rich taste of sea urchins will tempt those who like their food spiky. Seafood is a forte, but meat dishes are also above average for this coast. Bickering staff could do better.

★**Quique Dacosta** MODERN SPANISH €€€

(☎965 78 41 79; www.quiquedacosta.es; Calle Rascassa 1, El Poblet; degustation menu €210, wine flight €99; ⏰1.30-3pm & 8.30-10.30pm Wed-Sun Feb-Jun & Sep-Nov, daily Jul & Aug) In sleek, white, minimalist premises near the beach 3km west of Dénia, this coolly handsome place is one of the peninsula's temples to modern gastronomy. The eponymous chef employs molecular and other contemporary techniques to create a constantly surprising cornucopia of flavours and textures.

Aitana SEAFOOD €€€

(☎965 78 60 69; Calle de Sandunga 53; seafood €10-60; ⏰1.30-4pm Tue-Thu, 1.30-4pm & 8.30-11.30pm Fri & Sat) Perhaps the best place in Dénia to try the famous local prawns and other crustaceans, this nondescript backstreet bar gets thronged, so try to book a table or get there early and wait for a spot at the bar. The gruff boss has been doing this for years and knows his seafood inside out. Delicious.

Information

Tourist Office (☎966 42 23 67; www.denia.net; Plaza Oculista Buigues 9; ⏰9.30am-1.30pm & 4-7pm Mon-Sat, 10am-2pm Sun Sep–mid-Jun, 9.30am-1.30pm & 5-8pm daily mid-Jun–Aug) Near the waterfront and ferry and also close to the tram/light-rail station.

Getting There & Away

Baleària (☎902 160180, from overseas 912 66 02 14; www.balearia.com; Moll de la Pansa) runs ferries year-round to/from Mallorca (passenger €70 to €100, car €100 to €150, five to seven hours, daily) and Ibiza (passenger €70 to €105, car €120 to €160, two to 3½ hours, daily), and from May to September directly to Formentera (passenger €70 to €100, car €80 to €110, 2½ hours, five weekly).

Hourly light-rail services follow the scenic route southwards via Calp and Altea to Benidorm, connecting with the tram for Alicante.

ALSA (www.alsa.es) buses run around a dozen times daily to Valencia (€11.05, 1½ to two hours) and Alicante (€11.40, 1½ to three hours). There are also services to Benidorm and other Costa Blanca towns.

Xàbia

POP 27,200

With a large expat resident population, Xàbia (Spanish: Jávea) is a gentle, family-oriented place that has largely resisted the high-rise tourist developments that blight so much of the Costa Blanca. Pleasant, relaxed and picturesque, it comes in three flavours: the small old town 2km inland; El Puerto (the port), directly east of the old town; and the beach zone of El Arenal, a couple of kilometres south. Picturesque headlands and coves reward further exploration of this section of coast.

Activities

Montgó HIKING

A popular walk is ascending Montgó, the craggy mountain looming over the town. It's a climb best started in the morning or late afternoon as it's fairly exposed to the sun. It's a stony and arduous but not difficult path to the top. Access the trail from the road between Xàbia and Dénia; it's about 8km return from the car park.

Sleeping & Eating

Hotel Triskel BOUTIQUE HOTEL €€

(☎966 46 21 91; www.hotel-triskel.com; Calle Sor María Gallart 3; d €110;) By the old-town market, this cordially run place is a standout. The five lovely rooms are subtly and beautifully decorated according to themes, with thoughtful details, objets d'art and pleasing handmade wooden furniture. Everything is done with a warm personal touch and the cosy bar downstairs does a cracking G and T. Pets welcome and prices nearly halve in low season.

Hotel Jávea HOTEL €€

(☎965 79 54 61; www.hotel-javea.com; Calle Pio X 5; d €75, with sea view €120;) This extra-friendly small hotel is in the heart of the port district, with bars and restaurants on the doorstep. Offbeat decor and smart modern rooms make it a top spot. The sea view costs a fair bit extra, but it's a lovely perspective over the whole sweep of the bay. The top-floor restaurant makes the most of the vistas, too.

Sotavent SPANISH €

(☎660 341226; Calle Cristo del Mar 8; dishes €5-13; noon-11pm) This friendly spot just near the waterfront in the port area gets everything right with sizeable, delicious portions of seafood, rices, liver and more at extremely reasonable prices. There's a patio space that is the place to sit on another balmy Xàbia evening.

★**La Renda** VALENCIAN €€

(☎965 79 37 63; www.facebook.com/rendajaveabyjoseluis; Calle Cristo del Mar 12; mains €10-22; 1-4pm & 7-11pm Tue-Sat, 1-4pm Sun) There's more than you think to a paella, and this well-priced but classy, welcoming place at the port has numerous different rice dishes, including a delicious *meloso* (with broth) rice with lobster. For most dishes a minimum of two people is required, but there's a set menu with a rice option always available.

Drinking & Nightlife

Taverna Octopus PUB

(Paseo del Tenista David Ferrer; 11am-3am;) In business for several decades now, this grungy spot keeps things likeably simple, with ice-cold beer in miniature tankards and a rocking soundtrack. Grab an outdoor table and watch the world walk by along the beachfront promenade. It's easily the Arenal's best bar.

Information

There are tourist offices at **El Arenal** (☎966 46 06 05; www.xabia.org; Avenida del Pla; 9.30am-1.30pm Mon-Fri mid-Sep–mid-Jun, 10am-2pm & 5-9.30pm daily mid-Jun–mid-Sep), the **old town** (☎965 79 43 56; Plaza de la Iglesia; 9am-1.30pm & 4-7pm Mon-Fri (5-8pm Jun-Sep), 10am-1.30pm Sat) and the **port** (☎965 79 07 36; Plaza Presidente Adolfo Suárez 11; 9.30am-1.30pm & 4-7pm Mon-Fri (5-8pm Jun-Sep), 10am-1.30pm & 4-7pm Sat (5-8pm Jun-Sep), 10am-1.30pm Sun).

Getting There & Away

ALSA (www.alsa.es) run at least six buses daily to Valencia (€12, two to three hours) and Alicante (€10.20, 2¼ to 2¾ hours). There are also services to Dénia, Madrid, Benidorm, Gandia and Calp, as well as direct buses to the Valencia and Alicante airports, the latter run by **Beniconnect** (☎965 85 07 90; www.beniconnect.com).

Getting Around

You can rent a cycle at **Xàbia's Bike** (☎966 46 11 50; www.xabiasbike.com; Avenida Lepanto 5; per day/week from €13/56; 9.30am-1.30pm & 4.30-8.30pm Mon-Fri, 9.30am-1.30pm Sat) in the port area. It also does weekend rides and can organise guided bike tours. The tourist office has a booklet of cycling excursions. Buses link the different zones of the town.

Calp

POP 19,600

The striking Gibraltaresque Peñon de Ifach, a giant limestone molar protruding from the sea, rears up from the seaside resort of Calp. Two large bays sprawl either side of the Peñon: Playa Arenal on the western side is backed by the central part of town, while Playa Levante (La Fossa) to the north is a glorious beach backed by tourist apartments.

Activities

Peñon de Ifach WALKING

From the Peñon's Aula de Naturaleza (Nature Centre), a fairly strenuous walking trail – allow two hours for the round trip – heads through a tunnel and then climbs towards the 332m-high summit, offering great seascapes from its end point. There's a limit of 150 people on the mountain at any one time, so in July and August you may have a short wait.

Sleeping & Eating

Hostal Terra de Mar BOUTIQUE HOTEL €€
(☎629 665124; www.hostalterrademar.com; Calle Justicia 31; r €79-129; ❄📶🐾) At this artistic and highly original hotel, a range of influences combine to exquisite effect. Each floor has its own style (via the stairs you can travel from Japan to Morocco to Africa and Paris). Some rooms have mini-balconies looking over the old-town street. There are numerous details such as intricately folded towels and a personal tea box.

★**El Bodegón** SPANISH €€
(☎965 83 01 64; Calle Delfín 8; mains €8-16; ⊙noon-4pm & 7-11pm Mon-Sat) Tried and true, this traditional Spanish restaurant hasn't changed in decades and is all the better for it. Reliably good classic meals such as rabbit, seafood and hearty steaks make this a favourite for locals and visitors alike.

Information

Beach Tourist Office (☎965 83 69 20; www.calpe.es; Avenida Ejércitos Españoles 44; ⊙9am-9pm Mon-Fri, 10am-3pm Sat Jul & Aug, 9am-4.30pm Mon-Fri, 10am-2pm Sat Sep-Jun) Near the lagoon.

Old Town Tourist Office (☎965 83 85 32; www.calpe.es; Plaza del Mosquit; ⊙8am-3.30pm Mon-Fri)

Getting There & Away

Buses connect Calp with Alicante (€7.25, 1½ hours, six to 10 daily) and Valencia (€13.55, 2¾ to 3¾ hours, six or seven daily). There are also regular services to other nearby coastal destinations, including Benidorm and Altea. The **bus station** (Avenida de la Generalitat Valenciana) is just off the ring road.

Trams travel daily northwards to Dénia (€2.50, 40 minutes) and south to Benidorm (€2.50, 30 minutes), connecting with trams for Alicante.

Benidorm

POP 66,600

Benidorm's nice side is its old town, set on a hill between the two beaches. From the platform where once a castle stood, the evening light and sunsets can be incredible. Benidorm is packed in summer, with happy throngs of sun-seekers and party animals, including a sizeable LGBT scene. The area is also popular with families for its excellent theme parks.

Benidorm is infamous for mass tourism along its two wide sandy beaches and the high-rise development that backs them. Bingo, karaoke, fish 'n' chips, all-day fry-ups... it's all here, while the profusion of expat bars where not a word of Spanish is spoken give it an atmosphere of its own.

Activities

Terra Mítica AMUSEMENT PARK
(☎902 020220; www.terramiticapark.com; adult/4-12 yr €39/28; ⊙10.30am-9pm or midnight Easter & mid-May–mid-Sep, Sat & Sun mid-Sep–Oct; 👪) Everything is bigger and brasher in Benidorm, so it should come as no surprise to learn that this is Spain's biggest theme park. A fun day out, especially if you're with children, it's Mediterranean (well, kind of) in theme, with plenty of scary rides, street entertainment and areas devoted to ancient Egypt, Greece, Rome, Iberia and the islands.

Opening days are complex, so check its website outside high season.

Aqualandia WATER PARK
(☎965 86 01 00; www.aqualandia.net; adult/child €38/29; ⊙10am-dusk mid-May–Sep; 👪) Aqualandia is Europe's largest water park and can easily entertain for a full day. It's quite a bit cheaper if you book online, and there's discounted combined entry with other attractions in the area.

Sleeping

Hostal Irati HOSTAL €€
(☎965 84 96 07; Calle Condestable Zaragoza 5; r incl breakfast €60-80; ❄📶) In the old town, this place has comfortable, neat rooms with excellent tiled bathrooms above a friendly bar. It's an excellent deal. It has one car-parking spot, but you'll be lucky to get it.

★**Villa Venecia** BOUTIQUE HOTEL €€€
(☎965 85 54 66; www.hotelvillavenecia.com; Plaza San Jaime 1; s €205-308, d €356-510; P❄@📶🏊) Up high opposite the old town's church and lording it over the seething beach crowds below, this plush five-star hotel has it all. Each room has sweeping sea views and ultramodern bathrooms. As you lounge beside its diminutive rooftop pool after a spa session, you could be nautical miles from Benidorm. Its bar and excellent restaurant are open to all comers.

WORTH A TRIP

GUADALEST

The little village of (El Castell de) Guadalest, reached by a natural tunnel and overlooked by the **Castillo de San José** (☎965 88 53 93; adult/child €4/2; ⊙10am-6pm, 7pm or 8pm), is marvellously picturesque, with stunning views down the valley to the sea and over a turquoise reservoir below. You'll be far from the first to discover it – coaches, heading up from the Costa Blanca resorts, disgorge millions of visitors yearly. But get here early, or stay around after the last bus has pulled out, and the place will be almost your own.

There are half a dozen or so novelty museums, including the completely bonkers **Museo de Saleros y Pimenteros** (Avenida de Alicante 2; adult/child €3/1; ⊙11am-6pm, to 8pm in summer), which is a museum of salt and pepper pots – more than 20,000 of them.

Cases Noves (☎965 88 53 09; www.casesnoves.es; Calle Achova 1; r with breakfast standard €85-98, superior €105-145; ❄@🛜) makes an exceptional place to stay. Run by brilliant Sofia and Toni, this is B&B taken to a whole new level and worth travelling a long way for. The five thoughtfully designed bedrooms come with fresh flowers and numerous excellent details such as a tablet on which to watch Netflix or order your dinner. The gorgeous terrace offers views of the distant sea and the floodlit village.

Llorente (www.llorentebus.es) buses run from Benidorm to Guadalest (€3.75, one hour) on weekday mornings and return early afternoon, with a day trip possible. In July and August they also run on Saturday and Sunday. If you drive you'll be charged €2 to park.

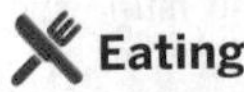

Eating

La Cava Aragonesa TAPAS €€
(☎966 80 12 06; www.lacavaaragonesa.es; Plaza de la Constitución; mains €10-18; ⊙noon-midnight, to 1.30am Jun-Sep) This has grown from origins as a tiny bar to a sprawling, dizzying array of tapas, fat canapés and plates of cold cuts, all arrayed before you at the bar. The sit-down restaurant offers wooden platters of mixed foods and a huge wine list. The zone is replete with tapas options so make a satisfying crawl of it.

Information

Old Town Tourist Office (☎965 85 13 11; www.benidorm.org; Plaza de Canalejas; ⊙9am-9pm Mon-Fri, 10am-5pm Sat, 10am-2pm Sun) In the old town, at the end of the eastern beach, this is the principal of several Benidorm tourist offices.

Getting There & Away

From Benidorm's bus station (served by local bus 41 and 47), ALSA (www.alsa.es) runs to the following destinations:

Alicante (€4 to €6, 45 minutes to one hour, frequent)

Alicante Airport (€9.45, 40 to 50 minutes, hourly)

Valencia (€16.55 to €16.90, 1¾ to 3¾ hours, frequent)

Some services also leave from the more central Avenida Europa 8 stop, a couple of blocks back from the beach.

The tram/light-rail runs to Alicante (€3.75, 1¼ hours, every 30 minutes) and in the other direction to Altea, Calp and Dénia.

Elche

POP 227,700

Thanks to Moorish irrigation, Elche (Valenciano: Elx) is an important fruit producer and also a Unesco World Heritage site twice over: for the *Misteri d'Elx*, its annual medieval play, and for its marvellous, extensive palm groves, which are Europe's largest and were originally planted by the Phoenicians. The palms, the mosque-like churches and the historic buildings in desert-coloured stone give the city, 23km southwest of Alicante, a North African feel in parts.

Sights

Around 200,000 palm trees, each with a lifespan of some 250 years, make the heart of this busy industrial town a veritable oasis. A signed 2.5km **walking trail** (ask at the tourist office for the leaflet) leads from the **Museu del Palmerar** (☎965 42 22 40; Porta de la Morera 12; adult/child €1/0.50, Sun free; ⊙10am-2pm & 3-6pm Tue-Sat, 10am-2pm Sun) through the groves.

★**Huerto del Cura** GARDENS
(☎965 45 19 36; http://jardin.huertodelcura.com; Porta de la Morera 49; adult/child €5/2.50, audio guide €2; ⊙10am-sunset Mon-Sat, 10am-3pm or 6pm Sun) In the Islamic world, a garden is

WORTH A TRIP

ALTEA

Separated from Benidorm only by the thick wedge of the Sierra Helada, **Altea** is an altogether quieter place, with a fishing harbour and beaches composed mostly of pebbles. The modern part is a pleasant enough, fairly standard low-rise coastal resort. By contrast, the whitewashed old town, perched on a hilltop overlooking the sea, is a delightfully pretty *pueblo*.

Altea Old Town is an easy 10-minute stroll back from the beach to this tight-knit hilltop warren of whitewashed houses. It's visually very beautiful and, though the main street and plaza are very touristy, you can find some quieter corners. Three miradors give different perspectives over the coast.

considered a form of Paradise. Elche's past and culture couldn't therefore be any more obvious than in these privately owned gardens, where humanity and nature have joined forces to produce something that truly approaches that ideal. The highlights are the water features and the cactus gardens.

Parque Municipal PARK

(Paseo Estación; 7am-9pm Nov-Mar, to 11pm Apr-Jul, Sep & Oct, to 11.45pm during Aug) This lovely park on the northern side of central Elche is one of several appealing places to stroll among the rustling palm trees. A small visitor centre within (open 10am to 3pm daily, plus 4pm to 7pm Friday to Sunday) has a multimedia presentation.

Museo Arqueológico y de Historia de Elche MUSEUM

(MAHE; 966 65 82 03; www.elche.es/museos/mahe; Calle Diagonal del Palau 7; adult/child €3/1, Sun free; 10am-6pm Mon-Sat, to 3pm Sun) This museum is a superb introduction to the town's long and eventful history. Everything is particularly well displayed and labelled, and it occupies both a purpose-built building and the town's castle. Starting with archaeological finds from the Neolithic, you progress into history of the Muslim occupation and Reconquest. In the castle's keep, a replica of the famous *Dama de Elche* statue holds pride of place; locals live in hope that the original will return from Madrid one day.

Festivals & Events

★Misteri d'Elx THEATRE

(www.misteridelx.com; 14-15 Aug, plus 1 Nov in even years) A lyric drama dating from the Middle Ages, this is performed annually in the **Basílica de Santa María** (965 45 15 40; Plaza de Santa María 2; tower adult/child €2/1; 7am-1pm & 5.30-9pm, tower 11am-7pm Jun-Sep, 10.30am-3pm Oct-May). The mystery's two acts, *La Vespra* (the eve of the Virgin Mary's death) and *La Festa* (the celebration of her Assumption), are performed in Valenciano by the people of Elche on 14 and 15 August respectively (with public rehearsals on the three previous days).

In even-numbered years, there's a single-day performance on 1 November, with two rehearsals in the days before.

One distant day, according to legend, a casket was washed up on Elche's Mediterranean shore. Inside were a statue of the Virgin and the *Consueta,* the music and libretto of a mystery play describing Our Lady's death, assumption into heaven and coronation.

The story tells how the Virgin, realising that death is near, asks God to allow her to see the Apostles one last time. They arrive one by one from distant lands and, in their company, she dies at peace. Once received into paradise, she is crowned Queen of Heaven and Earth to swelling music, the ringing of bells, cheers all round and spectacular fireworks.

You can see a multimedia presentation and learn more about the Misteri in the **Museu de la Festa** (965 45 34 64; Carrer Major de la Vila 25; adult/child €3/1; 10am-2pm & 3-6pm Tue-Sat, 10am-2pm Sun).

Sleeping & Eating

★Hotel Huerto del Cura BOUTIQUE HOTEL €€

(966 61 00 11; www.hotelhuertodelcura.com; Porta de la Morera 14; r €90-165; P) A sublime hotel with stylish white rooms and antique wooden furnishings. The accommodation is in trim bungalows within lush, palm-shaded gardens. It's a family-friendly place with a playground, large pool and babysitting service. Complete the cosseting at Elche's oldest luxury hotel by dining in its renowned Els Capellans restaurant. If you aren't so mobile, request a room close to reception.

★El Granaino SPANISH €€

(☎966 66 40 80; www.mesongranaino.com; Carrer Josep María Buck 40; mains €14-22; ⊙10am-4pm & 8pm-midnight Mon-Sat; 📶) Across the river from the centre, El Granaino, with its bar lined with people scarfing down a quick, quality lunch, is worth the 10-minute walk. Top seafood, delicious stews and a fine range of tapas showcase a classic, quintessentially Spanish cuisine. Fuller meals can be enjoyed outside or in the adjacent dining room. Excellent service and quality.

Dátil de Oro VALENCIAN €€

(☎966 45 34 15; www.datildeoro.com; Paseo de la Estación; set menus €12-31; ⊙9am-11pm; 📶) Within the Parque Municipal, the Golden Date is set up for weddings, with its own chapel and room for 800 diners. At other times it's a lovely spot to dine in a glass pavilion with palmy surrounds. Try local dishes such as *arroz con costra* (rice dish with a crusty egg topping); there's also date flan and date ice cream.

Information

Tourist Office (☎966 65 81 96; www.visitelche.com; Plaza Parque 3; ⊙9am-6pm or 7pm Mon-Fri, 10am-6pm or 7pm Sat, also 10am-2pm Sun May-Dec) By the palm grove that is the Parque Municipal.

Getting There & Away

Elche is on the Alicante–Murcia *cercanía* train line. About 20 trains rattle through daily, bound for Alicante (€2.70) or Murcia (€3.70) via Orihuela (€2.70). Train and bus stations are beside each other on Avenida de la Libertad (Avenida del Ferrocarril).

From the bus station, destinations include the following:

DESTINATION	COST (€)	TIME	FREQUENCY
Alicante	2.25	35min	every 30min
Murcia	4.51	45min-2hr	12-13 daily
Valencia	13.22	2½-4hr	10-12 daily

Buses also run to Alicante airport. See www.aerobusalicante.es for details.

Villena

POP 34,200

Pleasant Villena, between Alicante and Albacete, is the most attractive of the towns along the corridor of the Val de Vinalopó. Plaza de Santiago is at the heart of its old quarter, which is topped by a castle. The town's archaeological museum is particularly notable. It feels a long way from the Costa Blanca here, with a more Castilian atmosphere.

Sights

★Museo Arqueológico MUSEUM

(www.museovillena.com; Plaza de Santiago 1; adult/child €2/1; ⊙10am-2pm Tue-Sun) Plaza de Santiago is at the heart of Villena's old quarter, and within the imposing 16th-century Palacio Municipal, seat of the town council, is this archaeological museum. There are some magnificent pieces in the normal collection, even before you get to the stunning late Bronze Age treasure hoards, with a series of bowls, bracelets and brooches made from solid gold. It's the most impressive sight in town.

Castillo de la Atalaya CASTLE

(www.turismovillena.com; Calle Libertad; adult/child €3/1.50; ⊙guided tours 11am, noon, 1pm, 4pm & 5pm Tue-Sat, 11am, noon & 1pm Sun) Perched above the old town, this 12th-century castle has been handsomely restored and is splendidly lit at night. Entrance is by guided visit, in Spanish with English asides. Tickets can be bought at the town's tourist office or at the visitor centre near the castle's base. A double wall encloses the central *patio de armas* courtyard, overlooked by a high square keep.

Sleeping & Eating

La Casa de los Aromas B&B €

(☎666 475612; www.hotelcasadelosaromas.com; Calle Arco 1; s/d €30/47; ❄📶) In the heart of the old centre, this place offers a very genuine welcome and five sweet rooms, all with an individual aroma scheme. It's got lots of charm, and staff can arrange winery visits and other activities. You get access to a fridge and microwave as well as an appealing common room with a vinyl collection to play. Breakfast is an extra €3 per person. Two of the rooms are great for families.

La Despensa VALENCIAN, SPANISH €€

(☎965 80 83 37; www.mesonladespensa.com; Calle Cervantes 27; mains €12-20; ⊙9am-5pm & 8-11pm Mon, 9am-5pm Tue, 9am-midnight Wed-Sat, 1-5pm Sun; 📶) Near the station, La Despensa offers handsome traditional decor and excellent cuisine. It does some great rices, including a very tasty one with rabbit and snails, as well as some impressive slabs of meat on the grill. For tapas, try the house special with ham, quail's egg and *sobrasada* (Mallorcan pork and paprika spread).

Information

Tourist Office (☎966 15 02 36; www.turismovillena.com; Plaza de Santiago 5; ⏲9am-2pm Mon-Fri, 11am-2pm Sat & Sun) Villena's tourist office is on the main square opposite the town hall.

Visitor Centre (☎965 80 38 93; www.turismovillena.com; Calle de General Prim 2; ⏲10am-2pm & 4-6pm Tue-Sat, 10am-2pm Sun) Near the castle.

Getting There & Away

Nine trains run daily between Alicante and Villena (€6 to €10, 35 to 50 minutes), as well as buses; there are also train services to Valencia. Note that the Villena AV station, served by fast trains, is 10km southwest of town.

Orihuela

POP 34,000

Beside the Río Segura and flush with the base of a barren mountain of rock, the historical heart of Orihuela, with superb Gothic, Renaissance and, especially, baroque buildings, well merits a detour. The old town is strung out between the river and a mountain topped by a ruined castle. The main sights are dotted along the district, more or less in a line, and are well signposted throughout.

Orihuela has a vibrant **Moros y Cristianos** (http://morosycristianosorihuela.es; ⏲mid-Jul) festival, and reprises the atmosphere with an enormous medieval market at the end of January.

Sights

★Catedral de San Salvador CATHEDRAL
(☎965 30 48 28; Calle Doctor Sarget; adult/child €2/1; ⏲10.30am-2pm & 4-6.30pm Mon-Fri, 10.30am-2pm Sat) Low slung but achieving an understated majesty nonetheless, this cathedral is built of light-coloured stone in the centre of the old town and features three finely carved portals. Unusually, the altar is enclosed at the front by an ornate Renaissance (the other three sides are Gothic) *reja* (filigree screen); another closes off the choir, while an earlier Gothic one, alive with vegetal motifs, screens a chapel behind the altar. The highlight, though, is the tiny, exquisite two-level Renaissance cloister on the street behind.

Museo Diocesano de Arte Sacro GALLERY
(☎966 74 36 27; Calle Mayor de Ramón y Cajal; adult/child €4/2; ⏲10am-2pm & 4-7pm Mon-Sat) This sizeable and sober episcopal palace next to the cathedral now holds a collection of religious art. There are some fine pieces but the undisputed highlight is the masterly *Temptation of St Thomas* by Velázquez. A sizeable early work, painted around 1632, it depicts the saint as a young man swooning after having resisted the temptations of a prostitute, seen in the background. Angels reward him with a white chastity ribbon.

Convento de Santo Domingo MONASTERY
(☎965 30 02 40; http://colegio.cdsantodomingo.com; Calle Adolfo Clavarana; adult/child €2/1; ⏲10am-1.30pm or 2pm & 4-7pm or 5-8pm Tue-Sat, 10am-2pm Sun) A 16th-century monastery and university with two fine Renaissance cloisters and a refectory clad in 18th-century tile work, Santo Domingo was built on a monumental scale and houses a school. The stern but noble lines of the building stretch towards one of the city gates.

Eating

★Bodega La Venganza TAPAS €
(☎661 542220; www.facebook.com/bodegalavenganzaorihuela; Calle Togores 3; tapas €4-15; ⏲12.30-4.30pm & 7.30-11pm or later Wed-Sat, 11.30am-5pm Sun) It's impossible not to love this tiny, sassy tapas joint, which expands out to tree-shaded tables on a pretty plaza behind the Iglesia de las Santas Justa y Rufina. It makes a point of procuring excellent seafood – crabs, cockles, tuna, mackerel – and cooks it very well. Check the blackboard for daily specials or go for a tapas degustation.

Information

Tourist Office (☎965 30 46 45; www.orihuelaturistica.es; Plaza de la Soledad; ⏲8am-2pm or 3pm Mon, 8am-2pm or 3pm & 4-7pm or 5-8pm Tue-Fri, 10am-2pm & 4-7pm or 5-8pm Sat, 10am-2pm Sun) In the heart of the old town near the back of the cathedral. There's also an office at the train station.

Getting There & Away

Orihuela is on *cercanía* train line C1 between Murcia (€2, 20 minutes) and Alicante (€4.20, one hour, hourly). The train and bus stations are 1km south of the old centre.

DON'T MISS

MOROS Y CRISTIANOS

More than 80 towns and villages in the south of the Valencia region hold their own Fiesta de Moros y Cristianos (festival of Moors and Christians) to celebrate the Reconquista, the region's liberation from Muslim rule.

The biggest and best known is in the town of **Alcoy** (22-24 Apr), when hundreds of locals dress up in elaborate traditional costumes representing different 'factions' – Muslim and Christian soldiers, slaves, guild groups, town criers, heralds, bands – and march through the streets in colourful processions with mock battles. Processions converge upon Alcoy's main square and its huge, temporary wooden fortress. It's an exhilarating spectacle of sights and sounds.

Each town has its own variation on the format, steeped in traditions that allude to the events of the Reconquista. So, for example, Villena's **festival** (www.turismovillena.com; 5-9 Sep) features night-time parades, while La Vila Joiosa's festival (24 to 31 July), near Benidorm, re-enacts the landing of Muslim ships on the beaches. Some are as early as February, so you've a good chance of finding one whenever it is that you visit the region.

MURCIA PROVINCE

Murcia

POP 441,000

Officially twinned with Miami, Murcia is the antithesis of the city of vice; it's a sizeable but laid-back provincial capital with a handful of interesting sights and a pleasant, strollable centre. Like Valencia, it is famous for its *huerta*, a surrounding zone of market gardens dating back to Moorish times, which supply the city's restaurants with excellent fresh produce and drive a thriving tapas scene. It makes a top spot to visit for a couple of days.

Sights

★Real Casino de Murcia HISTORIC BUILDING

(www.casinodemurcia.com; Calle de la Trapería 18; adult/child €5/3; 10.30am-7pm) Murcia's resplendent casino first opened as a gentlemen's club in 1847. Painstakingly restored to its original glory, the building is a fabulous combination of historical design and opulence, providing an evocative glimpse of bygone aristocratic grandeur. Beyond the decorative facade are a dazzling Moorish-style patio; a classic English-style library with 20,000 books; a magnificent ballroom with glittering chandeliers; and a compelling *tocador* (ladies' powder room) with a ceiling fresco of cherubs, angels and an alarming winged woman in flames.

Catedral de Santa María CATHEDRAL

(968 35 87 49; Plaza del Cardenal Belluga; 7am-1pm & 5-8pm Tue-Sat, 7am-1pm & 6.30-8pm Sun & Mon Sep-Jun, 7am-1pm & 6.30-8pm Mon-Fri, 7am-1pm & 7-9pm Sat & Sun Jul & Aug) FREE Murcia's cathedral was built in 1394 on the site of a mosque. The initial Gothic architecture was given a playful baroque facelift in 1748, with a stunning facade facing on to the plaza. The 15th-century **Capilla de los Vélez** is a highlight; the chapel's flutes and curls resemble icing. The **Museo Catedralicio** (Plaza de la Cruz 1; adult/child €3/2; 10am-5pm Tue-Sat, 10am-1pm Sun) displays religious artefacts, but is most noteworthy for the excavations on display.

Museo Arqueológico MUSEUM

(968 23 46 02; www.museosregiondemurcia.es; Avenida Alfonso X El Sabio 7; 10am-2pm Tue-Fri, 11am-2pm Sat & Sun Jul & Aug, 10am-2pm & 5-8pm Tue-Sat, 11am-2pm Sun Sep-Jun) FREE The Museo Arqueológico has exceptionally well-laid-out and well-documented exhibits spread over two floors, starting with Palaeolithic times and including audiovisual displays. The trendy cafe with pleasant outdoor seating is a popular spot.

Festivals & Events

Semana Santa RELIGIOUS

(Mar/Apr) The city's Easter processions are of the traditional kind and are considered some of Spain's best, due especially to their excellent sculptural ensembles. Several notable baroque artists worked on them, and they are full of life and heart-on-sleeve emotion.

Bando de la Huerta FIESTA

(Mar/Apr) Two days after Easter Sunday, the mood changes from sombre to joyful as the city celebrates this annual spring festival with parades, food stalls, folklore and carafe-fulls of fiesta spirit.

Murcia City

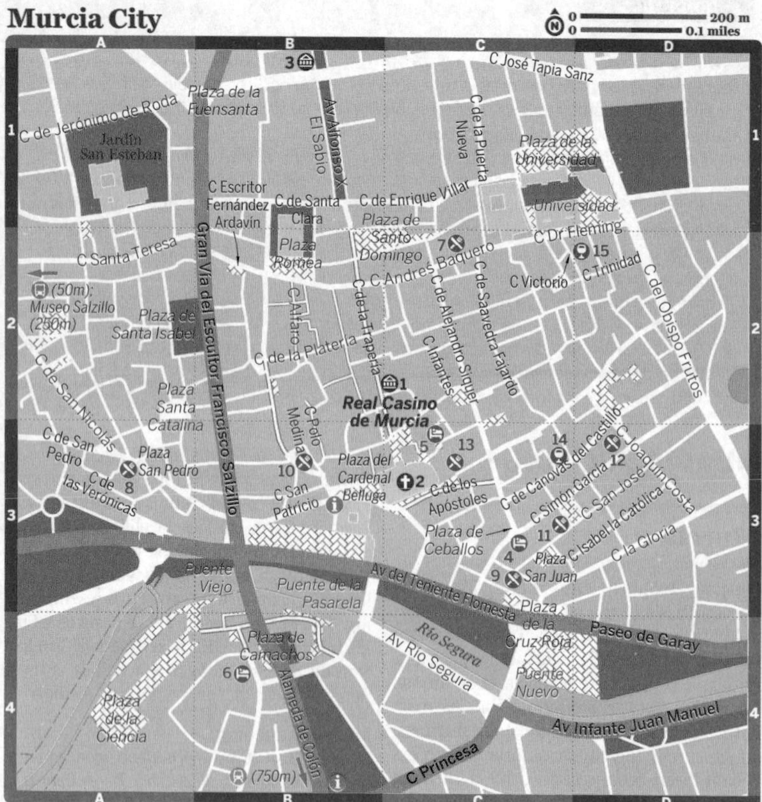

Murcia City

Top Sights
1 Real Casino de Murcia C2

Sights
2 Catedral de Santa María C3
3 Museo Arqueológico B1
Museo Catedralicio .... (see 2)

Sleeping
4 Arco de San Juan C3
5 Hotel Cetina C3
6 Pensión Segura B4

Eating
7 Alborada C2
8 El Pasaje de Zabalburu A3
9 La Pequeña Taberna C3
10 Los Zagales B3
11 Pura Cepa C3
12 Salzillo D3
13 Vacanal C3

Drinking & Nightlife
14 La Ronería y La Gintonería C3
15 Sala Revolver D2

Sleeping

★Pensión Segura HOSTAL €
(☎968 21 12 81; www.pensionsegura.es; Plaza de Camachos 14; r €38-48; ❄📶) Just across a bridge from the heart of town, this makes for a fine budget base. Staff go the extra mile to make you feel welcome, and the rooms are decent and shining clean, though bathrooms are generally tiny.

★Hotel Cetina HOTEL €€
(☎968 10 08 00; www.hotelcetina.com; Calle Radio Murcia 3; r €55-80; ❄📶) A total renovation has left this old city-centre hotel unrecognisable. It now offers unbeatable value for its

spacious, stylish, commodious rooms, which have eye-catching colour schemes, Smeg bar fridges and smart toiletries. Staff are very helpful; the only issue is that it's quite a walk to their associated car park (Paseo del Teniente Flomesta).

Arco de San Juan HOTEL €€
(☎968 21 04 55; www.arcosanjuan.com; Plaza de Ceballos 10; d €60-80; P ❄ @ 📶) In a former 18th-century palace, this hotel hints at its past with a massive 5m-high original door and some hefty repro columns. The rooms are classic and comfortable, with hardwood details and classy fabrics, and the low prices and top location – for both central sights and the best eating zone – are a big plus. Service is professional and welcoming.

Eating

★El Pasaje de Zabalburu TAPAS €
(☎622 622167; www.facebook.com/elpasajedezabalburu; Plaza San Pedro 3; tapas €4-10; ⏱noon-5pm & 8pm-midnight Mon-Sat, noon-5pm Sun; 📶) It's difficult to imagine tastier tapas than the inventive, exquisite creations at this bar on the west side of the centre. Grab a pew at the long bar and enjoy fabulous fare presented with flair. Seafood is especially good here, with stellar grilled calamari, and you have to try the house speciality, *pelochos* – ham croquettes with a spiky noodle coating…yum.

Los Zagales SPANISH €
(☎968 21 55 79; www.facebook.com/barloszagales.murcia; Calle Polo de Medina 4; dishes €3-12; ⏱9.30am-4pm & 7pm-midnight Mon-Sat) Handy to stop by after a cathedral visit, old-style, traditional Los Zagales dishes up superb, inexpensive tapas, *raciones, platos combinados* (mixed platters), homemade desserts (and homemade chips). It's locally popular so you may have to wait for a table. It's worth it.

★La Pequeña Taberna SPANISH €€
(☎968 21 98 40; www.lapequenataberna.com; Plaza San Juan 7; mains €10-21; ⏱1-5pm & 8pm-midnight Mon-Sat, 1-5pm Sun) Look for the cascade of market vegetables outside the door when locating this quality restaurant, which isn't quite as small as it claims. Excellent service furnishes its tables, divided by boxes of tomatoes, melons and the like, with dishes such as fish carpaccio, *huevas de mújol* (preserved fish eggs), *codillo* (pork knuckle), and quality salad and vegetable platters. Delicious, as are the wines.

★Vacanal ARGENTINE, GRILL €€
(☎968 71 58 93; www.vacanal.es; Plaza de los Apóstoles 5; mains €11-28; ⏱1-11pm Mon-Sat, 1-7pm Sun) Smart, spacious and modern, this Argentine restaurant focuses on meat. There are some great mixed-grill specials, but the real highlights are the sizeable steaks, perfectly cooked over coals. They get it all right here, with faultless service, sharp knives, hand-cut chips and numerous other details. There's enough on the menu for a top meal on most budgets. There's a big terrace, too.

Pura Cepa TAPAS €€
(☎968 21 73 97; www.puracepamurcia.com; Plaza Cristo del Rescate 8; dishes €6-15; ⏱1-4.30pm & 8pm-midnight Tue-Sat, 1-4.30pm Sun; 📶) Though the menu is full of typical Spanish ingredients, there's always an innovative kick to the dishes here, which shine out for their quality. Artichokes, octopus and other local, delicious morsels appear in everything from stir-fries to salads to exquisite appetisers. Eat outside on the heated terrace, at high tables in the bar area, or in the smart dining room.

DON'T MISS

TAPAS IN MURCIA

Surrounded by a *huerta* (area of market gardens), Murcia has great fresh produce and is excellent for tapas, with plenty of variety, generous portions and a considerable vegetarian choice for non-carnivorous folk. Many of the city's restaurants are fronted by tapas bars or serve *raciones* (large/full-plate tapas servings), which are great for sharing. Overall, *murciano* tapas are more inventive than the norm and reflect the province's comprehensive agriculture with their use of fresh seasonal ingredients. A local classic is the *marinera*, a scoop of Russian salad served on a loop of breadstick and topped by an anchovy. Delicious.

The network of streets on and northeast of Plaza San Juan are particularly fertile ground, and there's a lively scene around Plaza Santa Catalina and Plaza de las Flores, a short distance west of the old town.

Alborada SPANISH €€

(☎968 23 23 23; www.alboradarestaurante.com; Calle Andrés Baquero 15; mains €15-22; ⏲noon-4.30pm & 8-11.30pm Mon-Sat, noon-4.30pm Sun) Not particularly noteworthy from outside, this high-ceilinged minimalist dining space offers reliably excellent cuisine using carefully selected natural products. Presentation is modern without being avant-garde, and the flavour combinations are all pleasing. During the week you can eat in the bright bar area out front for just €12. Expect regular doses of air freshener.

Salzillo SPANISH €€€

(☎968 22 01 94; www.restaurantesalzillo.com; Calle de Cánovas del Castillo 28; mains €20-24; ⏲1-5.30pm & 9pm-midnight Mon-Sat, 1-5.30pm Sun) Favoured by well-heeled conservative Murcians, this elegant but comfortable spot has a lively bar and truly excellent eating in its split-level restaurant area. Starters run to elaborate creations with local artichokes, and the quality of the meaty mains is sky-high: order *a la brasa* for the flavoursome barbecue aromas.

Drinking & Nightlife

La Ronería y La Gintonería BAR

(☎968 90 00 05; www.la-roneria-y-la-gintoneria.com; Calle de Cánovas del Castillo 17; ⏲3pm-3am Tue-Sat, 3pm-2am Sun & Mon) A quite incredible selection of rums greets you on entering this bar. There are nearly a thousand available, with Caribbean travel videos playing to get you in the mood. Once you've tried them all, stagger up the stairs and start on the gin and tonics. Hundreds of gins, dozens of tonics. And you.

Sala Revolver BAR

(☎868 12 49 17; www.facebook.com/salarevolver.murcia; Calle Victorio 36; ⏲3.30pm-3.30am; 📶) The interior of this bar in the heart of the university-driven nightlife zone is a rock 'n' roll classic with red-vinyl booth seating, curios and photos on the walls and regular live music. It's very atmospheric with real rock-bar cred.

Information

Floridablanca Tourist Kiosk (www.turismodemurcia.es; Jardín Floridablanca; ⏲4.30-8.30pm Mon-Fri, 10am-2pm & 4.30-8.30pm Sat, 10am-2pm Sun) In a park across the river from the old town.

Tourist Office (☎968 35 87 49; www.murciaturistica.es; Plaza del Cardenal Belluga; ⏲10am-2pm & 5-8pm Mon-Sat, 10am-2pm Sun; 📶) On the cathedral square.

Getting There & Away

Murcia-San Javier airport (☎913 21 10 00; www.aena.es; Carretera del Aeropuerto, Santiago de la Ribera) is situated beside the Mar Menor, closer to Cartagena than Murcia. There are budget connections to the UK and other European nations, and direct Iberia flights from Madrid. A taxi between the airport and Murcia costs €65 (40 minutes). The airport is scheduled to be superseded by the **Aeropuerto Internacional de Murcia** (Aeropuerto de Corvera; www.aeropuertointernacionalmurcia.com; Avenida de España, Lo Jurado), 27km south of the city off the A30, by 2019.

At least 10 buses run daily from Murcia's bus station, 1km west of the centre, to both Cartagena (€4.75, 45 minutes to 1¼ hours) and Lorca (€5.75, 1½ hours).

Up to six trains travel daily to/from Madrid (€47, 4¼ hours). *Cercanía* trains run to Alicante (€5.75, 1¼ hours) and Lorca (€5.75, 50 minutes).

Getting Around

Several bus lines running a circular route pass the bus station and can take you into the centre. Number 14 will get you there quickest. From the train station, hop aboard bus C5.

Murcia has a tram line, but it's not of much use for visitors, mainly serving to bring people into town from the extensive northern suburbs.

Cartagena

POP 214,800

Cartagena's fabulous natural harbour has been used for thousands of years. Stand on the battlements of the castle that overlook this city and you can literally see layer upon layer of history spread below you: the wharf where Phoenician traders docked their ships; the street where Roman legionaries marched; the plaza that once housed a mosque where Islamic Spain prayed to Allah; the hills over which came the armies of the Christian Reconquista; the factories of the industrial age; the Modernista buildings; and the contemporary warships of what is still an important naval base.

As archaeologists continue to reveal a long-buried – and fascinating – Roman and Carthaginian heritage, the city is finally starting to get the recognition it deserves as one of Spain's most historically fascinating places. Its extensive network of pedestrian streets and lovely waterfront make it eminently strollable.

History

In 223 BC, the Carthaginian general Hasdrubal the Fair marched his invading army into what had been the Iberian settlement of Mastia, refounding it as Qart Hadasht. The town prospered as Carthago Nova during Roman occupation and, under Muslim rule, became the independent emirate of Cartajana, finally reconquered by the Christians in 1242. Though badly bombed in the civil war – it was the principal Republican naval harbour – industry and the population flourished during the 1950s and '60s.

Sights

★Museo Nacional de Arqueología Subacuática — MUSEUM

(ARQUA; 968 12 11 66; http://museoarqua.mcu.es; Paseo de Alfonso XII 22; adult/child €3/free, Sat afternoon & Sun free; 10am-8pm or 9pm Tue-Sat, 10am-3pm Sun) This excellent, attractive space delves into the depths of the fascinating world of underwater archaeology. It starts off by explaining the work of those delvers in the deep and then sails on into the maritime history and culture of the Mediterranean. There's lots of old pots, flashy lights, buttons to press, films to watch and a replica Phoenician trading ship to marvel over.

Museo del Teatro Romano — MUSEUM, RUIN

(www.teatroromanocartagena.org; Plaza del Ayuntamiento 9; adult/child €6/5; 10am-6pm Tue-Sat, 10am-2pm Sun Oct-Apr, 10am-8pm Tue-Sat, 10am-2pm Sun May-Sep) This impressive complex was designed by top Spanish architect Rafael Moneo. The tour transports visitors from the initial museum on Plaza del Ayuntamiento, via escalators and an underground passage beneath the ruined cathedral, to the recently restored Roman theatre dating from the 1st century BC. The layout of the museum is minimalist, taking you back through Cartagena's fascinating layers of urban history with a careful selection of statuary, pottery and other artefacts.

Barrio del Foro Romano — RUINS

(www.cartagenapuertodeculturas.com; Calle Honda; adult/child €5/4; 10am-5.30pm Tue-Sun Nov-Mar, 10am-7pm Tue-Sun Apr-Jun & mid-Sep–Oct, 10am-8pm daily Jul–mid-Sep) Set alongside the Molinete hill are the evocative remains of a whole town block and street linking the port with the forum, dating from the 1st century BC and including an arcade and thermal baths. One of the houses preserves a courtyard and important fragments of wall paintings.

Casa de la Fortuna — RUINS

(Plaza Risueño; adult/child €2.50/2; 10.30am-3.30pm Tue-Sun, Sat & Sun only Dec-Mar) The Casa de la Fortuna consists of the fascinating remains of an aristocratic Roman villa dating back to the 1st century BC, complete with some well-preserved murals and mosaics, and part of an excavated road. Access it down some steps on the plaza.

Museo Refugio de la Guerra Civil — MUSEUM

(www.cartagenapuertodeculturas.com; Calle de Gisbert; adult/child €3.50/2.50; 10am-7pm Tue-Sun Apr-Jun & mid-Sep–Oct, 10-8pm daily Jul–mid-Sep, 10am-5.30pm Tue-Sun Nov-Mar) Cartagena, as base of the Republican fleet and with an important arms industry, was the target of heavy bombing during the Spanish Civil War. This atmospheric air-raid shelter dug into the castle hill, one of many that protected the city's citizens, brings back those days with personal testimonies, posters, good Spanish-English information and a Charlie Chaplin clip.

Castillo de la Concepción — CASTLE

(www.cartagenapuertodeculturas.com; adult/child €3.75/2.75; 10am-5.30pm Tue-Sun Nov-Mar, 10am-7pm Tue-Sun Apr-Jun & mid-Sep–Oct, 10am-8pm daily Jul–mid-Sep) For a sweeping panoramic view, stride up to Castillo de la Concepción, or hop on the **lift** (Calle de Gisbert; adult/child €2/1, with Castillo de la Concepción €4.25/3.75). Within the castle's gardens, decorated by strutting peacocks, the **Centro de Interpretación de la Historia de Cartagena** offers a potted history of Cartagena through the centuries via audio screens and a 10-minute film (in English and Spanish).

Muralla Púnica — RUINS

(www.cartagenapuertodeculturas.com; Calle San Diego 25; adult/child €3.50/2.50; 10am-5.30pm Tue-Sun Nov-Mar, 10am-7pm Tue-Sun Apr-Jun & mid-Sep–Oct, 10am-8pm daily Jul–mid-Sep) The Muralla Púnica, built around a section of the old Punic wall, concentrates on the town's Carthaginian and Roman legacy. It also contains the tumbledown walls of a 16th-century hermitage complete with tombs filled with human bones.

Museo Arqueológico Municipal MUSEUM
(968 12 89 68; www.museoarqueologicocartagena.es; Calle Ramón y Cajal 45; 10am-2pm & 5-8pm Tue-Fri, 11am-2pm Sat & Sun) FREE Built above a late-Roman cemetery with a rich display of Carthaginian, Roman, Visigoth and Islamic artefacts. To get here, head northwest of the city centre, via Calle La Palma.

Festivals & Events

Semana Santa RELIGIOUS
(http://semanasanta.cartagena.es; Mar/Apr) During Easter week, Cartagena's haunting, elaborate processions are quite a sight.

Carthagineses y Romanos FIESTA
(Cartagineses y Romanos; www.cartaginesesyromanos.es; Sep) For 10 days during September, locals play war games in a colourful fiesta that re-enacts the battles between rival Carthaginian and Roman occupiers during the Second Punic War.

Sleeping

★**Pensión Balcones Azules** HOSTAL €
(968 50 00 42; www.pensionbalconesazules.com; Calle Balcones Azules 12; s €36-42, d economy/superior €50/60;) On a quiet central street overlooking the ruins of the forum, this modern option offers plenty of quality for the price. The superior rooms have bigger bathrooms, but there are some spacious 'economy' ones, too. It's all very comfortable, and the dedicated staff keep this, which is effectively a small hotel, absolutely spotless. Closes for a month around February.

> **DISCOUNTED ENTRY**
>
> Visiting all the different archaeological sites and museums in Cartagena can work out to be quite expensive. Fortunately help is at hand in the form of a variety of passes that provide cheaper admission (entry to four/five/six museums adult €12/15/18, child €9/12/14). A pass to all of them costs €22. They are valid for 15 days. Passes are available from the tourist office or the sites themselves. The Museo del Teatro Romano (p839) counts as two museum entries. Other options include a tourist boat and/or bus trip.

NH Cartagena HOTEL €€
(968 12 09 08; www.nh-hotels.com; Calle Real 2; r €85-125;) The location of this business hotel can't be bettered, steps from the waterfront and the Roman theatre and just behind the town hall. Rooms are spacious, and superior chambers come with balcony or a sizeable terrace. As usual with this chain, free wi-fi is frustratingly slow and to speed it up costs a fortune. The overpriced breakfast is best avoided.

Eating

La Fuente TAPAS €
(868 04 73 22; www.bodegalafuente.com; Calle Jara 17; 1 drink & tapas €1.90; 10am-5pm & 7.30pm-midnight Mon-Fri, 11am-5pm & 7.30pm-midnight Sat, 11am-5pm Sun;) Bright and busy, this place, which lives up to its name by indeed featuring a fountain, makes a top stop for a quick drink and a tapas. The speciality is anchovies, long and tasty, from the Bay of Biscay. A knot of similar bars here also offer a cheap drink-and-snack deal. The street number of 17 is also misleadingly numbered as 27.

El Barrio de San Roque SPANISH €€
(968 50 06 00; www.elbarriodesanroque.es; Calle Jabonerías 30; mains €12-20; 1.30-4pm & 8.30-11pm Mon-Sat) Done Roman and it's time for a decent central meal? Much of the pedestrian area is taken up with fairly mediocre restaurants pulling in cruise-ship visitors with frozen paellas, but this discreet, elegant place offers real quality. The €20 lunchtime *menú* is excellent, and the exposed brick, sizeable tables and polite service make this a pleasant haven.

★**Magoga** SPANISH €€€
(968 50 96 78; www.restaurantemagoga.com; Plaza Doctor Vicente García Marcos; mains €15-26; 1.30-4pm & 8.30-11.30pm Tue-Sat, 1.30-4pm Sun;) Elegant dining areas and an open kitchen characterise this smart white-exteriored local on a nondesript pedestrian boulevard off Calle Carlos III. The gastronomic enthusiasm of the young owners shines through in the food, which is far above most of Cartagena's culinary offerings. Good-value rices and stews take their place alongside superbly prepared and presented fish and meat mains.

La Marquesita SPANISH €€€
(968 50 77 47; www.lamarquesita.net; Plaza Alcolea 6; mains €13-24; 1-4.30pm & 8-11.30pm

Tue-Sat, 1-4.30pm Sun;) On a tucked-away plaza just off the pedestrian main drag, this place is easily spotted by its riot of pot plants. Sit in or out to enjoy quality fish dishes in particular, with other traditional plates on offer. It's a family affair, and genuinely welcoming.

Shopping

Centro para la Artesanía ARTS & CRAFTS
(www.carm.es; Calle Honda 10; 10am-2pm & 5-8.30pm Mon-Fri, 11am-1.30pm Sat) This government-funded shop displays the works of local artisans. There's an excellent range of everything from paintings to honey. It's a great spot to browse.

Information

Most of the Roman sites can furnish you with a city map and information; handy if you arrive outside tourist-office hours.

Ayuntamiento Tourist Office (968 12 89 55; www.cartagenaturismo.es; Plaza del Ayuntamiento 1; 10am-1.30pm & 4-6pm (5-7pm May-Sep) Mon-Sat, 10.30am-1.30pm Sun) Near the waterfront in the heart of town.

Puertas de San José Tourist Office (968 12 89 55; www.cartagenaturismo.es; Plaza Basterreche; 10am-2pm & 4-6pm Mon-Fri, 10am-1.30pm Sat Oct-Apr, 10am-2pm & 5-7pm Mon-Fri, 10am-1.30pm Sat May-Sep) Plenty of excellent information near the bus station. If it's shut, go to the desk in the **Muralla Púnica** (p839) opposite.

Getting There & Away

Buses run six to seven times daily to Alicante (€9, 2¾ hours), and roughly hourly to Murcia (€4.75, 45 minutes to 1¼ hours) from the **bus station** (Avenida Trovero Marín).

For Renfe train destinations, you'll mostly have to change in Murcia (from €5.45, 50 minutes, eight to 11 daily), though there are some through trains. If getting off in Murcia, take the local train as the slightly faster Altaria/Talgo trains can cost substantially more.

A taxi to or from Murcia-San Javier Airport costs approximately €50 (30 minutes).

Costa Cálida

Stretching westwards to the border with Andalucía, the Costa Cálida (Warm Coast) is aptly named. It offers a hot, dry climate with more than 300 days of annual sunshine. While the sprawling resort of La Manga is unappealing, quieter seaside towns offer a more engrossing experience.

Águilas

POP 34,700

Nearing the border with Andalucía, and 30km further along the coast from Mazarrón, you'll reach low-key Águilas, with a slowish vibe and pleasant centre. The waterfront in town is beautiful, and still shelters a small fishing fleet; back from here is lovely Plaza de España, with dignified trees. Town beaches are divided from each other by a low headland topped by an 18th-century **fortress**. The really charming beaches, though, are the **Cuatro Calas** a few kilometres south of town.

Festivals & Events

★**Carnaval de Águilas** CARNIVAL
(www.carnavaldeaguilas.org; Feb/Mar) One of Spain's most interesting Carnavals, featuring four characters who represent various aspects of humanity, virtues and vices. There are parades from the Friday through to Shrove Tuesday, as well as the following weekend.

Sleeping

Pensión Rodríguez PENSION €
(968 41 06 15; http://aguilaspensionrodriguez.blogspot.com; Calle Ramón y Cajal 7; s with shared/private bathroom €23/27, d with shared/private bathroom €37/42;) In a relatively central part of town and a short stroll to the beach, Pensión Rodríguez offers spotless rooms for a low price. Matilde the boss is very helpful and kind. A good deal.

★**Hotel Mayari** HOTEL €€
(964 41 97 48; www.hotel-mayari.com; Calle Río de Janeiro 14, Calabardina; s/d incl breakfast €65/98; Mar-Nov; P) In the seaside settlement of Calabardina, 7km from Águilas, this airy villa offers exceptional hospitality among dry, handsome hillscapes. Rooms are simple and comfortable and all different, with cool, fresh decor. Some have sea views, and there are brilliant home-cooked dinners available by request, as well as helpful hill-walking advice and bikes to explore the area.

Hotel Puerto Juan Montiel HOTEL €€
(968 49 34 93; www.hotelpuertojuanmontiel.com; Avenida del Puerto Deportivo 1; r incl breakfast €90-176; P@) This place occupies an ugly building by the marina, although it's substantially better than the hotels in the centre. The beach is paces away, and rooms

are of very good size, airy and functionally modern. Facilities are good, with a summer pool, on-site restaurant and lots of lounging space. Sea views cost slightly more. Prices drop substantially outside of high summer.

Eating

El Pimiento SPANISH €

(Calle Joaquín Tendero 1; tapas €1-12; ⊙6.30pm-1am) Cheerfully super-Spanish decor of horse paraphernalia, tiles and hanging hams makes this an upbeat place from the get-go; the colourful tables inside and sprawling down the steps outdoors are always packed, adding plenty of atmosphere. The tapas are simple – think big, generous chunks of meat, bread, potatoes, tomato – very tasty and extremely well priced. An enjoyable spot.

★El Poli SEAFOOD €€

(☎968 41 34 21; www.facebook.com/elpolirest; Calle Floridablanca 23; dishes €5-15; ⊙1.30-4pm & 8.30-11pm Wed-Mon) With a traditional varnished wood interior, albeit with a shipboard feel, this looks like another *barrio* cafe until you realise that the menu is all locally caught fish and shellfish. Don't spend too much time browsing it though, as only what was available in the fish market is offered. It's cooked simply and is delicious, served by brilliant staff at generous prices.

Information

Tourist Office (☎968 49 32 85; www.aguilas.es; Plaza Antonio Cortijos; ⊙10am-2pm & 5-7pm Mon-Sat, 10am-2pm Sun mid-Sep–Apr, to 8pm May & Jun, 9.30am-2pm & 5-9pm Mon-Fri, 10am-2pm & 5-9pm Sat, 10am-2pm Sun Jul–mid-Sep) Near the water in the heart of town.

Getting There & Away

Buses go to Lorca (€3, 30 minutes, three to seven daily) and Murcia (€8.90, 1½ hours, two to four daily) as well as Cartagena (€7.20, 1¾ hours, two to three daily) and Almería (€9.60, 2¼ hours, two to three daily).

Cercanía trains on the C2 line run from Murcia (€7.95, 1¾ hours) via Lorca three times daily.

Lorca

POP 91,700

The market town of Lorca has long been known for its pretty old town crowned by a 13th-century castle and for hosting Spain's most flamboyant Semana Santa (Holy Week) celebrations. In 2011 an earthquake struck here, leaving nine people dead, and many injured and homeless. It caused significant material damage, with the old town affected particularly badly. Lorca has bounced back now and there's a tangible air of optimism again in the town, which makes it a great place to visit.

Sights

★Plaza de España SQUARE

The highlight of the old town is a group of baroque buildings around Plaza de España, including the **Pósito**, a 16th-century former granary; the 18th-century **Casa del Corregidor**; and the **town hall**. Lording over the square is the golden limestone Colegiata de San Patricio, finally reopened in 2017 after substantial damage in the 2011 earthquake.

★Colegiata de San Patricio CHURCH

(☎968 46 99 66; Plaza de España; adult/child €2/free; ⊙11am-1pm & 6-7pm Mon-Sat) This stately and beautiful gem of a church presides in golden-stone majesty over Lorca's central square. The sober and handsome triple-tiered baroque facade conceals a triple-naved interior Renaissance interior with a fine altarpiece and other paintings. It was heavily damaged in the 2011 earthquake and only reopened recently. Work is still underway; as well as reconstruction, it's been a process of investigation, because the disaster's silver lining was the discovery of previously unknown paintings and crypts. Buy tickets in the adjacent tourist office (p846).

Museo de Bordados del Paso Azul MUSEUM

(MASS; ☎968 47 20 77; www.pasoazul.com; Calle Cuesta de San Francisco; adult/child €3/free; ⊙10.30am-2pm & 5-8pm Mon-Sat, 10.30am-2pm Sun) Attached to the San Francisco monastery, this is the modern museum of the Azul (Blue) Holy Week brotherhood, and gives an excellent idea of what Semana Santa (p843) means to the locals. As well as stirring videos and background information, the marvellous costumes are on display. If you go on a weekday, you may find people at work on them in the embroidery workshop upstairs – a great chance to see the work up close.

Some cloaks are up to 5m in length and all are elaborately hand-embroidered in silk, depicting colourful religious and historical scenes.

One of the museum sections takes you into the galleries of the church, an interesting outlook. To visit the church from ground level, it's an extra €1.

Museo de Bordados del Paso Blanco MUSEUM
(muBBla; ☎968 46 18 13; www.mubbla.org; Calle Santo Domingo 8; adult/child €2.50/free; ⏲10.30am-2pm & 4.30-7pm or 5-8pm Mon-Sat, 10.30am-2pm Sun) Attached to the church of Santo Domingo, this is the museum of the Blanco (White) Semana Santa brotherhood. Here you can see a collection of the beautifully elaborate robes worn by them during the passionately supported Holy Week processions. They are well displayed and extraordinary, depicting scenes from the Bible and antiquity. You might be advised to put the sunglasses on for the shiny baroque gold of the adjacent chapel of the Virgen del Rosario.

Castillo Fortaleza del Sol CASTLE
(Castillo de Lorca; ☎968 47 90 03; www.lorcatallerdeltiempo.com; Carretera de la Parroquia; adult/child €5/4; ⏲10.30am-dusk;) The town's castle, high over town, is an impressive place, a huge medieval complex characterised by two towers. The basic entry includes an audio guide and access to the **Torre del Espolón**, reconstructed after the earthquake, various cisterns and ramparts as well as exhibition spaces.The handsome **Torre Alfonsina** and the reconstructed synagogue plus **ruins of the Jewish quarter** can be visited twice or more daily by recommended guided tour (€4 each). A combined €10 entrance fee includes both tours.

Festivals & Events

★Semana Santa RELIGIOUS
(http://semanasantalorca.com; ⏲Mar/Apr) If you're from Lorca, you're probably passionately Blanco (White) or Azul (Blue), the colours of the two major brotherhoods that have competed since 1855 to see who can stage the most lavish Semana Santa display. Lorca's Easter parades are very distinctive; while still deeply reverential, they're full of colour and vitality, mixing figures from antiquity and Old Testament tales with the Passion story.

Each brotherhood has a statue of the Virgin (one draped in a blue mantle, the other in white, naturally), a banner and a spectacular museum (Museo de Bordados del Paso Azul and Museo de Bordados del Paso Blanco). The result of this intense and mostly genial year-round rivalry is just about the most dramatic Semana Santa you'll see anywhere in Spain. Processions feature horses, theatrical set pieces, colourful characters – gods, emperors and heroes – stirring music and plenty of emotion.

Sleeping & Eating

★Parador de Lorca HERITAGE HOTEL €€
(☎968 40 60 47; www.parador.es; Castillo de Lorca; r €90-170;) Memorably situated in the castle complex way above town is this modern, spick-and-span *parador* (luxurious state-run hotel, often set in a historic building). Rooms are tip-top, there's an indoor pool and spa and the views are just stunning. Various archaeological fragments are integrated into the hotel, including a reconstructed synagogue next to the car park.

Rates are normally around the €90 mark but tend to be much higher on Saturdays.

Jardines de Lorca HOTEL €€
(☎968 47 05 99; www.hoteljardinesdelorca.com; Alameda de Rafael Méndez; r €65-80;) A short walk from the centre, and handy for bus and train stations, this large complex has something of a resort feel. Its spacious rooms are comfortable and marble-tiled, though there's some echoing noise from passageways. They come with a balcony. Facilities are excellent, including a spa, summer-only pool, gym and tennis courts. Prices are variable but very reasonable.

Albedrío TAPAS €
(☎660 409702; http://albedrio.es; Plaza Calderón de la Barca 2; tapas €1-7; ⏲11am-12.30am, kitchen closed 4.30-8pm;) Below the level of the square, this bright and buzzy spot is a very welcome addition to the Lorca eating scene. A mural of Bogart and Hepburn overlooks chunky wooden tables where you can order from a wide range of locally inflected tapas. They are extraordinarily good value, with homemade croquettes, spicy *morcilla* (blood pudding) and fishy snacks among the delights.

Casa Roberto SPANISH €€
(☎968 44 25 58; Calle Corredera 21; mains €12-18; ⏲noon-4pm & 8-11pm) In an attractive pink house on the principal pedestrian street, this likeable family-run restaurant is a sound bet. There's a series of rooms converted into intimate dining areas, as well as a pleasant courtyard. Dishes cover a good range of traditional and contemporary Spanish ingredients and prices are fair.

THE BALEARICS

The Balearic Islands (Illes Balears in Catalan) adorn the glittering Mediterranean waters off Spain's eastern coastline. Beach tourism destinations par excellence, each of the islands has a distinct identity and each has managed to retain much of its individual character and beauty. All boast beaches second to none in the Med, but each offers reasons for exploring inland, too.

Getting There & Around

Charter and regular flights head to Mallorca and Ibiza from all over Europe. Ferries are the other main way of getting to and between the islands. Barcelona, Dénia, Gandia and Valencia are the mainland ports, with boats operated by Baleària (p828) and Trasmediterránea (p817).

Mallorca

The ever-popular star of the Mediterranean, Mallorca has a sunny personality thanks to its ravishing beaches, azure views, remote mountains and soulful hill towns.

PALMA DE MALLORCA

Rising in honey-coloured stone from the waters of the Badia de Palma, this stunning city dates back to the 13th-century Christian reconquest of the island, and to the Moors, Romans and Talayotic people before that. A diadem of historical sites, Palma also offers a huge array of galleries, restaurants,and bars – it's without doubt Mallorca's greatest treasure.

SIGHTS

Catedral de Mallorca (La Seu; www.catedraldemallorca.org; Carrer del Palau Reial 9; adult/child €7/free; ⏲10am-6.15pm Mon-Fri Jun-Sep, to 5.15pm Apr, May & Oct, to 3.15pm Nov-Mar, 10am-2.15pm Sat year-round) Palma's vast cathedral ('La Seu' in Catalan) is the city's major architectural landmark. Aside from its sheer scale and undoubted beauty, its stunning interior features, designed by Antoni Gaudí and renowned contemporary artist Miquel Barceló, make this unlike any cathedral elsewhere in the world. The awesome structure is predominantly Gothic, apart from the main facade, which is startling, quite beautiful and completely mongrel.

Palau de l'Almudaina (https://entradas.patrimonionacional.es; Carrer del Palau Reial; adult/child €7/4, audio guide €3, guided tour €4; ⏲10am-8pm Tue-Sun year-round) Originally an Islamic fort, this mighty construction opposite the cathedral was converted into a residence for the Mallorcan monarchs at the end of the 13th century. The King of Spain resides here still, at least symbolically. The royal family is rarely in residence, except for the occasional ceremony, as they prefer to spend summer in the Palau Marivent (in Cala Major). At other times you can wander through a series of cavernous stone-walled rooms that have been lavishly decorated.

Palau March (☎971 71 11 22; www.fundacionbmarch.es; Carrer del Palau Reial 18; adult/child €4.50/free; ⏲10am-6.30pm Mon-Fri Apr-Oct, to 5pm Nov-Mar, to 2pm Sat year-round) This palatial house was one of several residences of the phenomenally wealthy March family. Sculptures by 20th-century greats including Henry Moore, Auguste Rodin and Barbara Hepworth grace the terrace. Within lie more treasures from Salvador Dalí and Josep Maria Sert. Don't miss the meticulously crafted figures of an 18th-century Neapolitan *belén* (nativity scene).

INFORMATION

Consell de Mallorca Tourist Office (☎971 17 39 90; www.infomallorca.net; Plaça de la Reina 2; ⏲8.30am-6pm Mon-Fri, to 3pm Sat; 📶) Covers the whole island.

AROUND MALLORCA

Mallorca's northwestern coast is a world away from the high-rises on the other side of the island. Dominated by the Serra de Tramuntana, it's a beautiful region of olive groves, pine forests and small villages. There are a couple of highlights for drivers: the hair-raising road down to the small port of Sa Calobra, and the trip to the island's northern tip, Cap Formentor.

Menorca

Renowned for its pristine beaches and archaeological sites, tranquil Menorca was declared a Biosphere Reserve by Unesco in 1993. **Maó** absorbs most of the tourist traffic. North of here, a drive across a lunar landscape leads to the lighthouse at Cap de Faváritx. South of the cape stretch sandy bays and beaches, including Cala Presili and Platja d'en Tortuga, reachable on foot. **Ciutadella**, with its smaller harbour and historic buildings, has a more distinctly Spanish feel. A narrow road leads south from here to some lovely beaches, for which you'll need your own transport. In the centre of the island, 357m-high **Monte Toro** has great views. On the northern coast, the picturesque town of **Fornells** is on a large bay popular with windsurfers.

Ibiza

Ibiza (Eivissa in Catalan) is an island of extremes. Its party reputation is justified, with some of the world's greatest clubs attracting hedonists from the world over. The interior and northeast of the island, however, are another world. Peaceful drives, green hills, laid-back beaches and coves, and some wonderful inland accommodation and eateries are light years from the pumping beats of the west.

IBIZA TOWN

The heart and soul of the island, this vivacious, stylish capital has a magical, fortified World Heritage–listed old quarter topped by a castle and cathedral and set against a spectacular natural harbour. It's also a shopaholic's dream and a world-famous party destination.

SIGHTS

Dalt Vila Its formidable 16th-century bastions visible from across southern Ibiza, Dalt Vila is a fortified hilltop first settled by the Phoenicans and subsequently occupied by a roster of others. Tranquil and atmospheric, many of its cobbled lanes are accessible only on foot. It's mostly residential, but contains medieval mansions and several key cultural sights. Enter via the Portal de Ses Taules and wind your way uphill: all lanes lead to the summit.

Ramparts Encircling **Dalt Vila**, Ibiza's colossal protective walls reach more than 25m in height and include seven bastions. Floodlit at night, these fortifications were constructed to protect Ibizans from north-African raiders and the Turkish navy. In under an hour, you can walk the entire 2km perimeter, enjoying great views over the port and south to Formentera.

DRINKING & NIGHTLIFE

Sa Penya is the centre of Ibiza Town's nightlife. Dozens of bars keep the port area buzzing from sunset until the early hours. Later on, hit the world-famous nightclubs such as **Pacha** (www.pachaibiza.com; Avinguda 8 d'Agost; admission from €20; ⌚midnight-6.30am May-Sep). Just south of town, Platja d'en Bossa heaves with bars and clubs.

INFORMATION

Oficina d'Informació Turística (☎971 30 19 00; http://ibiza.travel; Avinguda de Santa Eulària; ⌚9am-8pm Mon-Sat, to 3pm Sun, reduced hours mid-Oct–Apr) Island-wide office next to the Formentera ferry terminal.

AROUND IBIZA

Ibiza has numerous unspoiled and relatively undeveloped beaches. Cala de Boix, on the northeastern coast, is the only black-sand beach on the island, while further north are the lovely strands of S'Aigua Blanca. On the north coast near Portinatx, Cala Xarraca is in a picturesque, secluded bay, and near Port de Sant Miquel is the attractive Cala Benirrás. In the southwest, Cala d'Hort has a spectacular setting overlooking two rugged rock islets.

The best thing about rowdy Sant Antoni, the island's second-biggest town, is heading to the small rock-and-sand strip on the north shore to join hundreds of others for sunset drinks at a string of chilled bars. The best known remains **Café del Mar** (☎971 80 37 58; www.cafedelmaribiza.es; Carrer de Lepant 27; ⌚5pm-midnight May–mid-Oct), a little further north.

Formentera

Off the south coast of Ibiza, a mere half-hour away by fast ferry, the island of Formentera is a beautifully pure, get-away-from-it-all escape designed for lazy days spent lounging on some of Europe's most exquisite beaches. Frost-white sand is smoothed by water in shades of azure, turquoise and lapis lazuli. Tourism here is tightly tied to environmental ethics, with hotel numbers restricted, construction controlled and most visitors exploring on two wheels. There are few sights and little nightlife, making Formentera perfect for revelling in blissful barefoot living.

Shopping

★Centro para la Artesanía ARTS & CRAFTS
(968 46 39 12; www.carm.es; Calle Lope Gisbert; 10am-2pm & 5-8.30pm Mon-Fri, 11am-1.30pm Sat) It's quite a surprise to go through the door here, and gradually descend into an enormous concrete structure replete with all kinds of handicrafts, from colourful rugs to wine and marvellous ceramics. A government initiative, it's a great place to browse and buy. No street number; it's opposite number 7 and next to the Palacio de Guevara.

Information

Centro de Visitantes (968 44 19 14; www.lorcatallerdeltiempo.es; Puerto de San Ginés; 10am-2pm) On the edge of the old town, this visitor centre has tourist information, sells visitor tickets and is a handy place to park.

Tourist Office (968 44 19 14; www.lorcaturismo.es; Plaza de España; 10am-2pm & 4-6.30pm Mon-Fri, 10am-2pm & 4-6pm Sat, 10am-2pm Sun, to 7pm or 7.30pm in summer) On the Plaza de España in the heart of the old town.

Getting There & Away

Hourly buses (€5.95, 1½ hours) and C2-line *cercanía* trains (€5.75, 50 minutes) run between Lorca and Murcia. Various bus services run into Almería province and beyond.

Parque Regional de Sierra Espuña

The Sierra Espuña, a 40-minute drive southwest of Murcia towards Lorca, is an island of pine forest rising high into the sky above an ocean of heat and dust. Sitting just north of the N340, the natural park that protects this fragile and beautiful environment has more than 250 sq km of unspoilt highlands covered with trails and is popular with walkers, climbers, cyclists and mountain bikers. Limestone formations tower above the sprawling forests. In the northwest of the park are many *pozos de la nieve* (ice houses) where, until the arrival of industrial refrigeration, snow was compressed into ice, then taken to nearby towns in summer.

Access to the park is best via **Alhama de Murcia**. The informative **Centro de Visitantes Ricardo Codorniu** (968 43 14 30; www.sierraespuna.com; 9am-2pm & 3-5.30pm Tue-Sat, 9am-3.30pm Sun Oct-May, 9am-3.30pm Sun & Tue-Thu, 9am-3.30pm & 5-8pm Fri & Sat Jun-Sep) is located in the heart of the park. A few walking trails leave from this visitor centre, and it can provide good maps for these and several other picturesque hikes.

The village of **El Berro** makes for a great base for the sierra. It has trailheads for a couple of good circular walks, a couple of restaurants and the friendly **Camping Sierra Espuña** (968 66 80 38; www.campingsierraespuna.com; Calle de Juan Bautista; site per person €5, tent €5, car €5, 2-/6-person bungalows €55-106;). For something altogether more luxurious, you can't beat the **Bajo el Cejo** (968 66 80 32; www.bajoelcejo.com; Calle El Paso; r incl breakfast €116-143;).

Another base for the sierra, and for northern Murcia in general, is the town of **Mula**. The town is a web of old streets squashed up against a pinnacle of dry rock topped by the very battered remnants of a **castle**. From a distance, the town actually looks like it's dropped straight out of a Middle Eastern fairy tale. Excellent accommodation is available at **El Molino de Felipe** (968 66 20 13; www.hotelruralmula.com; Carretera Ribera de los Molinos 321, Mula; d €48, apt for 2/4/6 €70/106/142;), about 4km from town.

Getting There & Away

The park is best accessed by car. The town of Alhama de Murcia is easily reached by bus from Murcia (€3.50, 45 minutes), but it's 19km from here to the visitor centre in the heart of the park. Mula is also accessible by bus from Murcia (€3.30, 45 minutes).

Understand Spain

Spain Today

Profound upheavals have shattered a status quo in Spanish public affairs that had endured since the country's return to democracy in the 1970s. A two-party domination of national politics has been split asunder by new parties born of popular anger at corruption and economic crisis; the push for independence in Catalonia has challenged assumptions of Spanish unity; and corruption finally came home to roost at the highest levels in 2018 with the unseating of the conservative Partido Popular (PP; Popular Party) government.

Best on Film

Jamón, jamón (1992) Dark comedy that brought Penélope Cruz and Javier Bardem to prominence.

Todo sobre mi madre (1999) Classic Pedro Almodóvar romp through sex and death.

Ocho apellidos vascos (Spanish Affair; 2014) Hugely successful comedy that takes a sideways glance at Spain and the Basque Country.

Mar adentro (The Sea Inside; 2004) Alejandro Amenabar's moving study of a Galician quadriplegic (Javier Bardem).

Best in Print

Three Plays (Federico García Lorca) Spain's greatest playwright's three great tragedies, about passion and trapped lives, written in the 1930s.

For Whom the Bell Tolls (Ernest Hemingway; 1941) Terse tale of the civil war, full of emotions and Spanish atmosphere.

A Late Dinner: Discovering the Food of Spain (Paul Richardson; 2007) Erudite journey through Spain's fascinating culinary culture.

Don Quijote (Miguel de Cervantes; 1605) Spain's best-known novel is a laugh-inducing journey with a lovably deluded knight.

Crisis in Catalonia

Many Catalans have long felt that the centralising tendencies of the Spanish state did not adequately respect their distinct culture, history and traditions. The push for Catalan independence that developed after economic crisis struck Spain in 2008 grew into a direct confrontation with the central government in Madrid, plunging modern democratic Spain into its biggest-ever crisis.

Catalonia is one of Spain's most prosperous regions, and resentment mounted about the size of its tax contribution to the national exchequer – by most estimates, €8 to €10 billion more per year than it gets back in services. In 2015 an alliance of pro-independence parties, led by Carles Puigdemont, came to power in Catalonia promising to hold a binding referendum on independence. Despite uncompromising opposition from Madrid, and a judgement by Spain's constitutional court that the referendum would be illegal, it went ahead on 1 October 2017. The Madrid government sent in national police to try to prevent voting at some polling stations, resulting in some violent scenes and injuries. According to the Catalan government, 43% of the electorate voted in the referendum, and 90% of those voted for independence.

In response to the referendum, a wave of support for Spanish national unity swept through much of Spain. Huge, peaceful demonstrations, both for and against independence, took place in Barcelona. On 27 October the Catalan parliament declared Catalonia independent, but the national parliament suspended Catalonia's regional autonomy and the Catalan parliament with it. A few days later Spain's attorney-general called for serious charges of rebellion and sedition against Puigdemont and 13 of his (now ex-) ministers; Puigdemont and four of them had slipped off to self-imposed exile in Brussels.

New Catalan elections in December 2017 saw separatist parties win 70 of the 135 seats in the regional parliament, giving them the opportunity to form Catalonia's new government. But by late March 2018, regional government had still not been restored, since all candidates who had been proposed for its presidency were either abroad (as in the case of Puigdemont) or in pre-trial detention. On 23 March Spain's supreme court dealt the separatists a new blow by ruling that 25 of them be tried for crimes including rebellion and embezzlement of public funds over their involvement in the referendum, with some facing jail terms of up to 30 years if convicted. Two days later Puigdemont was arrested in Germany, whose courts were due to rule within 60 days on Spain's request for his extradition.

While Spain's major political parties had made some noises about possible constitutional reform, the Madrid government was in no mood for any meaningful concessions to the independence movement, perhaps betting that support for it would wane over the coming months and years.

A New Politics

At a national level, Spain's political spoils had for decades been divided between the left-of-centre PSOE and the conservative PP. In 2015 and 2016, a groundswell of popular anger from the years of economic crisis changed all that, with two new anti-corruption parties – the radical, anti-austerity Podemos ('We Can') and the centrist, pro-business Ciudadanos (Citizens) – winning scores of seats in general elections. The PP managed to form a minority government – but this came to a dramatic end in June 2018 when the PP was unseated by a parliamentary vote of no confidence, following a high court judgement in one of numerous long-running corruption cases that have embroiled Spanish political circles. In the so-called Gürtel case, over events which mostly took place in the early 2000s, more than a dozen former PP members were sentenced for taking bribes for government contracts and other crimes, and the judges referred to the party's involvement with 'institutionalised corruption'.

The new prime minister, Pedro Sánchez of the PSOE, gave early signals of stability, but with his party holding just 84 of the 350 parliamentary seats and a spectrum of varied allies to keep happy, plenty more twists and turns in the political picture were in the offing.

Economy on the Up

By the end of 2017, unemployment in Spain was down to 16% – there were still 3.7 million people out of work, but this was a big improvement on the depths of the economic crisis five years previously, when joblessness reached 27%. Spain was the fastest-growing large economy in Europe, with tourism, car-making and digital startups all booming. There is still a way to go, and critics say too many of the new jobs are temporary and unstable, but despite the political upheavals Spain's economic picture is certainly far rosier than just a few years ago.

AREA: **505,370 SQ KM**

POPULATION: **48.96 MILLION**

GDP PER CAPITA: **US$36,400**

UNEMPLOYMENT: **16.7%**

ANNUAL INFLATION: **2%**

if Spain were 100 people

74 would speak Castilian (Spanish)
17 would speak Catalan
7 would speak Galician
2 would speak Basque

belief systems

(% of population)

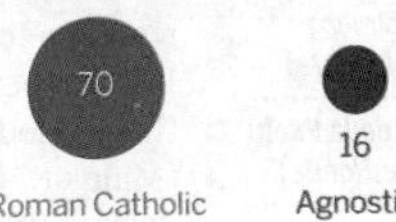

population per sq km

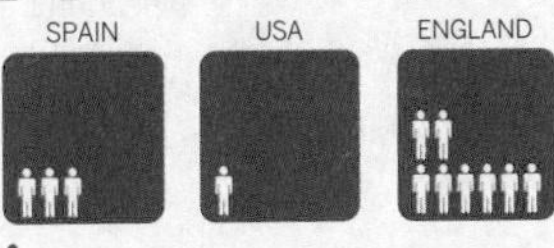

History

Spain's story is one of Europe's grand epics. It embraces the great struggles between Muslims and Christians of the Middle Ages, one of the world's biggest-ever empires, and, in the 20th century, civil war, dictatorship and a stunning return to democracy. As you travel around the country it's delightfully easy to get in touch with Spain's fascinating past through its countless well-preserved monuments and historical sites, and excellent museums.

Spain & the Ancient Civilisations

Spain can make a convincing claim to be the cradle of humanity in Western Europe: in 2007, Western Europe's oldest confirmed remains – 1.2 million years old – of the genus *Homo* were discovered at Atapuerca, near the northern city of Burgos. But it was not until around 3000 years ago that Spain entered history's mainstream.

Top Prehistoric Sites

- *Cueva de Altamira*
- *Atapuerca (near Burgos)*
- *Cueva de Tito Bustillo (Ribadesella)*
- *Dolmens (Antequera)*
- *Cueva de la Pileta (near Ronda)*
- *Siega Verde (near Ciudad Rodrigo)*

Phoenicians, Celts & Greeks

The Phoenicians were the first of the major civilisations of the ancient world to set their sights on Spain. From their base along what is now the southern Lebanese coast, the Phoenicians may have been the world's first rulers of the sea. They were essentially traders rather than conquerors, and it was commerce that first brought them to Spain around 1000 BC. They arrived on Spanish shores bearing perfumes, ivory, jewellery, oil, wine and textiles, which they exchanged for Spanish silver and bronze.

Conquest may not have been the Phoenicians' aim, but as their reach expanded, so too did their need for safe ports around the Mediterranean rim. One of these was Carthage in modern-day Tunisia, founded in 814 BC; in Iberia they established coastal trading colonies at Cádiz (which they called Gadir), Almuñécar (Ex or Sex), Huelva (Onuba) and Málaga (Malaka). Cádiz, that breezy and thoroughly Andalucian city in Spain's deep south, can as a result make a pretty strong claim to be the oldest continuously inhabited settlement in Europe.

After the Phoenicians, Greek traders began to arrive further north along the coast. In the 7th century BC, the Greeks founded a series of

TIMELINE

c 39,000–10,000 BC

Palaeolithic (Old Stone Age) hunters paint beautiful, sophisticated animal images in caves at Altamira and other sites along Spain's northern coastal strip.

218 BC

Roman legions arrive in Spain during the Second Punic War against Carthage, initiating the 600-year Roman occupation of the Iberian Peninsula; it takes two centuries to subdue all local resistance.

1st to 3rd centuries AD

Pax Romana (Roman Peace), a period of stability and prosperity. The Iberian Peninsula is divided into three provinces: Baetica (capital: Córdoba); Lusitania (Mérida) and Tarraconensis (Tarragona).

trading settlements mainly along the Mediterranean coast – the biggest was Emporion (Empúries) at L'Escala in Catalonia.

The most important gifts of the Phoenicians and Greeks to Spain were not cities, only fragments of which remain today, but rather what they brought with them. The technology of working iron and several things now considered quintessentially Spanish – the olive tree, the grapevine and the donkey – arrived with the Phoenicians and Greeks, along with other useful skills and items such as writing, coins, the potter's wheel and poultry.

Around the same time as the Phoenicians brought iron technology to the south, Celts, originally from Central Europe, brought that knowledge – and beer making – to the north. Celts in the northwest typically lived in hill fort-villages known as *castros*, many of which can be visited today in Galicia and northern Portugal. On the *meseta* (the high tableland of central Spain) Celts merged with Iberians (the general name given to most inhabitants of the Iberian Peninsula at this time) to become what are known as Celtiberians.

Madrid's Museo Arqueológico Nacional (National Archaeology Museum) is a great place to get a feel for the depth of Spanish history, with collections running through the Iberians, Romans and Visigoths right up to the Middle Ages.

The Romans

From about the 6th century BC, the Phoenicians and Greeks were pushed out of the western Mediterranean by newly independent Carthage, a former Phoenician colony that established a flourishing settlement on Ibiza. The next new Mediterranean power to arise was Rome, which defeated Carthage in the First and Second Punic Wars, and fought for control over the Mediterranean in the 3rd century BC. Between the two wars, Carthage conquered southern Spain. The Second Punic War (218–201 BC) saw Carthaginian general Hannibal march his elephants on from here and over the Alps to threaten Rome, but Rome's victory at Ilipa, near Seville, in 206 BC ultimately gave it control over the Iberian Peninsula. The first Roman town in Spain, Itálica, was founded near the battlefield soon afterwards.

The Romans held sway on the Iberian Peninsula for 600 years. It took them 200 years to subdue the fiercest of the local tribes, but by AD 50 most of Hispania (as the Romans called the peninsula) had adopted the Roman way of life.

Rome's legacy to Spain was incalculable, giving Hispania a road system, aqueducts, temples, theatres, amphitheatres and bathhouses, along with the religion that still predominates today – Christianity – and a Jewish population that was to play a big part in Spanish life for more than 1000 years. The languages now most widely spoken on the Iberian Peninsula – Castilian Spanish, Catalan, Galician and Portuguese – are all versions of the colloquial Latin spoken by Roman legionaries and colonists, filtered through 2000 years of linguistic mutation; the Basques,

4th to 7th centuries AD
Germanic tribes enter the Iberian Peninsula, ending the Pax Romana. The Visigoths establish control in the 6th century and bring 200 years of relative stability in which Hispano-Roman culture survives.

711
Muslims invade Iberia from North Africa, overrunning it within a few years, and becoming the dominant force on the peninsula for nearly four centuries and then a potent one for four centuries more.

718
Christian nobleman Pelayo establishes the Kingdom of Asturias in northern Spain. With his victory over a Muslim force at the Battle of Covadonga around 722, the Reconquista begins.

756
Abd ar-Rahman I establishes himself in Córdoba as the emir of Al-Andalus (the Islamic areas of the peninsula) and launches nearly three centuries of Cordoban supremacy.

Top Roman Remains

- *Mérida*
- *Segovia*
- *Itálica (Santiponce, near Seville)*
- *Tarragona*
- *Baelo Claudia (Bolonia, near Tarifa)*
- *Lugo*
- *Villa Romana La Olmeda (Montaña Palentina)*
- *Villa Romana La Dehesa (near Soria)*

though defeated, were never romanised like the rest and hence their language never came within the Latin orbit.

It was also the Romans who first began to cut (for timber, fuel and weapons) the extensive forests that in their time covered half the Spanish *meseta*. In return, Hispania gave Rome gold, silver, grain, wine, fish, soldiers, emperors (Trajan, Hadrian, Theodosius) and the literature of Seneca, Martial, Quintilian and Lucan.

The Roman centuries were something of a golden age for Spain, but the Pax Romana (Roman Peace; the long, prosperous period of stability under the Romans) in Spain began to crumble in the 3rd and 4th centuries AD when Germanic tribes began to sweep down across the Pyrenees. The Visigoths, another Germanic people, sacked Rome itself in 410 but later became allies. When the Germanic Franks pushed the Visigoths out of Gaul in the 6th century, they settled in the Iberian Peninsula, making Toledo their capital.

Throughout their rule, the roughly 200,000 Visigoths maintained a precarious hold over the millions of more sophisticated Hispano-Romans, to the extent that the Visigoths tended to ape Roman ways. Nonetheless, the Roman era had come to an end.

Moorish Spain & La Reconquista

A recurring theme in early Spanish history is Spain's susceptibility to foreign invasion – to empires that rose and fell on Spanish soil but invariably came from elsewhere. In time, that pattern would transform into a struggle for the soul of Spain.

The Muslim Arrival

The death of the Prophet Mohammed in far-off Arabia in 632 sent shock waves far and wide, and Spain, too, would soon feel the effects. Under Mohammed's successors, known as caliphs (from the Arabic word for 'follower'), the new religion spread with extraordinary speed. Much of the Middle East was theirs by 656, and by 682 Islam had reached the shores of the Atlantic in Morocco. Spain, and with it Europe, now lay within sight.

Best Moorish Monuments

- *Alhambra (Granada)*
- *Mezquita (Córdoba)*
- *Albayzín (Granada)*
- *Alcázar (Seville)*
- *Giralda (Seville)*
- *Aljafería (Zaragoza)*
- *Alcazaba (Málaga)*

The Muslims had chosen a good moment to arrive: with the disintegration of the Visigothic kingdom through famine, disease and strife among the aristocracy, the Iberian Peninsula was in disarray and ripe for invasion.

For all its significance, there is an element of farce to what happened next. If you believe the myth, the Muslims were ushered into Spain by the sexual misadventures of the last Visigoth king, Roderic, who reputedly seduced Florinda, the daughter of the governor of Ceuta on the Moroccan coast. The governor, Julian, sought revenge by approaching the Muslims

929

Abd ar-Rahman III inaugurates the Córdoba caliphate, under which Al-Andalus reaches its zenith and Córdoba, with up to half a million people, becomes Europe's biggest and most cultured city.

1031

The Córdoba caliphate disintegrates into dozens of *taifas* (small kingdoms) after a devastating civil war. The most powerful *taifas* include Seville, Granada, Toledo and Zaragoza.

1035

Castilla, a county of the northern Christian kingdom of León (successor to the kingdom of Asturias), becomes an independent kingdom and goes on to become the leading force of the Reconquista.

1085

Castilla captures the major Muslim city of Toledo in central Spain after infighting among the *taifas* leaves them vulnerable to attack.

with a plan to invade Spain, and in 711 Tariq ibn Ziyad, the Muslim governor of Tangier, landed at Gibraltar with around 10,000 men, mostly Berbers (indigenous North Africans).

Roderic's army was decimated, probably near Río Guadalete or Río Barbate in western Andalucía, and he is thought to have drowned while fleeing the scene. Visigothic survivors fled north and within a few years the Muslims had conquered the whole Iberian Peninsula, except for small areas behind the mountains of the Cordillera Cantábrica in the north. Their advance into Europe was only checked by the Franks at the Battle of Poitiers in 732.

Richard Fletcher's *Moorish Spain* is an excellent short history of Al-Andalus (the Muslim-ruled areas of the peninsula) and assumes little prior knowledge of the subject. Other titles include *Homage to al-Andalus* by Michael B Barry and *The Ornament of the World* by María Rosa Menocal.

Al-Andalus: The Early Years

The enlightened Islamic civilisation that would rule much of the Iberian Peninsula for centuries would be called Al-Andalus.

Initially Al-Andalus was part of the caliphate of Damascus, which ruled the Islamic world. Once again, as it had been in ancient times, Spain had become a distant outpost of someone else's empire. In 750, however, the Umayyads were overthrown in Damascus by a rival clan, the Abbasids, who shifted the caliphate to Baghdad. One aristocratic Umayyad survivor made his way to Spain and established himself in Córdoba in 756 as the independent emir of Al-Andalus, Abd ar-Rahman I. It was he who began construction of Córdoba's Mezquita, one of the world's greatest Islamic buildings. Just as importantly, Córdoba was the capital of an empire that relied on no foreign powers. For almost the first time, Spain (in this case, Al-Andalus) was both powerful and answerable only to itself.

Córdoba's Golden Age

From the middle of the 8th century to the mid-11th century, the frontier between Muslim and Christian territory lay across the north of the peninsula, roughly from southern Catalonia to northern Portugal, with a protrusion up towards the central Pyrenees. South of this line, Islamic cities such as Córdoba, Seville and Granada developed with beautiful palaces, mosques and gardens, universities, public baths and bustling *zocos* (markets). Al-Andalus' rulers allowed freedom of worship to Jews and Christians (known as Mozarabs) under their rule. Jews mostly flourished, but Christians had to pay a special tax, so most either converted to Islam or left for the Christian north. The Muslim settlers themselves were not a homogeneous group: beneath the Arab ruling class was a larger number of North African Berbers, and Berber rebellions weren't infrequent.

In 929, the ruler Abd ar-Rahman III gave himself the title caliph, launching the caliphate of Córdoba (929–1031), during which Al-Andalus

Medieval Jewish Sites

- *Judería (Toledo)*
- *The Call (Girona)*
- *Ribadavia (Galicia)*
- *Judería (Córdoba)*
- *Hervás (Extremadura)*
- *Centro Didáctico de la Judería (Segovia)*

1091

North African Muslim Almoravids invade the peninsula, unifying Al-Andalus, ruling it from Marrakesh and halting Christian expansion. Almoravid rule crumbles in the 1140s; Al-Andalus splits again into *taifas.*

1160–73

The Almohads, another strict Muslim sect from North Africa, conquer Al-Andalus. They make Seville their capital and revive arts and learning.

1195

The Almohads inflict a devastating defeat on Alfonso VIII of Castilla at the Battle of Alarcos, near Ciudad Real – the last major Christian reverse of the Reconquista.

1212

Combined armies of northern Christian kingdoms defeat the Almohads at Las Navas de Tolosa in Andalucía, and the momentum of the Christian–Muslim struggle swings decisively in favour of the Christians.

In the 12th century Córdoba, despite being past its caliphate golden age, produced the two most celebrated scholars of Al-Andalus: the Muslim Averroës (1126–98) and the Jewish Maimonides (1135-1204), multitalented men best known for their efforts to reconcile religious faith with Aristotelian reason.

reached its peak of power and lustre. Córdoba in this period was the biggest and most dazzling city in Western Europe. Astronomy, medicine, mathematics and botany flourished and one of the great Muslim libraries was established in the city.

Later in the 10th century, the fearsome Cordoban general Al-Mansur (or Almanzor) terrorised the Christian north with 50-odd forays in 20 years. He destroyed the cathedral at Santiago de Compostela in northwestern Spain in 997 and forced Christian slaves to carry its doors and bells to Córdoba, where they were incorporated into the great mosque. There was, it seemed, no limit to Córdoba's powers.

Al-Andalus: The Later Years

Just when it seemed that Córdoba's golden age would last forever, Al-Andalus turned the corner into a long, slow decline.

After Al-Mansur's death the caliphate collapsed into a devastating civil war, ending Umayyad rule, and in 1031 it finally broke up into dozens of *taifas* (small kingdoms).

Political unity was restored to Al-Andalus by the invasion of a strict Muslim Berber sect from North Africa, the Almoravids, in 1091. The Almoravids had conquered North Africa and were initially invited to the Iberian Peninsula to support Seville, one of the strongest *taifas,* against the growing Christian threat from the north. Seventy years later a second Berber sect, the Almohads, invaded the peninsula after overthrowing the Almoravids in Morocco. Both sects roundly defeated the Christian armies they encountered in Spain, and maintained the Muslim hold over the southern half of the peninsula.

THE MOORISH LEGACY

Muslim rule left an indelible imprint upon Spain. Great architectural monuments such as the Alhambra in Granada and the Mezquita in Córdoba are the stars of the Moorish legacy, but thousands of other buildings large and small are Moorish in origin (including the many churches that began life as mosques). The tangled, narrow street plans of many a Spanish town and village, especially in the south, date back to Moorish times, and the Muslims also developed the Hispano-Roman agricultural base by improving irrigation and introducing new fruits and crops, many of which are still widely grown today. The Spanish language contains many common words of Arabic origin, including the names of some of those new crops – *naranja* (orange), *azúcar* (sugar) and *arroz* (rice). Flamenco, though brought to its modern form by Roma people in post-Moorish times, has clear Moorish roots. It was also through Al-Andalus that much of the learning of ancient Greece and Rome – picked up by the Arabs in the eastern Mediterranean – was transmitted to Christian Europe, where it would exert a profound influence on the Renaissance.

1218

The University of Salamanca is founded by Alfonso IX, King of León, making it the oldest – and still the most prestigious – university in the country.

1229–38

King Jaume (Jaime) I of the Crown of Aragón, which includes Catalonia, takes the Balearic Islands and Valencia from the Muslims, making his kingdom the western Mediterranean's major power.

1248

Having captured Córdoba 12 years earlier, Castilla's Fernando III takes Seville after a two-year siege, leaving the Nasrid emirate of Granada as the last surviving Muslim state on the peninsula.

1469

Isabel, the 18-year-old heir to Castilla, marries Fernando, heir to Aragón and one year her junior, uniting Spain's two most powerful Christian states.

Almohad power eventually disintegrated in the early 13th century because of internal infighting and continuing Christian military pressure from the north. Seville fell to the Christians in 1248, leaving the emirate of Granada (about half of modern Andalucía) as the last Muslim territory on the Iberian Peninsula. Ruled from the lavish Alhambra palace by the Nasrid dynasty, Granada saw Islamic Spain's final cultural flowering as the Christian armies of the Reconquista were closing in.

La Reconquista

The Christian reconquest of the Iberian Peninsula began in about 722 at Covadonga, Asturias, and ended with the fall of Granada in 1492. Between these two dates lay almost eight centuries of misadventures, stirring victories and missed opportunities, during which different Christian kingdoms were almost as often at war with each other as with Muslims.

An essential ingredient in the Reconquista was the cult of Santiago (St James), one of the 12 Apostles. In about the 820s, the saint's supposed tomb was discovered in Galicia. The city of Santiago de Compostela grew around the site, becoming the third-most-popular medieval Christian pilgrimage goal, after Rome and Jerusalem. Christian generals experienced visions of Santiago before forays against the Muslims, and Santiago became the inspiration and special protector of soldiers in the Reconquista, earning the sobriquet *Matamoros* (Moor-slayer). Today he is the patron saint of Spain.

Castilla Rises

Covadonga lies in the Picos de Europa mountains in Asturias, where some Visigothic nobles took refuge after the Muslim conquest. Christian versions of the 722 battle there tell of a small band of fighters under their leader, Pelayo, defeating an enormous force of Muslims; Muslim accounts make it a rather less important skirmish. Whatever the facts of Covadonga, by 757 Christians had clawed back nearly a quarter of the Iberian Peninsula.

The Asturian kingdom eventually moved its capital south to León and became the kingdom of León, which spearheaded the Reconquista until the Christians were set on the defensive by Al-Mansur in the 10th century. Castilla, initially a small principality within León, developed into the dominant Reconquista force as hardy adventurers set up towns in the no man's land of the Duero basin. It was the capture of Toledo in 1085, by Alfonso VI of Castilla, that led the Seville Muslims to call in the Almoravids from North Africa.

In 1212 the combined armies of the Christian kingdoms routed a large Almohad force at Las Navas de Tolosa in Andalucía (near the modern town of Santa Elena). This was the beginning of the end for Al-Andalus: León took key towns in Extremadura in 1229 and 1230; Aragón took Valencia

Reconquista Castle Websites

www.castillosnet.org

www.castlesofspain.co.uk

For an entertaining journey into the modern legacy of Moorish Spain, read Jason Webster's *Andalus: Unlocking the Secrets of Moorish Spain*.

1478

Isabel and Fernando, the Reyes Católicos (Catholic Monarchs), stir up religious bigotry and establish the Spanish Inquisition that will see thousands killed between now and its abolition in 1834.

January 1492

Isabel and Fernando capture Granada, completing the Reconquista. Boabdil, the last Muslim ruler, is scorned (legend has it) by his mother for weeping like a woman over the loss.

April 1492

Isabel and Fernando expel Jews who refuse Christian baptism. Some 200,000 leave, establishing Jewish communities around the Mediterranean; Spain's economy suffers from the loss of their skills and knowledge.

October 1492

Christopher Columbus, funded by Isabel and Fernando, lands in the Bahamas, opening up the Americas to Spanish colonisation and tilting the balance of Spanish sea trade from Mediterranean to Atlantic ports.

THE CATHOLIC MONARCHS

Few individuals in any time or place have had such an impact on their country's history as Spain's Reyes Católicos (Catholic Monarchs), Isabel of Castilla and Fernando of Aragón. Indeed, Spain owes its very existence to their marriage in 1469 (which effectively united the Iberian Peninsula's two biggest Christian kingdoms) and to their conquest of Granada (1492) and annexation of Navarra (1512).

Isabel, by all accounts, was pious, honest, virtuous and very determined, while Fernando was an astute political operator – a formidable team. Isabel resisted her family's efforts to marry her off to half a dozen other European royals before her semi-clandestine wedding to Fernando at Valladolid – the first time the pair had set eyes on each other. They were second cousins; she was 18 and he 17. Isabel succeeded to the Castilian throne in 1474, and Fernando to Aragón's in 1479. By the time Isabel died in 1504, the pair had:

- set up the Spanish Inquisition (1478)
- completed the Reconquista by conquering Granada (1492)
- expelled all Jews (1492) and Muslims (1500) who refused to convert to Christianity
- helped to fund Columbus' voyage to the Americas (1492), opening the door to a vast overseas empire for Spain
- crushed the power of Castilla's rebellious nobility.

Today Isabel and Fernando lie side by side in the beautiful Gothic church they commissioned as their own mausoleum, Granada's Capilla Real.

The Crown of Aragón was one of the most powerful kingdoms in medieval Spain, created in 1137 when Ramón Berenguer IV, count of Barcelona, was betrothed to Petronilla, heiress to the kingdom of Aragón, creating a formidable new Christian power block in the northeast, with Barcelona as its power centre.

in the 1230s; Castilla's Fernando III El Santo (Ferdinand the Saint) took Córdoba in 1236 and Seville in 1248; and the Muslims were expelled from Portugal in 1249. The sole surviving Muslim state on the peninsula was now the emirate of Granada.

Granada Falls

In 1476 Emir Abu al-Hasan of Granada refused to pay any more tribute to Castilla, spurring the Reyes Católicos (Catholic Monarchs) – Isabel, queen of Castilla, and her husband, Fernando, king of Aragón – to launch the Reconquista's final crusade, against Granada. With an army largely funded by Jewish loans and the Catholic Church, the Christians took full advantage of a civil war within the Granada emirate, and on 2 January 1492 Isabel and Fernando entered the city of Granada at the beginning of what turned out to be the most momentous year in Spanish history.

The surrender terms were fairly generous to Boabdil, the last emir, who got the Alpujarras valleys south of Granada and 30,000 gold coins. History has been less kind. Whether true or not, it is often recounted

1494

The Treaty of Tordesillas (near Valladolid) divides recently discovered lands west of Europe between Spain and Portugal, giving the Spanish the right to claim vast territories in the Americas.

1512

Fernando, ruling as regent after Isabel's death in 1504, annexes Navarra, bringing all of Spain under one rule for the first time since Roman days.

1517–56

Reign of Carlos I, Spain's first Habsburg monarch, who comes to rule more of Europe than anyone since the 9th century, plus rapidly expanding areas of South and Central America.

how Boabdil turned for one last tearful look at his beloved Granada as he headed into exile, whereupon his mother scolded him by saying: 'Do not weep like a woman for what you could not defend like a man!' The remaining Muslims were promised respect for their religion, culture and property, but this didn't last long.

Eight centuries after it began, Al-Andalus was no more.

Spain's Empires

Having secured the Iberian Peninsula as their own, the Catholic Monarchs turned their attention elsewhere. The conquest of Granada coincided neatly with the opening up of a whole new world of opportunity for a confident Christian Spain. Columbus' voyage to the Americas, in the very same year as Granada fell, presented an entire new continent in which the militaristic and crusading elements of Spanish society could continue their efforts.

Conquering a New World

In April 1492 the Catholic Monarchs granted the Genoese sailor Christopher Columbus (Cristóbal Colón in Spanish) funds for his voyage across the Atlantic in search of a new trade route to the Orient.

Columbus sailed from the Andalucian port of Palos de la Frontera on 3 August 1492, with three small ships and 120 men. After a near mutiny as the crew despaired of sighting land, they finally arrived on the island of Guanahaní, in the Bahamas, and went on to find Cuba and Hispaniola. Columbus returned to a hero's reception from the Catholic Monarchs in Barcelona, eight months after his departure. Columbus made three more voyages, founding the city of Santo Domingo on Hispaniola, finding Jamaica, Trinidad and other Caribbean islands, and reaching the mouth of the Orinoco and the coast of Central America. But he died impoverished in Valladolid in 1506, still believing he had reached Asia.

Brilliant but ruthless conquistadors such as Hernán Cortés and Francisco Pizarro followed Columbus' trail, seizing vast tracts of the American mainland for Spain. By 1600 Spain controlled nearly all of present-day Mexico and Central America, a large strip of South America, all the biggest Caribbean islands, and Florida. The new colonies sent huge cargoes of silver, gold and other riches back to Spain, where the crown was entitled to one-fifth of the bullion (the *quinto real*, or royal fifth). Seville enjoyed a monopoly on this trade and grew into one of Europe's richest cities.

Entangled in the Old World

It wasn't just the Americas that the Catholic Monarchs thought should be theirs. Isabel and Fernando embroiled Spain in European affairs by

Echoes of Spain's American Colonies

- *Trujillo (Extremadura)*
- *Lugares Colombinos (near Huelva)*
- *Casa-Museo de Colón (Valladolid)*
- *Columbus' Tomb (Seville Cathedral)*
- *Tordesillas (near Valladolid)*
- *Palacio de Sobrellano (Comillas)*
- *Museo de América (Madrid)*

Giles Tremlett's *Catherine of Aragón: The Spanish Queen of Henry VIII* brings to life all the scheming and intrigue of royal Europe in the 16th century through the story of Isabel and Fernando's daughter.

1521

Hernán Cortés, from Medellín, Extremadura, conquers the Aztec empire, in present-day Mexico and Guatemala, with a small band of conquistadors, in the name of the Spanish crown.

1533

Francisco Pizarro, from Trujillo, Extremadura, conquers the Inca empire in South America with a small band of conquistadors, in the name of the Spanish crown.

1556–98

Reign of Felipe II, the zenith of Spanish power. The American territories reach from Florida to Chile, and enormous wealth arriving from the colonies is used for grandiose architectural projects.

1561

The king makes the minor country town of Madrid the capital of his empire. Despite many new noble residences, the overwhelming impression of the new capital is one of squalor.

THE SPANISH INQUISITION

Spain's new Catholic rulers made it clear from the beginning that any enlightened policies of religious coexistence were a thing of the past.

Not content with territorial conquest, the Catholic Monarchs' zeal led to the founding of the Spanish Inquisition to root out those believed to be threatening the Catholic Church. The Inquisition's leading figure was Grand Inquisitor Tomás de Torquemada, who was appointed Queen Isabel's personal confessor in 1479. He was, centuries later, immortalised by Dostoevsky as the articulate Grand Inquisitor who puts Jesus himself on trial in *The Brothers Karamazov*, and satirised in *Monty Python's Flying Circus*.

The Inquisition focused first on *conversos* (Jews converted to Christianity), accusing many of continuing to practise Judaism in secret; in an interesting footnote to history, Torquemada was himself born to *converso* parents.

During the Inquisition, the 'lucky' sinners had their property confiscated (this served as a convenient fund-raiser for the wars against Granada). The condemned were then paraded through towns wearing the *sambenito*, a yellow shirt emblazoned with crosses that was short enough to expose their genitals, then marched to the doors of the local church and flogged.

If you were unlucky, you underwent unimaginable tortures before going through an *auto-da-fé*, a public burning at the stake. Those who recanted and kissed the cross were garrotted before the fire was set, while those who just recanted were burnt quickly with dry wood. If you stayed firm and didn't recant, the wood used for the fire was green and slow-burning.

In the 15 years that Torquemada was Inquisitor General of the Castilian Inquisition, he ran some 100,000 trials and sent about 2000 people to burn at the stake. On 31 March 1492, Fernando and Isabel, on Torquemada's insistence, issued their Edict of Expulsion, as a result of which all Jews who refused Christian baptism were forced to leave Spain within two months on pain of death. Up to 100,000 converted, but some 200,000 – the first Sephardic Jews – left Spain for other Mediterranean destinations. The bankrupt monarchy seized all unsold Jewish property. A talented middle class was gone.

Cardinal Cisneros, Torquemada's successor as overseer of the Inquisition, tried to eradicate Muslim culture, too. In the former Granada emirate he carried out forced mass baptisms, burnt Islamic books and banned the Arabic language. After a revolt in Andalucía in 1500, Muslims were ordered to convert to Christianity or leave. Most (around 300,000) underwent baptism and stayed, becoming known as *moriscos* (converted Muslims), but their conversion was barely skin deep and they never assimilated. The *moriscos* were finally expelled between 1609 and 1614.

marrying their five children into the royal families of Portugal, the Holy Roman Empire and England. After Isabel's death in 1504 and Fernando's in 1516, their thrones passed to their grandson Carlos I (Charles I), who

1571

The Holy League fleet, led by Spain and Venice and commanded by Felipe II's half-brother Don Juan de Austria, defeats the Ottoman Turkish fleet at Lepanto, ending Ottoman expansion into Europe.

c 1580–1660

Spain enjoys a cultural golden age, with the literature of Cervantes and the paintings of Velázquez, Zurbarán and El Greco scaling new heights of artistic excellence as the empire declines.

1609–14

The *moriscos* (converted Muslims) are expelled from Spain in a final purge of non-Christians that undermines an already faltering economy.

1676

The devastation caused by the third great plague to hit Spain in a century is compounded by poor harvests. In all, more than 1.25 million Spaniards die through plague and starvation during the 17th century.

arrived in Spain from Flanders in 1517, aged 17. In 1519 Carlos also succeeded to the Habsburg lands in Austria and was elected Holy Roman Emperor (as Charles V) – meaning he now ruled all of Spain, the Low Countries, Austria, several Italian states, parts of France and Germany, and the expanding Spanish colonies in the Americas.

For all Spain's apparent power, European conflicts soaked up the bulk of the monarchy's new American wealth, and a war-weary Carlos abdicated shortly before his death in 1556, retiring to the Monasterio de Yuste in Extremadura and dividing his many territories between his son Felipe II (Philip II; r 1556–98) and his brother Fernando.

Felipe got the lion's share, including Spain, the Low Countries and the American possessions, and presided over the zenith of Spanish power, though his reign is a study in contradictions. He enlarged the American empire and claimed Portugal on its king's death in 1580, but he lost Holland after a long, drawn-out rebellion. His navy defeated the Ottoman Turks at Lepanto in 1571, but the Spanish Armada of 1588 was routed by England. He was a fanatical Catholic who spurred the Inquisition to new persecutions, yet he readily allied with Protestant England against Catholic France. He received greater flows of silver than ever from the Americas but went bankrupt.

Like his father, Felipe died in a monastery – the immense one at San Lorenzo de El Escorial, which he himself had commissioned, and which stands as a sombre monument to his reign and to the contradictions of Spain's colonial era.

Pre-Civil War Books

- *As I Walked out One Midsummer Morning* by Laurie Lee
- *South from Granada* by Gerald Brenan
- *The Spanish Labyrinth* by Gerald Brenan
- *Sketches of Spain* by Federico García Lorca

Riches to Rags

In Spain's finest hour, at a time when it ruled large swaths of the world, the country's rulers sowed the seeds of its disintegration. So much of the fabulous wealth that accrued from Spain's American and other colonies was squandered on lavish royal lifestyles and on indulgences that did little to better the lives of ordinary Spaniards. The result was a deeply divided country that would for centuries face repeated battles of royal succession and its fair share of external wars, while the bulk of the population got poorer and poorer.

Out of Step with Europe

At one level, a flourishing arts scene in 17th-century Spain created the illusion of a modern European nation. Spain was being immortalised in paint by great artists such as Velázquez, El Greco, Zurbarán and Murillo, and in words by the likes of Miguel de Cervantes (author of *Don Quijote*) and the prolific playwright Lope de Vega.

And yet weak, backward-looking monarchs, a highly conservative Church and an idle nobility allowed the economy to stagnate, leading to

Echoes of the Napoleonic Wars

- *Cabo de Trafalgar (Los Caños de Meca)*
- *Trafalgar Cemetery (Gibraltar)*
- *Museo de las Cortes de Cádiz (Cádiz)*
- *Xardín de San Carlos (A Coruña)*
- *Cementerio de la Florida (Madrid)*

1700

Felipe V, first of the Bourbon dynasty, takes the throne after the Habsburg line dies out with Carlos II. Felipe is second in line to the French throne, which causes concern across Europe.

1702–13

Rival European powers support Charles of Austria against Felipe V in the War of the Spanish Succession; Felipe survives as king, but Spain loses Gibraltar and the Low Countries.

1793

Spain declares war on France after Louis XVI is beheaded, but within a couple of years the country is supporting the French in their struggles against the British.

1805

A combined Spanish-French fleet is defeated by British ships under Nelson at the Battle of Trafalgar. Spanish sea power is effectively destroyed; discontent about King Carlos IV's pro-French policies grows.

During the First Republic some Spanish cities declared themselves independent states, and some, such as Seville and nearby Utrera, even declared war on each other.

food shortages and gross inequalities between the haves and the have-nots. Spain lost Portugal and faced revolts in Catalonia, Sicily and Naples. Silver shipments from the Americas shrank disastrously. And the sickly Carlos II (Charles II; r 1665–1700), known as El Hechizado (the Bewitched), failed to produce children, a situation that led to the War of the Spanish Succession (1702–13). Felipe V (Philip V; r 1700–46), to whom Carlos II had bequeathed the Spanish throne, managed to hold on to it, but during the war Spain lost its last possessions in the Low Countries to Austria, and Gibraltar and Menorca to Britain. Felipe V was the first of the Bourbon dynasty, still in place today.

This was Europe's Age of Enlightenment, but Spain's powerful Church and Inquisition were at odds with the rationalism that trickled in from France. Two-thirds of the land was in the hands of the nobility and Church, and inequality and unrest were rife.

France Invades

When France's Louis XVI, cousin to Spain's Carlos IV (Charles IV; r 1788–1808), was guillotined in 1793 in the aftermath of the French Revolution, Spain declared war on France, only to make peace with the French Republic two years later. In 1805 a combined Spanish-French navy was beaten by the British fleet, under Admiral Nelson, off Andalucía's Cabo de Trafalgar, putting an end to Spanish sea power.

In 1807, French forces poured into Spain, supposedly on the way to Portugal, but by 1808 this had become a French occupation of Spain, and Carlos IV was forced to abdicate in favour of Napoleon's brother Joseph Bonaparte (José I).

In Madrid crowds revolted, as immortalised by Goya in his paintings *El dos de mayo* and *El tres de mayo,* which now hang in Madrid's Museo del Prado. Across the country Spaniards took up arms guerrilla-style, reinforced by British and Portuguese forces led by the Duke of Wellington. A national Cortes (parliament) meeting at Cádiz in 1812 drew up a new liberal constitution, incorporating many of the principles of the American and French prototypes. The French were finally driven out after their defeat at Vitoria in 1813.

Spain's Decline

Although momentarily united to see off the French, Spain was deeply divided, not to mention increasingly backward and insular. For much of the 19th century, internal conflicts raged between liberals (who wanted vaguely democratic reforms) and conservatives (the Church, the nobility and others who preferred the earlier status quo).

Uncertainties over royal succession resulted in the First Carlist War (1833–39). During the war, violent anticlericalism emerged, religious

1808–13

French forces occupy Spain; Carlos IV abdicates in favour of Napoleon's brother, José I. The ensuing Peninsular War sees British forces helping the Spanish defeat the French.

1809–24

Most of Spain's colonies win independence as Spain is beset by problems at home. By 1824 only Cuba, Puerto Rico, Guam and the Philippines are under Spanish rule.

1814

Fernando VII becomes king and revokes the 1812 Cádiz Constitution (an attempt by Spanish liberals to introduce constitutional reforms) just weeks after agreeing to uphold its principles.

1833–39

The First Carlist War, triggered by disputes over the succession between backers of Fernando VII's infant daughter, Isabel, and his brother, Don Carlos. Isabel eventually becomes queen in 1843.

orders were closed and, in the Disentailment of 1836, church property and lands were seized and auctioned off by the government. It was the army alone that emerged victorious from the fighting. Another Carlist War (1872–76) followed, this time between the supporters of not just two but three claimants to the throne.

In 1873 the liberal-dominated Cortes proclaimed the country a federal republic. But this First Republic could not control the regions, and the army put Queen Isabel II's son Alfonso on the throne as Alfonso XII (r 1874–85), in a coalition with the Church and landowners.

Barely able to hold itself together, Spain had little chance of maintaining its few remaining colonies. In 1898, Spain lost Cuba, the Philippines, Guam and Puerto Rico after being defeated in the Spanish-American War by the USA.

For a country that had ruled one of the greatest empires of the age, this sealed an ignominious fall from grace.

The Spanish Civil War

The Spanish Civil War (1936–39) was a long time coming. In many ways, the seeds of division were sown centuries before in the profound inequalities that flowed from Spain's colonial riches, and in the equally profound social divisions that began to surface in the 19th century.

Seeds of War

By the early years of the 20th century, Spain was locked in an unending power struggle between left-wing and conservative forces, with neither able to maintain the upper hand for long.

For a time, the left seemed ascendant. Anarchism and socialism both gained large followings and founded powerful unions. In the 1890s and the 1900s, anarchists bombed Barcelona's Liceu opera house, assassinated two prime ministers and killed 24 people with a bomb at King Alfonso XIII's wedding to Victoria Eugenie of Battenberg in May 1906. Parallel to the rise of the left came the growth of Basque and Catalan separatism. In Catalonia this was led by business interests who wanted to pursue policies independent of Madrid; in the Basque Country, nationalism emerged in the 1890s in response to a flood of Castilian workers into Basque industries: some Basques considered these migrants a threat to their identity. In 1909 a contingent of Spanish troops was wiped out by Berbers in Spanish Morocco. The government's decision to call up Catalan reservists sparked the so-called Semana Trágica (Tragic Week) in Barcelona, which began with a general strike and turned into a frenzy of violence. The government responded by executing many workers.

Spain stayed neutral during WWI but remained a deeply troubled nation. In 1921, 10,000 Spanish soldiers were killed by Berbers at Anual in

The village of Belchite in central Aragón, reduced to shattered ruins by a fierce civil-war battle in 1937, was preserved in its devastated state after the war. The haunting ruins, including what's left of four churches, can be visited on daily tours with the local tourist office.

1872–76
The Second Carlist War, between three monarchist factions, brings Isabel II's son, Alfonso XII, to the throne after the brief, chaotic First Republic of 1873.

1898
Spain loses Cuba, Puerto Rico, Guam and the Philippines, its last remaining colonies, after being defeated in the Spanish–American War by the US, which declared war in support of Cuban independence.

1923–30
General Miguel Primo de Rivera launches an army rising in support of King Alfonso XIII and then establishes himself as dictator. He retires and dies in 1930.

1931
Alfonso XIII goes into exile after Republicans score sweeping gains in local elections. Spain's Second Republic is launched, left-wing parties win a national election, and a new constitution enfranchises women.

Morocco, and two years later General Miguel Primo de Rivera, an eccentric Andalucian aristocrat, led an army uprising and established a mild dictatorship, resigning in 1930 in the midst of an economic downturn following the Wall Street Crash. King Alfonso XIII departed for exile in 1931 and Spain's Second Republic was launched.

National elections in 1931 brought in a government composed of socialists, republicans and centrists. A new constitution gave women the vote, granted autonomy-minded Catalonia its own parliament, legalised divorce, stripped Catholicism of its status as the official religion, and banned priests from teaching. But Spain lurched back to the right in elections in 1933. One new force on the right was the fascist Falange, led by José Antonio Primo de Rivera, son of the 1920s dictator.

By 1934, violence was spiralling out of control. Catalonia declared itself independent (within a putative federal Spanish republic), and workers' committees took over the northern mining region of Asturias. A violent campaign against the Asturian workers by the Spanish Legion (set up to fight Moroccan tribes in the 1920s), led by generals Francisco Franco and José Millán Astray, split the country firmly into left and right.

In the February 1936 elections, the right-wing National Front was narrowly defeated by the left-wing Popular Front, with communists at the fore. Something had to give.

The Civil War Begins

On 17 July 1936, the Spanish army garrison in Melilla, North Africa, rose up against the left-wing Popular Front government, followed the next day by garrisons on the mainland. The leaders of the plot were five generals, among them Francisco Franco. The civil war had begun.

The war would split communities, families and friends, kill an estimated 350,000 Spaniards (some writers say 500,000), and cause untold damage and misery. Both sides committed atrocious massacres and reprisals. The rebels, who called themselves Nationalists because they believed they were fighting for Spain, shot or hanged tens of thousands of supporters of the Republic. Republicans did likewise to Nationalist sympathisers, including some 7000 priests, monks and nuns.

At the start of the war many of the military and the Guardia Civil police force went over to the Nationalists, whose campaign quickly took on overtones of a crusade against the enemies of God. In Republican areas, anarchists, communists or socialists ended up running many towns and cities, and social revolution followed.

Civil War Reads

For Whom the Bell Tolls by Ernest Hemingway

Homage to Catalonia by George Orwell

The Spanish Civil War by Hugh Thomas

Spain in Our Hearts by Adam Hochschild

Nationalist Advance

Most cities with military garrisons fell immediately into Nationalist hands – this included almost everywhere north of Madrid except Cat-

1933–35	1936	1936–39	1938
Right-wing parties win a new election, political violence spirals and a ruthless army operation against workers in Asturias irrevocably polarises Spain into left- and right-wing camps.	The left-wing Popular Front wins a national election. Right-wing 'Nationalist' rebels led by General Francisco Franco rise up against it, starting the Spanish Civil War.	The Spanish Civil War: the Nationalist rebels, under Franco, supported by Nazi Germany and Fascist Italy, defeat the USSR-supported Republicans. About 350,000 people die in fighting and atrocities.	The Nationalists defeat the Republicans' last major offensive, in the Ebro Valley, with 20,000 killed. The USSR ends its support for the Republican side.

alonia and the north coast, plus parts of Andalucía. Franco's force of legionnaires and Moroccan mercenaries was airlifted to Seville by German war planes in August. Essential to the success of the revolt, the force moved north through Extremadura towards Madrid, wiping out fierce resistance in some cities. At Salamanca in October, Franco pulled all the Nationalists into line behind him.

Madrid, reinforced by the first battalions of the International Brigades (armed foreign idealists and adventurers organised by the communists), repulsed Franco's first assault in November and then endured, under communist inspiration, over two years' siege. But the International Brigades never numbered more than 20,000 and couldn't turn the tide against the better-armed and -organised Nationalist forces.

Nazi Germany and Fascist Italy supported the Nationalists with planes, weapons and men (75,000 from Italy, 17,000 from Germany), turning the war into a testing ground for WWII. The Republicans had some Soviet planes, tanks, artillery and advisers, but other countries refused to become involved (although some 25,000 French fought on the Republican side).

Republican Quarrels

With Madrid besieged, the Republican government moved to Valencia in late 1936 to preside over the quarrelsome factions on its side, which encompassed anarchists, communists, moderate democrats and regional separatists.

In April 1937 German planes bombed the Basque town of Gernika (Guernica), causing terrible casualties; this became the subject of Picasso's famous pacifist painting, which now hangs in Madrid's Centro de Arte Reina Sofía. All the north coast fell to the Nationalists that year, while Republican counter-attacks near Madrid and in Aragón failed. Meanwhile, divisions among the Republicans erupted into fierce street fighting in Barcelona, with the Soviet-influenced communists completely crushing the anarchists and Trotskyites, who had run the city for almost a year. The Republican government moved to Barcelona in autumn 1937.

Nationalist Victory

In early 1938, Franco repulsed a Republican offensive at Teruel in Aragón, then swept eastward with 100,000 troops, 1000 planes and 150 tanks, isolating Barcelona from Valencia. In July the Republicans launched a last offensive in the Ebro Valley. This bloody encounter, won by the Nationalists, cost 20,000 lives. The USSR withdrew from the war in September 1938, and in January 1939 the Nationalists took Barcelona unopposed. The Republican government and hundreds of thousands of supporters fled to France. The Republicans still held Valencia and Madrid, and had

1939

The Nationalists take Barcelona in January. The Republican government flees to France, Republican forces evaporate and the Nationalists enter Madrid on 28 March. Franco declares the war over on 1 April.

1939–50

Franco establishes a right-wing dictatorship, imprisoning hundreds of thousands. Spain stays out of WWII but is later excluded from NATO and the UN and suffers an international trade boycott.

1955–65

Spain is admitted to the UN after agreeing to host US bases. The economy is boosted by US aid and mass tourism on the Costa Brava and Costa del Sol.

1959

Euskadi Ta Askatasuna (ETA; Basque Homeland and Freedom) is founded to fight for Basque independence. The terrorist group will murder more than 800 people before ending armed activity in 2011.

Paul Preston's searing *The Spanish Holocaust: Inquisition and Extermination in Twentieth-Century Spain* lays bare the brutality of Spain's civil war (neither side comes out well) and the oppression by victorious Franco forces after the war.

500,000 people under arms, but in the end their army simply evaporated. The Nationalists entered Madrid on 28 March 1939 and Franco declared the war over on 1 April.

Franco's Dictatorship

Bloodied and battered Spain may have been after the Civil War, but there was no peace dividend: Spain's new ruler, General Francisco Franco, began as he meant to continue.

The Early Franco Years

An estimated 100,000 people were killed or died in prison in the years immediately following the war. The hundreds of thousands imprisoned included many intellectuals and teachers; others fled abroad, depriving Spain of a generation of scientists, artists, writers, educators and more.

Though Franco promised Hitler an alliance, Spain remained on the sidelines of WWII. In 1944 Spanish leftists launched an attack on Franco's Spain from France; this attack failed. Small leftist guerrilla units continued a hopeless struggle in parts of the north, Extremadura and Andalucía until the 1950s.

After WWII Franco's Spain was excluded from the UN and NATO, and suffered a UN-sponsored trade boycott that helped turn the late 1940s into Spain's *años de hambre* (years of hunger). But with the onset of the Cold War, the US wanted bases in Spain, and Franco agreed to the establishment of four, in return for large sums of aid. In 1955 Spain was admitted to the UN.

Franco's Spain

Franco ruled absolutely, never allowing any one powerful lobby – the Church, the army, the Movimiento Nacional (the only legal political party) or the bankers – to dominate. Regional autonomy aspirations were not tolerated. The army provided many government ministers and enjoyed a most generous budget. And Catholic supremacy was fully restored.

In 1959 a new breed of technocrats in government, linked to the Catholic group Opus Dei, engineered a Stabilisation Plan, which brought an economic upswing. Spanish industry was modernised, transport was updated, and new dams provided irrigation and hydropower.

The recovery was funded in part by US aid and remittances from more than a million Spaniards who had gone to work abroad, but above all it was funded by tourism, which was developed initially along Andalucía's Costa del Sol and Catalonia's Costa Brava. By 1965 the number of tourists arriving in Spain was 14 million a year. These were the so-called *años de desarrollo* (years of development). Industry took off, foreign investment

Films Set in Franco's Spain

- *Pan's Labyrinth* (2006)
- *The Spirit of the Beehive* (1973)
- *¡Bienvenido, Mr Marshall!* (*Welcome, Mr Marshall!*; 1953)
- *Las 13 rosas* (*The 13 Roses*; 2007)

1960s

After two decades of extreme economic hardship, the decade becomes known as the *años de desarrollo* (years of development), with investment and rural immigrants flooding into Madrid and other cities.

1975

Franco dies and is succeeded by King Juan Carlos I. The monarch had been schooled by Franco to continue his policies but soon demonstrates his desire for change.

1976

The king appoints Adolfo Suárez as prime minister. Suárez engineers a return to democracy. Left-wing parties are legalised, despite military opposition, and the country holds free elections in 1977.

1978

A new constitution, overwhelmingly approved by referendum, establishes Spain as a parliamentary democracy with no official religion and the monarch as official head of state.

poured in, and the services and banking sectors blossomed. In 1960 fewer than 70,000 cars were on the road in Madrid. Ten years later, more than half a million clogged the capital's streets.

Spaniards' standard of living was improving, but the jails were full of political prisoners and large garrisons were still maintained outside every major city. From 1965 opposition to Franco's regime became steadily more vocal. The universities were scenes of repeated confrontation, and clandestine trade unions began to make themselves heard. In the Basque Country the terrorist group Euskadi Ta Askatasuna (ETA; Basque Homeland and Freedom) began to fight for Basque independence. Its first significant action outside the Basque Country was the 1973 assassination in Madrid of Admiral Carrero Blanco, Franco's prime minister and designated successor.

In what seemed like a safe bet, Franco then chose as his successor Prince Juan Carlos, the Spanish-educated grandson of Alfonso XIII. In 1969 Juan Carlos swore loyalty to Franco and the Movimiento Nacional. Cautious reforms by Franco's last prime minister, Carlos Arias Navarro, provoked violent opposition from right-wing extremists, and Spain seemed to be sinking into chaos when Franco died on 20 November 1975.

Paul Preston's *Franco* is the big biography of one of history's little dictators – and it has very little to say in the man's favour. Conspiracy theorists will love Peter Day's *Franco's Friends: How British Intelligence Helped Bring Franco to Power in Spain.*

Democratic Spain

Spain's way forward was hard to discern on Franco's death. The country remained as divided as ever and at its helm was an untested Franco protégé. But, not for the first time in Spanish history, not all was as it seemed.

The Transition

Juan Carlos I, aged 37, took the throne on 22 November 1975, two days after Franco's death. The new king's links with the dictator inspired little confidence in a Spain now clamouring for democracy, but Juan Carlos had kept his cards close to his chest. In July 1976 he appointed Adolfo Suárez, a 43-year-old former Franco apparatchik with film-star looks, as prime minister. To general surprise, Suárez got the Cortes (parliament) to approve a new, two-chamber parliamentary system, and in 1977 political parties, trade unions and strikes were all legalised. Franco's Movimiento Nacional was abolished.

Suárez' centrist party, the Unión de Centro Democrático (UCD; Central Democratic Union), won nearly half the seats in the new Cortes in 1977. A new constitution in 1978 made Spain a parliamentary monarchy with no official religion. In response to a fever for local autonomy, principally in Catalonia, the Basque Country and Galicia, by 1983 the country was divided into 17 'autonomous communities' with their own regional governments controlling a range of policy areas. Personal and social life

1981

On 23 February a group of armed Guardia Civil led by Antonio Tejero attempts a coup by occupying the parliament building. The king denounces them on national TV; the coup collapses.

1982–96

Spain is governed by the centre-left PSOE, led by Felipe González. The country experiences an economic boom, but the government becomes increasingly associated with scandals and corruption.

1986

Spain joins the European Community (now the EU). Along with its membership of NATO since 1982, this is a turning point in the country's post-Franco international acceptance.

1992

Barcelona holds the Olympic Games, putting Spain in the international spotlight and highlighting the country's progress since 1975. Madrid is European Capital of Culture and Seville hosts a world expo.

Bourbon Baubles

Palacio Real (Madrid)

Palacio Real (Aranjuez)

La Granja de San Ildefonso (near Segovia)

enjoyed a rapid liberation after Franco. Contraceptives, homosexuality and divorce were legalised, and the Madrid party and arts scene known as *la movida madrileña* formed the epicentre of a newly unleashed hedonism that still reverberates through Spanish life.

The Suárez government granted a general amnesty for deeds committed in the civil war and under the Franco dictatorship. There were no truth commissions or trials for the perpetrators of atrocities. For the next three decades, Spain cast barely a backward glance.

A Maturing Democracy

The main left-of-centre party, the Partido Socialista Obrero Español (PSOE; Spanish Socialist Workers' Party), led by a charismatic young lawyer from Seville, Felipe González, came second in the 1977 election and

LA MOVIDA

After the long, dark years of dictatorship and conservative Catholicism, Spaniards, especially those in Madrid, emerged onto the streets with all the zeal of ex-boarding-school teenagers as Spain returned to democracy in the late 1970s. Nothing was taboo in the phenomenon known as *la movida* (the scene) or *la movida madrileña* (the Madrid scene), as young Spaniards discovered the '60s, '70s and early '80s all at once. All-night partying was the norm, drug taking in public was not a criminal offence and Madrid in particular howled. Summer terraces roared to the chattering, drinking, carousing crowds, and young people from all over Europe (not to mention cultural icons such as Andy Warhol) flocked to join the revelry.

What was remarkable about *la movida* in Madrid is that it was presided over by Enrique Tierno Galván, an ageing former university professor who had been a leading opposition figure under Franco and was affectionately known throughout Spain as 'the old teacher'. A socialist, he became mayor in 1979 and, for many, launched *la movida* by telling a public gathering '*a colocarse y ponerse al loro*', which loosely translates as 'get stoned and do what's cool'. Unsurprisingly, he was Madrid's most popular mayor ever and when he died in 1986, a million *madrileños* turned out for his funeral.

La movida was also an explosion of creativity among the country's musicians, designers and film-makers. The most famous of these was director Pedro Almodóvar, whose riotously colourful films featured larger-than-life characters who pushed the limits of sex and drugs. Although his later films became internationally renowned, his first films, *Pepi, Luci, Bom y otras chicas del montón* (Pepi, Luci, Bom and the Other Girls; 1980) and *Laberinto de pasiones* (Labyrinth of Passion; 1982) are where the spirit of the movement really comes alive. When he wasn't making films, Almodóvar immersed himself in the spirit of *la movida*, doing drag acts in smoky bars that people in the know would frequent.

Other important cultural figures to emerge from *la movida* include actor Antonio Banderas, fashion designer Agatha Ruiz de la Prada and film director Fernando Trueba.

1996

Disaffection with PSOE sleaze gives the centre-right Partido Popular (PP), led by José María Aznar, a general-election victory at the start of a decade of sustained economic growth.

11 March 2004

A terrorist bombing kills 191 people on 10 Madrid commuter trains. The following day, an estimated 11 million people take to the streets across Spain.

14 March 2004

The PSOE led by José Luis Rodríguez Zapatero sweeps to power and ushers in 7½ years of Socialist rule, characterised by sweeping changes to social legislation.

October 2008

Spain's unemployment rate soars from less than 6% to 12.3% in a single month. Spain's finance minister admits that Spain has entered 'its deepest recession in half a century'.

then won power with a big majority in 1982. González was to be prime minister for 14 years. The PSOE's young and educated leadership came from the generation that had opened the cracks in the Franco regime in the late 1960s and early 1970s. Unemployment rose from 16% to 22% by 1986, but that same year, Spain joined the European Community (now the EU), bringing on a five-year economic boom. The middle class grew ever bigger, the PSOE established a national health system and improved public education, and Spain's women streamed into higher education and jobs.

In 1992 – the 500th anniversary of the fall of Granada and Columbus' first voyage to the Americas – Spain celebrated its arrival in the modern world by staging the Barcelona Olympics and the Expo 92 world fair in Seville. The economy, however, was in a slump and the PSOE was mired in scandals. It came as no surprise when the PSOE lost the 1996 general election.

The party that won the 1996 election was the centre-right Partido Popular (PP; People's Party), led by José María Aznar, a former tax inspector from Castilla y León. Aznar promised to make politics dull, and he did, but he presided over eight years of solid economic progress, winning the 2000 election as well. The PP cut public investment and sold off state enterprises, and liberalised sectors such as telecommunications; during the Aznar years Spain's economy grew a lot faster than the EU average, while unemployment fell dramatically.

Troubled Times

On 11 March 2004, Madrid was rocked by 10 bombs on four rush-hour commuter trains heading into the capital's Atocha station. When the dust cleared, 191 people had died and 1755 were wounded, many of them seriously. Perpetrated by an Islamic group with links to al-Qaeda, this was the biggest such terror attack in the nation's history.

In a stunning reversal of pre-poll predictions, the PP, which insisted that the ETA was responsible despite overwhelming evidence to the contrary, was defeated by the PSOE in elections three days after the attack.

The new socialist government of José Luis Rodríguez Zapatero gave Spain a makeover by introducing a raft of liberalising social reforms. Gay marriage was legalised, Spain's arcane divorce laws were overhauled, almost a million illegal immigrants were granted residence, and a law seeking to apportion blame for the crimes of the Civil War and Franco dictatorship entered the statute books. Although Spain's powerful Catholic Church cried foul over many of the reforms, the changes played well with most Spaniards. Spain's economy was booming – the envy of Europe.

And then it all fell apart.

July 2010

After decades of underachievement, Spain's national football team wins the World Cup for the first time, two years after its first European Championship trophy.

November 2011

The conservative Partido Popular, led by Mariano Rajoy, sweeps to power in national elections, announcing austerity measures to combat Spain's economic crisis.

2014

The economy experiences a full year of growth for the first time since 2007; unemployment dips below 25%.

June 2014

After a series of scandals that envelop the Spanish royal family, King Juan Carlos, who had reigned since 1975, abdicates and his son begins his reign as Felipe VI.

Spain's economy went into free fall in late 2008 with the global credit crunch, the bursting of the country's property bubble, and the international slump. In an economy heavily dependent on tourism and construction, two exceptionally vulnerable industries during economic downturns, unemployment rose above 27% (six million people) by 2013, and catastrophic youth-unemployment rates nudged 60%. Young professionals fled the country in unprecedented numbers. A wave of anger at corruption and the political and financial elite spread across Spain, spearheaded by a protest movement known as Los Indignados (The Indignant Ones), who camped out in central Madrid for months from 15 May 2011 in what was the forerunner to many similar movements around the world, including Occupy Wall Street.

Zapatero's government waited painfully long to recognise the severity of the crisis and was replaced, in the elections of November 2011, by a PP government led by Mariano Rajoy that launched a deep austerity drive that cut into the generous welfare state on which Spaniards had come to depend. Spanish banks were bailed out by the EU to the tune of €100 billion. The conservative government also turned back the liberalising reforms of the socialists, introducing some of Europe's strictest anti-abortion laws and restoring the role of the Catholic Church in education.

That the country remained firmly democratic, and the protests largely peaceful, however, were encouraging signs of how far Spain has come, given its tumultuous modern history.

Modern Spain Reading

Ghosts of Spain by Giles Tremlett

The New Spaniards by John Hooper

Juan Carlos by Paul Preston

Roads to Santiago by Cees Nooteboom

Driving Over Lemons by Chris Stewart

December 2015

The Partido Popular loses its majority in national general elections, with strong gains for the left-wing Podemos party and centrist Ciudadanos. No party or parties are able to form a government.

June 2016

A new general election again fails to produce a clear winner; in October the PSOE abstains in a parliamentary confidence vote, allowing the Partido Popular to form a minority government.

October 2017

Catalonia holds an independence referendum, disrupted by national police. Citing 90% voter support the regional parliament declares independence. The national government dismisses it and suspends regional autonomy.

December 2017

Pro-independence parties win a parliamentary majority in Catalonia's regional elections, leaving the way open for them to form the new regional government in 2018.

Art & Architecture

Spain's artistic and architectural landscapes are among the richest in Europe. A star-studded lineage of painters – El Greco, Velázquez, Goya, Picasso, Miró, Dalí – is one of the country's cultural hallmarks, while Spain's architecture narrates the full sweep of its history, from glorious Moorish creations in Andalucía to soaring cathedrals to the singular imagination of Gaudí to wacky contemporary creativity.

Architecture

You can almost see centurions marching beneath the great Roman aqueduct in Segovia, while the Alhambra similarly conjures up Spain's Islamic era. Elsewhere, the Middle Ages comes alive amid Santo Domingo de Silos' Romanesque cloisters, castles dot the countryside from Catalonia to Extremadura, and great Gothic cathedrals adorn Burgos, Palma de Mallorca and Toledo. And who in Barcelona isn't carried away by Gaudí's Modernista fantasies? Welcome to Spain, one of Europe's most intriguing architectural stories.

The Introduction of Islam

By AD 784 Córdoba was well established as the new capital of the Umayyad dynasty, which in 750 had been deposed as caliphs (supreme rulers of the Muslim world) in Damascus by the Abbasids. Syrian architects set to work on the grand Mezquita, conjuring up their homeland with details that echo the Umayyad Mosque in Damascus, such as delicate horseshoe arches and exquisite decorative tiles with floral motifs. But the building's most distinctive feature – more than 500 columns that crowd the interior of the mosque – was repurposed from Roman and Visigothic ruins.

In the centuries that followed, Moorish architecture incorporated trends from all over the Islamic world. The technique of intricately carved stucco detailing was developed in 9th-century Iraq, while *muqarnas* (honeycomb) vaulting arrived via Egypt in the 10th century. Square minarets, such as the Giralda in Seville (now a cathedral tower), came with the Almohad invasion from Morocco in the 12th century.

The finest remnants of the Islamic era are in Andalucía, although the Aljafería in Zaragoza is a beautiful exception. Perhaps the most magnificent creation is the core of Granada's Alhambra, the Palacios Nazaríes (Nasrid Palaces). From the 13th to the 15th centuries, architects and artisans achieved new heights of elegance, creating a study in balance between inside and outside, light and shade, spareness and intricacy. Eschewing innovation, the Alhambra refined well-tried forms, as if in an attempt to freeze time and halt the collapse of Moorish power, which had already been pushed back to an area smaller than today's Andalucía.

Roman Relics

- *Segovia aqueduct*
- *Teatro Romano (Mérida)*
- *City walls (Lugo, Galicia)*
- *Museu d'História de Tarragona (Catalonia)*
- *Itálica (Santiponce, near Seville)*
- *Baelo Claudia (Bolonia, Andalucía)*

Hybrid Styles: Mozarabic & Mudéjar

By the 10th century, Moorish rule had produced a class of people called Mozarabs – practising Christians who lived in Islamic territory and spoke Arabic. When Mozarab artisans moved or travelled north into Christian Spain, they took elements of classic Islamic construction with them.

Only a few small parts of northern Spain were never conquered by the Muslims. In one of these, Asturias, a unique building style (known as pre-Romanesque) emerged during the 9th century, exaggerating Visigothic styles. Oviedo's Palacio de Santa María del Naranco, for instance, has dramatically elongated proportions, delicate relief carvings and tall, thin arches.

For example, the Monasterio de San Miguel de Escalada, east of León, imitates the Mezquita, with horseshoe arches atop leafy Corinthian capitals reused from Roman buildings. Many arches are boxed in by an *alfiz* (rectangular decorative frame) around the upper portion of the arch. This became a signature detail in Mozarabic architecture.

Later, as the Reconquista started to gain ground, another border-crossing class emerged: Mudéjars (Muslims who stayed on in now-Catholic parts of Spain). Mudéjar artisans, largely disenfranchised, offered cheap labour and great talent. The Mudéjar style, in evidence from the 12th century on, is notable first for the use of relatively inexpensive materials – gone were the days of lavish government commissions, and the Roman stones had all been used up. Instead, brick, tile and plaster were worked with incredible skill to conjure opulence. Teruel in Aragón in particular is dotted with intricate brick towers, trimmed in glazed tiles.

Another tell-tale Mudéjar feature is extravagantly decorated timber ceilings done in a style called *artesonado*. They can be barrel vaults, but the most typical style is a flat wood ceiling made of interlocking beams that are inset with multicoloured wood panels in geometric patterns.

Romanesque & Gothic

As the tide turned against the Muslims, the Romanesque style was sweeping medieval Europe, taking root in Spain in part because it was the aesthetic opposite of Islamic fashions – the Catalan architect and art historian Josep Puig i Cadafalch posited that each Romanesque detail was a systematic riposte to an Islamic one. These buildings were spare, angular and heavy, inspired by the proportions of classical structures.

Romanesque structures had perfectly semicircular arches – none of the stylised horseshoe look that had come before. In churches, this was expressed in a semicylindrical apse (or, in many cases, triple apse), a shape previously found in Byzantine churches. The round arch also graced doorways, windows, cloisters and naves. Entrances supported stacks of concentric arches – the more eye-catching because they were often the only really decorative detail. The pilgrimage cathedral of Santiago de Compostela is arguably Spain's greatest Romanesque building; great, lesser-known examples include the Iglesia de San Martín in Frómista, and Sant Climent de Taüll, one of many fine examples in the Catalan Pyrenees.

Later, during the 12th century, Spanish architects began to modify these semicircles, edging towards the Gothic style, as they added pointed arches and ribbed vaults. The cathedrals in Ávila, Sigüenza and Tarragona all display transitional elements.

The Camino de Santiago was one of the chief avenues by which Romanesque architecture entered Spain, bringing such beauties as the Abadía de Santo Domingo de Silos, the smaller cloister in the Monasterio de las Huelgas in Burgos, and the cathedral itself in Santiago de Compostela.

The trend elsewhere in Europe towards towering cathedrals made possible by the newfangled flying buttresses caught on in Spain by the 13th century, when the cathedrals at Burgos, León and Toledo were begun. Some changes were subtle, such as placing choir stalls in the centre of the nave, but one was unmissable: the towering, decorative *retablo* (altarpiece) that graced the new churches. Spanish Gothic architects also devised the star vault, a method of distributing weight with ribbed vaults projecting out from a central point. Many great buildings were begun at the height of Romanesque fashion but not completed until long after the Gothic style had gained the upper hand. The cathedral in Burgos, for instance, was begun in 1221 as a relatively sober construction, but its 15th-century spires are a product of German-inspired late-Gothic imagination. Mudéjar influences also made themselves felt. Toledo boasts many gloriously original buildings with Gothic-Mudéjar flair.

Gothic is scattered liberally across Andalucía, where the Reconquista arrived just when Gothic was coming into fashion. The massive, mainly 15th-century, Gothic cathedral of Seville is one of the largest churches in the world. Most of the innumerable castles scattered across the country also went up in Gothic times – an extraordinary example is the sumptuous castle at Coca, not far from Segovia.

At the end of the 15th century, the Isabelline Gothic look, inspired by the Catholic queen, reflected her fondness for Islamic exotica and heraldic imagery. It's on display in the Capilla Real in Granada, where Isabel and her husband, Fernando, are buried. The Gothic fascination lasted into the 16th century, when there was a revival of pure Gothic, perhaps best exemplified in the new cathedral in Salamanca, although the Segovia cathedral was about the last, and possibly most pure, Gothic structure raised in Spain.

Ildefonso Falcones' best-selling historical novel *La catedral del mar* (The Cathedral of the Sea) tells the juicy tale of the construction of the Santa María del Mar cathedral in Barcelona in the 13th century.

Renaissance to Baroque

Arising from the pan-European Renaissance, the uniquely Spanish vision of plateresque drew partly on Italian styles and was also an outgrowth of the Isabelline Gothic look. It is so named because facade decoration was so ornate that it looked as though it had been wrought by *plateros* (silversmiths). To visit Salamanca, where the Spanish Renaissance first took root, is to receive a concentrated dose of the most splendid work in the genre.

A more purist Renaissance style, reflecting classical proportions and styles already established in Italy and France, prevailed in Andalucía, as seen in the Palacio de Carlos V in Granada's Alhambra. The Renaissance wild card was Juan de Herrera, whose work bears almost no resemblance to anything else of the period because it is so austere. His masterpiece is the palace-monastery complex of San Lorenzo de El Escorial.

Aside from the late-18th-century Cádiz cathedral, there are very few from-scratch baroque buildings in Spain. But exuberant baroque decoration is so eye-catching that it easily overtakes the more sober earlier buildings to which it's usually attached. The leading exponents of this often overblown style were the Churriguera brothers, three sons of a respected sculptor who specialised in *retablos*, the enormous carved-wood altar backdrops.

The hallmark of Churrigueresque is the so-called Solomonic (or Salomonic) column, a delightful twisting pillar that, especially when covered in gold leaf or vines, seems to wiggle its way to the heavens.

Leading examples of the Churrigueresque style are found in the Palacio de los Cepeda in Osuna; the Iglesia del Carmen in Antequera; Madrid's Antiguo Cuartel del Conde Duque; and the Catedral Nueva, Plaza Mayor and Convento de San Esteban, all in Salamanca.

Modernisme & Art Deco

At the end of the 19th century, Barcelona's prosperity unleashed one of the most imaginative periods in Spanish architecture. The architects at work here, who drew on prevailing art-nouveau trends as well as earlier Spanish styles, came to be called the Modernistas. Chief among them, Antoni Gaudí sprinkled Barcelona with jewels of his singular imagination. They range from his immense Sagrada Família (which is still being built) to the simply weird Casa Batlló and the only slightly more sober La Pedrera. Gaudí's structural approach owed much to the austere era of Catalan Gothic, which inspired his own inventive work with parabolic arches. The works of two other Catalan architects, Lluís Domènech i Montaner and Josep Puig i Cadafalch, are also Barcelona landmarks.

While Barcelona went all wavy, Madrid embraced the rigid glamour of art deco. This global style arrived in Spain just as Madrid's Gran Vía was laid out in the 1920s. One of the more overwhelming caprices from that era is the Palacio de Comunicaciones on Plaza de la Cibeles.

The 1936–39 civil war and more than three decades of dictatorship brought such frivolities to an abrupt end.

Best Baroque

- *Monasterio de la Cartuja (Granada)*
- *Plaza Mayor (Salamanca)*
- *Santiago de Compostela cathedral west facade*
- *Catedral de Santa María (Murcia)*
- *Real Academia de Bellas Artes (Madrid)*

Contemporary Innovation

After Franco, Spain has made up for lost time and, particularly since the 1990s, the unifying theme appears to be that anything goes.

Local heroes include Santiago Calatrava, who built his reputation with swooping, bone-white bridges. In 1996 he designed the futuristic Ciudad de las Artes y las Ciencias complex in Valencia. In 2000 he built the Sondika Airport, in Bilbao, which has been nicknamed La Paloma (the Dove) for the winglike arc of its aluminium skin. Catalan Enric Miralles had a short career, dying of a brain tumour in 2000 at the age of 45, but his Mercat de Santa Caterina in Barcelona shows brilliant colour and inventive use of arches. His Gas Natural building, also in Barcelona, is a poetic skyscraper that juts both vertically and horizontally.

Robert Hughes' *Barcelona* is a thorough, erudite history of the city, with an emphasis on architecture. The Gaudí chapters provide special insight into the designer's surprisingly conservative outlook.

In 1996 Rafael Moneo won the Pritzker Prize, the greatest international honour for living architects, largely for his long-term contributions to Madrid's cityscape, such as the revamping of the Atocha railway station.

In the years since, Spain has become something of a Pritzker playground. It's perhaps this openness – even hunger – for outside creativity that marks the country's built environment today. Norman Foster designed the metro system in Bilbao, completed in 1995; the transparent, wormlike staircase shelters have come to be called *fosteritos*. But it was Frank Gehry's 1998 Museo Guggenheim Bilbao in the same city that really sparked the quirky-building fever. Now the list of contemporary landmarks includes Jean Nouvel's spangly, gherkin-shaped Torre Glòries in Barcelona; Richard Rogers' dreamy, wavy Terminal 4 at Madrid's Barajas airport; and Jürgen Mayer's Metropol Parasol in Seville.

Art

Spain has an artistic legacy rivalling that of any country in Europe. In centuries past, this impressive portfolio (dominated by Goya and Velázquez, in particular) owed much to the patronage of Spanish kings who lavished money upon the great painters of the day. In the 20th century, however, the true masters were relentlessly creative artists such as Pablo Picasso, Salvador Dalí and Joan Miró, all of whom thumbed their noses at the establishment and artistic convention.

Though he predated the golden-age peak, the Cretan Doménikos Theotokópoulos, known as El Greco (The Greek; 1541–1614), ranks among Spain's great artists for his inspired, unconventional, colourful canvases populated by gaunt figures. See his highly recognisable work in the Museo del Prado and around Toledo, where he made his career.

The Golden Century: Velázquez & Friends

The star of the 17th-century art scene, which became known as Spain's artistic golden age, was the genius court painter Diego Rodríguez de Silva Velázquez (1599–1660). Born in Seville, Velázquez later moved to Madrid as court painter and composed scenes (landscapes, royal portraits, religious subjects, snapshots of everyday life) that owe their vitality not only to his photographic eye for light, contrast and the details of royal finery but also to a compulsive interest in the humanity of his subjects so that they seem to breathe on the canvas. With Velázquez, any trace of the idealised stiffness that characterised the previous century's spiritless mannerism fell by the wayside. His masterpieces include *Las meninas* (Maids of Honour) and *La rendición de Breda* (Surrender of Breda), both in Madrid's Museo del Prado.

The mystically inclined Francisco de Zurbarán (1598–1664), a friend and contemporary of Velázquez', ended his life in poverty in Madrid, and it was only after his death that he received the acclaim that his masterpieces deserved. He is best remembered for the startling clarity and light in his portraits of monks, a series of which hangs in Madrid's Real Academia de Bellas Artes de San Fernando, with other works in the Museo del Prado.

Other masters of the era whose works hang in the Museo del Prado include José (Jusepe) de Ribera (1591–1652), who was influenced by Caravaggio and produced fine chiaroscuro works, and the Sevillan Bartolomé

Esteban Murillo (1618–82), whose soft-focus beggar images and baroque Immaculate Conceptions struck a popular chord.

Goya & the 19th Century

There was nothing in the provincial upbringing of Francisco José de Goya y Lucientes (1746–1828), who was born in a tiny village in Aragón, to suggest that he would become one of the towering figures of European art. Goya began his career as a cartoonist in the Real Fábrica de Tapices (Royal Tapestry Workshop) in Madrid. Illness in 1792 left him deaf; many critics speculate that his condition was largely responsible for his wild, often merciless style that would become increasingly unshackled from convention. By 1799 Goya was appointed Carlos IV's court painter.

Several distinct series and individual paintings mark his progress. In the last years of the 18th century he painted enigmatic masterpieces, such as *La maja vestida* (The Young Lady Dressed) and *La maja desnuda* (The Young Lady Undressed), identical portraits but for the lack of clothes in the latter. The Inquisition was not amused by the artworks, which it covered up. Nowadays all is bared in Madrid's Museo del Prado.

The arrival of the French and the war in 1808 had a profound impact on Goya. Unforgiving portrayals of the brutality of war are *El dos de mayo* (The Second of May) and, more dramatically, *El tres de mayo* (The Third of May). The latter depicts the execution of Madrid rebels by French troops.

Goya saved his most confronting paintings for the end. After he retired to the Quinta del Sordo (Deaf Man's House) in Madrid, he created the nightmarish *Pinturas negras* (Black Paintings), which now hang in Madrid's Museo del Prado. *Saturno devorando a su hijo* (Saturn Devouring His Son) captures the essence of Goya's genius, and *La romería de San Isidro* (The Pilgrimage to San Isidro) and *El akelarre* (*El gran cabrón*; The Great He-Goat) are profoundly unsettling. The former evokes a writhing mass of tortured humanity, while the latter two are dominated by the compelling individual faces of the condemned souls of Goya's creation.

Velázquez so much wanted to be made a knight of Santiago that in *Las meninas* he cheekily portrayed himself with the cross of Santiago on his vest, long before his wish was finally fulfilled.

Picasso, Dalí & Miró

In the early years of the 20th century, the genius of the mischievous *malagueño* (Málaga native) Pablo Ruiz Picasso (1881–1973) came like a thunderclap. A teenager when he moved with his family to Barcelona, Picasso was formed in an atmosphere laden with the avant-garde freedom of Modernisme.

Picasso must have been one of the most restless artists of all time. His work underwent repeated revolutions as he passed from one creative phase to another. From his gloomy Blue Period through the brighter Pink Period and on to cubism – in which he was accompanied by Madrid's Juan Gris (1887–1927) – Picasso was nothing if not surprising. Cubism, his best-known form, was inspired by his fascination with primitivism,

Outside Spain, architect Rafael Moneo is best known for the 2002 Cathedral of Our Lady of Angels, in downtown Los Angeles, California.

WHERE TO SEE GOYA

Reach into the tortured mind of one of Spain's greatest artists with the help of Robert Hughes' riveting work *Goya*. To see what all the fuss is about, Madrid's Museo del Prado has the richest collection of Goyas, but the city's Real Academia de Bellas Artes de San Fernando is also good, while the Ermita de San Antonio de la Florida has fabulous ceiling frescoes painted by the artist. Beyond Madrid, Zaragoza's Museo Goya – Colección Ibercaja has an outstanding collection of Goya prints, while Fuendetodos, the village south of Zaragoza where Goya was born, has the Casa Natal de Goya and the Museo del Grabado de Goya.

PICASSO'S GUERNICA

It was market day in the small Basque town of Gernika (Spanish name: Guernica) on the morning of 26 April 1937. At the same time that market-goers poured into the town from outlying villages, a squadron of aeroplanes was making its way to Gernika. Over the next few hours Hitler's Condor Legion, in agreement with Franco, dropped hundreds of bombs on the town and killed somewhere between a couple of hundred and well over 1000 civilians.

After the Spanish Civil War broke out in 1936, Picasso was commissioned by the Republican government in Madrid to do a large-scale painting for the Spanish pavilion at the 1937 Paris Exposition Universelle. As news filtered out about the bombing of Gernika, Picasso committed his anger to canvas. To understand the painting's earth-shattering impact at the time, it must be remembered that the attack on Gernika represented the first use of airborne military hardware to devastating effect. Thus it was that this signature work of cubism's disfiguration of the human form would become an eloquent symbol of a world's outrage at the horrors wrought upon the innocent by modern warfare.

Guernica has always been a controversial work and was initially derided by many as being more propaganda than art. The 3.5m by 7.8m painting subsequently migrated to the USA and only returned to Spain in 1981, in keeping with Picasso's wish that the painting return to Spanish shores once democracy had been restored (it went first to Picasso's preferred choice, the Museo del Prado, then to its current home, Madrid's Centro de Arte Reina Sofía). Basques believe that its true home is in the Basque Country and calls to have it moved there continue unabated. Such a move is, however, unlikely to happen any time soon, with the Reina Sofía arguing that the painting is too fragile to be moved again.

primarily African masks and early Iberian sculpture. This highly complex form reached its peak in *Guernica*, which hangs in Madrid's Centro de Arte Reina Sofía. Picasso consistently cranked out paintings, sculptures, ceramics and etchings until the day he died. A good selection of his early work can be viewed in Barcelona's Museu Picasso, while the Museo Picasso Málaga has more than 200 Picasso works.

Every February, the Madrid exhibition centre IFEMA (www.ifema.es) hosts one of the world's major contemporary art fairs, named ARCOmadrid, with around 200 Spanish and international galleries participating.

Separated from Picasso by barely a generation, two other artists reinforced the Catalan contingent in the vanguard of 20th-century art: Dalí and Miró. Although he started off dabbling in cubism, Salvador Dalí (1904–89) became more readily identified with the surrealists. This complex character's 'hand-painted dream photographs', as he called them, are virtuoso executions brimming with fine detail and nightmare images dragged up from a feverish and Freud-fed imagination. Preoccupied with Picasso's fame, Dalí built himself a reputation as an outrageous showman and shameless self-promoter. The single best display of his work can be seen at the Teatre-Museu Dalí in Figueres, but you'll also find important works in Madrid's Centro de Arte Reina Sofía, and often in exhibitions at the Museu de Cadaqués, while the Casa Museu Dalí at nearby Port Lligat gives fascinating insight into the man's eccentric private life.

Slower to find his feet, Barcelona-born Joan Miró (1893–1983) developed a joyous and almost childlike style that earned him the epithet 'the most surrealist of us all' from the French writer André Breton. His later period is his best known, characterised by the simple use of bright colours and forms in combinations of symbols that represented women, birds (the link between earth and the heavens) and stars (the unattainable heavenly world, source of imagination). The Fundació Joan Miró in Barcelona and the Fundació Pilar i Joan Miró in Palma de Mallorca are the pick of the places to see his work, with some further examples in Madrid's Centro de Arte Reina Sofía.

People & Culture

Spain's iconic forms of entertainment and public cultural expression capture the powerful passions of a nation. Flamenco is one of the world's most recognisable musical styles, an uplifting combination of sorrow and joy, while the controversial and quintessentially Spanish realm of bullfighting may leave you angry or spellbound but never indifferent. And then there's football, that obsession of a large proportion of the country's people. Put them all together and you'll find yourself looking through a window into the Spanish soul.

Flamenco

Flamenco's passion is clear to anyone who has heard its melancholic strains in the background of a crowded Spanish bar or during an uplifting live performance. At times flamenco can seem like an impenetrable world, but if you're lucky, you'll experience that uplifting moment when flamenco's raw passion and rhythm suddenly transport you to another place (known as *duende*), where joy and sorrow threaten to overwhelm you. If you do, you'll quickly become one of flamenco's lifelong devotees.

The Essential Elements

A flamenco singer is known as a *cantaor* (male) or *cantaora* (female); a dancer is a *bailaor* or *bailaora*. Most of the songs and dances are performed to a blood-rush of guitar from the *tocaor* or *tocaora* (male or female flamenco guitarist). Percussion is provided by tapping feet, clapping hands, the *cajón* (a box beaten with the hands) and sometimes castanets.

Jason Webster's book *Duende: A Journey into the Heart of Flamenco* (2013) is a gripping journey through the underbelly of flamenco.

Flamenco *coplas* (songs) come in many types, from the anguished *soleá* or the intensely despairing *siguiriya* to the livelier *alegría* or the upbeat *bulería*. The first flamenco was *cante jondo* (deep song), an anguished instrument of expression for a group on the margins of society. *Jondura* (depth) is still the essence of pure flamenco.

The traditional flamenco costumes – shawl, fan and long, frilly *bata de cola* (tail gown) for women, and flat Cordoban hats and tight black trousers for men – date from Andalucian fashions in the late 19th century.

Birth of Flamenco

Flamenco's origins have been lost to time, but most musical historians agree that it probably dates back to a fusion of songs brought to Spain by the Roma people, with music and verses from North Africa crossing into medieval Muslim Andalucía.

Flamenco as we now know it first took recognisable form in the 18th and early 19th centuries among Roma people in the lower Guadalquivir valley in western Andalucía. The Seville, Jerez de la Frontera and Cádiz axis is still considered flamenco's heartland and it's here, purists say, that you'll encounter the most authentic flamenco experience.

Flamenco Legends

The great singers of the 19th and early 20th centuries were Silverio Franconetti and La Niña de los Peines, from Seville, and Antonio Chacón and

Flamenco Playlist

- *Camarón de la Isla, La leyenda del tiempo (1979)*
- *Pata Negra, Blues de la frontera (1987)*
- *Paco de Lucía, Antología (1995)*
- *Chambao, Flamenco chill (2002)*
- *Diego El Cigala & Bebo Valdés, Lágrimas negras (2003)*
- *Paco de Lucía, Cositas buenas (2004)*
- *Enrique Morente, Sueña la Alhambra (2005)*
- *Diego El Cigala, Indestructible (2016)*

Manuel Torre, from Jerez de la Frontera. Torre's singing, legend has it, could drive people to rip their shirts open and upturn tables.

After a trough in the mid-20th century, when it seemed that the *tablaos* (touristy flamenco shows emphasising the sexy and the jolly) were in danger of taking over, *flamenco puro* got a new lease of life in the 1970s through singers such as Terremoto, La Paquera, Enrique Morente and, above all, Camarón de la Isla (p877) from San Fernando near Cádiz.

Paco de Lucía (1947–2014), from Algeciras, was the doyen of flamenco guitarists. In 1968 de Lucía began flamenco's most exciting partnership, with his friend Camarón de la Isla; together they recorded nine classic albums. De Lucía would go on to transform the flamenco guitar into an instrument of solo expression with new techniques, scales, melodies and harmonies that have gone far beyond traditional limits.

Flamenco Today

Rarely can flamenco have been as popular as it is today, and never so innovative.

Some say that Madrid-born Diego El Cigala (b 1968) is Camarón de la Isla's successor, although he turns his talent as much to flamenco-Latin crossover as to pure flamenco. This powerful singer launched onto the big stage with the extraordinary *Lágrimas negras* (2003), a wonderful collaboration with Cuban virtuoso Bebo Valdés.

Universally acclaimed is singer José Mercé (b 1955), from Jerez. Estrella Morente from Granada and Miguel Poveda from Barcelona (b 1973) are younger singers who have already carved out niches in the first rank of performers.

Dance, often the readiest of flamenco arts to cross boundaries, has reached its most adventurous horizons in the person of Joaquin Cortés, born in Córdoba in 1969. Cortés fuses flamenco with contemporary dance, ballet and jazz in spectacular shows all over the world with music at rock-concert amplification. Top-rank, more purist dancers include Sara Baras (who performs internationally with her own company) and Antonio Canales.

Among guitarists, listen out for Manolo Sanlúcar from Cádiz, as well as Vicente Amigo from Córdoba and Moraíto Chico from Jerez, who both accompany today's top singers.

Seeing Flamenco

Flamenco is easiest to catch in Seville, Jerez de la Frontera, Granada and Madrid.

Seeing flamenco can be expensive – at the *tablaos* (restaurants where flamenco is performed, often geared to a tourist audience) expect to pay €20 to €35 just to see the show and have one drink. These shows are often magnificent, spine-tingling stuff – but they sometimes lack the raw emotion of real flamenco.

Local bars are your best bet to see flamenco on the cheap, although the music and dancing in these places is sometimes more akin to mad jamming sessions than authentic *cante jondo*. Well-known flamenco neighbourhoods such as Triana in Seville or Santiago in Jerez are known as places where dancers and musicians come together to talk, drink and, if you're lucky, perform.

The best places for live performances are generally *peñas* (clubs where flamenco fans band together). The atmosphere in such places is authentic and at times very intimate, proof that flamenco feeds off an audience that knows its stuff. Most Andalucian towns have several *peñas*, and many tourist offices have lists of those that are open to visitors.

Top Flamenco Festivals

- *Festival de Jerez, Jerez de la Frontera*
- *Suma Flamenca, Madrid*
- *Noche Blanca del Flamenco, Córdoba*
- *Bienal de Flamenco, Seville*

Football

Watching *fútbol* seems to be many a Spaniard's main hobby. Hundreds of thousands of fans attend the games in the *primera división* (first division) of La Liga (the League) every weekend from August to May, with millions more following the games on TV. Spain's national team sent the country into a state of delirium by winning the World Cup in 2010 and the European Championship in 2008 and 2012.

La Liga is one of the world's best football leagues, and almost any match is worth attending, if only to experience the Spanish crowd.

Matches between eternal rivals Real Madrid and FC Barcelona – this fixture is known as El Clásico – stir even greater passions, not just because they are Spain's two biggest clubs but also because of the political relationship between Catalonia and Spain's central government. These two clubs have something approaching a duopoly on the silverware: between them they had carried off the league title 58 times by 2018 – Real Madrid 33 times, Barcelona 25. Barça, inspired by Argentine Lionel Messi, had a dream run from the mid-2000s, winning La Liga in nine out of the 14 years from 2005 to 2018.

Real Madrid, inspired by Portuguese Cristiano Ronaldo – battling Messi for the accolade of the world's best player over the past decade (they won five Ballon d'Ors apiece between 2008 and 2017) – has been giving Barça more of a run for its money of late, and it remains the most successful club in European history, having won the UEFA Champions League and its predecessor the European Cup a record 13 times, including in 2014, 2016, 2017 and 2018.

Flama (www.guiaflama.com) is a good resource for upcoming live concerts, festivals and background information.

Atlético de Madrid, Madrid's second team and Spain's third most successful club, has enjoyed something of a revival in recent years. Its La Liga title in 2014 was its 10th, and in 2014 and 2016 it reached the UEFA Champions League final, only to lose to city rivals Real on both occasions.

Bullfighting

An epic drama of blood and heroism or a cruel form of torture that has no place in modern Europe? This most enduring and controversial of Spanish traditions is all this and more: for some, an ancient ritual, an essential part of Spanish culture and compelling theatre; for others, a violent, gory spectacle that sees many thousands of bulls painfully killed

THE SHRIMP FROM THE ISLAND

Possibly the most important flamenco singer of all time, José Monge Cruz (1950–92), aka Camarón de la Isla (the Shrimp of the Island), did more to popularise flamenco in the second half of the 20th century than anyone else. One of eight children born to Roma parents – a blacksmith and a basket weaver – in the town of San Fernando (known as La Isla) near Cádiz, Camarón started his career at a young age by singing in local bars. Eventually he met that other great of flamenco, guitarist Paco de Lucía, with whom he recorded nine much-praised albums between 1969 and 1977. Later in his career Camarón worked with one of Paco's students, Tomatito.

Camarón was an intense introvert and hated publicity, but so extraordinary was his talent that publicity was to hound him everywhere he went and, so many say, eventually led him to an early grave in live-fast, die-young rock-star fashion. He was idolised for his voice by flamenco fans across the world, and it was his fellow Roma who really elevated him almost to the status of a god.

He died of lung cancer at the age of just 42. It's estimated that more than 100,000 people attended his funeral. The Shrimp's best recordings include *La leyenda del tiempo*, *Soy gitano* and *Una leyenda flamenca*.

in public in Spain every year. Ernest Hemingway – a bullfighting fan – described it as a 'wonderful nightmare'.

The Basics

The matador (more often called the *torero* in Spanish) is the star of the team. Adorned in his glittering *traje de luces* (suit of lights), he provides the fancy footwork, skill and bravery before the bull that have the crowd in raptures or in rage, depending on his (or very occasionally her) performance. A complex series of events takes place in each 20- to 30-minute clash (there are usually six fights in a program). *Peones* (the matador's 'footmen', whose job it is to test the strength of the bull) dart about with grand capes in front of the bull; horseback *picadores* (horsemen) drive lances into the bull's withers; and *banderilleros* (flagmen) charge headlong at the bull in an attempt to stab its neck. Finally, the matador kills the bull, unless the bull has managed to put him or her out of action, as very occasionally happens.

If you do plan to attend a bullfight, it's important to understand what you're about to witness. The bull's back and neck are repeatedly pierced by the lances, resulting in quite a lot of blood, as well as considerable pain and distress for the animal. The bull gradually becomes weakened through blood loss before the *torero* delivers the final sword thrust. If done properly, the bull dies instantly from this final thrust, albeit after bleeding for some time from its other wounds. If the *coup de grâce* is not delivered well, the animal dies a slow death. When this happens, the scene can be extremely disturbing.

Bullfighting Books

Death in the Afternoon by Ernest Hemingway

Death and Money in the Afternoon: A History of the Spanish Bullfight by Adrian Shubert

On Bullfighting by AL Kennedy

Into the Arena: The World of the Spanish Bullfight by Alexander Fiske-Harrison

Making Sense of Bullfighting by Reza Hosseinpour

The Bullfighting Debate

Whether or not you watch a bullfight is very much a personal decision. Aficionados say the bull is better off dying at the hands of a matador than in the *matadero* (abattoir), but detractors say the whole thing is little short of torturing the animal to death.

While bullfighting remains strong in some parts of Spain, notably Andalucía, Madrid and the two Castillas, an opinion poll in December 2015 found that only 19% of Spaniards aged between 16 and 65 supported bullfighting, while 58% opposed it.

The anti-bullfighting movement in Spain has grown steadily during the 21st century, but the pro-bullfighting lobby is strong. The governing Partido Popular explicitly supports bullfighting as part of Spain's cultural heritage. A 2012 ban on bullfighting in Catalonia was overturned by Spain's constitutional court in 2016, but bullfights did not restart in Catalonia. A number of mainly left-wing local councils in various regions have stopped bullfighting in their areas. In 2017 the Balearic Islands' regional parliament approved measures making it impossible to hold bullfights, and bullfighting has been de facto banned in the Canary Islands since 1991.

The number of bullfights in Spanish bullrings has fallen dramatically, from 3651 in 2007 to 1598 in 2016, according to government figures – a decline that the bullfighting industry attributes partly to economic recession. There has, however, been a rise in the number of cheaper *festejos populares* – other events involving varying degrees of bull torment, such as *toros embolados* (setting fire to bunches of inflammable material attached to bulls' horns).

Much of the anti-bullfighting impetus has come from groups beyond Spanish shores, among them PETA (www.peta.org.uk). But home-grown Spanish organisations are ever more active, including a political party, PACMA (www.pacma.es); the vets-against-bullfighting association AVATMA (https://avatma.org); and the animal-rights NGO ADDA (www.addaong.org).

Survival Guide

Directory A–Z

Accommodation

Seasons

What constitutes low or high season depends on where and when you're looking. Most of the year is high season in Barcelona or Madrid, especially during trade fairs that you're unlikely to know about. August can be dead in the cities, but high season along the coast.

Winter is high season in the ski resorts of the Pyrenees and low season along the coast (indeed, many coastal towns seem to shut down between November and Easter).

Weekends are high season for boutique hotels and *casas rurales* (rural homes), but low season for business hotels (which often offer generous specials) in Madrid and Barcelona.

Reservations

Reserving a room is always recommended in the high season. Finding a place to stay without booking ahead in July and August along the coast can be difficult and many places require a minimum stay of at least two nights during high season. Always check out hotel websites for discounts.

Although there's usually no need to book ahead for a room in the low or shoulder seasons (Barcelona is a notable exception), booking ahead is usually a good idea, if for no other reason than to avoid a wearisome search for a room. Most places will ask for a credit-card number or will hold the room for you until 6pm unless you have provided credit-card details as security or you have let them know that you'll be arriving later.

Online booking services such as Airbnb (www.airbnb.com) offer a range of accommodation types, from apartments and houses to private rooms in somebody's house.

Prices

Accommodation in Spain can be outrageously good value by European standards. All deals are off, however, during big festivals, when prices skyrocket – sometimes quadrupling (or more) during major events such as Pamplona's San Fermín festival.

At the lower end of the budget category there are

PRACTICALITIES

Weights & Measures The metric system is used.

Smoking Banned in all enclosed public spaces.

Newspapers The three main newspapers are the centre-left *El País* (www.elpais.com), centre-right *El Mundo* (www.elmundo.es) and right-wing *ABC* (www.abc.es); the widely available *International New York Times* includes an eight-page supplement of articles from *El País* translated into English, or check out www.elpais.com/elpais/inenglish.html.

Radio Radio Nacional de España (RNE) has Radio 1, with general interest and current-affairs programs; Radio 5, with sport and entertainment; and Radio 3 (Radio d'Espop). Stations covering current affairs include the left-leaning Cadena Ser and the right-wing COPE. The most popular commercial pop and rock stations are 40 Principales, Kiss FM, Cadena 100 and Onda Cero.

TV National channels are the state-run Televisión Española (TVE1 and La 2) and the independent Antena 3, Tele 5, Cuatro and La Sexta. Regional governments run local stations, such as Madrid's Telemadrid, Catalonia's TV-3 and Canal 33 (both in Catalan), Galicia's TVG, the Basque Country's ETB-1 and ETB-2, Valencia's Canal 9 and Andalucía's Canal Sur.

dorm beds (from around €12 per person) in hostels or private rooms with shared bathrooms in the corridor. If you're willing to pay a few euros more, there are many budget places, usually *hostales,* with good, comfortable rooms and private bathrooms. In relatively untouristed or rural areas, the prices of some boutique or other hotels can sometimes drop into the budget category, especially during low season.

Spain's midrange hotels are generally excellent; you should always have your own private bathroom, and breakfast is sometimes included in the room price. Boutique hotels, including many that occupy artistically converted historical buildings, largely fall into this category and are almost always excellent choices.

Top-end hotels range from stunning, character-filled temples to good taste to reliably luxurious international chains.

And a final word about terminology. An *habitación doble* (double room) is frequently just that: a room with two beds (which you can often shove together). If you want to be sure of a double bed *(cama matrimonial),* ask for it!

Accommodation Types

HOTELS

Spain's *hoteles* run the gamut of quality, from straightforward roadside places, bland but clean, through to charming boutique gems and on to super-luxurious hotels. Even in the cheapest hotels, rooms are likely to have an attached bathroom and there will probably be a restaurant or, at the very least, a breakfast room.

Among the more tempting hotels for those with a little fiscal room to manoeuvre are the 90 or so **paradores** (☎902 547979; www.parador.es), a state-funded chain of hotels in often stunning locations, among them towering castles and former medieval convents. Similarly, you can find beautiful hotels in restored country homes and old city mansions, and these are not always particularly expensive.

A raft of cutting-edge, hip design hotels with cool staff and a New York feel can be found in the big cities and major resort areas. At the top end you may pay more for a room with a view – especially sea views or with a *balcón* (balcony) – and will often have the option of a suite.

Many places have rooms for three, four or more people where the per-person cost is lower than in a single or double, which is good news for families.

Many of the agencies listed under Apartments, Villas & Casas Rurales (p882) also have a full portfolio of hotels.

CAMAS, FONDAS & HOSPEDAJES

At the budget end of the market, places listing accommodation use all sorts of overlapping names to describe themselves. In broad terms, the cheapest are usually places just advertising *camas* (beds), *fondas* (traditionally a basic eatery and inn combined, though one of these functions is now often missing) and *casas de huéspedes* or *hospedajes* (guesthouses).

Most of these places will be bare and basic. Bathrooms are likely to be shared, although if you're lucky you may get an in-room *lavabo* (washbasin). In winter you may need to ask for extra blankets.

PENSIONES

A *pensión* is usually a small step up from the *camas, fondas* and *hospedajes* in standard and price. Some cheap establishments forget to provide soap, toilet paper or towels. Don't hesitate to ask for these necessities. On the other hand, many are charming, family-run places with clean rooms and willing service.

HOSTALES

Hostales are a step up from *pensiones* and operate as simple, small hotels – you'll find them everywhere across the country and the better ones can be bright and spotless, with rooms boasting full en-suite bathrooms – *baño privado,* most often with a *ducha* (shower) rather than bathtub, and usually a TV, air-conditioning and/or heating.

HOSTELS

Spain has more than 350 hostels. These are often the cheapest places for lone travellers, but two people can usually get a better double room elsewhere for a similar price.

The hostel experience in Spain varies widely. Some hostels are only moderate value, lacking in privacy, often heavily booked by school groups, and with night-time curfews and no cooking facilities (although if there's nowhere to cook there's usually a cafeteria). Others, however, are conveniently located, open 24 hours and composed mainly of small dorms, often with a private bathroom. An increasing number have rooms adapted for people with disabilities.

Some even occupy fine historic buildings.

Prices at hostels often depend on the season, and vary from about €15 to €30. In some hostels the price includes breakfast. A few hostels require you to rent sheets (around €2 to €5 for your stay) if you don't have your own or a sleeping bag.

Keep in mind that some of Spain's hostels are geared towards Spain's youth market: the **Red Española de Albergues Juveniles** (www.reaj.com) require you to have an HI card or a membership card from your home country's youth hostel association, though you can obtain an HI card in Spain at most hostels.

Generally more appealing for foreign travellers are hostel-style places not connected with HI or REAJ. These have individual rooms as well as the more typical dormitory options. A good resource for seeking out hostels, affiliated or otherwise, is **Hostel World** (www.hostelworld.com).

Finally, you will sometimes find independent *albergues* offering basic dormitory accommodation for around €10 to €20, usually in villages in areas that attract plenty of Spanish walkers and climbers. These are not specifically youth hostels – although the clientele tends to be under 35. They're a kind of halfway house between a youth hostel and a *refugio*. Some will rent you sheets for a couple of euros, if you need them.

REFUGIOS

Refugios (hostels) for walkers and climbers are liberally scattered around most of the popular mountain areas (especially the Pyrenees), except in Andalucía, which has only a handful. They're mostly run by mountaineering and walking organisations.

Accommodation, usually bunks squeezed into a dorm, is often on a first-come, first-served basis, although for some *refugios* you can book ahead. In busy seasons (July and August in most areas) they can fill up quickly, and you should try to book in advance or arrive by mid-afternoon to be sure of a place. Prices per person range from nothing to €15 or more a night.

Many *refugios* have a bar and offer meals (dinner typically costs €10 to €16), as well as a cooking area (but no cooking equipment). Blankets are usually provided, but you'll have to bring any other sheets or sleeping bag (or rent it at the *refugio*). Bring a torch too.

The Pyrenees are particularly well served with *refugios;* check out the following:

Albergues & Refugios de Aragón (www.alberguesyrefugiosdearagon.com) To make reservations in *refugios* and *albergues.*

Catalan Pyrenees Several organisations are worth checking out for info and bookings: the Federació d'Entitats Excursionistes da Catalunya (FEEC; www.feec.cat), the Centre Excursionista de Catalunya (CEC; http://cec.cat) and La Central de Refugis (www.la centralde refugis.com).

APARTMENTS, VILLAS & CASAS RURALES

Throughout Spain you can rent self-catering apartments and houses from one night upwards. Villas and houses are widely available on the main holiday coasts and in popular country areas.

A simple one-bedroom apartment in a coastal resort for two or three people might cost as little as €40 per night, although more often you'll be looking at nearly twice that much, and prices jump even further in high season.

More luxurious options with a swimming pool might come in at anything between €200 and €400 for four people.

Rural tourism has become immensely popular, with accommodation available in many new and often charming *casas rurales*.

These are usually comfortably renovated village houses or farmhouses with a handful of rooms – check whether you're renting a room or the whole house (which is more common) for *casas rurales*.

They often go by other names, such as *cases de pagès* in Catalonia, *casas de aldea* in Asturias, *posadas* and *casonas* in Cantabria and so on. Some just provide rooms, while others offer meals or self-catering accommodation.

Lower-end prices typically hover around €30/50 for a single/double per night, but classy boutique establishments can easily charge €100 or more for a double. Many are rented out by the week.

Agencies include the following:

Associació Agroturisme Balear (www.rusticbooking.com)

SLEEPING PRICE RANGES

The following price ranges refer to a double room with private bathroom:

€ less than €65

€€ from €65 to €140

€€€ more than €140

The price ranges for Madrid and Barcelona are inevitably higher:

€ less than €75

€€ from €75 to €200

€€€ more than €200

Casas Cantabricas (www.casas.co.uk)

Cases Rurals de Catalunya (www.casesrurals.com)

Escapada Rural (www.escapadarural.com)

Fincas 4 You (www.fincas4you.com)

Owners Direct (www.ownersdirect.co.uk)

Ruralka (www.ruralka.com)

Rustic Rent (www.rusticrent.com)

Rusticae (www.rusticae.es)

Secret Places (www.secretplaces.com)

Top Rural (www.toprural.com)

Traum Ferienwohnungen (www.traum-ferienwohnungen.de)

Villas 4 You (www.villas4you.co.uk)

Vintage (vintagetravel.co.uk)

CAMPING & CARAVAN PARKS

Spain has around 1000 officially graded *campings* (camping grounds). Some of these are well located in woodland or near beaches or rivers, but others are on the outskirts of towns or along highways. Few of them are near city centres, and camping isn't particularly convenient if you're relying on public transport.

Tourist offices can always direct you to the nearest camping ground. Camping grounds are officially rated as 1st class (1ªC), 2nd class (2ªC) or 3rd class (3ªC). There are also some that are not officially graded, usually equivalent to 3rd class.

Facilities generally range from reasonable to very good, although any camping ground can be crowded and noisy at busy times (especially July and August). Even a 3rd-class camping ground is likely to have hot showers, electrical hook-ups and a cafe. The best ones have heated swimming pools, supermarkets, restaurants, laundry service, children's playgrounds and tennis courts.

Camping grounds usually charge per person, per tent and per vehicle – typically €5 to €10 for each. Children usually pay less than adults.

Many camping grounds close from around October to Easter. You occasionally come across a *zona de acampada* or *área de acampada*, a country camping ground with minimal facilities (maybe just tap water or a couple of barbecues), little or no supervision and little or no charge.

If it's in an environmentally protected area, you may need to obtain permission from the local environmental authority to camp there. With certain exceptions – such as many beaches and environmentally protected areas and a few municipalities that ban it – it is legal to camp outside camping grounds (but not within 1km of official ones).

Signs usually indicate where wild camping is not allowed. If in doubt, you can always check with tourist offices. You'll need permission to camp on private land.

Useful websites:

Campings Online (www.campingsonline.com/espana) Booking service.

Campinguía (www.campinguia.com) Comments (mostly in Spanish) and links.

Guía Camping (www.guiacampingfecc.com) Online version of the annual *Guía Camping* (€15), which is available in bookshops around the country.

MONASTERIES

An offbeat possibility is staying in a monastery. In spite of the expropriations of the 19th century and a sometimes rough run in the 20th, numerous monastic orders have survived across the country.

Some offer rooms to outsiders – often fairly austere monks' or nuns' cells.

Monastery accommodation is generally a single-sex arrangement, and the idea in quite a few is to seek refuge from the outside world and indulge in quiet contemplation and meditation. On occasion, where the religious order continues ancient tradition by working on farmland, orchards and/or vineyards, you may have the opportunity (or there may be the expectation) to work, too.

Useful resources include the following:

Alojamientos en Monasterios (www.alojamientomonasterios.com)

Alojamientos Monásticos de España A guidebook to Spain's monasteries by Javier de Sagastizabal and José Antonio Egaña, although it's in desperate need of an update (the latest edition dates to 2003).

Customs Regulations

Duty-free allowances for travellers entering Spain from outside the EU include 2L of wine (or 1L of wine and 1L of spirits), and 200 cigarettes or 50 cigars or 250g of tobacco.

There are no restrictions on the import of duty-paid items into Spain from other EU countries for personal use. You *can* buy VAT-free articles at airport shops when travelling between EU countries.

Discount Cards

At museums, never hesitate to ask if there are discounts for students, young people, children, families or seniors.

Seniors Reduced prices for people over 60, 63 or 65 (depending on the place) at various museums and attractions (sometimes restricted to EU citizens) and occasionally on transport.

Student cards Discounts (usually half the normal fee) for students. You will need some kind of identification (eg an International Student Identity Card; www.isic.org) to prove student status. Not accepted everywhere.

Youth cards Travel, sights and youth-hostel discounts with the European Youth Card (www.eyca.org), known as Carné Joven in Spain.

Electricity

Spain uses the two-pin continental plugs in use elsewhere in Europe. In Gibraltar, both these and the three-square-pin plugs from the UK are used, though the latter is more common.

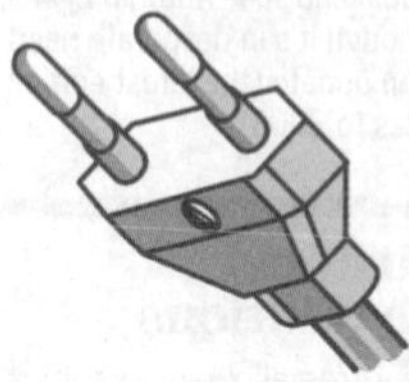

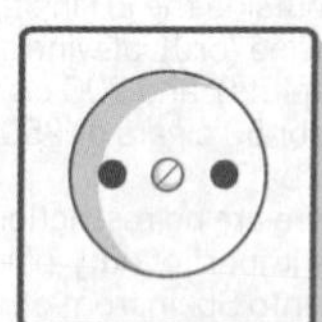

Type C
230V/50Hz

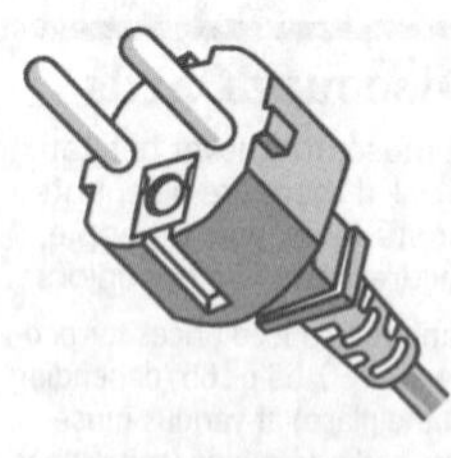

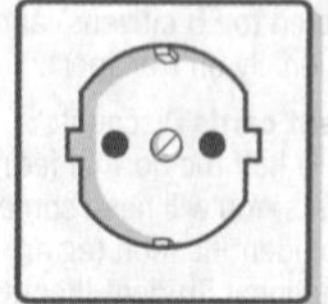

Type F
230V/50Hz

Embassies & Consulates

The embassies are located in Madrid. Some countries also maintain consulates in major cities, particularly in Barcelona.

Australian Embassy (☎91 353 66 00; www.spain.embassy.gov.au; 24th fl, Torre Espacio, Paseo de la Castellana 259D, Madrid)

Canadian Embassy (☎91 382 84 00; www.canadainternational.gc.ca/spain-espagne; Torre Espacio, Paseo de la Castellana 259D, Madrid)

Canadian Consulate (☎93 270 36 14; www.canadainternational.gc.ca; Plaça de Catalunya 9, Barcelona; ⊙9am-12.30pm Mon-Fri; Ⓜ Catalunya)

Canadian Consulate (☎95 222 33 46; Plaza de la Malagueta 2, Málaga; ⊙10am-1pm Mon-Fri)

Dutch Embassy (☎91 353 75 00; www.paisesbajosmundial.nl/paises/espana; Torre Espacio, Paseo de la Castellana 259D, Madrid)

French Embassy (☎91 423 89 00; www.ambafrance-es.org; Calle de Salustiano Olózaga 9, Madrid; Ⓜ Retiro)

French Consulate (☎93 270 30 00; www.barcelone.consulfrance.org; Ronda de la Universitat 22bis, Barcelona; ⊙9am-1pm Mon-Fri; Ⓜ Catalunya) Further consulates in Bilbao and Seville.

German Embassy (☎91 557 90 00; www.spanien.diplo.de; Calle de Fortuny 8; Ⓜ Rubén Darío)

German Consulate (☎93 292 10 00; www.spanien.diplo.de; Torre Mapfre, Calle de Marina 16-18, Barcelona; ⊙8.30am-noon & 2-3.30pm Mon-Thu, 8.30am-noon Fri; Ⓜ Ciutadella Vila Olímpica) Further consulates in Málaga and Palma de Mallorca.

Irish Embassy (☎91 436 40 93; www.dfa.ie/irish-embassy/Spain; Paseo de la Castellana 46, Madrid; Ⓜ Rubén Darío)

Japanese Embassy (☎91 590 76 00; www.es.emb-japan.go.jp; Calle de Serrano 109; Ⓜ Gregorio Marañon)

Moroccan Embassy (☎91 563 10 90; www.embajada-marruecos.es; Calle de Serrano 179, Madrid; Ⓜ Santo Domingo) Further consulates-general in Algeciras, Almería, Bilbao, Seville, Tarragona and Valencia.

New Zealand Embassy (☎91 523 02 26; www.mfat.govt.nz; 3rd fl, Calle de Pinar 7, Madrid; Ⓜ Gregorio Marañon)

UK Embassy (☎91 714 63 00; www.gov.uk/government/world/spain; Torre Espacio, Paseo de la Castellana 259D, Madrid)

UK Consulate (☎93 366 62 00; www.gov.uk; Avinguda Diagonal 477, Barcelona; ⊙8.30am-1.30pm Mon-Fri; Ⓜ Hospital Clínic) Further consulates in Alicante, Bilbao, Ibiza, Palma de Mallorca and Málaga.

US Embassy (☎91 587 22 00; https://es.usembassy.gov/es; Calle de Serrano 75, Madrid; Ⓜ Nuñez de Balboa)

US Consulate (☎93 280 22 27; www.usembassy.gov/spain; Passeig de la Reina Elisenda de Montcada 23, Barcelona; ⊙9am-1pm Mon-Fri; Ⓡ FGC Reina Elisenda) Consular agencies in A Coruña, Fuengirola, Palma de Mallorca, Seville and Valencia.

Health

Spain has an excellent health-care system.

Availability & Cost of Health Care

If you need an ambulance, call 061 or the general emergency number 112. For emergency treatment, go straight to the *urgencias* (casualty) section of the nearest hospital.

Farmacias offer valuable advice and sell over-the-counter medication. In Spain, a system of *farmacias de guardia* (duty pharmacies) operates so that each district has one open all the time.

When a pharmacy is closed, it posts the name of

the nearest open one on the door.

Medical costs are lower in Spain than in many other European countries, but can still mount quickly if you are uninsured. Costs if you attend casualty range from nothing (in some regions) to around €80.

Altitude Sickness

➡ If you're hiking at altitude, altitude sickness may be a risk. Lack of oxygen at high altitudes (over 2500m) affects most people to some extent.

➡ Symptoms of Acute Mountain Sickness (AMS) usually develop during the first 24 hours at altitude but may be delayed by up to three weeks.

➡ Mild symptoms include headache, lethargy, dizziness, difficulty sleeping and loss of appetite.

➡ AMS may become more severe without warning and can be fatal.

➡ Severe symptoms include breathlessness, a dry, irritative cough (which may progress to the production of pink, frothy sputum), severe headache, lack of coordination and balance, confusion, irrational behaviour, vomiting, drowsiness and unconsciousness.

➡ Treat mild symptoms by resting at the same altitude until recovery, usually for a day or two.

➡ Paracetamol or aspirin can be taken for headaches.

➡ If symptoms persist or become worse, immediate descent is necessary; even 500m can help.

➡ Drug treatments should never be used to avoid descent or to enable further ascent.

Bites & Stings

➡ Be wary of the hairy reddish-brown caterpillars of the pine processionary moth – touching the caterpillars' hairs sets off a severely irritating skin reaction.

➡ Some Spanish centipedes have a very nasty but non-fatal sting.

➡ Jellyfish, which have stinging tentacles, are an increasing problem at beaches along the Mediterranean coastline.

➡ Lataste's viper is the only venomous snake that is even relatively common in Spain. It has a triangular head, grows up to 75cm long, and is grey with a zigzag pattern. It lives in dry, rocky areas, away from humans. Its bite can be fatal and needs to be treated with a serum, which state clinics in major towns keep in stock.

Hypothermia

➡ The weather in Spain's mountains can be extremely changeable at any time of year.

➡ Proper preparation will reduce the risks of getting hypothermia: always carry waterproof garments and warm layers, and inform others of your route.

➡ Hypothermia starts with shivering, loss of judgment and clumsiness; unless warming occurs, the sufferer deteriorates into apathy, confusion and coma.

➡ Prevent further heat loss by seeking shelter, wearing warm dry clothing, drinking hot sweet drinks and sharing body warmth.

Tap Water

Tap water is generally safe to drink in Spain, although there are exceptions (Ibiza among them). If you are in any doubt, ask, *¿Es potable el agua (del grifo)?* (Is the (tap) water drinkable?).

Do not drink water from rivers or lakes as it may contain bacteria or viruses that can cause diarrhoea or vomiting.

Insurance

A travel-insurance policy to cover theft, loss, medical problems and cancellation or delays to your travel arrangements is a good idea.

Paying for your ticket with a credit card can often provide limited travel-accident insurance and you may be able to reclaim the payment if the operator doesn't deliver.

Worldwide travel insurance is available at www.lonelyplanet.com/travel-insurance. You can buy, extend and claim online anytime – even if you're already on the road.

Internet Access

Wi-fi is almost universally available at hotels, as well as in some cafes, restaurants and airports; usually (but not always) it's free.

Connection speed often varies from room to room in hotels (and coverage is sometimes restricted to the hotel lobby), so always ask when you check in or make your reservation if you need a good connection.

Some tourist offices may have a list of wi-fi hot spots in their area.

Language Courses

Among the more popular places to learn Spanish are Barcelona, Granada, Madrid,

EATING PRICE RANGES

The following price brackets refer to a standard main dish:

€ less than €12

€€ from €12 to €20

€€€ more than €20

Salamanca and Seville. In these places and elsewhere, Spanish universities offer good-value language courses.

The **Escuela Oficial de Idiomas** is a nationwide language institution where you can learn Spanish and other local languages. Classes can be large and busy but are generally fairly cheap. There are branches in many major cities.

Private language schools as well as universities cater for a wide range of levels, course lengths, times of year, intensity and special requirements. Many courses have a cultural component as well as language. University courses often last a semester, although some are as short as two weeks or as long as a year.

Private colleges can be more flexible. One with a good reputation is **donQuijote** (www.donquijote.com), with branches in Barcelona, Granada, Madrid, Salamanca and Valencia.

It's also worth finding out whether your course will lead to any formal certificate of competence. The Diplomas de Español como Lengua Extranjera (DELE) are recognised by Spain's Ministry of Education.

Legal Matters

If you're arrested, you will be allotted the free services of an *abogado de oficio* (duty solicitor), who may speak only Spanish. You're also entitled to make a phone call. If you use this to contact your embassy or consulate, the staff will probably be able to do no more than refer you to a lawyer who speaks your language. If you end up in court, the authorities are obliged to provide a translator.

In theory, you are supposed to have your national ID card or passport with you at all times. If asked for it by the police, you are supposed to be able to produce it on the spot. In practice it is rarely an issue and many people choose to leave passports in hotel safes.

The Policía Local or Policía Municipal operates at a local level and deals with such issues as traffic infringements and minor crime.

The Policía Nacional (091) is the state police force, dealing with major crime and operating primarily in the cities.

The military-linked Guardia Civil (created in the 19th century to deal with banditry) is largely responsible for highway patrols, borders, security, major crime and terrorism. Several regions have their own police forces, such as the Mossos d'Esquadra in Catalonia and the Ertzaintza in the Basque Country.

Cannabis is legal but only for personal use and in very small quantities. Public consumption of any illicit drug is illegal.

Travellers entering Spain from Morocco should be prepared for drug searches, especially if you have a vehicle.

LGBTI Travellers

Spain has become perhaps the most gay-friendly country in southern Europe. Homosexuality is legal, and same-sex marriages were legalised in 2005 – the move was extremely popular but met with opposition from the country's powerful Catholic Church.

In rural areas, lesbians and gay men generally keep a fairly low profile, but are quite open in the cities. Madrid, Barcelona, Sitges, Torremolinos and Ibiza have particularly lively scenes.

Sitges is a major destination on the international gay-party circuit; gays take a leading role in the wild **Carnaval** (www.carnavaldesitges.com; ⌚Feb/Mar) there.

There are also gay parades, marches and events in several cities on and around the last Saturday in June, when Madrid's **gay and lesbian pride march** (www.orgullolgtb.org; ⌚Jun) takes place.

Madrid also hosts the annual **Les Gai Cine Mad** (☎915 930 540; www.lesgaicinemad.com; ⌚late Oct/early Nov) festival, a celebration of lesbian, gay and transsexual films.

Resources

In addition to the following resources, Barcelona's tourist board publishes *Barcelona: The Official Gay and Lesbian Tourist Guide* biannually, while Madrid's tourist office has useful information on its website (www.esmadrid.com/lgtb-madrid).

Chueca (www.chueca.com) Useful gay portal with extensive links.

GayBarcelona (www.gaybarcelona.com) News and views and an extensive listings section covering bars, saunas, shops and more in Barcelona and Sitges.

Gay Iberia (www.gayiberia.com) Gay guides to Barcelona, Madrid, Sitges and 26 other Spanish cities.

Gay Madrid 4 U (www.gaymadrid4u.com) A good overview of Madrid's gay bars and nightclubs.

Gay Seville (www.patroc.com/seville) Gay guide to Andalucía's capital.

NightTours.com (www.nighttours.com) A reasonably good guide to gay nightlife and other attractions in Madrid, Barcelona and 18 other Spanish locations.

Shangay (www.shangay.com) For news, upcoming events, reviews and contacts. It also publishes *Shanguide*, a Madrid-centric biweekly magazine jammed with listings (including saunas and hard-core clubs) and contact ads. Its companion publication *Shangay Express* is better for articles with a handful of listings and ads. They're available in gay bookshops, and gay and gay-friendly bars.

Universo Gay (www.guia.universogay.com) A little bit of everything.

Organisations

Casal Lambda (Map p266; ☎93 319 55 50; www.lambda.cat; Avinguda del Marquès d'Argentera 22; ⏲5-9pm Mon-Sat; ⓂBarceloneta) A gay and lesbian social, cultural and information centre in Barcelona's La Ribera.

Colectivo de Gais y Lesbianas de Madrid (Cogam; ☎91 523 00 70, 91 522 45 17; www.cogam.es; Calle de la Puebla 9; ⏲5-9pm Mon-Fri, 6-8pm Sat; ⓂCallao, Gran Vía) Offers activities and has an information office and social centre.

Federación Estatal de Lesbianas, Gays, Transexuales & Bisexuales (☎91 360 46 05; www.felgtb.org; 4th fl, Calle de las Infantas 40; ⏲8am-8pm Mon-Thu, 8am-3.30pm Fri; ⓂGran Vía) A national advocacy group, based in Madrid, that played a leading role in lobbying for the legalisation of gay marriage.

Fundación Triángulo (☎91 593 05 40; www.fundaciontriangulo.org; 1st fl, Calle de Meléndez Valdés 52; ⏲10am-2pm & 4-8pm Mon-Fri; ⓂArgüelles) One of several sources of information on gay issues in Madrid.

Maps

Spain has some excellent maps if you're driving around the country – many are available from petrol stations. Topographical and hiking maps are available from specialist stores.

Small-Scale Maps

Some of the best maps for travellers are by Michelin, which produces the 1:1,000,000 *Spain Portugal* map and six 1:400,000 regional maps covering the whole country. These are all pretty accurate and are updated regularly, even down to the state of minor country roads. Also good are the **GeoCenter maps** published by Germany's RV Verlag.

Probably the best physical map of Spain is *Península Ibérica, Baleares y Canarias* published by the **Centro Nacional de Información Geográfica** (☎91 597 95 14; www.cnig.es; Calle del General Ibáñez de Ibero 3; ⓂGuzmán El Bueno), the publishing arm of the Instituto Geográfico Nacional (www.ign.es). Ask for it in good bookshops.

Walking Maps

Useful for hiking and exploring some areas (particularly in the Pyrenees) are **Editorial Alpina's** *Guía Cartográfica* and *Guía Excursionista y Turística* series.

The series combines information booklets in Spanish (and sometimes Catalan) with detailed maps at scales ranging from 1:25,000 to 1:50,000. They are an indispensable tool for hikers (and some come in English and German), but they have their inaccuracies.

The **Institut Cartogràfic de Catalunya** puts out some decent maps for hiking in the Catalan Pyrenees that are often better than their Editorial Alpina counterparts.

Remember that for hiking only, maps scaled at 1:25,000 are seriously useful. The **CNIG** (www.cnig.es) also covers most of the country in 1:25,000 sheets.

You can often pick up Editorial Alpina publications and CNIG maps at bookshops near trekking areas, and at specialist bookshops such as the following:

Altaïr (Map p278; ☎93 342 71 71; www.altair.es; Gran Via de les Corts Catalanes 616; ⏲10am-8.30pm Mon-Sat; 📶; ⓂCatalunya) In Barcelona.

De Viaje (Map p104; ☎91 577 98 99; www.deviaje.com; Calle de Serrano 41; ⏲10am-8.30pm Mon-Fri, 10.30am-2.30pm & 5-8pm Sat; ⓂSerrano) In Madrid.

La Tienda Verde (☎91 535 38 10; www.tiendaverde.es; Calle de Maudes 23; ⏲10am-2pm & 5-8pm Mon-Fri, 10am-2pm Sat; ⓂCuatro Caminos) In Madrid.

Librería Desnivel (Map p88; ☎91 429 12 81; www.libreriadesnivel.com; Plaza de Matute 6; ⏲10am-8.30pm Mon-Fri, 11am-8pm Sat; ⓂAntón Martín) In Madrid.

Money

The most convenient way to bring your money is in the form of a debit or credit card, with some extra cash in case of an emergency.

Many credit and debit cards can be used for withdrawing money from *cajeros automáticos* (ATMs) that display the relevant symbols such as Visa, MasterCard, Cirrus etc. There is usually a charge (around 1.5% to 2%) on ATM cash withdrawals abroad.

Cash

Most banks and building societies will exchange major foreign currencies and offer the best rates. Ask about commissions and take your passport.

Credit & Debit Cards

These can be used to pay for most purchases. You'll often be asked to show your passport or some other form of identification. Among the most widely accepted are Visa, MasterCard, American Express (Amex), Cirrus, Maestro, Plus and JCB. Diners Club is less widely accepted.

If your card is lost, stolen or swallowed by an ATM, you can call the following (mostly freecall) telephone numbers to have an immediate stop put on its use: **Amex** (☎900 814500), **Diners Club** (☎902 401112), **MasterCard** (☎900 971231) and **Visa** (☎900 991124).

Moneychangers

You can exchange both cash and travellers cheques at *cambio* (exchange) offices. Generally they offer longer opening hours and quicker service than banks, but worse exchange rates and higher commissions.

Taxes & Refunds

➡ In Spain, value-added tax (VAT) is known as IVA (ee-ba; *impuesto sobre el valor añadido*).

➡ Hotel rooms and restaurant meals attract an additional 10% (usually included in the quoted price but always ask); most other items have 21% added.

Visitors are entitled to a refund of the 21% IVA on purchases costing more than €90.16 from any shop, if they are taking them out of the EU within three months. Ask the shop for a cash-back (or similar) refund form showing the price and IVA paid for each item, and identifying the vendor and purchaser. Present your IVA refund form to the customs booth for refunds at the airport, port or border when you leave the EU.

Post

Correos (☎902 197197; www.correos.es), the Spanish postal system, is generally reliable, if a little slow at times.

Delivery times are erratic but ordinary mail to other Western European countries can take up to a week (although often as little as three days); to North America up to 10 days; and to Australia or New Zealand between 10 days and three weeks.

➡ *Sellos* (stamps) are sold at most *estancos* (tobacconists; look for 'Tabacos' in yellow letters on a maroon background), as well as at post offices.

➡ A postcard or letter weighing up to 20g costs €1.25 from Spain to other European countries, and €1.35 to the rest of the world.

➡ For a full list of prices for *certificado* (certified) and *urgente* (express post), go to www.correos.es and click on 'Tarifas'.

Public Holidays

The two main periods when Spaniards go on holiday are Semana Santa (the week leading up to Easter Sunday) and July and August. At these times accommodation in resorts can be scarce and transport heavily booked, but other places are often half-empty.

There are at least 14 official holidays a year – some observed nationwide, some locally. When a holiday falls close to a weekend,

Spaniards like to make a *puente* (bridge), meaning they take the intervening day off too. Occasionally when some holidays fall close, they make an *acueducto* (aqueduct)! Here are the national holidays:

Año Nuevo (New Year's Day) 1 January

Viernes Santo (Good Friday) March/April

Fiesta del Trabajo (Labour Day) 1 May

La Asunción (Feast of the Assumption) 15 August

Fiesta Nacional de España (National Day) 12 October

La Inmaculada Concepción (Feast of the Immaculate Conception) 8 December

Navidad (Christmas) 25 December

Regional governments set five holidays and local councils two more. Common dates include the following:

Epifanía (Epiphany) or **Día de los Reyes Magos** (Three Kings' Day) 6 January

Jueves Santo (Good Thursday) March/April; not observed in Catalonia and Valencia.

Corpus Christi June; the Thursday after the eighth Sunday after Easter Sunday.

Día de Santiago Apóstol (Feast of St James the Apostle) 25 July

Día de Todos los Santos (All Saints Day) 1 November

Día de la Constitución (Constitution Day) 6 December

Safe Travel

Most visitors to Spain never feel remotely threatened, but enough have unpleasant experiences to warrant some care. The main thing to be wary of is petty theft (which may not seem so petty if your passport, cash, travellers cheques, credit card and camera go missing).

➡ In cities, especially Madrid and Barcelona, stick to areas with plenty of people around and avoid deserted streets.

➡ Keep valuables concealed or locked away in your hotel room.

➡ Try not to look like a tourist (eg don't consult maps in crowded tourist areas).

➡ Be wary of pickpockets in areas with plenty of other tourists.

Scams

There must be 50 ways to lose your wallet. As a rule, talented petty thieves work in groups and capitalise on distraction. Tricks usually involve a team of two or more (sometimes one of them an attractive woman to distract male victims). While one attracts your attention, the other empties your pockets.

More imaginative strikes include someone dropping a milk mixture onto the victim from a balcony. Immediately a concerned citizen comes up to help you brush off what you assume to be pigeon poo, and thus suitably occupied, you don't notice the contents of your pockets slipping away.

Beware: not all thieves look like thieves. Watch out for an old classic: the ladies offering flowers for good luck. We don't know how they do it, but if you get too involved in a friendly chat with these people, your pockets almost always wind up empty.

On some highways, especially the AP7 from the French border to Barcelona, bands of thieves occasionally operate. Beware of men trying to distract you in rest areas, and don't stop along the highway if people driving alongside indicate you have a problem with the car. While one inspects the rear of the car with you, his pals will empty your vehicle.

Another trick has them puncturing tyres of cars stopped in rest areas, then following and 'helping' the victim when they stop to change the wheel. Hire cars and those with foreign plates are especially targeted. When you do call in at highway rest stops, try to park close to the buildings and leave nothing of value in view. If you do stop to change a tyre and find yourself getting unsolicited aid, make sure doors are all locked and don't allow yourself to be distracted.

Even parking your car can be fraught. In some towns fairly dodgy self-appointed parking attendants operate in central areas where you may want to park. They will direct you frantically to a spot. If possible, ignore them and find your own. If unavoidable, you may well want to pay them some token not to scratch or otherwise damage your vehicle after you've walked away.

You definitely don't want to leave anything visible in the car (or open the boot – trunk – if you intend to leave luggage or anything else in it) under these circumstances.

Theft

Theft is mostly a risk in tourist resorts, big cities and when you first arrive in a new city and may be off your guard. You are at your most vulnerable when dragging around luggage to or from your hotel. Barcelona, Madrid and Seville have the worst reputations for theft and, on very rare occasions, muggings.

Anything left lying on the beach can disappear in a flash when your back is turned. At night avoid dingy, empty city alleys and backstreets, or anywhere that just doesn't feel 100% safe.

Report thefts to the national police – visit www.policia.es for a full list of *comisarías* (police stations) around the country. You are unlikely to recover your goods but you need to make a formal *denuncia* for insurance purposes.

To avoid endless queues at the *comisaría*, you can make the report by phone (902 102112) in various languages or online at www.policia.es (click on 'denunciar por Internet') although the instructions are in Spanish only. The following day you go to the station of your choice to pick up and sign the report, without queuing.

Telephone

Local SIM cards can be used in European/Australian phones. Other phones must be set to roaming to work – be wary of roaming charges, although these should no longer apply if you have an EU phone.

Collect Calls

Placing *una llamada a cobro revertido* (an international collect call) is simple. Dial 99 00 followed by the code for the country you're calling.

Mobile Phones

Spain uses GSM 900/1800, which is compatible with the rest of Europe and Australia but not with the North American system unless you have a GSM/GPRS-compatible phone (some AT&T and T-Mobile cell phones may work), or the system used in Japan. From those countries, you will need to travel with a tri-band or quadric-band phone.

You can buy SIM cards and prepaid time in Spain for your mobile phone, provided you own a GSM, dual- or tri-band cellular phone. This only works if your national phone hasn't been code-blocked; check before leaving home.

All the Spanish mobile-phone companies (Telefónica's **MoviStar**, **Orange** and **Vodafone**) offer *prepagado* (prepaid) accounts for mobiles. The

GOVERNMENT TRAVEL ADVICE

The following government websites offer travel advisory services and information for travellers:

Australian Department of Foreign Affairs and Trade (www.smartraveller.gov.au)

Global Affairs Canada (www.voyage.gc.ca)

Ministère de l'Europe et des Affaires étrangères (www.diplomatie.gouv.fr/fr/conseils-aux-voyageurs)

Auswärtiges Amt, Länder und Reiseinformationen (www.auswaertiges-amt.de/de/)

Italian Ministero degli Affari Esteri e della Cooperazione Internazionale (www.viaggiaresicuri.mae.aci.it)

Ministerie van Buitenlandse Zaken (www.rijksoverheid.nl/ministeries/ministerie-van-buitenlandse-zaken#ref-minbuza.nl)

New Zealand Ministry of Foreign Affairs and Trade (www.safetravel.govt.nz)

UK Foreign & Commonwealth Office (www.gov.uk/foreign-travel-advice)

US Department of State (www.travel.state.gov)

SIM card costs from €10, to which you add some prepaid phone time. Phone outlets are scattered across the country. You can then top up in their shops or by buying cards in outlets, such as *estancos* (tobacconists) and newspaper kiosks.

Pepephone (www.pepephone.com) is another option.

If you're from the EU, there is now EU-wide roaming so that call and data plans for mobile phones from any EU country should be valid in Spain without any extra roaming charges. If you're from elsewhere, check with your mobile provider for information on roaming charges.

Phone Codes

Mobile (cell) phone numbers start with 6. Numbers starting with 900 are national toll-free numbers, while those starting with 901 to 905 come with varying costs. A common one is 902, which is a national standard rate number, but which can only be dialled from within Spain. In a similar category are numbers starting with 800, 803, 806 and 807.

International access code 00

Spain country code 34

There are no local area codes.

Phonecards

Cut-rate prepaid phonecards can be good value for international calls. They can be bought from *estancos*, small grocery stores, *locutorios* (private call centres) and newspaper kiosks in the main cities and tourist resorts.

If possible, try to compare rates. Many of the private operators offer better deals than those offered by Telefónica. *Locutorios* that specialise in cut-rate overseas calls have popped up all over the place in bigger cities.

Once widespread, but now almost non-existent, blue payphones are easy to use for international and domestic calls. They accept coins, *tarjetas telefónicas* (phonecards) issued by the national phone company Telefónica and, in some cases, various credit cards.

Time

Time zone Same as most of Western Europe (GMT/UTC plus one hour during winter and GMT/UTC plus two hours during the daylight-saving period).

Daylight saving From the last Sunday in March to the last Sunday in October.

UK, Ireland, Portugal & Canary Islands One hour behind mainland Spain.

Morocco Morocco is on GMT/UTC year-round. From the last Sunday in March to the last Sunday in October, subtract two hours from Spanish time to get Moroccan time; the rest of the year, subtract one hour.

USA Spanish time is USA Eastern Time plus six hours and USA Pacific Time plus nine hours.

Australia During the Australian winter (Spanish summer), subtract eight hours from Australian Eastern Standard Time to get Spanish time; during the Australian summer, subtract 10 hours. For most of October, it's nine hours.

12- and 24-hour clock Although the 24-hour clock is used in most official situations, you'll find people generally use the 12-hour clock in everyday conversation.

Toilets

Public toilets are rare to non-existent in Spain and it's not really the done thing to go into a bar or cafe solely to use the toilet; ordering a quick coffee is a small price to pay for relieving the problem.

Otherwise you can usually get away with it in larger, crowded places where they can't really keep track of who's coming and going.

Another option in some larger cities is to visit the department stores of El Corte Inglés.

Tourist Information

All cities and many smaller towns have an *oficina de turismo* or *oficina de información turística*. In the country's provincial capitals you will sometimes find more than one tourist office – one specialising in information on the city alone, the other carrying mostly provincial or regional information.

National and natural parks also often have their own visitor centres offering useful information.

Turespaña (www.spain.info) is the country's national tourism body, and it operates branches around the world. Check the website for office locations.

Travellers with Disabilities

Spain is not overly accommodating for travellers with disabilities, but some things are slowly changing. For example, disabled access to some museums, official buildings and hotels represents a change in local thinking.

In major cities more is slowly being done to facilitate disabled access to public transport and taxis; in some cities, wheelchair-adapted taxis are called 'Eurotaxis'.

Newly constructed hotels in most of Spain are required to have wheelchair-adapted rooms.

With older places, you will need to be a little bit wary of hotels that advertise and market themselves as being disabled-friendly, as this can mean as little as wide doors to rooms and bathrooms, or other token efforts.

Some tourist offices – notably those in Madrid and Barcelona – offer guided tours of the city for travellers with disabilities.

Inout Hostel (☎93 280 09 85; www.inouthostel.com; Major del Rectoret 2; dm €22; @☎≋; ⓇFGC Baixador de Vallvidrera) Worthy of a special mention is Barcelona's Inout Hostel, which is completely accessible for those with disabilities, and nearly all the staff that work there have disabilities of one kind or another. The facilities and service are first-class.

Museo Tifológico (Museum for the Blind; ☎91 589 42 19; www.museo.once.es; Calle de la Coruña 18; ⏲10am-2pm & 5-8pm Tue-Fri, 10am-2pm Sat, closed Aug; ⓂEstrecho) FREE This attraction is specifically for people who are visually impaired. Run by the Organización Nacional de Ciegos Españoles (National Organisation for the Blind, ONCE), its exhibits (all of which may be touched) include paintings, sculptures and tapestries, as well as more than 40 scale models of world monuments, including Madrid's Palacio Real and Cibeles fountain, as well as La Alhambra in Granada and the aqueduct in Segovia. It also provides leaflets in Braille and audio guides to the museum.

Organisations

Madrid Accesible (Accessible Madrid; www.esmadrid.com/madrid-accesible) Your first stop for more information on accessibility for travellers in Madrid should be the tourist section known as 'Madrid Accesible', where you can download a PDF of their excellent *Guía de Turismo Accesible* in English or Spanish. It has an exhaustive list of the city's attractions and transport and a detailed assessment of their accessibility, as well as a list of accessible restaurants. Most tourist offices in Madrid have a *mapa turístico accesible* in Spanish, English and French

Accessible Travel & Leisure (☎01452-729739; www.accessibletravel.co.uk) Claims to be the biggest UK travel agent dealing with travel for people with a disability, and encourages independent travel. Spain is one of the countries it covers in detail.

Barcelona Turisme (☎93 285 38 34; www.barcelona-access.com) Website devoted to making Barcelona accessible for visitors with a disability.

ONCE (Organización Nacional de Ciegos Españoles; Map p108; ☎91 532 50 00, 91 577 37 56; www.once.es; Calle de Prim 3; ⓂChueca, Colón) The Spanish association for those who are blind. You may be able to get hold of guides in Braille to Madrid, although they're not published every year.

Society for Accessible Travel & Hospitality (www.sath.org) A good resource, which gives advice on how to travel with a wheelchair, kidney disease, sight impairment or deafness.

Transport

Metro or tram lines, or stations built (or upgraded) since the late 1990s, generally have elevators for wheelchair access, but the older lines can be ill-equipped (including many of Madrid's lines; check the map at www.metromadrid.es).

Even in stations with wheelchair access, not all platforms necessarily have functioning escalators or elevators.

The single-deck *piso bajo* (low floor) buses are now commonplace in most Spanish cities. They have no steps inside and in some cases have ramps that can be used by people in wheelchairs.

If you call any taxi company and ask for a 'Eurotaxi' you should be sent one adapted for wheelchair users.

Visas

Spain is one of 26 member countries of the Schengen Convention, under which 22 EU countries (all but Bulgaria, Cyprus, Ireland, Romania and the UK) plus Iceland, Norway, Liechtenstein and Switzerland have abolished checks at common borders.

The visa situation for entering Spain is as follows:

Citizens or residents of EU & Schengen countries No visa required.

Citizens or residents of Australia, Canada, Israel, Japan, New Zealand & the USA No visa required for tourist visits of up to 90 days out of every 180 days.

Other countries Check with a Spanish embassy or consulate.

To work or study in Spain A special visa may be required – contact a Spanish embassy or consulate before travel.

Extensions & Residence

Schengen visas cannot be extended. You can apply for no more than two visas in any 12-month period and they are not renewable once you are in Spain.

Nationals of EU countries, Iceland, Norway, Liechtenstein and Switzerland can enter and leave Spain at will and don't need to apply for a *tarjeta de residencia* (residence card), although they are supposed to apply for residence papers.

People of other nationalities who want to stay in Spain longer than 90 days have to get a residence card, and for them it can be a drawn-out process, starting with an appropriate visa issued by a Spanish consulate in their country of residence. Start the process well in advance.

ACCESSIBLE TRAVEL ONLINE RESOURCES

Download Lonely Planet's free *Accessible Travel* guides from http://lptravel.to/AccessibleTravel.

Volunteering

Volunteering possibilities in Spain:

Earthwatch Institute (www.earthwatch.org) Occasionally Spanish conservation projects appear on its program.

Go Abroad (www.goabroad.com) Dozens of different volunteering opportunities in Spain.

Sunseed Desert Technology (☎950 52 57 70; www.sunseed.org.uk; Los Molinos del Río Agua) This UK-run project, developing sustainable ways to live in semi-arid environments, is based in the hamlet of Los Molinos del Río Agua in Almería.

Transitions Abroad (www.transitionsabroad.com) A good website to start your research.

Women Travellers

Travelling in Spain as a woman is as easy as travelling anywhere in the Western world.

That said, foreign women *can* attract unwanted male attention, especially when travelling solo and in small, remote places.

You should also be choosy about your accommodation. Bottom-end fleapits with all-male staff can be insalubrious locations to bed down for the night. Lone women should take care in city streets at night – stick with the crowds. Hitching for solo women travellers is never recommended.

Spanish men under about 40, who've grown up in the liberated post-Franco era, conform far less to old-fashioned sexual stereotypes, although you might notice that sexual stereotyping becomes a little more pronounced as you move from north to south in Spain, and from city to country.

Work

Nationals of EU countries, Switzerland, Liechtenstein, Norway and Iceland may freely work in Spain. If you are offered a contract, your employer will normally steer you through any bureaucracy.

Virtually everyone else is supposed to obtain a work permit from a Spanish consulate in their country of residence, and if they plan to stay more than 90 days, a residence visa. These procedures are well-nigh impossible unless you have a job contract lined up before you begin them.

You could look for casual work in fruit picking, harvesting or construction, but this is generally done with imported labour from Morocco and Eastern Europe, with pay and conditions that can often best be described as dire.

Translating and interpreting could be an option if you are fluent in Spanish and have a language in demand.

Language Teaching

Language-teaching qualifications are a big help when trying to find work as a teacher, and the more reputable places will require TEFL qualifications.

Sources of information on possible teaching work – in a school or as a private tutor – include foreign cultural centres such as the British Council and Alliance Française, foreign-language bookshops, universities and language schools. Many have noticeboards where you may find work opportunities or can advertise your own services.

Tourist Resorts

Summer work on the Mediterranean coasts is a possibility, especially if you arrive early in the season and are prepared to stay a while.

Check any local press in foreign languages, such as the Costa del Sol's *Sur in English* (www.surinenglish.com), which lists ads for waiters, nannies, chefs, babysitters, cleaners and the like.

Yacht Crewing

It is possible to stumble upon work as crew on yachts and cruisers. The best ports at which to look include (in descending order) Palma de Mallorca, Gibraltar and Puerto Banús.

In summer the voyages tend to be restricted to the Mediterranean, but from about November to January, many boats head for the Caribbean.

Such work is usually unpaid and about the only way to find it is to ask around on the docks.

Transport

GETTING THERE & AWAY

Spain is one of Europe's top holiday destinations and is well linked to other European countries by air, rail and road.

Regular car ferries and hydrofoils run to and from Morocco, and there are ferry links to the UK, Italy, the Canary Islands and Algeria.

Flights, cars and tours can be booked online at www.lonelyplanet.com/bookings.

Entering Spain

Immigration and customs checks (which usually only take place if you're arriving from outside the EU) normally involve a minimum of fuss, although there are exceptions.

Your vehicle could be searched on arrival from Andorra. The tiny principality of Andorra is not in the European Union (EU), so border controls remain in place. Spanish customs look out for contraband duty-free products destined for illegal resale in Spain.

The same may apply to travellers arriving from Morocco or the Spanish North African enclaves of Ceuta and Melilla. In this case the search is for controlled substances. Expect long delays at these borders, especially in summer.

Passports

Citizens of other EU member states as well as those from Norway, Iceland, Liechtenstein and Switzerland can travel to Spain with their national identity card alone. If such countries do not issue ID cards – as in the UK – travellers must carry a valid passport. All other nationalities must have a valid passport.

In the aftermath of the UK's decision to leave the EU, the future requirements for UK citizens travelling in Spain and the rest of the EU remains unclear – check with your local Spanish embassy or consulate for the latest rules.

By law you are supposed to carry your passport or ID card with you in Spain at all times.

Air

There are direct flights to Spain from most European countries, as well as from North America, South America, Africa, the Middle East and Asia. Those coming from Australasia will usually have to make at least one change of flight.

High season in Spain generally means Christmas, New Year, Easter and roughly June to September. The applicability of seasonal fares varies depending on the specific destination. You may find reasonably priced flights to Madrid from elsewhere in Europe in August, for example, because it is stinking hot and everyone else has fled

CLIMATE CHANGE & TRAVEL

Every form of transport that relies on carbon-based fuel generates CO_2, the main cause of human-induced climate change. Modern travel is dependent on aeroplanes, which might use less fuel per kilometre per person than most cars but travel much greater distances. The altitude at which aircraft emit gases (including CO_2) and particles also contributes to their climate change impact. Many websites offer 'carbon calculators' that allow people to estimate the carbon emissions generated by their journey and, for those who wish to do so, to offset the impact of the greenhouse gases emitted with contributions to portfolios of climate-friendly initiatives throughout the world. Lonely Planet offsets the carbon footprint of all staff and author travel.

to the mountains or the sea. As a general rule, November to March (aside from Christmas and New Year) is when airfares to Spain are likely to be at their lowest, and the intervening months can be considered shoulder periods.

Airports & Airlines

All of Spain's airports share the user-friendly website and flight information telephone number of **Aena** (☎902 404704, 91 321 10 00; www.aena.es), the national airports authority. To find more information on each airport, choose 'English' and click 'Airports'.

Each airport's page has details on practical information (including parking and public transport) and a full list of (and links to) airlines using that airport. It also has current flight information.

Iberia (www.iberia.com) is Spain's national carrier and it has an extensive international network of flights and a good safety record.

Madrid's **Adolfo Suárez Madrid-Barajas Airport** (☎902 404704; www.aena.es; Ⓜ Aeropuerto T1, T2 & T3, Aeropuerto T4) was Spain's busiest (and Europe's sixth-busiest) airport in 2016, while Barcelona's **El Prat Airport** (☎902 404704; www.aena.es) comes in 7th. Other major airports include Málaga, Palma de Mallorca, Alicante, Girona, Valencia, Seville, Vigo and Bilbao.

Land

Spain shares land borders with France, Portugal and Andorra.

Apart from shorter cross-border services, **Eurolines** (www.eurolines.com) is the main operator of international bus services to Spain from most of Western Europe and Morocco.

For information on trains connecting Spain with France and Portugal, and onward services between France and other countries, visit the Viajes Internacionales (International Journeys) section of www.renfe.com, the website of the Spanish national railway company, Renfe.

Andorra

Regular buses connect Andorra with Barcelona (including winter ski buses and direct services to the airport) and other destinations in Spain (including Madrid) and France. Regular buses run between Andorra and Barcelona's Estació d'Autobusos de Sants (€31, three hours) or Barcelona's El Prat Airport (€34, 3½ hours).

France

BUS

Eurolines (www.eurolines.com) heads to Spain from Paris and more than 20 other French cities and towns. It connects with Madrid (from €84, 17¾ hours), Barcelona (from €72, 14¾ hours) and many other destinations. There's at least one departure per day for main destinations.

CAR & MOTORCYCLE

The main road crossing into Spain from France is the highway that links up with Spain's AP7 tollway, which runs down to Barcelona and follows the Spanish coast south (with a branch, the AP2, going to Madrid via Zaragoza). A series of links cuts across the Pyrenees from France and Andorra into Spain, and there's a coastal route that runs from Biarritz in France into the Spanish Basque Country.

TRAIN

The principal rail crossings into Spain pierce the Franco-Spanish frontier along the Mediterranean coast and via the Basque Country. Another minor rail route runs inland across the Pyrenees from Latour-de-Carol to Barcelona.

In addition to the options listed below, two or three TGVs (high-speed trains) leave from Paris-Montparnasse for Irún, where you change to a normal train for the Basque Country and on towards Madrid. Up to three TGVs also put you on track to Barcelona (leaving from Paris Gare de Lyon), with a change of train at Montpellier or Narbonne.

For more information on French rail services, check out the **OuiSNCF** (https://en.oui.sncf/en/) website.

There are plans for a high-speed rail link between Madrid and Paris. In the meantime, high-speed services travel via Barcelona. These are the major cross-border services:

Paris to Barcelona (from €39, 6½ hours, two to four daily) A high-speed service runs via Valence, Nîmes, Montpellier, Beziers, Narbonne, Perpignan, Figueres and Girona. Also high-speed services run from Lyon (from €39, five hours) and Toulouse (from €35, three to four hours).

Paris to Madrid (from €185 to €210, 9¾ to 12½ hours, eight daily) The slow route runs via Les Aubrais, Blois, Poitiers, Irún, Vitoria, Burgos and Valladolid. The quicker route uses high-speed French TGV trains between Paris and Barcelona, where you change to a high-speed Spanish AVE to reach Madrid.

Portugal

BUS

Avanza (☎902 020999; www.avanzabus.com) runs daily buses between Lisbon and Madrid (€41 to €45, seven hours, two to three daily).

Other bus services run north via Porto to Tui, Santiago de Compostela and A Coruña in Galicia, while local buses cross the border from towns such as Huelva in Andalucía, Badajoz in Extremadura and Ourense in Galicia.

CAR & MOTORCYCLE

The A5 freeway linking Madrid with Badajoz crosses the Portuguese frontier and continues on to Lisbon. There are many other road connections up and down the length of the Spain–Portugal border.

TRAIN

From Portugal, the main line runs from Lisbon across Extremadura to Madrid.

Lisbon to Irún (chair/sleeper class €69/94, 13½ hours, one daily)

Lisbon to Madrid (chair/sleeper class from €61/84, 10½ hours, one daily)

Porto to Vigo (€15, 2½ hours, two daily)

Sea

A useful website for comparing routes and finding links to the relevant ferry companies is www.ferrylines.com.

Algeria

Algérie Ferries (www.algerieferries.dz) Operates year-round services from Alicante to Oran (11 hours, one to three weekly) as well as summer services from Alicante to Algiers and Barcelona to Mostaganem.

Trasmediterránea (☎902 454645; www.trasmediterranea.es) Runs year-round ferries between Almería and Ghazaouet (weekly) and Oran (weekly).

Italy

Most Italian routes are operated by **Grimaldi Lines** (www.grimaldi-lines.com) or **Grandi Navi Veloci** (www.gnv.it).

Civitavecchia (near Rome) to Barcelona (20 hours, six weekly)

Genoa to Barcelona (19 hours, three or more per week)

Livorno (19½ hours, three weekly)

Porto Torres (Sardinia) to Barcelona (12 hours, daily)

Savona (near Genoa) to Barcelona (20 hours, two weekly)

Morocco

Ferries run to Morocco from mainland Spain. Most services are run by the Spanish national ferry company, **Trasmediterránea** (☎902 454645; www.trasmediterranea.es). You can take vehicles on most routes. Other companies that

RAIL PASSES

Interrail Passes

Interrail (www.interrailnet.eu) passes are available to people who have lived in Europe for six months or more. They can be bought at most major stations, student travel outlets and online.

Youth passes are for people aged 12 to 25, and adult passes are for those 26 and over. Children aged 11 and under travel for free if travelling on a family pass.

Global Pass Encompasses 30 countries and comes in seven versions, ranging from five days' travel in 15 days to a full month's travel. Check out the website for a full list of prices.

One-country Pass Can be used for three, four, six or eight days within one month in Spain. For the eight-day pass you pay €339/255/192 for adult 1st class/adult 2nd class/youth 2nd class.

Eurail Passes

Eurail (www.eurail.com) passes are for those who've lived in Europe for less than six months. They are supposed to be bought outside Europe, either online or from leading travel agencies.

Be sure you will be covering a lot of ground to make your Eurail pass worthwhile. To be certain, check the **Renfe** (www.renfe.com) website for sample prices in euros for the places where you intend to travel.

For most of the following passes, children aged between four and 11 pay half-price for the 1st-class passes, while those aged under 26 can get a cheaper 2nd-class pass. The Eurail website has a full list of prices, including special family rates and other discounts.

Eurail Global Passes Good for travel in 28 European countries; forget it if you intend to travel mainly in Spain. There are nine different passes, from five days within one month to three months' continuous travel.

Eurail Select Pass Provides between five and 10 days of unlimited travel within a two-month period in two to four bordering countries (eg Spain, France, Italy and Switzerland).

Spain Pass With the one-country Spain Pass you can choose from three to eight days' train travel in a one-month period. The eight-day Spain Pass costs €325/261/213 for adult 1st class/adult 2nd class/youth 2nd class.

connect Spain with Morocco include the following:

Baleària (www.balearia.com)

FRS Iberia (www.frs.es)

Grandi Navi Veloci (www.gnv.it)

Grimaldi Lines (www.grimaldi-lines.com)

Naviera Armas (www.navieraarmas.com)

Services between Spain and Morocco include the following:

Al-Hoceima to Motril (3½ hours, weekly)

Nador to Almería (four to seven hours, daily)

Nador to Motril (3½ hours, weekly)

Tangier to Algeciras (one to two hours, up to 12 daily) Buses from several Moroccan cities converge on Tangier to make the ferry crossing to Algeciras, then fan out to the main Spanish centres.

Tangier to Barcelona (26 to 35 hours, one to two weekly)

Tangier to Motril (eight hours, daily)

Tangier to Tarifa (35 to 40 minutes, up to 15 daily)

UK

Brittany Ferries (☎in the UK 0871 244 0744; www.brittany-ferries.co.uk) runs the following services:

Plymouth to Santander (20 hours, weekly) Mid-March to November only.

Portsmouth to Bilbao (24 to 32 hours, two weekly)

Portsmouth to Santander (24 to 32 hours, three weekly)

GETTING AROUND

Spain's network of train and bus services is one of the best in Europe and there aren't many places that can't be reached using one or the other. The tentacles of Spain's high-speed train network are expanding rapidly, while domestic air services are plentiful over longer distances and on routes that are more complicated by land.

Air

Spain has an extensive network of internal flights. These are operated by both Spanish airlines and a handful of low-cost international airlines. Carriers include the following:

Air Europa (www.aireuropa.com) Madrid to A Coruña, Vigo, Bilbao and Barcelona, as well as other routes between Spanish cities.

Iberia (www.iberia.com) Spain's national airline and its subsidiary, Iberia Regional-Air Nostrum, have an extensive domestic network.

Ryanair (www.ryanair.com) Some domestic Spanish routes.

Volotea (www.volotea.com) Budget airline that flies domestically and internationally. Domestic routes take in Alicante, Bilbao, Málaga, Seville, Valencia, Zaragoza, Oviedo and the Balearics (but not Madrid or Barcelona).

Vueling (www.vueling.com) Spanish low-cost company with loads of domestic flights within Spain, especially from Barcelona.

Bicycle

Years of highway improvement programs across the country have made cycling a much easier prospect than it once was, although there are few designated bike lanes.

Cycling on *autopistas* (tollways) is forbidden. Driver attitudes on open roads are generally good; less so in the cities where cycling is not for the faint-hearted.

If you get tired of pedalling, it is often possible to take your bike on the train. All regional trains have space for bikes (usually marked by a bicycle logo on the carriage), where you can simply load the bike.

Bikes are also permitted on most *cercanías* (local-area trains around big cities such as Madrid and Barcelona).

On long-distance trains there are more restrictions. As a rule, you have to be travelling overnight in a sleeper or couchette to have the (dismantled) bike accepted as normal luggage. Otherwise, it can only be sent separately as a parcel. It's often possible to take your bike on a bus – usually you'll just be asked to remove the front wheel.

Hire & Bike-Sharing Schemes

Bicycle hire is not as widespread as in some European countries, though it's becoming more so, especially in the case of *bicis todo terreno* (mountain bikes) and in Andalucía, Barcelona and popular coastal towns.

Costs vary considerably, but expect to pay around €8 to €10 per hour, €15 to €20 per day, or €50 to €60 per week.

A number of cities have introduced public bicycle systems with dozens of automated pick-up and drop-off points. These schemes involve paying a small subscription fee, which then allows you to pick up a bicycle at one location and drop it off at another.

Madrid (☎010, 91 529 82 10; www.bicimad.com; 1/2hr €2/4; ⏲24hr)

Seville (☎900 900722; www.sevici.es)

Boat

Ferries and hydrofoils link the mainland (La Península) – or more specifically, Barcelona, Valencia and Denia – with Palma de Mallorca and/or Ibiza. There are also services to Spain's North African enclaves of Ceuta and Melilla.

Baleària (www.balearia.com) Runs between the mainland and Palma de Mallorca. On overnight services, you can opt for seating or sleeping accommodation in a cabin.

Trasmediterránea (☎902 454645; www.trasmediterranea.es) The main national ferry company runs a combination of slower car ferries and modern, high-speed, passenger-only fast ferries and hydrofoils.

Bus

There are few places in Spain where buses don't go. Numerous companies provide bus links, from local routes between villages to fast intercity connections. It is often cheaper to travel by bus than by train, particularly on long-haul runs, but also less comfortable.

Local services can get you just about anywhere, but most buses connecting villages and provincial towns are not geared to tourist needs. Frequent weekday services drop off to a trickle, if they operate at all, on Saturday and Sunday. Often just one bus runs daily between smaller places during the week, and none operate on Sunday.

It's usually unnecessary to make reservations; just arrive early enough to get a seat.

On many regular runs – say, from Madrid to Toledo – the ticket you buy is for the next bus due to leave and *cannot* be used on a later bus. Advance purchase in such cases is generally not possible. For longer trips (such as Madrid to Seville or to the coast), and certainly in peak holiday season, you can (and should) buy your ticket in advance. On some routes you have the choice between express and stopping-all-stations services.

In most larger towns and cities, buses leave from a single *estación de autobuses* (bus station). In smaller places, buses tend to operate from a set street or plaza, often unmarked. Locals will know where to go and where to buy tickets.

Bus travel within Spain is not overly costly, but there's a vast range of prices. The trip from Madrid to Barcelona starts from around €21 one way but can cost more than double that. From Barcelona to Seville, which is one of the longest trips (15 to 16 hours), you can pay €88 one way.

People under 26 should inquire about discounts on long-distance trips.

Among the hundreds of bus companies operating in Spain, the following have the largest range of services:

ALSA (☎902 422242; www.alsa.es) The biggest player, this company has routes all over the country in association with various other companies. Check online for discounts for advance ticket purchases.

Avanza (☎902 020999; www.avanzabus.com) Operates buses from Madrid to Extremadura, western Castilla y León and Valencia via eastern Castilla-La Mancha (eg Cuenca), often in association with other companies.

Socibus (☎902 229292; www.socibus.es) Operates services between Madrid, western Andalucía and the Basque Country.

BUS PASSES

Travellers planning broader European tours that include Spain could find one of the following passes useful.

Busabout (☎in the UK 084 5026 7514; www.busabout.com) A UK-based hop-on, hop-off bus service aimed at younger travellers. Its network includes more than 30 cities in nine countries, and the main passes are of interest only to those travelling a lot beyond Spain. However, they do have a handful of Spain-specific itineraries, such as the seven-day Iberian Adventure (per person including six nights' accommodation from €579).

Eurolines (www.eurolines.com) Offers a high-season pass valid for 15 days (adult/under 26 years €320/270) or 30 days (€425/350). This pass allows unlimited travel between 51 European cities, including a handful of Spanish ones.

Car & Motorcycle

Every vehicle should display a nationality plate of its country of registration and you must always carry proof of ownership of a private vehicle. Third-party motor insurance is required throughout Europe. A warning triangle and a reflective jacket (to be used in case of breakdown) are compulsory.

Driving Licences

All EU member states' driving licences are fully recognised throughout Europe.

Those with a non-EU licence are supposed to obtain a 12-month International Driving Permit (IDP) to accompany their national licence, which your national automobile association can issue. In practice, however, car-hire companies and police rarely ask for one.

If you have held residency in Spain for one year or more, you should apply for a Spanish driving licence or check whether your home licence entitles you to a Spanish licence under reciprocal agreements between countries.

Fuel

- *Gasolina* (petrol) is pricey in Spain, but generally slightly cheaper than in its major EU neighbours (including France, Germany, Italy and the UK); *gasóleo* is diesel fuel.
- Petrol is about 10% cheaper in Gibraltar than in

Spain and 15% cheaper in Andorra.

➡ You can pay with major credit cards at most service stations.

Hire

To rent a car in Spain you have to have a licence, be aged 21 or over and, for the major companies at least, have a credit card; note that some car-hire companies don't accept debit cards.

Smaller firms in areas where car hire is particularly common sometimes waive this last requirement. Although those with a non-EU licence should also have an IDP, you will find that national licences from countries such as Australia, Canada, New Zealand and the US are usually accepted without question.

With some of the low-cost companies, beware of 'extras' that aren't quoted in initial prices.

Avis (902 180854; www.avis.es)

Enterprise Rent-a-Car (902 100101; www.enterprise.es)

Europcar (902 105030; www.europcar.es)

Firefly (www.fireflycarrental.com)

Hertz (91 749 77 78; www.hertz.es)

Pepecar (807 414243; www.pepecar.com)

Sixt (902 491616; www.sixt.es)

Other possibilities include the following:

Auto Europe (www.autoeurope.com) US-based clearing house for deals with major car-rental agencies.

BlaBlaCar (www.blablacar.com) Car-sharing site that can be really useful for outlying towns, and if your Spanish is up to it, you get to meet people too.

Holiday Autos (900 838014; www.holidayautos.com) A clearing house for major international companies.

Ideamerge (www.ideamerge.com) Car-leasing plans, motor-home hire and much more.

Insurance

Third-party motor insurance is a minimum requirement in Spain and throughout Europe. Ask your insurer for a European Accident Statement form, which can simplify matters in the event of an accident. A European breakdown-assistance policy such as the AA Five Star Service or RAC Eurocover Motoring Assistance is a good investment.

Car-hire companies also provide this minimum insurance, but be careful to understand what your liabilities and excess are, and what waivers you are entitled to in case of accident or damage to the hire vehicle.

Road Rules

Blood-alcohol limit The limit is 0.05%. Breath tests are common, and if found to be over the limit, you can be judged, condemned, fined and deprived of your licence within 24 hours. Fines range up to around €600 for serious offences. Nonresident foreigners may be required to pay up on the spot (at 30% off the full fine). Pleading linguistic ignorance will not help – the police officer will produce a list of infringements and fines in as many languages as you like.

Legal driving age (cars) Minimum age is 18 years.

Legal driving age (motorcycles & scooters) Minimum age is 16 (80cc and over) or 14 (50cc and under) years. A licence is required.

Motorcyclists Must use headlights at all times and wear a helmet if riding a bike of 125cc or more.

Overtaking Spanish truck drivers often have the courtesy to turn on their right indicator to show that the way ahead of them is clear for overtaking (and the left one if it is not and you are attempting this manoeuvre). Make sure, however, that they're not just turning right!

Roundabouts (traffic circles) Vehicles already in the circle have the right of way.

Side of the road Drive on the right.

Speed limits In built-up areas, 50km/h (and in some cases, such as inner-city Barcelona, 30km/h), which increases to

BEATING PARKING FINES

If you've parked in a street parking spot and return to find that a parking inspector has left you a parking ticket, don't despair. If you arrive back within a reasonable time after the ticket was issued (what constitutes a reasonable time varies from place to place, but it is rarely more than a couple of hours), don't go looking for the inspector, but instead head for the nearest parking machine.

Most machines in most cities allow you to pay a small penalty (usually around €5) to cancel the fine (keep both pieces of paper just in case). If you're unable to work out what to do, ask a local for help.

It's also worth noting that metered street-parking zones (*zonas azules*, indicated by blue lines on the road or roadside) are generally free of charge at the following times, although always check the signs:

- from about 2pm to 4pm or 5pm
- through the night from about 8pm to 9am or 10am
- on Saturday afternoons and evenings
- all day on Sundays and public holidays

100km/h on major roads and up to 120km/h on *autovías* and *autopistas* (toll-free and tolled dual-lane highways, respectively). Cars towing caravans are restricted to a maximum speed of 80km/h.

Hitching

Hitching is never entirely safe, and we don't recommend it. Travellers who hitch should understand that they are taking a small but potentially serious risk. People who do choose to hitch will be safer if they travel in pairs and let someone know where they are planning to go.

Hitching is illegal on *autopistas* and *autovías*, and difficult on other major highways. If you must, choose a spot where cars can safely stop before highway slipways, or use minor roads. The going can be slow on the latter, as the traffic is often light.

Local Transport

Most of the major cities have excellent local transport. Madrid and Barcelona have extensive bus and metro systems, and other major cities also benefit from generally efficient public transport. By European standards, prices are relatively cheap.

Bus

Cities and provincial capitals all have reasonable bus networks. You can buy single tickets (usually between €1 and €2) on the buses or at *estancos* (tobacconists), but in cities such as Madrid and Barcelona, you are better off buying combined 10-trip tickets that allow the use of a combination of bus and metro, and which work out cheaper per ride.

These can be purchased in any metro station and from some tobacconists and newspaper kiosks.

Regular buses run from about 6am to shortly before midnight and even as late as 2am. In the big cities, a night bus service generally kicks in on a limited number of lines in the wee hours. In Madrid they are known as *búhos* (owls) and in Barcelona more prosaically as *nitbusos* (night buses).

Metro

Madrid has the country's most extensive metro network. Barcelona has a reasonable system. Valencia, Zaragoza, Bilbao and Seville have limited but nonetheless useful metro (or light rail) systems.

- Tickets must be bought in metro stations (from counters or vending machines), or sometimes from *estancos* (tobacconists) or newspaper kiosks.
- Single tickets cost the same as for buses (around €1.50).
- Visitors wanting to move around the major cities over a few days are best off getting 10-trip tickets, known in Madrid as Metrobús (€13) and in Barcelona as T-10 (€11).
- Monthly and seasonal passes are also available.

Taxi

You can find taxi ranks at train and bus stations, or you can telephone for radio taxis. In larger cities, taxi ranks are also scattered about the centre, and taxis will stop if you hail them in the street – look for the green light and/or the *libre* sign on the passenger side of the windscreen.

The bigger cities are well populated with taxis, although you might have to wait a bit longer on a Friday or Saturday night. No more than four people are allowed in a taxi.

- Daytime flagfall (generally to 10pm) is, for example, €2.40 in Madrid, and up to €2.90 after 9pm to 7am, and on weekends and holidays. You then pay €1.05 to €1.20 per kilometre depending on the time of day.
- There are airport and (sometimes) luggage surcharges.
- A cross-town ride in a major city will cost about €10 – absurdly cheap by European standards – while a taxi between the city centre and airport in either Madrid or Barcelona will cost €30 with luggage.

As elsewhere in Europe, Uber's presence in Spain has been controversial, leading to taxi strikes and court orders banning the company. At the time of writing, Uber operates services (either as Uber or UberX) in Madrid and Barcelona.

Tram

Trams were stripped out of Spanish cities decades ago, but they're making a minor comeback in some. Barcelona has a couple of new suburban tram services in addition to its tourist Tramvia Blau run to Tibidabo. Valencia has some useful trams to the beach, while various limited lines also run in Seville, Bilbao, Murcia and, most recently, Zaragoza.

Train

Renfe (☎91 232 03 20; www.renfe.com) is the excellent national train system that runs most of the services in Spain. A handful of small private railway lines also operate.

You'll find *consignas* (left-luggage facilities) at all main train stations. They are usually open from about 6am to midnight and charge from €4 to €6 per day per piece of luggage.

Spain has several types of trains, and *largo recorrido* or *Grandes Líneas* (long-distance trains) in particular have a variety of names.

Alaris, Altaria, Alvia, Arco & Avant Long-distance intermediate-speed services.

Cercanías (*rodalies* in Catalonia) For short hops and services to outlying suburbs and satellite towns in Madrid, Barcelona and 11 other cities.

Euromed Similar to the Tren de Alta Velocidad Española (AVE) trains, they connect Barcelona with Valencia and Alicante.

FEVE (Ferrocarriles de Vía Estrecha) Narrow-gauge network along Spain's north coast between Bilbao and Ferrol (Galicia), with a branch down to León.

Regionales Trains operating within one region, usually stopping all stations.

Talgo & intercity Slower long-distance trains.

Tren de Alta Velocidad Española (AVE) High-speed trains that link Madrid with Albacete, Alicante, Barcelona, Córdoba, Cuenca, Huesca, León, Lleida, Málaga, Palencia, Salamanca, Seville, Valencia, Valladolid and Zaragoza. There are also Barcelona–Seville, Barcelona–Málaga and Valencia–Seville services. In coming years, Madrid–Bilbao should also come on line, and travel times to Galicia should fall. The same goes for Madrid–Granada and Madrid–Badajoz.

Trenhotel Overnight trains with sleeper berths.

Classes & Costs

All long-distance trains have 2nd and 1st classes, known as *turista* and *preferente*, respectively. The latter is 20% to 40% more expensive.

Fares vary enormously depending on the service (faster trains cost considerably more) and, in the case of some high-speed services such as the AVE, on the time and day of travel. Tickets for AVE trains are by far the most expensive.

A one-way trip in 2nd class from Madrid to Barcelona (on which route only AVE trains run) could cost as much as €108 (it could work out significantly cheaper if you book well in advance).

Children aged between four and 12 years are entitled to a 40% discount; those aged under four travel for free (except on high-speed trains, for which they pay the same as those aged four to 12). Buying a return ticket often gives you a 10% to 20% discount on the return trip.

Train Routes

MEMORABLE TRAIN JOURNEYS

The romantically inclined could opt for an opulent and slow-moving, old-time rail adventure with numerous options across the peninsula.

Al-Andalus (☎902 555902; www.renfe.com/trenesturisticos) This is a luxurious train journey that loops through Andalucía, taking the slow route between Seville, Ronda, Granada and Córdoba among other stops. Options vary from three to six nights. Prices for the seven-day/six-night itineraries start at €3600 per person in high season; the single supplement costs €1800.

Transcantábrico (☎902 555902; www.renfe.com/trenesturisticos) For a journey on a picturesque narrow-gauge rail route, from Santiago de Compostela (by bus as far as O Ferrol) via Oviedo, Santander and Bilbao along the coast, and then a long inland stretch to finish in León. The eight-day trip costs from €3600 per person in high season; there's a €1800 single supplement. The trip can also be done in reverse or in smaller chunks. There are 11 departures from April to October. Check if your package includes various visits along the way, including the Museo Guggenheim Bilbao, the Museo de Altamira, Santillana del Mar, and the Covadonga lakes in the Picos de Europa. The food is exceptional, with some meals being eaten on-board but most in various locations.

The trains don't travel at night, making sleeping aboard easy and providing the opportunity to stay out at night.

Students and people up to 26 years of age with a Euro<26 Card (Carnet Joven in Spain) are entitled to 20% to 25% off most ticket prices.

If you're travelling as a family, ask for a group of four seats with a table when making your reservation.

On overnight trips within Spain on *trenhoteles*, it's worth paying extra for a *litera* (couchette; a sleeping berth in a six- or four-bed compartment) or, if available, single or double cabins in *preferente* or *gran clase* class. The cost depends on the class of accommodation, type of train and length of journey. The lines covered are Madrid–A Coruña, Barcelona–Granada, Barcelona–A Coruña–Vigo and Madrid–Lisbon, as well as international services to France.

Reservations

Reservations are recommended for long-distance trips, and you can make them in train stations, **Renfe** (☎91 232 03 20; www.renfe.com) offices and travel agencies, as well as online. In a growing number of stations, you can pick up prebooked tickets from machines scattered about the station concourse.

Language

Spanish *(español)* – or Castilian *(castellano)*, as it is also called – is spoken throughout Spain, but there are also three co-official, regional languages: Catalan *(català)*, spoken in Catalonia, the Balearic Islands and Valencia; Galician *(galego)*, spoken in Galicia; and Basque *(euskara)*, which is spoken in the Basque Country and Navarra.

The pronunciation of most Spanish sounds is very similar to that of their English counterparts. If you read our coloured pronunciation guides as if they were English, you'll be understood. Note that kh is a throaty sound (like the 'ch' in the Scottish *loch*), r is strongly rolled, ly is pronounced as the 'lli' in 'million' and ny as the 'ni' in 'onion'. You may also notice that the 'lisped' th sound is pronounced as s in Andalucía. In our pronunciation guides, the stressed syllables are in italics.

Where necessary in this chapter, masculine and feminine forms are marked with 'm/f', while polite and informal options are indicated by the abbreviations 'pol' and 'inf'.

BASICS

Hello.	*Hola.*	o·la
Goodbye.	*Adiós.*	a·*dyos*
Yes./No.	*Sí./No.*	see/no
Excuse me.	*Perdón.*	per·*don*
Sorry.	*Lo siento.*	lo *syen*·to
Please.	*Por favor.*	por fa·*vor*

WANT MORE?

For in-depth language information and handy phrases, check out Lonely Planet's *Spanish Phrasebook*. You'll find it at **shop.lonelyplanet.com**, or you can buy Lonely Planet's iPhone phrasebooks at the Apple App Store.

QUESTION WORDS

How?	*¿Cómo?*	ko·mo
What?	*¿Qué?*	ke
When?	*¿Cuándo?*	*kwan*·do
Where?	*¿Dónde?*	*don*·de
Who?	*¿Quién?*	kyen
Why?	*¿Por qué?*	por ke

Thank you.	*Gracias.*	*gra*·thyas
You're welcome.	*De nada.*	de *na*·da
How are you?	*¿Qué tal?*	ke tal
Fine, thanks.	*Bien, gracias.*	byen *gra*·thyas

What's your name?
¿Cómo se llama Usted? ko·mo se *lya*·ma oo·*ste* (pol)
¿Cómo te llamas? ko·mo te *lya*·mas (inf)

My name is ...
Me llamo ... me *lya*·mo ...

Do you speak English?
¿Habla inglés? a·bla een·*gles* (pol)
¿Hablas inglés? a·blas een·*gles* (inf)

I don't understand.
No entiendo. no en·*tyen*·do

ACCOMMODATION

hotel	*hotel*	o·*tel*
guesthouse	*pensión*	pen·*syon*
youth hostel	*albergue juvenil*	al·*ber*·ge khoo·ve·*neel*
I'd like a ... room.	*Quisiera una habitación ...*	kee·*sye*·ra *oo*·na a·bee·ta·*thyon* ...
single	*individual*	een·dee·vee·*dwal*
double	*doble*	*do*·ble
air-con	*aire acondicionado*	*ai*·re a·kon·dee·thyo·*na*·do

bathroom	*baño*	*ba*·nyo
window	*ventana*	ven·*ta*·na

How much is it per night/person?
¿Cuánto cuesta por noche/persona? — *kwan*·to *kwes*·ta por *no*·che/per·*so*·na

Does it include breakfast?
¿Incluye el desayuno? — een·*kloo*·ye el de·sa·*yoo*·no

DIRECTIONS

Where's ...?
¿Dónde está ...? — *don*·de es·*ta* ...

What's the address?
¿Cuál es la dirección? — kwal es la dee·rek·*thyon*

Can you please write it down?
¿Puede escribirlo, por favor? — *pwe*·de es·kree·*beer*·lo por fa·*vor*

Can you show me (on the map)?
¿Me lo puede indicar (en el mapa)? — me lo *pwe*·de een·dee·*kar* (en el *ma*·pa)

at the corner	*en la esquina*	en la es·*kee*·na
at the traffic lights	*en el semáforo*	en el se·*ma*·fo·ro
behind ...	*detrás de ...*	de·*tras* de ...
in front of ...	*enfrente de ...*	en·*fren*·te de ...
left	*izquierda*	eeth·*kyer*·da
next to ...	*al lado de ...*	al *la*·do de ...
opposite ...	*frente a ...*	*fren*·te a ...
right	*derecha*	de·*re*·cha
straight ahead	*todo recto*	*to*·do *rek*·to

EATING & DRINKING

What would you recommend?
¿Qué recomienda? — ke re·ko·*myen*·da

What's in that dish?
¿Que lleva ese plato? — ke *lye*·va e·se *pla*·to

I don't eat ...
No como ... — no *ko*·mo ...

Cheers!
¡Salud! — sa·*loo*

That was delicious!
¡Estaba buenísimo! — es·*ta*·ba bwe·*nee*·see·mo

Please bring us the bill.
Por favor, nos trae la cuenta. — por fa·*vor* nos *tra*·e la *kwen*·ta

I'd like to book a table for ...	*Quisiera reservar una mesa para ...*	kee·*sye*·ra re·ser·*var oo*·na *me*·sa *pa*·ra ...
(eight) o'clock	*las (ocho)*	las (*o*·cho)
(two) people	*(dos) personas*	(dos) per·*so*·nas

NUMBERS

1	*uno*	*oo*·no
2	*dos*	dos
3	*tres*	tres
4	*cuatro*	*kwa*·tro
5	*cinco*	*theen*·ko
6	*seis*	seys
7	*siete*	*sye*·te
8	*ocho*	*o*·cho
9	*nueve*	*nwe*·ve
10	*diez*	dyeth
20	*veinte*	*veyn*·te
30	*treinta*	*treyn*·ta
40	*cuarenta*	kwa·*ren*·ta
50	*cincuenta*	theen·*kwen*·ta
60	*sesenta*	se·*sen*·ta
70	*setenta*	se·*ten*·ta
80	*ochenta*	o·*chen*·ta
90	*noventa*	no·*ven*·ta
100	*cien*	thyen
1000	*mil*	meel

Key Words

bottle	*botella*	bo·*te*·lya
breakfast	*desayuno*	de·sa·*yoo*·no
(too) cold	*(muy) frío*	(mooy) *free*·o
dinner	*cena*	*the*·na
food	*comida*	ko·*mee*·da
fork	*tenedor*	te·ne·*dor*
glass	*vaso*	*va*·so
highchair	*trona*	*tro*·na
hot (warm)	*caliente*	ka·*lyen*·te
knife	*cuchillo*	koo·*chee*·lyo
lunch	*comida*	ko·*mee*·da
market	*mercado*	mer·*ka*·do
(children's) menu	*menú (infantil)*	me·*noo* (een·fan·*teel*)
plate	*plato*	*pla*·to
restaurant	*restaurante*	res·tow·*ran*·te
spoon	*cuchara*	koo·*cha*·ra
vegetarian food	*comida vegetariana*	ko·*mee*·da ve·khe·ta·*rya*·na

CATALAN

The recognition of Catalan as an official language in Spain is the end result of a regional government campaign that began when the province gained autonomy at the end of the 1970s. Until the Battle of Muret in 1213, Catalan territory extended across southern France, taking in Roussillon and reaching into the Provence. Catalan was spoken, or at least understood, throughout these territories and in what is now Catalonia and Andorra. In the couple of hundred years that followed, the Catalans spread their language south into Valencia, west into Aragón and east to the Balearic Islands. It also reached Sicily and Naples, and the Sardinian town of Alghero is still a partly Catalan-speaking outpost today. Catalan is spoken by up to 10 million people in Spain.

In Barcelona you'll hear as much Spanish as Catalan. Your chances of coming across English speakers are also good. Elsewhere in the province, don't be surprised if you get replies in Catalan to your questions in Spanish. However, you'll find that most Catalans will happily speak to you in Spanish, especially once they realise you're a foreigner. This said, the following Catalan phrases might win you a few smiles and perhaps help you make some new friends.

Hello.	*Hola.*
Goodbye.	*Adéu.*
Yes.	*Sí.*
No.	*No.*
Please.	*Sisplau./Si us plau.*
Thank you (very much).	*(Moltes) gràcies.*
You're welcome.	*De res.*
Excuse me.	*Perdoni.*
May I?/Do you mind?	*Puc?/Em permet?*
I'm sorry.	*Ho sento./Perdoni.*
What's your name?	*Com et dius?* (inf)
	Com es diu? (pol)
My name is ...	*Em dic ...*
Where are you from?	*D'on ets?*
Do you speak English?	*Parla anglès?*
I understand.	*Ho entenc.*
I don't understand.	*No ho entenc.*
Could you speak in Castilian, please?	*Pot parlar castellà sisplau?*
How do you say ... in Catalan?	*Com es diu ... en català?*
I'm looking for ...	*Estic buscant ...*
How do I get to ...?	*Com puc arribar a ...?*
Turn left.	*Giri a mà esquerra.*
Turn right.	*Giri a mà dreta.*
near	*a prop de*
far	*a lluny de*

Monday	*dilluns*
Tuesday	*dimarts*
Wednesday	*dimecres*
Thursday	*dijous*
Friday	*divendres*
Saturday	*dissabte*
Sunday	*diumenge*

1	*un/una* (m/f)
2	*dos/dues* (m/f)
3	*tres*
4	*quatre*
5	*cinc*
6	*sis*
7	*set*
8	*vuit*
9	*nou*
10	*deu*
11	*onze*
12	*dotze*
13	*tretze*
14	*catorze*
15	*quinze*
16	*setze*
17	*disset*
18	*divuit*
19	*dinou*
20	*vint*
100	*cent*

Meat & Fish

beef	*carne de vaca*	*kar*·ne de *va*·ka
chicken	*pollo*	*po*·lyo
duck	*pato*	*pa*·to
lamb	*cordero*	kor·*de*·ro
lobster	*langosta*	lan·*gos*·ta
pork	*cerdo*	*ther*·do
prawns	*camarones*	ka·ma·*ro*·nes
tuna	*atún*	a·*toon*
turkey	*pavo*	*pa*·vo
veal	*ternera*	ter·*ne*·ra

Fruit & Vegetables

apple	*manzana*	man·*tha*·na
apricot	*albaricoque*	al·ba·ree·*ko*·ke
banana	*plátano*	*pla*·ta·no
beans	*judías*	khoo·*dee*·as
cabbage	*col*	kol
capsicum	*pimiento*	pee·*myen*·to
carrot	*zanahoria*	tha·na·*o*·rya
cherry	*cereza*	the·*re*·tha
corn	*maíz*	ma·*eeth*
cucumber	*pepino*	pe·*pee*·no
fruit	*fruta*	*froo*·ta
grape	*uvas*	*oo*·vas
lemon	*limón*	lee·*mon*
lettuce	*lechuga*	le·*choo*·ga
mushroom	*champiñón*	cham·pee·*nyon*
nuts	*nueces*	*nwe*·thes
onion	*cebolla*	the·*bo*·lya
orange	*naranja*	na·*ran*·kha
peach	*melocotón*	me·lo·ko·*ton*
peas	*guisantes*	gee·*san*·tes
pineapple	*piña*	*pee*·nya
plum	*ciruela*	theer·*we*·la
potato	*patata*	pa·*ta*·ta
spinach	*espinacas*	es·pee·*na*·kas
strawberry	*fresa*	*fre*·sa
tomato	*tomate*	to·*ma*·te
vegetable	*verdura*	ver·*doo*·ra
watermelon	*sandía*	san·*dee*·a

Other

bread	*pan*	pan
cheese	*queso*	*ke*·so
egg	*huevo*	*we*·vo
honey	*miel*	myel
jam	*mermelada*	mer·me·*la*·da
rice	*arroz*	a·*roth*
salt	*sal*	sal
sugar	*azúcar*	a·*thoo*·kar

GALICIAN

Galician is the official language of the Autonomous Community of Galicia and is also widely understood in the neighbouring regions of Asturias and Castilla y Léon. It's very similar to Portuguese. Galicians are likely to revert to Spanish when addressing a stranger, especially a foreigner, but making a small effort to communicate in Galician will always be welcomed.

Hello.	*Ola.*
Good day.	*Bon dia.*
Goodbye.	*Adeus./Até logo.*
Many thanks.	*Moitas grácias.*
Do you speak English?	*Fala inglés?*
I don't understand.	*Non entendo.*
Could you speak in Castilian, please?	*Pode falar en español, por favor?*
What's this called in Galician?	*Como se chama iso en galego?*

Drinks

beer	*cerveza*	ther·*ve*·tha
coffee	*café*	ka·*fe*
(orange) juice	*zumo (de naranja)*	*thoo*·mo (de na·*ran*·kha)
milk	*leche*	*le*·che
red wine	*vino tinto*	*vee*·no *teen*·to
tea	*té*	te
(mineral) water	*agua (mineral)*	*a*·gwa (mee·ne·*ral*)
white wine	*vino blanco*	*vee*·no *blan*·ko

EMERGENCIES

Help!	*¡Socorro!*	so·*ko*·ro
Go away!	*¡Vete!*	*ve*·te
Call ...!	*¡Llame a ...!*	*lya*·me a ...
a doctor	*un médico*	oon *me*·dee·ko
the police	*la policía*	la po·lee·*thee*·a

I'm lost.
Estoy perdido/a. es·toy per·dee·do/a (m/f)

I'm ill.
Estoy enfermo/a. es·toy en·fer·mo/a (m/f)

It hurts here.
Me duele aquí. me dwe·le a·kee

I'm allergic to (antibiotics).
Soy alérgico/a a (los antibióticos). soy a·ler·khee·ko/a a (los an·tee·byo·tee·kos) (m/f)

Where are the toilets?
¿Dónde están los servicios? don·de es·tan los ser·vee·thyos

SHOPPING & SERVICES

I'd like to buy ...
Quisiera comprar ... kee·sye·ra kom·prar ...

I'm just looking.
Sólo estoy mirando. so·lo es·toy mee·ran·do

Can I look at it?
¿Puedo verlo? pwe·do ver·lo

I don't like it.
No me gusta. no me goos·ta

How much is it?
¿Cuánto cuesta? kwan·to kwes·ta

That's too expensive.
Es muy caro. es mooy ka·ro

Can you lower the price?
¿Podría bajar un poco el precio? po·dree·a ba·khar oon po·ko el pre·thyo

There's a mistake in the bill.
Hay un error en la cuenta. ai oon e·ror en la kwen·ta

ATM	*cajero automático*	ka·khe·ro ow·to·ma·tee·ko
internet cafe	*cibercafé*	thee·ber·ka·fe
post office	*correos*	ko·re·os
tourist office	*oficina de turismo*	o·fee·thee·na de too·rees·mo

TIME & DATES

What time is it?	*¿Qué hora es?*	ke o·ra es
It's (10) o'clock.	*Son (las diez).*	son (las dyeth)
Half past (one).	*Es (la una) y media.*	es (la oo·na) ee me·dya
At what time?	*¿A qué hora?*	a ke o·ra
At ...	*A la(s) ...*	a la(s) ...

morning	*mañana*	ma·nya·na
afternoon	*tarde*	tar·de
evening	*noche*	no·che

yesterday	*ayer*	a·yer
today	*hoy*	oy
tomorrow	*mañana*	ma·nya·na
Monday	*lunes*	loo·nes
Tuesday	*martes*	mar·tes
Wednesday	*miércoles*	myer·ko·les
Thursday	*jueves*	khwe·bes
Friday	*viernes*	vyer·nes
Saturday	*sábado*	sa·ba·do
Sunday	*domingo*	do·meen·go

TRANSPORT

Public Transport

boat	*barco*	bar·ko
bus	*autobús*	ow·to·boos
plane	*avión*	a·vyon
train	*tren*	tren

first	*primer*	pree·mer
last	*último*	ool·tee·mo
next	*próximo*	prok·see·mo

BASQUE

Basque is spoken at the western end of the Pyrenees and along the Bay of Biscay – from Bayonne in France to Bilbao in Spain, and inland, almost to Pamplona. No one quite knows its origin, but the most likely theory is that Basque is the lone survivor of a language family that once extended across Europe, and was wiped out by the languages of the Celts, Germanic tribes and Romans.

Hello.	*Kaixo.*
Goodbye.	*Agur.*
How are you?	*Zer moduz?*
Fine, thank you.	*Ongi, eskerrik asko.*
Excuse me.	*Barkatu.*
Please.	*Mesedez.*
Thank you.	*Eskerrik asko.*
You're welcome.	*Ez horregatik.*
Do you speak English?	*Ingelesez ba al dakizu?*
I don't understand.	*Ez dut ulertzen.*

a ... ticket	*un billete de ...*	oon bee·*lye*·te de ...
1st-class	*primera clase*	pree·*me*·ra *kla*·se
2nd-class	*segunda clase*	se·*goon*·da *kla*·se
one-way	*ida*	*ee*·da
return	*ida y vuelta*	*ee*·da ee *vwel*·ta

aisle seat	*asiento de pasillo*	a·*syen*·to de pa·*see*·lyo
station	*estación*	es·ta·*thyon*
ticket office	*taquilla*	ta·*kee*·lya
timetable	*horario*	o·*ra*·ryo
window seat	*asiento junto a la ventana*	a·*syen*·to *khoon*·to a la ven·*ta*·na

I want to go to ...
Quisiera ir a ... kee·*sye*·ra eer a ...

At what time does it arrive/leave?
¿A qué hora llega/sale? a ke o·ra *lye*·ga/*sa*·le

Does it stop at (Madrid)?
¿Para en (Madrid)? pa·ra en (ma·*dree*)

Which stop is this?
¿Cuál es esta parada? kwal es es·ta pa·*ra*·da

Please tell me when we get to (Seville).
¿Puede avisarme cuando lleguemos a (Sevilla)? *pwe*·de a·vee·*sar*·me *kwan*·do lye·*ge*·mos a (se·*vee*·lya)

I want to get off here.
Quiero bajarme aquí. *kye*·ro ba·*khar*·me a·*kee*

Driving and Cycling

I'd like to hire a ...	*Quisiera alquilar ...*	kee·*sye*·ra al·kee·*lar* ...
4WD	*un todo-terreno*	oon *to*·do·te·*re*·no
bicycle	*una bicicleta*	*oo*·na bee·thee·*kle*·ta
car	*un coche*	oon *ko*·che
motorcycle	*una moto*	*oo*·na *mo*·to
child seat	*asiento de seguridad para niños*	a·*syen*·to de se·goo·ree·*da* pa·ra *nee*·nyos
helmet	*casco*	*kas*·ko
mechanic	*mecánico*	me·*ka*·nee·ko
petrol	*gasolina*	ga·so·*lee*·na
service station	*gasolinera*	ga·so·lee·*ne*·ra

How much is it per day/hour?
¿Cuánto cuesta por día/hora? *kwan*·to *kwes*·ta por *dee*·a/*o*·ra

SIGNS

Abierto	Open
Cerrado	Closed
Entrada	Entrance
Hombres	Men
Mujeres	Women
Prohibido	Prohibited
Salida	Exit
Servicios/Aseos	Toilets

BASQUE SIGNS

In many towns in the Basque region street names and signs are changing from Spanish to Basque. Not everyone uses these new names though, and many maps remain in Spanish, which can make navigating a little tricky for travellers. In this book we've provided the most commonly used version or have included both Spanish and Basque. Here are some Basque words commonly used in signs, followed by their Spanish counterpart and English translation:

aireportua	*aeropuerto* (airport)
erdialdea	*centro* (city centre)
jatetxea	*restaurante* (restaurant)
kalea	*calle* (street)
kale nagusia	*calle mayor* (main street)
komunak	*servicios* (toilets)
kontuz	*atención* (caution/beware)
nekazal turismoak	*casas rurales* (village/farmstead accommodation)
ongi etorri	*bienvenido* (welcome)
turismo bulegoa	*oficina de turismo* (tourist office)

Is this the road to (Barcelona)?
¿Se va a (Barcelona) por esta carretera? se va a (bar·the·*lo*·na) por es·ta ka·re·*te*·ra

(How long) Can I park here?
¿(Por cuánto tiempo) Puedo aparcar aquí? (por *kwan*·to *tyem*·po) *pwe*·do a·par·*kar* a·*kee*

The car has broken down (at Valencia).
El coche se ha averiado (en Valencia). el *ko*·che se a a·ve·*rya*·do (en va·*len*·thya)

I have a flat tyre.
Tengo un pinchazo. *ten*·go oon peen·*cha*·tho

I've run out of petrol.
Me he quedado sin gasolina. me e ke·*da*·do seen ga·so·*lee*·na

GLOSSARY

Unless otherwise indicated, the following terms are from Castilian Spanish. The masculine and feminine forms are indicated with the abbreviations 'm/f'.

ajuntament – Catalan for *ayuntamiento*
alameda – tree-lined avenue
albergue – refuge
albergue juvenil – youth hostel
alcázar – Muslim-era fortress
aljibe – cistern
artesonado – wooden Mudéjar ceiling with interlaced beams leaving a pattern of spaces for decoration
autopista – tollway
autovía – toll-free highway
AVE – Tren de Alta Velocidad Española; high-speed train
ayuntamiento – city or town hall

bailaor/bailaora – m/f flamenco dancer
baile – dance in a flamenco context
balneario – spa
barrio – district/quarter (of a town or city)
biblioteca – library
bici todo terreno (BTT) – mountain bike
bodega – cellar (especially wine cellar); also a winery or a traditional wine bar likely to serve wine from the barrel
búhos – night-bus routes

cabrito – kid
cala – cove
calle – street
callejón – lane
cama – bed
cambio – change; also currency exchange
caña – small glass of beer
cantaor/cantaora – m/f flamenco singer
capilla – chapel
capilla mayor – chapel containing the high altar of a church
carmen – walled villa with gardens, in Granada
Carnaval – traditional festive period that precedes the start of Lent; carnival
carretera – highway
carta – menu
casa de huéspedes – guesthouse; see also *hospedaje*
casa de pagès – *casa rural* in Catalonia
casa rural – village, country house or farmstead with rooms to let
casco – literally 'helmet'; often used to refer to the old part of a city; more correctly, *casco antiguo/histórico/viejo*
castellano/a (m/f) – Castilian; used in preference to *español* to describe the national language
castellers – Catalan human-castle builders
castillo – castle
castro – Celtic fortified village
català – Catalan language; a native of Catalonia
catedral – cathedral
cercanías – local train network
cervecería – beer bar
churrigueresco – ornate style of baroque architecture named after the brothers Alberto and José Churriguera
ciudad – city
claustro – cloister
CNIG – Centro Nacional de Información Geográfica; producers of good-quality maps
cofradía – see *hermandad*
colegiata – collegiate church
coll – Catalan for *collado*
collado – mountain pass
comarca – district; grouping of *municipios*
comedor – dining room
comunidad – fixed charge for maintenance of rental accommodation (sometimes included in rent); community
conquistador – conqueror
copa – drink; literally 'glass'
cordillera – mountain range
coro – choir: part of a church, usually the middle
correos – post office
Cortes – national parliament
costa – coast
cruceiro – standing crucifix found at many crossroads in Galicia
cuesta – lane, usually on a hill
custodia – monstrance

dolmen – prehistoric megalithic tomb

embalse – reservoir
encierro – running of the bulls Pamplona-style; also happens in many other places around Spain
entrada – entrance
ermita – hermitage or chapel
església – Catalan for *iglesia*
estació – Catalan for *estación*
estación – station
estación de autobuses – bus station
estación de esquí – ski station or resort
estación marítima – ferry terminal
estany – Catalan for *lago*
Euskadi Ta Askatasuna (ETA) – the name stands for Basque Homeland & Freedom
extremeño/a (m/f) – Extremaduran; a native of Extremadura

fallas – huge sculptures of papier mâché (or nowadays more often polystyrene) on wood used in Las Fallas festival of Valencia
farmacia – pharmacy
faro – lighthouse
feria – fair; can refer to trade fairs as well as to city, town or village fairs that are basically several days of merrymaking; can also mean a bullfight or festival stretching over days or weeks
ferrocarril – railway
festa – Catalan for *fiesta*
FEVE – Ferrocarriles de Vía Estrecha; a private train company in northern Spain
fiesta – festival, public holiday or party
fútbol – football (soccer)

gaditano/a (m/f) – person from Cádiz
gaita – Galician version of the bagpipes
gallego/a (m/f) – Galician; a native of Galicia
gitanos – Roma people
glorieta – big roundabout (traffic circle)
Gran Vía – main thoroughfare
GRs – *(senderos de) Gran Recorrido*; long-distance hiking paths
guardia civil – military police

hermandad – brotherhood (including men and women), in particular one that takes part in religious processions
hórreo – Galician or Asturian grain store
hospedaje – guesthouse
hostal – cheap hotel
huerta – market garden; orchard

iglesia – church
infanta/infante – princess/prince
IVA – *impuesto sobre el valor añadido*, or value-added tax

jamón – cured ham
jardín – garden
judería – Jewish *barrio* in medieval Spain

lago – lake
librería – bookshop
lidia – the art of bullfighting
locutorio – private telephone centre

madrileño/a (m/f) – person from Madrid
malagueño/a (m/f) – person from Málaga
manchego/a (m/f) – La Manchan; a person from La Mancha
marcha – action, life, 'the scene'
marismas – wetlands
marisquería – seafood eatery
medina – narrow, maze-like old section of an Arab or North African town
mercado – market
mercat – Catalan for *mercado*
meseta – plateau; the high tableland of central Spain
mihrab – prayer niche in a mosque indicating the direction of Mecca
mirador – lookout point
Modernista – an exponent of Modernisme, the architectural and artistic style influenced by art nouveau and sometimes known as Catalan Modernism, whose leading practitioner was Antoni Gaudí
monasterio – monastery
morería – former Islamic quarter in a town
movida – similar to *marcha;* a *zona de movida* is an area of a town where lively bars and discos are clustered
mozárabe – Mozarab (Christian living under Muslim rule in early medieval Spain)
Mozarabic – style of architecture developed by Mozarabs, adopting elements of classic Islamic construction to Christian architecture
Mudéjar – Muslims who remained behind in territory reconquered by Christians; also refers to a decorative style of architecture using elements of Islamic building style applied to buildings constructed in Christian Spain
muelle – wharf or pier
municipio – municipality, Spain's basic local administrative unit
muralla – city wall
murgas – costumed groups
museo – museum
museu – Catalan for *museo*

nitbus – Catalan for 'night bus'

oficina de turismo – tourist office; also *oficina de información turística*

parador – luxurious state-owned hotels, many of them in historic buildings
parque nacional – national park; strictly controlled protected area
parque natural – natural park; protected environmental area
paseo – promenade or boulevard; to stroll
paso – mountain pass
pasos – figures carried in *Semana Santa* parades
pelota vasca – Basque form of handball, also known simply as *pelota*, or *jai-alai* in Basque
peña – a club, usually of flamenco aficionados or Real Madrid or Barcelona football fans; sometimes a dining club
pensión – small private hotel
pinchos – tapas
pintxos – Basque tapas
piscina – swimming pool
plaça – Catalan for *plaza*
plateresque – early phase of Renaissance architecture noted for its intricately decorated facades
platja – Catalan for *playa*
playa – beach
plaza – square
plaza de toros – bullring
port – Catalan for *puerto*
PP – Partido Popular (People's Party)
PRs – *(senderos de) Pequeño Recorrido;* short-distance hiking paths
PSOE – Partido Socialista Obrero Español (Spanish Socialist Workers Party)
pueblo – village
puente – bridge; also means the extra day or two off that many people take when a holiday falls close to a weekend
puerta – gate or door
puerto – port or mountain pass
punta – point or promontory

ración/raciones – large/full-plate-size tapas serving; literally 'rations'
rambla – avenue or riverbed

rastro – flea market; car-boot sale

REAJ – Red Española de Albergues Juveniles; the Spanish HI youth hostel network

real – royal

Reconquista – Christian reconquest of the Iberian Peninsula from the Muslims (8th to 15th centuries)

refugi – Catalan for *refugio*

refugio – mountain shelter, hut or refuge

Renfe – Red Nacional de los Ferrocarriles Españoles; the national rail network

retablo – altarpiece

Reyes Católicos – Catholic monarchs; Isabel and Fernando

ría – estuary

río – river

riu – Catalan for *río*

rodalies – Catalan for *cercanías*

romería – festive pilgrimage or procession

ronda – ring road

sacristía – sacristy; the part of a church in which vestments, sacred objects and other valuables are kept

sagrario – sanctuary

sala capitular – chapter house

salinas – salt-extraction lagoons

santuario – shrine or sanctuary

Semana Santa – Holy Week; the week leading up to Easter Sunday

Sephardic Jews – Jews of Spanish origin

seu – cathedral (Catalan)

sidra – cider

sidrería – cider bar

sierra – mountain range

tablao – tourist-oriented flamenco performances

taifa – small Muslim kingdom in medieval Spain

tasca – tapas bar

techumbre – roof

teleférico – cable car; also called *funicular aéreo*

terraza – terrace; pavement cafe

terrazas de verano – open-air late-night bars

tetería – teahouse, usually in Middle Eastern style, with low seats around low tables

torero – bullfighter

torre – tower

trascoro – screen behind the *coro*

turismo – means both tourism and saloon car; *el turismo* can also mean 'tourist office'

urgencia – emergency

vall – Catalan for *valle*

valle – valley

villa – small town

VO – abbreviation of *versión original;* a foreign-language film subtitled in Spanish

zarzuela – Spanish mix of theatre, music and dance

Behind the Scenes

SEND US YOUR FEEDBACK

We love to hear from travellers – your comments keep us on our toes and help make our books better. Our well-travelled team reads every word on what you loved or loathed about this book. Although we cannot reply individually to your submissions, we always guarantee that your feedback goes straight to the appropriate authors, in time for the next edition. Each person who sends us information is thanked in the next edition – the most useful submissions are rewarded with a selection of digital PDF chapters.

Visit **lonelyplanet.com/contact** to submit your updates and suggestions or to ask for help. Our award-winning website also features inspirational travel stories, news and discussions.

Note: We may edit, reproduce and incorporate your comments in Lonely Planet products such as guidebooks, websites and digital products, so let us know if you don't want your comments reproduced or your name acknowledged. For a copy of our privacy policy visit lonelyplanet.com/privacy.

OUR READERS

Many thanks to the travellers who used the last edition and wrote to us with helpful hints, useful advice and interesting anecdotes:
Alfonso Iturbe, Andres Ceuterick, Darius Pavri, Elyas Rouhban, Jackie Gurrie, John Cushing, Jorge Marina, Lucia Carrera, Maureen O'Leary, Megan Holmstrom, Michael Kraus, Michael Leonesio, Peter Stoppa, Ross Marquardt, Ross Whamond, Simon Mansfield, Steve Lamming, Steve Weisberg, Vince Calderhead.

WRITER THANKS

Gregor Clark

Muchísimas gracias to the many Spaniards and resident expatriates who shared their love of country and local knowledge with me, especially Isabella, Eneida, Nigel, Emma, Domingo, Lucy, Ángel, Peter Jan, Monica, Charles, Justine, Aideen and Marcel. Back home, *besos y abrazos* to Gaen, Meigan and Chloe, who always make coming home the best part of the trip.

Sally Davies

Thanks to all those on the ground fielding my queries – in no particular order: Maria Parrilla, Dolors Bas, Vera de Frutos, Stefanie Roth, Mónica Homedes, Enrichetta Cardinale, Cristina Rodenas, Gustavo Sánchez and Vanessa Ferrer. Thanks to Mary-Ann Gallagher for suggestions, to Tom Stainer for his patience and, most of all, to my untiring research companion, Tess O'Donovan.

Duncan Garwood

I owe a lot of thanks, starting with my favourite travel companions, Lidia, Ben and Nick. Thanks also to fellow writer John Noble for his generous advice and Tom Stainer at Lonely Planet for his support. In Spain, *gracias* to Carmen Prado, Vincente del Moral, María April, Paco Parra, Antonia Requena, Yolanda Magán, Encarni Gutiérrez, Carmen Plazas, Mercedes Aguilar Pérez, Paula, Alcayada García, Irene Godoy, Paula Dominguez and the team at Mojácar tourist office.

Anthony Ham

A life built in Spain encompasses so many relationships that extend far beyond one trip. Heartfelt thanks to Sandra, Javi, Dani, Lucia, Marina, Alberto, Jose, Bea and so many others. *Gracias* also to Eli Morales. At Lonely Planet, I am grateful to my editor Tom Stainer and numerous editors who brought focus and much wisdom to the book. To my family – Marina, Carlota and Valentina – who have always made Madrid a true place of the heart: *con todo mi amor*. And to Jan: we hope to see you in Madrid again soon.

Catherine Le Nevez

Moltes gràcies/muchas gracias/merci beaucoup first and foremost to Julian, and to all of the locals, tourism professionals and fellow travellers who provided insights, inspiration and good times. Huge thanks, too, to Destination Editor Tom Stainer, my Barcelona co-author Sally Davies and Spain co-authors, and all at Lonely Planet. As ever, *merci encore* to my parents, brother, *belle-sœur*, *neveu* and *nièce*.

Isabella Noble

In Catalonia, thanks to Sally and Damien; Javi and Olga in Girona; Josep and Ana in Espot; Llucia in Deltebre; and the team who fixed my car brakes in Begur. For Ibiza, *gracias* to Louis, Andrew, Becky, Doug, Val, Andy, Martin and Iain. Back in Andalucía, thanks to Jack, Dan, Annie, Pepi, Helen, Eugenia, Monika, Tessa, and the Grazalema and Tarifa tourism teams. Extra-special *gracias* to my fabulous co-writers, especially John, Gregor, Duncan and Brendan.

John Noble

Thanks to so many people for their help but extra-special thanks to Isabella Noble, Iain Colquhoun, Colin Richardson, Pablo and Manolo Canosa, Adrián Costa García and the Liñares family.

Josephine Quintero

Special thanks to the especially helpful tourist offices in Cuenca and Almagro, as well as the local experts in Toledo, who introduced me to some great places and provided invaluable advice. A mega *gracias* to the Lonely Planet editing staff, especially Tom Stainer, for pulling the whole thing together.

Brendan Sainsbury

Muchas gracias to all the bus drivers, tourist information staff, hoteliers, chefs, hiking guides and innocent passers-by who helped me, unwittingly or otherwise, on my research trip.

Regis St Louis

I'm grateful to many people who gave advice and offered insight into one of Spain's most fascinating regions. I'd like to thank Aitor Delgado and Carlos in Bilbao, Veronica Werckmeister of IMVG, and countless tourist office employees, barkeeps and restaurant staff who provided helpful tips. Warm thanks to Cassandra, our daughters Magdalena and Genevieve, and my niece Anna for joining on the great Basque Country road trip.

Andy Symington

I am lucky enough to have great friends in Valencia who help enthusiastically with research and provide brilliant hospitality. I'm grateful to all, but especially to Rosa Martínez Sala, Delfina Soria Bonet, Dolors Roca Ferrerfabrega and Enrique Lapuente Ojeda, who went out of their way to assist me. Thanks also to Gloria López Carro and Richard Prowse for a great stay in Alicante and to Vik Kritharelis and Rob Davies for excellent company. I also owe gratitude to many others who helped along the way.

ACKNOWLEDGEMENTS

Climate map data adapted from Peel MC, Finlayson BL & McMahon TA (2007) 'Updated World Map of the Köppen-Geiger Climate Classification', Hydrology and Earth System Sciences, 11, 163344.

Illustrations pp98-9, pp262-3, pp276-7, pp290-1, pp638-9, pp708-9, pp724-5 by Javier Zarracina

Cover photograph: Alhambra, Richard Taylor/4Corners ©

THIS BOOK

This 12th edition of Lonely Planet's *Spain* guidebook was researched and written by Gregor Clark, Sally Davies, Duncan Garwood, Anthony Ham, Catherine Le Nevez, Isabella Noble, John Noble, Josephine Quintero, Brendan Sainsbury, Regis St Louis and Andy Symington.

This guidebook was produced by the following:

Destination Editor Tom Stainer

Senior Product Editor Genna Patterson

Product Editors Grace Dobell, Heather Champion, Alison Ridgway

Senior Cartographer Anthony Phelan

Book Designer Virginia Moreno

Assisting Editors Sarah Bailey, Andrew Bain, Samantha Forge, Emma Gibbs, Carly Hall, Trent Holden, Gabrielle Innes, Anita Isalska, Ali Lemer, Jodie Martire, Rosie Nicholson, Christopher Pitts, Sarah Reid

Assisting Cartographers Anita Banh, Laura Bailey, Mark Griffiths, James Leversha

Cover Researcher Naomi Parker

Thanks to Ronan Abayawickrema, Katie Connolly, Gemma Graham, Shona Gray, Sandie Kestell, Tanya Parker, Joe Bindloss, Fiona Flores Watson, Rachel Rawling, Kathryn Rowan, Jessica Ryan, Maja Vatrić, Sam Wheeler, Amanda Williamson

Index

A

Map Pages **000**
Photo Pages **000**

D

E

Map Pages **000**
Photo Pages **000**

Map Pages **000**
Photo Pages **000**

Map Pages **000**
Photo Pages **000**

R

Map Legend

Sights

- Beach
- Bird Sanctuary
- Buddhist
- Castle/Palace
- Christian
- Confucian
- Hindu
- Islamic
- Jain
- Jewish
- Monument
- Museum/Gallery/Historic Building
- Ruin
- Shinto
- Sikh
- Taoist
- Winery/Vineyard
- Zoo/Wildlife Sanctuary
- Other Sight

Activities, Courses & Tours

- Bodysurfing
- Diving
- Canoeing/Kayaking
- Course/Tour
- Sento Hot Baths/Onsen
- Skiing
- Snorkelling
- Surfing
- Swimming/Pool
- Walking
- Windsurfing
- Other Activity

Sleeping

- Sleeping
- Camping
- Hut/Shelter

Eating

- Eating

Drinking & Nightlife

- Drinking & Nightlife
- Cafe

Entertainment

- Entertainment

Shopping

- Shopping

Information

- Bank
- Embassy/Consulate
- Hospital/Medical
- Internet
- Police
- Post Office
- Telephone
- Toilet
- Tourist Information
- Other Information

Geographic

- Beach
- Gate
- Hut/Shelter
- Lighthouse
- Lookout
- Mountain/Volcano
- Oasis
- Park
- Pass
- Picnic Area
- Waterfall

Population

- Capital (National)
- Capital (State/Province)
- City/Large Town
- Town/Village

Transport

- Airport
- Border crossing
- Bus
- Cable car/Funicular
- Cycling
- Ferry
- Metro station
- Monorail
- Parking
- Petrol station
- S-Bahn/Subway station
- Taxi
- T-bane/Tunnelbana station
- Train station/Railway
- Tram
- Tube station
- U-Bahn/Underground station
- Other Transport

Routes

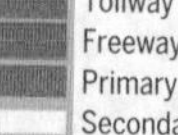

- Tollway
- Freeway
- Primary
- Secondary
- Tertiary
- Lane
- Unsealed road
- Road under construction
- Plaza/Mall
- Steps
- Tunnel
- Pedestrian overpass
- Walking Tour
- Walking Tour detour
- Path/Walking Trail

Boundaries

- International
- State/Province
- Disputed
- Regional/Suburb
- Marine Park
- Cliff
- Wall

Hydrography

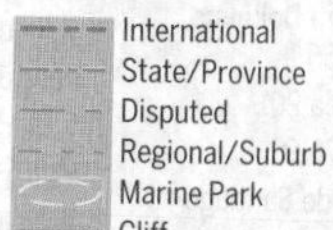

- River, Creek
- Intermittent River
- Canal
- Water
- Dry/Salt/Intermittent Lake
- Reef

Areas

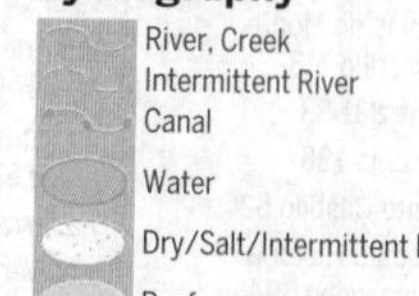

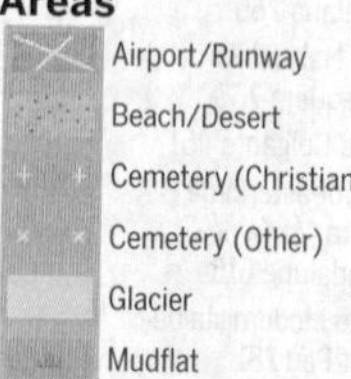

- Airport/Runway
- Beach/Desert
- Cemetery (Christian)
- Cemetery (Other)
- Glacier
- Mudflat
- Park/Forest
- Sight (Building)
- Sportsground
- Swamp/Mangrove

Note: Not all symbols displayed above appear on the maps in this book

Isabella Noble

Andorra, Cádiz Province, Catalonia, Formentera, Gibraltar, Ibiza, Menorca English-Australian on paper but Spanish at heart, Isabella has been wandering the globe since her first round-the-world trip as a one-year-old. Having grown up in a whitewashed Andalucian village, she is a Spain specialist travel journalist, but also writes extensively about India, Thailand, the UK and beyond for Lonely Planet, the Daily Telegraph and others. Find Isabella on Twitter and Instagram @isabellamnoble.

John Noble

Aragón, Córdoba Province, Galicia, Jaén Province John has been travelling for Lonely Planet since the 1980s. The number of LP titles he's written is well into three figures, on numerous countries scattered across the globe. He's still as excited as ever about unfamiliar destinations. Above all, he loves mountains, from the Pyrenees to the Himalaya. See his pics on Instagram: @johnnoble11. John also contributed to the Understand section of this book.

Josephine Quintero

Castilla-La Mancha Josephine launched her journalism degree at a wine and lifestyle magazine followed, ironically, with a move to 'dry' Kuwait where she worked as the Editor of the *Kuwaiti Digest* until the day Iraq invaded. After six weeks as a hostage, Josephine moved to the relaxed shores of Andalucía in southern Spain. Josephine has worked as a ghostwriter for crooks and minor celebrities, while also regulalry writing for in-flight magazines and Lonely Planet. She primarily covers Spain and Italy; other titles include *Mexico City*, *Australia*, *Portugal* and *Mediterranean Europe*.

Brendan Sainsbury

Málaga Province, Andalucía Born and raised in the UK, Brendan didn't leave Blighty until he was 19. He's since squeezed 70 countries into a sometimes precarious existence as a writer and professional vagabond. He has written over 40 books for Lonely Planet from Castro's Cuba to the canyons of Peru. When not scribbling research notes, Brendan likes partaking in ridiculous 'endurance' races, strumming old Clash songs on the guitar, and experiencing the pleasure and pain of following Southampton Football Club.

Regis St Louis

Basque Country, La Rioja, Navarra Regis grew up in a small town in the American Midwest – the kind of place that fuels big dreams of travel – and he developed an early fascination with foreign dialects and world cultures. He spent his formative years learning Russian and a handful of Romance languages, which served him well on journeys across much of the globe. Regis has contributed to more than 50 Lonely Planet titles, covering destinations across six continents. His travels have taken him from the mountains of Kamchatka to remote island villages in Melanesia, and to many grand urban landscapes. When not on the road, he lives in New Orleans.

Andy Symington

Valencia & Murcia Andy has written or worked on over a hundred books and other updates for Lonely Planet (especially in Europe and Latin America) and other publishing companies, and has published articles on numerous subjects for a variety of newspapers, magazines and websites. He part-owns and operates a rock bar, has written a novel and is currently working on several fiction and non-fiction writing projects. Andy, from Australia, moved to Northern Spain many years ago. When he's not off with a backpack in some far-flung corner of the world, he can probably be found watching the local football side or tasting local wines after a long walk in the nearby mountains.

Contributing Writers

Esme Fox contributed to the Barcelona chapter.

OUR STORY

A beat-up old car, a few dollars in the pocket and a sense of adventure. In 1972 that's all Tony and Maureen Wheeler needed for the trip of a lifetime – across Europe and Asia overland to Australia. It took several months, and at the end – broke but inspired – they sat at their kitchen table writing and stapling together their first travel guide, *Across Asia on the Cheap*. Within a week they'd sold 1500 copies. Lonely Planet was born.

Today, Lonely Planet has offices in Franklin, London, Melbourne, Oakland, Dublin, Beijing and Delhi, with more than 600 staff and writers. We share Tony's belief that 'a great guidebook should do three things: inform, educate and amuse'.

OUR WRITERS

Gregor Clark

Asturias, Cantabria, Huelva Province, Picos de Europa Gregor is a US-based writer whose love of languages and curiosity about what's around the next bend have taken him to dozens of countries on five continents. Since 2000, Gregor has contributed to Lonely Planet guides, with a focus on Europe and the Americas. Titles include *France*, *Portugal* and *Mexico*, among many others. Gregor has lived in California, France, Spain and Italy prior to settling with his wife and two daughters in Vermont.

Sally Davies

Barcelona Sally landed in Seville in 1992 with a handful of pesetas and five words of Spanish, and, despite a complete inability to communicate, promptly snared a lucrative number handing out leaflets at Expo '92. In 2001 she settled in Barcelona, where her daily grind involves nose-to-tail eating, getting lost in museums and finding ways to convey the beauty of this spectacular city.

Duncan Garwood

Almería Province, Granada Province, Seville From facing fast bowlers in Barbados to sidestepping hungry pigs in Goa, Duncan's travels have thrown up many unique experiences. These days he largely dedicates himself to Spain and Italy, where he's been living since 1997. He's worked on more than 30 Lonely Planet titles, covering Rome, Sardinia, Sicily, Bilbao and San Sebastián, among others, and has contributed to books on food and epic drives.

Anthony Ham

Castilla y León, Extremadura, Madrid & Around Anthony is a writer and photographer who specialises in Spain, East and Southern Africa, the Arctic and the Middle East. In 2001, after years of wandering the world, Anthony fell irretrievably in love with Madrid. When he finally left ten years later, he was married to a local and Madrid had beocme his second home. Now back in Australia, he continues to travel in search of stories. Anthony also contributed to the Plan Your Trip and Survival Guide sections of this book.

Catherine Le Nevez

Barcelona Catherine's wanderlust kicked in when she roadtripped across Europe from her Parisian base aged four, and she's been hitting the road at every opportunity since, travelling to around 60 countries and completing her Doctorate of Creative Arts in Writing, Masters in Professional Writing, and postgrad qualifications in Editing and Publishing along the way. She's written scores of Lonely Planet guides and articles covering Paris, France, Europe and beyond.

Published by Lonely Planet Global Limited
CRN 554153
12th edition – November 2013
ISBN 978 1 78657 2 660

10 9 8 7 6 5 4 3 2 1
Printed in China